INTERNATIONAL HANDBOOK OF ENGLISH LANGUAGE TEACHING

Springer International Handbooks of Education

Volume 15

A list of titles in this series can be found at the end of this volume.

International Handbook of English Language Teaching

Part I

Edited by

Jim Cummins
The University of Toronto, Canada

and

Chris Davison
The University of Hong Kong, China

Jim Cummins
Ontario Institute for Studies in Education/Canada

Chris Davison
The University of Hong Kong/China

Library of Congress Control Number: 2006932383

ISBN -13: 978-0-387-46300-1
ISBN -10: 0-387-46300-3

e-ISBN-13: 978-0-387-46301-8
e-ISBN-10: 0-387-46301-1

Printed on acid-free paper.

© 2007 Springer Science+Business Media, LLC.
All rights reserved. This work may not be translated or copied in whole or in part without the written permission of the publisher (Springer Science+Business Media, LLC., 233 Spring Street, New York, NY 10013, USA), except for brief excerpts in connection with reviews or scholarly analysis. Use in connection with any form of information storage and retrieval, electronic adaptation, computer software, or by similar or dissimilar methodology now known or hereafter developed is forbidden.
The use in this publication of trade names, trademarks, service marks and similar terms, even if they are not identified as such, is not to be taken as an expression of opinion as to whether or not they are subject to proprietary rights.
While the advice and information in this book are believed to be true and accurate at the date of going to press, neither the authors nor the editors nor the publisher can accept any legal responsibility for any errors or omissions that may be made. The publisher makes no warranty, express or implied, with respect to the material contained herein.

9 8 7 6 5 4 3 2   Corrected at 2nd printing, 2007

springer.com

Table of Contents

PART I

List of Authors	xiii
Preface	xxi
Acknowledgments	xxvii

SECTION 1. The Global Scope and Politics of ELT: Critiquing Current Policies and Programs

	Introduction: The Global Scope and Politics of ELT: Critiquing Current Policies and Programs *Jim Cummins and Chris Davison*	3
1	ELT and Colonialism *Alastair Pennycook*	13
2	Ideology, Language Varieties, and ELT *James W. Tollefson*	25
3	Tensions Between English and Mother Tongue Teaching in Post-Colonial Africa *Margaret Akinyi Obondo*	37
4	A Critical Discussion of the English-Vernacular Divide in India *Vaidehi Ramanathan*	51
5	ELT Policy Directions in Multilingual Japan *Yasuko Kanno*	63

6	English Language Teaching in Korea: Toward Globalization or *Glocalization*? Hyunjung Shin	75
7	The National Curriculum Changes and Their Effects on English Language Teaching in the People's Republic of China Qiang Wang	87
8	ELT and Bilingual Education in Argentina Agustina Tocalli-Beller	107
9	English, No Longer a Foreign Language in Europe? Robert Phillipson	123
10	Common Property: English as a Lingua Franca in Europe Barbara Seidlhofer	137
11	Teaching English as a Third Language Ulrike Jessner and Jasone Cenoz	155
12	Protecting English in an Anglophone Age Joseph Lo Bianco	169
13	Adult Immigrant ESL Programs in Canada: Emerging Trends in the Contexts of History, Economics, and Identity Douglas Fleming	185
14	Focus on Literacy: ELT and Educational Attainment in England Jill Bourne	199
15	Methods, Meanings and Education Policy in the United States Lois M. Meyer	211

SECTION 2. The Goals and Focus of the ELT Program: Problematizing Content and Pedagogy

	Introduction: The Goals and Focus of the ELT Program: Problematizing Content and Pedagogy Chris Davison and Jim Cummins	231
16	The Goals of ELT: Reproducing Native-Speakers or Promoting Multicompetence Among Second Language Users? Vivian Cook	237
17	Integrating School-Aged ESL Learners into the Mainstream Curriculum Constant Leung	249
18	Communicative Language Teaching: Current Status and Future Prospects Nina Spada	271

Table of Contents vii

19	Language Instruction Through Tasks *Peter Skehan*	289
20	Knowledge Structures in Social Practices *Bernard A. Mohan*	303
21	Accelerating Academic Achievement of English Language Learners: A Synthesis of Five Evaluations of the CALLA Model *Anna Uhl Chamot*	317
22	Predicting Second Language Academic Success in English Using the Prism Model *Virginia P. Collier and Wayne P. Thomas*	333
23	Four Keys for School Success for Elementary English Learners *Yvonne Freeman and David Freeman*	349
24	Collaborating in ESL Education in Schools *Sophie Arkoudis*	365
25	Organization of English Teaching in International Schools *Maurice W. Carder*	379
26	English for Specific Purposes: Some Influences and Impacts *Ken Hyland*	391
27	An Interdisciplinary Approach to Teaching Adults English in the Workplace *Jane Lockwood*	403

SECTION 3. Assessment and Evaluation in ELT: Shifting Paradigms and Practices

	Introduction: Assessment and Evaluation in ELT: Shifting Paradigms and Practices *Chris Davison and Jim Cummins*	415
28	Standards-Based Approaches to the Evaluation of ESL Instruction *David Nunan*	421
29	The Standards Movement and ELT for School-Aged Learners: Cross-National Perspectives *Penny McKay*	439
30	High-Stakes Testing and Assessment: English Language Teacher Benchmarking *David Coniam and Peter Falvey*	457

31	New Directions in Testing English Language Proficiency for University Entrance *Alister Cumming*	473
32	The Impact of Testing Practices on Teaching: Ideologies and Alternatives *Liz Hamp-Lyons*	487
33	Classroom-Based Assessment: Possibilities and Pitfalls *Pauline Rea-Dickins*	505
34	The Power of Language Tests, the Power of the English Language and the Role of ELT *Elana Shohamy*	521
35	Different Definitions of Language and Language Learning: Implications for Assessment *Chris Davison*	533

Author Index	549
Subject Index	575

PART II

List of Authors	xiii
Preface	xxi
Acknowledgments	xxvii

SECTION 1. The Learner and the Learning Environment: Creating New Communities

	Introduction: The Learner and the Learning Environment: Creating New Communities *Jim Cummins and Chris Davison*	615
36	ESL Learners in the Early School Years: Identity and Mediated Classroom Practices *Kelleen Toohey, Elaine Day and Patrick Manyak*	625
37	The Adolescent English Language Learner: Identities Lost and Found *Linda Harklau*	639

Table of Contents ix

38	What About the Students? English Language Learners in Postsecondary Settings *Sarah Benesch*	655
39	Imagined Communities, Identity, and English Language Learning *Aneta Pavlenko and Bonny Norton*	669
40	Academic Achievement and Social Identity Among Bilingual Students in the U.S. *Shelley Wong and Rachel Grant*	681
41	Sociocultural Theory: A Unified Approach to L2 Learning and Teaching *James P. Lantolf*	693
42	Mediating Academic Language Learning Through Classroom Discourse *Pauline Gibbons*	701
43	Creating a Motivating Classroom Environment *Zoltán Dörnyei*	719
44	Autonomy and Its Role in Learning *Philip Benson*	733
45	Creating a Technology-Rich English Language Learning Environment *Denise E. Murray*	747
46	The Internet and English Language Learning: Opening Up Spaces for Constructivist and Transformative Pedagogy Through Sister-Class Networks *Vasilia Kourtis-Kazoullis and Eleni Skourtou*	763

SECTION 2. Constructs of Language in ELT: Breaking the Boundaries

	Introduction: Constructs of Language in ELT: Breaking the Boundaries *Chris Davison and Jim Cummins*	777
47	Psycholinguistic Perspectives on Language and Its Acquisition *Jan H. Hulstijn*	783
48	Academic Language: What Is It and How Do We Acquire It? *Jim Cummins and Evelyn Man Yee-Fun*	797
49	Teaching Implications of L2 Phonology Research *John Archibald*	811
50	Current Perspectives on Vocabulary Teaching and Learning *Norbert Schmitt*	827

51	Changing Approaches to the Conceptualization and Teaching of Grammar *Beverly Derewianka*	843
52	Extending Our Understanding of Spoken Discourse *Michael McCarthy and Diana Slade*	859
53	New Directions in Student Academic Writing *Sue Starfield*	875
54	From Literacy to Multiliteracies in ELT *Heather Lotherington*	891
55	Technology and Writing *Mark Warschauer*	907
56	Multimodal Pedagogies, Representation and Identity: Perspectives from Post-Apartheid South Africa *Pippa Stein and Denise Newfield*	919
57	Approaches to Genre in ELT *Brian Paltridge*	931
58	Researching and Developing Teacher Language Awareness: Developments and Future Directions *Stephen Andrews*	945

SECTION 3. Research and Teacher Education in ELT: Meeting New Challenges

	Introduction: Research and Teacher Education in ELT: Meeting New Challenges *Jim Cummins and Chris Davison*	963
59	Qualitative Approaches to Classroom Research with English Language Learners *Patricia A. Duff*	973
60	Action Research: Contributions and Future Directions in ELT *Anne Burns*	987
61	Narrative Inquiry and ELT Research *JoAnn Phillion and Ming Fang He*	1003
62	Conversation Analysis: Issues and Problems *Numa Markee*	1017

63	Poststructuralism and Applied Linguistics: Complementary Approaches to Identity and Culture in ELT *Brian Morgan*	1033
64	What Shapes Teachers' Professional Development? *Amy B.M. Tsui*	1053
65	Appropriating Uncertainty: ELT Professional Development in the New Century *Michael P. Breen*	1067
66	Teacher Education for Linguistically Diverse Communities, Schools, and Classrooms *Tara Goldstein*	1085
67	Challenges and Opportunities for the Teaching Profession: English as an Additional Language in the UK *Charlotte Franson*	1101
68	Teachers' Roles in the Global Hypermedia Environment *Chris Corbel*	1113
69	Preparing Teachers for Technology-Supported ELT *Michael K. Legutke, Andreas Müller-Hartmann and Marita Schocker V. Ditfurth*	1125

Author Index	1139
Subject Index	1165

List of Authors

Stephen Andrews, Faculty of Education, The University of Hong Kong, Pokfulam Road, Hong Kong, SAR, China. Email: sandrews@hku.hk

John Archibald, Department of Linguistics, Language Research Centre, The University of Calgary, Calgary, Alberta, T2N 1N4, Canada. Email: john.archibald@ucalgary.ca

Sophie Arkoudis, Faculty of Education, The University of Melbourne, Parkville, Victoria, 3010, Australia. Email: s.arkoudis@unimelb.edu.au

Sarah Benesch, Department of English, Speech and, World Literature, The City University of New York, College of Staten Island, 2800 Victory Boulevard, Staten Island, New York, USA. Email: benesch@mail.csi.cuny.edu

Phil Benson, The Hong Kong Institute of Education, 10 Lo Ping Road, Tai Po, Hong Kong, SAR, China. Email: pbenson@hkucc.hku.hk

Jill Bourne, Centre for Research on Pedagogy and the Curriculum, School of Education, The University of Southampton, Highfield, Southampton, SO17 1BJ, United Kingdom. Email: j.bourne@soton.ac.uk

Michael P. Breen, Sutton House, Auchterarder, Perthshire PH3 1ED, Scotland. Email: m.breen@hotmail.co.uk

Anne Burns, Department of Linguistics, Division of Linguistics and Psychology, Macquarie University, NSW 2109, Australia. Email: anne.burns@mq.edu.au

Maurice Carder, Vienna International School, Strasse der Menschenrechte 1, A-1220, Vienna, Austria. Email: mcarder@vis.ac.at

Jasone Cenoz, Department of Research Methods in Education, FICE, The University of the Basque Country, Avda Tolosa 70, 01006 San Sebastian, Spain. Email: jasone.cenoz@ehu.es

Anna Uhl Chamot, George Washington University, 2121 Bye Street, N.W., Washington, USA. Email: auchamot@gwu.edu

Virginia P. Collier, Graduate School of Education, George Mason University, 4400 University Drive MS4B3, Fairfax, VA 22030, USA. Email: vcollier@gmu.edu

David Coniam, Department of Curriculum and Instruction, The Chinese University of Hong Kong, Shatin, New Territories, Hong Kong, SAR, China. Email: coniam@cuhk.edu.hk

Vivian Cook, School of Education, Communication and Language Sciences, King George VI Building, The University of Newcastle upon Tyne, Newcastle upon Tyne, NE1 7RU, England. Email: Vivian.Cook@newcastle.ac.uk

Chris Corbel, Manager Research and Development, NMIT, 77-91 St Georges Rd, Preston, Victoria 3072. Email: chrisc-rd@nmit.vic.edu.au

Alister Cumming, Modern Language Centre, Ontario Institute for Studies in Education, The University of Toronto, 252 Bloor Street West, Toronto, Ontario, M5S 1V6, Canada. Email: acumming@oise.utoronto.ca

Jim Cummins, Modern Language Centre, 10th Floor, Ontario Institute for Studies in Education, The University of Toronto, 252 Bloor St, West Toronto, Ontario, M5S 1V6 Canada. Email: jcummins@oise.utoronto.ca

Chris Davison, Faculty of Education, The University of Hong Kong, Pokfulam Rd, Hong Kong, SAR, China. Email: cdavison@hku.hk

Elaine Day, Faculty of Education, Simon Fraser University, 8888 University Drive, Burnaby, BC V5A, 1S6, Canada. Email: Elaine_Day@sfu.ca

Beverly Derewianka, Faculty of Education, The University of Wollongong, NSW 2522, Australia. Email: bevder@uow.edu.au

Zoltán Dörnyei, School of English Studies, The University of Nottingham, UK. Email: Zoltan.Dornyei@nottingham.ac.uk

Patricia A. Duff, Department of Language and Literacy Education The University of British Columbia, 2125 Main Mall, Vancouver, BC, V6T 1Z4, Canada. Email: patricia.duff@ubc.ca

Peter Falvey, University of Cambridge Local Examinations Syndicate, 4, Bramcote Lane, Chilwell, Beeston, Nottingham, NG9 5EN, UK. Email: falveyphk@gmail.com

List of Authors

Douglas Fleming, The University of British Columbia, 9500 Glenacres Drive Richmond, BC, V7A 1Y7, Canada. Email: fleming_douglas@sd36.bc.ca

Charlotte Franson, Canterbury Christ Church University, North Holmes Road, Canterbury, CT1 1QU, Kent, England. Email: cmf6@canterbury.ac.uk

David Freeman, School of Education, The University of Texas at Brownsville, 80 Fort Brown, Brownsville, TX 78520, USA. Email: david.freeman@utb.edu

Yvonne Freeman, School of Education, The University of Texas at Brownsville, 80 Fort Brown, Brownsville, TX 78520, USA. Email: yvonne.freeman@utb.edu

Pauline Gibbons, Faculty of Education, The University of Technology Sydney, PO Box 123, Broadway, NSW 2007, Australia. Email: Pauline.Gibbons@uts.edu.au

Tara Goldstein, Department of Curriculum, Teaching and Learning, Ontario Institute for Studies in Education, The University of Toronto, 252 Bloor Street, Toronto, Ontario, M5S 1V6, Canada. Email: tgoldstein@oise.utoronto.ca

Rachel Grant, Center for Language and Culture, College of Education and Human Development, George Mason University, 4400 University Drive, MS4B3, Fairfax, VA 22030, USA. Email: rag022@aol.com

Liz Hamp-Lyons, Faculty of Education, The University of Hong Kong, Pokfulam, Rd, Hong Kong, SAR, China. Email: lizhl@hku.hk

Linda Harklau, Department of Language Education, 125 Aderhold Hall, The University of Georgia, Athens, GA 30602, USA. Email: lharklau@uga.edu

Ming Fang He, Department of Curriculum, Foundations, and Reading, College of Education, Georgia Southern University, Post Office Box 8144, Statesboro, GA, 30460-8144, USA. Email: mfhe@georgiasouthern.edu

Jan H. Hulstijn, Faculty of Humanities, The University of Amsterdam, 134 Spuistraat, 1012 VB Amsterdam, The Netherlands. Email: j.h.hulstijn@uva.nl

Ken Hyland, Institute of Education, The University of London, 20 Bedford Way, London, WC1H OAL, UK. Email: K.Hyland@ioe.ac.uk

Ulrike Jessner, Department of English, The University of Innsbruck, Innrain 52/III, A-6020 Innsbruck, Austria. Email: Ulrike.Jessner@uibk.ac.at

Yasuko Kanno, The University of Washington, Department of English, Box 354330, Seattle, WA 98195-4330, USA. Email: ykanno@u.washington.edu

Vasilia Kourtis Kazoullis, Department of Mediterranean Studies, The University of the Aegean, 1 Demokratias Ave. GR-85100 Rhodes, Greece. Email: kazoullis@rhodes.aegean.gr

James P. Lantolf, Penn State University, Centre of Language Acquisition, 304 Sparks Building, University Park, PA 16802, USA. Email: jpl7@psu.edu

Michael K. Legutke, Justus-Liebig-Universität Giessen, Institut für Anglistik, Otto-Behaghel-Str, 10, B, IV, 35394 Giessen, Germany. Email: Michael.K.Legutke@anglistik.uni-giessen.de

Constant Leung, Department of Education and Professional Studies, School of Social Science and Public Policy, King's College, The University of London, Franklin-Wilkins Building, Waterloo Road, London, SE1 9NH, UK. Email: constant.leung@kcl.ac.uk

Joseph Lo Bianco, Department of Language and Literacy Education, The University of Melbourne, Parkville, Victoria 3010 Australia. Email: j.lobianco@unimelb.edu.au

Jane Lockwood, The Hong Kong Institute of Education, 10 Lo Ping Road, Tai Po, Hong Kong, SAR, China. Email: lockwood@ied.edu.hk

Heather Lotherington, Faculty of Education, York University, 4700 Keele Street, Toronto, Ontario, M3J 1P3, Canada. Email: hlotherington@edu.yorku.ca

Evelyn Man Yee-fun, Department of Curriculum and Instruction, The Chinese University of Hong Kong, Shatin, New Territories, Hong Kong, SAR China. Email: eyfman@cuhk.edu.hk

Patrick Manyak, College of Education, Department of Elementary and Early Childhood, The University of Wyoming, P.O. Box 3374 Laramine, WY 82071-3374, USA. Email: pmanyak@uwyo.edu

Numa Markee, Division of English as an International Language, The University of Illinois at Urbana-Champaign, 3070 Foreign Languages Building, 707 South Mathews, Urbana, IL 61801, USA. Email: nppm@uiuc.edu

Michael McCarthy, School of English Studies, The University Nottingham, University Park, Nottingham, NG7 2RD, UK. Email: mactoft@dial.pipex.com

Penny McKay, School of Cultural and Language Studies in Education, Queensland University of Technology, Kelvin Grove Campus, Brisbane, Queensland 4059, Australia. Email: pa.mckay@qut.edu.au

Lois M. Meyer, College of Education, Department of Language, Literacy & Sociocultural Studies, The University of New Mexico, Albuquerque, NM 87131, USA. Email: lsmeyer@unm.edu

Bernard A. Mohan, The University of British Columbia, 4640 West 13th Avenue, Vancouver, British Columbia, Canada V6R 2V7. Email: bernard.mohan@ubc.ca

List of Authors

Brian Morgan, Department of Languages, Literatures and Linguistics, York University, Canada. Email: bmorgan@yorku.ca

Andreas Müller-Hartmann, Department of English as a Foreign Language Pädagogische Hochschule Heidelberg, Im Neuenheimer Feld 561, D-69120 Heidelberg, Germany. Email: Andreas.Mueller-Hartmann@anglistik.uni-giessen.de

Denise E. Murray, National Centre for English Language Teaching and Research, Macquarie University, NSW 2109, Australia. Email: denise.murray@mq.edu.au

Denise Newfield, Department of English, School of Literature and Language Studies, University of the Witwatersrand, PO WITS 2050, South Africa. Email: dnewfield@languages.wits.ac.za

Bonny Norton, Department of Language and Literacy Education, The University of British Columbia, 2125 Main Mall, Vancouver, BC, Canada V6T 1Z4. Email: bonny.norton@ubc.ca

David Nunan, The English Centre, The University of Hong Kong, Pokfulam Rd, Hong Kong, SAR, China. Email: dcnunan@hku.hk

Margaret Obondo, Rinkeby Institute of Multilingual Research, P.O. Box 5028, 163 05, Spåna, Sweden. Email: margaret.obondo@rinkeby-multiling.stockholm.se

Brian Paltridge, Faculty of Education, The University of Sydney, NSW 2006, Australia. Email: b.paltridge@edfac.usyd.edu.au

Aneta Pavlenko, CITE Department, College of Education, Temple University, Philadephia, PA 19122, USA. Email: apavlenk@temple.edu

Alastair Pennycook, The University of Technology Sydney, City Campus Haymarket; PO Box 123, Broadway, NSW 2007, Australia. Email: alastair.pennycook@uts.edu.au

JoAnn Phillion, Department of Curriculum and Instruction, BRNG 4144, Purdue University, West Lafayette, IN 47907-2098. USA. Email: phillion@purdue.edu

Robert Phillipson, Department of English, Copenhagen Business School, Dalgas Have 15, 2000 Frederiksberg, Denmark. Email: rp.eng@cbs.dk

Vaidehi Ramanathan, Linguistics Program, The University of California, One Shields Ave., Davis, CA 95616, USA. Email: vramanathan@ucdavis.edu

Pauline Rea-Dickins, Graduate School of Education, The University of Bristol, 35 Berkerley Square, Clifton, Bristol BS8 1JA, UK. Email: p.rea-dickins@bristol.ac.uk

Norbert Schmitt, School of English Studies, The University of Nottingham, Nottingham NG7 2RD, UK. Email: norbert.schmitt@nottingham.ac.uk

Marita Schocker v. Ditfurth, Pädagogische Hochschule Freiburg, Institut für Fremdsprachen/Abteilung Englisch, Kunzenweg 21D-79117 Freiburg, Germany. Email: schocker@ph-freiburg.de

Barbara Seidlhofer, Institut für Anglistik, Universität Wien, Universitaetcampus AAKH/Hof 8, Spitalgasse 2-4, A-1090 Vienna, Austria. Email: barbara.seidlhofer@univie.ac.at

Hyunjung Shin, Ontario Institute for Studies in Education, The University of Toronto, 252 Bloor Street West, Toronto, Ontario, M5S 1V6, Canada. Email: shyunjung@hotmail.com

Elana Shohamy, Tel Aviv University, School of Education, Tel Aviv 69978, Isarel. Email: elana@post.tau.ac.il

Peter Skehan, English Department, Fung King Hey Building, The Chinese University of Hong Kong, Shatin, New Territories, Hong Kong, SAR, China. Email: pskehan@arts.cuhk.edu.hk

Eleni Skourtou, Department of Primary Education, The University of the Aegean, 1 Demokratias Ave. GR-85100, Rhodes, Greece. Email: skourtou@rhodes.aegean.gr

Diana Slade, The University of Technology Sydney, Faculty of Education, PO Box 123, Broadway, NSW 2007, Australia. Email: diana.slade@uts.edu.au

Nina Spada, Ontario Institute for Studies in Education, The University of Toronto, Modern Language Centre, Department of Curriculum, Teaching and Learning, 252 Bloor Street West, Toronto, Ontario, M5S IV6, Canada. Email: nspada@oise.utoronto.ca

Sue Starfield, The Learning Centre, The University of New South Wales, Sydney, NSW 2052, Australia. Email: s.starfield@unsw.edu.au

Pippa Stein, Department of Applied English Language Studies, School of Literature and Language Studies, University of Witwatersrand, PO WITS 2050, South Africa. Email: pippa@languages.wits.ac.za

Wayne P. Thomas, Graduate School of Education, George Mason University, 4400 University Drive MS4B3, Fairfax, VA 22030, USA. Email: wthomas@gmu.edu

Agustina Tocalli-Beller, El Montículo 153, La Planicie, La Molina, Lima 12, Peru. Email: atocalli-beller@oise.utoronto.ca/agustina@cogeco.ca

James W. Tollefson, The University of Washington, 5307 S. Langley Road, Langley, WA 98260, USA. Email: tollefso@u.washington.edu

Kelleen Toohey, Faculty of Education, 8888 University Drive, Simon Fraser University, Burnaby, BC V5A 1S6, Canada. Email: toohey@sfu.ca

List of Authors

Amy B. M. Tsui, Faculty of Education, The University of Hong Kong, Pokfulam Road, Hong Kong, SAR, China. Email: bmtsui@hku.hk

Qiang Wang, Department of Foreign Languages, Beijing Normal University, Beijing, China. Email: wang_qiang99@yahoo.com

Mark Warschauer, The University of California, Irvine, UCI Department of Education, 2001 Berkeley Place, Irvine, CA 92697-5500, USA. Email: markw@uci.edu

Shelley Wong, Center for Language and Culture, College of Education and Human Development, George Mason University, 4400 University Drive MS4B3, Fairfax, VA 22030, USA. Email: swong1@gmu.edu

Preface

This two-volume handbook provides a comprehensive examination of policy, practice, research, and theory related to English language teaching (ELT) in international contexts. Nearly 70 chapters highlight the research foundation for the best practices, frameworks for policy decisions, and areas of consensus and controversy in the teaching and development of English as a second and/or additional language for kindergarten through to adult speakers of languages other than English. In doing so it problematizes traditional dichotomies and challenges the very terms that provide the traditional foundations of the field.

A wide range of terms has been used to refer to the key players involved in the teaching and learning of the English language and to the enterprise of English language teaching as a whole. At various times and in different contexts, the following labels have been used in countries where English is the dominant language to describe programs, learners, or teachers of English: *English as a second language* (ESL), *English as an additional language* (EAL), *limited English proficient* (LEP), and *English language learners* (ELL). In contexts where English is not the dominant language, the following terms have been used: *English as a foreign language* (EFL), *English as an international language* (EIL), and *English as a lingua franca* (ELF). The international professional organization that supports and advocates for English language teaching calls itself *Teachers of English to Speakers of Other Languages* (TESOL) and the term *English to speakers of other languages* (ESOL) is also used in some contexts around the world to refer to programs, students, and teachers.

None of these labels is sociopolitically neutral; they each highlight certain features of the phenomenon of English language teaching and those who engage in it, and de-emphasize other features. For example, all of the labels listed above foreground *English* as the focus of attention, thereby obscuring the fact that the learners are bilingual or multilingual with fully functioning abilities in their home languages. This risks contributing to a deficit view of the learner, particularly in English-speaking contexts involving immigrant and refugee students. The term *limited English proficient* used by the US federal government is particularly problematic in this regard. Other terms are problematic for different reasons; for example, *ESL* makes the assumption, rooted in a monolingual perspective, that English is the second language of the student whereas in reality it may be the third, fourth, or fifth language that an individual has learned. *ELL* is currently the favored term among many professional organizations and educational agencies in North America but it obscures some key differences between programs for English mother tongue learners and those who are learning English as an additional language.

Attempts to use 'positive' terminology to refer to students and programs can also be problematic. For example, in the United Kingdom students have frequently been referred to as *bilingual* learners but this label obscures the fact that many of these students are still in great need of English language development (and were usually afforded few opportunities and little encouragement for mother tongue maintenance). In the United States, advocates for bilingual programs and some educational agencies have frequently referred to students as *bilingual* or *bilingual/bicultural*; however, it is arguable that this labeling may have contributed to the widespread assumption among the media and some policy-makers and educators that bilingualism represents a linguistic deficit and that the bilingual student is 'limited English proficient.' In contexts where English is not the dominant language, the label *EFL* has traditionally been used but *EIL* and *ELF* have been promoted as alternatives. The latter is seen as a much more accurate sociolinguistic descriptor to describe many learning and teaching situations outside predominantly English–speaking countries. The problem with adopting all such labels, however, is that by definition they create a single category in which people from many different linguistic and cultural backgrounds, language levels, socio-economic positions, aspirations, and perceived identities are treated as a collectivity.

In this handbook we have not attempted to reconcile this multiplicity of identities and ideologies; rather, we have generally remained faithful to whatever term has been provided by the author of each chapter, assuming that it is an accurate reflection of their context and history, with the exception of the term *LEP* which we have generally changed to *ESL* or *ELL*. The field as a whole, in all its richness and diversity, we have called *English language teaching* (ELT), despite the limitations of the term, hence the title of this handbook. As this discussion of labels illustrates, language intersects with societal power relations in multiple and complex ways and this reality is reflected in the entire field of English language teaching. Thus, it is not surprising that many of the chapters in this handbook explore the ideological dimensions of ELT and their implications for language policies and classroom practice.

The handbook is intended to provide a unique resource for policy makers, educational administrators, teacher educators and researchers concerned with meeting the increasing demand for effective English language teaching while, at the same time, supporting institutions and communities concerned with the survival and development of languages other than English. Its publication is timely in view of the continuing spread of English as a global language and the associated expansion of ELT in countries around the world. Policy decisions regarding ELT that will be made during the next five years will influence the lives of individuals and the development of societies for the next 25 years or more. Policies and practices relating to ELT are, unfortunately, just as likely to be motivated by political pressure backed up by plausible but flawed assumptions as they are by research and careful evaluation of alternative options. For example, many parents and policy makers just assume that earlier and more intensive instruction will result in higher levels of

English proficiency. As the research reviewed in this handbook demonstrates, this assumption is not necessarily valid—the issues are considerably more complex than the rush to English would suggest.

Even a cursory examination of the spread of English demonstrates the ecological nature of the phenomenon. The introduction or expansion of English language teaching in any particular environment exerts multidimensional influences on the status and even prospects for survival of other languages in that environment. Social and linguistic groups within these environments are similarly affected—either advantaged or disadvantaged—by the policies adopted in relation to English.

To illustrate, it is clear that in countries around the world, English is replacing other languages as the second language taught most frequently and intensively in school. The perceived social and economic rewards associated with English have propelled parents to demand earlier and more intensive teaching of English. For example, in Japan, pilot projects have been instituted to start teaching English in the primary grades. In Hong Kong there is spirited public debate about the value of English–medium education and the most appropriate age to start learning English. English-medium universities are expanding rapidly in traditionally non-English speaking contexts, not just through the establishment of off-shore campuses, but through local universities shifting to English as the main language of instruction. For example, universities in mainland China have been required to teach 10% of their curriculum in English since 2004; in Japan entire degree programs are being offered in English in an attempt to maintain student numbers as the university–age population rapidly dwindles. In Norway and Sweden English is rapidly displacing the national languages as the medium of teaching and learning in science and engineering faculties. Finland has the largest proportion of higher education courses taught in English outside English-speaking countries. In the European community in general, there are concerns that the drive to teach English is turning it into the de facto official language of the new Europe. Similar developments and debates about the accelerating spread of English are underway in countries around the world. Expansion and intensification of ELT by means of an earlier start, increased time allotment, and experimentation with immersion and bilingual or trilingual programs are evident both in private sector and public sector schools in many countries.

Demand for English has also escalated among adult learners including immigrants to English-speaking countries, business people involved in the global economy, and those who just want to travel as tourists. In many countries, large-scale ELT programs for adult learners have been established in the community and workplace as a result of the globalization of the workforce, the perceived need to increase economic competitiveness, and a move towards life-long learning.

In some contexts, English has displaced not only competing second languages but also first languages. In many former British colonies and other recently independent countries in Africa and Asia, for example, English is used almost exclusively as the medium of instruction in schools, thereby constricting the institutional space available for indigenous languages and creating immense challenges for students to learn academic content through a language they do not understand. Is this the best policy option? What are the alternatives? Who benefits from these policies and who is disadvantaged? Clearly, policies and practices associated with English language teaching must be considered not only in relation to effectiveness and efficiency but also with respect to the moral dimensions of decisions and initiatives. Who benefits from particular expenditures of resources and what are the hidden costs with respect to what these resources might have been spent on? Is external aid for language teaching programs promoting the development of home-grown expertise or inducing long-term dependency on external support? In short, power and status relationships between social groups both within and across societies are intertwined in obvious ways with language teaching policies and practices.

Increased focus on English language teaching has also occurred in countries where English is the dominant language. Many English-speaking countries have experienced dramatic increases in immigration during the past 30 years (e.g. the United States, Australia, and Canada). For example, about 40% of students in California have learned English as a second language and 25% of these are classified as *limited English proficient* by government agencies. In Canada, about 50% of students in the Toronto and Vancouver urban areas have learned English as an additional language. In Australia, more than 25% of the population use a language other than English as the main language of communication in the home. The rapid spread of the new knowledge economies and the decline in demand for traditional manual labor are creating even greater pressure for newcomer populations to be highly proficient in English. There is also much more transmigration with people moving to English-speaking countries for temporary periods seeking further education and/or work, a trend accelerated by developments such as the expansion of the European Union. The number of foreign university students in the United Kingdom, the United States, Australia, New Zealand, and Canada has increased steadily during the past 20 years.

Increasing cultural and linguistic diversity in English-dominant countries has given rise to concerns among some groups that English might be under threat from competing languages. These concerns have given rise to fierce debates, often with racist overtones, about how English should be taught to immigrant and second generation children as well as adults. In several US states, for example, referenda have mandated that only English be used in schools for instructional purposes. The goal has been to restrict or eliminate bilingual programs that are seen as conferring status on other languages. Clearly, debates on language policy issues in many countries have been characterized by the confounding of ideological and research-based perspectives. There is considerable research that can inform policy in these areas but it is frequently ignored and/or distorted as a result of entrenched ideological positions.

The *International Handbook of English Language Teaching* provides authoritative perspectives on these issues from many of the leading researchers, theorists, and policy-makers around the world. The handbook synthesizes the inter-disciplinary knowledge base for effective decision making and highlights directions for implementing appropriate language policies at both instructional and societal levels. Each volume is divided into three main sections and chapters are clustered to address common topics and themes. The focus of Volume I is on *Policies and Programs in ELT: Changing Demands and Directions* while Volume II addresses *Language, Learning and Identity in ELT: Reconceptualizing the Field*.

Volume I includes a critical examination of current policies and programs in a variety of contexts around the world (Section 1). The chapters in this section identify empirical, theoretical, and ideological foundations of ELT policies and their effects on learners and organizational structures. Section 2 of this Volume focuses specifically on the development of curriculum content for ELT programs and the pedagogical approaches that have been implemented to teach this content, while Section 3 examines policies and practices in assessment and evaluation. All of these dimensions of ELT—curriculum content, pedagogy, assessment, and evaluation—involve complex sets of decisions made by multiple actors (e.g. policy makers, curriculum developers, publishers, teachers, parents, researchers) who interact with each other in dynamic and often unpredictable ways. Increasingly, these actors span the international stage. Initiatives adopted in one or more contexts (e.g. standards-based curriculum development and high-stakes testing) influence decisions taken elsewhere, often through the mediation of international experts who consult with publishers and government agencies to identify 'best practices.' The chapters in all three sections of Volume I highlight the complex interplay between global and local perspectives and the need for policy decisions that take account of local linguistic contexts rather than just importing formulaic "off-the-shelf" solutions that may be highly inappropriate for a particular context.

In Volume II, the focus shifts to the changing conceptions of the learner, the teacher, the learning environment, and the English language itself that are implied by particular approaches to program development, curriculum, pedagogy, and assessment. *Identity* has emerged as a key construct in recent research and theory within ELT, reflecting the fact that learners and teachers are engaged in multiple social relationships both with each other and with peers and colleagues. Learning is conceived as a social endeavor rather than simply an individualistic cognitive and linguistic process. Identities are being constantly negotiated as learners learn language and this process of identity negotiation is strongly influenced by patterns of power relationships in the broader society. Language itself is being reconceptualized as a result of this process, with an increasing concern with shifting and emerging genres and multimodal texts. The final chapters focus on the development of the ELT profession in a broad sense, both in terms of cutting edge research and in terms of teacher growth and change in an increasingly complex and demanding global environment.

The spread of English is often presented as an inexorable and natural expansion, outside the control of government and non-government agencies, similar to the ideology of 'manifest destiny' that rationalized US imperialist expansion in the 19th and 20th centuries. At the same time its teaching is often assumed to be an inherent good, or at the other extreme, vilified as a threat to fragile and precarious linguistic ecologies. Our hope is that this handbook will, in some way, contribute to building the knowledge base and capability of various agencies and individuals to direct and control this expansion and shape its impact on complex and multiple linguistic and pedagogic communities, both local and global. Effectiveness and efficiency of ELT, and provision of equitable opportunities to all learners to acquire English (and other languages), are clearly important goals embedded throughout the handbook. However, informed and careful planning in ELT needs to focus not only on maximizing such elements in an increasingly complex, shifting and changing environment, but on ensuring balance and harmony among multiple elements. This is also a central goal of this handbook.

Acknowledgements

This two-volume handbook would not have been possible without the cooperation and enthusiasm of a large number of people. First and foremost we would like to express our appreciation to the 84 authors from all over the world who contributed in such original and insightful ways to the 69 chapters of the handbook. Their attention to detail and responsiveness to our editorial requests and suggestions helped enormously in completing this ambitious project.

A particular debt of gratitude goes to our friends, colleagues, and graduate students in both Hong Kong and Toronto who assisted in multiple ways during the editorial process. Eila Thomas helped establish contacts with prospective authors and was also responsible for the initial formatting and content and reference checking of the chapters. Hyunjung Shin continued this process at a later stage and helped in particular with the final proofreading. Xinmin Zhang and Jane Lockwood played a major role in developing the subject index. Special thanks also to Scarlet Poon for her work on the early formatting of the chapters and to Eunice Jam who took on the daunting task of getting the whole manuscript ready for the printer. We deeply appreciate their contributions, especially since they devoted time, energy, and enthusiasm to the project at demanding times in their professional lives—and even claimed to enjoy it!

We would also like to acknowledge the support (and patience!) of our editors at Kluwer Academic Publishers and later at Springer. In the initial stages of the project Joy Carp's encouragement provided a major impetus, and Renée De Boo's help was invaluable in identifying authors and topics and compiling the Table of Contents. Marie Sheldon put the wind back in our sails mid-way through the project and her unflagging support enabled us to bring the project to completion. Mary Panarelli was always available to answer questions about the finer points of style and format and shepherded the manuscript into the final production stages, with Kristina Wiggins offering invaluable support to complete the project. Finally, we would like to acknowledge the anonymous reviewers who made extremely useful suggestions on the initial proposal for the handbook and the copy editors who helped shape the final manuscript in a thousand small ways.

Financial support for the editorial process was provided by the Education Faculty of the University of Hong Kong as well as through support for graduate assistantships from both the University of Hong Kong and the University of Toronto. We would also like to express our deep appreciation to colleagues at the Faculty of Education, University of Hong Kong, and the Modern Language Centre of the Ontario Institute for Studies in Education of the University of Toronto, whose advice and encouragement was invaluable.

Last, but not least, our love and gratitude to our families for their understanding and support. This project has also been a part of their lives over a period of several years and they will no doubt be extremely happy to see it bound and dispatched so that we can all move on to additional personal opportunities and professional challenges.

In conclusion, as editors, we feel privileged to have had the opportunity to bring together this comprehensive survey of issues and trends in the field of English language teaching (ELT). The dialogues with authors and between ourselves, and the in-depth reading and re-reading of chapters, have extended our own appreciation of both the empirical basis for policy and practice, and the theoretical constructs that jostle for position in this still emerging field. However, what stands out as particularly significant for us at this point is the complexity of the moral dimensions of ELT in the context of the unrelenting spread of English. Teachers, policy-makers, and researchers—we are all implicated in the shaping of social and linguistic spaces where identities are being negotiated and personal and professional opportunities are being constructed or constricted. Our heartfelt thanks once again to all those who have contributed to our own growth in understanding of, and sensitivity to, the complexity of these issues. We hope that the handbook acts as a catalyst for reflection and dialogue aimed not only at increasing the effectiveness of ELT, but also at creating ecologically viable and sustainable multilingual societies.

Jim Cummins
Chris Davison

July 2006

Section 1:

The Global Scope and Politics of ELT: Critiquing Current Policies and Programs

SECTION 1

THE GLOBAL SCOPE AND POLITICS OF ELT:

Critiquing current policies and programs

JIM CUMMINS AND CHRIS DAVISON

INTRODUCTION

Language teaching research and theory have traditionally focused on issues of effectiveness and efficiency: What is the best method for teaching a second or foreign language? What is the optimal age for starting the teaching of a new language? What emphasis should be placed on each of the "four language skills"—speaking, listening, reading, and writing—for optimal outcomes? And more recently, the effectiveness of literature has expanded to include the role of technology in second or foreign language teaching: Is computer assisted language learning (CALL) effective in improving proficiency? Is CALL cost-effective? How should teachers use computers in the classroom to promote learning?

These are all legitimate issues for policy makers and educators to consider. However, when considered in isolation from the contexts, purposes, and politics of language teaching and learning, these questions of technical efficiency are naïve and unhelpful. Many educators and applied linguists might initially concur with statements such as *"language teaching should attempt to promote authentic communication in the target language,"* or *"better outcomes will result from starting language teaching as early as possible in children's schooling,"* or *"bilingual instruction will produce better outcomes in the target language than teaching the language as a school subject."* When presented in isolation, statements such as these may appear persuasive and almost common sense. However, as the chapters in this first section of the handbook make clear, language teaching cannot be reduced to a one-dimensional set of prescriptions. We use language in complex and constantly evolving ways depending on whom we are communicating with, the purposes of our communication, the history of our relationship, and the varieties of language to which we have access.

In a similar way, the teaching of languages will vary according to sociopolitical and economic contexts in ways that defy simplistic prescriptions that focus on effectiveness in a vacuum. For example, when English is taught in former colonial contexts, the language carries complex baggage related to its historical role in establishing and reinforcing patterns of power relations both between colonizer and colonized and within the colonized population. In non-colonial contexts, access to English is also associated with social stratification both with respect to who gets access and the social advantages of access. However, in other respects the sociopolitical dynamics and pedagogical realities are quite different than in former colonial contexts. In non-colonial contexts where it is seen as a "foreign" language, English has traditionally been regarded as the polite guest that knows its place and does not obviously intrude into the sphere of the dominant language; by contrast, in former colonial contexts, English has frequently been proclaimed the only language with educational and economic legitimacy with the result that students' mother tongues have been largely banished from educational and economic life.

Regardless of the sociopolitical and historical context, the embrace of English is increasingly characterized by a certain ambivalence. The instantaneous culture of an Information Age global economy has taken English out of the box—it can no longer be neatly packaged and controlled by governments or even publishing companies. At the same time as they commit vast amounts of money to expand the teaching of English in schools, governments around the world also express concern that English words are infiltrating the lexicon of the national language(s) and English-medium cultural artifacts (films, music, books, Internet content, etc.) are constricting the space available for indigenous cultural expression. The rapid spread of English is seen as threatening cultural sovereignty, particularly in light of the demand by the United States that cultural "products" be treated no differently than any other commodity within a "free" global market.

The papers in this first section all acknowledge that the teaching of English is as much an ideological as a pedagogical enterprise. In the opening chapter, Pennycook traces the historical relationships between ELT and colonialism. He points out that ELT originated as a professional discipline within the British empire and, in many respects, contemporary ELT reproduces colonial relations of Self and Other. He suggests that post-colonial theory has begun to articulate ways whereby marginalized groups can resist the neo-colonial power of English. However, for critical applied linguists and English language teaching professionals, there is still no clear resolution to the paradoxical requirement to teach English and about the English language, but also to develop in learners a critical awareness of the neo-colonial impact of English and encourage resistance to this impact.

Tollefson extends discussion of the ideological roots of ELT in the context of policy and pedagogical decisions regarding which language or variety of language is deemed appropriate for teaching in a range of sociopolitical and sociolinguistic contexts. He explicates the central characteristics of critical approaches and ideological orientations to medium of instruction policies in ELT. A critical approach moves beyond pedagogical issues to highlight how dominant ethnolinguistic groups use particular medium of instruction policies to retain their system of privilege, as well as how social and economic hierarchies may be challenged by alternative policies that better serve the interests of subordinated language groups. The term *ideology* in ELT tries to capture the implicit and usually unconscious assumptions about language and language behavior that fundamentally determine how human beings interpret events. Analysis of medium of instruction policies that remains at the pedagogical level is inadequate to understand the dynamics of policy options and academic outcomes. Tollefson points out, for example, that policies supporting mother tongue education can serve to maintain the social, economic, and political advantages of dominant groups (e.g. in apartheid-era South Africa) or they can represent an attempt to reclaim identities and resist dominant group hegemony (e.g. in the United States).

The chapters by Obondo and Ramanathan highlight the tensions between English medium instruction and mother tongue teaching in Africa and India. Both chapters also illustrate the necessity to examine how medium-of-instruction policies and practices intersect with the broader societal power structure. The central issue is not whether English-medium or vernacular-medium instruction is inherently superior but rather how best to provide access to strong educational development, together with English literacy, for students across social class and income boundaries.

Obondo presents examples drawn from different African countries that show the negative consequences of imposing a monolingual "English only" language policy in multilingual and multicultural Africa. She suggests that the African experience illustrates the operation of *linguicism* (Phillipson, 1992) that ensures educational success and social advancement only for speakers of the language that dominates political and economic structures. Linguicism operates in such a way that those who are excluded from access to the power structure believe that they will gain access only by acquiring the relevant European colonial language. Thus, they develop negative perceptions about their own indigenous languages and often protest vehemently against attempts to promote indigenous languages as languages for education and social empowerment. Obondo argues for an inclusive multilingual language policy in which indigenous African languages are used as the primary languages of schooling. English would be taught effectively but primarily as a subject rather than a medium of instruction. This policy direction would also make possible an inquiry-oriented transformative approach to pedagogy where students are enabled to participate much more actively and critically than is possible when their knowledge of the language of instruction is limited.

Ramanathan, focusing on Gujarati-speaking communities in India, examines how English, and the privileges associated with it, remain inaccessible to those who have been schooled through their vernacular language. This is due not to vernacular-medium schooling, in itself, but rather to the ways in which the social structure of the society is reinforced by pedagogical practices and curricular materials. She highlights the role of three inter-related socio-educational practices: (a) educational policies at national and state levels regarding medium of instruction, (b) curricular practices involving a focus on English literature to the exclusion of English language, (c) different pedagogical assumptions evident in the textbooks available in Gujarati-medium and English-medium classrooms. In English-medium classrooms populated largely by students from middle-class backgrounds, textbooks foster the voices and opinions of students, whereas the opposite is the case for the English textbooks used in Gujarati-medium classrooms. Thus, middle-class students in English-medium classrooms are encouraged to see themselves as individuals with perspectives that matter and that should be articulated, while students in Gujarati-medium classrooms remain in a passive role within the classroom. Thus, both medium of instruction and the content of instruction reinforce the structure of power and status in the wider society.

The next set of chapters deals with the rapid expansion of ELT in countries where English has traditionally been regarded as a foreign language: Japan, Korea, China, and Argentina. As Kanno's title indicates, despite its persistent stereotype as a homogeneous country, contemporary Japan is increasingly multilingual and multicultural. There are significant populations of people from Korean, Chinese, Brazilian, and Filipino backgrounds as well as a number of indigenous communities. Kanno points out that there has been extremely active public policy debate on ELT in recent years and sometimes the rationale for intensifying ELT (e.g. introducing it at elementary school level) is expressed in terms of "international understanding." However, the linguistic resources of minority populations are typically ignored and viewed implicitly as irrelevant to "international understanding." One gets the impression from Kanno's account of ELT policy and practice in Japan that the issues are very much in a state of flux. A strong government push to improve English language teaching (even to the extent of proposals to make English an official language) is countered by concerns that the infiltration of English will undermine Japanese culture and "corrode" the Japanese language. Newly implemented elementary school curriculum that reflects "communicative" language teaching principles is negated by secondary school curriculum firmly entrenched in a grammar-translation orientation designed to prepare students for university entrance examinations. These debates about policy and practice mirror those in other countries and undoubtedly will play themselves out over the coming decades.

Shin highlights the huge amount of money, time, and effort spent in studying English in Korea and the nationwide desire to be fluent in English. As in many other countries, more affluent parents arrange for their children to have private lessons in English to supplement the instruction they receive in the education system. She points out that the increased expectations of students and parents have brought enormous social and institutional pressure on Korean English teachers to turn out highly proficient speakers of English. In its pursuit of "authentic" English, the government has mandated that English be used as the medium of instruction in English classes to the greatest extent possible. According to Shin, the new Korean English-only policy went beyond the mere discussion of language of instruction and perpetuated the notion of the native speaker as the ideal language teacher. Korean English teachers, however, have resisted the dominant ideology embedded in the policy and recreated themselves as ELT professionals who know how to teach English to Korean students more effectively than do native speakers who frequently lack teacher qualifications and knowledge of the local context. Drawing from the work of Wallace (2002), Shin argues for a focus on developing a "global literate English" through critical forms of pedagogy that would harness English to address issues that resonate locally but have global implications. Clearly, implementation of this pedagogical approach to ELT might be advanced significantly if more case studies were available in different national contexts that documented the concrete pedagogical realities of critically-oriented classroom instruction.

Wang traces the gradual shift of ELT instruction in China during the past 30 years from grammar-translation and audio-lingual approaches through a more communicative-oriented approach which is currently shifting towards an emphasis on task-based teaching. Teaching of English now begins at the elementary (primary) school level and a range of textbooks are being developed to address the specifications of the new curriculum. Teachers are being encouraged to take advantage of technological tools such as TV and radio programs, English language magazines, computers, the Internet, distance language teaching, and other multimedia resources. Obviously, for these changes to be implemented successfully, extensive professional development of teachers is required. Wang's account suggests that while expanded teacher training is a central part of the implementation plan for the new curriculum, there is also the expectation that teachers will take the initiative in changing their traditional role definition from being simply the transmitter of knowledge and skills to a very different conception of what it means to teach English. She points out, for example, that the teaching objectives postulated in the new curriculum specify that language teaching is more than just teaching knowledge and skills. It includes caring for students' affective needs, developing their learning strategies, widening their cultural horizons, and establishing international perspectives through the process of language learning.

The situation of ELT in Argentina differs from that of the Asian countries discussed above insofar as there is a long tradition of English teaching within the private school system. Tocalli-Beller points out that within the private sector there is a large number of Spanish-English bilingual schools, some of which were established in the 19th century as ethnic schools by the first British settlers. Education legislation passed in 1996 has made English compulsory in all Argentine schools. The implementation of the new education law has been challenging for many schools in Argentina. The law mandates a content-based curriculum but the infrastructure with respect to both resources and teacher training has been inadequate to fully implement this mandate. As in many other countries, there is also pressure on teachers to shift from traditional transmission-oriented instructional approaches to student-centered approaches, a shift resisted by many teachers. Despite the change in instructional emphasis at the policy level, Tocalli-Beller points out that there is considerable uncertainty as to how to integrate language and content and how that integration could be most effectively realized in terms of curriculum and actual classroom practice. The gap in ELT provision between the private and public sectors with respect to age of introduction of the language, the resources available, time allocation, and number of years of instruction is likely to remain for many years to come.

The next set of chapters analyze the complex and rapidly changing situation of ELT in the European Union (EU). Phillipson argues that English is rapidly becoming a "second" rather than a "foreign" language in Europe. He highlights the tensions between the stated commitment of the EU to maintaining linguistic diversity and the escalating expansion in the functions that English serves within the EU. This expansion potentially reduces the range of functions that other languages serve and the cultural and institutional space available to them. Phillipson notes that it is still unclear whether the learning and use of English will remain an additive process, one that increases the repertoire of language competence of individuals and the society, or whether English threatens the viability of other languages through processes of domain loss and linguistic hierarchization. In the latter case, the spread of English together with its political and cultural baggage represents a threat to the linguistic ecology of Europe. The change in this ecology can be appreciated in the context of 2005 data from the United Kingdom that shows a sharp decline in the numbers of secondary level students studying modern languages. In 2004, approximately one-third of secondary schools required students to study a modern language beyond age 14, but by 2005 that figure had declined to one-quarter (http://news.bbc.co.uk/1/hi/education/4404998.stm). The fact that speakers of the dominant language see little need to acquire other languages reinforces Phillipson's concern about the rapid hierarchization of languages within the EU. He argues that restoration of a healthy linguistic ecology requires a renewed and more active commitment to multilingualism in education and other institutional spheres.

While Phillipson expresses reservations about conceptualizing English as a *lingua franca* because of the power imbalances inherent in the economic and cultural scope of contemporary English, Seidlhofer adopts a more positive perspective on the potential of English to serve as at least a temporary *lingua franca,* potentially available to all on an equitable basis. She argues that English can function in complementary rather than competitive relation to other languages. For this to happen, English as a Lingua Franca (ELF) must be conceptualized as *common property,* distinct from and independent of English as a native language. This, in turn, requires scientific description of how English is used as a *lingua franca*. The urgency of this reconceptualization is derived from the fact that second language acquisition policy, practice, and research typically operate from the basis of a native-speaker model and tends to construct non-native speakers as defective communicators. Seidlhofer's research in the context of the *Vienna-Oxford International Corpus of English* (VOICE) project aims to position ELF as a legitimate variety of English that is not in competition with other languages and thus does not occupy cultural and institutional space that other languages currently claim. This is a hugely ambitious project whose ultimate impact will not be fully realized for decades. It is intriguing, however, to see empirical lexicographic research mobilized, with the full support of "establishment" institutions such as Oxford University Press, publisher of the Oxford English Dictionary, to counter the hegemony of the "standard" variety of English that carries "establishment" values. Only time will tell whether the reservations that Phillipson expresses about the recognition of English as *lingua franca* or the legitimation of English as *lingua franca* that Seidlhofer proposes will lead to a healthier linguistic ecology in Europe and other parts of the world.

Jessner and Cenoz extend this discussion by noting that English is increasingly being taught as a *third* language both in Europe and other parts of the world. In some cases, English instruction takes place in the context of a bilingual program involving the national language and a minority language. For example, in the Basque Autonomous Community in Spain, English instruction is added to various forms of Basque/Spanish bilingual education. In other contexts, students speak a minority language in their homes and school instruction takes place primarily through the national language with English taught as a foreign language. Jessner and Cenoz review recent psycholinguistic research on third language acquisition and trilingualism showing that the acquisition of an L3 shares many characteristics with the acquisition of an L2 but there are also some significant differences. For example, the L3 acquisition process is influenced not just by L1 (as in second language acquisition) but also by L2. In addition, the cognitive and linguistic systems of multilingual speakers are clearly distinct from those of monolingual speakers as a result of the interaction and interdependence of the multiple languages. Research into the educational dimensions of third language acquisition is in its infancy but a number of studies carried out in the Basque Autonomous Community report that higher levels of bilingualism are positively related to higher levels of proficiency in English, taught as a third language. This suggests that the positive transfer of knowledge, skills, and strategies across languages observed in bilingual contexts operates also in trilingual contexts. Many issues that have been debated over decades in second language acquisition research and policy are now resurfacing in the context of third language acquisition: for example, what is the optimal age to introduce the teaching of a third language? Is instruction through the medium of three languages organizationally feasible and educationally sound? Natural laboratories such as the Basque Autonomous Community and many other contexts around the world will undoubtedly provide at least partial answers to these questions in coming years.

The next set of chapters in this section address issues related to ELT in countries in which English has long dominated and controlled public life and in which its pre-eminent status has been traditionally taken for granted, that is the United States, Canada and the United Kingdom (UK). Lo Bianco analyzes the concern, even paranoia, that grips a significant segment of the US population about the stability and status of English in the face of increasing immigration, primarily from Spanish-speaking countries, and the partial recognition of Spanish in some institutional contexts (e.g. voter information and bilingual education in some states). He points out that the US Congress has been requested on many occasions to declare English the official language of the United States. There is clearly no rational basis to the perceived need to protect the English language "in the world's most powerful political assembly, in the world's most powerful commercial economy, in the world's heartland of entrepreneurialism, and the world's greatest deployer of cultural products (especially English-mediated music and film)." However, the process is instructive for understanding processes of language planning and their intersections with societal power relations. In the US context, persuasive discourse, broadcast throughout the media, associates English with particular social and economic benefits (e.g. national belonging, patriotic citizenship, opportunity and progress) in contrast to the "stifling ethnic collectivisms" associated with language maintenance. A false "either-or" dichotomy is established and consent is manufactured among the general population for social and educational policies (e.g. English-only instruction) that legitimize schooling provision that produces students with minimal levels of literacy in L1 and literacy levels in English which lead only to poverty-level jobs (or crime and jail).

Fleming's chapter directs the spotlight to the United States' northern neighbor, Canada, and shifts the focus from school-age learners of English to adults. The Canadian government has been unequivocal in its pursuit of immigrants, particularly those who are highly educated and already speak one of the two official languages, English or French. Canadian aspirations for immigration project a one-third increase from 2005 to 2010, from approximately 220,000 per year to 330,000 per year. In this respect, Canada distinguishes itself from countries that view immigration ambivalently as a potential threat to social cohesion. The Canadian government views immigration as the fuel that drives the economic engine in an era of ageing population and declining birthrate.

Canada provides language programs for adult immigrants that compare very favorably to those provided by other settlement countries. However, as Fleming points out, Canadian provision is sometimes accompanied by a certain smugness that fails to critically engage with the limitations of its immigration policy in general and the limitations of its English language provision in particular. Fleming suggests that the focus of instructional provision on the lower levels of English language learning and on language instruction oriented towards job creation is overly narrow. It fails to engage with broader issues of identity formation and the struggles of New Canadian adults to recreate their personal and professional identities in a context that is discriminatory on multiple fronts (English "accent," recognition of qualifications, insistence on "Canadian experience" for employment opportunities, etc.). From the perspectives of both social justice and economic productivity, Canadian policies, according to Fleming, should broaden their focus to include identity as a dynamic constituent of social and economic participation.

Bourne focuses on recent attempts in the UK to align policy and practice in relation to students who are learning English as an additional language (EAL) with the comprehensive educational reforms introduced in the late 1990s. These reforms have included development of a national curriculum, a centrally-driven focus on literacy instruction, and the monitoring and setting of targets for student attainment. Educational policy has recognized that cultural and linguistic diversity is the norm rather than the exception in UK schools and has attempted to mainstream provision for ELT so that it becomes the responsibility of all teachers and school leaders rather than the responsibility only of specialist language teachers. The focus is on raising educational attainment for *all* students. Numerous specific initiatives have been undertaken at a national level to provide teachers and school leaders with the support they need to implement appropriate instruction in mainstream classes to enable EAL students to access the curriculum.

Although the process is in its early stages, the commitment to "mainstream" ELT provision in the UK is impressive and goes beyond what most other English-speaking countries have attempted. In both Canada and the United States, for example, the teaching of English to newcomers is still largely seen as the responsibility of specialist ESL teachers. At the secondary level, most subject matter teachers have received minimal support in integrating the teaching of content and language for English learners (or other students). Consequently, they typically know very little about how to teach their subjects to students who are in the process of learning English. Policy and practice in relation to ELT frequently represent little more than footnotes to broader educational initiatives. In these contexts, the generic student reflected in curriculum documents and assessment mandates is still white, middle-class, monolingual, and monocultural. Bourne recognizes the immense challenge that the UK has undertaken in its attempt to change this mindset but her documentation of the recent initiatives suggest that other countries might learn from the UK experience.

One area where more could be achieved in the UK context, she suggests, is in exploring ways in which students' home languages might be incorporated into instruction. As in the case of ELT, such initiatives should be undertaken as part of a broader strategy to raise student achievement and combat the impact of poverty and exclusion rather than as an end in itself.

The chapter by Meyer also examines how the diversity represented by ELL and minoritized students is addressed in the context of large-scale top-down educational reform. The *No Child Left Behind* (NCLB) legislation in the United States mandated that schools be held accountable for ensuring that all students make "adequate yearly progress" as measured by standardized tests. This mandate extends not only to the overall progress of students in a school but also to the progress of subgroups of students such as English learners, low-income students, etc. These centralized mandates are backed up by punitive accountability requirements. On the positive side, NCLB has put ELL and other marginalized groups of students on the accountability map. However, it has also resulted in narrowing of curricula, excessive testing, and extensive teaching to the test. Some school districts have even eliminated recess so that more instructional time can be squeezed into the day.

Meyer's concern with the one-size-fits-all mandate of NCLB is that local realities and their historical contexts are dismissed as irrelevant to the overall goal of boosting students' academic achievement. She reviews ethnographic accounts of four English language teaching contexts and shows the inherent difficulty of trying to address complex local instructional circumstances with uniform policies, abstract theories, packaged methodologies, and national or state standards. She argues that definitions of quality education in particular settings, and the ways in which these definitions are realized in schools and classrooms, must be co-constructed by communities and educators within the local and historical context of each school and community. Quality education must be community-based education.

Meyer's argument is not against educational reform in itself but against top-down micromanagement of instruction and assessment that ignores local realities and aspirations. She notes the parallels between the US situation (the 'Center' imposing a one-size-fits-all frame on local realities) and the ongoing debates in the teaching of English internationally regarding the dominance of instructional policies and methodologies imposed by academic and commercial interests in Western English-speaking countries. Pre-packaged "solutions" are exported from the Center to the Periphery with the presumption that they are valid, universally applicable, and culturally appropriate. Thus, Meyer suggests that educators and policy-makers in English-speaking Center countries have much to learn from the insights of Periphery scholars who have alerted us to the coercive power relations inherent in, and the counter-productive nature of, one-way transmission of "expertise" from Center to Periphery. Students' language learning and academic achievement will be furthered much more effectively by a collaborative process in which policy and practice are co-constructed through dialogue and equitable exchange.

Collectively the chapters in this first section highlight the fact that facile prescriptions and formulaic solutions regarding "best methods" fail to take account of the complex social and historical contexts of ELT around the world. Research, theory, and international experience are all relevant to language planning and educational policy-making; however, they must be interpreted in light of local sociopolitical and educational realities. It is insufficient, for example, to identify an approach to teaching English that promises to be effective in a particular context without simultaneously considering issues such as the impact of this approach on other languages of a community or on existing patterns of social stratification. Language planners and educators must be concerned not only with planting the seeds of English in soil with proper nutrients, they must also take account of interactions with other plants so that the ecology of the entire garden is enhanced. If English thrives by choking the roots of other plants or by denying them sunlight then the garden as a whole suffers. Thus, ELT must be planned and implemented in such a way that it enhances rather than undermines the social ecology of the entire community.

CHAPTER 1

ELT AND COLONIALISM

ALASTAIR PENNYCOOK

The University of Technology Sydney, Australia

ABSTRACT

There are several significant ways in which we need to understand the relationships between ELT and colonialism. The first and perhaps most obvious, is historical: If we wish to understand the development of ELT beyond the narrow confines of Europe and North America, we clearly have to engage with its history within the British and American Empires. The second is political and economic: There are many ways in which the current spread of English, teaching methods, and textbooks can be seen as a recapitulation, if not an intensification, of (neo-)colonial relations. And the third is cultural, by which I mean that the conjuncture between ELT and colonialism has had long-lasting effects on the theories, practices, and beliefs of ELT: From classroom practices to beliefs about the cultural makeup of our students, many aspects of ELT reproduce cultural constructs of colonialism. This chapter will give an overview of these concerns and will also discuss how postcolonial perspectives on ELT may provide a way out of these cycles.

INTRODUCTION

English expanded from a language spoken by about 6 million people in 1600, a little over 8 million in 1700, around 30 million in 1800, to about 120 million in 1900. Thus its growth can be seen first in the context of the growth of England as an imperial power, and second in the context of the spread of English as an imperial language. But the massive expansion in the global use of English, from just over 100 million in 1900 to a vast number (perhaps one billion) of users of English as a second language around the world, occurred in the context of decolonization, the decline of Britain as an imperial power, and the rise of the US as the new global power. This neo-colonial expansion of ELT will be discussed in the next section. In this section, I shall discuss some important concerns to do with ELT and colonialism. First of all, in spite of the expansion in the number of English users by 1900, it is important to understand that British colonial language policy was not massively in favor of spreading English.

Colonial language policies can be seen as constructed between four poles (for much greater detailed analysis, see Pennycook, 1998; 2000): First, the position of colonies within a capitalist empire and the need to produce docile and compliant workers and consumers to fuel capitalist expansion; second, the discourses of Anglicism and liberalism with their insistence on the European need to bring civilization to the world through English; third, local contingencies of class, ethnicity, race, and economic conditions that dictated the distinctive development of each colony; and fourth, the discourses of Orientalism with their insistence on exotic histories, traditions, and nations in decline. By and large, these competing discourses on the requirements for colonial education produced language policies broadly favoring education in local languages (Brutt-Griffler, 2002): Vernacular education was seen as the best means of educating a compliant workforce and of inculcating moral and political values that would make the colonial governance of large populations more possible. English was seen as a dangerous weapon, an unsafe thing, too much of which would lead to a discontented class of people who were not prepared to abide by the colonial system.

There are, of course, ample examples of imperial rhetoric extolling the virtues of English, from Charles Grant's argument in 1797 that:

> the first communication, and the instrument of introducing the rest, must be the English language; this is a key which will open to them a world of new ideas, and policy alone might have impelled us, long since, to put it into their hands... (Bureau of Education, 1920, p. 83)

through Macaulay's infamous Minute of 1835 (1972), to Frederick Lugard's views on the use of English at Hong Kong University in the early part of the 20th century:

> I would emphasize the value of English as the medium of instruction. If we believe that British interests will be thus promoted, we believe equally firmly that graduates, by the mastery of English, will acquire the key to a great literature and the passport to a great trade. (1910, p. 4)

These arguments, however, had more to do with the construction of English as a language with particular benefits, an issue that will be discussed below, than with the expansion of English beyond a narrow elite.

The weight of argument by colonial administrators was much more in favor of education in local languages. In the 1884 report on education (Straits Settlements), E. C. Hill, the Inspector of Schools for the colony, explained his reasons against increasing the provision of education in English that went beyond concerns about the costs and the difficulties in finding qualified teachers to teach English:

> As pupils who acquire a knowledge of English are invariably unwilling to earn their livelihood by manual labour, the immediate result of affording an English education to any large number of Malays would be the creation of a discontented class who might become a source of anxiety to the community. (p. 171)

This position was extremely common and is echoed, for example, by Frank Swettenham's argument in the *Perak Government Gazette*:

> I am not in favour of extending the number of 'English' schools except where there is some palpable desire that English should be taught. Whilst we teach children to read and write and count in their own languages, or in Malay...we are *safe* (emphasis in original). (6 July 1894)

Thus, as Loh Fook Seng (1970) comments, "modern English education for the Malay then is ruled out right from the beginning as an unsafe thing" (p. 114).

In an article on vernacular education in the State of Perak, the Inspector of Schools, H. B. Collinge (cited in Straits Settlements, 1894), explained the benefits of education in Malay as taking "thousands of our boys...away from idleness," helping them at the same time to "acquire habits of industry, obedience, punctuality, order, neatness, cleanliness and general good behaviour." Thus, after a boy had attended school for a year or so, he was "found to be less lazy at home, less given to evil habits and mischievous adventure, more respectful and dutiful, much more willing to help his parents, and with sense enough not to entertain any ambition beyond following the humble home occupations he has been taught to respect" (p. 177). And not only does the school inculcate such habits of dutiful labor but it also helps colonial rule more generally since:

> if there is any lingering feeling of dislike of the 'white man', the school tends greatly to remove it, for the people see that the Government has really their welfare at heart in providing them with this education, free, without compulsion, and with the greatest consideration for their Mohammedan sympathies. (p. 177)

Similarly, in Hong Kong, E. J. Eitel (Report, 1882), the Inspector of Schools, argued that by studying Chinese classics, students learn "a system of morality, not merely a doctrine, but a living system of ethics." Thus, they learn "filial piety, respect for the aged, respect for authority, respect for the moral law." In the Government schools, by contrast, where English books are taught from which religious education is excluded, "no morality is implanted in the boys" (p. 70). Thus, the teaching of Chinese is:

> of higher advantage to the Government…boys strongly imbued with European civilization whilst cut away from the restraining influence of Confucian ethics lose the benefits of education, and the practical experience of Hong Kong is that those who are thoroughly imbued with the foreign spirit, are bad in morals. (p. 70)

The implications of this understanding of colonial language policy are several. Education in vernacular languages was promoted both as a means of colonial governance and as an Orientalist project for the maintenance of cultural formations. While this has many implications for an understanding of mother tongue education and modes of governance (see Pennycook, 2002), it is also significant for the role of English both before and after the formal ending of colonialism. The effects of Anglicist rhetoric did not produce widespread teaching of English, but did produce widespread images of English as a superior language that could bestow immense benefits on its users, a topic to which I shall turn below. Meanwhile the language had been coveted and acquired by social and economic elites with whom the British were now negotiating independence. This was to have significant implications for the neo-colonial development of English in the latter half of the 20th century. Finally, however, although English teaching was relatively limited as an imperial project, the very scale of the empire and the ELT that did occur within it has ironically often been overlooked.

Thus, in spite of the relatively limited role of ELT within the British Empire, this new global position of English nevertheless had significant implications for the development of ELT. Indeed, the origins of a great deal of thinking about English and English language teaching have their origins in the colonial context rather than in what is often assumed to be their provenance in Britain itself. In his history of English language teaching, Howatt (1984, p. 71) comments that ELT forked into two streams at the end of the 18th century; one being the development of ELT within the Empire, the other being the influence of continental Europe on ELT. Although Howatt is no doubt right in suggesting that to study the development of ELT throughout the British Empire would entail a vast and separate series of studies, it is a shame that he opts so completely for the European side of the fork, and even more so if one considers that it may indeed have been the imperial fork that was more significant. That is to say, it was not so much that theories and practices of ELT were developed in Britain (with a strong European influence) and then exported to the Empire, but rather that the Empire became the crucial context of development of ELT, from where theories and practices were then imported into Britain.

This argument is akin to Gauri Viswanathan's (1989) observation that although "the amazingly young history of English literature as a subject of study (it is less than a hundred and fifty years old) is frequently noted," far less appreciated is "the irony that English literature appeared as a subject in the curriculum of the colonies long before it was institutionalized in the home country" (pp. 2-3). Viswanathan shows that because of the existence of an educated class of Indians who already exerted considerable control over their people, and because of the policy of religious neutrality in education, which prevented the British from promoting a firmer program of moral discipline through the educational system, English literature was called into service "to perform the functions of those social institutions (such as the church) that, in England, served as the chief disseminators of value, tradition, and authority" (p. 7). The development of English literature as a subject, then, was a response to the particular needs of the colonial administration in India. It was only later that this newly developed cultural curriculum of English literature, designed to develop moral and traditional views in a secular state, was imported into Britain and used to fulfill similar functions.

When Howatt (1984) opts for the European rather than the Imperial path of ELT development—after mentioning the publication of John Miller's *The Tutor* in Bengal in 1797—he thus lets the crucial 19th century colonial path of ELT development grow cold until he picks it up again with reference to the influential Michael West, the author of the *New Method Readers* (1927 onwards). The development of these readers was a result of an experiment also conducted in Bengal and reported in West's (1926) *Bilingualism (with Special Reference to Bengal)*. West (1888-1973), who worked in the Indian Education Service, and many other English language educators such as Thomas Prendergast (1806-1886) before him who worked in the Indian Civil Service, were highly influential in the development of ELT. More recently, the "Bangalore Project," or "Communicational Teaching Project," which ran from 1979 to 1984 under the guidance of the Madras British Council Officer, N. S. Prabhu, and was an attempt to explore the belief that the development of second language competence requires not so much systematized second language input as conditions under which learners cope with communication through a "procedural syllabus" (see Prabhu, 1987), has had a significant effect on the development of task-based learning elsewhere.

While at one level it is tempting to view this project as yet another in the long line of inappropriate and self-interested British Council-brokered projects (see Rajan, 1992; Thikoo, 2001), at another level it is important to acknowledge that such examples suggest that it was ELT that spread from India rather than in some other direction. What I am therefore suggesting here is that it is not merely the case that British colonial administrators tried out their teaching schemes in the empire rather than in Britain, nor merely that the empire was a more obvious site for developing English teaching than was Europe, but rather that the development of ELT was profoundly influenced by such contexts. Europeans have always attempted to write the colonized, and what they perceive as the periphery, out of the histories of what happened in the colonies (aside, of course, from treacheries, debaucheries, duplicities, and so forth), making all that has been deemed progressive to be only a product of European endeavor. Yet the development of English, the development of ELT, the development of English literature could not have happened without the colonial encounter. As I argue below, this has had profound and often pernicious effects on ELT.

THE NEO-COLONIAL POLITICS OF ELT

While, as I have suggested above, it is important to understand the relationships between ELT and colonialism in terms of the historical development of ELT in the colonial context, it is equally or more important to understand the ways in which relationships between ELT and colonialism continue into the present. This happens in two principal ways: the material and the cultural. By cultural relations, I mean the discursive effects of colonialism, the ways in which images of the Self and Other, the Occident and Orient, have become closely allied with the ELT project. This will be the topic of the following section. In this section, I shall look at the economic and political relations of ELT in terms of neo-colonial relations around ELT. I shall only give a brief overview of this position, however, since it is also expounded in some of the following articles.

Tollefson (2000) introduces some of the concerns about English as a neo-colonial language by pointing to a paradox: "At a time when English is widely seen as a key to the economic success of nations and the economic well-being of individuals, the spread of English also contributes to significant social, political, and economic inequalities" (p. 8). Thus, on the one hand some see English as fulfilling "the perceived need for one language of international communication. Through English, people worldwide gain access to science, technology, education, employment, and mass culture, while the chance of political conflict is also reduced"; on the other hand, amongst other things, "the spread of English presents a formidable obstacle to education, employment, and other activities requiring English proficiency" (p. 9). Phillipson's (1992) book, *Linguistic Imperialism*, remains the clearest articulation of this position. As Tollefson explains:

> Phillipson's analysis places English squarely in the center of the fundamental sociopolitical processes of imperialism, neo-colonialism, and global economic restructuring. In this view, the spread of English can never be neutral but is always implicated in global inequality. Thus Phillipson, in contrast to Kachru, argues that the spread of English is a positive development for some people (primarily in core countries) and harmful to others (primarily in the periphery). The spread of English, in this view, is a result of policies adopted by core countries to bring about the worldwide hegemony of English, for the benefit of core country institutions and individuals. (p. 13)

What Phillipson (1992) is arguing, then, is that English is interlinked with the continuing neo-colonial patterns of global inequality. He explains:

> We live in a world characterised by inequality—of gender, nationality, race, class, income, and language. To trace and understand the linkages between English linguistic imperialism and inequality in the political and economic spheres will require us to look at the rhetoric and legitimation of ELT (for instance, at protestations that it is a 'neutral', 'non-political' activity) and relate what ELT claims to be doing to its structural functions. (pp. 46-47)

Phillipson (1992) is therefore arguing that ELT plays an important role in the structure of global inequality. The notion of *imperialism* in *linguistic imperialism* thus refers not only to the imperialism of English (the ways in which English has spread around the world), but also to imperialism more generally (the ways in which some parts of the world are dominated politically, economically, and culturally by other parts of the world). It is not a coincidence, therefore, that English is the language of the great imperial power of the 19th century (Great Britain) and also of the great imperial (or neocolonial) power of the 20th (and probably 21st) century, the USA.

Phillipson (1994) convincingly shows how, for example:

> A vast amount of the aid effort has...gone into teacher education and curriculum development in and through English, and other languages have been neglected. A Western-inspired monolingual approach was adopted that ignored the multilingual reality and cultural specificity of learners in diverse 'Third World' contexts. (p. 19)

He goes on to argue:

> In the current global economy, English is dominant in many domains, which creates a huge instrumental demand for English. There has therefore already been a penetration of the language into most cultures and education systems. (pp. 20-21)

But the challenge here is to show not only that the global spread of English can be seen as a form of imperialism that is particularly threatening to other languages and cultures, nor only that this spread of English correlates with other forms of political and economic domination and thus reflects global inequality, but rather that there is also a *causative* relationship between the promotion of English and forms of global inequality: that English helps produce and maintain inequitable global power relationships. This is of course a harder case to make on this global scale, though it is certainly possible to see, for example, how the promotion of English and the global marketing of textbooks continually reproduce a cycle of dependency.

ELT AND THE CULTURAL CONSTRUCTS OF COLONIALISM

I suggested in the first section that one of the lasting effects of ELT under colonialism was the production of images of English and of its learners. Simply put, the point here is that English, like Britain, its empire and institutions, was massively promoted as the finest and greatest medium for arts, politics, trade, and religion. At the same time, the learners of English were subjected to the imaginings of Orientalism, with its exoticized, static, and derided "Others." Thus, on the one hand, we have the cultural constructs of Orientalism—the cultures and characters of those who learn English—and on the other hand the cultural constructs of Occidentalism—the benefits and glories of the English language. As many writers on colonialism have argued (see for example, Mignolo, 2000; Singh, 1996), such discourses have continued long beyond the formal end of colonialism. Thus, not only can we see the current spread of English in terms of economic and political neo-colonial relations, but also in terms of cultural neo-colonial relations. As Bailey (1991) comments:

> The linguistic ideas that evolved at the acme of empires led by Britain and the United States have not changed as economic colonialism has replaced the direct, political management of third world nations. English is still believed to be the inevitable world language. (p. 121)

It is to a brief overview of these Occidentalist and Orientalist images that I now turn.

The 19th century was a time of immense British confidence in their own greatness, and writing on English abounded with glorifications of English and its global spread. Guest (1838; 1882) argued that English was "rapidly becoming the great medium of civilization, the language of law and literature to the Hindoo, of commerce to the African, of religion to the scattered islands of the Pacific" (p. 703). According to Read (1849, p. 48):

> Ours is the language of the arts and sciences, of trade and commerce, of civilization and religious liberty....It is a store-house of the varied knowledge which brings a nation within the pale of civilization and Christianity....Already it is the language of the Bible....So prevalent is this language already become, as to betoken that it may soon become the language of international communication for the world. (Cited in Bailey, 1991, p. 116)

According to George (1867):

> Other languages will remain, but will remain only as the obscure Patois of the world, while English will become the grand medium for all the business of government, for commerce, for law, for science, for literature, for philosophy, and divinity. Thus it will really be a universal language for the great material and spiritual interests of mankind. (p. 6)

It is not hard to see the continuity between such pronouncements and more recent rhetoric on the global spread of English: from Bryson's (1990) statement that "more than 300 million people in the world speak English and the rest, it sometimes seems, try to" (p. 1); to a dossier on *International English* (1989) for language learners that tells us that "one billion people speak English. That's 20% of the world's population" (p. 2). Consider also the statement, "many foreign leaders speak in English to international journalists" (p. 4) and the sentiments expressed in following statements: "There are millions of Christians on every continent. It's the world's most international religion. But when Christian leaders from different countries meet, the language they use is English" (p. 5). In newspaper articles such as Jenkins (1995), we are told:

> When the Warsaw Pact was wound up it was wound up in English. When the G7 meets, it meets in English...English is the global computer language. It is the language of news gathering and world entertainment. The only substantial world body that struggles to keep going in a "foreign" tongue is the French-speaking European Commission in Brussels. With luck, enlargement will put an end to that.

In many such examples we can see the continuing glorification of the spread of English.

Similar arguments suggest that people are deprived if they do not speak English, that English is the language of civilization, or that Standard English is a more developed language than any other (see Bailey, 1991; Pennycook, 1998, for more examples). There are also many claims for the superiority of English itself. Thus, the Reverend James George (1867), for example, arguing that Britain had been "commissioned to teach a noble language embodying the richest scientific and literary treasures," asserted that:

> As the mind grows, language grows, and adapts itself to the thinking of the people. Hence, a highly civilized race, will ever have a highly accomplished language. The English tongue, is in all senses a very noble one. I apply the term noble with a rigorous exactness. (p. 4)

More recently, a similar type of argument underlies Honey's (1997) contention that because of the "elaborated vocabulary and syntax" (p. 175) of Standard English, "the world has effectively decided that English is the world language" (p. 249).

One of the most bizarre and common claims is that English has more words than any other language and thus is a better medium for expression or thought than any other language. Claiborne (1983), for example, asserts, "For centuries, the English-speaking peoples have plundered the world for words, even as their military and industrial empire builders have plundered it for more tangible goods." This plundering has given English:

> ...the largest, most variegated and most expressive vocabulary in the world. The total number of English words lies somewhere between 400,000—the number of current entries in the largest English dictionaries —and 600,000—the largest figure that any expert is willing to be quoted on. By comparison, the biggest French dictionaries have only about 150,000 entries, the biggest Russian ones a mere 130,000. (p. 3)

The MacMillan dossier on *International English* (1989) reproduces the same ideas for a wider audience, claiming, "There are more than 500,000 words in the Oxford English Dictionary. Compare that with the vocabulary of German (about 200,000) and French (100,000)" (p. 2). Claiborne (1983) goes on to explain the implications of this large vocabulary:

> Like the wandering minstrel in *The Mikado*, with songs for any and every occasion, English has the right word for it—whatever 'it' may be...[Thus]...It is the enormous and variegated lexicon of English, far more than the mere numbers and geographical spread of its speakers, that truly makes our native tongue marvellous—makes it, in fact, a medium for the precise, vivid and subtle expression of thought and emotion that has no equal, past or present. (p. 4)

In case the implications of this are not clear, Claiborne goes on to claim that English is indeed "not merely a great language but the greatest" (p. 4).

Othered Learners

These, then, are the tip of the iceberg of Occidentalist discourses on English. Meanwhile, the other side of the colonial coin, the Orientalist discourses on the Other, construct cultures and language learners in particular ways. There is not space here to elaborate on these multiple discourses, so I shall focus on one element, the construction of Asian learners as passive, rote, uncreative memorizers. Located in larger discourses on Asia and other colonies that viewed other cultures as static, traditional, and unchanging, the discourses on education then started to construct learners and education systems in the same way. Thus, in an article on Chinese education in *A Cyclopedia of Education* published in 1911 (Monroe), Isaac Headland, professor in the Imperial University, Peking, explains:

> There is nothing in the Chinese course of study in the way of mathematics or science, or indeed in any line of thought, which will tend to develop the thinking faculties, such as reason or invention, and hence these faculties have lain dormant in the Chinese mind. They have never invented anything. They have stumbled upon most of the useful, practical appliances of life, and among these upon the compass, gunpowder, and printing, and, though noted for their commercial astuteness, have lacked all power to develop them into a commercial success. (p. 635)

Such views on Chinese learners were, and still are, extremely common in contexts such as Hong Kong. As Frederick Stewart wrote in his education report for 1865, "The Chinese have no *education* in the real sense of the word. No attempt is made at a simultaneous development of the mental powers. These are all sacrificed to the cultivation of memory" (p. 138). The Rev. S. R. Brown, Headmaster of the Morrison Education Society School, wrote in a report in 1844 (cited in Sweeting, 1990) that Chinese children are usually pervaded by "a universal expression of passive inanity…The black but staring, glassy eye, and open mouth, bespeak little more than stupid wonder gazing out of emptiness." This view is linked to Brown's view of Chinese schools, where a boy may learn "the names of written characters, that in all probability never conveyed to him one new idea from first to last" (p. 21). In an article on Chinese education, Addis (1889) wrote:

> In truth Chinese education is—*pace* the sinologues—no education at all. It is no 'leading out of' but a leading back to. Instead of expanding the intelligence, it contracts it; instead of broadening sympathies, it narrows them; instead of making a man honest, intelligent and brave, it has produced few who are not cunning, narrow-minded and pusillanimous. (p. 206)

These views on Chinese education and the Chinese are remarkably consistent with more current stereotypes of Chinese and other Asian students. It is hard not to see the parallel between Bateson Wright's (headmaster of the Central School in Hong Kong after Stewart) comment that the average Chinese student was "incapable of sustaining an argument, starting with false premises and cheerfully pursuing a circuitous course to the point from which he started," for which he prescribed a "rigid course of geometrical study" (cited in Sweeting, 1990, p. 322), and the widely popularized "cultural thought patterns" described by Kaplan (1966), in which Asian students thought and wrote in spirals, while Westerners wrote in straight lines. Susser's (1998) review of the ESL/EFL literature on Japan concluded that it contained "considerable Orientalism" (p. 63). It is not just that there are occasional stereotypes or factual errors; rather "these fictions have been woven into a pervasive discourse that shapes our descriptions and then our perceptions of Japanese learners and classrooms" (p. 64). Kubota (1999) makes a similar point when she shows how writing on Japanese education has:

> …tended to dichotomize Western culture and Eastern culture and to draw rigid cultural boundaries between them. They have given labels such as *individualism, self-expression, critical and analytic thinking,* and *extending knowledge* to Western cultures on the one hand, and *collectivism, harmony, indirection, memorization,* and *conserving knowledge* to Asian cultures on the other. (p. 14)

As Kubota points out, such views are based on a form of cultural determinism that reproduces colonial relations of Self and Other. Distinctions such as extending knowledge versus conserving knowledge, for example, reproduce the distinction between changing, developing, and modern cultures on the one hand, and static, conservative, and traditional cultures on the other. As I have been suggesting throughout this section, such Orientalist and Occidentalist constructions were developed in, and reproduce colonial relations.

CONCLUSIONS: POSTCOLONIAL STRATEGIES FOR ELT

The sections above suggest a cycle of reproduction of colonial relations in ELT that looks virtually impossible to break out of. Yet while it is important to consider these very real relations of material and cultural neo-colonialism in ELT, it is equally important to understand how such conditions can be changed. As Canagarajah (1999; 2000) argues, from the very beginning of colonialism, there have always been acts of resistance, not necessarily large strategies of opposition but rather "simple acts of false compliance, parody, pretence, and mimicking" that served as "strategies by which the marginalized detach themselves from the ideologies of the powerful, retain a measure of critical thinking, and gain some sense of control over their life in an oppressive situation" (2000, p. 122). Canagarajah (2000) suggests four strategies of resistance: *Discursive appropriation*, by which he means "transforming the sign system of English to represent a discourse alien to it" (p. 125); *reinterpretation strategies*, referring to the ways in which people used dominant Western discourses (such as Christianity, liberalism, humanism) to articulate their own interests and ideologies; *accommodation strategies* through which local elites started "invoking English and its discourses to accommodate their vested interests" (p. 127); and *linguistic appropriation*, where the use of different languages constructs a "system of hybrid codes" that destabilize "the integrity of the language we call English" (p. 128).

But as Canagarajah points out, such strategies of appropriation and resistance always need to be understood in the context of the very real and continuing neo-colonial power of English. There is a tendency in some domains to celebrate these processes of appropriation as if the global imperialism of English was thereby rendered irrelevant. Thus, pedagogically, we are faced with some interesting questions. How can we teach English and teach about English teaching in a way that both acknowledges the colonial and neo-colonial implications of ELT yet also allows for an understanding of the possibilities of change, resistance, and appropriation? Is it possible to teach English in such a way that we can emphasize its post-colonial possibilities without ignoring its neo-colonial limitations? Is it a contradiction to try to teach English or teach about English teaching in a way that promotes appropriation? Can we teach in order to be resisted? These are some of the dilemmas we need to confront in order to deal with the postcolonial problem of English.

REFERENCES

Addis, C. S. (1889). Education in China. *The China Review*. *XVIII*, 205–212.
Bailey, R. (1991). *Images of English: A cultural history of the language*. Ann Arbor: The University of Michigan Press.
Brutt-Griffler, J. (2002). *World English: A study of its development*. Clevedon: Multilingual Matters.
Bryson, B. (1990). *Mother tongue: The English language*. London: Hamish Hamilton.

Bureau of Education (H. Sharp, Ed.). (1920). *Selections from educational records, Part 1, 1781–1839*. Calcutta: Superintendent of Government Printing.
Canagarajah, S. (1999). *Resisting linguistic imperialism in English teaching*. Oxford: Oxford University Press.
Canagarajah, S. (2000). Negotiating ideologies through English: Strategies from the periphery. In T. Ricento (Ed.), *Ideology, politics and language policies: Focus on English* (pp. 121–132). Amsterdam: John Benjamins.
Claiborne, R. (1983). *The life and times of the English language: The history of our marvelous tongue*. London: Bloomsbury.
Education Commission Report. (1883). *Report of the Education Commission appointed by His Excellency Sir John Pope Hennessy, K.C.M.G....to consider certain questions connected with Education in Hong Kong*, 1882. Hong Kong: Hong Kong Government.
George, J. (1867). *The mission of Great Britain to the world, or some of the lessons which she is now teaching*. Toronto: Dudley and Burns.
Guest, E. (1882). *A history of English rhythms*. London: George Bell and Sons. (Original version published 1838).
Honey, J. (1997). *Language is power: The story of standard English and its enemies*. London: Faber and Faber.
Howatt, A. P. R. (1984). *A history of English language teaching*. Oxford: Oxford University Press.
International English (1989). London: MacMillan.
Jenkins, S. (1995, February 25). The Triumph of English. *The Times*.
Kaplan, R. (1966). Cultural thought patterns in intercultural education. *Language Learning*, *16*, 1–20.
Kubota, R. (1999). Japanese culture constructed by discourses: Implications of English for applied linguistics research and ESL. *TESOL Quarterly*, *33*(1), 9–35.
Loh Fook Seng, P. (1970). The nineteenth century British approach to Malay education. *Journal Pendidekan*, *1*(1), 105–115.
Lugard, F. D. (1910). *Hong Kong University. Objects, history, present position and prospects*. Hong Kong: Noronha.
Luk Hung-Kay, B. (1991). Chinese culture in the Hong Kong curriculum: Heritage and colonialism. *Comparative Education Review*, *35*(4), 650–668.
Macaulay, T. B. (1835/1972). Minute on Indian Education. In J. Clive & T. Pinney (Eds.), *Thomas Babington Macaulay. Selected writings*. Chicago: University of Chicago Press.
Mignolo, W. (2000). *Local histories/global designs: Coloniality, subaltern knowledges, and border thinking*. Princeton, NJ: Princeton University Press.
Monroe, P. (1911). *A cyclopedia of education*. New York: The MacMillan Company.
Pennycook, A. (1998). *English and the discourses of colonialism*. London: Routledge.
Pennycook, A. (2000). Language, ideology and hindsight: Lessons from colonial language policies. In T. Ricento (Ed.), *Ideology, politics and language policies: Focus on English* (pp. 49–66). Amsterdam: John Benjamins.
Pennycook, A. (2002). Language policy and docile bodies: Hong Kong and governmentality. In J. Tollefson (Ed.), *Language policies in education: Critical issues* (pp. 91–110). Mahwah, NJ: Lawrence Erlbaum.
Phillipson, R. (1992). *Linguistic imperialism*. Oxford: Oxford University Press.
Phillipson, R. (1994). English language spread policy. *International Journal of the Sociology of Language*, *107*, 7–24.
Prabhu, N. S. (1987). *Second language pedagogy*. Oxford: Oxford University Press.
Rajan, R. S. (1992). Brokering English studies: The British Council in India. In R. S. Rajan (Ed.), *The lie of the land: English literary studies in India* (pp. 130–155). Delhi: Oxford University Press.
Singh, J. (1996). *Colonial narratives/Cultural dialogues: Discoveries of India in the language of colonialism*. London: Routledge.
Stewart, F. (1865). The annual report on the state of the Government Schools for the year 1865. *Hong Kong Blue Book*. Hong Kong: Hong Kong Government.
Straits Settlements (1884). *Straits settlements annual departmental reports*. Singapore: Government Printing Office.
Straits Settlements (1894). *Straits settlements annual departmental reports*. Singapore: Government Printing Office.
Susser, B. (1998). EFL's Othering of Japan. *JALT Journal*, *20*(1), 49–82.
Sweeting, A. E. (1990). *Education in Hong Kong, pre-1841 to 1941: Fact & opinion*. Hong Kong: Hong Kong University Press.
Swettenham, F. (1894, July 6). In *Perak Government Gazette*. Perak.

Thikoo, M. (2001). Sociocultural blindspots in language curriculum renewal: Causes, consequences, cures. In W. Renandya & N. Sunga (Eds.), *Language curriculum and instruction in multicultural societies* (pp. 107–122). Singapore: SEAMEO RELC.

Tollefson, J. (2000). Policy and ideology in the spread of English. In J. K. Hall & W. Eggington (Eds.), *The sociopolitics of English language teaching* (pp. 7–21). Clevedon: Multilingual matters.

Viswanathan, G. (1989). *Masks of conquest: Literary study and British rule in India*. London: Faber & Faber.

CHAPTER 2

IDEOLOGY, LANGUAGE VARIETIES, AND ELT

JAMES W. TOLLEFSON

The University of Washington, USA

ABSTRACT

The question of which language variety should be used as a medium of instruction in ELT involves two different issues: the variety used by teachers and students in the classroom, and the target language of the learners. Both issues are usually framed as pedagogical: Which variety (or varieties) will best serve learners' educational needs? In contrast, a critical perspective views pedagogical rationales for alternative ELT policies and practices as mechanisms for justifying conventions of language teaching. Thus, critical ELT research explores the underlying ideological orientations of alternative policies and practices. This chapter summarizes research, describes current debates, and suggests future directions for research on the ideology of medium of instruction issues. It suggests that medium of instruction issues are often called into service of social agendas that determine which language groups enjoy particular economic, political, and social benefits.

INTRODUCTION

The discussion of ideology, language varieties, and ELT involves two separate questions. The first is which variety or varieties should be used by teachers and students in their day-to-day teaching and learning activities. This question focuses on the value of exclusive use of the target language (English) versus a bilingual approach that permits some use of the students' native language. The second question is which variety of English should be the target language of learners in ELT classes. Most textbooks assume that the target language is one of the major standardized varieties, usually American or British English. Both questions are usually framed as fundamentally pedagogical; that is, their answers are assumed to depend upon decisions about which variety (or varieties) will best serve learners' educational needs. Thus, the best rationales for particular classroom practices are assumed to be pedagogical ones. For example, if English-only instruction is believed to be the most effective means for increasing English proficiency, then English-only instruction is justified. One example of this line of reasoning is Porter (1990), who claims that time-on-task (i.e. the time spent using English) is the key variable in determining success in English language learning, and therefore exclusive use of English is pedagogically justified. The central pedagogical issue is the validity of her claim about the effect of time on task. Similarly, if the use of Standard English rather than students' non-standard varieties is believed to more effectively aid students in learning the standard variety, then teachers are expected to speak the standard and to encourage students to do so as well. One example of this line of reasoning is Charpentier (1997), who argues against bilingual classroom language by claiming that classroom use of English and Bislama (a vernacular spoken in

Vanuatu) "seems to lead to social, psychological, and pedagogical blockage" because students "cannot seem to figure out the respective roles and characteristics of the two codes" (p. 236).

In contrast, a critical perspective toward these medium of instruction questions seeks answers not in narrow pedagogical terms, but rather by examining the underlying ideological orientation of pedagogical rationales for alternative policies and practices. Two key concepts—critical and ideological—require explanation. Though critical language studies entail a wide range of research methodologies, theories, and perspectives, in general it refers to work that is influenced by critical theory and that foregrounds the links between language, power, and inequality (e.g. see Fairclough, 1989; Forester, 1985; Foucault, 1972; Habermas, 1985; Pennycook, 1998; Tollefson, 1991). Critical analysis of language varieties in ELT investigates how dominant ethnolinguistic groups use particular medium of instruction policies to retain their system of privilege, as well as how social and economic hierarchies may be challenged by alternative policies that better serve the interests of subordinated language groups.

The term *ideology* in language studies refers to a shared body of commonsense notions about the nature of language, the nature and purpose of communication, and appropriate communicative behavior; these commonsense notions and assumptions are seen as expressions of a collective order (Woolard, 1992). This means that the ways human societies communicate both reflect and shape fundamental assumptions about individuals as members of collective identities. Though the term *ideology* is used in many ways in ELT, it is important to keep in mind what the term tries to capture: namely, the implicit, usually unconscious assumptions about language and language behavior that fundamentally determine how human beings interpret events.

Particularly important in a critical approach to medium of instruction questions is *standard language ideology*. Lippi-Green (1997) defines standard language ideology as "a bias toward an abstract, idealized homogenous spoken language, which is imposed and maintained by dominant bloc institutions and which names as its model the written language, but which is drawn primarily from the spoken language of the upper middle class" (p. 64). This definition foregrounds three key points. First, standard languages are in fact idealized constructs; the speech of speakers of Standard English includes significant variation that is largely ignored within ELT theory and practice. Second, though standard languages are usually considered to be politically neutral, equally accessible to everyone, and inherently superior to other varieties, in fact they are based upon whatever variety is spoken by the upper middle class. Third, educational institutions play a crucial role in imposing the standard, through systematic sanctions against those who do not speak the standard, and rewards (e.g. good grades in school) for those who do. An example of standard language ideology is the commonsense belief that communication is more efficient if everyone speaks a standard language variety. Another example is the belief that standard language varieties are uniform, typical, and normal.

A critical approach to ELT examines the impact of standard language ideology upon decisions about the pedagogical value of particular ELT practices. From a critical perspective, pedagogical rationales for medium of instruction policies are always viewed skeptically. In particular, second language acquisition (SLA) theory and formal teaching methods, which are major sources of pedagogical rationales for ELT practices, are viewed as a set of rules for determining the situated meaning of teaching acts. In an important analysis of the ideological function of SLA theory and teaching methodology, Stephan (1999) argues that SLA theory and ELT methodology combine with sociocultural values, such as participation, student involvement, and individualism, to valorize certain policies and practices as "effective" or (to use a currently popular term) best practices. Thus, particular practices come to be seen as pedagogically sound, while other practices are sanctioned with labels such as *outdated* or *not theoretically justified*. In particular, approaches to ELT that foreground questions of ideology and inequality are often labeled *political* rather than *pedagogical*, and thus outside the core realm of SLA theory and ELT methodology (Phillipson, 1992). In contrast, a critical approach seeks to unpack the implicit assumptions about language learning and use that shape ELT theory and practice, and the ways in which those assumptions benefit some groups while creating disadvantage for others.

Using a critical approach, I explore in the remainder of this chapter the question of how medium of instruction debates in ELT are shaped by standard language ideology.

SELECTED RESEARCH FINDINGS

The following summary of selected critical research on ideology, language varieties, and ELT is divided into two sections. The first section examines issues raised by research on the question of which variety or varieties should be used by teachers and students in their daily classroom activities. The second section examines issues raised by selected research on the question of which variety should be the target language in ELT.

The Language of the Classroom

Critical research on the language of the classroom examines two key issues: the exclusive use of English compared to bilingual approaches in ELT classes, and the use of stigmatized, non-standard varieties.

English-only versus Bilingual Approaches to ELT
In a series of critical publications, Auerbach has explored the ideological nature of pedagogical practices, particularly the widely held assumption that excluding students' primary languages from the classroom is the most efficient route to English proficiency (Auerbach, 1993, 2000; Auerbach et al. 1996). Auerbach points out that claims about the value of English-only instruction have virtually no research support, while literacy and schooling in the first language (L1) have long been associated with successful SLA (see Krashen, 1996). In adult literacy, though there is surprisingly little research comparing the value of initial first language literacy with English-only literacy, what research has been conducted suggests that initial L1 literacy has a beneficial effect on the acquisition of English literacy (Gillespie, 1994). Like Street (1984), Auerbach (2000) argues that instructional approaches that exclude varieties other than Standard English on pedagogical grounds reflect ideological assumptions with little support in research. Moreover, they serve to blind ELT professionals to the social, economic, and political consequences of English-only practices.

Other critics of English-only instruction have explored its impact on students. For example, Klassen (1991) found that English-only classes offered to Spanish-speaking immigrants in Toronto isolated students from one another and their teachers and were associated with high dropout rates. Snow (1990) examined the evidence that L1 use can significantly enhance the effectiveness of a wide range of language and educational programs. Particularly important is the growing body of "practitioner research" (Auerbach, 2000), namely, research conducted by teachers about their own students, classes, and programs. The rise of practitioner research is an important development in ELT: Much of this research suggests that English-only approaches in ELT are often detrimental to learners (see Gegeo, 1994; Gegeo & Watson-Gegeo, 1999, 2002; Strei, 1992; Watahomigie, 1995; Wrigley & Guth, 1992). Moreover, practitioner research reflects an implicit critique of the traditional separation of practitioners from researchers, who are often working in university positions that do not include actual ELT instruction. For instance, Earl (1994) describes her dissatisfaction with SLA research that generally ignores the special problems facing students with minimal literacy. The traditional debasement of teachers' judgment and experience as well as students' voices in SLA research is now being challenged by critical practitioner researchers, who foreground questions such as the following: Whom is the research intended to help? Who decides what research questions should be asked? What should be the involvement of students and teachers in the research process?

In reviewing practitioner research, Auerbach (2000) found five major advantages to the judicious use of students' home languages in ELT classes:

1. Using L1 opens classes to learners who know little English.
2. Using L1 attracts underserved populations, such as students who previously dropped out of classes.
3. Using L1 improves retention and progress in English.
4. Using L1 encourages communicative, learner-centered approaches.
5. Using L1 at school supports the cultures of families in which parents do not speak English.

Despite these advantages, English-only instruction continues to be widely advocated by policymakers and ELT professionals alike. In the final section of this chapter, I will consider the question of why research on medium of instruction has had so little impact upon medium of instruction policies.

Stigmatized Varieties in the ELT Class

The second important aspect of classroom language is the use of stigmatized varieties. Stigmatized varieties include social dialects marked as poor or working class, or as ethnic or "racial," such as African American Vernacular English; regional varieties associated with economically impoverished areas, such as Appalachian varieties in the United States; and pidgins and creoles, such as Hawaiian Creole English. Medium of instruction policy in most ELT settings requires the use of standard varieties, which are in fact the varieties of the upper middle class that have come to be considered more precise, more scientific, and more expressive than other varieties. In contrast, stigmatized varieties are widely considered to be unattractive, corrupted versions of the standard: Their use is widely believed to be responsible for the limited educational and employment opportunities of groups speaking them.

While there is ample evidence that negative attitudes towards stigmatized varieties are an expression of racism and other forms of bias (see Lippi-Green, 1997), their exclusion from ELT classrooms is usually justified on pedagogical grounds, namely, that they interfere with effective ELT instruction and restrict English language learning. In a review of research on such claims of interference, Siegel (1999) examines the use of stigmatized varieties in three types of educational programs that incorporate their use in systematic ways: instrumental programs, accommodation programs, and awareness programs. In instrumental programs, stigmatized varieties are used as medium of instruction for L1 literacy as well as subject content in mathematics, science, and other fields. In accommodation programs, stigmatized varieties are used by students for classroom activities, but not as medium of instruction. In awareness programs, stigmatized varieties are the focus of class discussion, often with contrastive analysis of stigmatized and standardized varieties. Siegel found overwhelming evidence in 22 separate research studies that the use of stigmatized varieties in all three types of programs has a positive effect on the acquisition of English and English literacy, as well as on students' participation, self-esteem, performance on standardized tests, and overall academic achievement. Particularly important is the finding that use of stigmatized varieties as medium of instruction does not restrict acquisition of English, but in many cases is associated with improved English language learning and use. Siegel concludes, "There is no basis for claims that using a stigmatized variety in the classroom increases interference or gets in the way of acquisition of the standard. On the contrary, research findings indicate that appropriate teaching methodology incorporating the students' vernacular may actually help them acquire the standard" (Siegel, p. 721). Despite these findings, most ELT programs preclude widespread use of stigmatized varieties. As was the case with research on L1 use in ELT, we find that research demonstrating the value of stigmatized varieties has limited impact upon ELT policy decisions.

Target Language in ELT

A second area of critical research on ELT classroom language explores the issue of which language variety should be the target language of language learners. A key component of standard language ideology is that language learners are (or should be) involved in the process of acquiring standard varieties. In most ELT textbooks and teachers' guides, the target of Standard English is depicted as fixed, consistent, and clear. For example, analyzing widely used books about teaching pronunciation, Tollefson (2000) found technical descriptions of an idealized version of Standard English, usually identified by terms that mask variability (e.g. *North American English*). Variability in English is acknowledged only narrowly, such as in general statements referring to British and American pronunciation. Completely ignored is the role of pronunciation in linguistic discrimination, and that the "target language" of many immigrants is a non-standard variety of English.

The belief in the fixity of Standard English entails what Cameron (1995) calls an "ideology of variation" that depicts variation as "deviant," the result of language users' "carelessness, idleness or incompetence" (p. 39). Indeed, grammar books, dictionaries, and most ELT textbooks are instruments of standard language ideology: They present the illusion of a uniform target (standard) language, assuming, despite evidence to the contrary, that uniformity is the norm (Milroy & Milroy, 1985). In this sense, ELT is largely unaffected by sociolinguistics, as all sociolinguists agree that variation is normal, necessary, and intrinsic to all language varieties, including standard languages. In Labov's words: "heterogeneity is an integral part of the linguistic economy, necessary to satisfy the linguistic demands of everyday life" (1982, p. 17). As Lippi-Green (1997) shows, human beings recognize and exploit variation in order "to send a complex series of messages about ourselves and the way we position ourselves in the world" (p. 30). That is, individuals vary their language in order to mark social, geographical, and other forms of associations and identities. Despite its fundamental importance, variation is largely absent from teachers' guides, ELT textbooks, and prescriptions for methodology. One noteworthy result is that teachers may have an idealized notion of their own spoken language. For example, the deletion of the auxiliary *have* is typical in the informal speech of many speakers of Standard English (e.g. "I been playing all day"). Yet most ELT instructors insist that their students produce the full or contracted form, despite the fact that many of the teachers themselves no longer produce the form in many contexts.

The obsession with errors and error correction in ELT reflects a second key component of the ideology of variation: the widely held assumption that students' failure to learn is behind the non-standard forms that they produce. Indeed, the notion persists that learners can and should produce Standard English, despite overwhelming evidence that nearly all adult language learners produce non-standard forms of interlanguage, even after many years of instruction (see research on fossilization in interlanguage in Selinker, 1991). In other words, standard language ideology is manifest in the persistent belief that a realistic target for English language learners is some version of Standard English. Thus, for example, the teacher's *job* is to reduce learners' errors, and to thereby move language learners' speech closer and closer to the ideal standard. Viewed through the lens of standard language ideology, student output that differs from the ideal standard is an error and accepting these errors ultimately is bad teaching.

In research demonstrating the ideological nature of these beliefs, Peterson's (1998) study of the Vietnamese-American community in Portland, Oregon, found that language variation was a fundamental mechanism used within the community to express its complex social identities. In a powerful critique of standard language ideology (what he calls *linguistic monism*), Peterson documents the complexity of social identities in the community, in which a range of standard and non-standard varieties are linked with complex, shifting, and multidimensional identities. Particularly striking is the emergence of new varieties of Vietnamese-English. Though usually viewed by ELT professionals merely as collections of errors, in fact these varieties are not the result of failure to adequately learn Standard English. Rather, they are newly emerging varieties of language that are considered to be appropriate for particular uses within the Vietnamese-American community. Moreover, for many young people, an important target variety is African-American English rather than an upper-middle-class standard. Thus, the complex relationship between language variety and social identity means that learners within the Vietnamese-American community are constantly creating, learning, using, and managing a range of non-standard varieties. The suggestion that Standard English is or should be the sole target language of this community reflects the simplistic and misleading assumptions of standard language ideology.

Other critical work on social identity also calls into question the key assumptions of standard language ideology. Norton (1997) argues that idealized visions of Standard English limit the "ownership" of English to white speakers of prestigious varieties of English. Leung, Harris, and Rampton (1997) argue that idealized notions of *native speaker* restrict employment opportunities for ethnolinguistic minorities in many professions, including ELT. Indeed, critical work has increasingly explored the ideological assumptions implicit in the concept of *native speaker* (Canagarajah, 1999).

The failure of ELT theory and practice to incorporate a notion of variation is particularly problematic because social and political agendas call ELT beliefs and practices into service (Stephan, 1999). In other words, social and political agendas, which allocate particular benefits and resources to different ethnolinguistic groups, exploit standard language ideology. One example in the United States is the use of standard language ideology to justify restrictions on language varieties other than Standard English in the public educational system. The exclusion of immigrants' home languages, African-American vernacular English, and other stigmatized varieties of English is routinely justified by standard language ideology. For example, when the Oakland California School Board in 1996 proposed a new policy requiring teachers to take their students' home language, African-American English, into account when teaching Standard English, there was a firestorm of protest that blocked this policy change (Baugh, 2000). Even this minimal effort to permit the schools to accommodate a stigmatized variety of American English was overwhelmed by the power of standard language ideology, which in this case was in the service of the social agenda of racism.

CURRENT DEBATES AND CONCERNS

Continuing critical work on ideology and language varieties in ELT focuses on four areas of concern. The first area is the relationship between language rights and medium of instruction. Critical work on language varieties in ELT has recently begun to explore widely held assumptions about the value of mother tongue education for ethnolinguistic minorities. Although many critical linguists support the right to education in the mother tongue (Phillipson, 2000), it is increasingly acknowledged that policies supporting mother tongue education can be part of strategies for maintaining the social, economic, and political advantages of dominant groups. Particularly important is analysis of language policies in South Africa, where mother tongue education was a key component of the apartheid system (Cluver, 1992), and more recently, mother tongue education has been constitutionally prescribed as part of a system to redistribute wealth and power (Blommaert, 1996; de Klerk, 2002). Thus, the impact of mother tongue promotion policies can vary significantly. In some instances, such policies are part of social and political agendas that have little to do with human rights, and instead are central to struggles for political power. (For detailed discussion of these issues, see Ricento, 2002.)

A second important area of current research is the economic and social value of standard varieties of English. Although standard language ideology entails an implicit belief in the value of learning Standard English, a growing body of research suggests that one important variable determining the value of English is a pattern of linguistic discrimination. In research on the economic value of English in three Latino communities in the United States, García (1995) concluded that shifting to English offers no advantage for individuals, unless Spanish is viewed as a "suspicious" variety that "must be eradicated" (p. 156). In other words, only when the minority community faces systematic discrimination is it to the community's advantage to shift to English. Obviously, the value of English will vary significantly from one context to another, but García's research demonstrates that claims about the value of English need to be critically examined. In some contexts, learning English is valuable precisely because speakers of other varieties are subject to patterns of discriminatory exclusion in education and employment.

A third area of current concern is the critique of key concepts in ELT. Increasingly, scholars have begun to explore the implicit ideologies of such terms as *target language*, *native* and *nonnative speaker*, *Standard English*, *accent*, and *error*. Indeed, the term *English* itself deserves scrutiny, as its use in many contexts entails standard language ideology, including a denial of variation. Just as the term *nation* is understood to refer to an "imagined community" (Anderson, 1983), the term *English* refers to an imagined, idealized construct (see Milroy & Milroy, 1985). Perhaps the most important area of research in this regard is the analysis of new varieties of English. Building on work by Kachru (1986, 1990), Lowenberg (1986), and Pride (1982), scholars have documented the diversity of new Englishes, as well as debates about the official status of new varieties (e.g. English in Singapore). One paradox of the spread of English as an international language is that it has become a "local" or "regional" language used for communication among speakers of languages other than English (e.g. in business in East Asia). As such, local use patterns become more common, regional varieties emerge, and American and British standards become less influential in ELT.

The fourth key area of concern is the link between language varieties in ELT and the processes of globalization. Indeed, language policies are increasingly affected by globalization. For example, global institutions such as the International Monetary Fund and the World Bank have had major impact on language education in developing regions of Africa, Asia, and Latin America (Mazrui, 2002). In many countries, programs of economic development include English language education (e.g. Vietnam, see Wright, 2002). Migration brought about by globalization (including economic migrants seeking employment, political refugees, and learners seeking training) is forcing changes in ELT policies in many contexts. Critical analyses of ELT and globalization continue to explore a range of topics, such as the institutions responsible for the spread of English internationally (Phillipson, 1992), the cultural politics of English as an international language (Pennycook, 1994), the dominance of British and American theories and practices in ELT (Canagarajah, 1999), and the loss of language diversity (Skutnabb-Kangas, 2000).

FUTURE DIRECTIONS

While debates continue about appropriate medium of instruction policies in different ELT settings, wide agreement has been reached on two key points. First, acquisition of English in many contexts is crucial for educational and economic opportunities. Given ongoing discrimination against speakers of other languages, including stigmatized varieties of English, the ability to speak English is associated in many settings with economic advantage. Yet, despite vast resources devoted to ELT worldwide, some groups have little access to effective English language instruction and therefore are cut off from its benefits. As different levels of access to English persist, English language proficiency (or lack of it) increasingly becomes a source of economic inequality. Therefore, a continuing concern of the ELT profession should be the question of access to English.

A second point of agreement is that maintaining the home language of many learners of English—particularly in immigrant communities—has enormous importance for individual and group identity. Research has shown that when learners shift to English monolingualism, there can be negative consequences for social identity and belonging (Fishman, 1991; Peterson, 1998). Thus, a central goal of medium of instruction policies should be to ensure maintenance of home languages and cultures, along with successful English language learning. Failure to adopt these dual goals will in many contexts increase the chance of economic inequality and sociopolitical conflict (see Tollefson, 2002). A central focus of the ELT profession should be to develop policies and programs that lead to both successful English learning and L1 maintenance.

In order to achieve this goal, it is helpful to examine programs that use English alongside learners' home languages. In recent years, methodologically sophisticated analyses of such programs have begun to accumulate. Particularly important is work by Cantoni (1996), Gegeo (1994), Gegeo and Watson-Gegeo (1999, 2002), Kamana and Wilson (1996), McCarty (2002), Reyhner (1997), Roessel (1977), Watahomigie and McCarty (1994, 1996), Watson-Gegeo and Gegeo (1994, 1995), and Wilson (1998). These important studies examine a variety of programs that seek to integrate English language learning with L1 language and literacy. The success of these programs, not only in teaching language but also in helping to shape the broader social development of linguistic minority communities, demonstrates that complex medium of instruction policies can be adopted to ensure both effective English language instruction and L1 maintenance.

Yet a major barrier to adopting such policies persists: the continuing impact of standard language ideology upon medium of instruction debates. Indeed, research on medium of instruction has had remarkably little impact upon policy, particularly in the United States (McQuillan & Tse, 1996). For example, discussion of California Proposition 227 (the Unz Initiative to ban most bilingual education in the State) was carried out largely without regard to the overwhelming evidence showing the benefits of bilingual education. Similarly, in ELT, the popularity of English-only instruction is widespread, regardless of research demonstrating the value of bilingual approaches that include significant use of learners' first languages. In his analysis of the bilingual education debate in the United States, Cummins (1999) describes what he terms "the process of doublethink" (p. 13), in which public discourse on language is characterized by contradiction, inconsistency, and manipulation. After reviewing contradictions in the writings of prominent opponents of bilingual education (e.g. Baker, 1992; Porter, 1990), Cummins concludes that their success in generating heated opposition to bilingual education "represents a process of mobilizing public discourse in the service of coercive relations of power" (p. 16). From a similar perspective, Donahue (1995, 2002) examines the unprincipled public discourse of prominent supporters of constitutional amendments to declare English the official language in the United States. Donahue argues that "individuals seeking political leadership can promote emotional divisions, masking or diverting attention from larger social problems" (2002, p. 137). English-only supporters "gain influence by crafting confusing and disputatious positions on such issues as...allegedly 'common sense' simplifications of educational policies" (p. 137). Both Cummins and Donahue call for a renewed focus on ethical issues in language policy, beginning with a concerted effort to undertake aggressive analysis of the ideological orientations of policy alternatives affecting medium of instruction. As long as standard language ideology continues to dominate the discourse of ELT, language policy, and the general public alike, research is likely to remain largely isolated from the policy making process. Therefore critical linguists have an ethical responsibility to identify and explore the underlying ideologies of alternative medium of instruction arguments, as well as the concrete economic, political, and social consequences of policy alternatives.

REFERENCES

Anderson, B. (1983). *Imagined communities: Reflections on the origins and spread of nationalism.* London: Verso.
Auerbach, E. (1993). Reexamining English only in the ESOL classroom. *TESOL Quarterly*, 27, 9–32.
Auerbach, E. (2000). When pedagogy meets politics: Challenging English only in adult education. In R. D. Gonzales with I. Melis (Eds.), *Language ideologies: Critical perspectives on the official English movement (Vol. I)*. Urbana, IL & Mahwah, NJ: NCTE and Lawrence Erlbaum.
Auerbach, E., Barahona, B., Midy, J., Vaquerano, F., Zambrano, A., & Arnaud, J. (1996). *From the community to the community: A guidebook for participatory literacy training.* Mahwah, NJ: Lawrence Erlbaum.
Baker, K. (1992, Winter/Spring). Review of Forked tongue. *Bilingual Basics*, 6–7.
Baugh, J. (2000). *Beyond Ebonics: Linguistic pride and racial prejudice.* Oxford: Oxford University Press.
Blommaert, J. (1996). Language planning as a discourse on language and society: The linguistic ideology of a scholarly tradition. *Language Problems and Language Planning*, 20, 199–222.
Cameron, D. (1995). *Verbal hygiene.* London: Routledge.
Canagarajah, A. S. (1999). *Resisting linguistic imperialism in English teaching.* Oxford: Oxford University Press.
Cantoni, G. (Ed.). (1996). *Stabilizing indigenous languages.* Flagstaff: Northern Arizona University Center for Excellence in Education.
Charpentier, J.-M. (1997). Literacy in a pidgin vernacular. In A. Tabouret-Keller, R. B. Le Page, P. Gardner-Chloros, & G. Varro (Eds.), *Vernacular literacy: A reevaluation* (pp. 222–245). Oxford: Clarendon Press.
Cluver, A. D. de V. (1992). Language planning models for a post-apartheid South Africa. *Language Problems and Language Planning*, 23, 133–156.
Cummins, J. (1999). The ethics of doublethink: Language rights and the bilingual education debate. *TESOL Journal*, 8(3), 13–17.
de Klerk, G. (2002). Mother tongue education in South Africa: The weight of history. *International Journal of the Sociology of Language*, 154, 29–46.
Donahue, T. S. (1995). American language policy and compensatory opinion. In J. W. Tollefson (Ed.), *Power and inequality in language education* (pp. 112–141). Cambridge: Cambridge University Press.
Donahue, T. S. (2002). Language planning and the perils of ideological solipsism. In J. W. Tollefson (Ed.), *Language policies in education: Critical issues* (pp. 137–162). Mahwah, NJ: Lawrence Erlbaum.
Earl, L. (1994). Necesitamos aprender bien el Español: The effect of literacy in Spanish on Latino students' acquisition of English. *Literacy Harvest: The Journal of the Literary Assistance Center*, 3(1), 4–20.
Fairclough, N. (1989). *Language and power.* London: Longman.
Fishman, J. A. (1991). *Reversing language shift.* Clevedon: Multilingual Matters.
Foucault, M. (1972). *The archaeology of knowledge.* New York: Pantheon.
Forester, J. (Ed.). (1985). *Critical theory and public life.* Cambridge: MIT Press.

García, O. (1995). Spanish language loss as a determinant of income among Latinos in the United States: Implications for language policy in schools. In J. W. Tollefson (Ed.), *Power and inequality in language education* (pp. 142–160). Cambridge: Cambridge University Press.
Gegeo, D. W. (1994). *Kastom and Bisnis: Towards integrating cultural knowledge into rural development in the Solomon Islands*. Unpublished Ph.D. dissertation, Department of Political Science, University of Hawaii, Manoa.
Gegeo, D. W., & Watson-Gegeo, K. A. (1999). Adult education, language change, and issues of identity and authenticity in Kwara'ae (Solomon Islands). *Anthropology and Education Quarterly, 30*, 22–36.
Gegeo, D. W., & Watson-Gegeo, K. A. (2002). The critical villager: Transforming language and education in Solomon Islands. In J. W. Tollefson (Ed.), *Language policies in education: Critical issues* (pp. 309–325). Mahwah, NJ: Lawrence Erlbaum.
Gillespie, M. (1994). *Adult native language literacy instruction for adults: Patterns, issues, and promises*. Washington: National Clearinghouse for ESOL Literacy Education.
Habermas, J. (1985). *The theory of communication action (Vol. I)*. London: Polity.
Kachru, B. B. (1986). *The alchemy of English*. Oxford: Pergamon Press.
Kachru, B. B. (Ed.). (1990). *The other tongue: English across cultures (2nd ed.)*. Urbana: University of Illinois.
Kamana, K., & Wilson, W. H. (1996). Hawaiian language programs. In G. Cantoni (Ed.), *Stabilizing indigenous languages*. Flagstaff: Center for Excellence in Education.
Klassen, C. (1991). Bilingual written language use by low-education Latin American newcomers. In D. Barton & R. Ivanic (Eds.), *Writing in the community* (pp. 38–57). London: Sage Publications.
Krashen, S. D. (1996). *Under attack: The case against bilingual education*. Culver City, CA: Language Education Associates.
Leung, C., Harris, R., & Rampton, B. (1997). The idealised native speaker, reified ethnicities, and classroom realities. *TESOL Quarterly, 31*, 543–560.
Lippi-Green, R. (1997). *English with an accent: Language, ideology, and discrimination in the United States*. London: Routledge.
Lowenberg, P. (1986). Non-native varieties of English: Nativization, norms, and implications. *Studies in Second Language Acquisition, 8*(1), 1–18.
Mazrui, A. M. (2002). The English language in African education: Dependency and decolonization. In J. W. Tollefson (Ed.), *Language policies in education: Critical issues* (pp. 267–282). Mahwah, NJ: Lawrence Erlbaum.
McCarty, T. L. (2002). Between possibility and constraint: Indigenous language education, planning, and policy in the United States. In J. W. Tollefson (Ed.), *Language policies in education: Critical issues* (pp. 285–307). Mahwah, NJ: Lawrence Erlbaum.
McQuillan, J., & Tse, L. (1996). Does research matter? An analysis of media opinion on bilingual education 1984–1994. *Bilingual Research Journal, 20*(1), 1–27.
Milroy, J., & Milroy, L. (1985). *Authority in language: Investigating language prescription and standardisation*. London: Routledge and Kegan Paul.
Norton, B. (1997). Language, identity, and the ownership of English. *TESOL Quarterly, 31*, 409–429.
Pennycook, A. (1994). *The cultural politics of English as an international language*. London: Longman.
Pennycook, A. (1998). *English and the discourses of colonialism*. London: Routledge.
Peterson, J. O. (1998). *Ethnic and language identity among a select group of Vietnamese-Americans in Portland, Oregon*. Unpublished M.A. thesis, Portland State University.
Phillipson, R. (1992). *Linguistic imperialism*. Oxford: Oxford University Press.
Phillipson, R. (Ed.). (2000). *Rights to language: Equity, power, and education*. Mahwah, NJ: Lawrence Erlbaum.
Porter, R. P. (1990). *Forked tongue: The politics of bilingual education*. New York: Basic Books.
Pride, J. (Ed.). (1982). *New Englishes*. Rowley, MA: Newbury.
Reyhner, J. (1997). *Teaching indigenous languages*. Flagstaff: Northern Arizona University Center for Excellence in Education.
Ricento, T. (2002). Revisiting the mother tongue question in language policy, planning and politics: Introduction. *International Journal of the Sociology of Language, 154*, 1–9.
Roessel, R. A., Jr. (1977). *Navajo education in action: The Rough Rock Demonstration School*. Chinle, AZ: Navajo Curriculum Center Press.
Selinker, L. (1991). *Rediscovering interlanguage*. New York: Addison Wesley.
Siegel, J. (1999). Stigmatized and standardized varieties in the classroom: Interference or separation? *TESOL Quarterly, 33*, 701–728.
Skuttnab-Kangas, T. (2000). *Linguistic genocide in education – Or worldwide diversity and human rights?* Mahwah, NJ: Lawrence Erlbaum.

Snow, C. (1990). Rationales for native language instruction: Evidence from research. In A. Padilla, H. H. Fairchild, & C. M. Valadez (Eds.), *Bilingual education: Issues and strategies* (pp. 60–74). Newbury Park, CA: Sage Publications.
Stephan, L. (1999). Political correctness versus freedom of speech: Social uses of language ideology. Unpublished doctoral dissertation, University of Washington.
Street, B. B. (1984). *Literacy in theory and practice*. Cambridge: Cambridge University Press.
Strei, G. (1992, Spring). Advantages of native language literacy programs: Pilot project. *TESOL Refugee Concerns Newsletter*, 7.
Tollefson, J. W. (1991). *Planning language, planning inequality: Language policy in the community*. London: Longman.
Tollefson, J. W. (2000). Language ideology and language education. In J. Shaw, D. Lubelska, & M. Noullet (Eds.), *Partnership and interaction: Proceedings of the Fourth International Conference on Language and Development* (pp. 43–52). Bangkok: Asian Institute of Technology.
Tollefson, J. W. (Ed.). (2002). *Language policies in education: Critical issues*. Mahwah, NJ: Lawrence Erlbaum.
Watahomigie, L. J. (1995). The power of American Indian parents and communities. *The Bilingual Research Journal*, *19*, 189–194.
Watahomigie, L. J., & McCarty, T. L. (1994). Bilingual/bicultural education at Peach Springs: A Hualapai way of schooling. *Peabody Journal of Education*, *69*, 26–42.
Watahomigie, L. J., & McCarty, T. L. (1996). Literacy for what? Hualapai literacy and language maintenance. In N. H. Hornberger (Ed.), *Indigenous literacies in the Americas: Language planning from the bottom up* (pp. 95–113). Berlin: Mouton de Gruyter.
Watson-Gegeo, K. A., & Gegeo, D. W. (1994). Keeping culture out of the classroom in rural Solomon Islands schools: A critical analysis. *Educational Foundations*, *8*, 27–55.
Watson-Gegeo, K. A., & Gegeo, D. W. (1995). Understanding language and power in the Solomon Islands: Methodological lessons for educational intervention. In J. W. Tollefson (Ed.), *Power and inequality in language education* (pp. 59–72). Cambridge: Cambridge University Press.
Wilson, W. H. (1998). The sociopolitical context of establishing Hawaiian-medium education. *Language, Culture, and Curriculum*, *11*, 325–338.
Wright, S. (2002). Language education and foreign relations in Vietnam. In J. W. Tollefson (Ed.), *Language policies in education: Critical issues* (pp. 225–244). Mahwah, NJ: Lawrence Erlbaum Associates.
Woolard, K. A. (1992). Language ideology: Issues and approaches. *Pragmatics*, *2*, 235–250.
Wrigley, H., & Guth, G. (1992). *Bringing literacy to life: Issues and options in adult ESL*. San Mateo, CA: Aguirre International.

CHAPTER 3

TENSIONS BETWEEN ENGLISH AND MOTHER TONGUE TEACHING IN POST-COLONIAL AFRICA

MARGARET AKINYI OBONDO

Rinkeby Institute of Multilingual Research, Sweden

ABSTRACT

This chapter examines the language of education policy situation in Africa focusing on the tensions created by the imposition of English and the other ex-colonial languages as the favored languages of education. It presents examples drawn from different African countries that show the negative consequences of imposing a monolingual 'English only' language policy of education in multilingual and multicultural Africa. It argues for a 'multilingual option,' an alternative approach for language and education in Africa, that explores the optimal conditions for promoting meaningful educational development in both the indigenous languages as well as in English, in their roles as the nations' first and second languages respectively.

INTRODUCTION

This chapter examines the tensions created by the imposition of the ex-colonial languages as languages of education in Africa. One distinctive feature of sub-Saharan Africa is its large number of indigenous languages. According to one classification Ruhlen (1991), between 1,300 and 1,500 languages are spoken by over 400 million people. Few of these languages are spoken by large numbers with less than 5% having more than a million speakers (Spencer, 1985). Added to this mosaic of indigenous languages, the ex-colonial languages of English, French, Portuguese, and Spanish have been superimposed on this complex multilingual situation. These ex-colonial languages constitute what Dirven (1993) refers to as the languages of secondary domain cluster used as official national languages in administration, judiciary, education, science and technology, trade and industry, and the media. The role of European languages as the official languages in post-colonial Africa has led to linguistic inequality and serious language conflict situations which Mateene (1985) characterizes as follows:

> The most obvious fact is that all African countries use European languages which are those of their former colonial masters, in nearly all their official business, and almost to the exclusion and to the detriment of their national African languages. Thus we are forced to admit that all African countries are today linguistically dependent on Western Europe from which they declare themselves to be politically independent. (p. 41)

The focus of this paper will be on the teaching and use of English and indigenous languages as media of instruction. The term media of instruction is used here to refer to the language of teaching and learning in the classroom. Unless otherwise stated the discussion will be limited to the countries in sub-Saharan Africa. According to Fafunwa (1990), there are 38 countries in Africa within this block: Seventeen are officially French-speaking or francophone states, 16 are officially English-speaking or anglophone states, and 5 are Portuguese-speaking or lusophone states. In each sub-Saharan African country, many different factors have influenced language educational policies and their implementation. The complexity of the individual countries' socio-economic needs, compounded with the multiplicity of languages and attitudes to these languages, has played an important role in the formulation of the language policies of the sub-Saharan states. However, to understand the dynamics of the post-colonial language policy, it is useful to go back to the history of colonial language policy and practices. The reason is that educational language policies in post-colonial Africa are, to a large extent, a heritage of colonial practices.

LANGUAGE POLICY IN POST-COLONIAL AFRICA: THE HEGEMONY OF ENGLISH

The current language policies in education in post-colonial African states provide the best illustration of what Bamgboşe (1991) has called inheritance situation, i.e., how the colonial experience continues to influence and define post-colonial practices. In other words, the attitude of the colonial authorities that ruled the respective countries has shaped post-colonial educational language policies and the current practices in schools (Bokamba, 1995; Obondo, 1994). According to Ansre (1978), we can divide these authorities into two groups: "pro-users" and "anti-users" depending on whether or not they allowed some use of the indigenous languages or rejected them. Belgium, Germany, and Britain were pro-users, while anti-users were France and Portugal.

The anti-users forbade the teaching of indigenous languages in their colonies because their colonial policy of assimilation was designed to encourage their own languages and discourage African languages. Togo, for example, which had started as a German colony and subsequently was ceded to France, experienced different policies under the two colonial powers. The Germans had earlier promoted the use of Ewe, one of the indigenous languages in the elementary schools, but when the French took over the colony after the Second World War, Ewe was completely banned from all government schools. Similarly, the Belgians had allowed the use of African languages in their former colony of the Congo but when France took over the colony the indigenous languages were abandoned. French continues to be the medium of instruction in the Congo Republic even today (Bamgboşe, 1991).

The pro-users led by Britain allowed the use of indigenous languages in the school system at the lower level of primary education. Education in the British colonies was initially left in the hands of the missionaries who were allowed the option of using the indigenous languages in their evangelical work including education. The missionaries were quick to realize that the vernacular languages were the most effective medium to lodge the word of God right into the hearts of their speakers. The English language was also taught but it was limited to a small number of schools and to very few Africans. The British did not find it necessary that everyone in the colonies should learn to speak English. The assumption was that a colony's needs could be well served by training a rather small cadre of natives in English and allowing these to mediate between the colonial power and the local population. This was in line with the British colonial policy of indirect rule. This system led to the creation of a new African class of elites, separating those who could speak English from those who could not. It was these local elites, functioning in their European languages and manning privileged positions, who became the new leaders and took over the affairs of the post-colonial African states (Obondo, 1996).

At independence, when these leaders were faced with the task of formulating the educational language policies for their liberated nations, their colonial linguistic inheritance had significant influence on their decisions. The debate about educational language policy in anglophone or pro-user countries was centered on whether the former colonial languages or one or more indigenous languages could serve as languages of education. The following statement made by Milton Obote, the first President of Uganda, soon after independence in the 1960s captures the flavor of that debate and the conflicts faced by these political leaders as they wrestled with the language issues. Addressing the question on national unity and the role of languages in Uganda, Obote hesitantly put forward the following argument:

> I am well aware that English cannot be the media [sic] to express Dingidingi songs, I have my doubts whether Lwo language can express in all its fineness Lusoga songs, and yet I consider that Uganda's policy to teach more and more English should be matched with the teaching of some of the other African languages. We are trying to think of a possible answer to the question of why we need an African language as a national language. Do we need it merely for political purposes, for addressing public meetings, for talking in Councils? Do we need it as a language for the workers; to enable them to talk and argue their terms with their employers? Do we need an African language for intellectual purposes? Do we need such a language to cover every aspect of our lives intellectually, politically, economically? I would not attempt to answer these questions but it appears to me that Uganda at least is faced with a difficult future on this matter and the future might confirm that a decision is necessary to push some languages deliberately and to discourage also the use of some languages also deliberately. (cited in Alexander, 2000, p. 7)

When Namibia became independent in the 1990s, one would have hoped that the implications of choosing one policy or another would be less problematic. Yet as Alexander (2000) notes, the fundamental questions regarding English remained exactly the same. Hage Geingob, a former Director of United Nations Institute for Namibia (UNIN), who became the country's first Prime Minister, made the following statement in 1981:

> In spite of the difficulties inherent in the task of implementing English as the official language for Namibia, the Namibian people will rise to the occasion. This decision, however, does not imply that the indigenous languages are being dismissed. Local languages have a vital role to play in society and there will be a need for an overall multilingual language planning policy, both long-term and short-term, in which various languages are institutionalized to their greatest advantage. The aim of introducing English is to introduce an official language that will steer the people away from linguo-tribal affiliation and differences and create conditions conducive to national unity in the realm of language. Inherent in the adoption of this policy are a number of issues and implications. Will English become an elitist language, thereby defeating the goals for which it was intended? Will Namibia be able to obtain a sufficient supply of teachers trained in English to teach English? How cost effective and cost beneficial will the choice of English prove to be for Namibia? (UNIN, 1981, cited in Alexander, 2000, pp. 8-9)

The views expressed by these leaders in support of English represent the typical arguments put forward in order to legitimize the choice of ex-colonial languages. Four main arguments, which Ansre (1978) characterizes as rationalizations, have been advanced by various political leaders to support their retention of the pre-independence language policies: (a) national unity (b) national development/ progress (c) efficiency of European languages of wider communication (d) cost-effectiveness. In Kenya, a commission instituted soon after independence in 1964 to advise the government on the educational language policy had this to say about the indigenous languages:

> The vernacular languages are essential languages of verbal communication and we recognize no difficulty in including one daily period for story-telling in the vernacular, or similar activities, in the curriculum of Primary I, II and III. We apprehend, therefore, that the vernaculars will continue to serve their historic role of providing a means of domestic verbal communication. We see no case for assigning to them a role for which they are ill adapted (my italics), namely the role of educational medium in the critical years of schooling. (Kenya Education Commission Report, Part 1, 1965, para. 171)

The Kenya Education Commission perception of African languages as being unsuitable as media of instruction is a view widely held by many of the leaders. A closely related argument maintains that the adoption of indigenously-based language policies would be extremely costly as they will necessitate the translation and writing of textbooks and the training of teaching personnel. The adoption of policies based on ex-colonial languages would be cost-effective, as the requisite pedagogical materials and personnel are available and can be imported from elsewhere, especially Western Europe (Bokamba, 1995). However as pointed out by Pütz (1995), these arguments are contradicted on the grounds that multilingual and multicultural nations, such as those in sub-Saharan Africa, cannot be accommodated by a one-nation, one-language approach. The decision by the leaders in newly independent African nations to accept the primacy of English as the language of education reflects the self-deprecating language attitudes of the vast majority of African people as they emerged out of the colonial era. However, these attitudes could not have been sustained if they were not reinforced by the political economy of the neo-colonial states or what has been called the ESL industry. Alamin Mazrui (1997) has described in the following terms the deleterious effects of World Bank policy on education in Africa:

> The European languages in which Africans are taught are important sources of intellectual control. They aid the World Bank's efforts to enable Africans to learn only that which promotes the agenda of international capitalism. Partly because of the European linguistic policy, intellectual self-determination in Africa has become more difficult. And, for the time being, the prospects of a genuine international revolution in Africa may depend in no small measure on a genuine educational revolution that involves, at the same time, a widespread use of African languages as media of instruction. (p. 46)

The role of the African elite in promoting the neo-colonial language policy and ESL industry has been analyzed in great detail by many African and European scholars (Alexander, N., 2000; Alexandre, P. 1972; Brock-Utne, 2000; Scotton, 1993; Skutnabb-Kangas, 1988). Scotton, for example, has termed the undemocratic situation created by the neo-colonial language policies as elite closure, which is accomplished when the small elite (i.e. the selected speakers of European languages, mostly upper-class members) successfully employ official language policies to limit access of non-elite groups (the overwhelming majority of the population) to political influence and socio-economic advancement. The undemocratic situation caused by the hegemony of European languages may point to what Phillipson (1992) describes as *linguicism*, which operates to ensure that only speakers of the language that dominates the working of political and economic structures succeed. The tragedy about the power of linguicism is that it operates in such a way that those against whom it is discriminating believe that the only way they will become empowered is by acquiring the European languages (Skutnabb-Kangas, 1988). In so doing they develop negative perceptions about their own non-dominant language. It is therefore not surprising that it is the most disempowered groups, for example parents with low economic and political power, who protest most vehemently about the promotion of indigenous languages as languages for education and empowerment (Obondo, 1996). Research shows that it is this category of parents who often prefer to speak to their children in a foreign language (despite limited competence in the language) in the belief that the earlier their children have access to English, for example, the more likely they will succeed in school and be able to compete for the jobs and advance their economic status (Obondo, 1966). However, as I will illustrate in the rest of this paper, the effects of using the European languages as media of instruction has not opened up the education system for children from such families. Instead, the use of ex-colonial languages has contributed to a deep crisis in the education of youth in Africa. In order to situate the discussion in its appropriate context, I will first give an overview of current practices with respect to the use of indigenous languages in education.

INDIGENOUS LANGUAGES AS MEDIA OF INSTRUCTION – AN OVERVIEW

Fafunwa (1990), in a report on the linguistic profile of Africa, notes that 22 out of 34 countries use African languages as media of instruction at primary (first) level; of these 22 only 3 countries have extended their use to secondary school. The use of indigenous languages in formal education in most sub-Saharan African countries is usually limited to the first 3 or 4 years of primary education. For example, the policies in Kenya, Ghana, and Malawi stipulate that mother tongue or the language of the schools' surrounding communities be used as the medium of instruction for the first 3 years of school. In Uganda, Zambia, Namibia, and Eastern States of Nigeria the mother tongue is to be used for the first 4 years of primary school (Obondo, 1996). These language practices have survived more or less unchanged from the British colonial period. In fact, the major innovation that has taken place in the post-independence period has been a move to extend the use of indigenous languages as media of instruction beyond the 3rd or 4th years of primary school. Tanzania provides an example of such an extension where Kiswahili is used as the medium of instruction for the entire primary education (Rubagumya, 1990). Somalia (before the 1990s civil war) provides another example of innovation in mother tongue education. Having inherited two systems of education (English in the north and Italian in the south) the country was able to break away from the inherited practices and embark on the use of Somali as a medium of instruction. Somali became the medium of instruction not only in primary but also secondary school.

Examples of other innovations are experimental projects in the use of indigenous languages. One project that has become famous in the literature of bilingual education in Africa is the Six Year Primary Project in Yoruba commonly known as the Ile-Ife Project in Nigeria. The objective of this project was to compare the traditional system of mixed media (mother tongue initially, then English) with a new system where Yoruba (one of the 3 major languages out of a total of 400 Nigerian languages) was used for the full 6 years of primary education. The experimental classes were taught all subjects in Yoruba and the control group was taught in Yoruba for 3 years, then later in English. When the two groups were evaluated, the results showed very clearly the superiority of the experimental groups in all areas: English, Yoruba, science, social studies and mathematics (Bamgboşe, 1991). The project proved that the experimental groups lost nothing cognitively and linguistically by this exposure to 6 years of primary school education through the medium of Yoruba.

The other project which was in effect complimentary to the Ile-Ife project was the Rivers Readers Project based in the River State of Nigeria, which is a highly multilingual state that has numerous minority languages. The project was designed to introduce initial literacy in 20 languages and to replace the practice of using only Igbo which constituted a dominant language in parts of the River states. This project demonstrated that the policy of using either the mother tongue or the language of the immediate community is possible in a multilingual state and that the cost of producing the materials need not be prohibitively expensive.

A similar innovation in mother tongue education is the Operational Research Project for Language Education in Cameroon (with acronym PROPELCA derived from the title in French). Cameroon is a unique country in Africa with two foreign languages—English (south) and French (north)—as official languages. This division follows the split of the country after the Second World War into a British and a French territory. PROPELCA was designed to experiment with the introduction of Cameroon languages into primary education in a context where the use of indigenous languages was prohibited during the colonial period (Tadajeu, 1995). Guinea is another francophone country that has attempted to introduce indigenous languages in education. At independence, Guinea named 8 of its 25 indigenous languages as national languages. In the late 1970s up to the 1980s, a mother tongue project was instituted. Guinean languages were introduced as media of instruction in the first 4 years of primary school and were taught as subjects from the 3rd year. Substantial progress was made in implementing the project and there was some advance in using the national languages beyond the 4th year (Ridge, 1999). However, the project floundered through lack of funds to provide books and teachers and through growing parent and pupil resistance to the use of indigenous languages. In the late 1980s, the government restored French as the only medium of instruction.

On the surface, these innovative projects give an indication that some effort has been made to use indigenous languages in education. This is particularly significant in the case of countries like Guinea and Cameroon moving from French as an initial primary medium to African languages. However, as the case of Guinea illustrates, any policy that seems to deny the people access to a language that they perceive as important for their advancement is likely to fail. Moreover, the majority of these projects were funded by foreign agencies. For example, the Ile-Ife project was funded by the Ford Foundation after a proposal by the Institute of Education at the University of Ife. The overall goal of the project was to improve English teaching. However, the assumption underlying this goal was that in order to improve English teaching, serious attention had to be paid to the teaching of Yoruba as well. Like other foreign-funded projects in Africa, the experiment ended when the flow of funds dried up. Hence, despite more than 30 years of independence for most African states, the situation of indigenous languages in education has remained as it was in the colonial period. In fact, in countries like Zambia and Kenya that instituted an English-only policy shortly after independence, the situation represents a reverse development from the British colonial policy. In actual fact, these practices are a reinforcement of the neo-colonial established practices, which are so overwhelming that it becomes virtually impossible for many states to break away from them (Bamgboṣe, 1991).

CONFLICTS BETWEEN ENGLISH AND INDIGENOUS LANGUAGES AS MEDIA OF INSTRUCTION

English, as we have noted, continues to enjoy a privileged position in most African countries. However, despite its status and the efforts made to promote it by foreign agencies (read ESL industry), English, like other ex-colonial languages, has remained a minority language in Africa. Heine (1992) estimates that less than 20% of Africans are competent in or make use of the official languages of their countries. Contrary to the expectation at independence that English would promote educational advancement for the African masses, the use of English as a sole medium of instruction has brought serious educational underdevelopment of the majority of the citizens of these states (Obondo, 1994, 1997; Pütz, 1995).

Take the case of Zambia as an example, which adopted a "straight for English" policy after independence. Researchers (e.g. Kashoki, 1990) analyzing the effects of this policy have concluded that it has been unsuccessful in terms of opening up the education system or improving access to jobs and participation in either political or social arenas in Zambia. In fact, it has exacerbated the high drop out rate from school and illiteracy in both English and mother tongue. It has also been reported that there is a shrinking minority of people who can speak English competently enough to participate as empowered members of the society. In other words, as in colonial times, Zambian "straight for English" language policy continues to ensure that only a small elite is empowered. As early as 1973, the Minister of Education of Zambia, at the time commenting on the impact of the English medium on the children's learning, warned that there was still no evidence that learning had been made easier nine years after the introduction of English as a medium of instruction in Zambian schools. In fact, in light of surveys published in 1973, it seemed clear that reading and mathematics in grade 3 were poorly developed (Obondo, 1994). The education situation in Zambia has not become any better despite the use of English as a medium of instruction for more than three decades.

This scenario is not unique to Zambia. Tanzania, which has often been cited as a good example of a country in which an indigenous language has been promoted, is today facing major pedagogical problems (Rubagumya, 2001). Tanzanian children receive seven years of primary education in Kiswahili, which is not the mother tongue of all, but the second language of most (an estimated 90% in 1971; Abdulaziz, 1971). Children begin learning English in 3rd year for about four hours per week. In secondary school, there is almost a complete and sudden switch to teaching entirely in English and this is continued throughout the tertiary level except in primary teacher education where there is a switch back to Kiswahili as a medium of instruction. An example of how bad the situation is in Tanzania is captured by an observation by one secondary school teacher who is credited with the following statement: "We have 105 pupils in Form 1 this year. Out of this only 12 can count up to 20 in English. Hardly anyone of them can form and understand a sentence in English. And this situation is said to be typical" (Criper & Dodd, 1984, p.14). Not only is students' English suffering in this situation but also their Kiswahili. According to Othman-Yahya (1990), the use of English in secondary school has meant that students do not have sufficient time to devote to the development of academic or literacy (decontextualized) skills in Kiswahili. Othman-Yahya further notes that, the use of no Kiswahili in secondary school and the switch to it later in teacher education, for example, constitutes a leap upward, skipping the intermediate stage. Kiswahili medium of instruction in Teacher Education in Tanzania constitutes a "grafting of a tertiary level experience on to a primary level literacy" (p. 61). The deleterious effects of this practice on Tanzanian education have given rise to many profound questions about the future of the country and its youth (cf. Höjlund, Mtana, & Mhando, 2001).

One question that immediately comes to mind is: If English has failed as a medium of education in Tanzania, why does the country find it difficult to change a course which is obviously so detrimental to its youth? The answer lies in the power of linguicism discussed earlier. As Rubagumya (2001) explains, "Any suggestions of changing the medium of instruction from English to Kiswahili in Tanzania is ignored by the policy makers and viewed with suspicion by ordinary parents" (p. 245). The reason, according to Rubagumya, is because it is in the interest of the elite to maintain the status quo by retaining English as a gate-keeping mechanism to exclude the majority of the people from power. The parents see English as the key to their children's future and assume that English medium education is the best way to achieve it.

South Africa provides yet another example of the growing acceptance of English as the dominant language in education. Unlike the other countries in the sub-continent, South Africa has formulated one of the most progressive language policies in post-colonial history. After the fall of the racist apartheid regime, 11 languages became official: Xhosa, Zulu, Swazi, Ndebele, Northern Sotho, Southern Sotho, Tswana, Tsonga, Venda, English, and Afrikaans. The Language Policy is derived from the Constitution, the Bill of Rights, Section, 29 (2), which states that:

> Everyone has the right to receive education in the official language or languages of their choice in public educational institutions where that education is reasonably practicable. In order to ensure effective access to, and implementation of, this right, the state must consider all reasonable educational alternatives, including single medium institutions, taking into account - (a) equity (b) practicability (c) the need to redress the results of past racially discriminatory laws and practices. (The South African Constitution, 1996, quoted in Vesely, 2000, p. 16)

The language policy marks a deliberate shift away from apartheid policy regarding the use of indigenous languages. For the first time, African languages can be used as languages of teaching and learning throughout schooling. The strength of this language policy in regard to the media of instruction is its commitment to additive bilingualism (cf. Cummins, 1996), i.e., the maintenance of the first language of the learner throughout his/her educational career while adding the second language. Thus English and Afrikaans are no longer given the favored status they enjoyed during apartheid. However, the strength of the policy of using indigenous languages in education is also its weakness. The reason is that under the apartheid regime, there was a link between mother tongue instruction and racial discrimination. Mother tongue instruction was used to indoctrinate black children with a racist curriculum for social inferiority. As a consequence, in the minds of black South Africans, the use of indigenous languages in education continues to be equated with inferior education and racial "ghettoisation" (Alexander, 2000). As a result, there is a growing demand for English in South African society because of the hatred for Afrikaans that is seen as the language of oppression, in contrast to English, which has become the language of power, unity, and liberation. The new status accorded to English is reflected in its increasing use as a language of instruction at all levels of the school system. Many parents send their children to private schools where "straight to English" policy is practiced. As Vukela (1994) confirms, "black parents believe that the earlier their children are exposed to English as a subject and English as a medium of instruction the better" (p. 4).

However, instruction in English poses serious challenges for educators in South Africa. In the black township schools, for example, where there were restrictions on the use of English during the apartheid regime, neither the teachers nor the students have the necessary competence in English to cope with the demands of the syllabus (Heugh, 1992). The difficulties of learning in English are compounded by the fact that, with the fall of the apartheid regime, there has been a population influx to the urban areas with black students moving into former white schools with a goal of learning in English. In a study of Xhosa-speaking students in two Cape Town townships, Vesely (2000) noted that:

> Migrating Xhosa-speaking students come to Cape Town with the goal of learning English, as they perceive people who don't know English to be 'uneducated' Because they generally speak very little English, their adaptation to English-language classes in Xhosa-language townships is particularly arduous and they often fail classes repeatedly. The sudden transition to an English medium of instruction for content subjects when most students do not have an adequate proficiency in English severely curtails the learning of African-language speakers in the classroom. (p. 24)

In conclusion, I have portrayed here a central problem in the general educational advancement of the African continent: the question of media of instruction and the consequences of the use of English as the sole medium of instruction. The chain of negative consequences of imposing a colonial language has put such a heavy burden on many countries that most African nations have realized that they are badly in need of a new concept of language of education.

A MULTILINGUAL PROPOSAL – A NEW CONCEPT OF LANGUAGE OF EDUCATION IN AFRICA

The disastrous consequences of the use of English for the education of the majority of African nations has led to a growing demand for an alternative concept of language and education in Africa, based on multilingualism. One of the attempts to provide a framework for a multilingual language policy for Africa is associated with the research project Languages in Contact and Conflict in Africa or LiCCA (Dirven & Webb, 1992). The immediate goal of LiCCA is to contribute to the optimal development of the multilingual and multicultural potential in sub-Saharan Africa. The project strives to define a criterion for the formulation of linguistic models that can result in optimal language policies beneficial to all the people in Africa. The

LiCCA program for anglophone African countries, for example, explores the optimal conditions for promoting both English and the indigenous languages in their roles as instruments serving in the secondary domain functions (e.g. education, media, etc.). The LiCCA multilingual framework represents many ideals that have become current in African sociolinguistic literature on the role of language in development. Sociolinguists in Africa (e.g. Bokamba, 1995; Bamgboşe, 1991; Fardon & Furniss, 1994; Mansour, 1993; Webb, 1998) generally support the greater use of indigenous languages (and therefore multilingualism) as a meaningful factor in economic, educational, and political development. These scholars argue in support of a multilingual approach to education on the grounds that meaningful educational development can, in practice, only occur in languages that learners know very well (see also Cummins, 2000; Thomas & Collier, 1997, for perspectives on the education of minority language students). Conversely, pupils perform poorly if a language that is not well known is used as a medium of learning and teaching, as is shown by the case of Tanzania discussed above. Sure (1997) has made similar observations with respect to Kenya where national examiners ascribe the poor results in Mathematics and Science to the use of English as the language of learning and teaching.

Until now, only a few countries have made practical attempts to formulate a language policy based on multilingualism or "additive multilingualism" as Alexander (2000) refers to it. South Africa and Eritrea are two of the few countries in the sub-continent that have declared indigenous languages as official media of instruction in their national education system. Like South Africa, Eritrea has declared nine indigenous languages as the official languages (Languages and Education in the Mother Tongue. The EFA 2000 Assessment: Country Reports, Eritrea). The Eritrean educational policy is officially understood to call for additive multilingualism so that languages complement one another in the experience of the learners. The most important achievement reported by the Minister of Education, Mr. Osman Saleh Mohammed with respect to the use of indigenous languages as media of instruction is the unshakable psychological confidence and self esteem it has given the learners (Mohammed Saleh, 2001).

According to the Minister, the opportunity to use the different languages of the learners has brought the users of these languages together and induced them to love, learn and tolerate each other. It has also enabled the learners to appreciate each other's languages as equally important to their own. Consequently, it has fostered unity in diversity through genuine and deep seated cultural tolerance.

These observations by the Minister reflect the qualitative consequences of adopting a multilingual attitude or what Webb (1998) calls "the spirit of multilingualism" characterized by the following sets of values and norms:

- an acceptance of the equal value of all languages and their speakers and a feeling of respect and tolerance towards them
- a positive attitude towards people who know more than two languages
- an acceptance of multilingualism as a national resource rather than as a problem
- a conscious rejection of linguistic and cultural imperialism and an acceptance that political stability is possible in non-European languages

- an understanding of the difficulties people may have in acquiring and using foreign languages and a tolerance (by teachers especially) of people who have an 'imperfect language knowledge' and make 'mistakes' e.g., use 'interlanguages' (thus also an acceptance of the legitimacy of local standards)

(Adapted from Webb, p. 143)

The antithesis of the spirit of multilingualism is the colonial attitude reflected in the bulk of colonial and post-colonial language policies presented in the earlier sections of this discussion. The belief that some languages are better or more effective than others, an attitude typical of communities and individuals that are dominated by single languages, is inappropriate in a multilingual and multicultural Africa. What are the implications of adopting a multilingual language approach for the effective use of mother tongue and English as languages of education in Africa? While space does not allow an exhaustive discussion of this question, I will briefly conclude this paper by highlighting how a multilingual approach can contribute to effective educational development including the teaching of English and indigenous languages. However, it is important to note that there are still a number of questions that need deeper investigation before the relationship between multilingualism and educational development can be fully understood. Hence the answer to the question above will be brief and speculative.

A MULTILINGUAL APPROACH – IMPLICATIONS FOR EDUCATIONAL DEVELOPMENT AND THE TEACHING OF ENGLISH AND INDIGENOUS LANGUAGES

Adopting a multilingual approach to educational development entails redefining the roles of English and indigenous languages as languages of teaching and learning. It needs a very clear, well-balanced policy on indigenous languages as the nations' first languages and English as the second language. It also entails developing a comprehensive and coherent stipulation on the ways indigenous languages can play their roles efficiently as languages of education. From the examples cited in this paper, it is obvious that if indigenous languages are to play a meaningful role in education, it is necessary to adapt them so that they can perform the functions they will be expected to perform. As we noted with the example of South Africa and Guinea, there continues to be a strong rejection of the African languages as languages of education by parents, teachers, and policy makers in many African countries (Obondo, 2001).

One of the main tasks in revalorization of the indigenous languages is their social promotion so that they can increasingly be regarded as instruments of value, instruments with which important tasks can be performed such as their use at all levels of education. The process of expanding the African languages into these domains begins with critical awareness of power structures and how language and power intersect. As Tollefson (1995) remarks in the context of language policies across the globe "language policies at all levels, from the national authority to the individual classroom, reflect relationships of unequal power" (p. 2).

As educators, a critical component of language teaching is placing emphasis upon asking questions about the social conditions that, for example, advance English and undermine the African languages. Connecting linguistic practices to power relationships in what Cummins (1996, 2000) has called transformative pedagogy must ground language teaching and other educational practices. Transformative pedagogy uses collaborative inquiry to enable students to analyze and understand the social realities of their own lives and their communities (Cummins, 2000). Africa is plagued by a variety of social problems and students are faced with many issues, some of which are connected to the language barrier in the classroom and others that arise directly from poverty (e.g. overcrowded classrooms, few resources, incompetent teachers, violence, AIDS, etc.). A language of education focused upon training in language skills without a critical component would seem to be failing in its responsibility to learners. As Fairclough (1992) underscores:

> People cannot be effective citizens in a democratic society if their education cuts them off from critical consciousness of key elements within their physical or social environment. If we are committed to education establishing resources for citizenship, critical awareness of the language practices of one's speech community is an entitlement. (p. 6)

A classroom following a multilingual policy is one of the foremost places to initiate critical transformative pedagogy. In such a classroom, critical awareness would include designing lessons where students would scrutinize the language practices that are taking place in their homes and communities and examine the hegemony of English in society and the impact of media of instruction within the classroom. An essential component of critical awareness is for educators to adopt strategies that enhance the students' participation. This involves making the classroom "a language-friendly place," where knowledge would be discussed and utilized through the media of the best-known languages. This practice would have the advantage of encouraging not only participatory/inquiry- based learning but also of raising the status of the different languages used in the classroom including English. For a multilingual policy to succeed there must be a strong emphasis on the effective teaching of English as a second language rather than using it as a medium of instruction. As the examples from the different countries cited in this paper have shown, the use of English as a medium of instruction creates an unnecessary and avoidable obstacle to academic performance and the development of students' proficiency in the language. If a multilingual language policy is to contribute effectively to educational development, effective teaching of English as a subject is a necessary prerequisite. Teaching English as a subject would eliminate the current practice of requiring children to struggle to achieve scholastic success in other subjects through a language they are still attempting to master.

CONCLUSIONS

This paper has highlighted some of the issues that have concerned African scholars and educators who genuinely want to see Africa educationally up on its feet again. Most of the changes recommended in this paper involve modifying deeply rooted attitudes and established practices. These changes require patience and perseverance. While advocating some of these changes, we must not underestimate the practical obstacles involved in modifying the existing practices. These obstacles include the prevalence of globally directed socio-cultural, political and economic forces associated with English as a global language as well as the asymmetric power relations brought about by the adoption of English as the sole medium of instruction in Africa. If multilingualism is to play an important role in educational development in Africa, then educators must be sensitive to the real needs of the communities by adopting an inclusive language policy. Only when a commitment towards language inclusiveness is made, when attitudes change, and multilingual policy is established, will education become accessible to all children.

REFERENCES

Abdulaziz, M. H. (1971). Tanzania's national language policy and the rise of Swahili political culture. In W. H. Whiteley (Ed.), *Language use and social change* (pp. 160–178). London: Oxford University Press.

Alexander, P. (1972). *An introduction to languages and language in Africa*. London: Heinemann.

Alexander, N. (2000). English unassailable but unattainable: The dilemma of language policy in South African education. PRAESA Occasional Papers No.3. Cape Town: PRAESA.

Ansre, G. (1978). The use of indigenous languages in education in Sub-Saharan Africa: Presuppositions, lessons, and prospects. In J. Alatis (Ed.), *Georgetown round table on language and linguistics* (pp. 285–301). Washington DC: Georgetown University Press.

Bamgboşe, A. (1991). *Language and the nation: The language question in Sub-Saharan Africa*. Edinburgh: Edinburgh University Press.

Bokamba, E. G. (1995). The politics of language planning in Africa: Critical choices for the 21st century. In M. Pütz (Ed.), *Discrimination through language in Africa?: Perspectives on the Namibian experience* (pp. 11–27). Berlin, New York: Mouton de Gruyter.

Brock-Utne, B. (2000). *Whose education for all?: The recolonialization of the African mind*. New York & London: Falmer Press.

Criper, C., & Dodd, N. (1984). Report on the teaching of English language and its use as a medium in education in Tanzania. Dar es Salaam: The British Council.

Cummins, J. (1996). *Negotiating identities: Education for empowerment in a diverse society*. Ontario, CA: California Association for Bilingual Education.

Cummins, J. (2000). *Language, power and pedagogy: Bilingual children in the crossfire*. Clevedon, UK: Multilingual Matters.

Dirven, R. (1993). The use of languages and language policies in Africa: Goals of the LiCCA program. *International Journal of Sociology of Language, 100/101*, 179–189.

Dirven, R., & Webb, V. N. (1992). *The LiCCA research and development programme*. Universities of Duisburg and Pretoria.

Fafunwa, A. B. (27–30 November 1990). Using national languages in education: A challenge to African educators. In *UNESCO-UNICEF, African thoughts on the prospects of education for all* (pp. 97–110). Selections from papers commissioned for the Regional Consultation on Education for All. Dakar.

Fairclough, N. (Ed.). (1992). *Critical language awareness*. Harlow: Longman.

Fardon, R., & Furniss, G. (Eds.). (1994). *African languages, development and the state*. London: Routledge.

Heine, B. (1992). Language, language policy and national unity in Africa: An overview. In B. Harlech-Jones (Ed.), *Language and National Unity* [Special Issue], 21–32.

Heugh, K. (1992). Enshrining elitism: The English connection. In K. Heugh (Ed.), *After apartheid: Dealing with diversity. Language Projects Review, Vol. 7*(3), 2–4.

Höjlund, G., Mtana, N., & Mhando, E. (Eds.). (2001). *Practices and possibilities in teacher education in Africa: Perspectives from Tanzania*. Dar es Salaam: Ministry of Education and Culture.

Kashoki, M. E. (1990). *The factor of language in Zambia*. Lusaka: Kenneth Kaunda Foundation.

Kenya Education Commission. (1965). Kenya Education Commission Report: Part 1. Para. 171. Nairobi.

Languages and Education in the Mother Tongue. The EFA 2000 Assessment: Country Reports, Eritrea. Retrieved from February 2002, from http://www2unesco.org/org/countryreports/rapport.

Mansour, G. (1993). *Multilingualism and nation building*. Clevedon: Multilingual Matters.

Mateene, K. (1985). Failure in the obligatory use of European languages in Africa and the advantages of a policy of linguistic independence, *Osnabrücker Beiträge zur Sprachtheorie [Osnabrücker Journal on Linguistic Theory]*. Osnabrück: OBST, 41–73.

Mazrui, Alamin. (1997). The world bank, the language question, and the future of African education. *Race & Class. A Journal for Black and Third World Liberation, 38*(3), 35–49.

Mohammed, S. O. (2001, September). *The role of languages for promoting education for all for learning to live together*. Paper presented at the Forty-Sixth Session of the International Conference on

Education, Geneva, 5–8 September, 2001. Retrieved February 2001 from, http://www.ibe.unesco.org/International/ICE/ministers/eritrea.htm.
Obondo, M. A. (1994). The medium of instruction and bilingual education in Africa: An appraisal of problems, practices and prospects. In I. Ahlgren & K. Hyltenstam (Eds.), *Bilingualism in deaf education* (pp. 274–295). Hamburg: Signum Verl.
Obondo, M. A. (1996). *From trilinguals to bilinguals? A study of the social and linguistic consequences of language shift on a group of urban Luo children in Kenya*, Unublished Ph.D. Thesis, Centre for Research on Bilingualism, Stockholm University.
Obondo, M. A. (1997). Bilingual education in Africa: An overview. In J. Cummins & D. Corson (Eds.), *Encyclopedia of Language and Education, Vol. 5* (pp. 25–31). Dordrecht: Kluwer Academy Publishers.
Obondo, M. A. (2001). Bilingual learners second and academic language development: Insights from education of immigrant minority children. In G. Höjlund, N. Mtana, & E. Mhando (Eds.), *Practices and possibilities in teacher education in Africa: Perspectives from Tanzania* (pp. 284–311). Dar es Salaam: Ministry of Education and Culture.
Othman-Yahya, S. (1990). When international languages clash: The possible detrimental effects on development of the conflict between English and Kiswahili in Tanzania. In C. M. Rubagumya (Ed.), *Language and education in Africa* (pp. 42–53). Clevedon: Multilingual Matters Ltd.
Phillipson, R. (1992). *Linguistic imperialism.* Oxford: Oxford University Press.
Pütz, M. (1995). Language and colonialism in Africa – Introduction. In M. Pütz (Ed.), *Discrimination through language in Africa?: Perspectives on the Namibian experience* (pp. 1–8). Berlin, New York: Mouton de Gruyter.
Ridge, S. G. M. (1999). Language education policy: Africa. In B. Spolsky (Ed.), *Concise encyclopedia of educational linguistics* (pp. 101–106). Oxford: Elsevier.
Rubagumya, C. (Ed.). (1990). *Language in education in Africa: A Tanzanian perspective.* Clevedon, Philadelphia: Multilingual Matters.
Rubagumya, C. (2001). The language of teaching and learning in Tanzania: Implications for teacher education. In G. Höjlund, N. Mtana, & E. Mhando (Eds.), *Practices and possibilities in teacher education in Africa: Perspectives from Tanzania* (pp. 241–254). Dar es Salaam: Ministry of Education and Culture.
Ruhlen, M. (1991). *A guide to the world's languages: Vol. 1.* London: Edward Arnold.
Scotton, C. (1993). Elite closure as a powerful strategy: The African case. *International Journal of the Sociology of Language, 103*, 149–163.
Skutnabb-Kangas, T. (1988). Multilingualism and the education of minority children. In T. Skutnabb-Kangas & J. Cummins (Eds.), *Minority education: From shame to struggle* (pp. 9–44). Clevedon, UK: Multilingual Matters.
Spencer, J. (1985). Language and development in Africa: The unequal equation. In W. Wolfson & J. Manes (Eds.), *Language of inequality* (pp. 387–397). The Hague: Mouton.
Sure, K. (1997, September). *Language development and integration in Kenya since independence: The breaking borders.* Paper presented at the African-Hispanic Encounters Conference. Durban.
Tadajeu, M. (1995). *National language education programme in Cameroon.* Yoande, Cameroon: Department of African Languages and Linguistics (DALL).
Thomas, W. P., & Collier, V. P. (1997). *School effectiveness for language minority students.* Washington, DC: National Clearinghouse for Bilingual Education.
Tollefson, J. (Ed.). (1995). *Power and inequality in language education.* Cambridge: Cambridge University Press.
Vesely, R. (2000). Multilingual environments for survival: The impact of English on Xhosa-speaking students in Cape Town. PRAESA Occasional Papers, No. 5. Cape Town: PRAESA.
Vukela, V.H. (1994, September). *The complexities of using English as a medium of instruction in South African "black" schools.* Paper presented at IVth International Conference on Law and Languages, Fribourg, Switzerland.
Webb, V. (1998). Multilingualism as a developmental resource: Framework for a research program. *Multilingua, 17*(2/3), 125–154. Berlin: Walter de Guyter.

CHAPTER 4

A CRITICAL DISCUSSION OF THE ENGLISH-VERNACULAR DIVIDE IN INDIA

VAIDEHI RAMANATHAN

The University of California, USA

ABSTRACT

This chapter offers a critical discussion of ELT-related practices in India to show how the middle class, with its relatively easy access to English, represents an inner circle of power and privilege that, for a variety of reasons, remains inaccessible to entire groups of people in India. Based on my extended seven-year project with English and vernacular-medium teachers in the city of Ahmedabad in Gujarat, India, the chapter offers a synthesized account of three inter-related local factors impacting English and vernacular educational scenes in Gujarat, namely: nation and state-wide educational policies regarding medium of instruction, a preference for teaching English literature vs. the English language, and some curricular practices as partially evidenced in English language textbooks in Gujarat. Each of these factors plays a crucial role in maintaining the status quo with the English-medium middle class and in shutting out the Gujarati-medium students from fully participating in schooling-related transactions.

INTRODUCTION

Studies of World Englishes in the last two decades have called attention to the growing number of Englishes used internationally (Kachru, 1985) by documenting features of the varieties of English (Pakir, 1991) and raising issues about the socio-ideological underpinnings of their use (Canagarajah, 1993). A key assumption has been that the inner circle of countries (Britain, the U.S., Canada, and Australia) with native speakers of the language sets English language standards for countries in the outer circle (e.g. India and parts of Africa), where English is used non-natively but extensively and has been given official language status. Research has largely concentrated on describing English language varieties or discussing the unequal power relations between inner and outer circles of countries resulting from the privileged standard-setting position of inner-circle countries (Pennycook, 1994, 1998; Phillipson, 1992), but little attention has been paid to examining how power relations operate within the outer circle itself.

Extending the study of hegemonic practices associated with English language use to the outer-circle country of India, this article examines how Indian English and the privileges associated with it remain inaccessible to those who have been schooled in the vernacular-medium (in the present case, Gujarati). Drawing on my extended exploration regarding English and vernacular education, I argue that the Indian middle-class assumes a position of relative power through its access to English. By selectively focusing on three specific educational and institutional practices influencing their access to Indian English, I show how students schooled in vernacular languages remain in less empowered positions.

The following are the three inter-related socio-educational practices I address: National and statewide educational policies regarding medium of instruction, an almost exclusive focus on the teaching of English literature instead of language, and inequities between English and vernacular medium students as reflected in textbooks. By no means a complete list, each of these social *cogs* or practices is part of a larger social machinery that is kept in place by the privileged assumptions of the middle- and upper-classes. A partial critical assessment of these aligned cogs (Wartenberg, 1990) allows us to see how certain assumptions get reflected, tied to, furthered, and embedded in others, thus sustaining the general social machinery and privileging the English-medium (EM) middle-class (For a fuller discussion see Ramanathan, 2005).

LOCATING THE CURRENT EDUCATIONAL SYSTEM IN INDIA

The current educational system in India has a long and complicated colonial history. Three famous, almost overcited measures include: (a) the East India Company being compelled to accept responsibility for the education of Indians in 1813, (b) Macaulay's infamous Minute (on 2 February 1835) wherein he denounced educating Indians in their mother tongue and upheld the intrinsic value of the English language and literature, and (c) Charles Wood's Dispatch of 1854 that imposed on the government the "task of creating a properly articulated scheme of education from primary school to the university" (Agarwal, 1984, p. 25). The system of education that the British introduced in India was modeled on the British system, especially in regard to higher education. The striking feature of this educational transplantation was English, which was not only taught as a language but also became a medium of instruction (Jayaram, 1993). Indeed, some scholars in India maintain that the emphasis on mastering the English language in schools and colleges became so firmly entrenched and continues to assume such importance that it has "encouraged mechanical learning through memorizing and discouraged inquisitiveness and an experimental bent of mind" (Jayaram, 1993, p. 85).

SOCIO-EDUCATIONAL PRACTICES THAT DISADVANTAGE VERNACULAR-MEDIUM STUDENTS (WHILE SIMULTANEOUSLY ADVANTAGING THEIR ENGLISH-MEDIUM COUNTERPARTS)

National Level Issues Related to the Medium of Instruction in India: Language-discipline Hierarchy

Language policies related to (differences in) mediums of instruction in India partially serve to sustain and reinforce the language-discipline hierarchy that currently exits in the educational system. There has been considerable controversy regarding what the medium of instruction should be at both the K-12 level and beyond. According to Jayaram (1993), a little more than half of the universities offer bilingual instruction in one or more courses, with English being one of the mediums of instruction. This availability of choice (regarding college education) in only certain mediums of instruction preordains a self-perpetuating language/medium-related exclusivity. Students schooled in the vernacular in the K-12 years—typically lower-income children—often have little choice but to go to vernacular-medium colleges, a development that limits their opportunities for social advancement, since English and English-medium institutions appear to be tickets to the key goods of the society.

A Critical Discussion of the English-Vernacular Divide in India 53

This language/medium-related exclusivity also plays itself out in heirarchizing disciplines in colleges. At the undergraduate level, most arts and commerce subjects are offered in the vernacular-medium as well as English, while all science and science-related subjects are typically offered only in English. Thus, fields such as engineering, medicine, physics, chemistry, biology, and pharmacy are taught only in English, while subjects such as psychology, economics, statistics, geography, history, and regional literature are available in all vernacular languages (Jayaram, 1993). This breakdown—where arts subjects are considered less "prestigious" than the sciences—dovetails with the language/medium in which they are taught, which in turn gets dovetailed with the class background of students. Middle-class, English-medium students have easier access to English medium colleges and, thus, to all disciplines. Because only some disciplines are taught in vernacular languages at the college-level, vernacular-medium students find themselves arriving at the college-scene in seriously disadvantaged positions, with their vernacular backgrounds being devalued. This is one intricate way in which the English-vernacular divide (Ramanathan 2004) is maintained and the status-quo is maintained with the Indian middle-class.

Statewide Educational Policies: Specific to K-12 in Gujarat

Ways in which vernacular-medium students remain disadvantaged become clearer when we consider the alignment between national and statewide language policy issues. Two such policies in the state of Gujarat are (a) the practice of tracking students based on their English language competence,[1] and (b) policies related to statewide exams and external assessment.

Tracking GM Students

English is typically introduced in the 5th grade as a foreign language in GM schools. However, it becomes an elective in the 10th grade, a feature that leads to GM students being tracked into separate streams—*a* and *b*—at college level (see Figure 1). Those students who opt to take English in 10th, 11th, and 12th grades end up entering college with 8 years of English instruction in school (from grades 5-12), and are placed in the *a stream* in English-medium colleges. On the other hand, students who drop English in the 10th grade and enter college with only 5 years of English instruction get placed into the *b stream* at college level. Most EM colleges in Gujarat will not admit *b* stream students.[2]

- English from 5th–9th grades = *b* stream at college level
- English from 5th–12th grades = *a* stream at college level

Figure 1. Tracking of Gujarati-medium students depending on years of English instruction in K-12

Statewide Exams and External Assessment

There are several state-wide exams built into the educational system. At the K-12 level students take common *Board exams*—exams scheduled, administered, and graded by the State Board of Education—at the end of their 10th and 12th grades. Twelfth grade scores, along with the years of English instruction students have had in school, determine, as we have just seen, not just the kinds of colleges they can apply to, but the streams they will get tracked into if they are Gujarati-medium students. At college level, all students have to take state board exams at the end of each year. These are set, administered, and graded by external examiners affiliated with the university (Gujarat University, in the present case), a practice that most institutionally affiliated personnel (administrators, faculty members, and students) that I have interviewed find seriously problematic. Faculty members consistently maintain that GM students—especially *b streamers*—are particularly disadvantaged by such policies. Not only have *b stream* students had English only for 5 years (from grades 5-9) before they get to college, they also have to take the same set of English language exams (in the final year of college) as their EM counterparts (who have had the advantage of having had their entire K-12 schooling in English). Furthermore, the exams of *b stream* students (like everybody else's) are also graded by external reviewers who have little or no idea of the kind of progress these students may have made in their English language development in their respective institutions.

Thus, both national and statewide language policy issues collude with each other in ways that privilege EM students over vernacular-medium ones. By having professional disciplines available only in the EM, national and statewide language policies seem to ensure that vernacular medium students do not have a fair chance to compete.

CURRICULAR PRACTICES

An Almost Exclusive Focus on English Literature Instead of English Language

Majoring in English literature—including British, U.S., and Indian writings in English—seems to be a popular way in which GM students feel they can master the English language. However, many students speak of the alienation and cultural dissonance from the literary texts they are reading (Ramanathan, 1999, 2004).

A second-year, *English special class* (for students majoring in English) in a very poor women's college with which I have had extensive contact is a case in point. A required text for the class is *The Importance of Being Earnest* (a comedy by the English playwright Oscar Wilde) and the syllabus requires that students be exposed both to theories of comedy as a form and to a close examination of the text itself. In each of the classes observed, the teacher taught primarily in Gujarati, and in instances when he did lapse into English, he typically followed it up with a direct translation in Gujarati ("How did drama begin? *Drama na udhbhog kevi rithe sharu thayu*?"). While reading the play aloud in English, the teacher laboriously translated each sentence, so that the larger comic scene seldom emerged. Students, likewise, seemed to concentrate too hard on figuring out the literal meaning of each sentence. Thus, while the teacher seemed to enjoy some of the comic scenes, laughing uproariously at moments, most of the students looked on uncomprehendingly. When the teacher tried to explain some of the comic elements in Gujarati in a scene, several of the students said that they couldn't see what was so funny. In one instance, the instructor spent about 15 minutes explaining sarcasm, a rhetorical turn that these students seemed unfamiliar with, but one that was crucial to some of the humor in the scene they were collectively reading. When asked about it in a group interview, several of the students maintained that although they realized they needed the explanation on sarcasm, they did not find any hilarity in what they were reading.

The poignancy of moments such as these and the general alienation that these students experience is caused by several competing factors, all tied to English-Vernacular Divide (Ramanathan, 2005): the content is culturally alien and far removed; the language in which the texts are written is one in which they are not fluent; and the language in which the content is explained reduces, in the above instance, a really funny literary scene to dullness and tedium, with traces of humor completely erased. The conflict between mediums of instruction—English in the text and Gujarati in class—among other things in such cases, serves to devoice the students, failing to help them gain fluency in either the language or the content/culture of what they are reading.

This preoccupation with English literature, both during the Raj (British Rule) and currently, was/is based on a simultaneous alienation from vernacular, regional literatures (Tharu, 1997), a practice that some scholars in India believe not only severs vital connections with local, indigenous cultures and literatures but also leaves students linguistically impoverished (Devy, 1997). A palliative to this trend has been a recent cry to integrate the literatures, to lead students from "an awareness of Shakespeare's artistry to a recognition of Bendre's genius" and to place them in a "global imaginary museum" that houses both Western and vernacular literatures (Tharu, p. 67). While this awareness of vernacular literatures is valuable in itself—inasmuch as it represents among other things, a marked anticolonial stance—it still, by and large, leaves the GM student out, since the vernacular literary pieces are themselves typically taught in their English translations. Thus, while the content of these texts may be more accessible, the medium in which they are translated still shuts them out.

PEDAGOGICAL MATERIALS: TEXTBOOKS

In Ramanathan (2002), I point out ways in which English language textbooks used in Gujarati and English medium K-12 classes draw on divergent cultural models of literacy regarding what it means to be "literate in English" in the Indian context, with EM textbooks advantaging one set of students, and parallel pedagogic practices in GM textbooks serving to disadvantage vernacular medium students. I offer here a summary of some points in that piece.

More Westernized Teaching Practices in EM Texts: Self-learning, Opinions, Compositions, and Voice

One noticeable way in which EM students are privileged is evident in the language-related exercises in textbooks that foster the voices and opinions of EM students and the complete lack of them in the GM counterparts. The inclusion and rehearsal of these activities—they occur systematically at the end of each reading—seem to encourage EM, middle-class students to see themselves as individuals with views that matter and that need to be articulated. Two exercises that particularly foster such qualities in EM texts are those entitled "self learning" and "compositions."

Self-learning

Related to themes in the readings and partially related to the exercises at the end of the readings, the following sections are like miniature puzzles that students are supposed to work on their own:

> Grade 5:
> 1. (At the end of a reading on different seasons) Make word-flowers for each season. Write the name of the season in the middle and words associated with it in the petals. One on summer is partly done for you.
>
> 2. Arrange the following events in proper order:
> Larry was in the next room doing his homework.
> Larry found the stamp from the 11th seat in row five.
> When Mr. Halperin was arrested, he whispered, "Seven, Alice, like in the old clock."
> Larry entered the theatre and went to the seat he wanted.
> Mr. Halperin had taken the stamp to help his wife.
> (Jadeja et al., 1999: 23)
>
> Grade 6: 'E' is one of the commonest letters in the English language. Insert the letter 'E' in the following, wherever required to make complete words: Examples, NTR—ENTER
> AGL, CHS, HR, VRY, SVN, STM, THR, FL, NDL, KPR
> (Purani et al., 1998: 68)
>
> Grade 7: (based on an excerpt from *The Diary of Anne Frank*)
> We think of some human qualities as positive and some others as negative. For example, 'love' as we all agree, is a positive quality. Enter a tick in the appropriate column against each adjective given in the following table:
>
> | Quality | Positive | Negative |
> |---|---|---|
> | love | | |
> | jealousy | | |
> | courage | | |
> | pride | | |
> | tolerance | | |
> | selfishness | | |
> | cowardice | | |
> | nobility | | |
>
> (Purani et al., 1999: 26)

As such exercises are included in "self-learning" sections, they seem to be based on the assumption that EM students will not need help with them and will be able to accomplish these tasks on their own: Seventh grade children should be able to specify that jealousy and cowardice are negative qualities, just as the 5th grade students should be able to arrange jumbled narrative events in a particular, chronological order. The preface for the texts in grades 5, 6, 7, and 8 (Gujarat State Board of Textbooks, 1999) insist "self learning …should be used for confidence-building as well as maximization of learning. The pupils should be…encouraged to do the work independently, and the outcomes of their efforts should be utilized for informal assessment" (p. vi). The noticeable absence of such exercises in GM texts, on the other hand, makes one wonder: Why aren't vernacular-medium students expected to "self-learn" and have a "voice"?

Voice or Opinions in Compositions

Along with "self-learning" sections are writing exercises that specifically ask EM students to articulate their opinions on certain topics. Entitled "composition," the writing prompts in almost all the EM textbooks expect students to present or manipulate their voices to suit the topic. The following are representative samples from textbooks for grades 5, 6, and 7:

Grade 5:
- Write a short paragraph of 10-12 lines on Madam Cama.
- Imagine you are Anabelle Nelson. Write a letter to Manisha saying how you celebrated the first anniversary of your friendship.
- Two boys go on a trip to the mountainside. They see a cave and go inside. To their great surprise, they find a treasure. As they are coming out, they come face to face with the chief of the robbers…. Now write 10-12 sentences to complete this story.
- If you could become invisible for a day, what would you do? Write about it 10-15 sentences.

(Jadeja et al., 1999)

Grade 6:
- Do you know a simple-minded person like Andy? Write ten sentences about him or her.
- Write two paragraphs about your plans for Christmas/Diwali/Id.
- You are traveling by bus/train. There is an accident on the way. Write two paragraphs describing your experience.
- Write an autobiography of a circus animal.
- Write a paragraph on "if I were a bird…"

(Purani et al., 1998)

Grade 7:
- Write a short autobiography of a dog.
- Write a short essay on: My favorite bird.
- Write an essay on the migration of birds and some reasons for it.
- Imagine that you were lost in a strange place. Write about your experiences.
- Do you know the difference between a portrait and a photograph? A photograph only shows us how a person looked at a particular time. A portrait, too, tells us about a person's appearance, but in addition, it may reveal traits of a person's character, personality, habits, etc. Prepare a word portrait of a nurse or a traffic policeman.

(Purani et al., 1999)

Several of these essay prompts ask that students assume another voice (to pretend they are a bird, or write an autobiography of a circus animal or imagine being Annabelle Nelson)—while others ask them to imagine make-believe situations ("imagine you were lost in a strange place" or to complete a story or narrative already begun). While the notion of *voice* does not seem to be overtly taught or emphasized in these texts, as it sometimes is in writing or rhetoric textbooks used in freshman composition classes in North American universities for instance (see Ramanathan & Atkinson, 1999; Ramanathan & Kaplan, 1996), prompts such as the above are already laying the groundwork for tertiary level academic work. Writing tasks in GM texts, on the other hand, especially from grades 5-7 are limited to "gaining control of the basic mechanics of writing like capital and small letters" (Grade 5), to "writing words and sentences neatly on a line with proper spacing" (Grade 6), to writing "answers to questions based on the text" (Grade 7)[3] (For an extended discussion of these divergent practices, see Ramanathan, 2004, 2005).

These different literacy practices point to at least two crucial assumptions being made of GM (and EM) students: GM students cannot work on their own (hence the absence of "self learning" sections), and the English language proficiency of a GM student at any grade level is not considered adequate to write extended compositions or to assume another character's voice. These assumptions seem to be embedded in another overarching one, namely that "individualized" ways of learning and articulating confident opinions in writing draw on westernized ways of being, thinking, and operating in the world, ways that are likely to be markedly different from the home lives of these students, and are deemed "irrelevant" for vernacular-medium students (For a fuller account, see Ramanathan 2003).

Differences Related to Readings or Content in the Two Sets of Textbooks

The readings in both sets of texts point to divergent English literacy models as well. GM texts, with their general focus on survival English, emphasize how language is used in particular Indian contexts (at the park, at the zoo, or sending a telegram). The readings in EM texts, in contrast, are more cosmopolitan, drawing as they do from British, American, and Indian literary texts. Table 1, partially drawn from the list of contents published by Gujarat State Board of Textbooks, charts out the readings for grades 6, 8, and 10.

Several interesting features emerge from a close comparison of the content in the two sets of textbooks. Poetry, a genre that draws heavily on metaphorical use of language, is relegated to the "optional" category in GM texts. Indeed, prefaces to the textbooks maintain that poetry for GM students is to be regarded as "supplementary reading" (Gujarat State Board of Textbooks, 1999: ii). EM texts, on the other hand, include essays and short readings from a relatively panoramic range of texts, with readings on Abraham Lincoln in grade 6, to those by Stephen Leacock and Tolstoy in grade 8, to ones by Hemmingway and Tagore in Grade 10. Also, poetry is not an optional category in these texts.

Other interesting details related to content also emerge: None of the prose sections in GM texts (which generally comprise most of the text) are identified by the authors who wrote them, giving the impression that because these pieces are not "creative" and literary, they do not need to by identified by authors. By contrast, all of the prose and poetry selections in the EM texts are "original" literary pieces that

Table 1. List of Contents for Grades 6, 8, and 10

A selection from GM texts	A selection from EM texts
Grade 6: GM: List of contents *Welcome, friends* *A Fancy Dress Show* *A Seashore* *A Park* *A Village Fair* *In the School Compound* *What Time is it Now?* *The Environment Day*	Grade 6: EM: List of contents *A Voyage to Lilliput* *Farewell to the Farm* *The Changing World* *Abraham Lincoln (Parts 1 and 2)* *Don Quixote Meets a Company of Actors* *The Poet's House* *Woodman, Spare that Tree!* *City Streets and Country Roads*
Grade 8: GM (no authors provided) Poetry: (optional) *Rhyme* *Rhyme* *Rhyme* *Only One Mother* *The Picnic* *Two Birds* Prose: *Let's Begin* *Hello! I am Vipul* *A Railway Station* *At the Zoo* *On the Farm* *Good Manners* *In the Kitchen*	Grade 8: EM Poetry: *Under the Greenwood Tree*: Shakespeare *She Dwelt among the Untrodden Ways*: William Wordsworth *To a Child Dancing in the Wind*: W. B. Yeats *The Listeners*: Walter de la Mare *Coming*: Phillip Larkin *A Blackbird Singing*: R.S.Thomas Prose: *Little Children Wiser than Men:* Leo Tolstoy *Do You Know?* Clifford Parker *My Financial Career*: Stephen Leacock *The Lady is an Engineer*: Patricia Strauss *The Judgment seat of Vikramaditya*: Sister Nivedita
Grade 10: GM Poetry (optional) *Laughing Song*: Blake *In the Night*: Naidu *Wander Thirst*: Gerald Gould *The Secret of the Machines*: Rudyard Kipling Prose (no authors provided) *An Act of Service* *Strange but True* *Have You Heard This One?* *Vaishali at the Police Station* *Prevention of Cruelty to Animals* *The Indian Village– Then And Now*	Grade 10: EM Poetry: *Blow, Blow, thou Winter Wind*: Shakespeare *London: Blake* *Upon Westminster Bridge*: Wordsworth *To–:* Shelley *La Belle Dame Sans Merci*: Keats *The Professor*: Nissim Ezekeil *The Fountain*: Lowell Prose: Ramanujam: C.P. Snow *On Saying Please*: A.G. Gardener *The Home Coming*: Tagore *Andrew Carnegie*: E. H. Carter *A Day's Wait*: Hemmingway *After Twenty Years*: O' Henry *Vikram Sarabhai*: M.G.K. Menon (Gujarat State Board of Textbooks, 1999)

are identified by the authors who wrote them. This relatively general importance placed on the author shows up in other instances as well: the comprehension-writing questions at the end of these readings (in EM texts) emphasize the importance of interpreting, questioning, and decoding authorial stances or intentions. The following are examples:

1. Does E. M. Forster describe tolerance? (Grade 12, based on E. M. Forster's essay, "Tolerance") (Khan et al., 2000: 74)

2. How does Churchill justify Britain's stand during the war? Do you agree with his views? (Grade 11, reference year, pp. 102-107, based on Churchill's essay, entitled "Speech to Congress") (Moses et al., 2000: 107)

3. Why, according to Joad, does money and power not make us civilized? Why do Shakespeare, Beethoven, and Raphael, matter for civilization? (Grade 10, based on C. E. M. Joad's essay, entitled "A dialogue on civilization") (Vamdatta et al., 2000: 158)

4. The poet, Keats, has asked several questions in this poem. Are they answered? What are your answers to these questions (Grade 6, based on a poem by John Keats entitled "song") (Purani et al., 1998: 127)

GM texts, on the other hand, for grades 5-9 evidence no such questions, leaving one with the impression that delving into authors' minds in order to capture authorial intentions or voice is a skill that is irrelevant for GM students. As mentioned previously, exercises at the end of readings in GM texts are limited to explanations of and exercises for grammatical points.

CONCLUSIONS

Each of the above ELT-related socio-educational practices shut doors on vernacular-medium students. The general devaluing of vernacular resources in this larger landscape is not to be missed at all. Some questions for us researchers and teachers, then, seem to be: What can we do to ensure that the vernacular backgrounds of students are valued and integrated? How can we change our (TESOL) realities to make this happen? In what ways can we make the distribution of power between languages (mediums of instruction) more just and equitable?

NOTES

[1] Other states vary in when they introduce English in vernacular-medium schools. As recently as June 2000, New Delhi passed a bill that would now introduce English in Hindi-medium schools at the first grade instead of the 5th.

[2] The EM institution studied in Ramanathan (1999) was an exception. A Jesuit institution, as part of its social welfare policy, it opened its doors to *b stream* students with the explicit aim of giving them some of the chances that *a stream* and EM students assume and get.

[3] The writing requirements for EM texts in contrast range from "writing answers to questions based on the text (grade 5) to "writing and building stories on given points"(Grade 6) to "writing essays based on the text" (Grade 7) (Purani et al., 1999: iv).

REFERENCES

Agarwal, J. C. (1984). *Landmarks in the history of modern Indian education*. New Delhi: Vikas Publishing House.

Canagarajah, S. (1993). Critical ethnography of a Sri Lankan classroom: Ambiguities in student opposition to reproduction in ESOL. *TESOL Quarterly, 27*, 601–626.

Devy, G. (1997). Some anthropological observations on the study of English literature prefaced by the confessions of an English teacher. In S. Tharu (Ed.), *Subject to change* (pp. 159–169). New Delhi: Orient Longman.

Holliday, A. (1994). *Appropriate methodology and social context*. Cambridge: Cambridge University Press.

Jadeja, R., Shrinivas, R., & Vansia, K. (1999). *English, standard 5*. Gandhinagar: Gujarat State Board of Textbooks.

Jayaram, N. (1993). The language question in higher education: Trends and issues. In S. Chitnis & P. Altbach (Eds.), *Higher education reform in India* (pp. 84–114). New Delhi: Sage Publications.

Kachru, B. B. (1985). *Standards, codifications, and sociolinguistic realism: The English language in the outer circle*. Cambridge: Cambridge University Press.

Khan, J., Desai, R., & Vyas, H. (2000). *English, standard 12*, Gandhinagar: Gujarat State Board of Textbooks.

Moses, D., Soni, P., Jadeja, R., & Kapadia, S. (2000). *English, standard 11*. Gandhinagar: Gujarat State Board of Texbooks.

Pakir, A. (1991). The range and depth of English-knowing bilinguals in Singapore. *World Englishes, 10*, 167–180.

Pennycook, A. (1994). *The cultural politics of English as an international language*. NY: Longman.

Pennycook, A. (1998). *English and the discourses of colonialism*. London: Routledge.

Phillipson, R. (1992). *Linguistic imperialism*. Oxford: Oxford University Press.

Purania, T., Nityadandanam, I., & Vansia, K. (1999). *English, standard, 7*. Gandhinagar: Gujarat State Board of Textbooks.

Purani, T., Nityanandanam, I., & Patel, S. (1998). *English, standard 6*. Gandhinagar: Gujarat State Board of Texbooks.

Ramanathan, V. (1999). "English is here to stay": A critical look at institutional and educational practices in India. *TESOL Quarterly, 33*(2), 211–31.

Ramanathan, V. (2002). What does "literate in English" mean? A critical examination of divergent literacy practices for vernacular vs. English-medium students in India. *Canadian Modern Language Review, 59*(3), 125–51.

Ramanathan, V. (2003). Written textual production and consumption (WTPC) in vernacular and English-medium settings in Gujarat, India. *Journal of Second Language Writing, 12*(2), 125–50.

Ramanathan, V. (2004). Ambiguities about English: ideologies and critical practice in vernacular-medium colleges in Gujarat, India. *Journal of Language, Identity and Education, 4*(1), 45–65.

Ramanathan, V. (2005). *The English-vernacular divide: Postcolonial language politics and practice*. Clevedon: Multilingual Matters.

Ramanathan, V., & Atkinson, D. (1999). Individualism, academic writing and ESL writers. *Journal of Second Language Writing, 8*(1), 45–75.

Ramanathan, V., & Kaplan, R. B. (1996). Some problematic "channels" in the teaching of critical thinking in current L1 composition textbook: Implications for L2 student-writers. *Issues in Applied Linguistics, 7*(2), 225–249.

Tharu, S., Ed. (1997). *Subject to change*. New Delhi: Orient Longman.

Vamdatta, D., Joshi, P., & Patel, Y. (2000). *English, standard 10*. Gandhinagar: Gujarat State Board of Textbooks.

Watenburg, T. (1990). *The forms of power: From domination to transformation*. Philadelphia: Temple University Press.

CHAPTER 5

ELT POLICY DIRECTIONS IN MULTILINGUAL JAPAN

YASUKO KANNO

The University of Washington, USA

ABSTRACT

ELT policies in Japan have been extremely controversial and not entirely consistent in recent years. An advisory panel to the Prime Minister proposed to make English Japan's official second language, which produced an enormous debate but not concrete steps to implement the proposal. Teachers at the secondary level continue to teach English in preparation for university entrance examinations, whereas in 2002 English was introduced in public elementary schools with a focus on communicative English. In this chapter, I analyze debates and concerns in each of these areas. Although there is a general call for a more effective, communicatively-oriented English education in Japan, some educators and policy makers argue that to allow more emphasis on English is to willingly subject Japan to English imperialism. On the other hand, the participants in these debates have limited their attention almost exclusively to the language majority population i.e. what the spread of English might mean for the Japanese. The question of how to reconcile the influence and power of English with the need to nurture other minority languages in Japan, crucial given Japan's increasing linguistic and cultural diversity, is rarely addressed.

INTRODUCTION

The purpose of this chapter is to provide an overview of ELT policy directions in Japan. A number of recent developments in Japan have focused public attention on English education in the country: Japan's long recession, a sudden increase of foreign migrant workers, the proposal by the prime minister's advisory panel to make English Japan's official second language, and introduction of English at the elementary school level. This chapter aims to demonstrate how these developments are interrelated and shape ELT policy directions in Japan.

Before I go into the discussion of ELT directions, I want to start with some background. First of all, despite its persistent stereotype as a homogeneous country, contemporary Japan is an increasingly multilingual and multicultural nation (Maher, 2002; Maher & Yashiro, 1995; Noguchi & Fotos, 2001). Currently, approximately 2 million foreign nationals, or 1.57% of the total population, live in Japan (Homusho, 2006). Fifty six percent are Korean and Chinese (including permanent residents who have made Japan their home for generations), followed by Brazilians and Filipinos. It is also now commonplace for Japanese citizens to spend some years abroad and then return to Japan proficient in English or other languages. In contemporary Japan, cultural and linguistic hybridity is a fact of life. Youths especially "listen to such black-derived music as rap, reggae, and hip-hop, accept Jamaican dreadlocks, and enjoy conversation with friends at Thai or Taiwanese restaurants in Shinjuku"

(Usui, 2000, p. 298). Understanding Japan as an increasingly multilingual and multicultural nation is an important starting point.

As part of this multilingualism, people in Japan are already exposed to a considerable amount of English. A quick glance at a national newspaper reveals the use of English loan words such as *client, bestseller, mystery, comment, member, center, suspense, artist, revenge, fan,* and *thrilling* (these words are spelled in *katakana,* one of three scripts in Japanese). In fact, although they are originally borrowed from English, these words are already part of the Japanese language. New words are constantly being borrowed from English and incorporated into Japanese, to the point where the meanings of many loan words are opaque to many Japanese speakers. There are several radio stations, such as J-WAVE, FM Yokohama, and Bay FM that air bilingual programs, in which DJs speak either in English or code-switch frequently between Japanese and English (Maher, 1991). And of course, Japan has been exposed to the Internet as much as any other developed nation. One could argue then that it is difficult to live in Japan these days without at least some knowledge of English.

Despite the ubiquity of English phrases in Japan, however, the average Japanese person cannot hold a basic conversation in English. That the Japanese education system has been stunningly unsuccessful in producing competent English speakers is not new information (Kato, 2000; Kunieda, 2000). What is new now is the sense of urgency about the problem, stemming not only from the field of education but also from the business world. A long-lasting recession in the country combined with the rise of other Asian nations such as China as new, and threateningly powerful, economic powers adds to this desperation. Of course, the fact that the average Japanese businessman cannot speak English fluently may not be a major cause of Japan's economic slump. However, when statistics show that Japan's average TOEFL score is among the lowest in Asian countries ("TOEFL saikai," 2000), however meaningless such a comparison may be, it is easy to interpret it as yet another sign that Japan is in decline. The demand that government and company employees learn to speak English is stronger than ever before. Opportunities for promotion are now often contingent upon attaining a specified level on the Test of English for International Communication (TOEIC) ("Eigo ga damenara," 2000; Nagashima, 2000).

In the following sections, I summarize recent developments in three areas: the government's proposal to make English an official second language, resistance among secondary level English teachers to communicative language teaching, and the introduction of English in elementary schools. All three topics have sparked much debate. Yet, most of these debates center on the question of what it means for the language majority population in Japan to learn English. Although the discourses surrounding English education relate English learning to international understanding, paradoxically they almost entirely ignore the fact that over 2 million non-Japanese nationals live in Japan. In the final section, then, I address the implications of an increasing emphasis on English education in public schools for the education of language minority students.

CURRENT DEBATES AND CONCERNS

English as an Official Language

In January 2000, an advisory panel to the then Prime Minister Keizo Obuchi issued a report on "Japan's Goals for the 21st Century" (The Prime Minister's Commission, 2000). Among many recommendations, the panel proposed to make English an official second language of Japan. The report stated:

> In the long term, it may be possible to make English an official second language, but national debate will be needed. First, though, every effort should be made to equip the population with a working knowledge of English. This is not simply a matter of foreign-language education. It should be regarded as a strategic imperative. (p. 10)

From the comments made by Hayao Kawai (2000), chair of the panel, it seems that the panel proposed the idea, not so much to actually implement the proposal in the near future but to provoke a debate. The hue and cry that ensued in the Japanese media suggests that this goal succeeded.

Vocal proponents of the proposal, many of them original members of the advisory panel, emphasize the importance of recognizing English as *the* international language. For this group, the power and importance of English in global society is a given, and they argue that if Japan does not make a concerted effort to elevate the English proficiency of the general public, "Japan will slip off the stage of history, its spirit and truth uncomprehended, its sympathies unfelt" (Funabashi, 2000/2002, p. 38). Behind the push to give English a more official status in Japan lies a strong sense of crisis about the future of Japanese economy. The report notes, "We share a sense of urgency. We fear that as things stand Japan is heading for decline. That is how harsh the environment both surrounding Japan and within Japan itself has become" (The Prime Minister's Commission, 2000, p. 1). Suzuki (2002) points out that similar moves in the past to adopt another language as the nation's official language also happened at times of national crisis: once right after the Meiji Restoration and once again after the Second World War. The proposal to make English an official second language was thus motivated by a desperate desire to make the nation economically more competitive again by promoting English proficiency among the general public.

Opponents of the proposal question the uncritical acceptance of the power of English as the international language, citing English imperialism (Phillipson, 1992). They claim that if English were made Japan's official second language, it would further corrode the Japanese language, which already has a number of loan words from English, and seriously threaten Japanese identity (Nakamura, 2000/2002; Tsuda, 1990, 2000/2002). In keeping with the metaphor of imperialism and colonization, Nakamura predicts that such a policy would turn many Japanese into "slaves of English (*eigo dorei*)" (p. 112).

It is easy to see the influence of *Nihonjinron*, a linguistic and cultural ideology long present in Japan that stresses the uniqueness of the Japanese and things Japanese, in the opponents' arguments. Nakamura (2000/2002), for instance, states in unambiguous terms, "the reason why the Japanese are Japanese is because they use the Japanese language" (p. 114). Tsuda (1990) also calls the Japanese language "the core of Japanese identity" (p. 92). As Usui (2000) points out, such nationalist thinkers pay little attention to the fact that some Japanese nationals with long overseas experiences may identify more strongly with other languages, or that naturalized Japanese living in Japan may continue to use and feel strong ties with their first language. Their scope of vision affords no room for a multilingual and multicultural Japan. But a similar Nihonjinron may also be a driving force in the pro-English camp. One of the most vocal proponents, Yoichi Funabashi in an exchange with the linguist Takao Suzuki (Funabashi & Suzuki, 1999/2002), argues, "Japanese expressions lack logic and avoid clear statements" (pp. 22-23). Suzuki concurs, adding, "the Japanese are an ethnic group who have spent 2000 years in an environment that does not require self-objectification" (p. 22). Their exchange is based on the shared assumption that Japanese is a vague language that shapes and is shaped by the homogeneous nature of the Japanese race.

Rather paradoxically, both camps refer to the increasing presence of foreign residents in Japan as a reason to promote, or to oppose, the English-as-an-official-language policy. Yet, they both seem to fail to notice the contradiction between their reference to the growing diversity in Japan and their "Japan as a homogeneous nation" assumption. Proponents of making English an official language argue that the general improvement of the average Japanese's English proficiency would facilitate the social integration of foreign immigrants into Japanese society (Funabashi, 2000/2002). What they fail to understand is that the vast majority of foreign immigrants and migrant workers in Japan are not English speakers. Improved general English proficiency on the part of Japanese citizens may help promote communication between Japanese company employees and Western company executives who are sent from North America and Europe. However it is unlikely to facilitate communication between Japanese small factory owners and non-Japanese assembly-line workers from Asia and South America. In this respect, the opponents of the official English language are closer to the mark. Some of them argue that giving English an official language status would sanction the dominance of Japanese and English over other languages and further advantage speakers of English and Japanese over speakers of other languages (Tsuda, 2000/2002). I will come back to this issue later in the section on future directions.

English Instruction at the Secondary Level

One of the consequences of the English-as-an-official-second-language debate is that the attention of the general public has turned once again to the state of English education in this country. Certainly, the kind of English education that does not allow learners to hold the most basic level of conversation after 6 years does not sit well with the ambitious goal of equipping the population with a working knowledge of English. There is sometimes a perception that the traditional methods of teaching English persist in Japan because that is what *Monbukagakusho* (the Ministry of Education, Culture, Sports, Science and Technology) wants. In fact, as Yoshida (2002) points out, the *Course of Study* (the curriculum guidelines that the Ministry revises and issues every decade) emphasizes the fostering of communicative competence in English. Even in as early as 1970, the emphasis was on "comprehending the foreign language" and "expressing oneself in the foreign language" (Yoshida, p. 198). The word *communication* appears in the Course of Study for the first time in the 1989 revision. The goals were set for both junior high school English and high school English to "understand a foreign language," to "develop a positive attitude to want to communicate in a foreign language," and to "develop the basis for international understanding" (p. 199). In order to further highlight the importance of communication, *Oral Communication* was introduced as one of the English courses at the high school level (Kunieda, 2000). In the latest version of the Course of Study, revised in 1998, an emphasis is placed on "fostering practical communicative abilities to comprehend information, to understand others' intentions and to express one's own ideas" (Monbukagakusho, 1998). Not only does the Ministry set the overall goal of English education, but it also suggests concrete instructional techniques such as group work, role-play, skits, team teaching, letter writing, and email exchange. It also discourages excessive linguistic and grammatical explanation in the classroom. In addition, through the Japan Exchange and Teaching (JET) Program, the Japanese government invites over 5,000 recent college graduates annually, mainly from Western countries, as Assistant Language Teachers (ALTs) to assist English instruction in secondary schools (McConnell, 2000; Monbukagakusho, 2002). Thus, it does seem that Monbukagakusho wants English teachers to focus on communicative competence (see Shin, this volume, for a similar discussion on ELT in Korea).

Yet, classroom teachers continue to teach using the grammar-translation method (Gorsuch, 2000). One newspaper article reports that concern with grammatical form and translation is still so paramount in even supposedly communicatively oriented *Oral Communication* that it is often nicknamed "Oral G"— G as in grammar ("Ikiru chikara," 2002). Gorsuch (2000) argues that university entrance examinations focus on the knowledge of grammatical points, vocabulary, and translation (from English to Japanese), and that high school teachers' priority is to prepare their students for university entrance exams. Academic high schools are ranked according to the number of students they can successfully send to top universities via entrance examinations (Gorsuch, 2000; Rohlen, 1983). The "effectiveness" of individual teachers is also gauged to a large extent by how successfully they can prepare their students to take the entrance exams. Since university entrance exams continue to emphasize grammar, vocabulary, and English translation, it is these aspects, not speaking and listening, that classroom teachers emphasize in their daily teaching. "It seems likely," Gorsuch (2000) writes, "teachers simply adapt the guidelines in *The Course of Study* to existing university preparation" (p. 682).

An analysis of the English components of university entrance exams by Brown and Yamashita (1995) supports Gorsuch's (2000) claims. Their analysis of 10 examinations, set by public and private universities as well as the nationwide "Center" examination, revealed a heavy reliance on reading passages and translation. Candidates are mostly asked to answer true/false, multiple choice, and matching questions and to translate short passages from English to Japanese. The result is that they are hardly required to produce English at all. Given that the ability to communicate in English is minimally relevant in the entrance exams, and that reading and translation are what get students into competitive universities, it is not surprising that students and their parents demand their English teachers to focus on these areas in their high school classes and that English teachers comply.

Elementary School English

The existing English education system at the secondary level has proved remarkably resistant to change. Monbukagakusho has thus decided to implement a new initiative that does not require the dismantling of the existing English education system. This new initiative focuses on English in elementary schools.

According to the new Course of Study (Monbukagakusho, 1998), which took effect in April 2002, public elementary schools may elect to teach English (or another foreign language) as part of the newly added "Period for Integrated Study (*sogo-teki na gakushu no jikan*)."[1] Each school is to take the initiative in setting a theme for the integrated study, such as local history, international understanding, health, environmental studies, or information technology. Those schools that elect to teach English will do so under the theme of international understanding (*kokusai rikai kyoiku*). However, because not all elementary schools teach English, junior high schools continue to assume zero proficiency when they start their programs.

Integrated Study starts in the third grade and is assigned three sessions a week (45 minutes a session). However, given that most elementary schools do not have classroom teachers who are trained to teach English and must therefore rely on ALTs or locally hired part-time instructors, it is more likely that at least for the next several years, students will receive at most one session of English a week. Classes are to focus on spoken English, leaving reading and writing to junior high school; activities center around singing, jazz chants, games, role-play, and skits (Monbukagakusho, 2001). The most recent statistics show that 93.6% of public elementary schools are teaching English in one form or another (Monbukagakusho, 2006c).

Introduction of English in the elementary grades has been hugely controversial, and remains so even though in reality, most children are already taking their English lessons. Proponents of elementary school English support the idea mainly for two reasons. First noting the rigid grammar-translation method in junior high schools, which often turns off students, they hope that genuinely communicative, experience-based English instruction—more games, singing, and conversation than grammar and reading—will foster a favorable attitude towards English on the part of young learners (Higuchi & Miura, 1997). Even if they encounter the grammar-translation method once they are in junior high schools, students who have been favorably disposed to English will continue to be motivated to learn English.

But one could argue that in this case, what needs to be changed is the English education in secondary schools. However, proponents of elementary school English education invoke another rationale for pushing English into the earlier grades: the Critical Period Hypothesis (Ito, 1997, 2000; Shirahata, 1997). They argue, citing studies such as Lenneberg (1967), Johnson and Newport (1989), and Larsen-Freeman and Long (1991), that there is a critical period for L2 learning and that starting in the first year of junior high school (12-13 years old) is too late for learning English. They particularly stress the importance of starting early for the acquisition of native-like pronunciation. Among them, Ito (2000) argues that given that the critical period for native pronunciation and syntax ends as early as age 6, starting in the third grade (8-9 years old) is already too late.

Opponents of early English education question the importance of native-like pronunciation. They argue that what is important is pronunciation that does not impede communication, which can be acquired even after puberty (Otsu & Torigai, 2002). Also, what often concerns the opponents is that the introduction of another language at an age when children are still in the process of acquiring their first language, Japanese, will confuse the learners and might negatively affect their Japanese development (Katagiri, Nakayama, Komazawa, Minoura, & Shirahata,

1994, as cited in Shirahata, 1997, p. 107). A third concern often raised is the issue of priority. Starting in 2002, all public schools adopted a 5-days-a-week schedule, ending the tradition of half a day on Saturdays. Opponents argue that, as there is simply too much to teach in the shorter period of time available, priority at the elementary level should be given to the development of first language literacy and numeracy and not to English (Otsu & Torigai, 2002).

Research in French immersion in Canada suggest that the opponents' concern about the negative impact on children's Japanese language development is probably unfounded. While French immersion students, who receive most of their instruction in French, initially lag behind, they eventually come to perform as well as or better than their English-educated peers on all aspects of English (Swain, 1997). A similar study at Kato Gakuen, the first school in Japan to offer an English immersion program, also found that immersion students learned English with no detriment to their Japanese (Bostwick, 1999). These are immersion students, who receive 50% to 100% of their instruction in an L2. One or two English lessons a week are highly unlikely to have an impact, either positive or negative, on students' Japanese language development.

The opponents' third point, that priority should be given to L1 development at the elementary school, however, is worth more attention especially when one considers an increasing public concern about the decline of students' academic abilities across all grades. Suzuki (2002) reminds us about the *zero-sum* nature of curriculum scheduling: time given to one subject is time taken away from others. Otsu and Torigai (2002) argue that time invested in English instruction can be more beneficially used to teach Japanese or other subjects at the elementary level. Their view is supported by Marinova-Todd, Marshall, and Snow (2000), who have recently challenged the critical period hypothesis. Marinova-Todd et al. caution:

> Decision to introduce foreign language instruction in the elementary grades should be weighed against the costs to other components of the school curriculum; as far as we know, there are no good studies showing that foreign language instruction is worth more than additional time invested in math, science, music, art, or even basic L1 literacy instruction. (p. 29)

Despite these reservations, however, English instruction in elementary schools has already begun, and once thus started, it is likely to stay.

FUTURE DIRECTIONS

As can be seen from the above discussion, debates on ELT policy directions in Japan have been extremely active in recent years. Yet these debates have focused almost entirely on what the spread of English and changes in English education mean for the language majority population. As Maher (2002) comments:

> In Japan many linguists and language education scholars, in concert with the media and political bodies, have mostly ignored the (abnormal) multilingual phenomena going on all around them, preferring the safety of (normal) national narratives, i.e. we are one people and one language (*tan'itsu minzoku, tan'itsu gengo*). (p. 165)

It is ironic that debates on English education have mostly ignored linguistic and cultural diversity within the nation when the language of the debates often invokes "international understanding."

The fact of the matter is that 2 million foreign nationals live in Japan. The number of Japanese as a second language (JSL) students in public schools (Grades 1-12) has more than quadrupled over the past 15 years and currently stands at 20,692 (Monbukagakusho, 2006b). These figures are growing every year, and "there is no path back to the old, cherished world" (Maher, 2002, p. 165). Discussion on ELT policies in Japan must explicitly address how to reconcile the influence and power of English with the need to nurture other minority languages within Japan. In the last section of this chapter, then, I would like to discuss this issue.

Monbukagakusho (1998) claims that the goal of introducing English in elementary schools is not language acquisition per se but international understanding. The case studies I conducted (Kanno, 2003, 2004) suggest that the International Understanding (i.e. English) class in public elementary schools can give language minority students a valuable opportunity to showcase their knowledge of other languages and cultures, or it can put them to further disadvantage, depending on how the class is taught. In a school that I call Sugino Elementary, International Understanding was taught by a Chinese part-time instructor who spoke fluent English. About a third of the student population in this school was of foreign origin, mainly Chinese. The goal of the class was to introduce Chinese culture to students through English. In theory one could argue that if international understanding was the real goal, the use of Chinese would be just as good as English, and in this setting more fitting. In practice this class did give language minority students some opportunities to shine. Because of their familiarity with Chinese culture, the Chinese members of the class understood the content of the class better than their Japanese peers. When the instructor introduced basic Chinese expressions or taught a Chinese song, they were able to provide a model for other students. Thus, although the class was mainly an English conversation class, it nonetheless helped promote other languages and cultures.

In a school in another prefecture that I call Midori Elementary, in contrast, the English class worked to further disadvantage language minority students. In Midori, about 8% of the students were South American, mostly Brazilian. The instructor of the English class was an American who spoke fluent Japanese. Because he had Japanese as a resource, the instructor naturally used it throughout the class to aid students' comprehension. His bilingual use helped Japanese members of the class; however, for Brazilian members of the class it imposed double translation. They did not understand the Japanese instruction that was offered as an aid to understand English instruction. During a task in which students were supposed to stand up and were allowed to sit down only when they had translated a number given in Japanese into English, a Brazilian boy who had recently arrived was among the last ones to sit down. Another Brazilian girl who was sitting close by looked worried and tried to help him by translating the number into Portuguese. Portuguese and English are linguistically much closer to each other than English and Japanese. Everything being equal—but of course it isn't—Brazilian students might potentially have an advantage over Japanese students in learning English. But because English had to be learned through Japanese, they were disadvantaged in this class just as in all other subject matters.

Concerns for English do not have to be pitted against concerns for minority languages. For example, practices at Sugino Elementary suggest the possibility of mutual enhancement. Canagarajah (1999) has pointed out that people can engage with both English *and* the vernacular and use each language to serve their own personal, ideological, and political purposes. Learning English is just as important for language minority students in Japan as it is for language majority students. However, the current education system in Japan works to promote additive (Japanese-English) bilingualism for Japanese students and subtractive bilingualism for language minority students (Kanno, 2004, forthcoming). Japanese students, especially those from upper and upper-middle classes whose parents can afford private schooling and after-school English conversation lessons, are given a cosmopolitan vision of Japan and are encouraged to learn Japanese and English. On the other hand, language minority students, who are predominantly of working class background, are given no support in public schools for first language (L1) maintenance while they are forced to learn Japanese in a submersion style (Kanno, 2003, 2004, forthcoming; Ota, 2000; Vaipae, 2001). Monbukagakusho (2006a) has recently designated 100 public high schools as "Super English Language High Schools" which focus on high-level English education. Some of these schools employ English as a medium of instruction for subject matter teaching (as in immersion programs). This is in a stark contrast to the refrain that I heard again and again from public school administrators and board of education personnel during my fieldwork that Japanese schools are to use Japanese as the medium of instruction and that they have no obligation to teach language minority students' L1s. Clearly, some versions of "international understanding" count more than others.

NOTES

[1.] It is important to point out that 87% of private elementary schools (about 1% of all elementary schools in Japan) have long been teaching English (Kitamura, 1997). What I am referring to here is the introduction of English instruction into public elementary schools.

REFERENCES

Bostwick, R. M. (1999). *A study of an elementary English language immersion school in Japan.* Unpublished doctoral dissertation, Temple University, Tokyo.
Brown, J. D., & Yamashita, S. O. (1995). English language entrance examinations at Japanese universities: What do we know about them? *JALT Journal, 17*(1), 7–30.
Canagarajah, A. S. (1999). *Resisting linguistic imperialism in English teaching.* Oxford: Oxford University Press.
Eigo ga damenara shoshin mo dame [No English, no promotion]. (2000, February 22). *Asahi Shimbun,* p. 1.
Funabashi, Y. (2000/2002). Eigo koyogo ron no shiso [The philosophy behind the English as an official language]. In Chuko Shinsho La Clef Henshubu & Y. Suzuki (Eds.), *Ronso: Eigo ga koyogo ni naru hi* [A debate: The day English becomes an official language] (pp. 38–47). Tokyo: Chuko Shinsho.
Funabashi, Y., & Suzuki, T. (1999/2002). Eigo ga nippon o sukuu [English will save Japan]. In Chuko Shinsho La Clef Henshubu & Y. Suzuki (Eds.), *Ronso: Eigo ga koyogo ni naru hi* [A debate: The day English becomes an official language] (pp. 5–33). Tokyo: Chuko Shinsho.
Gorsuch, G. J. (2000). EFL educational policies and educational cultures: Influences on teachers' approval of communicative activities. *TESOL Quarterly, 34*(4), 675–710.
"Ikiru chikara" e kabe imada [Obstacles to a "zest for living"]. (2002, April 11). *Asahi Shimbun,* p. 25.
Ito, K. (1997). Shogakko ni okeru gaikokugo kyoiku no igi to yakuwari [The significance and role of foreign language education in elementary schools]. In T. Higuchi (Ed.), *Shogakko karano gaikokugo kyoiku* [Foreign language education in elementary schools] (pp. 94–101). Tokyo: Kenkyusha.
Ito, K. (2000). Soki gaikokugo kyoiku donyu no bunka shinri teki haikei [The cultural-psychological background for early foreign language education]. *Ibunkakan Kyoiku, 14,* 17–32.
Higuchi, T., & Miura, I. (1997). Shogakusei jidai ni eigo o gakushu-shita seito to shinakatta seito no hikaku [A comparison between students who studied English in elementary grades and those who

did not]. In T. Higuchi (Ed.), *Shogakko karano gaikokugo kyoiku* [Foreign language education in elementary schools] (pp. 116–126). Tokyo: Kenkyusha.

Homusho (Japanese Ministry of Justice). (2006). *Heisei 17 nendomatsu genzai ni okeru gaikokujin torokusha tokei ni tsuite* [Results of the 2005 survey on registered foreign residents]. Retrieved July 13, 2006, from http://www.moj.go.jp/PRESS/060530-1/060530-1.html.

Johnson, J., & Newport, E. (1989). Critical period effects in second language learning: The influence of the maturational state on the acquisition of English as a second language. *Cognitive Psychology, 21*, 60–99.

Kanno, Y. (2003). Imagined communities, school visions and the education of bilingual students in Japan. *Journal of Language, Identity, and Education, 2*(4), 285–300.

Kanno, Y. (2004). Sending mixed messages: Language minority education at a Japanese public elementary school. In A. Blackledge & A. Pavlenko (Eds.), *Negotiation of identities in multilingual settings* (pp. 316–338). Clevedon, England: Multilingual Matters.

Kanno, Y. (forthcoming). *Language and education in Japan: Unequal access to bilingualism*. London: Palgrave/Macmillan.

Kato, S. (2000, February 17). Futatabi eigo kyoiku nitsuite [English education revisited]. *Asahi Shimbun*, p. 11.

Kawai, H. (2000, April 4). Kokusai shakai de fukaketsu na "shudan" [An indispensable "tool" in global society]. *Asahi Shimbun*, p. 13.

Kitamura, T. (1997). Anketo ni miru sanpi [A survey on elementary school English]. In T. Higuchi (Ed.), *Shogakko karano gaikokugo kyoiku* [Foreign language education in elementary schools] (pp. 20–27). Tokyo: Kenkyusha.

Kunieda, M. (2000). Shogakko no eigo kyoiku [A framework of English education at elementary schools in Japan]. *Ibunkakan Kyoiku, 14*, 4–16.

Larsen-Freeman, D., & Long, M. (1991). *An introduction to second language acquisition research*. London: Longman.

Lenneberg, E. (1967). *Biological foundations of language*. New York: Wiley.

Maher, J. (1991). Masu media ni okeru eigo [English in the mass media]. In J. Maher & K. Yashiro (Eds.), *Nihon no bairingarizumu* [Bilingualism in Japan] (pp. 17–33). Tokyo: Kenkyusha.

Maher, J. (2002). Language policy for multicultural Japan: Establishing the new paradigm. In S. Baker (Ed.), *Language policy: Lessons from global models* (pp. 164–180). Monterey, CA: Monterey Institute of International Studies.

Maher, J. C., & Yashiro, K. (1995). Multilingual Japan: An introduction. *Journal of Multilingual and Multicultural Development, 16*(1&2), 1–17.

Marinova-Todd, S. H., Marshall, D. B., & Snow, C. E. (2000). Three misconceptions about age and L2 learning. *TESOL Quarterly, 34*(1), 9–34.

McConnell, D. (2000). *Importing diversity: Inside Japan's JET Program*. Berkeley, CA: University of California Press.

Monbukagakusho [Ministry of Education, Culture, Sports, Science and Technology]. (1998). *Gakushu shido yoryo* [The course of study]. Retrieved April 23, 2002, from http://www.mext.go.jp/a_menu/shotou/youryou/index.htm.

Monbukagakusho. (2001). *Shogakko eigo katsudo jissen no tebiki* [Practical handbook for elementary school English activities]. Retrieved May 24, 2002, from http://www.mext.go.jp/b_menu/houdou/13/02/010212.htm.

Monbukagakusho. (2002). *Gaikokugo kyoiku jujitsu no tame no shisaku* [Initiatives for improving foreign language education]. Retrieved May 25, 2002, from http://www.mext.go.jp/b_menu/shingi/f_020201.htm.

Monbukagakusho. (2006a). *Heisei 18 nendo Super English Language High School no kettei ni tsuite* [On the 2006 implementation of Super English Language High Schools]. Retrieved November 25, 2006, from http://www.mext.go.jp/b_menu/houdou/18/04/06041201.htm.

Monbukagakusho. (2006b). *Nihongoshido ga hitsuyo na gaikokujin jido-seito no ukeire jokyoto ni kansuru chosa (Heisei 17 nendo) no kekka* [Results of the 2002 survey on the acceptance and instruction of foreign children and students needing Japanese language education]. Retrieved July 13, 2006, from http://www.mext.go.jp/b_menu/houdou/18/04/06042520/001.htm.

Monbukagakusho. (2006c). *Shogakko eigo katsudo jisshi jokyo chosa (heisei 17 nendo) no onona kekka gaiyo* [Summary of the 2005 survey of English activities in elementary schools]. Retrieved November 25, 2006, from http://www.mext.go.jp/b_menu/houdou/18/03/06031408/001.htm.

Nagashima, Y. (2000, April 7). Bijinesu ni fukaketsu [English indispensable for business]. *Asahi Shimbun*, p. 15.

Nakamura, K. (2000/2002). "Eigo koyogo-ka" kara "nihongo" o mamoru no wa iwaba "kokubo" mondai dearu [To protect "Japanese" from the "English as an official language" movement is a matter of "national defense"]. In Chuko Shinsho La Clef Henshubu and Y. Suzuki (Eds.), *Ronso: Eigo ga koyogo ni naru hi* [A debate: The day English becomes an official language] (pp. 109–116). Tokyo: Chuko Shinsho.

Noguchi, M. G., & Fotos, S. (Eds.). (2001). *Studies in Japanese bilingualism*. Clevedon, England: Multilingual Matters.

Ota, H. (2000). *Newcomer no kodomo to nihon no gakko* [Newcomer children in Japanese public schools]. Tokyo: Kokusai Shoin.

Otsu, Y., & Torigai, K. (2002). *Shogakko de naze eigo?* [Why study English in elementary schools?]. Tokyo: Iwanami Shoten.

Phillipson, R. (1992). *Linguistic imperialism*. Oxford: Oxford University Press.

The Prime Minister's Commission on Japan's Goals in the 21st Century. (2000). *The frontier within: Individual empowerment and better governance in the new millennium*. Retrieved May 20, 2002, from http://www.kantei.go.jp/21century/report/pdfs/3chapter/pdf.

Rohlen, T. (1983). *Japan's high schools*. Berkeley: University of California Press.

Shirahata, T. (1997). Gengo shutoku riron no shiten kara [From the perspective of language acquisition theory]. In T. Higuchi (Ed.), *Shogakko karano gaikokugo kyoiku* [Foreign language education in elementary schools] (pp. 101–109). Tokyo: Kenkyusha.

Suzuki, Y. (2002). Kaisetsu: eigo koyogo-ka ronso [Commentary: Debate on English as an official language]. In Chuko Shinsho La Clef Henshubu & Y. Suzuki (Eds.), *Ronso: Eigo ga koyogo ni naru hi* [A debate: The day English becomes an official language] (pp. 293–330). Tokyo: Chuko Shinsho.

Swain, M. (1997). French immersion programs in Canada. In J. Cummins & D. Corson (Eds.), *Encyclopedia of language and education, Volume 5: Bilingual education* (pp. 261–269). Dordrecht, The Netherlands: Kluwer Academic Press.

TOEFL saikai dasshutsu [Japan's TOEFL score escapes the bottom ranking]. (2000, January 26). *Asahi Shimbun*, p. 1.

Tsuda, Y. (1990). *Eigo shihai no kozo* [The structure of English dominance]. Tokyo: Daisan Shokan.

Tsuda, Y. (2000/2002). Eigo daini koyogoka "mittsu no otoshiana" ga matteiru [Three "pitfalls" of English as a second official language]. In Chuko Shinsho La Clef Henshubu & Y. Suzuki (Eds.), *Ronso: Eigo ga koyogo ni naru hi* [A debate: The day English becomes an official language] (pp. 117–122). Tokyo: Chuko Shinsho.

Usui, N. (2000). The anti-English linguistic imperialism movement: Savior of Japanese identity or Harbinger of petit nationalism? *Educational Studies, 42*, 277–303.

Vaipae, S. (2001). Language minority students in Japanese public schools. In M. Noguchi & S. Fotos (Eds.), *Studies in Japanese bilingualism* (pp. 184–233). Clevedon, England: Multilingual Matters.

Yoshida, K. (2002). Fish bowl, open seas and the teaching of English in Japan. In S. Baker (Ed.), *Language policy: Lessons from global models* (pp. 194–205). Monterey, CA: Monterey Institute of International Studies.

CHAPTER 6

ENGLISH LANGUAGE TEACHING IN KOREA:

Toward Globalization or *Glocalization*?

HYUNJUNG SHIN

The University of Toronto, Canada

ABSTRACT

This chapter presents a critical examination of current issues and controversies in English Language Teaching (ELT) in Korea, focusing on the recent Korean "English-only" educational policy, which requires that English be taught without L1 support in certain school grades. Drawing from a study I conducted with Korean English teachers and students, I investigate how the policy goes beyond the mere discussion of language of instruction and perpetuates the notion of the Native Speaker (NS) as an ideal language teacher. The conflict between the government's goal for English education (influenced by the discourse of globalization) and English teachers' goals for English education (constructed through daily interactions with the students in the local classrooms) suggests that Koreans should reconceptualize ELT in Korea. Drawing on Wallace's (2002) notion of *global literate English* and Robertson's (1995) notion of *glocalzation*, I argue that when the global English is *glocalized* through critical pedagogy, English can work as a language of opportunity for Koreans. A critical understanding of the complex relationship between ELT and colonialism and a reconceptualization of the ownership of English in Korea will have implications for ELT practices in other countries.

INTRODUCTION

The status of English as a global language is undisputed, and the impact of globalization on English education is pervasive in ELT practices in different parts of the world. Gray (2002) argued that the increasing number of transational corporations, the rise of world organizations with global networks, and the influence of the Internet are mainly responsible for the conjunction of globalization and English. As represented in Jung & Norton's (2002) discussion of Korea's new national elementary English program, recent language policies in Korea have been created within the discourse of globalization, as an effort of the Korean government to globalize the economy for further growth. Consequently, languages are often considered as economic commodities (cf. Heller, 2002) and education is treated as a tool to keep up with the rapid globalization of the world economy. The following article from a Korean newspaper is indicative of this:

> Universities ... will face mergers and acquisitions just like private businesses, and those failing to meet government criteria will be forced to close their doors ... They are a part of education policies to be pursued in the next five years, as reported by Education and Human Resources Development Minister Yoon Deok-hong to President Roh Moo-hyun yesterday ... In another initiative, a legal base will be established to force 'incompetent' universities to shut down voluntarily. (Na, 2003, p. 1, original in English)

In this chapter, I provide a critical examination of current issues and controversies in ELT in Korea, focusing on the debate around recent Korean "English-only" educational policy, which requires that English be taught without L1 support in certain school grades. I investigate how the policy, endorsed by the supporters of economic globalization, goes beyond the mere discussion of language of instruction and perpetuates the notion of the native speaker (NS) as an ideal language teacher. In doing so, I draw from a larger study I conducted with Korean English teachers and students in a large city in Korea, to be reported more fully elsewhere (cf. Shin, 2004).

I first provide some background context with an overview of the impact of the global spread of English on Korea and move to a discussion of the ideological orientation of the English-only policy. I then explore how teachers and students in Korean English as a Foreign Language (EFL) classrooms have responded to this policy. Finally, I discuss the implications of my study for the future of ELT in Korea and around the world, drawing on Robertson's (1995) notion of *glocalization*, which he introduces as a counterargument to common, monolithic understanding of the relationship between the global and the local in the discussion of globalization:

> I have tried to transcend the tendency to cast the idea of globalization as inevitably in tension with the idea of localization. I have instead maintained that globalization ... has involved and increasingly involves the creation and the incorporation of locality, processes which themselves largely shape, in turn, the compression of the world as a whole. Even though we are, for various reasons, likely to continue to use the concept of globalization, it might well be preferable to replace it for certain purposes with the concept of glocalization. (p. 40)

THE GLOBAL SPREAD OF ENGLISH AND ELT IN KOREA

> Learning English as a global language means learning how to understand and speak a variety of Englishes with speakers who are not necessarily native speakers of the language ... while the official rhetoric claims that English has become the *lingua franca* of the world and is not "owned" by any one nation in particular (Widdowson: 1994), everybody knows that not all English accents are equally prestigious, nor are all English ways of speaking. (Kramsch, 1999, p. 134, emphasis in original)

The global spread of English bound up with the spread of capitalism and its dominance in higher education in many parts of the world has made it the language of power and prestige in many countries. Indeed, the global use of English inherently serves the interests of some over those of others and often results in exacerbating the unequal relationship between the *Center* and *Periphery* in ELT, and between different groups within the Periphery countries (Canagarajah, 1999a, 2002; Pennycook, 1994, 1998, 2001). Accordingly, although the subtlety of the political nature of education often makes it invisible in everyday local contexts, ELT and colonialism are inherently intertwined (see Pennycook, this volume; Phillipson, 1992). It is clear then that ELT is not a neutral business and "those who wish to deny the political nature of schooling are clearly articulating an ideological position in favor of the status quo" (Pennycook, 1989, p. 591).

South Korea definitely belongs to a group of countries where the intimate relationship between language, language teaching, and power is clearly evident. English was brought into Korea initially with Christianity, which was a symbol of egalitarianism and democratism to undermine the corrupt feudal ruling class of the late Choson dynasty (1392-1910) (Lee, 1999; Sung, 2002). After the period of Japanese colonization (1910-1945), English reentered Korea with the U.S. army and the U.S. Military Government (1945-1948) in the South. Since the Korean War (1950-1953), there has been a great deal of military tension between communist North and capitalist South (and sometimes between the U.S. and North Korea) as evidenced in the recent nuclear crisis on the Korean Peninsula. Consequently, the ideological tension from the cold-war period is often still visible in the country, and the hegemonic role of the U.S. in politic, economic, and cultural domains in Korea has created an unequal relationship between the U.S. and Korea. This, in turn, legitimizes the status of English, American English in particular, as cultural capital in Korean society, and English has long maintained its status as the most popular and important foreign language, at least in the South.

According to Kwon (2000), the official English teaching in Korea began in 1883, although it was limited to diplomats and official interpreters. Sung (2002) maintained that during the Japanese colonial period, foreign languages were taught only scarcely and mainly by rote learning, and teaching of foreign languages other than Japanese was suppressed or sometimes prohibited. Hence, Grammar-Translation was the dominant method in English teaching in Korea even after the Japanese colonial period. A dramatic turn of ELT in Korea came with the development of the sixth National Curricula, implemented in middle schools and high schools in 1995 and 1996 respectively. A shift in focus in English teaching had occurred and fluency and communicative competence, instead of accuracy, were emphasized, which continues in the current, seventh Curricula. Accordingly, the English section of the College Scholastic Ability Test, the official, national college entrance examination since 1993, mainly consists of a reading comprehension test and a listening comprehension test, which is a different emphasis from measuring students' phonological, lexical and grammatical knowledges, as in the old college entrance exam. Furthermore, in 1996, the Ministry of Education initiated innovation in the curricula of pre-service teacher education program to foster English teachers' linguistic and pedagogical competence, moving away from traditional emphasis on knowledge of theoretical linguistics and literature in the curricula (Kwon, 2000).

Since English was first taught as a regular subject in secondary schools in 1945 (Jung & Norton, 2002, p. 246), one of the characteristics of ELT practices in Korea has been that they are often government-initiated, national operations. In the early 1990s, Kim Young-Sam, former President of Korea, promoted the policy of *segyehwa* (the Korean term for globalization[1]), urging the Korean ministry of education to shift from traditional grammar instruction to a communicative English curriculum. In 1996, the Ministry of Education launched EPIK (English Program in Korea) to recruit NSs of English to teach in Korean secondary schools (Kwon, 2000). NS teachers entered to invigorate the ineffective traditional English teaching system in Korea, whose weakness has often been attributed to the inadequate speaking abilities of Korean English teachers. After going through the Asian financial crisis in 1997 and the intervention by the International Monetary Fund,

Koreans again realized the importance of English for Korea to survive the severe competition in the international markets. As a result, South Korea is currently witnessing an unprecedented obsession among the population to attain a better command of English.

For example, expensive English kindergartens are ubiquitous. The desire to begin English education at an early age led to the introduction of English as a regular subject in elementary schools in 1997 (cf. Jung & Norton, 2002; Kwon, 2000). An increasing number of young Koreans leave the country to study abroad in the hope of gaining at least a good command of English, which they believe will guarantee them a prestigious job in the future. As of 2002, Koreans comprised the second largest group of international students studying in intensive English programs in the U.S. (Seo, 2003). There is a much contested idea of turning the southern resort island of Cheju into an international duty-free city that would have English as an official language; the government's ambition to promote Korea as "the business center of Northeast Asia" leads to another reckless plan to create three "special economic zones" in the west of Seoul with English as an official language (Choi, 2002; Park, 2002). The stunning, extreme obsession with English education among a few Korean parents have even led them to pay for "tongue surgery" for their children, in the hope that they would pronounce *r* and *l* sounds more distinctly, often considered a symbol of authentic American English pronunciation in Korea (Demick, 2002). The huge amount of money, time, and effort spent in studying English and the nationwide desire to be fluent in English are closely related to the social and economic prestige afforded by English (see Kanno, this volume, for a discussion of similar issues in ELT in Japan).

In an EFL context, where English is taught as a subject in classrooms, the relatively limited access to the target language and culture in natural settings remains a challenge, despite increasing opportunities for exposure to foreign countries and cultures now possible. In addition, English teaching in Korean schools usually involves large classes with students of multiple interests, a curriculum mandated from above, and the need to prepare students for the college entrance exam. The kind of flexibility fostered in natural language learning settings is rarely expected due to such institutional constraints. This often results in demands for "correct" English as a pedagogical norm. Kubota (2002b) reported that *foreign language* was frequently equated with *English* in Japan, standard North American and British varieties in particular. Similarly, the respect for a certain kind of English (i.e. so-called Standard American English) is prevalent in Korea. This, combined with the political dominance of the U.S.,[2] leads to the notion that the ideal English teacher is a NS of American English (so-called Standard American English), and non-native speaker (NNS) teachers of English are often marginalized in the ELT business in Korea. It is to the ideological context of this myth of the NS as an ideal teacher that I now turn, along with the discussion of the ideological nature of the new English-only policy.

"ENGLISH-ONLY" IN KOREA AND NNS TEACHERS OF ENGLISH IN EFL CLASSROOMS

The pervasiveness of the communicative language teaching (CLT) approach to ELT is evident around the world (Wallace, 2002). However, according to Norton Peirce's (1989) criticism of the hegemony of communicative competence as a goal for ELT practices internationally, CLT lacks the ability to help students challenge and transform the status quo. Accordingly, the attempt to "enable communication with native speakers in natural, everyday environments" (Wallace, 2002, p. 110) in CLT often results in "the empty babble of the communicative language class" (Pennycook, 1994, p. 311; also see Spada, this volume, for a useful discussion of common myths and misconceptions around CLT).

Nevertheless, in line with the government's globalization policy, the major purpose of English teaching in Korea has been to improve students' oral communicative abilities, since the sixth curriculum was promoted (Kwon, 2000; Jung & Norton, 2002). As a result, the craving for "authentic" English language and culture is immense in Korea. Without considering what kind of ELT could best serve the needs of the students in Korean EFL secondary school contexts, many Koreans now disregard "the value of sustained engagement with written text" (Wallace, 2002, p. 105). Many wealthy Korean parents send their children to expensive private language schools to study English with NS teachers, who they believe possess "authentic" English language and culture. The increased expectations of students and parents for English instruction in Korea have brought enormous social and institutional pressure on Korean English teachers to turn out highly proficient speakers of English. Under the sociopolitical circumstances, a new Korean language policy was announced in 2001: Beginning in that year, English classes should be taught in English only for the third, fourth, and seventh graders:

> Mr. Song Youngsup in the Ministry of Education and Human Resources Development said, '…. every school should *first* assign *those teachers who can do so* [who can teach English using English only] to the third, fourth, and seventh grade.'. … The Ministry of Education and Human Resources Development is planning to gradually expand 'English-only classes' into the higher grades. (Seoul/Yonhap News, 2001, my translation, emphasis added)

Given relatively little chance for students to use English outside the classrooms in EFL contexts, facilitating wider use of a target language in classroom contexts seems justifiable at first glance. However, the rhetoric of the policy favors linguistic proficiency over other qualifications of a good English teacher through hierarchical categorization of Korean English teachers into two groups: those who *can* teach English using English only, and therefore will be *first* assigned to the English-only classrooms, and those who *cannot*. The expertise of NNS teachers as bilinguals is not adequately acknowledged, given that many NS teachers are often monolinguals (Cook, 1999). With various challenging institutional constraints in the background, the question of effective English instruction is reduced to the issue of the teacher's oral proficiency in English. This in turn leads to the often contested and yet still prevalent myth of the NS as an ideal teacher. In addition, by institutionalizing the requirement that English be taught only in English, the policy implies that English can best be taught in English only, depriving NNS teachers of one of their advantages of using a shared mother tongue with their students (cf. Auerbach, 1993; Cook, 1999; Tang, 1997).

Pennycook (1998) maintains that the myth of the NS as an ideal teacher (both linguistically and culturally) is extended from the colonial discourse of orientalism (cf. Said, 1979). The rhetoric of the NS as an ideal teacher legitimizes the substitution of language politics for racial politics in ELT, creating a practically unattainable standard imposed by national origin and accent (cf. Amin, 1997;

Pennycook, 1994). This is analogous to the linkage between the English-only movement in the United States and anti-immigration sentiment (cf. Auerbach, 1993; Crawford, 1989). As Halliday (1968) argues:

> A speaker who is made ashamed of his own language habits suffers a basic injury as a human being: to make anyone, especially a child, feel so ashamed is as indefensible as to make him feel ashamed of the colour of his skin. (p. 165, cited in Cook, 2002, p. 331)

Nevertheless, L2 users "have continually been made ashamed by their inability to meet the native-based aims of language teaching" (Cook, 2002, p. 331).

However, the rhetoric of the link between race and language ability works in covert ways in the contemporary world in most cases (e.g. "cultural racism," cf. Hall, 1992), and is often unrecognized by the privileged, just as white privilege and male privilege are normally invisible to those who benefit from them (Kubota, 2002a). The struggle to resolve the dilemma between "language as a mark of authenticity and belonging or identity, and language as an acquirable technical skill and marketable commodity" (Heller, 2002, p. 47) is often left to the NNS teachers themselves. Yet, failing to understand the wider ideological context of the NS and NNS issue will perpetuate inequalities, as reflected in the ironic discrimination against NNS teachers in their home countries while discrimination against NNS teachers in Center Countries still remains (Canagarajah, 1999b). A report on my own investigation of how the Korean EFL teachers and the students responded to this complicated issue implied in the new Korean English-only policy is the focus of the next section.

RESISTANCE IN KOREAN EFL CLASSROOMS

The study was conducted in a large city in Korea during May through August 2001. The participants in the study included 39 Korean English teachers, 98 students, and 30 teachers who taught subjects other than English in the city. Data collection for the study included survey questionnaires, interviews, and classroom observations. The questionnaires and the interviews were written and conducted in Korean and were translated by me (cf. Shin, 2004). All the names of the participants in this chapter are pseudonyms.

The results from both the questionnaires and the interviews suggested that the Korean English teachers resisted the notion that oral proficiency was the most important qualification for a good English teacher. They conceived of the qualifications for a good English teacher as consisting of pedagogical expertise suiting local needs and professional consciousness combined with adequate professional training. A representative written response was: "There are many Native Speakers [of English] in Korean schools these days but not many Native Speaker teachers [of English]."

The responses from the students in the questionnaires also supported this: most of the students (85%) were against hiring external experts such as Korean-Americans as English teachers, saying that being good at speaking English was different from being a good teacher. A representative remark about Kim Kunmo, a famous Korean popular singer, was: "Isn't it the same as saying Kim Kunmo is not necessarily a good music teacher?"

Although almost half of the teachers (49%) acknowledged the need for increased use of English in classrooms, they did not think English could be best taught using English-only in Korean classrooms (81%) nor did they support the policy (79%). In response to the emphasis on oral English proficiency implied in the policy, the Korean English teachers valued localized pedagogical expertise over English speaking ability. In their responses in the questionnaires, the Korean English teachers chose "solid teaching philosophy and commitment to the profession" as the most important qualification for a good English teacher (32%), which was followed by "pedagogical expertise" (27%). Student surveys indicated that the students valued "pedagogical expertise" as the most important qualification for a good English teacher (33%), not oral English proficiency. To further illustrate this, consider the extract from the interview with Junki, a male high school teacher who had been teaching English for 3 years at the time of the study:

> I don't think I am less qualified compared to a NS teacher [although my English ability may not be as good as theirs]. I know the Korean educational system, how to prepare students for the entrance exam, and how to make things meaningful for the students. . . . It's often more than teaching English and they [NS teachers] don't understand this. (Interview, July 3, 2001)

The conflict between the government's conception of effective English teaching (influenced by the discourse of globalization) and English teachers' conception of effective English teaching (constructed through daily interactions with the students in the local classrooms) was also evident in comments made by Yujung, a female junior high school teacher with 5 years of teaching experience:

> I don't think that my major job is teaching English itself. The students learn more than enough knowledge of English at private institutes. I pay more attention to providing them with learning context where they can learn English with other students so that they learn how to get along well with others in the society. (Interview, June 20, 2001)

Several possible explanations for this conceptual conflict include the traditional emphasis on teacher's moral and parental role in Korean society, and the consequent importance of the role of the homeroom teacher in Korean secondary schools (often considered more important than the role of the teacher of the subject area). In addition, professional classroom management and pedagogical expertise are often valued over knowledge of the discipline in their workplaces (i.e. secondary schools where they were teaching beginning to low-intermediate level learners in large classrooms).

In relation to this, different expectations of a good teacher in different cultures warrant better recognition (Shin & Crookes, 2005). Cortazzi & Jin (1996) reported that Chinese students in their study listed being a role model as a friend, a parent, or sometimes as a strict teacher as qualifications for a good teacher. Accordingly, the students expected teachers to listen to their personal issues even outside the classroom and to share knowledge of society with them. Reagan (2000) suggested Confucian educational thought could work as a possible common value in educational philosophy in East Asian countries. In Confucianism, education is the very tool to lead people to reach the ideal of *Chun-tzu*, the ideal person in Confucian thought. Consequently, teachers have been highly respected in these countries[3] and have been expected to show moral behavior like *Chun-tzu* (Kim, 1996).

Nonetheless, rapid social change and economic development in Korea provide the students with a significantly different English learning environment from that of their teachers. The disparity between the material resources available to students in and out of school in contemporary Korean EFL classrooms, exacerbated by lack of administrative support for teacher education, has induced a sense of identity crisis even in some of the more conscientious Korean English teachers. Miju, a female teacher with 7 years of teaching experience at the time of the study, presented an illustrative case:

> The students' expectations [about the quality of the English education] are too high these days. When the expectation was low, it was OK, but the teaching methods I am familiar with don't work anymore. I feel that I'm losing confidence drastically for last couple of years as a teacher. Particularly in this year, I often feel that there is no reason I have to stay here. . . . My identity as a teacher is in crisis. (Interview, June 4, 2001)

The junior high school she was working for was located in a middle-class residential area. The parents there were very enthusiastic and even competitive about their children's English education. About 20 students in each class study English in English speaking countries every vacation. In Miju's school, the students' and parents' craving for "authentic" English was obvious, which led to her sense of inadequacy and incompetence.

Jung & Norton (2002) illustrated that enthusiastic teachers supported by a local teacher's group were successful with the implementation of their new curriculum. Similarly, interview data from Jongsu, a young male teacher with 3 years of teaching experience at the time of the interview, suggests the importance of the role of networking in empowering teachers as agents of change. Jongsu was teaching at a junior high school that had relatively high academic standards. He was also working as an active member of an innovative teacher development group in the city. The interview indicated that he was very articulate in his critique of the English-only policy and perceived himself as a very progressive, enthusiastic professional in Korean English classrooms:

> We are not just 'teachers of a language' but are more responsible for education in general. I think Korean English teachers suit Korean English classrooms better [than NS teachers] as we know what the students want and what they need. And I don't care about the policy—they [the policy makers] don't know how things are in the real classrooms. (Interview data, June 20, 2001)

> I really enjoy what I do at the teachers' group ... the students really want to have fun in English class these days. They are tired of attending too many English classes here and there. We focus on developing activities and materials for the junior high school students and share them and evaluate them together so that we can make a different English class ... When they enjoy the activity I developed and have fun in class, I am so happy. (Interview, July 14, 2001)

Through intimate interaction with his students and through networking with other like-minded teachers, Jongsu rejected the dominant ideology embedded in the English-only policy, which legitimized the myth of the NS as an ideal teacher. Through his understanding of the local context and student needs and his dedication to educational innovation, he could recreate himself as a competent educator with localized expertise.

As the data indicated, the goal for English education implied in the government's policy (i.e. improving students' oral conversational abilities to foster national competitiveness in a global market) was not congruent with the English teachers' immediate goals for English education (i.e. understanding and supporting students and facilitating a broader scope of learning experiences for them). In addition, a lack of proper preparation to implement the new policy into actual classroom settings (e.g. through curriculum development and adequate teacher development programs) caused confusion and conflicts in the classrooms. The unsuccessful implementation of the policy and resistance from the English teachers suggest that Koreans should reconceptualize ELT in Korea: what kind of English do Koreans need to learn and what kind of English education should Korea strive for? I conclude the chapter with a discussion about the issue of the ownership of English and the future of ELT in Korea.

CRITICAL PEDAGOGY AND GLOCALIZATION OF GLOBAL ENGLISH

In this chapter, I investigated the complex relationship between ELT and colonialism by examining how the new Korean English-only policy went beyond the mere discussion of language of instruction and perpetuated the notion of the native speaker as the ideal language teacher. The Korean English teachers in my study resisted the dominant ideology embedded in the policy and recreated themselves as ELT professionals who know how to teach English to Korean students more effectively (Brutt-Griffler & Samimy, 1999). The conflict between the government's goal for English education and English teachers' goals for English education resulted in the failure of policy implementation at the school level. This leads Koreans to question what kind of English should be taught in Korea and to what purposein this global era.

Wallace (2002) presents a possible answer to this question; she argues for teaching a particular kind of English that she calls "global literate English" (p. 106), to promote "a global critical literacy through the medium of English" (p. 111):

> My defence is not of English but of a particular kind of literate English. This more widely contextualized form of English ... coexists with vernacular literacies, with each occupying distinct domains. For its users, literate English offers a form of secondary socialization into the world of global English. ... learners of English as a foreign and second language can participate in its critique and recreation. Models of resistance to English are available through English, but a critically nuanced literate English. We resist global tyranny with global means. (p. 114)

Wallace goes on to argue that this global English needs to be taught through critical pedagogy (cf. Freire, 1993) to deal with "issues which may resonate locally but which have global implications" (p. 111). In response to Canagarajah's (1999a) argument for "pedagogies of resistance ... rooted in the everyday life of our students" (p. 194), she claims that English teachers should pursue a pedagogy for challenging social inequity in a broader way (Wallace, p. 111). She maintains that critical and creative use of this new form of literate English will "challenge the hegemony of English in its conventional forms and uses" (p. 112). This resonates with Norton Peirce's (1989) discussion of People's English in South Africa as a language of possibility for South Africans. Through a pedagogy of possibility, South Africans successfully appropriated English for freedom and possibility for all South

Africans "in terms of the way they perceive themselves, their role in society, and the potential for change in their society" (pp. 402-403).

Wallace's (2002) comments suggest how we can conceptualize ELT in order to transform English to a tool for resistance:

> English language teaching, like globalization itself, does not need to be seen to bring only negative consequences ... our resistance as language teachers need not be to the teaching of the language itself so much as to the grosser kinds of cultural and linguistic imperialism which continues to characterize some ELT discourse and practices. (p. 108)

In relation to the future direction of ELT in Korea, we can draw an analogy to Gray's (2002) critique of so-called global textbooks: Although the attempt to include the global necessarily led such textbooks to exclude the local, they could be an emancipatory site when successfully glocalized. Similarly, when global English is glocalized through critical pedagogy, English can work as a "language of opportunity" (cf. Pennycook, 1994, 2001) for Koreans. Although I acknowledge that "there are many different modes of practical glocalization" (Robertson, 1995, p. 40), reconceptualization of the ownership of English in Korea will have implications for ELT practices in other countries.

NOTES

[1] This Korean term has often been translated into both *globalization* and *internationalization* in English. I translated the term into *globalization* in this chapter.

[2] However, because of the very dominant political role of the U.S. on the peninsula, there has been an interesting co-existence of anti-American sentiment and the idealization of the U.S. among Koreans. Recent nationwide candlelight vigils and protest to mourn the tragic death of two teenage schoolgirls run over by a U.S. military vehicle in June 2002 represents this. The acquittals of the two American soldiers who controlled the vehicle by a U.S. military court and the insincere attitude of the U.S. toward the case created the proliferation of anti-American sentiment among Koreans. The protest has extended to a campaign to revise unequal Status of Forces Agreement (SOFA) governing the legal status of U.S. soldiers in Korea (Today's Editorial, 2002).

[3] Teachers in Korea, female teachers in particular, still have prestigious status and accordingly have high self-esteem in general. Although many participants indicated they endured less favorable social attitude toward the profession (72%), they still believed students had respect for their competence (56%) and felt fulfillment and commitment as professionals (62%).

REFERENCES

Amin, N. (1997). Race and the identity of the nonnative ESL teacher. *TESOL Quarterly, 31*, 580–583.
Auerbach, E. (1993). Reexamining English only in the ESL Classroom. *TESOL Quarterly, 27*, 9–32.
Brutt-Griffler, J., & Samimy, K. (1999). Revisiting the colonial in the postcolonial: Critical praxis for nonnative-English-Speaking Teachers in a TESOL Program. *TESOL Quarterly, 33*, 413–431.
Canagarajah, S. (1999a). *Resisting linguistic imperialism in English teaching.* Oxford: Oxford University Press.
Canagarajah, S. (1999b). Interrogating the 'Native Speaker Fallacy': Non-linguistic roots, non-pedagogical results. In G. Braine (Ed.), *Non-native educators in English language teaching* (pp. 77–92). Mahwah, NJ: Lawrence Erlbaum.
Canagarajah, S. (2002). Globalization, methods, and practice in periphery classrooms. In D. Block & D. Cameron (Eds.), *Globalization and language teaching* (pp. 134–150). London: Routledge.
Choi, I. (2002, April 7). Yeong-eo gongyonghwa munje itta [Problems with English as an official language]. *Internet Hankyoreh.* Retrieved November 9, 2002, from http://www.hani.co.kr/section-005100025/2002/04/005100025200204072132001.html.
Cook, V. (1999). Going beyond the native speaker in language teaching, *TESOL Quarterly, 33*, 185–209.
Cook, V. (2002). Language teaching methodology and the L2 user perspective. In V. Cook (Ed.), *Portraits of the L2 user* (pp. 325–343). Buffalo, NY: Multilingual Matters.

Cortazzi, M., & Jin, L. (1996). Cultures of learning: Language classrooms in China. In H. Coleman (Ed.), *Society and the language classroom* (pp. 169–206). Cambridge: Cambridge University Press.

Crawford, J. (1989). *Bilingual education: History, politics, theory and practice.* Trenton, NJ: Crane Publishing.

Demick, B. (2002, March 31). The world; Some in S. Korea opt for a trim when English trips the tongue; Asia: Parents are turning to specialty preschool and even surgery to give their children a linguistic advantage. *The Los Angeles Times.* Retrieved May 7, 2003, from http://www.latimes.com.

Freire, P. (1993). *Pedagogy of the oppressed.* New York: Continuum (M.B. Ramos, Trans.).

Gray, J. (2002). The global coursebook in English Language Teaching. In D. Block & D. Cameron (Eds.), *Globalization and language teaching* (pp. 151–167). London: Routledge.

Hall, S. (1992). The question of cultural identity. In S. Hall, D. Held, & T. McGrew (Eds.), *Modernity and its futures* (pp. 273–325). Cambridge, UK: Polity Press.

Halliday, M.A.K. (1968). The users and uses of language. In J. Fishman (Ed.), *Readings in the sociology of language.* The Hague: Mouton.

Heller, M. (2002). Commodification of bilingualism in Canada. In D. Block & D. Cameron (Eds.), *Globalization and language teaching* (pp. 47–63). London: Routledge.

Jung, S., & Norton, B. (2002). Language planning in Korea: The new elementary English program. In J. Tollefson (Ed.), *Language policies in education: Critical issues* (pp. 245–265). Mahwah, NJ: Lawrence Erlbaum.

Kim, K. (1996). The reproduction of Confucian culture in contemporary Korea. In W. Tu (Ed.), *Confucian traditions in East Asian modernity: Moral education and economic culture in Japan and the four mini-dragons* (pp. 202–227). Cambridge, MA: Harvard University Press.

Kramsch, C. (1999). Global and local identities in the contact zone. In C. Gnutzmann (Ed.), *Teaching and learning English as a global language: Native and Non-Native perspectives* (pp. 131–143). Tübingen: Stauffenburg Verlag.

Kubota, R. (2002a). The Author Responds: (Un)Raveling racism in a nice field like TESOL. *TESOL Quarterly, 36,* 84–92.

Kubota, R. (2002b). The impact of globalization on language teaching in Japan. In D. Block, & D. Cameron (Eds.), *Globalization and language teaching* (pp. 13–28). London: Routledge.

Kwon, O. (2000). Korea's English education policy changes in the 1990s: Innovations to gear the nation for the 21st century. *English Teaching* [Korea], *55*(1), 47–91.

Lee, J. (1999). Historic factors affecting educational administration in Korean higher education. *Harvard Educational Review, 32,* 7–23.

Na, J. (2003, April 10). Uncompetitive colleges may face shutdown. *The Korea Times,* p. 1.

Norton Peirce, B. (1989). Toward a pedagogy of possibility in the teaching of English internationally: People's English in South Africa. *TESOL Quarterly, 23,* 401–420.

Park, Y. (2002, April 5). 3 special Economic Zones to be designated next yr. *The Korea Times,* Retrieved May 7, 2003, from http://www.hankooki.com/times/200204/ t2002040500220440110.htm.

Pennycook, A. (1989). The concept of method, interested knowledge and the politics of language teaching. *TESOL Quarterly, 23,* 589–618.

Pennycook, A. (1994). *The cultural politics of English as an international language.* London: Longman.

Pennycook, A. (1998). *English and the discourses of colonialism.* London: Routledge.

Pennycook, A. (2001). *Critical applied linguistics: A critical introduction.* Mahwah, NJ: Lawrence Erlbaum.

Phillipson, R. (1992). *Linguistic imperialism.* Oxford: Oxford University Press.

Reagan, T. (2000). *Non-Western educational traditions: Alternative approaches to educational thought and practice.* Mahwah, NJ: Lawrence Erlbaum.

Robertson, R. (1995). Glocalization: Time-space and homogeneity-heterogenity, In M. Featherstone, S. Lash, & R. Robertson (Eds.), *Global Modernities* (pp. 25–44). London: Sage.

Said, E. (1979). *Orientalism.* New York: Vintage Books.

Seo, J. (2003, April 28). 62,000 Koreans studying in US. *The Korea Times,* p. 9.

Seoul/Yonhap News. (2001, February 18). Gyoyuk; Jung 1, Chodeung 3, 4, Yeong-eo sueop Yeong-eoroman jinheng [Education; English should be taught only in English for the third, fourth, and seventh graders]. *Internet Hankyoreh.* Retrieved February 21, 2003, from http://www.hani.co.kr/section-005000000/2001/005000000200102181230191.html.

Shin, H. (2004). *"English-only" in Korea and Korean English teachers: Hegemony of English and local resistance.* Manuscript submitted for publication.

Shin, H., & Crookes, G. (2005). Indigenous critical traditions for TEFL? A historical and comparative perspective in the case of Korea. *Critical Inquiry in Language Studies, 2*(2), 95–112.

Sung, K-W. (2002). Critical theory and pedagogy: Remapping English teaching in Korea. *English Teaching* [Korea], *57*(2), 65–89.

Tang, C. (1997). The identity of the nonnative ESL teacher: On the power and status of nonnative ESL teachers. *TESOL Quarterly, 31,* 577–580.
Today's Editorial. (2002, December 4). Spread of anti-American movement. *The Korea Times.* Retrieved May 5, 2003, from http://times.hankooki.com/lpage/opinion/200212/kt2002120416470011300.htm.
Wallace, C. (2002). Local literacies and global literacy. In D. Block & D. Cameron (Eds.), *Globalization and language teaching* (pp. 101–114). London: Routledge.
Widdowson, H. (1994). The ownership of English. *TESOL Quarterly, 28,* 377–388.

CHAPTER 7

THE NATIONAL CURRICULUM CHANGES AND THEIR EFFECTS ON ENGLISH LANGUAGE TEACHING IN THE PEOPLE'S REPUBLIC OF CHINA

QIANG WANG

Beijing Normal University, China

ABSTRACT

In China, the national curriculum, which applies to both primary and secondary schools, is the most influential foundation for educational practice. The Ministry of Education (MOE) is responsible for the development of the national curriculum across all subject areas. The national English curriculum, in the past 20 years, has seen some major changes along with the country's social, political, and economic developments. Changes in the English curriculum have had a profound influence on the methodological approaches to ELT in Chinese schools. This chapter, by providing an overview of the development of foreign language teaching in China over the last century, looks particularly into the ELT curriculum changes in the last 20 years with a focused examination of the different approaches taken in teaching and in materials development. The article gives special attention to the recent curriculum innovations and discusses the future directions of ELT in China.

INTRODUCTION

Of all the foreign languages taught in schools, English undoubtedly enjoys the largest number of learners. By the end of 2002, there were about 66.9 million junior secondary school students and 16.8 million senior secondary school students in the formal education sector (Yearbook of Chinese Education, 2003). This does not include college students and students doing vocational studies or studying in private schools. Among the figures mentioned above, over 99% were studying English. The number of students who were learning Russian and Japanese was 350,000 and 120,000 respectively, comprising less than 1%, scattered mainly in the northeast provinces and Inner Mongolia (Liu & Gong, 2001). At the same time, there were millions of part-time students learning the language in the non-formal education sector for career purposes or job benefits. There was an estimated number of 500,000 teachers of English involved in the teaching of English at secondary and tertiary levels in the whole country, of which 470,000 were teaching at secondary level and 30,000 at tertiary level. The formidable number of learners and teachers with one prescribed national curriculum and, for a long time, one prescribed set of textbooks make China a unique country for the provision of English language education.

In primary schools, the teaching of English was not standardized prior to 2001, due to its unrecognized position in the national curriculum, limited availability of qualified teachers, and lack of appropriate teaching materials. Previously, some teaching of English was to be found, especially in those schools designated as key schools and private schools in major cities over 27 provinces. It was estimated that there were about 8,000,000 primary school pupils studying English in 1998, and the number was growing rapidly, with an increase of around one million pupils every year since 1994 (Liu & Gong, 2001). In September 2001, English became a recognized subject in the primary school curriculum from grade 3 with the Basic Requirement for Primary School English designed and issued by the Ministry of Education (MOE Document, 2001). It is difficult to estimate the number of primary school children and teachers who are presently involved in learning or teaching English as the total number of primary pupils was over 121 million by the end of 2002 (Yearbook of Chinese Education, 2003) and it is just the beginning of a large-scale development of English language provision in the primary sector.

An Historical Overview

Foreign language teaching in schools has enjoyed a long history in China. English was established as a compulsory course in middle schools as early as the late Qing Dynasty in 1902 with eight periods of lessons a week totaling 1,444 hours throughout the middle school years. That was the time when some patriots, who initiated the Self-Strengthening Movement, advocated the learning of English and other Western languages in order to gain access to the technology of the West (Adamson & Morris, 1997). Since then, the study of a foreign language has always been regarded as one of the fundamental subjects in the curriculum of middle schools. However, due to political and social unrest, and the low living standards of the majority of the working people during the first half of the century, foreign language teaching had not achieved very much, although foreign language syllabi were issued in 1913, 1923, 1932, and 1948 by the Kuomintang government (Zhang & Shen, 2001). In all these syllabi, there was a stress on the importance of teaching English in schools with a time allocation of 4-5 hours a week throughout the middle school years.

Since the founding of the People's Republic of China in 1949, the first 15 years saw Russian as the predominant foreign language in both secondary schools and colleges. In the early 1960s, due to the diplomatic breakdown between China and the former USSR, Russian language was no longer a favored choice. Hundreds of thousands of secondary school and university teachers had to transfer their subject major from Russian to English. However, the Cultural Revolution between 1966 and 1976 witnessed a much decentralized situation for foreign language teaching: Some materials were developed by some local schools or agencies, and there was only sporadic teaching of a foreign language, mainly English. The materials were usually very simple and often contained political messages and slogans. When schools resumed teaching in the early 1970s, English replaced Russian as the required foreign language in secondary schools.

Following the Cultural Revolution, English was gradually restored to the secondary curriculum. Since 1978, English language teaching in China underwent increasingly rapid development in spite of continuous experience of great changes. The open-door policy has enabled broader exchanges between China and other countries, particularly in science, technology, business, and tourism. The development of ELT over the past two decades has gone through four major phases: the Restoration Phase, the Rapid Development Phase, the Reform Phase, and the Innovation Phase.

The Restoration Phase (1978-1985)

Following the Cultural Revolution, a national syllabus named *The Primary and Secondary English Syllabus for Ten-year Full-time Schools* was issued by MOE in 1978 (Zhou, 1995). The syllabus actually allowed two beginning levels, one from Primary 3, the other from Junior Secondary 1. As there were not enough teachers at that time, the actual offering of English in almost all the schools began from junior secondary school. The general aims and requirements of teaching were stated in the syllabus as follows (Li, Zhang, & Liu, 1988): Students should master basic phonetics and grammar, a certain number of words (2200 words for those beginning from Junior Secondary 1 and 2800 for those beginning from Primary 3), be able to read simplified reading materials on general topics with the help of dictionaries, and possess a preliminary ability in listening, speaking, writing, and translation. The time allocation was 656 hours in total for secondary schools. Following the syllabus, a new set of textbooks was published by the People's Education Press (PEP), which was then the only designated publisher under the MOE to publish textbooks for schools in China. The textbook was based on the principles of audiolingualism with one part characterized by oral and written drills of sentence patterns, and another part concentrated on literacy, principally reading texts to be learned through grammar-translation. The grammar of the textbooks followed the graded sequence of tenses and other grammatical items advocated by Zhang Daozhen in *A Practical English Grammar,* which was based on Soviet practices prevalent in the PRC during the 1950's (Adamson & Morris, 1997).

From 1978 to 1982, with efforts from all parties concerned, English was restored into the secondary curriculum and the teaching quality began to be given more attention. There were a lot of teaching experiments undertaken by teachers from all over the country to explore better ways for teaching. As a result, Foreign Language Teaching and Research Associations were set up one after another, in different provinces. Then, in 1981, the National Foreign Language Teaching and Research Association (NAFLTRA) was established, which aimed to organize all the English teachers from different parts of China to discuss issues related to teaching and to provide a forum for research and debate. NAFLTRA has held its bi-annual conference ever since then.

In 1983, test scores of a foreign language became a formal requirement for admission into higher education, whereas between 1978 and 1982, its scores were used only as a partial reference by the universities for admission. The establishment of a foreign language into the formal entrance requirements of universities not only gave the right status to foreign languages but also higher status to all the foreign language teachers in schools. The syllabus and textbooks were revised in 1982 in response to feedback from teachers. The revision was carried out by editors from PEP—the curriculum development section of MOE—in consultation with specialists from Beijing Foreign Languages Institute. They reduced the difficulty level of the 1978 series, texts were made more interesting and informative, and supplementary readings were added to each lesson. Despite these changes, the new series followed a similar pedagogical approach. The beginning levels of the course focused on short dialogues and sentence patterns for oral drilling. As the course developed, reading passages assumed greater prominence. The pedagogy was once more a blend of audiolingualism and the grammar-translation method.

The Rapid Development Phase (1986-1992)

The beginning of the second phase was symbolized by the issue of the 1986 English Syllabus followed by a plethora of teaching approaches and models developed by classroom teachers and teacher educators as a result of their persistent effort to explore better ways for teaching the language to Chinese learners. In 1985, a large-scale national survey on secondary school English teaching led by the State Education Commission (as the MOE was then called), revealed that most secondary school graduates were unable to use even very simple language to express themselves after spending almost 900 hours in learning the language (Li, Zhang, & Liu, 1988). The main factors identified as hampering the effectiveness of both teaching and learning were the grammar-based audio-lingual teaching method, rigid written examination requirements, shortage of qualified teachers, and extremely limited resources. As a result, a revised English syllabus for secondary schools was issued in the autumn of 1986, followed by the rewriting of the textbooks by PEP. The revised syllabus was based on the experiences of the past years and on the integration of the current international theories on language teaching and learning. It postulates in its aims that English does not only have instrumental utility, but more importantly, communicative and educational values. Therefore, English teaching should not only focus on developing students' knowledge about the language but also on developing students' cognitive ability, positive attitude, and personality. As far as pedagogy is concerned, it is stated that teaching should focus more on the students' ability to use the language.

During this period, quite a number of different approaches and models were developed which have had a national impact on ELT in China. Among these was Zhang, Sizhong's teaching method, with its core principles synthesized in four phrases with sixteen Chinese characters, namely, using blocks of time for teaching vocabulary and structures; recycling constantly what is learned; reading authentic texts; catering for individual needs (Zhang, 1993). Zhang Zhengdong's three-dimensional teaching approach (Zhang & Du, 1995) centers on the importance of the social, economic, and school contexts in which learning and teaching take place, valuing learning as opposed to acquisition. The "word, sentence, and discourse" model (Yu, 2004), developed by a classroom teacher in Beijing, stresses the teaching of vocabulary and structures within meaningful contexts, i.e. new words are taught within a sentence with many examples for learners to listen and repeat. Then the sentences are put into a short discourse by the teacher as a model followed by students' own creations of a discourse using as many words learned as possible. Another approach developed by a teacher in Beijing is known as the "harmonious teaching model" (Hao, 1999), which aims at satisfying children's learning needs and affective demands by providing differentiated levels of teaching for which children are allowed to choose the most appropriate level for themselves. In this way, teaching is made more assessable to different levels of learners and thus more interesting and enjoyable for most learners. It stresses strongly the idea of building up the learners' trust and confidence, aiming to change the situation from *I go to school because you want me to* into a situation in which *I go to school because I want to learn*. There are also many other models developed such as the whole-text approach to teaching reading (Zhang, 2000) and the 'three breakthroughs' model (Zhang, 2000, p. 284) which advocates that teaching should go beyond the teacher, the classroom and the textbook. The model also breaks with the traditional view that a good English teacher has to be knowledgeable and fluent in the language to be able to teach well. Instead, Zhang argues that "a good teacher can use a cup of water to elicit or draw out from the students endless water" (p. 287), which means that with the right method, one can be a good teacher without being absolutely fluent in the language; by inviting students to exercise their maximum potential and by using many different types of resources available, children can become even better speakers of English than the teacher (Wei & Sun, 2000). Unlike the communicative approach which is, to many Chinese teachers, a very vague and general term and a far away reality, these methods developed by Chinese teachers are more transparent and more easily adaptable to different contexts in China despite controversial views about them.

With the rapid social and economic development, changes also took place in educational policy. Firstly, the Nine-year Basic Education Law, which was promulgated in 1986, envisaged providing basic education to all citizens in phases: the richer seaboard areas first, followed by the industrial hinterland, and then the remote rural areas (Adamson & Morris, 1997). Secondly, the policy of decentralization permitted agencies at a regional level to develop and publish their own resources in competition with those produced by PEP (Zhao & Xu, 2002). Thirdly, the communicative approach became the bandwagon internationally, and there was a genuine concern in the profession to consider where we should be going. Obviously, the 1986 syllabus and textbooks could no longer adequately address the changes. Therefore, it was superseded by a new syllabus issued in 1993 seeing ELT in China move into the reform phase.

The Reform Phase (1993-2000)

In contrast with the previous syllabi, the 1993 syllabus stresses the value of English for modernization and for communication. It pays more attention to the study of foreign culture and the development of learning methods besides basic training in the four linguistic skills. In addition, it emphasizes the importance of stimulating students' interest in learning, helping them formulate good learning habits, educating them in aspects of virtues, patriotism, and socialism, and developing their thinking and self-study abilities. The teaching guidelines also call for the study of overseas theories of language and language teaching and for a synthesis of Western and Chinese ideas. They elucidate the policy for selecting appropriate pedagogical approaches (English Syllabus, 1993).

It was in the 1993 syllabus that the word *communication* was used in the objectives of teaching for the first time. A list of phrases for 30 situations, labeled *Daily Expressions in Communication* was also included, indicating a shift of paradigm from the grammar translation and audio-lingual method rooted in behaviorist psychology toward more communication-oriented language teaching. The contents of the syllabus reflected a synthesis of the new and the old approaches with discrete phonetic, grammatical, and lexical items specified. Also, in response to the policy of decentralization of materials development, some sets of teaching materials were produced to cater to the needs of schools in different regions according to the new syllabus. Among them are *Junior English for China (JEFC)* and *Senior English for China (SEFC)* compiled by PEP and Longman; textbooks for the four-year junior secondary school system compiled by Beijing Normal University with Shandong Province geared for less developed areas in the northern part of China; textbooks compiled by Sichuan Province geared for less developed areas in the West, and Guangdong Province, geared for coastal areas; and Beijing and Shanghai textbooks for Beijing and Shanghai.

Unlike the previous teaching materials that adhere to one pedagogy, these textbooks absorbed the current theories of language and language teaching and were adapted for Chinese contexts. That is, on the one hand, they stress communicative use of English in a social context; on the other hand, they emphasize the teaching of structures and the training of basic language skills. The content of the texts is also more closely related to the context in which students are living. Among the textbooks, JEFC and SEFC are the most widely used textbooks in secondary schools, taking over 95% of the market. The actual intention to decentralize textbook publication was not widely practiced as most local educational authorities, school principals, and teachers were unwilling to take risks by using books published by publishers other than PEP. This was because firstly, over the past 50 years, PEP had been the most authoritative publisher of school textbooks and it enjoyed a high reputation. Secondly, it had Longman as its collaborator for the new series of textbooks, adding more authority to the content and language used in the textbook. Thirdly, most schools and teachers were worried about regional and national examinations, which they believed would be based on PEP's textbook.

A research team from Beijing Normal University noted that ELT in China had seen a gradual breakaway from the traditional grammar-translation method, moving into a more functional-structural, more practice-focused and learner-centered era (Research team of Department of Foreign Languages, Beijing Normal University, 1999, 2001a, 2001b & 2002). However, the reform followed an eclectic approach rather than a revolutionarily communicative one, taking into consideration the diversified needs and local conditions as well as the experiences of teachers throughout China (Adamson, 1997). With the 1993 English Syllabus and the new sets of textbooks, ELT in China has yielded promising results. This can be reflected by a large scale English language teaching and research investigation led by Professor Zhang Zhengdong et al. in 1999 to the first group of senior secondary school leavers who used JEFC and SEFC. The study showed that the English proficiency levels of senior secondary school graduates had improved by a large margin compared to a similar study carried out in 1985 by MOE (Project team for research on senior secondary school English language teaching in China, 2001, p. 110). Although JEFC and SEFC have taken a very cautious step forward towards a more communication-oriented approach, the acceptance of its approach has varied from city to countryside, and from teacher to teacher. Their research also showed that out of all the teachers investigated who were using JEFC, only less than one third of them used English as their medium of instruction. Some unfavorable comments about the textbook came to be the vocabulary input, presentation of grammar and the supplementary materials provided. Some teachers commented that it was not because the number of vocabulary words was large, but because it was difficult for the students to recycle the words in meaningful ways. Over 50% of the teachers were dissatisfied with the presentation of grammar. The textbook claimed a recursive way of introducing the grammatical items, while teachers and students found the grammar points "not systematic" and "disorganized" (p. 128). It was also noted by many teachers that their students could understand and speak the language better but performed badly in tests on structures and writing tasks.

The Innovation Phase (2000 onwards)

The phase beginning from 2000 is characterized by a firm and urgent call from the government for quality-oriented education. It was generally felt by the government, the national educational authorities, as well as teachers and parents that there was something wrong with the current educational practices. That is, our students were being spoon-fed a lot of knowledge and spending a tremendous amount of time memorizing facts for examinations. They lacked the ability to think independently, to cope with things in real life, to care for others, and to learn by themselves. For many children and young adults, learning is not a happy experience but a miserable ordeal. As far as English language teaching is concerned, despite the achievements arising from reforms during the third phase, there remained significant problems needing to be addressed. Many teachers still put more emphasis on the delivery of knowledge about the vocabulary and structure of the language while ignoring the development of students' ability in using the language for communication. Classroom teaching continued to be largely teacher-centered, which did not foster students' interest and motivation for learning or develop their individuality. The major problems with language teaching in China are summarized as follows (Wang, 1999):

- Development of language ability is overlooked in both curriculum design and in teaching.
- In many secondary schools, beginning students have to relearn what they had learned in primary schools, wasting resources and meanwhile damaging student motivation.
- The vocabulary requirement in the 1993 syllabus (a mastery of 600 words after 426 hours of learning in junior secondary school) is inadequate for students to develop the four language skills.
- Evaluation of learning is heavily tilted towards pencil-and-paper tests, not conducive to developing students' communicative competence.
- There is a great variation in the quality of teachers in terms of their language proficiency and teaching ability.

In order to solve the problems raised above and to meet the challenges and changes in the 21st century, the government felt a strong pressure to revive the school curriculum. Following the government's *Strategic Plans for Reviving Education for the 21st Century* issued in early 1998 (MOE, 1998) and the Third National Conference on Education in June 1999, MOE launched the nationwide curriculum innovation projects. The English curriculum innovations were represented by the revision of the 1993 syllabus in the year 2000, the design and issue of the *Basic Requirement for Primary School English* in 2001, and the embarkation on the design of a new National English Curriculum that unifies primary and secondary (junior and senior) into one continuous entity. The following provides a detailed introduction to the revised 1993 syllabus and the Basic Requirement for Primary School English.

The Revision of the 1993 English Syllabus

To ensure a smooth transition period, the structure of the 1993 syllabus was generally followed, but the objectives, requirements, and some contents have been changed to a large extent to reflect a new understanding of teaching and learning. The revised syllabus has re-evaluated the English course in relation to quality education. It states, "English, in particular, has become an important means of carrying out the Open Policy and communication with other countries. Learning a foreign language is one of the basic requirements for 21st century citizens" (English Syllabus, 2000, p. 1). The overall aims of teaching English in schools are to develop students' study interest, confidence, good study habits, and effective learning strategies. It emphasizes helping students to acquire a specified amount of language knowledge, master basic language skills, and establish some language sense and an initial ability to use English so as to set a foundation for real communication. It also includes helping students develop their intellect, learn about different cultures, and nurture their personality so as to enable them to develop further. The following are the major changes in the objectives and requirements:

- To satisfy students' affective demands becomes the first priority for English language teaching, such as caring for students interests and motivation in learning, building up their confidence, helping them develop effective learning strategies and form good learning habits.
- It sets higher requirements for the use of language as stated in the objective descriptors.
- It increases vocabulary size, adding 220 more words, leading to a total of 830 words for mastery at junior secondary level.
- It stresses the importance of learning language knowledge, such as phonetics, grammar, vocabulary, and discourse, for communication rather than learning about the knowledge for the sake of the knowledge or for passing examinations.
- It requires an increase in the amount of input in listening and reading tasks. For example, students are required to complete 40 hours extensive listening and conduct 100,000 words of extensive reading outside class during the three-year junior secondary school.

As for assessment, the revised syllabus proposes that both formative and summative assessment should be used to determine students' overall language ability, which includes not only language knowledge and skills but also attitudes and motivation, strategies, participation and cooperation with others. It is postulated in the revised syllabus that summative assessment should include listening, written and oral tests. Written tests should measure students' ability to use English rather than purely measure their grammatical knowledge. Also the number and difficulty level of the questions on grammar points should be reduced.

In addition, the revised syllabus advocates a more student-centered approach to language teaching. It states that teachers should adjust their views on language and language teaching and foster students' creativity in language use. To ensure students' participation in class, it suggests that teachers' talking time should not exceed more than one third of class time, leaving the rest of the time for students' practice. Language input should be authentic, interesting, and practical. The revised syllabus also states that teachers are expected to make good use of modern teaching technology and develop effective teaching resources.

Following the revised syllabus, major textbook publishers for junior high schools set out to revise the textbooks according to the revised syllabus. Teacher training workshops were conducted in every province to introduce the changes in the syllabus. At the same time, national research projects were set up to evaluate school-leaving tests for junior secondary school. Analysis reports were disseminated and training of test designers were organized to make sure that such tests provide a positive wash back to the implementation of the revised syllabus (e.g. National Evaluation Team on School Leaving Tests, 2001, 2002; MOE Evaluation Team on School Leaving Tests, 2003).

The New Primary School English Requirement

Entering the new millennium, upgrading the level of English of all Chinese citizens has become a real concern for the Chinese government. It was decided in early 2001 that English would be offered at primary level at grade 3, first in cities and counties, then gradually in towns and villages. MOE requires each province to work out its strategic plan for implementing primary school English in terms of timeframe, beginning age, strategic provisional plan and teacher training schemes (MOE Document, 2001). The government is also very concerned about the teaching method to be used for primary school English. Although the Basic Requirement does not suggest any specific teaching methods, the principles and performance descriptors postulated reflect an activity-based approach to provide children opportunities to experience the language and facilitate their own discovery of meaning as a first-hand experience. For example, the framework of strands for Level 1 (grade 3 and 4) is designed as: Listen and Do, Speak and Sing, Play and Act, Read and Write, Audio and Visual. For Level 2 (grade 5 and 6), the strands are: Listening, Speaking, Reading, Writing, Play and Act, and Audio and Visual. A time allocation of 4 short periods (20-30 minutes each) a week is recommended on a regular and frequent basis to ensure sustained progress. The Basic Requirement also states that assessment for primary school English should focus on enhancing pupils' overall development and teachers' effectiveness in teaching. Formative assessment should be the major form for assessing pupils' achievement in English. Variety and selectivity should be the characteristics for ways of assessment in primary schools. Test-oriented evaluation is not encouraged for the primary phase.

To ensure success of primary school English teaching, MOE encourages the utilization of Satellite TV to support both teachers and pupils in teaching and learning the language. A separate channel on satellite TV is used to broadcast teacher training sessions and actual English lessons for use in classrooms where needed. All textbooks produced for use in the primary school have to be reviewed by the national textbook review committee under the MOE. Textbooks that pass the review are then formally recommended to schools. From September 2002, textbooks without passing reviews are not allowed in schools. Up until the end of 2004, more than 20 sets of textbooks have passed reviews and are now in use in different parts of China. Most of them are joint-venture productions between a Chinese publisher and a foreign publisher. The government does not encourage the complete import of foreign textbooks but cooperation is encouraged, as foreign textbooks have to be localized to meet the needs of the Basic Requirement and the needs of learners in Chinese contexts.

Introducing English into primary schools is not a temporary policy. It is rather a long-term goal and an enterprise to enable future generations to face the challenges of globalization in every sphere of human life. MOE expects that educational departments at all levels resolve to take effective measures in training primary school English teachers. Both pre-service and in-service courses are to be developed to meet the needs of primary English provision in the new century (MOE Document, 2001).

In order to ensure success, MOE emphasizes that research in primary school English teaching is to be enhanced and supported. This requires the inclusion of full time ELT advisors on primary school English teaching in local educational departments, who are to take responsibility for guiding teaching and research in the area. Demonstration schools and regions are encouraged to carry out experiments and reforms so as to lead the whole area in teaching and research. To protect other foreign languages taught in schools, a special policy will be issued that ensures schools presently teaching Russian and Japanese or other foreign languages may continue doing so (MOE Document, 2001).

LOOKING INTO THE FUTURE: THE DESIGN OF THE NEW NATIONAL ENGLISH CURRICULUM FOR THE 21ST CENTURY

To meet the challenges and demands of a technological economy and the rapid social development in the new century, the Ministry of Education launched a project which aimed to re-establish modern curricula for basic education over the next decade. The English curriculum project team was formed in June 1999 with 13 members representing a wide range of scholars, teacher educators, research fellows, and ELT advisors. Three national consultation meetings were organized at different stages of the project development. In addition, a large scale nation-wide consultation involving 10 provinces and hundreds of people representing different walks of life such as scientists, entrepreneurs, scholars, classroom teachers, members from political consultative committees and the people's congress was organized by MOE prior to the publication of the pilot version of the curriculum.

Main Characteristics of the New English Curriculum

The overall structure of the new English curriculum is the most comprehensive ever designed. It is based on the principles of quality education and focuses on developing students' creativity and practical language abilities. Fundamental changes have been made in terms of the views of English teaching and learning with regards to the objectives, content, methods, and assessment. The following points summarize the main characteristics of the new curriculum.

An Emphasis on Whole-Person Education through Language Teaching

The overall objective described in the new curriculum indicates a change in the understanding of the nature of English education. It moves from a focus on teaching the language to a focus on educating the students through the experiences of learning the language. The ultimate goal of English is to promote the students' overall ability in language use, which is based on the comprehensive development of their language skills, language knowledge, affect, learning strategies and cultural awareness. Figure 1 illustrates the framework of the overall objectives of the curriculum.

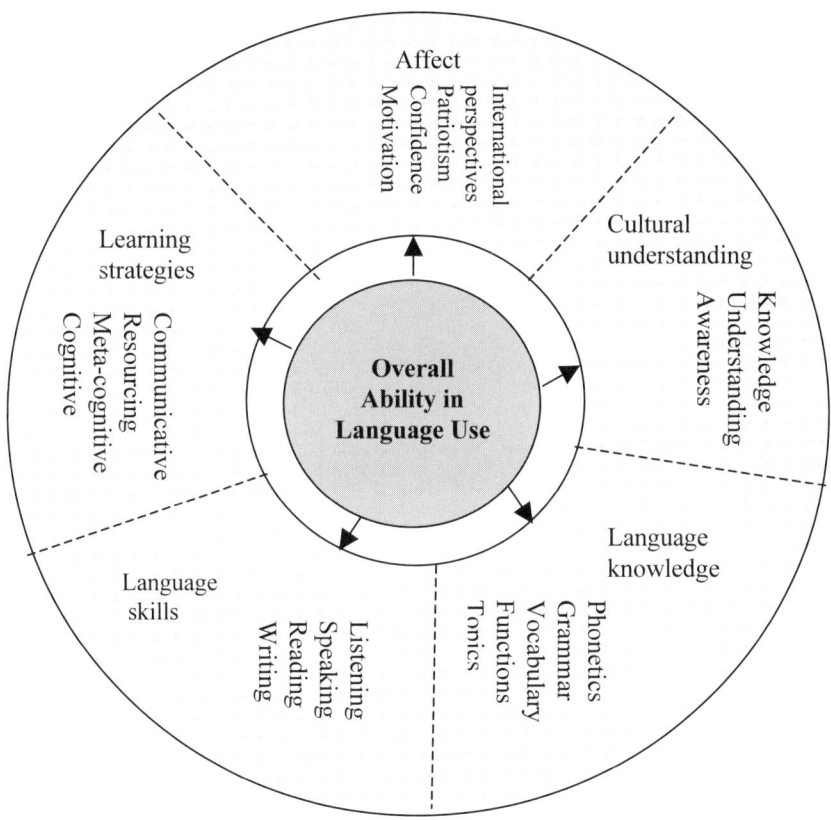

Figure 1. Framework of Objectives in the new English Curriculum (National English Curriculum Standards, 2001)

A New Design to Ensure Continuity, Flexibility and Selectivity

The design of the new English curriculum unifies both primary and secondary school English into one continuum of development and divides English language teaching and learning into nine competence-based levels with a required component for every student from Level 1 in primary 3 to Level 7 in senior secondary school. Detailed performance objectives for each level are given in addition to the overall aims of the course. The course adds an elective component with two optional tracks after the completion of the nine-year compulsory education with an intention to provide opportunities for different routes of development and individuality (see Figure 2).

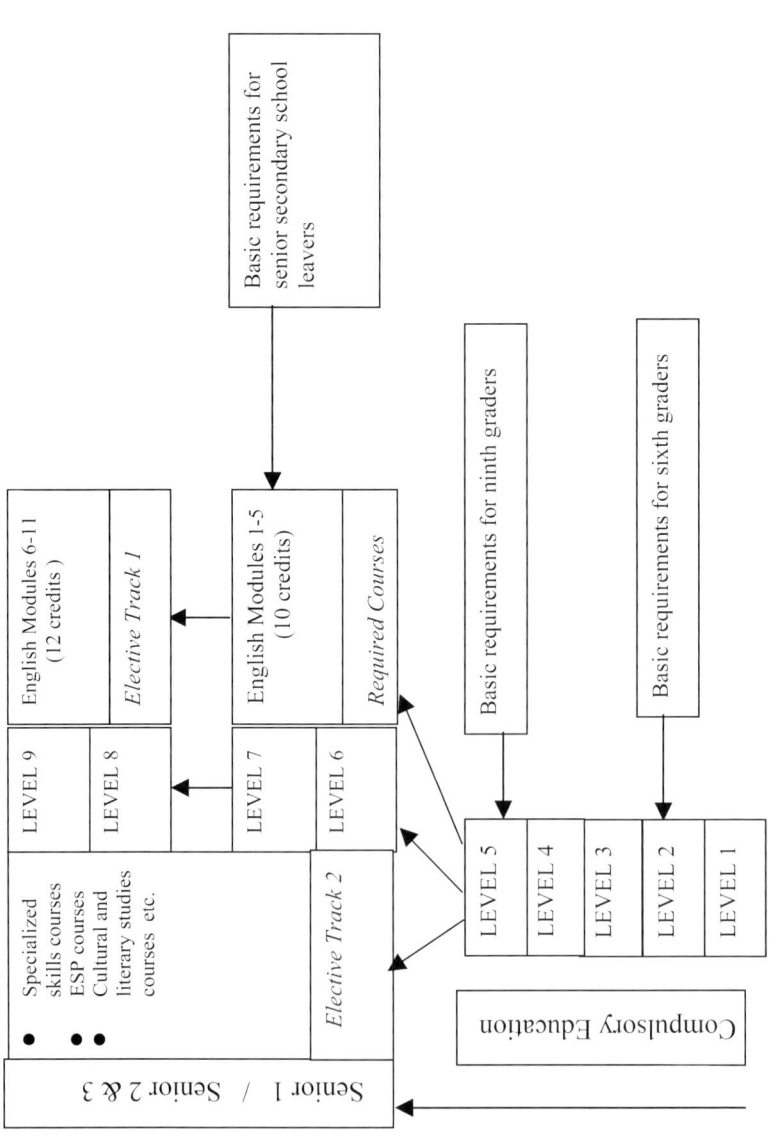

Figure 2. The Design of the New English Curriculum (Based on National English Curriculum Standards, 2001 & National English Curriculum Standards For Senior Secondary School 2003)

The unity of and continuity between primary and secondary English language teaching is to ensure effective learning and better utilization of teaching and learning resources. It also allows flexibility and practicality in the curriculum as local educational authorities retain control of decision-making regarding when to start the English course in primary schools and what level should be reached, and on time allocations (4 periods a week is recommended). By changing the design from a grade-based to a competence-based one gives the flexibility to both schools and students starting at different ages to follow the levels progressively. For example, schools with better teaching conditions can reach levels higher than Level 2 or 5 or 7 at grade 6, grade 9 or senior 2 respectively. Those with poorer teaching conditions or in ethnic minority regions may reach levels lower than the required. The flexibility is also exemplified in its design through an inclusion of both a required and an elective component after the period of compulsory education. Level 7 is required for all senior secondary students, which is designed as the common core foundation for life-long learning. After students reach Level 7 with certain required credits, the course becomes completely elective.

Advocating Student-centred and Task-based Teaching with a Proper Increase in Vocabulary

Although no particular teaching approach is specified in the new curriculum, it clearly aims to develop students' overall ability in language use. Detailed performance objectives for each level are described in terms of what the students should be able to do with the language rather than what the teachers should teach, putting the students at the center of learning. To help students achieve such objectives, task-based teaching is recommended with an emphasis on integrated skills development, language use in context, problem solving, and cooperative learning. As far as vocabulary is concerned, the new curriculum requires that students demonstrate an ability to use 600-700 words and 50 phrases at Level 2; 1,500-1,600 words and 200-300 phrases at Level 5; about 2,500 words and 300-400 phrases at Level 7; 3,300 words at Level 8; and 4,500-5,000 at Level 9.

Establishing a New Assessment System

The new curriculum establishes new principles for assessment with a shift of focus from a purely exam-based to a more performance and progress-based one. It encourages teachers to use formative assessment to assess students' learning progress. Level 2 is to be assessed by individual schools based on students' progress and performance in using the language according to the performance descriptions. At the secondary schools level, both formative assessment and summative assessment are to be used in evaluating students' achievement. As far as proficiency levels are concerned, it is currently planned that tests of Level 5, 7, 8, and 9 will be organized and certified by MOE recognized testing authorities. Test results will determine eligibility to transfer from corresponding schools or to graduate to a higher school of learning. For example, Level 5 is required for graduation from a junior secondary school into a senior secondary school. Level 7 together with some required course credits are required for graduation from a senior secondary school. Level 8 is required for entering into colleges and universities. Level 9 may allow students to be exempted from college English courses.

Emphasizing the Use of Technology for Language Teaching

The new curriculum puts a very strong emphasis on teachers' ability to make good use of modern educational resources and expand the use of multimedia technology in teaching. It encourages teachers to take advantage of modern educational technology such as TV and radio programs, English language magazines, computer, Internet, distance language teaching, and multimedia resources to create optimal conditions for students' learning.

Along with the design of the new curriculum, the policy of textbook production also changed to allow more publishers to bid for national textbook projects. Once approved by the MOE textbook review committee, they are recommended to schools. This marks the beginning of an unprecedented era of textbook development to allow a variety of textbooks for use in different regions for different needs. At present, there are more than 20 titles for primary English, and 7 titles for junior and senior English respectively. What is significant about such a change is that for many years teachers in classrooms have been quite ignorant of the national syllabus. What they are concerned about is what appears in textbooks and in examination papers. As a result, teachers rely heavily on the textbook writers to translate the aims, contents, and suggested methodology from the syllabus into the textbook. This also results from the way the syllabus is designed, as what is required is usually too general for teachers in the classrooms to follow. Therefore, textbooks have played a dictating role in English language teaching. With the new English curriculum and a number of textbooks available, the situation is expected to change. Tests will no longer be based on one particular textbook but on the level descriptions depicted in the new curriculum. Therefore, teachers will need to know about the requirements of the new curriculum, be familiar with the level specifications, and use them as a guide for teaching, although textbooks will continue to play a crucial role.

Piloting and Implementing the New Curriculum

Piloting of the new curriculums with a variety of new textbooks across 19 subjects started from September 2001. Thirty-eight districts, counties, and cities were involved in the whole country with 700,000 students (Newsletter for piloting the new curriculums, 2001). In 2002, over 500 regions joined in the piloting scheme and in 2003, over 1,000 counties and regions, comprising 40% of the students at the beginning grade both in primary and secondary schools. Training at all levels (educational administrators, teaching and research advisors, school principals, as well as classroom teachers) began throughout 2001 to 2004 and is still continuing.

A report from China Education Daily (9 December 2004) reveals that the piloting of the new curriculum for nine-year compulsory education has led to a smooth transition and further development based on the third MOE evaluation of the new curriculum in six provinces. New concepts and beliefs in education are beginning to be seen in classrooms. The main changes lie in the improved ecology for teaching and learning in schools, more harmonious relationships established between teachers and learners, and learners' more active engagement in activities. Most importantly, learners are finding learning a more enjoyable experience as they are playing a more active role in the learning process. At the same time, a school-based research system is being established with teachers' increased awareness of professional development. As a result, a lively, versatile, democratic and effective teaching environment is being formed, and a new assessment system for learning is being established. The school exit tests for junior secondary school for piloting regions have also seen substantial reform to meet with the requirements of the new curriculum. The expected outcomes are beginning to be seen in schools, despite many problems to be tackled in the future.

Preparing Teachers for the Change

For any educational change, teachers are the crucial factors as they are the implementers of the new ideas. Their contributions to and participation in the innovation are essential. Without their willingness, understanding, cooperation, and participation, there can be no change (Brown, 1980; White, 1988). However, for many teachers, change is a rather slow and stressful experience as during this transitional period, they are bound to "cope with both the mental and emotional demands of relearning aspects of their professional culture in order to be recognized as a competent professional using the new approach" (Wedell, 2001, p. 3). With the implementation of the new curriculum, English teachers in China are expected to change in many ways (Wang, 2003). First, they are expected to change their views about language teaching from a knowledge-based one to a competence-based one. Second, they are expected to change their traditional role as a knowledge transmitter to a multi-role educator, as the teaching objectives of English postulated in the new curriculum require that language teaching is more than just teaching knowledge and skills; it includes caring for students' affective needs, developing their learning strategies, widening their cultural horizons, and establishing international perspectives through the process of language learning. Third, teachers are expected to develop new teaching skills, i.e. skills for motivating learners in language learning, skills for developing their learning strategies, skill in designing more task-based, cooperative and problem-solving activities in order to make students the center of learning. Fourth, teachers are expected to change their ways of evaluating the students, learning to apply formative assessment in addition to using tests, which they are already very familiar with. Teachers also need to develop the ability to adapt the textbooks they use to meet the requirement of the curriculum and the needs of their learners. Last but not least, teachers are expected to use modern technology in teaching, creating more effective resources for learning and for using the language. These changes that teachers face may create a lot of emotional and professional pressure on them. In addition, teachers' own language proficiency needs to be improved, without which no other roles can be successfully fulfilled.

A preliminary survey on 200 key primary and secondary school English teachers by myself from Beijing, Shandong, Anhui, Hainan, Yunnan, and Tianjin immediately after the new curriculum training sessions between 2001 and 2002 reflected their initial reactions towards the change. Over 90% of the teachers surveyed overwhelmingly welcomed the change and expressed certain degrees of confidence in their ability to cope with it. At the same time, many of them expressed the need for support. Many of them felt pressured and worried about the management of change and the current assessment systems. A number of them expressed their worries about their own language proficiency as the new curriculum sets a much higher level on the students' ability in using the language for communication.

At the same time, teachers expressed strongly both internal and external needs in dealing with the new curriculum. The internal needs include a full understanding of the new English curriculum on the part of the teachers themselves, a need for improvement of their own language proficiency, a need to improve their own ability in thinking and reflections as well as their ability in developing new teaching skills. The external needs expressed by the teachers include, first, a full understanding of and support for the new curriculum from the public, school principals, parents and students. Second, school assessment systems need to be reformed in line with the objectives of the new curriculum. Third, effective communication and the provision of adequate information and resources are needed. Fourth, there is a need among teachers to cooperate in the implementation process. Other points made include providing talks and seminars on the new curriculum; training teachers on how to use the new textbook(s); providing model lessons; organizing seminars for teachers to discuss particular issues and guide teachers to do research on their teaching.

The following are some of the comments by the teachers in the survey which reflect teachers' typical feelings towards curriculum change:

T1: I feel extremely pressured. I feel I need to re-learn a lot of things. I feel I am lagging behind everyday if I do not learn more. I must attend training courses to improve myself.

T2: I am willing to try new things but I'm afraid that my students or their parents would not agree and accept me.

T3: I think we need support and understanding from all parties, including the public, the school principals, other teachers, parents and students themselves.

T4: All these changes come too quickly and there are too many new requirements. I feel I am overpowered and do not know what to do and where to start.

T5: I feel excited about NEC but at the same time I see a lot of difficulties and problems. First is the change of views of all the teachers and change of teaching methods and techniques. The exam system is the biggest obstacle.

T6: I think NEC is really good and necessary. It needs to be implemented as quickly as possible. I think I have been trying to teach following a lot of the same ideas, but I was not able to conceptualize or theorize. So, I sometimes succeed and sometimes fail. Now I know why. I really need to learn more.

As many writers (Fullan, 1991; Hutchinson 1991; Markee, 1997) who write about ELT curriculum change have all pointed out, during this transition period teachers will often feel insecure, vulnerable, and under pressure. They have to accommodate new beliefs and see themselves in new roles and this can be very demanding (Wedell, 2001). Furthermore, they have to teach within different constraints and satisfy different demands coming from the curriculum, the school, parents, as well as students. The change required of teachers can only be supported through involving them in their professional doings and reflections within very supportive environments, as Fullan (1992) points out, it "is what people develop in their minds and actions that counts. People do not learn or accomplish complex changes by being told or shown what to do. A deeper meaning and solid change must be born over time" (p. 115). We need to be fully aware of the fact that conceptual change is a difficult and lengthy process (Fullan, 1993; Karavas-Doukas, 1998), and needs supports from all levels. As for teachers, the new beliefs or ideas will have to be gradually incorporated into the teachers' own belief structures through continuous practice and reflections so that adjustments can be made in their own thinking (Lamb, 1995).

CONCLUSIONS

English language teaching in China has witnessed a rapid development since China opened its door to the world in the late 1970s. Curriculum changes over the last two decades have had a profound impact on the methodological approaches undertaken in ELT in China. In fact, change has been a constant effort and has been incremental following a gradual shift of paradigm from grammar-translation to audio-lingual approaches and then to a more functional-structural based communication-oriented approach and now moving towards a global approach to language education through task-based teaching. The ideology of the current curriculum has been welcomed in general by most teachers in China but many practical problems remain to be solved or overcome in many teaching situations and strong support and understanding at all levels are needed. In response to the continued top-down efforts in ELT innovations with the revision of the 1993 syllabus, the design of the primary English requirement, and piloting of the new English curriculum, an increasing number of teachers and researchers are now devoting themselves to the study of language teaching, especially in primary and secondary schools. At present, new textbooks are being developed and teacher training programs at primary and secondary levels are being funded by both the national and local governments. Many teachers are beginning to realize the need to change their beliefs about language and language learning, which enable them to see the possibility of modifying their teaching methods according to the new concepts in teaching and the needs of their students.

The newly designed English curriculum will play a vital role in enhancing the quality of English language teaching of the 21st century in China. However, there is still a long way to go in order to make the aspirations a classroom reality. The piloting of the new English curriculum is already underway with the training of teachers and the writing of textbooks being identified as crucial factors to the success of the implementation. Teachers' perceptions about the changes, their attitudes towards the changes, their subsequent changes in teaching behaviors, teacher training effectiveness as well as the impacts that the new curriculum and materials may bring about, will all need to be carefully evaluated after the nationwide implementation in 2005.

ACKNOWLEDGEMENTS

I would like to express my gratitude to Dr. Bob Adamson for his suggestions on revising the article and assistance in trimming it to an acceptable length.

REFERENCES

Adamson, B. (1997, October). *The English language curriculum since 1976*. Plenary presentation at the National Foreign Language Teaching and Research Association, China Education Society, Ninth Annual Conference, Jinan, PRC.

Adamson, B., & Morris, P. (1997). The English curriculum in the People's Republic of China. *Comparative Education Review, 41*(1), 3–26.

Brown, S. (1980). Key issues in the implementation of innovations in schools. *Curriculum, 1*(1), 32–39.

China Education Daily (2004-Dec-09). The third evaluation of the nine-year compulsory education curriculum reform indicates smooth and healthy development. Retrieved September 12 2005, from http://www.moe.edu.cn/edoas/website18/info7370.htm.

English syllabus for nine-year compulsory education in full-time junior secondary schools. (1993). Beijing: People's Education Press.

English syllabus for nine-year compulsory education in full-time junior secondary schools [Revised Edition]. (2000). Beijing: People's Education Press.

Fullan, M.G. (1991). *The new meaning of educational change*. London: Casell.

Fullan, M.G. (1992). Causes and processes of implementation and continuation. In N. Bennet, M. Crawford, & C. Riches (Eds.), *Managing change in education: Individual and organizational perspectives*, (pp. 109–131). London: Paul Chapman.

Fullan, M.G. (1993). *Change forces*. London: Falmer Press.

Hao, Y. (1999, August). *Differentiating teaching to maximize learning opportunities for different learners*. Plenary talk given at the Tenth Annual Conference of the National Foreign Language Teaching and Research Association, China Education Society, Harbin, PRC.

Hutchinson, T. (1991). The management of change. *Teacher Trainer, 5*(3), 19–21.

Karavas-Doukas, K. (1998). Evaluating the implementation of educational innovations: Lessons from the past. In P. Rea-Dickins & K. P. Germaine (Eds.), *Managing evaluation and innovation in language teaching: Building bridges* (pp. 25–50). Essex: Longman.

Lamb, M. (1995). The consequences of InSET. *ELT Journal, 49*(1), 72–79.

Li, L., Zhang, R., & Liu, L. (1988). *A history of English language teaching in China*. Shanghai: Foreign Language Education Press.

Liu, D., & Gong, Y. (2001). English language teaching development in schools in China. In *Retrospect and Prospect – Memoirs for the 20th Anniversary of the National Foreign Language Teaching and Research Association, China Education Society* (pp. 35–39). Beijing: People's Education Press.

Markee, N. (1997). *Managing curricular innovation*. Cambridge: Cambridge University Press.

Ministry of Education (1998). *Action plans for revitalizing education for the 21st century*. Beijing: Ministry of Education.

MOE Document (2001). Guidelines from the Ministry of Education for promoting primary school English. Ministry of Education. *Basic Education*, 2.

MOE Evaluation Team on School Leaving Tests (2003). *National evaluation report for the year 2002 school leaving tests of junior secondary schools*. Nanjing: Jiangsu Education Press.

National English curriculum standards for nine-year compulsory education and senior high schools (Piloting Edition). (2001). Beijing: Beijing Normal University Press.

National English curriculum standards for senior secondary school (Piloting Edition). (2003). Beijing: People's Education Press.

National Evaluation Team on School Leaving Tests. (2001). *National evaluation report for the year 2000 school leaving tests of junior secondary schools*. Beijing: Beijing Normal University Press.

National Evaluation Team on School Leaving Tests. (2002). *National evaluation report on test management and test evaluation for the year 2001 school leaving tests of junior secondary schools*. Beijing: Capital Normal University Press.

Newsletter for piloting the national curriculums. (2001, No. 4). Beijing Normal University, Center for School Curriculum Studies.

Research team of the Department of Foreign Languages, Beijing Normal University (1999). Observation analysis report of the National Senior Secondary School English Language Teaching Contest. *Foreign Language Teaching in Schools, 8,* 4–8; *9*, 1–4.

Research team of the Department of Foreign Languages, Beijing Normal University (2001a). Observation analysis report of the National Primary School English Language Teaching Contest. *Foreign Language Teaching in Schools, 8,* 6–10; *9*, 1–4.

Research team of the Department of Foreign Languages, Beijing Normal University (2001b & 2002). Observation analysis report of the National Junior Secondary School English Language Teaching Contest. *Foreign Language Teaching in Schools, 12,* 8–12; *1*, 12–15.

Wang, Q. (1999). Some thoughts on the 21st century foreign language curriculum reform for nine-year compulsory education. *Foreign Language Teaching in Schools, 7,* 1–4; 8, 1–3.

Wang, Q. (2003). New developments in primary English education in China–Opportunities and challenges. *Journal of Basic Education, 12*(2), 243–253.

Wedell, M. (2001, May). *ELT curriculum changes in the 21st century: Planning to support the implementers in their wider and local contexts.* Paper presented at the International Conference on College English Teaching, organized by China College English Language Teaching and Research Association and Foreign Language Teaching and Research Press, Beijing, China.

Wei, L., & Sun, C. (2000). *Modern English language teaching: Principles and practice.* Jilin: Jilin People's Press.

White, R.V. (1988). *The ELT curriculum.* Oxford: Blackwell.

Year book of Chinese education 2003. Beijing: Ministry of Education.

Yu, T. (2004). *Word, sentence, and discourse teaching model applied in junior English teaching.* An experimental research report. Retrieved September 12 2005.

Zhang, S. (1993). (Ed.). *Zhang Sizhong's foreign language teaching method: Theory and practice.* Shanghai: Shanghai Jiaotong University Press.

Zhang, Y., & Shen, B. (2001, October). *A general overview of the English course materials development in China.* Paper presented at the National Foreign Language Teaching and Research Association, China Education Society, 11th Annual Conference. Hangzhou, China.

Zhang, Z. (2000). *Theories and schools of foreign language teaching methodology in China.* Beijing: Science Press.

Project team for research on senior secondary school English language teaching in China (2001). Overall report investigating senior secondary school English language teaching in China. In Z. Zhang, Z. Chen, & L. Li. (Eds.). (2001). *The status quo and development of English language teaching: Investigations into senior secondary school English language teaching.* Beijing: People's Education Press.

Zhang, Z., & Du, P. (Eds.). (1995). *The principles and models of 3-dimension foreign language approach.* Chongqing: Chongqing Publishing House.

Zhao, J., & Xu, J. (2002). *Twenty years of curriculum reform in China: Retrospect and prospect.* China Education and Research Network. Retrieved September 12 2005.

Zhou, L. (1995). *Encyclopedia of secondary school English education in China.* Shenyang: Northeast University.

CHAPTER 8

ELT AND BILINGUAL EDUCATION IN ARGENTINA

AGUSTINA TOCALLI-BELLER

The University of Toronto, Canada

ABSTRACT

The English language has a long history and prestigious status in Argentina. Its presence as a foreign language is closely linked to the birth of the country as a nation. As a consequence, the teaching of English has always been widely encouraged in Argentina. Today, English is part of the curriculum of private and state-run schools. Within the private sector, there is a large number of bilingual schools, some of which were established as ethnic schools by the first English settlers in the 19th century. The success of the first bilingual schools has encouraged many other schools to copy, to varying degrees, their bilingual curriculum and thus create a large network of English-Spanish schools in the country. Education in Argentina has undergone extensive changes in the last decade. The new Federal Law of Education of 1996 has had a special impact on the teaching of foreign languages. Based on this law, English is now compulsory in all Argentine schools—a clear sign of the government's recognition of the importance of mastering the world's lingua franca. In this chapter, the implementation of the new education law and its impact on the teaching of English in public schools is discussed.

INTRODUCTION

The English language has a long history and prestigious status in Argentina. Its presence as a foreign language dates from the early years and is closely linked to the birth of the country as a nation. As a consequence, the study of English has always been widely encouraged in Argentina.

Today English is part of the curriculum of all schools in the country. In this sense, special attention must be paid to the 1993 educational reform, one of the premises of which claims "a systematic-linguistic construct for language development, which is able to accommodate mother tongue acquisition, second and foreign languages, pidgin and Creole varieties, alongside English as a global language" (Dirección General de Investigación y Desarrollo Educativo, 1998a, 1998b). Following the distinction by the linguist Braj Kachru (1985), we can say in Crystal's (1997) words that Argentina belongs to the *expanding* circle "which recognises the importance of English as an international language though they do not have a colonization by members of the *inner group* (UK, USA, etc.), nor have given English special administrative status" (p. 54).

Within the private sector of the Argentine educational system, there is a large number of bilingual schools, the origin of which lies in the first 20 British-founded schools (British Council Argentina, 2000). The first part of this chapter will discuss the success of these early bilingual schools, which has encouraged many other schools to copy, to varying degrees, their bilingual curriculum and thus create a large network of private English/Spanish schools in the country. The main features of bilingual schools will be presented.

Education in Argentina has undergone extensive changes in the last decade. The new Federal Law of Education (Ley Federal de Educación N° 24.195), enacted in 1993, brought about a long-awaited reform that would decentralize education and outline a curriculum in light of global trends as well as in the national context (see Pini & Cigliutti, 1999; Rhoten, 2000). The educational reform has also reflected a greater awareness of the different linguistic and cultural realities not only in the country but also in the world, a perspective that made the ministries of education of each province think both locally and globally. A global perspective highlights the importance of implementing EFL throughout the entire educational system. Based on the new Federal Law of Education, English is now compulsory in all Argentine schools—a clear sign of the government's recognition of the importance of mastering the world's lingua franca. The second part of this chapter will present the law and discuss its implementation and impact on the teaching of English.

ENGLISH IN THE PRIVATE SECTOR

The southernmost and second-largest country in South America, Argentina, covers an area of almost 4,000,000 km^2 and is divided into 24 provinces. The overall population, 36 million inhabitants, is dispersed with varying rates of density throughout the country. Strikingly, one third of the population lives in one city, Buenos Aires, the country's federal capital (Instituto Nacional De Estadística y Censos, INDEC, 2002).

Private schools in Argentina constitute an important part of the educational system. Out of a total student population of 10 million, 24% of the students attend privately run schools. The percentage of private schools is higher in the wealthier provinces. In the city of Buenos Aires itself, almost half of the schools are private (46%) (INDEC, 2002). Unfortunately, many Argentineans do not view the public education system as adequate and they are willing to pay for higher standards of instruction, especially when it comes to learning English. Even though, as will be discussed later, ELT has recently become compulsory for both the private and public sectors, the latter still lags behind the former in the mind of most Argentineans. Moreover, the large network of English/Spanish private bilingual schools provides an attractive option to those who want their children to achieve a high proficiency in English.[1]

The English Side of Argentine History

The Argentine population has been greatly influenced by European immigration that arrived in the country between 1860 and 1940. The two largest immigrant groups came from Spain and Italy towards the end of the 19th century, but the presence of English-speaking people dates from earlier times. Besides some aboriginal languages (see Baker & Prys Jones, 1998; Ethnologue, 2003; Hornberger, 1994), English is the second most widely spoken language in Argentina after Spanish, the official language. English is deeply rooted in the country's history of independence struggles and its political relations with Great Britain.

Historical, professional, cultural, and commercial factors have always encouraged Argentina's connection with English-speaking countries. Britain provided aid in arms and supplies in the independence wars which culminated in Argentina securing its independence from Spain in 1824. In 1825, the Friendship, Commerce, and Navigation Treaty brought Argentina and Britain even closer by not only recognizing Argentina's independence, but also by allowing the British in Argentina the same commercial freedom and expression of their creed and culture as that of the Argentine population. This treaty encouraged the arrival of many British settlers and a few years later a total of 3,500 English-speaking people lived in Argentina (Moyano, 1997).

As a result of poor harvests and extended famine in Ireland, the Irish also decided to emigrate in 1840 and settled in the west of the province of Buenos Aires, concentrating on the raising of sheep and the wool industry and keeping to themselves. This attitude favored the maintenance of their native language. Welsh and Scottish expeditions to Argentina were also undertaken in search of better prospects in the new continent. The first Welsh ventured to South America in the hope that there they would be able to defend their ideals and save their language and culture (Moyano, 1997). In a similar vein, the Scots settled in Patagonia (the southern part of the country) to rear sheep.

Further immigration from Europe and foreign investments continued in subsequent years. Investments were primarily British and came in areas such as railways and ports, shipping companies, banks and insurance companies, all of which became important pillars of the nation's wealth (Subcomisión de la Historia de la Escuela Escosesa San Andrés, 1988). Without a doubt, this boost in the Argentine economy increased the power of the English language.

The Birth of Bilingual Schools

As noted above, the presence of English-speakers in Argentina has influenced many fields including trade, banking, and transportation. It has also left a legacy of many bilingual schools. The first English-speaking communities in Argentina were very concerned about educating their children according to their own traditions and culture and thus founded their own schools. The Scottish settlers, in particular, were pioneers in terms of educational initiatives.

In 1838, 13 years after the arrival of the first Scots, the Scottish community set up, at the premises of their Presbyterian church, an ethnic group school (Fishman & Nahirny, 1966) called St. Andrew's Scots School. Their instructional methods became popular and the number of students increased rapidly. In 1860, they decided to add the teaching of Spanish to the regular curriculum. By 1909, 1.5 hours a day were devoted to Spanish instruction while 3.5 hours a day were for English, including time spent preparing for Cambridge Local examinations. In 1938, the state mandated that the official curriculum be taught and that classes taught in Spanish be extended to 3 hours per day. That year, all students sat for official examinations in Spanish. Out of 261 students, 244 (93%) passed the exam (Subcomisión de la Historia de la Escuela Escosesa San Andrés, 1988). Such results and ensuing interest in bilingual education encouraged the founding of many other Spanish/English schools and further enrollment in St. Andrew's. Over the years, however, the characteristics of the student body changed. Whereas in 1899 the school reported a majority of first and second generation immigrant students (82%), in 1944, those students represented only 28% of the school population (Subcomisión de la Historia de la Escuela Escosesa San Andrés, 1988). This change in student demographics resulted in a new student community with respect to language background and thus presented a new challenge to the school.

In recent years, St. Andrew's Scots School has become more integrated into the wider Argentine community. Monolingual families started to recognize English as a world language and bilingual proficiency as an asset in their children's upbringing. In 1963, a kindergarten in English was established and, in this way, the school became a viable option for non-English speaking parents (St. Andrew's Scots School, 1999). Implementing total immersion in the second language in kindergarten was the key stepping-stone for students to move into the bilingual curriculum in later years. St. Andrew's is the oldest and most vivid testimony of English schooling in Argentina. It has striven for high quality of education and for the maintenance and appreciation of English as have other bilingual schools, such as St. George's College, St. Hilda's College, Northlands, Belgrano Day School, to name but a few. These schools were also founded to teach according to the methods and discipline of schools in England.

English-Spanish Bilingual Schools Today

Bilingual schools in Argentina fall under two of the types of immersion education as defined by Swain and Johnson (1997): immersion in a foreign language and immersion in a language of power. The latter refers to the fact that, as discussed earlier, the English language is linked to the economic growth of the country. It is recognized as the international lingua franca and a good command of English is regarded as essential both for the upward mobility of individuals and for the economic development of the country. Notwithstanding this, since Argentina has only one official language, English is officially a foreign language (though it has been granted special treatment in the new law of education as will be discussed later). Bilingual schools in Argentina can therefore also fall within the category of immersion in a foreign language. Thus, in a similar way to countries such as Hungary (see Duff, 1997), the current impetus toward learning English in Argentina is oriented towards instrumental goals and has international reference (Johnson & Swain, 1997). In short, the ever-burgeoning interest in Spanish/English bilingual education responds to a desire to boost students' proficiency in a foreign language that is highly regarded, needed, and used worldwide.

The success of the original British-founded schools spawned other private schools and nowadays there is a large network of schools that run both Spanish and English curricula. Bilingual schools need, of course, to abide by the new education law and thus they are required to submit a *programa educativo institucional* [institutional educational program] (PEI). Therefore, their curricula are evenly divided between what is officially required and what an English curriculum can offer, namely, to teach a second language through content area subjects and not only as a subject itself. Moreover, second language development is reinforced through activities that are common in schools in the UK but are relatively unusual in Argentine schools, for example, sports, music, drama, debate, and other cultural interchanges and competitions (British Council Argentina, 2000).

Generally speaking, bilingual programs in Argentina strive to implement the following core features of prototypical immersion programs as outlined by Swain and Johnson (1997, p.15):

1. *The L2 is a medium of instruction.* English is used as the language of instruction for some school subjects. The ratio of instruction in English and in Spanish varies from school to school and even from year to year within one school (though schools that conform the most to the bilingual ideals offer equal instruction time in each language).
2. *The immersion curriculum parallels the local L1 curriculum.* The English curriculum follows the Spanish curriculum and is defined in terms of the educational norms, goals, needs, and aspirations as outlined by the Federal Law of Education. This law requires that all school subjects be taught in both languages. Notwithstanding this, as will be discussed later, there are a number of schools that also offer an international curriculum, the medium of instruction of which is English.
3. *Overt support exists for the L1.* As outlined earlier, Spanish is one of the languages of instruction and the only medium of instruction for subjects that are part of the Argentine curriculum exclusively, such as *Lengua Castellana* [Spanish Language], *Literatura Española* [Spanish Literature], *Educación Cívica y Ciudadana* [Civic Education].
4. *The program aims for additive bilingualism.* Although the level of proficiency varies, by the end of the program students in bilingual schools graduate with superior English to those who study English only as a school subject.
5. *Exposure to the L2 is largely confined to the classroom.* Students in bilingual programs in Argentina have little or no conversational exposure to English outside the school. However, because English is rapidly becoming the world's lingua franca, students have easy access to sources of authentic input such as movies, TV programs, the Internet, books, magazines, etc.
6. *Students enter with similar levels of L2 proficiency.* As noted earlier, even schools that were originally created for the English-speaking community in Argentina are no longer restricted to English-speaking families. There may still be some families who speak English at home (see Cortés-Conde, 1994) and other English-speaking families that come from abroad temporarily that send their children to bilingual schools; however, a large majority of the students enter the program with very limited proficiency in English.
7. *(Some of) the teachers are bilingual.* The linguistic qualifications of the teaching faculty of Argentine bilingual schools are quite varied. Spanish teachers are not required to know English. Teachers and heads of departments are, in some cases, brought from English-speaking countries; however, they may have little or no command of Spanish, their students' L1. Schools also hire Spanish-speaking teachers trained to teach English as a subject, teachers of particular subject matter who have a good command of English, as well as graduates of their own school, all of whom have varying degrees of proficiency in English. All these teachers are required, however, to hold the appropriate qualifications for teaching the language. Despite the variation in English proficiency, school subject teachers

generally know the course subject matter very well. However, they may not know about second language teaching/learning theory and pedagogy. Needless to say, without this knowledge and systematic planning, teachers may provide inconsistent or random information about language forms, pragmatics, discourse, and culture (Genesee, 1994).
8. *The classroom culture is that of the local L1 community.* Even when schools hire expatriate English-speaking faculty, these teachers (try to) adjust instruction to the students' Argentine culture and community.

Despite these common features, because bilingual schools are privately run and there is no blanket law that regulates these programs, each school is essentially a law unto itself. Therefore, they may differ considerably from other schools in terms of administration and planning and, most importantly, outcomes related to the learning of English and other subject matter. In fact, most of the features that Swain and Johnson (1997) outline as differentiating international immersion programs from each other are similar to features that differentiate the different English/Spanish schools in Argentina. That is, bilingual programs in Argentina differ in terms of the grade level at which immersion begins, extent of immersion, the ratio of L1 to L2 at different stages, continuity across levels within the educational system, resources, commitment to bilingual schooling, and ways of measuring success. What most bilingual schools seem to have in common, however, is a bilingual school ethos and international English exams. These two features constitute requirements for schools to become affiliated with the English Speaking Scholastic Association of the River Plate (ESSARP). This is an association of bilingual schools founded in 1926 to provide a forum for discussion for Heads of the bilingual schools and which now also offers professional development courses for teachers. In 1998, ESSARP undertook responsibility for providing University of Cambridge Local Examinations Syndicate exam services and assessment products to schools in Argentina. The association administers exams such as the International Certificate of Secondary Education (IGCSE), Advanced International Certificate of Education (AICE), and EFL exams.

An increasing number of private schools in Argentina have begun to endorse the English language immersion (bilingual) approach and the introduction of international certificates of education rather than simply EFL examinations as the benchmarks of their English curricula. The IGCSE, which has rapidly replaced the traditional General Certificate of Education-Ordinary (GCE-O), is usually integrated with the contents and requirements of the national curriculum. According to the British Council Argentina, "since the introduction of IGCSE, the number of schools offering these examinations has grown from 20 to 96 in 1996" (British Council Argentina, 2000, p. 2). Moreover, the number of candidates has grown from 162 in 1988 to 4,189 in 1997.

With such a great interest in IGSC, consideration has also been given to the development of an advanced course as a continuation of this certificate and a substitute for the GCE A level. In 1996, the first candidates sat for the AICE, and by 1998, 18 schools had already implemented this new set of pre-university examinations (see Garvie, 1998 for an example). Some schools, however, have not opted for the AICE curriculum and have implemented the International Baccalaureate (IB) instead. IB diploma holders are expected to graduate with a sound background to enter university anywhere in the world and, of course, with an excellent command of English, since the IB curriculum is, in most cases, taught in English.

English Language Schools and EFL Examinations

Because tuition fees in British-type bilingual schools are usually high, many parents are satisfied with the more traditional teaching of English as a foreign language. Therefore, outside the bilingual school system, there are also private schools where English is taught as a foreign language for 2 or more hours per week in the official school timetable. Some of these schools provide more curricular hours to achieve higher standards of English proficiency. Moreover, there is a large number and wide range of institutes outside of the public or private school systems that offer EFL courses of varying degrees of quality. As well, these institutes offer professional development courses and promote the transmission of English culture. There is a national network of approximately 30 Argentine-English/British cultural institutes that teach about 35,000 students (British Council Argentina, 2000). These institutes are independent of each other but are directed by the Coordinated British Cultural Institutes, which works closely with the British Council. Argentina also holds a strong linguistic connection with the U.S. through Instituto Cultural Argentino Norteamericano (ICANA) [North American Argentine Cultural Institute]. Both institutions teach English through modules or cycles with an average frequency of 2 to 3 hours per week. Both British and American English are taught in language institutes in Argentina, but the former seems to prevail because most of the teaching material is British. However, American English seems to be favored in the business arena (Moyano, 1997; 2000).

These cultural institutes and other associations together with the private language schools prepare students to sit for international EFL exams. English exam tuition and publishing constitute a significant business in Argentina. Cambridge EFL examinations such as First Certificate of English, Preliminary English Test, Certificate of Advanced English, etc., are very popular. The overall total of 18,618 candidates for 1995 placed Argentina fourth in the number of candidates sitting for these examinations (after Greece, UK, and Spain) (British Council Argentina, 2002). University of Cambridge Local Examinations Syndicate (UCLES) EFL as well as Education Testing Service (ETS) exams are the most common international exams in the country. Year after year, an increasing number of candidates sit for the TOEFL. Between July 1999 and June 2000, 2,861 students took the computer-based test and 388 students sat for the paper-based exam (ETS, 2002).

ENGLISH IN THE PUBLIC SECTOR

The English language also has a long history in the public sector of Argentine education. In 1818, the first English lesson was taught in the *Colegio de la Unión del Sud*. In 1826, the University of Buenos Aires inaugurated its first English course (Cardenas De Cantiello, 1997), and 1904 saw the foundation of the Profesorado en Lenguas Vivas, which still boasts one of the finest state-run training colleges for teachers of EFL.

In 1968, some public schools in the city of Buenos Aires started to teach foreign languages, English being the most popular. In 1982, the first *Centro Educativo Complementario de Idioma Extranjero (CECIE)* [Complementary Educational

Centre for Foreign Languages] was founded to teach foreign languages, mainly English, in those schools that had not yet incorporated them in their curricula. Ten years later, a CECIE was founded in each school district—21 in total—to teach EFL (and, to a lesser extent, French, Italian, and Portuguese) to 7,500 children from grade 4 onwards. These language classes were not and are still not compulsory. They are extracurricular and free of charge ("Sin vacantes en...", 2000b).

In 2001, the city of Buenos Aires, with the sponsorship of the British Council and the embassies of the U.S, France, Italy, Brazil, Portugal and the government of Quebec, launched the pilot of a foreign language teaching project in 12 public schools of low-income neighborhoods designed to enhance students' learning in ways similar to those offered by private schools. The number of hours of instruction in a foreign language increased to a total of 12 hours per week. Half of these schools teach EFL. These so-called "bilingual schools" do not have a bilingual curriculum per se but aim at teaching content in the foreign language. Whereas first graders start their language instruction through songs and play, it is expected that soon school subjects will be taught in the foreign language ("En busca de una...", 2001a; "Escuelas bilingües", 2000a; "La enseñanza bilingüe atrae...", 2001b; Lanusse, 2001).

Language Policy in the New Federal Law of Education

The educational reform of 1993 brought about long-awaited changes for the Argentine education system. For the first time in the history of the country, the federal government worked in tandem with the Ministry of Education of each province on a curriculum appropriate for the entire country, and each province became economically responsible for its internal education system.

The law guarantees free and compulsory education for citizens from 5 to 14 years of age. The organization and names for each stage have changed but the actual number of years of education has remained the same. Mandatory education, however, has been increased from 7 to 10 years, all organized in levels and cycles that form the new structure of the educational system. There are three main levels:

1. *Educación Inicial* [Initial Education]. Though kindergarten years are from age 3 to 5, attendance is only compulsory for the last year of this level.
2. *Educación General Básica* (EGB) [General Basic Education]. This level is compulsory and is organized into three cycles, each lasting 3 years, and focuses on teaching basic competencies.
3. *Educación Polimodal* [Polimodal Education]. This cycle is optional for all the provinces but mandatory for the province of Buenos Aires. It focuses on the skills and competencies that will equip students best for employment and/or post-secondary education (see Table 1).

The reform has had a special impact on the teaching of foreign languages. The *Acuerdo-Marco para la Enseñanza de Lenguas* [Agreement-Framework for the Teaching of Languages] is a document designed to give a framework for the implementation of the New Federal Education Law (1993) in terms of the teaching of languages in Argentina. It is based on both local and international agreements and declarations of human, economic, social, and cultural rights and it deals with the following issues: multilingualism, linguistic policy and equity, the teaching and learning of Spanish, the teaching and learning of aboriginal languages, the teaching and learning of foreign languages.

The foreign language project of the educational reform acknowledges the need for students to learn foreign languages and to become aware of different linguistic and cultural realities around the world. Foreign languages used to be included within a section of the Language (Spanish) Chapter of the Argentine Law of Education, but now they are handled as a separate and special case. EFL has always been considered important but was previously taught as an extracurricular activity. Nowadays, English is regarded as the language of international communication and is therefore given special treatment. "The decision to change recognizes the complexity of the processes of teaching, learning and acquisition, although in no way implies that Foreign Languages should be disassociated from Spanish as a mother tongue or second language" (Dirección General de Investigación y Desarrollo Educativo, 1998a, 1998b). The proposal of the Foreign Language Project is based on the following principles:

> An approach that integrates apparently irreconcilable differences, both theoretical and methodological, between language as competence or knowledge and language as use.
>
> A clear position that the languages of the world are essentially similar, although with organized sets of differences that give each one its unique reality.
>
> A systematic-linguistic construct for language development, which is able to accommodate mother tongue acquisition, second languages, foreign languages, pidgin and Creole varieties, alongside English as a global language. ...
>
> The logical reconsideration of the value of the mother tongue (Spanish or otherwise) in the processes of teaching and learning foreign languages, while at the same time assessing the phenomenon of transfer in both positive and negative terms.
>
> A shift of focus from teaching to acquisition and learning and to considering the age factor as decisive in the determination of what linguistic and communicative material should be incorporated.
>
> A new look at literary discourse in terms of how culture is currently conceived in the process of globalization.
>
> The incorporation of technology as a necessary component in the development of new communicative abilities. (Lenguas extranjeras –Dirección General de Investigación y Desarrollo Educativo, 1998a)

EGB, which is the compulsory education, is divided into three cycles of 3 years each. Each cycle implies levels or units of learning that are appropriate to the age concerned. Each level represents a unit of learning and implies the attainment of the contents and skills acquired in the previous level. It respects the student's cognitive and social development. Levels are designed to integrate previous knowledge in order to enhance the development of the linguistic and communicative competence expected to be achieved at the next level.

It is recommended that a progressive introduction of foreign languages starts in the second cycle of the EGB, but there is no deterrent to start earlier if deemed appropriate and advantageous to some students in particular. When foreign language instruction is started in the second cycle, at least two levels of foreign languages must be taught, one of which must be English. Because the school guarantees the teaching of three levels of a foreign language, in some situations the third level will be taught in the Polimodal level. A fourth level could also be taught when deemed feasible and appropriate (see Table 1). The levels do not necessarily coincide with the cycles, and the teaching of the first level could be implemented in any of the three years of any given cycle. In sum, the three options or situations for the three levels of foreign language learning proposed by the new law are:

1. one level of English as an International Language and two levels of another foreign language of choice;
2. two levels of English for International communication and one level of another foreign language of choice; and
3. three levels of English.

(Ministerio de Cultura y Educación de la Nación, 1998).

Content-based and Student-centered Instruction: A New Challenge for ETL in Argentina

The Federal law of Education establishes Common Basic Contents (CBC) that emphasize the use of English (or any other foreign language) for international communication. These guidelines outline the methodology, basic curriculum content, and training expectations for EFL teachers. As Snow, Cortés, and Pron (1998) explain, there are three categories for the content to be covered. These are procedural, attitudinal, and cross-curricula:

> The Procedural content refers to the "how to" of language: skills, processes, strategies, and methods. The Attitudinal content refers to the set of rules, values, virtues, and attitudes, both personal and social, that will underlie all the activities in the English classroom. Cross-Curricular content refers to topics or themes that do not belong to any special discipline but reflect the whole of the National Currículo. (p. 10)

Furthermore, contents have been organized into five teaching blocks:

> *Block 1 – Oral Language.* This block refers to the teaching of speaking and listening activities that will develop and enhance both student comprehension and production of the language(s) concerned.
>
> *Block 2 – Written Language.* As with block 1, block 2 emphasizes the development of both comprehension and production. However, this block deals with the teaching of reading and writing; that is, it focuses on written texts.
>
> *Block 3 – Literary Discourse.* This block focuses on the teaching of discourse features and language awareness through various and varied examples of language use.

Table 1. Educational Levels and ELT in Argentina

Age	3	4	5	6	7	8	9	10	11	12	13	14	15	16	17
				\multicolumn{3}{c}{1st cycle}	\multicolumn{3}{c}{2nd cycle}	\multicolumn{3}{c}{3rd cycle}			
				\multicolumn{9}{c}{Compulsory Education}			
Level	\multicolumn{3}{c}{Initial Level}	\multicolumn{9}{c}{General Basic Education}	\multicolumn{3}{c}{Polimodal}
ELT	\multicolumn{3}{c}{Not required but can be included}	\multicolumn{9}{c}{As of the 2nd cycle, two levels of foreign languages must be taught, one of which must be English}	\multicolumn{3}{c}{Another language or a higher level of EFL must be taught}

Block 4 – Procedures related to the comprehension and production of oral and written texts. Besides reflecting the processes and nature of learner input and output, this block focuses on the process of learning a new language and on the language itself. That is, in addition to cognitive and linguistics skills, metacognitive and metalinguistic skills are to be instilled in language learners.

Block 5 – General attitudes related to both written/oral input and written/ oral output. This block is intended to foster positive attitudes and motivate learners not only to learn the new language but also to learn about the target culture. Together with block 4, it should be integrated with the teaching of blocks 1 to 3.

Teachers in Argentina have been traditionally teacher-centered and are now facing the great challenge of following the mandates of a content-based, student-centered curriculum as outlined by the new education law. Indeed, the implementation of the new Federal Law of Education has been a difficult task for most schools in Argentina (see Snow, Cortés, & Pron, 1998 for examples). Not only has there been a profound change in the pedagogical approach to ELT but there has also been a lack of information and training and a shortage of appropriate resources for teaching. Moreover, some teachers are reluctant to explore new ways of teaching. Classes can have up to 35 to 40 students with varying degrees of language proficiency, and thus some teachers feel more confident and comfortable with the old ways of teaching for fear of losing control of classroom dynamics.

As Rossetti (1997) points out, some steps are necessary to make the EFL curriculum consistent with the new education law and also to keep up with recent pedagogical trends. For example, teachers require training in designing syllabi that reflect the aims, objectives, and evaluation of the EFL pedagogical theory; pedagogical resources must be appropriately designed for ELT in a developing country, with cultural content that is accessible to both teachers and students; and networking among teachers and administrators should be promoted both within the country as well as with other developing countries to encourage reflection on common practices, challenges, and solutions.

FUTURE DIRECTIONS

This chapter has discussed two very different realities for English instruction in Argentina. The distinction between private and public education is a reality in almost every country in the world and it is clearly present in Argentina. There is a sizable proportion of the Argentine population that demands and is willing to pay for more effective English language instruction for the advantages a good command of English confers (e.g. bilingual schools, private schools with more English instruction and/or language institutes). The Ministry of Education has recently acknowledged these advantages and shown its commitment to ELT by mandating its implementation in all schools in the country. However, research is required to assess the extent of English instruction in both public and private sectors and its impact on Argentina as a whole.

A positive move towards greater emphasis on English within the public system and even a radical change in pedagogical approach are probably not enough to make

ELT provision within the public and private sectors comparable. The discrepancies between public and private sectors in terms of age of introduction of the language, the resources available, time allocation, and number of years of instruction—to name but a few variables—seem insurmountable at the present time. Notwithstanding this, teachers represent a point of convergence between public and private sectors. The teaching faculty is indeed "the force driving the whole enterprise towards its educational aim because good teachers make good programs" (Pennington, 1989, p. 91).

While almost every teaching context in Argentina currently favors content-based instruction, and thus follows one of the latest trends in ELT worldwide, there is still some uncertainty as to how to integrate language and content and how that integration could be most effectively realized in terms of curriculum and actual classroom practice. Despite the fact that the law now requires an appropriate degree to teach English, the popular belief that anyone who speaks the language can teach it and/or teach in it, still prevails in Argentina. There is insufficient appreciation of the challenges faced by most EFL teachers in Argentina in helping learners understand content in a language they are still learning. Thus, there is an urgent need to address crucial issues in English language teacher training in Argentina. Regardless of the teaching context, language teaching (and more so content-based language teaching) requires a combination of knowledge and skills that is always hard to find. Training teachers who have the necessary linguistic and academic background to develop this specific knowledge and appropriate instructional skills should be the first concern for national and local policy in Argentina.

ACKNOWLEDGEMENTS

I wish to thank the following people for reading this chapter (or an earlier version of it) and providing feedback and/or further information to complete the paper: Mariana Aldave de Miquelarena, Cristina Banfi, Lindsay Brooks, Teresa Davis, María Luján Figueredo, Sharon Lapkin, Merrill Swain and Jane Turner de Beller.

NOTES

[1] The "bilingual" schools in the city of Buenos Aires have been greeted with enthusiasm by both students and parents. Of 900 students who registered in 2001, 622 have been able to receive language instruction in the first year of this project. Overall school registration has increased between 20% and 50% and six more "bilingual" schools will open in 2002 (La Nación, 2001b). Moreover, as reported by Lanusse (2001), 4 months after launching the first school year, the teaching of EFL (and the other languages) had already had a positive impact on the overall school performance of the students. Furthermore, the parents themselves took more interest in their children's schooling and requested language classes for themselves.

REFERENCES

Baker, C., & Prys Jones, S. (1998). *Encyclopedia of bilingualism and bilingual education*. Clevedon, England: Multilingual Matters.

British Council Argentina. (2002). *Education and the English language in Argentina*. Retrieved January 22, 2002 from the website of the British Council Argentina, 1–6. http://www.britishcouncil.org.ar/english/education/educ_el.htm.

Cardenas de Cantiello, M. S. (1997, February 21). The Teaching of English. *La Nación, Sec.1*, 26. Buenos Aires, Argentina.

Cortés-Conde, F. (1994). English as an instrumental language: Language displacement in the Anglo-Argentine community. *Bilingual Review/Revista Bilingüe, 19* (1), 25–38.
Crystal, D. (1997). *English as a global language*. Cambridge University Press.
Dirección General de Investigación y Desarrollo Educativo. (1998a). *Agreement framework for the teaching of languages (A-15).* Retrieved April 15, 1998 from http://www.dgid.mcye.cgov.ar/html/lenex/a-15.html.
Dirección General de Investigación y Desarrollo Educativo. (1998b). *Foreign languages in the new eductional system. The short and eventful life of the Foreign Languages Project.* Retrieved April 15, 1998.
Dirección General de Planeamiento y Dirección de Curricula. (2001). *Diseño Curricular de Lenguas Extranjeras - Niveles 1, 2, 3 y 4* [Foreign Language Syllabus Design – Levels 1, 2, 3 y 4]. Secretaría de Educación, Subsecretaría de Educación, Gobierno de la Ciudad Autónoma de Buenos Aires.
Duff, P. (1997). Immersion in Hungary: An EFL experiment. In R. K. Johnson & M. Swain (Eds.), *Immersion education: International perspectives* (pp. 19–42). Cambridge: Cambridge University Press.
English Speaking Scholastic Association of the River Plate (ESSARP) *History.* (2001). Retrieved January 22, 2002 from http://www.essarp.org.ar/about.html.
Educational Testing Services (ETS). (2002). *TOEFL test scores and data summaries.* Retrieved January 22, 2002 from http://www.toefl.org/educator/edsumm.html.
En busca de una segunda lengua [In search for a second language]. (2001, July 17). *La Nación-Cultura, 14.* Buenos Aires, Argentina.
Escuelas bilingües [Bilingual schools]. (2000, December 12). *La Nación-Cultura. 7,* Buenos Aires, Argentina.
Ethnologue, (2003). *Argentina.* [Electronic version] Retrieved January 26, 2003 from http://www.ethnologue.com/show_country.asp?name=Argentina.
Fishman, J. A., & Nahirny, V. C. (1966). The ethnic group school and mother tongue maintenance. In J. Fishman (Ed.), *Language loyalty in the United States* (pp. 206–252). The Hague: Mouton.
Garvie, M. (1998). A new pathway for advanced learning: A bilingual school adopts the Advanced International Certificate of Education. *International Schools Journal, 18*(1), 58–64.
Genesee, F. (1994). *Integrating language and content: Lessons from immersion.* California: The National Centre for Research on Cultural Research and Second Language Learning (Content, ESL and Rainbow).
Hornberger, N. H. (1994). Language policy and planning in South America. *Annual Review of Applied Linguistics, 14,* 220–239.
Instituto Nacional De Estadística y Censos (INDEC). (2002). *Población.* Retrieved January 22, 2002 from http://www.INDEC.mecon.ar/.
Johnson, R. K. & Swain, M. (1997). *Immersion education: International perspectives.* Cambridge, UK: Cambridge University Press.
Kachru, B. B. (1985). Standards, codification and sociolinguistic realism: The English language in the outer circle. In R. Quirk &. H. Widdowson (Eds.), *English in the World* (pp. 11–30). Cambridge: Cambridge University Press.
La enseñanza bilingüe atrae más alumnos [Bilingual education attracts more students]. (2001b, August 3). *La Nación-Cultura, 4.* Buenos Aires, Argentina.
Lanusse, A. (2001, Junio 12). Estudiar un segundo idioma mejora el rendimiento general [Learning a second language improves overall performance]. *La Nación,Cultura, 9.* Buenos Aires, Argentina.
Ministerio de Cultura y Educación de la Nación. Consejo Federal de Cultura y Educación. (1998). *Basic Common Contents for the Polimodal Education. Foreign Languages.* Retrieved January 22, 2002 from http://www.dgid.mcye.cgov.ar/html/lenex/le03.html.
Moyano, G. C. (1997). English in Argentina. A report on the history and current condition of English in South America. *English Today, 49,* 36–39.
Moyano, G. C. (2000). *Inglés @ info. La enseñanza del idioma inglés: para conocer las opciones de estudio del inglés en la Argentina.* F.A.A.P.I. [Federación Argentina de Asociaciones de Profesores de Inglés] Buenos Aires: Argentina.
Pennington, M. (1989). Faculty development for language programs. In R. K. Johnson (Ed) *The second language curriculum* (pp. 91–110). Cambridge: Cambridge University Press.
Pini, M., & Cigliutti, S. (1999, Autumn). Participatory reforms and democracy: The case of Argentina. *Theory into Practice, 38*(4), 196–202.
Rhoten, D. (2000). Education decentralization in Argentina: A 'global-local conditions of possibility' approach to stake, market, and society change. *Journal of Education Policy, 15*(6), 593–619.

Rossetti, M. (1997, Nov-Dec). Education reform brings new challenges to Argentina. *Language Magazine*. [Electronic version] Retrieved April 15 2000, from http://www.languagemagazine.com/Nov-Dec 97.

Sin vacantes en las escuelas bilingües [No more vacancies in bilingual schools]. (2000b, December 27). *La Nación-Cultura*. 5. Buenos Aires, Argentina.

Snow, A. M., Cortés, V., & Pron, A. (1998). EFL and educational reform: Content-based interaction in Argentina. *Forum, 36*(1), 10–13.

St. Andrew's Scot School. (1999). *Our history*. Retrieved April 15, 1999 from St. Andrew's Scot School http://www.sanandres.esc.ar/history.html.

St. Hilda's College. (2000). *History of the school*. Retrieved April 15, 2000 from St. Hilda's College http://www.sthildas.esc.edu/ar/files/history.html.

Subcomisión de la Historia de la Escuela Escosesa San Andrés. (1988). *Un siglo y medio después*. Buenos Aires: Escuela Escosesa.

Swain, M., & Johnson, R. K. (1997). Immersion education: A category within bilingual education. In R. K. Johnson & M. Swain (Eds.), *Immersion education: International perspectives* (pp. 1–16). Cambridge: Cambridge University Press.

CHAPTER 9

ENGLISH, NO LONGER A FOREIGN LANGUAGE IN EUROPE?

ROBERT PHILLIPSON

Copenhagen Business School, Denmark

ABSTRACT

English dovetails with globalisation and now serves so many purposes in continental European countries and in the institutions of the European Union that it is becoming a second language. Some of the political, journalistic and academic marketing of English, is false. There are fundamental paradoxes in the ostensible commitment of the EU to maintaining linguistic diversity and the expansion of the uses of English. Many of the variables affecting the goals and forms of English learning are contrasted in a Global English Paradigm and a World Englishes Paradigm. The conflicting pressures and interpretations of what is at stake in changed uses and forms of English can be traced in its evolving hybridity, in trends towards diglossia, and mythology about how English functions as a 'lingua franca.' Research into the increased use of English in Germany and Scandinavia is reported on. Moves towards seeing English as detached from Anglo-American norms are scrutinized, and limitations in the existing research are identified. Efforts nationally and in the EU directed towards strengthening multilingualism in education need to address the political, economic and cultural aspects of Englishization and to engage with these more actively in language policy formation and the reform of language pedagogy if the language ecology of Europe is to flourish.

INTRODUCTION

Contemporary Europe is no exception to the worldwide trend of English being used and learned more widely. Europe is undergoing an intensive process of integration. Language, education and culture are no longer the exclusive prerogative of each state but are also policy concerns of the European Union (EU), which is constantly expanding its range of activities. In addition, the enlargement process is bringing many more states into closer union, a total of 25 since May 2004. English figures prominently in these processes both within countries and as the dominant international language. In each country, English is intruding into domains in which other European languages have been unchallenged hitherto. There is a major challenge in the analysis of language policy in Europe to tease out the links between Englishization, Europeanization, globalization, and Americanization. The centrality of English learning in facilitating and constituting these ongoing processes requires language pedagogy and language policy to be situated within wider political, social and cultural contexts.

WHY IS THERE A PROBLEM IF CONTINENTAL EUROPEANS ARE ABLE TO FUNCTION IN ENGLISH?

English is increasingly prominent in continental Europe in such key domains as business, education, and the media. Its privileged position has evolved quite differently from the way the primacy of English was established in Europeanized states to which English was transplanted in North America and Australasia (countries inaccurately referred to as 'English-speaking' when the United States, for instance, is "one of the most linguistically and culturally diverse countries in the world", McCarty, 2004, p. 74). Nor has the consolidation of English in Europe followed the same route as in former colonies of the US and the UK, such as the Philippines, India, or Nigeria, in which the language of colonization was retained for elite formation and high-prestige functions internally and externally. In continental Europe, English has thus not been imposed through settlement by native speakers or through colonial dominance. Until recently English was a foreign language. Its increasing use in public, professional and private life, and in education means that for some it fulfills more the role of a second language.

In Europe, many languages have been consolidated as the key state language over the past two centuries. All domestic functions have been carried out in the key 'national' language, Danish, Estonian, French, Greek, etc. Foreign languages were learned for external communication purposes and familiarity with the cultural heritage associated with 'great' powers. Since 1945, and more intensively in recent years, there has been a gradual shift towards English becoming by far the most widely learned foreign language on the continent of Europe, taking over space, both in western and eastern Europe, occupied earlier by other foreign languages, French, German and Russian in particular.

There is massive exposure to Hollywood throughout Europe: "70-80% of all TV fiction shown on European TV is American ... American movies, American TV and the American lifestyle for the populations of the world and Europe at large have become the lingua franca of globalization, the closest we get to a visual world culture" (Bondebjerg, 2003, p. 79, 81). These US products are transmitted with the original soundtrack in the Nordic countries and the Netherlands, which strengthens the learning of English, and are generally dubbed elsewhere. By contrast in the US the market share of films of foreign origin is 1%.

The position of English is also strengthened by a proficiency requirement in many countries for access to higher education and for many kinds of employment. The triumphalist marketing of English is characteristically flagged on the cover page of *Business Week* (European edition) of 13 August 2001, which portrays twin executives, one communicating successfully, the English speaker, the other without a mouth, speechless. The accompanying text *Should everyone speak English?* flags the article "The great English divide. In Europe, speaking the lingua franca separates the haves from the have-nots." It deals with two symbiotically unified topics, English as a professional skill, and the mushrooming of English language schools. Such language schools, largely staffed by native speakers, are mostly a feature of countries in southern Europe in which the learning of English in state education tends to be less successful. In Scandinavia all university students are expected to be able to read texts in English; in Italy only 1% are able to do so (Renato Corsetti, University of Rome, personal communication).

English is increasingly the primary corporate language of transnational enterprises wherever they are based geographically. Top European executives tend to be multilingual, unless they come from the UK or the US (and it is arguable that monolingualism may in future be a liability (Graddol, 1998; Nuffield Languages Inquiry, 2000; Grin, 2001).

Academics and researchers in virtually all fields are expected to publish in English, either exclusively or as well as in the local language, depending on disciplinary pressures and the discourse communities that scholars contribute to (Petersen & Shaw, 2002). They are also increasingly required to teach through the medium of English in higher education, since universities seek to recruit more foreign students. This development is a key feature of the so-called *internationalisation* of higher education, and is obliging continental universities to address how best to function multilingually, which generally means in the national language and English. Conferences are being held to exchange experience (Wilkinson, 2004) and university administrators are being encouraged to address the language policy implications (for instance in policy statements in 2004 on internationalization from the Danish Rectors' Conference, which is what the assembly of university Vice-Chancellors in Denmark call themselves, in a literal translation from Danish into words that are manifestly a sample of 'European English').

In English-speaking countries, there is currently a boom market in foreign students. The British Council is worried about competition from other countries, and warned in 2004 that the UK economy is at risk if it doesn't invest more in international education. The UK economy benefits by £11 billion p.a. directly, and a further £12 billion indirectly, from international education. The goal is 8% annual growth across the sector, and to double the present number of 35,000 research graduates contributing to the UK's knowledge economy by 2020. In addition over 500,000 attend language learning courses each year (www.britishcouncil.org/mediacentre/apr04/vision_2020_press_notice.doc).

Expansion has been so rapid (and commercially driven) that some language schools and universities that offer pre-sessional language proficiency courses appreciate that they are ill-equipped to provide culturally and linguistically appropriate teaching for students from Asia, primarily China.

However, what is at stake is not merely the local question of whether Chinese students are getting good value for money when opting for English-medium higher education, whether in the UK or a continental European country. An article in the British *The Guardian Weekly*, 13-19 August 2004, p. 9 (citing *The Observer*) claims that the 'Scramble for lucrative foreign students is corrupting universities' by dropping academic standards. This is perhaps not surprising if the content of teaching and its delivery have remained unchanged, even if students have a radically different cultural and linguistic starting-point. What is at stake globally is the role of the English as a Second/Foreign Language business and its practitioners, and higher education in general, as an integral dimension of the global economy. English learning and use are preconditions for the functioning and legitimating of the global system. They are not merely an epiphenomenon that can be evaluated on its own terms, divorced from its indispensable role in servicing the global economy, the financial circuit supporting it, and the educational institutions that validate credentials.

In authorizing and imprinting particular norms of use and discourse, English teachers function as professional midwives to the "legitimate and illegitimate offspring of English," to use Mufwene's (2001) vivid image when characterizing those forms of English that are considered authentic: maximal legitimacy for British English, despite its creole origins, and for English transported by native speakers to Europeanized states in America and Australasia; dubious status for 'new' English that only has local validity (Singapore, Malaysia, Nigeria), and complete illegitimacy for creoles which are beyond the linguistic pale (in the Caribbean or West Africa). Discourses, pedagogical practices and institutions maintain norms. As Alexander puts it (2003), policing the language of the world goes hand in hand with policing the world. 'Global' English is a normative project, not a reality but a vision that powerful forces are keen to bring about.

There are major risks in considering that as English now functions outside many of its original sites, it is detached from social forces:

> English being disembedded from national cultures can never mean that it floats culture-free (or) is culturally neutral. The point may be simple, but it is often elided; and this elision constitutes a politics of English as a global language which precisely conceals the cultural work which that model of language is in fact performing. (Kayman, 2004, p. 17)

Kayman also makes the intriguing point that the prophets and proponents of English as a global language can be compared to the occupation by Europeans of other continents that were falsely seen as *terra nullius*. Contemporary linguists who proclaim the neutrality of English treat the language as a cultural *terra nullius* (Kayman, p. 18).

This is an influential tradition in writings on global English. Crystal (1997), identifying many factors in the past that account for English being widely used, sees the language as "independent of any form of social control" (p. 137). Yet he foresees global diglossia, world standard spoken English functioning alongside national English dialects. Presumably such a standard language will have guardians: Is it likely that a globally valid form of spoken English will be anything other than some sort of CNN/BBC hybrid?

Similarly Brutt-Griffler (2002, reviewed in Phillipson, 2004) sees World English as doing away with hierarchy among speech communities, non-Western nations taking equal part in the creation of the world econocultural system and its linguistic expression. At the same time she acknowledges that the US and UK dominate the world market and that World English is the dominant socio-political language form. Her attempt to explain the growth of English worldwide is therefore internally inconsistent and based on argumentation that ignores the reality of the market forces that strengthen some languages at the expense of others locally and globally. It ignores the political, economic and military forces behind English in the current neo-imperial, US-dominated world 'order' (Phillipson, 2005).

What is unclear in continental Europe is whether the learning and use of English remains an additive process, one that increases the repertoire of language competence of individuals and the society, or whether English threatens the viability of other languages through processes of domain loss and linguistic hierarchization. In theory there ought to be no problem, because of the strong position of national languages such as German, Italian and Polish, and because of the declared policies of the EU. Article 22 of The Charter of Fundamental Rights of the EU, which forms

English, No Longer a Foreign Language in Europe? 127

part of the constitutional treaty endorsed in 2004, and which represents principles that all member states are committed to, states: "The Union shall respect cultural, religious and linguistic diversity." In reality there are fundamental paradoxes:

- The first is that although the EU is essentially a Franco-German project, since France and Germany were founding member states and continue to occupy the political high ground in shaping the integration of Europe, English is expanding, and the French and German languages are on the defensive both at home and abroad. English is increasingly the dominant language both in EU affairs and in many societal domains in continental European countries.
- The second paradox is that EU rhetoric proclaims support for multilingualism and cultural and linguistic diversity in official texts, and the equality of all official and working languages in the EU, but in practice there is *laissez faire* in the linguistic marketplace (Phillipson, 2003). At the supranational level of EU institutions (the European Parliament, Commission, and Council), multilingualism is managed by the world's largest translation and interpretation services, but there is paralysis on broader language policy issues. The rhetoric of diversity and linguistic equality is pitted against the unfree market and the forces that strengthen English.
- The third paradox is that in the view of some scholars, multilingualism is synonymous with more English. Chaudenson (2003) from France concludes that no one is fooled by fiery declarations in favor of multilingualism, which he sees simply as a smoke screen for the spread of English. In somewhat similar vein, de Swaan (2001) from the Netherlands asserts that in the European Union the more languages, the more English, which he favors, but his analysis of language policy is excessively selective (Phillipson, 2004).
- The fourth paradox is that though we all live in a multilingual world, the monolingually-oriented English as a second language (ESL) profession thrives. However, the widespread faith in native-speaker teachers of English, and in expertise, teaching materials, postgraduate degrees, and theories of language learning deriving from the Anglo-American world, and in the mythology of global English is not widely influential in education systems in Europe. Here foreign language teaching presupposes deep familiarity with the linguistic and cultural background of the learners, and has never embraced a monolingual approach.

Many of the competing and conflicting trends in the analysis of English in the modern world, and norms for teaching the language, are brought together in two paradigms, a global English paradigm and a world Englishes paradigm, summarized in Table 1. The variables range from macro-level dimensions of economic and cultural globalization and language ecology to micro-level matters of equitable communication and target norms for language learners. The juxtaposition of a substantial number of variables serves to highlight the complexity of the tasks facing analysts of language policy and theorists of language pedagogy. Many of the dimensions are explored in the ongoing European context in the rest of this article.

Table 1. Diffusion of English vs. Ecology of Languages Paradigms

GLOBAL ENGLISH PARADIGM	WORLD ENGLISHES PARADIGM
assimilationist	celebrates and supports diversity
monolingual orientation	multilingual, multi-dialectal
'international' English assumes US/UK norms	'international' a cross-national linguistic common core
World Standard Spoken English	English as a Lingua Franca
Anglo-American linguistic norms	local linguistic norms, regional and national
exonormative English	endonormative Englishes
post-national, neo-imperial expansionist globalization	local appropriation, and resistance to linguistic imperialism
apparently *laissez faire* language policy strengthens market forces, hence English	proactive language policies serve to strengthen a variety of languages
English monopolizes prestige domains	local languages have high prestige
linguicist favoring of English	balanced language ecology
ideology stresses individual 'choice'	addresses the reality of linguistic hierarchies
no concern for languages other than English	a linguistic human rights approach
subtractive English learning	additive English learning
uni-directional intercultural communication	equitable bi-directional intercultural communication
standard language orientation	learning multiple forms of competence
target norm the 'native speaker'	target norm the good ESL user
reproductive curriculum	learner-created knowledge
external syllabus	learner-centred activities and discourses
teachers can be monolingual	bilingual and bicultural teachers
dovetails with the *diffusion of English* paradigm (Tsuda 1994, Skutnabb-Kangas 2000)	dovetails with the *ecology of languages* paradigm (Tsuda 1994, Skutnabb-Kangas 2000)

THE EVOLVING HYBRIDITY OF 'ENGLISH'

The intensification of contacts between the citizens of EU states involves an ongoing process of 'building' and 'imagining' Europe, of strengthening European identity as a complement to national identity. This unification was impelled by two agendas, one European and one American. The visionary European founding fathers of the 1940-50s wished to create forms of economic integration that would make the blood-letting of the past an impossibility, a goal which has been largely achieved at least within the EU, even if Northern Ireland and the Basque territory provide tragic exceptions (which incidentally confirm the principle that linguistic unification through an imposed language does not guarantee peace or justice). The twin agenda has been the determination of the US to impose its vision of society and economy on the world. Funds under the Marshall plan were made conditional on the integration of European economies. The most significant achievements of the EU, the common market and the common currency, represent the implementation of plans formed by the European Round Table of Industrialists, which is intimately linked with the Transatlantic Business Dialogue, which aims at a Transatlantic Economic Partnership that would make the Americas and Europe a single market (Monbiot, 2000).

Condoleezza Rice (2000) is continuing a century-old tradition by famously proclaiming that the rest of the world is best served by the USA pursuing its own interests because American values are universal (see also www.newamericancentury.org). Language, and the cultural universe and ways of thought it embodies, is a key dimension of this global mission. David Rothkopf, of Kissinger Associates, wrote in the US establishment journal *Foreign Policy* (1997): "It is in the economic and political interest of the United States to ensure that if the world is moving toward a common language, it be English" (p. 45). Englishization is manifestly a dimension of both Americanization and globalization. Americanization gradually gathered speed over the 20th century, and has been marketed in recent years as globalization, from which it is indistinguishable (Bourdieu, 2001). Globalization is, however, not a uniform, unidirectional process; there are many supply and demand, push and pull factors. Cultural and linguistic products and processes undergo local transformation processes wherever they become embedded. Many factors, structural and ideological, contribute to the strengthening of English in Europe and to language policy paralysis (Phillipson, 2003).

In a recent article on *The globalization of language. How the media contribute to the spread of English and the emergence of medialects*, a Danish researcher invents the term *medialect*, by logical extension from dialect and sociolect, to refer to new variants of language and cultural form that generally originate in the Anglo-American world, such as computer games, email and Internet interaction, SMSs, television programs (whether transmitted in the original language or the local one), advertising for the younger generation, and so on), and which are creatively adapted in continental European contexts and languages. In addition to English being the language in which these media products were evolved and marketed, English is the linguistic vehicle for meta-communication about mediated communication. The medialects consolidate the position of English, while excluding other international languages, and open up for "linguistic differentiation and innovation" (Hjarvad, 2004, p. 92) in the way language is used. Englishization affects the form and content of other languages.

University degrees in 'English' at continental European universities typically include American Studies and British Studies. The teaching of English in schools has traditionally been connected to familiarization with the culture of Britain and other traditional English-speaking countries. The study of literature is still strong in many parts of Europe, just as a degree in 'English' at most British universities means a degree in English literature. The need of continental universities to cover the language, literature and cultures of the 'English-speaking world' has led to the addition of Postcolonial Studies, World Englishes, and a wide range of topics (see the electronic *Annotated Bibliography of English Studies* (ABES), and the website of the *European Society for the Study of English* (ESSE), www.essenglish.org).

In some countries English can be seen as a second rather than a foreign language because of its functions locally and the meshing of the use of English by second language speakers with the globalizing of commerce, finance, politics, military affairs, scholarship, education, and many grassroots networks. Some networks, particularly among the young, represent bottom-up sub-cultural influences that mesh with the more formal learning of English top-down in state education (Preisler, 1999). The teaching of English should be adjusting to the changing nature of English use outside the classroom.

Referring to English as a 'second' language is perhaps terminologically unfortunate, because the position of ESL users and learners in continental Europe is radically different from that of learners of ESL in the US or the UK, just as it also significantly differs from English in postcolonial countries such as Singapore or Kenya, where the same label is sometimes used.

The fact that English is used for a wide range of intercultural communication that is unconnected to a British or US context may lead to English being seen as a *lingua franca*. However, this should not mislead one into believing that English is disconnected from the many 'special purposes' it serves in key societal domains, and where it might be more accurately described as a *lingua economica* (in business and advertising), a *lingua academica* (in research and higher education), or a *lingua cultura* (in entertainment and formal education). The ubiquitous function of English as a *lingua americana* is due to the massive economic and cultural impact of the US, and English as a *lingua bellica* and empire is increasingly visible. There are clear ideological dangers in labelling English as a lingua franca if this is understood as a culturally neutral medium that puts everyone on an equal footing.

The risk in English teaching is that "the dissemination of global communicative norms and genres, like the dissemination of international languages, involves a one-way flow of expert knowledge from dominant to subaltern cultures" (Cameron, 2002, p. 70). In addition, as Kramsch (2002) argues, given much intercultural communication itself typifies a certain Anglo-Saxon culture, discourse and worldview, "the concept of intercultural communication as it is currently used can be easily highjacked by a global ideology of 'effective communication' Anglo-Saxon style, which speaks an English discourse even as it expresses itself in many different languages" (pp. 283-284).

Being at the receiving end of cultural forces and under the influence of Anglo-American norms, linguistic and pedagogic, is vividly expressed by Dendrinos (1999), who bewails the monolingualism and monoculturalism of English language teaching (ELT) discourse in Greece:

> There is a systematic construction of reality whereby, by not knowing English, one is excluded from anything of social importance... Greek ELT practitioners persistently evaluate their proficiency in English against the English of the native speaker... *This underlying contradiction of a 'culturally neutral' language used in a 'culturally appropriate way'...* the claim that the native speaker is the ideal ELT practitioner construes Greek ELT practitioners as 'knowledge deficient'. (p. 713)

Comparable worries are expressed in the post-communist world, by Miklós Kontra of Hungary:

> Until 1989 there was little serious danger of English-American cultural and linguistic imperialism in Hungary but today there are unmistakable signs of such penetration and voices of concern are heard from a growing number of Hungarians... Most ELT materials produced in and exported from the United Kingdom and the United States disregard the learners' L1, and in this respect we might question their professionalism... business interests override a fundamental professional interest, or: business shapes our profession in ways that we know are unprofessional. This puts us, both native and nonnative teachers of English into quite a schizophrenic position. The challenge that we

are faced with is to keep the professionalism and get rid of the embarrassment. (Kontra, 1997, p. 85)

Others (e.g. House, 2003, drawing on some provisional empirical results in Germany) do not see the advance of English as problematic, but as merely the addition of a culturally neutral tool that has no impact on the German language, even if competence in English is spreading. Others from Germany stress the marginalization of German speakers in the scientific community (Ammon, 2000), and are seeking to persuade German policy-makers to be more proactive in strengthening German nationally and in the EU (Gawlitta & Vilmar, 2002).

At present there are many symptoms of diglossia. The rise of English has been of concern to many European states, leading to legislation to curb English in several of them. The effects of a switch to English in specific domains are generally considered to be more threatening than the borrowing of lexical items. Widespread or exclusive use of English may mean that expertise in the natural sciences, technology or medicine is no longer transmitted in the local language. Swedish research suggests that being obliged to operate extensively in a diglossic division of labor can lead to less efficiency and appropriacy in thought, expression, and communication; to dehumanization, and cold rationality, when operating in Anglo-American discourse norms; a loss of intertextuality when the local language is no longer used for certain purposes (e.g. fiction cannot draw on domains that operate in English); and ultimately to a loss of prestige for the local language (Melander, 2001). There is anecdotal evidence from several countries (Denmark, Greece, Serbia) that individual scholars who have used English successfully for decades experience a feeling of liberation when they shift to writing in the mother tongue.

The governments of the Nordic countries have commissioned research to assess whether domain loss is taking place, and whether Nordic languages run the risk of being downgraded into second-class languages (Höglin, 2002, which contains a 15-page summary in English of the Nordic findings). The studies are far from comprehensive, but they do indicate that there is a strong possibility of domain loss in technology and the natural sciences. There is definitely a need for language policy formation to counteract this. The Swedish government has gone a long way in undertaking a systematic analysis of the language policy issues, and consulting all relevant stake-holders. In government policy documents produced in Sweden in 2002 (and replicated on a much more modest scale in Denmark in 2003) on how to strengthen the national language in view of the increasing importance of English, the declared goal is to cultivate parallel linguistic competence. This would mean that Swedes and Danes active in business, politics, higher education, science and the media should be able to function equally well in the national language and in English. This might mean that domain loss and linguistic hierarchization are counteracted, through ensuring resource allocation to the language that now risks marginalization, and through fostering awareness of the need to provide conditions for all languages to thrive as well as English. Whether an increased use of English will serve as a catalyst for biculturalism or monoculturalism is a completely open question. But at least the question is being asked today.

SOME ONGOING RESEARCH AND ADVOCACY

Research that could represent a major contribution towards realizing a change of paradigm in English teaching includes analysis of the phonology of English as an

International Language (Jenkins, 2000). Work has also begun on clarifying the distinctive lexical and grammatical features of English when used by L2 speakers (see Seidlhofer, 2004, also this volume), in a project which labels this communication as English as a *lingua franca* (ELF), a term that is unfortunately open to many interpretations (see above), and is also often used to refer to communication between people speaking English as an L1 and as an L2. Quite apart from the potential of this research to make teaching more appropriate, it might, when combined with critical discourse analysis, help to unmask some of the spurious advocacy of English as a neutral *lingua franca* for the whole of Europe. It is impossible to reconcile the argument that English now belongs to everyone (a constant refrain from British government figures and British Council staff and which also occurs in writers like David Crystal and Tom McArthur, editor of *English Today*) with the major significance of the ELT business to the British economy, as stressed by the British establishment from the Prime Minister downwards. No British government has ever doubted that the privileged position of English also brought with it political and cultural influence. (On the duplicity of some of the professional advocacy for ELT, see Pegrum, 2004, and on the falsity of some scholarly marketing of 'global English,' see Phillipson, 1999 and 2004)

A pioneer study of Englishization such as House (2003) presents some empirical studies and reflections on the nature of ELF in Europe. I have major reservations about the validity of the three types of empirical ELF data presented in the study (see Phillipson, forthcoming for details) and about the features that are seen as characteristic of this variant of English. In the table below I list the characteristics she attributes to ELF, alongside which are my reservations about each trait, which, in my view, demonstrates how difficult it is to make theoretical headway in this field.

Table 2. Proposed Characteristics of ELF and a Critique

Characteristics of ELF (House, 2003)	**Critique**
functional flexibility, openness to integration of forms from other languages	it is false to claim that such traits are specific to ELF
not restricted or for special purposes	this conflicts with House referring to diglossic 'pockets of expertise'
negotiable norms	it is *use* of the code rather than the code itself that is negotiable
bereft of collective cultural capital	the global utility of English, often diglossically high, is significant linguistic capital
similar to English diversity in postcolonial countries	here English equals power, and there is no codification of local forms
non-identificational	English = cosmopolitanism, and House states that English in Germany has positive connotations of liberation from Nazi past
non-native ownership	a concern of the analyst, not the user

When House argues that English is a language for communication rather than a language for identification, the binary pair is tempting, as a way of separating English as a national language from English as an instrument for international communication that is less culturally shaped. The distinction is seen by Blommaert (2003), commenting on House's use of the terms, as "a metapragmatic dichotomisation that allocates specific indexicalities to particular speech varieties. ... matters are considerably more complex" (p. 620). He sees them as deriving from a functionalist-referential ideology and an ideological perception that results in uses of language being seen as 'instrumental.'

Hüllen was earlier an advocate of the binary distinction in a far from simplistic way, his initial analysis addressing the social functions of English, the risk of a monoculture, and acknowledging that competence in foreign languages can lead to identification with them (1992, pp. 313-5). Hüllen has explored some of these tensions in more recent work (2003), and to some extent distances himself from the dichotomy. He admits that seeing English as neutral, unrelated to the cultural identity of speakers, is problematic, since we are in an age where the United States is a new kind of empire:

> This makes it difficult to believe in the hypothesis that English as a national language and English as an international language are two separate systems, the latter being equidistant to all other languages and cultures. (Hüllen, 2003, p. 121)

The advance of English in continental Europe is associated with particular functions of the language, in specific domains, some of them formal, others informal. This is why the language can be seen as a second, rather than a foreign language. Many of its uses can therefore not be detached from societal functioning. Indeed the widespread attraction of English as a learning goal, referred to by Kachru (1986) as its alchemy, the magic of which continues to enthral, is to a large extent explicable because of the significant linguistic and cultural capital that competence in English entails. The global system is seen by some as empire that transcends states and is dominated by corporate interests that create subjectivities as well as products (Hardt & Negri, 2000). It functions through communication networks that can and do strengthen a lot of languages, but English most of all.

The recognition of English as a threat to the languages and cultures of EU member states is beginning to influence the formulation and synchronization of language policy at the supranational level. The Commission document *Promoting language learning and linguistic diversity: An Action Plan 2004-2006* is designed to curb an excessive focus on English in continental education systems and the wider society. It states: "learning one lingua franca alone is not enough... English alone is not enough... In non-anglophone countries recent trends to provide teaching in English may have unforeseen consequences on the vitality of the national language" (pp. 4, 8). The policy statement advocates life-long foreign language learning, including two foreign languages in the primary school. It strives to bring language policy higher up on national agendas, and to raise awareness of linguistic diversity. It endorses the notion of an inclusive 'language-friendly environment,' and states that this openness should include minority languages, those of both local regions and recent immigrants. Representatives of member states attend meetings in Brussels every three months, and are required to respond to questions on the implementation of the Action Plan and obstacles to it. Such activity takes place in the secrecy of the

EU bureaucratic system, and may or may not influence national policy formation, but the very existence of international pressure of this kind can serve to force states to address language policy issues that they would prefer to ignore. The EU's position is in many respects similar to what the Council of Europe, which brings together nearly twice as many European states, has been advocating for decades. It has undertaken a great deal of activity to promote language learning (see the *Common European Framework of Reference for Languages*, and related documents, www.coe.int). The Council of Europe has also taken the lead in attempting to ensure respect for the rights of national minorities (see, for instance, the contributions of Duncan Wilson and Tove Skutnabb-Kangas on educational rights in Council of Europe, 2004).

All these measures may have little impact when the reasons for young people to become competent in English, and perhaps ignore other languages, are so manifest in the present-day world, and when governments that may have reservations about English expanding are simultaneously attempting to ensure through the education system that their citizens are competent in English. English is such a chameleon in the modern world that it can serve countless purposes and be learned in countless ways. At the same time the interlocking of Englishization with globalization and Europeanization processes makes it possible in many contexts to specify what particular purposes an increased use of English is serving. There is a manifest need for more energetic language policy formulation both in European states and in the EU (Phillipson, 2003). If the advancement of English is to strengthen and enrich the ecology of language in Europe, many of the dimensions of the Global English paradigm need to be challenged and resisted. When much of the use and learning of English no longer serves foreign language purposes, language pedagogy can advance in new dynamic ways, and language policy can strive to ensure that all languages thrive.

REFERENCES

Alexander, R. J. (2003). G.lobal L.anguages O.ppress B.ut A.re L.iberating, Too: The dialectic of English. In Mair, C. (Ed.), *The politics of English as a world language: New horizons in postcolonial English studies* (pp. 87–96). Amsterdam & New York: Rodopi.

Ammon, U. (2000). Towards more fairness in international English: Linguistic rights of non-native speakers? In Phillipson, R. (Ed.), *Rights to language. Equity, power, and education* (pp. 102–110). Mahwah, NJ: Lawrence Erlbaum.

Blommaert, J. (2003) Commentary: A sociolinguistics of globalization. *Journal of Sociolinguistics* 7(4), 607–623.

Bondebjerg, I. (2003). Culture, media and globalisation. In *Humanities – essential research for Europe* (pp. 71–88). Copenhagen: Danish Research Council for the Humanities.

Bourdieu, P. (2001). *Contre-feux 2. Pour un mouvement social européen*. Paris: Raisons d'agir.

Brutt-Griffler, J. (2002). *World English: A study of its development*. Clevedon: Multilingual Matters.

Cameron, D. (2002). Globalization and the teaching of 'communication' skills. In Block, D. and Cameron, D. (Eds.), *Globalization and language teaching* (pp. 67–82). London: Routledge.

Chaudenson, R. (2003). Geolinguistics, geopolitics, geostrategy: The case for French. In J. Maurais & M. A. Morris (Eds.), *Languages in a globalising world* (pp. 291–297). Cambridge: Cambridge University Press.

Commission of the European Union (2003). *Promoting language learning and linguistic diversity: An Action Plan 2004–2006*, (COM(2003) 449). Retrieved September 20 2005, from http://europa.eu.int/.

Council of Europe (2004). *Filling the frame. Five years of monitoring the Framework Convention for the Protection of National Minorities*. Strasbourg: Council of Europe.

Council of Europe (2005). *Common European Framework of Reference for Languages*. www.coe.int, language policy division.

Crystal, D. (1997). *English as a global language*. Cambridge: Cambridge University Press.

De Swaan, A. (2001). *Words of the world. The global language system*, Cambridge: Polity.
Dendrinos, V. (1999). The conflictual subjectivity of the periphery ELT practitioner. In A.-F. Christidis, (Ed.), *'Strong' and 'weak' languages in the European Union. Aspects of linguistic hegemonism* (pp. 711–717). Proceedings of an international conference, Thessaloniki, 26–28 March 1997. Thessaloniki: Centre for the Greek Language.
Gawlitta, K., and Vilmar, F. (eds.) (2002). *'Deutsch nix wichtig'? Engagement für die deutsche Sprache.* Paderborn: IBF Verlag.
Graddol, D. (1998). *The future of English?* London: The British Council.
Grin, F. (2001). English as economic value: Facts and fallacies. *World Englishes 20*(1), 65–78.
Hardt, M., & Negri, A. (2000). *Empire.* Cambridge, MA: Harvard University Press.
Hjarvad, S. (2004). The globalization of language. How the media contribute to the spread of English and the emergence of medialects. *Nordicom Information Gothenburg 2,* 75–97 (original also published in Danish).
Höglin, R. (2002). *Engelska språket som hot och tillgång i Norden.* Copenhagen: Nordiska Ministerrådet.
House, J. (2003). English as a lingua franca: A threat to multilingualism? *Journal of Sociolinguistics 7*(4), 556–578.
Hüllen, W. (1992). Identifikationssprache und Kommunikationssprache. Über Probleme der Mehrsprachigkeit. *Zeitschrift für germanistische Linguistik 20*(3), 298–317.
Hüllen, W. (2003). Global English: Desired and dreaded. In R. Ahrens (Ed.), *Europäische Sprachenpolitik. European language policy* (pp. 113–122). Heidelberg: Universitätsverlag Winter.
Jenkins, J. (2000). *The phonology of English as an international language.* Oxford: Oxford University Press.
Kachru, Braj B. (1986). *The alchemy of English: The spread, functions and models of non-native Englishes.* Oxford: Pergamon.
Kayman, M. A. (2004). The state of English as a global language: Communicating culture. *Textual practice 18*(1), 1–22.
Kontra, M. (1997). *English linguistic and cultural imperialism and teacher training in Hungary.* Report on the 2nd ELT Conference on Teacher Training in the Carpathian Euro-region, Debrecen, Hungary, 25–27 April 1997. Budapest: British Council, English Language Teaching Contacts Scheme, 83–88.
Kramsch, C. (2002). In search of the intercultural. Review article, *Journal of Sociolinguistics, 6*(2), 275–285.
McCarty, T. L. (2004). Dangerous difference: A critical-historical analysis of language education policies in the United States. In Tollefson, J. & Tsui, A. B. M. (Eds.) *Medium of instruction policies. Which agenda? Whose agenda?* (pp. 71–93). Mahwah, NJ: Lawrence Erlbaum.
Melander, B. (2001). Swedish, English and the European Union. In Boyd, S. and Huss, L. (Eds.), *Managing multilingualism in a European nation-state. Challenges for Sweden* (pp. 13–31). Clevedon: Multilingual Matters.
Monbiot, G. (2000). *Captive state: The corporate take-over of Britain.* Basingstoke: Macmillan.
Mufwene, S. S. (2001). *The ecology of language evolution.* Cambridge: Cambridge University Press.
Nuffield Languages Inquiry (2000). *Languages: The next generation.* The Final Report and Recommendations of the Nuffield Languages Inquiry, Retrieved December 21 2005, from http://www.nuffield.org.
Pegrum, M. (2004). Selling English: Advertising and the discourses of ELT. *English Today 77, 20*(1), 3–10.
Petersen, M and Shaw, P. (2002). Language and disciplinary differences in a biliterate context. *World Englishes, 21*(3), 357–374.
Phillipson, R. (1999). Voice in global English: Unheard chords in Crystal loud and clear. *Applied Linguistics, 20*(2), 265–276.
Phillipson, R. (2003). *English-only Europe? Challenging language policy*, London: Routledge.
Phillipson, R. (2004). English in globalization: Three approaches. *Journal of Language, Identity and Education, 3*(1), 73–84.
Phillipson, R. (2005). Language policy and linguistic imperialism. In Ricento, T. (Ed.), *An introduction to language policy: Theory and method,* (pp. 346–361). Oxford: Blackwell.
Phillipson, R. (2006) Figuring out the Englishization of Europe. In J. Jenkins, & C. Leung (Eds.), *Reconfiguring Europe: The contribution of applied linguistics,* (pp. 65–85). London: Equinox and the British Association of Applied Linguistics.
Preisler, B. (1999). Functions and forms of English in a European EFL country. In Bex, T. & Watts, R. J. (Eds.) *Standard English: The widening debate* (pp. 239–267). London: Routledge.
Rice, C. (2000). Campaign 2000: Promoting the national interest. Cited in the Danish daily *Information*, 14 June 2001.
Rothkopf, D. (1997). In praise of cultural imperialism? *Foreign policy, 107,* 38–53.

Seidlhofer, B. (2004). Research perspectives on teaching English as a lingua franca. *Annual Review of Applied Linguistics, 24*, 209–239.
Skutnabb-Kangas, T. (2000). *Linguistic genocide in education–or worldwide diversity and human rights?* Mahwah, NJ: Lawrence Erlbaum.
The Guardian Weekly, 13–19 August 2004.
Tsuda, Y. (1994). The diffusion of English: Its impact on culture and communication. *Keio Communication Review, 16*, 49–61.
Wilkinson, R. (Ed.) (2004). *Integrating content and language. Meeting the challenge of a multilingual higher education.* Maastricht: Maastricht University Press.

CHAPTER 10

COMMON PROPERTY:
ENGLISH AS A LINGUA FRANCA IN EUROPE

BARBARA SEIDLHOFER

University of Vienna, Austria

ABSTRACT

This chapter is concerned with the role English plays as a lingua franca in Europe used by Europeans as a means of communication among themselves and with others. This extension of the use of English and its de facto status as an auxiliary language for global communicative purposes rather than as a traditional foreign language is widely acknowledged and discussed. However, current ways of thinking about English and its learning and use have yet to take this radical change in the role of the language fully into account. If the European ideals of individual plurilingualism and societal multilingualism are to be realized, it is crucial to understand how English as a lingua franca (ELF) functions in complementary rather than competitive relation to other languages. Such an understanding will depend on the fulfillment of two interrelated conditions: a) a proper conceptualization of ELF as *common property*, essentially distinct from and independent of English as a native language; and b) an empirically-based description of the linguistic properties of actual ELF usage. Such conceptualization and description will be prerequisites for adequately responding to the changing demands and directions that European language policy and language education face at the beginning of the 21st century.

INTRODUCTION

In the context of the continuing enlargement of the European Union the role of English as a lingua franca in Europe (ELFE) both inside and outside the Union is a particularly topical as well as a controversial issue. While this chapter endeavors to address issues that are relevant for the whole of Europe, what is said will be particularly true of the 25 member states of the European Union.

The impact of English is certainly pervasive in the whole of Europe, but it is uneven. With respect to the use and knowledge of the language, Europe is a very heterogeneous area. As Görlach (2002) points out, there are "enormous differences in the knowledge of English...between, say, Norwegians and Albanians, both in the number of speakers, and the range, expressiveness, fluency and correctness of the English produced" (p. 152).

One explanation of this, as Phillipson and Skutnabb-Kangas (1999) demonstrate, is that "Englishization" is "one dimension of globalization," and it follows that the more "developed," industrialized European countries are more firmly in the grip of globalization and thus also more firmly in the grip of Englishization—or, as Berns, de Bot, and Hasebrink (in press) put it more neutrally, "in the presence of English."

For a handbook of English language teaching, the following four perspectives on ELFE suggest themselves: functional, conceptual, linguistic, pedagogy and policy.

THE FUNCTIONAL PERSPECTIVE: THE ROLE OF ENGLISH IN THE WORLD, AND ITS DE FACTO STATUS AS AN INTERNATIONAL MEANS OF COMMUNICATION

English in Europe appears in at least three guises: as a first/native and national language in Britain and Ireland (ENL), as a foreign language in language education in non-English speaking countries (EFL), and thirdly, but most frequently, and with most speakers, as a lingua franca both for intra-European and for global communication (ELF).[1] As the title of this chapter indicates, its focus will be on this third function, English as a lingua franca.

But what do we mean by the term *English as a lingua franca*? The term *lingua franca* is usually taken to mean "any lingual medium of communication between people of different mother tongues, for whom it is a second language" (Samarin, 1987, p. 371). In this definition, then, a lingua franca has no native speakers, and this notion is carried over into definitions of English as a lingua franca, such as in the following example: "[ELF is] a 'contact language' between persons who share neither a common native tongue nor a common (national) culture, and for whom English is the chosen *foreign* language of communication" (Firth, 1996, p. 240).

Clearly, the role of English as the chosen foreign language of communication in Europe is an extremely important one, and one that is on the increase. Graddol (2001, p. 49) offers projections of L2 English use in EU countries up to the year 2050. These give an estimate of about 130 million speakers for 2005 and peak in 2030-2035 at nearly 200 million speakers. Graddol concludes that "English...is fast becoming a second language in Europe" (1999, p. 65; see also Phillipson, this volume). It is important to note that this means that both in Europe as well as in the world as a whole, English is now a language that is mainly used by bi- and multilinguals, and that its (often monolingual) native speakers are a minority.[2]

So both in society at large as well as in education, the role of English as an international lingua franca is generally acknowledged as a fact, welcomed by some and deplored by others. The question arises as to how this recognized status of English is reflected in European language curricula for institutions for primary, secondary, and tertiary education. The current general picture here is that curricula typically mention the global role of English as an econocultural fact and offer either (or both) of two kinds of motivation for learning it. One is utilitarian, and here what is stressed is the importance of English for international communication in business, science, etc.; and the other is idealistic, and here the emphasis is on the potential it affords for furthering international cross-cultural understanding. But how these two quite different kinds of motivation might be reconciled is apparently not considered. The acknowledgement of this lingua franca role of English sits uncomfortably with the way the subject English is treated in most curricula, which is really not different in kind from the treatment of other foreign languages, such as Italian in Sweden or Modern Greek in France.

As for the distinction between ENL, EFL, and ELF drawn above, one might respond by claiming that it does not matter, as in all three cases we are dealing with English. But upon closer scrutiny, the assumption "English = English = English" does not hold.[3] The differences between ENL, EFL, and ELF are conceptual and linguistic ones, and these differences are bound to have consequences for pedagogy and language policy. These will be addressed in the respective sections in this chapter. But first we need to consider the conceptualization and the linguistic description of ELF in general and ELFE in particular.

THE CONCEPTUAL PERSPECTIVE: POSITIONS ON THE GLOBAL ROLE OF ENGLISH

Two questions arise from the observations made thus far: Have ways of thinking about English kept pace with the rapid development in the functions of the language? And how far does such development call for a radically new concept of ELF(E)?

At present, the answer to the first question would have to be a resounding "no." Probably because we are used to the notion of any language being so closely and automatically tied up with its native speakers, it is very difficult to open up conceptual space for ELF. The observation Coulmas (1981) made a quarter of a century ago still holds:

> The nativeness criterion is maintained across theoretical boundaries and contrasts…Within the framework of field linguistics, the native speaker is a human being who is able to give information about his or her language. In theoretical linguistics, by contrast, he often figures as an abstract idealization. Yet, notwithstanding these fundamental differences, the speaker whom the linguist is concerned about is invariably claimed to be a *native* speaker. He is the one who can legitimately supply data, and his language is what grammatical analyses are meant to account for. Thus, nativeness is *the* only universally accepted criterion for authenticity. (p. 5)

In European history, of course, native languages have figured very prominently in the construction of social identities and of nation states. However, Europe is now at a juncture where it is seeking economic, cultural, and political integration and the transcending of national boundaries. It would therefore seem to be a timely move to reconsider—to reconceptualize indeed—what it means "to speak a language," and to call into question the control of native speakers over a language that is predominantly used by non-native speakers.

But this process is slow in getting started. The realization of the global role of English, so hotly debated on the meta-level (e.g. Canagarajah, 1999; Pennycook, 1994; Phillipson, 1992) has not so far led to any radical reconceptualization of this English. Instead, we are faced with what has been termed a "conceptual gap" (Seidlhofer, 2001a) in the place where ELF should be getting established in people's minds—of course, alongside existing notions of English as a native language.

This non-recognition of ELF may also explain why, despite certain dissenting voices (e.g. Cook, 1999; Firth & Wagner, 1997; Kasper, 1998; Sridhar & Sridhar, 1986) virtually all SLA research operates with a native-speaker model and tends to construct non-native speakers as defective communicators. It is also one reason why learner corpus research (see e.g. Granger, 1998) has so far been geared towards highlighting the difficulties specific L1 groups have with native English in order to make it easier for those learners to conform to ENL, and why dictionaries and grammars based on the large native-speaker corpora can lay claim to a monopoly of "real English."

This is not to say, however, that no conceptual progress has been made in recent years. A public discussion about a conceptualization of English in its role as a lingua franca has been gathering momentum (for an overview, see Seidlhofer, 2004). In a book-length study boldly entitled "*World English*," Brutt-Griffler (2002) argues that bi- or multilingualism is an intrinsic design feature of World English. She provides a carefully argued basis for acknowledging the active role of ELF users as *agents* in the spread and development of English: They are not just at the receiving end, but contribute to the shaping of the language and the functions it fulfils and so, as speech communities, take possession of the language in a process she terms "macroacquisition." Clearly, this is a perspective that contributes to theories of language spread and language change and has considerable implications for the conceptualization of English as a lingua franca.

For a view from within Europe, and by an expert commentator on the European sociolinguistic landscape, we can turn to the German sociolinguist Ulrich Ammon. In his editor's introduction to the book *The Dominance of English as a Language of Science* (2001), he has the following to say about ELF norms and description:

> A number of contributions to the present volume point out real advantages of the English-speaking world, or its scientists, and disadvantages of the other language communities and their scientists. Here the question of dominance in the literal sense arises, namely dominance of **the native speakers of the world lingua franca** by means of their language over the non-native speakers, let alone the non-speakers. In order to raise awareness of these problems I have postulated, in my contribution to this volume as well as elsewhere (Ammon, 2000), the "non-native speakers' right to linguistic peculiarities". It may appear a rather hopeless postulate considering the well-founded linguistic veneration of the native speaker, but I believe it deserves close examination, also re the possibilities of a political campaign to gather support similar to that for female linguistic rights. The feminist campaign too was far from being taken seriously at the beginning but has certainly had considerable success meanwhile. I am aware that *the postulate of equity for non-native speakers of English*, to put it in another way, faces far more formidable obstacles than did, or does, linguistic gender neutrality. It *needs, first of all, adequate specification before it can be taken seriously*. (p. vii f., emphases added)

What we find in the current situation, then, is a disparity between two positions. On the one hand, there is recognition of the significance and relevance of English as an international language and its necessary functional variation. On the other hand, descriptions of English continue to be focused on the core native-speaker countries. There are two opposing positions: one embracing pluralism, the other ignoring it. It may well be, however, that the balance of power in this unstable equilibrium is about to change, and an important factor in this will be the availability of descriptions of ELF. In the quotation above, Ammon insists on "adequate specification" of ELF as a crucial prerequisite for redressing the imbalance of sociolinguistic power between native and non-native users of English. Work in this area has been gathering momentum over the last few years, and this is what will be summarized in the following section.

THE LINGUISTIC PERSPECTIVE: WHAT DOES ELFE ACTUALLY LOOK LIKE AND SOUND LIKE?

The linguistic question—and it has to be an empirical one—is how English as a European lingua franca is actually spoken and written in various contexts of use, and whether salient linguistic features can be identified that characterize ELFE. It is entirely appropriate that this section should be placed at the center of this chapter, preceded by a consideration of functional and conceptual perspectives, and followed by matters of pedagogy and policy. For as long as there is no linguistic reality that is identified as ELFE, named, described, and codified in dictionaries and grammars, there is very little chance of it gaining acceptance as a concept existing alongside the familiar concept of ENL, of it being a factor in language pedagogy and language policy. Taking account of the actual visible and audible manifestations of the language is crucial.

What this amounts to is the extending of the same kind of descriptive service to ELF as has already been provided in the case of English in postcolonial contexts, more generally in what Kachru (e.g., 1992) has called the Outer Circle.[4] In these contexts, the realization has taken root that indigenized varieties of English are legitimate Englishes in their own right, accordingly emancipating themselves vis à vis British and American Standard English.

Descriptions and codification have been recognized as crucial prerequisites for the emergence of endonormative standards in these indigenized varieties (cf. Bamgboșe, 1998), and important research programs are underway in order to provide language descriptions as a basis for dictionaries and grammars (notably the International Corpus of English, cf. Greenbaum, 1996). Outer Circle language variation and change has, on the whole, been given the linguistic seal of approval.

In the Expanding Circle, however, a totally different situation presents itself. There is a recognition both of the all-pervasive use of English throughout what many like to term the *international community* and the fact that interactions using English as a lingua franca constitute a regular feature of many "influential frameworks" such as global business, science, politics, and media discourse (House, 1999, p. 74). Similarly, there are countless anecdotes about emerging varieties such as *Euro-English*. It is clear that English is therefore in transition from foreign-language to second-language status in many Expanding Circle countries (Graddol, 1997, p. 11) and yet the desire to make actual descriptions of this variation available has hardly even been articulated. The received wisdom seems to be that only when English is a majority first language or an official additional language, does it warrant description.

A closing of the conceptual gap, that is to say a conceptualization of ELF as outlined in the preceding section as distinct from a vague acknowledgement of its existence, is unlikely to happen as long as no comprehensive and reliable descriptions of salient features of ELF are available. Description is also crucial as a precondition for acceptance: ELF needs to be made visible as a "linguistic reality" that can be named and captured in reference works alongside ENL and so-called indigenized varieties of English such as Nigerian English and Indian English. This is indeed the lesson that can be learned from work on Outer Circle varieties of English. As Bamgboșe (1998) points out when discussing "the ambivalence between recognition and acceptance of non-native norms":

> The importance of codification is too obvious to be belaboured. ...one of the major factors militating against the emergence of endonormative standards in non-native Englishes is precisely the dearth of codification. Obviously, once a usage or innovation enters the dictionary as correct and acceptable usage, its status as a regular form is assured. (p. 4)

The same point is extended to ELF by Juliane House: She emphasizes the current rapid increase in ELF interactions, particularly in the previously mentioned influential networks. Significantly, the conclusion House (1999) draws from her observation is, again, the overriding importance of description:

> [I]t seems vital to pay more attention to the nature of ELF interactions, and ask whether and how they are different from both interactions between native speakers, and interactions between native speakers and non-native speakers. An answer to this question would bring us closer to finding out whether and in what ways ELF interactions are actually *sui generis*. (p. 74)

At present, the idea that some time in the future there may be a descriptive basis for an eventual codification of ELF may seem far-fetched, but in fact some empirical work has already been done to pave the way. The particular aims of these studies vary, but taken together this growing body of work will lead to a better understanding of the nature of ELF, which, as has been pointed out above, is a prerequisite for making informed decisions on any of the levels discussed in this chapter.

ELF is of course a very topical concern in Europe, particularly in the European Union (Seidlhofer, Breitender & Pitzl, in press). There are a number of studies on meta-level issues that obviously need to be understood as a backdrop to any descriptive work, variously focusing on the spread and all-pervasiveness of English in Europe (e.g. Berns, de Bot, & Hasebrink, in press; Erling, 2004; Graddol, 2001; Preisler, 1999; see also Gnutzmann & Intemann, 2005.), motivations for learning English in relation to and in competition with other languages (e.g. Cenoz & Jessner, 2000; Deneire & Goethals, 1997; Dörnyei & Csizér, 2002), and issues of language policy (e.g. van Els, 2005; Phillipson, 2003; and several contributions to Hartmann, 1996; see also Wright, 2003).

As far as the descriptive level is concerned, Görlach (1999), in a paper on varieties of English and language teaching, identifies "a few topics worthy of a Ph.D. student's dedicated efforts," that includes the following:

> Justification of the linguistic identity of English as an international language (EIL) as used for communication by non-native speakers; how much regularity/stability is there and under what communicational conditions. (p. 16)

There are, in fact, efforts underway already that address precisely these issues and seek to establish whether there may be a distinct regional ELF developing in Europe. Penz (2003) discusses instances of successful intercultural communication among speakers from a variety of European languages. Jenkins, Modiano, and Seidlhofer (2001) describe recurrent features that they have observed in this Euro-English while pointing out that more empirical work in this area is urgently needed. Such work is currently being undertaken in various regions, on various levels of language and in various domains, of which more will be said later in the chapter.

Mollin (2006) is based on a Ph.D. thesis conducted at that directly addresses the question of an emerging non-native variety of English in Europe. Some researchers have already ventured opinions as to whether ELF in general, or ELFE in particular, can be described as a variety in its own right: Meierkord and Knapp (2002) feel that English as a lingua franca is a variety in its own right, and refer to Meierkord (1996) and Gramkow Andersen (1993) as studies that support their view. Chambers (2000) predicts "a supranational standard" (p. 285) for Global English in less than a century from now. Others are more skeptical (e.g. Görlach, 1999, 2002; Gnutzmann, 1999). Everything, of course, hinges on the definition of the term *variety* and, importantly, on what emerges from the empirical work described in this chapter.

A geographically more focused project within Europe is a corpus of "English as a *lingua franca* in the Alpine-Adriatic region," currently in its pilot phase (James, 2000). This project aims to capture the English used in casual conversations among young people whose first languages are German, Italian, Slovene, and Friulian. James does not report empirical findings, but rather sets out hypotheses as to what the future analysis of this use of English might yield and links these up with current work in such areas as bi/multilingualism, (native English) casual conversation, and pidgin and creole linguistics.

Outside the European Union, in officially quadrilingual Switzerland there is now a lively debate about English as a lingua franca for Switzerland, referred to as "Pan Swiss English" (Droeschel, Durham, & Rosenberger, 2005; Murray, 2003; Watts & Murray, 2001).

Obviously, empirical research contributing to an understanding and a description of ELFE is also being undertaken within the framework of more general ELF projects that are not limited to, but include European ELF users. This research is, at the moment, being undertaken primarily on spoken data for two main reasons: Firstly, the language used is at one remove from the stabilizing and standardizing influence of writing; and secondly, spoken interactions are overtly reciprocal, allowing studies to capture the on-line negotiation of meaning in the production and reception of utterances, thus facilitating observations regarding mutual intelligibility among interlocutors.

In fact, mutual intelligibility rather than native-speaker norms seems to be the most apt summary formulation of the first comprehensive study of characteristics of ELF interaction available for one level of language, namely Jenkins' *The Phonology of English as an International Language* (2000). The reason why Jenkins decided to focus attention on phonological features was that in her data, pronunciation was by far the most frequent cause of intelligibility problems in ELF interactions. Jenkins' work (see also Jenkins, 1998, 2002), culminating in what she has termed the phonological "Lingua Franca Core" (LFC), thus takes as its starting point the need for empirical data drawn from interactions between L2 speakers of English in order to assess which phonological features are (and which are not) essential for intelligible pronunciation when English is spoken in lingua franca contexts. The analysis of her data enabled Jenkins to identify which pronunciation errors led to intelligibility problems for interlocutors from different L1 backgrounds and which did not. Those which caused such problems were then incorporated into the LFC while those which did not were considered, as far as ELF is concerned, to be non-core—different from ENL production, but not for that reason, wrong.

Jenkins has repeatedly pointed out that her LFC may need to be modified in the light of more data, maybe from additional L1s; but to date no studies that investigated her findings from the perspective of such additional L1s have falsified her results. But whether or not modifications become necessary as more research becomes available, Jenkins' work is groundbreaking in the genuine difference (rather than deficit) perspective she takes: Divergences from native speaker realizations in the non-core areas are regarded as perfectly acceptable instances of L2 sociolinguistic variation.

Working on phonology has, of course, the distinct advantage that one is dealing with a relatively closed system, which is not the case with the other levels of language. This may be the case why no definitive findings can be reported to date on ELF pragmatics and ELF lexicogrammar. However, this merely means that more time will be required for results to emerge from such work, as larger databases are needed to enable useful generalizations to be made.

Interestingly in the context of the present chapter, most of the empirical work on ELF pragmatics and ELF lexicogrammar has been, and is being, conducted in Europe. Several authors have analyzed data from a wide range of first language backgrounds (Firth, 1996; House, 1999, 2002; Lesznyak, 2002, 2004; Meierkord, 1996, 2002; Pölzl, 2003; Wagner & Firth, 1997). Their findings obviously vary with the research questions posed and the contexts in which the data were captured (e.g. dinner conversations, group discussions, simulated conferences, and business telephone calls). Nevertheless, some generalizations about the pragmatics of ELF can be made. Misunderstandings are not frequent in ELF interactions; when they do occur, they tend to be dealt with either by topic change or, less often, by overt negotiation using communication strategies such as rephrasing and repetition. Interference from L1 interactional norms has been found to be rare, maybe because a kind of suspension of expectations regarding norms is in operation in many ELF conversations. What is often observed is that as long as a certain threshold of understanding is obtained, interlocutors appear to adopt what Firth (1996) has termed the "let-it-pass principle" that gives the impression of ELF talk being overtly consensus-oriented, cooperative, and mutually supportive, and thus fairly robust. However, House (1999, 2002) does sound a more skeptical note, pointing to the danger that superficial consensus may well hide sources of trouble at a deeper level, a caveat that certainly needs to be taken seriously and, above all, investigated further by work on a much broader empirical base than has been available to date.

An area where findings are even scarcer so far is lexicogrammar. This may be surprising as lexicogrammatical features are probably the most noticeable, intuitively accessible ones in people's idea of *language*. But in order to arrive at reliable results, a large corpus would be necessary.

A new research initiative that attempts to meet this need is the *Vienna-Oxford International Corpus of English* (VOICE) (http://www.univie.ac.at/voice/; see e.g. Seidlhofer, 2001b, 2002; Breiteneder et al., in press). This project aims to compile a sizeable corpus dedicated to capturing the use of ELF from a variety of first language backgrounds and a range of settings and domains. Like the other data referred to so far, what is captured in VOICE is spoken ELF—unscripted, largely face-to-face interaction among fairly fluent speakers whose primary and secondary socialization did not take place through English. The recorded and transcribed speech events range over a variety of settings (professional, informal, educational), functions (exchanging information, enacting social relationships), and roles and relationships of participants (acquainted/unacquainted, symmetrical/asymmetrical). They are realized as private and public dialogues, private and public group discussions and casual conversations, and one-to-one interviews.

The primary aim of VOICE is to provide a basis for whatever empirical research is required to further extend the description of ELF. For example, due to the dearth of lexicogrammatical descriptions of ELF use, a useful first research focus might be to complement the work already done on its phonology and the initial findings on its pragmatics summarized in this chapter by concentrating on lexicogrammar, especially since this is an aspect that tends to be regarded as particularly central to language pedagogy. A general corpus such as VOICE should make it possible to take stock of how the speakers co-construct English for communication across cultures. The overall objective will thus be to find out what, if anything, notwithstanding all the diversity, emerges as salient common features of ELF use, irrespective of speakers' first languages and levels of proficiency.

At this stage, no reliable findings based on quantitative investigations can be reported. But quite a number of thesis and seminar projects conducted on VOICE data at the University of Vienna (e.g. Breiteneder, 2005; Hollander, 2002; Kordon, 2003; Pitzl, 2005; Pölzl & Seidlhofer, 2006; Strasser, 2004) have brought to light certain regularities that at least point to some hypotheses that in turn are proving useful for formulating more focused research questions. In particular, typical errors that most English teachers would consider in urgent need of correction and remediation, and that consequently often get allotted a great deal of time and effort in English lessons, appear to be generally unproblematic and no obstacle to communicative success. These include dropping the third person present tense *–s*, using the relative pronouns *who* and *which* interchangeably, omitting definite and indefinite articles where they are obligatory in ENL, or inserting them where the do not occur in ENL. There tends to be a heavy reliance on certain verbs of high semantic generality, such as *do, have, make, put, take*. What also happens frequently is that extra redundancy is added, for instance through the preposition in expressions like *We discussed about...*, or through increased explicitness in e.g. *black color* rather than just *black*. Such examples suggest the intriguing possibility that ELF users remove the redundancy of Standard English in certain areas and, in compensation, increase it in others.

While these features do not seem to interfere with intelligibility, other recurrent events in these interactions do cause communication problems and misunderstandings: Unsurprisingly, not being familiar with certain vocabulary items can give rise to problems, particularly when speakers lack paraphrasing skills. Most interesting perhaps are cases of "unilateral idiomaticity" (Seidlhofer, 2002), where particularly idiomatic speech by one participant can be problematic when the expressions used are not known to the interlocutor(s). Characteristics of such unilateral idiomaticity are, for example, metaphorical language use, idioms, phrasal verbs, and other fixed ENL expressions, such as *the ball is in your court* or *I like chilling out*.

Work being undertaken in Britain (Dewey, 2003 on lexicogrammar; Prodromou, 2003 on phraseology, particularly idiomaticity) seems to corroborate these initial findings from the VOICE project.

There are also research efforts underway that cut across different levels of language in that they focus on the use of ELF in particular domains of use, such as international business (Dresemann, 2004; Firth, 1996; Gramkow Andersen, 1993;

Haegeman, 2002; Hollqvist, 1984; Louhiala-Salminen, 2002; Meeuwis, 1994). Another domain in which ELF is prominent, is academic communication. At Tampere University in Finland a corpus of English as a Lingua Franca in Academic settings (ELFA) is now being compiled that captures spoken interactions among speakers of different, mostly European, L1s in international degree programs and other university activities regularly carried out in English (see Mauranen, 2003). English has, of course, become international across modes of written discourse as well, particularly as these have developed to serve specific institutional purposes. These modes of written ELF have, so far at least, conformed to the norms of standard ENL grammar. It stands to reason that in written language use, where there is no possibility of the overt reciprocal negotiation of meaning typical of spoken interaction, there is more reliance on established norms, and these are naturally maintained by a process of self-regulation whereby these norms are adhered to in the interests of maintaining global mutual intelligibility (Widdowson, 1997a). However, as these written modes become increasingly used and appropriated by non-native users, one might speculate that, in time, self-regulation might move towards less dependence on native norms so that these written modes also take on the kind of distinctive features that are evident in spoken ELF (cf. Meierkord, 2006).

PEDAGOGIC AND POLICY PERSPECTIVE: CAN, AND SHOULD, ELFE BE TAUGHT?

From the preceding section it seems clear that linguistic descriptions of ELFE are likely to become available in the near future. The question arises, then, what implications this might have for the teaching of English in Europe, and how teaching ELFE would differ from teaching English as a foreign language or English as a second language. These questions concern both the pedagogy of English teaching and the policy of European language education.

The idea of taking pedagogic account of the lingua franca function of English has been discussed in Europe for quite some time. However, compared to the vast number of publications on English teaching based on ENL norms, only a small number of scholars has been engaged in reflecting on the pedagogic potential of ELF (but see Beneke, 1991; Hüllen, 1982; Piepho, 1989; Smith, 1984; Widdowson, 1994, 2003; and some contributions to the early collections edited by Brumfit in 1982 and by Smith in 1983). However, as discussed previously, these rare exhortations to rethink the teaching of English have had minimal impact on mainstream curriculum planning over the last two decades or so (see e.g. Council of Europe, 2001). It would be interesting to speculate why this is the case. One factor to be taken into account in this respect is certainly the enormous influence of research in ENL countries that has been (somewhat uncritically) assumed to be of a priori relevance to teaching English in Europe. This research includes work on second language acquisition and corpus linguistics in the US and the UK that generally takes the primacy of standard native speaker norms as self-evident (cf. the discussion between Carter, 1998 and Cook, 1998). This attitude may have led, to use Widdowson's terms (1980, 2000), to "linguistics applied" taking precedence over developments in applied linguistics that otherwise might have evolved continuously from the early 1980s.

As seems clear from the predictions regarding the global role of English in the next half century discussed in the early part of this chapter, the demand for English in Europe will be self-sustaining. However, one could argue—as has been done—that this demand cannot, and need not, be met within the confines of a school subject. What can be done is to provide a basis from which students can learn, fine-tuning subsequently (usually after leaving school) to any native or non-native varieties and registers that are relevant for their individual requirements (cf. Widdowson, 2003). Such an approach would be supported by relevant work in intercultural communication (e.g. Bremer, Roberts, Vasseur, Simonot, & Broeder, 1996; Buttjes & Byram, 1990; Byram & Fleming, 1998; Byram & Grundy, 2003; Gumperz & Roberts, 1991; Knapp & Knapp-Pothoff, 1990; Vollmer, 2001) and language awareness (e.g. Bolitho et al., 2003; Doughty, Pearce, & Thornton, 1971; James & Garrett, 1991; Hawkins. 1991, van Lier, 1995; Widdowson, 1997b).

Abandoning unrealistic notions of achieving perfect communication through native-like proficiency in English would free up resources for focusing on skills and procedures that are likely to be useful in EIL talk, such as communication strategies (e.g. Kasper & Kellerman, 1997) and accommodation skills (e.g. Giles & Coupland, 1991; Jenkins, 2000). Thus, more learning time might usefully be spent on skills such as drawing on extralinguistic cues, gauging interlocutors' linguistic repertoires, supportive listening, signaling non-comprehension in a face-saving way, asking for repetition, paraphrasing, etc. Needless to say, exposure to a wide range of varieties of English and a multilingual, comparative approach (in the spirit of the Language Awareness/*Eveil aux Langues* project of the Council of Europe (Candelier & Macaire, 2000; Masats, 2003) are likely to facilitate the acquisition of these communicative abilities. The focus here would be on teaching language rather than languages (see Edmondson, 1999). Synergies achieved through linking the languages that learners bring to their classrooms would make a greater contribution to the Council of Europe's ideal of individual plurilingualism and societal multilingualism (cf. Beacco & Byram, 2003) than extended instruction in English, particularly when English is conceptualized exclusively as ENL.

With this last observation we have already moved into issues concerning European language policy. Given the EU's insistence on plurilingualism and diversification of languages as declared aims of European language policy, the question arises how English relates to these proclaimed ideals: Is English a threat to diversity or a lingua franca as a utility language, alongside national and regional languages, for the expression of socio-cultural identity (cf. House, 2003)?

The most obvious implication of the developments outlined above will be that in regard to what is often perceived as 'the vexed question' of English it will soon be possible, in principle at least, to move on from a reactive stage of "conjectures and refutations" (in Popper's terms) to a proactive one in which international users of English will be able to make a legitimate contribution to the development of the language. After all, the use of English as a lingua franca forms an important part of how Europeans conduct their everyday lives, and the existence of such a widespread use of English will have to be acknowledged as common and appropriate linguistic behavior. It will, therefore, be inappropriate to simply decry this means of communication as bad English and to dismiss the users of ELF as mere language learners striving to emulate endonormative models of English. Instead, these users of English should have a say in the definition of standards and norms of ELF that are relevant to them.

The advantages of a conceptualization, codification and acceptance of ELF for European language policy could be considerable. At present, Europe is faced with a situation in which various languages are in competition for resources in the pursuit of the European ideal of individual plurilingualism and societal multilingualism. But the different languages serve different functions, and can be grouped accordingly. Languages have been categorized under labels such as community language, official language, minority language, neighboring language, language of identification, regional lingua franca, global lingua franca, etc. The problem here is that while for all but one of these categories, different languages will be relevant in different settings, the category *global lingua franca* is occupied by only one language, English. Since the utility of the global lingua franca is universally recognized, English always wins out when it is in direct competition with other languages in the same pool. It follows, then, that English needs to be treated as what it is: a unique phenomenon, and therefore set apart from the rest. For many people, it would be sufficient to learn English *only* as a lingua franca, without studying the native English cultures, literatures, etc. (Seidlhofer, 2003). But this option will only be available when the preconceived idea has been overcome that that any notion of *language* has to equal *native language*.

It should be emphasized again, however, that suggesting that English should be adapted to European needs does not mean the same as suggesting that the language should simply be taught and learned badly, with a kind of "anything goes" attitude. What forms of English might be maximally useful as a European, and global, lingua franca is an empirical question, and the bulk of the empirical work sketched above is yet to be undertaken. The potential of such a description for pedagogy would reside in knowing which features tend to be crucial for international intelligibility and thus should be taught for production and reception, and which (non-native) features tend not to cause misunderstandings and thus do not need to constitute a focus in the teaching for production. There is, after all, no point in striving for fine nuances of native-speaker language use if such forms are communicatively redundant in lingua franca settings.

What is gaining acceptance, albeit slowly, is the conceptualization of English as a lingua franca that is distinct from other languages, and for which a unique model of learning might feasibly be formulated. Along these lines, the Swiss linguist Georges Lüdi (2002) very clearly and helpfully discusses what the consequences of such a conceptualization would be for European language policy. He demonstrates how the conscious decision to assign to English the role of a lingua franca (and thus, accordingly, reducing the number of years spent on learning it) could be an important step towards making the plurilingual repertoire envisaged for every European citizen a much more attainable target.

CONCLUSIONS

From the considerations outlined above, it follows that the most crucial concern for the teaching of English in Europe in the 21st century will be to understand how English functions in relation to other languages. Sociolinguistic research suggests that if—and this is a vital condition—English is appropriated by its users in such a way as to serve its unique function as ELF, it will not constitute a threat to other languages but leave other languages intact, precisely because of its delimited role and distinct status. Properly conceptualized as ELF, English can be positioned, quite literally, out of competition with other languages. Or, to modify a phrase by Neville Alexander (quoted in Phillipson & Skutnabb-Kangas, 1999), the task will be to find a way of "reducing English to equality."

NOTES

[1] There are some interesting cases where English is the official or co-official language, such as Gibraltar and Malta, but despite the official status of English, it is actually Spanish and Maltese that are predominantly used for general communication. And in Cyprus, English does not have official status but is widely used for official purposes (see Hoffman, 2000).

[2] And their monolingualism is, of course, supported by the spread of English as an international language.

[3] For more on the "English=English=English" fallacy see Seidlhofer and Jenkins (2003).

[4] In this respect, we can of course benefit from comparable, though by no means identical, developments that have been unfolding for a long time in postcolonial settings in Africa and Asia, where so-called indigenized, or nativized, varieties of English have formed and have gained widespread acceptance. It is thus conceivable that, partly due to the sheer numbers of people involved, the international ELF speech community will eventually no longer be regarded as what Braj Kachru, the most prominent pioneer of Indian English has termed "norm-dependent," but as "norm-developing" and, ultimately, "norm-providing" (Kachru, 1985).

REFERENCES

Ammon, U. (Ed.). (2001). *The dominance of English as a language of science. Effects on other languages and language communities*. Berlin & New York: Mouton de Gruyter.

Bamgboṣe, A. (1998). Torn between the norms: Innovations in world Englishes. *World Englishes, 17*, 1–14.

Beacco, J.-C., & Byram, M. (2003). *Guide for the development of language education policies in Europe. From linguistic diversity to plurilingual education*. Strasbourg: Language Policy Division, Council of Europe.

Beneke, J. (1991). Englisch als lingua franca oder als Medium interkultureller Kommunikation. In R. Grebing (Ed.), *Grenzenloses Sprachenlernen* (pp. 54–66). Berlin: Cornelsen.

Berns, M., de Bot, K., & Hasebrink, U. (Eds.). (in press). *In the presence of English: Media and European youth*. Amsterdam: John Benjamins.

Bolitho, R., Carter, R., Hughes, R., Ivanic, R., Masuhara, H., & Tomlinson, B. (2003). Ten questions about language awareness. *ELT Journal, 57*, 251–259.

Breiteneder, A. (2005). The naturalness of English as a European lingua franca: The case of the 'third person -s'. *Vienna English Working PaperS, 14*(2), 3–26. http://www.univie.ac.at/Anglistik/Views 0502ALL.pdf.

Breiteneder, A., Pitzl, M., Majewski, S., Klimpfinger, T. (in press). "VOICE recording – Methodological challenges in the compilation of a corpus of spoken ELF". *Nordic Journal of English Studies*.

Bremer, K., Roberts, C., Vasseur M.-T., Simonot M., & Broeder, P. (Eds.). (1996). *Achieving understanding: Discourse in intercultural encounters*. London: Longman.

Brumfit, C. J. (Ed.). (1982). *English for International Communication*. Oxford: Pergamon.

Brutt-Griffler, J. (2002). *World English. A study of its development*. Clevedon: Multilingual Matters.

Buttjes, D., & Byram, M. (Eds.). (1990). *Mediating languages and cultures: Towards an intercultural theory of foreign language education*. Clevedon: Multilingual Matters.

Byram, M., & Fleming, M. (Eds.). (1998). *Language learning in intercultural perspective*. Cambridge: Cambridge University Press.

Byram, M., & Grundy, P. (Eds.). (2003). *Context and cultures in language teaching and learning*. Clevedon: Multilingual Matters.

Canagarajah, S. (1999). *Resisting linguistic imperialism in English teaching*. Oxford: Oxford University Press.

Candelier, M., & Macaire, D. (2000). L' éveil aux langues a l' école primaire et la construction de compétences—pour mieux apprendre les langues et vivre dans une société multilingue et multiculturelle. Actes de colloque de Louvain *Didactique des langues romanes: Le développement des compétences chez l'apprenant*. Bruxelles: De Boek.

Carter, R. (1998). Orders of reality: CANCODE, communication, and culture. *ELT Journal, 52*, 43–56.

Cenoz, J., & Jessner, U. (Eds.). (2000). *English in Europe. The acquisition of a third language*. Clevedon: Multilingual Matters.
Chambers, J. K. (2000). World enough and time: Global enclaves of the near future. *American Speech, 75*, 285–287.
Cook, G. (1998). The uses of reality: A reply to Ronald Carter. *ELT Journal, 52*, 57–63.
Cook, V. (1999). Going beyond the native speaker in language teaching. *TESOL Quarterly, 33*, 185–209.
Coulmas, F. (Ed.). (1981). *A festschrift for native speaker*. The Hague: Mouton.
Council of Europe (2001). *Common European framework of reference for languages: Learning, teaching, assessment*. Cambridge: Cambridge University Press.
Deneire, M., & Goethals, M. (Eds.). (1997). Special issue on English in Europe. *World Englishes, 16*(1).
Dewey, M. (2003, April). *Codifying lingua franca English*. Paper presented at the IATEFL Conference Brighton, England.
Dörnyei, Z., & Csizér, K. (2002). Some dynamics of language attitudes and motivation: Results of a nationwide survey. *Applied Linguistics, 23*, 421–462.
Doughty, P., Pearce, J., & Thornton, G. (1971). *Language in use*. London: Edward Arnold.
Dresemann, B. (2004). *Merkmale englischer Lingua Franca-Kommunikation in professionellen Kontexten*. Unpublished manuscript, University of Münster.
Droeschel, Y., Durham, M., & Rosenberger, L. (2005). Swiss English or simply non-native English? A discussion of two possible features. In D. J. Allerton, C. Tschichold, & J. Wieser (Eds.), *Linguistics, language learning and language teaching. ICSELL 10*. Basel: Schwabe.
Edmondson, W. (1999). Die fremdsprachliche Ausbildung kann nicht den Schulen überlassen werden! *Praxis, 46*, 115–123.
van Els, T. (2005). Multilingualism in the European Union. *International Journal of Applied Linguistics, 15*, 263–281.
Erling, E. (2004). *Globalization, English and the German university classroom*. PhD thesis, Freie Universität Berlin. Retrieved November 23, 2005, from http://userpage.fu-berlin.de/~berling/Final%20Draft%20pdf.pdf.
Firth, A. (1996). The discursive accomplishment of normality. On 'lingua franca' English and conversation analysis. *Journal of Pragmatics, 26*, 237–259.
Firth, A., & Wagner, J. (1997). On discourse, communication, and (some) fundamental concepts in SLA research. *Modern Language Journal, 81*, 285–300.
Giles, H., & Coupland, N. (1991). *Language: Contexts and consequences*. Milton Keynes: Open University Press.
Gnutzmann, C. (1999). English as a global language. Perspectives for English language teaching and for teacher education in Germany. In C. Gnutzmann (Ed.), *Teaching and learning English as a global language. Native and non-native perspectives* (pp. 157–169). Tübingen: Stauffenburg.
Gnutzmann, C., & Intemann, F. (Eds.). (2005). *The globalisation of English and the English language classroom*. Tübingen: Narr.
Görlach, M. (1999). Varieties of English and language teaching. In C. Gnutzmann (Ed.), *Teaching and learning English as a global language. Native and non-native perspectives* (pp. 3–21). Tübingen: Stauffenburg. Görlach, M. (2002). *Still more Englishes*. Amsterdam: John Benjamins.
Graddol, D. (1997). *The future of English?* London: British Council.
Graddol, D. (1999). The decline of the native speaker. *AILA Review, 13*, 57–68.
Graddol, D. (2001).The future of English as a European language. *The European English Messenger, 10*, 47–55.
Gramkow Andersen, K. (1993). *Lingua franca discourse: An investigation of the use of English in an international business context*. Unpublished MA thesis, Aalborg University, Denmark.
Granger, S. (Ed.). (1998). *Learner English on computer*. London: Longman.
Greenbaum, S. (Ed.). (1996). *Comparing English worldwide. The international corpus of English*. Oxford: Clarendon.
Gumperz, J., & Roberts, C. (1991). Understanding in intercultural encounters. In J. Blommaert & J. Verschueren (Eds.), *The Pragmatics of International and Intercultural Communication* (pp. 51–90). Amsterdam: Benjamins.
Haegeman, P. (2002). Foreigner talk in lingua franca business telephone calls. In K. Knapp & C. Meierkord (Eds.), *Lingua franca communication* (pp. 135–162). Frankfurt a.M.: Peter Lang.
Hartmann, R. R. K. (Ed.). (1996). *The English language in Europe*. Oxford: Intellect.
Hawkins, E. (1991). *Awareness of language: An introduction* (Rev. ed.). Cambridge: Cambridge University Press.

Hoffmann, C. (2000). The spread of English and the growth of multilingualism with English in Europe. In J. Cenoz & U. Jessner, (Eds.), *English in Europe. The acquisition of a third language* (pp. 1–21). Clevedon: Multilingual Matters.
Hollander, E. (2002). *Is ELF a Pidgin? A corpus-based study of the grammar of English as a lingua franca*. Unpublished MA thesis, University of Vienna.
Hollqvist, H. (1984). The use of English in three large Swedish companies. *Studia Anglistica Upsaliensia 55.*
House, J. (1999). Misunderstanding in intercultural communication: Interactions in English as a *lingua franca* and the myth of mutual intelligibility. In C. Gnutzmann, (Ed.), *Teaching and learning English as a global language* (pp. 73–89). Tübingen: Stauffenburg.
House, J. (2002). Pragmatic competence in lingua franca English. In K. Knapp & C. Meierkord (Eds.), *Lingua franca communication* (pp. 245–267). Frankfurt a.M.: Peter Lang.
House, J. (2003). English as a lingua franca: A threat to multilingualism? *Journal of Sociolinguistics, 7,* 556–578.
Hüllen, W. (1982). Teaching a foreign language as 'lingua franca'. *Grazer Linguistische Studien, 16,* 83–88.
James, A. (2000), English as a European lingua franca. Current realities and existing dichotomies. In J. Cenoz & U. Jessner (Eds.), *English in Europe. The acquisition of a third language* (pp. 22–38). Clevedon: Multilingual Matters.
James, C., & Garrett, P. (Eds.). (1991). *Language awareness in the classroom*. London: Longman.
Jenkins, J. (1998) Which pronunciation norms and models for English as an International Language? *ELT Journal, 52,* 119–126.
Jenkins, J. (2000). *The phonology of English as an international language. New models, new norms, new goals*. Oxford: Oxford University Press.
Jenkins, J. (2002). A sociolinguistically based, empirically researched pronunciation syllabus for English as an International Language. *Applied Linguistics, 23,* 83–103.
Jenkins, J., Modiano, M., & Seidlhofer, B. (2001). 'Euro-English'. *English Today, 17,* 13–19.
Kachru, B. (1985), Standards, codification and sociolinguistic realism: the English language in the outer circle. In R. Quirk & H. G. Widdowson (Eds.), *English in the world: Teaching and learning the languages and literatures* (pp. 11–30). Cambridge: Cambridge University Press.
Kachru, B. (Ed.). (1992). *The other tongue.* (2nd ed.). Urbana and Chicago: University of Illinois Press.
Kasper, G. (1998). A bilingual perspective on interlanguage pragmatics. In J. H. O'Mealy & L. E. Lyons (Eds.), *Language, linguistics and leadership* (pp. 89–108). Honolulu: University of Hawai'i Press.
Kasper, G., & Kellerman, E. (Eds.). (1997). *Communication strategies: Psycholinguistic and sociolinguistic perspectives*. London: Longman.
Knapp, K., & Knapp-Pothoff, A. (1990). Interkulturelle Kommunikation. *Zeitschrift für Fremdsprachenforschung, 1,* 62–93.
Kordon, K. (2003). *Phatic communion in English as a lingua franca*. Unpublished MA thesis, University of Vienna.
Lesznyák, A. (2002). From chaos to the smallest common denomiator. Topic management in English lingua franca communication. In K. Knapp & C. Meierkord (Eds.), *Lingua franca communication* (pp. 163–193). Frankfurt a.M.: Peter Lang.
Lesznyák, A. (2004). *Communication in English as an international lingua franca. An exploratory case study*. Norderstedt: Books on Demand.
van Lier, L. (1995). *Introducing language awareness*. Harmondsworth: Penguin.
Louhiala-Salminen, L. (2002). The fly's perspective: Discourse in the daily routine of a business manager. *English for Specific Purposes, 21,* 211–231.
Lüdi, G. (2002). Braucht Europa eine lingua franca?, *Basler Schriften zur europäischen Integration, 60,* 7–29.
Masats, D. (2003). *Language awareness: An international project*. Retrieved November 19, 2003 from http://jaling.ecml.at/english/welcome_page.htm.
Mauranen, A. (2003). Academic English as lingua franca—a corpus approach. *TESOL Quarterly, 37,* 513–527.
Meierkord, C. (1996). *Englisch als Medium der interkulturellen Kommunikation. Untersuchungen zum non-native-/non-native speaker—Diskurs*. Frankfurt a.M.: Peter Lang.
Meierkord, C. (2002). 'Language stripped bare' or 'linguistic masala'? Culture in lingua franca communication. In K. Knapp & C. Meierkord, (Eds.), *Lingua franca communication* (pp. 109–133). Frankfurt a.M.: Peter Lang.
Meierkord, C. (Ed.). (2006). Lingua franca communication—standardization versus self-regulation. [Special issue]. *International Journal of the Sociology of Language*.

Meierkord, C., &. Knapp, K. (2002). Approaching lingua franca communication. In K. Knapp & C. Meierkord, C. (Eds.), *Lingua franca communication* (pp. 9–28). Frankfurt a.M.: Peter Lang.

Meeuwis, M. (1994). Nonnative-nonnative intercultural communication: An analysis of instruction sessions for foreign engineers in a Belgian company. *Multilingua, 13*, 59–82.

Mollin, S. (2006). *Euro-English. Assessing variety status*. Tübingen: Narr.

Murray, H. (2003). Swiss English teachers and Euro-English: Attitudes to a non-native variety. In H. Murray (Ed.). *anglais, English, inglese, Englais...English! bulletin vals-asla, 77*, 147–165.

Pennycook, A. (1994). *The cultural politics of English as an international language*. London: Longman.

Penz, H. (2003). Successful intercultural communication. In B. Kettemann & G. Marko (Eds), *Expanding circles, transcending disciplines, and multimodal texts* (pp. 229–247). Tübingen: Narr.

Phillipson, R. (1992). *Linguistic imperialism*. Oxford: Oxford University Press.

Phillipson, R. (2003). *English-only Europe? Challenging language policy*. London: Routledge.

Phillipson, R., & Skutnabb-Kangas, T. (1999). Englishisation: One dimension of globalisation. *AILA Review, 13*,19–36.

Piepho, H.-E. (1989), Englisch als *lingua franca* in Europa. Ein Appell zur didaktischen Bescheidenheit an das Fach Englisch und seine Vertreter. In E. Kleinschmidt (Ed.), *Fremdsprachenunterricht zwischen Sprachenpolitik und Praxis* (pp. 41–49). Tübingen: Narr.

Pitzl, M.-L. (2005). Non-understanding in English as a lingua franca: Examples from a business context. *Vienna English Working PaperS, 14*(2), 50–71. http://www.univie.ac.at/Anglistik/Views0502mlp.pdf.

Pölzl, U. (2003). Signalling cultural identity: The use of L1/Ln in ELF. *Vienna English Working Papers, 12*, 3–23.

Pölzl, U., & Seidlhofer, B. (2006). In and on their own terms: The "habitat factor" in English as a lingua franca interactions. *International Journal of the Sociology of Language*.

Preisler, B. (1999). Functions and forms of English in an EFL country. In T. Bex & R. J. Watts (Eds.), *Standard English: The widening debate* (pp. 239–268). London: Routledge.

Prodromou, L. (2003). In search of the successful user of English. *Modern English Teacher, 12*, 5–14.

Samarin, W. (1987). Lingua franca. In U. Ammon, N. Dittmar, & K. Mattheier (Eds.), *Sociolinguistics. An international handbook of the science of language and society* (pp. 371–374). Berlin & New York: Walter de Gruyter.

Seidlhofer, B. (2001a). Closing a conceptual gap: The case for a description of English as a lingua franca. *International Journal of Applied Linguistics, 11*, 133–158.

Seidlhofer, B. (2001b). The case for a corpus of English as a lingua franca. In G. Aston & L. Burnard (Eds.), *The roles of corpora of contemporary English in language description and language pedagogy* (pp. 70–85). Bologna: CLUEB.

Seidlhofer, B. (2002). *Habeas corpus* and *divide et impera*: 'Global English' and applied linguistics. In K. Spelman Miller & P. Thompson (Eds.), *Unity and diversity in language use* (pp. 198–217). London: Continuum.

Seidlhofer, B. (2003). *A concept of 'international English' and related issues: From 'real English' to 'realistic English'? Autour du concept d' "anglais international": de l' "anglais authentique" à l' "anglais réaliste"?* Strasbourg: Council of Europe.

Seidlhofer, B. (2004), Research perspectives on teaching English as a lingua franca. *Annual Review of Applied Linguistics, 24*, 209–239. Cambridge: Cambridge University Press.

Seidlhofer, B., & Jenkins, J. (2003). English as a lingua franca and the politics of property. In C. Mair, (Ed.), *The politics of English as a world language. New horizons in postcolonial cultural studies* (pp. 139–154). Amsterdam—New York: Rodopi.

Smith, L. E. (Ed.). (1983). *Readings in English as an international language*. Oxford: Pergamon.

Smith, L. E. (1984). Teaching English as an international language. *Studium Linguistik, 15*, 52–59.

Sridhar, K., & Sridhar, S. N. (1986). Bridging the paradigm gap: Second language acquisition theory and indigenised varieties of English. *World Englishes, 5*, 3–14.

Vollmer, H. (2001). Englisch und Mehrsprachigkeit: Interkulturelles Lernen durch Englisch als *lingua franca*? In D. Abendroth-Timmer & G. Bach, (Eds.), *Mehrsprachiges Europa* (pp. 91–109). Tübingen: Narr.

Wagner, J., & Firth, A. (1997). Communication strategies at work. In G. Kasper & E. Kellerman (Eds.), *Communication strategies: Psycholinguistic and sociolinguistic perspectives* (pp. 323–344). London: Longman.

Watts, R., & Murray, H. (Eds.). (2001). *Die fünfte Landessprache? Englisch in der Schweiz*. Akademische Kommission der Universität Bern.

Widdowson, H. G. (1980). Models and fictions. *Applied Linguistics, 1*, 165–170.

Widdowson, H. G. (1994). The ownership of English. *TESOL Quarterly, 28*, 377–389.

Widdowson, H. G. (1997a). EIL, ESL, EFL: Global issues and local interests. *World Englishes*, *16*, 135–146.
Widdowson, H. G. (1997b). The pedagogic relevance of language awareness. *Fremdsprachen Lehren und Lernen*, *26*, 33–43.
Widdowson, H. G. (2000). On the limitations of linguistics applied. *Applied Linguistics, 21*, 3–25.
Widdowson, H. G. (2003). *Defining issues in English language teaching.* Oxford: Oxford University Press.
Wright, S. (2003). *Language policy and language planning. From nationalism to globalization.* London & New York: Palgrave.

CHAPTER 11

TEACHING ENGLISH AS A THIRD LANGUAGE

ULRIKE JESSNER

The University of Innsbruck, Austria

JASONE CENOZ

The University of the Basque Country, Spain

ABSTRACT

In many countries in the world, English is identified as a foreign language with no official status but is increasingly used as the language of wider communication. In a number of these countries it is common that English is learned as a third language. Recent psycholinguistic research on third language acquisition and trilingualism has made clear that the acquisition of an L3 shares many characteristics with the acquisition of an L2 but it also presents differences. Accordingly, the educational aspects of teaching English as an L3 differ from those of teaching English as an L2 and have more implications concerning the optimal age for the introduction of the different languages and the desired level of proficiency in each. In the Basque Country there are two official languages, Basque and Spanish, and English is taught as a third language. Several projects have been carried out in order to improve proficiency in English: the early introduction of English in kindergarten, the use of content based approaches, and the use of English as one of the languages of instruction. This chapter describes the characteristics of these projects and discusses their outcomes as they relate to specific research conducted on third language acquisition.

INTRODUCTION

Whereas teaching English as a second language has become a very common part of language education in many countries, as the chapters in this handbook clearly show, teaching *English as a third language (henceforth ELT; in contrast to teaching English as a second language or ESL)* presents a rather young, albeit growing area of interest that shares many characteristics with the former but also shows important differences that will be highlighted in this chapter. These differences are linked to the differences between second and *third language acquisition* (TLA) and the changing nature of English in the world, in particular on the European Continent. In the Basque Country several projects on English as a third language (henceforth E3) have been carried out and this chapter describes the characteristics of these projects and discusses their outcomes in relation to research conducted on TLA.

An important issue in studies of TLA is related to terminology. When we use L1 and L2 to describe the relationship of the two languages involved in a bilingual system, L1 is usually interpreted not just as the first language learnt but also as the dominant language. It is implicitly assumed that the level of proficiency in L2 must necessarily be lower than in L1. When acquiring a third language the chronological order of languages learned does not necessarily correspond to the frequency of use of these languages or the levels of competence in the languages used by the trilingual speaker. For example, language proficiency in the individual languages usually changes over time and in addition, skills within the languages can vary from one time to another according to sociolinguistic contexts (Hufeisen, 1998, 169-70). For the future, it is has to be noted that we need to readdress this issue to find a terminological basis for discussions of multilingualism. However, in this chapter, E3 corresponds to chronological ordering because English is the third language that a speaker comes in contact with in her/his biography.

THE SPREAD OF E3

In many countries in the world, English is identified as a foreign language with no official status. However, English is increasingly used as the language of wider communication as a result of the British colonial legacy and the emergence of the United States as a major power in the 20th century. In multilingual countries that already have two or more national languages, English is increasingly being learned as a third language

According to Kachru (1985; 1992), the spread of English can be visualized in terms of three circles. The *inner circle* includes those countries where English is the L1 for the majority of the population such as UK, USA, Ireland, Canada, Australia, and New Zealand. However, in these countries, English is in contact with heritage languages or languages of the immigrant population and is thus not the only language spoken. The *outer circle* includes those countries where English is used as a second language at the institutional level as the result of colonization (India, Nigeria, Philippines, etc). The *expanding circle* includes those countries where English has no official status and is taught as a foreign language (Continental Europe, Japan, China, South America, etc).

The contact between English and other languages in the three circles and the spread of English in the outer and expanding circles carries important sociolinguistic and psycholinguistic implications. Sociolinguistically, the spread of English has important implications regarding the ownership of English and the varieties of English. For example, the spread of English as a lingua franca threatens the traditional ownership of English as a property of native speakers (Berns, 1995; Widdowson, 1997). At the same time, new non-native varieties of English, such as Nigerian English, have been developed as the result of the contact between English and other languages in different parts of the world. At a psycholinguistic level, English is acquired by many individuals not only as a second language but also as a third or fourth language, and in many cases English is one of the languages in the multilingual's linguistic repertoire. This is very often the case in Continental Europe, where the spread of the English language certainly shares some characteristics with the spread of English in other parts of the world. Most European countries are located in the expanding circle where English is a foreign language with no official status but it is increasingly used as a language of wider communication.

It is important to emphasize that the spread of English in Europe cannot be considered a uniform phenomenon. While English has a long tradition in most Northern European countries, its importance is growing steadily in Southern and Eastern European countries where other languages have been traditionally learned as foreign languages. Within the European Union, English is becoming a second rather than a foreign language as a result of the fact that it is the main language of communication among European citizens. The influence of American English and the increasing use of English among non-native speakers appear to be challenging the ascendancy of British English as the only model in the European context and a European non-native variety of English called *Euro-English* seems to be emerging (Crystal, 1995; Modiano, 1996). This variety shares characteristics of British and American English but presents some differences when compared to native varieties.

In the European context, English is in contact with other languages because most European countries are bilingual or multilingual. English is a second language for a large number of Europeans but it is also learned as a third language in a number of typical situations in the European context:

1. Native speakers of minority indigenous languages who are also proficient in the majority language and study E3. This is the case of native speakers of languages such as Basque, Breton, Sardinian, Catalan, Frisian, and Sami.
2. Native speakers of a majority language who learn a minority indigenous language at school and study E3. This is the case of native speakers of Spanish who learn Catalan or Basque at school, or native speakers of Dutch who learn Frisian at school and also study English as a foreign language.
3. Native speakers of less widespread European languages who acquire a second and a third language. For example, native speakers of Dutch in Belgium who learn French as a second language and E3 or native speakers of Swedish in Wasa who learn Finnish and English.
4. Native speakers of widespread European languages whose first language is a minority language at the national level and also learn E3. For example, speakers of German in Italy, France, or Belgium.
5. Immigrants from non-European countries who learn the official language of the new country and study E3. For example, Turkish immigrants in Germany or the Netherlands.
6. Other Europeans who learn E3, for example, an Italian who learns French and English or German and English.

However, as already mentioned, the acquisition of E3 is also common in other parts of the world. For example, English is a third language for many school children who are speakers of heritage languages (Guarani, Quechua, Mohawk, etc.) and live in Central America, South America or French speaking Canada. English is also a third language for many African speakers living in countries where French is widely used as a second language (Mozambique, Mauritius) and also for those children who live in African countries where English is widely used at the institutional level (Kenya, Nigeria, etc) but who already speak two languages before they enter school. English is also an L3 for many speakers in other parts of the world such as the Asia-Pacific region where a large number of languages are spoken but English is needed for wider communication. And English is the third language for a large number of immigrants who have established themselves in countries where English is learned as a second language (French speaking regions of Canada, Israel, Japan, etc.) and also for immigrants who already spoke two languages before they established themselves in English speaking countries that are part of the inner circle (US, Australia, New Zealand, etc).

Characteristics of E3

At first sight E3 might be seen simply as a variant of English as a foreign language (EFL) but actually it seems to develop differing characteristics from EFL as English is increasingly used as a lingua franca in many contexts on a more or less daily basis. Seidlhofer (1999, p. 54) describes it as "spreading, developing independently, with a great deal of variation but enough stability to be viable for lingua franca communication." This also means that it loses its "foreignness" (McArthur, 1996, p. 10) and that it develops features of a different kind, for example on the phonological level as discussed by Jenkins (2000). Drawing on the trilingual context in the Alpine-Adriatic region of Carinthia-Friuli-Slovenia where English is used as a lingua franca, James (2000) suggests that the variety of English used shows characteristics of a register rather than a dialect. Thus investigations into the linguistic nature of EFL certainly offer new perspectives for future research (see also Gnutzmann, 1999; Gnutzmann/Intemann, 2005). But it should be kept in mind that this kind of study should ideally be backed up by research on third language acquisition (Cenoz & Jessner, 2000b, p. 257) and considered in relation to a theory of multiple language acquisition that is not based on a monolingual norm.

THE STUDY OF THIRD LANGUAGE ACQUISITION

As already mentioned in the introduction, the acquisition of English as L3 shares many characteristics with the acquisition of English as L2 but it also presents differences. TLA is a more complex phenomenon than second language acquisition (SLA) because, apart from all the individual and social factors that affect SLA, the process and product of acquiring a second language can potentially influence TLA. In particular, learners of a third language have prior language learning knowledge and in this respect develop metalinguistic skills and metacognitive strategies that a monolingual learner lacks.

The study of third languages and trilingualism represents a recent focus within linguistics but one that has been gaining interest in recent years (see Cenoz & Genesee, 1998; Cenoz & Jessner, 2000a; Clyne, 1997; Hufeisen & Lindemann, 1998). Although the number of studies on third or multiple language acquisition is still limited, this research area has already established itself as a distinct field where the main focus is on the differences and similarities between TLA and SLA. In second language acquisition, the two linguistic systems can influence each other in a bidirectional way. However, the contact between three language systems in a multilingual speaker is more complex. In addition to the bidirectional relationship between L1 and L2, L3 can influence L1 and vice versa, and L2 and L3 can influence each other. Thus within studies of TLA and trilingualism, the crosslinguistic aspects of TLA and trilingualism represent an important focus (e.g. Cenoz, Hufeisen, & Jessner, 2001a, b, 2003; Clyne, 1997). Williams and Hammarberg (1998) present several criteria that they consider influential in the relationship between the languages in L3 production and acquisition: typological similarity, cultural similarity, proficiency, recency of use, and the status of L2. The role of L2 in TLA has turned out to be of greater importance than originally suggested (Cenoz, Hufeisen, & Jessner, 2001b).

Child trilingualism forms another important focus of recent research on TLA (Arnberg, 1987; Barron-Hauwaert, 2000; Hoffmann, 1985; Hoffmann &

Widdicombe, 1998; Quay, 2001; Barnes, 2006). Another developing field is trilingual education in primary school (Cenoz & Lindsay, 1994; Ytsma, 2001). The question of whether bilingual speakers experience advantages in acquiring additional languages has emerged as a central aspect of the research conducted in this context (Cenoz, 2003 for a review). One of the pioneers of research on TLA, Ringbom (1987), describes the advantages of Swedish speaking Finns over monolingual Finnish students when acquiring English in Finland. He relates the results to language typology and the prior language learning experience of the trilingual group.

Suggestions of a Multilingual Norm

Recent theorizing regarding the trilingual speaker has clearly been influenced by Grosjean's and Cook's ideas on the bilingual speaker. Based on his criticism of the widespread use of a monolingual norm in language proficiency measures commonly employed in language contact studies, Grosjean (1985) characterized the bilingual speaker as a competent speaker-hearer with a specific linguistic configuration. Cook (1993, pp. 3-4) proposed the construct of *multicompetence* on the basis of Grosjean's work. He argued that in contrast to monolinguals, bilinguals and multilinguals have a different knowledge of both their first language and their second language as well as a different kind of language awareness and language processing system. Cook (1999) also drew on the construct of multicompetence to critique the use of the native speaker as the norm in language teaching.

Herdina and Jessner (2002) adopted Grosjean's and Cook's critique of *double monolingualism* but also emphasized the dynamics of multilingual proficiency. They argued that the stages of development in a multilingual system have to be taken into account in multilingualism research. Their research is based on dynamic systems theory which is necessarily linked to a holistic approach and thus stresses emergent properties in multilingual systems. They emphasize in their dynamic model of multilingualism that the conditions of language learning undergo a change of quality in the multilingual speaker that is related to the development of an enhanced multilingual monitor. Whereas a second language learner's prior experience of learning a language can be related only to a monolingual norm, a third language learner can relate to a bilingual norm (Herdina & Jessner, 2000, p. 94).

The topic of interdependence between the language systems in a bilingual speaker has not only presented an issue in psycholinguistic research where we have an ongoing debate concerning the question of interdependence or independence between the languages in the brain (see Singleton, 2000), but the *interdependence hypothesis* as formulated by Cummins (1979, 1981) has exerted enormous influence in the field of applied linguistics, in particular in bilingual teaching. Cummins points out that a bilingual speaker develops a common underlying proficiency that represents a kind of linguistic reservoir enabling transfer of concepts and strategies across languages and results in potentially enhanced metalinguistic abilities. A number of studies have not only reported a bilingual superiority on measures derived from various cognitive skills but in some cases, positive crosslinguistic relationships, i.e. also from L2 to L1, have been found for pragmatic or conversationally-oriented language abilities as reported by Cummins (2000) in addition to literacy-related abilities as suggested by Kecskes and Papp (2000). Many studies have strongly indicated that bilinguals show definite advantages on measures of metalinguistic awareness, cognitive flexibility, and creativity (see Baker, 2006, p. 143-165) and therefore differ in thinking styles from their monolingual counterparts. Additional insight into the relationship between metalinguistic behavior and bilingualism can also be gained from research on the translation skills of bilinguals (Malakoff, 1992).

In short, the dynamic concept of "multilingual proficiency" proposed by Herdina and Jessner (2002) clearly distinguishes the cognitive and linguistic systems of multilingual speakers from those of monolingual speakers. Multilingual proficiency is conceptualized as composed of the individual language systems, the crosslinguistic interaction between the language systems, and other components such as an enhanced multilingual monitor that are developed as a result of the interdependence between the systems involved in the language learning process (Jessner, 2006).

EDUCATIONAL ASPECTS

Learning a third language in the school context is a common experience for many children all over the world. In European countries there are specific multilingual schools, such as the European schools, in which several languages are used as languages of instruction (Baetens Beardsmore, 1993; Baker & Prys Jones, 1998; Hoffmann, 1998). Similarly, in Canada, double immersion programs involving three languages of instruction have been implemented (Genesee, 1998). However, it is much more common around the world to study two or more foreign languages as school subjects. In Europe, with the exception of the United Kingdom and Ireland, English is generally the first foreign language and German and French tend to be the most popular second foreign languages (Ammon, 1996). Third and fourth language acquisition is also common in bilingual and multilingual communities all over the world. For example, learning E3 is common in the bilingual communities of Catalonia, the Basque Country, Friesland, Brittany, and Wasa and languages such as German and French are commonly learned as third languages in Ireland, Wales, and Scotland.

Outside Europe, English or French are learned as third languages by many immigrant and some aboriginal communities in Canada or in many areas of South America where speakers of Quechua, Aymara, Guarani, and many other languages also learn Spanish and English at school (Baker & Prys Jones, 1998; Hornberger & Lopez, 1998). TLA and the acquisition of additional languages is also common in multilingual communities in Africa and Asia where children speak one or more languages at home and in the community and use a different language as the language of instruction at school (Dutcher, 1998; Rubagumya, 1994; Tickoo, 1996). An increasingly common situation in countries where immigration has increased in recent years (e.g. Europe, the United States, Canada, Australia) is that children's home language is different from the major societal language(s), and children learn both the societal language and additional languages at school (Broeder & Extra, 1999).

In sum, TLA in the school context and trilingual education are not new phenomena but are becoming more widespread because of the increasing use of minority languages in education in many parts of the world and the trend to teach additional languages both at the elementary and secondary levels of education. In the following section we describe in more detail different aspects of the acquisition of E3 in a bilingual community, the Basque Country.

TEACHING ENGLISH AS A THIRD LANGUAGE IN THE BASQUE COUNTRY

The Basque Country covers an area of approximately 20,742 square kilometers bordering the Pyrenees and the Bay of Biscay, between France and Spain. The total Basque population is approximately 3 million with 92% being Spanish citizens. In this section we focus on the acquisition of E3 in the Basque Autonomous Community (BAC) in Spain where 73% of the Basque population live. Basque (Euskara) is a unique non Indo-European language in Western Europe and, as such, is typologically distant from Spanish.

Although Basque and Spanish are both official languages of the BAC, Basque is really a minority language spoken by approximately 27% of the population. Political repression during the Franco regime (1939-1975) contributed to the demographic weakness of Basque, but the political and social changes that have taken place during the last decades of the 20th century in Spain have favored attempts to maintain and revive the Basque language. Currently, Basque has a co-official status in the BAC. At the same time, Spanish continues to be the dominant language in most regions of the Basque Country, and virtually all Basque-speakers also speak Spanish and therefore are bilingual. At present, almost 40% of children between 5 and 14 years of age living in the BAC are bilingual. Although these data represent a relative improvement for the Basque language, it continues to be threatened since Spanish remains the dominant language in most regions of the country while the use of Basque in everyday life is limited to areas of the BAC that are dominated by Basque speakers.

BILINGUAL EDUCATION

Even though Basque was banned from education during the Franco regime, a number of Basque-medium schools (or *ikastolak*) were opened in the 1960s. These schools were not officially recognized in the beginning, but as the number of students increased they had to be eventually accepted. In 1979, with the new political situation, Basque, along with Spanish, was recognized as an official language in the BAC. The law on the Normalization of the Basque Language (1982) made Basque and Spanish compulsory subjects in all schools in the BAC and there are different bilingual programs that differ with respect to the language or languages of instruction, their linguistic aims, and their intended student population.

In recent years, an increasing number of students have enrolled in programs that use Basque as an instructional medium and currently most schoolchildren have Basque as the language of instruction for some or all subjects both in elementary and secondary school. When the bilingual models were established, approximately 25% of the students in the BAC attended Basque-medium schools; at present, approximately 80% of elementary schoolchildren, and approximately 60% of secondary schoolchildren have Basque as a language of instruction.

Several evaluations of the Basque bilingual programs have been carried out and more than 25,000 students have taken part in these evaluations. The evaluations have focused on both overall academic development and proficiency in Basque and Spanish (Etxeberria, 1999). The results indicate that instruction through Basque (the minority language) is strongly related to higher levels of achievement in this language while proficiency in Spanish tends to be unrelated to the language of instruction. It seems likely that since Spanish is the majority language, opportunities for extensive exposure to it outside school compensate for reduced exposure in school. Most studies have also found that there are no group differences in overall academic development.

THE TEACHING OF E3

Apart from the two official languages, English is studied as a foreign language by over 95% of schoolchildren. The status of English in the Basque Country is different from the status of Basque because English is regarded as a foreign language and is not used at the community level.

Traditionally, students in the BAC have achieved relatively low levels of proficiency in English at school but the increasing role of English in Europe (and in the world in general) has increased interest in learning English. This interest is reflected in demands for more English instruction and better quality English instruction in schools. In response to these demands, considerable effort has been expended in recent years by public and private institutions to reinforce and improve the teaching of English within the context of bilingual education. For example, the Department of Education of the Basque Government has subsidized intensive language learning and instructional methods courses for English teachers and has encouraged the adoption of new instructional approaches, especially those that emphasize the acquisition of oral skills, the use of learner-centered syllabi, and the integration of curricula for the three languages (Cenoz & Lindsay, 1994).

The Spanish educational Reform (that has been adapted to the Basque educational system) also pays specific attention to the role of foreign languages in the curriculum. In accordance with the Reform, foreign languages are introduced in the third year of primary school at the age of 8 (3 years earlier than previously). The Reform also promotes important changes at the methodological level including a focus on communicative competence, positive attitudes, and metalinguistic awareness as desired goals for foreign language teaching.

THE EFFECT OF BILINGUALISM ON E3

Research findings on the acquisition of E3 in the BAC indicate that higher levels of bilingualism are positively related with higher levels of proficiency in English (Cenoz & Valencia, 1994; Lasagabaster, 1997; Sagasta, 2001). The first of these studies (Cenoz & Valencia) analyzed the level of proficiency in English of 321 students in the last year of secondary school. The results indicated that bilingual students outperformed monolingual students once the effect of other variables (intelligence, motivation, or exposure to English) had been controlled. Lasagabaster compared proficiency in English in different programs in primary school and confirmed that proficiency in English was influenced by the degree of bilingualism in Basque and Spanish. Sagasta examined writing skills in English as related to the degree of bilingualism in Basque and Spanish and found that a higher level of bilingualism is associated with higher scores in general writing proficiency and specific areas such as syntactic complexity, lexical complexity, fluency, or error production.

These results are compatible with the folk wisdom belief that the more languages you know the easier it is to learn an additional language. They are also compatible with the threshold and interdependence hypotheses proposed by Cummins (1976, 1981) and also with research reporting higher levels of metalinguistic awareness associated with bilingualism and more highly developed learning strategies associated with L3 acquisition (Cenoz & Genesee, 1998; Jessner, 1999; Missler, 1999).

The Early Introduction of English

Traditionally, English was not taught until grade 6 (11-12 year olds), but the Spanish Educational Reform instituted in 1993 made a foreign language compulsory in grade 3 (8-9 year olds). The early introduction of English in the 2nd year of kindergarten (4-5 year olds) was initiated on an experimental basis in several Basque medium schools, or ikastola, in 1991. English is taught in kindergarten for 2 hours a week in four 30 minute sessions. The teacher of English only uses English in the classroom and all the activities are oral. The method is based on story-telling and requires the children's active participation by means of collective dramatization and playing. Enthusiasm for these experimental schools has spawned similar initiatives in many other ikastolak (Basque speaking schools) and also in a large number of public schools.

Research studies indicate that children have very positive attitudes toward early instruction in English in kindergarten and primary schools and that learning English from age 4 has no negative effects on the acquisition of Basque or Spanish or on overall cognitive development (Cenoz, 1997; Cenoz & Lindsay, 1994). Nevertheless, the results of research studies comparing different areas of English language achievement by different age groups who have received the same number of hours of instruction indicate that older learners obtain significantly higher results than younger learners (Cenoz, 2003; García Lecumberri & Gallardo, 2003; García Mayo, 2003; Lasagabaster & Doiz, 2003). These findings could be due to several reasons. Cognitive maturity can explain the higher linguistic development of the older group and their more highly developed test-taking strategies, but the differences could also be related to the type of input. An alternative interpretation is that younger learners do not present advantages because they are still in the first stages of third language acquisition. It could be that third language learners need to acquire a higher degree of cognitive academic language proficiency (Cummins, 2000) in the two languages they already know in order to benefit from the positive effects of bilingualism on third language acquisition.

On the other hand, younger learners show significantly better attitudes towards learning English than older learners (Cenoz, 2002). These differences could be linked to psychological and educational factors. Psychological factors associated with age could explain a rejection of the school system on the part of older learners and educational factors include the use of more traditional and less active methods with older learners.

English as an Additional Language of Instruction

So far we have referred to bilingual schools in which two languages (Basque and Spanish) are used as media of instruction and English as a subject. However, some schools have gone one step further and are using Basque and English or Basque, Spanish, and English as media of instruction. For example, Lauro Ikastola is a

Basque-medium school in which Spanish is introduced as a subject in the 1st year of primary school. English is introduced as a subject in the 2nd year of primary school but becomes the language of instruction of three subjects in secondary school: science, history of religion, and computer science.

These projects entail some organizational problems. Teachers need to have a high level of proficiency both in English and in the subject matter. It is not always clear whether it is better for the subject teacher or the language teacher to teach a subject in English or whether content teachers have to be trained in English or teachers of English trained in specific subjects. Moreover, students have to achieve the same level of knowledge in subjects taught in English as students who receive this instruction in Basque or Spanish. The school also has to make important decisions regarding the specific subjects to be taught in English. Finally, the use of English as the language of instruction implies the development of specific materials in accordance with the curriculum. These difficulties explain why experiments of this type are not as common as the early introduction of English in kindergarten, and why the most important projects have taken place in private schools. In spite of these difficulties, the use of English as an additional language of instruction provides the opportunity to increase the extremely limited time typically devoted to English. This approach is also being used as a follow-up to the early introduction of English when children who started learning English in kindergarten go to secondary school.

FINAL REMARKS

TLA in the school context shares many characteristics with SLA but also builds on SLA and is influenced by the degree of bilingualism already attained by the individual. SLA in the school context usually refers to the teaching of L2 as a subject while bilingual education usually refers to the use of two languages as languages of instruction. Nevertheless, this distinction cannot be taken as a dichotomy but rather as a continuum because there are approaches such as content based teaching that use the L2 as the medium of instruction for different types of content but very frequently within the L2 subject classes (Met, 1998). The great variety of models of bilingual education and particularly the so called "weak forms" of bilingual education bring SLA and bilingual education together (see Baker, 2001).

The distinction between TLA and trilingual education is also blurred. Basically, as we have seen in the Basque example, TLA in the school context refers to learning L3 as a subject and trilingual education refers to the use of three languages as languages of instruction. Nevertheless, the boundaries between these two poles of a continuum are necessarily soft and there are different possibilities according to the methodological approach used for the different languages, the educational aims for the different languages, and their relative weight in the curriculum. For example, a double immersion program for speakers of the majority language can use two languages as languages of instruction and the students' mother tongue as a subject rather than three languages of instruction, and can still be regarded as a trilingual program.

In spite of being a common phenomenon, TLA and trilingualism at school have received relatively little research attention in comparison to the extensive literature on bilingual education and SLA in the school context. The results of research studies on SLA and bilingualism and their educational implications are certainly relevant for the study of both TLA and trilingual education. However, in order to follow up on the studies reported in this chapter, it is necessary to conduct additional research to answer some basic questions such as the following: What is the influence of bilingualism on TLA? Do children mix languages when they learn more than one foreign language? How does the status of the L1 affect the acquisition of additional languages? What is the most desirable pedagogical approach when several languages are taught at school? What specific strategies do learners use in L3 acquisition? What is the optimal age to introduce different languages in the curriculum? What attitudes do children develop in relation to the different languages? Are there specific aspects of English that should be emphasized in order to teach E3? Which norms should be used in ETL if not native speaker norms? As ETL is increasingly acknowledged as a common phenomenon in the world, research will undoubtedly contribute answers to these questions.

REFERENCES

Ammon, U. (1996). The European Union: Status change of English during the last fifty years. In J. A. Fishman, A. W. Conrad & A. Rubal-Lopez (Eds.), *Post-Imperial English* (pp. 241–267). Berlin: Mouton de Gruyter.

Arnberg, L. (1987). *Raising children bilingually: The pre-school years*. Clevedon: Multilingual Matters.

Baetens Beardsmore, H. (Ed.). (1993). *European models of bilingual education*. Clevedon: Multilingual Matters.

Baker, C. (2006). *Foundations of bilingual education and bilingualism*. Clevedon: Multilingual Matters.

Baker, C., & Prys Jones, S. P. (1998). *Encyclopedia of Bilingualism and Bilingual Education*. Clevedon: Multilingual Matters.

Barnes, J. (2006). *Early Trilingualism*. Clevedon. Multilingual Matters.

Barron-Hauwaert, S. (2000). Issues surrounding trilingual families: Children with simultaneous exposure to three languages. In J. Cenoz, B. Hufeisen, & U. Jessner (Eds.), Trilingualism—Tertiary Languages—German in a multilingual world [Special issue]. *Journal of Intercultural Learning, 5*, 1 (electronic journal). http://epe.lac-bac.gc.ca/100/201/300/zeitschrift/2002/02-05/barron.htm.

Berns, M. (1995). English in Europe: Whose language, which culture? *International Journal of Applied Linguistics, 5*, 193–204.

Broeder, P., & Extra, G. (Eds.) (1999). *Language ethnicity and education*. Clevedon: Multilingual Matters.

Cenoz, J. (1997), L'acquisition de la troisième langue: bilinguisme et plurilinguisme au Pays Basque. (The acquisition of the third language: Bilingualism and multilingualism in the Basque Country). *Acquisition et Interaction en Langue Etrangère, 10*, 159–180.

Cenoz, J. (2002). Three languages in contact: Language attitudes in the Basque Country. In D. Lasagabaster & J. Sierra (Eds.), *Language Awareness in the Foreign Language Classroom*. Bilbao: University of the Basque Country.

Cenoz, J. (2003). The influence of age on the acquisition of English: General proficiency, attitudes and code mixing. In M. P. García Mayo & M. L. García Lecumberri (Eds.), *Age and the acquisition of English as a foreign language: Theoretical issues and field work* (pp. 77–93). Clevedon: Multilingual Matters.

Cenoz, J. (2003). The additive effect of bilingualism on third language acquisition: A review. *The International Journal of Bilingualism 7*, 71–88.

Cenoz, J., & Genesee, F. (1998). Psycholinguistic perspectives on multilingualism and multilingual education. In J. Cenoz & F. Genesee (Eds.), *Beyond bilingualism: Multilingualism and multilingual education* (pp. 16–32). Clevedon: Multilingual Matters.

Cenoz, J., Hufeisen, B., & Jessner, U. (Eds.). (2001a). *Beyond second language acquisition: Studies in tri- and multilingualism*. Tübingen: Stauffenburg.

Cenoz, J., Hufeisen, B., & Jessner, U. (Eds.). (2001b). *Cross-linguistic influence in third language acquisition: Psycholinguistic perspectives*. Clevedon: Multilingual Matters.

Cenoz, J., Hufeisen, B. & Jessner, U. (eds.) (2003). *The Multilingual Lexicon*. Dordrecht: Kluwer Academic.

Cenoz, J., & Jessner, U. (2000a). *English in Europe: The acquisiton of a third language*. Clevedon: Multilingual Matters.

Cenoz, J., & Jessner, U. (2000b). Expanding the scope: Sociolinguistic, psycholinguistic and educational aspects of learning English as a third language in Europe. In J. Cenoz & U. Jessner (Eds.), *English in Europe: The acquisiton of a third language* (pp. 248–260). Clevedon: Multilingual Matters.

Cenoz, J., & Lindsay, D. (1994). Teaching English in primary school: A project to introduce a third language to eight year olds in the Basque Country. *Language and Education, 8*, 201–210.

Cenoz, J., & Valencia, J. (1994). Additive trilingualism: Evidence from the Basque Country. *Applied Psycholinguistics, 15*, 157–209.

Clyne, M. (1997). Some of the things trilinguals do. *The International Journal of Bilingualism,* 1, 95–116.

Cook, V. (1993). Wholistic multi-competence: Jeu d'esprit or paradigm shift? In B. Kettemann & W. Wieden (Eds.), *Current issues in European second language acquisition research* (pp. 3–9). Tübingen: Narr.

Cook, V. (1999). Going beyond the native speaker in language teaching. *TESOL Quarterly,* 33, 185–209.

Crystal, D. (1995). *The Cambridge Encyclopedia of the English Language.* Cambridge: Cambridge University Press.

Cummins, J. (1976). The influence of bilingualism on cognitive growth: A synthesis of research findings and explanatory hypotheses. *Working Papers on Bilingualism*, No. 9, 1–43.

Cummins, J. (1979). Linguistic interdependence and the educational development of bilingual children. *Review of Educational Research, 49*, 222–251.

Cummins, J. (1981). The role of primary language development in promoting educational success for language minority students (pp. 3–49). *Schooling and language minority students: A theoretical framework.* Los Angeles: National Dissemination and Assessment Center.

Cummins, J. (2000). Putting language proficiency in its place: Responding to critiques of the conversational/academic language distinction. In J. Cenoz & U. Jessner (Eds.) *English in Europe: The acquisition of a third language* (pp. 54–83). Clevedon: Multilingual Matters.

Dutcher, N. (1998). Eritrea: Developing a programme of multilingual education. In J. Cenoz & F. Genesee (Eds.), *Beyond bilingualism: Multilingualism and multilingual education* (pp. 54–83). Clevedon: Multilingual Matters.

Etxeberria, F. (1999). *Bilingüismo y Educación en el País del Euskara* (*Bilingualism and education in the Country of the Basque Language*). Donostia: Erein.

García Lecumberri, M. L., & Gallardo, F. (2003). English FL pronunciation in school students of different ages. In P. Garcia Mayo & M. L. García Lecumberri (Eds.), *Age and the acquisition of English as a foreign language: Theoretical issues and field work* (pp. 115–135). Clevedon: Multilingual Matters.

García Mayo, M. P. (2003). Age, length of exposure and grammaticality judgments in the acquisition of English as a foreign language. In M. P. García Mayo & M. L. García Lecumberri (Eds.), *Age and the acquisition of English as a foreign language: Theoretical issues and fieldwork* (pp. 94–114). Clevedon: Multilingual Matters.

Genesee, F. (1998). A case study of multilingual education in Canada. In J. Cenoz & F. Genesee (Eds.), *Beyond bilingualism: Multilingualism and multilingual education* (pp. 243–258). Clevedon: Multilingual Matters.

Gnutzmann, C. (Ed.). (1999). *Teaching and learning English as a global language*: Native and non-native perspectives. Tübingen: Stauffenburg.

Gnutzmann, C. & Intemann, F. (eds.) (2005). *The Globalisation of English and the English Language Classroom.* Tuebingen: Gunter Narr.

Grosjean, F. (1985). The bilingual as a competent but specific speaker-hearer. *Journal of Multilingual and Multicultural Development, 6*, 467–477.

Herdina, P., & Jessner, U. (2000). Multilingualism as an ecological system. The case for language maintenance. In B. Kettemann & H. Penz (Eds.), *ECOnstructing language, nature and society. The Ecolinguistic Project revisited* (pp. 131–144). Tübingen: Stauffenburg.

Herdina, P., & Jessner, U. (2002). *A dynamic model of multilingualism: Perspectives of change in psycholinguistics.* Clevedon: Multilingual Matters.

Hoffmann, C. (1985). Language acquisition in two trilingual children. *Journal of Multilingual and Multicultural Development, 6*, 479–495.

Hoffmann, C. (1998). Luxembourg and the European Schools. In J. Cenoz & F. Genesee (Eds.) *Beyond bilingualism: Multilingualism and multilingual education* (pp. 143–174). Clevedon: Multilingual Matters.

Hoffmann, C., & Widdicombe, S. (1998). The language behaviour of trilingual children: Developmental aspects. *Acquisition et Interaction en Langue Etrangère, 1*, 51–62.

Hornberger, N., & Lopez, L. E. (1998). Policy, possibility and paradox: Indigenous multilingualism and education in Peru and Bolivia. In J. Cenoz & F. Genesee (Eds.), *Beyond bilingualism: Multilingualism and multilingual education* (pp. 206–242) Clevedon: Multilingual Matters.

Hufeisen, B. (1998). L3—Stand der Forschung—Was bleibt zu tun? In B. Hufeisen & B. Lindemann (Eds.) *Tertiärsprachen. Theorien, Modelle, Methoden (Tertiary languages. Theories, models, methods)* (pp. 169–183). Tübingen: Stauffenburg.

Hufeisen, B., & Lindemann, B. (Eds.). (1998). *Tertiärsprachen. Theorien, Modelle, Methoden (Tertiary languages. Theories, models, methods)*. Tübingen: Stauffenburg.

James, A. (2000). English as a European *Lingua Franca*: Current realities and existing dichotomies. In J. Cenoz & U. Jessner (Eds.), *English in Europe: The acquisiton of a third language* (pp. 248–260). Clevedon: Multilingual Matters.

Jenkins, J. (2000). *The phonology of English as an international language*. Oxford: Oxford University Press.

Jessner, U. (1999). Metalinguistic awareness in multilinguals: Cognitive aspects of third language learning. *Language Awareness, 8*, 201–209.

Jessner, U. (2006). *Linguistic Awareness in Multilinguals: English as a Third Language*. Edinburgh: Edinburgh University Press.

Kachru, B. B. (1985). Standards, codification and sociolinguistic realism: The English language in the outer circle. In R. Quirk & H. Widdowson (Eds.) *English in the world* (pp. 11–30). Cambridge: Cambridge University Press.

Kachru, B. B. (1992). Models for non-native Englishes. In B. B. Kachru (Ed.), *The other tongue* (pp. 48–74). Urbana: University of Illinois Press.

Kecskes, I., & Papp, T. (2000). *Foreign language and mother tongue*. Mahwah, NJ: Lawrence Erlbaum.

Lasagabaster, D. (1997). *Creatividad y Conciencia Metalingüística: Incidencia en el Aprendizaje del Inglés como L3 (Creativity and meatlaguistic awareness: Their effect on the acquisition of English as an L3)*. Leioa: University of the Basque Country.

Lasagabaster, D., & Doiz, A. (2003). Maturational constraints on foreign language written production. In M. P. García Mayo & M. L. García Lecumberri (Eds.), *Age and the acquisition of English as a foreign language: Theoretical issues and fieldwork* (pp. 136–170) Clevedon: Multilingual Matters.

Malakoff, M. (1992). Translation ability: A natural bilingual and metalinguistic skill. In R. Harris (Ed.), *Cognitive processing in bilinguals* (pp. 515–530). Amsterdam: North-Holland.

McArthur, (1996). English in the world and in Europe. In R. Hartmann (Ed), *The English Language in Europe* (pp. 3–15). Oxford: Intellect.

Met (1998). Curriculum decision-making in content-based language teaching. In J. Cenoz and F. Genesee (Eds.), *Beyond bilingualism: Multilingualism and multilingual education* (pp. 35–63). Clevedon: Multilingual Matters.

Missler, B. (1999). *Fremdsprachenlernerfahrungen und Lernstrategien (Foreign language learning experience and learning strategies)*. Tübingen: Stauffenburg.

Modiano, M. (1996). The Americanization of Euro-English. *World Englishes, 15*, 207–215.

Quay, S. (2001). Managing linguistic boundaries in early trilingual development. In J. Cenoz & F. Genesee (Eds.), *Trends in bilingual acquistion* (pp. 149–199). Amsterdam: John Benjamins.

Ringbom, H. (1987). *The Role of the first language in foreign language learning*. Clevedon: Multilingual Matters.

Rubagumya, C. M. (1994). *Language in education in Africa*. Clevedon: Multilingual Matters.

Sagasta, P. (2001). *La Producción Escrita en Euskara, Castellano e Inglés en el Modelo D y en el Modelo de Inmersión (Writing in Basque, Spanish and English in model D and the immersion model)*. Unpublished doctoral dissertation, University of the Basque Country.

Singleton, D. (2000). *Exploring the second language mental lexcion*. Cambridge: Cambridge University Press.

Tickoo, M. L. (1996). English in Asian bilingual education: From hatred to harmony. *Journal of Multilingual and Multicultural Development, 17*, 225–240.

Widdowson, H. G. (1997). EIL, ESL, EFL: Global issues and local interests. *World Englishes, 16*, 135–146.

Williams, S., & Hammarberg, W. (1998). Language switches in L3 production: Implications for a ployglot speaking model. *Applied Linguistics, 19*, 295–333.

Ytsma, J. (2001). Towards a typology of trilingual primary education. *Journal of Bilingual Education and Bilingualism, 4*, 11–22.

CHAPTER 12

PROTECTING ENGLISH IN AN ANGLOPHONE AGE

JOSEPH LO BIANCO

The University of Melbourne, Australia

ABSTRACT

The official English movement in the United States is unique in the world in that the discourse of protection is directed towards English, because of multilingualism, and not against English, in defense of minority languages. This chapter discusses the exceptional character of the official English movement, devoting particular attention to the 104th Congress (1995-1996) when, under the first Republican Party (GOP) majority for 40 years, the status of English in the United States achieved its much hoped for floor action resulting in a successful vote on 1 August 1996. The Bill Emerson Language Empowerment Act (1996) subsequently lapsed, but the official English movement remains, powerful and determined, pursuing energetically its controversial aim of inscribing English into the nation's legal register. That official English is a movement in the United States, with its global economic dominance and cultural influence, invites curiosity as to its aims, origins, politics, and ideologies. The chapter discusses bilingual education as a key site of struggle in language policy in the US. The chapter concludes with a critique of language policy and planning theory in relation to official English.

INTRODUCTION

Few have encapsulated the cultural associations of contemporary English quite so succinctly as former Italian Prime Minister Silvio Berlusconi who in a 2001 election slogan linked: *inglese, impresa, internet*. *Impresa* refers to entrepreneurial spirit and culture; *internet* expresses unfettered global connectedness; and *inglese* is the language pre-eminently expressive of liberal, consumerist modernity. The associations Berlusconi claims for *inglese* are neither strange nor new, and in Italy, as elsewhere, such enthusiasm for English, commerce, and cultural instrumentalism gives rise to both embrace and alarm. The triumvirate of words is, of course, deeply ideological with each 'i' giving rise to a contest of values and ideologies, ultimately forming a cultural politics around English as international language (Pennycook, 1994).

Much contemporary writing about English divides into two broad streams. In one, there is an unremarked and unproblematic acceptance of the global tongue. As a result, technique, method, and approaches for making its acquisition more effective predominate. The alternate stream seems obsessed with the cultural, critical, and political consequences of English, and sometimes imputes naiveté or false consciousness to those who teach, promote, support, or simply describe its seemingly inexorable demand.

However the global presence of English defies singular, or even bi-polar, characterization. The teachers, agencies, and others who work within the immense global English language teaching enterprise are engaged in an historically unprecedented endeavor that has come close to yielding the world meta-lect that artificial language idealists thought no natural language could ever fulfill. The inventors of artificial languages knew a global age was inevitable and wanted to provide it with a suitable medium of communication, believing natural languages were incapable of transcending ethnic and national associations. What has happened, however, is not that English has become neutral of culture, ideology, and worldview but that international English constitutes a repertoire of culturally and ideologically multiple styles, a matrix of mutual intelligibility built around practices of negotiation. In its expansion of forms and modes, English is both marked for the global and the local. The multiple forms of English include identity markings for its old native speaker communities.

It is important to emphasize that not all global communication occurs now, or ever will, only in English, and much uses no English at all. Inter-ethnic communication is often multi-lingual, involving code-switching, combining variable proficiencies, script and speech, gesture and word, in complex processes bringing together separate productive and receptive proficiencies. That English carries multiple cultural identities, values, and ideologies expands our understanding of what intercultural communication processes involve. They are not neutral practices of unproblematic message transfer, but dialogical, sometimes conflicted, practices of continual negotiation of meaning.

In fact, English does bring material and sometimes negative, consequences into societies and cultures that adopt it (Jernudd, 1992). This is particularly the case when its acquisition is asymmetrical and exacerbates existing social inequalities. No generalizations are warranted with respect to the overall effects of the spread of English. Its effects on any particular society will be unique depending on the specific local circumstances and histories. The particular impact of adoption of English also depends on local prospects of stable, functionally differentiated, multilingualism resulting from including English in local, possibly expanded, communication practices.

A major study of English in the world commissioned by The British Council (Graddol, 1997) found that more than one billion people either speak or are learning to speak English. Crystal's 1997 study concurs. It is unsurprising, then, that much language planning today looks either like protection against the incursions of English, perceived or actual, or energetic schemes to enhance and improve its acquisition. Just as for Berlusconi, English is seen as an integral part of ongoing modernization under globalization, so in Japan concerns about real or perceived "declining standards of English" have led to calls to make English co-official with Japanese (Kobayashi, 1999; also see Kanno, this volume, for a fuller discussion of this issue). Like Japan and Italy, developed nations with secure national languages that do not enjoy international status now opt universally for English as their language for communication with multiple others, replacing past foreign language policies that were multilingually differentiated. Alongside such instrumentalism, there remains anxiety about the effects of English, resulting in debate about the value of local varieties in post-colonial settings, compared to international, or selected "native" standards. Sri Lanka is an excellent example of these many settings where, in scholarship and language planning, sociolinguistic variation is addressed (Parakrama, 1995).

It seems that the sun never sets on English, though there are shadows as well as bright light. The exceptional, even astonishing, counter to English as problem-causer or desired-commodity is the decades long pursuit of official sanction for the language in, of all places, the United States, itself the greatest generator of entrepreneurial culture, of language-mediated technology and, of course, of English itself. While much of the rest of the world grapples with cultural, ideological, and material consequences of English as *Lingua Mundi* (Jernudd, 1992), or *global language* (Crystal, 1997), the US Congress has been requested on many occasions to legislatively declare English *official*. That this happens in the world's most powerful political assembly, in the world's most powerful commercial economy, in the world's heartland of entrepreneurialism, and the world's greatest deployer of cultural products (especially English-mediated music and film) makes this phenomenon important. That much of the discourse justifying moves to legislate English deploys a vocabulary of protection and defense (Birkales, 1986) renders it strange: but when advocates for the revival of America's dying indigenous languages (many spoken by fewer than 100 individuals) also advance their case with talk of protection and conservation (Hinton, 1994; Krauss, 1998) the strange merges with the bizarre.

Making it Official

So why does English need a legal bolster in the United States? According to the 1990 Census some 95% of the US population spoke English *well* or *very well*, with most speaking only English. Only 0.8% reported speaking no English at all (US Census Bureau, 1993, 1994). New arrivals learn English relatively quickly (Macias, 2000; Stevens, 1994). Spanish speakers transfer to English at rates equal to, and sometimes higher than, most earlier immigrant groups (Veltman, 1983, 1998). Of those who speak Spanish at home, about half speak English very well (US Department of Commerce, 1993), and the demand for English classes outstrips supply (Ewen, Wrigley, & Chisman, 1993). Results from the 2000 census appear to confirm the sense that minority language claimants typically speak English and that the real concern in language demography in the USA should not be for un-acquired English but for dying indigenous, non-maintained immigrant, and non-acquired foreign languages (Crawford, 2002).

Historically language-planning theory has used "self-evident" or concrete language problems as the starting point of research and theorization. How can the absence of a concrete language problem be reconciled with the immense effort to protect the United States from other languages? After all, most official status attribution for languages occurs as a consequence of political reconstitution in post-colonial settings. What tools do we have to explain such elusive, complex, and strange phenomena? Faced with this dilemma even eminent scholars have made recourse to ghosts and myths, asking, "Why are facts so useless in this discussion?" (Fishman, 1988, p. 127). When the facts don't help explain things, representation and symbolic politics become crucial.

On 1 August, 1996, the Bill Emerson English Language Empowerment Act of 1996 (104-723)[1] was passed by 259 votes to 169 in the House of Representatives after 15 years of failed attempts at floor action. The Act contained two chapters: "Title I: English Language Empowerment" and "Title II: Repeal of Bilingual Voting Requirements," declaring English official, making it the language of state (or at least of the Federal government). The specific provisions were the repeal of bilingual voting provisions, the banning of citizenship swearing-in ceremonies not conducted in English, a declaration that government business would take place only in English, and the granting of a private right of litigation to citizens if any government service were denied them *because* they spoke English. Omitted from the Bill was the most cherished target of the official English movement: the Federal mandate for bilingual education.

During the debate that preceded the Bill's passage, Speaker Gingrich commented that public schools' instruction in many languages would eventually lead "to the decay of the core parts of our civilization." Opponents, of course, satirized the Bill; Thomas Foglietta suggested, for example, that "since we're legislating an official language, how about an official religion to go along with it?" (cited in Lo Bianco, 2001, p. 44). Others claimed the Bill destroyed the First Amendment (Lo Bianco, 2001). These associations with American civilization and constitutional safeguards of freedom of religion and speech make official English especially interesting and important.

The 104th (1994-1996) was the first Republican dominated Congress in 40 years. The Speaker and architect of that conservative restoration, Newt Gingrich, made *English* a high-order issue (Gingrich, 1995) associating access to English not only with opportunity for the disadvantaged and improved social relations, but also with American civilization. Language in general formed part of his program of reconstituting the semantic as well as the political order, believing that discourse was biased towards the meanings of social democratic ideology. Claims that recent immigrants were refusing to learn English imbued the issue with a sense that key meanings in American political life, ideals of personal freedom especially, would be eroded. Woolard (1998, p. 19) has argued, "A crude version of Whorfian thinking that treats English as the *sine qua non* of democratic thought runs through the tradition of American language policy and at times has enabled attacks on the rights of minority language citizens" (see also Nunberg, 1992).

When in 1995 Senator Bob Dole challenged Bill Clinton for the Presidency, he too made officializing English a cause célèbre. For the first time since its modern revival in 1981, the movement secured Congressional floor action. But its House glory of 1 August 1996 was not consummated when the Bill lapsed in the Senate. Although official English has re-emerged in every Congress since and is backed by large, well-funded organizations whose sole purpose is defending English by defeating "official multilingualism," it lost momentum at the Federal level, making a spirited revival only in 2001. At the state level, things were more positive: 27 states had declared English official more or less assertively by mid 2002. At the county level, official English has enjoyed a florescence too, sometimes stimulating bitter controversy as in Green Bay Wisconsin (Wilgoren, 2002). Under the name of *English for the Children,* it achieved its greatest success so far: the June 2, 1998, 61% to 39% vote in California thereby approving Proposition 227, which was designed to severely restrict bilingual education in the state. Subsequent anti-bilingual education referenda in Arizona and Massachusetts also passed by large margins.

Action has turned away from specific attention to English to embedding English provisions in other laws. Most recently, in May 2006 the US Senate passed two competing amendments to the Senate Immigration Reform Act (S. 2611), declaring English as the National (S. A. 4064) or the Common Unifying (S. A. 4073) language of the US (see http://languagepolicy.org).

The Federal Mandate

Perhaps the most provocative measure for official English supporters has been the Federal mandate for bilingual education, from 1968 to 2002. The Federal mandate emerged from direct Congressional law making, supplemented and extended by class-action litigation drawing on the principles of the Civil Rights Act of 1964, which banned discrimination on the basis of national origin (Baron, 1990; Piatt, 1990). It also used the legal standard "education on equal terms" from Brown vs. Board of Education of 1954 (Crawford, 1995, 2000).

Both ways to make policy (legislating and litigating) are steeped in a distinctive practice of American governance that Kagan (1991) called *adversarial legalism*. The Congressional moves arose from politicians' concern about the poor education outcomes of Mexican-American children. The 1960 census had revealed dramatically unequal education outcomes for children with Spanish last names in southwestern states. On January 17, 1967, Texas Democrat Senator Ralph Yarborough proposed Federal measures to assist these children to learn English, including the possibility of using some Spanish. Together with Congressman James Scheuer of New York, Yarborough prepared a Bill to include all non-English speaking groups. This resulted in the *Bilingual Education Act* (BEA, Public Law 20-24), that took the form of Title VII of the Elementary and Secondary Education Act (signed into law on January 2, 1968). Yarborough declared in the Senate on December 1, 1967:

> My purpose in doing this is not to keep any specific language alive. It is not the purpose of the Bill to create pockets of different languages throughout the country... not to stamp out the mother tongue, and not to try to make their mother tongue the dominant language, but just to try to make those children fully literate in English. (Congressional Record, 1967, p. 34703)

From the passage of the Bill until its demise, the role of Federal agencies became progressively more legalistic, dominated by compliance supervision, and over time this practice gained considerable negative baggage. Legal cases pushed the Federal government into to a compliance-demanding role. The 1974 Supreme Court ruling in Lau vs. Nichols found that "sink-or-swim," effectively doing nothing particular for language minority children, violated their Civil Rights. After an Office of Civil Rights investigation found little compliance with the ruling, the Federal government issued the Lau remedies in August 1975. These named bilingual education and ESL as acceptable interventions, and specified when bilingual teaching was to be mandatory. It should be kept in mind, however, that the BEA programs were never intended to produce bilingual proficiency. The native language was to be used for a strictly limited period until students' English was sufficient to enable them to participate in mainstream classes. The result was a proliferation of strictly transitional programs. Political agitation for *bilingual enrichment* (for a literate capacity in the first language plus English) grew but the bulk of federally funded programs remained steadfastly transitional.

By 1977, a three-decade long dispute had commenced about research findings characterized by definitional differences, conflict about appropriate goals and methods, pedagogical and measurement issues about the value of students' first language, and disagreement about the role of affective, social, familial, ethnic, and self-esteem variables in children's educational progress (Baker & de Kanter, 1981; Crawford, 1995; Cummins, 1992, 2001; Porter, 1995; Ramirez, Yuen, Ramey, &

Pasta, 1991; Willig, 1985). Krashen's (1999) examination of the politicization and misuse of research findings is instructive. Carefully controlled and systematically defined examinations of two-language teaching, in many countries, consistently find evidence of positive educational and linguistic outcomes for learners (Cummins, 2000). But this research did not change the course of thinking about the BEA. The heavy weight of negative cultural and political baggage made that impossible. Opponents construed the BEA as advancing segregation for minorities, undermining assimilation ("the first salvo in Hispanics' war to preserve their ethnic identity," Chavez, 1991, p. 10), threatening the melting pot (Hayakawa, 1985), and spawning a self-serving and politicized bureaucracy that systematically concealed methodological failure (Porter, 1995).

In its 1978 reauthorization of Title VII, Congress clarified the intention of the law as strictly transitional, the native language being permitted only to the "extent necessary" to enable English proficiency to develop. It also allowed English-speaking children to join bilingual programs so that non-English speakers could learn English from them too, but also to assuage public concern about segregation. An attempt to strengthen the Federal regulations in August 1980 by mandating two-language teaching under certain conditions was rejected after a strong public reaction. As a result, the Federal role shrank to compliance enforcement. The association of bilingual education with negative cultural messages became deeper with the election of Ronald Reagan as President. He declared in 1981 that it was "against American concepts" to preserve native languages in state schooling (Ricento, 1998, p. 96).

While electoral calculations and political compromise softened the Reagan administration's opposition to the 1984 reauthorization, the Office of Civil Rights (OCR) retreated further to a new legal position requiring Federal intervention only in cases of *discriminatory intent*, rather than the previous test of *discriminatory effect*. The policing role of the OCR remained low under President George Bush, Senior and increased only slightly during the Clinton administration. At no time was the ever more maligned BEA re-imagined along more appropriate instructional models, such as an overarching national language policy based on language enrichment for all, with complementary two-language outcomes along distinctive pathways: ESL and language maintenance for minority children and second languages for majority children. Although there are many seriously intentioned second language and immersion programs in US schools (Christian, Montone, Lindholm, & Carranza, 1997), the BEA was mired in a compensatory ethos, negative characterization, and the residues of its adversarial birth. In an 8-year ethnographic study of a 40-year practice of bilingual education in the southwestern United States, Shannon (1999) documented the effects of inadequate models on teachers, concluding "the absence of a language policy in bilingual education leads teachers to practice it on the basis of a dominant language ideology" (p. 185). This observation is confirmed from the Southeast as well where language minority groups "typically have been perceived as people who pose language and cultural problems and difficulties for English-speaking monolinguals and for North American society" (Roca, 1999, p. 298). Fishman agrees that much of the vision of the BEA is not bilingualism but Anglification and even "anti-bilingualism" (1988, p. 405).

And yet, this same BEA became the prime justification for officializing English, based on claims that the BEA was official multilingualism. The initial anti-poverty bias of the BEA also left residues. Income criteria governed access to many language programs conceded to minority groups, leading Sonntag (1995) to argue that these are measures "ameliorating the circumstances of the uneducated poor" and therefore the counter moves to make English official are "part of an attempt to replace the old liberal... agenda with the right-wing, Reaganite ... agenda" (p. 99).

The BEA was even absorbed into the celebrated American culture wars of the 1980s and 1990s, accused of undermining the "cultural literacy" of the nation. The exemplary exponent of cultural literacy discourse was E. D. Hirsch (1988) whose position was that: "Linguistic pluralism enormously increases cultural fragmentation, civil antagonism, illiteracy, and economic-technological ineffectualness" (p. 91). The breadth of the claim, the vast distance it tracks away from in-class educational issues of pedagogical effectiveness, epitomizes the infusion of language questions into debates about wider cultural, political, and social cohesion. Bernstein (1994) similarly expressed the connection between language education policy and the wider social compact, ridiculing the idea that Cherokee might be taught in public schools and characterizing bilingual education as an "act of rebellion against white, Anglo-cultural domination" no less than a "multicultural animus against European culture and its derivatives" (p. 245).

These judgments do not get applied to the efforts of majority language children to acquire additional languages. Lambert (1992), Simon (1981/1992), and the 1979 *President's Commission on Foreign Language and International Studies,* which described US foreign language study as "nothing short of scandalous" (Perkins, 1979, p. 5), criticize American education for "neglecting" foreign languages. This sometimes involves efforts to distinguish *ethnic* from *foreign* language policy: "Linguistic policy is hostage to ethnic politics. Foreign language policy, in contrast...induce[s] or enable[s] citizens to master languages of other countries...trying to add to or sustain a national competency" (Lambert, 1992, p. 5). Foreign language study of this kind is readily absorbed into justification based on "the national interest." This pattern has accelerated in the wake of the terrorism of September 11, 2001 as expressed by both Congress and commentators: "The most pressing such need is for greater numbers of foreign language-capable intelligence personnel, with increased fluency in specific and multiple languages" (House of Representatives Report 107-219 on the Intelligence Authorization Act of 2002, p. 18).

In Congress, official English commenced in 1981 through Senator Hayakawa, founder of US English and one of the first to call the BEA *official bilingualism* (Hayakawa, 1985). Six states had passed official English declarations before California's Proposition 63 in November 1986. Some jurisdictions adopted bilingual statements: Hawaii in 1978 designated English and Hawaiian as official languages and New Mexico opted for English-plus. But "Prop 63" was critical in the modern revival of official English. Voting three to one, Californians instructed public officials to ensure that "the role of English as the common language of the State of California is preserved and enhanced" (Crawford, 2000, p. 43).

More extreme was the November 4, 1980 Dade County Florida citizen initiative Ordinance 80-128, repealing a decade-old bilingual-bicultural measure. The Ordinance forbade the use of County funds "for utilizing any language other than English, or promoting any culture other than that of the United States" (Donahue, 1995, p. 125). Although it was made less restrictive in 1984, its success stimulated other jurisdictions to consider similar legislation. During this period, public policy reflected what has been termed "the bilingual double standard" (Zelasco, 1991): Bilingualism resulting from mainstream Americans learning foreign languages is represented as a skill, while bilingualism resulting from minorities learning English is represented as cohesion-threatening.

Among the many victories for official English, however, there have also been setbacks. District Judge Paul Rosenblatt's February 6, 1990 striking down of Arizona's official English amendment (on the grounds of unconstitutionality) was the most significant. The Arizona law which required state officers and employees to "act in English and in no other language" (Donahue, 1995, p. 124; Combs, 1999) was considered by the judge to violate First Amendment free speech guarantees (Draper & Jiminez, 1992, p. 93; also Miner, 1998).

American

Although official English directed its energies against immigration-stimulated language provisions, in fact it continues a longer history of language laws involving English and marking the American polity: the desire to distinguish American Republicanism from British monarchical culture. This desire had to work with ambivalent raw material. English was the language in which the libertarian idealism of the new polity was fashioned through the philosophy of John Locke and others, but it was also the language of the rejected state. Anti-monarchical republicanism needed distance from Britain, but Britain's English was the repository of the philosophical traditions of the new polity. In relation to new immigrants, images of multiculturalism alarmed many who felt American distinctiveness resided in values expressed in English.

In 1780, John Adams urged the first Congress to bolster "liberty, prosperity, and glory" by devoting "an early attention to the subject of eloquence and language" (cited in Lo Bianco, 2001, p. 45). Nine years later, Noah Webster's *Declaration of Linguistic Independence* called for Americans to "adorn" English but separate American from English (in Crawford, 1992, p. 32-36). Webster's approach was conventional language corpus planning, issuing reading programs and dictionaries, to bring about John Adams' "more democratical" English—freed of class-based dialect stratification, sycophancy, and divisions of privilege—as democratic cultural capital (Bourdieu, 1991). Such a language would allow persons "of all social ranks" access to common public meanings, sustaining the democratic and classless imagery of early republican idealism. Webster's project, like Adams', was for English reform in the interests of both democracy and nationalism.

Probably the first official language measure in Congress was Washington J. McCormick's failed 1923 proposal to declare *American* official. McCormick's aim was to free American thought in a "mental emancipation" to accompany the political emancipation of 1776 (McCormick, 1923/1992, p. 41). In 1923, Illinois Senator Ryan, with "virulently anti-British" sentiment (Baron, 1992, p. 39), succeeded in having American declared official in that state, a provision that remained until the language was changed to *English* in 1969.

H. L. Mencken's exposition of the 'American or English' problem notes with disdain the "cultural timorousness" of 'social aspirants' who look to England for linguistic esteem (1936) observing that American was expanding, reaching as far as the "crude dialects of Oceanica." Mencken's hope was not for an Academy, after Adams, nor for micro-reforms, after Webster, but for a Chaucer or Dante who would venture into the mire of ordinary discourse and provide "dignity" to American speech.

Tradition, Phases, or Moments?

The Congressional history of language legislation oscillates between a pluralizing and a restricting tendency. At the pluralist end are the extensions of Civil Rights principles to language minority groups as well as the promulgation of the Native American Languages Act (NALA) of 1990. The latter, in intent if not effect, is arguably the most explicitly pluralist language law in US history, stating: "It is the policy of the United States to preserve, protect, and promote the rights and freedom of Native Americans... to use, practice and develop Native American languages" (Congressional Record 15024-30, 11 October, 1990). Whereas the BEA used children's first languages only as a bridge to English, NALA articulates a pluralist ideology, aiming to conserve languages. But NALA comes at a dismal time, is poorly resourced, and largely ineffective, as scores of languages have become extinct and most are threatened (Krauss, 1992).

The language restriction tendency is found in the repeated attempts to curtail language rights by moves to officialize English, including attempts (unsuccessful in this case) to impose an English-only amendment to the 1996 Puerto Rico Plebiscite Bill (H.R. 856).

For supporters of official English, the past establishes a tradition of conservative caution, of cohesion validated in a single, uncontested language associated with the precise political culture of the founding liberalism of the polity. By contrast, for opponents of official English, the American past, the constitution, and other founding documents (Rossiter, 1961) legitimize a pluralist or laissez faire modern language policy with official English seen as disrupting a 200-year history of language tolerance. This position is consistent with Kloss' (1998) influential conclusion, based on research conducted in the 1940s, that American language policy constitutes a tradition of toleration.

Wiley (1999) challenges Kloss' depiction as overly optimistic, offering the following phases:

- 1779-1880: No explicit designation of English by government; tolerance of *use* of other languages;
- 1880-1920; and then until WWII: Official English at State and Federal levels; language based restrictions, exclusion and discrimination against various minorities and immigrants;
- WWII to 1980s (especially during 1960s): Relaxation of restrictions; encouragement of other languages until the mid-1980s; and
- 1980s to the Present: A tendency back towards restrictionism.

Further insight into these phases of language policy is provided by Collins (1999) who identifies three sets of ideologies relevant to the "importance of literacy, print, and schooling in the American project of self-construction" (p. 216). During the "early national phase" (1780s-1880s), a colonial concept of citizenship and print-based public life merged with Jeffersonian Republicanism stressing equality of small producers as part of literate civic-virtuous governance. This gave way to an industrial economy with class divisions and calls for an American English to "express the democratic impulse." In the southern agrarian economy, literacy was denied to slaves in recognition of its politically empowering potential. Emancipation after the Civil War (1861-1865) and southern Reconstruction Period (1865-1976) were undermined by *de facto* segregation until the Civil Rights era of the 1960s (Zinn, 1995).

The "mature national phase" followed (1880s-1960s), dominated by the end of national expansion, and entrenchment of social stratification and skilling. The closing of the Western Frontier coincided with and helped produce a standardizing within many aspects of the economy. As technical efficiency and quantification became critical, the industrial economy's requirements produced a greater emphasis on the need for schools to produce adequate levels of 'schooled English' and literacy. A technical economy of Standard English literacy replaced the "character-formation moral economy." A restriction of language diversity inaugurated an officially sanctioned hierarchy among languages.

The "late national phase" embraces the Civil Rights era of the 1960s, the Conservative Restoration and globalization. During this period, social stratification has persisted but there have been demands for recognition of cultural differences and rejection of sameness; these pluralizing trends have been countered by conservative reaction deploying a standard English/literacy skills orientation and an anti-multicultural "cultural literacy" within a unitary literary canon.

Principles of Policy Response

As Wiley and Collins show, the national and colonial phases defy singular characterization because of highly differentiated practices. Public institutions accommodate to unthreatening languages and speech forms with place-territory association by making use of a discourse of heritage. Home identity in territory, or associations with the land, can mobilize a discourse of belonging. This is found in public adoption of words from native languages for marking local identity, for example, tourism's use of Aloha in Hawaii. The contrast with Canada's Quebec underscores that such accommodations to minority languages are much easier when the language is weak and has no separate statehood claims, or conversely, when it is strong but can, by accommodating policy, be contained. Most often only weak symbolic recognition is offered to minority languages, usually accorded in ceremonial functions.

The NALA was built on heritage discourse (preserving what is left of the past) but it is more difficult for immigrant languages to utilize heritage associations, since they have a 'price to pay' (Kloss, 1971) for being admitted to the nation. National cohesion ideologies predominate and heritage concessions to minorities usually occur when their languages are not communicatively vibrant. The most common accommodation to minority speech comes from public judgment of quaintness and folk-interest in dialect variations.

A radically different kind of response, *acquisition planning*, is applied to the languages of distant others when these have social or cultural prestige, or are languages of "economically significant others." In *strategic skills discourse,* languages are promoted to sharpen economic competitiveness, or to advance geopolitical or economic interests. The learners of strategically important languages are apparently considered to be less likely to become excessively culturally attached to the target language community, since foreign languages don't require the domestic institutional infrastructures of immigrant or indigenous languages, and therefore a sense of intellectual or economically useful bilingualism prevails. Strategic skills thinking aims to fill national capability shortfalls. The Russian launch of Sputnik in the late 1950s, and the terrorism of September 11, 2001, have stimulated major efforts to upgrade US language capability in this way.

Distinctive language planning operates for English. Mainstream attitudes towards various English varieties and dialects are influenced by their relation to prestige British norms and their American substitutes. While regional dialects can be appropriated as quaint and characteristically local, class dialects and "racialised" Englishes are often stigmatized, even calling forth ridicule in Congress such as during the Ebonics controversy of 1996 to 1997 (Baugh, 2000; Morgan, 1999). British standard forms attract ambivalent evaluation: simultaneously a separate variety and, to some, the authoritative original (Honey, 1997; Knowles, 1997; Leith, 1997). Declinist thinking is a hardy perennial with four areas identified: correctness of grammar, clarity and precision of expression, logic, and vividness or originality. "The belief in the decline of English is widely held and constitutes a significant element in the total set of shared beliefs about language in our society" (Ferguson, 1979, p. 52). Rubin (1978/1979) agrees commenting that "most Americans are quite anxious about their language usage" (p. 4).

Finally, public institutions and public attitudes often combine to marginalize some languages, and official English is part of this process. Immigrant languages are vulnerable because, unlike indigenous languages, they lack association to place within the country and therefore cannot mobilize appeal to heritage; they are unable to recruit associations of prestige, foreignness, or economic muscle. Indigenous languages that have vitality and territory associations, however, are also vulnerable to marginalization, and languages of domestic minorities that are official in proximal states can sometimes introduce new elements that make them problematical for policymakers.

In summary, strong immigrant languages, territory-based indigenous languages with vitality, and languages of proximate countries that coincide with local immigrant languages create difficulties for policy makers. The possibility of a rival "national" culture, the large numbers within particular minority groups, and the institutional nature of the supports required for intergenerational vitality can be perceived to challenge mainstream priorities.

CONCLUSIONS

Official status can be allocated in three ways: (a) juridically, via laws made by legislators, or in court decisions; (b) through various informal but authoritative social processes, such as dictionary stabilization, social emulation of prestige literature, and the propagation of standard forms in public education; and (c) through persuasive and authoritative talk and writing.

Unlike legislating or litigating that impose a language preference by mandate, or informal modelling that seeks to have particular norms adopted over rival norms, persuasive talk and writing seek to make a language official by *performing* the result they aim for. Persuasive discourse aimed at bringing about changes in language status rely on authoritative individuals performing acts of speech that continually associate English with particular social or economic benefits. In a multilingual environment this means associating English continually as the required and natural choice, the appropriate behavior for national belonging, patriotic citizenship and economic progress. One of the most potent connections used has been to link intergenerational maintenance of minority languages to 'stifling ethnic collectivisms' contrasted to a liberating ideology of 'free individuals,' for whom English represents opportunity and progress.

The moves to make English official in law have been bolstered by the reiteration of key messages by politicians and the media that continually make associations between citizenship, economy, place, national loyalty and English. Institutional sites, such as English classes and citizenship swearing-in ceremonies where the sole use of English is desired, are selected and the choice of English is displayed together with the paraphernalia of patriotic duty and symbols. Over time, these behaviors and associations come to function as performative allocation of authority to English (Lo Bianco 1999, 2001). They contribute to the larger assimilative cultural agenda by inscribing crucial messages into a national narrative: America, economy, modernity, capitalist opportunity and individualism. A key modality is argument—repeated, accumulated and remembered.

As a cultural and persuasive process, powerful talk for English and its intimate association with expected national behavior accompanies and makes possible juridical regulation and enforcement. The inscription of English in national ideology serves to legalize by cultural authority, by habitus (Bourdieu, 1991), and by expectations.

NOTES

[1.] Congressman Emerson was the key Bill sponsor.

REFERENCES

Adams, J. (1780/1992). Proposal for an American Language Academy. In J. Crawford, J. (Ed.). (1992) *Language loyalties: A source book on the official English controversy.* (pp. 31–33). Chicago and London: The University of Chicago Press.

Baker, K., & de Kanter, A. (1981). *The effectiveness of bilingual education programs.* Washington, D.C.: U.S. Department of Education.

Baron, D. (1990). *The English-only question, an official language for Americans?* New Haven and London: Yale University Press.

Baron, D. (1992). Federal English. In J. Crawford (Ed.), *Language loyalties: A source book on the official English controversy.* (pp. 36–40). Chicago and London: The University of Chicago Press.

Baugh, J. (2000). *Beyond Ebonics, Linguistic pride and racial prejudice.* New York and Oxford: Oxford University Press.

Bernstein, R. (1994). *Dictatorship of virtue: Multiculturalism and the battle for America's future.* New York: Knopf.

Birkales, G. (1986). About this book [Foreword]. In A. P. Blaustein & D. Blaustein-Epstein, *Resolving language conflicts: A study of the world's constitutions.* Washington, D.C.: U.S. English.

Bourdieu, P. (1991). *Language and symbolic power.* Cambridge, MA: Harvard University Press.

Chavez, L. (1991). *Out of the barrio: Towards a new politics of Hispanic assimilation.* Basic Books. New York: Harper Collins.

Christian, D., Montone, C. L., Lindholm, K. J., & Carranza, I. (1997). *Profiles in two-way immersion education.* Washington, D.C.: Center for Applied Linguistics and Delta Systems.

Collins, J. (1999). The Ebonics controversy in context: Literacies, subjectivities, and language ideologies in the United States. In Blommaert, J. (Ed.), *Language ideological debates* (pp. 201–235). The Hague: Mouton de Gruyter.

Combs, M. C. (1999). Public perceptions of official English/English only: Framing the debate in Arizona. In T. Huebner & K. A. Davis (Eds.). *Socio-political perspectives on language policy and planning in the USA.* (pp. 131–155). Amsterdam: Benjamins.

Congressional Record, 1967, p. 34703. Washington, D.C.: United States Congress.
Congressional Record 15024-30, 11 October, 1990. Washington, D.C.: United States Congress.
Crawford, J. (Ed.). (1992). *Language loyalties: A source book on the official English controversy.* Chicago and London: The University of Chicago Press.
Crawford, J. (2000). *At war with diversity: US language policy in an age of anxiety.* Clevedon, England: Multilingual Matters.
Crawford, J. (2002). Making sense of Census 2000. University of Arizona, Language Policy Research Unit.
Crystal, D. (1997). *English as a global language.* Cambridge: Cambridge University Press.
Cummins, J. (1992). Bilingual education and immersion education: The Ramirez Report in theoretical perspective. *Bilingual Research Journal, 16,* 91–105.
Cummins, J. (2000). *Language, power and pedagogy: Bilingual children in the crossfire.* Clevedon, England: Multilingual Matters.
Donahue, T. S. (1995). American language policy and compensatory opinion. In Tollefson, J. W. (Ed.) *Power and inequality in language education* (pp. 112–142). Cambridge: Cambridge University Press.
Draper, J. B., & Jiminez, M. (1990/1992). A chronology of the official English movement. In Crawford, J. (Ed.) *Language loyalties: A source book on the official English controversy.* (pp. 89–94). Chicago and London: The University of Chicago Press.
Ewen, D. T., Wrigley, H. S., & Chisman, F. P. (1993). *ESL and the American dream: A report on an investigation of ESL service for adults.* Washington, D.C.: The Southport Institute of Policy Analysis.
Ferguson, C. A. (1979/96). National attitudes to language planning. In Huebner, T. (Ed.) *Sociolinguistic perspectives: Papers on language in society, 1959–1994.* New York: Oxford University Press.
Fishman, J. A. (1988). 'English Only': Its ghosts, myths and dangers. *International Journal of the Sociology of Language, 74,* 125–140.
Gingrich, N. (1995). *To renew America.* New York: Harper Collins.
Graddol, D. (1997). *The future of English?* London: British Council.
Hayakawa, S. I. (1985). (*The English Language Amendment*) *One nation...indivisible?* Washington, D.C.: Institute for Values in Public Policy.
Hinton, L. (1994). *Flutes of fire: Essays on Californian Indian languages.* Berkeley, CA: Heyday Books.
Hirsch, E. D. (1988). *Cultural literacy: What every American needs to know.* New York: Vintage Books.
Honey, J. (1997). *Language is power: The story of Standard English and its enemies.* London: Faber and Faber.
House of Representatives Report 107-219 on the Intelligence Authorization Act of 2002.
Huebner, T., & Davis, K. A. (1999). (Eds.). *Sociopolitical perspectives on language policy and planning in the USA.* Amsterdam: Benjamins.
Jernudd, B. H. (1992). Culture planning in language planning, what do we know about culture loss, survival and gain in relation to language loss, survival and gain? In G. Jones & C. Ozog (Eds.) *Bilingualism and national development* (Vol. 2) (pp. 491–531). Universiti Brunei Darussalam.
Kachru, B. B. (Ed) (1992). *The other tongue: English across cultures* (2nd ed.). Urbana: University of Illinois Press.
Kagan, R. A. (1991). Adversarial legalism and American government. *Journal of Policy Analysis and Management, 10*(3), 369–407.
Kloss, H. (1971). Language rights of immigrant groups. *International Migration Review, 5,* 250–268.
Kloss, H. (1998). *The American bilingual tradition* (2nd ed.). Washington DC: ERIC Clearinghouse on Languages and Linguistics.
Knowles, G. (1997). *A cultural history of the English language.* London: Arnold.
Kobayashi, S. (August 3, 1999). English can save Japan, p. 16. *The Japan Times.*
Krashen, S. D. (1999). *Under attack: The case against bilingual education.* Culver City, CA: Language Education Associates.
Krauss, M. (1992). The world's languages in crisis. *Language, 68,* 6–10.
Krauss, M. (1998). The condition of native North American languages. *International Journal of the Sociology of Language, 132,* 9–21.
Lambert, R. D. (1992). *Foreign language planning in the United States* (Occasional Paper). Washington, D.C.: National Foreign Language Center, Johns Hopkins University.
Leith, D, (1997). *A social history of English.* London: Routledge.
Lo Bianco, J. (1999). The language of policy: What sort of policy making is the officialization of English in the United States? In Huebner, T. & K. A. Davis (Eds.), *Sociopolitical perspectives on language policy and planning in the USA.* (pp. 39–65). Amsterdam: Benjamins.
Lo Bianco, J. (2001). Language policies: State texts for silencing and giving voice. In P. Freebody, S. Muspratt, S. Devlin, B. Devlin, & B. Difference (Eds.), *Silence and textual practice: Studies in critical literacy* (pp. 31–71). Cleveland, University of New Hampshire: Hampton Press.

Lo Bianco, J. (2002) Uncle Sam and Mister Unz. *Australian Language Matters, 4*, 1 & 3–8.
Macias, R. F. (2000). The flowering of America: Linguistic diversity in the United States. In S. L. McKay & S. C. Wong (Eds.), *New immigrants in the United States* (pp. 11–58). New York: Cambridge University Press.
McCormick, W. J. (1923/1992). "American" as official language. In J. Crawford (Ed.) *Language loyalties: A source book on the official English controversy.* Chicago and London: The University of Chicago Press.
Mencken, H. L. (1936). *The American language*. New York: A. Kopf.
Miner, S. (1998). Legal implications of the official English declaration. In T. Ricento, & B. Burnaby (Eds), *Language and politics in the United States and Canada: Myths and realities*. (pp. 171–185). New Jersey and London: Erlbaum.
Morgan, M. (1999). US language planning and policies for social dialect speakers. In T. Huebner, & K. A. Davis (Eds.), *Sociopolitical perspectives on language policy and planning in the USA*. (pp. 173–193). Amsterdam: Benjamins.
Nunberg, G. (1992). Afterword: The official language movement: Reimagining America. In J. Crawford, (Ed.) *Language loyalties: A source book on the official English controversy.* (pp. 479–495). Chicago and London: The University of Chicago Press.
Parakrama, A. (1995). *De-hegemonizing language standard: Learning from (post)colonial Englishes about "English"*. Basingstoke and New York: Macmillan.
Porter, R. (1995). *Forked tongue: The politics of bilingual education.* New Brunswick: Transaction Books.
Pennycook, A. (1994). *The cultural politics of English as an international language.* New York and London: Longman.
Perkins, J. (Chair). (1979). *US President's commission of foreign languages and international studies, strength through wisdom, A critique of US capability (Final Report).* Washington, D.C.: Government Publications Office.
Phillipson, R. (1992). *Linguistic imperialism.* Oxford: Oxford University Press.
Phillipson, R., & Skutnabb-Kangas, T. (1996). English-only worldwide or language ecology? *TESOL Quarterly 30*, 429–452.
Piatt, B. (1990). *Only English? Law and language policy in the United States.* Albuquerque: University of New Mexico Press.
Ramirez, J., Yuen, S., Ramey, D., & Pasta, D. (1991). *Final report: Longitudinal study of structured English immersion strategy, early exit and late-exit bilingual education programs for language minority children (Vol. 1) (US Department of Education).* San Mateo, CA: Aguirre International.
Ricento, T. (1998). National language policy in the United States. In T. Ricento, & B. Burnaby (Eds.), *Language and politics in the United States and Canada: Myths and realities.* (pp. 85–103). New Jersey and London: Erlbaum.
Roca, A. (1999). Foreign language policy and planning in higher education: The case of the State of Florida. (pp. 297–313). In T. Huebner, & K. A. Davis (Eds.), *Sociopolitical perspectives on language policy and planning in the USA.* Amsterdam: Benjamins.
Rossell, C., & Baker, K., (1996). The educational effectiveness of bilingual education. *Research in the Teaching of English, 30*(1), 7–74.
Rossiter, C. (Ed.). (1961). *Alexander Hamilton, James Madison, and John Jay. The federalist papers.* New York and Scarborough: Penguin.
Rubin, J. (1978/1979). The approach to language planning within the United States. *Language Planning Newsletter* (East-West Center, Honolulu), *4*(4), 1 & 3–6 and "Continued" *5*(1), 1 & 3–6.
Schneider, S. G. (1976). *Revolution, reaction or reform: The 1974 bilingual education act.* New York: L.A. Publishing Company.
Shannon, S. M. (1999). The debate on bilingual education in the US: Language ideology as reflected in the practices of bilingual teachers. In J. Blommaert (Ed.), *Language ideological debates* (pp. 171–201). Berlin: Mouton de Gruyter.
Simon, P. (1981/1992). *The tongue-tied American, Confronting the foreign language crisis.* New York: Continuum Press.
Skutnabb-Kangas, T. (Ed) (1995). *Multilingualism for all*. Swets and Zeitlinger B.V.
Skutnabb-Kangas, T., Phillipson, R., & Rannut, M., (Eds.). (1994). *Linguistic human rights: Overcoming linguistic discrimination.* Berlin: Mouton de Gruyter.
Sonntag, S. K. (1995). Elite competition and official language movements. In J. W. Tollefson (Ed.) *Power and inequality in language education* (pp. 91–112). Cambridge University Press.
Stevens, G. (1994). Immigration, emigration, language acquisition, and the English language proficiency of immigrants in the U.S. In B. Edmonston & J. S. Passel (Eds.), *Immigration and ethnicity: The integration of America's newest arrivals* (pp. 163–181). Washington, D.C: The Urban Institute Press.

Tarver, H. (1989). Language and politics in the 1980s: The story of US English. *Politics and Society 17*(2), 220–239.
United States Census Bureau. (1993, April 28). *Number of non-English language speaking Americans up sharply in 1980s, Census Bureau says* [Press Release]. Washington, D.C.: U.S. Census Bureau.
United States Department of Commerce. (1993, Nov.). *We the American ... Hispanics*. Washington DC: U.S. Department of Commerce, Bureau of the Census.
United States Census Bureau. (1994). *1990 Census of Population* (CP-2-1A). Washington, D.C.: U.S. Government Printing Office.
Veltman, C. (1983). *Language shift in the United States*. Berlin: Mouton.
Veltman, C. (1998). Quebec, Canada, and the United States: Social reality and language rights. In T. Ricento, & B. Burnaby (Eds.), *Language and politics in the United States and Canada: Myths and realities*. (pp. 310–317). New Jersey and London: Erlbaum.
Wiley, T. G. (1999). Comparative historical analysis of U.S. language policy and language planning: Extending the foundations. In T. Huebner, & K. A. Davis (Eds.), *Sociopolitical perspectives on language policy and planning in the USA*. (pp. 17–39). Amsterdam: Benjamins.
Willig, A. (1985). A meta-analysis of selected studies on the effectiveness of bilingual education. *Review of Educational Research, 55*, 269–317.
Wilgoren, J. (2002, July 19). Divided by a call for a common language. *New York Times*, p. 13.
Woolard, K. A. (1998). Introduction: Language ideology as a field of inquiry. In B. B. Schieffelin, K. A. Woolard, & P. V. Kroskrity (Eds.), *Language ideologies: Practice and theory* (pp. 3–47). Oxford University Press.
Zelasko, N. F. (1991). *The bilingual double standard: Mainstream Americans' attitudes toward bilingualism*. Unpublished PhD dissertation, Georgetown University, Washington DC: University Microfilm International; Dissertation Information Service, Ann Arbor Michigan.
Zinn, H. (1995). *A people's history of the United States*. New York: The New Press.

CHAPTER 13

ADULT IMMIGRANT ESL PROGRAMS IN CANADA:

Emerging Trends in the Contexts of History, Economics, and Identity

DOUGLAS FLEMING

The University of British Columbia, Canada

ABSTRACT

The Canadian government likes to indulge in self-congratulatory and often smug statements about how generous it is to the large numbers of newcomers who immigrate into the country. Individual Canadians do indeed seem to be generous and welcoming to immigrants, but these tendencies should not mask the fact that the national government's policy developers support high levels of immigration primarily because this is vital to their perception of Canada's long-term economic and political interests. Canada obtains the full financial benefits of immigration only if newcomers can be integrated into the fabric of the nation's economic life. In that regard, second language education programs are central to the removal of barriers to newcomer integration, especially the inability to speak English or French, the country's two official languages. However crucial the economic contributions provided by these programs might be, it is also important to note they play a crucial role in identity formation, both in terms of what it means to individuals and the nation-state. The ability of these programs to foster identity construction is being limited by funding decisions that limit English language learning to basic levels of proficiency and increasingly place greater emphasis on the limited goal of job preparation.

> Canadian history and traditions have created a country where our values include tolerance and respect for cultural differences, and a commitment to social justice. We are proud of the fact that we are a peaceful nation and that we are accepted in many places around the world as peacekeepers. As a small population occupying a vast northern land enriched by immigration throughout its history, Canadians have developed a kind of genius for compromise and co-existence. (Citizenship and Immigration Canada, 2002a) Canada faces demographic challenges. Birth rates are at a historic low, and Canada's largest age cohort—the baby boomers—is ageing...Immigration will likely account for all net labour force growth by 2011, and projections indicate it will account for total population growth by 2031. For these reasons, ensuring that immigrants and refugees have the skills to succeed in the labour market is key to Canada's future prosperity. (Citizenship and Immigration Canada Immigration Plan, 2002c).
>
> Each and every form of ethnic, linguistic, religious, racial and indeed national social identity in Canada has been fabricated into a certain nationality through maintaining the dominance of some social identity (a certain patriarchal Englishness) against and under which...all others are subordinated. (Young, 1984, pp. 10-12)
>
> For all its rhetoric about a cultural 'mosaic', Canada refuses to renovate its national self-image to include its changing complexion. It is a New World country with Old World concepts of a fixed, exclusionist national identity... Canadians of colour were routinely treated as 'not real' Canadians. (Mukherjee, 1997)

INTRODUCTION

As indicated by the first quotation that introduces this chapter, the Canadian government often seems to make self-congratulatory, even smug statements about how generous it is to the large numbers of newcomers who immigrate into the country. Individual Canadians do indeed seem to be generous and welcoming to immigrants, as is shown in recent polling (Migration News, 2002) and exemplified by newspaper editorials (Toronto Star, 2002a). However, as the second quotation reveals, these tendencies should not mask the fact that the national government's policy developers support high levels of immigration primarily because this is vital to their perception of Canada's long-term economic and political interests. Canada obtains the full financial benefits of immigration only if newcomers can be integrated into the fabric of the nation's economic life. Second language education programs are central to the removal of barriers to newcomer integration (Wong, Duff, & Early, 2001) especially the inability to speak either English or French, the country's two official languages.

However crucial the economic contributions provided by these programs might be, it is also important to note they play a crucial role in identity formation, both in terms of what it means to individuals (Harris, Leung, & Rampton, 2002; Ilieva, 2000; Kubota, 2001; Morgan, 1997; Norton, 2000) and the nation-state (B. Anderson, 1991; Burt, 1986; Courchêne, 1996; Fleming, 2003; Hall, 1992; Kaplan, 1993; Kymlicka, 1992; McNamara, 1997; Mitchell, 2001; Murphy, 1971; Schecter & Bayley, 1997; White & Hunt, 2000). As I argue later, however, the ability of these programs to foster identity construction is being limited by funding decisions that limit English language learning to basic levels of proficiency and increasingly place greater emphasis on the limited goal of job preparation.

Canadian national identity is a highly contested and notoriously slippery entity. Up to the present time, most ESL programs have served to strengthen the privilege enjoyed by British-based culture in the ways criticized by Young (1984) and Mukherjee (1997) in the introductory quotations. The current challenge is to break this mould and design programming that helps recreate Canadian national identity in a truly egalitarian manner and fulfills the real promise of multiculturalism in its more critical forms (Chicago Cultural Studies Group, 1992; Cummins, 1988; McLaren, 2001).

In this chapter, I first sketch the historic context of immigration before outlining bilingualism and multiculturalism, the two policy initiatives that represent the Canadian government's strategic responses to pressing demographic and political pressures. In my third section, I provide a brief history of second language education program development in Canada. This is followed by a summary of how the more important features of current adult ESL policy and provision developed. I conclude with references to emerging trends in Canadian adult ESL programs and comment on the implications for nation-state identity formation in Canada.

THE HISTORIC CONTEXT OF IMMIGRATION

Some of the countries that currently make immigration an important part of state planning are Canada, the United States, Australia, and New Zealand. However, almost all economically developed countries are reassessing the benefits of immigration in the face of declining birth rates, ageing populations and globalization (Churchill, 1986). This trend is occurring at the same time that at least 150 million people are on the move on the globe at any one time, more than ever before in human history. Many of these emigrants are fleeing increased levels of war and violence, while others hope to escape the grinding forces of poverty that is deepening in many parts of the world. Increasingly, developed countries are competing with one another to attract skilled immigrants and take advantage of these vast diasporas (Citizenship and Immigration Canada, 2002c).

Immigration has always played a major role in Canadian demographics. According to the latest census data (Statistics Canada, 2003), out of a total current population of 31.5 million, only a little more than 1 million Canadians claim some form of aboriginal heritage. The vast majority of Canadians, on the other hand, have either descended from immigrants or are immigrants themselves.

In the aftermath of European contact and the devastation of native populations, the number of people in the French-speaking colonies of what would become Canada grew until it was approximately 1700. Soon after the British conquest of Quebec in 1759, however, large numbers of French-speaking Acadians were expelled from present-day Nova Scotia to Louisiana. Many of these exiles returned in large enough numbers to ensure the bilingual character of present-day New Brunswick, but not enough to turn the tide against successive waves of English-speaking immigration to what was now known as British North America. Not long after the American War of Independence, when those loyal to the British crown fled the United States, the English-speaking population became the majority in what would become Canada.

By 1900, the English-speaking majority made up 57% of the total Canadian population of 5,374,026. French speakers, both in and out of Quebec, amounted to 30%. Native peoples made up only 2.4% of the population. The remainder were principally immigrants from Central Europe recruited to populate the western prairies and those Chinese laborers (possibly up to 15,000) brought in to build the trans-continental railways.

Much of the history of 20th century Canadian immigration makes for upsetting reading (Knowles, 2000). There were strong preferences expressed by government for British immigrants. Those from Ireland or continental Europe were accepted for strategic reasons if those from the United Kingdom couldn't be found, particularly when the Canadian government moved to counteract American expansionism and Métis separatism in the West. These immigrants were often provided with significant land grants as incentives to immigrate. On the other hand, Asian applicants were either explicitly excluded or subject to prohibitive entry fees and regulations, even when holding British passports. The notorious *head tax* created a significant economic barrier to Asians who wished to enter the country or reunite their families. Other immigration procedures discouraged black applicants and made it nearly impossible for Jews fleeing war-torn Europe to enter the country. Even those racial minorities already in Canada faced serious forms of discrimination. Many racial groups were barred from practicing some professions, living in certain neighborhoods, or explicitly denied voting rights. Native peoples, to cite the worst example, only gained the federal franchise in 1960.

This sad history is littered with violence and the capricious exercise of power by government officials. A few of the worst examples demonstrate that Canadian history has not been the progress of sweetness and light that is often portrayed. In 1907, whites rampaged through Chinese and Japanese neighborhoods in Vancouver threatening its residents and smashing storefronts. In 1914, the Komogata Maru, a ship containing 440 emigrants from India, was refused entry to British Columbia under various arbitrary pretexts even though it had adhered to the ridiculous regulations used at the time to prevent the entry of South Asians, even if they held British passports. Later in the century, most Canadians of Japanese descent had their possessions confiscated during the Second World War because they shared the same ethnicity as the enemy of the time.

In 1947, a long process of change in citizenship and immigration policies was inaugurated. Chinese and South Asian citizens were allowed to vote in that year and Japanese citizens 2 years later. Canadian citizens were made distinct from British subjects. Married women gained the right to citizenship separate from their husbands. The ability to claim dual citizenship, a privilege enjoyed particularly by British citizens, was restricted. Residency requirements were instituted for all applicants, including those from Britain. In the 1960s, Canada removed quotas and racial criteria from its immigration selection process and adopted a "point system," in which applications were assessed on the basis of a set of objective criteria.

These changes in immigration policy occurred in the context of important demographic changes in Canadian society that started soon after the end of the Second World War. After the short but significant jump immediately following 1945, the Canadian birth rate steadily declined. The growth rate in births now stands at less than 1% annually and continues to fall. In the 1990s it became apparent that the Canadian labor force and tax base were declining to such a degree that it threatened the pensions and other state supports, such as state-run medical insurance, for the 'baby-boomers' born just after the war. To answer that threat, significant increases in immigration were inaugurated.

These trends are continuing. In 2003, Canada again increased its immigration targets to between 220,000 and 245,000 newcomers. Immigrants now account for over 70% of the total national labor force growth. If current trends continue, immigration will account for 100% of total labor force growth within 10 years and all population growth by 2031 (Citizenship and Immigration Canada, 2002c). The government's ability to account for expansion or inflation will thus soon be totally dependent on immigration.

It is important to note that these new immigrants increasingly tend to come from countries where the dominant language is neither English nor French. In recent years, up to 43% of all immigrants arriving in Canada have not been able to speak either of the official languages beyond a marginal level. There have also been changes in the ethnic origins of immigrants. In 1966, 87% of all immigrants to Canada were from Europe. Today, 80.3% of all immigrants originate from Asia and the Pacific, Africa, the Middle East, and South and Central America. The need for adult language education is also clear, given the fact that over 70% of all immigrants to Canada are adults.

These immigrants arrive at a time when over 16% of the country's population already claim a mother tongue other than English and French. Recent immigrants make up large percentages of the population of the three largest urban regions: Toronto (42%), Montreal (18%) and Vancouver (35%). These percentages will only increase if current trends continue (Statistics Canada, 2003).

These newcomers will face many of the challenges previous generations of immigrants faced, not the least of which will be racism. This is because racism is not simply a "historical fact" in Canada. As a number of scholars have made quite plain, it is still very much part of the nation's present condition (Bannerji, 2000; Henry, Tator, Mattis, & Rees, 2000; Li, 1990; Ng, 1993).

BILINGUALISM AND MULTICULTURALISM: THE POLICY CONTEXT

Since the 1970s, the Canadian government has embarked on two major policy initiatives to remake the nation-state: bilingualism and multiculturalism. The first of these, bilingualism, is a central part of the federal strategy to maintain national unity in the face of one of the greatest political challenges facing the modern Canadian nation state: Quebec separatism (Esses & Gardiner, 1996). The second, multiculturalism, is designed as a way to integrate the increased numbers of immigrants discussed above. Few nations have ever before attempted a project on this scale. Some have argued that Canada is the first country to remake itself in the contexts of post-modernism and globalization (Fulford, 1993).

Before the advent of bilingualism and multiculturalism in Canada, language policies centered on the interactions (or lack thereof) between the two "founding peoples," the English and the French. In most jurisdictions across the country, separate school systems were introduced for both language groups and little interaction occurred. The particular language education needs of other linguistic populations were not taken into account and they were simply expected to assimilate.

Bilingualism was instituted as official government policy as a result of the 1969 Official Languages Act, and was enshrined in the *Canadian Constitution Act* and *Charter of Rights and Freedoms* in 1982. It strengthened the role of both English and French as the official languages for the country, ensured equal access to government services and regulated the labeling of consumer goods in both languages. Bilingualism also financed the creation of English and French second language education programs in elementary and secondary schools throughout the country.

Bilingualism was instituted in answer to the *silent revolution* that occurred in Quebec during the 1950s and 1960s. Long-simmering grievances on the part of the French-speaking majority in the province led to movements for greater autonomy and even independence. Many Quebecois expressed bitterness over the discrimination they faced in the workplace and government, noting the degree of privilege enjoyed by the English-speaking minority. More importantly, they expressed fears about their eventual complete assimilation into an English-speaking continent, citing the slow decline of French in other parts of North America where it was once more commonly spoken, such as Louisiana, Manitoba, Saskatchewan, and northern Ontario.

Bilingualism developed in the context of the violent 1970 October Crisis in Quebec and the elections of separatist provincial governments in that province not long afterwards. As federal policy, bilingualism was designed to make French-speaking Canadians feel more at home in their own country by providing equal access to power structures. After the adoption of bilingualism, for example, it became difficult to have a career in the top levels of the federal civil service without a working knowledge of both official languages.

Multiculturalism, launched only one year after the October Crisis in Quebec, was developed quite clearly within the framework of bilingualism. It was adopted in response to increased immigration, the need to develop a distinct national identity in the face of an increasingly aggressive American cultural presence and the discontent expressed by immigrant groups to the designation of French and English as official languages (Esses & Gardner, 1996). In a speech at the time, Prime Minister Trudeau (1971) explicitly made the links between creation of an officially bilingual and multicultural state to national unity and economic development. Principles related to multiculturalism, such as respect for diverse cultures and races and the full and equitable participation of all ethnic groups in Canadian social life were also subsequently enshrined in the Canadian Constitution. On a practical level, multiculturalism released funds for the support of cultural activities and, more importantly, advocacy organizations in a multitude of ethnic communities.

Given the historic and political contexts that went into the creation of the policies of bilingualism and multiculturalism, it is not surprising that multilingualism was not part of the agenda (Corson, 1990). Multiculturalism was not designed to compromise the privileged position enjoyed by French and English, the languages of the two "founding peoples" or their corresponding cultures.

ADULT ESL PROGRAM DEVELOPMENT

No priority was given to the development of national ESL programs, either for children or for adults, prior to the Second World War (Ashworth, 2001; Burnaby, 1996). Separate jurisdictions, such as individual school districts or provincial ministries of education administered second language programs, but usually on an ad hoc basis.

There are some interesting historical examples of how second languages, dialects, and cultures were treated by educational institutions as things to be eradicated from Canadian social life. The first school in what would become Canada, founded in 1632 by the Jesuit order in Quebec, exposed its multicultural student body to an explicitly Christian training. This tradition continued with residential schools, a notorious system in which aboriginal children were forcibly taken from their parents and communities for the express purpose of eradicating their languages and cultures. The residential school system, responsible for an enormous amount of sorrow in native communities, were administered by various Christian churches and supported by the federal government.

The racist attitudes of many administrators were evident in every part of the country. In 1844, Egerton Ryerson, the first Chief Superintendent of Schools in what would become Ontario, helped found an educational system explicitly mandated to assimilate the newly arrived Catholic Irish and promote protestant "Anglo-conformity" (Tomkins, 1977).

On the prairies, one of the most influential educators of new Canadians, James Anderson, emphasized the need for teachers to adopt a "missionary spirit" for the task of stamping out bilingualism and promoting Anglo-Canadian values and culture (Anderson, 1918). Anderson, later elected premier of Saskatchewan, headed a notoriously conservative government that restricted French and minority language rights until being defeated at the polls in 1934, accused of corruption and having links with the Ku Klux Klan.

British Columbia has also had a long history of racial conflict over education. The most important example of this is the local school authority's 1922 attempt to segregate Chinese-Canadian children in Victoria, the provincial capital. The Chinese community in that city, one of the oldest immigrant enclaves in the country, organized a boycott that ended the practice a year later (Stanley, 1991). The Vancouver School Board opened the first ESL programs for children in British Columbia in 1907, but no provincial body sponsored adult ESL programs until the advent of federal multicultural policy, over 60 years later.

Multicultural policy quickly opened the door for programs that promoted heritage languages for children but did not lead immediately to the systematic provision of adult ESL. Many difficulties arose over conflicts between federal and provincial jurisdictions. Under the Canadian Constitution, education is a provincial responsibility. Immigration and citizenship is federal. Both jurisdictions claimed that adult second language education was the responsibility of the other. Ontario and Quebec developed provincial funding formulas that allowed various bodies, such as school districts, colleges, and community agencies to provide limited access to English and French language education, respectively. This led to some innovative and far-reaching program planning, most notably by the Toronto School Board, which had to cope with the enormous demographic changes of a city subject to a massive influx of immigrants. Few other jurisdictions in the country acted.

In 1978, the federal government, through the Employment and Immigration Canada (EIC), created the first national language training project as part of the Canadian Job Strategies (CJS) program. This program provided language training for adult migrants and native Canadians who could not find employment because they lacked proficiency in English or French. It did this through the use of *training seats*, where the federal government purchased the rights to enroll students they sponsored from the ranks of the unemployed. This training was usually full time with basic living allowances or unemployment insurance benefits provided to trainees who met certain criteria. The instructors, typically hired through community colleges, provided language instruction at a basic level of proficiency. Institutional providers applied for the funds, hired instructors, determined curricula, selected materials, and conducted assessments on their own, sometimes on an ad hoc basis. It is interesting to note that many of these programming features are still extant in current Canadian language training programs. Canadian governments, whether federal or provincial, have provided the funds but have not provided much direct guidance historically on ESL methodology, curriculum development, or teacher training. As I discuss later, however, this situation has changed.

Over time, several deficiencies of the CJS program became apparent. The total number of students enrolled in its language training components was never very large, rarely numbering more the 15,000 in any 1 year. This was far fewer than the estimated number of people in the country who needed language training, a fact undoubtedly due to the restricted nature of its eligibility requirements. More importantly, due to the fact that the program was geared for re-employment, only *heads of households* (i.e. the principal family wage earner) were eligible. Given the long-standing wage gap between the genders, this meant that almost all the participants in the program were men. In addition, recent immigrants with little or no Canadian work experience were ineligible because they were not on the unemployment insurance rolls.

As a result of a court challenge sponsored by several immigrant organizations in regard to these inequities, the federal government created three new language-training programs that had broader community foci. Two of these, the Secretary of State Citizenship and Language Training Program and the Citizenship and Community Participation Program were short-lived. They subsidized the wages of instructors in selected citizenship programs and provided money for textbooks. Both programs were part-time and offered no living allowances for participants.

The third program, the Settlement Language Training Program (SLTP), was more substantial. Created in 1986, it was designed to meet the needs of adult immigrants, primarily women and seniors, who were not destined for the labor force. The SLTP had the advantages of being flexible and the ability to provide onsite childcare and the reimbursement of out-of-pocket expenses such as bus fares. Immigrant organizations received substantial funding to enter the field with school districts and colleges as language training providers. Many formed alliances with already existing providers in the development of new and innovative programming, particularly in the Toronto region with the local school boards.

Over time, deficiencies also became apparent in the SLTP. Many immigrant organizations and providers complained that the program was chronically under-funded, with a variety of inequities in application, inferior facilities, poorly trained staff, and inconsistent curricula and methodology (Health and Welfare Canada, 1988).

THE CURRENT STRUCTURE OF ADULT ESL PROVISION

The string of events that led to the creation of the current structure of adult ESL programming in Canada started in 1990, with the release of the federal government's 4 year immigration plan (Government of Canada, 1991). The plan was a major change in direction for the federal government and came at a time when the demographic changes in Canadian society discussed earlier were becoming more evident.

The plan garnered a great deal of press at the time because it increased levels of immigration while extolling the associated economic benefits. The plan also prioritized the procurement of immigrants who had particular business and career skills, called for a streamlining of the immigration process, and indicated a need for greater provincial/federal co-operation. Most importantly, the plan set immigrant language training as a major national priority for the first time.

Responding to the need for greater provincial/federal cooperation, Quebec negotiated an accord with Ottawa in 1991 that gave the province immigration selection powers and the responsibility to provide integration services and French language training. The federal government turned over the funds apportioned for immigrants in Quebec to the province and retained only the power to set general guidelines.

In the rest of the provinces, however, no agreements regarding language policy were immediately forthcoming. In 1991, the federal government took the initiative and formed a special advisory council made up of various stakeholders in immigration and settlement. This body provided a set of recommendations that called for greater consistency in adult ESL provision, the development of professional development and training standards for teachers, valid language assessment tests, an increase in training periods, limits to class sizes, and national curriculum documents.

The following year, two adult immigrant training programs were initiated that attempted to implement the recommendations of the advisory council: Labour Market Language Training (LMLT) and Language Instruction to Newcomers to Canada (LINC). LMLT focused on higher levels of English proficiency and was modeled on language training programs in Australia that were career specific. It was short-lived, however. LINC and the provincial counterparts it has spawned, however, has become the dominant adult ESL structure in Canada. It has gradually replaced almost all other English training programs in the country and has been instrumental in the development of a myriad of national assessment and curriculum projects.

LINC has been designed for basic language training and can be accessed by any recently landed immigrant (official resident) of Canada. It features better levels of funding than those that existed in previous programs and more consistent assessment and placement procedures. A greater degree of accountability in regards to attendance and record keeping has also been set up. Like in other programs that preceded it, LINC providers have to apply yearly for funds, hire instructors, arrange classroom space, and determine curricula and materials. However, important differences in the funding application processes have led to a much wider range of providers. Community agencies (especially in Ontario), and for-profit businesses (especially in British Columbia) have become bigger players, much to the chagrin of more traditional providers such as community colleges. In order to compete with these new players, traditional providers have had to cut costs to survive, principally by restricting the salary demands of their professional staff.

Except in rare and isolated instances, LINC learners are not eligible for living allowances or significant subsidies. In some jurisdictions, learners are provided transportation allowances and access to childcare. A very small minority, with the co-operation of other government service agencies, can draw on welfare or unemployment benefits while attending classes. The vast majority, however, either attend evening classes while working during the day or depend on the financial resources of family members while taking day programs.

On average, depending on their level of English language proficiency, LINC learners are eligible for up to roughly 900 hours of instruction (close to 1 year of full-time classes or 3 years of part-time classes) from the time they start (Citizenship and Immigration Canada, 2002b). They are assessed prior to entering the program by an independent agency and placed in one of three levels of English language proficiency. These levels correspond to the most basic of the 12-level Canadian benchmark system to be discussed later. Some variation in program delivery models exist, but in most cases, LINC and the provincial programs associated with it, feature continuous enrolment, unilingual instruction, limited access to computer assisted learning, and frequent changes of instructor. In some cases, however, circumstances permit the same instructor at all levels, and staggered or semestered enrolment. Occasionally, classes are tailored for particular ethnic communities or women.

Although some of these programs are sponsored by community agencies and have a good grounding in neighborhoods and workplaces, the vast majority of LINC programs are housed in institutional settings, such as secondary schools and libraries. The model used most often emphasizes individualism and personal achievement. Programs often set college or university entrance as eventual goals for its learners.

LINC provided only limited amounts of guidance in terms of methodology and delivery, much like previously existing programs. There have been a few exceptions, however, such as when the Ontario region of Canada Immigration and Citizenship developed province-wide curricula and materials. Most aspects of provision, however, became decentralized, as part of the federal government's cost-saving divestiture of responsibilities for direct service.

Although most aspects of the program have remained uniform and consistent, LINC has occasionally been fine-tuned. The level of English proficiency it covers has been expanded in some programs in Ontario. In other isolated examples, more flexible forms of delivery have been developed to cover the special needs of women or seniors in certain jurisdictions.

Since the creation of LINC, several provincial and territorial governments in addition to Quebec have signed formal agreements with the federal government in regards to language policy. The federal goal is to have agreements in place with all provinces in the near future. To date, the Yukon, Saskatchewan, and Prince Edward Island have signed general agreements around processes of consultation and planning. British Columbia signed an agreement in 1998 that transferred federal responsibility for settlement services to the province. LINC programs in B.C. are now known as English Language Service to Adults (ELSA) and operate under a different funding structure. Manitoba signed a similar agreement in 1996, renaming its programs *Adult English as a Second Language Services* (A/ ESL).

These transfers of responsibility have been controversial. In Canada, most tax revenue is collected by the federal government, which transfers a large percentage of these funds to the provinces. Many disputes have occurred about whether or not these funds should be "earmarked" for specific purposes. For example, in regards to healthcare, a provincial responsibility constitutionally, federal/provincial agreements state that money transferred to the provinces is to be spent in that area. In the case of immigrant services such as language training, however, no such stipulation exists. The provinces of Manitoba and British Columbia put funds transferred for these programs into general revenue and then allot the money to ELSA and A/ ESL that they feel is appropriate. In British Columbia, the provincial government provides a significantly smaller amount of money per capita than provinces such as Ontario, where language training is still under the direct control of the federal government.

At the time of writing, the total national cost of integrating immigrants is $334.6 million per year (Citizenship and Immigration Canada, 2002d). Of that figure, LINC costs the federal government $100.4 million. The money transferred to Quebec, Manitoba, and British Columbia for their language training and immigrant settlement programs amounts to $45.1 million. Immigrants pay a substantial portion of the costs of these programs themselves, principally through payment of the Canadian permanent residence fee that currently stands at $975 each.

At the same time as LINC was being developed, the federal government initiated a process that led to the creation of the Canadian Language Benchmarks (CLB). In response to recommendations made by the immigration advisory council and a wide-ranging set of consultations conducted subsequently, the federal government set up a representative national working group in 1993 to facilitate the creation of a set of language proficiency benchmarks to inform assessment and curriculum development (Pierce & Stewart, 1997). The benchmarks were released as a working document in 1996 and finalized in 2000.

The CLB covers the full range of English proficiency (from beginning to full fluency), incorporates literacy and numeracy, emphasizes tasks and stand-alone descriptors for each level, encourages local curriculum development, and includes proficiencies related to learning strategies, socio-cultural and strategic competencies (Citizenship and Immigration Canada, 1996).

Associated with the CLB are implementation documents, curriculum guidelines, instructional resources pertaining to literacy and numeracy, sets of assessment materials and a representative national centre in Ottawa that coordinates a wide-range of language training curriculum initiatives. Publishers have also used the CLB as a basis for a wide variety of instructional materials.

It is difficult to determine the exact number of programs that exist and learners serviced in Canada. The only attempt to collect data was conducted by the federal government in 1999 (Heritage Canada, 1999). Unfortunately, the principal focus of the survey was the large commercial market that provides academic English training to overseas students on temporary visas to Canada. Projections completed by the researchers indicate that something in the order of 177,000 Canadian citizens and immigrants are taking English language training at any one time. LINC practitioners often cite anecdotal evidence related to high dropout and low attendance rates. It is difficult at the time of writing to ascertain hard facts about these claims, however. Better statistical gathering processes, being put in place for both LINC and its provincial equivalents, should provide us with a better picture in the near future.

EMERGING TRENDS AND THE CONSTRUCTION OF IDENTITY

Adult ESL programs, as they currently exist, are designed to bring most newcomers up to a minimal level of English language proficiency. In most jurisdictions, little consideration to date has been given to the provision of instruction beyond levels 3 and 4 of the Canadian Language Benchmark's 12-level scale. Most newcomers without independent means have had difficulty accessing programs that could give them the English language proficiency to gain non-menial employment. Higher levels of training and education have been available, but at increasingly greater costs. In addition, like in other social service sectors, financial cutbacks in the last decade have been common to all government funded adult ESL programs. These cuts have had devastating effects (Toronto Star, 2002b).

There has been recent increased pressure to expand ESL programming to train and re-license immigrants in specific professions in which labor shortages are developing. The demographic trends I have outlined earlier are having their effects. A major development occurred in 2002, when the Ontario provincial government earmarked $15 million for bridge training projects to re-license and train newcomers in the specific fields of health care, education, the machining, millwright, and tooling trades, financial services programming, engineering, life sciences, and welding (Ontario Ministry of Education, 2002). There has also been an expansion in funding for workplace specific literacy training that goes beyond survival needs (Preparatory Training Program of Toronto, 2002). At the present time, these are the kinds of programs that are receiving increases in government funding.

These examples are part of a trend in adult ESL programming that emphasizes skills and work-related training. Government funding priorities in adult ESL are clearly turning to workplace specific programming. While these programs are certainly practical, I would argue that they atomize learners into sets of marketable skills. This is a shift that has occurred in both Canada and Australia from learning skills and educational service models to an undesirable rationalized industry orientation (Cumming, 1998). Moore (1996) criticizes the trend towards rationalization in the Australian ESL context for the way in which it homogenizes programming, and ignores individual learner differences. I also contend that these programming policy decisions fail to take into account the entire individuality of our learners and their identities. The multifaceted and complex process of identity construction in the types of educational settings I have described cannot be fully realized without opportunities for intermediate and advanced language learning that engages the entire individual. Basic level language learning and work specific training may be practical, but they are severely limited.

Even though national identity and culture often appear to be unchanging and unidimensional systems of symbols, behaviors, and values that are somehow immutable or even ethereal, every modern nation-state must actively work on its creation (Teeple, 2000, p. 164). Like individual identity construction, this process is multifaceted, complex, and dynamic. Canadian cultural identity cannot be viewed as a pristine set of immutable facts to be transmitted to the immigrants in our ESL classes. Nor should our history be represented as an unproblematic and inevitable progress towards our status as the world's "best place to live." Our practice as ESL educators in countries like Canada must reflect the fact that newcomers are dynamically reconstructing identity, both in terms of their own personal and nation-state identities. In very real ways, they are transforming what they encounter both in and out of classes into new visions of what it means to be a citizen of a particular country, or even, in fact, the world as a whole.

ESL programs can make a significant contribution to this process if they are given the scope to do so. Limiting these programs in the ways they are presently only helps perpetuate the situation that Young and Mukherjee (1997) criticize. The privileged position of British-based culture is now an anachronism, given Canada's emerging demographics. Our challenge now is to expand and design adult ESL programming that helps recreate Canadian national identity in a truly egalitarian manner.

REFERENCES

Anderson, B. (1991). *Imagined communities: Reflections on the origins and spread of nationalism*. London: Verso.
Anderson, J. T. M. (1918). *The education of the new Canadian*. Toronto: Dent.
Ashworth, M. (2001). ESL in British Columbia. In B. Mohan, C. Leung, & C. Davison (Eds.), *English as a second language in the mainstream: Teaching, learning and identity* (pp. 93–106). London: Longman.
Bannerji, H. (2000). *The dark side of the nation: Essays on multiculturalism, nationalism and gender*. Toronto, Ontario, Canada: Canadian Scholars' Press.
Burnaby, B. (1996). Language policies in Canada. In M. Herriman & B. Burnaby (Eds.), *Language policies in English-dominant countries* (pp. 159–217). Philadelphia: Multilingual Matters.
Burt, E. C. (1986). Citizenship and social participation: Grounded theory in civic education. In R. R. Gadacz (Ed.), *Challenging the concept of citizenship* (pp. 46–75). Edmonton: CSC Consulting.
Chicago Cultural Studies Group. (1992). Critical multiculturalism. *Critical Inquiry, 18*, 531–555.
Churchill, S. (1986). *The education of linguistic and cultural minorities in the OECD countries*. Clevedon, Avon: Multilingual Matters.
Citizenship and Immigration Canada. (1996). *Canadian language benchmarks: ESL for adults and ESL for literacy learners*. Retrieved February 26, 2003, from http://www.cic.gc.ca/english/newcomer/esl%2De.html.
Citizenship and Immigration Canada. (2002a). *A look at Canada*. Retrieved February 26, 2003 from http://www.cicnet.ci.gc.ca/english/citizen/look/look-02e.html.
Citizenship and Immigration Canada. (2002b). *Fact sheet: Language instruction to newcomers to Canada*. Retrieved March 3, 2003, from http://www.cic.gc/english/newcomer/linc-fs1.html.
Citizenship and Immigration Canada. (2002c). *Immigration plan for 2002*. Retrieved February 26, 2003, from http://www.cic.gc.ca/english/pub/anrep02.html.
Citizenship and Immigration Canada. (2002d). *Report on plans and priorities in 2002–2003 Estimates*. Ottawa: Canadian Government Publishing.
Corson, D. (1990). *Language policy across the curriculum*. Clevedon: Multilingual Matters.
Courchêne, R. (1996). Teaching Canadian culture: Teacher preparation. *TESL Canada Journal, 13*(2), 1–16.
Cumming, A. (1998). Skill, service or industry? The orientation of settlement programs for adults learning English in Canada and Australia. *Prospects, 13*(3), 36–42.
Cummins, J. (1988). From multicultural to anti-racist education: An analysis of programmes and policies in Ontario. In T. Skutnabb Kangas & J. Cummins (Eds.), *Minority education: From shame to struggle* (pp. 127–157). Clevedon, Avon: Multilingual Matters.
Esses, V., & Gardner, R. C. (1996). Multiculturalism in Canada: Context and current status. *Canadian Journal of Behavioural Science, 28*(3), 145–152.
Fleming, D. (2003). Linking personal and nation-state identities: Research and practice. *TESL Canada Journal*, pp. 65–79.
Fulford, R. (1993). A post-modern dominion: The changing nature of Canadian citizenship. In W. Kaplan (Ed.), *Belonging: Essays on the meaning and future of Canadian citizenship* (pp. 104–122). Montreal: McGill-Queen's University Press.
Government of Canada. (1991). *Annual report to parliament: Immigration plan for 1991–1995*. Ottawa: Immigration Canada.
Hall, S. (1992). The question of cultural identity. In S. Hall, D. Held, & T. McGrew (Eds.), *Modernity and its futures* (pp. 273–326). Cambridge: Polity Press.
Harris, R., Leung C., & Rampton, B. (2002). Globalization, diaspora and language-teaching in England. In D. Block & D. Cameron (Eds.), *Globalization and language teaching* (pp. 29–46). London: Routledge.
Health and Welfare Canada. (1988). *Report of the Canadian task force on mental health issues affecting immigrants and refugees*. Retrieved February 26, 2003, from http://ceris.metropolis.net/Virtual%20Library/health/candian_taskforce/canadian1.html.
Henry, F., Tator, C., Mattis, W., & Rees, T. (2000). *The colour of democracy: Racism in Canadian society*. Toronto: Harcourt Brace.
Heritage Canada. (1999). *New Canadian perspectives: A profile of the providers of training in English and French as a second language*. Ottawa: Training and Continuing Education Section, Centre for Education Statistics, Statistics Canada.

Ilieva, R. (2000). Exploring culture in texts designed for use in adult ESL classrooms. *TESL Canada Journal, 17*(2), 50–63.
Kaplan, W. (1993). Who belongs? Changing concepts of Canadian citizenship. In W. Kaplan (Ed.), *Belonging: Essays on the meaning and future of Canadian citizenship* (pp. 245–264). Montreal: McGill-Queen's University Press.
Knowles, V. (2000). *Forging our legacy: Canadian citizenship and immigration, 1900–1977*. Ottawa: Public Works and Government Services Canada.
Kubota, R. (2001). Discursive construction of the images of U.S. classrooms. *TESOL Quarterly, 35*(1), 9–38.
Kymlicka, W. (1992). *Recent work in citizenship theory*. Ottawa: Multiculturalism and Citizenship Canada.
Li, P. (1990). *Race and ethnic relations in Canada*. Toronto: Oxford Press.
McLaren, P. (2001). Wayward multiculturalists: A reply to Gregor McLennan. *Ethnicities, 1*(3), 408–420.
McNamara, T. (1997). What do we mean by social identity? Competing frameworks, competing discourses. *TESOL Quarterly, 31*(3), 561–566.
Migration News. (2002). *Canada: Polls, data*. Retrieved March 3, 2003, from http://www.migration.ucdavis.edu/mn/archive_mn/apr_2002-04mn.html.
Mitchell, K. (2001). Education for democratic citizenship: Transnationalism, multiculturalism and the limits of liberalism. *Harvard Educational Review, 71*(1), 51–78.
Moore, H. (1996) Telling what is real: Competing views in assessing ESL development. *Linguistics and education, 8*, 189–228.
Morgan, B. (1997). Identity and intonation: Linking dynamic processes in an ESL classroom. *TESOL Quarterly, 31*(3), 431–450.
Mukherjee, B. (1997) *American dreamer*. Retrieved March 3, 2003, from http://www.mojones.com/mother_jones/JF97/mukherjee_jump.html.
Murphy, R. (1971). *Dialectics of social life*. New York: Basic.
Ng, R. (1993). Sexism, racism, Canadian nationalism. In H. Bannerji (Ed.), *Returning the gaze: Essays on racism, feminism and politics* (pp. 182–196). Toronto: Sister Vision Press.
Norton, B. (2000). *Identity and language learning*. Harlow: Pearson.
Ontario Ministry of Education. (2002). *Backgrounder to bridge training programs*. Retrieved March 4, 2003 from http://www.edu.gov.on.ca/eng/document/nr/02.11/bg1115.html.
Pierce, B., & Stewart, G. (1997). The development of the Canadian Language Benchmark Assessment. *TESL Canada Journal, 8*(2), 17–31.
Preparatory Training Program of Toronto. (2002). *About PTP*. Retrieved on March 4, 2003 from htp://ptp.ca/about.html.
Schecter, S., & Bayley. R. (1997). Language socialisation practices and cultural identity: Case studies of Mexican descent families in California and Texas. *TESOL Quarterly, 31*(3), 513–542.
Stanley, T. (1991) *Defining the Chinese other: White supremacy, schooling and social structure in British Columbia before 1923*. Vancouver: University of British Columbia.
Statistics Canada. (2003). *2001 census data*. Retrieved February 26, 2003, from http://www12.statcan.ca/english/census01/release/index.cfm.
Teeple, G. (2000). *Globalisation and the decline of social reform*. Aurora: Garamond.
Tomkins, G. (1977). Canadian Education and the Development of a National Consciousness: Historical and Contemporary Perspectives. In A. Chaiton and N. McDonald (Eds.), *Canadian Schools and Canadian Identity* (pp. 6–28). Toronto: Gage Educational Press.
Toronto Star. (2002a). *Editorial: Let Canada speak out at racism summit*. Retrieved March 3, 2003, from http://www.thestar.com/NASApp/cs/ContentServer?pagename=thestar/Layout/Article-PrintFriendly&c=Article&cid=998648066823.
Toronto Star (2002b). *Cuts hit ESL hard, survey finds*. Retrieved June 1st, 2002 from http://www.thestar.com/NASApp/cs/ContentServer?pagename=thestar.
Trudeau, P. E. (1971). *Multiculturalism*. Retrieved August 16, 2005 from http://northernblue.ca/canchan/cantext/speech2/1971ptmu.html.
White, M., & Hunt A. (2000). Citizenship: Care of the self, character and personality. In *Citizenship Studies, 4*, 93–115.
Wong, P., Duff, P., & Early, M. (2001). The impact of language and skills training on immigrants' lives. *TESL Canada Journal, 18*(2), 1–31.
Young, J. (1987). *Breaking the mosaic: Ethnic identities in Canadian schooling*. Aurora: Garamond.

CHAPTER 14

FOCUS ON LITERACY:

ELT and Educational Attainment in England

JILL BOURNE

The University of Southampton, UK

ABSTRACT

This chapter outlines the background to policy and practice in relation to learners of English as an additional language in England. It examines the ways in which mainstream educational policy and practice have attempted to adapt in recognizing that linguistic diversity is the norm rather than the exception in modern British society. Policy and practice for meeting the varied and specific needs of second language learners are set in the context of the introduction of a national curriculum, a focus on literacy, and of developing national processes of monitoring and target setting for raising the attainment of all students.

INTRODUCTION

In England, children from families with linguistic minority backgrounds form a substantial proportion of the school population, with more than 9% nationally recorded as having English as their second or additional language (DFES, 2003b). In some urban areas and in some schools, such students are in the majority, and it is worth noting that there is not one local education authority area in England, even for the most rural area, that has not recognized the need to reappraise its pedagogy in the context of global and national population mobility and the linguistic diversity this brings with it at the school level. In the last large scale national research study on provision for pupils' languages other than English (Bourne, 1989), every local education authority was making some provision for English language support. Furthermore, 11 different languages were reported as being supported in some way (either by community language teaching or by providing bilingual support for curriculum learning) within English schools: Punjabi, Urdu, Bengali, and Gujarati being the languages most mentioned, but also Turkish, Greek, Hindi, Chinese, Italian and Arabic. In recent years, the language profile of UK schools has diversified further, with pockets of substantial numbers of Somali, Kurdish, Bosnian, Romanian, Afghani, and other refugee groups from world trouble spots in different areas within cities across the country. At the same time, suburban schools with little experience of working with linguistic minority pupils increasingly find their intake changing to reflect the multilingual nature of the country, as more established groups make the traditional shift from the inner cities to more comfortable areas, consolidating their economic position in the country. Only 5% of all the secondary schools in England report having no ethnic minority pupils at all (DES, 1999). This chapter outlines the background to policy and practice in relation to learners of English as an additional language in England. It examines the ways in which mainstream educational policy and practice have attempted to adapt in recognizing that linguistic diversity is the norm rather than the exception in modern British society. Policy and practice for meeting the varied and specific needs of second language learners are set in the context of the introduction of a national curriculum, a focus on literacy, and of developing national processes of monitoring and target setting for raising the attainment of all students.

CONTINUING GLOBALIZATION AND POPULATION MOBILITY IN ENGLAND

Ethnic identities in the context of globalization and population mobility are highly complex. It is important to avoid viewing language minorities uni-dimensionally as having English as a second or additional language needs, and as potentially the objects of special policy and provision. Rather, it is essential to recognize the diversity of origins, of values, of lifestyles, and of socio-economic positions that impact on educational attainment. Across the world, there are now more second language speakers of English than those born into families using it as their main medium of communication (Graddol, 1997). Thus new arrivals from different parts of the world entering an English-speaking environment such as the UK bring with them different levels of contact with English, in different domains of use, with different senses of ownership of the language; and globalization is increasing contact with English. Length of settlement in an English dominant environment, previous level of education, age, gender, the closeness of the ethnic community within the neighborhood, and the educational history of family elders are just some of the other factors that play a part in creating diversity within as well as between language minority groups; and factors seem to play out differently within different minority communities (see Madood, et al., 1997).

So in trying to raise attainment levels among EAL students, the issue is not a simple one of general under-attainment, but a question of which of these students is successful and which unsuccessful. According to government data, students recorded as learning English as a second language in England are more likely to come from low-income families than other children, with 31% of English as an additional language (EAL) learners eligible for free school meals compared to just 15% of all other children (DFES, 2003b). Socio-economic background cannot be ignored when looking at differential levels of attainment. There remains a strong and direct association between social class background and success in education in England, right across ethnic groups (Gillborn & Mirza, 2000).

Comparing the reading development of young learners (half of whom had home backgrounds where languages other than English were dominant) in their 2nd year of schooling in an inner city urban context in the UK, Collins (1999) found that differences in contributory areas of learning and experience (e.g. the availability of books in the home; understanding and involvement by teachers of pupils' parents in school reading programs, etc.) outweighed the influence of the children's differing linguistic backgrounds. Having English as an additional language is only one among many factors that influence children's attainment at school—and it is salutory for English as a second language (ESL) specialists to remember that. Manjula Datta (2000), herself brought up in a multilingual context in India with experience of teaching in a multilingual English medium school in Calcutta, writes of her experience of entering teaching in London in 1976:

> I became aware of the perception and status of bilingualism or multilingualism of children in schools in England. I went through an enormous cultural shock, my whole world of education and schema of multilingualism was in turmoil.... In classrooms I found children's bilinguality equated with 'low ability', and their first language was regarded as a 'barrier' to excellence in education. ...I was confused and quite disturbed to see bilingual children withdrawn from class to be given facile exercises in English grammar and vocabulary rather than learning the whole language through the curriculum alongside their peers. (p. 2.)

I was recently asked to research attainment in relation to ethnicity rather than language background (see Blair & Bourne, 1998). This experience raised important issues for me as someone whose focus had always been on language development. Working with a colleague whose research background focused on educational provision for students of African-Caribbean family background, we began to ask ourselves why contextual issues such as prejudice and racism, so dominant in the literature in relation to African-Caribbean children, were so rarely the focus of research when examining causes of underachievement in relation to children of Asian minorities in the UK. Indeed, in our focus group interviews with parents and pupils, issues of low teacher expectations, lack of respect of schools towards minority group parents and pupils, and of unfair treatment were voiced as readily by Asian background parents and students as by those of African-Caribbean origin. Indeed, both parents and students from different linguistic and ethnic group backgrounds in the different focus groups we organized in different parts of England focused on these issues, rather than raising concerns about provision for English as a second or additional language (Blair & Bourne, 1998).

It is important, then, for educational researchers and policy makers not to adopt a monolingual perspective and assume that operating in a second or third language is necessarily difficult and problematic. As Crystal (1987) put it, "Multilingualism is the natural way of life for hundreds of millions all over the world" (p. 360). In the UK, there is evidence to suggest that over half of 16-29 year old students of Indian origin, and nearly half of those of Pakistani origin have English as their main language, although still tend to use a familial language in speaking to the older generation. In contrast, only a fifth of another minority group, those of Bangladeshi origin, had English as their main language (Madood, et al., 1997). These differences between large and well-established minority groups are amplified when we come to look at the diversity of language use and language needs among more recently arrived minority groups such as asylum seekers and refugees from areas of the world suffering war and famine, from a range of different socio-economic backgrounds and levels of educational attainment, and with differing political orientations and aspirations, including different levels of motivation to integrate into English dominant society.

There has therefore been some criticism in the UK of the ready categorization of children who come to school from backgrounds in which languages other than English are in use as *English as a second language learners*. In recent years, Her

Majesty's Inspectors (HMI) have adopted (and therefore legitimized) the term *bilingual learners*, explaining:

> 'bilingual' refers to children who are in regular contact with more than one language for the purposes of daily living. Their competence may be in one or all of the four skills (listening, speaking, reading, writing) in either or both languages and is likely to be at varying levels. 'Bilingual' or 'developing bilingual' are descriptors which encompass a wide range of starting points and levels of proficiency. 'English as a second language' (ESL) and 'English as an additional language' (EAL) are terms which refer to only one aspect of an individual's language repertoire. For most pupils, English will quickly become their main language for education, career and life chances, but their first or community language will remain a crucial dimension of their social and cultural identity. (OFSTED, 1999. p. 9)

It seems clear that EAL learners are not easily distinguished as a group requiring some sort of common program. As a social construct, the category *EAL learner* is highly problematic, raising a number of questions: At what level of proficiency does one pass out of the category of EAL learner? If being categorized as EAL depends on the results of testing, do all pupils take the same tests of language proficiency? If not, if only some school entrants are tested on their English language competence, is this not discriminatory? On what basis are certain children chosen to undergo special English language testing? And if language testing is applied to all children, are native speakers of English who score poorly in the same tests (and it seems possible that some will) also to be categorized as *second language speakers*, too? If not, why not?

Furthermore, how far is it possible to talk of *ESL teaching* as if referring to common provision at all? As far back as 1989, reporting on a national study of ESL provision in England, I concluded that the simple designation of teachers and programs as *ESL* had outlived its usefulness (Bourne, 1989). I argued that only when it becomes more usual to detail exactly the types of provision that are required in different schools for different pupils would we be able to be specific enough about the very different sorts of skills, training, qualifications and experience teachers would need to meet the different objectives entailed. A summary of some of the different types of additional provision that might be required in schools from time to time, depending on intake, in order for them to provide equal opportunities for linguistic minority students from different backgrounds and with different experiences might include the following:

1. Training and support for class and subject teachers in making the curriculum accessible to all pupils, and supporting pupils in meeting the demands of the curriculum;
2. procedures for the reception of students newly arrived in the country with little or no English, and their induction into the school;
3. additional classes (preferably intensive on arrival and thereafter after school hours and in vacations, so that pupils continue to have access to the curriculum) teaching basic literacy to newly arrived older students who have missed out on educational opportunities in their homelands and who have not yet learned to read and write to the level of their peer group;

4. extra support in providing access to and developing standard written forms of English for older pupils;
5. pastoral support for those refugee pupils who have experienced the traumas of war and terror and consequently have particular and pressing needs that must be met as a priority if they are to benefit from their education;
6. providing access to the spoken and written forms of the first language or standard written language of the pupil's home and community.

Local authorities might even, where practicable in terms of numbers, provide the choice of a fully bilingual education, a form of provision that is not yet available anywhere in the state sector in England.

Clearly there is no reason why one person should be able to fulfill all these different roles. Indeed, it is likely that each would call for rather different sorts of skills and expertise. Instead of expecting one postholder (an ESL teacher) to fulfill all such roles, schools could call on the most appropriate experience and expertise throughout the school and in the local community to staff the different areas found to be necessary in each particular school at any particular time for different groups or individuals. These needs would be expected to change, and provision would need to be flexible to meet them.

In the remainder of this chapter, I want to focus on the first of the types of provision identified in the list above—that of providing support for class and subject teachers in making the curriculum accessible to all pupils, and supporting pupils in meeting the demands of the curriculum. This is a crucial issue for all schools and for all teachers in multiethnic, multilingual societies if all students are to have real opportunities to succeed in modern "knowledge economies," and is the foundation upon which the success of all other forms of additional, special provision rest.

MAINSTREAMING POLICY AND PROVISION IN ENGLAND

In the 1980s and early 1990s, the emphasis was on oracy and on developing group work strategies to encourage talk for learning. The emphasis of specialist ESL staff was on supporting teachers in reorganizing their classrooms and implementing strategies to encourage such collaborative small group work (Levine, 1990). Wider partnerships in improving educational provision for all pupils in multilingual contexts were attempted through the development of *Partnership Teaching* inservice materials (Bourne & McPake, 1991) aimed at whole school training for diversity. These government funded materials, which had a national impact, addressed diversity of needs by encouraging patterns of working and institutional structures based on a form of action research. This action research involved pairs and groups of teachers working together in a *partnership cycle* to research their own local context and current patterns of pupil achievement and underachievement; to plan specific strategies to address these; to implement the strategies; monitor progress; then disseminate the outcomes to other teachers, leading to new questions for investigation.

While there remain continuing difficulties in terms of status, professional relationships and unclear roles between mainstream and ESL teachers (Creese, 2000), the aim of the Partnership Teaching project was not simply to get specialist ESL staff and mainstream teachers working together to address diversity, but also to get mainstream staff themselves to focus on meeting the needs of multilingual classrooms, working together within and across departments, identifying and sharing good practice, and to involve head teachers as leaders in supporting partnership practice. The focus was investigative and collaborative school improvement at the local level, to meet the specific needs of each school's own intake through maximizing the particular strengths available in each school's staff and local community. Rather than categorizing certain pupils as ESL and thus subjecting them to different pedagogic regimes and practices conducted by a separate group of differently trained teachers, the aim was to revise mainstream structures and pedagogic practices to make each school and each teacher responsible for meeting the needs of his/her own specific, diverse pupil population, at the same time setting up networks to share ideas of "what works for which pupils and when."

From the late 1990s, the development of the National Curriculum has offered further opportunities for intervention to raise attainment for bilingual learners of English, through opening up the possibility of ethnic monitoring of attainment in national test results. This has enabled the identification of schools that have "bucked the trend" of underachievement for pupils of certain ethnic and linguistic group backgrounds, and thus enabled investigation of the sorts of teaching and learning processes and whole school strategies that those schools are using (Blair & Bourne, 1998; Gillborn & Mirza,2000; OFSTED 1999b). Furthermore, monitoring has helped to raise teachers' levels of expectation for ESL learners, as schools are enabled to compare the outcome of their teaching with that of other schools in similar circumstances and with a similar pupil intake, using government supplied data on pupil attainment by gender, ethnicity, and indicators of socio-economic background (Bourne, 2000 a).

The results of early studies (Blair & Bourne, 1998) suggested that those schools in multilingual contexts that are most successful with students from minority language group backgrounds have strong leadership commitment to raising the attainment levels of all students, clear pastoral support systems with good parental liaison, careful progress monitoring systems, as well as an emphasis on mainstream teaching and learning processes at classroom level. Classroom teachers in successful primary schools showed strong awareness of students' ESL needs; but this was less evident in the secondary schools studied. At the same time, models of specialist ESL support in those same secondary schools were also found to be disappointing, suggesting a need at secondary level for trained specialists capable of working as advisers to help mainstream staff move forward. I shall return to this point later in this chapter.

LITERACY INSTRUCTION FOR LEARNERS OF ENGLISH AS AN ADDITIONAL LANGUAGE

Since the late 1990s, there has been a national focus on raising attainment for all children, but particularly for those who were found to be underachieving, through strengthening levels of literacy, especially in the years before secondary school. The National Literacy Strategy (NLS), introduced in 1998, is a sustained major national initiative that has resulted in the employment of a number of regional literacy coordinators together with centrally funded literacy advisors in every local authority. Each school receives regular inservice training, including training on leadership for literacy for every headteacher, and each is expected to nominate a literacy coordinator who remains in regular touch with the central development team. This is a centrally driven, high profile initiative, working top down, but increasingly involving schools and teachers in the development of the strategy, and growing more open to adaptation and innovation as experience develops. It offers, in Bernstein's (1990) terms, a highly visible pedagogy; one with a simple structure and clear procedures that can be shared with both parents and students and thus, according to Bernstein, one that offers greater potential for success with children from backgrounds which do not share the culture of the school. This is because the rules of procedure and of success are explicit and open to all, rather than having to be inferred and interpreted on the basis of schooled understandings handed down from the family.

The NLS has had a major impact on all schools in the country, and has brought about a major shift in awareness of the role of literacy in learning, and of the language skills necessary for developing initial and higher order skills in literacy. The result is a shift from an emphasis on the teacher as a "hands off" facilitator of learning towards a greater emphasis on explicit pedagogy, on the active role of the teacher in students' learning, whether interacting with the whole class, groups, or individuals. It has served to focus mainstream primary teachers' attention more closely on how written English works than ever before, making the rhetoric of "every teacher a language teacher" more of a reality.

In its pedagogic structure, the practice recommended by the NLS mirrors in interesting ways some of the prescriptions for good literacy practice analyzed by Gregory (1996) for supporting students learning to read in a new language. Gregory sets out two complementary approaches: *starting from the known*, and *introducing the unknown*. In *starting from the known*, teachers draw on the knowledge, experience, and emotions of the students themselves, including drawing on their knowledge of how both first and second languages work:

> The child's cultural knowledge is used rather as a springboard for comparing differences and similarities between languages and cultural practices, for showing children that stepping into a new world provides access to exciting experiences but need not mean abandoning the language and culture of the home. (p. 101)

This involves a language experience approach, joint construction of texts, explicit introduction of new lexis and language chunks, modeling chunks of language orally, using puppets, songs and drama, and devising home/school reading programs with which parents feel comfortable.

In *introducing the unknown*, the teacher not only leads the children into the new cultural worlds opened up by story and non-fiction, but also into the new written language and genres of books. Gregory (1996) identifies a sequence of introduction that facilitates literacy learning: orientation to collaborative reading through songs, poems, and chants; introduction to the subject of the new book, and the arousal of interest in reading it; collaborative reading, with the teacher modeling first; then *talk around text* in an exploration of meanings; a period of consolidation when children are offered "structured opportunities to deal directly with print" (p. 129) in small groups, with one group gaining intensive teacher interaction each day; and finally a number of extension reading and writing activities.

The NLS recommends a period of focused literacy teaching each day that follows very similar lines: a period of whole class orientation and talk around text with a focus on meaning, followed by attention to some selected specific features of the text. This is supplemented by group work dealing directly with print, with the teacher working intensively with one group, and the other groups working individually or in pairs or as a group, sometimes on follow-up activities, sometimes on extension activities, and sometimes with a bilingual assistant in preparation for the next day's whole class session. Literacy and language learning are not limited to the focused literacy session, of course, but are intended to be supported and enhanced in activities across the curriculum. However, the aim is to include a daily period of regular, explicit attention to both the meanings and forms of different types of text. Within this context, the strategy attempts to make the demands of the literacy curriculum clear and unambiguous to parents. Parental involvement and support are seen as key to the success of the program.

While most of the video training materials reflect instruction in multi-ethnic classroom contexts, examples of interesting practice have had to be identified and disseminated as they evolve. Supplementary packs of training materials (NLS, 1999) have emerged in an attempt to raise teacher awareness of the potential of the strategy for EAL learners, and particularly the importance of its principles of careful orientation to meaning-making alongside explicit modeling of the text for learners of English. More and better examples of real practice are still needed, especially as the emphasis moves on to other curriculum areas, since the strategy was renamed the *Primary Strategy* in 2003.

At the time of this writing, an equally focused national strategy, the Key Stage 3 Strategy, is being introduced into secondary schools. Again, the focus is on raising whole class achievement through modeling valued practices, focusing on forms as well as meanings and involving students in their own assessment and target setting. It will be interesting to see how far this strategy will be developed, as it is intended to be, to the advantage of learners of ESL.

As Bernstein (1990) has argued, we need to ask of every change, what has not changed? And in this unchanged context, in whose interests are the changes likely to be? In relation to the Literacy Strategy, I have argued (Bourne, 2000b) that while the pedagogic strategies of the Literacy Strategy have made a major impact on classroom practice, there has been less understanding of the underlying principles at school and classroom level. The Literacy Strategy is based on the notion that teaching matters, that a wide range of performance is not inevitable, that children do not have fixed and innate levels of intelligence or ability. It challenges the acceptance of continuing failure in the school system for children from socially disadvantaged groups. However, observations of what is happening in some schools alongside the introduction of the strategies appear to show a continuation of traditions in which underperformance is seen either as lack of "ability," or as an unfortunate but nevertheless understandable effect of home background, where raising attainment is "not possible for our kids." In this context, the national curriculum and national strategies appear to have led to increased setting and grouping of students by teacher assessments of their ability, in some cases resulting in the placing of early stage learners of ESL in "low ability" groups and often alongside children with behavioral and other problems. In this way, these students are trapped into a remedial curriculum of facts and basic skills, while others are introduced to ways of accessing, interpreting, and questioning knowledge, learning to control and produce the symbolic order. As I have argued elsewhere:

> There is a positive opening in the introduction of the Literacy Strategy in raising expectations for the achievement of all children, but only if we can avoid the danger of setting by estimations of 'ability', leading to a rich education for some, and a limited, narrow curriculum based in facticity for others. (Bourne, 2000b, p. 40)

Provided we do not trap EAL learners in contexts that deny them access to models of problem solving and interpretation, the prognosis is positive. Evidence from national data indicates that while nationally young EAL learners are often at a lower starting point in literacy tests in English than other students, they appear to make greater progress: that is, in mainstream settings they appear to "catch up" (DFES, 2003c). Of course, research from the USA (Thomas & Collier, 1997) suggests that progress would be greater if pupils were taught bilingually, a point I will return to later in this chapter.

LINGUISTIC DIVERSITY AND MAINSTREAM CHANGE

There has been an increasing focus in the 2000s on ensuring that students with home and first languages other than English are fully included in teachers' thinking, and their specific needs considered in teachers' planning, classroom practice, and assessment strategies. It is interesting to note that while mainstreaming strategies for teaching learners of ESL have been put in place, experienced specialist ESL staff have also mainstreamed themselves. For example, until recently, the Head of the National Literacy Strategy was a former ESL teacher, some of whose research has already been referred to in this chapter (see Collins, 1999). Others are found in key positions in the inspectorate, in the Department for Education and Skills, in the Teacher Training Agency, in the National College for School Leadership, and in university teacher training departments. This has supported an emphasis across national programs on recognizing the multicultural and multilingual nature both of modern British society and the student intake. As one example, the NLS (1998) materials stress:

> The NLS Framework and Literacy Hour are appropriate for children who speak EAL. The national Literacy Strategy emphasis on careful listening, supported reading and writing, phonological awareness, access to formal styles of written English and the participative nature of whole class and group work are all perfectly consistent with teaching children who speak English as an additional language. Literacy is a primary route to fluent and confident spoken English for second language learners. (p. 77)

These materials take an uncompromising view of teachers' responsibility for EAL learners, arguing that "working with pupils learning English as an additional language is not a job for additional staff in isolation," but rather that "the language and literacy development of pupils learning EAL is the responsibility of the whole staff," and that "it is the responsibility of school management to ensure that all staff are fully equipped to meet the needs of pupils learning EAL" (NLS, 1998, p. 9).

In support of this stance, the DFES/TTA (2002) Professional Standards for Qualified Teacher Status require all new teachers—wherever they are located—to provide evidence of their competence in planning for, teaching, and assessing learners of EAL. These requirements ensure that all teacher training providers include work on meeting the needs of bilingual learners in their curricula and, depending on their own local contexts, find appropriate ways of giving trainee teachers appropriate experience. Training providers themselves are subject to inspection and need to show how they are meeting the Standards effectively for all trainees. As with schools, this has meant that the issue cannot be treated as marginal, regardless of the proportions of EAL learners within the institutions and within the locality.

At the time of this writing, government funding has been made available to establish a network of teacher trainers to develop an Internet platform from which to share materials and good practice in relation to preparing new teachers for working in multilingual contexts. Other similar networks, for example on training teachers in the different subject areas and in cross-curricula themes such as citizenship have also been required as part of their remit to include a specific focus on the inclusion of learners of EAL.

In order to prepare school inspectors for their role in raising minority ethnic group achievement, new materials and training courses have been prepared for the inspectorate in order to provide exemplar materials illustrating recommended forms of practice. Inspector video-training materials I have seen include examples of literacy and numeracy lessons in multilingual schools where pupils are encouraged to use their stronger languages in "partner talk" during whole class teaching as well as in group work, as well as classrooms where adults have been recruited who share first languages with pupils, and who are deployed to support problem solving and meaning-making in a rich literacy environment. These materials make it clear that the promotion of first languages does not depend solely on the presence of bilingual adults, but that all teachers need to recognize and draw on the first languages of pupils to support their learning across the curriculum and in the learning of English.

The same examples are presented to teachers and teacher trainers themselves in a case study included within a consultation document sent to all schools on raising the attainment of minority ethnic group pupils (DFES, 2003a). This document also stresses the need for schools to consider ways of meeting the needs of more advanced learners of English in relation to academic writing. It recognizes that this requires close attention to student texts and ongoing assessment of EAL learners, and thus offers an important role for properly trained specialist teachers of English in academic writing.

Other training materials making their way into schools at this time include modules on linguistic diversity and supporting bilingual learners for teaching assistants who support teachers in the classroom. Training materials have also been developed for non-teaching staff (DFES, 2003d), including a focus on the induction of new arrivals, so that the whole school is aware of diversity and of strategies for including and supporting bilingual learners.

A SPECIFIC FOCUS ON LEARNERS OF ENGLISH AS AN ADDITIONAL LANGUAGE

At the same time as mainstream provision continues to be made more sensitive to linguistic diversity and the particular needs of EAL learners, the shift to more explicit forms of pedagogy in the national primary and secondary school strategies has opened the way for more focused and targeted specialized EAL support within mainstream schooling. For example, supplementary materials have been published to illustrate the ways in which the strategies are meant to include learners of EAL, and how activities may be extended to draw on other language skills as well as to address specific language learning needs (NLS, 1999). A new pilot scheme has been put in place within the Primary Strategy with the appointment of an EAL coordinator in each of a number of regions. This coordinator supervises a newly appointed and centrally funded EAL consultant in each of the region's local education authorities to focus specifically on disseminating strategies for the literacy development of EAL learners, from the beginner to the most advanced. Other interested education authorities not included in the pilot scheme are welcome to join in professional development activities as associate members. If the scheme is successful, it may be extended.

It is slowly being recognized that these new initiatives will need senior teachers with expertise in analyzing the language needs of different subject areas and of different types of bilingual learners. While the DFES plans to continue to develop training and support for mainstream staff 'to improve their competence and confidence in meeting the needs of bilingual learners' (DFES, 2003a, p. 29), it is now exploring the possibilities of establishing a nationally recognized inservice qualification in this area. Recent research (OFSTED, 2001) has established that in some regions, fewer than 30% of those in ESL posts had any type of specialist qualification. From 2003, funding has been made available to support courses in developing pilot schemes as models of a possible national accreditation. These courses will prepare experienced teachers to act as well-informed leaders in supporting school staff in meeting the needs of English language learners.

Future mainstream educational directions that promise points of intervention for those concerned to improve ELT and the success of learners of English indicate a resumption of interest in the development of oracy, and a new focus on analyzing and improving teacher talk (Alexander, 2000). New methods of research are also helping us to examine the ways in which teachers operate multimodally, using all the resources available to them (gesture, gaze, position, movement) to make meaning for their students, rather than relying only on the linguistic means (Bourne & Jewitt, 2003). These initiatives may help both students and teachers to understand and to support ELT in multilingual contexts in new and exciting ways.

CONCLUSIONS

In this chapter, I have outlined a national, centrally driven attempt to place ELT firmly within a focus on raising educational attainment. Initiatives to upgrade specific provision for English language learners are never isolated or marginalized but rather are being developed within other mainstream national initiatives, such as headship training and the national strategies. The overall focus is on providing support for class and subject teachers to make the curriculum accessible to all pupils and support pupils in meeting the demands of the curriculum.

There are dangers in adopting a mainstream approach, of course. One is that specific language learning needs may simply be overlooked. Another is that the initial underachievement of English language learners may be seen as an indication of "low ability," leading to placement in low level learning contexts. The development of clear assessment methods that make sense to class and subject teachers is therefore a priority. Still greater efforts also need to be made in paying more than lip-service to developing the place of other languages within the school system, including moving to more bilingual ways of teaching and learning where that is possible. However, unless the mainstream is addressed, all such specific provision will remain marginalized. ELT within the school context always needs to be seen within the wider frame of raising attainment and combating poverty and exclusion, not as an end in itself.

REFERENCES

Alexander, R. (2000). *Culture and Pedagogy*. London: Blackwell.
Bernstein, B. (1990). *The structuring of pedagogic discourse*. London: Routledge.
Blair, M., & Bourne, J. (1998). *Making the difference: Teaching and learning strategies in successful multi-ethnic schools*. London: DFEE.
Bourne, J. (1989). *Moving into the mainstream: Local education authority provision for bilingual pupils*. Windsor: NFER-Nelson.
Bourne, J. (2000a). A plea for ethnic monitoring of attainment in multi-ethnic schools. *Westminster Studies in Education, 23*, 5–18.
Bourne, J. (2000b). New imaginings of reading for a new moral order: A review of the production, transmission and acquisition of a new pedagogic culture in the UK. *Linguistics and Education, 11*, 31–45.
Bourne, J., & Jewitt, C. (2003). Orchestrating debate: A multimodal analysis of classroom interaction. *Reading, Literacy and Language, 37*(2), 64–72.
Bourne, J., & McPake, J. (1991). *Partnership teaching: Co-operative teaching strategies for language support in multilingual classrooms*. London: HMSO.
Collins, K. (1999). *A comparative analysis of early reading development in first language English speakers and children for whom English is an additional language*. Unpublished Ed.D. thesis, University of Leeds.
Creese, A. (2000). The role of language specialists in disciplinary teaching: In search of a subject. *Journal of Multilingual and Multicultural Development, 21*, 451–470.
Crystal, D. (1987). *The Cambridge encyclopaedia of language*. Cambridge: Cambridge University Press.
Datta, M. (2000). *Biliguality and literacy*. London: Continuum.
DES. (1999). *Ethnic minority pupils and pupils for whom English is an additional language: England 1996/7*. Statistical Bulletin 3/99. London: The Stationery Office.
DFES/TTA. (2002). *Qualifying to teach: Professional standards for initial teacher training*. London: DFES.
DFES. (2003a). *Aiming high: Raising the achievement of minority ethnic pupils*. London: DFES.
DFES. (2003b). *Minority ethnic attainment and participation in education and training: The evidence*. Research Topic Paper RTP01-03. London: DFES.
DFES. (2003c). *Pupil progress by pupil characteristics*. London: DFES.
DFES. (2003d). *The curriculum and EAL: Introductory training for teaching assistants*. London: DFES.
Gillborn, D., & Mirza, H. (2000). *Educational inequality: Mapping race, class and gender*. London: OFSTED.
Graddol, D. (1997). *The future of English?* London: The British Council.
Gregory, E. (1996). *Making sense of a new world: Learning to read in a second language*. London: Paul Chapman.
Levine, J. (1990). *Bilingual pupils and the mainstream curriculum*. London: Falmer.
Madood, T., Berthoud, R., Lakey, J., Nazroo, J., Smith, P., Virdee, S., et al. (1997). *Ethnic minorities in Britain: Diversity and disadvantage*. London: Policy Studies Institute.
National Literacy Strategy. (1998). *The management of literacy at school level*. London: DFES.
National Literacy Strategy. (1999). *Supporting pupils learning English as an additional language*. London: DFES.
OFSTED. (1999). *Raising the attainment of minority ethnic pupils*. London: OFSTED.
OFSTED. (2001). *Support for minority ethnic achievement: Continuing professional development*. London: OFSTED.
Thomas, W., & Collier, V. (1997). *School effectiveness for language minority students*. Washington: National Clearinghouse for Bilingual Education.

CHAPTER 15

METHODS, MEANINGS AND EDUCATION POLICY IN THE UNITED STATES

LOIS M. MEYER

The University of New Mexico, USA

ABSTRACT

What is the relationship between national education policy and local educational realities in the United States within the context of the *No Child Left Behind* (NCLB) legislation? NCLB imposed a centralized set of mandates, backed up by punitive accountability requirements, on US schools. In the process, local realities and their historical contexts are dismissed as irrelevant to the overall goal of boosting academic achievement. This chapter notes the parallels between the US situation (the 'Center' imposing a one-size-fits-all frame on local realities) and the ongoing debates in the teaching of English internationally regarding the dominance of instructional policies and methodologies imposed by academic and commercial interests in Western English-speaking countries (the 'Center') with little regard for the histories and contexts of local non-Western communities and classrooms in the 'Periphery.' Contrasting four ethnographic accounts of English language teaching contexts in the United States with the mandates of NCLB, the author suggests that English language learners will be left behind if the definition and implementation of quality education in a given setting are not co-constructed by the communities and educators within the local and historical context of each school and community.

INTRODUCTION

America's schools enroll the world's children, but do the world's children learn in American classrooms? If so, why? If not, why not?

Because English language learners (ELL) in US schools (usually termed "limited English proficient" in legislation and other official documents) achieve significantly below their English proficient classmates on standardized academic tests administered in English, they are labeled "disadvantaged" in the Bush Administration's education agenda, the No Child Left Behind Act of 2001 (NCLB). Traditionally, blame for English learners' lower academic achievement has been placed on the English learners themselves and on their minoritized[1] parents and communities. By contrast, researchers have focused on the role of a variety of intersecting social and pedagogical factors. Cummins (2001), for example, identifies a major source of the achievement gap to be the reproduction within schools of the unequal power and status relations between dominant and subordinated groups that exist outside of schools in the wider society. Poor children of color, including most non-English speakers, arrive at school already marked for likely failure, as though the "disadvantaged" label that mainstream society applies to their homes and communities were emblazoned on their backpacks like a second-rate brand name. Rather than blame their non-English languages and minoritized cultures for ELLs' lower academic achievement, Wiley and Lukes (1996) argue that English monolingual and Standard English ideologies expressed through educational policies, teacher attitudes, and school structures, systematically frustrate and truncate English learners' possibilities for academic achievement.

Research findings in the United States speak directly to these issues. Thomas and Collier (2002), for example, have tracked the academic achievement of ELLs over time, from school entry at kindergarten or first grade until eleventh grade. Their massive, nationwide research indicates that program choices provided for ELLs in the first years of schooling, especially the choice between early all-English or sustained bilingual instruction, greatly influence whether or not the English learner will succeed at closing the academic achievement gap with fluent English speakers by high school. Those few ELLs who receive a sustained, well implemented bilingual program from kindergarten through fifth grade or beyond generally close the gap; by contrast, the gap persists for the many who begin their early schooling in all English programs or bilingual programs of limited duration.

As documented below, *NCLB*'s approach to correcting the unequal educational outcomes of English learners is to hold states, school districts, and local schools accountable for two fundamental goals. First, these entities must achieve measurable improvements in the English proficiency of limited English proficient children each year. Second, the academic achievement gap between "disadvantaged" ELLs and their English proficient peers, as measured on English standardized tests, is to be reduced annually in specified increments, called Adequate Yearly Progress (AYP), until the gap is entirely eliminated within 12 years. Professional recognition and financial rewards are promised to schools and even individual teachers who succeed at meeting these goals. If the two goals are not met, the state runs the risk of losing federal funds, and a process of corrective action is begun against failing districts and schools.

Classrooms have long been considered the domain of teachers' professional decision-making and instructional competence. But with so much at stake, many states are now overriding teachers' professional judgments to require the use of packaged instructional programs in key curricular areas (e.g. English reading, math), though the effectiveness of these programs for enhancing ELLs' academic achievement and English language acquisition is largely untested. Outside of the instructional blocks of time when packaged programs are mandated, teachers are generally left to their own devices to adapt mainstream instruction – or not – for ELL students. Though they may be "highly qualified" as defined by NCLB, most teachers lack the specific skills needed to adapt their instruction across the curriculum to effectively meet the learning needs of ELL students. This is illustrated by the account of Janice, a middle school teacher in New Mexico, who describes her frustrations toward others and toward herself when faced with an English learner's struggle to makes sense of instruction:

> A sixth grader (I'll call him Juan) approached me during after-school tutoring in the library. He held a language arts worksheet in one hand. "Help me, Ms. Hart?" he asked. I studied the piece of paper and began to question Juan about the assignment to figure out how much he understood. Within seconds I realized that he understood nothing about the worksheet on nouns, adjectives, verbs and adverbs. It was double-sided with forty-five sentences written in English. Juan was supposed to circle nouns and underline adjectives on some of the sentences, then circle verbs and underline adverbs on the rest. He speaks almost no English and reads even less. We spent the hour painstakingly filling out the worksheet, with me gesturing and speaking broken Spanish to attempt

> some translation of the sentences. At the end of tutoring we were mostly finished. Juan thanked me for my help and went home. At first, I became furious with the teacher who assigned such a homework assignment to a student who could not possibly read or comprehend its content! Later, I used this experience to assess my own effectiveness at helping second language learners. (Hart, 2002, p. 1-2)

Janice's account is a single instance of the extremely varied and complex instructional dilemmas presented by English learners. Teachers like Janice in American classrooms cope with increasing linguistic diversity and demands for high-stakes accountability by improvising instructional strategies to compensate for curricular support and professional development that are missing or woefully inadequate.

Paradoxically, international English teaching professionals complain of a seemingly contrasting problem: pedagogical micromanagement of their instruction by English language teaching interests in English-speaking Western countries, which they call the "Center." Instead of feeling they have been abandoned to invent their own survival instructional strategies, classroom teachers in so-called "Periphery" countries – the English-using former colonies of English-speaking colonial powers – find their methodological choices overwhelmingly imposed by "Center" interests. Theories, methodologies, "expert" consultants, and packaged instructional materials – what Holliday (1994) calls "English language teaching technology" – are exported from the powerful English-speaking Center countries with the presumption that they are valid, universally applicable and culturally appropriate, ignoring the unique characteristics of the "Englishes" that are spoken and the teaching practices that are valued in non-Western but English-using Periphery communities and classrooms.

> Periphery scholars call for an end to such "pedagogical imperialism" (Canagarajah, 1999), the virtually one-way flow of English language teaching technology from the Westernized Center outward. Just as the English language no longer belongs to the West but has been "indigenized" into diverse global "Englishes", so, too, the theories and practices of English teaching must be "indigenized", that is, adapted or reconstructed to meet the needs of local non-Western communities and classrooms. Scholars such as Kachru have decried generalized theories and generic methodological prescriptions as entirely inadequate on the grounds that "there are no simple answers, no easy solutions, and no methodological remedies which apply to all users of English across cultures" (1992, p. xxiv).

These critiques by Periphery researchers are powerful and thought-provoking. They deserve serious reflection by Center language educators. Still, as a second language teacher, researcher, and teacher educator with experience across the years in diverse Center contexts and now in indigenous education settings in rural Mexico, I find these critiques unfortunately shortsighted, or at least unnecessarily constrained. The misapplication of presumed "universal" pedagogical solutions to culturally embedded language teaching contexts is not a frustration unique to the Periphery. English language teaching at the Center subsumes a complex diversity of instructional circumstances and culturally-embedded contexts. While this diversity at the Center seems to be largely unrecognized by Periphery scholars, it is entirely erased by *NCLB*. The *Act* claims to seek "equal educational opportunity" for limited English proficient students by incorporating them within its expectations and requirements for standards-based schooling. In reality, it homogenizes English learners' backgrounds and educational needs, assuming that their communities are willing and even eager to relinquish their own histories, languages, cultural values, and decision-making prerogatives to achieve *NCLB*'s version of success: English language proficiency and academic success at a par with that of mainstream students.

In this paper I describe why the inquiry "how to teach?" is a loaded question, answerable only in relationship to other more fundamental questions such as "what to teach?", "who teaches?", "to whom?", "for what purpose?", "in what language?", "in what context?", and crucially, "who decides?" Only in the presence of these more basic questions can we interrogate instructional methods for their meanings. That is, to truly investigate the meanings that adhere to instructional methods for English language teaching, we must be willing to abandon generality and theoretical abstraction in order to probe in detail the ways that pedagogical decisions about English instruction are inextricably embedded in *time, place, power relationships*, and *sociocultural contexts*. English language teaching methods convey more than merely linguistic messages to English learners and their families and communities, or to the teachers who implement them and to the curriculum decision-makers who select or generate them. Rarely are the meanings of an instructional method intrinsic or predetermined; rather, meanings depend on the lived experience of the user and the receiver, that is, they are deeply embedded in the local scenes and histories of human interaction known as teaching and learning. As we shall see, the meanings in this larger sense, that educators in US schools communicate through their teaching strategies, often disable English learners and their communities, contributing to rather than relieving these students' educational "disadvantage."

The perspective I develop here is that methods of English instruction must always be "relentlessly local" (Levinson & Holland, 1996) if they are to engender positive responses in English learners. They must be rooted in the needs, hopes, histories and discourse purposes of specific communities. Periphery scholars have convincingly argued the cultural embeddedness of language instruction, but have applied this important insight only to their own instructional contexts. My intention is to import the wisdom of Periphery scholars back from the English language teaching margins so that it can educate and enlighten pedagogy at the Center itself.

WHERE IS THE CENTER, AND WHAT ARE ITS MEANINGFUL METHODS?

Implicit in the claims of Periphery scholars are certain assumptions that underestimate the diversity and complexity of English language teaching contexts at the Center. Some of these assumptions are: 1) the circumstances and challenges of English language usage and instruction are uniform across all Center contexts; 2) the local model of oral and written English at the Center is always the Standard; 3) Standard English is heard and used, both informally and formally, to transact daily affairs at the Center; 4) English language learners interact with native English speakers and are taught by native English teachers in Center classrooms; 5) English language instruction at the Center makes use of interactive process approaches that generate many opportunities for natural language use.

In this section, these assumptions by Periphery scholars about Center instructional uniformity are questioned in light of five accounts of English language teaching at the US Center. Four of these accounts are "contextualized alternative versions" based on extensive ethnographic documentation in specific Center school settings. Two focus on schooling for urban immigrants (Olsen, 1997; Valdés; 2001) and two on schooling for native minoritized students (McCarty, 2002; Roberts, 2001). Olsen's (1997) *Made in America: Immigrant Students in our Public Schools* is a study of the contemporary Americanization of immigrants from many countries in a comprehensive urban high school in California. Valdés' (2001) *Learning and Not Learning English: Latino Students in American Schools* documents the schooling experiences of four newly arrived Latino immigrants in three primarily white middle schools in the San Francisco Bay area. The descriptions in these two accounts identify *immigration, segregation, assimilation*, and *Americanization* as salient elements in the schooling experience of ELLs at the urban Center. By contrast, McCarty's (2002) *A Place to be Navajo: Rough Rock and the Struggle for Self-Determination in Indigenous Schooling*, and Roberts' (2001) *Remaining and Becoming: Cultural Crosscurrents in an Hispano School* consider *place, identity, community*, and *self-determination*, more than *immigration, segregation, assimilation, and Americanization,* to be salient.

The local complexities of English language instruction in these four highly diverse Center contexts are contrasted with the "official version," a synthesis of the instructional implications for English learners of the Bush administration's No Child Left Behind Act of 2001 (NCLB). In contrast to the "official version" that proposes to define ELL instructional issues and remedies nationally and to "proceed as though the meanings people make of their lives are without significance" (McCarty, 2002, p. xvii), the four alternative versions begin as intentionally contextualized accounts of specific people's lived experience of English language learning and teaching, as well as the meanings they make of this lived experience within the complexity of local, historicized, and culturally-embedded instructional contexts. A comparison of the alternative and "relentlessly local" versions of English language teaching at the Center with each other and with the official version poses the following questions: What does it mean to teach from a Center perspective? Where is the Center? How should English language be developed across these diverse Center contexts? Is there a best teaching pedagogy for English learners at the Center? If so, what is it? If not, how can decisions about meaningful methods for English language instruction be made?

Madison High School, Bayview, California

Bayview's Madison High School was built in the 1960s with a capacity for 1,800 students, who at that time were almost all white. However, by 1990 this primarily working class high school enrolled 1,783 students in grades 9 through 12, of whom 32.8% were white, 26.1% Hispanic, 13.5% African American, 13.3% Asian, 11.1% Filipino, 2.4% Pacific Islander, and less than 1% Native American. Close to half the students in the school spoke a mother tongue other than English at home, a reflection of the diversity now apparent in the community.

Olsen acknowledges the perspective that guides her study: America's schools are "contested territory," struggling with whether their role will be to democratize society, making it more inclusive and providing more equal access, or to racialize it[2] by maintaining and reproducing current class, racial, and language relations (1997, p. 17). The latter orientation was clearly in evidence at Madison High School. Newcomers were required not merely to set aside their ethnic identities but to entirely recast them, eliminating whatever was considered excess baggage by the largely white and English-speaking mainstream, and reshaping whatever remained to fit the racial and linguistic categories considered appropriate for them in American society. According to Olsen, the new Americanization project in US public schools such as Madison High includes three components: 1. marginalizing and separating immigrant students academically; 2. requiring immigrant students to become English-speaking (despite huge barriers) and to drop their native languages in order to participate in the academic and social life of the high school; and, 3. pressuring each immigrant student to find and take his or her place in the racial hierarchy of the United States.

Olsen describes the "language shock" experienced by new immigrants when they encounter the social and structural inadequacy of Madison High to enable them to achieve what it relentlessly demands: rapid acquisition of flawless, accentless standard English. Peer rejection and ridicule, learning to stay silent, exclusion from academically challenging courses – each dimension of their isolation and loneliness is both cause and consequence of their lack of English proficiency (Olson, 2000). Given the pain and ridicule brought on by being limited in English proficiency, and craving the acceptance of American high school classmates, most new immigrants not only become "English seekers," they "abandon their mother tongues relatively quickly, becoming English preferers" (Olsen, 1997, p. 99). Nevertheless, their keen desire to learn English rarely translates into successful academic learning, due to the failure of mainstream teachers to provide appropriate instructional supports, as well as English learners' isolation from native English speaking peers and from academically challenging classes while in the rarely-exited ESL track.

Tied closely to the democratization vs. racialization contest at Madison High is the question of "how to teach?" For most of the teachers the immediate answer is "just as I always have." Despite Bayview's transformed demographics during the last two decades, Olsen found that most teachers do not believe they need any additional training to address these new realities. Few have sought out professional development related to the teaching of ELL students. Pedagogically, democratization to many Madison High teachers means instructional color-blindness, that is, "seeing all our students as the same" and making no distinctions to address specific needs. When racial and linguistic differences between the "skills" and "college bound" groups are too stark to overlook or dismiss, "teachers explain these distinctions as products of individual student abilities and motivation" (1997, p. 188). The school and its teaching staff take little responsibility for the resulting inequality in graduation rates.

Olsen offers only a brief glimpse of a "multicultural and inclusive alternative" to this urban immigrant version of teaching at the Center. This alternative would involve dismantling the system of "institutional sorting and tracking of students into different futures," providing full support for newcomers' language development in English and in the home language, and enabling immigrant students to connect with and affirm one another's linguistic and cultural identities (p. 252).

GARDEN MIDDLE SCHOOL, CRENSHAW SCHOOL, AND J.F.K. MIDDLE SCHOOL, MISSION VISTA, CALIFORNIA

The community studied by Valdés (2001), called Mission Vista, was also experiencing rapid demographic shift with large numbers of Latino immigrants primarily of Mexican background moving into what had once been a largely middle-class community. Valdés' intention is to document how ESL was taught to four Latino newcomers or, more specifically, these students' experiences "learning and not learning English" in three Mission Vista middle schools. All four students attended Garden Middle School during the first year of the study; two of them, Elisa and Bernardo, completed the second year at Garden while the other two transferred to other local schools, Lilian to Crenshaw School and Manolo to J.F.K. Middle School. The three schools have experienced Mission Vista's demographic diversification in different ways. Garden had experienced a significant influx of Latino students whereas Crenshaw had few ESL students. As a result, only one newcomer classroom was formed, into which all English learners in the school were placed, regardless of their level of English proficiency. J.F.K. Middle School, by contrast, was located in a more affluent community where the ethnic-minority population (African American and Latino) was less than 2%. The ESL program was designed and implemented for the children of professionals, primarily from Asian and European backgrounds.

Instructional confusion, or unacknowledged instructional ambivalence and bias, was exemplified in the structure of the ESL programs and the pedagogical approaches at the three schools. At Garden, there was little mobility into more advanced ESL or mainstream classes, and consequently, ELL students had little intellectual challenge or social or academic contact with native English speakers. Advanced ESL classes were made up of "LEP lifers" (Olsen 1997, p. 154), who, despite years of schooling in English, still were not deemed acceptable for mainstream classes. They often were retained in the beginning ESL classes as language models and translators for newcomers. This enabled the teacher to instruct solely through English without having to modify her own oral language to be understood. In general, classes for ELL beginners followed a traditional grammatical syllabus and involved little peer interaction, much skills-oriented seatwork, frequent time fillers like the board game "hangman," and few academically challenging learning experiences. Consequently, almost all ELL students at Garden continued on into the ESL track in high school. The ESL experience was similar at Crenshaw for Latino students, although Asian students often were exited from ESL into mainstream classes after only one year, apparently because they were perceived to be more competent than the Latinos.

In contrast, at J.F.K. Middle School English limitations were considered a "temporary handicap" for an otherwise motivated and capable mainstream-minded newcomer. ESL classes focused on the academic language skills that were immediately needed to succeed in the mainstream classes in which newcomers were simultaneously enrolled, classes that also would be important later in college. Tutors were available in several languages to assist newcomers in their mainstream classes. ESL instruction focused on elements of the core curriculum (e.g. the novel *Tom Sawyer*) with the goal of mainstreaming advanced English Language Development students *before* they got to high school. ELL students used their developing English to write about their experiences and views, in this process learning the forms of English academic writing.

Despite these instructional contrasts, the academic outcomes of the four students were somewhat discouraging. Elisa, who remained in ESL at Garden both years, chose to attend high school outside of Mission Vista in order to enroll, successfully, in mainstream courses, only to be reassessed after graduation as "ESL" by a California community college. Bernardo, who unlike the other three had received in Mexico a strong academic background in Spanish, also stayed at Garden in the ESL track. He then endured four years in the ESL track at Mission Vista High, graduated with few academically challenging mainstream courses, and has no plans to attend college. Lilian continued in ESL after her move to Crenshaw and again in high school until she dropped out after her sophomore year.

These three students' experiences of "not learning" academic English, "not receiving" instruction modified appropriately for their language needs, and "not accessing" quality academic content in school, set the critical tone of Valdés' study. However, the fourth student, Manolo, who according to Valdés, did receive more engaging and academically challenging instruction at J.F.K. fared no better. He went on to attend high school in the same affluent community, was placed in the "general" courses for "less motivated" students, and now works in a small grocery store run by his family. Valdés ascribes his academic limitations to personal factors such as his lack of study habits, his newness to the school, and the mediocre prior education he had received in Mexico.

Based on her frustration with the learning experiences of these four Latino immigrant students and their unsuccessful assimilation into the academic mainstream, Valdés recommends devising ESL courses that develop academic English skills, teaching language-learning and meta-cognitive strategies, and acknowledging students' primary language competence by "demanding ESL textbooks that have L1 support." The feasibility of this latter suggestion is questionable in view of the large number of home languages represented in schools (for example, in California more than fifty home languages are spoken by ELLs in grades K-12) and the fact that a significant number of students may not be highly literate in their L1.

Rough Rock Community School, Arizona

Diné Bi'ólta', The People's School as it is known in Navajo, or Rough Rock Community School in English, is historic in Native American education as the site of "the first American Indian community-controlled school" (McCarty, 2001, p. 72), as well as "the first school to have an all-Navajo governing board and the first to teach Navajo language and cultural studies" (p. 2). McCarty lovingly describes both the physical and the human geography of this "place to be Navajo." Unfortunately, during the past forty years, *Tse Ch'izhi* (Rough Rock) has experienced massive sociocultural change, including "a tidal wave of language shift" (p. 179). In the early 1960s only 37% of the population was able to speak and understand communications in English. Recently, however, "there has been an alarming shift in children's use of and proficiency in Navajo" (p. 15), and while it is English that is displacing the community language, it is a local variation of English rather than the Standard. Children who no longer communicate comfortably in Navajo are still stigmatized as "limited English proficient" and they experience considerable difficulty in school.

The experimental community-based school at Rough Rock was established in 1966 at a time when the focus on Civil Rights in the United States had exposed the hidden reality that public schools on the Navajo reservation were segregated, elitist, English-only institutions that served primarily the children of white trading post employees together with a smattering of Indians, those few who were approximately at grade level. Many of the community's elders had experienced the physical and cultural abuse meted out in years past in Bureau of Indian Affairs schools and embraced the possibility to create a school where children would be helped to succeed because of, not despite, who they are. The goal was to organize a school based on Navajo community principles of kinship, family and communalism, that would value, develop and care for the talents, resources, informal knowledge, health and spirituality of the entire community.

Instruction in both Navajo and English was a fundamental part of the radical vision for schooling at *Tsé Ch'izhi*. Bilingual education at Rough Rock was not directed toward rapid assimilation to the English-speaking mainstream, nor toward creation of a fast track toward uniform academic achievement. Instead, its goal was cultural reclamation, unseating of historical relations of authority and control, valuing one's own language, equality with non-native teachers, and a means to attract Navajo young adults back home as uniquely competent role models with skills of great worth inside the community.

While English was always a key instructional priority, especially given the students' status as limited English proficient, decisions about *how much* English to include, and *how to teach* English, vacillated in response to competing pressures that were financial, ideological, and political, as much as pedagogical. *Who* wielded the major decision-making power at a particular point in time – the community, or white school administrators – directly influenced the instructional and curricular decisions that were made. The first ESL program at Rough Rock, devised by a white external consultant, was "skills-driven, remedial, and explicitly unconcerned with natural language experiences, focusing entirely on correct syntax and phonology" (p. 95). A program introduced in the late 1970s, again by a white curriculum specialist, involved 4½ hours of Basic Skills instruction in English as the core of the K-12 curriculum, reducing the use of Navajo to periodic 30-minute language lessons. In contrast, Native teachers working within the Rough Rock English-Navajo Language Arts Program (RRENLAP), initiated in 1987, devised their own language development approaches, bringing English literacy to life through culturally-based activities. McCarty's observations in a third grade RRENLAP classroom in 1994 give a sense of the pedagogical approach:

> A bulletin board displays students' English texts on their Diné forebears. Insects and insect people are central to these stories, and the teacher uses this as an opportunity to connect literature study to science investigations. Another link is to social and political studies: The class is researching and writing stories about the creation of the Navajo Nation. Evaluation of this work includes student portfolios. (p. 156)

In the RRENLAP project, *all* students were viewed as writers and readers, regardless of their level of English proficiency. In time, teachers came to see the importance of introducing Navajo literacy hand-in-hand with English literacy development.

The issue of an appropriate English language teaching methodology at Rough Rock, while important, is secondary to McCarty's central questions: What does it mean to be Navajo, and educated, and living in the English-speaking Center as well as in the heart of the Navajo Nation in 21st century America? And crucially, what is the role of Navajo language instruction in a school that seeks to be "a place to be Navajo"? To be sure, it is identity that is at stake in the answers to these questions, for "[b]eing Navajo in Navajo is qualitatively different from constructing and enacting a Diné identity in English" (p. 189). Opinions from the Rough Rock community are split. A Native grandmother cautions, "If a child learns only English, you have lost your child" (p. 178). But other parents disagree. "'Why should we learn our language?' our children say...My kids are having a hard enough time trying to learn English" (p. 181). Rough Rock's experience would suggest that an instructional program that does the former – teaches children their Navajo language and literacy – is also the most likely to help them do the latter – overcome their difficulties in learning Standard English and achieve the greatest gains on local and national measures of academic achievement.

> RRENLAP students consistently outperformed a local comparison group who had not participated in RRENLAP or any other form of consistent bilingual/bicultural schooling. RRENLAP students also were assessed by their teachers as having stronger oral Navajo and Navajo literacy abilities than their non-bilingual education peers. Overall, our data showed that bilingual students who had the benefit of cumulative, uninterrupted initial literacy experiences in Navajo made the greatest gains on both local and national measures of achievement. (p. 160)

Without strong Native school leadership, however, even positive test indicators were not enough to protect the community vision of this "place to be Navajo." Decisions taken by the White school leadership, mainly males, distanced the school from its community until, in 1995, one White administrator described the school as "generally operating separately from the community, almost like an embassy" (p. 169). McCarty believes the likelihood is fading that the community will be free again to determine locally what kind of Navajo identity will be constructed in the Rough Rock Community School.

> Standards and accountability are national obsessions that strike at the heart of Indigenous self-determination and minoritized community control. The very existence of Indigenous community schools depends on their compliance with standards that not only devalue Indigenous knowledge, but jeopardize children's life chances by threatening to deny them a high school degree. That children are subjected to these pressures in preschool is among the more perverse manifestations of a national education system that, while masquerading as an equalizing force, in fact begins to stratify and segregate the moment children enter school. (p. 198)

Norteño High School, Norteño, New Mexico

Roberts, like McCarty, documents a community that has been "minoritized." The Hispanos who live in "Norteño" have had minority status conferred on them by the mainstream outside world, though they are a majority in their own world. Their immigration to Northern New Mexico goes back more than a century to Spanish colonial times; their story of Americanization begins when America crossed their borders, not vice versa, after Mexico's defeat by the US in 1848. As flags and governments changed, the Norteños' constant loyalty across generations was to "family, faith, land, and language." These fundamental values are still present, though Roberts documents the many ways in which the fabric of life and loyalties in Norteño has now become considerably more complex, especially for the young.

Poverty in Norteño is a fact of daily life. Thirty percent of Norteños live below the poverty level, while 78% of Norteño students are living in low-income families. According to Roberts, "[i]n Norteño School District, the elevation exceeds the population" (p. 13); the poverty is not so immediately visible since hundreds of students commute daily from still-isolated mountain villages. Though seemingly defined and sustained by tradition, under the surface Norteño is a community swept by cultural change. As in Rough Rock, there has been a "tidal wave of language shift." The parents' generation spoke little English when they first went off to school; their children, in general, speak little Spanish.

Attitudes toward the shift in dominant language preference from Spanish to English are divided, revealing the community's ambivalence toward two competing goals. Following Peshkin (1997), Roberts calls the first of these goals *remaining*, the encouragement given the community's youth to value their heritage and remain tied to local places and traditional ways, including use of the Spanish language. The other goal, *becoming*, focuses on "exposing students to the outside world as much as possible and emphasizing English to enhance the students' competitive edge"; in other words, helping students become something other than what they are, more English-speaking and mainstream (p. 10-11). Intensifying this debate is the fact that presently, few Norteño students appear competitive in either language. Language proficiency testing in the school district indicates that "nearly 70% lack proficiency in English, and more are inadequate in Spanish. Many speak English using the Spanish linguistic structure" (p. 111). The School District has long pursued funding to provide bilingual programs and many parents support bilingual education for their children. But increasingly the question is asked: "If the school district defines itself as bilingual, will it be going backward or forward?" (p. 11).

Roberts intended to document "who Norteño students are learning to be." In the process, she uncovered "the community's concern about who the students are *not* learning to be" (p. 87). Traditional community voices, and some teachers, question the cost of *becoming*, whether the "tangible gains may cause intangible losses" (p. 83). The question to which Roberts returns again and again is not so much "What are the students learning in school?" but rather, "Is what the students are learning worth as much as what they are forgetting? (p. 2-3).

The teachers vary in the messages they convey to students and in their instructional priorities, depending on what they feel the students need most – community-embedded Hispano history and culture, or more effective assimilation to the English-speaking and Anglo-oriented mainstream.

> Teachers who endorse the Anglo orientation want a rigorous curriculum that will prepare their students to cope with life in contexts larger than Norteño; they want young Norteños to be on par with Anglos in college and in the workforce. Teachers who endorse the Hispano orientation see cultural distinctness as an advantage, as well as a necessity for cultural revival, the viability of the villages, and the well-being of each individual. In their view, being different from the Anglo mainstream is worth the potential social, economic, and political costs. Other educators prefer a bicultural orientation that teaches adolescents to function competently in both cultures and "to distinguish situations where traditional ethnic behaviors are appropriate from those where a mainstream system is more useful." (p. 113)

Roberts describes the instructional approaches of several teachers at Norteño High, relating *how* they carry out instruction with *what future* they desire and anticipate for Norteño youth. Rather than espouse a particular methodology for English language instruction or even a preference for instruction through English, she displays the connection between instructional methods and intended goals, and thereby illuminates a far more fundamental question: What is the purpose of schooling in a minoritized community like Norteño, and who should decide? Roberts suggests that effective educational planning requires a shift from discussing students in a generic sense to a focus on their embeddedness in the communities in which they live:

> The ethnic composition of the community, the community's settlement pattern, changing lifestyles of the community, the way education came to the community, who controls the schools, being a community of faith, being a poor school district – How do these all shape what becoming educated means in this Hispano community in Northern New Mexico? (p. 3)

The Official Version: The No Child Left Behind Act of 2001

In contrast to the "relentlessly local" and deeply contextualized perspectives of the four alternative versions presented above, *NCLB's* legislated requirements for the instruction of English learners at the Center are national in scope and intended impact. Presented as "an Act to close the achievement gap with accountability, flexibility, and choice, so that no child is left behind," *NCLB* states as its purpose to "insure that all children have a fair, equal, and significant opportunity to obtain a high-quality education and reach, at a minimum, proficiency on challenging state academic achievement standards and state academic assessments" (*NCLB*, Purpose, Title I). In the name of "improving the academic achievement of the disadvantaged," *NCLB* places special emphasis on meeting the educational needs of "low-achieving children in our Nation's highest-poverty schools, limited English proficient children, migratory children, children with disabilities, Indian children, neglected or delinquent children, and young children in need of reading assistance" (Sec. 1011).

In exchange for allocating grant monies and decision-making flexibility to the states, *NCLB* sets a deadline for states to close the achievement gap between LEP students and their peers (within twelve years from the end of the 2001-2002 school year) and specifies that measurable "adequate yearly progress"(AYP) must be achieved during each intervening year. States must institute a system of "sanctions and rewards" to "hold local educational agencies and public elementary schools and secondary schools accountable for student achievement" (Title I, Part A, Sec. 1111 (b) 2.a.iii). If the disparities in LEP children's academic achievement are not demonstrably addressed within 2 years by accomplishing AYP on academic tests and English language measures, the state is required to identify the school for improvement; if AYP is not addressed adequately within 2 more years, states must take "corrective action" against "failing schools" in the form of state-controlled management, curriculum revision, or wholesale staff replacement (Sec. 1116). *NCLB* requires that ELL students with three consecutive years of US schooling be tested against the same rigorous content standards as English proficient students, employing the same English assessments, with only limited exceptions and accommodations permitted.

Ultimately, it is the classroom teacher who is held accountable for enabling ELL students to meet the *Act's* imposed requirements and timelines. Based on student test results, *NCLB* institutes rewards for those teachers whose students "move forward" by annually achieving the state's academic and English language development standards, while sanctioning those whose English learners "fall behind" by consistently failing to meet state standards.

NCLB offers no guidance to teachers regarding *how* to accomplish its mandated goal of successful performance by English learners on high-stakes standardized tests in English, nor are any programs, curricula, or teaching strategies recommended for developing English proficiency. The only stipulation is that a language teaching curriculum be used that is "tied to scientifically based research on teaching limited English proficient children and that has been demonstrated to be effective" (Sec. 3113.b.6). This apparent openness to innovation and diverse strategies is deceiving, however. The *Act*'s stated purposes and definitions, its unwavering focus on uniform academic standards and achievement measured through English standardized assessments, its narrow interpretation of what counts as "scientifically based research," its rigid and arbitrary timeline for English acquisition and for mainstreaming students into regular classrooms, and the threat of teacher and school sanctions, reveal a set of beliefs and commitments about the teaching of English learners that constrains the types of program models and curricular and instructional approaches that *NCLB* considers acceptable.

Where, then, is the Center?

Extracting from these widely contrasting settings and teaching circumstances one homogenous essence of "English language teaching at the Center" is a daunting, and I would suggest futile, task. Where is the Center? When the uniform requirements of *NCLB* are overlaid onto these highly diverse contexts, one glimpses the inherent difficulty of attempting to address complex local instructional circumstances with abstract theories, packaged methodologies, "one-goal-fits-all" policies, or national or state standards.

NCLB mirrors the naïve assumptions of homogeneity across Center contexts that appear in some Periphery scholars' work, and encodes them into law. This homogeneity is defended as an expression of the belief that all students, if taught well, are capable of achieving the same high standards. But such assumptions of national sameness ignore the reality of tremendous local diversity and beg a critical question: What educational outcomes do these communities desire for themselves and their children? Countless local varieties of English are spoken in communities – minoritized, immigrant and mainstream – across the nation. In many communities, the English spoken by native English speakers is the local variety, and therefore virtually the only English that ELLs hear and learn. Also overlooked in *NCLB*'s assumptions of ELL homogeneity are the racial and linguistic divides that separate ELLs from native English speakers in many US schools, greatly diminishing students' chances for successful English acquisition and the likelihood that they will be placed in challenging mainstream content classes. In short, *NCLB* obliterates the web of intricately woven factors that have been identified as promoting or inhibiting English language learning in any given local context. Rather than acknowledge local complexity, *NCLB* instead mandates state, school and especially teacher accountability for uniform outcomes.

While each of the alternative English language teaching contexts described previously is unique, a clear divide exists between the issues and concerns of immigrants, especially in urban settings, and those of native minoritized, and often rural, student populations. These distinctions are nowhere evident in *NCLB*. Yet even urban settings with large immigrant populations display distinct local histories and circumstances, and their needs and suggested remedies can be perceived differently. There are similarities in Olsen's and Valdés' accounts of English language teaching in the urban Center, especially the shared themes of *immigration, segregation, assimilation and Americanization*. But the similarities should not mask important differences. Beyond obvious contrasts of social class and ethnic mix, Olsen and Valdés look to US schools to achieve distinct goals for older immigrant students. Consequently, these researchers evaluate immigrant students' experiences in school, and specifically the instruction they receive, through different lenses.

Olsen strives for the creation of a "multicultural and inclusive alternative" to the exclusionary, racialized and intolerantly monolingual high school reality she encountered at Madison High. She calls for a new Americanization project in US schools, one that would be essentially democratic and multicultural and bilingual, laying the foundation for a more just, respectful and inclusive US society. Equality of educational opportunity for Olsen requires a reconceptualization of the basic assimilationist goals of American schooling.

Valdés' focus is more overtly pedagogical than Olsen's. She is not primarily concerned with reconceptualizing the basic assimilationist goals of American schooling, but rather with documenting in detail how instructional practices employed by ESL and other teachers close out opportunities for English learners to succeed within those mainstream goals. We glimpse in Valdés' descriptions that her four immigrant students, like Olsen's, experience racialization and language-shock in their encounters with American schooling and English-speaking students, but Valdés does not dwell on these wider realities. Rather than critique the assimilationist ends of schooling that propel education in this community, her concern is with the inappropriate and "dumbed down" methodologies used in the ESL track, and the unadapted sink-or-swim methodologies used in regular content classrooms, both of which foreclose students' chances of acquiring English or successfully achieving schooling's mainstream academic ends. Because the teachers are ignorant of immigrant students' levels of academic competence in their own languages, they frequently underestimate these students' academic capabilities, even as they rarely accommodate appropriately to their English language needs. Students' learning opportunities, and ultimately their life potentials, are wasted by instructional activities and teaching strategies that reveal the low expectations teachers hold for them.

Still, despite their internal differences, Olsen's and Valdés' urban immigrant versions of English language teaching at the Center present a striking contrast to McCarty's and Roberts' native minoritized versions. In both minoritized communities, a large majority of students are now English dominant, though most are assessed to be "English limited" on tests of standard language proficiency. This "linguistic limbo" – neither Standard English proficient nor heritage language proficient – is deeply significant for the question of an appropriate English language pedagogy in these communities. Which should be seen as the greater barrier to students' acquisition of academic English and consequent chances for success in school and in life? Is it the community's *loss of the heritage language*, the language that has traditionally grounded the community's identity, cultural knowledge and values? In the past the heritage language served as the emotional, linguistic, and conceptual base from which a learner drew the confidence to defend herself within the unfamiliar and English-requiring mainstream school culture. What provides that crucial base for identity and learning now that the heritage language is being lost? Can and should it be revitalized? Or, alternatively, is the real barrier to the children's academic achievement the community's use of a local non-standard variety of English, resulting in the children's *limitations in Standard English* and consequent poor achievement on language proficiency tests and academic assessments? The vacillation between these competing choices – heritage language revitalization or loss? Standard English ambivalence or preoccupation? – is the linguistic side of the remaining and becoming debate in Roberts' Norteño.

Now *NCLB* has weighed in on this debate, generating intense, assessment-driven pressure for overwhelmingly-English instruction. *NCLB* places no priority on the programs found to be most effective in helping ELL students close the academic gap by 12th grade–bilingual programs that are well implemented, sustained (5-6 years), and which promote language and literacy development in the students' native language as well as English (Thomas & Collier, 2002). Rough Rock's experience supports the Texas Education Agency (2000) and Thomas and Collier findings, and directly refutes the English-only ideology of the *NCLB*.

Overshadowing the debate over an appropriate English language pedagogy in Rough Rock and Norteño, however, are broader issues of *place, identity, community* and *self-determination*. Can schools in minoritized Center communities truly be places "where children are helped to succeed because of, not despite, who they are" (McCarty, 2002, p. 194)? Is it possible for minoritized children to accept new identities as Standard English speakers and "become" mainstream academic achievers, as Valdés proposes, without being forced in the process to leave behind their own familiar locales, languages and identities? Roberts' question is relevant here: Is what the students are learning in school worth as much as what they are forgetting, or more accurately, what they are being forced to forget? Questions about identity, cultural integrity, and community self-determination are not prominent in Olsen's or Valdés' accounts of urban immigrant schooling. Only in minoritized Rough Rock and Norteño are questions raised about community voice and local determination of the appropriate goals and methods of schooling.

THE MESSY MATTER OF MEANINGFUL METHODS

If a single image of English language teaching at the US Center is illusive, what can be said about the question of the best and most meaningful methods of language instruction? According to Canagarajah (1999), the field of English language teaching has been "obsessed" with the question of best instructional methods. While this obsession may be understandable within positivistic scientific traditions, Canagarajah asserts that it isn't always productive or useful. According to Periphery language educators, methods that are claimed to be "best" and imposed by Center language teaching interests can be counterproductive and even offensive in non-Center instructional settings.

Relevant in this regard is Stevick's (1976) argument that "the quality of personal activation" (p. 122), rather than any particular method, is critical in effective second language teaching. Canagarajah and other Periphery scholars contend that learners outside the Center are personally activated when English language teaching adapts to their own purposes and contexts; indeed, they resent and reject instruction based on external and imposed priorities, practices and materials. Extending these claims, or rather, bringing them home, I suggest that the power of language teaching methods to captivate or alienate English language learners here at the US Center is equally dependent on their "fit" within the particular goals, histories and values of the learners and their immigrant or minoritized communities.

Three years ago, unencumbered by so many pressing concerns about the local and cultural embeddedness of appropriate language teaching pedagogy, I felt comfortable to write about generic barriers to meaningful instruction for English learners, and to suggest possible solutions (Meyer, 2000). A deeper look at the complexity of English language teaching contexts in the US and elsewhere has eroded that level of comfort. It is not that the barriers I identified three years ago are *wrong*. Frankly, I continue to believe that some version of the four barriers to meaningful English language instruction (cognitive load, culture load, language load, and learning load) are relevant to teaching English in any local context. What has become clearer to me in these intervening years is that the barriers aren't caused by or inherent in certain teaching methods (Method A), nor are they "solved" by other methods (Method B). Instead, the barriers are constructed and take their specific forms locally, within just this group of learners and teachers, and within the details of our lives and learning experiences together in classrooms. Equally, the spark that can propel English learners to acquire and achieve despite these barriers must be discovered anew and ignited within each instructional setting.

THE CHILDREN LEFT BEHIND

Just as there are competing versions of English language teaching at the US Center, there are different interpretations of how to solve the vexing problem of unequal educational outcomes and the consistent finding that limited English proficient children are "left behind" on most measures of schooling success. According to *NCLB*, no limited English proficient child will be left behind if states, schools and individual teachers are made accountable by means of sanctions and rewards for adequate and incremental improvement in these students' academic achievement and English language proficiency, as measured on standardized tests administered in English.

Both Olsen and Valdés introduce complexity into this simplistic account. Olsen would involve students in redefining what it means to be an educated American, in order to assure that their views, values, and identities are respected and supported in the process of American schooling, and that their cultural strengths, home languages, and English learning needs are acknowledged in the institutional structures and teaching methods of school. Valdés, on the other hand, faults the design of ESL programs and their instructional methodologies for physically and mentally warehousing ELLs in a segregated and rarely-exited ESL track. According to Valdés, with appropriate instruction, Latino students will gain the academic English competencies necessary to compete within the existing mainstream and English-only goals of schooling.

Significantly, McCarty and Roberts find the definition of the problem, that limited English proficient children are "left behind" because they are failing in the rush to English and to mainstream academic success, to be deeply problematic itself for minoritized children and communities. When educational success is defined and measured in terms of speedy transition to English, how can English learners be said to have succeeded if, in the process, their parents, communities, and even their own cultural identities are made to appear as failures?

The nationwide demand for quality education for ELLs is legitimate and defensible. The definition of quality education in a given setting, however, and the processes and methods that construct this definition, must be co-constructed by communities and educators within the local and historical context of each school and community. Rather than being marginalized and left behind by top-down, decontextualized education policies, children are more likely to be nurtured and enriched when quality education is understood to be community-based education, that is, education for ourselves and for our own children implemented in ways we value here in this place. This is the powerful insight of Periphery scholars, brought home to challenge educational policies and instructional practices of English language teaching at the Center.

NOTES

[1] McCarty (2002, Footnote 1, p. xv) explains the use of the term "minoritized": "As a characterization of a people, 'minority' is stigmatizing and often numerically inaccurate. Navajos living within the Navajo Nation are, in fact, the numerical majority. 'Minoritized' more accurately conveys the power relations and processes by which certain groups are socially, economically, and politically marginalized within the larger society. This term also implies human agency."

[2] Olsen defines "racialization" in this way: "The term rests on an understanding that 'race' has neither a biological nor a natural basis, but is a social construct that is constantly being taught, learned, recreated, and renegotiated. The process of the social construction of race is termed 'racialization.' As people learn the expectations and beliefs that others have for them because of their skin color, they are becoming 'racialized.' As our society decides on new categories of 'race,' and determines the importance and implications of those categories, we are engaged in 'racializing'." (1997, p. 254)

REFERENCES

Canagarajah, A. S. (1999). *Resisting linguistic imperialism in English teaching.* Oxford, UK: Oxford University Press.
Crawford, J. (1995). *Bilingual education: History, politics, theory and practice.* Los Angeles, CA: Bilingual Educational Services, Inc.
Cummins, J. (2001). *Negotiating identities: Education for empowerment in a diverse society.* (2nd ed.). Los Angeles: California Association for Bilingual Education.
Hart, J. (2002). *The need for increased collaboration between ESL teachers and content teachers in middle school settings.* Unpublished Masters comprehensive paper, CIMTE 590, Department of Language, Literacy and Sociocultural Studies. University of New Mexico, Albuquerque, NM.
Holliday, A. (1994). *Appropriate methodology and social context.* Cambridge, UK: Cambridge University Press.
Kachru, B. (Ed.). (1992). *The other tongue: English across cultures* (2nd ed.). Urbana and Chicago, IL: University of Illinois Press.
Levinson, B.A., & Holland, D. (1996). The cultural production of the educated person: An introduction. In B. A. Levinson, D. E. Foley, & D. C. Holland (Eds.), *The cultural production of the educated person: Critical ethnographies of schooling and local practice* (pp. 1–54). Albany: State University of New York Press.

McCarty, T. (2002). *A place to be Navajo: Rough Rock and the struggle for self-determination in indigenous schooling*. Mahwah, NJ: Lawrence Erlbaum Associates.

Meyer, L. (2000). Barriers to meaningful instruction for English learners. *Theory into Practice, 39*(4), 228–236.

Olsen, L. (1997). *Made in America: Immigrant students in our public schools*. New York: The New Press.

Olsen, L. (2000). Learning English and learning America: Immigrants in the center of a storm. *Theory Into Practice, 39*(4), 196–202.

Peshkin, A. (1997). *Places of memory: Whiteman's schools and Native American communities*. Mahwah, NJ: Lawrence Erlbaum Associates.

Public law 107-110. (2002). *No Child Left Behind Act of 2001*. Washington, DC: Government Printing Office, Jan. 8, 2002.

Roberts, S. (2001). *Remaining and becoming: Cultural crosscurrents in an Hispano school*. Mahwah, NJ: Lawrence Erlbaum Associates.

Stevick, E. (1976). *Memory, meaning and method: Some psychological perspectives on language learning*. Rowley, MA: Newbury House Publishers.

Texas Educational Agency. (2000). *The Texas Successful Schools Study: Quality education for Limited English Proficient students*. Program Evaluation Unit, Office for the Education of Special Populations, Austin, TX.

Thomas, W., & Collier, V. (2002). *A national study of school effectiveness for language minority students' long-term academic achievement*. Santa Cruz, CA: Center for Research on Education, Diversity and Excellence, University or California-Santa Cruz. http://www.crede.ucsc.edu/research/llaa/1.1_final.html.

Valdés, G. (2001). *Learning and not learning English: Latino students in American schools*. New York & London: Teachers College, Columbia University.

Wiley, T., & Lukes, M. (1996). English-only and Standard English ideologies in the U.S. *TESOL Quarterly, 30*(3), 511–535.

Section 2:

The Goals and Focus of the ELT Program: Problematizing Content and Pedagogy

SECTION 2

THE GOALS AND FOCUS OF THE ELT PROGRAM:

Problematizing Content and Pedagogy

CHRIS DAVISON AND JIM CUMMINS

INTRODUCTION

In the English language teaching field, it seems self-evident that the goal of every ELT program must be to learn English, and hence the focus must be on teaching the English language. Although at some fundamental level such assumptions are undoubtedly valid, they have been severely tested by recent paradigm shifts in the field of second language acquisition and applied linguistics which have given much greater emphasis to the role of context in English language teaching development.

Many researchers and teacher educators, influenced by earlier Vygotskian work in first language socialization, are adopting a strongly sociocultural view of teaching and learning which highlights the role of interaction and social context in ELT. Another group of researchers, drawing heavily on poststructuralist and postmodernist notions of social identity and power, foreground the interplay in ELT between individual agency and institutional and societal structures. Thus, attempts to classify and describe the goals and focus of ELT have led to increasingly complex definitions of English language learners, purposes and frameworks for learning and teaching. There have also been significant critiques of what are now seen as overly narrow views of the English language learning task. Language is increasingly seen as inseparable from its social functions, and language learning and teaching as a specific field of curriculum activity, a community of practice, potentially involving many different professional, institutional, and/or disciplinary interactions and conflicts.

The interesting thing about these more recent interpretations of English language learning and teaching is that they define what is to be taught and learnt not as a fixed body of linguistic knowledge or even a set of autonomous skills to be mastered, but as the product of the dynamic interaction between learners, teachers and their social context. Thus, what is considered to be the purpose and focus of ELT is always shifting and changing, and may be contested or co-opted by different communities.

The first two chapters explicitly address the problem of defining the goals of ELT programs, albeit from very different perspectives. In the opening chapter of this section Cook proposes that the language teaching goals can be divided into *external* goals that relate to actual second language (L2) use outside the classroom, traditionally evaluated against the achievement of monolingual native-speaker competence, and *internal* goals that are evaluated against progress towards achieving the educational aims of the language curriculum itself. Yet it is almost always external goals that are privileged over internal goals, irrespective of classroom context and purpose. Cook argues that, compared with monolinguals, L2 users have different purposes for learning second languages, in particular, the increasingly strong need to be able to interact with different types of non-native speakers. Hence, compared with native speakers of the language, L2 users have different strengths and weaknesses, deploy different cognitive processes, possess different knowledge about their languages, and utilize different skills. Thus, Cook argues that direct comparisons between ESL and mother tongue English users are very misleading. He proposes that the goals of ELT should be to develop the linguistic and cognitive bilingual potential of English language users, including their language awareness, more systematically and effectively so that they can better function as multilingual individuals in the diverse L2 situations they may encounter outside the classroom.

Leung takes this debate over the issue of labels and norms further in his chapter which looks at current issues in integrating school ESL learners into the mainstream curriculum. He argues that the label of *ESL* itself increasingly appears to be a hybrid or catch-all for a very diverse set of learning and teaching expectations, partly linguistic, partly educational, partly social, and partly political. Leung analyses developments in ESL curriculum and pedagogy within the mainstream education system in English speaking countries, including the UK, Australia and the USA. He demonstrates how issues such as the goals of ESL education are difficult to disentangle from wider social and ideological concerns such as government policies on the integration of linguistic minorities, the use of languages other than English, and access and equity issues. He presents an analytical framework that may be useful to critically examine ESL curriculum and practice, to identify more clearly the specific orientation and goals of ESL education in schools.

The next set of chapters look more closely at questions of pedagogy and content, exploring the selection and balance of the different elements that need to be included in an English language curriculum. Different methodologies or approaches to English language teaching and learning are presented, based on somewhat varied interpretations or theories of language and language learning, often incorporating quite different features of instructional design (that is, objectives, syllabus specifications, types of activities, roles of teachers and learners, materials, and so forth), thus resulting in considerable variation in actual teaching and learning practices. However, all approaches explicitly acknowledge that sociocultural factors as well as psycholinguistic processes can have a strong impact upon what happens inside the classroom.

In the first chapter in this set Spada traces the development of what is now the dominant approach to teaching and learning in ELT, communicative language teaching (CLT). She analyses its evolution since the late 1970s, demonstrating that while most descriptions of CLT emphasize the communication of messages and meaning, there has been widespread disagreement as to whether CLT should include a focus on the analysis and practice of language forms. There has also been some debate and uncertainty as to whether the inclusion of literacy skills, the use of the L1, and vocabulary instruction are compatible with the principles and practice of CLT. Spada argues that these differences in the interpretation and implementation of CLT have become so significant that the term itself has become problematic. Spada concludes that CLT needs to be redefined to allow for the integration of more direct instruction of language (including grammatical, lexical, and socio-pragmatic features) with communicative skills.

In the following chapter Skehan explores a closely related and also well-established concept in ELT, that is, task-based language teaching (TBLT). Skehan begins his survey by making explicit the link between TBLT and communicative approaches to language teaching. Research in TBLT is then linked to studies of focus on form. He then classifies and compares research on tasks into four different areas or perspectives, each emphasizing different aspects of learning and teaching. The first perspective, a psycholinguistic approach to interaction emphasizes the quality of feedback that can be generated by well-designed interactions. The second more cognitive perspective explores how different task characteristics and task conditions influence attentional demands, and how much direct attention to form is possible without undermining meaningful communication. The third approach to research into tasks adopts a sociocultural perspective, examining how task participants collaborate on tasks and reinterpret them as they are being completed. The final area of research explores how to incorporate particular language structures into tasks without losing a focus on meaning. The chapter concludes with a discussion of some of the key methodological issues and areas for future research.

In the next chapter Mohan takes us even further into sociocultural theory, arguing that to meet the needs of our English language learners we must go beyond the acquisition of the L2 system and redefine English language learning and teaching as language socialization. Drawing on systemic functional linguistics, Mohan models social practices as frameworks of knowledge structures that link cultural meanings of the practice to meanings in discourse. He also explores a range of educational applications of such a framework, including integrated approaches to language and content; the connection of language and content standards in education; bridges between learners' languages and cultures; and links to strategies for comprehension in reading and discourse awareness in writing. He concludes by identifying future areas for research, including discourse research strategies to support the potential convergence of multimodal literacy, critical thinking skills, and computer technologies; and connections with metaphor and 'the body', and with critical linguistics.

In the following chapter, Chamot describes the cognitive academic language learning approach (CALLA), which provides instruction through a combination of academic content, language development, and learning strategies through a five-phase instructional sequence which is used to integrate these components in materials design and instruction. Chamot then reports on the results of five evaluations conducted in different school settings with various content emphases, and shows how successive cohorts of school-aged English language learners have benefited form the approach in terms of increased content knowledge and skills, English language proficiency, and learning strategies.

In the final chapter in this set, Collier and Thomas explore the kinds of school-based programs that are successful in enabling students to achieve peer-appropriate proficiency in the English language, at the same time learning a range of often unfamiliar academic content. They describe in detail the components and dimensions of a model they have created which enables predictions to be made regarding English language learners' degree of second language development in a variety of different academic context.

The final set of chapters in this section deal with the interplay between English language learning and teaching and its wider institutional and disciplinary context, with the chapters loosely ordered according to the age of the learners and the sector of education, that is, from elementary to secondary to tertiary to the workplace. All look at issue of disciplinary knowledge, institutional practices, and the barriers facilitating or inhibiting collaboration between ELT practitioners and other academic and professional workers.

In the first chapter Freeman and Freeman explore the implications of increasingly large numbers of students entering English-medium elementary schools speaking little or no English. They provide a brief review of the research on second language acquisition and effective schooling which reveals widespread agreement on the principles that underlie successful programs for these student, and the factors which may undermine their development, including an over-emphasis on standards and testing, a lack of mother tongue language support, a failure to distinguish among types of English learners, and a shortage of qualified teachers able to work effectively with English learners. Four keys for academic success for English language learners are explained and illustrated, that is, ensure students engage in challenging, theme-based curriculum to develop academic concepts; draw on students' background—their experiences, cultures, and languages; organize collaborative activities and scaffold instruction to build students' academic English proficiency; and create confident students who value school and value themselves as learners.

In the next chapter Arkoudis explores how ESL and mainstream teachers working in English-medium schools can cross traditional disciplinary boundaries to negotiate new understandings through sustained and productive dialogue. Arkoudis argues that underlying most dominant views of collaborative teaching has been the somewhat naïve presumption that an ESL teacher can easily influence the mainstream content-area teacher's pedagogy. In contrast, Arkoudis shows how ESL and mainstream teachers' views of language learning and teaching are shaped by their existing epistemological assumptions, and proposes a model to redress the pedagogical relations between mainstream and ESL teachers within the mainstream curriculum.

Carder's chapter on international schools reflects many of the same concerns raised in the previous two chapters, but in a very different educational context. After providing a brief introduction to the international schools network, he goes on to discuss how the linguistic needs of students from many different language backgrounds can be met in international schools. He proposes a four-point organizational model incorporating a content-based explicit English language syllabus, equality of certification for all ESL students, ESL awareness for all subject matter teachers, and mother tongue development for ESL students as a core component of their studies. The chapter concludes with directions for policy and professional development for international schools and suggestions for future research.

In the next chapter Hyland explores some of the same issues of disciplinary boundaries and the ESL/content interface in the tertiary and adult sectors through a discussion of *English for specific purposes* (ESP), which focus on the communicative needs and practices of particular professional or occupational groups. Hyland suggests that ESP draws its strength from an eclectic theoretical foundation and a commitment to research-based language learning and teaching which aims to reveal the constraints of social contexts on language use and the ways learners can gain control over these. He examines a number of current issues and influences in ESP, including needs analysis, ethnography, critical approaches, contrastive rhetoric, social constructivism, and discourse analysis. He argues that ESP has encouraged teachers to emphasize communication rather than language, to employ collaborative pedagogies, to attend to discourse variation, to adopt a research orientation to their work, and to consider the wider political implications of their role.

In the final chapter in this section, Lockwood explores the positive contribution that ideas and constructs from both the business and management training and the adult education literature can make to the theory and practice of workplace ELT curriculum design. She highlights how adult learning research can help ESP workplace practitioners better understand the English language needs of individual professionals at work, and how workplace practitioners can benefit from embracing the cross-disciplinarity inherent in their work.

This section as a whole provides a wide-ranging and comprehensive review of the goals and focus of ELT, highlighting common trends across sectors and regions, but also much contextual variation. The need for more research to provide general guidance and direction on curriculum and pedagogy is clear, but also needed is a recognition of the importance of understanding the particular and the local, especially the individual variation within a community, an institution, a school.

CHAPTER 16

THE GOALS OF ELT:

Reproducing Native-speakers or Promoting
Multicompetence among Second Language Users?

VIVIAN COOK

Newcastle University, UK

ABSTRACT

Goals of language teaching can be divided into *external* goals that relate to actual second language (L2) use outside the classroom and *internal* goals that relate to the educational aims of the classroom itself. Typically, external goals have been measured against the abilities of monolingual native speakers; internal goals have scarcely featured in modern language teaching apart from some alternative methods. Yet, externally, L2 users have different uses of second languages from monolinguals, have a different command of the language, and utilize different skills: L2 users of English in particular need to interact with different types of non-native speakers. Internally, L2 users are different types of people with different cognitive processes and different knowledge of both languages. Language teaching is creating L2 users with mental and linguistic potentials that monolinguals lack. The goals should be to help them on the one hand to function as multilingual individuals in whatever capacity they choose in the diverse situations of L2 use outside the classroom, on the other to acquire the benefits of bilingualism in cognitive ability and language awareness.

INTRODUCTION

Why do people learn a second language? One answer comes from the students themselves; for example, Coleman (1996) found that the six most popular reasons given by UK university students of modern languages were "for my future career," "because I like the language," "to travel in different countries," "to have a better understanding of the way of life in the country or countries where it is spoken," and "because I would like to live in the country where it is spoken." Another answer comes from the expectations of the educational systems in various countries, for example, the UK Modern Language Curriculum (DfEE, 1999) wants pupils to "understand and appreciate different countries," and to "learn about the basic structures of language" and how it "can be manipulated." A third perspective comes from second language acquisition research, which sometimes states the target of second language (L2) learning overtly, for example, "the ability to use language in communicative situations" (Ellis, 1996, p. 74). However, more often the goal is expressed covertly. For example, discussion of age and SLA focuses on "whether the very best learners actually have native-like competence" (Long, 1990), i.e. the unspoken assumption is that successful L2 learners are those that become like first language (L1) native speakers. The purposes of second language teaching are far from straightforward. The multifarious goals include benefits for the learner's mind, such as those gained through the manipulation of language; benefits for the learner's future career; opportunities to emigrate; and the effects on society whether through the integration of minority groups, the creation of a skilled work-force, the growth of international trade, or indeed, in the case of Malaysia, for example "good citizenship, moral values and the Malaysian way of life" (Kementerian Pendidikan Malaysia, 1987). Cook (2002) made an open-ended list of the goals of language teaching that includes the following:

1. *Self-development.* The student becomes in some way a better person through learning another language. This goal is unrelated to the fact that some people actually use the L2, as in the group-related dynamics of community language learning.
2. *A method of training new cognitive processes.* By learning another language, students acquire methods of learning or new perspectives on themselves and their societies.
3. *A way in to the mother tongue.* The students' awareness of their first language is enhanced by learning a second language.
4. *An entrée to another culture.* Students can come to understand other groups in the world and to appreciate the music and art of other cultures.
5. *A form of religious observance.* For many people, an L2 is part of their religion, whether Hebrew for Judaism, Arabic for Muslims, or indeed English for Christians in some parts of the world.
6. *A means of communicating with those who speak another language.* We all need to deal with people from other parts of the world whether for business or pleasure.
7. *The promotion of intercultural understanding and peace.* For some, the highest goals of language teaching are to foster negotiation rather than war and changes in the society (see for example Gomes de Matos, 2002).

None of these goals directly state that the learners should approximate native speakers, even if they are "waiting in the wings." They are instead concerned with the educational values of the L2 for the learner. Indeed many of them might be achieved without actually learning the new language per se. For example, degree courses in literature may be carried out through translations; courses in French civilization have been taught in English schools through the mother tongue.

INTERNAL AND EXTERNAL GOALS

These goals can be divided into two main groups – *external* and *internal* (Cook, 1983, 2002):

1. External goals relate to the students' use of language outside the classroom: traveling, using the second language in shops and trains, reading books in another language, attending lectures in a different country, or surviving as refugees in a strange new world.

2. Internal goals relate to the students' mental development as individuals: They may think differently, approach language in a different way, be better citizens, because of the effects that the L2 has on their minds. So-called traditional language teaching often stressed the internal goals. Learning Latin trained the brain; studying L2 literature heightened people's cultural awareness.

External goals dominated language teaching methodology for most of the last century, first through situational teaching and later through audiolingualism with its emphasis on external situations. Then communicative language teaching (see Spada, this volume) introduced syllabuses based on language functions and interactions in the world outside, not the world inside the student. Lists of language functions such as Wilkins (1976) ignored the internal functions that L2 users accomplish in the L2, like self-organization (keeping a diary, etc.), memory tasks (phone numbers), and unconscious uses (singing to oneself) (Cook, 1998).

The task-based learning approach, strongly influenced by the classroom based schemes of Prabhu (1987), has recognized that classroom tasks do not necessarily have external outcomes in the world outside. Skehan (1998), for example, thinks it desirable that tasks have real-world relevance but believes this to be "difficult to obtain in practice" (p. 96) (see Skehan, this volume for a fuller discussion). Task-based learning has, however, seldom tried to see what long-term internal goals such tasks might have for the student beyond the sheer acquisition of linguistic knowledge.

The platitude that has obsessed language teaching for 30 years has been that the goal of language teaching is communication. On the one hand, this skirts the issues of where, with whom, and for what purpose this communication takes place; communication is too vague a term to bear the weight that has been given to it in language teaching. If the goal is indeed external communication with other people who do not speak your first language, this is beside the point for many EFL students. Few students in China, Cuba or Chile, for instance, regularly speak with people in English outside the classroom. On the other hand, equating language with communication misses its other functions: Communication is only one role of language in human life, as proclaimed by linguists from Malinowski's phatic communion to Halliday's interpersonal function, and Chomsky's pragmatic competence. Enabling students to use an L2 does not just give them a tool for talking to people through a different language but changes their lives and minds in all sorts of ways (Cook, 2002).

THE NATIVE SPEAKER AS THE TARGET OF LANGUAGE TEACHING

The external goal implicit in much language teaching has been to make the students approximate to native speakers: "After all, the ultimate goal—perhaps unattainable for some—is, nonetheless, to 'sound like a native speaker' in all aspects of the language" (González-Nueno, 1997, p. 261). Students are judged on success according to how close they resemble native speakers: "The native speaker's 'competence' or 'proficiency' or 'knowledge of the language' is a necessary point of reference for the second language proficiency concept used in language teaching" (Stern, 1983, p. 341). The best teacher is therefore a native speaker who can represent the target the students are trying to emulate. A language school in London invites one to "Learn French from the French"; a school in Greece proclaims "all our teachers are native speakers of English."

Within the past decade, the term *native speaker* has been deconstructed, partly by recognizing that people are multi-dimensional; the role of native speaker is a comparatively minor part of one's identity compared to citizenship, membership of ethnic minorities, football supporters, social classes, professional groups, and so on (Rampton, 1990). Its basis in power has also been deconstructed; native speakers assert power over their language and insist that only they can control its destiny. Unlike DNA, nobody has copyrighted a natural language (computer languages and Klingon are a separate issue as they do not have native speakers). The denial of the right of L2 users to sound as if they come from a particular place is an issue of power; native speakers are not treated in the same way. It is acceptable for a speaker of English to sound as if he/she comes from London, Chicago, or Auckland but not from Paris, Beijing, or Santiago. As la Rochefoucauld wrote in 1678, "L'accent du pays où l'on est né demeure dans l'esprit et dans le coeur comme dans le langage" (The accent of the country where you were born lives on in your spirit and heart as it does in your speech.) Why should L2 users be the only ones to have to conceal it? An example is the denigration of Joseph Conrad for having a Polish accent, despite his status as one of the key stylists of English prose in the 20th century. The native speaker concept has contributed to the denial of the rights for some human beings to show their membership of particular groups.

The concept of native speaker has little meaning as an L2 goal. In the literal sense, it is impossible for an L2 user to become a native speaker, since by definition you cannot be a native speaker of anything other than your first language. Phrasing the goal in terms of the native speaker means L2 learning can only lead to different degrees of failure, not degrees of success: "Relative to native speaker's linguistic competence, learners' interlanguage is deficient by definition" (Kasper & Kellerman, 1997, p. 5). In a wider sense, accepting the native speaker goal still does not specify which native speaker in what roles: Native speakers of English come from all parts of the globe, classes of society, genders, and ages.

Indeed, many L2 users speak to people who are *not* native speakers, whether it be the German businessman negotiating contracts with a Dane, the Chinese air-line pilot talking to the control tower in Singapore, or the Japanese tourist buying a film for her camera in Spain. English is a useful lingua franca for much of the globe (see Seidlhofer, this volume, for a fuller discussion). The Israeli National Curriculum (2001) makes this explicit: It "does not take on the goal of producing near-native speakers of English, but rather speakers of Hebrew, Arabic or other languages who can function comfortably in English whenever it is appropriate" (p. 4). In fact, the majority of communication in English does not involve native speakers. While the native speaker goal can have a limited currency for some students, it has no relevance as an internal goal since learning a second language makes people different from monolingual native speakers.

THE L2 USER CONCEPT

An alternative to the native speaker goal is the concept of the *L2 user*, which refers to people who know and use a second language at any level. This is similar to functional definitions of *bilingualism*: "the point where a speaker can first produce complete meaningful utterances in the other language" (Haugen, 1953, p. 7). The term L2 user is however preferred to *bilingual* because of the diverse definitions of bilingualism, many of which refer to the native speaker – "*bilingualism*, native-like control of two languages" (Bloomfield, 1933, p. 56) – which assume the bilingual is the sum of two monolinguals rather than something distinct.

The majority of people in the world may even be L2 users. While accurate figures are impossible to cite, it is certainly suggested by countries like the Congo with 213 languages, or Singapore, where 56% of the population are literate in more than one language, or indeed Europe, where 53% of the population can speak at least one additional language (European Commission, 2001). The British Council (1999) estimates there are one billion learners of English in the world. Everyday life in many societies demands more than one language, for example in Cameroon or India. Other L2 users are members of linguistic minorities who need another language for education or health, like Bengali speakers in the East End of London, businessmen using a language other than their own, such as Luc Vandevelde, the former Belgian head of Marks and Spencers, or international sports personalities using English in interviews with the mass media, such as Maria Sharapova, Fernando Alonso, or Frankie Dettori. In short, the L2 increases rather than diminishes human diversity.

Linguistics, SLA research, and second language teaching have traditionally taken the monolingual native speaker as their starting point. Chomsky (1986) set the goals of linguistics as accounting for knowledge of language, not knowledge of language*s*. Both language teachers and students have traditionally seen their goal as getting close to native speaker competence. For people who treat L2 users as deviating from native speaker norms, the important questions are the cognitive problems of bilingualism, not the cognitive deficits of monolingualism, and why L2 students can't speak like native speakers, rather than why monolinguals can't speak two languages.

The L2 user concept, following Labov (1969), is rooted in difference rather than deficit. It recognizes that L2 users are different kinds of people from monolingual native speakers, and need to be evaluated as people who speak two languages, not as inefficient natives. The L2 user concept arose in the context of the multi-competence approach to SLA. *Multi-competence* is the knowledge of two or more languages in the same mind. It extends the concept of interlanguage by recognizing the continual presence of the L1 in the learner's mind alongside the second language, assuming that there is little point in studying the L2 as an isolated interlanguage system since its raison d'être is that it is added to a first language. Indeed, it may be wrong to count languages in people's minds—L1, L2, L3—as the language system exists in a single mind as a whole, akin to Chomsky's notion that the mental reality is a grammar, not a language (Chomsky, 1986). If the L2 user is the norm in the world, the monolingual mind has a more basic system because of its impoverished exposure to languages.

The term *L2 user* is conceptually different from *L2 learner* even when it refers to the same person. L2 *users* are exploiting whatever linguistic resources they have for a real-life purpose, whether that be ordering a CD on the Internet, talking about Manchester United, translating a letter, or visiting the doctor. L2 *learners* are acquiring a system for later use; they interact in information-gap games, they make up sentences, they plan activities in groups. Sometimes learner and user overlap: A student learning English in a classroom can also use it over coffee five minutes later. It is demeaning, however, to call a person who has been using an L2 for perhaps half their life, a learner.

THE NATURE OF THE L2 USER

So what is the purpose of L2 teaching? To put it simply, there are some qualities in people who use second languages that society or the individual student values; language teaching serves to foster these qualities in students. The following section described these qualities of L2 users that students can strive to emulate.

L2 Users Have Different Uses of Language from Monolinguals

If the aim of language teaching were to clone the native speaker, this would limit the functions of an L2 to those that native speakers can carry out in their L1. While some L2 users may indeed need to speak to native speakers, the language that native speakers use to non-native speakers is a specific variety. The presence of a non-native speaker alters the behavior of native speakers, changing their syntax and the information they provide (Arthur, Weiner, Culver, Young, & Thomas, 1980). The L2 user needs to master the skill of conversing with native speakers in this particular mode. Databases of native speaker speech, such as COBUILD and the BNC, have not provided any information about the native to non-native English the L2 user will actually encounter (let alone any insight into the non-native speakers they are more likely to talk to). Continental businessmen have no problems speaking English to fellow non-native speakers; it is the English person who gives them problems.

L2 users also have distinctive uses for language unavailable to monolinguals, most obviously, when two languages are on-line. Translation is an everyday activity for many L2 users, for instance, children translating for their non-native parents in consultations with doctors (Malakoff & Hakuta, 1991). Some L2 users are indeed professional interpreters, foreign correspondents or bilingual secretaries, but most L2 users are expected to translate something at one time or another. Even if translation is discouraged as a teaching technique, this does not negate its validity as an external goal. Indeed, "translation provides an easy avenue to enhance linguistic awareness and pride in bilingualism" (p. 163).

Another distinctive L2 use of language is code-switching. L2 users commonly switch from one language to the other according to a variety of rules depending on social roles, the topics that are being discussed, the grammatical overlap between the two languages, and so on (Auer, 1998). One example might be a Japanese university student remarking, *Reading sureba suruhodo, confuse suro yo. Demo, computer lab ni itte, article o print out shinakya* (The more reading I have, the more I get confused, but I have to go to the computer lab and need to print out some articles.) Another example might be T.S. Eliot's *The Waste Land:* 'London Bridge is falling down*, Poi s'ascose nel foco che gli affina, Quando fiam uti chelidon*—O swallow swallow*, Le Prince d'Aquitaine á la tour aboli.'*

Code-switching is a highly skilled L2 use. Grosjean (1989) distinguishes two modes of language in L2 users, a *monolingual* mode in which one language is used at a time, and a *bilingual* mode in which both are used simultaneously. Whether or not code-switching should be encouraged in the classroom is a separate issue. Traditionally the teacher was supposed to frown upon students using their L1 in group and pair-work, though Jacobson (1990) has described a teaching method based on systematic code-switching. Clearly most effective L2 users are capable of using two languages at once.

Paradis (1997) has argued that these L2 uses are simply extensions of what monolinguals do; translation is the same as paraphrase on a larger scale; code-switching is a more complex form of dialect or register-switching. From a multi-competence perspective, the monolingual uses restricted forms of the language functions available to the L2 user.

As will be discussed later in this chapter, compared to native speakers, L2 users demonstrate more subtle differences in their use of both their first and second languages mostly due to the links between the two languages in their minds. Whichever language they are using, they are still to some extent affected by the other language they know—its rules, concepts, and cultural patterns. An L2 user is essentially a product of *métissage*—"the mixing of two ethnic groups, forming a third ethnicity" (Canada Tree, 1996; see also Lionnet, 1989). The danger is not seeing themselves as fully members of either culture, rather than as fully-paid up L2 users. L2 users form the majority in many countries of the world where it is taken for granted that everyone uses whatever languages are necessary for their everyday lives. Both their first and second languages may differ from those of monolingual native speakers but this is not important for L2 users.

L2 Users Have a Different Command of the Second and First Languages

Some researchers have argued that people can speak an L2 like a native speaker (Bongaerts, Planken, & Schils, 1997); others have denied this possibility. This is, however, the wrong comparison. An L2 user should be compared with another successful L2 user, a member of the same group, not with a native speaker, who by definition is a member of a group that the L2 user can never join.

Arguments based on the achievements of a select few should be set to one side. Despite the achievements of a tiny minority, the knowledge of the second language of the vast majority of L2 users differs from that of native speakers. These differences are usually obvious. For example, although many spelling mistakes are common to all users of English spelling, be they native, non-native, young, or old, L2 users soon reveal their first language through their errors: *volontary* and *tissu* (French), *theese* and *precios* (Italian), *lavel* (i.e. *level*) and *congratale* (Urdu), and so on (Cook, 2004). Also, the voice onset time (VOT) of L2 users' plosive consonants deviates slightly from that of native speakers (Nathan, 1987). Even at advanced "passing for native" levels, there are still concealed differences between L2 users and native speakers revealed in grammaticality judgments (Coppetiers, 1987).

Recent research has been discovering that the L2 user also has a different command of the L1 from a monolingual native speaker (Cook, 2003). The knowledge of vocabulary in the L1 is affected by the second so that, for example, when a French person who knows English encounters the French word *coin,* they are aware of the English meaning *money* as well as the French meaning *corner* (Beauvillain & Grainger, 1987). With regards to syntax, L2 users process their *first* language differently so that, for instance, Japanese, Spanish, and Greek users of

English look for the subject of the L1 sentence in slightly different ways (Cook, Iarossi, Stellakis, & Tokumaru, 2003): Some L2 users can be said, more appropriately, to have an extended L1 competence than a declining L1 competence (Jarvis, 2003). In other words, the first language competence of L2 users is not the same as that of monolinguals. Within the multi-competence approach, such changes are seen as inevitable. At some level, the two languages form a single complex system within the individual mind; the totality of the L2 user is more than just adding a second language to a mind that has a first. While an overt goal of second language teaching may not be to alter the first language of the learner, this is an inevitable consequence.

L2 Users Have Different Minds from Monolinguals

The distinctive characteristics of L2 users extend outside what is normally thought of as language knowledge and use. L2 users also differ from monolinguals in terms of interior aspects of mind that go beyond the external uses of language detailed so far. Indeed this is implicit in the concept of internal goals of language teaching; as well as enabling students to communicate with other people, language teaching also affects their minds in ways that society may find beneficial—the traditional virtues of classical language teaching.

One such aspect is language awareness. Bilingually educated children are sharper at making grammaticality judgments about sentences than monolinguals (Bialystok, 2001). Afrikaans/English children aged 4-9 who know a second language are ahead of monolinguals in developing semantic awareness of words (Ianco-Worrall, 1972). Hungarian children who know English produce Hungarian sentences that are more structurally complex (Kecskes & Papp, 2000). Yelland, Pollard, and Mercuri (1993) employed all possible combinations of big and small objects with big and small words (e.g. *ant, caterpillar, airplane, whale*) to show that bilingual children are better aware that big words do not necessarily denote big things. The wider world of English literature soon shows us L2 users who have demonstrated this extra facility with language such as Milton, Beckett, and Nabokov.

A variety of measures have also shown that the actual processes of cognition are affected by the knowledge of a second language. Contrary to early findings about cognitive deficit in bilinguals, research has usually shown that bilingual children perform better than monolinguals on both verbal and non-verbal IQ tests (Peal & Lambert, 1962); bilingualism in 5-year-olds showed advantages for object constancy, naming objects and the use of object names in sentences (Feldman & Shen, 1971). Ianco-Worrall (1972) showed that bilingual children think more flexibly. Even code-switching by bilingual children is not a sign of deficit but according to Genesee (2002), a kind of linguistic competence that surpasses that which is demonstrated by monolinguals. Diaz (1985) lists other benefits from knowing a second language for conceptual development, creativity, and analogical reasoning. The only negative findings seem to be a slight deficiency on certain short term memory (STM) tasks. For example, Makarec & Persinger (1993) found that male L2 users, but not women, had some memory deficiencies compared to monolinguals.

L2 User Goals in Language Teaching: Problems and Issues

The goal of becoming an L2 user is thus more valid and more achievable for most L2 students, emphasizing both external and internal goals of language teaching. Let us bring together the threads.

Most importantly L2 users have to be credited with being what they are—L2 users. They should be judged by how successful they are as L2 users, not by their failure compared to native speakers. L2 students have the right to become L2 users, not imitation native speakers. If there is constant pressure to be like native speakers, students are likely to accept this as their role rather than understanding the advantages of L2 users. In my own experience with talking to groups of teachers about the shift from native speaker to L2 user goals, some feel insulted because I have undermined a life-time goal, others feel liberated by knowing that they have value in their own right rather than in relationship to native speakers. In education, one always has to acknowledge Peters' (1973) aphorism: "What interests the students may not be in the students' interests." The L2 user goal may not be the most popular among students or teachers, but this is more through ignorance than deliberate choice. As we have seen, the problem with the native speaker goal is that it is essentially unachievable for most students. As Kramsch (1998) concludes, "traditional methodologies based on the native speaker usually define language learners in terms of what they are *not,* or at least *not yet*" (p. 28). We need at least to explain the alternative goals to the students.

One major problem is to spell out what the L2 user goal actually means. Because linguistics has been concerned almost exclusively with natives, there are no descriptions of L2 users. By default, the only adequate descriptions in education are those of native speakers. The ultimate requirement, then, is descriptions of what L2 users are actually like, for instance their basic common grammars (Perdue, 2001), their phonological systems (Jenkins, 2000), the types of use that they actually make of the L2, the cognitive and processing differences, and so on. Teachers can start by building on their own experiences as L2 users. Native speaker teachers were formerly those who spoke with authority because of their ownership of the language; now non-native teachers are the authentic sources of knowledge about what it is like to be an L2 user (Llurda, 2005). Descriptions of native speaker English are a temporary measure until proper descriptions of L2 users are made.

Another problem is that L2 users differ considerably in their attainments and in their needs. Often this variability has been held against L2 users but one may become a perfectly adequate L2 user for one's own purposes with only a small system. For example, my few words of Italian enable me to go to a restaurant or a concert in Italy but I can't read anything in Italian; my knowledge of French lets me read Piaget in the original but I can't have a conversation in French. Yet, my L2 needs are adequately served in both cases despite their intrinsic limitations. In the first language, native speakers mostly have a greater range of uses, though reading Piaget may not be typical. In short, once the native speaker norm is abandoned, there is no need to aim at superfluous uses of language. In some ways, this is the philosophy of English for specific purposes (ESP), that is, teach the aspects of language appropriate to the students' anticipated uses and regard them as successes when they can carry them out, not as failures for still having a foreign accent.

One important lesson is recognizing the importance of internal goals. Part of the value of acquiring another language is the benefit internally, whether it be a greater awareness of language, a more flexible approach, different cognitive strategies, or whatever. This is already mentioned in some official syllabuses and curriculums: "Through the study of a foreign language, pupils ... begin to think of themselves as citizens of the world as well as of the United Kingdom" (DfEE, 1999). Most teaching methods and course-books are nevertheless still designed to foster external goals. Yet language teaching can enhance people's lives in many ways, even if they never meet a native speaker. One extreme example is the use of community language learning (Curran, 1976) as a form of therapy for patients with mental illnesses; talking about your problems in another language may help you to solve them. Language teaching should emphasize internal, not just external, educational goals for the individual L2 user.

As far as external goals are concerned, despite their prominence in language teaching methodology, they have usually not been related to the actual L2 uses of language. The only exception is the vast number of situations in course-books where apparent L2 users seek help or guidance from native speakers in shops, surgeries, stations, and so on. In as much as these actually reflect L2 use, they show low-level communication by powerless L2 users; the native speakers are almost invariably the experts in control. Teaching the L2 user goal means teaching for the situations that L2 users encounter, and modeling L2 roles and situations.

REFERENCES

Arthur, B., Weiner, M., Culver, J., Young, L., & Thomas, D. (1980). The register of impersonal discourse to foreigners: Verbal adjustments to foreign accent. In D. Larsen-Freeman, (Ed.), *Discourse analysis in second language research* (pp. 111–24). Rowley, Mass.: Newbury House.
Auer, P. (Ed.). (1998). *Code-switching in conversation: Language, interaction and identity*. London: Routledge.
Beauvillain, C., & Grainger, J. (1987). Accessing interlexical homographs: Some limitations of a language-selective access. *Journal of Memory and Language, 26*, 658–672.
Bialystok, E. (2001). *Bilingualism in development*. Cambridge: Cambridge University Press.
Bloomfield, L. (1933). *Language*. Holt: New York.
Bongaerts, T., Planken, B., & Schils, E. (1997). Age and ultimate attainment in the pronunciation of a foreign language. *Second Language Research, 19*, 447–465.
British Council. (1999). *Frequently asked questions*. Online document accessed 29.07.2005 at http://www.britishcouncil.org/english/engfaqs.htm#hmlearn1).
Canada Tree. (1996). *Genealogy to History*. Retrieved July 29, 2005, from http://users.rttinc.com/~canadatree/.
Chomsky, N. (1986). *Knowledge of language: Its nature, origin and use*. New York: Praeger.
Coleman, J. A. (1996). *Studying languages: A survey of British and European students*. London: CILT.
Cook, V. J. (1983). Some assumptions in the design of courses. *University of Trier Papers* (Series B), *94*.
Cook, V. J. (1998). Internal and external uses of a second language. *Essex Research Reports in Linguistics*, 100–110. http://homepage.ntlworld.com/vivian.c/Writings/Papers/InternalUses.htm.
Cook, V. J. (2002). Language teaching methodology and the L2 user perspective. In V. J. Cook (Ed.), *Portraits of the L2 user* (pp. 325–344). Clevedon: Multilingual Matters.
Cook, V. J. (Ed.). (2003). *Effects of the L2 on the L1*. Clevedon: Multilingual Matters.
Cook, V. J. (2004). *The English writing system*. London: Edward Arnold.
Cook, V. J., Iarossi, E., Stellakis, N., & Tokumaru Y. (2003). Effects of the second language on the syntactic processing of the first language. In V. J. Cook (Ed.). *Effects of the L2 on the L1* (pp. 214–233). Clevedon: Multilingual Matters.
Coppetiers, R. (1987). Competence differences between native and near-native speakers. *Language, 63*(3), 545–573.

Curran, C. A. (1976). *Counselling-learning in second languages.* Apple River Press, Apple River Illinois.
Department for Education and Employment (DfEE). (1999). *The National Curriculum for England: Modern foreign languages.* London: Department for Education and Employment. Retrieved July 29, 2005, from www.hmso.gov.uk/guides.htm.
Diaz, R. M. (1985). The intellectual power of bilingualism. *Quarterly Newsletter of the Laboratory of Comparative Human Cognition, 7*(1), 16–22.
Ellis, R. (1996). SLA and language pedagogy. *Studies in Second Language Acquisition, 19,* 69–92.
European Commission. (2001). *Special Eurobarometer Survey 54: Europeans and languages.* Retrieved July 29, 2005, from http://europa.eu.int/comm/education/policies/lang/languages/barolang_en.pdf.
Feldman, C., & Shen, M. (1971). Some language-related cognitive advantages of bilingual five-year-olds, *Journal of Genetic Psychology, 118,* 235–244.
Genesee, F. (2002). Portrait of the bilingual child. In V. J. Cook (Ed.), *Portraits of the L2 user* (pp. 161–179). Clevedon: Multilingual Matters.
Gomes de Matos, F. (2002). Second language learners' rights. In V. J. Cook (Ed.), *Portraits of the L2 user* (pp. 305–323). Clevedon: Multilingual Matters.
González-Nueno, M. (1997). VOT in the perception of foreign accent. *International Review of Applied Linguistics,* 24, 275–286.
Grosjean, F. (1989). Neurolinguists, beware! The bilingual is not two monolinguals in one person. *Brain and Language, 36,* 3–15.
Haugen, E. (1953). *The Norwegian language in America.* Philadelphia: University of Pennsylvania Press.
Ianco-Worrall, A. (1972). Bilingualism and cognitive development. *Child Development, 43,* 1390–1400.
Israeli National Curriculum. (2001). [Electronic version]. Retrieved July 29, 2005 from http://www.education.gov.il/tochniyot_limudim/ang3.htm.
Jacobson, R. (1990). Allocating two languages as a key feature of a bilingual methodology. In R. Jacobson & C. Faltis (Eds.), *Language description issues in bilingual schooling* (pp. 3–17). Clevedon: Multilingual Matters.
Jarvis, S. (2003). Probing the effects of the L2 on the L1: A case study. In V. J. Cook (Ed.), *Effects of the L2 on the L1* (pp. 81–102). Clevedon: Multilingual Matters.
Jenkins, J. (2000). *The phonology of English as an international language.* Oxford: Oxford University Press.
Kasper, G., & Kellerman, E. (Eds.). (1997). *Communication strategies: Psycholinguistic and sociolinguistic perspectives.* Harlow: Longman.
Kecskes, I., & Papp, T. (2000). *Foreign language and mother tongue.* Hillsdale, NJ: Lawrence Erlbaum.
Kementerian Pendidikan Malaysia (Malaysian Ministry of Education) (1987). *Sukatan Pelajaran Sekolah Menengah: Bahasa Inggeris.* Malaysia: PPK. (Secondary school syllabus: English language).
Kramsch, C. (1998). The privilege of the intercultural speaker. In M. Byram & M. Fleming (Eds.), *Language learning in intercultural perspective* (pp. 16–31). Cambridge: Cambridge University Press.
Labov, W. (1969). The logic of non-standard English. *Georgetown Monographs on Language and Linguistics, 22,* 1–31.
Lionnet, F. (1989). *Autobiographical voices: Face, gender, self-portraiture.* Ithaca, NY: Cornell UP.
Llurda, E. (Ed.) (2005). *Non-Native Teachers.* New York: Springer.
Long, M. (1990). Maturational constraints on language development. *Studies in Second Language Acquisition, 12,* 251–286.
Makarec, K., & Persinger, M. (1993). Bilingual men, but not women display verbal memory weakness but not figural memory differences compared to monolinguals. *Personality and Individual Differences, 15*(5), 531–536.
Malakoff, M., & Hakuta, K. (1991). Translation skills and metalinguistic awareness in bilinguals. In E. Bialystok (Ed.), *Language processing in bilingual children* (pp. 141–166). Cambridge: Cambridge University Press.
Nathan, G. S. (1987). On second-language acquisition of voiced stops. *Journal of Phonetics, 15,* 313–322.
Paradis, M. (1997) The cognitive neuropsychology of bilingualism. In A. M. B. de Groot & J. Kroll (Eds.), *Tutorials in bilingualism. Psycholinguistic perspectives* (pp. 331–354). Mahwah, NJ: Lawrence Erlbaum.
Peal, E., & Lambert, W. (1962). The relation of bilingualism to intelligence. *Psychological Monographs, 76*(27), 1–23.
Perdue, C. (2001). Development of L2 functional use. In V. J. Cook (Ed.), *Portraits of the L2 user* (pp. 161–179). Clevedon: Multilingual Matters.
Peters, R. S. (1973). *The philosophy of education.* Oxford: Oxford University Press.
Prabhu, N. S. (1987). *Second language pedagogy.* Oxford: Oxford University Press.

Rampton, M. B. H. (1990). Displacing the 'native speaker': Expertise, affiliation and inheritance. *ELT Journal, 44*(2), 338–343.
Skehan, P. (1998). *A cognitive approach to language learning*. Oxford: Oxford University Press.
Stern, H. (1983). *Fundamental concepts of language teaching.* Oxford: Oxford University Press.
Wilkins, D. A. (1976). *Notional syllabuses: A taxonomy and its relevance to foreign language curriculum development*. Oxford: Oxford University Press.
Yelland, G. W., Pollard, J., & Mercuri, A. (1993). The metalinguistic benefits of limited contact with a second language. *Applied Psycholinguistics, 14*, 423–444.

CHAPTER 17

INTEGRATING SCHOOL-AGED ESL LEARNERS INTO THE MAINSTREAM CURRICULUM

CONSTANT LEUNG

King's College London, UK

ABSTRACT

The concept of *integrating ESL learners into the mainstream curriculum* has been the subject of debate amongst educationalists and policy makers in many parts of the English-speaking countries in the past 30 years. The issues concerning the integration of ESL students into the mainstream curriculum are multi-dimensional—the label of *ESL* itself appears to be part linguistic, part educational, part social, and part political. The main purpose of this chapter is to give an account of the multidimensionality of ESL curriculum and practice. The developments in ESL curriculum and pedagogy within the mainstream education system will be looked at first. The influences of wider concerns such as social integration, and rights and entitlements to equal opportunity in public provision will be discussed next. Recent experiences in California, England, and Victoria will be drawn on to illustrate the multi-dimensional nature of ESL policy and practice. This chapter will conclude with some deliberations on the formulation of an analytical framework that may be used to critically examine any ESL curriculum and practice. The central assumption throughout this chapter is that ESL in mainstream schooling can only be understood properly if we pay attention to its unique position at the crossroads of educational, social, and ideological movements.

INTRODUCTION

The integration of ESL students into the mainstream schooling provision in the publicly funded school system has been an established educational policy position for some time now in ethnically and linguistically complex and diverse countries such as Australia, the UK, and the United States[1]. However, this apparently common educational commitment has been realized by a whole host of different national and/or local policies and practices in terms of English language teaching. The wide-ranging discussion on integration in this area of education has oriented towards:

1. linguistic and ethnic minority students who are (sometimes newly arrived) citizens and/or members of settled local communities: e.g. Vietnamese communities in Australia, Hispanic communities in the US, Chinese communities in English-speaking parts of Canada, and Asian (with community links to the Indian subcontinent) communities in Britain
2. educational integration in the general sense as much as English language learning
3. social integration and inclusion, and citizens' rights and entitlements as much as individual achievement in school
4. language policy/policies on English and other languages.

This chapter will argue that integration of ESL students into the mainstream (which is itself a metaphor) is as much a pedagogic issue as a social and ideological one: Beyond its basic reference to a *common* curriculum and viewed in a long(er) term perspective, the idea of the *mainstream* is actually a contestable and contested set of curriculum choices and pedagogic practices. ESL is in some sense an educational arena where various, sometimes competing and sometimes overlapping, expectations and demands meet one another. In other words, ESL is an ideologically charged discipline. A useful way of seeing the complex and "loaded" nature of ESL is to compare it with other more "insulated" school curriculum subjects such as mathematics and French (or indeed the more traditionally-minded varieties of English as a Foreign Language), which are generally less directly exposed to non-discipline-based pressure and influence. It is therefore a complex and non-static phenomenon requiring multi-faceted analysis. In order to understand the varieties of systemic responses in different locations we will need to look at lines of articulation between curriculum developments, and social values and beliefs. The purpose of examining the relationship between language education policy and practices and social values is not to claim any causal explanation but to show the need to go beyond pedagogic considerations if we are to understand why certain policy and pedagogy are adopted and not others at any one time. Beyond analytical understanding, there is a place for educationally and socially responsible critical questioning so that we do not stop at relativistic description. For that reason, the final section of this chapter will raise principled questions of clarification that can be used to critically examine some of the claims and equally important areas of confusion and omission of integration policies and practices. Many of the observations and questions raised in this chapter will be influenced by the trajectory of developments in ESL in England (and the UK more generally) in the past 30 years. It is hoped that this ethno-aware perspective will allow for a heightened consciousness of the underlying poignancy and analytical relevance of the seemingly diverse developments in other world locations.

INTEGRATION: CURRICULUM LEVEL DEVELOPMENTS

Broadly speaking, at the curriculum level, the integration of ESL students into the mainstream can be seen to have developed in two directions: (a) attempts at making the English-medium schooling environment inclusive and beneficial for language minority students; and (b) attempts at making the curriculum accessible by actively using students' first language (other than English) as a medium of learning and wider curriculum communication. The first is discussed as *ESL pedagogy* and the second as *bilingual education*.

ESL Pedagogy

For a variety of historical, demographic, social, and legislative reasons, the past 30 years or so have seen a high level of initiatives and activities in places such as Australia, Canada, and England in integrating ESL learners, who are either new to the education system or from an ethnic minority community background with a home language other than English, into the mainstream English-medium educational provision. (See Ashworth, 2000, p. 17-32 for a concise international overview.) The central idea behind the integration policies has been a concern with equal opportunities and entitlements in education. This invariably means an effort at accommodating or including ESL students into the mainstream across-subject content classes and/or extending the timetabling arrangements to provide access to mainstream curriculum-related but separate English language classes[2]. We will now look at a range of selective examples of pedagogic ideas and developments in ESL within the mainstream in the past 3 decades[3].

In broad terms, many of the ideas and developments can be seen as falling into one of the following four categories: (a) *language-content orientation*, (b) *content-language orientation*, (c) *trans-curriculum language orientation*, or (d) *student orientation*. These categories are used here partly because they signal different pedagogic concerns in different contexts, and partly because they are convenient labels to represent historically separate efforts by teachers and researchers. However, these categories should not be seen as mutually exclusive and, as it will be seen, they have some overlapping concerns[4].

1. Language-content Orientation

Many of the early attempts at developing specialist programmers for ESL students were based on a structural approach. For instance, the Scope materials (1978) advised teachers: "from the very beginning you have to see to it that your pupils learn correctly organised language, not a makeshift kind of pidgin....They have to master the way words are put together and the correct form of those words" (p. i). In some sense, under this kind of approach, the content of learning is the language system itself. However, there is often a *functional reality content* organized as themes in these kinds of materials. For instance, the Scope beginners materials were organized around the themes of shopping, and farm animals and farming.

An example of a specifically mainstream, curriculum-derived, language-content oriented syllabus is the topic approach (Cleland & Evans, 1984). This approach was initially developed out of a sense of dissatisfaction with the traditional grammar or structure-based teaching (Evans & Cleland, n.d.) for ESL students who were in the process of being integrated into mainstream classes. It was felt that ESL pedagogy should pay attention to students' English language competence with reference to their communicative requirements when studying curriculum subjects such as science and humanities. The conventional concerns of language teaching, e.g., grammar knowledge and the ability to use spoken and written language, are manifested through the content of topics such as *The Life Cycle of an Animal*. The topic content terms (vocabulary) and language expressions (structure and discourse) are presented and rehearsed through a teaching sequence that includes visuals and group activities (see Davison, 2001, for or a fuller discussion).

2. Content-language Orientation

The work of Crandall and her colleagues (Crandall, 1987; Crandall, Spanos, Christian, Simich-Dudgeon, & Willetts, 1987) can be seen as an example of curriculum content-oriented ESL, sometimes referred to as *content-based language instruction*. This approach is built on the observation that if school-aged ESL students are to participate in mainstream classroom learning, then it makes sense to focus "on the ways in which the language is used to convey or represent particular thoughts or ideas" (Crandall, p. 4)[5]. Subject-specific uses of vocabulary and discourse expressions are identified and classroom strategies are built around these in order to promote both understanding of the subject content and learning of English at the same time. For example, it is pointed out that mathematics uses English language vocabulary and structures in particular ways: e.g., the notion of subtraction can be expressed by *subtract from*, *decreased by*, *less*, *take away*, and so on, and language expressions such as "If a is a positive number, then $-a$ is a negative number" to represent the axioms of opposites (Dale & Cuevas, 1987, p. 17). Classroom activities designed to promote ESL development are built around the identified content-language.

Working within a theoretically explicit systemic functional linguistics perspective, Mohan (1986, 1990, 2001) proposes a content-language integration approach that ties language expressions and curriculum content together via a set of underlying knowledge structures. These knowledge structures, such as description and sequence, are argued to be cross-curricular. So, one may find sequence in narratives, in ordering historical events, and when following procedural steps in science experiments. This schema is intended to help teachers analyze the key knowledge structures in different subject areas and tasks and identify appropriate language expressions for teaching and for learning by students at different stages of ESL development. Mohan also suggests that knowledge structures can be visually represented in graphic forms such as charts and diagrams. Thus, the use of visual representations and other forms of graphics such as flow chart can assist students' understanding of the key language and content meaning.

3. Trans-curriculum Language Orientation

ESL pedagogy has also been discussed as a trans-curriculum issue. The first of the two examples we will look at is the work of Cummins (e.g. 1992, 1996, 2000; Cummins & Swain, 1986). Cummins suggests that language proficiency can be analyzed in terms of *basic interpersonal communicative skills* (BICS) and *cognitive/academic language proficiency* (CALP). *BICS* is understood to mean "the manifestation of language proficiency in everyday communicative contexts"; *CALP* is conceptualized as "manipulation of language in decontextualized academic situations" (1992, p. 17). BICS tends to occur in situations where the meanings communicated are broadly familiar to the participants and/or the immediate context or action provides supportive clues for understanding. Greeting friends and getting food in a student canteen are examples of context-supported BICS. A class discussion on the merits and demerits of the use of pesticide in farming—without any supporting print, visual, or video materials—is an example of context-impoverished CALP. These two conceptual categories do not yield precise linguistic descriptions nor do they map on to any specific area of the curriculum directly. However, they can be used to estimate the language and cognitive demands of a variety of communicative situations in school. It is understood that predicted language and cognitive demands have to be worked out with reference to the learning needs of specific students. In general, ESL students tend to acquire BICS relatively easily, whereas the development of CALP used in decontextualized situations is a more complex and long-term process. Pedagogically, it is suggested that ESL students, particularly those in the beginning stages, would benefit from context-embedded communication: e.g. learning new information and language expression through hands-on activities and/or with the support of visuals or realia, whenever the curriculum language is inaccessible.

The second example of the trans-curriculum development of ESL pedagogy to be examined is the conceptual framework proposed by Snow, Met, and Genesee (1992). This framework has been formulated specifically to enable ESL and content teachers to share a common teaching agenda. It is assumed that in a content-based approach to second language (L2) development, the language learning objectives are derived from "(a) the ESL curriculum, (b) the content-area curriculum, and (c) assessment of the learners' academic and communicative needs and ongoing evaluation of their developing language skills" (p. 30). Working with these three concerns, Snow et al. propose two types of language objectives: content-obligatory objectives and content-compatible objectives. *Content-obligatory objectives* specify the language—both structural elements as well as other features of discourse—that must be taught and learned as an integral part of any specific content topic: e.g. technical vocabulary such as *vibration* and *frequency* when studying the properties of sound and the associated discourse features of a formal scientific definition. Without learning these language items and features of discourse, content learning cannot be said to have taken place effectively. *Content-compatible language objectives* are language knowledge and skills that can be taught opportunistically, in a strategic sense, in the context of a particular topic or subject. For instance, if it is felt by teachers that some students would benefit from more guidance on the use of the past tense, then a history or humanities project on, for instance, Victorian clothing may provide the appropriate content environment. (For a further discussion of the varieties of content-language integration, see Davison & Williams, 2001.)

Thus, it can be seen that the ideas proposed by Cummins and Snow et al. are pedagogically relevant to L2 development within the mainstream curriculum but they are not tied to any specific areas of language and content. Cummins' BICS and CALP can be used to map out classroom strategies and the conceptual framework proposed by Snow et al. lends itself to both language and subject content analysis and planning.

Perhaps we should mention a specific aspect of one other relevant development that is also trans-curricular in nature: the *cognitive academic language learning approach* (CALLA) (Chamot & O'Malley, 1987). The CALLA was designed to be used for students in the transitional stage between attending separate ESL classes and mainstream schooling. Both language and subject content are addressed; it explicitly incorporates elements of Cummins' (1984 and others) and Mohan's (1986 and others) work on language and content learning. A distinguishing feature of this approach is that it pays attention to learning strategies. Chamot and O'Malley argue the following points:

1. Mentally active learners are better learners…
2. Strategies can be taught…
3. Learning strategies transfer to new tasks…
4. Academic language learning is more effective with learning strategies (p. 240)

The CALLA encourages students to use metacognitive strategies such as selective attention and self-monitoring; cognitive strategies such as grouping and classifying words according to their attributes, and visual imaging to understand and remember new information; and social-affective strategies such as co-operating with peers to solve problems, and asking teachers or peers to provide additional explanation or rephrasing. Quite clearly, these learning strategies are neither language nor curriculum oriented in any direct way, but it is argued that they assist both content and language learning.

Perhaps it should be pointed out that the examples of curriculum level developments described above can be, in principle, adopted in a variety of modes of delivery. For instance, teachers may use the content-obligatory and content-compatible objectives to guide their planning for ESL students who are within an *integrated* class (i.e. with English proficient students) and for ESL students who are enrolled in integrated schools but are attending some separate English or sheltered content lessons.

4. Student Orientation

The liberal humanistic perspective on language development has also had an influence on ESL pedagogic development, particularly in the development of a particular kind of student-oriented ESL pedagogy. An early proponent of this perspective was Levine (published posthumously, edited by Meek, 1996) who saw mixed ability teaching in mainstream classrooms as a potentially effective response to meeting the language learning needs of ESL students. Levine (Meek, p. 15) emphasizes the importance of "letting children have *their own voice*". In the English (subject) classroom, this means, inter alia, setting a teaching context whereby ESL students are encouraged to engage with ideas and projects that reflect their own interests as well as to work collaboratively in small groups with one another. In this perspective, social interaction between students and between students and teachers is seen as pivotal to L2 development. While the importance of the curriculum and teacher's instruction is acknowledged, the focus of attention is on the "dynamic and dialectical learning relationships" (p. 118). In contrast to the language and content oriented approaches mentioned earlier, the specific language to be learned is often not discussed explicitly. The notion of *language* is expressed either in terms of the "underlying systems of rules which govern native speakers' use of English" and *structure*, e.g. sentence level grammar (p. 22-23), or *communicative competence* in an abstract process sense:

> In so far as communicative competence equates with having learned language behaviour which is both appropriate and effective for the context of our lives, we all probably learn what we are able to do—no matter how different that is in kind or extent—in much the same way. That is to say, we are, and have been, open to external stimulae and motivation to learn the code and its appropriate use while, at the same time, having the opportunity to exercise an innate drive to learn on the code and on the situations and contexts in which particular parts of it are used….
>
> If these observations are applied to the communicative teaching of an additional language, it must surely suggest a more active role for learners in the learning-teaching process, and a more interactive one, allowing development from the data of the environment. (p. 123-124)

The language teaching agenda for the teacher in this conceptualization is essentially reactive in that the kind of teacher intervention made is dependent on the needs or problems shown in the active work of the ESL student. Classroom pedagogy is conceptualized in terms of learner active engagement. This perspective has been further elaborated in the officially promoted Partnership Teaching model (Bourne, 1989; DES, 1991; DfEE, 2001) in Britain:

> Learning is best achieved through enquiry-based activities involving discussion….To learn a language it is necessary to participate in its meaningful use….The curriculum itself is therefore a useful vehicle for language learning….A main strategy…for both curriculum learning and language learning is the flexible use of small group work. (Bourne, p. 63)

(For a more detailed discussion, see Leung, 2001.)

Bilingual Education[6]

The use of language minority students' first language (L1) as a medium of learning and curriculum communication has played a significant, if small in terms of student numbers[7], part in the effort to provide effective mainstream response to linguistic diversity. In the United States, where the use of students' L1 in the curriculum has received some federal and state level legislative support (Crawford, 1997), the concept of *bilingual education* is found to be expressed through three main programmed models:

1. Transitional/early exit bilingual education—the use of students' L1 is intended to help them keep up with curriculum subject learning; English is phased in as soon as possible; its primary goal is to mainstream students to all English classrooms.
2. Developmental/maintenance bilingual education—the use of students' L1 is maintained through active curriculum-related use even after English has been introduced gradually and successfully learned; its aim is to produce fluent bilingualism and a high level of academic success for language minority students.
3. Two-way bilingual education/dual language instruction—this type of program is designed to cater to both language minority and English proficient students: The curriculum is taught in a community minority language, e.g. Spanish, for up to half of the subjects and in English for the rest. The claimed effect is L1 maintenance and L2 acquisition for language

minority students and second/foreign language immersion for language majority students. This model has been favourably supported in the research literature[8]. The aim is to produce fluent bilingualism and high levels of academic achievement for both groups of students.

The arguments for two-way bilingual education are consistent with the L1-L2 interdependent hypothesis advanced by Cummins (1992, p. 22):

> To the extent that instruction in Lx is effective in promoting proficiency in Lx, transfer of this proficiency to Ly will occur provided there is adequate exposure to Ly...and adequate motivation to learn Ly.
>
> In concrete terms...Spanish instruction that develops L1 reading skills for Spanish-speaking students is not just developing Spanish skills; it is also developing a deeper conceptual and linguistic proficiency that is strongly related to the development of English literacy and general academic skills.

The effectiveness of developmental and two-way bilingual education in producing high levels of bilingualism and cross-curricular achievement has been reported by Krashen (1996), Ramírez (1992), and Thomas and Collier (1997) among others.

It should be noted here that there are a number of education systems which use students' first or home language as the medium of instruction, e.g. Welsh in Welsh-medium schools in Wales (see Williams, 2000), Basque in the Basque country (see Azurmendi, Bochoc, & Zabaleta, 2001), and the multilingual curriculum in European Schools (see Beardsmore, 1993). The first two cases are examples of efforts to revitalize and to support indigenous national minority languages. The European School approach to languages is an attempt to promote a trans-national identity and multilingualism within a European Union context. Although these systems and programs are also discussed as forms of bilingual education, they are not directly concerned with the integration of more recently settled ethnic and linguistic minorities[9]. Therefore, they fall outside the scope of the present discussion.

CURRICULUM ORIENTATIONS: KNOWLEDGE BASE AND PEDAGOGIC CHOICES

The collective efforts of researchers and practitioners in the past 30 years or so have led to a corpus of organized information and documented experience in the field of ESL. It would be reasonable to assume that there is now sufficient accumulated development of ideas and professional experience for education systems to choose and adopt pedagogic approaches and curriculum arrangements (particularly in terms of modes of delivery) that would, at least on the basis of available knowledge, promise the most effective response to the language and learning needs of ESL students. However, current experience in different parts of English speaking countries suggests that making pedagogic and curriculum decisions is neither a disinterested intellectual exercise nor a simple technical matter of choosing the most efficient means to achieve the desired ends. The common sense idea of choosing "the best deal" does not necessarily apply because there are multiple end-point consumers and there are different best deals for different parties. In linguistically and ethnically complex societies, language education policy decisions reflect the intricate interplay between demographic shifts, social values, political processes, and (often unevenly distributed) political power. The policy of educational integration of ESL students is arguably more exposed to these wider social and political developments than most other curriculum issues. We will now look at some key moments of recent experiences of integrating ESL students in three locations, England, Victoria, and California and attempt to understand the differences with reference to local ideological environments and political processes. These places have been chosen here not because they represent manifestations of some universal development, but because they can be seen as experiences that illustrate the nexus between integration of ESL students and wider social and ideological processes.

England

The mainstreaming initiatives in England since the 1980s have been largely expressed through a student-oriented pedagogy. ESL students are expected to be placed in mainstream age-appropriate classes as soon as possible upon joining school[10]. Pedagogically (all) teachers are expected to provide ESL development opportunities through engagement with curriculum activities that allow active hands-on participation and small group based learning (see the earlier discussion on the tenets of Partnership Teaching). ESL specialist teachers, where they are available, have multiple roles that include offering mainstream/subject teachers advice and guidance on how to generate English language learning opportunities in content lessons (including the use of students' L1 where possible and appropriate as a transitional facility into English), and doing collaborative "support" teaching in classes where ESL students are present (see Bourne, 1989, p. 107-108 for further discussion). There is relatively little *second language-specific* discussion on second language students learning English. For instance, there is currently no dedicated ESL curriculum; the mainstream English and literacy (mother tongue) curricula are presented as suitable for ESL development[11]. Professionally, ESL as a discipline is not offered as a main subject in pre-service teacher education: Indeed, there is no officially required credential for ESL teachers. Under these circumstances, ESL mainstreaming appears to have resulted in full structural integration for students, i.e. ESL students attending ordinary classes and, at the same time, under-provisioning in terms of curriculum infrastructure (e.g. the absence of explicit ESL curriculum specifications and mandatory specialist teacher education). (For a fuller discussion, see Leung, 2001.)

The current ESL policy and practice seem to be *student*-oriented but the mainstream curriculum itself is not *ESL*-oriented. This de-emphasizing of ESL has to be explained if we are to understand the current policy-practice configuration. The lineage of the current integration approach can arguably be traced back to a moment in the mid-1980s occasioned by the publication of two landmark documents. In 1986, the Commission for Racial Equality (CRE) published a report on the practice of teaching English to ESL students in separate language centers in one local education authority and found this practice tantamount to racial discrimination in terms of outcome (1986)[12]. The publication of this report led to the effective termination of the provision of separate ESL centers in the state-funded sector. The impact of this report was a reflection of the gathering strength of an emergent view on social integration of ethnic and linguistic minorities captured in the report of an official committee of enquiry, generally referred to as the *Swann Report* (DES, 1985).

> We believe that a genuinely pluralist society cannot be achieved without the social integration of ethnic minority communities and the ethnic majority community within a common whole. Whilst we are *not* looking for the assimilation of the minority communities within an unchanged dominant way of life, we are perhaps looking for the 'assimilation' of *all* groups within a redefined concept of what it means to live in British society today. (op.cit. p. 8)

Swann projected a vision of nested communities within a framework of a stable nation-state: Britain as a community of communities[13] engaged in the process of reconciling itself to the legacy of its imperial past (see Harris, Leung, & Rampton, 2001 for a further discussion). This shift from assimilation of ethnic and linguistic minorities to pluralist integration is articulated to a policy statement that emphasizes attitudinal change linked to a particular kind of educational inclusiveness:

> Language and language education...[have] usually been perceived in narrow and discrete terms, initially as concerning the 'problem' of teaching English to children for whom it is not a first language... We believe that the language needs of an ethnic minority child should no longer be compartmentalised in this way and seen as outside the mainstream of education since language learning and the development of effective communication skills is a feature of every pupil's education...Linguistic diversity provides the opportunity for all schools...to broaden the linguistic horizons of all pupils by ensuring that they acquire a real understanding of the role, range and richness of language in all its forms. (DES, 1985, p. 385-386)

The call for social integration, articulated to an inclusive education as defined by the Swann Report, signals the need to end the "compartmentalized" teaching of English to ethnic and linguistic minority pupils. By treating second/additional language learning as part of a broader communication issue, ESL can now be seen as an integral part of a generalized and common curriculum process, i.e. mainstreamed ESL. As Bourne (1989) observes, the Swann Report found a policy position that "was able to return English language learners to the mainstream classroom" (p. 64). Thus, in educational terms, this redefined vision of a pluralist society in a multi-ethnic and multilingual context has led to a view that favors social integration through common and undifferentiated membership in mainstream processes; conceptualizing ESL as a part of the more general communication issue provides a perspective that allows a toning down of distinctiveness and difference. The prioritizing of the social and socializing aspects of education in the rhetoric of this form of pluralism made it possible to downplay the significance of the different language and language learning needs of ESL students and to direct attention to the common communication needs. In other words, mainstreaming ESL students takes priority over the adapting and extending the mainstream curriculum for ESL students. The pedagogic option that makes immediate sense in this primarily social integration agenda is a student-oriented one that, above all, aims at helping the individual student benefit from the mainstream classroom activities, dispensing the need to address ESL as a distinct curriculum issue[14]. ESL, as it is currently conceptualized in the official educational literature, can be seen as a continuation of that line of thinking[15].

Victoria

ESL in Victoria, as in Australia more generally, has been mainstreamed[16]. Unlike the situation in England however, the Victorian mainstream system works with a range of structural (time-tabling) options that, according to Davison (2001), include fully integrated mainstream multi-ethnic classes with ESL support (similar to the situation in England), mainstream multi-ethnic classes with some separate ESL classes, ESL classes combined with some mainstream classes and intensive English classes in separate English language centers. These structural options are accompanied by variable curriculum concerns that range from a high language (integrated with content) focus for those who are ESL beginners to a high content (integrated with language) focus for those who are at more advanced stages of ESL development. In other words, the mainstreaming of ESL is simultaneously language-content-oriented, content-language-oriented, and student-oriented. Furthermore, the Victorian mainstream curriculum includes a dedicated ESL "companion" curriculum (Board of Studies, 1999). In total, the Victorian notion of *mainstream* appears to be quite different from the one adopted in England.

The idea that the mainstream curriculum itself should be open to adjustment and change to take account of ESL students' language and language learning needs emerged in public policy discourse in the 1980s in Australia. The central proposition was that public institutions should address the needs of ethnic minorities as part of their core services, not as an additional or marginal activity. In relation to the federal level provision for ESL in Australia, Campbell and McMeniman (1985) argue; "it should not be a question of 'NESB [non-English speaking background] versus the rest', but of acknowledging that, having been brought into Australia, NESB persons are 'us'" (p. 32). Davison (2001) reports that in Victoria there was an early recognition that mainstreaming ESL and curriculum design for ESL students in the mainstream are not the same thing: "The ESL profession has strongly resisted any reductionist tendencies, arguing that in a mainstream environment, ESL programming is necessarily complex. It involves…interrelated decisions about curriculum focus, first language input, modes of delivery, learner groupings and teacher roles" (p. 31).

However, the level of ESL provision and even the particular kind of ESL responses that we have just discussed are reported to have been under pressure across different parts of Australia in the past few years[17]. The policies of a "multicultural" Australia, once regarded as part of an accepted national value, and continuing immigration from non-English speaking parts of the world do not appear to receive unquestioned public support as they once did. At the same time, the introduction of economic rationalism in public finances has meant downwards pressures on public expenditure in general and, in education services in particular, value for money measures (see Williams, 1998). The education system in this new dispensation is meant to produce the human resources required for the nation's economic competitiveness. Under this political climate, ESL has been affected by a number of policy initiatives that have emerged. Broadbanding and benchmarking literacy appear to have been most significant. *Broadbanding* is an administrative device that can lead to adverse consequences for ESL provision:

> Broadbanding involves collapsing specific purpose programs into general purpose programs. This is done via the creation of categories broader than those of the specific purpose programs. ...Producing fewer programs means lowering administration costs and imposing fewer constraints on the use of funds by recipient jurisdictions. However, broadbanding can result in (across Australia this is now happening) a narrowing of ESL's scope and a reduction in ESL provision. In some places there is even a collapse of general support for ESL altogether. (Lo Bianco, 1998, p. 15)

The demand for the education system to produce the necessary human resources for economic competitiveness is translated into a concept of accountability through quantifiable measures of attainment in, *inter alia*, literacy, defined in terms of standards or benchmarks to be achieved at different stages of school education by all students. These benchmarks assume "mother tongue fluency in English and formal learning of English from Kindergarten" (Hoddinott, 1998, p. 24). This push for literacy as a national educational priority, accompanied by broadbanding as an implementation device to enhance administrative efficiency, can have the effect of blurring the differences between first and second languages, and the differences between developing mother tongue literacy (however defined) and learning a L2 and the associated literacy practices involved. As McKay (1998) points out:

> The incorporation of ESL under 'literacy' carries with it the danger of the ESL learner being constructed and taught as just one of the many learners of literacy in our classrooms. Inclusion rather than marginalisation is certainly crucial for ESL learners in our schools, but submersion rather than ESL-informed and ESL-specialist teaching is something we have successfully fought against for many years in Australia. (p. 9)

California

Nowhere is the complex nature of integrating ESL students into the mainstream educational provision and the choice of curriculum response illustrated more dramatically and vividly than by the political events in California in 1997-1998. California, as in some other parts of the USA, has responded to the educational needs of a linguistically and ethnically diverse student population with a number of different approaches and programs that range from English language medium schooling with little or no ESL support to bilingual education[18]. Of particular interest to this discussion is bilingual education. García and Curry-Rodriguez (2000) define *bilingual education* in the Californian context as "the application of specialized educational techniques utilizing a student's native language to enhance the learning opportunities of students who come to school speaking a native language other than the predominant language of the school process" (p. 2); and the term bilingual education in this context normally refers to the use of two particular languages: Spanish and English[19]. This particular conceptualization of bilingual education takes a variety of forms in terms of the balance of use between the two languages for curriculum purposes and the length of time/duration (see Crawford, 1997). In general bilingual education is not available to all students, for instance, in 1997-1998, only 29% of California's school students were officially classified as attending bilingual classrooms (Gándara, 2000). The published research on the strongest forms of this kind of bilingual education, e.g. maintaining a 40/60 or 50/50 split between Spanish and English up to Grade 6, has consistently pointed to the long-term overall educational benefits in terms of students' language and across the board curriculum achievement (e.g. Cummins, 2000; Ramirez, 1992; Thomas & Collier, 1997 & 2002). Given the clearly demonstrated benefits and the comparative small percentage of students involved, one would have thought that this would be a program type in line for further support and promotion. However, events turned out quite differently.

In 1998, the voters of California supported Proposition 227 *English for Children* (also known as the *Unz Initiative*, named after its promoter) that was designed to severely restrict the use of linguistic minority students' first or native language for curriculum learning purposes[20]; Proposition 227 also mandated the introduction of a transitional ESL program referred to as *structured English immersion* that was not normally to last more than 1 year. In other words, under this program ESL students are expected to have developed sufficient English language knowledge and skills within 1 year to be able to participate in all-English-medium schooling without further ESL assistance. During the campaign leading up to the vote, the pedagogic efficacies of different kinds of language education for linguistic minorities were debated by the proponents and opponents of Proposition 227. For reasons of focus, the case for and against the initiative will not be rehearsed here[21]; nor will we enter into the debate on the success or failure of the so-called structured English immersion since 1998[22]. What is of interest here is the background thinking behind Proposition 227. Unz's own writings (1997) offer some interesting insight that may help to clarify the underlying arguments. First, there appears to be an instrumental argument for learning English:

> If other languages such as Chinese or Spanish are of growing world importance, English ranks in a class by itself...over the past 20 years it has rapidly become the entire world's unofficial language, over the past 20 years it has...[dominated] the spheres of science, technology and international business...lack of literacy in English represents a crippling almost fatal disadvantage in our global economy. (p. M6)

In addition, there seems to be an interesting ideological articulation of a pro-immigration and an anti-affirmative action stance, i.e. against ethnic preferences for jobs in public sector employment, leading to an English language-only view of social and ethnic assimilation (Unz, 1999):

> It is...a tragedy of the first order that, even as the reality of the American melting pot remains as powerful as ever, the ideology behind it has almost disappeared, having been replaced by the 'diversity' model...A social ideology that allots to blacks and Latinos and Asians their own separatist institutions and suggested shares of society's benefits cannot long be prevented from extending itself to whites as well, especially as whites become merely one minority among many minorities...the diversity prescription contains the seeds of national dissolution. (p. 18)

In this view, the English language is seen as a sort of cement capable of binding all individuals, from whatever ethnic and language background, in the common endeavor of the American melting pot.

INTEGRATING ESL STUDENTS: CLARIFYING POLICY GOALS AND PEDAGOGY

We have seen that the integrating of ESL students into the mainstream curriculum has received public policy support in the past 30 years or so. In this same period, we have also seen a number of highly innovative and practicable pedagogic and curricular ideas designed to explore and exploit language development within a mainstream curriculum context. However, as our earlier discussion suggests, the policy and practice of integration of ESL students can be sometimes strongly shaped, some may even say determined, by wider social and ideological developments. In many ways, it is difficult to imagine ESL as a totally autonomous area of schooling for as long as public education is part of democratic political processes. Initiatives and movements for change in education are often triggered by perceived problems or deficiencies in the existing policy and practice. However, the proposed alternative/s may involve not just "fixing" the perceived problem at a professional or technical level, e.g. adjusting the amount of curriculum content if the teaching/learning load is judged to be too great, but also wholesale shifts in the fundamental analysis and framing of the issues. The re-defining and re-framing of ESL within a particular notion of literacy in Australia is a case in point. In any case, ESL educators and researchers themselves, like fellow professionals working in other areas of education, often have educational, social, and ideological commitments that may be more favorably disposed towards a particular kind of policy and practice than others. Questions concerning educational values, epistemology, and empirical evidence can get caught up in a whirlpool of policy contest. Some very important analyses and observations may be lost or not heard in the process. The recent discussion on the merits and demerits of the bilingual education triggered by Proposition 227 in California bears witness to this (see for example, Cummins, 2000, and Krashen, 2001). This seemingly unavoidable messiness when education enters the public policy arena, however, can be understood better with an analysis comprising principled abstraction and comparison of relevant experiences.

Educational policies and practices are multidimensional and the dimensions involved may or may not fit together as pieces of a puzzle at any one time[23]. Therefore, it would be useful to adopt a multidimensional view on any discussion on existing and/or proposed policy and practice for integrating ESL students[24]. If we look at the cases of England, Victoria, and California, we can extract the following dimensions from the earlier discussion:

Table 1. Abstracted Dimensions of ESL Policy and Practice in California, England, and Victoria

A. Public social and educational policy stance	B. Desired/possible outcome	C. Underlying language education assumption	D. Mainstream curriculum provision	E. Pedagogic approach to language in classroom
1. Equal access and equal opportunities for all, with English as the preferred school language for minority language students 2. Equal access and equal opportunities for all, with promotion of English (minority L2) and community language/s (minority L1s)	1. Monolingualism in English; minority bi/multilingualism not encouraged 2. Monolingualism in English; *laissez faire* position on minority bi/multilingualism 3. Monolingualism in English, recognizing minority bi-/multilingualism as worthwhile 4. Minority bi-/multilingualism in English and minority community languages	1. Priority on developing English (minority L2); minority L1 not addressed 2. Priority on developing English; minority L1 useful as transitional aid to English (L2) development 3. Priority on developing English (L2) and minority L1; both important as part of overall intellectual development for individuals	1. English-medium universal curriculum, with no dedicated L2 English extension for minorities; student-oriented ESL (England) 2. English-medium universal curriculum, with dedicated L2 English extension for minorities; language-content, content-language and/or trans-curriculum-oriented ESL (parts of California before and after Proposition 227; Victoria) 3. Bilingual (minority L1-L2) medium curriculum (parts of California before Proposition 227; and post-Proposition 227 where special local dispensation is granted)	1. English L2 focused; minority L1 not addressed 2. English L2 focused; minority L1 may be used opportunistically 3. English L2 focused; minority L1 used as transitional aid in a structured way (e.g. early-exit bilingual programs) 4. Both minority L1 and L2 addressed in a systematic way (e.g. two-way bilingual programs)

It is quite clear that the five dimensions and the characterizations included in Table 1 by no means represent an exhaustive empirical account of the complexities of ESL policies and practices even in just the three locations under discussion. It is certainly not claimed here that the relationship between policy and practice is a straightforward one (see Yanow, 1996 for a fuller discussion). The key argument here though is that policy rhetoric and curriculum statements often conflate social aspiration, desired/possible outcomes, policy declarations, curriculum provision, and classroom pedagogy as if they were one and the same thing. At times, policy rhetoric or curriculum statements may make aspirational claims that are circumscribed by the actual curriculum and pedagogic provision. To borrow a phrase from Cooper (1989), ESL policy and practice "can be a messy affair—ad hoc, haphazard, and emotionally driven" (p. 41). There is a need for greater conceptual and analytical clarity.

By conceptually separating the social from the pedagogic and the desired outcome from the curriculum provision and so on, there is a better chance of achieving some clarity in the way policy and practice are discussed and understood. For instance, in England there is a frequently rehearsed pro-multilingualism public rhetoric in local and national educational documents that suggests that the use of both English and minority community languages are or should be considered languages of the mainstream curriculum. One example of this is a statement in the English (subject) National Curriculum document: Teachers are advised that, in relation to the development of spoken and written English, they should be "building on pupils' experiences of language at home and in the wider community, so that their developing uses of English and other languages support one another" (DfEE & QCA, 1999, p. 49). A closer examination of the current policy and curriculum infrastructure would show that students' L1 can only be used opportunistically in the classroom (E2) because the mainstream curriculum is mediated through English (D1); the use of students' L1 is seen as, at best, an aid for transition to English (C2) when teachers and students (accidentally) share common language backgrounds; bi-/multilingualism in English and minority languages is rarely recognized in any systematic way beyond recognition of individual efforts and/or talent (B2); and curriculum achievement is measured only in terms of English-mediated attainments (A1) except in language subjects such as French. This example shows that by paying attention to the multidimensionality of policy and practice, it is possible to begin to understand the contextualized meaning of policy declaration in relation to actual curriculum possibilities.

The value of paying attention to the multidimensional nature of policy and practice can also be demonstrated by, for instance, examining the use of economic rationalism, i.e. efficiency in producing a productive work force, as a key argument against bilingual education in California. The rhetoric of the need to produce an English-proficient work force being best served by an exclusively English-medium curriculum is premised on a common sense argument, "the more time on learning English, the better the English proficiency." But the long-term research evidence (e.g. Cummins, 2000; Thomas and Collier, 1997 & 2002) suggests that two-way bilingual education actually produces the best academic and scholarly achievements, as measured by standardized testing, across the curriculum for linguistic minority students including achievement in English. This shows that if the dimensions in the policy and practice arena are examined carefully in terms of their contribution to students' academic attainment and their relationships with one another, it is possible to identify the heavily ideological nature of the pro-Proposition 227 arguments. This offers all parties involved in the debate, proponents, and opponents alike, a clearer sense of where the contest is located. In this case, it is clearly not located in the actual bilingual schooling provision itself if achievement in English language competence is the only issue at stake.

The analytical approach taken here can be useful in real-world practice in the more *here-and-now* sense. By paying attention to the multidimensionality of policy and practice, policy makers can be shown the kinds of examination of issues and actions they should be engaged with if their social and educational goals are to be translated into curriculum provision and classroom practice. The carrying over of policy positioning into ideologically comfortable curriculum options will be made to look less "natural" or common-sensical. For teachers a careful analysis of their curriculum and policy environment with reference to the five dimensions would produce a knowledge of the types of pedagogic freedoms and constraints with which they work. At the same time, such an analysis would provide them with an understanding of their own pedagogic and ideological position in relation to the wider curriculum and policy environments, and where changes, if changes were desired, should be made.

CONCLUSIONS

Historically, the integration of ESL students into the mainstream curriculum is an ideologically laden process. Over the past 3 decades or so, there have been a large number of developments in language curriculum and pedagogy that have attempted to address some of the teaching and learning issues concerned with ethnic and linguistic minority students. However, the curriculum options and approaches adopted by policy makers and education systems have not always been influenced by professional experience and research-based arguments. The recent experiences in California, England, and Victoria strongly indicate that arguments emanating from other spheres of society often hold sway and policy decisions on ESL can be made on non-language education grounds. This suggests that there is a need for analytical clarity in understanding the multidimensionality of ESL policy and practice. Such clarity, if nothing else, will serve to help identify what is being argued for and against.

NOTES

[1] In England, the preferred term in the official educational documents for ESL is English as an additional language (EAL). In this chapter, the more internationally common term ESL is used.
[2] These kinds of classes are sometimes referred to as sheltered English classes.
[3] These examples are used to illustrate the kind of innovations and developments that have emerged; no evaluation is intended. There are other concomitant developments related to the idea of mainstreaming that are not the subject of this discussion, e.g. multiculturalism in the curriculum.
[4] It should be noted out that a number of ideas emerged from the field of second language acquisition (SLA) research, e.g. Krashen (1981, 1985) and Widdowson (1979, 1983) have been part of the backdrop of the intellectual landscape of mainstreaming ESL. See further references in the discussion on bilingual education.
[5] There were similar developments in adult and university sectors, generally known as English for specific purposes (ESP). For a discussion, see Johns (1997).

6. There is a variety of bilingual education programs in different parts of the world (see e.g. Skutnabb-Kangas (1995). The discussion here is limited to those relevant developments with reference to ESL students in mainstream schooling.
7. Crawford (1997) points out that in the United States, where this form of education has been practiced in some areas/states, only a small number of students are involved. For instance, in California in 1994-95 "fewer than 30 percent of LEP [limited English proficiency] students were taught academic subjects in their native language. ...And of these students, only about half were in classrooms staffed by certified bilingual and ESL teachers" (p. 16).
8. For a detailed discussion of immersion education for language majority students see Cummins (2000, Ch. 8) and Johnson and Swain (1997).
9. It is recognized that the distinction between indigenous minorities and more recently settled minorities is fraught with ethical, epistemological, and ideological difficulties (see May, 2001; Taylor, 1992). The use of these terms here is intended to signal the thematic focus of this discussion.
10. There are some induction classes in school for newly arrived ESL beginners. But these classes or courses can best be described as tolerated (rather than encouraged) by curriculum authorities and the official educational inspectorate. See Leung (2002) for further discussion.
11. Although some guidance and advice on how to work with ESL students are available in a number of official curriculum, teacher training and inspections publications, e.g. DfEE (2001), DfES (2002), OFSTED (2001), and SCAA (1996).
12. In the 1970s, ESL provision, often very patchy and short-term, for school-aged students was mostly organized as a separate provision in addition to the mainstream school curriculum or in the form of separate English language centers (Townsend, 1971).
13. This can be seen in its view of language: "The English language is a central unifying factor in 'being British', and is the key to participation on equal terms as a full member of this society. There is, however, a great diversity of other languages spoken among British families in British homes" (DES, 1985, Ch. 7.1.1).
14. A corollary of this line of thinking is that teachers are often reminded that teaching techniques that enable ESL students to participate in lesson activities, such as breaking up complex texts and asking students to re-assemble the parts, are good for all students (e.g. DfEE, 2001).
15. It is interesting to note that, while ESL has not been conceptualized as a curriculum issue, the statutory National Curriculum (comprising school subjects) and the officially promoted National Strategies for Literacy and Numeracy for primary and secondary schools provide explicit curriculum content specifications.
16. There is inter-state variation in ESL provision and organization within Australia. For a detailed account of developments in Australia as a whole since the 1960s, see Davison (2001).
17. Australian ESL professionals would argue that ESL provision has been undermined in a series of government funding cuts since the 1980s. Focus and scope preclude a fuller discussion here. See Williams (1998) and Lo Bianco (1998) for a fuller discussion.
18. For a full discussion on program types see Crawford (1997), García (2000), and Thomas and Collier (1997).
19. The shortage of suitably qualified bilingual teachers has made it impossible to offer bilingual education to all minority language students. For instance, Crawford (1997) reports that "in 1994 California enrolled recently arrived immigrants from 136 different countries, but bilingual teachers were certified in only 17 languages—96 percent of them in Spanish" (p. 15–16).
20. Exemption from the mandate can be granted where local parents can demonstrate the benefits of bilingual education in relation to their own children's needs.
21. The documents and papers for and against the Proposition can be found on a number of websites, e.g. see the TESOL website http://www.tesol.edu. Also see Cummins (2000) for a view on the different evaluations of the empirical evidence.
22. See Krashen (2001) and Gándara (2000) for a view on the reported results of structured English immersion.
23. For a related discussion see Ball (1997) and Yanow (1996).
24. For an earlier discussion on social goals and educational outcomes, see Churchill (1986).

REFERENCES

Ashworth, M. (2000). *Effective teachers, effective schools: Second language teaching in Australia, Canada, England and the United States*. Toronto: Pippin Publishing Corporation.

Azurmendi, M.-J., Bachoc, E., & Zabaleta, F. (2001). Reversing language shift: The case of Basque. In J. Fishman (Ed.), *Can threatened languages be saved?* (pp. 234–259). Clevedon: Multilingual Matters.

Ball, S. J. (1997). Policy sociology and critical social research: A personal review of recent education policy and policy research. *British Educational Research Journal, 23*(3), 257–274.
Beardsmore, H. B. (1993). The European School model. In H. B. Beardsmore (Ed.), *European models of bilingual education* (pp. 121–154). Clevedon: Multilingual Matters.
Board of Studies (1999). *The ESL Companion to the English Curriculum and Standards Framework* (2nd ed.). Melbourne: Board of Studies.
Bourne, J. (1989). *Moving into the mainstream: LEA provision for bilingual pupils*. Windsor: NFER-Nelson.
Campbell, W. J., & McMeniman, M. (1985). *Bridging the language gap: Ideals and realities pertaining to learning English as a second language (ESL)*. Canberra: Commonwealth Schools Commission.
Chamot, A., & O'Malley, J. (1987). The cognitive academic learning approach: A bridge to the mainstream. *TESOL Quarterly, 21*(2), 227–249.
Chamot, A., & O'Malley, M. (1992). The cognitive academic language learning approach: A bridge to the mainstream. In P. Richard-Amato & M. A. Snow (Eds.), *The multicultural classroom: Readings for content area teachers* (pp. 39–57). White Plains, NY: Longman.
Churchill, S. (1986). *The education of linguistic and cultural minorities in the OECD countries*. Clevedon: Multilingual Matters.
Cleland, B., & Evans, R. (1984). *ESL topic books: Learning English through general science*. Melbourne: Longman Cheshire.
Commission for Racial Equality. (1986). *Teaching English as a second language*. London: CRE.
Cooper, R. L. (1989). *Language planning and social change*. Cambridge: Cambridge University Press.
Crandall, J. (1987). *ESL through content-area instruction*. Englewood Cliffs, NJ: Prentice Hall Regents.
Crandall, J., Spanos, G., Christian, D., Simich-Dudgeon, C., & Willetts, K. (1987). *Integrating language and content instruction for language minority students*. Washington, DC: National Clearing House for Bilingual Education.
Crawford, J. (1997). *Best evidence: Research foundations of the Bilingual Education Act*. Washington, DC: National Clearinghouse for Bilingual Education.
Cummins, J. (1984). *Bilingualism and special education: Issues in assessment and pedagogy*. Clevedon, Avon: Multilingual Matters Ltd.
Cummins, J. (1992). Language proficiency, bilingualism, and academic achievement. In P. A. Richard-Amato & M. A. Snow (Eds.), *The multicultural classroom: Readings for content-area teachers* (pp. 16–26). New York: Longman.
Cummins, J. (1996). *Negotiating identities: Education for empowerment in a diverse society*. Ontario: California Association of Bilingual Education.
Cummins, J. (2000). *Language, power and pedagogy: Bilingual children in the crossfire*. Clevedon: Multilingual Matters.
Cummins, J., & Swain, M. (1986). *Bilingualism in education*. New York: Longman.
Dale, T. C., & Cuevas, G. J. (1987). Integrating language and mathematics learning. In J. Crandall (Ed.), *ESL through content-area instruction: Mathematics, science, social studies* (pp. 9–54). Englewood Cliffs, NJ: Prentice Hall.
Davison, C. (2001). Current policies, programs and practice in school ESL. In B. Mohan, C. Leung, & C. Davison (Eds.), *English as a second language in the mainstream: Teaching, learning and identity* (pp. 30–50). London: Longman.
Davison, C., & Williams, A. (2001). Integrating language and content: Unresolved issues. In B. Mohan, C. Leung, & C. Davison (Eds.), *English as a second language in the mainstream: Teaching, learning and identity*. London: Longman.
Department for Education and Employment. (2001). *Key Stage 3 National strategy – Framework for teaching English: Years 7, 8 and 9*. London: DfEE.
Department for Education and Employment. (2001). *Key Stage 3 National Strategy – Literacy across the curriculum (Chapter 12 – All inclusive: Supporting EAL learners)* [Videotape]. London: DfEE.
Department for Education and Employment. (2001). *Key Stage 3 National Strategy – literacy across the curriculum*. London: DfEE Publications.
Department of Education and Skills. (2002). *Key Stage 3 National Strategy – Grammar for writing: Supporting pupils learning EAL*. London: DfES.
Department for Education, Employment, and Qualifications and Curriculum Authority. (1999). *English – The national curriculum for England*. London: DfEE and QCA.
Department of Education and Science. (1985). *Education for all: The report of the Committee of Inquiry into the Education of Children from Ethnic Minority Groups* – (Chair: Lord Swann). London: HMSO.

Department of Education and Science. (1991) *Partnership teaching*. London: DES.
Evans, R., & Cleland, B. (n.d.). *The topic approach to E.S.L.* [Video]. Victoria: Ministry of Education.
Gándara, P. (2000). In the aftermath of the storm: English learners in the post-227 era. *Bilingual Research Journal, 24*(1 & 2).
García, A. (2000). Informed parent consent and Proposition 227. *Bilingual Research Journal, 24*(1 & 2).
García, E. E., & Curry-Rodriguez, J. E. (2000). The education of limited English proficient students in California schools: An assessment of the influence of proposition 227 in selected districts and schools. *Bilingual Research Journal, 24*(1 & 2).
Harris, R., Leung, C., & Rampton, B. (2001). Globalisation, diaspora and language education in England. In D. Block & D. Cameron (Eds.), *Globalisation and language teaching* (pp. 29–46). London: Routledge.
Hoddinott, D. (1998). *Literacy—Meeting the needs of all learners*. Australian Council of TESOL Associations.
Johns, A. M. (1997). English for specific purposes and content-based instruction: What is the relationship? In M. A. Snow & D. Brinton (Eds.), *The content-based classroom: Perspectives on integrating language and content* (pp. 363–366). Reading, MA: Addison Wesley Longman.
Johnson, R. K., & Swain, M. (Eds.). (1997). *Immersion education: International perspectives*. Cambridge: Cambridge University Press.
Krashen, S. (1981). *Second language acquisition and second language learning*. Oxford: Pergamon.
Krashen, S. (1985). *The input hypothesis*. New York: Longman.
Krashen, S. (1996). A gradual exit, variable threshold model for limited English proficient children. *NABE News, 19*(1), 15–18.
Krashen, S. (2001). Are children ready for the mainstream after one year of structured English immersion? *TESOL Matters, 11*(1), 4.
Leung, C. (2001). English as an additional language: Distinctive language focus or diffused curriculum concerns? *Language and Education, 15*(1), 33–55.
Leung, C. (2002). Reception classes for immigrant students – England. *TESOL Quarterly, 36*(1), 93–98.
Lo Bianco, J. (1998, April/May/June). ESL ... Is it migrant literacy? ... Is it history? *Australian Language Matters*, pp. 1, 6–7.
McKay, P. (1998). *The literacy benchmarks and ESL*. Australian Council of TESOL Associations.
May, S. (2001). *Language and minority rights: Ethnicity, nationalism and the politics of language*. London: Longman.
Meek, M. (Ed.). (1996). *Developing pedagogies in the multilingual classroom: The writings of Josie Levine*. Stoke-on-Trent: Trentham Books.
Mohan, B. (1986). *Language and content*. Reading, MA: Addison-Wesley.
Mohan, A. (1990). LEP students and the integration of language and content: Knowledge structures and tasks. In C. Simich-Dudgeon (Ed.), *Proceedings of the first research symposium on limited English proficient students' issues* (pp. 113–160). Washington, DC: Office of Bilingual Education and Minority Languages Affairs.
Mohan, B. (2001). The second language as a medium of learning. In B. Mohan, C. Leung, & C. Davison (Eds.), *English as a second language in the mainstream: Teaching, learning and identity* (pp. 107–126). London: Longman.
Mohan, B., Leung, C., & Davison, C. (Eds.). (2001). *English as a second language in the mainstream: Teaching, learning, and identity*. London: Longman.
Office for Standards in Education. (2001). *Inspecting English as an additional language: 11–16 with guidance on self-evaluation*. London: OFSTED.
Ramírez, J. D. (1992). Executive summary. *Bilingual Research Journal, 16*, 1–62.
School Curriculum and Assessment Authority. (1996). *Teaching English as an additional language: A framework for policy*. London: SCAA.
Scope. (1978). *An introductory English course for immigrant children*. London: Longman.
Skutnabb-Kangas, T. (Ed.). (1995). *Multilingualism for all*. Lisse, NL: Swets and Zeitlinger B.V.
Snow, M. A., Met, M., & Genesee, F. (1992). A conceptual framework for the integration of language and content instruction. In P. A. Richard-Amato & M. A. Snow (Eds.), *The multicultural classroom: Readings for content-area teachers* (pp. 27–38). New York: Longman.
Taylor, C. (1992). *Multiculturalism and the 'politics of recognition'*. Princeton, NJ: Princeton University Press.
Thomas, W. P., & Collier, V. (1997). *School effectiveness for language minority students*. Washington, DC: Center for the Study of Language and Education, The George Washington University.
Thomas, W. P., & Collier, V. P. (2002). *A national study of school effectiveness for language minority students' long-term academic achievement*. Retrieved 4th September 2004, from http://www.crede.ussc.edu/research/llaa/1.1_final.html.

Townsend, H. (1971). *Immigrant pupils in England: The LEA response*. Windsor: NFER-Nelson.
Unz, R. K. (1997, October 19). Bilingualism vs. bilingual education. *Los Angeles Times*.
Unz, R. K. (1999). *California and the end of white America*. Retrieved 4th October, 2004, from http://www.onenation.org/9911/110199.html.
Widdowson, H. (1979). *Explorations in applied linguistics*. Oxford: Oxford University Press.
Widdowson, H. (1983). *Learning purpose and language use*. Oxford: Oxford University Press.
Williams, A. (1998). *Finding and showing the way: Teaching ESL in the late 1990s*: Australian Council of TESOL Associations.
Williams, C. (Ed.). (2000). *Language revitalization: Policy and planning in Wales*. Cardiff: University of Wales Press.
Yanow, D. (1996). *How does a policy mean? Interpreting policy and organizational action*. Washington, DC: Georgetown University Press.

CHAPTER 18

COMMUNICATIVE LANGUAGE TEACHING:

Current Status and Future Prospects

NINA SPADA

The University of Toronto, Canada

ABSTRACT

Since the introduction of communicative language teaching (CLT) in the late 1970s, there have been different definitions and interpretations of the communicative approach to second language (L2) instruction. Not surprisingly, this has resulted in several misconceptions of CLT and how it is implemented in the L2 classroom. While most descriptions of CLT emphasize the communication of messages and meaning, there is disagreement as to whether CLT should include a focus on the analysis and practice of language forms. There is also some debate (and confusion) as to whether the inclusion of literacy skills, use of the first language (L1), and vocabulary instruction is compatible with the principles and practice of CLT. These differences in interpretation and implementation of CLT are sufficiently problematic to suggest that CLT has become a rather vacuous term. Indeed, some have argued that, as a label for a language teaching method, CLT has lost its relevance to L2 teaching. In this chapter, I will describe some of the developments in CLT theory, research, and practice that point to the conclusion that a balance needs to be struck within CLT—one that allows for the integration of more direct instruction of language (including grammatical, lexical, and socio-pragmatic features) with communicative skills.

INTRODUCTION

Communicative language teaching (CLT) is described by some applied linguists as having reached a turning point—one in which "explicit direct elements are gaining significance in teaching communicative abilities and skills" (Celce-Murcia & Dörnyei, 1997, p. 141). In fact, for quite a few years now, words like *balance, integration,* and *equilibrium* have appeared in the CLT literature indicating that most second language (L2) educators agree that CLT is undergoing a transformation—one that includes increased recognition of and attention to language form within exclusively or primarily meaning-oriented CLT approaches to second language (L2) instruction (Celce-Murcia, 1991; Larsen-Freeman, 1991; Lightbown & Spada, 1999; Spada & Fröhlich, 1995; Williams, 1995).

While most L2 educators view CLT as in a state of transition, some have argued that because there have been so many different interpretations and implementations of CLT since it was introduced, it is no longer a useful concept and should probably be discarded. This concern is directed not only to CLT but also to the fundamental concept of method in L2 teaching—a concern that has been raised in the applied linguistics and second language teaching literature for quite some time. This is due to the fact that different methods overlap in several ways (Bosco & Di Pietro, 1970; Krashen & Seliger, 1975; Nunan, 1991; Richards, 1989; Stern, 1983, 1992) and on the observation that teachers who report using the same method do not implement it in the same way (Long, 1980, 1991; Spada, 1987). Additional evidence comes from the increased skepticism and reluctance on the part of L2 teachers to "jump on the bandwagon" of a particular method when experience and common sense indicate that all methods have instructional techniques and strategies that differ in their effectiveness according to different contexts and groups of learners. All of this has led some applied linguists to call for the abolition of the term *method* (Kumaravadivelu, 1994; Long, 1991; Pennycook, 1989; Richards, 1990; Stern, 1983) and to talk instead of specific macro- and micro-level instructional procedures as we enter into what Kumaravadivelu (2001) refers to as a *postmethod pedagogy*.

In this chapter, I will describe the current status and future prospects of CLT. A brief description of the history of CLT and how it has evolved in terms of theory, research, and practice will help to establish the context. As indicated above, CLT has become the cover term for a wide range of different approaches to L2 teaching, and some of these manifestations of CLT will be described. In the 20 years or so of its existence, several myths and misconceptions have developed around CLT and these will also be examined. Since the widespread implementation of CLT in the 1980s, considerable research has been done in communicative classrooms. This work, some of which will be reviewed here, provides empirical support for theoretical and pedagogical arguments that a balance needs to be struck between language-focused and meaning-focused L2 instruction regardless of what cover term may be attached to a set of pedagogical procedures intended to accomplish this. A discussion of the central questions and issues concerning the re-conceptualization and future implementation of CLT concludes the paper.

WHAT IS COMMUNICATIVE LANGUAGE TEACHING?

The answer to this question seems to depend on whom you ask. When I recently asked the question to a group of experienced second and foreign language instructors, the general consensus was that CLT is a meaning-based, learner-centered approach to L2 teaching where fluency is given priority over accuracy and the emphasis is on the comprehension and production of messages, *not* the teaching or correction of language form. When I asked my colleagues the same question, they typically responded by saying that CLT is an approach to L2 instruction which is primarily meaning-based and includes attention to both fluency and accuracy. The essential difference between the two definitions seems to be the presence or absence of attention to language form. This corresponds to Howatt's distinction (1984) between *strong* and *weak* versions of CLT.[1]

This is not to imply that the descriptions of CLT within each group are uniform. On the contrary, within the practitioner group, it is not uncommon to find that second language instructors (particularly in North America) differ from foreign language instructors. The former are more likely to describe CLT as exclusively meaning-based with no attention to language form, while the latter tend to characterize CLT as some combination of formal and functional aspects of language.[2] There are also different interpretations of CLT at the theoretical level. For example, while British applied linguists have been fairly consistent in their conceptualization of CLT as an approach to L2 teaching that incorporates form and meaning, there has been more divergence of opinion in North America. Again, the main difference is whether one's conceptualization of CLT includes attention to language form, either through direct instruction and/or through feedback.

In order to better understand why and how CLT has been interpreted and implemented differently by L2 educators, it is useful to consider some aspects of the history and development of CLT.

INFLUENCES ON CLT: THEORY, RESEARCH, AND PRACTICE

Language teaching has often turned to linguistics for guidance on how to teach languages. This is undoubtedly due to the fact that for most of the history of language teaching, linguistics has been one of the most influential disciplines. Furthermore, given that the central concern of linguistics for the past 50 years has been on the structures of language, it is not surprising that the emphasis in L2 teaching has also been on the mastery of the structures of language. The audio-lingual method influenced by structural linguistics and behavioral psychology, focused on the inductive learning of grammar via repetition, practice, and memorization. Later, the cognitive code method influenced by cognitive psychology and transformational grammar, was based on deductive learning principles associated with rule learning and hypothesis testing. Although the two methods represented fundamentally different views of linguistics, they both emphasized language structure sometimes to the virtual exclusion of other features of language.

In the 1970s, other more comprehensive conceptualizations of language began to lay the theoretical groundwork for CLT. In North America, Hymes' theory of communicative competence and the notion that knowing a language includes more than a knowledge of the rules of grammar (i.e. *linguistic competence*) but also a knowledge of the rules of language use (i.e. *communicative competence*) had a significant impact on CLT. Hymes (1971) introduced his theory of communicative competence in an effort to broaden current conceptualizations of language—specifically those proposed by Chomsky (1957) which dealt strictly with linguistic competence. Hymes' work raised important questions about an exclusive focus on the accurate use of grammatical forms in L2 teaching when it was evident that knowledge of a language (first or second) includes knowing how to use forms appropriately in different contexts. Following from Hymes, different models of communicative competence were proposed by other North American researchers and efforts were made to empirically validate them (Bachman & Palmer, 1981; Canale, 1983; Canale & Swain, 1980; Harley, Allen, Cummins, & Swain, 1990). The underlying assumption of these models was that language proficiency is not a unitary concept but consists of several different components including linguistic competence (e.g. grammar, phonology, and lexis), pragmatic competence (e.g. cohesion and coherence), sociolinguistic (e.g. formal/informal registers), and strategic competence (e.g. compensatory strategies). The recommendations for L2 pedagogy were that all components should be included in L2 curricula and instruction.

Without question, the primary influence on the development of CLT, certainly in its earliest days, comes from the work of British applied linguists whose ideas led to fundamental changes in the way in which second and foreign languages were taught. Their work, based on the linguistic theories of Firth (1957), Austin (1962), Searle (1969), and Halliday (1973), consistently included formal and semantic features within their conceptualization of language and language teaching. The development of the notional functional syllabus (Wilkins, 1976) was one of the first efforts to demonstrate what a shift from an exclusive focus on language forms (e.g. verbs, pronouns, adjectives) to a specification of its meanings and functions (e.g. greeting, describing, inviting) would look like. This novel approach to L2 syllabus construction represented an entirely different way of organizing language from its "structural" predecessor. Its emphasis on communicative functions led some L2 educators to conclude that the notional-functional syllabus was synonymous with CLT. However, the notional functional syllabus is an approach to syllabus design, not a method of instruction. The challenge of specifying guidelines and procedures for the delivery of a communicative methodology was taken up by several other applied linguists including Brumfit (1984), Johnson (1982), and Littlewood (1981). Throughout their considerable efforts to develop a CLT methodology, the fundamental assumptions were that form and meaning are inextricably linked and that both require attention in L2 instruction (Widdowson, 1978, 1990).

In the 1980s, two areas of research in the field of second language acquisition (SLA) began to play central roles in shaping our understanding of CLT. This included the work of North American researchers investigating two separate but related hypotheses about SLA: the comprehensible input hypothesis (Krashen, 1984b) and the interactionist hypothesis (Long, 1983, 1996). Both emphasize the central role of meaningful communication in language acquisition.

Comprehensible Input Hypothesis

Based on the observation that first language and second language learners of English go through similar sequences and stages of development in their acquisition of certain morphological and grammatical features, Krashen (1982) concluded that the process of L2 acquisition was similar to L1 acquisition. Despite this underlying similarity, Krashen also pointed to the fact that while most L2 learners (particularly classroom learners) do not succeed in mastering their L2, virtually all L1 learners are successful. He suggested that the reason for this discrepancy is differences in learning conditions. Traditionally, L2 learners have been taught rules of grammar and receive correction when they make grammatical mistakes while L1 learners receive neither grammatical instruction nor explicit correction when they make errors. This led Krashen to hypothesize that if the conditions for L2 acquisition were more similar to those of L1 acquisition, L2 development would be more successful. He proposed that the way to accomplish this is to expose learners to meaningful and motivating input that is just slightly beyond their current level of linguistic competence but sufficiently comprehensible for the learner to understand (Krashen, 1984b). In this way, L2 learners would be able to integrate the input into their developing interlanguage systems and successfully acquire their second language in much the same way as children acquire their L1.

Although Krashen's theory of SLA has been widely criticized for failing to propose hypotheses that can be empirically tested, most teachers (and many researchers) find his views intuitively appealing. There is little doubt that Krashen's work has been highly influential in shaping and supporting CLT, particularly in North America.

Interaction Hypothesis

While Krashen's focus was on the linguistic input to which learners are exposed, another group of SLA researchers with close ties to Krashen's theoretical framework became increasingly interested in how the input becomes comprehensible to the learner. Long (1983) hypothesized that conversational modifications (e.g. clarification requests, confirmation checks) that learners make when they "negotiate meaning" create comprehensible input and that this in turn promotes acquisition. One of the earliest advocates of interactionist theory was Evelyn Hatch (1978) who made the somewhat controversial claim that L2 learners do not need to be taught the grammatical forms of language so that they can "do conversations." Rather, L2 learners, like L1 learners, need to participate in conversational interactions, and it is through this process that they learn the grammar. Many L2 teachers came to believe that creating opportunities for their students to engage in conversational interaction in the classroom would be sufficient for successful and complete SLA.[3]

The combined impact of the comprehensible input hypothesis and the interaction hypothesis on the evolution of CLT was significant. Since both emphasized meaning-based instruction without attention to language form and/or corrective feedback, this reinforced the notion that CLT was exclusively meaning-based.[4] The interaction hypothesis also lent support to the view that CLT is a learner-centered approach to L2 instruction. Many teachers interpreted both hypotheses to mean that CLT focuses exclusively on listening and speaking. This misconception of CLT is discussed below.

MYTHS AND MISCONCEPTIONS OF CLT

Over the years, several myths about CLT have developed. They have become part of the CLT culture partly as the result of the vagueness of the term and the different ways in which it has been interpreted within the theoretical and empirical literature. Some of the myths have also naturally evolved from the ways in which teachers have chosen to implement CLT often for practical reasons. Some of the commonly held misconceptions of CLT, most of which have been documented elsewhere in the literature (e.g. Johnstone, 1999; Sato & Kleinsasser, 1999; Thompson, 1996) are:

1. CLT means an exclusive focus on meaning
2. CLT means no explicit feedback on learner error
3. CLT means learner-centered teaching
4. CLT means listening and speaking practice
5. CLT means avoidance of the learners' L1

CLT Means an Exclusive Focus on Meaning

Without question, the most pervasive misconception within CLT is that it is an approach to L2 instruction that focuses on meaning to the exclusion of any attention to language form. As indicated above, this characterization of CLT is not consistent with the view of most applied linguists—particularly British applied linguists—who, throughout the evolution of CLT theory and pedagogy, have recognized the importance of a formal language component within CLT. Indeed, CLT was not conceptualized as an approach that was intended to exclude form but rather one that was intended to *include communication*. Nevertheless, it is not surprising that many (indeed most) L2 teachers made this assumption about CLT particularly when they read the works of applied linguists such as Prahbu (1987), who argued that grammar is too complex to be taught, and second language acquisition researchers like Krashen (1982), who claimed that grammar can only be acquired unconsciously through exposure to the target language.

What does classroom research on L2 learning and teaching have to say about this? Since the early 1980s, classroom researchers and program evaluators have carried out a great deal of research on the effectiveness of CLT. Prior to that, the only experimental study that examined the contributions of CLT to L2 learning was done by Savignon (1972). Her research investigated the effects of adding a communicative component to university-level audio-lingual classes in French. Comparisons of learners who had received the additional communicative component with those who received either an additional cultural component or further audio-lingual practice revealed that learners in the communicative group performed better on the communicative tests than those in the cultural or audio-lingual group. Learners in the communicative group also performed at least as well on the linguistic tasks as learners in the other two groups. These results demonstrated the benefits of adding a communicative component to structure-based teaching. Unfortunately, the findings were sometimes misinterpreted as support for an exclusive focus on meaning rather than evidence to support a combination of form- and meaning-based instruction.

Since Savignon's study, other classroom research has indicated that CLT contributes positively to the L2 learners' fluency and communicative abilities. Furthermore, in some instances (e.g. Canadian French immersion programs), CLT has enabled L2 learners to develop comprehension abilities that parallel those of native speakers (Genesee, 1987). At the same time, however, observational research in CLT classrooms, particularly those in which no (or very little) attention is given to language form, has shown that students often fail to reach high levels of development and accuracy in many aspects of language (Harley & Swain, 1984; Spada & Lightbown, 1989). Experimental research to address this problem has incorporated some attention to language form (explicitly or implicitly) within exclusively (or primarily) meaning-focused CLT programs (Harley, 1989; Lyster, 1994; Spada and Lightbown, 1993; White, Spada, Lightbown, & Ranta, 1991). The results have indicated that the inclusion of form-focused instruction leads to improvement in students' knowledge and their ability to use that knowledge. (For reviews of this research see Norris & Ortega, 2000 and Spada, 1997.)

It is important to note that L2 teachers have not waited for SLA research to make decisions about what to do in their classrooms. Over the past 20 years, L2 teachers and program developers have had enough experience with CLT to decide for themselves that more of a balance is needed between form and meaning. This may be particularly true of L2 teachers who have been using a strong version of CLT. Nonetheless, there are still many L2 instructors who firmly believe that an exclusive focus on meaning via comprehensible input and interaction activities is sufficient for second/foreign language learning to succeed.

CLT Means No Explicit Feedback on Learner Error

Another myth about CLT is that it should not include corrective feedback. This is likely due to the fact that many teachers have been educated to believe that errors are evidence that the learner is testing hypotheses about the target language and in the process, progress is being made. The assumption is that with sufficient time and opportunities to hear and practice the target language, the learners' errors will eventually be replaced with target-like forms.

While some researchers have argued for the total rejection of any type of corrective feedback (Truscott, 1996, 1999), this represents an extreme view and is not typical of how most CLT teachers and researchers view feedback on learner error (Lyster et al., 1999). Instead, the type of corrective feedback that is widely encouraged and accepted in CLT is implicit and indirect and does not interfere with communication. For example, a particular type of feedback, referred to as a *recast*, has been observed to occur more frequently in CLT classrooms than other types of feedback (Lyster & Ranta, 1997; Panova, 1999; Havranek, 1999). A recast is the teacher's reformulation of a learner's incorrect utterance while maintaining a focus on meaning: for example, the L2 learner says, "His foots are cold," and the teacher responds by saying, "Yes, his *feet* are cold—he stayed outside too long!" The recast serves as corrective feedback by providing the learner with the correct form while at the same time confirming the content of the learner's utterance and continuing with the conversation.

Some researchers have argued that recasts are an effective way of providing learners with an opportunity to see how their interlanguage differs from the target language—that the recast enables L2 learners to notice the difference between what they say and how this compares with what native speakers say (Doughty & Varela, 1998; Long & Robinson, 1998). However, descriptive studies of the different types of feedback provided in communicative classrooms have shown that L2 learners do not recognize recasts as feedback on form (Havranek, 1999; Lyster, 1998). Instead, they perceive it as feedback on the content of their utterances (Mackey, Gass, & McDonough, 2000). Recent experimental classroom studies have revealed that more explicit types of feedback can lead to higher levels of accuracy and development than implicit types of feedback in the form of recasts (Ammar & Spada, 2006; Lyster, 2004). In addition, recasts have been observed to be more effective when they are accompanied by a clear signal to the learner that an error has been made (Doughty & Varela, 1998). Thus, there is insufficient evidence to support the claim that implicit forms of correction are most effective in CLT classrooms. In fact, there is growing evidence to demonstrate just the opposite; that more explicit forms of corrective feedback may be required in CLT classes where the learners' attention is primarily focused on meaning and content (for a review, see Nicholas, Lightbown, & Spada, 2001).

CLT Means Learner-centered Teaching

One of the primary themes of CLT is that learners should be given more control and autonomy for their language learning. This has led to opportunities for learners to provide input into decisions about course content (Breen & Candlin, 1980). It has also resulted in greater opportunities for student-initiated discourse in CLT classrooms (Allwright, 1980; Fröhlich, Spada, & Allen, 1985). One of the ways in which this has been accomplished is via learner-centered activities. In fact, groupwork has become so closely associated with CLT that for some L2 educators, CLT is simply not CLT unless it is learner-centered and in some cases, learner-directed.

In the mid-1980s, an influential article about the benefits of groupwork interaction was published in the *TESOL Quarterly* (Long & Porter, 1985). In that paper, the researchers outlined several pedagogical arguments for groupwork and offered evidence from SLA research to further support groupwork in L2 classrooms. This included studies that had revealed that in groupwork interaction, adult L2 learners produce not only more speech but also a greater variety of speech functions (and forms) than they do in teacher-centered interaction (Long, Adams, McLean, & Castaños, 1976). It also described research that had compared the language produced by adult L2 learners in pair work with other more and less advanced learners and with native speakers (Porter, 1983). The findings revealed that "although learners cannot provide each other with the accurate grammatical and sociolinguistic input that [native speakers] can, learners can offer each other genuine communicative practice, including the negotiation for meaning that is believed to aid SLA" (p. 217). Porter also observed that the accuracy levels of the L2 learners were the same regardless of whether they were speaking to a native or a non-native speaker. This last finding suggested that L2 instructors need not be concerned that groupwork interaction would lead to more errors than teacher-fronted instruction.

In their conclusions, Long and Porter (1985) were careful to emphasize that groupwork needs to be combined with other teacher-fronted activities in L2 classrooms. Furthermore, they raised the important issue of how one might organize groupwork interaction to encourage L2 learners to provide one another with feedback on accuracy. Nonetheless, many L2 educators interpreted the positive findings for groupwork as evidence that it is the central feature of CLT and for many years, instruction in CLT classrooms has been characterized by an almost exclusive focus on the exchange of messages and meanings in groupwork interaction. Although some early research investigated ways of focusing on language form in group-work interaction (Bruton & Samuda, 1980), it is only recently that more studies have explored this question. For example, Fotus (1994) investigated how adult L2 learners can make progress in the L2 by completing tasks that require them to think about, discuss, and share metalinguistic information. Swain and her colleagues (Kowal & Swain, 1994; Swain & Lapkin, 2002) have investigated the extent to which young adolescent L2 learners can provide each other with information about language and corrective feedback when engaged in collaborative interaction involving the reconstruction of texts.

CLT Means Listening and Speaking Practice

The view that CLT emphasizes speaking and listening—often to the exclusion of reading and writing—may have arisen in part from the fact that listening and speaking have been the focus of L2 instruction for quite some time. In particular, the strong influence of the audio-lingual method with its primacy of listening over reading and speaking over writing dominated the field of L2 teaching for over 30 years. The importance assigned to phoneme-grapheme relationships by structural linguists (Lado, 1964; Fries, 1945) led to the false assumption that aural-oral proficiency would automatically lead to reading and writing competency. However, when "dissatisfaction was growing with the audio-lingual method and teachers were becoming aware that aural-oral proficiency did not automatically produce reading or writing competency, L2 reading researchers began to call for teaching reading in its own right" (Carrell, 1988, p. 3). This led to more interactive approaches to reading based on psycholinguistic models of first language reading (Goodman, 1967; Smith, 1971). Around the same time, changes were also underway in the field of L2 writing characterized by a movement away from product-oriented approaches in an attempt to better understand the processes involved in L2 writing. This work was (and continues to be) influenced by theoretical frameworks across a wide range of disciplines including cognitive psychology (Bereiter & Scardamalia, 1982) and educational theory (Britton, 1970).

Thus, in many ways, the developments in L2 reading and writing research and pedagogy took place separately from CLT theory and practice. Nonetheless, it is important to note that from the beginning, many theorists agreed that one of the basic tenets of CLT was that linguistic skills and communicative abilities should not be treated in isolation from each other (Savignon, 1997). In his discussion of the importance of attention to discourse in CLT, Widdowson (1978) claimed: "What the learners need to know how to do is to compose in the act of writing, comprehend in the act of reading, and to learn techniques of reading by writing and techniques of writing by reading" (p. 144). Influenced by Widdowson and others, CLT materials writers have produced reading texts that are much more varied in terms of their content than in those typical of traditional structure-based instruction. Also, texts that have been specifically designed to meet the needs of particular groups of L2 readers (e.g. English for academic/scientific purposes) are abundant in CLT pedagogical libraries. Furthermore, the expectations that L2 learners need to keep in mind the relevant contextual and social factors contributing to their comprehension (i.e. listening and reading) and production (i.e. speaking and writing) has always been part of the fundamental principles and practices of CLT.

One area of reading research that is sometimes associated with CLT is extensive reading. This is because one of the underlying assumptions of extensive reading is that learners learn to read by reading, that is, by comprehending messages and meanings. This view is compatible with Krashen's comprehensible input hypothesis (1984b) and the claim that if learners are exposed to sufficient amounts of comprehensible input (e.g. via reading), not only will they learn how to read in the L2, but they will also acquire the linguistic features of the target language along the way. Considerable research has been done to investigate the impact of extensive reading on L2 reading abilities and the overall results indicate that second or foreign language readers at different ages and different levels of proficiency benefit from extensive reading (Elley, 1991). However, there is concern about how much progress second/foreign language learners can make without any assistance (Lightbown, Halter, White, & Horst, 2002). Furthermore, it is not clear from the research "the extent to which extensive reading should be balanced with an intensive reading program containing well-considered reading instruction/pedagogy" (Carrell & Grabe, 2002, p. 247). Once again, we hear the call for more of a balance between form and meaning.

CLT Means Avoidance of the Learners' L1

Avoidance of the use of the L1 or what Howatt (1984) refers to as the "monolingual principle" has been adopted by most L2 teaching methods ever since the direct method replaced the grammar translation method in the late 19th century. A particularly strong rejection of the use of the L1 in L2 classrooms was evident in 20th century audio-lingual teaching influenced by the contrastive analysis hypothesis (Lado, 1957), which viewed the L1 as a negative influence and an interference in the course of L2 development. While there are a few contemporary approaches to L2 instruction that encourage learners to use their L1 as an aid to their L2 learning such as community language learning (Curran, 1976), these are exceptions.

The argument against the use of L1 in L2 classrooms is obvious: Learners need as much exposure to the target language as they can get in order to become successful learners of that language. This is supported by considerable evidence that both the quantity and quality of target language input are crucial factors in L2 learning (Gass, 1997; Lightbown, 1991). However, in a recent paper that calls for a re-examination of the restrictions on L1 use in L2 classrooms, Cook (2001) argues that while "no one will quarrel with providing models of real language use for the students...[this is] not necessarily incompatible with L1 use in the classroom" (p. 409).

Sensible arguments can be (and have been) made for the principled use of L1 in L2 classrooms and there is theoretical, empirical, and pedagogical support for it. For example, the belief that first and second (or subsequent) languages exist in separate compartments in the mind and therefore should be kept separate in the classroom has not received empirical support. Neurolinguistic (Obler, 1982), psycholinguistic (Harris, 1992), and linguistic (Romaine, 1989) research has shown that knowledge of two languages is interwoven in the mind. Cummins (1991, 2001) refers to the overlap of the basic components of linguistic (and cognitive) information from two languages as *common underlying proficiency*. The notion of a common underlying proficiency has pointed to important benefits of L1 knowledge and use particularly for minority language children in bilingual education programs (Ramirez, 1992). This work has shown that there is significant transfer of conceptual knowledge and skills across languages. Thus, when a Spanish-speaking child learns how to read in Spanish, the skills being developed are not exclusive to Spanish but also to the child's underlying knowledge—conceptual and linguistic—about literacy. This knowledge then becomes accessible for the learning of a second or any subsequent language.

Other evidence that has been used to support L1 use in L2 learning comes from research influenced by Vygotsky's (1978) sociocultural theory. From this perspective, the L1 is viewed as providing crucial scaffolding support as learners negotiate form and meaning. For example, in a recent study of the L2 development of French immersion students engaged in collaborative tasks, Swain and Lapkin (2002) report that the use of the L1 enabled students to continue with the task and in the process to move forward in achieving their linguistic goals. In addition, Turnbull (2001) points to several pedagogic benefits of L1 use in the classroom (e.g. saving time, providing clearer and more concise explanations).

Despite the evidence that the L1 can have an important and positive role to play in L2 learning, one must be careful about exactly how much L1 use is productive.

Turnbull (2001) argues for a "judicious" use of the L1 in L2 classrooms, calling for more research to explore how different combinations and alternations of L1 and L2 use contribute to L2 learners' proficiency in different educational contexts. Although there is compelling evidence that L1 use should not be completely banned, it is crucial to keep in mind that decisions about whether and how much L1 use is encouraged in L2 classrooms is dependent upon the broader linguistic context. In foreign language settings, where the learners' exposure to the target language is restricted to the classroom, it is advisable to maximize target language exposure and minimize L1 use. For minority language learners who are at risk of losing their L1 as they are mainstreamed into the majority language and culture, maximizing opportunities for L1 use as a basis for L2 learning is recommended.

DIFFERENT MANIFESTATIONS OF CLT

As indicated in the introduction, one of the reasons for the lack of clarity and consistency in the definitions and conceptualizations of CLT is that the same label has been used to describe several different ways in which L2 instruction has been delivered over the past 20 years or so. Included among these are *content-based teaching,*[5] *task-based teaching, and participatory-based teaching.* Although there are differences in their instructional foci and goals, all have two common features or principles that grant them entry into the CLT family: an emphasis on meaning and learner-centered interaction. What appears to distinguish them from one another is the content of the instruction rather than the methodology. For example, in content-based teaching, the instructional focus is often on a school subject (e.g. mathematics, history). L2 learners are expected to learn the target language as they study mathematics and history, which are delivered via the target language. Krashen (1984a) has referred to this type of instruction, typical of French immersion classes as 'communicative language teaching par excellence' because the emphasis is on meaning and comprehensible input. Ideally, the content of task-based teaching (TBT) is based on an analysis of the learner's specific needs and interests in the target language (e.g. for professional purposes). In TBT, learners engage in different tasks (oral and written) requiring them to solve problems and/or negotiate meaning in order to achieve a particular purpose or goal. The assumption is that as learners work together, they will have opportunities to interact and that this interaction will facilitate their L2 learning (Long & Crookes, 1992). From the beginning, the emphasis in TBT has been on the negotiation of meaning. However, TBT has increasingly incorporated tasks in which learners are given opportunities to focus on form (Samuda, 2001). The content of participatory-based teaching differs considerably from the others in that it is motivated by social and political factors. Guided by Freire's (1970) use of dialogues as a basis for literacy development with the poverty-stricken in Brazil, the content is directly related to the personal lives of students and to notions of empowerment (Auerbach, 1992).

Not everyone would agree that the above-mentioned approaches to L2 teaching represent different versions of CLT. In Larsen-Freeman's (2000) review of 14 different methods of L2 teaching, a clear distinction is made between task-based, content-based, participatory-based, and communicative language teaching. CLT is defined as an approach to L2 instruction that focuses on language functions. However, because task-based, content-based, and participatory-based teaching are not organized in terms of language (i.e. forms or functions), Larsen-Freeman does not include them under the CLT label. It is true that in the early days of CLT it was considered to be different from previous L2 methods precisely because the emphasis was on language functions rather than language forms. Over the years, this distinction has become blurred. Indeed, as more contemporary approaches to L2 instruction have arrived on the scene—most of them with an emphasis on content other than language—CLT has gradually become the cover term for all of them.[6] It is precisely this problem of defining a clear set of instructional practices and procedures to characterize CLT that has led some researchers to suggest that it is time to discard the term CLT and along with it the global concept of method. While some might interpret this recommendation as radical and perhaps even premature, Stern (1983) put out a call for a "break with the method concept" almost 20 years ago arguing that:

> Neither from a theoretical nor a practical point of view are such contrasting pairs of concepts as audio-lingual versus grammar-translation, language laboratory versus non-laboratory, immersion versus non-immersion as clearly distinct from each other as the labels suggest. In experimental research it is not sufficient to accept these labels at their face value. (p. 492)

He went on to say, "the net effect of the different approaches to teaching…is now no longer conceptualized in terms of a single undifferentiated methodological prescription. Language teaching theorists at the present time shun the simple formula" (p. 494).

Interestingly, the assumption in Stern's writing in the early 1980s is that the break with the method concept had already been made. Perhaps it had in the minds of some language teaching theorists but certainly not all and to be sure, not in the minds of many, indeed most language teachers. As indicated in the introduction, among the voices of contemporary applied linguists who are reiterating this call is Kumaravadivelu (1994, 2001). He argues that the field of L2 teaching has reached a point where the accumulation of theoretical, empirical, and pedagogical knowledge is too sophisticated to be conceptualized in terms of methods. This has placed us in what he refers to as a postmethod condition—one which requires new conceptualizations and terminology to talk about language teaching (i.e. macrostrategies and situation-based microstrategies). Kumaravadivelu (2001) outlines an agenda as to how L2 educators might proceed to work within a postmethod pedagogy.

One of the arguments that is often used against a recommendation to abandon the notion of teaching method is that the *concept* of method is not the problem, but rather, how it is used. Larsen-Freeman (2000) argues that methods should not be understood as prescriptions for classroom behavior and imposed on teachers as a strict set of procedures to follow. Rather, they should be used to help "expand a teacher's repertoire of techniques" and "provide an avenue for professional growth" (p. x). Furthermore, if teachers are taught about different methods in ways that encourage them to reflect critically on their use and the underlying principles of learning and teaching associated with them, this should enable teachers to make their own choices as to what to do in their classrooms (For further discussion of this, see Freeman, 1991; Freeman & Richards, 1993; Richards, 1990).

In reaction to Kumaravadivelu's (1994) suggestion that macro- and micro-level instructional strategies that are neutral should serve as the guiding principles in the postmethod pedagogy, Celce-Murcia and Dörnyei (1997) argue that if the concept of

CLT is "construed as a general approach rather than a specific method," it could serve the same purpose and not be "inconsistent with the postmethod perspective" (p. 149). This is consistent with Savignon's (1997) description of CLT as a *philosophy* of language teaching rather than a *method*. For further discussion of the postmethod debate, see Bell (2003).

FUTURE DIRECTIONS

Notwithstanding the difficult issues of definition and implementation of CLT, there has been sufficient research in CLT classrooms (i.e. content-based, task-based) since the early 1980s to arrive at some conclusions about the contributions of CLT to L2 learning. As indicated above, there is an emerging consensus in the classroom research literature that the inclusion of form-focused instruction is needed within exclusively or primarily meaning-based approaches to CLT if learners are to develop higher levels of knowledge and performance in the target language. This has been demonstrated in descriptive, experimental, and quasi-experimental studies with adult, adolescent, and child learners in different second/foreign language contexts.

Of course, many questions remain unanswered—one of them is about the appropriate time in a communicative lesson to draw learners' attention to language form. This question has been lingering in the CLT literature for quite some time. In fact, as early as 1982, Johnson wrote about two different positions on this and described them in the following way: "The…separationist [position] seems to imply a divorce between the teaching of forms and use [whereas within] the unificationist position, the divorce of form and use is seen as undesirable and probably also untenable on linguistic and psycholinguistic grounds" (p. 129). Many teachers believe that the integration of attention to language form in communicative activities increases the likelihood that learners will attend to, notice, and be able to use that information later. Other teachers, however, fear that learners' motivation will decrease if attention is drawn to language form in the midst of communicative practice. While little research has been done to investigate isolated versus integrated form-focused instruction within CLT, there is a promising avenue of research to investigate this question. Within cognitive psychology, the concept of *transfer appropriate learning* predicts that we remember something best when we try to recall it in the context in which we originally understood it. Thus, it may be that language features are more readily available in spontaneous communicative interaction if they have been acquired in such a context (Segalowitz & Lightbown, 1999).

CONCLUSIONS

CLT is the most influential approach to arrive on the second/foreign language teaching scene since the so-called scientific method (i.e. audio-lingual method) in the 1960s. Some might even argue that CLT is the most influential approach in the history of second/foreign language instruction because it represents an effort to explore ways in which attention to language form and meaning can be *combined* in different areas of L2 education (i.e. syllabus design, methodology, materials development, and testing). CLT is undoubtedly the most researched approach to second/foreign language teaching in the history of language teaching. A count of the number of studies which have investigated the impact of CLT on L2 teaching and learning would be a difficult task. Such a productive program of L2 classroom research is unparalleled in the history of language teaching.

CLT is not without its problems. There is confusion in the definitions and interpretations of CLT and this confusion has resulted in a variety of myths and misconceptions regarding CLT. This points to the need for more efforts in teacher preparation and in-service teacher education programs to make teachers aware of the different ways in which CLT is interpreted and implemented. Equally important is the need to introduce teachers to the findings from classroom research that have examined the impact of the different versions of CLT on L2 learning—emphasizing that the research to date supports the advantages of a balance of form and meaning in L2 classrooms. It will take time to discover more precisely what that balance is. Nonetheless, it is likely that CLT will be around long enough to permit investigations of these questions. This process should provide theorists, researchers, and teachers with more information about how to continue to improve teaching and learning in second and foreign language education.

ACKNOWLEDGEMENT

The author would like to thank Jim Cummins, Chris Davison, Patsy Lightbown and Merrill Swain for their helpful comments on earlier versions of this paper.

NOTES

[1] According to Howatt, the "weak" version of CLT "stresses the importance of providing learners with opportunities to use [the target language] for communicative purposes and attempts to integrate such activities into a wider programme of language teaching." The "strong" version of CLT, on the other hand, "advances the claim that language is acquired through communication." Put simply and in the context of learning English, Howatt (1984) claims that the weak version of CLT can be described as "learning to use English" and the strong version as "using English to learn it" (p. 279).

[2] Of course, one's definition is not always consistent with one's practice. While some teachers describe CLT as exclusively meaning-based and view themselves as CLT teachers, this does not necessarily mean that they avoid any attention to language form (via correction and/or instruction) in their actual practice.

[3] Another theory that views interaction as crucial in learning and that has been applied to SLA is Vygotsky's sociocultural theory. This is not discussed here because Vygotskian theories of SLA are more recent contributions to the field and thus, were not influential in the early development of CLT.

[4] But see Long's (1996) revised interaction hypothesis for a discussion of how attention to form takes place in conversational interaction.

[5] *Subject-matter instruction* is a type of content-based instruction. This term has been used most often within the context of Canadian French immersion programs.

[6] See for example, Wesche and Skehan (2002) who describe task-based and content-based instruction as fitting Howatt's (1984) characterization of the strong version of CLT.

REFERENCES

Allwright, R. L. (1980). Turns, topics and tasks: Patterns of participation in language learning and teaching. In D. Larsen-Freeman (Ed.), *Discourse analysis in second language Research* (pp. 165–187). Rowley, Mass: Newbury House.

Ammar, A. & Spada, (2006). One size fits all? Recasts, prompts and L2 learning. *Studies in Second Language Acquisition*, 28(4), 543–574.

Auerbach, E. (1992). *Making meaning, making change: A guide to participatory curriculum development for adult ESL and family literacy*. McHenry, IL: Centre for Applied Linguistics and Delta Systems.

Austin, J. L. (1962). *How to do things with words?* Oxford: Clarendon Press.

Bachman, L., & Palmer, A. (1981). A multitrait-multimethod investigation into the construct validity of six tests of speaking and reading. In A. Palmer (Ed.), *The construct validation of tests of communicative competence* (pp. 149–165). Alexandria, Virginia: TESOL.

Bell, D. (2003). Method and postmethod: Are they really so incompatible? *TESOL Quarterly, 37,* 325–336.

Bereiter, C., & Scardamalia, M. (1982). From conversation to composition: The role of instruction in a developmental process. In R. Glaser (Ed.), *Advances in instructional psychology. Vol. 2.* (pp. 1–64) Hillsdale, NJ: Erlbaum.

Breen, M., & Candlin, C. (1980). The essentials of communicative curriculum in language teaching. *Applied Linguistics, 1,* 89–112.

Bosco, F. J., & Di Pietro, J. R. (1970). Instructional strategies: Their psychological and linguistic bases. *IRAL, 8,* 1–19.

Britton, J. (1970). *Language and learning.* Harmondsworth: Penguin.

Brumfit, C. J. (1984). *Communicative methodology in language teaching: The Roles of Fluency and Accuracy.* Cambridge: Cambridge University Press.

Bruton, A., & Samuda, V. (1980). Learner and teacher roles in the treatment of oral error in group work. *RELC Journal, 11,* 49–63.

Canale, M. (1983). From communicative competence to communicative language pedagogy. In J. C. Richards & R. W. Schmidt (Eds.), *Language and communication* (pp. 2–27). London: Longman.

Canale, M., & Swain, M. (1980). Theoretical bases of communicative approaches to second language teaching and testing. *Applied Linguistics, 1,* 1–47.

Carrell, P. (1988). Introduction: Interactive approaches to second language reading. In P. Carrell, J. Devine, & Eskey, D. (Eds.), *Interactive approaches to second language reading* (pp. 1–8). New York: Cambridge.

Carrell, P., & Grabe, W. (2002). Reading. In N. Schmitt (Ed.), *An introduction to applied linguistics* (pp. 233–249). London: Edward Arnold.

Celce-Murcia, M. (1991). Language and communication: A time for equilibrium and integration. In J. E. Alatis (Ed.), *Georgetown University Round Table on Language and Linguistics 1991: Linguistics and Language Pedagogy* (pp. 223–237). Washington, DC: Georgetown University Press.

Celce-Murcia, M., & Dörnyei, Z. (1997). Direct approaches in L2 instruction: A turning point in communicative language teaching? *TESOL Quarterly, 31,* 141–152.

Chomsky, N. (1957). *Syntactic structures.* The Hague: Mouton.

Cook, V. (2001). Using the first language in the classroom. *Canadian Modern Language Review, 57,* 402–423.

Cummins, J. (1991). Interdependence of first-and second-language proficiency in bilingual children. In E. Bialystok (Ed.), *Language processing in bilingual children* (pp. 70–89). Cambridge: Cambridge University Press.

Cummins, J. (2001). *Language, power and pedagogy: Bilingual children in the crossfire.* Toronto: Multilingual Matters.

Curran, C. A. (1976). *Counselling-learning in second languages.* Cliffside Park, NJ: Counselling Learning Institutes.

Doughty, C., & Varela, E. (1998). Communicative focus on form. In C. Doughty & J. Williams (Eds.), *Focus on form in classroom second language acquisition* (pp. 114–138). Cambridge: Cambridge University Press.

Elley, W.G. (1991). Acquiring literacy in a second language: The effect of book-based programs. *Language Learning, 41,* 375–411.

Firth, J. R. (1957). *Papers in linguistics: 1934–1951.* London: Oxford University Press.

Fotus, S. (1994). Integrating grammar instruction and communicative language use through grammar consciousness-raising tasks. *TESOL Quarterly, 28,* 323–351.

Freeman, D. (1991). Mistaken constructs: Re-examining the nature and assumptions of language teacher education. In J. E. Alatis (Ed.), *Georgetown University Round Table on Languages and Linguistics 1991: Linguistics and Language Pedagogy* (pp. 25–39). Washington, DC: Georgetown University Press.

Freeman, D., & Richards, J. (1993). Conceptions of teaching and the education of second language teachers. *TESOL Quarterly, 27,* 193–216.

Freire, P. (1970). *Pedagogy of the oppressed.* New York: Continuum.

Fries, C. (1945). *Teaching and learning English as a foreign Language.* Ann Arbor: University of Michigan Press.

Fröhlich, M., Spada, N., & Allen, P. (1985). Differences in the communicative orientation of L2 classrooms. *TESOL Quarterly, 19,* 27–56.

Gass, S. (1997). *Input, interaction and the second language learner*. Mahwah, NJ. Lawrence Erlbaum Associates.
Genesee, F. (1987). *Learning through two languages*. Rowley, Mass: Newbury House.
Goodman, (1967). Reading: A psycholinguistic guessing game. *Journal of the Reading Specialist, 6*, 126–135.
Halliday, M.A. K. (1973). *Explorations in the functions of language*. London: Edward Arnold.
Harley, B. (1989). Functional grammar in French immersion: A classroom experiment. *Applied Linguistics, 10*, 331–359.
Harley, B., & Swain, M. (1984). The interlanguage of immersion students and its implications for second language teaching. In A. Davies, C. Criper, & A. Howatt (Eds.), *Interlanguage* (pp. 291–311). Edinburgh: Edinburgh University Press.
Harley, B., Allen, P., Cummins, J., & Swain, M. (Eds.). (1990). *The development of second language proficiency*. Cambridge: Cambridge University Press.
Harris, R. J. (Ed.) (1992). *Cognitive processing in bilinguals*. Amsterdam: North-Holland.
Hatch, E. (1978). Discourse analysis and second language acquisition. In E. Hatch (Ed.), *Second language acquisition: A book of readings* (pp. 401–435). Rowley, Mass.: Newbury House.
Havranek, G. (1999). The effectiveness of corrective feedback: Preliminary results of an empirical study. *Acquisition et Interaction en Langue Étrangère, 2*, 189–206.
Howatt, A. (1984). *A history of English language teaching*. Oxford: Oxford University Press.
Hymes, D. (1971). *On communicative competence*. Philadelphia, PA: University of Pennsylvania Press.
Johnson, K. (1982). *Communicative syllabus design and methodology*. Oxford: Pergamon Press.
Johnstone, R. (1999). Research on language teaching and learning: 1999. *Language Teaching, 23*, 165–189.
Kowal, M., & Swain, M. (1994). Using collaborative language production tasks to promote students' language awareness. *Language Awareness, 3,* 73–93.
Krashen, S. (1982). *Principles and practice in second language acquisition*. Oxford: Pergamon Press.
Krashen, S. (1984a). Immersion: Why it works and what it has taught us. *Language and Society, 12*, 61–64.
Krashen, S. (1984b). *The input hypothesis: Issues and implications*. London: Longman.
Krashen, S., & Seliger, H. (1975). The essential contribution of formal instruction in adult second language learning. *TESOL Quarterly, 13*, 573–582.
Kumaravadivelu, B. (1994). The postmethod condition: (E)merging strategies for second/foreign language teaching. *TESOL Quarterly, 28*, 27–48.
Kumaravadivelu, B. (2001). Toward a postmethod pedagogy. *TESOL Quarterly, 35*, 537–560.
Lado, R. (1957). *Linguistics across cultures: Applied linguistics for language teachers*. Ann Arbor MI: University of Michigan Press.
Lado, R. (1964). *Language teaching: A scientific approach*. New York: McGraw-Hill.
Larsen-Freeman, D. (1991). Research on language teaching methodologies: A review of the past and an agenda for the future. In K. de Bot, R. B. Ginsberg, & C. Kramsch (Eds.), *Foreign language research in cross-cultural perspective* (pp. 119–132). Amsterdam: John Benjamins.
Larsen-Freeman, D. (2000). *Techniques and principles in language teaching* (2nd ed.). Oxford: Oxford University Press.
Lightbown, P. M. (1991). Getting quality input in the second/foreign language classroom. In C. Kramsch & S. McConnell-Ginet (Eds.), *Text and context: Cross-disciplinary perspectives on language study* (pp. 187–197). Lexington, Mass: D.C. Heath and Company.
Lightbown, P. M., Halter, R., White, J., & Horst, M. (2002). Comprehension-based learning: The limits of 'do it yourself'. *Canadian Modern Language Review, 58*, 427–464.
Lightbown, P. M., & Spada, N. (1999). *How languages are learned*. Oxford: Oxford University Press.
Littlewood, W. (1981). *Communicative language teaching: An Introduction*. Cambridge: Cambridge University Press.
Long, M. (1980). Inside the 'black box': Methodological issues in classroom research on language learning. *Language Learning, 30*, 1–42.
Long, M. (1983). Linguistic and conversational adjustments to non-native speakers. *Studies in Second Language Acquisition, 5*, 177–193.
Long, M. (1991). Focus on form: A design feature in language teaching methodology. In K. de Bot, R. B. Ginsberg & C. Kramsch (Eds.), *Foreign language research in cross-cultural perspective* (pp. 39–52). Amersterdam/Philadelphia: John Benjamins Publishing.
Long, M. (1996). The role of the linguistic environment in second language acquisition. In W. Ritchie & T. Bhatia (Eds.), *Handbook of second language acquisition* (pp. 413–454). New York: Academic Press.

Long, M., Adams, L., McLean, M., & Castaños, F. (1976). Doing things with words: Verbal interaction in lock-step and small group classroom situations. In R. Crymes & J. Fanselow (Eds.), *ON TESOL '76* (pp. 137–153). DC: TESOL.
Long, M., & Crookes, G. (1992). Three approaches to task-based syllabus design. *TESOL Quarterly, 26*, 27–56.
Long, M., & Porter, P. (1985). Group work, interlanguage talk, and second language acquisition. *TESOL Quarterly, 19*, 207–228.
Long, M., & Robinson, P. (1998). Focus on form: Theory, research and practice. In C. Doughty & J. Williams (Eds.), *Focus on form in classroom second language acquisition* (pp. 15–41). Cambridge: Cambridge University Press.
Lyster, R. (1994). The effect of functional-analytic teaching on aspects of French immersion students' sociolinguistic competence. *Applied Linguistics, 15*(3), 263–287.
Lyster, R. (1998). Recasts, repetition, and ambiguity in L2 classroom discourse. *Studies in Second Language Acquisition, 20*, 51–81.
Lyster, R. (2004). Differential effects of prompts and recasts in form-focussed instruction. *Studies in second language acquisition, 26*, 399–432.
Lyster, R., Lightbown, P. M., & Spada, N. (1999). A response to Truscott's 'What's wrong with oral grammar correction.' *Canadian Modern Language Review, 55*(4), 456–467.
Lyster, R., & Ranta, L. (1997). Corrective feedback and learner uptake: Negotiation of form in communicative classrooms. *Studies in Second Language Acquisition, 19*, 37–66.
Mackey, A., Gass, S., & McDonough, K. (2000). How do learners perceive implicit negative feedback? *Studies in Second Language Acquisition, 22*(4), 471–497.
Nicholas, H., Lightbown, P. M. & Spada, N. (2001). Recasts as feedback to language learners. *Language Learning, 51*, 719–758.
Norris, J. M., & Ortega, L. (2000). Effectiveness of L2 instruction: A research synthesis and quantitative meta-analysis. *Language Learning, 50*, 417–528.
Nunan, D. (1991). *Language teaching methodology*. London: Prentice Hall.
Obler, L. (1982). The parsimonious bilingual. In L. K. Obler & L. Menn (Eds.), *Exceptional language and linguistics* (pp. 339–346). San Diego, CA: Academic Press.
Panova, I. (1999). *Corrective feedback and learner responses: An observational study in an adult ESL classroom*. Unpublished master's monograph. McGill University, Montreal, Quebec, Canada.
Pennycook, A. (1989). The concept of method, interested knowledge, and the politics of language teaching. *TESOL Quarterly, 23*, 591–615.
Prahbu, N. S. (1987). *Second language pedagogy*. Oxford: Oxford University Press.
Porter, P. (1983). How learners talk to each other: Input and interaction in task-centred discussions. In D. Day (Ed.), *Talking to Learn: Conversation in second language acquisition* (pp. 200–222). Rowley, Mass: Newbury House.
Ramirez (1992). Executive summary. *Bilingual Research Journal, 16*, 1–62.
Richards, J. (1989). Beyond methods: Alternative approaches to instructional design. *Prospect, 3*, 11–30.
Richards, J. (1990). *The language teaching matrix*. Cambridge: Cambridge University Press.
Romaine, S. (1989). *Bilingualism*. Oxford: Blackwell.
Samuda, V. (2001). Guiding relationships between form and meaning during task performance. The role of the teacher. In M. Bygate, P. Skehan, & M. Swain (Eds.), *Researching pedagogic tasks, second language learning, teaching and testing* (pp. 119–140). New York: Longman.
Sato, K., & Kleinsasser, R. C. (1999). Communicative language teaching (CLT): Practical understanding. *The Modern Language Journal, 83*, 494–517.
Savignon, S. (1972). *Communicative competence: An experiment in foreign language teaching*. Philadelphia: Center for Curriculum Development.
Savignon, S. (1997). *Communicative competence: Theory and classroom practice* (2nd ed.). New York: McGraw-Hill.
Searle, J. R. (1969). *Speech acts: An essay in the philosophy of language*. Cambridge: Cambridge University Press.
Segalowitz, N., & Lightbown, P. M. (1999). Psycholinguistic approaches to SLA. *Annual Review of Applied Linguistics, 19*, 43–63.
Smith, F. (1971). *Understanding reading: A psycholinguistic analysis of reading and learning to read*. New York: Holt, Rinehart and Winston.
Spada, N. (1987). The relationship between instructional differences and learning outcomes: A process-product study of communicative language teaching. *Applied Linguistics, 8*, 137–155.
Spada, N. (1997). Form-focused instruction and second language acquisition: A review of classroom and laboratory research. *Language Teaching, 30*, 73–87.

Spada, N., & Fröhlich, M. (1995). *The communicative orientation of language teaching observation scheme (COLT): Coding conventions and applications*. Sydney Australia: NCELTR, Macquarie University.
Spada, N., & Lightbown, P. M. (1989). Intensive ESL programs in Quebec primary schools. *TESL Canada Journal, 7*, 11–32.
Spada, N., & Lightbown, P. M. (1993). Instruction and the development of questions in the L2 classroom. *Studies in Second Language Acquisition, 15*, 205–221.
Stern, H. H. (1983). *Fundamental concepts of language teaching*. Oxford: Oxford University Press.
Stern, H. H. (1992). *Issues and options in language teaching*. Oxford: Oxford University Press.
Swain, M., & Lapkin, S. (2002). Talking it through: Two French immersion learners' response to reformulation. *International Journal of Educational Research, 37*, 285–304.
Thompson, G. (1996). Some misconceptions about communicative language teaching. *ELT Journal, 50*, 9–15.
Truscott, J. (1996). The case against grammar correction in L2 writing classes. *Language Learning, 46*, 327–369.
Truscott, J. (1999). What's wrong with oral grammar correction? *Canadian Modern Language Review, 55*, 437–456.
Turnbull, M. (2001). There is a role for the L1 in second and foreign language teaching, but... *Canadian Modern Language Review, 57*, 531–540.
Vygotsky, L. S. (1978). *Mind in society: The development of higher psychological processes*. Cambridge, MA: Harvard University Press.
Wesche, M., & Skehan, P. (2002). Communicative, task-based, and content-based language instruction. In R. B. Kaplan (Ed.), *The Oxford handbook of applied linguistics* (pp. 207–228). Oxford: Oxford University Press.
White, L., Spada, N., Lightbown, P. M., & Ranta, L. (1991). Input enhancement and L2 question formation. *Applied Linguistics, 12*, 416–432.
Widdowson, H. G. (1978). *Teaching language as communication*. Oxford: Oxford University Press.
Widdowson, H. G. (1990). *Aspects of language teaching*. Oxford: Oxford University Press.
Wilkins, D. (1976). *Notional syllabuses*. Oxford: Oxford University Press.
Williams, J. (1995). Focus on form in communicative language teaching. Research findings and the classroom teacher. *TESOL Journal, 4*, 12–16.

CHAPTER 19

LANGUAGE INSTRUCTION THROUGH TASKS

PETER SKEHAN

The Chinese University of Hong Kong, China

ABSTRACT

The chapter provides a survey of research into task-based foreign language instruction, spanning the last twenty years or so. At the outset, it contextualises task research within communicative approaches to language teaching, and argues that optimistic interpretations of communicative activities as vehicles for language development lack research support. Task instruction research is then linked to a more realistic underlying account stressing a Focus-on-Form. Subsequently, four perspectives on task research are discussed: a psycholinguistic approach to interaction; a cognitive approach to attentional use during tasks; a sociocultural perspective; and the use of focused tasks. The first emphasizes the quality of feedback that can be generated by well-designed interactions. The second explores how different task characteristics and task conditions influence attentional demands, and the scope there is to direct attention to form without compromising meaningful communication. The third explores how task participants collaborate on tasks and reinterpret them as they are being completed. Finally, the fourth approach examines whether it is possible to "seed" tasks with particular language structures without losing the benefits of a primacy for meaning. After the different perspectives have been described, they are compared with one another. Next, a series of controversies within the task literature are examined and the chapter concludes by proposing some future directions for task instruction research.

INTRODUCTION

The 1970s and part of the 1980s represented a significant period of change within language teaching, both theoretically and practically. During this period, communicative language teaching grew enormously in importance. Practically, changes could be seen in the range of materials that became available, both as supplementary materials (e.g. Blundell & Stokes, 1982; Geddes & Sturtridge, 1982) and, at the end of the decade, new course book series (e.g. Abbs & Freebairn, 1977, 1981). Theoretically, communicative language teaching was linked to more meaning-based accounts of language (Halliday, 1978) which contrasted with Chomsky's (1965, and earlier) structuralist approach. Such accounts strongly influenced analyses of language teaching as primarily aimed at developing the ability to communicate (Widdowson, 1978).

Most of the developments in the U.K. at this stage derived, essentially, from linguistic analyses, and influenced commercial language teaching materials and procedures. Interestingly, in North America, the focus was more on exploring the joint significance of acquisitional dynamics and the role empirical research might play in understanding how language development occurs. Theoretically, this meant that researchers (and practitioners) looked to insights and advances in first language acquisition, which broadly suggested that the child brings a great deal of "pre-wired" capacity to the task of acquiring a language (Pinker, 1994). This suggested that the conditions of first language acquisition might be relevant for the second language case. Empirically, researchers sought to explore universals of second language development (Dulay & Burt, 1974; Ellis, 1985), and especially the role of input as a driving force in language development (Krashen, 1985). They also explored how different communicative classroom activities might make a difference to the language that is produced, the interaction patterns that occur, and the implications these might have for acquisition (Long, 1985). Practically, this was the period when the educational innovation of immersion education in Canada was very influential. Immersion suggested that *content-based instruction*, where school lessons in a variety of subjects were delivered in the target language by bilingual teachers, would lead to significantly higher achievement than conventional language instruction (Swain & Lapkin, 1982). In other words, as in the first language case, meaning-driven work would bring with it structural development, even though there had been no explicit focus on structure. In brief, this period saw a consensus emerging that linked communicative language teaching, second language acquisition (SLA) theory, and educational innovation.

Three major developments during the 1980s, though, caused a re-evaluation of what might otherwise have been seen as a fairly comfortable state of affairs:

> Practically, evaluations of immersion education indicated that it was not as successful as had originally been thought. In particular, comprehension abilities were shown to be much higher than production abilities, and time (i.e. more years of instruction) did not seem to redress this imbalance (Harley & Swain, 1984). Input alone, in other words, was not enough.

> Theoretically, it was realized that providing learners with input and interactive opportunities was not sufficient for acquisition *unless there was some concern for form*. Learners, in other words, prioritize meaning, and structure can be by-passed in the interests of communication. Interaction, in other words, is not enough in itself (Long, 1991).

> Empirically, it became increasingly clear that not all communicative activities are the same, and that it is productive to devise research studies to explore the consequences of using one type of activity rather than another. In other words, researching task characteristics and the conditions under which tasks are done is useful in exploring when form is more likely to come into focus within the context of communicative language teaching (Long, 1989).

These developments roughly coincided with a labeling change, as the broader term *communicative language teaching* was replaced with the term *task-based instruction*. Although the former is still very widely used, a task-based approach to language teaching is more associated with (a) an acceptance that a Focus-on-Form (FonF) is essential (Long & Robinson, 1998; Doughty & Williams, 1998a, 1998b); (b) the belief that it is not enough to explore the creativity and engagement of tasks, rather they need to be related to acquisition and language development; and (c) the belief that tasks and the conditions under which tasks are implemented also need to be researched and claims about them subjected to testing.

Given these developments, and the emergence of the term *task* within language teaching, it is necessary to offer a definition that captures the way most (but not all) task researchers operate. Drawing on Bygate, Skehan, and Swain (2001), a task is defined as "an activity which engages learners to use language, with emphasis on meaning, to attain an objective" (p. 11).

This minimalist approach to definition is meant to capture the essential qualities of tasks, i.e. the meaning emphasis and their linkage to an objective. Such criteria separate tasks from other classroom activities where there is a strong and more explicit concern with the form of language. The definition, though, does not include reference to a real-world relationship, i.e. that comparable tasks are done by native speakers in the real world, since the emphasis is on the *response* of the learner and his/her engagement with meaningful language use. That does not mean, of course, that a real-world relationship is inappropriate, and indeed, many tasks will have such a relationship. But it is the acceptance, on the part of the learner, that language should be used meaningfully that is the major factor.

CURRENT TASK RESEARCH

Broadly, there are four contrasting approaches to research with tasks. Each has a different theoretical foundation, and tends to explore different sets of variables. I describe each of them briefly, and then relate them to one another.

A Psycholinguistic Approach to Interaction

This approach derives from Long's (1983, 1989) analysis of the potential that interactive tasks contain to support and drive forward second language development. Long (1991; Long & Robinson, 1998) is the most influential advocate of a FonF, and he proposes that interaction itself, if properly designed and organized, contains what is necessary for form to come into focus. In earlier work, he proposed that the more learners who are doing tasks negotiate meaning (asking for clarification, confirming comprehension, etc.), the more they are likely to receive personalized and helpful feedback from other interlocutors, whether these are native or non-native speakers. The acquisitional dynamic he proposes is: good tasks bring about more negotiation of meaning, producing more feedback, which leads to faster acquisition. In other words, a FonF is engineered by the use of tasks that make negotiation of meaning more likely. In more recent work, Long (Long & Robinson, 1998) has modified this position slightly to argue more selectively for the usefulness of *recasting*, i.e. occasions when interlocutors rephrase an incorrectly formed contribution by a non-native speaker so that it is correct. In this way, they are providing the learner with feedback about the correct form of an utterance at a very helpful moment. Much research has been done within negotiation of meaning/recasting perspectives. This suggests that indeed, tasks and task use can provoke greater amounts of these interactional moves, e.g. convergent tasks, i.e. tasks which require an agreed outcome or decision by participants (Duff, 1986), or information exchange tasks (Doughty & Pica, 1986). Similarly, Doughty and Varela (1998) have shown how intensive recasting can occur in a science lesson, and have an impact upon learner language. (See Pica, 1994; and Gass, 2002, for reviews of this work.)

Two broad lines of questioning exist with respect to this body of work: whether negotiation of meaning and recasting occur in the way proponents claim it does, and whether, if it occurs, it has an effect on acquisition. It has been claimed that negotiation of meaning can be irritating to learners (Aston, 1986); that it does not occur in real classrooms with the frequency it occurs in laboratory situations (Foster, 1998); and that it is primarily lexical rather than structural (Foster). There are also claims that recasting does not occur as much as is claimed (Lyster, 1998, Lyster & Ranta, 1997); that it is often not recognized in reality as the potential feedback that it is (Mackey, Gass, & McDonough, 2000); and that, since it is not incorporated very much in learner utterances, its usefulness for acquisition has to be questioned (Lyster). The recasting literature has been reviewed recently (Nicholas, Lightbown, & Spada, 2001). These authors argue that recasting needs to be timed carefully in relation to learner readiness, and that not all areas of language are equally susceptible to recasting based feedback.

Cognitive Approaches to Tasks

The Negotiation of Meaning/ Recasting approach assumes that feedback (and so a FonF) arises naturally in well-designed interactions and drives forward language development. An alternative perspective to tasks, but still drawing upon the FonF construct, is to take a more attention-allocation perspective and ask how different tasks and different task conditions lead learners to prioritize different language areas (Skehan, 1996). Researchers of this persuasion tend to look at learner performance on a task as a function of task characteristics or task conditions, but do not emphasize what might be termed *process* variables such as negotiation of meaning. Instead, they tend to view performance in terms of complexity of language, accuracy, and fluency (Skehan & Foster, 1997). These three areas are considered to have acquisitional implications, in that more complex language is seen as reflecting learners attempting to change their underlying interlanguage and so make system-linked progress. Accuracy and fluency are then different aspects not of changing the underlying system but of achieving control over an existing system. Accuracy and error elimination concern greater "computational" control to apply interlanguage rules during communication, while fluency is seen as having a greater meaning orientation and as reflective of a capacity to use a more lexicalized mode of performance (Skehan, 1998). A range of measures have been developed for these areas, some generalized and some specific.

A key part of this approach is research into task difficulty, and also the effects of task characteristics on particular areas of performance. Tasks are seen as more difficult when they are based on abstract or dynamic information (rather than concrete), when they draw upon many elements rather than fewer (Brown, Anderson, Shilcock, & Yule, 1984), and when they require transformation of the elements that compose them rather than simply retrieval of information (Skehan & Foster, 1997). Task characteristics that have selective influences on performance can be summarized as follows:

1) *Structured tasks* (i.e. those tasks that have a clear time-line or causal macrostructure) produce markedly greater fluency in performance, and somewhat greater accuracy. It appears that knowledge of the general macrostructure of a task focuses the learners' attention away from

complexifying the task, and as a result, attention is diverted to achieving control (Foster & Skehan, 1996; Skehan & Foster, 1997, 1999) both with error avoidance and especially with coping with real-time performance.
2) *Familiar information* has similar effects, for similar reasons of easing attentional demands and enabling learners to focus on fluency and accuracy (Foster & Skehan, 1996; Skehan & Foster, 1997).
3) *Outcomes requiring justifications* operate in the reverse direction. They push learners to complexify the task, and as a result, language complexity increases, but fluency and accuracy suffer (Foster & Skehan, 1996; Skehan & Foster, 1997, 1999).
4) *Remoteness of information* influences task complexity and accuracy. Robinson (2001, 2003) claims that these two areas are both advantaged when tasks are based on what he terms "there and then" information, relative to "here and now" tasks.
5) *Interactive tasks* favor complexity and accuracy, but at the expense of fluency (Foster & Skehan, 1996, 1999; Skehan & Foster, 1997, 1998). It is not entirely clear why this is so, but the effect is dependable and strong. It may be that interactive tasks push learners to be more precise so that interlocutors understand more clearly; it may be that interaction actually provides more time (while an interlocutor is speaking) and enables mid-task on-line planning (Ortega, 1999); or it may be that learners scaffold one another's performance, recycling and even expanding more complex and accurate contributions.

Research into the conditions under which tasks are done has also proved enlightening. A number of studies have explored the role of pre-task planning, following studies by Crookes (1989) who proposed that planning advantages complexity and fluency but not accuracy, and Ellis (1987) who, in contrast, argued for an accuracy effect for planning. Most of the studies confirm Crookes' claims, demonstrating consistent and appreciable planning effects, generally operationalized in these studies as a period (10 minutes being typical) during which learners can plan for a task, alone (e.g. Mehnert, 1998; Ortega, 1999; Foster & Skehan, 1996, 1999; Wigglesworth, 1997). Less frequently, effects are also found for accuracy, although here the effects are not so strong and are often associated with the use of generalized rather than specific measures of accuracy (e.g. Foster & Skehan, 1996; Mehnert; Skehan & Foster, 1997; Wigglesworth, 1997), but not Ortega (1999) or Wigglesworth (2001). Recently Yuan and Ellis (2003) have argued for the distinction between pre-task planning (as in most of the studies currently completed) and on-line planning, i.e. learners who are able to effect some degree of planning while a task is running (see also Wendel, 1997, and Ortega, 1999). Ellis argues that on-line planning is associated with accuracy, where pre-task planning is not.

Post-task conditions have also been researched. Generally speaking, such conditions fall into two categories: those that attempt to increase accuracy and those that focus on complexity. With the former, Skehan and Foster have explored the consequences for performance of conditions such as requiring some learners in a class, chosen after a task is done, to re-do the task publicly afterwards (1997), or of requiring learners to transcribe 1 minute of their own performance on a task (1998). In each case, the post-task condition is hypothesized to selectively push learners to allocate attention towards accuracy, because the condition is meant to make them more aware of errors they might make, as well as the importance of pedagogic norms. In both these cases, the prediction was confirmed but only for an interactive task. Monologic tasks, i.e. where only one speaker is involved, as in a narration, do not lead to significantly different results in this area. It appears that attention can be channeled towards accuracy, but only under the supportive conditions of an interactive encounter.

Post-task conditions that are meant to increase complexity have not been extensively researched. Task repetition (Bygate, 1996, 1999, 2001) has been shown to lead to greater syntactization, as learners, on re-doing a task, are more able to pack denser syntax into the way they provide narrative accounts of a video-based cartoon. But the potential for post-task conditions to capitalize upon gaps which have been noticed during task completion (Swain, 1995) so that interlanguage restructuring is more likely to occur has not been translated into research studies, although pedagogic suggestions are available (Willis, 1996). This is an area of promise for the future.

Even so, the task condition research that has been completed, coupled with the task characteristic research, provides an interesting picture. Provided one is interested in performance characterized in terms of complexity, accuracy, and fluency, one can now point to a range of characteristics and conditions that can be chosen from to promote each one of these performance areas or of combinations of them. In other words, research results provide, for teachers, interesting suggestions that can feed into their decision making as to which tasks to use, when, and how.

Sociocultural Approaches to Tasks

Earlier we explored a psycholinguistic approach to interaction, where the focus was on the potential a task contains to provide relevant and personalized feedback to assist interlanguage development. In contrast, a range of other researchers draw explicitly on sociocultural work and explore how interaction itself is important for the collaborative building of meanings, i.e. the focus is not on the individual within interaction but on the joint interaction that develops as learners co-construct meanings (Lantolf, 2000). Some researchers of this type explore how tasks are re-interpreted by learners, jointly, (e.g. Duff, 1993; Coughlan & Duff, 1994) leading to the claim that it is unrealistic to expect tasks to have predictable and dependable qualities. For sociocultural researchers, such a view would make tasks wooden in nature, and deny the way meanings emerge unpredictably when people work together.

Other sociocultural theorists though are closer to the aims of FonF theorists, but take the view that psycholinguistic viewpoints have an impoverished view of what interaction can contribute to learning. Van Lier and Matsuo (2000) explore how interaction may be measured more effectively, focusing on how learners develop symmetrical interaction patterns and work together rather than seek to dominate. Nakahama et al. (2001) use a sociocultural framework to explore the potential of different task types. In this, they follow exactly the same strategy as more psycholinguistically oriented approaches, even contrasting two similar tasks to those explored within other frameworks. However, in their case, they use their measurement of interaction and of the emerging discourse to argue that it is the discussion task that provides more learning opportunities than does the information exchange task (cf. Duff, 1986). Finally, Swain and Lapkin (2001) explore how co-

construction of meaning, in the case of dictogloss and jigsaw tasks, provide learners with a scaffold that can help them, collaboratively, notice aspects of the target language grammar only through the collaborative activities they engage in. The focus, in this case, is psycholinguistics and how form is brought into focus, but the means connect with sociocultural theory.

Focused Tasks

All approaches considered so far assume that the structures that are used while doing a task are the structures that emerge naturally. In contrast, other approaches push for activities that meet the definition of task proposed earlier but which nonetheless enable specific structures to be "forced" into use (cf. Loschky & Bley-Vroman's, 1993, "necessary" condition). Ellis (2003) distinguishes between three types of *focused task*. The first category consists of *structure-based production tasks*, i.e. tasks that "finesse" the use of a particular structure. Samuda (2001) illustrates this with a task that uses input materials and task requirements, such that the use of modality is unavoidable. The task of the teacher, in this case, who works *with* the students while they are doing the task, is to try to insinuate more complex forms of modality (i.e. modal verbs in this case) into the learner's language when they are trying to express modality themselves, but with simpler forms, e.g. words like *maybe* or phrases like *it is possible*. In this way, the teacher can prepare ahead of time but then has to work very carefully with learners to induce the use of the desired forms, but without compromising the 'taskness' of the activity.

Ellis' (2003) second category consists of *comprehension tasks*. Observing that the majority of tasks that have been researched have focused on oral communication tasks, Ellis draws attention to the range of work which emphasizes comprehension-based activities (e.g. Ellis, 2001; Trahey & White, 1993) and also comprehension processing (Van Patten, 1996, 2002). The third type of focused task is the *consciousness-raising task*. In this case, language itself is the point of the task, and learners are drawn into interaction and language work about language. Such tasks can be used to promote vocabulary (Ellis, 2001; Newton, 2001) or language structure (Fotos, 1994; Fotos & Ellis, 1991).

Contrasting Approaches – An Assessment

What unites the four approaches to tasks that we have examined is their concern to ground claims in research. This is not as trivial as it sounds: It represents a significant move towards a researched pedagogy, implicitly rejecting claims that are supported simply on the basis of experience. All the approaches take a structured approach to gathering data, and then relate these data to questions that have connection with theory. But beyond that, there is considerable diversity. The approach to definitions exemplifies this. Three approaches take a fairly strong approach to implementing the definitions provided earlier. The fourth, that of focused tasks, is less clear. In this case, we cannot be so sure that there is a primacy of meaning; whether this is so seems to depend a lot on teacher activity. The other approaches all seem to see meaning and outcome and naturalness of response as more fundamental.

Perhaps the sharpest differences, though, concern the nature of acquisition and performance, and the relationship between these two. The psycholinguistic approach to interaction focuses on how instruction can be organized so that feedback is provided naturally and in a personalized manner. In other words, progress is seen as arising out of feedback provided at the point in performance when it is most relevant. Assumptions are then made about the learner noticing such feedback, recognizing it for what it is relevant to, incorporating it, and subsequently acting upon it. Development then proceeds through interaction, and in whatever route is appropriate to the learner. The cognitive approach shares this view of learning coming from within, as it were, but is not concerned with feedback, tacitly assuming that feedback does not function in the same way in second language development as it may do in first. In contrast, the key assumption is that development is a continual cycle of noticing aspects of language, restructuring a developing interlanguage, and gaining control of this developing system. The focus is on availability of attention to ensure that these things occur, and designing and using tasks to maximize the chances that they will. A sociocultural approach makes no apologies for not focusing on the nature of acquisition. Instead, it is concerned with the nature of interaction itself, and its capacity to help learners to co-construct meanings. It is assumed that out of such co-construction, in some unspecified way, language development will occur. Even so, some researchers in this tradition (e.g. Swain & Lapkin, 2001), as we have seen, have explored how learners can collaboratively bring form into focus in ways that are more difficult for the solitary learner (who is the focus for the previous two approaches). Finally, it is interesting that those who advocate focused tasks are, potentially, taking a fairly traditional approach to instruction in terms of syllabus. Unlike the other approaches, whose use of task-based methodologies are associated with procedural syllabi, the advocates of focused tasks are compatible with White's (1988) Type A, structural syllabus. They too are concerned with achieving progressive mastery over an emerging structure, but in this case take the view that it is open for the teacher or syllabus designer to choose what this structure will be.

CONTROVERSIES

One set of controversies concerns disputes between task researchers and non-task researchers. Most broadly, this derives from an attack on SLA in general (of which tasks are then but a part). The critique is most forcefully seen in the set of articles in *Modern Language Journal*, where it is argued that SLA researchers ignore the social dimension of language use (Firth & Wagner, 1997; Seedhouse, 1997, 1999). When this is applied to tasks, it is clearest in the critique that there is an excessive focus on *referential* tasks (Cook, 2000). Task researchers would respond by claiming, (a) while not denying social dimensions of language use, they are focusing on *acquisition*, and this legitimizes the use of referential tasks; (b) there are many task studies that do not use referential tasks. Other critics of task-based work similarly misrepresent the area by attacking studies based on what was described above as the psycholinguistic approach to interaction, i.e. the negotiation of meaning and recasting studies. They then go on to dismiss the entire task-based enterprise. As seen above, though, it is clear that task-based work goes well beyond this one line of inquiry. In any case, it is noteworthy that the critics of this one approach are remarkably data-free in their claims, simply making assertions, rather than substantiating them. Finally, in this category of controversies, Bruton (2002) argues that tasks should be seen only as an adjunct to conventional language teaching. This is an interesting point. Most task research demonstrates, in passing, two things. First, research-based progress is necessarily slow, and because of the need to focus and build findings cumulatively, cannot easily be applied as a complete solution to practical problems. Second, pedagogic, real-world applications of task insights, especially when these are the basis of longitudinal research, are the most difficult of all to do. Hence, it is certainly fair to claim that the case for tasks is not proven. But then, it is not unproven either. In fact, it could be argued that the case for *any* form of language instruction is unproven, and that this alone justifies a need to massively increase research endeavor.

There are also lively debates within the task-oriented literature. We have seen one already: arguments and counter-arguments relating to the existence and function of negotiation of meaning and recasting accounts. This controversy, it is worth noticing in passing, differs from those covered in the previous paragraph because although there are disagreements, the basis for the argument is not controversial: gathering data, and subjecting claims to test. But three debates are worth mentioning and also have implications for the next section on likely future developments: exploration of task characteristics; interpretations of the role of attention and of the nature of acquisition; and the functioning of planning. We have touched on issues concerning task characteristics already, and also noted that critics outside task research have claimed that referential tasks (which of course are not notably social) have played too prominent a role in research. We are currently in the position that a range of findings exist on task characteristics, but we have no convincing and comprehensive model of how these characteristics inter-relate and influence performance. Various programmatic suggestions have been made (Pica, Kanagy, & Falodun, 1993; Skehan, 1996), and many researchers are attempting to propose models that cover a range of, if not all, characteristics (Robinson, 2003). But this area is ready for significant progress and systematization of research findings, and we will have to await developments.

Perhaps linked to this is the disagreement on how attention functions in task use. Skehan (1998) advocates a limited capacity system such that the limitations in capacity and consequent need to establish processing priorities pervades all aspects of task performance. Robinson (2001, 2003) proposes a much less constrained functioning for attention, and so is able to claim that functional task demands will push performance so that more difficult tasks lead to greater complexity of language *and accuracy*. If we are to design tasks effectively, resolution of this disagreement is important, because it will clarify whether one chooses more complex tasks to drive forward language development (Robinson), or uses less complex tasks (and task conditions) to nurture particular aspects of performance less ambitiously but more realistically (Skehan). In the former case, acquisition will be pushed by the task, "dragging" more complex language and a need for accuracy, while in the latter, there is a version of the proceduralization argument at work: restructuring, nurtured into greater control for accuracy, develops into greater control in real-time performance and fluency.

A final controversy links the effects of planning to the development of accuracy. We have seen that research into pre-task planning consistently shows complexity and fluency effects, but inconsistency with respect to accuracy. In addition, some researchers (Yuan and Ellis, 2003; Ortega, 1999; Wendel, 1997) advocate the use of on-line planning as a basis for higher accuracy. Given that accuracy is an important aspect of language acquisition, this is an important area of dispute. A clear factor here is that our understanding of the details of the effects of planning on second language performance are very limited. One hopes that additional research, possibly using more qualitative research techniques, may uncover the conditions which produce accuracy effects for pre-task planning, and also clarify what is involved in on-line planning, i.e. how learners can be helped to create attentional space while completing a task.

FUTURE DIRECTIONS

The issues covered in the previous section (models of task characteristics, understanding attentional functioning and planning) are areas where progress would be welcome, and so they are also relevant to this section on future directions. However three additional areas will be covered here where findings are currently rudimentary, but which have promise.

First, there is a strong need for more longitudinal research. This is a common call at this point in a review of an area, but no less important as a result. Most of the research into tasks, from whichever paradigm, is cross-sectional and interprets research results for their implications for development. These are clearly interpretations, and so we urgently need research with a longer timescale that probes directly whether the effects that can be produced in the short-term have implications for acquisition over time. Inferences in this area are not enough.

Second, and as a development of this, there is an urgent need to relate task-based research to pedagogic situations. Tasks and what has been learned about the ways tasks can be implemented need to be made teacher-friendly. But beyond that, task research needs to be conducted within pedagogic contexts, to establish whether or not the research findings have relevance for classroom reality. Within this, it is clear, especially when one is considering focused tasks, that we need to make progress in understanding what the role of the teacher can most effectively be, as well as how relevant insights on tasks can be incorporated into teacher training. Most ambitiously of all, it will be interesting to see if current initiatives incorporating tasks into textbooks (Cunningham & Moor, 1999; Kay & Jones, 2001; Willis & Willis, 1988) are maintained and are successful as judged by the most demanding and influential criterion of all: publisher sales.

Finally, there is scope to relate tasks to assessment, and indeed, if this is not done, it is likely that tasks will remain a minority interest, used only in favorable teaching circumstances. In other words, unless a communicative approach to language teaching is "validated" by the use of tasks in public and international assessment, it is unlikely that they will have much impact upon language teaching worldwide. And for this to be achievable, we need more research into the effects of task characteristics upon test performance, and into any changes in task conditions that might also influence test scores (Skehan, 2001). There is also likely to be potential in relating what can be learned about the dimensions of performance on tasks, specifically the relative independence of complexity (usually interpreted as *range* in a testing context), accuracy, and fluency, for rating scale use in a testing context. Potentially, task-based research could pose a considerable challenge to testing procedures. For this potential to be translated into reality, significant research needs to be done.

REFERENCES

Abbs, B., & Freebairn, I. (1977). *Starting strategies*. London: Longman.
Abbs, B., & Freebairn, I. (1981). *Developing strategies*. London: Longman.
Aston, G. (1986). Trouble-shooting in interaction with learners: The more the merrier? *Applied Linguistics, 7*, 128–143.
Blundell, L., & Stokes, J. (1982). *Task listening*. Cambridge: Cambridge University Press.
Brown, G., Anderson, A., Shilcock, R., & Yule, G. (1984). *Teaching talk: Strategies for production and assessment*. Cambridge: Cambridge University Press.
Bruton, A. (2002). From tasking purposes to purposing tasks. *English Language Teaching Journal, 56*(3), 280–288.
Bygate, M. (1996). Effects of task repetition: Appraising the developing language of learners. In J. Willis & D. Willis (Eds.), *Challenge and Change in Language Teaching* (pp. 136–146). London: Heinemann.
Bygate, M. (1999). Task as context for the framing, reframing, and unframing of language. *System, 27*, 33–48.
Bygate, M. (2001). Effects of task repetition on the structure and control of oral language. In Bygate, M., Skehan, P., & Swain, M. (2001). (Eds.). *Researching pedagogic tasks: Second language learning, teaching, and testing* (pp. 23–48). London: Longman.
Bygate, M., Skehan, P., & Swain, M. (2001). (Eds.). *Researching pedagogic tasks: Second language learning, teaching, and testing*. London: Longman.
Chomsky, N. (1965). *Aspects of the theory of syntax*. Cambridge, Mass.: MIT Press.
Cook, G. (2000). *Language play, language learning*. Oxford: Oxford University Press.
Coughlan, P., & Duff, P. (1994). Same task, different activities: Analysis of a second language acquisition task from an activity theory perspective. In J. Lantolf & G. Appel (Eds.), *Vygotskian approaches to second language research* (pp. 173–193). Norwood, NJ: Ablex.
Crookes, G. (1989). Planning and interlanguage variation. *Studies in Second Language Acquisition, 11*, 367–383.
Cunningham, S., & Moor, P. (1999). *Cutting edge*. London: Longman.
Doughty C., & Pica, T. (1986). 'Information gap' tasks: Do they facilitate second language acquisition. *TESOL Quarterly, 20*, 305–325.
Doughty, C., & Varela, E. (1998). Communicative focus on form. In Doughty, C. & Williams, J. (Eds.). *Focus on form in classroom second language acquisition* (pp. 114–138). Cambridge: Cambridge University Press.
Doughty, C., & Williams, J. (1998a). *Focus on form in classroom second language acquisition*. Cambridge: Cambridge University Press.
Doughty, C., & Williams, J. (1998b). Pedagogic choices in focus on form. In C. Doughty & J. Williams (Eds.), In Doughty, C. & Williams, J. (Eds.). *Focus on form in classroom second language acquisition* (pp. 197–262). Cambridge: Cambridge University Press.
Duff, P. (1986). Another look at interlanguage talk: Taking task to task. In R. Day (Ed.), *Talking to learn*. Rowley, Mass.: Newbury House.
Duff, P. (1993). Tasks and interlanguage performance: An SLA perspective. In G. Crookes & S. Gass (Eds.), *Tasks and language learning: Integrating theory and practice* (pp. 57–95). Clevedon, Avon: Multilingual Matters.
Dulay, M., & Burt, H. (1974). Natural sequences in child second language acquisition. *TESOL Quarterly, 24*, 37–53.
Ellis, R. (1985). *Understanding second language acquisition*. Oxford: Oxford University Press.
Ellis, R. (1987). Interlanguage variability in narrative discourse: Style shifting in the use of the past tense. *Studies in Second Language Acquisition, 9*, 12–20.
Ellis, R. (2001). Non-reciprocal tasks, comprehension, and second language acquisition. In Bygate, M., Skehan, P., & Swain, M. (Eds.). *Researching pedagogic tasks: Second language learning, teaching, and testing*. London: Longman.
Ellis, R. (2003). *Task-based language learning and teaching*. Oxford: Oxford University Press.
Firth, A., & Wagner, J. (1997). On discourse, communication, and (some) fundamental concepts in SLA research. *Modern Language Journal, 81*(3), 285–300.
Foster, P. (1998). A classroom perspective on the negotiation of meaning. *Applied Linguistics, 19*(1), 1–23.
Foster, P., & Skehan, P. (1996). The influence of planning on performance in task-based learning. *Studies in Second Language Acquisition, 18*(3), 299–324.
Foster, P., & Skehan, P. (1999). The effect of source of planning and focus of planning on task-based performance. *Language Teaching Research, 3*(3), 185–214.

Fotos, S. (1994). Integrating grammar instruction and communicative language use through grammar consciousness-raising tasks. *TESOL Quarterly, 28*(2), 323–351.

Fotos, S., & Ellis, R. (1991). Communicating about grammar: A task-based approach. *TESOL Quarterly, 25,* 605–628.

Gass, S. (2002). Interactionist perspectives in second language acquisition. In R. Kaplan (Ed.), *Handbook of applied linguistics* (pp. 170–181). Oxford: Oxford University Press.

Geddes, M., & Sturtridge, G. (1982). *Reading links.* London: Heinemann.

Halliday, M. (1978). *Language as a social semiotic.* London: Arnold.

Harley, B., & Swain, M. (1984). The interlanguage of immersion students and its implications for second language teaching. In A. Davies, C. Criper, & A. Howatt (Eds.), *Interlanguage* (pp. 291–311). Edinburgh: Edinburgh University Press.

Kay, S., & Jones, V. (2001). *Inside out.* London: Heinemann.

Krashen, S. (1985). *The input hypothesis.* London: Longman.

Lantolf, J. (2000). *Sociocultural theory and second language learning.* Oxford: Oxford University Press.

Long, M. (1983). Native speaker/non-native speaker conversation and the negotiation of comprehensible input. *Applied Linguistics, 4*(2), 126–141.

Long, M. (1985). A role for instruction in second language acquisition: Task-based language training. In K. Hyltenstam & M. Pienemann (Eds.), *Modelling and assessing second language acquisition* (pp. 77–100). Clevedon, Avon: Multilingual Matters.

Long, M. (1989). Task, group, and task-group interaction. *University of Hawaii Working Papers in English as a Second Language, 8*(2), 1–26.

Long, M. (1991). Focus on form: A design feature in language teaching methodology. In K. De Bot, R. Ginsbert, & C. Kramsch (Eds.), *Foreign language research in cross-cultural perspective* (pp. 39–52). Amsterdam: John Benjamins.

Long, M., & Robinson, P. (1998). Focus on form: Theory, research, and practice. In C. Doughty & J. Williams (Eds.), *Focus on form in classroom SLA* (pp. 15–41). Cambridge: CUP.

Loschky, L., & Bley-Vroman, R. (1993). Grammar and task-based methodology. In G. Crookes & S. M. Gass (Eds.), *Tasks and language learning: Integrating theory and practice* (pp. 123–167). Clevedon, UK: Multilingual Matters.

Lyster, R. (1998). Recasts, repetition, and ambiguity in L2 classroom discourse. *Studies in Second Language Acquisition, 20,* 51–81.

Lyster, R., & Ranta, L. (1997). Corrective feedback and learner uptake: Negotiation of form in communicative classrooms. *Studies in Second Language Acquisition, 19*(1), 37–66.

Mackey, A., Gass, S., & McDonough, K. (2000). Do learners recognize implicit negative feedback as feedback? *Studies in Second Language Acquisition, 22*(4), 471–497.

Mehnert, U. (1998). The effects of different lengths of time for planning on second language performance. *Studies in Second Language Acquisition, 20,* 83–108.

Nakahama, Y., Tyler, A., & Van Lier, L. (2001). Negotiation of meaning in conversational and information gap activities: A comparative discourse analysis. *TESOL Quarterly, 35*(3), 377–405.

Newton, J. (2001). Options for vocabulary learning through communication tasks. *English Language Teaching Journal, 55*(1), 30–37.

Nicholas, H., Lightbown, P., & Spada, N. (2001). Recasts as feedback to language learners. *Language Learning, 51*(4), 719–758.

Ortega, L. (1999). Planning and focus on form in L2 oral performance. *Studies in Second Language Acquisition, 21,* 109–148.

Pica, T. (1994). Research on negotiation: What does it reveal about second language learning, conditions, processes, outcomes? *Language Learning, 44,* 493–527.

Pica, T., Kanagy, R., & Falodun, J. (1993). Choosing and using communicative tasks for second language instruction. In G. Crookes & S. M. Gass (Eds.), *Tasks and language learning: Integrating theory and practice* (pp. 9–34). Clevedon, UK: Multilingual Matters.

Pinker, S. (1994). *The language instinct.* London: Penguin.

Robinson, P. (2001). Task complexity, cognitive load, and syllabus design. In Robinson P. (Ed.), *Cognition and second language instruction* (pp. 287–318). Cambridge: Cambridge University Press.

Robinson, P. (2003). Attention and memory during SLA. In C. Doughty & M. Long (Eds.), *Handbook of second language acquisition* (pp. 631–678). Oxford: Blackwell.

Samuda, V. (2001). Guiding relationships between form and meaning during task performance: The role of the teacher. In Bygate, M., Skehan, P., & Swain, M. (Eds.). *Researching pedagogic tasks: Second language learning, teaching, and testing* (pp. 119–140). London: Longman.

Seedhouse, P. (1997). Combining form and meaning. *English Language Teaching Journal, 51*(4), 336–344.

Seedhouse, P. (1999). Task-based interaction. *English Language Teaching Journal, 53*(3), 149–156.
Skehan, P. (1996). A framework for the implementation of task based instruction. *Applied Linguistics, 17*(1), 38–62.
Skehan, P. (1998). *A cognitive approach to language learning*. Oxford: Oxford University Press.
Skehan, P. (2001). Tasks and language performance assessment. In M. Bygate, P. Skehan, & M. Swain (Eds.), *Researching pedagogic tasks* (pp. 167–185). London: Longman.
Skehan, P. (2003). Task based instruction. *Language Teaching, 36*(1), 1–14.
Skehan, P., & Foster, P. (1997). The influence of planning and post-task activities on accuracy and complexity in task based learning. *Language Teaching Research, 1*(3).
Skehan, P., & Foster, P. (1999). The influence of task structure and processing conditions on narrative retellings. *Language Learning, 49*(1), 93–120.
Skehan, P., & Foster, P. (1998, March). *The effects of post-task activities on the accuracy of language during task performance*. Paper presented at AAAL Conference, Seattle, WA.
Swain, M. (1995). Three functions of output in second language learning. In Cook, G. & Seidlhofer, B. (Eds.), *Principle and practice in applied linguistics* (pp. 245–256). Oxford: Oxford University Press.
Swain, M., & Lapkin, S. (1982). *Evaluating bilingual education: A Canadian case study*. Clevedon, Avon: Multilingual Matters.
Swain, M., & Lapkin, S. (2001). Focus on form through collaborative dialogue: Exploring task effects. In Bygate, M., Skehan, P., & Swain, M. (Eds.). *Researching pedagogic tasks: Second language learning, teaching, and testing* (pp. 99–118). London: Longman.
Trahey, M., & White, L. (1993). Positive evidence in the second language classroom. *Studies in Second Language Acquisition, 15*(2), 181–204.
Van Lier, L., & Matsuo, N. (2000). Varieties of conversational experience: Looking for learning opportunities. *Applied Language Learning, 11*(2), 265–287.
Van Patten, B. (1996). *Input processing and grammar instruction*. New York: Ablex.
Van Patten, B. (2002). Processing instruction: An update *Language Learning, 52*(4), 755–803.
Wendel, J. (1997). *Planning and second language narrative production*. Unpublished doctoral dissertation. Temple University, Japan.
White, R. (1988). *The ELT curriculum*. Oxford: Blackwell.
Widdowson, H. G. (1978). *Teaching language as communication*. Oxford: Oxford University Press.
Wigglesworth, J. (1997). An investigation of planning time and proficiency level on oral test discourse. *Language Testing, 14*(1), 85–106.
Wigglesworth, J. (2001). Influences on performance in task-based oral assessments. In Bygate, M., Skehan, P., & Swain, M. (Eds.). *Researching pedagogic tasks: Second language learning, teaching, and testing* (pp. 186–209). London: Longman.
Willis, J. (1996). *A framework for task-based learning*. London: Longman.
Willis, J., & Willis, D. (1988). *The Cobuild course: Book 1*. London: Collins.
Yuan, Y., & Ellis, R. (2003). The effects of pre-task planning and on-line planning on fluency, complexity, and accuracy in L2 monologic oral performance. *Applied Linguistics, 24*(1), 1–29.

CHAPTER 20

KNOWLEDGE STRUCTURES IN SOCIAL PRACTICES

BERNARD A. MOHAN

The University of British Columbia, Canada

ABSTRACT

To address the issue of education systems that are increasingly multilingual and multicultural, we must look beyond the acquisition of the second language (L2) system and consider education as language socialization into social practices. This chapter models social practices as frameworks of knowledge structures that link cultural meanings of the practice to meanings in discourse. The model is situated within systemic functional linguistics and focuses on field (or popularly, *content*) of discourse, showing typical relations between meanings of knowledge structures and language form, the role of atypical or metaphorical relations in constructing advanced knowledge, and how graphics and nonlinguistic media generally can be interpreted as knowledge structures. Some educational implications addressed in the chapter include integrated approaches to language and content, the connection of language and content standards in education, bridges between learners' languages and cultures, and links to strategies for comprehension in reading and discourse awareness in writing. Current concerns include failures of language assessment to deal adequately with the linguistic construction of content in discourse. Future directions include discourse research strategies to support the potential convergence of multimodal literacy, critical thinking skills, and computer technologies; and connections with metaphor and 'the body,' and with critical linguistics.

INTRODUCTION

As urban education throughout the world becomes increasingly multilingual and multicultural, we must look beyond the individual learning the language system of English and consider language as a medium of learning, the coordination of language learning and content learning, learning through multiple media, language socialization as the learning of language and culture, the relation between the learners' languages and cultures, learning by the social group and institution and discourse in the context of social practice. Education is the language socialization of learners into the social practices of communities. This chapter will discuss a model of social practice as a framework of knowledge structures, showing how knowledge structures are a link between cultural meanings in social practices and features of language and discourse.

SOCIAL PRACTICE, KNOWLEDGE STRUCTURES, AND FORM-MEANING RELATIONS

A *social practice* is a unit of culture that involves cultural knowledge and cultural action in a theory/practice, reflection/action relation. *Knowledge structures* (KSs) are semantic patterns of the discourse, knowledge, actions, artifacts, and environment of a social practice (Spradley, 1980, p. 93). Examples of various knowledge structures in discourse, such as *description, classification, sequence, principles, choice* and *evaluation* are shown in Figure 1 below.

Description:
(1) Mother: What cars have you got there?
(2) Stephen (about 2:6 years) *There's a fire engine one with a ladder on.*

Classification (taxonomy):
(1) Stephen (about 3:6), examining animal jigsaw puzzle pieces: There isn't a fox and there isn't – *is a platypus an animal?*
(2) Mother: Yes.
(Halliday & Matthiessen, 1999, p. 74)

Sequence:
(1) Nigel (2:11) thinking about 'The House that Jack Built': *Does the rat go when the cat has killed it?*
(2) Father: No, *it doesn't go anymore then.*
Principles:
(3) Nigel: *Why did the cat kill the rat?*
(4) Father: *Cats do kill rats.*

Talking about *choice* (e.g., to eat the grape or not) and *evaluation* (e.g., food preferences of cats)
(1) Nigel (3:2): *Will the cat eat the grape?*
(2) Father: I don't think so. *Cats like things that go, not things that grow.*
(Halliday & Matthiessen, 1999, p. 78)

Enacting *choice* (e.g., to lie down to sleep or not) and *evaluation* (e.g., bad behavior)
In this "pretend" play, the boy is the parent telling the baby to sleep and the girl is the "bad" baby who chooses to refuse.
(1) Boy (2:9): *Put your head down.* (sternly)
(2) Girl (3:3): *No.*
(3) Boy: *Yes.*
(4) Girl: *No.*
(5) Boy: Yes. OK. I will spank you. *Bad* boy. (spanks her)
(6) Girl: *My head's up* (giggles). I want my teddy bear (petulant voice).
(Garvey, 1977, p. 84)

Figure 1. Knowledge Structures in Discourse

A typical unit of work in schools shows the integration of social practices and knowledge structures (KSs) in a systematic way. For example, consider the high school ESL social studies class studying the following news item (Mohan, Leung, & Davison, 2001): "Quebeckers are taking part in what is perhaps the most momentous vote in the country's history….Prime Minister Chretien and his wife Aline cast their ballots in their home town of Shawinigan" (p. 111). By reflection on the action of voting, the class is being socialized into the social practice of voting in Canada, and its political context. They learn about ballots and also about cultural artifacts like ballot boxes and voting booths. They come to understand that the description of Mr. Chretien, as *Prime Minister,* classifies him as a politician and a member of the party in power. They note that the sequential procedure of voting is designed to conform to the principle of a secret ballot. They learn how the choice of vote in this case is related to the values surrounding federalism or separatism. Throughout their education, learners engage with many kinds of social practices, but it is only relatively recently that researchers have begun to study reading and writing as social practices (e.g., Barton, 1994; Gee, 2002).

Knowledge structures in social practices are situated within a *systemic functional linguistics (SFL)* approach to language, which views discourse in sociocultural context, learning as a linguistic process, and language learning as language socialization. SFL is oriented to the description of language as *a resource for meaning* rather than as a system of rules (see Halliday & Martin, 1993). Learners are seen as expanding their resources for meaning, their meaning potential, rather than making a transition from errors in rules to the correct form of rules. This has major implications for language assessment as will be discussed later in the chapter.

Halliday (1994) offers a model of discourse to characterize the relations between *text* (discourse) and *context*. A text relates to its context through *field*, the subject matter of the text or the social practice that is taking place at the time; through *tenor*, the social relationships that hold among the various participants in the interaction; and through *mode*, the role of language in the interaction. These three aspects—field, tenor, and mode—are realized in three corresponding types of meaning: *ideational*, which represents experience, i.e. expresses content, the speaker's experience of the world; *interpersonal*, which enables interaction; and *textual*, which achieves coherence and connectedness in discourse.

The chapter will focus on field (see Hasan, 1999) though without excluding mode and tenor. Halliday and Matthiessen (1999) note that many texts have two fields: subject matter and social activity. In the news item text, the teacher is instructing the class about voting in Canadian politics. The subject matter of the text (the *second order field*) is voting in Canadian politics and the social activity (the *first order field*) is classroom instruction. Both fields contain KSs, but in the first order field, they are enacted rather than discussed e.g., the teacher both discusses choices (voting) and makes (enacts) choices (e.g., which student to question).

There are major differences between field and genre. Field groups texts by topic/social practice; genre groups texts by type. As Martin (1997, pp. 12-13) notes, with a field approach, for instance, instructions for an experiment are grouped with doing the experiment, the recount of the experiment, and the explanation the experiment illustrates. With a genre perspective, by contrast, the instructions are grouped with similar procedural texts with closely related *texture* (i.e. a sequence of commands, etc.) dealing with any topic. Of course, the science learner relating the explanation of an experiment to the procedure for doing the experiment must not only group texts by field but must also build scientific understanding by fitting the meaning of these texts together (Mintzes et al., 1998). Similarly the researcher in field must explain how a learner can construct a model of a topic or social practice from its texts. How do learners relate explanations of scientific principles to the steps of an experiment? Other field/genre contrasts include: field accounts for KSs, while genre accounts for the unfolding of text; anthropologists use the KSs of field for cross-cultural comparison (Werner & Schoepfle, 1987), whereas genres are typically local to a culture.

The way that various knowledge structures can be related to social practices using SFL theory is illustrated in Table 1. This heuristic framework, presented in full in Mohan (1986), describes six core KSs of typical social practices, including at a general level *classification*, *principles*, and *values*, and at a specific level, *description*, *sequence*, and *choice*.

Table 1. Form-Meaning Relations in the Field of a Social Practice

Classification	Principles (e.g., norms, cause-effect, means-end)	Evaluation
Generic reference	Generic reference	Generic reference
Being process	Doing process	Sensing process
Additive conjunction	Consequential conjunction	Comparative conjunction
Taxonomy lexis	Consequence lexis	Evaluation lexis
Specific reference	Specific reference	Specific reference
Being process	Doing process	Sensing process
Additive conjunction	Temporal Conjunction	Alternative conjunction
Attribution lexis	Sequence lexis	Alternative/Choice lexis
Description	Sequence	Choice

Drawing on the four systems of English reference, transitivity, conjunction, and lexis (Halliday, 1994; Martin, 1992), the two rows (description vs. classification, sequence vs. principles, and choice vs. evaluation) in the framework in Table 1 are distinguished by the contrast between specific reference and generic reference (e.g., *the cat, the rat* vs. *cats, rats*). The three columns (description and classification vs. sequence and principles vs. choice and evaluation) are distinguished by the contrast in transitivity of the three main process types of Halliday: processes of being (*Is* a platypus animal?); doing (Does the rat *go*?); and sensing (the mental world of consciousness), including processes of liking and wanting (Cats *like* things, I *want* my teddy bear). The types of conjunction (e.g., additive: *And* is a seal...?, temporal: *when* the cat has killed it) are based on Martin (1992) but separate out the subclass of alternation, *either...or* (p. 205).

The lexical categories of the framework in Table 1 are inspired by Martin (1992), for example, taxonomy lexis in "Is a *platypus* an *animal*?" Listeners and readers use these categories to understand a text as a cohesive whole. Martin grounds his lexical categories explicitly on field and particularly on his notion of field as sets of activity sequences oriented to some global institutional purpose. This gives rise to the following categories that he illustrates for the field of tennis: taxonomy—part-whole relations among *game-set match*; configuration—agent-process-medium structure, *player-serve-ball*; activity sequence—*player serve - opponent return - player volley*. Our model of social practice leads to additional categories (again illustrated for tennis): attribution—numerative-thing structure, *second serve*; consequence—*let - replay*; evaluation—*foot-fault*; alternative or choice—*server/receiver*. In tennis, umpire or referee judgments reflect the institutional order underlying the social activity; they judge foot-faults and lets, call for replays, and monitor the selection of server and receiver roles.

Many of the categories and language systems of the first two columns of the framework in Table 1 are fairly standard in systemic functional studies of text and have been written about extensively. The third column, the field KSs of evaluation and choice, is not standard, but rather is argued for here and therefore requires further explanation. This column is associated with the mental processes of sensing as analyzed by Halliday and Matthiessen (1999, p. 139): desire (wanting, needing, etc.), cognition (thinking, knowing, understanding), emotion (liking, fearing), and perception (seeing, hearing, etc.). It is these processes that provide the dynamic link between social practice and human needs and interests. Choice is particularly related to desire and cognition: Desire includes planning, intending, and deciding, and both desire and cognition (unlike emotion and perception) can creatively project ideas into existence and can thus explore possible futures. It must be pointed out, though, that sensing is not limited to choice and evaluation but deals with a much wider area.

Evaluation and choice relate in a complex way to ideational and interpersonal meaning. The framework relates evaluation and choice to field and ideational meaning in a number of ways, for example, through transitivity. However, when evaluation and choice are enacted between speaker and addressee, as in the final example in Figure 1, systemicists usually analyze them in terms of interpersonal meaning. The same issue arises in relation to the considerable recent body of work on evaluative discourse that generally relates it to the interpersonal rather than the ideational (Martin, 2001).

GRAMMATICAL METAPHOR AND THE CONSTRUCTION OF ADVANCED KNOWLEDGE

The typical form-meaning relations shown in Table 1 are rendered more complex through the role of grammatical metaphor. *Grammatical metaphor* is defined by Halliday (1998) as a substitution of one grammatical class, or one grammatical structure, by another, such as *his departure* instead of *he departed*. Departure deviates from the typical or congruent pattern where processes are realized as verbs, participants as nouns, properties as adjectives, and logical relations as conjunctions. Grammatical metaphor is central to the construction of knowledge in the disciplines, it is central to written academic discourse, and it places major demands on the language resources of learners, amounting to a requirement for success in education (Halliday, 1998).

Halliday (1998) studied the register of scientific English, showing how it uses grammatical metaphor (specifically ideational metaphor) to reorganize commonsense experience and construct scientific knowledge. One benefit of grammatical metaphor is to create new classifications and technical taxonomies. For example, a process such as *move* is theorized about so that it becomes a theoretical abstraction, *motion*, and can be expanded into a taxonomy such as *linear motion, orbital motion, parabolic motion* (Halliday, p. 200). Another benefit is to create chains of reasoning from sequential processes related in time, that is, constructing a line of argument leading from one step to the next based on principles (e.g., cause-effect) as in this example from Newton's *Opticks* (1705/1952): "If the Humours of the Eye by old Age decay, so as by shrinking to make the Cornea and Coat of the Crystalline Humour grow flatter than before, the Light will not be refracted enough...This is the reason of the decay of sight in old Men" (pp. 15-16). In chains of reasoning, the causal relation, typically or congruently realized by a conjunction like *so*, may be lexicalized as a verb (eg., *cause, prove, result in*) or be nominalized (eg., *the cause, the proof, the result, the reason*).

Martin (cited in Halliday & Martin, 1993) applies this analysis of classification/taxonomy and causality to secondary school textbooks in science and history. He connects these with genres, showing how classification/taxonomy appears in the genre of descriptive report and how causality appears in the genre of explanation. He illustrates how classification and causality are central to both science and history, but shows that technical taxonomy plays a special role in science, whereas history uses relatively few technical terms, with the exception of terms for referring to periods of time, like the Middle Ages.

Veel (1997) provides an analysis of the main genres in secondary science textbooks. In addition he shows that texts work to construct certain kinds of meaning and argues that these texts construct an idealized knowledge path for students that apprentices them into the social practices of science. This knowledge path progresses from the genres related to *doing science* (procedure, procedural recount), to *organizing scientific information* (descriptive and taxonomic reports), to *explaining science* (sequential, causal, theoretical, factorial, consequential explanation and exploration), to *challenging science* (exposition and discussion that try to persuade a reader by presenting arguments for or against an issue). This progression shifts from the grammar of speaking to the grammar of writing, and an increasing use of grammatical metaphor. In part, it moves from specific sequences of events in specific places at specific times, to general sequences of events in timeless settings, to cause-effect sequences involving abstract phenomena.

Coffin (1997) maps a similar pathway that apprentices students into the written text types or genres of school history. The pathway moves from narrative genres to argument genres. There is a move from the past as story (with particular concrete events) through the genres of explanation to "constructing the past as argument" (p. 196). The pathway moves towards abstraction from mainly human participants to participants that are generic; from specific to general and from concrete to abstract. It moves from temporal links to causal links and the resources of appraisal for evaluation.

Viewing Veel (1997) and Coffin's (1997) results from a KS perspective, their evidence suggests that secondary textbooks in science or history construct a learning path for the student from the following KSs of their fields, roughly ordered (a) descriptions of the participants in the field (e.g., metals and other substances or people in historical context); (b) time sequences of events that include these participants (e.g., natural processes in science or historical processes in history); (c) classifications of the participants or processes in the field (creating taxonomies in science or abstractions in history); (d) causal patterns of conditions and consequences or chains of reasoning that explain or interpret events and processes; and (e) evaluations of such explanations or interpretations. Textbooks assume that the learner will create a model of the social practice from these elements.

KNOWLEDGE STRUCTURES AND MEANINGS IN MULTIMEDIA

Each of our groups of KSs has widely known graphic conventions for representing it, and these appear regularly in academic textbooks. Sequence has time lines and sequence charts; classification has trees and Venn diagrams, and so on. To explain these conventions we can extend our account of the linguistic construction of field or content meaning with the concept of *lines of meaning*. Longacre (1990, 1996) argues that different discourse types have different mainlines of development, or lines of meaning. In narrative discourse the line of meaning is a storyline. Similarly, in procedural discourse, the line of meaning is a line of procedure. Any adequate theory of discourse and literacy has to account for how writers/speakers construct lines of meaning and how readers/listeners interpret them. KSs can be viewed as lines of meaning.

When a reader draws a time sequence line to represent a story (e.g., about hiking, climbing, and then skiing), one can say, drawing on standard work in semantics, that the reader represents the sequence of events in the story in a graphic as a series of nodes of words connected with lines, where typically a node represents an event and a line represents the relation of time sequence:

$$\text{Hike}\longrightarrow\text{Climb}\longrightarrow\text{Ski}$$

In this way, the semantic relation of time sequence is represented in the story-line of the text and in the drawn line of the graphic.

A storyline is built using the resources outlined in Table 1 and grammatical metaphor; sequence features build the line of action, and description features build the setting. However, as Longacre shows, narrators elaborate on this basis, for example, backgrounding events and activities relative to the main storyline and creating secondary storylines, all of which are signaled linguistically, for example, by verbal aspect in English. At present, then, it is possible to account for many linguistic features of time sequence in storylines, but more research will be required to provide a fully adequate analysis. The same may be said for all KSs.

Storylines represent the time sequence of events that the story is about. They do not represent the unfolding of a story text, which is accounted for by a genre analysis of narrative. Martin (1999) makes a contrast between the text order of the story (*text time*) and the order of events of the story (*field time*). Literary techniques in narrative like flashback depend on this distinction between text time and field time, and readers must interpret linguistic signals to keep them distinct. All KSs are like storylines in the sense that they represent the semantic relations of field, not the unfolding of text, when the field is 'subject matter', not "social activity".

This approach to graphic representation, which applies to all of the KSs, has been widely used in linguistic semantics as a way of representing semantic relations, and its general theory is provided by graph theory in mathematics. In the form of transition networks, it has been used in SFL (e.g., Halliday & Martin, 1993; Halliday & Matthiessen, 1999). As a way of relating language to socio-semiotic systems such as the visual arts, music, and dance, and other forms of meaning-making behavior including charts, maps, diagrams, etc. (see Halliday & Matthiessen, p. 602ff.), it treats graphics as a complementary nonlinguistic resource that realizes linguistic meanings; and it differs from other approaches within SFL that treat socio-semiotic systems on the model of language, as if they had their own grammar and semantics (e.g., Kress & Van Leeuwen, 1996).

EDUCATIONAL IMPLICATIONS

The KS model outlined above was the basis for an integrated approach to language and content which was developed collaboratively across schools in Vancouver, Canada (for details, see Mohan, Leung, & Davison 2001). Ashworth (2001) describes the sociohistorical and policy context, Mohan (2001) explains the theory behind the approach, Tang (2001) gives detailed accounts of classroom action, and Early and Hooper (2001) document the implementation of two major project initiatives, particularly in staff development and teacher action, over a 10-year period in the schools. These initiatives required major and complex changes in the operation of schools, but nevertheless, three quarters of the teachers and over 90% of administrators and district staff rated the later project as moderately to very successful. Further contextual details are provided in a case study where Early (2001), contrasting two pairs of teachers in a project school, showed how teachers used the KS model in creatively different and reflective ways consistent with social constructivist principles.

KS analysis provides a model for the connection of language and content standards, which has been applied across the curriculum. As a result of the work of the international TESOL association in the area of ESL K-12 standards (particularly the goal for students to use English to achieve academically in all content areas), there have been increasing efforts to explore ways to engage English language learners with academic content learning and to connect ESL standards to subject matter content standards, so that English language learners can meet the grade-appropriate content standards in all areas of the curriculum (Center for Applied Linguistics, 2002; TESOL, 2005). In an examination of curriculum statements of core thinking skills for Grade 1-10 in Science and Social Studies in British Columbia, Early et al. (1986) demonstrated that most statements could be grouped under the six main KS categories, which therefore provided an important bridging role between language and content. In a later, more detailed study of curriculum goal statements, Mohan et al. (1994) showed a similar result and further showed that there was the potential to link common goals of subject areas such as classification and choice (decision-making) in science, social studies, mathematics, and language, so that learners could benefit from more integrated learning. More recently, extending the standards work of the New Jersey State Board of Education (2001), Huang (2002) has produced a KS analysis of New Jersey content standards that offers a promising base on which to build.

KSs offer vital bridges between languages and cultures in the globalizing educational environment. Tang (1997) has examined graphic literacy across languages and shown how certain KS graphics (e.g., the water cycle) occur in school textbooks across several languages and cultures and offer potential bridges to scaffold language development for bilinguals. Mohan and Huang (2002) describe a KS approach to the integration of language, content, and culture in Mandarin. Elementary school Anglophone students were enabled to discuss their daily lives in Mandarin, describing and classifying themselves, their classmates, and their families, and stating their everyday routines, and comparing their lives to that of a Chinese elementary student. An analysis of student writing illustrates how these KSs appear in the grammar and lexis of Mandarin discourse. For an account of the graphic scaffolding process of this course, see Huang (2003). In an account of academic discourse use in bilingual cooperative learning interactions of Mandarin-

English bilingual students, Liang and Mohan (2003) describe how students bilingually correlated their prior knowledge of classifications in their first language and culture with those in their second language and culture.

With respect to reading, the model encapsulates many text structure strategies that improve comprehension in the L1 and the L2, as noted by Grabe (1995; see also Grabe & Stoller, 2001). Grabe identifies two main strategy research strands: those that develop student awareness through graphic representations or graphic organizers, and those that develop student awareness of features of text. Because it addresses the links between graphics and features of text, the KS model suggests how these two research strands can be combined. In addition, KS research clarifies the difference between field relations and genre relations in text structure, and offers a way to relate prior knowledge (field 'in the mind') and the text (field 'in the text').

The KS model offers insights into field, mode, and tenor in writing. In our analysis of graphic representation of KSs, the graphic represents the semantic relations of field, not mode or tenor. Simply put, when someone reads such a graphic and writes about it, the graphic specifies the content but it leaves the writer free to construct text in a variety of ways. Mohan (1989) compared two students who were given a chart of the events of early European exploration and asked to write an essay about it. One was a grade 10 ESL student with limited education, a basic writer. The other was a native speaker university student, a skilled writer. Both writers covered essentially the same content, but they shaped it into discourse in very different ways: The native speaker used much richer resources to create the texture of the discourse—creating cohesion using lexical harmony—and showed much greater control of thematic development. Similar comparisons have been made by teachers guiding student peer discussions of their own writing.

CURRENT DEBATES AND DIRECTIONS

What kinds of discourse analysis are needed for research and assessment appropriate to the integration of language and content and the development of advanced literacy in L1 and L2 (see Pica, 2000; Short, 1993; TESOL, 2001)? Evidence points to a widespread and largely unrecognized failure to assess quality of linguistic construction of content meaning in discourse. How then can we research learning as a linguistic process?

The *TESOL Standards K-12* (TESOL 1997) point to the urgent need for language teachers and content teachers to collaborate to assess the work of ESL students in mainstream classes on an ongoing basis. Traditionally, a student essay may be assessed by the science teacher and by the language teacher in totally unrelated ways, despite the fact that the science teacher must interpret the content of the discourse to make the judgment. Mohan and Low (1995) and Low (1999) report on a study of teachers who engaged in collaborative assessment of student writing on such topics as the AIDS epidemic. Amid general difficulty, most of these teachers assumed a separation between the assessment of language and the assessment of content: "I mark language and content separately, equal marks for both, but sometimes I have trouble deciding which one to mark down when the ideas aren't clear." None were able to arrive at an integrative evaluation of how discourse constructed content.

Mohan and Huxur (2001) analyzed the grammatical scaffolding by teacher and L2 learner(s) of causal explanations that formed part of the work by a group of L2 students in a project on the human brain in a content-based language learning classroom. A 'focus on form' analysis of teacher recasts of learner errors in grammatical form was originally proposed, but this failed to address the issues of content in discourse raised by this approach to language learning. Mohan and Huxur showed how a functional analysis reveals quite different aspects of the recast sequences of these data than does a more focus on form approach: Teacher and students actively scaffolded and reconstructed explanations as more adequate academic discourse and specifically as KSs of ideational meaning.

Mohan and Slater (2005) examined the evaluation of two written causal explanations of the watercycle: one of which constructed a temporal sequence only, the other of which constructed an explicitly causal chain whose superior quality was demonstrated using Halliday's analysis of causal language in science and Halliday's notion of language as a resource for meaning rather than as a system of rules that determine correctness. One group of evaluators evaluated the explanations using a protocol based on Canale and Swain's model of communicative competence, and a second group of evaluators used the protocol of the *Test of Written English* (TWE). Both groups intuitively recognized the explicitly causal explanation as superior, but both groups rated the explanations as similar based on their protocols because they had the same number of errors. Both protocols assume a view of language as rules of correctness and are unable to account for text differences related to language as a resource for making meaning. In other words, standard approaches to the assessment of discourse recognize error but are unable to recognize differences in the quality of linguistic construction of content meaning in discourse.

The difficulties in assessing the quality of the discoursal construction of content are conceptual not practical. Mohan (1998) studied *Oral Proficiency Interview* (OPI) assessment and showed the natural presence of KSs in the interview interaction. The OPI interview was designed to elicit grammatical structures, but in order to do so, the interviewer elicited content information from the interviewee about familiar topics, and this information tended to fall into KS patterns. Thus the interviewer led the interviewees to talk about sequences such as their daily and weekly schedule, how to cook a meal, to make comparisons between China and Canada, and to explain the principles of football. Of course, the OPI does not analyze these KSs, but Mohan showed that such interviews can and should analyze them, for they influence the discourse of the interviewee.

Perhaps the most immediate directions of interest for KS analysis concern the new multimodal literacies, critical thinking skills, and computers. A KS perspective provides a discoursal link between these areas to support future convergence.

Interest in multimodality, for instance, the role of graphic organizers, has increased enormously with the development of the Internet as a web search for the phrase will show, though the quality of information is highly variable. Bibliographies on graphic organizers in elementary schools and secondary schools are available from the ERIC Clearinghouse (see eric.indiana/www/indexbd.html). Information for K-12 teachers can be accessed at the websites of a number of school boards in North America and elsewhere (e.g., www.broward.k12.fl.us). An informative website is www.graphic.org that, along with much else, provides a link to commercial software for creating graphic organizers such as *Inspiration*. A useful overview of graphic organizers is offered by Hyerle (1996). Hyerle emphasizes the constructivist role of learners using graphics to organize and communicate about their knowledge, fundamental patterns of thinking, and a common visual language where different patterns of thinking are consistently represented in corresponding graphic primitives. Hyerle's list of basic graphic elements (Hyerle, pp. 98, 101) includes most of the KSs above, as do a number of other writers. Related work on thinking is offered by Costa (2001). Similarly, Swartz and Parks (1994) approach classification, for instance, as thinking skills. The connection between graphics, critical thinking, and understanding science is illustrated by the work of Novak (1999). This can be extended to computer use. Jonassen (1999) argues for those computer-based technologies and programs that go beyond superficial computer use and use more generic applications (e.g., of databases and spreadsheets) that foster and facilitate critical thinking of the topic under study. Databases, for example, are programs that organize descriptions into classifications and present the results graphically. All of these strands can be brought together in a powerful convergence. For example, Hooper (1996) describes how ESL students in a biology class created and discussed a computer database of mammals and illustrates a KS analysis of their descriptions, classifications, and definitions. Thus for researchers, a KS analysis offers a discourse approach that integrates these strands; for language educators, it provides support for the coherent development of the potential of the new media.

Other future directions include how KS analysis can be extended in relation to the work of Lakoff and Johnson (1999) on how metaphor coherently structures experience and how bodily experience gives rise to container and path schemas that underlie our notions of classification and sequence; and how KS analysis can be applied in critical linguistics (see, for instance, the discussion of classification in Hodge & Kress, 1993; and the example of racist classification in Van Dijk, 1991).

CONCLUSIONS

This analysis of the broad range of research in the field shows the way in which a model of social practices as frameworks of knowledge structures connects with an SFL analysis of discourse, supports theory-based assessment of the integration of language and content, and includes discourse research strategies that illuminate the potential convergences of multimodal literacies, critical thinking and computer resources. Such a framework has also proved very useful for curriculum development and evaluation and for teaching at all levels of education.

REFERENCES

Ashworth, M. (2001). ESL in British Columbia. In B. Mohan, C. Leung, & C. Davison (Eds.), *English as a second language in the mainstream* (pp. 93–106). Harlow, Essex: Pearson Education.

Barton, D. (1994). *Literacy*. Oxford: Blackwell.

Center For Applied Linguistics. (2002). *ESL Standards for Pre-K-12 Students*. Retrieved 2 September, 2005, from www.cal.org/eslstandards/.

Coffin, C. (1997). Constructing and giving value to the past. In F. Christie & J. Martin (Eds.), *Genre and institutions* (pp. 196–230). London: Continuum.

Costa, A. (Ed.). (2001). *Developing minds: A resource book for teaching thinking* (3rd ed.). Alexandria, Virginia: Association for Supervision and Curriculum Development.

Early, M. (2001). Language and content in social practice: A case study. *Canadian Modern Language Review, 58*(1), 156–179.

Early, M., & Hooper, H. (2001). Implementation of the Vancouver School Board's ESL Initiatives. In B. Mohan, C. Leung, & C. Davison (Eds.), *English as a second language in the mainstream*. (pp. 138–150). Harlow: Pearson Education.

Early, M., Thew, C., & Wakefield, P. (1986). *English as a second language, K-12: Resource book* (Vol. 1). Victoria, B.C. Ministry of Education, British Columbia.

Gee, J. (2002). Literacies, identities and discourses. In M. Schleppegrell & C. Colombi (Eds.), *Developing advanced literacy in first and second languages* (pp. 159–176). New Jersey: Mahwah, NJ: Erlbaum.
Garvey, C. (1977). *Play*. Cambridge, MA: Harvard U.P.
Grabe, W. (1995). Discourse analysis and reading instruction. *The Journal of TESOL France, 1*, 5–20.
Grabe, W., & Stoller F. (2001). *Researching and teaching reading*. New York: Longman.
Halliday, M. (1994). *An introduction to functional grammar* (2nd ed.). London: Edward Arnold.
Halliday, M. (1998). Things and relations: Regrammaticising experience as technical knowledge. In J. Martin & R. Veel (Eds.), *Reading science* (pp. 185–235). London: Routledge.
Halliday, M., & Martin, J. (1993). *Writing science: Literacy and discursive power*. Washington D.C.: The Falmer Press.
Halliday, M., & Matthiessen, C. (1999). *Construing experience through meaning*. London: Cassell.
Hasan, R. (1999). Speaking with reference to context. In M. Ghadessy, (Ed.), *Text and context in functional linguistics* (pp. 219–328). Amsterdam: Benjamins.
Hodge, R., & Kress, G. (1993). *Language as ideology*. (2nd ed.). London: Routledge.
Hooper, H. (1996). Mainstream science with a majority of ESL learners. In J. Clegg (Ed.), *Mainstreaming ESL: Case studies in integrating ESL students into the mainstream classroom* (pp. 217–236). Clevedon, UK: Multilingual Matters.
Huang, J. (2002). *Academic literacy skills and ESL students in regular classrooms: What are content area teachers facing when implementing curriculum content standards?* International Journal of Learning, 9.
Huang, J. (2003). Activities as a vehicle for linguistic and sociocultural knowledge at the elementary level. *Language Teaching Research, 7*(1), 3–33.
Hyerle, D. (1996). *Visual tools for constructing knowledge*. Alexandria, VA.: Association for Supervision and Curriculum Development.
Jonassen, D. (1999). *Computers as mindtools for schools: Engaging critical thinking* (2nd ed.). New York: Prentice Hall.
Kress, G., & Van Leeuwen, T. (1996). *Reading images: The grammar of visual design*. London: Routledge.
Lakoff, G., & Johnson, M. (1999). *Philosophy in the flesh*. New York: Basic Books.
Liang, X., &. Mohan, B. (2003). Dilemmas of cooperative learning and academic proficiency in two languages. *Journal of English for Academic Purposes, 2*(1), 35–51.
Longacre, R. (1990). *Storyline concerns*. Los Angeles: UCLA Dept. of Linguistics.
Longacre, R. (1996). *The grammar of discourse*. (2nd ed.). New York and London: Plenum Press.
Low, M. (1999). *Difficulties' of integrative evaluation practices: Instances of language and content as/in contested spaces*. Unpublished doctoral dissertation, University of British Columbia, Vancouver, B.C., Canada.
Martin, J. (1992). *English Text: System and structure*. Amsterdam: Benjamins.
Martin J. (1997). Analysing genre: Functional parameters. In F. Christie & J. Martin (Eds.), *Genre and institutions: Social processes in the workplace and school*. (pp. 3–39). London: Continuum.
Martin J. (1999). Modelling context. In M. Ghadessy (Ed.), *Text and context in functional linguistics* (pp. 25–62). Amsterdam: Benjamins.
Martin J. (2001). Beyond exchange: Appraisal systems in English. In S. Hunston & G. Thompson (Eds.), *Evaluation in text* (pp. 142–175). Oxford: Oxford U.P.
Mintzes, J., Wandersee J., & Novak J. (Eds.). (1998). *Teaching science for understanding*. San Diego: Academic Press.
Mohan, B. (1986). *Language and content*. Reading, MA: Addison-Wesley.
Mohan, B. (1989). Knowledge structures and academic discourse. *Word, 40*(1–2), 89–105.
Mohan, B. (1998). Knowledge structures and oral interviews of international teaching assistants. In A. He & R. Young (Eds.), *Talking and testing: Discourse approaches to the assessment of oral proficiency* (pp. 173–204). Hillsdale, N.J.: Erlbaum.
Mohan, B. (2001). The second language as a medium of learning. In B. Mohan, C. Leung & C. Davison (Eds.), *English as a second language in the mainstream* (pp. 107–126). Harlow, Essex: Pearson Education.
Mohan, B., Early M., & Tang G. (1994). *Integration and 'thinking skills': A review of British Columbia curricular frameworks, K-12*. Report to the Ministry of Education, British Columbia. Unpublished manuscript.
Mohan, B., & Low, M. (1995). Collaborative teacher assessment of ESL writers: Conceptual and practical issues. *TESOL Journal, 5*(1), 28–31.
Mohan, B., & Huxur, G. (2001). A Functional approach to research on content-based language learning: Recasts in causal explanations. *Canadian Modern Language Review, 58*(1), 133–155.

Mohan, B., & Huang J. (2002). Assessing the integration of language and content in a Mandarin as a foreign language classroom. *Linguistics and Education. 13*(3), 405–433.

Mohan, B., Leung C., & Davison C. (Eds.). (2001). *English as a second language in the mainstream.* Harlow, Essex: Pearson Education.

Mohan, B., & Slater, T. (2005). The evaluation of causal discourse and language as a resource for meaning. In J. Foley (Ed.), *Language, education and discourse: Functional Approaches.* (pp. 171–187). London, UK: Continuum.

New Jersey State Board of Education. (2001). *Academic and Professional Standards.* Retrieved 9 February 2005, from http://www.state.nj.us/njded/aps/cccs/.

Newton, I. (1704/1952). *Opticks.* New York: Dover Editions.

Novak, J. (1999). *Learning, creating and using knowledge.* Mahwah, NJ: Erlbaum.

Pica, T. (2000). Tradition and transition in English teaching methodology. *System, 28*, 1–18.

Short, D. (1993). Assessing integrated language and content instruction. *TESOL Quarterly, 27*, 627–66.

Spradley, J. (1980). *Participant observation.* New York: Holt, Rinehart, Winston.

Swartz, R., & Parks, S. (1994). *Infusing the teaching of critical and creative thinking into content instruction.* Pacific Grove, CA: Critical Thinking Press.

Tang, G. (1997). From graphic literacy across languages to integrating English and content teaching in vocational settings. *Hong Kong Journal of Applied Linguistics,* (1)2, 97–114.

Tang, G. (2001). Knowledge framework and classroom action. In B. Mohan, C. Leung, & C. Davison (Eds.), *English as a second language in the mainstream* (pp. 127–137). Harlow, Essex: Pearson Education.

TESOL (1997). *ESL Standards for Pre-K-12 students.* Alexandria, VA: TESOL.

TESOL (2001). *Scenarios for Standards-Based Assessment.* Alexandria, VA: TESOL.

TESOL (2005). *ESL Standards for Pre-K-12 Students.* Retrieved 9 June, 2005, from www.tesol.org.

Van Dijk, T. (1991). *Racism and the press.* London: Routledge.

Veel, R. (1997). Learning how to mean—scientifically speaking. In F. Christie & J. Martin (Eds.), *Genre and institutions* (161–195). London: Continuum.

Werner, O., & Schoepfle, G. (1987). *Systematic fieldwork* (Vols. 1 & 2). Newbury Park, CA: Sage.

CHAPTER 21

ACCELERATING ACADEMIC ACHIEVEMENT OF ENGLISH LANGUAGE LEARNERS:[1]

A Synthesis of Five Evaluations of the CALLA Model

ANNA UHL CHAMOT

George Washington University, USA

ABSTRACT

This chapter reports the results of five evaluations of the Cognitive Academic Language Learning Approach (CALLA) conducted in different school settings with various content emphases. CALLA provides instruction through a combination of academic content, language development, and learning strategies in which a five-phase instructional sequence is used to integrate these components in materials design and instruction. Results indicated that English language learning (ELL) students enrolled in CALLA classrooms made substantial progress in acquiring content knowledge and skills, English language proficiency, and learning strategies. These results were sustained with successive cohorts of students. The effects in these evaluations had a high degree of educational significance and were supported by multiple measures of program impact across different school contexts with students from varied grade levels and language backgrounds.

INTRODUCTION

Students learning English as a new language face a number of challenges in American schools. Probably the most critical is the attainment of the knowledge and skills needed for success in academic subjects. Achieving academic competence requires far more than merely becoming proficient in English, as students also need knowledge about the subject matter taught in school, skilled literacy, and the ability to learn successfully. Abundant research has documented that students require a considerable amount of time, as much as 7 or more years, to become academically competent in English (Collier, 1989; Cummins, 1981). Since this length of time is not available to many students and requires extra expenditure of school resources, educators seek ways to improve instruction so that it will help students develop academic competence in a shorter period of time.

In the mid-1980s we began developing an instructional model that sought to accelerate the academic achievement of English language learning (ELL) students (Chamot & O'Malley, 1986, 1987, 1989). This model, the Cognitive Academic Language Learning Approach (CALLA), continues to be developed and refined as research and practice provide new insights into the interactions between learning and teaching processes (Chamot, 1994, 1995; Chamot & O'Malley, 1994). CALLA has

---

[1] The original version of this chapter was co-authored with J. Michael O'Malley.

been implemented by a number of school districts in a variety of program contexts, including both English as a second language (ESL) programs and bilingual programs at elementary and secondary levels. By adapting the model to meet the needs of their students and teachers, these programs have shown that CALLA principles can be applied to different contexts and language learners.

While many CALLA programs have been implemented in recent years, a few have been operating for longer periods and have conducted program evaluations to document the effects of CALLA. These evaluations have focused mainly on student achievement in content subjects and language development, though some of the evaluations have also provided information on learning strategies assessment, curriculum design and materials preparation, teacher development, and parental involvement. This chapter describes the program evaluations of five CALLA projects from geographically diverse parts of the United States.

THEORETICAL BACKGROUND

Many, if not most, ELL students encounter difficulties in achieving academic success in school. These difficulties have been attributed to various causes including the longer period required to catch up to peers in academic (as contrasted with social) language development, the interruption of native language cognitive development, the mismatch between students' prior linguistic and cultural knowledge and the curriculum and instructional practices of schools, and a general lack of understanding by teachers and others of the learning processes of students acquiring knowledge and skills through the medium of a new language (Cummins, 2001; Wong Fillmore & Meyer, 1992).

Our own initial research on the learning strategies of ELL students provided the impetus to explore the role of an instructional model that would help students progress more rapidly in school. This research revealed that successful ELL students were active, strategic language learners who could focus on the requirements of a task, transfer previously learned concepts and learning strategies to the demands of the English as a second language (ESL) or general education content classroom, and reflect on their own learning processes (O'Malley, Chamot, Stewner-Manzanares, Russo, & Küpper, 1985). This study also found that the success of vocabulary learning strategies was related to students' ethnicity: Hispanic students in the strategies groups outperformed those in the control group, while the opposite held true for Asian-background students, who preferred their previously perfected memory strategies.

In a further investigation of listening comprehension, we compared the learning strategy profiles of more and less successful students in ESL classrooms and discovered significant differences in the learning approaches of the two groups (O'Malley, Chamot, & Küpper, 1989). The more effective students displayed the same type of strategies that characterize good readers in native English-speaking *contexts* (e.g. Pressley, Woloshyn, & Associates, 1995), pointing to possible processing similarities between modalities as well as between first and second language learning.

From research in first-language contexts and our own initial studies we learned much that guided the development of CALLA and its underlying theoretical model. As in first-language contexts, both cognitive processes and social context are critical in the academic development of ELL students. Cognitive learning models emphasize the conscious and strategic nature of learning processes and the importance of prior knowledge in developing more complex schemata, among other theoretical assumptions (see, for example, Anderson, 1990). Social learning theories and the role of self-regulation in learning (e.g. Bandura, 1997; Zimmerman & Schunk, 2001; Vygotsky, 1978) have also contributed to the continuing development of the theoretical model underlying CALLA.

Our initial studies clearly indicated that undifferentiated instruction, no matter how innovative, will not be effective for all students. Individual differences need to be considered in all instruction, including the teaching of learning strategies. Students' interests and prior knowledge need to be identified and used actively by the teacher if learning is to be successful. We realized that the initial phase of instruction needs to be devoted to eliciting the prior knowledge of content, language, and learning strategies related to the new lesson. When students' prior knowledge is identified and made public, teachers can plan learning activities compatible with individual needs.

Thus, CALLA was developed in response to two major needs identified for ELL students: the need for instruction that focuses on academic (rather than only social) language learning, including both content and language; and the need for students to learn strategies that would assist them in learning more efficiently. CALLA's theoretical framework is based on a cognitive-social model that focuses on a combination of learners' mental activity and the social context of learning. We realize that some learners will tend to have a more pronounced internal locus of control, while others will be more strongly committed to a social-interactive approach to learning. We believe that learners can profit from a combination approach and that teachers can provide the necessary scaffolding to make this possible.

THE CALLA MODEL

The design of CALLA is simple in construction and complex in execution. The construction consists of three components: high priority academic content, academic language development with a focus on literacy, and explicit learning strategies instruction. By high priority academic content, we mean concepts and skills from subject areas such as science, mathematics, social studies and English language arts that are representative of national, state, and local curriculum standards. By academic language, we mean the type of language used to acquire new information in school, including the language of teacher explanations, textbooks, other input sources, and student language output such as discussions and writing about what is being learned. By learning strategies, we mean the techniques that students can learn to use to make their own learning more efficient. Examples of learning strategies are: planning before speaking or writing, selective attention to key words or ideas, making inferences while listening or reading, using imagery (visualization) to assist understanding or recall, cooperating with others on a learning task, and evaluating one's own learning.

While this structure is straightforward in design, the combination of the three components can present difficulties in actual instruction. Some teachers, for example, have little difficulty integrating content and language but are uncertain how to add learning strategies instruction. Other teachers can integrate language and learning strategies but feel hesitant about choosing and planning content. There are also some ESL teachers who decide to integrate content into their classrooms and who find the content so interesting that they may provide less than optimal attention to academic language and learning. We have concluded that the difficulty in executing CALLA instruction lies in the need to address three different components—content, academic language, learning strategies—rather than only one or two.

In order to help teachers integrate the three components of CALLA, we developed an instructional design sequence to assist teachers incorporate CALLA components and principles in their planning, instruction, and assessment. The CALLA instructional design is task-based and has five phases in which teachers combine the three components of content, language, and learning strategies. In the first phase, *preparation*, teachers focus on finding out what prior knowledge students have about the content topic to be taught, level of language proficiency, and their current learning strategies for the type of task. In the second phase, *presentation*, teachers use a variety of techniques to make new information and skills (including learning strategies) accessible and comprehensible to students, such as demonstrations, modeling, and visual support. This is followed by or integrated with the third phase, *practice*, in which students use the new information and skills in activities that involve collaboration, problem-solving, inquiry, and hands-on experiences. The fourth phase of the CALLA instructional design sequence *is evaluation*, in which students self-evaluate their understanding and proficiency with the content, language, and learning strategies they have been practicing. Finally, in the fifth phase, *expansion*, students engage in activities that apply what they have learned to their own lives, including other classes at school, families and community, and their cultural and linguistic background. These five phases are recursive allowing for flexibility in lesson planning and implementation.

The CALLA instructional sequence has much in common with lesson planning sequences already familiar to teachers. However, the CALLA instructional model features elements that are new to many teachers. The first of these is the equal importance given to content, language, and learning strategies. The second is the explicit learner-centered focus of the design that helps to ensure that teachers consistently elicit students' prior knowledge (preparation phase), encourage reflection and self-evaluation (evaluation phase), and make what is learned in school relevant to students' own lives (expansion phase). The third element, new to many teachers, is the stated goal of developing students' *metacognition*; that is, their ability to think about their own thinking and learning.

Our experience in working with CALLA projects has shown that the instructional design of CALLA is the key to implementing the model successfully. Each of the three components needs to be included and integrated into curriculum, materials, and instruction. The five-phase, recursive instructional sequence provides a framework in which teachers can integrate the components successfully and meet individual learner needs while developing students' academic knowledge.

PROJECT DESCRIPTIONS

Programs and Student Population

Each of the five CALLA projects described in this section included appropriate staff development and monitoring that provided some assurance that teachers were implementing the model as designed (see Table 1 for the basic descriptive features and goals of the projects).

The projects incorporated instruction in the three major components of CALLA, that is, one or more content areas, academic language, and learning strategies. These projects were directed by ESL educators with one or more prior workshops in CALLA, familiarity with the literature on CALLA, and a commitment to CALLA implementation. Academic content in each project was aligned with the district's grade-level curriculum. Content specialists worked together with ESL teachers to provide staff development and develop curricula using CALLA's five-phase instructional sequence. Teachers providing instruction in the classroom varied depending on the project and may have been ESL teachers or grade-level subject area teachers.

Arlington Math Project

This CALLA project was initiated in 1988 to serve the academic needs in math of approximately 450 ELL students annually in 15 classrooms distributed across grades 3-5 (about 15% of the students), 6-8 (50%), and 9-10 (35%). The principal focus of the project was on mathematics concepts and the application of learning strategies to word problems. Beginning and intermediate ELL students needing special assistance in math received one CALLA math period daily. CALLA math was taught in the elementary and middle schools primarily by the regular ESL classroom teachers. Typical exposure to the project was about 1 year due to students exiting from the program and student mobility.

Arlington Science Project

This project began in 1990 to prepare ELL students for grade-level language, concepts, and processes in science. The project served just over 410 ELL students annually in one target middle school (grades 6-8) who had little or no background in science plus about 350 ELL students in three other middle schools. CALLA science classes were taught by 10-12 teachers (depending on enrollments) who provided instruction to approximately 20 classrooms of students in these schools. Beginning and intermediate ELL students received one CALLA science period daily. Instruction in the CALLA Science Project was provided by ESL teachers who had received special staff development in science and CALLA methods through workshops, demonstrations, mentoring, and a for-credit course on CALLA taken by both ESL and grade-level teachers.

Boston Project

The Boston CALLA project began in 1990 and included instruction in math, science, and social studies for ELL students in grades 6-12. Over 700 Haitian Creole students were served annually in five schools (two middle and three high schools) and 41 classrooms. The goals of the project were to develop students' English language skills and to ensure successful participation in grade-level classrooms. Students received ESL for two periods daily and either content ESL or transitional bilingual instruction in math, science, and social studies. Students in transitional bilingual classrooms received learning strategies instruction in both Haitian Creole

Table 1. CALLA Project Features and Goals

Location	Emphasis	Grade Levels	Schools/ Classrooms/ Students	Languages	Goals
Arlington	Math	3-5 6-8 9-12	4 Schools 14 Classrooms 450 Students	75% Spanish	To reduce the gap in mathematics computation and concepts/applications between ELL students and native English speaking students within six years.
Arlington	Science	6-8	4 Schools 20 Classrooms 410 Students	75% Spanish	To prepare students for mainstream language, concepts, and processes in science.
Boston	Math Science Social Studies	6-8 9-12	5 Schools 41 Classrooms 700 Students	100% Haitian Creole	To develop English language skills and ensure successful participation in grade-level classes.
Fargo	Math Science Social Studies	K-5	16 Schools 40 Classrooms 290 Students	20% Asian 27% Middle East 17% Native Am. 12% Spanish 6% African 18% Other	To improve the English ability and academic language proficiency of students as measured by a gap reduction between the ELL students and a comparison group (norm sample on a standardized test).
New York	Math Science Social Studies	K-6	9 Schools 22 Classrooms 600 Students	34% Spanish 30% Chinese 36% Other	To improve English language reading and reading-related achievement; and to increase science, social studies, and math skills.

and in English. Project staff provided intensive staff development on demand including teacher meetings, classroom observations, and modeled lessons to a small number of schools for half a year then moved on to other schools in the project. Teachers often requested staff development on specific subjects or CALLA units, which then became the focus of pre-post criterion-referenced tests.

Fargo CALLA Project

The Fargo CALLA Project was initiated in 1994 and served 290 ELL students from mixed language backgrounds in 16 grade K-5 elementary schools during 1995-1996. The goals of the project were to improve students' English proficiency and to enhance their performance in language arts, math, science, and social studies. Students received CALLA instruction in these subjects, accompanied by hands-on instruction, demonstrations, and visual supports. CALLA instruction was provided for 75 minutes each day for beginning and intermediate level students and 50 minutes each day for upper level students. Instruction was provided by ESL teachers who received seven 32-hour workshops on teaching/learning strategies used in the program plus two credit-bearing workshops of 20 hours each. Teaching assistants were used in all classrooms, and students worked in small groups of 3-6 (Di Cola, 1996). Supplementary materials were developed in English in the content areas using the CALLA instructional sequence.

New York City Project

The CALLA project in New York City was initiated in 1990 to provide content ESL instruction in math, science, and social studies to over 600 ELL students annually in grades K-6 across 9 schools and 22 classrooms in Community School District #2. The goals of the project were to improve English language reading and achievement in science, social studies, and math. Students received CALLA instruction 4-5 times weekly. The project developed CALLA teacher manuals for language arts, mathematics, science, and social studies that were organized following the CALLA instructional sequence. The manuals were used by staff in professional development workshops for teachers and to model classroom instruction. CALLA teachers attended at least four full-day training sessions accompanied by weekly individual meetings, in-class modeling, observations of master teachers, and a one-week summer institute (Casale, 1995).

EVALUATION DESIGNS AND INSTRUMENTS

The projects reviewed here used a variety of evaluation designs and instruments that were selected based on specific project features as well as school contexts, information needs, and requirements of the federal government granting agency. The evaluations were conducted by outside evaluators or, in one case, by an evaluation office in the school district. In the following discussion, three common evaluation designs (Cook & Campbell, 1979) are outlined and matched to the projects in which they were used.

Pre-Posttest Non-Equivalent Comparison Group

Evaluations of CALLA using this design employed a standardized test of student achievement in the content area emphasized in the project. The test was administered at the beginning of a school year, or prior to the introduction of CALLA instruction, and at the end of a school year, following instruction in the project. In some cases, the test was administered again in the spring of each succeeding year to determine ongoing progress associated with project participation. National norms from the standardized test were used as a non-equivalent comparison group, typically with Normal Curve Equivalent (NCE) scores. Within this design, students in the project are expected to show progress and reduce their pretest score difference with respect to the norm group by the time of the posttest. The norm group on a standardized test will have a mean NCE of 50, and ELL students should move closer to the mean of the norm group with exposure to the project. The expected level of annual improvement should be at least .25 standard deviations for standardized tests in order to have a minimal level of educational significance (Cohen, 1977). Since the standard deviation of NCEs is 21.06, the expected improvement should be about 5 NCEs or more.

The pre-post non-equivalent comparison group design was used in evaluating the CALLA mathematics project in Arlington, VA (e.g., Thomas, 1993, 1996). A functional level form of the California Achievement Test (CAT-5) in mathematics was used to measure student progress against the national norm group

The pre-post non-equivalent comparison group design was also used with the CALLA project in New York City. In New York, the outcome measure was the Language Assessment Battery (LAB), using the oral proficiency score for earlier grades and a close reading assessment beginning in grade 3. Pre-post gains were interpreted using NCEs from a fluent English speaking normative sample in New York City that included a proportionate representation of language minority students.

A third project using the pre-posttest non-equivalent comparison group design was Fargo's CALLA project. The test used to assess project outcomes was the *Woodcock-Muñoz Language Survey* (WMLS) that has been normed on a national population of native English speakers. The WMLS has subtests on picture vocabulary, verbal analogies, letter-word identification, and dictation.

Post-test Only With Non-Equivalent Comparison Group

This design uses data collected following students' exposure to the treatment and makes comparisons to a similar group of students. In the application of this design reported here, the term *non-equivalent* is misleading because the project sought to locate a comparison group that was, in fact, as similar to the treatment group as could be identified. The project using this design was the CALLA science project in Arlington, VA. The outcome measure was grades obtained in grade-level classrooms because no suitable test of science knowledge and skills that matched the content to which students had been exposed during instruction could be identified.

One Group Pre-Posttest Design

In this design, a test is administered both before and after instruction and there is no comparison group. Either a standardized or other test such as a criterion-referenced test is used in the analysis. Students are expected to show progress over time on the test or to achieve some pre-established criterion level of performance. The project using this type of analysis was the Boston CALLA Project. The outcome measures were criterion-referenced tests in English based on the *Building Bridges* series (Chamot, O'Malley, & Küpper, 1992) and on various project-developed curriculum units, also in the content areas.

LIMITATIONS

None of the evaluation designs described above provides unequivocal evidence of project impact. A variety of threats to the validity of each design could prevent the results from being clearly attributed to the success of the project. For example, the procedures used in selecting the comparison group may unintentionally produce differences with the treatment group on the outcome measures. This could have affected the results of the Arlington science project. Also, use of the same instrument for selection of students and for assessment of outcomes could produce a regression effect in which students with initially low scores (those selected for the program) score higher at the posttest due only to measurement error. This could have affected scores for the New York City and Fargo projects.

While the threats to the validity of these designs are potentially serious, a number of mitigating circumstances in the nature of the designs, the instructional programs, and the type of data collected in these projects give greater confidence in attributing the results to the program interventions than would otherwise be evident. There are four such factors operating in these evaluations: a well-defined program, the strength of the effects, the use of varied measures of program impact, and the existence of qualitative evidence to support quantitative results.

RESULTS

Analyses of the results are based on existing evaluation reports submitted by each project to the Office of Bilingual Education and Minority Languages Affairs (now the Office of English Language Acquisition) in the U.S. Department of Education. The results are presented in relation to the three major components of CALLA: academic content, language development, and learning strategies. The evaluation designs and outcomes for each project are summarized in Table 2.

Academic Content

Goals for academic content were described in all five CALLA projects. However, only the two Arlington CALLA projects and the Boston CALLA project provided measures of content knowledge outcomes in their evaluation reports.

In the Arlington CALLA mathematics project, NCEs on the computation pretest (1992-1993 data, 4th year of project) ranged from 1 to 43 across the different grade levels, with a mean of 13.24, while NCEs at the posttest ranged from 12 to 60 and had a mean of 25.25. While correlated t-tests were not computed, the overall effect size was .62. Results over the same period on the concepts and applications subtest on the CAT showed a similar pattern of findings. NCEs on the pretest ranged from 1 to 32 across grade levels, with a mean of 5.18; NCEs at the posttest ranged from 9 to

Table 2. CALLA Evaluation Designs, Instruments, and Outcomes

Location/Emphasis	Evaluation Design	Instruments		Outcomes
Arlington/ Math	Pre-Post Non-Equivalent Comparison Group	CAT Form 5; grades in post-project academic courses; uses of learning strategies	X	Statistically and educationally significant gains of 11-12 NCEs on the CAT in math computation from fall to spring and similar gains in math concepts and applications. Gains maintained on successive cohorts over three years.
			X	CALLA graduates maintained C average in math courses.
			X	Significantly more students in high implementation CALLA classrooms used metacognitive strategies.
Arlington/ Science	Post-Test Only With Non-Equivalent Comparison Group	Grades in post-project academic courses; progress in English skills	X	CALLA students made significantly higher percentage of A/B course grades than non-CALLA students at both middle and high school levels.
			X	CALLA students who entered below grade level made more progress than students who entered at or above grade level.
			X	86% of CALLA students progressed to next English proficiency classification.
Boston/ Math, Science, Social Studies	One Group Pre-Posttest Design	Criterion-Referenced Tests (CRTs); course grades	X	CALLA students made statistically and educationally significant pre-post gains on 16 out of 16 CRTs used, including language arts, social studies, and science. For high school students, 87% passed their courses and 58% received C or better.
Fargo/ Math, Science, Social Studies	Pre-Post Non-Equivalent Comparison Group	Woodcock-Muñoz Language Survey (WLMS)	X	In 15 of 24 groups (4 WLMS subtests x 6 language groups), at least 70% of CALLA students had educationally significant gains.
			X	In 23 of 24 groups, at least 50% of CALLA students had educationally significant gains.
New York City/Math Science, Social Studies	Pre-Post Non-Equivalent Comparison Group	Language Assessment Battery (LAB)	X	Average gains for random sample of CALLA students were statistically and educationally significant.
			X	Statistical tests were significant in all 8 project schools with data.
			X	78% of students progressed at least one level in English proficiency.

37, with a mean of 16.02. The overall effect size for concepts and applications was .52. Thus, the project experienced substantial gains in concepts and applications as well as in computation, consistent with the learning strategy and problem solving emphasis in the project.

The project was able to maintain these sizeable effects on successive cohorts over a period of four years (Thomas, 1996). However, with an average NCE of 16 at the end of the first program year, gains of 10 NCEs or about half a standard deviation would need to be sustained over a period of 3-4 additional years before the average score of these students would approach the national mean (Thomas, 1993, 1996). In subsequent analyses, Thomas (1996) examined the performance of a sample of these students on an 11th grade standardized test and found that the early gains in CALLA were not sustained once the students were in classrooms that did not receive ESL support.

In the Arlington CALLA science project, data were collected on 79 ELL students who had attended the project middle school in which CALLA science was taught during the period 1990-1994 and who had completed at least one grade-level science course. The outcome measure was final course grade in this first post-CALLA science course, which consisted of eighth grade science for middle school students and a selection from ninth grade courses for high school students. The comparison group was 33 ELL students from the same school and a similar middle school who had been enrolled in the year prior to the onset of the project.

Results for middle and high school students combined showed that 48% of the CALLA students received an A or B in their first grade-level science course compared to 27% in the comparison group (Chamot, Gallard, & Gough, 1995). Twenty-seven percent of the CALLA students received D or below compared to 28% of the non-CALLA group. Results were comparable for both middle school and high school students. Thus, the benefit of the program appeared to be in moving a portion of the students who otherwise would receive a C into the A or B range.

The Boston CALLA project evaluation relied on pre- and post criterion-referenced tests in English administered to selected students who received various curriculum units and materials used in the project. The tests covered a variety of topics including science, mathematics, social studies, and literature. On these curriculum-based tests, the range of effect sizes on the pre- to posttest comparisons was .91 to 3.02 and the overall effect size was 1.39. On six criterion-referenced tests administered to assess other parts of the curriculum, covering topics that included math, science, and social studies, the effect sizes ranged from .90 to 7.96 with an average of 3.37. Thus, students showed substantial gains in academic language skills across a variety of content areas.

Language Development

All five of the CALLA projects monitored students' progress in English language development through project, district, and/or state language assessment instruments. However, two of the projects reported student growth in English skills using standardized tests.

The evaluators of the New York City CALLA project selected a random sample of 200 out of the 618 students in the project on whom to analyze LAB data (Casale, 1995). Average participation in the project was 10 months, or 1 school year. NCEs on the LAB were aggregated across schools to obtain an overall mean and standard deviation for the pre- and posttest. NCEs at the pretest were in the range of 6.5 to 25.6, while at the posttest the range was 26.5 to 52.9. A t-test for paired samples on the pre-post difference on the NCEs was statistically significant (t = 14.8, p<.001). Across schools, the effect sizes (computed using 21.07, the standard deviation of the norm group) ranged from .70 to 2.34, with an average of 1.55, well beyond the criterion of .25 suggested for educational significance. The project evaluation also reported that 78% progressed at least one level in the difficulty of the materials they were using in class.

The Fargo CALLA project measured English proficiency with the Woodcock-Muñoz Language Survey (WLMS). As with the New York City and Arlington math projects, Fargo used the gap-reduction design *Gap scores*, or the difference between the project group and the national norm, were determined at pretest and posttest and a weighted average was computed across the 16 elementary schools participating in the project. The gap reduction was determined by subtracting the pretest gap from the posttest gap. Data for each of six racial/ethnic groups were analyzed separately to identify the percentage of gap reduction (the ratio of the gap reduction to the pretest gap multiplied by 100) for each of the four WMLS scores. The percentage of gap reduction varied from 12 to 76 with a median on the 24 comparisons (four scores and six language groups) of 36%. An analysis of the educational significance of these changes was conducted to determine the percentage of students with gains equal to or greater than .25 standard deviations within each racial/ethnic group. This analysis revealed that gains on the four scores were educationally significant for 47 to 93% of the students with a median of 77%. In 15 out of the 24 groups (four subtests x six languages), at least 70% of the students had educationally significant gains, and in 23 out of 24 groups, at least 50% of the students had educationally significant gains. Thus, as with the New York City project, CALLA students showed substantial gains in English language skills.

Learning Strategies

While all of the CALLA projects had learning strategy objectives and described learning strategy lessons and their implementation, only the Arlington math and science projects provided any reliable assessment of strategies used by students. This is no doubt due to the complexity of measuring learning strategies in a typical project evaluation.

In the context of the Arlington CALLA mathematics project, a research study on strategy use was conducted separately from the program evaluation. A sample of 32 ELL students stratified by math performance participated in think-aloud and retrospective interviews in which students were asked to describe their thoughts while actively solving math problems (Chamot, Dale, O'Malley, & Spanos, 1993). Students came from classrooms that were classified as either high vs. low CALLA implementation based on observations of teachers by project staff and teacher participation in CALLA staff development.

ELL students in the high-implementation classrooms performed significantly better than those in low-implementation classrooms on the following indicators: use of metacognitive strategies, use of a sequential problem-solving procedure, and correct solution of the problem. Metacognitive strategies included planning, monitoring, and evaluating one's own learning.

Varela (1997) conducted a quasi-experimental study with students in two classrooms in the Arlington CALLA science project. The study was designed to examine the effects of explicit learning strategies instruction on students' use of strategies and performance in presenting an oral report on a science project. This project was being prepared for a science fair as part of the CALLA science class. The students in each classroom were all intermediate proficiency in English and were matched on language and socioeconomic background. Both teachers followed scripted CALLA lessons over a 2-week period and taught strategies appropriate for an oral presentation, e.g., using graphic organizers, selective attention, self-assessment, and self-talk. However, one teacher taught the strategies explicitly, including modeling, discussion, and peer and self-evaluation, while the other allowed students to read pointers and view videos that included the same strategies for strengthening their presentation. Both groups of students presented their oral reports as a pretest and again at the conclusion of the two weeks of learning strategies instruction. The oral presentations were followed by audio-taped retrospective student interviews on strategies used in their presentation. The videotapes and audiotapes were scored blindly by independent raters. Students receiving explicit strategy instruction significantly increased their reported use of strategies and their performance on the oral presentation, while the control group showed no increase in strategy use or in performance. Strategy use had a moderately strong correlation with performance on the oral report consistent with the hypothesis of a relationship between strategy use and improved performance.

DISCUSSION

The five project evaluations suggest that CALLA projects have been successful in improving content knowledge and processes, academic language, and use of learning strategies. However, the results should be examined to determine if counteracting features are present to offset potential threats to the internal validity of the evaluations. These features include a well-defined program, the strength of the effects, the use of varied measures of impact, the existence of qualitative evidence to support quantitative results, and the consistency of the effects across a variety of different settings and students.

As described above, the CALLA program has a clearly defined structure and, in these projects, was implemented by trained teachers in an appropriate and consistent way. The projects used multiple indicators of program impact and a number of evaluations also included qualitative evidence of program impact that supports and extends the quantitative findings.

In addition, the strength of effects was well beyond the lower limit of .25 standard deviations established for educational significance, whether the outcome was measured with a standardized test or curriculum-referenced test. It was not unusual for the effect sizes to be over 1.0, or a full standard deviation on the outcome measure. On a standardized test such as the CAT, the effect sizes in mathematics were about .50 overall, or about 10 NCEs, which corresponds to 4-6 raw score points on the test in the range at which most scores would fall. These results are sufficiently robust to suggest that the findings should be considered valid reflections of program impact since effects so large are unlikely to result from non-program influences. These meaningful increases in student knowledge and skills in math, while impressive, still mean that ELL students would need to spend, on average, an additional 4 years making comparable gains in order to reduce fully the gap with their grade-level native English-speaking peers.

The results supportive of CALLA have been evident across a variety of different sites and school contexts with students from different language backgrounds, different grade levels, different levels of prior education, and with both ESL and grade-level content teachers exposed to varying levels and intensity of CALLA staff development.

One feature that seems to have contributed to the success of these projects was the presence of a single project leader who was committed to staff development and implementation of CALLA. Other features are the presence of ongoing professional development for teachers and the adaptation and development of instructional materials embodying CALLA procedures. The materials were used to provide teachers with sample lesson plans on the subject areas targeted in the project, distributed in workshops, and used by staff developers to model lessons in classrooms. All projects also had a strong parent component that provided sample home activities in addition to information about the project.

What program developers can derive from these findings is assurance that ELL students in projects implemented in a manner consistent with the CALLA instructional design have a good chance of acquiring content knowledge, academic language skills, and learning strategies successfully. Further, projects can expect that gains on CALLA outcome measures will be substantial and that the time required to achieve an English language norm will be less than in a typical program.

CALLA projects should pay special attention to ensuring the continuity of early gains resulting from the project and the success of potentially low-performing students after they leave the program. This requires careful articulation between the ESL or bilingual program and grade level curriculum and instruction. Among the approaches we recommend are sustained staff development with grade-level teachers, attention to learning strategies in grade-level classrooms, and continuing assessments to identify students who do not maintain their initial progress. Both authentic assessments and district-wide standardized tests are useful for this purpose.

In summary, the evaluations we have analyzed provide evidence that schools can accelerate the academic achievement of ELL students, thus improving their educational prospects and life opportunities. The amount of time required for these students to reach grade level norms and the costs of district instruction can both be reduced substantially by adhering to the principles suggested in CALLA programs.

REFERENCES

Anderson, J. (1990). *Cognitive psychology and its implications* (3rd ed.). New York, NY: Freeman.
Bandura, A. (1997). *Self-efficacy: The exercise of control.* New York, NY: Freeman.
Casale, J. (1995). *The Cognitive Academic Language Learning Approach (CALLA) in Community School District 2.* Final evaluation report submitted to the U.S. Office of Bilingual Education and Minority Languages Affairs by the Office of Educational Research, New York City Schools.
Chamot, A. (1994). CALLA: An instructional model for linguistically diverse students. *English Quarterly, 26*(3), 12–16.
Chamot, A. (1995). Implementing the Cognitive Academic Language Learning Approach: *CALLA* in Arlington, Virginia. *Bilingual Research Journal, 19*(2), 221–247.
Chamot, A., Dale, M., O'Malley, J., & Spanos, G. (1993). Learning and problem solving strategies of ESL students. *Bilingual Research Journal, 16*(3–4), 1–38.

Chamot, A., Gallard, P., & Gough, L. (1995). *The Cognitive Academic Language Learning Approach (CALLA) project for science.* Final evaluation report submitted to the U.S. Office of Bilingual Education and Minority Languages Affairs by the Arlington County Schools.

Chamot, A., & O'Malley, J. (1986). *A cognitive academic language learning approach: An ESL content-based curriculum.* Washington, DC: National Clearinghouse for Bilingual Education.

Chamot, A., & O'Malley, J. (1987). The Cognitive Academic Language Learning Approach: A bridge to the mainstream. *TESOL Quarterly, 21*(2), 227–249.

Chamot, A., & O'Malley, J. (1989). The cognitive academic language learning approach. In P. Rigg & V. Allen (Eds.), *When they don't all speak English: Integrating the ESL student into the regular classroom* (pp. 108–125). Urbana, IL: National Council of Teachers of English.

Chamot, A., & O'Malley, J. (1994). The CALLA Handbook: Implementing the Cognitive Academic Language Learning Approach. Reading. MA: Addison-Wesley.

Chamot, A., O'Malley, J., & Küpper, L. (1992). *Building bridges. Books 1–3.* Boston, MA: Heinle & Heinle.

Cohen, J. (1977). *Statistical power analysis for the behavioral sciences.* New York: Academic Press.

Collier, V. (1989). How long? A synthesis of research on academic achievement in a second language. *TESOL Quarterly, 23*(3), 509–531.

Cook, T. D., & Campbell, D. T. (1979). *Quasi-Experimentation: Design and Analysis for Field Settings.* Rand McNally, Chicago, Illinois.

Cummins, J. (1981). Age on arrival and immigrant second language learning in Canada. A reassessment. *Applied Linguistics, 2*, 132–149.

Cummins, J. (2001). *Negotiating identities: Education for empowerment in a diverse society.* 2nd ed. Los Angeles: California Association for Bilingual Education.

Di Cola, J. (1996). *The BOOST (Better Instructional Options for an Optimal Start) Model.* Final evaluation report submitted to the U.S. Office of Bilingual Education and Minority Languages Affairs by Fargo Public Schools, Fargo, ND.

O'Malley, J., & Chamot, A. (1990). *Learning strategies in second language acquisition.* New York: Cambridge University Press.

O'Malley, J., Chamot, A., & Küpper, L. (1989). Listening comprehension strategies in second language acquisition. *Applied Linguistics, 10*(4), 418–437.

O'Malley, J., Chamot, A., Stewner-Manzanares, G., Russo, R., & Küpper, L. (1985). Learning strategy applications with students of English as a second language. *TESOL Quarterly, 19*, 285–296.

Pressley, M., Woloshyn, V., & Associates (1995). *Cognitive strategy instruction that really improves children's academic performance.* 2nd ed. Cambridge, MA: Brookline Books.

Thomas, W. (1993). *The Cognitive Academic Language Learning Approach (CALLA) project for mathematics.* Final evaluation report for 1989–90 submitted to the U.S. Office of Bilingual Education and Minority Languages Affairs by Arlington County Schools, Virginia.

Thomas, W. (April, 1996). *The long-term effects of the Cognitive Academic Language Learning Approach (CALLA) on minority student achievement.* Paper presented at the Annual Meetings of the American Educational Research Association, New York City.

Varela, E. (1997). *The effects of language learning strategies instruction on students' oral report production in a Cognitive Academic Language Learning Approach (CALLA) English as a second language science class.* Unpublished doctoral dissertation, Georgetown University.

Vygotsky, L. (1978). *Mind in society: The development of higher psychological processes.* Cambridge, MA: Harvard University Press.

Wong Fillmore, L., & Meyer, L. (1992). The curriculum and linguistic minorities. In P. Jackson (Ed.), *Handbook of research on curriculum* (pp. 626–659). New York: Macmillan.

Zimmerman, B. J., & Schunk, D. H. (2001). *Self-regulated learning and academic achievement: Theoretical perspectives.* 2nd ed. Mahwah, NJ: Lawrence Erlbaum Associates.

CHAPTER 22

PREDICTING SECOND LANGUAGE ACADEMIC SUCCESS IN ENGLISH USING THE PRISM MODEL

VIRGINIA P. COLLIER AND WAYNE P. THOMAS

George Mason University, Fairfax, USA

ABSTRACT

Many students in English-speaking contexts who are new to the English language have to acquire proficiency in the language, and at the same time learn a range of academic content, some of which is very unfamiliar. The Prism model defines factors that allow for predictions to be made regarding English learners' degree of second language acquisition in an academic context. In this chapter, the authors describe in detail the components and dimensions of the Prism model and describe several currently popular types of education programs for English language learners in the United States in terms of their degree of adherence to the model. Finally, we compare the predictions of the Prism model, using predicted rankings of relative program success, to the actual measured effectiveness of each program in producing varying degrees of English learners' achievement gap closure with mother tongue-English speakers.

INTRODUCTION

The Prism model, first published in Collier (1995a, 1995b, 1995c) and expanded in Thomas and Collier (1997), was initially conceived in a dialogue with a group of Hispanic parents concerned about their children's education in the USA. The parents spoke of their passions and concerns, and several of the elements of the prism emerged as we jotted down issues on the chalkboard. Over the following year, these same issues continued to surface in the research on academic achievement in a second language (L2) context. The general categories initially identified by the Hispanic parents matched closely with emerging theories based on research in SLA (Ellis, 1994; Larsen-Freeman & Long, 1991; Wong-Fillmore, 1991). The Prism model also closely connects to other social science theories, such as Cummins' theories on negotiating identities and the interdependence of a student's first and second languages (Cummins, 2000). As we studied the lists of variables that we were examining in our research on the long-term academic achievement of students acquiring ESL in school, to organize the variables into major categories, the components of the Prism model began to take shape.

The research synthesis, upon which the Prism model is based, can be found in Collier (1995a, 1995b, 1995c) and Ovando et al. (2003). Overall, the Prism model defines major developmental processes that children experience during their school years that need to be supported at school for language acquisition and learning to take place. The model can be applied to mother tongue-English speakers learning an L2 as well as to students acquiring English as their L2. The model can be used to predict the major school factors that help to close the academic achievement gap in L2, a current topic of considerable importance in English-speaking countries, as increasing numbers of children who do not know English arrive in schools.

THE PRISM MODEL: LANGUAGE ACQUISITION FOR SCHOOL

The Prism model has four major components that drive language acquisition for school: sociocultural, linguistic, academic, and cognitive processes. To experience success in L2 academic contexts, L2 students who are not yet proficient in English need a school context that provides the same basic conditions and advantages that the English-speaking group experiences. This includes attention to the ongoing developmental processes that occur naturally for any child through the school years. For students from a language other than English home background, these interdependent processes—cognitive, academic, and linguistic development—must occur in a supportive sociocultural environment through both their first language (L1) and their L2 to enhance student learning.

The Prism model has eight dimensions, comprising these sociocultural, linguistic, academic, and cognitive processes in L1 and L2. This is illustrated in Figure 1.

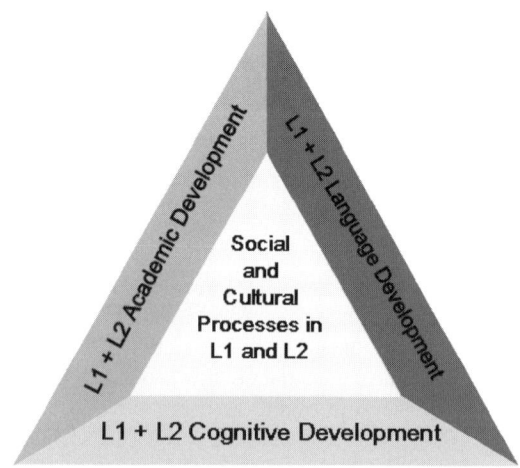

Figure 1. Language acquisition for school

As you examine this figure, which looks triangular on the flat surface of the page, visualize instead that you are looking down through a complex multi-dimensional prism, with the student in the center. Connected to the student's emotional responses to learning are the sociocultural processes that influence the learning process. Interconnected to this component are the other three major interdependent and complex components—linguistic, academic, and cognitive processes. Each of these dimensions will be described in turn.

Sociocultural Processes

At the heart of the Prism model is the individual student acquiring a L2 in school. Central to that student's acquisition of language are all of the surrounding social and cultural processes occurring in everyday life within the student's past, present, and future, in all contexts—home, school, community, and the broader society. For example, sociocultural processes at work in SLA may include individual students' emotional responses to school such as self-esteem or anxiety or other affective factors. At school, the instructional environment in a classroom or administrative program structure may create social and psychological distance between groups. Community or regional social patterns such as prejudice and discrimination expressed towards groups or individuals in personal and professional contexts, as well as societal patterns such as the subordinate status of a minority group or acculturation versus assimilation forces at work can all influence students' achievement in school. These factors can negatively affect the student's response to the new language and learning through the L2, unless the student is in a very socioculturally supportive environment.

Language Development

Linguistic processes, a second component of the model, consist of the subconscious aspects of language development (an innate ability all humans possess for acquisition of oral language), as well as the metalinguistic, conscious, formal teaching of language in school, and the acquisition of the written system of language. This includes the acquisition of the oral and written systems of the student's first and second languages across all language domains, such as phonology (the pronunciation system), vocabulary, morphology and syntax (the grammar system), semantics (meaning), pragmatics (how language is used in a given context), discourse (stretches of language beyond a single sentence), and paralinguistics (nonverbal and other extralinguistic features). To assure cognitive and academic success in the L2, a student's L1 system, oral and written, must be developed to a high cognitive level at least throughout the elementary school years.

Academic Development

A third component of the model, academic development, includes all school work in language arts, mathematics, the sciences, social studies, and the fine arts for each grade level, K-12 and beyond. With each succeeding grade, academic work dramatically expands the vocabulary, sociolinguistic, and discourse dimensions of language to higher cognitive levels. Academic knowledge and conceptual development transfer from the L1 to the L2. Thus, it is most efficient to develop academic work through students' L1, while teaching the L2 during other periods of the school day or week through meaningful academic content that reinforces and expands on the knowledge developed but does not repeat the academic work in L1. In earlier decades in the USA teaching L2 was recommended as the first step and the teaching of academic content postponed. However, research has shown that postponing or interrupting academic development while students work on acquiring the L2 is likely to lead to academic failure in the long-term. In an information-driven society that demands more knowledge processing with each succeeding year, English language learners cannot afford to lose time, especially when their English-speaking peers are steadily making one year's progress in one year's time.

Cognitive Development

The fourth component of this model, the cognitive dimension, is a natural, subconscious process that occurs developmentally from birth to the end of schooling and beyond. An infant initially builds thought processes through interacting with loved ones in the language of the home. All parents (including those non-formally schooled) naturally stimulate children's L1 cognitive growth through daily interaction and family-based problem solving in the language the parents know best. Students bring 5-6 years of cognitive development in their L1 to their first day of school. This is a knowledge base, an important stepping stone to build on as cognitive development continues. It is extremely important that cognitive development continues through a child's L1 at least through the elementary school years. Extensive research has demonstrated that children who reach full cognitive development in two languages (generally reaching the threshold in their L1 by around age 11-12) enjoy cognitive advantages over monolinguals. Cognitive development was mostly neglected by L2 educators in the USA until the past decade. Language teaching curricula were simplified, structured, and sequenced during the 1970s, and when academic content was added to language lessons in the 1980s, academic content was watered down into cognitively simple tasks, often under the label of *basic skills*. Too often neglected was the crucial role of cognitive development in the L1. Now we know from the growing research base that educators must address linguistic, cognitive, and academic development equally through both first and second languages if they are to assure students' academic success in the L2. This is especially necessary if English language learners are ever to reach full parity in all curricular areas with L1 English speakers.

Interdependence of the Four Components

All of these four components—sociocultural, academic, cognitive, and linguistic—are interdependent. If one is developed to the neglect of another, this may be detrimental to a student's overall growth and future success. The academic, cognitive, and linguistic components must be viewed as natural developmental processes. For the child, adolescent, and young adult still attending formal schooling, development of any one of the three academic, cognitive, and linguistic components depends critically on the simultaneous development of the other two through both first and second languages. Also, sociocultural processes strongly influence students' access to cognitive, academic, and language development in both positive and negative ways. It is crucial that educators provide a socioculturally supportive school environment, allowing natural language, academic, and cognitive development to flourish in both L1 and L2.

THE INSTRUCTIONAL SITUATION FOR THE ENGLISH LANGUAGE LEARNER IN AN ENGLISH-ONLY PROGRAM

Using all the components of the Prism model, we can apply this research knowledge base to the varying school programs provided for English language learners in the United States. This comparison will make clear where the school experience of English language learners is different from that of L1 English speakers, the source of achievement gaps. The common view of many education policy makers in English-speaking countries such as the USA, that students must learn English first, is portrayed in Figure 2.

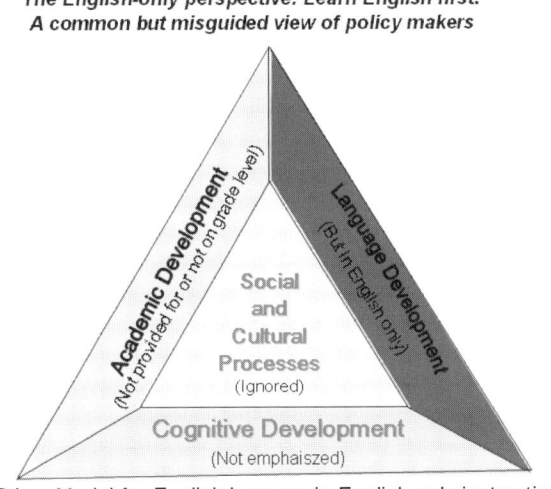

Figure 2. Second language acquisition for school

From a common-sense perspective, it would seem obvious that the first step anyone should take when entering a new country is to learn the language of that country. This may indeed be a wise decision for an adult immigrant who has been formally schooled and who has completed development in two of the prism components—cognitive and academic development—and lacks only one dimension of the linguistic component, acquisition of the L2, having already acquired the L1 to an adult level of proficiency. However, the school-aged child is in a very different situation. Developmental processes must continue without interruption through the school years in order for a child to reach the cognitive maturity of an adult.

Academic development must also continue without interruption for full adult mastery of the academic curriculum to occur. English is only one part of the learning process. When learning English is the first goal, during the period that this goal is the priority, the Prism model of language acquisition for school is reduced to mainly one dimension, development of one language (L2) and the other half of that component is missing—the continuing development of L1. This has unhappy consequences for the student in three out of four of the Prism model's components.

Firstly, meaningful academic development is not provided for in the initial years, because the highest priority is learning English rather than academic content. In succeeding years, academic development is often not at grade level, because students studying entirely in the L2 have missed at least two years of academic work while acquiring a basic knowledge of the L2. Secondly, cognitive development is not emphasized in the L2 and is not provided for in the L1 at school. Students enter school having completed six years of cognitive development in their L1. These students must continue to develop cognitively at the same rate as do other mother tongue English-speaking students in their first language. Switching a student's language of instruction to all-English causes a cognitive slowdown for English language learners that can last for several years. During this period, the English mother tongue speakers continue to develop cognitively at normal rates but the English language learners fall behind in cognitive development and may never catch up to their continually advancing mother tongue English peers. Thirdly, in an English-only environment, sociocultural processes may be largely ignored or less well provided for, and thus, as students feel that they are not in a supportive environment, less learning takes place.

In contrast, from kindergarten on, mother tongue-English speakers are instructed in all their school subjects through their L1, the language in which they are cognitively developed appropriate to their age. Even those who choose to participate in a bilingual class do not fall behind in other school subjects while learning another language during the school years. Thus, for most English mother tongue speakers, all four dimensions of the Prism model are in place in L1, including schooling in a socioculturally supportive environment and continuous cognitive and linguistic development in L1.

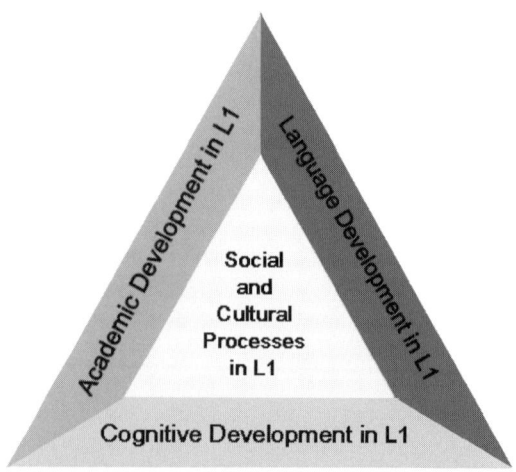

Figure 3. Language acquisition for school

HOW ACADEMIC PROGRESS IS MEASURED FOR BOTH MOTHER TONGUE AND SECOND LANGUAGE SPEAKERS OF ENGLISH

Typical mother tongue speakers of English in the USA make 10 months' progress in school achievement for each 10-month school year. This performance defines the 50th percentile or *normal curve equivalent* (NCE—an equal-interval percentile) on standardized norm-referenced tests and the average score on criterion-referenced tests as the students progress from grade to grade. Likewise, on a state or school district performance assessment, the standards developed for each grade level are also based on typical performance of groups of mother tongue English speakers on these tests. These tests measure continuous linguistic, cognitive, and academic growth in English, and the tests change weekly, monthly, and yearly to reflect that growth. It is on these school tests administered in English that English language learners are unrealistically expected to be able to demonstrate miraculous growth. Policy makers assume that non-English-proficient students should somehow be able to leap from the 1st percentile or NCE to the 50th (as compared to mother tongue speakers of English) in one to two years. During this period, mother tongue speakers continue to make 10 months' progress over a period of 10 months. Yet, if English learners are being taught only in English, a language they do not yet understand, they need at least two to three years to reach a high enough level of proficiency in L2 to attempt to keep up with the pace of the mother tongue-English speaker in school. For example, students in one group who are not yet proficient in English might study English intensively, and by the end of their first two years, make an enormous leap from the 1st to the 20th NCE when the students first take a standardized test in English reading, English language arts, and mathematics. To score at the level of the typical mother tongue-English speaker (50th percentile or NCE) in all school subjects, these English language learners must then continue to make *more* than one year's progress in one year and do so for several consecutive years to close the initial gap of 25-30 NCEs. Figure 4 visually illustrates this point.

For English language learners, progress at the typical rate of mother tongue-English speakers means only maintaining the initial large gap, not closing it, as the mother tongue-English speakers continue to make additional progress in all Prism components with each passing year. If English language learners make less than typical mother tongue-English speaker progress (e.g., English language learners might make 6 months' progress in one 10-month school year while typical mother tongue speakers make 10 months' progress), the initial large achievement gap will widen even further.

To illustrate further, if a group of English language learners experiences an initial 3-year gap in achievement assessed in English (math, science, social studies, language arts, reading, writing), they must make an average of about 1 ½ years' progress in the next 6 consecutive years (for a total of 9 years' progress in 6 years—a 30-NCE gain, from the 20th to the 50th NCE) to reach the same long-term performance level that a typical mother tongue-English speaker reaches by making 1 year's progress in 1 year for each of the 6 years (for a total of 6 years' progress in 6 years—a zero-NCE gain, staying at the 50th NCE). This is a difficult task indeed, even for an English language learner who has received excellent formal schooling before entering USA schools and whose achievement is on grade level for his/her

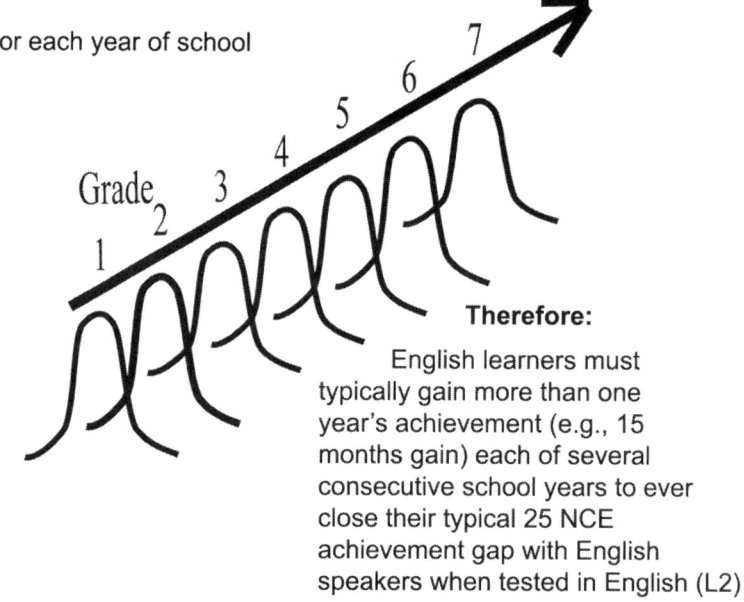

Figure 4. An important understanding

age when tested in his/her mother tongue. Still more daunting is the task of the English learner whose schooling has been interrupted by social or economic upheaval or warfare. Learning English while keeping up with mother tongue speakers' progress in other school subjects *and* while making up the material lost to interrupted or non-existent schooling in the student's country of origin is a truly formidable undertaking.

It is for these reasons that peer-equivalent grade-level bilingual schooling is essential to these students' long-term academic success. While the student is making the gains needed with each succeeding year to close the gap in performance on the tests in English, that bilingual student is not falling behind in cognitive and academic development. Once the bilingual students' average achievement reaches the 50th percentile or NCE (the average achievement level of mother tongue-English speakers) on school tests in English, the cognitive and academic work in L1 has kept these students on grade level and they sustain grade-level performance in English even as the academic work gets increasingly complex with each succeeding year in middle and high school.

Furthermore, L1 language development at school is deeply interrelated with cognitive development. Children who stop cognitive development in L1 before they have reached the final Piagetian stage of formal operations (somewhere around puberty) run the risk of suffering negative consequences as measured by school tests. Many studies indicate that if students do not reach a certain threshold in their L1, they may experience cognitive difficulties in the L2. Furthermore, developing cognitively and linguistically in L1 at least throughout the elementary school years provides a knowledge base that transfers from L1 to L2. When schooling is provided in both L1 and L2, both languages are the vehicle for strong cognitive and academic development. Linguistically, deep structure in L1 transfers to L2. Literacy skills transfer from L1 to L2 even when L1 is a non-Roman-alphabet language and L2 is English. Cognitive processes developed in L1 transfer to L2 (Ovando, Collier, & Combs, 2003).

Thus, the simplistic notion that all we need to do is to teach English language learners the English language does not address the needs of the school-age child. Furthermore, when we teach only the English language, we are literally slowing down a child's cognitive and academic growth (as well as ignoring the sociocultural aspects of learning), and that child may never catch up to the constantly advancing mother tongue-English speaker.

PREDICTIONS ON PROGRAM EFFECTIVENESS USING THE PRISM MODEL

In our series of longitudinal research studies (Thomas & Collier, 1997, 2002) conducted from 1985 to the present in 23 school districts in 15 states of the United States, we have collected data on English language learners' academic achievement across grades K-12. With each study, we have added to our understanding of what happens to these students across time and which school program and student background variables have the most influence on their academic success. We have examined the wide variety of USA school services provided for English learners and have been able to identify characteristics of school programs that distinguish one program from another. Figure 5 provides an overview of major program models developed for English language learners in the USA and their distinguishing characteristics based on the components of the Prism model.

The major types of programs for English language learners in the USA are illustrated on a continuum from left to right, from those programs with the least amount of support for the eight Prism dimensions to those programs with the most complete support for all of the Prism dimensions. For example, in the far left column is the program developed in response to Proposition 227 of California, as described in the referendum passed by voters in 1998. This program has to date demonstrated the least amount of success in closing the achievement gap, with the achievement gap between English language learners and mother tongue-English speakers remaining constant or even slightly widening during the first three years of its implementation. In the far right column is *two-way enrichment dual language education* (also called *bilingual immersion*), the program with the broadest coverage of the Prism dimensions. In the remainder of this chapter, we will examine the features of each program for its adherence to the four components of the Prism model in both L1 and L2. Finally, we will use large-scale data-based research findings to compare English language learners' progress over time in school systems where each of the different program types has been well implemented, as measured by fidelity to the definition of the program model. In other words, we will answer

While in these programs ➡ students receive:	REMEDIAL					ENRICHMENT	
	As in law	As well implemented				As well implemented	
	Proposition 227 in California	ESL Pullout	ESL Taught Through Content	TBE* with Traditional Teaching	TBE* with Current Teaching	One-way DL/DBE** -one group taught in two languages	Two-way DL/DBE** -two groups taught in their two languages
Cognitive Emphasis	None	Little	Some	Some	Moderate	Strong	Strong
Academic Emphasis (in all school subjects)	None	None	Yes	Yes	Yes	Yes	Yes
Linguistic Emphasis L1=primary language, L2=English	Only Social English (only in L2)	Only Social English (only in L2)	Academic English (only in L2)	Develops Partial L1 + L2 Academic Proficiency	Develops Partial L1 + L2 Academic Proficiency	Develops Full L1 + L2 Academic Proficiency	Develops Full L1 + L2 Academic Proficiency
Sociocultural Emphasis C1=1st culture C2=2nd culture	None	Little	Some	Some	Moderate	Strong C1+C2	Strong C1+C2
Program Length	Transitory 1 year	Short-term 1-2 years	Short-term 2-3 years	Short-term 2-3 years	Intermediate 3-4 years	Sustained 6-12 years	Sustained 6-12 years
Native Language Academic Support	None	None	None	Some	Moderate	Strong	Strong
Exposure to English Speakers	No	Yes	Yes	No	Yes Half-day	Yes Half-day	Yes All day
Extra Instructional Cost	High (extra teachers needed)	High (extra teachers needed)	High (extra teachers needed)	Small-to-moderate (special curriculum)	Small-to-moderate (special curriculum)	Least expensive: Standard mainstream curriculum	Least expensive: Standard mainstream curriculum
Percent of Achievement Gap With Native-English Speakers Closed by End of Schooling (based on data-analytic research)	Unresearched longitudinally but no evidence of gap closure by ELLs since 1998 start	None final average scores at 11th national percentile -max is 18th	Less than 50% final average scores at 22nd national percentile - max is 32nd	Less than 50% final average scores at 24th national percentile	More than 50% final average scores at 32nd national percentile (but 90-10 TBE at 45th percentile)	100% of gap fully closed by end of school – average scores at or above 50th national percentile	100% of gap fully closed by end of school -- average scores above 50th national percentile

* TBE stands for *transitional bilingual education*   ** DL/DBE stands for *dual language/ developmental bilingual education*

Copyright © 2003, Wayne P. Thomas & Virginia P. Collier

Figure 5. Summary of characteristics and effectiveness of common U.S. programs for English learners

the question of how well students do in school in their L2 depending upon the particular school program in which they are placed when they first arrive in the school system with no English proficiency. This will illustrate the predictive power of the Prism model by demonstrating a direct relationship between each program's coverage of the Prism dimensions and the degree of educational effectiveness for that program.

One Year Intensive English Only

Proposition 227, approved by California voters through a referendum in 1998, specifies that students not proficient in English should be placed in a one-year program to learn intensive English. This plan segregates the students in a classroom separate from the English mainstream and does not address how the students are to be given access to the rest of the curriculum—math, science, and social studies. The strongest principle stated in the referendum is that students are not to be instructed using their L1—only English instruction is allowed. Following passage of the referendum, few schools in California chose to deny students access to the curriculum, but many felt obligated to follow the principal purpose of the referendum to eliminate bilingual instruction. Only in schools where parents requested waivers have students been given continuing instruction through both L1 and L2. Some schools chose to continue or develop two-way dual language programs as another alternative to the referendum, a program supported by English-speaking parents who choose for their children to participate in the bilingual classes. As a result of the referendum, only approximately 15% of English learners in California continue to be taught through both L1 and L2.

The program mandated in Proposition 227 provides the least support for the eight dimensions of the Prism model as represented in the English-only Prism presented in Figure 2. Sociocultural support is not addressed in this program—the teachers are expected to teach only in English and respond to the students only in English. In these intensive English classes, a bicultural curriculum that would address some of the emotional/affective side of learning is not encouraged. Cognitive development is not addressed in the language of the referendum. Since students are to be taught exclusively in English in a segregated context where they do not have access to mother tongue English-speaking peers, there is little stimulus for cognitive development which best occurs in interactions with same-aged peers in the L2 or through age-appropriate problem-solving tasks done in L1. Since the students are denied use of their L1 in school, little cognitive development is stimulated in this one-year program. Even academic development is ignored, with heavy emphasis on English development rather than teaching English through meaningful academic content. Finally, the referendum clearly dictates that all instruction will be in English, so students in this program are denied access to academic, cognitive, and linguistic development through their mother tongue. This eliminates half of the Prism dimensions—all four dimensions developed through L1.

The Prism model predicts that bilingual learners receiving accelerated learning through their two languages develop socioculturally, linguistically, cognitively, and academically through each language—eight dimensions in all. In contrast, Proposition 227 supports students in only one dimension, i.e. acquiring the English language and only for one year. This is extremely minimal support. Our analyses (see Figure 6) as well as other researchers' studies have found that English learners in this program have not made any progress towards closing the achievement gap and the gap has widened in the secondary years. Thus, this program has resulted in the lowest achievement for English learners of any program in the USA (Parrish, et al. 2002; Thompson et al., 2002).

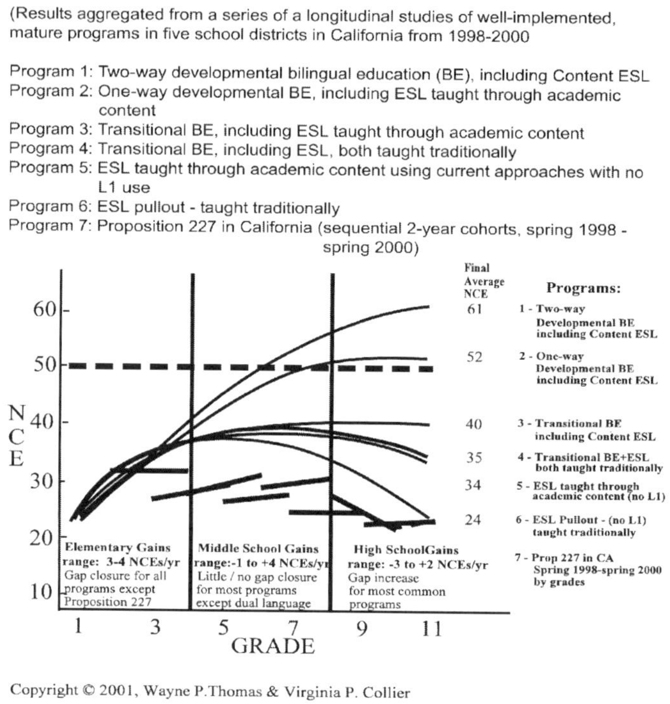
(Results aggregated from a series of a longitudinal studies of well-implemented, mature programs in five school districts in California from 1998-2000
Program 1: Two-way developmental bilingual education (BE), including Content ESL
Program 2: One-way developmental BE, including ESL taught through academic content
Program 3: Transitional BE, including ESL taught through academic content
Program 4: Transitional BE, including ESL, both taught traditionally
Program 5: ESL taught through academic content using current approaches with no L1 use
Program 6: ESL pullout - taught traditionally
Program 7: Proposition 227 in California (sequential 2-year cohorts, spring 1998 - spring 2000)
Final Average NCE
61
52
40
35
34
24
Programs:
1 - Two-way Developmental BE including Content ESL
2 - One-way Developmental BE including Content ESL
3 - Transitional BE including Content ESL
4 - Transitional BE+ESL both taught traditionally
5 - ESL taught through academic content (no L1)
6 - ESL Pullout - (no L1) taught traditionally
7 - Prop 227 in CA Spring 1998-spring 2000 by grades
NCE
60
50
40
30
20
10
Elementary Gains range: 3-4 NCEs/yr Gap closure for all programs except Proposition 227
Middle School Gains range: -1 to +4 NCEs/yr Little / no gap closure for most programs except dual language
High School Gains range: -3 to +2 NCEs/yr Gap increase for most common programs
1 3 5 7 9 11
GRADE
Copyright © 2001, Wayne P. Thomas & Virginia P. Collier

Figure 6. English learners' long-term K-12 achievement in normal curve equivalents (NCEs) on standardized tests in English reading compared across seven program models

ESL Pullout or ESL Taught as a Subject at Secondary Level

This most commonly encountered program for English learners in the USA places these students in a mainstream class in the elementary school, with an ESL resource teacher pulling the English learners out of their classrooms to focus on ESL lessons for generally one or two hours per day. At middle and high school level, English learners are assigned to ESL as one of their subjects for one or two classes per day, and the ESL teacher is mainly responsible for teaching the structure of the English language. Examining the Prism model dimensions, this model again provides minimal support for students. While with the ESL teacher, there is little time for focus on cognitive development. Academic subjects are not taught by the ESL teacher, and no support for development of academic skills through students' first language is provided. Program length is minimal, generally one to two years. As with Proposition 227, one Prism dimension is being developed during the ESL support time—the English language. A second Prism dimension, sociocultural support, may be addressed while students are with the ESL teacher but that is for a minimal amount of time. Our research findings across numerous school districts in the USA indicate that the average achievement levels of high school graduates who were initially placed in ESL pullout programs is the 11th percentile (24th NCE), not high enough achievement to continue in higher education, and this is the program with the largest number of high school dropouts (Thomas & Collier, 1997). Little or no long-term gap closure is associated with ESL pullout.

ESL Taught through Academic Content, also called Sheltered Instruction

Taking ESL instruction one step further by adding academic content to the responsibilities of the ESL teacher, or an ESL teacher teaming with a content teacher, adds two significant Prism components—academic and cognitive development in L2. All the instruction is still in English in this program, and thus four Prism dimensions are missing (sociocultural, linguistic, cognitive, and academic development through the first language). At least during English instruction, students are accelerating their growth through lessons that teach English through meaningful academic content, and the ESL classes are more cognitively complex, an important dimension that is missing from ESL pullout and Proposition 227 support services. In ESL content classes, as in ESL pullout, sociocultural support is provided: The teachers understand the SLA process, and aspects of bicultural curricular learning may be incorporated into these ESL classes. ESL content classes are usually provided for at least one more year than ESL pullout support so that both the Prism dimensions supported by the ESL content teacher are extended and the students' achievements are accelerated for one more year before students move into the mainstream for the full school day. English language learners need acceleration to achieve gap closure. While mother tongue-English speakers are making 10 months' progress with each school year, English language learners, who initially perform low on curricular tests in English, must make more than 10 months' progress for many years in a row to eventually catch up to the constantly advancing mother tongue-English speakers on grade level. We have found in our research studies that English language learners who received a quality ESL content program can close half of the achievement gap, graduating high school in the 22nd national percentile (34th NCE) (Thomas & Collier, 1997, 2002). Addressing half of the Prism model dimensions raises students' achievement levels significantly, but represents only half of the way to grade-level achievement, and these ESL graduates remain in the bottom quartile of student achievement across the USA.

Transitional Bilingual Education

Transitional bilingual education is, like ESL pullout, a commonly encountered program in the USA for the states with very large numbers of English language learners of one language background such as Spanish speakers. Among the various types of bilingual programs, transitional bilingual schooling is the program most often supported by state funding, when state legislation for bilingual instruction has been provided. This type of bilingual schooling is a remedial model designed to move students into all-English instruction as soon as possible with only two to three years of some instructional support through students' L1 combined with a portion of time in ESL content instruction. This program significantly increases the number of Prism dimensions addressed within the short duration of the program. Academic, cognitive, and linguistic development are provided through both L1 and L2 in a socioculturally supportive environment, with all of the eight dimensions addressed when the classes are well implemented.

However, transitional bilingual classes are typically self-contained, separate from the mainstream, and often perceived by mother tongue English-speaking peers as remedial, meant for students who have "problems." The same is true of separate ESL classes. The low social status of students in the program can lead to subtle but powerful influences on English language learners' achievement. This in turn affects the sociocultural processes in learning, lessening the effectiveness of this component. Even when bilingual/bicultural teachers are warm, caring and supportive emotionally and cross-culturally, students become increasingly aware of their low social status within the whole school community. Another Prism dimension that may be reduced in less effective transitional bilingual classes is the amount and type of L1 support. We have found that the classes that provide for very little L1, shifting into mostly L2 instruction within the first two years, lead to lower academic achievement in L2.

This raises an additional factor that must be taken into account in the Prism model. The number of Prism dimensions covered by a program is one aspect of the model, but length of the program also strongly influences student achievement. So the Prism dimensions must be implemented for a sufficient time to have a sustained effect on student achievement. Even when all eight dimensions of the model are addressed in transitional bilingual classes, after three years of support, students have only closed half of the achievement gap in their L2 (similar to the achievement levels of students attending ESL content). They may be on grade level in their L1 but not yet on grade level in their L2. In our latest research (Thomas & Collier, 2002), we found that once students leave their special support program and move into the mainstream, they no longer continue to close the achievement gap, but at their best, make one year's progress in each remaining year of school. Thus, students in the best implemented transitional bilingual programs by the end of high school were able to reach the 32nd percentile (40th NCE) in their English achievement, higher than ESL content but still not at the typical 50th percentile performance of mother tongue-English speakers (Thomas & Collier, 1997, 2002).

One-way and Two-way Dual Language Education

To avoid the negative social perceptions of transitional bilingual education, USA schools that have worked on enriching their bilingual programs are increasingly using the term *dual language education* to refer to an enrichment model of bilingual schooling. While these programs were the least common model a decade ago, they are rapidly increasing in number as educators discover the power of these programs to raise academic achievement for all students who choose to enroll. Dual language education is the curricular mainstream, taught through two languages. Students are educated together throughout the day in cognitively challenging, grade-level academic content in interactive, discovery-learning classes. Alternating between the two languages takes place not by translation but by subject or thematic unit or instructional time, so that after several years students become academically proficient in both languages of instruction, able to do academic work on grade level in either language. In this model, English learners can close the gap fully in their L2, reaching high attainment at or above the 50th percentile (grade-level achievement) in both L1 and L2 by middle school years and graduating above grade level by the end of high school (see Figure 6, Thomas & Collier, 1997, 2002).

One-way refers to one language group being schooled through two languages, while *two-way* refers to two language groups being schooled through their two languages. Two-way classes include mother tongue-English speakers who have chosen to be schooled bilingually, and their achievement is also typically at or above grade level when enrolled in these classes (Lindholm-Leary, 2001; Thomas &

Collier, 2002). Thus, all of the eight Prism dimensions are fully covered in the dual language program, for both English learners and mother tongue-English speakers. In two-way bilingual classes, the English learners are not segregated in a remedial program, but instead they are respected and valued as peer teachers when the instruction is in their home language, and they are given support by their peers to acquire full academic proficiency in English, their L2, across the curriculum. The dual language teachers support both groups socioculturally through a bilingual/bicultural curriculum and provide a context for students to develop cognitively, linguistically, and academically through both languages, for at least six years during the elementary school years (Grades PK-5). Increasingly, the middle schools and high schools that serve these students are developing coursework to continue the academic challenge in both languages.

CONCLUSIONS

We have examined several major types of programs for English learners in terms of the number of Prism model components and dimensions addressed, their degree of coverage of the factors included in the Prism model dimensions, and the length of time that each program operates. As a result, we predicted a ranking for each program, from lowest to highest in terms of the amount of achievement gap closure produced by each.

We also conducted research in school districts around the country from 1991 to 2002, following the longitudinal progress of English learners in each program type. Before comparing programs, we were careful to ascertain that each school district had fully and faithfully implemented the programs to the greatest extent possible so that implementation factors would be controlled, yielding a more valid comparison of program effects. In addition, our program descriptions specified initial conditions of student achievement, described specific program features and strategies, and linked these program descriptions to measured achievement and gap closure outcomes for each program. Finally, we evaluated each program type over a sufficiently long period of time to allow typically small program effect sizes, ranging from 0 to .25 (0-5 NCEs) per year, to accumulate to levels detectable by measures of practical and statistical significance.

The results of our program comparisons over time indicate that the long-term achievement of English learners in each program is indeed directly related to the Prism model dimensions addressed, the degree of coverage of these dimensions, and the duration of the program in years. We interpret this as evidence that the Prism model has construct validity, as well as predictive validity. Clearly, the Prism model can be used as a template for programmatic design, so that programs fully addressing the Prism components and dimensions, and that are sustained long enough, can be expected to produce full achievement gap closure.

As the next step in the refinement of the Prism model, we intend to further develop the Prism model to allow multiple regression-based predictions of long-term achievement of English learners, based on weights determined by observations of program characteristics in school classrooms. In this way, we will continue to investigate the potential for each program type to produce some degree of gap closure, and we will further improve the basis for our program recommendations based on the Prism components and dimensions.

REFERENCES

Collier, V. P. (1995a). *Acquiring a second language for school*. Washington, DC: National Clearinghouse for English Language Acquisition. [Electronic version: http//www.ncela.gwu.edu].

Collier, V. P. (1995b). *Promoting academic success for ESL students: Understanding second language acquisition for school*. Woodside, NY: Bastos Educational Publications.

Collier, V. P. (1995c). Second language acquisition for school: Academic, cognitive, sociocultural, and linguistic processes. In J. E. Alatis et al. (Eds.), *Georgetown University Round Table on Languages and Linguistics 1995* (pp. 311–327). Washington, DC: Georgetown University Press.

Cummins, J. (2000). *Language, power and pedagogy: Bilingual children in the crossfire*. Clevedon, England: Multilingual Matters.

Ellis, R. (1994). *The study of second language acquisition*. Oxford: Oxford University Press.

Larsen-Freeman, D., & Long, M. H. (1991). *An introduction to second language acquisition research*. New York: Longman.

Lindholm-Leary, K. (2001). *Dual language education*. Clevedon, England: Multilingual Matters.

Ovando, C. J., Collier, V. P., & Combs, M. C. (2003). *Bilingual and ESL classrooms: Teaching in multicultural contexts* (3rd ed.). New York: McGraw-Hill.

Parrish, T. B., Linquanti, R., Merickel, A., Quick, H. E., Laird, J., & Esra, P. (2002). *Effects of the implementation of Proposition 227 on the education of English learners, K-12: Year 2 report*. Palo Alto, CA: American Institutes for Research.

Thomas, W. P., & Collier, V. P. (1997). *School effectiveness for language minority students*. Washington, DC: National Clearinghouse for English Language Acquisition. [Electronic version: http//www.ncela.gwu.edu].

Thomas, W. P., & Collier, V. P. (2002). *A national study of school effectiveness for language minority students' long-term academic achievement*. Santa Cruz, CA: Center for Research on Education, Diversity and Excellence, University of California-Santa Cruz. [Electronic version: http//www.crede.ucsc.edu].

Thompson, M. S., DiCerbo, K. E., Mahoney, K., & MacSwan, J. (2002, January). Exito en California? A validity critique of language program evaluations and analysis of English learner test scores. *Education Policy Analysis Archives, 10*(7). Retrieved 26 February 2006 from http//www.epaa.asu.edu/epaa/v10n7.

Wong-Fillmore, L. (1991). Second-language learning in children: A model of language learning in social context. In E. Bialystok (Ed.), *Language processing in bilingual children* (pp. 49–69). Cambridge: Cambridge University Press.

CHAPTER 23

FOUR KEYS FOR SCHOOL SUCCESS FOR ELEMENTARY ENGLISH LEARNERS

YVONNE FREEMAN AND DAVID FREEMAN

The University of Texas at Brownsville, USA

ABSTRACT

Large numbers of students in English-speaking countries enter elementary schools speaking little or no English. A review of the research in second language acquisition and effective schooling reveals widespread agreement on the principles that underlie successful programs for these students. However, several factors have limited the implementation of such programs. This chapter reviews the theory and research that supports programs that lead to academic success for English learners. The factors that prevent the development of successful programs are then considered. These include an emphasis on standards and testing, a lack of primary language support, a failure to distinguish types of English learners, and a shortage of teachers prepared to work with English learners. Four keys for academic success for English learners are presented: engage students in challenging, theme-based curriculum to develop academic concepts; draw on students' background—their experiences, cultures, and languages; organize collaborative activities and scaffold instruction to build students' academic English proficiency; and create confident students who value school and value themselves as learners. Each key is explained and illustrated. A curriculum based on these keys provides elementary English learners with the greatest likelihood of academic success.

INTRODUCTION

Over the past 20 years the number of English language learners in schools in North America has increased dramatically. In North America, this increase has most affected elementary classrooms. In Europe, Asia, and South America as well, many more schools have opened to teach English as a second or additional language to elementary age children. Once the concern of English as a second language (ESL) specialists, English language learners are now every teacher's concern in many schools in North America. This is true in areas that have traditionally had high numbers of English learners, such as California, Florida, and Toronto, but now it is also true in locations that have had few English language learners in the past, such as Iowa and Idaho. Worldwide, the demand for qualified teachers of English continues to increase. In North America, as the number of English learners has grown, so has the sophistication of the teachers working with these students. More teachers now have had training in the areas of linguistics, second language acquisition, and second language teaching methods. However, in parts of North America and in many other areas of the world, despite a greater knowledge base for successful teaching of English learners, many teachers do not receive adequate preparation for working with English language learners. In many parts of the world, the only qualification for many elementary teachers hired to teach English is their English language proficiency and subject area knowledge. Often, these teachers have limited or no knowledge of second language acquisition, cross-cultural communication, or methods of teaching a second language.

Even teachers with some background in teaching ESL students have not fully developed an understanding of the differences among their English language learners, nor have they adopted current methods for teaching them. In the following sections, we identify three types of English learners and consider differences in their language proficiencies. Then we summarize the research for effective teaching of English learners, presenting it as four keys for school success. We conclude by providing an extended example of one teacher applying the four keys with her English learners in an elementary class in North America.

TYPES OF ENGLISH LANGUAGE LEARNERS

The range of backgrounds of English language learners is often not acknowledged. Programs designed for these students are often based on the assumption that they are all alike; nevertheless a careful examination of students learning English as an second or additional language reveals significant differences among types of students based on the time they have spent in a context in which English is frequently used and on their previous schooling. Many researchers have classified English language learners into three broad groups (Freeman & Freeman, 2002; Olsen & Jaramillo, 1999). Table 1 summarizes the characteristics of these three groups.

Table 1. Types of Older English Learners (adapted from Olsen and Jaramillo, 1999)

Learner Types	Description
New to English with adequate schooling	• Recent arrivals and/or less than 5 years in an English speaking setting) • Adequate schooling in mother tongue/country of origin • Soon catch up academically • May still score low on standardized tests given in English
New to English with limited formal schooling	• Recent arrivals and/or less than 5 years in an English-speaking setting • Interrupted or limited schooling in mother tongue/country of origin • Limited mother tongue literacy • Below grade level in math • Poor academic achievement
Long term ESL learner	• 7 or more years in an English-speaking setting • Have had ESL or bilingual instruction, but no consistent program • Below grade level in reading and writing • Mismatch between student perception of achievement and actual grades • May get adequate grades but score low on tests

The first group includes those students who have come to a school within the last five years, where English is the medium of instruction and who have strong educational backgrounds and literacy in their first language and sometimes in other languages as well. They have developed academic language and skills in their first language that will transfer to their content area studies in English. However, although many have studied English in their countries of origin, most lack conversational fluency in English. These students often achieve academic success in their classes in a short period of time although they may struggle for several years to compete with native English speakers on standardized tests. These new arrivals fit into traditionally organized programs for English learners, and they often are integrated into mainstream classes after one or two years.

Elementary students with adequate formal schooling generally catch up fairly quickly. Middle school and high school students may need more time to develop the level of academic language needed for school success since with each year, the academic demands increase. For example, Korean students entering high school in an English medium school in Hong Kong reported that they needed to study many more hours each week than their classmates, many of whom were mother tongue English speakers, if they hoped to do well in classes. These students came to Hong Kong with a good academic background, but the school they entered was one of the best in the city, and, as a result, there was a gap between the academic level of these Korean students and their new classmates. In addition, although they had studied English, they now received all their schooling in English, and it took them extra time to complete assignments in a second language.

Another example is in Lithuania where students from Lithuania, Latvia, Russia, and the Ukraine with adequate formal schooling and an advanced level of English proficiency entered a small English medium liberal arts college. The students achieved a high level of academic success, in part due to their strong backgrounds and good work ethic. However, very few mother tongue English speakers attended the college, so the students did not have to compete with mother tongue English-speaking peers. Although they did very well in college, some of these students struggled when they attended graduate school in English speaking countries.

The second group of students described in Table 1 are recent arrivals to an English-speaking setting who come to school with interrupted or limited formal schooling backgrounds as well as limited English proficiency. These students struggle with reading and writing in their first languages or do not read or write their home languages at all. In addition, because of their limited experiences in school, they lack basic concepts in the different subject areas, often operating at least two years below grade level in math. They are faced with the complex task of developing conversational English, becoming literate in English, and gaining the academic knowledge and skills they need to compete academically with mother tongue English speakers. Because they do not have the academic background to draw upon in their native languages, these students often struggle with course work and do not score well on standardized tests. They also may lack an understanding of how schools are organized and how students are expected to act in schools; they are not familiar with school culture.

In international settings, most English medium schools require incoming students to have adequate schooling. Students with limited or interrupted schooling are generally not admitted. However, in some cases students who are significantly behind their classmates enroll in these schools. For example, in Hong Kong some local Cantonese speakers are admitted to English medium schools. The Cantonese speakers have attended school, but the classes in the English medium school follow a different curriculum and teachers often organize group work and independent research projects, two types of pedagogic approaches many Cantonese students have not experienced. In addition, some of the Cantonese speakers enter school with limited literacy in Cantonese. Many of these students struggle in the English medium school.

A third group consists of English learners who, for an extended period of time, have lived in an English-speaking setting and attended schools in which the medium of instruction is English. Indeed, many have had their entire schooling in an English-speaking school system. Usually, they have been in and out of various ESL and/or bilingual programs without ever having received any kind of consistent support. Older students may also have missed school during extended periods at different times because their families were migrant workers or because they returned to the parents' homeland to visit relatives. These students are below grade level in reading and writing and usually in math as well. Often, they get passing grades when they do the required work. Because teachers may be passing them simply because they turn in the work, their grades give many of these students a false perception of their academic achievement. However, on standardized tests, their scores are low. These students usually have conversational fluency in English and also may be fluent speakers of their parents' first language, but they lack the academic English language proficiency they need to compete with native English speakers.

In some international settings students are schooled entirely in English. They do not receive first language literacy instruction and do not develop the ability to read in their first language despite the presence of environmental print in that language. For example, in both Argentina and Uruguay parents may enroll their preschool children in prestigious English medium schools. The students are instructed entirely in English. While some of these students succeed, others struggle and may drop out of the school. Students who do continue to study are often behind their classmates academically. Although they speak Spanish, they do not read and write well, and their written English is often significantly below the level of classmates who developed first language literacy.

The first group of students, the newly arrived English learners with adequate first-language schooling, do need support. They need effective bilingual or ESL programs that will allow them to continue to develop subject matter knowledge and skills as they acquire English. They need knowledgeable teachers who can make the English instruction comprehensible. They also need support as they go through culture shock and the adjustments involved in living in a new culture and speaking a new language. This is particularly true for students who enter school at the upper primary, middle school, and high school grades. Students in the other two groups face even greater challenges in trying to succeed academically in a new language. They may lack the academic concepts and academic language needed for school success. The difference between academic and conversational language registers is a key in understanding the needs of the three types of English learners.

CONVERSATIONAL AND ACADEMIC LANGUAGE PROFICIENCY

Based on the research of Skutnabb-Kangas (1979) with Finnish students in Sweden and his own research with immigrant students in Canada, Cummins (1981) observed that many teachers, administrators, and school psychologists assumed that children had overcome all difficulties with their new language when they could converse easily in the language. Because these same students struggled with academic tasks, they were often assigned to special education classes or labeled as lazy or unmotivated.

His research led Cummins to develop a distinction between *basic interpersonal communicative skills* (BICS) or conversational language *and cognitive academic language proficiency* (CALP), academic language. Cummins (2000) found that it takes longer for English learners to develop academic language in English than to gain conversational language proficiency:

> Conversational aspects of proficiency reached peer-appropriate levels usually within about two years of exposure to L2 but a period of five to seven years was required, on average, for immigrant students to approach grade norms in academic aspects of English (p. 58).

Subsequent research by Collier (1989, 1992, 1995, this volume) and others has supported Cummins' early findings. Students need about two years to develop conversational language, but academic language takes at least twice as long to develop.

Cummins (2000) has explained that the difference between conversational and academic language is not the same as the difference between oral and written language. Reading a picture post card from a friend could be an instance of conversational language while listening to an academic lecture would involve academic language. The distinction between the two is really a difference in register. As Cummins puts it,

> Oral classroom discussions do not involve reading and writing directly, but they do reflect the degree of students' access to and command of literate or academic registers of language. This is why CALP [cognitive, academic language proficiency] can be defined as expertise in understanding and using literacy-related aspects of language (p. 70).

DIFFERENCES IN LANGUAGE PROFICIENCY AMONG TYPES OF ENGLISH LEARNERS

Students coming from non-English-speaking families and new arrivals may enter school speaking little or no English even for conversational purposes. Most of these students develop conversational language fairly quickly as they interact with English speakers both in and out of school, although older students may not gain native-like pronunciation. If the new arrivals have developed academic proficiency in their first language, the task of developing academic proficiency in English is facilitated. They still need to develop the English vocabulary and syntax that characterizes academic English, but they already have an implicit knowledge of how academic language works.

Most new arrivals with limited or interrupted formal schooling lack both conversational and academic English. They face an especially difficult challenge to develop academic English. There is a significant gap between their academic knowledge and skills and the knowledge and skills of many of their classmates.

They are faced with learning both content knowledge and the academic registers of English needed to discuss the concepts.

Long-term English learners, those who have been in schools in English-speaking countries for an extended time, have generally acquired conversational English. As a result, they are often placed in mainstream classes. If they do poorly in school, they may be recommended for special education classes since the assumption is that English is not their problem. Although they may have developed conversational language, long-term English learners face the task of developing academic language. They do not know how to talk, read and write about school subjects in their first language or in English. In fact, teachers sometimes conclude that some English learners have 'no language,' when actually the problem is that they lack the language that is appropriate for and valued in the school setting.

Table 2 shows the kinds of language proficiency each of the types of English learners has typically acquired.

Table 2. Language Proficiency

	Conversational language		Academic language	
	English	L 1	English	L 1
Newly-arrived with adequate schooling	X	X	–	X
Newly-arrived with limited formal schooling	–	X	–	–
Long-term English learners	X	X	–	–

As teachers develop greater awareness of the differences in language proficiency among their English learners, they can better tailor instruction to meet their needs. In particular, teachers need to consider their students' background academic knowledge and their levels of academic and conversational English proficiency as they assess and place students.

RESEARCH-BASED KEYS FOR SUCCESS

English learners differ in a number of ways. These include differences in their academic background, their level of primary language literacy, and their level of English proficiency. Careful assessment and placement of English learners in appropriate classes enhances their potential for school success. When the classes are organized around research-based principles, all students can succeed. In the following sections, we summarize the research on effective classes for English learners as four keys for success.

Key #1 Engage Students in Challenging, Theme-Based Curriculum to Develop Academic Concepts

The U.S. Department of Education (Excellence, 1996) has issued a set of principles to guide state and local school districts in considering reform for the education of linguistically and culturally diverse students. These include having high expectations in both language and content, building on the previous experiences of students, taking their language and cultural backgrounds into consideration when assessing students, and being cognizant of the fact that the success of English learners is a responsibility shared by all educators, the family and the community. When educators challenge students by setting high expectations and then provide curricula that allow students to meet those challenges, they show a belief in students' potential.

In the U.S. nearly 80% of all English learners come from Spanish-speaking backgrounds. Moll (1988) explains that these Latino students need "challenging, innovative, and intellectually rigorous curriculum" (p. 467) that is meaningful and draws on personal experiences. He is opposed to ability groups, which he says degrade students and show a lack of respect for them. Moll's research shows that English learners thrive in classrooms where teachers are given autonomy and opportunities to reflect upon their teaching in order to better meet students' needs.

Teachers who believe in their students often become advocates for them. Moll (1988) identified three key characteristics of effective teachers working with English learners: a) They were able to articulate theory and defend their classroom practices; b) They were able to argue with administrators to allow them to select materials and implement curriculum according to their professional judgment; and c) they drew on support from colleagues who shared their approach to teaching.

These effective, knowledgeable teachers found ways to show both students and fellow educators that they believed in the potential of all the students they taught. They did this by implementing innovative student interactions including dramatization, crossage tutoring, and multiple opportunities to develop oral and written languages drawing on first language strengths. Such classroom practices enable students to develop their potential.

Gersten and Jiménez (1994) observed successful teachers during reading instruction. They looked particularly at ways teachers supported intermediate students who lacked first language literacy and experienced difficulties in reading in English. The researchers concluded that effective instruction for language minority students was challenging, encouraged involvement, provided opportunities for success, and included scaffolding and a variety of graphic organizers to draw on background knowledge and give students access to content. In addition, they found that effective teachers give frequent feedback, make the content comprehensible, encourage collaborative interactions, and show respect for cultural diversity. All these practices show a belief in student potential.

García (1999) conducted research on attributes of effective teachers. One of his findings was that the teachers focused on meaningful instruction and organized curriculum around themes. He explains that "students became 'experts' in thematic domains while also acquiring the requisite academic skills" (p. 311). Teachers show a belief in student potential when they create conditions in which students can become "experts." Further, García reported on a special program for high school students that featured student-generated themes. As one teacher commented:

> Having student-generated themes formalized student input for curriculum [because] they create the theme, [and] we [teachers] let them imagine what they want to study. They write the curriculum at the start of the six-week unit. From assignment to assessment, they are more involved" (p. 362).

This program was successful in part because teachers provided challenging curriculum by involving their students in choosing and developing the themes around which the curriculum was based.

Key #2 Draw on Students' Background – Their Experiences, Cultures, and Languages

In a large, urban California school district provides a series of all day inservices for all teachers. Teachers are provided a substitute and given professional development credit and can choose among sessions, which feature the language, culture, and history of the primary immigrant groups in the district. The presenters include members of the groups. Often, students from the group being featured are brought in, and a moderator asks questions of a student panel.

In the district, the Hmong people of Southeast Asia form a large proportion of the English learners. For that reason, each year several sessions highlight Hmong students. In this way, the district follows Vang's (2000) observation that preservice and inservice teacher training about Hmong culture helps teachers reach these students. By allowing teachers to choose the sessions they wish to attend, paying for a substitute, and giving professional development credit, the district encourages teachers to study the language and culture of their students.

Jiménez (2001) points out that the struggling Latino/a students he worked with thrived when their specific background and national origin were recognized and when the challenge these students face at becoming competent bilinguals was acknowledged. In the school that Jiménez studied, the Spanish-speaking students were not all lumped together and treated alike. Those who were not proficient in their native Spanish were not critiqued. Students from El Salvador or Guatemala were validated for their specific national origin, and students who served as language brokers for their monolingual Spanish-speaking relatives were given recognition. All the students were encouraged to connect their reading and writing in English to their own cultural backgrounds and to value the literacy of their communities, including the oral literary traditions. In these ways, educators at the school showed respect for the students' cultures, languages, and backgrounds.

Moran et al. (1993) point out that overage students (students who are older than their classmates) do well when "they are accepted, respected, made to feel that they belong, and given opportunities to be in charge of their own learning" (p. 117). It is especially important to show older elementary students that they are accepted, and one way schools can do this is to validate their linguistic and cultural backgrounds. These students need teachers who build personal relationships with them and connect to their families. Effective teachers use students' first languages and background knowledge as a base for what they are teaching and hold high expectations for all their students.

Shifini (1997) has also looked at struggling, immigrant students, including those with limited formal schooling. He makes specific suggestions for improving their literacy. These involve helping students feel part of the classroom community, drawing on students' background knowledge, and encouraging skill development through successful engagements with texts. A key is to build on what students bring to the classroom—their language, culture, and previous experience—to help them develop the knowledge and skills they need to succeed academically.

Key #3 Organize Collaborative Activities and Scaffold Instruction to Build Students' Academic English Proficiency

Much of the research reported in the previous sections points to the need for student collaboration and scaffolded instruction. For example, Chang (2001), whose research focused on struggling, immigrant Asian Pacific American students, calls for collaboration and scaffolding to help students build academic English proficiency. Chang presents a checklist for effective teaching and for creating a positive learning environment for immigrant students. To create the checklist, Chang drew on standards for effective teaching developed by the Center for Research on Education, Diversity, and Excellence (CREDE, see www.crede.ucsc.edu) and Gardner's (1983) theory of multiple intelligences. Chang has developed Gardner's idea of diverse entry points and applied this concept specifically to immigrant students. Immigrant students have different strengths, interests, and backgrounds that can be drawn upon by sensitive, knowledgeable teachers as they teach. When teachers know their students, they can teach effectively starting where the student is and moving the student to new understandings.

Chang (2001) suggests that teachers should consider the following six topics in planning lessons:

1. Joint productive activities: Students are encouraged to work with each other and the teacher as well as parents to reach instructional goals and objectives.
2. Language development: Teachers provide students with opportunities to use conversational and academic language appropriately in a variety of settings adjusting the language to students' experience with English and providing first language support.
3. Contextualization: Teachers draw upon students' background and culture and bring in guests who can foster respect for multicultural perspectives.
4. Challenging activities: Teachers plan for and implement activities that encourage academic concept development drawing on cultural funds of knowledge and using culturally appropriate approaches to teaching.
5. Instructional conversations: Teachers organize their classrooms to insure that conversation between the teacher and peers develops academic concepts and language.
6. Diverse entry points: In all content areas and in all interactive activities, the teacher is sensitive to the students' needs, interests, talents, and understandings and is able to use that information to extend students' learning.

Chang's list reflects both of the first two keys: the importance of providing challenging curriculum that shows a belief in student potential as well as building on students' culture, language, and background. In addition, her ideas of joint productive activities, diverse entry points, contextualization, and instructional conversations are consistent with the third key: all are ways teachers can organize collaborative activities and scaffold instruction to help students reach their potential.

Key #4 Create Confident Students Who Value School and Value Themselves as Learners

In their guide for educators and other advocates for immigrant students Olsen and Jaramillo (1999) describe in detail how schools can institute changes to enable immigrant students to build their confidence and come to value school. When schools implement these changes, English learners can succeed. The changes involve professional development and advocacy, communication and action. Olsen and Jaramillo point out that teachers and others working with immigrants must be involved in ongoing, sustained professional development that encourages both collaboration and individual reflection. There must be systems in place in schools to analyze data about student achievement and progress that goes beyond looking at standardized test scores. Olsen and Jaramillo call for strong advocates at school sites who can meet together and implement innovative forms of assessment and curriculum. They point out that educators need to understand the complexities of the lives of their students' and must listen to and learn from their English language learners in order to provide them with the opportunities they need to achieve at high levels academically.

Professional development for all school staff and special training for teachers and counselors is the key. Often teachers feel overwhelmed as they attempt to meet the needs of their students. Surveys of support staff working with overage English learners have reported the need for several types of support to enable their students to gain self-confidence and academic competence: a) professional development workshops on relevant topics specific to this population; b) curriculum development to produce instructional resources geared to meet the instructional needs of students; c) intervisitation among programs and replication of promising practices; d) policy and guideline development; and e) networking (Paiewonsky, 1997). In schools and districts where these supports are provided, students have experienced academic success.

Walsh (1991) provides guidelines to help school leaders develop programs that provide all students with opportunities to succeed. In order to help English learners meet academic challenges, school administrators must provide leadership in the development of appropriate programs. They must be knowledgeable about recent research and practice in bilingual and ESL education at the upper levels and must put into place programs that meet these students' special needs. Programs should be flexible and ungraded to allow students to move at their own pace. Classes should be small, and literacy and content should be taught thematically. In addition, placement and exit criteria should be well defined.

Walqui (2000) studied a successful academic program for immigrant students. Based on her observations, she lists 10 characteristics of schools that provide all students opportunities to become confident, competent learners. In such schools:

1. The culture of the classroom fosters the development of a community of learners, and all students are part of that community.
2. Good language teaching involves conceptual academic development.
3. Students' experiential backgrounds provide a point of departure and an anchor in the exploration of new ideas.
4. Teaching and learning focus on substantive ideas that are organized around themes with concepts presented cyclically.
5. New ideas and tasks are contextualized.
6. Academic strategies, sociocultural expectations, and academic norms are taught explicitly.
7. Tasks are relevant, meaningful, engaging and varied.
8. Complex and flexible forms of collaboration maximize learners' opportunities to interact while making sense of language and content.
9. Students are given multiple opportunities to extend their understandings and apply their knowledge.
10. Authentic assessment is an integral part of teaching and learning.

(p. 1-2)

The four keys are interrelated. In schools where teachers provide challenging curriculum, build on students' backgrounds, languages, and cultures and organize collaborative, scaffolded instruction to help student build academic English proficiency, the students become more confident. They begin to value themselves as learners and to value school. In the process, they develop the academic content knowledge and the academic language register they need to succeed in school. The following brief case study of Sandra demonstrates this process.

IMPLEMENTING THE FOUR KEYS

Sandra teaches a fourth through sixth grade newcomer class. Many of her students are recent arrivals with limited formal schooling. She also has some newcomers who arrive with adequate formal schooling and a few long-term English learners. All of her students speak Spanish although some speak Triqui or Mixteco as their first language. Sandra develops effective curriculum for these English learners by following the research-based keys described above.

Sandra's Immigrant Theme

Sandra begins her year with a theme study on immigrants since her newcomer students are, themselves, recent immigrants. Her students feel marginalized in their school because they are different, and even other Spanish-speaking students at the school tease them or ignore them because they do not speak English. Many of her limited formal schooling students do not understand school routines or see themselves as successful learners.

Sandra bases her themes on big questions and then engages her students in answering these questions by drawing on information from the different academic content areas. She wants her students to value their roots and their experiences and to begin to build confidence in themselves as learners so her big question for the theme study is, "How do I fit in as an immigrant?" Sandra explains how the topic helps her students:

> Talking about the issues involved in being an immigrant makes my students feel comfortable in the classroom. It helps them to feel that they are not alone. A lot of people through the years have been immigrants in this country in different situations.

The first thing Sandra does in the class is to talk with her students about why people come to a new country. She writes on the board, 'How did my family come to this country?' This question allows students to consider not only how they arrived but also how some of their relatives got here. After discussing this question as a whole class, the students take home an interview sheet with a series of questions they can ask their families. The questions are designed to elicit family members' stories about coming to America.

The next day the students share their findings. Most of her students have never thought about the various reasons others have come here or how they got here; so as each student shares his or her family story, their classmates fill out a chart listing why people come to the United States. Then, the students write, as best they can in Spanish or in English, their own story or the story of a relative. They write in third person and cast their story as an adventure.

Sandra expands their thinking about why immigrants come to a new country by reading several immigrant stories to them including *Grandfather's Journey* (Say, 1993) and *How Many Days to America* (Bunting, 1988). The idea of coming to America for adventure and learning more about the world as described in *Grandfather's Journey* is completely new for most of Sandra's students. Books like *Who Belongs Here?* (Knight, 1993) and *Our Trip to Freedom* (Nguyen and Abello, 1997) relate the struggles of those coming to this country for various reasons, including the freedom from the fear of being killed in war.

When the books are also available in Spanish, Sandra sometimes reads a story one day in Spanish and then comes back to it in English. Since students come to Sandra's classroom with various levels of English proficiency, this preview in her students' first language gives them access to the English text. The second reading also offers a chance to build a more complete understanding. So, for example, Sandra reads the Spanish version of *Grandfather's Journey* to her students before reading the English version.

Sandra connects all the activities for her theme to literature because she recognizes the importance of helping her students develop high levels of literacy. She also wants to be sure that her students are constantly building concepts and making conceptual connections. For example, in the story *Dear Abuelita* (Dear Grandmother) (Keane, 1997) (Spanish version: *Querida abuelita*), the main character is a young boy writing to his grandmother comparing his new life as an immigrant in the city in the United States to his life in rural Mexico. For the young boy, the language, the sounds, the school, the food, and even the sky at night are different.

As one of their first projects, Sandra has her students complete an art project with black construction paper and chalk, comparing the night sky in the country to the night sky with bright lights and tall buildings in their town. This hands-on art project helps Sandra's students feel comfortable in the classroom. In addition, they can express some of their feelings about being in a new and different place. After doing this activity, the students write real letters to relatives in Mexico comparing their new home with the area where they lived in Mexico, and, in this way, replicating the actions of the boy in the story.

Two other early books that Sandra uses are *The Keeping Quilt* (Polacco, 1988) and *The Tortilla Quilt* (Tenorio-Coscarelli, 1996). Both of these books show the importance of recollecting important life events. After reading these two books, Sandra and the students talk about memories they have of their families and their homelands. She then connects math and art to the reading:

> I also do some math instruction connected to the books we read. I teach patterns. I show the students different pictures of quilts, and then as a group we compare the different patterns. We discuss what patterns are and talk about patterns in math. We use manipulatives to get the idea, and then the students start a project where they create a patterned quilt with different shapes and colors of construction paper. In the white slots the students can write memories of their families, friends and country. This is a very powerful activity, and I use it to help my new arrivals share some of the emotions they are feeling.

Each day, the students write for 20 to 40 minutes. Because so many of her students have had limited reading and writing experiences, Sandra needs to find ways to support their emerging literacy and to involve her students in the writing process. After reading and discussing several immigrant books and charting their own and other immigrants' experiences, Sandra puts students into heterogeneous groups and gives them a form to use as they brainstorm together what their group's immigrant story will include. Each group is asked to think of a title, the setting, some characters, the main events for the story, and a conclusion.

Then, the entire class comes together, and each group shares the ideas they have developed. The class then composes a whole class story as a language experience activity with Sandra writing on the overhead. This first story usually takes about six weeks to complete and when finished, the students illustrate the story, bind it, and take home a copy to share with their families.

Sandra constantly weaves geography lessons with a multicultural emphasis into the theme study to expand her students' worldview. She and the students read an article about the many different Hispanic groups living in the United States which fascinated her students:

> We discussed the idea of other groups of Hispanics living here. Some of my students were amazed that, first of all, there was such a large number and then that there was such a long list of countries that Hispanics come from. It was a surprise to them to see the large number of immigrants who struggle just like they do. For most of my students their world starts and ends with Mexico. It was a real eye opener.

Sandra's students locate on a map the different countries the Hispanics in the article came from, then they choose several of these countries to research on the Internet.

To reinforce the geography concepts and connect to math, Sandra has students work together to make a bar graph on a large piece of butcher paper showing the countries that Hispanics come from and how many come from each country. This activity introduces the idea of grouping by thousands, another concept new to the students. To help her students develop social studies concepts, Sandra puts up a wall chart that contains a map of the world. This map has arrows to indicate the different countries from which people have immigrated to the United States and when they immigrated. Using this wall chart as a model, Sandra's students mark on a map where the immigrants in the different stories and poems they read came from. They also indicate when they came. In this way, Sandra is able to connect the literature to important social studies concepts.

Sandra's goal is to build new vocabulary and concepts through studying content areas such as math, social studies and geography. Keeping in mind that her students have not developed some concepts because they missed years of schooling, she spends time with her students studying basic concepts:

> We also do a study on continents, oceans and basic land forms such as mountains, river beds, deltas, canyons and so forth. We do this by making an ABC book where students can draw pictures and write short definitions of the concepts.

The students also do a related art project; they make a globe in the same way that a piñata is often made. They cover an inflated balloon with newspaper strips dipped in paste, let them dry, and paint the globe blue, then students cut out shapes of the continents and label them. Through cooperative discussion looking at maps and the classroom globe, students help each other place the continents and label the oceans. A piece of yellow yarn marks the equator. This globe-making project supports Sandra's students' learning about geography, and the globes are referred to in other subject areas including science and math as the class studies weather, the effects of water on land masses, and the percentage of water that makes up the earth.

For their final project in the immigrant theme study, Sandra's students create an international recipe book which helps her students extend their geography concepts and serves as a celebration. Sandra has developed a text set of Cinderella stories from around the world. Students enjoy comparing and contrasting versions of this classic tale. For each of the Cinderella stories, Sandra has the students find a recipe for a traditional dish from that culture and then actually make and eat the food. So for example, the class learns how to prepare teriyaki chicken with rice with an Asian Cinderella, tostadas with the Mexican Cinderella, pizza with the European Cinderella, and humus with the Egyptian Cinderella. Sandra gives the students books with a world map on one page and a blank space for writing the recipe on the facing page. The students color in the country on the world map that goes with each recipe. Naturally, they also bring in the ingredients and prepare the recipes. The excitement in the room as the students cook and eat dishes that, for the most part, are completely new to them is enough to show Sandra that her students have begun to feel comfortable in their classroom community and have begun to gain the confidence they need for school.

CONCLUSIONS

Sandra's unit puts into practice the four research-based keys for school success. She develops an extended theme that challenges her students. She builds on their background knowledge and culture. She organizes collaborative activities and scaffolds instruction to build students' academic English proficiency. In the process of studying about immigrants, Sandra's students begin to build confidence in themselves as learners, and they come to value school.

The increasing number of English learners in elementary schools poses a challenge to teachers. No longer are these students the sole responsibility of the ESL specialist. Instead, every teacher needs to work effectively with all their students, including their English learners. This involves recognizing differences among the students and providing them with appropriate curriculum. By following the four keys for success, effective teachers like Sandra provide their English learners with the skills and knowledge necessary for academic success.

REFERENCES

Bunting, E. (1988). *How many days to America?* Boston, MA: Clarion Books.
Chang, J. (2001). Monitoring effective teaching and creating a responsive learning environment for students in need of support: A checklist. *NABE News, 24*(3), 17–18.
Collier, V. (1989). How Long? A synthesis of research on academic achievement in a second language. *TESOL Quarterly, 23*(3), 509–532.
Collier, V. (1992). A synthesis of studies examining long-term language-minority student data on academic achievement. *Bilingual Research Journal, 16*(1 & 2), 187–212.
Collier, V. P. (1995). Acquiring a second language for school. *Directions in Language and Education, 1*(4).
Cummins, J. (1981). The role of primary language development in promoting educational success for language minority students. In *Schooling and language minority students: A theoretical framework* (pp. 3–49). Los Angeles: Evaluation, Dissemination and Assessment Center, California State University, Los Angeles.
Cummins, J. (2000). *Language, power and pedagogy: Bilingual children in the crossfire.* Tonawanda, NY: Multilingual Matters.
The George Washington University Center for Equity and Excellence. (1996). *Promoting excellence: Ensuring academic services for limited proficient students.* Arlington, VA: Evaluation Assistance Center East.
Freeman, Y., & Freeman, D. (2002). *Closing the achievement gap: How to reach limited formal schooling and long-term English learners.* Portsmouth, NH: Heinemann.
García, E. (1999). *Student cultural diversity: Understanding and meeting the challenge* (2nd ed.). Boston: Houghton Mifflin.
Gardner, H. (1983). *Frames of mind.* New York: Basic Books.
Gersten, R., & Jiménez, R. (1994). A delicate balance: Enhancing literature instruction for students of English as a second language. *The Reading Teacher 47*(6), 438–449.
Jiménez, R. (2001). 'It's a difference that changes us': An alternative view of the language and literacy learning needs of Latina/o students. *The Reading Teacher, 54*(8), 736–742.
Keane, S. (1997). *Dear Abuelita.* Crystal Lake, IL: Rigby.
Knight, M. (1993). *Who belongs here? An American story.* Gardiner, Maine: Tilbury House.
Moll, L. (1988). Some key issues in teaching Latino students. *Language Arts, 65*(5), 465–71.
Moran, C., Tinajero, J., Stobbe, J., & Tinajero, I. (1993). Strategies for working with overage students. In A. F. Ada (Ed.), *The power of two languages* (pp. 117–131). New York: MacMillan/McGraw Hill.
Nguyen, A., & Abello, P. (1997). *Our trip to freedom, greetings.* Crystal Lake, IL: Rigby.
Olsen, L., & Jaramillo, A. (1999). Turning the tides of exclusion: A guide for educators and advocates for immigrant students. Oakland, CA: California Tomorrow.
Paiewonsky, E. (1997). Summary of statewide preliminary pilot survey on programs for over-age limited English proficient students with interrupted formal schooling. *Idiom, 27*(3), 1 & 16.
Polacco, P. (1988). *The keeping quilt.* New York: Simon and Schuster Books for Young Children.
Say, A. (1993). *Grandfather's journey.* Boston: Houghton Mifflin.
Schifini, A. (1997). Reading instruction for the preliterate and struggling older student. *Scholastic Literacy Research Paper, 3*(13).
Skutnabb-Kangas, T. (1979). *Language in the process of cultural assimilation and structural incorporation of linguistic minorities.* Washington, DC: National Clearinghouse for Bilingual Education.
Tenorio-Coscarelli, J. (1996). *The tortilla quilt.* Lake Elsinore, CA: Quarter Inch Publishing.
Vang, T. (2000, May). *Hmong youth problems and its causes in the United States.* Paper presented at the 5th Annual Interprofessional Collaboration Conference, Fresno, CA.

Walqui, A. (2000). *Strategies for success: Engaging immigrant students in secondary schools, 1,2.* Washington, DC: Center for Applied Linguistics.

Walsh, C. (1991). Literacy for school success: Considerations for programming and instruction. In *Literacy development for bilingual students* (pp. 1–11). Boston: New England Multifunctional Resource Center for Language and Culture Education.

CHAPTER 24

COLLABORATING IN ESL EDUCATION IN SCHOOLS

SOPHIE ARKOUDIS

The University of Melbourne, Australia

ABSTRACT

This chapter explores how ESL and mainstream teachers can share understandings, not by abandoning their subject prejudices but by achieving a fusion of horizons, where new understandings emerge as individuals adjust their interpretations in light of the interpretations of others. One of the main issues in collaborative teaching has been how teachers from different discourse traditions and concerns can engage in sustained and productive dialogue. Inherent within the notion of collaborative teaching has been the unproblematic view that an ESL teacher can influence the mainstream teacher's pedagogy. Given the different status and power that ESL and academic subjects have within the social context of schools, this would seem a naive assumption. It will be argued that collaborative teaching is a profound journey of epistemological reconstruction, because ESL and the mainstream teachers' views of language and teaching are embedded within their own disciplinary prejudices and biases. This chapter proposes a model that redresses the pedagogical relations between mainstream and ESL teachers and allows the ESL teacher to have epistemological authority within the mainstream curriculum.

INTRODUCTION

This chapter will discuss issues relating to the development of collaborative teaching practices between mainstream classroom and subject specialists and ESL teachers. For ESL students enrolling in English-medium schools, attending school means entering a new culture, learning a new language, and learning to use it for the purposes of cognitive, academic, and social development (Cummins, 1996). ESL students may take up to 7 years to develop the level of academic language proficiency required to be able to successfully complete the tasks required at upper secondary school (Collier, 1987; this volume). The majority of school-age ESL learners spend most of their time in mainstream classes where they need to develop their English language proficiency at the same time as their subject specific knowledge. The development of collaborative teaching practices between ESL and mainstream teachers has been viewed by educational policy developers in Australia, England and certain states in the USA as a logical way to cater to the language learning needs of ESL students within mainstream subject contexts. In Australia and in England collaborative teaching has been established to integrate the ESL curriculum into mainstream programs, with the ESL teacher and the mainstream teacher working together to plan curriculum. While this may seem like a simple idea, the reality is that ESL teachers and subject specialists have found such collaboration very problematic (Arkoudis, 2002; Davison, 2001). The nature of collaborative work requires the ESL teacher to offer suggestions about the mainstream teacher's existing teaching practices, developing new pedagogic relations as they work together. Implicit in the notion of collaboration is the idea that the ESL teacher has the authority to influence the mainstream curriculum. As part of their collaborative work ESL teachers have been encouraged to work more closely with subject specialists in planning mainstream content. This may appear to be a relatively simple reframing of ESL teachers' work, a sharing of their pedagogical content knowledge, however in practical terms it has proved to be very difficult to implement in secondary schools (Arkoudis, 1994) for a number of reasons that will be outlined in the next section of this chapter.

Understanding how ESL and subject specialists can work collaboratively in schools requires an understanding of work on content-based instruction, which has been very important in linking ESL pedagogy to mainstream education (see Leung, this volume, for a more detailed discussion). Brinton, Snow, and Wesche (1989) have explored the adjunct model, the pairing of an ESL course with a university content course, at the college level in the USA. More recently, Brinton and Jensen (2002) have developed an alternative to the adjunct model which they refer to as the *simulated adjunct model*. This model imports authentic content from an existing university course into the ESL curriculum. Mohan's (1986) knowledge framework has also been influential in demonstrating ways to combine language and content teaching (see Mohan, this volume). What the above frameworks have contributed to secondary education is to more closely align the ESL and subject specific curriculum. This has been important in assisting ESL teachers as they attempt to cater to the language and learning needs of ESL students.

However, such work has not explicitly addressed how the ESL and the content teachers can develop collaborative practices, and tends to assume the responsibility for teaching ESL learners rests with the ESL teacher. The issue of how ESL and subject specialists can negotiate their goals and practices when planning curriculum together is a very under researched but important area. This chapter will explore this issue, review current debates and concerns and identify future directions, drawing on three different case studies of collaborative teaching experiences in schools in Australia, England and Asia.

MAIN RESEARCH FINDINGS

Within collaborative teaching, the role of the ESL teacher has been conceptualized differently among the various English-speaking countries. In Canada and the USA, there are sheltered or content-area curricula for ESL classes (Crandall, 1993; Harklau, 1994; Mohan, 1986); in England there is partnership teaching where the ESL teacher (known as the language support teacher) and the mainstream class teacher work together on planning, teaching, and assessment (Leung, 2001, this volume); and in Australia there are separate ESL classes as well as ESL teachers working with subject specialists (Davison, 2001; Department of Education, 2003; Herrimann, 1991). While different policies on collaborative work practices exist in these countries due to their different histories and different perceptions of the issues (Mohan, Leung, & Davison, 2001), what they share is the quest to cross the rough ground that at times can separate ESL and subject specialist teachers as they attempt to plan curriculum together to enhance the educational opportunities of ESL learners.

Within both the elementary and the secondary school context, ESL as a subject discipline generally has lower status within the academic subject hierarchy, even in an elite international school (see Carder, this volume). The institutional practices of schools are themselves a product of government policies which usually position ESL as a support subject. In England ESL as a distinct pedagogy has been diffused within the mainstream curriculum, with most discussion focusing on how to make the mainstream classroom a helpful environment for second language development (Leung, 2001). In the USA the issues are about clarifying pedagogical and social values and objectives in different learning contexts (Harklau, 1994). More recently, however, the focus in secondary schools has shifted from viewing collaboration as the ESL teacher offering teaching strategies to subject specialists, to viewing collaboration as the ESL teacher working with the mainstream curriculum. However, in most contexts ESL is still constructed as an adjunct to the mainstream curriculum (Davison, 2001), hence in any collaborative work the mainstream teacher has more power than the ESL teacher because he/she is the subject specialist (Arkoudis, 2000). This raises the question of what authority the ESL teacher has over the subject specific curriculum, and the rights and responsibilities of the ESL teacher and the mainstream teacher.

Attempts have been made to answer the above question by neatly trying to divide the role of ESL and subject specialists (Arkoudis, 1990; Davison, 1992). However, conceptualizing the collaborative relationship as simply one where the individual teachers have clear and specific roles does not seem to resolve the tensions and misunderstandings that can occur in such work. As Arkoudis (1994) has illustrated in her retrospective account of working with subject specialists, the professional relationship is a very complex one. Clarifying roles and responsibilities only solves part of the issue. Different teaching philosophies and the privileging of subject content over language needs can also exacerbate difficulties with collaborative work.

Another barrier to collaboration is that secondary teachers in particular tend to identify with their subject discipline and often form distinct discourse communities within their subject areas. They identify, and are identified, as subject specialists (Lieberman & Lorsch, 1984; Lortie, 1975). Subcultures are formed within subject disciplines (Siskin, 1991), playing a critical role in shaping and supporting teachers' identities within the context of their school (Grossman & Stodolsky, 1995; Gutiérrez, 1998; Sarangi & Baynham, 1996; Siskin, 1994). While this might seem obvious when one thinks about the typical teaching environment, it is only in recent research into the social organization of teachers' work that there has been a focus on subject departments as the unit of analysis for research in understanding teachers' working contexts (Sarangi & Baynham, 1996; Siskin & Little, 1995).

The idea that subject disciplines are distinct discourse communities, where teachers talk to one another and provide assistance to each other, is a useful concept to apply to conceptualizing the collaborative relationship between ESL and subject specialists. Membership of a department means being part of a collective community. This community has views about the canons of knowledge within the subject discipline, a sense of the importance of their discipline within the school curriculum, and a shared understanding of what needs to be taught and when. In these social worlds, Siskin (1994) has found that teachers limit conversations about their school to their department and refer to their department as *we*. Teachers within their subject departments identify very strongly to their subject discipline. This poses a problem for ESL teachers working with subject teachers, in that the ESL teachers need to have some understanding of the collective view of teachers working within the subject discipline. It also means that ESL teachers need to gain some credibility with the department, if they are to be accepted as someone who will give advice on the teaching of the discipline.

Siskin's research (1994), while relevant to collaborative teaching, has only focused on whom teachers talk to in schools. Their work has not considered the structural cross-departmental relationships between academic and other subject areas (Gutiérrez, 1998), nor how the epistemological assumptions that are entrenched within the nature of subject disciplines, can influence cross disciplinary discourse. Compounding the issue of subjects as discourse communities within the school is the fact that the institutional practices of the secondary school value traditional academic subjects, such as Science, as core learning areas within the school, invested with certain rights and responsibilities that are not shared by other subject areas. Indeed, the nature of the schools is such that subject knowledge and content are viewed as belonging to the teachers in that discipline. This has been one of the main difficulties in developing language across the curriculum programs, as most secondary teachers see the role of teaching writing as the English teachers' responsibility. While subjects such as Science and Mathematics are established academic subjects, the status of ESL as a subject is problematic. ESL is clearly not a traditional academic subject in the same sense, thus problematizing the credibility of the ESL teacher's authority to influence the academic curriculum of the subject specialist.

Roberts (1996) proposes that teachers' epistemological assumptions are structured by their beliefs about their students' learning. In other words, the individual beliefs of the teacher influence what is taught and how the curriculum is delivered to the students, and these beliefs are framed by teachers' identification of their subject discipline. Teachers vary in their approaches to teaching and learning, adopting, for example, constructivist or transmission approaches to teaching depending on their own experiences and their beliefs about good teaching in their subject discipline. Roberts argues that it is from the teacher's position as a subject specialist that they support and justify their beliefs. These beliefs have epistemological authority within teaching communities and the teachers' professional conversations could be regarded as their attempts to understand different dialects within their teaching world. This raises the question of how ESL and subject specialists justify their pedagogic beliefs to each other and the extent to which this can lead to developing shared understandings about addressing both language and content needs in the mainstream curriculum.

In negotiating the curriculum with the subject specialist so that language understanding is promoted in mainstream teaching and hence students' language is developed, the ESL teacher has to have a firm understanding of his/her own subject discipline. ESL teachers also need some understanding of the pedagogical content knowledge of other subject teachers. Knowledge about the nature of the pedagogical relationship between ESL and subject specialist teachers has been anecdotal rather than based on documented studies or researched understandings (Freeman & Johnson, 1998), leading to an oversimplification of the professional relationship in collaborative work. Teachers usually have strong pedagogic beliefs about their subject area and what good teaching means to them that are embedded within their professional identity. What ESL teachers should perhaps be more concerned with is not so much in defining their roles in the collaborative process, although this is important, but to explore how they can engage in professional discussions that result in developing shared understandings about how to best cater to the language and learning needs of ESL students in mainstream classes. The next section will describe some recent research on collaboration which has addressed this issue.

CURRENT DEBATES AND CONCERNS

Both curriculum as institution and curriculum as practice need to be taken into account in any discussion about subject disciplines in secondary schools (Reid, 1992). *Curriculum as institution* refers to the traditions and claims of content, and *curriculum as practice* focuses on the teaching and learning processes. Curriculum as practice can be transformed within planning conversations and in the process curriculum as institution is changed. Educational policy has proposed the mainstreaming of ESL as an institutionalized curriculum, with claims that ESL teachers should share their pedagogical understandings with subject specialists. Very little has been offered to ESL teachers about what this means in terms of the ESL curriculum as practice within the mainstream context. ESL teachers have felt uneasy about working with subject specialists, as the professional relationship is fraught with misunderstandings and misconceptions, where the subject specialist has the power to accept or reject suggestions and where ESL teachers feel increasingly frustrated in their work. At the same time it has been assumed that subject teachers can easily integrate so-called ESL strategies into their work. For example, the *ESL Annotations to the Science Curriculum and Standards Framework* (Department of Education, 1997) provides examples of ESL strategies embedded within descriptions of units of work for the science classroom. This is seen by the Victorian Department of Education as an effective way of sensitizing science teachers to the educational needs of their ESL students, but assumes that the underlying epistemological knowledge can be read off the page with no opportunities for collaboration or dialogue. Recent research into collaborative practices in schools in Australia, England, and Asia highlight the complexity of the collaboration between subject specialists and ESL teachers.

Collaboration in an Australian Secondary School

The following exemplar is drawn from a larger longitudinal study which explored the professional relationship between an ESL and a science teacher in a secondary school context through a detailed linguistic analysis of the teachers' regular planning conversations (for a more detailed discussion, see Arkoudis, 2000). In the sample extract the teachers have been discussing the topic of *Motion* in a senior science class. The science teacher, Alex, has asked the ESL teacher, Victoria, to offer him some ideas for teaching the ticker-tape experiment in his science class. In the extract below the two teachers reach a shared understanding of how this can be done. The extract also highlights the difficult nature of this type of professional collaboration because Victoria's ESL knowledge and skills are represented simply as techniques or strategies. The teaching of language is not addressed in this extract, nor anywhere else in their one hour planning conversation. However, unlike in other places in the conversation, the extract below indicates an increased awareness between the two teachers that can offer us glimpses of the complex and ongoing nature of collaborative work.

Note: A = Alex, the science teacher, V = Victoria, the ESL teacher; capital letters indicates emphatic stress and/or increased volume, == indicates overlap between speakers

143 A: So, in terms of presentation of this PARTICULAR UNIT, I mean what can you suggest? Let's say I was going to use those worksheets you've got there as basic instructions for two experiments.

144 V: I'd like to know, you know when they're doing their experiments, what are they saying? Are they just working in groups or pairs and doing something, or are they actually TALKING? To set up some task where they are articulating what they are doing, I think, would be an important THING, and another thing that I would say is that some of the stuff I've noticed that they're doing is really OBSERVATIONAL, where they're really observing stuff, DESCRIBING what's happening, but that other step of APPLYING and analyzing is something really interesting.

145 A: Right... so WHAT would I actually do on Monday when I teach this? If I just were to give them those sheets, HOW would I introduce the activity?

146 V: Well, what I would be thinking about, is that, instead of just acting on what's on the sheet and following the instruction, that there's some sort of dialogue between them, that there's some sort of you know instruction giving, or some sort of ARTICULATION of what's happening, so that they're actually TALKING WHILE THEY'RE DOING IT. Either talking about WHAT they're doing, or else talking about WHY they're doing it, or whatever. The main thing is that they are actually talking about it, that they are getting to articulate you know what they're doing and == what it means.

147 A: == How will I get them to do that? Will I just go around and say to all of them, I would like you to discuss == in your group beforehand, why you

148 V: == Well maybe one of them, or probably not, because I don't know that that works, but maybe you would get one of the, would they work in pairs or

149 A: Twos or threes.

150 V: Twos or threes. So give one of them the instructions and one of them gives the instructions, then another one is the person who asks the questions or is sort of observer or something and the other one is the person who does whatever has to be done. But,

there's just some sort of TALKING that happens while they're doing it. And then maybe the person who is the observer or the recorder or whatever umm has got a role of asking questions, to jot down questions that they don't UNDERSTAND, what's happening. Just so that there's some sort of dialogue happening.

151 A: So you're talking about a prac group with ROLES within the group, (yeah) so they have particular roles. That's umm that's really interesting.

152 V: Yes, I think so. And also, so the dialogue, the CONVER-SATION between themselves, but also with you as well, I think is very important. So that they're somehow jotting down the questions, the things that they're not sure of and stuff. So that it's not left to them to have the confidence you know to sort of stick up their hand and say, "But sir, what does this mean? Why did this happen?" or whatever. But, you've actually set up some structure INVITING THEM to ask. I think that's really important, (mmm) because, PARTICULARLY with ESL students who might see it as disrespectful to have to ask the teacher.

153 A: Yes, that's something that I'm really recently learning much more than I ... I mean it's very DIFFICULT to get some ESL students or some students, in general, but some ESL students in particular, to ask a question, because you're right, it SEEMS TO BE an admission that, either that they have disrespected you by not knowing it or understanding it when you first said it, or by revealing something about ignorance, (yeah) which is really distressing,(mmm) because there's a so much palpable (mmm) help for them there if they need help.

154 V: YES, so if there is a structure there which actually invites them, almost sort of mandates, (mmm yeah) that they ask questions that can often work. It really LEGITIMISES something that they might feel uncomfortable about otherwise.

155 A: So, the roles you just mentioned would be, umm I guess, == one person is like an equipment handler

156 V: == the instructor==

157 A: ==The person who runs the experiment, == a doer

158 V: ==Yeah the doer==

159 A: == There's an observer and==

160	V:	== There's an observer, well maybe not, even more a scribe and a recorder and a question-asker too.
161	A:	So, is that four?
162	V:	Well, it could be three, you said that you worked in twos and threes. (yes) So maybe the recorder and question-asker is the one person that could work.
163	A:	Well right, that's a SIMPLE sort of idea to set up, but it's a really intriguing one. I'll be interested to see how it goes. It would be, I will be going around, obviously as they're doing it, I ALWAYS DO, asking them questions, but this will really, this time they'll be asking me questions. (Arkoudis, 2000, p. 145)

Part of the reason that Victoria and Alex have reached shared understandings in this extract is due to the nature of the curriculum task they are discussing. Their discussion concentrates on how to organize the group discussion around the experiment, which is an activity that was seen as a ideal teaching tool from both a science and language perspective. The nature of a science experiment is one whereby individual students participate and contribute to the development of science practices established by the classroom teacher (Cobb & Bowers, 1999). Participation in these practices involves the immediate social context of the students' science development and apprenticeship into the world of science (Veel, 1997). A scientific experiment is social in nature and congruent with Victoria's dialogic approach to teaching (Roberts, 1996), requiring the students to talk to each other and construct their interpretation of what happens in the ticker-tape experiment. For various reasons the scientific experiment links their teaching worlds. For Alex, it involves a scientific procedure and reflects his iconic image of science teaching. For Victoria, the experiment is a physical process that engages students in talk and encourages them to reconstruct understandings of the concept of force within the scientific world. The teachers both view the symbol of the experiment as important.

Victoria's deliberate self positioning as supportive of the conversation (Harré & van Langenhove, 1999) allows opportunities for her to reposition Alex's views of teaching. Even though Victoria has greater authority than Alex in terms of their institutional standing in the school, when it comes to planning science lessons together, Victoria positions herself and is positioned by Alex as less powerful. This positioning reflects, in part, the status of the subject disciplines, their gender, and the teachers' own perceptions and experiences of working together. Victoria does not have the authority in the school to force Alex to reposition the science curriculum, but she is nevertheless forceful in her positive positioning by constantly questioning Alex's consideration of the ESL students. She has elicited Alex's responses to her questions and then supplemented and complemented his knowledge and experiences with teaching strategies that he can use in the classroom. Howie (1999) has referred to this as *positive positioning*. The way Victoria engages Alex, at the same time claiming some epistemological authority within the planning conversation, is through being supportive and positioning herself as offering professional development to Alex.

Secondary School Collaboration in England

Creese (2002) has also explored the discursive construction of power in teaching relationships. In England there are no separate ESL classes, unlike Australia, Canada, and the USA, and the only option for ESL teachers is to work with subject specialists in the mainstream classroom. In a longitudinal ethnographic study in three schools in London, Creese investigated how subject and ESL teachers' discourses position them in the classroom as central or peripheral to the school's agendas. She audio-taped lessons, shadowed subject and ESL teachers working together, and conducted individual teacher interviews. Her findings suggest that ESL teachers have a different institutional status from the subject teachers, with students viewing the ESL and subject teacher as different but not equal. Furthermore, while subject teachers felt a sense of ownership of their own subject area, ESL teachers did not discursively project a similar level of ownership: ESL teachers' "expertise in facilitation and their awareness of the role of language in learning and social life were positioned as peripheral within the classroom and were supported at the institutional level" (Creese, 2002, p. 611).

Creese argues that the teachers' discourses were most likely a reflection of the wider educational discourses. ESL teachers were firmly positioned in the role of facilitating learning rather than as having their own language content to teach in the classroom. While the subject teacher was perceived as the one teaching the 'real' curriculum, the ESL teacher was delegated to the role of a support person in the classroom. As secondary school teachers are identified within subject disciplines (Grossman and Stodolsky, 1995; Siskin, 1994), this led to the ESL teachers becoming disempowered pedagogically within the classroom and the school.

Creese's work highlights the difficulty of developing collaborative practices between teachers when the discourse at both the policy level and the institutional level continues to position ESL teachers as supporting the mainstream curriculum and lacking any pedagogy that is distinctly its own. In the last 20 years we have not seen much of a shift in the status of ESL teachers who attempt to work in collaboration with subject specialists. Creese's research has made the dynamics of collaborative practices more visible, helping us to understand the power relations within collaboration and thus begin to explore potential ways of transforming the professional relationship between ESL and subject teachers.

Collaboration in International Schools

The work of Davison (2002, 2006; Hurst & Davison, 2005) with international schools in Asia has also helped to illuminate the collaborative process in ESL and mainstream team teaching. In a study of a large international elementary school in Taiwan, Davison (in press) focused on exploring the process of co-planning and co-teaching and the various levels of partnership between ESL and content teachers, using systemic functional linguistics to analyze the different positioning of the teachers in relation to their evolving collaboration. Given the home language of 90% of the student population was a language other than English, the administration was very interested in developing more collaborative teaching between classroom and ESL teachers. They implemented an extensive professional development program that explored issues such as the role of language and learning, and the nature of best practice in ESL and content-area teaching. One of the results of the professional development work was the establishment of a draft document that outlined the roles and responsibilities of the ESL and content teachers, and the development of a planning proforma for units of work that encouraged both ESL and classroom teachers to develop common goals and activities, at the same time affirming the expertise that each teacher had to offer. However, even when the infrastructure supported collaborative teaching and teachers were encouraged to renegotiate their roles, there were still varying levels of success with collaborative teaching. Davison argues that this was due to the different views and expectations. There were some classroom teachers who demonstrated passive resistance to the idea, commenting "it seems obvious to me that only classroom teachers with ESL training will feel comfortable in this role." Other classroom teachers believed that they should support the idea as "it's best for the children," although they were not convinced that it was best for them. Other classroom teachers felt that they had benefited greatly from the experience: "we are constantly trying different strategies to accommodate the various learning styles." There was also a mixed reaction from the ESL teachers. Davison argues that partnership between ESL and classroom teachers is neither easy nor unproblematic, even in a well-resourced elementary school in which ESL student needs are seen as paramount and teachers appear to have a relatively loose identification with their teaching areas. Teacher attitudes and effort varied depending on the level of collaboration, with distinct stages, from survival self-concerns, where teachers struggled to adapt to routines and were reluctant to change, to a gradual awareness of the impact of collaboration on students, to a readiness to respond to feedback on teaching. This is also reflected in the teachers' perceptions of their achievements, with a clear move from teacher emphasis on relatively superficial strategies to a concern with curriculum content. The nature of the institutional and professional development support expected also seemed to be very different at different stages of collaboration, with preferences shifting from very concrete, externally constructed support to more internally-directed activity as the collaborations are perceived to be more successful. One of the implications for professional development is that collaborating teachers may benefit from more action-orientated teacher research with built-in opportunities for critical reflection and discussion of different views and perceptions of the nature of learning and teaching.

What is interesting about Davison's research is that it presents the evolutionary and ongoing nature of collaborative work, a point that comes out of the work cited above with Alex and Victoria. Collaboration appears to be a dialogical process as teachers negotiate, challenge, redefine and work through their views of teaching and language learning, in an attempt to reach shared understandings.

Conceptualizing the Collaborative Relationship

This discussion has attempted to highlight the complex nature of collaborative work. Collaborative teaching is an epistemology where pedagogic content knowledge is negotiated between ESL and subject specialists through their lived experiences of learning and teaching within their specific subject discipline. As we have seen from the examples in this paper, teachers from different subject disciplines often do not share the same epistemological beliefs, thus effective negotiation between a subject specialist and an ESL teacher requires the questioning of disciplinary assumptions on both sides in order to see each other's point of view. Effective collaboration necessitates a certain degree of conflict, as teachers explain and justify their positions to each other in an attempt to develop new practices and understandings. Collaboration is about changing teaching practices and conflict can assist in the process. As Fullan (1999) observes: "Conflict, if respected, is positively associated with creative breakthroughs under complex, turbulent conditions. Consensus would be pleasant, but actually is impossible to achieve except through superficial agreement" (p. 27).

Developing collaborative practice is a dialogical process where a fusion of horizons is sought. Achieving understandings is the first goal in bringing different disciplinary discourses together, but this assumes a major reconceptualization of the nature of this work. If collaborative work emphasizes pedagogical relations, that is, the processes that sustain conversations, such conversations then becomes less concerned with articulating views for or against certain practices and more concerned with creating new practices. The central question is how we can best bring together teachers with different disciplinary traditions and concerns and engage them into sustained and productive dialogue.

Figure 1 is a visual representation of how subject specialists, a science teacher in this case, and ESL teachers can develop new practices. In the knowledge quadrant is the public knowledge of the teacher to do with the routines in the school. Movement to the understanding quadrant occurs when teachers have appropriated knowledge from the school context that is developed into habits of teaching, for example, where working and teaching becomes a routine; where the content and teaching of Year 10 Science is the same year after year. In sharing ideas and perceptions about teaching with another teacher, the pedagogical assumptions of the teacher can change. The mainstream teacher reflects on how the new ideas presented by the other teacher relate to his existing teaching practices. When the mainstream teacher has internalized the new ideas, he is able to publicize them by presenting them as information to others. Once the information is public, then it becomes part of the knowledge base within the discourse and culture of each subject discipline. For example once Alex tried Victoria's suggestions for the groupwork activity and experienced success with it, this activity became part of his teaching knowledge that he used in his science classroom. In this way Victoria can claim some epistemological authority within their collaborative practices. The aim would be for ESL and mainstream teachers to be able to work in all four quadrants to develop curriculum that focuses on language and content teaching.

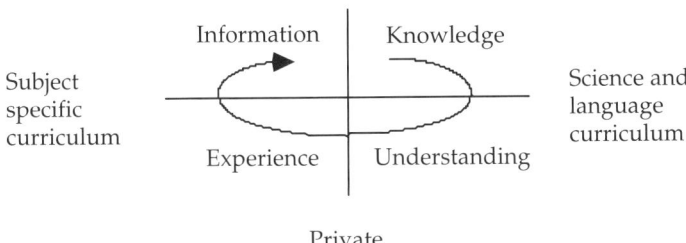

Figure 1. Mainstream ESL: The Personal/Professional Development Project (Arkoudis, 2000, p. 149)

The model supports the development of effective pedagogical relations between mainstream and ESL teachers, and allows the ESL teachers to establish epistemological authority within the mainstream curriculum. It provides a way to conceptualize and appraise teacher learning within the personal/professional development project implicit in collaborative teaching.

FUTURE DIRECTIONS

This chapter has concentrated on discussing collaboration between subject specialists and ESL teachers in secondary schools. It has been argued that collaboration involves reconceptualizing the professional relationship to emphasize the pedagogic relations between the professional teachers. This means that, in part, the focus would need to be on the dialogic nature of collaborative knowledge building. Part of empowering ESL teachers involved in collaborative work is to assist them in understanding how to manage the complex and conflicting nature of collaborative work. Therefore, further empirical research exploring the nature of the professional relationship in collaborative work is required. We need to explore different teaching contexts and develop frameworks that will better support effective collaboration.

This chapter has also argued that collaborative work by its very nature challenges the epistemological assumptions of the subject specialist and aims at developing new understandings about catering to the educational needs of the ESL learners in their classes. The process is ongoing, long term, and costly in terms of teacher time. Such work is often in conflict with outcomes-based education and state mandated standards, and may be undermined by prescriptive educational policies and a top-down approach to both preservice and inservice teacher education. Teachers need to be prepared for cross disciplinary conversations by learning how to collaborate as part of their core training.

REFERENCES

Arkoudis, S. (1990). *The ESL Handbook*. Melbourne: SMECU.
Arkoudis, S. (1994). Changing the role relationship between classroom teacher and ESL teacher. *Prospect, 9*(3), 47–53.
Arkoudis, S. (2000). *The epistemological authority of an ESL teacher in science education.* Unpublished Ph.D. thesis, University of Melbourne, Australia.
Arkoudis, S. (2003). Teaching English as a second language in science classes: Incommensurate epistemologies. *Language and Education, 17*(3), 161–173.
Brinton, S., & Jensen, L. (2002). Appropriating the adjunct model: English for academic purposes at the university level. In D. Kaufman (Ed.), *Content-based instruction in higher education settings* (pp. 125–138). Arlington, VI: TESOL.
Brinton, S., Snow, M., & Wesche, M. (1989). *Content-based second language instruction.* Boston, MA: Heinle & Heinle.
Crandall, J. (1993). Current directions in curriculum development for culturally and linguistically diverse children. In G. R. Tucker (Ed.), *Policy and practice in the education of culturally and linguistically diverse students: Views from language educators* (pp. 13–25). Alexandria, VA: TESOL.
Creese, A. (2002). The discursive construction of power in teacher partnerships: Language and subject specialists in mainstream schools. *TESOL Quarterly, 36*(2), 597–616.
Davison, C. (1992). Eight fatal flaws in team teaching. *TESOL in Context, 3*(2), 12–13.
Davison, C. (2001). Current policies, programs and practices in school ESL. In B. Mohan, C. Leung & C. Davison, (Eds.), *English as a second language in the mainstream: Teaching, learning and identity.* (pp. 30–50). Harlow: Pearson Education.

Davison, C. (2002, March). Collaborative education for ESL and content teachers: A developmental continuum. Paper presented at TESOL 2002, Salt Lake City, USA.
Davison, C. (2006). Collaboration between ESL and content teachers: How do we know when we are doing it right? *International Journal of Bilingualism and Bilingual Education, 9*(4), 454–475.
Department of Education. (1997). *Course advice: Science*. Melbourne: Department of Education.
Department of Education. (2003). *The ESL report 2002*. Melbourne: Department of Education and Training.
Freeman, D., & Johnson, K. E. (1998). Reconceptualising the knowledge-base of language teacher education. *TESOL Quarterly, 32*(3), 397–417.
Fullan, M. (1999). *Change forces: The sequel*. Philadelphia: Falmer Press, Taylor and Francis Inc.
Grossman, P. L., & Stodolsky, S. S. (1995). Content as context: the role of school subjects in secondary school teaching. *Educational Researcher, 24*(8), 5–11, 23.
Gutiérrez, R. (1998). Departments as contexts for understanding and reforming secondary teachers' work: Continuing the dialogue. *Journal of Curriculum Studies, 30*(1), 95–103.
Harklau, L. (1994). ESL versus mainstream classes: Contrasting L2 learning environments. *TESOL Quarterly, 28*(2), 241–272.
Harré, R., & van Langenhove, L. (1999). The dynamics of social episodes. In L. van Langenhove (Ed.), *Positioning theory: Moral contexts of intentional action* (pp. 1–13). Great Britain: Blackwell Publishers.
Herrimen, M. (1991). *An evaluative study of the Commonwealth ESL Program*. Unpublished report for the Federal Department of Education, Employment and Training: University of Western Australia.
Howie, D. (1999). Preparing for positive positioning. In L. van Langenhove (Ed.), *Positioning theory: Moral contexts for intentional action* (pp. 53–59). Great Britain: Blackwell Publishers.
Hurst, D., & Davison, C. (2005). Collaborating on the curriculum: Focus on secondary ESL. In J. Crandall & D. Kauffman (Eds.), *Case studies in TESOL: Teacher education for ESL and content area teachers* (pp. 41–66). Alexandria, VI: TESOL.
Leung, C. (2001). Mainstreaming: ESL as a diffused curriculum concern. In C. Davison (Ed.), *English as a second language in the mainstream* (pp. 165–176). Harlow: Pearson Education.
Lieberman, P. R., & Lorsch, J. W. (1984). *Teachers, their world and their work*. VA: Association for Supervision and Curriculum Development.
Lortie, D. (1975). *Schoolteacher: A sociological study*. Chicago: University of Chicago Press.
Mohan, B., Leung, C., & Davison, C. (2001). (Eds.). *English as a second language in the mainstream: Teaching, learning and identity*. Harlow: Longman Pearson.
Mohan, B. A. (1986). *Language and content*. USA: Addison-Wesley Publishing Company.
Reid, W. A. (1992). *The pursuit of curriculum: Schooling and the public interest*. Norwood, N.J.: Ablex.
Roberts, D. (1996). Epistemic authority for teacher knowledge: the potential role of teacher communities: A response to Robert Orton. *Curriculum Inquiry, 26*(4), 417–431.
Sarangi, S., & Baynham, M. (1996). Discursive construction of educational identities: Alternative readings. *Language and Education, 10*(2&3), 77–81.
Siskin, L. S. (1991). Departments as different worlds: Subject subcultures in secondary schools. *Educational Administrative Quarterly, 27*(2), 134–160.
Siskin, L. S. (1994). *Realms of knowledge: Academic department in secondary schools*. London: Falmer Press.
Siskin, L. S., & Little, J. W. (1995). Introduction The subject department: Continuities and critiques. In J. W. Little (Ed.), *The subjects in question* (pp. 1–22). New York: Teachers College Columbia University.
Veel, R. (1997). Learning how to mean – scientifically speaking: Apprenticeship into scientific discourse in the secondary school. In J. R. Martin (Ed.), *Genres and institutions: Social processes in the workplace and school* (pp. 161–195). London: Cassell.

CHAPTER 25

ORGANIZATION OF ENGLISH TEACHING IN INTERNATIONAL SCHOOLS

MAURICE W. CARDER

Vienna International School, Austria

ABSTRACT

This chapter provides a brief introduction to the international schools network and goes on to discuss how the linguistic needs of students from many different language backgrounds are met in an English-speaking educational environment. The focus is on the secondary level (Grades 6–12, ages 11–18) with particular attention paid to the orientation of students' bilingualism in both the types of program offered and the assessment system embedded in these programs. Specifically, the chapter explores the extent to which these programs promote additive as opposed to subtractive bilingualism among students whose home language is a language other than English. The paper proposes a four-point organizational model incorporating a content-based explicit English language syllabus, equality of certification for all ESL students, ESL awareness for all subject matter teachers, and mother tongue development for ESL students as a core component of their studies. The chapter concludes with directions for policy and professional development for international schools and suggestions for future research.

INTRODUCTION

International schools developed originally from the initiative of some national groups who needed schooling for their children abroad that would enable them to continue their education in their country of origin at a later date (for example, the Dutch in Indonesia, French in Africa and south-east Asia). English presented a somewhat different case initially as the traditional British approach to educating families working abroad was to send the children to boarding school in the United Kingdom. However after the Second World War, schools were set up to service the families of British and American military personnel stationed abroad, with curricula based on those of the British and American national systems.

From 1945 to the present there has been a gradual development to today's international schools. Global demographic trends and the desire to attract a wider clientele have resulted in the gradual erosion of national identifiers associating the school with a particular country. International schools are nearly all private and they depend on student numbers to balance the budget, hence they have become increasingly market-driven (Bunnell, 2005). The majority of international schools have a British or American based curriculum, but many also offer the International Baccalaureate (IB) curriculum either in whole or in part. School administrators are almost universally from the English-speaking world, a denomination that encompasses principally the United Kingdom, the United States, Canada, Australia and New Zealand. School staff, often referred to as 'expatriate' staff, are also principally from these countries, with some locally hired teachers from the host country who are generally fluent in English.

The number of students attending international schools around the world has been accelerating since the early 1990s when it was characterized as being equivalent to a nation of three to four million (Jonietz & Harris, 1991, p. 3). Enrollment numbers are rapidly expanding, not only in city-states like Hong Kong and Singapore which are reliant on a highly-educated multinational workforce, but also in traditional EFL countries such as Japan and Thailand, where demand from local elites for an English–medium international education is driving increased supply (MacDonald, 2006). For example, in 1991 there were only a handful of international schools in Thailand; now there are more than 80 (Hanchanlash, 2004). In the past enrollment in international schools by local students and returnees was often prohibited by the governments of the country concerned, but the rhetoric of internationalization, plus the impact of increasing globalization, with the accompanying transnational flow of human capital, have relaxed such traditional restraints, leading to even greater diversity in the linguistic and cultural composition of international schools (Bunnell, 2006).

There are various umbrella bodies, such as the European Council for International Schools (ECIS) and the East Asian Regional Council of Overseas Schools (EARCOS) that provide administrative support in areas such as school accreditation, teacher and executive recruitment, in-service training, fellowships in international education, and specialist publications. Schools differ considerably in the national composition of the student body, ranging from 85% British and/or American enrollment to fewer than 10% from any one country. Anywhere from 10 to 90 different nationalities may be represented. Such schools may be accredited by only one umbrella organization (such as the ECIS) or by two or more such organizations and/or by a local education authority.

This chapter focuses on the organization of ESL programs in international schools. The experience of the Vienna International School in Austria is highlighted to illustrate the broader issues. This school grew from the English School, which was set up after the Second World War for the children of British military personnel. In 1978 it was reorganized and renamed as the Vienna International School. It provides schooling for students whose parents work in organizations such as the United Nations, the Organization of Petroleum Exporting Countries (OPEC), the Diplomatic Community, the international business community, and the local business community.

The Status of ESL in International Schools

Current provision for ESL students in international schools can be evaluated against the findings of the broader research literature on the learning and teaching of English as an additional language. Three themes are prominent in this literature. First, the development of English for academic purposes to the level of native speakers typically requires at least five years, and academic progress in English is enhanced when students are supported in developing literacy in their mother tongues (Baker, 2001; Baker & Prys Jones, 1998; Collier & Thomas, this volume; Cummins, 2000; Thomas & Collier, 2002). In international schools where the language of instruction is predominantly English, this requires a program of instruction in each child's mother tongue. Given the fact that some international schools enroll students from up to 70 different mother tongues, provision for mother tongue literacy development is clearly challenging. However, the consequences of ignoring students' mother tongues are highly problematic. Carder (1993, in press), for example, has highlighted the ethical, theoretical and practical considerations in accepting non-speakers of English to schools named 'international' with no provision for mother tongue literacy support. He suggested that in our enthusiasm to teach fluent English we may be creating students with no firm foundation in any language.

Although rare, some examples of effective mother tongue support do exist. One such example is the mother tongue program in operation at the Vienna International School since 1978. This is largely an after-school program taught by private tutors, involving 170 students, 30 teachers, and 25 languages. Every year some 35 (out of 100 or more) students take their mother tongue as Language A1 (their strongest language) for the International Baccalaureate Diploma (see Carder, 2006, for a more detailed analysis of the delivery of bilingualism in the IB in international schools).

A second theme that emerges from the research literature is that content-based ESL instruction (e.g. ESL History, ESL Geography, ESL English, etc.) and various team teaching arrangements between ESL and mainstream content teachers (Davison, 2006, Hurst & Davison, 2005) generally yield superior results compared to the teaching of English as a pull out program in isolation from academic subject matter (Chamot & O'Malley, 1986, this volume; Collier & Thomas, this volume). Within international schools, this implies various degrees of articulation with mainstream programs, or for students with very low language proficiency, a parallel program to the mainstream, using the same content but presented in language more readily accessible to second language learners. The great number of teachers and smaller classroom groups that are likely to be involved in these types of teaching typically entail higher costs, a factor that must be considered by school administrators.

A third theme concerns the importance of effective professional development for all staff and administrators related to supporting ESL students' academic progress. A majority of administrators and staff in international schools have neither formal qualifications nor professional development experience in issues related to teaching ESL students, which undermines their capacity to provide an effective learning environment for the full range of students in the school. In recent years, steps have been taken to address this issue. For example, a number of international schools have subscribed to the scheme developed by the Department of Education, Training and Employment of South Australia called *ESL in the Mainstream* (Department of Education and Children's Services, 1999). This professional development course is described in more detail later in this chapter.

Even in schools in which there is some attempt to address these three areas, ESL provision is often fragmentary, haphazard and fails to fulfill the requirements of educational equity. In some schools, parents of beginning ESL students are required to pay additional fees and in others ESL is viewed as a remedial endeavor. This is in spite of the economic rationale for investing in ESL provision in schools being expressed very clearly more than 15 years ago (Murphy, 1990):

> (A strong ESL program) is a sound investment for a number of reasons. First, it relieves the pressure placed on mainstream teachers when confronted with students with very limited proficiency in English. Second, it allows the mainstream class to progress at its normal rate, 'unencumbered' by such students. And third, at a time when many English-

medium schools around the world appear to be experiencing a gradual decline in the numbers of native English-speaking students, and a fairly steady increase in the proportion of non-English L1 students, a good ESL program will attract students to the school who might otherwise go elsewhere for their education. (p. 9)

Although there has been minimal research conducted on language provision in international schools, what does exist suggests that parents whose home language is not English prioritize the acquisition of English as a major goal (Hayden and Thompson, 1997, 1998; Mackenzie et al., 2001). They recognize the importance of English for their children's economic and social mobility and frequently assume that continued use of the mother tongue in the home will be sufficient to ensure its development. Thus, many parents choose the international school precisely because of its emphasis on English-medium instruction and are not particularly well informed about possible alternative bilingual education options. They are also frequently not well informed about models of ESL provision and thus do not pressure the school with respect to the quality of this provision. Hence, the quality of ESL provision in international schools remains mixed and in many cases ESL remains on the periphery of administrators' concerns (Allan, 2002; Carder, 1991, 1993, 1995, 2002, 2006 in press; Jonietz & Harris, 1991).

CURRENT DEBATES AND CONCERNS

Given the multilingual composition of student enrollment in international schools, the quality of English instruction for ESL students constitutes a major determinant of the overall quality of the educational provision in these schools. Four directions for improving the quality of educational provision in international schools are outlined below:

1. There should be a well-planned and effectively integrated ESL program based on current research;
2. ESL students' progress in acquiring English should be acknowledged and rewarded with certificates and diplomas just as the academic progress of native English-speaking students is acknowledged and rewarded;
3. All international school staff *and* administrators should be professionally trained in order to provide appropriate instruction for ESL students;
4. The importance of maintaining students' mother tongues should be acknowledged and realized in programmatic support.

The ESL Program

A starting point for considering ESL provision is to ask whether ESL students have the same rights to an appropriate program as other students. As pointed out by Murphy (1990), it is very much in the interests of international schools to provide an equitable and high quality program for ESL students, apart altogether from ethical considerations. Adequate ESL provision requires the institutionalization of the program on an equal footing with other departments in the school. In the Vienna International School, Secondary, for example, there is an *ESL and Mother Tongue Department*. The department is responsible for the teaching of ESL to students in Grades 6–12. It is necessary to emphasize this institutionalization, otherwise ESL teachers, and thus by implication ESL students, become marginalized. When this institutionalization does not occur, ESL staff tend to be treated as 'shadows of the timetable' and ESL students are frequently patronized and referred to as those who need language support.

Without a firm base, centered at the hub of the school, ESL provision will not thrive. When ESL is considered peripheral and low-status, well-qualified ESL staff become de-motivated and either leave or move to another discipline because they are taken more seriously as Math or History or English teachers. The next stage is that unqualified staff are appointed, leading to a downward spiral of poor instruction, poor facilities, the last slots on the timetable, and in some cases the charging of additional tuition for ESL classes.

A frequent problematic decision is to include ESL teaching within an English (or Language Arts) department. Mainstream English teachers are qualified in their areas, but usually know little or nothing about second language acquisition and bilingualism (and the pedagogical skills of language teaching), with the result that they treat ESL students as 'slow learners' or those 'who need helping out with their English.' ESL becomes a peripheral concern when submerged into a larger department. There is currently an increasing number of teachers available for recruitment with formal qualifications related to ESL. It would seem obvious that international school administrators should be on the look-out for these well-qualified teachers at their yearly recruitment fairs.

If part of the solution is an ESL department, what should its role be? The answer, of course, is not simple. Having won the battle (and it *is* a battle) to be recognized as a discipline and a department, then the serious (and rewarding) work of planning how to proceed can begin. ESL students arrive at various times of the year with varying levels of competence in English. Every international school is different with respect to syllabus, mix of nationalities, host country language, number of students, etc., but a basic model at the secondary level will have a beginners' class and a regular ESL program in Grades 6–10 (but see Hurst & Davison, 2005, for alternatives to this traditional model).

At the Vienna International School, the ESL beginners' class contains students from Grades 6–9. The combination of grade levels in one class results from the relatively small numbers of beginning ESL students. The beginners are withdrawn or extracted for ESL from English, History, Geography, Science, and the 'third' foreign language. They attend regular Math, Physical Education, Art, Music, and Options (Technology, Textiles, Food, etc.) as well as German (the host country language). The latter decision was made after much debate; the argument being that if "they hear it so much in the playground, in the streets, on TV, then it would be better for them to have instruction in it than to only learn the slang."

The regular ESL program consists of a parallel ESL English class in Grades 6–10 taught by ESL staff, using simplified texts and videos of original texts in order to enable the ESL students to articulate with the mainstream when their English level is sufficient. The majority of the texts are based on the mainstream English syllabus so students will become familiar with the same content. Students also participate in another ESL class, offered when fluent English speakers are learning French or Spanish, in which the focus is on grammar, vocabulary, and all the basic or intermediate English language skills. In Grades 9 and 10 there is an extracted ESL class for History and Geography. Here the ESL teacher parallels the mainstream History and Geography syllabus (for useful resources related to ESL provision in international schools see the Frankfurt International School website: www.fis.edu/eslweb).

Currently there is a concern to reduce the number of pull-out classes for ESL students, with alternatives such as team-teaching being actively encouraged. However, this is not always practical in many international schools, which have complex timetables and schedules and do not always block all parts of a subject together at the same time. There is a strong argument for new ESL students to have a separate, pull-out group on pastoral grounds. Years of experience have shown how most ESL students value having an ESL teacher who understands their needs–linguistic, social, emotional–and is always ready to lend a sympathetic ear. This is a key element of international education and should not be ignored.

It has required a major effort over many years to achieve this program at the Vienna International School (see http://school.vis.ac.at/esl), but it still might be viewed as inadequate insofar as it does not offer ESL Science or ESL Math. However, these subjects are more readily accessible to most ESL students. As in many international schools, the timetabling of the school has been a major factor working against adequate ESL provision. In some international schools there is little pressure to implement more adequate provision because parents of ESL students often do not have strong English skills themselves and do not like to 'make a fuss.' Similarly, if ESL teachers do not feel confident in their position in the school, and the administration does not appreciate the value of ESL expertise, then the ESL teacher will find it very difficult, if not impossible, to advocate for better programs.

Equality of Certification for ESL Students

International schools have different ways of grading students and motivating them to succeed. ESL students need motivation at least as much as other students. Often they have been high achievers in their prior education in their country or language of origin. These students can experience deep disappointment and damage to their self-esteem as a result of their apparent diminished academic performance.

Many international schools offer the International Baccalaureat (IB) program that provides options designed to accommodate to some extent the multilingual realities of the student composition in international schools. Tosi (1987) identifies three language learning situations relevant to the IB:

1. Mother tongue learning for the native as well as the non-native speakers of the school language;

2. Foreign language learning for the native speakers of the school language;

3. Second language learning for the non-native speakers of the school language.

The third situation reflects the learning of English as the school language for ESL students. In recognition of the specific needs of this group, the IB organization instituted three categories of *Language* for Grades 11 and 12: *Language A1* is students' mother tongue or their best academic language, and the course contains a high literature content; *Language A2* is a language in which the student has attained a sufficiently high standard to be examined at virtually a native-speaker level. There is also a high literature content in this course. Success in both A1 and A2 leads to the award of a Bilingual Diploma. *Language B* is a foreign language and the course content focuses more on language rather than literature. A wide variety of languages can be taken for credit in these three categories with the result that ESL students can, in principal, take their mother tongue for credit as either A1 or A2 when the school is prepared to organize mother tongue classes. However, relatively few schools currently offer such provision.

The IB currently offers a Middle Years Program (MYP) for Grades 6–10. This program contains the usual subject content plus *Areas of Interaction* that address skills central to human society in today's world. As regards languages, there is *Language A*, which includes a focus on humanities as well as teaching literature at a native speaker level, and *Language B*, a foreign language. To obtain full MYP certification students must obtain a certain number of points in Language A.

The IB MYP does not adequately address the situation of ESL students at the present time (Carder, 2006). They fall between the cracks of Language A (intended for fluent speakers of the language) and Language B (a foreign language). Their English skills are not sufficiently developed to take English as Language A while English as Language B does not encompass the range of linguistic skills ESL students must achieve in order to function through the medium of English in the rest of the program. Clearly, because they are immersed in the language during the entire school day, ESL students usually make better progress in English as Language B than students typically do in foreign language programs. However, the 'foreign language' focus of the course does not sufficiently address the academic language proficiencies required for students to catch up academically in English during their time in the MYP.

This situation might be resolved by specifying a set of specific language objectives for ESL students in the MYP, clearly defined as such. These language objectives would require a higher level than Language B but would recognize the fact that students are not native speakers of Language A. This direction would be entirely consistent with the principles articulated in the IB MYP. The program emphasizes the interrelatedness of various academic subjects, the fostering of intercultural awareness, and promoting a better understanding of and respect for other cultures. It is hard to see how these objectives are consistent with the exclusion of ESL students from a significant part of the program because of their lack of competence in English. Rather than organizing evaluative structures to reward students' bilingualism, the current structure penalizes students in an arbitrary way. Because few international schools organize mother tongue programs, most ESL students are not able to take their mother tongue as Language A for MYP purposes and thus will not be able to qualify for the full MYP certificate.

In summary, ESL students should be on the center stage of any international curriculum. Instead they are frequently subjected to a process of subtractive bilingualism in which English replaces their mother tongue as their best academic language. If the word *international* is to mean anything more than an English-medium curriculum oriented to the needs and interests of native English-speaking students, then ESL students' needs must be considered and a proper curriculum (with appropriate aims, objectives and assessment criteria) put in place. Serious consideration should also be given to awarding a Bilingual Certificate within the MYP to those who meet specific criteria of proficiency in two languages.

ESL Awareness Training for All Staff and Administrators

International schools had their origins in the idealistic *internationalist education model*, which promoted a liberal education and an international worldview (Bunnell, 2006). However, in an increasingly market-driven globalist environment, the term *international* seems to be losing these connotations. Increasingly English–medium schools seem to be demanding "acculturation into western culture in order to achieve self-esteem and academic success" (Allan, 2006, p. 82). Many long-serving administrators and teaching staff in international schools have made minimal efforts to learn any language other than English and some exhibit patronizing attitudes towards speakers of other languages. What is urgently needed is appropriate professional development to enable staff to design and implement programs that address the learning challenges and opportunities of a multilingual context, and at the same time develop high levels of academic and English language proficiency.

As noted above, the *ESL in the Mainstream* course developed by the Department of Education and Children's Services of South Australia represents one significant attempt to provide the professional development that school staff need to address the learning and social needs of ESL students more effectively. The aims of the course are to:

- Enhance understanding of the language-related needs of learners from non-English speaking backgrounds and of ways of meeting those needs;
- Develop awareness of approaches to learning materials and teaching practices which take account of the diversity of cultural backgrounds and experiences of learners in all classes across the school curriculum;
- Further develop collaborative working relationships between classroom and subject educators, ESL specialists and bilingual support staff in schools;
- Increase awareness more generally in schools of the need for specialist personnel, training, programs and materials to support ESL learners. (Department of Education and Children's Services, 1999, p. 7)

Representatives of international schools (usually experienced ESL teachers) enroll in a one-week intensive course that trains them to deliver the professional development package to their school staffs. The professional development course is designed to be delivered at the local school level by the tutor to groups of 12 participants. The tutor's manual contains comprehensive information including videos, overhead transparencies, keys to worksheets, and discussion topics. Each participant receives two comprehensive folders of resources consisting of reading materials, workshop feedback sheets, reflection sessions, worksheets, homework tasks, bibliographies, websites, etc. The course is typically taught over ten sessions totaling 25 hours. An additional 25 hours is required for homework and reading tasks. The entire package (including the participants' manuals) consists of about 400 pages of materials that provide a balance between theory and practice. Ideas are presented in the context of a consistent conceptual framework with a variety of interactional formats and activities to cater to different learning styles. Teachers engage in collaborative learning with opportunities to research issues in their own classrooms. The course is aimed at those who are not ESL specialist, but who deal with ESL students on a daily basis in school. Specific workshops focus on how to make the language of each subject more accessible for students and also address the broader experience of ESL students coming from a language and cultural background different from that of their English-speaking peers. Such a course should be seen as essential for all those embarking on a career in international education, especially for those responsible for the curricula and the daily running of the schools.

This course had a lasting and positive effect on colleagues at the Vienna International School. Every international school could benefit from this type of well-conceptualized combination of theory and practice, cultural and language awareness techniques and hands-on application. Such courses have the potential to reduce prejudice and ignorance, sweep away much time-and-energy-wasting discussion, and put in place successful pathways for ESL students, as both staff and administrators take ownership of the need to provide appropriate instruction for these students.

The Importance of Developing Students' Mother Tongue Literacy

As noted above, there is clear research evidence to show that development of literacy in the mother tongue leads to more successful progress and achievement in the second language. Where literacy in the mother tongue is not maintained there is correspondingly less progress and achievement in the second language. This potentially results in subtractive rather than additive bilingualism, with its negative consequences of poor results in school work, low self-esteem, loss of identity, and perhaps drop-out from school (Collier & Thomas, this volume).

English is currently in demand throughout much of the world as the widely perceived language of career opportunities, economic reward, and social success. This should not be allowed to obscure the importance of developing all the linguistic resources that students bring to the school. Literacy in the mother tongue permits thoughts and emotions to be verbalized in finer nuances, multiple identities to be developed, and deeper levels of communication within the family to be realized, without conflicting with the need to acquire conversational and academic English literacy.

The low priority assigned to mother tongue programs in the international school system can be explained by the fact that schools tend to respond to the expressed needs and demands of their clientele. Unfortunately many parents see "more English" as the sole requirement for success and thus do not demand mother tongue programs. The few schools, such as the Vienna International School, that do offer such programs usually require students to pay more money. However, without a mother tongue development program many students will never achieve their educational potential with respect to literacy in both English and their mother tongue. To address this issue, it is thus important, first, to establish awareness among the entire community—parents, administrators, students and staff—of the importance of maintaining literacy in the students' mother tongue, and then to explore every possible avenue for providing a program of instruction in the relevant languages.

CONCLUSIONS

Adequate education for ESL students requires international schools to fulfill several key aims. First, there should be a well planned and institutionalized ESL program with structures operating within the school to integrate students effectively into the mainstream as their English literacy, cultural awareness and confidence levels increase. The ESL program should be staffed by professionals trained and qualified in the discipline, as is the case for other school subjects. Such teachers should have comprehensive knowledge of issues relating to second language acquisition and bilingualism. The program should have the same structures as other subjects, and should be at the hub of the school, not on the periphery. Among the responsibilities of ESL staff should be the teaching of English as Language B of the IB Diploma Program in Grades 11 and 12, if it is offered. ESL instruction should not involve extra payment by parents and there should be a clear distinction between ESL and *special educational needs* (SEN) students. These groups have entirely different learning and instructional needs and should not be grouped together. Furthermore, if its status is to be fully acknowledged, the ESL department should be independent, not subsumed within an English or Language Arts department.

A second key goal is to ensure that all staff and administrators follow a course of linguistic and cultural awareness, as described above. Recruitment of new staff should entail an active search for candidates who already have these qualifications and/or relevant instructional experiences. New staff who lack these qualifications or experiences should be obliged to take such a professional development course on arrival. Part of the institutional commitment to adequate ESL provision is that each school should ensure it has an on-site tutor trained to deliver such courses. There should be frequent communication with the entire school community about such matters, pointing out the time it takes for ESL students to reach the same level of proficiency as those who are already fluent in English, the importance of maintaining literacy in the mother tongue, the advantages of additive bilingualism, and the pitfalls and potentially lifelong negative consequences of subtractive bilingualism.

Finally, the research of Collier and Thomas (this volume) shows clearly that, at least in the US context, ESL pull-out models lead to short-term gains but long-term serious decline in English literacy development. In their research, the only models that clearly benefited ESL students were bilingual ones, an outcome that reinforces the importance of mother tongue support. Every effort should be made to establish a mother tongue program so that all students who are not mother tongue speakers of English receive instruction in their language. If teachers for some languages cannot be found, then students should be encouraged to read widely in their first language. This proactive encouragement would be part of the remit of all teachers, not just ESL teachers. The overall goal should be to move ESL students to the center of international school programs, to be treated equally and rewarded for their bilingual talents, not marginalized nor rendered invisible. Although progress has been slow, the IB MYP program support documents now contain clear statements on the benefits of bilingualism but more needs to be done to provide coherent articulation of the IB Primary Years Program, Middle Years Program and Diploma Program to ensure that they all carry the same message and offer structures that acknowledge and reward students' bilingualism and support mother tongue development.

REFERENCES

Allan, M. (2002). Culture borderlands: A case study of cultural dissonance in an international school. *Journal of Research in International Education, 1*(1), 63–90.
Baker, C. (2001). *Foundations of bilingual education and bilingualism* (3rd ed.). Clevedon: Multilingual Matters.
Baker, C., & Prys Jones, S. (Eds.). (1998). *Encyclopedia of bilingualism and bilingual education.* Clevedon: Multilingual Matters.
Bunnell, T. (2005). The growing momentum and legitimacy behind an alliance for international education *Journal of Research in International Education, 5*(2), 155–176.
Carder, M. W. (1991). The role and development of ESL programs in international schools. In P. Jonietz & D. Harris (Eds.). *World Yearbook of Education 1991: International Schools and International Education.* (pp. 108–124). London: Kogan Page.
Carder, M. W. (1993). Are we creating biliterate bilinguals? *International Schools Journal, 26*(1), 19–27.
Carder, M. W. (1995). Language(s) in international education: A review of language issues in International Schools. In T. Skutnabb-Kangas (Ed.) *Multilingualism for all.* (pp. 113–157) Lisse, The Netherlands: Swets and Zeitlinger.
Carder, M. W. (2002) Intercultural awareness, bilingualism, and ESL in the International Baccalaureate, with particular reference to the MYP. *International Schools Journal, 20*(2), 45–54.
Carder, M. W. (2006). Bilingualism in International Baccalaureate programmes, with particular reference to international schools. *Journal of Research in International Education, 5*(1), 105–122.
Carder, M. (2007) *Bilingualism in International Schools: A Model for Enriching Language Education.* Clevedon: Multilingual Matters.
Chamot, A. U., & O'Malley, J.M. (1986) *A cognitive academic language learning approach: An ESL content-based curriculum.* Washington, DC: National Clearinghouse for Bilingual Education.
Cummins, J. (2000). *Language, power and pedagogy: Bilingual children in the crossfire.* Clevedon, UK: Multilingual Matters.
Davison, C. (2006). Collaboration between ESL and content teachers: How do we know we are doing it right? *Journal of Bilingual Education and Bilingualism, 9*(4), 454–475.
Department of Education and Children's Services. (1999). *ESL in the mainstream: Tutor's manual.* Adelaide, South Australia. www.unlockingtheworld.com.
Hanchanlash, C. (2004). International cultural overpass: Its relation to an alienation from an indigenous culture. *International Schools Journal, 18*(2), 7–16.
Hayden, M., & Thompson, J. (1998). International education: Perceptions of teachers in international schools. *International Review of Education, 44*(5/6), 549–568.
Hayden, M., & Thompson, J. (1997). Student perspective on international education: A European dimension. *Oxford Review of Education, 23*(4), 459–478.
Hurst, D., & Davison, C. (2005). Collaboration on the curriculum: Focus on secondary ESL. In Crandall, J. & Kauffman, D. (Eds.), *Case Studies in TESOL: Teacher education for ESL and content area teachers* (pp. 41–66). Alexandria, VI: TESOL.
Jonietz, P. L., & Harris, D. (Eds.). (1991). *World Yearbook of Education 1991: International Schools and International Education.* London: Kogan Page.
MacDonald, J. (2006). The international school industry: Examining international schools through an economic lens. *Journal of Research in International Education, 5*(2), 191–213.
Mackenzie, P., Hayden, M., & Thompson, J. (2001). The third constituency: Parents in international schools. *International Schools Journal, 20*(2), 57–64.
Murphy, E. (Ed.). (1990). *ESL: A handbook for teachers and administrators in international schools.* Clevedon, UK: Multilingual Matters.
Thomas, W.P., & Collier, V.P. (2002). *A national study of school effectiveness for language minority students' long-term academic achievement.* Santa Cruz, CA: Center for Research on Education, Diversity and Excellence, University of California-Santa Cruz.
Tosi, A. (1987). *First, second or foreign language learning?* Unpublished Ph.D. thesis, Institute of Education, University of London, UK.

CHAPTER 26

ENGLISH FOR SPECIFIC PURPOSES:

Some Influences and Impacts

KEN HYLAND

Institute of Education, The University of London, UK

ABSTRACT

The field of English for specific purposes (ESP), which addresses the communicative needs and practices of particular professional or occupational groups, has developed rapidly in the past forty years to become a major force in English language teaching and research. ESP draws its strength from an eclectic theoretical foundation and a commitment to research-based language education which seeks to reveal the constraints of social contexts on language use and the ways learners can gain control over these. In this chapter, I will briefly point to some of the major ideas and practices that currently influence ESP, focusing on needs analysis, ethnography, critical approaches, contrastive rhetoric, social constructionism, and discourse analysis. I then go on to look briefly at some of the effects ESP has had on language teaching and research, arguing that it has encouraged teachers to highlight communication rather than language, to adopt a research orientation to their work, to employ collaborative pedagogies, to be aware of discourse variation, and to consider the wider political implications of their role. Together these features of ESP practice emphasise a situated view of literacy and underline the applied nature of the field.

INTRODUCTION

English for specific purposes (ESP) refers to language research and instruction that focuses on the specific communicative needs and practices of particular social groups. Emerging out of Halliday, MacIntosh, and Strevens' (1964) groundbreaking work nearly 40 years ago, ESP started life as a branch of English language teaching, promising a stronger descriptive foundation for pedagogic materials. In the years since, ESP has consistently been at the cutting-edge of both theory development and innovative practice in applied linguistics, making a significant contribution to our understanding of the varied ways language is used in particular communities. Drawing on a range of interdisciplinary influences for its research methods, theory, and practices, ESP has consistently provided grounded insights into the structures and meanings of texts, the demands placed by academic or workplace contexts on communicative behaviors, and the pedagogic practices by which these behaviors can be developed. In this chapter I will sketch out what I see as some of the major ideas which currently influence work in ESP, and briefly comment on some of the effects it has had on language teaching and research.

SOME INFLUENCES ON ESP

It is its interdisciplinarity, an openness to the approaches and insights of other fields, which helps distinguish ESP and underlies its understandings and practices. Its closest connections, of course, are to applied linguistics and particularly to discourse analysis. We can, however, also see strong links between ESP and pragmatics, communicative language teaching, corporate communications, writing across the curriculum, rhetoric, critical literacy, sociocognitive theory, and the sociology of scientific knowledge. This willingness to embrace and unite different disciplinary perspectives gives ESP its distinctiveness and helps to identify what it stands for. In this chapter I want to briefly introduce six of the most salient aspects of these perspectives as key influences: (a) needs analysis, (b) ethnography, (c) critical perspectives, (d) contrastive rhetoric, (e) social constructionism, and (f) discourse analysis.

This is perhaps an idiosyncratic list, but these are the core ideas which define what ESP seeks to do and the ways it currently chooses to do it, assisting practitioners to interpret how aspects of the real communicative world work and to translate these understandings into practical classroom applications.

Needs Analysis

While not unique to ESP, needs analysis is a defining element of its practices and a major source of its interdisciplinarity (e.g., Dudley-Evans & St John, 1998). The use of systematic means to define the specific sets of skills, texts, linguistic forms, and communicative practices that a particular group of learners must acquire is central to ESP, informing its curricula and materials and underlining its pragmatic engagement with occupational, academic, and professional realities. It is a crucial link between perception and practice, helping ESP to keep its feet on the ground by tempering any excesses of academic theory-building with practical applications.

Analysis presupposes an understanding of what must be analyzed and a theoretical framework for describing it. Both have changed over time. Early needs analyses focused on the lexical and syntactic features of texts of particular registers, or domains with discernible linguistic features, by establishing the distinctiveness of scientific and technical varieties of English. Interest then moved to the rhetorical macro-structure of specialist texts (Trimble, 1985) to describe expository writing as nested patterns of functional units. In Europe this approach was informed by functional-notional syllabi and attempts to specify, in functional terms, the competence levels students needed for particular activities (Munby, 1978). This interest in locating texts more deeply in their social contexts has continued through to the present as work has increasingly sought to develop an understanding of the social processes in which academic and workplace writing is sited. The use of genre analysis pioneered by Swales (1990) and Bhatia (1993), for instance, has provided a useful tool for understanding community situated language use and describing specific target texts required by learners.

Both pragmatic and rhetorical analyses have become more sophisticated and diverse, but simultaneously, the concept of *need* has been expanded beyond the linguistic skills and knowledge required to perform competently in a target situation. On one hand, it has moved to include *learner needs*, or what the learner must do in order to learn, incorporating both the learner's starting point and his/her perceptions of need (Hutchison & Waters, 1987). Most recently, the question of 'who's needs?' has been asked more critically, raising questions about target goals and the interests they serve rather than assuming they should exclusively guide instruction. The term *rights analysis* has been introduced to refer to a framework for studying power relations in classrooms and institutions and for organizing students and teachers to bring about greater equality (Benesch, 2001). Clearly however, the imperative of need, to understand learners, target contexts, discourses, and socio-political context, means that the starting point for any ESP activity must be a strong research base.

Ethnography

The second major influence on ESP has emerged more recently but has begun to make a significant impact on the ways we understand both language use and language learning. The movement away from an exclusive focus on texts to the practices that surround their use has been enormously facilitated by ethnographic studies. *Ethnography* is a type of research that undertakes to give a participant-oriented description of individuals' cultural practices. The term remains fuzzy and is often used loosely to refer to any qualitative method, but essentially it focuses on a holistic explanation of communicative behavior by drawing on the conceptual frameworks of insiders themselves. Members of discourse communities and the physical settings in which they work thus become the primary focus of study, with detailed observations of behaviors together with interviews and the analysis of texts, to provide a fuller picture of what is happening.

Ethnography has been important in ESP in three main ways. First, it has begun to provide valuable insights into target contexts, helping to identify the discursive practices involved in the production, distribution, and consumption of texts. So, for example, this approach was used by Gollin (1999) to analyze a collaborative writing project in a professional Australian workplace, and by Flowerdew and Miller (1995) to study L2 academic listening in Hong Kong. Second, ethnographic techniques have also been useful in exploring student practices, revealing how they participate in their learning, engage with their teachers, and experience their engagement as peripheral members of new communities. An excellent example of this kind of work is provided in Prior's (1998) studies of the disciplinary enculturation of graduate students through writing and their interactions with peers and professors. Third, ethnography has been used to argue for pedagogic appropriacy in contexts where overseas students study in Anglo countries or where Anglo teachers and curricula are employed in overseas settings. Holliday's (1994) ethnographic study of a large scale English for academic purposes (EAP) project in Egypt, for instance, underlines the need for sensitivity to local teaching models and expectations.

Critical Perspectives

Critical perspectives have only recently begun to have much of an influence on ESP, but they are now having an increasing impact on the ways teachers see and practice their profession. I noted above that, in its early years, ESP was largely concerned with identifying and describing formal, quantifiable text features without a great deal of social awareness. The growth of a more socially informed approach, however, has also brought a greater willingness to interrogate the assumptions on which theory and practice are based. This is apparent in various ways, but I think it is important to mention two.

First, it has helped to develop a growing sense in ESP that a social-theoretical stance is needed to fully understand what happens in institutions to make discourses the way they are. Increasingly, studies have turned to examine the ideological impact of expert discourses, the social distribution of valued literacies, access to prestigious genres, and the ways control of specialized discourses are related to status and credibility (Hyland, 2000). The values, beliefs, and ideologies of speakers and writers are seen in the distribution of particular features in texts and the ways texts are used, and are taken into account to understand and explain discourse practices. Issues such as individual competitiveness, alliances among particular groups, the role of gatekeepers, and vested interests in institutional reward systems have therefore become legitimate areas of ESP research.

Second, critical perspectives remind us that ESP teaching itself is not a politically neutral activity. Phillipson (1992), for instance, argues that marketing English as a global commodity is essentially ideological as it not only threatens local languages but also works to maintain socio-political elites. More directly, Pennycook (1997) believes that ESP should not simply accept the demands of global business and the academy. Instead, it should question the status quo and help students to develop a critical awareness of how language works to support institutional hierarchies and inequalities. More recently, Benesch (2001) has argued that ESP in universities can achieve its aims more effectively by engaging with issues of power, describing a teaching approach that tries to modify target context arrangements rather than reinforcing conformity. The main view here then is that our teaching practices should be less *accommodationist* to dominant political and institutional orders, helping students to perform the best they can while "encouraging them to question and shape the education they are getting" (Benesch, p. xvii).

Contrastive Rhetoric

The influence of *contrastive rhetoric*, the ways that first language and culture affect second language writing, has been particularly significant in EAP. Contrastive rhetoric has contributed a great deal to our understanding of the preferred patterns of writing of different cultural groups (Connor, 1996) and has also influenced the study of academic and professional cultures.

Only in the last 10 years has the field of Academic English taken the issue of students' culture seriously. This is partly because early formulations of contrastive rhetoric were seen as rather ethnocentric and prescriptive, and partly because of a well-established attitude that, in the fields of science and technology, there is an independent scientific culture expressed by a universal rhetoric. There are still reservations about contrastive rhetoric as it is often difficult to establish equivalent writing tasks across cultures and to distinguish the effects of first language from those of limited proficiency on the writing of non-native learners (Hyland & Milton, 1997). However, a growing number of studies has provided considerable evidence for cultural-specificity in preferred structures of exposition and argumentation across a large number of languages. These cultural preferences include different organizational patterns, different persuasive appeals, different ways of incorporating material, different uses of cohesion and metadiscourse, and different uses of linguistic features (Connor, 1996; Hinkel, 1999). It seems reasonable to assume that such differences may influence how students write in English.

The view that discoursal and rhetorical features of writing might reflect the cultural experiences of individuals has been enthusiastically taken up by ESP in other areas, revealing the discursive homogeneity of social and professional communities. Each discipline or profession can be seen as constituting a separate culture with its particular norms, nomenclature, bodies of knowledge, sets of conventions, and modes of inquiry (Bartholomae, 1986; Swales, 1990). Within each culture, individuals acquire specialized discourse competencies that allow them to participate as group members. These cultures differ along both social and cognitive dimensions, offering contrasts not only in their fields of knowledge, but in their aims, social behaviors, power relations, political interests, ways of talking, and structures of argument. Contrastive rhetoric also draws attention to the fact that we are members of several such cultures simultaneously and critically highlights the conflicts inherent in these multiple memberships. In particular it emphasizes the potential clashes between the discourse conventions of professional and ethnic cultures. The question of who establishes the linguistic conventions of professional communities and whose norms are used to judge them is a central issue in ESP, and researchers have questioned the traditional view that those familiar with other conventions need to conform to Anglo-American norms when engaging in professional and particularly academic genres (e.g., Ventola, 1992). Many post-colonial countries have developed thriving indigenous varieties of English, which are widely used and accepted locally but which diverge from international standards. ESP teachers now take the issue of appropriate models for EAP and English for occupational purposes (EOP) seriously, exploring how far the professions, corporations, and disciplines in which they work tolerate differences in rhetorical styles.

Social Constructionist Theory

Originating in the symbolic interactionism of Mead (1934) and developed within social psychology and post-modern philosophy, *social constructionism* is probably the mainstream theoretical perspective in ESP and EAP research today. The perspective mainly gained prominence in ESP through research on scientists' lab activities by those working in the sociology of scientific knowledge (e.g., Gilbert & Mulkay, 1984; Latour & Woolgar, 1979) and the rhetorical analyses of scientific texts by Bazerman (1988), Myers (1990), and Swales (1990).

Basically social constructivism suggests that knowledge and social reality are created through daily interactions between people and particularly through their discourse. It takes a critical stance towards taken-for-granted knowledge and, in opposition to positivism and empiricism in traditional science, questions the idea of an objective reality. It says that everything we see and believe is actually filtered through our theories and our language, sustained by social processes, which are culturally and historically specific. Discourse is therefore central to relationships, knowledge, and scientific facts as all are rhetorically constructed by individuals acting as members of social communities. The goal of ESP is therefore to discover how people use discourse to create, sustain, and change these communities; how they signal their membership; how they persuade others to accept their ideas; and so on. Stubbs (1996) succinctly combines these issues into a single question:

> The major intellectual puzzle in the social sciences is the relation between the micro and the macro. How is it that routine everyday behavior, from moment to moment, can create and maintain social institutions over long periods of time? (p. 21)

Social construction has thus become a central theoretical underpinning of work in ESP. It sets a research agenda focused on revealing the genres and communicative conventions that display membership of academic and professional communities, and a pedagogic agenda focused on employing this awareness to best help learners critique and participate in such communities. Swales (2001) points out that social constructionism is attractive to those working in ESP as it gives them "an enhanced place in the study of academic tribes and territories" (p. 48), putting discourse at the center of human endeavor and elevating the role of those who study it. The fact that this view makes truth relative to the discourses of social groups has not, however, always endeared ESP practitioners to those who prefer a less tenuous connection between reality and accounts of it, not least the scientists, academics, and professionals they study.

Nor have constructionists yet managed to agree on precisely what the term *community* means, despite its importance in this approach. Harris (1989), for example, argues we should restrict the term to specific local groups, and labels other uses as "discursive utopias" (p.18). Clearly if communities are regarded as real, stable groups conforming to certain shared and agreed upon values and conventions, there is a risk of representing them as static, abstract, and deterministic. Discourse communities, however, are not monolithic and unitary structures but involve interactions between individuals with diverse experiences, commitments, and influence. As a result, Porter (1992) understands a community in terms of its *forums* or approved channels of discourse, and Swales (1998) sees them as groups constituted by their typical genres, of how they get things done, rather than existing through physical membership. For the most part, recent research has sought to capture the explanatory and predictive authority of the concept by replacing the idea of an overarching force that determines behavior with that of systems in which multiple beliefs and practices overlap and intersect (Hyland, 2000).

Discourse Analysis

Finally, discourse analysis, probably the most important item in the ESP toolbox is discussed. *Discourse analysis* takes a variety of different forms, but in ESP it has traditionally involved attention to features of texts and their rhetorical purposes as a basis for pedagogical materials. This approach has been strongly influenced by *Systemic Functional Linguistics* (e.g., Halliday, 1994), a sophisticated theory of language concerned with the relationship between language and the functions it is used to perform in social contexts. In this view, language consists of a set of systems from which users make choices to most effectively express their intended meanings, and this fits neatly with ESP's aims to demystify the academic and professional genres that will enhance or determine learners' career opportunities. Genre analysis has thus become the principal form of discourse analysis in ESP, providing a very focused methodology and enabling researchers to identify the structural and rhetorical features that distinguish the texts most relevant to particular communities and contexts.

Genres are abstract, socially recognized ways of using language that we draw on to respond to perceived repeated situations. In ESP a fruitful line of research has been to explore and identify the characteristic lexico-grammatical features and rhetorical patterns of particular genres. This has helped to reveal how texts are typically constructed and how they relate to their contexts of use through specific social purposes, as well as providing valuable input for genre-based teaching. Genre analyses also characterize the processes by which texts and events are mediated through relationships with other texts, drawing on the concept of *intertextuality* (Bakhtin, 1986). The idea that any instance of discourse is partly created from previous discourses and reflected in subsequent ones is an important way of conceptualizing cultures. It also helps us to understand the ways that texts cluster to constitute particular social and cultural practices, networked in a linear sequence, as in the case of a formal job offer for instance, or more loosely cohering as a repertoire of options, say in the choice of a press advertisement, poster campaign, or mail shot to announce a product launch. Analyses have been greatly facilitated in recent years by the use of large text corpora and computer concordancing programs, which make reliable quantitative analysis more feasible. Researchers can now collect representative samples of texts differentiated by both genre and field and, with frequency counts and collocational analyses, produce more targeted and more plausible linguistic descriptions.

This is not the only way to see genre however, and analyses have broadened in recent years beyond the study of discoursal features to investigate the contexts in which they are produced and used. This involves studying genre "as the motivated, functional relationship between text type and rhetorical situation" (Coe, 2001, p. 195) and aims to extend text analyses to uncover something of the attitudes, values, and beliefs of the communities of text users that genres imply and construct.

In addition to being a valuable research tool, discourse analysis has also become a central teaching method in ESP, with a commitment to exploiting relevant and authentic texts in the classroom through tasks which increase awareness of their purpose and their linguistic and rhetorical features. More generally, providing students with an explicit knowledge of relevant genres is seen as a means of helping learners gain access to ways of communicating that have accrued cultural capital in particular communities. Genre approaches, in fact, also seem to offer the most effective means for learners to critique cultural and linguistic resources (Hyland, 2002b). The provision of a rhetorical understanding of texts and a metalanguage to analyze them allows students to see texts as artifacts that can be explicitly questioned, compared, and deconstructed, so revealing the assumptions and ideologies that underlie them.

SOME IMPACTS OF ESP

By way of balance, I would like to complete this chapter with a brief consideration of what all this amounts to and where these influences have taken ESP by looking at some of the effects ESP has had on language teaching. Basically, ESP coheres around a general acceptance that institutional practices and understandings strongly influence the language and communicative behaviors of individuals. It also stresses that it is important to identify these factors in designing teaching tasks and materials to give students access to valued discourses and the means to see them critically. I want to draw attention to five aspects of this characterization: (a) the study of communication rather than language, (b) the role of teacher as researcher, (c) the importance of collaborative pedagogies, (d) the centrality of language variation, and (e) the view that language represents broader social practices.

The Study of Communication not Language

Clearly ESP has moved some way from its original exclusive focus on text features. In the past, materials were often based solely on the lexical and grammatical characteristics of scientific and business discourses in isolation from their social contexts. Today these materials have largely been replaced by those that acknowledge wider interactional and semiotic contexts, where language and tasks are more closely related to the situations in which they are used. ESP practitioners now address wider communicative skills in their teaching. In the area of research, ESP attempts to go beyond texts to understand how they work in particular disciplines or professions, seeing genres, for instance, as recognizable kinds of social activity embedded in particular kinds of interaction rather than just arrangements of forms.

To understand language and the functions it performs for people, we have to appreciate how it is used within particular contexts, identifying the purposes and participants that are integral to the construction of particular communicative processes and products. We need, for instance, to understand the interpersonal conventions a sales manager might observe when giving a client presentation or the knowledge a chemist assumes of his or her audience when writing up a lab report. In the classroom, these concerns translate into finding ways of preparing students to participate in a range of activities and to see ESP as concerned with communicative practices rather than more narrowly with specific aspects of language.

The Teacher as Researcher

ESP is, fundamentally, research-based language education: a pedagogy for learners with identifiable professional, academic, and occupational communicative needs. This means that teachers cannot simply be the consumers of materials and research findings but must follow the imperative of specificity. They must consider the relevance of studies to their own learners and conduct their own target situation analyses and their own research into local contexts. While ESP textbooks and so called "English for General Academic Purposes" or "English for General Business Purposes" courses are still widespread, there is a growing awareness in the field of the limited transferability of skills, forms, and discourses across situations (Hyland, 2002a). In addition, teachers have not only become researchers of the genres and communicative practices of target situations, but also of their classrooms. As I mentioned above, teachers have used qualitative techniques such as observations and interviews to discover students' reactions to assignments, the ways they learn, and content instructors' reactions to learners' participation and performance. This information then feeds back into the design of ESP courses in the materials, tasks, and problems that are employed in the classroom.

Collaborative Pedagogies

A third major impact is the distinctive methodological approach that ESP has developed as a result of its view of specificity. ESP necessarily works in tandem with the specialist fields it seeks to describe, explain, and teach, bringing an expertise in communicative practices to the subject specific skills and knowledge of those working in particular target areas. It is a central tenet of ESP that professional communities possess their own distinguishing discoursal practices, genres, and communicative conventions, which arise from different ways of carrying out their work and of seeing the world. Because ESP learners need to acquire competence in particular genres and specific communicative skills along with the knowledge and tradecraft of their professions, this knowledge becomes the context for learning. The topics, content, and practices of the profession thus act as vehicles for teaching particular discourses and communicative skills. The fact that the ESP practitioner is generally a novice in these areas means that collaboration with both students and subject specialists is essential.

Students bring to their ESP classes some knowledge of their specialist fields and the kinds of communication that go on within them, and this latent communication knowledge is important in a number of ways. Importantly, it means that ESP teachers need to negotiate their courses with learners drawing on their specialist expertise to promote relevant communicative activities in the classroom. An imperative of ESP has always been a reliance on tasks and materials that display authenticity or faithfulness to real-world texts and purposes, and learners themselves are among the best arbiters of this kind of appropriacy. Another way that teachers often collaborate with learners is to employ this specialist knowledge as a learning resource. Much current ESP is strongly focused on rhetorical consciousness-raising, helping students to become more aware of the language, discourses, and communicative practices in their fields. This means the teacher is closely involved in assisting learners to activate and build on their latent understandings perhaps harnessing the methods of their fields to explore the ways that communicative intentions are expressed (Dudley-Evans & St John, 1998).

Teachers also often need to collaborate with subject experts, and there are a number of ways this can operate. The specialist can assist as an informant, providing teachers, or students, with background and insights into the kinds of practices that experts engage in and their understandings of the texts they use (Johns, 1997). Alternatively such collaboration can involve the specialist acting as a consultant, assisting the ESP teacher to select authentic texts and tasks. More centrally, ESP courses often involve the direct collaboration of subject specialists, either through team teaching or by *linked courses*, integrating an ESP course with the activities of a specialist course by jointly planning tasks and coordinating instruction (e.g., Haas, Smoke, & Hernandez, 1991).

The Importance of Discourse Variation

While the argument for a "common core" of generic skills and linguistic forms is still occasionally made, ESP research has strongly reinforced the view that professional and academic discourses represent a variety of specific literacies. A recurring theme through this chapter has been that each community has different purposes and ways of seeing the world, which are closely related to distinct practices, genres, and communicative conventions. As a result, investigating and teaching the communicative practices of those disciplines inevitably takes us to greater specificity. The idea of linguistic variation has been central to ESP since its inception and owes its origins to Michael Halliday's work on register in the 1970s, but it has gathered momentum as a result of a number of factors.

One contributing factor has been a growing awareness of the complexities of community literacies and the training that leads to professional membership. In universities a large body of survey research carried out during the 1980s and early 1990s revealed the considerable variation of discourses across the curriculum (e.g., Horowitz, 1986). This work showed that not only did different disciplines employ different genres but that the structure of common genres, such as the experimental lab report, differed completely across disciplines (Braine, 1995). The growth of modular degrees and interdisciplinary courses has made matters even more linguistically demanding for students, and recent case studies of individual students and courses reinforce this picture revealing marked diversities of task and texts in different fields (e.g., Candlin & Plum, 1999; Prior, 1998). In the workplace, discursive competence is increasingly recognized as a marker of professional expertise. References to specific communicative abilities are now often seen in the professional competency statements of nursing, law, and accountancy while caregivers, therapists, doctors, and other professionals are often judged in terms of their ability to gather and give information effectively in their particular contexts.

As I have noted, the idea of multiple literacies is supported by text analysis research. Successful communication depends on the projection of a shared context. Communication is effective to the extent that participants draw on knowledge of prior texts to frame messages in ways that appeal to appropriate cultural and institutional relationships. This directs us to the ways professional texts vary not only in their content but also in different appeals to background knowledge, different means of persuasion, and different ways of engaging with readers. In sum, this research shows that professional discourses are not uniform and monolithic differentiated only by specialist topics and vocabularies. It also undermines the idea that there is a single literacy that can be taught as a set of discrete, value-free technical skills across all situations. This helps teachers to see that weaknesses in English has little to do with a deficit of literacy skills which can be topped up in a few English classes and leads ESP to find ways of integrating the teaching and learning of language with the teaching and learning of disciplines and professions.

Language and Institutional Practices: Replication or Contestation?

Together with work in New Literacy Studies (e.g., Barton & Hamilton, 1998), ESP has begun to provide textual evidence for the view that language use is always socially situated and indicative of broader social practices. With the emergence of critical pedagogies, it has also raised questions about whether the teacher's responsibility lies in replicating and reproducing existing forms of discourse (and thus power relations) or of developing these in principled ways.

ESP's previous lack of engagement with critical issues was partly a result of its pragmatic origins in the 1970s oil boom and its tendency to "follow the dollar" through a global migration of teachers and students. While promoting an international outlook, this background may have encouraged a certain complacency or unquestioning acceptance of the value of this enterprise and the ways it was carried out. Practitioners rarely gave much thought to, and almost never sought to challenge, the power structures that erected and supported the prestigious literacy practices they taught. There is now greater awareness of critical issues and of the relationships between language and power, but the discipline has still to seriously confront these issues. This is partly a factor of the institutional constraints acting on ESP contexts themselves. In universities, ESP staff are frequently employed as vulnerable, short-term instructors in marginalized "service units." In the private sector, their status is normally greater, but here they are often contracted to provide a commercially evaluated product such as a course or materials for a paying client. Ways of facilitating change in such environments remain to be explored.

CONCLUSIONS

This brief overview has been necessarily selective, as limitations of space prevent a fuller coverage of the disciplines and theories that have influenced the growth of ESP and of the influences it has itself had on applied linguistics. Nor has it been possible to do justice to those areas that have been included, and the key ideas and contributors mentioned are worth following up in the literature.

There are, however, two clear ideas that emerge from this survey and which might stand for a synopsis of the field. First is the fact that ESP is clearly founded on the idea that we use language as members of social groups. This in turn means that it is concerned with communication rather than language and with the ways texts are created and used, rejecting an autonomous view of literacy to look at the practices of real people communicating in real contexts. The second point is that ESP is unashamedly applied. It should be clear that the term *applied* does not mean lacking a theory. It means gathering strength by drawing on those disciplines and ideas that offer the most for understanding and for classroom practice. Not only is there an interdisciplinary research base at the heart of ESP, but this eclecticism results in a clear theoretical stance that distils down to three main commitments: to linguistic analysis, to the principle of contextual relevance, and to the classroom replication of community-specific communicative events.

REFERENCES

Bakhtin, M. (1986). *Speech genres and other late essays.* Austin: University of Texas Press.
Bartholomae, D. (1986). Inventing the university. *Journal of Basic Writing, 5,* 4–23.
Barton, D., & Hamilton, M. (1998). *Local literacies.* London: Routledge.
Bazerman, C. (1988). *Shaping written knowledge.* Madison: University of Wisconsin Press.
Benesch, S. (2001). *Critical English for academic purposes: Theory, politics and practice.* Mahwah, NJ: Erlbaum.
Bhatia, V. K. (1993). *Analysing Genre: Language use in professional settings.* London: Longman.
Braine, G. (1995). Writing in the natural sciences and engineering. In D. Belcher, & G. Braine (Eds.), *Academic writing in a second language: Essays on research and pedagogy,* (pp. 23–46). Norwood, NJ: Ablex.
Candlin, C. N., & Plum, G. A. (1999). Engaging with challenges of interdiscursivity in academic writing: Researchers, students and teachers. In C. N. Candlin, & K. Hyland (Eds*.), Writing: Texts, processes and practices* (pp. 193–217). London & New York: Longman.
Coe, R. M. (2001). The new rhetoric of genre: Writing political briefs. In A. M. Johns (Ed.), *Genre in the classroom,* (pp. 195–205). Mahwah, NJ: Erlbaum.
Connor, U. (1996). *Contrastive rhetoric.* Cambridge: CUP.
Dudley-Evans, T., & St. John, M.-J. (1998). *Developments in English for specific purposes.* Cambridge: Cambridge University Press.

Flowerdew, J., & Miller, L. (1995). On the notion of culture in second language lectures. *TESOL Quarterly, 29*(2), 345–374.
Gilbert, G., & Mulkay, M. (1984). *Opening Pandora's box: A sociological analysis of scientific discourse.* Cambridge: CUP.
Gollin, S. (1999). 'Why? I thought we'd talked about it before': Collaborative writing in a professional workplace setting. In C. N. Candlin, & K. Hyland (Eds.), *Writing: Texts, processes and practices*, (pp. 267–90). London: Longman.
Haas, T., Smoke, T., & Hernandez, J. (1991). A collaborative model for empowering non-traditional students. In S. Benesch (Ed.), *ESL in America: Myths and possibilities*, (pp. 112–39). Portsmouth, NH: Heinemann.
Halliday, M. (1994). *An introduction to functional grammar* (2nd ed.). London: Edward Arnold.
Halliday, M., MacIntosh, A., & Strevens, P. (1964). *The linguistic sciences and language teaching.* London: Longman.
Harris, J. (1989). The idea of a discourse community in the study of writing. *College Composition and Communication, 40*, 11–22.
Hinkel, E. (Ed.). (1999). *Culture in second language teaching and learning.* Cambridge: CUP.
Holliday, A. (1994). *Appropriate methodology and social context.* Cambridge: CUP.
Horowitz, D. M. (1986). What professors actually require: Academic tasks for the ESL classroom. *TESOL Quarterly, 20*(3), 445–62.
Hutchison, T., & Waters, A. (1987). *English for specific purposes.* Cambridge: CUP.
Hyland, K. (2000). *Disciplinary discourses: Social interactions in academic writing.* London: Longman.
Hyland, K. (2002a). Specificity revisited: How far should we go now? *English for Specific Purposes, 21*(4), 385–395.
Hyland, K. (2002b) Genre: Language, context and literacy. *Annual Review of Applied Linguistics 22*, 113–135.
Hyland, K., & Milton, J. (1997). Hedging in L1 and L2 student writing. *Journal of Second Language Writing, 6*(2), 183–206.
Johns, A. M. (1997). *Text, role and context: Developing academic literacies.* Cambridge: CUP.
Latour, B., & Woolgar, S. (1979). *Laboratory life: The social construction of scientific facts.* Beverly Hills: Sage.
Mead, G.H. (1934). *Mind, self, and society, ed. C.W. Morris.* Chicago: University of Chicago.
Munby, J. (1978). *Communicative syllabus design.* Cambridge: CUP.
Myers, G. (1990). *Writing biology: Texts in the social construction of scientific knowledge.* Madison: University of Wisconsin Press.
Pennycook, A. (1997). Vulgar pragmatism, critical pragmatism and EAP. *English for Specific Purposes, 16*, 253–69.
Phillipson, R. (1992). *Linguistic imperialism.* Oxford: OUP.
Porter, J. (1992). *Audience and rhetoric: An archaeological composition of the discourse community.* Englewood Cliffs, NJ: Prentice Hall.
Prior, P. (1998). *Writing/disciplinarity: A sociohistoric account of literate activity in the academy.* Mahwah, NJ: Erlbaum.
Stubbs, M. (1996). *Text and corpus analysis.* Oxford: Blackwell.
Swales, J. (1990). *Genre Analysis: English in academic and research settings.* Cambridge: CUP.
Swales, J. (1998). *Other floors, other voices: A textography of a small university building.* Mahwah, NJ: Erlbaum.
Swales, J. (2001). EAP-related linguistic research: An intellectual history. In J. Flowerdew & M. Peacock (Eds.), *Research perspectives on English for academic purposes*, (pp. 42–54). Cambridge: CUP
Trimble, L. (1985). *English for science and technology.* Rowley, MA: Newbury House.
Ventola, E. (1992). Writing scientific English: Overcoming cultural problems. *International Journal of Applied Linguistics, 2*(2), 191–220.

CHAPTER 27

AN INTERDISCIPLINARY APPROACH TO TEACHING ADULTS ENGLISH IN THE WORKPLACE

JANE LOCKWOOD

The Hong Kong Institute of Education, China

ABSTRACT

This chapter explores the positive contribution that ideas and constructs from both the business and management training and the adult education literature can make to the theory and practice of workplace ELT curriculum design. Specifically, the chapter looks at how workplace stakeholders can provide a business voice to the ELT curriculum processes, how business-training planning and evaluation frameworks can assist ESP workplace practitioners in reconceptualizing the curriculum process, and how a review of adult learning research can help ESP workplace practitioners better understand the English language needs of professionals in the workplace. Unfortunately, the applied linguistic literature is, for the most part, school-based, leaving workplace ELT programs poorly researched and documented in terms of curriculum theory and practice. The chapter will report on studies of workplace English carried out in Hong Kong and the Philippines. The first Hong Kong study (Lockwood, 2002) investigated the way in which frameworks from business management and training can be used in ESP workplace training to ensure workplace stakeholders and thus the organization as a whole are better represented in the process. The second Hong Kong study (Hamp-Lyons et al., 2002) provides insights into how different stages in a professional career (in this case accountants) impact the kind of written language expectations of that professional. Two studies conducted in the Philippines in the business processing outsourcing (BPO) industry, specifically within call centers in Manila, illuminates further the language demands of the increasingly globalized workplace.

INTRODUCTION

Despite the increase in demand for more and better business English language programs in the workplace, the theoretical tenets upon which they are based remain under-researched (Nickerson, 1998; St. John 1996). Workplace language trainers, armed with applied linguistic skills and knowledge and teaching experience in schools and universities, face new challenges in the workplace environment and often report feeling ill-equipped to deal with language training in the business context. For example, workplace trainers at the Centre for Professional and Business English at the Hong Kong Polytechnic University, mostly trained in the humanities to work in school based institutions, bemoan their own lack of knowledge of business practices and business needs for workplace English language training. There is a dearth of research literature to assist them.

This chapter argues that by looking at the interdisciplinary literature of business management and training and adult education for the professions, new ideas and approaches may emerge and thus lend more support to ESP trainers in the workplace. The implications of the business context for ELT curriculum design are described and frameworks from the literature of business management and training used to show how new and more effective workplace English training programs may be developed (Brinkerhoff, 1998; Cummings, 1998; Kirkpatrick, 1994). This chapter also discusses how adult learning education research, particularly that which explores how professional knowledge and competence develops (Eraut, 1994), may help to inform and guide workplace ELT trainers in their program development. This will be illustrated in the outcomes of two different sets of workplace ELT research projects, one set of studies based in Hong Kong (Hamp-Lyons et al., 2002; Nunan & Forey, 1996) and one set of studies in Manila (Lockwood 2004; Lockwood & Forey, 2004).

Such interdisciplinary research into approaches to ELT course design and evaluation, and into language assessment design, can better equip teacher trainers in the workplace to carry out this very challenging area of specialized English for specific purposes (ESP), and can improve language teaching services to businesses and workplaces.

THE LANGUAGE NEEDS OF ADULTS AT WORK

Typically, during the life span of the adult professional, s/he spends in excess of double the time at work as s/he has spent in formal education. This situation raises a number of important questions for the recent promotion of life-long education in Asia. First, given the fact that adult professionals spend so much time at work, the question arises as to whether it is possible to analyze and articulate the stages of knowledge and competence acquired throughout their careers. If we are able to articulate these stages in professional knowledge and competence, then ESP language training curriculum processes and programs can be mapped onto such frameworks, thus increasing the transparency and relevance of ELT workplace training to the professional in the workplace. Although there is fragmented research in this area in Asia, there is, as yet, nothing large scale and systematic being carried out with the possible exception of the consultancy completed recently on the language benchmarking of primary and secondary school teachers in Hong Kong (see Coniam & Falvey, this volume).

Assuming a reasonable degree of success and fulfillment in our chosen areas of work, we know we get better at what we do and most professionals accept, even enjoy, the on-going challenges of 'moving up the ladder' in a successful career. Developing a model to analyze and exemplify these steps/stages/phases has however, been the subject of much work in adult education (Argyris & Schon, 1974; Calderhead, 1988; Dreyfus & Dreyfus, 1986; Eraut, 1994; Fuller, 1970). Eraut (1994) believes that an attempt to define and detail levels of professionalism in the workplace across industry types and professions worldwide is a fundamental step in being able to conceptualize curriculum models for life-long learning and training within the workplace:

> Behind the numerous policy issues which have enlivened the debate about the appropriate form and structure for professional education, lies a remarkable ignorance about professional learning. Apart from the limited though valuable literature on professional socialisation, we know very little about what is learned during the period of initial qualification besides the content of formal examinations. Still less is known about subsequent learning, how and why professionals learn to apply, disregard or modify their initial training immediately after qualification: and to what extent continuing education on-the-job or even off-the-job learning contributes to their professional maturation, updating, promotion or reorientation. Yet without such knowledge, attempts to plan or evaluate professional education are liable to be crude and misdirected. (p. 40)

Other researchers have made earlier attempts at this kind of conceptualization. For example, Dreyfus and Dreyfus (1986) identified five levels of skills acquisition in the workplace: novice, advanced beginner, competent, proficient and expert. Fuller (1970) has also developed a model that suggests three benchmark levels of professional development for teachers, specifically:

Level 1: Early phase (beginner)–where the concern is about self and how the teacher presents her/himself.
Level 2: Middle phase (competent)–where the teacher feels more in control of both the classroom and the content and becomes more concerned about the rapport that can be established with students.
Level 3: Late phase (professional)–where the teacher becomes more reflective about what can and should be taught to the students and how the program might change.

In two Hong Kong based research projects investigating the language needs of accountants (Hamp-Lyons et al., 2000; Nunan & Forey, 1996), researchers had to establish pathways of English language competencies for accountants from junior accountant through to partner in typical multinational and accounting firms. These pathways then informed the development of language assessment tasks and training materials at different levels of accounting work. It was found that accountants enter and advance through the professional hierarchy in a large multinational accounting firm from junior, to senior, to manager, and then to partner. At each level there are specific written tasks that they are responsible for, ranging from the creation of new documents, synthesizing information, and making judgements and interpretations to proofreading and editing. Interestingly, it was found that junior accountants, in their first three years of their careers in fact do very little writing in the Hong Kong workplace and typically collect and collate information before passing it on to their supervisors. However once promoted to the next stage, the senior level, accountants are suddenly required to write a variety of demanding and complex texts involving synthesizing information from a range of sources and making recommendations. Not surprisingly the Hong Kong Society of Accountants is very concerned about the quality of writing in English amongst its senior, manager, and partner membership. The training manager within that professional association also recently reported that she felt junior accountants in fact lose some of their English skills when they begin their careers in Hong Kong as accountants. Nunan & Forey (1996) suggest that:

> One conclusion that can be drawn from this research is the need for the development of tailor-made courses which match the requirements of the profession. The findings clearly demonstrate that even within, what appears to be a homogeneous professional group, there are quite diverse writer roles which need to be recognised and addressed.... From the findings of the survey and interviews it appears that senior accountants (managers and partners) are spending a large amount of their valuable time editing and rewriting documents produced by their subordinates. An improved writing training programme will help alleviate the time spent by seniors on editing and rewriting. (p. 52)

A human resources (HR) manager of a large multinational retail outlet in Hong Kong captured the complexity of designing well-targeted programs for adults when she said in an interview with the author (Lockwood, 2002):

> Senior professional members in our organisation will only come to English language training if they know it's going to be 'spot on'- otherwise they will drop out early on. To be 'spot on' means you need to know and find out what they write and why, and how the language training will help them reach the high standard of written communication at their specific level of professional expertise. It requires knowing them as professional adults; knowing us as an organisation and knowing the profession. Then the language trainer has to be able to analyse the kinds of texts they produce...In my experience this is poorly done by language teacher...it's hard to find a provider who can do this competently.

THE PROBLEMS OF CURRICULUM DESIGN IN WORKPLACE ELT

Although there is an abundance of research literature in adult English language teaching curriculum design going back many decades (e.g., Candlin, 1984; Hutchinson & Walters, 1987; Nunan, 1988; Markee, 1997; Wilkins, 1976), this is of limited use in workplace ELT program design because of the fundamental differences between the educational and workplace contexts. While some substantial research (Barbara et al., 1996; Bhatia, 1993; Boswood, 1992, 1997; Marriott, 1995; Nickerson, 1998; Nunan & Forey, 1996; Poon, 1992; Swales & Rogers, 1995) has been carried out over the last decade in identifying specific genres and discourse features of workplace and business texts world wide, very little research has been carried out in the field of course design and evaluation for such training. Although there is a great deal of applied linguistic literature that looks at the role of needs analysis in the design of language programs in educational institutions (Brindley, 1984; Munby, 1978; Nunan, 1988; Richterich, 1983; Willing, 1988), studies in the applied linguistic literature into the language needs of workplaces are scarce. Similarly in the applied linguistic literature dealing with language assessment and program evaluation (Douglas, 1998; Lynch, 1996), the workplace contexts appear under-researched.

The effective design and evaluation of workplace ELT programs depends on an insider knowledge of the business context driving the language training program, as well as an ability to gain access to the appropriate stakeholder group within the business community beyond the teacher and the learners. The problem that currently exists is that of access to the relevant stakeholders (e.g., line managers and other senior departmental managers, not just the participants themselves). Such access is needed to establish a clear view from a managerial perspective of the training needs and how they may be addressed. As businesses and workplaces increase their requirements for accountability for the expenditure of their training budgets, needs and outcomes for ELT workplace language programs must be more clearly specified, monitored, and evaluated. ELT workplace trainers who are typically outsourced for the particular language training project therefore have a great deal of information to gather from the workplaces contracting their services and a number of stakeholders need to be consulted. The business management and training literature is clear about this paradigm of need and accountability:

> The focus of training is moving away from the individual to the organisation. This manifests itself in various ways. We now speak of organisational learning. We tend to be interested in the organisational impact of training, not individual learning...training will have to change to be effective. There is a demand for justification of training expenditures and initiatives. Importantly it has also led to the need to demonstrate training activities' impact on strategic initiatives, core organisational capabilities, organisational effectiveness, and the bottom line. (Brown & Seidner, 1998, p. 10)

The problem for ELT workplace practitioners is to understand this paradigm and how it might inform and systematize language planning and evaluation processes for business and workplace training and ensure positive outcomes of the training.

One framework from the business management and training literature used for a Hong Kong study (Lockwood, 2002) of stakeholder involvement in ELT curriculum program design is the *levels of evaluation* framework (Bramley & Pahl, 1996; Easterby–Smith, 1994; Hamblin, 1974; Kirkpatrick, 1994). The framework provides a multi-level evaluation model that explores the outcomes of training from a variety of business and training stakeholder perspectives. Kirkpatrick (1994) presents a framework for training evaluation that consists of four levels:

Level 1: The reaction level.
At this level of training evaluation the participants are often asked to comment on various aspects of the training event itself such as the attitude of the trainer, the method of the presentation, the quality of the venue and handouts, and their general enjoyment of the training. This level of evaluation is most commonly done in the form of an evaluation form and often provides useful information to the trainer about how the session may be improved. Most evaluation is still done at this level of reaction. In a study carried out in the UK in 1989 by the UK Training Agency (Bramley & Pahl, 1996), only a small minority of organizations go beyond this level of evaluation.

Level 2: The learning level.
At this level of training evaluation the participants are tested on the content of the course as evidence that facts, skills, or, in the case of language learning, that language proficiency has improved.

Level 3: The performance level.
At this level of training evaluation the participants are assessed on how they apply or transfer what they have learned on the course to their jobs. Workplaces need to know if participants have used their newly acquired knowledge, skills, or attitudes in the context of their jobs. This third level of training evaluation is an attempt to measure the transfer of learning to workplace performance.

Level 4: The results level.
At this level of training evaluation the results of the training are related to general organizational improvement. Kirkpatrick (1994) suggests looking at areas such as staff turnover, absenteeism, and morale of employees. Evaluating this level of training can also incorporate a cost benefit analysis of the training, which is sometimes dealt in the literature as a fifth and separate level of evaluation.

The value of this model of training evaluation to the ELT curriculum designer is that it unfolds layers of stakeholder needs within the business training environment. To design and evaluate effectively at Level 3 for example requires an ELT trainer to understand the needs of line managers and department heads in terms of the job performance improvement required in the workplace.

An investigation of language program design and evaluation processes used in Hong Kong workplaces that commission highly specialized English language training (Lockwood, 2002) concluded that the involvement (or lack of involvement) of key business-based stakeholders in the ELT curriculum process significantly affected training outcomes. In this study, the business and management training framework described earlier was used as the basis for data collection about current design and evaluation practice from HR managers and ELT workplace language training specialists. The study found that both HR managers and ELT trainers thought that the most important levels to be incorporated into curriculum design and reported on in evaluation of workplace ELT training were the Level 3 (performance) and Level 4 (results) as described above. Their reasons for nominating these two higher levels as most important reflected the fact that workplace ELT training is most often driven by business needs, e.g., customer dissatisfaction with communication level and gaps in job performance.

As one of the HR managers in a large Hong Kong investment bank said when interviewed for the study (Lockwood, 2002):

> My aim is to have every English language course 'tailor-made' to the specific needs of the bank. They (the courses) should be competency based, and employees should enter at a reasonable level of English so that they can participate in and benefit from this highly targeted training. But language training can be tricky to deliver, and there's no more efficient way of wasting money than a misconceived training programme. Training in the bank must be measurably productive. A training programme can't just be nice for the employees. It's got to add to the bottom line, it's got to enhance the performance of the individual and therefore the bank.

This view of the workplace language program was further supported by the ELT workplace trainers, one of whom said:

> Although language programmes are run for different reasons, most are about improving performance in the workplace rather than importing a lot of language content in isolation.... Job performance improvements demonstrate a 'payback' to the workplace. What most organisations want to see is why they are paying for the course...that is improve performance at the workplace...this is why line managers should be more involved at the beginning and the end of the course.

However, it became evident later in the study that although both groups gathered plenty of evidence for evaluation at Levels 1 and 2 (normally in the form of end-of-course evaluation sheets and test score results), very little evidence for evaluation was gathered at Levels 3 and 4. In other words, language program success could be demonstrated from within the walls of the classroom, but not in terms of the wider workplace needs and expectations. Clearly this was a problem from the business point of view as accountability for training budgets is becoming increasingly stringent and training more focused on the business requirements. It was also a problem for ESP curriculum development as business and organizational needs are fundamental to the planning of an appropriate program. Ultimately, the quality of workplace ELT curriculum design will depend on being able to incorporate effectively the needs of workplace with the needs of the employee. Cooper (1992) was critical of workplace ELT course quality provision when she reported:

> The decision to commission ELT workplace training is often made on the strength of past practice or a course title and a brief description of the course. It is difficult for the employers to assess a course's suitability, except in broad terms, and to assess its content as to effective applicability in the workplace... present employers have no effective means of judging whether the English courses they sponsor are effective, nor indeed are they likely to have a clear picture of what employees will be able to do at the end of the course. (p. 226)

CASE STUDIES IN WORKPLACE ELT IN HONG KONG AND THE PHILIPPINES

There is no easy answer or formulaic response to how ESP workplace curriculum development should take place. It would appear however, that the more complex the subject matter (e.g., legal, accounting, medical, engineering) the more desirable it is to have subject matter experts heavily involved, or actually writing the materials. However, in all cases of ELT workplace curriculum development and training, there needs to be sustained and effective interface with a range of stakeholders in the workplace.

The Hong Kong government recently sponsored a materials development project entitled *Advanced Writing Skills for Tax Specialists and Advanced Writing Skills for Auditors* (Hamilton et al., 2002). This project was jointly managed by the Centre for Professional and Business English at the Hong Kong Polytechnic University and The Hong Kong Society of Accountants. The ELT writers selected for the project were not accounting experts and therefore needed considerable contact time with the HKSA and accounting professionals to ascertain the contextual writing needs of tax specialists and auditors. Just as importantly however, the writers needed to get authentic samples of written documents in accounting that they could analyze before beginning the materials writing phase. During this project, it became clear that contextual information, access to worksites and authentic documentation were critical to success. It also became evident that without professional accounting knowledge it is difficult to ascertain what matters and what does not in constructing meaningful texts. For example, when writing to the tax office, what constitutes an excuse for not filing a corporate tax return on time? What is the appropriate tone and style? How long should the letter be? Does only an experienced and senior accountant generate this kind of text?

On completion of this project, it was felt that professional subject matters experts with an ELT background would have been more able to 'short circuit' the process and produce materials that were more contextually sensitive in this professional arena. It was extremely difficult for the writing team to condense years of professional accounting knowledge into a comprehensive set of ESP materials.

Two different studies into ELT workplace design and evaluation (Lockwood 2004; Lockwood & Forey, 2004) were undertaken in the Philippines based in the business processing outsourcing (BPO) industry, specifically within the call centers in Manila. Most of these call centers service US based customers and there is an extremely high level of expectation that these calls will be handled by Filipino agents who have excellent levels of English and who sound American.

The first study examined the language needs of call center agents and how language performance can be effectively measured in the workplace after training. The study revealed that although on-the-job evaluations revealed impressive quality scores for communication, the evidence in the authentic data (the calls) showed a different story. This finding highlights important issues in the kind of job performance measures that are made, in the way they are administered and the ability of the people who carry them out. Call center scorecards are devised and administered by non-language experts and their judgments are inevitably flawed. Assessors are essentially being invited to make broad and subjective assessments of characteristics like 'energy,' 'confidence' and 'sincerity' whose linguistic correlates are either not defined at all, or else are defined in a way that is vague or difficult to understand. Many of the job performance scorecards dissected language into meaningless and fragmented parts e.g., *voice texture; professional grammar; pace of talking; allowed customer to vent; polite when put on hold; uses customer's name; avoids jargon and slang; exhibits balanced firmness; organizes conversation statements systematically and structurally; shows a lively and non-monotonous opening line to the customers; speaks with a smile*, and so on, in the hope that it will all add up to good communication. Clearly there is a role for the language specialist in the design and administration of the 'scorecard' as a measure of communication competence. Call center workplaces, like all workplaces are still oblivious of frameworks and expertise that could really help them in solving some of their communication problems.

The second study investigated the generic structure and linguistic features of a range of authentic calls. The study demonstrated the importance for workplace ELT specialists to be able to access authentic data upon which to base their training materials and assessment criteria. Preliminary analysis of transcriptions of authentic call center calls revealed a generic structure to these kinds of calls, with the 'moves' and the attendant linguistic features able to be described. Access to a range of calls across a range of industry types also revealed that some categories of calls were inherently more difficult than others. These findings are of importance not only to the design of ELT curriculum, but equally to language assessment evaluation, in particular the use of scorecards.

Language research into call center transactions is in its infancy and much of the early work done (Cameron, 2000) is now out of date. Graduates from some of the best universities in Manila are currently employed in this industry and view job prospects and the chances for promotion optimistically. The work is becoming more complex and is moving beyond the traditional customer care role to areas such as complex technical and computer support, financial, legal and insurance advice and emergency travel and hospitality care. Research into the attendant language needs as the agent moves up this new industry value chain has not yet started. Gone are the days when the choice was between Walmart and call center work for the high school graduate. In the new call center industry there need to be definitions of professional competence across an increasing complexity of work and accounts. This work will in turn inform applied linguistic research and ELT training program design and evaluation.

Current research based in Hong Kong and the Philippines into workplace ELT training highlights two separate but related questions. Firstly, how does the ESP specialist derive a better understanding of the nature of the organization or workplace requesting language training? This chapter has argued that the answer lies within the business management and training literature. The second key question relates to the working professionals themselves: How does the ESP specialist develop an understanding of the individual professional operating within his/her own professional community? This chapter has argued that the answer lies within some of the recent adult education literature that explores the developmental stages of professional knowledge and competence. New models and ways of thinking about workplace ELT training and curriculum development therefore need to engage much more with disciplinary knowledge outside applied linguistic theory and practice.

CONCLUSIONS

Using interdisciplinary constructs to analyze the problems and processes of curriculum design in ELT workplace training have resulted in a broader view of stakeholder needs and expectations for training as well as a better understanding of the business imperatives underpinning the desire for training. The collaborative negotiation of a curriculum for workplace ELT training depends on the effective involvement of business-based as well as training stakeholders. An understanding of the professional stage of the individual within this context is also important in ensuring the level and the focus of the language training is appropriate.

The implications of this research for the ESP workplace practitioner in the workplace are numerous and cannot be described in detail in this chapter. However, a reexamination of the knowledge and skills required of the ESP practitioner working in a business environment is clearly overdue. This need was captured in a statement made by an experienced ELT workplace trainer interviewed as part of Lockwood's (2002) study:

> One of the things that can hold workplace ELT trainers back is their dogmatism about what should and shouldn't be on the course based on their narrow view of what works in a school based classroom. The other trap in this highly specific kind of training is kidding yourself that a session on email writing for example can be taken off the shelf and simply delivered….this kind of training is going well beyond teaching generic skills from course books…it is the ability to ask questions of the workplace, listen carefully, think on your feet and be constantly creative about the training.

This raises the question of what then constitutes a better workplace ELT curriculum approach. From the limited research carried out in this area to date, it would seem that the ESP/ELT practitioner needs to draw on disciplines beyond applied linguistics and education to understand the business/organization context; the practitioner needs to understand the workplace stakeholders needs and expectations for language training; and finally the practitioner needs to understand where the individuals being trained fit into their own professional stage of development. The answers unfortunately do not lie in the applied linguistic and education disciplines alone. Mapping business management and training knowledge and adult education knowledge will provide a rich source of support for workplace ESP practitioners.

REFERENCES

Argyris, C., & Schon, D. (1974) *Theory in practice: Increasing professional effectiveness*. San Francisco: Jossey Bass.

Barbara, L., Celani, M. A. A., Collins, H. & Scott, M. (1996). A survey of communication patterns in the Brazilian business context. *English for Specific Purposes, 15*(1), 57–71.

Bhatia, V. (1993). *Analysing genre: Language use in professional settings*. London: Longman.

Boswood, T. (1992). *English for professional communication: Responding to Hong Kong employers' needs for English graduates*. Research Report No. 20. Hong Kong: City Polytechnic of Hong Kong.

Boswood, T. & Marriott, A. (1994). Ethnography for special purposes: Teaching and training in parallel. *English for Specific Purposes, 13*(1), 47–59.

Bramley, P & Pahl, J. (1996). *The evaluation of training in the social services*. London: National Institute for Social Work.

Brindley, G. (1984). *Needs analysis and objective setting in the adult migrant education program*. Sydney, NSW: Adult Migrant Education Services.

Brinkerhoff, R.O. (1998). Clarifying and Directing Impact Evaluation. In S. Brown & C. Schneider, *Evaluating corporate training: Models and* issues (pp. 141–166). Norwell, MA: Kluwer Academic Press.

Cameron, D. (2000). *Good to talk? Lliving and working in a communication culture.* London, Sage.
Calderhead, J. (1988). The development of knowledge structures in learning to teach. In J. Calderhead (Ed.), *Teachers' professional training* (pp. 51–64). London: Falmer Press.
Candlin, C. N. (1984). Applying a systems approach to curriculum innovation in the public sector. In J. Read (Ed.), *Trends in language syllabus design* (pp. 151–179). Singapore: SEAMO Regional Language Centre.
Cummings, O. (1998). What stakeholders want to know. In S. Brown & C. Seider (Eds.), *Evaluating corporate training: Models and* issues (pp. 102–123). Norwell, MA: Kluwer Academic Publishers.
Cooper, A. (1992). *Technical institute graduates: English in the workplace.* Hong Kong: Hong Kong Language Development Fund/Institute of Language Education.
Dreyfus, H.L. & Dreyfus, S.E. (1986). *Mind over machine.* New York: The Free Press.
Easterby-Smith, M. (1994). *Evaluating management development training and education.* Cambridge, UK: Gower Publishing.
Ellis, M. & Johnson, C. (1994). *Teaching business English.* Oxford: Oxford University Press.
Eraut, M. (1994). *Developing professional knowledge and competence.* New York: The Falmer Press.
Douglas, D. (1999). *Assessing language for specific purposes.* Cambridge: Cambridge University Press.
Dudley-Evans, N. & St. John, M. J. (1998). *Developments in English for special purposes: A multidisciplinary approach.* Cambridge: Cambridge University Press.
Forey, G. & Lockwood J. (2004). *Yes Maam: Call Centre Conversations.* International Systemic Functional Congress, Kyoto, Japan.
Fuller, F. (1970). *Personalised education for teachers: One application of the teacher concerns model.* Austin. Houston: University of Texas.
Hamblin, A. (1974). *Evaluation and control of training.* New York: McGraw-Hill.
Hamp-Lyons, L., Hamilton, J., Lockwood, J., & Lumley, T. (2000). *A context-led English language assessment system.* (Research Report). Hong Kong: Hong Kong Research Council.
Hamp-Lyons, L., Hamilton, J., Lockwood, J., & Lumley, T. (2001). A new approach to competency based language assessment in professional contexts – Hong Kong Institute of Company Secretaries (Research Report). Hong Kong: Hong Kong Research Council.
Hutchinson, T., & Walters, A. (1987). *English for specific purposes: A learning-centred approach.* Cambridge: Cambridge University Press.
Kirkpatrick, D. (1994). *Evaluating training programs: The four levels.* San Francisco: Berrett-Koehler Publishers.
Lockwood, J. (2002). *Language programme training design and evaluation processes in Hong Kong workplaces.* Unpublished PhD. dissertation, The University of Hong Kong.
Lynch, B.K. (1996). *Language program evaluation: Theory and practice.* Cambridge: Cambridge University Press.
Markee, N. (1997). *Managing curriculum innovation.* Cambridge: Cambridge University Press.
Mumby, J. (1978). *Communicative syllabus design.* Cambridge: Cambridge University Press.
Nickerson, C. (1999). The use of English in electronic mail in a multinational corporation. In F. Bargiela-Chiappini & C. Nickerson (Eds.), *Writing business: Genres, media, and discourses* (pp. 35–56). Singapore: Addison-Wesley.
Nickerson, C. & Van Nus, M. (1999). Teaching intercultural business communication research. In M. Hewings & C. Nickerson (Eds.), *Business English: Research into practice* (pp. 25–34). London; Longman.
Nunan, D. (1988a). *Syllabus design.* Oxford: Oxford University Press.
Nunan, D. (1988b). *The learner-centred curriculum.* Cambridge: Cambridge University Press.
Nunan, D. & Forey, G. (1996). *Communication in the professional workplace: A study of the writing needs of junior accountants in Hong Kong.* (Research Report No. E/012/96,), Hong Kong: Education and Manpower Bureau. Retrieved 13 June 2006 from http://cd1.emb.hkedcity.net/cd/scolar/html/projects/eng/e01296/report.pdf.
Poon, W. (1992). *An analysis of the language needs of accountants and company administrators in Hong Kong* (Research Report No. 21). Hong Kong: City Polytechnic of Hong Kong.
Richterich, R. (1983). *Case studies in identifying language needs.* Oxford: Pergamon.
St. John, M. J. (1996). Business is booming: Business English in the 1990s. *English for Specific Purposes, 15*(1), 3–18.
Swales, J. M. & Rogers, P. S. (1995). Discourse and the projection of corporate culture: The mission statement. *Discourse and Society 6*(2), 223–242.
Wilkins, D. A. (1976). *Notional syllabuses.* London: Oxford University Press.
Willing, K. (1988). *Learning styles in adult migrant education.* Sydney: National Centre for English Language Teaching and Research.

Section 3:

Assessment and Evaluation in ELT: Shifting Paradigms and Practices

SECTION 3

ASSESSMENT AND EVALUATION IN ELT:

Shifting Paradigms and Practices

CHRIS DAVISON AND JIM CUMMINS

INTRODUCTION

Assessment and evaluation have always been important areas of policy and practice in ELT, inextricably linked with many other aspects of TESOL, including language policy, language teaching methodology and curriculum design, teacher development, and second language acquisition, to name just a few. Assessment and evaluation are common concerns in different ELT sectors and levels, from mainstream schooling to specialist EAP courses, from kindergarten to adult, and in both traditional EFL and ESL contexts. However, for much of the history of ELT, assessment and evaluation have been seen as the responsibility of specialists, divorced from the business of teaching and learning. Assessment and evaluation judgments have usually been delivered long after the event, formulated in often mysterious and non-negotiable terms, with a heavy reliance on technical terminology and statistics. As a consequence, assessment and evaluation have always been taken for granted in ELT, but often misunderstood by practitioners, rarely included as a component in English language teacher training, and never really challenged by key stake-holders.

In the last ten to fifteen years, however, the ELT field has been experiencing a major paradigm shift in assessment and evaluation, with dramatic effects on teachers, learners and classrooms around the world. This paradigm shift has been driven partly by the dramatic rise in expectations (and forms) of accountability required by government bodies and funding agencies as a result of economic restructuring and globalization. It has also been influenced by a major questioning of traditional forms of testing and the underlying psychometric principles of measurement in the ELT field. Paradigm shifts in other areas of ELT have also contributed to the reconceptualization of English language assessment and evaluation policy and practice, in particular shifts in our constructs of language (and the challenge to standardization of new genres, multimodalities, world Englishes and English as a lingua franca) and our constructs of language learning (and the increasing influence of sociocultural theory and critical perspectives in ELT).

In many ways ELT has lagged behind the rest of the educational field in exploring new theories and methods of assessment and evaluation, partly because of the lack of integration with mainstream educational theory and practice in many areas of ELT, and partly because of the entrenched and powerful positions of traditional English language tests and testing agencies, as Shohamy highlights later in this section. However, now it is often the examination boards and testing agencies who are the leaders in researching and funding major reforms of the traditional evaluation and assessment systems used in ELT, leading to a resurgence of interest in the connection between teaching, learning and assessment and a much stronger focus on validity, authenticity, and test impact. The theoretical shifts described above and the international trend away from input-oriented norm-referenced to outcomes-based standards-referenced assessment has led to a strong interest in the role of the learner and teacher in assessment, and the problems and contradictions involved in trying to reconcile an increasing focus on common standards with individual variation and local communities of practice. In Asia and Africa, for example, educational systems are grappling with the introduction of substantial school–based assessment components into traditional testing cultures, while in the USA the introduction of the *No Child Left Behind* (NCLB) legislation has undermined the capacity of many ELT programs to develop assessment systems tailored for the needs of their English language learners (and teachers). In many parts of Europe tensions between standardized testing and teacher-based assessment are escalating, with Wales, for example, deciding to abandon formal standardized testing in favour of teacher-based assessment for all pedagogic, reporting, and public accountability purposes from 2008 onwards.

The term *standards* has several meanings in the English language teaching field, and is applied not only to learners, but to curricula, programs, teachers, and teacher certification and training and even the English language itself (e.g., content standards, program outcomes, language teacher competencies, teacher benchmarks, professional standards, language standards, etc). The term is used to denote both expected types and levels of achievement (a prescriptive sense) and the shared understanding of a particular type and level of achievement (a descriptive sense). In the first, usually top-down sense, the term is often used by administrators and policy-makers to convey a sense of the performance that should be reached by students, teachers and/or programs–both as a form of guidance for what is assumed is systematic and comparable progress towards successful achievement, and as a form of accountability to exhort schools and institutions to ensure that these levels of performance are reached. In the second sense, standard has less of a top-down connotation, being used more as a descriptive and formative statement of the achievement that has been attained. In both cases, standards are usually presented as stages of progress, attempting to provide diverse stake-holders (i.e., funding agencies, administrators, teachers, learners, parents, and the public) with a set of common descriptors or pathways that are assumed to applicable in all contexts. Both top-down and descriptive purposes have often been conflated in standards documents.

The standards-setting movement is part of a worldwide shift to a managerial culture in government and quasi-government agencies, and an exemplification of the application of economic rationalism and micro-economic reform to education. With rapid globalization has come the introduction of competition into the marketplace, and the use of outcomes-based measuring tools to establish and compare gains in achievement. Clear information about effectiveness through the measuring tools is designed to give clients or users the opportunity to make an informed choice about where to go to buy what they need. In education, competition ensures (theoretically) that students and parents have the opportunity to access the best services. Outcomes-based measuring tools help government bodies and funding agencies to set the achievement standards and to know who is achieving or not achieving according to these standards. They also allow funding to be tied to indicators of achievement. However, an over-reliance on inaccurate or over-simplified standards can lead to less, not more accurate reporting, and establish, even disguise, one view of language teaching and/or learning as the only reality. Not surprisingly, then, the widespread adoption of standards as a key concept in ELT over the last decade or so has been accompanied by much controversy and conflict.

The first two chapters of this section look at the standards movement in ELT in some detail, both from the assessment and evaluation perspectives. Both chapters emphasize the underlying ideology and problems of applying managerial concepts to English language teaching, but also highlight some of the important benefits for the field that have resulted from the standards-based movement. Nunan's chapter begins by tracing the history of the development and implementation of standards for the design and evaluation of English language teaching. He shows how the standards movement has had a significant impact on ELT developments in Europe, North America and Australia and is now increasingly being adopted in non-English speaking countries. He describes the proliferation of standards documents being disseminated by the international TESOL association, including content and assessment standards for kindergarten to end of secondary school, intensive English programs, adult education programs, community college employment, workplace language training, English language teacher education standards, teacher education standards for community college non-credit and credit programs, and adult education, and university programs. He then traces the close relationship between the evolution of standards, and the objectives movement and competency-based education, and explores the ideological aspects of standards-based assessment and evaluation.

In the following chapter, McKay highlights a number of issues in the application of the concept of standards to school-aged English language learners and programs. She looks at both English as a foreign language (EFL) standards written for contexts in which English is a subject in the school curriculum, studied by the majority of students, and ESL standards designed for students studying in an English-speaking environment, generally with English as the medium of instruction. The central thesis in her chapter is that despite variations amongst ELT standards, inevitable because of different policies, purposes, and contexts, there is a common core of issues and understandings that can and should result in greater integration of the field. An overview of recent research and suggestions for further collaboration are presented around three focal areas: standards development, critique and validation.

The following two chapters in this section look at the uncertainty and concerns that accompany innovation and reform in high-stakes language testing and assessment, in this case the introduction of a standards-based assessment of the English language proficiency and accreditation of English language teachers, and the reform of one of the leading English language tests used for university entrance around the world.

Coniam and Falvey's chapter takes as a case study the assessment of the English language competencies of teachers of English in Hong Kong, and, in particular, the innovative performance test of teacher classroom language assessment (CLA). Their case study highlights examples of major issues in the field such as the validity and reliability of the assessments, and the advantages and disadvantages of performance and criterion-referenced testing. It highlights the problems inherent in standards-based assessment and reporting, the need for close consultation between policy-makers, administrators, and practitioners, and the training and standardization of assessors. In the following chapter, Cumming reviews recent trends in the conceptualizations and formats of tests used to determine whether non-native speakers of English have sufficient proficiency in English to study at English-medium universities in English-speaking countries. The review focuses on recent research underpinning the development of a new version of the Test of English as a Foreign Language (TOEFL), but Cumming argues that many of the same concerns and issues have arisen in a range of other international tests. Test developers are now grappling with a whole range of questions relating to construct validation, particularly the description of testing purposes, evaluations of the discourse produced in the contexts of testing, and surveys of relevant stake holders. They are also actively investigating consistency, including fairness in opportunities for test performance across differing populations, reliability through field-testing and equating of test forms, and through the sampling of multiple forms of administration, including various forms of computer and other technological adaptations to see if they elicit comparable performances from examinees.

In fact, the term *assessment* embraces a wider set of parameters than the term *testing*, as Coniam and Falvey emphasize in their chapter. They argue that the latter term conjures up a formal, testing-room setting in which paper-and-pencil tests, usually of the multiple-choice variety, are attempted by the test takers, so the outcomes of such tests can be deemed reliable. Such tests were the dominant form of language assessment for many years, even though they usually contained no form of direct testing of communication through speaking (e.g., an interview) or writing (e.g., an extended piece of prose). In contrast, the current paradigm in educational assessment foregrounds the importance of validity and reconceptualizes reliability as just one component of validity. Current research interest in both old and new assessment contexts increasingly values various forms of classroom-based assessment integrated into the teaching and learning process, with teachers involved at all stages of the assessment cycle, from planning the assessment programme, to identifying and/or developing appropriate assessment tasks right through to making the final judgments. When assessments are conducted by the students' own teacher in their own classroom, students can also play an active role in the assessment process, particularly when self and/or peer assessment is used in conjunction with teacher-based assessment. However, although teacher-based assessment is established practice in a number of educational systems internationally, including Australia, New Zealand, and the United Kingdom, as well as in some developing countries, there has been comparatively little specific research into the teacher-based assessment of English as a second or additional language, partly because of the uncertain status of TESOL as a discrete curriculum area in schools and tertiary institutions, and partly because of the traditional dominance of the field by large-scale English language tests, and their research priorities and needs.

The research that has been done in teacher-based assessment in TESOL reveals much variability, a lack of systematic principles and procedures and a dearth of information as to the impact of teacher-based assessments on learning and teaching. Several studies of the use of large-scale criterion-referenced English as second language assessment frameworks in Australia and the United Kingdom have revealed a great diversity in teachers' approaches to assessment, influenced by the teachers' prior experiences and professional development, by the assessment frameworks and scales they used, and by the reporting requirements placed on them by schools and systems. Concerns have also been raised about, on the one hand, the ad-hoc or impressionistic nature of many teacher judgments and on the other hand, mechanistic criterion-based approaches to teacher-based assessment, which are often implemented in such a way that they undermine, rather than support teachers' classroom-embedded assessment processes.

Research into teacher-based assessment in ELT is further complicated by the considerable uncertainty and disagreement around the concept of teacher-based assessment itself, and by its intrinsically co-constructed, and context-dependent nature. In some ways teacher-based assessment is the opposite to traditional testing in which context is regarded as an extraneous variable that must be controlled and neutralized and the assessor as someone who must remain objective and uninvolved throughout the whole assessment process. Teacher-based assessment, in contrast, derives its validity from its location in the actual classroom where assessment activities are embedded in the regular curriculum, and assessed by a teacher who is familiar with the student's work. In fact, it could be argued that traditional conceptions of validity and reliability associated with the still dominant psychometric tradition of testing are themselves a potential threat to the development of the necessarily highly contextualized and dialogic practices of teacher-based assessment. For example, in a traditional exam-dominated culture, formative and summative assessment are seen as distinctly different in both form and function, and teacher and assessor roles clearly demarcated, but in teacher-based assessment, even summative assessments of the students' language skills can and should also be used formatively to give constructive feedback to students and improve learning. More interventionist and dynamic approaches to assessment can also be utilized to increase the validity of the assessment, without undermining consistency. However, there is much debate in the field, with some researchers arguing that the evaluation criteria traditionally associated with psychometric testing such as reliability and validity need to be reinterpreted, or even jettisoned, in teacher-based assessment, but others insisting that traditional test criteria do apply to alternative assessment. When the principles and procedures underlying teacher-based assessment are not clear, the basis for research and development is even muddier, hence the need for more discussion of the issues.

The next two papers in this section of the handbook look closely at the shift towards more classroom-based teacher-directed assessment. Hamp-Lyons examines the impact of testing on teaching, and the way in which two somewhat contradictory cultures are created from different approaches to assessment: a *learning culture* and an *exam culture*, derived from differing ideologies and underlying assumptions. Hamp-Lyons argues that because the exam culture is the dominant ideology in the discourse of educational economics and politics, conscious attention should be paid to teachers' voices, particularly through professional development activities during the process of establishing value systems for educational assessment. She concludes that planned innovation in assessment is unlikely to be successful without vastly improved attention to teacher assessment preparation. Rea-Dickins extends this discussion by exploring the possibilities and pitfalls of classroom-based English language assessment, drawing on both the language testing and classroom assessment literature in English language education as well as educational assessment more generally. The chapter begins with a brief sketch of the different contexts for language testing and assessment: external, classroom-based, and second language acquisition research. Different facets of classroom-based assessment are then highlighted, including the different meanings of and purposes for assessment, the relationship between formative and summative assessment, different approaches and frameworks used in teacher assessment, teacher perceptions and implementation of assessment, and the appropriacy of conventional measurement paradigms. Some current concerns and issues, as well as some of the potential pitfalls of classroom-based assessment, are explored. The final part of the chapter outlines future directions for the field and summarizes some of the challenges for both research and professional practice in relation to classroom-oriented assessment.

Shohamy returns to the broader context of evaluation and assessment in ELT, arguing that English language teachers play a major role in extending the dominion of the English language and the power of the English tests, but not necessarily to the advantage of learners. Alternative assessments, driven by teachers and based on pedagogical considerations, are encouraged as it is argued that such strategies can result in more democratic, ethical and humane approaches to English language testing and teaching, as well as more sensitivity to contextual variation in English language and second language learning. In the final chapter in this section Davison picks up the implications for assessment of changes in our conceptualization of English language learning, arguing that different models of language and language learning result in very different perceptions of language learning goals and hence, different judgements of success and failure.

Taken together, the chapters in this section of the handbook highlight three broad themes and directions in research in assessment and evaluation. Firstly, more research is needed into key theoretical constructs in English language assessment and evaluation, in particular core concepts such as standards, ethics, trustworthiness, and fairness, the relationship between testing, assessment, and evaluation, and the interaction between validity and reliability. Secondly, more detailed classroom-based studies of teacher-based alternative assessment practices and their effects on student learning are needed, including longitudinal studies of the relationship between formative assessment, feedback and learning, and evaluations of innovative assessment practices, including portfolio assessment, peer conferencing, self-assessment, and interactive or dynamic assessment. Finally, there is an urgent need for more research into professional development and system-level change, including the impact on teachers and learners of the adoption, implementation or evaluation of new assessment and evaluation systems, and comparative perspectives on assessment and evaluation policies and programs, including the effects of the importation of approaches from other contexts.

CHAPTER 28

STANDARDS-BASED APPROACHES TO THE EVALUATION OF ESL INSTRUCTION

DAVID NUNAN

The University of Hong Kong, China

ABSTRACT

A major thrust within the language teaching profession at the present time is the development and deployment of standards for instructional design. The standards movement has had a significant impact on curriculum development in Europe, North America and Australia. Within the International TESOL Association, standards have recently been developed for the following: Pre-K-12 content and assessment standards; standards for Intensive English Programs; adult education program standards; community college employment standards; standards for workplace language training; P-12 teacher education standards; teacher education standards for community college non-credit and credit programs; and adult education, and university programs. In this chapter, I will trace the evolution of the standards movement and relate it to the other two major performance-based movements: the objectives movement and competency-based education. I will then describe and exemplify three different types of standards: content, program, and teacher standards, before concluding the chapter by looking at ideological aspects of standards-based instruction.

INTRODUCTION

In this chapter, I will look at standards-based approaches to instructional design and at how these have been deployed in the evaluation of ESL instruction over the last 20 years. These approaches, which were developed within a behavioral (but not behaviorist) paradigm, include the objectives movement, competency based education, and the standards movement.

Standards-based instruction supports many of the most significant developments in education. In Europe, North America, and Australia it underpinned competency-based immigrant and workplace education. In Europe, it is the basis for the *Common European Framework of Reference for Languages: Learning, Teaching, Assessment* (Council of Europe, 2001). In North America, it has had a tremendous impact in all areas of both school and adult education as the ideological underpinning of the standards movement.

A number of professional associations in different parts of the world have drawn heavily on the behavioral paradigm for their work. Of particular note is the Council of Europe and the work that it has done in developing frameworks and defining performance levels for different languages within the European Union. The paradigm also underpins the work being commissioned by the TESOL Association within which standards are currently being written for developing and evaluating instruction in the following areas: Pre-K-12 content and assessment standards; standards for Intensive English Programs; adult education program standards;

community college employment standards; standards for workplace language training; P-12 teacher education standards; and teacher standards for adult education. In addition, TESOL has recently established a new standing committee on standards.

In the chapter, after looking at the genesis and evolution of the standards movement, I will illustrate the movement with reference to some of the aforementioned developments. Of particular interest is the way that a behavioral approach is being extended beyond content and assessment. At present, for example, standards are being developed for the development and evaluation of program specifications, setting criteria for professional employment, and describing and evaluating effective teacher behavior. In the final section of the chapter, I will look at some of the ideological and political issues associated with the paradigm.

THE OBJECTIVES MOVEMENT

It was the objectives movement that ushered in a behavioral approach to education. This movement has been very influential and highly contentious both in general education and also in language education. Most of the controversy has to do with the use of behavioral (or as they soon came to be called), *performance objectives*:

> During the early sixties we talked about behavior rather than about performance. This turned out to be an unfortunate choice of terms. A number of people were put off by the word, thinking that objectives necessarily had to do with behaviorism or with behaviorists. Not so. Objectives describe performance, or behavior, because an objective is specific rather than broad or general and because performance, or behavior, is what we can be specific about. (Mager, 1984, p. 23)

Objectives have been characterized in a number of different ways. Valette and Disick (1972) suggest they should stress output rather than input and that such output should be specified in terms of performance. It has been suggested that articulating precise statements of what the learner is to be able to do at the end of a course is an essential step in the curriculum design process, because it greatly facilitates a number of other steps.

In the field of general education, the work of Mager (1962, 1984) and Dick and Carey (1978) in North America, and Rowntree (1981) in the United Kingdom, was particularly influential. Mager, and Dick and Carey sit squarely within the systems approach to education first championed by Tyler (1949), and the cornerstone of their approach was the articulation of goals that were then elaborated as objectives. The key characteristic of a behavioral objective is that it describes what the learner rather than the teacher is to do. It may seem obvious that the instructional process should focus on the learner, but even today, it is possible to find programs with objectives for the teacher of the program such as, "To review the simple past" or "To teach prepositions of place." It is possible for objectives such as these to be achieved without any learning taking place.

Another characteristic of a behavioral objective is that it must specify observable learner behavior. "To appreciate Shakespeare's historical plays" is not a performance objective because the behavior is invisible. One cannot see *appreciation* or *understanding*. Mager (1984) lists the following words as being "dangerous" because they do not describe observable behavior and are open to many interpretations: *to know, to understand, to really understand, to appreciate, to fully appreciate, to grasp the significance of, to enjoy, to believe, to have faith in, to internalize* (p. 20).

Formal performance objectives are meant to include three elements: (a) a *performance* or *task* statement, (b) a *conditions* statement, and (c) a *standards* or *criterion* statement. The task element specifies what learners are to do, the conditions statement specifies the circumstances and conditions under which learners are to perform the task, and the standards statement specifies how well the task is to be performed.

The following statements illustrate three-part objectives:

- In a classroom role-play (condition), learners will exchange personal information (task). Four pieces of information will be exchanged (standard), and utterances will be comprehensible to someone unused to dealing with a second language speaker (standard).
- In an authentic interaction (condition), the student will request prices of shopping items (task). Utterances will be comprehensible to a sympathetic native speaker (standard).

In objectives-driven curricula, conditions and standards have an important bearing on difficulty, and a given task can be made more or less difficult by varying the conditions under which the learners will perform and the standards they are expected to reach. These include both (a) the degree to which the language event is embedded in a context that facilitates comprehension, and (b) the degree to which the language event makes cognitive demands on the learner.

Although they provided a more transparent basis for assessing student performance and evaluating program effectiveness, objectives-driven curricula were heavily criticized in the 1970s. Criticisms included the idea that trivial learning behaviors are the easiest to operationalize, hence the really important outcomes of education will be under-emphasized. In addition, many people feel that pre-specification of precise objectives prevents the teacher from taking advantage of instructional opportunities occurring unexpectedly in the classroom. It has also been noted that outcomes other than behavior change are important in education. In terms of language teaching, an additional criticism relates to the creative nature of language proficiency. Proficient language users know multiple ways of achieving communicative ends through language, and therefore identifying objectives *a priori*, or the standards that indicate how well the objective has been met, may be problematic. Another problem is that, taken to its logical conclusion, the approach spawns hundreds of detailed, micro-level performance statements. Finally, despite the emphasis on objectives in teacher education programs in the 1970s, they failed to take root in teachers' practices:

> Most teachers are trained to plan instruction by specifying behavioral objectives... While this prescriptive model of planning may be one of the most consistently taught features of teacher education programs, the model is consistently not used in teachers' planning in schools. Obviously, there is a mismatch between the demands of the classroom and the prescriptive planning model. (Shavelson & Stern, 1981, p. 477)

Despite these criticisms, objectives, used appropriately, did bring tangible benefits to the learning process. In work cited in my 1988 book on curriculum, the use of objectives, when conveyed to learners in ways that made sense to them, played an important part in sensitizing learners to what it is to be a language learner: (a) In particular, learners came to have a more realistic idea of what could be achieved in a given course; (b) learning came to be seen as the gradual accretion of achievable goals; (c) learners developed greater sensitivity to their roles as language learners, and their vague notions of what it is to be a learner became much sharper; (d) self-evaluation became more feasible; (e) classroom activities could be seen to relate to real-life needs; and (f) development of skills was seen as a gradual rather than all-or-nothing process.

THE COMPETENCY-BASED LANGUAGE TEACHING MOVEMENT

During the 1980s, competency-based instruction developed as an alternative to the use of objectives in program planning. As with the objectives movement, *Competency Based Language Teaching* (CBLT) focuses on what learners should be able to do at the conclusion of a course (as opposed, for example, to the specification of content). Competencies are also generally couched at a higher level of generality than performance objectives. There are therefore fewer of them, and they enable the development of more coherent programs. As with performance objectives, they provide a tangible basis for curriculum evaluation and improvement:

> Competency based training is concerned with the attainment and demonstration of specified skills, knowledge, and application to minimum specified standards rather than with an individual's achievement relative to that of others in a group. It is 'criterion-referenced' rather than 'norm-referenced'. (NSW Adult Migrant Education Service, 1993)

According to Leung and Teasdale (1998), performance-based approaches to competence can be placed into one of three categories (see also Reynolds & Salter, 1995). The first of these;

> ...regards competence as a list or combination of discrete parts. Tasks are analysed into components and each component part is stated as desired behaviour. A competent teacher is one who can perform the behaviours involved in the pre-specified tasks. The second model focuses on the ability to transfer previous learning to new situations...The third model looks at competence as the application of a combination of knowledge, understanding, experience and executive ability to task performance in specific contexts. (Leung & Teasdale, 1998, p. 17)

Standards are an important dimension to CBLT, and share the same characteristics of the concept as defined by the objectives movement. Competency-based programs have had a major impact on curriculum development and evaluation in workplace training, particularly in Australia, the United Kingdom, and New Zealand (Brindley, 1994), as well as in the United States:

> CBLT first emerged in the US in the 1970s and was widely adopted in vocationally-oriented education and in adult ESL programs. By the end of the 1980s CBLT had come to be accepted as 'the state-of-the-art' approach to adult ESL by national policymakers and leaders in curriculum development (Auerbach, 1984, cited in Richards, 2001, p. 46).

The following is an example of a competency statement:

> The learner can negotiate complex/problematic spoken exchanges for personal business and community purposes. He or she: achieves purpose of exchange and provides all essential information accurately uses appropriate staging, e.g. opening and closing strategies provides and requests information as required explains circumstances, causes, consequences, and proposes solutions as required sustains dialogue e.g. using feedback, turn taking uses grammatical forms and vocabulary appropriate to topic and register and grammatical errors do not interfere with meaning pronunciation/stress/intonation do not impede intelligibility interprets gestures and other paralinguistic features. (NSW Adult Migrant Education Service, 1993, p. 76)

From this example, it is apparent that competencies bear a strong family resemblance to performance objectives and reside squarely within the behavioral tradition. It can also be seen that competencies contain a task and a number of "how well" statements—"achieves purpose of exchange," "provides all essential information accurately," "uses appropriate staging," "errors do not interfere with meaning," "pronunciation is intelligible." However, as already noted, one difference is the level of generality in which each is couched, objectives being more specific than competencies.

In terms of evaluation, it is also interesting to compare the supposed benefits of CBLT with those listed earlier for performance objectives:

1. Teachers' and learners' attention becomes more focused on language as a tool for communication rather than on language knowledge as an end in itself.
2. Assessment is integrated into the learning process through the use of attainment targets that are directly linked to course content and objectives.
3. Learners are able to obtain useful diagnostic feedback on their progress and achievement since explicit criteria are provided against which they can compare their performances. (Bottomly, Dalton, & Corbel, 1994)

In Europe, the most ambitious attempt at applying a performance approach to the design and development of language programs has come from the Council of Europe. In fact, the very first documents emerging from their work make explicit the ideology underlying their work,

> (It) tries to specify foreign language ability as a *skill* rather than *knowledge*. It analyzes what the learner will have to be able to *do* in the foreign language and determines only in the second place what *language-forms* (words, structures, etc.) the learners will have to be able to handle in order to *do* all that has been specified. In accordance with the nature of verbal communication as a form of behaviour the objectives defined by means of [our] model are therefore *behavioural* objectives. (van Ek, 1977, p. 5)

van Ek hastens to reassure the reader that a behavioral syllabus does not entail a behaviorist methodology. He then suggests that verbal behavior can be atomized into two components: the performance of language functions and the expression of conceptual notions. Thus, we see one of the earliest manifestations of a functional-notional syllabus (Wilkins, 1976). We also see that functional-notionalism resides within the performance paradigm. (See Munby's (1978) exhaustive blueprint for the production of needs-based, communicative syllabus based on performance criteria.)

Twenty-five years after van Ek's initial set of specifications, the same paradigm is evident in the most recent work of the Council of Europe, although now the focus shifts from behavioral objectives to language competencies. Thus, in the introduction to the *Common European Framework* (CEF) the authors (Council of Europe, 2001) suggest that,

> (The framework) provides a common basis for the elaboration of language syllabuses, curriculum guidelines, examinations, textbooks etc. across Europe. It describes in a comprehensive way what language learners have to learn to do in order to use a language for communication and what knowledge and skills they have to develop so as to be able to act effectively. The description also covers the cultural context in which the language is set. The Framework also defines levels of proficiency which allow learners' progress to be measured at each stage of learning and on a life-long basis. (p. 1)

The CEF defines three broad levels of language use (Basic User, Independent User, and Proficient User) each of which is broken down into two further levels giving six levels in all. Table 1 provides global, behavioral descriptors for learners at each of these six levels.

These global descriptors are greatly elaborated, both in terms of the four macro-skills and also in terms of subskills. For example, in terms of spoken interaction, separate scales are provided for the following:

- Overall spoken interaction
- Understanding a native speaker interlocutor
- Conversation
- Informal discussion with friends
- Formal discussion and meetings
- Goal-oriented co-operation (e.g., repairing a car, discussing a document, organizing an event)
- Transactions to obtain goods and services
- Information exchange
- Interviewing and being interviewed.

It is worth noting that the more general level in which competency statements are couched has led to a situation that would be frowned upon by proponents of performance objectives such as Mager, and Dick and Carey. The competencies use vague and imprecise language that, in some instances, describes unobservable behavior. For example, to what extent would it be possible for an independent observer to discriminate between someone who "can express him/herself spontaneously, very fluently and precisely" (a C2 user) from someone who "can express him/herself fluently and spontaneously" (a C1 user)? This lack of precision has obvious implications when it comes to their use for assessing students and evaluating programs.

Table 1. General Levels of Language Use

Proficient user (C2)	Can understand with ease virtually everything heard or read. Can summarize information from different spoken or written sources, reconstructing arguments and accounts in a coherent presentation. Can express him/herself spontaneously, very fluently and precisely, differentiating finer shades of meaning even in more complex situations.
Proficient user (C1)	Can understand a wide range of demanding, longer texts, and recognize implicit meaning. Can express him/herself fluently and spontaneously without much *obvious* searching for expressions. Can use language flexibly and effectively for social, academic, and professional purposes. Can produce clear, well-structured, detailed text on complex subjects, showing controlled use of organizational patterns, connectors, and cohesive devices.
Independent user (B2)	Can understand the main ideas of complex text on both concrete and abstract topics, including technical discussions in his/her field of specialization. Can interact with the degree of fluency and spontaneity that makes regular interaction with native speakers quite possible with strain for either party. Can produce clear, detailed text on a wide range of subjects and explain a viewpoint on a topical issue giving the advantages and disadvantages of various options.
Independent user (B1)	Can understand the main points of clear standard input on familiar matters regularly encountered in work, school, leisure etc. Can deal with most situations likely to arise whilst traveling in an area where the language is spoken. Can produce simple connected text on topics that are familiar or of personal interest. Can describe experiences and events, dreams, hopes and ambitions and briefly give reasons and explanations for opinions and plans.
Basic user (A2)	Can understand sentences and frequently used expressions related to areas of most immediate relevance (e.g. very basic personal and family information, shopping, local geography, employment). Can communicate in simple and routine tasks. Can describe in simple terms aspects of his/her background, immediate environment, and matters in areas of immediate need.
Basic user (A1)	Can understand and use familiar everyday expressions and very basic phrases aimed at the satisfaction of needs of a concrete type. Can introduce him/herself and others and can ask and answer questions about personal details such as where he/she lives, people he/she knows and things he/she has. Can interact in a simple way provided the other person talks slowly and clearly and is prepared to help.

Note. From *Common European Framework of Reference for Languages: Learning, Teaching, Assessment* (p. 24), by Council of Europe, 2001, Cambridge: Cambridge University Press. Reprinted with permission.

BEYOND CBI: THE STANDARDS MOVEMENT

One influential current trend in performance-based curriculum development is the standards movement. While this is receiving most of its momentum in the United States, where it is approximately 10 years old, it is also popular elsewhere. It is the latest iteration of the behavioral approach to instructional design, and thus has close links with both the objectives movement and the competency movement. The confusing thing about this movement, is that it has appropriated the term 'standard' and used it in a broader sense than the objectives movement and CBI.

The strong family resemblance can be seen in the work that has been done in other subject areas such as Math and Language Arts. For example, the National Council for Teachers of English standards document for English language arts states: "By content standards, we mean statements that define what students should know and be able to do" (n.d. pp. 1–2). Again, the principal difference is the level of generality at which the performance statements are couched.

Here are two examples of Language Arts Standards:

- *Students read a wide range of literature from many periods in many genres to build an understanding of the many dimensions of human experience.*
- *Students adjust their use of spoken, written, and visual language to communicate effectively with a variety of audiences and for different purposes.*

In terms of the characterization given in the discussion of performance objectives, the first of these examples is a task while the second is a standard. By collapsing the different parts of performance objectives, NCTE (n.d.) has ended up with a confused and confusing list. These statements are from a set of content standards. I would argue that for all intents and purposes, these are indistinguishable from competencies, as will be apparent from the discussion that follows.

Content Standards

One of the most comprehensive and detailed sets of content standards yet developed within the field of language education are the Pre-K–12 standards commissioned by TESOL and developed by a team of specialists working within the United States (TESOL, 1997).

The ESL Pre-K-12 ESL standards are framed around three goals and nine standards. The standards are fleshed out in terms of descriptors, progress indicators, and classroom vignettes. *Standards* are defined as follows: "The nine content standards indicate more specifically (than the goals) what students should know and be able to do as a result of instruction" (TESOL, 1997, p. 15). It can be seen from this definition, that standards now encompass what students should be able to do in addition to how well they should perform. *Descriptors* are "broad categories of discrete, representative behaviors" (p. 15). *Progress indicators* "list assessable, observable activities that students may perform to show progress toward meeting the designated standard. These progress indicators represent a variety of instructional techniques that may be used by teachers to determine how well students are doing" (p. 16).

These standards, which are broken down into three broad areas by grade level (Pre-K-3; grades 4–8, and grades 9–12), are organized around three broad goals, each of which has three standards, as follows:

Goal 1: To use English to communicate in social settings
Standards for Goal 1
Students will:
use English to participate in social interaction
interact in, through and with spoken and written English for personal expression and enjoyment
use learning strategies to extend their communicative competence

Goal 2: To use English to achieve academically in all content areas
Standards for Goal 2
Students will:
use English to interact in the classroom
use English to obtain, process, construct and provide subject information in spoken and written form
use appropriate learning strategies to construct and apply academic knowledge

Goal 3: To use English in socially and culturally appropriate ways
Standards for Goal 3
Students will:
use the appropriate language variety, register, and genre according to audience, purpose, and setting
use nonverbal communication appropriate to audience, purpose, and setting
use appropriate learning strategies to extend their sociolinguistic and sociocultural competence. (TESOL, 1997, p. 9–10)

Here are the descriptors relating to standard 1 to exemplify how the standards are elaborated.

Descriptors

- Sharing and requesting information
- Expressing needs, feelings, and ideas
- Using nonverbal communication in social interactions
- Getting personal needs met
- Engaging in conversations
- Conducting transactions

Sample Progress Indicators set out observable behaviors that can be used to determine whether students have met designated standards. For example, in relation to standards 1, students in grades 9–12 will:

- Obtain, complete, and process application forms, such as driver's license, social security, college entrance
- Express feelings through drama, poetry, or song
- Make an appointment
- Defend and argue a position
- Use prepared notes in an interview or meeting
- Ask peers for their opinions, preferences, and desires
- Correspond with pen pals, English-speaking acquaintances, friends
- Write personal essays
- Make plans for social engagements
- Shop in a supermarket
- Engage listener's attention verbally or non-verbally
- Volunteer information and respond to questions about self and family
- Elicit information and ask clarification questions
- Clarify and restate information as needed
- Describe feelings and emotions after watching a movie
- Indicate interests, opinions, or preferences related to class projects
- Give and ask for permission
- Offer and respond to greetings, compliments, invitations, introductions, and farewells
- Negotiate solutions to problems, interpersonal misunderstandings, and disputes
- Read and write invitations and thank you letters
- Use the telephone

One of the most useful aspects of these standards is a series of vignettes. These are drawn from a wide range of classroom contexts and describe instructional sequences. From them, the reader gets a clear idea of what the standards might look like in action.

A somewhat different, although related approach has been adopted by a task force charged with developing national standards for foreign language education (National Standards in Foreign Language Education, 1994):

Goal one: communicate in languages other than English
Standard 1.1
Students will:
use the target language to participate in social interactions
and to establish and maintain personal relationships in a variety of settings and contexts.

They will:

discuss topics of interest through the expression of thoughts, ideas, opinions, attitudes, feelings, and experiences
participate in social interactions related to problem solving, decision making, and other social transactions.

Does this mean that the standards movement is a case of old wine in new bottle? To a certain extent, I would say that it is. As I have argued in this section, I see no salient distinction between competencies and content standards. However, the standards movement goes beyond performance statements for learners and applies behavioral criteria to other aspects of the educational system: most importantly, to the areas of program development and management and to teachers and teacher education. It therefore provides a much more comprehensive set of tools for evaluating educational systems and programs as a whole than was offered by earlier behavioral models. It is to these two areas that I now turn.

Program Standards

Program standards, as the name implies, provide indicators for evaluating the quality of programs as a whole. As might be imagined, such standards cover a wide range of areas and contexts. In places where English is taught as a second language (for example, Great Britain, the United States, Canada, and Australia), the range of program types is vast. In addition to the many public and private programs for educating children, there is a range of different program types for adult education. These include general English programs focusing on immediate survival and settlement needs, family literacy programs, vocational and workplace programs, English for specific purpose (ESP), and English for academic purpose (EAP) programs for learners requiring English for professional and/or study purposes, and content-based programs where content and language are integrated. In addition, in some countries, such as the United States, citizenship programs offer language and content classes for students who want to become naturalized.

Given the breadth of program types, it is hardly surprising that the substantive areas addressed by program standards are also wide-ranging and overlap with other types of standards. For example, the Adult Education ESOL Program standards in the United States cover the following areas: program structure, administration, and planning; curriculum; instruction; recruitment, intake, and orientation; retention and transition; assessment and learner gains; staffing/professional development/staff evaluation; support services.

Sample quality indicators for each of these areas are set out in Table 2, and illustrate the range and comprehensive nature of such indicators.

Table 2. Sample Quality Indicators for Program Areas (TESOL, 1999)

Program area	Sample quality indicator
Program structure, administration, and planning	The ESOL program has a mission statement, a clearly articulated philosophy, and goals developed with input from internal and external stakeholders. Internal stakeholders may include administrators, instructional staff, support staff, program volunteers, and learners. External stakeholders may include boards or advisory groups, community and agency leaders, business leaders, employment and training agencies, other educational service providers, state, federal, and local legislators, support services and funders.

Curriculum	The curriculum includes goals, objectives, outcomes, approaches, methods, activities, materials, technological resources, and evaluation measures that are appropriate for meeting learners' needs and goals as identified by needs assessment activities. The curriculum reflects learners' goals while considering their roles as individuals, family members, community participants, workers, and/or lifelong learners.
Instruction	Instructional activities adhere to principles of adult learning and language acquisition. These principles include the following: - Adult learners bring a variety of experiences, skills, and knowledge that need to be acknowledged and included in lessons. - Language acquisition is facilitated through providing a non-threatening environment in which learners feel comfortable and self-confident and are encouraged to take risks to use the target language. - Adult learners progress more rapidly when the content is relevant to the learners' lives. - Language learning is cyclical, not linear, so learning objectives need to be recycled in a variety of contexts.
Recruitment, intake, and orientation	The program takes steps to insure that culturally and linguistically appropriate recruitment and program information materials and activities reach the targeted populations in multiple languages as needed. Recruitment materials suitable for persons with special needs should be available (e.g. larger print, audio tapes).
Retention and transition	The program supports retention through enrollment and attendance procedures that reflect program goals, requirements of program funders and demands on the adult learner (e.g. flexible enrollment options, flexible transfer, and short-term courses).
Assessment and learner gains	The program uses a variety of appropriate assessments, including authentic performance based assessments, standardized tests, learner self-assessment, and assessment on non-linguistic outcomes (e.g. perceived improvement in self-esteem, participation in teamwork activities.)
Staffing/ professional development/ staff evaluation	The program recruits and hires qualified instructional staff with training in the theory and methodology of teaching ESOL. Qualifications may vary according to local agency requirements and type of instructional position (e.g. paid instructor, volunteer). Examples of qualifications include a Bachelor's or Master's degree in TESOL, TESOL certificate from an accredited institution, adult education credential with authorization to teach TESOL, a certificate of completion from a provider's pre-service TESOL training program, or a combination of adult level ESOL teaching experience and training determined to be equivalent.
Support services	The program provides access to a variety of services directly or through referrals to cooperating agencies. Examples of services include childcare, transportation, health services, employment counseling, assessment of learning disabilities, native language translators and interpreters, and services related to other barriers to learning.

In order to be used for purposes of evaluation, the quality indicators need to be operationalized as performance standards. Consider, for example, the quality indicator: *Curriculum and instructional materials are easily accessible, up-to-date, appropriate for adult learners, culturally sensitive, and oriented to the language and literacy needs of the learners.* This is operationalized as follows:

1. The program documents program assessment measures, including classroom-based needs assessments, target population surveys, census data, etc.
2. The program documents the implementation of curriculum change based on learner or target population needs.
3. The program houses or provides easy access to a materials library for teachers.
4. The program references current instructional materials in curricular documents.
5. The program pilot tests new materials on representative student groups.
6. The program staff/textbook committee periodically obtains and pilots the use of review copies of new materials that are consistent with curricular objectives and the needs of the learners, making recommendations for the adoption of texts on a regular basis (e.g., annually).
7. ____% of the faculty indicate that they have access to current and appropriate materials.

Teacher Standards

An exciting, albeit controversial, development currently under way in both Europe and North America is the development of professional standards for teachers. *Teacher standards* describe the skills that teachers should be able to demonstrate within certain defined areas. In Australia, a set of teacher standards (or, as they were then termed, *competencies*) were developed in the early 1990s to guide universities on how to structure their teacher education courses and to provide similar guidance to employers on "the development and implementation of induction and on-going professional development" (Strong & Hogan, 1994, p. 4). This performance-based approach to teaching and teacher education stands in contrast with the traditional *credentialing* approach in which the certificates, diplomas, and degrees that a teacher holds form the criterion for determining an individual's professionalism.

In Europe, the University of Cambridge Local Examinations Syndicate (UCLES) has established performance standards for teachers at different stages of professional development in a number of key areas. For example, the Certificate in English Language Teaching to Adults articulates statements in the following areas: (a) language awareness; (b) the learners, the teacher, and the teaching/ learning context; (c) planning for effective teaching of adult learners of English; (d) materials and resources for teaching; (e) professional development (UCLES, 1996).

In North America, a TESOL Task Force has developed a conceptual framework and set of teaching standards for post-secondary ESL teachers. This framework articulates standards in 10 different domains to support and sustain student learning. These areas are as follows: identity and setting, language, learning, professional community, content, professionalism, advocacy, planning, instructing, and assessing. Like other kinds of standards, these are behavioral in nature. In other words, the teacher should be able to demonstrate mastery of the standards through observable behavior in and out of the classroom. These behaviors are fleshed out as performance indicators. Table 3 sets out the standards for eight of these and provides sample indicators.

Table 3. Standards and Performance Indicators for TESOL Teachers (TESOL, 2002)

Domain	Standard	Sample performance indicators
1. Planning	Teachers plan instruction to promote learning and meet learner goals, and modify and adjust instruction plans in relation to learner engagement and achievement.	- identify and articulate learning goals for both language and other content - design short-term and long-term plans to promote learning - select appropriate resources
2. Instructing	Teachers create supportive environments that engage all learners in purposeful learning and that promote respectful interactions among learners and between learners and their teachers.	- create physical and virtual environments that engage all learners - organize and manage constructive interactions among learners - engage learners in decision-making about their learning
3. Assessing	Teachers recognize the importance of and are able to gather and interpret information about learning and performance to promote the continuous intellectual and linguistic development of each learner. Teachers use knowledge of student performance to make decisions about planning and instruction "on-the-spot" and for the future.	- gather, interpret, and document information about learner performance before, during, and at the end of instruction - engage learners in self-assessment - use assessments that allow learners to demonstrate their learning - use assessment instruments that are equitable
4. Identity and setting	Teachers understand the importance of who learners are and how their communities, heritages, and goals shape learning and expectations of learning. Teachers recognize the importance of the sociocultural and sociopolitical settings – home, community, workplace, and school – that contribute to the identity formation and therefore influence learning. Teachers use this	- create an environment conducive to adult learning - establish classroom outines that encourage learners' appreciation for each other - model impartial attitudes towards cross-cultural differences

		knowledge of identity and settings in planning, instructing, and assessing.	and/or conflicts - take information from learners' communities to guide planning, instructing and assessing
5. Language		Teachers demonstrate proficiency in English	- demonstrate proficiency in oral, written, and nonverbal English - serve as English language models for learners
6. Learning		Teachers draw on their knowledge of language and adult learning to understand the processes by which learners acquire a new language in and out of classroom settings. They use this knowledge to support adult language learning.	- create situations where meaningful messages are exchanged - provide learning experiences that promote autonomy and choice - provide learning experiences that respond to differential rates of learning
7. Content		Teachers use their understanding of the structure and function of language to support language learning. Teachers also use their understanding of the connections among concepts, procedures, and applications from content areas relevant to learners to further learners' language development	- design contextualized activities to provide practice with English discourses and texts - provide input and practice of socially and culturally appropriate language - use content as a vehicle for language instruction
8. Commitment to professionalism		Teachers continue to grow in their understanding of the relationship of second language teaching to the community of English language teaching professionals, the broader teaching community, and communities at large, and use these understandings to inform and change themselves and these communities.	- take information from the communities at large and the broader teaching community to inform the English language teaching profession - develop personal professional development plans - reflect on teaching practice to continue to grow professionally

Standards-based evaluation is not without its problems and controversies. Firstly, the criticism of the objectives movement, that it led to fragmentation of the curriculum as well as to an atomistic approach to instruction and learning, may well come to haunt proponents of standards-based curriculum evaluation.

Another related criticism that may well-prove pertinent is that of "death-by-checklist." The criticism here is that evaluating the overall worth of a program by tallying lists of items on a checklist is problematic because it assumes that the whole is simply the sum of its parts. While checklists of standards have the potential to provide valuable quantitative information, in most cases these will need to be augmented by qualitative data. (See similar criticisms by McKay, this volume, in relation to assessment.)

A third criticism has to do with the extent to which one can infer underlying competence from samples of observable behavior. This is an issue that has bedeviled the field of language assessment for years and is unlikely to be settled here. It is also a fundamental problem in many aspects of language research in which the researcher has to infer the existence of constructs such as *intermediate speaking proficiency* or *master teacher* from observable behavior. (For a detailed discussion of this issue in relation to proficiency rating scales, see Nunan, 1988).

IDEOLOGICAL ASPECTS OF THE STANDARDS-BASED INSTRUCTION

In this final section, I will discuss some of the ideological aspects of a standards-based approach to education. Where has it come from? Not surprisingly, the central impetus has been political. The initiatives I have described all fit into a much larger ideological picture. In the United States, for example, Glaser and Lin (1993, cited in Richards, in press) write:

> In recounting our nation's drive towards educational reform, the last decade of this century will undoubtedly be recognized as the time when a concerted press for national educational standards emerged. The press for standards was evidenced by the efforts of federal and state legislators, presidential and gubernatorial candidates, teacher and subject matter specialists, councils, governmental agencies, and private foundations.

In fact, there is legislation in place that requires performance-based content specifications for subjects in elementary, secondary, and adult curricula. For example, the Adult Education and Literacy Act (1991) requires Adult Basic Education programs in all states to develop indicators of program quality and to attach performance standards to these quality indicators.

Even a cursory examination of the standards and performance indicators presented in this chapter reveal their ideological bases. Consider the following:

- engage learners in self-assessment
- model impartial attitudes towards cross-cultural differences and/or conflicts
- provide learning experiences that promote autonomy and choice
- develop personal professional development plans

These four indicators, selected more or less at random, from the TESOL teacher standards, reveal that individual responsibility and self-direction, as well as tolerance for pluralism are important values for the creators of these standards, and it is against these that TESOL teachers are to be judged.

I would also like to return to the criticisms that were made many years ago of the objectives movement. These were many and varied, from the belief that prespecifying behavior was somehow "undemocratic," to the assertion that the purposes of education could, by definition, not be specified in advance. Of course, it could be argued that foreign language learning is a skill and, therefore, is a training rather than an educational endeavor. Set against that view are current notions of *communication* as necessarily imprecise and *meaning* as a variable and negotiable commodity. Thus, Widdowson (1983) writes, that

> A person educated in a certain language, as opposed to one who is trained only in its use for a restricted set of predictable situations, is someone who is able to relate what he or she knows to circumstances other than those which attended the acquisition of that knowledge. To put it another way, education in a language presupposes the internalization of what Halliday calls 'meaning potential'. (p. 17)

Rowntree, one of the strongest proponents of performance-based curriculum development later changed his mind, although he never became an outright opponent of objectives. In fact, he was to assert (1981) that:

> I still believe they (objectives) are extremely valuable in course development. Asking oneself what students should be able to do by the end of the course that they could not do (or not do so well) at the beginning can be illuminating. Many teachers (and I am one) would claim that teaching has been far better since they were introduced to objectives. (p. 35)

As I have already indicated, the standards-based education movement and the various standards projects around the world that it has spawned have greatly broadened our concept of performance-based learning and thereby obviated many of the criticisms of the narrow-band behavioral objectives approach criticized by Widdowson and Rowntree. My own view is that standards-based evaluation will play an increasingly important part in both learner assessment and in program- and teacher-evaluation, and whether we like it or not, allocation of public funds to educational institutions and entities will increasingly be determined by the application of content, teacher, and program standards to the evaluation of those institutions and entities.

REFERENCES

Adult Migrant Education Service. (1993). *Certificate in spoken and written English*. Sydney: NSW Adult Migrant Education Service (AMES).

Bottomly, Y., Dalton, J., & Corbel, C. (1994). *From proficiency to competencies: A collaborative approach to curriculum innovation.* Draft project report, Melbourne Victoria: AMES.

Brindley, G. (1994). Competency-based assessment in second language programs. *Prospect, 9*(2), 41–53.

Council of Europe. (2001). *Common European framework of reference for languages: Learning, teaching, assessment*. Cambridge: Cambridge University Press.

Dick, W., & Carey, L. (1978). *The systematic design of instruction*. Glenview Ill: Scott, Foresman and Company.

Leung, C., & Teasdale, A. (1998). ESL teacher competence: Professionalism in a social market. *Prospect, 13*(1), 4–23.

Mager, R. (1962). *Preparing objectives for programmed instruction*. Belmont CA: Pitman Learning Inc.

Mager, R. (1984). *Preparing instructional objectives*. Belmont CA: Pitman Learning Inc.

Munby, J. (1978). *Communicative syllabus design*. Cambridge: Cambridge University Press.

National Standards in Foreign Language Education. (1994). Unpublished draft.

Nunan, D. (1988). *The Learner-centred curriculum*. Cambridge: Cambridge University Press.

Reynolds, M., & Salters, M. (1995). Models of competence and teacher training. *Cambridge Journal of Education, 25*(3), 349–359.

Richards, J. C. (in press). *Curriculum development in language teaching*. New York: Cambridge University Press.

Rowntree, D. (1981). *Developing courses for students*. London: McGraw Hill.

Shavelson, R., & Stern, P. (1981). Research on teachers' pedagogical thoughts, judgments, and behavior. *Review of Educational Research, 51*(4).

Strong, R., & Hogan, S. (1994, March). *TESOL teacher competencies document.* Paper presented at the 28th Annual TESOL Convention, Baltimore, USA.

TESOL. (1997). *ESL standards for Pre-K-12 students.* Alexandria VA: TESOL.

TESOL. (1999). *Adult education program standards.* Alexandria VA: TESOL.

TESOL. (2002). *TESOL standards for teachers of adult learners.* Alexandria VA: TESOL

Tyler, R. (1949). *Basic principles of curriculum and instruction.* New York: Harcourt Brace.

University of Cambridge Local Examinations Syndicate. (1996). *Cambridge integrated language teaching schemes: Certificate in English language teaching to adults.* Cambridge UK: UCLES.

Valette, R., & Disick, R. (1972). *Modern language performance objectives and individualization.* New York: Harcourt Brace Jovanovich.

Van Ek, J. (1977). *The threshold level for modern language learning in schools.* London: Longman.

Widdowson, H. G. (1983). *Learning purpose and language use.* Oxford: Oxford University Press.

Wilkins, D. (1976). *Notional syllabuses.* Oxford: Oxford University Press.

CHAPTER 29

THE STANDARDS MOVEMENT AND ELT FOR SCHOOL-AGED LEARNERS:

Cross-National Perspectives

PENNY MCKAY

Queensland University of Technology, Australia

ABSTRACT

This chapter describes and discusses issues in the standards movement in ELT in relation to school-aged learners. Two broad types of standards are addressed: Firstly, English as a Foreign Language (EFL) standards that are written for English as a subject in the school curriculum, which is studied along common pathways by the majority of students; secondly, ESL standards that are written for ESL learners studying in an English-speaking environment, generally with English as the medium of instruction. Common "literacy" standards used to assess ESL learners are also discussed. Research in ELT standards is conceptualized as being three areas of work: the development of ELT standards, the critiquing of ELT standards, and empirical research into ELT standards. References to ELT standards from around the world are provided throughout, as are references to literature in the area. A central thesis in the chapter is that despite variations amongst ELT standards, inevitable because of policy, purpose, and contextual factors, there is a common core of issues and understandings that can and should draw the area of work together. Suggestions for further research, emphasizing the need for sharing of activity, are given.

INTRODUCTION

English language learners in schools around the world can be categorized into two broad groups: Those who are learning English as a foreign language (EFL learners) and those who are learning English in an English speaking environment and often as the medium of instruction (English as a second language or ESL learners). Examples of ELT standards exist for both groups around the world. The different contexts for English language learning dictate some broad variation between the construction of EFL and ESL standards. Broadly, EFL standards, being written for English as a subject in the school curriculum and studied along common pathways by the majority of students, are built to accommodate linear and common progression from Kindergarten (or beginning of EFL learning) to end of school. The construction of ESL standards is complicated by the factors of multiple entry points, mixed language and curriculum background experiences, and an immediate need for communication and language for learning across the curriculum. Beyond these two broad categorizations of ELT standards though, many different manifestations amongst ELT standards exist; these result from variations in local development—

differences in policy, purpose, and context, and differences in the perspectives of those involved in their construction. The common factor that makes the "standards movement in ELT for school-aged learners" worthy of common investigation, relates to the issue of validity underpinned by understandings of second language acquisition: Validity promotes the opportunity for learners' progress in English to be mapped fairly and ideally, enhanced by these standards.

While not all ELT standards have originated from government-initiated policy and curriculum changes, but rather from professional interest in furthering teaching and assessment (as in the case of the Australian *ESL Bandscales* and the *ESL Standards for Pre-K-12 Students*), a brief introduction to the wider standards movement provides the context for developments that have occurred in recent years. The standards movement was well entrenched in the United States and England (through the National Curriculum) by the early 1990s and was soon adopted and promoted by many governments around the world who saw in standards a means of instigating change and taking greater control of education. The standards movement, it was believed, would enable governments to redress perceptions of falling standards (some suggest these are manufactured perceptions) and address equity. The movement would improve community and government input into education, and increase data about student progress on which governments would be able to address issues of accountability of teachers, schools, and education systems. Prototype steps in a standards-based reform from the Title I program in the USA are set out by Yu and Taylor (1998):

> Set high standards that all students, including low-income and limited-English proficiency students, must meet in all subjects.
>
> Develop new assessments that measure the progress of students, schools, and school districts in meeting high standards.
>
> Hold school districts and individual schools accountable for showing continuous improvements in student performance, until all students achieve at high levels.
>
> Target resources to schools and districts with the highest concentrations of children from low-income families.
>
> Encourage school-wide improvements in schools where more than half the children are from low-income families.
>
> Ensure that eligible schools and districts have the capacity to teach to high standards, including adequate professional development, and, where necessary, the provision of extra resources to needy schools. (p. 11)

Content standards specify broad curriculum goals, defining the skills and knowledge that should be taught and learned. Content standards may or may not be staged into levels. *Performance standards,* set within the frame of the content standards, specify what ought to be achieved at one level or another. Other terms used for standards are *outcomes-based curriculum and assessment, benchmarks, bandscales, scales* and *profiles.* A major change brought about through the introduction of standards is a move from an *intentions-based curriculum*, where the curriculum is stated in terms of goals and objectives, to a curriculum where the outcomes are established and the school, the teacher, and the student are responsible for teaching towards those objectives. Thus in a government-initiated standards document (Curriculum Corporation, 1994), a typical descriptor, set under broader short statements of goals or outcomes, reads as follows:

Write for a variety of purposes (to give information such as personal information, to keep records, to display, to express opinions)

Understand and use some of the terminology of reading (author, title, letter, word, sentence, page)

Standards may take up the whole or part of a curriculum statement (as in content standards) or may consist of a set of staged descriptions of expected progress (as in performance standards). Education authorities use their standards to monitor program delivery, and individual and system-wide progress. Schools use standards for planning curricula and programs, communicating expectations, helping teachers know what to teach, co-ordinating different classes, choosing materials, and determining what students need to achieve (Porter, 2000).

Those who support standards believe that they "take the mystery" (Lachat, 1999, p. 3) out of what is expected of students, that they can provide guidelines for good practice (Scarino, 2001, p.11), and give consistent opportunity for instruction for students in different localities. Standards can assist governments to raise achievement by monitoring and giving feedback through systematic reporting and assessment. Supporters believe that comparisons with other individuals, other schools, other systems, and even other countries can provide information about relative progress and, indeed, a spark of motivating competition. The publication of standards can also help to define a field and give it status, as in the case of the TESOL's *ESL Standards* (1997) in the United States (Short, 2000).

Critics of standards, on the other hand, believe the use of standards by governments can take on "administrative, political, and at times, even moralistic value" (Ingram, 2001, p. 5). Commentators such as Broadfoot (1996) and McKay (2001) have critiqued the standards approach: Its underpinnings of *individualism* (responsibility to the individual), *rationalism* ('bean counting'), and *competition* can lead to a "blame the victim" mentality. Many teachers find that standards are intrusive on their professionalism. Thomas (2001), for example, places rubric-driven written assessment under the same standards paradigm as objective testing and suggests that both narrow the curriculum, reduce creativity, and take time away from teaching and learning. Fullan (2000) stresses the importance of change mechanisms when standards are implemented, saying that "accountability systems are effective only when they are connected to mechanisms and processes for making changes" (p. 24). Many parents in the general community appear to support close monitoring of students' progress (Phelps, 1998). Given the range of users and their needs and interests, it is not surprising that a common and continuing theme in the literature is the tension between the pedagogic and administrative purposes of standards (Brindley, 1998; McKay, 2000b, 2001).

MAIN RESEARCH FINDINGS

It is useful to classify the research work done in ELT standards for schools into three areas:

- The writing and publication of ELT standards documents that has been in itself an important research endeavor
- The critiquing of ELT standards (and those standards that are intended to act as ELT standards) that has taken the field forward and can be viewed as research
- Empirical research itself that is making only its first tentative steps

The Writing of ELT Standards

Writers of ELT Standards are becoming aware of international ELT standards work in other countries but mainly write for their own context. One of the challenges in the search for some sense of validation in ELT standards is that there has been mostly local development, not only across countries but within countries, and therefore a lack of comparability across standards. Lack of comparability, however, may not signal validity problems as much as framework differences and variations in what is considered salient by the writers for that context. The usual writing procedure is that experienced teachers are withdrawn from classroom teaching and, with curriculum experts and administrators, establish a series of levels describing progress or required progress, sometimes with accompanying guidelines and samples of work. Often in government-initiated standards, the *framework* (that is, the number of levels, the strands, the nature of the descriptors, the degree of detail) is set by the education system. In others, there is more professional choice in the formatting of the standards. McKay (2000b) has discussed the different ways that frameworks are organized and the way descriptors are formulated. Descriptions are usually moderated amongst groups of teachers and experts, and may or may not be checked against actual progress in the classroom (though this latter process, if it happens at all, often happens after the publication of the documents). The full process of development of the Australian *ESL Bandscales*, including theoretical underpinnings and consultative processes, has been described by McKay (1995).

EXAMPLES OF EFL STANDARDS

A range of EFL standards have been implemented in education systems where English is taught as a foreign language, usually as a separate subject in the curriculum. Because English is taught increasingly around the world, EFL standards are likely to exist wherever standards-based reform has been adopted.

For example, in Hong Kong the *Target-Oriented Curriculum* (Clark et al., 1994) was introduced in primary schools in the early 1990s and aimed towards the development of EFL standards (*targets*) embedded within a well conceptualized curriculum. Adopting a holistic view that learning through English would contribute to all-around development, targets for English were identified in key stages organized around an *interpersonal dimension*, a *knowledge dimension*, and an *experience dimensio,* the 'horizontal organizers' across the range of knowledge to be covered. Bands of performance, 'vertical organisers' building up stages of development of performance provide target descriptions for English language for educators and parents. A new secondary school English curriculum, introduced in 2001, also incorporates bands of performance for English language development. Both these curriculum documents embed standards within a broader curriculum approach rather than adopt the standards as the basis for the curriculum description. In Malaysia there is also an outcomes-based approach to the English language curriculum: Standards for learning developed by the Ministry of Education are accompanied by targeted textbook and student materials and workbooks.

Besides a number of independently prepared ELT standards in member States, Europe has worked towards adopting a shared approach to language standards through a European framework of reference for modern languages (Council of Europe, 1998). The framework for all languages, including English, divides learners into three target groups, each with two levels: Basic User (A1, A2), Independent Users (B1, B2), and Proficient Users (C1, C2). For each level, there are standards for understanding (listening), reading, spoken interaction, spoken production, and writing. The development of these standards has been accompanied by professional development projects. Coppare and Lopriori (cited in McKay et al., 2001a, 2001b) describe the European framework and discuss issues with other developers of ELT Standards. However, more information about how authorities have approached the writing of EFL standards needs to be collected.

EXAMPLES OF ESL STANDARDS

It is in the area of ESL (as opposed to EFL) standards where most examples of ELT standards can be found. A selection of ESL standards is described here. Only a small number of overview articles are known (for example, Davison and Williams, 2002; Derewianka, 1997; Leung, 1996; McKay, 2000b) which provide references to a number of other ESL standards documents.

The *ESL Standards for Pre-K-12 Students* (TESOL, 1997) are the result of the effort of the Association of TESOL (Teachers of English to Speakers of Other Languages) in the United States. The *ESL Standards* take their conceptual basis from sets of goals and principles of ESL learning. They are organized around three goals and nine standards. Each standard is further explicated by descriptors, sample progress indicators, and classroom vignettes with discussions. The standards section of the document that follows is organized into grade-level clusters: pre-K-3, 4-8, and 9-12 (p. 15). Accompanying the standards has been much activity related to the development of assessment guidelines and scenarios, teacher education and curriculum development materials, and professional development opportunities. A number of professional articles (for example, McKay et al., 2001a, 2001b; Short, 2000; Short et al., 2000) and sister publications support the document. The *ESL Standards* are, in the main, content and professional standards, giving guidelines to educators about the curriculum needs of ESL learners in schools and about ways to approach teaching (as in the vignettes). They do, however, include lists of descriptors, with sample progress indicators, which, as a result of the focus on the content and teaching standards, appear to be somewhat under-developed performance standards.

Other examples of ELT standards in the USA are the *New York Learning Standards for English as a Second Language* (The University of the State of New York, 2001), commonly referred to as the *New York ESL Standards* and the *California Pathways* (ESL Intersegmental Project team, 1995).

In Australia, the National Languages and Literacy Institute of Australia (NLLIA) *ESL Bandscales* (McKay, Hudson, & Sapuppo, 1994) exist alongside a number of other ESL standards documents, including the *ESL Scales* (Curriculum Corporation, 1994) and the *Victorian ESL Companion to the English Curriculum Standards Framework* (Board of Studies Victoria, 1996). Derewianka in Breen et al. (1997) provide an overview of all Australian ESL standards documents, together with a report of an investigation into their use by teachers. The *ESL Bandscales* have been in use across Australia by individual ESL teachers and by several education authorities for assessment and reporting for mainly pedagogic purposes. Like the *ESL Standards,* the *ESL Bandscales* are primarily professional documents prepared through university research and teacher collaboration rather than through a government reform initiative. Teachers and authorities have produced reporting formats, overviews, lists of key indicators, and a CD Rom for easier use of and reporting purposes. The *ESL Bandscales* have also been adapted by teachers in north Queensland for use with indigenous students (Education Department, 2000). *The Bandscales for Aboriginal and Torres Strait Islanders* are filling a gap for teachers of these students in, amongst other places, Queensland and Western Australia, where there is dissatisfaction with the use of common literacy standards for indigenous learners and a perceived need to use but adapt the *ESL Bandscales*. Further work is needed on the development of standards for *standard English as a second dialect*.

A curriculum for English as a second language and English literacy has also been produced in Ontario, Canada (Ministry of Education and Training, 1999). The curriculum provides concise, bullet-pointed, outcomes-based statements of what students will do and learn in a given course. There are five levels, called *courses*, and four strands per course: *oral and visual communication, reading, writing,* and *social and cultural competence*. For each strand there are *overall expectations* followed by *specific expectations*. Cumming (1999) has critiqued these ESL curriculum and standards following research into their impact (see also McKay et al., 2001a, 2001b).

ESL standards have also been developed by a number of education districts in the United Kingdom. Leung (1996) has discussed the separate development of these different standards documents, suggesting that variations in descriptors of progress from one district's standards to another raise some concerns regarding validity. ESL educators in the United Kingdom have long called for a national document, similar to the ESL standards documents available in Australia. An earlier set of descriptors for ESL development of primary learners (Barrs et al., 1988) was for a long time the only widely known set of descriptors of ESL learner progress in the United Kingdom. Following many years of lobbying by professional associations and others, *A Language in Common* (2000) was made available by the Qualifications and Curriculum Authority to give guidelines and standards for beginning ESL learners. The perennial question of whether to have an independent ESL Standards (therefore requiring two accounting systems) was therefore addressed by using ESL standards only to articulate with the National Curriculum. Continuing ESL support for students who have 'moved' onto the National Curriculum standards then becomes a common curriculum issue.

Many English-speaking countries grapple with the question of whether freestanding ESL standards should be created and used. Many English-speaking education systems, not just England, have taken a common approach to content and performance standards development. South Africa's English curriculum (Department of Education, 1997) is written for all children, irrespective of first or additional language background. Australia has introduced common *Literacy Benchmarks* (Department of Education, 1998) to provide directions and guide assessment in literacy for all learners for accountability purposes. However, the strength of the ESL profession may have had an influence on the retention of ESL standards, albeit attached to subject English, in the common curriculum standards. The *Ontario Benchmarks* (see Ontario Institute of Studies in Education, 1993), which describes through tasks related to curriculum goals and objectives, also includes all learners. The use of common English or literacy standards for all raises many concerns for ESL professionals, some of which are discussed below.

THE CRITIQUING OF ELT STANDARDS

Research into ELT standards has been advanced through critical analyses of documents produced, but such work is still somewhat embryonic. Moore (1995a, 1995b) was one of the first researchers to make a connection between policy and the nature of literacy standards documents. She compares two juxtaposing literacy policies in Australia and ties this analysis to comparisons of two major ESL standards documents for schools (the *ESL Bandscales* and the *ESL Scales*) that were produced under the auspices of each policy. Her thesis is that the two documents reflect the multicultural or English-centered policy respectively (Moore, 2004).

Brindley (1998) examines ELT standards under the label of outcomes-based curriculum and assessment, a term more commonly used in Australia to refer to standards. He describes several adult ELT and school standards documents in the USA, England, and Australia. His critique considers the interplay of political, technical, and practical factors in the development and use of standards. He recognizes the administrative requirements of policy-makers but suggests that tensions between purposes of policy-makers, administrators, and practitioners impact on the validity of standards documents in their use. He advocates closer consultation with and stronger professional development of teachers to enable more effective use of standards. He suggests directions for further research into the validity and effects of outcomes-based assessment and reporting on student learning. Brindley (2001) then examined the issue of standards further, emphasizing the role of teachers in assessment and, thus, the need for professional development as an integral strategy in an effective standards-based approach.

McKay (2000b, 2006) examines issues in policy, development, and use of a number of ELT standards for schools. A central theme in McKay's critique (as in Brindley, 1998) is the tension between administrative and pedagogic purposes and the influence of this tension on the construction and use of the standards. She classifies ELT standards into three types: Standards for planning, for professional understanding, and multi-purpose ELT standards (see Table 1). She suggests that in some cases, confusions evident in the presentation and format of the framework and the descriptors cause confusion for teachers and can threaten validity.

McKay (2000b) asserts K–12 ESL standards must contain separate bands for younger learners. Beginning younger and older learners cannot be described together; nor can younger advanced and older advanced learners be placed together on a scale. The tasks the learners are required to participate in, and differences in cognitive abilities require at least two separate scales or bands of progress. The effectiveness of ELT standards is evaluated by asking the following questions:

- Are the purposes for the ESL standards clear?
- Do the ESL standards provide separate descriptions for younger learners?
- Have principled decisions informed the construction of the ESL standards?
- Is the choice of descriptor-type appropriate to the purpose and appropriate for ESL description?
- Do the descriptors convey a sense of what we know about second language learning of school ESL learners learning in mainstream contexts?
- Are accompanying assessment procedures valid?

Table 1. *Questions to be Asked Regarding Choice and Scaling of Descriptors in ESL Standards (McKay, 2000, p. 195)*

Purposes	Questions		
	1. Do the descriptors reflect the language students need to be taught to move towards successful study in mainstream classrooms?	2. Do the descriptors give useful and sufficient detailed information for teachers to understand progress and, from this, to make teaching decisions?	3. Do the descriptors reflect progress that *should* be achieved as students progress in their ESL learning? Will they differentiate between those who are succeeding and those falling behind?
ESL Standards for *planning*	*		
ESL Standards for *professional understanding*		*	
Multi-purpose ESL Standards 1. Planning 2. Professional understanding 3. Reporting	*	*	*

Table 2. *Characteristics of Long-term Maps of Progress (McKay, 2000a)*

PROMOTING 'WELL-ROUNDEDNESS' →	
Measurable	Abstract
	Complex
Specific	Integrated
Analytic	Holistic
Dot-points	Paragraph descriptions and 'cameos'
Flat	Alive ("I can see the learner")
Message free	Message rich
'Can do' statements (context-reduced)	'Can do under certain conditions' statements (i.e. context-embedded)
Level = the majority of items are 'achieved'	Level = a teacher's sense of 'levelness'
←More administrative	More pedagogic→

In another paper, McKay (2000a) expands on a concept of *well-roundedness* put forward by Sizmur and Sainsbury (1997) who write:

> Level descriptions are intended to be descriptions of the typical performance of a **well-rounded** pupil at a given level. They retain much of the abstraction and complexity of the underlying educational notions to which they are linked, and eschew any attempt at precise, exhaustive behavioural definition. (p. 11)

McKay suggests there are different types of long-term maps of learning for the school language learning context. These characteristics can be placed on a continuum of well-roundedness, which in turn might be related to pedagogic and administrative purposes.

Statements on both sides may be short and concise or long and detailed. The left side of the chart reflects the characteristics of many long-term maps that have been developed firstly for administrative purposes. These characteristics reflect the need for simplicity required for accountability-driven standards.

McKay (2000b) suggests that long-term maps with characteristics on the left are problematic because it is difficult for teachers to pull together lists of dot-points (often in three or four strand lists) into a holistic and well-rounded map of progress in their mind. This can lead to assessing the learner as a list of abilities achieved or not, rather than as a well-rounded individual with interrelated abilities. The maps on the left are also less helpful for teachers because they say what the student can do regardless of the context; yet in effect, the context (i.e. the degree and nature of support, the background knowledge needed) is crucial to the ability of the student to demonstrate an ability in language. Where the left hand side tends to encourage ticking off item-by-item, the right encourages the holistic rating of progress. Standards that have characteristics set out on the right side of the chart are, McKay (2000a) suggests, optimal for long-term pedagogic and formative assessment, since the teachers then have mind-maps that reflect the complexity and well-roundedness they see in real life.

Well written, long-term, pedagogically oriented maps can, in the ideal world, help teachers to internalize a long-term mind-map and also to gain understandings about the following:

1. The interrelationship of the language being learned and the knowledge, understandings and skills required to grow towards success in the school context.
2. A developmental view of language and learning—how second language develops across time given the context of learning and the growing maturity of the learners, and how it interacts with other growing knowledge, understandings, and skills.
3. The learner as a social being, learning over time, developing in confidence, in learning strategies, and in abilities to make sense of his/her world.
4. Current conceptions of language and second language learning, and current knowledge about influences (like the L1) on learning.

The Critiquing of Common Literacy Standards Used For ESL Reporting

One of the challenges for ESL assessment is that ESL learners are commonly included in common literacy assessments because of the administrative requirement for accountability fuelled by the appeal of having comparable data on progress. The move to common literacy standards for all has been accompanied by a shift in the meaning of *literacy*, a description of required benchmarks or standards, and identification of *students at risk* (rather than *ESL learners, indigenous learners,* and so on) as those who do not meet the standards.

Lo Bianco (1999) has written about the Australian government's promotion of "sameness" to push its policies in relation to indigenous students in schools. The

Northern Territory Government has abolished bilingual programs and promoted ESL programs to push "students at risk" towards achieving the Benchmarks:

> Equity that is based on sameness, on assimilation, on narrow and prescriptive criteria for belonging is a defective and an essentially unequal kind of 'equality'. Even in a culturally homogenous society I imagine that we might stress individual differences and not claim that equality implies rigid equalisation, or narrow normalisation, or individuals and their lifestyles, values, occupational patterns or preferences. In a society where the differences are not simply individual ones, but group differences, more complex issues arise. (p. 65)

Lo Bianco (1999) calls for continuing a bilingual approach to education for Aboriginal students and for all ESL children.

> I think we need to reject notions of English literacy that negate complementary development of two languages for bilingual Australians, especially Australian speakers of Australian languages in a multi-cultural Australia. I also think we need to repudiate the logic that makes cultural assimilation a condition of 'educational equity. (p. 6)

Thus the definition of literacy supported through standards documents, whether in EFL or ESL contexts, is a matter for serious critique in its impact on equity for students and student groups.

An international comparison of ELT standards for schools compares USA's Title I and recent Australian policy in relation to their support for ESL learners in assessment and reporting processes (McKay, 1999a). Title I provision for ESL learners (as described in Yu & Taylor, 1998) represented at least a policy intent, in the United States to recognize the ESL population and to attend to their particular needs in assessment procedures. This type of attention to the needs of ESL students in schools is not always observed, for example, in the common assessments conducted in the UK (Leung, 1996), in Australia (Davison, 1999; Hammond & Derewianka, 1999) and in Canada (Cumming, 1999). Further critiques and analyses of how this can and should be done are needed in the ELT field.

EMPIRICAL RESEARCH INTO ESL STANDARDS

Limited empirical research has been undertaken into ESL standards. In their overview of ELT standards, a group of international researchers (McKay et al., 2001b) report that they do not know of any research that has systematically evaluated the effects of language standards. They suggest that it is vital that this is done, particularly in the variety of contexts in which language standards are being implemented:

> Without any indications of whether standards affect language education positively, there is little empirical basis on which to argue for their values or benefits. (p. 15)

The following is a summary of research that is known to have been carried out in relation to ELT standards.

Leung's comparison of ESL standards documents in England has already been described briefly. Butler and Stevens (1998) are amongst the few researchers who have approached the question of validity of ELT standards through an empirical process. Butler and Stevens worked on developing and refining a process for the validation of the aspects of the *California Pathways* (ESL Intersegmental Project team, 1995). Butler and Stevens examine writing by collecting samples of student writing. They asked team members to select typical writing tasks at the Intermediate-Mid level, and then they compared segments and tasks to see if there were similarities in the samples for one specific level:

> Since guidelines do not exist for validating language proficiency descriptors of this kind, a major part of the work described in the plan involved developing and refining a validation process that can be used for the descriptors from all four skill areas, noting that modifications may be needed for some steps in the process due to differences in modalities. For example, listening and reading performance will be more difficult to capture because these skills cannot be observed in isolation from others. It may be necessary to use established tests to help tap listening and reading ability. Irrespective of how performance is captured, to validate the descriptors, samples of language performance must be obtained for each skill area. (p. 2)

Griffin and McKay (1992) describe a 'bottom-up consultative' process for the construction of ESL standards: practitioners are asked to provide descriptions of both tasks and descriptors. End users (students) are then observed and rated on each of the descriptors in order to obtain calibration data. An expert group comments and edits the scales. The edited scales are trialled and calibrated against existing language instruments and against basic research results: A sample of students are selected to be rated on the scales and to undertake specific language tasks. The data should help to establish properties of the scales. At the time of proposal, there was resistance from ESL practitioners who felt that the process needed to address construct validity more thoroughly. This was done in a subsequent project.

The use of Rasch analysis in language assessment and in the validation of language scales (to date, mostly in adult scales) is addressed in detail by McNamara (1996) and Baker (1997). Strong-Krause (2001) reports on its application to questions of scale development, types, and difficulty of tasks in relation to a scale of speaking ability. In Australia, McKay & Bond (2002) propose research using quantitative analysis of teachers' reporting data (using Rasch analysis) combined with qualitative investigation of teachers' decision-making.

Research into Teachers' Application of ELT Standards

Since reporting against standards happens at the end of a process of assessment and decision-making by teachers, a critical consideration in relation to the validity of ELT standards is teacher decision-making at this stage of the process. Breen et al.'s (1997) lengthy report on teachers' use of ESL standards in Australia provides multiple insights into teachers' reactions to and interpretations of Australian ELT standards.

Scarino (2001) is currently researching, through teachers' introspections, how they judge learners' writing in language assessment. In attempting to draw out teachers' maps of standards and the interplay of aspects that come together in making judgements, she explains that:

> The transcripts show how teachers bring together multiple strands of their own professional knowledge, personal theories, experiences, practices, and values in making judgements. ... These strands contribute to their own system of standards. (p. 15)

She draws attention to the variability of decisions of teachers who hold different conceptions of standards.

Sainsbury (1997) has investigated the suitability of three common literacy assessment schemes in the UK. She has analyzed children's results, conducted a teacher questionnaire, and undertaken a program of visits to a subsample of 30 schools. She found:

> A...pervasive criticism was dissatisfaction on the part of teachers with the 'yes-no' nature of the checklist criteria. When a child failed to attain an item on the checklist, this gave no indication as to their actual level of attainment below that. One teacher wrote: *A blanket 'no' to tasks does not indicate the level of success a child may have achieved within the task.* (p. 16)

Research of this nature is needed in both EFL and ESL contexts, where fine-tuned data collection on, and analysis of, teachers' assessment and reporting decisions (either in formative or summative assessments) can lead to insights into what happens in the "black box" between the written ELT Standard document and the teacher's report.

CURRENT DEBATES

Many of the issues and debates in the literature are touched upon in the preceding discussion. Most debates return to the issue of validity, which in turn relate to questions of purpose. The issue of validity underpins all considerations about ELT standards: This section discusses four of many interrelated issues: (a) validity, (b) the nature of descriptors, (c) assessment and reporting practices, and (d) the impact of ELT standards.

The Issue of Validity

The validity of level descriptors in ELT standards for schools is an ongoing source of concern, as it is for all standards documents. Many accountability-driven standards do not reflect any effort expended on establishing construct validity. Scarino (2001) calls for explicit descriptions of the *deep structure* of standards, "specifically the origin, nature, organization and purpose of each key concept and the framework as a whole" (p. 12). Some standards refer to frameworks such as those developed by Bachman (1990), Bachman and Palmer (1996), and Cummins (1983) for their conceptual base (for example, the *ESL Bandscales*); others use curriculum-related goals as their conceptual base (e.g., the *ESL Standards*). The input of experienced teachers (experts) agreeing on the descriptors and their ordering provides a degree of content validity, though some commentators question descriptors "that are derived from experience and intuition rather than research" (Brindley, 1998, p. 63).

Whether a set of ESL standards for schools can lay claim to validity depends on a myriad of other issues related to their construction; to their purpose and subsequent use; to the teachers' interpretation of the descriptors; and to the teachers' assessment and reporting practices. Ingram (2001) emphasizes the need for purpose to match use: Standards "are inappropriate and generally harmful if they have little relationship to the nature of language, language behaviour, and language learning if they are set and imposed without being properly matched against desirable purposes" (p. 5). Validity is a complex issue that cannot be addressed fully here. Brindley's writing (for example, 1998, 2001) provides important insights into issues and summaries of work to date in relation to the validity of ELT Standards.

The Nature of Descriptors

A range of different formats, organizing frameworks and descriptor-types have been used to construct ELT standards. McKay (2000b, 2006) has discussed in some depth the nature of formats and descriptors in ELT standards. Validity of standards can be threatened because of administrators' requirements for simplicity, designed to lead to clarity in accountability procedures. However, descriptors can be less ambiguous if listed with contextual information (for example, information relating to the length of the book, the degree of support from the interlocutor) and with professional information (for example, on the nature of the silent period), and they have more chance of assisting the teacher to provide a valid and reliable assessment. Thus, in the *New York ESL Standards* (The University of the State of New York, 2001), writers have wisely included at least a small amount of illustrative information for teachers in descriptors:

> Standard 5: Students will demonstrate cross-cultural knowledge and understanding.
>
> Elementary (2-4)
>
> Interpret and demonstrate knowledge of nonverbal communication, and understand the contexts in which they are used appropriately. Such features include gestures, body language, volume, stress and intonation (Listening and speaking) (p. 28)

Context-embedded standards are valuable in that they promote an approach to teaching that recognizes the need for support and scaffolding. O'Malley and Valdez Pierce's assessment examples (1996, p. 167) show how descriptors can include the context within them (see Table 3).

Table 3. *Extract from Assessment with/without Scaffolded Prompts*

Assessment examples	Without scaffolding	With scaffolding
Retell or summarise text	Write 5 main ideas from an article and give examples	Complete a word problem **given examples and an outline of a sample problem**
Summarise a science experiment	Write a summary of procedures in a science experiment following scientific principles.	Complete a summary **given a list** of procedures in science experiments, including questions, materials, a plan, observations, and conclusions, or **demonstrate** the steps using actual materials.

Note. From *Authentic Assessment for English Language Learners* (p. 167), by J. M. O'Malley & L. Valdez Pierce, 1996, New York: Addison-Wesley. Adapted with permission.

A current debate concerns the inclusion of descriptors relating to *cross-cultural knowledge and understanding*. Aspects of sociocultural competence are very difficult to scale (Education Committee, 1996, cited in Ingram, 2001). The *New York ESL Standards* include Standard 5 "to develop [students'] familiarity with their new social and cultural environment in the United States, as well as to foster cross-cultural awareness in the multicultural American society" (The University of the State of New York, 2001). They are able to do this, however, in content standards rather than developmentally scaled performance standards. Development in sociocultural competence may include thinking skills (O'Malley & Valdez Pierce, 1996) and intellectual depth, however, if such characteristics are to be included, they clearly need to be dealt with from the beginning of the document. In fact, debate concerning the nature of descriptors in ELT standards has hardly begun.

Assessment and Reporting Practices

Assessment practices have a critical influence on the validity of reporting of progress against ELT standards. In EFL contexts, assessment is generally being carried out by schools through tests set by central authorities. Some teachers in EFL situations seem to prefer this method because then they are not answerable to parents and principals if complaints arise about fairness. This type of response is more likely to be expressed by teachers who work in high stakes assessment contexts.

In ESL contexts, assessment against ESL standards is commonly teacher- and performance-based. Assessment is often carried out by teachers through observation across tasks and across a length of time. Brindley (1998) summarizes issues raised by performance-based assessment in relation to assessment and reporting against standards:

> *Task comparability*: the relative difficulty of assessment tasks aimed at tapping the same competency and the relative severity of rater judgements of task difficulty (p. 61).
>
> *Rater consistency*: the consistency with which judges are able to classify performances. "Since the consistency of measurement may vary according to the number of judges and tasks used, we also need to know how many tasks and how many judges are necessary to achieve dependable measurement (pp. 61-62).
>
> *Generalisability*: the relationship between competency and proficiency, that is, to what extent tasks aimed at assessing the same competency draw on common components of language ability and thus can be generalised beyond the assessment context (p. 62).

Brindley summarizes research findings concerning these issues and recommends that banks of tasks, with detailed specifications for each type of assessment task, might be built in order to provide reliable information on learner outcomes, with regular moderation sessions to improve reliability and professional expertise.

Samples of work collected to represent levels and moderated by teachers can support teachers' decision-making as well as provide an effective focus for professional development. McKay (1999b) has commented on issues in the use of samples of work for assessment and reporting in languages teaching, and reminds teachers that one or two samples of work cannot represent a level, since the decision on whether a level is reached should be taken after multiple readings over time of the students' level.

Reporting against standards is done differently for different audiences and purposes. In teacher-based assessment contexts, teachers' record keeping and reporting for teaching and learning purposes can be detailed and multifaceted, and often is (see for one example Barrs et al., 1988). Administrators, however, desiring less complexity and more manageability (Pusey, 1981), require reporting by numbers rather than through detailed, qualitative reports. Reducing student progress to numbers is not pedagogically useful for teachers (except as information about broad trends), nor is it a true reflection of the multifaceted progress (cultural knowledge, gains in confidence, and so on) that learners, especially ESL learners, make as they gain proficiency in English. Administrators need to be persuaded to collect qualitative information (concerning group progress, school progress, etc.) as well as statistical information. They also need to consider collecting base-line (i.e. entry) data for ESL learners, since otherwise, even though ESL learners progress at a faster rate than their English-speaking-background counterparts, their ranking on common report statements still appears deficient. Thus, the administrative-pedagogic tensions in the purposes and uses of standards flow into assessment and reporting practices.

Where assessment is carried out through standardized assessment, as for example in many EFL contexts, validity and reliability issues are no less salient. The ability of a necessarily very small sample of assessment tasks to represent the range of abilities described in the ELT Standards (Brindley's *generalizability* issue, described earlier in this section), presents just one of the myriad reservations about standardized assessment represented in current debates. Lachat (1999) has published professional development guidelines for teachers reporting against standards, and reporting formats and guidelines accompany some standards (e.g. the TESOL *ESL Standards, ESL Bandscales*; *Patterns of Learning,* Barrs et al., 1988). However, assessment and reporting against ELT standards, whether through teacher judgement or standardized assessment, will require major research attention for many years to come.

Impact of ELT Standards

A most pressing issue for those concerned with ELT standards relates to consequential validity or impact of the assessment and reporting practices on the lives of the ESL or EFL students being monitored (Bachman, 1990; Messick, 1989). McKay (1999a) reports on research in the United Kingdom and Canada that shows the deleterious effect on the morale of teachers of pupils who do not fit easily into the common standards of academic achievement and who consequently are perceived as failures. Students and their parents are inevitably affected by this type of reporting, believing often erroneously that their child is failing to progress well. They are affected further when league tables comparing school results are published in the general press, leading to, in some reported cases in England, deliberately hidden pockets of non-achieving ESL learners in otherwise successful schools (Gillborn & Gipps, 1996). The effect of accountability-driven ELT standards on indigenous populations is an area for further serious consideration, both with regard to appropriateness of language pathways and cultural content in descriptors (see Lo Bianco, 1999). Inevitably, in many countries where education is a limited commodity, the use of EFL standards will continue to be implicated in the raising of student and parent stress. These environments necessitate ongoing attention to the construction as well as assessment and reporting practices around ELT standards.

CONCLUSIONS

Since ELT standards are a relatively recent phenomenon, all of the issues raised in this chapter provide signposts to future directions for research. In order to recognize the scope of work currently being undertaken and advance this field of study, it is worth classifying research into ELT standards in the way it has been defined in this chapter: that is, research into the writing of ELT standards, the critiquing of ELT standards, and empirical research itself. An important direction for future research is the collating and sharing of this work.

However, it needs to be recognized that differences will inevitably exist amongst ELT standards since they (like language itself) will be adapted to local requirements, including the particular educational polices and purposes, the learner groups, the parental requirements, teacher abilities, and resources available in the local context. Despite these contextual variations, a common core of work around standards can be identified and needs to be investigated. McKay and Ferguson (2000) have suggested that the concept of a third place (after Kramsch, 1993) might be adopted to share knowledge and experience of ELT standards across contexts, including cultural and national boundaries. They suggest that professionals from different cultural and educational contexts can forge a new space for ideas by exchanging experiences and ideas through a professional third place. They can do this by recognizing and setting aside the culturally and contextually specific characteristics of their work (as far as this is possible) in order to offer a set of underlying principles to be discussed and considered further by the other professionals. From these third place ideas, we can perhaps investigate and seek clarity about the common issues.

REFERENCES

Bachman, L. F. (1990). *Fundamental considerations in language testing*. Oxford: Oxford University Press.
Bachman, L. F., & Palmer, A. S. (1996). *Language testing in practice*. Oxford: Oxford University Press.
Baker, R. (1997). *Classical test theory and item response theory in test analysis*. Lancaster: Lancaster University.
Barrs, M., Ellis, S., Hester, H., & Thomas, A. (1988). *Patterns of learning: The Primary Language Record and the National Curriculum*. London: Centre for Language in Primary Education.
Board of Studies Victoria. (1996). *ESL companion to the English curriculum standards framework (CSF)*. Melbourne: Board of Studies, Victoria.
Breen, M. P., Barratt-Pugh, C., Derewianka, B., House, H., Hudson, C., Lumley, T., & Rohl, M. (1997). *Profiling ESL children: How teachers interpret and use national and state assessment frameworks*. Canberra: Department of Employment, Education, Training and Youth Affairs.
Brindley, G. (1998). Outcomes-based assessment and reporting in language learning progammes: A review of the issues. *Language Testing, 15*(1), 45–85.
Brindley, G. (2001). Outcomes-based assessment in practice: Some examples and emerging insights. *Language Testing, 18*(4), 393–408.
Broadfoot, P. M. (1996). *Education, assessment and society: A sociological analysis*. Buckingham: Open University Press.
Butler, F. A., & Stevens, R. (1998). *Initial steps in the validation of the second language proficiency descriptors for public high schools, colleges, and universities in California: Writing*. Los Angeles: Center for the Study of Evaluation, Graduate School of Education and Information Studies, University of California, Los Angeles.
Clark, J. L., Scarino, A., & Brownell, J. A. (1994). *Improving the quality of learning: A framework for target-oriented curriculum renewal in Hong Kong*. Hong Kong: HongkongBank Language Development Fund/Institute of Language in Education.
Council of Europe. (1998). *Modern languages: Learning, teaching, assessment. A common European framework of reference*. Strasbourg: Council for Cultural Cooperation.

Cumming, A. (1999). The difficulty of standards, for example in L2 writing. In T. Silva & P. Matsuda (Eds.), *On second language writing* (pp. 209–229). Hillsdale, N.J.: Lawrence Erlbaum Publishers.

Cummins, J. (1983). Language proficiency and academic achievement. In J. Oller (Ed.), *Issues in language testing research* (pp. 108–126). Rowley, Mass.: Newbury House.

Curriculum Corporation. (1994). *ESL scales*. Melbourne: Curriculum Corporation.

Davison, C. (1999). Missing the mark: The problem with benchmarking of ESL students in Australian schools. *Prospect, 14*(2), 66–76.

Davison, C., & Williams, A. (2002). *Learning from each other: Critical connections. Studies of child English language and literacy development K-12,* Vol. 1. Melbourne: Language Australia.

Department of Education, Education, Training and Youth Affairs. (1998). *Literacy for all: The challenge for Australian schools*. Canberra: Australian Government Publishing Service.

Department of Education, South Africa. (1997). *Language, literacy and communication* (*Intermediate phase*). Pretoria: Department of Education, South Africa.

Department of Education, South Africa. (1997, October). *Intermediate phase policy document* (*Grades 4 to 6*). Pretoria: Department of Education, South Africa.

Derewianka, B. (1997). National developments in the assessment of ESL students. In M. P. Breen, C. Barratt-Pugh, B. Derewianka, H. House, C. Hudson, T. Lumley, & M. Rohl (Eds.), *Profiling ESL children: How teachers interpret and use national and state assessment frameworks* (pp. 15–65). Canberra: Department of Employment, Education, Training and Youth Affairs.

Education Department, Queensland. (2000). *Bandscales for Aboriginal and Torres Strait Islander learners*. Brisbane: Education Department, Queensland.

ESL Intersegmental Project Team. (1995). *California pathways: The second language student in public high schools, colleges and universities*. Los Angeles: California College Chancellor's Office, Intersegmental Joint Faculty Project.

Fullan, M. (2000). The return of large-scale reform. *Journal of Educational Change, 1,* 5–28.

Gillborn, D., & Gipps, C. (1996). *Recent research on the achievements of ethnic minority pupils*. London: Office for Standards in Education.

Griffin, P., & McKay, P. (1992). Assessment and reporting in the ESL Language and literacy in schools project. *NLLIA ESL development: Language and literacy in schools project: Vol. 2*. Canberra: National Languages and Literacy Institute of Australia.

Hammond, J., & Derewianka, B. (1999). ESL and literacy education: Revisiting the relationship. *Prospect, 14*(2), 24–40.

Ingram, D. (2001). Setting standards and measuring outcomes. *Babel. Journal of the Australian Federation of Modern Language Teachers Associations Inc, 36*(1), 4–9.

Kramsch, C. (1993). *Context and culture in language teaching*. Oxford: Oxford University Press.

Lachat, M. A. (1999). *Standards, equity and cultural diversity*. Rhode Island: Brown University (LAB): The Education Alliance.

Leung, C. (1996). English as an additional language within the National Curriculum: A study of assessment practices. *Prospect, 11*(2), 58–58.

Lo Bianco, J. (1999). Struggle to speak: Talking bilingual education and ESL into English literacy. *Prospect, 14*(2), 40–52.

McKay, P. (1995). Developing ESL proficiency descriptions for the school context. In G. Brindley (Ed.), *Language Assessment in Action* (pp. 31–63). Sydney: National Center for English Language Teaching and Research.

McKay, P. (1999a). Standards-based reform through literacy benchmarks: Comparisons between Australia and the United States. *Prospect, 14*(2), 52–65.

McKay, P. (1999b). The effectiveness of work samples as elaborations of profiles. Some comments based on the ACT LOTE work samples. *Babel. Journal of the Australian Federation of Modern Language Teachers Associations Inc, 34*(3), 21–25.

McKay, P. (2000a). *Innovation in English language assessment: Looking towards long-term learning.* In C. Davison, V. Crewe, & J. Hung (Ed.), Selected papers from the International Language in Education Conference (ILEC) 2000 Conference [CD Rom]. Hong Kong: The University of Hong Kong.

McKay, P. (2000b). On ESL standards for school-age learners. *Language Testing, 17*(2), 185–214.

McKay, P. (2001). Why standards? Looking beyond the technicalities of standards-based assessment. *Babel. Journal of the Australian Federation of Modern Language Teachers Associations Inc, 36*(1), 16–21.

McKay, P. (2006). *Assessing young language learners*. Cambridge: Cambridge University Press.

McKay, P., & Bond, T. (2002). *Validation and calibration of language Australia ESL bandscales. Research proposal to Australian Research Council*. Brisbane: Queensland University of Technology.

McKay, P., Coppari, P., Cumming, A., Graves, K., Lopriore, L., & Short, D. J. (2001a). Language standards: An international perspective, Part 1. *TESOL Matters, 11*(2), 1, 4.

McKay, P., Coppari, P., Cumming, A., Graves, K., Lopriore, L., & Short, D. J. (2001b). Language standards: An international perspective, Part 2. *TESOL Matters, 11*(3), 11, 15.

McKay, P., & Ferguson, R. (2000). English language standards for schools in Australia and China: Finding the 'third place'. In V. Berry & J. Lewkowicz (Eds.), *Assessment in Chinese contexts* (pp. 108–128). Hong Kong.

McKay, P., Hudson, C., & Sapuppo, M. (1994). *The NLLIA ESL Bandscales. ESL development: Language and literacy in schools: Vol. 2*. Canberra: National Languages and Literacy Institute of Australia.

McNamara, T. (1996). *Measuring second language performance*. London: Longman.

Messick, S. (1989). Validity. In R. L. Linn (Ed.), *Educational measurement* (pp. 13–104). New York: Macmillan.

Ministry of Education and Training. (1999). *The Ontario curriculum, Grades 9 to 12: English as a second language and English literacy development*. Toronto: Queen's Printer for Ontario.

Moore, H. (1995a). Telling the history of the 1991 Australian language and literacy policy. *TESOL in Context, 5*(1), 6–20.

Moore, H. (1995b). Telling what is real: Competing views in assessing ESL development. *Linguistics and Education, 8*, 189–228.

Moore, H. (2004). *Identifying the target population: A genealogy of policy-making for English as a second language (ESL) in Australian schools*. Unpublished doctoral thesis, Ontario Institute of Studies in Education, University of Toronto.

O'Malley, J. M., & Valdez Pierce, L. (1996). *Authentic assessment for English language learners*. New York: Addison-Wesley.

Ontario Institute of Studies in Education (OISE). (1993). Standards, benchmarks, and Ontario curriculum. A Special Report on Standards and Accountability [Special Issue]. *Orbit, 24*(2).

Phelps, R. (1998, Fall). The demand for standardized student testing. *Educational Measurement: Issues and Practice, 17*, 5–23.

Porter, R. P. (2000). Accountability is overdue: Testing the academic achievement of limited English proficient students. *Applied Measurement in Education, 13*(4), 403–410.

Pusey, M. (1981). The control of education in the 1980's. *Politics, 16*, 223–224.

Qualifications and Curriculum Authority. (2000). *A language in common: Assessing English as an additional language*. London: Qualifications and Curriculum Authority.

Sainsbury, M. (1997). Baseline assessment: How well did SCAA's three schemes work? *British Journal of Curriculum and Assessment, 7*(2), 14–19.

Scarino, A. (2001). The concept of standards. *Babel. Journal of the Australian Federation of Modern Language Teachers Associations Inc, 36*(1), 10–15.

Short, D. J. (2000). *The ESL standards: Bridging the academic gap for English language learners. Publisher details?* (ERIC Digest No. EDO-FL-00-13).

Short, D., Gomez, E., Cloud, N., Katz, A., Gottlieb, M., & Malone, M. (2000). *Training others to use the ESL standards: A professional development manual*. Alexandria, VA: TESOL.

Sizmur, S., & Sainsbury, M. (1997). Criterion-referencing and level descriptions in national curriculum assessment. *British Journal of Curriculum and Assessment, 7*(1), 9–11.

Strong-Krause, D. (2001). *English as a second language speaking ability: A study in domain theory development*. Unpublished doctoral dissertation, Brigham Young University, Salt Lake City.

TESOL. (1997). *ESL standards for pre-K-12 students*. Alexandria, VA: Teachers of English to Speakers of Other Languages.

The University of the State of New York, The State Education Department, & Office of Bilingual Education. (2001). *The teaching of Language Arts to limited English proficient/English language learners: Learning standards for English as a second language*. New York: The University of the State of New York.

Thomas, A. (2001). All they care about is the PACT test; they don't care if we learn anything. *Orbit, 31*.

Yu, C. M. & Taylor, W. L. (Eds.). (1998). *Title I at midstream: The fight to improve schools for poor kids*. Report of the Citizens' Commission on Civil Rights. Washington, D.C.: Citizens' Commission on Civil Rights.

CHAPTER 30

HIGH-STAKES TESTING AND ASSESSMENT:

English Language Teacher Benchmarking

DAVID CONIAM

The Chinese University of Hong Kong, China

PETER FALVEY

University of Cambridge Local Examinations Syndicate, UK

ABSTRACT

This chapter highlights the uncertainty, concerns, and approbation that accompany high-stakes language testing and assessment. It takes as a case study the language assessment of teachers of English in Hong Kong, and, in particular, the innovative performance test of teacher Classroom Language Assessment (CLA). The case study provides examples of major issues such as the validity and reliability of the assessments, the advantages and disadvantages of performance and criterion-referenced testing, and considers, within the issue of stakeholder involvement and reaction, the feedback from professional bodies and the concerns of those being assessed. Topics such as the relationship between academic concerns and the wishes of the clients (the Hong Kong SAR Government) are also discussed in order to explain the somewhat contradictory decisions that sometimes occur. The case study reveals how vital it is to consult and involve as many stakeholders as possible. The chapter ends with a summary of lessons that have been learned and areas for future research.

INTRODUCTION

At the beginning of the 21st century more attention than ever before is being paid to issues such as the efficiency and quality of personnel, the assessment of performance, cost-benefit analysis of human resources, and accountability in all walks of life. As a consequence, high-stakes assessment has been extended to an increasing number of contexts worldwide. High-stakes assessment occurs whenever an assessment or battery of assessment instruments is used to make decisions that affect individuals' lives in significant ways: for example, entry tests for tertiary institutions; assessments of professional competence that can affect matters such as substantiation, promotion, or termination of employment contracts; and access to membership of professional bodies, including the setting of standards for teacher certification. Standards in this context are defined as documented agreements containing technical specifications or other precise criteria to be used consistently as rules, guidelines, or definitions of characteristics, to ensure that materials, products, processes, and services are fit for their purpose (see Nunan, this volume, for a fuller discussion of the evolution of standards in English language teaching).

This chapter first introduces the concept and history of teacher language certification and its assessment. It then highlights the uncertainty, concerns, and approbation that accompany such high-stakes testing and assessment. It then focuses on the language assessment of teachers of English in Hong Kong, and, in particular, the innovative performance test of teacher Classroom Language Assessment (CLA). The case study explores major issues such as the validity and reliability of the assessments, the advantages and disadvantages of performance and criterion-referenced testing, and considers, within the issue of stakeholder involvement and reaction, the reaction of professional bodies and the concerns of those being assessed. Topics such as the relationship between academic concerns and the wishes of the clients (the Hong Kong SAR Government) are also discussed in order to explain the somewhat contradictory decisions that sometimes occur. The case study reveals how vital it is to consult and involve as many stakeholders as possible. The chapter ends with a summary of lessons that have been learned and the announcement that a project for the revision of the benchmark test (now renamed the Language Proficiency *Assessment for Teachers (English) [LPAT])* has been initiated five years since the first administration of the test. It is hoped that the revision project will allow issues discussed in this chapter to be addressed.

LANGUAGE TEACHER CERTIFICATION

The setting of standards for teacher certification is not a recent phenomenon. The most striking event in the history of certification occurred in 1980 when *Time Magazine,* cited in Soled (1995), published an authentic letter, written by a teacher in the USA: "Scott is dropping in his studies he acts as if he don't Care. Scott want to pass in his assignment at all, he had a poem to learn and fell to do it." In the furore that followed, the Holmes Group (1986) was established to address the concerns of parents and professionals in education and was instrumental in introducing teacher assessment, stating that one of the goals of assessment was to create professionally relevant and intellectually defensible standards for entry into the teaching profession. In 1998, 59% of 1,800 prospective teachers in Massachusetts failed their tests, and controversy erupted again (Massachusetts Department of Education, April 1998, p. 1). In the English language area there are also many examples of situations where tests have been introduced to address community concerns. For example, in Guam, when the quality of English language education was questioned by the US military, whose children attended local schools, tests of reading, writing, listening, and speaking were created for non-native speakers of English by a team led by Stansfield, Karl, and Kenyon (1990) to ensure that minimum agreed standards were reached by the non-native English-language-speaking teachers of English.

In any country, because of the very nature of professional evaluation, teacher assessment remains a high-stakes, sensitive issue. Soled (1995) notes that, in a survey of public attitudes, 85% of the general public in the USA thought that teachers should be required to pass competency tests. For public opinion to be acceptable, however, some rational justification needs to be presented. Thus, Soled argues that teacher assessment must be addressed for two reasons: to prevent incompetence in the classroom, and as part of the solution for an educational system with problems in both teacher preparation and professional practice.

In the USA, the National Board for Professional Teaching Standards investigated the implications of introducing procedures for the voluntary certification of teachers to a standard of "advanced competence" in levels of knowledge and skill (Sykes and Wilson, 1988). Most states now have some measure of certification for ESL instructors in place (see, e.g., Grant, 1995; Thomas & Monoson, 1993). Most of the certification tests focus on subject content knowledge, rather than on language ability per se, although Thomas and Monoson report, in relation to International Teaching Assistants (ITAs) who supervise undergraduate classes for their research supervisors, that "student complaints to legislators led to 20 states mandating higher educational institutions develop policy on oral English language proficiency of international teaching assistants" (p. 195). The 1989 annual conference of the National Association for Bilingual Education approved a number of issues relating to the advancement of bilingual education in the USA, one of which related to "language proficiency in English and non-English languages and abilities to teach in those languages." In a more recent paper, Grant (1995), however, notes that while methodology and theories of bilingual education are required in many states, "the 'second' language proficiency of the teacher is only sometimes addressed" (p. 2). In Australia, with regard to the teaching of languages other than English (LOTE), Elder (1994), describes her work with LOTE teachers and argues that assessing teachers' classroom language is a vital part of any form of language proficiency assessment for teachers using and teaching through that language. Commins (1996), in discussing minimum standards for LOTE teachers, describes what constitutes minimum skills/competency in language proficiency and professional practice for entry into the LOTE teaching profession (see also Iwashita, 1997; Brown, Hill, & Iwashita, 2000).

In the USA, teacher competency testing continues to be a major growth area in educational assessment, although language teacher competency assessment remains relatively underdeveloped. Education Testing Service (ETS, 2005) has developed the *Praxis Series* of certification tests for beginning teachers. This three-level series consists of (a) basic skills tests of literacy and numeracy; (b) subject-content tests; (c) Classroom Performance Assessments that measure a teacher's in-class ability as a practicing teacher.

In the difficult area of assessing pedagogical content knowledge, Carlson (1986, pp. 157-163) discusses early work that attempted "to create test items that require *application* of pedagogical knowledge to specific content areas" (pp. 159-160). In Canada, Harrold (1995) provides an overview of the certification/accreditation situation for ESL instructors of adults, and Lewin, Flewelling & Gagné (1996) propose the introduction of a teacher certification test to assess the language proficiency of second language teachers before being admitted to teacher education programs in Canada or being hired as an ESL teacher. Sanaoui (1998) reports on a project to develop a protocol and uniform standards for the certification of instructors who teach ESL to adults (in non-credit programs) in Ontario. Alderson, Clapham & Steel (1997) report on a project with university students of French in the UK to examine their subject content knowledge in French. In Asia, teacher certification is much less in evidence, although the call for standards is beginning to be made (e.g., Sadtono, 1995).

It is claimed that the setting of and adherence to standards in any industry lends the product or service credibility, providing consumers with assurances about the quality of the product or service (see McKay, this volume, for a fuller discussion of the ideology underpinning corporate managerialism and its applications to education). If the product/service is human (e.g., doctors, lawyers, and teachers), it is clearly vital that the assessment procedures, especially in high-stakes situations, have credibility. The notion of *due process* requires that full documentation is available to all stakeholders, including an effective mechanism for appeals against assessor judgments. This implies certain shared assumptions about the assessment process, which will be explored in the next section.

CHANGING ASSUMPTIONS AND ASSESSMENT PARADIGMS

The major testing and assessment paradigm for over 50 years stressed the reliability of test items over their validity because of concerns about consistency and fairness in testing and marking. In this paradigm, language tests often test segments of language (slot and gap filling exercises and multiple-choice items) rather than discourse-based "chunks" of language. Adherents assert that testing segments of language avoids testing elements of language other than the construct or skill being assessed. It is a paradigm that has focused more on the act of testing than on the more holistic paradigm of assessment.

The connotation of the term *assessment* and, in particular, *high-stakes assessment* embraces a wider set of parameters than the term *testing* which conjures up a formal, testing-room setting in which paper-and-pencil tests, usually of the multiple-choice variety, are attempted by the test takers, so the analysis of such tests can be deemed reliable. Reliability-focused testers feel that unless a test is reliable, questions about its validity are not worth considering. Such tests dominated the language testing arena for many years because the tests were deemed reliable, even though the tests contained no form of direct testing of communication through speaking (e.g., an interview) or writing (e.g., an extended piece of prose) (see Cumming, this volume, for a fuller discussion). However, amid late 20th century concerns about an over-emphasis on reliability, examination authorities such as the University of Cambridge Local Examinations Syndicate (UCLES) and its advocates asserted that there was a place for valid, direct tests, balanced with shorter multiple-choice segments.

Two trends in assessment are now increasingly dominant in the English language teaching field: criterion-referenced assessment (often linked to a task-based curriculum and assessment procedures in English language assessment); and competency-based assessment (often linked to vocational, and, increasingly, professional-based training and assessment). In discussing such developments in assessment, Griffin and Nix (1991) report that:

> There are various approaches to scoring tests and tasks set for the assessment (of students). It is not necessary to set tasks that have only a right/wrong or true/false scoring routine. Other modes of scoring are possible, some of which do not involve enumeration at all but instead, depend on *benchmark tasks or samples with which performances are compared.* The interpretation is made in terms of like performances. (p. 173) (emphasis added)

Brindley (1995, pp. 1-2) highlights the necessity for test developers to begin with a clear theoretical conceptualization of the abilities they are assessing and to "reality-test" their constructs against data from the target language use situation, a method used in the case-study discussed in this chapter. Brindley (1998) also argues that problems inherent in outcomes-based assessment and reporting on language learning programs can be alleviated by close consultation between policy-makers, administrators, and practitioners. Countries that have established an academically and professionally trained language teaching workforce (such as Australia) require teachers to undergo professional training before new forms of assessment can be exploited successfully, and descriptors of performance are made as explicit and transparent as possible.

This changed attitude to assessment, and the tools that have been developed to help assessors, appeals to those (testers, test-takers, and employers) who believe that the validity of assessment should have priority over concerns about reliability. Nevertheless, reliability should not be discounted or ignored. Although the validity of language performance takes precedence, the reliability of the assessors of language performance is also given great prominence. Such forms of direct assessment against known and agreed standards/ criteria/ benchmarks require the regular training and standardization of assessors. Furthermore, whenever new assessments are to take place, further training must be provided, particularly if there has been a significant time-gap between initial training and the administration of a new batch of assessments (see Lumley & McNamara, 1995).

THE HONG KONG CASE STUDY

In Hong Kong, less than 20% of the secondary workforce of English language teachers are both academically and professionally qualified (Tsui et al., 1994). Thus, the government has deemed it essential that teachers of English develop their second language skills as one of the prerequisites for being able to teach and adapt to new assessment methods and curricular objectives in their classrooms.

The use of standards in Hong Kong education has caused concern since its inception (Bickley, 1997). In the late 1980s, however, the language standards of teachers in Hong Kong, particularly teachers of English, became a pressing issue. The business community felt English language standards were dropping among the workforce (Au, 1998; Choi, 1998). This was worrying because higher standards were required as commerce moved from a predominantly manufacturing base to a service-led economy, dealing with the world through the medium of English every working day.

Significant findings emerged in Tsui (1993) and Tsui et al. (1994) where, of the full cohort of 3,700 secondary school teachers of English in 1993, only 14.2% were both subject and professionally trained. This clearly demonstrated that many teachers of English in secondary schools had received neither subject content nor professional training or were teachers of other subjects, forced to teach English because of a shortage of qualified staff. Many initiatives were therefore implemented to improve English language standards, and to improve the curriculum and examination systems. One such initiative by the Education Commission (established 1982), requested the Advisory Committee on Teacher Education and

Qualifications (ACTEQ) to investigate language benchmarks under two recommendations, C1 and C2, (Education Commission, 1996, p. 11):

> C1: The concept of 'benchmark' qualifications for all language teachers should be explored by the Advisory Committee on Teacher Education and Qualifications (ACTEQ) with a view to making proposals to the Government as early as possible in 1996.
>
> C2: Minimum language proficiency standards should be specified, which all teachers (not just teachers of language subjects) should meet before they obtain their initial professional qualification. The standards should be designed to ensure that new teachers are competent to teach through the chosen medium of instruction.

This meant that accepted and agreed standards, or benchmarks, were to be established both for teachers of languages and for teachers of subjects other than languages.

THE INITIAL 1996 CONSULTANCY STUDY AND FOLLOW-UP

In early 1996, Education and Manpower Bureau (EMB)—the policy branch of the educational arm of the Hong Kong Government—commissioned a short study to investigate the feasibility of benchmarks for teachers of the English language, Putonghua, and Chinese subjects. The study began in mid-April 1996, with the formation of a consultancy team. From the outset, the study was conceived as a collaborative venture between the tertiary institutes responsible for teacher education in Hong Kong. Other consultants and investigators were drawn from secondary, vocational, and tertiary institutions, as well as from the UK and the USA. The consultancy team was constituted to reflect a broad spectrum of expertise and experience from local and international language teachers and language teacher educators at primary and secondary levels, thus including as many stakeholders or their representatives as possible.

1996 Consultancy Study – Major Elements

The consultancy team viewed and analyzed many videos that had been collected by the consultants over 20 years of working with and observing English language teachers. The purpose of analyzing the videos was to define the underpinning constructs and skills that an English language teacher requires to attain a minimum standard in the target language in the English language classroom.

In addition, the expertise of UCLES and its Cambridge English Examination for Language Teachers, Level 1 (CEELT1) provided a variety of task types on which English language teachers could be assessed. As the study was a mere four months, a detailed case study approach was employed using the entire English language teaching cohort of three schools together with one cohort of postgraduate teachers in training. The four-month process consisted of video viewing to identify key constructs and skills; creating prototype specifications for assessment instruments; piloting a broad battery of tests; developing scales and descriptors; and conducting investigations in order to set preliminary prototype benchmark levels.

Survey data was collected at both local and international levels. Responses indicated widespread agreement for the establishing of minimum-standard language assessment (see Coniam & Falvey, 1999a).

Measures to promulgate the development of minimum-standard tests, involved public forums for teachers in July 1996, where there was a general acceptance of the government's desire to establish minimum standards for language ability, subject content knowledge, and teaching qualifications. The responses to both the questionnaire and public forums underpinned the initiatives of the Education Commission and ACTEQ to set benchmarks for minimum standards of language ability, subject content knowledge, classroom teaching ability, and teaching qualifications for the teaching profession in Hong Kong. The Professional Teachers' Union (PTU) initially reacted slowly to language benchmarks in 1997, conducting just one small-scale survey. However, once Government policy on the benchmark tests was finally declared in 2000, the PTU became much more vocal in its opposition to the mandatory imposition of language benchmarks for its serving teacher-certificated members.

One flaw in the process of consulting stakeholders in respect of the whole study was the assumption of the other major stakeholders that primary school teachers would react in ways similar to secondary school teachers, i.e. in broad agreement with the need to create and set standards. It is clear, in retrospect, that this large number of stakeholders (the most anxious as it later turned out) was not incorporated into the process as much as they should have been.

1996 Consultancy Study – Development of the Test Battery

In the construction of any assessment mechanism, it is useful if existing assessment material is available for reference and, if possible, adaptation. As consultancy team members had been involved in the development of the instruments for language teacher assessment at UCLES—CEELT1—this test formed the backbone for the initial battery of test types. In addition, a number of new test types—particularly for oral assessment and classroom language assessment—were developed and tested. Changes also occurred after feedback from the teachers and conceptual advice, assessment instrument moderation, and feedback from the group of consultants. This advice and feedback was particularly valuable for forming the constructs assessed in the different benchmarks, and, in particular, with regard to the validity of the tests.

While investigating classroom spoken discourse, Bachman (personal communication, March, 1996) suggested that analysis of teachers' classroom discourse may reveal language traits that lend themselves—from an assessment perspective—to task types that can be developed into live classroom language test types. This is operationalized in the 1996 report (Coniam & Falvey, 1996) under *Task-specific Specifications*, where the final specification (the *classroom oral language component*) requires teachers, under the "input format," to demonstrate language competence in presenting to and interacting with students.

The initial test battery comprised a three-part paper-and-pencil formal test component; an oral component; and an observation of two live lessons (the CLA performance test of an English teacher teaching two English lessons). The latter test is considered the most valid part of the test battery since it consists of a performance test during a genuine *target language use* situation (described in depth in Coniam & Falvey, 1999c).

Study – Recommendations on Language Ability Benchmarks

The 1996 consultancy study had a number of objectives, including how language benchmarks for lower secondary English language teachers might be formulated; the type(s) of assessment instruments appropriate for use with English language teachers; and the nature of the training programs needed, including length, course provider constitution, selection, and evaluation. In their report Coniam & Falvey (1996), the consultancy team therefore restated the exploratory nature and the limitations of the small-scale initial study—that the study was not to determine minimum language standards at the initial stage, but to investigate the feasibility of establishing minimum language standards for English language teachers. While it was important to make recommendations to the Hong Kong Government, it was also important that Government not take it for granted that setting minimum language standards had been accomplished in the initial study.

The questionnaire responses indicated that the vast majority of teachers believed that minimum standards for language ability should be a prerequisite for all teachers of English. It was therefore recommended to ACTEQ that in establishing *language ability* benchmarks, consideration should be given to benchmarking English language teachers in the following areas: (a) reading, (b) writing, (c) listening, (d) speaking, and (e) classroom language assessment. It was recommended that the first three of these areas be assessed through formal examinations; the fourth area (speaking) by interview and interaction; the final area by *direct assessment* in a live classroom setting.

The Language Benchmark Subject Committee: Purpose and Brief

The report was sent to ACTEQ in late 1996. One of the recommendations was that the next phase in developing benchmarks be undertaken by a broad-based committee, representative of all stakeholders in the teacher, teacher education, and education fields in Hong Kong. This committee, the English Language Benchmark Subject Committee (ELBSC), was convened in October 1997 under the auspices of the Hong Kong Examinations Authority (HKEA) to produce language benchmarks specifications and an assessment syllabus for promulgation to Hong Kong teachers of English language prior to a large-scale pilot exercise—the Pilot Benchmark Assessment (English), known as the *PBAE*.

Although the ELBSC was broad-based, one group of stakeholders was omitted. These were the representatives of the teachers' union, the PTU, whose main constituents are primary school teachers. They were excluded because Hong Kong Government policy makers felt that including the PTU and negotiating with them would render their benchmark timetable unmanageable.[1] Given the importance of including as many stakeholders as possible, this omission clearly breached the principle of stakeholder involvement and had severe consequences later on, especially when the benchmark test went "live." This represents a major issue in high-stakes assessment—policy considerations versus assessment principles.

It should be stressed that although the ELBSC was prepared to accept the 1996 Consultancy Study report and many of its recommendations, they considered it a working document rather than one to be merely endorsed. They subsequently held 32 meetings and demonstrated that their role was not merely to rubber-stamp the 1996 Consultancy Study report. Consequently, many amendments and changes were made to the recommendations of the 1996 Consultancy Study report.

Classroom Language Assessment

One major objective in developing the Hong Kong Classroom Language Assessment (CLA) criterion-referenced scales (with accompanying descriptors) was the desire for transparency so that teachers and informed lay persons, could, with appropriate training, reach similar grades when viewing videos of English teachers and rating them on the four CLA scales.

The CLA was discussed at length in the ELBSC. As Sanaoui (1999) notes, attempting to define what is fair, yet what also needs to be assessed in a performance test such as the CLA, lies in the assessment being determined by consensus across a group of informed stakeholders. Although English language teachers are accustomed to paper-and-pencil tests (having spent so long preparing their students for public examinations), and formal tests would be acceptable to local teachers of English language, live classroom testing was more threatening. The constructs assessed would need to be broad in terms of language skills to be assessed. In addition, the constructs to be established had to assess language only and not pedagogical skills or personality traits.

A Working Party for CLA was formed under the main ELBSC to examine the constructs, scales and descriptors formulated in the 1996 Consultancy Study report. The Working Party met six times, viewed a large number of videos, and identified the skills and constructs they felt appropriate to English language teachers. There was strong agreement that the four constructs, formulated in the 1996 Consultancy Study report, incorporated the essential English language skills required of teachers of English language to underpin the effective teaching of English. *Grammatical Accuracy* and *Pronunciation, Stress, and Intonation* are the two "formal" elements that define an English language teacher's ability in English. The other two elements, *The Language of Presentation/Practice* and *The Language of Interaction,* are functional realizations of a teacher's formal ability in English in terms of communicating with students and getting things done in the classroom. They might therefore be construed as the *specific purpose* language skills required by an English language teacher. Language skills which require the use of an appropriate register, the ability to select vocabulary appropriate to the level of students, to provide appropriate linguistic feedback in response to student initiations, to give instructions that are clear and unambiguous, etc. were identified, discussed, and prioritized. Scales and their descriptors were then formed to reflect those skills at various levels of ability.

The four scales and their associated descriptors of language performance were reached by the following methods:

1. observation of videoed English language lessons and the creation of a taxonomy of teacher language tasks;
2. development of prototype constructs, their moderation by experts and practitioners and the creation of scales and descriptors;
3. validation of the constructs and descriptors through moderation and empirical study;
4. submission of the prototypes to the ELBSC

The outcome of the study was a proposal by the ELBSC to ACTEQ for a five-level scale in which the mid-point—Level 3—was identified as a tentative benchmark level.

By June 1998, after considerable and detailed examination of videos to investigate the operationalizability of the scales and descriptors, the specifications of the scales after revision, modification, and amendment were resolved as follows: (a) grammatical accuracy; (b) pronunciation, stress, and intonation; (c) the language of interaction; and (d) the language of instruction.

ELBSC—Commentary

The working party subgroups examined, discussed, moderated, and refined the constructs, scales, and descriptors, and the texts and tasks that comprised each test type. It was apparent, however, that the tests and test material needed to be trialed and validated. For some of the test types, validation exercises of the test material or of the training and standardization of assessors were conducted, the subjects consisting of in-service and pre-service teachers. To assist the ELBSC in its deliberations, a number of studies were conducted by the consultants focusing on the validation of the assessment instruments and the training and standardization of assessors for the criterion-referenced tests (Coniam & Falvey, 1998a, 1998b, 1998c; Falvey & Coniam, 1999a, 1999b). Nonetheless, it was not possible to trial all test types that the ELBSC recommended. No trialing or piloting of any of the test material for the listening test was possible. The listening test that emerged suffered, not surprisingly, from deficiencies. The writing test similarly underwent several changes and, although it was piloted, it was still being reformulated as Government policy was being made public in mid 2000. Once again, time constraints and policy needs vied with assessment principles. The syllabus specification document, produced by the ELBSC, was published by ACTEQ (1998) as an orientation document for those who would participate in the PBAE pilot test.

THE PILOT BENCHMARK ASSESSMENT (ENGLISH)

Introduction

The PBAE ran from November 1998 to January 1999, and involved large-scale testing of all the assessment instruments proposed and developed by the ELBSC. This exercise formed the test-bed for all the constructs, the benchmarks, and the assessment instruments that had been developed by the consultants and then the ELBSC in the 2 ½ years prior to its administration. It lasted 4 months because each teacher had to be observed teaching his/her own English language class twice, as called for by the CLA component of the benchmark test. A Benchmark Assessment Unit, working under the HKSAR Government's Education Department and rigorously trained by the consultants, began assessing over 320 teachers for the CLA component of the PBAE in November 1998, finishing in January 1999. The paper-and-pencil tests were then administered in early February 1999.

The PBAE was the focal point for the development of the benchmark initiative thus far. The prototype constructs, scales and descriptors—in the context of the whole test battery—were field tested on an intended representative sample of lower secondary teachers of English and the results reported to the ELBSC. The ELBSC were satisfied that the CLA and the Speaking Test had high validity (as perceived by both test makers and test takers) and good rater reliability between raters. The ELBSC recommended that further research was needed to produce a more valid writing test in terms of teacher writing tasks and further research to ascertain what was achievable in 90 minutes (their preferred time frame). The ELBSC were not satisfied with the format of the reading and listening tests. These traditional *read-and-answer-the-questions* tests had received criticism from teachers for being discrete tests of listening or reading—formats abandoned in the local Hong Kong public examinations for more integrated skills tests. Recommendations to trial new formats were forwarded to Government, but the policy needed to go public with the examinations and lack of time for research prevented further development.

Teacher Performance on the PBAE

Prior to the PBAE, the ELBSC felt that no exemptions from any of the benchmark tests should be allowed. The results of the PBAE were, however, surprising and, to an extent, gratifying in relation to results, qualifications, and relevant background. On all tests, the highest scoring group comprised secondary school teachers with a relevant degree and postgraduate professional training. On CLA, this group achieved close to the level designated "above the benchmark." Similarly, on the paper-and-pencil tests, this group of teachers achieved the best results on all the tests. As a result, it was recommended that this group of teachers should be exempt from the paper-and-pencil tests. This recommendation was not, however, accepted when the benchmark requirements were published; the lack of exemptions caused strong resentment and an immediate backtrack by Government.

A further option, adopted by Government was that each scale of each test must be passed (referred to by Alderson, Clapham, & Wall, 1995, p. 154, as having to jump "hurdles"). This also had serious consequences for pass rates when the test first went "live" (see Coniam & Falvey, 2001).

Going Live: The First Administration of the Benchmark Test

This section looks at developments following the PBAE, issues related to the publishing of the benchmark policy, and associated matters such as the granting of exemptions. It also focuses on official benchmark policy; the HKSAR Government's intention to raise standards, including resources for upgrading; language enhancement programs; and, in 2005, a policy decision to initiate a review and revision study of the benchmark test.

The benchmark examination syllabus was published in mid-2000, and a series of six seminars was held to explain government policy. The seminars were attended by approximately 10,000 teachers. It was, however, the first time that the PTU had been able to comment publicly on the benchmark issue. Consequently, the seminars managed to convey little of the spirit of the government's intention to upgrade the English of the teaching profession. Rather, the benchmark tests were viewed by teachers, especially primary school teachers, as a stick with which Government intended to beat English language teachers. It should be noted, however, that the achievement of the benchmark did not rely solely on test-taking. Instead, a considerable amount of Government resources ($30 million) were earmarked to allow "at risk" teachers (later, most teachers) to attend language enhancement courses.

In the years since its first administration in 2001, the benchmark test has been investigated and discussed by a number of researchers – from the perspectives of the test's advantages (McGrath, 2000), as well as its perceived problems (Glenwright, 2002; Glenwright, 2005). The problems associated with the overall pass mark—one which has caused grave dissatisfaction amongst test takers—have been investigated and discussed in Coniam and Falvey (2001). Whether or not standards as currently set actually reflect the need of the current English language teaching profession in Hong Kong is therefore one of the key issues which needs to be investigated.

After five years of administration of the test, the HKSAR Government recognized that some of the issues warranted further investigation. As a result, in mid 2005, the Government issued a brief for consultants to investigate the current situation and propose what, if any, changes should be made to the English language benchmark test. This will enable the consultants appointed to consider all the issues that have arisen since the first administration.

CONCLUSIONS

The benchmark test is merely one element in the HKSAR Government's desire to upgrade teacher levels of English. In addition to considerable resources for teachers' enhancement programs, teachers who enroll in them can choose to be "benchmarked" by the institution running the program rather than by the HKEA-provided benchmark test. Serving teachers had until 2005 to be benchmarked. Possibly because of the adverse public reaction to the first live test, many teachers decided either to wait and see how government policy on benchmarks would develop or chose to enroll in an enhancement program instead.

In retrospect, the two major factors that damaged the overall assessment project were time constraints and lack of consultation with one large stakeholder constituency, that is, primary teachers. However, one success has been the acceptance by all stakeholders of the classroom language assessment component of the CLA as a valid assessment instrument.

In spite of problems with the English language benchmark test itself, attention has been focused on the large number of teachers teaching English who are not capable of doing so effectively. The benchmark test is one method for deciding who should be permitted to teach English in Hong Kong's classrooms, and all pre-service teachers will be benchmarked in the future.

The time frame for the test was over-ambitious and the test suffered inevitable developmental and teething problems. However, the HKSAR Government's language policy and language benchmark policy in particular will benefit from the decision to revise this high-stakes examination, and will lead to higher English language standards in Hong Kong schools.

NOTES

[1] There was a very tight time frame in which to implement the benchmark policy. In large part, this was due to the inauguration of the Chief Executive of the new Hong Kong Special Administrative Region (HKSAR), who stated in his October 1997 address (Tung, 1997, paragraph 87) that all new teachers would be required to meet the benchmarks before they join the profession in 2000.

REFERENCES

Advisory Committee on Teacher Education and Qualifications. (1998). *Syllabus specifications: Specimen questions and notes for classroom language assessment.* Hong Kong: Government Printer.
Alderson, J. C., Clapham, C., & Steel, D. (1997). Metalinguistic knowledge, language aptitude and language proficiency. *Language Teaching Research, 1*(2), 93–121.
Alderson, J. C., Clapham, C., & Wall, D. (1995). *Language test construction and evaluation.* Cambridge: Cambridge University Press.
Au, A. (1998). Language standards and proficiency. In B. Asker (Ed.), *Teaching language and culture: Building Hong Kong on education* (pp. 179–183). Hong Kong: Longman.
Bachman, L. (1996). Personal communication, March 1996.
Bickley, G. (1997). *The golden needle: The biography of Frederick Stewart (1836–1889).* Hong Kong: David C. Lam Institute for East West Studies.
Brindley, G. (Ed.). (1995). *Language assessment in action.* Sydney: NCELTR.
Brindley, G. (1998). Outcomes-based assessment and reporting in language learning programmes: A review of the issues. *Language Testing, 15*(1), 45–85.
Brown, A., Hill, K. & Iwashita, N. (2000). Is learner progress in LOTE learning comparable across languages? *Australian Review of Applied Linguistics, 23*(2), 35–60.
Carlson, R. E. (1986, April 16–20). *Field-test data vs. real-test data.* Paper presented at the 67th Annual Meeting of the American Educational Research Association, San Francisco, CA.
Choi, C-C. (1998). Language standards: An HKEA perspective. In B. Asker (Ed.), *Teaching language and culture: Building Hong Kong on education* (pp. 184–192). Hong Kong: Longman.
Commins, L. (1996). *Minimum Competency Standards for LOTE Teaching.* Nathan, Qld: The National Languages and Literacy Institute of Australia; Language Testing and Curriculum Centre. (NLLIA-LTACC); Griffith University.
Coniam, D., & Falvey, P. (1996). *Setting language benchmarks for English language teachers in Hong Kong secondary schools.* Hong Kong: Advisory Committee on Teacher Education and Qualifications.
Coniam, D., & Falvey, P. (1998a). *Piloting the multiple-choice cloze test: The Hong Kong English language benchmarking initiative.* Hong Kong: Advisory Committee on Teacher Education and Qualifications.
Coniam, D., & Falvey, P. (1998b). *Validating the classroom language assessment component: The Hong Kong English Language benchmarking initiative.* Hong Kong: Advisory Committee on Teacher Education and Qualifications.
Coniam, D., & Falvey, P. (1998c). *Validating the reading test: The Hong Kong English Language benchmarking initiative.* Advisory Committee on Teacher Education and Qualifications: Hong Kong.
Coniam, D. & Falvey, P. (1999a). Setting standards for teachers of English in Hong Kong—The teachers' perspective. *Curriculum Forum, 8*(2), 1–27.
Coniam, D., & Falvey, P. (1999b). The English language benchmarking initiative: A validation study of the Classroom Language Assessment component. *Asia Pacific Journal of Language in Education, 2*(2), 1–35.

Coniam, D., & Falvey, P. (1999c). *The English language benchmarking initiative: Pre-pilot benchmark assessment validation studies and assessor training programmes—An overview.* Hong Kong: Advisory Committee on Teacher Education and Qualifications.

Coniam, D., & Falvey, P. (2001). Awarding passes in the Language Proficiency Assessment of English Language Teachers: Different methods, varying outcomes. *Education Journal, 29*(2), 23–35.

Education Commission. (1996). *Education Commission Report No. 6.* (ECR 6). Hong Kong: Government Printer.

Elder, C. (1994). Performance testing as a benchmark for LOTE teacher education. *Melbourne Papers in Language Testing, 3*(1), 1–25.

ETS. (2005). *The Praxis Series: Professional Assessments for Beginning Teachers®.* Retrieved 25 September 2005, from http://www.ets.org/praxis/.

Falvey, P., & Coniam, D. (1998). *Report on the pre-pilot exercise for the rewriting and speaking components of the English language benchmark project.* Hong Kong Examinations Authority.

Falvey, P., & Coniam, D. (1999a). *Assessor training and standardisation for the speaking test: The Hong Kong English Language Benchmarking Initiative.* Hong Kong: Advisory Committee on Teacher Education and Qualifications.

Falvey, P., & Coniam, D. (1999b). *Assessor training and standardisation for the writing test: The Hong Kong English language benchmarking initiative.* Hong Kong: Advisory Committee on Teacher Education and Qualifications.

Glenwright, P. (2002). Language proficiency assessment for teachers: The effects of benchmarking on writing assessment in Hong Kong schools. *Assessing Writing, 8*(2), 84–109.

Glenwright, P. (2005). Grammar error strike hard: Language proficiency testing of Hong Kong teachers and the four "noes". *Journal of Language, Identity and Education, 4*(3), 201–226.

Grant, L. (1995). *Testing bilingual teachers' language proficiency: The case of Arizona.* Educational Testing Service: Princeton, N.J.

Griffin, P., & Nix, P. (1991). *Educational assessment and reporting: A new approach.* Marrickville, NSW: Harcourt Brace Jovanovich.

Harrold, D. K. (1995). Accreditation/certification for adult ESL instructors in Canada: An overview. *TESL Canada Journal, 13*(1), 37–62.

Holmes Group. (1986). *Tomorrow's teachers.* East Lansing, MI: The Holmes Group, Inc.

Iwashita, N. (1997). Assessment of oral communication skills in LOTE settings in Australia. *Melbourne Papers in Language Testing 6*(2), 37–44.

Lewin, L., Flewelling, J., & Gagné, A. (1996). Meeting the challenge: The creation of a communicative test for evaluating the proficiency of second language teachers. *Mosaic, 4*(1), 9–14.

Lumley, T., & McNamara, T. F. (1995). Rater characteristics and rater bias: Implications for training. *Language Testing, 12*(1), 54–71.

Massachusetts Department of Education. (1998, July 2). *Board in brief on the Massachusetts teacher tests.* Report on the special meeting of the Board held 1 July 1998. Retrieved 23 July 2002 from http://www.doe.mass.edu/boe/bib/bib98/7298a.html.

McGrath, I. (2000). Language and the pre-service practicum. In J. Hung, V. Berry, V. Crew & C. Davison (Eds.), D*iscourses and development in language education* (pp. 157–172). Hong Kong: International Language in Education Conference.

Sadtono, E. (1995, April 12–15). *The standardization of teacher trainees in EFL countries.* Paper presented at the 2nd International Conference on Language in Development: The Stakeholders' Perspectives. Denpasar, Bali.

Sanaoui, R. (1998). Recommendations for a protocol and uniform certification standards for non-credit adult ESL instructors in Ontario. *Contact, 24*(3), 6–9.

Sanaoui, R. (1999, February 2). *Defining certification standards for ESL instructors in Ontario.* Talk delivered to the Advisory Committee on Teacher Education and Qualifications. Hong Kong.

Soled, S. W. (1995). The role of assessment in teacher education. In S. W. Soled (Ed.), *Assessment testing and evaluation in teacher education* (pp. 1–8). Norwood, NJ: Ablex.

Stansfield, C. W., Karl, J., & Kenyon, D. M. (1990). *The Guam educators' test of English proficiency (GETEP).* Final project report [revised]. Washington, D.C.: Center for Applied Linguistics.

Sykes, G., & Wilson, S. M. (1988). *Professional standards for teaching: The assessment of teacher knowledge and skills.* Washington, D.C.: Office of Educational Research and Improvement (ED).

Thomas, C. F., & Monoson, P. K. (1993). Oral English language proficiency of ITAs: Policy, implementation, and contributing factors. *Innovative Higher Education, 17*(3), 195–209.

Tsui, A. B. M. (1993). *Report to the Hong Kong Language Campaign.* Hong Kong: Hong Kong Language Campaign.

Tsui, A. B. M., Coniam, D., Sengupta, S., & Wu, K. Y. (1994). Computer-mediated communication and teacher education: The case of TELENEX. In N. Bird, P. Falvey, A. B. M. Tsui, & A. McNeill (Eds.), *Language and learning* (pp. 352–369). Hong Kong: Government Printer.

Tung, C. H. (1997, October 8). *Policy address: Building Hong Kong for a new era.* Hong Kong: Government Printer.

CHAPTER 31

NEW DIRECTIONS IN TESTING ENGLISH LANGUAGE PROFICIENCY FOR UNIVERSITY ENTRANCE

ALISTER CUMMING

The University of Toronto, Canada

ABSTRACT

This chapter reviews recent trends in the conceptualizations and formats of tests used to determine whether non-native speakers of English have sufficient proficiency in English to study at English-medium universities in English-dominant countries. The review focuses on published research informing a new version of the Test of English as a Foreign Language (TOEFL), but a range of similar tests internationally is also considered. Prominent among the issues guiding research and development on these tests are the following: construct validation, particularly refinements in the description of testing purposes, evaluations of the discourse produced in the contexts of testing, and surveys of relevant domains and score users; consistency, including fairness in opportunities for test performance across differing populations, reliability through field-testing and equating of test forms, and sampling of multiple, comparable performances from examinees; and innovations in the media of test administration, including various forms of computer and other technological adaptations.

INTRODUCTION

How can we know if a person whose dominant language is not English has sufficient proficiency in English to be able to study effectively in an academic program at an English-medium university, or at least to do so without undue disadvantages related to language proficiency? How might this decision be made fairly, on a regular and consistent basis many times each year, and without inordinate expenses for people from diverse language and cultural backgrounds around the world wishing to study at universities in the United States, Canada, the United Kingdom, Australia, or New Zealand? Can the decision be sufficiently trustworthy and reliable to satisfy university registrars, program administrators, and professors in these countries as well as over a million adults around the world who wish to have their English assessed for these purposes each year? Can the decision be equally appropriate for people wishing to study in different institutions, different academic disciplines, or different types of degree programs?

These are the principal demands associated with tests that screen candidates internationally for their English language proficiency for university admissions. As Spolsky's (1995) history of language testing amply demonstrates, screening students' English proficiency for university entrance increasingly over the past century has assumed the foreground of developments in language testing, but it is a situation that has always involved controversies, compromises, and innovations. For a single test to be able to provide information that indicates whether people have achieved high levels of proficiency in a second language—and to do so comprehensively, validly, reliably, regularly, economically, and fairly throughout the world—is exceptionally demanding. This is true in conceptualizing the appropriate content of a test as well as in the technical, logistical, and political aspects of producing and administering it consistently.

For tests such as the Test of English as a Foreign Language (TOEFL), the past decade has been the most active period of deliberation, research, and innovation since the test was first developed in the early 1960s. The purpose of this chapter is to review key trends associated with these innovations, as documented in recently published reports and articles. I first outline some of the factors that motivated or informed the new directions in these tests. Then I discuss three major issues defining these new directions.

BACKGROUND TO TEST REVISIONS

The impetus to reconceptualize English language tests for university admissions has arisen from a combination of interrelated factors. These factors include evident limitations in existing tests and educational practices associated with them; continuing expectations for high professional standards in these tests (because of the important consequences they exercise for examinees and institutions of higher education alike); the increasing spread of English globally; demands for universities and colleges to accommodate greater numbers of students from diverse backgrounds and around the world; requests for pedagogically useful information about the abilities of students tested; and opportunities provided by new technologies for test delivery and analyses.

Over the past decade, there have been many published criticisms and reviews of current testing practices, theoretical conceptualizations or models, and relevant empirical research. For instance, Spolsky (1995) traced the history of decisions leading to the current specifications for the TOEFL and International English Language Testing Service (IELTS) critiquing the fundamental idea that "language proficiency can be measured simply" (p. 346). Likewise, Alderson and Clapham (1992) reviewed the history of the English Language Testing Service's test, outlining how and why in the 1980s the test's notional/functional model of English proficiency was modified into the IELTS, now widely used for university admission decisions in the U.K., Australia, New Zealand, and Canada (Charge & Taylor, 1997). Various critical analyses of particular components of these tests have appeared: for instance, of the reading components in the TOEFL (Peirce, 1992) or IELTS (Clapham, 1996; Wallace, 1997), writing tasks for the TOEFL previously known as the *Test of Written English* (Connor-Linton, 1995; Greenberg, 1986; Raimes, 1990), or IELTS's oral interviews (Brown, 2003; Ross & Berwick, 1992; Young & He, 1998). Perhaps the strongest criticisms to emerge are that the testing formats emphasize single, simple genres of language performance (i.e. multiple-choice questions on brief reading passages, writing a simple, single-draft essay, or responding in an oral interview) or discrete types of knowledge about English (i.e. grammar or vocabulary) that can easily be coached, leading students to study or practice formal or restricted features of English—related to the narrow range of the test items, and thus producing an undesirable washback—to "pass the test" rather than to develop their proficiency broadly for university studies or their future careers

(Alderson & Hamp-Lyons, 1996; Bailey, 1999; Elson, 1992; Hamp-Lyons, 1998; Roberts, 2000). Other problematic issues that have emerged are discussed in the following section.

Research Informing New Test Formats

The most extensive and programmatic analyses related to English proficiency tests for university admissions have been co-ordinated through a long-term project at Educational Testing Service (ETS), initially called *TOEFL 2000*, that started in the early 1990s and continues at present, aimed at the development and validation of a new TOEFL. Jamieson et al. (2000) described the guiding purpose of the project:

> a new TOEFL test that: (1) is more reflective of communicative competence models; (2) includes more constructed-response tasks and direct measures of writing and speaking; (3) includes more tasks that integrate the language modalities tested; and (4) provides more information than current TOEFL scores do about international students' ability to use English in an academic environment. (pp. 3-6)

Initiatives in Europe, Australia, and elsewhere have also appeared but have been less extensive. These include, for example, revisions to IELTS (e.g., as described by Charge & Taylor, 1997; Clapham, 1996), numerous books appearing in the series *Studies in Language Testing* produced by the University of Cambridge Local Examinations Syndicate (UCLES) as well as Research Notes published since 2000 (www.cambridgeesol.org/rs_notes/index.cfm) and research reports published by IELTS Australia since 1998 (www.ielts.org/teachersandresearchers/research/default.aspx), or studies related to the development of a common framework for language studies in the European Community (e.g., North, 2000). Cross-national concerns for analyzing these English proficiency tests are evident in Bachman et al.'s (1995) systematic comparison of the content and format of the TOEFL with Cambridge's *First Certificate in English*.

Leading up to these initiatives, fundamental criticisms of the current version of the TOEFL started to emerge in the early 1990s. These were expressed distinctly by the test's own Committee of Examiners who argued that the model of language proficiency underpinning the test did not conform to theoretical concepts of communicative competence predominant in applied linguistics (Chapelle, Grabe, & Berns, 1997; Spolsky, 1995). In response to these concerns, ETS commissioned a number of scholars of language testing to review recent research that might identify theoretical constructs relevant to the test's assessments of reading (Hudson, 1996), speaking (Douglas, 1997), and writing (Hamp-Lyons & Kroll, 1997) as well as to review recent surveys of the needs associated with students using English in universities in North America (Ginther & Grant, 1996; Waters, 1996), psychometric issues associated with performance assessment (Carey, 1996), and issues of washback in language testing (Bailey, 1999). No definitive answers about test design emerged from these reviews because the full scope of the issues had not previously been investigated, but these reviews did identify many concerns and perspectives for future inquiry and development. About the same time, staff at ETS and other scholars were conducting various research projects into specific issues that might likewise inform revisions to the TOEFL. For example, Hale et al. (1996) surveyed writing tasks in academic courses at U.S. universities. Schedl et al. (1996) analyzed the dimensionality of the reading component of the TOEFL, and Wainer and Lukhele (1997) assessed comparable subsections (i.e. *testlets*) for reading and listening comprehension in the TOEFL for their reliability.

The framework for TOEFL 2000 prepared by Jamieson et al. (2000) consolidated many of these emerging ideas while establishing a basis to conceptualize and organize the domain of a new version of the TOEFL, to identify and operationalize relevant task characteristics and variables, and to validate and interpret these. Their framework was elaborated further by teams of experts (from within as well as outside of ETS) that proposed parallel developments to the test for the components of listening (Bejar et al., 2000), speaking (Butler et al., 2000), reading (Enright et al., 2000), and writing (Cumming et al., 2000). While these projects were underway in the late 1990s, ETS also converted the existing version of the TOEFL to a computer format in many parts of the world. This move was preceded by studies of computer familiarity among the population of TOEFL examinees (Kirsch et al., 1998; Taylor et al., 1999).

PROMINENT ISSUES

Three issues have figured centrally in discussions, research, and development for new versions of these tests: construct validation, consistency, and new media. Each of these issues remains, however, in a process of development as new advances appear, new research data accumulate, and prototype tasks are piloted, evaluated, and refined. At the time of publication of the present volume, the content of a new TOEFL has been outlined in the form of a handbook for teachers and assessors (ETS, 2002); validation studies are in progress to establish equivalencies of scores between the former and new components of the test and for local universities to set new admission standards correspondingly; and a new form of the test, as an Internet-based test (TOEFL iBT), is to be launched in North America in the autumn of 2005, then other parts of the world in phases through 2006.

Construct Validation

The conceptual foundation guiding revisions to TOEFL, IELTS, and other such tests has been to improve their construct validity. This follows a major trend in test design over the past decade, building on the theoretical frameworks for establishing evidence for test validity outlined by Messick (1988, 1989) and Moss (1992), consolidated into professional standards for educational and psychological assessment (AERA, APA, & NCME, 1999), and adopted widely for language testing (as described by Alderson & Banerjee, 2002; Bachman, 2000; Chapelle, 1998; Cumming, 1996; Kunnan, 1998; and Weir, 2005). Key questions from this viewpoint are: *Does the test assess what it claims to assess? What evidence exists for this in the interpretations and uses of the test?* Looking critically at the current TOEFL and IELTS, the professional consensus was that these questions could not be answered with certainty. So these tests require new specifications and frameworks that will allow their construct validity to be evaluated or demonstrated, to align them with current, relevant theories such as communicative competence or academic language proficiency (that describe people's performance abilities rather than abstract specifications of knowledge such as *grammar* or *vocabulary*), and to develop programs of research to establish evidence of various kinds to demonstrate that the tests actually fulfill their purposes.

Three complementary approaches have been taken to develop the construct validity of the tests. The principal approach has been to identify precisely the content and purpose of the tests, the tasks suitable for realizing these constructs, the rationales for them, and the variables that might influence them. This step aims to clarify what the test intends to assess so that test scores can be interpreted meaningfully, analyses can verify whether the intentions are realized or not, and adjustments can be made accordingly (i.e. to eliminate irrelevant sources of variation in test scores that are not directly related to the chief construct). Jamieson et al. (2000) spelled out a detailed, long-term program for developing a new TOEFL along these lines, proposing methods for specifying and validating variables empirically in the manner established recently for various tests of adult literacy. In turn, to implement this framework, teams of testing experts and educational researchers from within ETS and various universities produced reports that—for the modalities of reading (Enright et al., 2000), writing (Cumming et al., 2000), speaking (Butler et al., 2000), and listening (Bejar et al., 2000), respectively—reviewed recent theories and research: (a) to conceptualize the relevant constructs of academic language proficiency, (b) to specify appropriate task domains and situational features, (c) to identify key variables and task characteristics integral to them, (d) to propose agendas for research and development, and (e) to exhibit prototypical task types to be field-tested for consideration for the test.

In the process, conventional expectations for language assessment have been refined considerably. For example, the assessments of reading proposed by Enright et al. (2000) for a new TOEFL focus on four purposes of text comprehension considered integral to academic studies: reading to find information, for basic information, to learn, and to integrate information. More radical are the redefinitions of constructs that integrate language modalities (e.g., reading-writing, reading-speaking, listening-speaking, etc. in conjunction) rather than assessing them as single modalities (i.e., as had been established as conventional practices since Carroll's 1975 general distinction between tests of reading, writing, speaking, and listening broadly but vaguely defined as *language skills*). That is, the constructs to be assessed are language modalities in combination, not just separate abilities, as deemed relevant to academic performance in English. Field testing and analyses of prototype tasks following this design for a new TOEFL are well under way (e.g., Enright & Cline, 2002). Ironically in view of these developments for the TOEFL, the thematic links between reading and writing modules that were once featured in the IELTS have been removed in the interests of improving the test's construct validity, that is, by eliminating "the potential for confusing the assessment of reading ability with the assessment of writing ability" (Charge & Taylor, 1997, pp. 375-376). Wallace (1997), among others, has argued that this step reduces the authenticity or educational relevance of the IELTS, despite the test designers' aim of clarifying the constructs assessed.

The second approach to construct validation evaluates whether test tasks actually elicit the discourse they are intended to elicit. This approach is particularly suited to performance evaluations that involve examinees in the extended production of speech or writing (McNamara, Hill, & May, 2002). For example, Sullivan, Weir, and Saville (2002) reported on applications of an observation checklist of language functions to evaluate whether interviews for UCLES' Main Suite of tests (e.g., First Certificate in English) elicited the range of speech functions among examinees that the tasks were designed to elicit. Likewise, Lazarton and Wagner (1996) and

Lazaraton (2002) conducted detailed discourse analyses to verify whether the speech functions intended in revisions to the *Test of Spoken English* (Douglas & Smith, 1997) actually appeared in examinees' speech, and how these functions varied among native and nonnative speakers of English taking the test. Iwashita, McNamara, and Elder (2001) similarly used discourse analyses to determine if varying the conditions of fluency, complexity, and accuracy (following Skehan, 1998) in prototype tasks being considered for the new TOEFL significantly affected examinees' speech performance. From a different perspective, Cumming, Kantor, and Powers (2001, 2002) analyzed the verbal reports of groups of raters of ESL compositions, finding that the decisions they made while scoring diverse text types written for prototype tasks for the new TOEFL compared, but involved some additional considerations, to the decisions they made for the TOEFL essay that now appears in the test. The empirical evidence emerging from this perspective on test validation requires sound theoretical conceptualizations about second language acquisition and performance abilities (e.g., Brindley, 1998; Fulcher, 1996; Harley et al., 1990).

The third approach to construct validity looks more broadly to the domains relevant to the test, seeking to refine or specify characteristics of the abilities needed for academic performance in English. As Fulcher (1999) has argued, ensuring the integrity of the constructs defining a language test (as prescribed by Messick's model of construct validation) is more vital than having content in a test that appears superficially to be specific to an academic field (as conventionally prescribed by needs analysis in specific-purpose testing and dismissed by Clapham's 1996 research for the IELTS). For this reason, the survey undertaken by Rosenfeld, Leung, and Oltman (2001) of various university professors and students used the metaphor of a *job analysis* (i.e. the job of being a student in English) to request people's evaluations of the task statements guiding the design of prototype tasks for a new TOEFL. Studies such as Elder (1993) have likewise looked to the viewpoints of subject matter specialists to determine their views on language proficiency. Numerous unique approaches are being taken from this perspective. For instance, Bridgeman, Cline, and Powers (2002) matched scores on prototype tasks for a new TOEFL against such indicators as placements in ESL and academic programs, teachers' judgments of their students' abilities, and students' self-assessments of their own abilities in English. Similarly, Cumming et al. (2004) asked experienced ESL instructors to evaluate the appropriateness of specifications for tasks for the new TOEFL then interviewed the instructors to see if they thought samples of their students' performance on prototype tasks for the test corresponded to the students' usual performance in their ESL classes. Studies such as Biber et al. (2002), Boyle and Booth (2000), or Hale et al. (1996) have taken major steps forward in describing characteristics of the spoken and written discourse used in university settings in North America. Such studies have provided vital, systematic data for the design of testing and teaching materials alike, starting to fill the gap that Waters (1996) observed to exist in the basic descriptive information relevant to the assessment of academic English.

Consistency

Consistency has been a necessary, guiding concept in revisions to the tests. As indicated earlier, the ethical principle of fairness is fundamental to high stakes, internationally administered tests (Hamp-Lyons, 1997; Kunnan, 2000; McNamara, 1998). People expect tests such as the TOEFL or IELTS, and scores deriving from them, to be consistent for each administration and version of the test. They expect examinees to have a comparable opportunity to perform any time the test is taken. Similarly, the tests cannot be perceived to contain biases against particular groups of test-takers, for example, related to their ethnicity, race, linguistic background, subject matter knowledge, gender, or other such defining characteristics. This is truly a challenge, given that the population of examinees represents the full range of diversity possible around the world, and the high demand for the tests requires them to be administered frequently. Extensive pilot testing, analyses, and equating of items or tasks for each version of the TOEFL are therefore necessary, because wholly new test items (and combinations of them) have to be created each time the test is administered, and these in turn must be equivalent to all previous versions of the test (for test scores to "mean" the same thing). Moreover, adherence to high standards in the construction and administration of these tests is necessary to avoid challenges to their credibility or legality (see Alderson, Clapham, & Wall, 1995, pp. 235-260; Davidson, Turner, & Huhta, 1997; De Jong, 1990).

Numerous challenges to consistency arise in the process of test revision. One challenge is to ascertain that, as the tests are revised, the scales used to rank people's performance remain consistent or can be interpreted in a comparably meaningful way. For example, each university has established levels or criteria for admissions to its academic programs, and such information needs to be available a year or so in advance of students applying to these university programs, particularly for applications from outside the country. As TOEFL moved from pencil and paper to computer-based formats, new scales for test scores needed to be created based on empirically equating these two versions of the test. This begs the empirical question of whether different tests, conceptualized and operationalized in unique ways, can truly be equated—a long-standing issue in the use of assessments for academic purposes (e.g., Epp & Stawychny, 2001). A second challenge is that examinees require ample orientation and practice material well in advance of taking the test in order for their performance not to be hampered by their familiarity (or lack of it) with the test format or its expectations for performance. Likewise, educators need such information, and to understand it well not only to help students to prepare for the test but also to make meaningful use of information about students' abilities from the test. For these reasons, decisions about exactly when and how to introduce a new version of the TOEFL are complex. A related point concerns economies of scale and accessibility. On the one hand, TOEFL and IELTS are successful internationally because the populations tested are enormous and demand is relatively consistent (Powell, 2001), facilitating investments in test administration and improvements that could not be sustained by a single university alone or even small consortia of them (e.g., as documented for one region of Canada by Wesche, 1987). In turn, these tests are administered around the world in standard ways and at fixed schedules, making them accessible to international populations wishing to study in English-medium universities. On the other hand, it is a major challenge to ensure that the conditions for test administration are comparable in all parts of the world, and that these conditions can be altered in an effective and timely manner to accommodate new test formats given the costs and commitments of computer equipment and maintenance, experienced staff, and facilities.

Within a test, a key aspect of consistency concerns the number and type of measurements of language performance necessary to obtain an adequate sample of an examinee's abilities in English. What constitutes a reliable and sufficient sample of language performance, while keeping the time and costs of test administration (and fees for the test taker) within reasonable limits? This point has been central as the frameworks for a new TOEFL have proposed to expand the scope of the test to sample more broadly from examinees in different types of relevant tasks, and while revisions to IELTS, conversely, have reduced and streamlined their scope. Studies that have started to address this point systematically include Lee, Kantor, and Mollaun (2002), using generalizability theory, to determine how information about examinees' abilities improves according to the number of written compositions they produce, and how many raters are optimally required to judge such samples of writing. This issue is crucial, as well, for the direct assessment of speech performance—perhaps the most radical change to the TOEFL (because the test presently does not solicit speech data)—though there are major technical and logistical challenges to establishing an optimal, reliable, and cost-effective means for obtaining and analyzing examinees' speech (Butler et al., 2000; Douglas, 1997; Lee, 2005).

New Media

A final, major issue featuring in revisions to these tests concerns the opportunities afforded by new technologies, such as computers and multi-media. As in other domains of human activity, the prospects for change are great but they also entail many new challenges (Chapelle, 2001). Changes in the delivery of TOEFL from pen-and-paper to computer media have already made one fundamental difference in the logistics of test administration: Rather than mass administrations of a pen-and-paper test in a single exam-type sitting, computer administration necessarily distributes examinees over time. Thus testing is administered continuously, while examinees have some flexibility in scheduling individual appointments to be tested. Perhaps the most exciting innovations concern the prospects for computer-adaptive testing that can facilitate test items to be pitched at individual examinees' abilities, based on initial samples of their performance (Chalhoub-Deville & Deville, 1999; Chapelle, 2001; Kenyon & Malobonga, 2001). However, the potential to do this on a large scale is constrained by the needs for consistency already described. As noted earlier, examinees' access to and abilities to use computers have been a focal point of concern, and this is obviously an area of variation internationally, despite the evident familiarity with computers that most university-bound students possess (Taylor et al., 1999).

Each language modality assessed poses unique opportunities and challenges in a computer or multi-media environment. For instance, for listening comprehension, the presentation of authentic, realistic speech, such as lectures and conversations, based on corpora from real university contexts is a guiding principle for the new TOEFL, but designing these to be comparable and in identifiable genres is a challenge (Bejar et al., 2000). Likewise, the appearance and uses of visual stimuli appear to have specific but complex effects on examinees' performance of listening comprehension tasks (Ginther, 2001) as does the condition of whether examinees take notes while listening or not (Carrell, Dunkel & Mollaun, 2002). For speaking, requiring TOEFL examinees to produce extended, meaningful samples of oral

English will be a major innovation, but establishing the optimal contexts and speech genres to facilitate, score, and interpret this is a challenge (Butler et al., 2000; Lee, 2005). The prospects for automatic speech recognition and analyses are exciting but similarly in need of extensive research and development. For reading, the options for new test formats are numerous, including issues such as the optimal type of interface and text display, how to facilitate the scrolling or reviewing of texts, uses of multiple texts simultaneously, the inclusion of various types of graphics, and speed of access (Enright et al., 2000). For writing, computers can facilitate the transmission of examinees' texts to central locations for scoring, various prospects for automatic text analyses, and uses of aids such as spell-checkers or online dictionaries or glossaries; but issues remain about how to treat cut and paste functions in integrated reading-writing tasks, the comparability of writing done by pen and paper with that done on computers, as well as variability in examinees' keyboarding skills (Cumming et al., 2000; Grant & Ginther, 2000; Shermis & Burstein, 2003).

CONCLUSIONS

Concerns for construct validation, consistency, and new media will surely continue to be featured in future innovations to and uses of these tests. Moreover, these matters need to continue to be evaluated systematically. Doing so is an important professional responsibility for the agencies that design and administer the tests, particularly as these tests have become major international enterprises with increasing demands for accountability and fairness as well as increasing conceptual and technical sophistication. It is also a professional responsibility for the universities and other institutions that make use of the test scores and other results, for example, by establishing (and evaluating) appropriate score levels for admission to particular academic programs and monitoring the relative, long-term success of populations of students within those programs (AERA, APA & NCME, 1999, pp. 111-118). Undoubtedly, English language proficiency is a vital element in the success of students studying in English-medium universities. But English language proficiency is not the only predictive variable in such success, which is also determined by students' previous academic achievements and orientations, individual intentions and efforts, as well as the opportunities to learn English academic discourse and for cultural adaptation within the contexts of university studies (Benesch, 1988; Elson, 1992; Fletcher & Stern, 1989; Graham, 1987; Zamel, 1995).

REFERENCES

AERA (American Educational Research Association), APA (American Psychological Association), & NCME (National Council on Measurement and Evaluation). (1999). *Standards for educational and psychological assessment*. Washington, DC: Authors.

Alderson, J. C., & Banerjee, J. (2002). State of the art review: Language testing and assessment (Part 2). *Language Teaching, 35*, 79–113.

Alderson, J. C., & Clapham, C. (1992). Applied linguistics and language testing: A case study of the ELTS test. *Applied Linguistics, 13*(2), 149–167.

Alderson, J. C., Clapham, C., & Wall, D. (1995). *Language test construction and evaluation*. Cambridge: Cambridge University Press.

Alderson, J. C., & Hamp-Lyons, L. (1996). TOEFL preparation courses: A study of washback. *TESOL Quarterly, 13*, 280–297.

Bachman, L. (2000). Modern language testing at the turn of the century: Assuring that what we count counts. *Language Testing, 17*(1), 1–42.

Bachman, L., Davidson, F., Ryan, K., & Choi, I. (1995). *An investigation into the comparability of two tests of English as a foreign language: The Cambridge-TOEFL comparability study*. Cambridge: Cambridge University Press.

Bailey, K. (1999). *Washback in language testing* (TOEFL Monograph No. 15). Princeton, NJ: Educational Testing Service.

Benesch, S. (Ed.). (1988). *Ending remediation: Linking ESL and content in higher education*. Washington, DC: TESOL.

Bejar, I., Douglas, D., Jamieson, J., Nissan, S., & Turner, J. (2000). *TOEFL 2000 listening framework: A working paper* (TOEFL Monograph Series, Report No. 19). Princeton, NJ: Educational Testing Service.

Biber, D., Conrad, S., Reppen, R., Byrd, P., & Helt, M. (2002). Speaking and writing in the university: A multidimensional comparison. *TESOL Quarterly, 36*, 9–48.

Boyle, A., & Booth, D. (2000, March). The UCLES/CUP learner corpus. *Research Notes: University of Cambridge Local Examinations Syndicate EFL, 1*, 10.

Bridgeman, B., Cline, F., & Powers, D. (2002, April). *Evaluating new tasks for TOEFL: Relationships to external criteria*. Paper presented at the Annual TESOL Convention, Salt Lake City, UT.

Brindley, G. (1998). Describing language development? Rating scales and second language acquisition. In L. Bachman & A. Cohen (Eds.), *Interfaces between second language acquisition and language testing research* (pp. 112–140). Cambridge: Cambridge University Press.

Brown, A. (2003). Interviewer variation and the co-construction of speaking proficiency. *Language Testing, 20*, 1–25.

Butler, F., Eignor, D., Jones, S., McNamara, T., & Suomi, B. (2000). *TOEFL 2000 speaking framework: A working paper* (TOEFL Monograph Series, Report No. 20). Princeton, NJ: Educational Testing Service.

Carey, P. (1966). *A review of psychometric and consequential issues related to performance assessment* (TOEFL Monograph Series, Report No. 3). Princeton, NJ: Educational Testing Service.

Carrell, P., Dunkel, P., & Mollaun, P. (2002). *The effects of notetaking, lecture length and topic on the listening component of TOEFL 2000*. (TOEFL Monograph Series, Report No. 23). Princeton, NJ: Educational Testing Service.

Carroll, J. B. (1975). *The teaching of French as a foreign language in eight countries*. John Wiley & Sons: New York.

Chalhoub-Deville, M., & Deville, C. (1999). Computer-adaptive testing in second language contexts. *Annual Review of Applied Linguistics, 19*, 273–299.

Chapelle, C. (1998). Construct definition and validity inquiry in SLA research. In L. Bachman & A. Cohen (Eds.), *Interfaces between second language acquisition and language testing research* (pp. 32–70). Cambridge: Cambridge University Press.

Chapelle, C. (2001). *Computer applications in second language acquisition: Foundations for teaching, testing and research*. Cambridge: Cambridge University Press.

Chapelle, C., Grabe, W., & Berns, M. (1997*). Communicative language proficiency: Definition and implications for TOEFL 2000.* (TOEFL Monograph Series Report No. 10). Princeton, NJ: Educational Testing Service.

Charge, N., & Taylor, L. (1997). Recent developments in IELTS. *ELT Journal, 51*, 374–380.

Clapham, C. (1996). *The development of the IELTS: A study of the effect of background knowledge on reading comprehension*. Cambridge: Cambridge University Press.

Connor-Linton, J. (1995). Looking behind the curtain: What do L2 composition ratings really mean? *TESOL Quarterly, 29*, 762–765.

Cumming, A. (1996). The concept of validation in language testing. In A. Cumming & R. Berwick, (Eds.), *Validation in language testing* (pp. 1–14). Clevedon, UK: Multingual Matters.

Cumming, A., Grant, L., Mulcahy-Ernt, P., & Powers, D. (2004). A teacher-verification study of speaking and writing prototype tasks for a new TOEFL. *Language Testing, 21*, 159–197.

Cumming, A., Kantor, R., & Powers, D. (2001). *Scoring TOEFL essays and TOEFL 2000 prototype tasks: An investigation into raters' decision making and development of a preliminary analytic framework* (TOEFL Monograph Series, Report No. 22). Princeton, NJ: Educational Testing Service.

Cumming, A., Kantor, R., & Powers, D. (2002). Decision making while scoring ESL/EFL compositions: A descriptive model. *Modern Language Journal, 86*, 67–96.

Cumming, A., Kantor, R., Powers, D., Santos, T., & Taylor, C. (2000). *TOEFL 2000 writing framework: A working paper* (TOEFL Monograph Series, Report No. 18). Princeton, NJ: Educational Testing Service.

Davidson, F., Turner, C., & Huhta, A. (1997). Language testing standards. In D. Corson (Series Ed.) & C. Clapham (Vol. Ed.), *Encyclopedia of language and education: Vol. 7. Language testing and assessment* (pp. 303–311). Dordrecht, Netherlands: Kluwer.

De Jong, J. (Ed.). (1990). Standardization in language testing [Special issue]. *AILA Review, 7,* 24–45.

Douglas, D. (1997). *Testing speaking ability in academic contexts: Theoretical considerations* (TOEFL Monograph Series, Report No. 8). Princeton, NJ: Educational Testing Service.

Douglas, D., & Smith, J. (1997). *Theoretical underpinnings of the Test of Spoken English revision project* (TOEFL Monograph Series, Report No. 9). Princeton, NJ: Educational Testing Service.

ETS (Educational Testing Service). (2002). *Language Edge courseware: Handbook for scoring speaking and writing.* Princeton, NJ: Educational Testing Service.

Elder, C. (1993). How do subject specialists construe classroom language proficiency? *Language Testing, 10,* 233–254.

Elson, N. (1992). The failure of tests: Language tests and post-secondary admissions of ESL students. In B. Burnaby & A. Cumming (Eds.), *Socio-political aspects of ESL education in Canada* (pp. 110–121). Toronto: OISE Press.

Enright, M., & Cline, F. (2002, April). *Evaluating new task types for TOEFL: Relationships between skills.* Paper presented at Annual TESOL Convention, Salt Lake City, UT.

Enright, M., Grabe, B., Koda, K., Mosenthal, P., Mulcahy-Ernt, P., & Schedl, M. (2000). *TOEFL 2000 reading framework: A working paper* (TOEFL Monograph Series, Report No. 17). Princeton, NJ: Educational Testing Service.

Epp, L., & Stawychny, M. (2001). Using the Canadian Language Benchmarks (CLB) to benchmark college programs/courses and language proficiency tests. *TESL Canada Journal, 18,* 32–47.

Fletcher, J., & Stern, R. (1989). Language skills and adaptation: A study of foreign students in a Canadian university. *Curriculum Inquiry, 19,* 293–308.

Fulcher, G. (1996). Does thick description lead to smart tests? A data-based approach to rating scale construction. *Language Testing, 13,* 208–238.

Fulcher, G. (1999). Assessment in English for academic purposes: Putting content validity in its place. *Applied Linguistics, 20,* 221–236.

Ginther, A. (2001). *Effects of the presence and absence of visuals on performance on TOEFL CBT listening-comprehensive stimuli* (TOEFL Research Report No. 66). Princeton, NJ: Educational Testing Service.

Ginther, A., & Grant, L. (1996). *A review of the academic needs of native English-speaking college students in the United States* (TOEFL Monograph Series, Report No. 1). Princeton, NJ: Educational Testing Service.

Graham, J. (1987). English language proficiency and the prediction of academic success. *TESOL Quarterly, 21,* 505–521.

Grant, L., & Ginther, L. (2000). Using computer-tagged linguistic features to describe L2 writing differences. *Journal of Second Language Writing, 9,* 123–145.

Greenberg, K. (1986). The development and validation of the TOEFL writing test: A discussion of TOEFL Research Reports 15 and 19. *TESOL Quarterly, 20,* 531–544.

Hale, G., Taylor, C., Bridgeman, B., Carson, J., Kroll, B., & Kantor, R. (1996). *A study of writing tasks assigned in academic degree programs* (TOEFL Research Report No. 54). Princeton, NJ: Educational Testing Service.

Hamp-Lyons, L. (1997). Ethics in language testing. In D. Corson (Series Ed.) & C. Clapham (Vol. Ed.), *Encyclopedia of language and education: Vol. 7. Language testing and assessment* (pp. 323–333). Dordrecht, Netherlands: Kluwer.

Hamp-Lyons, L. (1998). Ethical test preparation practice: The case of TOEFL. *TESOL Quarterly, 32,* 329–337.

Hamp-Lyons, L., & Kroll, B. (1997). *TOEFL 2000–writing: Composition, community, and assessment* (TOEFL Monograph Report No. 5). Princeton, NJ: Educational Testing Service.

Harley, B., Cummins, J., Swain, M., & Allen, P. (Eds.). (1990). *The development of second language proficiency.* Cambridge: Cambridge University Press.

Hudson, T. (1996). *Assessing second language academic reading from a communicative competence perspective* (TOEFL Monograph Series, Report 4). Princeton, NJ: Educational Testing Service.

Iwashita, N., McNamara, T., & Elder, C. (2001). Can we predict task difficulty in an oral proficiency test? Exploring the potential of an information-processing approach in task design. *Language Learning, 51,* 401–436.

Jamieson, J., Jones, S., Kirsch, I., Mosenthal, P., & Taylor, C. (2000). *TOEFL 2000 framework: A working paper* (TOEFL Monograph Series Report No. 16). Princeton, NJ: Educational Testing Service.

Kenyon, D., & Malobonga, V. (2001). Comparing examinee attitudes toward computer-assisted and other oral proficiency assessments. *Language Learning and Technology, 5*(2), 60–83.

Kirsch, I., Jamieson, J., Taylor, C., & Eignor, D. (1998). *Computer familiarity among TOEFL examinees* (TOEFL Research Report Series, No. 59). Princeton, NJ: Educational Testing Service.

Kunnan, A. (1998). Approaches to validation in language assessment. In A. Kunnan (Ed.), *Validation in language assessment* (pp. 1–18). Mahwah, NJ: Lawrence Erlbaum.

Kunnan, A. (2000). Fairness and justice for all. In A. Kunnan (Ed.), *Fairness and validation in language assessment*. Cambridge: Cambridge University Press.

Lazaration, A. (2002). *A qualitative approach to the validation of oral language tests*. Cambridge: Cambridge University Press.

Lazarton, A., & Wagner, S. (1996). *The revised TSE: Discourse analysis of native and nonnative speaker data* (TOEFL Monograph Report No. 7). Princeton, NJ: Educational Testing Service.

Lee, Y-W. (2005). *Dependability of scores for a new ESL speaking test: Evaluating prototype tasks.* (TOEFL Monograph Series No. 28). Princeton, NJ: Educational Testing Service.

Lee, Y-W., Kantor, R., & Mollaun, P. (2002, April). Score reliability as an essential prerequisite for validating new writing and speaking tasks for TOEFL. Paper presented at the Annual TESOL Convention, Salt Lake City, UT.

McNamara, T. (1998). Policy and social considerations in language assessment. *Annual Review of Applied Linguistics, 18*, 304–319.

McNamara, T., Hill, K., & May, L. (2002). Discourse and assessment. *Annual Review of Applied Linguistics, 22*, 221–242.

Messick, S. (1988). The once and future issues of validity: Assessing the meaning and consequences of measurement. In H. Wainer & H. Braun (Eds.), *Test validity* (pp. 33–45). Hillsdale, NJ: Erlbaum.

Messick, S. (1989). Meaning and values in test validation: The science and ethics of assessment. *Educational Researcher, 18*(2), 5–11.

Moss, P. (1992). Shifting conceptions of validity in educational measurement: Implications for performance assessment. *Review of Educational Research, 62*(3), 229–258.

North, B. (2000). *The development of a Common Framework Scale of language proficiency*. Oxford: Peter Lang.

Peirce, B. (1992). Demystifying the TOEFL reading test. *TESOL Quarterly, 26*, 665–689.

Powell, W. (2001). *Looking back, looking forward: Trends in intensive English program enrollments* (TOEFL Monograph 14). Princeton, NJ: Educational Testing Service.

Raimes, A. (1990). The TOEFL Test of Written English: Causes for concern. *TESOL Quarterly, 24*(3), 427–442.

Roberts, M. (2000). *An examination of the way a group of Korean language learners prepare for the Test of English as a Foreign Language (TOEFL)*. Unpublished Masters' dissertation, Department of Curriculum, Teaching and Learning, University of Toronto.

Rosenfeld, M., Leung, S., & Oltman, P. (2001). *The reading, writing, speaking, and listening tasks important for academic success at the undergraduate and graduate levels* (TOEFL Monograph 21). Princeton, NJ: Educational Testing Service.

Ross, S., & Berwick, R. (1992). The discourse of accommodation in oral proficiency interviews. *Studies in Second Language Acquisition, 14*, 159–176.

Schedl, M., Gordon, C., Carey, P., & Tang, K. L. (1996). *An analysis of the dimensionality of TOEFL reading comprehension items*. TOEFL Research Report 53. Princeton, NJ: Educational Testing Service.

Shermis, M., & Burstein, J. (Eds.). (2003). *Automated essay scoring: A cross-disciplinary perspective*. Mahwah, NJ: Erlbaum.

Skehan, P. (1998). *A cognitive approach to language learning*. Oxford: Oxford University Press.

Spolsky, B. (1995). *Measured words: The development of objective language testing*. Oxford: Oxford University Press.

Sullivan, B., Weir, C., & Saville, N. (2002). Using observation checklists to validate speaking-test tasks. *Language Testing, 19*, 33–56.

Taylor, C., Jamieson, J., Eignor, D., & Kirsch, I. (1998). *The relationship between computer familiarity and performance on computer-based TOEFL test tasks* (TOEFL Research Report Series, 61). Princeton, NJ: Educational Testing Service.

Taylor, C., Kirsch, I., Jamieson, J., & Eignor, D. (1999). Examining the relationship between computer familiarity and performance on computer-based language tasks. *Language Learning, 49*, 219–274.

Wainer, H., & Lukhele, R. (1997). *How reliable is the TOEFL test?* (TOEFL Technical Report 12). Princeton, NJ: Educational Testing Service.

Wallace, C. (1997). IELTS: Global implications of curriculum and materials design. *ELT Journal, 51*, 370–373.

Waters, A. (1996). *A review of research into needs in English for academic purposes of relevance to the North American higher education context*. (TOEFL Monograph Report 6). Princeton, NJ: Educational Testing Service.

Weir, C. (2005). *Language testing and validation: An evidence-based approach.* New York: Palgrave Macmillan.

Wesche, M. (1987). Second language performance testing: The Ontario Test of ESL as an example. *Language Testing, 4*, 28–47.

Young, R., & He, A. (Eds.). (1998). *Talking and testing: Discourse approaches to the assessment of oral proficiency.* Amsterdam: John Benjamins.

Zamel, V. (1995). Stangers in academia: The experiences of faculty and ESL students across the curriculum. *College Composition and Communication, 46*, 505–521.

CHAPTER 32

THE IMPACT OF TESTING PRACTICES ON TEACHING:

Ideologies and Alternatives

LIZ HAMP-LYONS

The University of Hong Kong, China/The University of Nottingham, UK

ABSTRACT

This chapter considers the current state of classroom assessment of English language proficiency and use, and argues for the existence of two often conflicting assessment cultures, a *learning culture* and an *exam culture*. This chapter characterizes the key principles and practices in each culture, and suggests that these two cultures stem from differing ideologies that pose great obstacles to reconciliation between effective selection instruments (usually called *tests*) and humanistic assessment. The chapter suggests that planned innovation in assessment is unlikely to be successful without vastly improved attention to teacher preparation in relation to assessment. It is further proposed that because the principles and practices of the exam culture reflect the dominant ideology in the discourse of educational economics and politics, this domination can only be altered by paying conscious attention to teachers' voices, particularly through professional development activities conducted as an integral part of the process of establishing value systems for educational assessment.

> *Not everything that counts can be counted and not everything that can be counted counts*
> Albert Einstein

INTRODUCTION

The contexts and needs of classrooms and teachers are not the same as those of large scale testing. The large scale needs to discriminate, to separate, to categorize and label. It seeks the general, the common, the group identifier, the scaleable, the replicable, the predictable, the consistent, and the characteristic. The teacher, the classroom, seeks the special, the individual, the changing, the changeable, the surprising, the subtle, the textured, and the unique. Neither is better but they are different. We have only started to realize the extent of the difference in recent years. They grow from different epistemologies and we should not be surprised that they take us to different places, in what Teasdale and Leung (2000) have called seemingly 'incommensurate discourses'.

This chapter focuses on the classroom assessment of English language proficiency. It argues for the existence of two often conflicting assessment cultures, a *learning culture* and an *exam culture*, and describes the key principles and practices in each culture. It is suggested that these two cultures stem from differing ideologies that pose great obstacles to reconciliation between effective selection instruments (usually called *tests*) and humanistic assessment. In a *learning culture* assessment is primarily shaped by considerations of learning and teaching, while in an *exam culture* classroom assessment is seen as simply preparation for an externally set and assessed examination. The chapter suggests that attempts to introduce innovations toward a greater role for classroom-based assessment are unlikely to be successful without vastly improved attention to teacher preparation in relation to assessment. It further proposes that because the exam culture is the dominant ideology in the discourse of educational economics and politics, conscious attention should be paid to teachers' voices in any assessment innovation, particularly through professional development activities conducted during the process of establishing value systems for educational assessment.

TWO CULTURES: SIMILARITIES AND DIFFERENCES

Learning and exam cultures have some similarities but many more differences, including their focus, their purposes, and the voices they ask us to listen to.

Language or Learner Focus

In the case of classical language testing compared to classroom-based language assessment, perhaps the most striking difference between a learning culture and an exam culture is the particular kind of content that is assessed when we assess language proficiency. Assessing language is not like assessing maths or geography or physics. Language is a construct that is hard to define, although we are surrounded by it and immersed in it, and we know it when we see/hear it. To take the well-known question from many foundation linguistics courses: Is the bees' dance language? If not, why not? How do we distinguish the characteristics of the bees' performance from the performance of a native English speaker who passes in a hallway someone she knows well and replies to the greeting "Hi, how are you?" with "See you"? The successful communication of meaning is a complex process that requires more than words simply strung together; non-verbal and contextual cues also play a critical role.

Because language is difficult to characterize, it follows that proficiency in the language will be difficult to measure. As we see in Nunan's chapter in this section, there has been considerable debate about whether language should be viewed as a body of knowledge, a set of skills or competencies, or a collection of performances viewed within more or less specified parameters. The debate may seem abstract and theoretical, but it is of considerable importance to classroom teachers of language because it impacts not only how learners are assessed, but how they are taught. It is also of considerable importance to the developers of large-scale tests of language proficiency, because they must seek to build tests on a construct of language that not only fits the reality of how language is used, but also, of how it is learned.

Classical language testing, as its name suggests, focuses on the language, and this is a difficult enough problem in testing terms. In contrast, *classroom-based* or *teacher-based language assessment* focuses on the learner, the teacher, and the classroom; however, it also has to assess the 'content' of study, that is, the learner's mastery of the language. This is not a set of opposites, but a more expansive view; a difference of perception about what matters, what is valuable and important—a cultural difference. In educational measurement, work around *curricular alignment* (which is very similar to the concept of washback in language assessment) has shown that the syllabus of the test may become the teaching syllabus, especially for teachers in a prescriptively oriented educational system. A learning culture rejects English tests that end up dictating what kind of English will be taught and learned, and instead puts the value of the learning experience at the heart of the curriculum and of the assessment. The learner is seen as more important than the language.

Group or Individual Focus

The second cultural difference between classical language testing and classroom-based language assessment is in the attention paid to the group compared to learners as individuals. The classroom teacher's concern is inherently individual and pastoral, driven by the desire to ensure that every learner will succeed to the best of her/his ability, and be rewarded for doing so. When we ask teachers to 'norm' their students—to create an artificial curve of performance where, by definition, half the children are below average—we ask them to contradict the teacherly role they have chosen. Driven by the view that classroom-based teacher assessment is more useful to teachers in their work than the more conventional forms of standardized language testing, English language teaching is seeing major changes in assessment at the chalkface. There is, for example, a move to a greater focus on formative assessment and feedback, alternative/performance assessment, and to uses of technology in assisting classroom-based assessment. As we will see later in this chapter, these developments aim to improve the ways in which we can assess the learning of individuals by incorporating views and understanding of learning processes into assessment.

Focus on Different Purposes of Assessment

Another important difference between the cultural values of teacher-based assessment versus those of large-scale testing is the purpose of assessment. Large-scale language tests typically assess proficiency, that is, the absolute level of mastery of the language that any person or group has reached. In contrast, assessments within local programs or classrooms typically assess achievement of or progress toward a curriculum or set of goals. Huhta (2003), writing on the LTEST-L listserve, says: "It seems that if you want to monitor progress in your courses, the best (the only?) way is to design your own tools of assessment based on the course content and objectives, be they tests, portfolios, learner diaries or whatever." What teachers want to know is how well their own students are doing, how far they have progressed, where they need to be re-taught and where they can forge ahead. When assessment tools are designed for specific audiences and needs they become very expensive per capita. Some education authorities (notably in China, where the learner numbers are extraordinarily large) have attempted to solve this by having set textbooks and building in assessment as well as instruction. If we move into fixed assessments we limit teachers' ability to decide when and how to assess; it also becomes pedagogically awkward to assess some learners on different syllabus areas than others. Thus, lockstep education becomes almost inevitable, and the voices that we hear in decision-making about learners become those of others and not of the teacher (see Shohamy, this volume, for a fuller discussion).

WHAT DOES A LEARNING CULTURE LOOK LIKE?

What Does It Mean to be Learner-focused?

Learners are individuals, and have individual learning styles, abilities, interests, and needs. Learners' differences need to be valued, seen as a resource for learning, not as a problem. Classroom-based assessment is valuable because it enables the differences among learners, as well as among teachers, to be preserved and valued while also providing the means for generalization and interpretation of the assessments made in classrooms. Carefully-designed portfolio assessments can offer this quality (Hamp-Lyons & Condon, 2000). However, the learner focus only comes through when the assessment process preserves the information about what learners can do and enjoy doing all the way through the system and report this to parents, system administrators, national review panels, and so on. The technology has existed for some time to make this type of fine-grained reporting possible, but there is inertia in the bureaucratic system, an over-reliance on just one number or one letter grade—and this inertia is very damaging to learners. Studies of parents (e.g., Fremer, 2001) show that they would like more information about the tests their children take, including opportunities to view the test itself, access to materials that will help them help their child prepare for the test, and ways to understand how to judge whether a test is fair to their own child. In the USA a survey by the National Academy of Science Research Council (2003) found common concerns and strategies being worked on by education research institutes around the country. A key trend was the development of specific descriptions of the expectations of student performance, with programs breaking down the learning process and performance expectations into elements with clear definitions, using frameworks and matrices. Examples of this approach in English language education can be seen in the *Canadian Language Benchmarks* and the Australian *ESL Bandscales*. Well-detailed descriptions necessitate a transparent assessment policy but also a clear framework of understanding about what and how people learn, and how they learn a language, thus, the need for underpinning research in second language acquisition is greater now than ever before.

What Does It Mean to be Process-focused?

When education focuses on the individual learner, it makes sense that assessment moves increasingly to include assessments of learning processes, so that support can be given to individuals in need by understanding where their learning processes are relatively strong and weak, and then providing intervention and support at critical points. For example, one of the areas that has been claimed, especially in the USA, to contribute positively to learning, and to help shift the assessment focus from summative to formative values is process writing. *Process writing* refers to a set of beliefs and strategies that enable teachers to work with student writers while they are writing, rather than waiting until a piece of writing is finished and then marking or critiquing it. However, implementing process writing or other process methodologies requires professional development for teachers focusing on reflective teaching and on ways to strengthen the links between teaching/learning and assessment. For example, Hamp-Lyons, Chen, and Mok (2001a) worked collaboratively with Form 5 teachers in Hong Kong, in a highly dominant exam culture, to develop a program of materials to support the implementation of a process approach in their classrooms. Teachers responded positively to the first year of the program but were only willing to implement one process cycle in the school year because of the pressure of the major exams that are the culmination of five years of high school. As a response to this problem, for the second year the research team developed materials that used exam prompts as the starting point for process activities. Some teachers successfully implemented this approach, but others were unwilling to risk censure by department heads or principals if it appeared that students did less well on the exam as a result of the innovation. The researchers attempted to ease these concerns by further developing learning materials for students. By the third year of the study, the entire English departments of some schools were using the new program, but in other schools only a few teachers were continuing with it by themselves, and a few schools had reverted to their more traditional approach. The results demonstrated that even with a strongly directive approach to professional development and a great deal of in-class support to teachers, process-orientated assessment programs will not flourish unless the teaching community as a whole supports the assessment innovation; the exam culture is too dominant.

Feedback is the Heart of a Process Focus

Within the learning culture, feedback plays a very important part. As Black and Wiliam (1998, pp. 36-37, 47-52) have argued, feedback is central to the effectiveness of classroom-based and formative assessment. Feedback is the point at which the teacher models and shapes appropriate performance and teaches the learner how to self-assess. Building feedback into all aspects of teaching and learning further benefits the education system as a whole because it provides information of non-threatening kinds about what is working well and where the problems may be for particular kinds of learners and programs.

If we contrast a product focus with a process focus and consider what this offers learners, teachers, and education systems, we see that it provides scores. Scores do have value, especially for making high-stakes decisions one person at a time: for example, for the award (or not) of a prestigious or valuable scholarship. Scores also have value for evaluating comparable elements within a larger system and for bestowing or withholding rewards. This is the fundamental approach behind the US *No Child Left Behind* (NCLB) legislation. The problem with this approach is that it lays all responsibility on learners and teachers, whereas we know that many other real-world variables impact individual and group levels of educational success. A product focus also does not offer windows of discovery into what learners do when they learn, or what blocks they may face when they are failing to learn; process data can, used well, provide such information.

Recent work (for example, see Hyland & Hyland, 2006) is leading the way for a 'feedback revolution' in our approaches to language education. However, introducing forms of feedback into language teaching does necessitate conscious professional development for teachers. Many teachers do not instinctively develop a sense of the value of feedback or the ways in which to use it, and need very overt and highly-supportive, practical training (Hamp-Lyons, Chen, & Mok, 2001b), hence the current movement toward the provision of more and better feedback, with teacher training programs for the first time beginning to include classes in giving feedback. Teachers whose own learning backgrounds have been highly product-focused and whose teaching contexts are very top-down and rigid (as is the case in Hong Kong) will find it especially difficult to implement a process approach where formative feedback is given and received without such training and support.

Whose Voices?

Teasdale and Leung (2000) conclude that "insufficient research has been done to establish what, if any, elements of assessment for learning and assessment as measurement are compatible" (p. 180). Until teachers receive much better preparation for their roles as assessors, they will not have a 'voice' that can articulate why they feel uncomfortable with domination by an exam culture, or why they instinctively feel that what learners need is a culture in which assessment serves learning, not the reverse. The view from the classroom and the voice of the teacher, and the view and voice of those representing large assessment systems will remain irreconcilable until teachers' voices are listened to and their needs for in-service as well as pre-service professional development are taken into account. A number of studies (eg., Alderson & Hamp-Lyons, 1996; Davison, 2004; Hamp-Lyons, Chen, & Mok, 2001b; Hamp-Lyons, Hood, & MacLennan, 2001) have each provided data showing that teachers are aware of the tensions in their own teaching between what they believe would be best for the children and what they feel compelled to do because of the system. Each of these studies has also shown that teachers probably overestimate the constraints and that there are more opportunities to make some positive change than many teachers believe. Yet because teachers feel powerless, like powerless people in other situations, they give up more quickly and demonstrate more subservience than the facts of the situation warrant (Freire, 1971; Wall, 2000). Pre-service and in-service professional preparation and development for teachers provides an essential opportunity for teachers to critique their position in the education society, identify points of opportunity and mechanisms to influence education planning, including assessment, and to find ways to contribute to positive change.

Assessment of Learning versus Teaching-to-the-Test

M.L. Smith (1991) points out the negative effects on schools of the use of multiple choice test items and provides evidence of the (negative) power of assessment, showing that such tests lead teachers to focus their efforts on test content and skills.

This results in a narrowing of the curriculum whereby particular complex thinking skills that are hard to assess discretely and other non-assessed skills (such as problem-solving processes) are neglected. This is the teaching-to-the-test effect, known to language testing researchers as washback. Resnick and Resnick (1992) have found that schools and teachers tend to use the test format as a model for curriculum and instruction, thus distancing instruction from the direct needs of the students and narrowing the curriculum. In Hong Kong, we have seen this in extremis with tests in various areas even before the age of formal schooling and in every year thereafter, usually with very high stakes attached to results (Hamp-Lyons, 1999).

What teachers want is a learning culture, that is, a culture in which we can expect that the educational experience will be learner-centered, will encourage initiative and critical thinking, emphasize knowledge-creation rather than knowledge reproduction, value curriculum and materials appropriate to local needs, and adopt forms of assessment that are congruent with educational objectives determined locally. In a learning culture, curriculum and materials and the skills of teachers will be relevant to the ages of learners, their abilities, and interests, and to the medium in which they are learning. Classroom activities will be valued if they contribute to students' learning and understanding of important concepts and skills. In a learning culture, assessment will mainly go on in the classroom with more formal periodic assessments designed to blend into the learning continuum and recognize what the student has learned and what progress s/he has made. A focus on supporting learners (as opposed to informing teaching) demands an assessment system which is learner-referenced, rather than just referenced to average levels of attainment. However, it is not easy to establish such an assessment system, as can be demonstrated by the experience of the Hong Kong Education and Manpower Bureau, whose own goals are being undermined by the competition for places in the higher-status schools, by the lack of a nuanced suite of measures to help older students reach success on some recognized qualification, and by the extreme limits on access to higher education. All these weaknesses maintain the dominance of an exam culture in Hong Kong, despite the espoused aim of educational leaders to develop a learning culture. The reality is that tests are real and dynamic social forces that cannot be easily controlled, and their impact cannot be limited only to their intended positive effects. Societies have complex and often competing educational needs, expectations, and interests; and tests—including language tests—are tempting tools for educational policy and reform.

What teachers also want (and what most parents assume tests already provide) are assessments that can provide sound judgments of learning based on an understanding of learners' needs and background. Such assessments only occur when there is high contextual awareness and responsiveness, and when those who are actually engaged in the teaching of the learners in question are closely involved in assessment. A good example of how this can happen lies in the now-popular alternative assessment approach of portfolio assessment. Hamp-Lyons and Condon (2000) draw on their long-term research and development agenda to argue that instruction and assessment can meet in portfolio-based assessment. Good portfolio assessment resides within and is iterative with the instructional values and curriculum. Good portfolio assessment of writing necessitates that teachers have skills in the following areas:

- conferencing and workshopping
- reflection and self assessment
- discussing student work on all dimensions
- developing assessment criteria
- judging portfolios
- applying specialist subject and pedagogical knowledge

Hamp-Lyons and Condon (2000) describe in detail how communities of practice around portfolio assessment may develop. The existence of such communities of practice is essential for the successful implementation of alternative assessment measures such as language inventories, portfolio assessment, conferencing over writing and speaking performances, peer response, journaling, and other self-assessments. However, effective communities of practice do not develop without systematic attention to teachers' professional development and reflection on the curriculum, the end goals of the program, and the validity of the measures applied. Professional development is also needed to help guide teachers to apply methods of self-consistency to their own assessments. Only with a teaching community who are expert in the methods they are asked to implement can we begin to build a bridge between exam cultures and learning cultures.

CULTURAL CHARACTERISTICS AND CHANGE

We are beginning to arrive at a picture of the two cultures – the learning and exam cultures – stereotypical though I acknowledge the picture is. In Table 1 I sketch out some of the cultural contrasts, as they play out in the context of the language curriculum area.

Table 1. The two ends of the assessment cultures continuum

Classroom-based assessment	*Classical testing*
Fluency-focused	Accuracy-focused
Individual-focused	Group- or 'norm'-focused
Achievement/progress-focused	Proficiency-focused
Learner-focused	Language-focused
Process-focused	Product-focused
Teachers'/students' voices	Rule-makers' voices
Leads to assessment of learning	Leads to 'teaching to the test'

This leads into the key question of how can we facilitate closer integration between exam and learning cultures, and to what extent this is possible, given they have been called 'incommensurable.' The contrasts between an exam culture and a learning culture are not static but dynamic and highly contextualized; they are also multi-dimensional. Substantive change will only occur by creating connections between members of the different cultures, so that they can meet and listen to each others' voices. Most contextual features that lead to the development of these differences between cultures are historical. In Hong Kong, for example, a short colonial history made teachers as well as many classes of civil servants highly subservient to authority, and this pattern must be broken before teachers can find the courage to self-actualize a new and more autonomous, responsible role for themselves. In China by contrast, a strong value placed over many centuries on education as a means to successful competition for advancement and social status has awarded teachers an honored status; yet it has also led to deeply entrenched ways of teaching and learning that are slow to change. A tradition of equality of opportunity in education and all spheres of life, as for example in Norway, means that teachers are respected not as authority figures but as educated professionals, and are expected to take responsibility for teaching and learning and to participate in educational innovations. In my view, one fundamental factor in success, or otherwise, in effectively introducing teacher-based and classroom-based assessment is, simply, the status accorded to teachers within the society. Status is not an easy factor to influence, but perhaps we can make a contribution by providing teachers with consistent programs of professional development timed and targeted to their needs at key career points and to key educational innovations in their schools. After all, anecdotal evidence often tells us that when teachers are working in contexts of low power and poor training and support, they fall back on the worst myths of classical norm-referenced testing that they recall from their own experiences. Will more attention to professional development empower teachers to speak up and help those who represent the dominant exam culture to understand not only the needs but also the pathways to a learning culture? It seems to me an experiment worth trying.

Building Bridges with Standards?

An apparent bridge between the culture of teaching and the culture of testing is offered by the standards movements that have grown so rapidly in Australia, the USA, and the UK (see McKay, and Nunan, this volume for a fuller discussion), and which seem to offer ways for teachers to maximize their own close knowledge of the learners they teach. However, a standards orientation can restrict teachers to the narrow framework of the standards statements and can limit the types of language activities that can be used in assessable moments. The standards approach is inherently group-oriented; driven by the demands of bureaucrats and funding bodies that fixed numbers (or proportions) of people reach pre-determined expectations. We see this unraveling of the educational goals for political ends most strongly in the USA with the *No Child Left Behind* policy, but in Australia ESL teachers also feel that much of the good work done in assessment in the 1980s and early 1990s is being undone by a top-down interpretation of standards, resulting in a shift in the system away from a learning culture towards a more exam-oriented culture. McKay (2000, this volume) argues that good standards, properly understood and properly used, can be a positive force in improving classroom practice and the resources available for teaching, and this assertion certainly has some validity. However, the overtly political nature of standards movements makes many teachers uneasy, since teachers often do not share the sociopolitical values and goals of the authorities setting the policies that assessments must put into operation. A similar unease among teachers was reflected in discussions in the spring of 2004 on the email network of the European Association for Language Testing and Assessment (EALTA). EALTA is attempting to balance some of the institutional forces dominating national-level language testing in Europe through its association of individuals concerned with language assessment at the classroom level. This new grassroots action may perhaps contribute to a narrowing of the gap between the large-scale and politicized forces of the standards movement and the child-centered, needs- rather than resource-focused values basis that underlies the philosophy of the classroom-based assessment movement. However, EALTA's association with the Common European Framework of Reference (CEFR) which is a major project of the European Commission and which again focuses on the group rather than the individual, may weaken the potential for a real classroom-based focus of this new organization. However, this conversation is worth engaging in, whether in Europe, Australia, in Hong Kong, or elsewhere.

Changing the Power Dynamic

Shohamy (1993) makes a strong argument for the debilitating power of tests, and in later work has taken this case further both empirically and rhetorically. In many places, Hong Kong being perhaps one of the clearest examples, teachers feel powerless to influence how assessment is conducted in their classrooms. Hong Kong has a very rigid curriculum and a tight structure of assessments throughout the educational system. Hong Kong is also a highly competitive society where education is seen as the essential key to any of life's chances. Parents begin competing for good school places for their children as soon as they are born, and it only gets more extreme as the school years progress. There is a culture of blame on the teachers for anything that goes wrong for an individual child and in the education system as a whole. Yet key aspects of educational planning in Hong Kong—and these are principally testing-related aspects—conspire to give teachers little freedom to engage in reforms. The current move in the Hong Kong Examinations and Assessment Authority (HKEAA) toward reform of the English language examination to include a specific component of 'school-based assessment' (Davison, 2006) is perhaps the first truly hopeful step toward assessment reform for the classroom because it offers the potential to change the power dynamic between teachers and education authorities.

Being powerless does not mean that teachers are not alert to 'teaching-to-the-test' demands on them. In fact, they are often very conscious of their own teaching to the test behavior (Hamp-Lyons, Chen, & Mok, 2001b). In fact, teaching-to-the-test seems to be unavoidable. Spolsky (1995) explains how this happens and how it may harm learning:

> Once the content of an examination has been broadcasted, it becomes a more or less precise specification of what knowledge or behaviour will be rewarded (or will avoid punishment). This may be appropriate when the goal is the rote learning of a specified body of material...but it is constraining and rigid when it pertains to the less defined and more creative aspects of a curriculum. The greater the uniformity, the more the danger of crystallization and stultification. (pp. 55-56)

We should not be surprised, therefore, when trainee teachers choose not to attend courses that have to do with assessment. They know about assessment already from personal experience and they instinctively feel that is one part of the role of a teacher where they are powerless. Teachers do not need to read the professional literature on test impact to understand the consequences of an exam culture. Testing is seen by many teachers as something to be avoided and by all as something that takes up important teaching time. Yet, only when teachers have a better understanding of how traditional testing works, and in what conditions it works best, will they be equipped to argue for a new culture of classroom-based assessment. As Crocker (2003) says, "[teachers] will ill-serve their students if they are dismissive, disdainful, or antagonistic about the significant role that tests will play in their students' lives beyond the classroom" (p. 10).

This raises a conundrum: How can teachers accept exams and tests when they know that in an exam culture the educational experience will be score-oriented, that is, will encourage *rote learning* (that is, an emphasis on reproduction of knowledge, not on analysis, synthesis, or evaluation), and will adopt a one-size-fits-all approach to curriculum, materials, and classroom methods (Cheah, 1998)? Teachers know that a consequence of an exam culture is that large numbers of people are judged to have failed because the one size does not fit all, regardless of the extent to which distant bureaucrats feel it should. I share the concerns of educators such as M.L. Smith (1993) and Black and Wiliam (1998) that we are increasingly seeing a movement to use 'assessment innovation' to bring about changes in curriculum and in educational practice; the tail officially wagging the dog. While in extreme cases, beneficial washback may arise from deliberate educational planning through testing (and the CET-SET[1] may be a case in point; time will tell), I am skeptical about the benefits claimed for measurement-driven instruction (MDI) (see for example, Noble & M.L. Smith, 1994). The NCLB political platform in the United States has led to great changes in educational policy and planning and in educational assessment in schools all over the US. Crocker (2003) points out that "some have referred to No Child Left Behind as 'the *Psychometricians' Full Employment Act*'" (p. 6), and she describes whole categories of 'assessment lifeboats' that specialists need to climb into. The sinking ship that Crocker describes is the attempt to raise educational standards in the USA, but it is deeply ironic that this task is given to assessment specialists, not to teachers. Here, too, teachers are viewed as powerless, treated as powerless, and hence become powerless. However, so far there is little evidence that the NCLB legislation and the astonishing expansion of standards-based assessments that have resulted have led to meaningful improvement in the educational experience for children or to greater access to material and intellectual good in society. Stiggins (2004) argues that "we will tap the immense potential of assessment for school improvement only when we deliver those tools into the hands of practitioners" (p. 14). This is a statement of faith, not the outcome of empirical research, but in many countries around us in the post-millennial decade, there is overwhelming evidence that putting more and more eggs into the testing and testing agencies' basket is not achieving the educational change that governments want and that parents and employers expect.

Changing the Focus: From Standards and Expectations to Professional Development

Wiliam (2001) argues that research into authentic assessment of educational performance has been based on a deficit model, because even in this approach the assessment of, for example, portfolios of students' work, is expected to reach the standards of reliability of standardized multiple-choice tests, and naturally falls short. Equally, starting from standards as targets to be reached necessarily ties every report of individual, group, or school performance to how close to the 'standard' the participants have come—and again, how far they have fallen short.

Stimulating assessment reform by giving value and meaning to classroom-based assessment gives some power to teachers (and to learners), but it also presupposes that teachers have the knowledge and expertise to exercise that power. Teachers need to be well-prepared in the knowledge base of their subject, in classroom skills, and in assessment methods and options. This was noticeably the case in ELT in Australia throughout the 1980s and early 1990s, and the result was teachers who were highly active in professional organizations and in personal professional development. In that climate, initiatives such as the *ESL Bandscales* (McKay & Scarino, 1991) flourished and teachers felt some ownership over assessment processes.

In Hong Kong, however, at least until now, a different picture has been seen. Teachers, certainly English language teachers, are as a group under-prepared for their work as a result of policies and resource allocations by government over a long period of years dating to well before the return of Hong Kong to China. Many do not have basic teaching qualifications, let alone language teaching qualifications. Preparation in assessment of any kind is almost unheard of except for the tiny proportion who go on to study for Masters degrees. These teachers are not ready to take on the kinds of roles called for in a learning culture; they are not skilled in working with their students as individuals and in small groups, nor are they skilled in giving formative feedback or designing context- and level-appropriate tasks and criteria. Such teachers are not even sufficiently skilled at working together to develop teaching goals and plans.

In responding to criticism from Newton (2003) who is a representative of government-level education policy in the UK, Wiliam (2003) has suggested *light sampling* as a way to decrease the narrowing of the curriculum that results from a wholesale reliance on formal tests by returning more of the decision-making power to teachers. Light sampling is a form of day-to-day record-keeping by teachers of students' learning for formative purposes. Wiliam argues that these formative notes should not be "aggregated to the summative level for reporting to students and their parents" (p. 132). Teachers would be free to use their professional skills and close knowledge of each learner to discount inadequate evidence if the reasons for aberrant performances were known to them. Their formative data would be 'moderated' by external tasks that would establish the range of levels that could be used within the class for summative reporting.

Despite its post-modern acceptance of tensions and uncertainties in the system, Wiliam's proposed approach is essentially a convergent one and, in line with almost all work in large-scale performance assessment in the past 50 years, has as its goal the bringing together of views. However, as Davison (2004) points out, the current view is that there are several problems with attempts to adopt convergent values in judgment processes that seek to capitalize on teacher knowledge. Firstly, the common assumption underlying such approaches is that criteria can be teacher- and context-free, whereas many studies show that assessment criteria are interpreted differently by teacher-assessors according to a whole range of individual and cultural variables (Hamp-Lyons, 1989; Lumley, 2000; Pula & Huot, 1993): the people themselves, the teacher-raters, are not convergent at all.

The second problem that Davison (2004) identifies is that attempts to bridge assessment cultures inevitably assume that teacher-based assessment is "essentially a technical activity, requiring little professional judgment or interpretation" (p. 309). However, assessment descriptors are only words and, like all text, can never be completely disambiguated. In recent years, considerable research has revealed that judging language performances is an experience-based skill susceptible to training but remaining subjective. As Davison says, "it is only through teacher interpretation and negotiation of judgments that judgments can be made valid and reliable" (p. 309). Furthermore, as Arkoudis and O'Loughlin (2004) found, when a conflict arises between standardized criteria and teachers' own personalized judgments, teachers are likely to manipulate and/or reject the criteria rather than to make judgments that their experience and values tell them are false. Over and above all this, if assessments are designed to circumvent and change teachers' values and beliefs, it is hard to argue that they are in fact teacher-based or classroom-based, or that they are in fact based in a learning culture. In the most recent work in educational assessment (e.g., McMillan, 2003), it is being argued that measurement specialists should adapt their technical principles to be more relevant to the realities of classroom assessment decision-making. Even reliability is being reconsidered from the perspective of the values and demands of learning cultures (Smith, 2003).

Torrance and Pryor (1998) have developed a conceptual framework for formative assessment that presents two approaches to assessment: *convergent* and *divergent*, from which work by Wiliam (2001) described earlier draws. The divergent approach is presented as the one that would have most positive impact on pupil learning because it seeks to discover *what* the learner knows, not *whether* they know something; it focuses on errors, hesitations and other miscues that reveal the learner's current understanding; and it evaluates learning in a descriptive rather than a judgmental way. Torrance and Pryor see this model of formative assessment as being based on a constructivist view of learning and as being accomplished jointly by teacher and pupil. Perhaps the great strength of their work in this book is the level of example and detail they supply to support their arguments; this work goes a considerable way towards locating itself within a learning culture.

As I commented above, in my own view the characteristics that Wiliam describes for light sampling belong more to the convergent paradigm than to the divergent. For me, a far more fruitful way into professional development for teachers is to involve them in performance assessment judgments and rater training (Hamp-Lyons & Condon, 2000). Since teachers are both interlocutors and raters in their own classrooms, professional development can capitalize on the variability of response to language performances and help teachers to, first, deconstruct their own preferred ways of responding to learners' language, and then to establish a consistent approach to responding to student work. Teachers' understanding of what students in their context know and can do informs their judgments of spoken and written texts; it also informs the feedback they give to their learners. Deeper understanding of the criteria of assessment being used beyond the classroom gives teachers something substantive to bring back to the classroom and use in their teaching and responding to learners. Meanwhile, in such a participatory model, teachers' judgments are informing the assessment programs that their students will eventually be entering—a positive feedback loop.

Research from large-scale testing contexts, such as that on interlocutor and rater behaviors (e.g., Brown, 2004; Brown & Lumley, 1997; Lumley, 2000; O'Loughlin, 2000; usefully summarized by Reed & Cohen, 2001), and on criteria development and scale construction such as that described by Alderson (1991) can help us to design better professional development for teachers. Work in Australia on speaking performance for example (Lumley, Raso, & Mincham, 1993) has enabled the articulation of the dimensions and at least some observable "levels" of speaking ability. Further developments have gone beyond the presentation of tools for the assessment of learner language to demonstrate ways in which learner assessment may be integrated and embedded within teaching and learning processes (Breen, et al., 1997). This work is potentially useful for adaptation to structured classroom-based assessment. However, in the typical classroom, a teacher may feel that she can observe many different levels of performance, where a scale or a part of a national scale suggests only one or two levels of differentiation exist. Teacher professional development in assessment, especially in the participatory model described above, can help teachers to see how the large-scale "norms" may enable them to put their class as a whole in the context of a larger group while acknowledging that there are many finer distinctions within any group—i.e. that the group is composed of individuals with different levels and styles of performance.

In the same tradition, Wiliam (2001) describes what he calls construct-referenced assessment, a mode of assessment in which no attempt is made to prescribe learning outcomes but which depends on the consensus of the teachers making the assessments. His work provides a deeper theoretical foundation for an increasingly common practice in locally-run writing assessment programs, first reported at the University of Pittsburgh (W. Smith, 1993), whereby decisions about whether individual writers have reached the necessary level of writing proficiency to take the standard freshman writing course are made only by teachers of that course. Instead of criteria and scales, several teachers/raters with the right experience (i.e. knowledge of the construct) give a *yes/no* judgment.

Lumley (2000) describes how and why raters of the *Special Test of English Proficiency*[2] (STEP) made judgments of student essays and found that there was no fixed and essential meaning to their decisions; when their own judgments contradicted the directives of the rating system, they subverted the system. This is reminiscent of the argument of Barritt, Stock, and Clark long ago (1986) that writing assessment raters in their program read the writer at least as much as they read the text, and trust their own judgments more than the program scoring guidelines. Studies like these tell us that whenever the learning and exam cultures clash, teachers will do all they can (very often without being conscious of what they are doing) to bring the values of the learning culture back in. It simply makes sense to use professional development to make sure they do this in an informed way.

WORRY ABOUT RELIABILITY

I have left the strongest cultural barrier to closer integration between the learning and exam cultures until last. We must challenge the common perception that classical language testing is reliable and that scores from traditional language tests are more trustworthy than scores from alternative assessments. An upsurge in research, not only in language testing but even more strongly in educational measurement, has shown the problems with underlying assumptions about the validity of standardized test scores. Alderson and Banerjee (2002) make the following point:

> Recent language testing research has attempted to uncover the processes and strategies that learners engage in when responding to test items, and the most clear message to emerge from this research is that how individuals approach test items varies enormously. What an item may be testing for one individual is not necessarily the same as what it might test for another individual. This, unfortunately, is the logical conclusion of an interactionalist perspective, one which Messick (1989) also recognized...Thus strategies, and presumably traits, can vary across persons and tasks, even when the same scores are achieved. The same test score may represent different abilities, or different combinations of abilities, or different interactions between traits and contexts, and it is currently impossible to say exactly what a score might mean. This we might term The Black Hole of language testing. (p. 101)

If we cannot say what a score might mean, why are we fixated so strongly on reliability? The field of educational measurement, for many years the conservative end of the assessment spectrum, has moved significantly in the last 5 or more years and is now engaging seriously as a profession with alternative conceptions of reliability. Smith (2003) points out that "teachers *want* their students to be different next week as compared to last week" (p. 29), and therefore some of the fundamental assumptions of reliability theory are not appropriate for classroom assessment. This might be seen as a breakthrough understanding that will enable those in the exam culture to at least look for the bridges across to the learning culture. Smith suggests that we consider "sufficiency of information" as an alternative to standard measures such as coefficient alpha and proposes a formula to do so. This work is in its infancy but we should look on it with hope, because teachers need assessment experts on their side in the battle for power regarding decisions about learners in classrooms.

CONCLUSIONS

The goal of this chapter has been to encourage a greater understanding of the complexities involved in moving from an exam culture to a learning culture. Both teachers and assessment specialists need to give more open-minded consideration of the ways in which the strengths of both cultures of assessment can be brought together so that the great majority of learner assessment—assessment by teachers in classrooms in support of individual students' learning—can benefit. Huot (2003) reminds us that "since its inception in ancient China assessment was supposed to disrupt existing social order and class system. However, as we all know, assessment has rarely delivered on this promise." (p. 7). In my own view, disrupting the social order is a good thing only when we understand what it is we disrupt and what we have to offer in its place. This is not yet sufficiently the case for the debate (such as it is) between teachers and assessment authorities and agencies. Knowledge is power, and so the members of these two cultures need to know each other better. For example, substantial research has revealed that if teachers are left to their own judgments, they will include student effort as well as achievement in their decisions (McMillan, 2003), and this practice is often criticized by designers of exams. Yet despite such research, exam agencies, even those who have implemented automated scoring technologies, continue to use human raters as the benchmark for their scoring programs and for automated scores in reliability studies. In this technological era, when rating of written work can be automated (for example, ETS' *e-rater*) and oral performance can be rated automatically over the phone using speech tools (for example, Ordinate's *PhonePass*) what is it about human judgments that we still value? What special characteristics do humans bring to the process of making judgments about language in use? It seems to me that this is the common ground on which both assessment cultures may meet.

NOTES

[1] CET-SET = College English Test-Spoken English: National College English Testing Committee of China.
[2] STEP was used in Australia for immigration-related decisions in the early 1990s.

REFERENCES

Alderson, J. C. (1991). 1990. Bands and scores. In J. C. Alderson and B. North (Eds.), *Language testing in the 1990s: The communicative legacy* (pp. 71–85). London: British Council/Macmillan.

Alderson, J., & Banerjee, J. (2002). State of the art review: Language testing and assessment, Part 2. *Language Teaching, 35*(2), 79–113.

Alderson, J., & Hamp-Lyons, L. (1996). TOEFL preparation courses: A study of washback. *Language Testing, 13*(3), 11–18.

Arkoudis, S., & O'Loughlin, K. (2004). Outcomes anxiety: ESL teachers assessing newly arrived ESL learners. *Language Testing, 21*(3), 283–303.

Barritt, L., Stock, P., & Clark, F. (1986). Researching practice: Evaluating assessment essays. *College Composition and Communication, 37*, 315–327.

Black, P., & Wiliam, D. (1998). Assessment and classroom learning. *Assessment in Education, 5*(1), 7–74.

Breen, M., Barratt-Pugh, C., Derewianka, B., House, H., Hudson, C., Lumley, T., & Rohl, M. (1997). *Profiling ESL children: How teachers interpret and use national and state assessment frameworks.* Canberra: Department of Employment, Education, Training and Youth Affairs.

Brown, A. (2004). *Interviewer variability in oral proficiency interviews.* Unpublished doctoral dissertation, University of Melbourne, Australia.

Brown, A., & Lumley, T. (1997). Interviewer variability in specific-purpose language performance tests. In A. Huhta, V. Kohonen, L. Kurki-Suonio, & S. Luoma (Eds.), *Current developments and alternatives in language assessment* (pp. 137–150). Jyväskyla: Centre for Applied Language Studies, University of Jyväskyla.

Cheah, Y-M. (1998). The examination culture and its impact on literacy innovations: The case of Singapore. *Language and Education, 12*(3), 192–209.

Crocker, L. (2003). Teaching for the test: Validity, fairness, and moral action. *Educational Measurement: Issues and Practice, 22*(3), 5–11.

Davison, C. (2004). The contradictory culture of classroom-based assessment: Teacher assessment practices in senior secondary English. *Language Testing, 21*(3), 304–334.

Davison, C. (2006). Views from the chalkface: School-based assessment in Hong Kong. *Language Assessment Quarterly, 3*(4).

Freire, P. (1971). *Pedagogy of the oppressed.* New York: Seaview.

Fremer, J. (2001, March). *Ten things parents want to know about testing.* Presidential Address, National Council on Measurement in Education.

Hamp-Lyons, L. (1989). *Raters respond to rhetoric in writing.* In H. Dechert and G. Raupach (Eds.), *Interlingual Processes* (pp. 229–244). Tubingen: Gunther Narr.

Hamp-Lyons, L. (1999). Implications of the "examination culture" for (English language) education in Hong Kong. In V. Crew, V. Berry, & J. Hung (Eds.), *Exploring diversity in the language curriculum* (pp. 133–141). Hong Kong: Hong Kong Institute of Education.

Hamp-Lyons, L., Chen, J., & Mok, J. (2001a). Introducing innovation incrementally: Teacher feedback on student writing. *ThaiTESOL Bulletin: Selected papers from the 21st Annual ThaiTESOL International Conference, 14*(2), 59–66.

Hamp-Lyons, L., Chen, J., & Mok, J. (2001b). Supporting secondary English language teachers and learners: Developing good teaching strategies for giving written feedback on student work; and good learning strategies for effective use of teacher feedback. Report of Project H-ZJ47, submitted to the Language Fund, Hong Kong.

Hamp-Lyons, L., & Condon, W. (2000). *Assessing the portfolio: Issues for research, theory and practice.* Cresskill, NJ: Hampton Press.

Hamp-Lyons, L., Hood, S., & Maclennan, C. (2001). Promoting quality teaching in the tertiary context. *Higher Education Review, 34*(1), 60–76.

Huhta, A. (2003). Contribution to LTEST-L. Retrieved October 12 2003 from LTEST-L@psu.edu.

Huot, B. (2002). *(Re)articulating writing assessment for teaching and learning.* Logan: Utah State University Press.

Hyland, K., & Hyland, F. (Eds.) (2006). *Feedback on ESL writing: Contexts and issues.* Cambridge: Cambridge University Press.

Lumley, T. (2000). *The process of the assessment of writing performance: The rater's perspective.* Unpublished doctoral dissertation. The University of Melbourne, Victoria, Australia.

Lumley, T., Raso, E., & Mincham, L. (1993). Exemplar assessment activities. In NLLIA (Ed.), *NLLIA ESL Development: Language and Literacy in Schools.* Canberra: National Languages and Literacy Institute of Australia.

McKay, P. (2000). Innovation in English Language Assessment: Looking Towards Long-Term Learning. *Selected Refereed Papers from the ILEC 2000 Conference (CD Rom),* The University of Hong Kong.

McKay, P., & Scarino, A. (1991). *The ESL Framework of Stages.* Melbourne: Curriculum Corporation.

McMillan, J. (2003). Understanding and improving teachers' classroom assessment decision-making: Implications for theory and practice. *Educational Measurement: Issues and Practice, 22*(4), 34–43.

National Academy of Science Research Council. (2003). Assessment in Support of Instruction and Learning: Bridging the gap between large-scale and classroom assessment: Workshop Report. The National Academies Press. Retrieved Apr. 12, 2004 from http://www.nap.edu/openbook/0309089786/html/.

Newton, P. (2003). The defensibility of national curriculum assessment in England. *Research Papers in Education, 18*(2), 101–127.

Noble, A., & Smith, M.L. (1994). *Measurement-driven reform: Research on policy, practice, repercussion (CSE Technical Report No. 381).* Los Angeles: UCLA, National Center for Research on Evaluation, Standards, and Student Testing.

O'Loughlin, K. (2000). The impact of gender in the IELTS oral interview. In R. Tulloh (Ed.), *IELTS Research Reports 2000* (Vol. 3, pp. 1–28). Canberra: IELTS Australia Pty Limited.

Pula, J., & Huot, B. (1993). A model of background influences on holistic raters. In M. Williamson & B. Huot (Eds). *Validating holistic scoring for writing assessment* (p. 237–265). Cresskill, NJ: Hampton Press.

Reed, D., & Cohen, A. (2001). Revisiting raters and ratings in oral language assessment. In C. Elder, A. Brown, E. Grove, K. Hill, N. Iwashita, T. Lumley, et al. (Eds.), *Experimenting with uncertainty: Essays in honour of Alan Davies. Studies in Language Testing Series* (Vol. 11, pp. 82–96). Cambridge: UCLES/Cambridge University Press.

Resnick, L., & Resnick, M. (1992). Assessing the thinking curriculum: New tools for educational reform. In B. Gifford & M. O'Connor (Eds.), *Changing assessment: Alternative views of aptitude, achievement and instruction* (pp. 37–76). London: Kluwer.

Shohamy, E. (June, 1993). The power of a test: The impact of language testing on teaching and learning. *NFL Occasional Papers.*

Smith, J. K. (2003). Reconsidering reliability in classroom assessment and grading. *Educational measurement: Issues and practice, 22*(4), 26–33.

Smith, M. L. (1991). Put to the test: The effects of external testing on teachers. *Educational Researcher, 20*(5), 8–11.

Smith, M. L. (1993). *Reforming schools by reforming assessment: Consequences of the Arizona student assessment program* (CSE Technical Report No. 425). Los Angeles: University of California Center for Research on Evaluation, Standards, and Student Testing (CRESST).

Smith, W. (1993). Assessing the reliability and adequacy of using holistic scoring of essays as a college composition placement technique. In M. Williamson & B. Huot (Eds.), *Validating holistic scoring for writing assessment: Theoretical and empirical foundations* (pp. 152–205). Cresskill, NJ: Hampton Press.

Spolsky, B. (1995). The examination-classroom backwash cycle: Some historical cases. In R. Berry, V. Berry, & D. Nunan (Eds.), *Bringing about change in language education* (pp. 55–66). Hong Kong: Dept of Curriculum Studies, The University of Hong Kong.

Stiggins, R. (2001). The unfulfilled promise of classroom assessment. *Educational Measurement: Issues and Practice, 20*(3), 5–15.

Teasdale, A., & Leung, C. (2000). Teacher assessment and psychometric theory: A case of paradigm crossing? *Language Testing, 17*(2), 163–184.

Torrance, H., & Pryor, J. (1998). *Investigating formative assessment: Teaching, learning and assessment in the classroom.* Buckingham: Open University Press.

Wall, D. (2000). The impact of high-stakes testing on teaching and learning: Can this be predicted or controlled? *System, 28*(4), 499–509.

Wiliam, D. (2001). An overview of the relationship between assessment and the curriculum. In D. Scott (Ed.), *Curriculum and assessment* (pp. 165–181). Westport, CT: Ablex Publishing.

Wiliam, D. (2003). National Curriculum assessment: How to make it better. *Research Papers in Education, 18*(2), 129–136.

CHAPTER 33

CLASSROOM-BASED ASSESSMENT: POSSIBILITIES AND PITFALLS

PAULINE REA-DICKINS

The University of Bristol, United Kingdom

ABSTRACT

This chapter examines the possibilities and pitfalls of classroom-based English language assessment, drawing on both the language testing and classroom assessment literature in English language education as well as educational assessment more generally. The chapter opens with a brief overview of different contexts for language testing and assessment: external, classroom-based, and second language acquisition research. The second part of the chapter presents research findings that highlight different facets of classroom-based assessment: the different meanings of and purposes for assessment, relationships between formative and summative assessment, approaches and frameworks used in teacher assessment, teacher perceptions and implementation of assessment, and the extent to which conventional measurement paradigms are appropriate for assessing the worth of instructional embedded assessment. These research findings lead into a discussion of current concerns and issues, as well as some of the potential pitfalls associated with classroom-based assessment. The final part of the chapter outlines future directions for the field and highlights some of the challenges for both research and professional practice in relation to classroom-oriented assessment.

INTRODUCTION

There is a long and well-established tradition of research in the area of testing as a measure of language proficiency. This continues to be the case, with significant developments in, for example, our understanding of validity (e.g., Kunnan, 1998; Read & Chapelle, 2001; Mislevy, Steinberg, & Almond, 2002; Bachman, 2004) influenced by Messick's now classic article (Messick, 1989), greater technical sophistication in the statistical analysis of test performance (e.g., Purpura, 1999) and multi-faceted Rasch measurement (e.g., McNamara, 1996; O'Loughlin, 2001), advances in the use of qualitative approaches in the test validation process (e.g., Banerjee & Luoma, 1997; Green, 1998), together with a greater understanding of the nature of test performance, its interpretation, and interactions in language assessment processes (e.g., O'Sullivan, Weir, & Saville 2002). There is also a well trodden path for tests in the measurement of language learning as outcomes from instruction—as evidence for the *goodness of fit* of a language program—and, as early landmarks, the program evaluations of the 1960s and 1970s are obvious examples. There are also much more recent examples such as the *school effectiveness movement* in the UK and other English-speaking countries where, in response to increasing concerns about accountability in education, the testing of school children is used as a means for making decisions about the effectiveness of schools (e.g., Scheerens, Glas, & Thomas, 2003).

Much of this research, focused on language proficiency or achievement testing, is referenced to a context that Shohamy (1994) identifies as *external*, defined as a context "in which standardized tests are used for making decisions about individuals and programs regarding, for instance, certificates, diplomas, acceptance, rejection and placement" (p. 133). There is, however, increasing recognition of the significant limitations of an exclusive focus on learning outcomes as a measure of learner performance and the importance of capturing relevant data within the lived curriculum not only as evidence of quality of the program but also, and importantly, of the language learning process itself. Shohamy (1994) identifies two other contexts in addition to the external context for language testing: "the classroom context, where tests are used as part of the teaching and learning process," and "the SLA research context, where language tests are used as tools for collecting language data in order to answer and test SLA research questions and hypotheses" (p. 133). This chapter explores in some detail the second of Shohamy's contexts, that of the language classroom (whether as a foreign or second/additional language); it also touches upon the relationships between assessment and SLA research, with specific reference to formative language assessment.

The next section introduces a number of different facets of classroom-based assessment and relates these to recent research and writing in the field. This is followed by a summary of current debates and concerns that, in turn, feed into the identification of a range of potential pitfalls in and inhibitors to the implementation of effective classroom assessment. The chapter concludes with an outline of future directions important in researching and implementing quality classroom assessment. In order to avoid connotations of *testing* with standardized measures of achievement or proficiency, and to attempt to situate the discussion within the socio-cultural context of the classroom, the term *assessment* is used to refer to approaches to the elicitation of learner language in the classroom.

FACETS OF CLASSROOM-BASED ASSESSMENT

The analysis of major aspects of classroom-based assessment that follows is organized around a number of key themes: meanings of classroom-based assessment; purposes for classroom-based assessment; assessment approaches, frameworks, and implementation; and paradigm-appropriate orientations.

Meanings of Classroom-based Assessment

In the same way that there is inconsistency in both the use and interpretation of the terms testing and assessment, there is also considerable variation surrounding the meanings of *classroom-based assessment*. For example, Valette (1994) distinguishes between assessment that is associated with school-based tests and large-scale proficiency tests. In contrast, Huerta-Macias (1995, p. 9) emphasizes that "there is little or no change required in classroom routines and activities in order to implement alternative assessment" (p. 9), which she sees as significantly different from standardized measures and pencil and paper test formats. Such assessment embedded within instruction claims validity in relation to both curricula and instructional relevance, and authenticity in terms of classroom teaching activities and processes. Huerta-Macias (1995, p. 9) draws parallels between alternative assessment and qualitative research (e.g., Guba & Lincoln, 1994), suggesting trustworthiness and triangulation of data are more relevant in determining quality in alternative assessment than the criteria associated with the psychometric testing tradition. However, she also cites Wilde, Del Vecchio and Gustke (1995) who suggest that to ensure reliability in alternative assessments, "use trained judges, working with clear criteria, from specific anchor papers or performance behaviours," and "monitor periodically to ensure that raters use criteria and standards in a consistent manner" (Huerta-Marcias, 1995, p. 9). Huerta-Marcias recognizes the tension that exists between "teacher as supporting language development" and "teacher as examiner and rater," both roles for which teachers need to adapt, as appropriate, within the classroom. However, Brown and Hudson (1998, p. 655, 656) criticize Huerta-Macias's approach to reliability and validity as if these alternative procedures were of the add-on proficiency type measure:

> These statements [referring to the comments on trustworthiness and triangulation of data] are too general and short sighted to fit with our experiences as decision makers who...rely on the guidelines set forth in the *Standards for Educational and Psychological Testing* (American Psychological Association, 1985, 1986) for designing measures that will be used to make responsible decisions about students' lives ... As in all other forms of assessment, the designers and users of alternative assessments must make every effort to structure the way they design, pilot, analyse, and revise the procedures so the reliability and validity of the procedures can be studied, demonstrated, and improved. The resulting decision-making process should also take into account what testers know about the standard error of measurement and standards setting.

Clapham (2000, p. 152) has also applied traditional test criteria to alternative assessment:

> A problem with methods of alternative assessment, however, lies with their validity and reliability: Tasks are often not tried out to see whether they produce the desired linguistic information; marking criteria are not investigated to see whether they 'work'; and raters are often not trained to give consistent marks.

Both Brown and Hudson (1998) and Clapham (2000) are referring primarily to formal assessment procedures—albeit administered and implemented within classes—which have a high stakes purpose of some kind. These procedures are very different from those in which classroom assessment is used to inform language learning and teaching, and where assessment is seamlessly integrated into teaching and learning. As McNamara (2001, p. 343, 344) comments, when teachers and learners "engage in systematic reflection on the characteristics of an individual performance as an aid to the formulation of learning goals in a variety of contexts":

> This then means that the kinds of difficulties with subjective assessment that are exposed through careful validation research are not really an issue with this approach. From a certain perspective, each instance of this kind of assessment is unique; it does not always have to be fitted into a larger framework of comparison across individuals or across occasions ... Nor does this kind of assessment activity necessarily involve record keeping and reporting to fulfill managerialist agendas.

This "emergent" view of classroom-based assessment where learner performance is analyzed in terms of learning goals and instructional processes rather than a finished product introduces an important interactional perspective into assessment, critical to effective formative classroom language assessment (see also Rea-Dickins, 2001, Rea-Dickins, 2006 and Gardner, 2000). As Harlen and James (1997) comment:

> The kind of information that is gathered by teachers is not tidy, complete and self-consistent, but fragmentary and often contradictory (p. 376) ... However, where the purpose is to inform teaching and help learning, the fact that a pupil can do something in one context but apparently not in another is a positive advantage, since it gives clues to the conditions which seem to favor better performance and thus can be the basis for taking action. In this way, the validity, and usefulness of formative assessment is demonstrated and enhanced ... Through this rapid loop of feedback and adjustment between teacher and learner, the informational inevitably acquires greater reliability. (p. 371)

This analysis of the meanings of classroom-based assessment reveals different understandings of assessment derived from the different *purposes* for which learners are assessed, and the selection of an appropriate paradigm by which the goodness of fit to assessment purpose is established. The next section examines the different purposes of assessment in instructional contexts to provide a firmer framework for deconstructing the different meanings and potential roles for classroom assessment.

Purposes for Classroom Assessment

Purposes for classroom assessment are diverse, ranging from meeting the bureaucratic demands placed on teachers for data on learner achievement levels to assessment that has a primarily supportive function in the formative assessment of language learners and is firmly embedded within routine instructional contexts. These purposes, in turn, also give rise to different teacher and learner positioning in assessment (see Arkoudis & O'Loughlin, 2004).

The distinction conventionally drawn has been between summative and formative purposes for assessment, invariably contrasting one with the other, with much oversimplification of both of these constructs and the relationships between them. For example, *summative assessment* has been defined as assessment that takes place at the end of a school year for administrative purposes "in order to assign grades for purposes of certification or promoting students to the next level" (Genesee & Upshur, 1996, p. 49) or to "provide useful information ... of students' achievement or progress at the end of a course of study" (Bachman & Palmer, 1996, p. 98). In contrast, *formative assessment* is presented as helping "students guide their own subsequent learning, or for helping teachers modify their teaching methods and materials so as to make them more appropriate for students' needs, interests, and capabilities" (Bachman & Palmer, 1996, p. 98). Much of the discussion on formative assessment, however, has been couched in terms of formal achievement tests, thus, the focus on accurate and comprehensive profiling of language achievement (e.g., Brown & Hudson, 1998) is unsurprising. More recently, with the pervasive concern for national school league tables (e.g., in the UK) and for accountability to government and other agencies, there is increasing reference to the managerialist and summative purposes for assessment (see for example, Brindley, 2001; South, Leung, Rea-Dickins, Scott, Erduran, in progress[1]), which for the schools or programs concerned is high stakes.

In fact, there is relatively little empirical work on assessment purposes. An early study into the functions of teacher assessment was conducted by Brindley (1989) who asked teachers to rank the importance of a list of assessment functions. In terms of perceived importance to the teachers, it is interesting to note that they ranked lowest "providing information to funding authorities for accountability purposes," whereas "placing learners in class" and "providing information on learners' strengths and weaknesses for course planning" were ranked 1 and 2 respectively (p. 25). With reference to teacher classroom assessment, Rea-Dickins and Gardner (2000) found a striking variety in classroom assessments implemented on a regular basis for the assessment of English language learners. From teacher self-reports they identified five main purposes for assessment: assessment used formatively to inform the management and planning of teaching to assessments used summatively to review learners' developing linguistic competence and skills, to provide feedback for bureaucratic purposes, to assess an individual's readiness to access the mainstream curriculum and to provide feedback on teaching. The idea that assessment might also be formative for the learners themselves did not emerge clearly as a major purpose in this analysis.

The blurring of the boundaries between formative and summative assessment is not as clear cut as usually represented. Teachers may use the same data obtained from assessments for different purposes at different time intervals, formative in one context (e.g., a child's language sample used to inform discussion at a teachers' planning meeting where action is agreed for language support for that individual learner) and summative in another (i.e. where that same language sample is used as part of a child's school Language Achievement Record). An analysis of ESL frameworks (South, Leung, Rea-Dickins, Scott, & Erduran, in progress[2]) also reveals the multi-purpose nature of teacher assessment as operationalized through assessment frameworks and standards (see also McKay, 2000). As Black (1998) comments: "The formative and summative labels describe two ends of a spectrum in school-based assessment rather than two isolated and completely different functions" (p. 35). In general, these purposes for classroom-based assessment remain largely unproblematized and unresearched.

ASSESSMENT APPROACHES, FRAMEWORKS, AND IMPLEMENTATION

Brown and Hudson (1998) provide a useful listing of assessment procedures beyond the familiar pencil and paper tests, including checklists, journals, video-tapes, portfolios, self- and peer-assessment. They also provide a synthesis of characteristics (drawing from Aschbacher, 1991; Herman, Aschbacher & Winter, 1992; Huerta-Macias, 1995) associated with these alternative assessments, e.g., "tap into higher level thinking and problem solving skills" (p. 654). As Shohamy (1998) comments: "Each procedure is aimed at capturing different aspects and domains of language knowledge, as it is assumed that language knowledge is exemplified differently in different contexts and situations" (p. 109). This perspective is also reinforced by a teacher, talking about her use of language sampling as an assessment tool (Gardner & Rea-Dickins, 2002):

> Once I sat down and the children were having dinner [midday meal], with a shy one at the beginning of the year, because she wouldn't speak. She didn't speak for weeks. And I caught her talking to a friend after a few weeks and I sat there in my lunch break and copied down two pages. It was just social chat. It wasn't academic type language, but it was the fact that she could talk at length if she was given the opportunity so, it's just— my system is ad hoc…it's just as and when I pick things (p. 6).

As Gardner and Rea-Dickins (2002) observe, it is not surprising that teachers rated language sampling as the least stressful form of assessment for learners, as it is usually fully contextualized in day-to-day work, "an example of continuous, naturalistic performance testing, *par excellence*" (p. 6).

Assessment innovations of a different order that have impacted significantly on modes of teacher assessment are those associated with the development of language assessment frameworks and standards. These are used in various part of the world primarily for the assessment of school-age children using English as an additional language (see McKay and Nunan, this volume).[3] Although, there is considerable variation across these frameworks, several of them incorporate detailed guidance for the teacher in important areas of classroom assessment. The ESL Bandscales (National Languages and Literacy Institute of Australia, 1994) and the TESOL Standards (TESOL, 1997), in particular, go well beyond a discussion of assessment tools and the interpretation of learner language to demonstrate ways in which learner assessment may be integrated within teaching and learning processes and embedded within instruction (see Short, 2003; South, Rea-Dickins, Scott, & Erduran, in progress).

There is a growing literature about different assessment approaches and procedures, but although issues of classroom assessment are not new (most notably, see Brindley, 1989, 1995, 2000), relatively little has been written about the actual engagement of teachers and their learners—as evidenced by research studies—in the implementation of specific approaches and assessment activities. A number of Australian research studies have examined how teachers work with assessment frameworks and how they develop an understanding of assessment issues. Breen et al., 1997) investigated the implementation of assessment in primary schools, focusing on the relationship between assessment frameworks and teachers' pedagogic practice in making judgments about the English language development of their learners. In a three year longitudinal study Davison and Williams (2002) compared teachers' use of different assessment frameworks, including the ESL Bandscales (NLLIA, 1994) and the *English Curriculum Standards Frameworks* (Board of Studies, 2000). Arkoudis and O'Loughlin (2004) have investigated teachers' understandings of reliability and validity through using assessment frameworks to produce a meaningful assessment of their students' progress. Through an analysis of teachers' stories, they illustrate how state mandated assessment policies are translated into teacher assessment practices and how the teachers develop an awareness of the limitations of such frameworks, in this case *English as a Second Language (ESL) Companion to the English Curriculum Standards Frameworks* (Board of Studies, 2000). Such research also raises quite poignantly the broader issue of teacher/examiner role conflict, which is a particular challenge where integration and embeddedness of assessment are viewed as necessary. A comparative study of Hong Kong and Australia (Victoria) by Davison and Tang (2001) investigated ESL teacher assessment practices (e.g., choice of assessment tasks, criteria, teacher feedback to students) and their beliefs about language, language development, and assessment. This research revealed a high level of teacher awareness and acceptance of the need for accountability, particularly in high stakes assessment contexts as well as a need for more opportunities for teacher interaction about assessment issues. In a later study, Davison (2004) explores the tensions faced by teachers and the types of decisions they make when assessing student work and suggests that traditional norms of validity may need to be re-conceptualized in high stakes teacher-based assessment. Cheng, Rogers, and Hu (2004) have also identified the complex and multifaceted roles that assessment plays in different language learning contexts based on a comparative survey of ESL/EFL instructors in Canadian, Hong Kong, and Chinese tertiary settings. Hamp-Lyons & Condon (2000) have researched the use of portfolios in helping "teachers help learners assume more responsibility for their own learning" and in providing "a rich source of information to teachers as they continually reconsider their theory and practice" (p. xv).

Rea-Dickins (2002) identified various influences on teacher assessment activities, revealing that English language teachers draw upon the mainstream curriculum (i.e. subject knowledge, learning objectives and outcomes), high stakes national tests, and psychometric notions of reliability and norming to inform their assessment activities. Some are also aware of an interactional perspective on classroom formative assessment and the importance of creating opportunities for sustained talk in the classroom.

Fewer studies still have adopted a learner and learning focus in instruction-embedded assessment. Within general educational assessment, there are notable exceptions. Tunstall and Gipps (1996), for example, have developed a typology to account for different types of teacher feedback to their learners that might lead to the promotion of curricula learning (i.e. not specifically language learning). This research is noteworthy as their feedback typology is grounded in the discourse of the classroom. A similar approach to researching classroom assessment was taken by Torrance and Pryor (1998) who investigated the impact of formative assessment on pupil learning.

In the field of language education, Rea-Dickins (2002) reports on the various ways in which learners may be scaffolded in their language and content learning, as they progress through their assessment activities. Drawing on Tunstall and Gipps (1996), a range of teacher feedback strategies were demonstrated: when teachers "specify" for the learner what needs to be worked on in order to improve their use of language, when they "encourage learner self-assessment," or when they are in dialogue with a child in "constructing next steps" within the learning activity. In addition, teachers were observed providing feedback of other kinds: encouraging children to elaborate and/or explain their utterances by use of questions or echoing strategies; and assisting language performance through teacher "recasts" (Nicholas, Lightbown, & Spada, 2001) as feedback on both the content and form of the children's utterances. The recasts observed included teacher "correction of errors," "recasting of a child's utterance," "expanding on learner contributions," "offering a target like model," and inviting the learner "to fill the gap." These scaffolding strategies support learners so that their awareness of language use across the curriculum is enhanced and their language and content learning further developed and enriched.

Recent and interesting work arising from early years' research in Holland and Germany has also drawn attention to teacher feedback and to the concept of a teacher's *diagnostic competence,* which the researchers define as "the ability to interpret foreign language growth in individual children" (Edelenbos & Kubanek-German, 2004). Data from both systematic observation and ethnographic classroom studies are used to identify and illustrate teachers' diagnostic activities and processes on the basis of which these researchers offer a preliminary description of levels of diagnostic competence and associated features.

In a university level language course, Spence-Brown (2001) investigated the construct of authenticity in an assessment activity designed "to optimise authenticity" (p. 463). Through interviews with students she identified a range of factors that compromised the authenticity of a learning task when used for purposes of formal assessment, leading her to the conclusion that authenticity must be viewed in terms of the implementation of an activity as well as a function of its design. This relationship between the purpose(s) and design of an assessment and features of its actual implementation is highly important in classroom assessment research.

In terms of washback effects on classroom assessment processes from national assessment policies and associated frameworks and standards, there is overall relatively little research in spite of the growing number and use of assessment frameworks and standards (cf., Breen et al., 1997; Scott, 2005; Scott & Erduran, 2004).

PARADIGM-APPROPRIATE ORIENTATIONS

Implicit in the various understandings of classroom-based assessment and linked to the different purposes for assessment is the way in which classroom-based teacher assessment is conceptualized. The traditional positivist position on language testing, with the tendency to map the standard psychometric criteria of reliability and validity on to the classroom assessment procedures, has been called into question, and the scope of validity has been significantly broadened (e.g., Chapelle, 1999; Lynch, 2001, 2003; McNamara, 2001) and taken further by a number of researchers. Teasdale & Leung (2000), for example, highlighted the need to clarify the epistemological bases of different types of assessment within the context of the assessment of spoken English in mainstream classrooms. Drawing on both the TESOL and general educational assessment literature, Leung (2005) problematizes some of the "constitutive issues concerning pedagogically oriented classroom-based teacher assessment" (p. 869) and the tensions that exist for teachers in their dual roles in assessing and scaffolding learning. Through an analysis of classroom episodes and teacher interview data, he argues, "attending to teachers' professional knowledge and practice ... would contribute towards understanding the 'construct' in construct-referenced assessment" (p. 884). It is this kind of understanding, requiring the critical engagement of researchers with teachers, which Leung argues is critical for the development of a grounded, dynamic and contextually sensitive research agenda and, furthermore, that the evaluation criteria traditionally associated with psychometric testing such as reliability and validity are not necessarily relevant, "especially when the outcomes of teacher assessment are not used for public comparison and reporting purposes" (p. 885).

Appropriate paradigm orientation directly links to purposes for assessment. For purposes of accountability and normative and comparative rankings across or within schools, or when important decisions about individual learners are being made, a conceptualization of assessment as standardized measurement and the role of the teacher as rater/examiner has relevance (but see Davison, 2004). However, where the teacher's main role is to support learning and to provide opportunities in which learners feel able to use and stretch their linguistic resources in an attempt to convey their meanings to others in class, the priorities are different and other criteria have resonance. Thus classroom-based assessment represents an epistemological departure from the practice of framing research within established paradigms and theoretical models in the psychometric tradition.

CLASSROOM-BASED ASSESSMENT: POTENTIAL PITFALLS

There are a number of pitfalls in the implementation of effective classroom-based assessment and a number of potential inhibitors to quality assessment practices. One rather obvious one is that classroom assessment may be operationalized as the testing of linguistic knowledge that achieves little more than presenting learners with a series of summative mini-achievement tests. There are several points to consider here in relation to the potential mismatch between teaching and learning goals and classroom assessment practices. The first has to do with the motivation and rationale for teaching a foreign language (see Karavas-Doukas & Rea-Dickins, 1997). Within the primary language curriculum, in particular, there is a range of reasons for introducing a foreign or additional language. The reasons span the acquisition of structures and lexis or of communicative language ability, goals linked to developing language awareness and intra- and inter-cultural awareness (Kubanek-German, 1997), or the need to access subject knowledge through the medium of an additional language. The question is to what extent assessment activities mirror these diverse purposes and achieve an appropriate matching and balance in terms of "content" with reference to stated curriculum goals.

A second point has to do with the pedagogic approach and language skills actually assessed. Evidence from a small-scale case study (Rea-Dickins & Rixon, 1999) suggested that even though teachers recognized the need to assess both speaking and listening skills, this did not always happen. Where speaking skills were assessed, there was evidence that this was realized through rehearsed dialogues with little or no opportunity for spontaneous language use (cf., Gardner & Rea-Dickins, 2002), and the tendency was for teachers to rely on the tried and tested written assessment of structure and lexis and writing skills. Although there is a range of elicitation tools and frameworks described in the literature and in research studies (e.g., Genessee & Upshur, 1996; Hamp-Lyons & Condon, 2000; NLLIA Bandscales, National Languages and Literacy Institute of Australia, 1994), there seems to be a continued over-reliance on the paper and pencil format in preference to more observation-driven approaches to assessment. Even assessment frameworks, such as the ESL Standards (TESOL 1997), may be used normatively, with an over-reliance on summative tests that might result in limited opportunities for teachers to provide their learners with the necessary linguistic and cognitive structuring within instructional sequences.

More generally, there is evidence of a tendency in both handbooks for teachers (e.g., Hughes, 1990; Weir, 1993) and amongst teachers themselves (e.g., Rea-Dickins, 2003) for classroom assessment practices to be referenced to criteria associated with a psychometric approach to test validation and to normative standards, which in most circumstances have little or no relevance for the bulk of classroom-based formative assessment (for examples of paradigm confusion, see Teasdale and Leung, 2000; McNamara, 2001; Lynch, 2001). Given the mixed discourses of assessment prevalent in curriculum policy documents (e.g., QCA, 2000) and the emphasis in some countries on outcomes-based assessment of performance (e.g., the National Curriculum in England) (see Brindley, 2001), it is thus unsurprising that teachers also fail to grasp some of the nuances of classroom-based assessment. The problems include teachers employing limited means to capture knowledge and develop understandings of their learners' language abilities and failing to grasp the potential of collaborative dialogue for formative assessment.

Spence-Brown (2001), summarized earlier, draws our attention to the distinction between assessment plans and specifications and actual implementation. Classroom assessments may be developed according to a specific blueprint but may be implemented by students in ways that fundamentally compromise the intended design and characteristics. This is something that has become forcibly apparent in my own research where six teachers implemented the same assessment activities in very different ways that, in turn, provided the learners with opportunities for different kinds of engagement within the activity and use of different linguistic resources, some much more formative than others (Rea-Dickins, 2003). In fact, an activity or elicitation procedure in itself is neutral. It is only in its implementation and the use to which the data that emerges from a given activity is put that then develops its formative or summative potential, a point that is rarely given enough emphasis in the language testing literature.

A final pitfall is the dual roles of teachers – as assessor/tester vs. facilitator of language support – and how learners come to understand and perceive these dual functions within instruction. A distinction has been made between high and low-stakes assessment contexts, which together with the language attainment levels/development dimensions impact on the role of the teacher, whether as rater and examiner versus language teacher and facilitator (Arkoudis & O'Loughlin, 2004; Leung, 2004). They also affect the inherent trustworthiness and comprehensiveness of assessment activities that are embedded within routine instruction developing over time for individual learners in the classroom (Davison, 2004) and the criteria evoked, whether that be psychometric criteria drawn from standardized measurement or notions of *construct-referenced assessment* and *communities of practice* (Davison, 2004; Leung, 2005).

FUTURE DIRECTIONS

A number of central directions for classroom-based assessment practice and research can be identified, although obviously these reflect my own particular orientation to researching assessment in the language classroom and what I consider to be important to the development of greater understandings of assessment processes and their effects in relation to both teachers and learners.

"Researching" Classroom-based Assessment

Given the desired embeddedness of assessment within classroom processes, "in-flight" vs. "add on" assessment, it is suggested that the most appropriate way of investigating assessment in action is situated within a broad socio-cultural approach. This would facilitate an understanding of assessment practices and the language learning potential of these practices within the social and cultural context in which they take place. This theoretical positioning implies a methodology in which assessment is studied in depth within the ecology of the classroom, and one in which multi-layering techniques combining ethnography, discourse analysis, and linguistic description are appropriate. A layered approach was adopted by Rea-Dickins (2003) in which learner engagement in assessment activities analyzed from an interactional perspective proved particularly revealing.

The Centrality of the Learner

In language proficiency testing, we may observe over the last decade increased attention to examination processes and, in particular, on the test taker in, for example, the oral interview (O'Sullivan, 2002). By the same token, I believe that the way forward in classroom-based assessment is not only on elaborating teacher assessment processes but also, and importantly, developing greater understanding of the facets of classroom-based assessment through the lens of the learners. The research of Spence-Brown (2002) and Rea-Dickins (2002) are examples of this orientation in the area of language assessment. Two further examples from research in educational assessment have positioned the learner at the center of the assessment process: the LEARN Project (Weeden et al., 1999) focused their research around learners' views of assessment; and the Effective Lifelong Learning Inventory project (Deakin-Crick, Broadfoot & Claxton, 2004[4]) is investigating empirically the concept of students' learning power and potential.

Embedding Assessment within Classroom Learning and Learning

McNamara (1998, p. 311) draws his readers' attention to Spolsky (1995) who stressed "that tests and examinations have historically been a means of control and power ever since the original shibboleth test in the Bible" (see also Shohamy, 2001a, 2001b). If classroom assessment is interpreted as a series of summative tests in the classroom, disembedded from the flow of teaching and learning, this can be criticized as being unfair and a denial of formative language learning opportunities. It represents further evidence of the stranglehold that prevails in the form of language testing practices associated with external measures of language performance. There is, thus, a need to be alert to a change in emphasis from what learners have achieved—this becomes less of a priority for most of the time—to how learners can be supported in their language learning in different classroom situations through varied activities. Inherent in much current classroom assessment discourse is a view of assessment as a technicist endeavor, very probably linked to a policy context that prioritizes the use of assessment data for bureaucratic purposes of accountability and standard setting across schools, as well as the operationalization of learner language performance as *achievement*. This contrasts with a view of assessment as embedded within the socio-cultural practices of the classroom (see McNamara, 2001), one that also supports emergent language development. In the words of Gipps (1994):

> Assessment is an interactive, dynamic and collaborative activity. Rather than being external and formal in its implementation, assessment is integral to the teaching process and is embedded in the social and cultural life of the classroom. Such an approach can be seen as constructive and enabling because of its focus on assessing the process of learning, its attempt to elicit elaborated performance, and its emphasis on collaborative activity, whether the collaboration is with the teacher or a group of peers. (p. 158)

Research that attends to the relationships between assessment and instruction will be an important future focus.

Exploring Relationships between Formative Assessment and Second Language Acquisition

A limited number of researchers has examined the interfaces between language testing and assessment as highlighted by Shohamy and described in the introduction of this chapter (for exceptions, see the summary by Bachman & Cohen, 1998; Brindley, 1998; Shohamy, 2000). In the case of classroom embedded assessment and, in particular, assessment that is intended to promote the development of language learning and learner language, there is a direct and explicit link to be made with processes of second language acquisition. As Shohamy (2000) argues:

> The disciplines of language testing (LT) and second language acquisition (SLA) belong to the same field, that of language learning. They share similar goals of understanding the process of language learning, assessing it and looking for ways to improve it. It is, therefore, expected that the two disciplines would interact, share and contribute to one another. (p. 542)

The quality of teacher feedback and the impact of this feedback on student uptake and output become important in this respect. However, few classroom assessment studies have explored the interaction between the two disciplines (for some examples see Edelenbos & Kubanek-German, 2004; Leung & Mohan, 2004; and Rea-Dickins, 2002). Thus, there remains a need for increased understanding and collaborative work between the two fields: The impact of formative classroom assessment on acquisition needs to be explored and tracked. SLA studies that have teacher feedback as their focus are particularly useful starting points (e.g., Doughty & Williams, 1998; Ellis, Basturkmen, & Loewen, 2001).

Quality in Classroom-based Assessment

What constitutes quality in classroom-based assessment is a key question and an area for further research. As observed earlier, the means by which to achieve consistency in making judgments about language samples are well rehearsed, but much uncharted territory remains in the development of quality formative language assessment. The types of criteria that become important in classroom assessment include "resonance with curricula goals and instructional processes" and the provision of a "rich variety of opportunities" for learners to use and stretch their linguistic resources, using language appropriate to different contexts. The Assessment Reform Group (1994; see also Clarke, 1998, 2001; Wiliam, 2001), drawing on research in educational assessment, has developed principles for good practice in recognition that assessment for learning has the following characteristics:

- It is part of effective planning.
- It reflects how students learn.
- It is central to classroom practice.
- It is a key professional skill.
- It has an emotional impact.
- It affects learner motivation.
- It promotes commitment to learning goals and assessment criteria.
- It helps learners know how to improve.
- It encourages self- and peer-assessment.
- It recognizes all achievements.

Given that preservice training and professional development in the area of language testing and assessment may be rather "hit and miss," and many teachers are unfamiliar with the intricate relationships between formative and summative assessment, there are significant implications for teacher education as well.

CONCLUSIONS

A number of the tensions surrounding classroom-based assessment have been raised in this chapter, including the question of what is actually meant by classroom-based assessment, and the tendency in the assessment discourse for sharp distinctions to be made between a summative assessment activity and a formative one, with most research focusing on the former rather than the latter. This may be to the detriment of assessment opportunities that support student language learning. Good teaching—where teachers respond to learners' language learning and needs, with different types of feedback of an appropriate kind, of learner involvement through collaborative learning activities and self- and peer-assessment, with ample opportunities for language practice—implies good formative assessment practice. The next decade should see an increase in research on classroom-based assessment and a closer investigation of the linkages between formative classroom language assessment and second language acquisition. This is not, however, proposing an either/or situation, and it will be interesting to explore ways in which there might be a greater integration between the areas of language testing, classroom language assessment and second language acquisition in Applied Linguistics.

NOTES

[1] A review and critical evaluation of different assessment frameworks and standards, funded by the Paul Hamlyn Foundation and the National Association for Language Development in the Curriculum (NALDIC), 2002-2003. The research team comprises Hugh South, Constant Leung, Pauline Rea-Dickins, Catriona Scott, and Sibel Erduran.

[2] This research—Classroom Assessment of English as an Additional Language: Key Stage 1 Contexts—was funded by the Economic and Social Research Council (ESRC Major Research Grant R000238196, 1999 – 2002). Further details from: P.Rea-Dickins@bristol.ac.uk.

[3] These are *Canadian Language Benchmarks 2000: English as a second language – for adults* (Centre for Canadian Language Benchmarks, 2000); *South Australian Curriculum, Standards and Accountability Framework: English as a second language* (Department of Education, Training and Employment (DETE), South Australia, 2002); *A Language in Common* (QCA, 2000); ESL Development: Language and Literacy in Schools (National Languages and Literacy Institute of Australia (NLLIA), 1994); ESL Standards for Pre-K-12 Students—TESOL (TESOL Task Force, 1997), *ESL Companion to the English CSF: Curriculum and Standards Framework II* (Board of Studies, Victoria, 2000).

[4] The Effective Lifelong Learning Project is based in the Graduate School of Education, University of Bristol.

REFERENCES

Arkoudis, S., & O'Loughlin, K. (2004). Tensions between validity and outcomes: Teachers' assessment of written work of recently arrived immigrant ESL students. *Language Testing, 20*(3), 284–304.

Assessment Reform Group. (1999). *Assessment for learning: Beyond the Black Box.* Cambridge: University of Cambridge School of Education. See also: arg.educ.cam.ac.uk.

Bachman, L. F. 2004. *Statistical analysis for language assessment.* Cambridge: Cambridge University Press.

Bachman, L., & Cohen, A. (1998). *Interfaces between second language acquisition and language testing research.* Cambridge: Cambridge University Press.

Bachman, L., & Palmer A. (1996). *Language testing in practice*. Oxford: Oxford University Press.
Banerjee, J., & Luoma, S. (1997). Qualitative approaches to test validation. In C. Clapham, & D. Corson (Eds.), *Encyclopedia of Language and Education: Vol. 7. Language testing and assessment* (pp. 275–287). Dordecht: Kluwer.
Black, P. (1998). *Testing: Friend or foe?* London: The Falmer Press.
Black, P., & Wiliam, D. (1998). Assessment and classroom learning. *Assessment in Education, 5*(1), 7–74.
Board of Studies. (2000). *ESL companion to the English CSF*. Victoria.
Breen, M., Barratt-Pugh, C., Derewianka, B., House, H., Hudson, C., Lumley, T., & Rohl, M. (1997). *How teachers interpret and use national and state assessment frameworks.* (Vols. 1–3). Canberra, Department of Employment, Education, Training and Youth Affairs.
Brindley, G. (1989). *Assessing achievement in the learner-centred curriculum*. NCELTR Research Series. Macquarie University Sydney: National Centre for English Language Teaching and Research.
Brindley, G. (1995). (Ed.). *Language assessment in action*. Research Series. Macquarie University Sydney: National Centre for English Language Teaching and Research.
Brindley, G. (1998). Describing language development: Rating scales and SLA. In L. Bachman, & A. Cohen (Eds.), *Interfaces between second language acquisition and language testing research* (pp. 112–140). Cambridge: Cambridge University Press.
Brindley, G. (2001). Outcomes-based assessment in practice: Some examples and emerging insights. *Language Testing, 18*(4), 393–408.
Brown, J., & Hudson, T. (1998). The alternatives in language assessment. *TESOL Quarterly, 32*, 653–675.
Canadian Language Benchmarks. (2000). *Canadian language benchmarks 2000: English as a second language for adults*. Ottawa, ON: Centre for Canadian Language Benchmarks.
Chapelle, C. (1999). Validity in language assessment. *Annual Review of Applied Linguistics, 19*, 254–272.
Cheng, L., Rogers, T., & Hu, H. (2004). ESL/EFL instructors' classroom assessment practices: Purposes, methods and procedures. *Language Testing, 21*(3), 360–389.
Clapham, C. (2000). Assessment and testing. Annual Review of Applied Linguistics, 20, 147–161.
Clarke, S. (1998). *Targeting assessment in the primary classroom.* Bristol: Hodder & Stoughton.
Clarke, S. (2001). *Unlocking formative assessment*. London: Hodder & Stoughton.
Davies, A. (1997). Introduction: The limits of ethics in language testing. *Language Testing, 14*(3), 235–241.
Davison, C. (2004). The contradictory culture of teacher-based assessment: ESL teacher assessment practices in Australian and Hong Kong secondary schools. *Language Testing, 20*(3), 304–334.
Davison, C., & Tang, R. (2001, February). *The contradictory culture of school-based assessment: Teacher assessment practices in Hong Kong and Australia.* Paper presented at the American Association for Applied Linguistics, St Louis, USA.
Davison, C., & Williams, A. (Eds.). (2001). *Learning from each other: Literacy, labels and limitations.* Studies of child English language and literacy development K-12, Vol. 2. Melbourne: Language Australia.
Deakin-Crick, R., Broadfoot, P., & Claxton, G. (2004). Developing an effective lifelong learning inventory: The ELLI project. *Assessment in Education, 11*(3), 247–272.
Doughty, C., & Williams, J. (1998). *Focus on form in classroom second language* acquisition. Cambridge: Cambridge University Press.
Edelenbos, P., & Kubanek-German, A. (2004). Teacher assessment: The concept of 'diagnostic competence'. *Language Testing, 21*(3), 259–283.
Ellis, R., Basturkmen, H., & Loewen, S. (2001). Learner uptake in communicative ESL lessons. *Language Learning, 51*, 281–318.
Gardner, S., & Rea-Dickins, P. (2002). *Focus on language sampling: A key issue in EAL assessment.* London: National Association for Language Development in the Curriculum (NALDIC).
Genesee, F., & Upshur, J. (1996). *Classroom-based evaluation in second language education*. New York: Cambridge University Press.
Gipps, C. (1994). *Beyond testing: Towards a theory of educational assessment*. London: The Falmer Press.
Green, A. (1998). *Verbal protocol analysis in language testing research* (Vol. 5). Cambridge: Cambridge University Press.
Guba, E., & Lincoln, Y. (1994). *Handbook of qualitative research.* Thousand Oaks, CA.: Sage.
Gunn, M. (1995). Classroom-based assessment in intensive English centres. In G. Brindley (Ed.), *Language assessment in action* (pp. 239–270). Macquarie University Sydney: National Centre for English Language Teaching and Research.

Hamp-Lyons, L. (1997). Washback, impact and validity: Ethical concerns. *Language Testing, 14*(3), 295–303.

Hamp-Lyons, L., & Condon, W. (2000). *Assessing the portfolio: Principles for practice, theory, and research.* Cresskill, New Jersey: Hampton Press, Inc.

Harlen, W., & James, M. (1997). Assessment and learning: Differences and relationships between formative and summative assessment. *Assessment in Education, 4*(3), 365–379.

Huerta-Macías, A. (1995). Alternative assessment: Responses to commonly asked questions. *TESOL Journal, 5,* 8–11.

Hughes, A. (1990). *Testing for language teachers.* Cambridge: Cambridge University Press.

Karavas-Doukas, K., & Rea-Dickins, P. (1997). (Compilers.). *Evaluating innovation and establishing research priorities.* Euroconference Proceedings. University of Warwick: Centre for English Language Teacher Education. (Contact: P.Rea-Dickins@bristol.ac.uk).

Kubanek-German, A. (1997). Modern foreign languages in German primary schools: a case study. In K. Karavas & P. Rea-Dickins (Compilers.), 217–225.

Kunnan, A. (1998). (Ed.). *Validation in language assessment.* Mahwah, N.J.: Lawrence Earlbaum Associates, Inc. Publishers.

Leung, C. (2001b, February). *Working with pupil talk: Assumptions and stances in teacher assessment of spoken interaction in the mainstream classroom.* Paper presented at the American Association for Applied Linguistics, St Louis, USA.

Leung, C. (2002, April). *Validity as social construction—Stability and flux.* Paper presented at the American Association for Applied Linguistics, Arlington, VA, USA.

Leung, C. (2005). Classroom teacher assessment of second language development: Construct as practice. In E. Hinkel (Ed.), *Handbook of research in second language learning and teaching.* Mahwah, N.J.: Lawrence Earlbaum Associates, Inc. Publishers.

Leung, C., & Mohan, B. (2004). Teacher formative assessment and talk in classroom contexts: Assessment *as* discourse and assessment *of* discourse. *Language Testing, 21*(3), 335–359.

Lynch, B. (2001). Rethinking assessment from a critical perspective. *Language Testing, 18*(4), 351–372.

Lynch, B. (2003). *Language assessment and programme evaluation.* Edinburgh: Edinburgh University Press.

McKay, P. (2000). On ESL standards for school-age learners. *Language Testing, 17*(2), 185–214.

McNamara, T. (1996). *Measuring second language performance.* Harlow, Essex: Addison Wesley Longman Ltd.

McNamara, T. (1998). Policy and social considerations in language assessment. *Annual Review of Applied Linguistics, 18,* 304–319.

McNamara, T. (2001). Language assessment as social practice: Challenges for research. *Language Testing, 18*(4), 333–350.

Messick, S. (1989). Validity. In R. Linn (Ed.), *Educational measurement* (3rd ed.) (pp. 13–103). New York: Macmillan.

Mislevy, R. J., Steinberg, L. S., & Almond, R. G. 2002. Design and analysis in task-based language assessment. *Language Testing,* 19(4), 477–496.

National Languages and Literacy Institute of Australia. (1994). *ESL development: Language and literacy in schools* (Vol. 1). Canberra: The National Languages and Literacy Institute of Australia.

Nicholas, H., Lightbown, P., & Spada, N. (2001). Recasts as feedback to language learners. *Language Learning, 51,* 719–758.

O'Loughlin, K. (2001). *The equivalence of direct and semi-direct speaking tests.* Cambridge: Cambridge University Press.

O'Sullivan, B. (2002). Learner acquaintanceship and oral proficiency test pair-task performance. *Language Testing, 19*(3), 277–295.

O'Sullivan, B., Weir, C., & Saville, N. (2002). Using observation checklists to validate speaking-test tasks. *Language Testing, 19*(1), 33–56.

Purpura, J. (1999). *Learner strategy use and performance on language tests: A structural equation modelling approach* (Vol. 8). Cambridge: Cambridge University Press.

Qualifications and Curriculum Authority (QCA). (2000). *A language in common.*

Read, J., & Chapelle, C. (2001). A framework for second language vocabulary assessment. *Language Testing, 18*(1), 1–32.

Rea-Dickins, P., & Gardner, S. (2000). Snares and silver bullets: Disentangling the construct of formative assessment. *Language Testing, 17*(2), 215–243.

Rea-Dickins, P. (2001). Mirror, mirror on the wall: Identifying processes of classroom assessment. *Language Testing, 18*(4), 429–462.

Rea-Dickins, P. (2002). Exploring the educational potential of assessment with reference to learners with English as an additional language. In C. Leung (Ed.), *Language and additional/second language issues for school education: A reader for teachers* (pp. 81–93). York: York Publishing Services.

Rea-Dickins, P. (2003a). *Classroom Assessment of English as an Additional Language: Key Stage 1 Contexts.* End of Project Report for ESRC Major Research Grant R000238196, 1999–2002.

Rea-Dickins, P. (2003b, September). *Framing assessment: Breaking the mould.* Plenary Paper presented at TESOL Symposium on ESL/EFL Standards for Young Learners, University of Rome. Alexandria, Virginia: TESOL, Inc.

Rea-Dickins, P. (2006). Currents and eddies in the discourse of assessment: A learning-focused interpretation. *International Journal of Applied Linguistics, 16*(2), 163–188.

Rea-Dickins, P., & Rixon, S. (1999). Assessment of young learners' English—Reasons and means. In S. Rixon (Ed.), *Young learners of English: Some research perspectives* (pp. 89–101). Addison Wesley Longman/The British Council.

Scheerens, J., Glas, C., & Thomas, S. (2003). *Educational evaluation, assessment and monitoring: A systemic approach.* Lisse, Abingdon, Exton (PA), Tokyo: Swets & Zeitlinger.

Scott, C. (2005). *Washback in the UK primary context with EAL learners: Exploratory case studies.* Unpublished PhD Dissertation. Bristol: Graduate School of Education, University of Bristol.

Scott, K., & Erduran, S. (2004). Learning from international frameworks for assessment: EAL descriptors in Australia and the USA. *Language Testing, 21*(3), 409–431.

Shohamy, E. (1994). The role of language tests in the construction of second-language acquisition theories. In E. Tarone, S. Gass, & A. Cohen (Eds.), *Research methodology in second language acquisition* (pp. 133–42). Hillsdale NJ: Lawrence Erlbaum.

Shohamy, E. (1998). Applying a multiplism approach. In E. Li & G. James (Eds.), *Testing and evaluation in second language education.* Hong Kong: Language Centre, The University of Science and Technology.

Shohamy, E. (2000). The relationship between language testing and second language acquisition revisited. *System, 28*, 541–553.

Shohamy, E. (2001a). Democratic assessment as an alternative. *Language Testing, 18*(4), 373–392.

Shohamy, E. (2001b). *The power of tests: A critical perspective on the uses of language tests.* London: Pearson.

Spence-Brown, R. (2001). The eye of the beholder: Authenticity in an embedded assessment task. *Language Testing, 18*(4), 463–481.

Spolsky, B. (1995). *Measured words.* Oxford: Oxford University Press.

Teasdale, A., & Leung, C. (2000). Teacher assessment and psychometric theory: A case of paradigm crossing. *Language Testing, 17*(2), 163–184.

TESOL. (1997). *ESL standards for pre-K-12.* Alexandria, VA: Teachers of English to Speakers of Other Languages.

Torrance, H., & Pryor, J. (1998). *Investigating formative assessment.* Buckingham: Open University Press.

Tunstall, P., & Gipps, C. (1996). Teacher feedback to young children in formative assessment: A typology. *British Educational Research Journal, 22*(4), 389–416.

Valette, R. (1994). Teaching, testing and assessment: Conceptualizing the relationship. In C. Hancock (Ed.), *Teaching, testing and assessment: Making the connection* (pp. 1–42). Lincolnwood, IL: National Textbook Company.

Weeden, P., & Winter, J. with Broadfoot, P., Hinett, K., McNess, E., Tidmarsh, C., Triggs, P., & Wilmut (September 1999). *The LEARN Project: Learners' Expectations of Assessment for Learning Nationally.* Report for the Qualifications & Curriculum Authority. Bristol: Graduate School of Education.

Weir, C. (1993). *Understanding and developing language tests.* Hemel Hempstead, Hertfordshire: Prentice Hall International (UK) Ltd.

Wiliam, D. (2001). An overview of the relationship between assessment and the curriculum. Scott, D. (Eds.). *Curriculum and assessment.* (pp. 165–181). Westport, CT: Ablex Publishing.

CHAPTER 34

THE POWER OF LANGUAGE TESTS, THE POWER OF THE ENGLISH LANGUAGE AND THE ROLE OF ELT

ELANA SHOHAMY

Tel Aviv University, Israel

ABSTRACT

This chapter argues that both language tests and the English language play powerful roles in today's world and that the combination of these two powerful entities has far reaching implications for policy and practice in English language teaching (ELT). It further claims that it is often the case that the English language teaching profession serves as a major mechanism through which these powerful entities are manifested as English language teachers are expected to carry out and implement language testing and English language teaching policies. This brings about a change in the status of teachers, from authoritative and responsible professionals to what many would regard as servants of the system. Alternative proposals, driven by teachers and based on pedagogical considerations are encouraged as such strategies can result in more democratic, ethical, humane and pedagogical approaches to English language testing and teaching.

INTRODUCTION

This chapter shows how both English language tests and the English language play dominant roles in the world today. When these two powerful entities are combined, the repercussions on policy and practice in English language teaching (ELT) are far reaching. The English language teaching profession serves as a major mechanism through which these powerful entities are manifested in that English language teachers are expected to take a major role in implementing language testing and English language teaching policies. This can result in a change, often a reduction, in the status of teachers, from authoritative and responsible professionals to servants of the system. This chapter proposes some alternative possibilities, determined by teachers and founded on pedagogical considerations which may lead to more democratic, ethical, humane and pedagogical approaches to English language testing and teaching.

ON THE POWER OF LANGUAGE TESTS

Over the past decade a new view of tests has emerged in the field of testing and educational measurement. Tests especially in the area of language, are not viewed as naïve tools aimed at measuring progress and carrying out exclusively pedagogical goals. Rather, the current view sees tests as tools that are embedded in political and social contexts. It was Messick (1981, 1994, 1996) who first introduced the notion of test consequences as part of a unified concept of construct validity. Accordingly, the act of language testing and the language tests themselves are not neutral but are strongly embedded in political, social and educational contexts. Although not explicitly stated, language tests are often introduced in a top-down manner as devices that define and impose language knowledge and create de facto language policies. At state and national levels language tests are often used as gatekeeping tools to exclude unwanted groups (Davies, 1997; Shohamy, 2001), especially immigrants, preventing them from entering new countries and/or obtaining citizenship and residence rights.

The emphasis on the political and social dimensions of tests stands in stark contrast to the traditional views of testing that have dominated since the emergence of the field of measurement. In the traditional psychometric view, the major criteria for high quality tests was the need to conform to specific norms and procedures of reliability, validity and item quality. Once a test was designed and developed, its items written, its format piloted, items statistics obtained and some types of reliability and evidence of validity reached, the role of the tester was complete as the test was ready to be delivered and administered to 'real' people leading to scores, grades and decisions. Issues of test consequences, the political and social implications of tests, as well as issues of values, were not of concern in such traditional testing approaches.

However, the past few years have witnessed a new emphasis in the field of testing shifting attention to the uses of tests in education, society and in the political realm (Hamp-Lyons, 1997; Lynch, 1997; Shohamy, 1997). *Use oriented testing* is concerned with what happens to test takers, to the knowledge that is created through tests, to the teachers who prepare students for tests as well as to the motivations of different stake holders such as politicians, principles, administrators and testing companies who introduce and administer tests. Use oriented testing poses questions about the effects and impact of tests on the teaching material taught and learned as a result of tests and the teaching methods applied in teaching as a reaction to testing. It evaluates the specific intentions and motivations for introducing tests by policy makers, bureaucrats, principles and especially politicians. It is concerned with the consequences of test results for parents whose children are subject to tests, ethical and fairness issues associated with the act of testing, and the short and long term consequences of tests to education and society. In other words, a use-oriented view of testing does not view tests as isolated events but rather as acts which are embedded in and connected to educational, pedagogical, bureaucratic, psychological, social and political variables that affect people, knowledge, curriculum, teaching, learning, ethicality, social classes, bureaucracy, politics, inclusion and exclusion. (Messick, 1981, 1994, 1996).

Research in the domain of test use focuses on the rationale and intentions behind the introduction of tests. Such research reveals that tests are often introduced by powerful organizations attempting to manipulate and control educational systems according to set agendas. According to Foucault (1979) tests possess unique features that allow them to be used for such purposes. For example, tests employ the language of numbers and science, written forms and documents and objective formats that evoke fairness, prestige and trust. Even tests which were originally developed as democratic tools to introduce equal opportunities to all, have generally been transformed over time into a range of powerful and controlling devices. This phenomenon is especially noticeable in centralized educational systems where tests are used as major devices to control and manipulate curricula, learning, teaching and knowledge, exemplified by the *No Child Left Behind* law which imposes a series of tests in all schools in the USA.

It is through narratives (Shohamy, 2001) obtained from test takers, in which they admit that tests affect their behaviors in many different ways, that one can see how test takers have internalized such powerful messages. In describing their experiences with language tests, test takers point to the low trust they have in such tests, claiming that the tests do not provide a true and correct reflection and indication of their actual knowledge. They also claim that tests are detached from real learning and from 'real life' performances. Test takers also claim they feel that success on tests is not under their control, yet at the same time they are fully aware that teachers in classrooms use tests as tools for punishment, control and discipline. Test takers in return adopt behaviors that 'play the testing game.' This means that they comply with the demands of the language tests by studying for the test according to the specifications; they are fully aware of the detrimental consequences that result from poor test scores, and the influential role of test scores on their lives, creating winners and losers, successes and failures, rejections and acceptances. Test scores are often the sole indicators for decisions such as acceptance to programs, placement in specific language courses, obtaining certificates, being allowed to continue with future studies, deciding on specific professions and gaining entrance to the workplace.

On the other hand, from the perspective of those who introduce tests, tests serve as efficient tools for perpetuating policies and for creating changes in behavior on the part of educational systems, schools, principals, teachers and test takers. Such uses of tests for dictating what test takers will learn and what teachers will teach, are often in contradiction with stated policies as specified in the formal curricula. However, it is the introduction of tests, often in contradiction to these curricula, that cause changes as test takers and other key stakeholders all attempt to maximize test scores. With *No Child Left Behind*, for example, low scores can lead to harsh sanctions such as the closure of schools and the dismissal of 'failing' teachers.

Given the power of tests, questions arise about the ethical aspects of creating and dictating policies through the use of particular testing instruments for disciplinary purposes, to carry out, often hidden policy agendas, to manipulate educational systems and to force compliance in implicit ways. In the USA where no national curricula exists due to the independence of education from the nation-state, *No Child Left Behind* and its associated tests act a powerful coercive influence on local educational decisions.

Over the years many research studies examining the uses of tests have been undertaken. Some of this research has focused on the intentions of test developers, exploring the rationale, purposes and expectations of those in charge of introducing tests. Considerable research has also focused on the impact, effects and washback of tests on learning and teaching as well as on other social and political dimensions.

In terms of intentions, a number of studies (Shohamy, 2001) have shown that policy makers explicitly state that they have introduced language tests in order to influence and control the educational practices of students, teachers and schools. For example, in the introduction of a new oral English test the policy makers claimed that the test would 'force' teachers to teach oral language in the classrooms. In another case, the introduction of a reading comprehension test, it was shown that even in situations when such intentions were not explicitly stated they still led to major changes in teaching practices.

In terms of the effect of language tests on learning it was shown in the example of the English oral test that the introduction of the test did, in fact, lead to changes in teaching practices, redefinition of language knowledge, teaching 'test language' and greater focus on the tested content. This led to a redefinition of the curricula so that it reflected the content that was tested. In general, the introduction of the tests has generally had negative effects on the quality of knowledge as it has created narrow 'test language' as well as parallel forms of education, often outside schools, in which the tested knowledge becomes the de facto curriculum. Shohamy et al. (1996), showed that the effects of language testing on language teaching were not uniform but varied according to various features, such as whether the language test was of high or low stakes, the status of language tested in the given context (i.e English high, Arabic low), the purposes of the test and the specific skill tested. Thus, it was shown that the introduction of an Arabic test did not lead to meaningful changes in teaching and learning in the classroom but only to procedural changes (i.e. preparation before the administration of the tests and a total switch in teaching strategies after the test had been administered), while the introduction of the English test led to more meaningful changes. Cheng (1998), Alderson and Wall (1993), Alderson and Hamp-Lyons (1996), and Hamp-Lyons (1997) have also shown that not all aspects of teaching are equally affected by the introduction of new tests. Other research has examined impact issues, for example, a study that examined the effect on the TOEFL tests on teaching and learning has recently been conducted by Hamp-Lyons while a series of studies on the effect of the IELTS had been carried out in the past few years.

Another dimension that has gained attention recently is the effect of language tests in multilingual and multicultural societies. When powerful tests are administered in a dominant language such as English in countries where the main language is not English or where English is the dominant and official language, they can suppress multi lingual realities and diversities. The power of tests is especially noticeable in multicultural societies where the use of high stakes standardized tests means that often the unique knowledge and languages of the different groups are overlooked, as standardized national tests are generally administered in the hegemonic language of the nation. This implies the other languages used in society, especially those used by immigrants and indigenous groups, are irrelevant, the tests conveying a direct message as to the legitimacy of certain languages and the illegitimacy of others (Evans and Hornberger, 2005, Byrnes, 2005, Shohamy, 2004), perpetuating the domination of certain languages and their speakers while denying and excluding groups whose languages are less powerful. Given that the different groups need to comply with the demands of the tests, these serve as gatekeepers and tools for eliminating unique linguistic and cultural knowledge of 'the others' (Shohamy, 2004). In the past few years the introduction of language tests as a condition for acquiring citizenship has been gaining prominence, especially in Europe, where immigrants must pass tests in the national languages in order to be granted citizenship and permission to reside in given territories. These tests also deliver messages regarding attitudes towards and the relevance of home languages, perpetuating monolingualism, but even more seriously, affecting personal rights and social benefits.

However, in spite of the above arguments regarding the power of tests, the motivations for introducing tests, and especially their consequences, the dominance of tests is unquestioned, unchallenged, unmonitored and uncontrolled. Tests often achieve a trust and acceptance in the community, in public institutions and in government, simply as a result of their status as tests. In most cultures the results of tests are used to make rites of passage from an early age. Bourdieu (1991) notes that tests create dependence, leading to the marginalization of those who do not pass them. Furthermore, those who introduce tests create myths and propaganda about their usefulness and lead the public to believe in their infallibility, fairness and meaningfulness (Milroy and Milroy, 1999, Evans and Hornberger, 2005). For example, the name 'No Child Left Behind' itself conveys certain myths, even propaganda, which is accepted without any real questioning by the public.

Bourdieu (1991) also claims that the power of tests is derived from the trust that those who are affected by tests place in them. There is an unwritten contract between those in power who want to dominate and those who want to be dominated and grant them the power and authority so they can perpetuate and maintain this power. Accordingly, tests are instrumental in reaffirming societal powers and in maintaining social order.

In most societies nowadays tests are powerful and widely used tools, leading to high stake decisions for individuals, groups and political systems. Tests are implicated in multiple agendas - educational, social, economic and political. Similarly, in the context of language learning, it is often through language tests that policy makers are successful in introducing language policies that determine language priorities, language correctness and language status and in creating de facto language policies and language hegemony as is evident from the increase in the use of language tests required by immigrant children and adults in schools and society (Evans and Hornberger, 2005; Shohamy, 2006).

ON THE POWER OF ENGLISH

In the same way that language tests are powerful, so is the English language. English is the language that is currently spoken most widely in the world; it is the language that includes the largest number of learners as a second language and has a monopoly in the language learning market (Pennycook, 1994, 1998, 2001; Tollefson, 2002). The English language is dominant in most national, educational, societal and technical systems, specifically in academia, business and commerce and it is directly associated with globalization, often referred to also as a 'world language' (Brutt-Griffler, 2000). According to de Swann (1998) it is predicted that English will expand and grow further. It is also the main language of technology as English has become the dominant choice for international and often national and regional communication. There are many explanations for this phenomenon and much has been written about it in literature (see Pennycook, this volume, for a fuller discussion).

English is often learned and used as a first language in countries where it is a national or official language (e.g. Canada, South Africa, New Zealand, Australia, USA, UK), although the linguistic diversity of the so-called 'English speaking' countries is often under-estimated (Edwards, 2004). Consequently, in educational systems in most countries in the world today, there is a high demand for the learning of English in schools and societies. These demands come from students, parents, teachers who demand that educational systems and governments intensify the teaching of English from an early age so that students can gain even higher proficiency. The English language is viewed as a valuable commodity, and is often explicitly referred to as a 'currency.' Students realize from a very young age the importance of the English language and its role in promoting their future opportunities. The status of English can be seen in most language policies nowadays which almost always include English as a compulsory language in schools from a very early age. The demand for English is so high that there is strong bottom-up pressure to include English, even at the cost of subjects that were traditionally considered important.

The dominance of the English language is often perceived as a problem, with concerns raised about the consequences of a situation when one particular language is in demand by such a large number of people, particularly when that single language has become the world's lingua franca. Questions are also raised as to the class differentiation as well as marginalization of those who do not have access to English (Phillipson, 1992, 2003, this volume).

Much has been written about the fact that with the spread of English, different varieties of English are emerging, different from those varieties used in nations and regions where English is considered the official or national language (Crystal, 2000). Once a language is the possession of a large number of groups, it develops different varieties which often result from the interaction of local and national languages and English. Some view these varieties as narrow, limited and telegraphic, others perceive them as efficient and effective communication devices that facilitate contacts among groups of people in different parts of the world. There are often situations in which those who consider English as their home language feel that 'their' language is being 'polluted' by others and its correct 'pure' standards are being manipulated.

Another argument against the power of English in countries where English is not considered the main language is that it threatens other, mostly local, languages as well as additional languages used in given territories. Thus, while English is becoming more powerful as the dominant language in the world, it may also be viewed negatively when it manages to compete and take over home languages and creates a new class of those who are left out as they do not have access to the English language and who have lost their own language status locally. Thus, the power and control of one language over other languages leads to a situation in which other languages are marginalized by English, or viewed as irrelevant. Such a phenomenon may lead to a situation where groups using other languages see themselves as marginal, often leading to their exclusion from higher education or the workplace. Thus, a situation in which English is the only powerful language may imply that other language groups are not respected and appreciated, resulting in an English elite associated with power on one hand and marginalization on the other. There is also a feeling of injustice that groups that were born into the English language and acquired it as 'native' have advantages over those who learned it as an additional language.

Further questions that are raised relate to whether English can provide the answers to all communicative needs of non-native speakers. Even in the world of high technology where English is the dominant language, it still cannot reach all populations. In fact international companies now realize that successful global marketing requires knowledge of the local languages of the consumer. In spite of the advantages of having a 'world language' there are strong arguments for maintaining other languages and there is a need to be aware of the dangers of the unlimited power and domination of the English language. While English may be necessary, it may not be sufficient as a number of languages are needed to fulfill various social, communicative and economic purposes. The situation today is that national and regional languages are needed for internal communication, indigenous and regional lingua franca are used for communicating within certain regions (e.g., Putonghua in Greater China) and English for international communication as well as a large number of other languages. In fact the boundaries between and among languages are not clearly marked any more as various types of hybrids and fusions, often involving English are continuously emerging in dynamic and fluid ways (Makoni and Pennycook, 2005).

CONNECTING THE POWER OF LANGUAGE TESTS WITH THE POWER OF ENGLISH

It is the combination of two powerful entities, language tests and the English language that is of concern here as they both affect one another. It is of special concern how the power of language tests perpetuates the power of English, and vice versa. This prevents non-standard varieties of the language developing and creates *de facto* language policies that prioritize English as a language of status, power and prestige, perpetuating hegemonic standards of correctness and suppressing diversity.

Tests are used as instruments to promote, upgrade or downgrade certain languages. In situations when political entities declare a test of English as a condition of graduation at the end of high school or as a conditions of inclusion and acceptance to specific programs of higher education or the workplace through school or entrance tests, this delivers a strong message that English language is important while the others languages are not. Testing provides the language with status as the message that is communicated is that this very language is what is valued. Likewise but in the opposite direction, when certain languages are not tested, the opposite message is delivered. The act of requiring students to be tested in English as a condition for entrance and/or graduation is a statement about the priority that the society grants to the language. This creates a situation whereby students demand the teaching of the language in schools, parents encourage it, more hours are devoted to it, funds are granted and so on, in a vicious circle. Thus, the English language is granted even more power than it already has. The testing of English in most countries today at all levels of the educational systems—elementary school, end of secondary education, and universities—remains unchallenged and guarantees continuous domination of the English language in school systems and often in society as well.

This situation is not unique to English, but also occurs when governments and educational authorities introduce tests of English as requirement for graduation and acceptance to educational programs and the workplace. In most nation states passing a test in the national official language is a requirement for all students, including immigrants. At the same time this sends a message of marginalization with regard to other languages that are not tested, including a variety of foreign languages. In Byrnes (2005) and Evans and Hornberger (2005), it is shown how the implementation of tests associated with *No Child Left Behind* in the USA led to a reduction in the teaching of foreign languages, suppressing other languages of immigrants and diversity and creating de facto monolingual language policies. It is often the case, even in situations when English is not declared the official language, that the requirement to be tested in English gives it such status. Thus testing policy becomes the de facto language policy, often more powerful than any declared policy (Shohamy, 2003). It is through such English language tests that the centralized authoritative educational systems communicate the priority, prestige and status of the power of English.

The influence of testing in English, however, goes beyond perpetuating *de facto* language priorities, status and prestige and policies; tests also dictate the type of English that will be learned and accepted as high quality. Thus, the English language that is most widely accepted is the 'native speaker' variety, the exclusive criterion of quality. It is through such criteria that language is defined and perpetuated in spite of the distance that exists among different English varieties. For example, the TOEFL test still uses the native speaker as the criterion for correctness, in spite of the increasingly vague definition of that construct. The idea of a multilingual TOEFL reflecting the fusions and hybrids existing in today's workplace with regard to the English language is still a dream. Testing determines not only the status of the English language but also the specific variety of the language itself in terms of what is considered 'good language,' referring therefore to both status and corpus.

THE ROLE OF ENGLISH LANGUAGE TEACHERS

English language teachers also play a major role in extending the dominion of the English language and the power of English tests. Given the far reaching consequences of tests for students and test takers, tests influence and shape instruction. For example, if English language tests use specific criteria for correctness it is obvious that in high stake situations, these criteria become the very criteria used as part of the teaching and learning English in schools. If the native speakers' variety continues to be used as the criterion on tests, this also becomes the criterion for teaching English. Given the high-stakes power of tests, those who introduce English language tests know that teachers and students will comply by changing their behaviors in order to succeed, dictating what to teach and what test takers will study, as teachers and tests takers comply with these demands so to maximize their scores. In such situations, teachers are not viewed as equal partners but rather as servants of the system.

The complex interaction between the English language, English language testing and the English language teacher is characterized by several key phases. First, an area is identified that policy makers believe should be taught, or taught in 'better' ways. This decision is often a reaction to public or media demands for action, but in the case of English language teaching, demand appears unlimited. Parents judge success of schools by the proficiency their children attain in the English language. To ensure that the English language is taught to the highest degree possible new English tests are introduced, since this is the easiest and quickest way for policy makers to demonstrate action and authority. Given the status and need for English, the English test is high stakes, often serving as the main criteria for graduating from secondary school and for entering higher education. In these situations English tests provide 'efficient' and 'quick' tools to change the behaviors of teachers and students. However, English language teachers often experience fear and anxiety as students, principals, and parents all demand intensive preparation for these high stakes English tests, especially since teachers are often judged by the success of their students on these tests. Hence, teachers change their behavior and start teaching for the test or teaching the test itself. The test then serves as the model of knowledge and as the main pedagogical source and guide. Over the years, new teaching materials are developed and workshops are designed to prepare teachers for these English tests. This is especially the case if no meaningful professional teacher training takes place, then the tests become the *de facto* curriculum. Even when a richer and more appropriate curriculum exists, it often becomes subordinate to the power of the test.

In this process teachers are not viewed as professionals but rather as agents used by the system to carry out the policies of those in authority. For those in authority, as was noted earlier, tests offer disciplinary tools for policy making. Tests are perceived by the public, especially parents, as authoritative, a guarantee of control and seemingly objective evidence of attainment. At the same time tests can themselves be used to redefine knowledge, through their high status and a flexible approach to cutting scores. For the policy makers, tests provide visible evidence of action, yet are cost effective as they do not in and of themselves require investment in teacher training, materials development and new curricula (Shohamy, 2001). Thus, it is through English tests that the language itself gets expanded power.

This interactive process does not involve teachers directly, but rather indirectly and in implicit ways. Teachers do not take part in the decisions to introduce national or state-wide tests, yet they are expected to carry out the task of teaching for the tests, and to adapt their pedagogical strategies according to the demands of the tests and its requirements. Teachers internalize these views and often view the success of their students on these very high stakes tests as an indication of their own success as teachers, not asking questions about the extent to which these tests (often administered on a single occasion) can actually provide a valid indication of their quality as teachers and whether the expectations for certain levels of English proficiency are at all realistic.

Thus, given the power of tests and the power of the English language, English language teachers become the agents through whom such powerful and controlling policies are exercised. This is compounded by the fact that teachers, who are responsible for implementing English language testing policies, have little or no power and authority to resist. Teachers in most countries around the world have been socialized into seeing themselves as implementing curricula and assessment that have been formulated by others; tests are prime tools for such a social engineering. Yet the demands on tests are often detached from reality. For example, in a study of the length of time it takes immigrants to arrive at equal levels of competence to those who were born in the country (Levin, Shohamy and Spolsky, 2003), it was found that the time taken ranges from 7 to 11 years. Yet, in the case of the *No Child Left Behind*, for example, as well as in many other national tests, immigrants are often expected to reach similar levels within one year. Thus, testing policies are detached from research on second language learning, with far reaching ramifications for teachers and schools.

CONCLUSIONS

Despite the power of tests, English language teachers can adopt more resistant roles in their own English language teaching context, demanding greater participation and representation in the decision making process, decisions not only about what is tested, but how and why.

Teachers can demand that tests include multiple types of English texts, represent the different types of English language varieties, as well as argue, for example, that a number of languages be included in tests of literacy, thus reflecting the reality of using language in many multilingual countries. Different language knowledge needs to be acknowledged in testing, not treated as deficient. Teachers can demand more diverse criteria and acceptability around notions of correctness, in particular challenging the assumption of the native speaker as the only criterion.

Teachers can also demand more democratic approaches to assessment so that decisions regarding the achievements and proficiency of students in the English language rely on authentic data, diverse student knowledge and multiple interpretations, not just a single language test and/or unrealistic views of how long it takes to acquire the language. Teachers can learn to become skilled and confident in multiple methods of assessment and in the planning and implementation of alternative assessment procedures based on and suitable for classroom learning (see Rea-Dickins, this volume, for a more detailed discussion). Applying such interactive models of assessment means that power is shared and decisions are based on contextualization of the evidence obtained from the different sources. Through constructive, interpretive and dialogical processes English language assessment procedures can be developed for different participants and used in interpretive and contextualized ways. This, rather than expecting a simple mechanical device to translate the complex data of individual language proficiency into a single measure, language testers (and teachers) can develop assessment which lead to intelligent and responsible interpretations. Such practices would build on the true power of tests, that is, to provide diagnostic information and feedback to students and teachers, thus leading to more effective learning and teaching. In this way language tests, as well as other assessment procedures, can be used for beneficial and constructive purposes, not just as a tool for agencies seeking unethical and undemocratic ways for power and control.

Another key point is the importance of English language teachers seeing their teaching as an integral part of the larger language community, concerned with languages in general, not just with English. English language teachers need to view the language they teach and the tests they use in political, contextual and ideological terms and resist the domination of one language over another. They need collaborate with teachers of other languages as well as reject rigid and separate language boundaries.

Lastly, English language teachers need to develop critical strategies to examine the uses and consequences of English language tests, to control the power of tests and minimize their detrimental impact. Teachers need to become more socially responsible and reflexive about the uses of language tests. They can also encourage test takers and the public at large to question the uses of tests, the material they are based on and, most importantly, the values and beliefs embedded in them. In this way English language teachers can also be involved in making language testing policies decisions.

REFERENCES

Alderson, C. & Wall, D. (1993). Does washback exist? *Applied Linguistics, 14*, 115–29.
Alderson, C. & Hamp-Lyons, L. (1996). TOEFL preparation courses: A study of washback, *Language Testing, 13*(3), 280–297.

Brutt-Griffler, J. (2000). *World English: A study of its development.* Clevedon, England: Multilingual Matters.
Byrnes, H. (2005). Perspectives. No Child Left Behind. *Modern Language Journal, 89*, 2.
Bourdieu, P. (1991). *Language and symbolic power.* Cambridge, Massachusetts: Harvard University Press.
Cheng, L. (1998). Impact of a public English examination change on students' perceptions and attitudes toward their English learning. *Studies in Educational Evaluation, 24,* 279–301.
Crystal, D. (2000). *Language death.* Cambridge: Cambridge University Press.
Davies, A. (1997). Demands of being professional in language testing. *Language Testing, 14*(3), 328–339.
de Swann, A. (1998). A political sociology of the world language system. *Language Problems and Language Planning, 22* (1&2).
Edwards, V. (2004). *Multilingualism in the English speaking world.* Malden, Mass: Blackwell.
Evans, B. & Hornerger, N. (2005). No child left behind: Repealing and unpeeling federal language education policy in the United States. *Language Policy, 4*(1), 67–85.
Foucault, M. (1979). *Discipline and punish.* New York: Vintage Books.
Hamp-Lyons, L. (1997). Washback, impact and validity: Ethical concerns, *Language Testing, 14*(3), 295–303.
Levin, T., Shohamy, E., & Spolsky, B. (2003). *Academic achievements of immigrants in schools.* Report submitted to the Ministry of Education. (in Hebrew).
Lynch, B. (1997). In search of the ethical test. *Language Testing, 14*(3), 315–327.
Makoni, S. & Pennycoook, A. (2005). Disinventing and (re)constituting languages. *Critical Inquiry in Language Studies, 2*(3), 137–156.
Messick, S. (1981). Evidence and ethics in the evaluation of tests. *Educational Researcher, 10,* 9–20.
Messick, S. (1994). The interplay of evidence and consequences in the validation of performance assessments. *Educational Researcher, 23,* 13–23.
Messick, S. (1996). Validity and washback in language testing. *Language Testing, 13*(4), 241–257.
Milroy, J. & Milroy, L. (1999). *Authority in language: Investigating standard English.* (3rd ed.) London: Routledge.
Pennycook, A. (1994). *The cultural politics of English as an international language.* London: Longman.
Pennycook, A. (1998). *English and the discourses of colonialism.* London: Routledge.
Pennycook, A. (2001). *Critical applied linguistics.* Mahwah, New Jersey: Lawrence Erlbaum Assoicates.
Phillipson, R. (1992). *Linguistic imperialism.* Oxford: Oxford University Press. Refer in text
Phillipson, R. (2003). *English-only Europe? Challenging language policy.* London: Routledge.
Shohamy, E., Donitsa-Schmidt, S. & Ferman, I. (1996). Test impact revisited: Washback effect over time. *Language Testing, 13*(3), 298–317.
Shohamy, E. (1997). Testing methods, testing consequences: Are they ethical? Are they fair? *Language Testing, 14*(3), 340–349.
Shohamy, E. (2001). *The power of tests: A critical perspective on the uses of language tests.* Harlow, England: Longman.
Shohamy, E. (2003). Implications of language education policies for language study in schools and universities. Perspective. *The Modern Language Journal, 87*(2), 276–286.
Shohamy, E. (2004). Assessment in multicultural societies: Applying democratic principles and practices to language testing. In Norton, B. and Toohey, K., *Critical pedagogies and language learning.* (pp. 72–93). New York: Cambridge University Press.
Shohamy, E. (2006). *Language policy: Hidden agendas and new approaches.* London: Routledge.
Tollefson, J. (2002). *Language policies in education.* London: Lawrence Erlbaum Associates.

CHAPTER 35

DIFFERENT DEFINITIONS OF LANGUAGE AND LANGUAGE LEARNING:

Implications for Assessment[1]

CHRIS DAVISON

The University of Hong Kong, China

ABSTRACT

This chapter discusses the implications for assessment of changes in our conceptualization of English language learning. The chapter begins by proposing that different models of language and language learning result in very different perceptions of language learning goals and hence, different judgments of individual success and failure. This is exemplified with reference to a two year longitudinal ethnographic study of Hong Kong-born Cantonese-speaking students completing their final two years of English in a Melbourne secondary school. The detailed linguistic analysis of the students' written argument revealed a shift in the students' preferred genre, a shift apparently linked to the very different expectations and socialisation practices of Australian and Hong Kong schools as well as to conflicting subject discourses. However, the evaluation, and the consequences, of this shift depended on which model of argument and its development was foregrounded by teacher-assessors. In the absence of any clear guidance from examination boards, teachers made their own implicit and, usually, negative judgments without realising their own involvement in the co-construction of the students' arguments. The chapter concludes with some implications for assessment policy and future research.

INTRODUCTION

Just as in second language acquisition (SLA) there are very different interpretations of what is meant by acquisition, depending on the view of what is to be learnt and how learning occurs (Seeley & Carter, 2004; Thorne, 2000; Zuengler & Miller, 2006), so there are very different views of development in English as a second or additional language, which in turn impacts on how we assess ESL. In many English-speaking countries, although there is still a lot of disagreement over terminology, most teachers use the term ESL to refer to those students from language other than English (LOTE) backgrounds whose English is still perceived to need development. By implication, other LOTE background students may be users *of* English as a second language and learners *in* English as a second language, but no longer, at least in pedagogic parlance, ESL learners. However, such pedagogic definitions are complex and somewhat circular, critically dependent on what is meant by *development* and *need* (Moore, 1995, 2004).

Development is usually equated with progress, or improvement towards a desirable end, although what this end is may be strongly contested (Jenkins, 2006;

Leung, Harris & Rampton, 1997). In the ELT field, it is not just our understandings of language learning that are being redefined through the 'social turn' (Block, 2003), it is also our constructs of language.

Need is usually defined by English language teaching specialists very broadly to include not just language but literacy, cultural and educational needs in both mother tongue and English language contexts (see Collier and Thomas, this volume, for a fuller discussion). Thus, definitions of ESL-ness in curriculum and professional development material in Australia tend to take into account the pedagogic context as well as personal characteristics such as first and second language and literacy background, learning experiences, competencies and practices, sociocultural background, familiarity with Anglo-Australian cultural practices and prior educational experiences and attitudes. This view of ESL-ness is seen as "a highly complex and shifting phenomenon ... likely to be different in nature and degree and change over time" (McKay, 1996, p. 13).

This variability around the basic constructs of ESL-ness has major implications for the assessment of English language learners, in particular, in school-based and teacher-directed assessment, as will be seen in this chapter. This chapter reports on a study of Hong Kong-born Cantonese-speaking students completing their final two years of English in a Melbourne secondary school in order to qualify for university entrance. The study focuses in particular on the development and assessment of the students' knowledge and skills in written argumentation, a central component of the requirements for their final certificate. The application of Martin's (1985) distinction between hortatory and analytical exposition to the analysis of the students' written argument revealed a shift in the students' preferred genre, a shift apparently linked to the very different expectations and socialization practices of Australian and Hong Kong schools as well as to conflicting subject discourses. However, the evaluation, and the consequences, of this shift depended on which model of argument and its development was foregrounded by the teacher-assessors, and how such models interact with notions of ESL-ness. The analysis shows that, not surprisingly, assessment which took into account only linguistic factors failed to capture much of what was happening in terms of the students' overall ESL development. The paper concludes that teachers and researchers need to take into account both the role of individual intentions and the socially and ideologically constructed nature of the textual practices in which the learners are engaged in any evaluation of ESL development.

THEORIZING THE PROBLEM: DEFINING DEVELOPMENT IN ESL WRITTEN ARGUMENT

To be able to construct a persuasive written argument is a highly-valued skill in all English-speaking societies, but the structure and purpose of such argument may vary and its linguistic features are often assumed, rather than explicitly taught. The effectiveness of the learning and teaching of written argument in schools has long been a concern in the United Kingdom. For example, a large-scale survey of 11-15 year olds in England and Wales (Gorman, 1988) found that students often responded to an argumentative task by writing a story, raising questions as to whether the students "have any capacity to abstract from the narrative frame" or whether they are "stuck in one mode of written discourse" (Gorman, 1988, p. 154). Younger students were also perceived to rely too heavily on oral strategies (Gorman, 1988). Students often seemed confused as to whether they should write a balanced, objective account or a hortatory statement to persuade a reader to share their point of view. Gorman (1988) concluded that:

> While there are few pupils who are not alert to the use of writing to argue a personal case, most would benefit from a systematic study of the great variety of linguistic techniques which speakers and writers draw on when taking an authoritative stand on matters of controversial interest (p. 158).

Andrews, Costello and Clarke (1993), in responding to Gorman's study, argue that the problems with argument are not inherent to the genre, but more likely the result of the way the genre is taught. They suggest that the greatest difficulty with writing argument is seen "when the structure is not 'given', that is to say, when the structure has to be created to suit the subject matter to be communicated" (p. 8). Gubb (1987) also observes that time spent by teachers developing and discussing stimulus topic material may be disproportionate to time spent on "the 'how' of discursive writing" (p. 182). He suggests that teachers provide more models of different types of argumentative writing and greater exploitation of the relationship between spoken and written argument.

Canadian researchers have also demanded more explicit instruction and modeling of argument after finding students far more competent at writing a story than argumentative writing (Freedman & Pringle, 1984), with a significant number of Grade 12 students "unable to write an argument that satisfied the minimal criteria" (Pringle & Freedman, 1985, p. ix). Freedman and Pringle (1984) argue for teaching students more varied ways to write an argument, to move them away from the ubiquitous five paragraph essay or the for/against model, which they suggest is often the only model taught to many students.

In Australia, Martin (1985) has also called for more explicit instruction in schools on how to write argument. Martin (1984) proposes a classification system for a range of written factual genres used in Australian schools, including argument which he labels as *exposition*. An exposition, according to Martin (1985, p. 14), presents more than one argument in favor of a judgment, or *thesis*. This thesis is the focal element of an exposition, but can be expressed either as a statement, or macroproposition, or as a command or exhortation to undertake a particular course of action, a macro-modulated proposition (Martin 1992, p. 563). According to Martin (1985), this distinction leads to two linguistically distinct varieties of exposition - *analytical*, in which the thesis and supporting arguments are presented more overtly as fact, and *hortatory*, which attempts to persuade the reader to do what the thesis recommends.

These different genres are associated with different linguistic features. In a systemic functional linguistics (SFL) framework (Halliday, 1985), these features can classified according to *field*, *tenor* and *mode*. Field refers to what the language is being used to talk about, the topic or content of the communication. Tenor refers to the roles and relationships constructed by the writer with the intended audience. Mode refers to how the language is organized to make it more spoken-like or more written-like. Martin (1992) highlights three specific ways in which aspects of field are realized in exposition: through lexical collocations (the co-occurrence of particular words), through references to people (as more or less abstract, more or less personal) and through the way in which processes are realized through the verbal system. Aspects of tenor are realized through features such amplification, reciprocity and elaboration. Amplification has to do with the intensity of the communication, and in written language it is manifested in intensification (e.g., exclamations, underlining) and repetition as well as through attitudinal lexis. Attitudinal lexis refers to the selection of lexis which communicates something of the writer's judgments, appraisal or feelings about an issue, and reveals their positive or negative attitudes towards their audience and/or topic. Affect is conceptualized as varying along a continuum from positive to negative, according to the degree of intensity. Reciprocity is marked by the use of more first and second personal reference (indicators of solidarity and agreement with an issue or person) through various choices from the mood and modal system, for example, through the use of more rhetorical questions and inclusive imperatives, as well as through the incorporation of more modulated appeals (e.g. we should do X). Elaboration reflects contact, the degree of involvement of the addresser with the addressee and is reflected in assumptions about shared knowledge, manifested in choices of topics within the text and in the degree of technical knowledge assumed about the topic. A more spoken-like mode is realized more thematization of human participants rather than things, making the discourse seem less abstract and less distant from the events being discussed, and through more incorporation of features associated with dialogue such as rhetorical questions.

Martin (1985) suggests that it is the analytical genre which is more highly valued in schools and society. This is reflected in official state curriculum documents in various Australian states. For example, the Queensland Department of Education (1994), following Martin, highlights the importance of this analytical genre:

> Genres in this category often become the means for individuals and groups to sway the public on major issues affecting society. Factual and academic in tone, it is highly valued in secondary and tertiary education. Success in examinations in some subject areas can depend on the students' experience and expertise in this genre. (p. 60)

The reasons for the greater value attached to analytical exposition demand further exploration. Looking at the issue from a socio-cognitive perspective, it could be argued that analytical exposition is perceived as the expression, even the construction of a more rational intellectual social being (Martin, 1985):

> In our culture, reason and emotion are felt to be diametrically opposed. Intellect must not be confused with feeling, and whenever it is we become suspicious ... Expositions are supposed to be rational (p. 25).

Alternatively, analytical exposition may be valued in schools precisely because it is more abstract and distanced, hence it is perceived as more complex, more 'written-like', thus more cognitively demanding, reflecting the 'great divide' view of spoken and written language. From a socio-political perspective, Martin's notion of ideology suggests that analytical exposition may be valued because it is oriented towards stasis, rather than change, towards the maintenance rather than critique of social order.

Unlike in Queensland, references to the linguistic form of argument in official documents relating to the senior secondary English curriculum in Victoria at the time of this study seemed vague and lacked exemplification, although teachers were

Different Definitions of Language and Language Learning 537

encouraged to raise student awareness of the role of language in shaping argument (Board of Studies, 1994):

> Argumentative or persuasive: here the writer is concerned with presenting a substantiated point of view. It includes writing to argue a point of view about texts, ideas and issues. In such writing the sequence and progression of ideas is critically important. The writer should present the point of view coherently, explain how it has been arrived at, substantiate key points and demonstrate that alternative points of view have been considered ... In critically analyzing the use of language in the issues in the media, students consider many different aspects of language, noting the choices writers and speakers make in order to achieve a wide range of purposes with many different audiences. These include structure, organization, sequencing, emphasis, tone, word choice, as well as ways in which an argument is developed and presented (p. 13, 29).

Like elsewhere, in Victoria there were similar concerns that English teachers were not explicit enough in their conceptualization of argument (Love, 1996; VATME, 1995), and that they relied too heavily what Bernstein (1996) calls "invisible pedagogies" (see Davison, 2005, for a fuller discussion). Difficulties reported were both linguistic (the language of argumentation is especially demanding for the language learner) and cultural (the linear argumentation required is highly culture-specific) (Board of Studies 1995, p. 12). These suggestions received some support in a study of senior secondary English by McLoughlin (1993), who found that significantly more ESL than English mother tongue students produced hortatory rather than analytical argument. McLoughlin suggested that as hortatory texts are closer to spoken language and are more context-situated than analytical texts, ESL students were most likely transferring their more developed oral strategies into their writing, using "a style of argument consistent with the language resources available to them" (p. 36). This explanation assumes that ESL students are stronger orally than in writing, and indicates an acceptance of Martin's assumption that hortatory genres are acquired earlier than analytical genres because they are less abstract and more spoken-like.

An alternative explanation is also proposed, namely, that "ESL students may be unaware of, or without sufficient cultural knowledge of persuasion written in an analytical style according to the normal conventions of English" (McLoughlin, 1993, p. 37). In other words, the analytical style is not in the students' cultural repertoire or the hortatory style is more culturally congruent. Like other researchers, McLoughlin (1993) suggests that this lack of awareness and/or knowledge could be readily addressed through explicit teaching of the analytical genre. However, few researchers raise the issue of the link between the students' existing genre choices and their instructional context, and fewer still explore the role of the teacher-as-assessor in the construction of "literate competence" (Baker & Freebody, 1989; Baker & Freebody, 1993).

In fact, there are as many different models of argument and its development as there are of teaching, ranging from argument as logic, argument as persuasion, argument as text/discourse, argument as genre, to argument as cultural practice. These different approaches to the description (and conceptualization) of written argument all assume one particular view of language and language learning and exclude (and occlude) other possibilities. Each of these models will be briefly described in turn.

In a construction of argument as *logic*, derived from Socratic dialogue, and introduced into subject English through the rise of philosophy and literary criticism, it is the writer's reasoning that is foregrounded. Argument is seen as the product of universal mental processes, a cognitively demanding genre, which develops in clear stages from the toddlers' egocentric non-verbal gestures of rejection to the disinterested Supreme Court judgment. The ability to maintain two or more sides of argument at same time and mediate between them is seen as more developed than the ability to argue one side of an argument to make something happen or change things. This construction of argument excludes concepts such as mode, purpose, audience and context, rendering invisible the culturally-constructed nature of logic, and presenting the arrangement or organization of text and the more analytical forms of argument as natural development.

In contrast, a view of argument as (per)*suasion* highlights the writer's relationship with and strategies towards the audience. Derived from Aristotelian rhetoric, and achieving prominence through the "rhetorical turn" (Toulmin, Rieke & Janik, 1979; Kinneavy, 1971), such argument is judged by appeals to *ethos* (foregrounding the personal character of the speaker), *pathos* (putting the audience into a certain frame of mind) and *logos* (proof or apparent proof offered in speech), as well as by language and its arrangement. Rationality is not seen as an abstract universal analytical category, rather argument is embedded in the historical, disciplinary and/or cultural context. Hence, what counts as appropriate or convincing varies across cultures (Hinds, 1983). Development is still seen in stages but is viewed more as a process of progressively enlarging the number of points of view the writer can identify with. That is, argument is more demanding if you are required to assume a number of perspectives on audience and an ethical subject divorced from personal experience (Miller, 1980). However, this view of argument tends to render invisible the communicative purpose and the power relations inherent in communication.

Another view of argument, as *text/discourse*, focuses attention on the whole text and/or the elements of the situation in which the text is embedded. Derived from text and systemic functional linguistics, it became established as a distinct field in the 1970s with the move away from Chomskyan transformational grammar towards greater emphasis on the social bases of communication. It includes both more cognitive analyses of text structure, especially coherence and cohesion, and analyses of top-level structures including a growing number of cross-cultural studies (e.g., Connor, 1996; Hinds, 1983) and studies of metadiscourse strategies such as connectives and hedges (eg., Crismore, 1993; Ventola, 1991) as well as studies drawing on systemic functional models, initially focusing on cohesion (Halliday, 1975) but since taken up in many other studies of the relationship between text and context. Such views assume argument has predictable characteristic textual structures and features, the product of predictable but varied social/institutional situations. Universal cognitive processes are assumed with a progression from simpler to more complex argumentative structures, but with a Vygotskian rather than Piagetian view of development, i.e., from the social to individual. Such views highlight not only the nature of the text, but also the context, including cultural as well as situational context. The preoccupation with linguistic analysis and quantification tends to lead to a focus on textual rather than contextual features such as task and purpose. Less visibility is given to the dynamic, socially and culturally-embedded construction of argument.

Argument as *genre* focuses on the social, institutional and ideological purposes of the text. Three distinct and somewhat conflicting branches of genre theory have been identified, all building on earlier models of text linguistics and Bakhtinian notions of intertextuality (see Paltridge, Volume 2, for a fuller discussion). The branches usually identified are Swalesian applied linguistics (e.g., Swales, 1990), Australian genre theory exemplified by the so-called Sydney school (e.g., Christie, 2002; Martin 1985, 1992) and the *new rhetoric* movement (Miller 1984; Freedman & Medway 1994). In these models of language and language learning, arguments are seen as having ordered, albeit dynamic and intertextual unified forms; however, there is disagreement among different schools of genre theory as to the extent to which genres are codifiable and determined by purpose. It is assumed development takes place within a genre, that is, from simpler to more complex forms, as well as from genre to genre. However, development is presumed to be strongly influenced by exposure, input and instruction, with 'immature' writers being scaffolded and apprenticed into new genres. This view of argument also assumes written-like modes are acquired later than spoken-like modes. Like text approaches, in genre-based approaches the argument linguistic structure is foregrounded, but even more important is the communicative or ideological purpose, and the relationship between argument and context. What is usually less visible is the individual writer and the relationship among text, writer, and audience or discourse community. Somewhat paradoxically, many approaches also do not take into account the socio-historic conditions in which writers act and interact.

The fifth view of argument, as *culturally-situated practice*, highlights writers (and their writing acts). Stimulated by social constructivism, this view foregrounds the notion of discourse or knowledge communities, including their linguistic and rhetorical conventions (Bazerman, 1994; Bhatia 1993; Swales 1990) and their induction of novices (Belcher, 1994; Berkenkotter, 1993; Prior, 1995; Casanave, 1995). Most L2 studies of argument as culturally-situated practice are concerned with how and where individuals learn what constitutes 'good' argument in a given culture. Effective writers of argument are seen as requiring both knowledge of textual features, and knowledge of social and cultural rules about argument. For example, in English there are certain conventions regarding the positioning of individual writers, the valuing of personal opinion and the contestation of text. The assumption is that argument varies within, not just across, cultures and institutions, and that learning to argue in a new discourse community requires not only learning of new language but developing a new identity and positioning in relation to audience, evidence and self. This view challenges cognitive notions of simplicity and complexity, seeing development as adding to one's repertoire of identities, although there is disagreement as to the role of explicit instruction in acquiring membership of a discourse community. However, such views may present cultures and disciplines as discrete, discontinuous and predictable (e.g., static and stereotypical conceptualizations of Chinese rhetorical styles and practices vs. 'Western' forms of argument). Few models attempt to link linguistic features and cultural practice in any coherent or systematic way.

In each model of argument outlined above certain features are foregrounded, others rendered less visible, or even invisible. This is problematic for teaching, but even more problematic for assessment, especially when the assessment is teacher-based, hence more contextualized and co-constructed, as will be seen in the following case study.

PROBLEMATIZING THE THEORY: ASSESSING CANTONESE-BACKGROUND STUDENTS AND WRITTEN ARGUMENT IN ESL

In a longitudinal ethnographic-style study of English as a second language development (Davison 1998), I followed ten Cantonese-speaking Hong Kong-background immigrant students with varying lengths of residence through their last two years of secondary school in Australia.[2] The students attended a government secondary college in a socioeconomically advantaged area of Melbourne in an area populated by many Hong Kong-born Chinese as well as a number of more established ethnic groups. The texts collected included the various drafts of the written arguments undertaken for the teacher assessed work requirements for subject English in Year 11 & 12 in the Victorian Certificate of Education (VCE), which comprised 25% of the students' final result. The text analysis was contextualized with reference to transcripts of unplanned student group discussion, unplanned student-teacher/whole class discussion, planned student presentations, student notes, teachers' feedback and comments on the drafts, and a series of teacher and student interviews.

The application of Martin's (1985b, 1986) model of genre analysis to the students' written arguments over the two year period revealed systematic shifts in their linguistic structures and features from more analytical to more hortatory. This shift was most marked through greater use of appeals, first and second person reference, rhetorical questions and more emotive lexis. However, in mode there appeared to be a contradictory shift towards more written-like features, with increasing lexical density, thematization of non-human participants, use of internal rhetorical markers and nominalization. The shifts also seemed to be loosely associated with length of residence, with the two most recently arrived students demonstrated the strongest shift overall, converging towards a more uniform hortatory-like genre.

However, contrary to expectations, teacher, peer and self evaluations of the Melbourne students' oral skills in English all revealed that their writing skills were superior to their oral skills, especially in the case of the more recently arrived students. In other words, the students' shift towards features associated with more hortatory-like genre contradicted McLoughlin's proposal that the unmarked developmental path for English language learners is from hortatory, more spoken-like to analytical, more written-like. Thus, we need to examine more closely not only the teachers' and students' views of what they were doing in developing an argument, but also their actual classroom interactions for other possible explanations for this shift. Some of the factors which emerged from the systematic and detailed analysis of the classroom data included a mismatch between the students' prior educational experiences and the demands of the VCE, a lack of familiarity with Anglo-Australian cultural practices in relation to argument and the profound influence of the pedagogic context, in particular the teachers' demand for an overt verbal display of opinion from the students with little or no scaffolding or explicit instruction. These factors will be briefly examined in turn.

The students' views of argument and its development were heavily influenced by their previous educational experiences in Hong Kong. For example, Kwong, a recently immigrant, had finished five years of secondary school, including English, in Hong Kong. However, although English was the language of textbooks, it was rarely used in the classroom. Not surprisingly, Kwong thought that he was much better in Cantonese than in English. Even though the quantity of writing required in his new school seemed overwhelming, he found it easier to write than to speak because the "pronunciation difficult." He appreciated the more relaxed environment though:

> Here it's pretty flexible if you forget to do the homework but in Hong Kong there is forty people in one class, the teachers teach - they have a lot of things–the feelings are a bit angry about things–stressed. If you don't hand in the homework they may go a little bit far with the reprimand.

English as a subject was also quite different to Hong Kong, in particular the demand for oral as well as written contributions to argument. As Victor (Interview 2) commented: "In Australia, you have to discuss your own opinion, the teacher expect us to ask the question ... It's good but I'm not used to this, you can sit in class and not say anything in Hong Kong" (p. 11). Leanne (Interview 2), another recent arrival, also commented on differences in expectations between the two school systems:

> It is hard to talk in class in Hong Kong, you don't have to speak for few questions, you just have to write an essay and do less, you don't speak in class much (p. 6)

Kwong (Interview 1, p. 3) also reflected this viewpoint: "In Hong Kong always learn about the grammar ... never read the newspaper or make a point of view ... never talks much."

In Kwong's first year in Australia, he was seen by his English teacher as making rapid progress (Chee, Interview 2, p. 13):

> Kwong is a reasonably intelligent person ... he is a bright kid. You show him the structure, he can take it on and he can reproduce a similar genre when he has to.

However, by his second and final year, despite his "obvious intelligence", Kwong was viewed by his teachers as "struggling with the language," with major problems working independently (Anna, Interview 3, p. 16). This shift in perception was in part linked to his unwillingness to participate orally in English, to talk in class. "Talk" appeared to be correlated with maturity, with the capacity to think. Nita (Interview 2, p. 12), another English teacher, explicitly equated these qualities in her evaluation of a longer term resident, Jenny, "Jenny would always talk, she always had opinions, she can think." When asked to rate the students, Anna, also commented she would give the highest rating to Jenny, "because Jenny is more vocal in my class. I hear her saying more things." In contrast, according to Anna (Interview 3, p. 21):

> Kwong when he was asked, the discrepancy between what he could do in his written work and what he could produce orally was just so great. It was a nerve type thing where language wouldn't come out.

Other students from Hong Kong were seen by their teachers as "offering nothing" (Di, Interview 3: 15):

> Ken doesn't take part in any discussion at all. He sits there and you get absolutely no feedback at all as to whether he understands, whether he is formulating his own ideas, whether he is formulating an opinion, whether he sees subtleties, you really don't get that sort of feedback because he just doesn't take part in any of it at all.

These comments suggest that the teachers valued a particular kind of talk, opinion, not just as a means of learning and thinking, and as a preparation for writing, but as an end in itself, as if wanting to create "a community of dialogic exchanges."

However, the teachers seemed to assume that the Cantonese-background students' failure to talk was due to individual factors, such as lack of motivation and interest, an over-reliance on L1, or, in Kwong's case, nerves. Hence, when students didn't talk they were labeled as "reluctant." This is exemplified in Anna's (Interview 3, p. 13) perception that Kwong and Leanne failed to take advantage of their small class situation to communicate:

> I was not able to get them involved in discussion informally, because they were just such reluctant speakers basically, both of them ... That group was a very vocal group. The majority of the students were very high marked kids, very loud, very opinionated boys, boys I say because I had nine boys and three girls, so the atmosphere was there but they didn't take advantage of it. They didn't become part of that class discussion that was going on. None of that chemistry that the others had, you know, they'd start a discussion and there would be an opinion here and an opinion there, extending, but those two didn't participate.

This comment reinforces the finding that it was a particular kind of talk that was valued in subject English, that is, asking questions and giving opinions.

Given their orientation towards education and desire to fit in, most students tried to comply with the demand to talk, despite their continual feelings of inadequacy and frustration. For example, Peter tried to copy his Australian peers, "try to ask the questions ... but it's hard." He observed that he didn't talk in class because "my English is not good ... embarrassed" (Interview 2, p. 12). Leanne (Interview 2, p. 10) also didn't talk in English other than in her ESL adjunct class "because they are mainly Australian, but I only go in front and ask the teacher how but not in front of the class." Like Peter, she also commented:

> [A good teacher] encourage us to talk more ... In Hong Kong the teacher only teach you how to do this, how to do that, they don't know whether you understand or not. The Australian teacher they will ask students many questions to make sure they understand.

However, these questions were never directed at her.

> CD: Do the teachers in the other classes say, Leanne, what's the answer to this? Do they ask you?
> Leanne: No.
> CD: What about in ESL?
> Leanne: Yes ... If I know the answer I'll tell the teacher.

Only in the ESL class was Leanne pushed to participate, and only in the ESL class, did she feel comfortable enough to respond. In other classes she was too apprehensive to claim "her right to speak" (Peirce, 1993), often not even understanding "when the teacher explain to us what they want... It's easy for an English student because they know how to speak."

Different Definitions of Language and Language Learning 543

The students' feelings of isolation appeared to lead to a sense of powerlessness and boredom, yet awareness of the need to speak didn't necessarily help them to do so, as the following exchange illustrates:

CD:	So, do you think your English is as good as Lee's, who has been here five years.
Leanne:	More or less the same.
CD:	So why isn't his English better?
Leanne:	Maybe he should speak English more in leisure time.
CD:	And do you?
Leanne:	No.

Leanne felt that "it's easier for the ESL students [who] come earlier … because when they are small they will make more friends and they will speak English more then." Many students commented that they had come to Australia at the 'wrong' time. Their resultant boredom and lack of friends seemed directly attributable to their sense of being unable or afraid to talk. These negative feelings about talk were even more pronounced amongst longer term residents such as Cathy and Ken. This negativity seemed to build over time. When asked in Year 11 how she felt about talking in class, Cathy responded: "I don't mind. You get more ideas and you share your feelings around. That's OK. I suppose." However, she saw her opportunities to "talk" as fairly restricted (Interview, 2, p. 13):

> As a Chinese I find …it feels more comfortable when you're discussing, it's because they are like you, but in English it's not as open … You tend to be a bit more quieter, there's more people in there and like people from mainstream English they like to tease. So, you get a bit afraid of speaking what you want to say.

She commented at the beginning of Year 12 (Cathy, Workbook Year 12, p. 4):

> When I speak in class, I feel apprehensive and terrified because if I speak things wrongly, people tend to laugh at me. I also feel uncomfortable when I speak and nervous because words run out of my mind.

She considered formal presentations were particularly difficult because "audiences often make funny faces at me." In response, her teacher, Di, responded: "Keep trying. Experience will lead to improvement" (Cathy, Workbook Year 12, p. 4). This comment exemplified the teacher-assessors' approach to talk, namely, that more use would naturally lead to development, an individual rather than pedagogic or structural problem. Not surprisingly, Cathy's proposed solution to her lack of talk was self-improvement rather than pedagogic change, listing amongst her priorities for Year 12 (Workbook Year 12, p. 4):

- participate in class discussions
- talk more in front of strangers and adults
- pay close attention to class discussions

The role of talk and the development of individuality have long influenced perceptions of success in subject English, as highlighted by Andrews, Costello and Clarke (1993):

> The subject (English) has been seen as primarily to do with the development of individual writers and speakers, with the cultivation of feeling and personal response, and with the expression of individual thoughts and feelings (p. 38).

The relationship between talk, individuality and the development of argument is foregrounded even more strongly by several of the teachers in the school, including Anna (Interview 3):

> One of the things I start off with issues is to say, I would prefer you to find an issue that you're committed to, something that you really strongly believe in, because that way you're going to be more persuasive, you're really going to become involved, you're going to talk about things that matter in your essay. Now not all students have got issues that they are interested in, so there's a problem there, but I always start off with, choose something that you are genuinely interested in, so that you can put yourself in the situation and talk about it in a more personal way (p. 16).

All teachers highlighted the need to develop a strong feeling, even passion about an issue: "You want them to have that sense of involvement and commitment, passion, if you like" (Di, Interview 3, p. 10); "It is wonderful when you get a student who becomes involved with their issue and writes passionately and strongly about it" (Nita, Interview 2, p. 9). Teachers saw this passion also manifested in student behavior, for example, Di commented that Cathy is "neither articulate nor fluent, but I still feel that she understands things better than (Ken) does, she's more excitable."

The teachers' valuing of feelings and passion seemed to suggest they valued an emotive, highly personalized hortatory-like challenge to the status quo, not a balanced, two sided discussion. However, when teachers were confronted with written work which exemplifed the features associated with Martin's hortatory genre, they downgraded it, giving students lower marks as their argument became increasingly personal and passionate. Hence, there were mixed messages, multiple discourses and ultimately, a lack of clarity as to what did count. Teachers assessed written argument but wanted 'real' spoken engagement, they created group-think while seeking individuality. Through the covert rhetoric of individual difference, argument acted as a mechanism for social reproduction and a means of maintaining commonality and conformity. The more recently arrived Hong Kong students' texts became far more emotive and spoken-like over the course of their final two years of school, in an apparent process of socio-psychological convergence. At the same time, the students tried to participate more in class, although they were not successful. Some students became invisible, because they were improving, because they were just coping, or because they had given up. All students' grades deteriorated. Jenny was the only one out of ten students who was consistently praised.

THE IMPLICATIONS FOR ASSESSMENT

This study shows that different assumptions about the purpose, audience, structure and development of argument not only affect teacher-assessors judgments of (in)competence, but also shape ESL students' linguistic 'choices' in critical and often unpredictable ways.

In a view of argument as logic, the Melbourne students can be seen as moving away from so-called 'balanced, objective argument' incorporating opposing viewpoints to one-sided opinion with little or no refutation. This is contrary to the shift expected (and desired) by many theorists in subject English and by ESL teachers more generally. This suggests that logical and supposedly more complex modes of reasoning are not being given as much emphasis in teaching, and students may be regressing.

In a view of argument as persuasion, the Melbourne students can be seen as developing a greater range of emotional appeals, and more overt rhetorical strategies. The movement from impersonal to personal reference and from 'I' to 'we' can be interpreted as a progressive enlargement of the number of points of view the writers can identify with, stage by stage. Experiments with adopting fictive roles in writing argument such as that of a foetus or a homosexual can be seen as attempts to develop understanding of another's viewpoint. However, the movement in the students' texts towards 'we' can also be read as a loss, rather than a gain, in rhetorical maturity, an assumption of union with the audience (Miller, 1980).

In a view of argument as text or discourse, the Melbourne students can be seen as developing a range of different cohesive features associated with the written mode, including greater use of internal rhetorical markers and nominalization, which are considered signs of development (Halliday, 1985). However, the move towards more hortatory, rather than analytical features in terms of tenor and field would be seen by many text linguists and systemic theorists as only a stage in the development towards more socially-valued written-like texts. Hence, Kwong may be judged as having attained only a partial competence. Martin himself, in his topology of development, appears to adopt this position, despite his acknowledgement of the existence of 'mature' hortatory forms.

In a more dynamic and evolving view of genre, the Melbourne students can be seen as developing within the expository genre, but playing with its linguistic possibilities to achieve multiple and different purposes. In doing so, their expression of 'opinion' was developed to such an extent that it could be described as a sub "sub-genre" (after Bhatia, 1993). The students' opinion, not their logic nor their consideration of other viewpoints, is what appeared to count in their school. Overt displays of opinion were what the teachers demanded as a way of getting students to feel. Once feelings were dominant in their writing, the push for opinion seemed to fade. In this view of argument, Kwong appeared to be successful. His fellow students all moved, often dramatically, towards greater displays of personal opinion over the course of the VCE. That they were not rewarded suggests that this notion of genre is necessary but insufficient to describe their development.

In other views of argument as genre which draw more strongly on the notion of discourse communities, the Melbourne students can be seen as aligning themselves more overtly with particular 'socio-rhetorical networks' (Swales, 1990) or 'sites of social and ideological action' (Freedman and Medway, 1994). In this view of argument, students are judged on how well their texts are recognised by the 'expert members of the parent discourse community' (Swales 1990, p. 58). However, the students' texts received increasingly negative comments and grades, suggesting that either the students texts' were ambiguous, or that the VCE English discourse community was itself composed of multiple and competing discourses and cultural-practices.

In a view of argument as culturally-situated practice, the Melbourne students can be seen as making major adjustments to their ideological and textual stance, and moving away from pre-existing textual preferences. This suggests progress in acculturation, although it is unclear whether this change is subtractive or additive.

In this view of argument, students can either be accredited with competence or 'becoming-competence' (after Baker and Freebody, 1993), or marginalized. Competence in persuasive and/or argumentative discourse in VCE English seemed to require both structure and passion. As was seen in the teachers' responses to individuals, passion was associated with talk rather than writing, with action rather than reflection, hence the teachers' insistence of student participation in a 'community of dialogic exchanges.' Students who were more oral in class, more outspoken in their opinions, more 'excitable,' were considered more competent. Within the official period of ESL-ness, there was some space given for ESL students to change and improve, but even with these ESL boundaries, judgments were formed almost immediately about the limits of students' competence.

CONCLUSIONS

Argument appears to have a range of different roles and purposes in education in general, and in subject English in particular. In the official guidelines for senior secondary English in Melbourne, argument was conflated with persuasion. However, the findings of this study suggest argument had three other, more covert roles in Melbourne schools: as a mode of critical thinking and reasoning (derived from views of argument as logic), as a mode of apprenticeship into the ways of thinking and writing in subject English in particular and the Anglo-Australian democratic literate community in general (foregrounding argument as culturally-situated practice) and as a mode of evaluation (foregrounding argument as text). There are apparent contradictions in educational discourses between the notion of argument as expression of personal viewpoint and argument as conforming to conventional requirements. Similarly, there are tensions in education in general and the subject English in particular between the notion of argument as expanding modes of thinking and critique and argument as the mechanism for high stakes assessment.

These findings also suggest that many terms given prominence in the description of written argument and its development, such as *opinion*, *purpose*, *audience*, and *response*, need to be problematized, because different interpretations may lead to different views of argument, and hence different views of assessment, learning and teaching. A text cannot be considered separately from its ideological context, for to do so obscures the essentially social nature of the text and makes the participants in its construction, the readers and writers and other texts invisible. ESL students are not just learning English but attempting to become competent members of the classroom and community culture. However, different and sometimes conflicting, highly localized sociological and ideological forces may push development in particular directions which might not be what the individual learner (or teacher) expects, wants or needs. This suggests that traditional notions of ESL development as simply the acquisition of English language proficiency are problematic, as are definitions of language and language learning which are based on an assumed set of common, fixed norms.

The implication for assessment, and especially for teacher-assessors, is that no judgments can be made of ESL development without first establishing what is actually being taught and learnt.

NOTES

1. A much earlier version of this chapter was presented at the International Language in Education Conference in Hong Kong in December 1999.
2. Because of the ambiguities over the concept, I have avoided the use of the term *ESL* to describe the student informants in this study.

REFERENCES

Andrews, R., Costello, P., & Clarke, S. (1993). *Improving the quality of argument 5–16 Final Report*: The University of Hull.
Baker, C., & Freebody, P. (1989). *Children's first school books: Introduction to the culture of literacy*. Oxford: Blackwell and Associates.
Baker, C., & Freebody, P. (1993). The crediting of literate competence in classroom talk. *The Australian Journal of Language and Literacy, 16*(4), 279–294.
Bazerman, C. (1994). Systems of genres and the enactment of social intentions. In A. Freedman & P. Medway (Eds.), *Genre and the new rhetoric* (pp. 79–101). London: Taylor and Francis.
Belcher, D. (1994). The apprenticeship approach to advanced academic literacy: Graduate students and their mentors. *English for Specific Purposes, 13*(1), 23–34.
Berkenkotter, & Huckin, T. (1993). Rethinking genre from a sociocognitive perspective. *Written Communication, 10*(4), 475–509.
Bernstein, B. (1996). *Pedagogy, symbolic control and identity*. London: Taylor and Francis.
Bhatia, V. K. (1993). *Analyzing genre: Language use in professional settings*. New York: Longman.
Block, D. (2003). *The social turn in second language acquisition*. Edinburgh: Edinburgh University Press.
Board of Studies. (1994). *English VCE Study Design*. Carlton: Board of Studies.
Casanave, C. P. (1995). Local interactions: Constructing contexts for composing in a graduate sociology program. In D. Belcher & G. Braine (Eds.), *Academic writing in a second language: Essays of research and pedagogy* (pp. 83–110). Norwood, NJ: Ablex.
Christie, F. (2002). *Classroom discourse analysis: A functional perspective*. London Continuum.
Connor, U. (1996). *Contrastive rhetoric: Cross-cultural aspects of second-language writing*. Cambridge: Cambridge University Press.
Crismore, A., Markkanen, R., & Steffensen, M. S. (1993). Metadiscourse in persuasive writing: A study of texts written by American and Finnish university students. *Written Communication, 10*(1), 39–71.
Davison, C. (1998). *'It's your opinion that counts': Written argument and ESL students in secondary English*. Unpublished PhD, La Trobe University, Melbourne.
Davison, C. (2005). Learning your lines: Negotiating language and content in subject English. *Linguistics and Education, 16*(4), 219–237.
Freedman, A., & Pringle, I. (1984). Why students can't write arguments. *English in Education, 18*(2), 73–84.
Gorman, T. (1988). *Language performances in schools: Review of APU Language Monitoring 1979–1983*. London: HMSO.
Gubb, J. (1987). Discursive writing: A small-scale observation study. In J. Gubb (Ed.), *The study of written composition in England and Wales*. Windsor: NFER/Nelson.
Halliday, M. A. K. (1975). *Learning how to mean: Explorations in the development of language*. London: Edward Arnold.
Halliday, M. A. K. (1985). *An introduction to functional grammar*. London: Edward Arnold.
Hinds, J. (1983). Contrastive rhetoric: English and Japanese. *Text, 3*(2), 183–195.
Jenkins, J. (2006). Points of view and blind spots: ELF and SLA. *International Journal of Applied Linguistics, 16*(2), 137–162.
Kinneavy, J. (1971). *A theory of discourse*. Englewood Cliffs, NJ: Prentice Hall.
Leung, C., Harris, R., & Rampton, B. (1997). The idealised native speaker, reified ethnicities, and classroom realities. *TESOL Quarterly, 31*(3), 543–560.
Love, K. (1996). Unpacking arguments: The need for a metalanguage. *Idiom,* (1), 60–75.
Martin, J. R. (1984). Types of writing in infants and primary school. In L. Unsworth (Ed.), *Reading, writing, spelling: Proceedings of the Fifth Macarthur Reading/Language Symposium* (pp. 34–55). Sydney: Macarthur Institute of Higher Education.
Martin, J. R. (1985). *Factual writing: Exploring and challenging social reality*. Geelong: Deakin University Press.
Martin, J. R. (1992). *English text: System and structure*. Amsterdam: John Benjamins.

McKay, P. (1996). ESL learners: How do we know them? *English in Australia,* (115), 13–23.
McLoughlin, R. (1993). *Persuasive writing: An analysis of English and ESL students' texts.* Unpublished MA Minor thesis, University of Melbourne.
Miller, S. (1980). Rhetorical maturity: Definition and development. In A. Freedman & I. Pringle (Eds.), *Reinventing the rhetorical tradition.* Careltown University, Ottawa: Canadian Council of the Teachers of English.
Moore, H. (1995). Telling what is real: Competing views in assessing ESL development. *Linguistics and Education, 8,* 189–228.
Moore, H. (2004). Identifying the target population: A genealogy of policy-making for English as a second language (ESL) in Australian schools. Unpublished doctoral thesis, Ontario Institute of Studies in Education, University of Toronto.
Peirce, B. (1993). *Language learning, social identity and immigrant women.* Unpublished PhD, University of Toronto.
Pringle, I., & Freedman, A. (1985). *A comparative study of writing abilities in two modes at Grade 5, 8 and 12 levels.* Toronto: Ministry of Education.
Prior, P. (1995). Redefining the task: An ethnographic examination of writing and response in six graduate seminars. In D. Belcher & G. Braine (Eds.), *Academic writing in a second language: Essays of research and pedagogy* (pp. 47–82). Norwood, NJ: Ablex.
Seeley, A., & Carter, B. (2004). *Applied linguistics as a social science.* London: Continuum.
Swales, J. (1990). *Genre analysis: English in academic and research settings.* Cambridge: Cambridge University Press.
Toulmin, S., Rieke, R., & Janik, A. (1979). *An introduction to reasoning.* New York: Macmillan.
VATME. (1995). Submission to the VCE English Review Panel Board of Studies. *VATME Newsletter, 58,* 7.
Ventola, E., & Mauranen, A. (1991). Non-native writing and native revising of scientific articles. In E. Ventola (Ed.), *Functional and systemic linguistics: Approaches and uses* (pp. 457–492). Berlin: Mouton de Gruyter.
Zuengler, J., & Miller, E. (2006). Cognitive and social perspectives: Two parallel SLA worlds. *TESOL Quarterly, 40*(1), 35–58.

AUTHOR INDEX

A
Abbs, B. 299
Abdulaziz, M. 49
Abello, P. 363
Abeysekera, R. 825
Accardo, A. 1082
Achebe, C. 678
Adams, G. 649
Adams, J. 180
Adams, L. 287
Adamson, B. 104
Addis, C. 22
Adolphs, S. 839
Agarwal, J. 61
Agnello, M. 904
Ahlgren, I. 50
Ahmed, M. 839
Akamatsu, N. 1050, 1099
Alatis, J. 49, 285, 348, 1001, 1027
Alderson, J. 469, 481, 502, 957
Alexander, B. 1029, 1047
Alexander, N. 40, 49
Alexander, P. 49
Alexander, R. 134, 210
Alfred, G. 1047
Allan, K. 856
Allan, M. 389
Allan, Q. 957
Allen, P. 285, 286, 483
Allwright, D. 984, 999, 1082
Almon, C. 678
Almond, R. 519
Altman, H. 742
Alvarez, A.

Alvarez, H. 637
Alvermann, D. 1014
Amin, N. 84, 689, 1047
Ammar, A. 284
Ammon, U. 134, 149, 165
Anderson, A. 299
Anderson, B. 34, 197, 678, 887
Anderson, G. 1000, 1047
Anderson, J. 197, 330
Anderson, M. 758
Andrew, D. 930
Andrews, S. 957
Angelil-Carter, S. 665
Angelova, M. 887
Ansre, G. 49
Anzaldúa, G. 1012, 1014
Aoki, N. 742
Aphek, E. 839
Appadurai, A. 1047
Appel, G. 690
Applebaum, S. 679, 1015
Archibald, J. 824
Argyris, C. 411, 1000
Arkoudis, S. 376, 502, 517
Arnaud, J. 34
Arnberg, L. 165
Arndt, V. 957, 1066
Arnett, J. 649
Arredondo, J. 652
Arthur, B. 246
Artin, G. 638
Arva, V. 957
Asato, J. 637
Ashworth, M. 197, 266, 313

Askehave, I. 940
Aston, G. 299
Atkey, S. 824
Atkinson, D. 61, 887, 889, 984, 986, 1047
Atkinson, J. 1026
Atkinson, P. 985
Atkinson, T. 1082
Au, A. 469
Au, K. 689
Auer, P. 246
Auerbach, E. 34, 84, 284, 689, 1000, 1047
August, D. 689
Austin, J. 284, 1047
Ayers, W. 1016
Azurmendi, M. 266

B

Bachman, L. 285, 454, 469, 482, 517, 518
Bachoc, E. 266
Baddeley, A. 839
Badger, R. 940
Bahns, J. 839
Bailey, B. 678
Bailey, K. 482, 984, 999, 1000, 1082
Bailey, R. 22, 1051
Baker, C. 119, 165, 389, 547
Baker, K. 34, 180, 182, 715
Baker, R. 454
Baker, S. 72, 73
Bakhtin, M. 401, 636, 887, 1047
Balazs, G. 1082
Balester, V. 915
Baley, R. 678
Ball, K. 1137
Ball, S. 267
Ballard, B. 887
Bamgboşe, A. 38, 49, 141, 149
Bamworth, R. 940
Bandura, A. 330
Banerjee, J. 481, 502, 518
Banks, C. 652, 689
Banks, J. 652, 689
Bankston, C. 645, 653
Bannan-Ritland, B. 758
Bannerji, H. 197
Baquedano-López, P. 637
Barahona, B. 34
Barfield, A. 742
Barker, T. 915
Barnes, A. 1137
Barnes, D. 715, 742, 889
Barnett, R. 1082
Baron, D. 180
Baron, N. 904

Barratt-Pugh, C. 454, 502, 518
Barritt, L. 502
Barro, A. 1051
Barron-Hauwaert, S. 165
Barrs, M. 454
Barry, H. 643, 652
Barson, J. 915
Barthes, R. 1047
Bartholomae, D. 401
Barton, D. 313, 401
Barton, L. 1083
Basena, D. 758
Bassano, S. 1000
Basturkmen, H. 518
Bates, E. 794
Bateson, M. 1014
Batson, T. 916
Baugh, J. 34, 180
Baumeister, R. 649
Bayley, R. 984
Baynham, M. 377
Baynham, N. 940
Bazerman, C. 401, 547, 887, 940, 1047
Beacco, J. 149
Beardsmore, H. 165, 267
Beasley, V. 887
Beaty, E. 744
Beauvillain, C. 246
Beck, I. 840
Beck, J. 761
Beck, U. 1082
Becker, W. 809
Beglar, D. 840
Behar, R. 1098
Bejar, I. 482
Belcher, D. 547, 887, 888
Bell, D. 285
Bell, J. 1014
Bellack, A. 715
Belmore, N. 915
Belsey, C. 1047
Belz, J. 1047, 1137
Beneke, J. 149
Benesch, S. 401, 482, 665, 666, 689, 887, 1047
Benner, P. 1065
Bennett, C. 1000
Benson, D. 1026
Benson, M. 666
Benson, P. 742
Bereiter, C. 285, 794, 1065
Berge, Z. 1123, 1137
Berkenkotter, C. 887, 940
Berliner, D. 1065

Author Index

Berns, M. 149, 165, 482
Bernstein, B. 210, 547, 1082, 1111
Bernstein, R. 180
Berry, J. 649
Berry, R. 957
Berthoud, R. 210
Berwick, R. 484
Beveridge, M. 718
Bhabha, H. 649, 1047
Bhatia, V. 401, 411, 547, 666, 940
Bialystok, E. 246
Biava, T. 679
Biber, D. 482, 715, 856, 871
Bickel, B. 1123
Bickley, G. 469
Biesenbach-Lucas, S. 758
Bigelow, B. 715
Biott, C. 1000
Birdsong, D. 824
Birkales, G. 180
Bissoondath, N. 1047
Black, P. 502, 518
Blackledge, A. 680, 1047, 1051
Blair, M. 210
Blaise, C. 1014
Blaustein-Epstein, A. 180
Bley-Vroman, R. 300
Bloch, J. 758
Block, D. 134, 547, 1047
Blommaert, J. 34, 134, 180
Bloomfield, L. 246
Bloor, T. 957
Blue, G. 743
Blum-Kulka, S. 871
Blundell, L. 299
Bock, H. 887
Boden, D. 1026
Boersma, P. 794
Boggs, G. 689
Bohman, J. 638
Bokamba, E. 49
Boling, E. 810
Bolitho, R. 149, 957, 959
Bolter, J. 758
Bonanno, H. 888
Bond, T. 455
Bondebjerg, I. 134
Bongaerts, T. 246, 824
Booth, D. 482
Borg, S. 957, 1065, 1082
Borg, W. 985
Borko, H. 1065
Borman, K. 649, 652

Bosco, F. 285
Bostwick, R. 71
Boswood, T. 411
Bottery, M. 1082
Bottomly, Y. 437
Boud, D. 743
Bourdieu, P. 134, 180, 531, 679, 689, 887, 904, 1047, 1082, 1098
Bourne, J. 210, 267, 636, 1111
Boxer, D. 871
Boykin, A. 1098
Boyle, A. 482
Brabazon, T. 1123
Braine, G. 401, 679, 887, 957, 1047
Bramley, P. 407, 411
Brazil, D. 856
Breen, M. 285, 454, 502, 518, 715, 743, 1000, 1082, 1137
Bremer, K. 149
Brennan, M. 1083
Brenner, J. 930
Bridgeman, B. 482, 483
Brilliant-Mills, H. 984
Brindley, G. 411, 437, 454, 469, 482, 518, 1000
Brinkerhoff, J. 1137
Brinkerhoff, R. 404, 411
Brinton, S. 376
Britton, B. 794
Britton, J. 285, 715
Broadfoot, P. 454, 518, 520
Brock, M. 1083
Brock-Utne, B. 49
Broeder, P. 149, 165
Broeselow, E. 824
Bronfenbrenner, U. 700
Brookes, A. 743
Brookfield, S. 743
Brookhart, S. 1065
Brooks, F. 715
Brophy, J. 731, 957
Broselow, E. 824
Brousseau, K. 1000
Brown, A. 469, 482, 502
Brown, C. 824
Brown, G. 299
Brown, H. 1047
Brown, J. 71, 518
Brown, K. 758, 809
Brown, S. 104
Brownell, J. 454
Brumfit, C. 149, 285, 957, 1000
Bruner, J. 689, 715, 718, 1014
Brush, T. 1137

Bruton, A. 285, 299
Brutt-Griffler, J. 22, 84, 134, 149, 531, 1047
Bryson, B. 22
Bryson, P. 1001
Bull, P. 1029
Bullough, R. 1065
Bunnell, T. 389
Bunting, E. 363
Burbules, N. 915
Burgess, S. 940
Burnaby, B. 197
Burns, A. 856, 1000, 1082
Burstein, J. 484
Burt, E. 197
Burt, H. 299
Burt, M. 636
Burton, D. 871
Butler, F. 454, 482
Butler, J. 1047, 1048
Butler, Y. 809
Buttjes, D. 149
Button, G. 1026
Byram, M. 149, 1047, 1048, 1051
Byrd, P. 482

C
Cadman, K. 887
Cadorath, J. 871
Cain, A. 1050
Cain, C. 637
Calderhead, J. 412, 1065, 1082, 1083
Calderón, M. 649
Calhoun, E. 1000
Cameron, D. 34, 134, 412, 904, 1048
Cameron, K. 758
Campbell, D. 331
Campbell, W. 267
Camps, D. 887, 889
Canagarajah, A. 34, 71, 227, 636, 666, 984, 1048
Canale, M. 285, 715
Candelier, M. 149, 957
Candlin, C. 285, 401, 412, 666, 887, 1000, 1048, 1082
Candy, P. 743
Cantoni, G. 34
Carder, M. 389
Carey, L. 437
Carey, P. 482, 484
Carger, C. 1014
Carlgren, I. 1082
Carlisle, R. 824
Carlson, R. 469

Carpenter, P. 794
Carr, D. 1026
Carr, J. 1048
Carr, W. 1000, 1083
Carranza, I. 180
Carrell, P. 285, 482
Carroll, J. 482
Carroll, S. 856
Carson, J. 483
Carter, K. 1014
Carter, R. 149, 839, 857, 871, 872, 957
Caruso-Shade, D. 1123
Carver, R. 794
Casale, J. 330
Casanave, C. 547, 666, 887, 888, 1048
Casey, K. 1014
Cash, D. 916
Casllister, T. 915
Castaños, F. 278, 287
Castells, M. 904
Cazden, C. 636, 715
Celce-Murcia, M. 285, 856, 871
Cenoz, J. 150, 165, 166
Centrie, C. 650
Chafe, W. 871
Chaika, E. 1048
Chaiklin, S. 637, 716
Chalhoub-Deville, M. 482
Chambers, J. 150
Chamoiseau, P. 1014
Chamot, A. 267, 330, 331, 389, 840
Chan, A. 1098
Chandler, P. 957
Chang, J. 363
Chang, P. 1014
Chang, Y. 888
Chang-Wells, G. 718
Chapelle, C. 482, 518, 519, 758, 984
Charge, N. 482
Charpentier, J. 34
Chascas, S. 809
Chase, G. 888
Chaudenson, R. 134
Chavez, L. 180
Cheah, Y. 497, 502
Chen, J. 503
Cheng, L. 518, 531
Cherry, R. 888
Cherryholmes, C. 1048
Chesla, C. 1065
Cheung, K. 1099
Chiseri-Strater, E. 888
Chisman, F. 181
Chiu, M. 637

Choi, C. 461, 469
Choi, I. 84, 482
Chomsky, N. 246, 285, 299, 794, 856
Christensen, C. 1123
Christensen, J. 1065
Christian, D. 180, 267
Christie, F. 547, 715, 716, 856, 940
Christison, M. 1000
Christopher, E. 872
Chu, W. 809
Chun, D. 758, 915
Churchill, S. 197, 267
Cicourel, A. 1026
Cisneros, S. 1014
Claiborne, R. 23
Clanchy, J. 887
Clandinin, D. 1014
Clapham, C. 469, 481, 482, 518, 957
Clark, C. 1083
Clark, E. 794
Clark, F. 502
Clark, H. 794
Clark, J. 454
Clark, R. 888, 957
Clarke, D. 1065
Clarke, S. 518, 547, 1137
Claxton, G. 518, 1082
Clayman, S. 1026
Clayton, J. 716
Cleland, B. 267, 268
Clifford, J. 650, 1099
Cline, F. 482, 483
Clive, J. 23
Cloud, N. 456
Cluver, A. 34
Clyne, M. 166, 904
Coady, J. 794, 839
Cobb, T. 957, 958
Cochran, C. 916
Cochran-Smith, M. 1000
Coe, R. 401
Coehlo, E. 1099
Coffin, C. 313, 858
Cohen, A. 503, 517, 743, 839
Cohen, E. 731
Cohen, J. 331
Cohen, L. 984
Cole, M. 637
Coleman, H. 85
Coleman, J. 237, 246
Coles, R. 1014
Colhoun, E. 1049
Collier, J. 1000

Collier, V. 50, 210, 228, 268, 331, 348, 363, 690, 715, 810
Collins, J. 180
Collins, K. 210
Collins, P. 689
Collot, M. 915
Combs, M. 180, 348
Commins, L. 469
Conchas, G. 650
Condon, W. 503, 519
Coniam, D. 4671, 810
Conle, C. 1014
Connelly, F. 1014
Connolly, J. 651
Connor, U. 401, 547, 666, 940, 1048
Connor-Linton, J. 482
Conrad, S. 482, 856
Constas, M. 1048
Cook, G. 150, 299, 871
Cook, T. 331
Cook, V. 84, 150, 166, 246, 285, 679, 856, 1048
Cooke, D. 1048
Cooper, A. 412
Cooper, R. 267
Cooper, S. 1138
Cope, B. 650, 774, 888, 904, 930, 940
Coppari, P. 455, 456
Coppetiers, R. 246
Corbel, C. 437, 758, 1123
Corbett, J. 1048
Corbin, J. 986
Corno, L. 731
Corsaro, W. 984
Corson, D. 197, 809, 1048, 1099
Cortazzi, M. 85
Costa, A. 313
Coté, J. 650
Cotterall, S. 743
Coughlan, P. 299
Coulmas, F. 150
Coulthard, R. 717, 873
Coupland, J. 871
Coupland, N. 150, 872
Courchêne, R. 186, 197, 1038, 1048
Covington, M. 731
Cowan, P. 1014
Crabbe, D. 743
Crabtree, B. 984
Craig, A. 888
Craig, C. 1014
Crandall, J. 267, 376, 389
Crawford, J. 85, 180, 181, 227, 267, 636

Creese, A. 210, 376, 1111
Creswell, J. 984
Criper, C. 49
Crites, S. 1014
Crocker, L. 502
Crookes, G. 85, 287, 299, 1001
Crow Dog, M. 1014
Crow, N. 1065
Crump, S. 1123
Crystal, D. 120, 134, 166, 181, 210, 531, 904, 915
Csizér, K. 150
Cuckle, P. 1137
Cuevas, G. 267
Culler, J. 1048
Cumming, A. 197, 455, 456, 482, 1001
Cummings, O. 412
Cummins, J. 34, 49, 166, 181, 197, 227, 267, 285, 286, 331, 348, 363, 389, 455, 483, 636, 650, 689, 715, 758, 769, 774, 809, 888, 904, 916, 1048, 1099, 1111
Cunningham, A. 809
Cunningham, D. 1123
Cunningham, S. 299
Curran, C. 247, 285
Currie, P. 888
Curry-Rodriguez, J. 268
Cutler, A. 794
Czarniawska, B. 1014

D

Dabbagh, N. 758
Dale, M. 330
Dale, T. 267
Dall'Alba, G. 740, 744
Dallas, D. 809
Dalton, J. 437
Dam, L. 743, 1000, 1082
Darder, A. 650, 715
Darling-Hammond, L. 958
Datta, M. 210
Davidson, A. 650
Davidson, F. 482, 483
Davidson, J. 1026
Davies, A. 518, 531, 716
Davies, B. 636
Davies, L. 760
Davis, B. 1123
Davis, J. 1015
Davis, K. 181, 984
Davis, N. 1137
Davison, C. 267, 268, 376, 377, 389, 455, 502, 518, 547, 986, 1100

Dawson, K. 1137
Day, C. 1083
Day, E. 636
de Bot, K. 149
de Jong, J. 483
de Kanter, A. 180
de Klerk, G. 34
de Silva Joyce, H. 856, 1000
de Smedt, K. 794
de Swaan, A. 135
Deakin-Crick, R. 518
Debski, R. 758, 915, 1123
DeCarrico, J. 857
Dehaene-Lambertz, G. 824
Dei, G. 1099
DeKeyser, R. 789, 794
Del Rio, P. 638
Deleuze, G. 1048
Delgado-Gaitan, C. 689
Delpit, L. 715, 1051, 1099, 1100
Demick, B. 85
Dendrinos, V. 135
Deneire, M. 150
Denicolo, P. 1083
Denzin, N. 984, 1014
dePyssler, B. 653
Derewianka, B. 454, 455, 502, 518, 715, 856, 940, 941
Derrida, J. 1048
Desai, R. 61
Deville, C. 482, 985
Devitt, S. 760
Devlin, B. 181, 716
Devy, G. 61
Dewey, J. 743, 1015
Dewey, M. 150
Di Cola, J. 331
Di Pietro, J. 285
Dias, P. 940
Diaz, R. 247
Diaz, S. 637
DiCerbo, K. 348
Dick, W. 437
Dicker, S. 1048
Dickinson, L. 743
Dijkstra, T. 794
Dillon, J. 715
DiMatteo, A. 916
Dirven, R. 49
Disick, R. 438
Dison, A. 888
Dison, L. 888
Dixon, C. 716, 717, 985

Doan, L. 905
Dodd, N. 49
Doiz, A. 167
Donahue, T. 34, 181
Donaldson, M. 715
Donato, R. 651, 690, 715
Donmall, G. 958
Donmall-Hicks, G. 958
Dorfman, A. 1015
Dörnyei, Z. 150, 285, 731, 743, 871
Doughty, C. 285, 299, 518, 758, 856, 1026, 1028, 1029
Doughty, P. 150
Douglas, D. 412, 482, 483
Draper, J. 181
Dresemann, B. 150
Drew, M. 930
Drew, P. 1026
Dreyfus, H. 758
Dreyfus, S. 758
Droeschel, Y. 150
Drucker, P. 1123
Drury, H. 889
Dryfoos, J. 650
du Gay, P. 637, 651
Du, P. 90, 105
Dudley-Evans, N. 412
Dudley-Evans, T. 401, 666, 940, 941
Duff, P. 120, 198, 299, 650, 984, 985, 1027, 1112
Dufficy, P. 941
Dugan, N. 794
Duke, N. 810
Dulay, H. 636
Dulay, M. 299
Dunkel, P. 482, 758
Dunn, W. 700
Dupoux, E. 824
Duran, R. 717
Duranti, A. 651, 1026
Durham, M. 150
Dutcher, N. 166
Dutertre, A. 1001
Dykman, E. 650
Dyson, A. 636

E
Earl, L. 34
Early, M. 198, 313, 985
Easterby-Smith, M. 412
Eckman, F. 824
Economou, D. 889
Edelenbos, P. 518
Edelsky, C. 689

Edge, J. 958, 985, 1001
Edmondson, W. 150
Edmonston, B. 182
Edwards, D. 715
Edwards, V. 531, 1112
Egan, K. 700
Eggington, W. 24, 691, 1047–1049, 1052
Eggins, S. 856, 872, 941
Ehrlich, S. 1048
Ehrman, M. 731
Eignor, D. 482, 484
Eimas, P. 794, 795
Eisner, E. 985
Elbaz, F. 1065, 1083
Elbaz-Luwisch, F. 1015
Eldaw, M. 839
Elder, C. 470, 483
Eliot, C. 761
Elley, W. B. 802, 809, 834, 839
Elley, W. G. 285
Elliott, J. 700, 1001
Ellis, A. 759, 809
Ellis, G. 1083
Ellis, M. 412
Ellis, N. 794
Ellis, R. 247, 2901, 348, 518, 840, 856, 958, 1027, 1137
Ellis, S. 454
Ellsworth, E. 1050
Elman, J. 794
Elson, N. 483
Ely, C. 759
Endres, S. 759
Engeström, Y. 637
English, L. 888
Enright, M. 483
Epp, L. 483
Epstein, A. 679
Eraut, M. 412
Erdoes, R. 1014
Erduran, S. 520
Erickson, M. 889
Ericsson, K. 1065
Erikson, E. 650
Erling, E. 150
Ernst, G. 872
Espinosa, P. 690
Esses, V. 197
Etxeberria, F. 166
Evans, L. 1123
Evans, R. 267, 268
Ewen, D. 181
Extra, G. 165

F

Faderman, L. 650
Fafunwa, A. 49
Faigley, L. 916
Fairclough, N. 34, 49, 650, 888, 930, 958, 985
Falodun, J. 300
Faltis, C. 689
Falvey, P. 469, 470
Fardon, R. 49
Feak, C. 942, 943
Featherstone, M. 85
Feez, S. 941
Feinberg, W. 650
Feldman, C. 247
Feldman, S. 652
Felix, U. 759
Ferguson, C. 181
Ferguson, P. 1001, 1082
Ferguson, R. 456
Fessler, R. 1065
Feuerverger, G. 1015
Fielding, L. 809
Fillmore, L. 331, 348, 638, 691, 810
Fine, G. 650
Fine, M. 652, 653
Finegan, E. 856
Finer, D. 824
Firmat, G. 1015
Firth, A. 150, 152, 299, 872, 1027
Firth, J. 285
Fishman, J. 34, 120, 181
Flavell, J. 743
Fleming, D. 197, 1048
Fleming, M. 149, 1047, 1048
Fletcher, J. 483
Flewelling, J. 470
Floriani, A. 715
Flower, L. 794
Flowerdew, J. 402, 872, 888, 1083
Flynn, L. 916
Fodor, J. 794
Fok, O. 809
Forester, J. 34
Forey, G. 412
Forman, E. 637, 638
Forsyth, D. 731
Foster, P. 299, 301
Fotus, S. 285
Foucault, M. 34, 531, 650, 1049, 1083
Fox, H. 666, 888
Fox, J. 1123
Fox, R. 1123
Fradd, S. 716

Francis, G. 872
Fránquiz, M. 635, 637
Franson, C. 1112
Fraser, B. 731
Freebairn, I. 299
Freebody, P. 547, 905
Freedman, A. 547, 548, 940, 941
Freeman, D. 72, 285, 286, 348, 363, 377, 958, 1001, 1015, 1065, 1083, 1137
Freeman, R. 985
Freeman, Y. 363
Freire, P. 85, 285, 502, 689, 743, 904, 1049
Fremer, J. 503
Fries, C. 285
Fröhlich, M. 285, 288
Frommer, J. 915
Fujishima, N. 666
Fulcher, G. 483
Fulford, R. 197
Fullan, M. 377, 455, 1137
Fuller, F. 412
Funabashi, Y. 71
Furlong, J. 1083
Furniss, G. 49

G

Gabel, P. 1137
Gabrielsen, G. 1000, 1082
Gagné, A. 470
Gairns, R. 839
Gall, J. 985
Gall, M. 985
Gallard, P. 331
Gallardo, F. 166
Gallas, K. 715
Gallego, M. 904
Gallegos, B. 1047
Gallimore, R. 638, 717
Gan, D. 1100
Gándara, P. 261, 266, 268
Ganderton, R. 759
García Lecumberri, M. 163, 165–167
García Mayo, M. 163, 165–167
García, A. 266, 268
García, E. 260, 268, 355, 363, 643, 650, 688, 690
García, O. 32, 35
Gardner, H. 363
Gardner, R. 197, 872
Gardner, S. 518, 519
Gardner-Chloros, P. 34
Garfinkel, H. 1027
Garrett, P. 151, 958
Gartner-Clough, P. 1124

Garton, J. 1123
Garvey, C. 314
Gaskill, W. 1027
Gass, S. 286, 287, 300, 794, 1027, 1030
Gates, P. 1082
Gawlitta, K. 135
Geddes, M. 300, 743
Gee, J. 314, 637, 650, 689, 888, 904, 1049, 1083, 1099, 1123
Gee, S. 941
Geertz, C. 888, 1015
Gegeo, D. 35, 36
Genesee, F. 120, 165, 166, 247, 268, 286, 518, 825
Geoghegan, W. 1123
George, J. 23
Gernsbacher, M. 794
Gersten, B. 1001
Gersten, R. 363
Geva, E. 809
Ghadirian, S. 759
Gibbons, P. 715, 856
Gibson, M. 650, 985, 1112
Giddens, A. 1082, 1083
Gilbert, G. 402
Giles, H. 150, 650
Gill, G. 840
Gillborn, D. 210, 455, 650, 1112
Gillespie, M. 35
Giltrow, J. 1049
Gimenez, T. 1083
Gingrich, N. 181
Ginther, A. 483
Ginther, L. 483
Gipps, C. 455, 518, 520
Giroux, H. 1049, 1083
Glas, C. 520
Glazewski, K. 1137
Glenwright, P. 470
Glesne, C. 985
Glynn, S. 794
Gnutzmann, C. 150, 166
Godwin-Jones, B. 754, 759
Goethals, M. 150
Goldstein, T. 652, 679, 985, 986, 1049, 1099
Golebiowski, Z. 759
Gollin, S. 402, 889
Golub, J. 1138
Gomes de Matos, F. 247
Gomez, E. 456
Gong, Y. 104
Gonzales, R. 34
González-Nueno, M. 239, 247

Good, T. 731
Goodfellow, R. 760
Goodman, K. 716
Goodman, S. 856
Goodman, Y. 716
Goodson, I. 1065
Goodwin, C. 1027
Goossens, L. 650
Gordon, C. 484
Gore, J. 690, 1001, 1066
Görlach, M. 150
Gorsuch, G. 71
Goswami, D. 1001
Gotanda, N. 637
Goto, S. 651
Gottlieb, M. 456
Gough, L. 331
Goulden, R. 839
Gout, A. 824
Grabe, W. 285, 314, 482, 794, 888, 941, 1049
Graddol, D. 135, 150, 181, 210, 904
Graham, J. 483
Grainger, J. 246, 794
Gramkow Andersen, K. 150
Granger, C. 905, 1049
Granger, S. 150
Grant, C. 1100
Grant, L. 470, 482, 483
Grant, R. 689, 691
Granville, S. 888
Graves, K. 455, 456, 1001
Gray, J. 85
Green, A. 518
Green, C. 868, 872
Green, J. 716, 717, 985
Greenbaum, S. 150, 857
Greenberg, K. 483
Greene, M. 689, 1015
Gregg, K. 1027
Gregory, E. 210
Gremmo, M. 743
Griffin, P. 455, 470
Grigorenko, E. 700
Grin, F. 135
Groom, N. 942
Grosjean, F. 166, 247, 679
Grossberg, L. 651
Grossman, P. 377, 1065
Grumet, M. 1015
Grundy, P. 149, 743
Grundy, S. 1001
Guattari, F. 1048
Guba, E. 518

Gudykunst, W. 651
Guest, E. 23
Gumperz, J. 150, 651, 1049
Gunn, M. 518
Guth, G. 36
Gutiérrez, K. 716, 985
Gutiérrez, R. 367, 368, 377

H

Haas, T. 402
Habermas, J. 35, 1083
Haegeman, P. 150
Hafner, K. 916
Haimd, N. 759
Hakuta, K. 247, 679, 689, 809
Halasek, K. 915
Hale, G. 483
Halio, M. 916
Hall, G. 651
Hall, J. 716, 985, 1049
Hall, K. 1049
Hall, S. 85, 197, 637, 651, 679, 1099
Halliday, M. 300, 314, 402, 547, 716, 856, 888, 930, 941
Halsey, A. 1001
Halter, R. 286
Hamblin, A. 412
Hamilton, J. 412
Hamilton, M. 401
Hammarberg, W. 167
Hammersley, M. 985
Hammond, J. 455, 716, 856, 941
Hamp-Lyons, L. 412, 481, 483, 502, 503, 519, 530, 531
Hanchanlash, C. 389
Hansen, J. 651, 666
Hao, Y. 104
Hardman, F. 959
Hardt, M. 135
Hargreaves, A. 1083
Harklau, L. 377, 651, 666, 985, 1049
Harlech-Jones, B. 49
Harlen, W. 519
Harley, B. 286, 300, 483, 824
Harré, R. 377, 636
Harrington, M. 794
Harris, D. 389
Harris, J. 402, 888, 1065
Harris, R. 35, 197, 268, 286, 547, 1049, 1112
Harris, S. 871
Harris, V. 691
Harris, Z. 1027
Harrold, D. 470

Hart, J. 227
Hartman, K. 916
Hartmann, R. 150
Hartup, W. 651
Harvey, P. 957
Hasan, R. 314, 774, 856, 872, 941
Hasebrink, U. 149
Hatch, E. 286, 872
Hatch, J.A. 1006, 1015
Hatcher, P. 809
Haugen, E. 247
Havranek, G. 286
Hawisher, G. 904, 916
Hawkins, E. 150, 958
Hawley, W. 1065
Hayakawa, S. 181
Haycraft, J. 958
Hayden, M. 389
Hayes, J. 794
Hazenberg, S. 839
He, A. 485, 1027
He, M. 1015, 1016
Healy, D. 743
Heath, C. 1027
Heath, S. 651, 904, 985
Hebdige, D. 651
Hegelheimer, V. 759
Heine, B. 49
Held, D. 85, 197, 679
Heller, M. 85, 651, 1049, 1099
Helt, M. 482
Hémard, D. 759
Henriques, J. 637
Henry, A. 941
Henry, F. 197
Henze, R. 651, 690
Herdina, P. 166
Heritage, J. 1026, 1027
Hermerschmidt, M. 888
Hernandez, J. 402
Hernández, R. 644, 651
Heron, J. 731
Herr, K. 1000
Herrimen, M. 377
Herrmann, A. 1123
Hester, H. 454
Heugh, K. 49
Hewlett, L. 888
Higa, M. 840
Higuchi, T. 71
Hiley, D. 638
Hill, K. 469, 484
Hinds, J. 547, 941
Hinett, K. 520

Author Index

Hingley, W. 1050
Hinkel, E. 402, 1049
Hinton, L. 181
Hird, B. 1082
Hirsch, E. 181
Hirvela, A. 888
Hitchcock, G. 985, 1001
Hjarvad, S. 135
Hoddinott, D. 268
Hodge, R. 314, 930
Hoey, M. 872
Hoffman, E. 679, 1015
Hoffmann, C. 151, 166
Hogan, S. 438
Höglin, R. 135
Höjlund, G. 49
Holec, H. 743, 759
Holland, D. 227, 637
Hollander, E. 151
Holliday, A. 61, 227, 402, 985, 1049, 1083
Hollingsworth, H. 1065
Hollingsworth, S. 904, 1015
Hollqvist, H. 151
Hollway, W 637
Holmes, J. 888
Honey, J. 23, 181
Hong, T. 1100
Hood, S. 503, 1000
Hook, P. 731
Hooks, B. 1015
Hooper, H. 313, 314
Hooper, J. 957
Hope, M. 1083
Hopkins, D. 1001
Hopper, R. 1027
Horenczyk, G. 651
Hornberger, N. 120, 167, 1049
Horowitz, D. 402, 666
Horst, M. 286
Houghton, D. 666
House, H. 454, 502, 518
House, J. 135, 151
Hoven, D. 759
Howard, U. 1123
Howatt, A. 23, 286
Howie, D. 377
Hsia, S. 1083
Hsu, J. 759
Hu, H. 518
Huber, J. 1015
Huberman, A. 986
Huberman, M. 1065
Huckin, T. 547, 839, 887, 940, 941

Huddleston, R. 857
Hudelson, S. J. 685, 689
Hudson, C. 454, 456, 502, 518
Hudson, T. 455, 483, 518
Huebner, T. 181
Huerta-Macías, A. 506, 509, 519
Hufeisen, B. 165, 167
Hughes, A. 519
Hughes, D. 985, 1001
Hughes, J. 1026
Hughes, R. 149, 872
Huhta, A. 483, 503
Hull, D. 1123
Hull, G. 888
Hüllen, W. 135, 151
Hulme, C. 809
Hulstijn, J. 794, 795, 840
Humphrey, S. 857
Hunston, S. 872
Hunt, A. 840
Hunter, J. 637, 1099
Huot, B. 503
Hurd, S. 743
Hurst, D. 377, 389
Hurtado, A. 650
Hutchby, I. 872
Hutchinson, T. 104, 412
Hutchison, B. 1001
Huxur, G. 314
Hyerle, D. 314
Hyland, F. 503
Hyland, K. 402, 503, 887, 888, 941
Hyltenstam, K. 50, 300
Hyman, R. 715
Hymes, D. 286, 872
Hyon, S. 941

I

Ianco-Worrall, A. 247
Ibrahim, A. 637, 679, 1049, 1099
Iedema, R. 857
Igoa, C. 1015, 1099
Ihnatko, T. 888
Ilieva, R. 198, 1049
Illich, I. 743
Inbar, O. 810
Intemann, F. 150, 166
Ip, K. 809
Ito, K. 71
Ivanič, R. 875, 877, 881, 882, 884–889, 1046, 1049
Iverson, G. 824
Iwashita, N. 469, 470, 483

J

Jackson, A. 650
Jacobs, A. 794
Jacobs, U. 930
Jacobson, R. 247
Jacoby, S. 1018, 1029
Jadeja, R. 61
James, A. 151, 167, 651
James, C. 151, 742, 958
James, I. 1099
James, M. 519
James-Williams, S. 1099
Jamieson, J. 4884, 758
Janks, H. 1049
Jaramillo, A. 363
Jarvis, J. 872
Jarvis, S. 247, 1001
Javed, S. 759
Jayaram, N. 61
Jayroe, T. 1137
Jefferson, G. 872, 873, 1029
Jenkins, I. 1137
Jenkins, J. 135, 151, 152, 167, 247, 547
Jenkins, S. 23, 941
Jensen, L. 376
Jernudd, B. 181
Jessner, U. 150, 1667
Jewitt, C. 210, 930
Jiménez, R. 363
Jiminez, M. 181
Jin, L. 85
Johansson, S. 856
John, S. 890
Johns, A. 268, 401, 402, 666, 857, 889, 941
Johnson, C. 412
Johnson, J. 72
Johnson, K. 286, 377, 958, 1052, 1065, 1083, 1137
Johnson, M. 314, 794, 1123
Johnson, P. 650
Johnson, R. 120, 121, 268
Johnston, B. 1049, 1052
Johnston, M. 857
Johnstone, R. 286
Jonassen, D. 314, 759
Jonasses, D. 759
Jones, B. 1123
Jones, C. 889, 1123
Jones, F. 731
Jones, J. 888, 889
Jones, K. 905
Jones, L. 731
Jones, S. 119, 165, 389, 482, 483
Jones, V. 300
Jonietz, P. 389
Jordan, S. 1051
Jordan, R. 931, 941
Joshi, P. 61
Jung, S. 85
Jusczyk, P. 795
Just, M. 794

K

Kachru, B. 35, 61, 120, 151, 167, 181, 227, 679, 958
Kachru, Y. 679
Kagan, R. 181
Kalantzis, M. 650, 774, 888, 904, 930, 940
Kamana, K. 35
Kanagy, R. 300
Kanfer, R. 731
Kanno, Y. 72, 679, 1015
Kantor, R. 4884
Kapadia, S. 61
Kaplan, A. 1015
Kaplan, R. 23, 61, 794, 888, 889, 941
Kaplan, W. 198
Karavas-Doukas, K. 104, 519
Karl, J. 470
Karmiloff-Smith, A. 794
Karp, S. 715
Karumanchery, L. 1099
Kasermann, M. 716
Kashoki, M. 49
Kasper, G. 151, 247, 1027
Kato, S. 72
Katz, A. 456
Katz, M. 985
Kay, H. 941
Kay, S. 300
Kayman, M. 135
Keane, S. 363
Kecskes, I. 167, 247
Keep, C. 1123
Kellerman, E. 151, 247
Kellner, D. 904
Kelly, G. 743
Kelm, O. 759, 916
Kember, D. 1001
Kemmis, S. 1000, 1001, 1083
Kemp, F. 915
Kempf, S. 689
Kempler, D. 638
Kenning, M. 1123
Kenny, B. 743
Kenyon, D. 470, 484
Kere-Levy, M. 810

Kern, R. 759, 916, 1123
Kerr, P. 958
Khan, J. 61
Khan, R. 1050
Kheimetz, N. 679
Kiang, P. 651
Kiesler, S. 916
Kim, K. 85
Kim, R. 651
Kincheloe, J. 1049
Kinginger, C. 679
Kingston, M. 1015
Kirkpatrick, D. 412
Kirsch, I. 483, 484
Kirshner, D. 638, 1052
Kitamura, T. 72
Kleinsasser, R. 287
Klesmer, H. 809
Kliebard, H. 715
Kloss, H. 181
Knapp, K. 150, 151, 152, 1049
Knapp, M. 689
Knapp, P. 940
Knapp-Pothoff, A. 151
Knight, M. 363
Knijnik, G. 1001
Knobel, M. 904
Knowles, G. 181
Knowles, J. 1065
Knowles, M. 743
Knowles, V. 198
Kobayashi, M. 985
Kobayashi, S. 181
Kobayashi, Y. 679
Koda, K. 483
Koedinger, K. 759
Kohonen, V. 743, 1137
Kolb, D. 743
Kommers, P. 759
Komter, M. 872
Kontra, M. 135
Kordon, K. 151
Koshik, I. 1027, 1029
Kouritzin, S. 679
Kourtis-Kazoullis, V. 763, 770, 771, 772, 774
Kowal, M. 286
Kozol, J. 689
Kozulin, A. 716
Krainer, K. 1137
Kramer, M. 666
Kramsch, C. 85, 135, 247, 455, 679, 872, 985, 1049, 1083, 1137

Krashen, S. 35, 181, 268, 286, 300, 636, 651, 795, 809, 857, 958, 1027
Krauss, M. 181
Kress, G. 314, 759, 857, 889, 904, 930, 940, 941, 1049
Kreuter, B. 716
Kroll, B. 483
Kroskrity, P. 651
Ku, H. 1137
Kubanek-German, A. 518, 519
Kubota, R. 23, 85, 198, 689, 889, 941, 1050
Kuczaj, S. 700
Kuhl, J. 731
Kumaravadivelu, B. 286, 1050
Kunieda, M. 72
Kunnan, A. 484, 519
Küpper, L. 331
Kwan, A. 809
Kwon, O. 85
Kymlicka, W. 198

L
Labov, W. 247, 872
Lachat, M. 455
Lachicotte, W. 637
Lado, R. 286
Ladson-Billings, G. 1050
Lafond, L. 1050
Lakey, J. 210
Lakoff, G. 314
Lam, C. 809
Lam, E. 916
Lam, J. 872
Lam, W. 759
Lamb, C. 994, 1002
Lamb, M. 104
Lamb, T. 744, 745
Lambert, R. 181
Lambert, W. 247, 809
Lamy, M. 760
Landsman, L. 700
Langston, M. 916
Lanier, J. 1065
Lankshear, C. 904, 1123
Lantolf, J. 300, 690, 700, 717, 1050, 1137
Lapkin, S. 288, 301, 717
Larsen-Freeman, D. 72, 286, 348
Larson, J. 637, 716
Lasagabaster, D. 167
Lash, S. 1082
Lather, P. 1050
Latour, B. 402

Laurillard, D. 760
Laver, J. 872
Lawrence-Lightfoot, S. 1015
Lazaraton, A. 984, 985, 1027, 1028
Lazarus, R. 651
Le Page, R. 34
Lea, M. 889
Leather, J. 985
Lebauer, R. 872
Lebiere, C. 794
Lee, C. 716
Lee, D. 872
Lee, I. 810
Lee, J. 85
Lee, O. 716
Lee, S. 651
Lee, Y. 480, 481, 484
Leech, G. 840, 856, 857, 958
Legenhausen, L. 743, 744
Legutke, M. 744, 1137, 1138
Leibhammer, N. 930
Leibowitz, B. 889
Leith, D. 179, 181
Leki, I. 666, 986
Lemke, J. 716, 930
Lenneberg, E. 72
Leontiev, A. 700
Lerner, G. 1028
Lesaux, N. 809
Lesznyák, A. 144, 151
Leung, C. 197, 315
Leung, K. 809
Leung, S. 484
Leung, W. 810
Levelt, W. 795
Levin, J. 905
Levine, J. 210, 1112
Levine, T. 810
Levinson, B. 214, 227
Levy, M. 758, 760, 810
Lewin, K. 731, 1001
Lewin, L. 470
Lewis, M. 837, 840, 1123
Li, E. 744
Li, L. 104
Li, P. 198
Li, X. 1015
Liang, X. 314
Libben, G. 744
Lidz, C. 700
Lieberman, A. 1065
Lieberman, P. 377
Liebkind, K. 651
Lightbown, P. 2888, 300, 519, 760

Lillis, T. 889
Lin, A. 690, 1050, 1099
Lin, L. 716
Lincoln, Y. 518, 984, 1014
Lincoln-Porter, F. 717
Lindblad, S. 1082
Lindemann, B. 167
Lindholm, K. 180
Lindholm-Leary, K. 348
Lindsay, D. 166
Linell, J. 717
Lionnet, F. 247
Lippi-Green, R. 35, 679, 1099
Lippitt, R. 731
Litowitz, B. 637
Little, D. 744, 760, 857
Little, J. 377, 1065, 1083
Littlejohn, A. 743, 1137
Littlewood, W. 286, 744
Liu, D. 104
Liu, J. 651
Liu, L. 104
Llurda, E. 247
Lo Bianco, J. 181, 182, 268, 455
Lockhart, C. 1002, 1083
Lockwood, J. 412
Loewen, S. 518
Logan, G. 789, 795
Loh Fook Seng, P. 23
Long, M. 72, 247, 286, 287, 300, 348, 716, 760, 857, 958, 1001, 1028
Longacre, R. 314
Longhi-Chirlin, T. 810
Lopez, L. 167
Lopriore, L. 455, 456
Lor, W. 742
Lorsch, J. 377
Lortie, D. 377, 1066, 1083
Loschky, L. 300
Losey, K. 986
Lotherington, H. 904, 905
Louhiala-Salminen, L. 151
Low, M. 314
Lowenberg, P. 35
Lubelska, D. 36
Lucas, T. 651, 690
Lüdi, G. 151
Lugard, F. 23
Luk Hung-Kay, B. 23
Luk, J. 1050
Luke, A. 905, 941, 1099
Luke, C. 690
Lukes, M. 228, 638
Lukhele, R. 484

Lumley, T. 412, 454, 470, 502, 503, 518
Luoma, S. 518
Luria, A. 857
Lynch, B. 519, 531, 1050
Lynch, T. 872
Lyotard, J. 1071, 1083
Lyster, N. 986
Lyster, R. 287, 300
Lytle, S. 1000

M

Mabrito, M. 916
Macaire, D. 149
Macaulay, T. 23
MacDonald, J. 389
Macias, R. 182
MacIntosh, A. 402
Macken, M. 942
Macken-Horarik, M. 856
Mackenzie, P. 389
Mackey, A. 287, 300
Mackrell, G. 840
Maclear, K. 1099
Maclennan, C. 503
MacPherson, S. 1050
MacSwan, J. 348
MacWhinney, B. 795
Madood, T. 210
Mager, R. 437
Maggisano, C. 1015
Magnan, S. 1000
Magoto, J. 1123
Maharaj, S. 651
Maher, J. 72
Mahoney, K. 348
Maier, P. 942
Mair, C. 134, 1050
Makarec, K. 247
Malakoff, M. 167, 247
Malderez, A. 731
Malobonga, V. 484
Malone, M. 456
Man, E. 810
Manes, J. 50
Manion, L. 984
Mann, S. 743
Mansfield, S. 760
Mansour, G. 49
Manyak, P. 637
Marchart, O. 905
Marchenkova, L. 1049
Marcovitz, D. 1137
Marcus, G. 1099

Marinova-Todd, S. 72
Markee, N. 104, 412, 1001, 1028
Markus, H. 679
Marrow, A. 1001
Marshall, C. 986
Marshall, D. 72
Marshall, S. 649
Martin, J. 314, 547, 716, 850, 856, 857, 940, 942
Martin-Jones, M. 905
Marton, F. 744
Masats, D. 151
Masters, J. 993, 1001
Masuhara, H. 149
Mateene, K. 49
Mathew, R. 1001
Matsuda, P. 889
Matsuo, N. 301
Matthiessen, C. 314
Mattis, W. 197
Matute-Bianchi, M. 651
Maungedzo, R. 930
Mauranen, A. 151, 548, 942
May, L. 484
May, S. 268, 1050
Maybin, J. 716
Mayes, J. 759
Mazrui, A. 35
McCarthy, L. 889
McCarthy, M. 840, 857, 871, 872
McCarty, T. 35, 36, 135, 228
McCombs, B. 731
McConnell, D. 72
McCormick, M. 690
McCormick, W. 182
McDermott, R. 637, 716
McDonough, K. 287, 300
McGrath, I. 470, 744, 745
McGrew, T. 85, 197, 679
McGroarty, M. 690
McHoul, A. 1028
McKay, P. 268, 455, 456, 503, 519, 548, 716
McKay, S. 637, 651, 690, 986, 1050, 1099
McKeown, M. 840
McLaren, P. 198, 716
McLaughlan, T. 1123
McLaughlin, M. 651
McLean, M. 287
McLeod, P. 795
McLuhan, M. 905
McMahill, C. 679
McMeniman, M. 267

McMillan, J. 503
McNamara, T. 198, 456, 470, 4884, 519, 700, 1050
McNeill, A. 957, 958
McNess, E. 520
McNiff, J. 1001
McPake, J. 210, 1111
McPherson, P. 760, 1001
McQuillan, J. 35
McTaggart, R. 1001, 1083
Meacham, S. 690
Meara, P. 840
Measor, L. 1066
Mechling, J. 650
Meddleton, I. 840
Medgyes, P. 679, 957, 958
Medway, P. 940, 941
Meek, M. 268
Meeuwis, M. 152
Mehan, B. 716
Mehan, H. 690, 916, 1028
Mehler, J. 794
Mehlinger, H. 1138
Mehnert, U. 300
Meierkord, C. 151, 152, 1049
Melander, B. 135
Melanson, Y. 1015
Melis, I
Meloni, C. 761, 917
Mencken, H. 182
Mennen, S. 824
Mercer, N. 715, 716, 718
Mercuri, A. 248
Merriam, S. 986
Merten, M. 890
Messick, S. 456, 484, 519, 531
Met, M. 268
Meyer, L. 228, 331
Mhando, E. 49
Michaels, S. 716
Midy, J. 34
Mignolo, W. 23
Miklosy, K. 679
Miles, M. 986
Miles, S. 1083
Miller, C. 942
Miller, E. 548, 1030
Miller, J. 679, 795, 986, 1001
Miller, W. 975, 984
Mills, S. 637
Milroy, J. 35, 531
Milroy, L. 35, 531
Milton, J. 402, 840
Milton, M. 1082

Min, P. 651
Mincham, L. 503
Miner, S. 182
Minick, N. 637, 638
Mintzes, J. 314
Mirza, H. 210, 1112
Mishler, E. 1001
Mislevy, R. 519
Missler, B. 167
Mistry, J. 638
Mitchell, K. 198
Mitchell, R. 700, 857, 957, 1000
Miura, I. 71
Modiano, M. 151, 167
Moerman, M. 1028
Mohammed, S. 49
Mohan, A. 268
Mohan, B. 268, 314, 315, 377, 519, 717, 986, 1100
Moje, E. 652
Mok, J. 503
Moll, L. 363, 637, 690, 717
Mollaun, P. 482, 484
Mollin, S. 152
Monbiot, G. 135
Monoson, P. 470
Monroe, P. 23
Montero-Sieburth, M. 653
Montone, C. 180
Moon, R. 840
Moor, P. 299
Moore, H. 198, 456, 548
Moran, C. 363, 916
Moran, P. 1050
Morbey, M. 905
Morgan, B. 198, 1050, 1052
Morgan, C. 1050
Morgan, M. 182
Mori, J. 986, 1028
Morita, N. 986
Morris, L. 958
Morris, P. 104
Mosenthal, P. 483, 1014
Moses, D. 61
Mosier, C. 638
Moss, P. 484
Motteram, G. 760, 1123
Moya, P. 652
Mtana, N. 49
Mufwene, S. 135
Mukherjee, B. 198
Mulcahy-Ernt, P. 482, 483
Muldoon, M. 1001
Mulkay, M. 402

Müller-Hartmann, A. 1137, 1138
Mumby, J. 412
Muñez, V. 643, 645, 652
Mura, D. 679
Muraven, M. 649
Murphey, T. 731
Murphy, D. 1002
Murphy, E. 389
Murphy, R. 198
Murray, D. 690, 760
Murray, H. 152, 958
Murray, L. 1137
Mustafa, Z. 942
Muth, D. 794
Myers, G. 402, 942
Myles, F. 700, 857

N

Na, J. 85
Nagashima, Y. 72
Nagy, W. 840
Nakahama, Y. 300
Nakamura, K. 72
Nakaone, T. 1028
Nardi, B. 1124
Nathan, G. 247
Nation, I. 840
Nation, P. 744, 829, 830, 839, 840
Nattinger, J. 857
Nazroo, J. 210
Ndebele, N. 679
Negri, A. 135
Nel, K. 930
Nelson, C. 1050
Nettle, D. 905
Neumann, A. 1015
Neuwirth, C. 916
Newfield, D. 930
Newmark, L. 958
Newport, E. 72
Newton, I. 315
Newton, P. 503
Ng, R. 198
Ng, S. 810
Nguyen, A. 363
Nguyen, H. 1030
Nias, J. 1066
Nicholas, H. 287, 300, 519
Nichols, R. 1002
Nicholson, A. 758
Nickerson, C. 412
Niemann, Y. 652
Nieto, S. 690, 717, 1051, 1100
Nightingale, P. 887

Nihlen, A. 1000
Nissan, S. 482
Nityadandanam, I. 61
Nix, M. 742
Nix, P. 470
Noble, A. 503
Noble, G. 652, 940
Noddings, N. 1016
Noguchi, M. 73
Norris, A. 1137
Norris, C. 1051
Norris, D. 794
Norris, J. 287
North, B. 484
Norton, B. 35, 85, 198, 531, 637, 666, 679, 680, 690, 700, 986, 1051, 1100
Norton Peirce, B. 85, 680, 1051
Noullet, M. 36
Novak, J. 314
Novakovich, J. 680
Novinski, M. 1137
Nowakowski, J. 1123
Noyes, P. 957
Nunan, D. 287, 412, 437, 742, 744, 760, 872, 984, 1000, 1002
Nunberg, G. 182
Nurius, P. 679
Nuttall, J. 957

O

O' Donnell-Allen, C. 707, 717
O' Loughlin, K. 499, 500, 502, 503, 505, 508, 510, 514, 517, 519
O' Malley, J. 253, 267, 317, 318, 325, 328, 330, 331, 381, 389, 451, 452, 456, 837, 838, 840
O' Malley, M. 267
O' Sullivan, B. 505, 515, 519
Oakes, J. 717
Obler, L. 287
Obondo, M. 50
Ochs, E. 638, 1029
Odlin, T. 857
Ogborn, J. 930
Ogbu, J. 652, 1112
Ogulnick, K. 650
Ohta, A. 1028
Oja, S. 1002
Oliver, R. 716, 1082
Olneck, M. 652
Olsen, J. 1083
Olsen, L. 228, 363, 690
Olsen, M. 1015
Olsher, D. 1029

Olshtain, E. 856
Olson, D. 717
Olson, L. 652
Oltman, P. 484
Omaggio-Hadeley, A. 1000
Omanson, R. 840
Or, C. 810
Or, W. 744
Orellana, M. 680
Orlikowski, W. 943
Ortega, L. 287, 300
Osborn, T. 1051
Ota, H. 73
Othman-Yahya, S. 50
Otsu, Y. 73
Ovando, C. 348
Owston, R. 902, 904
Oxford, R. 760

P
Pahl, J. 411
Paiewonsky, E. 363
Pakir, A. 61, 1051
Palfreyman, D. 744, 958
Palloff, R. 760
Palmer, A. 285, 454
Palmquist, M. 916
Paltridge, B. 857, 889, 942
Palys, T. 986
Panova, I. 287
Papp, T. 167, 247
Paradis, J. 940
Paradis, M. 247, 795
Parakrama, A. 182
Pare, A. 940
Parisi, D. 794
Park, Y. 85, 760
Parks, S. 315
Parmar, R. 1123
Passel, J. 182
Pasta, D. 182
Patel, S. 61
Patel, Y. 61
Pattinois, D. 717
Pavlenko, A. 679, 680, 700, 1047, 1051
Pawley, A. 840
Pea, R. 760
Peal, E. 247
Pearce, J. 150
Pearson, P. 809
Pease-Alvarez, L. 638, 690, 759, 1016
Peck, A. 1002
Peck, J. 869, 872
Pegrum, M. 135

Peirce, B. 85, 484, 548, 680, 1051, 1100
Pelham, L. 809
Pemberton, R. 744
Pennycook, A. 23, 35, 61, 85, 152, 182, 287, 402, 531, 666, 690, 889, 905, 916, 1051
Penz, H. 152
Percy, A. 890
Perdue, C. 247
Perez, B. 690
Perkins, J. 182
Perrett, G. 856, 942
Perry, T. 1051, 1100
Persinger, M. 247
Peshkin, A. 228, 985
Peters, R. 247
Petersen, A. 652
Petersen, M. 135
Peterson, B. 715
Peterson, J. 35
Peterson, N. 915
Peterson, P. 1015, 1083
Peyton, J. 916
Phelps, R. 456, 759
Phillion, J. 1015, 1016
Phillips, D. 1016
Phillips, M. 1124
Phillips, T. 717
Phillipson, R. 23, 35, 50, 61, 73, 85, 134, 135, 152, 182, 402, 531, 905, 958
Phinney, J. 650, 652
Piatt, B. 182
Pica, T. 291, 297, 299, 300, 311, 315, 705, 717, 1023, 1026, 1028, 1029
Pick, S. 652
Pickering, L. 871
Pienemann, M. 857
Piepho, H. 152
Pierce, B. 198
Pierson, H. 744
Piller, I. 680, 1051
Pimsleur, P. 840
Pinar, W. 1016
Pinker, S. 300, 795
Pinney, T. 23
Pintrich, P. 731
Planken, B. 246, 824
Plass, J. 758
Plum, G. 401, 856, 887
Plunkett, K. 794, 795
Polacco, P. 363
Polanyi, L. 873
Polkinghorne, D. 1016
Pollard, J. 248

Pölzl, U. 152
Pomerantz, A. 1029
Pon, G. 652, 986
Poon, W. 412
Pope, C. 1138
Popham, D. 840
Popkewitz, T. 1083
Pople, M. 840
Porter, J. 402, 889
Porter, P. 287, 1028
Porter, R. 35, 182, 456
Portes, A. 652
Posch, P. 1137
Postlethwaite, T. 810
Powell, W. 484
Powers, D. 482
Poynting, S. 652
Poynton, C. 1051
Prabhu, N. 23, 247, 873, 958
Pratt, E. 916
Pratt, K. 760
Pratt, M. 889
Preisler, B. 135, 152
Pressley, M. 331, 810
Price, S. 1051
Pride, J. 35
Prior, P. 402, 548, 666, 889
Prodromou, L. 152
Pryor, J. 504, 520
Prys Jones, S. 119, 165, 389
Psathas, G. 1029
Puetter, S. 760
Pula, J. 503
Pullum, G. 857
Purani, T. 61
Purania, T. 61
Purpura, J. 519
Pusey, M. 456
Putnam, R. 1065
Putney, L. 691, 717
Pütz, M. 50

Q
Quay, S. 167
Quirk, R. 120, 151, 167, 845, 857, 958

R
Raimes, A. 484
Rajan, R. 23
Ramanathan, V. 61, 889, 984, 986, 1051
Ramey, D. 182
Ramirez, J. 182
Rampton, B. 35, 197, 268, 547, 652, 1049, 1051, 1112

Rannut, M. 182
Ranta, L. 287, 288, 300
Raphael, T. 689
Rasmussen, C. 1123
Raso, E. 503
Raymond, P. 656, 663, 664, 666
Rayson, P. 840
Raz, J. 744
Read, J. 519, 839
Rea-Dickins, P. 5120
Reagan, T. 85, 1051
Redfern, A. 1112
Redman, S. 839, 840
Reed, D. 503
Reed, M. 718
Rees, T. 197
Reich, R. 1124
Reid, W. 377
Reiman, A. 1066
Renandya, W. 24
Reppen, R. 482, 942
Resnick, L. 503
Resnick, M. 503
Reyes, A. 652
Reyes, M. 637
Reyhner, J. 35
Reynolds, M. 437
Riazantseva, A. 887
Riazi, A. 1050
Riazi, M. 1099
Ribé, R. 744
Rice, C. 135
Ricento, T. 35, 135, 182
Richards, J. 285, 287, 437, 873, 1002, 1083
Richards, K. 985, 986, 1001
Richterich, R. 412
Rickford, J. 760
Ridge, S. 50
Riley, P. 743, 744
Ringbom, H. 167
Risager, K. 1048
Rixon, S. 520
Rizzo, T. 984
Roberge, B. 1016
Roberts, B. 745
Roberts, C. 149, 150, 857, 1051
Roberts, D. 377
Roberts, M. 484
Roberts, S. 228
Robertson, R. 85
Robinson, J. 872, 1029, 1050
Robinson, M. 872
Robinson, P. 287, 300, 958
Robinson, W. 957

Robson, M. 1065
Roca, A. 182
Rochín, R. 644, 651
Rodriguez, R. 1016
Rodriguez, V. 652
Rodriguez-Brown, F. 637
Roelofs, A. 795
Roessel, R. 35
Roger, D. 1029
Rogers, C. 731, 744
Rogers, E. 760
Rogers, J. 1002
Rogers, P. 412
Rogers, T. 518
Rogoff, B. 638
Rohl, M. 454, 502, 518
Rohlen, T. 73
Rolls, E. 795
Romaine, S. 287, 905
Romero, A. 652
Ronowicz, E. 1051
Roschelle, J. 760
Rose, M. 888
Roseberry, R. 941
Rosenau, P. 1051
Rosenberger, L. 150
Rosenfeld, M. 484
Rosenthal, D. 652
Rosewell, L. 744
Rosiak, J. 1014
Rösler, D. 1138
Ross, G. 718
Ross, K. 810
Ross, S. 484
Rossell, C. 182
Rossiter, C. 182
Rossman, G. 986
Roth, A. 1027
Rotheram-Borus, M. 653
Rothery, J. 716, 942
Rothkopf, D. 135
Rouse, J. 1051
Routh, M. 840
Rowe, M. 717
Rowntree, D. 437
Rubagumya, C. 50, 167
Rubin, J. 182
Ruhlen, M. 50
Ruiz, R. 690
Rumbaut, R. 652
Russell, P. 840
Russo, R. 331
Rutherford, J. 637
Ryan, K. 482

Ryle, G. 958
Rymes, B. 716

S
Sacks, H. 873, 1029
Sadtono, E. 470
Sagasta, P. 167
Said, E. 85, 1051, 1100
Sainsbury, M. 456
Salaberry, R. 760
Salomon, G. 700
Salters, M. 437
Samarajiwa, C. 825
Samarin, W. 152
Samimy, K. 84
Samuda, V. 285, 287, 300
Sanaoui, R. 470, 840
Santiago, E. 1016
Santos, M. 637
Santos, T. 482, 889
Sapuppo, M. 456
Sarangi, S. 377
Sarap, M. 1051
Sato, K. 287
Sauvé, V. 1051
Savignon, S. 287
Saville, N. 484, 519
Saville-Troike, M. 700, 986
Say, A. 363
Sayers, D. 758, 774, 809, 916
Scardamalia, M. 285, 794, 1065
Scarino, A. 454, 456, 503
Schafer, R. 1016
Schecter, R. 1051
Schecter, S. 198, 652, 984, 986
Schedl, M. 483, 484
Scheerens, J. 520
Schegloff, E. 873, 1029
Schellekens, P. 744
Schieffelin, B. 183
Schiffrin, D. 873
Schifini, A. 363
Schils, E. 246, 824
Schlegel, A. 652
Schmid-Schoenbein, G. 1124
Schmidt, K. 651
Schmidt, R. 795
Schmitt, D. 840
Schmitt, N. 839, 840
Schmuck, P. 731
Schmuck, R. 731
Schneider, B. 649, 652
Schneider, M. 666
Schneider, S. 182

Schocker-v. Ditfurth, M.   970, 1125–1127, 1129, 1131, 1134, 1137, 1138
Schoepfle, G.   315
Scholes, R.   1051
Schön, D.   1000, 1083
Schonell, F.   840
Schultz, J.   916
Schunk, D.   331, 731
Schutz, A.   1029
Schutz, E.   1029
Schwab, J.   1002, 1016
Schwartz, J.   1029
Schwartz, M.   915
Schwarz, H.   1124
Schwienhorst, K.   760
Scollon, R.   690, 889, 942, 1051
Scollon, S.   690, 942, 1051
Scott, C.   520
Scott, K.   520
Scott, M.   411, 942
Scotton, C.   50
Scovel, T.   652, 825
Searle, J.   287
Seedhouse, P.   300, 301, 873, 1030
Segalowitz, N.   287, 795
Segul, J.   794
Seidlhofer, B.   136, 151, 152, 959
Selfe, C.   904
Seliger, H.   286
Selinker, L.   35, 794
Sengupta, S.   471
Senior, R.   731
Seo, J.   85
Shanahan, T.   637
Shannon, S.   182, 638, 1016
Shapard, R.   680
Shavelson, R.   437
Shaw, B.   840
Shaw, J.   36
Shaw, P.   135, 959
Shea, C.   1052
Sheeran, Y.   889
Shemesh, M.   810
Shen, B.   105
Shen, F.   890
Shen, M.   247
Shermis, M.   484
Sherwood, C.   1138
Shetzer, H.   761, 916, 917
Shield, L.   760
Shih, T.   652
Shilcock, R.   299
Shin, H.   85
Shirahata, T.   73

Shohamy, E.   503, 520, 531, 810
Shorrock, S.   1065
Short, D.   315, 455, 456, 690
Shrinivas, R.   61
Shubert, W.   1016
Shulman, L.   959, 1084
Shulz, R.   760
Shusterman, R.   638
Siegal, M.   666, 941
Siegel, J.   35
Siegel, L.   800, 809
Sikes, P.   1066
Silc, K.   758
Siles, M.   651
Silva, T.   889, 890, 942
Silverman, D.   986
Simich-Dudgeon, C.   267
Simmons, D.   744
Simon, P.   182
Simonot, M.   149
Simons, H.   1112
Simpson, J.   882, 884, 889
Sinclair, B.   745
Sinclair, J.   717, 857, 873
Singh, M.   1124
Singh, R.   825
Singleton, D.   167, 760
Siskin, L.   377
Sizmur, S.   456
Skehan, P.   248, 288, 2901, 484
Skillen, J.   890
Skinner, D.   637
Skourtou, E.   622, 763, 766, 774
Skutnabb-Kangas, T.   50, 136, 152, 182, 268, 363, 690, 905
Slade, D.   856, 872, 942
Slater, T.   315
Sleeter, C.   1016, 1100
Slimani, A.   873
Smagorinsky, P.   716, 717
Smith, C.   1137
Smith, D.   1016
Smith, F.   287, 715
Smith, J.   483, 503, 1065
Smith, L.E.   146, 152
Smith, L.M.   1016
Smith, M.   412, 492, 497, 503, 504, 1000, 1006
Smith, N.   857
Smith, P.   210
Smith, R.   744
Smith, W.   504
Smoke, T.   402, 666
Smulyan, L.   1002

Snow, C. 36, 72, 1100
Snow, M. 268, 376
Snyder, I. 760
Sökmen, A. 841
Soled, S. 470
Solomon, R. 652
Solsken, J. 638, 690, 986
Somekh, B. 1002
Soni, P. 61
Sonntag, S. 182
Soto, L. 1016
Sower, C. 1052
Spack, R. 666, 890
Spada, N. 2888, 300, 519, 760, 986
Spanos, G. 267, 330
Spence-Brown, R. 520
Spencer, J. 50
Spencer, M. 652
Spodark, E. 1124
Spolsky, B. 484, 504, 520, 531, 810
Spradley, J. 315
Sprinthall, L. 1066
Sprinthall, N. 1066
Sproull, L. 916
Sridhar, K. 152
Sridhar, S. 152, 680
Stanley, T. 198
Stansfield, C. 470
Starfield, S. 666, 890, 1052
Stawychny, M. 483
Steel, D. 469, 957
Stein, P. 930, 1052
Steinberg, L. 519
Steinberg, S. 1049
Steinkopf, M. 1124
Stenglin, M. 857
Stenhouse, L. 1002, 1138
Stephan, L. 36
Stephens, C. 840
Stephens, L. 690
Stern, H. 248, 288
Stern, M. 761
Stern, P. 437
Stern, R. 483
Sternberg, R. 700
Stevens, G. 182
Stevens, R. 454
Stevick, E. 228
Stewart, F. 23
Stewart, G. 198
Stewner-Manzanares, G. 331
Stierer, B. 716
Stiggins, R. 504
Stillman, J. 1001

Stivers, T. 1030
St. John, E. 910, 916
St. John, M. 392, 399, 401, 403, 412, 655, 666, 931, 940
Stobbe, J. 363
Stock, P. 502
Stodolsky, S. 377
Stokes, J. 299
Stoller, F. 1049
Stone, C. 700
Stone, L. 716
Strauss, A. 986
Street, B. 36, 889, 905, 1051, 1052
Strei, G. 36
Strevens, P. 402
Strickland, D. 1002
Strong, R. 438
Strong-Krause, D. 456
Stubbs, M. 402, 1030
Sturtridge, G. 300, 743
Suárez-Orozco, C. 640–645, 652
Suárez-Orozco, M. 637, 640–645, 652
Sugimoto, T. 905
Sullivan, B. 484, 519
Sullivan, N. 916
Sullivan, P. 1083
Sun, C. 105
Sung, K. 85
Sunga, N. 24
Suomi, B. 482
Sure, K. 50
Susser, B. 23
Sussex, R. 1124
Suzuki, Y. 73
Svartvik, J. 857
Swaffer, J. 1000
Swain, M. 73, 120, 121, 267, 268, 285, 286, 288, 2901, 483, 717, 856, 857
Swales, J. 402, 412, 548, 667, 888, 890, 940, 942, 943
Swanson, D. 652
Swartz, R. 315
Sweeting, A. 23
Syder, F. 829, 840
Sykes, G. 470, 958

T
Tabar, P. 652
Taborn, S. 873
Tabors, P. 1100
Tabouret-Keller, A. 34
Tadajeu, M. 50
Tajfel, H. 652, 1052
Tang, C. 86

Tang, G. 315
Tang, K. 484
Tang, R. 518, 890
Tanner, C. 1065
Tao, H. 872
Tao, P. 810
Tapia, J. 637
Tardy, C. 1049
Tarver, H. 183
Tator, C. 197
Taylor, C. 268, 4884, 638
Taylor, G. 887
Taylor, L. 482
Teasdale, A. 437, 504, 520
Teel, K. 731
Teeple, G. 198
Tejeda, C. 637
Tella, S. 916, 917, 1138
Tenorio-Coscarelli, J. 363
Terdiman, R. 1052
Teuben-Rowe, S. 691
Teutsch-Dwyer, M. 680
Thaler, M. 1002
Tharp, R. 638, 717
Tharu, S. 61
Thavenius, C. 745
Theodoridis, T. 774
Thesen, L. 667, 680, 890
Thew, C. 313
Thikoo, M. 24
Thomas, A. 454, 456
Thomas, C. 470
Thomas, D. 246
Thomas, H. 744, 1137
Thomas, J. 1138
Thomas, S. 520
Thomas, W. 50, 210, 228, 268, 331, 348, 690, 810
Thompson, G. 288, 864, 873
Thompson, J. 389
Thompson, M. 348
Thompson, P. 152, 942
Thornbury, S. 873, 959
Thorne, S. 700, 857, 1137
Thornton, G. 150
Thurrell, S. 871
Thwaite, A. 1082
Tickoo, M. 167
Tidmarsh, C. 520
Tigchelaar, A. 1050
Tinajero, J. 363
Tinker Sachs, G. 1002
Tinkham, T. 841
Tlusty, N. 1001

Tochon, F. 1016
Tollefson, J. 24, 36, 50, 135, 181, 531
Tomasello, M. 700
Tomkins, G. 198
Tomlin, R. 857
Tomlinson, B. 149, 957
Tonkyn, A. 856
Toogood, S. 734, 742, 744
Toohey, K. 531, 638, 700, 717, 986, 1002, 1016, 1051, 1052, 1100, 1112
Torigai, K. 73
Torr, J. 717
Torrance, H. 504, 520
Torres-Guzman, M. 690
Tosi, A. 389
Tough, A. 745
Tough, J. 717
Townsend, H. 269
Trahey, M. 301
Triggs, P. 520
Trimble, L. 402
Trivett, N. 890
Trudeau, P. 198
Truscello, D. 1123
Truscott, J. 288
Tsatsarelis, C. 930
Tse, L. 35
Tsuda, Y. 73, 136
Tsui, A. 135, 470, 471, 873, 959, 1066
Tu, W. 85
Tucker, G. 809
Tung, C. 471
Tunstall, P. 520
Turbee, L. 745
Turkle, S. 1124
Turnbull, M. 288
Turner, C. 483
Turner, D. 1050
Turner, J. 482
Turner, T. 760
Turner-Bisset, R. 959
Tyler, A. 300
Tyler, R. 438

U
Uchida, Y. 985
Umaña-Taylor, A. 640, 643, 652
Unsworth, L. 718
Unz, R. 269
Upshur, J. 518
Urwin, C. 637
Ushioda, E. 745
Usui, N. 73

V

Vaipae, S. 73
Valdés, G. 228, 653, 810, 1016
Valdes, J. 1052
Valdez, G. 1123
Valdez Pierce, L. 456
Valencia, J. 166
Valenzuela, A. 1100
Valette, R. 438, 520
Valli, L. 1065
Valsiner, J. 700
Vamdatta, D. 61
van Dam, J. 985
van der Silk, F. 824
van der Veer, R. 700
van Dijk, T. 315
van Ek, J. 438
van Els, T. 150
van Essen, A. 959
van Langenhove, L. 377
van Leeuwen, T. 314, 857, 930
van Lier, L. 151, 300, 301, 718, 873, 986, 1002, 1030
van Manen, M. 1016
van Nus, M. 412
van Patten, B. 301
Vandenberghe, R. 1065
Vandrick, S. 1052
Vang, T. 363
Vansia, K. 61
Vaquerano, F. 34
Varela, E. 285, 299, 331
Vargas, L. 653
Varghese, M. 1052
Varonis, E. 1030
Varro, G. 34
Vasquez, O. 638, 1016
Vass, A. 731
Vasseur, M. 149
Veel, R. 315, 377, 716, 858
Veltman, C. 183
Venezky, R. 905
Venn, C. 637
Ventola, E. 402, 548, 873
Verduin, J. 1002
Verhoeven, L. 810
Vidal, N. 744
Vieira, F. 745
Vigil, J. 653
Villarruel, F. 653
Villenas, S. 653
Vilmar, F. 135
Vincent, D. 905
Virdee, S. 210
Visser, J. 1124
Viswanathan, G. 24
Vitanova, G. 1049
Vocate, D. 700
Voller, P. 742, 745
Vollmer, G. 653
Vollmer, H. 152
Von Hoene, L. 679
Vukela, V. 45, 50
Vyas, H. 61
Vygotsky, L. 288, 331, 638, 690, 700, 718, 745, 774, 1138

W

Wadsworth, Y. 1002
Wagner, J. 150, 152, 299, 1027
Wagner, S. 484
Wagner, J. 139, 144, 150, 152, 296, 299, 1022, 1023, 1027
Wainer, H. 484
Wakefield, P. 313
Walberg, H. 731
Walkerdine, V. 637, 638, 1052
Wall, D. 469, 481, 504, 530
Wallace, C. 86, 484
Wallace, M. 1002, 1084
Walqui, A. 364
Walsh, C. 364, 718
Walsh, S. 873, 959
Walters, A. 412
Wandersee, J. 314
Wang, Q. 105
Wang, W. 1050, 1099
Wang, Y. 917
Ware, P. 917
Waring, R. 829, 840, 841
Warschauer, M. 745, 760, 761, 905, 916, 917, 1138
Watahomigie, L. 36
Watenburg, T. 61
Waters, A. 402, 485
Watson-Gegeo, K. 35, 36, 986
Watts, R. 135, 152, 873
Weasenforth, D. 758
Webb, C. 888
Webb, V. 49, 50
Weber, R. 810
Webster, A. 718
Wedell, M. 105
Weeden, P. 520
Weedon, C. 638, 653, 690, 1052
Wegerif, R. 718
Wei, L. 105
Weiner, M. 246

Weininger, M. 760
Weinstein, G. 690
Weinstein, N. 1124
Weir, C. 484, 485, 519, 520
Weir, R. 700
Weis, L. 653
Wells, G. 718, 774, 986, 1052
Wendel, J. 301
Wenden, A. 743, 745
Wenger, E. 637, 638, 680, 700, 941, 1050, 1112
Wennerstrom, A. 943
Werner, O. 315
Werry, C. 1124
Wertsch, J. 638, 700
Wesche, M. 288, 376, 485
West, C. 690
West, M. 841
Wheeler, S. 744
Whelan, K. 1015
Whisler, J. 731
White, G. 940
White, J. 286
White, L. 288, 301, 825
White, M. 198
White, R. 301, 731, 1066
Whiteley, W. 49
Whiting, C. 1083
Whitmore, K. 637
Whittaker, S. 1124
Whitty, G. 1083, 1084
Widdicombe, S. 166
Widdowson, H. 86, 152, 153, 167, 269, 288, 301, 438, 873, 943, 1052, 1138
Wideman, H. 902, 904
Wigglesworth, J. 301
Wiley, T. 183, 228, 638
Wilgoren, J. 183
Wiliam, D. 502, 504, 518, 520
Wilkins, D. 248, 288, 412, 438
Wilkinson, A. 718
Wilkinson, R. 136
Willett, J. 638, 690, 986, 1112
Willetts, K. 267
Willey, B. 1030
Williams, A. 267, 269, 455, 518
Williams, C. 269, 1052
Williams, E. 856
Williams, G. 857, 858, 941
Williams, J. 288, 299, 518, 856
Williams, S. 167, 1099
Williamson, J. 959
Willig, A. 183
Willing, K. 412

Willis, A. 691
Willis, D. 301, 858
Willis, J. 301, 1138
Willows, D. 809
Wilmut, J. 520
Wilson, A. 840
Wilson, S. 470
Wilson, T. 1030
Wilson, W. 35, 36
Wilson-Keenan, J. 690, 986
Wink, J. 691
Winter, J. 520
Winter, R. 1002
Wisniewski, R. 1015
Witherell, C. 1016
Witt, D. 809
Wlodkowski, R. 731
Wolfson, W. 50
Woloshyn, V. 331
Wong, A. 810
Wong, C. 810
Wong, J. 1030
Wong, K. 809
Wong, P. 198
Wong, S. 637, 651, 689, 691, 986, 1052, 1099
Wong, S.C. 182, 1099
Wong Scollon, S. 1051
Wong, S.L. 651, 690
Wong-Fillmore, L. 348, 691
Wong-Scollon, S. 942
Woods, D. 1084
Woods, P. 1066
Woodward, T. 1084
Woodward-Kron, R. 890
Woolard, K. 36, 183
Woolf, B. 761
Woolgar, S. 402
Woolverton, S. 689
Worswick, C. 810
Wortham, S. 986
Wray, A. 841
Wray, D. 959
Wright, S. 36, 153
Wright, T. 959
Wrigley, H. 36, 181
Wu, K.Y. 471
Wulff, H. 653

X
Xiong, G. 650
Xu, J. 105
Xu, Y. 893, 896, 897, 904, 905

Y

Yager, T. 653
Yallop, C. 1051
Yamashita, S. 71
Yang, J. 1100
Yanow, D. 269
Yashiro, K. 72
Yates, J. 943
Yates, S. 917
Yeager, B. 717
Yee, P. 1100
Yelland, G. 248
Yngve, V. 873
Yon, D. 1100
Yoshida, K. 73
Young, J. 198
Young, L. 246
Young, R. 485, 745, 1029, 1030, 1052
Yow, V. 1016
Ytsma, J. 167
Yu, H. 1087, 1089, 1097, 1100
Yu, T. 105
Yuan, Y. 293, 297, 301
Yuen, S. 182
Yule, G. 299
Yung, H. 810

Z

Zabaleta, F. 266
Zambrano, A. 34
Zamel, V. 485, 890, 1052
Zammit, S. 716
Zeichner, K. 1001, 1066, 1084
Zelasko, N. 183
Zentella, A. 653
Zhang, R. 104
Zhang, S. 105
Zhang, Y. 105
Zhang, Z. 105
Zhao, J. 105
Zhenhua, H. 905
Zhou, L. 105
Zhou, M. 653
Zimmerman, B. 331
Zimmerman, C. 840
Zimmerman, D. 1026
Zine, J. 1099
Zinn, H. 183
Zoppis, C. 744
Zuber-Skerritt, O. 1002
Zubrow, D. 916
Zuengler, J. 548, 653, 986

SUBJECT INDEX

A
aboriginal students   448
academic   211, 212, 216–220, 222–228, 233, 234, 317–321, 329–331, 333–341, 343–355, 357–359, 391–396, 475–479, 655–660, 665–667, 681–689, 701–707, 709, 797–810, 875–891, 940–942, 1086–1090
  concepts   234, 319, 321, 325, 327, 349, 351, 352, 354, 355, 357, 359, 658, 702, 779, 797, 800, 801, 803, 806, 890, 917
  coursework   347
  development   161–163, 233, 234, 253, 317–321, 327, 328, 334–338, 340, 341, 343–345, 357–359, 365, 380, 381, 412, 616, 619, 681, 685–688, 701, 702, 797–802, 807, 808, 888–890
  disciplines   307, 368, 395, 400, 473, 709, 854, 877, 878, 883, 937, 973, 1034, 1070
  discourse   233, 309, 310, 312, 314, 315, 335, 368, 395, 396, 619, 620, 655, 662, 663, 665–667, 701–707, 709–715, 781, 873, 875–879, 884–886, 888–890, 916, 917, 976, 977
  discourse communities   368, 393, 869, 877–879, 886, 890
  discourse socialization   980, 986
  English   211–214, 216–220, 222–228, 233, 234, 264–267, 317–319, 333–355, 357–359, 380–382, 385–387, 401–403, 455–458, 483–485, 632–635, 665–667, 797–801, 803–810, 887–891, 940–943, 1086–1090
  genres (*see also* genre structure; genre-based approach)   377, 395, 396, 398, 400, 401, 536, 547, 620, 655, 659, 665, 666, 702, 716, 869, 876–879, 883, 884, 886, 887, 931, 932, 934, 937, 938, 942, 943
  language   222–226, 252–256, 317–321, 329–331, 333–341, 343–349, 351–355, 384–387, 475–479, 483–485, 632–636, 665, 666, 679–685, 700–705, 713–717, 797–810, 824, 876–880, 887–891, 937–942
  language development   50, 69, 166, 217, 223, 233, 310, 317–319, 325, 327, 335, 336, 340, 357, 363, 367, 412, 454, 619, 634, 701
  language learning   233, 234, 253, 254, 286, 287, 312, 317–319, 330, 331, 348, 384, 389, 483, 484, 616, 617, 632, 633, 666, 669, 679–681, 701–703, 707–709, 713–715, 763, 809
  learning   218, 224–226, 233, 234, 253–255, 267, 314, 315, 317–321, 327–331, 333, 334, 337, 338, 384–386, 615–617, 619, 620, 632–635, 679–681, 701–705, 707–709, 711–717, 802–805, 888–891
  literacies   399, 401, 402, 666, 781, 875–877, 883, 884, 886, 888–891, 900, 902, 905, 917, 941
  registers   352–354, 392, 635, 701, 702,

798, 800, 804, 808
researchers 195, 211, 395, 396, 398, 401, 477, 619, 645, 655, 656, 665, 706, 781, 886, 887, 968, 978, 995, 997, 998, 1034, 1070, 1078
writing 58, 61, 279, 350–353, 392–394, 401, 402, 477, 483, 484, 547, 548, 662, 663, 666, 781, 794, 797–801, 807, 808, 875–891, 912–914, 934, 940–943, 980
accent discrimination 9, 32, 35, 679, 825, 1094, 1099
accountability 10, 193, 211, 213, 220, 222, 223, 260, 406, 408, 415, 416, 440, 441, 444, 447, 450, 451, 453, 456, 457, 508, 967, 968, 998, 999, 1103
accountability-driven standards 447, 450
acculturation 335, 386, 545, 641, 643, 644, 646, 649, 651
acoustic
  information 787, 791
  input 791
acquired systems 949
acquisition (*see also* L1 acquisition; second language acquisition studies) 8, 155, 157, 158, 160–163, 165–167, 274–276, 284–292, 296–301, 333–335, 348–350, 516–518, 625, 626, 633–639, 716, 717, 783–795, 824, 825, 839–841, 848, 849, 856, 857, 1025–1028
  academic knowledge of English 335
  of ESL (*see* English as a second language) 350, 382, 383, 388, 416, 440, 490, 619, 625, 631, 633
  of language and literacy 633, 758
acquisition-rich 949
action research (*see also* ethnographic research; experimental research; qualitative research; quantitative research) 203, 759, 760, 911, 965, 977, 987–1002, 1067, 1074–1077, 1082, 1083
activity 133, 134, 290, 291, 295, 305–307, 361, 374, 375, 393, 394, 511, 512, 514, 515, 619, 629, 630, 635, 637, 638, 640, 641, 693–699, 705, 727–729, 947, 948, 976, 1046
adjacency pair 867
adolescence 616, 639–643, 649–652
adolescent
  identity 641–643, 645, 648, 649

immigrants 641, 646, 1049
adult
  education 34, 35, 235, 403, 404, 410, 411, 417, 421, 422, 431, 432, 436, 438, 657, 743
  literacy 27, 477, 689
Adult Migrant Education Services (AMES), Australia 411
Advisory Committee of Teacher Education and Qualifications (ACTEQ), Hong Kong 461–464, 466
affective filter 949
African-Caribbean 201
agent of change (*see* change agent) 688, 1059, 1131, 1133, 1059, 1064
alternative 4, 25, 26, 34, 37, 45, 85, 163, 215, 216, 222, 224, 306, 307, 419, 420, 493, 494, 501, 506, 507, 519–521, 537, 1042, 1043, 1073–1075, 1077, 1078
  assessment (*see* assessment) 419, 420, 493, 494, 501, 506, 507, 509, 519, 530
  pedagogies 1043, 1073, 1074
American Educational Research Association (AERA) 331, 469, 481, 1014, 1016
American War of Independence 187
Americanization 123, 129, 167, 215, 216, 220, 224, 1093
analytical thinking 1075
anecdotes 141, 869, 933, 975
applied
  linguistics (AL) 135, 136, 150–153, 284–288, 299–301, 331, 391, 392, 401, 402, 481–484, 517–520, 716, 717, 839, 840, 871, 872, 940–942, 957, 958, 966, 967, 984–987, 1000, 1001, 1027–1030, 1033–1035, 1047–1052
  research 337, 419, 963
apprenticeship 372, 377, 546, 547, 638, 686, 690, 704, 882, 887, 890, 1054, 1056
Argentina 5, 7, 107–121, 352
articulation 17, 250, 261, 330, 370, 381, 388, 422, 500, 790, 795, 813, 921, 986, 1074, 1075
Asian Americans 644, 645, 647, 648, 651, 652
Asian Canadian 647
assessment (*see also* benchmarks; testing) 94–96, 99, 101, 102, 206–209, 311–315, 415–422, 431–434, 436, 437,

Subject Index

443–445, 447–471, 475–478, 480–485, 487–520, 529–531, 533, 534, 697–700, 928–930, 939, 1101–1104, 1106, 1107
  alternative   419, 420, 489, 493, 494, 501, 503, 506, 507, 509, 519, 520, 530
  dynamic assessment   419, 420, 494, 496, 512, 515, 619, 684, 699, 700, 898, 1110
  formative assessment (*see also* summative assessment)   94, 95, 99, 101, 419, 420, 447, 450, 489, 491, 492, 498, 499, 504–509, 511, 513–520, 1102
  frameworks   313, 314, 410, 418–421, 454, 455, 476, 490, 502, 505, 506, 509, 510, 512, 513, 517, 518, 520, 684
  functions   508, 509, 514
  innovations   488, 495, 502, 510
  instruction-embedded assessment   511
  instruments   327, 434, 449, 457, 462–464, 466, 487, 488, 656, 894, 1045
  paradigm   415, 418, 421, 422, 441, 460, 499, 504, 506, 508, 512, 513, 520, 684, 699
  performance   99, 298, 328, 329, 339, 417, 418, 421, 425, 432–434, 436, 437, 452, 456–459, 461, 477, 478, 482–485, 489–491, 497–500, 502, 503, 507, 508, 515, 698–700
  practices   49, 52, 198, 206, 313, 315, 366, 413, 419, 420, 449, 450, 452, 453, 487–489, 502, 503, 510, 513–515, 518, 530, 531, 534, 922, 928, 929
  procedures   193, 325, 418, 419, 432, 445, 448, 451, 459, 460, 507, 509, 510, 512, 518, 530, 1103, 1134
  summative assessment   94, 99, 419, 420, 450, 491, 498, 505, 508, 509, 513–515, 517, 519, 1102
Assessment Reform Group, UK   516, 517
assimilation   38, 174, 180, 189, 215, 218, 219, 221, 224, 258, 261, 335, 363, 448, 641, 650, 985
assimilationist   128, 224, 631, 645
assisted performance   619, 628, 703
asynchronous
  communication   762, 779
  environments   896, 900
attention   33, 63, 87, 107, 143, 164, 206, 208, 233, 254, 264, 265, 319, 320, 329, 330, 419, 487, 488, 792, 793, 931–933, 935, 945, 946, 1019, 1020
attentive silence   1093–1095
attitudinal roles   970, 1113, 1114, 1116
attraction   133, 720, 729
attribution   171, 306, 729
audience expectations   932, 937
auditory discrimination task   815, 817
Australia   156, 157, 196, 197, 249, 250, 259, 260, 266, 365, 366, 376, 377, 417, 418, 421, 443–445, 448, 449, 455, 456, 469, 470, 473–475, 495, 496, 502, 503, 517–520, 540, 541, 759, 760, 875, 876
Australian Council of TESOL Associations (ACTA)   268, 269, 1123
Austria   137, 155, 379, 380, 824
authentic
  communication   3, 754, 922
  language   621, 748, 752, 753, 873
  literacy tasks   979
  tasks   1114
authenticity   35, 80, 139, 399, 416, 477, 506, 511, 512, 520, 615, 718, 742, 752, 753, 824, 870, 1073, 1074, 1136
authorial
  meanings   1036
  self   881
authoring systems   1119, 1124
authoritarian leadership   724
autobiographical self   881
autocratic leadership   724
automatic word recognition   793
automatization   789, 795
autonomous
  classrooms   738
  learners   621, 744, 1129
  learning   621, 706, 739–741, 743–745, 915, 1071, 1128
  mode   620, 725, 726
  models of literacy   892, 900
autonomously-controlled tasks   738
autonomy   189, 277, 355, 435, 436, 620, 621, 623, 718, 725, 726, 728, 733–745, 750, 759, 760, 806, 946, 1002, 1036, 1046, 1051, 1069, 1079
  in English language teaching   733, 736, 741
  in language learning   733, 734, 738, 739, 742–745
autonomy-related practices   734, 735

B

back-channel utterances 866
backtracking 792
Bangalore Project 16
basic interpersonal communicative skills (BICS) 252, 353
behavioral objectives 423, 426, 437
behaviorism (*see also* cognitivism; constructivism) 422
behaviorist approaches 421
behaviorist-based teaching 1132
benchmark test (*see also* assessment) 458, 464, 467, 468
benchmarks 112, 195, 197, 260, 268, 416, 440, 444, 447, 448, 455, 456, 461–464, 466, 468–470, 483, 490, 502, 517, 518, 955, 1072
benchmark-setting 955
bilingual
 class 338, 343, 1088
 contexts 8, 1046
 education 8, 9, 33–36, 49, 50, 109–111, 119–121, 161, 162, 164, 165, 167, 172–175, 180–183, 219–221, 255, 256, 260–262, 264–269, 330, 331, 345, 346, 389, 459, 688–690, 809, 810
 principles 894
 programs 8, 64, 111, 112, 161, 174, 212, 221, 225, 263, 318, 330, 345, 346, 352, 448
 students 72, 162, 220, 311, 340, 364, 618, 634, 678, 679, 681–685, 687, 1107
 and trilingual programs xxiii
bilingualism 8, 16, 50, 71–73, 162–167, 174–176, 189–191, 241, 242, 246, 247, 255, 256, 267, 379, 385, 387–389, 676, 679, 680, 685, 794, 795, 894, 895, 901, 902
 additive bilingualism 44, 71, 111, 165, 166, 379, 387, 388, 895, 901, 902
biliteracy 635, 690, 1049
biographical methods 741
biolinguistic diversity 894
Black Stylized English (BSE) 675
branching onsets 820
British Council 16, 23, 49, 107, 110, 112–114, 119, 125, 132, 135, 150, 170, 181, 210, 241, 246, 502, 520, 742, 743, 1000
British National Corpus (BNC) 870

BSE (*see* Black Stylized English) 675

C

CA (*see* conversation analysis) 864, 865, 867–870, 1017–1026, 1031
CACD (*see* computer-assisted classroom discussion) 908–910, 914
CALL (*see* computer-assisted language learning) 3, 621, 622, 743, 747–749, 751, 752, 757–761, 915, 1113, 1117, 1118, 1120, 1122–1124
Cambodian 648
Canada 9, 10, 156, 157, 160, 182, 183, 185–198, 249, 250, 287, 288, 303, 304, 459, 470, 473, 474, 483, 674–677, 770, 771, 809–811, 1015, 1039–1042, 1047–1050, 1085, 1086, 1098, 1099
Canadian Constitution Act (CCA) 189
Canadian Language Benchmarks (CLB) 195, 197, 483, 490, 517, 518
Cantonese 352, 533, 534, 540–542, 631, 803, 968, 1011, 1012, 1057, 1065, 1086–1094, 1097
case studies 6, 70, 198, 314, 366, 377, 389, 400, 409, 412, 520, 615, 640, 658, 665, 666, 876, 877, 922, 923, 973, 979, 982, 983
casual conversation 143, 856, 860, 865, 866, 869, 872, 936, 966
Center for Applied Linguistics, USA 180, 310, 313, 364, 470, 689, 690
certification tests 459
change agent 1059
chat rooms 798
No Child Left Behind (NCLB) 10, 211, 215, 222, 228, 416, 491, 495, 497, 523, 525, 527, 529, 531
China (also PRC) 5, 6, 22, 64, 85, 87–93, 95, 100, 101, 103–105, 125, 156, 239, 289, 312, 403, 456, 457, 501, 502, 809, 810, 980, 1003, 1004, 1015
Chomsky 239, 241, 246, 273, 285, 289, 299, 694, 777, 779, 784, 785, 794, 846–849, 852–857, 1034
Chomsky's Universal Grammar 1034
chunking 880
class discussions 543, 658, 977, 979, 991, 1004
classificatory systems 535
classroom 280–288, 372–376, 417–420,

Subject Index 579

487–520, 625–638, 700–709, 713–731, 907–910, 912–917, 968–971, 973–979, 981–986, 994–996, 999–1005, 1027, 1028, 1050–1058, 1075–1077, 1089–1094, 1104–1108, 1125–1138
approaches 6, 7, 27, 90, 287, 419, 420, 505, 506, 509, 510, 706, 757, 758, 843, 883, 937, 939–941, 949, 950, 964, 973–975, 985, 986, 1069, 1075, 1076, 1127
assessment 193, 206–208, 267, 268, 314, 315, 329, 417–420, 433, 434, 443, 457–459, 463–465, 468–470, 487–520, 530, 619, 700, 929, 930, 939, 1101, 1102, 1104, 1107
communication 239, 258, 399, 401, 402, 700, 715, 717, 748, 759, 760, 779, 888, 907, 908, 910, 913–917, 920, 942, 943, 969, 970, 976, 977, 984–986, 1125
context 206, 231, 232, 314, 402, 419, 420, 442, 499, 500, 506, 514, 515, 622, 634, 700–702, 706, 714–717, 719, 720, 941, 969, 970, 987, 1001–1003, 1005
discourse 90, 299, 300, 311, 312, 315, 402, 463, 514, 515, 519, 520, 547, 619, 620, 634–637, 701–715, 717, 718, 862–864, 871–873, 888, 889, 909, 910, 916, 917, 976, 977, 982–986
discourse processes 866
environment 48, 253, 255, 265, 286, 335, 367, 411, 620, 622, 716, 717, 719–721, 723, 725–727, 729–731, 760, 761, 763, 799, 1085, 1128, 1129
ethos 713, 888
interaction 275, 286, 287, 464, 465, 633, 634, 700, 701, 707–709, 714, 715, 717, 721, 741, 754, 863, 864, 872, 873, 908, 909, 915, 916, 963, 964, 966, 975–977, 985, 986, 1027, 1028
learning 252–255, 280–287, 299–301, 433–435, 487–497, 499–504, 510–520, 619, 620, 625–638, 700–709, 711–720, 733–735, 741–744, 757–761, 968–971, 984–987, 999–1005, 1050–1052, 1125–1128, 1131–1138
management 81, 222, 509, 720, 731, 735, 739, 943, 988, 1002, 1056, 1060, 1085, 1105
management strategies 1082
observations 61, 80, 206, 219, 255, 323, 358, 398, 661, 664, 963, 976, 977, 979, 981, 983, 990, 1010, 1092
pedagogy 6, 34, 48, 85, 89, 112, 232, 254, 255, 264, 267, 285, 635, 636, 715, 716, 763, 767, 926, 941, 942, 1050, 1081, 1082, 1104–1107
practices 13, 25, 47, 48, 355, 372, 373, 375, 392, 398, 399, 401, 419, 420, 487–489, 502, 503, 513–515, 518, 625–637, 706, 707, 922, 963–965, 982–986, 1075, 1076
research (*see* classroom-based research) 276, 283, 284, 629, 747, 757, 914, 964, 973, 974, 975, 977, 978, 982, 983, 985, 994, 995, 1000–1082
teaching 90, 150, 151, 254, 255, 281–289, 372–376, 462, 463, 491–497, 502–504, 715, 856, 857, 915–917, 939–941, 957, 958, 968–971, 999–1003, 1050–1058, 1064, 1065, 1075–1077, 1104–1108, 1129–1132
Classroom Action Research Network (CARN) 992
classroom-based
 courses 735
 research 922
 studies 420, 978, 983
clinical psychology 617, 639–641
CLT (*see* communicative language teaching) 78, 79, 232, 271–284, 287, 1071, 1127
clusters 443, 618, 669, 671, 748, 821–824, 964, 974, 988
CMC environments 752
coaches 1115
codas 820
code choices 647
coded data 983
code-switching 170, 242–244, 246, 635, 778, 1097
coercive relations of power 33, 706, 972, 1037
cognitive
 activity 619, 705, 855
 development 163, 247, 318, 336, 338, 340, 343–345, 629, 630, 638, 690, 788, 791
 learning models 318
 processes of language acquisition 631
 psychology 72, 273, 279, 283, 330
 science 779, 783, 786, 792, 793

cognitive academic language proficiency (CALP) 163, 353
cognitively complex questions 712
cognitively-challenging tasks 704, 969, 1105
cognitive-social model 319
cohesive
  devises 694
  linguistic references 909
collaboration (*see also* interaction) 227, 234, 320, 357–359, 363, 365–367, 369, 373–377, 389, 399, 417, 443, 515, 621, 629, 637, 752, 753, 967, 968, 1046, 1047, 1076, 1077
collaborative
  activity 515, 629, 630, 635
  basis 999
  critical inquiry 753, 765, 911
  dialogue 301, 513, 705, 717, 857
  learning 387, 517, 717, 739, 744, 753, 754, 760, 765, 802, 902, 903, 909, 1061, 1123
  pedagogies 235, 391, 398, 399
  relations of power 903, 972
  roles 235, 368, 374, 635, 969, 1105, 1115
  support 1068
  teaching 234, 365, 366, 368, 373, 374, 376, 915, 1104, 1105
  work 365–369, 374–376, 516
collegial development 1078, 1080, 1082
collegiality 997, 1061, 1080
collocation 830, 833, 857, 953
colonial
  language policy 13, 15, 38, 40
  privilege 1044
colonialism 4, 13, 15, 17–19, 21–23, 35, 50, 61, 75, 76, 83, 85, 531, 672, 1051, 1088, 1097, 1098
colonialist discourses 23, 35, 61, 79, 85, 531, 1051
colonization 65, 77, 107, 124, 156
command of English 78, 110, 111, 113, 118, 674
commitment control strategies 728
common literacy standards 444, 447
communication 66–68, 91–94, 127–134, 136–138, 144–147, 149–152, 155–158, 170, 239, 240, 398–402, 408–412, 694, 748, 749, 777–779, 887–899, 907–917, 920–922, 1048–1052, 1111–1113, 1125–1128
communicative
  abilities 67, 79, 115, 147, 271, 276, 279, 400, 928
  action 1076
  activity 694, 705, 845
  approach 91, 271, 298, 753, 760, 804, 1083
  behavior (*see also* behaviorism) 26, 393, 936
  competence 66, 67, 77, 78, 93, 115, 162, 254, 255, 273, 285–287, 312, 429, 475, 476, 483, 622, 672, 715, 717, 758, 779, 868, 893
  competencies 898, 903
  flexibility 659
  functions 274, 861, 862, 872
  language learning 742
  language pedagogy 285, 868
  language teaching (CLT) 64, 78, 232, 239, 271–273, 275, 277, 279, 281, 283, 285–290, 392, 751, 760, 804, 857, 869, 871, 872, 922, 967
  methodology 274, 285, 1126
  needs 234, 253, 391, 398, 526, 780, 855, 898, 932
  options 647
  practices 278, 283, 392, 398–400, 647, 779, 920, 928
  problems 694
  strategies 1030
  styles 647
community
  literacies 400, 892
  of practice (COP) 231, 633, 638, 670, 1046
comparative education 23, 104, 658, 689
competencies 114, 195, 227, 278, 279, 395, 405, 408, 412, 416, 417, 421, 424–426, 428, 431, 433, 437, 438, 452, 459, 736, 898, 1132, 1133
  in education 1071
competency-based programs 424
comprehensible input 274–276, 279, 281, 300, 717, 752, 769, 848, 949, 1023, 1028
comprehension-based activities 295
compulsory education 97, 99, 100, 104, 105, 114, 115

Subject Index 581

computer 242, 313, 476, 479, 480, 482–484, 621, 622, 747–760, 762, 767, 768, 781, 863, 864, 899, 904, 905, 907–910, 912–917, 953, 954, 1114, 1115, 1117, 1118, 1123–1125, 1130–1134
  adaptive testing 480, 482
  corpora 397, 480, 953, 954, 1070
  labs 749
  literacy 233, 303, 313, 622, 747, 749, 756, 758–760, 781, 904, 905, 907, 914–916, 1123
  support teacher 1117
  technology 3, 100, 484, 621, 622, 747–751, 753, 755–760, 904, 907, 915–917, 954, 1071, 1114, 1121, 1123–1125, 1127, 1130, 1131, 1133, 1137
computer-assisted
  classroom discussion (CACD) 781, 907, 908, 910
  instruction 622, 747, 749–751, 753, 756–758
  language learning (CALL) 621, 742, 747, 752, 758–760, 1117
computer-based
  activities 1127
  approaches 748, 755
  instruction (CBI) 748, 753, 755
  technologies 313, 747, 750, 751, 755, 756, 758
  training 748
computerized spellchecking 899
computer-mediated
  communication (CMC) 471, 748, 757, 762, 767, 781, 905, 907, 912–917
  communication literacy 914
  language learning 1132
  messages 909
  writing 781, 907
computer-supported
  learning environments 1125
  project seminars 1131
  projects 1133
concordancing tools 954, 956
connectionism 785, 793, 794
connectionist
  approach to learning 785
  architecture 785, 786
conscious knowledge 787, 813
consciousness 48, 80, 169, 198, 250, 285, 295, 300, 306, 399, 669, 689, 693, 695, 992
consciousness-raising tasks 285, 300
consonant 787, 789, 813, 821–823
  clusters 821–823
constructivism (*see also* behaviorism; cognitivism) 235, 395, 539
constructivist
  approaches 622, 737, 758, 1114
  view of learning 499, 750
  views of teaching 1126
consultants 213, 399, 462, 463, 466–468, 1115
content 58, 59, 114–116, 118–121, 231–234, 251–254, 266–268, 281–284, 303, 309–315, 317–321, 323–325, 345, 346, 357–359, 366–369, 373–377, 428, 429, 431–437, 803–808, 1119–1122, 1126–1129
  analysis (*see also* discourse analysis) 29, 253, 262, 281, 284, 310–313, 325, 381, 400, 478, 868, 869, 931, 942
  and assessment standards 417, 421
content-based
  instruction 119, 268, 284, 290, 366, 376
  language teaching 119, 167, 1085
content-language integration approach 252
context 6–11, 157–160, 199–201, 231–234, 252–256, 402, 403, 446, 447, 506, 537–540, 621, 622, 714–717, 734–740, 777–781, 797–800, 849–852, 856, 857, 937–942, 1005, 1021–1023, 1069–1073
  of culture 303, 649, 933, 935, 1037
context-dependent 419
context-free 498
context-sensitive 1039
contextual features 494, 538, 861, 975
contingency 710, 853, 915, 1119
contingent responses 712
contrastive rhetoric 235, 391, 392, 394, 395, 401, 547, 938, 940, 1039, 1047, 1048
control 219, 220, 240, 241, 292, 293, 296, 297, 318, 319, 329, 330, 522, 523, 529, 530, 615, 695, 708, 713, 724–726, 728, 729, 737, 738, 743, 744, 750, 851, 990, 1056
conversation 63, 64, 70, 71, 245, 246, 369, 371, 372, 715, 716, 752–754, 798, 799, 801, 802, 804–806, 859, 860, 863–866,

868, 869, 872, 873, 900, 966, 1017–1019, 1021–1023, 1025, 1027–1032
analysis (CA)   143, 150, 246, 647, 781, 859, 864, 865, 868, 869, 872, 873, 966, 975, 978, 983, 1017–1019, 1021–1023, 1025, 1027–1031
analysts   865, 869, 1018, 1019, 1021, 1022
conversational
 competence   868
 exposure   111
 fluency   351, 352, 701, 779, 797, 799–801, 805
 style   860
conversation-analysis-for-second-language-acquisition (CA-for-SLA)   1022
cooperative
 action research   992
 learning   99, 310, 314, 970, 1085, 1128, 1134
 learning activities   1085
core identities   65
coronal node   816, 817
corpora of language data   954
corporate
 position   1116
 universities   1119, 1124
corpus
 linguistics   146, 954
 of spoken language   870
 studies   853
corpus-based   151, 777, 840, 870, 871, 917
corrective feedback   275, 277, 278, 286, 287, 300, 760, 845, 948
Council of Europe   134, 146, 147, 149, 150, 152, 421, 425–427, 437, 442, 454, 734, 743, 759
covert error correction   790
Creole   28, 107, 115, 126, 143, 321, 644, 646, 1013
critic   1115
critical   25–29, 31, 32, 34–36, 47–49, 61, 83–85, 312–315, 391–395, 615–619, 650–653, 655, 656, 660–662, 665, 666, 685, 686, 689–691, 713–716, 763–766, 769–773, 1036–1052, 1097–1100
 applied linguistics   61, 85, 313, 315, 392, 402, 517, 519, 530, 531, 615, 650, 652, 689, 690, 824, 941, 967, 986, 992, 1048, 1050–1052

approaches   4, 6, 27, 36, 85, 169, 233, 235, 303, 391, 392, 531, 615–617, 690, 691, 706, 855, 883, 971, 1034, 1041, 1045
contrastive rhetoric   235, 391, 392, 394, 938, 1048
curriculum   36, 40, 69, 83, 250, 267, 313, 314, 392, 408, 444, 455, 493, 619, 665, 686, 714, 764, 765, 971, 972, 1000, 1015, 1016
discourse analysis   132, 235, 391, 392, 615, 650, 748, 976, 977, 1049–1051
discourse studies   645
EAP (*see* English for academic purposes)   402, 656, 665, 883, 1044
engagement   400, 512, 650, 911, 1046, 1116
ethnography   61, 235, 391–393, 617, 636, 651, 655, 656, 658, 660, 666, 905, 977, 978, 984, 986, 1045, 1098, 1099, 1112
language awareness   49, 854, 888, 947, 957, 958, 1094
language studies   26, 85, 531, 666, 1051
language testing   455, 474, 493, 517, 519, 520, 530, 531, 616, 1050
linguistics   49, 61, 85, 233, 303, 313–315, 392, 488, 517, 519, 531, 615, 650, 652, 689, 690, 824, 856, 938, 1048, 1050–1052
literacy   27, 28, 34–36, 178, 400, 401, 444, 445, 455, 689, 691, 749, 763–766, 769, 856, 876, 887, 888, 891–893, 901, 902, 905, 971, 972, 1012, 1014, 1015
multiculturalists   1042
pedagogy   6, 23, 34, 48, 75, 83–85, 250, 401, 616, 618, 636, 666, 686, 689–691, 715, 716, 753, 763–766, 971, 972, 1041–1044, 1050, 1051
period   40, 68, 69, 72, 178, 652, 747, 814, 824, 825, 832
period hypothesis   68, 69, 814, 824
reflexive practices   1043, 1044
reflexivity   966, 1041, 1043–1045, 1078
stance   395, 660, 707, 1074, 1076
theory   4, 26, 27, 31, 34, 35, 85, 197, 228, 313, 392, 401, 415, 639, 689, 742, 743, 824, 825, 855, 905, 1034, 1046–1048, 1050, 1051
thinking skills   233, 303, 312, 313, 452, 706, 713, 807

cross disciplinary conversation 376
cross-cultural
  communication 350, 1085
  comparison 306
cross-generational 642
crossings 650, 1035, 1079
cross-institutional communication 1128
cross-national 128, 439, 475, 642
cultural
  capital 77, 132, 133, 176, 397, 688, 875, 1088, 1093
  competence 444, 851, 1022
  congruence 709
  determinism 21
  difference 489, 650, 765, 919, 921, 922, 928, 941
  formations 15
  hybridity 1035
  identities 85, 133, 170, 197, 198, 202, 216, 227, 637, 645–647, 651, 679, 706, 893, 895, 898
  inequality 661
  instrumentalism 169
  meanings 233, 303
  ownership 870
  practices 205, 393, 397, 515, 534, 537, 539, 540, 698, 1039, 1042, 1051
  resources 629, 637
  specificity 18
  studies 152, 186, 197, 218, 538, 639, 645–647, 651, 679, 778, 1049, 1050, 1099, 1133, 1134, 1136
culturally
  appropriate curricula 1079
  specific context 706
culture 49, 50, 78, 79, 112, 113, 175–177, 196–198, 356–359, 394, 395, 419, 487–503, 637–641, 648–653, 921–924, 933, 984, 985, 1009, 1011–1016, 1021, 1022, 1033–1035, 1037–1052, 1098–1100
curriculum 87–89, 95–105, 107–114, 199–204, 206–210, 246–269, 355, 356, 365–369, 372–377, 406–412, 437–445, 454–456, 493, 494, 517–520, 684–687, 757–760, 807–809, 999–1002, 1014–1016, 1101–1112
  approaches 6, 7, 36, 87, 103, 162, 219, 232, 254, 256, 260, 368, 420, 421, 424, 425, 432, 433, 622, 706, 757, 758, 939, 940, 971, 992, 993
  change 7, 10, 82, 90, 96, 100–104, 118, 120, 165, 203, 259, 262, 284, 440, 441, 987, 999, 1001, 1069, 1110, 1111, 1126
  de facto curriculum 524, 529
  dynamic curriculum 10, 231, 254, 496, 979, 1080, 1110
  evaluation 93, 100, 104, 118, 253, 265, 268, 313, 320, 325, 327, 407, 408, 412, 413, 415, 420, 421, 424, 425, 431–433, 435, 517, 518, 992
  inquiry-based curriculum 619
  materials 87, 88, 103, 105, 164, 191, 195, 206, 208, 232, 251, 252, 318, 320, 327, 355, 386, 409, 410, 432, 433, 441–443, 484, 493
  planning 35, 105, 146, 253, 254, 301, 319, 366, 369, 372, 403, 407, 408, 423, 424, 431, 441, 497, 509, 1080, 1085, 1109
  practices 16, 77, 89, 93, 204, 206, 232, 250, 262, 355, 365–369, 372, 373, 510, 513, 534, 618, 622, 684, 685, 928, 1063
  theory 105, 118, 120, 235, 287, 313, 349, 355, 377, 392, 403, 410, 412, 454, 456, 503, 504, 511, 939, 940, 992, 1002
customization 1122

D

data-based language analysis 953
declarative knowledge 955
decolonization 13, 35
decolonized 1040
deconstructionism 1044
deep structure 341, 450, 1034
  of mind 1034
  of standards 450
default practices 1017
deficit model 497, 676
delayed communication 907
democratic
  approaches to assessment 530
  leadership 725
demographic
  changes 188, 191, 192
  research 617, 655–657
denominator 1024, 1025
descriptive ethnography 660

developmental
  path 540, 799, 1054, 1058, 1062, 1064
  stage 639, 1115
dialects 28, 126, 129, 158, 176, 179, 190, 243, 368, 444, 627, 647, 845, 870
diasporic identities 1035
digital
  divide 622, 755, 761, 917
  interfaces 891
  literacies 893, 897, 902
  text 899
disciplinary
  microworlds 884
  problems 1057, 1058
discoursal
  self 881
  strategies 884
discourse 303–305, 309–315, 391–400, 536–539, 545–547, 619, 620, 662, 663, 701–715, 777–781, 859–873, 875–880, 884–886, 888–891, 908–910, 930–932, 934–940, 975–977, 982–986, 1026–1030, 1049–1052
  analysis 33, 34, 235, 310–314, 391–393, 396, 397, 402, 484, 662, 663, 717, 861, 864, 868, 869, 872, 873, 888, 931, 975–977, 982, 983, 986, 1027–1031, 1049–1051
  classroom discourse 252, 287, 299, 300, 373, 401, 402, 419, 463, 511, 514, 515, 519, 520, 619, 620, 634–637, 701–709, 713–718, 862–864, 871–873, 909, 910, 976, 977, 982–986, 1027, 1028
  community 34, 112, 141, 178, 367, 396, 399, 402, 539, 545, 546, 635–637, 666, 764, 778, 781, 873, 875–878, 885, 886, 889, 890, 1068
  context 9, 81, 150, 210, 253, 284, 303, 305, 314, 514, 515, 701, 702, 706, 714, 715, 777, 778, 850, 851, 856, 857, 872, 873, 879, 880, 935, 937–940
  in English 9, 34, 75, 79, 111, 124, 125, 130, 131, 146, 149, 151, 214, 300, 314, 315, 400, 401, 418, 419, 473, 477, 478, 828, 894, 896
  of globalization 75, 81, 115, 893, 1070
  markers 545, 861, 862, 872, 873, 983
  of meetings 738
  norms 126, 130, 131, 146, 179, 395, 709, 713, 781, 869, 877, 878, 885, 891, 897, 898, 900, 1041, 1046, 1076
  practices 75, 84, 303–305, 313–315, 373, 375, 391–394, 396, 397, 400, 487, 514, 515, 634, 635, 637, 707, 876–879, 975–977, 982–986, 1043, 1058, 1080, 1081
  structure 251, 279, 307, 311, 314, 538, 539, 546, 708, 717, 778, 780, 806, 853, 859, 861, 864, 872, 873, 876, 878, 1030
  systems 284, 303, 314, 335, 394, 396, 419, 487, 488, 659, 861, 868, 878, 930, 938, 947, 966
discourse-based contexts 935
discursive
  construction 198, 373, 376, 377, 1047, 1050
  perspectives 1046
disengagement 1054
disintermediation 1121
display-based teaching 863
disruptive technology 1121
distance learning 735, 743, 749, 750, 758
domain 7, 37, 46, 126, 131, 146, 212, 434, 456, 476, 522, 699, 814, 857, 894, 909, 922, 929, 983, 1023–1025
dominance of tests 524
dominant variety of English 1042
dual language instruction 255
dynamic qualifications 1133

E
EAL (*see* English as an additional language) xxi, 10, 200, 202, 206–209, 265, 921, 928, 968, 969, 1101–1111
EAP (*see* English for academic purposes) 393–395, 415, 431, 617, 655, 656, 658–660, 663–665, 735, 751, 876, 883–887, 1044
  curricula 658, 659
early
  adopter group 1119
  majority 1116
ecological validity 974
economic globalization 76
education 20–23, 31–52, 103–105, 107–121, 164–167, 195–203, 255–269, 386–389, 421–425, 452–456, 469–471, 685–690, 715–719, 963–976, 1047–1055, 1082–1089, 1097–1107, 1110–

Subject Index 585

1120, 1123–1127, 1136–1138
educational
  anthropology 639
  attainment 10, 199–201, 203, 205, 207, 209, 656
  computing 1114, 1119
  disadvantage 663
  discourse 704, 742, 872
  integration 249, 257
  linguists 948
  opportunities 202, 366
  psychology 693, 698, 699, 720, 725, 729, 740, 759, 794, 1007
  reform 10, 11, 107, 108, 114, 115, 121, 162, 163, 436, 503, 618, 631, 637, 656, 681, 734, 735, 764, 999, 1083, 1137
  sectors 1119
  studies 73, 620, 719, 1003, 1013
EFL (*see* English as a foreign language) xxi, xxii, xxv, 21, 76, 78–80, 82, 108, 112–116, 118, 119, 121, 138, 139, 158, 167, 239, 380, 415, 417, 439, 442, 443, 448, 450, 452, 453, 462, 511, 661, 763, 834, 845, 895, 951, 952, 954, 956, 970, 971, 983–985, 1035, 1072, 1126, 1127, 1130–1134, 1136
  learners 439
  standards 417, 439, 442, 443, 453
electronic 120, 121, 129, 165, 247, 348, 412, 748, 749, 755, 758–761, 767, 773, 781, 808, 896, 904, 905, 907–910, 912–917, 939, 1123, 1124, 1137, 1138
  discourses 412, 908
  feedback 755, 909, 910, 917
  literacy 749, 758–760, 781, 808, 904, 905, 907, 914–916, 1123
  text types 1120
electrophysiological data 822
elementary schools 38, 63, 64, 68–73, 78, 222, 234, 312, 323, 328, 344, 349, 363, 527, 905
ELF (*see* English as lingua franca) xxi, xxii, 8, 132, 137–142, 144, 145, 147–149
ELLs (*see* English language learners) 211, 212, 215, 218, 223, 226, 227, 639, 640, 642–649, 655–657, 660, 661, 663–665, 806, 973, 974–976, 978, 979, 982, 983
ELT (*see* English language teaching) xxi, xxv, xxviii, 3–7, 9, 10, 13, 15–17, 19, 22, 25–33, 63, 67, 69, 70, 75–79, 83, 84, 87, 88, 90–92, 96, 102, 103, 107, 108, 118, 119, 130, 132, 155, 199, 209, 210, 231–235, 238, 403, 404, 406–410, 414–417, 419, 420, 439, 449, 441–445, 448–454, 498, 521, 534, 655, 656, 658, 733, 734, 735, 736, 741, 749, 777–782, 843–845, 849, 891, 893, 894, 896–898, 901–903, 919, 928, 929, 931, 946, 951, 954, 955, 963–968, 970–972, 987, 992, 994, 996, 999, 1003, 1033, 1037, 1038, 1040–1047, 1067, 1068, 1070, 1072–1074, 1114, 1118–1120, 1125
  classroom 29, 897, 928, 929
  curriculum design 235, 403, 408
  professional discourse community 951
  standards 417, 439–443, 445, 448–454
  workplace design and evaluation 409
e-mail 754, 755, 758, 760, 772, 860, 907, 908, 910–917, 1127, 1134, 1135
  communication 760, 907, 910–913, 915–917
  exchanges 908, 910–912, 916
emancipatory models 992
emerging demographics 196
EMI (*see* English medium instruction) 803, 804, 805, 807, 808
emic perspectives 973, 974, 977
emoticons 896, 899, 913
emotion control strategies 729
empirical research 143, 145, 289, 376, 439, 441, 448, 454, 474, 497, 625, 636, 737, 977, 987, 1000
empirical-analytical techniques 1043
empirically grounded understanding 1023
employment standards 421, 422
enculturation 393, 666, 902
England 13, 16, 72, 73, 110, 181, 199–203, 209, 210, 249, 250, 257, 259, 262–269, 348, 364–367, 373, 444, 445, 531, 647, 1049, 1100–1104, 1109–1111
English
  for Academic Purposes (EAP) 314, 376, 380, 393, 401, 402, 483, 485, 617, 655, 666, 689, 735, 798, 876, 887, 888, 890, 917, 941, 942, 1044, 1047
  as an additional language (EAL) 10, 163, 164, 199, 200, 202, 204, 207, 208, 210, 265, 268, 380, 455, 456, 510, 517, 520, 618, 735, 921, 968, 1101, 1111, 1112
  as an official language 65, 71–73, 78, 84

deficiency 657
education 14, 63, 64, 66–69, 71, 72, 75, 78, 82, 83, 85, 96, 105, 669, 929
as a European lingua franca 141, 149, 151, 167
as a foreign language (EFL) 76, 113, 146, 157, 158, 165–167, 250, 285, 417, 418, 439, 473, 474, 482, 484, 774, 825, 895, 945, 983, 1004
for general purposes 661
as a global language 48, 75, 76, 85, 107, 115, 120, 126, 134, 135, 150, 151, 166, 181, 671, 672, 893, 895, 900, 904, 967, 1049
grammar 89, 201, 954
imperialism 63, 65, 1048
language education 32, 87, 419, 458, 490, 505, 748, 940, 973, 974, 1080
language immersion 71, 112, 657
language learners (ELLs) 30, 209, 211, 214, 226, 231, 233, 234, 310, 336–339, 341, 345, 346, 349, 350, 416, 417, 456, 630–634, 655, 663, 665, 666, 675, 676, 973, 974
language teaching (ELT) 15, 83–85, 92–94, 103–105, 213–215, 223–227, 231, 232, 299–301, 416, 417, 518, 521, 747, 855–857, 931, 1000, 1003–1007, 1009, 1013, 1014, 1047–1050, 1123, 1124
as a lingua franca (ELF) 7, 8, 128, 130, 132, 135–141, 143, 145–149, 151–153, 156, 415, 870
medium instruction (EMI) 5, 1055
medium school 201, 351, 352
monolingual ideologies 644
proficiency 17, 25, 27, 65, 66, 81, 92, 111, 113, 174, 193–195, 212, 216, 217, 219, 223, 351, 354, 357, 359, 360, 473–475, 798
as a second language (ESL) 13, 48, 72, 127, 146, 155, 200–202, 267, 268, 313–315, 318, 331, 376, 377, 443, 444, 456, 517, 518, 533, 809, 895, 1100, 1111, 1112
sociolects 870
for Specific Purposes (ESP) 151, 234, 245, 265, 268, 391, 393, 395, 397, 399, 401, 402, 404, 411, 412, 547, 665, 782, 887, 888, 890, 931, 940–942
Englishization 123, 129, 132, 134, 135, 137
English-only 6, 9, 25, 27, 28, 33, 34, 43, 75, 76, 78–83, 85, 135, 152, 177, 180, 182, 219, 225, 227, 228, 337, 338, 343, 1089, 1090
environment 336, 338, 1089
instruction 6, 9, 25, 27, 28, 33, 34, 43, 75, 76, 79, 83, 225, 226, 338, 682
policy 6, 33, 34, 43, 73, 75, 76, 78–83, 135, 152, 177, 182, 219, 227, 337, 531, 684, 1089
English-speaking 10, 11, 108, 109, 111, 112, 124, 125, 129, 174, 187, 189, 213, 216, 219–221, 249, 333, 334, 337, 338, 343, 349–354, 379, 382, 674–677, 799, 800
ability 453, 799, 1093
contexts 123, 211, 221, 318, 330, 333, 334, 417, 418, 453, 674, 799, 968, 1003, 1005
environment 200, 334, 338, 345, 379, 417, 439, 701, 799, 834, 1013, 1102
environment control strategies 729
epistemological
assumptions 234, 368, 376
foundations of applied linguistics 1034
framework 1024
grounds 891, 893
practices 883
shift 891
epistemology (*see also* naturalistic enquiry) 262, 374, 844
error correction 30, 790, 791
ESL
bandscales 440, 442–445, 450, 453, 455, 456, 490, 498, 510
classroom 84, 198, 287, 321, 402, 666, 678, 689, 758, 760, 872, 926, 979, 1001, 1050
educators 196, 262, 321, 444
learners 204, 232, 249–251, 253, 255, 257, 259–261, 263, 265, 267, 269, 314, 365, 366, 376, 439, 443–445, 447, 448, 453, 631, 704
learning 443, 446, 625, 631, 633, 636, 637, 679, 903, 1049, 1099
pedagogy 250–254, 366
programs 185–187, 189–191, 193, 195–197, 217, 219, 226, 288, 352, 380, 382, 388, 389, 424, 448, 1040, 1050

Subject Index 587

teachers   10, 86, 203, 207, 227, 234, 257, 266, 320, 321, 323, 344, 345, 365–370, 373–376, 383, 384, 386, 388, 433, 443, 688, 1055
ESP (*see* English for Specific Purposes)   234, 235, 245, 265, 391–401, 403, 404, 408–411, 431, 751, 782, 828, 931–933
 genre analysis   931
 language training curriculum   404
essayist-text literacy   876
ethical review boards   977
ethics   15, 34, 420, 483, 484, 518, 531, 1045, 1049, 1065
ethnic
 affiliations   617, 641, 664
 identity formation   641
ethnography   61, 235, 391–393, 411, 514, 617, 636, 647, 649–651, 655, 656, 658, 660, 665, 666, 975, 977, 978, 984–986, 1005–1007, 1023, 1027–1029, 1098, 1099
 case studies   658, 666
 data   660, 968, 977, 978, 986, 1019, 1098
 descriptions   656, 658, 1097
 findings   657, 1098
 methods   975, 984–986, 1097
 monitoring   204, 992
 research   234, 235, 391, 393, 411, 617, 649, 655–658, 968, 975, 977, 978, 984–986, 1005–1007, 1014, 1015, 1019, 1023, 1027–1029, 1099
 study   61, 393, 650, 660, 666, 872, 977, 978, 985, 986, 1029, 1045, 1047
 techniques   393, 514, 660, 986, 1019, 1023
ethnolinguistic
 identity   640, 649, 650
 minority groups   31, 642
ethnomethodological approach   1018
etic perspectives   977, 1018
EU (*see* European Union)   7, 123, 126–129, 131, 133, 134, 138
European immigration   108
European Union (EU)   7, 123, 127, 134, 135, 137, 142, 143, 150, 156, 165, 256, 421, 673
Europeanization   123, 134
evaluation strategies   740, 1085
evaluative   307, 377, 385, 670, 720, 748, 988, 1027

evidence-based practices   1071
exchange structure
 analysis   861, 868
 models   864
exchanges   66, 88, 222, 278, 314, 423, 425, 542, 543, 546, 622, 708, 710, 712–714, 725, 781, 862–865, 867, 907, 908, 910–912, 1132
ex-colonial languages   37, 39–41, 43
exemplary practices   994
expectancy of success   727
experience-based
 decision-making   1078
 skill   499
experiential
 function   849
 learning   706, 739, 743, 1132
 metafunctions   706, 846
expert teacher   1055
explicit   205, 206, 233, 234, 274, 275, 277, 290, 291, 319, 320, 329, 425, 535, 537, 539, 540, 778, 779, 783, 787, 788, 791–795, 831–833, 853, 854, 878, 879, 938, 939, 950, 951
 grammar instruction   779, 783, 793, 800
 knowledge   205, 252, 320, 397, 425, 537, 619, 714, 779, 783, 787, 788, 791–793, 795, 823, 833, 836, 938, 946, 950, 951, 957
 language instruction   290, 291, 794, 795, 979
 learning   205, 206, 276, 277, 319, 320, 328, 329, 516, 539, 619, 620, 698, 723, 753, 754, 768, 779, 783, 784, 788, 792–795, 831–833, 836, 837, 854, 938, 939, 1004, 1005
 pedagogy   205, 208, 766, 783, 809, 833, 885, 1106, 1111
 roles   1113, 1114
exploratory   151, 464, 520, 651, 690, 713, 810, 872, 902, 903, 967, 968, 976, 995, 1007, 1076–1078, 1082, 1083, 1114
 media   1114
 practice   713, 967, 968, 1076–1078, 1082, 1083
 talk   713, 872
 work   872, 967, 1076–1078, 1082, 1083
Exploratory Practice Centre   1077, 1082
expositions   536, 933
expression plane   850

external examiners 54
extracurricular activities 721
extralinguistic
  differences 1039
  factors 1036
extrinsic conditions 1036

F

face-to-face discussion 908–910, 970
facilitator 205, 514, 620, 725, 726, 731, 750, 998, 1108, 1114, 1115, 1117, 1122, 1123, 1129
faculty resistance 1116
familial conflict 641
Federal Law of Education (FLE) 107, 108, 111, 114, 116, 118
feedback 275, 277, 278, 286, 287, 291, 292, 296, 300, 419, 420, 425, 463, 491, 492, 498–500, 503, 508–511, 516, 517, 519, 520, 712, 729, 730, 845, 846, 862, 909, 910
female linguistic rights 140
feminism (also feminist) 198, 677, 1047, 1048
field 158, 159, 231, 305–309, 311, 391, 392, 394, 395, 397–401, 415–420, 477, 478, 534, 535, 739–743, 747–749, 843–846, 851, 852, 964–966, 980–983, 994–997, 999, 1007, 1008, 1010–1012
filter 673, 722, 949, 950
first
  class 912, 1116, 1134, 1135
  language (L1) 27, 44, 68, 69, 144, 173, 238–241, 243–246, 258, 259, 289, 290, 344, 345, 351–355, 359, 360, 394, 780, 813, 823, 936, 1070, 1072, 1090, 1091
FLE (*see* Federal Law of Education)
fluency 55, 77, 137, 162, 175, 195, 260, 272, 276, 285, 292–294, 297, 298, 301, 351, 352, 427, 478, 494, 783, 792–795, 799–801
  and accuracy 272, 276, 285, 293, 297, 301, 478
  promoting activities 792, 793
focus on form (FonF) 233, 281, 285–288, 299–301, 312, 518, 845, 856, 857, 932, 948, 956, 958, 1071
follow-up 164, 206, 462, 862, 864, 865, 909, 950, 1018, 1022, 1080, 1127
Ford Teaching Project 992

foreign language 66, 71–73, 87–89, 104, 105, 110, 113–116, 123–125, 133–135, 137, 138, 155–158, 162, 163, 165–167, 175, 283–289, 383–385, 673, 742–744, 915–917, 1124–1127, 1137, 1138
  classroom 3, 5, 68, 116, 165, 166, 283, 284, 286–288, 300, 513, 731, 735, 744, 763, 915–917, 985, 1000, 1004, 1005, 1050, 1125–1127, 1137, 1138
  education 41, 66–69, 71–73, 87–89, 104, 105, 107, 110, 113–116, 124, 125, 164–167, 181, 182, 283–285, 314, 315, 417, 915–917, 984, 985, 1049–1051, 1083, 1084, 1124–1127, 1137, 1138
  teacher 78, 103, 104, 284, 285, 287, 288, 417, 436–438, 511, 742, 744, 840, 916, 917, 945, 952, 984, 985, 1000, 1049, 1050, 1057, 1083, 1084, 1124–1127, 1137, 1138
  teacher education 284, 285, 389, 417, 471, 744, 916, 917, 952, 984, 1015, 1083–1085, 1125–1127, 1137, 1138
foreign-born students 657
formal register 876, 881
form-focused instruction 276, 283, 287
frequency 113, 155, 253, 292, 397, 778, 785, 790, 794, 798, 799, 801, 805, 806, 828, 830, 833, 836, 839, 840, 867, 1025
fricative 821
full
  access 813, 820, 822, 823, 848
  transfer 813, 820, 823
function 8, 26, 124–126, 130, 131, 138, 146, 148, 180, 221, 232, 237, 239, 240, 296, 297, 695–698, 722, 723, 726, 727, 828, 844, 849, 850, 1131, 1132
functional
  linguistic analyses 983
  roles 970, 1113, 1114, 1116, 1117, 1119
  roles for teachers 1116
  variation 140, 853
functional/notional model of English proficiency 474

G

gang affiliations 645
gendered identities 618, 641, 669, 671, 677
generalist teachers 1120
generalizability theory 480

Subject Index

generative
  grammar 786
  linguistics 784, 785
  theory 846, 848
generic
  approach 660
  structures 702
genre 58, 305, 308, 309, 311, 313–315, 392, 396, 397, 401, 402, 533–541, 544, 545, 547, 548, 716, 778, 781, 782, 851, 852, 856, 857, 869, 870, 887–890, 931–943, 1061
  structures 1061
genre-based approach 935–938, 941, 942
genres 305, 306, 308, 313–315, 394–402, 428, 429, 480, 481, 535–539, 545, 547, 716, 778, 781, 782, 856, 857, 869, 870, 876–879, 883, 884, 886, 887, 913, 926, 927, 931–943
gestures 170, 209, 425, 451, 538, 838, 920–922, 1019, 1020, 1028, 1036
global
  communications 1040, 1118
  community 672, 676, 870, 1068
  English 75, 83, 84, 123, 126–128, 132, 134, 135, 143, 152, 169, 895
  hypermedia 1113, 1115, 1117, 1119, 1121, 1123
  imperialism of English 22
  inequality 17, 18
  language 48, 75, 76, 85, 107, 115, 120, 126, 134, 135, 150, 151, 166, 171, 181, 671, 672, 871, 891, 893, 895, 900, 904, 967
  networks 75, 781, 891
  spread of English 18, 19, 76
globalization 32, 75–77, 79, 81, 84–86, 96, 115, 123, 124, 127–129, 134, 135, 137, 150, 153, 170, 178, 197, 200, 415, 416, 904, 905, 1047–1049
goals 33, 45, 65–67, 83, 211, 212, 221, 222, 224–227, 231–233, 237–241, 243–247, 280, 281, 320–323, 428–432, 434, 440, 443, 444, 493–496, 513, 721, 722, 726–729
government-initiated
  policy 440
  standards 440, 442
grades 53, 54, 56–60, 68–71, 75, 76, 79, 95, 99, 100, 163, 212, 310, 311, 321, 323, 324, 352, 383–385, 429, 729, 730, 768, 799–801, 923, 924, 1092–1094
grammar 6, 67, 68, 77, 89–92, 140, 141, 273–276, 285–288, 300, 301, 308–310, 314, 777–780, 783–786, 793–795, 813, 814, 843–858, 869–871, 932, 933, 939–941, 950–958, 1070, 1071
  checkers 1115
  instruction 6, 67, 68, 77, 92, 254, 273–275, 279, 280, 285, 287, 288, 295, 300, 301, 314, 622, 744, 753, 779, 783, 793, 800, 848, 849
grammar-translation method 67, 68, 89, 92
grammatical
  information 793, 847
  metaphor 307–309, 1035
  patterns 702
  terminology 951, 957
graphic
  literacy across languages 310, 315
  representation 309, 311
gratifying function 730
grounded
  accounts 983
  analysis 975, 1021
  theory (*see also* empirical research) 197, 986, 1074
  understanding 1023
group 201–208, 275, 276, 324, 325, 327–329, 351, 352, 361, 370–372, 467, 620, 640–648, 656, 657, 719–727, 731, 919, 920, 927, 1001, 1002, 1028, 1092–1097, 1104–1108, 1134, 1135
  cohesiveness 620, 719–723, 726, 1129
  dynamics 4, 238, 620, 642, 719, 720, 726, 731, 991, 1001, 1093, 1095
  norms 144, 324, 395, 500, 620, 645, 647, 719, 722, 723, 726, 1046
  roles 144, 257, 285, 371, 405, 498, 617, 620, 647, 712, 717, 719, 722–724, 969, 1096, 1114, 1119
  work 144, 145, 203, 206–208, 351, 352, 495, 496, 498, 640, 642, 645, 647, 712, 720–724, 772, 1028, 1057, 1058, 1091, 1092, 1094–1097, 1102, 1105–1108, 1134, 1135
group-orientedness 724
group-sensitive teaching practice 726
guided participation 628, 638
guides 29, 30, 215, 247, 1115

H

Hallidayan linguistics 1034
hedging 402, 868, 888
heritage language 224, 225
hierarchical mode 620, 725
higher education 52, 61, 76, 85, 89, 124, 125, 130, 131, 136, 182, 344, 376, 470, 474, 482, 485, 493, 503, 526–528, 547, 887–890
high-proficiency 791
high-stakes 213, 223, 417, 457–461, 463–465, 467, 469, 471, 491, 504, 528, 618, 684, 900, 972, 1096
  assessment 417, 457–471, 504, 505
  tests 223, 417, 457, 458, 460, 462, 463, 467, 528, 900, 972
high-track classes 979
Hong Kong 14, 15, 23, 351, 403–405, 407–412, 454–458, 461–465, 467–471, 491–494, 496, 502–504, 533, 534, 540–542, 742–745, 797, 798, 802, 803, 806–810, 1086–1089, 1091, 1092, 1098, 1099
Hong Kong Examination and Assessment Authority (HKEAA) 496
hybrid
  learning context 634
  register 709, 710
hypermedia 759, 907, 908, 959, 1113, 1115, 1117, 1119, 1121, 1123
  text types 1113
hypertext 756

I

ICT (see Information and Communication Technologies) 748, 749, 778, 891, 898, 899, 902, 969, 970 1113, 1114, 1116–1120, 1122, 1125–1136
  environment 1113, 1118
ICT-supported
  classrooms 1128, 1136
  context 1128
  EFL classroom 1127, 1131, 1132
  environments 1128, 1129
  learning environments 1127, 1131
  school-based projects 1135
ideational meanings 305, 307, 312, 868, 869
identity 185, 186, 195–198, 616–620, 625–633, 635–653, 655, 656, 660–666, 669–671, 673–675, 677–685, 705, 706, 887–890, 925–928, 985, 986, 1011–1016, 1041–1044, 1046–1052, 1071–1073, 1099, 1100, 1108–1112
  functions 133, 135, 152, 178, 231, 778, 923, 925
  negotiation 72, 170, 616, 625, 627, 670, 678–680, 706, 876, 965, 1046, 1047
  positioning 539, 616, 618, 627, 628, 632, 636, 646, 648, 661, 778, 1046
  processes 170, 195, 198, 435, 625, 626, 636, 640–643, 646, 648, 649, 705, 763, 887, 888, 1043, 1068, 1072, 1073, 1081
ideological models of literacy 892
IELTS (see International English Language Testing System) 474–480, 524
imagined communities 32, 34, 72, 197, 617, 618, 669–673, 675, 677–680, 887
imitation 245, 693, 696, 697, 880, 885, 1132
immersion education 110, 120, 121, 180, 181, 266, 268, 290
immigration 9, 80, 108, 109, 160, 172, 176, 182, 185–188, 190–195, 197, 198, 215, 220, 224, 259, 261, 502, 631, 641–643, 651, 652, 656, 657
  policy 9, 188
imperial
  language 13
  power 13, 18
imperialism 17, 18, 22, 23, 34, 35, 46, 50, 61, 63, 65, 71, 73, 84, 85, 128, 130, 135, 149, 152, 182, 213, 893, 894, 1097, 1098
implicit 4, 26–28, 31, 32, 214, 239, 244, 277, 287, 300, 353, 366, 376, 427, 512, 698, 699, 779, 783, 788, 789, 791–795, 1117, 1118
  knowledge 239, 244, 353, 354, 366, 376, 529, 764, 779, 783, 786, 788, 789, 791–793, 795, 936
  learning 27, 31, 32, 277, 287, 300, 354, 376, 533, 698, 757, 764, 779, 783, 784, 788, 792–795, 856, 1104
  roles 722, 1113, 1114
independent 8, 37, 39, 40, 113, 126, 137, 193, 195, 329, 352, 388, 394, 426, 427, 443, 444, 621, 721, 735, 736, 744, 788, 903

Subject Index 591

construction 195, 788, 790, 851
learning 37, 194, 329, 388, 426, 427,
    620, 621, 735, 736, 744, 745, 788, 800,
    837, 903, 1037, 1059
India 5, 16, 23, 24, 51–53, 55, 57, 59, 61,
    124, 156, 188, 201, 241, 672, 1044
indigenous
  languages 5, 34, 35, 37–47, 49, 157, 171,
    179, 672, 755, 972
  populations 453
individual
  cognitive phenomenon 1024
  plurilingualism 137, 147, 148
individualism 21, 27, 61, 180, 194, 441,
    739, 889, 976, 1040
individualization 438, 739, 742, 743, 1114
individualized voice 881
individualizing discourse 1037
inductive analysis 980, 983
information 291–294, 312, 318–320, 405–
    407, 425–427, 429, 430, 434–436,
    451–454, 477–480, 490–492, 507, 508,
    688, 689, 766, 767, 771, 772, 784–793,
    801, 897–904, 1113, 1114, 1118, 1137,
    1138
Information and Communication
    Technologies (ICT) 622, 781, 891,
    898, 907, 969, 1113
information
  economy 4, 9, 621, 735, 893, 1113, 1114,
    1118, 1121, 1122
  literacy 319, 634, 704, 749, 756, 760,
    764, 772, 791, 891, 895, 898–904, 914,
    915, 972, 1015, 1052, 1122
  revolution 492, 891, 897, 899
  superhighway 895, 899
inhibitive silence 1093–1095
initial survival and exploration phase 1053
initiating 712, 850, 862, 865, 886, 890, 909,
    1107
initiation-response-evaluation (IRE) 975
initiation-response-feedback (IRF) 708,
    864
inner circle of countries 51
insider-outsider dichotomy 663
inquiry-based teaching 754
in-service 96, 284, 380, 466, 492, 687, 745,
    953, 956, 959, 1058, 1067, 1072–1074,
    1079, 1083, 1097, 1131, 1136
  professional qualification program 1058

provision 96, 1072, 1073, 1079
trainees 953, 956, 1131
training 96, 380, 466, 745, 1073, 1074,
    1131
institutional
  discourses 648, 1043
  talk 966, 1017, 1018
  varieties of talk 966, 1017, 1025
instruction 3–11, 24–38, 40–46, 50–55,
    66–72, 111, 112, 160–164, 212–215,
    271–276, 278–291, 299–301, 319–321,
    323, 324, 345–347, 380–383, 431–439,
    696–699, 747–760, 797–800, 807–810
instructional
  conversations 357, 358, 709
  designers 1115, 1120
  materials 195, 213, 330, 433, 738
  methods 109, 162, 214, 222, 225, 915
  technologies 756
instrumental value 727
integrated digitalization 902
integration 7, 50, 66, 90, 119, 123, 127,
    128, 132, 139, 151, 185, 186, 232,
    249–253, 256–258, 268, 271, 310, 311,
    313–315, 1125, 1126, 1130
integrative 311, 314, 727, 751
  evaluation 311, 314
  value 727
integrator 1122
intelligence quotient (IQ) 244, 698, 699,
    783, 794
intentions of introducing tests 522
interaction 275, 276, 278, 283, 284, 286,
    287, 289–291, 293–296, 299–301,
    627–629, 633, 634, 700–703, 707–710,
    714–718, 751–755, 872, 873, 908, 909,
    966, 975–977, 985, 986, 1017–1020,
    1023–1030
interactional
  behaviors 1017
  hypothesis 275, 284
  options 708
  patterns 709, 716
  scaffolding 705
interactionist sociolinguistics 1097
interactive 214, 255, 279, 285, 290, 291,
    293, 294, 319, 346, 357, 420, 515, 529,
    530, 658, 702, 707, 758–760, 765–767,
    854, 855, 1026, 1027, 1128
  approaches 214, 279, 285, 291, 357, 420,

421, 854, 855
process   214, 255, 515, 529, 658, 851, 855, 937, 952
teaching   215, 255, 279, 285, 357, 515, 529, 658, 702, 759, 766, 855, 937, 952, 1106
intercultural communication   128, 130, 142, 147, 150–152, 170, 639, 640, 646, 685, 690, 942, 1051, 1052, 1079, 1126
interculturality   1035, 1042
interdisciplinary   391, 400, 401, 403–405, 407, 409, 411, 719, 886, 1034
  approach   403, 405, 407, 409, 411, 719
  research   391, 400–404, 719, 886
interethnic communication   1079, 1081
intergenerational conflict   641
intergroup competition   722
interlanguage (IL)   30, 35, 47, 151, 240, 241, 274, 277, 286, 287, 292, 294, 296, 299, 300, 676, 785, 813, 824, 947–949, 1023, 1025, 1028
  knowledge   241, 947, 948, 1023
  speakers   240, 241, 277, 676, 824
internalization   437, 619, 631, 693, 695–698, 700
international   6–8, 19, 20, 34–36, 49, 50, 64, 65, 67–73, 77, 78, 110–116, 120, 121, 128–130, 132–135, 138, 140–152, 165–167, 169, 170, 181–183, 234, 379–389, 648–653, 1203, 1204
  communication   17, 19, 32, 64, 66, 67, 115, 116, 129, 130, 132, 133, 138, 142, 146, 147, 149–152, 170, 247, 387, 525, 527, 685, 690, 911, 912
  language   6–8, 19, 23, 32, 34–37, 49, 50, 64–66, 68–73, 110–113, 115, 116, 132–135, 140–152, 165–167, 181–183, 379–389, 455, 456, 520, 521, 525–527, 895, 896, 958
  students   70, 71, 90, 96, 101, 112–115, 234, 314, 351, 352, 362, 379–389, 448, 474, 475, 651, 652, 658, 659, 664, 665, 690, 799, 804, 911, 912, 980
International English Language Testing System (IELTS)   474
internationalization   84, 125
Internet   4, 6, 64, 75, 84, 85, 100, 111, 169, 749, 755, 759–763, 765–774, 894–897, 901, 904, 905, 907, 913–917, 1114, 1117–1123, 1133–1135

communication   129, 673, 748, 749, 759, 762, 767, 861, 894, 896–898, 901, 904, 905, 907, 913, 915–917, 1127
interpersonal   239, 252, 305, 307, 353, 398, 430, 442, 616, 619, 620, 622, 706, 713, 714, 719, 720, 724, 731, 849, 850, 866, 869, 876
  function   239, 619, 849, 850, 876
  language   239, 252, 305, 353, 398, 442, 619, 620, 622, 623, 706, 713, 714, 719, 731, 849, 868, 869, 871, 876, 878, 879, 996, 1072, 1079
  meanings   252, 868, 869
  metafunctions   706, 849, 850
interpretative activity   1126
intertextual   539, 778, 876, 879, 880, 888, 1036
intertextuality   131, 397, 539, 756, 778, 781, 875, 879, 881, 883, 887–889, 930, 1047
intrinsic value   52, 727
intuitive practice   1075
investment   381, 408, 529, 625, 627, 628, 637, 651, 662, 669, 671, 678, 690, 986, 1041, 1051, 1054, 1089, 1099, 1100
involuntary minority groups   644
IQ (*see* intelligence quotient)   244, 698, 699, 783, 784
IRE (*see* Individual-Response-Evaluation)   915, 975, 979
IRF (*see* Individual-Response-Feedback)   708, 709, 711–713, 716, 909
  sequence   712, 909, 986
IT industry professional   1115
iterative
  analysis   983
  process   995
IT-supported English language teaching   1127

J

Japan   5, 6, 21, 23, 63–67, 69–73, 78, 85, 156, 157, 170, 181, 301, 380, 412, 677–679, 742, 1028
Japanese identity   65, 73
joint construction   205, 851

K

K-12 school years   52
kindergartens (also pre-schools)   78

Subject Index

knowledge   303–309, 311–315, 317–320, 349–357, 365–369, 374–377, 397–404, 493–498, 522–524, 701–705, 739–741, 782–789, 791–795, 828–831, 938–942, 945–959, 965–969, 1068–1075, 1107–1112, 1125–1132
  about language (KAL)   101, 112, 282, 714, 740, 938, 946, 950, 953–959, 1005, 1006, 1108
  in action   469, 965, 995, 1070, 1075
  construction   130, 205, 303, 307, 309, 377, 396, 398, 402, 469, 537, 616, 650, 689, 697, 701, 705, 764, 765, 985, 1048, 1049
  economies   203
  framework   97, 190, 233, 301, 303, 306, 313, 315, 319, 320, 366, 369, 426, 495, 725, 766, 779, 792, 798, 883, 1105
  providers   1115
  structures (KSs)   92, 190, 233, 252, 268, 303–307, 309, 311, 313–315, 388, 395, 412, 425, 513, 621, 702, 707, 744, 766, 813, 814

L

L1 (*see* first language)   8, 9, 27–29, 33, 69, 71, 75, 76, 111, 112, 130, 132, 139, 143, 144, 152, 155, 156, 158, 159, 165, 218, 232, 238, 241–244, 246, 247, 255–257, 263, 264, 271, 274, 275, 280, 281, 311, 334–338, 340, 341, 343, 345, 346, 382, 402, 447, 542, 696, 697, 783, 785, 790, 791, 793, 794, 799, 802, 813–816, 818, 820, 821–824, 838, 846, 848, 885–887, 915, 950, 984
  acquisition   274, 790, 791
L2 (*see* second language)   x, 8, 61, 68, 69, 72, 80, 111, 112, 132, 138, 143, 144, 155, 158, 159, 164, 231–233, 237–246, 253–256, 260, 263, 271–284, 303, 311, 333–339, 341–343, 345–347, 353, 393, 539, 615, 619, 639, 674, 676, 677, 693, 699, 701, 703–705, 708, 710, 712–714, 719–721, 727, 728, 753, 757, 763, 779, 780, 782–785, 788, 790–794, 800, 802, 811, 813–815, 817, 820, 821–824, 834, 838, 843, 845, 848, 854, 855, 885–887, 915, 945–947, 949–952, 954–956, 977, 980, 984, 1037, 1039, 1046, 1087
la langue   1034

la parole   1034
LA (*see* Language Awareness)   945–947, 950–954, 956
labial   813, 818
laggards   1116
laissez-faire leadership   724
language   3–11, 22–56, 63–73, 75–97, 107–116, 123–153, 155–167, 169–183, 188–228, 237–269, 271–293, 295–301, 333–341, 343–361, 379–389, 391–412, 415–440, 442–471, 473–485, 498–519
  acquisition   8, 155, 157, 158, 160–163, 165–167, 274–276, 284–290, 296–301, 333–335, 348–350, 516–518, 625, 626, 633–639, 783–787, 791–795, 824, 825, 839–841, 848, 849, 856, 857, 1025–1028
  acquisition process   8, 947
  analysis   31–36, 104, 286, 287, 310–314, 391, 392, 396, 449, 508–510, 517–519, 547, 548, 670–672, 868–870, 872, 873, 931–934, 952, 953, 966, 981–983, 1017, 1022–1025, 1027–1030
  analyst   132, 947, 1032
  assessment processes   419, 498, 505, 512, 514, 515
  awareness (LA)   49, 116, 147, 149, 151, 153, 159, 165, 167, 232, 237, 244, 286, 387, 433, 513, 945–949, 951–953, 955, 957–959
  benchmarking   404, 455, 457, 464, 469, 470
  choice   39, 44, 52, 88, 116, 128, 180, 203, 245, 260, 305–307, 310, 410, 445, 446, 460, 646, 647, 677, 847, 920, 921, 1127
  competence   66, 67, 115, 131, 133, 202, 239–241, 243, 244, 254, 255, 273, 274, 285–287, 317, 404, 410, 429, 436, 437, 475, 476, 672, 673, 717, 921, 922, 947
  context   6–9, 157–160, 199–201, 231–234, 252–256, 402, 403, 447, 454–457, 506, 621, 622, 637–639, 714–717, 737, 738, 777–781, 797–800, 849–851, 856, 857, 933, 937–942, 1005
  curriculum   6, 7, 87–89, 95–105, 110–114, 247–269, 365–369, 375–377, 403, 404, 406–408, 410–412, 437–440, 442–444, 454–456, 503, 504, 517–520, 757–760, 807–809, 1000–1002, 1015,

1016, 1101–1107
development 15, 16, 45–50, 87–91, 252–259, 286–292, 317–321, 334–338, 343–345, 372–377, 454–456, 481–484, 514–519, 697–702, 739–745, 797–802, 807–811, 967–972, 1067–1072, 1074–1083, 1101–1107
diversity 32, 127, 128, 132–134, 181, 182, 199–201, 208, 213–215, 261, 527, 666, 685, 690, 717, 767, 809, 810, 894, 921, 968, 969, 1000, 1001, 1099, 1100
ecology 7, 8, 11, 123, 127, 128, 134, 135, 182, 514, 632, 700, 893, 895, 985
education 31–52, 71–73, 103–105, 109–121, 164–167, 179–183, 255–258, 265–269, 453–456, 469–471, 688–690, 715–719, 957–959, 965–976, 984–986, 1047–1052, 1082–1085, 1097–1107, 1123–1127, 1136–1138
of empowerment 281, 666, 677, 689, 912, 996
features 111, 112, 141–146, 148, 232, 233, 253, 273, 274, 311, 320–322, 329, 330, 396–398, 410, 535, 538–540, 778, 789, 790, 812, 813, 851, 859–861, 933–938, 1078
function 8, 26, 124, 125, 131, 138, 146, 221, 232, 237, 239, 240, 292, 296, 297, 385, 419, 435, 508, 512, 619, 844, 849, 850
ideology 4, 6, 23–27, 29–36, 65, 82, 83, 103, 128, 130, 133, 170, 172, 174, 177, 180, 182, 183, 225, 261, 854, 856
of instruction 4–7, 11, 14, 25–34, 37, 38, 40–46, 48, 50–52, 55, 71, 75, 76, 111, 160, 161, 163, 164, 380, 439, 763, 798, 799, 808–810, 1085–1087
instructor 70, 194, 909, 1129
knowledge 93, 94, 243–246, 303–305, 311–315, 317–320, 352–355, 401–404, 522–524, 701–703, 739–741, 764–766, 782–789, 791–795, 811–814, 828–830, 945–951, 953–959, 965–969, 1068–1072, 1125–1127
learning 246–261, 283–288, 317–321, 327–331, 432–439, 510–520, 619–623, 625–640, 693–720, 733–745, 747–755, 757–761, 763–769, 934–943, 999–1007, 1009–1016, 1047–1052, 1099–1107, 1123–1128, 1131–1138

learning tasks 719, 738, 744
minority status 220, 642, 651
norms 35, 111, 123, 126–128, 130, 131, 140, 143, 146, 147, 149, 151, 165, 179, 232, 241, 330, 620, 722, 723, 781, 895, 897, 898
output 30, 118, 301, 319, 516, 615, 705, 708, 711, 717, 753, 757, 789, 848, 851, 857, 950
points 4–7, 9, 22, 26, 27, 32, 55, 65, 66, 92, 356–358, 537, 538, 626, 627, 632, 660, 661, 702, 705, 706, 708, 802, 803, 806, 807, 948, 949, 964, 965
policy 3–11, 33–40, 42–50, 71–73, 75, 76, 78, 79, 81–83, 127–129, 133–135, 146–149, 174, 175, 177, 178, 180–183, 199–201, 249, 250, 257–259, 262–265, 267–269, 467–471, 527–529
practices 5, 25–27, 38, 47–52, 232–234, 303, 313–315, 365–368, 391–394, 396–403, 487–489, 513–515, 616, 617, 625–637, 645–648, 887–889, 928, 929, 982–986, 1042–1044, 1049–1051
proficiency 65, 66, 101, 102, 110, 111, 155, 156, 158–166, 193–195, 223–226, 278–281, 349–354, 435–437, 458, 459, 469, 470, 473–479, 481–485, 487–489, 505–507, 528–530, 797–804, 806–809, 947, 948
proficiency testing 221, 470, 515
as a resource for meaning 305, 312, 315
socialization 83, 144, 231, 233, 303, 305, 633, 638, 641, 651, 652, 666, 670, 674, 759, 781, 854, 891, 892, 968, 978, 981–986
as system 950
systems 101, 102, 133, 158–160, 204, 256, 309, 416, 418–420, 444, 522, 523, 525, 527, 528, 688, 689, 753, 754, 786, 827, 847, 848, 895–897, 947, 1123, 1124
teacher 365–370, 415–423, 457–459, 461–471, 507–512, 514–520, 630–635, 707–713, 741–745, 861–864, 898–901, 945–959, 966–972, 994–996, 999–1002, 1066–1072, 1074–1085, 1102–1108, 1123–1129, 1136–1138
teacher development programs 83, 1074, 1079
teacher education 49, 50, 257, 284, 285,

Subject Index 595

376, 377, 417, 421–423, 433, 461, 462, 469–471, 916, 917, 957–959, 963–972, 1002, 1015, 1016, 1082–1085, 1097–1099, 1125–1127, 1129, 1131–1133, 1136–1138
  teaching 37–52, 77–97, 99–105, 111–116, 146–153, 223–227, 231–234, 271–291, 297–301, 365–369, 517–525, 930–942, 945–959, 967–972, 999–1007, 1009–1016, 1047–1052, 1075–1085, 1099–1112, 1123–1129
  user 39, 84, 128, 132, 152, 214, 240–247, 426, 443, 748, 754, 762, 871, 896, 913, 947, 953, 966, 1051
  varieties 3, 25–33, 35, 51, 78, 107, 115, 133, 141, 142, 147, 149, 150, 152, 156, 157, 250, 526–528, 767, 859, 863, 895, 896, 966
large scale testing (*see also* assessment) 487
large-scale corpora 854
late majority 1116
leadership styles 719, 724, 726
learner 274, 275, 277, 278, 291, 292, 422–425, 431–434, 488–491, 498–501, 506–511, 514–519, 615–617, 619–623, 724–728, 736–745, 750, 752–754, 833–835, 845, 846, 902, 903, 948–953, 1127–1129
  achievement 212, 225, 321, 337, 339, 348, 350, 434, 489, 494, 506, 508, 509, 515, 518, 616, 626, 650, 719, 730, 731, 1101
  autonomy 277, 620, 621, 728, 734, 736–745, 750, 759, 760
  beliefs 725, 727, 739, 740, 743, 745, 950, 952
  development 159, 238, 255, 274, 277, 292, 296, 320, 336, 424, 425, 431, 432, 444, 500, 515–519, 546, 616, 618, 619, 717, 739–743, 745
  identities 196, 616, 617, 620, 629, 632, 636, 639, 642, 644–646, 648, 649, 670, 671, 676, 898, 900, 1111
  learnability 784
  training 196, 432, 437, 517, 518, 621, 734, 739, 742, 743, 745, 951–953, 955, 1120
  learner-centered 28, 92, 162, 272, 275, 277, 278, 281, 320, 493, 731, 742, 902, 910,

1042, 1127, 1129
  activities 278, 493, 902
  approaches 28, 162, 1127
  teaching 128, 275, 277
learner-centeredness 750
learner-computer interaction 754
learner-learner interaction 754
learner-text interaction 754
learning 246–255, 299–301, 317–321, 327–331, 432–439, 487–503, 510–520, 619–623, 625–637, 699–720, 733–745, 747–755, 757–761, 763–769, 836–841, 999–1006, 1009–1013, 1099–1111, 1120–1129, 1131–1138
  activity 115, 134, 231, 259, 511, 512, 515, 619, 629, 630, 635, 637, 638, 693–695, 697–699, 705, 727, 728, 765, 766, 845, 855, 947, 948, 953, 976
  contexts 10, 11, 32, 33, 90, 203, 204, 207–209, 215, 317, 318, 367, 377, 393, 506, 507, 519, 520, 616, 617, 633–635, 672, 714–716, 891, 892, 934, 935, 1005–1007, 1126–1128
  management systems 1117
  strategies 94, 97, 101, 203, 204, 208–210, 233, 246, 247, 252–254, 317–321, 328–331, 429, 511, 728, 729, 739, 740, 759, 760, 802, 803, 833, 834, 837–840, 1107, 1108, 1110, 1111
  style coordinators 1115
  styles 207, 374, 387, 412, 490, 500, 627, 716, 719, 735, 750, 759, 861, 937, 950, 1123
  teaching 90, 91, 93–97, 99–101, 231–234, 280–288, 299–301, 491–496, 747–754, 831–837, 855–858, 934–942, 967–972, 999–1007, 1009–1016, 1047–1052, 1055–1057, 1061–1065, 1075–1081, 1099–1108, 1123–1128
learning-to-teach studies 1126, 1131
legibility conditions 847, 848
legitimate peripheral participation 628, 637, 700, 941, 1050
LEP (*see* limited English proficiency) xxi, xxii, 217, 222, 266, 683, 971, 1037
level of development 725, 849
lexemes 789, 790, 829
lexical
  entry 789
  feedback signals 866

items 91, 131, 697, 790, 847, 853
knowledge 793, 830, 831, 839
lexico-grammar 850
lexicon 4, 20, 165, 635, 789, 790, 795, 841, 847, 866, 867, 898
lexis 205, 273, 306, 310, 513, 536, 540, 710, 777, 853, 869, 876
lifelong learning 515, 517, 518, 743, 1203
Likert-scale 640
limited English proficiency (LEP) 266, 351, 676, 1037, 1093
linear
 order 790
 reading 792
lingua franca 7, 8, 76, 107, 108, 110, 111, 123, 124, 128, 130, 132, 133, 135–141, 143, 145–153, 156, 158, 167, 240, 415, 526, 527, 777, 870, 895
linguistic 6–8, 32–35, 113–115, 125–142, 158–161, 199–202, 273–276, 279–281, 334–339, 399–403, 533–540, 681, 682, 688–691, 843–846, 851–854, 893, 894, 907–911, 1085, 1086, 1088–1091, 1096–1099
 anthropology 646, 1034
 awareness 47, 108, 131, 133, 140, 147, 151, 159, 160, 167, 232, 234, 237, 242, 303, 388, 782, 945, 948, 949, 957–959, 1094
 capital 132, 133, 176, 380, 397, 688, 893, 1036, 1088, 1089, 1093
 colonialism 17–19, 23, 35, 50, 61, 85, 531, 1088, 1097, 1098
 competence 7, 67, 77, 115, 126, 128, 131, 133, 240, 244, 273, 274, 285, 392, 410, 509, 544, 545, 632, 676, 779, 823, 824
 corpora 397, 777, 779
 and cultural backgrounds 356
 description 137, 139, 141, 305, 309, 514, 840, 844, 861, 936, 1039
 discrimination 29, 32, 50, 182, 257, 335, 815, 825, 968, 1085, 1098, 1099
 diversity 7, 10, 35, 63, 69, 123, 127, 128, 132–134, 136, 149, 182, 199, 200, 207, 208, 213, 223, 684, 685, 690, 767, 893, 894, 968, 969
 factors 129, 201, 223, 334, 335, 400, 534, 755, 948, 1036
 features 108, 141, 146, 158, 273, 279, 309, 320, 392, 395, 397, 410, 534, 535, 538–540, 778, 845, 846, 851, 852, 861, 933, 935, 936
 identities 30, 198, 200, 216, 227, 387, 539, 616, 618, 625, 626, 646, 648, 671, 675, 682, 689, 690, 706, 778, 1098, 1099, 1111
 imperialism 17, 18, 22, 23, 34, 35, 46, 50, 61, 63, 65, 71, 73, 84, 85, 128, 130, 135, 149, 152, 182, 227, 893, 894, 1097, 1098
 input 163, 274, 275, 279, 539, 630, 754, 757, 778, 802, 848, 851, 949, 1028
 models 34, 45, 73, 135, 147, 161, 167, 255, 273, 410, 512, 533, 534, 539, 786, 958, 1046, 1099, 1115
 pluralism 175, 1040
 practices 41, 47, 48, 50, 61, 77, 84, 305, 392, 400–403, 513, 514, 533, 534, 625, 626, 630, 632, 634, 635, 646, 647, 684, 893, 894, 1088, 1098, 1099
 profile 41, 199
 repertoires 147, 630
 resources 6, 7, 79, 147, 209, 241, 305, 309, 387, 397, 512, 514, 618, 625, 626, 630, 634, 635, 684, 685, 704, 851, 852, 920, 1088
 socialization 305, 534, 641, 651, 854, 968
 tensions 7, 47, 1085, 1086, 1088, 1089, 1091, 1093, 1096, 1097
 units 115, 392, 694, 812, 844, 935
 variation 29, 30, 140, 141, 399, 400, 940, 941
linguistically deficient 673
linguistically-mixed groups 1092, 1095, 1096
linguists 3, 4, 31, 34, 69, 126, 139, 239, 271–276, 278, 282, 545, 699, 702, 783, 784, 787, 844, 856, 859, 1025, 1026, 1033
listening
 comprehension 77, 318, 331, 476, 480, 658, 759
 skills pedagogy 866
literacies (also multiple literacies) 36, 83, 86, 180, 312–314, 394, 399–402, 650, 666, 690, 749, 758, 761, 781, 875–877, 883, 884, 888–895, 897, 898, 900–905, 1122, 1123
literacy 27–29, 33–36, 199–210, 260–262,

350–358, 387, 388, 399–402, 443–445, 455, 456, 517–519, 632–638, 681–686, 689–691, 716–718, 763–767, 875–878, 883–905, 914–916, 940–942, 1011–1015
  acquisition 27, 29, 210, 284, 285, 388, 518, 547, 626, 633, 634, 636, 637, 666, 716, 717, 758, 800, 839, 857, 878, 886, 890, 984
  to adults 9, 1122
  education 34–37, 42, 44, 196, 197, 209, 210, 227, 259, 260, 267, 268, 313, 444, 455, 456, 689, 690, 716–718, 809, 887–891, 898, 902–905, 930, 1014, 1015, 1110–1112
  learning 204–210, 260–262, 284, 285, 303, 447, 517–519, 615, 616, 626, 629, 632–638, 690, 691, 716–718, 749, 757–760, 763, 764, 773, 774, 856–858, 890–892, 900–905, 1011–1014
  pedagogy 34, 85, 205, 208, 225, 285, 547, 616, 618, 635, 637, 650, 666, 686, 689–691, 763–767, 774, 887, 888, 903–905, 971, 972
  practices 27, 55, 58, 61, 391, 392, 400, 401, 518, 534, 618, 629, 633–637, 646, 647, 684, 685, 876, 877, 883–886, 891–893, 903–905, 922, 928, 982–984
local articulations 1035, 1037
localization 76
localized pedagogical expertise 81
logocentric context 922
longitudinal study 182, 369, 510, 840
low-proficiency 791
low-track mainstream classes 979

M

mainstream 10, 203–205, 207–212, 216–221, 223–225, 234, 249–255, 257–269, 313–315, 343–346, 365–369, 373, 375–377, 381, 383, 384, 674–677, 978, 979, 985, 986, 1104–1109, 1111, 1112
  approach 209, 251–253, 257, 265, 267, 314, 331, 389, 1026, 1104
  curriculum 10, 146, 199, 200, 204, 207, 209, 210, 212, 232, 234, 248–253, 255–269, 313, 314, 343, 365–369, 375–377, 701, 979, 980, 1101, 1104, 1111, 1112
mainstreaming 207, 217, 257–259, 314, 369, 377, 969, 979, 1101, 1104, 1108, 1109, 1112
managerial role 1129
mandated assessment policies 510
marginalization 131, 179, 525–527, 617, 641, 642, 644, 810, 965, 981, 983, 1037, 1068, 1074, 1079
meaning-based instruction 275, 276
meaning-focused activity 948
measure of language proficiency 505
mediated
  action 628–630
  classroom practices 625
medium
  of communication 138, 170, 200
  of education 44, 701
  of instruction 4–6, 14, 25–29, 31–34, 38, 41–45, 48, 50–52, 71, 92, 111, 135, 164, 256, 351, 352, 417, 439, 462, 803, 809, 810
mentor teacher 321, 754, 1064, 1118
mentoring 321, 754, 1061
message redundancy 710
metacognitive 118, 158, 254, 328, 728, 738, 740, 745, 839, 884, 886, 948
  awareness 738, 884, 948
  control strategies 728, 729
  knowledge 158, 740, 745, 947, 948
metadiscourse 394, 538, 547, 778, 864
metalanguage 397, 547, 766, 938, 951
metalinguistic
  awareness 162, 163, 167, 247, 705, 948, 951, 957
  knowledge 469, 705, 791, 957, 958
metaphoric roles 969, 1113–1115
methodology 27, 29, 30, 61, 84, 100, 105, 116, 191, 192, 194, 220, 246, 247, 274, 285–287, 300, 759, 760, 973, 974, 1002, 1017, 1018, 1082, 1083, 1120
microcontexts 875
micro-ethnographic approach 1022
micro-level
  acts 864
  analyses 973, 974, 976, 977, 983
middle ground 1038
migration (see also immigration) 32, 57, 181, 186, 198, 400, 653, 656, 657, 666, 1079
minimalist program 846–848

minimum language standards   464
minority stereotype   648
mixed
  methods   983
  mode   1121
mode   242, 292, 305, 311, 500, 534–536,
    538, 540, 545, 546, 620, 704, 710, 725,
    726, 737, 741, 778, 779, 849, 850,
    920–922, 924, 925, 929
  continuum   704, 710, 778
model
  minority   644, 648, 651, 1099
  texts   937
modeling   205, 206, 246, 320, 323, 329,
    535, 704, 722, 723, 759, 794, 795, 851,
    914, 942, 1034
modernism   189, 891
modes of facilitation   725
modifier   1122
modularity issue   784
monitoring
  acquisition   621, 736
  work   1096
monocultural instruction   707
monoculturalism   130, 131, 618, 678
monolingual   5, 8, 10, 18, 37, 110, 127, 128,
    138, 158–160, 162, 201, 211, 224, 231,
    237, 240–243, 280, 634, 635, 675, 676,
    683, 684
monologic instruction   707
morphology   335, 697, 705, 753, 780, 814,
    823, 844, 846
mother tongue (*see* language)   xxii, 4, 5, 15,
    22, 31, 34, 35, 37, 41–43, 46, 47, 49,
    52, 107, 115, 131, 138, 164, 167, 173,
    188, 215, 216, 232, 234, 238, 247, 257,
    260, 333, 338, 339, 340, 341, 343,
    345–347, 350, 351, 379, 380, 381–385,
    387, 388, 534, 787, 790, 861
motivating classroom
    environment   719–721, 723, 725, 727,
    729, 731
motivation   93, 94, 138, 142, 150, 162, 201,
    216, 255, 256, 283, 522, 620, 621, 652,
    669, 670, 707, 726–729, 731, 742, 743,
    752, 911, 912, 1063, 1064
motivational
  dimensions   728
  psychology   620, 719, 726, 729
  teaching practice   719, 726, 729

motivators   1115
moves   4, 65, 96, 123, 171, 173, 175, 177,
    180, 206, 291, 308, 410, 490, 616, 712,
    716, 855, 862–864, 883
multicultural
  contexts   348
  education   652, 689, 690, 706, 713, 717,
    1100, 1102
  language   690, 986
  urban classrooms   632
multiculturalism   176, 180, 186, 189, 190,
    197, 198, 265, 268, 893, 895, 901, 976,
    1006, 1015, 1016, 1039, 1040, 1044,
    1047, 1049, 1050, 1102
multiethnic schools   203, 1093
multilingual
  approach   46, 47
  authors   677
  classrooms   210, 268, 678, 941, 1093,
    1094, 1111
  communities   160, 689, 1088
  contexts   201, 203, 204, 208, 209, 258,
    386, 894, 1047, 1051, 1086
  education   165–167, 1097
  literacies   892, 905
  and multicultural   5, 37, 40, 45, 47, 63,
    64, 66, 72, 166, 167, 210, 303, 524,
    618, 679, 688
  policy   48, 49
  schools   160, 208, 968, 1049, 1085–1088,
    1091, 1093, 1094, 1097–1099
  speaker   158, 159, 676
multilingualism   7, 45–47, 49, 50, 64, 114,
    123, 127, 135, 137, 147, 148, 150, 151,
    159, 165–167, 169, 170, 201, 263, 264,
    679, 680, 892–894, 901, 902, 1051
multiliteracies   650, 683, 684, 690, 764,
    766, 767, 774, 778, 781, 808, 891–893,
    895, 897–901, 903–905, 919, 920,
    927–930, 939, 940
Multiliteracies Project   808, 920, 928, 929
multimedia   6, 100, 309, 735, 748, 751, 758,
    760, 767, 781, 901, 905, 907, 912–914,
    929, 939, 984, 1117, 1118, 1128
  center teacher   1117
  literacies   914
multimodal
  assessment   929
  classrooms   921, 930
  contexts   891

Subject Index

discourse 781, 919, 930
pedagogies 779, 782, 919–923, 925–929, 1052
work 928
multimodalism 893, 896, 902
multimodality 312, 415, 778, 781, 854, 897, 904, 919, 922, 926–929
multiple 8, 9, 158, 170, 256, 257, 395, 396, 418, 449, 460, 530, 544, 545, 632, 636, 637, 645–647, 656, 657, 892, 893, 904, 905, 919–922, 975, 976, 984–986, 1098, 1099
choice questions 474, 656
cultural identities 170, 645, 646
identities 9, 170, 387, 616, 618, 625, 626, 632, 636, 637, 645–647, 649, 651, 657, 669, 671, 677, 885, 985, 986, 1033, 1098, 1099, 1111
language 8, 9, 158, 170, 256, 257, 303, 317, 423, 460, 469, 525, 529, 530, 627, 628, 632, 669, 767, 779, 857, 919–922, 941, 1098, 1099
linguistic codes 625, 634
literacies 400, 877, 892, 904, 905, 941, 1099, 1122
semiotic modes 779, 919, 920
sources of authority 1068
worlds 626, 637, 893, 904, 921, 968, 1087, 1089, 1098
multiskilled individuals 1120
mundane conversation 1017

N

narratives 23, 69, 252, 523, 627, 630, 635, 648, 650, 651, 653, 869, 879, 895, 933, 980, 1003, 1005, 1009, 1012–1015, 1043
nasal 813, 821
national assessment 193, 512
National Council for Accreditation of Teacher Education (NCATE) 1125, 1138
for Language in Education (NCLE) 946
national identities 671, 672
National Literacy Strategy (NLS) 204, 207, 210, 1111
native speaker competence 241
native-like pronunciation 68, 353, 815
native-speaker (NS) (*see also* near-native speakers) 8, 127, 139, 140, 143, 148, 231, 385, 756, 782, 801, 945, 954, 957, 1037, 1072
fallacy 954
nativism 784, 793
naturalistic 510, 824, 863, 864, 870, 964, 974, 994, 1034, 1121
enquiry 994
patterns 864, 964
spoken materials 870
nature of test performance 505
NCATE (*see* National Council for Accreditation of Teacher Education) 1125, 1138
NCLB (*see* No Child Left Behind) 10, 11, 211, 212–215, 222–226, 416, 491, 497
NCLE (*see* National Council for Language in Education) 946, 958
near-native speakers (*see also* native-speakers) 240, 246, 815
needs analysis 235, 391, 392, 406, 411, 478, 617, 658, 665, 883
research 658
negotiation of meaning 143, 146, 170, 281, 291, 292, 296, 297, 299, 300, 634, 705, 708, 711, 754, 851, 1030, 1060, 1127
neo-behaviorist discipline 694
neo-colonialism 17, 22
neologisms 898, 1035
Netherlands 73, 124, 127, 157, 389, 483, 758–760, 783, 824, 959, 984, 986
neurobiological function 786
neurocognitive
mechanics 793
studies 788
new literacies 891, 892, 900, 904, 905, 1099
New London Group 684, 690, 766, 767, 774, 892, 903, 905, 920
new rhetoric 401, 539, 547, 778, 782, 931–934, 936, 941, 942
New Zealand 156, 157, 186, 379, 418, 424, 473, 474, 525, 1050
nihilism 1044
NNS (*see* non-native speaker) 78, 79, 80, 945, 947, 949, 950, 952, 954, 955, 956, 1037, 1042
nomadology 1035, 1048
non-accent 1094
non-native 84, 85, 134, 135, 139–143, 146–148, 150–152, 156, 157, 166, 167,

242, 243, 291, 384, 458, 676, 814–817, 870, 871, 876, 877, 880, 881, 885, 942, 957, 958, 1027, 1028
  dialects 870
  speaker (NNS) 78, 151, 242, 278, 291, 300, 676, 820, 885, 1027, 1028
  speaker (NNS) teachers 78, 886
  users 140, 146, 867, 871
norm 10, 30, 78, 128, 149, 158, 159, 199, 200, 241, 245, 324, 328, 330, 339, 416, 424, 489, 494, 495, 617, 722, 723, 968, 969
norm-building procedure 723
norm-referenced testing 495
North American functionalists 849
noun phrase (NP) 784, 847
NP (*see* noun phrase) 784, 847
NS (*see* native-speakers) 75–82, 945, 949, 954, 955, 956, 1027
nuclear exchange 712
numerator 1024, 1025

O

objectives-driven curricula 423
observation 16, 43, 104, 139, 142, 147, 174, 252, 272, 274, 288, 315, 356, 452, 642, 643, 659, 988, 1013, 1044, 1045, 1061
Office for Standards in Education (OFSTED), England 268, 455, 1103, 1112
official
  curricula (*see* curriculum) 109
  language of instruction 1087
  language (*see* language) xxiii, 6, 9, 33, 37, 39, 40, 42, 43, 44, 46, 51, 65, 66, 71–73, 78, 84, 108, 110, 148, 155, 157, 161, 162, 172, 175, 176, 180, 182, 185, 186, 188, 189, 190, 524, 525, 527, 921, 1087
  participatory rights 707
online 246, 481, 748–750, 753–755, 758–761, 777, 784, 786, 787, 829, 833, 840, 860, 896, 897, 899, 900, 905, 907–909, 913–917, 951, 1114–1123, 1137, 1138
  communications 896, 913, 916, 1118, 1137
  contact 1119
  degree programs 1115
  discussion 749, 755, 908, 909, 914, 915, 1114, 1115, 1117
  education 759–761, 899, 905, 915, 917, 1114–1116, 1118, 1119, 1137, 1138
  learning environments 1117, 1120
  tutorial 1115
online-forum 900, 1135
open-ended questions 979
opposition 22, 33, 61, 174, 395, 463, 636, 661, 664, 666, 672, 937, 984, 1039, 1098
oppositional stance 1116
optimal
  language learning 701
  leadership style 620, 724
oral
  academic presentations 977
  assessment 463
  proficiency 79, 80, 278, 279, 312, 314, 324, 483–485, 502, 519, 868, 873
  proficiency interview 312, 868
ordinary conversation 966, 1017–1019, 1025
orientalism 13, 18, 21, 79, 85, 1051, 1098, 1100
orthographic input 791
outcomes-based
  approach 442
  assessment 445, 454, 461, 469, 513, 518, 999
  curriculum 440, 445
outer circle 51, 61, 120, 141, 151, 156, 167, 958
overt correction 790

P

packages 386, 702, 1118, 1119
palatal 811, 818, 819, 824
  fricatives 819
  stops 818, 819, 824
panel chair 1058–1061, 1064
paper-and-pencil tests 418, 460, 465, 467
paradigmatic assumptions 1034
paralinguistic 425, 1039
parallel distributed processing (PDP) 786
parameters theory 846
participatory
  action research 992, 995, 999, 1000, 1002
  model 500
patterns 3, 17, 21, 89, 243, 290, 294, 303,

Subject Index 601

308, 312, 335, 361, 394, 453, 454, 616, 709, 716, 785, 786, 853, 854, 975, 976
pedagogic 55, 130, 146, 153, 204–206, 210, 250, 251, 254, 256, 261–265, 294, 297–301, 368, 391, 445–447, 533, 534, 543, 948, 949, 1070, 1071, 1073–1075
  appropriacy 393
  content knowledge (PCK) 366, 368, 374, 948
  freedom 265
  grammars 787, 844, 845
  imperialism 1070, 1073
  knowledge 205, 256, 261, 265, 303, 366, 368, 374, 376, 447, 513, 787, 948, 949, 951, 967, 1069–1071, 1073–1075
  potential 146, 294, 951, 1075
  relations 366, 376
  structure 205, 299, 301, 844
pedagogies of transformation 1037, 1043
pedagogy 48, 49, 83–85, 249–255, 285–287, 618, 619, 684–687, 689–691, 715, 716, 763–768, 774, 840, 841, 866–871, 903–905, 919–921, 926–929, 970–972, 1041–1044, 1046–1051, 1081–1083, 1104–1107
peer 202, 216, 217, 233, 311, 329, 340, 347, 353, 418, 516, 517, 628–630, 642, 645, 647, 651, 909–911, 981, 983–985, 1087–1089, 1104, 1105
  groups 329, 347, 628, 642, 645
  social capital 1087–1089
  teaching 202, 418, 494, 517, 661, 726, 801, 916, 969, 1085, 1104, 1105
peer-feedback 909, 910
perception 40, 66, 133, 185, 186, 201, 247, 307, 350, 352, 392, 489, 501, 541, 542, 621, 660, 694, 695, 780, 794, 795, 817–819, 822–824
performance 99, 292–294, 296–301, 327–329, 339, 340, 407–410, 416–418, 421–426, 428, 431–434, 436–438, 440–444, 452, 456–461, 473–480, 482–485, 488–491, 497–500, 505–508, 698–700
  criteria 425, 431, 461, 479, 498, 500, 507, 513, 1096
  standards 97, 98, 120, 223, 339, 416, 417, 421–424, 428, 431, 433, 434, 436–444, 447, 449, 452, 458, 461, 479, 497, 498, 507, 510, 513

performance-based curriculum 428, 437
performative utterances 1037
performativity 984, 1035–1037, 1051, 1071, 1074, 1077, 1082
permanent residents 63, 657
personal
  autonomy 733, 745
  literacies 892
phatic exchanges 864
phenomenological approach 1018
phonemes 786, 787, 790, 815–817, 821
  coronal phonemes 817
phonetic information 791
phonetics 89, 94, 97, 247, 791, 824, 1059
  epenthetic vowel 822, 823
phonological
  structure 811, 812
  theory 811, 821, 825
phonology 131, 135, 143–145, 151, 167, 219, 247, 273, 335, 616, 777, 779, 780, 799, 800, 811, 813, 815, 817, 819, 821, 823–825
  allophones 815
  alveolar distinction 818, 819
  alveolar ridge 818
pivot move 712
place of articulation 813
placement 193, 209, 354, 358, 478, 504, 506, 523, 655, 664, 665, 683, 1104
plagiarism 781, 875, 876, 879, 880, 883, 885, 887–889, 907, 909, 913, 914, 916
plan 6, 78, 95, 128, 133, 134, 185, 192, 197, 203, 242, 293, 319, 343, 357, 365, 366, 404, 423, 789, 790, 1075, 1135, 1136
policy directions 63, 65, 67, 69, 71, 73
political 4, 5, 17–19, 31–36, 39–41, 76–78, 87, 88, 123, 126, 127, 161, 171–178, 185, 186, 257, 393–395, 521–523, 630, 631, 662, 663, 893–897, 996, 1040, 1044, 1045
population mobility 199, 200
portfolio assessment (*see* assessment) 420, 490, 493, 494, 498, 509
positivism (*see also* empirical research) 395, 1035, 1071
positivist research 1039
positivistic
  assumptions 966, 1034
  inquiry 1034

postcolonial
  contexts 141, 661, 671, 672
postcolonialism (*see also*
  colonialism) 1044
Postgraduate Certificate in Education
  (PCED) 1058
post-alveolar segments 817
post-method pedagogy 272, 282, 286
postmodern
  literacies 898, 902
  perspectives 645, 1040, 1083
postmodernism 645, 646, 652, 669, 891,
  1035, 1044, 1046, 1048, 1051, 1052
postsecondary
  contexts 655
  institutions 617, 655–657, 660, 665
  settings 655–657, 659–661, 663, 665,
  667
poststructural
  ideas 1037, 1041, 1046
  researchers 1042
  teachers 1043, 1045
poststructuralism 639, 669, 976,
  1033–1035, 1037–1039, 1041,
  1043–1047, 1049, 1051
poststructuralist theory 632, 638, 653, 690,
  1052
practical classroom teaching 1054
practice 199, 200, 204–208, 262–265, 271–
  273, 275–279, 303–308, 502–505,
  516–519, 625–630, 635–638, 716–719,
  741–744, 758–760, 892–895, 953–959,
  963–965, 997–999, 1044–1052, 1073–
  1084, 1108–1112
practitioner research 28, 987, 1000
pragmatic
  competence 151, 239, 273, 717
  functionalism 849
PRC (*see* China) 89
prefix 813, 836
preschools (*see* kindergarten) 85, 220, 352,
  675, 982, 1100
prescriptive 376, 394, 416, 423, 448, 812,
  937, 967, 1064, 1110
preservice 356, 376, 517, 687, 777,
  951–953, 956, 1001, 1016, 1097, 1125,
  1131, 1137
  courses 777, 952, 953, 956, 1125, 1131
  teachers 356, 376, 517, 951, 953, 1001,
  1097, 1125, 1131, 1137

TEFL training (*see* teaching English as a
  foreign language) 951
  trainees 951, 953, 956, 1131
  training 356, 376, 517, 777, 951–953,
  1131, 1137
primary
  language 166, 218, 349, 354, 363, 454,
  513, 880, 1085, 1086, 1095, 1096
  schools (*see* elementary schools) 6, 41,
  42, 87, 88, 93, 95, 96, 99, 104, 133,
  159, 162–164, 166, 204, 288, 442, 463,
  464, 468, 510, 519, 547, 798, 803–805,
  807, 869, 923, 946, 957, 1055, 1062,
  1066, 1111, 1112
Prism Model 333–335, 337, 338, 341–347
private speech 693, 696, 697, 700
problem-based learning 903
problem-posing 618, 686, 902, 1043
procedural
  dimensions 953, 955, 956
  TLA (*see* teacher language awareness)
  955
procedures 118, 147, 187, 193, 202, 205,
  272, 274, 282, 289, 298, 418, 419, 451,
  459, 460, 507, 509, 510, 530, 1076–
  1078, 1103, 1104, 1126–1128
process of self-regulation 146
process-oriented 713, 719, 1077, 1104
professional
  autonomy 946, 1079
  development 112, 113, 209, 210, 356,
  358, 372–376, 381, 386, 418–420,
  431–433, 435, 436, 443, 491, 492, 494,
  495, 497–500, 967, 968, 1052–1057,
  1059–1068, 1070, 1076–1078, 1083
  evaluation 458
  identity 368, 967, 969, 1067, 1071, 1073,
  1078–1081, 1111
  knowledge 404, 410, 412, 449, 512, 846,
  957, 968, 969, 1015, 1082, 1101, 1105,
  1108–1111
  participation 1043
  relationships 203
  standards 207, 210, 315, 416, 433, 443,
  470, 474, 476, 946, 953–955, 969,
  1107
professionalism 130, 131, 404, 433, 435,
  437, 441, 946, 968, 1067, 1069, 1072,
  1074, 1076, 1079, 1080, 1082, 1083
proficiency 65, 66, 79–81, 110, 111, 155,

Subject Index 603

156, 158–166, 193–195, 216–219, 221–226, 278–281, 349–354, 435–437, 452–455, 458, 459, 469, 470, 473–479, 481–485, 487–489, 505–507, 797–804, 806–809
program standards 421, 431, 437, 438
project learning 739
pronunciation 29, 68, 78, 143, 151, 166, 246, 335, 353, 425, 465, 466, 541, 634, 780, 800, 812, 814, 815, 822–825, 829, 1057
proposition 33, 172, 175, 259, 261–263, 265, 266, 268, 341, 343–345, 348, 535, 695, 798, 843, 852
prosody 781, 859
prototypicality 932
psychoanalytic theories 632, 641
psycholinguistics 151, 152, 166, 247, 248, 280, 295, 694, 794, 795, 843, 855, 1034
  psycholinguistic approach, perspective 233, 289
psychometric 415, 419, 475, 482, 504, 507, 511–514, 520, 522, 640, 973
psychosocial
  processes 640
  theorists 641
public examinations 465, 467, 1088
pushed language 712

Q

qualitative research 298, 506, 518, 760, 886, 964, 965, 973–975, 978, 983–986, 994, 1014, 1016, 1027, 1097, 1126
quality assurance 945, 1060, 1061, 1086
quantitative research 964, 974–976, 1024
queer theory 1041, 1050

R

racial
  conflict 191
  minority groups 642
  tensions 1085, 1086, 1088, 1092–1095, 1097
racialized discourses 1093
racism 29, 31, 80, 85, 189, 197, 198, 201, 315, 644, 650, 926–928, 968, 976, 982, 1044, 1085, 1095, 1097, 1098, 1102
rational thinking 695
real-time communication 779, 907

recounts 305, 869, 933
reductionist curriculum (*see* curriculum) 703, 706
reference grammars (*see* grammar) 844, 845
reflection 118, 213, 215, 258, 303, 304, 320, 358, 373, 374, 386, 453, 494, 507, 523, 546, 621, 686, 698, 1035, 1074–1077, 1082, 1083
reflective
  conversation 754, 760, 1075
  methods 741
  practice 873, 959, 1067, 1074–1078, 1084
  practitioner 741, 1066, 1083
  thinking 1075
reflexivity 966, 978, 1041, 1043–1045, 1069, 1078, 1080
regional variation 950
register 158, 169, 243, 246, 307, 353, 359, 400, 425, 429, 465, 704, 705, 709, 710, 715, 716, 830, 833, 845, 857, 871, 941, 942
  of science 705
register-meshing 709
re-imagining 689
re-intermediation 1121, 1122
relational imitation 1132
remedial 206, 219, 345, 347, 381, 644, 682, 883
  students 345, 883
repair practices 966, 1017, 1018
representation 171, 309, 311, 644, 645, 647, 648, 651, 663, 664, 759, 781–785, 787, 788, 792, 793, 817, 823, 847, 881, 919–922, 924, 925, 928, 929, 984, 1033
representational resources 684, 779, 919, 920, 922, 924, 928, 929
research 25–29, 104, 105, 286–291, 297–301, 393–406, 410–412, 481–484, 517–520, 633–637, 655–658, 715–720, 757–760, 963–968, 972–979, 981–1003, 1005–1011, 1013–1016, 1023–1029, 1074–1077, 1130–1136
resistance 4, 22, 42, 64, 80, 83–85, 128, 374, 449, 637, 648, 651, 652, 661, 664, 669, 671, 678, 679, 689, 980–982, 1043–1045
response 80, 81, 178, 254–256, 287, 288,

475, 543, 544, 666, 708, 807, 862, 864, 872, 889, 897, 898, 915, 916, 920, 921, 932–934, 987, 1027–1029, 1074, 1075
responsibility   10, 34, 48, 52, 96, 112, 191, 192, 194, 207, 216, 355, 363, 366, 481, 742, 743, 1069, 1070, 1079, 1103, 1107, 1128, 1129
retrospective self-evaluation   620, 727, 729
rewards   26, 212, 222, 223, 226, 491, 721, 728–730, 833, 878, 998
rhetoric   14, 15, 17, 19, 58, 76, 79, 80, 127, 264, 391, 392, 394, 395, 401, 402, 538, 539, 547, 844, 931–934, 936, 938, 940–942, 1047, 1048, 1119, 1120
rhetorical
  analyses   392, 395
  purpose   852, 932
  structure   933
role identity   1097
roleplay   749
rules of pronunciation   812

S

scaffolding   280, 310, 311, 319, 355, 357, 451, 511, 512, 540, 619, 623, 686, 703, 705, 711, 715, 716, 726, 754, 807, 851, 856
schema   201, 252, 1054
schematic structure   933
school   6–11, 41–45, 66–72, 87–102, 104, 105, 109–114, 159–166, 199–212, 215–228, 265–269, 317–321, 333–369, 372–377, 379–389, 439–443, 797–801, 1054–1065, 1085–1092, 1096–1104, 1108–1112
  curriculum   6, 7, 87–89, 93, 97–105, 109–111, 202–204, 248–253, 255–259, 263–269, 318–320, 355, 356, 358, 359, 365–368, 403, 404, 439–442, 686, 687, 701, 702, 803–805, 807, 808, 1101–1106
  literacies   314, 650, 892, 900, 902, 904, 905, 914, 1049
school-aged learners   439–441, 443, 445, 447, 449, 451, 453, 455, 710
school-based
  assessment   496, 502, 509, 518
  curriculum development   999
  materials development   1059
school-wide pedagogical interventions   1096
science discourse   702
scientific
  concepts   702
  method   283, 975
Scotland   160, 1082, 1102
SCT (*see* socio-cultural theory)   693–695, 697, 699
second language (L2)   155–159, 237–241, 265–268, 284–288, 298–301, 347–351, 516–520, 700, 701, 715–719, 758–760, 794, 795, 809–811, 822–825, 887–890, 914–917, 939–942, 957–959, 1000–1004, 1026–1029, 1047–1051
  education programs   185, 186, 189
  acquisition (SLA)   8, 157, 158, 165, 166, 247, 274, 284–291, 298–301, 348–350, 482, 516–518, 625, 626, 638, 639, 716, 717, 783, 792–795, 824, 825, 839–841, 856, 857, 966, 1026–1028
  classrooms   198, 201, 213, 285, 287, 300, 318, 347–349, 446, 461, 616, 625, 632, 633, 856, 857, 916, 917, 936, 937, 939, 941, 984, 985, 1049, 1050
  competence   16, 115, 166, 202, 207, 231, 237, 239, 241, 244, 246, 274, 285–287, 317, 437, 444, 483, 717, 823, 824, 984, 985
  curriculum   110, 247–249, 253, 257, 267, 268, 366, 367, 376, 377, 439, 440, 443, 444, 454–456, 484, 485, 517–519, 687, 701, 758–760, 809, 915–917, 939, 940, 1000–1002, 1111, 1112
  grammar   241, 267, 274, 276, 285–288, 300, 301, 310, 314, 402, 705, 783, 794, 795, 813, 822, 823, 843, 856, 857, 939, 940, 957, 958, 1048, 1050, 1051
  learning   267, 268, 284–288, 299–301, 317–319, 331, 515–520, 631–633, 669–671, 679, 680, 700, 701, 715–719, 743, 758–761, 792–795, 839–841, 856–858, 915–917, 939–942, 1010–1013, 1048–1051
  literacy   199–201, 207, 210, 267, 268, 313–315, 387, 388, 443, 444, 447, 455, 456, 517–519, 626, 632, 633, 689, 690, 716–718, 758–760, 856, 857, 887, 888, 914–916, 940–942, 1011, 1012

Subject Index 605

phonology 616, 779, 780, 799, 811, 815, 823–825
syllabus 16, 120, 247, 274, 286, 287, 300, 402, 437, 743, 809, 941, 959
user 240, 241, 243–247, 871, 966, 1051
writing 61, 394, 401, 402, 454, 455, 482–484, 491, 547, 548, 666, 760, 783, 794, 875, 876, 880, 881, 887–890, 907–910, 912, 914–917, 940–942, 984, 985, 1047, 1048
secondary schools 7, 67, 68, 77, 81, 87–90, 92, 93, 99, 100, 103, 104, 189, 194, 200, 204, 206, 222, 266, 312, 364, 366, 367, 376, 377, 807–810
segmental 812, 823
segments 9, 449, 460, 812, 813, 815–818, 868, 870, 1022
segregation 174, 178, 215, 224, 641, 647, 969, 1107
self-access 734, 735, 738, 739, 743–745, 954, 956, 969, 1118
   centre 734, 744
   learning 735, 738, 739, 743–745, 969, 1118
   multimedia resource centers 735
self-assessment 329, 420, 432, 434, 436, 511
self-correction 711, 873, 1029
self-directed speaking 694
self-evaluation of teacher talk (SETT) 952
self-management of learning 736, 738, 739
self-motivating strategies 728
semantic
   activity 860
   plane 850
semiotic 300, 309, 398, 617, 638, 646–648, 774, 779, 782, 851, 854, 872, 897, 919–921, 925, 928, 930, 941, 966, 1014
   activity 309, 398, 779, 920, 928, 966, 1036
   practices 398, 617, 646–648, 779, 782, 920, 928, 1036
   production 928, 1036
separation 28, 35, 311, 641, 1095, 1132
sibilant 813
signalling 152
signifier 1035
silent period 451, 700, 1091
simplification 708, 806, 1039

simplified tasks 703
site 16, 84, 169, 218, 388, 656, 682, 687, 701, 750, 760, 808, 921, 922, 966, 970, 999, 1033, 1041, 1042, 1046, 1052
situated learning theory 670
skilled work force 238
skills-based instruction 634
SLA (see second language acquisition) 26–28, 139, 150, 158, 164, 237, 241, 247, 265, 274–276, 278, 284, 287, 290, 296, 299, 300, 333, 335, 345, 506, 516, 533, 626–628, 630, 633, 636, 639, 649, 670, 676, 701, 705, 748, 753, 757, 789, 811, 848, 851, 855, 1017, 1019, 1022–1026, 1034, 1037
social 30, 31, 261–267, 303–311, 391–398, 615–620, 625–643, 645–653, 681–691, 694–701, 715–720, 763–766, 853–857, 891–898, 919–925, 930–942, 970–976, 1026–1030, 1033–1037, 1048–1053, 1087–1089
   awareness 47, 48, 233, 242, 373, 386, 393, 396, 452, 537, 641, 708, 713, 718, 808, 912, 942, 959, 973, 974, 996, 1094
   construction 130, 139, 185, 198, 227, 309, 319, 396, 398, 402, 519, 536, 538, 546, 616, 627, 641, 764, 765, 1018, 1019, 1027
   context 9, 92, 231, 305, 314, 318, 319, 402, 447, 538, 539, 638, 639, 642, 643, 649, 650, 715, 716, 856, 857, 891, 892, 920–922, 933, 935, 937–942, 987, 988
   differences 139, 158, 173, 178, 185, 200, 224, 257, 305, 319, 395, 615, 616, 639, 643, 647, 673, 963, 964, 990, 1033, 1036
   integration 66, 139, 232, 249, 250, 257, 258, 262, 304, 313, 315, 641, 673, 679, 905, 978, 1126
   practices 5, 25–27, 47, 48, 170, 249, 250, 303–309, 313–315, 391, 392, 400, 401, 514, 515, 616–618, 625–630, 632–636, 646–648, 684, 685, 876, 883, 891–895, 1018, 1042
   processes 9, 116, 123, 170, 257, 258, 307, 308, 318, 319, 335, 397, 398, 514, 625, 626, 642, 643, 646, 648, 649, 705, 892, 987, 988, 1023, 1068, 1072, 1073
   psychology 395, 617, 620, 637, 639–641,

646, 649, 651, 690, 695, 698, 699, 716, 718–720, 731, 857, 1007, 1034
relationships 13, 47, 48, 144, 145, 254, 305, 386, 395, 397, 430, 515, 516, 615, 617, 619, 626, 636, 661, 682, 695, 707, 764, 765
roles 26, 144, 242, 307, 617, 618, 627, 629, 632, 633, 678, 707, 715, 741, 964, 971, 1030, 1052, 1096, 1113, 1114, 1117, 1122, 1123
semiotics 781, 873, 919, 930, 1051
theory of language 396, 699, 854, 919, 933
variation 30, 31, 235, 391, 398, 853, 940, 941, 950
social-contextual 975
socially
  constructed 626, 628, 636, 655, 656, 665, 693, 877, 934
  distributed cognition 1024
  oriented research 644
socially-mediated cognitive development 630
social-semiotic systems 851
societal multilingualism 137, 147, 148
society for information technology and teacher education (SITE) 1130
sociocognitive
  psychological 703
  traditions 701
sociocultural 24, 27, 214, 218, 231–233, 294–296, 334–336, 343–346, 452, 615, 619, 625–632, 637, 638, 693, 699–701, 705, 715–718, 766, 857, 1046
  approach 232, 233, 289, 294, 296, 305, 693, 695, 697, 699, 700, 716, 854, 1022
  identity 231, 434, 619, 625–628, 631, 632, 635, 637, 638, 640, 643, 705, 1041, 1046
  perspectives 233, 289, 415, 625, 626, 628, 631, 691, 700, 716, 718, 742, 857, 941, 985, 1046
  processes 232, 334–336, 338, 341, 346, 348, 625, 626, 640, 700, 705, 774, 855, 941, 952
  theoretical framework 640, 952
  theory (SCT) (*see also* Vygostkian theory) 26, 27, 227, 233, 280, 284, 295, 300, 415, 615, 619, 628, 629, 640,

693, 699, 700, 717, 718, 766, 855, 857, 1046, 1050
socio-educational 5, 52, 60
  contexts 976
  practices 5, 51, 52, 60
  problems 973
sociohistorical theories 626
sociolinguistics 30, 134, 135, 151, 152, 156, 166, 273, 335, 429, 647, 672, 674, 860, 872, 976, 983, 1034, 1039, 1041, 1048, 1049, 1097
  norms 1039
  perspectives 976, 1048
  practices 976, 983
sociology 23, 34, 35, 49, 50, 85, 151, 152, 181, 267, 392, 395, 531, 547, 639, 643, 650, 651, 666, 723, 860, 878, 889, 890, 1018, 1019
sociopolitical 3, 4, 11, 17, 33, 36, 79, 181–183, 434, 495, 631, 661, 690, 706, 707, 717, 964, 976, 985, 1100
  conflict 17, 33
  context 4, 11, 36, 660, 690, 717, 985, 1100
  elites 394
  statement 707
sociopsychological frames 1041
socio-rhetorical communities 875
South Africa 4, 31, 34, 44–47, 83, 85, 444, 455, 525, 661, 672, 676, 680, 781, 782, 875, 876, 919, 921, 922, 926, 927, 929, 930, 984
South Korea 77, 78
Southampton KAL project 950
Spanish-speaking ethnic groups 643
speaking rights 713, 862
specialist 10, 203, 204, 207–209, 219, 251, 257, 260, 286, 363, 366–369, 374, 376, 386, 387, 399, 400, 410, 704, 1101, 1105, 1107, 1108, 1119, 1120
  discourse 399, 704
  language teachers 10, 285, 1085, 1119
  teaching software 1120
speech 30, 144, 145, 149, 150, 176–179, 278, 477, 478, 480, 481, 634, 635, 693–697, 700, 786, 787, 789–795, 844, 860, 861, 869–872, 894–896, 979, 980, 1017, 1018, 1025, 1091–1093
  behavior 180, 242, 627, 696, 1025
  communities 48, 126, 140, 149, 170, 635,

Subject Index

869, 887, 895, 896, 921, 1081, 1093
  exchange systems 1017, 1025
  segmentation 791, 793
spiraling curriculum 979
spoken 25, 26, 37, 126, 143, 144, 146, 156, 157, 223, 237, 425–429, 443, 535–537, 702–704, 714, 715, 780–782, 804, 805, 854–857, 859–861, 865–873, 923–925, 936
  corpora 781, 845, 854, 859, 870, 953
  discourse 146, 149, 171, 251, 463, 478, 536, 539, 619, 620, 702–704, 714, 715, 780, 781, 828, 829, 839, 854, 856, 857, 859, 861–863, 865, 869–873
  interaction 143, 144, 146, 426, 427, 429, 443, 519, 778, 855, 859, 864, 868, 870, 872, 1017
  language 25, 26, 126–128, 143–146, 156, 157, 237, 251, 426–429, 463, 483, 525, 535–537, 619, 620, 714, 715, 778–782, 795, 799, 800, 854–861, 868–873, 921–925, 979, 980
  language use 146, 426, 427, 697, 828, 859, 860, 938, 979
spread of English 4, 7, 13, 17–19, 24, 32, 63, 69, 76, 127, 129, 135, 149, 151, 156, 170, 474, 526, 967, 972
stabilization phase 1053
stakeholder involvement 407, 457, 458, 464
standard 19, 20, 25–34, 61, 78, 79, 126, 128, 145, 146, 178, 179, 181–183, 203, 214, 224, 225, 307, 324, 327–329, 423, 427–430, 450–452, 462, 463, 647
  deviations 324, 328, 329
  English 8, 19, 20, 23, 25–34, 61, 78–80, 126, 128, 145–147, 152, 178, 179, 181, 182, 214, 218–220, 224, 225, 462, 527, 672, 673, 677, 870, 871
  language 19, 20, 25–34, 51, 61, 78–80, 126–128, 178, 179, 181–183, 214, 224, 225, 247, 385, 427–430, 462, 463, 527, 531, 672, 673, 763, 764, 1091, 1099–1101
  language ideology 26, 27, 29–34, 183, 1094
  written English 214, 312, 429, 921
standardized 10, 25, 29, 35, 87, 211, 212, 223, 226, 264, 324, 327, 329, 330, 339, 344, 350–352, 416, 453, 498, 499, 506, 524
  assessment 327, 339, 358, 416, 432, 453, 456, 489, 497–499, 506, 507, 512, 514, 898, 915
  measures of achievement 506
  multiple-choice tests 498
  test scores 358, 501
standards 97, 98, 222, 223, 310, 311, 313–315, 416, 417, 420–425, 427–431, 433–464, 469, 470, 495–498, 507, 509, 510, 512, 513, 517, 519, 520, 895, 946, 953–955, 998, 999, 1103, 1104
  approach 267, 310, 376, 422–424, 428, 430, 433, 435–437, 441–445, 448, 451, 495, 497, 507, 513, 953, 969, 999, 1002
  for literacy 260
  for teacher certification 457, 458
  for workplace 421, 422
standards-based 213, 315, 417, 421, 423, 425, 427, 429, 431, 433, 435–437, 440, 442, 445, 455, 497
  approaches 420, 421, 423, 425, 427, 429, 431, 433, 435, 437
  movement 417, 421, 428, 431, 435–437, 440
  reform 417, 436, 440, 442, 455
state-wide exams 54
statistical processes 195
stereotype 5, 63, 644, 648, 651
stigmatization 632, 647, 648
stigmatized varieties 28, 29, 31, 32
strategies 22, 23, 94, 151, 152, 203–210, 213, 214, 223, 224, 233, 252–255, 317–321, 328–331, 728, 729, 739, 740, 759, 760, 833, 834, 836–840, 884, 885, 980–983, 1078–1080, 1095, 1107–1111
strategy training 742, 838
stretched language 712
structural accuracy 846
structure 5, 93, 94, 192–194, 205, 251, 290, 295, 296, 306, 307, 311, 371, 410, 534, 535, 537–539, 806, 807, 811, 812, 820–823, 843–847, 859–861, 931–933, 971, 972
structure-based
  production tasks 295
  teaching 251, 276
student 257–260, 310, 311, 333–336, 355–

360, 502–504, 540, 616–618, 626–628, 662–664, 697, 698, 703, 705–712, 725–731, 764, 765, 799, 800, 875–890, 907–911, 968–972, 979–981, 1129–1138
  agency   207, 323, 660, 663, 927
  interaction   82, 278, 420, 423, 465, 510, 516, 627, 658, 703, 705, 707, 709, 710, 712, 714, 716, 721, 752, 908, 909, 1028
student-centered
  educational thought   733
  learning   753, 1114, 1115
student-student interaction   703
subject   16, 110–112, 163, 164, 208–210, 251–255, 365–369, 372–377, 384–387, 399, 463, 464, 533–538, 540–547, 701, 702, 803–808, 813, 945–948, 950, 951, 953–956, 1070, 1104–1107
  content   10, 164, 234, 251–253, 281, 284, 310, 319, 321, 366–369, 373–376, 381, 385, 428, 429, 459, 463, 702, 803, 804, 806–808, 948
  disciplines   367–369, 372–374, 709, 878, 1070
  positions   372, 375, 1037
  specialists   210, 321, 365–369, 373–376, 386, 399, 409, 436, 478, 483, 1072
subjectivity   133, 135, 180, 645, 682, 850, 854, 978, 998, 1014, 1036, 1037, 1042, 1047, 1049
subject-matter knowledge   945–947, 950, 953–956
subject-related
  discourse   704, 714
  registers   704
subject-specific approach   950
subjugated knowledges   1037
summative feedback   419, 509
Sweden   37, 131, 135, 138, 352
syllabic segmentation   791
syllabification   820
syllable   789, 791, 812, 820–822, 844
  boundaries   791, 822
  structure   789, 812, 820–822
symbolic
  architectures   784
  capital   669, 1036
symbolism   784, 793, 923
symmetrical interaction patterns   294

synchronous communication   762, 909
syntax   20, 68, 219, 242, 243, 294, 299, 335, 353, 705, 753, 769, 777, 780, 801, 812, 814, 823, 824, 846, 853, 1028, 1029
systematic   26, 29, 32, 92, 107, 112, 115, 130, 131, 191, 243, 263, 264, 304, 315, 392, 404, 416, 418, 539, 540, 844, 845, 1059
  analysis   29, 131, 392, 540, 975, 983
  descriptions   975
systemic functional linguistics (SFL)   233, 252, 303, 305, 306, 309, 313, 373, 396, 535, 538, 619, 701, 702, 851, 887, 933, 941, 983, 1051

T

talk-in-interaction   966, 1017–1019, 1023–1025, 1028, 1029
target language   3, 25, 27, 29, 31, 32, 78, 79, 178, 276, 277, 279–281, 283, 284, 461, 462, 627, 628, 639, 640, 752, 753, 807, 808, 848, 949, 950, 955, 956, 970, 1127, 1128
task   233, 280, 281, 283, 284, 287–301, 318–320, 423–425, 452, 462, 463, 476–478, 483, 519, 520, 619, 666, 703, 704, 721–725, 729, 730, 738, 752–754, 815–817, 1136–1138
task-based
  assessment (TBA)   320, 460, 519
  learning (TBL)   16, 239, 299, 301, 1138
  research   298
teachability hypothesis   849
teacher   75–84, 203–210, 365–377, 415–424, 457–459, 461–471, 507–512, 707–717, 739–745, 861–864, 898–903, 945–959, 963–972, 994–1002, 1052–1057, 1061–1089, 1093–1099, 1102–1108, 1117–1134, 1136–1138
  assessment   311, 404–406, 412, 413, 415–422, 436, 437, 449–453, 457–459, 463, 464, 466, 467, 469–471, 487–492, 495, 496, 498–500, 502, 504, 505, 507–520, 533, 534, 929, 1103, 1104, 1106, 1107
  autonomy   436, 620, 621, 725, 733, 739–745, 750, 946, 1002, 1069, 1079
  cognition   300, 636, 782, 952, 956, 957, 1052, 1082, 1084
  courses   209, 266, 399, 415, 433, 437,

489, 496, 659, 777, 952–954, 956, 958, 970, 979, 1012, 1054, 1055, 1085, 1125, 1126, 1130, 1131
curriculum   6, 7, 95, 96, 103, 104, 206, 257, 266, 355, 356, 365–368, 372–377, 437, 438, 440, 503, 504, 509–511, 709, 710, 958, 959, 970–972, 992, 999–1002, 1014–1016, 1103–1108
development   49, 50, 82, 83, 318, 319, 323, 344, 345, 356, 357, 374–377, 418–422, 433, 516–519, 533, 534, 543, 544, 739–743, 952–954, 956, 967, 968, 999–1001, 1052–1057, 1059, 1061–1083
education   49, 50, 81–83, 375–377, 389, 421–424, 436–438, 458–462, 469–471, 741–745, 957–959, 963–972, 1001, 1002, 1014–1016, 1052–1055, 1064–1066, 1082–1089, 1097–1100, 1125–1127, 1129–1133, 1136–1138
as entrepreneur   1115
feedback   277, 278, 296, 374, 419, 420, 457, 463, 465, 489, 491, 492, 503, 508–511, 516, 520, 542, 708, 712, 729, 730, 845, 846, 862, 917
interaction   82, 205, 217, 231, 254, 278, 296, 301, 305, 420, 464, 465, 510, 707, 709, 710, 714, 741, 872, 873, 908, 909, 1026–1028, 1127
intervention   204, 209, 255, 620, 719, 965, 1095
language awareness (TLA)   782, 945, 947, 949, 951, 953, 955, 957, 959
metalinguistic awareness   163, 948, 951, 957
professionalism   433, 437, 946, 968, 1067, 1069, 1072, 1074, 1076, 1079, 1080, 1082, 1083
programs   6, 83, 103, 284, 285, 406, 416, 417, 421–423, 431, 436, 437, 459, 491, 492, 749, 750, 952, 954, 955, 968, 1043, 1077–1079, 1097, 1098, 1125, 1126, 1129–1131
reflection   213, 373, 374, 453, 708, 965, 968, 972, 1001, 1074–1076, 1082, 1085
research   418–420, 453, 454, 510–512, 515–517, 741, 742, 757, 919, 950–952, 956–958, 963–965, 967–973, 991–1002, 1014–1016, 1065–1067, 1069–1071, 1074–1077, 1082–1087, 1097–1099, 1124–1127, 1130–1136
as researcher   398, 916, 996, 1002
roles   259, 285, 1114, 1127, 1129
standards   207, 208, 222, 223, 416, 417, 420–424, 431, 433, 434, 436–438, 440, 441, 443, 449–454, 457–463, 469, 470, 509, 510, 512, 519, 520, 946, 954, 955, 958, 959, 969, 1103, 1104
thinking   207, 314, 509, 713, 945, 994, 1004, 1008, 1045, 1065, 1067, 1069, 1074–1076, 1082–1084, 1092
training providers   207, 208
teacher-based assessment   416, 418, 419, 453, 489, 499, 510, 518
teacher-centered methods   1128
teacher-student interactions   616, 627, 703, 709, 851
teaching
English as a foreign language (TEFL)   146, 945
English as a second language (TESL)   155, 267, 376, 958, 1111
literature   271, 385, 926
methodology (*see also* teaching methods)   27, 29, 84, 105, 220, 239, 246, 286, 287, 300, 315, 415, 719, 857, 994, 1002
style   1063
technical
economy   178
language   702
technologies   233, 303, 313, 474, 480, 502, 621–623, 629, 630, 747, 748, 750, 751, 755–758, 781, 891, 898, 907, 915, 916, 937, 969, 970, 1113, 1114, 1120–1123
technology
enhanced language learning   748
integration   1130
resource people   1115
TEFL (see teaching English as a foreign language)   945, 947, 951, 952, 954, 955, 1060
metalanguage   951
tenor   305, 311, 535, 545, 849, 852
tertiary settings   511, 876, 1116, 1119
TESL (*see* teaching English as a foreign language)   197, 288, 470, 483, 679, 905, 951, 986, 1015, 1048
TESOL Quarterly   34, 35, 84–86, 198,

285–287, 299, 300, 331, 376, 377, 481–484, 636–638, 665–667, 679, 680, 856, 857, 871–873, 889, 890, 941, 983–986, 998–1002, 1026–1028, 1049–1052, 1098–1100

TESOL (*see* teaching English to speakers of other languages) xxi, 23, 34, 60, 84, 150, 166, 182, 198, 266, 278, 299, 310, 311, 415, 417, 418, 421, 422, 428, 431–434, 436, 441, 443, 453, 510, 512, 513, 678, 801, 978, 983, 994, 995, 998, 1038, 1041, 1085,

Test of English as Foreign Language (TOEFL) 64, 113, 418, 473–483, 524, 528

tests 10, 92–95, 99–101, 104, 222–226, 323–325, 327, 339–341, 350–352, 417, 418, 457–460, 462–470, 473–484, 487–490, 492–494, 496–498, 501–506, 519–525, 527–531, 951

text 205, 206, 305–309, 311, 312, 314, 397, 398, 536–540, 545–547, 752–757, 777–781, 797, 798, 801, 802, 804–808, 828, 829, 849–855, 879–881, 913–916, 932–936, 940–942, 1010, 1011, 1120–1122

   analysis 309, 311, 397, 400, 402, 538, 540, 548, 748, 853, 872, 888, 910, 916, 932–934, 940, 1007, 1022, 1023, 1058, 1136

   coherence 305, 538, 778, 792

   types 206, 305, 306, 308, 477, 478, 481, 547, 755, 756, 778, 807, 850, 860, 861, 914, 933, 936, 984, 1113, 1120–1122

textbooks 5, 6, 13, 18, 25, 29, 30, 40, 51, 52, 55, 57–59, 61, 84, 89–92, 95, 100–103, 308–310, 661, 766–768, 770, 771, 804, 805, 974, 975

textual 61, 135, 181, 305, 400, 534, 538, 539, 545, 622, 715, 759, 764, 778, 849, 850, 869, 879, 880, 883–887, 928, 929, 934–937, 1046, 1047

   function 849, 850

   information 764, 849, 850, 937

   meanings 622, 764, 850, 868, 869

theory 26, 27, 271–275, 299, 300, 309, 310, 391, 392, 538–540, 619, 636–640, 650–653, 689–691, 693–695, 697–700, 715–718, 741–743, 794, 795, 845–848, 851–857, 939–941, 963, 964, 1050–1052

thinking 21–23, 61, 160, 172, 179, 233, 261, 303, 310, 312–315, 452, 493, 503, 509, 546, 765, 807, 940, 1075, 1083, 1084

third
   ground 919, 921, 922, 928
   party 1122

TLA (*see* teacher language awareness) 782, 945–956

traditional 6, 7, 77, 221, 379, 380, 415, 416, 418, 419, 522, 622, 623, 698, 699, 763, 764, 766, 768–770, 774, 777, 779–782, 843–846, 863, 864, 910, 923–925, 1127–1130

   grammar 77, 92, 251, 402, 622, 661, 738, 744, 764, 768, 769, 777, 779, 780, 843–847, 853, 855, 924, 939

   grammar teaching 661, 768

   testing 221, 415, 416, 419, 497, 501, 512, 522, 619, 698, 699

transactions 51, 182, 410, 426, 429, 430, 862, 863, 869

transcript 924, 1019–1021, 1026, 1031, 1032

transcription 410, 781, 859, 865, 1020, 1022, 1031, 1032

transcultural identities 645

transculturation 1035, 1042, 1052

transformational grammar 273, 538, 778

transformative 5, 48, 622, 669, 684, 689, 696, 707, 753, 763, 765–768, 774, 903, 924, 928, 971, 972, 997, 1043, 1044, 1052, 1079–1081

   language pedagogy 669, 766

   pedagogy 5, 48, 669, 707, 753, 763–768, 774, 903, 928, 971, 972, 1043, 1044

transitional bilingual education 345, 346

transitions 663, 889, 979, 982, 1068, 1073

transmission 7, 11, 113, 210, 368, 481, 637, 751, 767, 768, 878, 902, 903, 953, 971, 972, 1114, 1126

   approaches 7, 368, 971, 1114

   education 7, 210, 637, 768, 902, 903, 1126

   knowledge transmitter 6, 101, 861, 971, 1132

transnational 125, 380, 646, 648, 1035, 1040

   identities 256

Subject Index 611

triangulation 507, 973–976
t-tests 325
turn-taking 709, 865–867, 873, 966, 979, 1017, 1018, 1029
two-way bilingual education 255, 256, 264

U
UK (also United Kingdom) 9, 10, 49, 50, 124–126, 199–201, 227, 237, 249, 250, 300, 314, 315, 389, 407, 520, 679, 735, 794, 795, 858, 859, 945, 946, 1047–1049, 1051, 1052, 1101, 1102
unilinear stage model 641
United Kingdom (UK) 7, 9, 130, 160, 187, 246, 379, 418, 422, 424, 444, 453, 505, 534, 650, 781, 875, 876, 903, 1101, 1102
United States of America (USA) 781, 875, 876, 895
universal grammar (UG) 784, 785, 813, 822, 844, 848, 856, 1034, 1048
universities 49, 52, 54, 67, 76, 89, 125, 129, 400–403, 454, 455, 473–477, 479, 481, 482, 656–659, 662–664, 878, 879, 887–889, 1057, 1058, 1130–1132, 1134, 1135
University of Cambridge Local Examinations Syndicate (UCLES) 112, 113, 433, 438, 457, 460, 475, 482, 959
university entrance 6, 63, 67, 194, 417, 473, 534

V
validity 325, 347, 348, 416–420, 440, 444, 445, 448–453, 456–458, 460, 461, 476–478, 482–484, 494, 495, 501, 502, 505–508, 510, 512, 517–519, 521, 522, 531, 974, 975, 998
variation 26, 29–32, 93, 111, 140, 141, 144, 158, 170, 193, 218, 232, 235, 398–400, 416, 417, 439, 642, 871, 937, 940, 941, 950
velum 818
verb phrase (VP) 843, 847
verbal
  description 1021, 1031
  narratives 925
  participation 1093

vernacular
  education 14, 51
  medium 52, 54, 55
Vietnam 32, 36, 1003
Vietnamese 30, 35, 249, 650, 653, 674, 1003
virtual
  information exchange 901
  space 894, 895, 899
visible pedagogy 205
visual literacy 622, 756, 854, 930
vocabulary 20, 67, 90, 92–94, 97, 99, 145, 171, 201, 251–253, 335, 742–744, 758, 759, 779, 780, 793–795, 797–808, 827–841, 910, 911, 935, 951
  profiles 318, 951, 958
  teaching and learning 97, 232, 764, 780, 827, 829, 831, 833, 835, 837, 839–841, 898, 935, 1000
voice 8, 55, 57, 58, 60, 135, 144, 145, 149, 181, 225, 243, 492, 686, 806, 881, 883–885, 887–889, 896, 897, 1031, 1043, 1111
voluntary immigrants 644
VP (*see* verb phrase) 847
Vygotskian theory (*see also* sociocultural theory) 716, 851

W
wash out effect 1054
web
  designer 1115
  pages 749, 773, 907, 912, 922, 1119–1121
  traffic 891
Web-based bulletin 907
web-based cultural studies 1134
web-conferencing 1127
well-formed sentences 784
Wits Multiliteracies Reasearch Group 919, 930
word retrieval skills 783
working conditions 967, 1053, 1069
workplace English 403, 404
World Englishes 51, 61, 123, 126–129, 135, 140, 149, 150, 152, 153, 167, 415, 672, 954, 958, 959, 1039, 1050
world language 19, 20, 110, 134, 152, 525, 526, 531, 672, 678, 1050

World Wide Web   749, 759, 762, 767, 856, 907, 912, 916
writing   57, 58, 60, 61, 278, 279, 392–395, 401, 402, 409, 474–477, 480–484, 545–548, 662, 663, 666, 781, 788–794, 797–801, 875–891, 907–917, 929–935, 940–943, 979–982, 1061, 1062
  assignments   659, 662, 878, 914, 980, 981, 1096
written language   26, 35, 116, 146, 203, 205, 251, 353, 355, 403, 536, 619, 714, 777, 856, 859–861, 871, 872, 896, 897, 923, 924, 979

X
xenophobic   646

Z
zero proficiency   68
zone of proximal development (ZDP) (*see also* Vygotsky)   619, 623, 628, 629, 634, 636, 686, 693, 697, 700, 703, 717, 764, 766, 857, 1132
ZPD (*see* zone of proximal development)   619, 620, 629, 630, 693, 697–699, 703, 710, 764, 766

Springer International Handbooks of Education

Volume 1

International Handbook of Educational Leadership and Administration
Edited by Kenneth Leithwood, Judith Chapman, David Corson,
Philip Hallinger, and Ann Hart
ISBN 0-7923-3530-9

Volume 2

International Handbook of Science Education
Edited by Barry J. Fraser and Kenneth O. Tobin
ISBN 0-7923-3531-7

Volume 3

International Handbook of Teachers and Teaching
Edited by Bruce J. Biddle, Thomas L. Good, and Ivor L. Goodson
ISBN 0-7923-3532-5

Volume 4

International Handbook of Mathematics Education
Edited by Alan J. Bishop, Ken Clements, Christine Keitel, Jeremy Kilpatrick,
and Collette Laborde
ISBN 0-7923-3533-3

Volume 5

International Handbook of Educational Change
Edited by Andy Hargreaves, Ann Leiberman, Micheal Fullan,
and David Hopkins
ISBN 0-7923-3534-1

Volume 6

International Handbook of Lifelong Learning
Edited by David Aspin, Judith Chapman, Micheal Hatton,
and Yukiko Sawano
ISBN 0-7923-6815-0

Volume 7

International Handbook of Research in Medical Education
Edited by Geoff R. Norman, Cees P.M. van der Vleuten, and David I. Newble
ISBN 1-4020-0466-4

Volume 8

Second International Handbook of Educational Leadership and
Administration
Edited by Kenneth Leithwood and Philip Hallinger
ISBN 1-4020-0690-X

Volume 9

International Handbook of Educational Evaluation
Edited by Thomas Kellaghan and Daniel L. Stufflebeam
ISBN 1-4020-0849-X

Volume 10

Second International Handbook of Mathematics Education
Edited by Alan J. Bishop, M.A., (Ken) Clements, Christine Keitel,
Jeremy Kilpatrick, and Frederick K.S. Leung
ISBN 1-4020-1008-7

Volume 11

The International Handbook of Educational Research in the Asia-Pacific Region
Edited by J.P. Keeves and R. Watanabe
ISBN 978-1-4020-1007-1

Volume 12

International Handbook of Self-Study of Teaching and Teacher Education Practices
Edited by J. John Loughran, Mary Lynn Hamilton, Vicki Kubler LaBoskey,
and Tom L. Russell
ISBN 978-1-4020-1812-1

Volume 13

International Handbook of Educational Policy
Edited by Nina Bascia, Alister Cumming, Amanda Datnow, Kenneth Leithwood,
and David Livingstone
ISBN 978-1-4020-3189-2

Volume 14

International Handbook of Virtual Learning Environments
Edited by Joel Weiss, Jason Nolan, Jeremy Hunsinger, and Peter Trifonas
ISBN 978-1-4020-3082-0

Volume 15

International Handbook of English Language Teaching
Edited by Jim Cummins and Chris Davison
ISBN 0-387-46300-3

Printed in the United States of America

INTERNATIONAL HANDBOOK OF ENGLISH LANGUAGE TEACHING

Springer International Handbooks of Education

Volume 15

A list of titles in this series can be found at the end of this volume.

International Handbook of English Language Teaching

Part II

Edited by

Jim Cummins
The University of Toronto, Canada

and

Chris Davison
The University of Hong Kong, China

 Springer

Jim Cummins
Ontario Institute for Studies in Education/Canada

Chris Davison
The University of Hong Kong/China

Library of Congress Control Number: 2006932383

ISBN-13: 978-0-387-46300-1
ISBN-10: 0-387-46300-3

e-ISBN-13: 978-0-387-46301-8
e-ISBN-10: 0-387-46301-1

Printed on acid-free paper.

© 2007 Springer Science+Business Media, LLC.
All rights reserved. This work may not be translated or copied in whole or in part without the written permission of the publisher (Springer Science+Business Media, LLC., 233 Spring Street, New York, NY 10013, USA), except for brief excerpts in connection with reviews or scholarly analysis. Use in connection with any form of information storage and retrieval, electronic adaptation, computer software, or by similar or dissimilar methodology now known or hereafter developed is forbidden.
The use in this publication of trade names, trademarks, service marks and similar terms, even if they are not identified as such, is not to be taken as an expression of opinion as to whether or not they are subject to proprietary rights.
While the advice and information in this book are believed to be true and accurate at the date of going to press, neither the authors nor the editors nor the publisher can accept any legal responsibility for any errors or omissions that may be made. The publisher makes no warranty, express or implied, with respect to the material contained herein.

9 8 7 6 5 4 3 2   Corrected at 2nd printing, 2007

springer.com

Table of Contents

PART I

List of Authors	xiii
Preface	xxi
Acknowledgments	xxvii

SECTION 1. The Global Scope and Politics of ELT: Critiquing Current Policies and Programs

Introduction: The Global Scope and Politics of ELT: Critiquing Current Policies and Programs 3
Jim Cummins and Chris Davison

1. ELT and Colonialism 13
   Alastair Pennycook

2. Ideology, Language Varieties, and ELT 25
   James W. Tollefson

3. Tensions Between English and Mother Tongue Teaching in Post-Colonial Africa 37
   Margaret Akinyi Obondo

4. A Critical Discussion of the English-Vernacular Divide in India 51
   Vaidehi Ramanathan

5. ELT Policy Directions in Multilingual Japan 63
   Yasuko Kanno

6	English Language Teaching in Korea: Toward Globalization or *Glocalization*? *Hyunjung Shin*	75
7	The National Curriculum Changes and Their Effects on English Language Teaching in the People's Republic of China *Qiang Wang*	87
8	ELT and Bilingual Education in Argentina *Agustina Tocalli-Beller*	107
9	English, No Longer a Foreign Language in Europe? *Robert Phillipson*	123
10	Common Property: English as a Lingua Franca in Europe *Barbara Seidlhofer*	137
11	Teaching English as a Third Language *Ulrike Jessner and Jasone Cenoz*	155
12	Protecting English in an Anglophone Age *Joseph Lo Bianco*	169
13	Adult Immigrant ESL Programs in Canada: Emerging Trends in the Contexts of History, Economics, and Identity *Douglas Fleming*	185
14	Focus on Literacy: ELT and Educational Attainment in England *Jill Bourne*	199
15	Methods, Meanings and Education Policy in the United States *Lois M. Meyer*	211

SECTION 2. The Goals and Focus of the ELT Program: Problematizing Content and Pedagogy

	Introduction: The Goals and Focus of the ELT Program: Problematizing Content and Pedagogy *Chris Davison and Jim Cummins*	231
16	The Goals of ELT: Reproducing Native-Speakers or Promoting Multicompetence Among Second Language Users? *Vivian Cook*	237
17	Integrating School-Aged ESL Learners into the Mainstream Curriculum *Constant Leung*	249
18	Communicative Language Teaching: Current Status and Future Prospects *Nina Spada*	271

Table of Contents vii

19	Language Instruction Through Tasks *Peter Skehan*	289
20	Knowledge Structures in Social Practices *Bernard A. Mohan*	303
21	Accelerating Academic Achievement of English Language Learners: A Synthesis of Five Evaluations of the CALLA Model *Anna Uhl Chamot*	317
22	Predicting Second Language Academic Success in English Using the Prism Model *Virginia P. Collier and Wayne P. Thomas*	333
23	Four Keys for School Success for Elementary English Learners *Yvonne Freeman and David Freeman*	349
24	Collaborating in ESL Education in Schools *Sophie Arkoudis*	365
25	Organization of English Teaching in International Schools *Maurice W. Carder*	379
26	English for Specific Purposes: Some Influences and Impacts *Ken Hyland*	391
27	An Interdisciplinary Approach to Teaching Adults English in the Workplace *Jane Lockwood*	403

SECTION 3. Assessment and Evaluation in ELT: Shifting Paradigms and Practices

	Introduction: Assessment and Evaluation in ELT: Shifting Paradigms and Practices *Chris Davison and Jim Cummins*	415
28	Standards-Based Approaches to the Evaluation of ESL Instruction *David Nunan*	421
29	The Standards Movement and ELT for School-Aged Learners: Cross-National Perspectives *Penny McKay*	439
30	High-Stakes Testing and Assessment: English Language Teacher Benchmarking *David Coniam and Peter Falvey*	457

31	New Directions in Testing English Language Proficiency for University Entrance *Alister Cumming*	473
32	The Impact of Testing Practices on Teaching: Ideologies and Alternatives *Liz Hamp-Lyons*	487
33	Classroom-Based Assessment: Possibilities and Pitfalls *Pauline Rea-Dickins*	505
34	The Power of Language Tests, the Power of the English Language and the Role of ELT *Elana Shohamy*	521
35	Different Definitions of Language and Language Learning: Implications for Assessment *Chris Davison*	533

Author Index	549
Subject Index	575

PART II

List of Authors	xiii
Preface	xxi
Acknowledgments	xxvii

SECTION 1. The Learner and the Learning Environment: Creating New Communities

	Introduction: The Learner and the Learning Environment: Creating New Communities *Jim Cummins and Chris Davison*	615
36	ESL Learners in the Early School Years: Identity and Mediated Classroom Practices *Kelleen Toohey, Elaine Day and Patrick Manyak*	625
37	The Adolescent English Language Learner: Identities Lost and Found *Linda Harklau*	639

Table of Contents ix

38	What About the Students? English Language Learners in Postsecondary Settings *Sarah Benesch*	655
39	Imagined Communities, Identity, and English Language Learning *Aneta Pavlenko and Bonny Norton*	669
40	Academic Achievement and Social Identity Among Bilingual Students in the U.S. *Shelley Wong and Rachel Grant*	681
41	Sociocultural Theory: A Unified Approach to L2 Learning and Teaching *James P. Lantolf*	693
42	Mediating Academic Language Learning Through Classroom Discourse *Pauline Gibbons*	701
43	Creating a Motivating Classroom Environment *Zoltán Dörnyei*	719
44	Autonomy and Its Role in Learning *Philip Benson*	733
45	Creating a Technology-Rich English Language Learning Environment *Denise E. Murray*	747
46	The Internet and English Language Learning: Opening Up Spaces for Constructivist and Transformative Pedagogy Through Sister-Class Networks *Vasilia Kourtis-Kazoullis and Eleni Skourtou*	763

SECTION 2. Constructs of Language in ELT: Breaking the Boundaries

	Introduction: Constructs of Language in ELT: Breaking the Boundaries *Chris Davison and Jim Cummins*	777
47	Psycholinguistic Perspectives on Language and Its Acquisition *Jan H. Hulstijn*	783
48	Academic Language: What Is It and How Do We Acquire It? *Jim Cummins and Evelyn Man Yee-Fun*	797
49	Teaching Implications of L2 Phonology Research *John Archibald*	811
50	Current Perspectives on Vocabulary Teaching and Learning *Norbert Schmitt*	827

51	Changing Approaches to the Conceptualization and Teaching of Grammar *Beverly Derewianka*	843
52	Extending Our Understanding of Spoken Discourse *Michael McCarthy and Diana Slade*	859
53	New Directions in Student Academic Writing *Sue Starfield*	875
54	From Literacy to Multiliteracies in ELT *Heather Lotherington*	891
55	Technology and Writing *Mark Warschauer*	907
56	Multimodal Pedagogies, Representation and Identity: Perspectives from Post-Apartheid South Africa *Pippa Stein and Denise Newfield*	919
57	Approaches to Genre in ELT *Brian Paltridge*	931
58	Researching and Developing Teacher Language Awareness: Developments and Future Directions *Stephen Andrews*	945

SECTION 3. Research and Teacher Education in ELT: Meeting New Challenges

	Introduction: Research and Teacher Education in ELT: Meeting New Challenges *Jim Cummins and Chris Davison*	963
59	Qualitative Approaches to Classroom Research with English Language Learners *Patricia A. Duff*	973
60	Action Research: Contributions and Future Directions in ELT *Anne Burns*	987
61	Narrative Inquiry and ELT Research *JoAnn Phillion and Ming Fang He*	1003
62	Conversation Analysis: Issues and Problems *Numa Markee*	1017

63	Poststructuralism and Applied Linguistics: Complementary Approaches to Identity and Culture in ELT *Brian Morgan*	1033
64	What Shapes Teachers' Professional Development? *Amy B.M. Tsui*	1053
65	Appropriating Uncertainty: ELT Professional Development in the New Century *Michael P. Breen*	1067
66	Teacher Education for Linguistically Diverse Communities, Schools, and Classrooms *Tara Goldstein*	1085
67	Challenges and Opportunities for the Teaching Profession: English as an Additional Language in the UK *Charlotte Franson*	1101
68	Teachers' Roles in the Global Hypermedia Environment *Chris Corbel*	1113
69	Preparing Teachers for Technology-Supported ELT *Michael K. Legutke, Andreas Müller-Hartmann and Marita Schocker V. Ditfurth*	1125
Author Index		1139
Subject Index		1165

List of Authors

Stephen Andrews, Faculty of Education, The University of Hong Kong, Pokfulam Road, Hong Kong, SAR, China. Email: sandrews@hku.hk

John Archibald, Department of Linguistics, Language Research Centre, The University of Calgary, Calgary, Alberta, T2N 1N4, Canada. Email: john.archibald@ucalgary.ca

Sophie Arkoudis, Faculty of Education, The University of Melbourne, Parkville, Victoria, 3010, Australia. Email: s.arkoudis@unimelb.edu.au

Sarah Benesch, Department of English, Speech and, World Literature, The City University of New York, College of Staten Island, 2800 Victory Boulevard, Staten Island, New York, USA. Email: benesch@mail.csi.cuny.edu

Phil Benson, The Hong Kong Institute of Education, 10 Lo Ping Road, Tai Po, Hong Kong, SAR, China. Email: pbenson@hkucc.hku.hk

Jill Bourne, Centre for Research on Pedagogy and the Curriculum, School of Education, The University of Southampton, Highfield, Southampton, SO17 1BJ, United Kingdom. Email: j.bourne@soton.ac.uk

Michael P. Breen, Sutton House, Auchterarder, Perthshire PH3 1ED, Scotland. Email: m.breen@hotmail.co.uk

Anne Burns, Department of Linguistics, Division of Linguistics and Psychology, Macquarie University, NSW 2109, Australia. Email: anne.burns@mq.edu.au

Maurice Carder, Vienna International School, Strasse der Menschenrechte 1, A-1220, Vienna, Austria. Email: mcarder@vis.ac.at

Jasone Cenoz, Department of Research Methods in Education, FICE, The University of the Basque Country, Avda Tolosa 70, 01006 San Sebastian, Spain. Email: jasone.cenoz@ehu.es

Anna Uhl Chamot, George Washington University, 2121 Bye Street, N.W., Washington, USA. Email: auchamot@gwu.edu

Virginia P. Collier, Graduate School of Education, George Mason University, 4400 University Drive MS4B3, Fairfax, VA 22030, USA. Email: vcollier@gmu.edu

David Coniam, Department of Curriculum and Instruction, The Chinese University of Hong Kong, Shatin, New Territories, Hong Kong, SAR, China. Email: coniam@cuhk.edu.hk

Vivian Cook, School of Education, Communication and Language Sciences, King George VI Building, The University of Newcastle upon Tyne, Newcastle upon Tyne, NE1 7RU, England. Email: Vivian.Cook@newcastle.ac.uk

Chris Corbel, Manager Research and Development, NMIT, 77-91 St Georges Rd, Preston, Victoria 3072. Email: chrisc-rd@nmit.vic.edu.au

Alister Cumming, Modern Language Centre, Ontario Institute for Studies in Education, The University of Toronto, 252 Bloor Street West, Toronto, Ontario, M5S 1V6, Canada. Email: acumming@oise.utoronto.ca

Jim Cummins, Modern Language Centre, 10th Floor, Ontario Institute for Studies in Education, The University of Toronto, 252 Bloor St, West Toronto, Ontario, M5S 1V6 Canada. Email: jcummins@oise.utoronto.ca

Chris Davison, Faculty of Education, The University of Hong Kong, Pokfulam Rd, Hong Kong, SAR, China. Email: cdavison@hku.hk

Elaine Day, Faculty of Education, Simon Fraser University, 8888 University Drive, Burnaby, BC V5A, 1S6, Canada. Email: Elaine_Day@sfu.ca

Beverly Derewianka, Faculty of Education, The University of Wollongong, NSW 2522, Australia. Email: bevder@uow.edu.au

Zoltán Dörnyei, School of English Studies, The University of Nottingham, UK. Email: Zoltan.Dornyei@nottingham.ac.uk

Patricia A. Duff, Department of Language and Literacy Education The University of British Columbia, 2125 Main Mall, Vancouver, BC, V6T 1Z4, Canada. Email: patricia.duff@ubc.ca

Peter Falvey, University of Cambridge Local Examinations Syndicate, 4, Bramcote Lane, Chilwell, Beeston, Nottingham, NG9 5EN, UK. Email: falveyphk@gmail.com

List of Authors

Douglas Fleming, The University of British Columbia, 9500 Glenacres Drive Richmond, BC, V7A 1Y7, Canada. Email: fleming_douglas@sd36.bc.ca

Charlotte Franson, Canterbury Christ Church University, North Holmes Road, Canterbury, CT1 1QU, Kent, England. Email: cmf6@canterbury.ac.uk

David Freeman, School of Education, The University of Texas at Brownsville, 80 Fort Brown, Brownsville, TX 78520, USA. Email: david.freeman@utb.edu

Yvonne Freeman, School of Education, The University of Texas at Brownsville, 80 Fort Brown, Brownsville, TX 78520, USA. Email: yvonne.freeman@utb.edu

Pauline Gibbons, Faculty of Education, The University of Technology Sydney, PO Box 123, Broadway, NSW 2007, Australia. Email: Pauline.Gibbons@uts.edu.au

Tara Goldstein, Department of Curriculum, Teaching and Learning, Ontario Institute for Studies in Education, The University of Toronto, 252 Bloor Street, Toronto, Ontario, M5S 1V6, Canada. Email: tgoldstein@oise.utoronto.ca

Rachel Grant, Center for Language and Culture, College of Education and Human Development, George Mason University, 4400 University Drive, MS4B3, Fairfax, VA 22030, USA. Email: rag022@aol.com

Liz Hamp-Lyons, Faculty of Education, The University of Hong Kong, Pokfulam, Rd, Hong Kong, SAR, China. Email: lizhl@hku.hk

Linda Harklau, Department of Language Education, 125 Aderhold Hall, The University of Georgia, Athens, GA 30602, USA. Email: lharklau@uga.edu

Ming Fang He, Department of Curriculum, Foundations, and Reading, College of Education, Georgia Southern University, Post Office Box 8144, Statesboro, GA, 30460-8144, USA. Email: mfhe@georgiasouthern.edu

Jan H. Hulstijn, Faculty of Humanities, The University of Amsterdam, 134 Spuistraat, 1012 VB Amsterdam, The Netherlands. Email: j.h.hulstijn@uva.nl

Ken Hyland, Institute of Education, The University of London, 20 Bedford Way, London, WC1H OAL, UK. Email: K.Hyland@ioe.ac.uk

Ulrike Jessner, Department of English, The University of Innsbruck, Innrain 52/III, A-6020 Innsbruck, Austria. Email: Ulrike.Jessner@uibk.ac.at

Yasuko Kanno, The University of Washington, Department of English, Box 354330, Seattle, WA 98195-4330, USA. Email: ykanno@u.washington.edu

Vasilia Kourtis Kazoullis, Department of Mediterranean Studies, The University of the Aegean, 1 Demokratias Ave. GR-85100 Rhodes, Greece. Email: kazoullis@rhodes.aegean.gr

James P. Lantolf, Penn State University, Centre of Language Acquisition, 304 Sparks Building, University Park, PA 16802, USA. Email: jpl7@psu.edu

Michael K. Legutke, Justus-Liebig-Universität Giessen, Institut für Anglistik, Otto-Behaghel-Str, 10, B, IV, 35394 Giessen, Germany. Email: Michael.K.Legutke@anglistik.uni-giessen.de

Constant Leung, Department of Education and Professional Studies, School of Social Science and Public Policy, King's College, The University of London, Franklin-Wilkins Building, Waterloo Road, London, SE1 9NH, UK. Email: constant.leung@kcl.ac.uk

Joseph Lo Bianco, Department of Language and Literacy Education, The University of Melbourne, Parkville, Victoria 3010 Australia. Email: j.lobianco@unimelb.edu.au

Jane Lockwood, The Hong Kong Institute of Education, 10 Lo Ping Road, Tai Po, Hong Kong, SAR, China. Email: lockwood@ied.edu.hk

Heather Lotherington, Faculty of Education, York University, 4700 Keele Street, Toronto, Ontario, M3J 1P3, Canada. Email: hlotherington@edu.yorku.ca

Evelyn Man Yee-fun, Department of Curriculum and Instruction, The Chinese University of Hong Kong, Shatin, New Territories, Hong Kong, SAR China. Email: eyfman@cuhk.edu.hk

Patrick Manyak, College of Education, Department of Elementary and Early Childhood, The University of Wyoming, P.O. Box 3374 Laramine, WY 82071-3374, USA. Email: pmanyak@uwyo.edu

Numa Markee, Division of English as an International Language, The University of Illinois at Urbana-Champaign, 3070 Foreign Languages Building, 707 South Mathews, Urbana, IL 61801, USA. Email: nppm@uiuc.edu

Michael McCarthy, School of English Studies, The University Nottingham, University Park, Nottingham, NG7 2RD, UK. Email: mactoft@dial.pipex.com

Penny McKay, School of Cultural and Language Studies in Education, Queensland University of Technology, Kelvin Grove Campus, Brisbane, Queensland 4059, Australia. Email: pa.mckay@qut.edu.au

Lois M. Meyer, College of Education, Department of Language, Literacy & Sociocultural Studies, The University of New Mexico, Albuquerque, NM 87131, USA. Email: lsmeyer@unm.edu

Bernard A. Mohan, The University of British Columbia, 4640 West 13th Avenue, Vancouver, British Columbia, Canada V6R 2V7. Email: bernard.mohan@ubc.ca

List of Authors

Brian Morgan, Department of Languages, Literatures and Linguistics, York University, Canada. Email: bmorgan@yorku.ca

Andreas Müller-Hartmann, Department of English as a Foreign Language Pädagogische Hochschule Heidelberg, Im Neuenheimer Feld 561, D-69120 Heidelberg, Germany. Email: Andreas.Mueller-Hartmann@anglistik.uni-giessen.de

Denise E. Murray, National Centre for English Language Teaching and Research, Macquarie University, NSW 2109, Australia. Email: denise.murray@mq.edu.au

Denise Newfield, Department of English, School of Literature and Language Studies, University of the Witwatersrand, PO WITS 2050, South Africa. Email: dnewfield@languages.wits.ac.za

Bonny Norton, Department of Language and Literacy Education, The University of British Columbia, 2125 Main Mall, Vancouver, BC, Canada V6T 1Z4. Email: bonny.norton@ubc.ca

David Nunan, The English Centre, The University of Hong Kong, Pokfulam Rd, Hong Kong, SAR, China. Email: dcnunan@hku.hk

Margaret Obondo, Rinkeby Institute of Multilingual Research, P.O. Box 5028, 163 05, Spåna, Sweden. Email: margaret.obondo@rinkeby-multiling.stockholm.se

Brian Paltridge, Faculty of Education, The University of Sydney, NSW 2006, Australia. Email: b.paltridge@edfac.usyd.edu.au

Aneta Pavlenko, CITE Department, College of Education, Temple University, Philadephia, PA 19122, USA. Email: apavlenk@temple.edu

Alastair Pennycook, The University of Technology Sydney, City Campus Haymarket; PO Box 123, Broadway, NSW 2007, Australia. Email: alastair.pennycook@uts.edu.au

JoAnn Phillion, Department of Curriculum and Instruction, BRNG 4144, Purdue University, West Lafayette, IN 47907-2098. USA. Email: phillion@purdue.edu

Robert Phillipson, Department of English, Copenhagen Business School, Dalgas Have 15, 2000 Frederiksberg, Denmark. Email: rp.eng@cbs.dk

Vaidehi Ramanathan, Linguistics Program, The University of California, One Shields Ave., Davis, CA 95616, USA. Email: vramanathan@ucdavis.edu

Pauline Rea-Dickins, Graduate School of Education, The University of Bristol, 35 Berkerley Square, Clifton, Bristol BS8 1JA, UK. Email: p.rea-dickins@bristol.ac.uk

Norbert Schmitt, School of English Studies, The University of Nottingham, Nottingham NG7 2RD, UK. Email: norbert.schmitt@nottingham.ac.uk

Marita Schocker v. Ditfurth, Pädagogische Hochschule Freiburg, Institut für Fremdsprachen/Abteilung Englisch, Kunzenweg 21D-79117 Freiburg, Germany. Email: schocker@ph-freiburg.de

Barbara Seidlhofer, Institut für Anglistik, Universität Wien, Universitaetcampus AAKH/Hof 8, Spitalgasse 2-4, A-1090 Vienna, Austria. Email: barbara.seidlhofer@univie.ac.at

Hyunjung Shin, Ontario Institute for Studies in Education, The University of Toronto, 252 Bloor Street West, Toronto, Ontario, M5S 1V6, Canada. Email: shyunjung@hotmail.com

Elana Shohamy, Tel Aviv University, School of Education, Tel Aviv 69978, Isarel. Email: elana@post.tau.ac.il

Peter Skehan, English Department, Fung King Hey Building, The Chinese University of Hong Kong, Shatin, New Territories, Hong Kong, SAR, China. Email: pskehan@arts.cuhk.edu.hk

Eleni Skourtou, Department of Primary Education, The University of the Aegean, 1 Demokratias Ave. GR-85100, Rhodes, Greece. Email: skourtou@rhodes.aegean.gr

Diana Slade, The University of Technology Sydney, Faculty of Education, PO Box 123, Broadway, NSW 2007, Australia. Email: diana.slade@uts.edu.au

Nina Spada, Ontario Institute for Studies in Education, The University of Toronto, Modern Language Centre, Department of Curriculum, Teaching and Learning, 252 Bloor Street West, Toronto, Ontario, M5S IV6, Canada. Email: nspada@oise.utoronto.ca

Sue Starfield, The Learning Centre, The University of New South Wales, Sydney, NSW 2052, Australia. Email: s.starfield@unsw.edu.au

Pippa Stein, Department of Applied English Language Studies, School of Literature and Language Studies, University of Witwatersrand, PO WITS 2050, South Africa. Email: pippa@languages.wits.ac.za

Wayne P. Thomas, Graduate School of Education, George Mason University, 4400 University Drive MS4B3, Fairfax, VA 22030, USA. Email: wthomas@gmu.edu

Agustina Tocalli-Beller, El Montículo 153, La Planicie, La Molina, Lima 12, Peru. Email: atocalli-beller@oise.utoronto.ca/agustina@cogeco.ca

James W. Tollefson, The University of Washington, 5307 S. Langley Road, Langley, WA 98260, USA. Email: tollefso@u.washington.edu

Kelleen Toohey, Faculty of Education, 8888 University Drive, Simon Fraser University, Burnaby, BC V5A 1S6, Canada. Email: toohey@sfu.ca

List of Authors

Amy B. M. Tsui, Faculty of Education, The University of Hong Kong, Pokfulam Road, Hong Kong, SAR, China. Email: bmtsui@hku.hk

Qiang Wang, Department of Foreign Languages, Beijing Normal University, Beijing, China. Email: wang_qiang99@yahoo.com

Mark Warschauer, The University of California, Irvine, UCI Department of Education, 2001 Berkeley Place, Irvine, CA 92697-5500, USA. Email: markw@uci.edu

Shelley Wong, Center for Language and Culture, College of Education and Human Development, George Mason University, 4400 University Drive MS4B3, Fairfax, VA 22030, USA. Email: swong1@gmu.edu

Preface

This two-volume handbook provides a comprehensive examination of policy, practice, research, and theory related to English language teaching (ELT) in international contexts. Nearly 70 chapters highlight the research foundation for the best practices, frameworks for policy decisions, and areas of consensus and controversy in the teaching and development of English as a second and/or additional language for kindergarten through to adult speakers of languages other than English. In doing so it problematizes traditional dichotomies and challenges the very terms that provide the traditional foundations of the field.

A wide range of terms has been used to refer to the key players involved in the teaching and learning of the English language and to the enterprise of English language teaching as a whole. At various times and in different contexts, the following labels have been used in countries where English is the dominant language to describe programs, learners, or teachers of English: *English as a second language* (ESL), *English as an additional language* (EAL), *limited English proficient* (LEP), and *English language learners* (ELL). In contexts where English is not the dominant language, the following terms have been used: *English as a foreign language* (EFL), *English as an international language* (EIL), and *English as a lingua franca* (ELF). The international professional organization that supports and advocates for English language teaching calls itself *Teachers of English to Speakers of Other Languages* (TESOL) and the term *English to speakers of other languages* (ESOL) is also used in some contexts around the world to refer to programs, students, and teachers.

None of these labels is sociopolitically neutral; they each highlight certain features of the phenomenon of English language teaching and those who engage in it, and de-emphasize other features. For example, all of the labels listed above foreground *English* as the focus of attention, thereby obscuring the fact that the learners are bilingual or multilingual with fully functioning abilities in their home languages. This risks contributing to a deficit view of the learner, particularly in English-speaking contexts involving immigrant and refugee students. The term *limited English proficient* used by the US federal government is particularly problematic in this regard. Other terms are problematic for different reasons; for example, *ESL* makes the assumption, rooted in a monolingual perspective, that English is the second language of the student whereas in reality it may be the third, fourth, or fifth language that an individual has learned. *ELL* is currently the favored term among many professional organizations and educational agencies in North America but it obscures some key differences between programs for English mother tongue learners and those who are learning English as an additional language.

Attempts to use 'positive' terminology to refer to students and programs can also be problematic. For example, in the United Kingdom students have frequently been referred to as *bilingual* learners but this label obscures the fact that many of these students are still in great need of English language development (and were usually afforded few opportunities and little encouragement for mother tongue maintenance). In the United States, advocates for bilingual programs and some educational agencies have frequently referred to students as *bilingual* or *bilingual/bicultural*; however, it is arguable that this labeling may have contributed to the widespread assumption among the media and some policy-makers and educators that bilingualism represents a linguistic deficit and that the bilingual student is 'limited English proficient.' In contexts where English is not the dominant language, the label *EFL* has traditionally been used but *EIL* and *ELF* have been promoted as alternatives. The latter is seen as a much more accurate sociolinguistic descriptor to describe many learning and teaching situations outside predominantly English–speaking countries. The problem with adopting all such labels, however, is that by definition they create a single category in which people from many different linguistic and cultural backgrounds, language levels, socio-economic positions, aspirations, and perceived identities are treated as a collectivity.

In this handbook we have not attempted to reconcile this multiplicity of identities and ideologies; rather, we have generally remained faithful to whatever term has been provided by the author of each chapter, assuming that it is an accurate reflection of their context and history, with the exception of the term *LEP* which we have generally changed to *ESL* or *ELL*. The field as a whole, in all its richness and diversity, we have called *English language teaching* (ELT), despite the limitations of the term, hence the title of this handbook. As this discussion of labels illustrates, language intersects with societal power relations in multiple and complex ways and this reality is reflected in the entire field of English language teaching. Thus, it is not surprising that many of the chapters in this handbook explore the ideological dimensions of ELT and their implications for language policies and classroom practice.

The handbook is intended to provide a unique resource for policy makers, educational administrators, teacher educators and researchers concerned with meeting the increasing demand for effective English language teaching while, at the same time, supporting institutions and communities concerned with the survival and development of languages other than English. Its publication is timely in view of the continuing spread of English as a global language and the associated expansion of ELT in countries around the world. Policy decisions regarding ELT that will be made during the next five years will influence the lives of individuals and the development of societies for the next 25 years or more. Policies and practices relating to ELT are, unfortunately, just as likely to be motivated by political pressure backed up by plausible but flawed assumptions as they are by research and careful evaluation of alternative options. For example, many parents and policy makers just assume that earlier and more intensive instruction will result in higher levels of

English proficiency. As the research reviewed in this handbook demonstrates, this assumption is not necessarily valid—the issues are considerably more complex than the rush to English would suggest.

Even a cursory examination of the spread of English demonstrates the ecological nature of the phenomenon. The introduction or expansion of English language teaching in any particular environment exerts multidimensional influences on the status and even prospects for survival of other languages in that environment. Social and linguistic groups within these environments are similarly affected—either advantaged or disadvantaged—by the policies adopted in relation to English.

To illustrate, it is clear that in countries around the world, English is replacing other languages as the second language taught most frequently and intensively in school. The perceived social and economic rewards associated with English have propelled parents to demand earlier and more intensive teaching of English. For example, in Japan, pilot projects have been instituted to start teaching English in the primary grades. In Hong Kong there is spirited public debate about the value of English–medium education and the most appropriate age to start learning English. English-medium universities are expanding rapidly in traditionally non-English speaking contexts, not just through the establishment of off-shore campuses, but through local universities shifting to English as the main language of instruction. For example, universities in mainland China have been required to teach 10% of their curriculum in English since 2004; in Japan entire degree programs are being offered in English in an attempt to maintain student numbers as the university–age population rapidly dwindles. In Norway and Sweden English is rapidly displacing the national languages as the medium of teaching and learning in science and engineering faculties. Finland has the largest proportion of higher education courses taught in English outside English-speaking countries. In the European community in general, there are concerns that the drive to teach English is turning it into the de facto official language of the new Europe. Similar developments and debates about the accelerating spread of English are underway in countries around the world. Expansion and intensification of ELT by means of an earlier start, increased time allotment, and experimentation with immersion and bilingual or trilingual programs are evident both in private sector and public sector schools in many countries.

Demand for English has also escalated among adult learners including immigrants to English-speaking countries, business people involved in the global economy, and those who just want to travel as tourists. In many countries, large-scale ELT programs for adult learners have been established in the community and workplace as a result of the globalization of the workforce, the perceived need to increase economic competitiveness, and a move towards life-long learning.

In some contexts, English has displaced not only competing second languages but also first languages. In many former British colonies and other recently independent countries in Africa and Asia, for example, English is used almost exclusively as the medium of instruction in schools, thereby constricting the institutional space available for indigenous languages and creating immense challenges for students to learn academic content through a language they do not understand. Is this the best policy option? What are the alternatives? Who benefits from these policies and who is disadvantaged? Clearly, policies and practices associated with English language teaching must be considered not only in relation to effectiveness and efficiency but also with respect to the moral dimensions of decisions and initiatives. Who benefits from particular expenditures of resources and what are the hidden costs with respect to what these resources might have been spent on? Is external aid for language teaching programs promoting the development of home-grown expertise or inducing long-term dependency on external support? In short, power and status relationships between social groups both within and across societies are intertwined in obvious ways with language teaching policies and practices.

Increased focus on English language teaching has also occurred in countries where English is the dominant language. Many English-speaking countries have experienced dramatic increases in immigration during the past 30 years (e.g. the United States, Australia, and Canada). For example, about 40% of students in California have learned English as a second language and 25% of these are classified as *limited English proficient* by government agencies. In Canada, about 50% of students in the Toronto and Vancouver urban areas have learned English as an additional language. In Australia, more than 25% of the population use a language other than English as the main language of communication in the home. The rapid spread of the new knowledge economies and the decline in demand for traditional manual labor are creating even greater pressure for newcomer populations to be highly proficient in English. There is also much more transmigration with people moving to English-speaking countries for temporary periods seeking further education and/or work, a trend accelerated by developments such as the expansion of the European Union. The number of foreign university students in the United Kingdom, the United States, Australia, New Zealand, and Canada has increased steadily during the past 20 years.

Increasing cultural and linguistic diversity in English-dominant countries has given rise to concerns among some groups that English might be under threat from competing languages. These concerns have given rise to fierce debates, often with racist overtones, about how English should be taught to immigrant and second generation children as well as adults. In several US states, for example, referenda have mandated that only English be used in schools for instructional purposes. The goal has been to restrict or eliminate bilingual programs that are seen as conferring status on other languages. Clearly, debates on language policy issues in many countries have been characterized by the confounding of ideological and research-based perspectives. There is considerable research that can inform policy in these areas but it is frequently ignored and/or distorted as a result of entrenched ideological positions.

The *International Handbook of English Language Teaching* provides authoritative perspectives on these issues from many of the leading researchers, theorists, and policy-makers around the world. The handbook synthesizes the interdisciplinary knowledge base for effective decision making and highlights directions for implementing appropriate language policies at both instructional and societal levels. Each volume is divided into three main sections and chapters are clustered to address common topics and themes. The focus of Volume I is on *Policies and Programs in ELT: Changing Demands and Directions* while Volume II addresses *Language, Learning and Identity in ELT: Reconceptualizing the Field*.

Volume I includes a critical examination of current policies and programs in a variety of contexts around the world (Section 1). The chapters in this section identify empirical, theoretical, and ideological foundations of ELT policies and their effects on learners and organizational structures. Section 2 of this Volume focuses specifically on the development of curriculum content for ELT programs and the pedagogical approaches that have been implemented to teach this content, while Section 3 examines policies and practices in assessment and evaluation. All of these dimensions of ELT—curriculum content, pedagogy, assessment, and evaluation—involve complex sets of decisions made by multiple actors (e.g. policy makers, curriculum developers, publishers, teachers, parents, researchers) who interact with each other in dynamic and often unpredictable ways. Increasingly, these actors span the international stage. Initiatives adopted in one or more contexts (e.g. standards-based curriculum development and high-stakes testing) influence decisions taken elsewhere, often through the mediation of international experts who consult with publishers and government agencies to identify 'best practices.' The chapters in all three sections of Volume I highlight the complex interplay between global and local perspectives and the need for policy decisions that take account of local linguistic contexts rather than just importing formulaic "off-the-shelf" solutions that may be highly inappropriate for a particular context.

In Volume II, the focus shifts to the changing conceptions of the learner, the teacher, the learning environment, and the English language itself that are implied by particular approaches to program development, curriculum, pedagogy, and assessment. *Identity* has emerged as a key construct in recent research and theory within ELT, reflecting the fact that learners and teachers are engaged in multiple social relationships both with each other and with peers and colleagues. Learning is conceived as a social endeavor rather than simply an individualistic cognitive and linguistic process. Identities are being constantly negotiated as learners learn language and this process of identity negotiation is strongly influenced by patterns of power relationships in the broader society. Language itself is being reconceptualized as a result of this process, with an increasing concern with shifting and emerging genres and multimodal texts. The final chapters focus on the development of the ELT profession in a broad sense, both in terms of cutting edge research and in terms of teacher growth and change in an increasingly complex and demanding global environment.

The spread of English is often presented as an inexorable and natural expansion, outside the control of government and non-government agencies, similar to the ideology of 'manifest destiny' that rationalized US imperialist expansion in the 19th and 20th centuries. At the same time its teaching is often assumed to be an inherent good, or at the other extreme, vilified as a threat to fragile and precarious linguistic ecologies. Our hope is that this handbook will, in some way, contribute to building the knowledge base and capability of various agencies and individuals to direct and control this expansion and shape its impact on complex and multiple linguistic and pedagogic communities, both local and global. Effectiveness and efficiency of ELT, and provision of equitable opportunities to all learners to acquire English (and other languages), are clearly important goals embedded throughout the handbook. However, informed and careful planning in ELT needs to focus not only on maximizing such elements in an increasingly complex, shifting and changing environment, but on ensuring balance and harmony among multiple elements. This is also a central goal of this handbook.

Acknowledgements

This two-volume handbook would not have been possible without the cooperation and enthusiasm of a large number of people. First and foremost we would like to express our appreciation to the 84 authors from all over the world who contributed in such original and insightful ways to the 69 chapters of the handbook. Their attention to detail and responsiveness to our editorial requests and suggestions helped enormously in completing this ambitious project.

A particular debt of gratitude goes to our friends, colleagues, and graduate students in both Hong Kong and Toronto who assisted in multiple ways during the editorial process. Eila Thomas helped establish contacts with prospective authors and was also responsible for the initial formatting and content and reference checking of the chapters. Hyunjung Shin continued this process at a later stage and helped in particular with the final proofreading. Xinmin Zhang and Jane Lockwood played a major role in developing the subject index. Special thanks also to Scarlet Poon for her work on the early formatting of the chapters and to Eunice Jam who took on the daunting task of getting the whole manuscript ready for the printer. We deeply appreciate their contributions, especially since they devoted time, energy, and enthusiasm to the project at demanding times in their professional lives—and even claimed to enjoy it!

We would also like to acknowledge the support (and patience!) of our editors at Kluwer Academic Publishers and later at Springer. In the initial stages of the project Joy Carp's encouragement provided a major impetus, and Renée De Boo's help was invaluable in identifying authors and topics and compiling the Table of Contents. Marie Sheldon put the wind back in our sails mid-way through the project and her unflagging support enabled us to bring the project to completion. Mary Panarelli was always available to answer questions about the finer points of style and format and shepherded the manuscript into the final production stages, with Kristina Wiggins offering invaluable support to complete the project. Finally, we would like to acknowledge the anonymous reviewers who made extremely useful suggestions on the initial proposal for the handbook and the copy editors who helped shape the final manuscript in a thousand small ways.

Financial support for the editorial process was provided by the Education Faculty of the University of Hong Kong as well as through support for graduate assistantships from both the University of Hong Kong and the University of Toronto. We would also like to express our deep appreciation to colleagues at the Faculty of Education, University of Hong Kong, and the Modern Language Centre of the Ontario Institute for Studies in Education of the University of Toronto, whose advice and encouragement was invaluable.

Last, but not least, our love and gratitude to our families for their understanding and support. This project has also been a part of their lives over a period of several years and they will no doubt be extremely happy to see it bound and dispatched so that we can all move on to additional personal opportunities and professional challenges.

In conclusion, as editors, we feel privileged to have had the opportunity to bring together this comprehensive survey of issues and trends in the field of English language teaching (ELT). The dialogues with authors and between ourselves, and the in-depth reading and re-reading of chapters, have extended our own appreciation of both the empirical basis for policy and practice, and the theoretical constructs that jostle for position in this still emerging field. However, what stands out as particularly significant for us at this point is the complexity of the moral dimensions of ELT in the context of the unrelenting spread of English. Teachers, policy-makers, and researchers—we are all implicated in the shaping of social and linguistic spaces where identities are being negotiated and personal and professional opportunities are being constructed or constricted. Our heartfelt thanks once again to all those who have contributed to our own growth in understanding of, and sensitivity to, the complexity of these issues. We hope that the handbook acts as a catalyst for reflection and dialogue aimed not only at increasing the effectiveness of ELT, but also at creating ecologically viable and sustainable multilingual societies.

Jim Cummins
Chris Davison

July 2006

Section 1:

The Learner and the Learning Environment: Creating New Communities

SECTION 1

THE LEARNER AND THE LEARNING ENVIRONMENT:

Creating New Communities

JIM CUMMINS AND CHRIS DAVISON

INTRODUCTION

Throughout the relatively short history of second language acquisition research there has been a clear division, and sometimes tension, between cognitive and socially-oriented approaches. Cognitive approaches view learners as individuals who process language input and produce language output. The major challenge for the researcher is to discover what happens in the 'black box' between input and output. In contrast, socially-oriented approaches see learners as part of a larger social matrix, affiliated with diverse communities and interacting in dynamic ways with members of these communities. Second language acquisition, and learning generally, is produced within communities of practice rather than reflecting an accomplishment of isolated individuals. Gibbons in this section expresses the distinction succinctly: learning is seen as occurring between individuals, not within them. Clearly, there is no absolute division here—all theorists acknowledge that learners are both cognitive and social beings, but there are certainly differences in emphasis accorded to these two dimensions in the research literature.

A cognitive orientation that focuses on the individual learner lends itself to experimental or quasi-experimental research in which characteristics of the L2 input can be carefully controlled and its impact on output or performance measured in quantifiable ways. Social environments, on the other hand, are much less easy to control, particularly if authenticity of interaction is desired, and as a result research has tended to draw on ethnographic and other qualitative methods (e.g., discourse analysis, case studies, and so on). The goal here is not to control variables and exclude extraneous influences but to observe and document the complexities of learners' interactions within their immediate social environment.

In recent years, sociocultural theory, strongly influenced by the work of early Soviet-era psychologist Lev Vygotsky, has emerged as perhaps the most prominent framework for conceptualizing the relationships between learners and the learning environment. Researchers vary, however, in the extent to which they extend sociocultural approaches into more critical spheres where power relations operating in the broader society, or across regions or countries, become the object of inquiry. A critical applied linguistics, or what Pennycook (2001) calls "applied linguistics with an attitude", broadens the analysis of the intersections between language and learning and language and society in order to bring into focus not only the *micro-*

interactions among individuals in various social contexts but also the historical and current *macro-interactions* among social groups. Regardless of the issue or topic—literacy development, language learning, second language pedagogy, the status and development of linguistic varieties, phonology, student academic achievement, language testing, and so on—a critical approach to the learner and the learning environment attempts to explore how patterns of linguistic interactions among individuals and between communities are structured by relations of power in the broader society. Critical approaches also inquire into the extent to which changes in patterns of linguistic interactions (e.g. between teachers and students in classrooms) might challenge the operation of inequitable power structures.

The first five chapters of this section of the handbook explore the intersections between social identity development and language learning among ELL students of varying ages in minority language situations. Toohey, Day, and Manyak address the issue of how ELL student identities are formed in the early years of schooling. They point to numerous research studies suggesting that learning takes place as a result of participation in social practices. Classroom instruction represents a set of social practices in which both students and teachers construct and negotiate identities, and these identities then mediate their experiences with English. Teacher-student interactions are not neutral with respect to the broader context of power relations—they reflect societal discourses in relation to diversity, patterns of cultural expectations, institutional categories (e.g. learning disabled), and assumptions about class and gender, all of which can position linguistically diverse students in problematic ways. This positioning excludes students from access to the kinds of social and instructional participation necessary for the development of expertise in carrying out academic tasks. Under these conditions, the identity options available to ELL students shrink so that they experience few opportunities or incentives to invest their identities in acquiring English and succeeding academically. Toohey and her colleagues also discuss the kinds of instructional and interpersonal spaces that can expand rather than reduce the identity options for linguistically diverse students. Drawing on Manyak's research among Latino students in California, they document the positive impact on learning that occurs in classrooms where students' social and cultural experiences are viewed as legitimate sources of knowledge and as valuable resources for literacy development. Students thrive in contexts of collaborative inquiry focused on challenging tasks where they have access both to demonstrations of expert performance and to identity positions of expertise, and where they can draw on the totality of their prior knowledge and experience as resources for learning.

In Harklau's chapter, the focus moves to adolescence and the ways in which identity negotiation influences patterns of English language learning. She points out that identity construction is challenging for all adolescents but particularly so for multilingual and multiethnic English language learners. For all adolescents, identities are shifting and mobile but ELL students are faced with an additional range of identity choices and pressures deriving from the linguistic, cultural, and often religious differences between their home environments and the social practices of the school and wider community. Harklau outlines three major approaches to the investigation of social identity formation among ELL adolescents. All three approaches—the psychological, the contextual, and the interactional—reject notions of stable and fixed adolescent identities in favor of conceptions that emphasize the multiple and dynamic nature of identity formation. Researchers working within the disciplines of social and clinical psychology have investigated constructs such as self-esteem, stress, coping, and resilience and their roles in the formation of ethnic affiliation and cultural identification among immigrant and minority youth. The second approach draws on sociological and anthropological research that investigates how schools and other social contexts contribute to the marginalization of identities that are constructed as deviant on the basis of race, language, culture, or religion. Finally, the interactional approach focuses on the semiotic practices (of which language behavior is just one) that express group affiliations and identities. Drawing on a wide variety of disciplinary perspectives, this approach explores how adolescent ELL students' identities and status are actively processed and negotiated in social interactions and discursive contexts that reflect broader patterns of societal power relations.

The ways in which the image of the learner interacts with the learning environment are also the focus of Benesch's chapter. In this case, the learners in question are ELL students participating in English for academic purposes (EAP) courses at the postsecondary level. Benesch draws attention to the tension between the definitions of ELL students in postsecondary institutions and they ways in which students define themselves. It is only in recent years that ethnographic research, and particularly critical ethnography, has begun to uncover the complexities of student identities that are obscured by survey or demographic research approaches. Demographic research is frequently conducted as part of a needs analysis process and tends to highlight commonalities in student populations through the use of broad general categories such as *foreign-born, first language,* etc. These results are intended to inform institutional planners about shifts in enrollment, attrition, attainment, and proficiency and enable the institution to respond to these changing realities. However, according to Benesch, this form of research raises questions such as: Who decides upon the categories? Which groups are highlighted as different and which are *not* marked as different and therefore accepted as the norm? During the 1990s, ethnographic research that focused on ELL students' experiences in postsecondary institutions began to be published, marking a shift from the positioning of students into broad general categories to the detailed description of student perspectives. However, much of this research focused on students as individuals struggling on their own to complete assignments and succeed in their courses. Little attention was paid to how student identities are positioned in the institution and larger society. Critical ethnographies have begun to address these issues by focusing on how student identities shift as students move across different discourses in their families, with peers, in classrooms, and the workplace. This research also examines how students are positioned in various ways by their race, class, ethnicity, and gender, and how they resist these external constructions of their identity in both overt and covert ways. When the learning of academic English is considered within this multi-dimensional social space, the complexities of the process and the challenges for both students and faculty can be better appreciated.

Pavlenko and Norton elaborate on the relationships between identity and English language learning by introducing the concept of *imagined communities*. These are communities or social groups to which learners aspire to belong (or avoid) and which influence their language learning behavior in powerful ways. Learning is seen as more than just the accumulation of skills and knowledge; it transforms who we are and what we can do and thus implicates our image of self. Learning inevitably entails identity changes because it is a process of becoming a certain kind of person (or rejecting a certain kind of positioning such as 'ESL student', which may have been externally imposed). Pavlenko and Norton highlight five identity clusters: (a) postcolonial, (b) global, (c) ethnic, (d) multilingual, and (e) gendered identities. These clusters illustrate how languages, and the identities linked to them, acquire and lose symbolic value in the linguistic marketplace. As one example within the global cluster, after the fall of the Soviet Empire, the newly emerged countries of Eastern Europe sought to refashion themselves as democratic and capitalist with language education reform playing a significant role. The establishment of English as the primary foreign or second language in schools (in place of Russian) is seen by these countries as key to national prosperity and global cooperation. Thus, the re-imagination of English is intertwined with the re-imagination of national, collective, and individual identities. Pavlenko and Norton highlight implications of the imagined communities concept for second language classrooms. For example, the work of successful bilingual writers can be appropriated within the classroom to challenge dominant ideologies of monolingualism and monoculturalism. These writers have learned English as an additional language, often after childhood, and their work opens up spaces for discussion of the potential congruence of different imagined communities, for example, the possibility of belonging fully to both original and dominant (English-speaking) imagined communities.

The notion of *imagined community* is also implicit in Wong and Grant's focus on how the life choices and life chances of low-income minority students in the United States are constricted by societal discourses that vehemently reject multilingual and multicultural identities. They point out that policies in relation to curriculum, teaching practices, and high-stakes testing are aimed at establishing and maintaining cultural homogeneity and an English-only conception of literacy that ignores the multiple literacy practices of bilingual and multilingual students outside the school system. Wong and Grant propose an instructional model designed to affirm ELL and bilingual students' identities and sense of agency and simultaneously promote academic achievement. The model specifically highlights the roles that educators can play in transforming educational and social inequities in relation to human resources, dialogic pedagogy, and curriculum reform. Human resources include the funds of knowledge represented by bilingual students and their families and communities. Wong and Grant point out that the current 'system of squandered bilingualism' must be replaced with educational policies and practices that construct linguistic and cultural diversity as a resource and enables students and their families to use this resource to contribute to their schools and the broader society. Effective use of human resources also requires more inclusive recruitment of professionals who speak multiple languages to work in schools and other social institutions. The second component of Wong and Grant's model—dialogic pedagogy—draws on Paulo Freire's work and is similar in orientation to critical pedagogy, critical literacy and participatory education. As implied by the term 'dialogic,' a central feature is a teacher-student relationship that emphasizes two-way communication and mutual respect within communities of learning. Dialogic pedagogy also emphasizes problem-posing and learning through social action and is aimed at giving voice to those who have been previously silenced. The third component of Wong and Grant's model involves the development of curricula that enable students and communities to participate in the democratic process and in the economic life of their societies. The overall model of educational reform proposed by Wong and Grant envisages the creation of new pedagogical spaces that are capable of promoting and sustaining dramatically different identity options for marginalized students and communities than those that currently dominate U.S. schools.

Lantolf's chapter brings us back to the fundamental tenets of sociocultural theory and their implications for L2 pedagogy. According to Lantolf, sociocultural theory resolves the tensions between cognitively-oriented and socially-oriented approaches to L2 pedagogy by insisting that all cognitive activity is fundamentally social in both its origins and operation. With respect to both social relationships and higher mental functions, human beings are fundamentally communicatively-organized. Speech (and writing) mediates both our social and cognitive activity. The interlocutors in the social sphere are *I* and *you* whereas in the cognitive sphere the interlocutors are *I* and *me*. Cognitive functions appear first in the *intermental* sphere and then, through internalization, in the *intramental* sphere. A central construct within sociocultural theory, and the one most relevant for understanding the relationship between the learner and the learning environment, is the *zone of proximal development* (ZPD). Vygotsky formulated the notion of the ZPD to capture the relationship between assisted and self-regulated performance. The ZPD represents the distance between what the learner can do individually without assistance and what he or she can do with assistance (e.g., through instruction or the mediation of cultural artifacts such as paper and pencil, calculators or computers). Learning occurs within the interpersonal space of the ZPD, in the context of assisted performance, while development results from the appropriation and internalization of that assistance and enables individuals to function independently of specific concrete circumstances. For language pedagogy, this perspective implies that instruction, learning, development, and assessment are inseparably linked and are essentially the same activity. Traditional approaches to testing are problematic because they focus on the learner in isolation rather than on what the learner can achieve within a supportive instructional context. By contrast, dynamic assessment focuses on what the learner can achieve within the ZPD and Lantolf concludes by urging second language educators and researchers to explore the relevance of dynamic assessment for L2 pedagogy.

Gibbons draws on sociocultural theory, systemic functional linguistics, and second language acquisition research in examining the relationship between classroom discourse and the development of ESL students' academic language learning. Within the mainstream content classroom, instruction (discourse) not only mediates students' learning but also constructs the sociocultural roles, relationships, and identities that teachers and students adopt. This mediation is effected within the zone of proximal development through *scaffolding*, a metaphor increasingly used to describe the kinds of support that enable learners to successfully complete a task that alone they would be unable to complete. Scaffolding, or assisted performance, enables learners not only to carry out the task but also to gain the expertise to know *how to* carry out the task. Thus, transfer to other contexts and situations is implied by the nature of the deep understanding that scaffolding attempts to develop. Gibbons concludes by highlighting the kinds of classroom discourse that are likely to be enabling of academic language development for L2 learners. She suggests that this discourse will be contextualized around scaffolded and intellectually challenging tasks and reflect a critical and inquiry-based curriculum. The discourse will connect with students' prior conceptual and linguistic knowledge while, at the same time, providing a bridge between what students already know and the new knowledge and skills embedded in the curriculum. Spoken and written language will be used and incorporated as tools for learning and there will be an explicit focus on pushing students' spoken language towards more writtenlike forms. Also taught explicitly will be the kinds of interpersonal language required for working collaboratively as well as the specific language features or genres of particular subject matter. Gibbons emphasizes that classroom discourse not only shapes learning but also shapes the identities of learners. To the extent that learners are constructed as capable of and committed to learning through classroom discourse, their actual academic expertise and capacity for learning increases.

What pushes learners to become engaged within the ZPD? Clearly, motivation is a crucial component of engagement for learning. However, motivation is not just an individual trait; the learner's motivation is intertwined with the micro-social environment of the classroom and the macro-social environment of the broader society. As discussed in several previous chapters in this section, the learner's social identity is constantly being negotiated in the classroom in relation to patterns of power relations in the broader society. Students whose identities are devalued in the classroom and wider society frequently withdraw from mental effort to achieve academically. These issues are taken up from a different perspective by Dörnyei. Drawing on research from group dynamics, motivational psychology, educational studies, and second language learning, he suggests that conscious intervention by the language teacher can dramatically affect the motivational character of the learning environment. Challenges for the language teacher (or any group leader) include building group cohesiveness where members of the group (or class) feel a sense of common purpose and acceptance of each other, and establishing appropriate group norms and specific roles for individual members. Norms refer to the general rules of behavior within the group. According to Dörnyei, potential norms should be formulated, discussed, and agreed upon early in the group's life with the consequences for violating the rules also specified. This should happen not in an autocratic manner but with input encouraged from all group members. Teachers should also encourage individual students to adopt constructive and complementary roles within the group, some of which may emerge naturally (e.g., the leader, the clarifier, etc.) and some of which may be assigned (e.g. the time-keeper, the secretary, etc.). The teacher's leadership plays a crucial role in establishing the motivational character of the learning environment. Dörnyei suggests that an optimal leadership style for encouraging motivation will tend to be somewhat hierarchical in the early stages of the group where the teacher or facilitator takes responsibility for designing the syllabus and providing explicit structures for learning. This hierarchical mode will shift to a more cooperative approach, where the teacher/facilitator begins to share power and responsibilities with the group and encourages members to increasingly self-regulate their learning. Finally, the teacher/facilitator can move into an autonomous mode where the group is given extensive autonomy to exercise their own judgment and organize their learning to achieve their personal goals. Dörnyei concludes by suggesting specific strategies whereby the teacher generates initial motivation, maintains and protects this motivation, and finally encourages positive retrospective self-evaluation on the part of students.

Related to motivation is the construct of *autonomy* which Benson suggests is concerned with learners' active and sustained participation in their learning. There is widespread agreement that autonomy involves both behavioral and psychological attributes. At the behavioral level, autonomy involves taking charge of one's own learning reflected in behaviors such as determining objectives, content, and progression, selecting methods and techniques, monitoring acquisition, and evaluating what has been acquired. The psychological attributes underlying autonomous learning involve the capacity for detachment, critical reflection, decision-making, and independent action. However, neither the behavioral nor psychological attributes associated with autonomy can be precisely pinned down because autonomy is likely to be displayed variably both from learner to learner and from context to context. Benson attributes the increased interest in learner autonomy and flexible modes of access to learning opportunities during the past 25 years to the changing nature of the international labor market, together with the influence of ideologies associated with globalization, the information age, and the knowledge economy. There has been a shift in the perception of what constitutes successful learning. Successful learners, he notes, are increasingly seen as capable of instructing and training themselves rather than as simply responsive to instruction. Benson notes that there is a reciprocal relationship between learner autonomy and teacher autonomy: in order to foster learner autonomy, teachers should possess capacities that correspond in some sense to those that they aim to develop within their students. However, teachers frequently operate in situations characterized by many constraints on autonomy which can range from immediate conditions of employment to pedagogical issues concerned with methods and ideologies of teaching and learning. For example, in many parts of the United States the mandating of 'teacher-proof' scripted curricula, which are applied predominantly to low-income and English language learning students, severely restricts teacher autonomy and minimizes students' opportunities to become autonomous learners. This example illustrates the complex and contradictory nature of pedagogical debate both in the specific area of ELT and the broader area of learning in general. Administrators frequently want top-down control over the delivery of teaching and learning and, as a result, they establish structures that foster instructional dependence and limit students' capacity to become autonomous learners capable of thriving in a knowledge-based society. It is in this context that Benson's suggestion that the idea of autonomy might serve as a compass to evaluate instructional or organizational initiatives is both intriguing and extremely valuable. Given the realities of 21st century learning, the information age, and the knowledge-based society, one could argue that initiatives fostering learner autonomy should be supported and those that limit autonomy should be critically scrutinized.

    Throughout the short history of the use of digital technologies in education, policy-makers and educators have assumed that these tools will not only increase learner autonomy but also result in enhanced learning and performance. Unfortunately, as Murray points out, these expectations remain to be fulfilled. Research on computer-assisted language learning tends to be small-scale and not generalizable beyond the specific context in which it was conducted. In addition, computer technology continues to develop so rapidly that research has difficulty keeping pace—frequently by the time results get reported the technology investigated has become largely obsolete. Murray argues that *pedagogy* rather than technology should be the appropriate focus for research and we should be asking the same questions of computer-assisted language learning (CALL) that we ask of language learning in general. Although limited in scope and generalizability, there *is* research evidence that computer-assisted technologies can increase motivation and collaboration among learners. Learners can also access more authentic language and benefit from opportunities for interaction and active use of the target language, all of which theoretically should support language learning. Among the issues that remain problematic within CALL and computer-assisted instruction generally, according to Murray, are the so-called digital divide, the need for on-going professional development of teachers, greater understanding of the grammar and semiotics of visual literacy, the need to better integrate technological advances into English language curriculum design, and the need for research approaches that can better address the emerging issues of computer-assisted instruction. Murray concludes that computer-assisted instruction can support the development of learners' communicative competence within the context of interactionist and constructivist approaches to language learning but considerable research and practical experimentation is still required to develop appropriate instructional practices that fully exploit this potential.

In the final chapter of this section, Kourtis-Kazoullis and Skourtou reinforce Murray's point that computer technologies can exert a significant impact on language teaching practices and outcomes. Their documentation of the Internet-based sister class exchange, entitled *DiaLogos*, between Rhodes, Greece, and Toronto, Canada, also illustrates the potential of technology to promote interactionist and social constructivist approaches to language instruction. The curriculum in Greece, including the English language teaching curriculum, is developed by the national government and is uniform across the country. Pedagogy tends to be highly traditional and teacher-centered with a focus on grammar and vocabulary instruction based on the nationally-mandated textbook. In the DiaLogos project, one of the three English lessons each week was devoted to the sister class exchange with the Canadian students. It was thus possible to contrast what students did in the regular English class with the kinds of language activities they engaged in as part of the sister class exchange. Kourtis-Kazoullis and Skourtou report that in the traditional classroom context, students did focus on both meaning and language itself but this typically involved the study of textbook language far removed from any context relevant to students' identity and experience. By contrast, within the context of DiaLogos, students engaged in more critical forms of literacy, analyzing textual meanings that were relevant to their lives and sense of self. They were also exposed to colloquial language that was very different from textbook language (e.g. *stuff like that*, *chilling out*, *with a really big bang*, *we had a blast, whaz up,* etc.) and they began to use this language themselves in their exchanges with their sister class partners. They also used English for authentic communicative and creative purposes, a practice that was virtually absent form the traditional classroom environment. Kourtis-Kazoullis and Skourtou conclude that sister class networks specifically, and technology-assisted instruction more generally, have the potential to shift language teaching from a traditional instructional orientation to more social constructivist (inquiry-based) and transformative (social justice focused) orientations.

In conclusion, we live in a rapidly-changing global environment where information and communication technologies have transformed every facet of human existence. In English language teaching, these technologies have changed both the learner and the learning environment, and we can only speculate about when the pace of change will slow down and what kinds of interpersonal spaces will have emerged at that point. Based on the chapters in this section, however, we can be reasonably confident of two dimensions of the relationship between the learner and the learning environment: Firstly, virtual forms of communication, mediated by digital technologies, will play an increasing role in language teaching and learning and increasingly encroach on traditional face-to-face language teaching environments and methodologies. Presumably, an optimal and complementary blend of virtual and face-to-face language teaching/learning environments will emerge in the coming decades. Secondly, regardless of the kinds of technologies that mediate the language teaching/learning relationship, policy, research, and theory, should focus primarily on *pedagogy* rather than technology in isolation. Constructs directly related to the teaching/learning relationship such as scaffolding, the zone of proximal development, motivation, identity, autonomy, and the impact of societal power relations, are all likely to remain more directly relevant for policy and practice than the forms of technology themselves.

CHAPTER 36

ESL LEARNERS IN THE EARLY SCHOOL YEARS:

Identity and Mediated Classroom Practices

KELLEEN TOOHEY

ELAINE DAY

Simon Fraser University, Canada

PATRICK MANYAK

University of Wyoming, USA

ABSTRACT

In this chapter, Toohey, Day, and Manyak discuss theoretical perspectives and empirical research that advance our understanding of the complex social processes involved in young children's acquisition of ESL. In the first two sections, they examine post-structuralist and sociocultural theories of identity and of mediated practice, highlighting constructs that provide insight into children's second language learning. In the last two sections, they review recent studies of young children's ESL learning that have applied these theoretical perspectives. The studies reveal how learners' identities, classroom practices, and learning resources interweave to inhibit or promote children's acquisition of English.

Classrooms represent complex social environments constructed through the interweaving of institutional and instructional practices; lived cultures; social relations, identities, goals, and purposes; and multiple linguistic codes, texts, and artifacts. Through participation in the social practices of the classroom, children develop a sense of the order of the academic world and their place within it, their status relative to teachers and peers, the nature of the tasks they face, and the relative legitimacy ascribed to their cultural and linguistic resources. For young second language learners, these broad lessons crucially influence investment in, access to, and acquisition of English. A number of contemporary scholars have demonstrated that the acquisition of English involves the negotiation of social goals, relations, and identities inside and outside of classrooms (Day, 2002; Gutiérrez, Baquedano-López, Alvarez, & Chiu, 1999; Manyak, 2000, 2001, 2002; Toohey, 1998, 2000; Vasquez, Pease-Alvarez, & Shannon, 1994; Willett, 1995). In this chapter, we examine the theoretical perspectives underlying and empirical findings issuing from this body of research. We begin by discussing critical and post-structural theories of identity (Hall, 1996; Holland, Lachicotte, Skinner, & Cain, 1998; Holland & Lave, 2001; Taylor, 1991; Weedon, 1987; Wenger, 1998) and sociocultural/sociohistorical theories of mediated practice (Lave & Wenger, 1991; Rogoff, 1995; Vygotsky, 1978; Wertsch, 1991, 1998), drawing out the conceptual tools that they provide for understanding the complex social processes involved in children's second language acquisition (SLA). Next, we survey recent studies of children's second language learning that examine teacher-student and peer relationships; the social organization of instructional activities; and the cultural, linguistic, and material resources that participants use to mediate these activities. In particular, we focus on how issues related to learners' identities and the structure of classroom practices influence the children's acquisition of ESL.

SOCIOCULTURAL AND POST-STRUCTURAL THEORIES OF IDENTITY

Sociocultural perspectives on learning share a common belief that individuals' acquisition of new knowledge and skills often results from the growing sense of belonging to and participation in particular communities and increasing identification with members of those communities. Lave and Wenger (1991) succinctly articulate this belief by describing a learner as "a practitioner...whose changing knowledge, skill and discourse are part of a developing identity" (p. 122). Making a parallel claim with regard to literacy learning, Solsken (1993) asserts that "questions about...the achievement of literacy cannot be addressed without taking into account that each and every literacy transaction is a moment of self-definition in which people take action within and upon their relations with other people" (p. 8). In this chapter, we suggest that young children's second language learning is similarly linked to and mediated by issues of identity.

The coupling of second language learning and identity necessitates a carefully theorized notion of *identity*. While the term generally refers to the view that individuals have of themselves and of their relationship to the social world, contemporary theorists have elaborated on this meaning in important ways. Here we distill five key points from sociocultural and post-structuralist efforts to theorize the complex relationship between the individual and the social that contribute powerfully to understanding children's acquisition of ESL. (We believe that these points roughly capture the thinking of theorists such as Bakhtin, 1981; Gee, 1999; Hall, 1990, 1996; Henriques, Hollway, Urwin, Venn, & Walkerdine, 1984; Holland, Lachicotte, Skinner, & Cain, 1998; Holland & Lave, 2001; Lave & Wenger, 1991; Norton, 2000; Ochs, 1993; Taylor, 1991; Weedon, 1987; Wenger, 1998.)

1. Identities are socially constructed within cultural worlds; therefore, they do not reflect unique and fixed essences assumed to reside at the core of individuals.
2. Identities are multiple, dynamic, and contradictory.
3. Identities are sites of struggle deeply influenced by the working out of power relations within inequitably structured social contexts.
4. The ways that individuals see themselves and their relationship to the social world are delimited by *discourses*—"[systematic groupings] of the ideas, opinions, concepts, ways of thinking and behaving which are formed within a particular context" (Mills, 1999, p. 17). In other words, people do not experience unlimited freedom in constructing identities but instead are

limited by the raw materials (beliefs, truths, categories, desires, etc.) that their sociocultural milieus provide.

5. Identities are not wholly socially or discursively determined, but rather, represent evolving products of participation in social practices through which social positions and discourses are actualized, created, mediated, and resisted. Punctuating this point, Wenger (1998) states, "What narratives, categories, roles, and positions come to mean...is something that must be worked out in practice" (p. 151). In other words, despite the thoroughly social nature of identity construction and the raw materials for that construction, individuals and communities nonetheless exert diverse forms of agency that contribute to the "authoring" of their own identities (Holland, Lachicotte, Skinner, & Cain, 1998; Holland & Lave, 2001).

These points reveal the complexity of identities and the highly situated and conflictive process of identity construction. Viewed from a sociocultural perspective, classroom instruction represents a set of social practices in which children (and teachers) construct identities—identities that in turn mediate their experience with English. To further articulate how children's identities interact with their language learning, we now further elaborate on the key constructs of *identity positioning* and *investment*.

Identity Positioning

The notion of *positioning* issues from the recognition that people always communicate more than semantic content through their speech and non-verbal behavior (Davies & Harré, 1990). Through our choices of languages, dialects, genres, styles, modes, intonations, and timing, we create certain social positions for ourselves and simultaneously position others in particular ways. These acts of positioning occur in and contribute to a dynamic and often inequitable social terrain. The concept of identity position refers to this ongoing process of positioning: Through what we say and do, we place ourselves and are placed by others in positions that influence our *identities* (the ways we view ourselves and our relationship to the world). Ethnographic research has documented how teacher-student interaction, colored by cultural expectations, institutional categories, and notions of class and gender, can create problematic identity positions for linguistically diverse students—positions loaded with the baggage of presumed incompetence, ignorance, and "benign deviance" (Gutiérrez, Rhymes, & Larson, 1995; Toohey, 1998; Willet, 1995). Thus, the formation and negotiation of identity positions represent an important dimension of classroom practices that contributes critically to students' evolving relationship with school communities and their investment in learning English.

Investment

Our understanding of *investment* draws on Norton's (2000) discussion of the concept. Concerned primarily with adult SLA, Norton states, "investment...signals the socially and historically constructed relationship of learners to the target language, and their often ambivalent desire to learn and practice it" (p. 10). As an alternative to more invariable conceptions of *motivation*, investment is grounded in a poststructuralist view of identity as socially constructed, dynamic, multiple, and conflictive. Drawing upon the notion of positioning, Norton emphasizes that language learners not only exchange information when speaking with target language speakers but also "[organize] and [reorganize] a sense of who they are and how they relate to the world" (p. 11). This identity work leads language learners to invest in strategic and often contradictory ways in the second language. In their study of adolescent Chinese immigrant students, McKay and Wong (1996) further elaborated the concept of investment. In particular, the authors stressed that the acts of speaking, reading, and writing English had distinct consequences for the students' identities and, as a result, that the same students invested in these uses of the language to widely varying degrees. Based on the work of Norton and McKay and Wong, we posit that children are active agents who invest strategically in learning English in specific social settings. These investments occur at the intersection of the identities children acquire through life in their families, communities, and peer groups and the identity positions made available to them by classroom practices. Thus, tracing students' investments in speaking English illuminates the complex ways in which children's historically, culturally, and socially constituted identities and desires contribute to or hinder their SLA.

SOCIOCULTURAL THEORIES OF MEDIATED PRACTICES

In our introduction, we stated that classrooms are complex social environments shaped largely by the interweaving of institutional and instructional practices. In this section, we elaborate on this statement by discussing the powerful ways that classroom practices—structured, recurring teacher student and student student interactions—shape children's opportunities to learn English. Sociocultural theories of learning have critiqued the notion that learning occurs within the heads of individual learners (Lave & Wenger, 1991; Moll, 1990; Rogoff, 1991, 1995; Vygotsky, 1978; Wenger, 1998; Wertsch, 1991, 1998). Constructs such as the zone of proximal development (Vygotsky), assisted performance (Tharp & Gallimore, 1988), guided participation (Rogoff, Mosier, Mistry, & Artin, 1993), legitimate peripheral participation (Lave & Wenger), and mediated action (Wertsch, 1998) have increased understanding of how people acquire knowledge, skills, and identities through participation in historically, culturally, and socially constituted practices. Here we survey several sociocultural perspectives on mediated practice and consider their relevance for understanding young children's SLA.

Learning as Participation

Lave and Wenger's (1991) theory of *legitimate peripheral participation* (LPP) conceptualizes learning as a process of evolving participation in numerous and overlapping communities of practice. These authors define *communities of practice* as informal social organizations resulting from mutual human engagement in joint enterprises. Over time, participants in these communities come to share ways of doing things, forms of interaction and discourse, beliefs and values, and ensembles of resources that include tools, concepts, and symbols. The theory of LPP focuses on newcomers' participation with and transformation into old-timers in these communities of practice.

In contrast to approaches that conceive of learning as an isolable experience in which individuals engage in order to gain specific knowledge and skills, LPP emphasizes that "learning, thinking, and knowing are relations among people in activity in, with, and arising from the socially and culturally structured world" (Lave & Wenger, 1991, p. 51). By locating learning in the processes of evolving participation in social practice, LPP shifts "analysis away from teaching and onto the intricate structuring of a community's learning resources" (p. 94). These resources include the social relations necessary for the development of identities of belonging; diverse forms of collaboration that enable participants to perform at levels beyond their individual capacity and thus grow into new levels of competence (Cazden, 1981); the community's shared history, tools, and understandings; and the unique knowledge possessed by individual members. A learner's access to such resources requires an evolving trajectory of participation in the community. Through engagement in increasingly central roles and responsibilities in practice, participants expand their access to community members, activities, discourses, and technologies, and they experience new opportunities to develop knowledge, skills, and identities. Conversely, confining learners to a narrow range of participation limits their access to learning resources and their chances for "absorbing and being absorbed in 'the culture of practice'" (Lave & Wenger, 1991, p. 95) of the community.

The theoretical insights provided by LPP stress the importance of young English learners' access to robust forms of participation within school and classroom practices, viable identity positions as students and English speakers, and valuable learning resources such as carefully structured collaborative activity with native speaking peers. Unfortunately, as we discuss in detail later, classroom research has documented how instructional and peer practices often exclude English learners from the kind of participation important for language and literacy development (Gutiérrez & Larson, 1994; Moll & Diaz, 1987; Toohey, 1996, 1998).

Learning as Mediated Action

The notion of *mediated action* combines synergistically with the theory of LPP to provide a more comprehensive understanding of the social nature of learning in classroom settings. Following Vygotsky's seminal insights, several contemporary sociocultural theorists emphasize the mediated nature of human learning (Moll, 1990; Tharp & Gallimore, 1988; Wertsch, 1991, 1998). These scholars detail how social interaction and cultural tools enable people to engage in activities and perform tasks beyond their individual level of competence. These views of mediated action contribute to a finer-grained understanding of the learning that occurs during social practice.

Vygotsky (1978) theorized that social interaction constitutes the genesis of higher cognitive functions. He conceived of joint activity within the *zone of proximal development* (ZPD), the space between what an individual can do alone and what s/he can do in collaboration with a more competent other, as the driving force of individual cognitive development. Moll (1990) argues that the ZPD has been narrowly interpreted as primarily applying to adult-child dyads in which the adult transmits skills to the child. Based on their research in an elementary classroom, Moll and Whitmore (1993) propose that a "'collective' zone of proximal development" resulting from "the interdependence of adults and children, and how they use social and cultural resources" (p. 20) better captures the dynamic spirit of Vygotsky's concept. Informed by this more expansive understanding of the ZPD, we argue that collaborative participation in community practice produces overlapping, multidirectional ZPDs that form the basis for socially mediated cognitive development and that also powerfully mediate SLA. For instance, in his study of young English language learners in an English immersion class in California, Manyak (2001, 2002) has demonstrated that densely collaborative activity involving the translation and scribing of personal narratives originally told in Spanish effectively promoted the children's acquisition of English.

Wertsch's (1991, 1998) notion of *privileging* further enhances the concept of mediated action and its use in understanding the classroom experiences of young English language learners. Privileging focuses analytic attention on how a community defines resources for learning. The term issues from Wertsch's theorizing on mediational means. Working in the Vygotskian tradition, Wertsch emphasizes the ubiquity of mediational means or cultural tools in human activity and points out that while many cultural tools may serve to accomplish a task, one tool is often privileged above others. He elaborates, "Privileging refers to the fact that one mediational means, such as a social language, is viewed as being more appropriate or efficacious than others in a particular sociocultural setting" (1998, p. 124). The concept of privileging raises questions about the learning resources considered appropriate for participation in classroom practices. Is the teacher defined as the sole source of knowledge in a practice or is peer input also considered a valued learning resource? Is so-called Standard English defined as the only appropriate code for a practice or are children's broad linguistic repertoires also viable resources for participation and meaning making? These questions address the delimiting of learning resources in classroom practices and, subsequently, children's access to legitimate forms of participation and viable identity positions.

Historical, Cultural, and Political Dimensions of Practice

While the theories of LPP and mediated action illuminate the ways in which the social organization of classroom practices shape children's learning, they often fail to account for the broader historical, cultural, political, and institutional forces that influence those classroom practices. McDermott (1993) succinctly articulates the effect of these broad forces on learning:

> The question of who is learning what and how much is essentially a question of what conversations they are a part of, and this question is a subset of the more powerful question of what conversations are around to be had in a given culture. (p. 295)

McDermott's "more powerful question" implies that if learning takes place as a result of participation in social practices, the types of practices available in a given community crucially influence what its members can learn and who they can become. Rogoff's (1995) discussion of the community plane of sociocultural activity elaborates on the need to analyze the broad historical, cultural, political, and institutional contexts of participation. In Rogoff's words, the *community plane of activity* involves "the institutional structure and cultural technologies of intellectual activity," including "purposes (defined in community or institutional terms), cultural constraints, resources, values relating to what means are appropriate for reaching goals… and cultural tools such as…linguistic and mathematical systems" (pp. 143-144). By considering these dimensions, analysis on the community plane makes clear the broad forces that impact local practice.

Numerous historical, cultural, societal, and political conditions currently exert a powerful influence on the schooling of English language learners in North America. Such conditions include the troubling history of assimilationist schooling for English language learners in North America (Crawford, 1995; Cummins, 1996), widely embraced ideologies opposed to language diversity (Wiley & Lukes, 1996), the current political backlash against immigration, and new educational policies directed at linguistically diverse children. These factors suggest the need for research that carefully links macrosocial analyses with close descriptions of the kinds of classroom practices available to young ESL learners. Guitiérrez and her colleagues (Gutiérrez, Baquedano-López, & Asato, 2000; Gutiérrez, Asato, Santos, & Gotanda, in press) have provided a blueprint for this type of work in two recent articles addressing the consequences of broad sociopolitical movements on the schooling of linguistically diverse children in California. We encourage additional studies providing detailed accounts of local instructional practices involving English language learners while simultaneously connecting such practices to broad historical, political, economic, and cultural conditions and significant educational reform movements.

ESL RESEARCH WITH YOUNG CHILDREN

Many early investigations of the second language learning of children attempted to explicate the individual internalization of second language knowledge. This work focused on the cognitive processes of language acquisition "by which language learners gradually organize the language they hear, according to the rules they construct to understand and generate sentences" (Dulay, Burt, & Krashen, 1982, p. 276) and on measuring individual personality traits of children and attempting to correlate these with language learning (e.g., Wong Fillmore, 1979). However, these studies frequently failed to examine how social relations with peers, teachers, and the second language community influenced children's "personalities" and to document the nature of the learning environments, the particular activities in which English learners engaged, or the resources to which these learners had access in these instructional contexts. Fortunately, recent research applying poststructural and sociocultural theoretical perspectives to the subject of young children's second language learning have begun to address these issues. We now move to a review of this research, examining a small group of studies that focus on issues of learners' identities, classroom practices, and learning resources.

Identities and ESL Learning

A number of studies have attended specifically to identity issues in young children's ESL learning. In this section, we briefly summarize the insights resulting from these studies and, based on those insights, suggest fruitful paths for further research.

Bourne (1992), Willet (1995), and Toohey (2000) each document ways in which young English language learners acquired problematic school identities that inhibited their ESL learning. Bourne reported on a year-long ethnographic study of a multilingual primary classroom of English-, Bengali- and Cantonese-speaking children. She reveals the importance of students' positioning in relation to the teacher's beliefs and classroom practices. Since the English language learners in her study were often isolated or placed with other beginners upon entry to the classroom, they had restricted access to the teacher and to other students. Over time, this condition seemed to lead to the students being perceived as having low status and to their more permanent isolation.

Willett (1995) reports on a year-long study of four English language learners (three girls and one boy) in a first grade elementary school classroom in the Northeastern United States. She demonstrates how the classroom's micropolitics of gender and class mediated the children's opportunities to acquire English. The three girls, allowed to sit together over the year, displayed competence and gained identities as good students by collaboratively supporting one another. In contrast, the boy was placed between two English-speaking girls who tended not to help him. Unable to complete his work alone, the boy was positioned as a problematic learner and sent out for additional ESL lessons that further enhanced his identity as a less-than-capable outsider in the classroom. Willett concludes that "the sociocultural ecology of the community, school, and classroom" powerfully "shaped the kinds of micro-interactions that occurred and thus the nature of [the children's] language learning over the course of the year" (p. 473).

Toohey (2000) investigated identity practices in a longitudinal ethnographic study that follows six English language learners in a Canadian elementary school from kindergarten through Grade 2. In particular, she analyzes classroom ranking and normalizing practices and demonstrates that three of the English language learners were constructed as deficient language learners due to their positioning along continuums in various dimensions of competence (i.e., academic, physical, behavioral, social, and linguistic). For example, one boy, although a competent English speaker, struggled to gain access to participatory roles because of his heavy accent, clumsiness with skills such as using scissors, and stigmatization by other children. As a result, he acquired a problematic identity within the class, he was denied access to social and material resources, and his English production decreased over time.

Noting that affiliation with peers, teacher approval, and a complex of "school-appropriate" behaviors permitted the other children access to desirable identities, Toohey (2000) points to the need for further research on how second language learners take up and/or resist identity positions in their everyday interactions.

Two additional studies highlight the multiple communities that young ESL students participate in and the conflict of identities that they experience (Day, 2002; Hunter, 1997). Drawing on a 2-year ethnographic study of English language learning in multicultural urban classrooms in Eastern Canada, Hunter uses poststructuralist theory to analyze the multiple and contradictory positioning of one pupil she calls Roberto, a Portuguese- and English-speaking bilingual child, in writing activities. She reveals how school expectations conflicted with identities valued in Roberto's peer group and points out how his negotiation of this conflict influenced his second language and literacy learning. Hunter concludes by calling attention to the multiple, shifting, and conflicting identities of English language learners (in contrast to the school's static construction of the students' identities based on ethnicity and language proficiency) and by stressing the complexity of students' investments in English learning and using English.

Day (2002) presents findings from her ethnographic case study of a Punjabi-speaking English language learner in kindergarten. The study shows how the child actively positioned himself in the diverse subcommunities in his class and how he experienced both constraints and possibilities in negotiating a powerful identity in and across those communities. Day's work draws on psychoanalytic theories (e.g.,

Henriques, Hollway, Urwin, Venn, & Walkerdine, 1984; Litowitz, 1997) to explore the role of identification and unconscious desires in the child's relationship with the teacher and thus suggests the importance of including such psychoanalytic understandings in frameworks of identity and second language learning.

The studies described here provide useful understandings of the complexities of young English learners' identities and the mediating role of those identities in acquiring English. In keeping with these findings, Ibrahim (1999) argues that we must be concerned with the interlocking question of identification and desire in education. He challenges scholars to ask questions that have not typically been raised in ESL and applied linguistics research: "Who do we as social subjects living within a social space desire to be or to become? And whom do we identify with, and what repercussions does our identification have on how and what we learn?" (p. 352). Grappling with such questions should constitute an important part of future research investigating the ESL learning of young children. In particular, further study is needed on how children are positioned and position themselves in the classrooms in which they are learning English. For instance, we believe it will be particularly interesting to consider the question of agency with respect to young children. Canagarajah (1993), Gutiérrez, Rymes, and Larson (1995), and McKay and Wong (1996) have alerted us to how older learners often resist the positions offered to them in academic contexts. We call for similar research examining young children's agency in negotiating identities in second language classrooms and the consequences of that agency for their acquisition of English. In conclusion, as Dyson (2000) has noted, children are currently growing into (and creating) cultural worlds and using (and creating) cultural tools that teachers frequently have not experienced. Thus, coming to understand the cultural worlds that linguistically and culturally diverse children inhabit seems critical to efforts to make second language teaching more helpful in equipping children for those worlds.

Practices and Mediating Artifacts

Classroom instruction represents a set of culturally and socially organized practices with underlying assumptions, values, and goals. As we previously discussed, instructional practices structure students' interaction with teachers and peers, their evolving identities, and their access to various forms, functions, and meanings of language and literacy. Consequently, the nature of classroom practices dramatically affects young English language learners' socialization to the academic community and their acquisition of language and literacy. In this section, we discuss a set of studies on young second language learners that place participation and mediation at the center of analyses of classroom language learning. While several of these studies describe situations in which English language learners accessed only a narrow scope of participatory roles, others portray classrooms operating as communities-of-learners in which young students participated vitally in meaning-centered activities.

Concerned with foregrounding the socially situated nature of SLA, Toohey (1998) applies the notion of community of practice to her study of English learners in a Canadian first grade class. Her analysis of ethnographic data reveals that the social structures and interactional routines of classroom practices served to place students within a stratified community in which the English learners were considered "benignly deviant" (p. 78). Toohey concludes that such practices resulted in "the exclusion of some students from certain activities, practices, identities, and affiliations" (p. 80). For example, the desks of the English learners were clustered at the front of the room near the teacher where the children had little opportunity to converse with either their English-speaking peers or others who spoke their own home language. In addition, strict rules regarding copying discouraged the English learners from imitating the speech and writing of fluent English speakers. Thus, classroom social practices kept English learners from the kind of participation important for language acquisition and the development of competent academic identities.

Focusing on Latina/o students in California, Gutiérrez and Larson (1994) describe how teachers' hegemonic discursive practices relegate children to "contexts for learning that limit participation in and access to the forms or practices of literacy that are central to language development and successful membership in academic communities" (p. 23). Drawing upon data from ethnographic research in a number of elementary classrooms, the authors emphasize the restrictive nature of the traditional recitation script as it functioned to close off student participation in the negotiation of meaning from texts. Instead, this form of classroom discourse socialized children to the role of "being a student" in which they attempted to guess the answers desired by the teacher.

Also studying Latina/o children in California, Moll and Diaz (1987) observed a group of bilingual students as they participated in Spanish reading in their own classroom and then went next door for English reading instruction. Although the children were capable readers in Spanish, they found that the English reading lessons were organized in ways that made them appear to be incompetent English readers. In particular, the lessons stressed oral reading and verbal recall in English. In this context, the students' pronunciation and limited English caused the teacher to misevaluate their reading ability and thus assign simple skills-based instruction. However, by discussing the stories in Spanish with the children, Moll and Diaz revealed that the students fully understood what they read in English.

In contrast to these cases in which English language learners suffered from limited access to participation, a number of researchers have documented classrooms in which children fulfill diverse participatory roles in classroom practices. Moll and colleagues (Moll, Tapia, & Whitmore, 1993; Moll & Whitmore, 1993) provide portraits of bilingual classrooms featuring highly collaborative literacy activities in which Latina/o students benefited from a variety of socially distributed resources for learning. In particular, bilingual children utilized their linguistic ability to facilitate interaction between monolingual participants and to access sources of information in Spanish and English. These settings prompted Moll and colleagues to conceptualize the rich potential for learning within a collective zone of proximal development in which "children become important, indispensable, thinking resources for one another" (Moll, Tapia, & Whitmore, 1993, p. 160).

Appropriating the construct of hybridity for research on diverse learning environments, Gutiérrez, Baquedano-López, and Tejeda (1999) underscore the dynamic possibilities for human development resulting from the interaction of multiple cultural and linguistic codes. While all classrooms contain a variety of spaces, practices, and linguistic codes, Gutiérrez et al. posit that many teachers suppress or ignore the hybrid moments or activities created by the interaction of diverse "scripts." However, they demonstrate that this hybridity, when embraced, creates fruitful contexts for development for young English language learners. Their study describes a *hybrid learning context* that occurred in an elementary-grade classroom in California when the teacher and a group of Latina/o students developed an instructional unit on the human body as a result of the children's name-calling. The hybrid language practices, or "commingling of, and contradictions among different linguistic codes and registers" (p. 289), of this learning community redefined the lexicon, humor, and local knowledge of the students' informal discourse as important meaning-making resources for classroom learning.

Fránquiz and Reyes (1998) similarly describe "inclusive learning communities" in which teachers and bilingual children employed "a range of language registers and codes (e.g., from standard to more colloquial forms of speech and from monolingual to more mixed language uses)" (p. 213) in the course of classroom activity. In these classrooms, the teacher focused on academic content and affirmed the children's choice of language for facilitating their learning. The authors particularly emphasize the strategic role code-switching played in developing the students' linguistic awareness and biliteracy as they moved in between languages and cultures. Urging teachers to meet children in a middle ground, Fránquiz and Reyes promote a "dialogic pedagogy in which diverse and even competing meanings and forms of knowledge exist" (pp. 216-217).

Patrick Manyak (2001, 2002) describes classroom language and literacy practices that promoted the bilingualism and biliteracy of Spanish-speaking children in a first and second grade classroom in a city on the outskirts of Los Angeles. In one practice, The Daily News, the teacher scribed children's stories of daily events in English and preserved these narratives in books that became part of the classroom's library. When the children shared stories in Spanish, the community collaborated to produce English translations, an activity which effectively scaffolded the students' acquisition of English. Later, the children took over the role of producing The Daily News by collaboratively writing one another's stories. Manyak notes that the activity provided the children with access to a wide range of participatory roles that evolved over time, involved densely collaborative activity in which the children shifted constantly between expert and apprentice roles, and "positioned the children's sociocultural experience as a legitimate source of knowledge and a valuable resource for acquiring literacy" (2001, p. 455). Based on his analysis, Manyak concludes that the following characteristics contribute to dynamic contexts of development for English learners: (a) challenging and multifaceted tasks that provide for numerous forms of participation and generate a need for collaborative activity, (b) access to expert performance of the task over time, (c) access to identity positions of expertise, and (d) opportunity to draw upon personal experience and a wide range of community resources (e.g., languages, knowledge, skills, and so on). Manyak's distillation of these characteristics emphasizes that instructional practices, identity positions, and resources for learning intertwine to compose classroom environments that can either promote or truncate opportunities for language acquisition.

The research reviewed in this section illuminates the social contexts of classroom language instruction and learning. In keeping with the theoretical perspectives we examined earlier, the studies demonstrate that access to legitimate forms of participation in school activities crucially defines children's opportunities for developing the skills and identities necessary for acquiring English and achieving academic success. In particular, the research we have discussed reveals that for English learners such access often hangs in the balance, dependent on the inclusiveness of classroom social practices and the range of cultural tools deemed acceptable as resources for learning. We believe that additional community research would contribute to a more robust understanding of the language and literacy practices in specific ESL communities and their interface with school instruction. At a time when school reform is high on national agendas, researchers also need to continually document the influence of new educational policies on the kinds of classroom literacy activities available to English learners. Finally, in addition to describing the social organization of classroom practices and the nature of children's participation in them, we believe that socioculturally oriented SLA research should document more carefully the language and literacy knowledge and skills that students acquire as by-products of their participation. This evidence would enable more compelling comparisons of the consequences of differently structured classroom language learning environments.

CONCLUSIONS

In this chapter, we have discussed theoretical perspectives and empirical research that envisions children's acquisition of English as a complex social phenomenon. In particular, we have stressed that young English learners are complex beings whose socially constructed, multiple, and dynamic identities mediate their investments in and opportunities to learn English and that classroom social practices crucially structure such learners' access to the relationships and resources necessary to do so. While we would not suggest that the theories and research that we have presented here provide definitive answers to all questions regarding ESL learning and pedagogy, we do feel that the insights they offer are too critical to ignore. Throughout the chapter, we have also pointed to areas for further research related to issues of young English learners' identity processes and to the social organization of classroom practices. We believe that such research, when considered alongside the studies that we have reviewed, will contribute powerfully to an understanding of young children's acquisition of English and to multifaceted efforts to facilitate that process.

REFERENCES

Bakhtin, M. M. (1981). *The dialogic imagination: Four essays* (C. Emerson & M. Holquist, Trans.). Austin, TX: University of Texas Press.

Bourne, J. (1992). Inside a multilingual primary classroom: A teacher, children and theories at work. Ph.D. thesis, University of Southampton.

Canagarajah, A. S. (1993). Critical ethnography of a Sri Lankan classroom: Ambiguities in student opposition to reproduction through ESOL. *TESOL Quarterly, 2,* 601–626.

Cazden, C. B. (1981). Performance before competence: Assistance to child discourse in the zone of proximal development. *The Quarterly Newsletter of the Laboratory of Comparative Human Cognition, 3,* 5–8.

Crawford, J. (1995). *Bilingual education: History, politics, theory, and practice.* Los Angeles: Bilingual Educational Services, Inc.

Cummins, J. (1996). *Negotiating identities: Education for empowerment in a diverse society.* Ontario: CABE.

Davies, B., & Harré, R. (1990). Positioning: The discursive production of selves. *Journal for the Theory of Social Behaviour, 20,* 43–63.

Day, E. (2002). *Identity and the young English language learner.* Clevedon, England: Multilingual Matters.

Dulay, H., Burt, M., & Krashen, S. (1982). *Language two.* New York: Oxford University Press.

Dyson, A. (2000). Linking writing and community development through the children's forum. In C. Lee & P. Smagorinsky (Eds.), *Vygotskian perspectives on literacy research* (pp. 127–149). Cambridge: Cambridge University Press.

Fránquiz, M., & Reyes, M. de la Luz, (1998). Creating inclusive learning communities through English language arts: From chanclas to canicas. *Language Arts, 75*(3), 211–220.

Gee, J. (1999). *An introduction to discourse analysis.* New York: Routledge.

Gutiérrez, K., Asato, J., Santos, M., & Gotanda, N. (in press). Backlash pedagogy: Language and culture and the politics of reform. In M. Suarez-Orozco (Ed.), *Latinos in the 21st century.* Berkeley: University of California Press.

Gutiérrez, K., Baquedano-López, P., Alvarez, H., & Chiu, M. M. (1999). Building a culture of collaboration through hybrid language practices. *Theory into Practice, 38*(2), 87–93.

Gutiérrez, K., Baquedano-López, P., & Asato, J. (2000). "English for the children": The new literacy of the old world order, language policy and educational reform. *Bilingual Research Journal, 24,* 1–26.

Gutiérrez, K., Baquedano-López, P., & Tejeda, C. (1999). Rethinking diversity: Hybridity and hybrid language practices in the third space. *Mind, Culture, and Activity, 6,* 286–303.

Gutiérrez, K., & Larson, J. (1994). Language borders: Recitation as hegemonic discourse. *International Journal of Educational Reform, 3*(1), 22–36.

Gutiérrez, K., Rymes, B., & Larson, J. (1995). Script, counterscript, and underlife in the classroom: James Brown versus Brown v. Board of Education. *Harvard Educational Review, 65,* 445–471.

Hall, S. (1990). Cultural identity and diaspora. In J. Rutherford (Ed.), *Identity: Community, culture, difference* (pp. 222–237). London: Lawrence and Wishart.

Hall, S. (1996). Introduction: Who needs identity? In S. Hall & P. du Gay (Eds.), *Questions of cultural identity* (pp. 1–17). London: Sage.

Henriques, J., Hollway, W., Urwin, C., Venn, C., & Walkerdine, V. (1984). *Changing the subject.* New York: Methuen.

Holland, D., Lachicotte, W., Skinner, D., & Cain, C. (1998). *Identity and agency in cultural worlds.* Cambridge, MA: Harvard University Press.

Holland, D., & Lave, J. (Eds.). (2001). *History in person: Enduring struggles, contentious practice, intimate identities.* Santa Fe, NM: School of American Research Press.

Hunter, J. (1997). Multiple perceptions: Social identity in a multilingual elementary classroom. *TESOL Quarterly, 31,* 603–611.

Ibrahim, A. (1999). Becoming black: Rap and hip-hop, race, gender, identity and the politics of ESL learning. *TESOL Quarterly, 33,* 349–369.

Lave, J., & Wenger, E. (1991). *Situated learning. Legitimate peripheral participation.* New York: Cambridge University Press.

Litowitz, B. (1997). Just say no: Responsibility and resistance. In M. Cole, Y. Engeström, & O. Vasquez (Eds.), *Mind,Culture, and Activity* (pp. 473–484). New York: Cambridge University Press.

Manyak, P. (2000). Borderlands literacy in a primary-grade English immersion class. In T. Shanahan & F. Rodriguez-Brown (Eds.), *National Reading Conference Yearbook, 49* (pp. 91–109). Chicago, IL: National Reading Conference.

Manyak, P. (2001). Participation, hybridity, and carnival: A situated analysis of a dynamic literacy practice in a primary-grade English immersion class. *Journal of Literacy Research, 33*(3), 423–465.

Manyak, P. (2002). 'Welcome to Salón 110': The consequences of hybrid literacy practices in a primary-grade English immersion class. *Bilingual Research Journal, 26,* 421–442.

McDermott, R. (1993). The acquisition of a child by a learning disability. In J. Lave & S. Chaiklin (Eds.), *Understanding practice: Perspectives on activity and context* (pp. 269–305). Cambridge: Cambridge University Press.

McKay, S., & Wong, S. (1996). Multiple discourses, multiple identities: Investment and agency in second-language learning among Chinese adolescent immigrant students. *Harvard Educational Review, 66,* 577–608.

Mills, S. (1999). *Discourse.* New York: Routledge.

Moll, L. (1990). Introduction. In L. Moll (Ed.), *Vygotsky and education: Instructional implications and applications of sociohistorical psychology* (pp. 1–27). New York: Cambridge University Press.

Moll, L. & Diaz, S. (1987). Change as the goal of educational research. *Anthropology and Education Quarterly, 18,* 300–311.

Moll, L., Tapia, J., & Whitmore, K. (1993). Living knowledge: The social distribution of cultural resources for thinking. In G. Salomon (Ed.), *Distributed cognitions: Psychological and educational considerations* (pp. 139–163). Cambridge, UK: Cambridge University Press.

Moll, L., & Whitmore, K. (1993). Vygotsky in classroom practice: Moving from individual transmission to social transaction. In E. Forman, N. Minick, & C. A. Stone (Eds.), *Contexts for learning: Sociocultural dynamics in children's development* (pp. 230–253). New York: Oxford University Press.

Norton, B. (2000). *Identity and language learning: Gender, ethnicity and educational change.* London: Longman.

Ochs, E. (1993). Constructing social identity: A language socialization perspective. *Research on Language and Social Interaction, 26,* 287–306.

Rogoff, B. (1991). *Apprenticeship in thinking: Cognitive development in social context.* New York: Oxford University Press.

Rogoff, B. (1995). Observing sociocultural activity on three planes: Participatory appropriation, guided participation, and apprenticeship. In J. Wertsch, P. Del Rio, & A. Alvarez (Eds.), *Sociocultural studies of mind* (pp. 139–164). New York: Cambridge University Press.

Rogoff, B., Mosier, C., Mistry, J., & Artin, G. (1993). Toddlers' guided participation with their caregivers in cultural activity. In E. Forman, N. Minick, & C. A. Stone (Eds.), *Contexts for learning: Sociocultural dynamics in children's development* (pp. 230–253). New York: Oxford University Press.

Solsken, J. (1993). *Literacy, gender, and work in families and in school.* Norwood, NJ: Ablex.

Taylor, C. (1991). The dialogical self. In D. Hiley, J. Bohman, & R. Shusterman. (Eds.), *The interpretive turn: Philosophy, science and culture* (pp. 304–314). Ithaca, NY: Cornell University Press.

Tharp, R., & Gallimore, R. (1988). *Rousing minds to life: Teaching, learning, and schooling in social context.* New York: Cambridge University Press.

Toohey, K. (1996). Learning English as a second language in kindergarten: A community of practice perspective. *The Canadian Modern Language Review, 52*(4), 549–576.

Toohey, K. (1998). 'Breaking them up, taking them away': ESL students in grade one. *TESOL Quarterly, 32,* 61–84.

Toohey, K. (2000). *Learning English at school: Identity, social relations, and classroom practice.* Philadelphia: Multilingual Matters.

Vasquez, O., Pease-Alvarez, L., & Shannon, S. (1994). *Pushing boundaries: Language and culture in a Mexicano community.* New York: Cambridge University Press.

Vygotsky, L. S. (1978). *Mind in Society.* Cambridge, MA: Harvard University Press.

Walkerdine, V. (1997). Redefining the subject in situated cognition theory. In D. Kirshner & J. Whitson (Eds.), *Situated cognition. Social, semiotic, and psychological perspectives* (pp. 57–70). Mahwah, NJ: Lawrence Erlbaum.

Weedon, C. (1987). *Feminist practice and poststructuralist theory.* New York: Basil Blackwell.

Wenger, E. (1998). *Communities of practice: Learning, meaning, and identity.* New York: Cambridge University Press.

Wertsch, J. V. (1991). *Voices of the mind.* Cambridge, MA: Harvard University Press.

Wertsch, J. V. (1998). *Mind as action.* New York: Oxford University Press.

Wiley, T. & Lukes, M. (1996). English-only and standard English ideologies in the U.S. *TESOL Quarterly, 30,* 511–535.

Willett, J. (1995). Becoming first graders in an L2: An ethnographic study of L2 socialization. *TESOL Quarterly, 29,* 473–503.

Wong Fillmore, L. (1979). Individual differences in second language acquisition. In C. Fillmore, D. Kempler, & W. Wang (Eds.), *Individual differences in language ability and behavior* (pp. 277–302). New York: Academic Press.

CHAPTER 37

THE ADOLESCENT ENGLISH LANGUAGE LEARNER:

Identities Lost and Found

LINDA HARKLAU

The University of Georgia, USA

ABSTRACT

Theory and research on second language acquisition have long acknowledged the significant influence of learner identities—that is, how learners see themselves and are seen by others in relation to the target language and culture. Learner age has likewise been a central theme in second language acquisition research. These two important factors intersect in the case of adolescent language learners. Adolescence is regarded as a particularly malleable and difficult age in the development of social identity and conception of self, and even more potentially problematic for multilingual and multiethnic English learners. In this chapter, I first briefly outline current debates and cross-cultural research about adolescence as a unique developmental stage in identity development and suggest potential implications for English language learning. I then outline major strands of investigation on the role of social context and social identity in adolescent English language learning, including research in social psychology and intercultural communication; research in social psychology, clinical psychology, and clinical health; research in educational anthropology and sociology; and research on critical theory, cultural studies, and poststructuralism. The chapter concludes with a summary of current debates and directions for further research.

INTRODUCTION

Theory and research on second language acquisition (SLA) have long acknowledged the significant influence of *learner identities*—that is, how learners see themselves and are seen by others in relation to the target language and culture. Learner age has likewise been a central theme in second language acquisition research. These two important factors intersect in the case of adolescent English language learners (ELLs).

In SLA research, adolescence has been seen primarily as a developmental watershed in which the child's neurological facility for learning languages is lost or altered (e.g., Scovel, 2000). At the same time, theorists have often portrayed maturing learners' changing views of self and social context as an important factor in age differences in second language (L2) attainment (e.g., Krashen, 1981). Accordingly, this chapter reviews research and theory on societal images and self-perceptions of adolescent ELLs and their interrelationships with language and academic learning.

The modern notion of adolescence can be traced to G. Stanley Hall, whose expansive 1904 opus on the subject launched a century of research on adolescence as a unique phase of human development. Scholarship on the nature of adolescence has focused primarily on youth in the dominant, American middle class, white culture. The experiences of adolescents outside of this group are considerably less understood and researched (Arnett, 1999). This review addresses identity development in first-generation, adolescent migrants to majority-English speaking societies. However, because the literature frequently aggregates this population with second-generation and indigenous minorities under pan-ethnic labels such as *Hispanic* (e.g., Niemann, Romero, Arredondo, & Rodriguez, 1999), this review will necessarily include some of that work. Since there is no universally understood period of adolescence, I define it somewhat arbitrarily here as ages 12-18. Finally, this review focuses on scholarship over the past 15 years (See Giles & Johnson, 1987; Gudykunst & Schmidt, 1987; Gumperz, 1982; Phinney, 1990; and Tajfel, 1981 for earlier work.)

While widely varying in perspective and emphasis, theory and research on adolescent ELL identity address at least one of three interrelated foci: (a) individual psychosocial processes that serve to recursively organize and construct the self; (b) sociocultural, political, economic, institutional, and historical structures or discourses that convey group values and beliefs to the individual about identity and are in turn affected by individual actions and beliefs; and (c) interaction and day-to-day contact among individuals through which constructions of identity are constantly asserted, monitored, and altered. In practice, there is overlap among these foci as well as work in which a theoretical framework is underspecified or missing entirely (Phinney, 1990). Nevertheless, these foci can serve as useful ways to organize a discussion of English language learning adolescents' experience of identity.

INDIVIDUAL PSYCHOSOCIAL PROCESSES OF IDENTITY FORMATION

Scholarship in this area spans several disciplines including social psychology, intercultural communication, counseling, and clinical psychology. Work in this area is typically characterized by the administration of Likert-scale-based multi-item inventories soliciting adolescent feelings, values, and self-reported behaviors relating to ethnolinguistic identity (see, e.g., Niemann et al., 1999; Phinney, 1992; Umaña-Taylor & Fine, 2001) and multivariate predictive models (e.g., Swanson, Spencer, & Petersen, 1998). Less common are in-depth case studies (e.g., Shih, 1998), focus groups (Niemann et al., 1999), and other psychometric measures (e.g., Suárez-Orozco & Suárez-Orozco, 1995).

In psychosocially oriented research, how adolescent ELLs see themselves in relation to the target language and culture is encapsulated in the notion of *ethnic identity*. Several facets of ethnic identity have been investigated, including how adolescents self-identify or self-label their ethnicity, the relative strength of the bond with a self-identified group, how favorably youth regard the group, and the degree to which youth participate in the social life of their self-identified group through language use, friendships, religious organizations and practices, ethnic clubs or associations, political activity, and living in ethnic enclaves (Phinney, 1990; Rosenthal & Feldman, 1996). While early work (e.g., Giles & Johnson, 1987; Tajfel, 1981) highlighted the role of language choice and use in ethnic identity, recent theorists consider its role less central and more ambiguous (e.g., Hansen & Liu, 1997; Liebkind, 1999). Theorists see strong links between ethnic identity, acculturation (Berry, 1997; Maharaj & Connolly, 1994; Phinney, 1990; Schönflug, 1997), socialization (Adams & Marshall, 1996), and constitution of the self (Baumeister & Muraven, 1996), although opinions vary widely on the exact nature of the relationship. Psychosocial theorists also vary on the extent to which they posit an essential self or identity existing autonomously from linguistic or social construction (Baumeister & Muraven, 1996).

Ethnic identity formation is seen as a dynamic process that is as much achieved as given and that changes over time. Phinney's (1990) model of acculturation, based upon psychoanalytic theories of identity (e.g., Erikson, 1968), proposes that individuals begin adolescence with a received or unexamined ethnic identity. Identity exploration, often triggered by a significant experience with another ethnic group, focuses awareness on one's own identity and ultimately results in a new examined or achieved ethnic identity. Berry (1997), however, contends that immigrant acculturation processes are too varied to characterize in a unilinear stage model. Instead, he focuses on strategies used by youth in acculturation and identity formation, characterizing them in one of four ways: assimilation (rejection of home culture in favor of adopted culture); marginalization (rejection of both home and adopted culture); integration (identification with both home and adopted culture); and separation/segregation (rejection of adopted culture in favor of home culture).

Following Erikson (1968), psychosocial researchers cast the achievement of a stable, coherent, positive sense of identity as the major task of adolescence (Phinney, 1990; Rosenthal & Feldman, 1996). Social and clinical psychology has therefore examined constructs such as self-esteem, stress, coping, and resilience and has focused on the formation of ethnic affiliations, self-concept, and cultural identification as variables intervening in adolescent "storm and stress" (Hall, 1904). Clinicians hypothesize links between adolescent identity formation and risks of parental conflict, mood disruptions, and behaviors (Arnett, 1999) including substance abuse, underage sexual activity, violence and criminality, depression, suicide, school underachievement, and dropping out (Dryfoos, 1998).

Researchers debate whether immigrant status enhances these risks (Berry, 1997; Lazarus, 1997). Rosenthal and Feldman (1996) propose that risk level is determined by the degree of similarity or difference between old and new cultures, the reason for the transition, the abruptness of the change, and the extent of immersion in the new culture. Others find that adolescent immigrants may have distinctively high levels of sadness and preoccupation with losses (Suárez-Orozco & Suárez-Orozco, 1995) and that refugee traumas (Kiang, 1995) affect psychological well-being and identity. Since adolescents may acculturate faster than their parents (Kiang), adolescent ELL identity formation is sometimes associated with familial and intergenerational conflict (Calderón, 1998; Shih, 1998). Affiliation with urban youth gangs has also been linked with immigration and attendant destabilization of familial and community support systems (Faderman, 1998; Fine & Mechling, 1993; Vigil, 1993). Immigrants, particularly female youth, may also face conflicts in gendered identities (Kiang, 1995; Lee, 1996; Olson, 1997). On the other hand, some researchers report that immigrant adolescents value family and tradition more than non-immigrant peers do (Rosenthal & Feldman, 1996) and experience less parental conflict (Suárez-Orozco & Suárez-Orozco, 1995).

Although Erikson's (1968) influential work hypothesized that parental influences on identity formation are eclipsed by peer associations in adolescence, empirical work suggests individual (Hartup, 1999) and cultural (Rosenthal & Feldman, 1996; Suárez-Orozco & Suárez-Orozco, 1995) variation in peer influences on adolescent identity. Moreover, while non-minority adolescents in Western contexts tend to be defined and define themselves in terms of the activities, interests, or reputation of their peer group, immigrants from ethnolinguistic and racial minority groups may find their identities and peer associations defined primarily in terms of similarities in ethnicity and race, and similarities in perceived distance and marginalization from the dominant group (Shih, 1998). Maharaj and Connolly (1994), however, suggest cross-national variation in tendencies for peers to self-segregate in racialized ethnic groups.

Adolescent ELLs' ethnic identities are shaped not only by the experience of immigration but also by the status of their identified group in the wider society. Following Tajfel's (1981) early work, many scholars suggest that the achievement of identity for ethnolinguistic or racial minority adolescents necessitates more complex cognitive and affective dynamics than that of the dominant cultural group (Rosenthal & Feldman, 1996; Swanson, Spencer, & Petersen, 1998). Adolescent ELLs may face psychological conflict bridging home and dominant cultures in societies where they are associated with a stigmatized subordinate group (Phinney, 1990). Swanson et al. believe that societal prejudices regarding language minority status work upon the individual by triggering stress and coping mechanisms (e.g., not participating in biased school practices) that may be effective in an immediate sense but lead ultimately to adverse "lifestage outcomes" (e.g., poor school achievement). As a result, minority youth might be more likely overall than majority youth to have a poorer sense of "personal efficacy" and to accept perceptions of limited social access rather than to challenge or circumvent them.

Psychosocial research on adolescent ELL identity is not without logistical and theoretical challenges. While theories abound, empirical work on general adolescent processes of identity formation, and on ethnolinguistic minority youth in particular, lags far behind and is as yet limited (Phinney, 1990). While some theorists regret the lack of a single overarching and universally accepted framework for the exploration of identity formation, they themselves may contribute to the proliferation of models (e.g., Côté, 1996; Phinney, 1990). Reliance on cross-sectional measures has hampered efforts to discern longitudinal developmental trends (Goossens & Phinney, 1996; Hansen & Liu, 1997). Self-report measures are not accompanied by confirmatory observation (Suárez-Orozco & Suárez-Orozco, 2001), and the reliability of some measures is low or unassessed (Phinney, 1990). Moreover, while the linkage between social context and intra-individual identity formation is widely acknowledged (Berry, 1997; Erikson, 1968; Swanson, Spencer, & Petersen, 1998), methodologies typically employed in psychosocial research have nonetheless emphasized individuals as the unit of analysis (Goossens & Phinney, 1996). The "storm and stress" orientation of research on adolescence tends to emphasize deviations and negative effects of ELL identity development and may be distorting our understanding of the process. Researchers note the need for more research on how ethnic identity changes situationally (Phinney, 1990) as well as more systemic cross-cultural research on how the size and status of the local and societal ethnic community influence adolescents' ethnic identities (Berry, 1997). Recent work is marked by cross-national and cross-generational comparisons of ethnic identity in adolescent ELLs (Rosenthal & Feldman, 1996; Suárez-Orozco & Suárez-Orozco, 1995).

A particular challenge is the use of broad ethnic categories in psychosocially oriented research on identity. Umaña-Taylor and Fine (2001) show that pan-ethnic designations, such as *Latino* or *Hispanic*, prevalent in identity research are of dubious validity, since responses to commonly used measures of ethnic identity vary considerably among Spanish-speaking ethnic groups. Moreover, an increasing number of individuals' backgrounds are not representative of one "pure" ethnolinguistic group (Phinney, 1990). Berry (1997) further cautions that research must contextualize ethnicity in the full constellation of cultural and psychological factors brought to acculturative processes, e.g., gender, race, and social class. For example, while extant research often fails to differentiate generational status of ethnolinguistic minority youth, there can be major differences and tensions among first and subsequent generations of adolescents in the same setting (Lee, 1996; Lee, 2001; Olson, 1997; Shih, 1998; Valdés, 2001). Moreover, even adolescent ELLs quite similar in ethnicity, socioeconomic status, and social context can experience considerably different processes of identity formation (Shih, 1998), resilience, and coping (Calderón, 1998). Additionally, because the host society is not monolithic either, immigrant youth necessarily favor some subgroups such as youth cultures (James, 1995) more than others in processes of acculturation and identity formation (Horenczyk, 1997). As a result of these difficulties, some psychosocially oriented scholars (Horenczyk, 1997; Pick, 1997; Swanson, Spencer, & Petersen, 1998) recommend a social constructionist perspective and more investigation of how immigration causes individuals and groups in contact to actively reconstruct and redefine representations of their own and other cultures.

INSTITUTIONAL AND SOCIETAL CONTEXTS OF IDENTITY FORMATION

Scholarship in this area draws primarily from the sociology and anthropology of education and is typically characterized by ethnographic and case study methodologies featuring unstructured, in-depth interviews and participant observation of informants in social settings (although see Portes & Rumbaut, 2001, for a large-scale survey approach). While there is considerable anthropologically and sociologically oriented work on the cross-cultural identity formation of immigrant children (e.g., García & Hurtado, 1995), scholarship on adolescents is less plentiful (Wulff, 1995b).

It must first be noted that anthropologists and sociologists dispute whether adolescent identity-seeking and even adolescence itself are universal or culturally specific phenomena (e.g., Baumeister & Muraven, 1996; Coté, 1994). Very little empirical work has addressed cultural differences in identity exploration (Goossens & Phinney, 1996), and cultures may define adolescence in different ways (Adams & Marshall, 1996; Arnett, 1999; Muñez, 1995; Schlegel & Barry, 1991). If notions of adolescence are culturally produced, socially oriented researchers argue that the nature of adolescent ELL identities cannot be studied or understood apart from their specific institutional and sociocultural contexts.

Adolescent ELLs enter societies in which images of immigrants are largely unfavorable (Vargas & dePyssler, 1998). Latinos in the U.S., for example, are portrayed in the media as *waves* or *tides* of criminal aliens or helpless victims

(Vargas & dePyssler, 1998) and Latino youth as gang-bangers, graffiti artists, and migrant fieldworkers (Hernández, Siles, & Rochín, 2000). Asian Americans are often perceived as unassimilable foreigners (Lee, 1996). Rampton (1995) identifies a prevalent racist "babu" stereotype of ESL/Indian English speakers in England— "deferential, polite, uncomprehending, and incompetent in English" (p. 52).

Schools are primary "arenas" (Olneck, 1995) for instilling or ameliorating societal notions of race, ethnicity, language, and identity. Thus, schooling has been a central focus of socially oriented research on adolescent ELL identity. In the U.S., studies report that schools operate on prevalent English monolingual ideologies, overlooking immigrant students' previous linguistic and academic accomplishments and casting students as linguistically and cognitively deficient (Harklau, 2000; McKay & Wong, 1996). Bilingualism or ELL status is often stigmatized as remedial (McKay & Wong, 1996), subjecting immigrants to harassment and ridicule from American-born peers (Lee, 1996; Olson, 1997) and marginalization in the classroom (McKay & Wong, 1996). Immigrants from white middle-class backgrounds (e.g., Russian immigrants; see Vollmer, 2000) may be perceived as more assimilable than Asian or Latino peers. Latino adolescents in U.S. schools may be subject to "benevolent racism" (Villenas, 2001), casting students as "academic underachievers, illiterates, dropouts, incompetents in reading, writing, and numeracy" (Villarruel & Montero-Sieburth, 2000, p. xviii) in need of special help. A *model minority* representation of Asian heritage students in the U.S. (Lee, 1996; McKay & Wong, 1996), Canada, and Australia (Rosenthal & Feldman, 1996) obscures differences in achievement and schooling problems among them by portraying them as uniformly successful. African Caribbean youth in British (Gillborn, 1997) and Canadian (Solomon, 1992) schools experience persistent harassment and discrimination, and their language is stigmatized by teachers who see Creole simply as non-standard or incorrect forms of English.

Ogbu's (1991) cultural ecological model of cultural identity development and minority academic achievement has been influential in explaining the variable effects of societal discrimination and stereotyping on immigrant youth identities. Ogbu proposes that *voluntary* immigrants tend to overlook discrimination and to learn English and succeed academically, while *involuntary* minority groups incorporated through conquest or slavery develop oppositional identities in which English and schooling are seen as vehicles of societal oppression. Ogbu's model has received qualified support in research on adolescent ELLs (see, e.g., Gibson, 1988; Lee, 1996; Matute-Bianchi, 1991; Suarez-Orozco, 1989). However, some researchers question whether all immigrant groups are equally successful (Portes & Rumbaut, 2001). Moreover, in recent years research on immigrant identity and school performance has shifted towards equally important patterns of intragroup variation (Davidson, 1996; Gibson, 1997; Goto, 1997; Lee). Researchers also note the interaction of immigrant status with other aspects of identity such as gender (Gibson, 1997; Lee; Olson, 1997; Poynting, Noble, & Tabar, 1999), class (Lee, 1996), and race (Cummins, 2000; Gillborn, 1997; Lee, 1996; Solomon, 1992).

Researchers have also noted changes in voluntary immigrant responses to the dominant society across generations and time (Gibson, 1997). Adult immigrants and their adolescent children's ethnic identities may develop quite differently during acculturation (Shih, 1998; Suárez-Orozco & Suárez-Orozco, 2001) and take on hybrid cultural characteristics as a result of contact with the dominant group (Darder, 1995; Lee, 1996). Davidson (1996) argues that adolescent ELLs can take on identities that are simultaneously academically engaged like voluntary minorities and oppositional in the sense of preserving home language and culture.

Researchers note the important role of educational institutions in adolescent ELL identity formation. Schools contribute to marginalized identities when they take a coercive (Cummins, 2000) role, enforcing assimilationist values (Feinberg, 1998) and practices such as negative academic expectations, impersonal and uncaring relationships with educators, and unequal access to information about and opportunities for their futures (Davidson, 1996; Conchas, 2001; Gillborn, 1990; Olson, 1997). Alternatively, schools can counter societal relations of power (Cummins) by actively engaging ELLs' divergent cultural identities (Feinberg), holding high academic expectations, and guiding them and their families in preparing for future opportunities (Lucas, Henze, & Donato, 1990). Adolescent ELLs may adopt a range of strategies in identity development, including ethnic flight and identification with the dominant group, adversarial identities rejecting the dominant group, and transcultural identities synthesizing elements of each (Suárez-Orozco & Suárez-Orozco, 2001). Some suggest that those with strong heritage cultural identities and those with transcultural identities fare best in school and society (Gibson, 1997; Suárez-Orozco & Suárez-Orozco, 2001; although see Lee, 2001, for a dissenting view).

Relatively little work has focused on immigrant adolescent identity formation in home, work, and community and in peer contexts (Heath & McLaughlin, 1993; Weis & Fine, 2000), although existing research shows the significant influences of family and community (Centrie, 2000; Suárez-Orozco & Suárez-Orozco, 1995; Zhou & Bankston, 1994), peer groups (Olson, 1997), gang affiliations (Moje, 2000; Valdés, 2001), and workplaces (Muñez, 1995).

Recent theorizing on adolescent ELL identity is situated in critiques of the very concepts of culture (e.g., Clifford, 1986) and identity (Hall, 1996). This "contextualist perspective" (McKay & Wong, 1996) draws variously from cultural studies (e.g., Bhabha, 1994; Hall, 1996; Weedon, 1997), postmodernisms (e.g., Foucault, 1977, 1995/1979), and critical discourse studies (e.g., Fairclough, 1995; Gee, 1996). Key notions in these perspectives include cultural identities (or subjectivities, e.g., Weedon 1997) as representational, power-laden, reciprocal, multiple and hybrid, mobile, and contested.

Identities are *representations* that fix upon attributes of the individual—physical phenotype, language, cultural beliefs, and practices and use them as shorthand to classify people (Hall, 1997). In doing so, however, they mask heterogeneity within and across individuals. Harklau (2000), for example, finds that the same individuals can take on very different identities as ELLs depending on the institutional context and the other students with whom they are grouped or with whom they are compared.

Identity categories are *power laden* because the dominant group defines itself by defining and excluding a cultural *Other* (Grossberg, 1996; Hall, 1996). For example, pan-ethnic identities such as *Latino* and *Asian American* are as much imposed by contact with a dominant white group as chosen by individuals (Lee, 1996). Immigrants of color internalize dominant U.S. norms equating *American* with *whiteness*, and cast themselves as foreigners (Harklau, 2000; Lee, 1996; Olson, 1997). Lee (1996) and McKay and Wong (1996) find that adolescents draw upon pan-ethnic identities such as *Asian* or *Chinese* for group solidarity in situations of interethnic and interracial contact and potential social vulnerability, while negotiating much more intricate and nuanced ethnolinguistic identities among themselves.

Processes of adolescent ELL identity formation are also *reciprocal*; that is, they both shape and are shaped by societal and institutional influences or discourses (Adams & Marshall, 1996; Foucault, 1995/1979). The individual's range of possible identities at any point in time is limited by preexisting societally and institutionally recognized differentiations in gender, language, ethnicity, and race. Adolescents always operate in reference to these discourses at the same time they are contributing to or resisting them. Adolescent immigrants, however, may experience acculturation and identity formation to be a one-way process in which they and not American-born peers are expected to change (Olson, 1997). Berry (1997) points out that the adjustments of the non-dominant group have been emphasized in both research and social policy and calls for increased attention to mutual accommodation in pluralistic societies.

Cultural identities in transnational multiethnic societies are *multiple and hybrid* (Grossberg, 1996). The notion of *core* unitary ethnolinguistic identities corresponding with geographic boundaries is in fact largely an invention of eighteenth and nineteenth century social science (Kroskrity, 2001) and is belied by current research. For example, Lee (1996) finds that ethnic Chinese students from Cambodia identified with both ethnic groups. McKay and Wong (1996) contend that the notion that immigrants commit to only one identity and one language or the other is xenophobic. Nevertheless, the notion of a unitary or authentic ethnicity is a powerful one (Reyes, 2002), and adolescent ELLs may therefore see ethnic identity as a choice between home and adopted cultures (e.g., Olson, 1997).

Adolescents' identities are also *shifting and mobile*, an ongoing and never completed process of the remaking of the self. For example, among British adolescents, the use of Creole has changed its meanings in relation to identity, becoming popularized among white youth, and in turn has changed the nature of the Creoles themselves (Gillborn, 1990).

Cultural identities are innately strategic and positional (Hall, 1996) and are therefore *sites of contestation* (McKay & Wong, 1996; Rampton, 1995). Adolescent ELLs do not simply accept their positioning by others but actively set about resisting their positioning and attempting to reposition themselves through counterdiscourses. For example, McKay and Wong show how a student resisted the subject position of *ESL student* by utilizing his greater command of Chinese cultural symbols to make an off-color joke that his friends but not the teacher would understand.

A nascent challenge to postmodern conceptualizations of culture and identity comes from Moya (2000), who expresses dissatisfaction with an oversimplistic binary between *essentialist* and *postmodern* conceptualizations of cultural identity. Moya also notes that postmodernism and cultural studies have negatively emphasized the violence of identification and subjectification at the expense of the enriching and enabling aspects of cultural identities. Some, particularly educators seeking change in educational or societal practices, seek greater emphasis on the role of personal agency in processes of cultural identity formation.

FOCUS ON INTERACTION AND SEMIOTIC PRACTICES

Scholarship in this area spans a number of disciplines, including intercultural communication, social psychology, linguistic anthropology, literacy education, and media and cultural studies. Methodological approaches vary, ranging from surveys of communicative styles and language attitudes to ethnography, microethnography, conversation analysis, and other approaches taking an intensive focus on recorded interactions. Recent work goes beyond the traditional realm of spoken language to investigate a broad range of semiotic and communicative practices (e.g., Moje, 2000).

One approach examines *communicative styles* cross-culturally. Yager and Rotheram-Borus (2000), for example, find evidence for differing expectations for social interactions among European American, Hispanic, and African American adolescents. They suggest that cultural differences in group orientation, assertiveness, and aggressiveness may help to explain self-segregation and conflict among adolescent ethnic groups in school settings. Likewise, Gillborn (1990) argues that culturally influenced interactional styles of Afro-Caribbean students in England were misinterpreted by teachers as disaffected or threatening, in turn shaping student identity.

Other researchers look at the roles of *code switching* and *language choice* in identity work. Zentella's (1997) influential work on Puerto Rican ELLs in New York follows in an interactionist tradition in anthropology and sociolinguistics (e.g., Gumperz, 1982). Zentella shows how members of the community construct multiple and shifting identities through the sometimes overlapping deployment of multiple languages and dialects, including standard and non-standard Puerto Rican Spanish, standard New York English, Puerto Rican and Hispanicized dialects of English, and African American vernacular English. Likewise, Heller (1999) shows complex negotiations of adolescent ELL school-based identities through the uses of French, English, and vernacular languages at a Francophone high school in Toronto. Zentella notes that this sort of complexity of communicative options and patterns is what one might expect in a community that is linguistically, ethnically, and racially diverse, and Heller further describes how particular code choices are made legitimate or illegitimate in power-laden discursive contexts. Working in a multilingual high school setting in England, Rampton (1995) finds that adolescents aspiring to full participation in the peer group acquire not simply the monolingual Standard English but rather a variable mastery of a repertoire of languages. Both Zentella and Rampton suggest therefore that adolescent ELLs' social identities and social status are actively processed and renegotiated in social interactions.

Work in this area also looks at language as symbolic resources used to include and exclude. Lee (1996), for example, notes that ELLs at one high school used Korean language as a means of excluding other Asian Americans from social events. Zentella (1997) argues that stigmatization of Puerto Rican identity in New York is associated with the stigmatization of bilinguals' synthetic language repertoire. Asian Americans and Asian Canadian ELLs may be subject to silencing in schools through peer ridicule of their English usage, but paradoxically their very silence may also invoke representations of cognitive and emotional immaturity (Duff, 2002; Lee, 1996; Pon, Goldstein, & Schecter, 2003). However, silence was also agentive when resisting unwanted representations of their cultural identities (Duff, 2002). James (1995) suggests that youth cultures possess distinctive communicative practices and dialects and contends that adolescents who are most competent in the generational style use talk to distinguish themselves from more marginal members of the group. Rampton (1995) shows that minority languages may be incorporated into community language norms and practices as adolescents cross ethnolinguistic groups and fashion new conceptualizations of ethnic identity. Moreover, Rampton shows how immigrant youth may revoice minority or learner linguistic codes as a means of resisting stigmatization. Adolescents in his study deployed stylized code-switches into ESL/Indian English to parody stereotypes of Asians they encountered in English society and to undermine the authority of white authority figures in school interactions. Reyes (2002) shows how Cambodian American students deploy talk to resist their positioning by educators as inauthentic bearers of Cambodian ethnic identity and instead counter with a notion of identity indexing ethnic and racial differentiation.

A small number of studies have noted the *production of identities in narrative*. Harklau (2000) suggests that adolescent ELLs draw upon societal and institutional discourses about immigrants to portray themselves positively in autobiographical texts as moral agents who overcome hardship and possess model behavior and special respect for educators. Likewise, Lee (1996) suggests those Asian refugees' self-disclosures about personal traumas in school-based written narratives invoked and reinstantiated the model minority stereotype. Research on adolescent ELL identity work in spoken narratives remains far less explored (see Rymes, 2001, for work with American-born adolescents.). Although untapped in current research on adolescent ELLs, diary studies and other autobiographical forms (e.g., Dykman, 2000; Min & Kim, 2000) hold potential for research on identity development.

A long tradition (e.g., Hebdige, 1979) links adolescent identity formation with media, consumption, and youth styles (Wulff, 1995a). Recent research has shown how a broad range of semiotic practices associated with youth styles, including gang tags, writing styles, music, and clothing styles (Lee, 1996; Moje, 2000), are used by ethnolinguistic minority youth to assert group affiliations and identities. Côté (1996) suggests that such practices are of increasing importance for managing one's social place in urbanized late-modern societies. With growth in media and adolescents as their primary targets and consumers, media images or representations of culture and of adolescents are perhaps more pervasive and more influential than ever before. Media images potentially carry stereotypes that can act to validate and normalize particular beliefs and notions of adolescent ELL identity (Zuengler, 2004).

Researchers also suggest that media growth has transnational and global implications for youth identities. Schlegel (2000) and Wulff (1995b) argue that ideas and commodities of youth culture flow most easily across cultural borders. They suggest that an adolescent culture oriented towards consumerism and emblematized in behaviors, clothing, and music is being spread globally through international media, touring entertainers, migrants, import-export markets, and travels of adolescents themselves. From this perspective, media make it ever more possible and even necessary to navigate across cultural and linguistic boundaries (Cope & Kalantzis, 2000). Some argue that the proliferation of media lends multiethnic adolescents access to media reflecting both the dominant youth cultures of English-speaking societies and alternative images in Latino (Vargas & dePyssler, 1998) and Asian American media, while others (Duff, 2002) argue that popular culture can be exclusionary to immigrant youth who do not share referents. Zuengler (2004) argues that adolescent ELLs do not simply take on identities available to them in consumer-oriented media but rather engage in a sophisticated process of appropriation and resistance.

Scholars in this area increasingly portray interaction and semiotic practices as mediating between intra-individual psychological processes and institutional and social contexts. Nevertheless, this remains perhaps the least researched area of inquiry on adolescent ELL identity formation.

CONCLUSIONS

From this review, it is clear that the notion of adolescent ELLs possessing a stable, bounded, and essential ethnolinguistic identity is no longer favored, if indeed it ever was. Theorists from across disciplines appear to agree that identities are multiple and dynamic in nature. There is also widespread agreement that ELL identity is an immensely complex construct, situated in a matrix of social interaction, intra-individual psychological processes, and broader institutional and societal contexts. All three perspectives—the psychological, the contextual, and the interactional—are required in order to get a holistic sense of the phenomenon. Rampton (1995), for example, argues for a need for research combining ethnography with close analysis of language use in order to capture connections between language use and higher levels of social structuring. Nevertheless, work on the same population that spans disciplinary perspectives and methodological paradigms remains quite rare. Additionally, in spite of the widespread view that identity is a continual work in progress, there is a paucity of longitudinal work following the same individuals over the course of several years (e.g., Zentella, 1997).

It is also important to note that language in most recent work is portrayed as only one of an array of symbolic resources through which identities are forged, tried on, accommodated, imposed, resisted, and changed. While researchers in SLA may see English learning as the central issue, as McKay and Wong (1996) note, it is important to remember that adolescents themselves may see English language learning as peripheral to the work of building and managing identities in a new social context. Thus, too narrow a focus on the role of language unnecessarily narrows the scope of research on ELL identity (Hansen & Liu, 1997).

Given the diversity of findings presented here, it seems likely that universally applicable theories or conclusions about adolescent ELLs and identity will always elude us. And if we should happen upon them, even stalwart seekers of such theories (e.g., Phinney, 1990) acknowledge that they may not be particularly useful when developing educational and counseling applications for specific individuals and groups in particular contexts. This admission does not diminish the value of the work to theorists and educators, however. Continuing growth in scholarship on identity is likely to provide more new insights and perspectives on adolescent identity formation and associated processes of additional language learning for the foreseeable future.

REFERENCES

Adams, G. R., & Marshall, S. K. (1996). A developmental social psychology of identity: Understanding the person-in-context. *Journal of Adolescence, 19*, 429–442.
Arnett, J. J. (1999). Adolescent storm and stress, reconsidered. *American Psychologist, 54*(5), 317–326.
Baumeister, R. F., & Muraven, M. (1996). Identity as adaptation to social, cultural, and historical context. *Journal of Adolescence, 19*, 405–416.
Berry, J. W. (1997). Immigration, acculturation, and adaptation. *Applied Psychology: An International Review, 46*(1), 5–34.
Bhabha, H. K. (1994). *The location of culture*. London: Routledge.
Calderón, M. (1998). Adolescent sons and daughters of immigrants: How schools can respond. In K. Borman & B. Schneider (Eds.), *The adolescent years: Social influences and educational

challenges. Ninety-seventh Yearbook of the National Society for the Study of Education. Part I (pp. 65–87). Chicago: University of Chicago Press.

Centrie, C. (2000). Free spaces unbound: Families, community, and Vietnamese high school students' identities. In L. Weis & M. Fine (Eds.), *Construction sites: Excavating race, class, and gender among urban youth* (pp. 65–83). New York: Teachers College Press.

Clifford, J. (1986). Introduction: Partial truths. In J. Clifford & G. E. Marcus (Eds.), *Writing culture: The poetics and politics of ethnography* (pp. 1–26). Berkeley, CA: University of California Press.

Conchas, G. Q. (2001). Structuring failure and success: Understanding the variability in Latino school engagement. *Harvard Educational Review, 71*(3), 475–504.

Cope, B., & Kalantzis, M. (Eds.). (2000). *Multiliteracies: Literacy learning and the design of social futures*. New York: Routledge.

Coté, J. E. (1994). *Adolescent storm and stress: An evaluation of the Mead-Freeman controversy.* Hillsdale, NJ: Lawrence Erlbaum Associates.

Côté, J. E. (1996). Sociological perspectives on identity formation: The culture-identity link and identity capital. *Journal of Adolescence, 19*, 417–428.

Cummins, J. (2000). *Language, power, and pedagogy: Bilingual children in the crossfire.* Clevedon, UK: Multilingual Matters.

Darder, A. (1995). The politics of biculturalism: Culture and difference in the formation of Warriers for Gringostroika and The New Mestizas. In A. Darder (Ed.), *Culture and difference: Critical perspectives on the bicultural experience in the United States* (pp. 1–20). Westport, CT: Bergin & Garvey.

Davidson, A. L. (1996). *Making and molding identity in schools: Student narratives on race, gender, and academic engagement.* Albany, NY: State University of New York Press.

Dryfoos, J. G. (1998). *Safe passage: Making it through adolescence in a risky society.* New York: Oxford University Press.

Duff, P. (2002). The discursive co-construction of knowledge, identity, and difference: An ethnography of communication in the high school mainstream. *Applied Linguistics, 23*(3), 323–347.

Dykman, E. (2000). The vagabond years. In K. Ogulnick (Ed.), *Language crossings: Negotiating the self in a multicultural world* (pp. 30–34). New York: Teachers College Press.

Erikson, E. H. (1968). *Identity: Youth and crisis.* New York: W.W. Norton & Company.

Faderman, L., & with Xiong, G. (1998). *I begin my life all over: The Hmong and American immigrant experience.* Boston: Beacon Press.

Fairclough, N. (1995). *Critical discourse analysis: Papers in the critical study of language.* New York: Longman.

Feinberg, W. (1998). *Common schools/Uncommon identities: National unity and cultural difference.* New Haven: Yale University Press.

Fine, G. A., & Mechling, J. (1993). Child saving and children's cultures at century's end. In S. B. Heath & M. W. McLaughlin (Eds.), *Identity and inner-city youth: Beyond ethnicity and gender* (pp. 120–146). New York: Teachers College Press.

Foucault, M. (1977). *Language, counter-memory, practice: Selected essays and interviews* (D. F. B. S. Simon, Trans.). Donald F. Bouchard (Ed.). Ithaca, NY: Cornell University Foucault Press. M. (1995). *Discipline and punish: The birth of the prison* (A. Sheridan, Trans.). New York: Vintage Books. (Original work published 1979.)

García, E. E., & Hurtado, A. (1995). Becoming American: A review of current research on the development of racial and ethnic identity in children. In W. D. Hawley & A. W. Jackson (Eds.), *Toward a common destiny: Improving race and ethnic relations in America* (pp. 163–184). San Francisco: Jossey-Bass.

Gee, J. P. (1996). *Social linguistics and literacies: Ideology in discourses* (2nd ed.). New York: Falmer Press.

Gibson, M. (1988). *Accommodation without assimilation: Sikh immigrants in an American high school.* Ithaca, NY: Cornell University Press.

Gibson, M. (1997). Complicating the immigrant/involuntary minority typology. *Anthropology and Education Quarterly, 28*(3), 431–454.

Giles, H., & Johnson, P. (1987). Ethnolinguistic identity theory: A social psychological approach to language maintenance. *International Journal of the Sociology of Language, 68*, 69–99.

Gillborn, D. (1990). *'Race,' ethnicity, and education: Teaching and learning in multi-ethnic schools.* London: Unwin Hyman.

Gillborn, D. (1997). Ethnicity and educational performance in the United Kingdom: Racism, ethnicity, and variability in achievement. *Anthropology and Education Quarterly, 28*(3), 375–393.

Goossens, L., & Phinney, J. S. (1996). Commentary. Identity, context, and development. *Journal of Adolescence, 19*, 491–496.

Goto, S. T. (1997). Nerds, Normal People, and Homeboys: Accommodation and resistance among Chinese American students. *Anthropology and Education Quarterly, 28*(1), 70–84.
Grossberg, L. (1996). Identity and cultural studies: Is that all there is? In S. Hall & P. Du-Gay (Eds.), *Questions of cultural identity* (pp. 87–107). London: Sage.
Gudykunst, W. B., & Schmidt, K. L. (1987). Language and ethnic identity: An overview and prologue. *Journal of Language and Social Psychology, 6*(3–4), 157–170.
Gumperz, J. J. (Ed.). (1982). *Language and social identity*. New York: Cambridge University Press.
Hall, G. S. (1904). *Adolescence: Its psychology and its relation to physiology, anthropology, sociology, sex, crime, religion, and education*. New York: D. Appleton and Company.
Hall, S. (1996). Introduction: Who needs identity? In S. Hall & P. Du-Gay (Eds.), *Questions of cultural identity* (pp. 1–17). London: Sage.
Hall, S. (1997). The work of representation. In S. Hall (Ed.), *Representation: Cultural representation and signifying practices* (pp. 13–64). London; Thousand Oaks, CA: Sage.
Hansen, J. G., & Liu, J. (1997). Social identity and language: Theoretical and methodological issues. *TESOL Quarterly, 31*(3), 567–576.
Harklau, L. (2000). From the "good kids" to the "worst"?: Representations of English language learners across educational settings. *TESOL Quarterly, 34*(1), 35–67.
Hartup, W. W. (1999). Constraints on peer socialization: Let me count the ways. *Merrill-Palmer Quarterly, 45*(1), 172–183.
Heath, S. B., & McLaughlin, M. W. (1993). Ethnicity and gender in theory and practice: The youth perspective. In S. B. Heath & M. W. McLaughlin (Eds.), *Identity and inner-city youth: Beyond ethnicity and gender* (pp. 13–35). New York: Teachers College Press.
Hebdige, D. (1979). *The meaning of style*. London: Methuen.
Heller, M. (1999). *Linguistic minorities and modernity: A sociolinguistic ethnography*. New York: Longman.
Hernández, R., Siles, M., & Rochín, R. (2000). Latino youth: Converting challenges to opportunities. In M. Montero-Sieburth & F. Villarruel (Eds.), *Making invisible Latino adolescents visible: A critical approach* (pp. 1–28). New York: Falmer Press.
Horenczyk, G. (1997). Commentary on immigration, acculturation, and adaptation. *Applied Psychology: An International Review, 46*(1), 34–38.
James, A. (1995). Talking of children and youth: Language, socialization and culture. In V. Amit-Talai & H. Wulff (Eds.), *Youth cultures: A cross-cultural perspective* (pp. 43–62). New York: Routledge.
Kiang, P. N.-c. (1995). Bicultural strengths and struggles of Southeast Asian Americans in school. In A. Darder (Ed.), *Culture and difference: Critical perspectives on the bicultural experience in the United States* (pp. 201–225). Westport, CT: Bergin & Garvey.
Krashen, S. (1981). *Second language acquisition and second language learning*. Oxford: Pergamon Press.
Kroskrity, P. V. (2001). Identity. In A. Duranti (Ed.), *Key terms in language and culture* (pp. 106–109). Malden, MA: Blackwell.
Lazarus, R. S. (1997). Acculturation isn't everything. *Applied Psychology: An International Review, 46*(1), 39–43.
Lee, S. J. (1996). *Unraveling the "model minority" stereotype: Listening to Asian American youth*. New York: Teachers College Press.
Lee, S. J. (2001). More than 'model minorities' or 'delinquents': A look at Hmong American high school students. *Harvard Educational Review, 71*(3), 505–528.
Liebkind, K. (1999). Social psychology. In J. A. Fishman (Ed.), *Handbook of language and ethnic identity* (pp. 141–151). New York: Oxford University Press.
Lucas, T., Henze, R., & Donato, R. (1990). Promoting the success of Latino language-minority students: An exploratory study of six high schools. *Harvard Educational Review, 60*(3), 315–340.
Maharaj, S. I., & Connolly, J. A. (1994). Peer network composition of acculturated and ethnoculturally-affiliated adolescents in a multicultural setting. *Journal of Adolescent Research, 9*(2), 218–240.
Matute-Bianchi, M. E. (1991). Situational ethnicity and patterns of school performance among immigrant and nonimmigrant Mexican-descent students. In M. A. Gibson & J. U. Ogbu (Eds.), *Minority status and schooling: A comparative study of immigrant and involuntary minorities* (pp. 205–247). New York: Garland.
McKay, S. L., & Wong, S.-L. C. (1996). Multiple discourses, multiple identities: Investment and agency in second-language learning among Chinese adolescent immigrant students. *Harvard Educational Review, 66*(3), 577–608.
Min, P. G., & Kim, R. (2000). Formation of ethnic and racial identities: Narratives by young Asian-American professionals. *Ethnic and Racial Studies, 23*(4), 735–760.

Moje, E. B. (2000). 'To be part of the story': The literacy practices of gansta adolescents. *Teachers College Record, 102*(3), 651–690.
Moya, P. M. L. (2000). Introduction: Reclaiming identity. In P. M. L. Moya & M. R. Hames-García (Eds.), *Reclaiming identity: Realist theory and the predicament of postmodernism* (pp. 1–26). Berkeley: University of California Press.
Muñez, V. I. (1995). *Where 'something catches': Work, love, and identity in youth*. Albany, NY: State University of New York Press.
Niemann, Y. F., Romero, A. J., Arredondo, J., & Rodriguez, V. (1999). What does it mean to be "Mexican"? Social construction of an ethnic identity. *Hispanic Journal of Behavioral Sciences, 21*(1), 47–60.
Ogbu, J. U. (1991). Immigrant and involuntary minorities in comparative perspective. In M. A. Gibson & J. U. Ogbu (Eds.), *Minority status and schooling: A comparative study of immigrant and involuntary minorities* (pp. 3–33). New York: Garland.
Olneck, M. R. (1995). Immigrants and education. In J. A. Banks & C. A. M. Banks (Eds.), *Handbook of research on multicultural education* (pp. 310–327). New York: Macmillan.
Olson, L. (1997). *Made in America: Immigrant students in our public schools*. New York: New Press.
Phinney, J. S. (1990). Ethnic identity in adolescents and adults: Review of research. *Psychological Bulletin, 108*(3), 499–514.
Phinney, J. S. (1992). The multigroup ethnic identity measure: A new scale for use with diverse groups. *Journal of Adolescent Research, 7*(2), 156–176.
Pick, S. (1997). Berry in Legoland. *Applied Psychology: An International Review, 46*(1), 49–52.
Pon, G., Goldstein, T., & Schecter, S. R. (2003). Interrupted by silences: The contemporary education of Hong Kong-born Chinese Canadians. In R. Bayley & S. R. Schecter (Eds.), *Language socialization in bilingual and multilingual societies* (pp. 114–127). Philadelphia: Multilingual Matters.
Portes, A., & Rumbaut, R. (2001). *Legacies: The story of the second generation*. Berkeley: University of California Press.
Poynting, S., Noble, G., & Tabar, P. (1999). 'Intersections of masculinity and ethnicity: A study of male Lebanese immigrant youth in western Sydney'. *Race Ethnicity and Education, 2*(1), 59–77.
Rampton, B. (1995). *Crossing: Language and ethnicity among adolescents*. New York: Longman.
Reyes, A. (2002). 'Are you losing your culture?': Poetics, indexicality, and Asian American identity. *Discourse Studies, 4*(2), 183–200.
Rosenthal, D. A., & Feldman, S. S. (1996). Crossing the border: Chinese adolescents in the West. In S. Lau (Ed.), *Growing up the Chinese way: Chinese child and adolescent development* (pp. 287–320). Hong Kong: Chinese University Press.
Rymes, B. (2001). *Conversational borderlands: Language and identity in an alternative urban high school*. New York: Teachers College Press.
Schlegel, A. (2000). The global spread of adolescent culture. In L. J. Crockett & R. K. Silbereisen (Eds.), *Negotiating adolescence in times of social change* (pp. 71–88). New York: Cambridge University Press.
Schlegel, A., & Barry-III, H. (1991). *Adolescence: An anthropological inquiry*. New York: Free Press Macmillan.
Scovel, T. (2000). A critical review of the critical period research. *Annual Review of Applied Linguistics, 20*, 213–223.
Shih, T. A. (1998). Finding the niche: Friendship formation of immigrant adolescents. *Youth & Society, 30*(2), 209–240.
Solomon, R. P. (1992). *Black resistance in high school: Forging a separatist culture*. Albany, NY: State University of New York Press.
Suárez-Orozco, C. & Suárez-Orozco, M. (1995). *Transformations: Immigration, family life, and achievement motivation among Latino adolescents*. Stanford, California: Stanford University Press.
Suárez-Orozco, C., & Suárez-Orozco, M. (2001). *Children of immigration*. Cambridge, MA: Harvard University Press.
Suárez-Orozco, M. (1989). *Central American refugees and United States high schools: A psychosocial study of motivation and achievement*. Stanford, CA: Stanford University Press.
Swanson, D. P., Spencer, M. B., & Petersen, A. (1998). Identity formation in adolescents. In K. Borman & B. Schneider (Eds.), *The adolescent years: Social influences and educational challenges. Ninety-seventh yearbook of the National Society for the Study of Education. Part I* (pp. 18–41). Chicago: University of Chicago Press.
Tajfel, H. (1981). *Human groups and social categories*. Cambridge: Cambridge University Press.
Umaña-Taylor, A., & Fine, M. A. (2001). Methodological implications of grouping Latino adolescents into one collective ethnic group. *Hispanic Journal of Behavioral Sciences, 23*(4), 347–362.

Valdés, G. (2001). *Learning and not learning English: Latino students in American schools* (Vol. 27). New York: Teachers College Press.

Vargas, L., & dePyssler, B. (1998). Using media literacy to explore stereotypes of Mexican immigrants. *Social Education, 62*(7), 407–412.

Vigil, J. D. (1993). Gangs, social control, and ethnicity: Ways to redirect. In S. B. Heath & M. W. McLaughlin (Eds.), *Identity and inner-city youth: Beyond ethnicity and gender* (pp. 94–119). New York: Teachers College Press.

Villarruel, F. A., & Montero-Sieburth, M. (2000). Introduction. Latino Youth and America: Time for a change. In M. Montero-Sieburth & F. Villarruel (Eds.), *Making invisible Latino adolescents visible: A critical approach* (pp. ix–xxii). New York: Falmer Press.

Villenas, S. (2001). Latina mothers and small-town racisms: Creating narratives of dignity and moral education in North Carolina. *Anthropology and Education Quarterly, 32*(1), 3–28.

Vollmer, G. (2000). Praise and stigma: Teachers' constructions of the "typical ESL student". *Journal of Intercultural Studies, 21*(1), 53–66.

Weedon, C. (1997). *Feminist practice and poststructuralist theory* (2nd ed.). Cambridge, MA: Blackwell.

Weis, L., & Fine, M. (2000). Construction sites: An introduction. In L. Weis & M. Fine (Eds.), *Construction sites: Excavating race, class, and gender among urban youth* (pp. xi–xiv). New York: Teachers College Press.

Wulff, H. (1995a). Inter-racial friendship: Consuming youth styles, ethnicity and teenage feminity in South London. In V. Amit-Talai & H. Wulff (Eds.), *Youth cultures: A cross-cultural perspective* (pp. 63–80). New York: Routledge.

Wulff, H. (1995b). Introduction: Introducing youth culture in its own right: The state of the art and new possibilities. In V. Amit-Talai & H. Wulff (Eds.), *Youth cultures: A cross-cultural perspective* (pp. 1–18). New York: Routledge.

Yager, T. J., & Rotheram-Borus, M. J. (2000). Social expectations among African American, Hispanic, and European American adolescents. *Cross-Cultural Research, 34*(3), 283–306.

Zentella, A. C. (1997). *Growing up bilingual: Puerto Rican children in New York*. Malden, MA: Blackwell.

Zhou, M., & Bankston-III, C. L. (1994). Social capital and the adaptation of the second generation: The case of Vietnamese youth in New Orleans. *International Migration Review, 28*(4), 821–845.

Zuengler, J. (2004). Jackie Chan drinks Mountain Dew: Constructing cultural models of citizenship. *Linguistics and Education, 14*(3/4), 277–304.

CHAPTER 38

WHAT ABOUT THE STUDENTS? ENGLISH LANGUAGE LEARNERS IN POSTSECONDARY SETTINGS

SARAH BENESCH

The College of Staten Island, The City University of New York, USA

ABSTRACT

This chapter examines research on English language learner identity in postsecondary contexts. It focuses first on how demographic research classifies students according to commonalities, overlooking significant differences. It then examines how ethnography and critical ethnography reveal more complex notions of identity, thereby offering insight into where institutional and pedagogical reform might be needed. The examples of critical ethnography, in particular, show students as active participants in their learning who should be consulted about institutional labels, testing, placement procedures, and teaching.

INTRODUCTION

English for academic purposes (EAP) is the subfield of English language teaching (ELT) devoted to the linguistic demands facing postsecondary English language learners. From its beginnings in the 1960s until the late twentieth century, EAP research was mainly concerned with defining and codifying academic English and developing ways to teach it. Very little attention was paid to the learners themselves. The result is that the strength of EAP has been its research and teaching materials in the discourse and genres of such fields as science and technology, business, medicine, and law. Its shortcomings have been in the social influences on both academic English and the academic lives of English language learners (ELLs) pursuing degrees. That is, though EAP researchers acknowledge that academic discourse is socially constructed (Bhatia, 1993; Dudley-Evans & St. John, 1998; Swales, 1990), reasons why postsecondary institutions favor certain types of knowledge and discourse over others have not been sufficiently examined. Nor have the varying socioeconomic and educational backgrounds of EAP students been taken into account when carrying out research and developing teaching materials.

Questions about who EAP students are, that is, how they are defined by postsecondary institutions and how they define themselves, did not arise until the late twentieth century, 30 years after EAP emerged as a field. Candlin (2000) attributes "the consistent anonymising, if not the actual eclipsing" of the learner in ELT as a whole, in part, to a concern about contaminating linguistic and pedagogical data with the "messiness and variability of everyday communication" (p. xiii). However, beginning in the early 1990s, in a move away from this empirical tradition, critical ethnographers, in EAP and other areas of ELT, turned their attention to learners, to investigate *identity*, defined by Norton (2000) as "how a person understands his or her relationship to the world, how that relationship is constructed across time and space, and how the person understands possibilities for the future" (p. 5). *Identity* in this research is assumed to be socially constructed, mediated by various discourses, and a "site of struggle" (Norton, 1997, p. 411), not fixed or unitary. Critical ethnographic studies of ELLs at the tertiary level investigate how institutions, curricula, textbooks, and assessment instruments construct learners identities and how learners construct their own, as well as conflicts between them (Angelil-Carter, 1997; Canagarajah, 1993; Harklau, 2000; Raymond & Parks, 2004; Thesen, 1997).

In later sections of this chapter, I discuss critical ethnography as a method investigating the complex identities of ELLs in postsecondary education. Before describing that body of work, however, I offer an example of demographic research sponsored by a U.S. university aiming to characterize its ELLs. Though this research was not carried out by ELT specialists, it illustrates how institutional research can shape perceptions of who ELLs are, thereby influencing curricula, funding, and access to education. The demographic survey described, with its attempt to group ELLs into a common identity, is a contrast to critical ethnography with its focus on identity as multiple, overlapping, and fluid across contexts.

Also included in the chapter is a discussion of ethnography in EAP and ways that it differs from critical ethnography. Though EAP ethnographies do not interrogate or theorize learner identity per se, they offer detailed descriptions of ELLs' experiences in postsecondary settings, revealing both the formidable challenges they faced in academic courses and the strategies they developed to navigate the difficulties.

DEMOGRAPHIC RESEARCH

Demographic research is undertaken by postsecondary institutions seeking to characterize their student bodies by dividing them into sub-groups assumed to have similar attributes. It is usually conducted through surveys composed of multiple choice questions, developed a priori by researchers looking for particular types of information. Data from demographic surveys of ELLs in postsecondary settings typically include country of birth, first language, additional languages, high school grade point average, employment situation, parents' educational attainment, employment goals, and educational goals. The results inform institutional planners about shifts in enrollment, retention, attrition, attainment, and proficiency and point to possible educational reforms or changes in funding from one population to another, depending on the institution's goals. Due to the highstakes consequences of this type of research, it is important to examine how it groups and defines ELLs in higher education, as in the following example from the City University of New York (CUNY).

An Example of Demographic Research

"Immigration/Migration and the CUNY" (1995) is a demographic research report issued by a publicly funded U.S. university of about 200,000 students. It summarizes the results of three separate surveys conducted in 1980, 1990, and 1992, respectively. The stated purpose of the research was to examine cultural and linguistic trends among foreign-born CUNY students "so as to better identify and prepare for changes in the composition of the student body between now and the year 2000" (p. 3).

One finding of the research appears in the report in bold lettering, signaling that it is the most significant one: "Extrapolating current trends, we estimate that more than half of CUNY first-time freshmen in the year 2000 will have been born outside of the United States" ("Immigration and Migration and the CUNY," 1993, p. 3). Indeed, this is the finding that was most often remarked upon during discussions and media accounts of the report. It led some to conclude that half of CUNY's students required ESL instruction, a notion disputed by research conducted by the CUNY ESL Task Force (1994) estimating that about 15% of entering students needed ESL courses.

Though similarities between foreign-born students, based on averages, are detailed, the report hedges about its own decision to group together all students born outside the United States. The heterogeneity of foreign-born students is discussed, in terms of length of residency and amount of U.S. education, and doubts are raised about the validity of clustering visa students, documented immigrants, undocumented immigrants, permanent residents, and citizens into a single category, *foreign-born*. However, the retention of this overarching label is defended by the following unsupported claim: "Nonetheless, as a group, they have distinct educational needs and interests that distinguish them from American-born students" ("Immigration/Migration and the CUNY," 1993, p. 19).

The political context of "Immigration/Migration and the CUNY" (1995) is that at the time of its publication, administrators were lobbying for funding to create English language immersion institutes that would move much of the university's ESL instruction from academic departments into continuing education, that is, pre-college, lower-cost adult education programs. The institutes were, indeed, funded by the New York State legislature in 1996 and continue to function to this day. Whether the 1995 report influenced the decision of legislators to dedicate funds to immersion institutes has not been investigated. However, it can be documented that New York City and State newspapers reported the CUNY survey, focusing on the purported English deficiency of foreign-born students ("Immigrants' needs," 1995; "Study: A more diverse CUNY," 1995).

Aside from serving as a window onto the local politics of a publicly funded, open enrollment U.S. university, subject to competing interests, the 1995 report is also political in a more global way. It reveals the politics of demographic research: making choices about how to group and label individuals and highlighting aspects of the findings when reporting them. All demographic research raises the following questions: Who decides upon the categories? Which groups are highlighted as different? Which are *not* marked as different and are therefore accepted as the norm? How does the highlighting of difference serve to marginalize those who are "othered"? In what ways does a single category erase individuals' multiple identities? What are the consequences of ignoring multiplicity?

I return to these questions later, in my discussion of Harklau's (2000) and Thesen's (1997) findings about conflicts between the labels for ELLs used by postsecondary institutions and ways the students view their participation in those institutions as well as in their lives outside. Their research can be read as a reaction to demographic categorization and therefore offers an interesting contrast to the CUNY report.

ETHNOGRAPHY IN EAP

Before, and alongside, the appearance of critical ethnography in ELT publications in the 1990s, case studies of individual EAP students were published. These studies offered detailed descriptions of ELLs' experiences in courses across the curriculum, representing a departure from earlier needs analysis research in EAP in which surveys of faculty from a variety of disciplines were carried out to discover the types of assignments given (Horowitz, 1986; Johns, 1981). Rather than simply surveying faculty members about assignments and relying on their answers to inform EAP curricula, as earlier needs analyses had done, ethnographers observed classes, interviewed faculty and students, and studied assignments and texts. Most of these ethnographies investigated graduate students (Benson, 1989; Casanave, 1992; Connor & Kramer, 1995; Fox, 1994; Hansen, 1999; Houghton, 1991; Prior, 1991, 1995, 1998; Schneider & Fujishima, 1995); a smaller number focused on undergraduates (Johns, 1992; Leki, 1999; Smoke, 1994; Spack, 1997). Though the contexts of these studies differed, they all sought to examine the demands of academic course work as well as how the participants reacted to and carried out assigned tasks. I summarize four of these studies next, two of graduate ELLs and two of undergraduates.

Benson (1989) conducted an ethnographic study of Hamad, a Saudi Arabian master's candidate in public administration at a U.S. university. In particular, Benson wanted to document the role listening played in Hamad's learning and performance in one course, comparative education. His data included taped lectures, his participant's lecture notes, and interviews with his participant, other students, and the professor. Benson's analysis showed, among other things, that Hamad took lecture notes only on what he viewed to be main points, those he believed would appear on the final exam. He ignored examples as well as information offered in teacher/student interaction and teacher asides, which the professor believed offered equally important information. In addition, Benson noted, "in a highly verbal and participatory class, Hamad never said a word" (p. 439). Despite Hamad's selective listening and lack of overt participation, he received a grade of A-, an average grade in this class.

In drawing implications for EAP instruction from his study, Benson (1989) recommends teaching listening comprehension as an interactive process. He also supports encouraging ELLs to ask for clarification and contribute to class discussions so that they might "participate in a manner that would do justice to their abilities" (p. 442). Benson claims that without overt participation, EAP students will not gain a deep enough understanding of academic concepts to retain them beyond the exams.

Prior's (1991, 1995) ethnographies are case studies of semester-long graduate seminars in second language education. The data included observations, interviews, and "text-based interviews" (Prior, 1991, p. 273), and reactions of the professor to particular student papers. Prior chronicled the history of selected assignments, from preliminary in-class explanations by the professor to clarification, negotiation, and enactment of the guidelines by the students in dialogue with the professor. He describes assignment making and fulfillment in the graduate seminars as complicated and interactive "indeterminate" processes characterized by "order, convention, and continuity," on the one hand, and "chance, anomaly, and rupture," on the other (Prior, 1991, p. 304). For example, Prior discovered that students relied less on the professor's initial guidelines in carrying out assignments than they did on their prior experience in school, the assigned readings, and their perceptions of the professors' interests and biases. He also noted that some of the international students in the seminar were able to prevail on the professor to reduce the number of reading assignments and drop one of the writing assignments, revealing a degree of flexibility that would not have surfaced if the data had only included the original syllabus and assignment guidelines.

Prior (1995) concludes from his research that "academic discourse and academic environments are complex, constructed, and unfolding events and not closed systems susceptible to taxonomic and rule-oriented description" (p. 77). His principal recommendation for EAP instruction is to help students achieve "communicative flexibility" (p. 77) so that they are prepared to meet the idiosyncrasies of any course.

Spack (1997) carried out a 3-year study of the reading and writing processes of Yuko, a Japanese undergraduate at a privately funded U.S. university. The data included interviews with the participant and two of her political science professors, classroom observation notes, and Yuko's writing from 10 courses in three disciplines. Because this study was longitudinal, Spack was able to document changes in Yuko's literacy habits and in her attitudes toward courses and assignments. She found that Yuko's discouragement in the first year was replaced by increased confidence in her ability to read a variety of texts and carry out writing assignments based on careful readings of those texts. Some of the strategies Yuko developed over the 3 years included "choosing professors who were accessible and who could best facilitate her learning and selecting courses and paper topics that tapped into the background knowledge and experience she brought to the academy" (p. 48). Spack speculated that these strategies may have developed, in part, from Yuko's participation in the case study, which allowed her to articulate her difficulties and devise ways to overcome them.

Like Prior (1995), Spack (1997) concluded from her study that EAP curricula should avoid a fixed notion of academic genres. In addition, she argues against an exclusive focus on non-fiction texts. Due to the unpredictable nature of academic assignments, Spack recommends a variety of texts, including literature. She also questions the assumption that the skills learned in an EAP class are transferable to other settings, pointing out that assignments differ, even those made in the same course. Above all, Spack concludes that EAP students need preparation not in particular discourse practices but, rather, in how to "productively...negotiate their way through diverse discourses" (p. 51) the type of flexible approach advocated by Prior.

Leki's (1999) longitudinal case study of Jan, an undergraduate ELL at a publicly funded U.S. university, analyzed interviews with the participant, his class notes, assignments, and course work as well as observation notes about his participation in courses, including his interaction with classmates. Leki was initially interested in investigating Jan's experiences with writing in college. However, she found that very little writing was assigned in his first 3 years of college, yet Jan was required to take ESL and English classes in which essay writing was the focus. Of additional interest was the finding that Jan had difficulty following lectures and taking notes in such courses as chemistry and psychology. He was also unable to read the lecture notes he had taken because of the lapses in comprehension and the spaces he had left.

After a demoralizing first year in which Jan received a low grade point average, he began to strategize ways to "beat the system" (Leki, 1999, p. 30) so that he could raise his average. These included leaving out steps in carrying out a research project, turning in one paper numerous times knowing the teacher only checked if the work had been done, taking a Russian language course out of which he had placed so that he would receive an A, and turning in papers done for one class to a different class. Jan's approach helped raise his grade point average, but it also seemed to have contributed to his perception of academic work as a game in which students outwit their teachers to win the highest number of points.

Leki (1999) stops short of theorizing identity and power as areas of exploration. Yet she does raise questions about the role of institutional expectations in Jan's schemes, cynical outlook, and perception of himself as a college student. She attributes Jan's stance, in large measure, to institutional failures: big and dehumanizing lecture classes, lack of support for ELLs, insufficient academic advisement, and an anti-intellectual environment in which grades rather than learning are stressed. The institution "abandoned him to his own resources" (p. 40) rather than offering the help he needed. U.S. higher education is implicated, she believes, in perpetuating a "not particularly praiseworthy educational environment" (p. 40) in which critical thinking is subordinated to competition for the highest marks.

Though the contexts and findings of these ethnographies differ, each describes the challenges for ELLs of navigating academic course work and the unpredictable and idiosyncratic nature of academic assignments. The ethnographies also demonstrate the place of student agency in actively strategizing ways to succeed, including Hamad's decision to record only the information he thought would be included in an exam; Prior's participants' requests for a reduction in the number of assignments; Yuko's choice of professors who would be willing to speak to her regularly; and Jan's techniques for raising his grade point average. Yet, the students' private struggles to succeed point to a lack of adequate support for ELLs in postsecondary institutions and a need for a more flexible, less generic approach to EAP. One implication for instruction might be to offer EAP linked directly to the academic courses students are taking rather than precourse EAP based on an assumption of skills transfer from one context to another (Benesch, 1996, 1999, 2001).

Ethnography in EAP has provided important insight into individual students' experiences in courses across the curriculum. However, it has not focused specifically on the question of learner identity in postsecondary settings as an area of investigation. Demographic data about the participants is offered, such as age, gender, ethnicity, and, in ESL contexts, country of birth and length of residency, but identity is neither theorized nor explored as a factor in academic language learning. For that, I turn to critical ethnography, first discussing how it differs from ethnography.

CRITICAL ETHNOGRAPHY IN EAP

In contrasting critical and descriptive ethnography, Canagarajah (1993) credits the latter with offering a way to "systematically study the students' own point of view of English language teaching in its natural context" (p. 605). However, he advocates, instead, a critical approach as a way to "analyze how the attitudes formed by students in daily classroom life are impinged upon by the more abstract sociopolitical forces outside the walls of the classroom" (p. 605). Pennycook's (1994) discussion of critical pedagogical approaches to research points to its "focus on questions of social and cultural inequality in education" (p. 691). Critical ethnographers, then, take into account poststructuralist notions of unequal power relations and their impact on social constructions of identity. They problematize received categories, such as *non-native*, and develop more complex portraits of students' identities, through extensive interviews, classroom observations, and examination of course materials and students' written work. Five critical ethnographies of ELLs in various settings are discussed next.

Canagarajah (1993) sought to discover how students in a postcolonial setting might experience the ambivalence exhibited in the larger society toward English as both economically beneficial and politically/culturally oppressive. To this end, he studied 22 first-year students at the University of Jaffna enrolled in an English for General Purposes class, a required course for all students in arts and humanities programs. The 13 female and 9 male Tamil students were from poor rural communities in Sri Lanka where families had limited education. Data included precourse questionnaires about English; postcourse interviews about the class, textbook, and English; field notes based on classroom observations; and students' written comments in their textbooks. The last data set revealed students' opposition to the characters and storylines in the American textbook on which the English lessons were based.

Canagarajah (1993) found that the students exhibited a "very active underlife" (p. 613) in the drawings and comments they made in their textbooks and shared with other students. These included drawings showing the struggle for a separate Tamil state, alterations of American characters in the textbook into Tamil characters, and drawings that seemed to "deliberately vulgarize sex" (p. 614), perhaps as a way to ridicule the middle-class U.S. values depicted in the stories and dialogues.

As to questions of identity, students expressed concerns about learning English because their peers might view this as an "attempt to discard their local rural identity and pass off as an anglicized bourgeois or even a foreigner" (Canagarajah, 1993, p. 616). On the other hand, they also worried that their use of English would be ridiculed by better-educated Sri Lankans with greater English proficiency. To protect themselves from English and U.S. culture, the students focused selectively on grammar and vocabulary while refusing to participate in role-playing, peer work, and exercises focused on such topics as shopping.

Canagarajah (1993) concluded that the students' strategies for shielding themselves from the cultural domination of the English language and American textbooks do not constitute *resistance*, a conscious commitment to social transformation, but, rather, *opposition*, "which is unclear, ambivalent, and passive" (p. 624). He did not, therefore, conclude that EFL teaching in postcolonial contexts should rely on traditional grammar teaching to comply with students' opposition. Rather, he calls for critical teaching that could make students aware of their ambivalence toward English so that they could act consciously.

Students' complex and shifting relationships with English, as well as their resistance to institutional positioning, are taken up in the four studies discussed next. The first two, one by Angelil-Carter (1997) and the other by Thesen (1997), were carried out at the University of Cape Town (UCT) at a time of enormous change in South Africa, when black students were being admitted to historically white

English-medium colleges in greater numbers than previously, following Nelson Mandela's release from prison. Both studies examined questions of identity and power in the acquisition of academic discourse.

Angelil-Carter (1997) interviewed a first student, Tshediso, a member of the African National Congress and native speaker of Zulu who had served time as a political prisoner before enrolling at the university. The interviews, conducted over 9 months, were part of an ongoing investigation into "how students develop an authorial voice within multivoiced text in academic writing" (p. 269).

When studying the interview transcripts, Angelil-Carter noticed that power shifted back and forth between her and Tshediso, depending on which one felt authorized to speak. She was struck by her own tendency in the early interviews to set the agenda and interrupt. Yet she also noticed that when the subject of discussion turned to areas in which the student had greater knowledge, for example, life in prison, he became the authorized speaker and spoke for longer periods. Angelil-Carter believes that these shifts of power between researchers and participants should be taken into account when analyzing and reporting data.

Aside from discussing power shifts within the interviews, Angelil-Carter also examined Tshediso's changing relationship to English from his school days, to his time in prison, to his experiences at the university. In school, he was taught by Irish nuns who imposed an English-only rule in the classroom and on school grounds. Yet the students did not use English outside of school and Tshediso did not consider himself strong in the language at that time. While in prison, however, English had currency because it was the language spoken among black prisoners but not well understood by the white, Afrikaans-speaking guards. Tshediso became custodian of the library, a status and morale booster, and his investment in learning English grew. Later, when he arrived at UCT, his status as an English speaker was challenged by his encounters with people who exhibited equal or greater proficiency than he, as well as higher standards of correctness. Yet he took these standards as an opportunity to improve rather than as signs of deficiency.

Tshediso's changing relationship to English and his identity as a student were also revealed in readings and discussions of his academic writing. His experiences with writing in prison - letters in English to those outside, describing conditions within - had been positive. The letters had a clear audience and a purpose that had been fulfilled. Assignments in political studies and psychology presented new difficulties: how to integrate sources within a written text and how to make his ideas clear to an audience that was not well defined. In fact, he told Angelil-Carter that he understood that the goal in acquiring academic discourse was to "write a dead paper" (p. 279), a departure from his impassioned letters from prison.

It is here that Angelil-Carter (1997) drops the critical ball. Rather than questioning the type of writing her participant, a first-year student, was asked to generate in his social science courses, she considers him responsible for becoming invested in that writing. She does not question the institution's sanctioning of "dead" author-evacuated prose, but, instead, assumes that Tshediso must remediate his accustomed style, which she characterizes as "descriptive, almost poetic discourse that is not appropriate academic writing" (p. 279).

Angelil-Carter's study (1997), then, offers an interesting examination of power relations between the researcher and her participant and of the student's changing relationship with English according to his investment at different times of his life. However, missing from the analysis of the participant's writing is an interrogation of institutional expectations for first-year students, especially those who have been previously excluded (see Starfield, 2001, 2002, for a discussion of these concerns in a different South African university). Academic discourse is redefined as monolithically unemotional and unpoetic. The institution's role in constructing Tshediso's prose as inadequate is not explored, even though such a discussion might have revealed conflicts between how the university construed its English language learners and how they perceived themselves. For this type of analysis, I turn to Thesen (1997), Harklau (2000), and Raymond and Parks (2004), each study presenting the tensions between varying identities.

Thesen (1997) interviewed 13 black English language learners at the University of Cape Town, aiming to discover how they viewed their participation in an institution. Because of their history of exclusion from the university, these first-year students were labeled *disadvantaged*. Thesen wanted to explore their prior literacy experiences, both in and out of school, to move "beyond an empty notion of educational disadvantage" (p. 492). Her goal was to interrogate both *disadvantaged* and *mainstream*, in light of the changing population at UCT, admitting that the predominately white, middle-class faculty and staff "had locked ourselves into seeing only the educational disadvantage" (p. 491).

To transcend institutional labels and received categories, such as race, gender, ethnicity, and language, Thesen (1997) theorized identity as a "dynamic interaction between the fixed identity categories that are applied to social groupings...and the way individuals think of themselves as they move through different discourses in which these categories are salient" (p. 488). To discover students' multiple and fluid identities, she interviewed them about their experiences at UCT and in other settings. The focus of the interviews was *transitions*, including from a rural school to an urban university, from political writing to academic writing, and from first language to other languages, and how these discourses coexist and inform each other.

Though Thesen (1997) reports some findings from her interviews, her concern is primarily with raising theoretical and methodological questions. First, she underscores the importance of conducting interviews with ELLs to discover how they locate and understand themselves in relation to received identities and discourses. The interviews, Thesen believes, allow students to "generate new categories" (p. 505) through the process of articulating, however tentatively, emergent identities. Second, Thesen stresses *student agency*, that is, their awareness of "being in or out of discourses" and their decisions about "where to merge and where to resist" (p. 504). Finally, Thesen challenges EAP researchers to reconsider their construction of the *mainstream* as a "reasonably coherent and commonly understood entity" (p. 505). She warns that this assumption entails an insider/outsider dichotomy that is overly deterministic and not necessarily upheld when students are consulted about their emerging identities.

Like Thesen, Harklau (2000) examined discrepancies between institutional constructions of secondary and postsecondary ELLs and students' perceptions of themselves. In seeking to discover why schools and colleges construct identity as unitary and stable despite its multiplicity and fluctuations, she contrasts *representation*—"temporary artifacts that serve to stabilize and homogenize images of identity"—and *identities*—"multiple, fragmentary, and subject to constant change" (p. 37). To study how representations of ELLs develop and are perpetuated, Harklau conducted three year-long case studies of immigrant students' transitions from a U.S. urban high school to a 2-year community college.

Harklau's (2000) data included interviews with the students and their high school and college teachers, classroom observations, and documents pertaining to class work, such as assignment guidelines and student essays. She found that in high school, the ELLs were mythologized as Ellis Island immigrants, fleeing persecution and coming to the Promised Land, where hard work and perseverance pay off. This myth was encouraged through assignments emphasizing personal disclosure and ethnic difference. The monolithic immigrant identity, though positive, was, nonetheless, essentializing and, in some cases, stultifying. ELLs were expected to be well behaved and diligent, an expectation Harklau's participants strove to fulfill, at least overtly.

The transition to college revealed a different mythology: ELLs need to be socialized into U.S. and college life, through language and cultural instruction. That is, they were constructed as "newcomers and cultural novices" (Harklau, 2000, p. 54), regardless of their length of residence. This construction was reinforced through assignments focusing on students' countries, foods, holidays, and so on, thereby denying the "hybridity and multiplicity of U.S. high school graduates ethnic affiliations" (p. 56).

During classroom observations and interviews, Harklau (2000) discovered her participants' *opposition*, to institutional representations, especially when the students were in college where the constructions were more negative. They acted out in various ways, including inattention, poor attendance, and negative comments to ESOL teachers. However, these behaviors only served to reinforce the representation of ELLs as linguistically and culturally deficient.

Raymond and Parks (2004), on the other hand, uncovered *resistance* to the ways the Chinese MBA students they observed and interviewed were constructed, as EAP students, and instructed at a Canadian University. This *resistance* demonstrated that the students viewed themselves as active participants who were "savvy in negotiating conditions which to them appeared more conducive to ensuring their success" (p. 200) and helped transform what they found to be pedagogically unsound practices. The authors claim that the students' "ability to resist certain aspects of their program [was] due to their financial power" (p. 200). That is, the university in which they were enrolled depended on the high tuition fees paid by international students, and these students' complaints were therefore taken seriously, including raising grades and dismissing instructors. The examples of student resistance, interpreted by Raymond and Parks (2004) as the exercise of "economic clout" (p. 199), show that when students are aware of the context of "education as commodity" (p. 199) and their identity as consumers, they can bring power to bear. This formulation, of course, raises new questions about the complexity of student/faculty relationships, an area of possible struggle and conflict requiring future research.

The above-cited studies show a need for greater dialogue with ELLs to arrive at more complex and nuanced understandings of identity and power relations. Above all, they demonstrate the need for discussion of how institutional representations affect decisions about testing, placement, and curricula so that reforms can take multiplicity into account.

FUTURE DIRECTIONS

EAP was driven mainly in its first 30 years by an *ideology of pragmatism* (Benesch, 1993), that is, developing ways of teaching academic discourse and genres regardless of institutional and social conditions. However, in the 1990s, with the emphasis shifting toward classroom experiences, away from what should happen to what does happen, learners began to come into focus. Methodologically speaking, the shift was from needs analysis surveys to ethnographic case studies.

Ethnographies have documented the experiences of ELLs in courses across the curriculum. By and large, they examine students as individuals, struggling on their own to make sense of assignments and succeed in their courses across the curriculum, without considering the various ways they are positioned in the institution and larger society. Yet, despite its individualistic focus, this research has yielded important findings that highlight the unpredictable and sometimes unreasonable nature of academic course work. These findings have led some EAP researchers to encourage ELLs to act as ethnographers who investigate particular courses and assignments to become aware of how they are socially constructed (Johns, 1997).

Critical ethnographies, on the other hand, have focused on ELLs within social contexts that extend beyond the classroom, studying how their positionality in the larger society, that is, their race, class, ethnicity, and gender, might affect their learning. Identity is theorized as multiply constructed and shifting, not unitary or fixed, allowing critical ethnographies to examine the ways in which students move through different discourses, in their families, with peers, in classrooms, and in the workplace. This rich theoretical construct of identity as shifting across contexts offers a dynamic model of the acquisition of academic English. It shows how various discourses compete with one another, presenting significant challenges to students.

Critical ethnographies of English language learners offer cautionary portraits of how these students are constructed by institutional labels, such as *disadvantaged, immigrant*, and *international*, and how those labels entail certain expectations. Yet they also show that students may be aware of these constructions and may resist them in overt and covert ways.

The findings of critical ethnographies in EAP point to a need for dialogue with ELLs to discover how they respond to institutional labels, testing, and placement, as well as how they view their participation in postsecondary institutions and in other areas of their lives. The findings also suggest a need for critical EAP that encourages students to articulate their attitudes toward academic English, negotiate assignments, ask questions during lectures, and organize with other students for institutional change.

REFERENCES

Angelil-Carter, S. (1997). Second language acquisition of spoken and written English: Acquiring the sceptron. *TESOL Quarterly, 31*, 263–287.

Benesch, S. (1993). ESL, ideology, and the politics of pragmatism. *TESOL Quarterly, 27*, 705–717.

Benesch, S. (1996). Needs analysis and curriculum development in EAP: An example of a critical approach. *TESOL Quarterly, 30*, 723–738.

Benesch, S. (1999). Rights analysis: Studying power relations in an academic setting. *English for Specific Purposes, 18*, 313–327.

Benesch, S. (2001). *Critical English for academic purposes: Theory, politics, and practice*. Mahwah, NJ: Lawrence Erlbaum Associates.
Benson, M. J. (1989). The academic listening task: A case study. *TESOL Quarterly, 23*, 421–445.
Bhatia, V. K. (1993). *Analyzing genres: Language use in professional settings*. Essex: Longman.
Canagarajah, A. S. (1993). Critical ethnography of a Sri Lankan classroom: Ambiguities in student opposition to reproduction through ESOL. *TESOL Quarterly, 27*, 601–626.
Candlin, C. (2000). General Editor's preface. In B. Norton (Ed.), *Identity and language learning: Gender, ethnicity, and educational change* (pp. xiii–xxi). Essex: Longman.
Casanave, C. P. (1992). Cultural diversity and socialization: A case study of a Hispanic woman in a doctoral program in sociology. In D. E. Murray (Ed.), *Diversity as resource: Redefining cultural literacy* (pp. 148–182). Alexandria, VA: TESOL.
Connor, U. M., & Kramer, M. G. (1995). Writing from sources: Case studies of graduate students in business management. In D. Belcher & G. Braine (Eds.), *Academic writing in a second language: Essays on research & pedagogy* (pp. 155–182). Norwood, NJ: Ablex.
CUNY ESL Task Force Report (1994). The City University of New York. CUNY Office of Academic Affairs.
Dudley-Evans, T., & St. John, M. J. (1998). *Developments in English for academic purposes: A multidisciplinary approach*. Cambridge: Cambridge University Press.
Fox, H. (1994). *Listening to the world: Cultural issues in academic writing*. Urbana, IL: NCTE.
Hansen, J. G. (1999). Interactional conflicts among audience, purpose, and content knowledge in the acquisition of academic literacy in an EAP course. *Written communication, 17*, 27–52.
Harklau, L. (2000). From the "good kids" to the "worst": Representations of English language learners across educational settings. *TESOL Quarterly, 34*, 35–67.
Horowitz, D. (1986). What professors actually require: Academic tasks for the ESL classroom. *TESOL Quarterly, 20*, 445–462.
Houghton, D. (1991). Mr. Chong: A case study of a dependent learner of English for academic purposes. *System, 19*, 75–90.
Immigrants' needs at CUNY to grow. (1995, March 20). *The Times Union*.
Immigration/Migration and the CUNY student of the future (1995). The City University of New York.
Johns, A. M. (1981). Necessary English: A faculty survey. *TESOL Quarterly, 15*, 51–57.
Johns, A. M. (1992). Toward developing a cultural repertoire. In D. Murray (Ed.), *Diversity as resource: Redefining cultural literacy* (pp. 183–201). Alexandria, VA: TESOL.
Johns, A. M. (1997). *Text, role, and context: Developing academic literacies*. Cambridge: Cambridge University Press.
Leki, I. (1999). "Pretty much I screwed up": Ill-served needs of a permanent resident. In L. Harklau, K. M. Losey, & M. Siegal (Eds.), *Generation 1.5 meets college composition: Issues in the teaching of writing to U.S.- educated learners of ESL* (pp. 17–43). Mahwah, NJ: Lawrence Erlbaum.
Norton, B. (1997). Language, identity, and the ownership of English. *TESOL Quarterly, 31*, 409–429.
Norton, B. (2000). *Identity and language learning: Gender, ethnicity, and educational change*. Essex: Longman.
Pennycook, A. (1994) Critical pedagogical approaches to research. *TESOL Quarterly, 28*, 690–693.
Prior, P. (1991). Contextualizing writing and response in a graduate seminar. *Written Communication, 8*, 267–310.
Prior, P. (1995). Redefining the task: An ethnographic examination of writing and response in graduate seminars. In D. Belcher & G. Braine (Eds.), *Academic writing in a second language: Essays on research & pedagogy* (pp. 47–82). Norwood, NJ: Ablex.
Prior, P. (1998). *Writing disciplinarity: A sociohistoric account of literate activity in the academy*. Mahwah, NJ: Lawrence Erlbaum Associates.
Raymond, P.M. (2004). Chinese students' enculturation into an MBA program: Issues of empowerment. *Critical Inquiry in Language Studies, 1*(4), 187–202.
Schneider, M., & Fujishima, N. K. (1995). When practice doesn't make perfect: The case study of a graduate ESL student. In D. Belcher & G. Braine (Eds.), *Academic writing in a second language: Essays on research & pedagogy* (pp. 3–21). Norwood, NJ: Ablex.
Smoke, T. (1994). Writing as a means of learning. *College ESL, 4*, 1–11.
Spack, R. (1997). The acquisition of academic literacy in a second language: A longitudinal case study. *Written Communication, 14*, 3–26.
Starfield, S. (2001). 'I'll go with the group': Rethinking 'discourse community' in EAP. In J. Flowerdew & M. Peacock (Eds), *Research Perspectives on English for Academic Purposes* (pp. 132–147). Cambridge: Cambridge University Press.
Starfield, S. (2002). 'I'm a second-language English speaker': Negotiating writing identity and authority in sociology one. *Journal of Language, Identity, and Education, 1*(2), 121–140.

Study: A more diverse CUNY Struggle to meet changing needs. (1995, March 20). *Newsday*, p. 13.
Swales, J. M. (1990). *Genre analysis: English in academic and research settings.* Cambridge: Cambridge University Press.
Thesen, L. (1997). Voice, discourse, and transition: In search of new categories in EAP. *TESOL Quarterly, 31*, 487–511.

CHAPTER 39

IMAGINED COMMUNITIES, IDENTITY, AND ENGLISH LANGUAGE LEARNING

ANETA PAVLENKO

Temple University, USA

BONNY NORTON

The University of British Columbia, Canada

ABSTRACT

This chapter introduces the notion of *imagined communities* as a way to better understand the relationship between second language learning and identity. It is argued that language learners' actual and desired memberships in imagined communities affect their learning trajectories, influencing their agency, motivation, investment, and resistance in the learning of English. These influences are exemplified with regard to five identity clusters: postcolonial, global, ethnic, multilingual, and gendered identities. During the course of this discussion, we consider the relevance of imagined communities for classroom practice in English education.

INTRODUCTION

This chapter discusses ways in which language learners' actual and desired memberships in "imagined communities" (Anderson, 1991) affect their learning trajectories. We will start out by explaining the notion of *imagined communities* with reference to language and identity. Then, we will show how the process of imagining and reimagining one's multiple memberships may influence agency, motivation, investment, and resistance in the learning of English in terms of five identity clusters: postcolonial, global, ethnic, multilingual, and gendered identities. We will argue that the notion of imagined communities has great potential for bridging theory and praxis in language education and for informing critical and transformative language pedagogy.

The theoretical framework adopted in the present chapter is best viewed as poststructuralist or postmodernist. While the terms *poststructuralism*, *postmodernism*, or *critical inquiry* serve as an umbrella for a variety of theoretical approaches adopted by different researchers (see Morgan, this volume, for a fuller discussion), in the present chapter we will use the terms interchangeably, emphasizing similarities that they all share. Of particular importance to us is the postmodernist focus on *language* as the locus of social organization, power, and individual consciousness, and as a form of symbolic capital (Bourdieu, 1991). *Learning*, in turn, will be seen as a situated process of participation in particular communities of practice, which may entail the negotiation of ways of being a person in that context (Wenger, 1998). Thus, "because learning transforms who we are and what we can do, it is an experience of identity" (p. 215), a process of becoming, or avoiding becoming a certain person, rather than a simple accumulation of skills and knowledge. While the situated view of learning as socialization has been productive in the second language acquisition (SLA) literature, so far it has focused predominantly on learning that takes place as a result of the learners' direct engagement in face-to-face communities. Learning that is connected to learner participation in a wider world has been little explored. Yet we humans are capable, through our imagination, of perceiving a connection with people beyond our immediate social networks. Our orientation toward such imagined communities might have just as much impact on our current identities and learning as direct involvement in communities of our everyday life. We argue that the notion of *imagination* as a way to appropriate meanings and create new identities, developed by Anderson (1991) and Wenger (1998), allows us to transcend the focus on the learners' immediate environment, as the learning of another language, perhaps more than any other educational activity, reflects the desire of learners to expand their range of identities and to reach out to wider worlds (Kinginger, 2004; Kramsch, 2000; Kramsch & von Hoene, 2001; Norton, 2001).

Our discussion of the role of imagination in second language learning draws on three complementary sources: Anderson's (1991) view of nation-states as imagined communities, Wenger's (1998) view of imagination as a form of engagement with communities of practice, and Markus and Nurius's (1986) view of possible selves as the link between motivation and behavior. In his work on the role of language in the creation of nation-states, Anderson traces ways in which the invention of printing technology in the capitalist world gave new fixity to language and created languages-of-power, different from older vernaculars. The nation-states, in turn, were conceived around these languages, as imagined communities "because the members of even the smallest nation will never know most of their fellow-members, meet them, or even hear of them, yet in the minds of each lives the image of their communion" (p. 6). Anderson's analysis presents imagination as a social process, emphasizing the fact that those in power oftentimes do the imagining for the rest of their fellow citizens, offering them certain identity options and leaving other options 'unimaginable'.

Wenger's (1998) situated learning theory provides a complementary perspective to that of Anderson, presenting imagination as both an individual and social process. In his view, imagination is a distinct form of belonging to a particular community of practice and a way in which "we can locate ourselves in the world and history, and include in our identities other meanings, other possibilities, other perspectives" (p. 178). In this, Wenger's insights converge with the well-known psychological theory of *possible selves* (Markus & Nurius, 1986), which represent individuals' ideas of what they might become, what they would like to become, and what they are afraid of becoming, thus linking cognition, behavior, and motivation. For both Wenger and Markus and Nurius, possible selves, linked to memberships in imagined communities, shape individuals' present and future decisions and behaviors and provide an evaluative and interpretive context for such decisions, behaviors, and their outcomes.

Norton (2000, 2001) has incorporated Wenger's (1998) views into the study of second language learning and education, suggesting that learners have different investments in different members of the target language community, and that the people in whom the learners have the greatest investment may be the very people who provide (or limit) access to the imagined community of a given learner. The goal of the present chapter is to build on the previous arguments, demonstrating how nation-states may shape the imagination of their citizens and how actual and desired memberships in various imagined communities mediate the learning of—or resistance to—English around the world.

IMAGINED COMMUNITIES AND IDENTITIES

In what follows, we will discuss membership in imagined communities in terms of five identity clusters that have relevance to English as an international language: (a) postcolonial, (b) global, (c) ethnic, (d) multilingual, and (e) gendered identities. While separating the identities into these five subcategories for purposes of clarity and better focus, we acknowledge that much of the time these multiple facets of learners' selves are inseparable. Thus, for example, postcolonial identities are centrally concerned with questions of ethnicity, while ethnicity may be implicated in the construction of multilingual identities. Our survey does not aim to be comprehensive or all-inclusive: rather, with a choice of one or two examples from diverse contexts, we aim to illustrate how languages—and identities linked to them—lose and acquire value in the linguistic marketplace through the work of imagination.

Postcolonial Englishes

Anderson's (1991) lucid analysis makes it clear that in the modern era, nations are no longer created in blood but imagined in language. Hebrew offers an extraordinary example of a language that served to unify Jews from all over the world who otherwise had little if anything in common, sometimes not even religion. At present, postcolonial contexts offer a particularly fertile area for examination, since newly imagined national identities and futures are often tied to language. Due to British colonial history and, more recently, to American cultural and linguistic imperialism, English is implicated in this process of reimagination more than any other language. In the era of globalization, postcolonial nations and subjects are forced to take a stance with regard to the role that English as a global language will play in their future.

Even a brief look at these decisions demonstrates that English—and identities that can be fashioned out of it—is imagined differently in different contexts. One of the key issues in Africa, for instance, is the language of literature and thus of the national narrative, and numerous African writers have expressed their views on this issue in press and at conferences on the role of English in African literature (Miller, 1996). This attention to the written word is not surprising, since, according to Anderson (1991, p. 134), nationalism is conceived in the print-language, not a language per se. What is surprising are the opposing stances taken by individuals in seemingly similar contexts. Thus, in 1977 a well-known Kenyan writer, Ngugi wa Thiong'o, publicly refused to write in English after having published four successful novels as well as numerous essays, plays, and short stories in that language. In doing so, Ngugi decried his allegiance with the language of Kenya's colonial past, in which the poorest and most oppressed citizens of the country could neither read nor communicate. Instead, to transcend the "colonial alienation" of the African intelligentsia from its own people, he chose to write in the local language Gikuyu, which at the time had not developed traditions of written narrative. In contrast, another famous African writer, Chinua Achebe (1965), argues that while English is a "world language which history has forced down our throats" (p. 29), it is also the language that made it possible for Africans to talk to one another and to create national rather than ethnic literatures.

Miller's (1996) insightful analysis indicates that these diametrically opposed visions of African national identities and English are not incidental, for they carry with them different visions of the future of African nation-states. While Ngugi imagines the Kenyan future as a revolutionary change within the country, Achebe's vision encourages African unity and places Africa on a par with other countries in a global community. Notably, Achebe's view does not entail an uncritical appropriation of English as spoken and written by some imaginary native speakers: rather, Achebe (1988) intends to indigenize the language, declaring, "Let no one be fooled by the fact that we may write in English for we intend to do unheard of things with it" (p. 50). Instead of reimagining themselves, Achebe and other like-minded writers reimagine English and refashion their relationship to it, creating hybrid work that, like Nuyorican bilingual poetry, can no longer claim allegiance to one language only and draws on multiple languages and literary traditions (Miller, 1996; for an in-depth discussion of the tensions between English and indigenous languages in postcolonial Africa, see Obondo's chapter in this Handbook).

A similar approach to the reimagination of English in postcolonial contexts is that undertaken in South Africa, where a focus on *People's English* represents a challenge to the hegemony of Standard English (Norton Peirce, 1989). Rather than dispensing with the use of English in public discourse, advocates of People's English take the position that English should be appropriated to serve the interests of the majority of people who use it. Central to the argument is that models of communicative competence should focus on what is *desirable*, rather than socially acceptable, in the learning and teaching of English. Recent research on world Englishes confirms the fact that appropriation and indigenization of English is the route taken in many postcolonial contexts, from India to the Caribbean (cf. Baley & Gorlach, 1982; Kachru, 1982).

In sum, recent explorations in language policy and sociolinguistics indicate that in postcolonial contexts, national identities are oftentimes fashioned in relation to English as a global language. While some countries may renounce English as a language of colonialism, others may take a neutral stance, neither privileging nor discouraging English, and yet others may choose to appropriate and indigenize English, constructing national identities simultaneously through and in opposition to English. The link between national identities and imagined communities plays an important role in language and educational policies, thus confirming Anderson's (1991) thesis about public media playing a key role in shaping the public imagination and creating identities for public consumption.

English and the Global Marketplace

In contrast to postcolonial contexts, in which developing countries are seeking to address their ambivalent relationship to English, other countries for which English is not a postcolonial language aim to promote Standard English in order to align themselves with the Western powers and gain an entry into the global market. A striking example of foreign language education as a mirror of national allegiances is seen in Eastern Europe, where, after the collapse of the Soviet Empire, the newly emerged countries aim to refashion themselves as democratic and capitalist. An important aspect of this social and economic change involves language education reform, which has eliminated or severely limited Russian as a primary foreign or second language and established English (followed by German and French) as key to national prosperity and global cooperation. While prior to 1989, international contacts of Eastern European and Soviet citizens were restrained and supervised, and the opportunity to use foreign languages was rather limited, the dissolution of communist regimes offered unlimited possibilities for international collaboration—and a pressing need to engage in them in view of the breakdown of the Soviet economy. New political and economic futures involve new national identity options—in particular those of "citizens of the world"—and, as a result, lead to a significant increase in foreign language learning motivation. While Russian, the language of the Big Brother, was often ridiculed and resisted in Eastern Europe, English is now receiving a warm welcome, and former teachers of Russian are being retrained as teachers of English.

Hungary provides an excellent example of this trend towards English and other European languages. The country's realignment with the West has resulted in a marked increase in the numbers of those enrolled in foreign language public and private schools as well as those who take certification exams in these languages. In 1996, three times as many people took foreign language proficiency exams as in 1987: this trend documents both the growing interest in foreign language education and the realization of the importance of certified knowledge (Medgyes & Miklosy, 2000). The growing preoccupation with foreign language competence is continuously in the public eye as the one and only issue on which three different Hungarian governments elected since 1990 came to an agreement. The media endlessly discusses the insufficient language competence of the average Hungarian; employers publish increasing numbers of job advertisements in English to filter out the "linguistically deficient"; the bookstore windows are adorned by language books and dictionaries; and the streets of major Hungarian towns display "Learn English Fast and Easy" language school ads (Medgyes & Miklosy, 2000). It is not surprising then that even Hungarians, who previously did not see the relevance of English—or any other foreign language—to their personal and professional future, are reconsidering their attitudes and reimagining themselves as sophisticated multilinguals, engaged members of the European Union. On the other hand, as citizens of any small nation, they also exhibit ambivalence as to the possible involvement with NATO and the West and fears that English may come to contaminate and displace their own language (Biava, 2001; Medgyes & Miklosy, 2000).

Research in Israel provides another example of the increased symbolic value of English within the global marketplace and the communities that are imagined by English language learners. Kheimetz and Epstein's (2001) study suggests that English is crucial in the professional and social integration of scientists from the former Soviet Union in Israel. As more and more professional meetings, Internet communication, and publications take place in English, it is English, rather than only Hebrew, that is instrumental for successful transformation of Soviet scientists into Israeli ones. Quantitative results of the study revealed significant differences between those who studied English and those who studied either German or French regarding feelings of personal self-actualization and job satisfaction, and both statistical tests and personal interviews demonstrated that command of English was the determining factor for risk of losing a job. A successful physicist the authors interviewed for their study said that he pities Russian scientists who don't speak English, as they have no professional future ahead of them, and advised all Russians who would like to continue being scientists in Israel to study English as intensively as they can. In turn, another scientist who lost his job admitted that his lack of mastery of English narrowed his professional and social options and ultimately cost him his first job. Even though initially he did get a professional job in Israel, he couldn't read professional literature in English, nor could he follow the conversations of his colleagues whose Hebrew abounded in English terms: instead, he suspected that they were laughing at him behind his back. He cited the difficulties in communication, which stemmed both from low English proficiency and from low self-esteem, among the main reasons for losing the job.

To sum up, recent research in sociolinguistics, language policy, and language education also suggests that, in the global marketplace, national—and individual—identities are often constructed in relation to English as the language of world economy. Some countries, like Hungary, may encourage a greater role for English as a way to enter the global marketplace and create a more visible national identity, while individual citizens in non-English speaking countries may invest in English for career advancement purposes.

Ethnicity and the Ownership of English

Even in countries in which English is the dominant mother tongue, research suggests that there exists much ambivalence about who constitutes a "legitimate" speaker of English. The American writer David Mura (1991), a third-generation Japanese-American, once remarked in despair that "in the world of the tradition, [he] was unimagined" (p. 77). The utter invisibility of second- and third-generation Asian-Americans in the media led his classmates, and later his coworkers, to constantly challenge his "ownership" of English, which clashed, in their mind, with his Asian features. To researchers in language education, this practice does not come as a surprise: in many English-speaking contexts, the ownership of English by white immigrants is contested to a significantly lesser degree than that by racialized newcomers. Miller's (2000) ethnographic study of ESL students' socialization into the mainstream in an Australian high school demonstrates that white and fair-haired Bosnian students assimilate quickly, establishing friendships with the English-speaking students and appropriating a range of discourses in English, while the dark-haired Chinese students remain isolated from the mainstream. The Chinese students in her study stated that they had felt discriminated against, because neither their peers nor their teachers acknowledged their legitimacy as L2 users of English in the same way they acknowledged the legitimacy of their European immigrant classmates who resemble Australians physically. Similarly, Norton's (2000) research with immigrant women in Canada documents the case of the Vietnamese woman Mai, who perceived a "perfect Canadian" as one who was both white and English-speaking. During the study, Mai described the alienation that her nephews experienced as Chinese/Vietnamese people in Canada and explained how the eldest child, Trong, had chosen to change his name from a Vietnamese one to an anglicized one. Mai had objected to this practice and had said to her nephews that they should not reject their heritage, explaining, "With your hair, your nose, your skin, you will never be perfect Canadians" (p. 149). Like Mura and the Chinese students in Miller's study, Trong would remain unimaginable as a mainstream Canadian.

It would be highly erroneous, however, to posit that all newcomers in Australia, Canada, the U.S., or Britain aim to speak Standard English and emulate its white middle-class speakers. Ibrahim (1999) found that African students in a high school in Toronto were learning to reimagine themselves as Black, rather than as Sudanese or Nigerian, and by speaking what he calls *Black Stylized English* (BSE) to position themselves with regard to the racial divide constructed by the North American society around them. Similar arguments are brought up by Bailey (2000) with regard to Dominican American students in the U.S. who adopt African American English vernacular as a language of solidarity with their African American peers while simultaneously using Spanish to differentiate themselves from the same peers. This and other work suggests that in order to understand the learners' investments, we need to examine their multiple communities and understand who can and who cannot be imagined as a legitimate speaker of a particular language variety in a specific context.

The extent to which identity options are seen to be publicly visible and politically valued is implicated in the kinds of communities that language learners imagine and desire for themselves. In this regard, the media is central in the shaping of ethnic and racial identities, in particular with regard to language: while powerfully presenting and endorsing some identity options, the media can also make some identity options "invisible" or, at least, devalue and delegitimize them. The work of Stuart Hall (1992a, 1992b) has been particularly influential in documenting the ways in which the media reproduces a limited range of identities for minority citizens. With respect to questions of race, he notes that it is the silences that are highly meaningful: what isn't there says a great deal about what is or is not valued in a given society. A poignant example of the ability of popular culture and the media to shape language attitudes comes from a groundbreaking ethnographic study by Orellana (1994) that demonstrates that even the youngest children are very sensitive to both negative and positive images offered by the media. Following three Spanish-speaking children enrolled in a bilingual preschool in the US, the researcher found that these children's initial spontaneous use of English occurred when playacting at being superheroes and other figures from children's popular culture. One child, Carlos, also explicitly stated that when he grows up, he will speak only English because this is the language spoken by Ninja Turtles, Batman, and Peter Pan. Like few other studies, Orellana's work demonstrates that monolingual English-speaking characters, which successfully capture children's imagination, transmit powerful ideas about which linguistic identities and possible selves are preferable to others. What remains unsaid is the fact that some speakers of English are, in unforgettable Orwellian words, "more equal than others"; and that down the road, Carlos' ownership of English may be challenged on the grounds of his ethnicity, first or last name, or the color of his skin.

In short, it appears that ethnicity and race play an important role in institutional and individual imagined communities of legitimate speakers of English. And as English language learners reimagine their futures in a changing world, the question "Who owns English?" will become ever more strident and contested (see Norton, 1997).

English Language Learner or Multilingual Speaker?

Complementary to debates over who may be considered a legitimate speaker of English are debates over the framing and positioning of English language learners. Given the power of English within the larger global community, English language learners, the "marked" case, are often positioned within a deficit framework that limits the kinds of identities and communities that can be imagined by and for these learners. In English-speaking countries, in particular, those who have learned English as a second, third, or fourth language are often seen as non-native speakers, limited English proficiency students, interlanguage speakers, or language learners. A Japanese learner of English in Canada in Kanno and Applebaum's (1995) study recalls that once a classmate yelled at her, "Are you deaf or ESL?" (p. 43). This classmate drew on a powerful—and ever-present in North America—discourse that equates bilingualism and non-native speaker status with disability and cognitive impairment (Hakuta, 1986).

As English language learners grow up, they become ever more sensitive to the label *ESL*. In contexts like South Africa, *second language* is often equated with *second class*. Thesen (1997) argues convincingly that the categories that are used to label English language learners in tertiary education in South Africa are highly political, and can have the unintended consequence of exacerbating the challenges these learners face. She draws on the work of Ndebele (1995) to make the case that the term *disadvantaged*, for example, is a cause for concern: "The namer isolates the named, explains them, contains them, and controls them. In this way a numerical majority can, in part through linguistic manipulation, simulate a majoritarian character" (p. 4).

Recently, several scholars challenged the deficit model, accusing mainstream linguistics and SLA theory of monolingual and ethnocentric biases and pointing out that in a world where more than half the population is bi- and multilingual, it is monolingual—and not bilingual—competence that is the marked case (Braine, 1999; Cook, 1992, 1999, 2002; Grosjean, 1998; Kachru, 1994; Lippi-Green, 1997; Sridhar, 1994). Instead of reproducing the native/non-native speaker dichotomy, these scholars proposed to bridge the fields of bilingualism and SLA and see previous *non-native speakers* as bilinguals (Grosjean, 1998) and as legitimate L2 users (Cook, 1999, 2002). However, while scholars continue battling against the monolingual bias on the pages of learned journals, the researchers' plight remains ignored by the general public, which typically doesn't read scholarly disquisitions. Thus, the monumental task of imagining diverse—but nevertheless legitimate—owners and users of English falls on the shoulders of public individuals: politicians, media personalities, and, in particular, writers.

Recent analyses demonstrate that the theme of reimagining language ownership dominates the pages of cross-cultural memoirs and fiction published in the United States, from Richard Rodriguez's *Hunger of Memory* and Hoffman's *Lost in Translation* to Chang Rae Lee's *Native Speaker* (Pavlenko, 1998, 2001). This is not surprising, since in 1999 alone, the U.S. National Book Award in Fiction for an English language novel went to Ha Jin, a native of China, who had begun learning English at the age of 21, and four out of eight Guggenheim fellowships for fiction went to foreign-born non-native speakers of English (Novakovich & Shapard, 2000). Award-winning prose and poetry by bilingual writers, such as Julia Alvarez, Andrei Codrescu, Jerzy Kosinski, Kyoko Mori, or Bharati Mukherjee, have completely changed the landscape of North American literature, redefining what it means to be an American writer.

The reimagining of linguistic membership and ownership takes place in the work of these and other bilingual writers in two ways. On the one hand, by composing their work in English, the authors appropriate the language, implicitly claiming their right to it. On the other, some also proclaim their linguistic rights and allegiances explicitly, stating, like Eva Hoffman (1989), that English is the language of their inner self. The written medium is ideal for this discursive battle over legitimate ownership: while in spoken interactions, opinions of some L2 users may be discounted by others due to their physical appearance or traces of non-standard accent in their speech, published texts constitute excellent equalizers and unique arenas where accents are erased and voices imbued with sufficient authority. Consequently, many contemporary bi- and multilingual authors and scholars explore the links between their multiple languages and selves in ways that were previously non-existent and/or impossible: challenging the essentialist notions of self; deconstructing various ethnic, national, colonial, and gender identities; creating new discourses of hybridity and multiplicity; and imagining new ways of "being American"—and bilingual—in the postmodern world. We can only hope that these hybrid and multilingual identities will find their way into the public media so that new generations can learn to imagine themselves as members of a linguistically diverse world, rather than one dominated by Standard English.

English and Gendered Identities

Cutting across postcolonial, global, and ethnic identities in relation to the learning of English is gender as a system of social and discursive relations (Pavlenko, Blackledge, Piller, & Teutsch-Dwyer, 2001). Recent research demonstrates that in different contexts, English may offer language learners the possibility of imagining different gendered identity options for themselves. On the one hand, many women around the globe see learning English as a way of liberating themselves from the confines of gender patriarchy (Kobayashi, 2002; McMahill, 1997, 2001). A survey of 555 high school students in Japan found that female Japanese students are significantly more positive toward—and more interested in—learning English, training for English-language related professions, and traveling to English-speaking countries than their male counterparts (Kobayashi, 2002). As a result, in 1998, according to the Japanese Ministry of Education, 67% of foreign language majors among the university students were female, with English being the most popular choice. This trend is not surprising, since young women continue to be marginalized in mainstream Japanese society, and English teaching and translation offer them a socially sanctioned occupational choice, a profession that is "ladylike," although not well paid. Further, McMahill argues that many young Japanese women consider English to be intrinsically linked to feminism and thus are motivated to learn it as a language of empowerment.

On the other hand, Goldstein (1997), Kouritzin (2000), and Norton (2000) suggest that immigrant women in Canada do not necessarily consider English to be the only key to social mobility and enhanced opportunity. At times, in particular workplaces, a greater mastery of English may lead to a decrease in productivity and lack of support from colleagues (Goldstein, 1997; Norton, 2000). In other contexts, immigrant women may choose not to attend English classes because of cultural constraints that require them to prioritize their roles as housekeepers, mothers, wives, and caretakers. Still others may choose not to attend English classes if they feel that the English curriculum is not consistent with their desires for the future. Norton (2001) makes that case for two immigrant women who removed themselves from their English classes because their teachers did not appear sympathetic towards their investments in particular imagined communities. While Felicia from Peru was heavily invested in the local Peruvian community, Katarina from Poland was anxious for validation by a community of professionals. The central point, Norton argues, is that an imagined community presupposes an imagined identity—one that offers an enhanced range of possibilities for the future.

REIMAGINING ENGLISH TEACHING

The discussion above allows us to draw a number of implications that the imagined communities perspective has for language classrooms. To begin with, recent research suggests that the work of bilingual writers can be successfully appropriated for both ESL classrooms (Almon, 2001) and TESOL teacher education classrooms (Pavlenko, 2003), where it serves to challenge the dominant notions of native speakerness and to give birth to discourses of resistance to dominant ideologies of monolingualism and monoculturalism. Writing appears particularly important in this approach, as written texts may represent uniquely safe spaces in which new identities can be invented and new multilingual voices "tried on" (Pavlenko, 2001). Norton's (2000, 2001) work demonstrates that students' non-participation in specific language practices can be explained through their investment in particular imagined communities and through their access (or lack thereof) to these communities. If we do not acknowledge the imagined communities of the learners, we may exacerbate their non-participation and impact their learning trajectories in negative ways. Kanno (2003) notes, further, that it is not only classrooms but also schools that have imagined communities. In her study of four schools in Japan that serve large numbers of bilingual students, she examines the relationship between the schools' visions for their students' future, their current policies and practices, and their students' identities. She makes the case that it is the least privileged bilingual students who are socialized into the least privileged imagined communities, when it is precisely this group that would benefit from an education that would dare to imagine a different set of options for the future. We conclude with the hope that English language teachers in different parts of the globe may consider the ways in which our own multilingual classrooms can be reimagined as places of possibility for students with a wide range of histories, investments, and desires for the future.

REFERENCES

Achebe, C. (1965). English and the African writer. *Transition: A Journal of the Arts, Culture, and Society, 4*, 18.
Achebe, C. (1988). *Hopes and impediments: Selected essays 1965–1987*. London: Heinemann.
Almon, C. (2001). *Identity stories in an ESL classroom*. Unpublished manuscript, Temple University.
Anderson, B. (1991). *Imagined communities: Reflections on the origins and spread of nationalism* (Rev. ed.). London: Verso.
Bailey, B. (2000). Language and negotiation of ethnic/racial identity among Dominican Americans. *Language in Society, 29*(4), 555–582.
Baley, R., & Gorlach, M. (Eds.). (1982). *English as a world language*. Ann Arbor: University of Michigan Press.

Biava, T. (2001, February). *Creating a post-Communist identity in English, "a small lane between optimism and pessimism."* Paper presented at the American Association of Applied Linguistics (AAAL) Conference, St. Louis, MO.
Bourdieu, P. (1991). *Language and symbolic power.* Cambridge: Polity Press.
Braine, G. (Ed.). (1999). *Non-native educators in English language teaching.* Mahwah, NJ: Lawrence Erlbaum.
Cook, V. (1992). Evidence for multicompetence. *Language Learning, 42,* 557–591.
Cook, V. (1999). Going beyond the native speaker in language teaching. *TESOL Quarterly, 33,* 185–209.
Cook, V. (Ed.). (2002). *Portraits of the L2 users.* Clevedon, UK: Multilingual Matters.
Goldstein, T. (1997). *Two languages at work: Bilingual life on the production floor.* Berlin/New York: Mouton de Gruyter.
Grosjean, F. (1998). Studying bilinguals: Methodological and conceptual issues. *Bilingualism: Language and Cognition, 1,* 131–149.
Hakuta, K. (1986). *Mirror of language: The debate on bilingualism.* New York: Basic Books.
Hall, S. (1992a). Race, culture, and communications: Looking backward and forward at cultural studies. *Rethinking Marxism, 5*(1), 10–18.
Hall, S. (1992b). The question of cultural identity. In S. Hall, D. Held, & T. McGrew (Eds.), *Modernity and its futures* (pp. 273–325). Cambridge, UK: Polity Press.
Hoffman, E. (1989). *Lost in translation. A life in a new language.* New York: Dutton.
Ibrahim, A. (1999). Becoming Black: Rap and Hip-Hop, race, gender, identity, and the politics of ESL learning. *TESOL Quarterly, 33*(3), 349–369.
Kachru, B. (1982). *The other tongue: English across cultures.* Urbana: University of Illinois Press.
Kachru, Y. (1994). Monolingual bias in SLA research. *TESOL Quarterly, 28,* 795–800.
Kanno, Y. (2003). Imagined communities, school visions, and the education of bilingual students in Japan. *Journal of Language, Identity, and Education, 2,* 241–249.
Kanno, Y., & Applebaum, S. (1995). ESL students speak up: Their stories of how we are doing. *TESL Canada Journal, 12*(2), 32–49.
Kheimetz, N., & Epstein, A. (2001). English as a central component of success in the professional and social integration of scientists from the former Soviet Union in Israel. *Language in Society, 30,* 187–215.
Kinginger, C. (2004). Alice doesn't live here anymore: Foreign language learning and identity reconstruction. In A. Pavlenko & A. Blackledge (Eds.), *Negotiation of identities in multilingual settings* (pp. 219–242). Clevedon, UK: Multilingual Matters.
Kobayashi, Y. (2002). The role of gender in foreign language learning attitudes: Japanese female students' attitudes toward English learning. *Gender and Education, 14*(2), 181–197.
Kouritzin, S. (2000). Immigrant mothers redefine access to ESL classes: Contradiction and ambivalence. *Journal of Multilingual and Multicultural Development, 21*(1), 14–32.
Kramsch, C. (2000). Social discursive constructions of self in L2 learning. In J. Lantolf (Ed.), *Sociocultural theory and second language learning* (pp. 133–153). New York: Oxford University Press.
Kramsch, C., & von Hoene, L. (2001). Cross-cultural excursions: Foreign language study and feminist discourses of travel. In A. Pavlenko, A. Blackledge, I. Piller, & M. Teutsch-Dwyer (Eds.), *Multilingualism, second language learning, and gender* (pp. 283–306). Berlin: Mouton de Gruyter.
Lippi-Green, R. (1997). *English with an accent: Language, ideology, and discrimination in the United States.* London: Routledge.
Markus, H., & Nurius, P. (1986). Possible selves. *American Psychologist, 41*(9), 954–969.
McMahill, C. (1997). Communities of resistance: A case study of two feminist English classes in Japan. *TESOL Quarterly, 31,* 612–622.
McMahill, C. (2001). Self-expression, gender, and community: A Japanese feminist English class. In A. Pavlenko, A. Blackledge, I. Piller, & M. Teutsch-Dwyer (Eds.), *Multilingualism, second language learning, and gender* (pp. 307–344). Berlin: Mouton de Gruyter.
Medgyes, P., & Miklosy, K. (2000). The language situation in Hungary. *Current Issues in Language Planning, 1*(2), 148–242.
Miller, J. (1996). A tongue, for sighing. In J. Maybin & N. Mercer (Eds.), *Using English: From conversation to canon* (pp. 275–298). London: Routledge.
Miller, J. (2000). Language use, identity, and social interaction: Migrant students in Australia. *Research on Language and Social Interaction, 33*(1), 69–100.
Mura, D. (1991). *Turning Japanese.* New York: Doubleday.
Ndebele, N. (1995). Maintaining domination through language. *Academic Development, 1,* 1–5.
Norton, B. (1997). Language, identity, and the ownership of English. *TESOL Quarterly, 31*(3), 409–429.
Norton, B. (2000). *Identity and language learning: Gender, ethnicity, and educational change.* London:

Longman/Pearson Education.
Norton, B. (2001). Non-participation, imagined communities and the language classroom. In M. Breen (Ed.), *Learner contributions to language learning: New directions in research* (pp. 159–171). London: Longman/Pearson Education.
Norton Peirce, B. (1989). Toward a pedagogy of possibility in the teaching of English internationally: People's English in South Africa. *TESOL Quarterly, 23*(3), 401–420.
Novakovich, J., & Shapard, R. (Eds.). (2000). *Stories in the stepmother tongue*. Buffalo, NY: White Pine Press.
Orellana, M. (1994). Appropriating the voice of the superheroes: Three preschoolers' bilingual language uses in play. *Early Childhood Research Quarterly, 9*, 171–193.
Pavlenko, A. (1998). Second language learning by adults: Testimonies of bilingual writers. *Issues in Applied Linguistics, 9*(1), 3–19.
Pavlenko, A. (2001). "In the world of the tradition I was unimagined": Negotiation of identities in cross-cultural autobiographies. *The International Journal of Bilingualism, 5*(3), 317–344.
Pavlenko, A. (2003). "I never knew I was bilingual": Reimagining identities in TESOL classes. *Journal of Language, Identity, and Education*, 2, 251–268.
Pavlenko, A., Blackledge, A., Piller, I., & Teutsch-Dwyer, M. (Eds.). (2001). *Multilingualism, second language learning, and gender*. Berlin/New York: Mouton de Gruyter.
Sridhar, S. (1994). A reality check for SLA theories. *TESOL Quarterly, 28*(4), 800–805.
Thesen, L. (1997). Voices, discourse, and transition: In search of new categories in EAP. *TESOL Quarterly, 31*(3), 487–511.
Wenger, E. (1998). *Communities of practice: Learning, meaning, and identity*. Cambridge, MA: Cambridge University Press.

CHAPTER 40

ACADEMIC ACHIEVEMENT AND SOCIAL IDENTITY AMONG BILINGUAL STUDENTS IN THE U.S.

SHELLEY WONG

RACHEL GRANT

George Mason University, USA

ABSTRACT

This chapter discusses academic achievement and social identity development among bilingual students with respect to changing demographics of increased linguistic diversity and poverty for school-aged children in the United States. Institutional policies and practices are described that lead to blaming the victims of institutional inequity for low test scores and high dropout rates. Contrasting paradigms in literacy research are also discussed in relation to how perspectives of monolingual meritocracy lead to language loss and perpetuation of deficit discourses that negatively affect social identity formation for bilingual students. The authors argue that educators can play an important role in transforming inequities in the politics and practices of schooling, and they provide a model for the successful academic achievement of English language learning (ELL) and bilingual students. The model includes three essential components for literacy development and academic achievement: (a) human resources, including ELL students, their families and communities, and ESL and bilingual education professionals; (b) dialogic pedagogy; and (c) a curriculum for democratic citizenship, and economic and community development.

INTRODUCTION

The academic underachievement of racial, linguistic, and cultural minority students has been documented consistently throughout the history of public education in the United States (see, for example, August & Hakuta, 1997; Kozol, 1991; Thomas & Collier, 1997). Despite intense educational reform efforts during the 1990s, the reading achievement gap between racial, linguistic, and cultural groups remained constant between 1992 and 2003: "At both grades 4 and 8, the average score gaps between White and Black students and between White and Hispanic students in 2003 were not found to differ significantly from those in 2002 or 1992" (National Center for Educational Statistics [NCES], 2004, p. 13).

Similarly, the NCES reported no reduction in the reading achievement gap between 1998 and 2003 for low-income students (eligible for free or reduced lunch) as compared to higher-income students (not eligible for free or reduced lunch). Poverty among school-age children has remained at high levels in the United States, with obvious and predictable effects on student achievement. How can children learn if they are hungry, are carrying out shift work with their parents, or have severe dental problems? The dire economic and social conditions under which too many Kindergarten-Grade 12 (K-12) English language learning (ELL) students live, the growing economic divisions in the society, and increased racial and linguistic polarization are important challenges to the entire educational community (Wong & Grant, 1995; Knapp & Woolverton, 2004).

In this chapter we explore the complex relationships between school achievement and social identity. Social identity is closely related to an individual's sense of belonging within particular social groups. Our identities are shaped by our families, the schools and neighborhoods we group up in, and the many life experiences we have. The way others view us plays a major role in constituting our identities. Gee (2001) refers to social identity as "being recognized as a certain kind of person." Too often, racial and linguistic minorities are positioned by educators as not the kind of people who can achieve academically. Low expectations based on characteristics such as skin color or language difference result in systematic devaluing that is reflected in tracking into lower-level classes, bias in assessment and testing, and various forms of remedial labeling (e.g., *culturally deprived*, *linguistic deficit*, etc.).

We examine the ways in which societal discourses (e.g., relating to English-only instruction, cultural and linguistic deficits, etc.) affect the ways in which bilingual students in the United States form their social identities. Specifically, socially and historically determined structures within the wider society identify minority communities as subordinate to the dominant group and position students from these communities for academic failure. The ways in which literacy is conceptualized, researched, and promoted in classrooms plays a central role in both the identity formation and academic engagement of racial and linguistic minority students. An alternative model is presented that outlines how educational professionals working with ELL and bilingual students can transform schooling and make a difference in the academic achievement of their students.

SOCIAL IDENTITY AND THE CREATION OF SOCIAL INEQUALITY

Norton (1997) uses "identity to refer to how people understand their relationship to the world, how that relationship is constructed across time and space and how people understand their possibilities for the future" (p. 410). Norton's framework for identity draws on critical race, feminist, and poststructuralist theories (Bourdieu, 1977; Cummins, 1996; Weedon, 1987; West, 1992, 1993). West emphasized that an analysis of an individual's desires for recognition, affiliation, and security and safety cannot be separated from an analysis of the material resources in society. Bourdieu pointed out that differences in symbolic power make the speakers in an interaction unequal partners (Grant & Wong, 2006). It cannot be assumed that a bilingual language minority speaker will be listened to: instead, s/he must claim the "right to speak." Norton has also drawn from Weedon's feminist, poststructuralist position that emphasizes subjectivity and agency. Subjectivity is seen as a dynamic force: multiple, non-unitary, and as a site for struggle. Language and subjectivity are seen as mutually constitutive and changing over time.

The operation of these constructs is illustrated in an ethnographic study of a multilingual multicultural high school in Northern California (Olsen, 1997). The study describes the complex and difficult path of becoming American experienced by ELL students as they negotiate conflicting social identities. These students are quickly "racialized" into various social identities in a school in which the student body is clearly divided and sorted according to categories such as language, race, and religion. Olsen suggests:

> There are many paths to and aspects of becoming American, though they all involve becoming English speaking... For newcomers the persistent question is whether or not the path to being American is one that is really open to them. (p. 43)

She points out that what clothing to wear, how to act, and how to respond are not easily negotiated. If a newcomer makes the wrong choice, s/he is open to ridicule. Newcomers navigate a difficult path between being accused of being "wannabees" and betraying their ethnic identity or remaining permanent outsiders.

Labels used to categorize students for purposes of funding, placement, and instruction can also introduce bias in the ways that students are perceived and the identity options open to them. The term *Limited English Proficient* (LEP), for example, is a problematic label because it emphasizes what second language learners can't do and ignores the home language that they already know. The label not only stigmatizes students, marking them as different from and inferior to the majority, but also sets unfair expectations of rates of second language learning, which are not applied to the majority monolingual students. When an Anglo child knows a few songs or colors in Spanish, it is seen as a great achievement, but when a Spanish-speaking child has made remarkable progress in second language learning, the standard s/he is measured by is the performance of the monolingual English child (Edelsky, 1991).

CONTRASTING PARADIGMS ON LITERACY AND ACADEMIC ACHIEVEMENT

Two contrasting paradigms operate in the United States with respect to literacy and academic achievement for bilingual students. The monolingual, meritocracy paradigm uses the white native-English speaker to establish the norm and to set guidelines on what constitutes achievement. The second paradigm acknowledges multilingualism and multiliteracies as well as the importance of preserving children's home languages and recognizing the negative consequences of language loss (Au & Raphael, 2000; Skutnabb-Kangas, 2000). Wong Fillmore has expressed clearly the challenges of maintaining minority languages in countries such as the United States:

> Language loss is not necessary or inevitable when children acquire second languages. Otherwise, the world would have no bilinguals. In the United States, however, and in other societies like it, powerful social and political forces operate against the retention of minority languages. To many and perhaps most Americans, English is more than a societal language; it is an ideology. (2000, p. 207)

Language loss results from both internal and external forces operating on the child: "The internal factors have to do with the desire for social inclusion, conformity and the need to communicate with others. The external forces are the socio-political ones operating in the society against outsiders, against differences, and against diversity" (Wong Fillmore, 2000, p. 208).

Central to the second paradigm is the belief that academic success for bilingual students can be achieved through culturally inclusive theoretical frameworks for research methods, literacy assessment, and literacy instructional practices. The pedagogy of multiliteracies extends definitions of literacy such that "language and other modes of meaning are dynamic representational resources, constantly being remade by their users as they work to achieve their various cultural purposes" (New London Group, 1996, p. 64). Or in Meacham's words, the conceptual parameters are expanded "to produce multiply constituted, interconnected, and broadly relevant cultural knowledge as it relates to literacy" (2000-2001, p. 183).

Throughout the history of schooling in the United States, efforts to incorporate linguistic and cultural diversity into conceptions of literacy have been viewed as chaotic and a threat to the social order (West, 1993). Willis and Harris (2000) noted that within the last century, literacy instruction and politics have worked hand in hand, creating barriers for many people of color, the poor, and females. As a result, the status quo has been maintained and many non-mainstream populations have been denied access to ownership of literacy. According to Meacham (2000-2001), this situation is reflected in current policy:

> Policymakers believed that it was necessary to promote literacy practices in keeping with a *single* [emphasis added] cultural and linguistic identity at the expense of cultural and linguistic diversity…. In other words, structural *singularity* [emphasis added] has been the structural hallmark of dominant social visions and literacy practices. (p. 182)

In order to maintain this structural singularity, literacy has been conceptualized, defined, taught, and assessed through the dominant white monolingual view of literacy (Willis & Harris, 2000). Willis and Harris note:

> The current disregard for the cultural politics of literacy research, which is being used to maintain an illusion of an equal educational system, has failed to suggest the importance of creating more culturally responsive, inclusive, and transformative literacy learning and teaching spaces. (p. 80)

In recent years, federal government institutions and policymaking groups have narrowed definitions of literacy research to include only experimental and quasi-experimental research as "scientific" and having relevance to policy. The result has been that many studies that have examined literacy in contexts of linguistic and cultural diversity do not meet these arbitrary criteria of "scientific rigor." This situation has effectively excluded much insightful and relevant work on literacy and diversity from policy consideration. In short, currently in the United States, curriculum reform policy is shaped, teaching practices are advanced, and high-stakes testing measures are employed to sustain a singular and English-only conception of literacy that ignores the multiple literacy practices of bilingual and multilingual students outside the school system (Grant & Wong, 2003).

FUTURE DIRECTIONS: TOWARDS A MODEL FOR LITERACY DEVELOPMENT AND ACADEMIC ACHIEVEMENT FOR ELL AND BILINGUAL STUDENTS

This final section discusses the role educators can play in transforming inequities in the politics and practices of schooling. An instructional model is outlined that is designed both to enhance students' agency and identity formation and to promote successful academic achievement among ELL and bilingual students (Wong, 2000). The model includes three essential components for transforming the politics of schooling:

1) Human resources: ELL students, their families, and educational professionals;
2) Dialogic pedagogy; and
3) Curriculum for democratic citizenship, and economic and community development.

Human Resources

The model of transformation must begin with human resources. Language minority students and their families bring a rich resource of languages and cultures to other students. Their diversity is much more appropriately viewed as a resource rather than as a problem (Murray, 1992; Ruiz, 1984). The system of squandered bilingualism must be replaced with a model of human resources that invests in linguistic and cultural diversity, sees home languages and cultures as an asset, and sees language minority students and their families as having important contributions to make to school and society (Perez & Torres-Guzman, 1992). In the global economy of the twenty-first century, bilingualism (and multilingualism) is not only a valuable asset but a vital necessity; bilingual people are needed in every profession, including business, medicine, law, and engineering: in every academic field and profession, knowledge of other international languages and intercultural communication plays an important role in overall success (Scollon & Scollon, 1995).

Reversing history's wasteful use of human resources will require a tremendous reallocation of resources. Schools can capitalize on the multilingual resources represented by the hundred different languages spoken by incoming kindergarten children (Faltis & Hudelson, 1998). Use of multilingual resources will not occur without a change in mission and educational leadership from the top. Successful minority recruitment requires creativity, planning, hard work, honest reporting, and evaluation. Professionals in ESL and bilingual education are in a unique position to advocate linguistic and cultural diversity because of their expertise in working with language minority students and their families. By including those who have been traditionally excluded, not only will schools be more culturally responsive to those who have been marginalized, but also all students will have a stronger democratic, critical, and less ethnocentric knowledge base (Banks, 1981, 1993).

Dialogic Pedagogy

A second component of the model for transforming the politics of schooling is dialogic pedagogy. Dialogic pedagogy is also called critical pedagogy (Benesch, 2001; Pennycook, 1994; Wink, 1997), critical literacy, and participatory education or participatory curriculum development (Auerbach, 1992, 1995). Paolo Freire (1970) pioneered this component in teaching Brazilian peasants how to read. Freire was critical of what he termed *banking* models of education, in which teachers "deposited" knowledge into students as if they were passive receptacles.

A central feature of dialogic pedagogy is a teacher-student relationship that stresses mutual respect, sharing, and learning in community. Learning is both social and cultural (Vygotsky, 1978). Sociocultural approaches to the teacher-student relationship have used metaphors such as apprenticeship and scaffolding to investigate how children learn with the assistance of adults (Bruner, 1985; Lantolf & Appel, 1994; Rogoff, 1990). Language is not learned in isolation. Dialogic pedagogy facilitates the expression of voices that have traditionally been excluded.

A second feature of dialogic pedagogy is its problem-posing orientation to learning. Dialogic pedagogy encourages students to develop self-awareness of their language learning strategies and meta-cognitive processes, rather than simply memorizing any particular set of material (e.g., vocabulary, grammar rules, etc.). It encourages an integrated approach to meaning, use, and form. Students learn within the zone of proximal development (Vygotsky, 1978) to solve problems with the assistance of an adult or a more competent peer. With assistance, they are able to learn to solve problems that they will later be able to solve independently (Wink & Putney, 2002).

Third, dialogic pedagogy stresses learning through doing. Students discover and learn principles by applying them in real-life situations. Learning through doing encourages students to learn through observing, constructing, building, and designing. After engaging in activity, students reflect on their experiences through dialogue and writing, thus developing a reflective, self-critical attitude towards *praxis* (a dialectical process involving theory, practice, and reflection).

Finally, dialogic pedagogy asks the question (Wong, 2006), "Who does knowledge serve?" Who benefits from this knowledge? Is it for the elite, for the privileged? Dialogic pedagogy serves the oppressed and the entire community rather than being for the benefit of the individual alone. Dialogic pedagogy gives voice to those who have been previously silenced; it gives voice to new social identities (McKay & Wong, 1996; Norton, 1997) and new *epistemologies* (theories of knowledge or ways of knowing) that were not part of the traditional, male-centered, Western curriculum (Greene, 1988; Hill, 2000; Kubota, 2004: Lin, 2004; Luke & Gore, 1992). By incorporating critical perspectives from Asia, Africa, the Americas, Australia, and the South Pacific, education is enriched and becomes more global (Amin & Kubota, 2004; Canagarajah, 1999).

Three-pronged Curriculum

A third component to the model for transforming the politics of schooling is a three-pronged curriculum that promotes successful academic achievement for (a) democratic citizenship, (b) economic development, and (c) community development. The first prong of this curriculum for academic achievement is to prepare ELL and bilingual students for democratic citizenship (Willett, Solsken, & Wilson-Keenan, 1999). Developing democratic citizenship may include helping middle and high school students, who are the future leaders of their communities, prepare for citizenship tests. It may also include working with young American-born children who are the first in their families to become American citizens.

Curriculum projects in environmental justice, such as calling attention to toxic waste dumping in minority communities or workplace safety conditions, are important democratic issues that elementary ELL students can tackle. The curriculum can include an investigative component, an advocacy component, and a community service component revolving around an issue such as a polluted area cleanup. By integrating dialogic pedagogy with a curriculum for democratic and community development, ELL students in K-12 can do something about poverty (Kempf, 1997). For example, students can work with children with special needs, make *Get Well* cards and visit the sick, perform for the elderly in rest homes, and create awareness about gender discrimination (McCormick, 1994); they can organize communities for change (Stephens, 1995).

The second prong of the curriculum for academic achievement is curriculum development to prepare ELL students for economic development. The ESL curriculum should help prepare students for skilled jobs in the global economy. High school Vocational English as a Second Language (VESL) programs can involve partnerships between schools and businesses for economic enterprises. Curriculum development can include minority businesses developing projects that respond to local markets and niches. For example, there might be a market for fresh shitake mushrooms, around which a successful VESL agricultural program could be built. Air conditioning repair, auto mechanics, or construction could all be outstanding VESL programs, depending on the interests and human resources of the ELL students, communities, and professionals.

The third and final prong of curriculum for successful academic achievement of ELL students is community development. Creating professional development programs, in which colleges of education work with schools within educational districts for preservice and in-service professional development, is an excellent way of developing an ESL and/or bilingual curriculum for community development. Some schools have social services, health clinics, and child-care programs on site. ELL students of all ages can serve as student interns. For example, ELL students in grades 4-6 could help nutritionists investigate culturally responsive alternatives to dairy products for pregnant and nursing mothers who are not accustomed to drinking milk. High school ELL students could help an AIDS prevention and treatment clinic do community outreach. Partnerships with local and national community organizations and civil rights groups could enhance the effectiveness of community development curriculum (McGroaty, 1998; Grant & Wong, 2004).

Curricula to revitalize inner city communities could have a humanities and performing arts component. Research indicates that successful academic achievement for language minority students includes "more than just the basics" (August & Hakuta, 1997, p. 162). Drama, playwriting, music, storytelling, and multicultural literature are all-important vehicles for community development and tap the strengths of ELL students and the emerging hybrid of mixed and hyphenated immigrant communities (Weinstein, 1999).

Just as grocery stores in immigrant communities may cater to an African, Latin, or Caribbean crossover market, urban schools in the United States are a rich heteroglossic, diverse mix of ethnic culture and new identities. Schools that incorporate the "funds of knowledge" from the community (Moll, 1990) are better able to revitalize communities and transform squandered resources into cultural capital and address the gap between the "haves" and "have-nots" through economic and community development (Boggs, 1998).

ESL and bilingual education professionals *can* develop curricula for democratic citizenship and economic and community development that will enable students to succeed academically. Collaboration among ESL and bilingual education professionals in the development of content-based ESL curricula is a growing and important trend (Short, 1994). Research has shown that ELL students succeed academically when teachers have high expectations of their students (Lucas, Henze, & Donato, 1990), classroom practices reflect the cultural and linguistic background of students (Pease-Alvarez, Garcia, & Espinosa, 1991), parents are involved in their children's education (Delgado-Gaitan, 1990), and a supportive atmosphere exists for learning and strong leadership for schoolwide change (Nieto, 1992).

Another important role for ESL teachers within schools is to help ELL students and their families gain access to information: access to information is power. It may include ensuring that parents know that translation is available for important meetings or that they can ask that information concerning college-bound programs, summer enrichment, and after-school programs be translated. For ESL teachers, advocacy often involves bridging cultural as well as linguistic barriers. For example, immigrant parents may be very concerned about the academic achievement of their children, but unlike middle class parents with the kind of cultural capital recognized by schools, may not "push" for their children to be in the classes with the best teachers (Wong & Teuben-Rowe, 1996).

ESL and bilingual education professionals may also find that they need to advocate for ELL students to be eligible for academic programs and to have access to computers and school activities. For example, in some high schools, ELL students are not eligible to take foreign language classes. In some middle schools, ELL students are not eligible for various kinds of enrichment programs. Counselors may steer ELL students away from college preparatory courses. Career days may not include language minority professional role models.

One of the most important lessons that ESL and bilingual education teachers can learn is how to use the resources around them to be effective social change agents. With a concerted effort and a clear plan for transforming the politics of schooling, ESL and bilingual education professionals can at least partially replace the systems and structures of inequality with creative strategies of inclusion. By utilizing the dialogic approach and including the multilingual and multicultural voices that have historically been excluded, educators can develop curricula for democratic participation and economic and community development. Together with students, their parents, and multicultural communities, ESL professionals can develop new models for the successful academic achievement of language minority students by addressing the problem of first language loss and creating new multilingual, multi-literate spaces for the emergence of new transformative subjectivities, sensibilities, and social identities.

REFERENCES

Amin, N., & Kubota, R. (2004). Native speaker discourses: Power and resistance in postcolonial teaching of English to speakers of other languages. In P. Ninnes & S. Mehta (Eds.), *Re-Imagining comparative education: Postfoundational ideas and applications for critical times* (pp. 107–127). New York: Routledge Falmer.

Au, K. H., & Raphael, T. E. (2000). Equity and literacy in the next millennium. *Reading Research Quarterly, 35*, 170–188.

Auerbach, E. (1992). *Making meaning, making change*. Washington, D.C.: Center for Applied Linguistics, and McHenry, IL: Delta Systems.

Auerbach, E. (1995). The politics of the ESL classroom: Issues of power in pedagogical choices. In J. W. Tollefson (Ed.), *Power and inequality in language education* (pp. 9–33). Cambridge: Cambridge University Press.

August, D., & Hakuta, K. (Eds.). (1997). *Improving schooling for language-minority children: A research agenda*. Washington, D.C.: National Academy Press.

Banks, J. (1981). *Multicultural education: Theory and practice*. Boston, MA: Allyn & Bacon Inc.

Banks, J. (1993). The canon debate: Knowledge construction, and multicultural education. *Educational Researcher, 22*, 4–14.

Benesch, S. (2001) Critical English for Academic Purposes: Theory, politics and practice. Mahwah, NJ: Lawrence Erlbaum Assoc.

Boggs, G. L. (1998). *Living for change*. Minneapolis, MN: University of Minnesota.

Bourdieu, P. (1977). The economics of linguistic exchange. *Social Science Information, 16*, 645–668.

Bruner, J. (1985). Vygotsky: A historical and conceptual perspective. In J. V. Wertsch (Ed.), *Culture, communication and cognition: Vygotskian perspectives* (pp. 21–34). New York: Cambridge University Press.

Canagarajah, S. (1999). *Resisting linguistic imperialism in English teaching*. Oxford: Oxford University Press.

Collins, P.H. (2000). *Black feminist thought: Knowledge, consciousness and the politics of empowerment* (2nd Ed.). New York: Routledge.

Cummins, J. (1996). *Negotiating identities: Education for empowerment in a diverse society*. Ontario: California Association for Bilingual Education.

Delgado-Gaitan, C. (1990). *Literacy for empowerment: The role of parents in children's education*. New York: The Falmer Press.

Edelsky, C. (1991). *With literacy and justice for all: Rethinking the social in language and education*. London: The Falmer Press.

Faltis, C. J., & Hudelson, S. J. (1998). *Bilingual education in elementary and secondary school communities: Toward understanding and caring*. Boston: Allyn and Bacon.

Freire, P. (1970). *Pedagogy of the oppressed*. New York: Herder and Herder.

Gee, J. (2001). Identity as an analytic lens for research in education. In W. Secada (Ed.), *Review of Research in Education*, Vol. 25, (pp. 99–126). Washington, DC: AERA.

Grant, R., & Wong, S. (2006). Critical race perspectives on Bourdieu for TESOL/BE and literacy education. In A. Luke and J. Albright (Eds.), *Bourdieu and literacy education*. Mahwah, NJ: Lawrence Erlbaum.

Grant, R., & Wong, S. (2004). Forging multilingual communities: School-based strategies. *Multicultural Perspectives, 6*, 17–23.

Grant, R., & Wong, S. (2003). Barriers to literacy for language-minority learners: An argument for change in the literacy education profession. *Journal of Adolescent and Adult Literacy, 46*, 386–394.

Greene, M. (1988). *The dialectic of freedom*. New York: Teachers College Press.

Kempf, S. (1997). *Finding solutions to hunger: A sourcebook for middle and upper school teachers*. New York: World Hunger Year.

Kozol, J. (1991). *Savage inequalities*. New York: Harper.

Knapp, M.S., & Woolverton, S. (2004). Social class and schooling. In J.A. Banks and C.A. McGee Banks (Eds.) *Handbook of Research on Multicultural Education* 2nd Ed., (pp. 656–681). San Francisco: Jossey-Bass.

Lantolf, J. P., & Appel, G. (1994). *Vygotskian approaches to second language research.* Norwood: NJ: Ablex Publishers.

Lin, A. M. Y. (2004). Introducing a critical pedagogical curriculum: A reflexive account from feminist perspectives. In B. Norton & K. Toohey (Eds.) *Critical Pedagogies and Language Learning* (pp. 271–290). Cambridge: Cambridge University Press.

Lucas, T., Henze, R., & Donato, R. (1990). Promoting the success of Latino language-minority students: An exploratory study of six high schools. *Harvard Educational Review, 60*, 315–340.

Luke, C., & Gore, J. (1992). *Feminisms and critical pedagogy.* London: Routledge.

McCormick, M. (1994). *Creating the non-sexist classroom.* New York: Teachers College Press.

McGroarty, M. (1998). Partnerships with linguistic minority communities. TESOL Professional Papers #4. Alexandria, VA: Teachers of English to Speakers of Other Languages.

McKay, S., & Wong, S-L. C. (1996). Multiple discourses, multiple identities: Investment and agency in second-language learning among Chinese adolescent immigrant students. *Harvard Educational Review, 66*(3), 576–608.

Meacham, S. (2000–2001). Literacy at the crossroads: Movement, connection, and communication within the research literature on literacy and cultural diversity. In W. G. Secada (Ed.), *Review of Research in Education, 25* (pp. 181–208). Washington, D.C.: AERA.

Mehan, H. (1991). *Sociological foundations supporting the study of cultural diversity.* Santa Cruz, CA: National Center for Research on Cultural Diversity and Second Language Learning.

Moll, L. (1990). Vygotsky and education: Instructional implications and applications of sociohistorical psychology. Cambridge University Press.

Murray, D. (1992). *Diversity as resource: Redefining cultural literacies.* Alexandria, VA: Teachers of English to Speakers of Other Languages.

National Center for Educational Statistics (2004). *The Nation's report card: Reading highlights 2003.* Washington, D.C.: U.S. Department of Education.

New London Group. (1996). A pedagogy of multiliteracies: Designing social futures. *Harvard Educational Review, 66*, 60–92.

Nieto, S. (1992). Affirming diversity: The sociopolitical context of multicultural education. White Plains, NY: Longman.

Norton, B. (1997). Language, identity and the ownership of English. *TESOL Quarterly, 31*, 409–429.

Olsen, L. (1997). Made in America: Immigrant students in our public schools, New York: The New Press.

Pease-Alvarez, L., Garcia, E. E., & Espinosa, P. (1991). Effective instruction for language-minority students: An early childhood case study. *Early Childhood Research Quarterly, 6*, 347–361.

Pennycook, A. (1994). The cultural politics of English as an international language. London: Longman.

Perez, B., & Torres-Guzman, M. (1992). Learning in two worlds: An integrated Spanish/English biliteracy approach. New York: Longman.

Rogoff, B. (1990). Apprenticeship in thinking: Cognitive development in social context. New York: Oxford University Press.

Ruiz, R. (1984). Orientations in language planning. *Journal of the National Association of Bilingual Education, 8*, 15–34.

Scollon, R. & Scollon, S. (1995). *Intercultural communication.* Oxford, UK: Blackwell.

Short, D. J. (1994). Expanding middle school horizons: Integrating language, culture and social studies. *TELL Quarterly, 28*, 581–608.

Skutnabb-Kangas, T. (2000). *Linguistic genocide in education or worldwide diversity and human rights?* Mahwah, N.J.: Lawrence Erlbaum, Associates.

Stephens, L. (1995). *The complete guide to learning through community service. (K-9).* Needham Heights, MA: Allyn and Bacon.

Thomas, W. P., & Collier, V. P. (1997). *School effectiveness for language minority students.* Washington, D.C.: National Clearinghouse for Bilingual Education.

Vygotsky, L. (1978). *Mind in society.* Cambridge, MA: Harvard University Press.

Weedon, C. (1987). *Feminist practice and poststructuralist theory.* London: Blackwell.

Weinstein, G. (Ed.). (1999). *Learners' lives as curriculum: Six journeys to immigrant literacy.* McHenry, IL: Center for Applied Linguistics/Delta Books.

West, C. (1992). A matter of life and death. *October, 61*, 20–23.

West, C. (1993). The cultural politics of difference. In C. McCarthy & W. Crichlow (Eds.), *Race, identity and representation in education* (pp. 11–23). New York: Routledge.

Willett, J., Solsken, J., & Wilson-Keenan, J. (1999). The (im)possibilities of constructing multicultural language practices in research and pedagogy. *Linguistics and Education, 10*(2), 165–218.

Willis, A. I., & Harris, V. J. (2000). Political acts: Literacy learning and teaching. *Reading Research Quarterly, 35*, 72–88.
Wink, J. (1997). *Critical pedagogy*. New York: Longman.
Wink, J., & Putney, L. (2002). *A vision of Vygotsky*. Boston, MA: Allyn & Bacon.
Wong, S. (2000). Transforming the politics of schooling in the U.S.: A model for successful academic achievement for language minority students. In Joan Kelly Hall and William Eggington (Eds.), *The sociopolitics of English language teaching*. (pp. 117–139). Clevedon: Multilingual Matters.
Wong, S. (2006). *Dialogic approaches to TESOL: Where the ginkgo tree grows*. Mahwah, NJ: Lawrence Erlbaum Associates.
Wong, S., & Grant, R. (1995). Addressing poverty in the Baltimore-Washington metropolitan area: What can teachers do? *Literacy Issues and Practices, 12*, 3–12.
Wong, S., & Teuben-Rowe, S. (1996). Critical perspectives on the language of family literacy research: Use of native language with involved parents from diverse linguistic backgrounds. *The Journal of Educational Issues of Language Minority Students, 16*, 235–261.
Wong-Fillmore, L. (2000). Loss of family languages: Should educators be concerned? *Theory into Practice, 39*(4), 203–210.

CHAPTER 41

SOCIOCULTURAL THEORY:

A Unified Approach to L2 Learning and Teaching

JAMES P. LANTOLF

Pennsylvania State University, USA

ABSTRACT

The chapter examines the pedagogical implications for English language teaching of the fundamental theoretical tenet of sociocultural theory: higher forms of human consciousness are semiotically mediated. In the first part of the chapter, I will discuss the specifics of what it means to make such a claim regarding human thinking. I will consider the following theoretical constructs: the zone of proximal development, internalization, imitation, and private speech. In the second part of the chapter, I will consider the implications of the theory for the English language classroom. In particular, I will focus on ways in which the theory compels us to reinterpret the relationship between learners and teachers, the role that activity as defined in sociocultural theory plays in learning, how we understand successful learning, and the relationship between learning, development, and assessment.

INTRODUCTION

The aim of this chapter is to present a brief overview of the major theoretical claims of the sociocultural theory (henceforth, SCT) of mind and mental development with particular attention to how it relates to the learning and teaching of second languages. Space does not permit a detailed analysis of the theory nor of the growing research literature on SCT and L2 learning (see Lantolf, 2000). I will limit my focus to three fundamental propositions of the theory and will consider how these can inform L2 research and teaching. The propositions are as follows: human mental activity is always and everywhere mediated; mediation develops through internalization of socially constructed activity; instruction, development, and assessment are inseparable processes dialectically unified in the Zone of Proximal Development (ZPD).

Although SCT has gained a good deal of popularity within educational psychology and more specifically within applied linguistics over the past two decades, a continuing problem has been that researchers have often borrowed its theoretical concepts, in particular the ZPD, without paying sufficient attention to the full theoretical framework in which the concepts are embedded. Consequently, this approach has frequently resulted in partial or complete misinterpretation of the theory and its affiliated concepts (see for example, Dunn & Lantolf, 1998; Lantolf, forthcoming). With this in mind, it will be helpful to situate SCT within the historical context of psycholinguistics. In this way, the reader will be better able to appreciate what the theory seeks to achieve and why it is important to deal with its claims in a unified rather than piecemeal way.

SCT: THIRD-GENERATION PSYCHOLINGUISTICS

A. A. Leontiev (1981), in his important but generally overlooked book on SCT and foreign language learning, points out that at the beginning of its history in the early 1950s, psycholinguistics was a neobehaviorist discipline interested in the acquisition and processing of discrete units of language (e.g., words). The second generation of psycholinguistics that emerged in the early 1960s, with Chomsky's rise to preeminence in linguistics coupled with George Miller's psychological perspective, overcame the atomism of the first generation through its claim that what is acquired are abstract rules rather than discrete units (Leontiev, p. 93). Consequently, researchers focused on perception and production of sentences, and occasionally on formal cohesive devises that link sentences into texts. Although Leontiev sees the second generation as representing progress, he nevertheless argues that its orientation was more linguistic than psychological (p. 93). Moreover, it shared the same interest in formal properties of language as manifested by its predecessor. Neither of the first two generations paid much attention to meaning; neither were they concerned with how language was actually deployed as a tool for communication or for thinking. To be sure, both generations studied the individual, but as an entity "isolated not only from society but also from any real process of communication, as such communication is reduced to the most elementary model of information transfer from speaker to listener" (p. 92).

The third generation of psycholinguistics, according to Leontiev (1981, p. 95), is less linguistic and more psychological in orientation and has moved away from interest in the processing and perception of sentences and texts and "towards a psychological analysis of the processes of communication and thought" (p. 96). For the third generation, "psycholinguistics does not deal with the process of actualizing psychological structures which serve 'speech behaviour' in the linguistic product, but explores the different strategies for using language (as a means) in activity" (p. 96). This activity may be aimed at influencing others or at influencing the self. When aimed at others, the activity is communicative; when aimed at the self, it is cognitive. Importantly, however, the two activities, as Vygotsky (1987) argued, are dialectically and therefore necessarily connected to each other in their genesis. That is, the activity of self-directed speaking is derived from the activity of other-directed speaking: in essence, both are forms of communication. In the first case, the interlocutors are *I* and *you*, and in the second, *I* and *me* (see Vocate, 1994).

In giving precedence to communicative activity over the acquisition and processing of abstract linguistic rules and representations, the third generation is interested in how speaking (and writing) mediates the concrete social and mental activity of human beings. Thus, speaking activity is "motivated and purposive. It represents a process of solving *communicative problems*" (Leontiev, 1981, p. 97), and these problems can be social as well as cognitive. Seen from this perspective, the learning and teaching of another language is not about learning and teaching rules and forms but about communication as a means of mediating "distinct types of intellectual and practical [i.e., social] activity" (p. 99).

Thus, the central proposition of SCT is that humans are fundamentally communicatively organized beings. This notion extends not only to the world of social relationships but also to the world of higher mental functions. Just as our social activity is mediated through speech, so too is our mental activity. Specifically, through speaking (and writing) we are able to gain control over our memory, attention, planning, perception, learning, and development, but this control is derived from the social activity we engage in not only with our contemporaries but also with those who have preceded us in time through the cultural artifacts, including language, they have created and left behind. Given this, a very interesting question presents itself with regard to learning additional languages—what effect, if any, does internalizing a new mediational system have not only on the way we interact with others but also on the way we think? SCT researchers have only begun to grapple with this important issue. For example, Pavlenko and Lantolf (2000) discuss the well-known case of Eva Hoffman, in which a young Polish-speaking immigrant to North America develops into an English-speaking adult intellectual. Hoffman writes about the struggle she went through to construct a new inner voice in English, as her first language, Polish, began to lose its power to mediate her relationship to the new culture and subsequently her own relationship to herself (see Norton & Toohey, 2001, for a discussion of the experiences of immigrants who, unlike Hoffman and her colleagues, have not documented in writing their struggle to mediate themselves socially and intellectually through a new language).

INTERNALIZATION

The second theoretical proposition I would like to consider is internalization, which is Vygotsky's insight into overcoming the mind-body Cartesian dualism that had fractured not only psychology but virtually all the disciplines comprising the humanities and social sciences of his time, including linguistics. Among other things, in Vygotsky's view, the dualism prevented psychology from developing an adequate theory of human mental activity, or as Vygotsky referred to it, *consciousness*. Vygotsky recognized that humans shared specific mental abilities with other animals and that these were part of our biological endowment. On the other hand, he also argued that we are able to organize and control our brains in ways that animals cannot. Thus, while animal and human behavior arises from instinct as well as from environmental influences, only humans develop the capacity to voluntarily and intentionally regulate their memory, attention, and planning and to engage in rational thinking. The innatists argue that our unique mental abilities can be accounted for primarily in terms of the genetically specified properties of the human brain. The social constructionists, on the other hand, maintain that the explanation resides in discourse and social interaction. In either case, the dualism that so concerned Vygotsky and others among his contemporaries is not overcome as much as it is dissolved, in the former case to the biological through downward reductionism, and in the latter to the social through upward reductionism (see Valsiner & van der Veer, 2000, for a full discussion).

Accepting that biology lays the foundation on which human mental activity is constructed, Vygotsky argued that it is participation in, and internalization of, culturally shaped activities that imbues humans with the power to regulate (i.e., mediate) our biological endowment. Internalization transforms the structure and function of social processes that we carry out in conjunction with others, while at the same time maintaining traces of their external origins (Wertsch & Stone, 1985, p. 163). What on the social plane is elaborate and other-directed activity becomes abbreviated and self-directed activity on the psychological plane. Through internalization, individuals develop the ability to extend what was at one point specific concrete activity, guided in some way by others, to similar though not identical activities in order to function independently of others.

IMITATION AND PRIVATE SPEECH

The key to internalization for Vygotsky (1987, p. 221) resides in imitation, which, according to Tomasello (1999), is not about repetition or parroting, as in the case of animals, but is a uniquely human capacity that relies on our ability to understand the intentionality that motivates others to act. In fact, imitation is potentially a transformative act, particularly in the case of children, who have not undergone the intense pressure that schools in particular impose on us to conform to culturally sanctioned knowledge and ways of doing things. Importantly, as Tomasello notes, imitation not only involves physical behavior, as happens in learning how to play tennis, golf, etc., but also encompasses symbolic forms of mediation, including, importantly, language.

Imitation of language behavior, as demonstrated in research on language play and so-called crib speech among children (Kuczaj, 1983; Weir, 1962), is frequently carried out when the children are alone as a form of private speech. Saville-Troike (1988) has uncovered evidence of imitative private speech among children learning ESL in a classroom setting. The following example is taken from Saville-Troike's study in which the teacher first tells the students in the class to brush their teeth and wipe their hands:

> You guys go brush your teeth. And wipe your hands on the towel.
> The child (4 years old, L1 Korean), instead of just following the teacher's instructions, responds by quietly saying to himself:
> Wipe your hand. Wipe your teeth (Saville-Troike, p. 584).

Based on lack of eye contact and the low volume with which the child's utterance was produced, Saville-Troike concludes that the child was not responding conversationally to the teacher, but was instead imitating the teacher's utterance. Notice that the imitation is not an exact repetition of the teacher's production but is a transformation in which 'wipe' collocates with 'teeth,' a pairing that would be inappropriate in native English in the intended meaning.

Saville-Troike's study (1988) found that six of the nine children she observed over about a 6-month period frequently generated private imitations of the language they heard around them as produced by their teacher as well as their English-speaking classmates. At the same time, the children refused to use English socially in the classroom. Eventually, they were willing to use English publicly, and as it turns out, much of the language they then used in their social speech involved many of the forms documented first in their private speech. It would appear that the children first built up a repertoire in English privately in order to then use the language socially. If so, then it might well be that private imitation is in essence language learning in flight (see Lantolf & Thorne, 2006, for an extended discussion).

As part of an ongoing project on private speech among adult language learners, we collected samples of private speech from a Korean L1 university ESL learner. The student, enrolled in an ESL literacy class, had been in the U.S. for approximately 6 months at the time of the data collection. As with Saville-Troike's (1988) study, the student agreed to wear a microphone connected to a minidisc recorder, which enabled us to record about 10 hours of talk over 2 weeks. Following Saville-Troike, any utterance that was produced at a very low volume and for which there was no response from an interlocutor, as, for example, when the teacher was interacting with another student, was classified as private speech.

In the first example, following work on a reading passage, the instructor is explaining the meaning of a new word, *significance*, which she defines for them as *Important or notable*. The learner, however, appears to encounter something else that is new, *notable*, which she produces in a low volume to herself: "Ah, notable (rising intonation). Notable (rising intonation). Mm (very softly)." The learner most likely knows the word *important* and therefore focuses instead on what she probably doesn't know, *notable*. Thus, it is likely that the student has the opportunity to learn not only the meaning of *significance* but also an additional word, *notable*. The analysis of private speech, thus, shows that learners often develop a learning agenda that is at times broader and at other times at odds with the instructional agenda of the teacher (see Ohta, 2001; Lantolf & Thorne, 2006).

In a second example, the same student focused her private speech on English morphology. The instructor, in explaining the meaning of *take a nap* to another student, produces the following utterance: "Were you taking a nap, a little sleep?" The Korean student quietly says to herself, "Nap, I take nap ... ing." This type of morphological experimentation is very similar to what Saville-Troike (1988) uncovered for her ESL children. Notice that in her imitation of the teacher's utterance, the learner substitutes the original *you* with *I* and instead of marking progressive on *take*, she appears to inflect what in the teacher's utterance is a noun, *nap*. It is, of course, possible in English to use *nap* as a verb, as in *I was napping*. The learner in this case could have been confused by the fact that in English many lexical items can cross form class boundaries and function either as a noun or as a verb. This confusion might well be indicated by the pause (...) between her production of *nap* and the progressive morpheme *-ing*. The result is that she ends up producing what looks like a hybrid construction: "I take napping."

Unlike in Saville-Troike's study (1988), to date, no one, to my knowledge, has been able to establish a connection between the forms learners produce during private imitation of linguistic affordances and the appearance of those forms in social language use (either spoken or written). This is an important area for future research to focus on, because if the connection can be made, it strengthens the argument that private speech plays a critical role in internalization, and we have suggested elsewhere, may in fact represent language learning in progress (Lantolf & Thorne, 2006).

INSTRUCTION, DEVELOPMENT, ASSESSMENT, AND THE ZPD

The concepts discussed in the previous sections come together in a unified way in perhaps what is the most well-known feature of SCT—*the Zone of Proximal Development*. According to Vygotsky (1978), the ZPD is the activity in which learning precedes and leads development. For some, the idea that instruction and learning construct the pathway along which development occurs is no doubt an odd claim, given that most educational settings assume the relationship between the two processes to be the other way around—for learning to occur, the individual must have developed the requisite cognitive capacities, which, of course, is the classic Piagetian perspective (see Egan, 1983). As with so much else in developmental and educational psychology, Vygotsky turns the standard assumptions on their heads. He did not do this capriciously, however. He based his theory on the Marxist contention that humans are always and everywhere social beings whose formation as humans depends necessarily and dialectically on joint social activity (e.g., labor), as well as on careful empirical observation of the link between IQ and schooling. Vygotsky noticed that children entering school with low IQs generally showed a significant increase in their scores as a result of instruction, while children that entered the same institution with high IQs usually did not show much improvement in their scores (van der Veer & Valsiner, 1991). Vygotsky developed the metaphor of the ZPD, or the activity in which instruction/learning leads development, to capture what he observed in the school setting.

To fully appreciate the relevance of the ZPD, it is important to understand what Vygotsky (1978) meant by learning and development. *Learning*, in Vygotsky's view, is what an individual is able to do with assistance of another person or an artifact created by others. Assistance may be in the form of direct and explicit instruction, as occurs in school; it may be indirect and implicit instruction, as occurs in the case of everyday unreflective activity (e.g., when someone is apprenticed into a particular cultural practice, such as a tailor, butcher, plumber, etc. (see Lave & Wenger, 1991), or into a social role, such as mother, father, student, supervisor, etc.). Assistance may also be provided by cultural artifacts, such as computers (see Salomon, 1991). Development, on the other hand, results from the appropriation and internalization of that assistance, which in turn, enables individuals to function independently of specific concrete circumstances and to therefore extend their abilities to a broader range of circumstances. Vygotsky formalized this notion in his often cited *law of cultural development*, which I paraphrase as follows: Every cognitive function appears twice: once on the intermental plane, when the person is performing with the overt external assistance provided by someone else, either in person, as in joint collaborative interaction, or vicariously through some artifact, such as a computer, calculator, or even paper and pencil; and again on the intramental plane, when the person is able to perform without external support (Vygotsky, 1978). Vygotsky captured this critical relationship between assisted and self-regulated performance with the concept of the ZPD. Described another way, the ZPD illustrates the process wherein mediation by cultural-historical resources (human and material) can be seen to create the present and transform the future.

An important implication of all this, particularly with regard to language pedagogy, is that instruction, learning, development, and assessment are inseparably linked in a dialectic unity. For Vygotsky they are no longer discrete activities as in standard classroom practice, but are in effect the same activity. According to Vygotsky, it is not enough to know what an individual can do alone without assistance, as reflected in traditional approaches to testing: it is necessary to discover what the person can do with help (i.e., instruction), because this is a reflection of what the person will eventually be able to do when that help has been internalized. A. N. Leontiev, one of Vygotsky's early colleagues, puts it as follows: The ZPD "discovers not how the child came to be what it is, but how it can become what it not yet is" (cited in Bronfenbrenner, 1977, p. 528). Two individuals, who score the same on a traditional test in which they act without overt assistance, may well perform completely differently when assistance is provided. One person may be able to do much more with help, while the other may not. Thus, according to Vygotsky, the two individuals have very different developmental trajectories. This is why Vygotsky insisted that the only good instruction was aimed at the future, at what the person cannot yet do.

Recently, researchers working within general education have begun to develop a new type of assessment instrument, *dynamic assessment,* based on the ZPD, which recognizes the significance of Vygotsky's claim on the dialectic unity of instruction, development, and assessment. Space does not permit me to delve into this exciting new approach where teaching and testing are integrated into a unified activity, but it essentially involves an assessment, intervention, and reassessment procedure. While dynamic assessment has been explored in other educational domains (IQ assessment, math, literacy development), to date, it has not been given much attention by applied linguists, although McNamara (1997) suggests ways in which language testing might incorporate a perspective based on the ZPD.

In brief, in dynamic assessment learners are first assessed using a traditional solo performance measure, whether it be an IQ test, a math assessment, or a science test. They are then provided with assistance, in the form of implicit hints, clues, or if necessary explicit instruction. The assistance is then withdrawn and the learners are reassessed, but not just on the original instrument; rather they are provided with a task that extends beyond the original task in order to determine whether they have indeed internalized the assistance, as per my earlier discussion of this process. Of course, I have simplified things considerably for present purposes, but I at least want to stress that an important aspect of dynamic assessment is that both rate and pathway of development are likely to be different for different individuals. That this should be the case, from Vygotsky's standpoint, is not at all surprising, despite the fact that it presents a challenge to the current way of thinking about L2 learning—that there is a common route and rate at which, on average, acquisition happens, an assumption that underlies Mitchell and Myles's (1998) critique of SCT research on L2 learning. For a fuller discussion of dynamic assessment, see the following sources: Sternberg and Grigorenko (2002), Lidz (1987, 1991, 1995), and Lidz and Elliot (2000).

SCT brings a new perspective to how researchers and teachers understand and promote language learning and teaching. While there is a great deal of interesting work to be carried out within this theoretical paradigm, an area that is especially exciting and relevant for L2 pedagogy is that which deals with the ZPD and dynamic assessment. While research in this domain has been flourishing in general education and educational psychology, it has not yet found its way into applied linguistics and in particular language pedagogy. This situation is unfortunate. On the other hand, general research in this area is in its early stages of development, and there is still time for language researchers and practitioners to get in on the ground floor, as it were. In this enterprise, the important point to keep in mind is that SCT is not a theory of language, language learning, or language processing. It is a theory that unites human social activity and human mental activity through communication, and as such, it is very much grounded in everyday experiences rather than controlled experiments—experiences that themselves are holistic activities.

REFERENCES

Bronfenbrenner, U. (1977). Toward an experimental ecology of human development. *American Psychologist, 32*, 513–551.
Dunn, W. E., & Lantolf, J. P. (1998). Vygotsky's zone of proximal development and Krashen's i + 1: Incommensurable constructs; incommensurable theories. *Language Learning, 48*, 411–442.
Egan, K. (1983). *Education and psychology. Plato, Piaget, and scientific psychology.* New York: Teachers College Press.
Kuczaj, S. A. II. (1983). *Crib speech and language play.* New York: Springer Verlag.
Lantolf, J. P. (Ed.). (2000). *Sociocultural theory and second language learning.* Oxford: Oxford University Press.
Lantolf, J. P. (2003). Intrapersonal communication and internalization in the second language classroom. In A. Kozulin, V. S. Ageev, S. Miller, & B. Gindis (Eds.), *Vygotsky's theory of education in cultural context* (pp. 349–370). Cambridge: Cambridge University Press.
Lantolf, J. P. (2005). Sociocultural theory and SLA: An exegesis. In E. Hinkel (Ed.). *Handbook of second language research* (pp. 335–354). Mahwah, NJ: Erlbaum.
Lantolf, J. P. & Thorne, S. L. (2006). *Sociocultural theory and the genesis of second language development.* Oxford: Oxford University Press.
Lave, J., & Wenger, E. (1991). *Situated learning: Legitimate peripheral participation.* Cambridge: Cambridge University Press.
Leontiev, A. A. (1981). *Psychology and the language learning process.* Oxford: Pergamon.
Lidz, C. S. (Ed.). (1987). *Dynamic assessment: An interactional approach to evaluating learning potential.* New York: Guilford Press.
Lidz, C. S. (1991). *Practitioner's guide to dynamic assessment.* New York: Guilford Press.
Lidz, C. S. (1995). Dynamic assessment and the legacy of L. S. Vygotsky. *Schools Psychology International, 16,* 243–153.
Lidz, C. S., & Elliott, J. G. (Eds.). (2000). *Dynamic assessment: Prevailing models and applications.* Greenwich, CT: Elsevier-JAI.
McNamara, T. F. (1997). 'Interaction' in second language performance assessment: Whose performance? *Applied Linguistics, 18,* 446–467.
Mitchell, R., & Myles, F. (1998). *Second language learning theories.* London: Edward Arnold.
Norton, B., & Toohey, K. (2001). Changing perspectives on good language learners. *TESOL Quarterly, 35,* 307–322.
Ohta, A. S. (2001). *Second language acquisition processes in the classroom: Learning Japanese.* Mahwah, NJ: Lawrence Erlbaum.
Pavlenko, A., & Lantolf, J. P. (2000). Second language learning as participation and the (re)construction of selves. In J. P. Lantolf (Ed.), *Sociocultural theory and second language learning* (pp. 155–179). Oxford: Oxford University Press.
Salomon, G. (1991). On the cognitive effects of technology. In L. T. Landsman (Ed.), *Culture, schooling and psychological development* (pp. 185–204). Norwood, NJ: Ablex.
Saville-Troike, M. (1988). Private speech: Evidence for second language learning strategies during the 'silent period.' *Journal of Child Language, 15,* 567–590.
Sternberg, R. J., & Grigorenko, E. L. (2002). *Dynamic testing. The nature and measurement of learning potential.* Cambridge: Cambridge University Pres.
Tomasello, M. (1999). *The cultural origins of human cognition.* Cambridge, MA: Harvard University Press.
Valsiner, J., & van der Veer, R. (2000). *The social mind. The very idea.* Cambridge: Cambridge University Press.
van der Veer, R., & Valsiner, J. (1991). *Understanding Vygotsky: A quest for synthesis.* Oxford: Blackwell.
Vocate, D. R. (Ed.). (1994). *Intrapersonal communication. Different voices, different minds.* Hillsdale, NJ: Erlbaum.
Vygotsky, L. S. (1978). *Mind in society.* Cambridge, MA: Harvard University Press.
Vygotsky, L. S. (1987). *The collected works, Volume 1, including Thinking and speaking.* New York: Plenum.
Weir, R. (1962). *Language in the crib.* The Hague: Mouton.
Wertsch, J. V., & Stone, C. A. (1985). The concept of internalization in Vygotsky's account of the genesis of higher mental functions. In J. V. Wertsch (Ed.), *Culture, communication and cognition: Vygotskian perspectives* (pp. 162–182). Cambridge: Cambridge University Press.

CHAPTER 42

MEDIATING ACADEMIC LANGUAGE LEARNING THROUGH CLASSROOM DISCOURSE

PAULINE GIBBONS

The University of Technology Sydney, Australia

ABSTRACT

For school-aged students who are learning ESL, the discourse of the classroom must simultaneously construct curriculum knowledge and be a site for second language development. This chapter focuses on academic language learning in the ESL school context, in particular on how language learning is mediated through classroom discourse. While linguistic, social, and sociocognitive traditions have interpreted the nature of interaction differently, it is seen in all of them as playing a major part in learning and language development. The chapter draws on research in sociocultural approaches to pedagogy, systemic functional linguistics (SFL), and second language acquisition (SLA) studies in examining the relationship between classroom discourse and the development of ESL students' academic language learning. It argues that interactions should be examined both for their effectiveness in fostering language development and also for the impact these interactions have on how students view themselves. The chapter concludes with some implications for classroom practice, which suggest how teachers can orchestrate classroom discourse for academic language learning.

INTRODUCTION

For students who are learning ESL in an English-medium school, English is both one of the aims and the medium of education: the students are not only learning English as a school curriculum subject but also learning in it and through it. Since the early 1980s, a number of studies have shown that despite rapid growth in conversational fluency, ESL students can take between 5 and 7 years to develop the more academic registers associated with school learning at a level concomitant with that of their native English-speaking peers, since, while English-speaking students are building on the foundations of their first language to develop these registers, ESL learners in English-medium schools are not (Collier, 1989; Cummins, 1984, 1986, 1996, 2000; McKay et al., 1997).

For such learners, the classroom environment and curriculum must allow for the construction of curriculum knowledge to progress hand in hand with the development of the student's second language (L2), in particular in relation to the academic registers of school learning. However, merely exposing L2 learners to the mainstream classroom is not an adequate response to their language development needs and "cannot be assumed to provide optimal language learning opportunities as a matter of course" (Mohan, 2002, p. 108). Rather, subject teaching must be planned to provide the specific contexts for the development of academic English.

This chapter focuses on how classroom discourse can mediate learning for ESL students but, particularly, how it can provide a site for L2 development in the context of the mainstream content classroom. It also addresses the equally important question of the roles, relationships, and identities that are being constructed in the instructional processes. The chapter concludes with a discussion of some of the implications for classroom practice.

DISCOURSE AND CLASSROOM LEARNING

The Characteristics of Academic Language

The registers associated with academic learning traditionally code knowledge in ways that are linguistically unfamiliar to many students. As Martin (1990) points out, for example, in relation to science discourse, "it codes an alternative perspective on reality to commonsense [knowledge], a perspective accumulated over centuries of scientific enquiry" (p. 86). Literacy in science has to be considered from the point of view of both the knowledge being constructed and the genres that, in Martin's terms, "package" that knowledge. Similarly, the development of literacy within any subject in the school curriculum involves learning to control the *registers*—the specific technical language and grammatical patterns—and generic structures particular to that subject. These school-related registers usually involve more "writtenlike" discourse, which tends to be less personal, more abstract, more lexically dense, and more structured than the face-to-face everyday language with which students are familiar. While more conversational texts tend to have high personal involvement, low explicitness of meaning, and interactive features, these more academic texts require a high explicitness of lexical content but allow for little interaction or personal involvement (Biber, 1986). In recent years, linguists working within SFL (see McCarthy & Slade, this volume) have described many of the genres of school subjects (Derewianka, 1990; Martin, 1984; Martin, Christie, & Rothery, 1987; Martin & Veel, 1998; Unsworth, 2000) and the registers and macrogenres of teaching (Christie, 1994; Gibbons, 2001; Hammond, 1990).

Vygotsky's (1978, 1987) notion of spontaneous and scientific concepts offers another perspective on academic language learning. *Spontaneous concepts* emerge from a child's everyday experiences: They may be rich, but they are embedded within specific situational contexts and instances and are therefore not systematic; thus they will vary from learner to learner. *Scientific concepts*, on the other hand, are located within the structured and specialized *discourse* of the subject, are relatively more fixed, and are systematically and logically organized and related (Kozulin, 1998). Cummins (2000) points out that other related theoretical distinctions between what can be thought of as *everyday* and *academic* language have been made by a number of writers, among them Bruner (1975), Olson (1977), Donaldson (1978), Canale (1983), and Mohan (1986).

Discourse and Learning

In the late 1960s and 1970s, especially in Britain with the publication of the Plowden Report, the importance of discourse to the development of understanding in the classroom began to be recognized; the work of Wilkinson (1965), Britton (1970), Barnes (1976), and Tough (1977) brought to attention the role and importance of spoken language across all areas of the school curriculum, which until that time had given prestige almost exclusively to the written form. While at that time attitudes towards student talk in the classroom changed from "something to be forbidden to something to be encouraged at all costs" (Phillips, 1985, p. 59), it has also been argued that the role of spoken discourse in the acquisition of academic knowledge, compared with research on written discourse, is still not as well recognized (Gallas, 1995).

However, more recently the particular role of classroom discourse in students' learning has been more critically examined. Much of this work has been located within the sociocognitive psychological frame developed out of the work of Vygotsky (see, for examples, Cazden, 1988; Edwards & Mercer, 1987; Goodman & Goodman, 1994; Hall, 1998; Lee & Smagorinsky, 2000; Mercer 1995; Moll, 1994; Tharp & Gallimore, 1988; Wells, 1999, 2000; Wells & Chang-Wells, 1992). Within this perspective, learning is seen as occurring within a *zone of proximal development* or ZPD (Vygotsky, 1978, 1987), which Vygotsky perceives as the distance between the actual development level of the individual and the level achieved with collaboration with a more expert "other." What is significant in this view of learning is that it is seen as occurring between individuals, not within them. As Wells (1999) suggests, the theory leads to a particular view of knowledge and understanding: "understanding ... comes into existence through participation in a particular activity." Furthermore, "by contributing to joint meaning making with and for others, one also makes meaning for oneself and, in the process, extends one's own understanding" (p. 108).

Within pedagogical approaches that draw on a social view of learning, the term *scaffolding* is increasingly being used as a metaphor for the particular kinds of support given to students to enable them to successfully complete a task. Scaffolding is the means whereby a student is able to carry out a task that, alone, he or she would be unable to complete. It thus operationalizes the notion of the ZPD (Wells, 1999). The notion of scaffolding has been used by educators in the fields of both mother tongue and L2 to describe the nature of this assisted performance, which involves not simply "help to do" but "help to know *how* to do," and while originally applied only to teacher-student interactions, it is also now seen as applying to certain forms of student-student interaction (Brooks, 1992; Cazden, 1988; Lee & Smagorinsky, 2000; Maybin, Mercer, & Stierer, 1992; Mercer, 1994; Webster, Beveridge, & Reid, 1996; Wells, 1999).

The term was originally used by Wood, Bruner, and Ross (1976) in their examination of parent tutoring in the early years. In the classroom, it can be defined as the temporary, but essential, assistance that helps teachers apprentice learners into new skills, concepts, or levels of understanding (Maybin, Mercer, & Stierer, 1992, p. 186). Sociocultural theory, encompassing the notion of the ZPD and the related pedagogical construct of scaffolding, challenges teachers to maintain high expectations of students but also to provide adequate scaffolding for tasks to be completed successfully. In terms of L2 learners, it suggests a somewhat different orientation to learning tasks that has often been the case in the past. Although it may still sometimes be necessary to simplify tasks, the use of simplified tasks as an ongoing strategy can lead to a reductionist curriculum. Instead, we should consider the nature of the scaffolding that is being provided for learners to carry out tasks:

> As far as possible, learners need to be engaged with authentic and cognitively challenging tasks: it is the nature of the support—support that is responsive to the particular demands made on children learning through the medium of a second language—that is critical for success. (Gibbons, 2002, pp. 10–11)

One of the major functions of classroom discourse is to socialize learners into the kinds of discourse associated with academic learning. Wells (1992) writes of the dual role of discourse in the development of understanding and of literacy in this way:

> Spoken discourse has an essential role to play in mediating the pupils' apprenticeship into the discipline, both as a medium in which to respond to and prepare for work on written texts (Barnes, 1976) and, more generally, as an opportunity for 'talking their way in' (Halliday, 1975) to ways of making sense of new information. (p. 291)

He adds that spoken discourse needs to include "forms that, with the assistance provided by the teacher, gradually incorporate the essential features of the discourse of the particular discipline" (Wells, 1992, p. 291).

Wells's (1992) comments have particular relevance for ESL learners, who are not only developing these new subject-related registers but are also doing so in their L2. Gibbons (2001), researching the learning of new registers by young ESL learners in a science classroom, describes how one teacher worked towards the gradual incorporation of subject-related discourse in her talk with students. The teacher based her program on a series of tasks sequenced along what Martin (1984) describes as the *mode continuum*. Rather than seeing texts as spoken or written, the mode continuum illustrates how text features vary along a spoken-written continuum: Face-to-face talk, which is related to what the participants are doing, requires fewer linguistic resources than a written piece where the writer may be writing for an unknown audience who has not shared in the experience. Thus the more removed the text is from a situation, the more linguistic resources are needed to create meaning through language alone. Based on this principle, the first of the classroom tasks required groups of students to carry out a range of experiments, each demonstrating magnetic repulsion, with each group of students carrying out a different experiment. The second task involved less situationally dependent language: Each group shared what they had done and learned with the class, a stage in the teaching program that Gibbons refers to as "teacher-guided reporting" since the teacher took an explicitly guiding role at this point. The third task required students to write in their science journals about what they had learned. Gibbons suggests that teacher-guided reporting was significant in assisting students to move beyond both their everyday understandings of the topic and their current linguistic levels in English, towards the educational discourse and specialist understandings of the subject. In talking together, children were able to explore their understandings of concepts and knowledge, and in talking with the teacher they were able to reflect on and recontextualize what they had learned in more register-appropriate ways. Through the mediation of the teacher in the teacher-guided sessions, students' contributions to the discourse were progressively transformed into the specialist discourse of the school curriculum. In this process, the teacher interacted with the students as they were reporting, supporting their efforts at making meaning through prompting. She used a number of strategies to achieve this: encouraging students to clarify or reword what they said; questioning; modeling aspects of the lexicogrammar associated with the register of science; talking explicitly about language; and at times, when students were at the outer limits of what they were able to say alone, recasting or reformulating student contributions in more register-appropriate ways.

Gibbons (2001) points out that these jointly constructed sequences of discourse were taken up in what the students wrote in their journals. Just as important, however, was the fact that the teacher-guided reporting sequences, because of the provision of highly responsive and contingent interactional scaffolding, resulted in the students being able to successfully articulate quite complex ideas, and thus they were positioned by the discourse as successful interactants and learners. This issue is taken up later in the section on Classroom Discourse and Identity.

Sociocultural Theory and Second Language Learning

Much research in SLA, until recent years, had been concerned largely with the acquisition processes around morphology and syntax. To a great extent, research and thinking about interaction have tended to focus simply on its role as a provider of input (Swain, 2000). However, a view of discourse as a collaborative medium in which learning is co-constructed between participants, in recent years, has begun to influence the field of SLA, and has focused researchers' attention on the social and cultural situatedness of language learning and use. Recently, broader interpretations of the role of interaction have been taken in SLA studies (Long, 1996; Pica, Lincoln-Porter, Patinois, & Linell, 1996; Swain, 2000), and sociocultural approaches to both research and teaching have been applied specifically to the L2 and bilingual classrooms. Cognitive processes, while not denied, are seen as connected to social processes.

These socioculturally oriented studies of L2 learning have shown how language learning is mediated by language use, both in the discourse between teacher and student and in that between students (Donato, 1994, 2000; Engstrom & Middleton, 1996; Gibbons, 2001; Putney, Green, Dixon, Duran, & Yeager, 2000; Ohta, 1995, 1997, 1999, 2000; Swain, 2000). The negotiation of meaning that occurs in authentic discourse contexts between interactants is seen as a way of both improving comprehensibility and encouraging further learner output (van Lier, 2000).

Many researchers in SLA now argue that collaborative dialogue deserves to be further examined for its contribution to L2 learning. Swain, for example, argues that the scope of output should be extended beyond communicative activity to include cognitive activity (Swain, 2000, p. 98). She describes the talk between pairs of students in a language-based activity that required the students to recreate a text they had listened to as a written piece. In their discussion, they attempted to create the problematic phrases for themselves, which they then reflected on, leading Swain to conclude that the act of producing language focused the learners' attention on what they did not know and led them to engage in the co-construction of metalinguistic knowledge. Such a situation, she suggests, represents an example of language learning being mediated by language use. It would seem that collaborative dialogue like this has the potential to allow students' current abilities to outstrip what would have been possible for any one of them to achieve alone (see also Donato, 1994). Swain's research also points to the importance for language development of both problem-based small group tasks and the development of metalinguistic awareness among learners.

CLASSROOM DISCOURSE AND IDENTITY

As Hall (1998) points out, there is now considerable research which shows that not only the content but also the processes of student learning are tied to the instructional practices created in their classroom interactions (Baker, 1992; Cazden, 1988; Delpit, 1988; Green & Dixon, 1994; Gutiérrez, 1994; Lemke, 1988; Lin, 1994; Michaels, 1981; Philips, 1983; Smagorinsky, 1993; Wells, 1996). As Halliday's (1985) work in systemic functional grammar demonstrates, the experiential and the interpersonal metafunctions of language exist in any instance of language use at one and the same time; language not only is the means by which experiential learning is constructed but also, through its interpersonal resources, constructs the role of relationships and the identities of interactants in a particular situational context.

Along with a focus on discourse as a tool for learning, then, has come a more critical perspective which focuses on how learners are positioned through the discourse of the classroom and how their identities are constructed though the interactions in which they are participants. As Walsh (1996) argues, while the centrality of identity negotiation has often been ignored in the mainstream literature on effectiveness, it must be a central issue among researchers focused on equity. This focus shifts discussion about student achievement from a purely linguistic and cognitive perspective to a sociological and sociopolitical one: Much research has now been done that links academic achievement not only to the pedagogical effectiveness of teaching programs but also to the institutional and societal power relations in which classroom communication occurs (see inter alia, Cummins, 1986, 1996, 2000; Walsh, 1991; Floriani, 1993; Green & Dixon, 1994; Gutiérrez, Larson, & Kreuter, 1995; Gutiérrez, Rymes, & Larson, 1995; Gutiérrez & Stone, 2000; McLaren, 1994; Toohey, 2000). Such studies view the classroom as a historically and culturally specific context within a societally governed institution. Identity negotiation has also been a significant and parallel theme among others concerned with equity and multicultural education (Darder, 1991; Nieto, 1996, 1999; Toohey, 2000; Walsh, 1996).

Cummins (2000) suggests that there is a need to problematize the power structures of society and to reverse, in the classroom, those societal macropatterns of interactions that result in coercive relations of power. Coercive relations of power include the expectation that minority groups deny their linguistic and cultural identity and work out of a narrow curriculum that results from approaches that take a reductionist approach to learning. Oakes's (1985) work illustrates how such approaches highlight the teaching of basic, low-level skills and fail to provide opportunities for students to develop higher-order, critical-thinking skills and autonomous learning strategies. In contrast, in a classroom that challenges coercive relations of power, interactions between students and teachers are such that students' identities are confirmed and extended, there are opportunities for collaborative critical enquiry, and the classroom becomes a micro-version of the kind of society "we hope our students will help form" (Cummins, 2000, p. 48). Cummins argues that to educate learners in a truly culturally and linguistically diverse context, it is necessary to nurture both intellect and identity equally in ways that "of necessity, challenge coercive relations of power." Since interactions are never neutral, they represent the direct determinant of ESL learners' success or failure in school: Such an approach focuses not only on the student as learner but also recognizes that the process of identity negotiation is fundamental to educational success for all students.

As McDermott (1993) argues, "the question of who is learning what and how much is essentially a question of what conversations they are part of, and this question is a subset of the more powerful question of what conversations are around to be had in a given culture" (p. 295). Creating opportunities to shape learning depends not only on the kinds of instructional practices constructed through discourse but on the larger institutional forces by which learners' voices are shaped in moment-by-moment interaction of the classroom: "Our every use of language serves as a sociopolitical statement indicating our stance toward the particular interactive moment, our place in that interaction and our positioning toward the others involved" (Hall, 1995, p. 214). A similar perspective comes from Delpit (1995) who argues for forms of pedagogy that not only develop necessary and fundamental skills but also expand students' personal, intellectual, and academic horizons in transformative ways.

Thus from a critical perspective on classroom discourse any set of interactions needs to be examined from two perspectives: the effectiveness of the instruction in fostering learning, and the impact of the instruction on the way students view themselves. Educators also need to be mindful that, no matter how positive may be the orientation of teachers to their students, it may amount to very little in comparison to the message communicated to them as a result of academic failure. In a study that analyzes the moment-by-moment interaction of one marginalized Latina student and her teacher, Gutiérrez, Larson, and Kreuter (1995) show how the monologic and monocultural instruction in the classroom "paralyses" students and teachers, and prevents the creation of a rich and vital classroom life, ultimately limiting students' potential for learning. A number of other studies based on a close analysis of interaction also illustrate how marginalized students may be offered differential opportunities for learning; through differential attention to their participation, students may be led along individual paths. Language learning does not depend only on students' abilities or motivation but is also tied to a teacher's motivation for and interest in providing learners with what Hall refers to as "official participatory rights" to engage in opportunities for learning (Hall, 1998, and see also Philips, 1983; Gutiérrez, Rymes, & Larson, 1995; Smagorinsky & O'Donnell-Allen, 2000; Toohey, 2000; Torr, 1993). Hall also argues that it is not simply students' participation patterns that are significant, but how students' contributions are responded to by the teacher and the consequence of such differential responses, which may result in "primary" and "secondary" groups of students. Differential responses include different rights to the floor and the roles participants are allowed to play: For example, certain students may not have their contributions responded to, or they may be less encouraged to bring in personal knowledge.

A discussion of how academic language learning can be orchestrated in the classroom, then, must take account not simply of the experiential content of the discourse itself, but also the participation structures and responses constituted in educational practices, within which participants play out particular roles and relationships. In the words of Gutiérrez and Stone (2000), learning contexts are "complex social spaces that are inextricably related to what gets learned and how" (p. 157).

INTERACTIONAL CHOICES

Van Lier (1996) makes the point that no one kind of discourse pattern alone is sufficient for all the purposes of education. He argues for the need for teachers to have a "map of pedagogical options" (p. 180), an awareness of a number of alternatives for classroom interaction and the probable effects and purposes for each. In this section we look at some of the interactional options and characteristics of discourse in the classroom in relation to L2 learners.

The IRF Exchange

Among the most documented and well-recognized pattern of classroom discourse is the Initiation-Response-Feedback (IRF) structure, first noted by Bellack, Kliebard, Hyman and Smith (1966) and later, among others, by Sinclair and Coulthard (1975), Mehan (1979), Edwards and Mercer (1987), Cazden (1988), Lemke (1990), and van Lier (1996), all of whom have noted its ubiquitous presence in classroom discourse. It is a three-part pattern consisting of an initiation move by the teacher (usually a question designed for the student to display their knowledge), a response from the student, and a feedback or evaluation move from the teacher.

While such exchanges almost never occur outside of a formal educational setting, it has been argued that in some ways it is well-designed for instruction where the aim is to deliver certain ideas or facts. Van Lier (1996) argues that it enables teachers to lead students in certain preplanned ways, akin to the Socratic dialogue. In addition, the student knows immediately if the answer is correct, it allows the teacher to better maintain control and, when used skilfully, can encourage students to think more deeply and critically about their answers. It may also facilitate the student's response, since the initial question may offer strong clues as to what is expected: it "strips away the work of turn taking and utterance design," (van Lier, p. 152) and this simplification of the exchange may be an important one for low-level L2 learners.

However, as van Lier also points out, in such exchanges, one third is given over to evaluation, and the student's response is "hemmed in" between a demand from the teacher to respond, and a judgment on the appropriateness of the response. The third move, when realized as an evaluation, can "close down" the exchange, preventing further exploration or reflection on the particular topic. Furthermore, from the point of view of a L2 learner, the IFR pattern may not provide many of the critical factors for language learning, such as extended student output and the negotiation of meaning. Work by Swain and Lapkin (1990) in French bilingual classrooms, for example, points to the negative effects for language learning of limited opportunities for extended student talk. Swain has argued that it is in the process of producing a L2 that learners develop language, since they are pushed to process language at a deeper level than is required in receptive situations. Output is not thus simply an indicator of language learning, it is the means by which learning occurs (Swain, 1985, 1995).

But as van Lier (1996) points out, the negative effects of IRF are not a necessary consequence of the structure, simply that its particular form favors these consequences. It may offer a more positive context for learning if it can be shifted away from a control orientation, towards a participation orientation that is aimed to stimulate clear thinking and clarity of expression. Cazden (1988) and Wells (1996,

1999), for example, have shown how quite minor changes in the IRF exchange can have quite significant effects on the discourse as a whole (see also Table 2).

Interaction as Congruent, Contingent, Synchronous

Many studies have illustrated considerable differences in the interactional patterns between the culture of mainstream teachers and the diverse cultures of their students. Two important areas have emerged from the body of research on teacher-student interactions: Cultural congruence and instructional conversations (Lee & Fradd, 1996). *Cultural congruence* in the classroom requires the use of the characteristic discourse of the particular minority group, which is often at odds with the typical discourse patterns of the classroom: Shared discourse by multiple speakers; similar types and lengths of turn-taking patterns; a focus on the social aspects of discourse and task engagement; and communication in language that is familiar. Lee and Fradd, however, argue that cultural congruence is not enough: Establishing cultural congruence without also attending to the nature of the academic discipline can result in interactional patterns that offer unequal opportunities for students to learn, since cultural congruence (requiring the use of students' particular interactional styles) may be incompatible with *instructional congruence* (the norms of academic discourses) and, hence, may lead to lower academic achievement.

The crucial question seems to be whether procedures that promote culturally congruent environments can be integrated with providing instruction that enhances academic achievement. In this kind of instructional congruence, shared cultures are used in combination with academic disciplines and build on students' prior knowledge and experience, while at the same time expanding students' repertoire to include new ways of participating in academic subjects (Lee & Fradd, 1996). This integration of cultural and academic congruence may result in discourse where there is a meshing of the everyday language of the students and the academic curriculum-related language of the subject discipline: A kind of hybrid register. The text in Table 1 illustrates one example of this "register-meshing."

Table 1. "Register-meshing"

Turn number	Student	Teacher
1	when we put it on one pole . em faces the other one it doesn't stick but when we turned the other one around . it sticks together	
2		OK can I just clarify something? you've got two magnets? they're in line/when you put . the two together
3	yes	
4		like that (*demonstrating*) they attracted to/each other/ is that right?

Text taken from Gibbons, 2003 (p. 258)

The teacher's discourse encapsulates a number of shifts along the mode continuum. It includes reference to a here-and-now demonstration (*like that*), the everyday language of the student (*sticks together*), and the standard lexis of school science (*attracted*). These mode shifts construct a hybrid register that has features of both the language of the student and the language of the science curriculum. Thus one way to conceptualize the ZPD for school-aged learners is to consider it as the zone where their everyday concepts and language interact with the "schooled" concepts within specific subjects (Kozulin, 1998). The closeness of fit between student and teacher contributions is clearly significant: too close a match between teacher and student contributions would suggest that students are not being provided with a context in which learning will occur, since there will be no access to as yet unknown language; too great a difference may lead to students failing to understand the teacher's discourse. In addition, because such hybrid registers code similar meanings in several modes, there is likely to be *message redundancy*, the coding of a meaning in a range of ways, which is an important aspect of discourse in facilitating access to the curriculum for L2 learners.

The notion of *contingency* appears also to be a major factor in effective teacher-student interaction. Contingency refers to the way in which the teacher (or other adult) judges the need and quality of assistance required by the learner, on the basis of moment-to-moment understanding. It requires interactants to be oriented towards collaboration and is anchored within the shared agenda of the participants (van Lier, 1996), requiring what Wells (1986) refers to as a rich interpretation of what the learner is attempting to communicate. Van Lier refers to the Janus-like quality of such interactions: The discourse looks both backwards, to the familiar, known, or *given*; and forward, to the language associated with curriculum learning, or *new*. In contingent interactions there is a sharedness of perspectives, which help ensure continued engagement (van Lier, p. 184). Contingent utterances, like those shown in the text of Table 1, are likely to relate new material to known material, set up expectancies for what may come next, validate (value and respect) both preceding and following utterances, and promote intersubjectivity (p. 184). Intersubjectivity tends to reduce overt power relations, since it requires "a constant oscillation between one's own role as an actor... and the role of one's counterpart in interactions" (Markova, 1982, cited in van Lier, 1996, p. 161).

Using a similar notion, Kasermann (1991) describes such contributions as *cooperative* or *synchronous* and suggests they are utterances that are called for at that particular moment, and that initiate or complete the exchange in expected ways: for example, teachers build on the knowledge embedded in the prior utterance in a way that extends or expands it (rather than evaluates it). Cooperative or synchronous utterances facilitate the creation of a shared perspective among participants and help in the joint process of knowledge construction and strengthening of social bonds. Thus participants are jointly focused on the activity and its goals, and draw each other's attention into a common direction.

The text in Table 2, taken from the same science lesson with young L2 learners, illustrates further what contingent and cooperative discourse might look like in practice and shows how meaningful participation by the learner becomes possible through the teacher's contingent and synchronous responses. Here, a student is trying to explain to the rest of the class that a magnet attracted a nail through a sheet of aluminium foil. Note that the teacher allows the student several attempts to explain what she wants to say (during which process, the utterances become increasingly more complete and comprehensible) before herself recasting. The teacher's recast does not in fact occur until turn 11, offering a greatly increased potential for student self-correction, language output, and negotiation of meaning than would be the case in a more truncated form of the IRF exchange. While the teacher's responses are short (note that the student says far more than the teacher), she provides sensitive and contingent scaffolding, which makes clear to the student the kind of information she needs to give her audience. Equally important is that at the end of this sequence, the student has been able to express what she wants to say, and thus has been positioned as a successful and effective contributor to the discourse.

Table 2. Teacher-student Collaborative Discourse

	Student	Teacher
1		what did you find out?
2	Tina: if you put a nail . onto the piece of foil . . and then pick it . pick it up . . the magnet will . . . . that if you put a . nail . under a piece of foil . and then pick . pick the foil up with the magnet . . still . still with the nail . . under it . . . it won't	
3		it what?
4	Tina: it won't/ it won't come out	
5		what won't come out?
6	Tina: it'll go up	
7		wait just a minute . . can you explain that a bit more Tina?
8	Tina: like if you put a nail and then foil over it and then put the nail on top . of the foil . . the nail underneath the foil/ Miss I can't say it	
9		no you're doing fine I/ I can see
10	Tina: Miss forget about the magnet/ em the magnet holds it with the foil up the top and the nail's underneath and the foil's on top and put the magnet in it and you lift it up . . and the nail will em . . .hold it/stick with the magnet and the foil's in between	
11		oh/ so even with the foil in between . the . magnet will 'still pick up the nail . alright does the magnet pick up the foil?
12	Tina: no	

(Taken from Gibbons, 2002, pp. 35-36)

The interaction here is essentially an extended IRF sequence, with the teacher initiating the exchange, the student responding, and the teacher providing feedback. However, in place of the third (feedback or evaluation) move, which typically might have occurred at turns 3, 5, 7, or 9, there is what Wells (1996) refers to as a *pivot move*. Rather than closing down the discourse, as often occurs in the third move of a single nuclear IRF exchange, a pivot move extends the discourse by continuing the participatory rights of the student. This occurs through moves that are *prospective*, that is, by moves which require a further response through a demand (for information). The teacher's probes for information, realized by the questions and the encouragement to continue in moves 3, 5, 7, and 9, are examples of this increase in prospectiveness. Making the feedback move more prospective modifies the IRF pattern in ways that foster collaborative and jointly constructed stretches of dialogue. In relation to L2 development, these longer sequences allow time for the student to have several attempts at explaining what she is trying to say, a process which encourages what Swain (1985, 1995) has referred to as *pushed* or *stretched* language. In the text above, it can be seen that the student's three attempts to give an explanation (2, 8, 10) are increasingly more complete and more "writtenlike."

The creation of a shared perspective, and synchronous and contingent responses, presupposes an environment in which students feel able to contribute more extended responses. It has been argued that often what foils discussion is the fast pacing and number of teacher-questions (Dillon, 1983, 1985), with most teachers waiting a second or less for students to reply and responding to what the student has said within a second of the student finishing speaking (Rowe, 1986). However, when teachers wait 3 seconds or more, "there are pronounced changes in student use of language and logic as well as in student and teacher attitudes and expectations" (Rowe, p. 443). Increased wait time tends to lead to teachers asking fewer but more cognitively complex questions; they become more adept at using student responses (possibly because they have greater listening time); expectations about certain students are raised; and "some previously invisible people become visible" (Cazden, 1988, p. 60). For students using their L2, increased wait time is especially important, since more time is needed for formulating how they will respond, not only to the experiential content of what they will say.

Progressive Discourse

For discourse to be worthwhile, it must involve more than simply the sharing of opinions, and this is particularly the case if small group work is to be effective for learning. It must also result in progress to "a new understanding that everyone involved agrees is superior to their own previous understanding of ideas" (Bereiter, 1994, in Wells, 1999, p. 112). Central to discourse that can be viewed as progressive are four commitments, which must be made by the participants: (a) to work towards common understanding; (b) to frame questions and propositions in ways that allow evidence to be brought to bear on them; (c) to expand the body of collectively valid propositions; and (d) to allow beliefs to be subjected to critique and criticism if this will advance the discourse. In contexts where the direction of the discourse and the relevance of contributions are jointly determined by the group, there is the potential to change learning situations and participant roles, and to create the possibilities for the direction of the discourse, and the agenda itself, to be shaped by all participants (van Lier, 1996).

For progressive discourse to occur, three conditions need to be met (Wells, 1999). First, exploratory talk needs to be based on enquiry and problem solving, where there is a need for ideas not simply to be shared but also to be questioned and revised. Students must also learn to pose critical questions relating to their own lives: "Who makes decisions and who is left out? Who benefits and who suffers? Why is a given practice fair or unfair? What alternatives can we imagine?" (Bigelow, Christiansen, Karp, Miner, & Peterson, 1994, cited in Cummins, 2000). As Nieto (1999) has argued, multicultural education will ultimately be judged by its effectiveness both in teaching subject content and in teaching critical thinking skills and social awareness.

Second, there needs to be a classroom ethos that encourages students to state opinions and engage with the ideas of others (Wegerif & Mercer, 1996). Contributions to the discourse must be treated seriously, both by the teacher and by peers, and treated as relevant and important for the other students to know (Hall, 1998).

Third, it becomes necessary to change the traditional speaking rights of classroom participants, to make changes in what Wells refers to as the division of labor within the discourse, moving it away from the sole control of the teacher. Changing the speaking rights may be represented in quite subtle but significant ways. Cazden (1988) remarks that discourse that is closer to conversation (but is unusual in schools) may involve students addressing each other directly (which she refers to as *cross-discussion*) rather than in the third person via the teacher. She suggests that it may be helpful, especially for young children, to have different physical arrangements for events where different discourse norms are expected, so that a change in a pattern of discourse (e.g., cross-discussion) is signaled visually (e.g., by students changing their seating so that they sit in a circle). Changing speaking roles and rights positions students as authoritative participants and constructs a very different identity from that which is constructed in discourse dominated by IRF exchanges.

I add here a fourth point that I believe is of particular relevance to ESL learners. What may be overlooked in L2 classrooms is the fact that progressive discourse requires learners to be able to control the interpersonal language needed to participate in productive ways in critiquing and revising ideas. Since most teachers' concerns are with the development of more obviously academically associated language, *modality* (that area of meaning that enables a speaker to express tentativeness, to make a polite suggestion, or to indicate respect for a speaker even while disagreeing with an idea) is frequently not explicitly taught. However, if discourse is to be progressive, if it is to be the vehicle by which new ideas are co-constructed, and if in this process learners are to be constructed as interactants who have ideas worthy of attention, then teaching must also include the interpersonal aspects of language that will enable this to occur (see Gibbons, 2002).

Students therefore need to be provided with opportunities to take part in discourse that is symmetrical, process-oriented, exploratory, self-determined, and contingent (van Lier, 1996). Breen (2001) also argues that teachers should be facilitating the kind of discourse "which is more challenging to its participants than it sometimes is," should ensure that much of it is generated by learners rather than the teacher, and should encourage risk taking "so that discursive pressure is seen by learners as genuine opportunities for creative use of emerging knowledge and skills" (p. 318).

ORCHESTRATING DISCOURSE FOR LANGUAGE LEARNING

The research discussed in this chapter carries many implications for classroom practice and for the kind of classroom discourse that will be enabling of academic language development for L2 learners. It concludes with some comments about what this classroom discourse might look like in practice.

Such discourse will be based around scaffolded and intellectually challenging tasks, and constructed through a critical and enquiry-based curriculum. It will be anchored in what learners already know, their current knowledge, and linguistic skills. At the same time it will provide a bridge between this familiar language and ways of thinking and knowing, and new curriculum knowledge and subject-related discourse. It will incorporate both spoken and written language as tools for learning and will consciously plan for contexts where students use more writtenlike spoken language, and in this process, it will incorporate the specific language features of subject-related discourse. It will include explicit teaching and talk about language, including the explicit teaching of the interpersonal language necessary for working collaboratively. It will be structured so that all students are accorded equal participant rights. Teachers will respond contingently and respectfully to students' contributions to this discourse. Thus sufficient wait time is given for students to respond when it is their turn to take the floor, and a discourse context is provided where students can become conversational partners in exchanges: Teachers will seek to increase the prospectiveness of the discourse rather than focusing only on evaluating the responses of students.

Arguing that students' capacity to learn is "intricately intertwined" with the context of the classroom, Lee and Smagorinsky (2000) write:

> The potential for learning is an ever-shifting range of possibilities that are dependent on what the cultural novice already knows, the nature of the problem to be solved or task to be learned, the activity structures in which learning takes place and the quality of the person's interaction with others. Context and capacity are intricately intertwined. (p. 2)

The classroom context includes the learning culture that the teacher and student create and is ultimately dependent on the discourse that occurs. As this chapter has argued, the nature of this discourse is critical for learning and for the way that students' identities as learners are shaped. The chapter concludes with a comment by van Lier (1996), who argues for an examination and transformation of classroom discourse in these terms:

> Starting by a close examination of interaction itself, and transforming it according to sound pedagogical principles, would necessarily (though not instantaneously) bring about a transformation of the institution itself. Reform thus occurs from the bottom up, one pedagogical action at a time. (p. 158)

These pedagogical actions, the particular ways that teachers choose to interact with their students, have the potential to lead to a more equitable and effective context for learning for minority and L2 learners.

REFERENCES

Baker, K. (1992, Winter, Spring). Review of forked tongue. *Bilingual Basics*, 6–7.
Barnes, D. (1976). *From communication to curriculum*. Harmondsworth: Penguin.
Bellack, A., Kliebard, H., Hyman, R., & Smith, F. (1966). *The language of the classroom*. New York: Teachers' College Press.
Biber, D. (1986). Spoken and written textual dimensions in English: Resolving the contradictory findings. *Language* 62, 384–414.
Bigelow, B., Christensen, L., Karp, S., Miner, B., & Peterson, B. (1994). *Rethinking our classrooms: Teaching for justice and equity*. Milwaukee, WI: Rethinking Schools Ltd.
Breen, M. (2001). Navigating the discourse: On what is learned in the classroom. In C. Candlin & N. Mercer (Eds.), *English language teaching in its social context*, (pp. 306–322). London: Routledge.
Britton, J. (1970). *Language and learning*. London: Allen Lane.
Brooks, F. (1992). Communicative competence and the conversation course: A social interaction perspective. *Linguistics and Education, 4*, 219–246.
Bruner, J. (1975). Language as an instrument of thought. In A. Davies (Ed.), *Problems of language and learning*, (pp. 61–68). London: Heimemann.
Canale, M. (1983). On some dimensions of language proficiency. In J. Oller (Ed.), *Issues in language testing research*, (pp. 333–342). Rowley, MA: Newbury House.
Cazden, C. (1988). *Classroom discourse: The language of teaching and learning*. Portsmouth, NH: Heinemann.
Christie, F. (1994). *On pedagogic discourse*. Melbourne: Australian Research Council.
Collier, V. (1989). How quickly can immigrants become proficient in school English? *Journal of Educational Issues of Language Minority Students, 5*, 26–28.
Cummins, J. (1984). *Bilingualism and special education: Issues in assessment and pedagogy*. Clevedon: Multilingual Matters.
Cummins, J. (1986). Empowering minority students: A framework for intervention. *Harvard Education Review, 15*, 18–36.
Cummins, J. (1996). *Negotiating identities: Education for empowerment in a diverse society*. Los Angeles: California Association for Bilingual Education.
Cummins, J. (2000). *Language, power and pedagogy. Bilingual children in the crossfire*. Clevedon: Multilingual Matters.
Darder, A. (1991). *Culture and power in the classroom: A critical foundation for bicultural education*. New York: Bergin and Garvey.
Delpit, L. (1988). The silenced dialogue: Power and pedagogy in educating other people's children. *Harvard Educational Review, 58*(3), 280–298.
Delpit, L. (1995). *Other people's children: Cultural conflict in the classroom*. New York: The New Press.
Derewianka, B. (1990). *Exploring how texts work*. Sydney: Primary English Teaching Association.
Dillon, J. (1983). *Teaching and the art of questioning*. Bloomington, IN: Phi Delta Cappa Educational Foundation.
Dillon, J. (1985). Using questions to foil discussion. *Teaching and Teacher Education, 1*, 109–121.
Donaldson, M. (1978). *Children's minds*. Glasgow: Collins.
Donato, R. (1994). Collective scaffolding in second language learning. In J. Lantolf & G. Appel (Eds.), *Vygotskian approaches to second language research*, (pp. 33–56). Norwood, NJ: Ablex Press.
Donato, R. (2000). Sociocultural contributions to understanding the foreign and second language classroom. In J. Lantolf (Ed.), *Sociocultural theory and second language learning*, (pp. 27–50). Oxford: Oxford University Press.
Edwards, D., & Mercer, N. (1987). *Common knowledge: The development of understanding in the classroom*. London: Methuen.
Engstrom, Y., & Middleton, D. (Eds.). (1996). *Cognition and communication at work*. Cambridge: Cambridge University Press.
Floriani, A. (1993). Negotiating what counts: Roles and relationships, texts and contexts, content and meaning. *Linguistics and Education, 5*, 241–273.
Gallas, K. (1995). *Talking their way into science: Hearing children's questions and theories, responding with curricula*. New York: Teachers College Press.
Gibbons, P. (2001). Learning a new register in a second language. In C. Candlin & N. Mercer (Eds.), *English language teaching in its social context* (pp. 258–270). London: Routledge.
Gibbons, P. (2002). *Scaffolding language, scaffolding learning: Teaching second language learners in the mainstream classroom*. Portsmouth, NH: Heinemann.
Gibbons, P. (2003). Mediating language learning: Teacher interactions with ESL students in a content-based classroom. *TESOL Quarterly 37*(2), 247–273.

Goodman, K., & Goodman, Y. (1994). Vygotsky in a whole language perspective. In L. Moll (Ed.), *Vygotsky and education: Instructional implications and applications of sociohistorical psychology* (pp. 223–250). Cambridge: Cambridge University Press.

Green, J., & Dixon, C. (1994). Talking knowledge into being: Discursive and social practices in classrooms. *Linguistics and Education, 5*(3–4), 231–239.

Gutiérrez, K. (1994). How talk, context and script shape contexts for learning: A cross-case comparison of journal sharing. *Linguistics and Education 5*, 335–365.

Gutiérrez, K., Larson, J., & Kreuter, B. (1995). Cultural tensions in the scripted classroom: The value of the subjugated perspective. *Urban Education, 29*(4), 410–442.

Gutiérrez, K., Rymes B., & Larson, J. (1995). Script, counterscript, and underlife in classrooms: James Brown vs. Brown vs. Board of Education. *Harvard Educational Review, 65*, 445–471.

Gutiérrez, K. & Stone, L. (2000). Synchronic and diachronic dimensions of social practice: An emerging methodology for cultural-historical perspectives on literacy learning. In C. Lee. & P. Smagorinsky, *Vygotskian perspectives on literacy research. Constructing meaning through collaborative enquiry* (pp. 150–164). Cambridge: Cambridge University Press.

Hall, J. (1995). (Re)creating our worlds with words: A sociohistorical perspective of face-to-face interaction. *Applied Linguistics, 16*, 206–232.

Hall, J. (1998). Differential teacher attention to student utterances: The construction of different opportunities for learning in the IRF. *Linguistics and Education 9*(3), 287–311.

Halliday, M. (1985). *An introduction to functional grammar*. London: Edward Arnold.

Hammond, J. (1990). Is learning to read and write the same as learning to speak? In F. Christie (Ed.), *Literacy for a Changing World* (pp. 26–53). Victoria: ACER.

Kasermann, M. (1991). Obstruction and dominance: Uncooperative moves and their effect on the course of conversation. In I. Markova & K. Foppa (Eds.), *Asymmetries in dialogue* (pp. 101–123). Hertfordshire: Harvester Wheatsheaf.

Kozulin, A. (1998). *Psychological tools: A sociocultural approach to education*. Cambridge, MA: Harvard University Press.

Lee, C., & Smagorinsky, P. (2000). *Vygotskian perspectives on literacy research. Constructing meaning through collaborative enquiry*. Cambridge: Cambridge University Press.

Lee, O., & Fradd, S. (1996). Interactional patterns of linguistically diverse students and teachers: Insights for promoting science learning. *Linguistics and Education, 8*, 269–297.

Lemke, J. (1988). Genres, semantics and classroom education. *Linguistics and Education, 1*(1) 81–89.

Lemke, J. (1990). *Talking science: Language, learning and values*. Norwood, NJ: Ablex.

Lin, L. (1994). Language of and in the classroom: Constructing patterns of social life. *Linguistics and Education, 5*, 367–409.

Long, M. (1996). The role of the linguistic environment in second language acquisition. In W. Ritchie & T. Bhatia (Eds.), *Handbook of second language acquisition* (pp. 413–468). San Diego, CA: Academic Press.

Martin, J. (1984). Language, register and genre. In F. Christie (Ed.), *Children writing, study guide*, 21–29. Geelong, Victoria: Deakin University Press.

Martin, J. (1990). Literacy in science: Learning to handle text as technology. In F. Christie (Ed.), *Literacy for a changing world* (pp. 79–117). Hawthorn, Victoria: ACER.

Martin, J., Christie, F., & Rothery, J. (1987). Social processes in education: A reply to Sawyer and Watson (and others). In I. Reid (Ed.), *The Place of genre in learning: Current debates* (pp. 58–82). Geelong, Victoria: Centre for Studies in Literary Education, Deakin University Press.

Martin, J. & Veel, R. (1998). *Reading science*. London: Routledge.

Maybin, J., Mercer, N., & Stierer, B. (1992). Scaffolding learning in the classroom. In K. Norman (Ed.), *Thinking voices: The work of the National Oracy Project* (pp. 186–195). London: Hodder and Stoughton.

McDermott, R. (1993). The acquisition of a child by a learning disability. In S. Chaiklin & J. Lave (Eds.), *Understanding practice: Perspectives on activity and context* (pp. 269–305). Cambridge: Cambridge University Press.

McKay, P., Davies, A., Devlin, B., Clayton, J., Oliver, R., & Zammit, S. (1997). *The bilingual interface project report*. Canberra: Department of Employment, Education, Training and Youth Affairs.

McLaren, P. (1994). *Life in schools: An introduction to critical pedagogy*. New York: Longman.

Mehan, B. (1979). *Learning lessons*. Cambridge, MA: Harvard University Press.

Mercer, N. (1994). *Neo-Vygotskian theory and classroom education*. Clevedon: Multilingual Matters.

Mercer, N. (1995). *The guided construction of knowledge: Talk amongst teachers and learners*. Clevedon: Multilingual Matters.

Michaels, S. (1981). 'Sharing time': Children's narrative styles and differential access to literacy. *Language in Society, 10*, 423–442.

Mohan, B. (1986). *Language and content*. Reading, MA: Addison-Wesley.
Mohan, B. (2002). The second language as a medium of learning. In B. Mohan, C. Leung & C. Davison (Eds.), *English as a second language in the mainstream* (pp. 107–126). New York: Longman.
Moll, L. (1994). *Vygotsky and education. Instructional implications and applications of sociohistorical psychology*. Cambridge: Cambridge University Press.
Nieto, S. (1996). *Affirming diversity: The sociopolitical context of multicultural education* (2nd Ed.). White Plains, NY: Longman.
Nieto, S. (1999). *The light in their eyes: Creating multicultural learning communities*. New York: Teachers College Press.
Oakes, J. (1985). *Keeping track: How high schools structure inequality*. New Haven: Yale University Press.
Ohta, A. (1995). Applying sociocultural theory to an analysis of learner discourse: Learner-learner collaborative interaction in the zone of proximal development. *Issues in Applied Linguistics, 6*, 93–121.
Ohta, A. (1997). The development of pragmatic competence in learner-learner classroom interaction. In L. Bouton (Ed.), *Pragmatics and language learning, Monograph Series, Vol. 8* (pp. 223–242). Urbana-Champaign, IL: University of Illinois.
Ohta, A. (1999). Interactional routines and the socialisation of interactional style in adult learners of Japanese. *Journal of Pragmatics, 31*, 1493–1512.
Ohta, A. (2000). From utterance to text: The bias of language in speech and writing. *Harvard Educational Review, 47*, 257–281.
Olson, D. R. (1977) From utterance to text: The bias of language in speech and writing. *Harvard Educational Review, 47*, 257–281.
Phillips, T. (1985). Beyond lip-service: Discourse development after the age of nine. In G. Wells & J. Nicholls (Eds.), *Language and learning: An interactional perspective* (pp. 59–82). East Sussex: Falmer Press.
Pica, T., Lincoln-Porter, F., Pattinois, D., & Linell, J. (1996). Language learners' interaction: How does it address the input, output, and feedback needs of language learners? *TESOL Quarterly, 30*, 59–84.
Putney, L., Green, J., Dixon, C., Duran R., & Yeager, B. (2000). Consequential progressions: Exploring collective-individual development in a bilingual classroom. In C. Lee & P. Smagorinsky, *Vygotskian perspectives on literacy research. Constructing meaning through collaborative enquiry* (pp. 86–126). Cambridge: Cambridge University Press.
Rowe, M. (1986). Wait time: Slowing down may be a way of speeding up. *Journal of Teacher Education, 37*, 43–50.
Sinclair, J., & Coulthard, R. (1975). *Towards an analysis of discourse: The English used by teachers and pupils*. London: Oxford University Press.
Smagorinsky, P. (1993). The social environment of the classroom: A Vygotskian perspective on small group process. *Communication Education, 42*(2) 159–171.
Smagorinsky, P., & O'Donnell-Allen, C. (2000). Idiocultural diversity in small groups: The role of the relational framework in collaborative learning. In C. Lee & P. Smagorinsky (Eds.), *Vygotskian perspectives on literacy research. Constructing meaning through collaborative inquiry* (pp. 1–18). Cambridge: Cambridge University Press.
Swain, M. (1985). Communicative competence: Some roles of comprehensible input and comprehensible output in its development. In S. Gass & C. Madden (Eds.), *Input in second language acquisition* (pp. 235–253). Cambridge, MA: Newbury House.
Swain, M. (1995). Three functions of output in second language learning. In G. Cook & B. Seidlehofer (Eds.), *Principle and practice in applied linguistics: Studies in honour of H.G. Widdowson* (pp. 125–144). Oxford: Oxford University Press.
Swain, M. (2000). The output hypothesis and beyond: Mediating acquisition through collaborative dialogue. In Lantolf, J. (Ed.), *Sociocultural theory and second language learning* (pp. 97–114). Oxford: Oxford University Press.
Swain, M., & Lapkin, S. (1990). Aspects of the sociolinguistic performance of early and late French immersion students. In R. Scarcella, E. Andersen, & S. Krashen (Eds.), *Developing communicative competence in a second language* (pp. 41–54). New Work: Newbury House.
Tharp, R., & Gallimore, R. (1988). *Rousing minds to life*. Cambridge: Cambridge University Press.
Toohey, K. (2000). *Learning English at school: Identity, social relations and classroom practice*. Clevedon: Multilingual Matters.
Torr, J. (1993). Classroom discourse: Children from English speaking and non-English speaking backgrounds. *Australian Review of Applied Linguistics, 16*(1), 37–56.
Tough, J. (1977). *Talking and learning: Schools council communication skills in early childhood project*. London: Ward Lock Educational in association with Drake Educational Associates.

Unsworth, L. (Ed.). (2000). *Researching language in schools and communities: Functional linguistics perspectives.* London: Cassell.
van Lier, L. (1996). *Interaction in the language curriculum: Awareness, autonomy and authenticity.* London: Longman.
van Lier, L. (2000). From input to affordance: Social-interactive learning from an ecological perspective. In J. Lantolf (Ed.), *Sociocultural theory and second language learning* (pp. 245–260). Oxford: Oxford University Press.
Vygotsky, L. S. (1978). *Mind in society.* Cambridge, MA: Harvard University Press.
Vygotsky, L. S. (1987). *The collected works, Volume 1, including Thinking and speaking.* New York: Plenum.
Walsh, C. (1991). *Issues of language, power and schooling for Puerto Ricans.* Toronto: OISE Press.
Walsh, C. (Ed.). (1996). *Education reform and social change: Multicultural voices, struggles and visions.* Mahwah, NJ: Lawrence Erlbaum Associates.
Webster, A., Beveridge, M., & Reed, M. (1996). *Managing the literacy curriculum.* London: Routledge.
Wegerif, R. & Mercer, N. (1996). Computers and reasoning through talk in the classroom. *Language and Education, 10*(1), 47–64.
Wells, G. (1986). *The meaning makers: Children learning language and using language to learn.* London: Hodder and Stoughton.
Wells, G. (1992). The centrality of talk in education. In K. Norman (Ed.), *Thinking voice: The work of the National Oracy Project.* London: Hodder and Stoughton.
Wells, G. (1996). Using the tool-kit of discourse in the activity of learning and teaching. *Mind, Culture and Language, 3*(2), 74–101.
Wells, G. (1999). *Dialogic inquiry. Towards a sociocultural practice and theory of education.* Cambridge: Cambridge University Press.
Wells, G. (2000). Dialogic inquiry in education: Building on the legacy of Vygotsky. In C. Lee & P. Smagorinsky (Eds.), *Vygotskian perspectives on literacy research. Constructing meaning through collaborative inquiry* (pp. 51–85). Cambridge: Cambridge University Press.
Wells, G., & Chang-Wells, G. (1992). *Constructing knowledge together: Classrooms as centers of inquiry and literacy.* Portsmouth, NH: Heinemann.
Wilkinson, A. M. (1965). *Spoken English.* Birmingham: University of Birmingham School of Education.
Wood, D., Bruner, J., & Ross, G. (1976). The role of tutoring in problem solving. *Journal of Child Psychology and Psychiatry, 17*(2), 89–100.

CHAPTER 43

CREATING A MOTIVATING CLASSROOM ENVIRONMENT

ZOLTÁN DÖRNYEI

The University of Nottingham, UK

ABSTRACT

This chapter addresses the complex question of what makes a classroom environment motivating. It will be argued that in order to understand the psychological tapestry of classroom life, we need to adopt an interdisciplinary approach and draw on research findings from a number of different areas within the social sciences, such as group dynamics, motivational psychology, educational studies, and second language research. The assumption underlying this chapter is that the motivating character of the learning context can be enhanced through conscious intervention by the language teacher, and accordingly the main facets of the environment will be discussed with such a proactive and practical objective in mind. Key concepts to be addressed include group cohesiveness and interpersonal relations, group norms and student roles, the teacher's leadership styles, and the process of facilitation, as well as the main phases of a proactive, motivational teaching practice within a process-oriented framework.

Researchers analyzing the effectiveness of second language (L2) education usually focus on issues such as the quality and quantity of L2 input, the nature of the language learning tasks, and the teaching methodology applied, as well as various learner traits and strategies. These are undoubtedly central factors in L2 learning, and they significantly determine the effectiveness of the process, particularly in the short run. If, however, we consider learning achievement from a longer-term perspective, other aspects of the classroom experience, such as a motivating classroom climate, will also gain increasing importance. Wlodkowski (1986) points out that although boring lessons can be very unpleasant and sometimes excruciatingly painful, boredom itself does not seem to affect the short-term effectiveness of learning. After all, much of what many of us currently know has been mastered while being exposed to some uninspiring presentation or dull practice sequence. Yet, no one would question that attempts to eliminate boredom from the classroom should be high on every teacher's agenda. Why is that? What is the significance of trying to create a more pleasant classroom environment?

The basic assumption underlying this chapter is that long-term, sustained learning—such as the acquisition of an L2—cannot take place unless the educational context provides, in addition to cognitively adequate instructional practices, sufficient inspiration and enjoyment to build up continuing motivation in the learners. Boring but systematic teaching can be effective in producing, for example, good test results, but rarely does it inspire a lifelong commitment to the subject matter. This chapter will focus on how to generate this additional inspiration, that is, how to create a motivating classroom environment.

The characteristics of the learning context can be studied from a number of different perspectives. In educational psychology there has been an established line of research focusing on a multidimensional concept describing the psychological climate of the learning context, termed the *classroom environment* (cf. Fraser & Walberg, 1991). Educational researchers have also focused on aspects of classroom management as an antecedent of the overall classroom climate (e.g., Jones & Jones, 2000). Adopting a different perspective to describe classroom reality, social psychologists have looked at the dynamics of the learner group as part of the vivid discipline of group dynamics (e.g., Schmuck & Schmuck, 2001). Motivational psychologists have taken yet another approach by focusing on the motivational teaching practices and strategies employed in the classroom (for example, Pintrich & Schunk, 2002). While all these lines of investigation represent slightly different priorities and research paradigms, in the end they concern the same larger picture and therefore show a considerable overlap. In the following overview, I will synthesize the various approaches by focusing on the different psychological processes that underlie and shape classroom life.

TOWARD A COHESIVE LEARNER GROUP

One of the most salient features of the classroom environment is the quality of the relationships between the class members. The quality of teaching and learning is entirely different depending on whether the classroom is characterized by a climate of trust and support or by a competitive, cutthroat atmosphere. If learners form cliques and subgroups that are hostile to each other and resist any cooperation, the overall climate will be stressful for teachers and students alike, and learning effectiveness is likely to plummet. How do such negative relationship patterns develop? And, once established, how can they be changed? These questions have been studied extensively within the field of group dynamics (for a review, see Forsyth, 1999), and recent work on the topic in the L2 field has produced detailed recommendations on how to develop cohesiveness in the language classroom (e.g., Dörnyei & Malderez, 1999; Dörnyei & Murphey, 2003; Ehrman & Dörnyei, 1998; Senior, 1997, 2002).

Intermember relations within a group are of two basic types: *attraction* and *acceptance*. Attraction involves an initial instinctive appeal, caused by factors such as physical attractiveness, perceived competence, and similarities in attitudes, personality, hobbies, living conditions, etc. An important tenet in group dynamics is that despite their initial impact, these factors are usually of little importance for the group in the long run, and group development can result in strong cohesiveness among members regardless of, or even in spite of, the initial intermember likes and dislikes. In a "healthy group," initial attraction bonds are gradually replaced by a deeper and steadier type of interpersonal relationship, acceptance.

Acceptance involves a feeling toward another person which is non-evaluative in nature, has nothing to do with likes and dislikes, but entails an unconditional positive regard toward the individual (Rogers, 1983), acknowledging the person as a complex human being with many (possibly conflicting) values and imperfections. One of the most important characteristics of a good group is the emergence of a high level of acceptance between members that powerful enough to override even negative feelings between some. This accepting climate, then, forms the basis of a more general feature of the group, group cohesiveness.

Group cohesiveness refers to the closeness and "we" feeling of a group, that is, the internal gelling force that keeps the group together. In certain groups it can be very strong, which is well illustrated by reunion parties held even several decades after the closure of the group. Cohesiveness is, obviously, built on intermember acceptance, but it also involves two other factors that contribute to the group's internal binding force: the members' commitment to the task/purpose of the group and group pride, the latter referring to the prestige of group membership (cf., elite clubs).

How can we promote acceptance and cohesiveness? There are a variety of methods, and from an L2 teaching perspective, Dörnyei and Murphey (2003) list the following main factors:

1. Learning about each other: This is the most crucial and general factor fostering intermember relationships, involving the students' sharing genuine personal information with each other. Acceptance simply does not occur without knowing the other person well enough—enemy images or a lack of tolerance very often stem from insufficient knowledge about the other party.
2. Proximity, contact, and interaction: Proximity refers to the physical distance between people, contact to situations where learners can meet and communicate spontaneously, and interaction to special contact situations in which the behavior of each person influences the others'. These three factors are effective natural gelling agents, which highlight the importance of classroom issues such as the seating plan, small group work, and independent student projects.
3. Difficult admission: This explains why exclusive club membership is usually valued very highly, and the same principle is intuitively acted upon in the various initiation ceremonies for societies, teams, or military groups.
4. Shared group history: The amount of time people have spent together and "Remember when we…" statements usually have a strong bonding effect.
5. The rewarding nature of group activities: Rewards may involve the joy of performing the activities, approval of the goals, success in achieving these goals, and personal benefits (such as grades or prizes).
6. Group legend: Successful groups often create a kind of group mythology that includes giving the group a name, inventing special group characteristics (for example, dress code), and group rituals, as well as creating group mottoes, logos, and other symbols such as flags or coats of arms.
7. Public commitment to the group: Group agreements and contracts as to common goals and rules are types of such public commitment, and wearing school colors or t-shirts is another way of achieving this.
8. Investing in the group: When members spend a considerable amount of time and effort contributing to the group goals, this increases their commitment toward these goals. That is, psychological membership correlates with the actual acts of membership.
9. Extracurricular activities: These represent powerful experiences—indeed, one successful program is often enough to "make" the group, partly becau-

se during such outings students lower their "school filter" and relate to each other as "civilians" rather than students. This positive experience will then prevail in their memory, adding a fresh and real feel to their school relationships.
10. Cooperation toward common goals: Superordinate goals that require the cooperation of everybody to achieve them have been found to be the most effective means of bringing together even openly hostile parties.
11. Intergroup competition (that is, games in which small groups compete with each other within a class): These can be seen as a type of powerful collaboration in which people unite in an effort to win. You may want to group students together who would not normally make friends easily, and mix up the subteams regularly.
12. Defining the group against another: Emphasizing the discrimination between "us" and "them" is a powerful but obviously dangerous aspect of cohesiveness. While stirring up emotions against an outgroup in order to strengthen ingroup ties is definitely to be avoided, it might be OK to occasionally allow students to reflect on how special their class and the time they spend together might be, relative to other groups.
13. Joint hardship and common threat: Strangely enough, going through some difficulty or calamity together (for example, carrying out some tough physical task together or being in a common predicament) has a beneficial group effect.
14. Teacher's role modeling: Friendly and supportive behavior by the teacher is infectious, and students are likely to follow suit.

TOWARD A PRODUCTIVE NORM AND ROLE SYSTEM IN THE CLASSROOM

When people are together, in any function and context, they usually follow certain rules and routines that help to prevent chaos and allow everybody to go about their business as effectively as possible. Some of these rules are general and apply to everybody, in which case we can speak about group norms. Some others, however, are specific to certain people who fulfill specialized functions, in which case they are associated with group roles.

Group Norms

In educational settings we find many classroom norms that are explicitly imposed by the teacher or mandated by the school. However, the majority of the norms that govern our everyday life are not so explicitly formulated, and yet they are there, implicitly. Many of these implicit norms evolve spontaneously and unconsciously during the interactions of the group members, for example, by copying certain behaviors of some influential member or the leader. These behaviors then become solidified into norms, and these "unofficial" norms can actually be more powerful than their official counterparts. The significance of classroom norms, whether official or unofficial in their origin, lies in the fact that they can considerably enhance or decrease students' academic achievement and work morale. In many contemporary classrooms, for example, we come across the norm of mediocrity that refers to the peer pressure put on students not to excel or else they will be called names such as "nerd", "swot", "brain", and so on.

One norm that is particularly important to language learning situations is the norm of tolerance. The language classroom is an inherently face-threatening environment because learners are required to take continuous risks as they need to communicate using a severely restricted language code. An established norm of tolerance ensures that students will not be embarrassed or criticized if they make a mistake and, more generally, that mistakes are seen and welcomed as a natural part of learning.

How can we make sure that the norms in our classroom promote rather than hinder learning? The key issue is that real group norms are inherently social products, and in order for a norm to be long-lasting and constructive, it needs to be explicitly discussed and accepted as right and proper. Therefore, Dörnyei and Malderez (1997) have proposed that it is beneficial to include an explicit norm-building procedure early in the group's life. They suggest formulating potential norms, justifying their purpose in order to enlist support for them, having them discussed by the whole group, and finally agreeing on a mutually accepted set of class rules, with the consequences for violating them also specified. These class rules can then be displayed on a wall chart.

Our norm-building effort will really pay off when someone breaks the norms, for example, by misbehaving or not doing something expected. It has been observed that the more time we spend setting, negotiating, and modeling the norms, the fewer people will go astray. And when they do, it is usually the group that brings them back in line. Having the group on your side in coping with deviations and maintaining discipline is a major help: members usually bring to bear considerable group pressure on errant members and enforce conformity with the group norms.

Group Roles

Role as a technical term originally comes from sociology and refers to the shared expectation of how an individual should behave. Roles describe the norms that go with a particular position or function, specifying what people are supposed to do. There is a general agreement that roles are of great importance with regard to the life and productivity of the group: if students are cast in the right role, they will become useful members of the team, they will perform necessary and complementary functions, and at the same time they will be satisfied with their self-image and contribution. However, an inappropriate role can lead to personal conflict and will work against the cohesiveness and effectiveness of the group. Thus, a highly performing class group will display a balanced set of complementary and constructive student roles.

Although listing all the possible roles is impossible (partly because some of them are specific to a particular group's unique composition or task), some typical examples include the leader, the organizer, the initiator, the energizer, the harmonizer, the information-seeker, the complainer, the scapegoat, the pessimist, the rebel, the clown, and the outcast. How do these roles emerge? They may evolve naturally, in which case it is to some extent a question of luck whether the emerged roles add up to a balanced and functional tapestry. Alternatively, by their own communications or through using certain teaching structures, teachers might encourage students to explore and assume different roles and adopt the ones that suit them best for strategies and activities. The most subtle way of encouraging role taking is to notice and reinforce any tentative role attempts on the students' part, and sometimes even to highlight possible roles that a particular marginal learner may assume. Alternatively, teachers can make sure that everybody has something to contribute by assigning specific roles for an activity, such as chair, time-keeper, task-initiator, clarifier, provocateur, synthesizer, checker, and secretary (Cohen, 1994; Dörnyei & Murphey, 2003). Having explicitly marked roles in the lessons has the further advantage that teachers can prepare the students to perform these roles effectively, including providing the specific language routines that typically accompany a role.

TOWARD AN OPTIMAL LEADERSHIP STYLE

Language teachers are by definition group leaders and as such they determine every facet of classroom life. The study of various leadership styles and their impact has a vast literature, but all the different accounts agree on one thing: leadership matters. As Hook and Vass (2000) succinctly put it, "Leadership is the fabled elixir. It can turn failing schools into centers of excellence … It is the process by which you allow your students to become winners" (p. 5).

The study of group leadership goes back to a classic study more than 60 years ago. Working with American children in a summer camp, Lewin and his colleagues (Lewin, Lippitt, & White, 1939) were interested to find out how the participants would react to three very different group leadership styles:

1. *Autocratic* (or *authoritarian*) leadership, which maintains complete control over the group
2. *Democratic* leadership, where the leader tries to share some of the leadership functions with the members by involving them in decision-making about their own functioning
3. *Laissez-faire* leadership, where the teacher performs very little leadership behavior at all

The results were striking. Of the three leadership types, the laissez-faire style produced the least desirable outcomes: the psychological absence of the leader retarded the process of forming a group structure, and consequently the children under this condition were disorganized and frustrated, experienced the most stress, and produced very little work. Autocratic groups were found to be more productive, spending more time on work than democratic ones, but the quality of the products in the democratic groups was judged superior. In addition, it was also observed that whenever the leader left the room, the autocratic groups stopped working whereas the democratic groups carried on. From a group perspective, the most interesting results of the study concerned the comparison of interpersonal relations and group climate in the democratic and autocratic groups. In these respects democratic groups significantly exceeded autocratic groups: the former were characterized by friendlier communication, more group-orientedness, and better member leader relationships, whereas the level of hostility observed in the autocratic groups was 30 times as great as in democratic groups, and aggressiveness was also considerably (eight times) higher in them.

Although leadership studies have moved a long way since this pioneering research, the main conclusion that a democratic leadership style offers the best potential for school learning is still widely endorsed. In educational psychology, therefore, an important research direction has been to operationalize this general style characteristic. Several models for the "democratic" leader/teacher have been offered in the past; the most influential metaphor used in contemporary educational research and methodology is the humanistic notion of the group leader as a *facilitator*.

A Situated Approach to Facilitation

The concept of the teacher as the facilitator highlights the important role the learner is to take in the learning process, while restricting the teacher's role to facilitating learning, that is, providing an appropriate climate and resources to support the student. Thus, the teachers are not so much "drill sergeants" or "lecturers of knowledge" as partners in the learning process. How should they behave to achieve this? It depends largely on the developmental phase of the learner group, that is, on how far the class has progressed toward becoming a mature and cohesive social unit. In *The Complete Facilitator's Handbook*, John Heron (1999) offers a relatively straightforward situated system of operation and control concerning the behavior of facilitators.

Heron (1999) argues that—contrary to beliefs—a good facilitator is not characterized by a "soft touch" or a "free for all" mentality. He distinguishes three different modes of facilitation:

1. *Hierarchical* mode, whereby the facilitator exercises the power to direct the learning process *for* the group, thinking and acting *on behalf of* the group, and making all the major decisions. In this mode, therefore, the facilitator takes full responsibility for designing the syllabus and providing structures for learning.
2. *Cooperative* mode, whereby the facilitator shares the power and responsibilities with the group, prompting members to be more self-directing in the various forms of learning. In this mode the facilitator collaborates with the members in devising the learning process, and outcomes are negotiated.
3. *Autonomous* mode, whereby the facilitator respects the autonomy of the group in finding their own way and exercising their own judgment. The task of the facilitator in this mode is to create the conditions within which students' self-determination can flourish.

Heron has found that the ideal proportion of the three modes changes with the level of development of the group. He distinguishes three stages:

1. At the outset of group development, the optimal mode is predominantly *hierarchical*, offering a clear and straightforward framework within which early development of cooperation and autonomy can safely occur. Participants at this stage may be lacking the necessary knowledge and skills to orientate themselves, and they rely on the leader for guidance. Within the hierarchical mode there should be, however, cooperative exchanges with the teacher and autonomous practice on their own. Also, even in this mode

the students' consent should be sought for the major leader-owned decisions.
2. Later, in the middle phase, more *cooperation* with group members may be appropriate in managing the learning process. The facilitator can negotiate the curriculum with the students and cooperatively guide their learning activities. The students' acquired confidence will allow them to take an increasing part in making the decisions about how their learning should proceed.
3. Finally, when the group has reached maturity and is thus ready for the *autonomous* mode, more power needs to be delegated to the members so that they can achieve full self-direction in their learning. Learning contracts, self-evaluation, and peer assessment may "institutionalize" their independence.

Thus, to synthesize Heron's (1999) system with the Lewin, Lippitt, and White (1939) study, a group-sensitive teaching practice begins more autocratically to give direction, security, and impetus to the group. Then as the students begin performing, teachers initiate more democratic control of the processes, increasingly relying on the group's self-regulatory resources. When the group further matures and begins to show its initiative, a more autonomy-inviting, almost laissez-faire, leadership style might be the most conducive to encouraging student independence—but of course, this is a well-prepared withdrawal of the scaffolding rather than an abandonment of leadership responsibilities.

ADOPTING A MOTIVATIONAL TEACHING PRACTICE

Although the title of this chapter identifies the motivating aspect of the classroom environment as the focal issue, the term *motivation* has hardly been mentioned in the previous sections. The main reason for this is that so far we have looked at the characteristics of the whole learner group rather than the individual learner. However, the term *motivation* has usually been associated with an individualistic perspective, focusing on the individual's values, attitudes, goals, and intentions. If we want to talk about the motivation of a whole learner group, it is necessary to also use group-level counterparts of the concept, such as group cohesiveness, group norms, and group leadership. After all, these latter factors all play an important role in determining the behavior of the learner group, and therefore they can be seen as valid motivational antecedents. In other words, when we discuss the learning behavior of groups of learners, motivational psychology and group dynamics converge. Having covered the most important group features, the rest of this chapter will draw on findings from more traditionally conceived motivation research.

What makes the classroom climate motivating and how can we increase this characteristic? To start with, let me propose that the motivational character of the classroom is largely a function of the teacher's motivational teaching practice, and is therefore within our explicit control. Therefore, the emphasis in the following analysis will be on proactive and conscious strategies that can be used to promote classroom motivation.

After the initial motivational conditions have been successfully created—that is, the class is characterized by a safe climate, cohesiveness, and a good student-teacher relationship—the motivational teaching practice needs to be established. This process comprises three phases: (a) generating initial motivation; (b) maintaining and protecting motivation; and (c) encouraging positive retrospective self-evaluation.

Generating Initial Motivation

Although many psychologists believe that children are inherently eager to expand their knowledge about the world and, therefore, the learning experience is by definition a source of intrinsic pleasure for them, classroom teachers tend to have perceptions that are in sharp contrast with this idyllic view. Instead of all those keen pupils, all they can often see is rather reluctant youngsters who are totally unaware of the fact that there should be an innate curiosity in them, let alone a desire to learn. And even if we are fortunate to have a class of students with a high degree of academic motivation, we cannot expect all the students to favor the L2 course over all the other subjects they study. Thus, unless we are singularly fortunate with the composition of our class group, student motivation will not be automatically there, and we will need to try to actively generate positive student attitudes toward L2 learning.

There are several facets of creating initial student motivation. Dörnyei (2001a) has divided these into five broad groups:

1. Enhancing the learners' language-related values and attitudes: Our basic value system greatly determines our preferences and approaches to activities. We can distinguish three types of language-related values: (a) *intrinsic value*, related to the interest in and anticipated enjoyment of the actual process of learning; (b) *integrative value*, related to our attitudes toward the L2, its speakers, and the culture it conveys; and (c) *instrumental value*, related to the perceived practical, pragmatic benefits that the mastery of the L2 might bring about.
2. Increasing the learners' expectancy of success: We do things best if we expect to succeed, and, to turn this statement round, we are unlikely to be motivated to aim for something if we feel we will never get there.
3. Increasing the learners' goal-orientedness: In a typical class, too many students do not really understand or accept why they are doing a learning activity. Moreover, the official class goal (that is, mastering the course content) may well not be the class group's only goal and in extreme cases may not be a group goal at all!
4. Making the teaching materials relevant for the learners: The core of this issue has been succinctly summarized by McCombs and Whisler (1997): "Educators think students do not care, while the students tell us they do care about learning but are not getting what they need" (p. 38).
5. Creating realistic learner beliefs: It is a peculiar fact of life that most learners will have certain beliefs about language learning, and most of these beliefs are likely to be (at least partly) incorrect. Such false beliefs can then function like time "bombs" at the beginning of a language course because of the inevitable disappointment that is to follow, or can clash with the course methodology and thus hinder progress.

Once the main aspects of creating initial student motivation have been identified, it is possible to generate or select a variety of specific classroom techniques to promote the particular dimension (for practical ideas, see Brophy, 1998; Dörnyei, 2001a).

Maintaining and Protecting Motivation

It is one thing to initially whet the students' appetite with appropriate motivational techniques, but unless motivation is actively maintained and protected, the natural tendency to lose sight of the goal, to get tired or bored of the activity, and to give way to attractive distractions will result in the initial motivation gradually petering out. Therefore, motivation needs to be actively nurtured. The spectrum of motivational strategies relevant to this phase is rather broad (since ongoing human behavior can be modified in so many different ways), and the following six areas appear to be particularly relevant for classroom application:

- making learning stimulating and enjoyable;
- presenting tasks in a motivating way;
- setting specific learner goals;.
- protecting the learners' self-esteem and increasing their self-confidence;
- creating learner autonomy;
- promoting self-motivating learner strategies.

These motivational dimensions, except for the last one, are more straightforward than the facets of initial motivation described above, and due to space limitations I will not elaborate on them here (for a theoretical and methodological discussion, see Dörnyei, 2001a, 2001b). Self-motivating strategies, however, are a relatively unknown and underutilized area, so let us look at them in more detail.

Self-motivating strategies can be characterized, using Corno's (1993) words, "as a dynamic system of psychological control processes that protect concentration and directed effort in the face of personal and/or environmental distractions, and so aid learning and performance" (p. 16). That is, they involve ways for the learners to motivate themselves and thereby sustain the action when the initial motivation is flagging. These strategies are particularly important in second language learning because due to the longlasting nature of the process, L2 learners need to maintain their commitment and effort over a long period, often in the face of adversity. Let us not forget that failure in language learning is regrettably a very frequent phenomenon worldwide.

Based on the pioneering work of Corno (1993), Corno and Kanfer (1993), and Kuhl (1987), Dörnyei (2001a) has divided self-motivating strategies into five main classes:

- *Commitment control strategies* for helping to preserve or increase the learners' original goal commitment (e.g., keeping in mind favorable expectations or positive incentives and rewards; focusing on what would happen if the original intention failed)
- *Metacognitive control strategies* for monitoring and controlling concentration, and for curtailing unnecessary procrastination (e.g., identifying recur-

ring distractions and developing defensive routines; focusing on the first steps to take when getting down to an activity)
- *Satiation control strategies* for eliminating boredom and adding extra attraction or interest to the task (e.g., adding a twist to the task; using one's fantasy to liven up the task)
- *Emotion control strategies* for managing disruptive emotional states or moods, and for generating emotions that will be conducive to implementing one's intentions (e.g., self-encouragement; using relaxation and meditation techniques)
- *Environmental control strategies* for eliminating negative environmental influences and exploiting positive environmental influences by making the environment an ally in the pursuit of a difficult goal (e.g., eliminating distractions; asking friends to help and not to allow one to do something)

An important part of a motivational teaching practice that has a considerable empowering effect is to raise student awareness of relevant strategies and to remind them at appropriate times of their usefulness.

Encouraging Positive Retrospective Self-Evaluation

A large body of research has shown that the way learners feel about their past accomplishments and the amount of satisfaction they experience after successful task completion will significantly determine how they approach subsequent learning tasks. Strangely enough, the students' appraisal of their past performance depends not only on the absolute, objective level of the success they have achieved but also on how they subjectively interpret their achievement (which is why, for example, we find so many people being regularly dissatisfied despite their high-quality work). However, by using appropriate strategies, teachers can help learners to evaluate their past performance in a more "positive light," take more satisfaction in their successes and progress, and explain their past failures in a constructive way. This latter area is related to the role attributions, which is an issue practicing teachers are usually unfamiliar with even though it has been a central topic in educational psychology.

The term *attribution* has been used in motivational psychology to refer to the explanation people offer about why they were successful or, more importantly, why they failed in the past. Past research had identified a certain hierarchy of the types of attributions people make in terms of their motivating nature. Failure that is ascribed to stable and uncontrollable factors such as low ability has been found to hinder future achievement behavior, whereas failure that is attributed to unstable and controllable factors such as effort is less detrimental in that it can be remedied. Thus, the general recommendation in the literature is to try and promote effort attributions and prevent ability attributions in the students as much as possible. In failure situations, this can be achieved by emphasizing the low effort exerted as being a strong reason for underachievement, and if failure occurs in spite of hard work, we should highlight the inadequacy of the strategies employed.

Finally, no account of classroom motivation would be complete without discussing the controversial but very salient effects of various forms of feedback, rewards, and grades dispensed by the teacher. As these are all forms of external evaluation by authority figures, they have a particularly strong impact on the students' self-appraisal. Feedback has at least three functions:

1. Appropriate motivational feedback can have a gratifying function, that is, by offering praise it can increase learner satisfaction and lift the learning spirit.
2. By communicating trust and encouragement, motivational feedback can promote a positive self-concept and self-confidence in the student.
3. Motivational feedback should be informative, prompting the learner to reflect constructively on areas that need improvement.

However, we should note that one common feature of educational feedback—its controlling and judgmental nature (that is, comparing students against peer achievement or external standards)—is considered very harmful (Good & Brophy, 2002).

While feedback is generally considered a useful motivational tool when applied sensitively, rewards and grades (the latter being a form of rewards) are usually disapproved of by educational psychologists. This is all the more surprising because most teachers feel that rewards are positive things and dispense them liberally for good behavior and praiseworthy efforts or accomplishments. So what's wrong with rewards?

The problem with rewards and with grades in particular is that they are very simplistic devices and they can do a great deal of damage. Rewards in themselves do not increase the inherent value of the learning task or task outcome, and neither do they concern other important learning aspects such as the learning process, the learning environment, or the learner's self-concept. Instead, all they do is simply attach a piece of "carrot or stick" to the task. By doing so, they divert the students' attention away from the real task and the real point of learning. When people start concentrating on the reward rather than on the task itself, they can easily succumb to the "mini-max principle" (Covington & Teel, 1996), whereby they attempt to maximize rewards with a minimum of effort. Indeed, we find that many students become grade driven, if not "grade grubbing," surprisingly early in their school career (Covington, 1999). Also, due to their ultimate importance in every facet of the education system, grades frequently become equated in the minds of school children with a sense of self-worth; that is, they consider themselves only as worthy as their school-related achievements, regardless of their personal characteristics such as being loving, good, or courageous. This is obviously a complex issue (for a more detailed discussion, see Dörnyei, 2001a; Good & Brophy, 2002; Pintrich & Schunk, 2001), but it is clear that we need to be cautious with rewards and grades and should try and rely on other forms of motivational practices as much as possible.

CONCLUSIONS

This overview has demonstrated that the quality of the classroom environment is made up of a number of varied ingredients. And just as in cooking, achieving an optimal, motivating outcome can be done using different combinations of spices: while some chefs rely on paprika and build the recipe around it, others prefer pepper and the herbs that go with it. The situation is exactly the same in developing a motivating teaching practice. As long as we are aware of the vast repertoire of techniques that are at our disposal, it is up to us to choose the specific ones that we will apply, based on the specific needs that arise in our concrete circumstances. There is only one thing we should not attempt: to try and apply all the techniques we know at the same time. This would be the perfect recipe for teacher burnout. What we need is quality rather than quantity; some of the most motivating teachers often rely on a few well-selected basic techniques.

REFERENCES

Brophy, J. E. (1998). *Motivating students to learn.* Boston, MA: McGraw-Hill.
Cohen, E. (1994). *Designing groupwork* (2nd ed.). New York: Teachers College Press.
Corno, L. (1993). The best-laid plans: Modern conceptions of volition and educational research. *Educational Researcher, 22,* 14–22.
Corno, L., & Kanfer, R. (1993). The role of volition in learning and performance. *Review of Research in Education, 19,* 301–341.
Covington, M. (1999). Caring about learning: The nature and nurturing of subject-matter appreciation. *Educational Psychologist, 34,* 127–136.
Covington, M., & Teel, K. (1996). *Overcoming student failure: Changing motives and incentives for learning.* Washington, DC: American Psychological Association.
Dörnyei, Z. (2001a). *Motivational strategies in the language classroom.* Cambridge: Cambridge University Press.
Dörnyei, Z. (2001b). *Teaching and researching motivation.* Harlow: Longman.
Dörnyei, Z. & Malderez, A. (1997). Group dynamics and foreign language teaching. *System, 25,* 65–81.
Dörnyei, Z., & Malderez, A. (1999). Group dynamics in foreign language learning and teaching. In J. Arnold (Ed.), *Affective language learning* (pp. 155–169). Cambridge: Cambridge University Press.
Dörnyei, Z., & Murphey, T. (2003). *Group dynamics in the language classroom.* Cambridge: Cambridge University Press.
Ehrman, M., & Dörnyei, Z. (1998). *Interpersonal dynamics in second language education: The visible and invisible classroom.* Thousand Oaks, CA: Sage.
Forsyth, D. (1999). *Group dynamics* (3rd ed.). Pacific Grove, CA: Brooks/Cole.
Fraser, B., & Walberg, H. (Eds.). (1991). *Educational environments: Evaluation, antecedents and consequences.* Oxford: Pergamon.
Good, T., & Brophy, J. (2002). *Looking in classrooms* (9th Ed.). Needham Heights, MA: Allyn & Bacon.
Heron, J. (1999). *The complete facilitator's handbook.* London: Kogan Page.
Hook, P., & Vass, A. (2000). *Confident classroom leadership.* London: David Fulton.
Jones, F., & Jones, L. (2000). *Comprehensive classroom management: Creating communities of support and solving problems* (6th ed.). Needham Heights, MA: Allyn & Bacon.
Kuhl, J. (1987). Action control: The maintenance of motivational states. In F. Halish & J. Kuhl (Eds.), *Motivation, intention, and volition* (pp. 279–291). Berlin: Springer.
Lewin, K., Lippitt, R., & White, R. (1939). Patterns of aggressive behavior in experimentally created 'social climate.' *Journal of Psychology, 10,* 271–299.
McCombs, B., & Whisler, J. (1997). *The learner-centered classroom and school: Strategies for increasing student motivation and achievement.* San Francisco, CA: Jossey-Bass.
Pintrich, P., & Schunk, D. (2002). *Motivation in education: Theory, research and applications* (2nd ed.). Englewood Cliffs, NJ: Prentice Hall.
Rogers, C. (1983). *Freedom to learn for the 80's.* Columbus, OH: Merrill.
Schmuck, R., & Schmuck, P. (2001). *Group processes in the classroom* (8th ed.). Boston, MA: McGraw-Hill.
Senior, R. (1997). Transforming language classes into bonded groups. *ELT Journal, 51,* 3–11.
Senior, R. (2002). A class-centred approach to language teaching. *ELT Journal, 56,* 397–403.
Wlodkowski, R. (1986). *Enhancing adult motivation to learn.* San Francisco, CA: Jossey-Bass.

CHAPTER 44

AUTONOMY AND ITS ROLE IN LEARNING

PHILIP BENSON

The Hong Kong Institute of Education, China

ABSTRACT

This chapter discusses the development of the concept of autonomy in ELT and makes particular reference to its role in helping teachers come to terms with changing landscapes of teaching and learning. It then goes on to outline what we know about autonomy and its implementation to date and to discuss three current issues of concern: the social character of autonomy, learners' knowledge of the learning process, and teacher autonomy. The chapter concludes by indicating possible future developments in the field.

AUTONOMY IN LEARNING: WHAT IT IS AND WHERE IT COMES FROM

In the field of political philosophy, autonomy signifies "the free choice of goals and relations as an essential ingredient of personal well-being" (Raz, 1986, p. 369). The fundamental idea in autonomy, according to Young (1986, p. 35), "is that of authoring one's own world without being subject to the will of others." In this broad sense, *personal autonomy* has long been an acknowledged goal of education systems that seek to develop individuals who are capable of free and critical participation in the societies in which they live. The acknowledgment of this goal does not, however, necessarily imply the exercise of autonomy within the learning process itself. As Boud (1988) observes, "as long as autonomy remains an abstract concept divorced from any particular situation, it can be an ideal to which we can aspire but it is not something that we can realistically expect to emerge from any given course" (p. 20).

Thus, although the concept of personal autonomy provides a point of reference, theorists of autonomy in learning are especially concerned with learners' active participation in the day-to-day processes of their learning. This participation is seen as being both essential to the development of personal autonomy and beneficial to the learning process itself. In this sense, the origins of the idea of autonomy in language learning lie more in the radically student-centered educational thought of writers such as Dewey (1916), Freire (1970), Illich (1971), and Rogers (1969); in work on adult self-directed learning by writers such as Brookfield (1986), Candy (1991), Knowles (1975), and Tough (1971); and in work on the psychology of learning by writers such as Kelly (1963), Barnes (1976), Kolb (1984), and Vygotsky (1978).

The theory and practice of *autonomy in language learning* was first developed systematically in the 1970s in the context of the Council of Europe's Modern Languages Project, which at that time aimed to provide adults with opportunities for lifelong foreign language learning. Since the early 1980s, autonomy has become an increasingly important concept in foreign language education, and a number of books, collections of papers, and journal special issues have appeared (e.g., Barfield & Nix, 2003; Benson, 2001; Benson & Toogood, 2002; Benson & Voller, 1997; Brookes & Grundy, 1988; Cotterall & Crabbe, 1999; Dam, 1995; Dickinson, 1987; Dickinson & Wenden, 1995; Holec, 1988; Little, 1991; Palfreyman & Smith, 2003; Pemberton, Li, Or, & Pierson, 1996; Riley, 1985; Sinclair, McGrath, & Lamb, 2000). Indeed, it is mainly within the field of language education that the theory and practice of autonomy in learning has developed in recent years. Before discussing the concept of autonomy in more detail, it is therefore worth pausing to consider why it has come to have a particular resonance for language teachers and researchers.

The Significance of Autonomy in ELT

Gremmo and Riley (1995) have suggested that the rise of the concept of autonomy in learning in the 1970s corresponded to an ideological shift away from consumerism and materialism towards an emphasis on the value of personal experience, quality of life, personal freedom, and minority rights. In its origins, therefore, autonomy was an antiauthoritarian idea, which was, even in the late 1980s, often "associated with a radical restructuring of language pedagogy, a restructuring that involves the rejection of the traditional classroom and the introduction of wholly new ways of working" (Allwright, 1988, p. 35). These new ways of working, as they were developed at the Centre de Recherches et d'Applications en Langues (CRAPEL) at the University of Nancy, France, and elsewhere, included self-access (Riley & Zoppis, 1985) and learner training (Holec, 1980), two modes of practice that were specifically intended to foster autonomy.

The more widespread current interest in the concept of autonomy could be seen as a sign of growing acceptance of its radical implications within the ELT community. However, this acceptance also has much to do with changes in the landscape of ELT as a social and economic practice over the past two decades. In particular, rapid increases in the number and variety of language learners in educational institutions and new conceptions of the successful learner are already making the radical restructuring of language pedagogy, to which Allwright (1988) referred, a reality. In particular, autonomy-related practices have been widely accepted by ELT providers for reasons that often have little to do with fostering autonomy in learning. In this context, the concept of autonomy serves less as a focal point for educational reform and more as a means of identifying the interests of learners within this changing landscape of teaching and learning.

The nature of the changes to which I am referring is illustrated by two articles on British ELT published in the *Guardian Weekly*. In the first of these, Schellekens (2001) observed that, in the previous year, approximately 600,000 adults had come to the UK to learn English and that a further 100,000 permanent settlers had received ELT. She also noted that 546,000 schoolchildren had been identified as speakers of English as an additional language, although the number actually receiving ELT support was not known. The implication of such figures is that very large numbers of individuals with varying needs (including ESL tourists, professionals, immigrants and their children, and asylum seekers) now receive ELT in a wide variety of commercial and non-commercial institutional contexts.

In this context, which has its parallels elsewhere in the world, language teaching institutions are increasingly open to "flexible" ways of meeting the diverse learning needs of growing student numbers. In a companion piece in the same issue of the *Guardian Weekly*, for example, Blue (2001) noted that many universities had recently created self-access multimedia resource centers and that, although English for academic purposes (EAP) classes still took place, "many students opt for independent language learning, either alongside support classes, or in some cases, as an alternative to attending classes" (p. 3). Distance learning, which increasingly involves Internet-based learning, is also an option for flexible delivery that is growing in importance—the Open University in the UK, for example, now offers foreign language diplomas to more than 5,000 distance students (Hurd, 2001). At the same time, there is a tendency for classroom-based courses to become shorter and more intensive. Whether these classroom courses are connected to some formalized process of independent learning or not, there is an increasing emphasis on support for independent learning as a legitimate use of classroom time.

The changing nature of the international labor market, combined with ideologies of globalization, the information age, and the knowledge economy is also leading to a focus on flexibility in learning. Successful learners are increasingly seen less as individuals who are responsive to instruction and more as individuals who are capable of instructing and training themselves. Little (1996) has noted, for example, a convergence between ideas of autonomy in learning and new management styles such as Total Quality Management. Learning-to-learn skills, in particular, are becoming a key theme of educational policy around the world. In Hong Kong, for example, the idea of learning to learn has been advertised on TV as one element in a proposed educational reform that is supported at the highest official levels (Benson, 2004).

One of the consequences of these changes is that autonomy-related practices and ideas are often imposed upon teachers from above. The reasons for change are often economic, either in the narrow sense of providing language learning opportunities at minimum cost or in the broader sense of a perceived need to meet the demands of changing labor markets. In this context, change may represent both an opportunity and a threat as valid concerns are raised about the quality of learning and the role of teachers in new modes of learning. Discussion of the concept of autonomy represents a way of making sense of these new modes of learning and of ensuring that their implementation genuinely serves the interests of their learners. Also, as Breen and Mann (1997) have suggested, interest in autonomy among teachers may be related to a much broader "sense that the locus of control over their work is shifting away from themselves and their immediate institutions to centralized bureaucracies." (p. 16). Personal uncertainty and feelings of powerlessness, they argue, may well be leading teachers to "question the culture of 'authority' as it manifests itself towards the end of the century, including that which they themselves represent as teachers."

To ascribe the current interest in autonomy in ELT exclusively to the success of the work of those who have advocated it in the past would therefore be a mistake. But it would be equally wrong to suggest that the idea of autonomy in learning has entirely lost its earlier radical character. The changing landscape of ELT presents us with a complex picture, in which the economic and pragmatic interests of ELT providers interact with teachers' perceptions of the nature of teaching and learning in the context of global debate over what it means to be an educated person in the twenty-first century. Within this changing and dynamic landscape, the concept of autonomy continues to play a role as a point of reference for the interests of the learner in ELT.

RESEARCH FINDINGS

A great deal of the research in the field of autonomy to date has focused on two questions: How should we define and describe autonomy? And how is autonomy best fostered through the teaching and learning process?

Defining Autonomy

Research aimed at the definition of autonomy in learning is important for the simple reason that, if we are to foster autonomy, we need know what it is that we are trying to foster. Holec (1979/1981) defined autonomy as "the ability to take charge of one's own learning" (p. 3). This often-quoted definition has stood the test of time and has worked well as a broad framework for research and practice. In order to define autonomy more delicately, however, we need to specify what *taking charge of one's own language learning* means. Elaborating on his definition, Holec (p. 3) mentioned determining objectives, content, and progression, selecting methods and techniques, monitoring acquisition, and evaluating what has been acquired—the key behaviors involved in the self-management of learning. Other researchers, however, have placed greater emphasis on the psychological capacities underlying these behaviors. A later definition of autonomy offered by Little (1991, based on a much longer definition agreed upon at a conference in Bergen, Norway, and reprinted in Dam, 1995, pp. 1-2), for example, argues that

> Autonomy is a *capacity*—for detachment, critical reflection, decision-making, and independent action. It presupposes, but also entails, that the learner will develop a particular kind of psychological relation to the process and content of his learning. The capacity for autonomy will be displayed both in the way the learner learns and in the way he or she transfers what has been learned to wider contexts. (p. 4)

Researchers are, however, broadly agreed that autonomy involves abilities and capacities that are both behavioral and psychological. One of the problems in defining autonomy in any concise way, however, lies in the sheer number of abilities and capacities that could be listed under the heading of autonomy. Candy (1991, pp. 459-466), for example, has identified more than 100 competencies associated with autonomy in the literature. Ultimately, there is also a concern that any competency associated with good learning could be listed as a competency involved in autonomy.

One alternative to attempting to define the construct of autonomy precisely is to accept that it can take a variety of forms. Elsewhere, I have suggested that autonomy might be located in any combination of directly or indirectly observable behaviors in which control over an aspect of the learning process is displayed (Benson, 2001). I have also suggested that, in the context of language learning, these behaviors can be concerned with control over the management of learning, the cognitive processes involved in second language acquisition, or the content of learning. Although this does not solve the problem of concise definition, it does allow for the coexistence of differences of emphasis and for the identification of observable behaviors associated with autonomy through empirical research.

Little (1990, p. 7) has also provided us with a remarkably useful definition of what autonomy is not. He argues that autonomy is (a) not a synonym for self-instruction, (b) not a matter of letting learners get on with things as best they can, (c) not a teaching method, (d) not a single easily described behavior, and (e) not a steady state. This definition of what autonomy is not is probably more widely accepted within the field than any definition of what autonomy is! Its value lies, in part, in its emphasis on attributes of the learner, as opposed to the learning situation, and, in part, on its emphasis on the fact that autonomy is likely to be displayed variably both from learner to learner and from context to context.

Fostering Autonomy

One of the questions often asked of advocates of autonomy is whether greater autonomy, in fact, leads to more effective language learning. This is a legitimate question because, in the context of language learning programs, autonomy is rarely an end in itself. It is, however, important to make a distinction between two issues: the relationship between autonomy and learning and the effectiveness of our attempts to foster autonomy in practice.

On the first of these issues, Little (1994) argues that "all genuinely successful learning is in the end autonomous" (p. 341). Support for this argument is found principally within constructivist approaches to the theory of learning, where it is assumed that knowledge leading to a change in the learner's systems of meaning is of a higher order than knowledge leading to the accumulation of facts or enhancement of skills. This higher-order knowledge, it is argued, cannot be taught and demands the learner's active participation in the learning process. In the context of language learning, it could be argued, the genuinely successful learners are those who succeed in constructing the target language system as a system for the interpretation and communication of their own meanings, a process that necessarily involves some degree of control over management, acquisition, and content. Thus, if we assume that the goal of language teaching and learning is not simply the accumulation of facts and technical skills, autonomous language learning is, almost by definition, equivalent to effective language learning.

But this theoretical premise does not imply that our efforts to foster autonomy will necessarily lead to more effective language learning in practice. Our efforts are necessarily mediated through modes of learning of various kinds, and it is principally the effectiveness of these modes of learning in fostering autonomy that is open to question. Studies that have succeeded in empirically demonstrating the effectiveness of any mode of teaching of learning in fostering autonomy are, in fact, few, and, as Sinclair (1999) has pointed out, there is currently "little evidence to suggest that learners who have followed a programme that promotes greater learner responsibility develop greater language proficiency than those who do not" (p. 97). One reason for this is that the assessment of gains in autonomy is problematic in itself. In particular, many of the psychological attributes associated with autonomy are not directly observable, and the display, or lack of display, of directly observable behaviors associated with self-management of learning can be misleading. Breen and Mann (1997, p. 52), for example, have suggested that learners who are explicitly expected to develop autonomy may simply "put on the mask of autonomous behaviour" in order to show they meet the goals of a course. Sinclair (1999), on the other hand, considers the case of a learner working on a reading task in a self-access, who gets up to ask the adviser on duty the meaning of a word. While this behavior may seem to represent a lack of autonomy, she argues, it could represent the opposite if it were the outcome of a careful consideration of various options for finding out the meaning of the word. The essence of autonomous behavior, in other words, does not lie in the behavior itself, but in the fact that it is authentic, self-initiated, and considered—factors that are extremely difficult to assess.

Researchers have, however, explored methods of measuring gains in autonomy with some degree of success. In a study of learners using self-instructional materials, for example, Rosewell and Libben (1994) devised an inventory of *autonomously controlled tasks* based on diary entries indicating when the learners deviated from the instructions in the materials. Simmons and Wheeler (1995) analyzed the discourse of meetings in which course content and procedures were discussed in order to find out the extent to which learners actually participated in the decision-making process. And Sinclair (1999) has devised a method of questioning students in order to discover the extent of their *metacognitive awareness*, or their awareness of the processes underlying their approach to learning tasks. Questions such as *What did you do?* and *What else could you have done?* might, for example, reveal more about the learner's capacity for autonomous behavior in the context of a task than direct observation of the way in which the task was actually performed. Each of these methods has succeeded in discriminating among individual learners and measuring change over time. At the same time, it should be emphasized that each method is context bound and measures a particular aspect of control over the learning process rather than the more global construct of autonomy itself.

Difficulties in assessing gains in autonomy clearly underlie difficulties in assessing the relationship between any such gains and language proficiency (to date the best indicator that we have of effective language learning). Important work in this area has, however, been carried out by Dam and Legenhausen, who found that students in autonomous classrooms in Denmark developed greater proficiency in aspects of vocabulary, grammar, and spoken communication than students in more traditional classrooms in Denmark and Germany (Dam & Legenhausen, 1996; Legenhausen, 1999a, 1999b, 1999c). Although Dam and Legenhausen acknowledge that their results are problematic from an experimental point of view (in particular, the comparability of the groups observed is questionable), they do show conclusively that the attempts of Dam and her colleagues to foster autonomy are not harmful to their students' language learning. This conclusion is all the more significant because their work (described in detail in Dam, 1995), represents the single most sustained attempt to foster autonomy in language learning reported in the literature to date. Much of the research in this area, it should be noted, is based on short-term interventions, which, if it is acknowledged that the development of autonomy is a long-term process, are unlikely to yield valid or reliable results.

CURRENT DEBATES AND CONCERNS

Important as the evaluation of our attempts to foster autonomy may be, current debates within the field tend to be related more to developing theoretical and philosophical issues. Here, I will discuss three of these issues: the social dimensions of autonomy, learners' knowledge of the learning process, and teacher autonomy.

The Social Dimensions of Autonomy

In its early days, the theory and practice of autonomy in language learning enjoyed an uneasy relationship with the notion of *individualization*, especially in collections of papers that covered both areas (Altman & James, 1980; Brookes & Grundy, 1988; Geddes & Sturtridge, 1982). The insistence that autonomy be defined as a capacity of the individual learner, an emphasis on methods of meeting individual needs, and the fact that the term *autonomy* was occasionally used loosely to describe situations in which learners studied on their own led to concern about an inherent individualism within the concept. Countering this concern, more recent work has tended to stress the social character of autonomy. Kohonen (1992), for example, has argued that autonomy involves "being responsible for one's own conduct in the social context: being able to cooperate with others and solve conflicts in constructive ways" (p. 19), while Little (1996) has argued that "a capacity to participate fully and critically in social interactions" is central to autonomy (p. 210).

Concerns about social dimensions of autonomy have largely been addressed in the context of a shift in the locus of the practice away from self-access and learner training towards classroom and curriculum-based approaches, including experiential learning (Kohonen, 1992, 2000), the process or negotiated syllabus (Breen & Littlejohn, 2000), project learning (Legutke & Thomas, 1991; Ribé & Vidal, 1993), and cooperative and collaborative learning (Littlewood, 2002). Debate has also begun on the more general nature of the social interactions within classroom and curriculum practice that are likely to foster autonomy. Crabbe (1993), for example, has emphasized the nature of the minute-by-minute interaction between teachers and learners in the classroom, while Kenny (1993) has emphasized the learner's role in the determination of curriculum tasks.

Learners' Knowledge of the Learning Process

In its early days, the theory and practice of autonomy were also largely concerned with the self-management of learning. More recently emphasis has shifted towards the cognitive capacities involved in autonomous learning and in particular towards learners' knowledge. Important developments in this respect have been the forging of links between work on autonomy and work on learning strategies (e.g., Cohen, 1998; Dickinson, 1992; Wenden, 1991) and learner beliefs (Benson & Lor, 1998, 1999; Cotterall, 1995, 1999; Riley, 1997; Wenden, 1995, 1998, 1999). The central assumption in research on learner beliefs is that systems of belief condition learning behavior. Cotterall (1995, p. 195) argues, therefore that the development of autonomy in a behavioral sense implies changes in the learner's beliefs. The area of learner beliefs has been described by Riley as "rather untidy," and research to date has been dogged by difficulties in defining exactly what beliefs about language learning are and how they are related to behavior. Research on metacognitive knowledge and conceptions of language learning offers some potential for a more systematic understanding of these issues.

The construct of *metacognitive knowledge* derives from work in the field of educational psychology by Flavell (1979). Wenden (1995) uses the term to describe the "stable, statable and sometimes fallible knowledge learners acquire about themselves as learners and the learning process" (p. 185). Metacognitive knowledge constitutes a specialized portion of the learner's knowledge base in regard to a particular subject matter and is distinct from the learner's knowledge of its content. Flavell classifies this knowledge in terms of three categories of *person, task,* and *strategic knowledge*. In the context of language learning, person knowledge includes general knowledge of factors that facilitate or inhibit learning and specific knowledge of the ways in which these factors apply in the learner's own experience. Task knowledge involves knowledge of the purpose, nature, and demands of the tasks involved in learning a language. Strategic knowledge involves general knowledge of what language learning strategies are and specific knowledge about how and when to use them (Wenden, 1998). The importance of the construct of metacognitive knowledge lies in an assumption that it is learners' knowledge of the language learning process that underlies their ability to employ the planning, monitoring, and evaluation strategies that are associated with autonomous learning behavior. "If they fail to make contact with a rich knowledge base," she argues, "these three strategies are weak" (pp. 518-519).

The construct of conceptions of language learning also derives from work in field of educational psychology by Marton and his associates. According to Marton, Dall'Alba, & Beaty (1993), a conception of learning refers to a distinct conception of the ontological status of learning, or what the objects and processes involved in learning are from the learner's point of view. Research by Benson and Lor (1998, 1999) has suggested that conceptions of learning may be also contextualized within conceptions of the phenomena towards which learning efforts are directed. In other words, learners' conceptions of what the target language is and what the process of learning it involves will tend to condition specific beliefs about language learning.

The constructs of metacognitive knowledge and conceptions of language learning both point to the importance of the development of learners' knowledge of the learning process in the development of autonomy. Also, because both of these constructs have been shown to be describable on the basis of learners' accounts of their learning, they appear to hold considerable potential for a better understanding of the long-term processes involved in the development of autonomy and of learners' responses to our attempts to foster autonomy through the teaching and learning process.

Teacher Autonomy

A third important area of current debate concerns the role of teachers in the development of learner autonomy. Discussion of teacher autonomy has two major origins. First, it has long been clear that in order to foster autonomy, teachers must possess capacities that correspond in some sense to those that they expect to develop within their learners. The ways in which these capacities are translated into teaching behavior has therefore become a matter of concern (Crabbe, 1993; Little, 1995; Voller, 1997). Second, as the theory and practice of autonomy has matured, it has become a matter of concern within teacher education, where it is strongly linked to the idea of the teacher as *reflective practitioner* (Lamb, 2000; McGrath, 2000; Thavenius, 1999; Vieira, 1999). As Aoki (2002) points out, teacher autonomy may mean one of two things: teachers' ability to help their learners towards autonomy, or their freedom to exercise their professional competence and judgment to teach what and how they think best. This second aspect of teacher autonomy, which involves what have been described as *constraints on autonomy*, is linked to the first aspect because teachers often find that constraints on their freedom restrict their opportunities to foster autonomy among their learners. Although Benson (2000) has made an initial attempt to model constraints on teacher autonomy (which range from immediate conditions of employment to broader issues concerned with methods and ideologies of teaching and learning), there is considerable potential for future research in this area.

FUTURE DIRECTIONS

The three areas of debate and concern discussed in the previous section are perhaps indicative of a fundamental shift in the focus of theory and practice in the field of autonomy that is likely to continue in the future. At the root of this shift is the fact that autonomy is now seen less as a clearly definable goal that can be achieved through clearly definable methods, and more as a guiding concept that is relevant to varied fields of practice within ELT. Better understanding of the social dimensions of autonomous learning, in particular, has established the relevance of the idea of autonomy to a wide range of modes of teaching and learning. Research into learners' knowledge of the learning process and teacher autonomy is also important in this respect because it helps us to understand both the roles in which learners and teachers are cast within particular modes of teaching and learning and the possibilities for modifying these roles. In this sense, the idea of autonomy serves as a compass within changing and increasingly varied landscapes of teaching and learning. The questions that researchers are now asking, therefore, are much less concerned with the modes of practice that are most likely to foster autonomy, and much more concerned with the possibilities for any given mode of practice to lead either in the broad direction of autonomy or away from it. In view of this development, we see considerable potential for dialogue between researchers in the field of autonomy and researchers in other fields of ELT in the future.

One aspect of this dialogue is likely to involve further development of research into the qualitative nature of teacher-learner interaction and the experience of language learning and language teaching. Here we may perhaps expect the field of autonomy to benefit especially from fields such as classroom interaction and teacher education, in which participatory, ethnographic, reflective, biographical methods have been used. We may also expect greater emphasis in research on the long-term development of autonomy as we begin to investigate the ways in which learners move through varied contexts of learning in the course of their language learning careers and the ways in which their knowledge and identities develop (see, for example, Benson & Nunan, 2002, 2004). This emphasis will inevitably lead us to pay much greater attention to out-of-class learning, an area that has, perhaps surprisingly, attracted little attention in the field of autonomy in the past. Here, links with sociocultural and critical perspectives on language learning may also be forged as we begin to look more closely at relationships between the long-term development of autonomy and social contexts of learning.

A second aspect of this dialogue is likely to involve greater prominence for the idea of autonomy in other fields of language learning research. When the idea of autonomy enters other fields, it often does so as a potential guiding concept for theory and practice. This has already been seen, for example, in the fields of strategy training (e.g., Cohen, 1998; Wenden, 1991), computer-assisted language learning (e.g., Healy, 1999; Warschauer, Turbee, & Roberts, 1996), the learner-centered approach (e.g., Nunan, 1996, 1997), communicative language learning (Breen & Mann, 1997; Littlewood, 1997, 1999), and motivation (Dörnyei, 2001; Ushioda, 1996). The inclusion of a chapter on autonomy in Nation's (2001) recent book on vocabulary learning, however, represents a new departure and perhaps the promise that the idea of autonomy will become as pervasive within the broader field of language learning as ideas such as communication and authenticity have become in the past.

REFERENCES

Allwright, R. L. (1988). Autonomy and individualization in whole-class instruction. In A. Brookes & P. Grundy (Eds.), *Individualization and autonomy in language learning* (pp. 35–44). ELT Documents, 131. London: Modern English Publications and the British Council.

Altman, H. B., & James, C. V. (Eds.). (1980). *Foreign language teaching: Meeting individual needs.* Oxford: Pergamon.

Aoki, N. (2002). Aspects of teacher autonomy: Capacity, freedom, and responsibility. In P. Benson & S. Toogood (Eds.), *Learner autonomy: Challenges to research and practice* (pp. 11–124). Dublin: Authentik.

Barfield, A., & Nix, M. (Eds.) (2003). *Learner and teacher autonomy in Japan 1: Autonomy you ask!* Tokyo: Learner Development Special Interest Group of the Japan Association of Language Teachers.

Barnes, D. (1976). *From communication to curriculum.* Harmondsworth: Penguin.

Benson, P. (2000). Autonomy as a learners' and teachers' right. In B. Sinclair, I. McGrath, & T. Lamb (Eds.), *Learner autonomy, teacher autonomy: Future directions* (pp. 111–117). London: Longman.

Benson, P. (2001). *Teaching and researching autonomy in language learning.* London: Longman.

Benson, P. (2002). Autonomy and communication. In P. Benson & S. Toogood (Eds.), *Learner autonomy: Challenges to research and practice* (pp. 10–28). Dublin: Authentik.

Benson, P. (2004). Autonomy and information technology in the educational discourse of the information age. In C. Davison (Ed.) *Information technology and innovation in language education.* (pp. 173–192). Hong Kong: Hong Kong University Press.

Benson, P., & Lor, W. (1998). *Making sense of autonomous language learning: Conceptions of learning and readiness for autonomy* (English Centre Monograph, No. 2). Hong Kong: University of Hong Kong, English Centre.

Benson, P., & Lor, W. (1999). Conceptions of language and language learning. *System, 27*, 459–472.

Benson. P., & Nunan, D. (Eds.) (2002). Special issue on the experience of language learning. *Hong Kong Journal of Applied Linguistics, 7*(2).

Benson. P., & Nunan, D. (Eds.) (2004). *Learners' stories: Difference and diversity in language learning.* Cambridge: Cambridge University Press.

Benson, P., & S. Toogood (Eds.). (2002). *Learner autonomy: Challenges to research and practice.* Dublin: Authentik.

Benson, P., & Voller, P. (Eds.). (1997). *Autonomy and independence in language learning.* London: Longman.

Blue, G. (2001, 27 September–3 October). Declaring campus independence. [Supplement on Learning English]. *Guardian Weekly.* p. 3.
Boud, D. (1988). *Developing student autonomy in learning.* London: Kogan Page.
Breen, M. P., & Littlejohn, A. (Eds.). (2000). *The process syllabus: Negotiation in the language classroom.* Cambridge: Cambridge University Press.
Breen, M. P., & Mann, S. (1997). Shooting arrows at the sun: Perspectives on a pedagogy for autonomy. In P. Benson & P. Voller (Eds.), *Autonomy and independence in language learning* (pp. 132–149). London: Longman.
Brookes, A., & Grundy, P. (Eds.). (1988). *Individualization and autonomy in language learning.* (ELT Documents No. 131). Modern English Publications / British Council.
Brookfield, S. (1986). *Understanding and facilitating adult learning.* San Francisco: Jossey-Bass.
Candy, P. C. (1991). *Self-direction for lifelong learning.* San Francisco: Jossey-Bass.
Cohen, A. D. (1998). *Strategies in learning and using a second language.* London: Longman.
Cotterall, S. (1995). Readiness for autonomy: Investigating learner beliefs. *System, 23,* 195–206.
Cotterall, S. (1999). Key variables in language learning: What do learners believe about them? *System, 27,* 493–515.
Cotterall, S., & Crabbe, D. (Eds.). (1999). *Learner autonomy in language learning: Defining the field and effecting change. Bayreuth Contributions to Glottodidactics, Vol. 8.* Frankfurt am Main: Lang.
Crabbe, D. (1993). Fostering autonomy from within the classroom: The teacher's responsibility. *System, 21,* 443–452.
Dam, L. (1995). *Learner autonomy 3: From theory to classroom practice.* Dublin: Authentik.
Dam, L., & Legenhausen, L. (1996). The acquisition of vocabulary in an autonomous learning environment-the first months of beginning English. In R. Pemberton, E. Li, W. Or, & H. Pierson (Eds.), *Taking control: Autonomy in language learning* (pp. 265–280). Hong Kong: Hong Kong University Press.
Dewey, J. (1916). *Democracy and education.* New York: The Free Press.
Dickinson, L. (1987). *Self-instruction in language learning.* Cambridge: Cambridge University Press.
Dickinson, L. (1992). *Learner autonomy 2: Learner training for language learning.* Dublin: Authentik.
Dickinson, L., & Wenden, A. (Eds.). (1995). Special issue on autonomy. *System, 23.*
Dörnyei, Z. (2001). *Teaching and researching motivation.* London: Longman.
Flavell, J. H. (1979). Metacognition and cognitive monitoring: A new area of cognitive-developmental inquiry. *American Psychologist, 34,* 906–911.
Freire, P. (1970). *Pedagogy of the oppressed.* New York: Herder & Herder.
Geddes, M., & Sturtridge, G. (Eds.). (1982). *Individualisation.* London: Modern English Publications.
Gremmo, M-J., & Riley, P. (1995). Autonomy, self-direction and self-access in language teaching and learning: The history of an idea. *System, 23,* 151–164.
Healy, D. (1999). Theory and research: Autonomy and language learning. In J. Egbert & E. Hanson-Smith (Eds.), *CALL environments: Research, practice and critical issues* (pp. 391–402). Alexandria, VA: TESOL.
Holec, H. (1980). Learner training: Meeting needs in self-directed learning. In H. B. Altman & C. Vaughan James (Eds.), *Foreign language learning: Meeting individual needs* (pp. 30–45). Oxford: Pergamon.
Holec, H. (1981). *Autonomy in foreign language learning.* Oxford: Pergamon. (Original work published 1979, Strasbourg: Council of Europe).
Holec, H. (Ed.). (1988). *Autonomy and self-directed learning: Present fields of application,* Strasbourg: Council of Europe.
Hurd, S. (2001). Managing and supporting language learners in open and distance learning environments. In M. Mozzon-McPherson & R. Visman (Eds.), *Beyond language teaching towards language advising.* London: CILT, in association with the University of Hull.
Illich, I. (1971). *Deschooling society.* New York: Harper & Row.
Kelly, G. (1963). *A theory of personality.* New York: Norton.
Kenny, B. (1993). For more autonomy. *System, 21,* 431–442.
Knowles, M. (1975). *Self-directed learning: A guide for learners and teachers.* New York/Cambridge: The Adult Education Company.
Kohonen, V. (1992). Experiential language learning: Second language learning as cooperative learner education. In D. Nunan (Ed.), *Collaborative language learning and teaching* (pp. 14–39). Cambridge: Cambridge University Press.
Kohonen, V. (Ed.) (2000). *Experiential learning in foreign language education.* London: Longman.
Kolb, D. (1984). *Experiential learning: Experience as the source of learning and development.* Englewood Cliffs, NJ: Prentice Hall.

Lamb, T. (2000). Finding a voice: Learner autonomy and teacher education in an urban context. In B. Sinclair, I. McGrath, & T. Lamb (Eds.), *Learner autonomy, teacher autonomy: Future directions* (pp. 118–127). London: Longman.
Legenhausen, L. (1999a). Language acquisition without grammar instruction? The evidence from an autonomous classroom, *Revista Canaria de Estudios Ingleses, 38*.
Legenhausen, L. (1999b). The emergence and use of grammatical structures in conversational interactions: Comparing traditional and autonomous learners. In B. Mißler & U. Multhaup (Eds.), *The construction of knowledge, learner autonomy and related issues in foreign language learning* (pp. 27–40). Tübingen: Stauffenberg.
Legenhausen, L. (1999c). Traditional and autonomous learners compared: The impact of classroom culture on communicative attitudes and behaviour. In C. Edelhoff & R. Weskamp (Eds.), *Autonomes fremdsprachenlernen* (pp. 166–182). Munich: Max Hueber Verlag.
Legutke, M., & Thomas, H. (1991). *Process and experience in the language classroom.* London: Longman.
Little, D. (1990). Autonomy in language learning. In I. Gathercole (Ed.), *Autonomy in language learning* (pp. 7–15). London: CILT.
Little, D. (1991). *Learner autonomy. 1: Definitions, issues and problems.* Dublin: Authentik.
Little, D. (1994). Learner autonomy: A theoretical construct and its practical application. *Die Neueren Sprachen, 93*, 430–442.
Little, D. (1995). Learning as dialogue: The dependence of learner autonomy on teacher autonomy. *System, 23*, 175–182.
Little, D. (1996). The politics of learner autonomy. *Learning Learning, 2*, 7–10.
Littlewood, W. T. (1997). Self-access: Why do want it and what can it do? In P. Benson & P. Voller (Eds.), *Autonomy and independence in language learning* (pp. 79–92). London: Longman.
Littlewood, W. T. (1999). Defining and developing autonomy in East Asian contexts. *Applied Linguistics, 20*, 71–94.
Littlewood, W. T. (2002). Co-operative and collaborative learning tasks as pathways to autonomous interdependence. In P. Benson & S. Toogood (Eds.), *Learner autonomy: Challenges to research and practice* (pp. 29–40). Dublin: Authentik.
Marton, F., Dall'Alba, G., & Beaty, E. (1993). Conceptions of learning. *International Journal of Educational Research, 19*, 277–300.
McGrath, I. (2000). Teacher autonomy. In B. Sinclair, I. McGrath, & T. Lamb (Eds.), *Learner autonomy, teacher autonomy: Future directions* (pp. 100–110). London: Longman.
Nation, P. (2001). *Learning vocabulary in another language.* Cambridge: Cambridge University Press.
Nunan, D. (1996). Towards autonomous learning: Some theoretical, empirical and practical issues. In R. Pemberton, E. Li, W. Or, & H. Pierson (Eds.), *Taking control: Autonomy in language learning* (pp. 13–26). Hong Kong University Press.
Nunan, D. (1997). Designing and adapting materials to encourage learner autonomy. In P. Benson & P. Voller (Eds.), *Autonomy and independence in language learning* (pp. 192–203). London: Longman.
Palfreyman, D. & Smith, R. C. (Eds.) (2003). *Learner autonomy across cultures: Language education perspectives.* Basingstoke: Palgrave Macmillan.
Pemberton, R., Li, E. S. L., Or, W. W. F., & Pierson, H. D. (Eds.). (1996). *Taking control: Autonomy in language learning.* Hong Kong: Hong Kong University Press.
Raz, J. (1986). *The morality of freedom.* Oxford: Oxford University Press.
Ribé, R., & Vidal, N. (1993). *Project work.* London: Heinemann.
Riley, P. (Ed.). (1985). *Discourse and learning.* London: Longman.
Riley, P. (1997). 'BATs' and 'BALLs': Beliefs about talk and beliefs about language learning. *Autonomy 2000: The Development of Learning Independence in Language Learning.* Conference Proceedings. Bangkok: King Mongkut's Institute of Technology Thonburi.
Riley, P., & Zoppis, C. (1985). The sound and video library. In P. Riley (Ed.), *Discourse and learning* (pp. 286–298). London: Longman.
Rogers, C. R. (1969). *Freedom to learn.* Columbus, OH: Charles E. Merrill.
Rosewell, L. V., & Libben, G. (1994). The sound of one-hand clapping: How to succeed in independent language learning. *Canadian Modern Language Review, 50*, 668–688.
Schellekens, P. (2001, September 27–October 3). Three ways to teach won't do [Supplement on Learning English]. *Guardian Weekly*, p. 3.
Simmons, D., & Wheeler, S. (1995). *The process syllabus in action.* Sydney: National Centre for English Language Teaching and Research.

Sinclair, B. (1999). Wrestling with a jelly: The evaluation of learner autonomy. In B. Morrison (Ed.), *Experiments and evaluation in self-access language learning* (pp. 95–109). Hong Kong: Hong Kong Association for Self-Access Learning and Development.

Sinclair, B., McGrath, I., & Lamb, T. (Eds.). (2000). *Learner autonomy, teacher autonomy: Future directions*. London: Longman.

Thavenius, C. (1999). Teacher autonomy for learner autonomy. In S. Cotterall & D. Crabbe (Eds.), *Learner autonomy in language learning: Defining the field and effecting change* (pp. 163–166). *Bayreuth Contributions to Glottodidactics, Vol. 8*. Frankfurt am Main: Lang.

Tough, A. (1971). *The adult's learning projects*. Toronto: Ontario Institute for Studies in Education.

Ushioda, E. (1996). *Learner autonomy 5: The role of motivation*. Dublin: Authentik.

Vieira, F. (1999). Pedagogy for autonomy: Teacher development and pedagogical experimentation-an in-service teacher training project. In S. Cotterall & D. Crabbe (Eds.), *Learner autonomy in language learning: Defining the field and effecting change* (pp. 153–162). *Bayreuth Contributions to Glottodidactics, Vol. 8*. Frankfurt am Main: Lang.

Voller, P. (1997). Does the teacher have a role in autonomous learning? In P. Benson & P. Voller (Eds.), *Autonomy and independence in language learning* (pp. 98–113). London: Longman.

Vygotsky, L. S. (1978). *Mind in society: The development of higher psychological processes*. Cambridge, MA: Harvard University Press.

Warschauer, M., Turbee, L., & Roberts, B. (1996). Computer learning networks and student empowerment. *System, 24*, 1–14.

Wenden, A. L. (1991). *Learner strategies for learner autonomy*. London: Prentice Hall International.

Wenden, A. L. (1995). Learner training in context: A task-based approach to promoting autonomy. *System, 23*, 183–194.

Wenden, A. L. (1998). Metacognitive knowledge and language learning. *Applied Linguistics, 19*, 515–537.

Wenden, A. L. (Ed.). (1999). Special issue on metacognitive knowledge and beliefs in language learning, *System, 27*.

Young, R. (1986). *Personal autonomy: Beyond negative and positive liberty*. London: Croom Helm.

CHAPTER 45

CREATING A TECHNOLOGY-RICH ENGLISH LANGUAGE LEARNING ENVIRONMENT

DENISE E. MURRAY

Macquarie University, Australia

ABSTRACT

The use of computer technology in English language teaching and learning is accepted, often uncritically, in many settings, even though in other settings, computers are not available, while in still other settings, teachers and learners often lack the necessary computer literacy skills to exploit the technology effectively for language teaching and learning. While many articles and books discuss tips for using computer-based technologies in the classroom, research studies tend to be small scale and seldom generalizable. Still lacking is a rigorous approach to the study of the implementation of computer-based technologies (both how the technologies are implemented and which technologies are chosen); the effects of computer-based technologies on instruction (including effects on the role of the teacher); the effects of computer-assisted instruction on language learning; and the integration of computer-assisted instruction into curriculum design. This chapter summarizes extant research in these areas, while identifying the assumptions underlying much of the literature on the use of new technologies. The chapter also predicts, from the existing research data, what would be necessary for computers to be ubiquitous and part of teachers' repertoire of instructional approaches.

INTRODUCTION

The use of computer technology in English language teaching and learning, while no longer new, is still sufficiently new that its very naming is contested. Its role in education, and in particular in English language teaching and learning, is also contested. Yet its inclusion in instruction is not contested, despite our primitive understanding of the value of technology, and of the extent to which it is readily available, especially in language learning contexts. While many articles and books discuss tips for using computer-based technologies in the classroom, research studies tend to be small scale (e.g., Ghadirian, 2002) and seldom generalizable. In a 1996 article, Basena and Jamieson report results of a survey of the computer-assisted language learning (CALL) research literature for the period 1990-1994, concluding that "research articles examined CALL use from a variety of perspectives—so many perspectives, in fact, that identification of a coherent research agenda for the field as a whole is impossible" (p. 19). They also note that while initial findings show promise, the studies do not lend themselves to reproduction or generalizability, a situation that has not changed in the period since then. There have, however, been attempts at defining a research agenda (e.g., Dunkel, 1991), the most comprehensive being that of Chapelle (1997, 1999), who considers the most critical research questions to be those that examine learners' work on CALL and that the research methods and approaches in interactionist second language acquisition (SLA) and discourse analysis provide useful tools for investigation of this work.

TOWARDS A DEFINITION

The use of computers in language education and in English language education in particular remains an emerging field of study, largely because technological advances introduce new instructional possibilities. The past two decades have seen computer-assisted approaches move from a cluster of learners grouped around one machine, trying to solve a text-only puzzle such as *Storyboard* or going through a text-only drilling exercise, to communication between learners via computers to networked multimedia programs where students can hear authentic language, record their own, and receive feedback on their language use. Outside the field of language teaching and learning (and sometimes even within the field, especially in Europe), Information and Communications Technology (ICT) is often used to refer to the range of computer-based programs and services. Here, being *computer-based* refers only to applications where the computer is transparently assisting or delivering the program or service. This definition, therefore, excludes the multitude of applications in which the computer is invisible to the user (for example, watches, car engines, toasters). The terminology for using ICT in language teaching and learning varies considerably. *CALL*, while still used and also the title of a prestigious journal, conjures up the drill-modes of early computer-based approaches or, for others, refers only to "programs designed especially to teach language" (Brown, 1999). Quite recently, Warschauer (2001) has called for a return to the term *CALL*, arguing that the term *cyberspace* "suggests that there exists a virtual, online world that is distinct from our real world" (p. 1). But Warschauer has also rejected the notion of CALL as being simply a tool, arguing that it can empower learners and provide a space for collaborative identity creation (see, for example, Warschauer 2000). Egbert and Hanson-Smith (1999) propose "CALL or technology-enhanced environments," insisting that electronic technology presents a learning environment that can encompass the world. *Technology enhanced language learning* (TELL) also appears in the literature; but this term is evaluative, not neutral, since it assumes that the mere use of technology enhances learning. In still other arenas, the terms *computer-based instruction* (CBI) or *computer-based training* (CBT) are used. These terms place the computer at the heart of the learning-teaching enterprise, which I believe is unfortunate since it focuses on the means of instruction, and often the computer is only one among many means. It is useful, however, to refer to the technologies now being used in instruction as computer-based to distinguish them from chalkboards, audiotapes, or videotapes. For the instructional enterprise, I have purposely chosen the more neutral term, *computer-assisted*, but also have attempted to invoke the reality that using technology is not the driving force in teachers' decisions about what to do in the classroom. Rather, teachers choose from a variety of approaches, methodologies, practices, and techniques, depending on the needs of their learners.

Other terminologies also exist, many referring to specific applications of computer technology to language instruction (or instruction in general). Computer-mediated communication (CMC) is used to cover a range of modes of communication such as chat, email, instant messaging (IM), MOOs, MUDs, IRC discussion lists, listservs, all of which provide channels of communication among learners (see Glossary for an explanation of these terms). They vary on several dimensions—whether synchronous (chat) or asynchronous (email); whether one-to-one (email) or one-to-many (discussion lists); and whether "real" world (IM) or role-playing worlds (MUDs).

The *web* is often used loosely to refer to all interaction on the Internet. It is more helpful to think about the Internet—that collection of networks through which people are connected to each other and online data—as consisting of two major functions: communication and information retrieval. Communication, as we saw above, can be conducted through a variety of different modes. Information retrieval refers to the ability to access the World Wide Web to find, select, and use data.

Another aspect of computer-assisted approaches is the use of applications such as word processing, spreadsheets, and databases. While these can be accessed via networks, they can also be installed on individual PCs.

Computer literacy is yet another term with many definitions. For some, it refers to the ability to work effectively with computers. As one text for learning computer literacy states, computer literacy means knowing how to orient to electronic texts, interact with electronic texts, modify electronic texts, and integrate electronic texts into other work (Corbel, 1999, p. 1). But the critical distinction is *which* electronic texts. Many courses and discussions of computer literacy refer to skills such as reading menus, using a mouse, pointing and clicking, dropping and dragging, and so on. However, we could equally include literacies required to work in an online world, such as reading of Web pages, being able to use the results from a Web search, being able to complete online forms, and even being able to create Webpages. The use of the Internet has vastly expanded our conceptualizations of computer literacy(ies) (see also Warschauer, this volume, for an expanded discussion on electronic, including computer, literacies).

Educators have exploited all these functions to facilitate language instruction and learning. Because names convey more than their denotative meaning, for this chapter, I refer to the field as *English language teaching and learning*, rather than the simpler ELT, because it is important to focus our attention on student learning. Much of the non-researched hype on computer-assisted instruction focuses on the teacher or the computer, not on how the tasks will facilitate learning. I also have chosen to use the term *computer-assisted instruction* as a short version, where *instruction* is meant to convey both teaching and learning. This choice frees the reader from narrow interpretations of CALL as stand-alone programs, and clearly includes all of the functions mentioned above.

While the focus of this chapter is on English language teaching and learning, we can learn much from research into computer-assisted approaches to instruction and learning in general and in languages other than English. We traditionally refer to cross-disciplinary studies to gain insights into student learning. But in the case of ICT, data on general learning are especially useful, since there have been no large-scale studies of ICT in English language learning. Therefore, this chapter will also draw from selected literature in general education.

One of the uses of computer-assisted approaches is for distance learning. While there is much extant research literature on distance learning, this subject would be a chapter in itself. Therefore, in this chapter, I have chosen to focus entirely on computer-assisted approaches in classrooms and computer labs.

THE EFFECTS OF COMPUTER-BASED TECHNOLOGIES ON INSTRUCTION

As Papert (1987) and Chappelle have pointed out, it is not so much the computer but "the kinds of tasks and activities that learners do on the computer that can make the difference" (Hoven, 1999, p. 149). However, classrooms that use computer-based technologies for tasks and activities do change the context for learning by adding an additional variable to traditional variables such as learners' age, aptitude, home language, and gender; the teacher's approach to instruction; the institution's support for language learning; and the national curriculum framework. This next section explores how the introduction of this additional variable affects teaching and learning.

Teacher and Leaner Roles

Learner-centeredness has been a theme in language learning for the past two decades (see, for example, Ely & Pease-Alvarez, 1996; Nunan, 1988). Concomitant with learner-centeredness is the notion of *learner autonomy* (see, for example, Benson, this volume; Holec, 1979): the ability of the learner to take charge of his/her own learning, to make his/her own "decisions about the content, modes, order, pace, level, and level of self-direction" (Hoven, 1999, p. 150). One of the advantages claimed for computer-assisted instruction is the ability for learners to work at their own pace in their own time. Computer-assisted programs often use as a selling point that the teacher will no longer be an instructor, but a facilitator. This shift is often summarized in the rather catchy phrase of changing from "the sage on the stage" to "the guide on the side." For some teachers, this constitutes a threat to their perceived role as instructor. To others, it supports their constructivist view of learning by providing opportunities for learners to take more control of their own learning. However, while computer-based technologies can facilitate learner autonomy, they can also be used for rote learning. Some amount of learner-centeredness can be built into programs in forms such as feedback and assistance, or problem solving, or freedom for learners to navigate their own paths through the program at will, for example. However, for such learner control to be effective, learners need instruction in learning strategies—how to understand their own learning styles and how to adapt their strategies for effective language learning (see, for example, Oxford, 1990). They also need scaffolded approaches to how to use the technology to support their learning (Murray and McPherson, 2004).

One result of using some computer-based technologies such as email, especially in distance learning, is that students consider they are Socrates on one end of the log with their teacher as Plato on the other. In other words, they expect immediate and individual responses to their questions and concerns. Such a situation increases the teacher's workload considerably. For instead of a class of 40 students, the teacher has 40 classes, each with one student. Palloff and Pratt (1999), for example, claim that while face-to-face instruction requires 6 ½ to 7 ½ hours preparation per week, preparation for online instruction requires 18 to 19 hours per week. One teacher (Puetter, 2002), who had been building his own Webpages since 1991, indicated that it takes him 8 to 10 hours to design and build a lesson page, with the building of the original site taking several weeks.

Pedagogy

Chapelle (2001) suggests that "the relationship between knowledge of classroom language teaching and CALL should be considered tentative" since CALL instruction provides a different context from that of the classroom (p. 3). However, using an historical approach, Warschauer (2001, p. 6) identifies pedagogical changes within CALL. As shown in Table 1, Warschauer characterizes the three stages of CALL as *structural* in the 1970s to the 1980s, *communicative* in the 1980s to the 1990s, and *integrative* in the twenty-first century.

Table 1. The Three Stages of CALL

Stages	1970s-1980s Structural	1980s-1990s Communicative	21st century Integrative
Technology	Mainframe	PCs	Multimedia and Internet
English-teaching paradigm	Grammar-translation and audio-lingual	Communicative Language Teaching	Content-based, ESP/EAP
View of language	Structural (a formal structural system)	Cognitive (a mentally-constructed system)	Sociocognitive (developed in social interaction)
Principle use of computers	Drill and practice	Communicative exercises	Authentic discourse
Principal objective	Accuracy	And fluency	And agency

(adapted from Warschauer, 2001, p. 6)

While twenty-first century CALL may indeed be characterized as integrative, this description may be more a potential than a reality, for, as Levy (1999) notes, "Once new hardware and software have been introduced, language teachers are often left to learn to use new computer software on their own. Consequently, patterns of use are highly individualistic" (p. 26). And those patterns of use include structural and communicative CALL.

The Effects of Computer-assisted Instruction on Language Learning

While educators and administrators argue about the effectiveness of computer-based technologies, we need to remember the following:

> Technologies do not directly mediate learning. That is, people do not learn from computers, videos, or any other devices that were developed to transmit information. Rather, learning is mediated by thinking ... therefore, we should concern ourselves less with the design of technologies of transmission and more with how learners are required to think in completing different tasks. (Jonassen, 1992, p. 2)

Therefore, while it could be useful to organize the data around the different technology types, it is more beneficial to examine the research literature from the perspective of pedagogy, rather than technology. We should therefore be asking the same questions we ask about language learning in general. Chapelle (2001, 2002) has discussed what we know about using CALL by identifying six qualities or criteria for what she calls "appropriate CALL": language learning potential, learner fit, meaning focus, authenticity, positive impact, and practicality. In her summaries of examples of extant research, she notes that, while there are studies that provide evidence of language learning potential (e.g., Chun & Plass, 1996; Doughty, 1991; Hegelheimer, 1998; Hsu, 1994), learner fit (e.g., Kern, 1995; Park, 1994), meaning focus (Kelm, 1992; Kern, 1995; Park, 1994), and authenticity (e.g., Kern, 1995; Warschauer, 1995, 1996), studies that would provide evidence for impact and practicality are still to be conducted. One recent study, however, examined practicality as well as language learning potential, learner fit, and authenticity (Murray and McPherson, 2002).

I have organized the following discussion on what we now know about computer-assisted language learning around salient themes from the research: motivation, collaboration, authentic language, interaction, and finally language learning. The first four themes link what we know about language learning in classroom settings with what we are beginning to discover through research on the use of computer-assisted teaching and learning.

Motivation

Many small-scale studies note that shy students are more encouraged to use the target language in computer-assisted learning than in face-to-face conversation. This outcome has been reported across different CMC environments—MOOs (e.g., Chun, 1994; Guest, 1995; Turner, 2001), chat (Lam, 2004), and email (e.g., Bloch, 2004; Warschauer, 1999). Other studies report that student motivation is heightened; students are more interested in learning and are more likely to stay in class (e.g., Felix, 2001; Javed, 1996). While this is generally accepted wisdom, we have found in a recent study (Murray & McPherson, 2001) that some male immigrant learners refused to use computers, seeing them as "women's work"; others found the task of designing and building one's own Webpage as irrelevant (Endres, 2002); and still others felt alienated from using email because, as refugees, they had no families and friends to correspond with in their home country. Such conflicting results should not be unexpected. However, it is a salutary lesson, since much has been made of increasing student motivation as a reason for adopting computer-assisted approaches to instruction.

Collaboration

From the earliest use of the computer, research and advocates have noted its potential to encourage collaboration. "A natural side-effect of computer use [is] the interaction among students ... this may promote language development as learners provide each other with comprehensible input and negotiation of input" (Golebiowski, 1994, p. 34). Even when learners were using mainframe or text-only early PCs for drilling, with insufficient computers for each student to have one, learners grouped around a computer to jointly perform the tasks. Authentic language interactions then took place as learners jointly constructed meaning. Researchers working with CMC have often found that when instruction is designed around the completion of a group task, learners collaborate using CMC, often when they are continents apart (e.g., Shield, Weininger, & Davies, 1999; Warschauer, Shetzer, &

Meloni, 2000). However, other research has found that online collaborative learning needs to be carefully planned and scaffolded for learners to be effective (Schwienhorst, 2003).

One of the best-articulated, research-based frameworks for how computer-assisted instruction can facilitate collaboration is the work of Cummins and Sayers (1995). They propose a "transformative pedagogy [that] uses collaborative critical inquiry to relate curriculum content to students' individual and collective experience and to analyze broader social issues relevant to their lives" (p. 153). They claim that the potential of networked computers can only be realized through such a transformative pedagogy.

Authentic Language

SLA and writing research have identified the importance of authentic language, as opposed to a text or conversation produced solely for the teacher, in facilitating language acquisition because learners find it more motivating; the focus is on content, not form; and such materials provide immersion in the target language (Little, Devitt, & Singleton, 1994). Researchers such as Felix (1999) note that web-based tasks provide just such authenticity. In the use of computer-assisted instruction, they argue that:

> There appears to be a gradual shift from teacher-centred approaches, largely reflected in the explicit teaching of grammar, which exploit the technical potential of the Web, to student-centered learning, reflected in meaningful task-based activities, which exploits the new medium's unique potential for authentic learning experiences. (p. 86)

Learners can search the web for information for a particular project; they can communicate with other learners or with native speakers to achieve particular goals of a task.

However, while students enjoy the authenticity of computer-based instruction, especially CD-ROM, they also find the amount of information, especially on the web, to be a distraction. They get lost navigating, they get to inappropriate sites, they have difficulty recognizing the different elements of a Webpage, they find the authentic language overwhelming because so much is beyond their current language proficiency, and they often do not have the linguistic or experiential expertise to identify sites whose data is reliable (see, for example, Felix, 2001; Ganderton, 2001; Mansfield, 2002; Murray & McPherson, 2001).

Interaction/Opportunities to Use the Language

The communicative approach to language teaching, as well as SLA research (for example, Long, 1985) has shown that language learning is facilitated through communication, that is, through interaction between speakers of the language and the language learner.

> The L2 is acquired through learners' interaction in the target language because it provides opportunities for learners to (a) comprehend message meaning, which is believed to be necessary for learners to acquire the L2 forms that encode the message; (b) produce modified output, which requires their development of specific morphology and syntax; and (c) attend to L2 form, which helps to develop their linguistic systems. (Chapelle, 1997, p. 22)

While some computer-assisted approaches to language instruction explicitly focus on authentic communication via chat, MOOs, or email, other approaches talk of the interactivity achievable. This interactivity may refer to simple user input with appropriate responses from the computer (see, for example, Felix, 2001; Godwin-Jones, 1998) or to a more complex definition that includes learner-computer, learner-text, learner-learner interaction (see, for example, Felix, 2001; Ganderton, 2001) that is tailored to the particular learner and his/her responses (see, for example, Laurillard, 1993). However, such interactivity requires intelligent systems. Thus far, the major application of artificial intelligence (AI) has been in intelligent tutoring systems in very limited domains such as the *Pump Algebra Tutor* for high school algebra developed by the Pittsburgh Cognitive Tutor Center at Carnegie Mellon University (see, for example, Koedinger, 2001). Most other domains have been in corporate situations, since using AI is both expensive and limited. Given the complexity of language, it is unlikely that intelligent language tutoring systems will be developed for some time, if at all (see, for example, Dreyfus & Dreyfus, 1986, on the feasibility of AI). For as Woolf, Beck, Eliot, and Stern (2001), who have developed successful intelligent tutoring systems, state;

> Current instructional technology research has succeeded in exploring many domains and some nontraditional pedagogical strategies, such as partnering, mentoring and scaffolding. However, many of the rich and detailed tutoring methods used by talented teachers, such as mentoring and inquiry-based teaching and collaborative learning, still elude researchers. (pp. 142-143)

CMC, however, does provide the potential for interaction. However, is that interaction similar to or different from that in oral and written classroom language that has been shown to facilitate language acquisition? Lamy and Goodfellow (1999), in analyzing the interactions among learners using CMC, identified differences between the interactions of social conversation and those focused on the learning task. For the former, they noted, little negotiation of meaning was required and learners stayed within their current linguistic competence: For the latter, which they call "reflective conversation," learners focused on language, which the researchers claim gave learners opportunity to negotiate understanding, refer explicitly to language, and negotiate control of the discourse. With CMC, as well as having explicit conversations about their language learning online, students can save their contributions and refer to them later, giving them opportunities to notice language structures and use, such noticing having been identified as contributing to language acquisition (e.g., Doughty, 1991; Lightbown & Spada, 1990).

Classes that use real-time conferencing software or synchronous chat software find that, since there is no silent time, shy students participate more (Kern, 1995; Warschauer, 1996). However, these synchronous modes facilitate fluency, rather than accuracy. Similarly, the use of asynchronous bulletin boards or email gives all students equal opportunity to express their views (see, for example, Dabbagh, Bannan-Ritland, & Silc, 2001).

Language Learning

Since much of the extant research is case study, it is rather difficult to draw generalizable conclusions about whether computer-assisted environments result in richer language learning. Studies have shown that students using e-mail

(Biesenbach-Lucas & Weasenforth, 2001; Wang, 1993) write more text than when writing on paper or using a word processor, respectively. Wang also noted that students using email asked more questions and used more language functions than did students writing on paper. Biesenbach-Lucas and Weasenforth, however, found that there was no difference in the cohesive devices students used in the two types of writing environments. In another study on writing, Schulz (2000) found that students applied more of the changes their peers suggested in electronic feedback to their writing than they did when engaged in face-to-face conferencing. However, in the face-to-face medium, they made more global changes, which research has shown to result in better writing.

But, despite the mixed research results, many teachers anecdotally report similar findings to the following: "Students' casual writing became at ease as most lessons gave them the opportunity to have a real and varied audience. They got excited to check in their e-mail and reply straight away and in ENGLISH!!!" (Haimd, 2002, p. 6).

CURRENT DEBATES AND CONCERNS

Uptake of computer-based approaches still remains determined by issues of infrastructure, in particular, access, and pedagogic and technical support. As a result, teachers' focus is largely local—what their students' needs are, what computer-based programs and facilities are available, when they can use the computers, what training is provided, and what support they'll receive. As teachers ask and answer these questions, they decide whether to embark on computer-based instruction. The early adopters, most of whom were willing to experiment and take risks, are already using computer-based approaches. When, and even whether, computer-based approaches will be adopted by others will depend on local infrastructure.

The Digital Divide

The *digital divide* is a catchy term that has gained wide currency to draw attention to the uneven and inequitable distribution of computer-based technologies both within and across nations. Much of the discussion around the digital divide refers to statistics of who is online, although other statistics relating to home computer ownership are also used. Recent statistics show, for example, that less than 12% of the world's population is online (Global Reach, 2004). Like all dichotomies, the division into haves and have-nots oversimplifies a very complex interaction of social, economic, political, and linguistic factors that result in differential access, which in its turn contributes to social, economic, and linguistic divisions (for a recent discussion of these complex factors, see Warschauer, 2002). However, despite the oversimplification of the term, the issue is still one of concern, especially for language educators. While there are numerous examples of the use of indigenous languages on the Web, of people in small rural villages accessing the Internet, and a recent increase in the numbers of minorities in the United States who are online, it still remains true that the language of the Internet is primarily English, people in the developing world are less likely to have access to computers, and in the more technologically advanced nations, the poor, elderly, rural dwellers, and minorities are least likely to have computers in their homes or be online (see, for example, Murray, 1999, 2004). Of additional concern for educators is that even in schools and other institutions where computers are available, English language learners may have less access to them than their native-speaker peers (Murray & McPherson, 2001).

In contradiction to this issue of access is the increasing sophisticated knowledge and use of computer-based technologies of many younger learners. This development has serious implications for one of the purported advantages of computer-assisted instruction, namely, motivation. Will learners continue to be motivated if computer-based technologies are already ubiquitous in their lives? Research indicates that learners are expecting and requiring sophisticated and professional design features in instructional technologies. Students want professionally designed screen displays that are reliable, attractive, uncluttered, and consistent (see Hémard, 1999), especially consistent with commercially available programs (Murray & McPherson, 2002). They particularly want to be able to navigate through the program with ease (Felix, 2001).

Professional Development

Until relatively recently, most teachers who have embraced computer-assisted instruction have been innovators and early adopters (Rogers, 1995), that is, teachers who either understood the technology or immediately were intrigued by its potential for language instruction. Since this group is usually around only 16% of the potential population of teachers, of major concern is whether and how other teachers will begin using computers in their instruction.

Researchers (e.g., Anderson & Nicholson, 1995; Ellis & Phelps, 2000) and practitioners (Corbel, 1996; Murray & McPherson, 2001) are unanimous in their insistence on appropriate and adequate training if teachers are to exploit the new technologies. Both Corbel and Murray and McPherson, in surveying and interviewing teachers, found that teachers needed training and technical support both before and during instruction. "Perhaps more than any other innovation it calls for support that is ready to hand, or, in the language of management, just-in-time" (Corbel, p. 57).

Visual Literacy and Hypertext

Computer-based technologies have resulted in changes to the structure of text types, with visual features increasingly becoming used to convey information, not just to support printed text, a situation that has been described as "a tectonic shift" (Kress, 1997) and "the breakout of the visual" (Bolter, 1996). To help learners navigate, comprehend, and even construct these new text types will require a clearer understanding of the grammar of visual literacy.

Similarly, many digital texts use hypertext, that system of explicitly branching and linking texts, as opposed to the often implicit intertextuality of print texts (Snyder, 1997). Just as we need a clearer understanding of visual literacy, so too we also need to examine the structure of hypertexts and how learners navigate through them.

The Integration of Computer-assisted Instruction into English Language Curriculum Design

"Finally, is it possible that students and their instructors sometimes focus only on the means (the computers) or the ends (learning the target language) rather than integrating the two?" (Basena & Jamieson, 1996, p. 19). Unfortunately, many uses of computer-assisted instruction take place in rooms separate from regular classrooms, with the result that both teachers and learners view the computer-assisted instruction as separate from what goes on in the regular classroom. This situation is exacerbated by the scheduling difficulties of being able to use computer-assisted instruction just in time and by the additional planning time it takes for a teacher to incorporate tasks and activities in the computer lab with those in the classroom. Research (e.g., Roschelle & Pea, in press) is just beginning on the use of *wireless Internet learning devices* (WILD), that is, handheld wireless computer-based devices that build on the portability of Palm devices. Such devices are neither affordable nor useable at present but will help provide physical affordability not possible with current desktops or even laptops. However, this new technology will not help solve the curriculum issue of how the teacher can seamlessly move from tasks on computer to tasks in printed text to face-to-face tasks.

Research Designs

A further common need addressed in the computer-assisted instruction literature has been to identify research questions and approaches that can describe and evaluate computer-assisted instruction (e.g., Cameron, 1995; Chapelle, 1997). This remains an issue of concern. In 1997, Chapelle called for a closer tie between research methods for instructed SLA and CALL research, arguing that

> the broad perspective of SLA classroom research holds the language of the classroom participants as central for evaluating the quality of learning. The results of such research in L2 classrooms and experimental settings have provided a clearer picture of the nature of language that occurs in classroom activities, in addition to hypotheses about the relative value for SLA of particular linguistic features." (p. 5)

More recently (1999, 2001), she has proposed a model in which she takes principles from SLA and posits parallel CALL research questions and methods. She identifies five principles as being known to be necessary for language acquisition: learners need to notice linguistic characteristics of input; learners need to have opportunities for language output; learners need to notice errors in their output; learners need to correct their output; and learners need to interact in situations where language can be modified for comprehension (adapted from Chapelle, 1999, p. 109). Other researchers have noted other areas of concern, calling for research into the sociocultural dimensions of the use of new technologies (e.g., Warschauer, 1998), local contexts (Levy, 1999), computer-mediated communication (Salaberry, 1999), classroom practices (Debski & Levy, 1999; Motteram, 1999), or learner tasks and activities (Hoven, 1999).

CONCLUSIONS

For computer-based technologies to be ubiquitous and part of teachers' repertoire of instructional approaches, educators and researchers will need to focus on learning, on what tasks and activities facilitate student learning. Computer-based technologies are neither "just a tool" nor intelligent tutors; they provide opportunities for developing the learners' communicative competence. But, to achieve that outcome, we need to understand the context (often a very local context) in which learning takes place and develop instructional activities that support interactionist and constructivist approaches to language instruction. And, once computer-assisted instruction has become integrated into instructional practice, rather than being seen as a separate instructional practice, research will focus on learning, rather than solely on the technology, as has so often been the case in CALL research over the past two decades.

REFERENCES

Anderson, M., & Nicholson, A. (1995). *New technology and curriculum design: A research project with NESB distance learning students*. Sydney: NCELTR.

Basena, D. & Jamieson, J. (1996). CALL research in second language learning: 1990–1994. *CAELL Journal*, 7(1/2), 14–22.

Biesenbach-Lucas, S., & Weasenforth, D. (2001). E-mail and word processing in the ESL classroom: How the medium affects the message. *Language, Learning & Technology*, 5(1), 135–165.

Bloch, J. (2004). Second language cyberrhetoric: A study of Chinese L2 writers in an online Usenet group. *Language, Learning and Technology*, 8(3), 66–82.

Bolter, J. D. (1996). Ekphrasis, virtual reality, and the future of writing. In G. Nunberg (Ed.), *The Future of the Book* (pp. 253–272). Berkeley: University of California Press.

Brown, K. (1999). *Using new technology in the classroom*. Sydney: NCELTR.

Cameron, K. (1995). Editorial. *Computer Assisted Language Learning*, 8(4), 293–294.

Chapelle, C. (1997). CALL in the year 2000: Still in search of research paradigms? *Language, Learning & Technology*, 1(1), 19–43. Retrieved January 11, 2002, from http://llt.msu.edu/vol1num1/chapelle/default.html.

Chapelle, C. (1999). Research questions for a CALL research agenda: A reply to Rafael Salaberry. *Language, Learning & Technology*, 3(1), 108–113.

Chapelle, C. (2001). CALL in the 21st century: Looking back on research to look forward for practice. In P. Brett (Ed.), *Call in the 21st century*. [CD-Rom]. Whitstable, Kent: IATEFL.

Chapelle, C. (2002). Computer-assisted language learning. In R. B. Kaplan (Ed.), *The Oxford Handbook of Applied Linguistics*. Oxford: Oxford University Press.

Chun, D. M. (1994). Using computer networking to facilitate the acquisition of interactive competence. *System*, 22(1), 17–31.

Chun, D. M., & Plass, J. L. (1996). Effects of multimedia annotations on vocabulary acquisition. *The Modern Language Journal*, 80, 183–198.

Corbel, C. (1996). *The computing practices of language and literacy teachers*. Sydney: NCELTR.

Corbel, C. (1999). *Computer literacies: Working effectively with electronic texts*. Sydney: NCELTR.

Cummins, J., & Sayers, D. (1995). *Brave new schools: Challenging cultural literacy through global learning networks*. New York: St. Martin's Press.

Dabbagh, N., Bannan-Ritland, B., & Silc, K. (2001). Pedagogy and Web-based course authoring tools: Issues and implications. In B. H. Khan (Ed.), *Web-based training* (pp. 343–354). Englewood Cliffs, NJ: Educational Technology Publications.

Debski, R., & Levy, M. (1999). Introduction. In R. Debski & M. Levy (Eds.), *World CALL: Global perspectives on computer-assisted language learning* (pp. 7–10). Lisse, Netherlands: Swets & Zeitlinger.

Doughty, C. (1991). Second language instruction does make a difference: Evidence from an empirical study of SL relativization. *Studies in Second Language Acquisition*, 13, 431–469.

Dreyfus, H. L., & Dreyfus, S. E. (1986). *Mind over machine*. New York: The Free Press.

Dunkel, P. (1991). The effectiveness of research on computer-assisted language learning. In P. Dunkel (Ed.), *Computer-assisted language learning and testing* (pp. 5–36). New York: Newbury House.

Egbert, & Hanson-Smith (Eds.). (1999). *CALL environments: Research, practice, and critical issues.* Alexandria, VA: TESOL

Ellis, A., & Phelps, R. (2000). Staff development for online delivery: A collaborative, team based action learning model. *Australian Journal of Educational Technology, 16*(1), 26–44. Retrieved May 28, 2002 from http://www.ascilite.org.au/ajet/ajet16/ellis.html

Ely, C. M., & Pease-Alvarez, L. (1996). Learning styles and strategies in ESOL: Introduction to the special issue. *TESOL Journal, 6*(1), 5.

Endres, S. (2002). Web page publishing and ESL. Unpublished action research report. Moreton Institute of TAFE, Queensland.

Felix, U. (1999). Web-based language learning. A window to the authentic world. In R. Debski & M. Levy (Eds.), *World CALL: Global perspectives on computer-assisted language learning* (pp. 85–98). Lisse, Netherlands: Swets & Zeitlinger.

Felix, U. (2001). *Beyond Babel: Language learning online.* Melbourne: Language Australia Ltd.

Ganderton, R. (2001). Interactivity in L2 Web-based reading. In R. Debski & M. Levy (Eds.), *World CALL: Global perspectives on computer-assisted language learning* (pp. 49–66). Lisse, Netherlands: Swets & Zeitlinger.

Ghadirian, S. (2002). Providing controlled exposure to target vocabulary through the screening and arranging of texts. *Language, Learning & Technology, 6*(1), 147–164.

Global Reach. (2004, October 19). *Global Internet statistics.* Retrieved October 19, 2004, from http://global-reach.biz/globalstats/index.php3.

Godwin-Jones, (1998). *Language interactive: Language teaching and the web.* Retrieved October 18, 2004, from http://www.fln.vcu.edu/cgi/1.html.

Golebiowski, Z. (1994). An evaluation of CALL in an advanced ESL communication skills program. *ON-CALL, 8*(3), 32–34.

Guest, (1995). An interview with a cat. *Learner to Learner: A Forum for Learners of Japanese and Other Languages, 3*, 3.

Haimd, N. (2002). Using the Internet in the AMEP class. Unpublished action research report, **acl**, Cabramatta, Australia.

Hegelheimer, V. (1998). *Effects of textual glosses and sentence-level audio glosses on reading comprehension and vocabulary recall.* Unpublished doctoral dissertation, Department of Educational Psychology, College of Education, University of Illinois, Urbana, IL.

Hémard, D. (1999). A methodology for designing student-centred hypermedia CALL. In R. Debski & M. Levy (Eds.), *WorldCALL: Global perspectives on computer-assisted language learning* (pp. 215–228). Lisse, Netherlands: Swets & Zeitlinger.

Holec, H. (1979). *Autonomy and foreign language learning.* Oxford: Council of Europe/Pergamon Press.

Hoven, D. (1999). CALL-in the learner into focus. In R. Debski & M. Levy (Eds.), *World CALL: Global perspectives on computer-assisted language learning* (pp. 149–167). Lisse, Netherlands: Swets & Zeitlinger.

Hsu, J. (1994). *Computer assisted language learning (CALL): The effect of ESL students' use of interactional modifications on listening comprehension.* Unpublished doctoral dissertation, Department of Curriculum and Instruction, College of Education, Iowa State University, Ames, IA.

Javed, S. (1996). Electronic mailing lists for teachers and learners: A Victoria experience. *Literacy Now, 1.*

Jonassen, D. (1992). What are cognitive tools? In P. A. M. Kommers, D. H. Jonasses, & J. T. Mayes (Eds.), *Cognitive tools for learning* (pp. 1–6). Berlin: Springer-Verlag.

Kelm, O. R. (1992). The use of synchronous computer networks in second language instruction: A preliminary report. *Foreign Language Annals, 25*(5), 441–454.

Kern, R. (1995). Découvrir Berkeley: Students' representation of their world on the World Wide Web. In M. Warschauer (Ed.), *Virtual connections: Online activities and projects for networking language learners* (pp. 355–356). Honolulu: University of Hawai'i, Second Language Teaching and Curriculum Center.

Koedinger, K. R. (2001). Cognitive tutors as modeling tools and instructional models. In K. D. Forbus & P. J. Feltovich (Eds.), *Smart machines in education* (pp. 145–167). Menlo Park, CA: American Association for Artificial Intelligence.

Kress, G. (1997). Visual and verbal modes of representation in electronically mediated communication: The potentials of new forms of text. In I Snyder (Ed.), *Page to screen: Taking literacy into the electronic era* (pp. 53–79). London: Routledge.

Lam, W. S. E. (2004). Second language socialization in a bilingual chat room: Global and local considerations. *Language Learning and Technology, 8*(3), 44–65.

Lamy, M-N, & Goodfellow, R. (1999). 'Reflective conversation' in the virtual language classroom. *Language Learning & Technology*, *2*(2), 43–61. Retrieved May 28, 2002, from http://llt.msu.edu/vol2num2/default.html.

Laurillard, D. (1993). *Rethinking university teaching—a framework for the effective use of educational technology*. London: Routledge.

Levy, M. (1999). Responding to the context of CALL: Directions for research. *Prospect*, *14*(3), 24–31.

Lightbown, P. M., & Spada, N. (1990). Focus-on-form and corrective feedback in communicative language teaching. *Studies in Second Language Acquisition*, *12*, 429–448.

Little, D., Devitt, S., & Singleton, D. (1994). The communicative approach and authentic texts. In A. Swarbrick (Ed.), *Teaching modern languages* (pp. 43–47). London: Routledge.

Long, M. H. (1985). Input and second language acquisition theory. In S. M. Gass & C. G. Madden (Eds.), *Input in second language acquisition* (pp. 113–142). New York: Newbury House.

Mansfield, S. (2002, March). Web site match filtering skills. Presentation at **acl** Professional Development Day, Bankstown, Australia.

Motteram, G. (1999). Changing the research paradigm: Qualitative research methodology and the CALL classroom. In R. Debski & M. Levy (Eds.), *World CALL: Global perspectives on computer-assisted language learning* (pp. 201–214). Lisse, Netherlands: Swets & Zeitlinger.

Murray, D. E. (1999). Access to information technology: Considerations for language educators. *Prospect*, *14*(3), 4–12.

Murray, D. E. (2004). The language of cyberspace. In J. Rickford & E. Finegan (Eds.), *Language in the USA* (pp. 463–479). Cambridge: Cambridge University Press.

Murray, D. E. (2005). Technology and L2 literacy. In M. McGroarty (Ed.), *Annual Review of Applied Linguistics*. Cambridge: Cambridge University Press.

Murray, D. E., & McPherson, P. (2001). Using multimedia in English language teaching. Paper presented at the Adult Migrant English Program (AMEP) Conference 2001, Adelaide, Australia.

Murray, D. E., & McPherson, P. (2002). *Using Planet English with AMEP learners*. Sydney: NCELTR.

Murray, D. E., & McPherson, P. (2005). *Navigating to read; reading to navigate*. Sydney: NCELTR.

Nunan, D. (1988). *The learner centred curriculum*. Cambridge: Cambridge University Press.

Oxford, R. L. (1990). *Language learning strategies: What every teacher should know*. Boston, MA: Heinle & Heinle Publishers.

Palloff, R. M., & Pratt, K. (1999). *Building learning communities in cyberspace: Effective strategies for the online classroom*. San Francisco: Jossey-Bass.

Park, Y. (1994). *Incorporating interactive multimedia in an ESL classroom environment: Learners' interactions and learning strategies*. Unpublished doctoral dissertation, Department of Curriculum and Instruction, College of Education, Iowa State University, Ames, IA.

Puetter, S. (2002). *Using the Internet in the classroom*. Unpublished action research report, Gold Coast College of TAFE, Queensland.

Rogers, E. M. (1995). *Diffusion of innovations*. New York: The Free Press.

Roschelle, J., & Pea, R. (in press). A walk on the WILD side: How wireless handhelds may change computer-supported collaborative learning. *International Journal of Cognition and Technology*.

Salaberry, R. (1999). CALL in the year 2000: Still developing a research agenda. *Language Learning and Technology*, *3*(1), 104–107.

Schwienhorst, K. (2003). Learner autonomy and tandem learning: Putting principles into practice in synchronous and asynchronous telecommunications environments. *Computer Assisted Language Learning*, *16*(5), 427–443.

Shield, L., Weininger, M. J., & Davies, L. B. (1999). A task-based approach to using MOO for collaborative language learning. In K. Cameron (Ed.), *CALL and the learning community* (pp. 391–401). Exeter: Elm Bank Publications.

Shulz (2000). Computers and collaborative writing in the foreign language curriculum. In M. Warschauer & R. Kern (Eds.), *Network-based language teaching: Concepts and practice* (pp. 121–150). Cambridge: Cambridge University Press.

Snyder, I. (1997). *Page to screen: Taking literacy into the electronic era*. London: Routledge.

Turner, T. A. J. (2001). Worlds of words; Tales for language teachers. In F. Uschi (Ed.) *Beyond Babel: Language learning online* (pp. 163–186). Melbourne, Vic: Language Australia Ltd.

Wang, (1993). E-mail dialogue journaling in an ESL reading and writing classroom. Unpublished doctoral dissertation, University of Oregon, Eugene.Warschauer, M. (Ed.). (1995). *Virtual connections: On-line activities & projects for networking language learners*. Honolulu, HI: Second Language Teaching & Curriculum Center, University of Hawai'i.

Warschauer, M. (1996). Comparing face-to-face and electronic communication in the second language classroom. *CALICO Journal*, *13*(2), 7–26.

Warschauer, M. (1998). Researaching technology in TESOL: Determinist, instrumental, and critical approaches. *TESOL Quarterly, 32*(4), 757–761.
Warschauer, M. (1999). *Electronic literacies: Language culture, and power in online education.* Mahawh, NJ: Lawrence Erlbaum Associates.
Warschauer, M. (2000). Language, identity, and the Internet. In G. Rodman (Ed.), *Race in cyberspace* (pp. 151–170). New York: Routledge.
Warschauer, M. (2001). The death of cyberspace and the rebirth of CALL. In P. Brett (Ed.), *Call in the 21st century* [CD-Rom]. Whitstable, Kent: IATEFL.
Warschauer, M. (2002). Technology and social inclusion: Rethinking the digital divide. Boston, MA: MIT Press.
Warschauer, M., Shetzer, H., & Meloni, C. (2000). *Internet for English teaching.* Alexandria, VA: TESOL Publications.
Woolf, B. P., Beck, J., Eliot, C., & Stern, M. (2001). Growth and maturity of intelligent tutoring systems. In K. D. Forbus & P. J. Feltovich (Eds.), *Smart machines in education* (pp. 99–144). Menlo Park, CA: American Association for Artificial Intelligence.

Glossary

chat	synchronous written communication between people who are logged onto computers that are networked
computer-mediated communication (CMC)	communication between people using computer networks; CMC includes email, chat, instant messaging, and discussion lists
discussion list	asynchronous communication where many people "post" messages to be read by everyone with access to the discussion list
email	written messages sent asynchronously across a computer network; email can be sent to one or many people if you know their email addresses
instant messaging (IM)	synchronous communication on a network, only sent to specific recipients
Internet	a network of computer networks that links computers around the world; often abbreviated to 'Net'
listserv	software that provides a forum or discussion for subscribers using email
MUD	Multi-user dungeon; an interactive virtual game played on the Internet by several people at the same time
MOO	Multi-object-oriented MUDs; this refers to the programming; however, MUDs and MOOs are almost indistinguishable from the user's point of view
World Wide Web	a hyperlinked database residing on the Internet, providing network-accessible information

CHAPTER 46

THE INTERNET AND ENGLISH LANGUAGE LEARNING:

Opening up Spaces for Constructivist and Transformative Pedagogy through Sister-Class Networks

VASILIA KOURTIS-KAZOULLIS AND ELENI SKOURTOU

The University of the Aegean, Greece

ABSTRACT

When the internet is added to the environment of the classroom, instructional changes inevitably take place. The intensity of these changes depends on how the internet is used, as it can be aligned with either traditional or innovative forms of instruction. With traditional forms of instruction, the benefits are limited, whereas with innovative forms of instruction, the results can be powerful. This chapter discusses how the internet can open up spaces for social constructivist and transformative pedagogy, even in traditional classroom settings, by using as an example an internet-based sister class project, entitled *DiaLogos*, designed for the teaching of English as foreign language (EFL) in Greece and Greek as a second language (L2) in Canada. In the Greek context where the teaching of English followed a very traditional textbook-oriented approach, *DiaLogos* demonstrated how this approach can be expanded to integrate critical thinking, creative writing, and identity exploration with language learning. Illustrative examples of these processes are discussed in relation to a framework for promoting academic language learning and conceptualizing the relationships between pedagogy and technology.

PEDAGOGICAL ORIENTATIONS AND LANGUAGE LEARNING

According to Cope and Kalantzis (2000), literacy pedagogy traditionally meant learning to read and write in standard forms of the national language and was restricted to "formalized, monolingual, monocultural, and rule-governed forms of language" (p. 9). In contrast, Cope and Kalantzis argue for an expanded notion of literacy pedagogy in which pedagogy is viewed as "a teaching and learning relationship that creates the potential for building learning conditions leading to full and equitable social participation" (2000, p. 9). In the classroom, it is difficult to describe the learning environment in relation to only one type of pedagogy, as different types of pedagogy combine in the teaching/learning process. However, for descriptive purposes, pedagogy will be discussed here with reference to three specific types: traditional, social constructivist, and transformative, each with different implications for literacy pedagogy. These categories represent different pedagogical orientations rather than totally autonomous or separate concepts. They have been distinguished with respect to their instructional assumptions, their social assumptions, and the student outcomes they envisage (Cummins, 2001; Cummins & Sayers, 1995).

Traditional Pedagogy

Within a traditional pedagogical orientation, language is assumed to consist of its component parts. These language components are taught individually and in sequence: first, simple elements are introduced, proceeding to complex forms of language. This sequence complies with how foreign languages are traditionally taught. Students learn phonics before they learn to read. They learn grammar, vocabulary, and spelling before they learn to write. The curriculum content is presented sequentially and learning is organized hierarchically from simple to complex, a process that renders knowledge static. The cultural knowledge or prior experience of the students is seldom utilized in teaching and learning.

The implicit social assumptions of traditional pedagogy are that the curriculum should reflect the cultural literacy of the society. This cultural literacy is aligned with the power relationships that exist in the society, with the result that students are not encouraged to become critical thinkers and question aspects of the social order.

Cope and Kalantzis (2000, p. 5) contrast this "mere literacy" with *multiliteracies*. The former is "centered on language only," which is conceived as a singular, standardized form of the national language. It is assumed that correct usage of language can be discerned and described. This view of language and the associated pedagogy is described as an "authoritarian kind of pedagogy" (p. 5). In contrast to this one-sided literacy, they propose a *pedagogy of multiliteracies* that "focuses on modes of representation much broader than language alone [and that]…differ according to culture and context, and have specific cognitive, cultural and social effects" (p. 5). The literacy that they propose, as opposed to the literacy linked to traditional pedagogy, implements various modes of meaning-making, including textual, visual, audio, spatial, behavioral, and multimodal, where written linguistic modes are combined with visual, audio, and spatial (characteristic of meanings on the web). Cope and Kalantzis question the validity of traditional pedagogies that represent a "formal, standard, written national language" (p. 6). As meaning is increasingly multimodal (in part due to information technology [IT]), and as local diversity and global connectedness are increasing, new types of literacy and pedagogy must be implemented in schools where educators and students are "active participants in social change" (p. 7).

Social Constructivist Pedagogy

Within the realm of social constructivist pedagogy are a variety of inquiry-based knowledge-construction approaches that are based on the social learning theory of Vygotsky and particularly on his notion of the *zone of proximal development* (ZPD). In these approaches, the cognitive advancement of the student is the primary goal. Wells (1999) places Vygotsky's social constructivist theory between two views of educational reform: progressive child-centered forms of education and structured teacher-directed education, emphasizing basic knowledge and skills. He claims that Vygotsky's social constructivist theory bridges these two views as it stresses dialogue and co-construction of knowledge, forming a collaborative community between teacher and student. Wells borrows from the theories of Vygotsky and Halliday (e.g. Halliday & Hasan, 1985) in order to define an approach to language learning and learning mediated by language that he terms *dialogic inquiry*. He proposes that a variety of modes of knowing are involved in human development with oral discourse playing a central role (in combination with other modes of semiosis). Wells emphasizes the creation of classroom communities of dialogic inquiry where "different kinds of meaning making…are enabled by different modes of discourse in such communities" (p. xvi).

Several principles of social constructivist pedagogy contributed to the design of the *DiaLogos* project to be discussed in this chapter. These principles focus on active student inquiry, collaborative learning, the importance of student experience (or prior knowledge), reading of authentic material, language learned holistically through communication with others, and the importance of social interaction for cognitive advancement (Cummins & Sayers, 1995). With reference to language and social activity, Vygotsky and Halliday consider language as a human invention that is used "as a means of achieving the goals of social living" (Wells, 1999, p. 6).

In summary, social constructivist pedagogy accepts cultural difference, but frequently curricula based on constructivist principles fail to focus on societal power relationships. The result is that the students may be liberal or tolerant, but uncritical of their own experiences and social realities (Cummins, 2000, 2001). Gee (2000) refers to cognitivist curricula in schools today as producing students "who can think critically, that is, engage in 'higher order thinking', but not *critiquely*." (Gee, 2000, p. 62). In other words, students are "unable to understand and critique systems of power and injustice in a world that they will see as simply economically 'inevitable'" (Gee, 2000, p. 62). He goes on to describe how students who cannot think *critiquely* are unable to empathize with the plight of people. Gee differentiates the two terms in that "critical" thinking is linked with higher-order thinking and thinking "critiquely" is linked to thinking critically about systems of power and injustice. In this sense, students are unable to understand or empathize with the plight of other people. Thus, social constructivist pedagogy is limited insofar as it fails to address societal power relations and the ways in which they intersect with learning.

Transformative Pedagogy

According to Cummins (2001), transformative pedagogy follows the instructional orientation of constructivist pedagogy to some extent. Language is taught as a whole, knowledge is catalytic, and learning involves joint interactive construction through critical inquiry. However, the social assumptions underlying transformative pedagogy differentiate it from constructivist pedagogy. Transformative pedagogy focuses on social realities relevant to students' experiences and incorporates *collaborative critical inquiry* in order to relate the curriculum content to students' individual and collective experiences. Broader social issues, relevant to students' lives, are analyzed, and students are encouraged to discuss ways in which social realities might be changed through social action and democratic participation (Cummins & Sayers, 1995). The result is that students develop critical literacy and a sense of empowerment.

Cummins and Sayers (1995) view transformative pedagogy as central in "realizing the potential of global learning networks" (p. 153). As the environment created in *DiaLogos* was an environment of collaboration between sister classes joined via Internet connections, it was vital that the pedagogy used was one that allowed for the potential of these connections to be realized.

The work of Wells (1999), grounded in sociocultural theory, incorporates the notion of *dialogic inquiry*. Cummins (2001), however, takes this notion further as he relates critical inquiry to existing social circumstances and power distribution, both of which intersect with how knowledge is constructed and learned (Skourtou, 2002). Cope and Kalantzis (2000) also refer to critical inquiry in the four components of pedagogy that they propose within the context of their multiliteracies framework, originally proposed by the New London Group (1996). This pedagogy is rooted in active design of meaning as well as active design of social futures. The key concept that is used as a basis of literacy pedagogy is *design,* in which people are "both inheritors of patterns and conventions of meaning while at the same time active designers of meaning" (Cope & Kalantzis, 2000, p. 7). They link *designers of meaning* to designers of social futures in the workplace and other public spheres (Cope & Kalantzis, 1997). Of the four components of pedagogy that they propose, *Transformed practice* can be linked to transformative pedagogy in which "students as meaning makers become designers of social futures" (Cope & Kalantzis, 2000, p. 7). The other components include:

> *Situated practice* which draws on the experience of meaning-making in life worlds, the public realm, and workplaces; *overt instruction*, through which students develop an explicit metalanguage of design; and *critical framing*, which interprets the social context and purpose of designs of meaning. (p. 7)

PEDAGOGY AND INFORMATION TECHNOLOGY

In the following sections, we argue that the ways in which IT will be used in the learning environment depend largely on the underlying pedagogical orientation.

Traditional Pedagogy and Information Technology

A traditional approach to second language pedagogy focuses on the teaching of language structures and forms with little emphasis on processing of meaning or active communicative or authentic use of the language (Cummins, 2001). Furthermore, because traditional pedagogy usually involves students learning predominantly from the textbook, IT used with this orientation would likely just reinforce the learning of content, vocabulary, and grammatical knowledge. IT used in this way is made more appealing to students than the textbook through the use of interactive games and activities; however, the basic aim is still reinforcement of information and skills.

Constructivist Pedagogy and Information Technology

As noted above, much of the research within the constructivist tradition has been framed within sociocultural theory with special emphasis on Vygotsky's zone of proximal development (ZPD). There is much activity in the field of language learning and technology that corresponds with this pedagogical framework. There are also many uses of IT that involve higher-order thinking skills and cognitive challenge that are designed to enable students to learn content, language structures, and functions. These activities are likely to be more motivating for students than simply learning about a topic from a textbook. Active, hands-on, cooperative activities tend to be more cognitively engaging and motivating for students than activities that flow from a transmission orientation.

Transformative Pedagogy and Information Technology

Cope and Kalantzis (2000) link transformative pedagogy to IT in two ways:

1. IT permits diversity in ways of expression. The New London Group uses the term *multimodal meaning* to refer to the diverse means through which meaning can be expressed. They use the meanings on the World Wide Web or interactive multimedia as examples, where written text is combined with audio, visual, and spatial expressions of meaning. Thus, the use of IT in the classroom expands the range of literacies or *modes of expression* available to the student. In the context of multiliteracies pedagogy, these different modes of expression are expanded in order to include expression or literacy in other languages. Just as IT can bridge geographical distance, it can also bridge linguistic differences.
2. Local diversity and global connectedness mean that a single standard version of a language is no longer sufficient. Local diversity and global connectedness change the nature of language learning, as it is necessary to be able to access and interact in multiple varieties of a language.

The latter point is linked with two issues related to the implementation of *DiaLogos*, namely, how participants communicate across different languages and how accuracy of language use is negotiated:

1. Just as IT can bridge geographic distance and facilitate communication between people with different first languages, it can also facilitate communication between people who use different varieties of the same language (for example, different forms of English).
2. People engaged in computer-mediated communication frequently are required to use a second language that they may not know very well. In face-to-face situations, they may be reluctant to use a language that they do not fully control, but in electronic communication this seems to pose much less of a problem.

In conclusion, pedagogies that assume a single correct version of language are insufficient to represent the diversity of language forms used in IT communication.

DIALOGOS: AN INTERNET-BASED SISTER CLASS PROJECT WITH MULTIPLE PEDAGOGICAL ORIENTATIONS

The title *DiaLogos* implies many things. In the simplest sense, as one word, "*dialogos*" means conversation or dialogue in Greek. However, with the "L" capitalized, *DiaLogos* is separated into two words and implies two different things: (a) "*dia logos*" or (b) "*diadiktuou logos.*" With reference to the first meaning, *Dia Logos* literally means *through words/through discourse/through logos*. The meaning of *logos* in Greek incorporates notions such as "speech," "discourse," and the system of rules underlying particular discourses. In reference to the second meaning, a *diadiktuou logos* means *logos on/through the Internet*.

DiaLogos was an Internet-based sister class project that was carried out over two school years between elementary school classes (4th, 5th, and 6th grades) in Canada and Greece. The initial objective was to create an environment of *dialogic inquiry* where two different languages (that is, English and Greek) could be learned. In cooperation with their sister classes, students in Greece were learning English and students in Canada (of Greek heritage) were learning Greek. The sister project of *DiaLogos* was *Metro-polis (*Theodoridis, 2000). *Metro-polis* focused its activities on the Canadian side, and hence the learning of Greek, while *DiaLogos* focused its activities on the Greek side, and hence the learning of English.

The pedagogical significance of *DiaLogos* was that it managed to combine the very traditional environment of the regular English class with new orientations to pedagogy, both social constructivist and transformative. Although, on the Greek side, *DiaLogos* was carried out within a traditional textbook-dominated educational setting the pedagogical orientation of the project attempted to be explicitly transformative. At different times the activities that took place in the context of the project ranged across the pedagogical space from transmission to transformative. Some activities were partly traditional, partly constructivist. At other times, they were constructivist, moving towards transformative. However, regardless of where the activities were located within the pedagogical space, the goal was always to move towards the transformative realm.

Combining Traditional Learning with New Learning Environments

At the elementary school level, all students in Greece use the same book that is published by the Ministry of Education, regardless of the student's actual language level. All students are grouped into three levels according to their grade (i.e., grades 4, 5, and 6). The methodology of the textbook is described by the authors as communicative, but in the actual classroom, teaching often involves a more traditional approach (i.e., explicit grammar teaching, memorization, etc.). Students in the Greek elementary school attend English lessons 3 hours per week. The *DiaLogos* students attended regular English lessons two times a week using the textbook published by the Ministry of Education. However, once a week the lesson was held in the *DiaLogos* computer room. This combination of traditional teaching and *DiaLogos* in reality combined the three foci of Cummins' academic expertise framework (2001) as shown in Figure 1.

The Internet and English Language Learning

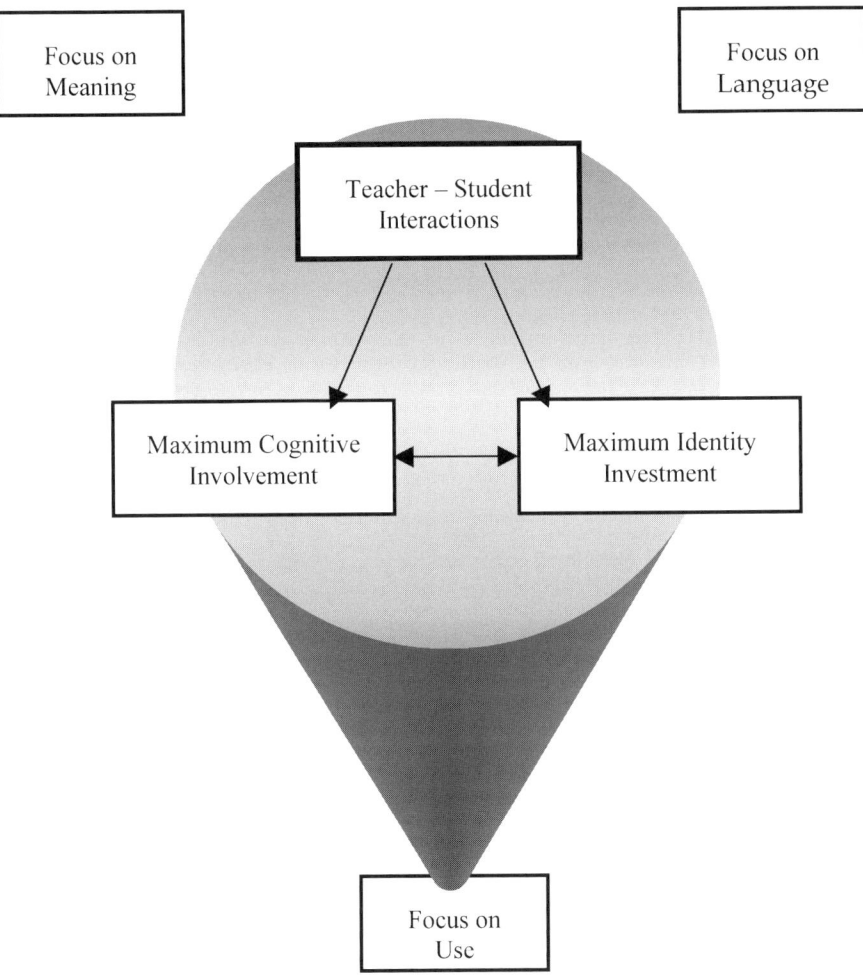

Figure 1. Classroom conditions for academic language learning. *(Adapted from Cummins, J. (2001). Negotiating identities: Education for empowerment in a diverse society. Los Angeles: California Association for Bilingual Education. p. 125*

With respect to the *focus on meaning* in Figure 1, students in the traditional classroom were receiving comprehensible input in English by reading texts or listening to other students or the teacher speaking. However, there was minimal focus on developing critical literacy. Critical literacy, however, *was* being developed through the use of IT and in combination with the sister class, as discussed below. The diversity of the two sister class pairs served to fuel critical literacy.

A *focus on language* was already apparent, with the teacher making the students aware of language forms and uses by explicitly teaching grammar, vocabulary, syntax, and other formal aspects of the language in a traditional manner. However, critical analysis of language forms and uses came only when the students compared different forms of language in the context of messages received from their sister class. The English language in their textbook was of a relatively consistent form: the English language on the Internet was diverse, and the English language used by their sister classes opened up an entirely new perspective on how the language could be used. For example, students from Canada were using expressions that were completely new to the students in Greece.

Table 1. Letters from Canada

Posted by Chester afternoon class for E1 and E2 Rhodes on February 18, 1999:

Katerina – I didn't have much of a Christmas this year because I was moviong and we didn't put up a tree and stuff like that but it was fun moving and stuff. On Christmas eve we went to my aunt's house and had a big feast and me and cousin Maria were chilling out. On New Years eve we went to my moms friends house and clebrated it there and we brought in 1999 we [with] a really big bang!!

BYE FOR NOW KATERINA!!!!!!!!!

Posted by Michael I. [student from Canada] on December 11, 1999:

Hi its me your penpal. My name is Michael I. What did it look like and how was it at the museum and threatre? What does your cousin look like? Was the parthenon aand the Acropolis cool?

I doubt it was bad.

Have a nice day

1998-1999 school year bulletin board entry from Diefenbaker [student from Canada] to ST2 Rhodes:

7. On my winter break I had a remarkable week. My sister had her 8th birthday party. We had a blast!

..

Hellen Vrysselas. Diefenbaker school

1998-1999 school year bulletin board entry from Chester to E1/E2 Rhodes:

9. Whaz up! My name is Katerina. I'm 10 years old but November 15th I'm turning 11 years old. . . . .

Expressions in the letters in Table 1, such as *stuff like that*, *and stuff*, *chilling out*, *with a really big bang*, *we had a blast* and *whaz up*, fueled the students' curiosity and resulted in critical analysis of language forms. *Cool* and *bad* were words that students in Greece were familiar with; however, they were not familiar with the different way in which they were used. The students were using English but a different type of English. The Greek students began using these new expressions in the English language as early as the first year of correspondence (Kourtis-Kazoullis, 2001).

Whereas activities in the traditional classroom reflected primarily a *focus on meaning* and *focus on language*, the computer-mediated activities also incorporated a *focus on use*. Students were using language to generate new knowledge, create literature and art, and act on social realities. With respect to cognitive engagement, the *DiaLogos* activities enabled students to work at their own levels and with a variety of materials, both of which increased engagement. Also, students' identities were invested in the sister class project, as what they were producing stemmed from their own identities and experiences in combination with the identities and experiences of the members of their sister classes. When students themselves generate knowledge and create materials through project work, their experiences and identities are inevitably integrated in the process.

Ancient Rhodes

In order to provide information to a student from Canada who was doing a project on Ancient Greece in his own school, the students from one school in Rhodes, Greece, began conducting research into the history of their own island and the areas around their homes and school. As all curriculum in Greek schools is appointed by the central government and all textbooks are the same, regional history is not specifically taught in school. The students began conducting their own research and embarked upon a project that was entitled *Ancient Rhodes*.

The significance of this project was that the students learned that they were able to "make waves" or act on social realities. The students were guided through the project with the help of a learning packet. This learning packet included suggestions to teachers about how to guide the students through critical research. This process was divided into a series of phases as outlined in Table 2 (Kourtis-Kazoullis, 2001).

Table 2. Critical Research

Phase 1: Setting questions

What do we want to know?

Phase 2: Using what we know and what others know to construct new knowledge

First we begin with what we already know. The students begin from themselves (i.e., what do they know about the topic), then what each member of the group knows, then what the class as a whole knows. Likewise, the same process (i.e., ourselves in relation to others) takes place with the sister class (i.e., What does the sister class know? Do they know something different?).

Once we utilize what we already know, we can gather new information.

Phase 3: Gathering information

a. Finding information.

Where can we find information? We find information by first looking at what is physically near us and then moving more and more distant. First we begin from our own environment. For example, in *Ancient Rhodes*, students can begin by what they see around their home and school. All through the city there are brown signs that provide archeological sites. Is there one near their school or home?

Then information is found from other sources (teachers, the Internet, visiting sites, performances, experts, textbooks, i.e., 4th and 5th grade history books, other books, etc.). Finally, see what information we can find from our sister classes.

> b. Taking notes.
>
> How do we store the material we find?
>
> c. Documenting our work.
>
> How do we state where we found the material?
>
> **Phase 4: Critically viewing our topic**
>
> Is the material we found all from one viewpoint? This can be discussed. Before we start writing, we can discuss things in class. We can also discuss our topics with our sister class and see what they think.
>
> **Phase 5: Production as process not as product**
>
> This is where we actually write our texts. We must remember what we learned about documenting our work.
>
> It is important that the text that students produce is not a product, i.e., a text that is written once and forgotten about. It is meant to be a process. The text once written can be changed at any time. More information can be added without time constrictions. The student can change his/her opinion. The text can be produced by one individual, but it can also be the combined efforts of a group.
>
> **Phase 6: Sharing our ideas with others both orally and in written form**
>
> Our articles can be shared between students, classes, and schools. They can be sent by e-mail to the sister classes.
>
> **Phase 7: Critically viewing our work with others**
>
> When we share our work with others, we can critically view our work by asking for other opinions and discussing issues with others.
>
> Kourtis-Kazoullis, 2001, pp. 276-277

The research that the students conducted was divided into three steps:

- **Step 1**: The students went out looking for information in their own neighborhood. For example, in the students' village, there were several archeological sites and signs put up by the archeology department giving information about these sites. In most cases, the students had not even noticed these signs or sites prior to the project.
- **Step 2**: The students visited the museum of Rhodes and the special exhibit commemorating the 2400-year history of the city of Rhodes. Preparation was done in advance in class on what the students could ask the guiding archeologist.
- **Step 3**: Finally, the students were asked to find information on the Internet dealing with ancient Greece and ancient Rhodes. The project was to be an exercise in critical literacy as the students were to examine whether the image of Greece in these texts was similar or different from their own image of Greece.

This third step led to several discoveries. The students discovered that the material on the Internet includes a variety of opinions and thus may contain perspectives that are different from what the students themselves believe. They also discovered that the depiction of their own culture on the Internet may be very different from how they view themselves. But more importantly, they discovered that they could take action and that this action could bring results. The action that the students took involved writing a letter to the editor of an electronic archeological magazine (*Dr. Dig*) protesting against the representation of their history in a way that was not acceptable to them.

In *Dr. Dig* the students completed a quiz dealing with historical and archeological facts. When the students answered the following question in this quiz, they were surprised to find that their answer was labeled incorrect:

> 2. The marble figures and sculptures from the Parthenon in Greece that have been owned by Britain since 1801 are called
> a. The Parthenon Artifacts
> b. The Greek Relics
> c. The Elgin Marbles
> d. The Olympic Artifacts (Dig Magazine, 2000, quiz 6)

Most of the students answered (a), as they knew that the marbles were from the Parthenon. However, this response evoked the following feedback:

> Your answer for question 2, Parthenon, is WRONG!
> The answer is c, the Elgin Marbles. The marbles were taken by a British ambassador named Lord Elgin in 1801 when Greece was ruled by Turkey's Ottoman Empire

This surprising answer motivated these grade 6 students to research the topic and, with the help of their teachers, write to the editor to present their perspectives. Their letter outlined the history of the Parthenon Marbles and the circumstances under which Lord Elgin took possession of them and shipped them to England. They concluded as follows:

> When you refer to these marbles on your web page, please do not refer to them as the Elgin Marbles. In reality, they are of Greek origin and should be called the Marbles of the Parthenon. Elgin profited by stealing them. He should not profit by having them named after him.
> We thank you very much. We would appreciate a reply from you with your own viewpoint on this matter.
>
> On behalf of the 6th grade class of the Kremasti Elementary School in Rhodes, Greece,

Two letters were received back from the editor and the "in-house" archaeologist of the magazine. These letters noted the complexity of the issue but also acknowledged the legitimacy of the students' concern.

In short, in the context of their critical inquiry, these students discovered that how others depict their own culture might be very different from how they view themselves. But more importantly, they discovered that they could take action and that this action could bring results.

CONCLUSIONS

Frequently, the introduction of IT into a traditional school environment dominated by traditional pedagogy exerts only a minimal impact on processes of teaching and learning. When IT is used only to support traditional pedagogy, its power is largely squandered. However, it is by no means easy to extend the pedagogical focus beyond traditional into social constructivist pedagogy, let alone transformative pedagogy (Skourtou, 2001, 2002).

DiaLogos demonstrated some directions for using IT to move from traditional to transformative pedagogy. Specifically, it demonstrated that it is possible to expand the limits of a traditional environment and integrate elements of a social constructivist orientation into the teaching of English as a foreign language. The project also illustrated both the challenges of planning for transformative outcomes and also how these outcomes can evolve when the conditions are appropriate, that is, when there is an actual need to think critically and take action, especially when the issue deals with the identities, experiences, and beliefs of the students.

REFERENCES

Cope, B., & Kalantzis, M. (Eds.). (1997). *Productive diversity: A new Australian model for work and management.* Annandale: Pluto Press Australia.

Cope, B., & Kalantzis M. (Eds.). (2000). *Multiliteracies: Literacy learning and the design of social futures.* London and New York: Routledge.

Cummins, J. (2000). *Language, power and pedagogy: Bilingual children in the crossfire.* Clevedon: Multilingual Matters.

Cummins, J. (2001). *Negotiating identities: Education for empowerment in a diverse society.* (2nd ed.). Los Angeles: California Association for Bilingual Education.

Cummins, J., & Sayers, D. (1995). *Brave new schools: Challenging cultural illiteracy through global learning networks.* New York: St. Martin's Press.

Gee. J. P. (2000). New people in new worlds: Networks, the new capitalism and schools. In B. Cope & M. Kalantzis (Eds.), *Multiliteracies: Literacy learning and the design of social futures* (pp. 43–68). London and New York: Routledge.

Halliday, M.A.K., & Hasan, R. (1985). *Language, context and text: Aspects of language in a social-semiotic perspective.* Geelong, Victoria: Deakin University Press.

Kourtis-Kazoullis. V. (2001). *DiaLogos: Bilingualism and the teaching of second languages on the Internet.* Unpublished doctoral dissertation, University of the Aegean, Rhodes.

New London Group (1996) A pedagogy of multiliteracies: Designing social futures. *Harvard Educational Review*, 66, 60–92.

Skourtou, E. (2001). Lernen und Zweitsprachlernen im Internet—Paedagogische Fragestellungen [Learning and second language learning via Internet—Pedagogical issues]. In Chr. Beck & Al. Sofos (Eds.), *Neue Medien in der paedagogischen Kontroverse* [New media in the pedagogical discourse] (pp. 185–194). Mainz: Logophon.

Skourtou, E. (2002). Connecting Greek and Canadian schools through an Internet-based sister class network. *International Journal of Bilingual Education & Bilingualism,* 5(2), 85–95.

Theodoridis, T. (2000). *Metro-polis.* Retrieved June 2, 2000 from http://www.metro-polis.net.

Wells, G. (1999). *Dialogic inquiry: Towards a sociocultural practice and theory of education.* Cambridge: Cambridge University Press.

Vygotsky, L. S. (1978). *Mind in society: The development of higher psychological processes.* Cambridge, MA: Harvard University Press.

Section 2:

Constructs of Language in ELT: Breaking the Boundaries

SECTION 2

CONSTRUCTS OF LANGUAGE IN ELT:

Breaking The Boundaries

CHRIS DAVISON AND JIM CUMMINS

INTRODUCTION

It is obvious that English language teaching must have as its primary focus the development of the English language, as Cummins and Man point out in their chapter in this section of the handbook, but the ELT field has not yet reached a common shared understanding of what is meant by *language*. (The issue of what is *English* is even more contentious, but the current controversies around its description and ownership are dealt with in other sections of this handbook). Traditionally in ELT programs and in many textbooks and teaching materials, the English language has been divided into four discrete language skills—speaking, listening, reading, and writing—and/or, particularly in preservice teacher training courses, into the traditional structural elements of language—phonology, vocabulary (or *lexis*), grammar (or *syntax*) and more recently, *discourse* and/or *text*. However, these traditional boundaries for classifying language are inherently problematic in that they represent language as a clearly demarcated and somewhat static construct that can be decontextualized and described without reference to its context and users. In reality (or virtual reality, as is increasingly the case) texts constructed via email or online chatrooms seem closer to conversational language than to written language, and they often make meaning through the incorporation of non-verbal references, digital images and other extralinguistic information. Increasingly, too, corpus-based studies of real language use are showing how language forms and functions are changing and are changed by users, especially when English is being used as a lingua franca.

Three clear interrelated themes are evident in current research into the nature of language and the implications for language learning and teaching. Firstly, the relationship between text and context is being reconceptualized and traditional boundaries are being redrawn, particularly under the influence of more functional views of language. Secondly, the emergence of increasingly mulitmodal texts is breaking down traditional distinctions between the four skills and reconstructing language as just one of a number of dynamic and unpredictable modes of communication. Thirdly, there is a marked change in how descriptions of language are being constructed, with insights and theories being built from practice up, utilizing growing linguistic corpora from real interactions between language learners and users, rather than, as in Chomsky's era, from theory down, based on the assumption of an ideal speaker. Each of these broad themes will be briefly described in turn.

The first theme, the relationship between *text* and *context*, is not new to English language teachers. Text/discourse studies were established as a distinct field in the 1970s with the move away from Chomskyan transformational grammar towards greater emphasis on the social bases of communication. Text/discourse studies include both more cognitive analyses of text structure, especially coherence and cohesion, and analyses of top-level structures including a growing number of cross-cultural studies and studies of metadiscourse strategies such as connectives and hedges as well as studies drawing on Hallidayan systemic functional models, initially on cohesion but since extended to many other aspects of the relationship between text and context. The related construct of *genre* focuses on the social, institutional and ideological purposes of the text. Three distinct and somewhat conflicting branches of genre theory are now clearly established, that is, Swalesian applied linguistics, Australian genre theory and the new rhetoric movement, all building on earlier models of text linguistics and Bakhtinian notions of intertextuality. Texts and genres are seen having ordered, unified forms, albeit dynamic and intertextual, but there is disagreement as to the extent to which they are codifiable and determined by purpose. Increasingly, however, studies within this broadly functional view of language are also trying to account for the role of the learner and the interlocutor, audience or discourse community, as well as the contextual and sociohistoric conditions in which such learners act and interact. Effective language users are seen as requiring both knowledge of textual and generic features, and knowledge of social and cultural rules about text (who, when, where, what about and how), for example, the positioning of individual writer, valuing of personal opinion and contestation of text. The assumption is that text varies within, not just across, cultures and institutions, and that learning to use language in a new discourse community requires not only the learning of new forms and functions, but the development of a new identity and positioning in relation to audience, topic and self. Such functional views of language assume development is within a text-type of genre, as well as from genre to genre, i.e. simpler and more complex forms. However, it is argued that what develops is strongly influenced by exposure/input/instruction, that is, developing speakers and writers are scaffolded or apprenticed into new text-types and genres. This view challenges cognitive notions of simplicity and complexity, seeing development as adding to one's repertoire of identities, although there is disagreement as to the role of explicit instruction in acquiring membership of a discourse community. However, little work so far has attempted to link linguistic features and practice in any coherent or systematic way.

The second interrelated theme, that of *multimodality*, or *multiliteracies*, highlights the ways in which rapid changes in information and communication technology (ICT) have resulted in new text types, with new structures and visual features increasingly used to convey information, not just to support printed text, but as text in its own right. ICT has transformed the nature of the language used by teachers and students, and by students themselves, through offering an enormous variety of ways to adjust the type, frequency and quantity of the interaction and interactants, and significantly increased opportunities to exploit the full mode continuum from most spoken-like to most written-like. As a result an enormous diversity of new text-types have been created, most not yet properly described, including many involving digitization and code-switching (using two or more languages and even modes of communication simultaneously) via chatrooms and real-time messaging as well asynchronous communication networks such as email and web forums. As a result, communication in the contemporary classroom has been reconceptualized as more than just the linguistic, with language increasingly viewed as one mode of communication amongst multiple semiotic modes, all of which function to communicate meanings in an integrated, multilayered way. There is a growing interest amongst researchers in studying the ways in which teachers and learners draw on a much fuller repertoire of representational resources to communicate their meanings: for example, how language, action, and visual images interact to produce meaning; how knowledge is transformed across different modes; and how learners use different modes in different ways. Thus, the fundamental paradigm shift is from a focus on *language* to a focus on *mode*, with multimodal pedagogy conceptualized as a multiple semiotic activity in which teachers and learners make selections from the representational resources available to them to represent their meanings within the context of communicative practices.

The third and final interrelated theme highlighted in this section is that of the importance of looking at real language use by real language users. Most ELT professionals and researchers have been heavily influenced by the notion of communicative competence, itself a critique of Chomsky's highly abstracted notion of competence. However, as a number of researchers have noted, in ELT there has been a gradual shift away from Hymes' original emphasis on the need to investigate and understand actual language use in specific social and cultural contexts to establishing a set of statements about what should be included in an idealized curriculum for L2 learning. With accelerating interest in and use of linguistic corpora, this trend is now being reversed, and with this reversal, an increasing interest in redefining traditional and taken-for-granted conceptualizations of language and language learning.

The first two papers provide an overview of current research relating to the nature of language and its implications for English language learning and teaching. Hulstijn describes recent developments in cognitive science which have redefined Krashen's influential original notions of acquisition and learning, resulting in a new definition of implicit and explicit learning. In relation to explicit grammar instruction, it is argued that although, neurophysiologically speaking, explicit knowledge cannot be transformed into implicit knowledge, explicit grammar instruction may indirectly contribute to the establishment of implicit knowledge. In particular, Hulstijn emphasizes the importance of English language learners being able to automatize their word recognition and retrieval skills. Cummins and Man's chapter looks at the issue of vocabulary in more detail, as part of their framework for conceptualizing the nature of academic language and the pedagogical conditions that foster its development. They distinguish academic language proficiency (defined as the ability to understand and express more abstract concepts and ideas in both oral and written modes) from both conversational fluency and discrete language skills. They argue that extensive reading is crucial for academic language development because grammatical constructions and discourse structures found in typical written text differ significantly from those found in conversational interactions. More technical vocabulary, mostly derived from Greek and Latin sources, is also found primarily in written text.

The next set of papers in this section explores recent developments in research into various aspects of language, ranging from phonology, to vocabulary, grammar and text/discourse. Given the discussion earlier, these categories might seem very traditional, but the views of language adopted and the research drawn on is cutting-edge. In the first paper in this set, Archibald looks at the implications of recent second language acquisition research in the field of phonology for second language teachers. He argues against the tendency in ELT to think of L2 phonology as being synonymous with pronunciation, hence just focusing on the production of consonants, vowels, stress, and so on, and making stereotypical generalizations about particular languages and their users. Rather, Archibald shows how learner behavior (both production and perception) is governed by the nature of their abstract phonological representations, and, like syntax and morphology and semantics, phonology is a subtle cognitive system. He shows that adult second language learners can develop new phonological structures that are not present in the first language. He argues that we do not know which methods or techniques work for which learners of which languages, but if we provide instruction which gives learners opportunities to both produce and perceive the sounds in question and to be exposed to metalinguistic information about the sounds to be learned, then this is likely to lead to successful phonological development.

In the next chapter of this set, Schmitt reviews key vocabulary research and its implications for teaching and learning. He describes the contribution of corpus research in revealing the amount of vocabulary required to use English, what it means to know and learn a word, and the huge amount of lexical patterning that exists in English. He demonstrates the incremental nature of vocabulary acquisition, the role of memory in vocabulary learning, incidental and intentional vocabulary learning, techniques for effective vocabulary teaching, and the role of learning strategies in vocabulary acquisition. He argues that when considering which vocabulary learning strategies to introduce to our students, we need to consider the learners themselves and their overall learning context. Proficiency level seems to be important, but so is the first language and culture of students, their motivation and purposes for learning English, the task and text being used, and the nature of the English language itself. The insights and techniques discussed in this chapter can help teachers develop more principled and effective vocabulary programs for their students.

In the next chapter Derewianka challenges the traditional view of grammar as simply a collection of word classes and rules for their combination, and shows how this view is being overturned by theories that construct grammar in terms of its cognitive and social origins. Such theories are being used in more sociolinguistically-oriented research into the learning and teaching of grammar, broadly defined. In her chapter Derewianka examines three different models of grammar that are representative of the major paradigms currently informing ELT research and practice: grammar as structure, grammar as mental faculty, and grammar as functional resource. She argues that grammar needs to be reconceptualized as a dynamic system of text-making choices relevant to the students' communicative needs. The chapter concludes with a look at some of the issues surrounding grammar and future directions for research and teaching.

The last two chapters in this set look at discourse, first spoken, then written. McCarthy and Slade summarize some of the major features of spoken language, and in doing so, highlight the differences between spoken and written language. They then describe some of the major approaches to analyzing spoken language, beginning with the approach taken by Sinclair and Coulthard (known as the

Birmingham School) and then moving to conversation analysis and to systemic-functional approaches. They also look at genre theory and how this has been underpinned by the development of spoken corpora. They identify a number of problems with current approaches to spoken discourse, including the lack of codification of spoken grammars and the absence of a 'canon' of spoken texts, the variation of English as a spoken language from assumed norms, debates over the ownership of English, and problems with transcription and the representation of context and prosody. The chapter concludes with a discussion of the potential contribution of technological advances to our understanding of spoken discourse.

The final paper in this set deals with written discourse, using an academic literacies approach. Like other researchers, Starfield adopts a view of writing not as a generic skill to be taught as a set of static rules, but rather as shaped by the complex interactions of unequal social, institutional, and historical forces. Her chapter reviews research into student academic writing in Australia, South Africa, the United Kingdom, and the United States of America, and demonstrates how students and teachers negotiate academic literacies within specific local contexts. The key themes highlighted are the changing notion of the concept of discourse community in academic writing; the significance of the inter-relationship between intertextuality and plagiarism; and the increasing significance writer identity plays in academic writing. The pedagogical implications and potential of approaches using academic literacies are considered and avenues for further exploration, particularly those that involve greater engagement of academic literacy practitioners and disciplinary specialists, briefly examined.

The next set of three chapters deal with multimodality, or *multimodal discourse*, a relatively new focus of research in social semiotics and associated areas of linguistics. In her chapter on multiliteracies, Lotherington demonstrates how the traditional boundaries of literacy are being stretched as the contexts in which we move become increasingly multicultural, multilingual, and multimodal. Language, text, and discourse norms and practices are being rapidly extended and reinvented in response to new media and global networks. Lotherington argues that the boundaries for English language socialization have been expanded from traditional geographical and social contexts to the entire virtual world. This creates major challenges for English language teachers who are themselves learners in this new environment. Warschauer reinforces the view that information and communication technologies are having a profound affect on all aspects of language use, especially in written communication. He argues that purposes of writing, the nature of written genres, and the positioning of audience and author are all changing rapidly with the establishment of computer-mediated communication. In his chapter focusing specifically on writing and multimodality, he provides an overview of research on the relationship between new technologies and writing, and highlights the implications of this for English language learning and teaching. Topics include the participatory dynamics and linguistic features of computer-assisted classroom discussion, the impact of e-mail exchanges on students' writing process, and the relationship of writing purpose to student outcomes in multimedia authoring. The chapter also addresses areas of increasing concern in ELT, such as whether the Internet fosters plagiarism, and whether new forms of computer-mediated writing serve to complement and enhance more traditional forms of writing or undermine them. The nature and importance of electronic literacy are also explored.

The third chapter in this set focuses on the applicability of *multimodal pedagogies* to multilingual, multicultural classrooms in Johannesburg, South Africa. Stein and Newfield demonstrate how multimodal pedagogies work across semiotic modes, including the visual, written, and spoken language, the gestural, the sonic, and the performative. Their research into early childhood, secondary, and tertiary classrooms reports on the limits and possibilities afforded through the use of different resources in the representation of meaning. They suggest that multimodal pedagogies can broaden the base for representation through the creation of symbolic identity objects and practices that lead to creative rapprochements in a society struggling to find a way to reconcile the demands of mainstream schooling and traditional cultural modes of representation.

The final two chapters step back to look at the impact of changes in our traditional definitions of language on English language teaching. Paltridge looks at the increased attention now given to the notion of genre in the area of English language teaching, particularly in the area of English for specific purposes (ESP), the teaching of English in Australia in the so-called Sydney School, and the teaching of composition studies, or new rhetoric, in North America. The chapter examines the similarities and differences in the way each of these perspectives defines and describes genre, and the origins of their underlying theoretical assumptions. The chapter concludes with some unresolved questions about genre-based approaches to language teaching, and future directions for genre-based language teaching and research.

In the final chapter in this section Andrews examines the increasingly important concept of teacher language awareness (TLA) in ELT. Although acknowledging the need for TLA to include a broad awareness of language in communication, this chapter concentrates specifically on TLA as it relates to the language systems. The chapter first briefly defines the nature of TLA and explores its potential significance in pedagogical practice, then examines the main research findings about the linguistic content of teaching revealed in studies of TLA and in related areas such as L2 teacher cognition. The chapter then considers current issues in the field, in particular the TLA of native-speaker and non-native-speaker teachers, before concluding with a discussion of future directions in researching and developing TLA.

This section of the handbook demonstrates that when it comes to the nature of language itself, our boundaries of knowledge and understanding are continually being twisted and bent, if not broken, in the pursuit of more relevant and authentic ways to describe what it is we are doing with language.

CHAPTER 47

PSYCHOLINGUISTIC PERSPECTIVES ON LANGUAGE AND ITS ACQUISITION

JAN H. HULSTIJN

The University of Amsterdam, The Netherlands

ABSTRACT

Knowing, using and learning a language are forms of what is often called cognition. Ideally, theories of cognition account for its representation, processing, and acquisition. Linguists in the generative school and connectionists give radically different accounts of these three dimensions of cognition, and therefore hold different views on the acquisition of speaking, listening, reading, and writing skills in a second language. Recent developments in cognitive science also result in new definitions of implicit and explicit learning, different from Krashen's notions of acquisition and learning that have influenced L2 pedagogy for more than 20 years. The chapter focuses on fluency, emphasizing the importance for L2 learners to automatize their word recognition skills in listening and reading and their word retrieval skills in speaking and writing. With regard to explicit grammar instruction, it is argued that although explicit knowledge cannot be transformed into implicit knowledge neurophysiologically, explicit grammar instruction may indirectly be beneficial to the establishment of implicit knowledge.

INTRODUCTION

Most people around the world, whether they are attending school or whether they are functioning as professionals or entertaining themselves as tourists, live with the desire to know one or more foreign languages. However, most people think that, whereas learning their mother tongue takes place naturally, incidentally, and without much effort, learning a foreign language is a long, laborious, and even boring enterprise, not unlike the learning of mathematics or physics—believed to require a high IQ. That is why, when foreign language learning is obligatory, students often begin to hate it, and, when it is voluntary, students soon drop out of classes. How realistic is the popular belief that L1 learning is easy and L2 learning is difficult? In this chapter, we look at this question from a psycholinguistic perspective. In the first part of the chapter, language acquisition is placed in a general framework of human cognition. Recent developments in cognitive science are described, leading to a conceptualization of *implicit* and *explicit learning*. These two notions are different in some essential respects from the well-known notions of *acquisition* and *learning*, proposed by Krashen (1981). The next few sections of the chapter give a brief description of the components of the processes involved in fluent speaking, listening, reading, and writing. The chapter ends with conclusions and implications for L2 instruction, focusing on fluency building.

A LINGUISTIC VIEW ON LANGUAGE ACQUISITION

Knowing, using, and learning a language are forms of what is often called *cognition*. Ideally, theories of cognition account for its *representation*, the *processing*, and the *acquisition*, three essential aspects to which we will return several times in this chapter. As we will see in the present and next section, linguists in the generative school and connectionists give different accounts of these three dimensions of cognition.

The big question, which has kept psychologists, linguists, biologists, neuroscientists, and philosophers busy for a long time, is, to what extent do we have to regard cognition as consisting of several modules, specialized in processing and storing specific kinds of information; to what extent do such modules depend on each other; and to what extent do they do their work independently of each other as if they were encapsulated or isolated (Elman et al. 1996; Fodor, 1983; Pinker, 1997)?

A major breakthrough in the discussion of this fundamental issue was produced some 50 years ago by Chomsky, the founder of generative linguistics. According to Chomsky (1986), one of the most remarkable characteristics of human languages is that they allow the generation of an infinite number of grammatical sentences. Every day, we hear and produce new sentences that we have never heard or produced before. For instance, we can, in principle, make sentences which have no end, such as "Yesterday I met the doctor's sister, who is married to a carpenter, who is the son of a teacher, who teaches in the school where ...." Chomsky also pointed out that, with elements such as words, one can generate a class of grammatical, well-formed sentences (such as *Did you order already?*), as well as a class of ungrammatical, ill-formed sentences (such as **Ordered you already?*), and that adult native speakers have intuitions concerning the grammaticality of sentences. To account for the infiniteness of language, Chomsky proposed recursive rules, operating on categories, which function as slots for items that are members of these categories. For instance, a grammar may (a) contain categories such as Sentence, Verb, and Noun Phrase (NP); (b) contain a rule stipulating that a sentence may contain a verb accompanied by one or several NPs; and (c) contain the rule that NPs can be expanded as sentences (such as the NP, *a carpenter*, expanded with the sentence, *who is the son of a teacher*). Generative linguistics, the school that grew out of Chomsky's epoch-making ideas, concerns itself with designing grammars, with which all and only the infinite set of grammatical sentences of a language can be generated. Although most linguists claim that grammars reflect the knowledge that native speakers have of their mother tongue (called *competence*), it is *not* their principal aim to account for the way language knowledge is actually (a) stored in the brain, (b) processed online, e.g., during speaking, or (c) acquired. However, they do claim that any serious theory addressing these three issues must be capable of accounting for the infiniteness of language. Chomsky, and many generative linguists with him, makes the following claims concerning language and cognition: language is a relatively encapsulated component of cognition, separate from other components (*modularity issue*); children can learn the language of their environment by virtue of an inborn Universal Grammar (*nativism*) that restricts the power of their grammars (*learnability*); and knowledge of language must be represented with *symbolic architectures*, i.e., systems of principles and rules operating on abstract categories (*symbolism*—a notion to which we will return in a later section). Most theories of L2 acquisition are based on Chomsky's school of thought. They regard L2 acquisition as a movement through successive grammars (*interlanguages*). There is, however, no consensus on the issues of whether Universal Grammar is still operative during L2 acquisition and how L1 knowledge affects L2 knowledge (Gass & Selinker, 2001, chap. 3-7).

COGNITIVE VIEWS ON LANGUAGE ACQUISITION

A view on language acquisition, in many ways radically different from that of generative linguistics, has been developed over the last 20 years by a school of thought commonly referred to as *connectionism*. A connectionist architecture or system is a network of interrelated units or nodes, representing knowledge. The connection between any two nodes is said to have a certain activation weight, reflecting the strength with which the two nodes are associated. When the system is exposed to new information (in the form of input nodes), the connection between some of its nodes may increase or decrease somewhat (acquisition or loss of knowledge). When asked to perform (use of knowledge), the system produces output nodes that reflect its current internode activation patterns (Dijkstra & de Smedt, 1996; McLeod, Plunkett, & Rolls, 1998). In most architectures, activation does spread upwards and downwards. For instance, in a simple network for the recognition of written words, if the system has recognized the word's first letter as being the letter *B*, it will activate all words beginning with a *B* while simultaneously deactivating all words not beginning with a *B*. There are many words whose first two letters are *BA,* but there are no words beginning with *BN*. The recognition of the second letter *A*, therefore, takes place not only upward but is also facilitated in a downward fashion. At the same time, the expectation that *N* will be the word's second letter is decreased.

One of the ambitions of connectionism is to tackle the representation, processing, and acquisition of cognition with a single model. Knowledge representation is the connection pattern of a network at a given moment; knowledge processing is the flowing of activation through the network when it receives new information; and knowledge acquisition is the changes in internode connection strengths, as the result of processing. After exposure to a large number of inputs, certain groups of nodes will eventually settle on more or less permanent connection weights (e.g., the group of nodes that together recognize the word *BALL*).

The notion of *frequency* is of crucial importance for an appreciation of the connectionist approach to learning. The more frequently the system is exposed to the letter string *BALL*, the more readily this string will form a strong bond, in contrast to strings which will never or seldom occur, such as *BLAL, LABL,* etc. Thus, in connectionist models, there is no absolute borderline between grammatical and ungrammatical strings. In a network representing the knowledge of a native speaker of English, the string *Ordered you already?* will not be categorically ruled out—although it will evoke an extremely low activation—whereas the sentence *Did you order already?* will have a high activation level.

Pinker (1997, 1999) and many other critics of the connectionist approach have argued that connectionist architectures may be good models of those areas of cognition that can be considered as finite, e.g., knowledge of a finite number of words and knowledge of relatively idiosyncratic phenomena such as "irregular" plurals (*mice, men*) and past tenses (*saw, took*), but that they are insufficient to account for phenomena of regularity and productivity (e.g., the fact that native speakers can easily understand new formations such as *ragas* as the plural of *raga*, and *flacked* as the past tense of *flack*, when heard for the first time). That is why so-called *hybrid models* have been proposed, consisting of connectionist architectures to handle finite forms of cognition and symbolic, rule-based architectures to handle phenomena of (infinite) regularity (e.g., Carpenter & Just, 1999; MacWhinney, 1999; Pinker, 1999). Perhaps children learn language, and other forms of cognition, first as a closed system, best represented by a connectionist architecture, and later develop open, productive forms of cognition, best represented by rule systems of the symbolic type. In a similar vein, it has been suggested that second language acquisition also proceeds in two stages. First, words and (frequent) word combinations are acquired, to be represented in architectures of the connectionist type. Later, prototype patterns of words and phrases are acquired. These patterns may first be represented in the form of connectionist networks but eventually take the form of rule-based networks, to account for their productivity (Ellis, 2002; Hulstijn, 2002).

WHAT IS THE FORM OF GRAMMATICAL KNOWLEDGE UNDERLYING FLUENT LANGUAGE USE?

It is not easy to assess the value of the arguments for and against symbolist and connectionist architectures in modern cognitive science, because it is often left implicit at which point of the so-called mind-brain continuum a certain architecture is proposed to have explanatory value. We must ask ourselves, is the architecture supposed to have a philosophical/mental, a psychological/behavioral, or a neurobiological/neurophysiological function? With this question in mind, let us look at three types of architectures.

1. A generative grammar can best be seen as an attempt to explain mental phenomena and must therefore be placed at the mind end of the continuum. Because of its serial nature (the generation of a sentence is a stepwise, serial, non-parallel procedure), such a grammar is not optimally suited to account for behavioral data, such as the speed with which we process linguistic information online during listening and speaking.
2. Connectionist architectures of the so-called *localist* type must be placed at the psychological/behavioral level of the mindbrain continuum. Such systems are networks of symbols (such as phonemes, letters, syllables, word stems, word endings, etc.). They have been mainly developed to account for the speed and accuracy of human language use. For instance, models of speaking (to which we will turn in a later section) aim to account not only for accurate speech but also for speech errors. If the model produces an error, the error should be a "human error." It may, for instance, allow for the production of the occasional human error *a pig bark* instead of the intended *a big park*, but not for the implausible error *a bag pirk*.
3. Proponents of connectionist models of the so-called *parallel distributed processing* (PDP) type have claimed both psychological and neurophysiological plausibility for these architectures. A PDP network does not have nodes that represent abstract, symbolic categories but consists, instead, of more elementary, subsymbolic units. For instance, in a

PDP network for reading, there is no single node representing the word *BALL*. *BALL* is represented in a distributed way over many nodes at levels lower than the word level (hence *subsymbolic*), as a constellation of four letters, each of which in turn consists of a number of letter features (straight-curved, long-short, horizontal-vertical, etc., lines). The neurophysiological plausibility of PDP networks rests on two claims. First, it has been claimed that there is a resemblance between PDP networks and the way neurons and their axons and synapses in brain tissue are interconnected. Second, the mechanics of activation spreading in PDP networks resembles the way in which electrochemical processes take place in the brain, involving the secretion and diffusion of neurotransmitters. However, these resemblances may only be superficial and without much significance. It is not certain, therefore, whether PDP networks have to be placed at the brain end of the continuum (Grainger & Jacobs, 1998; McLeod, Plunkett, & Rolls, 1998, p. 10).

Notwithstanding differences in view concerning the type of phenomena along the mind-brain continuum that different types of architectures purport to model, most scholars do agree on the following two claims:

Claim 1: There are some forms of cognition of which we can't have conscious, explicit, knowledge. We simply do not know how our brains and the dozens of muscles in our speech organs work together to allow us to articulate a word or a phrase. Similarly, in the realm of language reception, we are not consciously aware of how our brains and ears work together in parsing the acoustic signal into phonemes, syllables, and words. Thus, at what we may call the lower levels of cognition, explicit, conscious knowledge is hardly possible. Furthermore, it is a matter of debate whether architectures of some connectionist type (localist or PDP), are best suited to account for the representation and processing of information at this level.

Claim 2: There are forms of cognition from which we can form conscious, explicit, knowledge. Linguists and psycholinguists have uncovered, empirically investigated, and documented an impressive amount of regularities in the knowledge and online processing of language. At school, in mother tongue and foreign-language classes, many students learn some of these regularities, couched in the terms of pedagogic grammars (e.g., "Say *a* and *an* when the following word begins with a consonant or vowel, respectively"). However, adult native speakers do not consciously apply such rules when they speak or listen to others. For instance, there is evidence that to understand a passive negative sentence (e.g., *The boy wasn't hit by the car*) does not necessarily take more time than to understand the active affirmative sentence (*The car hit the boy*), although, in linguistic theories of the 1970s, the derivation of the passive negative sentence involved the application of more rules than the derivation of the active affirmative sentence (Clark & Clark, 1977, p. 143).

It is safe to conclude then that, although it remains an unresolved issue how grammatical knowledge can best be modeled in order to account for fluent speaking, listening, reading, and writing behavior, fluent language use does not involve the rapid, serial application of explicit rules. Fluency emanates from a form of implicit cognition that is not open to conscious inspection.

IMPLICIT AND EXPLICIT KNOWLEDGE AND LEARNING

On the basis of the previous discussion, we may now introduce and define the notions of implicit and explicit linguistic knowledge and learning (see Hulstijn, 2005, for a more elaborate exposition).

Implicit knowledge is knowledge that is represented in a way that allows for rapid, parallel processing. To date, connectionist networks might be the best candidates for the representation and processing of implicit knowledge. It is implicit knowledge that underlies the normal, fluent speaking, listening, reading, and writing behavior of skilled native speakers. At the phenomenological level, it can be observed that implicit knowledge is not open to conscious inspection; its processing components cannot be verbalized. Recent neurocognitive studies suggest that implicit knowledge resides not in a particular, restricted area of the brain but is spread out over various regions of the neocortex (Paradis, 1994; Reber, Allen, & Reber, 1999). *Implicit learning* is the forming of implicit knowledge. This is an autonomous, non-conscious process taking place whenever information is processed receptively (through hearing and seeing), be it intentionally and deliberately or unintentionally and incidentally. That is, once we have decided to listen, read, speak, or write, we cannot choose *not* to encode and store information, or, technically speaking, *not* to adjust the connection weights in our network.

Explicit knowledge is knowledge in the form of symbols (concepts, categories) and rules, specifying intersymbol relationships. Explicit knowledge, including many aspects of vocabulary knowledge, has been claimed to reside, or at least be processed, in a particular area of the brain (the medial temporal lobe, including the hippocampus), independent of the areas where implicit knowledge resides (Squire & Knowlton, 2000; Ullman, 2001). *Explicit learning* is the construction of explicit, verbalizable knowledge—a conscious, deliberative process of concept formation and concept linking. This process may either take place when learners are being taught concepts and rules by an instructor or textbook, or when they operate in a self-initiated searching mode, trying to develop concepts and rules on their own. Explicit learning, therefore, requires a certain cognitive development, and will generally not occur in early childhood. In most instructional settings around the world, explicit teaching and learning are the preferred modes of instruction and knowledge acquisition. This is true for many school subjects, including foreign languages.

THE INTERFACE ISSUE: CAN EXPLICIT KNOWLEDGE TRANSFORM INTO IMPLICIT KNOWLEDGE?

A burning question that is as old as the history of L2 instruction is whether the goal of establishing fluent L2 use, based on implicit L2 knowledge, can, or even must, be reached through the learning of explicit knowledge. According to Anderson and his associates, implicit knowledge can come into existence through the proceduralization of explicit knowledge (Anderson & Lebiere, 1998). According to

Logan (1988), learners may start off with a rule (e.g., "Use *a* and *an* when the following word begins with a consonant or vowel, respectively"), but each time they produce or perceive a phrase in which this rule is instantiated, they store that phrase as an *instance* in their memory. With increasing experience, these instances will become stronger in memory, raising their activation levels. Eventually, retrieval of a stored instance will be faster than rule application.

Empirical evidence, so far, does not unequivocally support either theory (for a discussion, see DeKeyser, 2001; Schmidt, 2001; Segalowitz, 2003; Segalowitz & Hulstijn, 2005). What is important in the present context, however, is that although there may be several routes of developing implicit knowledge (*automatization*), automatized processing eventually takes place in parallel and not under conscious control.

PROCESSES OF SPEAKING, LISTENING, READING, AND WRITING

What are the characteristics of skilled, fluent, implicit language behavior? This question has been studied by psycholinguists over the last 40 years with considerable success, as documented, for instance, by Gernsbacher (1994) and Miller and Eimas (1995). We will briefly review some of the robust findings of this research, relevant to SLA.

Speaking

According to the most prominent theory of speaking (Levelt, Roelofs, & Meyer, 1999), the transformation of thoughts into spoken utterances comprises a number of stages. First, there is the emergence of nonverbal thoughts. In the second stage, a search is undertaken in the mental lexicon for so-called *lexemes* that match some of the key elements of these thoughts. A lexeme is a word without information concerning its phonological form; the latter information is carried by the *lexical entry*. Lexemes and lexical entries form, as it were, two sides of the coin *word*. For instance, if a speaker wants to give a verbal expression to the thought that she visually perceived a road accident, the search in the mental lexicon may result in the activation of lexemes that correspond to the lexical entries *see, perceive, observe, view, witness*. If the speaker has opted for the lexeme *witness*, she has selected a conglomerate of semantic and grammatical features, such as the meaning *to hear or see something* and the fact that it is a verb that can take a grammatical subject and object with certain obligatory and optional features. The next stage involves the search for the lexical entry, i.e., the phonological form of the lexeme. It is not until this stage that the phoneme string /wItnəs/ is activated. One of the reasons to distinguish the lexeme from the lexical entry is the so-called *tip-of-the-tongue phenomenon*. The speaker may definitely know the word or name she wants to express but may momentarily be unable to retrieve its full form; for instance, she may be able to say, "It begins with a /w/ and it has two syllables."

The next stage in the speaking process involves the construction of an articulatory plan, which requires a phonetic specification of the lexical entries in terms of syllable structure, phonetic features, and the arrangement of the lexical entries in the right utterance order. The final stage consists of the implementation of the articulatory plan by the speech organs. The output of the articulatory plan is fed back into the language system, enabling speakers to monitor their speech plan, detect any errors in the planned utterance, and plan the utterance once more (*covert error correction*). Speakers also listen to the utterance after it has been articulated and may then detect errors, which may motivate them to plan and produce the utterance once again (*overt correction*).

Note that the stages in the production of an utterance partially overlap each other. Thus, at some point in the process of producing an utterance, a speaker may be simultanesously doing three things: articulating the first phrase, formulating the second, and contemplating about the contents of the third.

In the context of L2 instruction, it is important to note two characteristics of speaking. The first one is the fact that speakers do not select an empty grammatical structure first, and subsequently fill its slots with lexical items. Speaking is primarily lexically driven. The key lexemes, which have been selected from the mental lexicon, are matched and arranged on the basis of their grammatical specification. In general, one could say that the lexicon comes first and grammar only second. (This is largely true as well for listening, reading, and writing.) The second characteristic to bear in mind is that the planning of utterances is a matter of *parallel processing,* running off automatically without the speaker's conscious awareness. Only the actual articulation itself is largely a matter of serial processing, as speech sounds are articulated consecutively, not simultaneously.

Listening

At first, one may be inclined to think that listening is basically the same thing as speaking but in reverse order. This, however, is not the case. Developing listening skills involves the construction of a cognitive system partly independent of the system that needs to be constructed for speaking. Speech perception is a complex process of abstraction, taking auditory data as its input and producing mental representations of abstract categories, such as phonological features, phonemes, and syllables, as its output (Boersma, 1999; Harrington, 2001). *Frequency* appears to be the main driving force in the construction of such categories, in both L1 and L2 acquisition (Ellis, 2002).

Understanding the meaning of utterances involves many stages (Rost, 2002). The most crucial one is the word-by-word understanding of what is being said. Only after one or more words have been identified can the higher order processes begin to operate. These processes involve sentence parsing, reorganization of the linear order of the incoming information into a nonlinear arrangement of grammatical and semantic information units, and finally the activation of nonverbal thoughts. Listening, like speaking, is largely a matter of automatic, parallel processing. The lower-order processes of word recognition play a crucial role in these automatic processes, as it is at the level of words (i.e., lexemes) that forms are matched with meanings.

Ontogenetically, listening comes before speaking. Infants acquire their mother tongue primarily by listening. During the first few months of their lives, they become tuned to the speech sounds that are characteristic of the language spoken in their environment (Eimas, 1985). There is even a brief period during which infants of up to 6 months old can discriminate between speech sounds that are present in languages other than the language of their parents (Jusczyk, 1997). The strengthening of features characteristic of the mother tongue may simultaneously imply the inhibition of features characteristic of other languages. Thus, L1 acquisition can, in and of itself, form an obstacle to L2 acquisition. The extent to which this may be so depends on the structural differences between L1 and L2.

This is illustrated in a remarkable study on syllable segmentation, conducted by Cutler, Mehler, Norris, and Segui (1989). Native speakers of French segment their language syllable-by-syllable, as French has relatively clear (phonetic) syllable boundaries. English, however, has relatively unclear syllable boundaries and uses, instead, stress-based timing. French-English bilinguals with French as their dominant language had no difficulty switching from the marked syllabic segmentation to the unmarked stress-based processing when listening to English. English-French bilinguals with English as their dominant language, however, were not able to develop the marked syllabic segmentation procedures when listening to French. According to the investigators, these results suggest that, at the level of speech segmentation, there appears to be a limit to bilingualism (see also Cutler, 2001).

The interfering role of L1, present in speaking, writing, listening, and reading, appears to be especially hard to overcome in the case of listening, because of the high degree of automaticity of speech segmentation processes in L1. Speech segmentation pertains to lower levels of cognition than morphological and syntactic processes. Whereas the latter lend themselves more to conscious monitoring (resulting in error correction in the case of speaking), the former can hardly be consciously monitored (allowing for the interference of highly automatic L1 processes, in the case of listening). Furthermore, because of its highly implicit nature, listening provides the listener with fewer opportunities to invoke time-consuming explicit knowledge than do the other skills, as listeners, in most communicative situations, cannot influence the speed with which they process incoming speech. L2 speakers with low to intermediate L2 knowledge, can, and often have to, slow down their speaking processes, allowing themselves more time to consciously pay attention to the formulation process. That is why the speech of low-proficiency L2 speakers exhibits more pausing than that of high-proficiency L2 speakers (Towell, Hawkins, & Bazergui, 1996). Listeners, on the other hand, are dependent on the speech to which they listen: they therefore have fewer possibilities to avail themselves of extra processing time.

Reading

Reading is similar to listening in many respects, but it is certainly not identical to it. The processing of acoustic and orthographic input requires different networks with different units to be constructed. Another difference is that literacy (reading and writing) requires a form of metalinguistic knowledge, which, in turn, requires a certain cognitive development. It is only at the age of 4 or 5 years that children develop a conscious awareness for literacy. It is at around that age that they acquire words such as *meaning*, *language*, *letter*, *sound*, and *word* itself. They then become consciously aware that the words that already belonged to their daily oral vocabulary can actually be *written down* and also be *read*. Word recognition is the most important factor in fluent reading (Perfetti, 1994). Most deficiencies in literary skills are caused by problems at the lowest cognitive levels, in particular in the coding of acoustic, phonetic, and phonemic information.

Writing

Due to its complex problem-solving nature, writing requires perhaps more attention to the highest levels of information than the other language skills. Writers, when writing a particular sentence, must be aware of where they are in the text, what has been written already, and what has and what has not already been planned (Bereiter & Scardamalia, 1994; Flower & Hayes, 1980; Grabe & Kaplan, 1996). This requirement normally exceeds the attentional capacity of the writer. That is why writers spend more time on pausing (for rereading and planning) than on the very act of producing strings of letters. However, to be able to devote pausing time to higher-order information, it is mandatory that word retrieval and spelling consume relatively little time. That is why writers with high verbal ability have been shown to spend more time on text coherence than low verbal-ability writers (Glynn, Britton, Muth, & Dogan, 1982).

THE NECESSITY OF AUTOMATICITY IN L2 LEARNING

Language use requires the processing of a large amount of information in a short time. Normal speech is produced with two to three words per second (Levelt, 1989, p. 22) and must hence be processed by listeners with the same speed. Normal *linear reading*, i.e., the reading of easy text that does not require backtracking, proceeds with the pace of five words per second (Carver, 1990, p. 20). If so much information has to be processed in such a limited time, it is mandatory that most of this information is processed automatically, in parallel, without conscious monitoring, as human beings possess a limited capacity to pay conscious attention to information. It is especially the recognition of words that must be automatized so as to free up attentional capacity for the processing of the meaning of the text that is being produced or perceived (Segalowitz & Hulstijn, 2005). L2 curricula often allow too little time to be devoted to the training of fluency skills. Moreover, fluency-promoting activities, when programmed at all, often do not meet the requirement that they must not pose lexical obstacles for their successful completion. If improving learners' listening and reading fluency is the aim of a task, texts should not contain (many) unfamiliar words, as the occurrence of an unfamiliar lexical item will bring the course of listening or reading to a halt. The fundamental requirement for fluency tasks can be stated in simple terms: words can only be "re-cognized" if they are already "cognized" (Coady, 1997; Hulstijn, 2001).

CONCLUSIONS

This chapter has placed the four language skills in a general framework of the representation, processing, and acquisition of cognition. It was shown that recent developments in cognitive science now allow us to give more precise definitions of implicit and explicit knowledge and learning of a second language than Krashen (1981) could provide for his influential notions of acquisition and learning, respectively. The following conclusions and implications emerge from the literature dealt with in this chapter:

1. Humans have a limited attentional capacity for information processing. The more the processing of information at the lower levels is automatized, the

more attention language users are able to give to the higher levels of linguistic information, i.e., to meaning. Fluency-promoting activities, therefore, must have a prominent place in the L2 curriculum. (Nation, 2001, suggests spending 25% of learning time to fluency.)

2. An important element of fluent language use is automatic word recognition (in listening and reading) and automatic word retrieval (in speaking and writing). Words cannot be recognized if they are not known. The acquisition of a large vocabulary should therefore constitute a key element in any L2 curriculum (see Chapter 50 by Schmidt in this volume).

3. Acquiring a large vocabulary, however, is not enough. The recognition and retrieval of words needs to be automatized. Activities that aim to promote fluency in these skills need to meet the requirement that their linguistic demands must be at, but not beyond, the learner's current lexical knowledge (see Skehan's chapter in Volume 1 for a fuller discussion).

4. There are good reasons to regard listening as the most implicit and least explicit of the four language skills. Speech segmentation hardly lends itself to conscious monitoring. Listeners can seldom determine the speed at which they process the speech they listen to. Furthermore, speech segmentation processes in L1 play an interfering role in L2 speech segmentation because of their automatic and implicit nature. These facts call for special attention to listening tasks in the L2 curriculum.

5. Recent developments in cognitive science, with the advent of connectionism and the current debate between symbolism and connectionism, the call for hybrid systems, and recent findings in brain imaging research, have significantly increased our understanding of implicit and explicit knowledge and learning. Although the underlying, fundamental issues of human cognition (modularity, nativism) still remain to be solved, the debate has opened our eyes to the distinction between representation and processing of information: most linguistic theories appear to be poorly suited for a psychological account of the representation and processing of grammatical information, as they consist of rules that apply sequentially. Architectures are needed that allow parallel processing, the hallmark of automatic, fluent language use. Furthermore, better definitions of implicit and explicit knowledge can now be given than before (see the above, Implicit and Explicit Knowledge and Learning).

6. Explicit grammar instruction may be beneficial to the acquisition of implicit knowledge, although the actual neurocognitive mechanics are still poorly understood. However, as humans can handle only a limited amount of explicit knowledge at a time, explicit rules must be as short and simple as possible. Windy rules, although valid, must be broken down into, and replaced by, simple rules of thumb for the sake of explicit, serial, information-processing capacity. For example, for many learners of English a rule like "Use *much* with words like *money* and *many* with words like *dollars*" may be just simple enough to consciously apply during speaking, although a linguistically valid generalization would require a much longer and more complex expression, including various classes of determiners and quantifiers and a formal distinction between count and mass nouns. However, although explicit grammar instruction may have a useful place in L2 acquisition, it is important to bear in mind that implicit knowledge comes into

existence *not* through the conscious use of explicit rules itself, but only by the frequency with which a to-be-acquired linguistic construction occurs in receptive and productive language use.

In the introduction to this chapter, a question was raised: How realistic is the popular belief that L1 acquisition is easy and L2 acquisition difficult? The thrust of argument in this concluding section is that L2 acquisition can be a lot easier, and a lot more fun, than many learners (and teachers) believe, when language courses provide ample opportunities to develop fluency in word-by-word understanding, for which high levels of IQ are not required.

REFERENCES

Anderson, J.R., & Lebiere, C. 1998: *The atomic components of thought*. Mahwah, NJ: Erlbaum.

Bereiter, C., & Scardamalia, M. (1994). *The psychology of written composition*. Hillsdale, NJ: Lawrence Erlbaum.

Boersma, P. (1999). On the need for a separate perception grammar. *Rutgers Optimality Archives*, 358. Retrieved September 2 2005 from http://www.fon.hum.uva.nl/paul/.

Carpenter, P. A., & Just, M. A. (1999). Computational modeling of high-level cognition versus hypothesis testing. In R. J. Sternberg (Ed.), *The nature of cognition* (pp. 245–293). Cambridge, MA: MIT Press.

Carver, R. P. (1990). *Reading rate: A review of research and theory*. San Diego, CA: Academic Press.

Chomsky, N. (1986). *Knowledge of language: Its nature, origin and use*. New York: Praeger.

Clark, H. H., & Clark, E. V. (1977). *Psychology and language*. New York: Harcourt Brace Jovanovich.

Coady, J. (1997). L2 vocabulary acquisition through extensive reading. In J. Coady & T. Huckin (Eds.), *Second language vocabulary acquisition* (pp. 225–237). Cambridge, UK: Cambridge University Press.

Cutler, A., Mehler, J., Norris, D., & Segul, J. (1989). Limits on bilingualism. *Nature, 340*, 229–230.

Cutler, A. (2001). Listening to a second language through the ears of a first. *Interpreting, 5*, 1–18.

DeKeyser, R.M. (2001). Implicit and explicit learning. In C. J. Doughty & M. H. Long (Eds.), *The handbook of second language acquisition* (pp. xx–yy). Cambridge, MA: Blackwell.

Dijkstra, T., & De Smedt, K. (1996). Computer models in psycholinguistics: An introduction. In T. Dijkstra & K. De Smedt (Eds.), *Computational psycholinguistics* (pp. 3–23). London: Taylor and Francis.

Eimas, P. (1985). The perception of speech in early infancy. *Scientific American, 252*, 34–40.

Ellis, N. (2002). Frequency effects in language processing: A review with implications for theories of implicit and explicit language acquisition. *Studies in Second Language Acquisition, 24*, 143–188.

Elman, J. L., Bates, E. A., Johnson, M. H., Karmiloff-Smith, A., Parisi, D., & Plunkett, K. (1996). *Rethinking innateness: A connectionist perspective on development*. Cambridge, MA: MIT Press.

Flower, L. S., & Hayes, J. R. (1980). The dynamics of composing: Making plans and juggling constraints. In L. W. Gregg & E. R. Steinberg (Eds.), *Cognitive processes in writing* (pp. 31–50). Hillsdale, NJ: Erlbaum.

Fodor, J. A. (1983). *The modularity of mind*. Cambridge, MA: MIT Press.

Gass, S., & Selinker, L. (2001). *Second language acquisition: An introductory course*. Mahwah, NJ: Erlbaum.

Gernsbacher, M. A. (Ed.). (1994). *Handbook of psycholinguistics*. San Diego: Academic Press.

Glynn, S. M., Britton, B. K., Muth, D., & Dugan, N. (1982). Writing and revising persuasive documents: Cognitive demands. *Journal of Educational Psychology, 71*, 557–567.

Grabe, W., & Kaplan, R. (1996). *Theory and practice of writing: An applied linguistic perspective*. Harlow, UK: Longman.

Grainger, J., & Jacobs, A. M. (1998). On localist connectionism and psychological science. In J. Grainger & A. M. Jacobs (Eds.), *Localist connectionist approaches to human cognition* (pp. 1–38). Mahwah, NJ: Erlbaum.

Harrington, M. (2001). L2 sentence processing. In P. Robinson (Ed.), *Cognition and second language instruction* (pp. 91–124). Cambridge: Cambridge University Press.

Hulstijn, J. H. (2001). Intentional and incidental second-language vocabulary learning: A reappraisal of elaboration, rehearsal and automaticity. In P. Robinson (Ed.), *Cognition and second language instruction* (pp. 258–286). Cambridge: Cambridge University Press.

Hulstijn, J. H. (2002). Towards a unified account of the representation, processing, and acquisition of second-language knowledge. *Second Language Research, 18*, xx–yy.
Hulstijn, J.H. (2005). Theoretical and empirical issues in the study of implicit and explicit second-language learning. *Studies in Second Language Acquisition, 27*, 129–140.
Jusczyk, P. W. (1997). *The discovery of spoken language*. Cambridge, MA: MIT Press.
Krashen, S. D. (1981), *Second language acquisition and second language learning*. Oxford, UK: Pergamon Press.
Levelt, W. J. M. (1989). *Speaking: From intention to articulation*. Cambridge, MA: MIT Press.
Levelt, W. J. M., Roelofs, A., & Meyer, A. S. (1999). A theory of lexical access in speech production. *Behavioral and Brain Sciences, 22*, 1–75.
Logan, G.D. (1988). Toward an instance theory of automatization. *Psychological Review, 95*, 492–527.
MacWhinney, B. (Ed.). (1999). *The emergence of language*. Mahwah, NJ: Erlbaum.
McLeod, P., Plunkett, K., & Rolls, E. T. (1998). *Introduction to connectionist modeling of cognitive processes*. Oxford, UK: Oxford University Press.
Miller, J. L., & Eimas, P. D. (Eds.). (1995). *Speech, language, and communication: Handbook of perception and cognition* (2nd Ed.) San Diego: Academic Press.
Nation, I.S.P. (2001). *Learning vocabulary in another language*. Cambridge: Cambridge University Press.
Paradis, M. (1994). Neurolinguistic aspects of implicit and explicit memory: Implications for bilingualisms and SLA. In N. Ellis (Ed.), *Implicit and explicit learning of languages* (pp. 393–419). London: Academic Press.
Perfetti, C. A. (1994). Psycholinguistics and reading ability. In M. A. Gernsbacher (Ed.), *Handbook of psycholinguistics* (pp. 849–894). San Diego: Academic Press.
Pinker, S. (1997). *How the mind works*. New York: Norton.
Pinker, S. (1999). *Words and rules: The ingredients of language*. London: Weidenfeld & Nicolson.
Reber, A. S., Allen, R., & Reber, P. J. (1999). Implicit versus explicit learning. In R. J. Sternberg (Ed.), *The nature of cognition* (pp. 475–513). Cambridge, MA: MIT Press.
Rost, M. (2002). *Teaching and research listening*. Harlow, UK: Longman.
Schmidt, R. (2001). Attention. In P. Robinson (Ed.), *Cognition and second language instruction* (pp. 3–32). Cambridge, UK: Cambridge University Press.
Segalowitz, N. (2003). Automaticity and second language learning. In C. Doughty & M. Long (Eds.), *The handbook of second language acquisition* (pp. 382–408). Oxford: Blackwell.
Segalowitz, N., & Hulstijn, J. (2005). Automaticity in second language learning. In J. F. Kroll & A. M. B. De Groot (Eds.), *Handbook of bilingualism: Psycholinguistic approaches* (pp. 371–388). Oxford: Oxford University Press.
Squire, L. R., & Knowlton, B. J. (2000). The medial temporal lobe, the hippocampus, and the memory systems of the brain. In M. S. Gazzaniga (Ed.), *The new cognitive neurosciences* (pp. 765–779). Cambridge, MA: MIT Press.
Towell, R., Hawkins, R., & Bazergui, N. (1996). The development of fluency in advanced learners of French. *Applied Linguistics, 17*, 84–119.
Ullman, M. T. (2001). The neural basis of lexicon and grammar in first and second language: The declarative/procedural model. *Bilingualism: Language and Cognition, 4*, 105–122.

CHAPTER 48

ACADEMIC LANGUAGE:

What Is It and How Do We Acquire It?

JIM CUMMINS

The University of Toronto, Canada

AND

EVELYN MAN YEE-FUN

The Chinese University of Hong Kong, China

ABSTRACT

This chapter proposes a framework for conceptualizing the nature of academic language and the pedagogical conditions that foster its development. Academic language proficiency is distinguished from both conversational fluency and discrete language skills and defined as the ability to understand and express, in both oral and written modes, concepts and ideas that are relevant to success in school. Extensive reading is crucial for academic language development because less frequent vocabulary, most of which derives from Greek and Latin sources, is found primarily in written text. Also, grammatical constructions and discourse structures found in typical written text differ significantly from those found in conversational interactions. The implications of this conceptualization of academic language for English language teaching in Hong Kong are discussed.

INTRODUCTION

English language teaching is obviously intended to develop English language proficiency. Policy makers and curriculum designers typically think of English language proficiency in terms of the four "language skills"—speaking, listening, reading, and writing. This conceptualization of language proficiency has the advantage of corresponding to obvious distinctions in how we use and experience language but it also suffers from significant limitations with respect to the development of policy for curriculum design and language instruction.

The problem comes from the fact that none of the four language skills represents a unitary construct. If we ignore the distinctions within the four language skills we risk designing curricula and language instruction practices that are poorly aligned with the needs of learners and the overall goals of the program. As we illustrate later in this chapter, in the Hong Kong context, for example, English curricula and textbooks at the primary school level have implicitly conceptualized "English proficiency" as relatively superficial conversational skills. However, this kind of proficiency is far removed from the use of English for academic purposes. Consequently, many pupils go on to English-medium secondary schools ill-prepared for the language demands of English literature, social studies, science, and mathematics.

Speaking skills can range from face-to-face conversation about familiar everyday topics that require only high frequency vocabulary to the ability to give an oral report of a science experiment, summarize the plot of an English novel, or debate a controversial topic. All of these speaking skills will require a much broader range of vocabulary knowledge, grammatical sophistication, and discourse competence than is the case with typical face-to-face conversation. In fact, these skills have much more in common with reading comprehension abilities than they do with face-to-face conversation insofar as the vocabulary required for successful completion of the tasks is typically found only in text or in classrooms where academic topics are being discussed and taught.

Similarly, the registers of writing often found in email or Internet chat rooms have as much in common with conversational language as they do with written language. Likewise, reading does not constitute a unitary construct. The decoding skills required to read a text represent a very different set of abilities than the skills and conceptual knowledge required to understand the text that we are reading. Not surprisingly, the forms of instruction that are effective in developing decoding skills may be quite limited in their capacity to promote sustained development of reading comprehension skills (Cummins, Brown, & Sayers, 2007).

In this chapter we discuss an alternative framework for conceptualizing academic language, and language proficiency more generally, and illustrate its applications in the context of English language instructional policy in Hong Kong. Although we focus on the Hong Kong context for illustrative purposes, the issues are of central importance in language education contexts around the world. We conclude with suggestions for developing language policies both at the level of the school and at the level of educational systems as a whole.

THE NATURE OF LANGUAGE PROFICIENCY

Educational policies in many different contexts are frequently based on assumptions about the nature of language proficiency and how long it takes to attain. For example, funding for English as a second language (ESL) and bilingual education classes in North America is based (at least in part) on assumptions about how long it takes English language learners (ELL) to acquire sufficient English proficiency to follow instruction in the regular classroom. These assumptions have significant implications for funding and level of support provided to ELL students. If we assume that English proficiency can be acquired within a year, then the funding burden is much less than if we assume that five years is likely to be required to catch up to grade expectations in English proficiency. For example, Proposition 227 that was passed by Californian voters in 1998 explicitly claimed that one year of intensive English support was sufficient to enable ELL students to catch up academically. Subsequent research has shown that this claim was "wildly unrealistic" (Hakuta, Butler, & Witt, 2000, p. 13). However, the persuasiveness of the claim was based on the common observation that many ELL students *do* acquire reasonably fluent conversational skills in English within one or two years. Thus, both policy and politics can be swayed by confusions between conversational and academic language skills.

A related contentious issue concerns the validity and appropriateness of administering state-mandated standardized tests to ELL students. Clearly, to administer English reading and writing measures to a grade 5 ELL student who has been learning English for only a few months is unlikely to yield any useful accountability data regarding the quality of instruction in that student's classroom. It is also ethically problematic to require a student to take a high stakes test that she or he has no possibility of passing. Such a procedure is likely to damage the student's academic confidence and self-esteem. But when does it become reasonable to administer state-mandated assessments to ELL students—after one year, two years, or three or more years? What accommodations in administration procedure or interpretation are required to make the test more meaningful?

Similar issues play themselves out within the international schools context. What forms of support should be provided for students who come to school with minimal English? How long should these supports be provided? What are the roles of the ESL teacher and classroom teachers in providing support for students? How should parents support their children's acquisition of English and their academic development generally? Misconceptions about these issues abound.

Research in both first and second language contexts suggests the need to distinguish three dimensions of language proficiency that become differentiated from each other as development progresses: (a) conversational fluency, (b) discrete language skills, and (c) academic language proficiency. The rationale for making these distinctions is that each dimension of proficiency follows a different developmental path among both first and second language students and each responds differently to particular kinds of instructional practices in school.

Conversational Fluency

This dimension of language proficiency represents the ability to carry on a conversation in familiar face-to-face situations. The vast majority of native speakers of English have developed conversational fluency when they enter school at age 5. This fluency involves use of high frequency words and simple grammatical constructions. ELL students generally develop fluency in conversational aspects of English within a year or two of intensive exposure to the language either in school or in the environment. Thus, immigrant students within an English-speaking country will often pick up sufficient native-like phonology and fluency in English to blend in to the mainstream classroom relatively quickly. However, this fluency frequently conceals significant gaps in their vocabulary knowledge and in other aspects of academic language proficiency. Students who do not have exposure to the target language in the environment will take much longer to develop fluency even when the language is used for instructional purposes within the school. In these contexts, students' spoken language tends to reflect a 'classroom dialect' that contains many influences from their first language (L1).

Discrete Language Skills

These skills involve the learning of rule-governed aspects of language (including phonology, grammar, and spelling) where acquisition of the general case permits generalization to other instances governed by that particular rule. Becker describes this process with respect to decoding as follows: "One can teach a set of sounds, blending skills, and rapid pronunciation skills, so that the student can read any regular-sound word composed from the sounds taught" (1977, p. 533).

Discrete language skills can be developed in two independent ways: (a) by direct instruction (e.g. systematic explicit phonics instruction, grammar instruction, etc.), and (b) through immersion in a literacy- and language-rich home or school environment. A combination of these two conditions appears to yield the most positive outcomes (e.g. Cunningham, 1990; Hatcher, Hulme, & Ellis, 1994). For example, in the case of reading and writing development, students exposed to a literacy-rich environment in the home generally acquire initial literacy-related skills, such as phonological awareness and letter-sound correspondences, with minimal difficulty in the early grades of schooling.

ELL students can learn the specific language skills associated with literacy development concurrently with their development of basic vocabulary and conversational fluency (Weber & Longhi-Chirlin, 2001). About two years is typically required for many ELL students in English-medium programs to acquire basic decoding skills in English to a level similar to that of their English-speaking classmates (e.g. Geva, 2000; Lesaux & Siegel, 2003). The acquisition of decoding (and encoding) skills is an important achievement. However, it is just the beginning step in the process of developing academic language proficiency. Little direct transference is observed to more academic aspects of oral language proficiency such as linguistic concepts, vocabulary knowledge, sentence memory, and word memory (see review by Geva, 2000). Similar findings are reported by Kwan and Willows (1998) for ELL students in the Canadian context, Verhoeven (2000) for minority language students in the Dutch context, and by Lambert and Tucker (1972) for English-speaking students in French immersion programs.

The distinction between discrete language skills and academic language proficiency is also evident in the case of writing instruction. Valdés (2004) notes that writing instruction frequently focuses only on the mechanics of writing with particular concern for spelling and grammatical accuracy. Even when the focus is broadened somewhat, concern with organization and mechanics predominates: "Teachers are being encouraged to expect that the presence of topic sentences, body paragraphs, introductions and conclusions, coupled with the absence of major mechanical and grammatical errors equals good writing" (2004, p. 122). She goes on to lament the fact that what is missing entirely from discussions of academic discourse to L2 learners is "the notion that writing is about ideas, that presentations are about ideas, and that when one engages in writing and speaking one also engages in a dialogue with others" (2004, p. 122).

Academic Language Proficiency

Academic language proficiency reflects the extent to which an individual has access to and command of the oral and written academic registers of schooling. In other words, it refers to students' ability to understand and express, in both oral and written modes, concepts and ideas that are relevant to success in school. Valdés (2004) summarizes the conception of academic language embedded in the TESOL Standards document (TESOL, 1997):

> In the *Standards* document, for example, we are told that to achieve academically students will use English to follow oral and written directions both implicitly and explicitly, request and provide clarification, request information and assistance, explain actions, negotiate and manage interactions, and ask and answer questions. They will also use English to obtain, process, construct, and provide subject matter information in written form. They will retell information, compare and contrast information, persuade, argue, and justify, analyse, synthesise and infer from information. They will also hypothesize and predict, understand and produce technical vocabulary and text features according to the content area. (2004, p. 121)

Thus academic language proficiency includes knowledge of the less frequent vocabulary of English as well as the ability to interpret and produce increasingly complex written and oral language. As students progress through the grades, they encounter far more low frequency words (primarily from Greek and Latin sources), complex syntax (e.g. passives), and abstract expressions that are virtually never heard in everyday conversation. Students are required to understand linguistically and conceptually demanding texts in the content areas such as literature, social studies, science, and mathematics, and to use this language in an accurate and coherent way in their own writing.

Acquiring academic language is challenging for all students. For example, schools spend at least 12 years trying to extend the conversational language that native-speaking children bring to school into these more complex academic language spheres. It is hardly surprising, therefore, that research has repeatedly shown that ELL students, on average, require at least 5 years of exposure to academic English to catch up to native-speaker norms (Cummins, 1981; Hakuta, Butler, & Witt, 2000; Klesmer, 1994; Thomas & Collier, 2002; Worswick, 2001). In Israel, research has shown that Russian and Ethiopian immigrant students require at least 9 years to catch up to their peers in academic Hebrew (Shohamy, Levine, Spolsky, Kere-Levy, Inbar, Shemesh, 2002). Many ELL students who have acquired conversational fluency and decoding skills in English are still a long way from grade-level performance in academic language proficiency (e.g. reading comprehension) (Cummins, 2000, 2001; Krashen, 2001; Weber & Longhi-Chirlin, 2001).

In short, the evidence for distinguishing these three dimensions of language proficiency is that their developmental trajectories are different among both first and second language learners, and minimal direct transfer is observed between the acquisition of conversational fluency and discrete language skills, on the one hand, and the development of academic language proficiency on the other. These findings have many implications for teaching.

TEACHING THE LANGUAGE OF ACADEMIC SUCCESS

Fielding and Pearson (1994, p. 62) highlight four instructional components that research suggests are strongly related to reading comprehension outcomes:

- Large amounts of time for actual text reading;
- Teacher-directed instruction in comprehension strategies;
- Opportunities for peer and collaborative learning; and
- Occasions for students to talk to a teacher and one another about their responses to reading.

Extensive reading is crucial for academic language development because less frequent vocabulary, most of which derives from Greek and Latin sources, is found primarily in written text. According to Corson:

> Printed texts provided much more exposure to [Graeco-Latin] words than oral ones. For example, even children's books contained 50% more rare words than either adult prime-time television or the conversations of university graduates; popular magazines had three times as many rare words as television and informal conversation. (1997, p. 677)

The research is unequivocal is showing strong relationships for both L1 and L2 learners between opportunities to read and development of vocabulary and reading comprehension abilities (e.g. Elley, 1991; Krashen, 2004; Postheltwaite & Ross, 1992). Research also supports the importance of explicit instruction in comprehension strategies and explanation of word meanings (Pressley, Duke, & Boling, 2004; Rand Reading Study Group, 2002).

With specific reference to second language learners, Wong Fillmore (1997, p. 4) has articulated the role that teachers should play in making texts work as input for language learning:

- Provide the support learners need to make sense of the text;
- Call attention to the way language is used in the text;
- Discuss with learners the meaning and interpretation of sentences and phrases within the text;
- Point out that words in one text may have been encountered or used in other places;
- Help learners discover the grammatical cues that indicate relationships such as cause and effect, antecedence and consequence, comparison and contrast, and so on.

Wong Fillmore points out that teachers transform written texts into usable input not only by helping children make sense of the text but by drawing their attention to how language is used in the materials they read. When students are reading extensively and when teachers are consistently focusing their attention on the intersections of meanings and linguistic features, the learners themselves will soon come to notice the way language is used in the texts they are reading. At this stage, everything they read becomes input for learning.

We illustrate the relevance of a clear understanding of the nature of academic language proficiency with reference to language policy and practice in the Hong Kong context.

THE HONG KONG CONTEXT

Most primary (elementary) schools in Hong Kong use Chinese as the medium of instruction (CMI). However, about a quarter of the students switch to English medium in secondary school. In 1997, the Hong Kong government issued a policy that allowed 112 secondary schools out of a total of over 400 to be English-medium (EMI) (Hong Kong Education Department, 1997). To qualify as an EMI secondary school, the schools have to satisfy three criteria: students have to attain a minimum threshold level of English language proficiency, teachers have to demonstrate that they can teach competently in the language, and there should be a rich English language environment in the school. Though standards for meeting such criteria are controversial, the public has generally acknowledged that these criteria should be met. Despite this, EMI schools find that students are experiencing increasing difficulties learning English and learning through English. A huge gap is evident between the primary and secondary English language curriculum, and between the language demands of the English subject and that of other content subjects (Man, 2004). Principals and teachers voice increasing concern with students' ability to cope with English academic content subjects in EMI schools.

A study was conducted by the Chinese University of Hong Kong (CUHK) and the Government's Education and Manpower Bureau (EMB) to examine the adaptation of first year secondary students as they switch from CMI primary to EMI secondary education. Five EMI schools participated in the project and questionnaires were received from about 1000 Form 1 students and 100 teachers. Focus group interviews were conducted with students as well as English language and content subject teachers. Teachers reported that many students could not follow a lesson conducted entirely in English, had difficulty expressing themselves in English, and were not capable of fully understanding reading material in the content areas. Students also had difficulty dealing with long and linguistically complex texts, and were incapable of writing academic texts coherently and in a well-organized manner. In class students often failed to express salient points in an oral presentation and showed little confidence speaking in English; many had received little phonics instruction and could hardly spell. Since the majority of students had not developed good English reading habits, they lacked the reading strategies and skills necessary for tackling academic tasks. As a result, many students appeared passive in class, felt English was extremely difficult and lost any motivation to learn in English as they moved into senior levels. Content subject teachers often had to use Cantonese to supplement their explanation and elaboration of concepts in subject areas (Man, Coniam, & Lee, 2004).

Interviews with students revealed that 35% of them found learning content-based subjects in English very difficult (Man, Coniam & Lee, 2002). Specific difficulties included:

- dealing with as many as 20 new English vocabulary words in various subjects every day, many of which they had never come across in primary school;
- inability to tackle complex grammatical structures in subject readings;
- inability to grasp abstract ideas and comprehend general meaning of texts;
- difficulty in writing continuous and lengthy texts;

- difficulty in expressing themselves in oral presentations;
- problems in spelling.

50% of the students felt that subject teachers were more concerned with transmitting academic content in subjects such as history, science, and mathematics than in helping them to understand the language associated with the content. They felt that both English teachers and content teachers should play a more active role in helping students adapt to EMI. The findings suggest that students' foundation in academic English is weak. They lack exposure to the different registers of academic text in both oral and written modes. Students are faced with significant challenges in using formal English to read, write and conduct oral presentations for different content-based subjects in an EMI learning environment when they are baffled by subject-specific vocabulary and the ways in which subject texts are organized.

Curriculum and Materials

The Primary English Curriculum (Curriculum Development Council, 1997) issued by the government stresses a communicative use of the language that is essentially task-based and activity-oriented (see Spada, Volume 1, for a fuller discussion of communicative language teaching). Unfortunately, many primary school teachers' interpretation of the communicative approach tends to be rather narrow and focuses largely on daily spoken communication and face-to-face conversation. Some even believe that grammar should not be stressed, possibly reflecting the fact that they may have weak grammatical competence themselves. During the primary school years, fun and pleasure in English learning are heavily emphasized. English learning activities include story-telling, songs, drama, big books and so forth. Since some primary school teachers have limited exposure to English and their English proficiency may not be high, textbooks often take on the role of the teacher. The English textbooks at the primary level contain a lot of pictures, single words in isolation, short phrases, matching exercises, simple and repetitive language structures, all in a very limited narrative context. Visuals abound and cartoon characters engage in daily conversation with artificial dialogues in speech bubbles. This pattern carries over to textbooks even at the Form 1 level.

The themes found in the Primary English Curriculum include daily topics like *Family, School, Friends, Food, Festivals*, and so on. For example, in a widely-used Grade 6 English textbook (Dallas & Pelham, 2000), there is a lesson on *At the international food festival* that teaches students some vocabulary related to food. There is a buyer and seller of food and the entire page is covered with pictures of different kinds of food and dialogues of everyday spoken English. Two question forms are taught and illustrated by the cartoon characters: "Hello, what food are you selling?" and "How much do they cost?" Students are then expected to answer with simple substitute structures like "I sell hamburgers/ fried rice/ chicken wings/ pizza" and so on, reflecting common food items that students are likely to encounter. Simple role-plays are suggested as class activities. Such artificial dialogues and daily conversation pieces are commonly found in primary level textbooks at all grade levels.

Consider another lesson entitled 'Visiting the doctor' from the same textbook. The page shows different people pressing parts of the body that require attention. A list of vocabulary describing various kinds of symptoms such as a headache, stomach ache, tooth ache, sore throat, or runny nose appears at the bottom of the page. Students learn these simple words through role playing a conversation with the doctor, and they match different characters with different symptoms. With clear visual cues, students have little difficulty completing the matching exercise correctly. The English they are required to produce is to repeat and substitute a simple sentence "Mr. X has a headache/stomach ache/ tooth ache" and so on. Again, a conversational role-play between a doctor and a patient is suggested.

In order to teach students how to describe people or objects, the English textbook makes use of the situation of a policeman identifying a thief with certain characteristics. Photos of six thieves are presented and students help the police to match the photos with certain descriptions. Again, there is a strong emphasis on everyday language and substitution exercises such as: 'Is it the man in the black coat/ green shorts/ blue jeans/ white T-shirt' etc. Where listening and writing are required of the students, they listen to a short description and fill in the blanks of the length, width and weight of certain objects.

A closer look at the content of the textbooks that students use in Grade 6 and Form 1 gives a clearer picture of the nature of the gap between the primary and secondary English curriculum, and between English for conversational fluency versus the English required for academic study. In EMI schools, what language demands are placed on students learning content subjects in English? What kind of language do students really need at Form 1 level and how does it differ from what has been taught at the primary level?

From a junior secondary Geography textbook (Ip, Lam, & Wong, 1999), there is a text about locating a place on a map by using grid reference. In contrast to primary school English texts, there are no cartoon pictures, no speech bubbles, no dialogues of spoken English and no repetition of simple sentences. Instead, the text is made up of a number of sentences with extensive nominalization as well as vocabulary that carries special meanings in a specific subject area. The following passage is extracted from the text:

> There are two sets of lines on the map. They are called **grid lines**. Each grid line is numbered by a two digit value. The vertical grid lines are called **eastings**. Their number values increase eastwards. The horizontal grid lines are called **northings**. Their number values increase northwards. A grid reference on a map is formed by the number of an **easting** and the number of a **northing**. It may be either four-figure or six-figure. (Ip et al. 1999, p. 8).

Students might be familiar with the meaning of a few single words such as 'line', 'number', 'north' and 'east' taught in primary school, but the meaning of 'two digit value', 'two sets of lines', 'vertical', 'horizontal', 'number values', or 'grid reference' would likely escape the students, not to mention the special terminology in bold. Students frequently would try to memorize words like 'vapor', 'evaporate', 'evaporation' and 'vaporization' as completely different words, not realizing that they all come from the same root (Man, 2004).

Take another example from a mathematics textbook for Form 1. The heading is *Notations for various numeral systems* (Leung, Chu, & Fok, 2001). It is likely that three words out of the five in the heading –'notation', 'numeral' and perhaps 'systems' would be unfamiliar to students whose previous learning of English has focused on simple everyday vocabulary. Other low frequency words not commonly used in everyday conversation are shown below in bold. In the introductory subheading *Numeral systems around us*, the passage reads:

> In everyday life, we prefer using **measuring** units in the **metric** system to simplify **calculation** and **conversion**. The **metric** system is a **decimal** (or denary) system, the conversion factors are either 10 or **powers** of 10... Numerals are **symbols** used to **denote** numbers, e.g. 0, 1, etc. are Arabic numerals and I, X, etc. are Roman numerals... (Leung, et al., 2001, p. 97)

An example taken from an Economics and Public Affairs textbook also has low frequency new words in every sentence. Again, vocabulary words that have probably not been taught at the primary level are in bold:

> **With effect from** July 1, 1997, Hong Kong became a **special administrative region** according to the **constitution** of the People's Republic of China. Hong Kong is **directly** under the Central People's Government. It enjoys a high **degree** of **autonomy**, which is even higher than that of the **provinces** (such as Guangdong), **autonomous regions** (such as Xinjiang) and **municipalities** (such as Shanghai). (Ng & Leung, 1999, p. 31)

Students mention that even though they may know the meaning of individual words, when these words are put together in a sentence, they have difficulty understanding the whole phrase or sentence and the related concepts. A common strategy that students adopt is to look up individual words in a bilingual dictionary. However, knowing the meaning of each word does not guarantee that they understand the associated concept. In addition, with unfamiliar words in every line, the lexical density, lexical variation and new word density within a short paragraph make it extremely difficult for the students to grasp the meaning and concepts easily. The frequent use of the passive form in formal texts is certainly not something that students would be familiar with from daily conversation.

Knowing that students have difficulty coping with the language, publishers and teachers try to reduce students' academic load by simplifying the English. In an attempt to help Secondary One students learn content subject matter through English, publishers produce simplified texts. For example, the following sentence found in a Form 1 science text *Many inventions and discoveries are the result of scientists asking and trying to find answers* (Chan, Hui, Luk & Kong, 2000, p. 60) appears in the simplified text as *Scientists ask questions and try to answer them. So they make new discoveries*. A complex sentence is broken down into two simple sentences and active voice is used rather than passive voice. Take another example, the passage *It would be very dangerous if you do not use a Bunsen burner properly and therefore safety measures need to be taken. Before starting to use a Bunsen burner you have to know its structure* is simplified to *To use the Bunsen burner safely, you have to know its structure*. Simplification of the language is reflected in shorter expressions, more frequent use of the active voice, more commonly used vocabulary words, and sometimes more abrupt organization of the language. Cause and effect expressions commonly found in academic discourse are regarded as being too difficult for students, and long texts with complex structures seen as inappropriate. Whether ELLs' language proficiency really develops from such language reduction in simplified texts is open to question.

Language reduction takes another form when students are expected to read only short phrases, fill in the blanks instead of having to write continuous text, or express ideas by constantly using bullet points. An example from a Form 1 chemistry text (Tao, Yung, Wong, Or, & Wong, 2000) is the following: After finishing a chemistry experiment, students are asked to answer the question of what happens to the color of a rod used as an indicator. Instead of allowing students to give open-ended answers, a very limited response to fill in a blank is provided: *Exhaled air contains ___ (less/more) carbon dioxide than fresh air.* When asked "Which splint burns more brightly?", again, only a very limited response is required: *Exhaled air contains ___ (less/more) oxygen than fresh air.* In answer to the more demanding question "Why does the flame go out?", students do not have to exercise their imagination or give their reasons, but only to fill in one blank: *Because the burning candle has used up ___ in the air.* Eliciting such responses from students does not encourage the development of imagination, creativity or critical thinking. In many content subject textbooks, academic language is simplified and diluted by extensive use of matching exercises, filling in the blanks, use of bullet points as well as short and simple phrases or sentences. Such language reduction is not conducive to developing higher-order thinking skills, and limits the chances for students to strengthen their academic language proficiency.

To develop proficiency in academic English, students need systematic scaffolding and instruction to deal with longer texts, structurally more complex sentences, more subject-specific new vocabulary, less visual material, and more creative and critical higher-order thinking skills. Furthermore, students need greater exposure to readings of different text types, such as narrative texts to provide a comforting linear structure for reading fluency, expository texts to provide useful repeated exposure to key vocabulary, and argumentative texts for developing reasoning and justification. Extensive reading and writing is essential for the development of academic English, which students need to acquire for academic success and for higher education. Students need to be engaged in knowledge construction in both oral and written form, be supported to understand rhetorical patterns in the language and basic linguistic cues such as prefixes, suffixes and root words, and become familiar with a variety of subject-specific examples. The new English Language Curriculum Guide for Primary School (Curriculum Development Council, 2004) recommends that 40% of the curriculum should be devoted to reading. This is a step in the right direction, but the reading needs to be better integrated with the other things that students are taught. In EMI schools, it is crucial to adopt a language across the curriculum approach in which English language teachers work together with content subject teachers to understand better the language necessary for academic success. Until educators recognize the importance of developing academic language proficiency and what is involved in it, students will still have a long way to go before they can attain the high levels of English proficiency required for educational success.

CONCLUSIONS

We have highlighted the fact that teaching through the medium of a second language is no panacea either for acquisition of that language or for learning content taught through the language. Carefully planned instruction is essential to help students acquire content knowledge and develop their target language proficiency. At the level of the school (e.g. EMI secondary schools in Hong Kong), policy should address the following questions:

- Do subject matter teachers see their role as *language* teachers in addition to content teachers? What resources or additional professional training do they require to fulfill this dual role adequately?

- Do language teachers systematically connect the target language to the vocabulary, grammatical structures and discourse features that students are encountering in the different content areas?
- Are students being provided with intrinsic and extrinsic incentives to read extensively (and critically) in the target language and to discuss the content of their reading with peers and teachers?
- Do language and content teachers draw students' attention systematically to how the target language works in the texts that students are reading? Is there a focus on building up students' language awareness across the curriculum?
- Are students being provided with opportunities and incentives to use the target language, in both written and oral forms, in ways that are meaningful and identity-enhancing to them? Examples might be the writing of dual language (e.g. Chinese and English) books for younger students, writing of poetry in both languages, sister class projects in content areas such as social studies, math and science in which students collaborate with students from other parts of the world through the Internet, etc. (see Cummins, Brown, & Sayers, 2007). Collaborative projects such as these encourage students to take ownership of the language as a tool that is relevant to their lives rather than simply an academic subject to be studied for examinations.

In the Hong Kong context, it would also be important to address at the primary school level the discontinuity between the conversational focus of the primary English curriculum and the academic focus of instruction in EMI secondary schools. There is a relatively straightforward way to do this. Because academic language is found primarily in written text, extensive reading is an essential means of gaining access to this language. At both secondary and primary levels, it is equally important to give students ample opportunities to encounter and use the oral and written registers of academic English. Students need to engage actively with literacy in the target language if they are to develop the kind of academic language proficiency required to succeed at the secondary school level.

In the context of students' reading and discussion (in Chinese or English) of these books, teachers can focus students' attention on lexical, grammatical, and discourse features of the language. Educators might also explore technological tools that scaffold English texts through built-in electronic voice and dictionary supports, thereby enabling students to read texts that might otherwise have been too difficult for them (Chascas & Cummins, 2005). In addition to promoting extensive reading of high-interest books of appropriate difficulty in English, students can also be encouraged to use the target language to create literature and art, for example through the creation of dual language books in Chinese and English. They can be provided with opportunities to participate in musical and dramatic performances and to use readily available technology (e.g. digital cameras, camcorders) to record these performances for sharing with sister classes. All of these instructional strategies have been implemented successfully (see, for example, the Dual Language Showcase, http://thornwood.peelschools.org/Dual/, and the Multiliteracies Project web site, www.multiliteracies.ca, for Canadian examples) and they illustrate a central prerequisite for academic language development: Students will learn and take ownership of a language to the extent that it opens up opportunities for them to communicate, either orally or in written form, their ideas, feelings, imaginations, and identities to others who matter to them.

REFERENCES

Becker, W. C. (1977). Teaching reading and language to the disadvantaged: What we have learned from field research. *Harvard Educational Review, 47*, 518–543.
Chan, W. K., Hui, Y. K., Luk, W. Y., & Kong, S. W. (2000). *Understanding integrated science for the 21st century (Form 1)*. Hong Kong: Aristo Educational Press Ltd.
Chascas, S., & Cummins, J. (2005). *e-Lective Language Learning*. (Computer program). www.e-Lective.net.
Corson, D. (1997). The learning and use of academic English words. *Language Learning, 47*, 671–718.
Cummins, J. (1981). Age on arrival and immigrant second language learning in Canada: A reassessment. *Applied Linguistics, 1*, 132–149.
Cummins, J. (2000). *Language, power, and pedagogy: Bilingual children in the crossfire*. Clevedon, England: Multilingual Matters.
Cummins, J. (2001). *Negotiating identities: Education for empowerment in a diverse society* (2nd ed.). Los Angeles: California Association for Bilingual Education.
Cummins, J., Brown, K., & Sayers, D. (2007). *Literacy, technology, and diversity: Teaching for success in changing times*. Boston: Allyn & Bacon.
Cunningham, A. (1990). Explicit versus implicit instruction in phonemic awareness. *Journal of Experimental Child Psychology, 50*, 429–444.
Curriculum Development Council. (1997). *Syllabus for English Language (Primary 1–6)*. Hong Kong: Hong Kong Education Department, HKSAR.
Curriculum Development Council. (2004). *English Language curriculum guide (Primary 1–6)*. Hong Kong: The Education and Manpower Bureau, HKSAR.
Dallas, D., & Pelham, L. (2000). *Longman new welcome to English (Primary 6)*. Hong Kong: Longman Hong Kong Education.
Elley, W. B. (1991). Acquiring literacy in a second language: The effect of book-based programs. *Language Learning, 41*, 375–411.
Fielding, L. G., & Pearson, P. D. (1994). Reading comprehension: What works. *Educational Leadership, 51*(5), 62–68.
Geva, E. (2000). Issues in the assessment of reading disabilities in L2 children: Beliefs and research evidence. *Dyslexia, 6*, 13–28.
Hakuta, K., Butler, Y. G., & Witt, D. (2000). *How long does it take English learners to attain proficiency?* Santa Barbara: University of California Linguistic Minority Research Institute.
Hatcher, P., Hulme, C., & Ellis, A. (1994). Ameliorating early reading failure by integrating the teaching of reading and phonological skills: The phonological linkage hypothesis. *Child Development, 65*, 41–57.
Hong Kong Education Department. (1997). *Firm guidance on secondary schools' medium of instruction.* Hong Kong: Hong Kong Education Department.
Ip, K. W., Lam, C. C., & Wong, K. F. (1999). *Exploring geography (Form 1)*. Hong Kong: Oxford University Press (China) Ltd.
Klesmer, H. (1994). Assessment and teacher perceptions of ESL student achievement. *English Quarterly, 26*(3), 8–11.
Krashen, S. D. (2001, September/October/November 2001). Are children ready for the mainstream after one year of structured English immersion? *TESOL Matters, 11*, 1, 4.
Krashen, S. D. (2004). *The power of reading: Insights from the research.* (2nd ed.). Portsmouth, NH: Heinemann.
Kwan, A. B., & Willows, D. M. (1998, December). *Impact of early phonics instruction on children learning English as a second language.* Paper presented at the National Reading Conference, Austin, TX.
Lambert, W. E., & Tucker, G. R. (1972). *Bilingual education of children: The St. Lambert experiment*. Rowley, MA: Newbury House.
Lesaux, N. K., Siegel, L.S. (2003). The development of reading in children who speak English as a second language. *Developmental Psychology, 39*, 1005–1019.
Leung, K. S., Chu, W. M., & Fok, O. K. (2001). *Exploring mathematics: An I.T. enhanced course (Form 1)*. Hong Kong: Oxford University Press (China) Ltd.

Man, E. Y. F. (2004, December). *Teaching and learning in English-medium classrooms.* Paper presented at the International Language in Education Conference, Hong Kong Institute of Education, Hong Kong.

Man, E.Y.F., Coniam, D., & Lee. I. (2004). *Development of support measures for student adaptation in English medium schools. Final report of the project.* Submitted to the Education and Manpower Bureau, HKSAR.

Man, E.Y. F., Coniam D., & Lee, I. (2002). Helping students to adapt to an English medium of instruction environment in Hong Kong secondary schools. *Education Journal, 30*(2), 63–81.

Ng, S. T. M., & Leung, W. (1999). *Hong Kong our home: A new approach to economic and public affairs (Form 1).* Hong Kong: Manhattan Press Ltd.

Postlethwaite, T. N., & Ross, K. N. (1992). *Effective schools in reading: Implications for educational planners. An exploratory study.* The Hague: The International Association for the Evaluation of Educational Achievement.

Pressley, M., Duke, N. K., & Boling, E. C. (2004). The educational science and scientifically-based instruction we need: Lessons from reading research and policy making. *Harvard Educational Review, 74*, 30–61.

Rand Reading Study Group (2002). *Reading for understanding: Toward an R&D program in reading comprehension.* Report prepared for the Office of Educational Research and Improvement. Santa Monica: RAND, http://www.rand.org/publications/MR/MR1465/MR1465.pdf.

Shohamy, E., Levine, T., Spolsky, B., Kere-Levy, M., Inbar, O., Shemesh, M. (2002). *The academic achievements of immigrant children from the former USSR and Ethiopia.* Report (in Hebrew) submitted to the Ministry of Education, Israel.

Tao, P. K., Yung, H. W., Wong, C. K., Or, C. K., & Wong, A. (2000). *Living science (Form 1).* Hong Kong: Oxford University Press (China) Ltd.

Thomas, W. P., & Collier, V. P. (2002). *A national study of school effectiveness for language minority students' long-term academic achievement.* Santa Cruz, CA: Center for Research on Education, Diversity and Excellence, University of California-Santa Cruz, http://www.crede.ucsc.edu.

Valdés, G. (2004). Between support and marginalization: The development of academic language in linguistic minority children. *International Journal of Bilingual Education and Bilingualism, 7*, 102–132.

Verhoeven, L. (2000). Components in early second language reading and spelling. *Scientific Studies of Reading, 4*, 313–330.

Weber, R., & Longhi-Chirlin, T. (2001). Beginning in English: The growth of linguistic and literate abilities in Spanish-speaking first graders. *Reading Research and Instruction, 41*, 19–50.

Wong Fillmore, L. (1997). *Authentic literature in ESL instruction.* Glenview, IL: Scott Foresman.

Worswick, C. (2001). *School performance of the children of immigrants in Canada, 1994–98* (No. 178; ISBN: 0-662-31229-5). Ottawa: Statistics Canada.

CHAPTER 49

TEACHING IMPLICATIONS OF L2 PHONOLOGY RESEARCH

JOHN ARCHIBALD

The University of Calgary, Canada

ABSTRACT

This chapter discusses the implications of recent second language acquisition research in the field of phonology for second language teachers, including the question of whether adult second language learners can trigger a new phonological structure that is not present in the first language. I will look at processes of Chinese and Japanese learners of English acquiring the [l]/[r] contrast, and then will follow this up by looking at the implications of Matthew's work on Japanese learners being instructed in acquiring a variety of English sounds and how phonological theory explains their results. Work by Atkey on the acquisition of Czech palatal sounds will also be described to illustrate the conditions under which people can perceive new sounds. The chapter will conclude with a list of the implications for second language teachers of recent research in phonology.

INTRODUCTION

One of the traditional preoccupations of the field of second language acquisition (SLA) research has been to understand the nature of second language grammars and the factors that influence the development of those grammars. While this is a wide-ranging area of interest, my emphasis here will be on the common patterns found and the nature of the mental representation of second language grammars, in particular their phonological aspects. English language teachers are also concerned with what their students come to know about English and why they may find learning some aspects of the language easy while other aspects are difficult. What I propose to do in this paper is to bring together these two worlds of research, although I will not have much to say about variation in the attainment of individual learners.

BASIC QUESTIONS

What Is Phonology?

The first question that must be addressed is 'What is phonology?' Phonology has to do with the rules and patterns of sounds in a language. The discipline of linguistics is concerned with describing what people know when they know a language. This knowledge is very complex, and largely unconscious. By unconscious, we mean that if native speakers of English are asked why the sentence 'Who do you think that arrived?' is ill-formed, they tend not to be able to identify the source of the violation. We may have been taught the grammatical bells and whistles of a particular language (e.g., don't end a sentence with a preposition; don't use *task* as a verb) but these "rules" are usually *prescriptive* (imposing on the speaker) rather than *descriptive* of what speakers actually do.

The sound system of a language is just as complex as the *syntax* (or sentence structure) and our knowledge of it is also largely unconscious. Again, we may be taught certain rules of pronunciation (which are often sociolinguistic rules) such as "say, *running* not *runnin*." But when asked to produce rules about English pronunciation that we have not been taught, we often are caught short. Why can the words *city* and *pretty* be pronounced with a d-like sound for the *t* ([sɪDi], [prɪDi]) but the word *attack* cannot (*[əDæk])?

When we know a language, we know very complex, abstract things about the combinations of sounds. One model of phonological structure is shown in Figure 1. This figure illustrates that an English word such as *backlog* has a rich linguistic structure at a variety of levels. In this chapter, we will focus primarily on *features* (e.g., [±voice]), *segments*, and *syllables* (represented by σ) but will virtually ignore *moras* (represented by μ) and *feet* (e.g. *iambic* or *troachaic*)).

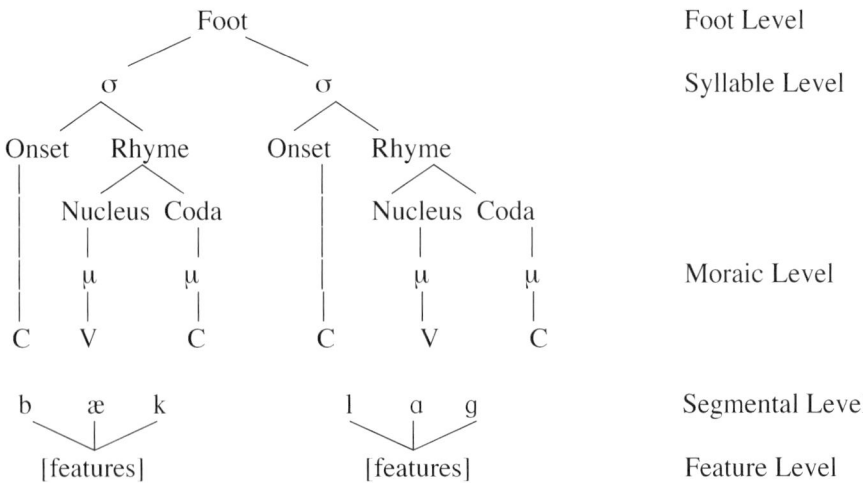

Figure 1. Levels of Phonological Structure

The segmental level may well be the most intuitively obvious. We know that words are made up of small units that we know as sounds or *segments* (a useful cover term that groups together consonants and vowels). We also know that segments can be grouped together to form syllables. The rules of syllable structure can vary from language to language, so that a Japanese speaker having to learn to pronounce the English word *strengths* may have difficulty, just as an English speaker learning to pronounce the Polish word *wybaczyc* may also have trouble.

Finally, we know that segments are not the smallest possible unit of analysis. They are more like molecules while the *features* below them are like atoms. We tend to have less conscious knowledge of the behavior of features, but consider the following example: English has a negative prefix *in-* that is often described as a negative prefix as in the word *in-tolerant*. However, note that the prefix can take a slightly different form in words like *im-possible*. There is a predictable pattern; it is not the case that we have a prefix *in-* that is used with some arbitrary set of words and a prefix *im-* that is used with some other arbitrary set of words. We find the variant with an [m] when the root of the word begins with a sound made with the lips (e.g. [m, b, p]) as in *im-perfect, im-mobile* and *im-balance*. The final consonant of the prefix is always a nasal consonant but it changes its *place of articulation* from *alveolar* to *labial*. Therefore, these terms (like *alveolar* and *labial*) are like the atoms that make up the molecules of the segments. A consonant can be broken down into smaller units like *voiced, nasal, labial, sibilant*, and so on. Later in the chapter we will see how these features affect second language learners.

Full Transfer/Full Access?

A broad issue concerning the nature of interlanguage (IL) grammars has been raised by White (2000) under the rubric of the *full transfer/full access* question. Essentially, this question seeks to address two basic concerns about a learner's grammar: What elements of it transfer from the L1 to the L2, and what can the learner do when attempting to learn structures that are absent from the first language? The term *full transfer* identifies a position that assumes that L2 learners will transfer *all* elements of their L1 grammar into their initial IL grammar. If your L1 has stress, you will start by trying to find stress in your L2. If your L1 has gender, you will start by trying to find gender in your L2. If your L1 has a voicing contrast, you will start by trying to find a voicing contrast in your L2. Of course, the IL grammar may change over time, but the question of full transfer refers primarily to the initial assumptions made by the learner.

The question of *full access* refers to whether or not adult second language learners' grammars are constrained by principles of *universal grammar*. Universal grammar (UG) is a linguistic theory that assumes that all human languages share certain basic structural properties in their grammatical design. UG captures the idea that there are possible human grammars and impossible human grammars. That is to say, there are some things that no human language does. This is relevant to L2 learners when we look at the nature of their IL grammars. Are those grammars subject to the same universal laws as other languages such French and Swahili and English? How would we know? Imagine the following kinds of thought experiments: First, let's imagine a subject whose first language is a tonal language like Chinese, and that subject is trying to learn a language like English, which is not a tonal language but rather a stress-timed language. Will the IL grammar that he or she sets up be governed by the universal principles we know govern the stress systems of the world's natural languages? Of course, this is an empirical question. A second thought experiment that might be relevant to this question is to think how a second language learner will fare when attempting to learn new structures. Imagine the subject trying to learn something that is not found in the L1. It could be an [l]/[r]

contrast, or gender, or optitive case. We could assume that if the learners had access to UG, they would know that those structures were part of the human linguistic arsenal. If their only source of knowledge is their L1 (and not UG), then they will not be able to automatically trigger linguistic knowledge that is not found in their L1. We will return to both these questions throughout the chapter.

Can Adult L2 Learners Acquire a New Language?

Many people are probably familiar with this general question in the literature on the critical period hypothesis (e.g., Birdsong, 1999; Harley, 1986; Scovel, 1988, 1995). In spite of the attention devoted to this topic, the question of whether proficient users of an L2 actually have knowledge or competence that is indistinguishable from native speakers had not been satisfactorily addressed. Coppieters (1987) looked at highly proficient second language learners and argued that none of them performed within the range of native speakers (acknowledging, of course, that native speakers will vary on their test performance too). Birdsong (1992) replicated this study (with modifications) and argued that some of his highly proficient L2 subjects *did* perform within the range of native speakers. White and Genesee (1996) looked at just this question in the domain of syntax. They looked at knowledge of facts about the movement of Wh-words in questions, the syntactic details of which do not concern us here. Consider these sample sentences:

*Who$_i$ did Mary meet the man who saw t$_i$?
*What$_i$ was a dish of t$_i$ cooked by Mary?

The principles governing syntactic movement are abstract and complex, and not taught in any second language class. Note that the semantics of the situation are fine. A man saw someone and Mary met this man. We want to ask a question about the someone that the man saw. This is a logically possible scenario but it is blocked by the rules of English syntax. Similarly, note that the syntax allows to move Wh-words in structures which seem very similar. For example, 'When did Mary meet the man who left?' is grammatical while 'Who did Marry meet the man who saw?' is ungrammatical. Native speakers' grammars capture this distinction. Therefore, the question of whether second language learners can arrive at knowledge of these principles that is within the range of knowledge we see in native speakers is an interesting question. White and Genesee (1996) looked at 89 subjects aged 16-66 who were interviewed extensively in English. Samples of their speech were evaluated by two judges for pronunciation, morphology, syntax, vocabulary, fluency, and overall impression of nativelike-ness. Each dimension was assessed on a 9 cm line, as shown in Figure 2.

Non-native _____ Native

Figure 2. Assessing Nativelike Proficiency

Each judge had to mark the line and the marks were measured to within the nearest half-centimeter, resulting in an 18-point scale.

Individuals who received scores of 17 or 18 on all scales by both judges were classified as *near-native* speakers. Forty-five of the original 89 subjects fell into this category. Subjects were given grammaticality judgment tasks (on a computer screen) and a pencil and paper question formation task. The subjects were compared to a control group of native speakers for both the accuracy and speed of their judgments, and to see if they produced grammaticality violations in their question formation. There were no significant differences between the native speakers and the near-native speakers with respect to their grammaticality judgments, their response times, or their question production. This was true even for those subjects who received their first intensive exposure to the L2 after the age of 16. In short, the near-natives performed just like the natives with respect to accuracy and speed on the grammaticality judgment tasks. This experiment demonstrates that the ultimate attainment of second language learners can be native-like.

Is this true of phonology as well? There have been a number of studies in Nijmegen, Holland, that have investigated this question. Bongaerts and his colleagues have argued that there are some late learners of a L2 who can achieve native-like pronunciation in both instructed and uninstructed settings. Bongaerts (1999) suggests that those people who did achieve native-like pronunciation all received intensive training in both the production and perception of the target language sounds. Bongaerts, Mennen, and van der Silk (2000) looked at uninstructed learners of Dutch as a second language. All speakers (both non-native speakers and native speaker controls) read 10 sentences out loud (e.g., *Alle exemplaren van de dichtbundel zijn uit de handle genomen*.). The samples were rated by 21 native speakers of Dutch (11 were teachers of Dutch) on a 5-point scale ranging from *very strong accent* to *no foreign accent*. The native speakers of Dutch were given ratings from 4.00 to 4.91 (mean: 4.73), while the non-native speakers were given ratings from 1.70 to 4.59 (mean: 3.50). While the mean scores of the two groups were significantly different, there were some non-native subjects who were assessed within the native speaker range.

THE ACQUISITION OF SEGMENTS

Brown (2000) looked at the acquisition of English /l/ and /r/ by speakers of Japanese and Mandarin Chinese (neither of which contrasts /l/ and /r/ phonemically). The Japanese situation is illustrated in Figure 3, and is explicitly contrasted with the representations for English. Note that SV stands for sonorant voice, a feature used by phonologists to capture the fact that typologically voicing behaves differently on sonorants than on obsturents.

[l] and [ɾ] are allophones of a single phoneme. This phoneme may appear only in a simple onset in Japanese. Mandarin Chinese also lacks the contrast, hence the structure is the same as shown in Figure 3 for Japanese speakers. If the segment is taken to be the level of explanation, then we might predict that both Mandarin and Japanese speakers should be unable to acoustically discriminate /l/ from /r/ (given their L1 feature geometries). The graph (see Figure 4) shows the overall performance of the subjects on the auditory discrimination task to test the subjects' discrimination of English /l/ and /r/.

(a) Japanese

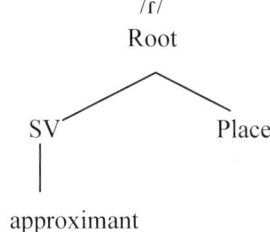

(b) English

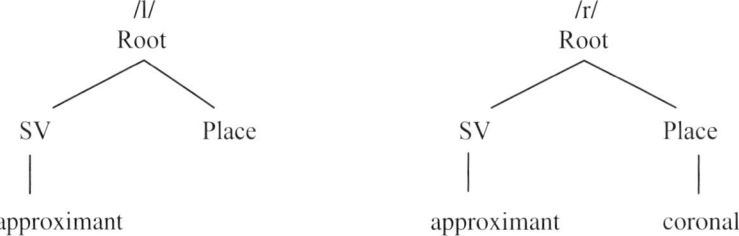

Figure 3. Cross-Linguistic Liquid Structure

In general, the Japanese speakers were unable to discriminate /l/ from /r/ both acoustically and phonologically in a lexical choice task, whereas the Chinese speakers discriminated the contrast in both tasks. The initial hypothesis that speakers of both languages would be unable to perceive the /l/ and /r/ distinction because one of the members of the contrast is an L1 phoneme is not supported by the Chinese subjects. So, what aspect of the L1 could be accounting for this difference? Brown (2000) suggests that a speaker may be able to perceive a non-native contrast if the feature that distinguishes the two segments is present in the L1 feature geometry, even if the feature is not utilized for the contrast in question. It is the coronal feature (that is, the sounds made with the tip of the tongue) that distinguishes /l/ from /r/. Chinese requires the coronal node for some features but Japanese does not. The inventories are given in Table 1.

Overall Performance on Auditory Task

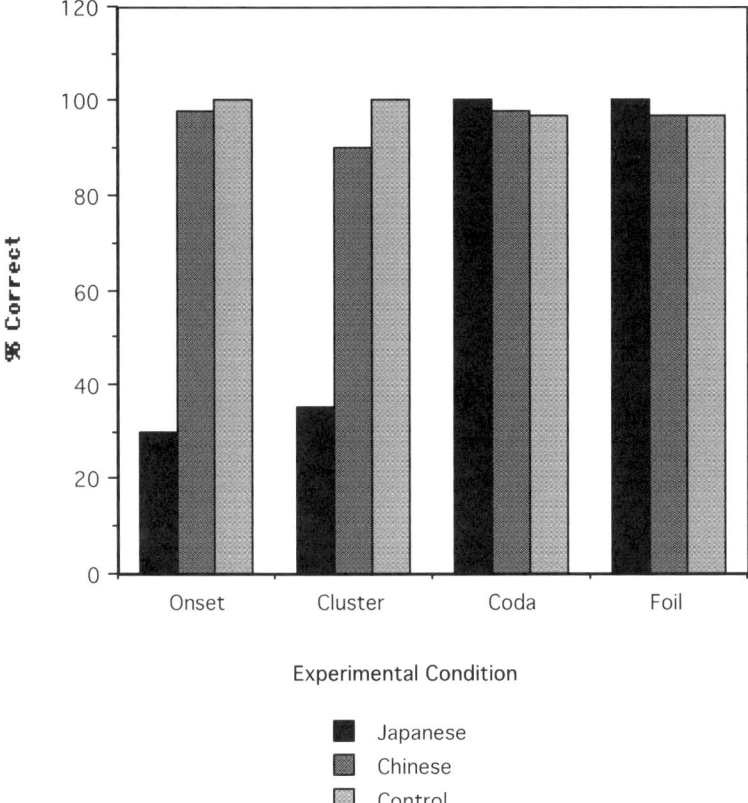

Figure 4. Overall Performance on Auditory Discrimination Task

Regardless, then, of the liquid inventory, the Chinese speaker will have a representation for the feature [coronal] somewhere in the phonological inventory (i.e., to contrast alveolar from post-alveolar segments shown in the box). The Japanese inventory, on the other hand, does not contrast any coronal phonemes and will, therefore lack a coronal node. Thus, Brown concludes that L2 speakers cannot build representations for segments that require features not present in their L1. They can, however, combine the features of their L1 in new ways to yield new segments.

Matthews (1997) investigated whether training can influence the perception of non-native contrasts. He looked at the well-known case of Japanese learners acquiring the [l]/[r] contrast. Many studies have shown that Japanese subjects can have difficulty in learning to perceive this contrast, which is not found in their L1. Matthews also tested other contrasts not found in Japanese such as ([b]/[v]; [s]/[θ]; [f]/[θ]. This focus on perceptual ability is important as it can be argued that perceptual studies are a better window onto linguistic competence as production tasks have many other factors involved (e.g., motor control).

Table 1. Japanese vs Chinese Phonemic Inventory

(a) Japanese Phonemic Inventory

p	t	k	ʔ
b	d	g	
	s		h
m	n	ŋ	
	ɾ		
w	y		

(b) Mandarin Chinese Phonemic Inventory

p	t		k	
	ts	tṣ		
	s	ṣ		h
		ẓ		
m	n		ŋ	
	l			
w	y			

Matthews' (1997) study comprised one group of students who received training and one who did not. The training took place once a week for 5 weeks. Each training session included training on all five of the sounds which are not found in Japanese: [f], [v], [l], [r] and [θ]. The subjects received no perceptual training or model pronunciations, but, rather, explicit instruction in the articulation of the five segments. During testing, the subjects heard stimulus pairs (drawn from familiar vocabulary) and had to indicate whether the words were the same or different. Over time, there was significant improvement in their perception of the [b]/[v] and [f]/[θ] contrasts but no significant change in their perception of [p]/[b], [s]/[f], or [l]/[r]. Thus, this training regimen caused improvement in some contrasts but not others. There was no improvement on [l]/[r] but there was improvement on [f]/[θ]. What could be causing the difference? Matthews, like Brown (2000), argues that the source of the behavior lies in the feature geometry. If the L1 utilizes the appropriate feature for a new contrast, then new contrasts can be acquired. To take just one example, Japanese lacks a [v] but contains the necessary features to build one.

Perception of New Segments

A similar example can be found in the work of Atkey (2001) who looked at English speakers acquiring palatal stops in Czech. While English has stops made at the lips ([p]/[b]), *alveolar ridge* ([t]/[d]), and *velum* ([k]/[g]), Czech has the *labial, alveolar*, and *palatal* stops ([c ɟ]). The feature required to make the distinction between alveolar and palatal stops is [posterior]. The relevant Czech sounds are given in Table 2.

Table 2. Alveolar versus Palatal Stops in Czech

Alveolar /t/, /d/	Palatal /c/, /ɟ/
Root	Root
|	|
Coronal	Coronal
	|
	[posterior]

English makes use of the feature [posterior] to distinguish alveolar and palatal fricatives, as shown in Table 3.

Table 3. Coronal contrasts in English

/s/ Alveolar	/ʃ/ Alveo-palatal	/θ/ Dental
root	root	root
|	|	|
coronal	coronal	coronal
	[posterior]	[distributed]

The perception results shown in Table 4 demonstrate that the adult subjects (all native speakers of English acquiring Czech as a foreign language) Atkey (2001) looked at were able to perceive the alveolar/palatal distinction very accurately.

Table 4. Percentage of Palatal Stop Tokens Perceived Correctly by Native-Speakers of English

Position	ML (0;3)	JD (0;5)	AD (0;11)	SW (0;11)	JA (1;0)	RK (10;0)
Initial	70	90	80	85	80	95
Medial	70	70	80	90	85	90
Final	20	30	50	70	70	80

THE ACQUISITION OF SYLLABLES

Let us turn now to another example of hierarchical structure at a higher level: the syllable. A common model of syllable structure is shown in Figure 5:

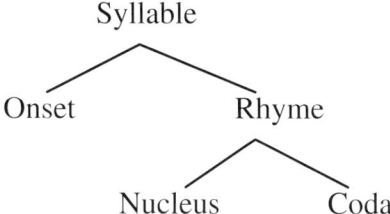

Figure 5. Syllable Structure

The languages of the world vary according to such things as whether syllabic nodes can branch. Some languages (e.g., Japanese) do not allow branching onsets or codas. Again, we can see the benefit of these types of models when it comes to the full transfer/full access issues. If we assume full transfer, then what the learner will be transferring will be the allowable syllable structures of the L1. Ignoring some complexities, let us assume for a particular L1 that all syllables must be CV or CVC. More complex syllables such as CCVCC are not allowed. A common phenomenon in L2 learning involves modifying an L2 word so that it fits the L1 syllable structure. Consider the words shown in Table 5 spoken by someone whose L1 is Arabic (adapted from Broselow, 1988):

Table 5. L2 Syllabification of English words by Arabic speakers

English target	Non-native speaker's version
plant	pilanti
Fred	Fired
translate	tiransilet

Arabic does not allow branching onsets or codas, so an English word like *plant* cannot be mapped onto a single Arabic syllable. As this example helps to show, we can explain why Arabic speakers pronounce English words in the way that they do by investigating the principles of syllabification in the L1. Especially at the beginning levels of proficiency, the structure of the IL is influenced by the structure of the L1. This would suggest that learners are clearly transferring the L1 principles of syllabification.

This raises the question of what learners do when they are faced with a situation where the mental representation of the structure of the L1 is not appropriate for the structure of the input perceived in the L2. Can they acquire new structures at the syllabic level? And do they have access to UG properties of syllable structure?

Clusters

Most of the consonant clusters in the worlds' languages obey what is known as the *sonority sequencing generalization* (shown in Figure 6) which captures the fact that the nucleus of a syllable is the most sonorous element and sonority diminishes towards the edges:

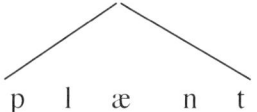

Figure 6. The Sonority Sequencing Generalization

There are, however, sequences of consonants that violate this generalization, and they tend to involve the phoneme /s/. In English, some s-clusters violate sonority sequencing (e.g., *st* since the fricative [s] is more sonorous than the stop [t]) while some do not (e.g., *sn* where the fricative [s] is less sonorous than the nasal [n]). The analysis of the structure of s-clusters is a complex and problematic area of phonological theory, so the details will not be elaborated here. Many researchers argue that [s] is what is known as *extrasyllabic*. In other words, [s] is not really part of the syllable, but somehow outside it. However, L2 learners are aware of this. Carlisle (1997) looked at how Spanish speakers deal with English onset clusters. He notes that three-consonant clusters are changed significantly more often than two-consonant clusters. Carlisle (1991) in a study on two-segment onsets, found that Spanish speakers modified onsets that violated the sonority sequencing generalization (e.g., st-) significantly more often than they did those that did not (e.g., sn-). They would, for example, be more likely to say [e]*stop* than [e]*snow*. Broselow (1988) also showed that Arabic speakers treat s-clusters that violate the sonority sequencing generalization differently than those that do not, as shown in Table 6.

Table 6. L2 Repairs of Consonant clusters

Needs a heading	Another heading here
sweater -> [siwɛtər]	study -> [istadi]
slide -> [silayd]	ski -> [iski]

Singh (1985) demonstrates the same pattern for Hindi speakers (see Table 7).

Table 7. L2 repairs of consonant clusters

Needs a heading	Another heading here
fruit -> [fɪrut]	school -> [ɪskul]
please -> [pɪliz]	spelling -> [ɪspɛliŋ]

Samarajiwa and Abeysekera (1964) show the same pattern by native speakers of Sinhalese speaking Sanskrit, as shown in Table 8.

Table 8. L2 repairs of consonant clusters

Sanskrit target pronuncitation	Pronunciation by Sinhalese speakers	English translation
Tyage	[tiyage]	*gift*
sriyavə	[siriyavə]	*grace*
stri	[istiri]	*woman*

These data suggest that L2 learners have full access to the principles of sonority sequencing, regardless of their L1 experience. The work of Broselow and Finer (1991) and Eckman and Iverson (1993) also clearly demonstrate that syllable structure can be changed in L2 learning. People can learn to pronounce new clusters that are not found in their L1. This means that even though a structure may be lacking from the L1, second language learners are able to acquire that structure, and to set up IL grammars that are constrained by the principles of universal grammar.

Perception of Clusters

Up to now, we have focused on the production data from subjects who are producing consonant clusters, and, as we have noted, sometimes modifying them. A related question that arises in this field has to do with these subjects perception of consonant clusters. Dehaene-Lambertz, Dupoux, and Gout (2000) have reported on both behavioral and *electrophysicological data* (i.e., data resulting from monitoring the electrical activity in a subject's brain during the processing of language) that argue that when second language learners are listening to linguistic items they are also modifying the consonant clusters. The relevant experiment looked at native speakers of French and Japanese. French allows consonant cluster quite freely across syllable boundaries while Japanese breaks up clusters with an epenthetic vowel. An example of this can be seen when Japanese borrows a word from another language. English *baseball* [beysbal] is pronounced something like [beysubaru] where the consonantal sequence *sb* is broken up by an epenthetic [u]. The question that Dehaene-Lambertz, Dupoux, and Gout address is whether Japanese subjects when listening to sequences like *gm* or *sb* will hear an epenthetic vowel. The results of their paper show that they do. The implications of this are that second language learners who break up consonant clusters by inserting a vowel may not be doing this as a late production routine but rather as a result of deep processes influenced by their first language.

CONCLUSIONS

So, where are we now? We have seen that at a variety of levels—segmental and syllabic—learners transfer their L1 phonological representations: full transfer. What about full access? Most of the studies that I have referred to suggest that the representations that the learners set up do not violate UG. Learners can change their existing representations given exposure to the target language, but can they trigger completely new structure? That evidence appears to be a little more mixed.

There are a number of conclusion and implications of this research for English language teachers and teaching. Firstly, phonological knowledge is abstract and complex. There is still a tendency to think of L2 phonology as being synonymous with pronunciation by focusing on the production of consonants, vowels, stress, etc. The literature reveals, however, that learners' behavior (both production and perception) is governed by the nature of their abstract phonological representations. This does not mean that L2 teachers need to become theoretical phonologists but rather need to be sensitive to the fact that, like syntax and morphology and semantics, phonology is a subtle cognitive system. Full access to UG means that new sounds can be acquired. Just because a certain sound is not found in the student's first language does not mean that they are doomed to never master the production or perception of that sound. Research has shown that learners have access to another source of knowledge beyond the structure of their first language. All human languages share a base of common building blocks that can be re-deployed to acquire new sounds. Full transfer means that subtle complexity will be transferred from the L1. For example, if your L1 allows coda consonants but only a certain class of coda consonants , then this is what will initially transfer to learning the L2. However, this in not necessarily the final state of the learner's grammar. Teachers cannot be lulled into believing stereotypical generalizations about a particular language

Secondly, a number of studies show that L2 learners can acquire linguistic competence that is indistinguishable from native speakers in terms of accuracy and response time (White & Genesee, 1996). In other words, L2 learners can successfully acquire a second language. Late L2 learners (both instructed and uninstructed) can achieve pronunciation that falls within the range of native speakers (Bongaerts, Mennen, & van der Silk, 2000). Pronunciation is not just a matter of motor ability. As we have said before, phonology is a symbolic system; just like any other area of knowledge, it can be acquired. New contrasts can be acquired if the L1 utilizes the necessary *features* (Brown, 2000; Matthews, 1997). Teachers need to be aware that just because a student lacks a particular *sound* in their L1 does not mean that they lack the building blocks to acquire new sounds.

Finally, the research demonstrates that explicit instruction can help with L2 phonological development, but won't always do so (Matthews, 1997). Instruction requires emphasis on perception and production. The literature on which method of instruction is the best is notoriously incomplete. We do not know which methods or techniques work for which learners of which languages. Nonetheless, if instruction takes place which provides the learners with opportunities to both produce and perceive the sounds in question and to be exposed to metalinguistic information about the sounds to be learned, then this is likely to be an environment that will be useful to the most learners.

REFERENCES

Archibald, J. (1993). *Language learnability and L2 phonology: The acquisition of metrical parameters.* Kluwer Academic Publishers.

Archibald, J. (1998). Second language phonology, phonetics, and typology. *Studies in Second Language Acquisition, 20,* 189–211.

Atkey, S. (2001). *The acquisition of Czech palatal stops.* M.A. dissertation. University of Calgary.

Birdsong, D. (1992). Ultimate attainment in second language acquisition. *Language, 68,* 706–755.

Birdsong, D. (1999). *Second language acquisition and the critical period hypothesis.* Mahwah, NJ: Lawrence Erlbaum.

Birdsong, D. (2004). Second language acquisition and ultimate attainment. In A. Davies & C. Elder (Eds.), *Handbook of applied linguistics* (pp. 82–105). London: Blackwell.

Bongaerts, T. (1999). Ultimate attainment in L2 pronunciation: The case of very advanced late L2 learners. In D. Birdsong (Ed.), *Second language acquisition and the critical period hypothesis* (pp. 133–159). Mahway, N.J.: Erlbaum.

Bongaerts, T., Mennen, S., & van der Silk, F. (2000). Authenticity of pronunciation in naturalistic second language acquisition: The case of very advance late learners of Dutch as a second language. *Studia Linguistica, 54*(2), 298–308.

Bongaerts, T., Planken, B., & Schils, E. (1995). Can late starters attain a native accent in a foreign language? A test of the critical period hypothesis. In Z. Lengyel & D. Singleton (Eds.), *The age factor in second language acquisition* (pp. 30–50). Clevedon, England: Multilingual Matters.

Broselow, E. (1988). Prosodic phonology and the acquisition of a second language. In S. Flynn & W. O'Neil (Eds.), *Linguistic theory in second language acquisition* (pp. 295–308). Dordrecht, Netherlands: Kluwer Academic Publishers.

Broselow, E., & Finer, D. (1991). Parameter setting in second language phonology and syntax. *Second language Research, 7,* 35–59.

Brown, C. (2000). The interrelation between speech perception and phonological acquisition from infant to adult. In J. Archibald (Ed.), *Second language acquisition and linguistic theory* (pp. 4–63). Malden, Mass: Blackwell.

Carlisle, R. S. (1991). The influence of environment on vowel epenthesis in Spanish/English interphonology. *Applied Linguistics, 12,* 76–95.

Carlisle, R. S. (1997). The modification of onsets in a markedness relationship: Testing the Interlanguage Structural Conformity Hypothesis. *Language Learning, 47,* 327–361.

Coppieters, R. (1987). Competence differences between native and fluent non-native speakers. *Language, 63,* 544–573.

Dehaene-Lambertz, G., Dupoux, E., & Gout, A. (2000). Electrophysiological correlates of phonological processing: A cross-linguistic study. *Journal of Cognitive Neuroscience, 12*(4), 635–647.

Eckman, F., & Iverson, G. (1993). Sonority and markedness among onset clusters in the interlanguage of ESL learners. *Second language Research, 9,* 234–252.

Harley, B. (1986). *Age in second language acquisition.* Clevedon, Avon: Multilingual Matters.

Matthews, J. (1997). The influence of pronunciation training on the perception of second language contrasts. In J. Leather & A. James (Eds.), *New sounds 97* (pp. 223–239). Klagenfurt, Austria: University of Klagenfurt Press.

Samarajiwa, C., & Abeysekera, R. M. (1964). Some pronunciation difficulties of Sinhalese learners of English as a foreign language. *Language Learning, 14,* 45–50.
Scovel, T. (1988). *A time to speak: A psycholinguistic inquiry into the critical period for human speech.* New York: Newbury House.
Scovel, T. (1995). Differentiation, recognition and identification in the discrimination of foreign accents. In J. Archibald (Ed.), *Phonological acquisition and phonological theory* (pp. 169–182). Hillsdale, N.J.: Erlbaum.
Singh, R. (1985). Prosodic adaptation in interphonology. *Lingua, 67,* 269–282.
White, L. (2000). Second language acquisition: From initial to final state. In J. Archibald (Ed.), *Second language acquisition and linguistic theory* (pp. 130–155). Malden, Mass: Blackwell.
White, L., & Genesee, F. (1996). How native is near native? The issue of ultimate attainment in adult second language acquisition. *Second Language Research, 12,* 238–265.

CHAPTER 50

CURRENT PERSPECTIVES ON VOCABULARY TEACHING AND LEARNING

NORBERT SCHMITT

The University of Nottingham, UK

ABSTRACT

This chapter reviews key vocabulary research and draws a number of teaching and learning implications from that research. Lexical areas addressed include the amount of vocabulary required to use English, what it means to know and learn a word, the incremental nature of vocabulary acquisition, the role of memory in vocabulary learning, incidental and intentional vocabulary learning, techniques for effective vocabulary teaching, and the role of learning strategies in vocabulary acquisition. The insights and techniques discussed in this chapter can help teachers develop more principled, and hopefully more effective, vocabulary programs for their students.

INTRODUCTION

Reflecting the generally buoyant state of second language vocabulary research at the moment, there have been a number of recent commentaries summarizing research-led pedagogical suggestions for vocabulary teaching (e.g., Hunt & Beglar, 1998; Nation & Meara, 2002; Sökmen, 1997). This chapter highlights some of the key insights from these and other sources and aims to provide tangible advice on how to teach vocabulary in a principled and effective manner.

THE VOCABULARY CHALLENGE FACING ESL LEARNERS

Before teachers can design principled vocabulary programs for their students, they first need to understand the vocabulary challenge facing learners of English. English probably contains the greatest number of words of any major language, which makes learning a sufficient amount of its vocabulary a formidable task. Many other languages routinely create new words by either combining two or more simpler words together into one longer compound word (like German) or by adding regular affixes to a word in order to make a new one (like Spanish). In these languages, learners can create and understand a large number of new words simply by knowing the systems underlying lexical construction. English utilizes similar systems to some degree, but to a large extent learners have to acquire considerable numbers of words that are not systematically transparent. For example, Germans might say *herzlich* (*herz* = heart and *lich* = like) to express the concept *warm-hearted*, while in English, learners would have to know and choose between a number of near-synonyms like *cordial, convivial, enthusiastic,* and others.[1] Learning this vocabulary will likely form a key constraint to how well English is eventually mastered (Nation & Meara, 2002).

However, the difficulty in learning English vocabulary should be put in context. Out of the 54,000 or so word families appearing in *Webster's Third New International Dictionary* (1961), even educated native speakers will know only a fraction, perhaps up to around 20,000 word families (Goulden, Nation, & Read, 1990). Although this is probably an unrealistic figure for all but the most motivated learners, the good news is that it is possible to function in English with vocabularies far smaller than this. We know that in order to participate in basic everyday oral communication, knowledge of the most frequent 2,000-3,000 word families in English provides the bulk of the lexical resources required (Adolphs & Schmitt, 2003; Schonell et al.,1956). The vocabulary in the 2,000-3,000 frequency band provides additional material for spoken discourse, but additionally, knowledge of around 3,000 families is the threshold that should allow learners to *begin* to read authentic texts. Most research indicates that knowledge of the most frequent 5,000 word families should provide enough vocabulary to enable learners to read authentic texts. Of course, many words will still be unknown, but this level of knowledge should allow learners to infer the meaning of many of the novel words from context and to understand most of the communicative content of the text. Second language learners with a knowledge of the most frequent 10,000 word families in English can be considered to have a wide vocabulary, and Hazenburg and Hulstijn (1996) found that a vocabulary of this magnitude may be required to cope with the challenges of university study in a second language.

The figures mentioned above are achievable, and many learners are successful in reaching such levels. These statistics are useful in giving size targets that students need to achieve in order to be able to function in English in various ways, but they don't tell us *which* words the students need to know. In some situations, the particular words to teach are obvious. For example, beginners in a classroom need, among other things, the words required to operate in a classroom setting, e.g., *book, pencil, read,* and *say.* ESP learners focusing on a specific field of study, e.g., medicine, will need to learn the technical vocabulary required in that field (*scalpel, femur*). This situationally based vocabulary and technical vocabulary are obvious targets for vocabulary teaching, but it is less obvious which vocabulary to teach if the goal is a general increase in vocabulary size. In this case, the best criterion we have to guide target word selection is frequency of occurrence. Words occurring frequently in English are typically the most useful and the first acquired by students. The usefulness of frequent words has much to do with text coverage. Nation and Waring (1997, p. 9) show how knowing a small number of words in English allows coverage of a large proportion of a typical written text (Table 1). Spoken discourse generally has less diversity when it comes to vocabulary, and so 2,000 word families will cover around 95% of typical speech (Adolphs & Schmitt, 2003). Clearly, the most frequent words in English are an essential foundation to all language use and need to be learned regardless of the effort.

Table 1. Vocabulary Size and Text Coverage of Written Discourse

Vocabulary size in Lemmas (stem words and inflected forms)	Text coverage
1,000	72.0%
2,000	79.7%
3,000	84.0%
4,000	86.8%
5,000	88.7%
6,000	89.9%
15,851	97.8%

Note: Adapted from Nation, P., and Waring, R. (1997). Vocabulary size, text coverage and word lists. In N. Schmitt & M. McCarthy (Eds.), *Vocabulary: Description, acquisition and pedagogy* (p. 9). Cambridge: Cambridge University Press. Copyright year by the name of the copyright holder. Adpated with permission.

In addition to learning a wide and varied vocabulary of individual words, English learners must also cope with a great number of multiword units (Moon, 1997, 1998; Wray, 2002). English has a large number of these multiple-word-item lexemes that behave as a single word with a single meaning (e.g., *pass away, bite the dust, kick the bucket,* and *give up the ghost* all meaning *to die*). There are a number of different kinds of multiword units, including compound words (*playpen*), phrasal verbs (*give up*), fixed phrases (*ladies and gentlemen*), idioms (*put your nose to the grindstone*), and proverbs (*A stitch in time saves nine*). Although it is certainly possible to be communicative without using these multiword units, they are a large part of what makes proficient English speakers sound natural. Once a learner reaches a proficiency level where appropriateness of usage becomes a major concern, then mastery of these multiword units becomes essential to understanding and producing nativelike idiomatic language. In addition, once these multiword units are in place in the memory as whole chunks, they can facilitate fluent language use, because they are preassembled and do not need to be generated online via grammar rules and lexical choice (Pawley & Syder, 1983).

ISSUES IN VOCABULARY LEARNING

What Does Learning a Word Entail?: Word Knowledge

Perhaps the first step to understanding vocabulary learning is to specify what it means to know a word. The average layperson would probably assume that if learners know a word's meaning and spelling/pronunciation, they know that word. In fact, learners may be able to use a word to a large extent with just such knowledge. However, in order to have full mastery of a word and to be able to employ it in any situation that the learner desires, then much more knowledge is necessary. Nation (2001, p. 27) gives the following description of truly knowing a word:

Form			
spoken	R	What does the word sound like?	
	P	How is the word pronounced?	
written	R	What does the word look like?	
	P	How is the word written and spelled?	
word parts	R	What parts are recognizable in this word?	
	P	What word parts are needed to express this meaning?	
Meaning			
form and meaning	R	What meaning does this word form signal?	
	P	What word form can be used to express this meaning?	
concept and	R	What is included in the concept?	
referents	P	What items can the concept refer to?	
associations	R	What other words does this make us think of?	
	P	What other words could we use instead of this one?	
Use			
grammatical	R	In what patterns does the word occur?	
functions	P	In what patterns must we use this word?	
collocations	R	What words or types of words occur with this one?	
	P	What words or types of words must we use with this one?	
constraints on use (register, frequency…)	R	Where, when, and how often would we expect to meet this word?	
	P	Where, when, and how often can we use this word?	
R = receptive knowledge			
P = productive knowledge			

Note: From Nation, P. (2001). *Learning vocabulary in another language* (p. 27). Cambridge: Cambridge University Press. Copyright year by the name of copyright holder. Reprinted with permission.

As can be seen by this listing, true mastery of a word involves knowing a variety of *word knowledge* aspects. The more aspects of word knowledge we know about a word, the more likely we will be able to use it in the right contexts in an appropriate manner.

The Incremental Nature of Vocabulary Learning

Complete mastery of all of the above kinds of word knowledge obviously cannot be achieved simultaneously. Although we have only the vaguest idea of how some of these word knowledge types are acquired (e.g., collocation and register), it seems clear that certain types are learned before others. For example, Bahns and Eldaw (1993) found that their subjects' collocational knowledge lagged behind their general vocabulary knowledge. Advanced learners studied by Schmitt (1998) had little problem with spelling regardless of what else they knew about the words, suggesting that this is one of the first aspects of lexical knowledge to be mastered by these students. Likewise, just because some word knowledge aspects are known doesn't necessarily mean that others will be. Schmitt and Zimmerman (2002) found that even advanced learners who knew one form of a word (e.g., *philosophy*) did not necessary know all of the other members of its word family (*philosophize, philosophical, philosophically*). Also, learners might know the core meaning sense of a word, but they are unlikely to know all of the other possible meaning senses (Schmitt, 1998). Thus, learning a word must be an incremental process, as the various types of word knowledge are mastered at different rates. It follows from this that each of the word knowledge types will be known at different degrees of mastery at any one point in time. One useful way to conceptualize this mastery is along a continuum for each word knowledge aspect. Even an aspect as seemingly basic as spelling is likely to be learned incrementally, along a cline something like the following (although progress along the cline may be swift):

Can't spell	knows some	phonologically	fully correct
word at all	*letters*	*correct*	*spelling*

-->

From this, we see that vocabulary acquisition is not only incremental but also incremental in a variety of ways. First, lexical knowledge is made up of different kinds of word knowledge, and not all can be learned simultaneously. Second, each word knowledge type may develop along a cline, which means that not only is word learning incremental in general; learning of the individual word knowledge aspects is as well. In addition, each word knowledge type may be receptively or productively known regardless of the degree of mastery of the others. Taken together, these conclusions indicate that word learning is a complicated but gradual process.

RECYCLING, REVISION, AND MEMORY

The fact that vocabulary is learned incrementally inevitably leads to the implication that words must be met and used multiple times to be truly learned. The number of exposures/usages necessary will depend on a number of factors, including how salient the word itself is, how necessary the word is for a learner's present needs, and whether the word is met incidentally while pursuing some other purpose or studied with the explicit goal of learning it. It is possible, however, to look at research and get some idea of the number of repetitions necessary. Certainly, once is not usually enough. For incidental exposure, the chances of learning and retaining a word from one exposure when reading are only about 5%-14% (Nagy, 1997). Nation (1990) reviewed a number of studies suggesting that from 5 to 16 or more repetitions are required for a word to be learned. Even a rich program of vocabulary instruction can require seven or more encounters with a word (McKeown, Beck, Omanson, & Pople, 1985). It should be noted that these and other vocabulary studies set a relatively restricted criterion for the achievement of learning (usually focusing on meaning), and mastery of all word knowledge aspects undoubtedly requires a much higher number of repetitions.

It follows that regardless of how vocabulary is presented, it must be recycled in order to be learned. One of the great mistakes many teachers make is to focus on a new word only once, leading to a high probability of that word being forgotten and the time spent on teaching it wasted. Nation (1990) suggests that it is as important to recycle older, partially known words as it is to teach new ones in order to avoid this waste. However, there are more efficient and less efficient schedules for recycling and revision. To understand the best timing for this recurring exposure to words, it is necessary to understand how the mind forgets new information. Typically, most forgetting occurs soon after the end of the learning session. After that major loss, the rate of forgetting decreases. This is illustrated in Figure 1.

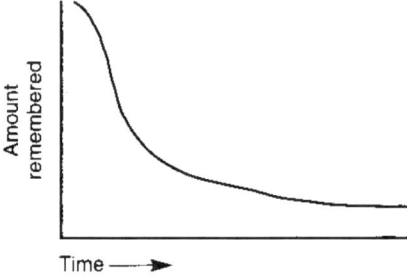

Figure 1. Typical Pattern of Forgetting

Note: From N. Schmitt, (2000). *Vocabulary in language teaching* (p. 131). Cambridge: Cambridge University Press. Copyright year of the name of the copyright holder. Reprinted with permission.

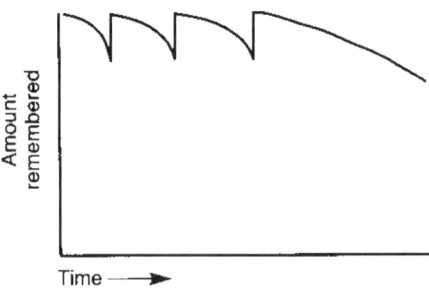

Figure 2. Pattern of Forgetting with Expanded Rehearsal

Note: From N. Schmitt, (2000). *Vocabulary in language teaching* (p. 131). Cambridge: Cambridge University Press. Copyright year of the name of the copyright holder. Reprinted with permission.

The forgetting curve in Figure 1 indicates that it is critical to have a review session soon after the learning session, but less essential as time goes on. This finding suggests that learners should rehearse new material soon after the initial meeting and then at gradually increasing intervals, as illustrated in Figure 2 (Baddeley, 1990, p. 156-158; Pimsleur, 1967). One explicit memory schedule proposes reviews 5-10 minutes after the end of the study period, 24 hours later, one week later, one month later, and finally six months later (Russell, 1979, p. 149). *Expanding rehearsal* schedules like this can aid teachers in recycling vocabulary in a principled manner but might be most helpful as a guide for students for their own revision (Schmitt & Schmitt, 1995).

VOCABULARY TEACHING AND LEARNING IN A PRINCIPLED WAY

The background in the above sections leads to several observations that are important for vocabulary pedagogy. First, a learner is unlikely to be able to acquire a wide vocabulary (around 10,000 word families) through explicit learning alone. There are simply too many words to learn. Second, learning a more achievable number of word families (2,000-5,000) can provide considerable rewards in the linguistic abilities they support. A significant percentage of this amount of vocabulary can be realistically addressed in an explicit manner over a period of time. Third, the most important words to target for explicit attention are the most frequent words in English.

Combining these points, one can make a cost/benefit calculation (Nation, 1995) concerning what vocabulary to teach. All teaching carries cost, mainly in classroom time, but also in teaching and learning effort. The most frequent words are worth this cost, because they are the essential foundation to any language use. The most frequent 2,000 word families certainly fall into the must-learn category. If learners wish to be able to read in English, then the vocabulary in the 2,000-5,000 frequency band could also be explicitly approached. Beyond this band, words occur less frequently, and learners should concentrate on the specific technical vocabulary they need for specific topics, for example, specialized engineering terminology for engineers. Other than this, time is better spent on developing strategies that enable learners to work with unknown lower-frequency vocabulary on their own. In other words, we should teach high-frequency vocabulary, because there is a high benefit for the cost, while teaching low-frequency vocabulary, which the learner will seldom meet, is not worth the cost. It is better to expend precious classroom time in teaching strategies to students so that they can tackle low-frequency vocabulary independently (frequency lists are available in Leech, Rayson, & Wilson, 2001; West, 1953; and online at http://www.comp.lancs.ac.uk/ucrel/bncfreq/flists.html).

In addition to this cost/benefit consideration, any single method of vocabulary learning will not address all of the word knowledge aspects that are required for full vocabulary use. We can explicitly address some aspects, like meaning and grammatical characteristics, but aspects like collocation, register, and intuitions of frequency are only ever likely to be mastered through extensive exposure to the target word in many different contexts. Thus any vocabulary program needs two strands: an explicit strand to present the teachable word knowledge aspects of high-value words and an incidental learning strand where (a) those words are consolidated and more is learned about them, and (b) a multitude of other new words are met.

Facilitating the Incidental Learning Strand

One key to facilitating incidental learning is to maximize learners' exposure to English. This can be done orally in a number of ways: (a) maximizing the amount of English used in the classroom; (b) using group work, where learners can learn new words from each other during their interactive discussions (not all members of a group will know the same words) (Newton, 2001); (c) encouraging communication with proficient English users whenever possible; and (d) spending time in an English-speaking country or environment.

The most effective way to learn English is undoubtedly to live in an English-speaking country for a period of time: Milton and Meara (1995) found that learners living in the UK for six months improved their vocabulary by an average of 1,326 words. However, this approach is unrealistic for most students. Moreover, in many EFL situations, access to any spoken English may be severely limited. Thus, reading has traditionally been promoted as the most practical way to increase a learner's exposure to English.

For beginning learners, graded readers are a good way to start. Although graded readers have been criticized in the past for being boring and containing stilted language, modern graded series are generally well written and contain a diverse enough range of titles to engage virtually any student (see, for example, the *Cambridge English Readers* series, the *Oxford Bookworms* library, and Pearson's *Penguin Readers*). These readers have the advantage of providing considerable language input at an early stage of a learner's development, helping to improve reading skills as well as vocabulary, and hopefully starting a long-term reading habit in the L2.

As their proficiency increases, learners will naturally wish to move on to authentic texts. The jump from graded readers to authentic texts can sometimes be a large one, and a good way of easing this transition is with *narrow reading*. Narrow reading entails reading numerous texts but all on the same topic. Reading on one subject means that much of the topic-specific vocabulary will be repeated throughout the course of reading, which both makes the reading easier and gives the reader a better chance of learning this recurring vocabulary (Schmitt & Carter, 2000). Narrow reading can be achieved by following a continuing story in a newspaper, by reading magazines focusing on a particular topic, or, longer term, by engaging in content-based teaching. Once students have a foundation of reading skills, the best way to increase language input is through *extensive reading*. Extensive reading simply means reading a lot, and research suggests that it is very effective in terms of increasing general language proficiency (Elley, 1991).

In addition to promoting language input, teachers can equip learners to cope with the vocabulary they meet in this input by helping them to develop appropriate strategies. Guessing from context and choosing which words to explicitly focus upon are two obvious strategies learners will need in their repertoire. Other vocabulary learning strategies will be discussed below in the Strategies section. In sum, both the promotion of reading and instruction in key strategies are vital parts of the incidental learning strand and will thus be important components of any principled vocabulary program.

Facilitating Intentional Learning of Vocabulary

The Learning of Word Pairs

Although vocabulary is incremental in nature, it is obvious that the learner has to start someplace. Since all word knowledge aspects cannot be learned on the initial meeting, one reasonable way to start is by focusing on the meaning and word form aspects of a word first. Using word pairs is a good way to achieve this. The word pairs could be translation equivalents (English *dog* – Japanese *inu*), paired associates in English (*spur – encourage*), or word-picture pairs. Research has shown that students can successfully learn large numbers of words using this technique and that the learning seems to be durable (Nation, 2001, p. 298). A good way to use word pairs is to look at only one word in the pair and try to retrieve the other, because each retrieval strengthens the connection between the form of the word and its meaning (Nation & Meara, 2002). Word pairs have often been criticized for not giving words in context, but it seems the main problem is the way they are often employed by teachers: assigning word pairs as homework, perhaps testing them the next session, and then never returning to them. There seems no reason why learners should not get their initial introduction to new words on their own time via word pair homework, but teachers should then consolidate and enrich this initial knowledge with contextualized practice in subsequent classroom sessions.

Teaching Groups of Words Together and Cross-association

A well-known psychological principle is that organized information is easier to learn than unorganized information. This finding would suggest that grouping similar words together when learning should be beneficial. However, this is only true if the words are already partially known. Teaching similar words together in the first instance can lead to learner confusion, because students learn the word forms and learn the meanings, but can confuse which goes with which (*cross-association*). For example, if learners are taught the antonyms *deep* and *shallow* together, most are likely to remember that one concept is *relatively great depth* and the other concept is *relatively little depth*, but a significant number of them may confuse which word goes with which concept. Even native speakers often cross-associate similar words like *affect* and *effect*, or *inductive* and *deductive*. Antonyms are particularly prone to cross-association, because they tend to come in pairs like *noisy/quiet* or *hard/soft*, but synonyms and other words from closely related semantic groupings (e.g. numbers, days of the week) are also at risk. Research shows that cross-association is a serious trap for learners (Higa, 1963; Tinkham, 1993; Waring, 1997), with Nation (1990, p. 47) suggesting that about 25% of similar words taught together are typically cross-associated. He suggests the way to avoid cross-association is to teach the most frequent or useful word of a pair first (e.g., *deep*), and only after it is well established introducing its partner(s) (e.g., *shallow*).

Teaching the Underlying Meaning of a Word

Many words are polysemous in English, and often some of their different meaning senses have a common underlying trait. *Fork*, as an example, can mean a *fork* to eat with, a *fork* in a road or river, a *tuning fork* for use with music, a *pitch fork* that farmers use to throw hay, or several other things. The *General Service List* (West, 1953) indicates that the meaning sense of *implement used for eating or in gardening* makes up 86% of the occurrences, while *anything so shaped*, like *a fork in the road*, makes up 12%. This would suggest that *eating fork* is the most important meaning sense, but in this case, we can capture all of the meaning senses by defining the word with a drawing like this: ⑴. By defining the underlying meaning concept, we maximize the effect of the teaching by enabling students to understand the word in a much wider variety of contexts. Similarly, Nation (1990, pp. 72-73) suggests that defining *run* with a definition like *go quickly, smoothly, or continuously* is best, because it covers meaning senses like *the girl ran*, *the road runs up the hill*, and *run a business*.

Teaching Word Families instead of Words

Teachers can also maximize vocabulary learning by teaching word families instead of individual word forms. Instructors can make it a habit when introducing a new word to mention the other members of its word family. In this way, learners form the habit of considering a word's derivations as a matter of course. To reinforce this habit, teachers may eventually ask students to guess a new word's derivatives at the time of introduction. Including a derivation section as part of assessment also promotes the idea that learning the complete word family is important.

Teaching Word Parts

Many words in English, particularly academic words, are made up of Latin- and Greek-derived affixes and word stems. Knowledge of the most frequent affixes and stems in English can be a valuable resource with which both to guess the meanings of new words and to help remember the meanings of partially known words. Using a cost/benefit analysis, the explicit teaching of such stems and affixes would appear to be well worth the cost, with Nation (1990) suggesting this is one of the three key strategies learners should know in order to handle low-frequency vocabulary (the other two are guessing from context and mnemonic techniques). He suggests a number of exercises focusing on word parts, ranging from the memorization of prefix lists to classroom exercises focusing on the use of word parts to create new words.

Present Sequences of Words Together

One of the great insights to come out of corpus research is the overwhelming amount of lexical patterning that exists in English (and probably most other languages as well). Some of these patterning constraints have long been obvious, such as those that exist in idioms and proverbs (*burn the midnight oil*, but not **burn the 2 am oil* or **consume the midnight oil*). Corpus evidence has now made it possible to see other kinds of lexical patterning as well. This patterning can take the shape of collocational ties between two words (*mingle freely*) where the connection seems to be sequence based rather than being meaning based (**mingle unhindered* would make perfect sense semantically, but is not commonly used). Moreover, we find that lexical patterning also exists at a much broader level, where the word choices in sometimes quite long strings of language are constrained lexically:

SOMEONE/SOMETHING *made it plain that* SOMETHING AS YET UNREALIZED WAS
(often with authority) INTENDED OR DESIRED
(Schmitt, 2000, p. 189)

Lewis (1997) suggests that the implication of this patterning is that teachers should present words in the classroom in sequences whenever possible. In his publications he provides numerous examples of how this can be done, including the following:

Exploring a Simple Word

Do you know the word *book*? Add as many collocates to the following as you can.

Verb	Adjective	Key Word	Preposition
read	interesting	BOOK	about
buy	expensive		on
borrow	academic		for
edit	illustrated		by
publish	absorbing		of
ban	controversial		
lend	amusing		
recommend	hilarious .		.

Note: From Lewis, M. (1993). *The lexical approach* (p. 119). Hove: LTP. Copyright year by the name of copyright holder. Adapted with permission.

Other Principles for Explicit Teaching

Vocabulary research is now booming, and we have many more insights into effective teaching than can be highlighted in this section. Interested readers are encouraged to refer to the following sources, which give a multitude of additional teaching principles: Carter, 1998; Coady & Huckin, 1997; Gairns & Redman, 1986; Hunt & Beglar, 1998; McCarthy, 1990; Nation, 1990, 2001; Nation & Meara, 2002; Schmitt, 2000; Schmitt & Schmitt, 1995; and Sökmen, 1997. A good source for numerous vocabulary teaching activities is *New Ways in Teaching Vocabulary* (Nation, 1994). Teachers may also find it profitable to browse through some of the newer student textbooks (e.g., the *A Way with Words* series), as many contain a wealth of different exercise types that teachers may be able to adapt to their own teaching situations.

Facilitating Independent Vocabulary Learning: Vocabulary Learning Strategies

The above section discusses what teachers can do to actively promote vocabulary learning by their students. However, learners can do much to learn vocabulary independently of the teacher and classroom. One of the ways teachers can aid this process is by helping learners become aware of and practiced in using a variety of vocabulary learning strategies. Research shows that many learners do use strategies for learning vocabulary, and some of the more common strategies are simple memorization, repetition, and taking notes on vocabulary. These more mechanical strategies are often favored over more complex ones requiring significant active manipulation of information, such as imagery and inferencing. Because psychologists believe that activities which require more engagement with and manipulation of the information to be learned (*deeper processing*) generally lead to better retention, it seems that instructing learners in deeper processing strategies could lead to more efficient learning. Indeed, research into some deeper strategies, such as forming associations (Cohen & Aphek, 1981) and using the keyword method (Hulstijn, 1997) have been shown to enhance retention better than rote memorization. However, even rote repetition can be effective if students are accustomed to using it (O'Malley & Chamot, 1990). If a generalization can be made, shallower activities may be more suitable for beginners, because they contain less material that may only distract a novice, while intermediate or advanced learners can benefit from the context usually included in deeper activities (Cohen & Aphek, 1981).

Rather than being used individually, multiple vocabulary learning strategies are often used concurrently. This means that active management of strategy use is important. Good learners do things like use a variety of strategies, structure their vocabulary learning, review and practice target words, and remain aware of the semantic relationships between new and previously learned L2 words. That is, they are conscious of their learning and take steps to regulate it. Poor learners generally lack this awareness and control (Ahmed, 1989; Sanaoui, 1995).

When considering which vocabulary learning strategies to introduce to our students, we need to consider the learners themselves and their overall learning context. Proficiency level seems to be important, with one study showing word lists to be better for beginning students and contextualized words to be better for more advanced students (Cohen & Aphek, 1981). It is also important to gain the cooperation of the learners, because another study showed that students who resisted strategy training learned worse than those who relied on their familiar rote repetition approach (O'Malley & Chamot, 1990). Other factors to consider include the L1 and culture of students, their motivation and purposes for learning the L2, the task and text being used, and the nature of the L2 itself.

There are a few listings of vocabulary learning strategies available, including Ahmed (1989), Cohen (1990), and Sanaoui (1995). One relatively comprehensive listing of these strategies is presented by Schmitt (1997), who includes 58 strategies, divided in five categories. The following sampling provides a flavor of the range of strategies available:

1. *Determination strategies* used by an individual when faced with discovering a new word's meaning without recourse to another person's expertise.

   - Analyze any available pictures or gestures
   - Guess meaning from textual context
   - Use a dictionary (bilingual or monolingual)

2. *Social strategies* involve interaction with other people to improve language learning.

   - Ask the teacher for a synonym, paraphrase, or L1 translation of new word
   - Learn and practice new words with a study group
   - Interact with native-speakers

3. *Memory strategies* (traditionally known as *mnemonics*) involve relating new words to previously learned knowledge, using some form of imagery or grouping.

   - Use semantic maps
   - Use the keyword method
   - Associate a new word with its already known synonyms and antonyms

4. *Cognitive strategies* entail manipulation or transformation of information about words to be learned, although they are not so specifically focused on mental processing as memory strategies.

- Written repetition
- Keep a vocabulary notebook
- Put English labels on physical objects

5. *Metacognitive strategies* involve a conscious overview of the learning process and making decisions about planning, monitoring, or evaluating the best ways to study.

- Use spaced word practice (expanding rehearsal)
- Test oneself with word tests
- Continue to study word over time

CONCLUSIONS

The ideas presented in this chapter are important to consider when developing any vocabulary program. Different learners will obviously need emphasis on different types of words (whether high-frequency or specialized vocabulary), but nearly all students can benefit from a judicious blend of intentional and incidental learning. Even advanced learners with large vocabularies can continue to fill out their lexical knowledge, as many (or most) of the words in their mental lexicons will only be partially mastered. After all, even native speakers continue to learn new words throughout their lifetimes.

NOTES

[1] Thanks to Christina Lee for this example.

REFERENCES

Adolphs, S., & Schmitt, N. 2003. Lexical coverage of spoken discourse. *Applied Linguistics, 24*(4), 425–438.
Ahmed, M. O. (1989). Vocabulary learning strategies. In P. Meara (Ed.), *Beyond words* (pp. 3–14). London: CILT.
Baddeley, A. (1990). *Human memory: Theory and practice*. Needham Heights, MA: Allyn and Bacon.
Bahns, J., & Eldaw, M. (1993). Should we teach EFL students collocations? *System, 21*(1), 101–114.
Carter, R. (1998). *Vocabulary: Applied linguistic perspectives* (2nd ed.). London: Routledge.
Coady, J., & Huckin, T. (Eds.). (1997). *Second language vocabulary acquisition*. Cambridge: Cambridge University Press.
Cohen, A. D. (1990). *Language learning*. New York: Newbury House.
Cohen, A. D., & Aphek, E. (1981). Easifying second language learning. *Studies in Second Language Acquisition, 3*(2), 221–236.
Elley, W. B. (1991). Acquiring literacy in a second language: The effect of book-based programs. *Language Learning 41*(3), 375–411.
Gairns, R., & Redman, S. (1986). *Working with words*. Cambridge: Cambridge University Press.
Goulden, R., Nation, P., & Read, J. (1990). How large can a receptive vocabulary be? *Applied Linguistics, 11*(4), 341–363.
Hazenberg, S., & Hulstijn, J.H. (1996). Defining a minimal receptive second-language vocabulary for non-native university students: An empirical investigation. *Applied Linguistics, 17*(2), 145–163.

Higa, M. (1963). Interference effects of intralist word relationships in verbal learning. *Journal of Verbal Learning and Verbal Behavior, 2*, 170–175.

Hulstijn, J. H. (1997). Mnemonic methods in foreign language vocabulary learning. In J. Coady & T. Huckin (Eds.), *Second language vocabulary acquisition* (pp. 203–224). Cambridge: Cambridge University Press.

Hunt, A., & Beglar, D. (1998). Current research and practice in teaching vocabulary. *The Language Teacher, 22*(1). Available online at http://langue.hyper.chubu.ac.jp/jalt/pub/tlt/98/jan/hunt.html.

Leech, G., Rayson, P., & Wilson, A. (2001). *Word frequencies in written and spoken English*. Harlow: Longman.

Lewis, M. (1993). *The lexical approach*. Hove: LTP.

Lewis, M. (1997). *Implementing the lexical approach*. Hove: LTP.

McCarthy, M. (1990). *Vocabulary*. Oxford: Oxford University Press.

McKeown, M. G., Beck, I. L., Omanson, R. C., & Pople, M. T. (1985). Some effects of the nature and frequency of vocabulary instruction on the knowledge and use of words. *Reading Research Quarterly, 20*, 522–535.

Milton, J., & Meara, P. (1995). How periods abroad affect vocabulary growth in a foreign language. *ITL Review of Applied Linguistics, 107–108*, 17–34.

Moon, R. (1997). Vocabulary connections: Multi-word items in English. In N. Schmitt & M. McCarthy (Eds.), *Vocabulary: Description, acquisition, and pedagogy* (pp. 40–63). Cambridge: Cambridge University Press.

Moon, R. (1998). *Fixed expressions in English: A corpus-based approach*. Oxford: Oxford University Press.

Nagy, W. (1997). On the role of context in first- and second-language vocabulary learning. In N. Schmitt & M. McCarthy (Eds.), *Vocabulary: Description, acquisition, and pedagogy* (pp. 64–83). Cambridge: Cambridge University Press.

Nation, P. (1995). The word on words: An interview with Paul Nation. [Interviewed by Norbert Schmitt.] *The Language Teacher 19*(2), 5–7.

Nation, I. S. P. (1990). *Teaching and learning vocabulary*. Boston, MA: Heinle and Heinle.

Nation, P. (Ed.). (1994). *New ways in teaching vocabulary*. Alexandria, VA: TESOL.

Nation, I. S. P. (2001). *Learning vocabulary in another language*. Cambridge: Cambridge University Press.

Nation, P., & Meara, P. (2002). Vocabulary. In N. Schmitt (Ed.), *An introduction to applied linguistics* (pp. 35–54). London: Arnold.

Nation, P., & Waring, R. (1997). Vocabulary size, text coverage and word lists. In N. Schmitt & M. McCarthy (Eds.), *Vocabulary: Description, acquisition and pedagogy* (pp. 6–19). Cambridge: Cambridge University Press.

Newton, J. (2001). Options for vocabulary learning through communication tasks. *English Language Teaching Journal, 55*(1), 30–37.

O'Malley, J. M., & Chamot, A. U. (1990). *Learning strategies in second language acquisition*. Cambridge: Cambridge University Press.

Pawley, A., & Syder, F.H. (1983). Two puzzles for linguistic theory: Native like selection and native like fluency. In J. Richards & R. Schmidt (Eds.), *Language and communication* (pp. 191–225). London: Longman.

Pimsleur, P. (1967). A memory schedule. *Modern Language Journal, 51*(2), 73–75.

Redman, S. & Ellis, R. *A way with words*. (Series 1989–). Cambridge: Cambridge University Press.

Russell, P. (1979). *The brain book*. London: Routledge and Kegan Paul.

Sanaoui, R. (1995). Adult learners' approaches to learning vocabulary in second languages. *Modern Language Journal, 79*, 15–28.

Schmitt, N. (1997). Vocabulary learning strategies. In N. Schmitt & M. McCarthy (Eds.), *Vocabulary: Description, acquisition, and pedagogy* (pp. 199–227). Cambridge: Cambridge University Press.

Schmitt, N. (1998). Tracking the incremental acquisition of second language vocabulary: A longitudinal study. *Language Learning, 48*(2), 281–317.

Schmitt, N. (2000). *Vocabulary in language teaching*. Cambridge: Cambridge University Press.

Schmitt, N., & Schmitt, D. (1995). Vocabulary notebooks: Theoretical underpinnings and practical suggestions. *English Language Teaching Journal, 49*(2), 133–143.

Schmitt, N., & Zimmerman, C. B. (2002). Derivative word forms: What do learners know? *TESOL Quarterly*.

Schonell, F., Meddleton, I., Shaw, B., Routh, M., Popham, D., Gill, G., Mackrell, G., & Stephens, C. (1956). *A study of the oral vocabulary of adults*. Brisbane and London: University of Queensland Press/University of London Press.

Sökmen, A. (1997). Current trends in teaching second language vocabulary. In N. Schmitt & M. McCarthy (Eds.), *Vocabulary: Description, acquisition, and pedagogy* (pp. 237–257). Cambridge: Cambridge University Press.
Tinkham, T. (1993). The effect of semantic clustering on the learning of second language vocabulary. *System, 21*(3), 371–380.
Waring, R. (1997). The negative effects of learning words in semantic sets: A replication. *System 25*(2), 261–274.
Webster's Third New International Dictionary. (1961). Springfield, MA: Merriam-Webster Inc.
West, M. (1953). *A general service list of English words*. London: Longman, Green & Co.
Wray, A. (2002). *Formulaic Language and the Lexicon.* Cambridge: Cambridge University Press.

CHAPTER 51

CHANGING APPROACHES TO THE CONCEPTUALIZATION AND TEACHING OF GRAMMAR

BEVERLY DEREWIANKA

The University of Wollongong, Australia

ABSTRACT

The traditional view of grammar as simply a collection of word classes and rules for their combination is being supplemented by theories that conceive of grammar in terms of its cognitive and social origins. Such theories are being used to support research from psycholinguistic and sociolinguistic perspectives into the learning and teaching of language and how grammar is implicated in such processes. This chapter looks at three models of grammar that are representative of the major paradigms currently informing ELT research and practice: grammar as structure, grammar as mental faculty, and grammar as functional resource. It concludes with a look at some of the issues surrounding grammar and future directions for research and teaching.

INTRODUCTION

Grammar is currently enjoying a vigorous revival of interest following a period when it had become virtually a taboo area. Given the centrality of grammar to ELT, this is a welcome return. But for those nostalgic for the "good old days," the new wave of grammar teaching will provide little solace. New approaches to grammatical description together with new ways of applying these in the classroom have challenged the rules and drills of yesterday.

This chapter will examine three models of grammar and associated pedagogies that are currently influential in the field of second language (L2) teaching. It does not pretend to be comprehensive—there are any number of approaches to grammar and the teaching of grammar. The purpose of the chapter is to distinguish between the various grammatical theories that teachers might encounter and to clarify some of their key features with a view to illuminating their relevance for the ELT field.

THE WESTERN TRADITION

In order to understand contemporary grammars, we need to see where they have come from. All grammars of English have their roots in the Western linguistic tradition. We can trace the beginnings of grammatical analysis to the ancient Greeks. It was Plato, for example, who recognized the sentence (*logos*) as a basic unit of language, representing a proposition. Propositions were seen as consisting of *onoma* (name/noun—corresponding to the topic or subject) and *rhema* (verb phrase—corresponding to the predicate: what is said about the subject). These were not empty categories but were early attempts at trying to describe the function of each unit from the perspective of logic. Plato was interested in the truth value of propositions, not in grammatical analysis as an end in itself.

These rudimentary categories were further developed by Aristotle, who lived around 384-322 BC, and who divided language into the following parts: letter, syllable, connecting word, noun, verb, inflection or case, sentence or phrase. As with Plato, Aristotle's primary concern was not with identifying discrete linguistic units but with exploring how language functions in particular ways in terms of the art of rhetoric, poetics, and reasoning. As Allan (2001) notes, the footprints of Aristotle are to be found throughout the linguist's garden. Most of the major themes of modern linguistics find their roots in Aristotle.

Aristotle's description of letters and syllables focuses on their sound qualities, arising out of his interest in the intonational patterns employed in poetics and rhetoric. The other categories relate more to his interest in *epistemology*—the nature of knowledge and knowing. He was intrigued by the possibility that the structure of language could reflect the structure of thought and that in categorizing language, we are also categorizing perceived reality. Aristotle contended that the mental experiences that the speech sounds represent are the same for all human beings. That is, meaning is given, unchanging, and universal, while the expression of meaning is conventional and differs according to the speech community.

An Alexandrian scholar, Dionysius Thrax, in the second century BC, produced the first systematic grammar of the Western tradition dealing with words and their morphology. He identified the eight word classes that persist in various ways through to today: the noun, verb, participle, article, pronoun, preposition, adverb, and conjunction.

From these early beginnings, we can identify three main themes that have continued to reverberate through history and that characterize the grammars presented in this chapter:

1. What are the basic constituents of a sentence and how are they organized into structures?
2. Is there a universal grammar that reflects human cognition?
3. How does language function to help us achieve our rhetorical purposes?

In relation to these questions, the following sections will look at language as structure, language as mental faculty, and language as functional resource, respectively.[1]

LANGUAGE AS STRUCTURE

Traditionally, grammar in the ELT field has been conceived of in terms of identifying the parts of speech and the rules for combining them into structures. The most enduring example of such an approach is traditional grammar, arguably still the most widely used model in ELT internationally. While we might encounter impoverished and even erroneous versions in certain pedagogic and school grammars, the rich tradition is sustained in the more scholarly reference grammars.

Reference grammars of English have been written for the past several decades, most of them by non-native speakers. Their aim is to provide a comprehensive, in-depth account of the constituents of the English sentence and how these combine to form larger units. Most of these grammars claim no overt theoretical allegiance, accepting the time-honored categories as self-evident. Perhaps the best known of the contemporary reference grammars is that of Quirk, Greenbaum, Leech, and Svartvik (1985), who draw both on the long-established tradition and on the insights of several contemporary schools of linguistics.

More recently, Longman has published an equally comprehensive reference grammar by Biber, Johansson, Leech, Conrad, and Finegan (1999). Whereas Quirk, Greenbaum, Leech, and Svartvik (1985) claimed to describe the "common core" of educated English regardless of dialect or register, Biber et al. have exploited the capacity of modern technology to analyze extensive corpora, allowing commentary on the occurrence of different structures in relation to different varieties of English (including spoken English). Despite this innovation, Biber et al. acknowledge that they have not departed to any great extent from the framework developed by Quirk et al.

Huddleston and Pullum (2002), in collaboration with a number of international experts, have also produced a major new reference grammar, still locating itself within the heritage of the great descriptive grammars of the past, while drawing systematically on linguistic research during the past 40 years, claiming to be sounder and more consistent than other large-scale grammars. Huddleston and Pullum are explicit about the grammatical rationale that informs their endeavor but claim, "the primary goal of this grammar is to describe the grammatical principles of Present-Day English rather than to defend or illustrate a theory of grammar" (p. 18).

These grammars play an important role in the ELT field, providing an authoritative, up-to-date, and comprehensive point of reference for the profession and a shared terminology for talking about language. They have been written by respected teams of academics and represent scholarly yet accessible accounts of contemporary views on grammar, without radically departing from the Aristotelian tradition.

Language as Structure: Implications for Teaching

The methodology typically associated with traditional grammar involved the explicit, systematic teaching of rules followed by decontextualized exercises. While this method can still be encountered (particularly in some EFL contexts), it is more common these days to take an approach more finely tuned to the needs of the learner and informed by what we know about learning an L2.

One such approach is most commonly referred to as *focus on form*.[2] Long (2001) distinguishes between *focus on formS* (where discrete items are taught in isolation) and *focus on form* (where linguistic features are attended to in the context of meaning-oriented activity). Rejecting the first option, he proposes that teachers draw students' attention to linguistic elements as they arise incidentally within a communicative activity. If, for example, a student makes a persistent error that is amenable to remedy, the teacher (or another learner) could draw attention to the problem. In this way, the focus is placed on specific features that arise from the learner's experience and is therefore relevant and motivating.

Research has been undertaken into the type of *corrective feedback* that can be provided. Carroll and Swain (1993), for example, studied the effect of different responses to learner errors (e.g., giving an explanation, recasting the learner's offering, inviting the learner to try again) and found that all these forms of feedback were more effective than no feedback at all. Difficulties with a reactive approach include its impracticality, especially if the class is large and includes students of different L1 backgrounds. It would also require a high level of professional knowledge on the part of the teacher to be able to make on-the-spot judgments as to which linguistic features to address and how.

At the other end of the spectrum to this reactive position are those who take a proactive stance. Such teachers might build into their lessons opportunities to address learner problems that have been frequently observed. This again requires a great deal from the teacher in terms of observation and recording of common errors and preparation of authentic activities and materials that address the language feature in question.

While focus-on-form can target any level of language (Doughty & Williams, 1998), it is generally restricted to matters of morphology and syntax, often with an emphasis on encouraging structural accuracy.

LANGUAGE AS MENTAL FACULTY

Whereas traditional grammarians tend to study linguistic structure as an end in itself, grammarians coming from a psycholinguistic perspective investigate grammar in order to know more about how it is implicated in cognitive processes. Here we will focus on the work of Noam Chomsky as one of the key figures in this field.[3]

For Chomsky (2000), knowledge of language is internal to the human mind/brain. It is a genetically determined property of the individual:

> The faculty of language can reasonably be regarded as a 'language organ' in the sense in which scientists speak of the visual system, or immune system, or circulatory system, as organs of the body. ...We assume further that the language organ is like others in that its basic character is an expression of the genes. ...Language acquisition seems much like the growth of organs generally; it is something that happens to a child, not that the child does. And while the environment plainly matters, the general course of development and the basic features of what emerges are predetermined by the initial state. But the initial state is a common human possession. It must be, then, that in their essential properties, languages are cast to the same mold. (p. 4)

Generative theory has undergone a number of phases. The standard theory (1950-1980) was concerned with phrase structure theory and transformations. In 1980, the government and binding theory was introduced, with such innovations as X-bar syntax, Wh-movement and NP-movement, case, and binding. Currently, two strands dominate: principles and parameters (1986) and the minimalist program (1995).

Principles and Parameters

Chomsky views the Principles and Parameters theory as constituting a major break with 2,500 years of linguistic tradition, inasmuch as it dispensed with the rules and constructions associated with traditional grammar. Instead, it developed a radically new conception of language. The mental representations of language that are seen as innate in the human species consist of two elements: sets of principles (which are the same for all languages) and sets of parameters (those elements that can differ across languages):

> We can think of the initial state of the faculty of language as a fixed network connected to a switch box; the network is constituted of the principles of language, while the switches are the options to be determined by experience. When the switches are set one way, we have Bantu; when they are set another way, we have Japanese. Each possible human language is identified as a particular setting of the switches—a setting of parameters, in technical terminology. (Chomsky, 2000, p. 8)

The most basic principle is that all languages have the two core components: noun phrase (NP) and verb phrase (VP)—generally corresponding to subject and predicate. The phrases of different languages, however, can have different internal structures depending on their parameters. Whereas infants are already hardwired for basic phrases such as NP and VP, they need exposure to a particular language to acquire the parameters (i.e., the distinct internal phrase structure). All the possible choices of parameters are preprogrammed in the infant in a hierarchical structure. When exposed to input, the child will set the parameters of his or her first language. At each choice point, there are only two options available (choose A or B), making the child's task relatively simple. For example, some languages have the structure NP (subject) followed by VP (predicate) whereas others have the structure VP followed by NP. The child will select the structure that is characteristic of the input received. Having made this basic choice, the next step is to analyze in finer detail the structure of the NP and VP (e.g., in terms of whether it is head-initial or head-final).

The Minimalist Program

In order to maximize the descriptive and explanatory power of his theory, Chomsky opts for a "parsimonious" approach, with the minimalist program now focusing its attention on the most basic unit of analysis, the morpheme, and the syntactic information it carries.

With the minimalist program, Chomsky (1997) embarks on an even more radical course. In an attempt to identify the bare essentials, he sheds "excess baggage" such as phrase structure rules, X-bar theory, and the levels of deep and surface structure:

> The minimalist program seeks to show that everything that has been accounted for in terms of these levels has been misdescribed, and is as well or better understood in terms of legibility conditions at the interface: for those of you who know the technical literature, that means the projection principle, binding theory, Case theory, the chain condition, and so on. (p. 32)

While principles and parameters holds that each parameter is tied to certain principles, the minimalist program now contends that parameters are not tied to principles but are instead part of the lexicon. Individual lexical items contain sufficient grammatical information for parameter setting.

Chomsky (2000) believes the faculty of language to be embedded within the broader architecture of the mind/brain. It engages with other systems, in particular the system related to sound and the system related to meaning. At the interface between these systems, Chomsky posits *legibility conditions* that language must satisfy. That is, an expression generated by the language contains a phonetic representation that must be legible to the sensorimotor systems and a semantic representation that must be legible to the conceptual system:

> The sensorimotor systems, for example, have to be able to read the instructions having to do with sound, that is the 'phonetic representations' generated by the language. The articulatory and perceptual apparatus have specific design that enables them to interpret certain phonetic properties, not others. These systems thus impose legibility conditions on the generative processes of the faculty of language, which must provide expressions with the proper phonetic form. The same is true of conceptual and other systems that make use of the resources of the faculty of language: they have their intrinsic properties, which require that the expressions generated by the language have certain kinds of 'semantic representations', not others. (p. 9)

The minimalist program is an attempt to explore these legibility conditions, calling into question previously held tenets of generative theory.

Language as Mental Faculty: Implications for Teaching

In attempting to explain the learning of language, Chomsky points to the speed and efficiency with which children are able to produce an inordinately large number of original utterances. He claims that the only way in which this can be explained is to assume that the fundamentals are already in place in the child's brain and exposure to a particular language triggers certain options from a prespecified set.

One interpretation of universal grammar (UG) theory is that because the principles and parameters are already available to the learner, all that is needed for the forms to emerge is the triggering evidence in the target language. Chomsky (1968) himself questions the usefulness of explicit instruction, urging instead that teachers create a rich linguistic environment for the "intuitive heuristics" that students bring to the learning task. Krashen (1992) also adopts a noninterventionist approach based on his monitor theory, which claims that unconscious acquisition results in greater fluency than learned knowledge. He believes that acquisition will be enhanced if the learner is exposed to comprehensible input. Subsequent research into second language acquisition (SLA) has focused on the nature of the input (and output) involved in the language learning process. Cook (1994, p. 46), for example, states that UG theory emphasizes the role of the teacher as provider of input and that this input can be optimalized using insights provided by the theory.

Another line of inquiry arises out of the Principles and Parameters research. If one accepts that learning an L1 involves setting the parameters through exposure to input, then one might assume that the same holds true for L2 learners, whose task might be to reset the parameters. Once the parameters of the target language have been identified, it would make it easier to develop teaching programs addressing these parameters and to compare the parameters of L1 and L2 (Cook, 1994). This approach rests on the assumption, however, that older learners still have access to the universal grammar. Mitchell and Myles (2002) point to four possible positions regarding UG mechanisms:

1. All L2 learners continue to have full access to universal grammar;
2. After the acquisition of L1 in early childhood, access to universal grammar disappears, and adult learners must resort to other non-language-specific means;
3. Adult L2 learners have indirect access to universal grammar through the model provided by their L1, particularly in terms of the principles (which are common to L1 and L2) and those parameters that are similar in L1 and L2; and
4. L2 learners have partial access to universal grammar: some parameters are reset and others aren't. (p. 17, enumeration added)

Other researchers are interested in the sequence and timing of acquisition. It has been observed, for example, that learners pass through predictable developmental stages in their acquisition of particular structures such as negatives, interrogatives, and relative clauses (see Johnston, 1985). From such findings, Pienemann (1989) has developed the *teachability hypothesis*: that learners appear to be unable to acquire a structure far beyond their level of development, so learning is maximized when the teacher is able to gear instruction to the learner's current stage. Such research could be helpful to the syllabus designer, the textbook writer, and the teacher in terms of developing instructional sequences based on expected learner progress. However, at this stage the research has not produced sufficient information on these sequences to underpin an ELT curriculum.

LANGUAGE AS FUNCTIONAL RESOURCE

There are many interpretations of the term *functional* and many theories of grammar claiming to be functional, including The Prague School, the functional grammar of Dik and colleagues, the North American functionalists (Chafe, Givón, Bates, and MacWhinney), pragmatic functionalism (Leech), and systemic functional grammar (Halliday and colleagues).[4] Here we will focus on the latter.

While Chomsky sees language as a biological phenomenon, Halliday is more interested in language as a social phenomenon. The nature of language is explained not in terms of a genetic blueprint located in the individual brain, but as a result of countless social interactions over the millennia.

According to Halliday, the language system has evolved as a complex network of choices. The choices we make in any particular situation are influenced by contextual factors:

1. the *field* (what is the subject matter being developed? e.g., everyday, personal, technical, abstract, specific, generalized);
2. the *tenor* (what are the social relations between the interactants? e.g., differences in terms of status, power, expertise, age, gender, familiarity);
3. the *mode* (what mode and medium are being used? e.g., written, spoken, face-to-face, distanced).

Obviously, the language used in a situation involving the writing of a highly technical text to persuade an academic audience will be quite different from that used by a child telling his mother what happened at school that day. Context is not given and deterministic. It is emergent, dynamic, and cumulative. Context and language are co-constructed: the context helps to shape our use of language and the language choices we make help to shape the context.

For Halliday, language is as it is because of what it does. Its structure reflects the functions it serves in our daily lives: representing our experience of the world (the *experiential* function), mediating interaction (the *interpersonal* function), and structuring the flow of information (the *textual* function). Halliday (1994) refers to these as *metafunctions*. There is a close relationship between the context and the various metafunctions. Depending on the field being developed, certain choices will be made from the experiential system. Depending on the tenor of the situation, certain choices will be made from the interpersonal system. And depending on the mode and medium, certain choices will be made from the textual system. In any given utterance, all three metafunctions operate simultaneously.

In looking at *experiential meaning*, we would be interested in how we use grammar to construe our experience of the world: What kinds of events are taking place? (e.g., *doing, thinking, feeling, saying, relating*); Who or what is participating in those events/processes? (e.g., who is initiating the action? who is affected by it? what is being thought/felt/said? what qualities and attributes do these participants have?); and What kinds of circumstances surround the activity? (e.g., when? where? how? with whom? why?).

Interpersonal meaning, on the other hand, is concerned with grammatical resources for interacting and the development of subjectivity (e.g., various types of speech function: statements, questions, commands; the adoption and allocation of speech roles; the assessment of probability, obligation, and commitment; the ways in which we address each other; the expression of opinion; and so on).

Finally, the *textual* resources function to make a text coherent and cohesive, organizing the flow of information in particular ways: what can be taken as given, what is new, the speaker's point of departure, and how the various parts of the discourse relate to each other (Hasan & Perrett, 1994).

Language also operates at three levels: the *semantic plane* (meaning), the *content plane* (lexico-grammar), and the *expression plane* (sounds and letters). These levels are related through a process of realization: meanings are realized by particular lexical and grammatical choices that are in turn realized by the phonological system.

We could summarize this model as shown in Figure 1.

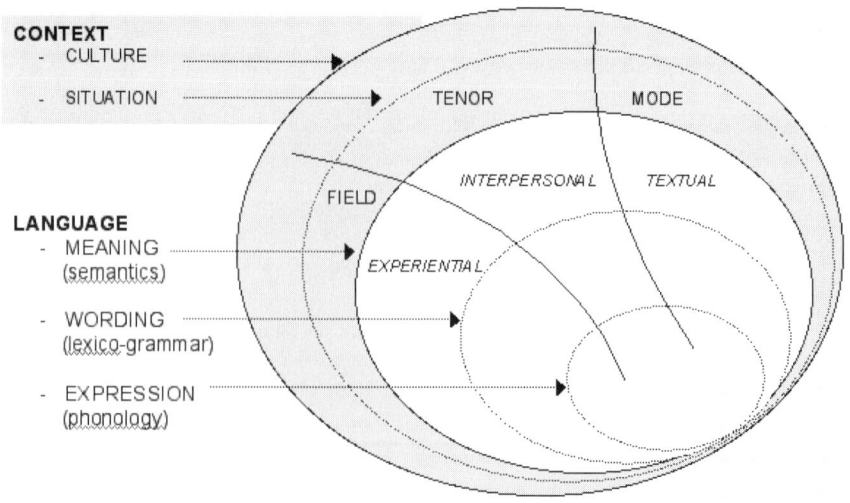

Figure 1. Halliday's Functional Model of Language

Adapted from Martin, J. (1999). Modelling context: the crooked path of progress in contextual linguistics. In M Ghadessy (Ed.), *Text and Context in Functional Linguistics* (pp. 25-61). Amsterdam: Benjamins (CILT Series IV). Adapted with permission of author.

Halliday describes his theory as "extravagant". It is multilayered and multidimensional in its efforts to capture the richness and complexity of language. Grammar is studied within the context of the whole text, as the meaning of an utterance is contingent upon the unfolding grammatical and semantic patternings at the discourse level (see McCarthy & Slade, this volume, for a fuller discussion).

Language as Functional Resource: Implications for Teaching

Halliday explains language development as a social phenomenon, where the infant initially uses meaningful sounds in order to satisfy basic needs: *give me that, help me, look at that*, and so on. These rudimentary functions gradually evolve into the metafunctions of the adult language through constant, contextualized interactions with caregivers who are acutely sensitive to the child's emergent linguistic system and who provide supported opportunities for the child to participate in the negotiation of meaning.

Thorne (2000) sees the work of Halliday as formative to the view of language as social-semiotic systems adopted by many socioculturally oriented SLA researchers. The Hallidayan model of language resonates with Vygotskian theory, which maintains that language learning occurs through situated interaction. In this view, language learners are not simply processors of input or producers of output, but speaker/hearers engaged in a collaborative process through which they build grammatical, expressive, interactional, and cultural competence (Ohta, 2000). It is the negotiation work involved in the interactive construction of meaning (e.g., repairs, clarifications, recastings) that provides affordances for language learning. According to Luria (1979, p. 174), such an approach seeks to maintain the richness and complexity of "living reality" rather than distilling it into its elementary components for the purposes of constructing abstract models that lose the properties of the phenomenon itself.

An example of the convergence of social interactionist theory and systemic functional linguistics in an ESL context can be found in the work of Gibbons (2002, also see Gibbons, this volume), who examined the microprocesses of teacher-student interaction to see how teachers scaffold learners' language development.

A further example is the *curriculum cycle* developed for use in schools with high migrant density in Australia to enable access to the powerful discourses of schooling. (See Christie, 1999, and de Silva Joyce & Burns, 1999, for further elaboration.) The cycle, based on the notion of *scaffolding*, consists of a number of recursive phases:

1. building up the field (developing learners' control over the subject matter and the lexicogrammatical resources needed to control the field);
2. modeling and deconstruction (familiarization with the genre and its linguistic features);
3. joint construction (the collaborative production of a text with explicit attention to the characteristic language features); and
4. independent construction (the autonomous production of a similar text by the learner, drawing on the support previously provided).

For teachers who choose to be proactive rather than reactive in their language teaching, functional grammar can provide a basis for predicting which linguistic features are likely to arise within a particular context. If the context entails, for example, the writing of an essay in the field of commerce by an undergraduate student on the effects of the global economy on developing countries, then we could predict some of the key linguistic resources that students would need in order to undertake such a task, as shown in Table 1.

Table 1. Using Context to Predict Linguistic Features

	Contextual factor	Potential linguistic focus
Purpose	Expository genre: causal explanation of a phenomenon	The distinctive functional stages that such a text needs to develop in order to achieve its rhetorical purpose
Field	The academic discipline of commerce (including cause and effect implication sequences)	E.g., lexicogrammatical resources for building field-specific technicality, and the nominalization of experience, the expression of causal relationships
Tenor	The construal of self as a knowledgeable, critical apprentice interacting with "the academy" (mediated by the lecturer as assessor)	E.g., the indirect expression of probability, the degree of commitment to a proposition, resources for critical evaluation, citing practices, and the choice of speech role pronouns
Mode	Written product (through a process of reading, discussion, and drafting)	E.g. cohesive devices typical of written text, and resources for manipulating the flow of information (e.g., foregrounding and backgrounding; signaling the development of the argument)

ISSUES AND FUTURE DIRECTIONS

Along with the renewed interest in grammar and its teaching come debates and issues. The following section comments on a few current and future directions with reference to the models of grammar discussed above.

The Way Grammar is Conceptualized

The way we conceptualize language has implications for the way we conceptualize learning and teaching. The relevance of a particular theory of language will depend on what we are interested in investigating and which theory will help to shed light on the phenomenon. The primary object of investigation for Chomsky, for example, is the properties of the language faculty as a biological entity located within the human brain. He differentiates the idealized, abstract *I-language* that is internal to the individual brain from the performance that is derived from this. *Performance—*

our use of language—is seen as not being amenable to serious study, as it contains imperfections and deviations. He believes that how we put competence to use in our performance is still largely a closed book, perhaps a mystery (Smith, 2000). For Halliday, on the other hand, the challenge is to explain the nature of language with reference to its use in social contexts. He sees language as a resource, a meaning-making system. It is through language that we interactively shape and interpret our world and ourselves. Halliday does not distinguish between competence and performance. In his view, we can only usefully deal with the evidence that we have from language in use and seek its explanation in relation to social, cultural, and historical contexts. Rather than *deviance*, he prefers to talk in terms of *functional variation*.

Chomsky (2000) comments that, even though each approach defines the object of its inquiry in the light of its special concerns, the various approaches are not in conflict, and each should try to learn what it can from other approaches in a mutually supportive way. Halliday (1994) admits that there are many cross-currents between formal grammars (with their roots in philosophy and logic) and functional grammars (with their roots in rhetoric and ethnography), but that they are different in their ideological orientations and assumptions, making it difficult to maintain a dialogue. While acknowledging that there can be no single universal truth, Thorne (2000) predicts that "truth(s) bringing together neurobiology and historical-contextual contingency may in fact be obtainable, but will require a plurality of efforts to be realized" (p. 238).

Unit of Analysis

While the clause remains the unit of analysis in most grammars, there is now interest below and beyond the clause. Below the clause, we find a growing awareness of the importance of lexical items. Referring to current UG theory, Cook (1994, p. 46) observes that the acquisition of syntax is minimized and the acquisition of vocabulary items with lexical entries is maximized. There is also a recognition of the lexical phrase as a significant unit in language development (e.g., Little, 1994; Nattinger & de Carrico, 1992; Willis, 1994), with learners regularly beginning with prefabricated "chunks" before becoming more analytical about their structure. Corpus studies such as the COBUILD project (Sinclair, 1991) will continue to reveal quite unsuspected collocational patternings of lexis and grammar that traditional descriptive frameworks are normally not able to account for.

At the other end of the spectrum, the unit of analysis is discourse (e.g., Celce-Murcia & Olshtain, 2000; McCarthy, 2001) with a focus on how grammatical meanings are contingent upon the unfolding text:

> A text is a semantic unit, not a grammatical one. But meanings are realized through wordings; and without a theory of wordings—that is a grammar—there is no way of making explicit one's interpretation of the meaning of a text. ...In order to provide insights into the meaning and effectiveness of a text, a discourse grammar needs to be functional and semantic in its orientation, with the grammatical categories explained as the realization of semantic patterns. Otherwise it will face inwards rather than outwards, characterizing the text in explicit formal terms but providing no basis on which to relate it to the non-linguistic universe of its situational and cultural environment. (Halliday 1994, p. xvii)

A great deal of recent research has focused on identifying the characteristic lexicogrammatical features of the discourses of various curriculum subjects and academic disciplines (e.g., Christie & Martin, 1997; Halliday & Martin, 1993; Paltridge, 2002; van Leeuwen & Humphrey, 1996; Veel & Coffin, 1996).

The Grammar of Spoken Language

Traditionally, grammars have been based on the written language due to the fact that it is more stable. Spoken language was perceived as a deviant version of the written, with its false starts, incomplete sentences, "mistakes," and so on. One of the great advances of recent times is the focus on spoken language and its own distinctive grammatical features (e.g., Brazil, 1995; Burns, 2001; Eggins & Slade, 1997; Halliday, 1989, 2001; McCarthy & Carter, 2002, McCarthy & Slade, this volume). It is now possible to analyze large-scale corpora of spoken discourse using computers and to identify the distinctive patterns of spoken language. This is of particular significance to ELT, providing support for approaches to language learning that are based on the negotiated construction of meaning in interactive oral contexts.

Multimodalities

With the increasing use of texts that combine a variety of modalities (written text, still graphics, animated graphics, video clips, icons), it has become apparent that we can't take it for granted that learners will automatically know how to understand, interpret, and even construct such texts. Efforts are now being made (e.g., Goodman, 1996; Kress & van Leeuwen, 1996; Stenglin & Iedema, 2001) to provide analytical tools in the form of "grammars" of these various modalities (as well as other semiotic systems such as music, architecture, film, and dance) with a view to enhancing students' visual literacy.

Grammar and Ideology

As can be seen from several titles in this collection, there is currently great interest in the political and ideological aspects of ELT. There is a need for a theory of language that is in sympathy with and provides support for these concerns. Despite his role as a radical social activist, Chomsky's theory of language is totally divorced from ideological considerations as he is only concerned with the internal workings of the individual brain. Conversely, Halliday, coming from a socialist background, believes that language is inherently ideological and locates the individual within collective, material, and historical contexts. He has a fervent interest in issues of social justice and draws heavily on the work of Bernstein in explicating the relationship between language and ideology. Research by colleagues such as Hasan (e.g., 1986) and Martin (e.g., 1993) demonstrates how particular discourses of power marginalize the less powerful and how these discourses can be disrupted and subverted when the linguistic resources are made explicit. Other studies demonstrate how a functional approach to grammar can be used to develop a critical literacy (e.g., Hammond & Macken-Horarik, 1999) or a critical language awareness (e.g., van Lier, 2001). If we believe that learning an L2 is a process of socialization where we are learning to construct new sociocultural realities and to reshape our subjectivity, then we need a theory of language that enables us to understand how grammar is implicated in such processes (Roberts, 2001).

Grammar and SLA

Perhaps the most critical question is what a theory of grammar can contribute to our understanding of how an L2 is learnt. Ellis (1997) acknowledges that the SLA field is predominantly psycholinguistic in its orientation, seeking to examine the mental processes involved in the creation and use of L2 knowledge, with the learner seen as "an information processor, receiving and autonomously processing input in the black box of the mind" (p. 241).

Formal approaches to SLA such as the above are brought into question by more socially oriented researchers:

> [T]he dominant core of current theories of SLA are for the most part defining a world of a-historical, decontextualized, and disembodied brains. It is my belief that such a theory does not fit the evidence. (Thorne, 2000, p. 220)

Hasan and Perrett (1994) also question the dominant paradigm:

> What the field needs as its foundation is not a model of language as an autonomous system which is taken to evolve in isolation from human interaction. Nor can it thrive on a physicalist theory of mental development where cognition is equated simply with some human biological equipment whose growth follows a preordained path laid out once for all by nature (Piaget, 1960, 1973; Brown, 1973; Krashen, 1987), as if the individual's interactive history played no part in the process. ... Such models of language and human cognition fail to accommodate the complex relations between teaching, learning and language, since the origin of this complexity is social rather than biological. (p.180)

Already there are moves towards a rapprochement, with researchers such as Swain (2000, p. 97) calling for a view of language learning that is both cognitive activity and social activity.

In summary, contemporary approaches to English language teaching and learning emphasize the need for learners to engage in purposeful interaction using spoken, written, and visual modes. Learners are expected to be critically literate and able to create accurate, contextually appropriate texts. A grammar that is responsive to such challenges needs to go beyond simply describing the "parts of speech" and their combination. It would require reconceptualizing grammar as a dynamic system of text-forming choices relevant to the students' communicative needs. The past few decades have seen promising developments in this direction.

NOTES

[1] For a fuller overview of these (and other) approaches to grammatical description, see Derewianka (2001).
[2] While this approach is not solely associated with a traditional model of grammar, many tend to take traditional categories and terminology as the default.
[3] It would be impossible to do justice to all the cognitivist, formal, and generative grammars currently in use. In focusing on Chomsky it is recognized that not all generative researchers would concur with Chomsky's philosophical agenda nor with Chomskyan formulations of generative systems (Odlin, 1994).
[4] See Tomlin (1994) for an account of various functional grammars.

[5.] Martin (2001), a colleague of Halliday, would add a fourth variable, *purpose*, which he locates in the cultural context. Different cultures use language in different ways to achieve their social purposes: persuading, recounting, instructing, narrating, informing, explaining, and so on.

[6.] For several useful articles addressing such questions, see Bygate, Tonkyn, & Williams (1994).

REFERENCES

Allan, K. (2001). *Aristotle's footprints in the linguist's garden*. Retrieved January, 20 2003, from the World Wide Web, http://www.arts.monash.edu.au/ling/ka/shtml.

Biber, D., Johansson, S., Leech, G., Conrad, S., & Finegan, E. (1999). *The Longman grammar of spoken and written English*. London: Longman.

Brazil, D. (1995). *A grammar of speech*. Oxford: Oxford University Press.

Burns, A. (2001). Analysing spoken discourse: Implication for TESOL. In A. Burns & C. Coffin (Eds.), *Analysing English in a global context: A reader* (pp. 123–148). London: Routledge.

Bygate, M., Tonkyn, A., & Williams, E. (Eds.). (1994). *Grammar and the language teacher*. Hertfordshire, UK: Prentice Hall.

Carroll, S., & Swain, M. (1993). Explicit and implicit negative feedback: An empirical study of the learning of linguistic generalizations. *Studies in Second Language Acquisition, 15*(3), 173–189.

Celce-Murcia, M., & Olshtain, E. (2000). *Discourse and context in language teaching: A guide for language teachers*. Cambridge: CUP.

Chomsky, N. (1968, May). Noam Chomsky and Stuart Hampshire discuss the study of language. *Listener*, pp. 687–691.

Chomsky, N. (1997). *Language and mind: Current thoughts on ancient problems (Part 1)*. Retrieved January 20 2003 from the World Wide Web, http://www.utexas.edu/courses/lin380l/nc-pap2.htm.

Chomsky, N. (2000). *New horizons in the study of language and mind*. Cambridge: CUP.

Christie, F. (1999). Genre theory and ESL teaching: A systemic-functional perspective. *TESOL Quarterly 33*(4), 759–763.

Christie, F., & Martin, J. R. (Eds.). (1997). *Genres in institutions: Social processes in the workplace and school*. Herndon, VA: Cassell Academic Press.

Cook, V. (1994). Universal grammar and the learning and teaching of second languages. In T. Odlin (Ed.), *Perspectives on pedagogical grammar* (pp. 25–48). Cambridge: CUP.

Derewianka, B. (2001). Pedagogical grammars: Their role in English language teaching. In A. Burns & C. Coffin (Eds.), *Analysing English in a global context: A reader* (pp. 240–269). London: Routledge.

de Silva Joyce, H., & Burns, A. (1999). *Focus on grammar*. Macquarie University, NSW, Australia: National Centre for English Language Teaching and Research.

Doughty, C., & Williams, J. (1998). Pedagogical choices in focus on form. In C. Doughty & J. Williams (Eds.), *Focus on form in classroom second language acquisition* (pp. 197–261). Cambridge: CUP.

Eggins, S., & Slade, D. (1997). *Analysing casual conversation*. London: Cassell.

Ellis, R. (Ed.). (1997). *SLA research and language teaching*. Oxford: Oxford University Press.

Gibbons, P. (2002). *Scaffolding language, scaffolding learning: Teaching second language learners in the mainstream classroom*. New Hampshire: Heinemann.

Goodman, S. (1996). Visual English. In S. Goodman & D. Graddol (Eds.), *Redesigning English: New texts, new identities* (pp. 38–72). London: Routledge.

Halliday, M. A. K. (1989). *Spoken and written language*. Oxford: OUP.

Halliday, M. A. K. (1994). *An introduction to functional grammar* (2nd ed.). London: Edward Arnold.

Halliday, M. A. K. (2001). Literacy and linguistics: Relationships between spoken and written language. In A. Burns & C. Coffin (Eds.), *Analysing English in a global context: A reader* (pp. 181–193). London: Routledge.

Halliday, M. A. K., & Martin, J. R. (1993). *Writing science: Literacy and discursive power*. London: The Falmer Press.

Hammond, J., & Macken-Horarik, M. (1999). Critical literacy: Challenges and questions for ESL classrooms. *TESOL Quarterly 33*(3), 528–544.

Hasan, R. (1986). The ontogenesis of ideology: An interpretation of mother child talk. In T. Threadgold, E. A. Grosz, G. Plum, G. Kress, & M. A. K. Halliday (Eds.), *Language, semiotics, ideology. Sydney Studies in Society and Culture 3* (pp. 125–146). Sydney: The Sydney Association for Studies in Society and Culture.

Hasan, R., & Perrett, G. (1994). Learning to function with the other tongue: A systemic functional perspective on second language teaching. In T. Odlin (Ed.), *Perspectives on pedagogical grammar* (pp. 179–226). Cambridge: CUP.

Huddleston, R., & Pullum, G. (2002). *The Cambridge grammar of the English language*. Cambridge: CUP.
Johnston, M. (1985). *Syntactic and morphological progressions in learner English*. Canberra, Australia: Commonwealth Department of Immigration and Ethnic Affairs.
Krashen, S. (1992). Formal grammar instruction: Another educator comments. *TESOL Quarterly, 26*(2), 409–411.
Kress, G., & van Leeuwen, T. (1996). *Reading images: The grammar of visual design*. London: Routledge.
Little, D. (1994). Words and their properties: Arguments for a lexical approach to pedagogical grammar. In T. Odlin (Ed.), *Perspectives on pedagogical grammar* (pp. 99–122). Cambridge: Cambridge University Press.
Long, M. (2001). Focus on form: A design feature in language teaching methodology. In C. Candlin & N. Mercer (Eds.), *English language teaching in its social context: A reader* (pp. 180–190). London: Routledge.
Luria, A. R. (1979). *The making of the mind. A personal account of Soviet psychology*. Cambridge, MA: Harvard University Press.
Martin, J. R. (1993). Technology, bureaucracy and schooling: Discursive resources and control. *Cultural Dynamics, 6*(1) 84–130.
Martin, J.R. (1999). Modelling context: the crooked path of progress in contextual linguistics. In M. Ghadessy (Ed.), *Text and context in functional linguistics (CILT Series IV)* (pp. 25–61). Amsterdam: Benjamins.
Martin, J. R. (2001). Language, register and genre. In A. Burns & C. Coffin (Eds.), *Analysing English in a global context: A reader* (pp. 149–166). London: Routledge.
McCarthy, M. (2001). Discourse. In R. Carter & D. Nunan (Eds.), *The Cambridge guide to teaching English to speakers of other languages* (pp. 48–55). Cambridge: Cambridge University Press.
McCarthy, M., & Carter, R. (2002) Ten criteria for spoken grammar. In E. Hinkel & S. Fotos (Eds), *New perspectives on grammar teaching in second language classrooms* (pp. 51–76). Mahwah, NJ: Lawrence Erlbaum.
Mitchell, R., & Myles, F. (2002). Second language learning: Concepts and issues. In C. Candlin & N. Mercer (Eds.), *English language teaching in its social context: A reader* (pp. 11–27). London: Routledge.
Nattinger, J., & DeCarrico, J. (1992). *Lexical phrases and language teaching*. Oxford: Oxford University Press.
Odlin, T. (Ed.). (1994). *Perspectives on pedagogical grammar*. Cambridge: Cambridge University Press.
Ohta, A. S. (2000). Rethinking interaction in SLA: Developmentally appropriate assistance in the zone of proximal development and the acquisition of L2 grammar. In J. P. Lantolf (Ed.), *Sociocultural theory and second language learning* (pp. 51–78). Oxford: OUP.
Paltridge, B. (2002). Genre, text type, and the EAP classroom. In A. Johns (Ed.), *Genre in the classroom: Multiple perspectives* (pp. 73–90). Mahwah, NJ: Lawrence Erlbaum.
Pienemann, M. (1989). Is language teachable? *Applied Linguistics, 10*(1), 52–112.
Quirk, R, Greenbaum, S., Leech, G., & Svartvik, J. (1985). *A comprehensive grammar of the English language*. London: Longman.
Roberts, C. (2001). Language acquisition or language socialisation in and through discourse? Towards a redefinition of the domain of SLA. In C. Candlin & N. Mercer (Eds.), *English language teaching in its social context: A reader* (pp. 108–121). London: Routledge.
Sinclair, J. (1991). *Corpus, concordance and collocation*. Oxford: OUP.
Smith, N. (2000). Foreword. In N. Chomsky (2000). *New horizons in the study of language and mind*. Cambridge: Cambridge University Press.
Stenglin, M., & Iedema, R. (2001). How to analyse visual images: A guide for TESOL teachers. In A. Burns & C. Coffin (Eds.), *Analysing English in a global context: A reader* (pp. 194–208). London: Routledge.
Swain, M. (2000). The output hypothesis and beyond: Mediating acquisition through collaborative dialogue. In J. P. Lantolf (Ed.), *Sociocultural theory and second language learning* (pp. 97–114). Oxford: OUP.
Thorne, S. (2000) Second language acquisition theory and the truth(s) about relativity. In J. P. Lantolf (Ed.), *Sociocultural theory and second language learning* (pp. 219–244). Oxford: OUP.
Tomlin, R. (1994). Functional grammars, pedagogical grammars, and communicative language teaching. In T. Odlin (Ed.), *Perspectives on pedagogical grammar* (pp. 140–178). Cambridge: Cambridge University Press.
van Leeuwen, T., & Humphrey, S. (1996). On learning to look through a geographer's eyes. In R. Hasan & G. Williams (Eds.), *Literacy in society* (pp. 29–49). London: Longman.

van Lier, L (2001). Language awareness. In R. Carter & D. Nunan (Eds.), *The Cambridge guide to teaching English to speakers of other languages* (pp. 160–165). Cambridge: Cambridge University Press.

Veel, R., & Coffin, C. (1996). Learning to think like an historian: The language of secondary school History. In R. Hasan & G. Williams (Eds.), *Literacy in society* (pp. 191–239). London: Longman.

Willis, D. (1994). A lexical approach. In M. Bygate, A. Tonkyn, & E. Williams (Eds.), *Grammar and the language teacher* (pp. 56–66). Hertfordshire, UK: Prentice Hall.

CHAPTER 52

EXTENDING OUR UNDERSTANDING OF SPOKEN DISCOURSE

MICHAEL McCARTHY

The University of Nottingham, UK

DIANA SLADE

University of Technology Sydney, Australia

ABSTRACT

This chapter aims to extend our understanding of spoken discourse by first outlining some of the major features of spoken language, and by doing so, highlighting the differences between spoken and written language. It will then describe some of the major approaches to analyzing spoken language, beginning with the approach taken by Sinclair and Coulthard (known as the Birmingham School) and then moving to conversation analysis and to systemic-functional approaches. We also consider recent work on genre theory and how this has been underpinned by the development of spoken corpora. The chapter will then center on some of the principal debates in the study of spoken language. These include problems of transcription and the representation of context, prosody, etc., and problems arising from the centrifugal tendency of spoken language away from standards and collective norms (as compared with the more homogenous nature of written varieties). The debate also includes critical issues of ownership of a language such as English, where many spoken varieties (both native and non-native) are in daily use around the world. Additionally, the problem of lack of codification of spoken grammars and the absence of a "canon" of spoken texts will be raised as an issue for pedagogy. The chapter concludes with a consideration of the contribution technological advances are likely to make in the future.

INTRODUCTION

The role spoken language plays in our formation as social beings starts from when we are very young. It is the form of language to which we are all first exposed—it is the prototypical kind of language use, so it provides a gateway into language. Fillmore, in relation to conversation, argued that "other types of discourse can be usefully described in terms of their deviation from such a base" (1981, p. 165). Lyons similarly argued that "there is much in the structure of languages that can be explained on the assumption that they have developed for communication in face-to-face interaction" (1977, p. 638). An account of spoken language is therefore integral to a systematic description of English. As Firth (1957) argued many years ago:

> Neither linguists nor psychologists have begun the study of conversation; but it is here we shall find the key to a better understanding of what language really is and how it works. (1957, p. 32)

Palmer, as early as 1932, argued that language is based on and is an extension of spoken language and added that it must be the starting point for a study of language.

However, in the decades that followed, the focus of descriptive studies was written language. Spoken language was seen as disorganized, ungrammatical, and formless and written language as highly structured and organized.

Only recently has there been a renewed interest and awareness of the importance of the study of spoken language and a realization that this study is essential for any real understanding of actual language use. Recent research from linguistics, sociolinguistics, and sociology has shed light on the nature and structure of spoken language, demonstrating that it does have a consistent and describable structure. In this chapter we will outline some of the characteristic features of spoken language, first outlining some of the differences between speaking and writing.

SPEECH AND WRITING

Spoken language is different from written language, but there is no simple, single way of demarcating the difference, and many factors need to be taken into account in describing the range of differences (see Hughes, 1996, pp. 6-15). One way of understanding the differences is to conceive of them as scales along which spoken and written texts can be compared, as depicted in Figure 1. For example, written public notices tend to be written in a detached style, typically stating laws and rules or giving warnings or important information. Everyday casual conversation, in contrast, tends to be very involved interpersonally, and distancing oneself from the talk is often perceived as unfriendly or problematic in some way. On the other hand, written advertisements might deliberately imitate a friendly, intimate conversational style (McCarthy, 1993), or a speaker may purposely attempt to sound "writerly" in making a speech or delivering a lecture. Another feature is the tendency for formal written texts to be explicit, while informal everyday conversation tends to be more implicit and more context dependent. Thirdly, conversation is typically created and produced *online* (with little or no preplanning) and received in real time. Writing is typically produced in one time and place and read in another time and place; writing can afford time for planning and revision. In terms of organization, written discourses typically reveal greater tightness or integration; conversation often appears bitty, fragmented, and unorganized, though this is usually a perception of the outside observer and may not correspond at all to how the conversational participants experience the talk. Despite the sometimes aimless appearance of conversation, it is, in fact, a highly structured, functionally motivated, semantic activity. These differences, viewed as scales, make it possible to plot the characteristics of individual texts as being, to a greater or lesser degree, typically written or typically spoken. For example:

- ✹ casual, intimate conversation between life-partners
- ◉ informal e-mail to a close friend
- ⌂ technical report

```
involved  <—✹—◉————————————⌂————> detached
implicit  <—✹————◉——————————⌂——> explicit
real time <—✹————————◉———⌂——> lapsed time
fragmented<—✹———————————◉————⌂——> integrated
```

Figure 1. Comparison of Some Spoken and Written Text Types

Scales like this have been used by linguists such as Chafe (1982) to describe the different potential modes of expression.

Similarly, Biber (1988, 1995), using computational techniques, shows how linguistic and contextual features cluster in different types of text (written and spoken). Biber's work is based on the idea that language features cluster or co-occur because they serve a similar communicative function (p. 101). His investigations show that in a range of written and spoken texts (e.g., personal and professional letters, fiction, phone calls, etc.), language features cluster differently, and this enables us to see general trends in differences between spoken and written texts. In this chapter, the special nature of spoken language and how it differs from written language will have implications not only for linguistic description (e.g., a grammar of speech may have some different features from a grammar of writing), but also for our conception of the roles of speaking and writing in our societies and cultures. Priorities in language teaching (vis-à-vis the different emphases given to writing and speech) may need to be reassessed in a world where orally influenced styles (e.g., the informality of e-mail discourse, Internet chat styles, text-messaging) and oral communication itself (e.g., telephones, voice recognition software systems) are increasingly becoming dominant in global communication. Much has been achieved on the descriptive level, which has greatly increased our understanding of spoken language to an extent that it is increasingly seen as a major component of any general language-learning program, and is seen as an equal partner with written language in terms of accurate and reliable lexical and grammatical description.

EXCHANGE STRUCTURE ANALYSIS

Sinclair and Coulthard (1975) developed a system for the description of spoken discourse derived from audio tape recordings of mother-tongue classrooms. Their approach has become known as the Birmingham School of Discourse Analysis and has been very influential in applied linguistics and language teaching contexts. The classes they studied were traditional, teacher-fronted lessons where knowledge was "on display," transmitted typically by pupils answering the teacher's *display questions* (questions functioning to impart knowledge or information, to which the teacher already knows the answer), engaging in some sort of task or activity, or just attending to the teacher talking and giving information via monologue. Sinclair and Coulthard also noted that teachers marked the boundaries between different phases of the lesson with *discourse markers* such as *right, now then, okay* (p. 40). Similar patterns of language are found in second-language classrooms. In the following extract, the class are looking at a picture, and the teacher asks questions:

> Teacher: Where are they, Renata, these two?
> Pupil 1: On the train?
> Teacher: On the train, on the train. Does anybody know, has anybody ever been to London? Yeah, what do you call the underground train in London?
> Pupil 2: The tube.
> Teacher: The tube or the underground.
> (Data from Walsh, 2001, p. 262)

It is clear that the teacher knows where the people in the picture are, and what the name for the London underground railway is; these are display questions. The teacher initiates the sequence with a question, the pupils answer, and the teacher follows up, indicating to the pupils that the answer is the right one by repeating it with falling intonation. This pattern is called a *three-part classroom exchange*, consisting of initiation, response, and feedback or follow-up moves:

speaker	utterance	move
Teacher	Where are they, Renata, these two?	Initiation
Pupil	On the train?	Response
Teacher	On the train, on the train	Follow-up

Such exchanges are at the core of language-teaching discourse in classrooms throughout the world (see Gibbons, this volume, for a fuller discussion). The public display tests the knowledge of the learners and confirms to them what the correct/desired language is. The teacher controls things, providing the feedback, and the topics follow his/her lesson plan. The pupils have minimal speaking rights in such exchanges, though that is not to say that good language teachers engage exclusively in this type of discourse. The teacher also controls the larger picture, dividing the lesson up into meaningful stages that Sinclair and Coulthard (1975) called *transactions* (whose boundaries are typically indicated by the discourse markers, *right*, *okay*,and so on). The moves can be subdivided into *acts*: individual stretches of language, which perform local communicative functions. In the extract above, the teacher's initiating move included selecting who should answer the question; thus the move is composed of two acts, one eliciting an answer, the other nominating the respondent:

speaker	Move	act(s)
Teacher	Where are they, [.....] these two? [Renata]	Elicitation Nomination

Typical classroom discourse, then, is organized at several different levels. The highest level is the lesson phases typically bounded by discourse markers such as *Now then* and *Right*: the transactions. The next level is exemplified in the question-answer-feedback sequence above, i.e., *exchanges*. The next level is represented by the single actions of questioning, answering, and following up, i.e., the *moves*. Finally, there are local actions such as nominating a pupil to speak, giving clues, acknowledging, etc., i.e., the acts. These different levels can be viewed as a rank-scale as shown in Figure 2.

TRANSACTIONS
EXCHANGES
MOVES
ACTS

CONSIST OF

COMBINE TO FORM

Figure 2. Rank-scale of the Different Levels of Classroom Discourse

Acts combine to form moves, which combine to form exchanges, which in their turn combine to form transactions, and, in reverse, transactions consist of exchanges, exchanges consist of moves, and moves consist of acts.

Such exchanges, along with teacher-monologues and activities of various kinds, are the stock-in-trade of language teaching, especially where large groups of learners are involved, and especially when curricular pressures militate against more imaginative communication in the classroom. This type of traditional, display-based teaching may be criticized as inauthentic (e.g., people asking questions to which they already know the answer; see Lynch, 1991; Nunan, 1988), but it can provide important support or *scaffolding* for learners struggling with new language (Jarvis & Robinson, 1997). Note here how the teacher provides such support:

[The class are discussing parking fines]
Pupil: ... or if my car
Teacher: **is parked**
Pupil: is parked illegally, the policeman take my car and ... er ... go to the police station, not police station, it's a big place where they have some cars, they
Teacher: L **Yes, where they collect the cars**=
Pupil: =collect the cars and if I have a lot of ... erm
Teacher: **stickers ... or fines**
Pupil: stickers ... or fines
Teacher: **yeah**
Pupil: erm I I don't know ... because no erm, if I have for example 100 fines [Teacher: **fines**] and I have money in the bank the government take the money from the bank [Teacher: **good**], no consult
(Walsh, 2001, p. 264)

Seedhouse (1996) argues that traditional classroom discourse has been unjustly pilloried by those advocating more "communicative" pedagogies. He argues that the goal of creating "natural" conversation in the second language classroom is basically unattainable and that it would be better to adopt an *institutional discourse approach*, where classroom discourse is seen as an institutional variety of discourse, alongside other institutional varieties and alongside non-institutional varieties, in which the character of the interaction corresponds appropriately to institutional goals (though see Nunan, 1987, for a more optimistic view of the potential for naturalistic discourse in the communicative classroom).

Attempts have been made to take the Sinclair-Coulthard model (1975) into the world of everyday conversation outside the classroom (see especially Hoey, 1991 Francis & Hunston, 1992), where transactions, moves, and exchanges can still be observed, albeit sometimes in a less clear-cut way. Transaction boundaries are often evident in *service encounters* (i.e., conversations between someone offering a service and a client); in the following extract, a salesperson marks the transition from general sales-talk to the specific phase of taking the customer's personal details, then again when the details are fed to the computer:

[Telephone call to a company about insurance and pension plans]
Salesperson: Would you like me to erm to get one of the advisers to give you a call sometime? And they can go over with you basically what pensions are available to you and what life insurance.
Customer: That would be good yeah.
Salesperson: Yeah?
Customer: Please.
Salesperson: **Okay that's fine. Erm what I'll do is I'll take all your details from you.**

Customer:	Uh-huh.
Salesperson:	And then we send it out to your closest branch and they give you a call in the next few days.
Customer:	Right okay.
Salesperson:	If I can just chat with you what's available through National General.
Customer:	Okay.
Salesperson:	Firstly may I take your surname please?
Customer:	Yes it's Horton.
Salesperson:	And your postcode please?
Customer:	FB9 6LN.
Salesperson:	Okay. Okay, the computer is just searching for your address.
(CANCODE[1] data)	

"What I'll do is I'll take all your details from you," and "The computer is just searching for your address," are examples of *metadiscourse* (i.e., discourse about the discourse) and are important signals of boundaries in talk.

The range of exchange types and the microlevel acts observed in traditional classrooms was rather impoverished compared with the wider range found in everyday conversation: where people ask a variety of different types of questions (see Tsui, 1994); where they challenge and accuse one another (Burton, 1980); and where exchanges often occur just to oil the social wheels, with no real content, known as *phatic* exchanges, e.g., exchanges about the weather, general *how-are-you*'s, etc. (Coupland, Coupland, & Robinson, 1992; Laver, 1975). Nonetheless, the general pattern of initiation-response-feedback underlies most everyday conversation but with important differences: outside of the classroom, response and follow-up moves typically include affective reactions (see *lovely* in the extract below) as well as acknowledgment or reply, and follow-up is not designed to evaluate the respondent's performance (except in restricted cases such as police and courtroom interrogations and quiz games), and various loops and checks might be necessary before the exchange can be closed:

speaker	utterance	move
customer	Erm when will you be able to let me know?	Initiation
travel agent	This afternoon.	Response 1
customer	Sorry?	Re-initiate (check)
travel agent	L= later on this afternoon	Response 2
customer	This afternoon?	Re-initiate (check)
travel agent	Yes.	Response 3
customer	Okay, **lovely**.	Follow-up

Exchange structure models are powerful tools for analyzing discourse inside and outside of the classroom, and for evaluating how closely concocted language such as coursebook dialogues approach or depart from naturalistic patterns (Carter, 1998), as well as providing the basis for a robust observational tool in reflective teacher education (e.g., Thompson, G., 1997; Thornbury, 1996; Walsh, 2001).

CONVERSATION ANALYSIS

Conversation analysis (CA) focuses on the detailed organization of everyday interaction. As Markeee (this volume) explains, CA owes much to researchers such as Sacks, Schegloff, Jefferson, and others (see, e.g., Jefferson, 1972; Sacks, 1992; Sacks, Schegloff, & Jefferson, 1974; Schegloff, 1972; Schegloff, Jefferson, & Sacks, 1977). CA focuses on banal, everyday conversation using fine-grain analyses, often of quite short conversational extracts. Pedagogically–related questions in CA include:

- How do speakers take orderly turns in conversation?
- How do speakers open and close conversations?
- How do speakers launch new topics, close exhausted topics, etc.?
- How is it that conversation generally progresses satisfactorily with little or no conflict or confusion?

Turn Taking

In CA, the basic unit of analysis is the individual speaker turn rather than a move. In the Sinclair and Coulthard exchange structure model (1975), one turn could contain, for example, the follow-up move of one exchange and the initiating move of the next one. In CA, a *turn* is each occasion that a speaker speaks, and a turn ends when another speaker takes the turn. Conversation analysts are interested in how speakers achieve smooth turn-taking, with relatively few overlaps and interruptions or breakdowns, and what the social norms are for who speaks when.

In any ordinary, informal everyday conversation, there may be overlaps but there will be hardly any true interruptions, and there will be only minimal silences between turns (on average, less than a second) if there is any silence at all. Sacks et al. (1974) noted that speakers typically take turns when they are selected or *nominated* by the current speaker, or else, if no one is directly selected, they may speak of their own choice (*self-selection*). If neither of these conditions apply, the current speaker may simply continue. The language system provides speakers with ways of securing the next turn. These vary in their appropriateness to different contexts and speaker relationships (in English, for example, among many other possible realizations, *If I may ask a question Madam Chair*, *Can I say something?*, *Shut up, will you, and listen to me!*). There are also ways of not taking the turn even when one could take it, for example by just saying *mmm* instead of giving a fuller reply. Vocalizations and short words uttered while another person is speaking, such as *mmm, uhuh, yeah, sure, right*, are called *back-channel responses* (see McCarthy, 2002; Yngve, 1970) and show that the listener is still following the speaker and wishes him/her to continue, as well as providing some indication of how the message is being received, but that the listener does not necessarily want to take up the speaker role. McCarthy calls this function *listenership*. Another important aspect of turn-taking is the way speakers predict one another's turns and often complete the other person's utterance or turn for them. Equally, there is often overlap between speakers as they complete each other's utterances. Back-channels, completions, and overlaps are not normally heard as interruptions or as rude. For CA analysts, they represent cooperative activity to facilitate communication. The following extract is typical of everyday casual conversation, and how fragmented it can look in transcription, though the *fragmentation* seems to present no problems for the actual participants:

[Speaker 1 is a radio ham recounting a coincidence of meeting someone he'd spoken to by radio]

Speaker 1: And I said Well I've got a feeling that your call sign is familiar too cos you get to know people's sort of call signs anyway.

Speaker 2: ⌊But you would have that logged

Speaker 1: ⌊That's right. And when I got home looked up in my log and I'd got a card from him and everything.

Speaker 2: ⌊*Yeah.*

Speaker 1: He lived in Wakatiri or somewhere you know in the+

Speaker 2: Somewhere out of the=

Speaker 1: +yeah. But amazing. And er+

Speaker 2: ⌊*Yeah.*

Speaker 1: +I had a great time and my wife wondered where I'd gone+

Speaker 2: And missing all the sights outside.

Speaker 2: ⌊ +I was away about an hour and a half you know. And erm=

Speaker 1: ⌊*Yeah.*

Turn-taking is a key feature of conversation by which participants negotiate the joint production of meanings. The implications of its description for language pedagogy are several. Most tempting is to assemble a lexicon of turn-taking gambits for teaching; however, these can sound peculiar if used inappropriately and normally only occur in rather specialized contexts (*Can I come in here?* and similar utterances are rare in casual conversation but may be useful in formal meetings). A second possibility is to see turn-taking in the classroom as a potential source of understanding of classroom discourse processes (van Lier, 1984): where the intrinsic motivation to listen to and observe the unfolding turn-taking processes in terms of one's own potential to participate is missing, opportunities for active participation and enhanced learning may be lost. Teachers can learn much, van Lier argues, from observing turn-taking patterns in their own classrooms. A third implication of the descriptions of turn-taking is seen in the importance of listener-signals such as back-channel utterances (e.g., *yeah, right, uhuh, mm*, etc., while listening). McCarthy (2002) sees these and a number of lexical feedback signals (e.g., *lovely, great, true, absolutely*) as central to good listenership and to the construction and maintenance of interpersonal relations. Much *listening skills pedagogy* focuses on comprehension of the message, with few opportunities afforded to the examination of appropriate reaction by the listener, who may not wish to take over the turn and become main speaker. The true integration of listening and speaking skills may require a reassessment of what listeners do.

Adjacency Pairs

In CA, the most basic pattern is the *adjacency pair*, which is a pair of turns that mutually condition one another. Examples of everyday adjacency pairs are *greeting-greeting, good wishes-thanks*, and *invitation-acceptance*. Adjacency pairs consist of two parts, namely, a *first pair-part* and a *second pair-part*:

First pair-part	Good evening	Congratulations, by the way.
Second pair-part	Hello/Good evening	Thanks

These adjacency pairs proceed smoothly and are well formed in terms of the contexts in which they typically occur in English: a greeting gets a greeting in return, and *congratulations* prompt a *thank-you*. These are examples of *preferred sequences*. But consider:

] A: Have you got the time?
    B: Get lost!

This exchange would normally be heard as a *dispreferred sequence*, a problematic event for the speakers. Sometimes we cannot avoid producing dispreferred second pair-parts (e.g., refusing an invitation). Where this happens, effort is usually undertaken by the speaker to make the response as little-threatening to the other's *face* (sense of personal esteem and dignity) as possible, with prefaces that soften the blow, or with accounts and reasons, such as, *I'd love to come, but I have a hospital appointment so I'll have to say no this time*, rather than a blunt and potentially hurtful *no*. Apart from ritual adjacency pairs (often connected with politeness, small talk, openings and closings, etc.), other everyday types include solidary routines (e.g., A: *I have a terrible backache;* B: *Oh, I'm sorry, do you want to lie down?*), and converging pairs (e.g., A: *I just love those roses*; B: *Oh, so do I, aren't they wonderful!*) (see Pomeranz, 1984). The same questions apply to adjacency pairs as applied to turn-taking in terms of the relationship between description and practice in language pedagogy: the opportunities for teaching a lexicon of useful phrases is limited to the more ritualistic pairs (e.g., high-frequency phrases for greetings, partings, well-wishing, condolences, etc.), and problems of contextual appropriateness equally apply. The main difficulties would seem to arise, for both native- and non-native users alike, in constructing dispreferred sequences; Dörnyei and Thurrell (1994) argue that such skills require practice.

Topic Management

CA analysts also examine openings and closings in conversations (see Schegloff & Sacks, 1973) and how speakers manage the topics they talk about or want to talk about (see Gardner, 1987). Topics generally shade smoothly into one another without unnatural jumps, and in conversations between equals, the right to launch a topic belongs to any speaker, but the other participants have to accept the topics and contribute to them before they can truly be said to be conversational topics. In short, topics are typically *negotiated* in everyday talk among equals. Again, questions relating to language pedagogy include the possibility of teaching a lexicon of topic-management expressions such as *Oh, by the way*, *Going back to ...,* and *As I was saying* (Dörnyei & Thurrell, 1994); the exercising of topical control (typically by the teacher); and the potential therein for losing opportunities for the introduction of topics of which learners have genuine knowledge (Cadorath & Harris, 1998). The question of motivation if topics are imposed on learners or whether it is preferable to allow learners to introduce and manage their own topics (Green, Christopher, & Lam, 1997; Slimani, 1989) is also one of interest. Other issues include whether raising awareness of topic-boundary phenomena (such as metastatements or discourse markers) can help learners to listen more selectively to discourses such as university lectures (Lebauer, 1984), and the way learners actually intervene in topical negotiation, including even in relatively traditional language classrooms (Ernst, 1994; Kramsch, 1985; Van Lier, 1984).

Summary

The strength of CA lies in part in the fact that it always uses actual recorded data of naturally occurring interactions, transcribed in meticulous detail (albeit often only extending over very brief segments of talk). CA has always rejected artificial methods of collecting data such as simulating dialogues or setting up experimental contexts, and has emphasized the data of banal, everyday life. CA studies have also helped to reduce prejudices about spoken language, for instance, that use of markers such as *like, you know, sort of,* and *see* are typical of bad or lazy conversational habits (Watts, 1989). Not only are such items part of the regular vocabulary of even the most educated speakers but also studying their use can often show that they are far from superfluous, realizing important functions such as signaling and confirming the state of shared knowledge among participants and/or hedging what might otherwise be too direct and possibly face-threatening to the listener.

The significance of CA, as with exchange structure analysis, is that it uses a terminology that is largely independent of that used in the study of written language. This fact has enabled a meaningful debate among applied linguists as to the applicability of specifically spoken research to language teaching (e.g., Bygate, 1987; Cook, 1989; Hatch, 1992; McCarthy, 1991; McCarthy & Carter, 1994). Richards (1980), in an early example of examining insights from CA, stresses the importance of "strategies of conversational interaction" (p. 431) in the development of conversational competence and refers to CA in support of his arguments. Van Lier (1989) deconstructs the oral proficiency interview and draws on CA to address the question of whether or not natural conversation should serve as an appropriate model for oral tests. More recently, some commentators have noted a shift in approaches to communicative language pedagogy and a growing interest in the bottom-up, local aspects of communicative competence, with discourse- and conversation analysis playing a significant role in the reassessment of what suitable teaching input should consist of (Celce-Murcia, Dörnyei, & Thurell, 1997).

SYSTEMIC FUNCTIONAL ANALYSIS (SFL)

Systemic functional analysis is firmly based on the work of Halliday (e.g., Halliday, 1978, 1989) and is a socially oriented model of analysis, describing the relationships between language, texts, and social systems. The functional approach inherent in systemic analysis seeks to explain language in terms of choices available within the basic systems of meaning that encode ideational (or content) meanings, interpersonal meanings, and textual meanings (see Derewianka, this volume, for a fuller discussion). SFL has particular relevance to the analysis of face-to-face spoken discourse owing to its insistence on raising interpersonal meaning (as realized by, for example, modal expressions and different clause types) to the same level of importance as ideational/content meaning, and its orientation shares common ground with CA in that both describe the relationship between language and social context. However, in SFL, the emphasis is on how the language system is organized to enable conversation to proceed. At any point in a discourse, speakers choose from the options the language system presents to create their desired ideational, interpersonal, and textual meanings. CA, on the other hand, focuses on social life, and conversation is seen as central in the construction and reinforcement of social identities and social practices. An example of a combination of the system-building description of SFL and the local, socially explicated descriptions of CA is Eggins and Slade (1997). Halliday's work has been extremely influential in mother tongue education, especially in the teaching of literacy in secondary and primary school contexts, and although the influence is not as widespread in second language pedagogy, it is apparent in recent developments such as communicative language teaching and discourse-based syllabuses (see Celce-Murcia, 1991).

GENRE ANALYSIS

Hymes (1972, p. 56) saw genres as "activities ... that are directly governed by rules or norms for the use of speech." In recent years, building on the work of written genre analysts who identify different types of written texts in terms of their communicative purpose within particular discourse communities (e.g., the role of journal articles in academic life, or technical reports within science or industry), spoken language analysts have attempted to identify different types of speech events in terms of their communicative purposes in particular social settings (see McCarthy, 1998, for an extended discussion). Most familiar is the storytelling genre, with its everyday spoken manifestations in personal narratives, anecdotes, recounts, tall tales, and other subtypes (Eggins & Slade, 1997; Labov, 1972; Polanyi, 1982). Other everyday genres include service encounters (e.g., in shops, restaurants, banks, travel agents, etc.; see Hasan, 1985; Ventola, 1987), argumentation (debates, quarrels, exchanges of opinion; see Lee & Peck, 1995; Hutchby, 1996; Schiffrin, 1985), interviews (political interviews, job interviews; see Blum-Kulka, 1983; Komter, 1991), and pedagogical genres (lectures, tutorials, classes; see Carter & McCarthy, 1997; Prabhu, 1992; Thompson, S.., 1997). Genre analysts are interested in regularities of patterning in such events, both in terms of larger phases or stages (e.g., a typical shop service encounter might follow the pattern: request for service → statement of availability of service → transaction of service → thanks) and the local grammar and lexis that characterize such events (e.g., the use of present-perfect tense/aspect in the concluding sections of anecdotes to "bridge" back to the present, such as *And ever since then I've always been scared of rabbits!*). Genre analysts are also concerned with the relationship between obligatory elements of genres (e.g., *request for service* in a travel agent's, and optional elements such as *greetings* in the same travel agent's setting, or small talk; see papers in Coupland, 2000). Casual conversation consists of a range of different genres and mixed genres, such as the storytelling genres (narratives, anecdotes, recounts, and exemplums), opinions, gossip, and joke. In conversations, participants weave in and out of telling stories, gossiping, etc., but in between these *chunks* or genres there are the highly interactive *chat* segments, which do not display a generic structure. These chat segments often involve multiple speakers who manage the interaction turn by turn (see Eggins & Slade, 1997, for a detailed discussion of these different genres and of the characteristic features of the *chunks* and *chat* of casual talk).

Spoken genre analysis has had less direct influence in second language pedagogy than written genre research, but its influence is becoming increasingly felt. Flowerdew (1993) sees written and spoken genres as central in the pedagogy of language for professional communication (e.g., professional presentations, negotiations, etc.), everyday genres have been examined in relation to how faithfully or otherwise they are reflected in typical teaching and materials (e.g., Boxer & Pickering, 1995; Taborn, 1983), and the relationship between grammar and spoken genres has been explored (Carter & McCarthy, 1995; McCarthy, 1998) (see (see Paltridge this volume, for a fuller discussion).

CORPUS INVESTIGATIONS AND IDEOLOGICAL ISSUES IN THE STUDY OF SPOKEN DISCOURSE

The study of spoken discourse has been greatly influenced in recent years by the development of large-scale spoken corpora, collections of texts that amount to millions of words (e.g., the 10-million-word spoken segment of the British National Corpus, or the 5-million-word CANCODE corpus that has been used in the present chapter, among others; see McCarthy, 1998, pp. 5-13 for an overview). Spoken corpora have confirmed many of the findings of CA and verified the widespread occurrences across many texts of features observed in single texts in CA analyses. Spoken corpora have also enabled observations of grammatical regularities across large numbers of speakers and varieties such that researchers have begun to posit an independent grammar for spoken interaction (Carter & McCarthy, 1995, 1999; McCarthy & Tao, 2001).

However, assembling a corpus of spoken language, or basing findings on any spoken texts, is an ideologically embedded activity: Whose speech, and whose English, is involved? The founders of the CANCODE corpus, for instance, set out to challenge the dominance of middle-class, southern-England English by recording speakers from across the geographical and social spectrum of Britain and Ireland.

However, this approach raises questions concerning the applicability of such data as a model of Standard English, and the status of a northern European set of English sociolects and dialects in a global community where English is multivoiced, including many native, postcolonial dialects, and non-native dialects that have evolved from the daily use of English as a *lingua franca*. These facts challenge the naïve use of corpus-based and other naturalistic spoken materials in the second language classroom and raise the issue of authenticity. Widdowson (1998) addresses authenticity, which he sees not as an objective characteristic of texts but as something that users bring to texts by their ability and willingness to recontextualize them, to recreate the world of their original utterance; his view is that this will be impossible with materials plucked directly from a corpus. The use of spoken texts, from whatever source, raises issues of cultural ownership and of the authority of speakers, since spoken texts tend much more towards diversity of form and tend to be much more linked to their situation of utterance than written ones. The notion of Standard English has traditionally been associated with the native speaker, and, in particular, with old-world, middle-class, educated native speakers. However, the reality in many parts of the world is that spoken English has come to serve differing functions, for example, the role of spoken English as a language of business negotiations between non-native users, as evidenced in the work of Firth (1995). Furthermore, if the speech samples are demographically representative, then many levels of competence (linguistic and communicative) will be displayed by the speakers in the corpus. The data will include speakers who seem clear, communicative, and expressive; it will also include those who stumble, who are poor communicators, who display eccentric usages, etc. Many of the native speakers in the corpus will be less proficient than many non-native speakers. The automatic claim of the native speaker to be the target user is therefore questioned.

Despite unresolved issues, the study of spoken discourse has advanced considerably in the last two decades, with corpus-based research pointing forward for the future. Second language pedagogy has already been partly reshaped by insights gained into the special nature of speech, and such reassessments of description and applications will undoubtedly gain momentum in the near future as global language-learning needs evolve.

NOTES

[1.] CANCODE stands for *Cambridge and Nottingham Corpus of Discourse in English*; the corpus was established at the School of English Studies, University of Nottingham, UK, and is funded by Cambridge University Press. The corpus consists of five million words of transcribed conversations, recorded in a variety of settings including private homes, shops, offices and other public places, and educational institutions in non-formal settings across the islands of Britain and Ireland, with a wide demographic spread. The CANCODE corpus forms part of the larger Cambridge International Corpus.

REFERENCES

Biber, D. (1988). *Variation Across Speech and Writing*. Cambridge: Cambridge University Press.
Biber, D. (1995). *Dimensions of Register Variation*. Cambridge: Cambridge University Press.
Blum-Kulka, S. (1983). The dynamics of political interviews. *Text, 3*(2), 131–153.
Boxer, D., & Pickering, L. (1995). Problems in the presentation of speech acts in ELT materials: the case of complaints. *ELT Journal, 49*(1), 44–58.
Burton, D. (1980). *Dialogue and Discourse*. London: Routledge.
Bygate, M. (1987). *Speaking*. Oxford: Oxford University Press.
Cadorath, J., & Harris, S. (1998). Unplanned classroom language and teacher training. *ELT Journal, 52*(3), 188–196.
Carter, R. A. (1998). Orders of reality: CANCODE, communication, and culture. *ELT Journal, 52*(1), 43–56.
Carter, R. A., & McCarthy, M. J. (1995). Grammar and the spoken language. *Applied Linguistics, 16*(2), 141–158.
Carter, R. A., & McCarthy, M. J. (1997). *Exploring spoken English*. Cambridge: Cambridge University Press.
Carter, R. A., & McCarthy, M. J. (1999). The English *get*-passive in spoken discourse: description and implications for an interpersonal grammar. *English Language and Linguistics, 3*(1), 41–58.
Celce-Murcia, M. (1991). Grammar pedagogy in second and foreign language teaching. *TESOL Quarterly, 25*(3), 459–480.
Celce-Murcia, M., Dörnyei, Z., & Thurrell, S. (1997). Direct approaches in L2 instruction: A turning point in communicative language teaching? *TESOL Quarterly, 31*(1), 141–152.
Chafe, W. (1982). Integration and involvement in speaking, writing and oral literature. In D. Tannen, (Ed.), *Spoken and written language: Exploring orality and literacy* (pp. 35–54). Norwood, NJ: Ablex.
Cook, G. (1989). *Discourse*. Oxford: Oxford University Press.
Coupland, J. (Ed.). (2000). *Small Talk*. London: Longman.

Coupland. J., Coupland, N., & Robinson, J. (1992). 'How are you?': Negotiating phatic communion. *Language in Society, 21*(2), 207–230.
Dőrnyei, Z., & Thurrell, S. (1994). Teaching conversational skills intensively: Course content and rationale. *ELT Journal, 48*(1), 40–49.
Eggins, S., & Slade, D. (1997). *Analysing Casual Conversation*. Cassell: London and Washington.
Ernst, G. (1994). "Talking circle": Conversation and negotiation in the ESL classroom. *TESOL Quarterly, 28*(2), 293–322.
Firth, A. (Ed.). (1995). *The discourse of negotiation: Studies of language in the workplace*. Oxford: Pergamon.
Flowerdew, J. (1993). An educational, or process, approach to the teaching of professional genres. *ELT Journal, 47/4*, 305–316.
Francis, G., & Hunston, S. (1992). Analysing everyday conversation. In R. Coulthard (Ed.), *Advances in Spoken Discourse Analysis* (pp. 123–161). London: Routledge.
Gardner, R. (1987). The identification and role of topic in spoken interaction. *Semiotica, 65*(1/2), 129–141.
Green, C.F., Christopher, E. R., & Lam, J. (1997). Developing discussion skills in the ESL classroom. *ELT Journal, 51*(2), 135–143.
Halliday, M.A.K. (1978). *Language as social semiotic: The social interpretation of language and meaning*. London & Baltimore: Edward Arnold & University Park Press.
Halliday, M.A.K. (1989). *Spoken and written language*. Oxford: Oxford University Press.
Hasan, R. (1985). The structure of a text. In M. A. K. Halliday & R. Hasan (Eds.), *Language, context and text: Aspects of language in a social-semiotic perspective* (pp. 52–69). Oxford: Oxford University Press.
Hatch, E. (1992). *Discourse and language education*. New York: Cambridge University Press.
Hoey, M. P. (1991). Some properties of spoken discourse. In R. Bowers and C. Brumfit (Eds.), *Applied linguistics and English language teaching* (pp. 65–84). Basingstoke: Macmillan/MEP.
Hughes, R. (1996). *English in speech and writing* (pp. 6–15). London: Routledge.
Hutchby, I. (1996). *Confrontational talk: Arguments, asymmetries, and power on talk radio*. Mahwah, NJ: Lawrence Erlbaum Associates.
Hymes, D. (1972). Models of the interaction of language and social life. In J. Gumperz & D. Hymes, (Eds.), *Directions in sociolinguistics: The ethnography of communication* (pp. 35–71). New York: Rinehart and Winston.
Jarvis, J., & Robinson, M. (1997). Analysing educational discourse: An exploratory study of teacher response and support to pupils learning. *Applied Linguistics, 18*(2), 212–228.
Jefferson, G. (1972). Side sequences. In D. Sudnow (Ed.), *Studies in social interaction* (pp. 294–338). New York: The Free Press.
Komter, M. (1991). *Conflict and cooperation in job interviews: A study of talk, tasks and ideas*. Amsterdam: John Benjamins.
Kramsch, C. (1985). Interaction processes in group work. *TESOL Quarterly, 19*(4), 796–800.
Labov, W. (1972). *Language in the inner city*. Oxford: Basil Blackwell.
Laver, J. (1975). Communicative functions of phatic communion. In A. Kendon, R. Harris, & M. Key (Eds.), *The organization of behaviour in face-to-face interaction* (pp. 215–238). The Hague: Mouton.
Lebauer, R. (1984). Using lecture transcripts in EAP lecture comprehension courses. *TESOL Quarterly, 18*(1), 41–54.
Lee, D., & Peck J. (1995). Troubled waters: Argument as sociability revisited. *Language in Society, 24*(1), 29–52.
Lynch, T. (1991). Questioning roles in the classroom. *ELT Journal, 45*(3), 201–210.
McCarthy, M. J. (1991). *Discourse analysis for language teachers*. Cambridge: Cambridge University Press.
McCarthy, M. J. (1993). Spoken discourse markers in written text. In J. M. Sinclair, M. Hoey, & G. Fox (Eds.), *Techniques of Description* (pp. 170–182). London: Routledge.
McCarthy, M. J. (1998). *Spoken language and applied linguistics*. Cambridge: Cambridge University Press.
McCarthy, M. J. (2002). Talking back: 'Small' interactional response tokens in everyday conversation. *Research on Language in Social Interaction* [vol. and page numbers to follow, not out yet].
McCarthy, M. J., & Carter, R. A. (1994). *Language as discourse: Perspectives for language teaching*. London: Longman.
McCarthy, M. J., & Tao, H. (2001). Understanding non-restrictive *which*-clauses in spoken English, which is not an easy thing. *Language Sciences, 23*, 651–677.
Nunan. D. (1987). Communicative language teaching: Making it work. *ELT Journal, 41*(2), 136–145.
Nunan, D. (1988). *The learner-centred curriculum*. Cambridge: Cambridge University Press.

Polanyi, L. (1982). Linguistic and social constraints on storytelling. *Journal of Pragmatics,* 6(5/6), 509–524.
Pomeranz, A. (1984). Agreeing and disagreeing with assessments: Some features of preferred/dispreferred turn shapes. In J. Atkinson, & J. Heritage (Eds.), *Structures of social action* (pp. 57–101). Cambridge: Cambridge University Press.
Prabhu, N. S. (1992). The dynamics of the language lesson. *TESOL Quarterly,* 26(2), 225–241.
Richards, J. (1980). Conversation. *TESOL Quarterly, XIV*(4), 413–432.
Sacks, H. (1992). *Lectures on Conversation. Volumes I & II.* Cambridge, MA: Blackwell.
Sacks, H., Schegloff, E. A., & Jefferson, G. (1974). A simplest systematics for the organisation of turn-taking for conversation. *Language,* 50(4), 696–735.
Schiffrin, D. (1985). Everyday argument: The organisation of diversity in talk. In *Handbook of discourse analysis, Vol. 3* (pp. 00–00). London: Academic Press.
Seedhouse, P. (1996). Classroom interaction: possibilities and impossibilities. *ELT Journal,* 50(1), 16–24.
Schegloff, E. A. (1972). Notes on a conversational practice: formulating place. In D. Sudnow (Ed.), *Studies in Social Interaction* (pp. 75–117). New York: The Free Press.
Schegloff, E. A., & Sacks, H. (1973). Opening up closings. *Semiotica,* 8(4), 289–327.
Schegloff, E. A., Jefferson, G., & Sacks, H. (1977). The preference for self-correction in the organisation of repair in conversation. *Language, 53,* 361–382.
Sinclair, J. McH., & Coulthard, R. M. (1975). *Towards an analysis of discourse.* Oxford: Oxford University Press.
Slimani, A. (1989). The role of topicalization in classroom language learning. *System, 17,* 223–234.
Taborn, S. (1983). The transactional dialogue: misjudged, misused, misunderstood. *ELT Journal, 37*(3), 207–212.
Thompson, G. (1997). Training teachers to ask questions. *ELT Journal, 51*(2), 99–105.
Thompson, S. (1997). *Presenting research: A study of interaction in academic monologue.* Unpublished Ph.D. Dissertation. University of Liverpool.
Thornbury, S. (1996). Teachers research teacher talk. *ELT Journal,* 50(4), 279–289.
Tsui, A. (1994). *English conversation.* Oxford: Oxford University Press.
Van Lier, L. (1984). Analysing interaction in second language classrooms. *ELT Journal, 38*(3), 160–169.
Van Lier, L, (1989). Reeling, writhing, drawling, stretching, and painting in coils: Oral proficiency interviews as conversation *TESOL Quarterly, 23*(3), 489–508.
Ventola, E. (1987). *The structure of social interaction: A systemic approach to the semiotics of service encounters.* London: Frances Pinter.
Walsh, S. (2001). *Characterising teacher talk in the second language classroom: A process model of reflective practice.* Unpublishd Ph.D. thesis. The Queen's University, Belfast.
Watts, R. J. (1989). Taking the pitcher to the 'well': native speakers' perception of their use of discourse markers in conversation. *Journal of Pragmatics, 13,* 203–237.
Widdowson, H. G. (1998). Context, community and authentic language. *TESOL Quarterly,* 32(4), 705–716.
Yngve, V. H. (1970). On getting a word in edgewise. *Papers from the 6th Regional Meeting, Chicago Linguistic Society.* Chicago: Chicago Linguistic Society.

CHAPTER 53

NEW DIRECTIONS IN STUDENT ACADEMIC WRITING

SUE STARFIELD

The University of New South Wales, Australia

ABSTRACT

Recent research into student academic writing adopts an *academic literacies* approach in which writing is no longer viewed as a generic skill to be taught as a set of static rules but rather as shaped by complex interactions of social, institutional, and historical forces in contexts of unequal power. This chapter reviews research into student academic writing in Australia, South Africa, the United Kingdom, and the United States of America, identifying how students and teachers negotiate academic literacies within specific local contexts. The key themes discussed are the changing notion of understandings of the concept of *discourse community* in academic writing; the significance of the interrelationship between *intertextuality* and *plagiarism*; and the increasing significance attributed to the role *writer identity* plays in academic writing. The pedagogical implications and potentialities of the academic literacies approach is considered and avenues for further exploration, particularly those that involve greater engagement of academic literacy practitioners and disciplinary specialists, are briefly examined.

INTRODUCTION

Over the last decade, research into academic writing, in line with developments in linguistics and applied linguistics, has taken what has become known as the *social turn*, responding to theoretical developments in the social sciences more broadly. As Candlin and Hyland (1999) point out, the view of writing as a "social act" has "achieved a certain orthodoxy" (p. 2). This chapter, while grounding itself in these social understandings (see Belcher & Braine, 1995) that locate written academic discourse within the sociorhetorical communities in which it is produced and interpreted, adopts a perspective that is both sociohistorical (Prior, 1991, 1995, 2001) and political – having to do with how power is distributed in society (Clark & Ivanič, 1997). These evolving understandings of the notion of social context in academic writing have implications for writing pedagogy as we move from functional views of the relationship between texts and context, which believe it is possible to predict from the social context the types of discourses and genres that will be used in a given situation and which tend to be unitary and mechanistic (Clark & Ivanič, 1997), to views that focus on the complex microcontexts in which academic literacies are negotiated and renegotiated in terms of the power relations between the participants.

Within this perspective, individual writing is seen as shaped by complex interactions of social, institutional, and historical forces (see Bakhtin, 1981, 1986) that shape access to the privileged discourses of the academy. As Bourdieu (1991) argues, a specific form of cultural capital is needed in order to produce written discourse worthy of being published, but while all speakers will recognize this authorized, prestige language, they will have very unequal knowledge of and access to its usage, prestigious rhetoric, and genres. In the "stylistic elaboration of literary writers, the references and apparatuses of scholars, the statistics of sociologists," Bourdieu (1977, p. 649) sees an *authority effect*, which confers legitimacy on those who speak the language of authority. Academic discourse or *essayist-text literacy* (see Gee, 1990) can therefore be considered as a very particular instance of a language that has been socially legitimated.

The typical student academic genres of essay, test, and exam set up and reflect asymmetrical power relations in part through the so-called impersonal language forms (passive, avoidance of personal pronouns, nominalization, aspects of modality) and formal register (adoption of the standard or high variety; complex thematic structure; coded citation practices; conventions of formal written language; field-specific lexis, lexical density) and therefore set up unequal social and identity relations in discourse (Fairclough, 1992a; Halliday, 1994; Hyland, 2002a; Jones, Gollin, Drury, & Economou, 1989). Kress (1993) identifies these features as central to the ideology of Western science and "the genre of scientific writing with its insistence on suppressing any mention of the individual" (p. 125).

Understandings of academic writing as being part of a set of institutionally bounded literacy practices that are subject to negotiation in contexts of asymmetrical power are changing both theoretical understandings of written academic discourse and pedagogical practices in the teaching of writing in tertiary settings in contexts as diverse as Australia, South Africa, the United Kingdom, and the United States of America.

Whereas the academic writing of professional academic writers in their disciplinary area has been the object of sustained study (see Bazerman, 1988; Berkenkotter & Huckin, 1995; Hyland, 1998, 2000; Swales, 1990), this chapter focuses on research into the written academic discourse of student writers in higher education settings, mainly, but not solely, students writing in English as a second language. Recent research into academic literacy development has been grounded in empirical case studies that use either ethnographic or a combination of qualitative methodologies. These studies are providing a richer understanding of the complex institutional, societal, and interpersonal contexts and processes that students, both undergraduate and post-graduate, native and non-native speakers of English, negotiate as they strive to acquire written academic discourse. This chapter identifies four key emergent and overlapping themes: (a) How research is contesting the notion of *discourse community* as it has been used to explain the function of the *social* in academic writing; (b) How the notions of *intertexuality* and *plagiarism* sit at the heart of academic literacy practices and mediate success and failure while challenging unquestioned assumptions about originality; (c) How research into *writer identity* is reshaping long-held beliefs about the personal and interpersonal in academic writing; (d) How new understandings of *academic literacy* and English for Academic Purposes (EAP) as a critical practice have implications for pedagogy in as much as "all literacies are, in fact, social, intertextual and historical" (Johns, 1997, p. 16).

MAIN RESEARCH FINDINGS

Reexamining Discourse Communities

Earlier socially-oriented studies of written academic discourse tended to focus on the identification of specific disciplinary discourses and of the specific genres that academic discourse communities utilize in the communicative furtherance of their aims (see, for example, Johns, 1992; Silva, 1992; Swales, 1990). While giving recognition to the socially constructed nature of the norms and conventions that regulate written communication in the disciplines (see Ballard & Clanchy, 1988), such work tended to present a view of discourse conventions as static and monolithic (Ivanič, 1998; Starfield, 2001). Learning to write was viewed as induction and socialization into a discourse community that is governed by a range of norms and conventions: "writers ... must use the communication means considered appropriate by members of particular ... discourse communities" (McCarthy, 1987, p. 234). Traditional usage of the term *discourse community* led to writing pedadgogies based on the identification of powerful discursive conventions and genres that can then be explicitly taught to new students entering the university (Ramanathan & Kaplan, 1996; Swales, 1990).

The recurrent use of the discourse community metaphor to explain students' academic discourse acquisition has been critiqued for being based on a set of assumptions involving the unilateral socialization of novices (students) by experts (teachers) into the dominant practices of the academic community. Such assumptions do not take into account the existing discourses students may bring into the academic community, at the same time they present academic discourse as unitary and monolithic rather than dynamic and contested (see Canagarajah, 2002; Chase, 1988; Clark, 1992; Grabe & Kaplan, 1996; Harris, 1989; Starfield, 2001; Woodward-Kron, 2004). The qualitative case studies of students' academic literacy development referred to earlier have begun to illustrate the complexities of the "induction" into academic discourse that students may undergo. These studies provide a counterpoint to descriptions of discourse communities that have "too often been reduced to identifying the language conventions, and generic forms that supposedly represent the various disciplines" (Zamel, 1993, p. 29) as they offer a thick description (Geertz, 1975) of the frequently unequal, local contexts in which literacies are negotiated. Carried out by academic literacy practitioners, these studies rely on multiple sources of data collection, including participant and non-participant observation; in-depth interviews with students and their teachers; the analysis of student texts and materials such as course handbooks, as well as student insights into their textual choices; and teacher feedback to students. While these studies vary as to the number of participants involved and whether the participants are native or non-native speakers of English, or undergraduate or postgraduate students (Angelova & Riazantseva, 1999; Belcher, 1994; Cadman, 1997; Casanave, 1995; Chiseri-Strater, 1991; Dison, 1997; Fox, 1994; Hewlett, 1996; Hirvela & Belcher, 2001; Ivanič, 1998; Lea & Street, 1988, 1999; Lillis, 1997; Prior, 1991, 1994; 1995; Spack, 1997a; Starfield, 2002, 2004a; Thesen, 1997), many of the findings stress the mismatch between student and teacher expectations, noting that it is often white, male, middle-class anglophone students who are successfully "inducted" into academic discourse communities. Many of the student participants in these studies struggle not only to understand the codified conventions of Western written academic discourse but also to negotiate identities for themselves that are recognized by the discourse communities they seek to enter.

Casanave's (1995) study is illustrative of the difficulties that students from outside of the U.S. mainstream may experience when seeking to successfully enter the established, frequently white and male, discourse community and how difficult it seems to be for senior members of this community to consider that culturally diverse students might have a significant contribution to make to the discipline. Richard, a white middle-class student, stays in the sociology graduate program, while Virginia, a Latina student, and Lu-Yun, from the People's Republic of China, leave. Richard's initially negative attitude changes "toward acceptance of the type of world he was being trained to enter" (p. 100) as he identifies the potential rewards at stake. On the other hand, Lu-Yun and Virginia, "perhaps coincidentally a foreign student and a minority student, each seemed to find it difficult to create contexts for writing from these local interactions" (p. 107).

"If you don't tell me, how can I know?," the title of one of the articles cited above, captures the induction approach, which seems to suggest that literacy acquisition is a matter of making explicit the hidden conventions that may differ across cultures. Whereas explicit pedagogies advocate the teaching of powerful genres as a response to the difficulties that students from historically excluded communities may face in academic writing (Cope & Kalantzis, 1993; Delpit, 1988), writers such as Lea and Street (1998) suggest that the normative categories of academic writing such as structure, argument, etc., be viewed as exercising a gatekeeping function rather than as "unproblematic generic requirements" (p. 169). Similarly, while handbooks and guidelines may present apparently clear and unambiguous departmental guidelines regarding generic expectations, in practice, discrepancies arise between what is stated and the variable kinds of feedback students receive on their assignments, suggesting a lack of consensus in assessment practices amongst members of the academic discourse community (Angélil-Carter, 2000; Starfield, 2001). The research further suggests that explicit induction should not be at the expense of devaluing the multiple discourses students bring with them to the university but that students (and the academy) may benefit from a recognition of these (Casanave, 1995; Dison, 1997; Thesen, 1997). Access to privileged discourse is not simply a matter of its transmission to all students but rather the outcome of complex processes of inclusion and exclusion regulating access to authoritative discourse. Meaning is not fixed in *a priori* academic genres but shaped via the interaction of the histories of student and teachers, the contexts in which they read and write texts, and the roles they engage in (Casanave, 1995; Johns, 1997; Prior, 1995): "academic discourse is not unitary, the disciplines themselves are not fixed, but, like all cultures are subject to continual reshaping as others enter the discourse community and change its terms" (Zamel, 1993, p. 31). If, as Prior has argued, "academic discourse and academic environments are complex, constructed and unfolding events and not closed systems susceptible to taxonomic and rule-oriented description, then we cannot simply specify and teach 'academic writing tasks'" (p. 77).

Rather than discourse communities real or imagined (Anderson, 1983), it may be useful to view our classrooms as "contact zones" (Pratt, 1991, p. 34). Pratt contrasts contact zones with the ways in which *community* has been used within the university to suggest a homogeneous social world in which language is a resource shared equally by all and in which all participants share a single set of norms and values.

Intertextuality and Plagiarism

Bakhtin (1981) describes the richly social and shared nature of all language, emphasizing its intertextual and interpersonal dimensions: "Language is not a neutral medium that passes freely and easily into the private property of the speaker's intentions; it is populated, even overpopulated, with the intentions of others." (p. 294). Academic discourse has been frequently described as decontextualized or context reduced (Cummins, 1996). While this understanding holds true when comparing face-to-face conversation with written texts in which immediate contextual cues to meaning are not readily available, what has been neglected is the highly intertextual nature of written academic discourse and the difficulties this may pose for student writers. Fairclough (1992b) identifies two main ways in which texts constantly draw on other texts, either through the explicit usage of manifest intertextuality, in which a text explicitly *manifests* the presence of other texts, typically through highly coded citation practices; or via *interdiscursivity*, the ways in which texts "selectively draw upon orders of discourse-the particular configurations of conventionalized practices (genres, discourses, narratives, etc.), which are available to text producers and interpreters in particular social circumstances" (p. 194). Within this understanding, for a student writer "expropriating it [language], forcing it to submit to one's own intentions and accents is a difficult and complicated process" (Bakhtin, p. 294).

Intertextuality and interdiscursivity are dynamic processes whereby genres and discourses from different times may intermingle in text production, particularly in student academic writing. Academic discourse communities can be seen as fundamentally intertextual communities – communities that share texts and discourses. In their study of U.S. freshman composition textbooks, Ramanathan and Kaplan (1996) claim that one of the assumptions underlying the approaches to teaching academic writing that they identified was that strong arguments make intertextual connections. They conclude that an absence of shared textual histories could further complicate ESL students' success in U.S. discourse communities. Starfield (2002) argues that the amounts of textual or intertextual capital students bring with them to the university may impact on their likely success.

Intertextuality problematizes the common academic practice of asking students to say things in their own words, as texts are no longer seen solely as the original works of talented individuals, and requires us to "rethink our ideas about plagiarism" (Porter, 1986, p. 42). For Hull and Rose (1989), a "fundamental social and psychological reality about discourse – oral *or* written – is that human beings continually appropriate each others' language to establish group membership, to grow, and to define themselves in new ways" (emphasis in the original, p. 151). In her struggle to summarize a text, Tanya [their student] produced a "patchwork" of the original text and of her own meanings – "trying on" (p. 151) the language of the original text but also a new academic identity. Howard (1995) renames *plagiarism* "patchwriting" – a survival strategy adopted by novice writers "working in unfamiliar discourse, when they must work monologically with the words and ideas of a source text" (p. 796). Hewlett (1996) found that her black South African students felt a "pressure to plagiarize," arising out of what they experienced as stringent disciplinary demands for linguistic accuracy and precision, which highlighted their difficulties with "put[ting] those words into our own words" (p. 91). In Angélil-Carter's (2000, p. 29) view, plagiarism is not so much the outcome of a conscious effort to deceive as a new student's response to encountering complex intertextual worlds in which words seem to belong to more powerful authorities and can only be "rented."

Students' understandings of what constitute plagiarism appear to differ widely from those held by their lecturers (Lea & Street, 1998; Pennycook, 1996). Whereas lecturers view the issue as being about the correct referencing of sources, for students plagiarism is linked to their developing identities as writers and their relative lack of authority vis-à-vis the authority of academic texts and is part of a complex process of learning to write according to unfamiliar norms and conventions in a language that is often not their primary language. One of Cadman's (1997) postgraduate students from China admitted that she had "never heard of referencing another scholar's work" (p. 9). Imitation may also be an important stage in a writer's development. Using formulaic language or *chunking* may be a productive strategy in language learning whereby learners internalize chunks of language and reproduce these word by word (Angélil-Carter, 2000; Pennycook, 1996). In fact, a number of textual strategies that students may be expected to engage in, such as paraphrasing, summarizing, copying down, etc., closely resemble plagiarism but are pedagogically legitimated in particular contexts that new students may have difficulty distinguishing (Angélil-Carter, 2000).

Traditionally, plagiarism is severely sanctioned in official university documents (see Angélil-Carter, 2000; Howard, 1995; Pennycook, 1994, 1996). In some quarters of the academy, however, the very construct of plagiarism is under critical review. Kress (1993), Pennycook (1996), and Scollon (1995) argue that the notion of plagiarism needs to be understood as linked to historically limited, peculiarly Western, essentially modernist constructs of authorship and originality that are used as a gatekeeping mechanism by those in power in academic communities over new students. Pennycook (1996) hypothesizes that the intensity of outrage that plagiarism generates needs to be understood within a context of increasing challenge to the traditional "authority of both teacher and text" (p. 214). The determination to stamp out plagiarism "may be seen as part of a desperate rearguard action against changing textualities" (p. 215) to preserve traditional Western notions of unique authorial selves.

Angélil-Carter (2000) also found that certain students, through their prior socialization into patterns of privileged discourse, were able to challenge the strict regulation of citation that the writing of other less privileged students was subjected to. Those students who came from more middle-class backgrounds, and were assumed to have authority, did not have to demonstrate the same degree of acknowledgment as others. In contrast, a degree of suspicion permeated the reading of less privileged students' essays, particularly when ideas or expression were judged too "sophisticated" in terms of the marker's perception of the student. What markers were prepared to accept as common knowledge or shared ground (i.e., not requiring referencing) varied, and whether students wrote English as a first or second language was also a factor in the degree of scrutiny of the referencing.

Angélil-Carter's (2000) findings clearly indicate the extent to which plagiarism is part and parcel of the students' *self-identities* as new writers. Plagiarism is not limited to non-native students but is a significant survival strategy of all students in the academic contact zone, where the discourses that the students bring with them to their academic writing tasks encounter the entirely textual, highly literate, overpopulated worlds of the academy.

Writer Identities

It is noteworthy that the term *identity* does not appear in Grabe and Kaplan's (1977) *Theory & Practice of Writing* and that intertextuality merits but two brief references, yet these two interrelated areas are of growing interest in the field of academic literacy. The typical characterization of academic writing as impersonal, objective, and using a formal register is still commonly adhered to by many students, teachers of writing, writing manuals, and academics and has helped to keep issues of writer identity off the academic writing agenda (see Canagarajah, 1996; Chang & Swales, 1999; Clark & Ivanič, 1997; Hyland, 1999; Ivanič, 1998; Lillis, 1997).

Recent research into both native speakers' and non-native speakers' writing has argued for greater attention to be paid to the significance of identity in academic writing and to the ways in which writers, through the linguistic and discursive resources on which they choose to draw as they write, convey a representation of the self (Cherry, 1988; Hyland, 1999; Ivanič, 1998; Ivanič & Camps, 2000; Tang & Johns, 1999). While earlier research into social aspects of the writing process tended to focus on the reader, and drew on notions of audience, recent research has identified the writer as an important focus (Ivanič, 1999). Ivanič (1994) claims that those analysts who have been concerned about how subjects are positioned in discourse have mainly looked at how readers "are positioned by discourse through texts" rather than at "how writers are positioned by the discourse(s) they draw on as they write" (p. 4). The lexical, syntactic, semantic, visual and material resources writers employ construct *writerly* identities, as do the various primary and secondary discourses that they bring to the academic writing process (Gee, 1990; Ivanič, 1998).

The notion of individualized voice as embodied in progressivist writing pedagogy drew on romantic notions of the creative self and ideologies of the autonomous author referred to in the previous section (see Ivanič, 1998). It has been further argued that teaching that encourages the development of a student's own voice can be seen to disadvantage students from cultures that are seen to de-emphasize the role of the individual in favor of the collective (Atkinson, 2001; Ramanathan & Atkinson, 1999). Social or sociohistorical views of voice, however, emphasize the socially available repertoires that writers draw on as they write and that condition the choices writers make, while allowing for agency within this positioning as writers attempt to force language to submit to their own intentions (Bakhtin, 1981; Ivanič, 1998; Lillis, 1997; Prior, 2001).

The *writerly self* or voice can be seen to be composed of several strands, which shape the writer's representation of self. These are not discrete but interact at the moment of utterance to shape the choices a writer makes when constructing a text (Ivanič, 1998). The *autobiographical self* refers to resources the writer brings from his or her life history, beliefs, values, and interests and the literacy practices with which he or she is familiar. The *discoursal self* refers to the ways writers textually convey an impression of who they are, and the discursive practices they are able to draw on, while the *authorial self* refers to the extent to which writers are able to project an identity for themselves as authoritative (Clark & Ivanič, 1997). A fourth, more abstract, aspect of writer identity concerns the "socially available possibilities for self-hood" (Ivanič, 1998, p. 28) within specific sociocultural and institutional contexts. Some of these *subject positions* or identities – ways of thinking, feeling, believing, valuing, and acting – will have higher status than others (Gee, 1990; Ivanič, 1998). First-year students, for example, may feel they cannot appear very authoritative in their essays, yet some students, through their personal histories, may be able to bring authority to their writing in ways in which other students cannot (Angélil-Carter, 2000; Starfield, 2002, 2004).

Traditional forms of academic discourse, particularly in the social sciences and sciences, require an impersonal style, and part of the "apprenticeship" process is the effacing of prior identities in academic writing in order to join the new discourse community (Clark, 1992). Clark provides examples of feedback in which the marker explicitly instructed the student not to use personal pronouns in essays and to avoid expressions such as "in my view," as the student was "not an established authority" (p. 120). Lea and Street (1998), however, found a good deal of uncertainty over the use of the first person pronoun in student writing: "Even within the same courses, individual tutors had different opinions about when or if it was appropriate" (p. 164). At an Australian university, while the Psychology Department actively discouraged the use of personal forms in the students' writing, in Computing originality and a personal stance were encouraged (Candlin & Plum, 1999).

Ivanič and Simpson (1992) see referencing conventions as setting up inferior subject positions for students, which reinforce students' feelings of inadequacy vis-à-vis the disciplinary authorities. They suggest that it may be legitimate for students to respond by resisting these subordinate identities and questioning these academic conventions. Clark (1992), Ivanič and Simpson, and Clark and Ivanič (1997) recount attempts to work with their students to develop self-identities that allow them to express other aspects of their values, beliefs, and prior experiences, which the academy may not traditionally value. Hewlett's (1996) interviews with black South African students revealed student anger at the perceived negation of their political identities by marker feedback that questioned the relevance of students' political comments to the given essay topic. This issue appeared to be particularly sensitive when the marker was "white and unfamiliar to the student" (p. 94). A number of South African writers emphasize the importance of understanding students' autobiographical selves in shaping their identities as academic writers, as the diverse discourses the writer is familiar with shape their engagement with university discourses and may be in conflict with them (Angelil-Carter, 2000; Dison, 1997; Leibowitz, 1995; Thesen, 1997).

Ivanič and Simpson (1992, p. 154) report on the struggles of a mature student, Simpson, to "find the 'I'" – to develop an identity as a writer of academic texts with which he is comfortable. One of the issues raised is the need for student writers to become aware of the *characters* who *populate* (in the Bhaktinian sense) not only the texts they read but also those they write. They contrast this view of academic literacy with the traditional one, in which academic writing is characterized as impersonal and objective. The student Simpson's essays are populated by the tutors who set the assignment, the people who wrote the texts he read and who they write about, Simpson himself, the people he writes about, and those who read what he has written. Between Simpson the student writer and these various characters, relationships exist that are mostly unequal, as the characters have greater academic authority or *capital* than he has. Unstated "ground rules" (Sheeran & Barnes, 1991, p. 1) may ensure that a "student writer has to back up what he [sic] says with quotations from sources, to show that 'it's not just an opinion,'" (Ivanič & Simpson, 1992, p. 161), even if the student's personal experience makes him or her a much greater authority than the cited writer. Students' struggles to position themselves and take ownership of their arguments in academic discourse may led to inadvertent plagiarism as their own voice blurs with the voice of those whose writings they are reviewing (Cadman, 1997).

Academic Literacies and Writing Pedagogy

EAP and writing pedagogies have typically focused on identifying – often through needs analyses – sets of transferable generic literacy skills that are seen to be applicable in the majority of academic settings (see Benesch, 2001; Hyland, 2000; Johns, 1997; Lea & Street, 1998; Prior, 1995; Starfield, 2001). Such approaches derive from the induction approach to teaching a set of monolithic rules described above. Lea and Street (1998, 1999), most clearly perhaps, identify three phases in the development of approaches to teaching writing within the university, which seem applicable to understanding the provision of writing teaching in a range of contexts. These approaches may exist concurrently within courses and programs and in individual tutor requirements and may be a source of confusion for students. In the study skills approach, often called remedial (see Benesch, 1988), students are viewed as lacking the skills necessary for success, and these *surface skills* (Lea, 1999) are then taught in discrete EAP/study skills courses, outside of the disciplines. In the *academic socialization* or *anthropological* approach (Ballard & Clanchy, 1988; Lea & Street, 1998), students are exposed to the textual conventions and written genres of disciplinary discourses, but this remains a one-way induction model with writing seen as a transparent medium for the representation of given disciplinary forms. In the third approach, consistent with the theoretical framework adopted in this chapter, academic literacies are viewed as diverse, contested social practices, and student writers and their teachers are viewed as adopting different identities and positions as they negotiate these contested practices, which construct meaning in a discipline rather than simply represent it (Lea, 1999; Lea & Street, 1988; Paltridge, 2002). Literacy practices are thus seen as integrally part of the knowledge-making (epistemological) practices of specific disciplines. The development of students' writing needs to be seen within its broader institutional setting, in terms of the dominant social and discursive practices that maintain and reproduce authority and power rather than as solely located within students themselves. Whereas traditional needs analysis tends to transform academic genres into "abstract, anonymous structures occurring anytime anywhere" (Prior, 1995, p. 55), academic literacies approaches allow us to understand the complex situatedness and particularity of each classroom (Casanave, 1995). Critical EAP (Benesch, 2001) further challenges needs analysis approaches by arguing that within specific social contexts, students can exercise their right to challenge dominant discourses and unilateral socialization into preexisting sets of expectations. Academic literacies approaches have been implemented in South African and Australian university contexts (English, Bonanno, Ihnatko, Webb, & Jones, 1999; Skillen, Merten, Percy, & Trivett, 1998; Starfield, 1994) in moves away from discrete study skills approaches.

In pedagogical terms, working within the third approach for teachers of writing who are not themselves disciplinary specialists presents a challenge, particularly within a context of the increasing intertextuality, hybridity, and instability of genres (Candlin & Plum, 1999; Kress, 1999). Aspects of the two other approaches may well underlie the repertoires of teachers as they assist students to engage with the dominant discursive practices of the institution. Many of the suggested approaches are novel but appear worth pursuing if we are to move students from reproductive, static approaches to ones that enable them to engage meaningfully with texts, within the contexts in which those texts are produced and interpreted, and to negotiate successful identities for themselves as writers. In Johns's (1997) terms, these latter approaches involve raising student writers' awareness of how the texts they write, the individual roles these texts imply, and the contexts within they write can be analyzed, critiqued, and negotiated.

Given the complexities involved in the processes of successful negotiation of complex disciplinary microworlds, a number of writers suggest developing students' strategic competence and/or metacognitive strategies to enable them to begin to negotiate entry into these contact zones (Cadman, 1997; Granville & Dison, 2005; Hyland, 2000; Johns, 1997; Jones, 1999, Starfield, 2004b). This approach involves developing an awareness of the functions of texts and genres within different disciplines and a familiarity with the discoursal strategies the students need to perform particular roles and sustain particular interactions. A major task of EAP teachers, according to Hyland, is to address students' prior perceptions and assumptions about writing and to build from these to help the students unpack the assumptions about writing that are embedded in the disciplines. This view is supported by Johns's (1997) encouragement of her students to approach the new communities they are seeking to join as ethnographic researchers studying the discursive practices of those communities. Johns's students are encouraged to compile literacy portfolios – reflective collections of the variety of texts and genres they bring from their primary cultures and languages as well as texts they encounter as they do this research. In this view, students should be helped to analyze authentic genres and be made aware of the choices writers are making, the consequences of these choices (Hyland, 2000), and what the textual possibilities are that writers have at their disposal to take ownership of and position themselves in their texts. Johns's view of an academic literacies approach to teaching writing is one in which "literacy classes become laboratories for the study of texts, roles and contexts ... in which students are able to assess their current practices and understandings and develop strategies for future rhetorical situations" (p. 19).

How writers come to represent their own voice while constructing a text based on the voices of the authorities is a key element of an academic literacies approach (Angélil-Carter, 2000). Prior (2001) suggests asking students to consider what kinds of people use particular discourses, in what ways and when, as part of an attempt to assist students to acquire disciplinary academic discourse. Cadman (1997) encourages students to express a personal voice, even though conventional genres may not allow this. However, she follows Ivanič and Simpson (1992, p. 147) in helping the student to find the "committed 'I'" or, where the impersonal is required, to move progressively from the personal in early, private drafts to more impersonal styles in the public, polished drafts. Students need to be helped to understand how writing is not only about constructing relevant field-specific arguments but also about constructing appropriate social relationships within that specific field–how to develop, through discourse, a *persona* and a *stance* (Hyland, 1999). Tang and John (1999) propose a pedagogy focused on sensitizing student writers to the differing uses of the first person pronoun in academic texts with the aim of developing in students greater presence and authority. They stress that students need to be shown that they can make choices around their representations of self in their academic writing and that the impersonal genres are shifting.

Currie (1998) acknowledges that a pedagogy for "apparent plagiarism" (p. 12) would include alerting students to the danger of institutional censure; skills for synthesizing course materials and writing from sources; and explicit instruction in citation, paraphrase, and effective reading strategies, but she concludes that these techniques, while popular in EAP courses, fail to recognize how ambiguous textual borrowing is and how fundamental it is to academic literacy practices and notions of authority and power. She suggests that using imitation explicitly in the initial stages may be useful in finding out from students what strategies they have used successfully, previously.

Hirvela and Belcher (2001) suggest that the concept of "situational voice" (p. 90) – how voice varies according to rhetorical context – may be helpful, particularly to L2 postgraduate students who already have repertoires of voices and identities as successful writers in their L1, and that the new contexts can be seen as extending these, rather than as a surrender to dominant L2 discourses.

Based on her experience of teaching a linked EAP Writing/Anthropology course in the U.S., Benesch (2001) argues for pedagogies that build community between students through a recognition of difference and of students' multiple and overlapping identities and goals, as she encourages her students to collectively negotiate with their professor over understandings of the professor's expectations.

CURRENT DEBATES AND CONCERNS

Are the problems related to ESL students' experience with writing largely due to clashes between cultural expectations around academic discourse, different national rhetorics, and approaches to authority and tradition,"a set of 'cultural norms'" (Ramanthan & Kaplan, 1996, p. 23), which many non-native speakers of English do not possess (see also Paltridge, 2004)? It has been argued that this approach may be slipping into an unfortunate *othering* of non-native speakers as lacking certain thinking and writing skills (Casanave, 2004; Kubota, 1999; Pennycook, 1996; Spack 1997b; Thesen, 1997). A number of studies of L1 speakers, particularly those from non-middle-class backgrounds, or of women or mature-age students, point to dominant Western norms as constructed (e.g., Chiseri-Strater, 1991; Hermerschmidt, 1999; Ivanič, 1998). Lea and Street (1998) also point to the difficulties students from a range of backgrounds have with dominant literacy practices such as citation, being original, developing an argument, and what counts as evidence, and suggest that identities and power relations are implicated in success. Reviewing various explanations for the poor success rates of black students in tertiary studies at South African universities, Craig (1991) states, "I favor an explanation which recognizes their [black students'] unfamiliarity with texts, textual analysis and the construction of meaning from texts" (p. 140). Rather than problems located within students' cultures, there may be a need to acknowledge the textual/intertextual nature of the cultural capital needed for academic literacy success. If student writing and learning are issues at the level of epistemology and identities, all students,' regardless of their cultural and linguistic backgrounds, may need support with their writing (Lea & Street, 1998).

Do dominant writing pedagogies expect non-native speaker students to "become someone else" (Atkinson, 2001, p. 115)? In Prior's (2001) view, "all activity involves becoming ... teaching and learning language can never be simply about transferring or acquiring skills, codes and rules" (p. 78). Similarly, Zamel and Spack

(1998) emphasize that ongoing negotiation between teachers and learners is at the heart of academic literacy acquisition. Ivanič's (1998) research with mature-age native speakers who are not from a culture that is "widely distant" (Ramanathan & Atkinson, 1999, p. 55) suggests that becoming someone else is a challenge they face too and that to reduce these struggles over voice and identity to ones of cultural difference is to neglect fundamental issues at the heart of academic literacy concerning how novices gain authorial voice. Shen's (1989) struggles to create a new "English self" (p. 461) seem to parallel those of Ivanič's (1998) and Lillis's (1997) native English speakers, some from non-middle-class backgrounds. One of Cadman's (1997) students came to see that "cross cultural differences are a matter of degree, not kind" (p. 11).

Spack's (1988) question to EAP teachers, "Initiating ESL students into the academic discourse community: How far should we go,?" remains topical. On the one hand, much of the research reported in this chapter emphasizes the situatedness of writing within very local contexts and suggests the need for teachers of writing to engage at this level not only with students but also with their disciplinary teachers (Prior, 1991, 1994, 1995; Skillen, Merten, Percy, & Trivett, 1998). On the other, the response of some academic literacy practitioners is to advocate approaches that focus on the metacognitive and the strategic with a view to enabling students to negotiate a multiplicity of diverse disciplinary contexts and texts (Johns, 1997). This issue relates to that of who can teach writing, the extent to which L2 writing is a discrete field of study with its own specialists (see Santos, Atkinson, Erickson, Matsuda, & Silva, 2000), and the extent to which both L1 and composition studies can inform L2 pedagogies (Matsuda, in Santos et al.,2000; Paltridge, 2004). This chapter has taken the view that there is much to be learned mutually by researchers in both fields and that what are perceived as differences explicable by culture or linguistic background may be occasioned by the complexities of the constitution of the literacy practices of the academy themselves and the ways in which access to these is socially regulated.

FUTURE DIRECTIONS

More ethnographic research into the local contexts in which academic literacies are negotiated is clearly called for (Flowerdew, 2002). More particularly, research is needed into the increasingly interdisciplinary contexts in which students and teachers find themselves engaged and into the increasingly hybrid discourses and genres that inhabit written academic discourse, further countering monolithic conceptions of academic discourse and discourse communities (Candlin & Plum, 1999). EAP practitioners need to be wary of traditional models, which may not represent the textual worlds students encounter on a daily basis (Lillis, 2001). Candlin & Plum (1999) also call for research using interdiscursive research methodologies, which can further illuminate participant perceptions of processes of student induction.

An examination of the traditional, powerful impersonal research genres, particularly in terms of the extent to which qualitative research with its very different notions of researcher objectivity requires new reporting genres (Canagarajah, 1996), seems called for, for example, to assist students to write qualitative theses and dissertations.

Ivanič and Camps's (2001) research into how student writer identity is textually represented, which uses systemic functional linguistics to examine the linguistic resources writers draw on as they compose and the identities and social relations they construct, seems an area of promising research for both L1 and L2 writing research.

In a recent paper, Holmes (2004) describes an approach to EAP in an African context, blending intertextuality and genre theory in ways that may have wider application. Currie's (1998) and Prior's (2001) suggestions that more sophisticated models than direct and indirect speech and paraphrase are needed to help deal with the use of sources and with plagiarism and which might draw on research into intertextuality, interdiscursivity, hybridity, and sociohistorical ideas of voice to assist student writers establish textual ownership and voice are worthy of detailed consideration. Above all, greater engagement in disciplinary discourses and negotiations between mainstream teachers and academic literacy specialists is needed (Hyland, 2002b; Skillen, Merten, Percy, & Trivett, 1998).

REFERENCES

Anderson, B. (1983). *Imagined communities*. London: Verso.
Angélil-Carter, S. (2000). *Stolen language*. London: Longman.
Angelova, M., & Riazantseva, A. (1999). "If you don't tell me, how can I know?" *Written Communication*, *16*(4), 491–525.
Atkinson, D. (2001). Reflections and refractions on the JSLW special issue on voice. *Journal of Second Language Writing, 10*, 107–124.
Bakhtin, M. (1981). *The dialogic imagination*. Austin: University of Texas Press.
Bakhtin, M. (1986). *Speech genres and other late essays*. Austin: University of Texas Press.
Ballard, B., & Clanchy, J. (1988). Literacy in the university: An anthropological approach. In G. Taylor, B. Ballard, V. Beasley, H. Bock, J. Clanchy, & P. Nightingale, *Literacy by degrees* (pp. 7–23). Milton Keynes: Society for Research in Higher Education/Open University Press.
Bazerman, C. (1988). *Shaping written knowledge*. Madison: University of Wisconsin Press.
Belcher, D. (1994). The apprenticeship approach to advanced academic literacy: Graduate students and their mentors. *English for Specific Purposes, 13*(1), 23–34.
Belcher, D., & Braine, G. (1995). Introduction. In D. Belcher & G. Braine (Eds.), *Academic writing in a second language: Essays on research and pedagogy* (pp. xiv–xxxi). Norwood, NJ: Ablex.
Benesch, S. (1988). *Ending remediation: Linking ESL and content in higher education*. Washington, DC: TESOL.
Benesch, S. (2001). *Critical English for academic purposes*. Mahwah, NJ: Lawrence Erlbaum.
Berkenkotter, C., & Huckin, T. (1995). *Genre knowledge in disciplinary communication: Cognition/culture/power*. Hillsdale, NJ: Lawrence Erlbaum.
Bourdieu, P. (1977). The economics of linguistic exchanges. *Social Sciences Information, 16*(6), 645–668.
Bourdieu, P. (1991). *Language and symbolic power*. Cambridge: Polity Press.
Cadman, K. (1997). Thesis writing for international students: A question of identity? *English for Specific Purposes, 16*(1), 3–14.
Canagarajah, S. (1996). From critical research practice to critical research reporting. *TESOL Quarterly, 30*(2), 321–330.
Canagarajah, S. (2002). *Critical academic writing and multilingual students*. Ann Arbor: University of Michigan Press.
Candlin, C., & Hyland, K. (1999). Introduction: Integrating approaches to the study of writing. In C. Candlin & K. Hyland (Eds.), *Writing: Texts, processes and practices* (pp. 1–17). London: Longman.
Candlin, C., & Plum, G. (1999). Engaging with challenges of interdiscursivity in academic writing: Researchers, students and tutors. In C. Candlin & K. Hyland (Eds.), *Writing: Texts, processes and practices* (pp. 193–217). London: Longman.
Casanave, C. (1995). Local interactions: Constructing contexts for composing in a graduate sociology program. In D. Belcher & G. Braine (Eds.), *Academic writing in a second language: Essays on research and pedagogy* (pp. 83–110). Norwood, NJ: Ablex.

Casanave, C. (2004). *Controversies in second language writing.* Ann Arbor: University of Michigan Press.
Chang, Y., & Swales, J. (1999). Informal elements in English academic writing: Threats or opportunities for advanced non-native speakers? In C. Candlin & K. Hyland (Eds.), *Writing: Texts, processes and practices* (pp. 145–167). London: Longman.
Chase, G. (1988). Accommodation, resistance and the politics of student writing. *College, Composition and Communication,* 39(1), 13–22.
Cherry, R. (1988). Ethos versus persona: Self-representation in written discourse. *Written Communication,* 5(3), 251–276.
Chiseri-Strater, E. (1991). *Academic literacies: The public and private discourse of university students.* Portsmouth, NH: Boynton/Cook.
Clark, R. (1992). Principles and practice of CLA in the classroom. In N. Fairclough (Ed.), *Critical language awareness* (pp. 117–140). London: Longman.
Clark, R., & Ivanič, R. (1997). *The politics of writing.* London: Routledge.
Cope, B., & Kalantzis, M. (Eds.). (1993). *The powers of literacy: A genre approach to teaching writing.* London: Falmer Press.
Craig, A. (1991). Adult cognition and tertiary studies. *South African Journal of Higher Education,* 5(2), 137–144.
Cummins, J. (1996). *Negotiating identities: Education for empowerment in a diverse society.* Ontario: CABE.
Currie, P. (1998). Staying out of trouble: Apparent plagiarism and academic survival. *Journal of Second Language Writing,* 7(1), 1–18.
Delpit. L. (1988). The silenced dialogue: Power and pedagogy in educating other people's children. *Harvard Educational Review,* 58(3), 280–298.
Dison, A. (1997). The acquisition and uses of literacies within social contexts: Tsholo Mothibi's story. *Academic Development,* 3(2), 53–73.
English, L., Bonanno, H., Ihnatko, T., Webb, C., & Jones, J. (1999). Learning through writing in a first-year accounting course. *Journal of Accounting Education,* 17, 221–254.
Fairclough, N. (1992a). *Discourse and social change.* Cambridge: Polity Press.
Fairclough, N. (1992b). Discourse and text: Linguistic and intertextual analysis within discourse analysis. *Discourse and Society,* 3(2), 193–217.
Flowerdew, J. (2002). Ethnographically inspired approaches to the study of academic discourse. In J. Flowerdew, *Academic discourse* (pp. 235–252). Harlow, UK: Longman.
Fox, H. (1994). *Listening to the world: Cultural issues in academic writing.* Portsmouth, NH: Boynton/Cook.
Gee, J. P. (1990). *Social linguistics and literacies: Ideology in discourses.* London: The Falmer Press.
Geertz, C. (1975). *The interpretation of cultures.* London: Hutchinson.
Grabe, W., & Kaplan, R. (1996). *Theory and practice of writing.* London: Longman.
Granville, S., & Dison, L. (2005). Thinking about thinking: Integrating self-reflection into an academic literacy course. *Journal of English for Academic Purposes,* 4, 99–118.
Halliday, M. A. K. (1994). *Introduction to functional grammar* (2nd Ed.). London: Arnold.
Harris, J. (1989). The idea of community in the study of writing. *College Composition and Communication,* 40(1), 11–22.
Hermerschmidt, M. (1999). Foregrounding background in academic learning. In C. Jones, J. Turner, & B. Street (Eds.), *Students writing in the university* (pp. 5–16). Amsterdam: John Benjamins.
Hewlett, L. (1996). How can you discuss alone?: Academic literacy in a South African context. In D. Baker, J. Clay & C. Fox (Eds.), *Challenging ways of knowing: In English, Mathematics and Science* (pp. 89–100). London: Falmer Press.
Hirvela, A., & Belcher, D. (2001). Coming back to voice: The multiple voices and identities of mature multilingual writers. *Journal of Second Language Writing,* 10, 83–106.
Holmes, J. (2004). Intertextuality in EAP: An African context. *Journal of English for Academic Purposes,* 3, 73–88.
Hull, G., & Rose, M. (1989). Rethinking remediation: Towards a social-cognitive understanding of problematic reading and writing. *Written Communication,* 6(2), 139–154.
Hyland, K. (1998). *Hedging in scientific research articles.* Amsterdam: John Benjamins.
Hyland, K. (1999). Disciplinary discourses: Writer stance in research articles. In C. Candlin & K. Hyland (Eds.), *Writing: Texts, processes and practices,* (pp. 99–121). London: Longman.
Hyland, K. (2000). *Disciplinary discourses: Social interactions in academic writing.* Harlow: Longman.
Hyland, K. (2002a). Options of identity in academic writing. *ELT Journal,* 56(4), 351–358.
Hyland, K. (2002b). Specificity revisited: How far should we go now? *English for Specific Purposes,* 21(4), 385–395.
Ivanič, R. (1994). I is for interpersonal: Discoursal construction of writer identities and the teaching of writing. *Linguistics and Education,* 6, 3–15.

Ivanič, R. (1998). *Writing and identity*. Amsterdam: John Benjamins.
Ivanič, R., & Camps, D. (2001). I am how I sound: Voice as self-representation in L2 writing. *Journal of Second Language Writing*, *10*(3), 3–33.
Ivanič, R., & Simpson, J. (1992). Who's who in academic writing? In N. Fairclough (Ed.), *Critical language awareness* (pp. 141–173). London: Longman.
Johns, A. (1992). L1 composition theories: implications for developing theories of L2 composition. In B. Kroll (Ed.), *Second language writing* (pp. 24–36). Cambridge: Cambridge University Press.
Johns, A. (1997). *Text, role, and context: Developing academic literacies*. Cambridge: Cambridge University Press.
Jones, C. (1999). The student from overseas and the British University. In C. Jones, J. Turner & B. Street (Eds.), *Students writing in the university* (pp. 37–59). Amsterdam: John Benjamins.
Jones, J., Gollin, S., Drury, H., & Economou, D. (1989). Systemic-functional linguistics and its application to the TESOL curriculum. In R. Hasan & J. R. Martin (Eds.), *Language development: learning language, learning culture* (pp. 257–328). Norwood, NJ: Ablex.
Kress, G. (1993). *Learning to write*. London: Routledge.
Kress, G. (1999). Genre and the changing contexts for English language arts. *Language Arts*, *76*(6), 461–469.
Kubota, R. (1999). Japanese culture constructed by discourses: Implications for applied linguistics research and ELT. *TESOL Quarterly*, *33*(1), 9–35.
Lea, M. (1999). Academic literacies and learning in higher education. In C. Jones, J. Turner, & B. Street (Eds.), *Students writing in the university* (pp. 103–124). Amsterdam: John Benjamins.
Lea, M., & Street, B. (1998). Student writing in higher education: An academic literacies approach. *Studies in Higher Education*, *23*(2), 157–172.
Lea, M., & Street, B. (1999). Writing as academic literacies: Understanding textual practices in higher education. In C. Candlin & K. Hyland (Eds.), *Writing: Texts, processes and practices* (pp. 62–81). London: Longman.
Leibowitz, B. (1995). Transitions: Acquiring academic literacy at the University of the Western Cape. *Academic Development*, *1*(1), 33–46.
Lillis, T. (1997). New voices in academia?" The regulative nature of academic writing conventions. *Language and Education*, *11*(3), 182–199.
Lillis, T. (2001). *Student writing: Access, regulation, desire*. London: Routledge.
McCarthy, L. P. (1987). A stranger in strange lands: A college student writing across the curriculum. *Research in the Teaching of English*, *21*(3), 233–265.
Paltridge, B. (2002). Academic literacies and changing university communities. *Revista canaria de estudios ingleses*, *44*, 15–28. Retrieved September 20 2005 from http://www.arts.usyd.edu.au/committees/ArtsTLCtee/Projects/CIWE/paltridge.htm.
Paltridge, B. (2004). State of the art review: Academic writing. *Language Teaching*, *37*(2), 87–105.
Pennycook, A. (1994). The complex contexts of plagiarism: A reply to Deckert. *Journal of Second Language Writing*, *3*(3), 277–284.
Pennycook, A. (1996). Borrowing others' words: Text, ownership, memory and plagiarism. *TESOL Quarterly*, *30*(2), 201–230.
Porter, J. (1986). Intertextuality and the discourse community. *Rhetoric Review*, *5*(1), 34–47.
Pratt, M. L. (1991). Arts of the contact zone. *Profession 91*. New York: Modern Languages Association.
Prior, P. (1991). Contextualising writing and response in a graduate seminar. *Written Communication*, *8*(3), 267–310.
Prior, P. (1994). Response, revision, disciplinarity: A microhistory of a dissertation prospectus in Sociology. *Written Communication*, *11*(4), 483–533.
Prior, P. (1995). Redefining the task: An ethnographic examination of writing and response in graduate seminars. In D. Belcher & G. Braine (Eds.), *Academic writing in a second language: Essays on research and pedagogy* (pp. 47–81). Norwood, NJ: Ablex.
Prior, P. (2001). Voices in text, mind, and society: Sociohistoric accounts of discourse, acquisition and use. *Journal of Second Language Writing*, *10*(3), 55–81.
Ramanathan, V., & Atkinson, D. (1999). Individualism, academic writing, and ESL writers. *Journal of Second Language Writing*, *8*(1), 45–75.
Ramanathan, V., & Kaplan, R. (1996). Audience and voice in current L1 composition texts: Some implications for ESL student writers. *Journal of Second Language Writing*, *5*(1), 21–34.
Santos, T., Atkinson, D., Erickson, M., Matsuda, P. K. & Silva, T. (2000). On the future of second language writing: A colloquium. *Journal of Second Language Writing*, *9*(1), 1–20.
Scollon, R. (1995). Plagiarism and ideology: Identity in intercultural discourse. *Language in Society*, *24*, 1–28.
Sheeran, Y., & Barnes, D. (1991). *School writing*. Milton Keynes: Open University Press.

Shen, F. (1989). The classroom and the wider culture: Identity as a key to learning English composition. *College, Composition and Communication, 40*(4), 459–466.

Silva, T. (1992). Second language composition instruction: Developments, issues and directions in ESL. In B. Kroll (Ed.), *Second language writing* (pp. 11–23). Cambridge: Cambridge University Press.

Skillen, J., Merten, M., Percy, A., & Trivett, N. (1998). The IDEAL approach to learning development: A model for fostering improved learning outcomes for students. In *Proceedings of the Australian Association for Research in Education Annual Conference*, Adelaide, SA. Retrieved September 20 2005 from http://www.swin.edu.au/aare/con98.htm.

Spack, R. (1988). Initiating ESL students into the academic discourse community: How far should we go? *TESOL Quarterly, 22*, 29–51.

Spack, R. (1997a). The acquisition of academic literacy in a second language: A longitudinal case study. *Written Communication, 14*, 3–62.

Spack, R. (1997b). The rhetorical construction of multilingual students. *TESOL Quarterly, 31*(4), 765–774.

Starfield, S. (1994). Multicultural classrooms in higher education. *English Quarterly, 26*(3), 16–21.

Starfield, S. (2001). "I'll go with the group": Rethinking 'discourse community' in EAP. In J. Flowerdew & M. Peacock (Eds.), *Research perspectives on English for academic purposes* (pp. 132–147). Cambridge: Cambridge University Press.

Starfield, S. (2002). "I'm as second–language English speaker": Negotiating writer identity and authority in Sociology One. *Journal of Language, Identity, and Education, 1*(2), 121–140.

Starfield, S. (2004a). Word power: Negotiating success in a first-year sociology essay. In L. Ravelli & R. Ellis (Eds.), *Analysing academic writing: Contextualized frameworks* (pp. 66–83). London: Continuum.

Starfield, S. (2004b). "Why does this feel empowering?": Thesis writing, concordancing, and the *corporatizing* university. In B. Norton & K Toohey (Eds.), *Critical pedagogies and language learning* (pp. 138–157). Cambridge: Cambridge University Press.

Swales, J. (1990). *Genre analysis.* Cambridge: Cambridge University Press.

Tang, R., & John, S. (1999). The 'I' in identity: Exploring writer identity in student academic writing through the first person pronoun. *English for Specific Purposes, 18*, S23–S39.

Thesen, L. (1997). Voices, discourses and transition: In search of new categories in EAP. *TESOL Quarterly, 31*(3), 487–511.

Woodward-Kron, R. (2004). 'Discourse communities' and 'writing apprenticeship': An investigation of these concepts in undergraduate Education students' writing. *Journal of English for Academic Purposes, 3*, 139–161.

Zamel, V. (1993). Questioning academic discourse. *College ESL, 3*(1), 28–39.

Zamel, V., & Spack, R. (1998). *Negotiating academic literacies: Teaching and learning across languages and cultures.* Mahwah, NJ: Lawrence Erlbaum.

CHAPTER 54

FROM LITERACY TO MULTILITERACIES IN ELT

HEATHER LOTHERINGTON

York University, Canada

ABSTRACT

The conceptual and epistemological grounds of literacy are being stretched as the encoded worlds we navigate increasingly interpenetrate multicultural, multilingual, and multimodal contexts. The twenty-first century finds us at a critical juncture for reevaluating English language and literacy teaching agendas. The technological revolution has facilitated and augmented human communication such that everyday interactions now essentially include digital interfaces. Language, text, and discourse norms and practices are being rapidly expanded and reinvented in response to new media and global networks. The language driving the majority of intercultural web traffic is English, which reinforces its position as a global language and adds an insidious dimension of cybercolonialism. Teachers are in crisis: domains for English language socialization now extend from known geographical and social contexts to the global panorama of the virtual world in which we, too, are learners. Information and communication technologies (ICT) have created new literacies that are required by learners of all ages if they are to fairly contend for academic and economic success. This chapter examines the evolution of literacy into multiliteracies and considers how this epistemological shift affects ELT. Digitally responsive, pedagogically strategic, ecologically sensitive English language and literacy teaching and learning practices are discussed in conclusion.

INTRODUCTION

From Literacy to Multiliteracies

Once upon a time, literacy was simply defined as reading and writing. Prior to the invention of the printing press, literacy was principally the province of clerics and scholars. Only high-prestige, classical languages were considered worthy of laborious hand inscription, fixing at an early historical juncture the understanding that literacy connotes particular language competencies. The dawning of the Industrial Revolution provided the social context for mass education, which transfigured literacy from social elitism into a commodity: measurable, marketable knowledge. The role of modern education was to prepare learners for the workforce (Agnello, 2001). Thus began the tradition of associating literacy with economic growth (Vincent, 2000).

As contemporary society moves away from Industrial era modernism, and towards postmodernism, spurred by the information revolution that began in the late twentieth century, operationalizing literacy has reopened very basic questions. Social worlds have become much more complex, and the conceptual grounds on which mass literacy was scaffolded have shifted, raising important questions such as: Who is a literate person in contemporary multicultural, multilingual, digitally infused communities? What is literacy in this day and age?

Given the immense and dynamic complexity of our present encoded and interconnected world, the notion of literacy as a monolith has been soundly disputed in the research literature, and various alternative constructions of *multiple literacies* have been proposed by theorists such as Street, Heath, Gallego and Hollingsworth, Martin-Jones and Jones, and the New London Group.

Street (1984, 1995) was one of the first to challenge the notion of a singular literacy, dichotomizing *autonomous* and *ideological* models of literacy. The autonomous model, which characterizes much of the historical study of literacy, approaches literacy as cognitive advancement: a skill or set of skills developed by the individual, detached from social context. He argues this conceptualization as an inherently ethnocentric and colonial view of human and cultural development, assuming a linear relationship of orality to literacy. The ideological model, which is oriented to the future of literacy, is a critical approach to literacy rooted in social agency that sees the individual as embedded in a social and cultural context within which the practices of literacy have meaning.

Heath (1983) also firmly situates emergent literacy in social practice, linking primary socialization, as realized in three communities marked by ethnicity and class differences, with literacy expectations held in schools. Building on the concept of literacy as situated social practice, Gallego and Hollingsworth (2000) propose a conceptual framework for discussion of *multiple literacies*, that is:

- *School literacies*–the learning of interpretive and communicative processes needed to adapt socially to school and other dominant language contexts, and the use or practice of those processes in order to gain a conceptual understanding of school subjects
- *Community literacies*–the appreciation, understanding, and/or use of interpretive and communicative traditions of culture and community, which sometimes stand as critiques of school literacies
- *Personal literacies*–the critical awareness of ways of knowing and believing about self that comes from thoughtful examination of history or experiential and gender-specific backgrounds in school and community language settings, which sometimes stands as a critique of both school literacies and community literacies (p. 5)

This framework splits the school literacies hegemony, fusing multicultural and gendered perspectives into community and personal domains. However, the place of multilingualism in structuring communication networks has not been so well delineated.

More recently, Martin-Jones and Jones (2000) have examined what they describe as *multilingual literacies*: literacies in contexts where different languages and language varieties, written and oral, script conventions, and social contexts are interwoven, refocusing the concept of community through a multilingual lens. Hawisher and Selfe (2000a) further probe the nature of community, exploring the Web as a distinct global environment in which new literacies and new identities are rapidly developing. Their work challenges the exclusivity of real-world, paper-based constructions of literacy as social practice.

The term *multiliteracies* was developed by the New London Group[1] (1996) as a framework for action, to return the field of English language teaching to the broader question of the social outcomes of language learning, given that "there was no singular canonical English that either could or should be taught any more" (Cope & Kalantzis, 2000, p. 5).

> We decided that the outcomes of our discussions could be encapsulated in one word: 'Multiliteracies'–a word we chose because it describes two important arguments we might have with the emerging cultural, institutional and global order. The first argument engages with the multiplicity of communications channels and media: the second with the increasing salience of cultural and linguistic diversity. (Cope & Kalantzis, 2000, p. 5)

The concept of multiliteracies assumes multiple worlds communicated in multiple ways. As Street (2000) points out, the concept of multiliteracies is dynamic and requires critical vigilance so as not to become itself a reification of form, focused on channels rather than on the multiple social practices that play out in continual, complex interrelationship.

SHIFTING EPISTEMOLOGICAL GROUNDS: CONSIDERATIONS FOR INFORMED ELT PRACTICE

Political and social conceptualizations of literacy position, drive, and define the education process. Fresh ways of thinking about multiliteracies are shattering old expectations and understandings of literacy and are inspiring critical thought about how multilingualism, multiculturalism, and multimodalism affect ELT policy and practice. Prominent issues and debates include inquiries as divergent as managing delicate language ecologies and subduing linguistic imperialism (Nettle & Romaine, 2000; Phillipson & Skutnabb-Kangas, 1999; Skutnabb-Kangas, 2000); exploring digital literacies (Gee, 2003; Kellner, 2002; Kress, 2003; Lankshear & Knobel, 2003; Lotherington, 2004b); negotiating concepts of language ownership with increasingly deterritorialized languages, such as English (Graddol, 1999); critically renegotiating cultural identities in complex postmodern digital landscapes (Castells, 2000; Hawisher and Selfe, 2000b); tracking innovative language and discourse conventions in digital environments (Baron, 2003; Crystal, 2001; Lotherington, 2004a; Lotherington & Xu, 2004; Werry, 1996); investigating the effects of globalization on language teaching (Cameron, 2002; Zhenhua, 1999); and problematizing changing communication needs in an information-based economy (Castells, 2000; Gee, 2000, 2001). These issues challenge ELT professionals to reconceptualize communicative competence to better meet the needs of contemporary postmodern society, and to reconsider the implications of multilingualism, multiculturalism, and multimodalism for ELT.

Multilingualism: Linguistic Capital, Linguistic Imperialism and Language Ecology

Literacies are politically constructed, whether explicitly or implicitly, as specific language competencies. In the field of ELT, literacies are focused on English. The position of English as a global language confers considerable linguistic capital on the fluent English speaker.

Crystal (1997) outlines the cultural foundations of English as a global language in the domains of international relations, mass and popular media, education, travel, and safety, indicating the dominant use of English interculturally, and even interlingually in awkward translation situations.[2] As Pennycook (1995) notes:

> Turn on the television news, and everywhere there will be something going on in English: signs and placards in English at a demonstration for Estonian independence or political change in China, an interview with King Hussein of Jordan in English, a speech by Nelson Mandela in English to a packed stadium in Soweto. (p. 35)

For example, in the domain of higher education, publication in academic journals (essential for academic promotion) is overwhelmingly in English. Crystal (1997) cites as an example that in 1995, 90% of the 1,500 papers listed in *Linguistics Abstracts* were published in English (p. 102). Warschauer (1999), looking at inequalities on the Internet, quotes that 82% of webpages were posted in English in 1997 (p. 19), though this has changed considerably with engineering advances that facilitate the use of diverse scripts in digital environments.

Contemporary policy, assessment instruments, and curriculum documents in ELT commonly assume that the globally hegemonic position of English makes it politically and economically attractive without necessarily acknowledging the ecological menace English and other such killer languages[3] present to global linguistic diversity. The impetus to learn English, particularly in a multilingual context, may be answered by teaching oriented to subtractive bilingualism. Even in nations where language policy is protective of multilingualism, such as Australia, balancing instruction through responsive bilingual principles is difficult. Education prioritizes the acquisition of English literacies, which are essential to economic and social survival: literacies in other languages tend to be treated as enrichment learning (Lotherington, 2001).

On a global scale, language education policy and practices that promote English above other languages fuel the current crisis in supporting linguistic diversity, which, in a worst-case scenario, forecasts the death of 90% of the world's oral languages within the century (Skutnabb-Kangas, 2000, p. ix). With the extinction of the majority of the world's languages comes traumatic loss of what Nettle and Romaine (2000) term "*biolinguistic diversity:* the rich spectrum of life encompassing all the earth's species of plants and animals along with human cultures and their languages" (p. 13). ELT becomes an unwitting party to such global destruction if a subtractive approach to language learning and maintenance is expressed in the classroom.

Linguistic Imperialism

English also continues to be the dominant language of virtual communication. The digital universe is in principle a global alliance (though not in practice due to economic constraints). However, the notion of the global village conceived by Canadian scholar Marshall McLuhan (1964) decades before the advent of the Internet is, in digital realization, flawed in many respects. As Hawisher and Selfe (2000b) explain:

> The global-village narrative, it is becoming clear, simply will not work for much of the world in the next century–it is too reductive, too western, too colonial in its conception. (p. 286)

The virtual space of Internet communication is not a global village in character. Despite its geographically and politically transcendent nature, the Internet originated in and embodies American values. It is, as Marchart puts it "the American new frontier" (1998, p. 56):

> The specific imagery of the Internet relies on what one could call the colonial discourse of the Net in general and on American New World narratives in particular: Gore's information superhighway, cyber-hippies and the so called Californian ideology ....
> (p. 56)

The Internet continues to be dominated by users in rich Western nations; it is a portal to the world through a lens fixed in those cultural values, materials, and notions of information (Hawisher & Selfe, 2000a). Virtual space is not culturally neutral territory: it is colonial. The cybercolonial forces of the Net fortify the position of English as lingua mundi to the continuing detriment of global language ecology. ELT needs to respond with good critical literacies and strong principles of additive bilingualism.

Multiculturalism: Whose English?

Current language teaching policy and practice tend to characterize English language and literacy as fitting into prestige varieties, such as American or British, that are treated as grammatically static, paper-based systems. This perspective is an oversimplification of the evolving, geopolitically fragmented language that, quite apart from its social, cultural, and regional variants in real-world usage, is rapidly growing new standards, registers, and literacy practices within the digital universe.

The classic distinction between *English as a second language* (ESL) and *English as a foreign language* (EFL) is based on the availability and desirability of local language norms: English as a second language is *intranational* and *endonormative*, that is, language norms are generated within the national context, whereas English as a foreign language is *international* and *exonormative*, with language norms imported from another country. This distinction works from a marketing point of view, but it is seriously flawed sociolinguistically. Global communication trends have introduced a number of complications that trouble the ESL/EFL distinction.

English is being increasingly recognized as a *lingua mundi*: a global language. Global English language use occurs in both real-world and digital contexts. *English as a global language* is used interculturally amongst international users, both native speakers and second language learners, whose standards of speech are rooted in different social and political traditions (Clyne, 1994).

As English grows in international prominence as a lingua franca, the profile of its speech communities is shifting. Graddol (1999) describes the trajectory of English as a language increasingly used by second language learners. As native-speaking populations decline in proportion to the numbers of second language users, interesting questions about language norms, cultural identity, and ownership of English emerge: Whose language is it?

The idea of *new Englishes* is not new. English left the shores of England hundreds of years ago. According to Crystal (1997), the largest English-speaking country in the world, the United States of America, is home to only about 20% of the world's English speakers (p. 130). The English language, which is highly pluricentric, is increasingly international and intercultural. This presents the teacher of English with the very real dilemma of attempting to fix acceptable language norms and standards in a world of rapidly shifting and splintering paradigms.

Multimodalism and Language Innovation

As McLuhan (1964) famously commented, the phrase "'the medium is the message,' means, in terms of the electronic age, that a totally new environment has been created" (p. vii). All ELT teachers are aware that language change is a natural and inevitable phenomenon. Over time and space, both geographically and socially configured, all languages morph into variants. The Roman Empire colonially transported Vulgar Latin across Europe to eventually regionalize as French, Spanish, Italian, Portuguese, Romanian, etc. English has not been renamed over political borders but an extensive, dynamic range of regional and social varieties exist, and, indeed, coexist in the repertoires of many individuals.

The Internet provides a channel for communication not limited by social or geopolitical space, or even time as customarily envisioned. Internet communication uses literacy conventions to create speech communities, in both synchronous environments, where participants are both/all physically present at their computers, such as instant messaging systems and chats; and asynchronous environments, where participants do not have to be present at the same time, such as email, conferences and listservs. In this way, no voice imprints, including accents, mark the identity of the user/s.

Because language is input via keyboard on screens that are variably sized, keystroke-saving conventions have become popularized to the point of creating a radically facelifted online orthography, particularly in synchronous environments (Lotherington & Xu, 2004). The possibilities of digital media have nurtured innovative means of expression, such as the use of *emoticons*, e.g., ;-), which are essentially logograms constructed of punctuation marks and diacritics to represent emotional states, intended to inject into written language some of the nonverbal meaning intrinsic in face-to-face encounters. Emoticons are not language specific; they are systemic throughout Internet communications. Interestingly, there are documented cultural variations, e.g., :) :((read perpendicularly in English); and (^o^) (+_+) (read "head on" from left to right in Chinese and Japanese) (Lotherington & Xu, 2004; Sugimoto & Levin, 2000).

These innovations in language use growing in Internet conversations among users who inhabit different areas of the globe are occurring in nanoseconds rather than over centuries. What we are seeing is truly a revolution in language conventions. Indeed, the spelling reform that important thinkers such as George Bernard Shaw,[4] Noah Webster, and Benjamin Franklin strove to induce, each in his own way, alas to minimal effect (Venezky, 1980), is occurring naturally and rapidly in grass-roots Internet conversations. The revolutionary changes in English orthography in online discourse provide confusing alternatives to conventional print usage for language learners (and teachers).

Four Skills?

ELT has conventionally described and taught language in four designated skill areas: reading, writing, listening, and speaking. These four skills, which have arguably formed the very cornerstone of ELT in the past, are inadequate descriptions of language use in Internet encounters, where the borders between orality and literacy have disintegrated and new conventions have emerged. Indeed, Crystal finds that communication in online environments cannot be pigeonholed within the classic four skills paradigm and terms online chat *NetSpeak* (2001).

Internet conversations have developed their own distinct procedural, politeness, and formality norms, which fall between the structured formality of printed text and the diaphanous, utterance-based nature of face-to-face talk. Internet-based communication is often labeled *chat*, yet the interface is written and read. However, what is written on screen is far more casual and colloquial than paper-based text, yet it also has some of the characteristics of formal, written language, such as opportunities to edit what has been "said" before it is sent, particularly in asynchronous encounters. The medium has inspired language and discourse norms that set digital literacies apart from spoken and written language and show them to be innovative and flexible, yet rule-governed (Lotherington, 2004a; Lotherington & Xu, 2004).

The Internet environment is disintermediated by design: computers are directly networked through software. This situation positions the reader of Internet texts as a consumer of directly available materials, displacing the traditional arbiters of quality, namely, publishers, editors, reviewers, librarians, and teachers, and offloading the critical and organizational functions of these highly educated specialists to readers of digital texts. The onus on the reader and the writer thus shifts in subtle ways: it is no longer the writer who is responsible for quality control but the reader. The development of the expanded critical skills needed to adequately prepare readers demands a reconceptualization of literacies in the ELT classroom, reconfiguring reading and writing to fundamentally include critical skills for digital as well as paper texts.

New Genres

Digital literacies have become pervasively and ineluctably institutionalized in contemporary social and economic life. Digital-human interfaces are invisibly woven into daily routines, from managing variously digitized messages (voice mail, pagers, automated telephone systems, email...) to banking and shopping with credit and debit cards vetted through small screens, to form-filling, bill-paying, information-seeking, communicating, shopping, blogging, and even looking for romance on the Internet. Such learned digital encounters for adults are in a universe native to contemporary children, particularly those born into wealthy countries within the past decade and a half, whose understanding of play fundamentally includes digital pop culture literacies, such as playing video games on different platforms; using Internet-based instant messaging systems; and downloading, sharing, and playing songs and movies.

Kress (2000, 2003) explores the concept of *multimodality*, questioning the boundaries of encoded text in our contemporary, wired world. He states that the information revolution has "dislodge[d] written language from the centrality which it has held, or which has been ascribed to it, in public communication" (2000, p. 182). Understanding what comprises textuality, human semiotic communication in its new range of possibilities forces a reconceptualization of educational agendas. Slow political response to educationally incorporating digital literacies is inexcusable if we believe that, as Kress (1997) states:

> Curriculum is a design for the future. The contents and processes put forward in curriculum and in its associated pedagogy are the design for future human dispositions. (p. 78).

Postmodern Literacies

Education reproduces the social order. Modern education demanded particular knowledges and skills of its educational systems, of which literacy was central. Postmodern education, too, anticipates preparation of the worker, but as capitalism and communication media have changed, so, too have educational priorities for future work demands.

According to Gee (2000, 2001), who looked at American schools, the social order being reproduced in current education is that of Industrial era, hierarchically shaped, old capitalism rather than the hierarchically flattened, distributed systems of new capitalism in the Information Age. Business in the new global "fast capitalism" (2000, p. 46) is knowledge-based, demanding of the worker dynamic and creative expertise and entrepreneurial flexibility. However, across North America, current trends towards accountability are steering curricula and assessment towards conservative modern-age literacies in a climate of controversial high stakes and standardized testing.

Education, including ELT, is indeed in crisis. The crisis, however, is not in strategically improving educational success for those who fall below current indicators, but in transforming education itself. ELT needs to rethink the place and nature of English language and literacy, and ways of teaching and learning that compatibly and proactively anticipate the world in which students engage.

CURRENT DEBATES AND CONCERNS IN ELT

Recognizing multiliteracies in ELT practice entails recognizing new genres and communicative needs; reexamining the fabric of the language to situate changing norms and conventions; integrating new modalities; and fostering complex linguistic and cultural identities.

Shifting Language Competencies

English is undergoing rapid innovation in many ways. New vocabulary, both alphabetic and iconic, is being coined and introduced into the lexicon. Orthographic conventions are changing in response to new communication environments. Discourse conventions are being reshaped by new media requirements and possibilities; and language and literacy "skills" are being reconfigured with new textualities. These changes require new communicative competencies of the learner and teacher alike. As Bourdieu (1991) argues:

> It follows that one cannot fully account for the properties and social effects of the legitimate language unless one takes account, not only of the social conditions of the production of literary language and its grammar, but also of the social conditions in which this scholarly code is imposed and inculcated as the principle of the production and evaluation of speech. (p. 61)

Information and communication technologies (ICT) driven neologisms have saturated the English lexicon. New alphabetic words have been coined, such as email, webpage, spellchecker, and Internet. Existing words have assumed new meanings, including send, undo, and chat. New collocations have come into use, such as information superhighway, virtual space, digital text, and real time. These new words and expressions are difficult for learners to trace in dictionaries, whether paper or online, as they are typically very recent constructions.

Although alphabetic constructions are tricky to look up in dictionaries, they are nonetheless reasonably transparent to the teacher who is immersed in contemporary ICT. A more grass-roots user guide is often required for rebus constructions such as *ICQ* (I seek you), *cu* (see you), and *gr8 1* (great one). This also goes for emoticons, such as ☺, and acronyms used in chat shorthand, such as *lol* (laugh out loud), and *btw* (by the way), as demonstrated by the following example:

> I will think up sum smiley faces that ppl use when they r describing emotions in a couple o' taps of the keyboard (when they r 2 lazy 2 describe their emotions 2 u). (Personal communication, Aimee[5])

Spelling and punctuation mechanics have been inspired by ICT possibilities and limitations as well. As the DOS environment was not case sensitive, capitals on names in email addresses were not needed. Capitalization in screen environments thus became stylistic rather than grammatical: a contemporary computer look is conferred by using word-medial capitals, such as *iBook* and *WordPerfect*. Indeed, capitals and annoying punctuation marks, such as apostrophes, may be discarded altogether, as is seen in this online chat between two university students[6]:

> *sk8Celine* (11:52:49 PM): uh............sorry - i 4got to think about it
> *honeygarli* (11:53:31 PM): :-(
> *honeygarli* (11:53:32 PM): me too
> *honeygarli* (11:53:41 PM): oh, and I forgot to ask michael
> *sk8Celine* (11:53:50 PM): hehe - thanx 4 the mail :-DO:-)
> *honeygarli* (11:53:57 PM): you are welcome :-)

Conversations with teachers indicate that such innovative spelling constructions are filtering into paper and pencil texts. How does the teacher handle instruction of canonical grammatical, spelling, and punctuation conventions, with such real examples to the contrary? Moreover, how does the learner sort out when to apply which set of conventions? Given that education has lagged behind in the Information Revolution, children are often still being taught cursive writing over keyboarding skills in schools. Many current computer users have poor keyboarding skills. As such, online usage may be riddled with typographic errors that provide anything but a good model of the language in use.

For the teacher of English, spellcheckers pose a double-edged blade. On the one hand, the availability of mechanical assistance in correcting conventional aspects of writing, such as spelling and punctuation, is liberating for the teacher, who can focus on more substantive aspects of composition. On the other hand, I question whether we are growing increasingly reliant on computerized spellchecking, and moving the burden of spelling as cultural memory into machine memory. This raises the possibility that society may eventually lose its cultural imperative for individuals to learn to spell.

New Conversations

The impossibility of neatly separating orality and literacy emerged clearly in early social practice investigations into literacy behaviors (Heath, 1983). The interplay of the oral and the literate is increasingly fused in virtual environments, where a literate interface is needed to engage in conversation. As a result, online discourse conventions have changed. In many ways, these changes make engaging in English conversations more welcoming for those learning the language, although it also raises the question of how does the "ordered space of the Web affect the literacy practices of individuals from different cultures – and the constitution of their identities – personal, national, cultural, ethnic through language?" (Hawisher & Selfe, 2000a, p. 1)

Online forums can assist learners in developing a voice in the language they are learning. In online conversations, the physical identity of the participants is masked. Each participant essentially writes his or her own identity. Whereas this is a situation of potential danger for children who may not grasp possible deceit in the sender's identity, it is an advantage to the language learner who is hesitant in speech, apprehensive in conversation, or simply shy.

Conversational threads in synchronous environments, such as chats, can be both cryptic and difficult to keep up with for participants not reading and writing at a pace sufficient to join into the flow of conversation. However, asynchronous environments, such as email, which tend to utilize more conservative print-oriented writing conventions, can provide many good practice opportunities for language learners, whose social, cultural, and physical information, including accent and ethnic identity, does not influence the conversational encounter. Language learners can comfortably edit their messages, with assistance from help options, such as spellcheckers, until they are ready to send. They can take the time they need to consider previous responses, and rest assured of not being interrupted while trying to get their thoughts down. In these ways the medium supports language learning by providing a low-anxiety forum for practicing conversational English.

New Literacies and Old Expectations

Flexible multiliteracies are required for academic, social, cultural, and economic navigation of real and virtual environments. The extent to which educational systems have moved towards preparing learners for life in the Information Age is variable, however, and successes are fragmented. For instance, there is an increasing prevalence of modern-era, autonomous-model, high-stakes testing of literacy at the grade school level in North America. This situation presents the teacher with the troubling prospect of having to prepare learners to pass inflexible tests that complement neither contemporary teaching objectives nor current and future workplace demands.

For learners in her class, the teacher is an authority; an essential guide to the discourse norms of the English language. Her knowledge and understanding of the appropriate use of English in society is part of the key to learner's successful attainment of the language. However, virtual requirements for English now reach beyond local usage and textually identifiable prestige models into newer genres of English as a global language that stretch any teacher's expected competencies into terra incognita. Is it then sufficient for the teacher to continue to teach and model

English according to regional use parameters? In this world of increasing virtual information exchange, how and where does the teacher's knowledge fit in? Does the teacher legitimate the English or Englishes that she is prepared to teach, and treat less formal (even if increasingly prevalent) registers of English as do-it-yourself territory?

There is a human rights issue embedded in this quandary. Teachers cannot simply decide to limit their classrooms to local language survival when the society in which we all live is increasingly global. To do so would be to create a subclass of modern-era paper literates in an increasingly postmodern world. This is not a responsible, moral choice for any teacher. As Kellner advises (2002):

> Critical educators need to theorise the literacies necessary to interact in these emergent multimedia environments and to gain the skills that will enable individuals to learn, work, and create in emergent cultural spaces and domains. (p. 164)

FUTURE DIRECTIONS IN ELT: NEW WAYS OF TEACHING AND LEARNING

An evolving reconceptualization of literacy as multiliteracies reconstructs the educational goals and outcomes of ELT to be more linguistically and culturally sensitive and inclusive, socially and linguistically repositioning the English language. Such changes in perspectives demand responsive ways of learning and teaching.

Responsive ESL Teaching: Nurturing Multilingualism and Multiculturalism

> Our vision is of a 'heteroglossic democracy', where in principle all voices and texts of difference have a right to be heard, critiqued, analyzed and constructed in the public forums of governments and schools, workplaces and community meetings, churches and corporations. (Luke & Freebody, 1997, p. 213)

Teaching towards additive bilingualism has never been more important. ELT cannot morally ignore the ecological debate about the relative status of English and its encroachment on other language domains. The teacher must ensure that her learners are learning English, at the same time complementing and maintaining the many literacies learners will need to engage in their complex, multicultural, and multilingual lives.

Interestingly one of the primary culprits in pushing English language and American cyberculture, the Internet, also provides a potential solution for establishing a viable postmodern multilingualism. Digital commuters, who work in a virtual office, can live wherever on the (wired) globe they choose. This provides opportunities for virtual-real diglossia, where English is used interculturally for digital office work, and other languages are used for communication in the family and/or community.

The opposite is also true. The Internet is becoming increasingly multilingual. As technology grows in sophistication, information searching and exchange is becoming more accessible to and more accommodating of other languages, including those using non-alphabetic scripts.

The principle remains the same: English is an auxiliary language for an increasing number of 'speakers.' ELT professionals must recognize that English confers academic, social, cultural, and economic accessibility at an ecological cost to the world's diminishing linguistic diversity, and must responsibly support critical literacies and additive bilingualism and multilingualism. The written word and its interpretation are not simply page or screen deep: English literacies must be questioning, not normalizing and colonizing.

Nurturing Multimodalism

In Freire's (1998/1970) banking concept of education,

> [e]ducation thus becomes an act of depositing, in which the students are the depositories and the teacher is the depositor. Instead of communicating, the teacher issues communiqués and makes deposits which the students patiently receive, memorize, and repeat. (p. 53)

This he contrasts with problem-posing education that

> affirms men and women as beings in the process of becoming–as unfinished, uncompleted beings in and with a likewise unfinished reality....Education is thus constantly remade in the praxis. (p. 65)

Freire's critical probing of literacy as enculturation is of great importance in contemporary classrooms: digital literacies, by their very nature, do not suit a transmission model of learning. Collaborations in the learning project are essential.

New learning collaborations call on the teacher as learner, and the learner as teacher. The teacher is a lifelong learner; this is simply more apparent in the Information Age. In instances of best practice, collaborative learning partnerships are forged between and among teachers for strategic, bottom-up, in-house professional development (Granger, Morbey, Lotherington, Owston, & Wideman, 2002; Lotherington, Morbey, Granger, & Doan, 2001). This allows teachers to share in reflective, on-going, contextualized learning, tailored to their collective knowledge. This sharing also includes the learner as teacher. ELT typically employs learner-centered activities: these can include learners sharing their knowledge of strategic digital literacies with others in the classrooms.

The digital universe, so threatening to adult notions of socially sanctioned literacies, is intuitive to children, who have been socialized into it, and for whom digital literacies are exploratory play. Adults may find new ways of communicating digitally to be quite baffling and confronting of our communicative expertise; children do not. Instant messaging systems, such as MSN, AOL, ICQ, for example, provide as natural a medium for communicating to them as telephones did for the baby-boomer generation. It is not fair for the teacher to treat ICT as auxiliary communication with learners for whom it is mainstream and primary.

Learning spaces are important. Although teachers seldom have much individual say in the layout of teaching spaces, collaborative relationships may help to encourage integrated digitization, where computers are not segregated in laboratories but are interspersed throughout the school environment. In digitally infused curricula, postmodern literacies do not supplant but complement modern literacies, so that access to information is driven by purpose and content rather than by the media available (Lotherington, Morbey, Granger, & Doan, 2001).

RESPONSIVE ESL LEARNING

Political engagement with the social practices of language has reconstructed literacy as emancipatory, and education as dialogue. Transmission education is simply not applicable to learning in the Information Age, where much of the responsibility for learning has been downloaded onto the learner. Both collaborative effort and greater independence in learning are called for. Responsive ESL learning fundamentally invokes what Cummins (2000) calls *transformative pedagogy*, which is "realized in interactions between educators and students that attempt to foster collaborative relations of power" (p. 246).

Digitally acculturated children have learned to become much more independent learners by problem solving within digital domains. They understand what it means to access help functions, and have learned strategies to navigate through digital chaos. These new communicative competencies are arrived at through independent and collaborative exploratory learning.

ELT typically nurtures collaborative learning through communicative exercises conducted in pairs and groups. However, many learners, new to the culture of problem-based learning, still have expectations of the language teacher as ultimate authority and guide. This expectation of transmission learning is not valid or useful to the learner, and learners holding such concepts must learn to learn again, with their own motivated learning as central to the endeavor. Help in this era is decentralized: it comes from software, manuals, peers, and individual explorations as well as from the traditional resources of teachers and reference books.

CONCLUSIONS

This chapter has explored the current social and economic reality in which teachers of English are educating children and adults, at the same time attempting to explore what our changing conceptions of literacy mean for ELT. Literacies in the twenty-first century have been described as fundamentally multicultural, multilingual, and multimodal. Issues and problems in ELT arising from a reconceptualization of literacy as multiliteracies have been posed and suggestions made to help create a better understanding and learning environment that prepares learners for responsive English language and literacy learning.

NOTES

[1] The New London Group comprised Courtney Cazden, James Gee, Sarah Michaels (United States); Bill Cope, Mary Kalantzis, Allan Luke, Carmen Luke, Martin Nakata (Australia); Gunther Kress, Norman Fairclough (United Kingdom).

[2] An example would be using English as an intermediary language in translations/interpretations of two smaller languages, e.g., Turkish to Finnish, where one translator translates Turkish into English and another English into Finnish (Crystal, 1997, p. 81).

[3] Skutnabb-Kangas defines killer languages as "the languages whose (native) speakers have arrogated to themselves and to their languages more structural power and (material) resources than their numbers would justify, at the cost of speakers of other languages" (2000, p. 46)

[4] The fabled alternative spelling of "fish" as "ghoti" ("gh" as in "enough", "o" as in "women," and "ti" as in "nation") is one of George Bernard Shaw's legacies.

[5] Aimee is a pseudonym for a 13-year-old girl in Toronto who participated in a study I conducted on children and digital popular culture.

[6] Authentic digital chat used with the permission of the interlocutors, two undergraduate students studying at a large Canadian university. These conversations form part of the data collected for the

project *Digitization and language change*, conducted by Heather Lotherington and Xu Yejun in 2003. We are indebted to the Faculty of Education at York University for funding assistance through a Minor Research Grant; and to the Graduate Program in Theoretical and Applied Linguistics in the Faculty of Arts for supporting this project through the allocation of an extended graduate assistantship.

REFERENCES

Agnello, M. F. (2001). *A postmodern literacy policy analysis.* New York: Peter Lang.
Baron, N. (2003). Why email looks like speech: Proofreading, pedagogy and public face. In J. Aitcheson & D.M. Lewis (Eds.), *New media language* (pp. 85–94). London: Routledge.
Bourdieu, P. (1991). *Language and symbolic power*. Cambridge, MA: Harvard University Press.
Cameron, D. (2002). Globalization and the teaching of 'communication skills.' In D. Block & D. Cameron (Eds.), *Globalization and language teaching* (pp. 67–82). London: Routledge.
Castells, M. (2000). *The rise of the network society* (2nd ed.). Malden, MA: Blackwell.
Clyne, M. (1994). *Inter-cultural communication at work: Cultural values in discourse*. Cambridge: Cambridge University Press.
Cope, B., & Kalantzis, M. (2000). Introduction. Multiliteracies: The beginnings of an idea. In B. Cope & M. Kalantzis (Eds.), *Multiliteracies: Literacy learning and the design of social futures* (pp. 3–8). London: Routledge.
Crystal, D. (1997). *English as a global language.* Cambridge: Cambridge University Press.
Crystal, D. (2001). *Language and the Internet.* Cambridge, UK/New York: Cambridge University Press.
Cummins, J. (2000). *Language, power and pedagogy: Bilingual children in the crossfire*. Clevedon: Multilingual Matters.
Freire, P. (1998). *Pedagogy of the oppressed* (M.B. Ramos, Trans.) (20th anniversary edition). New York: Continuum. (Original work published 1970).
Gallego, M. A., & Hollingsworth, S. (2000). Introduction. The idea of multiple literacies. In M.A. Gallego & S. Hollingsworth (Eds.), *What counts as literacy: Challenging the school standard* (pp. 1–23). New York: Teachers College Press.
Gee, J. P. (2000). New people in new worlds: Networks, the new capitalism and schools. In B. Cope & M. Kalantzis (Eds.), *Multiliteracies: Literacy learning and the design of social futures* (pp. 43–68). London: Routledge.
Gee, J. P. (2001). Literacies, schools and kinds of people: Educating people in the new capitalism. In M. Kalantzis & B. Cope (Eds.), *Transformations in language and learning: Perspectives on multiliteracies* (pp. 81–98). Australia: Common Ground.
Gee, J.P. (2003). *What video games have to teach us about learning and literacy*. New York: Palgrave Macmillan.
Graddol, D. (1999). The decline of the native speaker. In D. Graddol & U. H. Meinhof (Eds.), *English in a changing world*. *AILA Review 13*, 57–68.
Granger, C.A., Morbey, M.L., Lotherington, H., Owston, R.D., & Wideman, H.H. (2002). Canada: Factors contributing to teachers' successful implementation of information technology. *Journal of Computer Assisted Learning, 18*(4), 480–488.
Hawisher, G. E., & Selfe, C. L. (2000a). Introduction: Testing the claims. In G.E. Hawisher & C.L. Selfe (Eds.), *Global literacies and the world-wide web* (pp. 1–18). London: Routledge.
Hawisher, G. E., & Selfe, C. L. (2000b). Conclusion: Inventing postmodern identities: Hybrid and transgressive literacy practices on the web. In G.E. Hawisher & C.L. Selfe (Eds.), *Global literacies and the world-wide web* (pp. 277–289). London: Routledge.
Heath, S. B. (1983). *Ways with words: Language, life and work in communities and classrooms*. Cambridge: Cambridge University Press.
Kellner, D.M. (2002). Technological revolution, multiple literacies, and the restructuring of education. In I. Snyder (Ed.), *Silicon literacies: Communication, innovation and education in the electronic age.* London: Routledge.
Kress, G. (1997). Visual and verbal modes of representation in electronically mediated communication: The potentials of new forms of text. In I. Snyder (Ed.). *Page to screen: Taking literacy into the electronic era* (pp. 53–79). St. Leonards, NSW: Allen & Unwin.
Kress, G. (2000). Multimodality. In B. Cope & M. Kalantzis (Eds.), *Multiliteracies: Literacy learning and the design of social futures* (pp. 182–202). London: Routledge.
Kress, G. (2003). *Literacy in the new media age.* London: Routledge.
Lankshear, C., & Knobel, M. (2003). *New literacies: Changing knowledge and classroom learning.* Buckingham: Open University Press.

Lotherington, H. (2001). A tale of four teachers: A study of an Australian late-entry content-based program in two Asian languages. *International Journal of Bilingual Education and Bilingualism, 4*(2), 97–106.

Lotherington, H. (2004a). What four skills? Redefining language and literacy skills in the digital era. *TESL Canada Journal, 22*(1), 64–78.

Lotherington, H. (2004b). Emergent metaliteracies: What the Xbox has to offer the EQAO. *Linguistics and Education, 14*(3–4), 305–319.

Lotherington, H., Morbey, M. L. Granger, C., & Doan, L. (2001). Tearing down the walls: New literacies and new horizons in the elementary school. In B. Barrell (Ed.), *Technology, teaching and learning: Issues in the integration of technology* (pp. 131–161). Calgary: Detselig.

Lotherington, H., & Xu, Yejun (2004) How to chat in English and Chinese: Emerging digital language conventions. *ReCALL, 16*(2), 308–329.

Luke, A., & Freebody, P. (1997). Shaping the social practices of reading. In S. Muspratt, A. Luke, & P. Freebody (Eds.), *Constructing critical literacies: Teaching and learning textual practice* (pp. 185–225). St. Leonards, NSW: Allen & Unwin.

Marchart, O. (1998). The east, the west and the rest: Central and Eastern Europe between techno-orientalism and the new electronic frontier. *Convergence, 4*(2), 56–75.

Martin-Jones, M., & Jones, K. (2000). Introduction: Multilingual literacies. In M. Martin-Jones & K. Jones (Eds.), *Multilingual literacies* (pp. 1–15). Amsterdam: John Benjamins.

McLuhan, M. (1964). *Understanding media: The extensions of man*. New York: McGraw-Hill.

Nettle, D., & Romaine, S. (2000). *Vanishing voices: The extinction of the world's languages*. Oxford: Oxford University Press.

Pennycook, A. (1995). English in the world/ The world in English. In J.W. Tollefson (Ed.), *Power and inequality in language education* (pp. 34–58). Cambridge: Cambridge University Press.

Phillipson, R., & Skutnabb-Kangas, T. (1999). Englishisation: One dimension of globalization. In D. Graddol & U. Meinhof (Eds.), *English in a changing world. AILA Review, 13*, 19–36.

Skutnabb-Kangas, T. (2000). *Linguistic genocide in education- or worldwide diversity and human rights*. Mahwah, N.J: Lawrence Erlbaum.

Street, B. (1984). *Literacy in theory and practice*. Cambridge: Cambridge University Press.

Street, B. (1995). *Social literacies: Critical approaches to literacy in development, ethnography and education*. London: Longman.

Street, B. (2000). Literacy events and literacy practices: Theory and practice in the New Literacy Studies. In M. Martin-Jones & K. Jones (Eds.), *Multilingual literacies* (pp. 17–29). Amsterdam: John Benjamins.

Sugimoto, T., & Levin, J. (2000). Multiple literacies and multimedia: A comparison of Japanese and American uses of the Internet. In G.E. Hawisher & C.L. Selfe (Eds.), *Global literacies and the world-wide web* (pp. 133–153). London: Routledge.

The New London Group (1996). A pedagogy of multiliteracies: Designing social factors. *Harvard Educational Review, 66* (1), 60–92.

Venezky, R. (1980). From Webster to Rice and Roosevelt: The formative years for spelling instruction and spelling reform in the U.S.A. In U. Frith (Ed.), *Cognitive processes in spelling* (pp. 9–30). New York: Academic Press.

Vincent, D. (2000). *The rise of mass literacy. Reading and writing in modern Europe*. Cambridge: Polity.

Warschauer, M. (1999). *Electronic literacies: Language, culture and power in online education*. Mahwah, NJ: Lawrence Erlbaum Associates.

Werry, C.C. (1996). Linguistic and interactional features of Internet relay chat. In S. Herring (Ed.), *Computer-mediated communication: Linguistic, social and cross-cultural perspectives*. Amsterdam/ Philadelphia: John Benjamins.

Zhenhua, H. (1999). The impact of globalization on English in Chinese universities. In D. Graddol & U. Meinhof (Eds.), *English in a changing world. AILA Review, 13*, 19–36.

CHAPTER 55

TECHNOLOGY AND WRITING

MARK WARSCHAUER

University of California, Irvine, USA

ABSTRACT

Information and communication technologies are having a profound affect on all aspects of language use, especially in written communication. The purposes of writing, the genres of written communication, and the nature of audience and author are all changing rapidly with the diffusion of computer-mediated communication, both for first and second language writers. This chapter reviews research on the relationship of new technologies to writing and discusses the implications of this research for English language learning and teaching. Issues addressed include the participatory dynamics and linguistic features of computer-assisted classroom discussion, the impact of e-mail exchanges on students' writing process, and the relationship of writing purpose to student outcomes in multimedia authoring. The chapter also addresses areas of debate and concern, such as whether the internet fosters plagiarism, and whether new forms of computer-mediated writing serve to complement and enhance more traditional forms of writing or detract from them. Finally, future trends in technology-intensive writing, such as the increased importance and nature of electronic literacy, are also discussed, as are the implications of these trends for teaching and research.

INTRODUCTION

The development and spread of the personal computer and the internet have brought the most significant changes in the technology of writing since the diffusion of the printing press. Changes in how and why people write are occurring so quickly that documentation is difficult, let alone analysis. Yet as difficult as such analysis is, it must be attempted if we are to understand the role that *computer-mediated communication* (CMC) can and should play in English language teaching, especially in the teaching and learning of writing.

This chapter looks at the relationship of CMC to English language writing. I will begin by reviewing research on classroom use of the main forms of CMC. I will then discuss current debates and concerns regarding the use of online communication in second language writing instruction. Finally, I will address future directions regarding research and practice of new technologies and the teaching of writing.

SUMMARY OF MAIN RESEARCH FINDINGS

CMC covers a wide range of technologies of writing. These include various forms of *synchronous* (or real-time) communication, such as that which takes place in instant messaging, on MOOs,[1] or via internet relay chat; *asynchronous* (or delayed) communication, such as that which takes place via e-mail or on Web-based bulletin boards; and *hypermedia* (multimedia, hypertextual) authoring, for example, through the creation and publication of World Wide Web pages. Each of these three types of

CMC, namely, synchronous, asynchronous, and hypermedia, has a corresponding use that is most popular in the writing classroom. These are computer-assisted classroom discussion (synchronous), e-mail exchanges (asynchronous), and Web page creation (hypermedia).

Computer-Assisted Classroom Discussion [2]

Computer-assisted classroom discussion (CACD) refers to synchronous computer-mediated interaction that takes place among students, with or without the instructor, in a single classroom. Though there are many possible interfaces for this type of discussion, most of the published research on CACD has involved the use of a commercial software program called *Daedalus Interchange* (Daedalus Inc., 1989). The program features a split screen interface, which encourages students to write long sentences or full paragraphs, as opposed to the typical interface of chat rooms and MOOs that instead privilege rapid-fire abbreviated comments.

CACD became popular in the English composition classroom in the 1980s, due to several purported benefits. Instructors reported that control of discussion shifted decisively in the direction of the students, as students could speak to each other without having to wait for the teachers' permission (Balester, Halasek, & Peterson, 1992; Barker & Kemp, 1990; Faigley, 1990). They claimed that this fostered student discussion and promoted cooperative relationships among students (Langston & Batson, 1990). Students reportedly become better writers by having an authentic audience and a purpose for their writing (Peyton, 1990) as well as more time on task. Electronic discussion allegedly encouraged a communal process of knowledge making (Barker & Kemp, 1990) and a critical awareness about how communication, or miscommunication, occurs (DiMatteo, 1991).

Research on CACD in the second language classroom has focused on several aspects. These include the amount of student participation, the linguistic characteristics of interaction, and the impact of CACD use on students' writing. Several studies included quantitative measures to evaluate the amount of student participation and compare it to face-to-face-discussions (Chun, 1994; Kelm, 1992; Kern, 1995; Sullivan & Pratt, 1996; Warschauer, 1996a). All studies found a greater amount of student participation in three measures-percentage of student talk vs. teacher talk, directional focus of student talk (toward other students or toward the teacher), and equality of student participation. Specifically, the total amount of student participation in electronic discourses ranged from 85% to 92% (85% in Sullivan and Pratt; 86% and 88% in two classes studies by Kern; and 92% in Kelm). In face-to-face discourse, student participation ranged from 35% (Sullivan & Pratt) to 37% (one class in Kern) to 60% (the second class in Kern).

Sullivan and Pratt (1996) found that 100% of the students participated in electronic discourse and only 50% in the face-to-face discussion. Kern (1996) and Kelm (1992) similarly found that some students said nothing face-to-face, while all participated online. Warschauer (1996a), in an experimental study comparing small group discussion online or face-to-face, found that the online groups were twice as balanced, principally because the most silent students increased their participation many-fold online. As for directional focus of comments, Chun (1994) found that 88% of student comments and questions online were directed to each other. Kern (1995) found in one class that 232 online comments were directed to specific students, whereas only one face-to-face comment was similarly directed.

This data suggests important directions toward the possibilities of promoting collaborative learning in the classroom. One of the main obstacles toward achieving a collaborative classroom is the teacher-centered nature of discussion, with classroom discourse dominated by the ubiquitous *IRF* sequence of an *initiating* move by the teacher, a *responding* move by a student, and a *follow-up* move by the teacher (Mehan, 1985).[3] While electronic discussion is certainly not the only way to break this pattern, it does appear to be a very effective way. Warschauer (1999, 2002a) conducted ethnographic research of students in an ESL composition course that used CACD extensively throughout the semester. The study found that the student-directed nature of the discussion—which contrasted greatly with the face-to-face discussions in the classroom, almost all of which were dominated by the teacher—allowed students to explore and develop their opinions on important topics related to second language writing, such as the nature of plagiarism and the value of networking with professors and fellow students.

Other studies have investigated the linguistic characteristics of students' discourse in CACD, comparing it to face-to-face interaction. Research has shown that students in CACD use language that is lexically and syntactically more complex than in face-to-face interaction (Warschauer, 1996a) and covers a wide range of communicative and discourse functions (Chun, 1994; Kern, 1995). The types of sentences they use required not only comprehension of the preceding discourse but also coherent thought and use of cohesive linguistic references and expressions (Chun, 1994). One instructor noted a significant improvement in the depth and strength of student arguments following online collaborative discussion (Kern, 1995). Based on her study, Chun claims that electronic discussion appears to be a good bridge between writing and speaking skills, with the strengths of each domain apparently helping the other.

Finally, at least one report (Kelm, 1992) indicated that synchronous communication can also be a useful tool for developing students' linguistic accuracy. Kelm, in a university intermediate Portuguese course, used students' own computer-mediated messages as a basis for review of particular grammatical points and noted an 80% reduction in certain grammatical errors (e.g., incorrect usages of gerunds and progressives) following this review. This type of post-hoc analysis is difficult for oral communication, which is generally not recorded and thus is less accessible for later review.

Two studies have attempted to analyze student's writing performance as a result of having participated in online discussions. Sullivan and Pratt (1996), comparing one ESL writing class using online discussion and one ESL writing class not using it, found a significant advantage for the online discussion course in writing improvement (using holistically scored essays) over the course of the semester. However, the results are questionable, both due to the small size of the sample (i.e., two classes) and also because of the unusual finding that the non-computer class actually decreased in writing proficiency over the course of the semester. A second study, by Schultz (2000), compared the revisions that students made to their writing after having participated in peer feedback sessions via CACD as compared to via face-to-face communication. The study found that advanced language students made more detailed, local revisions after feedback via CACD, whereas they made more extensive, global revisions after feedback via face-to-face discussion. Students made the greatest number of revisions, and appeared to improve the papers the most, when they were able to combine peer feedback via both CACD and face-to-face discussion.

In summary, research on CACD supports the view that it can be an important component of the second language writing classroom, especially when judiciously combined with, rather than replacing, face-to-face discussion.

E-Mail Exchanges

Electronic mail, similarly to computer-assisted classroom discussion, has been a tool in both first-language and second-language education. It is used both for communication between teacher and student and for long-distance exchanges between students in different locations. In first-language studies, Hartman et al. (1991) found (a) that teachers using e-mail substantially increased their communication with students over time compared with teachers using traditional modes (face-to-face, paper, and phone); (b) that teachers using e-mail interacted substantially with lower-performing students compared with teachers using traditional modes who interacted overwhelmingly more with higher-performing students; (c) that students in computer networked sections communicated more with each other than did students in non-networked sections; (d) that students with lower SAT verbal scores made use of e-mail most frequently; and (e) that writing anxiety limited participation less in e-mail than it did in traditional modes. Mabrito (1991, 1992) found that that high-apprehensive writers (a) contributed more equally to e-mail discussions than they did to face-to-face discussions, (b) made more text-specific comments in e-mail discussions than in face-to-face discussions (1991), (c) offered more ideas for revision during e-mail discussions than in face-to-face discussions (1992), (d) were influenced more by group comments received during e-mail discussions than during face-to-face discussions (1992), and (e) produced better papers after e-mail discussions than after face-to-face discussions (1992).

In second language learning, Wang (1993) compared the discourse of ESL students' dialogue journals written in both e-mail and traditional paper format. She found that the students using e-mail journals wrote greater amounts of text, asked more questions, and used different language functions more frequently than did students writing on paper.

St. John and Cash (1995) used linguistic analysis and learn reports to describe the learning process and results achieved by an adult learner of German who carried out a lengthy e-mail exchange with a native speaker. Their research found that the learner systematically studied the new vocabulary and grammatical structures in his incoming e-mail and used this information to improve his own letter writing, with dramatic results by the end of six months. The learner compared the results he achieved via the e-mail exchange to what he was getting out of a language course taken simultaneously, and noted that in the language course there was no automatic record of classroom discourse that he could draw on and learn from.

Tella (1991, 1992a, 1992b) carried out an ethnographic study based on a semester-long series of e-mail exchanges between several high school classes in Finland and England. Tella's (1992b) well-documented study found that

1. Emphasis switched from teacher-centered, large-group sponsored teaching toward a more individualized and learner-centered working environment,

while the content of the class shifted from that of a standard syllabus to the students' own writings (Tella, 1992b).
2. The e-mail communication gave a good opportunity for practicing language in open-ended linguistic situations. A shift from form to content was achieved, a free flow of ideas—and with it expressions, idioms, and vocabulary (Tella, 1992b).
3. The whole writing process changed to some extent. Rather than writing their compositions only once, as is the norm, the Finnish students naturally edited and revised their compositions, poems, and other messages to make them appropriate for their English peers. Instead of writing most of their compositions and other work alone, they increasingly made use of peer tutoring and other collaborative methods in order to compose their e-mail messages together (Tella, 1992b).
4. The quality of writing improved as writing changed from teacher-sponsored and led that was only to be marked and graded, to real-purpose writing with genuine audiences around the world (Tella, 1992b).
5. The modes of writing became more versatile, including not only the narrative and descriptive genres usually found in regular class but also personal, expressive, and argumentative use of language (Tella, 1992b).
6. Reading also became more public and collaborative, with students actively assisting each other in studying incoming messages. Students also used different reading strategies to read the wide variety of messages, notices, and documents that came in.

Many of Tella's results were confirmed by Barson, Frommer, and Schwartz (1993), who carried out an action research study of a project-oriented e-mail exchange between language students at three universities. Their study found that students developed free and spontaneous communication using complex structures in the exchange, due in large part to the students' sense that the communication was real rather than pedagogical.

Cummins and Sayers (1995) provide eight portraits of e-mail exchanges between diverse groups of learners from around the world. These exchanges involve students of different languages (e.g., Spanish and English); different "abilities" (e.g., hearing and deaf); different ethnic groups (African-American, Mexican-American, and Afro-Caribbean); different life experiences (Croatian refugees and suburban and urban Americans); and different viewpoints (Palestinians and Israelis). They conclude that these projects have allowed students "to amplify literacy and intellectual skills collaboratively with peers in culturally and geographically distant settings" (p. 21). In their view, the key to the success of these projects includes the engagement of students and teachers in collaborative critical inquiry around issues of importance to students' lives.

A study by Kern (1996) further supports the idea that e-mail exchanges can bring broad benefits of cultural and historical knowledge as well as enhanced student motivation. Kern organized and investigated a French-English exchange between students in the United States and France based on e-mail communication and an exchange of essays on topics related to the immigrant experience. He noted the following:

> While ostensibly an exercise in communicative language use, this e-mail exchange has been at least as significant in enhancing students' cultural and historical awareness as well as their overall motivation in learning French. For example, in discussing "the French family" students are not restricted to studying textbook descriptions of fictional families—they learn about real families of various social backgrounds and traditions, living in different environments, each with their own particular perspective on the world. Students have expressed great satisfaction in learning about important historical events of which they had little or no previous knowledge, such as the Algerian war or the Armenian massacre of 1915. Many students have been pleasantly surprised to find that what they are learning in French class connects with what they are learning in their other courses in history, sociology, and anthropology. (p. 118)

The motivational benefits of e-mail communication were further explored by Warschauer (1996b), who carried out an international survey of 167 students in 12 university language classes in three countries. The survey found that three factors explained students' heightened motivation due to participation in e-mail exchanges: their enjoyment of international communication, their sense of empowerment (and possible career benefit) due to the development of new technological skills, and their belief that communication via e-mail assisted their language learning. The study also found that these benefits were heightened in courses in which the e-mail exchanges were well integrated into the overall goals and structure of the course, rather than included as a marginal add-on to course activities.

WEB-PAGE AUTHORING

The development and publication of World Wide Web pages represents a qualitatively different type of computer-mediated communication. Unlike the previous two categories, Web page authoring does not feature a type of direct interaction between pairs or a group of interlocutors. Rather, it represents a type of writing (or, more correctly, multimedia authoring) for publication to a broad public audience.

Most of the writing about language learners' Web page creation has been anecdotal or descriptive in nature (see, for example, Barson & Debski, 1996; Shetzer & Warschauer, 2001). The most in-depth research on Web page authoring in the second language classroom was conducted by Warschauer (1999, 2000). His two-year ethnographic study focused on three classes that made extensive use of Web page authoring, including a university graduate ESL writing course, a university writing-intensive Hawaiian language course, and an English composition course at a community college (in which two-thirds of the students were second language speakers of English). The processes and results in the three courses varied dramatically. Warschauer (2000) interpreted this variation according to four factors related to the purposefulness of the writing: (a) whether students understood the purpose, (b) whether students found the purpose socially or culturally relevant, (c) whether the electronic medium was appropriate for achieving the purpose, and (d) whether students were encouraged and enabled to use medium-appropriate rhetorical features to fulfill the purpose.

In the first class, students designed professional home pages that were meant to highlight their academic accomplishments and research interests. However, since most of the students were first-year master's students, they had few academic accomplishments and were unclear about their research direction. They thus failed to grasp the purpose of the assignment and put little time and effort into it, with correspondingly poor results. In the second class, students worked together to develop a class Website with links to their individual pages based on research projects related to the life and history of the Hawaiian people. The students found the assignment highly relevant and important to their own community; they were also allowed and encouraged to develop multimedia works of art, rather than merely cutting and pasting their essays from a word processor onto the Web. The students put a great deal of time and effort into all aspects of the assignments—both in terms of text development and broader artistic design—and appeared to benefit greatly from it. In the third class, students developed English-language Websites and other multimedia products (such as brochures) for local community organizations in a service learning assignment. In this case, the value of the assignment varied greatly from group to group, and depended largely on whether students felt the purpose was authentic (i.e., if they sensed that the local organization was actually going to use the product).

Few other studies have been carried out on Web page authoring in the language classroom, though Lam (2000) has carried out a very interesting investigation into an ESL student's production of a Website outside the classroom. In her study, she analyzed the in-class and out-of-class English writing experiences of a Chinese immigrant to the United States. Though he was struggling with academic English in school, he was quite a proficient user of English on the internet, having produced his own English-language Website about Japanese pop music and communicating about it with people around the world via e-mail. Lam's study highlights the wide variety of genres that online writing includes as well as the new forms of hybrid identity that are emerging in the era of electronic communication.

CURRENT DEBATES AND CONCERNS

Much of the debate and concern around the use of online communications in the English language classroom focuses on the ways in which writing changes in the electronic realm, and whether these changes are beneficial or harmful to the teaching of writing. Three particular concerns have been raised about online writing: (a) that it is informal, (b) that it is graphic (rather than text) dominant, and (c) that it facilitates plagiarism.

A number of works have analyzed the style, genre, and special features of computer-mediated texts, comparing them to other forms of writing, as well as oral communication (Collot & Belmore, 1996; Crystal, 2001; Moran & Hawisher, 1998; Yates, 1996). Some of the features that are common in many electronic texts pointed out by Crystal include the use of repeated letters (*aaaaaahhhhh, ooooops*) or punctuation marks (*hey!!!!!, no more!!!!!*) for a prosodic affect; the use of all capitals (I SAID SO), extra spacing (*w h y n o t ? ?*), or asterisks (*the *real* effect*) for emphasis; the use of emoticons, or *smileys*, to convey a feeling (*:-), :-(*); the use of special abbreviations or acronyms (*lol* for *laughing out loud*, *tafn* for *that's all for now*); reduced use of capitalization or punctuation (*an excerpt from a tommy cooper forward i got*); and abbreviated and informal language (*where r ya from?*).

However, as Moran and Hawisher (1998) point out, computer-mediated communication includes a wide variety of more formal and informal styles and genres, just as other forms of writing (think of anything from a shopping list to a formal essay) and speech (anything from a chat with a friend to a public speech). Just because many forms of CMC are informal, more formal genres can be chosen for classroom use, when appropriate. For example, students can interact by CACD or e-mail in an informal conversational voice, but then collaborate together to write and publish an electronic journal, magazine, or newspaper on the Web.

A related concern of many educators is that online communication is dominated by graphics rather than texts and that students that produce multimedia will get distracted from writing and instead waste a great amount of time on perfecting fonts, colors, or images (Halio, 1990). Classroom research (e.g., Warschauer, 1999) indicates that students largely respond in this regard to the expectations set by the instructor. Teachers that set up assignments demanding a product that includes both sophisticated writing and a highly professional look are more likely to achieve both. In contrast, to overemphasize the design of a Website can result in students paying little attention to texts, whereas to underemphasize design issues can limit students' opportunities to develop important new multimedia literacies.

Finally, there is little doubt that the rapid diffusion and growth of the internet facilitates students' plagiarism by making available millions of texts around the world for easy cutting and pasting, many of them commercially provided and tailored to high school and college students' needs. Online plagiarism takes a variety of forms from the blatant and intentional (e.g., purchasing an essay online) to the accidental and ill-informed (e.g., quoting small amounts of online material without proper citation; see discussion in Burbules & Casllister, 2000). However, the internet also provides instructors the opportunities to check for plagiarism, either informally through search engines or through special commercial antiplagiarism sites (Hafner, 2001). And Internet-based discussion can even be an excellent realm for exploring students' ideas about plagiarism (Warschauer, 1999). As Pennycook (1996) points out, plagiarism for second language learners is a complex and challenging issue; at the same time that they are encouraged to improve their language through modeling and copying the words of others, they are prohibited from doing so in certain instances. The new challenges of plagiarism in the online era can provide instructors with a valuable opportunity to address this issue head on in the classroom, and thus to help students advance their understanding of the nature of academic research and writing.

FUTURE DIRECTIONS

The nature of writing can be expected to continue changing in coming decades, as new forms of audiovisual communication complement or challenge the importance of the written word in a variety of realms. Because of these changes, many university English departments are altering their curricula and even their names in order to better reflect the nature of communication in today's world (Flynn, 1997). In the future, computers will be used in the English language classroom not to teach the same types of writing as before in a new way, but rather to teach the new types of writing that are emerging in the online era. The special characteristics of text production and interpretation in computer-mediated realms has been referred to as *electronic literacy*, which, according to Warschauer (2002b), includes four main components: (a) *computer literacy,* comfort and fluency in using hardware and software; (b) *information literacy,* the ability to find, analyze, and critique information available online; (c) *multimedia literacy*, the ability to interpret and produce documents combining texts, sounds, graphics, and video; and (d) *computer-mediated communication literacy*, the mastery of the pragmatics of synchronous and asynchronous CMC. Shetzer and Warschauer (2000) discuss a strategic approach toward the promotion of electronic literacy through an emphasis on communication, construction, research, and autonomous learning (see also Warschauer, Shetzer, & Meloni, 2000).

The continued growth of electronic communication for writing will likely change the nature of second language learning research as well. The archived and easily searchable nature of electronic texts will allow for far more sophisticated forms of linguistic and corpus analyses, including comparisons of L1 and L2 writing, developmental comparisons among groups of L2 learners, and comparisons among different categories of L2 learners (e.g., from different countries, or taught through different instructional methods).

Finally, the expanded use of *automated writing evaluation* software will likely have a major impact on second language writing instruction, assessment, and research. Software engines developed by Educational Testing Service, Vantage Learning, and other companies can now provide almost instantaneous holistic scoring of essays, as well as feedback on a number of mechanical, stylistic, and organizational features (see discussion in Warschauer & Ware, 2006). These engines are already being used to score standardized tests and have recently been incorporated into commercial online services designed for classroom instruction.

In summary, the digital era has just begun. As online communication continues to develop and expand, it will pose challenges not only to how we teach writing, but also to how we conceptualize writing and its role in education and society.

NOTES

[1] Technically, Multi-user Object Oriented. MOOs refer to a type of text-based virtual reality that allows interpersonal interaction and the development and exploration of objects and spaces.

[2] This section and the following draw in part on my previous discussion of these topics in Warschauer, 1997.

[3] Also referred to as IRE: initiation, response, and evaluation.

REFERENCES

Balester, V., Halasek, K., & Peterson, N. (1992). Sharing authority: Collaborative teaching in a computer-based writing course. *Computers and Composition, 9*(3), 25–39.

Barker, T., & Kemp, F. (1990). Network theory: A postmodern pedagogy for the written classroom. In C. Handa (Ed.), Computers and community: Teaching composition in the twenty-first century (pp. 1–27). Portsmouth, NH: Heinemann.

Barson, J., & Debski, R. (1996). Calling back CALL: Technology in the service of foreign language learning based on creativity, contingency and goal-oriented activity. In M. Warschauer (Ed.), *Telecollaboration in foreign language learning* (pp. 49–68). Honolulu, HI: University of Hawai'i Second Language Teaching and Curriculum Center.

Barson, J., Frommer, J., & Schwartz, M. (1993). Foreign language learning using e-mail in a task-oriented perspective: Interuniversity experiments in communication and collaboration. *Journal of Science Education and Technology, 4*(2), 565–584.

Burbules, N. C., & Casllister, T. A. J. (2000). *Watch IT: The risks and promises of information technologies for education.* Boulder, CO: Westview Press.

Chun, D. (1994). Using computer networking to facilitate the acquisition of interactive competence. *System, 22*(1), 17–31.

Collot, M., & Belmore, N. (1996). Electronic language: A new variety of English. In S. C. Herring (Ed.), *Computer-mediated communication: Linguistic, social, and cross-cultural perspectives* (pp. 13–28). Amsterdam: Benjamins.

Crystal, D. (2001). *Language and the Internet.* Cambridge: Cambridge University Press.

Cummins, J., & Sayers, D. (1995). *Brave new schools: Challenging cultural illiteracy through global learning networks*. New York: St. Martin's Press.

Daedalus Inc. (1989). *Daedalus Integrated Writing Environment*. Austin, TX: The Daedalus Group.

DiMatteo, A. (1991). Communication, writing, learning: An anti-instrumentalist view of network writing. *Computers and Composition, 8*(3), 5–19.

Faigley, L. (1990). Subverting the electronic workbook: Teaching writing using networked computers. In D. Baker & M. Monenberg (Eds.), *The writing teacher as researcher: Essays in the theory and practice of class-based research* (pp. 290–311). Portsmouth, NH: Heinemann.

Flynn, L. J. (1997, November 9). College English departments embracing cyber-studies. *New York Times*. Retrieved February 20, 2002, from the World Wide Web: http://www.nytimes.com/library/cyber/week/110997georgia.html.

Hafner, K. (2001, June 28). Lessons in Internet plagiarism. *New York Times*. Retrieved February 20, 2002, from the World Wide Web: http://www.nytimes.com/2001/06/28/technology/28CHEA.html.

Halio, M. P. (1990). Student writing: Can the machine main the message. *Academic Computing, 4*, 16–19, 45.

Hartman, K., Neuwirth, C., Kiesler, S., Sproull, L., Cochran, C., Palmquist, M., & Zubrow, D. (1991). Patterns of social interaction and learning to write: Some effects of networked technologies. *Written Communication, 8*(1), 79–113.

Kelm, O. (1992). The use of synchronous computer networks in second language instruction: A preliminary report. *Foreign Language Annals, 25*(5), 441–454.

Kern, R. (1995). Restructuring classroom interaction with networked computers: Effects on quantity and quality of language production. *Modern Language Journal, 79*(4), 457–476.

Kern, R. (1996). Computer-mediated communication: Using e-mail exchanges to explore personal histories in two cultures. In M. Warschauer (Ed.), *Telecollaboration in foreign language learning* (pp. 105–119). Honolulu, HI: University of Hawai'i Second Language Teaching and Curriculum Center.

Lam, E. (2000). Second language literacy and the design of the self: A case study of a teenager writing on the Internet. *TESOL Quarterly, 34*, 457–482.

Langston, M. D., & Batson, T. (1990). The social shifts invited by working collaboratively on computer networks: The ENFI project. In C. Handa (Ed.), *Computers and community: Teaching composition in the twenty-first century* (pp. 149–159). Portsmouth, NH: Boynton/Cook.

Mabrito, M. (1991). Electronic mail as a vehicle for peer response: Conversations of high- and low-apprehensive writers. *Written Communication, 8*(4), 509–532.

Mabrito, M. (1992). Computer-mediated communication and high-apprehensive writers: Rethinking the collaborative process. *The Bulletin* (December), 26–30.

Mehan, H. (1985). The structure of classroom discourse. In T. A. van Dijk (Ed.), *Handbook of discourse analysis* (pp. 120–131). London: Academic Press.

Moran, C., & Hawisher, G. E. (1998). The rhetorics and languages of electronic mail. In I. Snyder (Ed.), *Page to screen: Taking literacy into the electronic era* (pp. 80–101). London: Routledge.

Pennycook, A. (1996). Borrowing others' words: Text, ownership, memory, and plagiarism. *TESOL Quarterly, 30*(2), 201–230.

Peyton, J. K. (1990). Technological innovation meets institution: Birth of creativity or murder of a great idea? *Computers and Composition, 7* (Special Issue), 15–32.

Schultz, J. (2000). Computers and collaborative writing in the foreign language curriculum. In M. Warschauer & R. Kern (Eds.), *Network-Based Language Teaching: Concepts and Practice*. New York: Cambridge University Press.

Shetzer, H., & Warschauer, M. (2000). An electronic literacy approach to network-based language teaching. In M. Warschauer & R. Kern (Eds.), *Network-based language teaching: Concepts and practice* (pp. 171–185). New York: Cambridge University Press.

Shetzer, H., & Warschauer, M. (2001). English through Web page creation. In J. Murphy & P. Byrd (Eds.), *Understanding the courses we teach: Local perspectives on English language teaching*. Ann Arbor, MI: University of Michigan Press.

St. John, E., & Cash, D. (1995). Language learning via e-mail: Demonstrable success with German. In M. Warschauer (Ed.), *Virtual connections: Online activities and projects for networking language learners* (pp. 191–197). Honolulu, HI: University of Hawai'i, Second Language Teaching and Curriculum Center.

Sullivan, N., & Pratt, E. (1996). A comparative study of two ESL writing environments: A computer-assisted classroom and a traditional oral classroom. *System, 24*(4), 491–501.

Tella, S. (1991). *Introducing international communications networks and electronic mail into foreign language classrooms* (Research report 95). Helsinki: Department of Teacher Education, University of Helsinki.

Tella, S. (1992a). *Boys, girls and e-mail: A case study in Finnish senior secondary schools.* (Research report 110). Helsinki: Department of Teacher Education, University of Helsinki.

Tella, S. (1992b). *Talking shop via e-mail: A thematic and linguistic analysis of electronic mail communication.* (Research report 99). Helsinki: Department of Teacher Education, University of Helsinki.

Wang, Y. M. (1993). *E-mail dialogue journaling in an ESL reading and writing classroom.* Unpublished Ph.D. dissertation, University of Oregon at Eugene.

Ware, P., & Warschauer, M. (2006). Electronic feedback and second language writing. In K. Hyland & F. Hyland (Eds.), *Feedback on ESL writing: Contexts and issues* (pp. 157–180). New York: Cambridge University Press.

Warschauer, M. (1996a). Comparing face-to-face and electronic communication in the second language classroom. *CALICO Journal, 13*(2), 7–26.

Warschauer, M. (1996b). Motivational aspects of using computers for writing and communication. In M. Warschauer (Ed.), *Telecollaboration in foreign language learning* (pp. 29–46). Honolulu, HI: University of Hawaii, Second Language Teaching and Curriculum Center.

Warschauer, M. (1999). Electronic literacies: Language, culture, and power in online education. Mahwah, NJ: Lawrence Erlbaum Associates.

Warschauer, M. (2000). Online learning in second language classrooms: An ethnographic study. In M. Warschauer & R. Kern (Eds.), Network-based language teaching: Concepts and practice (pp. 41–58). New York: Cambridge University Press.

Warschauer, M. (2002a). Networking into academic discourse. *Journal of English for Academic Purposes, 1*(1), 45–58.

Warschauer, M. (2002b). *Technology and social inclusion: Rethinking the digital divide.* Cambridge, MA: MIT Press.

Warschauer, M., Shetzer, H., & Meloni, C. (2000). *Internet for English Teaching.* Alexandria, VA: TESOL Publications.

Warschauer, M. & Ware, P. (2006). Automated writing evaluation: Defining the classroom research agenda. *Language Teaching Research*, 157–180.

Yates, S. J. (1996). Oral and written linguistic aspects of computer conferencing: A corpus-based study. In S. C. Herring (Ed.), *Computer-mediated communication: Linguistic, social and cross-cultural perspectives* (pp. 29–46). Amsterdam: John Benjamins.

CHAPTER 56

MULTIMODAL PEDAGOGIES, REPRESENTATION AND IDENTITY: PERSPECTIVES FROM POST-APARTHEID SOUTH AFRICA

PIPPA STEIN AND DENISE NEWFIELD

University of the Witwatersrand, South Africa

ABSTRACT

Since 1994 South Africa has been transformed from an isolated, apartheid state into an Afro-modernist democracy linked to the rest of the world. Our chapter locates itself within this post-apartheid historical moment and reports on the findings of an ELT teacher research group, the Wits Multiliteracies Research Group that has focused, since 1996, on the applicability of *multimodal pedagogies* to multilingual, multicultural classrooms in Johannesburg (Cope and Kalantzis 2000; Kress and van Leeuwen 1996, 2001). Multimodal pedagogies work across semiotic modes, including the visual, written and spoken language, the gestural, the sonic, and the performative. In South Africa, writing culture is underdeveloped, except in educational institutions where success is unattainable without access to written language skills in English. Our research in early childhood, secondary, and tertiary classrooms reports on the limits and possibilities afforded through the use of different *representational resources* in the representation of meaning, suggesting that multimodal pedagogies can broaden the base for representation by opening up the third ground in the struggle between mainstream schooling literacy demands and cultural difference. In their multiple configurations, such pedagogies have the power to unleash creativity, intelligence, and agency through the creation of symbolic identity objects and practices that lead to creative rapprochements in a society struggling to heal itself after a painful, traumatic past.

INTRODUCTION

Since 1994, South Africa has been transformed from an isolated, apartheid state into an Afro-modernist democracy linked to the rest of the world. During this period, South Africans have been engaged in various forms of nation-building and identity-quests in which the past is being constantly brought into perspective in "a drama of self-definition" (Jacobs, 1992, p. 73). This chapter locates itself within this post-apartheid historical moment and reports on the findings of an ELT teacher-research group, the Wits Multiliteracies Research Group, which has focused since 1996 on the applicability of what we call "multimodal pedagogies" to multilingual, diverse classrooms in Johannesburg. Through the use of such pedagogies, we explore issues of identity, representation, and pedagogy in the English classroom.

Multimodality or *multimodal discourse* is a relatively new focus of research in social semiotics and allied forms of linguistics (Hodge & Kress, 1988; Kress, 1997; Kress and van Leeuwen, 1996, 2001; Lemke, 2000; van Leeuwen, 1999). Social semiotics arises out of Halliday's (1985) social theory of language, which conceptualizes meaning as choice from a network of interlocking options. The concept of meaning as choice is extended by theorists working in multimodal communication to modes other than language. A *mode* is defined as a semiotically articulated means of representation and communication that has materiality and particular conventions that have been socially and culturally produced over time, for example, images or gesture. Each mode has its own grammar, which is being constantly reshaped by human beings according to their cognitive and affective interests in social contexts of use. Thus, concepts of choice and change through human agency are at the heart of this model of representation (Kress in Cope and Kalantzis 2000; Kress and van Leeuwen 2001).

FROM LANGUAGE TO MODE

The term *multimodal pedagogies* signals a paradigm shift in relation to forms of representation and meaning making in classrooms. In broad terms, it reconceptualizes communication in the contemporary classroom beyond the linguistic, locating language as one mode of communication amongst multiple semiotic modes, all of which function to communicate meanings in an integrated, multilayered way. Until recently, those interested in education have focused on teaching and learning as mainly mediated through the linguistic mode. However, there has been a growing interest in studying the ways in which teachers and learners draw on a much fuller repertoire of representational resources to communicate their meanings: for example, how language, action, and visual images interact to produce meaning; how knowledge is transformed across different modes; how learners use different modes differently; and the potentialities and limitations of specific modes (Kress, Jewitt, Ogborn, & Tsatsarelis, 2001). Thus, the fundamental paradigm shift is from a focus on *language* to a focus on *mode* and the linguistic mode is seen relationally as one option within multiple options for communication.

In the paradigm shift from language to mode, pedagogy is conceptualized as a multiple semiotic activity in which teachers and learners make selections from the representational resources available to them to represent their meanings within the context of communicative practices. Central to this reconceptualization is the idea of learning as transformation and meaning making as 'design'. The concept of designing and redesigning the available designs comes from the New London Group's Multiliteracies Project (Cope & Kalantzis, 2000), which explores multimodal communication in relation to the changing communication landscape, multicultural diversity, and globalization. In the redesigning of available semiotic resources, meaning making is constantly in flux as learners make signs in response to other signs in a never-ending relation of initiation and responsiveness, arising out of their interests in the social context of power in which the meanings are being made. In this theory, human beings are positioned as active and creative makers of signs. Representation in classrooms is semiotically determined by the available representational resources that are redesigned by teachers and learners in relation to their cognitive, affective, and social interests. In this redefining of the pedagogical environment as resource-based, the nature of the resources available, the constraints and possibilities operating around the use of such resources, the degree of access to such resources by learners and teachers, and the assessment of learners' use of available resources are fundamental issues in an analysis of the effects of such pedagogies on learners.

Our particular perspective on multimodal pedagogies has developed in response to our location in southern Africa. We have been concerned that mainstream pedagogies in schools and universities in South Africa define learning within very narrow bands; successful learning is ultimately measured in terms of proficiency in standard written English. South Africa is a multilingual country with 11 official languages and a huge diversity across race, cultures, and histories. The majority of learners speak English as an additional language (EAL) and come from communities where predominantly oral and visual forms of communication and media (radio and television) thrive and where literacy levels, in the sense of competence in reading and writing, are low.

Central to our work in multimodal pedagogies is the repositioning of identity, language, creativity, history, and memory within an authentic social context of learning in which multiple modes of representation (including the visual, written, and spoken language, the gestural, sound, and action), rather than language alone, become the matrix through which meanings are made (Newfield, Andrew, Maungedzo and Stein 2003; Stein and Newfield 2004). Multimodal pedagogies redefine the semiotic space in classrooms by shifting the narrow focus on written language to explorations of multiple semiotic worlds of meaning. This pedagogy is radical in the sense that it reshapes what the language and literacy classroom looks like. The notion of a self-contained language and literacy classroom disappears and what emerges is something more like *a multimodal classroom* in which different modes are explored for their potentialities and limitations in relation to specific contexts of meaning. We argue that through their capacity to open up the space for the investigation of alternative semiotic worlds of meaning making, multimodal pedagogies broaden the base for representation in classrooms. We call this potential for freeing up of semiotic zones a form of opening up the "third ground" in the struggle between mainstream schooling and cultural difference. In their multiple configurations, such pedagogies have the power to produce learning through the unleashing of creativity, intelligence, and agency. From a social justice and equity perspective, such pedagogies can lead to creative rapprochements in a society like South Africa, which is struggling to heal itself after a painful, traumatic past.

THE BODY AS MULTIMODAL SIGN

Multimodal pedagogies are concerned with the use and transformation of modes of communication in classrooms. Modes are produced in and by the body, for example, gesture, speech and writing. The body is the articulation of meaning; simultaneously a multimodal sign as well as a site of multimodal resources for making meaning. Multimodal pedagogies view the relations between body, cognition, and affect as integrated rather than split. The diverse ways in which individuals and communities engage with different forms of materiality and the sensory in the representation of their meanings are shaped by culture, history, memory, gender, class, and affect.

Bodies are repositories of knowledge, but these knowledges are not always knowable in and through language: they can be sensed, felt, performed, imagined, imaged, or dreamed. Language itself as a mode of communication is subject to constraints around what is unthinkable and unsayable within the context of existing cultural forms. If teaching for diversity is an acknowledgement of difference, then what is the relation between language and experience that a culture has evolved? We argue that the choice of mode of communication in areas of social tension and taboos can be motivated by the constraints and possibilities operating within the dominant culture. For example, the silences around HIV/AIDS, rape, and sexual abuse in South Africa is an ongoing site of contestation between the government and HIV/AIDS activists.

Theories of multimodality claim that each mode of communication has its own distinct materialities, structures, affordances, and constraints (Kress & Van Leeuwen, 2001). In the same way that images or gestures have the potential to do certain kinds of work and not others, so language alone is limited in its capacity to express the full range of human experience. As a group of literature students said to their teacher in one of our case studies reported in the next section, "Sir, we struggle to describe Maru through words. Just have a look at our drawing. It says it all"[1]. The same learners, deeply moved by an extract in the novel, *Maru*, by Bessie Head showing xenophobia and racial prejudice, asked their teacher if they could respond to the text by singing songs, because "when they are sad, depressed or down, they sings songs to ease their pain or sorrow. They simply cannot talk." In this example, learners used multimodality in the integration of language, gesture, and sound to give expression to their cognitive and affective interests.

In language and literacy classrooms, words in their multiple realizations are the focus of study and the means through which communication is achieved. In this logocentric context, an uncritical relation exists between words and authentic communication. Communicative language teaching is built on notions of communicative competence in which talk and volubility are central to how teachers measure this competence. We argue that cultural and social differences exist in the relations between language and authentic communication: A focus on language alone can restrict learners from using the range of representational resources available to them in the expression of their authentic meanings.

We acknowledge that the points we have made regarding the limits of language are a fundamental challenge to our work as language and literacy teachers. Language teachers may argue that their aim is to develop learners' linguistic skills and the work of Arts teachers to develop their visual and body language (Brenner & Andrews, 2001). We are not saying that language does not matter; we believe that is it is central to what we do. What we are saying, however, is that we do not view these skills as discrete categories. In cultural contexts outside the classroom domain, language and music, for example, are so bound up together in the expression of longing or pain, that separating the two modes is an artificial wrenching apart of a completely evolved cultural form of meaning making. In the same way, it is obvious that designing a web page nowadays cannot be de-linked from questions of design, visual aesthetics, language, and space.

Our work in multimodal pedagogies has focused on exploring the effects of implementing multimodal pedagogies at different levels with multilingual learners in diverse classrooms (Stein & Newfield, 2004). On the basis of our classroom-based research, we claim that multimodal pedagogies unleash creativity and agency in learners and teachers in unexpected ways, recontextualize the representation of learners' identities, reframe concepts and practices of existing curricula, foreground issues of equity and value in relation to assessment practices, and open up the third ground in the struggle between mainstream language and literacy practices and cultural difference.

We present two case studies from different Johannesburg classroom contexts and levels to provide evidence for the above claims.

THE OLIFANTSVLEI FRESH STORIES PROJECT

This case reports on an early years project in narrative that worked systematically across visual and three-dimensional modes, spoken and written language, and multimodal performance. The aim was to produce a body of fresh stories, as distinct from traditional folkloric stories, with a Grade 1 and 2 class of multilingual African children attending the Olifantsvlei Primary School on the outskirts of Johannesburg. The children all live in the surrounding informal settlement communities, popularly known as *squatter camps*. Many of them come from single parent, female-headed households with very few material resources. In this project children were asked by their teachers, Ntsoaki Senja and Tshidi Mamabolo, to invent fresh stories rooted in and arising out of their social worlds. As a stimulus to the creative process, children were asked to think of someone in their neighborhood who interested them. This was followed by improvisational activities in which they acted out how this person walked, talked, ate food, and behaved in the world. They then drew these characters on paper. In preparation for making the same characters as three dimensional figures, the teachers decided to make papiér maché but it turned into what the children called "a kind of porridge!" The children turned to their teachers and said, "Don't worry, we'll make our own figures." Over the next few days, the children brought in from their homes an extraordinary collection of doll-like figures which they had constructed from the resources available to them in their environments: various forms of waste material like plastic bags in different colors, Coke bottles filled with stones and sand, pieces of discarded dishcloth, cardboard, wire, buttons, and old stockings. A 7-year-old African girl from the Grade 2 class who lives in a shack next to a rubbish dump on the outskirts of the city, made a doll out of a glass Coke bottle (its body), bubble wrap (its flowing clothes) and a discarded plastic bag (its head and scarf or *doek*). That which cannot be eaten on the dump can be fashioned into a doll. Another doll has a body made from a plastic Coke bottle, around which has been delicately and artfully woven an old stocking. Her arms are sticks and her breasts are stones.

Most of these doll-like figures are transformed traditional child figure objects in which the children have drawn on materials and designs which are part of African fertility doll making culture. These fertility dolls or child figures produced in the Southern African region are usually small, anthropomorphic figures fabricated by women, for young girls and women. Such dolls have specific cultural, symbolic and identity functions relating to women's fertility, puberty, and marriage rituals. As pointed out by Nel and Leibhammer (1998), their symbolism in form and materials is talisman-like, suggestive, and affective. Traditionally, such dolls are cylindrical or conical in shape, made from available materials such as gourds and tins that are filled with powders and seeds, then wrapped in cloth and adorned with glass beads, safety pins, leather, and metal. Many of these materials appear ordinary but their iconic visual power is linked to the human body, its potential for fertility, and the male and female principle (the cloth—female—which is woven around the conical phallic centre). Thus, the child figures become metaphors for the procreative act.

The children's doll-like figures demonstrate how they had at their disposal, through their families, histories, cultural memories, and available people in the community, a range of representational resources for constructing these figures (the available designs), within an urban informal settlement, and how they had redesigned these figures for a new context; that is, to make three dimensional characters for a story to be told at school. Both materially and in form, their doll figures demonstrate conscious, motivated choices by their makers around the use of texture, shape, cloth, color, and adornments each of which has mythical, social, and symbolic significance bound to particular life processes and social codes of behavior. These three dimensional figures illustrate the hybridity and fluidity of contemporary urban cultural life and the degree to which cultural and generic transformation have taken place at multiple levels. At the level of making, it is traditionally women who make such dolls but in this project, boys participated in the making of their own dolls. The traditional boundaries around what constitutes fertility dolls within ethnic and gender classifications have collapsed, and what we witness in this process is the redesigning of the traditional, in all its multiplicity of forms and materiality, into contemporary dolls using available contextual materials. These doll figures illustrate how individuals have many layers of representational resources available to them, not only from one culture, but from many cultures. This children's process of remaking is not reproductive but innovative and transformative both of the objects, which are extending the grammar of doll making culture, and in relation to the children's identities.

In the next stage of the story making process, the mode shifted from three dimensional representation to spoken and written language. The children were asked to talk to or make up a dialogue about their dolls in any language they wanted. Even though English is the language of teaching and learning in the school, all the children chose to talk to their dolls in their home languages. Here is a transcript of a Grade 1 child, Sonti, who created a fantasy play in Sotho using her doll whom she has named *Ntswaki*. Ntswaki is a conical shaped female doll, wearing a red cloth dress and adorned with bright plastic beads and black traditional African beads strung around her neck (see Figure 4).

SONTI: Lebitso la hae ke Ntswaki. Ntswaki o ne a rata ho bapala le bana. Jwale a itebala a fihla bosiu. Ntate a ba a mo fihlele pele. Mme ke hona a kenang ka tlung.
[Her name is Ntswaki. Ntswaki likes to play with the children. She used to be relaxed while she played and used to come back home late. Her husband would get home first. It's then that the mother, Ntswaki, came into the house.]
FATHER/HUSBAND: (in a deep voice) Mme o tswa kae ka nako e?
[Mother/wife, where do you come from at this time?]
NTSWAKI: (trembling) A...a....a../nna ke ne ke ilo bapala le bana.
[A..ah...ah.. I went to play with the children.]
FATHER/HUSBAND: Why o rata ho bapala le bana?
[Why do you like to play with children?]
NTWSAKI: Nna ke rata bana. *[I like children.]*
(A ba a setse a mo mathisa.) *[He chases her out of the house.]*
FATHER/HUSBAND: Mme, why o itebala hore o tlo pheha?
[Mother/wife, why do you forget that you have to cook?]

> **NTSWAKI:** Ha ke a itebala. Ke ne ke tlile. Ke ne ke nahana hore wena ha wa mphihlela pele. A ba a re.
> *[I am not relaxed. I came here. I thought that you would not be home before me. (She said)]*
> **FATHER/HUSBAND:** O-[Oh.]
> **NTSWAKI**: A ba a re nna ha ke sa tla hlola ke bapala le bana.
> *[I'm not going to play with the children again.]*

Different modes provide different views of the world and different potentials for learning. Each mode enables the expression of certain kinds of knowledge and creativity that are intrinsic to that mode. The use of three dimensional representation in the doll figures gave the children an opportunity to design a tactile, visual object using shape, color, different kinds of cloth, and decorative objects in particular spatial arrangements, which are imbued with cultural and aesthetic significance. In the case of Sonti, her doll figure provides a concrete body as the pivotal point and stimulus for a verbal narrative text, which creates a fictionalized interior life story for the doll. Sonti gives her a name, a gender, a language, a mind, a history, a set of relationships, emotions, behaviors, and actions within a social context. In other words, Sonti brings her doll into being as a dynamic, speaking character. The mode of spoken language enables her to do this and to provide a different view of the three dimensional doll figure—an interiorized view as distinct from an exteriorized image. This example demonstrates how the child as a sign maker has used the modes of three dimensional representation and spoken language to build different aspects of the character called Ntswaki that inflect on one another in an accretive, multilayered way. It thus becomes impossible to think of Ntswaki without simultaneously seeing the visual image of Ntswaki and hearing the character of Ntswaki in dialogue with her husband.

We have stated earlier that each mode enables the expression of certain kinds of knowledge and creativity that are intrinsic to representation in that mode. What is striking about Sonti's use of modes is how she uses her verbal narrative to further investigate the identity functions of fertility, marriage, and procreativity traditionally associated with the doll figures. This investigation takes the form of a conflictual dialogue between Ntswaki and her husband. Ntswaki is represented as a child-bride who is being instructed by her husband-father to "stop playing", and to take seriously her role as a mother-wife, to "start cooking". In this extract, Sonti is extending the iconic power of the male and female principles symbolized in the doll figures in a self-reflexive and playful enactment of the notions of play; the consequences of being a child bride are that the time for play, in every sense of the word, is over as you enter into patriarchy, marriage, and motherhood. The dialogue begins with the doll/character Ntswaki challenging her status as wife and ends with her submission to the power of her husband and the traditional role of women in marriage. We would argue that through the making of a symbolic identity object (the doll figure), the learner has established a relationship to her history and identity, which then provides a rich resource for the exploration of further identity texts in a semiotic chain across multiple representational forms. These multimodal, symbolic identity texts produce motivated learners who produce texts because there is a deeply felt reason to produce them.

"I FELL IN LOVE WITH MULTIMODALITY": MULTIMODAL PEDAGOGIES IN A SECONDARY SCHOOL CLASSROOM IN SOWETO

Our second case study discusses Robert Maungedzo's account of his implementation of multimodal pedagogy in an ESL classroom in a high school in Soweto, as rendered in an interview. Robert is a young black male teacher in an impoverished area of Soweto. As for many teachers in South Africa, teaching English Literature is a difficult chore. Robert's school has no library and few sets of literature books. His students come from different socio-cultural backgrounds, speaking a range of African languages as their home language (for example, Isixhosa, Xitsonga, Sepedi, Setswana, Isizulu), with no student having English as a home language. Morale is low: "Learners openly told me that they are wasting their time because people who are educated are unemployed and those who are driving the posh cars are criminals."

For the final school-leaving examination, Robert had to teach the novel, *Maru* by Bessie Head. He was delighted to have *Maru,* an African novel set in Botswana, as a set work, rather than, for example, Hardy's *Tess of the d'Urbevilles ,* a work set in the days when the literature curriculum was dominated by the Western canon. Robert found *Maru* relevant to post-apartheid South Africa, with its themes of racism, xenophobia, love, and reconciliation. However, although he expected his learners to enjoy it, they would not engage with it:

> My approach to teaching literature was characterized by me reading the novel to the learners, and in some instances, the learners themselves read the novel. I literally taught them the themes and fed them what I thought was important. I did my best to teach the learners but to no avail, as the learners did not perform well in their exams. I began a soul-searching of some kind.[2]

Robert's pedagogic intervention that year was less an experiment than an act of desperation. His own reflections on the multimodal journey he undertook with his students reveal the teaching program he instituted as well as the work his students produced. More than that, however, they show his courageous attempt to participate in a project of educational transformation, of himself, his learners, their attitudes to schooling, and, ultimately, of the nature of learning itself. The key to understanding *Maru*, for Robert, lay in understanding that the novel was not simply about the arrival of a foreigner at the school—Margaret Cadmore, a Masarwa or Bushman—and about the emotions she set loose in the community, but about identity, exclusion, racism, and reconciliation. The characters were both emblematic and complex, their Setswana names suggesting their qualities: for example, Maru, the main character, whose name means *clouds*, Moleka, *the one who tries*, Dikeledi, *tears*, and Ranko, *Mr. Nose*. For two years, Robert had tried in vain to get his learners to appreciate the significance of the names.

Robert's implementation of multimodal pedagogy involved a bold reframing of his existing beliefs and practices in relation to teaching literature. He allowed his learners to find their own meanings in the novel, and play with them, articulating them in whatever modes and genres they liked rather than in the solely linguistic genres of comprehension tests, questions, and summaries that he had previously used. Within a few weeks, Robert's classroom became a hive of activity. Students read the novel; wrote about their own African names having researched these with parents, grandparents, or other family members; represented their understandings of key scenes and central characters in the form of drawings, composed and performed plays and songs on central themes; and created resistance art in the form of sculptural installations and other art genres.

One group produced a complex pencil drawing of the main character. It shows Maru resting on the mountains like a cloud, part of nature, with a moon and stars to his left and a sun on his right. He is a mysterious, half-man, half-demon, and yet god-like, tender yet frighteningly powerful. The group said: "Sir, we struggle to describe Maru through words. Just look at our drawing. It says it all." Three other groups, shocked by the description of the corpse of Margaret's mother lying unwashed on the hospital floor soon after giving birth to Margaret, drew the scene in pencil crayons. Students found it difficult to believe that the nurses had refused her a stretcher, and to wash her, because she was of the lowly Masarwa tribe. Discussion of these drawings led to the writing and performance of two eight-page plays and three songs on the themes of xenophobia in contemporary settings. Even though neither art, music, nor drama had been taught to the students, they demonstrated a facility with the basic conventions, such as in the case of plays, the conventions of dialogue, voice, and scene changes. The students who wrote the song said that they had been affected emotionally by the description of the hospital ward. They wrote the song because, in their culture, when they are sad or depressed they escape from their pains through songs. The group that wrote the play indicated that their preference for dancing and acting because, they said, "in our culture dancing is a cathartic process. Sometimes one can run out of words but not out of body language."

According to Robert, "one mode led to the usage of other modes." Having watched the plays and listened to the songs, another group decided to work with the theme of *identity* and make something that would express their view of non-racism. They redesigned a giant, Western-style, white doll into something that was beyond racial or ethnic definitions. The girls did this by draping it in different cloths that represented different ethnic and racial groups. They also painted half the doll black. Through this conscious transformation of the three dimensional object, the group created a potent metaphor for representing the myth of the 'rainbow nation', one of the key nation building metaphors used by the government in the imagining of a new South Africa. In another exploration of black and white social relations, a student, alluding to a recently publicized case of a white farmer murdering a black laborer by dragging him behind a truck, critiqued the behavior of white farmers in a carefully executed pencil drawing.

Robert's soul searching had led to an explosion of creativity and agency in his usually disaffected students. In the final ESL examination, his students showed a dramatic improvement: Of 140 candidates, only one failed. On reflection, Robert said:

> One may conclude by saying that the pedagogy of multimodality and multiliteracies is not restricted by material conditions on the part of the learner. Instead, it is more interesting, innovative and original in learning environments characterized by lack of resources. Although mine was a kind of pilot study, I could see that with good planning on the part of the educator this could be a pedagogical approach that could change the conception of literature and literacy for learners, and for educators as well. The approach brought back a sense of urgency into my lessons. I was spared the pains of explaining everything to learners. It was the learners who were creating and constructing their own meaning. They used modes and designs of their own choice. Their drawings, sculptures, and plays reflect a wide variety of sources: learners' knowledge of popular culture, their knowledge of current events and of global and

national politics. Their products were not just literal illustrations of the novel: rather they functioned as concentrated visual emblems and signs of the written work. What surprised me was the creativity of some of the learners who, when a monomodal approach was adopted, would never say a word. It was, however, evident that even if an educator implements a multimodal approach, there is no way that language is relegated. Language and the other modes work in tandem.[3]

Robert's account vividly captures the sense of excitement and productivity generated in his class. We think that this new energy was produced through a complex mix of risk-taking on the part of the teacher that opened up untapped longings in the students to explore issues of the personal and the political (identity, racism, and xenophobia) in whatever forms of representation they felt comfortable with. Through this engagement with multimodality, students were able to recontextualize their identities in a pedagogic space. We claim that by broadening the base for representation in this class, Robert and his students succeeded in opening up the third ground between mainstream language and literacy practices and cultural difference. Together, they forged a community in which all participants were free to draw on representational resources from their cultures and histories in acts of transformation that spoke of them and to them. The semiotic production across modes stimulated a complex chain of activity and creativity that led to an increase in semiotic production in quality and quantity, contributed to their learning, and enhanced their understanding of the novel as well as of themselves[4].

CURRENT ISSUES, DEBATES, AND FUTURE DIRECTIONS

A common critique of multimodal work in the ELT classroom is that the use of multimodal pedagogy is an abdication of the English teacher's prime responsibility, which is to provide learners with access to dominant discourses in oral and written English. One form this argument takes is that not enough time exists in the ELT curriculum to cope satisfactorily with the demands of the language syllabus, let alone with the demands of multimodal forms of communication. Fairclough (2000) argues that:

> The creative and transformative mixing of discursive practices can be a difficult achievement which people quite commonly do badly. The complex communicative practices which are put in focus with the Multiliteracies Project constitute heavy demands on the communicative abilities of people. (p. 181)

While we would agree that multimodal pedagogies place complex demands on the communicative abilities of both teachers and learners, we have found learners excited and motivated by the opportunity to express parts of themselves that have been made invisible or silenced. We think that the kind of learning that transpires outweighs the problems and that we are investing time rather than wasting time.

Implementing multimodal pedagogies in the language and literacy curriculum has profound consequences for assessment practices (Drew, 2001; Newfield, Andrew, Maungedzo and Stein 2003). Such pedagogies illuminate in stark ways the narrowness of current assessment practices in relation to literacy, which determine what literacy is and how it is taught. In the examples we have shown, learners of ESL/EAL who do not have flexibility with their language resources, have shown sensitivity, creativity, and insight in their multimodal textual products, which constitute evidence of real learning within a context that makes sense to them and speaks of them. In post-apartheid South Africa, constitutional principles of non-racism, non-sexism, democracy, and redress are inseparable from the promotion of equity and justice in assessment practices. If students live in communities and cultural contexts that value modes other than writing, then how can the worldview of the school integrate these multiple modes of representation in order to give students the best opportunities to demonstrate their abilities? We argue that multimodal pedagogies can broaden the base of representation, constituting a wider base for making meaning. Setting multimodal tasks in which each mode has a particular assessment weighting in relation to the whole is a more equitable assessment procedure that also gives different learners opportunities to work with their cultural and representational resources available to them beyond the classroom walls. Such processes of recontexualizing their identities provide learners with new ways of seeing who they are within the context of a classroom community.

Assessment of multimodal texts in the English classroom is a complex, multilayered task that makes new demands on teachers' competencies and has important implications for teacher education. Multimodal assessment in language classrooms involves assessing what was learned, understood, and expressed—it is always more than looking for recall of facts. Assessing a drawing or a three dimensional figure requires a specific set of criteria which are contextually sensitive and appropriate: For example, the hierarchy of criteria used by the Arts teacher in assessing a drawing or three dimensional figure would be inappropriate for the English class as well as unfair in terms of the kinds of knowledge learners are required to develop in each domain. Developing assessment criteria for multimodal texts is a direction for future research. However, this should not overly control what learners are required to produce. Part of the energy of this work derives, we feel, from the tension between policed and unpoliced activities in the classroom. Some are kept loose, flexible, free, while others are more tightly controlled. Explicit criteria should not reduce the complex mix of freedom and restraint that is required to work playfully and innovatively with new concepts, ideas, and languages.

CONCLUSIONS

Multimodality is a key aspect of representation. All texts are multimodal and prominently so in the multiplicity of textual forms in the contemporary multimedia environment. In this chapter, we have focused on how multimodal pedagogies have evolved in our context and historical moment as pedagogies that allow learners and teachers to represent their histories, identities, and cultural forms through and beyond language. Multimodality is a fundamental challenge to the ELT classroom's emphasis on language as the central mode through which representation occurs. We think that it is a challenge that is impossible to ignore.

ACKNOWLEDGEMENTS

We wish to thank Tshidi Mamabolo, Ntsoake Senja, Thandiwe Mkhabela, Olifantsvlei Primary School, Robert Maungedzo, the Wits Multiliteracies Project and the many Gauteng teachers and graduate students in English Education at the University of the Witwatersrand who have worked with us in the field of multimodality. We have been enriched by all of you.

NOTES

[1] Maungedzo, Robert in an interview with Denise Newfield in Johannesburg, November 2001.
[2] Maungedzo, Robert in an interview with Denise Newfield in Johannesburg, November 2001.
[3] Maungedzo, Robert, in an interview with Denise Newfield in Johannesburg, November 2001.
[4] Robert's subsequent work with poetry supports these claims. See Newfield and Maungedzo's *Thebuwa, Poems from Ndofaya*, an anthology of poems written by his students, which he co-edited and which was published in 2005.

REFERENCES

Brenner, J., & Andrews, D. (2001, July). *Aluta continua: Weapons from the Visual Literacy Foundation Course at Wits University*. Paper presented at the Eighth International Literacy and Education Research Network Conference on Learning (LERN), Spetses, Greece.

Cope, B., & Kalantzis, M. (Eds.) (2000). *Multiliteracies*. London: Routledge.

Drew, M. (2001). *Thinking multimodally: An exploration of the use of multimodal, three-dimensional objects as an assessment task in tertiary education*. Unpublished Research Report, University of the Witwatersrand, Johannesburg, South Africa.

Fairclough, N. (2000). Multiliteracies and language: Orders of discourse and intertextuality. In B. Cope & M. Kalantzis (Eds.), *Multiliteracies: Literacy learning and the design of social futures* (pp. 162–181). London: Routledge.

Halliday, M. A. K. (1985). *An introduction to functional grammar*. London: Arnold.

Hodge, R., & Kress, G. R. (1988). *Social semiotics*. Cambridge: Polity Press.

Jacobs, U. U. (1992). Narrating the island: Robben Island in South African literature. *Current Writing*, 4(1), 73–84.

Kress, G. R. (1997). *Before writing: Rethinking the paths to literacy*. London: Routledge.

Kress, G. R., Jewitt, C., Ogborn, J., & Tsatsarelis, C. (2001). *Multimodal teaching and learning*. London: Continuum.

Kress, G. R., & Van Leeuwen, T. (1996). *Reading images: The grammar of visual design*. London: Routledge.

Kress, G. R., & Van Leeuwen, T. (2001). *Multimodal discourse*. London: Arnold.

Lemke, J. (2000). Introduction: Language and other semiotic systems in education. *Linguistics and Education*, 10(3), 307–34.

Nel, K., & Leibhammer, N. (1998). Evocations of the child. In E. Dell (Ed.), *Evocations of the child: Fertility figures of the Southern African region*. Cape Town: Human and Rousseau (Pty) Ltd and Johannesburg: The Johannesburg Art Gallery.

Newfield, D., Andrew, D., Maungedzo, R., & Stein, P. (2003). 'No number can describe how good it was': Assessment issues in the multimodal classroom. *Assessment in Education*, 10 (1), 61–81.

Newfield, D., & Maungedzo, R. (Eds.). 2005. *Thebuwa, Poems from Ndofaya*. Johannesburg: Denise Newfield Publishers for the WITS Multiliteracies Research Group.

Stein, P., & Newfield, D. (2004). Shifting the gaze in South African classrooms: New pedagogies, new publics, new democracies. *Thinking Classroom*, 5(1), 28–36.

Van Leeuwen, T. (1999). *Speech, music, sound*. London: Macmillan.

CHAPTER 57

APPROACHES TO GENRE IN ELT

BRIAN PALTRIDGE

The University of Sydney, Australia

ABSTRACT

Recent years have seen increased attention being given to the notion of genre in the area of English language teaching. This is especially the case in the teaching of English for specific purposes (ESP), the teaching of English in Australia, and the teaching of composition studies in North America. The main approaches to the analysis of genres in these areas are *the ESP perspective*, the work of the *Sydney school*, and the composition studies view of genre in what is sometimes called the *new rhetoric*. There are a number of ways in which each of these perspectives on genre overlap and ways in which they are different from each other. Much of this is due to the different goals of each of these views of genre and the differing theoretical positions and concerns that underlie the various perspectives. This chapter discusses insights that have been gained in each of these areas and what they might mean for English language teaching. It discusses debates and concerns about genre-based approaches to language teaching, and also considers future directions for genre-based language teaching and research.

INTRODUCTION

The term *genre* was first introduced in the area of English for specific purposes (ESP) in the early 1980s. The Australian work on genre dates back to a similar time and originates in the examination of children's writing in Australian elementary school classrooms. Genre studies in composition studies in North America and what has been called the *new rhetoric* have been influenced, in particular, by Miller's 1984 seminal paper, "Genre as social action" (reprinted in Freedman & Pedway, 1994). This chapter discusses insights that have been gained in each of these areas and what they might mean for English language teaching.

THE ESP PERSPECTIVE

ESP genre analysis is based largely on Swales' (1981, 1990) studies of the discourse structure and linguistic features of scientific research articles. This work has had a strong influence in the area of ESP and especially in the teaching of graduate writing to ESL students (see Dudley-Evans & St John, 1998; Jordan, 1997; Paltridge, 2001b; Swales, 2001; Swales & Feak, 1994, 2000).

Genres and *part-genres* that have been examined in this perspective include the introduction and results sections of research articles, the introduction and discussion sections of theses and dissertations, research article abstracts, job application and sales promotion letters, grant proposals, legislative documents, the graduate seminar, academic lectures, and lecture and poster session discussions at conferences. In this *ESP perspective* on genre analysis, discourse structures are most often described as series of *moves*, analyzed in terms of rhetorical purpose, content, and form. Many ESP genre studies have also examined linguistic aspects of genres as well.

The ESP perspective on genre has been influenced by work in the new rhetoric and, in particular, Miller's (1984) notion of *genre as social action*. In this view, a genre is defined not in terms of "the substance or the form of discourse but on the action it is used to accomplish" (Miller, p. 151). Miller's view, that the types of genres that members of a discourse community "have names for in everyday language" (p. 155) tells us something important about discourse, is also reflected in ESP genre studies: that is, the view that the names used for genres by those who are most familiar with them provide important information for the identification and description of genres (Dudley-Evans, 1989; Swales, 1990).

ESP (and new rhetoric) genre analysts argue that genres are not static but rather change and evolve in response to changes in particular communicative needs. They also discuss the notion of *prototypicality*: that is, the way in which properties such as communicative purpose, form, structure, and audience expectations operate to identify the extent to which a text is prototypical as an example of a particular genre (Swales, 1990).

Hyon (1996) provides an overview of the history of ESP genre studies while Johns (2002) provides a summary of key issues in ESP (and other) approaches to genre analysis. As Hyon explains, many ESP genre studies have been particularly form-focused due, in part, to their connection with the teaching of English to non-native speakers and its inevitable attention to surface-level patterns of grammar and vocabulary. Hyon also suggests that this focus on form may derive from the fact that most leading ESP teachers and researchers have a background in formal language study, rather than literary or rhetorical theory. This situation, however, has begun to change as ESP genre studies have been influenced by genre theories in other areas such as rhetoric and the sociology of science. Swales' own work, for example, changed as his move from Great Britain to the United States in 1985 brought him more in contact with the work of rhetoric and composition studies scholars working there (Hyon, 1996). His (1990) book, *Genre Analysis. English in Academic and Research Settings*, thus considers sociocontextual aspects of genres as well as their historical nature, at the same time discussing the more formal features of genres.

In his (1990) book, Swales argued that the most important aspect of a genre was communicative purpose, the key factor that leads us to decide whether a text is an instance of a particular genre or not. He has since, however, revised this view, saying that it's now clear that genres may have multiple purposes, and these may be different for each of the participants involved. Communicative purpose, then, cannot always be taken at face value and be used, by itself, to quickly and incontrovertibly decide which genre category a text belongs to (or not) (Askehave & Swales, 2001). Kress (1989, 1994) suggests that genres, rather than being determined by social (or communicative) purpose, "are in fact formed out of the dynamics of social interactions involving participants in particular social relations" (Scott & Groom, 1999, p. 24).

THE SYDNEY SCHOOL

Australian genre work is based on the work of linguists living in Sydney such as Michael Halliday (1994), Ruqaiya Hasan (Halliday & Hasan, 1989), and Jim Martin (1984, 1992). This work has been taken up mostly in school writing programs and the teaching of English to adult migrants in Australia (see Christie, 1995; Christie & Martin, 1997; Cope & Kalantzis, 1993; Feez, 1998; Paltridge, 2001a).

The Australian view of genre draws for its model of description on the theory of language known as *systemic functional linguistics* (Eggins, 1994; Halliday, 1994; Halliday & Hasan, 1989). Systemic functional linguistics considers language primarily as a resource for making meaning rather than as a set of rules. The *systemic* component of systemic functional grammar derives from the fact that the grammar describes language as being made up of systems of choices. The *functional* dimension of systemic functional grammar aims to describe what language is doing in a particular context. Labels given to language features in systemic functional analyses are, thus, described in terms of what they are doing in functional, rather than grammatical, terms.

Martin's (1984, p. 25) definition of *genre* as "a staged, goal-oriented, purposeful activity in which speakers engage as members of our culture" has been extremely influential in the work of the Sydney school. This definition draws on the view "that contexts both of situation and of culture [are] important if we are to fully interpret the meaning of a text" (p. 25). For Martin, as for the majority of systemic functional genre analysts, the notion of genre corresponds to the *context of culture* and is responsible for the schematic or the rhetorical structure of a text. The *register* (Halliday, 1989b) of a genre corresponds to the *context of situation* (Halliday, 1989a) and is responsible for the language features of a text. Genres are, thus, described as being culture specific and as having particular purposes, stages, and linguistic features associated with them, the meanings of which need to be interpreted in relation to the cultural and social contexts in which they occur.

A number of different ways of describing genres have emerged in systemic genre analyses. The most influential of these are the descriptions presented by Martin and Rothery (1986) and Martin (1989) in which the analysis of the schematic structure of texts involves the identification of the organizational stages of a text and the typical linguistic features that accompany them. Examples of types of texts that have been examined from this perspective include *narratives, anecdotes, recounts, reports, procedures, descriptions, explanations,* and *expositions* (see Derewianka, 1991, for examples of these).

THE NEW RHETORIC

The term *rhetoric* has a long history reaching back to the work of Aristotle in ancient Greece, who defined rhetoric as "ways of convincing an audience of a subject": that is, the examination of different types of *rhetorical argument*. The new rhetoric emerged in response to the *current-traditional* model of teaching writing that was dominant in North American composition classrooms in the mid-twentieth century with its emphasis on the product, or form, of writing (Silva, 1990; Paltridge, 2001a), rather than considerations such as context, audience, demands of the occasion, and writing as a social activity.

The notion of genre has been given particular attention in North American first language composition studies, rhetoric, and professional writing studies. Genre studies in the new rhetoric differ from ESP and systemic genre studies in that they have focused more on the relationship between text and context and the *actions* that genres fulfill within particular situations. Researchers of this perspective, thus, have been less concerned with the analysis and teaching of formal textual features and more with understanding the social functions of genres and the contexts in which they are used (Hyon, 1996).

Examples of new rhetoric genre studies include Bazerman's (1988) study of scientific research reports, Myers' (1990) study of biologists' writing, Bazerman and Paradis' (1991) book on writing in professional communities, Dias, Freedman, Medway, and Pare's (1999) book on writing in academic and workplace settings, Berkenkotter and Huckin's (1995) *Genre Knowledge in Disciplinary Communication*, and the collections of papers edited by Freedman and Medway titled *Genre and the New Rhetoric* (1994a) and *Learning and Teaching Genre* (1994b). A key figure in this area is Carolyn Miller and, in particular, her (1984) paper "Genre as social action."

Miller (1984) describes genres as responses to social situations that are part of a socially constructed reality. Genres, in this view, both respond to and contribute to the constitution of social contexts, as well as contribute to the socialization of individuals. Miller (p. 165) argues that genres "serve as keys to understanding how to participate in the actions of a community" and that the failure to understand genre as social action turns activities such as writing instruction from "what should be a practical art of achieving social ends into ... [an] art of making texts that fit formal requirements" (Miller, 1994, p. 67).

Attention is given in the new rhetoric to exploring sociocontextual aspects of genres and the action a particular genre aims to accomplish. Studies in the new rhetoric also consider how aspects of genres change through time. Bazerman (1988), for example, examines developments in scientific writing in response to changes in scientific knowledge. Yates (1989) and Yates and Orlikowski (1992) examine change and development in office memos in response to changes in sociocultural phenomena such as the philosophy, organization, and conditions of business management and communication.

Within this perspective on genre, formal features of a text both derive from and relate to a writer's social motive in responding to a recurring type of social situation. Berkenkotter and Huckin (1995) use the term *genre knowledge* to refer to these repertoires of *situationally appropriate responses to recurrent situations*: that is, the knowledge that is needed in order to participate in the activities of particular discourse communities.

GENRE AND THE LANGUAGE-LEARNING PROGRAM

A number of people have argued for the use of genre as an organizing principle for language learning programs. Widdowson (1983), for example, suggests that the notion of genre has a number of advantages over other frameworks for analysis in that it takes us beyond the level of functions and notions into larger units of work on which to base our teaching and learning programs. Swales (1986) has argued that the units in a genre-based program are neither too small, as in a structural or functional syllabus, nor too large, as in a skills-based syllabus. Dudley-Evans (1989) argues that a language-learning program based on the notion of genre means texts that are similar in terms of purpose, organization, and audience can be grouped together in a way that can usefully be drawn to learners' attention.

A genre-based language-learning program takes us beyond grammatical or functional units yet excludes neither from the overall program. A genre-based approach to language program development *starts* with genre as the overall organizing principle yet still includes other elements, such as grammar, functions, vocabulary, language skills, situation, topics, and communicative tasks, according to the particular genre and the setting in which it occurs. A genre-based approach to syllabus design focuses on language at the level of whole text and also takes into account the social and cultural context in which the genre is used (Feez, 1998). Genre-based language-learning programs place grammar instruction in discourse-based contexts that are both meaningful and recognizable for learners. Genre-based language teaching also provides a basis for cross-cultural comparisons of the use of genres in different linguistic and cultural settings.

A genre-based approach to language teaching and learning links together discourse, cultural, and situational aspects of language use that may be given less attention in programs based on lower-level, organizational units of language such as structures, functions, or vocabulary (alone). A genre-based approach should not, however, ignore language features such as structures, functions, and vocabulary. Indeed, such aspects of language use are an essential and fundamental part of a genre-based language-learning program (Callaghan, Knapp, & Noble, 1993). Nor should it exclude a focus on specific reading, writing, listening, and speaking skills. A genre-based perspective focuses on these aspects of language use within the social and cultural contexts of particular genres. This perspective needs to include a flexible view of genre and one that takes as its starting point the context of culture and the context of situation of the particular genre rather than patterns of textual and linguistic features of the texts (alone). That is, genres need to be considered not as patterns of texts in isolation, but in relation to the cultural and situational context of the particular genre and the aims and assumptions of the particular discourse community in which it occurs.

One of the aims of a genre-based language-learning program, then, is to enable students to participate in and respond to new and recurring genres. This outcome includes the ability to construct, use, and exploit generic conventions to achieve particular communicative goals (Bhatia, 1999). Taking part in a genre means much more than just producing a text that looks like the ones that are usually produced in a particular situation (Dias, Freedman, Medway, & Pare, 1999). It also involves understanding the social and cultural contexts in which the genre occurs and how these factors impact upon the language choices that a speaker or writer makes. Using a genre also includes an understanding of what it is appropriate to talk or write about in such settings (Berkenkotter & Huckin, 1995). This understanding is especially important in that many descriptions of genres might focus on the language and structure of a text but pay much less attention to the issue of appropriate content (Connor, 1996). (See Burns, 2001; Hammond & Derewianka, 2001; Hyland, 2002, 2003, 2004; Swales, 2004; Wennerstrom, 2003, for further discussions of genre-based teaching.)

DEBATES AND CONCERNS

Writers such as Hammond and Macken-Horarick (1999) argue that genre-based teaching can help students gain access to texts and discourses, which will, hopefully, help them to participate more successfully in second language spoken and written interactions. Others, such as Luke (1996), argue that teaching *genres of power* leads to uncritical reproduction of the status quo and does not necessarily provide the kind of access we hope it might provide for our learners. Others, such as Christie (1993) and Martin (1993), argue that not teaching genres of power is socially irresponsible in that it is the already disadvantaged students who are especially disadvantaged by programs that do not address these issues. In Hammond and Macken-Horarick's (1999) view, teaching about genres does not exclude critical analysis of them. It, rather, provides learners with the necessary tools for analyzing and critiquing them.

Gee (1997) argues that it is simply good teaching to help learners learn what they need to know. She sees the explicitness of genre-based teaching as one of its strengths in that it provides a framework for learners to draw on, as they need. She argues that a development of genre awareness, in terms of types of genres and their characteristic features, is essential for learners so that they are aware of "the purposes that different genres serve in society and culture" (p. 39).

It is important to consider, however, what might be the limitations of a genre-based language-learning program. One might be: How do we identify a spoken or written text as an instance of particular genre? (See Askehave & Swales, 2001; Paltridge, 1997, for a discussion of this issue.) And in turn, what are the genre's characteristic features? Can these be described in linguistic terms alone, or does this description require a broader set of categories? (See Paltridge, 1994 for further discussion on this issue.) Genre knowledge not only involves linguistic and textual knowledge but also includes social and cultural knowledge (Bhatia, 1999). Exactly what this knowledge is can be difficult to identify, especially if teachers are teaching a genre that they, themselves, do not regularly use or, indeed, have never used. This situation becomes even more complex if teachers are not native speakers of English and if they are teaching in a setting in which English is not used around them. There is also the problem of getting authentic examples of spoken and written genres, especially if a teacher is working in a foreign rather than a second language setting.

There is also the difficulty of using a genre-based approach in classrooms where there are no common goals amongst learners. In this kind of setting, more everyday genres might be more usefully focused on, such as casual conversation and the kinds of genres people use in everyday interactions, rather than some of the more specific-purpose ones that tend to be focused on in genre-based classrooms.

A number of people in the new rhetoric have expressed reservations as to whether genres can and should be taught at all. Berkenkotter and Huckin (1995), for example, argue that what native speakers know about genres and appropriate communicative behavior is not explicitly taught but rather results from participation in the activities of our lives. Much of the discussion of the teaching of genres in the new rhetoric refers, however, to first rather than second language settings. First language speakers clearly do have much naturally acquired genre knowledge in their first language. It is not at all clear, however, that second language learners have the same implicit knowledge of the genres they need to be able to understand and use (Grabe & Kaplan, 1996).

Other issues include the extent to which a genre-based approach might limit student expression through its use of model texts and its focus on audience expectations. This issue is clearly something teachers need to keep in mind when they are teaching particular genres. Teachers equally need to help students see how they can bring their own individual voices into their use of particular genres (Swales, 2000). Students need to be careful not to overgeneralize what they have learnt about one genre and apply it inappropriately to their use of other genres (Hyon, 2001).

Genres, further, are constantly changing. In some cases this may be a slow and gradual process, and in others it may be quite rapid. The email message is an example of a genre that has evolved and changed over a relatively short space of time. University lectures are a further example of genre that is changing, especially with the introduction of new technologies in higher education and the move towards more interactive teaching and learning styles in academic settings. Academic writing in some disciplines is also changing, especially in new and emergent areas of study and in what have been termed *new universities* (Baynham, 2000).

Kay and Dudley-Evans (1998) discuss teachers' views on genre and its use in second language classrooms. Some of the teachers they spoke to were concerned that a genre-based approach might become too prescriptive. The teachers pointed to the need to highlight the kind of variation that occurs in particular genres as well as to consider why this variation might occur. Care, then, needs to be taken to avoid a reductive view of genres and of the textual information that is given to students about them (see Hyon, 2001 for further discussion on this point). Kay and Dudley-Evans' teachers also stressed the importance of contextualizing genres in the classroom by discussing purpose, audience, and underlying beliefs and values before moving on to focus on language features. They said learners should be exposed to a wide range of sample texts and that these should be both authentic and suitable for their learners. They also felt a genre-based approach should be used in combination with other approaches, such as process and communicative approaches to language teaching and learning. They said, however, they thought a genre-based approach was especially suitable for beginner and intermediate-level students in that the use of model texts gave them confidence as well as something to fall back on. They concluded that genre provided a useful framework for language teaching and learning as long as it was made clear that the examples of genres they presented were just possible models and not rigid sets of patterns. Scott and Groom (1999) present a similar view, saying that genres are not fixed codes but just one of the resources students need for the expression and communication of meaning. The teaching of generic forms, for Scott and Groom, does not eschew the use of models but rather sees models as part of a wider repertoire of resources that students can draw on and adapt, as appropriate, to support their meaning making.

A further issue is the tension between process approaches to teaching writing, where individual expression is encouraged, and genre-based approaches that focus more on audience and discourse-community expectations. Writers such as Bamworth (1993) and Badger and White (2000) argue that these two approaches are complementary rather than in opposition with each other. Badger and White suggest that the potential weakness of a genre-based approach could be the limited attention given to process skills, such as planning, drafting, and reworking texts. They argue that a key strength of a genre-based approach is its focus on social context and communicative purpose. In their view, process and genre-based approaches can be usefully drawn together. As they argue, effective communication involves knowledge about language (as in a genre-based approach), knowledge about social context and purpose (as in a genre-based approach), and skills in using language (as in a process-based approach). Teachers need to focus on each of these aspects of genre knowledge in order to help learners participate in and respond to particular communicative situations.

FUTURE DIRECTIONS

Genres, then, provide a frame that enables learners to take part in and interpret particular communicative events. Making this genre knowledge explicit can provide learners with the knowledge and skills they need to communicate successfully in particular situations. It can also provide learners with access to socially powerful forms of language.

Clearly, however, much more research still needs to be carried out into genre-based language teaching and learning. We need to understand better the effect of genre-based instruction. Studies carried out, for example, by Reppen (1995), Mustafa (1995), Henry and Roseberry (1998), Johns (1999), and Hyon (2001, 2002) are starting to show the benefits of genre-based instruction. More of these studies are still needed. We also need to better understand the nature of genre-specific language if we are to helpfully focus on this in our language learning classrooms. And we need to better understand the settings of particular genres as well as how we can focus on complex social relations, expectations, and assumptions in ways that are useful and accessible to our learners.

Teachers and students need a metalanguage for describing what people 'do' with language, how they make meanings, and how they get things done. They also need theories of text and context for describing how the social, cultural, and communicative context, which surrounds a genre, impacts upon the language choices that people make. Teachers and students also need tools of description to help them understand how texts aim to position intended readers and listeners. Systemic functional linguistics provides one way of doing this.

Teachers also need an understanding of what Scollon and Wong-Scollon (2001, pp. 5-6) call *discourse systems* to help them unpack the historical, social, and ideological underpinnings of particular genres, and how these impact on what people say and what people do in their use of particular genres. We also need further analyses of the use of language in particular communities of practice (Lave & Wenger, 1991) that look at language and context, and ask what are the features of that context that impact on language use.

The area of research known as *contrastive rhetoric* (see Connor, 1996) compares written and spoken genres in different languages and cultural settings. Although many studies in this area have focused on academic writing, studies have also been carried out that examine other genres as well. For example, studies have been carried out which examine Finnish and English economic reports (Mauranen, 1993), business letters in Japanese, French, and English (Jenkins & Hinds, 1987), business letters written by native and non-native speakers of English (Maier, 1992), and linguistics articles in Spanish and English (Burgess, 1997). Kubota (2000), more recently, has called for studies into *critical contrastive rhetoric*. By this she means studies that examine cultural differences in language and communication but do not essentialize the notion of culture and cultural differences as if they were neutral and permanent truths. Rather, she argues, we need to see cultural differences as dynamic and situated in relations of power and ideologies. There is clearly a need for many more studies to be carried out in this particular area.

We also need to better understand the multiliteracies (Cope & Kalantzis, 2000) requirements of our *changing worlds* (Christie, 1990), the expanding use of electronic, visual, and multimedia in our lives, in our classrooms, in the workplace, in our homes, at university, and in the professions, and the expanding range of genres that people need to be able to participate in these particular settings, as well as how language constructs and communicates knowledges within these genres. We especially need second language acquisition studies that move beyond traditional descriptions of grammar to functional descriptions of grammar, pragmatics, and discourse and examine how these are acquired over time within the context of learning particular genres. These studies need to be based on complete rather than isolated samples of learner language, and they need to examine learners in the process of learning rather than single-moment studies of learners' grammatical abilities and performance (Perrett, 2001).

We need to look for patterns of interaction in genre-based classrooms that foster language learning (Dufficy, 2000), and we need to look at the social nature of learning particular genres (Perrett, 2001). We need both quantitative and qualitative studies to help us understand what is happening in genre-based classrooms and what goals are being achieved that will help us to evaluate, assess, and refine our classroom practices. We need to understand the range of ways of providing explicit instruction, at the same time accepting that there is no best way. We need to understand how the relationship between language and context can best be drawn to learners' attention.

In the area of second language curriculum development, we need ongoing evaluation and refinements of genre-based approaches to second language teaching, considering issues such as the relationship between theory and the way it is taken up in the classroom, the role of teachers as curriculum developers, the role of learners in curriculum development, the place of needs-based programming in a genre-based model of curriculum development, and accountability of genre-based language-learning programs.

In the area of second language assessment, we need to examine the kinds of assessment we use in our classrooms, working with principles of assessment such as those outlined by Macken and Slade (1993). This includes making assessment criteria explicit to learners, explaining criteria in terms and at a level learners will understand, relating assessment to the aims and objectives of the program or the purpose for which students are undertaking the assessment, and reporting the assessment in terms that are common to teachers, curriculum writers, and program managers.

Much research then still needs to be done in the area of genre-based language teaching. Much has, however, already been done that points to the value of this approach to second language teaching and learning.

REFERENCES

Askehave, I., & Swales, J. M. (2001). Genre identification and communicative purpose: A problem and possible solution. *Applied Linguistics, 22*, 195–212.

Badger, R., & White, G. (2000). A process genre approach to teaching writing. *ELT Journal, 54*, 153–160.

Bamworth, R. (1993). Process versus genre: Anatomy of a false debate. *Prospect, 8*, 89–99.

Baynham, N. (2000). Academic writing in new and emergent discipline areas. In M. R. Lea & B. Stierer (Eds.), *Student writing in higher education: New contexts* (pp. 17–31). Buckingham: Open University Press.

Bazerman, C. (1988). *Shaping written knowledge.* Madison: University of Wisconsin Press.

Bazerman, C., & Paradis, J. (Eds.). (1991). *Textual dynamics and the professions: Historical and contemporary writing in professional communities.* Madison: University of Wisconsin Press.

Berkenkotter, C., & Huckin, T. N. (1995). *Genre knowledge in disciplinary communication: Cognition/culture/power.* Hillsdale, NJ: Lawrence Erlbaum.

Bhatia, V. K. (1993). *Analyzing genre: Language use in professional settings.* London: Longman.

Bhatia, V. K. (1995). Recent developments in genre theory: Problems and perspectives. In S. Gill (Ed.), *Proceedings of the international English language education conference: National and international challenges and responses* (pp. 352–361). Kuala Lumpur: Universiti Kebangsaan Malaysia.

Bhatia, V. K. (1997). Genre-mixing in academic introductions. *English for Specific Purposes, 16*, 181–195.

Bhatia, V. K. (1999, August). *Analyzing genre: An applied linguistic perspective.* Keynote presentation at the 12th World Congress of Applied Linguistics, AILA 1999, Tokyo.

Burns, A, (2001). Genre-based approaches to writing and beginning adult ESL learners. In C.N. Candlin & N. Mercer (Eds.), *English language teaching in its social context.* London: Routledge.

Burgess, S. (1997). *Discourse variation across cultures: A genre-analytic study of writing on linguistics.* Unpublished Ph.D. thesis, Centre for Applied Language Studies, The University of Reading.

Callaghan, M., Knapp, P., & Noble, G. (1993). Genres in practice. In B. Cope & M. Kalantzis (Eds.), *The powers of literacy: A genre approach to teaching writing* (pp. 179–202). London: Falmer Press.

Christie, F. (Ed.). (1990). *Literacy for a changing world.* Hawthorn, Victoria: Australian Council for Educational Research.

Christie, F. (1993). The "received" tradition of literacy teaching: The decline of rhetoric and the corruption of grammar. In B. Green (Ed.), *The insistence of the letter: Literacy studies and curriculum theorizing* (pp. 75–106). London: Falmer Press.

Christie, F. (1995). Genre-based approaches to teaching literacy. In M. L. Tickoo (Ed.), *Reading and writing theory into practice* (pp. 300–320). Singapore: SEAMEO Regional English Language Centre.

Christie, F., & Martin, J. R. (Eds.). (1997). *Genre and institutions: Social processes in the workplace and school.* London: Continuum.

Connor, U. (1996). *Contrastive rhetoric: Cross-cultural aspects of second language writing.* Cambridge: Cambridge University Press.

Cope, B., & Kalantzis, M. (Eds.). (1993). *The powers of literacy: A genre approach to teaching writing.* London: Falmer Press.

Cope, B., & Kalantzis, M. (Eds.). (2000). *Multiliteracies: Literacy learning and the design of social futures.* London: Routledge.

Cope, B., Kalantzis, M., Kress, G., & Martin, J. R. (1993). Bibliographical essay: Developing the theory and practice of genre-based literacy. (Compiled by L. Murphy.) In B. Cope & M. Kalantzis (Eds.), *The powers of literacy: A genre approach to teaching writing* (pp. 231–247). London: Falmer Press.

Derewianka, B. (1991). *Exploring how texts work* (Revised impression). Sydney: Primary English Teaching Association.

Dias, P., Freedman, A., Medway, P., & Pare, A. (1999). *Worlds apart: Acting and writing in academic and workplace contexts.* Mahwah, NJ: Lawrence Erlbaum.

Dudley-Evans, T. (1989). An outline of the value of genre analysis in LSP work. In C. Lauren & M. Nordman (Eds.), *Special language: From humans thinking to thinking machines* (pp. 72–79). Clevedon: Multilingual Matters.

Dudley-Evans, T. (1995). Genre models for the teaching of academic writing to second language speakers: Advantages and disadvantages. *The Journal of TESOL France, 2*, 181–192. (Reprinted in Miller, T., Ed., 1997, *Functional approaches to written text: Classroom applications*, pp. 150–159, Washington, DC: United States Information Agency.)

Dudley-Evans, T., & St John, M. J. (1998). *Developments in English for specific purposes.* Cambridge: Cambridge University Press.

Dufficy, P. (2000). Through the lens of scaffolding: Genre pedagogy and talk in multilingual classrooms. *TESOL in Context, 10*, 4–9.

Eggins, S. (1994). *An introduction to systemic functional linguistics*. London: Pinter.

Feez, S. (1998). *Text-based syllabus design*. Sydney: National Centre for English Language Teaching and Research, Macquarie University.

Freedman, A., & Medway, P. (Eds.). (1994a). *Genre and the new rhetoric*. London: Taylor & Francis.

Freedman, A., & Medway, P. (Eds.). (1994b). *Learning and teaching genre*. Portsmouth, NH: Boynton/Cook Publishers.

Gee, S. (1997). Teaching writing: A genre-based approach. In G. Fulcher (Ed.), *Writing in the English language classroom*. (pp. 24–40). Hertfordshire, UK: Prentice Hall Europe ELT.

Grabe, W., & Kaplan, R. (1996). *Theory and practice of writing. An applied linguistic perspective*. London: Longman.

Halliday, M. A. K. (1989a). Context of situation. In M. A. K. Halliday & R. Hasan. (Eds.), *Language, context and text: Aspects of language in a social-semiotic perspective* (pp. 3–14). Oxford: Oxford University Press.

Halliday, M. A. K. (1989b). Register variation. In M. A. K. Halliday & R. Hasan, *Language, context and text: Aspects of language in a social-semiotic perspective* (pp. 29–43). Oxford: Oxford University Press.

Halliday, M. A. K. (1994). *An introduction to functional grammar* (2nd ed.). London: Edward Arnold.

Halliday, M. A. K. & Hasan, R. (1989). *Language, context and text: Aspects of language in a social-semiotic perspective*. Oxford: Oxford University Press.

Hammond, J., & Macken-Horarick, M. (1999). Critical literacy: Challenges and questions for ESL classrooms. *TESOL Quarterly, 33*, 528–544.

Hammond, J., & Derewianka, B. (2001). Genre. In R. Carter & D. Nunan (Eds.), *The Cambridge guide to teaching English to speakers of other languages*. Cambridge: Cambridge University Press.

Henry, A., & Roseberry, R. L. (1998). An evaluation of a genre-based approach to the teaching of EAP/ESP writing. *TESOL Quarterly, 32*, 147–156.

Huckin, T. (1997). Cultural aspects of genre knowledge. *AILA Review, 12*, 68–78.

Hyland, K. (2002). Genre: language, context and literacy. *Annual review of applied linguistics, 22*, 113–136.

Hyland, K. (2003). Genre-based pedagogies: a social response to process. *Journal of Second Language Writing, 12*, 17–29.

Hyland, K. (2004). *Genre and second language writing*. Ann Arbor: University of Michigan Press.

Hyon, S. (1996). Genre in three traditions: Implications for ESL. *TESOL Quarterly, 30*, 693–722.

Hyon, S. (2001). Long term effects of genre-based instruction: A follow up study of an EAP reading course. *English for Specific Purposes, 20*, 417–438.

Hyon, S. (2002). Genre and ESL reading: A classroom study. In A. M. Johns (Ed.), *Genre in the classroom: Multiple perspectives* (pp. 121–141). Mahwah, NJ: Lawrence Erlbaum Publishers.

Jenkins, S., & Hinds, J. (1987). Business letter writing: English, French, and Japanese. *TESOL Quarterly, 21*, 327–354.

Johns, A. M. (1995). Genre and pedagogical purposes. *Journal of Second Language Writing, 4*, 181–190.

Johns, A. M. (1997). *Text, role and context: Developing academic literacies*. Cambridge: Cambridge University Press.

Johns, A. M. (1999). Opening our doors: Applying socioliterate approaches (SA) to language minority classrooms. In L. Harklau, K. M. Losey & M. Siegal (Eds.), *Generation 1.5 meets college composition. Issues in the teaching of writing to US-educated learners of ESL* (pp. 159–171). Mahwah, NJ: Lawrence Erlbaum Publishers.

Johns, A. M. (Ed.). (2002). *Genre in the classroom: Multiple perspectives*. Mahwah, NJ: Lawrence Erlbaum Publishers.

Jordan. R. R. (1997). *English for academic purposes*. Cambridge: Cambridge University Press.

Kay, H., & Dudley-Evans, T. (1998). Genre: What teachers think. *ELT Journal, 52*, 308–314.

Kress, G. (1989). *Linguistic processes in sociocultural practice*. Oxford: Oxford University Press.

Kress, G. (1994). *Learning to write* (2nd ed.). London: Routledge.

Kubota, R. (2000). *Politics of cultural difference in second language writing*. Keynote presentation at Symposium on Second Language Writing, Purdue University, USA.

Lave, J., & Wenger, E. (1991). *Situated learning: Legitimate peripheral participation*. Cambridge: Cambridge University Press.

Luke, A. (1996). Genres of power? Literacy education and the production of capital. In R. Hasan & G. Williams (Eds.), *Literacy in society* (pp. 308–338). London: Longman.

Macken, M., & Slade, D. (1993). Assessment: A foundation for effective learning in the school context. In B. Cope & M. Kalantzis (Eds.), *The powers of literacy: A genre approach to teaching writing* (pp. 203–230). London: Falmer Press.

Maier, P. (1992). Politeness strategies in business letters by native and non-native English speakers. *English for Specific Purposes, 11,* 189–205.

Martin, J. R. (1984). Language, register and genre. In F. Christie (Ed.), *Language studies: Children's writing: Reader* (pp. 21–30). Geelong, Victoria: Deakin University Press.

Martin, J. R. (1989). *Factual writing: Exploring and challenging social reality.* Oxford: Oxford University Press.

Martin, J. R. (1992). *English text: System and structure.* Amsterdam and Philadelphia: John Benjamins.

Martin, J. R. (1993). Genre and literacy: Modeling context in educational linguistics. *Annual Review of Applied Linguistics, 13,* 141–172.

Martin, J.R., & Rothery, J. (1986). What a functional approach to the writing task can show about 'good writing'. In B. Couture (Ed.), *Functional approaches to writing,* Norwood, NJ: Ablex.

Mauranen, A. (1993). Contrastive ESP rhetoric: Metatext in Finnish-English economics text. *English for Specific Purposes, 12,* 3–22.

Miller, C. R. (1984). Genre as social action. *Quarterly Journal of Speech, 70,* 151–167. Reprinted in A. Freedman & P. Medway (Eds.) (1994). *Genre and the new rhetoric* (pp. 23–42) London: Taylor and Francis.

Miller, C. R. (1994). Rhetorical community: The cultural basis of genre. Reprinted in A. Freedman & P. Medway (Eds.), *Genre and the new rhetoric* (pp. 67–78). London: Taylor and Francis.

Mustafa, Z. (1995). The effect of genre awareness on linguistic transfer. *English for Specific Purposes, 14,* 247–256.

Myers, G. (1990). *Writing biology: Texts in the social construction of scientific knowledge.* Madison, WI: University of Wisconsin Press.

Paltridge, B. (1997). *Genre, frames and writing in research settings.* Amsterdam and Philadelphia: John Benjamins.

Paltridge, B. (2001a). *Genre and the language learning classroom.* Ann Arbor: University of Michigan Press.

Paltridge, B. (2001b). Linguistic research and EAP pedagogy. In J. Flowerdew & M. Peacock (Eds.), *Research perspectives on English for academic purposes* (pp. 55–70). Cambridge: Cambridge University Press.

Perrett, G. (2001). Researching second and foreign language development. In L. Unsworth (Ed.). *Researching language in schools and communities* (pp. 87–110). London: Cassell.

Paltridge, B. (1994). Genre analysis and the identification of textual boundaries. *Applied Linguistics, 15,* 288–299.

Reppen, R. (1995). A genre-based approach to content writing instruction. *TESOL Journal, 4,* 32–35.

Scollon, R., & Wong-Scollon, S. (2001). *Intercultural communication: A discourse approach* (2nd ed.). Oxford: Blackwell.

Scott, M., & Groom, N. (1999). Genre-based pedagogy: Problems and possibilities. In P. Thompson (Ed.), *Issues in EAP research and writing instruction.* Reading: Centre for Applied Language Studies, University of Reading.

Silva, T. (1990). Second language composition instruction: Developments, issues, and directions in ESL. In B. Kroll (Ed.), *Second language writing: Research insights for the classroom* (pp. 11–23). Cambridge: Cambridge University Press.

Swales, J. M. (1981). *Aspects of article introductions.* (Aston ESP Research Reports, No. 1). The University of Aston at Birmingham, Language Studies Unit.

Swales, J. M. (1986). A genre-based approach to language across the curriculum. In M. L. Tickoo (Ed.), *Language across the curriculum* (pp. 10–22). Anthology Series 15. Singapore: SEAMEO Regional Language Centre.

Swales, J. M. (1990). *Genre analysis. English in academic and research settings.* Cambridge: Cambridge University Press.

Swales, J. M. (2000). Further reflections on genre and ESL academic writing. Keynote presentation at the Symposium on Second Language Writing, Purdue University, USA.

Swales, J. M. (2001). EAP-related linguistic research: An intellectual history. In J. Flowerdew & M. Peacock (Eds.), *Research perspectives on English for academic purposes* (pp. 42–54). Cambridge: Cambridge University Press.

Swales, J. M., & Feak, C. B. (1994). *Academic writing for graduate students. A course for non-native speakers of English.* Ann Arbor: University of Michigan Press.

Swales, J.M. (2004). *Research genres: explorations and applications.* Cambridge: Cambridge University Press.

Swales, J. M., & Feak, C. B. (2000). *English in today's research world.* Ann Arbor: University of Michigan Press.
Wennerstrom, A. (2003). *Discourse analysis in the classroom. Volume 2: Genres of writing.* Ann Arbor: University of Michigan Press.
Widdowson, H. G. (1983). *Learning purpose and language use.* Oxford: Oxford University Press.
Yates, J. (1989). *Control through communication.* Baltimore, MD: Johns Hopkins University Press.
Yates, J., & Orlikowski, W. J. (1992). Genres of organizational communication: A structurational approach. *Academy of Management Review, 17,* 299–326.

CHAPTER 58

RESEARCHING AND DEVELOPING TEACHER LANGUAGE AWARENESS:

Developments and Future Directions

STEPHEN ANDREWS

The University of Hong Kong, China

ABSTRACT

Teacher language awareness (TLA) is receiving increased attention among researchers, teacher educators, and those responsible for quality assurance in language education. This chapter aims to summarize current thinking and research about TLA and to consider future directions for work in the area. Whilst acknowledging the need for TLA to encompass a broad awareness of language in communication, the chapter concentrates specifically on TLA as it relates to the language systems. The first section of the chapter outlines the nature of TLA and explores its potential significance in pedagogical practice. The next section examines the main research findings within TLA and also in interconnected areas such as L2 teachers' cognitions about the linguistic content of their teaching. This is followed by an outline of current approaches to the development of TLA in teaching English as a foreign language (TEFL) programs. The chapter then considers issues of current debate, in particular the TLA of native-speaker (NS) and non-native-speaker (NNS) teachers, before concluding with a discussion of future directions in researching and developing TLA.

INTRODUCTION

Teacher language awareness (TLA) has been defined by Thornbury as "the knowledge that teachers have of the underlying systems of the language that enables them to teach effectively" (1997, p. x). Those who work in the area of TLA are therefore researchers interested in the nature of the L2 teacher's subject-matter knowledge and the impact of that knowledge on pedagogical practice, and/or teacher educators seeking to develop the subject-matter knowledge of L2 teachers in ways that may have a positive influence on the quality of the teaching and learning that takes place in classrooms.

TLA AND LANGUAGE AWARENESS

TLA is closely associated with the so-called *language awareness* (LA) "movement" (e.g., Donmall-Hicks, 1997; Hawkins, 1984; James, 1999; James & Garrett, 1991). LA had its precursors in mainland Europe (see, for example, the discussion in van Essen, 1997), but the movement came to the fore in the UK in the early 1980s, when a National Council for Language in Education (NCLE) Working Party defined LA as "a person's sensitivity to and conscious awareness of the nature of language and its role in human life" (Donmall, 1985, p. 7).

The major focus of LA is explicit knowledge about language and the role of such knowledge in language learning, language teaching, and language use. The associated term, *knowledge about language* (KAL), appears in much of the related literature, reflecting a broadly similar focus (see, for example, Carter, 1990). The LA movement, embracing both mother tongue and second/foreign language teaching, has been particularly influential in the UK and also in other parts of Europe (see, for instance, Candelier, 1999, for discussion of the European EVLANG project, focused on developing "l'éveil aux langues" among children in the last 2 years of primary school).

Those who seek to improve the language awareness of students and of their teachers assume that there is a direct relationship between knowledge of formal aspects of language and performance when using the language. They believe that students who can analyze and describe language accurately are likely to be more effective users of that language. They also believe that teachers' understanding of the language they teach and their ability to analyze it will contribute significantly and directly to their effectiveness as teachers.

TLA, SUBJECT-MATTER KNOWLEDGE, AND PROFESSIONAL STANDARDS

The recent growth of interest in TLA can also be linked to the increased attention currently being paid to the knowledge-base of second language teacher education (e.g., Freeman & Johnson, 1999; Andrews, 2003) and the professionalization of ELT, as well as to the generic notion of the teacher as professional (see, for example, the various papers in Darling-Hammond & Sykes, 1999), and attempts to set professional standards for teachers (see Coniam & Falvey's chapter in Volume 1 for discussion of standards setting for L2 teachers). According to Shulman (1999), teachers are professionals because they need to take thoughtful, grounded actions under conditions that are inherently uncertain and complex. Shulman argues that for those actions to be effective, they need to be grounded in a deep knowledge of subject matter.

Subject-matter knowledge is thus seen as an essential component of teacher professionalism, underpinning the teacher's professional autonomy and responsiveness. At the same time, however, the teacher needs to be "a knowledge worker oriented towards the interpretation, communication, and construction of such knowledge in the interests of student learning" (Shulman, 2000, p. xiii). This view of pedagogy places teachers in a central mediating role in their classrooms, both in relation to what students learn and also to how they learn (Freeman, 2001, pp. 608-609). Within the context of the L2 classroom, such a view of the teacher's role highlights the need to focus attention on the teacher's subject-matter knowledge and its potential impact on the effectiveness with which that teacher mediates input for learning. These are the principal concerns of TLA research.

The core of any teacher's language awareness is subject-matter knowledge. However, as Turner-Bisset (2001) observes, "subject knowledge means different things to different people, and it is important to determine exactly what is meant by subject knowledge" (p. 21). The L2 teacher's subject-matter knowledge base in principle embraces the full range of LA-related issues, including not only grammar but also "other aspects of language in use, including those relating to culture and context, to discourse, to variety, to change and to power" (Arndt, Harvey, & Nuttall, 2000, p. 11). While not denying the importance, for teachers as well as learners, of these broader aspects of LA, including those associated with "critical language awareness" (e.g., Clark & Ivanic, 1999; Fairclough, 1992), the present discussion has a narrower focus, concentrating on teachers' knowledge and understanding of the language systems, in particular grammar and vocabulary, in the belief that those systems are at the heart of the language acquisition process, and that they must therefore form the core of teachers' subject-matter knowledge and of their language awareness.

TLA AND PEDAGOGICAL PRACTICE

What is TLA?

In relation to English language teaching, Wright and Bolitho (1993) assert, "the more aware a teacher is of language and how it works, the better" (p. 292). But what is the nature of such awareness, and how does awareness of language differ from knowledge? The following paragraphs will address these issues.

Edge (1988), writing about NNSs of English, identifies three roles that the TEFL trainee must learn to take on: those of language user, language analyst, and language teacher. Competence as a *language user*, which determines a teacher's adequacy as a model for students, is dependent on that teacher's language proficiency. Competence as a *language analyst* refers to the teacher's ability to understand the workings of language in general and the target language in particular, and is therefore dependent on the teacher's language systems knowledge base. Competence as a *teacher of the language* relates to the teacher's creation and handling of opportunities for language learning, including that teacher's mediation of input for learning.

TLA is centrally related to the second of those two roles: however, it is more than just subject knowledge about the language systems. In pedagogical practice, the three roles identified by Edge (1988) interact, and the harmony of their interaction is dependent upon the extent to which the teacher is "language aware." Wright (2002) relates TLA to the teacher's overall sensitivity to language and illustrates how the different domains of TLA (Edge's three roles) interact:

> A linguistically aware teacher not only understands how language works, but understands the student's struggle with language and is sensitive to errors and other interlanguage features. The linguistically aware teacher can spot opportunities to generate discussion and exploration of language, for example by noticing features of texts which suggest a particular learning activity. (Wright, 2002, p.115)

In other words, TLA is at the heart of successful language teaching. As Wright's (2002) characterization of the language-aware teacher suggests, however, the relationship between subject-matter knowledge and classroom teaching is very complex. One factor contributing to that complexity is the relationship between knowledge of subject matter (i.e., the teacher as language analyst) and language proficiency (the teacher as language user). In those teaching situations where the L2 is taught through the medium of the L2, the relationship is in part one of mediation, with the teacher's knowledge of subject matter being mediated through her language proficiency. At the same time, TLA is also, as Wright implies, metacognitive, involving an extra cognitive dimension of reflections upon both knowledge of subject matter and language proficiency that provides a basis for the tasks of planning and teaching. Brumfit (1997) makes a similar point when he refers to "the central role of teachers as educational linguists (i.e. as conscious analysts of linguistic processes, both their own and others')" (p. 163). Because of its metacognitive nature, TLA has sometimes been referred to as *teacher metalinguistic awareness* (e.g., Andrews, 1997, 1999b, 1999c). TLA also, as Wright suggests, encompasses an awareness of language from the learner's perspective, an awareness of the learner's developing interlanguage, and an awareness of the extent to which the language content of materials/lessons poses difficulties for students.

TLA is therefore very closely linked to the more generic construct of *pedagogic content knowledge*, or *PCK* (e.g., Brophy, 1991; Gess-Newsome, 1999; Shulman, 1986, 1987; Turner-Bisset, 2001). Turner-Bisset outlines a model of PCK as an amalgam of all the interacting knowledge bases that underpin expert teaching. TLA is concerned with a subset of those knowledge bases: specifically, substantive and syntactic subject knowledge (Schwab, 1964), i.e., "knowing that" and "knowing how" (Ryle, 1949), and beliefs about the subject. TLA has been proposed as a major subcomponent of PCK rather than as a synonym for the language teacher's PCK because of its specific focus on subject matter and also because of the uniqueness of the process of language teaching in which language is taught through language (see, for example, the discussion in Andrews, 2001, 2003).

Why is TLA important?

In order to understand why TLA is important, it may be helpful to consider the relevance of TLA to each of the three options in language teaching outlined by Long and Robinson (1998), options that are linked to different teaching/learning foci: (a) "focus on formS" (concentrating on the teaching of discrete points of language); (b) "focus on form" (where the emphasis is on meaning-focused activity, with attention switching to language as the need/opportunity arises in the course of communication); and (c) "focus on meaning" (the "non-interventionist" approaches associated, for example, with Krashen, 1985; Newmark, 1966; and Prabhu, 1987, which advocate abandoning a focus on language forms).

If we take the first option, it should be clear that TLA can potentially play a crucial role in determining the success of any focus-on-formS approach designed to help develop learners' explicit knowledge. Whatever the nature of the focus-on-formS approach adopted, if the syllabus is broadly linguistic, then TLA will necessarily be a significant factor at each stage from lesson preparation through to the provision of corrective feedback.

Less obviously, perhaps, the second option, focus on form, poses no less of a challenge to a teacher's language awareness, because of the teacher's need to consider such factors as the potential linguistic demands of the task and the linguistic capacity of the learners to cope with those demands. In fact, a focus-on-form approach may actually increase the demands on a teacher's language awareness because of the emphasis on language-related activity arising spontaneously out of the tasks rather than being determined in advance. TLA would significantly affect both the teacher's judgment of whether and when to intervene and also her ability to intervene in ways likely to promote learning.

It is with the third option, focus on meaning, that the importance of TLA is perhaps the least obvious. However, even within the most non-interventionist of approaches, one could argue that TLA is significant in determining the effectiveness or otherwise of what takes place in the classroom. If, for example, a teacher (following Krashen, 1981, 1985) wanted the classroom to be a major source of comprehensible input and therefore an "acquisition-rich" environment, then she would presumably need to make decisions about the current stage of development of the students' acquired systems (or interlanguage) and select texts providing comprehensible input, devise tasks entailing an appropriate level of linguistic challenge, and control her own language to a level a little beyond the students' current level of competence. All of these tasks would pose considerable challenges to the teacher's language awareness.

From this it would appear that although TLA is of particular importance where teachers are employing focus-on-formS or focus-on-form approaches, it can also have an impact upon a teacher's effectiveness even within the most extreme of meaning-focused approaches. It therefore seems reasonable to argue that TLA is an essential part of any language teacher's knowledge/skills base.

How Does TLA Affect Teacher Behavior?

In recent years, there have been various attempts to characterize how language awareness affects teacher behavior. Wright and Bolitho (1993) identify a number of pedagogic tasks where TLA may have a significant positive impact, including preparing lessons; evaluating, adapting, and writing materials; understanding, interpreting, and designing syllabuses; and assessing learners' performance. They suggest that a lack of awareness most typically shows itself at the classroom level: "for example when a teacher is unable to identify and compensate for shortcomings in a coursebook, or is 'caught out' by a learner's question on the language" (Wright & Bolitho, p. 292). They emphasize that these points about TLA apply equally to NS and NNS teachers. Thornbury (1997) extends the list of potential consequences of a weakness in TLA to include the teacher's inability to anticipate learners' learning problems and therefore to plan lessons that are pitched at the right level, and "a general failure to earn the confidence of the learners due to a lack of basic terminology and ability to present new language clearly and efficiently" (p. xii).

Leech's (1994) profile of the language-aware teacher outlines the knowledge, awareness, and ability that the teacher brings to the task of dealing with issues relating to *input*—"the target language samples to which the learner is exposed" (Ellis, 1990, p. 96). According to Andrews (2001), the significance of TLA comes from its impact upon the ways in which input is made available to learners. Andrews (p. 80) uses the metaphor of *a filter* to show how a teacher's language awareness can affect the way in which input from each of the three main sources—teaching materials, other learners, and the teacher—is made available to the learner in the L2 classroom.

TLA-RELATED RESEARCH

Wright and Bolitho (1997), echoing James and Garrett (1991), point out that LA remains in general an underresearched area. This continues to be the case, although recently there has been an increase in TLA-related research. This section outlines the nature of such research, with specific reference to L2, and highlights some of the more significant findings.

Early research relating to teachers' KAL (or TLA) was mainly conducted in relation to primary teachers, teachers of English as an L1, and teachers of modern foreign languages (e.g., Chandler, Robinson, & Noyes, 1988; Williamson & Hardman, 1995; Wray, 1993). Much of this research was concerned with measuring aspects of teachers' KAL and finding out about teachers' understandings of KAL, rather than with examining the effects of their KAL on classroom teaching. However, the Southampton KAL project (e.g., Brumfit, Mitchell, & Hooper, 1996) switched the focus of research attention to the classroom. The Southampton project, designed to investigate how language is talked about in UK classrooms, gathered empirical evidence regarding L1 and L2 teachers' beliefs and classroom practices in relation to five dimensions of KAL: language as system, language learning and development, styles and genres of language, social and regional variation, and language change through time. According to Brumfit et al, (1996), although there were individual variations in teacher style, there seemed to be distinctive subject-specific approaches to KAL. The approach of the L1 teachers was text focused, and their KAL-related classroom comments were mainly concerned with features of whole texts. The L2 teachers, in contrast, focused their KAL work on language as system, their rationale being the potential contribution of such activity to the development of students' proficiency in the target language.

More recent research (e.g., Andrews, 1999b) has concentrated specifically on the nature of the subject-specific approach to KAL among L2 teachers. Andrews investigated the TLA of 17 teachers of English (all NNSs working in Hong Kong secondary schools), exploring their beliefs, knowledge, and instructional practices relating to grammar, with a particular focus on the interaction between subject-matter knowledge (the *declarative dimension* of TLA) and pedagogical practice (the *procedural dimension*). The study found that while explicit knowledge of grammar is vital to the consistently successful application of TLA in practice, the possession of such knowledge is not sufficient to ensure that the teacher will deal with grammar-related issues in ways most likely to be conducive to learning. Language proficiency was shown to play a crucial role in the application of TLA in pedagogical practice, not only affecting the quality of teacher reflections about language but also impacting the quality of teacher output and the teacher's mediation of all three potential sources of input for learning: teaching materials, other learners, and the teacher. There was also considerable evidence to suggest that the TLA filter has a marked effect upon the teacher's performance of a number of tasks widely believed to facilitate learning: for instance, making salient the key grammatical features within input, providing examples and explanations, helping learners to make useful generalizations, and limiting potential sources of learner confusion. A follow-up study (Andrews, 2005) investigated the TLA of three of the original 17 teachers after a gap of seven years, and found that their knowledge and beliefs about grammar were largely unchanged.

Andrews's work (from Andrews, 1994, onwards) has focused specifically on TLA as it relates to grammar (although Andrews and McNeill, 2005, report a study focusing on TLA as it relates to both grammar and vocabulary). Research by Morris (e.g., Morris 2002; 2003) has also looked at grammatical knowledge, specifically of pre-service teachers, in order to identify correlations between participant traits and their pre-service learning. Morris (2002) suggests that age is a very good predictor of responses to different pedagogical approaches in TESL training.

McNeill's research (e.g., 1999) has concentrated on teachers' knowledge of vocabulary, in particular their awareness of lexical difficulty. McNeill's work is noteworthy for highlighting the role of awareness of the learner in any conceptualization of both TLA and of the language-aware teacher (see also Wright, 2002). McNeill argues that, given the text-based nature of so much EFL pedagogical practice, the effectiveness of such teaching may be crucially affected by teachers' ability to identify the vocabulary content of texts that their students find difficult. As McNeill shows, awareness of learners' vocabulary difficulties varies widely among teachers.

Tests of metalinguistic awareness have been used by a number of researchers, to measure the LA of both students (e.g., Alderson, Clapham, & Steel, 1996; Bloor, 1986) and teachers (Andrews, 1999a, 1999b, 2004; Andrews & McNeill, 2005). LA tests are also commonly used by centers offering preservice TEFL training for the practical purpose of screening applicants. Recently, the predictive value of such testing has become the subject of research in TLA. Morris and Cobb (2004), for example, report on a study forming part of a broader project (see also Morris, 2002, 2003) to examine the relationship between the metalinguistic awareness of preservice TESL trainees and their performance on their initial training program. Morris and Cobb's study investigates the predictive power of trainees' vocabulary profiles, based on analysis of their entrance essays using a modified, online version of Hwang and Nation's *Vocabulary Profiler* (Cobb, 2002). According to Morris and Cobb (2004), the results indicate that vocabulary profiles have great potential as predictors of academic and pedagogic success on TEFL programs.

Knowledge of metalanguage, though not synonymous with metalinguistic awareness, has formed the basis for the aforementioned tests of metalinguistic awareness, because, as Alderson, Clapham, and Steel (1996) observe, "whatever explicit knowledge is, it must include metalanguage" (p. 2). A number of TLA-related research studies have also focused on metalanguage. Murray (1998), for example, has investigated ELT trainees' acquisition of TEFL metalanguage, which she suggests is part of their professionalization, helping them to become members of the ELT professional discourse community. Borg (1999c) focuses specifically on teachers' practices in using grammatical metalanguage and the motivation for their decisions about how metalinguistically explicit to be. Meanwhile, Berry (1997) has investigated teachers' awareness of learners' knowledge of grammatical terminology, basing his research on the premise that, if metalinguistic terminology is used in L2 classrooms, teachers need to be aware of their student's knowledge of metalanguage. Berry's research, which, like McNeill's (1999), highlights the importance for TLA of awareness of the learner, revealed major discrepancies between students' knowledge of terminology and teachers' estimates of that knowledge, with teacher overestimation of that knowledge being far more common than underestimation.

The area of L2 teachers' cognitions (their beliefs, knowledge, assumptions, theories, and attitudes) in relation to grammar has recently become an increasingly important part of TLA-related research (see, for example, Andrews, 1999b; Borg, 1998, 1999a, 1999b, 2003; Palfreyman, 1993). Borg (1999a) makes a powerful case for researching this area, given our lack of understanding of teachers' practices and cognitions in L2 grammar teaching and of the reasons for their instructional decision-making, and he argues that improved understanding could have a significant impact on the process of teacher education. Borg's 1998 study is an example of such research, providing a detailed examination of the personal pedagogical system that shapes the approach to grammar pedagogy of one experienced EFL teacher. A recurrent theme in Borg's work is the interactive, and sometimes potentially conflicting, nature of the cognitions informing teacher decisions about grammar pedagogy. Borg (2003) provides an overview of studies of teacher cognition in relation to the teaching of grammar in first, second, and foreign language classrooms.

Recent research by Walsh (e.g., 2001, 2003) has focused on the *teacher talk* aspect of TLA and has suggested the need to add an additional dimension to the conceptualization of TLA: L2 teachers' interactional awareness. Walsh's work employs a sociocultural theoretical framework to investigate teacher's own use of language in teacher-fronted, multiparticipant L2 classes. The study uses the constructs *quality teacher talk* and *L2 classroom interactional competence* to describe how teachers' enhanced understanding of interactional processes can facilitate learner involvement and increase opportunities for learning. According to Walsh, training in interactional awareness, making use of procedures such as the self-evaluation of teacher talk (SETT) grid, can help teachers to develop appropriate teacher language and strategies for potentially enhancing learning opportunities in the L2 classroom. Training to enhance interactional awareness is premised on the belief that, as Walsh observes, "so much of what 'good' teaching is about…depends on developing L2 classroom interactional competence and making the most of the interactional choices available" (p. 337).

APPROACHES TO THE DEVELOPMENT OF TLA

Language awareness work has formed an integral part of TEFL courses ever since John Haycraft set up his pioneering preservice courses for NSs at International House (IH) in London in the 1960s (see Haycraft, 1988). Language work in TEFL programs, variously labeled in syllabus documents as *language analysis*, *language awareness*, or, ambiguously, *LA*, has become an area of increasing interest and debate (beginning with Shaw, 1979). This section outlines some of the issues relating to LA work on teacher development courses.

The IH "four-week" courses provided a blueprint for similar programs in many parts of the world, via the RSA/Cambridge CTEFLA preservice training scheme (now known as CELTA, and targeted at both NSs and NNSs). From the outset, the IH courses included a certain amount of language analysis because it was felt that the NSs for whom the courses were designed had no experience of analyzing language from the perspectives of learning and the learner.

According to Kerr (1993), much of the LA work on courses following the IH or CTEFLA model has emphasized the analytical process of studying language at the expense of the application of any insights that might be gained from such analysis.

As a result, LA activity has typically focused on the transmission of knowledge about language rather than on fostering an awareness of implications for the learner or the teaching/learning process (p. 41). In 1996, the CTEFLA scheme gave way to CELTA, which had a more enlightened Language Awareness syllabus than its predecessor. However, Kerr (1998) found that the LA component of training courses in 30 CELTA centers was largely unchanged, with recent developments in the analysis of computer corpora, of collocation, of spoken grammar, and of discourse having had "very little impact in the way that CELTA trainers have conceived of and packaged language awareness for their trainees" (p. 5).

The problem noted by Kerr (1998) is, at least in part, the result of a dilemma in preservice training: on the one hand, trainees need the security of predigested "facts" about language that will enable them to survive their initial classroom experience without their confidence being too severely dented; on the other hand, if they are to develop professionally, they must be ready to question and reflect on the adequacy of such facts. As Wright and Bolitho (1993) point out, basic knowledge about language may be a necessary part of TLA work, but it is not in itself sufficient to produce a language-aware teacher. For Wright and Bolitho, LA is a process intended to help both preservice and in-service trainees "to develop their sensitivity towards language, as part of a strategy aimed at enhancing classroom teaching and learning" (p. 302). LA activity therefore needs to focus on the procedural dimension of TLA as well as the declarative dimension.

The first published LA materials aimed primarily at teachers (Bolitho & Tomlinson's "Discover English") appeared in 1980, to be followed by Wright (1994), the second edition of "Discover English" (Bolitho & Tomlinson, 1995), and Thornbury (1997). These materials consist in the main of data-based language analysis tasks intended to stimulate the user's reflections on the workings of different parts of the language systems. Many of the activities in these materials focus primarily on the declarative dimension of TLA, encouraging the user to question predigested facts and preconceptions about language. Wright (2002) suggests that the materials published up to now do not always make a successful link between the declarative dimension and the procedural dimension of pedagogical practice. Arndt, Harvey, and Nuttall (2000) take a broader view of LA (see section on *TLA, Subject-matter Knowledge, and Professional Standards* earlier in the chapter) and attempt to link the declarative and procedural dimensions of TLA through tasks that explicitly encourage the user to relate information and ideas to their individual teaching situations. However, the success of any materials in integrating the declarative and procedural dimensions of TLA is inevitably dependent on how those materials are used.

Wright and Bolitho (1997) outline an "experiential" approach to LA work, which is intended to make that link between the declarative and procedural dimensions. In proposing this approach, which they see as especially appropriate for in-service work, they associate TLA with more general views of teachers' professional development, arguing that "no teacher of any language should ever stop learning about their subject" (p. 173). This experiential approach requires teachers to focus on a language problem deriving from their own experience, to analyze and review that experience, to explore the problem in order to gain deeper insights into the particular area of language, and to plan for subsequent classroom action. The approach is seen as having a number of benefits, with the increased knowledge about language and the ability to link such knowledge to pedagogical practice giving teachers increased confidence in their subject-matter knowledge and a consequent readiness to be a discriminating, critical master of textbook materials, rather than an uncritical slave.

A number of the most recent proposals for developing TLA derive from research, for example, Walsh's (2001, 2003) training in interactional awareness, Murray's (2002) activities to promote error detection, and Borg's (1999b) strategies for encouraging teachers to explore the theories underlying their pedagogical practice when teaching grammar. Increasingly, approaches to developing TLA are also making use of the ease of access to large corpora of language data and the development of powerful concordancing tools. Such developments as the Telenex computer network, for instance, which links hundreds of teachers in Hong Kong schools, make use of corpus data both in online grammar files and in responses to queries from teachers about language points (e.g., Allan, 1999; Tsui & Nicolson, 1999). The impact of corpus linguistics on TLA is undoubtedly set to grow in the coming years as technology opens up new opportunities for LA work, both on courses and via self-access.

ISSUES IN TLA

A number of the major issues in TLA, in both research and teacher development, were discussed earlier. These include the nature of the subject-matter knowledge of the L2 teacher, the impact of such knowledge on pedagogical practice, and how best to handle language work at different stages of the L2 teacher's professional development. The aim in this section of the chapter is therefore to focus on another issue only briefly touched upon earlier: the TLA of NS and NNS teachers and professional standards.

The relative merits of NS and NNS teachers of English have been increasingly debated in recent years (e.g., Andrews, 1999a; Medgyes, 1994; Seidlhofer, 1999; and the papers in Braine, 1999). Conventional wisdom in the early days of the ELT profession held the ideal teacher of English as L2 to be an NS of that language. This view, the so-called *native-speaker fallacy* (Phillipson, 1992, pp. 193-199), has been seriously questioned as part of the ongoing debate, stimulated by Kachru (for example, Kachru, 1985, 1990), about the status of non-native World Englishes and the implications of using them as pedagogical models in the classroom. It was, however, a fallacy that was widely accepted in the 1960s and 1970s, making NS graduates of that era easily employable as EFL teachers.

The inclusion of an LA component in the first, previously mentioned, IH TEFL courses in the 1960s was already an indication of the potential limitations of the NS graduate as a teacher of EFL. The need for increased attention to TLA on such programs became more and more apparent in the 1980s and 1990s, particularly as providers of training realized that most NSs of English below a certain age had no experience of studying English grammar, even at school (see Andrews, 1994). The experience of one NS teacher of English working in Hungary is perhaps typical: "Most native teachers I know never really came across grammar until they started teaching it. So you have to learn it as you go along" (Arva & Medgyes, 2000, p. 361).

Fewer doubts have generally been voiced about the TLA of NNS teachers of English. According to Arva and Medgyes (2000), there may indeed be a common perception that such teachers "speak poorer English, use 'bookish' language, and use English less confidently" than NS teachers (p. 357). However, it has also been assumed that NNS teachers have "more insight into and better meta-cognitive knowledge of grammar" than their NS counterparts (p. 364), because of their educational background and training. Seidlhofer (1999) also emphasizes the strengths of NNS teachers, not just in terms of the high level of declarative knowledge of the internal organization of the language that they possess as a result of their own language learning experience, but also because of their ability to "get into the skin of the foreign learner" (pp. 242-243).

In recent years, however, assumptions about the high level of subject-matter knowledge of NNS teachers have been called into question in many parts of the world because the demand for appropriately qualified teachers of English has far outstripped the supply. The inevitable result of this shortage in those countries affected is that there are large numbers of NNS teachers of English in both the public and private sectors who lack the necessary educational background and training. The consequences for their TLA, both the declarative and procedural dimensions, are highlighted in studies such as Andrews (1999b).

Given the importance of TLA in pedagogical practice and the potential TLA limitations of both NS and NNS teachers, as noted above, it is hardly surprising that TLA has become an increasingly important component of the professional standards expected of the L2 teacher. Recognition of the importance of TLA in professional standards setting can be seen in the greater emphasis accorded to the teaching and assessment of language awareness within such TEFL programs as the CELTA and DELTA (UCLES, 1996, 1998). At the same time, it is noteworthy that CELTA and DELTA are unifications of previously separate training schemes for NS and NNS teachers of English. A major aim behind the unification of these schemes was to focus on the similarities between NS and NNS teachers, and on the need for all teachers of English to achieve certain professional standards. TLA has therefore been highlighted as an area of crucial importance for every L2 teacher, whether an NS or NNS of the target language.

There are, however, a number of challenges relating to TLA and NS/NNS teachers. One such challenge arises in situations where NS and NNS teachers are working together as colleagues, namely, the challenge of making the best possible use of the often complementary strengths of such teachers, particularly in relation to their knowledge of language and knowledge about language, in ways that are maximally beneficial to the students and also of mutual benefit to the NS and NNS teachers.

Another major set of challenges faces those charged with implementing the wish of policymakers to assess the language knowledge and language proficiency of L2 teachers to ensure that they meet minimum professional standards. These challenges, which affect both NS and NNS teachers, concern what to assess (language proficiency, declarative TLA, and/or procedural TLA) and how to assess, as well as the crucial issue of how and where to set the benchmark, or minimum acceptable standard, in each of the assessed performance dimensions (see Coniam & Falvey's chapter in Volume 1 for further discussion of some of these issues). As professional standard setting becomes more widespread, these issues are set to assume even greater importance for the ELT profession.

FUTURE DIRECTIONS

As indicated in the earlier discussion, many of the future directions in TLA development are likely to be associated, at least in part, with advances in technology. Those responsible for the LA component of teacher development courses will be able to make full use of the possibilities opened up by easy access to corpora and concordancing tools, and to set up improved networks of communication allowing trainees (both preservice and in-service) to interact electronically with each other and/or the trainer on language-related issues. Increasingly, too, technological developments will allow self-access work on TLA to become a focal point for the L2 teacher's ongoing professional development.

In research, TLA is such an underinvestigated area that there is enormous scope, as well as a great need, for TLA-related research activity of all kinds. Freeman (2001) outlines a number of the key questions, such as the role of subject-matter knowledge in instruction, what it is that L2 teachers need to know about language in general and the target language in particular in order to teach, and the amount and type of subject-matter knowledge needed to teach different levels of learner. Some of the studies discussed earlier have attempted to address these questions, but they and other questions remain to be investigated further, including the issue raised by Borg (2003): the relationship between teacher cognition, classroom practice and learning. The following are examples of TLA-related issues that would all warrant further investigation:

1. The TLA profiles of different types of teacher (i.e., with different language, educational and professional backgrounds)
2. The impact of TLA in contexts where the prevailing approach to language pedagogy emphasizes a focus on form or focus on meaning approach
3. Systematic comparison of the TLA of NS and NNS teachers
4. Influences upon the development of TLA, including the potential impact of professional training
5. Dimensions of TLA other than grammar, and the links between grammar-related TLA and teacher awareness of other aspects of the language systems
6. The impact of TLA upon learners and learning
7. The relationship between the declarative and procedural dimensions of TLA, and between TLA and general teaching competence
8. How TLA might best be developed, both the declarative dimension and, more especially, the procedural dimension
9. Factors affecting the impact of TLA upon pedagogical practice, including the teacher's willingness to "engage" with language-related issues and teacher confidence
10. The relationship between the L2 TLA of the NNS teacher and that same teacher's LA in L1.

Above all, it is to be hoped that future directions in TLA bring research and practice in TLA closer together, so that practice becomes a focus for research and is also informed by research. Creating such a bridge between research and practice can only serve to strengthen the professionalization of EFL teachers.

REFERENCES

Alderson, J., Clapham, C., & Steel, D. (1996). Metalinguistic knowledge, language aptitude and language proficiency. *CRLE, University of Lancaster Working Papers*, 26.

Allan, Q. (1999). Enhancing the language awareness of Hong Kong teachers through corpus data: The Telenex experience. *Journal of Technology and Teacher Education*, 7(1), 57–74.

Andrews, S. (1994). The grammatical knowledge/awareness of native-speaker EFL teachers. In M. Bygate, A. Tonkyn, & E. Williams (Eds), *Grammar and the language teacher* (pp. 69–89). Hemel Hempstead: Prentice Hall.

Andrews, S. (1997). Metalinguistic awareness and teacher explanation. *Language Awareness*, 6(2 & 3), 147–161.

Andrews, S. (1999a). 'All these like little name things' – a comparative study of language teachers' explicit knowledge of grammar and grammatical terminology. *Language Awareness*, 8(3 & 4), 143–159.

Andrews, S. (1999b). *The metalinguistic awareness of Hong Kong secondary school teachers of English*. Unpublished Ph.D. thesis, University of Southampton, U.K.

Andrews, S. (1999c). Why do L2 teachers need to 'know about language'?: Teacher metalinguistic awareness and input for learning. *Language and Education*, 13(3), 161–177.

Andrews, S. (2001). The language awareness of the L2 teacher: Its impact upon pedagogical practice. *Language Awareness*, 10(2 & 3), 75–90.

Andrews, S. (2003). Teacher language awareness and the professional knowledge base of the L2 teacher. *Language Awareness*, 12(2), 81–95.

Andrews, S. (2005). The evolution of teacher language awareness. *Language Awareness*, 15(1), 1–19.

Andrews, S., & McNeill, A. (2005). Knowledge about language (KAL) and the 'good language teacher'. In N. Bartels (Ed.), *Applied linguistics and language teacher education* (pp. 159–178). New York: Springer.

Arndt, V., Harvey, P., & Nuttall, J. (2000). *Alive to language*. Cambridge: Cambridge University Press.

Arva, V., & Medgyes, P. (2000). Native and non-native teachers in the classroom. *System*, 28, 355–372.

Berry, R. (1997). Teachers' awareness of learners' knowledge: The case of metalinguistic terminology. *Language Awareness*, 6(2 & 3), 136–146.

Bloor, T. (1986). What do language students know about grammar? *British Journal of Language Teaching*, 24(3), 157–160.

Bolitho, R., & Tomlinson, B. (1980). *Discover English*. London: George Allen and Unwin.

Bolitho, R., & Tomlinson, B. (1995). *Discover English* (2nd ed.). Oxford: Heinemann.

Borg, S. (1998). Teachers' pedagogical systems and grammar teaching: A qualitative study. *TESOL Quarterly*, 32(1), 9–37.

Borg, S. (1999a). Studying teacher cognition in second language grammar teaching. *System*, 27, 19–31.

Borg, S. (1999b). Teachers' theories in grammar teaching. *ELT Journal*, 53(3), 157–167.

Borg, S. (1999c). The use of grammatical terminology in the second language classroom: a qualitative study of teachers' practices and cognitions. *Applied Linguistics*, 20(1), 95–126.

Borg, S. (2003). Teacher cognition in grammar teaching: a literature review. *Language Awareness*, 12(2), 96–108.

Braine, G. (Ed.). (1999). *Non-native educators in English Language teaching*. Mahwah, NJ: Lawrence Erlbaum.

Brophy, J. (Ed.). (1991). *Advances on research on teaching* (Vol. 2). Greenwich, CT: JAI Press.

Brumfit, C. (1997). The teacher as educational linguist. In L. van Lier & D. Corson, (Eds.), *Encyclopedia of language and education*, (Vol. 6): *Knowledge about language* (pp. 163–171). Dordrecht: Kluwer Publications.

Brumfit, C., Mitchell, R., & Hooper, J. (1996). "Grammar", "language" and classroom practice. In M. Hughes (Ed.), *Teaching and learning in changing times* (pp. 70–87). Oxford: Blackwell.

Candelier, M. (1999). En quelques lignes: L'éveil aux langues à l'école primaire dans le programme européen 'Evlang' [In brief: language awareness in primary schools in the European EVLANG program]. *Language Awareness*, 8(3 & 4), 237–239.

Carter, R. (1990). *Knowledge about language and the curriculum: The LINC reader*. London: Hodder and Stoughton.

Chandler, P., Robinson, W., & Noyes, P. (1988). The level of linguistic knowledge and awareness among students training to be primary teachers. *Language and Education*, 2(3), 161–173.

Clark, R., & Ivanic, R. (Eds.). (1999). Critical language awareness [Special issue]. *Language Awareness*, 8, 2.

Cobb, T. (2002). Web VocabProfile. Available at http://www.er.uqam.ca/nobel/r21270/cgibin/webfreqs/web_vp.cgi.

Darling-Hammond, L., & Sykes, G. (Eds.). (1999). *Teaching as the learning profession*. San Francisco: Jossey-Bass.
Donmall, G. (Ed.). (1985). Language Awareness. *NCLE Reports and Papers, 6*. London: CILT.
Donmall-Hicks, G. (1997). The history of language awareness in the United Kingdom. In L. van Lier & D. Corson (Eds.), *Encyclopedia of language and education (Vol. 6): Knowledge about language* (pp. 21–30). Dordrecht: Kluwer Publications.
Edge, J. (1988). Applying linguistics in English language teacher training for speakers of other languages. *ELT Journal, 42*(1), 9–13.
Ellis, R. (1990). *Instructed second language acquisition*. Oxford: Blackwell.
Fairclough, N. (Ed.). (1992). *Critical language awareness*. London: Longman.
Freeman, D. (2001). Teacher learning and student learning in TESOL. *TESOL Quarterly, 35*(4), 608–609.
Freeman, D., & Johnson, K. (1999, May). *Towards a new knowledge-base of second language teacher education*. Paper presented at the International Conference on Language Teacher Education (ILTE), CARLA, University of Minnesota.
Gess-Newsome, J. (1999). Pedagogical content knowledge: An introduction and orientation. In J. Gess-Newsome & N. Lederman (Eds.), *Examining pedagogical content knowledge* (pp. 3–20). Dordrecht: Kluwer.
Hawkins, E. (1984). *Awareness of language: An introduction*. Cambridge: Cambridge University Press.
Haycraft, J. (1988). The first International House Preparatory Course: A historical overview. In T. Duff (Ed.), *Explorations in teacher training – problems and issues* (pp. 1–9). London: Longman.
James, C. (1999). Language awareness: Implications for the language curriculum. *Language, Culture and Curriculum, 12*(1), 94–115.
James, C., & Garrett, P. (Eds.). (1991). *Language awareness in the classroom*. London: Longman.
Kachru, B. (1985). Standards, codification and sociolinguistic realism: The English language in the Outer Circle. In R. Quirk & H. Widdowson (Eds.), *English in the world: Teaching and learning the language and literatures* (pp. 11–30). Cambridge: Cambridge University Press.
Kachru, B. (1990). World Englishes and applied linguistics. *World Englishes, 9*(1), 3–20.
Kerr, P. (1993). Language training on pre-service courses for native speakers. *Modern English Teacher, 2*(4), 40–43.
Kerr, P. (1998). Language awareness: practices and progress. *English Language Teacher Education and Development, 4*(1), 1–7.
Krashen, S. (1981). *Second language acquisition and second language learning*. Oxford: Pergamon.
Krashen, S. (1985). *The input hypothesis: Issues and implications*. London: Longman.
Leech, G. (1994). Students' grammar – Teachers' grammar – Learners' grammar. In M. Bygate, A. Tonkyn, & E. Williams (Eds.), *Grammar and the language teacher* (pp. 17–30). Hemel Hempstead: Prentice Hall.
Long, M., & Robinson, P. (1998). Focus on form: Theory, research, and practice. In C. Doughty & J. Williams (Eds.), *Focus on form in classroom second language acquisition* (pp. 15–41). Cambridge: Cambridge University Press.
McNeill, A. (1999). *Teachers' awareness of lexical difficulty in ESL reading texts*. Unpublished Ph.D. thesis, University of Wales.
Medgyes, P. (1994). *The non-native teacher*. London: Macmillan.
Morris, L. (2002). Age and uptake in TESL training: Differing responses to declaratively- and procedurally-oriented grammar instruction. *Language Awareness, 11*(3), 192–207.
Morris, L. (2003). Linguistic knowledge, metalinguistic knowledge and academic success in a language teacher education programme. *Language Awareness 12*(2), 109–123.
Morris, L., & Cobb, T. (2004). Vocabulary profiles as predictors of the academic performance of Teaching English as a Second Language trainees. *System, 32*(1), 75–87.
Murray, H. (1998, Spring). The development of professional discourse and language awareness in EFL teacher training. *IATEFL Teacher Trainers SIG Newsletter, 21*, 3–7.
Murray, H. (2002). Developing language awareness and error detection: What can we expect of novice trainees? In H. Trappes-Lomax & G. Ferguson (Eds.), *Language in language teacher education* (pp. 187–198). London: John Benjamin.
Newmark, L. (1966). How not to interfere in language learning. *International Journal of American Linguistics, 32*, 77–87.
Palfreyman, D. (1993). "How I got it in my head": Conceptual models of language and learning in native and non-native trainee EFL teachers. *Language Awareness, 2*(4), 209–223.
Phillipson, R. (1992). *Linguistic imperialism*. Oxford: Oxford University Press.
Prabhu, N. (1987). *Second language pedagogy*. Oxford: Oxford University Press.
Ryle, G. (1949). *The concept of mind*. London: Hutchinson.

Schwab, J.J. (1964). The structure of disciplines: Meanings and significance. In G.W. Ford & L. Pugno (Eds.), *The structure of knowledge and the curriculum* (pp. 6–30). Chicago: Rand McNally.

Seidlhofer, B. (1999). Double standards: Teacher education in the Expanding Circle. *World Englishes, 18*(2), 233–245.

Shaw, P. (1979). Handling a language component in a teacher training course. In S. Holden (Ed.), *Teacher Training* (pp. 12–15). London: Modern English Publications.

Shulman, L. (1986). Those who understand: Knowledge growth in teaching. *Educational Researcher, 15*(2), 4–14.

Shulman, L. (1987). Knowledge and teaching: Foundations of the new reform. *Harvard Educational Review, 57*(1), 1–22.

Shulman, L. (1999). Foreword. In L. Darling-Hammond & G. Sykes (Eds.), *Teaching as the learning profession* (pp. xi–xiv). San Francisco: Jossey-Bass.

Thornbury, S. (1997). *About language.* Cambridge: CUP.

Tsui, A., & Nicholson, S. (1999). Hypermedia database and ESL teacher knowledge enrichment. *Journal of Information Technology for Teacher Education, 8*(2), 215–237.

Turner-Bisset, R. (2001). *Expert teaching.* London: Fulton.

UCLES. (1996). *CELTA: Pilot syllabus and assessment guidelines.* Cambridge: University of Cambridge Local Examinations Syndicate.

UCLES. (1998). DELTA: Pilot syllabus guidelines for course tutors and assessors and DELTA: Pilot assessment guidelines for course tutors and assessors. Cambridge: University of Cambridge Local Examinations Syndicate.

van Essen, A. (1997). Language awareness and knowledge about language: An overview. In L. van Lier & D. Corson (Eds.), *Encyclopedia of Language and Education (Vol. 6): Knowledge about Language* (pp. 1–9). Netherlands: Kluwer Publications.

Walsh, S. (2001). *Characterising teacher talk in the second language classroom: A process model of reflective practice.* Unpublished Ph.D. thesis, Queen's University, Belfast.

Walsh, S. (2003). Developing interactional awareness in the second language classroom through teacher self-evaluation. *Language Awareness, 12*(2), 124–142.

Williamson, J., & Hardman, F. (1995). Time for refilling the bath?: A study of primary student-teachers' grammatical knowledge. *Language and Education, 9*(2), 117–134.

Wray, D. (1993). Student-teachers' knowledge and beliefs about language. In N. Bennett & C. Carre (Eds.), *Learning to teach* (pp. 51–72). London: Routledge.

Wright, T. (1994). *Investigating English.* London: Arnold.

Wright, T. (2002). Doing language awareness: Issues for language study in language teacher education. In H. Trappes-Lomax & G. Ferguson (Eds.), *Language in language teacher education* (pp. 113–130). London: John Benjamin.

Wright, T., & Bolitho, R. (1993). Language awareness: A missing link in language teacher education? *ELT Journal, 47*(4), 292–304.

Wright, T., & Bolitho, R. (1997). Language awareness in in-service programs. In L. van Lier & D. Corson (Eds.), *Encyclopedia of language and education (Vol. 6): Knowledge about language* (pp. 173–181). Dordrecht: Kluwer Publications.

Section 3:

Research and Teacher Education in ELT: Meeting New Challenges

SECTION 3

RESEARCH AND TEACHER EDUCATION IN ELT:

Meeting New Challenges

JIM CUMMINS AND CHRIS DAVISON

INTRODUCTION

The purpose of research in the social sciences is to generate data that contribute to our understanding of social phenomena. In education, research provides information on multiple phenomena such as the efficacy of various instructional approaches, achievement differences between social groups and across countries, and the many factors that contribute to school improvement generally. It is common to assume that there is a direct relationship between research and both policy and practice. Policy-makers and practitioners are usually seen as consumers of research insofar as they apply research findings to the generation of policy and the implementation of more effective practice. Clearly political considerations enter into all stages of this process—in decisions about what research gets funded, what research methodologies are considered "scientific" or relevant to policy, in the conclusions drawn from the research, and the policies and practices that are ultimately promoted. Analysis of the relationship between research and policy/practice in virtually any context will reveal the complex intersections between empirical data and ideology.

Less clearly understood is the role of *theory* in mediating the relationship between research and both policy and practice. Popular conceptions of theory view it either as standing alone, aloof from practice, or alternatively, as being irrelevant to practice and the real world. It is common to hear ideas being dismissed as "just theory" followed up by demands to just "show me the facts." This perspective reflects an inadequate understanding of the role that theory plays in making "facts" or research data interpretable for policy and practice. In fact it is theory rather than research that speaks directly to policy and practice. Theory, rather than individual research findings, permits the generation of predictions about program outcomes and the effects of various interventions under different conditions. Research findings themselves cannot be directly applied across contexts. Theory permits generalizations across contexts based on understanding of the underlying processes that give rise to specific phenomena in particular contexts. Theory also integrates observations and practices into coherent perspectives and, through dialogue, feeds these perspectives back into practice and from practice back into theory. Theory addresses educational practice not only in the narrow sense of what happens in the classroom but also in terms of how classroom interaction is influenced by the societal discourses that surround educational practices. Theory can challenge inappropriate or coercive policies, practices, and associated discourses by pointing both to inconsistencies with empirical data and also to internal logical contradictions within these discourses. It can also propose alternative understandings of phenomena and chart directions for change. Thus, the relationship between theory and practice is two-way and ongoing: practice generates theory, which, in turn, acts as a catalyst for new directions in practice, which then inform theory, and so on. Theory and practice are infused within each other. The role of researchers and policy-makers is to mediate this relationship. Research provides a lens through which practice can be seen and brought into theoretical focus for particular purposes and in particular contexts. Policy-makers interpret the research findings and set guidelines for practice on the basis of both the research and sociopolitical and fiscal realities.

The chapters in this section examine various approaches to research in ELT and explore how research interacts with theory and sociopolitical considerations in the development of teacher education policies and practices. The influence of broader epistemological discourses is also addressed by Brian Morgan in contrasting how applied linguists and poststructuralists frame ELT issues and phenomena. The chapters on research focus on various approaches to qualitative research in ELT. We have chosen to focus on qualitative approaches rather than quantitative approaches because, while both are legitimate and important, recent qualitative research has emerged as a fruitful source of insight and theory generation in the field of ELT. This is partly because issues that have preoccupied researchers in recent years, such as the roles of identity and societal power relations in language learning, do not lend themselves to quantification. Furthermore, much of the experimental and quasi-experimental research in ELT has proven to be quite limited in its ability to answer questions about program effectiveness (see Cummins, 2000). This derives primarily from ethical and practical constraints in applying a medical model of double blind experimentation to complex educational and social phenomena. Even well-designed large-scale analyses of quantitative data that have succeeded in overcoming many of the ethical and practical constraints of program comparison, such as the Collier and Thomas study (see Volume 1 of this Handbook), only provide us with a starting point for inquiry into the underlying causes of the program differences observed. These underlying causes are more likely to be elucidated by qualitative than by quantitative research. In short, both qualitative and quantitative research data have important, and often complementary, roles to play in generating understanding (theory) and thereby informing policy and practice.

Duff's chapter provides an overview of qualitative approaches to classroom research in ELT. She points out that qualitative research represents a cluster or continuum of approaches that seek naturalistic, holistic understandings and interpretations of phenomena that occur in particular types of contexts. Qualitative research conducted in classrooms has typically focused on instructional behaviors, interaction patterns among teachers and students, and the teaching/learning processes and outcomes associated with different types of language and literacy activities. A significant advantage of qualitative approaches is that they are capable of exploring *insider* perspectives and interpretations rather than relying only on what can be observed or measured from the outside, as in more traditional research paradigms. Teachers, as inside participants in educational relationships, have the potential to "see inside" these relationships; their "in-sights" cannot be duplicated by those who gaze at these processes from the outside (e.g. typical university researchers). At the same time there are dimensions of issues and problems that are not apparent to those in the middle of a situation but potentially identifiable to those who are somewhat distanced from it. Thus, while often logistically and conceptually challenging, as Duff points out, qualitative research has the potential to bring together macro- and micro-analyses and insider and outsider perspectives on issues and phenomena. Duff illustrates the kinds of insights that can be derived from qualitative research by reviewing three exemplary studies of English language learning and teaching in classroom contexts. These studies range from the early grades of public school to college level and provide insight into how certain kinds of language and literacy practices can unwittingly contribute to the marginalization of English language learners.

Burns extends the discussion of qualitative research into the more specific area of *action research* that focuses simultaneously on *action* and *research*. Although typically qualitative in orientation, the approach can also include the collection of quantitative data. Action research involves the initiation of a planned intervention that implements concrete strategies, processes, or activities in response to a perceived problem or issue that policy-makers or practitioners wish to address and resolve. Systematic data are collected about the implementation and outcomes of the intervention, typically with a focus on understanding the conditions necessary for change to occur. Thus, the process involves reflection by participants focused on how to improve practice and informed by data collected in the specific action research context. Action research may be undertaken by individuals (e.g. a teacher in her classroom), groups (e.g. a partnership between school-based and university-based researchers), or by larger institutions (e.g. an entire school or school district). Burns points out that there is considerable debate in the ELT field about how to ensure methodological rigor in action research. However, the core question to be asked of action research is similar to the criteria for judging other forms of research, namely, "Are the claims being made on the basis of the data meaningful, believable, and trustworthy?" She suggests that action research will expand its influence on ELT practice and policy both because of its flexibility and potential for broad application and because it positions ELT professionals as agents, rather than recipients, of knowledge.

Phillion and He address another form of qualitative research, narrative inquiry, that is rapidly gaining credibility in the general field of education as well as in the specific area of language teaching and learning. Narrative inquiry focuses on the stories that make up people's lived experience. The stories are the phenomena that are studied by means of narrative inquiry. The goal, in the context of English language learning and teaching, is to gain insight into the complex life experiences of individuals as they engage in the process of acquiring a new language or helping others learn a new language. Because it focuses on the totality of experience, narrative inquiry can address issues such as the intersections between language learning and identity negotiation, the challenges of gaining access to a new culture, and the impact of societal power relations on language learning. Phillion and He point out that there are no particular hypotheses or ideas being demonstrated or tested. Rather than attempting to control variables, narrative inquiry welcomes the range of influences on individuals' experience and behavior into the research setting and attempts to understand the dynamics of their intersections. As in much qualitative research, the goal is to gain insight through the in-depth study of one particular set of phenomena, in this case the stories that constitute experience.

Markee's description of *conversation analysis* takes us far from the experiential realm of narrative inquiry discussed by Phillion and He. Conversation analysis emerged as a significant methodological tool within applied linguistics in the mid-1990s, although its roots go back much further. The goal of conversation analysis is to develop a grounded interpretation of participants' culturally and contextually situated behaviors as they engage in the production of "talk-in-interaction". Talk-in-interaction encompasses two broad categories: ordinary everyday casual conversation and institutional talk that includes varieties of talk such as debates, classroom interaction, broadcast news interviews, press conferences, doctor-patient exchanges, courtroom interaction, emergency telephone calls, etc. Institutional varieties of talk become more ritualized as their distance from ordinary conversation increases. Markee describes conversation analysis as a "militantly behavioral discipline" very different from the cognitivist and psycholinguistic orientation that characterizes much second language acquisition research. Conversation analysis provides empirically-based accounts of individuals' observable sequential, turn-taking and repair practices. According to Markee, these analyses are *emic* in orientation insofar as they attempt to interpret social actions from the perspective of the language user rather than from the researcher's perspective. This orientation is similar to that of most other forms of qualitative inquiry in the social sciences. Perhaps not surprisingly for a still-emerging methodological approach, there is considerable debate about the contributions that conversation analysis is capable of making to the broader field of second language acquisition; some researchers have argued, for example, that techniques originally developed to analyze language *use* are inappropriate for the purpose of analyzing language *acquisition* processes. Markee concludes that conversation analysis is clearly a growth area but only time will tell how much influence it will exert on theory and research within second language acquisition.

Morgan's chapter steps back from consideration of research methods *per se* to the epistemological foundations and assumptions that frame the kinds of research questions that are asked. He contrasts the approaches adopted by applied linguists and poststructuralists in addressing issues of ELT. Applied linguistics research has often been guided by positivistic and structuralist assumptions that fuel a search for ultimate rules or universals regarding second language acquisition. Furthermore, it is assumed that such rules exist independently of the research methods and inquiry tools used to discover them. These positivistic and structuralist assumptions are rejected by poststructuralists who view language categories as provisional and indeterminate, and identity as inseparable from the enactment or "play" of language. Knowledge as the outcome of scientific inquiry is similarly always partial, and notions of "objective validity" give way to conceptions of knowledge as dialogical and situated. Furthermore, language as a site for social exchange is never neutral—meanings are always embedded within discourses, understood as systems of power/knowledge (Foucault), that regulate and assign value to all forms of semiotic activity. Thus when ELT and teacher education are viewed from a poststructuralist perspective, teachers do not acquire common objective "truths" about ELT as much as they attain a particular understanding of their field—a discourse comprised of both insights and blind spots. Critical reflexivity is required to enable teachers to explore the partiality of their knowledge and the naturalized or normalized nature of their assumptions and ideas. This critical reflexivity is particularly important whenever theories and methods are exported across cultural settings. In concluding,

Morgan advocates constructive dialogue between applied linguistics and poststructuralist perspectives and he suggests that each has important contributions to make to the improvement of English language teaching. Regardless of which perspective might predominate in any language teaching or teacher education setting, further insight into effective and empowering forms of pedagogy will be gained only by means of equitable collaboration with teachers. Breen's chapter, discussed below, extends this perspective further, arguing that collegial exploratory inquiry carried out by teachers, rather than academic research, must take the lead in generating insights about effective ELT practice.

With Tsui's chapter the focus shifts squarely onto teacher professional development. The rapid spread of English as a global language and the search by policy makers for more effective approaches to teaching English, has generated new challenges for teachers in many countries to meet the increasing expectations of policy-makers, parents, and the students themselves. Professional development clearly plays an essential role in helping teachers meet these challenges. Tsui identifies the following factors that influence teachers' conceptions of teaching and learning: their personal background and life experiences, their disciplinary training, their teaching and learning experiences, and their professional teacher education. She describes a case study of one teacher, Marina, whose professional development illustrates the influence of these factors. Tsui characterizes Marina's professional development as a process of constant renewal, of looking for and responding to opportunities for learning, seeking challenges that enabled her to work at the edge of her expertise, and reflecting on and reframing her understanding of her work as a teacher. Tsui concludes that while teacher professional development will follow certain predictable trajectories, the phases of development are not linear. Teachers will move in and out of phases as a result of their life experiences, social environment, and organizational influences in schools or tertiary institutions. Thus, she argues, it is essential for teacher educators to recognize the situated and personal nature of teachers' professional growth and not be overly prescriptive.

Related themes are discussed by Breen in analyzing contemporary pressures on English language teachers and strategies for addressing these pressures. He identifies four key aspects of teachers' work that are being challenged or destabilized in the present context: (a) the knowledge that teachers may apply; (b) acceptable ways of teaching; (c) accountability; and (d) working conditions. Teachers are confronted with the fact that new developments in applied linguistics have rendered knowledge transient; recent descriptions of the English language with respect to notions of grammar, communicative competence, genre, etc. have called into question the certainties of the past. Pedagogic imperatives have also shifted in recent years requiring teachers to reconstruct their roles according to the fickle mandates of governments and/or textbook publishers anxious to exploit the latest developments in communicative language teaching or computer assisted language learning. Accountability requirements, according to Breen, have also increased on the basis of two unproven assumptions: that whatever teachers achieved before is no longer adequate and that the bureaucratic surveillance of teachers' work will improve their students' performance. Finally, teachers' professional identity is further destabilized by the contractual insecurity that characterizes many ELT positions. Breen highlights the potential of *exploratory practice* as a model of professional development that can respond to the contemporary pressures faced by English language teachers. Exploratory practice involves teachers and learners working together towards a situated understanding of life in the classroom. Its inquiry operates not through the use of conventional research procedures but through collaboration among teachers and learners that is driven by local concerns and needs and integrated into everyday teaching-learning activities. Accountability is addressed by means of a collegial process whereby teachers give an account of or share with other groups of teachers their achieved understandings of classroom issues or "puzzles". This process might also involve academic researchers and teacher educators not as external experts, but as colleagues working in a collaborative power relationship with the teacher *insiders* to further develop or elaborate shared understandings. Breen concludes that the collegial endeavor represented by exploratory practice can enable teachers to grapple with and participate as agents in the change process. Part of the change process will entail challenging the current construction of professionalism as an individual rather than a collective attribute.

Goldstein extends the focus from ELT in a narrow sense to the more general question of how to prepare teachers to teach effectively in contexts where a significant proportion of the students come from non-English-speaking backgrounds. This situation is typical of urban schools in North America, and increasingly in other English-dominant contexts. Up to this point, teacher education programs have been content to prepare teachers to teach the "generic" student of 40 years ago—white, middle-class, monolingual, monocultural, and heterosexual. Currently in many urban contexts, multiple forms of diversity are apparent for all to see and hear. Diversity is the norm and, in many schools, the student who is learning English as an additional language *is* the mainstream. Goldstein argues that effective teacher education in linguistically diverse communities must help teachers develop a sophisticated understanding of issues associated with language choice, bilingualism, linguistic discrimination, and racism. Furthermore, critical ethnographic research on language use and pedagogy in multilingual schools has much to offer teacher education programs located in linguistically diverse communities. Goldstein's own ethnographic study of a linguistically-diverse high school documented the stresses Cantonese-speaking students experienced in meeting contradictory socialization agendas and negotiating the difficulties of living in "multiple worlds". The dilemma for these students, according to Goldstein, was how to find opportunities to practice English (which would benefit them in the long term) at the same time as they used Cantonese to gain social capital among peers and achieve more immediate social and academic goals. She also briefly notes the possibilities for innovative dissemination of the insights generated in this kind of ethnographic research. In her ethnographic play, *Hong Kong, Canada,* she transformed her ethnographic data and texts into scripts and dramas that have been read and performed for various audiences of educators and the general public. This "ethnographic playwriting" or "performed ethnography" has considerable potential to promote reflection and dialogue among educators, researchers, and policy-makers and can exert a potentially important role in teacher education and professional development contexts.

Franson's focus is also on provision for school-age learners of English as an additional language (EAL). She describes how the rapid pace of educational change in England during the past decade has resulted in uncertainty about the role to be played by specialist language support teachers and the professional knowledge base required to fulfill that role. In some respects the model of EAL provision is more clearly delineated than in other contexts (e.g. North America) insofar as withdrawal of pupils from the mainstream classroom is strongly discouraged and mainstreaming of pupils with their age peers is the accepted norm. The *Partnership Teaching* model of practice for mainstreaming EAL learners and EAL support teachers provides for EAL and classroom teachers to work together to support pupils in acquiring both the English language and academic content taught through that language (see Jill Bourne's chapter in Volume 1 of this Handbook). Franson points out that mainstreaming was intended to provide the EAL learner with opportunities to participate with his or her peer group in cognitively challenging tasks with contextualized language support, to promote mutual respect and understanding of linguistic and cultural diversity, and to provide communicatively purposeful opportunities for language learning. However, implementation of partnership teaching is not without problems and challenges, including the lower status that sometimes accrues to the EAL support teacher, ambiguity in relation to the respective roles and responsibilities of the subject matter and EAL teacher, and the potential for segregation of EAL pupils within the classroom. These challenges may limit the range of comprehensible language experience made available to EAL pupils despite the fact that they are in a mainstream classroom with peers who are fluent speakers of English. Another issue identified by Franson that is related to the ill-defined nature of the EAL teacher's role and the professional expertise necessary to fulfill that role is the increasing employment of teaching assistants to support EAL pupils. Teaching assistants typically have significant gaps in professional knowledge and practical experience but these gaps are less apparent to policy-makers because a set of professional standards for EAL teaching has not yet been established. The knowledge base associated with such standards should, according to Franson, specify appropriate pedagogical responses to learners at different stages or levels of EAL development in different phases of education, and also establish a systematic and principled approach to the integration of curriculum content and language. She concludes that EAL teachers themselves need a stronger professional identity and greater status within the teaching profession in order to be effective in supporting EAL learners to construct identities that will enable confident classroom participation and sustained academic achievement.

    The issue of professional identity is also taken up by Corbel in the context of the rapid emergence of information and communication technologies (ICT) onto the educational landscape. With the prospect that face-to-face teaching may be eroded or possibly even largely disappear under pressure from the economic rationalization made possible through ICT-mediated self-access learning, the teaching profession is being forced to examine its role and the nature of the teaching/learning relationship generally in a radically changed environment. Corbel's chapter focuses on the question of how effective use of technology for learning will change the roles of all professions involved in mediating the teaching/learning relationship including teachers, university lecturers, the guidance professions, trainers in business environments, librarians, and learning resource professionals. He distinguishes three categories of teacher role definition–the metaphoric, the attitudinal, and the functional.

    Metaphoric roles invoke a familiar existing role or metaphor to describe how teachers integrate their work with ICT. These metaphoric roles include the supportive (e.g. facilitating student learning through ICT), the collaborative (e.g. the teacher as a co-producer of knowledge and learning together with students), the economic (e.g. the teacher as designer of materials and courses), and the professional (e.g. the teacher as a learning or training consultant within a business environment). *Attitudinal roles* refer to the attitudes adopted by teachers in relation to the changes in their environment associated with ICT. These attitudes range across the spectrum from skeptical and oppositional stances to the uncritical promotion of ICT and attempts to identify and exploit the transformational potential of the new technologies. *Functional roles* are those imposed by the ICT itself on those who engage with it. Teachers, for example, may be required to manage web-based or other ICT learning environments, organize student activities and tasks within that environment, and moderate on-line discussion that differs significantly from the face-to-face discussion that takes place in classrooms. Corbel concludes that ICT will require ELT professionals to adopt a wider range of roles than might previously have been the case and to become flexible and adaptable in managing their work in a context where change is likely to be a constant.

The final chapter in this section by Legutke, Müller-Hartmann, and Schocker-v. Ditfurth, also addresses the challenges and potential of ICT for English language teachers and learners. Their focus is on the EFL context and their overall message is optimistic. They suggest that with appropriate support and preparation, ICT can be integrated into language classrooms, thereby opening up opportunities for enhanced access to a wide variety of learning resources and for communicative interaction through the target language beyond the classroom. The authors describe their work in preparing student teachers to work effectively in a technology-supported English language classroom environment. The teacher preparation process models the kind of instruction that the student teachers themselves are expected to implement in the EFL classroom. Student teachers work cooperatively to choose a research question; they use ICT to research, discuss, and publish (on the course web site) the results of their projects; they cooperate with other student teachers working on the same research question at different universities; they use English as their language of communication both in face-to-face and virtual groups; and they evaluate selected aspects of the process and the overall outcomes of their projects. This process enables student teachers to experience both the challenges and immense potential of project-based ICT-supported learning. This approach to teacher education for ICT is powerful, according to the authors, because it simultaneously addresses the concerns of school-based English language learning, of university-based initial teacher education, and of professional development for established teachers. However, they caution that based on their experience and the research literature, effective use of ICT in the classroom is impossible within a behaviorist or teacher-centered orientation to curriculum and instruction. Rather a social constructivist approach to the teaching/learning relationship involving cooperative learning and project work is required to truly exploit the potential of ICT.

In reminding us of the importance of teachers' orientation to pedagogy, Legutke, Müller-Hartmann, and Schocker-v. Ditfurth help us to re-focus on themes that have resonated throughout this Handbook. Many chapters have emphasized that ELT involves more than just teaching a particular target language. The language teaching endeavor, or "enterprise" when viewed through an economic lens, is always located in a complex and dynamic social and historical context. In every language classroom, echoes of power relations from the past merge with the envisaged entitlements of present and future packaged with the language and culture being transmitted. In many countries, gaining access to English is seen as gaining access to economic and social power. And access is inevitably rationed. Typically, access is distributed according to the social capital that learners and their families already possess.

The embedding of language teaching in a matrix of societal and global power relations plays itself out within classrooms in the concrete interactions between teachers and students. These interactions transmit not only conceptual knowledge and language/literacy competencies but also messages about identity, belonging, opportunities, and entitlement. An image of the learner is constructed in classroom interactions. Students from marginalized communities frequently internalize an image of themselves defined by what they lack: they are "limited English proficient" (LEP) or English-as-a-second-language (ESL), rather than bilingual. The language and cultural knowledge they bring into the classroom is devalued in comparison to what others already possess. In EFL contexts, global power relations play themselves out in the perceived necessity to acquire English without any expectation that reciprocal language learning will occur.

None of this is surprising. And the reign of English as the world's *lingua franca* may be more short-lived than seems apparent at the moment. However, the point we wish to emphasize here is that English language teachers are not just passive cogs in a deterministic wheel of global power relations, destined to play out scripts penned by the economic czars of our time; in other words, *English language teachers have choices*.

There are obviously many constraints that affect the choices that teachers may pursue. But there are always degrees of freedom in language teaching situations whereby teachers can identify and challenge the images of the learner imposed by textbooks, curricula, and the broader social structure. This is where the discussion of orientations to pedagogy becomes relevant. The detailed discussions of ELT pedagogy contained in this Handbook range across three broad orientations: *transmission, social constructivist, and transformative*. These orientations are not discrete alternatives; rather they are each more appropriately conceived as legitimate, but nested within each other. They differ in the kinds of learning they hope to promote and in the image of the learner they imply.

Transmission-oriented pedagogy, with the narrowest focus, aims to transmit information and skills articulated in the curriculum directly to students. ELT, and language teaching generally, has historically located itself within this traditional orientation. Social constructivist pedagogy incorporates the "direct instruction" focus of transmission approaches but broadens it to include the development among students of higher-order thinking abilities based on teachers and students co-constructing knowledge and understanding. The extension of ELT from exclusively language-focused instruction into broader spheres of content-based and bilingual instruction has generated the potential, and in many cases the expectation, that cognitive as well as language goals will be pursued. Finally, transformative approaches to pedagogy broaden the focus still further by emphasizing the relevance not only of transmitting the curriculum and constructing knowledge but also of promoting critical literacy among students to enable them to analyze societal discourses and to influence these discourses by means of social action. Only transformative orientations directly address the power relations that are embedded in ELT.

Each of these orientations entails ideological presuppositions related to teacher and student roles in addition to assumptions about effective approaches to language teaching. These ideological presuppositions intersect with images of the learner that are enacted and communicated within different orientations. Transmission orientations construct images of the teacher as expert and student as passive recipient; social constructivist orientations highlight the cognitive and imaginative abilities of teacher and learner as co-constructors of knowledge and learning; transformative orientations highlight the potential and responsibility of teachers to prepare students to use language not just to read the surface structure of texts but also to "see through" the surface structure to the social realities and power relations underlying the text. These "reading skills" seem particularly relevant in an era of global propaganda and information overload.

So which of these orientations (or combinations of these orientations) is likely to predominate in teacher education and the professional development of teachers? How do different research methodologies intersect with pedagogical orientations in ELT or education generally? To what extent are quantitative experimental and quasi-experimental research designs capable of assessing curriculum objectives that defy simplistic measurement (e.g. critical literacy)? If particular forms of high-stakes standardized tests or examinations focused on narrow curriculum objectives are used exclusively to judge student and teacher performance, to what extent will the learning outcomes of social constructivist and transformative orientations to pedagogy become visible?

All of these issues, and the many others reflected in this Handbook, are currently "in play" in the ongoing drama of ELT. We have assembled commentators and critics, actors and directors, to illuminate sections of the trail but the ultimate destination is still unclear. As editors of this volume, we hope that the spread of English draws inspiration from collaborative relations of power rather than from coercive relations of power. Within the former construct, power is generated through interactions such that more power is available for all to share. Coercive relations of power, by contrast, are subtractive in a typical colonial sense: the more power that accrues to one participant, the less is available for others to share. For example, as English has spread historically in colonial contexts, indigenous languages have been devalued and erased. The notion of collaborative relations of power reflects the dictionary meaning of "being enabled or empowered" while coercive relations reflect the notion of exerting "power over" another.

Every English language teacher aspires to help students master the codes of English. We hope that this Handbook encourages teachers to exercise their choice to help students also use the codes of English to promote reflection, insight, and social action.

CHAPTER 59

QUALITATIVE APPROACHES TO CLASSROOM RESEARCH WITH ENGLISH LANGUAGE LEARNERS

PATRICIA A. DUFF

The University of British Columbia, Canada

ABSTRACT

This chapter provides an overview of recent qualitative research in classrooms examining English language learners (ELLs). I first present common features of qualitative research and review debates regarding research paradigms in the social sciences and humanities. I also discuss the role of triangulation and capturing participants' insider or *emic* perspectives in qualitative research and highlight various data collection methods and ways of combining macrolevel and microlevel analyses, particularly in ethnographic research. Ethical issues, difficulties obtaining informed consent in classroom research, and criteria for evaluating qualitative research are then considered. Three qualitative studies that have been deemed exemplary and meritorious by scholars in English language education are then presented, and some common themes in current qualitative classroom research with ELLs are identified. The chapter concludes with some directions for future qualitative research.

INTRODUCTION

Over the past two decades, research in language education, as in other academic disciplines, has witnessed a major shift in the types and methods of research that are accepted as valid, important, and useful. Whereas quantitative studies of a psychometric nature or involving (quasi-) experimental designs might previously have been viewed as more legitimate forms of research within education and the social sciences, rigorous qualitative studies in classrooms and other learning environments are now increasingly accepted as an important way of generating new knowledge and moving disciplines in innovative directions. They are also receiving more validation and support through competitive grant funding and research awards than before.

Reasons for the shift or expansion of research orientations to include more qualitative perspectives might include the following:

1. the current availability of more methodology books, special issues of journals, and courses that provide in-depth explanations and models of exemplary qualitative research in education;
2. an acceptance of the value and power of well-presented case studies, ethnographic descriptions, and discourse and content analyses of speech, writing, and interaction patterns to shed light on educational issues and to seek solutions to socioeducational problems;
3. an awareness that conducting a limited number of detailed small-scale studies, ideally longitudinally, can in some cases be just as effective and

insightful as larger-scale studies of different groups' performance on standardized tests, for example (see Duff, 2007);
4. a recognition that teachers' and learners' perceptions of their educational experiences can be extremely revealing and instructive;
5. a growing interest in "ecological validity," and the social, cultural, situational, embodied, and enacted nature of language, knowledge, and learning (e.g., Kramsch, 2002; Leather & van Dam, 2003; van Lier, 1997);
6. an awareness that the categories and interpretations that participants from different backgrounds provide in relation to their activities or knowledge—which may differ from those of outsiders—can be just as meaningful as those that are developed by researchers;
7. a greater interest in having teachers become more integrally involved in many aspects of the research process as coinvestigators, from planning stages to the interpretation of results; and
8. recognition of the difficulties posed by conducting experimental studies in classrooms, for ethical and practical reasons, and difficulties applying certain statistical tests to smaller sets of non-parametric or not normally distributed data.

Indeed, the number of qualitative and mixed-method studies combining qualitative and quantitative approaches has surged in recent years, a phenomenon clearly reflected in the journals and books published in language education and applied linguistics today (e.g., Bailey & Nunan, 1996; Davis & Lazaraton, 1995; Duff, 2002a; Lazaraton, 2000, 2003). Naturally, quantitative research still plays an important role in generating knowledge connected with teaching and learning and is preferred by many funding agencies and stakeholders, such as ministries or departments of education as well as by parents.

This chapter provides an overview of current qualitative research in classrooms examining English language learners (ELLs). The purpose of the chapter is threefold: first, to provide an overview of qualitative research as method; second, to present some studies that have been deemed exemplary and meritorious by scholars in English language education; and third, to identify some common themes addressed in current qualitative classroom research with ELLs.

QUALITATIVE CLASSROOM RESEARCH: FOUNDATIONS AND ISSUES

In this section, I consider briefly the following issues: some properties of qualitative research; paradigm debates in research methodology; the role of triangulation, participants' insider or *emic* perspectives, and various data collection methods used in qualitative research; combining macrolevel and microlevel analyses, particularly in ethnographic research; ethical issues and informed consent; and criteria for evaluating qualitative research.

What is Qualitative Research?

Qualitative research is not a unitary construct but a cluster or continuum of approaches that generally seek contextualized, naturalistic, holistic understandings and interpretations of phenomena that occur in particular types of contexts (Duff, 2002a). A growing number of qualitative methodology textbooks in education and the social sciences serve as helpful reference manuals (e.g., Denzin & Lincoln, 2005; Cohen & Manion, 1994; Crabtree & Miller, 1999; Creswell, 1994, 1998; Glesne & Peshkin, 1992; Hammersley & Atkinson, 1995; Hitchcock & Hughes, 1995; Holliday, 2002; Marshall & Rossman, 1995; Merriam, 1998; Silverman, 1993; Strauss & Corbin, 1998). Almost no textbooks in language education and applied linguistics, in comparison, are devoted to a far-reaching discussion of qualitative research methods exclusively (Richards, 2003, is one of the few).

In classrooms, the typical focus is instructional behaviors, interaction patterns among teachers and students such as Initiation-Response-Evaluation (IRE) routines, and the teaching/learning processes and outcomes associated with different types of language and literacy activities (e.g., Duff, 2002b; Hall & Verplaetse, 2000; Wells, 1993). Generally, qualitative research also includes the triangulation of perspectives of insiders, such as students and teachers, and those of outsiders, such as university researchers. However, the methods used also depend on the type of qualitative research being conducted, the accepted conventions associated with that approach, and the research questions being addressed. As Lazaraton (2003) and Chapelle and Duff (2003) report, conversation analysis is based on a very different set of assumptions than those in ethnography about how to interpret observed behavior and how much contextual information is relevant or important within an analysis. For ethnography, participants' explicit reflections on their own practices, values, and utterances are sought; on the other hand, speakers' perspectives and social-contextual features of discourse are only inferred in most conversation-analytic research from transcribed face-to-face and telephonic oral interactions.

The Research Paradigm Debates

Despite the gradual acceptance of qualitative research noted in the introduction, it is still often contrasted and compared with quantitative research and characterized as a less robust or less mature form of scholarly inquiry (Duff & Early, 1996). Part of the blame for such misconceptions originates with studies that do not reflect a theoretically grounded, systematic, methodical, in-depth, or original analysis or appear to simply contain a few anecdotes or vignettes. Blame also stems from old biases from the biological and physical sciences regarding the goals of research and the procedures that constitute "the scientific method." While space does not permit a review of the quantitative/qualitative research "paradigm debates" here, they continue to influence descriptions and evaluations of qualitative research and of theory building in our field (Creswell, 1994; Duff, 2006; Gall, Borg, & Gall, 1996; Palys, 1997). For example, in Eisner and Peshkin's (1990) edited volume entitled *Qualitative Inquiry in Education: The Continuing Debate*, authors address recurring themes in debates about the strengths, weaknesses, and validity of different approaches to research and the problems with imposing quantitative constructs on qualitative studies or asserting that quantitative research is necessarily objective, generalizable, reliable, and so on.

Triangulation: Incorporating Multiple Perspectives, Methods, and Data Sources

Whereas observational classroom research with ELLs in the process-product tradition often involves quantification and real-time coding of interaction among teachers and students (Spada & Lyster, 1997), scholars now emphasize the value of understanding interaction from participants' perspectives as well (e.g., Allwright, 1997; Bailey & Nunan, 1996; van Lier, 1997). The need to ask students about their behaviors and beliefs may be particularly important in situations where they are outwardly silent (e.g., Morita, 2002; Pon, Goldstein, & Schecter, 2003). There is less emphasis on the triangulation of methods, perspectives, theories, sites, and interpretations in quantitative research. Moreover, unlike quantitative research, which often sets out to establish causal relationships or strengths of relationships among variables of a more general nature, qualitative classroom research may be more exploratory and interpretive, and designed to examine the complex relationships among factors in a learning situation.

In classroom research on the experiences of ELLs, for example, the following elements might be involved: observations and narrative accounts of what students are doing during a particular type of focal activity and what behaviors, knowledge, and written products result from that activity; and observations of what teachers are doing during the same focal activity or in the instructional phases leading up to or following it. These observations ideally are videotaped or audiotaped, so that researchers can easily review the activities and transcribe and analyze portions of the discourse in activities of greatest interest. In some cases, however, a discourse analysis of transcripts may be of less interest than a general understanding of the activity setting, interviews with participants about the activities, and then possibly a discussion of how students' participation in the activities relates to their progress in English or in a particular subject area. Careful field notes and a synthesis of multiple data sources pertaining to a situation may be sufficient.

Combining Macro- and Microanalyses

Some classroom research incorporates both macro- and microlevels of analysis in studies of classroom discourse (Duff, 1995, 2002a; Watson-Gegeo, 1988, 1997). Obtaining a macroscopic perspective requires studying the social, cultural, and historical contexts of communicative events and uncovering attitudes and behavioral patterns within schools and local communities. This approach is often found within ethnographies of communication (Saville-Troike, 1989). Studies combined with interactional sociolinguistics or critical theory (e.g., Fairclough, 1989) may address issues connected with ideologies of school reform, individualism, bilingualism, multiculturalism, racism, and power relations (e.g., Freeman, 1996; Willett, 1995; Willett, Solsken, & Wilson-Keenan, 1999). Drawing on poststructuralism, they may also explore the multiple, and sometimes contested, identities, perspectives, values, and practices of individuals and groups; the discourses and tensions associated with observed practices; and the sociohistorical factors that gave rise to them (Canagarajah, 1993; Goldstein, 1997; Katz, 2000; McKay & Wong, 1996; Norton, 2000).

Macroethnographic studies of school settings are often far-ranging works that may or may not include discourse analysis or excerpts of recorded discourse, but examine the discourse contexts and ideological worlds in which members of a culture or group operate, often over a substantial period of time (e.g., Gibson, 1988; Harklau, 1994; Heath, 1983). Book-length reports of large-scale studies often combine macro- and microanalyses, noting the larger socioeducational and sociopolitical contexts and issues surrounding language education and use and academic achievement. They may also analyze how the macro is constituted in or by microexchanges and how points of tension between native and imported (or local vs. newcomer) orientations to schooling are manifested. For example, my ethnographic classroom research in Hungary (Duff, 1993, 1995, 1996) revealed how a combination of macro- and microlevel analyses of communication within classrooms—and within schools and society—helped capture the evolution of discourse practices there and the tensions sometimes accompanying such changes at both the macro/societal and micro/classroom discourse levels.

However, bringing together macro and microanalyses and etic and emic perspectives can be very challenging logistically, in terms of data collection, analysis, and concise reporting. As in all empirical research, data reduction is necessary, often achieved by the principled selection of a limited number of representative activities, discourse samples, and focal research participants from a much larger study, sometimes in combination with a quantification of general patterns across the dataset and more macroscopic contextualization. One strategy is to track focal activities, participants, and types of discourse across time and settings (Green & Dixon, 1993a, 1993b). For example, McKay and Wong (1996) and Willett (1995) focused on the sociolinguistic practices, experiences, and identities (or discourses) of three to four immigrant students. Another strategy is to present data from a small number of lessons or activities from a much more extensive corpus in order to address specific theoretical issues (e.g., Gutiérrez, 1994; Wortham, 1992). Some studies focus on just the first days of exposure to and participation in new activities—that is, the critical, initial induction of students into new practices, situated within a larger ethnographic study (Brilliant-Mills, 1994).

Examples of activities examined in L2 research using a combination of ethnography and discourse analysis include oral academic presentations in graduate school seminars (Kobayashi, 2003; Morita, 2000), class discussions (e.g., Hall, 1998; Losey, 1995; Morita, 2002), and literacy activities in various academic fields (e.g., Atkinson & Ramanathan, 1995; Ramanathan & Atkinson, 1999).

Ethical Issues

Permission to conduct observations in classroom research (whether recorded or not) and to interview participants and examine other kinds of oral/written performance is normally required, according to widely accepted ethical guidelines. However, these permissions may be difficult to obtain from all parties because of the perceived invasiveness of such practices or reluctance to draw attention to one's abilities and actions. Furthermore, those individuals (or their parents/guardians) most reluctant to provide their permissions are sometimes the ones of greatest interest and concern to researchers; for example, immigrant or international students who are struggling with limited L2 proficiency (Duff, 2002a). It is actually becoming increasingly difficult to negotiate and obtain permissions for some types of classroom research from university ethical review boards and from educational institutions; this difficulty is especially apparent when audio- and video-recorded observations are proposed for the purpose of discourse or interaction analysis but not all parents, teachers, and students agree to participate or be recorded. Action research projects may also face ethical hurdles, as university human-subjects research boards, such as the one at my own university, consider it to be coercive to seek informed consent from one's own students (Duff, 2007).

Criteria and Guidelines for Qualitative Research

Recently, because of the recognition that not all research can realistically be evaluated using the same criteria, there has been greater clarification about appropriate criteria for assessing both quantitative and qualitative research in TESOL—including classroom research (Edge & Richards, 1998). Examples of recent guidelines for some common types of qualitative research—(critical) ethnography, case study, and conversation analysis specifically—can be found in the *TESOL Quarterly* (Chapelle & Duff, 2003) and in Lazaraton (2003). Importantly, the guidelines underscore the need to situate research within a theoretical context, to select an issue of wide relevance and significance to the field, plus the need to collect and analyze data appropriate to the research questions being asked. Finally, sufficient evidence (e.g., data) must be provided for the interpretations and conclusions that are drawn, and counterexamples, if any, should be explained. Furthermore, an explicit account by researchers (often referred to as *reflexivity* and *subjectivity*) about their own role or history in a project and unanticipated influences over the findings are expected in many types of ethnographic research nowadays. The intent is not for researchers to apologize for "contaminating" research sites by their presence but to recognize that researchers are themselves participants or instruments as well as learners in projects, who should not pretend to be dispassionate, arms-length, impersonal, and invisible research agents.

In the following section, I review three exemplars of qualitative classroom research in some detail. Each reports on one piece of a larger program of research conducted by the authors, in which issues of the integration and academic performance and social well-being of immigrant language learners in North America are addressed.

EXAMPLES OF QUALITATIVE CLASSROOM RESEARCH IN APPLIED LINGUISTICS

Three qualitative classroom-based studies awarded the annual TESOL Distinguished Research Award over the past decade[1] of so illustrate some of the principles and procedures of rigorous qualitative research and at the same time deal with important topics and potentially vulnerable populations of learners. Two of the studies took place in the United States (Harklau, 1994; Leki, 1995), and one took place in Canada (Toohey, 2001). All three involved ELLs and addressed issues connected with students' variable forms of language and literacy socialization in classrooms and the general outcomes of their schooling in terms of their academic success, language/literacy development, and sense of well-being within the educational system.

ESL vs. Mainstream Learning Environments

First among them chronologically, Harklau (1994) is one of the best known studies to examine differences in learning environments for secondary-level immigrant students in ESL classes versus mainstream courses in North America. In her longitudinal ethnographic study initially situated in a northern California high school, Harklau tracked four newcomer students of ethnic Chinese backgrounds (three from Taiwan and one from Hong Kong) in their transition from ESL classes to mainstream courses over a period of from 4 to 7 semesters. Later, she also examined their school-to-college transitions and contradictory ways in which the students were represented in high school and college (Harklau, 1999, 2000). Harklau (1994) observed that, unfortunately, teachers in mainstream courses tended not to modify their speech for the sake of ELLs to render it more comprehensible, either through verbal adjustments to the rate and complexity of speech or through non-verbal support such as the provision of graphic organizers. Rather, rapid speech, and the use of puns, humor, sarcasm, and asides were common in teacher talk, elements that posed many difficulties for learners; similar observations have been made in studies in other countries as well (see Mohan, Leung, & Davison, 2001, for summaries of other, mostly qualitative, research on optimal conditions for the mainstreaming of ELLs). In addition, with a pervasive interaction format of IRE between teachers and students in large mainstream classes, Harklau observed that students were unlikely to have more than 1 turn in 30 (if any), and generally were required to produce only short responses. Opportunities to negotiate turn-taking, nominate and develop topics, produce extended discourse, and manipulate linguistic forms related to tense, nominal reference, cohesion, and complex syntax were therefore limited.

These findings were especially noticeable in *low-track* mainstream classes—those in which recently mainstreamed ELLs were likely to be placed, which were academically less demanding and also interactionally less varied than *high-track* classes. In 12 days of classes, Harklau observed very few instances (just eight) of ESL learners talking in mainstream class discussions. In ESL classes, on the other hand, which had fewer students in them, students had more opportunities to interact, with teachers calling on them more frequently, using different seating arrangements and more open-ended questions; a dynamic, spiraling curriculum; and different, often more creative and authentic literacy tasks involving different genres. Harklau's (1994) findings mirror those subsequently reported in completely different geographical contexts in Australia and Canada but with similar populations of ethnic Chinese immigrant students (Duff, 2001, 2002b; Miller, 2000).

In summary, Harklau's (1994) article provides a very complete, well-situated and synthesized account of the focal students, classes, and school over a 3.5-year period. Notably missing from the article is the presentation of transcribed classroom discourse involving teachers and students or any writing produced by the students. Rather, the primary data included, other than the rich observational data, were interviews. Each focal student was interviewed regularly, and a number of other Chinese immigrants at the school were also interviewed and observed in the final year of the study to ensure that the case studies were representative of this larger population. In total, Harklau reported collecting 315 hours of observations (roughly half of them spread across 56 mainstream classes ranging from the sciences to humanities, and half in ESL classes) and 38 formal interviews in addition to many informal ones. Her article includes 21 short excerpts from interview data taken primarily from students to support her observations, which are organized around the themes of spoken language use in the (mainstream) classroom, spoken language use in the ESL classroom, written language use in the mainstream, written language use in the ESL classroom, structure and goals of instruction, explicit language instruction, and socializing functions of schooling.

Second-language Writing across the University Curriculum and Campus

The second study, by Leki (1995), examines a different population of learners and somewhat different issues as well. The focus is the challenges faced by three graduate and two undergraduate international (visa) students from Europe and Asia in their first semester at an American university. Of interest was the English writing requirements in their disciplinary courses across the curriculum and their coping strategies as newcomers to the local academic culture. That is, unlike most articles on English L2 writing, the study was not situated in writing courses and was not simply an analysis of the writing they did. It looked at the students' approaches to completing their writing assignments based on interview narratives of their academic discourse socialization. Data included weekly interviews with students, document analysis (e.g., students' writing), students' journals about their academic experiences, and interviews with some of the students' professors. Leki presented a profile of each of the five students in terms of their backgrounds and the writing requirements that stymied them in certain courses. For example, she described one student, Ling, who had to write an essay for a course in Behavioral Geography, that would

> place a hypothetical group of people into fictional neighborhoods by determining in broad terms their socioeconomic class through an examination of certain personal characteristics, whether, for example, they drink Budweiser or Heineken, read *GQ magazine* or *Track and Field*, drive a Dodge or a Saab. (p. 241)

Noting how difficult this task would be for a newcomer from Taiwan, because of their lack of cultural background knowledge, Leki went on to describe how Ling overcame her difficulties by appealing to classmates or professors for help, incorporating more information about Taiwan or China in her essays, or comparing Chinese and American cultures. In some cases, Ling resisted the professor's request that she not incorporate Chinese content into each assignment. In fact, she was not the only focal student to use a strategy of resistance to a professor's demands or requirements, as Leki later explains. A case in point was a student who made up her observations for a field assignment in Speech Pathology (for which students were supposed to pretend to be a stutterer on campus for 4 hours) because of her potential embarrassment of being perceived both as a non-native English speaker and a stutterer by strangers. In another case, a student named Yang described the dilemmas he had writing critical reviews of articles on international relations: he felt that he did not yet have the expertise to presume to make authoritative, critical comments about articles. Yang also related how he had been socialized into one American professor's academic expectations when in China, only to encounter quite contradictory expectations when he went on to study in Zimbabwe, prior to coming to America. In Zimbabwe, for example, he had been expected to rely more heavily on the authority of the original authors and not to inject his own ideas, and was graded accordingly.

In her section on strategies, in which Leki (1995) discussed themes that had emerged from her inductive analysis of the data, she noted the ten different strategies that students employed, such as "Looking for Models" of good writing assignments or essays of the genre/rhetorical structures required that would help students complete their own assignments effectively. Unfortunately, none of the courses the students took provided models for students, so the students relying on this strategy had to try to find suitable models themselves. Another strategy was "Using Current or Past ESL Writing Training," which, with only one exception, no students mentioned as helping them with their current writing needs.

In summary, the data presented in Leki's (1995) article include well-rounded student profiles, followed by a description and discussion of general themes (strategies) that surfaced across the five students' experiences as well as differences across the five cases. Nine short quotations or excerpts from the students' interviews, journals, or assignments were included from the corpus of transcribed data. She concludes the article by reviewing some of the strategies that did or did not serve students particularly well and also by considering things that the professors seemed totally unaware of. These included types of student resistance—and reasons underlying the resistance—as well as the apparent success of the strategy; students' lack of necessary cultural schemata; the ineffectiveness of group work, which Leki (2001) later documents more fully; and lack of explicit links between their ESL course strategies and those used in their other courses. She also suggests how university-level ESL instructors might better prepare students for the intellectually and rhetorically complex tasks that await them in mainstream courses.

Marginalization and Conflict in Classes with Young Children

The third study (Toohey, 2001), examined the intersection of language and power in "peer disputes" among children in Western Canadian classrooms. From Toohey's larger longitudinal ethnographic study of six children's language, literacy, and identity socialization between kindergarten and Grade 2 (Toohey, 2000), she selected two focal students for this article. Data were collected through weekly classroom observations and field notes, with observations also recorded on videotape one morning a month for the 3-year period. Interviews were conducted with parents and teachers as well, and home visits were also arranged by bilingual research assistants.

Toohey analyzes the videotaped data that had been transcribed and coded, from a corpus based on 80 hours of video, using a qualitative software program. The unit of analysis was disputes that occurred privately among the children—that is, without knowledge or intervention by their teachers—and the implications or consequences of children's variable participation in these private peer disputes for their subsequent language learning and self-esteem. Toohey contrasted the linguistic backgrounds and current experiences of two Canadian-born children from her larger sample of focal students: Julie, a Polish girl who, despite having had limited proficiency in English upon entering kindergarten had made rapid and effective progress in English and was considered an "average student" by her teacher; and Surjeet, a Punjabi girl who, despite living in a bilingual Punjabi- and English-speaking home and becoming English-dominant by age 5, "by the end of Grade 2 had acquired a school identity as an ESL learner with learning disabilities" (p. 264).

Using Corsaro and Rizzo's (1990) classification of different types of disputes (e.g., concerning children's possession and use of materials, engagement in play activities, opinion-giving), Toohey presents seven excerpts of classroom interaction among children that contrast the girls' different responses to three types of dispute incidents: for example, whereas Julie resists attempts to prevent her from using the computer (e.g., through strategic use of her allies and the compliance of others), Surjeet was much less successful negotiating disputes, usually deferring to the demands or hostility of domineering classmates and being undervalued by them as a result. Toohey argues that the ways the two children differentially negotiated disputes either enabled them to gain personal validation and opportunities to practice and improve their English (Julie) or, conversely, to be shut down by students and be positioned repeatedly as subordinate and incompetent and excluded from further opportunities to use English. The different outcomes were not only attributed to the children's personalities: also relevant, in Toohey's assessment, were their prior socialization into schooling practices (e.g., through Polish-medium Sunday School and English preschool activities, in Julie's case, with no equivalent formal preschool experience in Surjeet's case), the larger sociohistorical context of racism against visible minorities in the region as well as in the school, and then the everyday interactions such as those reported in disputes that reproduced existing inequalities. Toohey concludes that, rather than simply impose "zero tolerance" policies toward racism in schools, schools should model effective conflict resolution strategies that children might emulate, address situations of potentially dangerous domination and subordination among students, and recognize areas of children's special expertise that might validate and position them more powerfully.

DISCUSSION

The preceding studies, all conducted by well-regarded language education researchers with established programs of research exploring related issues, provide a kind of "raw data" for an inductive exploration of qualitative classroom research in our field. The commonalities among the studies, beyond their having been published in the same journal, are that they each employed ethnographic methods and conducted case studies of focal ELLs in mainstream North American classroom contexts. All three studies involved sustained observation of classes by the researchers, interviews with participants (teachers, students, and parents in some cases), and a concern about the well-being of newcomers in their new English-mediated learning communities. All three also addressed issues and course contexts not previously examined adequately: ESL-to-mainstream transitions, the role of disputes in learning/socialization, and students' perceptions of, and successes dealing with, writing demands across university disciplines. Two of the studies (by Toohey, 2001, and Harklau, 1994) took place over at least a 3-year period, and two of them (Harklau and Leki, 1995) included excerpts from students' interviews or journals as their only primary, quoted, source data. Only one of the studies (Toohey's) also included an analysis of excerpted classroom discourse, although in her case it was not sanctioned or public discourse, which most classroom research investigates, but rather private interactions among children. Finally, all three make some recommendations as to how ELLs might better be accommodated and supported in their early years of classroom language/literacy socialization, with some critical discussion of the practices that least support that goal. Furthermore, they all point out ways in which teachers may be oblivious to the needs, resistance, or concerns of their minority students.

Most qualitative studies end with cautionary notes and disclaimers about their limited sample size and thus problems of generalizability (Duff, 2006). None of these three did so, but Harklau (1994) verified the representativeness of her sample of focal students by later surveying a much larger sample of students from similar backgrounds. Rather than to attempt to generalize to the larger population of all

ELLs, the point of studies such as those reviewed here is to understand deeply, through a thorough, systematic, iterative analysis, a small number of participants and events considered sufficiently representative or emblematic of the larger phenomenon to be discussed. Then, instead of choosing research participants who all share exactly the same attributes and experiences, contrastive cases are sometimes selected so as to highlight variable experiences and outcomes; this sampling, selection, and reporting strategy was evident in Leki's (1995) and Toohey's (2001) case studies.

By presenting three "case studies" of qualitative classroom research with ELLs, I similarly need to provide a disclaimer to readers about the generalizability of my observations: although these studies may be very good—indeed, award-winning—examples of qualitative research published in recent years, they do not represent the methods or issues addressed in *all* such studies, or with the many different types of learners and instructional contexts featured in the *TESOL Quarterly* or other peer-reviewed journals. To do so would require collecting a corpus of all such studies and then doing a careful inductive analysis of the similarities and differences (or key patterns and elements) among them. Missing from these three studies, for example, was any quantification of coded data or the use of mixed methods and data matrices (e.g., Miles & Huberman, 1994), or scores showing the relationship between students' behaviors and their assessed performance at the end of the year, although Leki does report on students' grades on certain written assignments. Also absent were in-depth microlevel analyses of particular language structures, such as verb types, registers, or discourse markers, the sort of analysis that is typically undertaken in Systemic Functional Linguistic studies of classroom interaction or in certain kinds of interactional sociolinguistics, conversation analysis, and in other functional linguistic analyses (e.g., Zuengler & Mori, 2002). Nevertheless, all three articles provided persuasive and clear analyses of the language/literacy practices that may unwittingly contribute to the marginalization and disadvantage of certain types of learners, findings that might be applicable or transferable to teachers in many other settings as well.

CONCLUSIONS

The purpose of this chapter was to examine the underpinnings of qualitative classroom research, to provide several examples of classroom-based studies, and to reflect on other concerns, such as ethical issues and practical constraints in undertaking such studies. Space did not permit a fuller discussion of the entire range of topics that have been investigated qualitatively in recent years, not even within the same general research domain of language socialization (but for other examples, see Bayley & Schecter, 2003, and Davis & Lazaraton, 1995). Learners' complex identity issues also surfaced in the three reviewed articles, and many other qualitative studies dealing with that theme have been published by others (e.g., Duff & Uchida, 1997; Norton, 1997). What is clear is that sound qualitative research has achieved an important status in the field and has contributed, in my view, to fuller, more textured, humanized, and grounded accounts of the experiences of teachers and learners in contemporary classrooms that are easily accessible to a wide and diverse readership. Less published qualitative research has featured the issues in English as a foreign language (EFL) settings, and particularly in developing regions of the world where issues of class size, multilingualism, gender (e.g., favoring the education of boys), and access to basic teaching and learning resources and to basic teacher education may be serious problems for schools and communities (e.g., see studies in Bailey & Nunan, 1996, that focus on EFL in Hong Kong, Hungary, Pakistan, Peru, and South Africa). Some of these issues are, fortunately, now being studied to a greater extent and offer promising new directions for future research internationally. The issues are also now being studied with the use of innovative qualitative methods adopted from the humanities, involving narrativity, performativity, and multimedia, including multiple types of text and data representation, contained on websites or CD-ROMS, and not just traditional forms of representation derived from the social sciences that have been the primary focus of this chapter.

NOTES

[1] The award is given annually to an empirical article published in the *TESOL Quarterly* in the previous calendar year (in some years, submissions from other journals are also considered) that is deemed to be meritorious by a research adjudication committee.

REFERENCES

Allwright, D. (1997). Classroom-oriented research in second language learning. In N. Hornberger & D. Corson (Eds.), *Encyclopedia of language and education. Vol. 8: Research methods in language and education* (pp. 63–74). Dordrecht, The Netherlands: Kluwer.

Atkinson, D., & Ramanathan, V. (1995). Cultures of writing: An ethnographic comparison of L1 and L2 university writing/language programs. *TESOL Quarterly, 29*, 539–568.

Bailey, K., & Nunan, D. (1996). *Voices from the language classroom*. New York: Cambridge University Press.

Bayley, R., & Schecter, S. (2003). *Language socialization in bilingual and multilingual societies*. Clevedon: Multilingual Matters.

Brilliant-Mills, H. (1994). Becoming a mathematician: Building a situated definition of mathematics. *Linguistics and Education, 5*, 301–334.

Canagarajah, A. (1993). Critical ethnography of a Sri Lankan classroom: Ambiguities in student opposition to reproduction through ESOL. *TESOL Quarterly, 27*, 601–626.

Chapelle, C. & Duff, P. (Eds.). (2003). Some guidelines for conducting quantitative and qualitative research in TESOL. *TESOL Quarterly, 37*, 157–178.

Cohen, L., & Manion, L. (1994). *Research methods in education* (4th ed.). London: Routledge.

Corsaro, W., & Rizzo, T. (1990). Disputes in the peer culture of American and Italian nursery school children. In A. Grimshaw (Ed.), *Conflict talk: Sociolinguistic investigations of arguments in conversations* (pp. 21–66). Cambridge: Cambridge University Press.

Crabtree, B., & Miller W. (Eds.). (1999). *Doing qualitative research* (2nd ed.). Thousand Oaks, CA: Sage.

Creswell, J. (1994). *Research design: Qualitative and quantitative approaches*. Thousand Oaks, CA: Sage.

Creswell, J. (1998). *Qualitative inquiry and research design: Choosing among five traditions*. Thousand Oaks, CA: Sage.

Davis, K. (1995). Qualitative theory and methods in applied linguistics research. *TESOL Quarterly, 29*, 427–453.

Davis, K., & Lazaraton, A. (Eds.). (1995). *Qualitative research in ESOL*. Special Issue. *TESOL Quarterly, 29*, 3.

Denzin, N., & Lincoln, Y. (Eds.). (2005). *Handbook of qualitative research* (3rd ed.). Thousand Oaks, CA: Sage.

Duff, P. (1993). *Changing times, changing minds: Language socialization in Hungarian-English schools*. Unpublished Ph.D. dissertation. University of California, Los Angeles.

Duff, P. (1995). An ethnography of communication in immersion classrooms in Hungary. *TESOL Quarterly, 29*, 505–537.

Duff, P. (1996). Different languages, different practices: Socialization of discourse competence in dual-language school classrooms in Hungary. In K. Bailey & D. Nunan (Eds.), *Voices from the language classroom: Qualitative research in second language acquisition* (pp. 407–433). New York: Cambridge University Press.

Duff, P. (2001). Language, literacy, content, and (pop) culture: Challenges for ESL students in mainstream courses. *The Canadian Modern Language Review, 59*, 103–132.
Duff, P. (2002a). Research methods in applied linguistics. In R. Kaplan (Ed.), *Handbook of Applied Linguistics* (pp. 13–23). Oxford: Oxford University Press.
Duff, P. (2002b). The discursive co-construction of knowledge, identity, and difference: An ethnography of communication in the high school mainstream. *Applied Linguistics, 23*, 289–322.
Duff, P. (2006). Beyond generalizability: Context, credibility and complexity in applied linguistics research. In M. Chalhoub-Deville, C. Chapelle & P. Duff (Eds.), *Inference and generalizability in applied linguistics: Multiple research perspectives* (pp. 65–95). Amsterdam: John Benjamins.
Duff, P. (2007). *Case study research in applied linguistics*. Mahwah, NJ: Lawrence Erlbaum.
Duff, P., & Early, M. (1996). Problematics of classroom research across sociopolitical contexts. In J. Schachter & S. Gass (Eds.), *Second language classroom research: Issues and opportunities* (pp. 1–30). Mahwah, NJ: Lawrence Erlbaum.
Duff, P., & Uchida, Y. (1997). The negotiation of teachers' sociocultural identities and practices in postsecondary EFL classrooms. *TESOL Quarterly, 31*, 451–486.
Edge, J., & Richards, K. (1998). May I see your warrant, please?: Justifying outcomes in qualitative research. *Applied Linguistics, 19*, 334–356.
Eisner, E., & Peshkin, A. (1990). *Qualitative inquiry in education: The continuing debate*. New York: Teachers College Press.
Fairclough, N. (1989). *Language and power*. New York: Longman.
Freeman, R. (1996). Dual-language planning at Oyster Bilingual School: 'it's much more than language.' *TESOL Quarterly, 30*, 557–583.
Gall, M., Borg, W., & Gall, J. (1996). *Educational research* (6th ed.). New York: Longman.
Gibson, M. (1988). *Accommodation without assimilation*. Ithaca, NY: Cornell University Press.
Glesne, C., & Peshkin, A. (1992). *Becoming qualitative researchers: An introduction*. White Plains, NY: Longman.
Goldstein, T. (1997). *Two languages at work: Bilingual life on the production floor*. Berlin/New York: Mouton de Gruyter.
Green, J., & Dixon, C. (Eds.). (1993a). Santa Barbara Classroom Discourse Group. Special Issue. *Linguistics and Education*, 5, 3 & 4.
Green, J., & Dixon, C. (1993b). 'Talking knowledge into being': Discursive practices in classrooms. *Linguistics and Education*, 5, 231–239.
Gutiérrez, K. (1994). How talk, context, and script shape contexts for learning: A cross-case comparison of journal sharing. *Linguistics and Education*, 5, 335–365.
Hall, J. (1998). Differentiated teacher attention to student utterances: The construction of different opportunities for learning in the IRF. *Linguistics and Education*, 9, 287–311.
Hall, J., & Verplaetse, L. (Eds.). (2000). *Second and foreign language learning through classroom interaction*. Mahwah, NJ: Lawrence Erlbaum.
Hammersley, M., & Atkinson, P. (1995). *Ethnography: Principles in practice* (2nd ed.). New York: Routledge.
Harklau, L. (1994). ESL versus mainstream classes: Contrasting L2 learning environments. *TESOL Quarterly, 28*, 241–272.
Harklau, L. (1999). Representing culture in the ESL writing classroom. In E. Hinkel (Ed.), *Culture in second language teaching and learning* (pp. 109–130). New York: Cambridge University Press.
Harklau, L. (2000). From the 'good kids' to the 'worst': Representations of English language learners across educational settings. *TESOL Quarterly, 34*, 35–67.
Heath, S. (1983). *Ways with words: Language, life and work in communities and classrooms*. Cambridge: Cambridge University Press.
Hitchcock, G., & Hughes, D. (1995). *Research and the teacher: A qualitative introduction to school-based research* (2nd ed.). New York: Routledge.
Holliday, A. (2002). *Doing and writing qualitative research*. Thousand Oaks, CA: Sage.
Katz, M-L. (2000). The intercultural construction of ideologies of competence. *The Canadian Modern Language Review*, 57, 144–172.
Kobayashi, M. (2003). The role of peer support in ESL students' accomplishment of oral academic tasks. *The Canadian Modern Language Review, 59*, 337–368.
Kramsch, C. (Ed.). (2002). *Language acquisition and language socialization*. New York: Continuum.
Lazaraton, A. (2000). Current trends in research methodology and statistics in applied linguistics. *TESOL Quarterly, 34*, 3.
Lazaraton, A. (2003). Evaluating criteria for qualitative research in applied linguistics: Whose criteria and whose research? *Modern Language Journal, 87*, 1–12.
Leather, J., & van Dam, J. (Eds.). (2003). *Ecology of language acquisition*. Dordrecht: Kluwer.

Leki, I. (1995). Coping strategies of ESL students in writing tasks across the curriculum. *TESOL Quarterly, 29*, 235–260.
Leki, I. (2001). 'A narrow thinking system': Nonnative-English-speaking students in group projects across the curriculum. *TESOL Quarterly, 35*, 39–67.
Losey, K. (1995). Gender and ethnicity as factors in the development of verbal skills in bilingual Mexican American women. *TESOL Quarterly, 29*, 635–661.
Marshall, C., & Rossman, G. (1995). *Designing qualitative research* (2nd ed.). Thousand Oaks, CA: Sage.
McKay, S., & Wong, S. (1996). Multiple discourses, multiple identities: Investment and agency in second-language learning among Chinese adolescent immigrant students. *Harvard Educational Review, 66*, 577–608.
Merriam, S. (1998). *Qualitative research and case study applications in education*. San Francisco: Jossey-Bass Publishers.
Miles, M., & Huberman, A. (1994). *Qualitative data analysis* (2nd ed.). Thousand Oaks, CA: Sage.
Miller, J. (2000). Language use, identity, and social interaction: Migrant students in Australia. *Research on Language in Social Interaction, 33*, 69–100.
Mohan, B., Leung, C., & Davison, C. (Eds.). (2001). *English as a second language in the mainstream: Teaching, learning and identity*. New York: Longman/Pearson.
Morita, N. (2000). Discourse socialization through oral classroom activities in a TESL graduate program. *TESOL Quarterly, 34*, 279–310.
Morita, N. (2002). Negotiating participation in second language academic communities: A study of identity, agency, and transformation. Unpublished doctoral dissertation, University of British Columbia.
Norton, B. (1997). Language and identity. Special Issue. *TESOL Quarterly, 31*.
Norton, B. (2000). *Identity and language learning: Gender, ethnicity, and educational change*. London: Longman/Pearson Education.
Palys, T. (1997). *Research decisions: Quantitative and qualitative perspectives* (2nd ed.). Toronto: Harcout Brace & Co. Canada.
Pon, G., Goldstein, T., & Schecter, S. (2003). Interrupted by silences: The contemporary education of Hong Kong-born Chinese Canadians. In R. Bayley & S. Schecter (Eds.), *Language socialization in bilingual and multilingual societies* (pp. 114–127). Clevedon: Multilingual Matters.
Ramanathan, V., & Atkinson, D. (1999). Ethnographic approaches and methods in L2 writing research: A critical guide and review. *Applied Linguistics, 20*, 44–70.
Richards, K. (2003). *Qualitative inquiry in TESOL*. New York: Palgrave Macmillan.
Saville-Troike, M. (1989). *The ethnography of communication* (2nd ed). New York: Basil Blackwell.
Silverman, D. (1993). *Interpreting qualitative data*. Thousand Oaks, CA: Sage.
Spada, N., & Lyster, N. (1997). Macroscopic and microscopic views of the L2 classroom. *TESOL Quarterly, 31*, 787–795.
Strauss, A., & Corbin, J. (1998). *Basics of qualitative research: Techniques and procedures for developing grounded theory* (2nd ed.). Thousand Oaks, CA: Sage.
Toohey, K. (2000). *Learning English at school: Identity, social relations and classroom practice*. Clevedon, England: Multilingual Matters.
Toohey, K. (2001). Disputes in child L2 learning. *TESOL Quarterly, 35*(2), 257–278.
van Lier, L. (1988). *The classroom and the language learner*. New York: Longman.
van Lier, L. (1997). Observation from an ecological perspective. *TESOL Quarterly, 22*, 783–787.
Watson-Gegeo, K. (1988). Ethnography in ESL: Defining the essentials. *TESOL Quarterly, 22*, 575–592.
Watson-Gegeo, K. (1997). Classroom ethnography. In N. Hornberger & D. Corson (Eds.), *Encyclopedia of language and education. Vol. 8: Research methods in language and education*). Dordrecht, The Netherlands: Kluwer.
Wells, G. (1993). Reevaluating the IRF sequence: A proposal for the articulation of theories of activity and discourse for the analysis of teaching and learning in the classroom. *Linguistics and Education, 5*, 1–37.
Willett, J. (1995). Becoming first graders in an L2: An ethnographic study of language socialization. *TESOL Quarterly, 29*, 473–504.
Willett, J., Solsken, J., & Wilson-Keenan, J. (1999). The (im)possibilities of constructing multicultural language practices in research and pedagogy. *Linguistics and Education, 10*, 165–218.
Wortham, S. (1992). Participant examples and classroom interaction. *Linguistics and Education, 4*, 195–217.
Zuengler, J., & Mori, J. (Eds.). (2002). Methods of micro-analysis in classroom discourse. Special issue. *Applied Linguistics, 23*, 3.

CHAPTER 60

ACTION RESEARCH:

Contributions and Future Directions in ELT

ANNE BURNS

Macquarie University, Australia

ABSTRACT

Action research focuses simultaneously on *action* and *research*. The action aspect requires some kind of planned intervention, deliberately putting into place concrete strategies, processes, or activities in the research context. Interventions in practice are usually in response to a perceived problem, puzzle, or question that people in the social context wish to improve or change in some way. These problems might relate to teaching, learning, curriculum or syllabus implementation, but school management or administration are also a possible focus. This chapter describes the origins of action research, its relationships to other forms of empirical research, its reach and development, its central characteristics, and the current debates that surround it. It also considers the scope of action research in the applied linguistics field and concludes by looking at future directions.

INTRODUCTION

Since the 1940s, the term *action research* and the associated terms *action science, action learning, practitioner research,* and *participatory research* have been used to identify a particular philosophical stance towards research inquiry. Although action research extends to many fields, including the health care professions (e.g., Kember, 2001; Nichols, 1997), business and management (Somekh & Thaler, 1997), organizational and human development (Biott, 1996), higher education (Zuber-Skerritt, 1992), vocational education and training and social work (Hutchison & Bryson, 1997), and community activism (Knijnik, 1997), my focus is on educational action research, specifically in the ELT field.

WHAT IS ACTION RESEARCH?

As the term implies, action research focuses simultaneously on *action* and *research*. The action aspect requires some kind of planned intervention, deliberately putting into place concrete strategies, processes, or activities in the research context. Interventions in practice are in response to a perceived problem, puzzle, or question that people in the social context wish to improve or change in some way. These problems might relate to teaching, learning, curriculum, or syllabus implementation, but school management or administration are also a possible focus. Areas for action cover a wide range of possibilities, as Wallace (1998, p. 19) suggests:

1. classroom management
2. appropriate materials
3. particular teaching areas (e.g., reading, oral skills)
4. student behavior, achievement, or motivation
5. personal management issues (e.g., time management, relationships with colleagues/higher management)

Action may be taken individually, in groups, or across wider institutional or organizational clusters. Working collectively has the obvious advantage of enabling others to be brought in at different stages, sharing and discussing ideas or findings, planning new actions, talking about data collection methods, and comparing results.

The research component of action research means systematically collecting data about the planned actions, analyzing what they reveal, reflecting on the implications of the data, and developing alternative plans and actions based on data analysis. Improvement and involvement are twin pillars underpinning action research. Table 1 outlines the various focuses, purposes, and outcomes in different approaches to action research.

The research process is less predictable than in most other research approaches, as it is characterized by a spiral of cycles that minimally involve planning, acting, observing, and reflecting, although like other forms of research the reality is likely to be much messier than this description suggests. The best-known model of action research is one devised by Kemmis and McTaggart (1988a), who refer to four "moments", evolving in a self-reflective spiral or loop that is reiterated according to the scope of the research:

- *Plan*–prospective to action, forward looking, and critically informed in terms of (a) the recognition of real constraints, and (b) the potential for more effective action
- *Action*–deliberate and controlled, but critically informed in that it recognizes practice as ideas in action mediated by the material, social, and political "struggle" towards improvement
- *Observation*–responsive, but also forward looking in that it documents the critically informed action, its effects, and its context of situation, using "open-eyed" and "open-minded" observation plans, categories, and measurements
- *Reflection*–evaluative and descriptive, in that it makes sense of the processes, problems, issues, and constraints of action and develops perspectives and comprehension of the issues and circumstances in which it arises
(Based on Kemmis & McTaggart, 1988a, pp. 11-14)

Table 1. Focus and Purpose of Different Approaches to Action Research

	Individual	Collaborative	Institutional	Organizational
Focus	Single classroom	Multiclassroom	Whole department or school	Whole district or organization
Purpose	Investigate personal classroom issues	Investigate complementary or common classroom issues	Investigate common schoolwide issues	Investigate organizational issues, factors, structures
Type of support needed	Colleague/mentor Assistance with data collection, organization, or analysis	Substitute teachers Release time Administrative support	Institutional involvement and commitment Effective in-school communication Administrative leadership	Organizational involvement and commitment Effective cross-organizational communication Cross-district partnerships
Potential outcomes	Changes in practice Continuing personal reflection on teaching	Improvements in curriculum or syllabus design and implementation Greater collaboration in professional development	Evaluation of school restructure/change Curriculum/program evaluation School policy reevaluation	Improved allocation of resources Educational policy evaluation Improved knowledge of new curriculum implementation Improved cross-district professional development opportunities

The critically informed, improvement-oriented components of this model take participants much further than they would normally go in daily teaching in reflecting on the effects of their actions. McPherson (1997) provides a good example of how the focus and purpose of action research might change with successive iterative cycles. McPherson worked with learners enrolled in Australian adult immigrant classes. The account below is summarized from her article (pp. 26-30):

> My group was diverse in all the ways that make adult immigrant classes so interesting to teach. Ages ranged from 22-58 with equal number of males and females. They came from 15 different countries and spoke 17 different languages. Most had come to Australia because their country of origin was now unsafe for them.... My concern was with the wide variation in the levels of spoken and written English.... I was uncertain how to manage the class and I felt my planning was very 'hit and miss'.... I decided to read the literature on managing mixed-ability groups and to talk to teachers in [my center] and in community organisations and primary school education about strategies they used....
>
> As a result I decided to focus on developing materials and activities at different levels and to observe the response of the learners to these materials. I documented these observations [using a journal and drawing up diagrams of classroom interaction] and began to realise how much I tended to 'control' their learning by dispersing materials at 'appropriate' levels. When I allowed the students to take control, they worked with the [materials] in different ways which they found personally effective....
>
> However, at this point I became concerned about another aspect of the class. I observed that the students would not cooperate to undertake joint activities. They were also starting to express exasperation, boredom, irritation and once, near hostility, as I brought to the classroom lessons and activities [about personal experiences] I thought were interesting and relevant, but which they were not prepared to participate in.... I decided on a strategy of individual consultation. I spoke to each student about what they were learning, how they were learning and how they could develop their skills. I documented their comments and followed with activities designed to enhance their requested learning areas. I also documented comments on their reactions to my classroom activities....
>
> I began to see emerging patterns and to uncover the reasons for the rejected activities. Student comments and reactions indicated that discussions that revolved around cultural or social difference were not acceptable.... On a class excursion, I learned that the students were aware of deep ethnic, religious and political differences because of their experiences of the part of the world they had just left [former Yugoslavia].... I suddenly realized how difficult it had been for them to maintain the veneer of courtesy and civility when I was introducing activities which demanded that they expose and discuss the differences they were attempting to ignore!

As McPherson (1997) illustrates, data collection procedures are principally, but not universally *qualitative* in nature. Burns (1999) categorizes the most commonly used methods as observational and non-observational:

Table 2. Observational and Non-observational Methods for Action Research

Observational	Non-observational
Examples: • brief notes or recorded comments made by the teacher while the class is in progress • audio or video-recordings of classroom interaction • observation by self or colleague on particular aspects of classroom action • transcripts of classroom interactions between teacher and students or students and students • maps, layouts, or sociograms of the classroom that trace the interactions between students and teacher • photographs of the physical context	Examples: • questionnaires and surveys • interviews • class discussions/focus groups • diaries, journals, and logs kept by teacher or learners • classroom documents, such as materials used, samples of student writing, or tests

To summarize the essential concepts and principles of action research:

1. Action research is localized and commonly small-scale. It investigates problems of direct relevance to the researchers in their social contexts, that is, it is based on specific issues of practice.
2. Action research involves a combination of action and research that means collecting data systematically about actions, ideas, and practices as they occur naturally in daily life.
3. Action research is a reflective process aimed at changes and improvements in practice. Changes come from systematically and (self-) critically evaluating the evidence from the data.
4. Action research is participatory, as the actor is also the researcher and the research is done most effectively through collaboration with others.

HISTORICAL AND PHILOSOPHICAL EVOLUTION OF ACTION RESEARCH

A number of writers (Kemmis & McTaggart, 1988b; McNiff, 1988; Zuber-Skerritt, 1992) argue that action research originated with Kurt Lewin, a social psychologist who applied theories of group dynamics and human relations training to his investigations of social problems in 1940s America (e.g., Lewin, 1947). Although Collier (1945) may have been the first to use the actual term (see McTaggart, 1991), Lewin's notable contribution was his construction of a theoretical model, consisting of action cycles of analysis, fact-finding, conceptualization, planning, implementation, and evaluation (Lewin, 1947). He also argued for including practitioners from the target research communities in the work of professional researchers. His student, Alfred Marrow (1969), referred to him as "a practical theorist".

During the 1950s, Stephen Corey led the growing interest in the U.S. in *cooperative action research* (Verduin, 1967), where teachers and schools worked with external researchers. By the late 1950s, however, action research was increasingly criticized for its lack of rigor and generalizability. Indeed, Corey's own arguments retained a strong flavor of the conventional scientific research paradigms of the time. The concepts of action research in this period have been characterized as essentially "*technical*" and individualistic (see Burns, 2005, for further discussion).

Action research received a new lease on life in the late 1960s and 1970s, as interest in curriculum theory (Schwab, 1969) and the teacher-researcher movement (Stenhouse, 1971) grew. In Britain, the work of Lawrence Stenhouse and others in the Humanities Curriculum Project (1967-1972) emphasized that curriculum theory, research, and evaluation could not be separated from teaching. Rather than focusing on how research could improve curricula, Stenhouse was interested in how teachers as researchers interacted with the curriculum. Thus, Stenhouse's work tended towards a *practical* model of action research (Grundy, 1982). Significant developments that followed were the Ford Teaching Project (1972-1975) directed by Stenhouse's colleagues, John Elliott and Clem Adelman, and the establishment of the *Classroom Action Research Network* (CARN).

Critical or *emancipatory* models emanate largely from the work of Stephen Kemmis and his colleagues at Deakin University in Australia (Kemmis & McTaggart, 1982). Critical action research "promotes a critical consciousness which exhibits itself in political as well as practical action to promote change" (Grundy, 1987, p. 154). Critical action research theorists question what they see as the passive foundations of technical and practical models. Critical action research is embedded in notions of the empowerment of practitioners as participants in the research enterprise, the struggle for more democratic forms of education, and the reform of education from the insider perspective. It is to this critical approach that participatory action research is most essentially related (see Auerbach, 1994).

These three broad approaches to action research differ, not so much in their methodologies but in the underlying assumptions of the participants. Table 3 summarizes the broad differences.

THE DEVELOPMENT OF ACTION RESEARCH IN ELT

In the applied linguistics field in the 1980s, action research was barely discussed. This is not to say that it was unrecognized or that calls for teacher involvement in research were not being made. In the early 1980s, Breen and Candlin's (1980) proposals that curriculum evaluation should be an integral aspect of classroom teaching and learning foreshadowed shifts towards an action research orientation, while calls for more active participation of teachers in classroom-centered research were increasing (e.g. Allwright, 1988; Long, 1983). Towards the end of the 1980s, van Lier (1988) was arguing for "ethnographic monitoring" of classroom curriculum processes and, like others, was pointing out that action research had "not so far received much serious attention as a distinct style of research in language teaching" (p. 67).

Table 3. *Approaches to Action Research*

	Technical AR	Practical AR	Critical AR
Philosophical base	Natural sciences	Hermeneutics	Critical theory
Nature of reality	Measurable	Multiple, holistic, constructed	Interrelated with social and political power structures
Nature of problem	Predefined, (problem-posing)	Defined in context (problem-solving)	Defined in context in relation to emerging values (problematizing)
Status of knowledge	Separate, deductive	Inductive, theory producing	Inductive, theory producing, emancipatory, participatory
Nature of understanding	Events explained in terms of real causes and simultaneous effects	Events described in terms of interaction between the external context and individual thinking	Events understood in terms of political, economic, and social constraints to improved conditions
Purpose of research	Discover "laws" of underlying reality	Discover the meanings people make of actions	Understand what impedes more democratic and equal practices
Change outcomes	Change is value free and short-lived	Change is value bounded and dependent on individuals involved	Change is value relative and leads to ongoing emancipation

Note:. From Masters, J. (2000), *The History of Action Research* (p. 7) Retrieved October 5, 2002, from http://www.fhs.usyd.edu/arer/003.htm. Copyright 1995-2000, The University of Sydney and Authors. Adapted with permission.

Nunan's publication, *Understanding Language Classrooms* (1989a), subtitled *A guide for teacher-initiated action*, offered, for the first time, a practical guide for the language teacher. "The intention is to provide a serious introduction to classroom research to language professionals who do not have specialist training in research methods... it is aimed specifically at the classroom teacher and teachers in preparation" (p. xiv). This book was quickly followed by another, *Language teaching methodology* (1991), where Nunan outlined methodological proposals for language teaching that departed from similar publications by including transcribed data from real classrooms. His purpose was "not to provide instances of exemplary practice, that is to show what *should be* done, but to demonstrate what actually *is* done in language classrooms" (p. xiv).

Work by others such as Peck (1988), Allwright and Bailey (1991), and Brindley (1990) was equally significant in opening up the concept of an active and reflective role for teacher educators and researchers. As Edge points out, this paradigm shift in our way of thinking about teacher education (Richards, 1987; Richards, 1990; Wallace, 1991) no longer seems controversial. However, at the time it stood in stark contrast to the applied science model, where research and practice were regarded as separate and teachers were expected to implement their practice based on findings from current research. Contemporary trends in teacher education and language teaching have reversed our perspectives from a uniquely "theory-applied-to-practice" approach towards a more "theory-derived-from-practice" approach (cf. Graves, 1996; Nunan & Lamb, 1996; Richards & Lockhart, 1994; Richards & Nunan, 1990). Specific treatments of action research within this paradigm shift have emerged in publications such as Wallace (1998), Burns (1999), and Edge (2001). Publications illustrating action research generally fall into two major categories. The first is the "how-to" type that outline ways of doing action research. These publications are usually written by academics, and may include illustrative examples of research done by teachers (e.g. Burns, 1997; Burns, 1999; Christison & Bassano, 1995; Freeman, 1998; Wallace, 1998). The second type, which are still relatively small in number, are action research case studies written by teachers, either working individually (e.g., Brousseau, 1996; Dutertre, 2000; Edge, 2001; Gersten & Tlusty, 1998) or in collaborative groups (e.g., McPherson, 1997; the accounts in Burns & Hood, 1995, and Burns & de Silva Joyce, 2001; Mathew, 2000; Tinker Sachs, 2002).

ACTION RESEARCH WITHIN ELT RESEARCH

In a plenary session at the New York TESOL Convention, Bailey (1999) referred to action research as *the road less traveled*, highlighting its status as an approach that is still relatively unrecognized (in both senses of the word) in the ELT field. The question of how action research is positioned in relation to the range of approaches adopted in research is one that confronts those new to action research. Action research is sometimes represented as a "third way" in research. Nunan (1992), for example, having outlined the traditional major paradigms of quantitative and qualitative research, devotes a separate discussion to action research. Bailey, Omaggio-Hadley, Magnan, and Swaffar (1991) distinguish action research from experimental studies, those that "emphasize careful isolation of variables functions and target subjects, a high degree of control over external variables and clearly defined research goal" and naturalistic enquiry, where "the general goal of enquiry is to understand the phenomenon under investigation" (pp. 94-95). Brindley (1991) discusses *basic* (concerned with knowledge for its own sake), *applied* (directed at specific problems), and *practitioner* (undertaken by participants in the context of their own work) research. Cumming (1994) categorizes orientations to TESOL research as *descriptive* (concerned with the goals of general scientific inquiry), *interpretive* (concerned with the purpose of interpreting local institutional issues in their cultural contexts), and *ideological* (concerned with advocating and fostering ideological change within particular contexts and broader domains), which includes participatory action research. It is worth noting also that the philosophical values and methods adopted in action research can be linked to a whole tradition of contextualized or ecological research reflected in the work of social psychologists such as Vygotsky, Bronfenbrenner, Cole, and Wertsch (van Lier, personal communication, 25 January, 2002).

Classroom research, teacher research, and *action research* have become familiar terms in recent applied linguistics literature. However, they are often used interchangeably so that the distinctions are not necessarily clear. Bailey (2001) comments that "[action research] is sometimes confused with teacher research and classroom research because in our field, action research is often conducted by teachers in language classrooms" (p. 490).

However, whereas classroom research denotes the focus of the research and teacher research refers to the people conducting the research, action research refers, as we have seen, to a distinctive methodological orientation to research, a "way of working," as Kemmis and McTaggart (1988b, p. 174) describe it. Allwright and Bailey (1991, p. 2) define classroom research as research that is centered on the classroom, as distinct from research that concerns itself with the inputs (curriculum, materials and so on) or the outputs (test scores). In its most narrow form, it emphasizes the study of classroom interaction. Allwright and Bailey take a broader view, defining classroom research as "a cover term for a whole range of research *studies on classroom learning and teaching. The obvious unifying factor is that the emphasis is solidly on trying to understand what goes on in the classroom setting"* (p. 2).

Teacher research, that is, research conducted by teachers, may well center on the classroom but does not necessarily do so. For example, a teacher might compile an autobiographical profile of her learners in order to understand affective factors in their learning (see Muldoon, 1997, for an example). Classroom research is primarily conducted by academic researchers whose studies relate to questions of classroom teaching and learning. Many of these studies have been conducted in experimental laboratory settings (Breen, 1985) set up for the testing of theoretical hypotheses, although in the last decade a greater number of exploratory and descriptive studies located in natural classroom settings have appeared (e.g., Toohey, 1998). Action research, on the other hand, is not confined to the classroom or to teachers. It is implemented in a wide range of settings, not focused exclusively on educational questions. It involves an iterative process of research rather than a specific type of researcher or research location. All three types of research may adopt a wide range of qualitative and quantitative methodological approaches to data collection, data analysis, and interpretation depending on the kinds of research issues under investigation.

THE NATURE OF ACTION RESEARCH IN ELT

Over the last decade, accounts of action research in the ELT literature have fallen largely into the technical or practical categories. Crookes (1993) argues that action research has primarily been motivated by *the teacher as researcher* concept (cf. Cochran-Smith & Lytle, 1990; Nunan, 1989a; Strickland, 1988). He characterizes this type of action research as (nominally) value free and conservative. In contrast, the more radically progressive, critical, and emancipatory orientation (Carr & Kemmis, 1986; Gore & Zeichner, 1991) "has gone almost without representation in SL discussions of this topic" (Crookes, 1993, p. 133).

Crookes' argument (1993) appears to be confirmed by analysis of the published literature over the last decade. The lack of accounts of critical action research could be attributable to the newness of this concept in the field, little opportunity for teachers in the (marginalized) world of ELT to work collaboratively and find time for reflection, or fear that a critical perspective might upset the prevailing institutional culture. Whatever the reasons, most publications focus on outlining techniques for conducting action research and/or providing individual illustrative case studies (e.g., Bailey & Nunan, 1996; Edge, 2001; Edge & Richards, 1993; Nunan, 1989b; Wallace, 1998). Where collaboration between researchers and teachers exists, it tends to be of the "flying visit" (Breen, Candlin, Dam, & Gabrielsen, 1989, p. 114) variety. Also, despite the arguments that action research provides a voice for teachers, collected accounts written by classroom teachers, who would not also consider themselves academics or teacher educators, do not yet figure very prominently in the ELT literature (but see the papers in Burns & Hood, 1995, 1998; Burns & de Silva Joyce, 2000; Edge, 2001; Richards, 1997). On the other hand, argues Edge (2001, p. 4), there may be limits to the extent ESOL teachers can or should engage in social justice action research. However, undertaking action research will ultimately contribute to a shift in values oriented towards concepts of social justice:

> The most basic idea of empowerment, participation, stakeholding are still news to a lot of people. But every little shift made by a language teacher, for example, from the fragile security of given knowledge to the robust uncertainty of emergent awareness is of a piece with the underpinning values of a sense of social justice that is shared. Or to express this in interpersonal terms, our individual responsibility is not to attempt to impose large-scale change, but to act in our everyday exchanges with others in ways that instantiate the values that we value. (Edge, 2001, p.4)

Edge's last comments echo the sentiments of others, that action research is inevitably a political process. "Politics will intrude," proclaims McNiff (1988, p. 72), arguing that because action research has to do with change, researchers may well find themselves at odds with established practices and policies. Although she does not term it critical action research, Ferguson (1998), for example, describes her growing political awareness of her role as a teacher, as she lobbied for continued funding of her adult ESL class:

> We, as ESL practitioners, can look at our field of work and easily say, "It's hopeless!" The inadequacies in the field are great: in recognition of the need for ESL service for adults, in funding for service delivery, in amount of services available, in employment opportunities for teacher and so on and on. However, we can just as easily say, "It's wide open!" There is so much room for improvement that small actions towards building political visibility can be significant. Any expertise we gain is valuable. Any progress we make is laudable. (p. 13)

CURRENT DEBATES

There is growing evidence, albeit sometimes anecdotal, that action research offers teachers a transformative rather than transmissive experience of professional development. As Bennett (1993, p. 69, cited in van Lier, 1994) notes:

> Experienced teacher-researchers stated that their research brought them many personal and professional benefits, including increased collegiality, a sense of empowerment, and increased self-esteem. Teacher-researchers viewed themselves as being more open to change, more reflective, and better informed than they had been when they began their research. They now saw themselves as experts in their field who were better problem solvers and more effective teachers with fresher attitudes toward education. They also saw strong connections between theory and practice.

Comments such as the following from an Australian teacher support these arguments:

> Collaborative action research is a powerful form of staff development because it is practice to theory rather than theory to practice. Teachers are encouraged to reach their own solutions and conclusions and this is far more attractive and has more impact than being presented with ideals which cannot be attained. (Linda Ross, cited in Burns, 1999, p. 7)

Wadsworth (1998) summarizes the benefits claimed to be offered by action research, saying we become:

- more conscious of "problematizing" an existing action or practice and more conscious of who is problematizing it and why we are problematizting it;
- more explicit about "naming" the problem, and more self-conscious about raising an unanswered question and focusing an effort to answer it;
- more planned and deliberate about commencing a process of inquiry and involving others who could or should be involved in that inquiry;
- more systematic and rigorous in our efforts to get answers;
- more carefully documenting and recording action and what people think about it and in more detail and in ways which are accessible to other relevant parties;
- more intensive and comprehensive in our study, waiting much longer before we "jump" to a conclusion;
- more self-skeptical in checking our hunches;
- attempting to develop deeper understanding and more useful and more powerful theory about the matters we are researching in order to produce new knowledge which can inform improved action or practice; and
- changing our actions as part of the research process, and then further researching these changed actions. (p. 4)

On the other hand, numerous criticisms have been raised. Commentators from Halsey (1972) onwards have pointed to the fundamental tension between action and research and to the differing, and inherently incompatible, interests and orientations of teachers and researchers. Others have questioned whether it is the business of teachers to do research at all, given that they usually have no specialist training (e.g., Jarvis, 2002a), while the academic status and the rigor of the methodological procedures have also been the subject of debate (e.g., Brumfit & Mitchell, 1989).

Winter (1982) and others draw attention to the lack of rigor in interpreting findings and the restricted nature of the data characterizing action research studies. Related to Winter's argument is the point that there is danger of overinvolvement by the researcher, leading to personal bias and subjectivity. Others raise question marks over accountability in experimentation with learner subjects (cf. Hitchcock & Hughes, 1995; Tinker Sachs, 2000).

The idea of teachers carrying out research is perhaps no longer so much in contention (although see the recent debates in the TESOL Research Interest Section Newsletter; Jarvis, 2002a, 2002b). Nevertheless, there are many aspects of action research that remain to be more fully understood. In a recent *TESOL Quarterly* discussion, Allwright (1997) and Nunan (1997) debated the following issues: What are the standards by which action research is to be judged, and should these be the same as for other forms of research? Should action research conform to existing academic criteria? What ethical considerations need to be brought to bear on research that is highly contextualized in practice? How should action research be reported? What tensions exist between the quality of action research and its sustainability by practitioners?

At a more pragmatic level, teachers themselves may well resist the current calls to become researchers. Action research imposes a double burden of teaching and research, which adds to the already complex lives of teachers. The rewards for doing action research must balance the time and additional efforts involved. Some teachers may also question whether the growing trend of encouragement by government ministries or other educational bodies to do action research is not another way to ensure they become compliant with organizational agendas, (as shown in the following comments by a teacher cited in Miller, 1990):

> Well, what I mean is that nothing would please some administrators I know more than to think that we were doing "research" in their terms. That's what scares me about the phrase "teacher-as-researcher"— too packaged. People buy back in to the very system that shuts them down. ... But I'm still convinced that if enough people do this, we could get to a point of seeing at least a bigger clearing for us. (p. 114)

The latter suggestion, that action research offers teachers a grass-roots opportunity that could be undermined, is taken up also by others who argue that the involvement of academic researchers might also take action research out of the hands of teachers (see Burns, 1999). Outside researchers could influence the research agenda, challenging in subtle ways the questions posed, the data collected or the interpretations made. On the other hand, academic researchers can provide an impetus in a climate where teachers' voices are unrepresented in educational decision-making. Tinker Sachs (2000), for example, points to the tensions over these issues that she experienced as an academic facilitator of action research in Hong Kong, a process she describes as "both 'pushing' and 'pulling'" (p. 37).

On the subject of rigor, validity, and appropriateness, Bailey (1998) suggests that action research should not be judged by the traditional criteria of random selection, generalizability, and replicability, as its central goals are to establish local understandings. A basic criterion for validity will rest on two questions: (a) Is what the researcher is claiming on the basis of the data meaningful, believable, and trustworthy (Anderson, Herr, & Nihlen, 1994; Mishler, 1990)? and (b) To what extent does this research resonate with my understandings of practice and have meaning in my context (see Burns, 1999)? In sum, a major, and continuing, challenge in action research will be "to define and meet standards of appropriate rigor without sacrificing relevance" (Argyris & Schön, 1991, p. 85).

FUTURE DIRECTIONS

Current educational philosophies of devolved management, quality improvement, accountability, and outcomes-based assessment emerging in many educational contexts are likely to contribute to the rapid spread of action research as a way of monitoring, evaluating, and improving practice. Because of its flexibility and broad application, it offers numerous implications for areas of the ELT field that are still relatively unexplored.

In terms of institutionwide educational reform, action research provides a way of stimulating overall renewal (Calhoun, 1994; Elliot, 1991; Goswami & Stillman, 1987) and a climate where teachers are enabled to accept rapid change more readily (Burns, 1999; Markee, 1997). School-based curriculum development benefits from teacher involvement that is underpinned by action research (Hopkins, 1993), meaning that change is more likely to be accepted and implemented (Fullan, 1996) as well as to be more rigorously evaluated (Murphy, 1996; Somekh, 1993). Immediate teaching or learning problems can be systematically addressed on an individual (Nunan, 1989a; Wallace, 1998) or collaborative (Burns; Oja & Smulyan, 1989) basis, while more reflective and personally meaningful forms of professional development can be made available to teachers (Richards & Nunan, 1990). In addition, action research holds promise as a major site for building more substantial theories about language teaching and learning, about which the ELT field still knows relatively little. As one teacher researcher recently put it:

> To the extent that any part of our language education work, from classroom teaching to large-scale policy planning, seeks to involve the informed choices of the people concerned, it is difficult to see how this work would not be enhanced by some elements of participatory action research. (Rogers, 2001, p. 55)

CONCLUSIONS

From this broad overview, it can be seen that action research is an approach that has long-term historical and methodological developments. However, only in the last decade has it become influential in the ELT field. At the moment, it enjoys widespread popularity in professional development, but its further impact remains to be seen. There are many questions about appropriate standards and forms of action research that remain to be answered. In the meantime, it is clear that there is a broad movement away from decontextualized and abstract forms of knowledge and enquiry in our field, as in other disciplines. There is a shift towards the concept of professionals as agents, rather than recipients, of knowledge. As the term *action* research implies, it appears to be an approach that is well suited to this movement.

REFERENCES

Allwright, D. (1988). *Observation in the language classroom*. London: Longman.
Allwright, D. (1997). Quality and sustainability in teacher-research. *TESOL Quarterly, 31*(2), 368–370.
Allwright, D., & Bailey, K. (1991). *Focus on the language classroom*. Cambridge: Cambridge University Press.

Anderson, G. L., Herr, K., & Nihlen, A. S. (1994). *Studying your own school: An educator's guide to qualitative practitioner research*. Thousand Oaks, CA.: Corwin Press.

Argyris, C., & Schön, D. (1991). Participatory action research and action science compared: A commentary. In W.F. Whyte (Ed.), *Participatory action science* (pp. 85–98). Newbury Park, CA: Sage.

Auerbach, E. (1994). Participatory action research. *TESOL Quarterly, 28*(4), 693–697.

Bailey, K. (1998). Approaches to empirical research in instructional settings. In H. Byrnes (Ed.), *Perspectives in research and scholarship in second language teaching*. New York: The Modern Language Association of America.

Bailey, K. (1999). What have we learned in two decades of classroom research? Plenary presentation at the 33rd TESOL Convention, New York, NY.

Bailey, K. (2001). Action research, teacher research, and classroom research in language teaching. In M. Celce-Murcia (Ed.), *Teaching English as a second or foreign language* (3rd ed., pp. 489–498). Boston: Heinle & Heinle.

Bailey, K., & Nunan, D. (Eds.). (1996). *Voices from the language classroom*. Cambridge: Cambridge University Press.

Bailey, K., Omaggio-Hadeley, A., Magnan, S., & Swaffer, J. (1991). Research in the 1990s: Focus on theory building, instructional innovation and collaboration. *Foreign Language Annals, 24*, 89–100.

Bennett, C. K. (1993). Teacher-researchers: All dressed up and no place to go? *Educational Leadership, 51*(2), 69–70.

Biott, C. (1996) Latency in action research: Changing perspectives on occupational and researcher identities. *Educational Action Research, 4*(2), 169–183.

Breen, M. P. (1985). The social context for language learning–a neglected situation? *Studies in Second Language Acquisition, 7*, 135–158.

Breen, M. P., & Candlin, C. N. (1980). The essentials of a communicative curriculum in language teaching. *Applied Linguistics, 1*, 89–112.

Breen, M. P., Candlin, C. N., Dam, L., & Gabrielsen, G. (1989). The evolution of a teacher training program. In R. K. Johnson (Ed.), *The second language curriculum* (pp. 111–135). Cambridge: Cambridge University Press.

Brindley, G. (1990). Towards a research agenda for TESOL. *Prospect: A Journal of Australian TESOL, 6*(1), 7–26.

Brousseau, K. (1996). Action research in the second language classroom: Two views of a writing process class. *Carleton Papers in Applied Language Studies, 13*, 1–20.

Brumfit, C., & Mitchell, R. (1989). The language classroom as a focus for research. In C. Brumfit & R. Mitchell (Eds.), *Research in the language classroom*. ELT Documents 133 (pp. 3–15). London: Modern English Publications and The British Council.

Burns, A. (1997). Valuing diversity: Action researching disparate learner groups. *TESOL Journal, 7*(1), 6–9.

Burns, A. (1999). *Collaborative action research for English language teachers*. Cambridge: Cambridge University Press.

Burns, A. (2005). Action research. In E. Hinkel (Ed.), *Handbook of research in second language teaching and learning* (pp. 241–256). Mahwah, NJ.: Lawrence Erlbaum.

Burns, A., & Hood, S. (1995). *Teachers' voices: Exploring course design in a changing curriculum*. Sydney: National Centre for English Language Teaching and Research.

Burns, A., & Hood, S. (1998). *Teachers' voices 3: Teaching critical literacy*. Sydney: National Centre for English Language Teaching and Research.

Burns, A., & de Silva Joyce, H. (2000). *Teachers' voices 5: A new look at reading practices*. Sydney: National Centre for English Language Teaching and Research.

Burns, A., & de Silva Joyce, H. (2001). *Teachers' voices 7: Teaching vocabulary*. Sydney: National Centre for English Language Teaching and Research.

Calhoun, E. R. (1994). *How to use action research in the self-renewing school*. Alexandria, VA.: Association for Supervision and Curriculum Development

Carr, W., & Kemmis, S. (1986). *Becoming critical: Knowing through action research*. London: The Falmer Press.

Christison, M., & Bassano, S. (1995). Action research: Techniques for collecting data through surveys and interviews. *The CATESOL Journal, 8*(1), 89–103.

Cochran-Smith, M., & Lytle, S. (1990). Research on teaching and teacher research: The issues that divide. *Educational Researcher, 19*(2), 2–11.

Collier, J. (1945, May). United States Indian administration as a laboratory of ethnic relations. *Social Research, 12*.

Cumming, A. (1994). Alternatives in TESOL research: Descriptive, interpretive and ideological orientations. *TESOL Quarterly, 28*(4), 673–676.
Crookes, G. (1993). Action research for second language teachers: Going beyond teacher research. *Applied Linguistics, 14*(2), 130–144.
Dutertre, A. (2000). A teacher's investigation of her own teaching. *Applied Language Learning, 2*(1), 99–122.
Edge, J. (Ed.). (2001). *Action research*. Alexandria, VA: TESOL.
Edge, J., & Richards, K. (Eds.). (1993). *Teachers develop teachers' research*. London: Heinemann.
Elliott, J. (1991). *Action research for educational change*. Milton Keynes: Open University Press.
Ferguson, P. (1998). The politics of Adult ESL literacy: Becoming politically visible. In T. Smoke (Ed.), *Adult ESL: Politics, pedagogy and participation in classroom and community programs* (pp. 3–16). Mahwah, NJ.: Lawrence Erlbaum.
Freeman, D. (1998). *Doing teacher research: From inquiry to understanding*. Boston: Heinle & Heinle.
Fullan, M, (1996). *The new meaning of educational change*. New York: Teachers' College Press.
Gersten, B. F., & Tlusty, N. (1998). Creating contexts for cultural communication: Video exchange projects in the EFL/ESL classroom. *TESOL Journal, 7*(5), 11–16.
Gore, J. M., & Zeichner, K. M. (1991). Action research and reflective teaching in preservice education: A case study from the United States. *Teaching and Teacher Education, 7*(2), 119–136.
Goswami, D., & Stillman, J. (1987). *Reclaiming the classroom: Teacher research as an agency for change*. Upper Montclair. NJ.: Boynton/Cook.
Graves, K. (1996). *Teachers as course developers*. Cambridge: Cambridge University Press.
Grundy, S. (1987). *Curriculum: Product or praxis*. London: Falmer Press.
Halsey, A. H. (Ed.). (1972). *Educational priority: Volume 1: E. P.A. Problems and policies*. London: HMSO.
Hopkins, D. (1993). *A teacher's guide to classroom research* (2nd ed.). Buckingham: Open University.
Hitchcock, G., & Hughes, D. (1995). *Research and the teacher* (2nd ed.). London: Routledge.
Hutchison, B., & Bryson, P. (1997). Video, reflection and transformation: Action research in vocational education and training in a European context. *Educational Action Researcher, 5*(2), 283–304.
Jarvis, S. (2002a). Research in TESOL Part I. *TESOL Research Interest Section Newsletter, 8*(3), 1–2.
Jarvis, S. (2002b). Research in TESOL Part II. *TESOL Research Interest Section Newsletter, 9*(1), 1–2.
Kember, D. (2001). *Reflective teaching and learning in the health professions*. Oxford: Blackwell.
Kemmis, S., & McTaggart, R. (Eds.). (1982). *The action research reader*. Geelong, Victoria: Deakin University Press.
Kemmis, S., & McTaggart, R. (Eds.). (1988a). *The action research planner* (3rd ed.). Geelong, Victoria: Deakin University Press.
Kemmis, S., & McTaggart, R. (Eds.). (1988b). *The action research reader* (3rd ed.). Geelong, Victoria: Deakin University Press.
Knijnik, G. (1997). Popular knowledge and academic knowledge in the Brasilian peasant's struggle for land. *Educational Action Research, 5*(3), 501–512.
Lewin, K. (1947). Frontiers in group dynamics: II. Channels of group life; social planning and action research. *Human Relations, II*, 142–153.
Long, M. (1983). Training the second language teacher as classroom researcher. In J. E. Alatis, H. H. Stern, & P. Strevens (Eds.), *Applied linguistics and the preparation of teachers: Towards a rationale* (pp. 281–297). Washington, DC: Georgetown University Press.
Markee, N. (1997). *Managing curricular innovation*. Cambridge: Cambridge University Press.
Marrow, A. (1969). The practical theorist: The life and work of Kurt Lewin. New York: Basic Books.
Masters, J. (2000). The history of action research. Retrieved October 5, 2002, from http://casino.cchs.usyd.edu.au/arow//arer/00.
Mathew, R. (2000). Teacher-research approach to curriculum renewal and teacher development. In R. Mathew, R. L. Eapen, & J. Tharu (Eds.), *The language curriculum: Dynamics of change. Volume I: The outsider perspective* (pp. 6–21). Hyderabad: Orient Longman.
McNiff, J. (1988). *Action research: Principles and practice*. London: Routledge.
McPherson, P. (1997). Action research: Exploring learner diversity. *Prospect, 12*(1), 50–62.
McTaggart, R. (1991). *Action research. A short modern history*. Geelong, Victoria: Deakin University Press.
Miller, J. (1990). *Creating spaces and finding voices: Teachers collaborating for empowerment*. Albany: State University of New York Press.
Mishler, E. (1990). Validation in inquiry-guided research: The role of exemplars in narrative study. *Harvard Educational Review, 60* (4), 415–442.
Muldoon, M. (1997). A profile of group diversity. In A. Burns & S. Hood (Eds.), *Teachers' voices: Teaching disparate learner groups* (pp. 18–23). Sydney: NCELTR.

Murphy, D. (1996). The evaluator's apprentices: Learning to do evaluation. *The International Journal of Theory, Research and Practice, 2*(3), 321–328.
Nunan, D. (1989a). *Understanding language classrooms: A guide for teacher-initiated action*. New York: Prentice Hall.
Nunan, D. (1989b). The teacher as researcher. In C. Brumfit & R. Mitchell (Eds.), *Research in the language classroom*. ELT Documents 133 (pp. 16–32). London: Modern English Publications and The British Council.
Nunan, D. (1991). *Language teaching methodology*. Cambridge: Cambridge University Press.
Nunan, D. (1992). *Research methods in language learning*. Cambridge: Cambridge University Press.
Nunan, D. (1997). Developing standards for teacher-research in TESOL. *TESOL Quarterly, 31*(2), 365–37.
Nunan, D., & C. Lamb (1996). *The self-directed teacher*. Cambridge: Cambridge University Press.
Nichols, R. (1997). Action research in health care: The collaborative action research network health care group. *Educational Action Researcher, 5*(2), 185–192.
Oja, S. N., & Smulyan, L. (1989). *Collaborative action research: A developmental approach*. London: The Falmer Press.
Peck, A. (1988). Language teachers at work. A description of methods. London: Prentice-Hall.
Richards, J. C. (1987/90). The dilemma of teacher education in second language teaching. In J. C. Richards & D. Nunan (Eds.). *Second language teacher education*. Cambridge: Cambridge University Press. (Reprinted from *TESOL Quarterly, 21*, 209–226.)
Richards, J. C. (Ed.). (1998). *Teaching in action*. Alexandria, VA: TESOL.
Richards, J. C., & Lockhart, C. (1994). *Reflective teaching in second language classrooms*. Cambridge: Cambridge University Press.
Richards, J. C., & Nunan, D. (Eds.). (1990). *Second language teacher education*. Cambridge: Cambridge University Press.
Rogers, J. (2001). Process courting context: Action research meets learner education. In J. Edge (Ed.). *Action Research* (pp. 45–56). Alexandria, VA: TESOL.
Schwab, J. (1969). *College curricula and student protest*. Chicago: University of Chicago Press.
Somekh, B. (1993). Quality in educational research – the contribution of classroom teachers. In J. Edge & K. Richards (Eds.), *Teachers develop teachers research*. London: Heinemann.
Somekh, B., & Thaler, M. (1997). Contradictions of management theory, organisational cultures and the self. *Educational Action Research, 5*(1), 141–160.
Stenhouse, L. (1971). The Humanities Curriculum Project: The rationale. *Theory into Practice, X*(3), 154–162.
Strickland, D. (1988). The teacher as researcher: Toward the extended professional. *Language Arts, 65*(8), 754–764.
Tinker Sachs, G. (2000). Teacher and researcher autonomy in action research. *Prospect: A Journal of Australian TESOL, 15*(3), 35–51.
Tinker-Sachs, G. (2002). *Action research. Fostering and furthering effective practices in the teaching of English*. Hong Kong: City University of Hong Kong.
Toohey, K. (1998). "Breaking them up, taking them away": ESL students in Grade 1. *TESOL Quarterly, 32*(1), 61–84.
Verduin, J. (1967). *Cooperative curriculum improvement*. Englewood Cliffs, NJ.: Prentice-Hall.
Wadsworth, Y. (1998). What is participatory action research? *Action Research International*. Retrieved October 5, 2002, from http://www.scu.edu.au/schools/gcm/ar/ari/p-ywadsworth.
Wallace, M. (1991). *Training foreign language teachers*. Cambridge: Cambridge University Press.
Wallace, M. (1998). *Action research for language teachers*. Cambridge: Cambridge University Press.
Winter, R. (1982). 'Dilemma analysis': A contribution to methodology for action research. *Cambridge Journal of Education, 12*(3), 11–74.
Zuber-Skerritt, O. (1992). *Improving learning and teaching through action learning and action research*. Higher Education RDSA Conference, University of Queensland.
van Lier, L. (1988). *The classroom and the language learner*. London: Longman.
van Lier, L. (1994). Action research. *Sintagma, 6*, 31–37.

CHAPTER 61

NARRATIVE INQUIRY AND ELT RESEARCH

JOANN PHILLION

Purdue University, USA

MING FANG HE

Georgia Southern University, USA

ABSTRACT

This chapter explores the contributions and potential of narrative inquiry in English language teaching. Two stories of experience are presented and used as a touchstone throughout the chapter. We begin by discussing key terms—*narrative inquiry* and *English language teaching and learning*—to set boundaries for the review. The latter term led to a literature of learning of English as a second, third, or other language in predominantly English-speaking cultures and environments. The former term led to an experiential literature focused on language learning in life contexts. The narrative inquiry research literature is traced through the social sciences, educational studies, and language learning literature. Experiential characteristics of narrative inquiry are brought forward, and a detailed narrative inquiry analysis is made of two specific studies. In addition, life-based literary narratives are named and described. The contribution of narrative inquiry lies in its potential to permit and encourage the study of English language teaching and learning in the context of life and in the pursuit of broad educational questions.

STORY 1

Pam is in the back of her grade 4/5 classroom in Room 23, on the second floor of Bay Street School—a community school in inner city Toronto. The children, seated at tables or on the carpet, were born in 12 different countries and speak 13 different home languages. Several children are working on a mural that portrays the theme of "Swinging on a Star." Paper, glue, and scissors litter the table. The children are making miniature stars, moonbeams, pigs, and fish. There is a soft hum of voices, mixed with laughter and the muted strains of classical music coming from Pam's radio in the closet behind her desk. Aisha comes from Somalia, and has never attended school before coming to Bay Street School. George's parents are from Vietnam; he appears to be a speaker of English as a second language (ESL), but his Vietnamese is, according to him, "only for simple things, not for talking about aliens." Annette is from the Caribbean. Dan-Dan arrived from Mainland China three days ago; she speaks no English. The four children continue to cut out pictures for the mural. How does Pam teach children from 12 countries with 13 home languages? How do they come together to learn English? How do Aisha, George, and Dan-Dan feel when they learn English at home and in school? How will their parents cope with the tension between maintaining their children's native language and their learning of English for a future in a new world? How will the mix of hopes of parents from such different lands be expressed in the classroom curriculum? What kinds of programs can Bay Street School provide to facilitate the language learning of these students?

STORY 2

Even though I, Ming Fang, was an English language teacher in a Chinese university for six years, the first time I sat in a literature class in a Canadian university I was overwhelmed by a mass of concepts and terminology never mentioned in my English as a foreign language education. I was incapable of keeping notes. I dared not speak in class. Sometimes my mind was really stimulated and I had a surge of ideas. However, it took me a long time to translate my Chinese thinking into English words and to figure out how I could cut into class discussions to express what I wanted to say. When I found the way, the opportunity was gone. I felt frustrated and helpless. I could not sleep at night and felt sleepy during class. Are concepts and terminology the only barriers in my English language learning? Are my feelings about learning English part of my language learning process? Why does learning the English language feel so different in China and North America? Do different cultures shape the way a person learns a second language? What is the impact of the specific place: Would it make any difference if the story were told about language learning in an everyday life situation rather than in a classroom setting? Do the ways immigrants learn English in their new countries have anything to do with their previous experiences?

At the heart of a narrative inquiry there is a quest for making meaning of the experiences of language learners such as Aisha, George, Dan-Dan, and Ming Fang. These stories of experience illustrate that language learning is a complex, contextualized, and narrativized experience. The questions asked of the stories illustrate that for narrative inquirers, language learning is intertwined with language teaching, influenced by past, present, and future experience, impacted by place, developed in relationship, and unfolded in a social milieu.

BOUNDARIES FOR THE LITERATURE REVIEW

The opening stories are informative of the kinds of life questions we wish to address in this chapter. They also highlight our dilemma in defining boundaries for including and excluding literature. How do we review the literature on English language teaching when language learning situations are so diverse and so embedded in everyday life? To develop a feasible plan, we needed to address the question of what literature would fall under the scope of our review. Furthermore, because narrative inquiry in English language teaching is so sparse, we needed to find ways to connect narrative inquiry in general to English language teaching. Our resolution of these matters sets the parameters for the chapter.

There is immense scope in the literature of English language teaching, ranging from learning the English language in early childhood to learning English as a second, third, or foreign language at any stage of life. The opening stories are telling of how we put boundaries on our review. We define our target literature as a literature of research on the learning of English as a second, third, or other language in predominantly English-speaking cultures and environments. We exclude the vast literature on English language and literature teaching in English environments and the learning of English in non-English contexts. Our explicit focus is on the learning of English language in life contexts. The significance of this focus will become clearer as we work our way through specific studies. What is important to note is that context, whether classroom, school, community, parents, family immigration history, or other, is considered central to our topic. Many of the works reviewed are primarily studies of context where language is not the focus but one of the factors in the context. Thus, our focus in this review is on the learning of language in context rather than on the learning and teaching of the English language per se.

Another aspect of our dilemma over boundaries, also highlighted by the stories, is how to address the contributions and future directions of narrative inquiry to English language teaching when there is little narrative work in the field as defined. Our approach to this matter is to underscore the experiential basis of narrative and, through this means, to include for review closely connected, experiential inquiries. We proceed by drawing on the general literature of narrative inquiry. We show how *experience* is the key term in narrative inquiry, and we illustrate the promise of narrative inquiry through a review of research in fields related to the purposes of this chapter.[1] We also briefly review two sets of literature closely connected to narrative by virtue of their reliance on experience. These two, important to future directions for English language teaching, are ethnography and a literature for which we have developed the term *life-based literary narratives*.

Finally, we wish to explain our emphasis on context. Returning to the opening stories, readers can see how language is interwoven throughout; however, some might not see these stories as primarily stories of language teaching and learning and thus wonder at their relevance. For narrative inquirers, these stories are directly relevant because our focus is on life and on language teaching and learning in life contexts. For the most part, it is an observer's abstraction to think of a student's life situation as a language learning situation. For a language learner, experiences are rarely solely experiences of language learning; they are experiences of life. With a narrative stance, we consider the learning of language as not the learning of the subject alone but as the learning of life.

As narrative inquirers, we also think of language as an elusive phenomenon that comes in and out of focus in a particular inquiry situation. For a moment, aspects of language learning dominate a teaching situation; moments later other matters, related but more significant, become the focus. Foreground and background keep shifting; the phenomenon can never, except in abstraction, be seen as a purely language matter. When studying life, as in a narrative inquiry, the researcher needs to attend to whatever happens in life. When language is uppermost, it is attended to as such; when language fades, it is seen in context. This, for us, is one of the potentials of narrative inquiry in English language teaching and learning, namely, the study of language in context where, in an inquiry, life context may assume prominence over specific language concerns.

This narrative stance translates into questions asked of our key illustrative texts: How did the study take place, and in what sense is it a narrative inquiry of language teaching and learning? If we shift our focus as readers entirely to the question of language, what do we learn about language teaching and learning? These questions bring forward another potential of narrative inquiry. By shifting our perspective to different positions on the language teaching and learning landscape, we see different things, ask different questions, and make different knowledge claims. For instance, the key narrative text discussed later in the chapter, Carger's (1996) study of a Mexican-American child's school years in inner city Chicago, is not purely a study of English language teaching and learning. However, by asking the two questions, we learn a great deal about language teaching and learning.

EXPERIENTIAL METHODS IN INQUIRY

There is an explosion of new methodologies in the social sciences (Denzin & Lincoln, 2000). Making sense of the array of methodologies and the overlapping, related labels used to name them is difficult. Schwab (1960/1978), commenting on the history of inquiry generally, referred to such periods of methodological development as *fluid inquiry*: a time when trial and error and imaginative exploration of new possibilities overrides the conservatism of established criteria and norms for the conduct of inquiry. Within this array of creative new work, we restrict our attention to research methods that focus on understanding experience. We review a set of narrative studies in the social sciences and educational research aimed at understanding personal experience.

Even with these restrictions, there is a large set of qualitative methodologies in educational research that are either narrative or closely related to the narrative, experiential focus of this chapter. The following, though not comprehensive, is illustrative: autobiography (Grumet, 1992; Pinar, 1988), biographical method (L. Smith, 1994), life history research (Hatch &Wisniewski, 1995), memoir (Neumann & Peterson, 1997), personal narrative and narrative inquiry (Clandinin & Connelly, 2000), narrative multiculturalism (Phillion, 2002a, 2002b, 2002c, 2002d), cross-cultural narrative (Conle, 2000; He, 2002a, 2002b, 2002c, 2003), oral history (Yow, 1994), phenomenology (Van Maanen, 1990), hermeneutics (D. Smith, 1991), and portraiture (Lawrence-Lightfoot & Davis, 1997).

Special attention needs to be paid to ethnography, not because it is a new methodology but because a number of people working in this area contribute to an understanding of language teaching and learning and because it overlaps with narrative inquiry in a focus on experience (e.g., Feuerverger, 2001; Soto, 1997; Toohey, 2000; Valdés, 1996, 2001; Vasquez, Pease-Alvarez, & Shannon, 1994). Recent ethnographic work in bilingual education (e.g., Soto 1997) and English language learning (e.g., Valdés, 2001) provides detailed narrations of the experiences of children's language learning and parents' struggles for quality education (see also participatory research on immigrant education, e.g., Igoa, 1995). This work demonstrates a transition from abstract formalistic research to research that develops an in-depth, nuanced understanding of the complexity of language learning and its embeddedness in interconnected social, cultural, and political contexts. In addition, though not limited to this literature, one feature that stands out is the respect for the knowledge held by the community: the community and its participants are authoritative voices mingling with the interpretations of the researcher. This knowledge, sometimes overlooked by policymakers, contributes to new ways of understanding language teaching and learning.

NARRATIVE INQUIRY IN THE SOCIAL SCIENCES AND EDUCATION

The explosion of methods that has accompanied Schwab's (1960/1978) fluid inquiry is behind the editors' request for a chapter on narrative approaches to English language teaching. Narrative is one of the new methodologies that have found fertile ground in the social sciences. Key texts, often written by leaders in their respective disciplines, make the case for narrative in different fields: Geertz's (1995) *After the Fact: Two Countries, Four Decades, One Anthropologist* and Bateson's (1994) *Peripheral Visions: Learning Along the Way* in anthropology, Denzin's (1997) *Interpretive Ethnography: Ethnographic Practices for the 21st Century* in ethnography, Polkinghorne's (1988) *Narrative Knowing and the Human Sciences* in psychology, Schafer's (1992) *Retelling a Life: Narrative and Dialogue in Psychoanalysis* in psychotherapy, Coles's (1989) *The Call of Stories: Teaching and the Moral Imagination* in psychiatry, Crites's (1971) *The Narrative Quality of Experience* in theology, and Czarniawska's (1997) *Narrating the Organization: Dramas of Institutional Identity* in organizational theory. What is it about these disparate fields that have led these scholars to narrative, or conversely, what is it about narrative that makes it a useful way of thinking in so many different fields?

These questions are impossible to explore adequately in this review. However, what does appear to be the case is that there is no single answer to the questions. Following an analysis of a set of these key texts, Clandinin and Connelly (2000) point out that each text has its own argument: the authors come to narrative by different routes, and with different justifications. Though this conclusion may seem surprising at first, it makes sense viewed from Schwab's (1960/1978) vantage point. Creative possibilities and exploratory methods in inquiry are taking hold in the social sciences. Different aspects of narrative inquiry are becoming important and developing in selected fields: for Geertz (1995), it is the historical continuity of the phenomena and tentativeness of research texts; for Crites (1971), it is the embededdness of local, personal stories in grand contextual sacred stories; for Coles (1989), it is the participant's perspective on experience; for Bateson (1994), it is relationship in changing life situations and cultural contexts; for Schafer (1992), it is collaborative meaning making; for Polkinghorne (1988), it is the contrast between the storied world of the practitioner and the abstract world of the theoretician; and for Czarniawska (1997), it is literary forms for imagining experience. These are important resources for exploring narrative inquiry in language teaching and learning not only because of the methodologies applied but, perhaps even more so, for the reasons that led the authors to adopt a narrative way of thinking in their work.

We believe that readers of this chapter will gain understanding of narrative inquiry and its potential for English language teaching and learning from the aforementioned literature. This literature has its own set of reasons, arguments, and characteristics that can inform language-teaching inquiries. It would be wrong, however, to think of this as a foundational literature. Important as these resources are, there is also an educational literature, closer to the purposes of this chapter, in which a similar picture vis-à-vis narrative inquiry emerges as described above for the social sciences more generally. People from different educational fields are using narrative inquiry: for instance, Carter (1993), Casey (1995), Hollingsworth (1994), and Olsen (2000) in teacher education; Witherell and Noddings (1991) in teaching and learning; Huber and Whelan (1999) in the study of teaching; Elbaz-Luwisch (2002) in the study of writing; Chang and Rosiak (2003) in science education; Shubert and Ayers (1999) in curriculum studies; Craig (2001) in school reform; Freeman (1996) in language teacher knowledge; Bruner (1986) in educational psychology; Hooks in Black feminist studies (1991); and Greene (1995) in educational philosophy. Narrative inquiry also appears in research review literature, for instance, in reading (Alvermann, 2000) and in multicultural teacher education (Sleeter, 2001).

Connelly and Clandinin (1988, 1990) were among the first to bring narrative inquiry to the field of education, and they have the longest sustained program of narrative research. Their work has influenced research in a wide array of educational fields. The main contribution of their work, best seen in *Narrative Inquiry* (Clandinin & Connelly, 2000), is what they call *thinking narratively*, by which they mean, in part, that people experience the world narratively. Every experience takes place in the context of a story: every experience is shaped by stories lived at the time of the experience. Consequently, when social science/educational researchers study experiential phenomena, they are studying the stories that shape experience, i.e., the stories are the phenomena. This leads to a technical distinction between *story* and *narrative* in that story is the phenomenon of inquiry and narrative is the method of inquiry. This distinction is illustrated in the opening stories in this chapter. The stories are the phenomena and carry a strong sense of being there in an experience. The questions at the end of each story initiate narrative inquiry into the phenomena.

This line of work draws heavily on the Deweyian theory of experience, where the idea of experience takes on a conceptual and analytic quality. *Experience*, for Dewey (1938), is not merely an empty or impenetrable term: it is a term with dimension. Experience has both temporal and existential dimensions: temporal, in that every experience, no matter how instantaneous or historical, has a quality of past, present, and future; existential, in that experience takes place in a personal and social dimension, not solely within a person. All experience, large or small, has past, present, and future aspects and is simultaneously personal and social. Thus, when I, JoAnn, pursue a narrative inquiry of Pam, as in the first story, I not only record experience while being there but also query Pam and her teaching situation temporally. I wonder and ask about what came before, where she taught, what life events might have made a difference to the events described. Similarly, I ask of Pam and Aisha questions having to do with the milieu in which they live, work, and play. It will make a difference for the inquiry into Aisha if I understand her refugee history, her home environment, her parents' hopes for her education, and her feelings about her education. Thus, the phenomena of narrative, the experiences described in the story, are explored in temporal, social, and experiential contexts.

Another key feature of narrative inquiry that we wish to bring forward in this chapter is the narrative idea of understanding experience in its own terms rather than categorizing experience according to predetermined structures and theories (Phillion, 1999). In the latter approach, experience is seen, shaped, and written about by the researcher using theoretically derived forms: in effect, the experience is determined by the theory. In contrast, experience is the starting point of a narrative inquiry (Clandinin & Connelly, 2000) and is in the forefront at every stage of the research. As such, narrative inquiries arise from experiences of researchers and participants rather than being formulated as abstract research questions, and they proceed by continual reference to experience as field texts are collected, analyzed, and interpreted, and as research texts are crafted. Pam and Aisha and their life and experiences, for example, remain in the foreground, as the inquiry into immigrant children's education is the background. One of the most direct signs of this feature of narrative inquiry is that its literature is "peopled" with characters such as Pam and Aisha.

NARRATIVE STUDIES OF THE EXPERIENCE OF LANGUAGE LEARNING

In this section we turn to the narrative literature of language teaching and learning. We wish to remind readers that the lengthy process of getting to this literature was necessitated by the fact that there is so little narrative inquiry literature that focuses explicitly on English language teaching and so much relevant, related work that has been done in associated fields. There is, however, a small body of narrative research that explores language, culture, and identity as interconnected phenomena and that contributes to an understanding of English language teaching and learning (e.g., Bell, 1997; Carger, 1996; Conle, 2000; Elbaz-Luwisch, 1997; Enns-Connolly, 1985; He, 1999, 2002a, 2002b, 2002c, 2003; Kanno & Applebaum, 1995; Li, 2002; Maggisano, 1999; Phillion, 1999, 2002a, 2002b, 2002c, 2002d; Roberge & Phillion, 1997). For this group of narrative inquirers, to study language is to study culture and identity: language, culture, and identity shift between foreground and background in the inquiries.

This literature does not directly focus on teaching and learning English in classroom settings, nor does it focus on the learning of English as an isolated subject. Rather, in a narrative focus on the interconnectedness of language, culture, and identity in life contexts, it broadens understanding of the complexity of English language teaching and learning. In this chapter, we analyze two studies that illustrate this potential that narrative inquiry has in research on English language teaching and learning: Carger's (1996) *Of Borders and Dreams: A Mexican-American Experience of Urban Education* and Bell's (1997) *Literacy, Culture and Identity*. We conclude this section with a discussion of life-based literary narratives.

Chris Carger—Of Borders and Dreams

Carger (1996) takes readers on a journey that begins with Alejandro's parents' perilous entry into the United States from Mexico. The uncertainties, tensions, and risks of the dangerous border crossing foreshadow Alejandro's language learning struggles. The story begins prior to the marriage of Alejandro's parents and continues on the west side of Chicago, a predominantly Mexican-American community with a mix of public and separate Catholic schools. The book focuses on a period of time 15 or so years following the border crossing and documents Alejandro's life at the borders between his family and community and the world of English America.

This is a from-the-heart story that documents Carger's relationship with Alejandro, his family, his teachers, and various schools he attended. Initially, Carger is Alejandro's ESL tutor. As she works with Alejandro she becomes increasingly aware of his family and community, and she grows into the role of advocate for Alejandro and chronicler of his life. We enter his family's life at home, in the community, and at school, especially in negotiations with school officials. We become acquainted with his neighborhood, his school, the school's philosophy, the principal's character, and the role of religion in the family's life and the place church authority plays in education, particularly in Alejandro's learning of English. We begin to sense his parents' dreams for his future, the same dreams that drove them to their border crossing years earlier. We begin to understand how deeply his parents care about his education and how they recognize education as the key to his success in the future, yet how hopeless they feel not knowing how to realize their dreams. The book, as with narrative inquiries generally, begins in the midst of life with tensions over Alejandro's language learning and ends in the midst of life with ongoing language learning tensions. We are left to wonder at what the future holds for Alejandro.

With this brief narrative of Carger's (1996) narrative work, we now turn to an account of what she does as a narrative inquirer. The most striking methodological features to a reader interested in narrative method are the extent of Carger's involvement in Alejandro's life, the time period over which it occurs, and the passion of her commitment. The book is filled with stories, some, as with the border crossing story, told in extensive conversations with the parents, and others as Carger relates her experience of tutoring Alejandro and advocating on his behalf in various settings—in school, in his home, in Carger's home, and in the community.

Yet another reading of this text reveals a great deal about the immigrant experience from the point of view of parents and children in the educational system. We understand the universality of immigrant experience that runs through this family's life, and we understand a great deal about the learning of a second language in a particular kind of cultural milieu. In the course of reading this book, we learn to think about English language learning in the context of immigrant experiences that brought particular learners to specific English language learning settings.

So far we have drawn attention to the focus on Alejandro's experience. But, as with most narrative writing, the experiences of researchers and participants are crucial to the ultimate meaning and central to the writing. Methodologically, a great deal is revealed by paying close attention to Carger's part in the story: who she interacted with, how she interacted with them, under what circumstances, and how she represented those experiences in the text. It is through Carger's experience of Alejandro's experience that his language learning comes to light. The nuanced detail of meaning that unfolds around Alejandro's language learning arises from Carger's passion, her intensive commitment to Alejandro's life, and the time she gives to her inquiry.

Readers of this chapter interested in raw narrative data, in what Clandinin and Connelly call *field texts* (1994, 2000), will find only hints. There is a strong sense of Carger being there in direct participation with Alejandro, in conversations with his parents, in everyday negotiations between school staff, parents, and teachers, and in classroom observations. But the field texts are not presented as such, nor is there an account of how Carger moves from her own experience in the study to the recording of field texts and to the writing of the research text—her book. In this sense her manuscript has the feel of a memoir where the weaving of memory strands takes precedence over explicit grounding in field texts.

Turning to the question of what is learned about language teaching and learning from Alejandro's story, we want to remind readers of the notion that narrative inquiry is first and foremost a way of thinking. Applied to Carger's (1996) work, it means that we are looking for different ways of thinking about language learning than might be found in traditional research texts. There is nothing in this work that approximates a controlled research setting. There are no particular hypotheses or ideas being demonstrated or tested. Rather, it is an inquiry into the total experience of an inner city child learning a second language in a Mexican-American community interpenetrated with other cultures and surrounded by still others, with parents who are also learning English and with a child who has learning disabilities. We learn to think of English language learning as a complex life experience shaped by multiple contexts, not easily categorized by labels and theories applied by the education system and the research literature.

The research literature on English language teaching and learning is, of course, relevant and is displayed throughout the text. But the display is shaded and complicated by Carger and Alejandro's stories of practice. For example, Carger tries to help Alejandro understand *The Ugly Duckling* by first explaining what a swan is and then by showing Alejandro a picture of a swan. As the story unfolds, this turns out to be an exceedingly complicated exercise, since Alejandro has never seen a swan. This particular part of the book reveals a teacher, Carger, puzzling over Alejandro's lack of comprehension of a text she carefully chose for its relevance, working out the reasons for the lack of comprehension, then entering into a lengthy story that entails a family visit to a zoo to look at swans, and ending in a dinner filled with language and culture learning lessons in Carger's home. Carger's struggle to help Alejandro understand *The Ugly Duckling* is one of the teachings of this text. However, it is not a teaching that can be formalized: a reader needs to follow the text closely, puzzle along with Carger, take the field trip with her, and imagine the complexities of the dinner experience in her home.

As we said above, a key feature of narrative is that it is a way of thinking about phenomena. With this stance, as seen in *The Ugly Duckling* story, every page of Carger's (1996) text is filled with suggestion, meaning, and insight into the teaching and learning of English. A narrative reading of this text shows how Carger's concern for Alejandro's literacy leads her into his parents' border crossing stories to provide meaningful context to his reading difficulties. Time spent in the family kitchen, in the principal's office, and elsewhere, expresses the parents' concern about and drive towards creating the right conditions for Alejandro's language learning. Individual stories, such as *The Ugly Duckling*, and the text as a whole need to be read with a narrative eye, an eye for the context, an eye for the personal, an eye for the situation, and an eye for the timeline. Readers who allow themselves to fall into this narrative mode of thinking will find surprising, enlightening, and provocative twists and turns in English language teaching and learning in *Of Borders and Dreams* (Carger, 1996). Some readers may even be surprised to find themselves developing compassion and empathy for Alejandro, for Mexican-American children, and for all English language learners.

Jill Bell—Literacy, Culture and Identity

Bell (1997) takes readers on a journey of a different sort to Carger: she autobiographically enters the inner world of an adult language learner. Bell's journey begins with her struggle to understand what literacy might mean to immigrants with no formal literacy experiences in their home language and culture. She grapples with an overriding question: What is literacy? Can these adult immigrants be said to be literate? If so, what idea or notion of literacy might make it possible to say so? To answer these questions, unlike Carger who began directly with Alejandro and his learning, Bell begins with reflections on the research literature connected to her own experiences as an ESL teacher. She puzzles over what actually happens during literacy experiences. This puzzle, joined with her ongoing wish to learn Cantonese and her desire to understand her students' experience of learning English as a second language, leads her to engage in an in-depth autobiographical study of her learning of Cantonese.

Throughout her study, Bell (1997) took courses in Cantonese and was tutored by Cindy, a Cantonese-speaking immigrant who taught ESL and appeared as a collaborative meaning maker in the book. The book is filled with detailed records of exchanges with Cindy, class conversations, journal-style reflections, and graphic images of Bell's development of learning to construct Chinese characters. A reader positively feels the weight of the extraordinarily detailed field texts collected by Bell and used as the basis for her narrative inquiry. Framed within her developing notion of literacy and through examination of these field texts, readers gain knowledge of the rigor of language learning.

Through cultural contextual comparisons of Cindy's Chinese background and Bell's English background, we also understand the tensions inherent in language learning in ostensibly straightforward language learning situations. Bell's language learning situation, in one-on-one tutoring or in a university class, dissimilar to students who have had few formal literacy experiences, is nonetheless filled with similar tensions born of different cultural settings. Bell and Cindy have vastly different notions of how Bell should learn Chinese characters. Bell writes Chinese by quickly filling as many character boxes as she can, while Cindy feels Bell has wasted her time and should practice quietly and slowly. Reflecting on this and similar situations, Bell came to understand how narrative histories of teachers and learners confound the idea of literacy and the teaching and learning of language.

Bell also came to understand that the feelings of language learners and the stories they hold of their language learning from previous experiences are a critical part of the language learning process. This point was also hinted at in Ming Fang's opening story of learning English. Her assumptions of how language should be learned, based on her experiences in China, are reflected in her feelings toward her learning of English in a Canadian classroom. As with Carger's (1996) work, Bell's *Literacy, Culture and Identity* (1997), read narratively, yields new insights into language teaching and learning from the beginning of her book to its end. Following Bell's insights into her story of learning Chinese, some readers may be surprised to find themselves questioning their taken-for-granted ways of thinking about the teaching and learning of language.

LIFE-BASED LITERARY NARRATIVES OF THE EXPERIENCE OF LANGUAGE LEARNING

Another literature that is explicitly narrative in focus but which differs significantly from Carger's work (1996) and yet again from Bell's work (1997), is a literature we term *life-based literary narratives*. This work shares qualities described for narrative and brings forward some of the key characteristics described in the sections on Carger and Bell. It is autobiographical as seen in Bell's work, but without the sense of field texts, and it is oriented to life stories as seen in Carger's work.

Life-based literary narratives such as autobiographies/memoirs/novels that portray the experiences of language learners in intimate detail contribute to understanding English language learning (e.g., Anzaldúa, 1987; Blaise, 1993; Chamoiseau, 1994; Cisneros, 1994; Cowan, 1982; Crow Dog & Erdoes, 1990; Dorfman, 1998; Firmat, 1994; Hoffman, 1989; Kaplan, 1993; Kingston, 1975; Melanson, 1999; Rodriguez, 1982; Santiago, 1993). For example, Patrick

Chamoiseau's *School Days* explores the inner world of a Creole-speaking child, his love of language and learning, and the dilemmas he experiences when thrown into a French-only environment in school. Readers feel the child's experiences from his perspective and see his experiences through his eyes. Eva Hoffman's *Lost in Translation: A Life in a New Language* creates a nuanced portrayal of her life as a Jewish teenage girl exiled from Poland to North America as she struggled to find her place, and express who she was, in an English-speaking world. She portrays the emotional cost, the losses, entailed in second language acquisition. For Hoffman, learning to speak a new language involves more than acquiring the language. It involves the reinvention of self, a self divided yet enriched by the exile experience.

These life-based literary narratives create in-depth understandings of the lived experience of language learning from the perspective of the learner. They portray the desires, fears, and hopes of language learners. These are stories that are best thought of as research stories, told not in teaching/learning situations, in most cases, but in life situations. These life-based literary narratives are clearly written with life in the foreground, and we, with our research interest in English language teaching and learning, read these texts in order to reveal the language in the background. This observation takes us full cycle and returns us to one of the key points noted above about narrative inquiry—that a narrative approach to language teaching and learning is concerned with life contexts.

CONCLUSIONS

In summary, we have brought forward a discussion of the place of narrative inquiry in social science research and have shown how widespread narrative inquiry is in educational studies. By reviewing aspects of this literature, we have presented key experiential features of narrative inquiry, and we have taken the view that it is important to learn about language learning from a wide range of experientially oriented studies, not all of which explicitly address English language teaching and learning questions. With that stance, we reviewed in detail two narrative inquiries, Carger's (1996) *Of Borders and Dreams* and Bell's (1997) *Literacy, Culture and Identity*. In addition, we identified a literature, life-based literary narratives, that we feel should be part of the literature on English language teaching and learning. Experientially focused, life-based work reveals a wealth of insight into the lived experiences of language learners and demonstrates a transition from abstract research to inquiries that develop in-depth, nuanced understandings of the complexity of language learning and its embeddedness in interconnected historical, social, and cultural contexts.

The potential of narrative inquiry lies in experiential qualities. Narrative inquirers explore experience by bringing personal experience to bear on inquiry, seeing research as having autobiographical roots, as connected to, rather than disconnected from life; by thinking narratively, seeing experience as the starting point of inquiry, as changing rather than fixed, as contextualized rather than decontextualized; by being in the midst of lives, seeing research as long-term, passionate involvement in daily lives of participants rather than short-term, in and out, detached observation; and by making meaning of experience in relationship, developing understanding in relationship rather than making meaning in isolation. Narrative inquiry, an approach that focuses on experience, humanizes research. The promise of narrative inquiry is that it permits and encourages the study of English language teaching and learning in the context of life and in the pursuit of broad educational questions of immigration, culture, identity, community, and literacy.

NOTES

1. In this review we have identified the possibilities of narrative inquiry in the study of English language teaching and learning. There are methodological limitations and questions that arise in using this method that we have not explicitly addressed in this review. Some of these questions relate to traditional issues of validity and reliability, solipsism and subjectivity; others relate to new methodological concerns of voice and authority, reification of the status quo and critical perspectives. Clandinin and Connelly (2000) have addressed what they call the risks, dangers, and abuses of narrative inquiry, and Phillion and He (2001) have examined concerns in using narrative, particularly the vulnerability of participants. There are also many critiques of narrative inquiry available in the research literature: for example, see Tochon (1994) on semiotic matters, Phillips (1997) on philosophical questions, and Freeman (1996) on the reduction of experience to interview data.

REFERENCES

Alvermann, D. E. (2000). Narrative approaches. In M. L. Kamil, P. B. Mosenthal, P. D. Pearson, & R. Barr (Eds.), *Handbook of reading research* (Chap. 9, pp. 123–139). Mahwah, NJ: Lawrence Erlbaum.
Anzaldúa, G. (1987). *Borderlands:La forontera*. San Francisco: Aunt Lute Books.
Bateson, M. C. (1994). *Peripheral visions:Learning along the way*. New York: HarperCollins.
Bell, J. S. (1997). *Literacy, culture and identity*. New York: Peter Lang.
Blaise, C. (1993). *I had a father: A post–modern autobiography*. Reading, MA: Addison-Wesley.
Bruner, J. (1986). *Acts of meaning*. Cambridge, MA: Harvard University Press.
Carger, C. (1996). *Of borders and dreams: Mexican-American experience of urban education*. New York: Teachers College Press.
Carter, K. (1993). The place of story in the study of teaching and teacher education. *Educational Researcher, 22*(1), 5–12, 18.
Casey, K. (1995). The new narrative research in education. In M. W. Apple (Ed.), *Review of research in education* (Vol. 21, pp. 211–254). Washington, DC: American Educational Research Association.
Chamoiseau, P. (1994). *School days*. Lincoln: University of Nebraska Press.
Chang, P., & Rosiak, J. (2003). Anti-Colonialist antinomies in a biology lesson: A Sonata-form case study of cultural conflict in the science classroom. *Curriculum Inquiry, 33*(3), 251–290.
Cisneros, S. (1994). *The house on Mango Street*. New York: A.A. Knopf. Distributed by Random House.
Clandinin, D. J., & Connelly, F. M. (1994). Personal experience methods. In N. K. Denin & Y. S. Lincoln (Eds.), *Handbook of qualitative research* (pp. 413–427). Thousand Oaks, CA: Sage.
Clandinin, D. J., & Connelly, F. M. (2000). *Narrative inquiry: Experience and story in qualitative research*. San Francisco, CA: Jossey-Bass.
Coles, R. (1989). *The call of stories:Teaching and the moral imagination*. Boston: Houghton Mifflin.
Conle, C. (2000). Thesis as narrative: What is the inquiry in narrative inquiry? *Curriculum Inquiry, 30*(2), 189–213.
Connelly, F. M., & Clandinin, D. J. (1988). *Teachers as curriculum planners: Narratives of experience*. New York: Teachers College Press.
Connelly, F. M., & Clandinin, D. J. (1990). Stories of experience and narrative inquiry. *Educational Researcher, 19*(5), 2–14.
Cowan, P. (1982). *An orphan in history: Retrieving a Jewish legacy*. Garden City, NY: Doubleday.
Craig, C. J. (2001). The relationships between and among teachers' narrative knowledge, communities of knowing, and school reform: A case of "The Monkey's Paw." *Curriculum Inquiry, 31*(3), 303–331.
Crites, S. (1971). The narrative quality of experience. *Journal of the American Academy of Religion, 39*(3), 291–311.
Crow Dog, M., & Erdoes, R. (1990). *Lakota woman*. New York: Harper Collins.
Czarniawska, B. (1997). *Narrating the organization: Dramas of institutional identity*. Chicago: University of Chicago Press.
Denzin, N. K. (1997). *Interpretive ethnography: Ethnographic practices for the 21st century*. Thousand Oaks, CA: Sage.
Denzin, N., & Lincoln, Y. (2000). *Handbook of qualitative research. Collecting and interpreting qualitative materials* (2nd ed.). Thousand Oaks, CA: Sage.

Dewey, J. (1938). *Experience and education.* New York: Collier Books.
Dorfman, A. (1998). *Heading south and looking north: A bilingual journey.* New York: Penguin Books.
Elbaz-Luwisch, F. (1997). Narrative research: Political issues and implications. *Teaching and Teacher Education, 13*(1), 75–83.
Elbaz-Luwisch, F. (2002). Writing as inquiry: Storying the teaching self in writing workshops. *Curriculum Inquiry, 32*(4), 403–428.
Enns-Connolly, E. (1985). *Translation as interpretive act: A narrative study of translation in university-level foreign language teaching.* Unpublished doctoral dissertation, The Ontario Institute for Studies in Education, University of Toronto, Toronto, Canada.
Feuerverger, G. (2001). *Oasis of dreams: Teaching and learning peace in a Jewish-Palestinian village in Israel.* New York: RoutledgeFalmer.
Firmat, G. P. (1994). *Life on the hyphen: The Cuban-American way.* Austin, TX: University of Texas Press.
Freeman, D. (1996). To take them at their word: Language data in the study of teachers' knowledge. *Harvard Educational Review, 66*(4), 732–761.
Geertz, C. (1995). *After the fact: Two countries, four decades, one anthropologist.* Cambridge, MA: Harvard University Press.
Greene, M. (1995). *Releasing the imagination: Essays on education, the arts, and social change.* San Francisco, CA: Jossey-Bass.
Grumet, M. (1992). Existential and phenomenological foundations of autobiographical method. In W. Pinar & W. Reynolds, *Understanding curriculum as phenomenological and deconstructed text* (pp. 28–43). New York: Teachers College Press.
Hatch, J. A., & Wisniewski, R. (1995). *Life history and narrative.* London: Falmer.
He, M. F. (1999). A life-long inquiry forever flowing between China and Canada: Crafting a composite auto/biographic narrative method to represent three Chinese women teachers' cultural experiences [Featured article], *Journal of Critical Inquiry into Curriculum & Instruction, 1*(2), 5–29.
He, M. F. (2002a). A narrative inquiry of cross-cultural lives: Lives in China [Special issue]. *Journal of Curriculum Studies, 34*(3), 301–321.
He, M. F. (2002b). A narrative inquiry of cross-cultural lives: Lives in Canada [Special issue]. *Journal of Curriculum Studies, 34*(3), 323–342.
He, M. F. (2002c). A narrative inquiry of cross-cultural lives: Lives in North American Academe. *Journal of Curriculum Studies, 34*(5), 513–533.
He, M. F. (2003). *A river forever flowing: Cross-cultural lives and identities in the multiculturall landscape.* Greenwich, CT: Information Age Publishing.
Hoffman, E. (1989). *Lost in translation: A life in a new language.* New York: Penguin Books.
Hollingsworth, S. (1994). *Teacher research and urban literacy education: Lessons and conversations in a feminist key.* New York: Teachers College Press.
Hooks, b. (1991). Narratives of struggle. In P. Mariani (Ed.), *Critical fictions: The politics of imaginative writing* (pp. 53–61). Seattle, WA: Bay.
Huber, J., & Whelan, K. (1999). A marginal story as a place of possibility: Negotiating self on the professional knowledge landscape. *Teaching and Teacher Education 15*(4), 381–396.
Kanno, Y., & Applebaum, S. D. (1995). ESL students speak up: Their stories of how we are doing. *TESL Canada Journal/REVUE TESL DU CANADA, 12*(2), 33–48.
Igoa, C. (1995). *The inner world of the immigrant child.* Mahwah, NJ: Lawrence Erlbaum.
Kaplan, A. (1993). *French lessons: A memoir.* Chicago: University of Chicago Press.
Kingston, M. H. (1975). *The woman warrior: Memoirs of a girlhood among ghosts.* New York: Random House.
Lawrence-Lightfoot, S., & Davis, J. H. (1997). *The art of and science of portraiture.* San Francisco, CA: Jossey-Bass.
Li, X. (2002). *The Tao of life stories: Chinese language, poetry, and culture in education.* New York: Peter Lang.
Maggisano, C. G. (1999). *A narrative inquiry into understanding the drama of encounter at the borders of identity: Six second generation Italian Canadian women teachers speak.* Unpublished doctoral dissertation, The Ontario Institute for Studies in Education/University of Toronto, Toronto, Canada.
Melanson, Y. (1999). *Looking for lost bird: A Jewish woman discovers her Navaho roots.* New York: Avon Books.
Neumann, A., & Peterson, P. L. (Eds.). (1997). *Learning from our lives: Women, research, and autobiography in education.* New York: Teachers College Press.
Olsen, M. (2000). Curriculum as a multistoried process. *Canadian Journal of Education, 25*(3), 169–187.
Phillion, J. (1999). Narrative and formalistic approaches to the study of multiculturalism. *Curriculum Inquiry, 29*(1), 129–141.

Phillion, J. (2002a). Becoming a narrative inquirer in a multicultural landscape. *Journal of Curriculum Studies, 34*(5), 535–556.

Phillion, J. (2002b). Narrative multiculturalism [Special issue]. *Journal of Curriculum Studies, 34*(3), 265–279.

Phillion, J. (2002c). Classroom stories of multicultural teaching and learning [Special issue]. *Journal of Curriculum Studies, 34*(3), 281–300.

Phillion, J. (2002d). *Narrative inquiry in a multicultural landscape: Multicultural teaching and learning.* Ablex/Greenwood Press.

Phillion, J., & He, M. F. (2001). Narrative inquiry in educational research. *Journal of Critical Inquiry Into Curriculum and Instruction, 3*(2), 14–20.

Phillips, D. C. (1997). Telling the truth about stories. *Teaching and Teacher Education, 13*(1), 101–109.

Pinar, W. (1988). Autobiography and the architecture of self. *Journal of Curriculum Theorizing, 8*(1), 7–36.

Polkinghorne, D. E. (1988). *Narrative knowing and the human sciences.* Albany, NY: State University of New York Press.

Roberge, B., & Phillion, J. (1997). A narrative exploration of language learning experiences through a letter exchange. *Canadian Modern Language Review, 54*(1), 110–119.

Rodriguez, R. (1982). *Hunger of memory: The education of Richard Rodriguez: An autobiography.* New York: Bantam Books.

Santiago, E. (1993). *When I was Puerto Rican.* New York: Vintage Books.

Schafer, R. (1992). *Retelling a life: Narrative and dialogue in psychoanalysis.* New York: Basic Books.

Schwab, J. J. (1978). What do scientists do? In I. Westbury & N. J. Wilkof (Eds.), *Science, curriculum, and liberal education: Selected essays (of) Joseph J. Schwab.* Chicago: University of Chicago Press. (Reprinted from *Behavioral Science, 5,* 1–17, 1960.)

Shubert, W. H., & Ayers, W. C. (Eds.). (1999). *Teacher lore: Learning from our own experience.* Troy, NY: Educator's International Press.

Sleeter, C. E. (2001). Epistemological diversity in research on preservice teacher preparation for historically underserved children. In W. G. Secada (Ed.), *Review of research in education* (Vol. 25, pp. 209–250). Washington, DC: American Educational Research Association.

Smith, D. (1991). Hermeneutic inquiry: The hermeneutic imagination and the pedagogic text. In E. Short (Ed.), *Forms of curriculum inquiry* (pp. 187–209). Albany, NY: State University of New York Press.

Smith, L. M. (1994). Biographical method. In N. K. Denzin & Y. S. Lincoln (Eds.), *Handbook of qualitative research* (pp. 286–305). Thousand Oaks, CA: Sage.

Soto, L. D. (1997). *Language, culture, and power: Bilingual families and the struggle for quality education.* Albany, NY: State University of New York Press.

Tochon, F. V. (1994). Presence beyond the narrative: Semiotic tools for deconstructing the personal story. *Curriculum Studies, 2*(2), 221–247.

Toohey, K. (2000). *Learning English at school: Identity, social relations and classroom practice.* Clevedon, UK: Multilingual Matters.

Valdés, G. (1996). *Con respeto: Bridging the distances between culturally diverse families and schools.* New York: Teachers College Press.

Valdés, G. (2001). *Learning and not learning English: Latino students in American schools.* New York: Teachers College Press.

Van Manen, M. (1990). *Researching lived experience: Human science for an action sensitive pedagogy.* Albany, NY: State University of New York Press.

Vasquez, O. A., Pease-Alvarez, L., & Shannon, S. M. (1994). *Pushing boundaries: Language and culture in a Mexicano community.* New York: The Press Syndicate of the University of Cambridge.

Witherell, C., & Noddings, N. (Eds.). (1991). *Stories lives tell: Narrative and dialogue in education.* New York: Teachers College Press.

Yow, V. R. (1994). *Recording oral history: A practical guide for social scientists.* Thousand Oaks, CA: Sage.

CHAPTER 62

CONVERSATION ANALYSIS: ISSUES AND PROBLEMS

NUMA MARKEE

The University of Illinois at Urbana-Champaign, USA

ABSTRACT

Conversational analysis (CA) is a methodology for analyzing a broad range of speech exchange systems, or spoken interaction. This chapter begins by briefly describing what ethnomethodologically oriented conversation analysis is and then considers the intellectual roots of CA. It then describes how CA researchers typically set about developing analyses of interactional behaviors, and shows how such analyses may be used to address questions that are of interest to specialists in applied linguistics (AL) and second language acquisition (SLA) studies. Finally, it outlines some of the major issues and problems that must be addressed if CA is to become widely accepted in AL and SLA studies.

INTRODUCTION

Conversational analysis (CA) is a methodology for analyzing a broad range of speech exchange systems that are collectively known as *talk-in-interaction*. Two main types of talk-in-interaction may be distinguished: *ordinary, mundane conversation,* and *institutional talk*. *Ordinary conversation* is the kind of casual, everyday talk that typically occurs between friends and acquaintances, either face-to-face or on the telephone, and is considered to be the default speech exchange system in all talk-in-interaction (Sacks, Schegloff, & Jefferson, 1974). Other speech exchange systems involve varying degrees of structural modification to the sequential, turn-taking, and repair practices of ordinary conversation. These other speech exchange systems are collectively known as *institutional* varieties of talk and include debates, classroom talk, broadcast news interviews, press conferences, doctor-patient interactions, courtroom interactions, emergency telephone calls, etc. As these institutional varieties of talk become structurally more distant from the default practices of ordinary conversation, they tend to become more and more ritualized. Debates, for example, are characterized by highly formalized, preallocated rules for turn taking, and these conventions for deciding who speaks when and to whom are markedly different from the locally managed turn-taking practices of ordinary conversation (Sacks, Schegloff, & Jefferson, 1974).

More specifically, in ordinary conversation, turn taking is done "on the fly." That is, the question of who gets to speak to whom, how, when, and about what is not predetermined. As a result, turn size, content, and type are all free to vary. Furthermore, there is a preference for turn length to be minimized (Sacks, Schegloff, & Jefferson, 1974) and for repair to be self-initiated and self-completed (Schegloff, Jefferson, & Sacks, 1977).

In institutional talk, however, the purposes of the interaction, its preference structure, and, thus, the distribution of members' sequential, turn-taking, and repair practices may be quite different from those found in ordinary conversation, although the basic practices of talk used by participants are the same as those used in ordinary conversation (Koshik, 2003; for examples of studies of institutional talk, see Boden & Zimmerman, 1991; Button, 1991; Clayman & Heritage, 2002; Drew & Heritage, 1992; Heath, 1986; Heritage & Roth, 1995; McHoul, 1978, 1990; Robinson, 1998; Stivers, 2002). For example, in press conferences, the purpose of this kind of talk is for one member (typically a government official or other "important" person) to communicate information to another collective party, in this case, many reporters). Reporters typically ask a short question to which the official may respond at considerable length. Reporters may then ask an optional follow-up question. After the official has finished responding to this optional follow-up question, he or she then has the right to select the next speaker, who then proceeds in the same fashion.

The analyses that conversation analysts develop consist of empirically based accounts of members' observable sequential, turn-taking, and repair practices. A fundamental characteristic of these analyses is that they are *emic* in orientation. That is, they attempt to interpret social actions from a member's rather than from an *etic* or researcher's perspective (Heritage, 1988; Psathas, 1995; Schegloff, 1987). Furthermore, they are minutely detailed. More specifically, CA aims to show how members *orient*, that is, observably pay attention, to the behavioral practices that underlie the co-construction of talk-in-interaction in real time. As I have already suggested, these practices—which are unconscious—include the sequential organization of talk, turn taking, and repair (Markee, 2000; Schegloff, Koshik, Jacoby, & Olsher, 2002). Furthermore, conversation analysts may also focus on topics such as the sequential organization of various "speech acts" in ordinary conversation (Davidson, 1984; Drew, 1984; Pomerantz, 1975, 1978a, 1978b, 1984a, 1984b; Psathas, 1986), the construction of syntax-for-conversation (Goodwin, 1979; Lerner, 1991; Schegloff, 1979, 1996), reference (Sacks & Schegloff, 1979), the structure of joke- and storytelling (Goodwin, 1984; Sacks, 1974; Stubbs, 1983) and other related issues.

INTELLECTUAL ROOTS OF CONVERSATION ANALYSIS

The intellectual roots of CA are to be found in the phenomenological approach of Edmund Husserl (see Carr, 1974) and Alfred Schutz (1962a, 1962b, 1962c, 1964a, 1964b) in philosophy, updated by Garfinkel's *ethnomethodological* approach in sociology (1967, 1974, 1984; see also Cicourel, 1968; Heritage, 1987; Mehan, 1979). According to Roger and Bull (1988):

> The term 'ethnomethodology' was coined by Garfinkel (1974). In combining the words 'ethno' and 'methodology,' Garfinkel was influenced by the use of such terms as 'ethnobotany' and 'ethnomedicine' to refer to folk systems of botanical and medical analysis. What is proposed is that any competent member of society (including the professional social scientist) is equipped with a methodology for analysing social phenomena; the term 'ethnomethodology' thus refers to the study of ways in which everyday common-sense activities are analysed by participants, and of the ways in which these analyses are incorporated into courses of action. The most prominent

development within ethnomethodology is undoubtedly that which has become known as conversation analysis, which examines the procedures used in the production of ordinary conversation. The influence of conversation analysis is being increasingly felt in disciplines outside sociology, notably psychology, linguistics[1] and anthropology. (p. 3)

Under the influence of analysts such as Harvey Sacks, Emanuel Schegloff, and Gayle Jefferson (see, for example, Sacks, 1995; Sacks, Schegloff, & Jefferson, 1974; Schegloff, Jefferson, & Sacks, 1977), CA itself emerged in the late 1960s and early 1970s. As Roger and Bull remark in the final sentence of the previous citation, the techniques of CA have been adopted by a number of fields other than sociology. I return to the issue of how CA may be used by applied linguists and SLA researchers in a later section of this chapter. First, however, let me address the issue of how CA is done.

METHODOLOGICAL CONSIDERATIONS

As already noted, CA adopts an emic approach to knowledge construction. In common with other qualitative approaches to understanding the world, such as ethnography, the typical research procedure used by conversation analysts is to allow research questions to slowly emerge from the data. These data consist of video- (or audio-) recorded[2] interactions that are then transcribed according to the microanalytic conventions of CA originally developed by Gail Jefferson and codified in Atkinson and Heritage (1984).

As shown in the fragment in Figure 1, these transcripts are extremely detailed. CA proposes that no detail of interaction, however small or seemingly trivial, may a priori be assumed to be irrelevant to members' social construction of talk-in-interaction (Heritage, 1988). For this reason, analysts seek to capture the quality of participants' talk by reproducing as accurately as possible pauses, hesitations, silences, cutoffs, overlaps, lengthenings of sounds, in-breaths, laughter tokens, the relative loudness of talk, and the relative speed of delivery. In addition, they also provide a more or less detailed record of participants' gestures and eye gaze, etc. (see Appendix 1 for an explanation of the symbols used in Figures 1 and 2).

What do such (fearsomely) detailed transcripts show us? The transcript in Figure 1 comes from an intermediate undergraduate ESL class at a university in the Midwestern United States. It allows us to see how L9 accomplishes the act of paying attention to the teacher (T) as the teacher makes an important class announcement, while simultaneously attending to the need to maintain his social relationship with a fellow student L11 (see the → signs at lines 412-414).

More specifically, in this fragment the learners (L9 and L11) have been engaging in some off-task talk during a small group activity in which they were supposed to have been talking about the prospect of German reunification in 1990. However, for 1 minute and 32 seconds, L11 tries to persuade L9 to accept an invitation to go to a party in one of the halls of residence on campus (see Markee, 2005a).

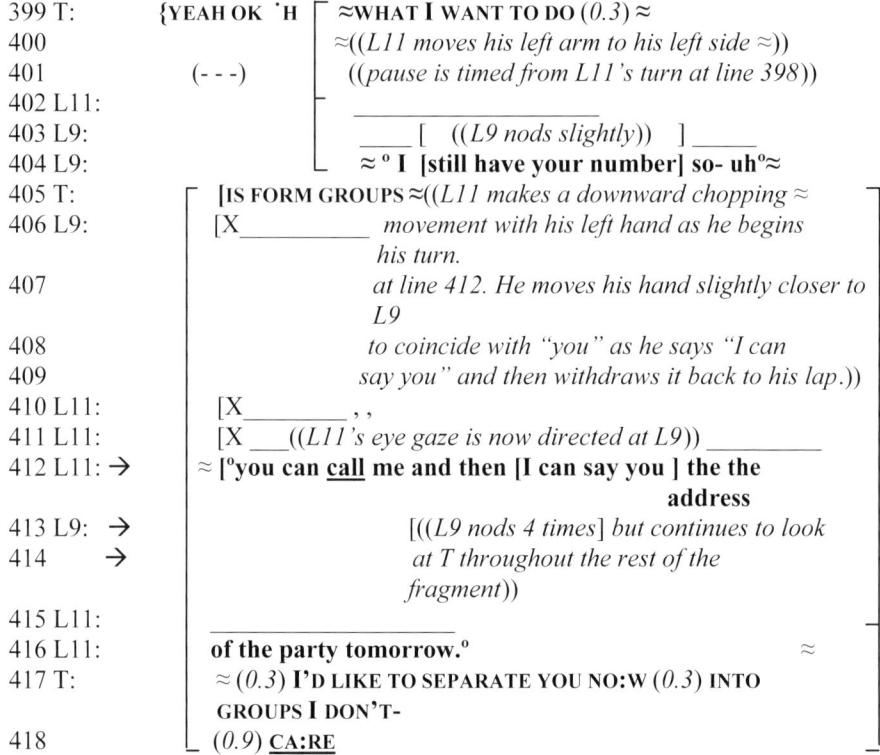

Figure 1. Fragment 1 from Class 1: Invitation to a Party

During most of this invitation talk, L9 has been quite coy about accepting L11's invitation, repeatedly avoiding taking up any of the many opportunities that L11 constructs for him to accept the invitation. By line 399 of the transcript, which is where we pick up the interaction, T has begun to make a public announcement to the whole class, during which she explains how students should start forming new groups for the next phase of the lesson. L9 and L11 have therefore almost run out of time to maintain their social relationship and have to wrap up their illicit invitation talk in a hurry. As shown by the transcription of L9's and L11's eye gaze behaviors in this fragment, L9 focuses his gaze on T at line 406. As L11 says "you can call me and then" at line 412, his gaze is focused on L9. As L11 continues his turn at line 412 and says "I can say you," L9 responds to L11 with four overlapping nods at line 413. However, note that, as L9 nods in response to L11's talk at line 412, L9's gaze remains fixed on *T*, not on *L11* (see lines 413-414). Thus, L9 uses eye gaze as a resource for signaling that he is paying attention to what *T* is saying, and simultaneously uses gesture (nodding) to indicate to L11 that he has taken note of L11's offer to call him after class.

In certain circumstances, CA transcripts may also include frame grabs from the original video recordings to illustrate what participants are doing at a particular moment during the interaction. Gestures that are visually simple to interpret are often difficult to describe through words alone. An elegant solution to this problem is to incorporate a video frame grab into the transcript. Such data, used either alone or in conjunction with a verbal description of the embodied behaviors under study (as in lines 3-5 of Fragment 2 in Figure 2, in which a student uses her fingers and the light of an overhead projector to project the shadow of an animal onto the screen) can be used very effectively to communicate to consumers of CA research how participants choreograph verbal and visual information into their interactions.

01 L11:   any comments?
02 L6:   no. great handwriting
03   →   (*L11 projects the shadow of an animal head onto*
04   →   *the screen using her hands and the light of the*
05   →   *OHP*)
06 L11:   animal
07 L10:   hhh huh h huh huh huh
08 L6:   yeah(h)
09 L11:   ok ok ·hh uh:m I'm talking about- . . .
          (Class 2, Group 3 presentation)

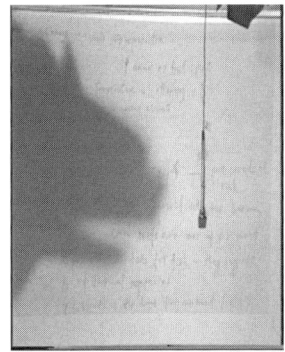

Figure 2. Fragment 2: Animal Head Shadow

As we can see from these two excerpts, CA is always based on in-depth, grounded analyses of single occurrences of behavior. As analysts sift through their transcripts, they may also make *collections* of individual fragments of talk that seem to be organized in the same way. The purpose of this collections-based methodology is to account for the organization of a practice in *all* instances in the corpus. In order to meet such a requirement, an analysis that holds for the majority of cases may have to be revised through the use of *deviant case analysis* (see Markee, 1995, for an example of this technique) in order to account for the apparent exceptions. The best-known example of this overall approach is Schegloff's (1968) analysis of sequencing in conversational openings on the telephone. The first analysis yielded 499 out of 500 cases in the collection. However, Schegloff had to reanalyze the entire corpus in order to account for all 500 cases of this phenomenon, and this analysis differed considerably from the first. Note, incidentally, that it is also quite possible that an analyst may ultimately come to the conclusion that what initially seemed to be a promising collection of a putative phenomenon turns out, after detailed microanalytical study of the object, to be a red herring. In such cases, the analysis may be abandoned and other issues that became foregrounded during the initial investigation will come into sharper focus and assume more importance.

We may summarize the discussion so far by noting that the aim of conversation analyses is to develop a grounded interpretation of participants' culturally and contextually situated behaviors. At this point, however, it is important to understand what conversation analysts mean by *context* and *culture*. As Heritage (1988) argues, CA is both context free and context renewing. More specifically, from a CA perspective, context and culture are phenomena that are observably achieved in real time by participants in and through talk. Thus, CA is context free in the sense that culture is not viewed as an a priori, exogamous variable that predisposes participants to act in particular ways. At the same time, CA is without contradiction also context renewing in that members (and therefore analysts) interpret their interlocutors' actions on the basis of what is said immediately before and immediately after a current turn. So, for example, we can see that members orient to a particular spate of talk as a question because the talk in next speaker's turn is observably constructed as an answer to this question. As Benson and Hughes (1991) conclude, therefore:

> the point of working with 'actual occurrences', single instances, single events, is to see them as the products of 'machinery' that constituted members' cultural competence enabling them to do what they do, produce the activities and scenes of everyday life...the explication, say, of some segment of talk in terms of the 'mechanism' by which that talk was produced there and then, is an explication of some part of culture. (p. 130)

CONVERSATION ANALYSIS IN APPLIED LINGUISTICS AND SECOND LANGUAGE ACQUISITION STUDIES

The use of CA as a methodological resource for researchers in AL and SLA studies is a comparatively recent phenomenon. Two studies on repair in second language contexts by Gaskill (1980) and Schwartz (1980) are among the earliest examples of CA that we have in AL and SLA studies. For approximately 15 years after 1980, however, there was little if any follow-up to these two publications. However, since 1994, there has been a renewal of activity and a burst of interest in the kinds of insights that CA potentially has to offer. I am calling this emerging trend conversation-analysis-for-second-language-acquisition (CA-for-SLA) (Markee, 2005b; see also Kasper, 2002).

A landmark publication that has significantly contributed to this development is the *Modern Language Journal*'s special issue on conversation analysis, which features a controversial lead article by Firth and Wagner (1997). This paper has prompted a number of interesting comments and rebuttals by Kasper (1997), Long (1997, 1998), and Gass (1998). Also noteworthy in this context are full-length monographs by Markee (2000) and Ohta (2001a), as well as articles, chapters, mimeos, talks, or conference presentations by He (2003), Kasper (2002, 2003), Lazaraton (2003a, 2003b, 2003c), Markee (1994, 1995, 2005a, 2005b), Mori (2002, 2003), Ohta and Nakaone (n.d), Seedhouse (1997, 1999), van Lier (1988, 1996), Young and Nguyen (2002), Young and Miller (2002), Willey (2001), and Wong (2000).

Note that while all these writers use CA transcription and analytic techniques to a greater or a lesser extent, not all regard themselves as being "pure" conversation analysts. For example, Lazaraton prefers to characterize her work as microanalysis. Van Lier calls his work a microethnographic approach. Furthermore, while Ohta and her collaborators frame their analytic work within a language socialization/ sociocultural theory perspective, Young and his students appeal to systemic grammar.

CURRENT ISSUES AND PROBLEMS

It is clear that CA-for-SLA is still an emerging phenomenon. Consequently, there are a number of issues that are the subject of vigorous, ongoing discussions. Some of these issues are methodological, while others are more substantive. For example, a perennially debated, and famously contentious, methodological issue is the extent to which CA's understanding of context as the immediate co-text of talk is a source of methodological rigor or whether it is a needless limitation on our ability to understand what members are doing. The "purist" approach to these questions is represented by Schegloff (1992), while writers such as Cicourel (1992), Moerman (1988), and Wilson (1991) illustrate a more ethnographically oriented approach to the formulation of context.

In AL and SLA studies, the same issue is alive and well, and it is probably safe to predict that neither side will carry the day any time soon (see Hopper 1990/1991). In this context, it is worth remembering that ethnography and CA have different research agendas. Ethnography ultimately seeks to develop a grounded understanding of *why* members act in particular ways (see Duff, 1995, 2002). CA, on the other hand, strives to provide sequential analyses of *how* participants achieve particular practices (see Sacks, Schegloff, & Jefferson, 1974; Schegloff, Jefferson, & Sacks, 1977). There is obviously a certain amount of room here for a methodological rapprochement between ethnography and CA. One potential solution involves ethnographic work beginning with a sequential analysis of how members co-construct talk, and then moving on to develop a broader analysis of why they co-constructed this talk in particular ways. In practice, however, this is often difficult to do well, because it is often impractical to do justice to both the CA and the ethnographic parts of the analysis equally well.

In CA-for-SLA, the contributions that the use of CA techniques can potentially make to our understanding of language learning issues are hotly debated. CA is a militantly behavioral discipline. In contrast, SLA has traditionally been a strongly cognitive, psycholinguistically defined field. Consequently, we may ask how viable it is to use techniques originally developed to analyze language *use* for the purpose of analyzing language *acquisition* processes (Markee, 2000). More specifically, this issue is at the heart of the exchanges between Firth and Wagner (1997), on the one hand, and the rebuttals of Firth and Wagner by Kasper (1997), Long (1997, 1998), and Gass (1998), on the other. Briefly, whereas Firth and Wagner argue that psycholinguistic learning processes cannot be divorced from their social context, Kasper, Long, and Gass counter that the proper domain of SLA studies is language *acquisition*, not *use*. Indeed, as shown in Figure 3, Gass (1998) argues that, despite the early work done by social cognitivists on the role of conversational repair as a catalyst for getting comprehensible input in SLA (Doughty & Pica, 1986; Ellis, 1985; Krashen, 1980, 1981, 1982, 1985; Long, 1980, 1981, 1983a, 1983b, 1985; Long & Porter, 1985; Pica, 1987; Pica & Doughty, 1985; Pica, Doughty, & Young, 1986; Varonis & Gass, 1985a, 1985b), an understanding of social context is only of incidental interest to SLA researchers.

My own position on this question is that:

> An empirically grounded understanding of how learners' interlanguage knowledge (as this is reflected *in* and *through* their talk-in-interaction) progresses from A to B, and what 'events promote or hinder such progress' (Kasper, 1997, p. 310) cannot be dismissed as a 'trivial' issue. It is a crucial foundation for the [interaction hypothesis] (IH). If this means that advocates of the IH have to accept that language acquisition and use are indivisible components of the SLA enterprise, then this is not to be seen as a threat to the disciplinary integrity of SLA studies. It is a consequence of the IH's own theoretical interests in social interaction as a resource for SLA (Markee, 2005b).

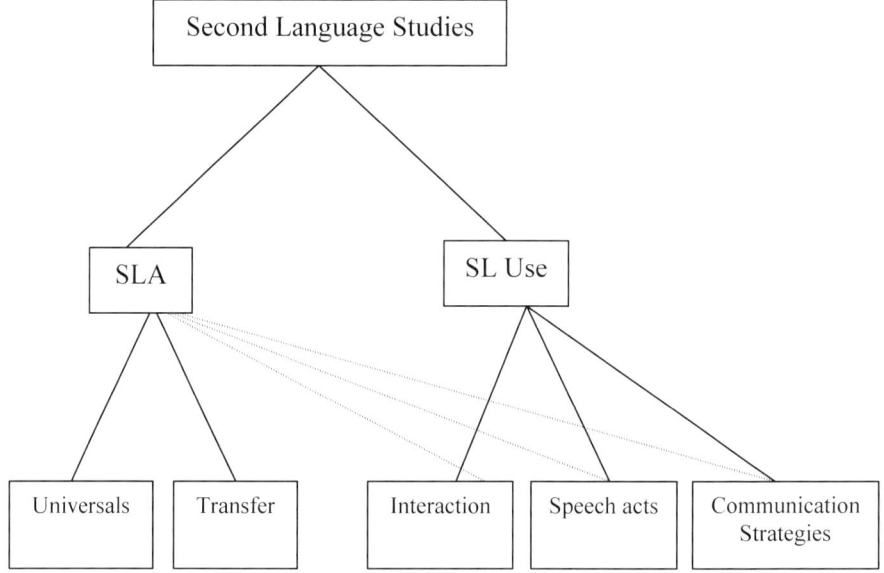

Figure 3. A characterization of Research in "SLA" (after Gass, 1998, p. 88)

This position has controversial implications, in that it leads us to view language learning as *socially distributed cognition* (Markee, 2000, drawing on Schegloff, 1991) rather than as an *individual* cognitive phenomenon. Since this issue has only just begun to be debated in AL and SLA studies, the jury is still out on which position will prove to be most persuasive.

Another important emerging area of controversy in CA-for-SLA focuses on the extent to which CA's reliance on analyses of single cases can ever yield significant, generalizable results. This problem—if it is indeed a problem—is a concern that is particularly relevant to researchers who are used to working within the relatively familiar epistemological framework of experimental, quantitative research (see, for example, Long, 1997). However, as argued by Schegloff (1993), framing the issues this way begs the question of whether such a question is relevant to qualitative researchers.

More specifically, Schegloff argues that the emic perspective of CA assumes that significance is not just a technical concept in statistics. Much more importantly, this notion also refers to what participants demonstrate, through their own observable behaviors, *to be important to them*. As we have already seen, the use of single-case analysis in CA (as illustrated by Schegloff's, 1968, comprehensive analysis of 500 opening sequences in telephone conversations) therefore precludes dropping "outliers" from an analysis just because they do not fit the general patterns that are captured through aggregated data. There are also issues concerning the *domain* or scope of CA-for-SLA and so-called *numerator* and *denominator* problems in the study of talk-in-interaction (Schegloff, 1993).

As we have already seen, the controversy surrounding the proper scope of SLA studies (see Figure 1 and the related discussion) is a *domain* issue. Other domain issues include whether SLA is a unitary phenomenon (i.e., all language learning is governed by universal psycholinguistic principles; (see, for example, Gregg, 1993, 1996; Long, 1998) or whether, as is also somewhat contradictorily implied by Long (1996), there is a fundamental distinction between ordinary conversation and other speech exchange systems, and whether this affects the type of learning opportunities to which learners have access: "Free conversation is notoriously poor as a context for driving interlanguage development ... in contrast, tasks that orient participants to shared goals and involve them in some work or activity produce more negotiation work" (Long, 1996, p. 448).

If such a distinction between ordinary conversation and other speech exchange systems (in the specific example drawn from the citation from Long, 1996, classroom talk) is an important factor in SLA studies—and I believe it is crucial—then we have to examine how different speech exchange systems differ from each other much more carefully than we have done so far. In particular, we must also be careful to limit the kinds of generalizations that we make about how particular acquisition resources (such as repair) work in SLA. For example, Varonis and Gass (1985b) indiscriminately conflate empirical data from different institutional varieties of talk and then proceed to make generalizations about language learning that are said to be relevant to SLA as a whole. This may well not be the case. SLA studies therefore needs to develop a better understanding of how different types of language use potentially provide different kinds of opportunities for language learning before we attempt make the kinds of generalizations that are so common in experimental research.

Finally, the *numerator* and *denominator* problems have to do with what raw frequency counts of a particular behavior (say, repair) tell us about that behavior and how such frequency counts can be contextualized within a viable analytic framework. So, for example, if we say that there were 87 examples of second-position repairs in a corpus, we are providing information about numerators. If, on the other hand, we say that 40 examples of second-position repairs occurred in the domain of a one-way task, and 47 second-position repairs occurred in the domain of two-way tasks, we are providing information about what types of speech exchange systems constitute viable denominators for our research. Broadly speaking, I would argue that much of so-called "mainstream" SLA has not paid sufficient attention to these kinds of questions, and that much more qualitative, grounded research on how members co-construct talk is needed in order to help us understand these crucial questions.

CONCLUSIONS

This chapter has addressed five basic questions:

1. What is conversational analysis (CA)?
2. Where does CA come from intellectually?
3. How do CA researchers analyze talk-in-interaction?
4. How may such analyses be used to address questions that are of interest to applied linguists and SLA researchers?
5. What are some of the major issues and problems that must be addressed if CA is to become widely accepted in AL and SLA studies?

As we can see from this brief review, CA-for-SLA has the potential to offer applied linguists and SLA researchers novel, often provocative insights into how second language users and learners organize their significant worlds. While the amount of CA-for-SLA research produced to date is tiny when compared to the vast amount of theoretical and empirical studies generated by "mainstream" SLA in the last 30 years or so, there are encouraging signs that CA-for-SLA is not just a passing, marginal phenomenon. CA-for-SLA is clearly on the verge of potentially influencing how we understand language use and language learning in important ways. What is less clear is how quickly this process will happen, and how deep, or how lasting, the influence of this approach will be. Only time will tell, but at the moment, CA-for SLA is certainly a growth area that welcomes new practitioners to its ranks.

NOTES

[1] See, for example, Zelig Harris (1951), whose work on the discourse level of language within the framework of structuralist linguistics also constitutes a direct methodological antecedent to CA.

[2] Early CA transcripts, such as the "Two Girls" transcript, were based on audio recordings of telephone conversations. As the field expanded, however, it became increasingly clear that video recordings were needed to show how participants choreographed talk with eye gaze and gestural phenomena (see, for example, Goodwin, 1981, 1996). In current CA, videotaped data are strongly preferred (Markee, 2005b), to the extent that audio-recorded data are usually viewed as being deficient (Markee, 2005b). Indeed, audio recordings are now only used in unusual circumstances, as when the material is so sensitive (for example, in therapy sessions) that participants or their guardians do not give researchers permission to use video equipment.

REFERENCES

Atkinson, J., & Heritage, J. (1984). Transcript notation. In J. Atkinson & J. Heritage (Eds.), *Structures of social action* (pp. ix–xvi). Cambridge: Cambridge University Press.

Benson, D., & Hughes, J. (1991). Method: Evidence and inference for ethnomethodology. In G. Button (Ed.), *Ethnomethodology and the human sciences* (pp. 109–136). Cambridge: Cambridge University Press.

Boden, D., & Zimmerman, D. (Eds.). (1991). *Talk and social structure.* Cambridge: Polity Press.

Benson, D., & Hughes, J. (1991). Method: Evidence and inference for ethnomethodology. In G. Button (Ed.), *Ethnomethodology and the human sciences.* Cambridge: Cambridge University Press.

Button, G. (Ed.). (1991). *Ethnomethodology and the human sciences.* Cambridge: Cambridge University Press.

Carr, D. (1974). *Phenomenology and the problem of history: A study of Husserl's transcendental philosophy*. Northwestern University studies in phenomenology & existential philosophy. Evanston: Northwestern University Press.

Cicourel, A. (1968). The social organization of juvenile justice. New York: Wiley.

Cicourel, A. (1992). The interpenetration of communicative contexts: Examples from medical contexts. In A. Duranti & C. Goodwin (Eds.), *Rethinking context: Language as an interactive phenomenon* (pp. 291–310). Cambridge: Cambridge University Press.

Clayman, S., & Heritage, J. (2002). *The news interview: Journalists and public figures on the air.* Cambridge: Cambridge University Press.

Davidson, J. (1984). Subsequent versions of invitations, offers, requests, and proposals dealing with potential or actual rejection. In J. Atkinson & J. Heritage (Eds.), *Structures of social action* (pp. 102–128). Cambridge: Cambridge University Press.

Doughty, C., & Pica, T. (1986). 'Information gap' tasks: An aid to second language acquisition? *TESOL Quarterly, 20*, 305–325.

Drew, P. (1984). Speakers' reportings in invitation sequences. In J. Atkinson & J. Heritage (Eds.), *Structures of social action* (pp. 129–151). Cambridge: Cambridge University Press.

Drew. P., & Heritage, J. (Eds.). (1992). *Talk at work: Interaction in institutional settings.* Cambridge: Cambridge University Press.

Duff, P. (1995). An ethnography of communication in immersion programs in Hungary. *TESOL Quarterly, 29*, 505–537.
Duff, P. (2002). The discursive co-construction of knowledge, identity, and difference: An ethnography of communication in the high school mainstream. *Applied Linguistics, 23*, 289–322.
Ellis, R. (1985). Teacher-pupil interaction in second language development. In S. Gass & C. Madden (Eds.), *Input in second language acquisition* (pp. 69–85). Rowley, MA: Newbury House.
Firth, A., & Wagner, J. (1997). On discourse, communication, and (some) fundamental concepts in SLA research. *The Modern Language Journal, 81*, 285–300.
Garfinkel, H. (1967). *Studies in ethnomethodology*. Englewood Cliffs, NJ: Prentice Hall.
Garfinkel, H. (1974). The origins of the term ethnomethodology. In R. Turner (Ed.), *Ethnomethodology* (pp. 15–18). Harmondsworth: Penguin.
Garfinkel, H. (1984). *Studies in ethnomethodology*. Cambridge: Polity Press.
Gaskill, W. (1980). Correction in native speaker-non-native speaker conversation. In D. Larsen-Freeman (Ed.), *Discourse analysis in second language research* (pp. 125–137). Rowley, MA: Newbury House.
Gass, S. (1998). Apples and oranges: Or, why apples are not oranges and don't need to be. A response to Firth and Wagner. *The Modern Language Journal, 82*, 83–90.
Goodwin, C. (1979). The interactive construction of a sentence in natural conversation. In G. Psathas (Ed.), *Everyday language: Studies in ethnomethodology* (pp. 97–121). New York: Irvington.
Goodwin, C. (1981). *Conversational organization: Interaction between speakers and hearers*. New York: Academic Press.
Goodwin, C. (1984). Notes on story structure and the organization of participation. In J. Atkinson, & J. Heritage (Eds.), *Structures of social action* (pp. 225–246). Cambridge: Cambridge University Press.
Goodwin, C. (1994). Professional vision. *American Anthropologist, 96*, 606–633.
Gregg, K. (1993). Taking explanation seriously; or, let a couple of flowers bloom. *Applied Linguistics, 14*, 276–294.
Gregg, K. (1996). The logical and developmental problems of second language acquisition. In W. Ritchie & T. Bhatia (Eds.), *Handbook of second language acquisition* (pp. 49–81). New York: Academic Press.
Harris, Z. (1951). *Methods in structural linguistics*. Chicago: University of Chicago Press.
He, A. (2003, March 22). Classroom talks. Paper given at the AAAL invited colloquium on Classroom Talks. American Association of Applied Linguistics Conference, Arlington, VA.
Heath, C. (1986). *Body movement and speech in medical interaction*. Cambridge: Cambridge University Press.
Heritage, J. (1987). Ethnomethodology. In A. Giddens & J. Turner (Eds.), *Social theory today* (pp. 224–272). Stanford: Stanford University Press.
Heritage, J. (1988). Current development in conversation analysis. In D. Roger & P. Bull (Eds.), *Conversation* (pp. 21–47). Clevedon: Multilingual Matters.
Heritage, J., & Roth, A. (1995). Grammar and institution: Questions and questioning in the broadcast news interview. *Research on Language and Social Interaction, 28*, 1–60.
Hopper, R. (Ed.). (1990/1991). Special section: Ethnography and conversation analysis after Talking Culture. *Research on Language and Social Interaction, 24*, 161–387.
Kasper, G. (1997). 'A' stands for acquisition: A response to Firth and Wagner. *The Modern Language Journal, 81*, 307–312.
Kasper, G. (2002, March 13). Conversation Analysis as an approach to second language acquisition: Old wine in new bottles? Invited talk, SLATE speaker series, University of Illinois at Urbana-Champaign.
Kasper, G. (2003, March 22). NNS-NS talk as chameleon: Participant orientations in conversation-for-learning. Paper given at the AAAL invited colloquium on Classroom Talks. American Association of Applied Linguistics Conference, Arlington, VA.
Koshik, I. (2003). Wh-questions used as challenges. *Discourse Studies, 5*, 51–77.
Krashen, S. (1980). The input hypothesis. In J. Alatis (Ed.), *Current issues in bilingual education* (pp. 168–180). Washington, DC: Georgetown University Press.
Krashen, S. (1981). *Second language acquisition and second language learning*. Oxford: Pergamon.
Krashen, S. (1982). *Principles and practice in second language acquisition*. Oxford. Pergamon.
Krashen, S. (1985). *The input hypothesis*. London: Longman.
Lazaraton, A. (2003a). Evaluative criteria for qualitative research in applied linguistics: Whose criteria and whose research? *The Modern Language Journal, 87*, 1–12.
Lazaraton, A. (2003b). Incidental displays of cultural knowledge in the NNEST classroom. *TESOL Quarterly*.

Lazaraton, A. (2003c). Gesture and speech in the vocabulary explanations of one ESL teacher: A microanalytic inquiry. *Language Learning, 87,* 1–12.
Lerner, G. (1991). On the syntax of sentences-in-progress. *Language in Society, 20,* 441–458.
Long, M. (1980). *Input, interaction and second language acquisition.* Unpublished doctoral dissertation, University of California at Los Angeles, Los Angeles, CA.
Long, M. (1981). Input, interaction and second language acquisition. In H. Winitz (Ed.), *Native language and foreign language acquisition* (pp. 259–278). Annals of the New York Academy of Sciences, 379, 259–278.
Long, M. (1983a). Linguistic and conversational adjustments of non-native speakers. *Studies in Second Language Acquisition, 5,* 177–193.
Long, M. (1983b). Native speaker/non-native speaker conversation and the negotiation of comprehensible input. *Applied Linguistics, 4,* 126–141.
Long, M. (1985). Input and second language acquisition theory. In S. Gass & C. Madden (Eds.), *Input in second language acquisition* (pp. 377–393). Rowley, MA: Newbury House.
Long, M. (1996). The role of the linguistic environment in second language acquisition. In W. Ritchie & T. Bhatia (Eds.), *Handbook of second language acquisition* (pp. 414–468). New York: Academic Press.
Long, M. (1997). Construct validity in SLA research: A response to Firth and Wagner. *The Modern Language Journal, 81,* 318–323.
Long, M. (1998, March). SLA: Breaking the siege. Plenary address, PacSLRF 3, Tokyo, Japan: Aoyama Gakuin University. *University of Hawai' Working Papers in ESL, 17*(1), 79–129. Revised and updated version to appear in M. Long, *Problems in SLA.* Mahwah, NJ: Lawrence Erlbaum Associates.
Long, M., & Porter, P. (1985). Group work, interlanguage talk and second language acquisition. *TESOL Quarterly, 19,* 207–228.
Markee, N. (1994). Toward an ethnomethodological respecification of second language acquisition studies. In E. Tarone, S. Gass, & A. Cohen (Eds.), *Research methodology in second language acquisition* (pp. 89–116). Hillsdale, NJ: Lawrence Erlbaum.
Markee, N. (1995). Teachers' answers to students' questions: Problematizing the issue of making meaning. *Issues in Applied Linguistics, 6,* 63–92.
Markee, N. (2000). *Conversation analysis.* Mahwah, N.J: Lawrence Erlbaum.
Markee, N. (2005a). The organization of off-task talk in second language classrooms. In K. Richards & P. Seedhouse (Eds.), *Applying conversation analysis* (pp. 197–213). Basingstoke: Palgrave-MacMillan.
Markee, N. (2005b). Conversation analysis for second language acquisition. In E. Hinkel (Ed.), *Handbook of Research in Second Language Teaching and Learning* (pp. 355–374). Mahwah, NJ: Lawrence Erlbaum.
McHoul, A. (1978). The organization of turns at formal talk in the classroom. *Language in Society, 7,* 183–213.
McHoul, A. (1990). The organization of repair in classroom talk. *Language in Society, 19,* 349–377.
Mehan, H. (1979). *Learning lessons: Social organization in the classroom.* Cambridge, MA: Harvard University Press.
Moerman, M. (1988). *Talking culture: Ethnography and conversation analysis.* Philadelphia: University of Pennsylvania Press.
Mori, J. (2002). Task design, plan, and development of talk-in-interaction: An analysis of a small group activity in a Japanese language classroom. *Applied Linguistics, 23,* 323–347.
Mori, J. (2003, 22 March). Classroom talks, discourse identities, and participation structures. Paper presented at the Colloquium on Classroom talks: A conversation analytic perspective. American Association of Applied Linguistics, Arlington, VA.
Ohta A. (2001a). *Second language acquisition processes in the classroom.* Mahwah, NJ: Lawrence Erlbaum.
Ohta, A. (2001b, March). Confirmation checks: A conversation analytic reanalysis. Paper presented as part of the Colloquium on Unpacking negotiation: A conversation analytic perspective on L2 interactional competence. Annual AAAL Conference, St. Louis, MI.
Ohta, A., & Nakaone T. (n.d.). When students ask language-related questions: Student questions and their answers in teacher-fronted and group work classroom interaction. Unpublished manuscript, University of Washington, Seattle.
Pica, T. (1987). Second language acquisition, social interaction and the classroom. *Applied Linguistics, 8,* 3–21.
Pica, T., & Doughty, C. (1985). The role of group work in classroom second language acquisition. *Studies in Second Language Acquisition, 7,* 233–248.

Pica, T., Doughty, C., & Young, R. (1986). Making input comprehensible: Do interactional modifications help? *IRAL, 72*, 1–25.
Pomerantz, A. (1975). *Second assessments: A study of some features of agreements/disagreements.* Ph.D. dissertation, University of California, Irvine, Irvine, CA.
Pomerantz, A. (1978a). Attributions of responsibility: Blamings. *Sociology, 12*, 115–121.
Pomerantz, A. (1978b). Compliment responses: Notes on the cooperation of multiple constraints. In J. Schenkein (Ed.), *Studies in the organization of conversational interaction* (pp. 79–112). New York: Academic Press.
Pomerantz, A. (1984a). Agreeing and disagreeing with assessments: Some features of preferred/dispreferred turn shapes. In J. Atkinson & J. Heritage (Eds.), *Structures of social action* (pp. 152–163). Cambridge: Cambridge University Press.
Pomerantz, A. (1984b). Pursuing a response. In J. Atkinson & J. Heritage (Eds.), *Structures of social action* (pp. 57–101). Cambridge: Cambridge University Press.
Psathas, G. (1986). Some sequential structures in direction-giving. *Human Studies, 9*, 231–246.
Psathas, G. (1995). *Conversation analysis: The study of talk-in-interaction.* Thousand Oaks, CA: Sage.
Robinson, J. (1998). Getting down to business: Talk, gaze and body orientation during openings of doctor-communication consultations. *Human Communications Research, 25*, 97–123.
Roger, D., & Bull, P. (1988). Introduction. In D. Roger & P. Bull (Eds.), *Conversation* (pp. 21–47). Clevedon: Multilingual Matters.
Sacks, H. (1974). An analysis of the course of a joke's telling. In R. Bauman & J. Sherzer (Eds.), *Explorations in the ethnography of speaking* (pp. 337–353). Cambridge: Cambridge University Press.
Sacks, H. (1995). *Lectures on conversation* (Vol. I and II). (Edited by G. Jefferson & E. Schegloff). Cambridge: Blackwell's.
Sacks, H., & Schegloff, E. (1979). Two preferences in the organization of reference to persons and their interaction. In G. Psathas (Ed.), *Everyday language: Studies in ethnomethodology* (pp. 15–21). New York: Irvington.
Sacks, H., Schegloff, E., & Jefferson, G. (1974). A simplest systematics for the organization of turn-taking in conversation. *Language, 50*, 696–735.
Schegloff, E. (1968). Sequencing in conversational openings. *American Anthropologist, 70*, 1075–1095.
Schegloff, E. (1979). The relevance of repair to syntax-for-conversation. In T. Givon (Ed.), *Syntax and semantics, Volume 12: Discourse and Syntax* (pp. 261–286). New York: Academic Press.
Schegloff, E. (1987). Between macro and micro: Contexts and other connections. In J. Alexander, B. Giesen, R. Munch, & N. Smelser (Eds.), *The micro-macro link* (pp. 207–234). Berkeley: University of California Press.
Schegloff, E. (1991). Conversation analysis and socially shared cognition. In L. Resnick, J. Levine, & S. Teasley (Eds.), *Socially shared cognition* (pp. 150–171). Washington, DC: American Psychological Association.
Schegloff, E. (1992). On talk and its instituutional occasions. In P. Drew & J. Heritage (Eds.), *Talk at work*, (pp. 101–134). Cambridge: Cambridge University Press.
Schegloff, E. (1993). Reflections on quantification in the study of conversation. *Research on Language and Social Interaction, 26*, 99–128.
Schegloff, E. (1996). Turn organization: One intersection of grammar and interaction. In E. Ochs, E. Schegloff, & S. Thompson (Eds.), *Interaction and grammar* (pp. 52–133). Cambridge: Cambridge University Press.
Schegloff, E., Jefferson, G., & Sacks, H. (1977). The preference for self-correction in the organization of repair in conversation. *Language, 53*, 361–382.
Schegloff, E., Koshik, I., Jacoby, S, & Olsher, D. (2002). Conversation analysis and applied linguistics. In M. McGroarty (Ed.), *ARAL, 22, Discourse and dialog.*
Schutz, A. (1962a). Commonsense and scientific interpretation of human actions. In *Collected papers, Volume 1* (pp. 3–47). The Hague: Martinus Nijhof.
Schutz, A. (1962b). Some leading concepts in phenomenology. In *Collected papers, Volume 1* (pp. 99–117). The Hague: Martinus Nijhof.
Schutz, A. (1962c). On multiple realities. In *Collected papers, Volume 1* (pp. 207–259). The Hague: Martinus Nijhof.
Schutz, A. (1964a). The social world and the theory of social action. In *Collected papers, Volume 2* (pp. 3–19). The Hague: Martinus Nijhof.
Schutz, E. (1964b). The problem of rationality in the social world. In *Collected papers, Volume 2* (pp. 64–90). The Hague: Martinus Nijhof.
Schwartz, J. (1980). The negotiation for meaning: Repair in conversations between second language learners of English. In D. Larsen-Freeman (Ed.), *Discourse analysis in second language research* (pp. 138–153). Rowley, MA: Newbury House.

Seedhouse, P. (1997). The case of the missing 'No': The relationship between pedagogy and interaction. *Language Learning, 47*, 547–583.

Seedhouse, P. (1999). The relationship between context and the organization of repair in the L2 classrooom. *IRAL, XXXVII*, 59–80.

Stivers, T. (2002). Presenting the problem in pediatric encounters: 'Symptoms only' versus 'candidate diagnosis' presentations. *Health Communication, 14,* 3, 299–338.

Stubbs, M. (1983). *Discourse analysis.* Oxford: Basil Blackwell.

van Lier, L. (1988). *The classroom and the language learner.* London: Longman.

van Lier (1996). Interaction in the language curriculum. London: Longman.

Varonis, E., & Gass, S. (1985a). Miscommunication in native/nonnative conversation. *Language in Society, 14*, 327–343.

Varonis, E., & Gass, S. (1985b). Non-native/non-native conversations: A model for negotiation of meaning. *Applied Linguistics, 6*, 71–90.

Willey, B. (2001). Examining a 'communicative strategy' from a conversation analytic perspective: Eliciting help from native speakers inside and outside of word search sequences. Unpublished master's thesis, University of Illinois at Urbana-Champaign.

Wilson, T. (1991). Social structure and the sequential organization of interaction. In D. Boden & D. Zimmerman (Eds.), *Talk and social structure* (pp. 22–43). Cambridge: Polity Press.

Wong, J. (2000). Delayed next turn repair initiation in native-nonnative speaker English conversation. *Applied Linguistics, 2*, 244–267.

Young, R., & Miller, E. (2002, December 16–21). *Learning as Changing Participation: Negotiating Discourse Roles in the ESL Writing Conference.* Paper presented at the 13th World Congress of Applied Linguistics, Singapore.

Young, R., & Nguyen, H. (2002). Modes of meaning in high school science. *Applied Linguistics, 23*, 348–372.

APPENDIX 1: TRANSCRIPTION CONVENTIONS

CA transcription conventions (based on Atkinson & Heritage, 1984).

IDENTITY OF SPEAKERS

SVH:	initials of an identified participant
?:	unidentified participant
SDN?:	probably SDN
LL:	several or all learners talking simultaneously

SIMULTANEOUS UTTERANCES

SVH: [yes
SDN: [yeh   simultaneous, overlapping talk by two speakers

SVH: [huh? [oh] I see]
SDN: [what]
MXS: [I dont get it   ]   simultaneous, overlapping talk by three (or more) speakers
≈   fortuitous overlap between another conversation and the one that is being analyzed

CONTIGUOUS UTTERANCES

=   indicates that there is no gap at all between the two turns

INTERVALS WITHIN AND BETWEEN UTTERANCES

(0.3)	a pause of 0.3 second
(1.0)	a pause of one second.

CHARACTERISTICS OF SPEECH DELIVERY

☺	smiley voice
☹	serious tone (contrasts with smiley voice in preceding or following environment)
#	creaky voice
?	rising intonation, not necessarily a question
!	strong emphasis, with falling intonation
yes.	a period indicates falling (final) intonation
so,	a comma indicates low-rising intonation suggesting continuation
go:::d	one or more colons indicate lengthening of the preceding sound; each additional colon represents a lengthening of one beat
no-	a hyphen indicates an abrupt cutoff, with level pitch
be<u>cau</u>se	underlined letters indicates marked stress
SYLVIA	large capitals indicate loud volume
sylvia	small capitals indicate intermediate volume
sylvia	lower case indicates normal conversational volume
°sylvia°	degree sign indicates decreased volume, often a whisper
˙hhh	in-drawn breaths
hhh	laughter tokens
> the next thing<	indicates speeded-up delivery relative to the surrounding talk
< the next thing>	indicates slowed-down delivery relative to the surrounding talk

COMMENTARY IN THE TRANSCRIPT

((coughs))	verbal description of actions noted in the transcript, including non-verbal actions
((unintelligible))	indicates a stretch of talk that is unintelligible to the analyst
. . . . (radio)	single parentheses indicate unclear or probable item

EYE GAZE PHENOMENA
The moment at which eye gaze is coordinated with speech is marked by an X and the duration of the eye gaze is indicated by a continuous line. Thus in the example below, the moment at which L11's eye gaze falls on L9 in line 412 coincides with the beginning of his turn at line 413

```
                     [X___((L11's eye gaze is now directed at L9))_____
412 L11:    [°you can call me and then [I can say you ] the the address
413 L9:                                 [((L9 nods 4 times]
```

Eye gaze transition is shown by commas
```
              [X_____ , ,
```
The moment at which there ceases to be eye contact (as when a participant looks down or away from his/her interlocutor) is shown by periods
```
              [X_____ . . .
```

OTHER TRANSCRIPTION SYMBOLS

{	talk from another conversation to the one that is currently being analyzed
Co/l/al	slashes indicate phonetic transcription
→	an arrow in transcript draws attention to a particular phenomenon the analyst wishes to discuss

CHAPTER 63

POSTSTRUCTURALISM AND APPLIED LINGUISTICS:

Complementary Approaches to Identity and Culture in ELT

BRIAN MORGAN

York University, Canada

ABSTRACT

Applied linguistics and poststructuralism offer varied perspectives on language, culture, and identity. The purpose of this chapter is to establish key theoretical and pedagogical contrasts, as well as to sketch out future areas of complementarity. Applied linguists tend to view language as a site in which social and cultural differences are displayed, whereas poststructuralists tend to view language as a vehicle through which differences between and within identity categories (e.g., gender, race, ethnicity) are created and realized. By extension, applied linguists often provide rigorous descriptions of particular features (e.g., pragmatic norms, literacy practices) that define minority identities and place students at potential risk. Such mappings, for poststructuralists, are illusory. Language is fundamentally unstable (cf. Derrida's notion of *différance*), and identities are multiple, contradictory, and subject to change across settings and through interaction. Representation becomes a crucial area of debate here. Many applied linguists rightfully claim that academic achievement and social justice are advanced when non-dominant varieties of language are systematically described and valorized in schools. Poststructuralists correctly warn, however, that power relations are always implicated when we formalize particular language/identity correlations. Such representations are always shaped by discourses, and are hence "dangerous," in that they potentially reify the marginal positions and practices that they name.

INTRODUCTION

Applied linguistics (AL) and poststructuralism bring to light divergent and at times conflicting perspectives on language and identity. Exclusive observance of either theoretical framework thus provides only a partial viewpoint on cultural and linguistic diversity. The purpose of this chapter will be to establish key theoretical differences, describe the types of pedagogy they suggest, and in the final sections, sketch out areas of complementarity that enhance theory and practice in the ELT profession.

Forming comparisons between AL and poststructuralism is problematic in several respects. Unlike poststructuralism, AL has a longstanding methodological tradition. Thus, ELT professionals might select aspects of poststructural thought to inform their practice, whereas the reverse would seem unimaginable at this time. Varied paths of development and the lack of consensus they engender further complicate comparison. In North America, for instance, Butler (1992, p. 4) notes a tendency to use poststructuralism as an umbrella term for an eclectic set of theories lacking coherence by continental standards. In Britain, as well, poststructuralism has been uniquely associated with Marxist thought through the writings of Louis Althusser (Culler, 1997, p. 125).

APPLIED LINGUISTICS: A BRIEF SURVEY

As with poststructuralism, AL should not be seen as a unitary or static concept. With growing interest in ideological and interdisciplinary theory, especially over the past decade, AL is experiencing unprecedented plurality in thought and regional/national variation. The preeminence and mainstreaming of Hallidayan systemic-functionalism in Australia, as one example, has yet to occur—if it ever will—in North America where cognitive, task-based, and communicative approaches predominate in ESL curricula.

This raises the critical question of which other academic disciplines, besides linguistics applied (Widdowson, 1980), might provide additional foundations for the future? Grabe, Stoller, and Tardy (2000) identify psychology, anthropology, educational theory, and sociology as particularly strong candidates for language teacher education. For other researchers the major questions relate to the implementation of language teaching approaches rather than to their theoretical foundations: Can teaching methods and materials be generalized across diverse cultural and linguistic contexts (see Holliday, 1994; Kumaravadivelu, 2003a)? Under what conditions and in which settings might social needs take priority over linguistic ones (Auerbach, 2000; Morgan, 1998; Sauvé, 2000)? Perhaps most important, in a world of social possibilities both conceived and concealed through language, can applied linguistics remain impartial? As Corson (1997) argues, the common "perception that 'language teaching' is its central function, may have distorted the epistemological foundations of applied linguistics" (p. 167).

Corson's (1997) insight underscores the positivistic, paradigmatic assumptions that have often guided AL research: a quest for ultimate rules or universals regarding SLA; a conviction that such rules have a measurable reality or ontology independent of the rational, scientific frames and tools used to discover them; and an assumption that such research methods, if not culturally and ideologically neutral, are at least controllable through experimental design (cf. *positivistic* vs. *naturalistic* inquiry, Lynch, 1996). Structuralist principles, as well, are firmly rooted in AL's modernist foundations. The "deep structure" of mind, unveiled by way of Chomsky's Universal Grammar, not only has influenced grammars of a pedagogical bent (e.g., Cook, 1994) but also has underpinned an SLA research agenda that is heavily psycholinguistic rather than ethnographic, sociolinguistic, or ideological in orientation (e.g., Norton, 2000; Rampton, 1995; Roberts et al., 2001). More generally, Saussure's descriptive privileging of a decontextualized, ahistorical system, *la langue,* over individual use and creativity, *la parole,* gives rise to a mindset in which system-building and comprehensive modeling (e.g., word corpuses, taxonomies of learner strategies, hierarchies of closely-specified task descriptors, etc.) are highly valued.

Arguably, this structuralist and positivist convergence is most responsible for "the consistent anonymising, if not the actual eclipsing, of the learner" (Candlin, 2000, p. xiii). By this is meant that the learner comes to stand for the system—be it mind, language, or culture—and the language he or she produces is abstracted, analyzed, and categorized as a reflection of the system's timeless and general properties. Lost in this "primordial" (Appadurai, 1996), "essentialized" (Kubota, 1999), or "received" (Atkinson, 1999) model is an understanding of how individuals use language to *differentiate* themselves or to resist and transform their categorization. By making the system more "real" than those who use it, language professionals yield to the epistemological trap identified by Corson: a preoccupation with language as an *end-in-itself*, rather than a vehicle for self-discovery and social transformation.

POSTSTRUCTURALISM: A CONCEPTUAL SURVEY

In defining *poststructuralism*, there is no small irony in attributing foundations to an intellectual field noted for its antifoundationalism and deep suspicion of system-building in any form (see Butler, 1992; Sarap, 1993; Weedon, 1987). Poststructuralism is "postmodern" in its critique of universal notions of objectivity, progress, and reason. A weakening of scientific hegemony marks this conceptual shift. Whereas modernist educators (i.e., conservative, liberal, or Marxist) tend to view science as a *tool* to challenge inequalities, postmodern educators tend to view science—or one version of science (i.e., positivism)—as partial knowledge, and if applied too generally, a potential *source* of injustice. This partiality, in turn, increases the validity of situated and dialogical forms of knowledge (see Benesch, 1999; Canagarajah, 2002, 2005; Carr, 2003; Hall, Vitanova, & Marchenkova, 2005; Lather & Ellsworth, 1996; Wells, 1999; Wong, 2000).

Poststructuralism is similarly postmodern in its attentiveness to the dynamics and disjunctures of social categories. Concepts such as *performativity* (Butler, 1990), *cultural hybridity* (Bhabha, 1994), *transnational, diasporic* identities (Appadurai, 1996), and *nomadology* (Deleuze & Guattari, 1986) highlight this focus on the creative and composite dimensions of experience, a perspective embraced by a growing number of language researchers. Zamel's (1997) use of *transculturation*, Kramsch's (1993) concept of *interculturality*, Rampton's (1995) study of *crossings*, and Johnston's (1999) depiction of expatriate EFL teachers as *postmodern paladins* are notable examples.

A postmodern preoccupation with language is also evident in the provocative use of grammatical metaphors and neologisms in publications. Street (1993), for instance, argues that culture needs to be de-nominalized, recast as a verb to counter its reification. Similarly, Kramsch (2000) details an immigrant experience that "gets *languaged* after the fact" (p. 136). And the hybrid term *glocalization* (Lin, Wang, Akamatsu, & Riazi, 2002; Pakir, 2000) serves to illustrate local articulations of global processes. Though such glosses might seem trivial or merely playful, they *are* a reflection of the so-called *linguistic turn* in postmodernism, an increased sensitivity to language-conditioned understandings.

While postmodern in spirit, poststructuralism is distinctively post-Saussurian (see Belsey, 1980; Cherryholmes, 1988; Weedon, 1987). In Saussure's semiotics, nothing inside the mind or outside language accounts for the "arbitrary" binding of signifier (a sound or graphic image) and signified (the concept designated) in a sign's operation. The meanings we attach to words/signs are produced within language through differences between other signs in a self-regulating language system. Poststructuralists, particularly through the work of Derrida (1982), utilize these ideas but radicalize them by amplifying the system's dynamism and instability: "In a language, in the system of language there are only differences...on the one hand, these differences play: in language...On the other hand, these differences are themselves effects. They have not fallen from the sky fully formed, ...[nor are they] prescribed in the gray matter of the brain" (p. 11). Through this "play of differences" (cf. *différance*, Derrida), neutrality and objectivity in Saussure's ordered system is undermined: meanings become provisional and the boundaries between linguistic and extralinguistic factors erased. Instead of focusing on intrinsic properties of words, or relations within a fixed system, poststructuralists often investigate extrinsic conditions—the social intentions of language users—in their critical analyses of texts.

Texts attain a similar provisional status, one tied closely to the process of their production rather than their reference to worldly phenomena. Texts are *deconstructed*, read against themselves in order to reveal their *aporias* (i.e., self-generated paradoxes) and to expose the techniques and social interests in their construction (e.g., Norris, 1982; Terdiman, 1985). A novel or theory that at first glance might appear to be the cohesive product of a single writer becomes pluralized, revealing a number of competing and complementary social voices that vie for a reader's attention (cf. *heteroglossia,* Bakhtin, 1981). The purpose of reading changes accordingly: no longer passive recipients of an author's intentions, readers become active producers of a text's "authorial" meanings (see Barthes, 1988; Cherryholmes, 1993; Scholes, 1985). The meanings created, however, are not unconstrained. Texts are always *intertextual* (Bazerman, 2004), their production and circulation taking place in a linguistic "marketplace" that values particular language practices and stigmatizes others (cf. *symbolic capital,* Bourdieu, 1991).

These ways of conceptualizing language and texts are then transposed upon identity. In so far as meanings are produced within language, "meanings" of self and others are produced within *discourses*—systems of *power/knowledge* (Foucault, 1982) that regulate and assign value to all forms of semiotic activity, for instance, oral/written texts, gestures, images, spaces, and their multimodal integration (e.g., Gee, 1996; Harklau, 2003; Kress, 2003; Kumaravadivelu, 1999; Pennycook, 2001; Stein, 2004; Toohey, 2000). In so far as language is provisional and indeterminate, self-understanding, or *subjectivity* (e.g., Foucault; Norton, 2000), is viewed as having comparable instability in its discursive realization. No longer the center or rational source of understanding, the individual becomes "de-centered"—in part, "spoken" by the language he or she uses, even at the level of the unconscious (cf. Lacan's psychoanalytics, in Sarap, 1993; Granger, 2004; Weedon, 1987). The individual similarly becomes *textualized*, his or her "private" experiences deconstructed to reveal the discourses that have produced them. Poststructuralists, however, conceptualize the determination of subjectivity as partial or incomplete in that discourses also create the possibilities for autonomy and resistance (cf. *agency*, Norton & Toohey, 2001; Pavlenko, 2002; Price, 1999).

The continual play of differences assigned to language serves as inspiration for an active and relational "politics of difference" (Pennycook, 2001) within and between social categories. Through Butler's (1990) concept of performativity, in particular, the "differencing" of identity becomes a permanent condition, whose significance for education has attracted growing research attention (Alexander, Anderson, & Gallegos, 2005; Morgan, 2004a; Nelson, 1999; Pennycook, 2004).

Performative utterances, following Austin (1975), do not describe prior or existing conditions (cf. constatives) but instead create that which they name in language (e.g., "let the games begin"). In a famous passage, Butler (1990) reworks Austin's concept to describe gender as "the repeated stylization of the body, a set of repeated acts within a highly rigid regulatory frame that congeal over time to produce the appearance of substance, of a natural sort of being" (p. 33). Simply put, gender is an effect of what we *do* (in large part with language) and not just who we are (e.g., Cameron, 1997; Ehrlich, 1997). Identity, by extension, is fundamentally a social practice.

These poststructural ideas on language and identity have several strategic implications for ELT. Firstly, theories of culture and identity should not be judged on their internal merits alone—as *things-in-themselves*—but also in relation to their origins, exclusions (i.e., "subjugated knowledges," Foucault, 1980, pp. 82-83), and local articulations (e.g., Lin & Luk, 2002). SLA theory, for example, is seen through Norton Peirce's (1995) landmark study as an *individualizing* discourse, one that has conceptually isolated the language learner from the language-learning context. Attitudinal and motivational profiles, in Norton's view, fail to capture the complex desires and social power relations that shape communication and restrict access to target language speakers and authentic speech situations. Drawing on Bourdieu, Norton (2000) reconceptualizes L2 learning as a *shared* responsibility and expands the definition of L2 competence to include claiming "the right to speak" and "the power to impose reception" (p. 8).

Similar strategies pertain to all methods and materials. The language rules and behaviors they claim to embody are no longer viewed as independent "facts" but, instead, as effects of discourses. Classrooms, thus, become sites of power relations that work on and through individuals as well as through the microtechnologies of ELT (e.g., Harklau, 2000; Kubota, 2001; Lynch, 2001; Toohey, 2000). Language standards, curricula, and assessment tools, in this perspective, are no longer appraised solely for the outcomes they enable but also for the identities or subject positions they constitute—the limited English proficiency (LEP) student or the non-native-speaking (NNS) teacher, as examples. Once made "visible" by discourse, prescribed "inadequacies" are then transferred onto those labeled, setting into motion a wide range of normalizing strategies (e.g., expert interventions, forms of remediation, professional marginalization). Although some resist, others *produce* forms of self-understanding that accord with the subject positions that a particular discourse presents: a student labeled LEP, for example, might come to accept the notion that the prior knowledge he or she brings to school is "backwards" and that a dead-end job is all that the future holds.

Concepts such as power/knowledge, discourse, subjectivity, and performativity clearly amplify the presence of power relations in ELT and underpin the need for critical pedagogies in language education (e.g., Norton & Toohey, 2004; Reagan & Osborn, 2002). This intensification of power, however, has both positive and negative ramifications. On the positive side, poststructural educators apply reflexive checks and balances on emergent power relations (cf. problematizing practice, Pennycook, 2001; Benesch, 2001) that more instrumental orientations would view as superfluous. The status of teachers is also enhanced in that the poststructural ontology of situatedness assigns teachers a decisive role in creating pedagogies of transformation (cf. collaborative vs. coercive relations of power, Cummins, 2001).

On the negative side, the pervasiveness of power, so theorized, can be destabilizing: new teachers, for example, may become overly cautious, worried that their next lesson may inadvertently silence minority students. Also, there is the danger that power becomes overdetermined, projected onto settings or activities in which its explanatory value may be marginal. What such concerns speak to is the need for a poststructuralism more grounded in the specifics of ELT research and practice.

Although desirable, a constructive dialogue between AL and poststructuralism is potentially problematic. Such collaboration, on the one hand, suggests an expansive and exciting range of conceptual possibilities. On the other, it may contribute to an excess of theoreticism and abstraction from which only a select few might seek guidance. In order to realize the former and minimize the latter, ELT professionals should keep in mind what is specifically at stake: how we understand and relate to those whose interests we claim to serve. The following sections will elaborate on this issue.

MAIN RESEARCH FINDINGS

Culture in ELT: Concepts and Definitions

The importance attached to the concept of culture is reflected in a growing wealth of journal articles, books, and anthologies that have addressed various aspects of cultural knowledge and interaction as they pertain to ELT (e.g., Alfred, Byram, & Fleming, 2003; Atkinson, 2004; Byram & Fleming, 1998; Corson, 2001; Courchêne, 1996; J. K. Hall, 2002; Hinkel, 1999; Ilieva, 2000; Kramsch, 1993, 1998; McKay, 2000; Moran, 2001; Morgan & Cain, 2000; Ronowicz & Yallop, 1999; Scollon & Scollon, 1995; Schecter & Bailey, 2002; Valdes, 1986). This recent expansion of cultural materials can be seen, on the one hand, as acknowledgment of the concept's importance in language education, while on the other, as a response to a tendency to invoke culture in commonsensical ways. This tendency, as Byram and Risager (1999) note, reflects the fact while "many curriculum documents urge [teachers] to develop cultural awareness and knowledge of other countries and cultures, ... there is no discussion of what concept of culture underpins the documents themselves" (p. 83).

Such concerns are addressed in Atkinson's (1999) comprehensive survey of the culture concept in TESOL. Three perspectives, in Atkinson's article, demarcate this field: (a) an earlier "received" view, which is still prominent in the profession; (b) a "middle ground" approach that questions many "received" assumptions; and (c) a postmodern-inspired, "critical" approach that fundamentally questions the basis and purpose of cultural knowledge in the field. The following discussion borrows and expands upon the first and third categories.

A received view, following Atkinson (1999), treats cultures as "geographically (and quite often nationally) distinct entities, as relatively unchanging and homogeneous, and as all-encompassing systems of rules or norms that substantially determine personal behavior" (p. 626). Culture understood in this way can become an explanatory crutch for those aspects of classroom experience beyond a teacher's current expertise. The problem can be even more acute for new teachers trained in a single methodological framework. Any "problems" that occur outside this frame are likely viewed as cultural in origin rather than pedagogical in effect. In this way, the "unteachable" student comes to reflect the exotic and inscrutable "Other" of orientalist tradition (Said, 1978), whose "limitations" are attributed to ingrained cultural traits inimical to progress. Kubota's (1999, 2004) work has been particularly insightful in alerting educators to the dangers inherent in the stereotypical dichotomies of cultures and classrooms often disseminated through AL research.

Students can be "Othered" or "exoticized" even by well-meaning teachers sensitized to notions of diversity. The "simplification of culture," Bissoondath's (1994) controversial critique of official multiculturalism in Canada, draws attention to a troubling pedagogical habit of reducing differences to superficial displays of food, fashion, and festivals. "Culture Disnified," Bissoondath's (1994) provocative description of Canadian practices, also portends global developments in the *lingua franca* functions of World English (e.g., Brutt-Griffler, 2002; Knapp & Meierkord, 2002), whereby culture increasingly becomes *commoditized*, conceived and taught as a "value-adding" set of sociopragmatic skills for cross-cultural entrepreneurship (e.g., Block, 2002; Cameron, 2002; Corson, 2002; Kramsch, 2000).

A received view of culture is discernible in many other areas of AL: in the description of paralinguistic (e.g., elements of style such as tone, pitch, volume) and extralinguistic differences (e.g., proxemics, kinesics, etc.) attributed to race, culture, and gender categories (e.g., Chaika, 1994); in the cataloging of cross-cultural or interracial pragmatic norms that contribute to miscommunication (cf. *interactional sociolinguistics*, Gumperz, 1986); in the explication of prototypical forms of writing based on cultural traditions (cf. *contrastive rhetoric* studies, Casanave, 2004, Ch. 2; Connor, 1996); or in the description of internal states and motivational inadequacies (e.g., "culture shock"), reference to which "explain" students' inabilities to acquire an L2 or *acculturate* to dominant norms (e.g., Brown, 1986).

Through the wisdom of postmodern hindsight, one might dismiss such work for its inattention to power relations and its overreliance on positivistic research, but this would be unfair, in many cases. Sociolinguists such as Gumperz and Labov, for example, set out to demonstrate that the academic underachievement of minority students was not the product of culturally and linguistically deprived home or community environments. Through systematic data collection and formal description—the hallmarks of scientificity—they hoped to convince the public of the legitimacy of non-dominant varieties of language and the need for schools to respect and support such differences (e.g., Corson, 2001, Ch. 3 & 4). Nonetheless, scientific rigor has not stemmed the fear of cultural, racial, and linguistic diversity that underpins opposition to bilingual education and Ebonics instruction in parts of the U.S.A. In this respect, a "received" view of national identity—a dominant ideology of homogeneity and monolingualism—supersedes its multilingual and multiracial realities (e.g., Cummins, 2000; Dicker, 2000; Perry & Delpit, 1998).

A critical view offers strong points of contrast, many of them distinctively postmodern. Cultural practices and forms are seen as dynamic and context sensitive rather than static and universal. Similarly, causal relations between language and culture are reversed or understood as mutually constitutive. Culture is seen as not simply the source of meaning-making activities, but also its effect. Modes of expression (i.e., words, images, rituals, etc.) come to shape, dialogically, how individual and collective experiences are conceptualized and retained (e.g., Morgan & Cain, 2000). These emphases on change, complexity, and locality take us away from conventional notions of cultures as homogeneous and bound to specific nations, regions, or languages on a one-to-one basis.

A critical view also seeks to understand students' cultural activity in a world progressively "shrinking" in fundamental ways: Money, information systems, and populations are more mobile than ever and increasingly concentrated in major cosmopolitan centers noted for their ethnic, racial, and linguistic pluralism (e.g., Blackledge, 2002; Goldstein, 2003; Pavlenko & Blackledge, 2004). In English-dominant metropolises such as London, New York, Toronto, and Sydney, ESL programs struggle to remain relevant for newcomers who, in a sense, live transnational, juxtaposed lives (e.g., Appadurai, 1996; Harris, Leung, & Rampton, 2002) in which geographical distances are instantaneously bridged through global communications media (i.e., the Internet, telephone, movies, newspapers) and life "abroad" is eased by an abundance of services and employment possibilities in students' L1.

The world is also shrinking in frightening and dangerous ways. Political violence against civilian populations seems to be escalating, and as recently demonstrated in Iraq, overwhelming military superiority and the political and cultural insularity it provides its owners can be unilaterally, if not decisively, imposed anywhere, followed closely by the symbols and values of the triumphant. For those without such power, assimilative pressures can be more acutely felt, and resistance, of necessity, is more covert and often cultural and linguistic in form. With English now globalized, the question that remains is the extent to which it can be "decolonized," locally appropriated in ways that challenge the political and economic hegemony of dominant nations, as well as respect vernacular forms of knowledge and literacy (e.g., Canagarajah, 1999, 2005; Cooke, 1999; Hornberger, 2003; Kumaravadivelu, 2003b; Mair, 2003; Pennycook, 1998; Ramanathan, 2005).

Cultural continuity, in the face of current realities, becomes an intensely active and relational process. Traditions are retraditionalized, acquiring new or additional meanings by which important differences are maintained. Yet the maintenance of such "differences," particularly in liberal democratic societies, can become strategically *extra-cultural* in response to national ideologies and globalization pressures (e.g. Fleming, 2003; K. Hall, 2002; Heller, 2003). In Canada, for example, Williams (1998) notes the growth of astute and well-organized groups who view official multiculturalism as "a set of institutional opportunities for individual and group advancement in a competitive environment" (p. 26). Liberal democracies, in general, tend to undermine traditional ties and encourage greater cultural experimentation and syncretism through the promotion of values such as individualism, secularism, and cultural relativism in legal and educational institutions. Second language teachers, who perceive or present such values as universal, unwittingly increase students' own sense of alienation and foreignness in their new surroundings (e.g., Johnston, 2003).

In contrast to its received precursor, a critical, postmodern perspective of culture is a highly complex notion, one that seeks to unveil "the fissures, inequalities, disagreements, and cross-cutting influences that exist in and around all cultural scenes, in order to banish once and for all that cultures are monolithic entities, or in some cases anything important at all" (Atkinson, 1999, p. 627). For ELT professionals, the images proffered here might appear so fleeting that their realization within language curricula would seem careless. Yet such perceptual obstacles reflect, in large part, SLA and AL traditions. To reiterate, a received view of culture in the form of timeless facts, reified learner profiles, and essentialized literacy and discourse norms is still pervasive and not easily overcome. In received approaches to pedagogy, students are encouraged to exchange what they already know (i.e., cultural facts). Critical approaches, in contrast, foreground cultural reflexivity as a pedagogical goal, encouraging students to discover what they *don't* know—about themselves, their cultural "others," and the social forces that shape intercultural understanding (e.g., Carr, 2003; Corbett, 2003; Cummins, 2001; Kramsch, 1993; MacPherson, et al., 2004; Nieto, 2002; Young, 1996).

Poststructural Critique: Culture or Identity?

As detailed by Belz (2002), Blackledge and Pavlenko (2001), McNamara (1997), Norton (2000), Pavlenko (2002), Pennycook (2001), and Varghese, Morgan, Johnston, and Johnson (2005), the construct of *identity* has been theorized in numerous ways, through *sociopsychological* frames (cf. Tajfel, 1974), *interactional sociolinguistics* (cf. Gumperz, 1986), and postmodern approaches such as *feminist poststructuralism* (cf. Weedon, 1987; Norton, 2000), and *queer theory* (cf. Butler, 1990; Nelson, 1999, 2002), as examples. Adding further complexity, identity is often aligned with premodifiers such as *social*, *cultural*, *sociocultural*, or *ethnic* in ELT publications, the substance of which only offer brief, if any, categorical distinctions.

In evaluating current developments, a critical, postmodern view of culture (Atkinson, 1999) has much in common with the poststructural framework outlined in this chapter. Indeed, Norton's (2000) often quoted depiction of identity as "multiple and contradictory" and "a site of struggle" (p.127) bears close resemblance to the cultural "fissures, inequalities, [and] disagreements" described by Atkinson (p. 627). Thus, a pertinent question would be, "Do poststructural theories of identity seek to replace the concept of culture or weaken its importance?" In recent publications such as the *Journal of Language, Identity, and Education*, and in special issues of *TESOL Quarterly* (1997, Vol. 31, No. 3; 1999, Vol. 33, No. 3) and the *International Journal of Bilingualism* (2001, Vol. 5, No. 3), those inspired by poststructural ideas tend to use identity not so much to replace culture but to broaden its implications or critique its use in ELT.

Norton's (1997) feminist poststructural construct of *investment* brings to light some of the subtle distinctions implied: "The construct of investment conceives of the language learner as having a complex history and multiple desires. An investment in the target language is also an investment in a learner's own social identity, which changes across time and place" (p. 411). The multiplicity and complexity of Norton's construct foregrounds heterogeneity. It reminds us that while culture is important, it is not necessarily primary, separable, or more salient than other experiences and desires. When students interact with native speakers, they are "constantly organizing and reorganizing a sense of who they are and how they relate to the social world" (Norton, 2000, p. 11). The "force" of culture in such reorganization may only be marginal or, in specific situations, so tightly interwoven with other influences as to be largely indistinguishable.

Ibrahim's (1999) study of African youth in Canada is a notable example. In Africa, his participants defined themselves through personal qualities and national, ethnic, and linguistic affiliations. Once in Canada, however, they are *racialized*, compelled to enter "a discursive space or representation in which they are already constructed, imagined, and positioned...as Blacks" (p. 353). Thus, they *become* Black, negotiating a new identity for themselves through the repeated "performance" (cf. Butler, 1990) of cultural practices such as rap, hip-hop, and Black English, which offer them a recognizable history, politics, and collective memory in the North American context. While creating new solidarities, however, these positionings also create new liminalities in that the women in Ibrahim's study "misrecognize" themselves in the misogynistic lyrics and videos of many rap songs.

Ibrahim's study is indicative of poststructural preferences: dynamic and overlapping categories (i.e., culture, race, class, and gender), contingencies over continuities, identities created in language and not just displayed, and power relations operating on and through the formation of subjectivities. These concerns are not exclusive to identity nor are their possible absence inherent to culture. But concepts, similar to identities, live discursive lives, and in spite of current postmodern trappings (i.e., transculturation, hybridity, interculturality, third spaces) the culture concept may always carry its "received" associations in ELT that potentially conceal more than they reveal.

For poststructural researchers in AL, the key question is not just "What is culture?" but rather "What does it do?" What forms of knowledge does it enable? And what does it diminish or hide? Poststructuralists, in common cause with critical multiculturalists (e.g., Kubota, 1999, 2004; May, 1999) and critical race theorists (e.g., Ladson-Billings, 1999), worry that a preoccupation with cultural issues can become a form of "power erasure" (e.g., Kincheloe & Steinberg, 1997), disguising systemic inequalities connected to race, class, sexual orientation, or gender relations in society.

Such inequalities mark the treatment of teachers defined as non-native speaking (NNS) in ELT (e.g., Braine, 1999). As Amin (1999) persuasively argues, many ESL students perceive the ideal teacher of English to be a white, Anglo male, irrespective of his actual TESL experience. Speaking a dominant variety of English, he is seen and heard as "accentless" and the natural possessor of the appropriate culture knowledge to teach the language. As a woman of color, and a speaker of Pakistani-English, Amin's legitimacy as an ESL teacher is often questioned, requiring her to adopt teaching strategies in which her authority is less likely to be challenged. This last point is instructive as to how white privilege is systematically organized and concealed within a profession. Specifically, the types of learner-centered, participatory practices that currently define an exemplary teacher in ELT are also the types of practices that are often the least available—or most dangerous—for NNS teachers and teachers of color.

For poststructural educators, then, culture is important insofar as it is understood in relation to wider sets of experiences and discursive practices. As Pennycook (1997) argues:

> Culture determines how social reality is understood; it is a site of primary importance. This is not to deny the importance of a material world, of social or economic relations, but to emphasize that these have no meaning outside their cultural interpretations. What I want to pursue ... is the notion of a *pedagogy of cultural alternatives*, an educational project that seeks to open up alternative ways of thinking and being in the world. (p. 47)

In Pennycook's project, culture serves pedagogy primarily through its illumination and translation of broader social processes. By acting on, or "problem-posing" (e.g., Freire, 1997), cultural experiences, critical practitioners hope to demystify social "realities" and the intimidating sense of permanence that fortifies existing inequities. The assumption guiding this strategy is that possibilities for change must first be imagined at a personal, experiential level before they can be achieved (e.g., Simon, 1992). Whether we explore the notion of culture or that of identity, a poststructural syllabus represents a major shift in priorities—from pedagogies of inclusion to pedagogies of transformation.

CURRENT DEBATES AND CONCERNS

Reflexivity and the Politics of Pedagogy

By recasting power as power/knowledge, and by its valorization of voice, resistance, and agency, poststructuralism places a notion of politics at the center of teaching around culture and identity formation. Poststructural teachers would argue that by "politicizing" pedagogy, they are addressing a reality that is part of all language education and one that many or most ELT professionals wish to deny. Nonetheless, pursuing "alternative ways of thinking and being" is not without potential repercussions for students. In-group members may be quite happy with the status quo and may resent fellow group members who publicly voice alternatives. Those who express such views risk isolation and loss of crucial support networks. Educators who engage in transformative pedagogies acknowledge these concerns and try to limit them through sustained reflection on their own assumptions and heightened awareness of unintended consequences that may arise from their teaching practices.

Critical reflexivity is a term used to describe this cautionary strategy, which "makes particular forms of knowledge themselves objects of study, asking where they came from, what they are like, and how they got that way" (Giltrow & Colhoun, 1992, p. 60). Reflexive techniques can vary, from introspection (e.g., personal narratives) to more empirical-analytical techniques (e.g., critical discourse analyses of program curricula and materials) (e.g., Benesch, 2001; Kumaravadivelu, 2001; Morgan, 2002; Pennycook, 2001; Ramanathan, 2002; Vandrick, 1999). Through poststructuralism, reflexive practices engage more closely with the formation of teacher identities through institutional discourses.

In much the same way we think of students being "cultural"—having particular worldviews and habits of thought—so are teachers as a result of their socialization into ELT through their teacher education programs and professional participation. As recent studies by Ramanathan (2002) and Varghese (2004) emphasize, language teacher education programs evolve in divergent ways, embodying internal conversations and disputes. The theoretical creativity that arises underpins a key poststructural tenet: Teachers do not acquire common "truths" about ELT as much as they attain a particular understanding of their field—a discourse composed of both insights and blind spots. The theories and methods teachers learn, accordingly, are a potential form of cultural politics when exported across settings. Critical reflexivity, in this perspective, encourages teachers to explore the partiality of their knowledge and to maintain a "skeptical eye towards assumptions, ideas that have become 'naturalized,' [and] notions that are no longer questioned" (cf. *problematizing givens*, Pennycook, 2001, p. 7).

Vandrick's (1999) personal narrative demonstrates the types of critical connections that reflexivity supports. Looking back on her missionary upbringing in India, Vandrick reevaluates her memories through her current experiences as an ESL teacher. She acknowledges "the unconscious racism that infects almost everyone with privilege, including 'colonial' privilege" (p. 70) and poses "the possibility of a 'colonial shadow' over our profession" (p. 63) in the form of condescending attitudes towards students and beliefs in the inherent superiority of English.

For Benesch (2001), reflexive, problematizing practices infuse every aspect of her critical approach to English for Academic Purposes (EAP). Cases of student resistance—several male students resented her selection of anorexia as a research topic—are addressed in a principled, self-reflective way that reinforms curricula (e.g., topic choices in critical EAP, Ch. 4). As she recognizes, "provoking a desire to interrogate the status quo…is not achieved by critical teachers imposing their vision or political agenda on students" (p. 51). Instead, Benesch's pedagogy emphasizes dialogue and the importance of balancing pragmatic issues with transformative ones in the university context (cf. "needs" vs. "rights" analyses). "Questioning the theory, practice, content and politics of one's own experiments," according to Benesch (2001, p. 142), is an essential aspect of critical pedagogy.

A question of intense debate can be posed in the following way: Do critical reflexive practices provide adequate safeguards for teachers that act on culture and identity in their classrooms? Sower (1999), in a critique of Kubota's (1999) article, is unreserved in his negative assessment:

> The application of postmodernism, poststructuralism, postcolonialism, and critical multiculturalism to English language teaching is just an exercise in word games….As for critical multiculturalism, introducing an explicitly political agenda into the classroom is dangerous. Of course, postmodernists would have us believe that everything is political, so abandoning any attempt at objectivity is only natural, but I beg to differ. (p. 742)

Sower is not alone in viewing postmodern theories as a license for irresponsibility in education (e.g., Constas, 1998). Indeed, Derrida's deconstructionism seems to invite, in some readers, a sense that there is nothing "real" outside of language and texts. Some of Foucault's ideas—the production of "truth" within discourse, for example (1980, p. 131)—have been narrowly perceived as condoning an "anything goes" antirealism. Such readings do provide an extreme form of relativism that underpins particular strands of postmodern thought (cf. *skeptical postmodernism*, Rosenau, 1992; *nihilistic deconstructive postmodernism*, Shea, 1998). But by reducing *all* postmodernism to particular elements, Sower demonstrates a highly selective understanding of that which he criticizes. Besides, Foucault was not interested in abandoning objectivity, *per se*, as much as he was concerned with how "objectivities" are discursively produced and circulated within specific fields such as ELT and how they act on people in ways that potentially restrict their freedoms (e.g., Foucault, 1982; Rouse, 1994).

These two views on objectivity bring to light fundamental paradigmatic distinctions. Sower's (1999) stance is decidedly positivistic, a bipolar world in which objectivity and relativism are counterposed: "If we are freed from the requirements of scientific observation and truth, then we are left with only stories"

(p. 737). Poststructuralists would argue that "scientific observation and truth" are themselves "stories," *cultural* stories of a Western European tradition—stories that can easily slide into a dangerous political agenda, especially when their general neutrality is presumed across different sites of practice.

A most striking example is Giltrow and Colhoun's (1992) chapter "The Culture of Power: ESL Traditions, Mayan Resistance," an incisive study of how ELT is sometimes perceived and, in this case, confronted by a specific group of students. What might appear "scientific" and benign was, for these students, ethnocentric and offensive, a "system which had captured them and their speech, for purposes of ranking, scoring, and screening.... Acutely sensitive to the political and colonial implications of language acquisition, our informants detected the operation of power" (Giltrow & Colhoun, p. 55). This reverse ethnography, of sorts, is a deeply troubling portrait of ELT, on the one hand, and noticeably ambivalent, on the other. The authors offer neither solutions nor broadsides to the effect "everything is political," nor do they pick "winners" in a head-to-head competition between competing ideologies. Moreover, Giltrow and Colhoun are skeptical regarding the claims to be made on behalf of critical reflexivity. Students "may become even more shadowy and negligible in new critical approaches than they are in traditional approaches which portray them in statistical and positivistic colors" (p. 61).

In this last quote we come to the crux of the matter. If poststructural educators do believe that "everything is political," then they are prone to an "unreflexive" complacency in which all students become, in effect, "shadowy" remnants of discourses. Certainly, a student's individuality is diminished, but so are his or her practical interests. When "everything is political," in an undifferentiated way, conceptual rigor is sacrificed. Without a sense of how the *internal* parts of a system—such as a university—are coordinated, teachers lose sight of the specificities of power, the particular subsystems that are the most responsive to positive changes at any given time (e.g., Benesch, 2001). Teaching, as a result, may have much less bearing on helping students negotiate their circumstances.

The counterargument, however, that neutrality can be predetermined or guaranteed, also breeds complacency. Such presumptions, following Giltrow and Colhoun (1992), are highly problematic. Drawing from poststructuralism, positivistic-minded teachers would do well to adopt a more situated ethics—an awareness of the contingencies by which instruments of "objectivity" (i.e. methods, materials, assessment tools, research techniques) become "technologies of power" (e.g., Foucault, 1997). Poststructural teachers, in turn, would do well to refine their own situated understanding. While learning about the specificities of power, for example, they might also explore the *limits* of power as a source of explanation and a guide to relations with students, an argument persuasively made by Bill Johnston (2003) in his wide-ranging study of values in ELT. The issue Johnston raises here should not be seen as a choice—one chooses to be either political or moral—but rather as a reminder that the centrality and intimacy of teacher-student relations in education, as Cummins (2000, 2001) also emphasizes, may require teachers to be both.

Whether we think of ourselves as poststructuralists or psycholinguists, ideologists or pragmatists, deterministic thinking can linger in various forms, many of which remain stubbornly unresponsive to the spirit of reflexivity. As ELT professionals, then, it is necessary to continuously ask ourselves which conceptual models or their combination help us address our students in all their uniqueness and complexity, rather than as purely instances of mental states, cultural rules, or effects of discourses.

FUTURE DIRECTIONS

Out of the linguistic turn, characteristic of postmodernism, a "pedagogical turn" specific to educational fields can be seen taking root. Giroux (1994), for example, raises the need to "understand pedagogy as a mode of cultural criticism for questioning the very conditions under which knowledge and identities are produced" (p. 280). For ELT, the implications of this "turn" are many, and they suggest several areas of constructive dialogue between poststructuralism and AL research.

From AL, poststructural educators might explore representational options that are more form-focused and linguistic, following the work of Janks (1997) and Poynton (1993), both of whom provide needed analytical rigor to understanding the lexical, grammatical, and textual elements that underpin the positioning of subjects in discourse. Regarding identity negotiation, poststructural educators might also examine the degree to which classroom instruction in an L2 constitutes different ways of being and knowing in the world. Such inquiry would build on a growing body of research that examines poststructural ideas in multilingual and bilingual contexts (e.g., Pavlenko & Blackledge, 2004; Pavlenko & Piller, 2001).

From poststructuralism, AL researchers are alerted to a plurality of coexisting goals in any pedagogical activity. An L2 grammar, vocabulary, or writing activity may, at one level, enunciate linguistic forms or textual prototypes; but at another, the same activity for participants becomes a site of identity negotiation in which engagement with formal genres and L2 forms shapes the self-perception and retention of students' experiences (e.g., Starfield, 2002; Ivanič, 1998; Kramsch, 2000; Morgan, 2002, 2004b). Discursive perspectives on student resistance and agency also benefit teachers in how they identify and respond to "problem" students. Again, there are several poststructural-informed studies in ELT to build upon (Benesch, 2001; Canagarajah, 1999; Giltrow & Colhoun, 1992; Harklau, 2003; Toohey, 2000).

These dialogic examples draw attention to the relative uniqueness of ELT settings and practices. Given this uniqueness, ELT professionals might consider the distinctive, theoretical contributions to be made through future collaboration. In conceptualizing language, culture, and cognition, for example, poststructural semiotics and psychoanalytics may provide critical insights that invigorate *sociocultural theory* (e.g. Lantolf, 2000) and *community of practice* (COP) models (e.g., Lave & Wenger, 1991).

Though complementary (e.g., Toohey, 2000, Ch. 1), each theory provides distinctive foci on power and agency. From a poststructural perspective, COP and sociocultural models might be criticized for exaggerating the internal cohesion and cooperation of collectivities and for understating the operation of discourse and power through the communication of group norms. In addition, sociocultural theorists may assign individuals a degree of autonomy and self-awareness greater than that assigned to poststructural subjects (e.g., Morgan, 2004a, pp. 183-184; Walkerdine, 1997). From COP and sociocultural perspectives, poststructural theories of identity might be criticized for overstating the dynamic, multiple, and contested nature of subjectivity. That is, while change has always been a recognized aspect of personal and collective experience, continuity and cohesion are far more prevalent phenomena and are thus more valid research priorities.

Future dialogue may emphasize points of convergence between these models. Still, the implications of their differences are worth investigating in the context of ELT pedagogy. If the past is any indication, however, future dialogue between ELT theorists will be less cumbersome than genuine dialogue between theorists and practitioners. For both poststructural and AL researchers, further insights to be gained from a "pedagogical turn" will be dependent on equitable collaboration with teachers.

REFERENCES

Alexander, B. K., Anderson, G. L., & Gallegos, B. P. (Eds.). (2005). *Performance theories in education: Power, pedagogy, and the politics of identity*. Mahwah, NJ: Lawrence Erlbaum Associates.

Alfred, G., Byram, M., & Fleming, M. (Eds.). (2003). *Intercultural experience and education*. Clevedon, UK: Multilingual Matters.

Amin, N. (1999). Minority women teachers of ESL: Negotiating White English. In G. Braine (Ed.), *Non-native educators in English language teaching* (pp. 93–104). Mahwah, NJ: Lawrence Erlbaum Associates.

Appadurai, A. (1996). *Modernity at large: Cultural dimensions of globalization*. Minneapolis, MN: University of Minnesota Press.

Atkinson, D. (1999). TESOL and culture. *TESOL Quarterly, 33*, 625–654.

Atkinson, D. (2004). Contrasting rhetorics/contrasting cultures: Why contrastive rhetoric needs a better conceptualization of culture. *Journal of English for Academic Purposes, 3*, 277–289.

Auerbach, E. (2000). Creating participatory learning communities: Paradoxes and possibilities. In J. Hall & W. Eggington (Eds.), *The sociopolitics of English language teaching* (pp. 143–164). Clevedon: Multilingual Matters.

Austin, J. (1975). *How to do things with words*. Cambridge, MA: Harvard University Press.

Bakhtin, M. (1981). *The dialogic imagination*. Austin, TX: University of Texas Press.

Barthes, R. (1988). The death of the author. In D. Lodge (Ed.), *Modern criticism and theory* (pp. 166–172). New York: Longman.

Bazerman, C. (2004). Intertextuality: How texts rely on other texts. In C. Bazerman & P. Prior (Eds.), *What writing does and how it does it: An introduction to analyzing texts and textual practices* (pp. 83–96). Mahwah, NJ: Lawrence Erlbaum Associates.

Belsey, C. (1980). *Critical practice*. London: Methuen.

Belz, J. (2002). Second language play as a representation of the multicompetent self in foreign language study. *Journal of Language, Identity, and Education, 1*, 13–39.

Benesch, S. (1999). Thinking critically, thinking dialogically. *TESOL Quarterly, 33*, 573–580.

Benesch, S. (2001) *Critical English for academic purposes*. Mahwah, NJ: Lawrence Erlbaum Associates.

Bhabha, H. (1994). *The location of culture*. London: Routledge.

Bissoondath, N. (1994). *Selling illusions: The cult of multiculturalism in Canada*. Toronto: Penguin.

Blackledge, A. (2002). The discursive construction of national identity in multilingual Britain. *Journal of Language, Identity, and Education, 1*, 67–87.

Blackledge, A., & Pavlenko, A. (2001). Negotiation of identities in multilingual contexts. *International Journal of Bilingualism, 5*, 243–257.

Block, D. (2002). 'McCommunication': A problem in the frame for SLA. In D. Block & D. Cameron (Eds.), *Globalization and language teaching* (pp. 117–133). New York: Routledge.

Bourdieu, P. (1991). *Language and symbolic power* (G. Raymond & M. Adamson, Trans.). Cambridge, MA: Cambridge University Press.

Braine, G. (Ed.). (1999). *Non-native educators in English language teaching*. Mahwah, NJ: Lawrence Erlbaum.

Brown, H. (1986). Learning a second culture. In J. Valdes (Ed.), *Culture bound: Bridging the culture gap in language teaching* (pp. 33–48). New York: Cambridge University Press.

Brutt-Griffler, J. (2002). *World English: A study of its development*. Clevedon, UK: Multilingual Matters.

Butler, J. (1990). *Gender trouble: Feminism and the subversion of identity*. New York: Routledge.

Butler, J. (1992). Contingent foundations: Feminism and the question of "postmodernism." In J. Butler & J. Scott (Eds.), *Feminists theorize the political* (pp. 3–21). New York: Routledge.
Byram, M., & Fleming, M. (Eds.). (1998). *Language learning in intercultural perspective: Approaches through drama and ethnography*. Cambridge: Cambridge University Press.
Byram, M., & Risager, K. (1999). *Language teachers, politics and cultures*. Clevedon, UK: Multilingual Matters.
Cameron, D. (1997). Performing gender identity: Young men's talk and the construction of heterosexual masculinity. In S. Johnson & U. Meinhof (Eds.), *Language and masculinity* (pp. 47–64). Cambridge: Blackwell.
Cameron, D. (2002). Globalization and the teaching of 'communication skills'. In D. Block & D. Cameron (Eds.), *Globalization and language teaching* (pp. 67–82). New York: Routledge.
Canagarajah, A. S. (1999). *Resisting English imperialism in English language teaching*. Oxford: Oxford University Press.
Canagarajah, A. S. (2002). Reconstructing local knowledge. *Journal of Language, Identity, and Education, 1*, 243–259.
Canagarajah, A. S. (Ed.). (2005). *Reclaiming the local in language policy and practice*. Mahwah, NJ: Lawrence Erlbaum.
Candlin, C. (2000). [General editor's preface]. In B. Norton (Ed.), *Identity and language learning* (pp. xiii–xxi). London: Longman.
Chaika, E. (1994). *Language: The social mirror* (3rd ed.). Boston: Heinle & Heinle.
Carr, J. (2003). Culture through the looking glass: An intercultural experiment in sociolinguistics. In A. J. Liddicoat, S. Eisenchlas, & S. Trevaskes (Eds.), *Australian perspectives on internationalizing education* (pp. 75–86). Melbourne: Language Australia.
Casanave, C. P. (2004). *Controversies in second language writing: Dilemmas and decisions in research and instruction*. Ann Arbor, MI: University of Michigan Press.
Cherryholmes, C. (1988). *Power and criticism: Poststructuralist investigations in education*. New York: Teachers College Press.
Cherryholmes, C. (1993). Reading research. *Journal of Curriculum Studies, 25*, 1–32.
Connor, U. (1996). *Contrastive rhetoric: Cross-cultural aspects of second-language writing*. New York: Cambridge University Press.
Constas, M. (1998). The changing nature of educational research and a critique of postmodernism. *Educational Researcher, 27*(2), 26–33.
Cook, V. (1994). Universal grammar and the learning and teaching of second languages. In T. Odlin (Ed.), *Perspectives on pedagogical grammar* (pp. 25–47). Cambridge: Cambridge University Press.
Cooke, D. (1999). Contending discourses and ideologies: English and agency. *Language & Communication, 19*, 415–424.
Corbett, J. (2003). *An intercultural approach to English Language Teaching*. Clevedon, UK: Multilingual Matters.
Corson, D. (1997). Critical realism: An emancipatory philosophy for applied linguistics? *Applied Linguistics, 18*, 166–188.
Corson, D. (2001). *Language diversity and education*. Mahwah, NJ: Lawrence Erlbaum.
Corson, D. (2002). Teaching and learning for market-place utility. *International Journal of Leadership in Education. 1*, 1–13.
Courchêne, R. (1996). Teaching Canadian culture: Teacher preparation. *TESL Canada Journal, 13*(2), 1–16.
Culler, J. (1997). *Literary theory: A very short introduction*. New York: Oxford University Press.
Cummins, J. (2000). *Language, power and pedagogy: Bilingual children in the crossfire*. Clevedon, UK: Multilingual Matters.
Cummins, J. (2001). *Negotiating identities: Education for empowerment in a diverse Society* (2nd ed.). Ontario, CA: California Association of Bilingual Education.
Deleuze, G., & Guattari, F. (1986). *Nomadology: The war machine* (B. Massumi, Trans.). New York: Semiotext(e).
Derrida, J. (1982). *Margins of philosophy* (A. Bass, Trans.). Chicago, IL: University of Chicago Press.
Dicker, S. (2000). Official English and bilingual education: The controversy over language pluralism in U.S. society. In J. Hall & W. Eggington (Eds.), *The sociopolitics of English language teaching* (pp. 45–66). Clevedon, UK: Multilingual Matters.
Ehrlich, S. (1997). Gender as social practice: Implications for second language acquisition. *Studies in Second Language Acquisition, 19*, 421–446.
Fleming, D. (2003). Building personal and nation-state identities: Research and practice. *TESL Canada Journal, 20* (2), 65–79.

Foucault, M. (1980). *Power/knowledge: Selected interviews and other writings, 1972–1977*. New York: Pantheon.
Foucault, M. (1982). The subject and power. In H. Dreyfus & P. Rabinow (Eds.), *Beyond structuralism* (pp. 208–226). Chicago, IL: University of Chicago Press.
Foucault, M. (1997). Various works. In P. Rabinow (Ed.), *Michel Foucault: Ethics, subjectivity and truth*. New York: The New Press.
Freire, P. (1997). *Pedagogy of the oppressed*. New York: Continuum.
Gee, J. (1996). *Social linguistics and literacies: Ideologies in discourse*. London: Taylor & Francis.
Giltrow, J., & Colhoun, E. R. (1992). The culture of power: ESL traditions, Mayan resistance. In B. Burnaby & A. Cumming (Eds.), *The socio-political aspects of ESL* (pp. 50–66). Toronto, Ontario: OISE Press.
Giroux, H. (1994). Doing cultural studies: Youth and the challenge of pedagogy. *Harvard Educational Review, 64*, 278–308.
Goldstein, T. (2003). *Teaching and learning in a multilingual school*. Mahwah, NJ: Lawrence Erlbaum.
Grabe, W., Stoller, F., & Tardy, C. (2000). Disciplinary knowledge as a foundation for teacher preparation. In J. Hall & W. Eggington (Eds.), *The sociopolitics of English language teaching* (pp. 178–194). Clevedon, UK: Multilingual Matters.
Granger, C. A. (2004). *Silence in second language learning: A psychoanalytic reading*. Clevedon, UK: Multilingual Matters.
Gumperz, J. (1986). Interactional sociolinguistics in the study of schooling. In J. Cook-Gumperz (Ed.), *The social construction of literacy* (pp. 45–68). Cambridge, England: Cambridge University Press.
Hall, J. K. (2002). *Teaching and researching language and culture*. London: Pearson.
Hall, J. K, Vitanova, G., & Marchenkova, L. (Eds.). (2005). *Dialogue with Bakhtin on second and foreign language learning*. Mahwah, NJ: Lawrence Erlbaum.
Hall, K. (2002). Asserting 'needs' and claiming 'rights': The cultural politics of community language education in England. *Journal of Language, Identity, and Education, 1*, 97–119.
Harklau, L. (2000). From the 'good' kids to the 'worst': Representations of English language learners across educational settings. *TESOL Quarterly, 34*, 35–66.
Harklau, L. (2003). Representational practices and multi-modal communication in US high schools: Implications for adolescent immigrants. In R. Bayley & S. R. Schecter (Eds.), *Language socialization in bilingual and multilingual societies* (pp. 83–97). Clevedon, UK: Multilingual Matters.
Harris, R., Leung, C., & Rampton, B. (2002). Globalization, diaspora and language education in England. In D. Block & D. Cameron (Eds.), *Globalization and language teaching* (pp. 29–46). London: Routledge.
Heller, M. (2003). Globalization, the new economy, and the commodification of language and identity. *Journal of Sociolinguistics, 7*, 473–492.
Hinkel, E. (Ed.). (1999). *Culture in second language teaching and learning*. Cambridge: Cambridge University Press.
Holliday, A. (1994). *Appropriate methodology in social context*. Cambridge: Cambridge University Press.
Hornberger, N. (Ed.). (2003). *Continua of biliteracy: An ecological framework for educational policy, research, and practice in multilingual settings*. Clevedon, UK: Multilingual Matters.
Ibrahim, A. (1999). Becoming black: Rap and hip hop, race, gender, identity and the politics of ESL learning. *TESOL Quarterly, 33*, 349–370.
Ilieva, R. (2000). Exploring culture in texts designed for use in adult ESL classrooms. *TESL Canada Journal, 17*(2), 50–63.
Ivanič, R. (1998). *Writing and identity: The discoursal construction of identity in academic writing*. Amsterdam: John Benjamins.
Janks, H. (1997). Critical discourse analysis as a research tool. *Discourse, 18*, 329–342.
Johnston, B. (1999). The expatriate teacher as postmodern paladin. *Research in the Teaching of English, 34*, 255–280.
Johnston, B. (2003). *Values in English language teaching*. Mahwah, NJ: Lawrence Erlbaum Associates.
Kincheloe, J., & Steinberg, S. (1997). *Changing multiculturalism*. Philadelphia: Open University Press.
Knapp, K., & Meierkord, C. (Eds.). (2002). *Lingua franca communication*. Frankfurt am Main: Peter Lang.
Kramsch, C. (1993). *Context and culture in language teaching*. Oxford: Oxford University Press.
Kramsch, C. (1998). *Language and culture*. Oxford: Oxford University Press.
Kramsch, C. (2000). Global and local identities in the contact zone. In C. Gnutzmann (Ed.), *Teaching and learning English as a global language* (pp. 131–143). Tübingen, Germany: Stauffenberg Verlag.
Kress, G. (2003). *Literacy in the new media age*. London: Routledge.

Kubota, R. (1999). Japanese culture constructed by discourses: Implications for applied linguistics research and ELT. *TESOL Quarterly, 33*, 9–35.

Kubota, R. (2001). Discursive construction of the images of U.S. classrooms. *TESOL Quarterly, 35*, 9–38.

Kubota, R. (2004). Critical multiculturalism and second language education. In B.Norton & K. Toohey (Eds.), *Critical pedagogies in language learning* (pp. 30–52). Cambridge: Cambridge University Press.

Kumaravadivelu, B. (1999). Critical classroom discourse analysis. *TESOL Quarterly, 33*, 453–484.

Kumaravadivelu, B. (2003a). *Beyond methods: Macrostrategies for language teaching.* New Haven, CT: Yale University Press.

Kumaravadivelu, B. (2003b). Critical language pedagogy: A postmethod perspective on English language teaching. *World Englishes, 22*, 539–550.

Ladson-Billings, G. (1999). Just what is critical race theory, and what's it doing in a *nice* field like education? In L. Parker, D. Deyle, & S. Villenas (Eds.), *Race is-race isn't: Critical race theory and qualitative studies in education* (pp. 7–30). Boulder, CO: Westview Press.

Lantolf, J. (Ed.). (2000). *Sociocultural theory and second language learning.* New York: Oxford University Press.

Lather, P., & Ellsworth, E. (Eds.). (1996). Situated pedagogies—classroom practices in postmodern times. *Theory into Practice* [Special issue], *35*(2).

Lave, J., & Wenger, E. (1991). *Situated learning: Legitimate peripheral participation.* New York: Cambridge University Press.

Lin, A., & Luk, J. (2002). Beyond progressive liberalism and cultural relativism: Towards critical postmodernist, sociohistorically situated perspectives in ethnographic classroom studies. *Canadian Modern Language Review, 59*, 97–124.

Lin, A., Wang, W., Akamatsu, N., & Riazi, A. (2002). Appropriating English, expanding identities, and re-visioning the field: From TESOL to teaching English for glocalized communication (TEGCOM). *Journal of Language, Identity, and Education, 1*, 295–316.

Lynch, B. (1996). *Language program evaluation: Theory and practice.* Cambridge: Cambridge University Press.

Lynch, B. (2001). Rethinking assessment from a critical perspective. *Language Testing, 18*, 351–372.

Mair, C. (Ed.). (2003). *The politics of English as a world language: New horizons in postcolonial cultural studies.* Amsterdam: Rodopi.

MacPherson, S., Turner, D., Khan, R., Hingley, W., Tigchelaar, A., & Lafond, L. D. (2004). ESL and Canadian multiculturalism: Multilingual, intercultural practices for the 21st Century. *TESL Canada Journal, Special Issue 4*, 1–22.

May, S. (Ed.). (1999). *Critical multiculturalism: Rethinking multicultural and anti-racist education.* London: Falmer Press.

McKay, S. L. (2000). Teaching English as an international language: Implications for cultural materials in the classroom. *TESOL Journal, 9*(4), 7–11.

McNamara, T. (1997). What do we mean by social identity? Competing frameworks, competing discourses. *TESOL Quarterly, 33*, 561–567.

Moran, P. (2001). *Teaching culture: Perspectives in practice.* Scarborough, Ontario: Nelson/Thomson Learning.

Morgan, B. (1998). *The ESL classroom: Teaching, critical practice, and community development.* Toronto: University of Toronto Press.

Morgan, B. (2002). Critical practice in community-based ESL programs: A Canadian perspective. *Journal of Language, Identity, and Education, 1*, 141–162.

Morgan, B. (2004a). Teacher identity as pedagogy: Towards a field-internal conceptualization in bilingual and second language education. *International Journal of Bilingual Education and Bilingualism, 7*, 172–188.

Morgan, B. (2004b). Modals and memories: A grammar lesson on the Quebec referendum on sovereignty. In B. Norton & K. Toohey (Eds.), *Critical pedagogies and language learning* (pp. 158–178). Cambridge: Cambridge University Press.

Morgan, C., & Cain, A. (2000). *Foreign language and culture learning from a dialogic perspective.* Clevedon: Multilingual Matters.

Nelson, C. (1999). Sexual identities in ESL: Queer theory and classroom inquiry. *TESOL Quarterly, 33*, 371–391.

Nelson, C. (2002). Why queer theory is useful in teaching: A perspective from English as a second language teaching. In K. H. Robinson, J. Irwin, & T. Ferfolja (Eds.), *From here to diversity: The social impact of lesbian and gay issues in education in Australia and New Zealand* (pp. 43–53). Binghamton, NY: Harrington Park Press.

Nieto, S. (2002). *Language, culture, and teaching: Critical perspectives for a new century*. Mahwah, NJ: Lawrence Erlbaum Associates.
Norris, C. (1982). *Deconstruction: Theory and practice*. New York: Methuen.
Norton Peirce, B. (1995). Social identity, investment, and language learning. *TESOL Quarterly, 29*, 9–30.
Norton, B. (1997). Language, identity, and the ownership of English. *TESOL Quarterly, 31*, 409–429.
Norton, B. (2000). *Identity and language learning: Gender, ethnicity and educational change*. London: Longman.
Norton, B., & Toohey, K. (2001). Changing perspectives on good language learners. *TESOL Quarterly, 35*, 307–322.
Norton, B., & Toohey, K. (Eds.). (2004). *Critical pedagogies and language learning*. Cambridge: Cambridge University Press.
Pakir, A. (2000). The developments of English as a 'glocal' language: New concerns in the old saga of language teaching. In H.W. Kam & C. Ward (Eds.), *Language in the global context: Implications for the language classroom* (pp. 14–31). Singapore: SEAMO Regional Language Centre.
Pavlenko, A. (2002). Poststructuralist approaches to the study of social factors in second language learning and use. In V. Cook (Ed.), *Portraits of the L2 user* (pp. 277–302). Clevedon, UK: Multilingual Matters.
Pavlenko, A., & Blackledge, A. (Eds.). (2004). *Negotiation of identities in multilingual contexts*. Clevedon, UK: Multilingual Matters.
Pavlenko, A., & Piller, I. (2001). New directions in the study of multilingualism, second language learning and gender. In A. Pavlenko, A. Blackledge, I. Piller, & M. Teutsch-Dwyer (Eds.), *Multilingualism, second language learning, and gender* (pp. 17–52). Berlin: Mouton de Gruyter.
Pennycook, A. (1997). Cultural alternatives and autonomy. In P. Benson & P. Voller (Eds.), *Autonomy and independence in language learning* (pp. 35–53). London: Longman.
Pennycook, A. (1998). *English and the discourses of colonialism*. New York: Routledge.
Pennycook, A. (2001). *Critical applied linguistics: A critical introduction*. Mahwah, NJ: Lawrence Erlbaum.
Pennycook, A. (2004). Performativity and language studies. *Critical Inquiry in Language Studies, 1*, 1–20.
Perry, T., & Delpit, L. (Eds.). (1998). *The real Ebonics debate: Power, language and the education of African-American children*. Boston: Beacon Press.
Poynton, C. (1993). Grammar, language and the social: Poststructuralism and systemic-functional linguistics. *Social Semiotics, 3*, 1–21.
Price, S. (1999). Critical discourse analysis: Discourse acquisition and discourse practices. *TESOL Quarterly, 33*, 581–595.
Ramanathan, V. (2002). *The politics of TESOL education: Writing, knowledge, critical pedagogy*. New York: Routledge Falmer.
Ramanathan, V. (2005). *The English-vernacular divide: Postcolonial language politics and practice*. Clevedon, UK: Multilingual Matters.
Rampton, B. (1995). *Crossing: Language and ethnicity among adolescents*. London: Longman.
Reagan, T. G., & Osborn, T. A. (2002). *The foreign language educator in society: Toward a critical pedagogy*. Mahwah, NJ: Lawrence Erlbaum.
Roberts, C., Byram, M., Barro, A., Jordan, S., & Street, B. (2001). *Language learners as ethnographers*. Clevedon, UK: Multilingual Matters.
Ronowicz, E., & Yallop, C. (Eds.). (1999). *English: One language, different cultures*. New York: Cassell.
Rosenau, P. (1992). *Postmodernism and the social sciences: Insights, inroads, and intrusions*. Princeton, NJ: Princeton University Press.
Rouse, J. (1994). Power/Knowledge. In G. Gutting (Ed.), *The Cambridge companion to Foucault* (pp. 92–114). New York: Cambridge University Press.
Said, E. (1978). *Orientalism*. New York: Random House.
Sarap, M. (1993). *An introductory guide to post-structuralism and postmodernism* (2nd ed.). Athens, GA: University of Georgia Press.
Sauvé, V. (2000). *Issues, challenges and alternatives in teaching adult ESL*. Don Mills, Ontario: Oxford University Press.
Schecter, R. S., & Bailey, R. (2002). *Language as cultural practice: Mexicanos en el norte*. Mahwah, NJ: Lawrence Erlbaum.
Scholes, R. (1985). *Textual power*. New Haven: Yale University Press.
Scollon, R., & Wong Scollon, S. (1995). *Intercultural communication: A discourse approach*. Malden, MA: Blackwell.

Shea, C. (1998). Critical and constructive postmodernism: The transformative power of holistic education. In H. Shapiro & D. Purpel (Eds.), *Critical social issues in American education: Transformation in a postmodern world* (2nd ed.) (pp. 337–354). Mahwah, NJ: Lawrence Erlbaum.

Simon, R. (1992). *Teaching against the grain.* Toronto: OISE Press.

Sower, C. (1999). Postmodern applied linguistics: Problems and contradictions. *TESOL Quarterly, 33,* 736–745.

Starfield, S. (2002). 'I'm a second-language English speaker': Negotiating writer identity and authority in Sociology One. *Journal of Language, Identity, and Education, 1,* 121–140.

Street, B. (1993). Culture is a verb: Anthropological aspects of language and cultural process. In D. Graddol, L. Thompson, & M. Byram (Eds.), *Language and culture* (pp. 23–43). Clevedon, UK: BAAL and Multilingual Matters.

Stein, P. (2004). Representation, rights, and resources: Multimodal pedagogies in language and literacy. In B. Norton & K. Toohey (Eds.), *Critical pedagogies and language learning* (pp. 95–115). Cambridge: Cambridge University Press.

Tajfel, H. (1974). Social identity and intergroup behavior. *Social Science Information, 13,* 65–93.

Terdiman, R. (1985). *Discourse/counter-discourse.* Ithaca, NY: Cornell University Press.

Toohey, K. (2000). *Learning English at school: Identity, social relations and classroom practice.* Clevedon: Multilingual Matters.

Valdes, J. (Ed.). (1986). *Culture bound: Bridging the culture gap in language teaching.* New York: Cambridge University Press.

Vandrick, S. (1999). ESL and the colonial legacy: A teacher faces her 'missionary kid' past. In G. Haroian-Guerin (Ed.), *The personal narrative: Writing ourselves as teachers and scholars* (pp. 63–74). Portland, ME: Calendar Islands Publishers.

Varghese, M. (2004). Professional development for bilingual teachers in the United States: A site for articulating and contesting professional roles. *International Journal of Bilingual Education and Bilingualism, 7,* 222–237.

Varghese, M., Morgan, B., Johnston, B., & Johnson, K. (2005). Theorizing language teacher identity: Three perspectives and beyond. *Journal of Language, Identity, and Education, 4,* 21–44.

Walkerdine, V. (1997). Redefining the subject in situated cognition theory. In D. Kirshner & J. Whitson (Eds.), *Situated cognition: Social, semiotic, and psychological perspectives* (pp. 57–70). Mahwah, NJ: Lawrence Erlbaum.

Widdowson, H. (1980). Models and fictions. *Applied Linguistics, 1,* 165–170.

Williams, C. H. (1998). Introduction: Representing the citizens—reflections on language policy in Canada and the United States. In T. Ricento & B. Burnaby (Eds.), *Language and politics in the United States and Canada* (pp. 1–32). Mahwah, NJ: Lawrence Erlbaum Associates.

Weedon, C. (1987). *Feminist practice & poststructuralist theory.* New York: Basil Blackwell.

Wells, G. (1999). *Dialogic inquiry.* Cambridge: Cambridge University Press.

Wong, S. (2000). Transforming the politics of schooling in the U.S.: A model for successful academic achievement for language minority students. In J. Hall & W. Eggington (Eds.), *The sociopolitics of English language teaching* (pp. 117–139). Clevedon, UK: Multilingual Matters.

Young, R. (1996). *Intercultural communication: Pragmatics, genealogy, deconstruction.* Clevedon, UK: Multilingual Matters.

Zamel, V. (1997). Towards a model of transculturation. *TESOL Quarterly, 31,* 341–352.

CHAPTER 64

WHAT SHAPES TEACHERS' PROFESSIONAL DEVELOPMENT?

AMY B.M. TSUI

The University of Hong Kong, China

ABSTRACT

Studies of teachers' professional development have identified phases or sequences that teachers go through in the course of their careers. Some of the commonly identified phases are an initial survival and exploration phase, a stabilization phase if the experience in the previous phase is positive, or a phase of self-doubt if the experience is negative, an experimentation and diversification phase in which they are highly motivated to try out new ideas and increase their impact inside as well as beyond the classroom, a phase of reassessment if they are disappointed with the outcome, and a phase of serenity in which teachers come to terms with themselves. These phases of development, however, are not linear. Teachers move in and out of phases because of a number of factors such as personal experiences, social environment and organizational influences. This chapter reports on a case study of one ESL teacher and the factors and sources of influence that have shaped her professional development. It discusses the implications of the findings for teacher education.

INTRODUCTION

Studies of teachers' professional development have identified phases that teachers go through in the course of their careers (see Fessler and Christensen, 1992; Huberman, 1993a). Typically, beginning teachers go through a "survival" phase in which they are pre-occupied with coping with the multi-faceted nature of their work in the classroom. This phase is also a phase of "discovery" where teachers are excited by the fact that they are now a teacher with their own students. The survival and discovery elements often go together. Huberman (1993a) refers to this phase as "exploration" (p. 5). Positive experiences in the first phase usually lead to a phase of "stabilization" where teachers consolidate their experience, become more concerned about the impact of their instructions on students, more flexible, and able to handle the unpredictable. Negative experience in this phase, however, could lead to a phase of self-doubt.

Following the stabilization phase, some teachers go through a phase of "experimentation" and "diversification" (Huberman, 1993b). They begin to experiment with new ideas for teaching to enhance the effectiveness of their teaching. They have a heightened awareness of problems with the system and a desire to go beyond their own schools to bring about change. However, the lack of impact of their efforts on the system could lead to disillusionment and a phase of self-doubt about their commitment to teaching (see Sikes, Measor and Woods, 1985). Factors like the monotony of classroom teaching and unpleasant working conditions could also lead to a phase of self-doubt. Huberman (1993b) refers to this phase as "reassessment". A phase of uncertainty or even a crisis could lead to another phase where teachers come to terms with themselves and hence have more peace of mind. This is a phase of "serenity" (Huberman, p.10), which is marked by a decline in professional investment and enthusiasm on the one hand, and by greater confidence, more tolerance and spontaneity in the classroom on the other.

Near the end of teachers' career cycles, a phase of "disengagement" can be identified. The disengagement can take the form of withdrawing and investing their time and effort elsewhere, as a result of disappointment with the system, or reconciling the discrepancy between what they had set out to achieve and what they have actually achieved.

The phases of development outlined above, however, are not linear. Studies have found that teachers go through the phases in different sequences and they also move in and out of the various phases (Sprinthall, Reiman, and Sprinthall, 1996). The questions that this chapter addresses are: What are the factors that shape teachers' professional development? What might contribute to teachers' moving in and out of a certain phase? Why are some teachers able to maintain their professional growth and become expert teachers whereas other teachers remain very much experienced non-experts? What implications do answers to these questions have for teacher education?

TEACHERS' PROFESSIONAL DEVELOPMENT AND CONTRIBUTING FACTORS

Research on teachers' professional growth has identified a number of possible factors and sources of influence that shape teachers' developmental path. One often mentioned factor is the "apprenticeship of observation" (Lortie, 1975). It refers to the experience of being taught as a student, which provides teachers with an image of what teaching is and should be like. This source of influence is particularly strong for teachers who join the profession without professional training (see also Brookhart and Freeman, 1992; Bullough, Knowles and Crow, 1992; Calderhead and Robson, 1991).

Another factor is the context of work. There is a complex interaction between the beliefs and values held by individual teachers and those held by the institution (see Calderhead and Shorrock, 1997; Johnson, 1996). The latter has a powerful "wash out effect"; they often eradicate what teachers have learnt in their professional training courses (Zeichner and Gore, 1990). However, school contexts in which teachers are able to pursue their values through their work and feel professionally rewarded can have a very positive effect on teachers' professional development (Huberman and Vandengerhe, 1999).

A third factor is teachers' own teaching experience. Teachers consider classroom experience the most important source of knowledge about teaching (Lanier and Little, 1986) and have gained immensely rich practical knowledge about teaching through practical classroom teaching (Elbaz, 1983). A fourth factor is the personal life experience of teachers that shape their 'substantial self' (Nias, 1984), which is the person that they bring into the classroom context. Beginning teachers often enter pre-service courses with partial but firmly held conceptions of themselves as teachers and a teaching schema which is developed over years of life experience. These conceptions not only influence the way they begin to teach, but also act as life-long references for their identity as teachers (see Goodson, 1991).

Finally, the professional training that teachers have had, or have not had, is a powerful factor. Despite the criticisms of teacher education courses as being ineffective, studies of the interrelationship between teacher education courses and teachers' beliefs and classroom practices have shown the former to be an important contributing factor (see Grossman, 1990; Borg, 1998).

To summarize, the factors that play an important part in shaping teachers' conceptions of teaching and learning include their personal background and life experiences, their disciplinary training, their teaching and learning experiences, and their professional training, if they have any. These conceptions have a powerful influence on the way teachers make sense of their work. They may be changed or modified as teachers gain experience or as they encounter critical incidents that challenge them. They may also be very resistant to change. The interaction between teachers' conceptions of teaching and learning and their world of practice is an important dimension that should be taken into consideration in understanding teachers' professional development.

In the rest of this chapter, I shall present the findings of a case study of the professional development of an experienced and highly competent ESL teacher, Marina, who would be referred to as an "expert teacher" in the expertise literature (Berliner, 1994). I shall discuss the phases of professional development that Marina went through, and the factors that shaped her development. The implications of the findings for teacher education will be discussed. The case study reported in this chapter is part of four detailed qualitative case studies conducted with ESL teachers in one Hong Kong school over an eighteen month period, all exploring the development of expertise in teaching. For the methodology used in the case study reported in this chapter, see Tsui (2003).

MARINA

Marina was in her early 30s when the study started and in her eighth year of teaching. She comes from a working class family and studied in a primary school in a working class housing estate. Her academic results were outstanding and she won a government scholarship in the public examination for secondary school entrance. She recalled having a teacher who was very kind to her and gave her a great deal of help. She said, "I had a teacher who was very nice to me. She was not a good teacher; she used mixed code,[1] but she helped me." Because of her excellent results, she entered one of the most prestigious secondary schools in Hong Kong, St. John's, where the majority of the students came from middle-class families and the medium of instruction and communication was English, even in school assemblies. The first two years in this school were "very tough" for Marina. She had great difficulties learning through English in the first few months, and her confidence was seriously undermined. To improve her English, she borrowed books from the school library and read voraciously. Reflecting on her secondary schooling, she observed that although it took her only several months to get used to English medium instruction, it took her several years to rebuild her self-confidence.

Marina did not have an English environment at home; her parents do not speak English. Apart from reading voraciously, she tried to maximize opportunities for learning English by paying attention to the English around her, including the media, posters, labels, signage, and so on. She said, "to survive in St. John's, I have to work on my English." Marina's struggle for survival at St. John's had a strong influence on her conception of learning English and the strategies that she developed for teaching English.

After St. John's, Marina entered the University of Hong Kong and took translation as her major discipline. Teaching had always been her aspiration since she was a child. Her image of a teacher was that he or she should be a figure of authority but kind to students. Marina did not go into teaching immediately after graduation because she felt that she needed more work experience in other settings. After working in the civil service for a year and in a hospital for another year, she joined St. Peter's as an English teacher.

In the following sections, I shall present the phases of professional development that Marina went through. We shall see how her life experiences and learning experiences impacted on Marina's development. We shall also see what other factors have come into play.

PROFESSIONAL DEVELOPMENT OF MARINA

Phase I: Learning Teaching

Surviving in the Classroom and Relating to Students

In the first 2 years of teaching, classroom management and relationship with students were two recurring concerns for Marina. Like all new teachers, she found it difficult to handle the multiple dimensions of classroom teaching and to exercise her judgment on when to be lenient and when to be strict. She simply followed the golden rule of "don't smile till Christmas" (Calderhead, 1984). However, this approach went against her personality and she was caught in a dilemma. After the first year of teaching, Marina was still unable to maintain what she considered to be good discipline in the classroom. She decided to be "more firm" and "more serious" so that the class would not "get out of control."

Being very strict with students "worked" for Marina: she was able to keep the students under control. However, her inflexibility in imposing penalty on students who broke the rules generated resentment among some students. On reflection, she felt that she was too strict and unable to see things from the students' perspectives. The problem of classroom management and handling her relationship with students persisted in her second year of teaching.

Making Learning Fun and Interesting

Contrary to managing students, in teaching methods, Marina was able to see things from her students' perspective even in her 1st year of teaching. In the first 2 years, she was engaged in "explorations" of ways to improve her teaching: how to make learning fun. Going into teaching without professional preparation, Marina relied heavily on the way she was taught, that is, what Lortie (1975) refers to as the "apprenticeship of observation." Her English teachers in her secondary school frequently involved students in activities. Therefore, she felt that "learning English didn't mean that the teacher had to do all the talking. Students should be involved." She also picked up the concept of working on tasks from her former teachers, "I feel that students need to produce things. We must give them the opportunity to work together, to produce."

Another source of influence was her German teacher at the Goethe Institute when she was an undergraduate. She recounted:

> I had a very good German teacher ... His methods were very communicative. There was a lot of talking, pair work, group work, discussion and he was very funny. If students spoke very softly, he would open a (Chinese) paper fan, which meant "speak louder". For teaching intonation, he brought a musical instrument. He had a lot of influence on me. When I started teaching, I borrowed a lot of his methods.

Apart from communicative language teaching, Marina also learnt how to teach grammar systematically from her German teacher. From her own experience of learning German, she is convinced that one can learn a foreign language without using the mother tongue. Therefore, in her classroom, students are not allowed to speak a word of Cantonese or to use mixed code.

In addition to relying on her past experiences, Marina paid attention to anything related to teaching. She often went to seminars and attended extramural courses offered by universities on specific teaching skills like reading, pronunciation, and vocabulary. She bought a lot of reference books and resource books on teaching. She felt that this was necessary because the school culture was very supportive of change and the teachers were keen to try out new ideas in their own teaching. These references and resource books gave her many good ideas for teaching and she was fully engaged in experimenting with different activities and different pedagogical designs.

The first phase of her development, which consists of the first 3 years of teaching, was a phase in which Marina experienced difficulties in reconciling her image of a teacher as a figure of authority but at the same time as being kind and caring to the students. It was a phase in which her experimentation with various ideas in teaching gave her immense satisfaction, especially when she saw students enjoying the lessons and making progress.

Phase II: Self-doubt and Reassessment

Marina was not happy about managing classroom discipline by fear. She said, "They would listen to you, and would do what you asked them to, but that doesn't mean they were willing to learn." At the end of the third year, despite her efforts, Marina felt that she was still unable to stamp out disciplinary problems. She was very frustrated and wanted to quit teaching to pursue further study in librarianship overseas. Though there were several reasons that made her change her mind, such as her family circumstances, the most important factor was the support that she received from her principal, who was the vice principal at that time. She said, "(She) has given me a lot of support. That was very important ... she cared about me." The school culture and the support system for new teachers established by the school were also important factors. The school has a double form-mistress (class teacher) system, in which a new teacher teams up with an experienced teacher to look after a class, as well as the provision of pastoral care for new teachers.

In her first year of teaching, Marina teamed up with her principal (then vice-principal) as form-mistresses. She received a great deal of help from her principal, particularly in settling disputes with students, and they became very good friends.

The moral support from her colleagues, her principal, and a collegial working environment helped her to make the decision to stay on. This phase of self-doubt and uncertainty about her commitment to teaching did not last very long. She told herself, "This is not the end of the world," and she moved on.

Phase III: Understanding and Mastering Teaching

Marina's decision to stay on marked a turning point in her developmental path. When describing her own development, Marina repeatedly referred to the fourth year as the turning point when she began to really deal with disciplinary problems and to see things from the students' perspective. It was also in the fourth year that she decided to make teaching her career and enrolled in an in-service professional qualification program, the Postgraduate Certificate in Education (PCED) Program, at the university. The PCEd program confirmed a lot of her own practices and provided the rationale for them. For example, she had been using communicative activities, but she did not understand the rationale behind these activities until she attended the PCEd program. She had always felt the need to distinguish between teaching and testing, and the PCEd program reaffirmed her belief. Aspects of language teaching that she was not aware of were introduced in the program, for example, discourse analysis and text analysis and their applications in teaching, the purpose of group work, and so on.

Apart from instructional practices in the classroom, the PCEd program also helped her to understand wider educational issues: for example, why streaming could have a negative effect on students, what contributed to students' sense of failure, and why it is important to see things from the students' perspective, to empathize, and to think positively. Positive thinking is something that she often referred to as an important element when she talked about teaching and about her colleagues. What she learnt from the program helped her not only in her relationship with students but also in coping with stress and depression.

This phase, which consists of the fourth and fifth years of teaching, was a period when Marina, having had 3 years' of teaching behind her, had built up a repertoire of instructional practices. She was able to draw on this repertoire in her teaching, thus allowing her time to explore new ideas, to "tinker" with her existing practices (Huberman, 1993b, p. 112), and to think about wider educational issues.

Phase IV: Taking on a New Role

In the fifth year, Marina was appointed Panel Chair of the English Panel (the equivalent of the head of English Department in a school in the UK). She accepted the appointment on the basis that she had already been an assistant to the English Panel Chair for two years. Her understanding of the responsibilities of a panel chair at the time was carrying out routine duties and administrative chores. Gradually she realized that the role of a panel chair was far more demanding than that. She did not like the job because she found administrative duties very time-consuming and dealing with personnel problems very unpleasant. She felt that her time would be better spent on teaching than on administration.

In the sixth year, Marina completed her professional training and was promoted to Senior Graduate Mistress, a rank above the initial teaching grade of university graduates. She had had one year behind her as English panel chair. She began to move from just handling administrative chores to involving the whole English panel to make changes to their teaching. She started small. One initiative was to get teachers to specify teaching objectives in the scheme of work, something she learnt in the PCEd program. Another initiative was to introduce the teaching of phonetics in oral English lessons. Phonetics was not widely nor systematically taught in schools at the time. She found that many of the students were tongue-tied in class not because they did not know the words but because they could not pronounce them. She felt that if students learnt the phonetic symbols, they would have a self-learning tool and they could figure out the pronunciation of new words themselves by looking up the phonetic transcriptions in the dictionary. In other words, instead of making a host of drastic changes, Marina focused on only changes which were manageable and which were much needed. The process of getting her fellow teachers to introduce phonetics teaching made her realize that as a panel chair, she could bring about change not only in her own teaching but also in other teachers'. However, she was not able to theorize her role until she attended a refresher course for panel chairs in the following year.

Phase V: Opportunities for Reflection

In the second half of the sixth year, Marina obtained leave for half a year to attend a government-funded refresher course for panel chairs. In this course, she was introduced to the concept of the panel chair as "an agent of change" for the first time. She identified with the concept immediately because she felt that she had already been playing the role of a change agent, though she was not able to articulate her role as such. An awareness of her role as a change agent helped her to formulate her goals for attending the course, which were as follows: "to streamline the work of the panel so everyone has breathing space to reflect on their teaching," "to think of a more systematic program for staff development," and "to explore means to promote independent learning." She also had the opportunity to read up on references on educational change and teacher development, and to reflect on her own development. After reading Grossman's book *The Making of a Teacher* (1990), she wrote the following in her reflective journal:

> This [Grossman's book] reminds me of my first few years of teaching. I didn't do the PCEd until the fourth year of my teaching profession. The reliance on past experiences was predominantly heavy, particularly in the first few months of teaching. Luckily, I came from a background where drama, role-play and discussions were the norm. The greatest influence on my style and approaches of teaching was the school culture. It was a time when St. Peter's was still having the pilot scheme and everyone was expected to select, adapt and evaluate teaching materials. When I did the PCEd course, I found that the methods recommended were in line with the approaches I adopted. In retrospect, wasn't that staff development? One of the objectives that I set in attending this course was to think of a more systematic program to help staff development. I began to see one way of achieving this goal is to engage my colleagues in school-based materials development.

Marina decided to get teachers involved in school-based materials development as a milieu for professional development. She zeroed in on the teaching and marking of compositions. She read up on writing and sent messages to TeleNex, an English teacher support website, to discuss her ideas and to consult teachers in other schools.

Though Marina was absorbing new input like a sponge in the refresher course, she had problems relating theory to practice, especially in the management of a subject panel. She learnt that for teachers to be committed, it was important to give them a sense of ownership by letting them take on responsibilities. However, she was not able to resolve the dilemma between delegating responsibilities and overburdening teachers with responsibilities. She felt that apart from assigning duties, she needed to give her teachers something more, but she was not clear exactly what that something was.

Spending half a year away from the classroom to attend the refresher course was critical to her professional development. It gave her the opportunity to obtain new professional input, to become aware of bigger educational policy issues, and, more importantly, to reflect on her work and her new role in the school and beyond. Marina graduated from the refresher course with new insights, but at the same time, with unresolved questions.

Phase VI: Reinvesting Resources

Seeking More Professional Input

Attending the refresher course made Marina crave for more. A year after she resumed teaching, she enrolled in a part-time master's program on Teaching of English as Foreign Language (TEFL). The program provided the theoretical bases of her work. For example, she was able to evaluate textbooks in a principled manner; she had a better understanding of group work as a means of getting students to engage in the negotiation of meaning; and she was not only able to distinguish between poorly designed and well-designed grammar activities, but also to articulate the reasons.

Doing a master's program was very tough for Marina. She often had to stay up very late to do her assignments and often had only one or two hours of sleep. Her students knew about this and called her "superwoman." So did her colleagues. Marina did extremely well in the course, often getting top grades for her assignments. She chose topics that were related to her teaching tasks and addressed issues that were pertinent to her context of work.

Exploring the Role of a Panel Chair

Marina had a different understanding of her role as panel chair after completing the refresher course. She no longer saw herself as merely carrying out administrative chores, but as steering the direction of the panel and helping staff members to develop professionally. However, as mentioned before, Marina was faced with the dilemma of setting targets and goals for them and not putting too much pressure on them. She said, "My colleagues are already exhausted; I just do not have the heart to push anything more down their throats." She did not have any formal plans for staff development. For those who were teaching the same level as her, she felt that she could do a lot more by sharing materials and discussing their teaching with them. Generally, she adopted "a personal approach" by talking to teachers individually.

An important aspect of the work of a panel chair is quality assurance. In her school, one quality assurance mechanism was lesson observations of new staff members. At first, Marina did not think there was much use in doing this because she felt that she would not be able to see what the teacher was really like behind closed doors. Instead of just rejecting the practice, she consulted the History panel chair. He pointed out to her that the lesson observation would enable her to see what a teacher could achieve. After observing some lessons, she encountered the problem of providing feedback to teachers whose lessons did not go well. Instead of telling them their weaknesses, she invited them to observe her teach and she also asked them to observe good models of teaching. Marina's willingness to open her classroom to anybody at any time changed the nature of lesson observation. It was no longer a quality assurance mechanism but an opportunity for learning. It also enhanced the culture of collegiality and collaborative learning.

Another quality assurance measure was the checking of the grading of homework and compositions by the panel chair. At first she focused on whether teachers made mistakes in marking and whether they were able to pick out students' mistakes. However, as she learnt more about genres and genre structures, she turned her attention to the students' writing – whether the style and genre were appropriate to the writing task, and how teachers could help students to improve. In the process of exploring of her role as panel chair, quality assurance was reinterpreted by Marina from monitoring to mentoring.

Phase VII: Taking on the Challenge—Adopting the Process Approach to Writing

The six-month refresher course gave Marina time to step back from her teaching and to ask questions about existing practices. In Bereiter and Scardamalia's (1993) words, it enabled her to problematize routines and asked questions about practices that had been taken for granted. In particular, it provided her with the opportunity to seek answers in an area that had troubled her for a long time - the inordinate amount of time spent on grading compositions and the lack of impact that this had on students' writing. She questioned whether the product approach to writing gave students opportunities to explore interesting ideas and to be creative in writing. She read up on the teaching of writing, for example Harris's (1994) *Introducing Writing*, and White and Arndt's (1991) *Process Writing*. She found the ideas useful because they corroborated her own experience of having to go through several drafts whenever she produces a piece of written work.

After a year's incubation, Marina embarked on a major experimentation with the process approach to writing in the eighth year. She started with junior forms. The experimentation took place throughout the whole school year where all staff members teaching S1 to S3 (Grades 7 to 9) were involved, some to a fuller extent than others. (For a detailed account of the implementation, see Chapter 9 in Tsui, 2003.) In a panel meeting in which the teachers reviewed the effectiveness of the implementation (a meeting in which I participated), it was clear that there was marked improvement in students' writing. The meeting ended with the teachers in high spirits and unanimously agreeing that the tryout was a success and a move in the right direction.

Looking back at the changes that she introduced, Marina felt that she was lucky to have colleagues who supported her whenever she introduced changes. Marina attributed this mainly to the school culture, which was collegial and supportive of collaborative endeavors to bring about change. The way she played her role as panel chair was an important factor as well. She said, "I try to be supportive and give my colleagues as much help as I can, like sharing good resources and ideas. I also show appreciation for their hard work. I try not to be bossy and I don't put on airs. My colleagues feel that I'll stand up for them and fight for them when necessary."

Marina also tried to be reasonable in the demands that she made on the teachers. When she initiated process writing, she was very much aware of the extra work that needed to go into grading students' multiple drafts. She persuaded the school authority to be flexible about the number of compositions that they required the teachers to give students each school year[2]. She avoided a top-down approach when introducing innovative practices. She tried them out first and invited colleagues to observe how she implemented them in her own classrooms. There was a great deal of informal sharing of ideas that she felt was very useful in changing beliefs.

Reflecting on her own professional development, Marina saw three broad stages. She said:

> The 1st year is a stage when I was very green. (I) didn't know what was going on. I just observed and followed others. The 2nd to the 4th year, I was already developing my own style of teaching. From the second year onwards, I used a lot more group work in teaching, which was (a) more active (style of teaching). It was a period when I learned how to handle students. The years following up to now (that is, from the fourth year onwards) ... I have entered a stage in which I am not just responsible for my own teaching, but I also have to give advice to other colleagues. I think I will divide it (her professional development) into these 3 broad stages.

DISCUSSION

From the above account of Marina's professional development, we can see how the factors and sources of influence outlined at the beginning of this chapter have shaped her developmental path. As Huberman (1993a) points out, the phases of professional development that an individual goes through, the ways in which these phases take shape, and the sequence in which they occur are very much dependent on the factors that come into play in the individual's professional life. In the case of Marina, it is clear that factors such as personal life experiences, learning experiences, teaching experiences, professional training, and the context of work figured prominently in her developmental path.

Marina entered teaching with a personal conception of teaching and learning. Her image of a teacher as having authority but kind and caring to students was shaped by her primary school experience. This served as a reference for her as she explored her role as a teacher (see Bullough et al., 1992). Being able to reconcile the seemingly conflicting qualities in her image of a teacher was one of the landmarks in her developmental path. She is no longer a figure of authority that has control over her students. She is described by her students as a teacher who is "totally integrated with the students," as well as one whom they respect and from who they can learn a lot. Marina said, "I can feel my own development through my relationship with my students."

Her conception of what language learning involves was shaped by her own learning experiences. The latter were the bases on which she formulated her personal practical theories of teaching. Going from a working-class housing estate school to a very prestigious middle-class school and having to struggle for survival in that school had a strong influence on her personal beliefs about learning in general and English language learning in particular. Reading and maximizing the available resources for learning English figured importantly in her teaching (for detailed accounts of Marina's teaching, see Chapters 6 and 7 in Tsui, 2003). Moreover, her struggle for survival influenced her personal belief in the importance of maximizing time for learning. This was reflected in her insistence on punctuality in attending classes, both for herself and her students, so that full use can be made of the time allocated to one lesson[3]. Her English and German learning experiences shaped her teaching style and approach.

The professional input that she obtained from various sources, and the integration of theory and her own learning experiences helped her to understand and to master teaching. The master's program that she was attending when the study was conducted provided the theoretical motivation for her practices and stimulated her to probe more deeply into questions relating to students' learning, the curriculum, and language policy. While her learning experiences helped her to develop techniques and strategies for teaching, the professional and theoretical input that she obtained helped her to theorize her practices.

The school context in which she worked and the way she responded to it played a crucial part in her professional development. On the one hand, she was able to benefit from a supportive, caring, and collaborative school culture, which helped her to move out of the phase of self-doubt and become a committed teacher. On the other hand, her positive responses were very much part of the school culture that shaped her own professional development as well as that of the teachers on the English panel.

In studying the factors predictive of career satisfaction, Huberman (1993b) found that teachers who engaged in classroom-level experimentation were more likely to be satisfied with their career later on than those who were heavily involved in structural reforms. Furthermore, Huberman (1993b) found that "recurring episodes in which the demands of the situation are slightly beyond one's existing repertoire" are crucial for professional development (p.112). He observed that career satisfaction was high "…when teachers felt 'pushed' or 'stretched' beyond their customary activity formats or materials and met this challenge through systematic revisions of their instruction repertoire" (p.113). Huberman's observations echo Bereiter and Scardamalia's (1993) theory of the development of expertise in all professions, including teaching. According to them, experts are those who work at the edge of their competence. It is when they refuse to get into a rut and go beyond the "customary" that their performance becomes exemplary. This view is shared by Ericsson and Smith (1991), who point out that "one should be particularly careful about accepting one's number of years of experience as an accurate measure of one's level of expertise." (p. 27). They maintain that the learning mechanisms that mediate the improvements from experience have a crucial role to play in the acquisition of expertise.

Huberman's observations and Bereiter and Scardamalia's theory of expertise were borne out in Marina's case. The professional development of Marina was a process where she was continuously working at the edge of her competence (Bereiter and Scardamalia, 1993). For example, in handling teacher-student relationship, she was unhappy about merely maintaining control over students; she was not complacent about her class being the best-behaved class in the school. She wanted to develop a relationship with students that was conducive to learning. She also wanted to make learning enjoyable for them. Her ability to become "totally integrated with the students" was the result of Marina's efforts over the years.

In classroom teaching, we can see a persistent search for renewal in small and big ways. She constantly questioned what she was doing and how she could make it better, and was aware of what she needed to know in order to do her job well. She felt that she was expanding her repertoire of pedagogical skills but that there were still areas of teaching that she needed to think about more. For example, her speaking lessons were well received by students, but she felt that there was a need to reexamine the materials that she developed three years earlier and see what needed to be changed. She constantly experimented with different ways of helping students to learn and closely scrutinized the learning outcomes. Hawley and Valli (1999) maintain that one source of motivation for teachers to engage in professional development is that it will improve student achievement. This is only one side of the coin. The other side of the coin is that professional development is also embedded in the process of improving student achievement, as demonstrated in Marina's case.

In playing her role as panel chair, Marina rose to the challenge of being an agent of change in her school. She looked for opportunities for gaining new ideas, knowledge, and instructional strategies within and beyond her own school, which is very important to professional growth (see Borko and Putnam, 1995; Lieberman, 1995). Through the process of leading her teachers to implement a new approach to teaching writing, Marina reconceptualized her role from a caretaker to a mentor.

The professional development of Marina can be summarized as a process of constant renewal: a process of looking for and responding to opportunities for learning, seeking and taking on challenges which allowed her to work at the edge of her competence, reflecting on and "reframing" (Schon, 1987) her understanding of her work as a teaching professional.

IMPLICATIONS FOR TEACHER EDUCATION

In this chapter, I have outlined the phases of professional development of Marina and the factors that shaped the path that she has taken. While the phases that Marina went through bear characteristics that have been identified in the teacher development literature, they varied from those outlined by Huberman (1993b) in terms of the ways in which the phases took shape as well as in term of the sequence. The non-linear and somewhat idiosyncratic and individual nature of professional development is very much due to the situated and personal nature of professional growth (see also Clarke and Hollingsworth, 2002). According to Benner, Tanner, & Chesla (1996), "being situated" means that one is neither totally determined by the specific context nor radically free to act in whichever way one wants. Rather, there are "situated possibilities." This means that "there are certain ways of seeing and responding that present themselves to the individual in certain situations, and certain ways of seeing and responding that are not available to that individual." (Benner et al., 1996, p. 352). Therefore, the developmental paths that teachers take depend on the ways in which they personally interact with their specific contexts of work, of which they are a part, and the ways in which they see the possibilities that can be opened up for their professional learning. It is essential for teacher educators to recognize the situated and personal nature of teachers' professional growth and not be prescriptive, to understand the "situated possibilities" that are opened up for each individual teacher, and to help them to maximize the opportunities for professional learning.

NOTES

[1] "Mixed code" refers to using English and Cantonese in teaching, which is still very common practice in many schools in Hong Kong because of students' limited ability to understand instructions in English. The Education and Manpower Bureau has made repeated attempts to stamp it out with little success.

[2] In Hong Kong, the Education and Manpower Bureau gives schools a rough guideline of how many compositions they should expect a teacher to give to students. Schools have the flexibility to decide on the number of compositions that they give to students, but they will be asked to justify the number when an inspection is conducted.

[3] The duration of a single lesson in Marina's school is 35 minutes. This is the norm for most secondary schools in Hong Kong although there is now a tendency to lengthen lessons to 50–60 minutes.

REFERENCES

Benner, P., Tanner, C. A., & Chesla, C. A. (1996). *Expertise in nursing practice—Caring, clinical judgment and ethics.* New York: Springer Publishing Company.

Bereiter, C., & Scardamalia, M. (1993). *Surpassing ourselves—An inquiry into the nature and implications of expertise.* Illinois: Open Court.

Berliner, D. (2000, November/December). A personal response to those who bash teacher education. *Journal of Teacher Education, 51*(5), 358–371.

Borko, H., & Putnam, R. T. (1995). Expanding a teacher's knowledge Base: A cognitive psychological perspective on professional development. In T. R. Guskey & M. Huberman (Eds.), *Professional development in education: New paradigms and practices* (pp. 35–65). New York: Teachers College.

Borg, S. (1998). Teachers' pedagogical systems and grammar teaching: A qualitative study. *TESOL Quarterly, 32*(1), 9–37.

Brookhart, S., & Freeman, D. (1992). Characteristics of entering teacher candidates. *Review of Educational Research, 62*, 37–60.

Bullough, R. V., Knowles, J. G., & Crow, N. A. (1992). *Emerging as a teacher.* London: Routledge.

Calderhead, J. (1984). *Teachers' classroom decision-making.* London: Holt, Rinehart and Winston.

Calderhead, J., & Robson, M. (1991). Images of teaching: Student teachers' early conceptions of classroom practice. *Teaching and Teacher Education, 7*(1), 1–8.

Calderhead, J., & Shorrock, S. (1997). *Understanding teacher education.* London: The Falmer Press.

Clarke, D., & Hollingsworth, H. (2002). Elaborating a model of teacher professional growth. *Teaching and Teacher Education, 18*, 947–967.

Elbaz, F. (1983). *Teacher thinking: A study of practical knowledge.* London: Croom Helm.

Ericsson, K. A., & Smith, J. (1991). Prospects and limits of the empirical study of expertise: An introduction. In K. A. Ericsson & J. Smith (Eds.), *Towards a general theory of expertise: Prospects and limits.* New York: Cambridge University Press.

Fessler, R., & Christensen, J. (1992). *The teacher career cycle: Understanding and guiding the professional development of teachers.* Boston: Allyn and Bacon.

Goodson, I. (1991). Teachers' lives and educational research. In I. F. Goodson & R. Walker (Eds.), *Biography, identity and schooling: Episodes in educational research* (pp. 135–152). Dordrecht: Kluwer. London: Falmer Press.

Grossman, P. (1990). *The making of a teacher.* New York: Teacher's College Press.

Harris, J. (1994). *Introducing writing.* London: Penguin.

Hawley, W., & Valli, L. (1999). The essentials of effective professional development. In M. Huberman & R. Vandenberghe (Eds.), *Understanding and preventing teacher burnout* (pp. 127–150). Cambridge: Cambridge University Press.

Huberman, M. (1993a). Steps towards a developmental model of the teaching career. In L. Kremer-Hayon, H. Vonk, & R. Fessler (Eds.), *Teacher professional development: A multiple perspective approach* (pp. 93–118). Amsterdam: Swets and Zeitlinger.

Huberman, M. (1993b). *The lives of teachers.* New York, Teachers' College Press.

Huberman, M., & Vendenberghe, R. (1999). Introduction: Burnout and teaching profession. In M. Huberman & R. Vandenberghe (Eds.), *Understanding and preventing teacher burnout* (pp. 1–12). Cambridge: Cambridge University Press.

Johnson, K. E. (1996). The role of theory in L2 teacher education. *TESOL Quarterly, 30*(4), 765–772.

Lanier, J. E., & Little, J. W. (1986). Research on teacher education. In M. C. Wittrock (Ed.), *Handbook of research on teaching* (pp. 527–569). New York: Macmillan.

Lieberman, A. (1995). *The work of restructuring schools: Building from the ground up.* New York: Teachers College Press.

Lortie, D. (1975). *Schoolteacher.* Chicago: University of Chicago Press.
Nias, J. (1984). The definition and maintenance of self in primary schools. *British Journal of Sociology of Education,* 5(3), 267–280.
Schon, D. A. (1987). *Educating the reflective practitioner.* San Francisco, CA: Jossey-Bass.
Sikes, P. J., Measor, L., & Woods, P. (1985). *Teacher careers: Crises and continuities.* London: Falmer Press.
Sprinthall, N. A., Reiman, A. J., & Sprinthall, L. T. (1996). Teacher professional development. In J. Sikula, T. Buttery, & E. Guyton (Eds.), *Handbook of research on teacher education* (pp. 666–703). New York, Macmillan.
Tsui, A. B. M. (2003). *Understanding expertise in teaching.* New York: Cambridge University Press.
White, R., & Arndt, V. (1991). *Process writing.* London: Longman.
Zeichner, K., & Gore, J. (1990). Teacher socialization. In W. Houston (Ed.), *Hand-book of research on teacher education* (pp. 329–348). New York: Macmillan.

CHAPTER 65

APPROPRIATING UNCERTAINTY:

ELT Professional Development in the New Century

MICHAEL P. BREEN

ABSTRACT

This chapter critically reviews three trends that exemplify Western perspectives on the professional development of English language teachers at the turn of the century. Both reflective practice and action research aim to engage teachers directly in their own professional growth, while investigations of teacher thinking represent a complementary research perspective. All three, it is argued, are responses to, and symptoms of, a loss of certainty in former grand narratives of English language teaching (ELT). All three are evaluated in relation to their cultural assumptions concerning appropriate support for teacher development. The chapter concludes with a discussion of possible future directions in the in-service professional development of teachers that may represent either an evolution or a rejection of current approaches.

INTRODUCTION

In focusing upon ELT practitioners, this chapter identifies wider influences upon teachers' work at the present time that may be undermining professional identity. It explores current approaches to teacher development that are symptomatic of such changes. The purpose is to consider aspects of teacher development that may be contributing to this appropriation of professionalism and to identify alternative approaches in which teachers may confront present uncertainties through strategies that enable them to create positive opportunities for change on their own terms. The chapter begins with a brief review of some of the pressures that teachers presently face. This is followed by an evaluation of currently influential approaches to teacher development as responses to these pressures. Finally, the chapter proposes possible future directions in teacher development that may overcome the present constraints upon professionalism and the limitations inherent in current approaches. The terms *teacher development* and *professional development* are treated as synonymous throughout the chapter. They are used to refer to any in-service program or course for experienced English language teachers, be these planned and provided by teacher educators or others or generated locally by and for teachers themselves in planned or spontaneous ways.

THE NEW MILLENNIUM: A CRITICAL MOMENT FOR TEACHER DEVELOPMENT?

It is widely recognized by those who closely study contemporary society that we live within a global culture that confronts us with unanticipated risks to our sense of equilibrium and with recurrent demands upon our adaptability that seem to sever our links with the conventional wisdom of previous generations. Traditional values and community ties that formerly sustained our sense of stability have been replaced by multiple sources of authority wherein increasingly intrusive media articulate on our behalf what we should regard as "common sense," economically desirable, and politically advantageous. While such global processes unify the human community, paradoxically, they may disrupt local and individual ways of living. Local communities, formerly sustainable through familial and other means of collaborative support, are experiencing fragmentation due to rapid changes in work opportunities, demography, and the demands upon public services to the extent that many become sites of deep social tension (Bourdieu, Accardo, Balazs & Ferguson, 1999).

Individual identity, framed in our participation in the global economy and, more directly, by our membership in local communities—including those in which we work—is being challenged and reconstructed by rapidly shifting values and by changes in the ways we conduct our lives that are beyond the imaginings of previous generations (Beck, Giddens, & Lash, 1994; Giddens, 1991). Most of us are obliged to take on a recurrently adaptable identity while, for increasing numbers of people, it becomes necessary to sever their community and cultural roots and move elsewhere. In parts of Asia, for example, the workforce at present is made up of hundreds of thousands of migrant families, and in Europe, one-third of all people under the age of 30 now work in a country in which they were not born. Temporary or permanent, voluntary or forced, transitions in community identity are a defining characteristic of our global community.

In education, it is not surprising that such transitions in personal and community identity reverberate in the discourse of pedagogy, which articulates our relationships with knowledge, with those in authority, with colleagues, and with students (Bernstein, 1996; Gee, 1996; Giroux, 1997; Popkewitz & Brennan, 1998). Although on a smaller scale and located within a particular community of professionals, we cannot expect that the working lives and, therefore, the development of English language teachers will be immune from these wider influences. On the contrary, teachers of English are confronted by a stark choice. Either we perceive ourselves as a teacher of language unconnected to wider social, cultural, and political processes and, thereby, participate in the marginalization of our profession, or we accept the formative role we play in these processes and confront the possibilities for beneficial change in the intercultural work that we do.

If we regard professional development as simultaneously providing benefit to the individual teacher and to the wider community of ELT practitioners, we can also see it as beneficial local action for the classroom community, the school or institutional community, and, indeed, the wider community from which our students come. And such local action is unavoidably contextualized within the global processes here briefly identified. Perhaps more than previously, strategies for confronting such processes may be seen to be essential in any program of professional development. And more than previously, we recognize that a teacher's development is not merely an individual matter. It is professional action that, while permeable to the impact of social, cultural, and political forces, also provides the opportunity for positive change emanating outwards to the communities within which a classroom is located. This dual process of external global influences impinges upon contemporary approaches to teacher development and how approaches to development may initiate creative responses and opportunities in such a context are the focus of this chapter. We need to begin by identifying some of the key challenges that confront English language teachers at the present time.

The Uncertain Practitioner

Towards the end of the twentieth century, an increasing body of research, mainly undertaken in countries where English is the dominant language, identified a crisis in the professionalism of teachers (Bottery, 1998; Furlong, Barton, Miles, Whiting, & Whitty, 2001; Hargreaves, 1994; Whitty, 1996). While the crisis clearly reflects emergent external pressures upon teachers, the research reveals that teachers and teacher educators are contributing to the undermining of their own professionalism. In essence, many are resisting inevitable changes on the basis of former stances and values that are no longer sustainable. Focusing upon the work of English language teachers, I suggest that there are four key aspects of our work that are being challenged in the present context: (a) the knowledge we may apply; (b) the ways we may teach; (c) our accountability; and (d) working conditions. Each of these is related, of course, so that change is palpable because it touches most aspects of our work in an aggregative way. In considering each in turn within the constraints of brevity, what I have to say may not apply equally across all teaching situations and for all teachers, although many English language teachers are experiencing the processes that are referred to here.

Transient Knowledge

Teacher knowledge has, of late, been the focus of close analysis (Clark & Peterson, 1986; Day, Hope, & Denicolo, 1990; Day, Calderhead, & Denicolo, 1993; Elbaz, 1983; Shulman, 1987; inter alia). A major recent development in language teaching research, strongly influenced by investigations of teacher knowledge in Western countries, is the study of how language teachers think about their work: their beliefs, their theories, and the principles that guide their practices (Breen, 1991; Breen, Hird, Milton, Oliver, & Thwaite, 2001; Burns, 1993; Freeman, 1991; Freeman & Richards, 1996; Gimenez, 1995; Johnson, 1989; Woods, 1996; [Borg, 2003, provides a comprehensive review]). This growth of interest is not merely coincidental. Echoing the extensive research on teacher thinking in the last two decades of the twentieth century, it is a particular investigative response to what might constitute language teachers' knowledge, responsibility, and autonomy at a time when significant change is impacting upon each of these. Because teachers' knowledge and principles are at the heart of curriculum change, they need to be revealed not least to discover their potential for adaptation. Giddens (1991), in his influential work on late modernity and self-identity, specifies *reflexivity* as a key attribute of the self and of wider society. For him, reflexivity is the process of incorporation—in the self and in society—of changes in beliefs and knowledge and changes that, in our present context, entail almost constant revision.

Simplifying somewhat, we may distinguish between language teachers' knowledge of the subject and their mainly experientially informed knowledge of how to teach the subject—their *pedagogic knowledge* or, in Schön's (1983) terms, their "knowledge in action." These two realms of knowledge are in constant relation, for what a teacher knows about the English language is likely to influence how she works with it and how she expects students to work upon it. Focusing only upon knowledge of English, the teacher whose first language is not English is highly sensitive to real or assumed limitations of students' subject knowledge, and this sensitivity, in turn, filters any innovations they are urged to undertake in practice by academic researchers or curriculum planners. However, their subject knowledge and that of their peers whose first language *is* English have also been the target of relatively constant revision in recent years due to developments in applied linguistics (see, for example, the chapters in Section II of the present volume). If we are to teach grammar, which model of grammar should it be? If we are to teach language as communication, which aspects of communicative competence must we focus upon? How might we base the syllabus on the growing reservoir of authentic computer corpora? And how can we disregard current studies of discourse and genre when they are said to offer our learners more revealing frameworks for uncovering how English is used? Of course teachers recognize the value of recent refinements in how subject matter may be defined and presented. But these refinements have entailed a shift in professional stance in terms of a readiness to mistrust prior knowledge and replace this with sustained reflexive alertness.

Meantime, a number of applied linguists have not merely challenged how English should be described and taught, but what English? And more significantly, whose English? (see chapters by Obondo, Pennycook, and Tollefson, in Volume I of the current Handbook). Patterns of globalization are revealingly articulated in present discussions of the linguistic imperialism of English. The issue directly confronts teachers' professional responsibility with the dilemma of seeking to provide learners with potentially emancipatory access to other cultures while simultaneously complying within a process that may be repressive in relation to other languages and cultures.

Role Reconstructions

Teachers' practical pedagogic knowledge regarding how language may be best taught has been subject to two major interventions in recent years that spring from academic theory and research and from innovations in technology. Disciplines contributory to ELT have been marked by rapid changes, thereby confronting teachers with shifting pedagogic imperatives. A key role of professional development is to mediate between academic exploration and classroom practice. Much of this mediation has sometimes contributed to teachers' perplexity rather than enlightenment, and a major cause of this has been the realignment of professional development to other agendas. State and regional governments, in the context of global competitiveness, have sought to implement curricula that are as at least as good as those of their nearest competitors. While this is understandable, such curricula are inevitably reinterpretations of innovations in theory and research assumed to be appropriate to local conditions. As English language teaching is a global business, publishing corporations are keen participants in this process so that their textbooks may be adopted on a large scale. Much professional development made available to teachers at present directly serves these interests, and such development positions the teacher as the recipient of "new" knowledge rather than as a contributor to it: as novice rather than expert. The resulting tension between innovations driven by theory and research and the inherent conservatism of governments and publishers has resulted in contradictory messages to teachers to mistrust new ideas coming from academics while being obliged to interpret and express what they do in classrooms through the discourse of contemporary applied linguistics. A salient example of this issue is the widely propagated assumptions that communicative language teaching (CLT) entailed replacing grammar work with speaking and listening activities and that more recent research identifying focus on form during negotiation as facilitative of language acquisition implied a rejection of CLT and a return to the explicit teaching of grammar. While both beliefs are misinterpretations of the original theory and research, the fragmentation of CLT at the present time—into task-based, collaborative, or autonomous learning—illustrates how pedagogic knowledge within the profession gravitates between established convention and ongoing reflexive adjustment.

Several chapters in this volume articulate the implications of current developments in technology for the language teacher (for example, see Corbel and Legutke et al.). Computer applications for language learning exemplify the tension between genuine opportunities for innovation and apparent shifts in the locus of control in teaching that directly challenge former professional identity. These changes are aggregative in their impact, and a major contributive factor in the present construction of teachers as merely "delivery systems" of centrally planned curricula is the assumption that computers have the capacity to do as good a job as they can. While computers will continue to revolutionize networked learning, the shift towards machines as both the sources of knowledge of a language and how that knowledge may be accessed by learners unavoidably contributes to a "de-skilling" of the experientially evolved pedagogy of the teacher and, thereby, the teacher's sense of worth.

Performativity

The concept of *performativity* has been proposed by Lyotard (1984) in his analysis of significant changes in contemporary society. He argues that the metanarratives guiding education until recently have been criteria related to truth and justice. His analysis reveals that both have been replaced by a preoccupation with action: with how things are done. This displacement has had a number of effects upon how we perceive our world, so that truth, for instance, is eroded into "regimes of truth" that legitimize the actions of powerful groupings in society and thereby disempower the "unknowing" (Foucault, 1980). Performativity entails that personal and professional worth is reduced to what individuals can be seen to do and to assessable criteria of how competent they are in doing it.

The implications for the teaching profession have been palpable in recent years, especially in economically advantaged societies. In the context of the wider performativity in economic competition, governments have mobilized standards of achievement and competencies in education, systems for the accountability of educators, and the new positivism of evidence-based practices. Such measures have been put in place on the basis of two unproven assumptions: that whatever teachers achieved before is no longer adequate and that the bureaucratic surveillance of teachers' work will improve their students' performance. More overt consequences in these societies have been the "re-skilling" of highly experienced teachers into managers and an escalating exodus from the profession. The reason most often given by teachers for their decision to leave is the intensification of workloads entailed in regular testing of students and related accounting and reporting processes. More covertly, assessing a teacher's worth primarily in relation to national benchmarks of the outcomes of learning include the displacement of teachers' broader educational aims and the complex interpersonal process of enabling learning to occur.

Insecurity

Although not especially recent, the particular contractual conditions of many English language teachers combine with current changes to intensify professional uncertainty. Generally speaking, there are differences between the circumstances of the itinerant native-speaker of English and teachers of EFL in their own countries whose first language is not English, a major difference being relative opportunities for choice. However, the need to be on the move either literally or intellectually impinges upon both. Native speakers of English enjoy a measure of internationally transferable intellectual capital, and those who choose to work in other countries largely accept a transience of teaching positions. The latter years of the twentieth century witnessed an increased professionalization of English language teaching through the provision of initial qualifications by institutions such as the Royal Society of Arts and International House in the United Kingdom, while many teachers increasingly sought access to postgraduate or postexperience courses in ELT offered by universities. Increasing professionalization occurred in the context of mobility and transitory local contractual arrangements and, paradoxically, facilitated both of these conditions.

Many teachers whose first language was not English also obtained access to such professional training, and there was a significant increase in in-country training and development funded by governments or organizations. A contributory factor influencing the contractual insecurity of English teachers, perhaps especially in post-school education, has been the internal status accorded to language teaching. It is often positioned as a "service" provision wherein teachers' knowledge of the language is perceived as lacking the disciplinary status accorded to the expertise of specialists in conventional subject departments. Many highly experienced teachers of EFL in their own countries are subject to different contractual arrangements compared with other teachers and are often required to undertake more than one job to make ends meet. However significant their classroom and prior teacher education experience, they frequently need to obtain higher academic qualifications in order to attain both career mobility and a more secure contractual position.

I have so far identified four interrelated processes of destabilization that impact upon the identity of the English language teacher. The key question, therefore, is how processes for professional development may enable teachers to engage strategies to deal with such circumstances and the wider social forces that generate them in a personally developmental way. In approaching this question, I will consider whether current influential modes of in-service provision have the potential either to appropriate the uncertainty of teachers in order to maintain compliance with processes that may undermine professionalism or to enable teachers to appropriate *for themselves* a resilient professional identity. The following two sections address this ambiguity in current approaches to teacher development. The first focuses upon the prevailing stance of much in-service provision and a particular reaction to it. The subsequent section evaluates three approaches that appear to offer positive directions.

TRAINABILITY OR VERNACULAR PEDAGOGIES?

It is not surprising that the majority of professional development opportunities available to teachers at present are short training courses largely serving policy imperatives or updating by the teaching resource industry. There is increasing evidence that such training, focusing piecemeal upon teachers' skills, is transient in its benefit because its effects are superficial (Hargreaves, 1995; Little, 1993). In a climate in which professional identity and the entailed relationships with colleagues and students are being redefined, Bernstein (1996) identified the resultant recontextualization of pedagogic knowledge as a pivotal process. He described how teachers' knowledge is most often positioned by in-service training that serves agendas other than those of teachers themselves:

> The concept of trainability places emphasis upon 'something' the actor must possess in order for that actor to be appropriately formed and re-formed according to technological, organisational and market contingencies. This 'something', which is crucial to the survival of the actor, the economy and presumably the society, is the ability to be taught, the ability to respond effectively to concurrent, subsequent, intermittent pedagogics. Cognitive and social processes are to be specifically developed for such a pedagogized future. However, the ability to respond depends upon a capacity, not an ability. The capacity for the actor to project him/herself *meaningfully* rather than relevantly, into this future, and recover a coherent past. (p. 73)

Meaningful adaptation therefore rests upon an identity, which, according to Bernstein, can readily integrate what may be required in the future with what has been achieved in the past. Bernstein goes on to suggest that:

> (This identity) cannot be constructed by lifting oneself up by one's shoelaces. It is not a purely psychological construction by a solitary worker as he/she undergoes the transitions which he/she is expected to perform on the basis of trainability. This identity arises out of a particular social order, through relations which the identity enters into with other identities of reciprocal recognition, support, mutual legitimization and finally through a negotiated collective purpose. (p. 73)

Therefore, the capacity to deal meaningfully with the challenges of recontextualization of knowledge in an era of change depends upon the ongoing interaction between the individual's unfolding career and its entailed social relationships in a collective context such as that of the school or community—including the community of colleagues in ELT.

Being positioned as someone to be trained in the latest innovations generated by theory and research has been the target of recent arguments against what may be described as pedagogic imperialism. The alternative perspective asserts the authenticity of local pedagogic principles and frameworks for classroom practice that are generated by teachers in real and diverse situations. Such vernacular pedagogies are argued to be more culturally and situationally sensitive than imported innovations and, thereby, justifiably resistant to them (Canagarajah, 1999; Ellis, 1996; Holliday, 1994; Kramsch & Sullivan, 1996; Kumaravadivelu, 1994).

Although indicative of the fertile ground for the seeds of future teacher development, the closing off of the potentials of interaction between such vernacular pedagogies, research-informed innovation, and alternative pedagogic innovations generated in other parts of the world may be non-developmental. While the assertion of the authenticity of local knowledge and practice is an understandable response to uncertainty, there is the risk of inertia and the privileging of conventional ways of thinking and acting in language education that fail to confront significant global and local changes or, more positively, grasp the opportunities that they present. We might perceive such appeals to local authenticity as paradoxically contributing to the marginalization of the ELT profession.

However, in addition to reminding us that teacher development must not only be integrated with what has been meaningful in the past but also grounded in situations of practice, this recent recognition of the integrity of vernacular pedagogies reminds us that professionalism across ELT is unavoidably hybrid. And one of the positive opportunities of the current unification of human society is the process of interchange that supports and generates hybrid solutions and the inclinations of ELT practitioners to cross boundaries between ways of thinking and acting professionally. Much in-service training fails in this regard because it positions teachers as deficient before it commences. The current romanticization of vernacular wisdom is similarly retrograde in positioning teachers as guardians of pedagogies that somehow lack the capacity for evolution. We need to turn to alternative perspectives on teacher development that appear to challenge both tendencies.

REFLECTIVE PRACTICE, ACTION RESEARCH, AND THE CRITICAL STANCE

Although distinctive in their own ways, the three approaches to teacher development briefly evaluated here share the late modern skepticism regarding the primacy of rationalism in our dealings with our environment and our relationships. It needs to be emphasized that such disillusionment is a characteristic of developed societies and might be regarded as symptomatic of their more direct participation in global economic, technological, and institutional processes that, paradoxically, destabilize former personal and community identities. Focusing upon teacher professionalism, this questioning of rationalism coupled with the emphasis upon performativity encourages us to place greater faith in the wisdom of experientially based practice rather than in theories that have formerly provided rational justifications for it. Contemporary language-teacher development programs that give primacy to modes of teacher reflection and action research locate practice as the source of understanding and, thereby, the crucible wherein problems may be solved, innovations accommodated, and uncertainties reduced.

Schön (1983, 1987), perhaps the most influential founder of the reflective practice movement, rejected the belief that professional people undertake their work by relying upon the systematic application of scientifically grounded theory and technique. For him, the complexities of day-to-day professional work render such reliance inappropriate: "The problems of real-world practice do not present themselves to practitioners as well-formed structures. Indeed they tend not to present themselves as problems at all but as messy indeterminate situations" (1987, p. 4).

It is precisely such "messy indeterminate situations" in language classrooms and the close consideration and, crucially, the articulation of the ways in which we act in them that exemplify the focus of reflective practice. For Schön (1987), reflection within action during classroom work, for instance, is most often a response to the unexpected and has the potential for a "reflective conversation" leading to on-the-spot experimentation (p. 28). Such reflective conversations may be facilitated and undertaken in various ways, just as the process of reflection itself may be variously defined (Calderhead & Gates, 1993). In language teacher development, the making-sense of practical problems through their identification, reflection upon them, and their articulation has been identified as processes towards developmental ways of acting (Flowerdew, Brock, & Hsia, 1992; Richards & Lockhart, 1994; Wallace, 1991; Woodward, 1991).

Kemmis, in the same tradition as Schön (1983, 1987), proposed action research as a methodical extension of reflective practice (Kemmis, 1985; Carr & Kemmis, 1986; Kemmis & McTaggart, 1988; see Burns, 1999, and her chapter in the present volume for a review of action research within language teaching). Action research entails the teacher's own investigative exploration of the implementation of alternative ways of acting in the face of identified practical problems. Focusing on an innovation to be implemented or a problematic aspect of practice, the teacher moves through a cycle from a particular plan for implementation or investigation to the collection of feedback on outcomes or other appropriate data and, thence, to a revised plan for action. Thence, the cycle may be repeated until the problem or issue is more clearly specified and resolved. As with reflective practice, action research addresses the teaching-learning process in a classroom as the location for teachers' refinement of pedagogic knowledge and for methodically implementing alternative practices. Both approaches can be seen as responses to change in terms of providing a means for enabling teacher adaptability.

There remains, however, an inherent paradox in these approaches. In engaging teachers in the articulation of their practices—a task that many teachers understandably find difficult—they replace the former rationalism of pedagogic theories with a localized process of rationalization that has the potential to displace other forms of knowing that permeate the teaching process. While it would be hard to find a teacher who was not *reflexive* during classroom work in the sense of imposing coherence on messy indeterminate situations, much research has deduced that teachers' decision-making is often not rational and, in contrast to Schön's perception of other professions (his research focused mainly upon architects, doctors, and psychologists), teaching can be seen as too complex an activity to be identified as action based upon reflection (Carlgren & Lindblad, 1991; Olsen, 1991). Lortie's (1975) classic account of the culture of teaching revealed that, generally, teachers are not analytical in the sense of stepping back from the taken-for-granted, experiential process of teaching. Introducing recent explorations of teacher knowledge, Atkinson and Claxton (2000) propose that teachers work on the basis of three ways of thinking, only one of which is grounded in action or practice. For them, *intuitive practice* typifies teachers' immediate classroom decision-making. This is distinctive from *rational* or *analytical thinking* that teachers may engage when planning for classroom work and from *reflective thinking,* which entails learning from experiences that are unavoidably contextualized within the teachers' local circumstances. Therefore teacher development based upon reflective practice and action research will access only ways of thinking that, on the one hand, can be more easily abstracted from actual practice while, on the other hand, tend to be oriented to the teachers' perceptions of the immediate context in which they work.

These approaches to professional development reconstruct teaching as primarily rational activity, and this within the boundaries of the individual teacher's own immediate circumstances.

There are a number of potential consequences of these approaches, one of which may be the reduction of professionalism rather than its enhancement. The onus for change is upon the individual teacher in her own classroom. Taking on the stance of a researcher is not merely an additional time-demanding role. It may displace those aspects of teachers' engagement in the classroom process with a disproportionate concern with effectiveness of delivery; with a primary focus upon means at the cost of content, broader learning outcomes, and wider educational and social processes. And both approaches entail the risk of legitimizing and reproducing classroom practices and routines that may be harmful to learning. There is a tension in both in that they may be mobilized either as an imported technology that can systematically appropriate the ways in which teachers *ought* to think about their work, or as procedures controlled by teachers to enable them to reform language education in the situations in which they work.

It is this latter concern that underlies proponents of a critical stance within teacher professionalism (Barnett, 1997; Furlong, 1992; Hargreaves, 1994). Zeichner (1994), a leading interpreter of reflective practice in teaching, identified the culture of schooling, in its broadest sense, as antipathetic to critical inquiry, while only reflection that *is* critical will enable teachers to directly address the historical, cultural, and structural conditions within which they work. Because of the institutional constraints upon the individual teacher, such an undertaking, he argues, will need to be a collaborative endeavor between teachers, teacher educators, and researchers. To be fair to Carr and Kemmis (1986), their original formulation of action research also argued for the collaborative implementation of a systematic critical approach to the conditions of teachers' work. Such proposals echoed the ideas of Habermas (1970, 1974), a leading critical theorist, and his distinction between *communicative action* and *discourse.* In order to facilitate communicative action, we uncritically take for granted the commonsense truths, norms, and social practices of everyday life. In genuine discourse, however, we may collaborate in overtly questioning the validity of our beliefs and norms, and our actions that are governed by these. For Habermas, the ideal speech situation is one that entails equality among participants and the space to overcome internal and external constraints in ways of thinking and acting. Reflective practice and action research remain ambiguous modes of teacher development unless they also entail the willing critique, in collaboration with fellow practitioners, of personal taken-for-granteds and the broader prevailing conditions of the context of one's work. It seems that we need to look further for new directions in teacher development that may reduce such ambiguity. The final two sections focus respectively on two alternatives.

EXPLORATORY PRACTICE

Partly developed out of a reaction against what were seen as the disproportionate demands of action research compared with its longer-term benefits for the working lives of language teachers, exploratory practice was first proposed by Allwright and Bailey (1991) as a means for teachers to confront the kinds of unanticipated "puzzles" in the language classroom that Schön had earlier identified as "surprises" in practice that generated opportunities for reflectively driven experimentation. As an alternative to action research, exploratory practice evolved out of the situated experiences of teachers in different situations, echoing earlier development programs that had been teacher-generated (Breen, Candlin, Dam, & Gabrielsen, 1989). Allwright and his colleagues in the Exploratory Practice Centre at Lancaster University define the approach as:

> (A)n indefinitely sustainable way for classroom language teachers and learners, while getting on with their learning and teaching, to develop their own understandings of life in the language classroom. It is essentially a way for teachers and learners to work together to understand aspects of their classroom practice that puzzle them, through the use of normal pedagogic procedures (standard monitoring, teaching, and learning activities) as investigative tools.
>
> (www.ling.lancs.ac.uk/groups/crile/EPCentre)

Allwright proposes that reflection on classroom work enables teachers, in collaboration with learners, to identify particular puzzles—such as issues in dealing with aspects of language, or adopted working procedures, or the challenges of heterogeneity, or size of classes, etc. Subsequent to reflection and before undertaking action to resolve such puzzles, a crucial stage in the process is to achieve a deeper understanding of them. And it is the attainment of a situated understanding of the life of the classroom, not through the use of conventional research procedures but through everyday teaching-learning activities, that exemplifies the approach. Allwright (2000, 2001) proposes six design features characterizing ongoing professional development that exploratory practice would provide:

1. Joint teacher-learner work towards understanding must precede/be undertaken instead of action for change.
2. Such work must not hinder teaching and learning, but rather make a positive contribution to it.
3. Whatever is focused upon in exploratory work must be seen to be relevant to those involved—learners in addition to teachers.
4. It must be indefinitely sustainable (unlike action research projects) by being integrated into the normal work of teaching and learning.
5. It must bring people together—teachers, learners, researchers, etc.—in a productive collegial relationship.
6. It must promote the development of understanding among all concerned.

Therefore exploratory practice appears to go beyond reflective practice and action research in being process-oriented, integrated within everyday ways of working, and driven by the local concerns and needs of teachers *and* learners. It is distinctive in explicitly resisting performativity or a preoccupation with effectiveness, replacing these with a focus upon teachers' quality of life or professional well-being through a cooperative understanding of everyday puzzles in practice.

However, Allwright and his colleagues do not dismiss teachers' responsibilities regarding accountability, and they are alert to the risk of the potential insularity of vernacular pedagogies. The approach, having evolved through a collegial process among teachers, entails the public sharing of achieved understandings of classroom puzzles with other groupings of teachers—including dissemination opportunities provided by computer networking. Furthermore, extending its collegial reach, such exploratory work might involve academic researchers and teacher educators, but in a different relationship to local practice than that typified by previous development programs and entailing a shift in power relations. Minimally, it may involve the researcher as a resource within the process of exploratory work serving the "insiders" agenda, while teacher educators would be positioned as participating in the understanding of what teachers and learners discover locally and as means for the wider dissemination of these discoveries and the procedures of exploratory practice. Each of these possibilities may reduce the risk of insularity and mere reproduction in local practices. What appears to be distinctive in exploratory practice is its concern with the quality of teachers' lives as the *primary* motive for teacher development. This motive may also provide the space for critical reflexivity in relation to the conditions of teachers' work although not a principle of the approach.

FUTURE DIRECTIONS AND COLLEGIAL DEVELOPMENT

Building upon the potentials of all of the above approaches, what may be the characteristics of future language teacher development that can be grounded in localized communities of practice while also generating strategies for engaging with regional and global issues that impinge upon teachers' work? From the foregoing analysis, I deduce seven desirable features of professional development, be these programs generated within situated practice or provided by or for groups of teachers. The seven features are interrelated and exemplify collegial development within language teaching. Four features address how the teacher may be positioned as an active participant in such development, while a further three are requirements upon the developmental process.

The Position of Teachers

As Integrated Individuals

One of the paradoxes of forms of reflective practice is their requirement that teachers rationalize about their work when such rationalization is difficult, often inappropriate, and can articulate only a part of the experience-based decision-making and actions that are engaged in language teaching. Teacher development needs to be holistic in addressing practitioners who enact imagination, values, alignments, intuitions, and diverse knowledge systems during the teaching-learning process. As Bernstein (1996) argued in his critique of training, for teachers to integrate alternative ways of working into current practice, they need to make *their own links* between what has been personally meaningful in their work so far and what can be seen to be meaningful in future ways of acting. Teacher development must therefore address all the attributes of professional identity and self-esteem grounded in ongoing achievements rather than merely the attainment of external imperatives: it must start where teachers have come to and why, assuming that their personal experience and knowledge are evolving rather than things to be superseded.

As Members of Communities

A teacher's professional identity is sustained by, and constituted of, relationships with others. A teacher is a major player in the community of the classroom and is, most often, highly sensitive to its evolution. Like the layers of an onion, the classroom community is contextualized within the institution, and its particular patterning of peer and authority relations serves and reflects the wider community in which it is situated, locally, regionally, and internationally. And teachers' lives contribute to, and are subject to, the conventions and changes that reverberate through these communal strata. Future teacher development must explore the dynamic that each of these layers entails for professional responsibility and action. The global phenomenon of increasing migration, for example, impinges directly upon the English teacher because classrooms represent "border crossings" between cultures and communities (Giroux, 1997). While some teacher development programs touch upon learners' communities of origin, the impact upon the teaching-learning process of the shifting identities of learners *and* teachers, and the communities that they represent and between which they move, are central to an understanding of language teaching at the present time.

As Cultural Workers

English language teachers can comply to their own marginalization as service providers delivering technical solutions to learners' linguistic needs or position themselves as people at the heart of an educational and social agenda for interethnic and intercultural communication. Much current teacher development gravitates uncertainly between these alternatives. Future work, although relating to the immediate agendas of teachers and learners in their classrooms, must actively support teachers in strategies that assert languages as pivotal in all educational provision for the benefit of regional and international understanding. Most current in-service provision is premised upon economic and instrumental objectives, displacing the educational and cultural motives of teachers. This tension needs to be addressed directly from the perspective of the socially transformative potential of language teaching. The implication for teacher development is that it actively engages teachers' alignment with broader social endeavors as generative of a diversity of culturally appropriate curricula.

As Responsible for Their Own Development

For teachers to develop in the present context, they will redefine their professionalism in dynamic ways, not least by reclaiming the wider educational agenda of their work. Teachers can articulate those things for which they are accountable beyond narrow learning outcomes. They can rise above uncertainty as a reaction to increased external intervention through their pivotal mediating role in language education and the dissemination of accounts of such mediation from their own situations of practice. And they can transcend external imperatives regarding "efficient" delivery through the negotiable space they occupy within those interpersonal relationships that the realization of any curriculum depends upon. Professional autonomy, accountability, and responsibility have to be addressed in these terms at the present time, and development programs need to explore diverse strategies for enacting the transformative expression of these aspects of professionalism in classroom, institutional, and wider communities of practice.

Requirements upon Teacher Development

Collegiality

Professional identity is not only constituted through classroom, local, and wider community membership. Teachers are also members of the community of fellow practitioners with a shared awareness of common demands and pressures in their work. A major failing of much teacher development in the past has been its short-termism. Mobilizing the networking potential of the practitioner community within school or institution, within the region, and internationally is crucial for English language teaching at the present time, not least because these levels of professional membership are sites for resistance to external pressures that may be undermining. Teachers consistently value networking and the benefits of collaborative follow-up work. While teacher development must be grounded in local practice—directly relevant to it and *all* the people involved—it has to be permeable to insights from elsewhere. Just as local action can be further sustained through its being made known across the profession, local explorations need to be framed within strategies for interchange so that they can be recontextualized for wider collegial access. Whilst more formal associations to which English language teachers belong provide opportunities for collegial participation, spontaneously emergent arenas for teacher development need to be fostered, including electronic communities of practitioners interacting regularly in more open-ended ways.

Collegial development for the future also entails overcoming boundaries between activities that constitute English language education in its broader sense. Teaching, learning, and researching are being seen now—occasionally rather superficially—as overlapping processes. Nevertheless, much current research is overlooked by teachers as irrelevant to their concerns, while some researchers assert immunity from practical matters. The gap between these activities and curriculum or materials planning appears to be greater than previously because of the current centralization of language policies. Clearly, future teacher development needs to restore dynamic interchange between *all* these activities and the people engaged in them, thereby reducing unnecessary spaces between them while also recognizing that each of the activities has its own integrity of purposes and procedures.

Discursiveness

We have seen that reflexivity, entailing an almost constant revision of beliefs and knowledge, currently permeates teachers' working lives. The uncertainty that this generates can be appropriated by external interests and agendas so that teachers' space for the negotiability of their own meanings becomes confined. A major goal for future teacher development should be the reclaiming of this space in terms of a collegial shift towards discursiveness or engagement in discourse that Habermas (1970) identified as the "ideal speech situation." Such a shift is challenging because teachers would be engaged in critically questioning their consensual beliefs, values, and practices. This undertaking goes beyond current approaches to development through explicitly confronting vernacular relativism, insularity, and mere reproduction of practices. It demands intellectual honesty and the recontextualization of local understandings so that these may be justified, compared, and reworked within a dialogue of critical evaluation among peers. It also demands that teachers identify those conditions in their work that are mutable by their own actions and those that are not, so that transformative effort is focused rather than dissipated. Such an endeavor can be seen as a key step towards what Bernstein (1996) identified as *negotiated collective purposes* and, thereby, the reassertion of individual professional identity through relationships within the wider community of language teachers. Because of likely institutional antipathy towards critique and a sense of individual powerlessness, this kind of discursiveness is necessarily collegial in its provision of mutual support.

Evolutionary

The future development of English language teachers requires their explicit recognition of the pivotal role they play at the heart of current educational, cultural, and political change and the responsibilities that such a role involves. The versions of English being taught and learned by many thousands across the world mediate those contradictions inherent in society wherein the potentials for interethnic and international communication exist alongside potentials for conflict between values and community identities. Learning English entails the ongoing tension between access and inclusion and between cultural hegemony and the diversity of local cultural systems. Teachers can address such issues in explicit ways by focusing upon how they are enacted locally in relation to more global processes. There are significant practical implications of, for example, learners' experienced shifts in identity between speech communities; the hybridity of Englishes and their evolving realizations in contemporary spoken and written texts; the negotiability of meanings, values, and norms; and so on. Professional development is now at a critical moment, for it is the arena in which teachers can freely explore ways of thinking and acting collegially that focus upon the positive opportunities of the present climate of change. Potentially it enables them to *exploit* the challenges it presents as a means towards collaboratively negotiated alternatives. It has to be evolutionary in continually reflecting and being permeable to beneficial influences from elsewhere—from other communities of practice, other disciplines, and other cultural realizations of pedagogy—and in having an ongoing reciprocal influence upon communities beyond the classroom.

CONCLUSIONS

In this chapter, I have reviewed some of the pressures upon English language teachers emerging from global processes at the turn of the century. I considered the ways in which current teacher development has reacted to these pressures. In identifying some of the limitations of current practices, I proposed certain aspects of future teacher development that may move beyond such limitations in the direction of collegial endeavor. My purpose has been to explore ways in which teachers may reclaim the process of teaching and learning as appropriate to all those involved in it, rather than its being appropriated by interests that may be non-educational. I have argued that future teacher development entails recognizing, grappling with, and participating in change, acknowledging that change itself has both negative and positive potentials. And I have suggested that collegial endeavor in particular can overcome the former and realize the latter. The practical implementation of collegial development, in whatever forms it takes, may not be easy because professionalism is currently constructed as an individual attribute subject to performativity criteria. Collegial endeavor is a reaction against this and is being exemplified by instances of spontaneous positive action by groups of teachers and teacher educators in different parts of the world. There is a growing recognition that identification and enactment of alternative strategies for appropriating change and making it work to the benefit of language education are urgent tasks at the present moment, not least because they may become more difficult in the future.

REFERENCES

Allwright, D. (2000). Exploratory practice: An appropriate methodology for language teacher development? Paper presented to the 8th IALS Symposium for Language Teacher Education, Edinburgh, Scotland, 2000.

Allwright, D. (2001). Three major processes of teacher development and the appropriate design criteria for developing and using them. In B. Johnson & S. Irujo (Eds.), *Research and practice in language teacher education: Voices from the field. CARLA Working Paper 19* (pp. 115–133), Minneapolis, MN.

Allwright, D., & Bailey, K. (1991). *Focus on the language classroom: An introduction to classroom research for language teachers*. Cambridge: Cambridge University Press.

Allwright, D., and colleagues. Exploratory Practice Centre at Lancaster University. Available at www.ling.lancs.ac.uk/groups/crile/EPCentre.

Atkinson, T., & Claxton, G. (Eds.). (2000). *The intuitive practitioner*. Buckingham: Open University Press.

Barnett, R. (1997). *Higher education: A critical business*. Buckingham: SRHE/Open University Press.

Beck, U., Giddens, A., & Lash, S. (1994). *Reflexive modernisation: Politics, tradition, and aesthetics in the modern social order*. Cambridge: Polity Press.

Bernstein, B. (1996). *Pedagogy, symbolic control and identity*. London: Taylor and Francis.

Borg, S. (2003). Teacher cognition in language teaching: A review of research on what language teachers think, know, believe and do. *Language Teaching, 36*(2), 81–109.

Bottery, M. (1998). *Professionals and policy: Management strategy in a competitive world*. London: Cassells.

Bourdieu, P., Accardo, A., Balazs, G., & Ferguson, P. P. (1999). *The weight of the world: Social suffering in contemporary society*. Cambridge: Polity Press.

Breen, M. P. (1991). Understanding the language teacher. In R. Phillipson, E. Kellerman, L. Selinker, M. Sharwood-Smith, & M. Swain (Eds.), *Foreign/Second language pedagogy research* (pp. 213–233). Clevedon: Multilingual Matters.

Breen, M. P., Candlin, C. N., Dam, L., & Gabrielsen, G. (1989). The evolution of a teacher training programme. In R. K. Johnson (Ed.), *The second language curriculum* (pp. 111–135). Cambridge: Cambridge University Press.

Breen, M. P., Hird, B., Milton, M., Oliver, R. & Thwaite, A. (2001). Making sense of language teaching: Teachers' principles and classroom practices. *Applied Linguistics, 22*(4), 470–501.

Burns, A. (1993). An exploration of the relationship between teacher beliefs and written language instructional practice in beginning ESL classes. Unpublished Ph.D. dissertation, Macquarie University, Sydney.

Burns, A. (1999). *Collaborative action research for English language teachers*. Cambridge: Cambridge University Press.

Calderhead, J., & Gates, P. (Eds.). (1993). *Conceptualising reflection in teacher development*. Lewes: Falmer Press.

Canagarajah, S. (1999). *Resisting linguistic imperialism in language teaching*. Oxford: Oxford University Press.

Carlgren, I., & Lindblad, S. (1991). On teachers' practical reasoning and professional knowledge: Considering conceptions of content in teachers' thinking. *Journal of Curriculum Studies, 7*, 507–516.

Carr, W., & Kemmis, S. (1986). *Becoming critical: Education, knowledge and action research.* London: Falmer Press.
Clark, C., & Peterson, P. (1986). Teachers' thought processes. In M. C. Whittrock (Ed.), *Handbook of research on teaching* (3rd ed.) (pp. 255–296). New York: MacMillan.
Day, C., Hope, M., & Denicolo, P. (1990). *Insights into teachers' thinking and practice.* London: Falmer Press.
Day, C., Calderhead, J., & Denicolo, P. (1993). *Understanding professional development.* London: Falmer Press.
Elbaz, F. (1983). *Teacher thinking: A study of practical knowledge.* New York: Nichols Publishing.
Ellis, G. (1996). How culturally appropriate is the communicative approach? *English Language Teaching Journal, 50*(3), 213–218.
Foucault, M. (1980). Truth and power. In C. Gordon (Ed. and Trans.), *Power/Knowledge: Selected interviews and other writing by Michel Foucault, 1972–1977* (pp. 109–133). New York: Pantheon.
Flowerdew, J., Brock, M., & Hsia, S. (Eds.). (1992). *Perspectives on second language teacher development.* Hong Kong: City Polytechnic of Hong Kong.
Freeman, D. (1991). The same things done differently: A study of the development of four foreign language teachers' conceptions of practice through an in-service teacher education programme. Unpublished Ph.D. Dissertation, Harvard University.
Freeman, D., & Richards, J. (Eds.). (1996). *Teacher learning in language teaching.* Cambridge: Cambridge University Press.
Furlong, J. (1992). Reconstructing professionalism: Ideological struggle in initial teacher education. In M. Arnot & L. Barton (Eds.), *Voicing concerns: Sociological perspectives on contemporary education reform.* Wallingford: Triangle.
Furlong, J., Barton, L., Miles, S., Whiting, C., & Whitty, G. (2001). *Teacher education in transition: Reforming teacher professionalism?* Buckingham: Open University Press.
Gee, J. P. (1996). *Social linguistics and literacies: Ideology in discourses.* London: Taylor and Francis.
Giddens, A. (1991). *Modernity and self-identity.* Cambridge: Polity Press.
Gimenez, T. N. (1995). Learners becoming teachers: An exploratory of beliefs held by prospective and practising EFL teachers in Brazil. Unpublished Ph.D. dissertation, Lancaster University.
Giroux, H. (1997). *Pedagogy and the politics of hope.* Boulder, CO: Westview Press.
Habermas, J. (1970). Towards a theory of communicative competence. *Inquiry, 13*, 89–113.
Habermas, J. (1974). *Theory and practice.* London: Heinemann.
Hargreaves, A. (1994). *Changing teachers, changing times: Teachers' work and culture in the postmodern age.* London: Cassell.
Hargreaves, A. (1995). Development and desire: A postmodern perspective. In T. R. Guskey & M. Huberman (Eds.), *Professional development in action.* New York: Teachers' College Press.
Holliday, A. (1994). *Appropriate methodology and social context.* Cambridge: Cambridge University Press.
Johnson, K. (1989). *The theoretical orientations of English as a second language teachers: The relationship between beliefs and practice.* Unpublished Ph.D. dissertation, Syracuse University.
Kemmis, S. (1985). Action research in the politics of reflection. In D. Boud, R. Keogh, & D. Walker (Eds.), *Reflection: Turning experience into learning.* London: Croom Helm.
Kemmis, S., & McTaggart, R. (Eds.). (1988). *The action research planner.* Geelong, Victoria: Deakin University Press.
Kramsch, C., & Sullivan, P. (1996). Appropriate pedagogy. *English Language Teaching Journal 50*(3), 199–212.
Kumaravadivelu, B. (1994). The postmethod condition: (E)merging strategies for second/foreign language teaching. *TESOL Quarterly, 28*(1), 127–148.
Little, J. W. (1993). Teachers' professional development in a climate of educational reform. *Educational Evaluation and Policy Analysis, 15*(2), 121–151.
Lortie, D. C. (1975). *School-teacher.* Chicago: University of Chicago Press.
Lyotard, J-F. (1984). *The postmodern condition: A report on knowledge.* Manchester: Manchester University Press.
Olsen, J. K. (1991). *Understanding teaching.* Milton Keynes: Open University Press.
Popkewitz, T. S., & Brennan, M. (Eds.). (1998). *Foucault's challenge: Discourse, knowledge and power in education.* New York: Teachers' College Press.
Richards, J. C., & Lockhart, C. (1994). *Reflective teaching in second language classrooms.* Cambridge: Cambridge University Press.
Schön, D. (1983). *The reflective practitioner.* San Francisco, CA: Jossey-Bass.
Schön, D. (1987). *Educating the reflective practitioner.* San Francisco, CA: Jossey Bass.

Shulman, L. (1987). Knowledge and teaching: Foundations of a new reform. *Harvard Educational Review*, 57, 1–12.
Wallace, M. J. (1991). *Training foreign language teachers: A reflective approach*. Cambridge: Cambridge University Press.
Whitty, G. D. (1996). Marketisation, the state and the re-formation of the teaching profession. In A. H. Halsey, H. Lauder, P. Brown, & A. S. Wells (Eds.), *Education, culture, economy and society* Oxford: Oxford University Press.
Woods, D. (1996). *Teacher cognition in language teaching*. Cambridge: Cambridge University Press.
Woodward, T. (1991). *Models and metaphors in language teacher training*. Cambridge: Cambridge University Press.
Zeichner, K. M. (1994). Research on teacher thinking and different views of reflective practice in teaching and teacher education. In I. Carlgren, G. Handal, & S. Waage (Eds.), *Teachers' minds and actions: Research on teachers' thinking and practice* (pp. 9–27). London: Falmer Press.

CHAPTER 66

TEACHER EDUCATION FOR LINGUISTICALLY DIVERSE COMMUNITIES, SCHOOLS, AND CLASSROOMS

TARA GOLDSTEIN

Ontario Institute for Studies in Education, The University of Toronto, Canada

ABSTRACT

Conceptualizing and implementing teacher education programming for teachers who work with students who do not use the school's language of instruction as their primary language is a complex task. The arrival of second or other language students often has an impact on a school's linguistic, cultural, and learning environment and can create linguistic and racial tensions within the school community. This chapter reviews current research and writing in the fields of education, TESOL, and applied linguistics that can help English language teachers respond to linguistic and racial tensions that arise in multilingual schools.

INTRODUCTION

The conceptualizion and implementation of teacher education programs for teachers who work with students who do not use the school's language of instruction as their primary language is complex. At the heart of this programming, we usually find a set of courses and materials that examine topics such as the teaching of listening, speaking, reading, and writing skills; content-based language teaching; curriculum planning; classroom management; and evaluation strategies.

Increasingly, these methodology courses also include observation of and reflection on language classrooms; peer teaching with feedback; cooperative learning activities; and work around cross-cultural communication. However, what isn't often discussed is the impact that the arrival of second or other language students has on a school's linguistic, cultural, and learning environment outside the classroom or the linguistic and racial tensions that sometimes arise as these students attempt to integrate into the school community.

Responding to changes in the school learning environment and to linguistic and racial tensions between students is not easy, and school staff members often turn to their specialist language teachers to help them think about effective ways of moving forward. This chapter focuses on what English language teachers need to know to provide leadership around such issues as language choice, bilingualism, linguistic discrimination, and racism. I focus on two types of linguistic and racial tensions that arise in multilingual schools. Part 1 of the chapter looks at linguistic and racial tensions and dilemmas related to speech. Part 2 describes tensions and dilemmas related to silence. At the heart of my discussions of speech and silence are findings from a four-year (1996-2000) critical ethnographic case study of an English-speaking Canadian high school that had recently enrolled a large number of immigrant students from Hong Kong (Goldstein, 2003).[1] At the end of each discussion in Parts 1 and 2, I describe a variety of pedagogical approaches that educators have used to respond to the tensions and dilemmas that have just been outlined. In Part 3, the chapter concludes with a discussion of the usefulness of critical ethnographic research for teacher education in multilingual contexts.

While it is not common to see a discussion of one particular study frame a handbook review, I believe that there is much to learn from the case of Northside and the ways that Northside students and teachers responded to the linguistic and racial tensions that arose in their school. A discussion of one multilingual school's efforts to work towards an effective equitable learning environment for all its students provides me with an interesting, grounded way to review other current research and writing in the fields of education, TESOL, and applied linguistics. It also allows me a way to include the voices of students and teachers who work in a multilingual school into the review (the names of all Northside students and teachers in this chapter are pseudonyms). Before turning to these voices, however, I want to conclude this introductory discussion with a brief description of Northside Secondary School. I offer this description to provide readers with a set of contextual understandings they can use in thinking about the dilemmas and tensions presented in the rest of the chapter.

The Case of Northside

Since opening in a mostly middle-and upper-middle-class suburb north of the city of Toronto in 1970, Northside Secondary School has established a reputation of academic excellence. The school's 1995-1996 *Quality Assurance School Review* reported that students achieved at levels above the system average in both mathematics and literacy testing. The *School Review* also reported that 86% of the students at Northside were immigrants to Canada and that 60% of the students reported that their primary language was a language other than English. The top five primary languages spoken by students were English, by 38% of the students; Cantonese, by 35%; Mandarin, by 6%; and Farsi and Korean, by 4%. The large percentage of bilingual and multilingual speakers at the school meant that while English was the language of instruction, everyday talk in classrooms, hallways, and the cafeteria took place in languages other than English as well as English. As discussed below, this created tensions for many people at the school.

The Cantonese-speaking Students at Northside

Between the years of 1991 and the first 4 months of 1996 (the year in which the study began), 48,535 people, about 11% of the city's population, immigrated to Toronto from Hong Kong.[2] As explained by historian, Paul Yee (1996), around the mid-1970s Canada began making efforts to attract foreign business immigrants who could bring in capital and entrepreneurial skills to help the Canadian economy. These efforts were particularly successful with Hong Kong Chinese who were beginning to worry about their economic and political future in light of the impending transfer of control from Britain to China in 1997. Many of the relatively affluent immigrants who settled in the Greater Toronto Area between 1991 and early

1996 bought houses in suburban areas outside the city and enrolled their children in schools like Northside.

Students such as the Cantonese-speaking students who attend Northside are very different from previous waves of immigrants. They are actively living in two or more cultures and are engaged in multiple language and literacy practices. They travel back and forth between their countries of settlement and their countries of birth to visit parents and other relatives who continue to live and work there. They access and consume pop culture from their countries of birth through the Internet, cable TV, CDs and videos. Learning to work effectively with students who call more than one place home and have strong affiliations in "multiple worlds" (Boykin, 1986; Phelan, Davidson, & Yu, 1998; Valenzuela, 1999) is critical to good teaching and effective teacher education programs.

TENSIONS, DILEMMAS, AND PEDAGOGIES RELATED TO SPEECH IN MULTILINGUAL SCHOOLS

The Case of Northside: Choosing to Use Cantonese at School

At Northside, most Cantonese-speaking students born in Hong Kong used Cantonese to speak to other students born in Hong Kong. The use of Cantonese was associated with membership in the Cantonese-speaking community at the school. It symbolized a Hong Kong Canadian identity. The choice to use Cantonese to seek and maintain membership in the Cantonese-speaking community was related to the students' goals of academic and social success at school. To illustrate, research in both a Finite Mathematics class and a Calculus class revealed that the use of Cantonese allowed students to gain access to friendship and assistance that helped them achieve good marks in the course. Having friends in the classroom was related to the goal of a getting high or passing mark in several ways.

First, friends explained things you didn't understand, for example, an explanation the teacher had given of a math concept or how to do a math problem. A second way having friends was important to academic success had to do with the way friends provided each other with an opportunity to discuss the marks they had received on an assignment or quiz. Negotiating a mark in an L2 was not always easy for Cantonese-speaking students. As English was the "legitimate" (Bourdieu, 1991) language or official language of instruction at Northside, those students who wanted a teacher to consider changing a mark needed to be able to articulate exactly why their answers were (partly) right and why they should receive more marks. Talking with friends about your case (in Cantonese) sometimes helped make the task of negotiating a mark easier.

The use of Cantonese to seek and maintain friendships within the Cantonese-speaking community at Northside can be understood as a strategy for developing peer social capital. As explained by critical educational theorist Angela Valenzuela (1999), the concept of social capital comes from exchange theory in sociology. It refers to an exchange of networks and trust and solidarity among people who wish to attain goals that cannot be attained individually. Understanding students' use of their primary languages at school as peer social capital allows us to see that it is possible for students to capitalize on ethnic forms of solidarity to build a support system that provides them with important forms of social and academic support. This can occur even when the school does not legitimize such solidarity.

The Case of Northside: Risks Associated with Using English

Importantly, while Cantonese was associated with building up peer social capital, the use of English was risky as it could jeopardize the access to friendship and assistance that was important to academic and social success in school. Cantonese-speaking students reported that other Cantonese students told them that they were "rude" if they spoke to them in English. When asked why, one student told us that some people thought that you were trying to be "special" if you spoke English or that you liked to "show off your English abilities."

To understand the reasons behind the association between the use of English and showing off, I turn to work undertaken by Angel Lin (2001), who talks about English as the language of power and the language of educational and socioeconomic advancement in Hong Kong. To illustrate her point, Lin writes that a student who wants to study medicine, architecture, and legal studies in Hong Kong, must have adequate English resources, what Bourdieu (1991) has called "linguistic capital". Adequate English must be acquired, in addition to subject knowledge and skills, in order to enter and succeed in English-medium professional training programs. After graduating from these programs, students also need to have adequate English resources to earn the credentials to enter these professions that are accredited by the British-based or British-associated professional bodies (Hong Kong was a British colony until July 1997). Students' access to linguistic capital that would provide them with the mastery of English needed to enter high-income professions in Hong Kong is uneven. Only a small elite group of Cantonese speakers has had the opportunity to obtain such mastery. The elite bilingual class in Hong Kong includes people who are wealthy enough to afford high-quality private English-medium secondary and tertiary education and a very small number of high-achieving students who get access to such education via their high scores in public examinations. It is the association of English with membership in this elite bilingual class in Hong Kong that helps explain why Cantonese-speaking students at Northside associated speaking English with showing off.

In Toronto, English is also the language associated with educational and socioeconomic advancement. Students at Northside passed courses and acquired "cultural capital" (Bourdieu, 1991) by demonstrating what they had learned in English. Students from Hong Kong who were first-generation immigrants to Canada used English with varying levels of proficiency and mastery. This meant they had varying levels of linguistic capital at school. When Cantonese-speaking students used English with other Cantonese students, they demonstrated their proficiency or mastery and could be seen as showing off their linguistic capital and flexing their linguistic power. Students who depended on peer social capital did not want to risk being considered "show-offs." The implications that this local analysis of "showing off" has for teacher education in multilingual communities in different parts of the world is this: Different legacies of colonialism (in this case, the legacy of British colonialism in Hong Kong) have an impact on students and teachers' current linguistic practices in schools.[3] Understanding the politics of linguistic practices in terms of legacies of colonialism and students' identities at school is the key to working through the linguistic and racial tensions arising in multilingual schools.

In summary, while the use of Cantonese at Northside was associated with peer social capital and important academic and social benefits, the use of English was associated with risk, and most students in the Hong Kong community at Northside avoided using it with each other. This linguistic strategy, demonstrating ambivalence in students' investment in English (Norton, 2000; Peirce, 1995), created several linguistic and academic dilemmas for the students.

The Case of Northside: Dilemmas, Tensions, and Pedagogies Associated with Using Cantonese

Choosing to use Cantonese only with other Cantonese speakers at Northside was problematic for some of the students. These students told us that while working and socializing almost exclusively in Cantonese provided them with friends and helped them succeed in their courses, it did not provide them with many opportunities to practice English. These students talked about the educational and socioeconomic benefits, the cultural and economic capital, associated with being able to use English well. Strong proficiency in English provided students with access to a wider range of programs and courses at university. The students also suggested that strong English skills were required in many of the local labor markets and in such high-status and high-influence professions as law, politics, and upper-management positions in both the private and public sector (see Delpit, 1998, and Maclear, 1994, on this issue).

Put a little differently, the students were trying to deal with the stresses of meeting contradictory socialization agendas and the difficulties of living in "multiple worlds" (see Boykin, 1986; Phelan, Davidson & Yu, 1998; Valenzuela, 1999, for examples of students from other communities negotiating multiple worlds). The dilemma for these students was how to find opportunities to practice English (which would benefit them in the long term) at the same time as they used Cantonese to gain peer social capital and achieve more immediate social and academic goals. One of the challenges for teachers at Northside, then, was finding ways to assist Cantonese-speaking students in developing their spoken English language skills without forcing them to assume the risks associated with showing off.

A second dilemma associated with using Cantonese at school was that many of the teachers and students didn't like hearing it in the classrooms and hallways of the school. Some teachers responded to the use of Cantonese by implementing classroom English-only rules or policies. One such teacher, Anne Yee, explained the reason behind her English-only policy in the following way. Mrs. Yee was a bilingual (Cantonese-English) speaker herself and had 17 years of teaching experience in Hong Kong and Toronto:

> I have a strong commitment to make sure that they speak only English in class because I think I understand the family backgrounds. Not just the Chinese kids' [backgrounds], the ESOL kids' [backgrounds]. I mean they don't speak English at home. Their parents don't usually speak English with them and their parents very often expect them to be able to retain their mother tongue. So, these kids, if we don't force them to speak English at school, they'd have no chance of speaking the target language or the language that they need to acquire. And if we cannot provide such an environment for them, I think we are doing them a disservice. (Interview, May 27, 1998)

While Mrs. Yee implemented an English-only classroom policy, others discussed their preferences with students at the beginning of their courses and reminded them to "Speak English, please" whenever they heard another language being used. Often, these teachers' preference for English was related to the fact that some students in their class reported that they felt excluded or "left out" when other students used languages they didn't understand, especially when they were working in small groups. These students also reported that they were worried that others were talking negatively about them in languages they couldn't understand. These feelings of being excluded and talked about often reflected the teachers' own feelings. Students who spoke Cantonese (or other languages) in classrooms where teachers had made their preference for English clear, risked their teachers' displeasure and disapproval. Students overheard using Cantonese in classrooms with English-only rules or policies risked being punished or disciplined. In all classrooms, students who spoke Cantonese risked the anger and resentment of classmates who felt excluded from their conversation. Yet, as discussed earlier, using English with Cantonese speakers was also costly. Once again, we see difficulties and stress of having to participate in two different language communities in the same school.

There were a number of ways Cantonese speaking students tried to work through this linguistic dilemma. Some tried to accommodate the language preferences of their English-speaking classmates and teachers whenever it was possible, censoring their use of Cantonese when necessary. Others code-switched from Cantonese to English and from English to Cantonese in an effort to accommodate both English and Cantonese speakers and work across linguistic differences in their classrooms. Still others resisted the insistence for English and chose to use Cantonese despite the anger of other students and their teachers. When asked to comment on the creation of classroom English-only policies as a pedagogical strategy to assist students to practice English, Lin (in Goldstein, 2003) rightly suggested that such policies do nothing to increase students' confidence and interest in using English despite their limited proficiency. English-only policies also fail to rally the first language resources that students might have to support their learning of English (see Cummins, 1989, 2000, for a review of research and writing on the ways that students' first language learning supports their second language learning and overall academic development).

A somewhat different critique of English-only policies and practices can be found in the literature on the American Ebonics Debate (cf., e.g., Perry & Delpit, 1998). African-American educator Carrie Secret (in Miner, 1998) has responded to the question of "allowing" students to use Ebonics (also known as Black English, and African American Vernacular English) in her classroom in the following way:

> The word that bothers me is 'allow'. Students talk. They bring their language to school. That is their right. If you are concerned about children using Ebonics in the classroom, you will spend the whole day saying, 'Translate, translate, translate'. So you have to pick times when you are particularly attuned to and calling for English translation (Miner, 1998, p. 82).
>
> Some days I simply announce: 'While you are working I will be listening to how well you use English. In your groups you must call for translation if a member of your group uses an Ebonic Structure.' Some days I say, 'Girls, you are at Spelman and boys, you are attending Morehouse College (historically Black American colleges). Today you use the language the professors use and expect you to use in your classes, and that language is English.' (Miner, 1998, p. 81).
>
> I once had some visitors come to my class and they said, 'We don't hear Ebonics here.' But that is because I had explained to my children that company was coming, and when company comes, we practice speaking English. Company is the best time to practice

because most of our visitors are from a cultural language context different from ours.
(Miner, 1998, p. 82)

In line with her beliefs that it is important for teachers not to imply that a student's language is inadequate but rather that different language forms are appropriate in different contexts, Carrie Secret also had her students become involved with the standard form of English through various kinds of role-play. For example, memorizing parts for drama productions provided her students with an opportunity to practice standard English while keeping their own linguistic identities and investments intact. These kinds of pedagogical activities meet the challenge of assisting students in developing target language skills without forcing them to break the sociolinguistic norms of their communities.

TENSIONS, DILEMMAS, AND PEDAGOGIES RELATED TO SILENCES IN MULTILINGUAL SCHOOLS

While much has been written about language development and language use in multilingual schools, much less has been written about silence. When the topic of silence appears in the literature on second language acquisition and language education, it is often discussed in terms of students entering or going through a *silent period* (cf., e.g., Igoa, 1995; Tabors & Snow, 1994). During this silent period, students who cannot communicate with those around in their first language stop talking. Tabors and Snow have written that this lack of speech does not necessarily mean that students stop communicating. Often, they find alternative, nonverbal, ways of communicating with others. The challenge for teachers and classmates working with such students is learning to be perceptive about what is being communicated non-verbally.

The discussion in this part of the chapter addresses the issue of silence from a different perspective. It looks at how students in a multilingual school view the importance of speech and silence differently. And it looks at the tensions and dilemmas that arise when these different understandings of speech and silence rub against each other in everyday classroom interaction. I begin this discussion with excerpts from two Northside student interviews. The first interview was with Cantonese-speaking student Victor Yu, while the second interview was with Mina Henry, a Canadian-born woman of Indo-Caribbean ancestry. The interview excerpts are followed by analysis of the different ways Victor, Mina, and other students have understood Asian silence at Northside. This analysis is followed by a pedagogical discussion about the ways teachers might assist their students in negotiating the dilemmas and tensions associated with silences in the classroom.

Victor Yu: "I can keep it in my heart"

> Tara: Tell me some of the differences between going to school in Hong Kong and going to high school here in Toronto.
>
> Victor: Oh, there's a big difference. In Hong Kong, right... the good students will have no questions... If, if you see a student, right? Like especially from Hong Kong or from Asia. Like, they, they do their work really good. But they're quiet, right? Don't blame them because this is like what they used to be in the school in Hong Kong, or in, in their country. Because they, they think that, "If I don't have any problems for the teacher, the teacher will think I am good." So they keep quiet. They don't know that if they

don't, like, answer questions, then they are not really participating in the class. Right? It's, it's, they will, like, the teachers will see them as not really good students. So this is, this would be a difference from the school in Hong Kong and here.

Tara: Was it very hard for you when you first came to Toronto to get used to the presentations and the group work and the speaking out in class?

Victor: Yeah. It was really, really hard. 'Cause, okay, 'cause I, when I want to answer some questions I was thinking about, "If I answer," right? "What will other Cantonese students or students from Hong Kong think about me?" If I, like, they may be thinking about how I am showing off my knowledge. I mean, yeah, I know the [answers to the] questions, right? I know it. That's, that's good. I can keep it in my heart. But then, if I put my hand up and then say, "Sir, I understand" and then answer the question, right? They will, they may think, think I am showing off. So it is really hard. (*Interview*, October 9, 1999)

Mina Henry: "Everyone has to contribute"

Tara: Group work is a very important topic for our work. In what ways is it good and in what ways is it bad?

Mina: I think group work is good, but you have to have people at the same level, you know what I mean? Everyone has to contribute. Of course, there is always going to be someone to take the lead…but you need other people to contribute, right? And they don't. Especially in this class, they don't. There's a lot of Chinese people, like, no offense, right? And they can't speak English properly, you know what I mean? And, like, she [Mrs. Yee] makes us, like, teach them. Well, like, I'm in a grade 12 Advanced English. My English is not that great myself, like, you know what I mean? I can speak proper English, but I am here to learn how to write properly for my OAC level [Ontario Academic Credit/high school leaving credit level]. I don't want to have to teach people, like, basic work. I need to learn how to write an essay properly. I need to learn the basic skills. In Math class, the Chinese people are all good. They don't teach me Math, you know what I mean? They sit there and do their own work. They go to private school and learn Math. None of them help me, you know what I mean? But here I have to teach them basic primary skills. And my English is not that good…

…In my other classes, I have other people [who] will say things, will disagree with me, will give me-in this class I have nothing. Everyone in that class just sits there like this. They're really quiet, they don't do nothing, like, you know what I mean? In other classes, I have other people that are on the same level in the same way as I am, so I have something to conflict with me. Seriously, I don't think half of those people in that class should be in a Grade 12 Advanced class. That's honestly what I'm saying. They shouldn't, they can't speak proper English. (Interview, May 6, 1998)

As Gordon Pon and I have written elsewhere (Goldstein 2003), in their interviews, Victor and Mina present two very different views of the importance of speech and silence in the classroom. Mina, who had always attended school in Toronto, desired conflict and debate in whole group classroom discussions and believed that everyone should contribute to smaller group discussions. Victor, who had completed most of his schooling in Hong Kong, worried about being perceived as "showing off" if he contributed to classroom discussions in the way Mina desired. The reluctance on the part of some of the students to speak English in a classroom where students were asked to work extensively in linguistically mixed groups gave rise to particular racial tensions between Hong Kong-born Chinese, Canadian-born Chinese, and non-Chinese students. As Mina asserted in her interview, our classroom observations revealed that in many sessions of small group work the Hong Kong–born Chinese students spoke little. In response, the Canadian-born Chinese and non-Chinese students assumed a leadership role in an attempt to elicit verbal participation from the quieter members. For Mina, the silence was burdensome ("I am left to do the work for them") and threatened the quality of her education ("In my other classes, I have other people [who] will say things, will disagree with me...in this class I have nothing").

Mina's comments equate silence with a lack of understanding and passivity. They also link silence with students' inability to work at a Grade 12 level. Such comments reflect the findings of other North American educational researchers, such as McKay and Wong (1996), who have argued that in multiethnic and multilingual schools such as Northside, colonialist and racialized views find daily expression. One such common expression is the belief that English-speaking ability not only is associated with academic success but also is an indication of cognitive maturity, sophistication, and degree of "Americanization" (or, in this case, "Canadianization"). Likewise, McKay and Wong note the common belief that immigrant status and limited English proficiency are considered states of deficiency and backwardness. Mina's comments about the inability of her Chinese Canadian classmates to speak "proper English" invoke such colonialist and racialist discourses. Mina's understanding of her classmates' silence as being part of their Asian nature and her use of the word *orientals* ("Orientals I find to be quieter people") also demonstrates the legacy of colonialist worldviews that North American teachers and students have inherited.[4]

In analyzing what is at stake in the linguistic and racial tensions in Mrs. Yee's classroom, there was a conflation of at least two things. First, there was an invocation of colonialist and racialized discourses that pathologized the quiet "Oriental" students in Mrs. Yee's class. Second, there was very real or material pressure for high grades and academic success (cultural capital) that weighed heavily on the minds of students like Mina ("I am here to learn how to write properly for my OAC level"). Thus, the silence of some Chinese Canadian students functioned to affirm, in the minds of some non-Chinese students, dominant negative stereotypes of Asians. These negative reactions became more strident when Asian reticence pulled down the collective marks of a group.

The comments offered by Mina show us that student silences can be disenabling for positive race relations in multilingual classrooms. Yet, what Mina and other students did not understand was the complex social and political forces that shaped the dynamics of speech and silence among their Cantonese-speaking classmates. As discussed above, these dynamics were often the result of linguistic dilemmas that trapped students into silences. Moreover, these dilemmas had little to do with being Asian, as suggested by Mina. They were peculiar to the immigration process that had created Cantonese-speaking communities in schools like Northside.

Inhibitive and Attentive Silences

After reading through a variety of literature on student silences, Pon and I found that the work of King-Kok Cheung offered us new ways of understanding the silences that troubled students like Mina. In her book *Articulate Silences*, Cheung (1993) proposes at least five differing, and often overlapping, modes or tonalities of silences, two of which, *attentive silence* and *inhibitive silence*, are of particular relevance to understanding the function of silence among Cantonese-speaking students at Northside.

Attentive silence is a form of silence in which there is acute listening, empathy for others, and awareness of even the subtlest signs from a speaker. In essence, attentive silence is a quiet understanding. Such a mode of silence, argues Cheung (1993), is empowering and thus the antithesis of passivity. An example of attentive silence at Northside is the choice Cantonese-speaking students make to remain silent in class because speaking English and answering questions could be perceived as showing off. Such attentive silence, however, traps students into a linguistic dilemma or double bind. They are caught in a "lose-lose" situation. On the one hand, they stand to lose grades and also risk the resentment of their non-Chinese and some Canadian-born Chinese classmates if they do not speak English, answer questions, and express their opinions in class. On the other hand, if they do use English with their Cantonese-speaking classmates in group work or answer the teacher's questions in front of other students, they stand to draw negative reactions from their Hong Kong-born friends.

Inhibitive silence is a self-imposed silence that at Northside is rooted in students' fears that their English pronunciation and Cantonese accent will be laughed at. As Cathy Lee, a Hong Kong-born student in Mrs. Yee's English class says:

> They're embarrassing of the English. They can't speak. They scared that people will laugh at them. Because I try that- I'm in that stage before-right? So I know how they think and how they feel. (Interview, April 30, 1998)

Working with Inhibitive and Attentive Silences

In thinking about what pedagogical maneuvers might alleviate the racial tensions described above, it is helpful for pedagogy to, first of all, acknowledge that various silences are at play in the multilingual classroom. Accordingly, each silence probably benefits from differing pedagogical engagements. In thinking about the ways teachers and students might work with different kinds of silences, I turn to the work undertaken by Northside English teachers Anne Yee, Greg Dunn, and Leonard Robertson.

In an interview about the silences in her classroom, Anne Yee commented that:

> Silence is a signal for lack of trust. It also means insecurity: 'I don't feel good about my English. I want to hide it, I don't want to hear it, I don't want to be picked on. It requires a lot of courage for me to say something in a language in which I know I have an accent, in which I know that I may not be able to use the right word. I may use it wrong and people may laugh at me. I am not going to show you something that I am not good at.' (Interview, May 27, 1998)

In the context of Mrs. Yee's understanding of inhibitive silences as being related to students' feelings about accents and language use, pedagogy can help students and teachers to negotiate inhibitive silences by deconstructing the myths and stereotypes they hold around accents and different varieties of English. Of particular interest to teachers in multilingual schools is Rosina Lippi-Green's (1997) examination of how the notions of *non-accent* and *standard language* are really myths used to justify social order and how language ideology affects students. She also examines how the media and the entertainment industry promote linguistic stereotyping and how employers discriminate on the basis of accent. The work that has been undertaken by Lippi-Green could be used to develop a classroom unit on language awareness that aims to engage students in critical analysis around issues of language, power, and racism.

Northside teacher Greg Dunn suggested direct teacher intervention as a way of responding to inhibitive silences that emerge in group work:

> I think the teacher has to be watching for the dynamics in the various groups and intervene when they see [silence] happening. And go and sort of find out and see what's going on and sometimes maybe talk to the students individually about what's happening. Suggest ways for the group leaders to encourage the students who feel they maybe don't have something to contribute. Have them prepare something, maybe even show it to me ahead of time. Show me what you are going to give your group today so that they have something to contribute and they know that it's okay. (Interview, May 13, 1998)

Mrs. Yee commented that one of her strategies in response to "dead silence" to a question is to ask students to talk about the question with a partner for a couple of minutes. When she asks the same question again, the students are able to answer the question with greater ease and she is able to elicit participation from students who were silent the first time. Another one of Mrs. Yee's strategies is calling on students who don't volunteer answers. When I suggested that calling on students in this manner may put them in "a bad position," both Mr. Dunn and Mrs. Yee commented that they had used the strategy with success.

> Tara: ...I've learnt to call on people who don't speak out because you recognize sometimes they need that space created for them. But when there is no answer, it's just, you feel like you've put somebody in a bad position.
>
> Greg: Yes. And what do you do? 'Cause if you just sort of come off and call on someone else, then they look bad. So how do you handle it? I used to say, "It's okay to say if you don't know right now. You can think about it and we'll come back and look at your response later." To give them that option rather than just saying, "You don't know, we'll go to someone else." (Interview, May 13, 1998)
>
> Tara: ...some teachers feel that they may embarrass the kids. If the kids don't volunteer, they are afraid to call on the kids' 'cause it will be embarrassing.
>
> Anne: I think the first time they may feel embarrassed, and the second, third, fourth, and the fifth, they'll get used to it. (Interview, May 27, 1998)

Imagining pedagogy that can assist students in negotiating attentive silence is more difficult than imagining a pedagogy for negotiating inhibitive silence, as it is rooted in issues of identity and the pursuit of friendship and academic success. Perhaps the most helpful way forward is working towards alleviating the racial tensions that emerge from the practice of attentive silence.

Alleviating Tensions in Small-group Work

One place to begin is to attempt to address the concerns of students like Mina who feel burdened by having to assume the responsibility for doing most, if not all, of the talking in group work. At Northside, several students suggested that group work would be more productive for them if the teacher could ensure that each member of a group had similar proficiency in English. This strategy, however, would result in placing ESOL students and students who use English as their primary language in separate groups. This kind of separation is problematic for teachers who purposefully establish linguistically mixed groups to provide opportunities for the

ESOL students in their classes to practice English. Yet, to effectively manage the tensions that can emerge in such mixed groups, it may be helpful to be flexible in grouping arrangements and alternate the kinds of groups we ask students to work in.

Alternating grouping arrangements provides teachers with a space to encourage rather than restrict the use of languages other than English during particular activities. While students working in their primary language lose an opportunity to practice English during these activities, they gain the opportunity to speak about academic material in ways that are enabling and might better prepare them for the kind of interaction, debate, even conflict, that Mina desires and is valued in North American classrooms. Thus, students can be given the opportunity to first work on a particular assignment in their primary language and then be asked to share their work in English with the teacher or others in a linguistically mixed group.

A second way to work towards alleviating tensions in small-group work is to give recognition to students who take on leadership roles and try to work effectively across linguistic differences. This is a strategy teacher Leonard Robertson used successfully in Northside by awarding extra marks to those who showed social leadership. Other forms of recognition recommended by Coehlo (1998) are a letter of commendation from the teacher or a school administrator (in a language that the students' parents can understand) or acknowledgment in a school assembly.

A third strategy for alleviating group work tensions involves the careful monitoring of the progress students are making on group work assignments. Mr. Robertson managed this monitoring work by asking students to document their individual responsibilities to the group in writing. By asking his students to document their responsibilities and progress on major group work assignments, Mr. Robertson knew when a particular student was not contributing to the group work. He could take action to alleviate the anxiety of the other group members who were worried that they would all be penalized for that student's lack of participation.

Before concluding this discussion, I'd like to touch on Mina's comment about being asked to work in groups in her English class, but having to solve math problems on her own without the support of students who might assist her when she runs into difficulty. If Mina had felt that she had access to assistance from classmates in her Math class, perhaps she would have felt less resentment in providing assistance to classmates in her English class. Engaging with such a possibility means thinking about schoolwide pedagogical interventions that encourage students to assist each other in a variety of classes. It means asking teachers and administrators to work across subject areas and departments to collectively plan ways of encouraging students to use their different academic strengths to assist others. Such planning can be complex and difficult, but may be a positive way to alleviate the resentment Mina demonstrates in her interview.

Lowering the Stakes of Small-Group Work

In view of the tensions that can surface in cooperative small-group activities that are connected to high-stakes projects, reserving group work for lower-stakes activities might be helpful. This can be done in at least two ways. First, group work can be reserved for activities that are not evaluated as part of the students' final grade but are designed to help students prepare for individually graded assignments. A second way of lowering the stakes of group work activity is to evaluate group processes rather than group products. Teachers can use specific performance criteria to provide students with feedback on how well they approach mixed group tasks; for example, seeking assistance from peers, providing assistance to peers, code-switching (e.g., from Cantonese to English or from English to Cantonese) to facilitate group communication; and participating in group problem solving.

Alternatives to Small-Group Work

In addition to lowering the stakes of the group work, teachers can also alleviate linguistic and racial tensions by alternating small-group work with whole-class work. Examples of whole-class work that could provide students with opportunities to practice English include reciting self-enhancing poetry or prose in chorus, and asking students to answer questions in unison. I noted that when students in Mr. Robertson' class answered questions in unison, several Cantonese speaking students who were usually silent responded to the question.

In summary, pedagogical suggestions have been made to enable teachers in multilingual schools to address silences, racial tensions, and the dynamics of identity by working directly with students' feelings of embarrassment, frustration, and anger. These pedagogical engagements also bring teachers face to face with everyday racism and the legacy of colonialism. Teacher education programming in linguistically diverse communities needs to provide preservice and in-service teachers with an understanding of the important role identity plays in teaching and learning (Cummins 1989, 2000; Norton 2000; see also Benesch, this volume; Gee, 2000; Harklau, this volume; Ibrahim, 1999; Ivanic, 1998; Norton, 1997; Norton & Pavlenko, this volume; Toohey, 2000; Toohey, Manyak, & Day, this volume; and Yon, 2000). It also needs to provide an understanding of how to challenge everyday racism at school (see Corson, 2001; Dei, James, Karumanchery, James-Williams, & Zine, 2000; Goldstein, 2003; Sleeter & Grant, 1999; Mohan, Leung, & Davison, 2001; and Nieto, 2000, 2002). Insofar as much of the everyday racism students experience in school can be related to different legacies of colonialism, teacher education programs should also address the history of linguistic colonialism and imperialism as it relates to linguistic communities in particular schools (see Canagarajah, 1993, 1999; Lin, 1997, 2001).

DIRECTIONS FOR FURTHER RESEARCH

Given the importance of the dynamics of identity, racism, and the legacy of colonialism to teaching and learning in multilingual schools, a very rich direction for further research involves conducting more critical ethnographic and qualitative studies on multilingual schooling in different communities. A strong critical ethnographic and qualitative research program on language, identity, and schooling has begun to grow in the fields of language education, multicultural/multilingual education, applied linguistics, and interactionist sociolinguistics (e.g., Canagarajah, 1993, 1999; Goldstein, 1997, 2003; Heller, 1994, 1999, 2001; Hunter, 1997; Ibrahim, 1999; Ivanic, 1998; Lin, 2001; Lin, Wang, Akamatsu, & Riazi, 2002; Nieto, 2000; Norton, 2000; Phelan, Davidson, & Yu, 1998; Toohey, 2000; and Valenzuela, 1999).

New critical ethnographic and qualitative research can build on the methods and writing strategies of traditional, modernist critical research (see the studies listed above for descriptions of these methods and examples of these writing strategies). It can also respond to the postmodern, postcolonial call (cf., e.g., Clifford and Marcus

1986; Behar 1993, 1995) for experimentation by exploring new ways of collecting ethnographic data and analyzing, representing, and disseminating ethnographic findings. My own response to this call has involved experimenting with "ethnographic playwriting" and "performed ethnography" (Goldstein, 2000, 2003). The project of turning ethnographic data and texts into scripts and dramas that are read and performed before audiences has been taken up by a number of writers and researchers in the disciplines of sociology and anthropology and in the fields of performance studies, theatre studies, and arts-based inquiry in education (see Denzin, 1997). The name of my first ethnographic play is *Hong Kong, Canada* and it disseminates many of the findings of the critical ethnographic study I describe in this chapter. The play is included in its entirety in Goldstein (2003).

In conclusion, I have argued that effective teacher education programming in linguistically diverse communities must help teachers develop a sophisticated understanding of issues associated with language choice, bilingualism, linguistic discrimination, and racism. Such an understanding recognizes that students often have strong affiliations in multiple linguistic and cultural worlds and that their linguistic practices are influenced by colonialism, racism, and the development of their student identities at school. Critical ethnographic research on language use and pedagogy in multilingual schools, such as the study described in this chapter, has much to offer teacher education programs located in linguistically diverse communities.

NOTES

[1] This research was undertaken with the assistance of a 3-year Social Sciences and Humanities Research Council of Canada (SSHRCC) grant (1996-1999).
[2] See Statistics Canada, available at www.statcan.ca ("Hong Kong immigration").
[3] See Pennycook's (1994, 2001) work for further discussion on the legacies of colonialism and linguistic imperialism.
[4] As Yang, Gan, and Hong (1997) have explained, the terms *orient* and *oriental* were popularized during the height of Western colonialism, when nations to the south and eeast of Europe were subjugated and exploited. While many people understand *Orient* to simply mean *The East*, over time particular ideas have become associated with the term: The Orient was seen as the farthest point from civilization (i.e., Europe) and a region of barbarism, exotic custom, and strange delight. Orientals have been conceived as mysterious and inscrutable, with traditions and beliefs so different as to be inhuman. As social historian Edward Said (1994) has explained, the intent and result of such orientalism was the objectification of cultures in Asia and the Middle East. This objectification provided a rationale for colonial subjugation, missionary conversion, and military adventure.

REFERENCES

Behar, R. (1993). *Translated woman: Crossing the border with Esperanza's story*. Boston: Beacon Press.
Behar, R. (1995). Introduction: Out of exile. In R. Behar & D. Gordon (Eds.), *Women writing culture* (pp. 1–29). Berkeley: University of California Press.
Bourdieu, P. (1991). *Language and symbolic power*. (John B. Thompson Ed.; Gino Raymond and Matthew Adamson, Trans.). Cambridge: Polity Press.
Boykin, A. W. (1986). The triple quandary and the schooling of Afro-American children. In U. Neisser (Ed.), *School achievement of minority children: New perspectives* (pp. 57–92). London: Lawrence Erlbaum.
Canagarajah, S. (1993). Critical ethnography of a Sri Lankan classroom: Ambiguities in student opposition to reproduction through ESOL. *TESOL Quarterly, 27*(4), 601–626.
Canagarajah, S. (1999). *Resisting linguistic imperialism in English teaching*. Oxford: Oxford University Press.
Chan, A. (1983). *Gold mountain: The Chinese in the new world*. Vancouver: New Star Books.

Cheung, K. K. (1993). *Articulate silences: Hisaye Yamamoto, Maxine Hong Kingston, Joy Kogawa.* Ithaca & London: Cornell University Press.
Clifford, J., & Marcus G. (Eds.). (1986). *Writing culture: The poetics and politics of ethnography.* Berkeley, CA: University of California Press.
Coehlo, E. (1998). *Teaching and learning in multicultural schools.* Clevedon: Multilingual Matters.
Corson, D. (2001). *Language diversity and education.* Mahwah, NJ: Lawrence Erlbaum.
Cummins, J. (1989). *Empowering minority students.* Sacremento: California Association for Bilingual Education.
Cummins, J. (2000). *Negotiating identities: Education for empowerment in a diverse society* (2nd ed.). Ontario, CA: California Association for Bilingual Education.
Dei, G., James, I., Karumanchery, L., James-Williams, S., & Zine, J. (2000). *Removing the margins: The challenges and possibilities of inclusive schooling.* Toronto: Canadian Scholars' Press.
Delpit, L. (1998). What should teachers do?: Ebonics and culturally responsive instruction. In T. Perry & L. Delpit (Eds.), *The real Ebonics debate: Power, language and the education of African-American children* (pp. 17–26). Boston: Beacon Press.
Denzin, Norman. (1997). Performance texts. In W. G. Tierney & Y. S. Lincoln (Eds.), *Representation and the Text: Re-framing the narrative voice.* Albany: SUNY Press.
Gee, J. (2000). Identity as an analytic lens for research in education. *Review of Research in Education, 25,* 99–125.
Goldstein, T. (1997). *Two languages at work: Bilingual life on the production floor.* New York/Berlin: Mouton de Gruyter.
Goldstein, T. (2000). Hong Kong, Canada: Performed ethnography for anti-racist teacher education. *Teaching Education Journal, 11*(3), 311–326.
Goldstein, T. (2003) *Teaching and learning in a multilingual school community: Choices, risks and dilemmas.* Lawrence Erlbaum.
Hall, S. (1996). The significance of new times. In D. Morley & K-H. Chen (Eds.), *Critical dialogues in cultural studies* (pp. 223–237). New York: Routledge.
Heller, M. (1994). *Crosswords: Language, education and ethnicity in French Ontario.* Berlin and New York: Mouton de Gruyter.
Heller, M. (1999). *Linguistic minorities and modernity: A sociolinguistic ethnography.* New York: Longman.
Heller, M. (2001). Legitimate language in a multilingual school. In M. Heller & M. Martin Jones (Eds.), *Voices of authority: Education and linguistic differences* (pp. 381–402). Westport, CT: Ablex.
Hunter, J. (1997). Multiple perceptions: Social identity in a multilingual elementary classroom. *TESOL Quarterly, 31*(3), 603–611.
Ibrahim, A. (1999). Becoming Black: Rap and hip-hop, race, gender, identity and the politics of ESL learning. *TESOL Quarterly, 33*(3), 349–369.
Igoa, C. (1995). *The inner world of the immigrant child.* New York: St. Martin's Press.
Ivanic, R. (1998). *Writing and identity: The discoursal construction of identity in academic writing.* Amsterdam/Philadelphia: John Benjamins.
Lin, A. (1997). Analyzing the "language problem" discourses in Hong Kong: How official, academic, and media discourses construct and perpetuate dominant models of language, learning and education. *Journal of Pragmatics, 28,* 427–440.
Lin, A. (2001). Symbolic domination and bilingual classroom practices in Hong Kong schools. In M. Heller & M. Martin Jones (Eds.), *Voices of authority: Education and linguistic differences* (pp. 139–168). Westport, CT: Ablex.
Lin, A., Wang, W., Akamatsu, N., Riazi, M. (2002). Appropriating English, expanding identities and re-visioning the field: From TESOL to teaching English for glocalized communication (TEGCOM). *Journal of Language, Identity and Education, 1*(4), 279–293.
Lippi-Green, R. (1997). *English with an accent: Language, ideology and discrimination in the United States.* New York: Routledge.
Luke, A. (1999, March). *New times, new identities, and new literacies.* Plenary Address at TESOL, 1999, New York, NY.
Maclear, K. (1994). The myth of the "model minority": Rethinking the education of Asian Canadians. *Our schools/our Selves, 5*(3), 54–76.
McKay, S. L., & Wong, S. C. (1996). Multiple discourses, multiple identities: Investment and agency in second-language learning among Chinese adolescent immigrant students. *Harvard Educational Review, 6*(3), 577–608.
Miner, B. (1998). Embracing Ebonics and teaching Standard English: An interview with Oakland teacher Carrie Secret. In T. Perry & L. Delpit (Eds.), *The real Ebonics debate: Power, language and the education of African-American children* (pp. 79–88). Boston: Beacon Press.

Mohan, B., Leung, C., & Davison, C. (Eds.). (2001). *English as a second language in the mainstream: Teaching, learning and identity.* Harlow, England/Don Mills, Ontario: Longman.

Nieto, S. (2000). *Affirming diversity: The sociopolitical context of multicultural education* (3rd ed.). New York: Longman.

Nieto, S. (2002). *Language, culture and teaching: Critical perspectives for a new century.* Mahwah, NJ: Lawrence Erlbaum.

Norton, B. (Ed.) (1997). Special issue on language and identity. *TESOL Quarterly 31*(3).

Norton, B. (2000). *Identity and language learning: Gender, ethnicity and educational change.* New York: Longman.

Peirce, B. (1995). Social identity, investment and language learning. *TESOL Quarterly, 29*(1), 9–31. Mahwah, NJ: Lawrence Erlbaum.

Perry, T., & Delpit, L. (Eds.). (1998). *The real Ebonics debate: Power, language and the education of African-American children.* Boston: Beacon Press.

Phelan, P., Davidson, A.L., & Yu, H.C. (1998). *Adolescents' worlds: Negotiating family, peers, and school.* New York: Teachers College Press.

Said, E. (1994). *Orientalism* (2nd ed.). New York: Vintage Books.

Sleeter, C., & Grant, C. (1999). *Making choices for multicultural education: Five approaches to race, class, and gender* (3rd ed.). Toronto: John Wiley and Sons.

Tabors, P., & Snow, C. (1994). English as a second language in preschool programs. In F. Genesee (Ed.), *Educating second language children* (pp. 103–125). New York: Cambridge University Press.

Toohey, K. (2000). *Learning English at school: Identity, social relations, classroom practice.* Toronto: Multilingual Matters.

Valenzuela, A. (1999). *Substractive schooling: U.S.-Mexican youth and the politics of caring.* New York: State University of New York Press.

Yang, J., Gan, D., & Hong, T. (1997). *Eastern standard time: A guide to Asian influences on American culture: From Astro Boy to Zen Buddhism.* Boston: Houghton Mifflin.

Yee, P. (1996). *Struggle and hope: The story of Chinese Canadians.* Toronto, Ontario: Umbrella Press.

Yon, D. (2000). *Elusive culture: Schooling, race and identity in global times.* Albany, NY: State University of New York Press.

CHAPTER 67

CHALLENGES AND OPPORTUNITIES FOR THE TEACHING PROFESSION:

English as an Additional Language in the UK

CHARLOTTE FRANSON

Canterbury Christ Church University, England

ABSTRACT

Provision for the EAL learner in England can offer a purposeful and communicative learning environment, that is, the mainstream classroom, where there is a prescribed curriculum from which teachers can derive both content and language learning objectives and appropriate activities and tasks to encourage meaningful language learning. However, continuing debate persists with respect not only to assessment for funding, curriculum achievement, and language proficiency but also to mainstreaming versus withdrawal, specialist language teaching versus provision to promote the inclusion of ethnic minorities, and school-based versus local education authority resourcing. EAL teachers must be prepared to respond in diverse ways to the needs of learners and to engage more proactively with mainstream pedagogy to assist schools in delivering inclusion and to empower learners. They will also need to continue to engage with and challenge government policies in order to increase understanding of EAL as a specialist field and to ensure that policies that relate to equality and educational access take full account of EAL learners. In order to do this, they will need the convictions of an informed professional knowledge base afforded by opportunities for further professional development and research. This chapter discusses the challenges that face the EAL profession and suggests possibilities for a future agenda.

INTRODUCTION

The EAL (English as an additional language) teaching profession and educational provision for EAL pupils in the United Kingdom (UK) face both challenges and opportunities in the coming years. The EAL pupil population is very diverse, as are the needs of EAL pupils; for example, significant numbers of asylum-seeking pupils arrive in schools with a range of social, educational, and linguistic needs, whereas children of settled ethnic groups arrive in school with distinctive and different EAL needs. In addition, families of international business employees working in England on short-term contracts often place their children in state education for 1 or 2 years. In 2005, the Department for Education and Skills (DfES) identified approximately 10.3% of the pupil cohort aged 5 to 16 years as having English as an additional language.

Current practice in state-maintained schools places the EAL learner in the classroom with monolingual English speaking peers. All children entering school, regardless of their English language proficiency or prior educational experiences, join the relevant age group in that school and participate in the curriculum designated for that cohort. Assessment, both formative and summative, is undertaken in relation to the National Curriculum in which all pupils are required to participate, and children progress automatically from year to year with their age cohort. Implicit in the process is the belief that English language can be acquired through participating in the National Curriculum. Additional language support within the context of the classroom and curriculum is provided at the discretion of the school and the local education authority (LEA) and is funded by a national grant for this purpose. Although the title of this chapter makes reference to the UK, most references will be to practice in England. The United Kingdom comprises four administrative regions, including Scotland, Wales, and Northern Ireland, all of which have developed distinctive approaches to the implementation of national policy. For example, in Wales, the situation is made more complex as a result of the Welsh-English bilingual education system.

THE CONTEXT OF EAL PROVISION IN ENGLAND

The historical background to the education of EAL learners can be seen in the wider context of educational provision in English State schools. In 1967, the publication of *The Plowden Report* (Department of Education and Science [DES]) was instrumental in establishing a basis for educational practice in the following decades. The report advocated the use of concrete activities and experiences as the best means of promoting learning; children were encouraged to work at their own level and were seen as agents of their own learning; and the teacher's role was that of a facilitating adult who would foster and extend children's learning through conversations, the exchange of ideas, and the use of appropriate language.

This conceptualization of teaching and learning emphasized child-centered educational practice, which included activity-based pupil participation, learning by discovery techniques, cooperative group work, and integrated teaching of subject- and topic-based work. Many of these practices have subsequently been advocated as equally important in the development of learning environments considered necessary for promoting successful EAL learning. And indeed, the current view in England emphasizes that well-managed and language-rich classrooms will naturally provide the best environment for the learning of English and subject content through the daily interaction of EAL learners with their English-speaking peers.

However, in the 1970s and 1980s it was recognized that additional efforts were needed to address cultural diversity, especially in larger urban centers. Some local authorities made significant efforts in tackling racism and promoting multiculturalism, acknowledging that more needed to be done to secure the linguistic and academic achievement of ethnic minority EAL pupils (Department of Education and Science, 1972, 1975, 1985). By the end of the 1980s, LEAs had been through a period in which multicultural and antiracist teaching policies and strategies had been implemented, government funding had been provided for multicultural education initiatives, and *equality of access* had become a populist phrase. A review of provision for EAL and ethnic minority learners had resulted in the restructuring and development of centrally managed teaching services for EAL learners (Home Office, 1988, 1990). Many EAL teachers argued that mainstreaming provided equality of access and saw their presence in the school as supporting their pupils' access to both language learning opportunities and the curriculum. This position was strengthened with the success of the legal action taken against a local education authority's program of separate provision for EAL pupils (Commission for Racial Equality, 1986).

But by the early 1990s in England, other issues were foregrounded in the government's educational agenda: a National Curriculum was implemented that highlighted regular pupil assessment, target setting, and the development of teacher training standards and national inspection procedures, all in the name of accountability and the raising of standards.

Greater emphasis is now placed on reducing the levels of underachievement amongst ethnic minority groups, and national policy is focused on *educational inclusion*, as evidenced in the guidance for school inspectors (Office for Standards in Education [OFSTED], 2000). Centrally funded EAL teaching services have been dismantled, and there has been a loss of expertise as EAL teachers have moved into other areas of education. As a result, the nature of EAL support within the curriculum and the school is changing, as individual schools take up the resources and the responsibility for EAL teaching support offered to their pupils. Anecdotal evidence would suggest that more and more frequently, schools are employing less qualified teaching assistants rather than experienced EAL teachers. At the same time as this dilution of EAL expertise, ESOL provision for adults has progressed significantly, with a new national ESOL curriculum and national training for ESOL teachers (Basic Skills Agency, 2001). However, at the level of primary and secondary schools, the fragmentation and loss of EAL teaching expertise and resources, both financial and otherwise, is challenging the profession to think in new ways.

FUNDING EAL PROVISION

For three decades, the funding for EAL provision came from the Home Office, under the Local Government Act (1966), to support pupils from New Commonwealth heritage. As a result of government scrutiny in the late 1980s, local education authorities were encouraged to bid for funding for new projects to support EAL pupils. In the mid-1990s, the remit of such projects was extended to include pupils from non-New Commonwealth heritage, but at the same time, the amount of the grant to LEAs was reduced. At the end of the 1990s, the remit of the work was again widened to include all ethnic minority pupils. The increasing number of refugee and asylum-seeking pupils, of whom many have limited English language skills, has also put additional demands on the available funding.

The rationale for funding of EAL provision also needs to be seen within the wider context of educational funding. In the past decade, the government has increased the financial responsibility of schools by delegating a large portion of the educational grant directly to schools. This has had a significant impact on EAL provision because the responsibility now rests with schools to ensure that the language and learning needs of EAL learners are appropriately addressed. However, with no obligatory system of accountability at the local level, EAL provision can be dependent upon the level of the Headteacher's knowledge and understanding of EAL learners' needs. Within a local education authority (LEA), there can be a wide range and disparity in EAL provision, with few monitoring procedures to ensure high-quality provision for all learners. This decentralization of funding has resulted in a loss of EAL teaching expertise, materials, and other resources.

The changes in educational provision since the early 1990s, the emphasis on raising standards, the erosion of mixed-ability teaching, and the continued uncertainty about funding and the professional status of the EAL teacher have made a significant impact on the field of EAL education. But the fundamental issues have not disappeared and remain areas of continuing debate. These issues include the conceptualization of appropriate EAL provision, the role of the EAL teacher, the distinctiveness of the EAL learner, effective EAL pedagogy and assessment, and professional development and research.

EAL PROVISION IN THE MAINSTREAM CLASSROOM

EAL teaching in England is predicated on collaboration and team teaching between a mainstream subject teacher and an EAL language support teacher to provide both language and curriculum content learning in the mainstream classroom (Bourne, 1989; Levine, 1990), and this view has been subsequently supported in government reports and professional publications (e.g., OfSTED, 1994; School Curriculum and Assessment Authority, 1996).

The model of practice for mainstreaming EAL learners and EAL support teachers is commonly known as *Partnership Teaching*, in which EAL and classroom teachers work together to "develop a curriculum response to the language needs and abilities of all pupils, whether monolingual, bilingual or multilingual" (Bourne & McPake, 1991, p. 8). It promotes both collaborative teaching in the classroom and a whole-school approach to meeting the learning needs of EAL learners. Implicit in this approach is the view that individual learning arises in process-oriented, mixed-ability groupings.

Collaborative teaching has been widely promoted as a pedagogic model that supports EAL learners; however, the focus of collaborative teaching has often been on managing the relationship between the subject or class teacher and language support teacher rather than on specific language teaching strategies that might benefit the EAL learner in the mainstream context. Edwards and Redfern (1992) refer to the "missionary zeal" with which mainstreaming has been pursued as a panacea for the needs of the EAL learner, but classroom ethnographic studies suggest that the complex interplay of variables in the classroom make that assumption less secure (Toohey, 1998; Willett, 1995).

Mainstreaming was intended to provide for the EAL learner opportunities to continue learning with his or her peer group, to promote mutual respect and understanding of linguistic and cultural diversity, and to provide communicatively purposeful opportunities for language learning. However, the placement of EAL pupils within the mainstream classroom has sometimes been carried out in the absence of appropriate support for the teacher and the EAL learner to optimize the teaching-learning relationship.

Nevertheless, collaborative or team teaching has meant far greater participation of the English language support teacher in the mainstream subject lesson (Bourne & McPake, 1991; OfSTED, 2001a, 2001b). The language support teacher is encouraged to work with the subject teacher in the planning and delivery of the lesson, providing input that will enhance the language learning opportunities afforded to EAL pupils. National inspection reports in the past decade have endorsed the collaborative role of the EAL support teacher in mainstream classrooms (e.g., OfSTED, 1994, 2001a, 2001b). The implementation of a national strategy for the teaching of literacy skills has also created opportunities for EAL teachers to take a leading role in developing strategies appropriate for EAL learners (DfEE, 2000). However, research reported in the Times Educational Supplement [May 3, 2002] suggested that during the Literacy Hour teacher-pupil oral interaction had declined. Both strategies are now supplemented by additional support programs to ensure that pupils attain the expected level.

However, one could argue that the zealous adoption of mainstreaming has constrained the development of a more explicit and rigorous conceptualization of EAL provision. Furthermore, the EAL profession has been distracted from this task by the lack of employment and career prospects and the demanding pace of curriculum that they are required to teach. Although the implementation of mainstreaming has varied in effectiveness, educators generally acknowledge the potential benefits for EAL pupils of being with their peer group and participating in cognitively challenging tasks with contextualized language support. Unfortunately, it would seem that the benefits of collaborative teaching practices are being jeopardized with the loss of EAL teaching expertise as this generation of EAL specialists gets older, moves into management and other aspects of education, or retires, and as schools, for a range of reasons, increasingly choose to appoint less qualified teaching assistants, rather than EAL specialist teachers, to work with EAL pupils.

EAL PEDAGOGY

Over the past two decades, much of what has happened in the classroom and in the policy that has directed EAL provision has been very much driven by practice, immediacy, and expediency. Both policy and pedagogy have in many ways reflected a *bottom-up approach*, an approach in which language support teachers viewed their roles as a moment-by-moment activity that was highly contextualized, and dependent upon the subject being taught, the relationship with the classroom teacher, and the needs of diverse learners.

Thus, a central point of the argument about EAL provision in English State schools is that there is no shared and agreed-upon theoretical foundation from which teachers can derive an appropriate conceptualization of EAL pedagogy. Unlike subject matter teachers, who typically hold a higher degree in their specialization (e.g., History, Science, etc.), many EAL teachers do not hold a specialist degree or postgraduate qualifications for the simple reason that there have been limited opportunities to pursue such qualifications. They continue to work within very generalized principles of learning, and many have only limited understanding of how they might address more advanced academic language learning needs of EAL learners, particularly as they relate to curriculum content. It is assumed that they have the expertise, but without training of a sufficiently high level, such knowledge that is available is often locally developed and is not embedded in a theoretical framework that would allow for expansion of their professional knowledge. For example, a recent national inspection report on EAL provision noted that "much of the support work focused on helping pupils access the curriculum and did not do enough to address their specific language needs directly at the same time" (OfSTED,

2001a, p. 26). Many EAL teachers continue to define their work in relation to outcomes such as pupil confidence, home-school liaison, and pupil participation in classroom activities, rather than attainment in curriculum-related tasks. Successful teaching is often defined in terms of social and affective outcomes (Leung & Franson, 2001b). This may be in part a result of the continuing difficulties in conceptualizing EAL pedagogy (Franson, 2001b).

The lack of agreed-upon principles of practice and a well-defined pedagogy often leaves EAL teachers without a working agenda on the day-to-day level. It is assumed that interactive group work and the discussion generated as a result of activities will provide language input for the EAL pupil. Other factors cited in determining good practice include joint planning between the mainstream and EAL teacher, activities that encourage pupils to rehearse and explore the language needed, continued support with writing through the use of graphic organizers and writing frames, and a focus on content, ensuring appropriate cognitive challenge as well as the necessary language to complete the task (OfSTED, 2001a, p. 27). However, these are quite general statements that could be applied to all learners and lack the specificity needed for EAL learners. It would seem that there are two areas of EAL pedagogy that need attention: (a) developing pedagogical responses to learners at different stages or levels of EAL development in different phases of education, and (b) development of a systematic and principled approach to the integration of curriculum content and language (Leung & Franson, 2001b, p. 174).

The absence of a more pedagogically explicit practice continues to need to be addressed in the face of the changing context of EAL teaching and learning. It would seem that in recent years international research and development into second language learning and pedagogy have been largely neglected at government level despite the various attempts to redress this situation by professional organizations. Guidance on the teaching of EAL learners tends to remain very general in nature, addressing the needs of beginners and only recently have there been initiatives to address the demands of more advanced EAL learners.

Research into provision for ethnic minority and EAL pupils has raised the awareness of EAL learners' needs, but the emphasis, more recently, has been on the academic achievement of all ethnic minority pupils, and issues related to EAL provision have been subsumed within the broader institutional issue of the ways in which schools are addressing the attainment of ethnic minority pupils in general (Blair & Bourne, 1998; Gillborn & Mirza, 2000; OfSTED, 2002).

Unresolved issues regarding assessment of pupils for whom English is an additional language highlight ongoing tensions in implementing a single National Curriculum directed at all pupils. Although teachers are expected to take account of and support the particular needs of some individuals and groups, the purpose is to enable them to participate effectively in curriculum and assessment activities (DfEE, 1999, p. 35). This overarching requirement that all pupils must be taught and assessed against the National Curriculum levels does not acknowledge the distinctiveness of EAL learning and the need to establish additional and complementary means of assessing EAL progression. Nor does it recognize that the issue concerns not simply the learning of English by EAL pupils but also impinges on the assessment of other curriculum subjects, for example, Science or History, where the pupil is learning EAL and subject content at the same time. Further direction to teachers is provided by the Qualifications and Curriculum Authority (QCA, 2000), which extends the English National Curriculum scale to include three additional steps by which teachers can assess beginners in EAL, but it does not resolve the issue for the Science teacher who knows that it is English language skills that are depressing an EAL pupil's Science results. Whereas the earlier work of individual EAL services in Local Education Authorities attempted to address the distinctiveness of stages in EAL development, the QCA scale attempts to integrate EAL development with the national levels and standards expected of English as a first language learners. From all perspectives, it would be helpful "to be clear about how curriculum provision, assessment of progress and the setting of targets for pupils learning EAL relates to broader national initiatives" (QCA, 2000, p. 7).

As the pressure on schools to reach their performance targets has increased, so too has the importance of establishing effective approaches to EAL pedagogy and assessment. Teachers continue to use a range of strategies that may be less than appropriate, including the withdrawal of pupils from lessons. For example, a recent inspection report (OfSTED, 2001a, p. 25) noted continued ineffective use of EAL teachers in the classroom and evidence of schools choosing to provide EAL support by withdrawing EAL pupils from mainstream classes. Despite the emphasis in the past decade on integrating EAL into mainstream curriculum pedagogy, a new generation of teachers is making other, potentially less informed choices. Without a professionally agreed upon theoretical framework and knowledge base upon which to draw, the aims and outcomes of EAL provision are likely to remain unclear. The raising of professional standards and improvement of quality of provision would be significantly advanced if EAL were established as a teaching specialty with minimum requirements of knowledge and skills (Leung & Franson, 2001a, p. 207).

THE ROLE OF THE EAL SPECIALIST TEACHER

Ambiguities and tensions surrounding the role of the EAL teacher have persisted for a considerable period of time. In an ideal classroom, the language support teacher works as the language specialist supporting and advising the class teacher; however, it is commonly known that for many EAL teachers, the role is mainly a passive one in which she tries to help the EAL learner through the language difficulties in the classroom. This situation is illustrated by Levine (1990), who writes about her efforts to integrate her group of EAL learners:

> Initially, I felt I could only accept responsibility for 'my' pupils, sitting with them separately and letting the English teacher carry on as before, initiating the work and taking the responsibility for the day-to-day assessment.... I was obviously in a subordinate role, one which signalled very clearly to all the members of the class that I was the lesser of the two teachers. That, combined with the fact that the 'weaker' of the two teachers looked after the children at most risk,... simply served to underline the separateness of the bilingual students. (p. 75)

The author identified problem areas in providing EAL support in the mainstream that have continued to persist more than two decades after the writing:

> 1. What are the respective roles and responsibilities of subject teacher and EAL teacher in the classroom?
>
> 2. How do we ensure that a range of language experience is made available within the classroom to students developing a use of English as a second language?
>
> 3. How do we avoid segregation of students within the classroom? (p. 75)

For many EAL teachers, the practice of mainstreaming that drew them into partnership with classroom teachers was to be welcomed. It strengthened their position and asserted their legitimate role in schools. However, the remit of their work widened over the years and, in their attempts to secure professional credibility for themselves and assist the pupils they supported, EAL teachers not only worked alongside colleagues but also contributed to various school activities. Some schools took advantage of their willingness to become part of the mainstream and used EAL teachers to act in a variety of roles. In many ways, the language teaching role became secondary to the role as facilitator of cultural and social inclusion (Franson, 2001b).

Another recent challenge to EAL provision and the EAL teacher has arisen with the national implementation of strategies promoting the deployment of teaching assistants (TAs). The number of TAs has increased significantly over the past few years, and more schools are employing teaching assistants to support their EAL pupils. Classroom assistants traditionally have been employed for a range of non-teaching tasks that were often characterized as *washing the paint pots and putting up displays*. More frequently, they helped by listening to pupils' reading, working with children with learning difficulties, and undertaking a range of similar supporting tasks in the classroom. TAs now lead small-group work to assist the implementation of the literacy and numeracy strategies that are integral to the National Curriculum; many work with children with special educational needs and, increasingly, TAs are being employed to provide EAL support teaching. A national initiative for specialist training of EAL teaching assistants is being piloted, and many LEAs have also developed local versions of training. Anecdotal evidence from TAs includes concerns similar to those expressed by EAL teachers: that is, lack of preparation time, insufficient detail about lesson objectives, lack of direction from the teacher, lack of knowledge about EAL development and practice, and being marginalized both by teachers and pupils. Despite the fact that TAs have large gaps in professional knowledge and practical experience, they are now increasingly becoming responsible for delivering EAL provision.

Creese (2001) points out that the terms *support* and *partnership* explain little of the complexities of the professional relationship between classroom and EAL teachers. The difficulties faced by the EAL specialist include isolation, lack of power, and the lack of understanding in schools about language and its relevance to power relations, culture, and identity (Creese, p. 85). As many EAL teachers have themselves reported, they continue to be marginalized in the same way as their pupils, and this simply reflects societal power relations. Similar issues were addressed by Franson (1995), and it would seem that the status of the EAL teacher, and increasingly, the EAL teaching assistant, has changed little since the mid-1990s.

EQUALITY, INCLUSION, AND EAL PROVISION

Very often the success of EAL learners and their teachers is reported and praised at an individual or school level, but there is continuing discussion at a national level regarding the cost effectiveness of EAL provision and its impact on raising attainment. The national focus on raising attainment emphasizes data collection and analysis, with increased targeting of resources and increased autonomy at school level to implement strategies to improve outcomes.

It could be argued, however, that neither improved data collection systems nor the setting of targets nor increased EAL teaching input in isolation will resolve the issues of raising attainment and securing equality of participation for EAL pupils. As emphasized by a recent OfSTED (2001b) report, there is a need for whole-school planning and commitment of the totality of school resources to improve provision for EAL and ethnic minority pupils. A similar perspective is evident in recent inspection reports on provision for Black Caribbean pupils that highlight the complexity of support needed and recommend strategies that are whole-school focused, including curriculum planning, teaching, and assessment that reflects cultural and ethnic diversity; and high-quality training for staff to meet the needs of minority ethnic pupils (OfSTED, 2002).

Furthermore, any discussion of achievement and ethnicity and EAL without consideration of variables such as class and socioeconomic factors has to be treated with caution, and research findings paint a very complex picture of achievement and ethnicity (see Cummins, 2000; Gibson, 1997; Ogbu & Simons, 1998). The links between language, identity, and class, especially for Black and Asian pupils living in working class communities, are often not explicitly expressed in teachers' discussions (Harris, 2001). The challenge for EAL teachers is to develop their professional knowledge about the diverse trajectories of language learning for these groups and to develop pedagogies that take account of their diverse learning needs.

In the wider educational debate about *inclusion* that permeates educational discussions in England, many educators feel that if all pupils with diverse learning needs were included within mainstream provision, then the feelings of difference and separateness associated with segregated provision would be reduced, and pupils within mainstream provision would learn to live more comfortably with diversity (Franson, 2001b). The word *inclusive*, like *mainstreaming* and the phrase *equal access*, is used widely and generically, meaning different things to different groups. National inspection guidance (OfSTED, 2000) offers a long list of groups that are to be recognized within the concept of inclusion. This is not to say that the intent behind the use of such terms is not sincere and worth pursuing, but rather that the particularity of the needs of certain groups of learners, such as EAL learners, may be lost in the generality of pedagogical approaches advocated to promote inclusion.

Recent legislation regarding the provision of racial equality in schools may result in more focused discussion of these issues. Schools are now mandated to promote racial equality, and the Commission for Racial Equality (CRE) (2000) takes the position that race equality is about enabling pupils of different ethnic and racial groups to participate fully in all aspects of schooling. Schools are legally required to monitor and review all aspects of school life, from admissions to the ways in which pupils are grouped in classes, and the monitoring of schools' implementation of race equality practice is now within the remit of national school inspection teams. This legislation will hopefully strengthen the arguments of educators of EAL and ethnic minority pupils for improved educational provision that challenges implicit beliefs and stereotypes and institutionally racist practices.

CHALLENGES FOR THE PROFESSION

Challenges for the profession have been raised throughout this chapter; however, there are two or three that should be emphasized, as they are critical to the continued debate about appropriate and effective provision for EAL and ethnic minority learners in the UK. In the first place, there is a need to institute a statutory entitlement to additional specialist teaching for EAL learners. This is an important challenge that must be addressed, especially in view of the changes in national educational policy and funding that have diffused the needs of EAL learners within the more general emphasis on inclusion and the raising of achievement of ethnic minority pupils.

There also needs to be a clearer conceptualization of the EAL learner. Such learners include those who are recently arrived asylum seekers totally new to English, those from an ethnic/linguistic minority in England who might not be conversant in spoken English (very young learners) or who might need support in developing academic English, or bilingual pupils whose English language ability is similar to monolingual native speakers. Their levels of literacy in the home language vary enormously, as will the level of spoken fluency. The identity of the EAL learner is not static but constantly changing, reflected, for example, in the growing numbers of asylum-seeking pupils in schools and the generational changes in settled populations. In the same way, the growing numbers of learners of mixed race heritage present challenges to the stereotypical notions of ethnic minority groups. These different types of learners have varied language learning needs that require a range of responses from their teachers in terms of differentiated teaching and learning strategies (Leung & Franson, 2001a).

Concomitant with this point is the need for greater recognition and provision for the first languages and cultures of EAL children. In the ongoing discussion over educational provision for EAL pupils, the arguments for bilingual teaching support and bilingual education are often subsumed and even neglected within the wider debate.

It may be that EAL teachers are at a point of critical change in identity in terms of their role in school and in terms of themselves as practitioners. In the changing educational context, they need to have a better understanding of equality, and of issues of identity, agency, and difference (Duff, 2002), which are fundamental to discussions of mainstreaming and EAL provision. Language socialization can also provide a useful theoretical framework by which practitioners can discuss the ways in which language, knowledge, and participation in educational activities are co-constructed and linked with identity. These debates can only happen within an informed and articulate profession, drawing upon a shared knowledge base, and thus the development of their own professional knowledge is vital to the continued professional role of EAL teachers. The development of postgraduate training and qualifications will lead to further research and development in the field and enhance the status of the EAL profession. EAL teachers also need to continue to challenge the thinking that has underpinned educational change over the past ten or more years. Changes in education have predicated success on the implementation, at the national level, of a prescriptive and content-driven curriculum, regular and frequent assessment practices, the setting of targets for schools and LEAs, and a demanding inspection regime. During the past decade, teaching has become bureaucratized and daily practice has become scripted, as illustrated by the guidance accompanying the national literacy and numeracy strategies. Yet EAL provision does not sit easily within this educational context, nor does a conceptualization of schools as dynamic, complex, and changing contexts in which adults and children can interact and new ideas, identities, and practices emerge.

Teachers know well that their pupils present different identities in different contexts: for EAL and ethnic minority learners, the reconciliation of the first language and community identity and their school identity, manifested through their competency in English and their ability to adapt to school life, can be a difficult and contentious process (see for example the work of Rampton, 1995). The challenge for the ethnic and linguistic minority learner is to establish a nexus in which there is some reconciliation across the multiple boundaries that is ongoing and intrinsic to the concept of identity (Wenger, 1998, pp. 160–161). Institutionally, the challenge is to make some of the invisible pedagogy (Bernstein, 1978) more explicit and open to questioning. EAL teachers themselves need a stronger professional identity and greater status if they are to help EAL learners construct identities that will enable fuller participation and increase their academic achievement.

Paradoxically, it could be argued that the lack of a nationally recognized identity within the curriculum has allowed the EAL profession to develop its own voice, to explore international perspectives on EAL provision, and, from the margins of the curriculum, to challenge educational changes. It has allowed EAL teachers to exploit the cross-curricular aspects of their work and develop their knowledge and experience of a wide range of institutional and classroom practice. Yet this independence has left the profession vulnerable, without gravitas or recognized authority, to challenge or support educational changes that affect EAL and bilingual pupils. Thus, the biggest challenge to EAL provision may be to ensure that the progress of the past decade in developing a distinct identity and a professional knowledge base and voice is not lost in face of seemingly relentless educational change. The need for a national strategy that would secure the EAL profession and bring together the myriad of initiatives that are appropriating EAL has never been more necessary.

REFERENCES

Basic Skills Agency (BSA). (2001). *Adult ESOL curriculum*. London: DfES.
Bernstein, B. (1977). Class and pedagogies: Visible and invisible. In J. Karabel & A. H. Halsey (Eds.), *Power and ideology in education* (pp. 511–534). New York: Oxford University Press.
Blair, M., & Bourne, J. (1998). *Making the difference: Teaching and learning strategies in successful multi-ethnic schools.* London: HMSO.
Bourne, J. (1989). *Moving into the mainstream: LEA provision for bilingual pupils*. Windsor, England: NFER-Nelson.
Bourne, J., & McPake, J. (1991). *Partnership teaching: Co-operative teaching strategies for English language support in multilingual classrooms*. London: HMSO.
Commission for Racial Equality (CRE). (1986). *Teaching English as a second language*. (*The Calderdale Report*). London: CRE.
CRE (2000). *The statutory code of practice on the duty to promote race equality.* London: CRE.
Creese, A. (2001). Teachers talking: Communication in professional partnerships. In C. Jones & C. Wallace (Eds.), *Making EMAG work* (pp. 73–86). Stoke on Trent: Trentham Books.
Cummins, J. (2000). *Language, power and pedagogy*. Clevedon: Multilingual Matters.
Department of Education and Science (DES). (1967). *Children and their primary schools* (*The Plowden Report*). London: HMSO.
DES (1972). *The continuing needs of immigrants*. Education Survey 14. London: HMSO.
DES (1975). *A language for life* (*The Bullock Report*). London: HMSO.
DES (1985). *Education for all: The report of the committee of inquiry into the education of children from ethnic minority groups* (*The Swann Report*). London: HMSO.
Department for Education and Employment (DfEE). (1999). *The national curriculum*. London: HMSO.
DfEE (2000). *Supporting pupils learning English as an additional language* (The National Literacy Strategy). Reading: The National Centre for Literacy and Numeracy.

Duff, P. (2002). The discursive co-construction of knowledge, identity and difference: An ethnography of communication in the high school mainstream. In J. Zeungler & J. Mori (Guest Eds.), *Microanalyses of Classroom Discourse: A Critical Consideration of Method* (Special Issue). *Applied Linguistics, 23*(3), 289–322.

Edwards, V., & Redfern, A. (1992). *The world in a classroom: Language in education in Britain and Canada.* Clevedon: Multilingual Matters.

Franson, C. (1995). The role of the English as a second/additional language support teacher: Necessary conditions for a new definition. *NALDIC Occasional Paper No. 4.* Watford: NALDIC.

Franson, C. (2000). *The EAL teacher: Descriptors of good practice.* Unpublished report for the DfEE.

Franson, C. (2001a). Additional language: Additional needs. (L. Evans, Ed.) *Including Special Children, 139,* 15–17.

Franson, C. (2001b). Repositioning EAL: The way forward. In C. Jones & C. Wallace (Eds.), *Making EMAG Work* (pp. 111–121). Stoke on Trent: Trentham Books.

Gibson, M. (1997). Complicating the immigrant/voluntary minority typology. *Anthropology and Education Quarterly, 28*(3), 431–454.

Gillborn, D., & Mirza, H. (2000). *Educational inequality: Mapping race, class and gender.* London: OfSTED.

Harris, R. (2001, July). The contribution of EAL to race equality. Paper presented at the National Association for Language Development in the Curriculum General Council Meeting, University College, London.

Home Office. (1988). *A scrutiny of grants under Section 11 of the Local Government Act: Final report.* London: HMSO.

Home Office. (1990). *Policy criteria for the administration of Section 11 Grant.* London: HMSO.

Leung, C., & Franson, C. (2001a). Curriculum identity and professional development: System-wide questions. In B. Mohan, C. Leung, & C. Davison (Eds.), *English as a second language in the mainstream: Teaching, learning and identity* (pp. 199–214). Harlow, Essex: Pearson.

Leung, C., & Franson, C. (2001b). Mainstreaming: ESL as a diffused curriculum concern. In B. Mohan, C. Leung, & C. Davison (Eds.), *English as a second language in the mainstream: Teaching, learning and identity* (pp. 165–176). Harlow, Essex: Pearson.

Levine, J. (1990). (Ed.). *Bilingual learners and the mainstream curriculum.* London: The Falmer Press.

Office for Standards in Education (OFSTED). (1994). *Educational support for minority ethnic communities: A survey of educational provision funded under section 11 of the 1966 Local Government Act.* London: OfSTED.

OfSTED. (1999). *Raising the attainment of minority ethnic pupils.* London: OfSTED.

OfSTED. (2000). *Evaluating educational inclusion.* London: OfSTED.

OfSTED. (2001a). *Inspecting English as an additional language 11–16.* London: OfSTED.

OfSTED. (2001b). *Managing support for the attainment of pupils from minority ethnic groups.* London: OfSTED.

OfSTED. (2002). *Achievement of black Caribbean pupils: Three successful primary schools.* London: OfSTED.

Ogbu, J., & Simons, H. (1998). Voluntary and involuntary minorities: A cultural-ecological theory of school performance with some implications for education. *Anthropology and Education Quarterly, 29*(2), 155–188.

QCA. (2000). *A language in common: Assessing English as an additional language.* London: QCA.

Rampton, B. (1995). *Crossing: Language and ethnicity among adolescents.* Harlow: Longman.

School Curriculum and Assessment Authority (SCAA). (1996). *Teaching and learning English as an additional language.* London: SCAA.

Teacher Training Agency. (2000). *Raising the attainment of ethnic minority pupils.* London: TTA.

Toohey, K. (1998). 'Breaking them up, taking them away': ESL students in grade 1. *TESOL Quarterly, 32*(1), 61–84.

Wenger, E. (1998). *Communities of practice: Language, meaning and identity.* Cambridge: CUP.

Willett, J. (1995). Becoming first graders in an L2: An ethnographic study of L2 socialization. *TESOL Quarterly, 29*(3), 473–503.

CHAPTER 68

TEACHERS' ROLES IN THE GLOBAL HYPERMEDIA ENVIRONMENT

CHRIS CORBEL

Northern Melbourne Institute of Technical and Further Education, Australia

ABSTRACT

This chapter provides an overview of the roles teachers are adopting as they engage with the increasingly complex web of digital texts and communications that compose the early twenty-first century economic and educational environment. It identifies and describes three main categories of roles in the literature on CALL and information and communication technologies (ICTs)—the metaphoric, the attitudinal, and the functional. *Metaphoric roles* are those assigned in order to capture some key aspect of changes in work practices. *Attitudinal roles* are those adopted by individuals in relation to the changes in their environment associated with ICTs. *Functional roles* are those imposed by the ICT itself on those who engage with it. The chapter goes on to present four key issues in relation to teachers' roles in the new ICT environment— the extent to which teachers can influence adoption and use, the change in teachers' work and status, the changes in teaching contexts and conditions, and the skills needed to engage with ICT effectively.

INTRODUCTION

Purpose

Teachers work in social and institutional environments of which technology has always been an integral part. Some technologies are so familiar that they are no longer seen as technology, but are experienced as part of our "natural" environment. Older communication technologies such as paper and telephones are seen by many as natural in this way. Over the past 20 years, computers have gone from being a new technology to becoming almost as ubiquitous, in some settings, as paper and telephones, and thus almost as invisible. For some teachers they are simply part of the natural environment of the twenty-first century. Two key characteristics of this complex mix of information and communication technologies (ICT) are the global nature of their reach and the rich new hypermedia text types that they contain (see Murray, this volume , for a fuller discussion).

This global hypermedia environment is intricately intertwined with global economic systems, which has led to the development of the information economy, in which value is generated through the virtual manipulation of symbols as well as the physical manipulation of goods and services. When teachers engage with ICTs, they engage with features of the new work order typical of "late" or "fast" capitalism (Gee, Hull, & Lankshear, 1996), which are the dominant drivers of economic growth in the information economy. The environment in which teachers work and the roles they have available are shaped as much by economics as technology (for a detailed background on the social, institutional, and educational environment, see Corbel,

1999a). While it is important to understand what is new about working in the information economy, it is also important to remember what existing practices and roles are still relevant.

Scope and Significance

The focus of the chapter is on the explicit and implicit roles that are emerging for teachers as the old technologies are interconnected with new ones. There is relatively little work directly on this issue in an ELT context, so the chapter draws from the wider literature on teachers' roles in using ICTs.

Much of the literature on roles in educational computing focuses on the role of the computer. In some cases the computer is said to take on the role of teacher. The focus here, however, will be on the people, not the machines. The discussion is intended for all teachers, not just the small number working exclusively online.

As part of a broad examination of the effect of ICT on education, Howard (2000) asks, "How will effective use of technology for learning change the roles of teachers/tutors/lecturers/advice and guidance professions/trainers/librarians and learning resource professional?" (p. 37). This chapter is intended to address this issue.

MAIN RESEARCH FINDINGS

Discussions of teacher roles in using ICT can be grouped into three categories: the metaphoric, the attitudinal, and the functional. Metaphoric roles are those assigned in order to capture some key aspect of changes in work practices. These roles are often described in the literature that addresses the potential rather than actual work of teachers. Attitudinal roles are those adopted by individuals in relation to the changes in their environment associated with ICT. Functional roles are those imposed by the ICT itself on those who engage with it.

Metaphoric Roles

Metaphoric roles attempt to capture features of the new environment by invoking a familiar existing role. There are four general types of metaphor identifiable in the literature—the supportive, the collaborative, the economic, and the professional.

The main group of metaphoric roles for the teacher in the new environment is based on the notion of *support*, with the term *facilitator* perhaps the most common. The facilitator and related support metaphors have emerged throughout teaching in general to accompany a shift in focus from transmission approaches in teaching to constructivist approaches. The supportive metaphors have grown at the same time as schools have taken up more complex exploratory media such as CD ROMs and the Internet. There is a widespread belief that computers facilitate student-centered learning and that there is the potential to maximize individualization through use of the Internet (see, for example, Bickel & Truscello, 1996), with the teacher facilitating student-centered learning. The following description of the facilitator role is typical: "As facilitators, teachers provide rich learning environments, experiences and activities; create opportunities for students to work collaboratively, to solve problems, do authentic tasks and share knowledge and responsibility"

(Jones, Valdez, Nowakowski, & Rasmussen, 1995, p. 1). Other supportive metaphors include motivators, coaches (Spodark, 2001), and guides. "Teachers play complex and varied roles as guides. They mediate, model, and coach" (Jones et al., p. 1).

Davis and Caruso-Shade (1994) relate these supportive metaphoric roles to stages of learner development. They propose four roles: instructor, coach, model, and critic each coinciding with a developmental stage. At the initial stage the teacher needs to actively guide and encourage use (*instructor*). As confidence increases, peers instruct and the teacher facilitates (*coach*). The teacher uses the computer in the way the students are encouraged to (*model*). The teacher helps students select the most appropriate software (*critic*).

A new sense of equality and shared experience in exploring the new medium is noticeable in the use of *collaborative* role metaphors. "A number of studies emphasize the new role of the teacher in a collaborative writing environment: No longer the central authoritarian evaluator, the pedagogue now becomes consultant, co-writer, coach and editor" (Keep, McLaughlan, & Parmar, 2000, p. 1). Jones, Valdez, Nowakowski, and Rasmussen (1995) suggest that "teachers are often co-learners and co-investigators right alongside students" (p. 1).

Johnson (2001) proposes another set of metaphors that explicitly relate to the underlying *economic* basis of teachers' work. These metaphors see teachers as learners, producers of knowledge, and as entrepreneurs. As learners, "(t)he wide proliferation of online tutorial as well as both free and for fee web-based professional development courses, including online degree programs, has allowed teachers to take control of their own learning" (p. 2); as producers of knowledge, "(t)echnology is also empowering teachers as instructional designers, authors and presenters" (p. 3). A third metaphor, teacher as entrepreneur, acknowledges that in certain contexts teachers are chasing seed funding grants, students are starting classroom businesses, schools are marketing curriculum materials, and teachers are acting as consultants.

Finally, the discussion of roles is sometimes couched in terms of teachers metaphorically taking on another *professional* role. One of the commonest metaphoric roles is that of the IT industry professional. In the early days it was programmer, and the issue was whether teachers should learn BASIC, for example. This perspective has been overtaken in recent years by the role of web designer (Magoto, 1997).

Spodark (2001) sees teachers adopting all these roles and more: "The role of the foreign language teacher is becoming increasingly complex. We are knowledge providers, activity designers, facilitators, motivators, grammar checkers, guides, linguistic models, sirens, learning style coordinators, technology resource people, and directors and creators of constructive learning environments" (p. 5).

Critiques of role metaphors are of two main kinds—those that accept their appropriateness but argue that practice is more complex than the metaphor makes it appear (see, for example, Jones, 1999), and those that question the appropriateness of the metaphor itself. Brabazon (2001), for example, sees the use of these terms as evidence that "the notion of effective education has morphed" and that "student-centered learning is not only rhetoric, but also an ideological mask to deflect attention away from the power that teachers hold, and the increased workload necessary to promote web-based education" (p. 4).

Attitudinal Roles

Attitudinal roles are those adopted by individuals or members of different teaching stakeholders groups in response to the changing environment. Fox and Herrmann (undated) identify five "stances" in relation to computers. *Stances* are "ways of thinking about the use of online technology in higher education" (p. 2). They are archetypes, not mutually exclusive categories, and individuals may adopt different ones at different times. They identify *neutralitarians* as those who see technology as just a tool. *Boosters* are those who see successive waves of technological change introducing improvement through efficiency. Those adopting an *oppositional* stance often see technology as replacing the human element in education. *Skeptics* are not concerned about the technology but by the extravagant claims made for it. *Transformationalists* acknowledge the changes taking place, see them as basically positive, and seek ways to engage with them.

Werry (2001) identifies four positions taken in debates about online education. The *administrative* position focuses on how online education can be used to increase student admissions, keep up with technological advancements, and manage costs. The *corporate* position is that "the digitisation of the university will bring about a leaner, flatter, more flexible and efficient institution, one that will more closely resemble the structure of the modern organisation" (p. 11). The *faculty resistance* position focuses on the negative side of corporatization and "the casualization of academic work" (p.11). However, this entails a withdrawal rather than contestation. The *critical engagement* position is "one that engages sympathetic administrators, provides them with an alternative to corporate models" (p. 12).

As computers are introduced into educational settings, individuals are likely to find themselves in one of five adopter roles. Geoghegan (1994) describes five categories of adopters. *Innovators* (2% to 3% of adopters) are interested in the technology as much as the application and may be members of broad, cross-disciplinary networks of like-minded individuals. *Early adopters* (about 10% of adopters) are interested in the possible application of the technology to professional tasks. They are project-oriented risk takers, willing to experiment, and are reasonably self-sufficient. The *early majority* are more pragmatic, wanting proven applications. Their networks are more vertically discipline-based, rather than cross-disciplinary. The *late majority* are similar to the early majority though perhaps less comfortable with technology. The last 15%, the *laggards*, may never take up the innovation at all.

Functional Roles

Just as the introduction of the car created new functional roles of driver and mechanics, so the increasing use of ICTs in education has led to the creation of new functional roles for teachers, created by the features and use of the technologies themselves.

A feature of ICT in education in the last 5 years or so has been the increased use of software that integrates the delivery, information, communication, and administration functions that previously were carried out by separate products. Teachers, particularly in tertiary settings, are now using products such as WebCT, Blackboard, and First Class, and many others. Such products are described as online learning environments or learning management systems and are seen as a huge growth market.

These products assign functional roles based on individual access rights. There are usually five or six levels, such as *guest, student, instructor, moderator, developer, administrator*. Each level is granted access to an increasingly greater range of features and the capacity to modify them. Much of the emerging discussion of online learning focuses, often implicitly, on the instructor, moderator, and developer role, as these are the ones most likely to be assigned to teachers (see, for example, Jones, 1999). Berge (1996) suggests that teachers working online (in the instructor or moderator role) may encounter yet another set of roles, each one of which may have to be taken on at different times. These roles are *pedagogical* (as a facilitator), *social* (creating an appropriate learning setting), *managerial* (managing conferencing), and *technical*.

Related types of functional roles are the *organizational* roles assigned by institutions to staff undertaking tasks and duties that have not previously existed. The use of increasingly complex online learning environments across multiple locations necessitates the creation of roles such as site coordinator, multimedia center teacher, computer support teacher, and so on (Corbel, 1999b).

CURRENT DEBATES AND CONCERNS

Adoption and Use

One of the most common features of the literature on *computer-assisted language learning* (CALL) and ICT has been concern about the capacity of the teacher to influence its adoption and use. The concern has been expressed differently in different eras, reflecting the different stages of adoption of ICT into education. In the 1980s, the questions were, "*Should* I use computers in my teaching?" "If so, why?" "Is there any evidence for their effectiveness?" "Are they here to stay?" The target audience being addressed was individuals who might wish to become involved, and who would have to argue the case for funding. A degree of choice and influence was implicit.

In the next era, from the late 1980s to the mid-1990s, the implicit question was, "*What* should I use?" It still assumed a degree of teacher control over implementation. Since the late 1990s, however, the implicit question has been, "*How* should I use what is there?" Computers are established, teachers use them to differing degrees, but they have little influence over software and hardware. They are concerned, as they always have been, to work most effectively.

Ironically, the more computers are adopted, the less an individual teacher may be able to affect adoption issues. This is because adoption now means not simply putting a few computers in a room and connecting them to a printer, but installing an increasingly complex set of computers networked internally and to the Internet. Standardization of software is necessary to keep technical support costs down. Some fear that adoption has an economic rather than an educational rationale, or that computer decisions may be made on technical grounds, with teachers assuming subordinate roles (see, for example Brabazon, 2001; Crump, 1999; Evans, 1998).

Work and Status

A continual theme in the literature on CALL and ICT has been the possibility that the teacher might, in some way, be replaced by the computer. Early writers addressed the emerging security fears of teachers by distinguishing the role of the teacher from that of the computer, concluding that, for example, "for most teaching activities, teachers will probably be better than computers" (Fox, 1985, p. 92). Phillips (1986) foresaw the computer replacing some of the teacher's management work, but suggested a central role for the teacher in managing, for example, complex simulations, and made a still-relevant call for "…the new equilibrium that will be brought about by the computer in the delicate balance among students, materials and the teacher" (p. 8).

It has often been said that any teacher who could be replaced by a computer should be (see, for example, Cunningham, 1990), with the implicit assumption that this could never be the case. Underlying this was the belief that the teacher would always be a richer source of information and experience than the computer, which was to be relegated to providing basic skills practice for students. In the 2000s, the Internet is now by many seen as a vastly richer source of information and inspiration than an individual teacher, and the issue is, not so much do we need a teacher as, do we need the current skill sets that teachers have? Evans (1998) sounds the alarm:

> Multimedia and the Internet are here to stay. Teachers must, therefore, grasp these tools and integrate them into their daily teaching or they may find that the teacher's role in the classroom is minimised or lost completely as more multimedia, self-contained packages are produced. Under economic rationalism, self-access learning can be achieved through computer laboratories with a tutor-supervisor (not necessarily with a teaching background), or at home. Face-to-face teaching, therefore, could disappear, although a limited mentor role might be required. (p. 58)

It is in this rearguard action context that the support metaphors described above are often used.

Corbel (1999a, 1999b) argues that although teachers may see themselves as knowledge workers in the new information economy, a closer analysis of teachers' work shows elements of the lower-status, in-person worker and routine-production worker categories of the information economy workforce (Drucker, 2001; Reich, 1991). This uncertainty is potentially exacerbated by the trends Evans (1998) refers to above.

It is not just information that students have access to via the Internet. Learners now also have access to the possibility of interaction with many other users of English besides than their teacher (Lewis, 2001). More broadly, the effect of the steady reduction of the relative proportion of English in global communications (Singh, 2000) may be an issue of interest for all those involved in ELT.

CONTEXTS AND CONDITIONS

The changes in the ICT environment have been matched and are interconnected with changes in the economic and social environments. Many industries and companies, including those in education, are seeking to become virtual not only in the online sense but in the structural and organizational sense. This trend is likely to have effects on workers in those industries:

> Accounts of the 'virtual' organisation and organisations with flattened hierarchies have stressed the benefits of the streamlined, nimble democratic workplace, responsive to contingency, empowering workers to make decisions quickly and independently. It seems, however, that these transformed organisations also mean reduced institutional support, and that individual workers incur some of the costs associated with corporate gain. (Nardi, Whittaker, & Schwarz, 2000, p. 31)

The ELT field is already highly casualized, so this issue is likely to be of relevance, particularly as teachers find themselves working in emerging educational sectors, such as corporate universities (Weinstein, 2000) and online schools. An issue for teachers in tertiary settings may be that their online work not only is time-consuming but also may not be valued in the same way as other academic work (Visser, 2000).

Administrators of schools and institutions face a new range of issues emerging from the changing educational and economic context. How should online contact be accounted for? How should rates of pay reflect the changing functional roles of teachers? What are the occupational health and safety implications of teachers working off-site? If teachers are indeed knowledge workers, who owns the results of teachers' work? Who should provide the tools of trade to online teachers? And how do you manage a workforce that may take its tools of trade home with it each night?

From a purely practical point of view, all of those in education are working in technical settings of greater or lesser sophistication, with varying levels of support. In spite of the basic premise of this chapter, that computers are no longer technology but are a transparent part of the environment, computers are often not as "invisible" as they should be. They are subject to problems, breakdowns, and a range of other time-consuming issues (see, for example, Debski, 2000).

SKILLS AND TRAINING

Given that engagement with ICT is no longer a matter of choice for most teachers, what skills are necessary, and what form should training take? One of the key debates has been the extent to which teachers should create the content that is used online. This issue has been pragmatically resolved in the case of print resources, where a balance has traditionally been achieved between commercially, locally, and individually produced resources according to local circumstances and needs. However, in keeping with the personal empowerment rhetoric accompanying computers, some writers have suggested that the Internet in particular could allow teachers to become writers more easily (see the economic roles above). From the earliest days of educational computing, writers asked whether teachers should learn to program. An influential early work (Kenning & Kenning, 1983) captures the mood of the early 1980s, claiming that, "whereas early developments were generally the work of a team comprising one or more professional programmers, materials are often now written by language teachers with little or no specialist assistance" (p. 144). Throughout the 1980s and early 1990s the discussion extended to the use of authoring systems and packages (see, for example, Motteram, 1990; Sussex, 1989, 1991).

In the late 1990s, this issue increasingly took the form of whether teachers should create web pages (Magoto, 1997). Much of the literature reports on the success of individuals in creating web resources. These are likely to be members of the early adopter group (see adopter roles above), who are not representative of the field as a whole. In a study of several hundred teachers in a national ELT program, Corbel (1996) found very little evidence of teachers modifying content in even the simplest of ways. Given the increasing complexity and high standard of resources, the capacity for generalist teachers to routinely modify content is limited. Where modification does take place, it is likely to be through the use of templates in online learning environments.

While it may be true that a few teachers now create web pages, almost none would singlehandedly create commercial quality content. In practice, teachers developing content are likely to be working as a member of a team rather than as an individual (for an early identification of this trend, see Schmid-Schoenbein, Gartner-Clough, & Steinkopf, 1986). Again, the individual empowerment rhetoric has tended to mask the social nature of computing. Just as virtual teams have emerged in other industries, many teachers will find the need for similar skills as well. Even if a teacher does become involved in a content development project, it is likely to be as a content specialist rather than, say, a web specialist or instructional designer. The key skill is to be able to work with the other team members, not for any one team member, including the teacher, to do all the work individually. In essence, the issue has to do with the development of skilled networkers rather than multiskilled individuals. The building of "intentional networks" (Nardi, Whittaker, & Schwarz, 2000, p. 31), networks of contacts consciously created and managed, is therefore likely to be an important skill for teachers.

Another type of skill is in the creation and manipulation of electronic text types (Corbel, 1997). Many teachers spend more time teaching the use of office-related applications than using specialist teaching software. They need the skills themselves before they can teach them to others.

A final issue has been the relationship between ICTs and methodology. Early manifestations of CALL tended to focus on discrete-item practice activities and text manipulation. Where communicative language teaching was established, these activities were seen by many as inappropriate and uninspiring. There were calls for a unique CALL or ICT methodology to emerge. In practice, it is really only the emergence of the use of the Internet that has led to the need for teachers to develop new methodology such as project-based CALL (Debski, 2000) and network-based language teaching (Kern & Warschauer, 2000).

Teacher education institutions and internal training departments face a continual challenge concerning the extent to which generalist teachers should develop computing skills or whether to create and support specialist computing roles (see Legutke et al, this volume, for further discussion). An additional issue for training institutions is whether to develop critics of computing practices as well as skilled practitioners. Garton (1990) suggests CALL training should be part of curriculum development as a "catalyst for the enhanced role of the teacher and learner in the curriculum" (p. 4).

FUTURE DIRECTIONS

ICTs and Intermediation

According to Christensen (1997), any new technology can be either sustaining or disruptive. *Sustaining technologies* are those that improve the performance of established products. They are often developed by existing leaders in an industry, possibly in close relations with their main clients. A *disruptive technology*, on the other hand, is usually a low-cost innovation that undermines the competitive advantage of existing players in the field. It may not appeal initially to established customers and indeed may not perform as well as existing products. The personal computer is a classic example. It was initially cheaper than existing computers but performed existing tasks less well. What it did do, however, was typical of disruptive technologies, which allow less skilled and less affluent people to do things previously done by specialists in centralized, inconvenient locations.

ICTs, and especially the Internet, have long been seen as potentially disruptive to intermediaries in any industry because they allow individuals to carry out roles that were previously mediated by others, such as making their own flight bookings. This effect is one of *disintermediation*. In the travel industry, it is now possible to make bookings in this way, and the cheapest flights are often those that are available only online. This trend is completely in accordance with the characteristics of a disruptive technology, since these flights are the least flexible and least likely to appeal to the airlines' main customers, the business travelers.

However, in spite of the availability of cheap flights online, or any other service including learning, it is still worth involving an intermediary in many cases. It can save time and it can be more focused and efficient. The mediation role is still useful. Rather than eliminating the mediation, we need to look at how to make it most effective. In other words, what form should *reintermediation* take?

One area in which there have been continual predictions of the effect of the Internet has been on the role of the teacher. The essential issue in determining whether a technology is disruptive, as we saw earlier, is whether the technology allows less skilled and less affluent people to do things done only by expensive specialists in centralized, inconvenient locations. The issue faced by teachers (and managers) is just the same as that faced by agents, publishers, and everyone else in the information economy: How can I mediate most effectively between my learners and the content of the Internet? And how can I use the communications options of the Internet to enhance that mediation? If there is potential disintermediation, how can I go about ensuring the most effective reintermediation?

To answer this question, we need to remind ourselves what form the current intermediation takes. Arguably, the essence of what a teacher does is to mediate between a learner and the environment in a way that enhances learning. The environment contains a huge number of text types in numerous and an increasingly wide range of delivery modes, in a complex mix of social contexts. Teaching language involves assisting learners to enter the discourse communities that value and use these text types.

In the absence of formal mediation, an individual learns directly from the environment in a naturalistic way. The advantage of formal mediation (teaching) is that the teacher enhances that process by selecting, shaping, and focusing elements of the environment towards an educational goal. This enhancement is usually in the form of communication around learning objects or resources.

In the information economy, the teacher's work remains essentially the same as it has always been. There is a wider range of text types (such as documents, web pages, presentations, email) emerging in more intricate and complex modes, but the work remains essentially the same, and the underlying set of skills and competencies needed by the user have much in common across all text types (Corbel, 1997). The experiences of teachers of ESL and of literacy to adults are uniquely placed to teach the skills associated with these text types.

In practice, then, the range of text types teachers now mediate on behalf of learners is expanding. Although the addition of new tasks is not always accompanied by the removal of old ones, it would be interesting to see whether some text types start to become taught less. At the same time, an increasing range of formal, informal, and assigned roles are emerging to accompany this expansion in text types, as was outlined above.

Intermediation Roles

In conclusion, a final set of roles is presented below, which are intended to reflect the forms of reintermediation being taken up by teachers. These roles do not exist in any formal way. They are tentative groupings of tasks, orientations to content, or ways of engagement. They are described in levels that are intended to reflect the effort involved in each particular form of engagement. It is not a hierarchy of value—any one of them may be appropriate to an individual teacher at different times.

The simplest level might be called *adviser*. An adviser is aware of the range of material available and makes it known as options to students. The next level might be called *integrator*. Teachers, here, use ICT materials and activities as part of a continuing sequence of learning activities, most of which are done in the classroom. The idea of project-based CALL is consistent with this approach. Helping students to post their work to the website can also be a part of this type of use.

The next two levels involve making changes to content that is already available. The first of these involves *framing* third party online content, typically by posting a lesson plan that relates to a third party site. This is the equivalent of a teacher bringing realia into the classroom (Corbel, 1999b). We might call this person a *modifier* of content. The fourth role, *developer*, involves the creation of new material. This is typically through the use of a template of some kind. A fifth role is what we might call a *customizer*. This person liases between partner organizations and internal support and delivery units, to develop courses in response to the particular need of a customer.

None of these ways of engagement with the ICTs involves what we have traditionally thought of as programming. Engagement with ICTs does not involve programming but networking. Teachers are more likely to find themselves as members of new types of networks, involving ICT-related people, rather than becoming ICT people themselves. Teachers remain experts in their core business, that of mediating between the learner and the environment in a principled way. They do not need to change occupations in order to engage with the Internet effectively and appropriately. However, they do need to extend their repertoire of literacies (Corbel, 1997) and become critically engaged (Werry, 2001). They also need to ensure that they do not become relegated to mere facilitators, but continue to work in ways that are valued in the information economy.

In any case, there may be no need for teachers to adopt just one role, just as in the rest of our lives we do not adopt a single identity. We adopt multiple identities and roles as teachers, parents, members of social groups, and so on. As Turkle (1995) puts it, "What matters now is the ability to adapt and change—to new jobs, new career directions, new gender roles, new technologies" (p. 225).

REFERENCES

Berge, Z. (1996). *The role of the online instructor/facilitator.* Available at http://www.emoderators.com/moderators/teach_online.html. Retrieved November 11, 2004.

Bickel, B., & Truscello, D. (1996). New opportunities for learning: Styles and strategies with computers. *TESOL Journal, 6*(1), 15–19.

Brabazon, T. (2001). Internet teaching and the administration of knowledge. [Electronic version.] *First Monday, 6*(6), http:// firstmonday.org/issues/issue6_6/brabazon/index.html.

Christensen, C. (1997). *The innovator's dilemma: When new technologies cause great firms to fail.* Boston: Harvard University Press.

Corbel, C. (1996). *The computing practices of language and literacy teachers.* Sydney: National Centre for English Language Teaching and Research.

Corbel, C. (1997). *Computer literacies: Working effectively with electronic texts.* Sydney: National Centre for English Languge Teaching and Research.

Corbel, C. (1999a). *ESL teaching in the global hypermedia environment.* Australian Council of TESOL Associations.

Corbel, C. (1999b). Task as tamagotchi: ESL teachers' work in the emerging hypermedia environment. *Prospect, 14*(3), 40–45.

Crump, S. (1999). "E-duction": Electronic, Emotionless, and Efficient. *Journal of Education Policy, 14*(6), 631–637.

Cunningham, D. (1990, November). Past predictions, current perspectives and future prospects in CALL. *Babel, 25*(2), 6–26.

Davis, B., & Caruso-Shade, D. (1994). *Integrate, don't isolate: Computers in the early childhood curriculum. Urbana, IL:* ERIC Clearinghouse on Elementary and Early Childhood Education.

Debski, R. (2000). Exploring the re-creation of a CALL innovation. *Computer Assisted Language Learning, 13*(4–5), 307–332.

Drucker, P. (2001, November). The next society: A survey of the near future. *The Economist,* 3.

Evans, L. (1998). CALL: What is the future for the EFL teacher? *EA Journal, 16*(2), 55–60.

Fox, J. (1985). Humanistic CALL: Teachers' needs and learners' needs in the design of computer–assisted language learning systems. In C. Brumfit (Ed.), *Computers in English Language Teaching* (pp. 91–97). Oxford: Pergamon.

Fox, R., & Herrmann, A. (n.d.). *Changing media changing times: Taking a stance on new technology adoption.* Retrieved September 21 2005, from http://www.ilce.edu.mx/icde_ilce/ponencia/viena/p00374.htm.

Garton, J. (1990). A place for CALL in the language curriculum. *On-CALL, 5*(3), 2–5.

Gee, J., Hull, D., & Lankshear, C. (1996). *The new work order.* St. Leonards: Allen and Unwin.

Geoghegan, W. H. (1994). *Whatever happened to instructional technology? Reaching mainstream faculty.* Norwalk, CT: IBM Academic Consulting.

Howard, U. (2000). Learning with IT: Towards a research agenda–questions and issues. *Alt-J, 8*(3), 31–40.

Johnson, M. (2001). *New roles for educators.* Milken Family Foundation. Retrieved Month date, Year from www.mff.org/edtech.

Jones, C. (1999). From the sage on the stage to what exactly? Description and the place of the moderator in co-operative and collaborative learning. *Alt-J, 7*(2), 29–36.

Jones, B., Valdez, G., Nowakowski, J., & Rasmussen, C. (1995). New times demand new ways of learning. In *Plugging in: Choosing and using educational technology.* North Central Regional Education Laboratory. Retrieved Month date, year from www.ncrel.org/sdrs/edtalk/toc.htm.

Keep, C., McLaughlan, T., & Parmar, R., (2000). *Computers, pedagogy and composition.* The Electronic Labyrinth. Retrieved from www.iath.Virginia.edu/elab/hfl0033.html.

Kenning, M., & Kenning, M. (1983). *An introduction to computer assisted language teaching.* Oxford: Oxford University Press.

Kern, R., & Warschauer M., (2000). Theory and practice of network-based language teaching. In M. Warschauer & R. Kern (Eds.), *Network-based language teaching: Concepts and practice* (pp. 1–19). New York: Cambridge University Press.

Lewis, M. (2001, February). Let's face it: ELT's a trade. *EL Gazette, 25*(3), 5.

Magoto, J. (1997, Fall). HTML and the teacher's role. *CAELL Journal, 8*(1), 23–26.

Motteram, G. (1990). Using a standard authoring package to teach effective reading skills. *System, 18*(1), 15–21.

Nardi, B., Whittaker S., & Schwarz, H. (2000). It's not what you know, it's who you know: Work in the information age. *First Monday,* 5(5). Available at www.firstmonday.org/issues/issue5_5/nardi/index.html.

Phillips, M. (1986). CALL in its educational context. In G. Leech & C. Candlin, *Computers in English language teaching and research* (pp. 2–10). Longman: London.

Reich, R. (1991). *The work of nations.* New York: Knopf.

Schmid-Schoenbein, G., Gartner-Clough, P., & Steinkopf, M. (1986). Don't wait, co-operate! (The team approach to software development). *System, 14*(2), 211–214.

Singh, M. (2000). Innovation in TESOL provision: Local responses and engagements with globalisation. *EA Journal, 18*(1), 12–21.

Spodark, E. (2001, January/February). The changing role of the teacher: A technology-enhanced, student-centred lesson on French fashion. *Foreign Language Annals, 34*(1), 1–6.

Sussex, R. (1989). Issues in computer-aided language learning: Towards an expert-systems learning environment. In C. Candlin & T. McNamara. *Language learning and community* (pp. 91–104). Sydney: National Centre for English Language Teaching and Research.

Sussex, R. (1991). Author languages, authoring systems and their relation to the changing focus of computer-aided language learning. *System, 19*(1/2), 15–27.

Turkle, S. (1995). *Life on the Screen.* London: Phoenix.

Visser, J. (2000). Faculty work in developing and teaching web-based distance courses: A case study of time and effort. *The American Journal of Distance Education, 14*(3), 21–31.

Weinstein, N. (2000, September/October). Corporate universities: A new frontier for ESL/EFL professionals. *ESL Magazine,* 14–16.

Werry, C. (2001). The work of education in the age of E-college. If viewed only in electronic form then insert [Electronic version] *First Monday,* 6(5). Available at www.firstmonday.org/issues/issue6_5/werry/index.html.

CHAPTER 69

PREPARING TEACHERS FOR TECHNOLOGY-SUPPORTED ELT

MICHAEL K. LEGUTKE

The Justus-Liebig-University of Giessen, Germany

ANDREAS MÜLLER-HARTMANN

The University of Education at Heidelberg, Germany

MARITA SCHOCKER V. DITFURTH

The University of Education at Freiburg, Germany

ABSTRACT

The availability of information and communication technology (ICT) in educational settings offers the chance to reconceptualize the second and foreign language classroom as a learning environment with a new quality of communicative and intercultural learning. If teachers are adequately prepared to handle the difficult task of incorporating ICT into the classroom, then these new environments have the potential for language encounters beyond the classroom, for enhanced access to a wide variety of resources, and for the communicative use of the target language. After a review of recent research on the integration of technology in teacher education programs, two model formats for integrating technology into preservice teacher courses are presented that can be emulated in a variety of national settings. Even though technology plays an important role, these formats extend far beyond technology by integrating different domains of relevant knowledge as identified by educational research on teacher learning, for example, knowledge pertaining to insights gained from previous and current research, the processes of language teaching and learning in actual classrooms, and student teachers' identities and their images of teaching and learning.

INTRODUCTION: A NEW KNOWLEDGE BASE FOR TEACHER EDUCATION

Access to computers in educational settings has increased steadily during the last ten years, but what should be considered appropriate education and training of teachers for computer-supported learning environments remains a major issue in the field of English language learning and teaching. As the National Council for Accreditation of Teacher Education's (NCATE) Task Force on Technology and Teacher Education has put it, "classroom teachers hold the key to effective use of technology to improve learning" (1997, p. 3). In their seminal survey of information and communication technology (ICT), Willis and Mehlinger (1996) also stress that teacher preparation is "critically important if U.S. schools are to use technology effectively" (p. 984).

At the same time, teacher education programs for second and foreign languages in general have come under growing criticism in recent years. It has been argued that they often fail to provide the relevant knowledge base that enables student teachers, once they have left the university classroom, to cope with the complex demands of the school setting and, more importantly, to become part of the social change process (Fullan, 1993). The ability to bring about change is especially relevant when schools are considering how to integrate technology into their curriculum.

In spite of huge resources that have been mobilized both to equip schools with technology and for language teacher education, very little is known about the effectiveness of these programs when it comes to improving language education in schools. There still is an obvious lack of learning-to-teach studies, particularly in foreign language teacher education. What Freeman and Johnson (1998) point out about the U.S., namely, that "teacher education has been much done but relatively little studied in the field" (p. 298), certainly applies to other contexts as well. What is known, however, supports personal anecdotal observation: The teaching formats at universities are still predominantly transmission oriented and therefore contradict long-established ideologies of student-centeredness and communicative methodology (Legutke & Thomas, 1991); the program components often lack a coherent curriculum framework within which the practicum, if provided at all, often remains an alien element among university courses (Gabel, 1997; Schocker-v. Ditfurth, 2001).

Consequently, Freeman and Johnson (1998) have called for a reconceptualization of the knowledge base of foreign language teacher education that aligns teacher education with teaching:

> In defining the knowledge base, one must recognize that language teacher education is primarily concerned with teachers as learners of language teaching rather than with students as learners of language. Thus teacher education focuses on teacher-learners ... as distinct from language learners. (pp. 407-409)

Based on this premise, we need to move from a behaviorist view of teaching where teachers "are portrayed as conduits to students" toward a social constructivist view. This is because language teachers work in institutions where "teaching is constructed as a highly situated and highly interpretative activity ... and teachers and students and teaching and learning are shaped by the institutional settings in which they work" (Johnson, 2002, p. 1). Therefore teachers have "a fundamental need for cogent analysis and self-understanding within the social, cultural, and political contexts and consequences of language teaching and language learning" (Freeman & Johnson, 1998, p. 407). The attitudes, knowledge, and skills it takes to be able to teach a foreign language as a means of intercultural communication thus become the core component of any teacher education curriculum. The contents and the procedures of teacher education then should be derived from an analysis of the complex competencies foreign language teachers need to develop so that they will be able to organize, support, and evaluate language learning in their prospective EFL classrooms.

While there is a need for qualitative research studies on ICT in teacher education to further delineate those contents and procedures, there have been a number of studies (e.g., Tella, 1991; Warschauer, 1996, 1999) focusing on the integration of technology into the foreign language classroom. With the *social turn* in educational research, i.e., the recognition that teachers, learners, learning, and teaching always form part of cultural, historical, institutional, and power-structured contexts, recent studies have also looked at the institutional affordances and constraints teachers face (Belz & Müller-Hartmann, 2003). All of these studies have sharpened our view as to the complexity of factors teachers and teachers-to-be are confronted with when working in IT-supported English language teaching and learning settings. The following section discusses the major changes at the classroom level that teacher education needs to address.

DIMENSIONS OF THE ICT-SUPPORTED EFL CLASSROOM— CHALLENGES FOR TEACHERS

There is no doubt that ICT has greatly enhanced the possibilities for learner-centered approaches of learning and teaching in the English language classroom, such as Communicative Language Teaching (CLT), and task-based and project-oriented approaches (Ellis 2003; Kohonen, 1992; Legutke & Thomas, 1991; Müller-Hartmann & Schocker-v. Ditfurth, 2004; Willis, 1996). Together with the recent focus on sociocultural approaches to foreign language learning (Lantolf, 2000), ICT-supported learning environments call for the development of a specific set of attitudes, skills, and knowledge in English language teacher education. These may be derived from the following dimensions of change that the availability of technology in classrooms seems to bring about: (a) encounters beyond classroom walls, (b) enhanced access to resources of various kinds, (c) settings, (d) learner roles, and (e) teacher roles.

Encounters Beyond Classroom Walls

ICT enables teachers and learners to overcome traditional constraints of classroom learning by providing them with various channels for interaction with speakers of the target language in different cultural environments. An authentic audience, which has been lacking in most traditional classrooms, is now easily accessible. This interaction, brought about by computer-based activities such as e-mail, web-conferencing, and chat, potentially enhances language learning and promotes communication. However, the negotiation of meaning and critical cultural awareness will depend on factors that go beyond technology. Their communicative success will be influenced by the choice of appropriate content that engages learners, by the choice of pedagogical goals to be pursued, and, of course, by meaningful tasks that structure such interactions, focus learners' attention, and challenge their points of view (Müller-Hartmann, 2000). "The medium is not the message because if people have nothing to say to each other then it doesn't really make any difference in which medium they don't say it" (Rösler, 2000, p. 18). The ease of access to speakers of English by no means guarantees that learners will be capable of dealing with misunderstandings, breakdowns in communication, and divergent views unless the teachers know how to initiate and lead follow-up discussions to Internet-mediated "key-pal" partnerships (Kramsch & Thorne, 2002). Finally, the outcome of such encounters will depend on the overall formats of teaching and learning, connecting content and procedures to form a coherent curriculum.

Enhanced Access to Resources of Various Kinds

The traditional textbook will not lose its significance in ICT-supported classrooms. For the first time, however, learners have unlimited access to a wide range of resources and target language texts. Therefore, they can play a decisive role as active agents in cocreating a rich learning environment when contributing texts they have gathered themselves to supplement the textbook or open new topics according to their interests and needs. In this way they might seize opportunities for overt negotiation about the classroom curriculum and become responsible members of the classroom community by being accountable for the learning content. The major challenge here is how the enhanced access to texts becomes knowledge to be used by students. They not only need to learn how to formulate questions for searching the web, how to evaluate resources, and how to make choices, but also, as Widdowson (1990) pointed out, how to actively transform such findings into coherent texts of their own. Learners will take full authorial responsibility for such transformational work if their contributions are relevant for an audience, be it members of their classroom community or of some other ICT-supported context. From a teacher's point of view, this again raises the issue of supporting autonomous learning contexts, i.e., appropriate content needs to be explored and meaningful tasks have to be developed that frame the use of resources and the production of learner texts.

Setting

Setting is important in at least three ways. Firstly, a noticeable trait of ICT-supported classrooms is that their potential to use language and language contacts cannot be unlocked within the confines of teacher-centered methods. Rather, they require cooperative learning formats and project work. This requirement entails not only effective modes of division of labor, such as more pair and group work, but also the taking on of teaching functions by the learners. This poses major challenges for the teacher not only in terms of his or her ability to initiate, manage, and monitor group processes but also because learners require pedagogically motivated interventions, strategy and media training, and teacher-led phases that foreground content and present procedures (Legutke & Thomas, 1991). The second dimension of setting refers to the physical learning space: the way it is equipped with hardware and software; the way it can be used for cooperative learning; and the way it is connected to other learning spaces within the institution and beyond, in the community and the students' homes. Thirdly, *setting* means the institutional specifics of a given context that have a major impact on the success of cross-institutional projects (Belz, 2002; Belz & Müller-Hartmann, 2003). Each of these three dimensions needs to be addressed in the preparation of teachers.

Learner Roles

If learners are to benefit from the potential of ICT-supported environments for cross-institutional communication, for the use and production of multimedia texts, and for the co-construction of the environment itself, interactive formats allowing for a negotiated curriculum have to be initiated (Breen & Littlejohn, 2000). Such interactive formats expand the role of learners who simultaneously need to act as researchers, as coproducers of diverse texts, as managers of their own learning, and last but not least as peer teachers. The challenge for student teachers is that the capacities of learners to act in these roles cannot be taken for granted; instead, these capacities must be developed and fostered. For this reason, issues of learner education for ICT-supported environments must hold a prominent position in any teacher education program.

Teacher Roles

As has become clear so far, the roles of the teacher are clearly multidimensional. The shift of responsibility to the individual learner and/or small cooperative groups and the use of project formats require a high degree of flexibility on the part of the teacher because the learning process is far less predictable. However autonomous learners may become in setting or executing their own tasks, the teacher carries the responsibility for the learning process as a whole and retains the right to intervene with help, advice, or setting fresh targets. For this reason, the most commonly used term describing the teacher as *facilitator* is too vague and misleading (see Barnes & Murray, 1999). Following Berge (1995), we propose four role categories that describe the new tasks of the teacher: pedagogical, social, managerial, and technical. In his *pedagogical* role, the teacher will, for example, promote interest in relevant topics, focus on content and on the processes of intercultural learning, and promote responsible and critical authorship. In her *social* role, she will promote human relationships and collaborate with learners in creating a productive and challenging learning climate and in maintaining group cohesiveness. In his *managerial* role, he will be in charge of the overall time frame; he will make sure that schedules are kept and plans followed, and that both institutional constraints as well as affordances to be utilized are taken into account. In her *technical* responsibility, the teacher must make participants comfortable with the system and the software, making the technology as transparent to learners as possible.

It goes without saying that the traditional role of the teacher as *language instructor* providing language resources and monitoring language use does not cease to be relevant. On the contrary, teachers have to be able to deal with the imponderability and complexity that the expanded space of action entails. Instead of simplifying what is to be approached and learned, they are called upon to maintain the complexity and help learners to approach and understand concepts and phenomena in the complex environment in which they find themselves (Legutke, 2001; Müller-Hartmann & Schocker-v. Ditfurth, 2004).

To prepare future teachers adequately for these complex demands seems a rather daunting task. A number of questions need to be answered to provide adequate formats for teacher education programs:

1. How can we offer teacher education experiences that will allow student teachers to meet the challenges of both the learner-centered language classroom and of new technology?
2. How can we provide a framework that will allow teacher educators to integrate and develop the knowledge base of teacher education as currently discussed? Following Freeman and Johnson (1998), we have argued that the knowledge base must focus on the activity of teaching itself, on the teacher who does it, and the contexts in which it is done.

3. How can we establish productive collaboration between the two traditionally separate areas in which relevant knowledge is created, that is, school and university?

Before we delineate two formats that take these questions into consideration, a review of the recent research on the integration of technology in teacher education programs is in order.

DEVELOPMENTS IN THE INTEGRATION OF TECHNOLOGY INTO TEACHER EDUCATION

Since Willis's and Mehlinger's (1996) comprehensive historical and theoretical overview of ICT and teacher education, a number of important developments have taken place. One of them is the firm establishment of several organizations that focus on teacher education and technology, such as the Society for Information Technology and Teacher Education (SITE), as well as the creation of four scholarly journals on information technology in teacher education (see Davis, 2000).

While the use of technology in the EFL classroom is slowly finding its way into German state curricula, the call for teacher education guidelines in this area can still only be detected at the programmatic level (Weilburger Erklärung, 2002). Other countries, such as Australia (Sherwood, 1993), France (Davis, 2000), Great Britain (Cuckle, Clarke, & Jenkins, 2000), and especially the United States (Milken Exchange, 1999) have undertaken comprehensive surveys of their teacher education institutions, and they have established guidelines (e.g., Pope & Golub, 2000) for the integration of technology into teacher education. The surveys' decisive finding is that student teachers and teacher education faculty feel insufficiently prepared by the training they have received (see also Willis & Mehlinger, 1996). Research has shown that student teachers might need four years or more to feel confident about the use of technology in the classroom (Willis & Mehlinger, 1996; see also Dawson & Norris, 2000). The fact that university faculty are unable to adequately model the integration of technology in the EFL classroom leads to low confidence on the part of the student teachers or to qualitatively inferior use of technology in the classroom, for example, drill and practice (Willis & Mehlinger, 1996). Consequently, studies at the turn of the millennium have come up with recommendations that are being implemented in a number of current programs:

1. The traditional stand-alone computer course "does not correlate well with scores on items dealing with technology skills and the ability to integrate IT into teaching" (Milken Exchange, 1999, p. 3). Instead, technology should be integrated into general methods courses, and it should form part of the whole teacher education curriculum. At the same time, the quality of technology use must improve to profit from the enormous potential of technology integration (see also Pope & Golub, 2000).
2. Apart from the improvement of university courses, many studies see the necessity to provide more field-based courses to promote "the creation of authentic technology-rich field experiences" in primary and secondary classrooms (Dawson & Norris, 2000, pp. 5; Brush, Igoe, Brinkerhoff, Glazewski, Ku, & Smith, 2001). University-school partnerships, such as the professional development schools in the U.S., facilitate these experiences,

ensuring at the same time an integrated model of teacher pre- and in-service training (Dawson & Norris, 2000; Jayroe, Ball, & Novinski, 2001).
3. The training of university faculty as well as school mentors to provide adequate models for preservice teachers is essential (Willis & Mehlinger, 1996; Thomas & Cooper, 2000). Trainees, for example, can be paired into novice/expert partnerships, and in the "cascade" model new experts can then "'cascade' what they have learnt to their own designated 'novices'" (Barnes & Murray, 1999, pp. 171). While in-service training is obviously necessary for both groups, the education of interested teachers can also be enhanced through various field-based course models. Student teachers then often act as change agents (Marcovitz, 1999).

Some principles that clearly reflect these findings form part of many of the new programs in different subject fields such as those based on the U.S. report, *Preparing Tomorrow's Teachers To Use Technology (PT3)* (2002). We would like to spell them out in relation to seminars for teaching EFL. Since most of the current studies refer to either large-scale programs such as the PT3 or general advances on the institutional level (e.g., Cuckle, Clarke, & Jenkins, 2000), we would like to present two model formats for integrating technology into preservice teacher seminars that can be emulated in individual courses in a variety of national settings without the necessity of a general organizational overhaul of the institution or the necessity of large-scale funding. The models also integrate teacher pre- and in-service training, and they obviously could function as crystallizing points for institutional change in the respective schools and universities.

PRINCIPLES OF COMPUTER-SUPPORTED PROJECT SEMINARS FOR EFL STUDENT TEACHERS

There are two basic premises we follow when we design ICT-supported learning environments: First, we prepare student teachers to *integrate technology into everyday teaching* rather than just using it sporadically as an additive tool (= *the principle of a classroom-oriented teacher education*). Second, we support them in developing local understandings of teaching. To do so, they develop projects for a particular classroom and research an aspect of the language learning potential that technology offers for that particular classroom (= *the principle of research-oriented teacher education*). To achieve both purposes, student teacher learning is based on three principles described below.

Research Approach to Learning: Developing a Multiperspective View of the EFL Classroom

Student teachers develop a research approach to learning that helps them understand the complex dynamics that determine language learning in ICT-supported EFL classrooms. To do so, they learn to integrate three relevant perspectives on teaching and learning (Schocker-v. Ditfurth, 2001):

1. Relevant published knowledge
2. Student teachers' own ideas on the potential of institutional language learning. Learning-to-teach studies have demonstrated that students' own

learning experiences affect both their awareness and images of learning in classrooms and their dispositions to behave, regardless of whatever cognitive knowledge they may have encountered during teacher education.
3. The perspective of practice as represented by the experiences of teachers and their students. We consider the inclusion of the perspective of practice to be crucial for various reasons: The relevance of research results depends on the value that teachers associate with them, as Freeman & Johnson, (1998) argue, "schools are powerful places that create and sustain meanings and values ... it is misleading to see them merely as settings in which educational practices are implemented ... schools and classrooms function as frameworks of value and interpretation in which language teachers must learn to work effectively" (p. 409). Furthermore, in accordance with Stenhouse (1975), we believe that any proposal needs to be evaluated and adapted by each teacher in their own classroom.

Experiential Learning: Developing Action-oriented Models for ICT-supported EFL Classrooms

Seminars are organized as projects to allow student teachers to experience the very processes that they are supposed to initiate with learners in their prospective classrooms: They choose a research question (see Figure 2); they use ICT to research, discuss, and publish the results of their projects; they cooperate in virtual teams in which they exchange and discuss ideas with student teachers working on the same research question in seminars at different universities; they use English as their language of communication at all levels of the exchange; and they evaluate selected aspects of the process and the product of their projects. In doing so, they experience the highlights and the drawbacks involved in cooperative ICT-supported learning. In other words, seminars follow an approach to learning that is based on reflected experience. This approach integrates the experiences of students in classrooms and the experiences of student teachers at university. It is obvious that, in both learning environments, a teacher's role may no longer be adequately defined as a transmitter of knowledge to passive recipients. Instead, both university and classroom teachers need to offer expert guidance and support to their respective students so that students will be able to cope with the multiple skills this learning environment involves. Teachers need to be positive role models from whom students gradually learn by appropriating the mutually agreed on purposes. This concept of teacher as model must not be confused with the mechanical imitation of behavior that characterized behaviorist-based teaching. Contrary to that, it is understood in the Vygotskyan sense of learning as *relational imitation,* which he expressed in his concept of the zone of proximal development (Vygotsky, 1978). This is yet another aspect of the principle of experiential learning.

Experimental Learning: Supporting School Development Competencies Through Cooperation in Cross-institutional Projects

The ability to develop a research approach to language classrooms implies that we overcome the traditional separation of school and university. For computer-mediated language learning, this is essential because the open structure of the medium is prone to clash with the traditions of language teaching at schools. There, lessons are usually textbook based and follow a routine sequence of presentation, practice, and production. In computer-supported projects, on the other hand, teachers need what has come to be called *dynamic qualifications*, that is, competencies and attitudes that are the basis for any innovation to be successful, such as "an appreciation of problems that one has identified during the process, student-orientation, process evaluation, an experiment attitude to practice, ... and the ability to cope with controlled risks" (Krainer & Posch, 1996, p. 25, translation by authors). This is why we support experimentation in that we ask student teachers to cooperate in teams to develop materials for various EFL classrooms, a process whose outcome can never be predicted and which involves intensive negotiation. Student teachers become proactive change agents who develop certain aspects of classroom language learning for a particular and clearly defined context (see also Marcovitz, 1999).

The pedagogical implications of these principles can be illustrated using two seminar types that we have developed and revised based on student feedback.

TWO MODELS FOR ICT-SUPPORTED TEACHER EDUCATION SEMINAR TYPES

Seminar Type I: Cultural Studies Internet Research Projects: Student Teachers as Direct Classroom Researchers

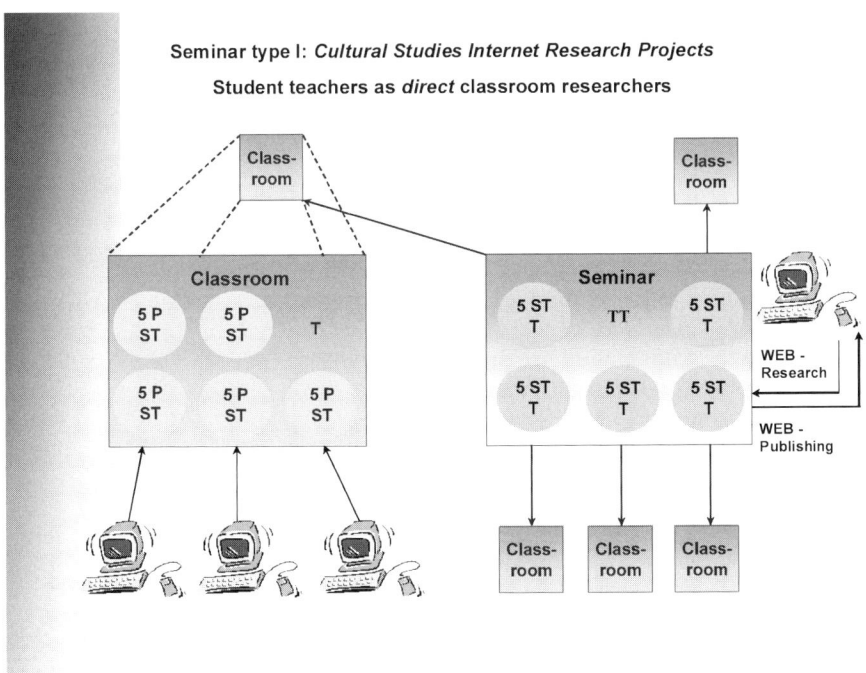

| ST = Student teacher | P = Pupil |
| T = Classroom teacher | TT = Teacher trainer |

Figure 1: Seminar Type I: Cultural Studies Internet Research Projects

Student Teachers as Direct Classroom Researchers

To begin with, we have attempted to implement our principles by defining student teachers' roles as *direct* classroom researchers. Teams of student teachers developed and taught web-based cultural studies research projects in cooperation with EFL teachers and their classrooms. In the process of doing so, they collected data to answer their research questions. These concerned different aspects of the added value that the availability of ICT offers for language learning. At the end of the term, student teachers presented their results at one of the universities involved, and they published their findings on our project's website (for a detailed description of our experiences with this seminar type, see Legutke, Müller-Hartmann, & Schocker-v. Ditfurth, 2001; Moving West, 2001; Schocker-v. Ditfurth & Legutke, 2002).

This seminar type differs considerably from the seminars universities conventionally offer. While the traditional arrangement of a graduate course as the central place for cooperative learning is maintained, it is extended by 5–7 school classrooms (see right-hand side of Figure 1). Classroom teachers [T] participate in a few key sessions of the university seminar, and they follow the general development of the seminar via the Internet (e-mail and special conferences in the *First Class* computer conferencing system). Project work on the seminar level follows four main phases:

Phase 1: Preparation of the School Projects

Teams of three to five student teachers [ST] design a project for a group of pupils [P]. The project is usually designed to last 3 days, and it focuses on work with web-based materials. To do so, student teachers research suitable websites, develop tasks, and suggest procedures for the presentation and assessment of the projects. All this is done in close cooperation with participating teachers and their pupils.

Phase 2: Realization of the Project and Collection of Data in an EFL Classroom

During the second phase, the student teachers leave the university and carry out the projects (see Figure 1). A team of student teachers works together with one teacher and her class. During this phase, one student teacher works with one group of pupils in the classroom. This way, the school projects mirror the project approach student teachers experience themselves in their university seminar, in that they include the preparation, research, presentation, and evaluation of projects.

Phase 3: Evaluation of the Project and Presentation

After the school phase, student teachers return to the university, where they evaluate their experiences in their respective groups. They analyze the data that they have collected (e.g., teacher interviews, recordings of group discussions or questionnaires with pupils, observation protocols, audio and/or video recordings). Findings are discussed at the end of the term in a public presentation at the university in which teachers who have participated take part.

Phase 4: Publication of Results

Finally each group designs a website on their project. This includes the project plan and their research report. For an overview of selected projects, go to http://www.vib-bw.de/tp7 (-> Unterrichtsprojekte).

Seminar Type II: Multinational Topic-Based E-Mail-Exchange Projects: Student Teachers as Indirect Classroom Researchers

In seminar type I, we asked student teachers to develop, teach, *and* research aspects of school-based Internet research projects. Obviously, this meant an enormous workload for student teachers as compared with the demands of traditionally structured seminars. At the same time, schools became more and more interested in doing multinational e-mail exchange projects, which could not be planned and carried out in any predictable way. To reduce the workload, making seminars institutionally more compatible, *and* to be able to meet growing demands from schools for long-term exchange projects, we included the following changes: In seminar type II, *we* as course organizers, supported by a research assistant, developed ICT-supported school-based projects in cooperation with teachers, and we collected classroom-based data ourselves. In each case, the e-mail project was based on a young adult novel, which provided the core content for the multinational exchange. Again, the data included interviews with teachers, group discussions with learners, project portfolios, and tasks and letters that pupils had exchanged in the course of their e-mail projects. When the projects had finished, we put all of the classroom-based data into *First Class,* our intranet server.

First Class serves two purposes in our seminars. First, it provides student teachers with the classroom-based information that allows them to get an idea of the processes an e-mail project triggered with pupils in a particular classroom and to understand the perspectives of pupils and teachers involved in the projects, without having to go to classrooms in person to do their research. At the same time, *First Class* organizes collaboration between student teachers who study at three different universities but cooperate in virtual teams on different research questions in *conferences.*

A *conference* is an online forum for user discussions that serves as a common mailbox for a group of people. It is a kind of container for a certain topic. Student teachers use these conferences as a forum for their collaborative and cross-institutional group work. Using this frame, they deal with the virtual exploration of a research question over the course of a semester. Figure 2 gives some examples of research questions student teachers could choose from in one term.

As with seminar type I, student teachers experience the very teaching approach they study because learners also use *First Class* to do their topic-based e-mail projects. Again, the data that student teachers use for their research includes the three perspectives on language learning mentioned previously, i.e., relevant published knowledge, student teachers' own personal ideas, and images of teaching and classroom-based data. And at the end of the term, student teachers meet face to face to present and discuss and their findings, which they then also publish on a website.

Examples of Research Questions Student Teachers May Choose From

1. What is there to consider when you plan and organize an e-mail project that intends to promote intercultural learning? (Data: use teachers' letters and interviews; results of pupils; questionnaires)

2. Which qualities does a teacher need to have to be able to set up and sustain an e-mail project that promotes intercultural learning? (Data: use teachers' letters and interviews; results of students' questionnaires)

3. Which task features are appropriate? How do they influence language and language learning in an EFL classroom? To what extent does language and language learning differ from traditional classrooms? (Data: use pupils' letters, teachers' letters, teachers' interviews)

4. Has intercultural learning taken place in the two projects? What was conducive to/ impeded promoting intercultural learning? (Data: use text analysis of pupils' letters, teachers' interviews)

5. What kind of role does the literary text play in such a setup? (You might want to consider aspects such as language help, language text difficulty, authenticity of input, cultural studies, etc.) (Data: use students' and teachers' letters, literary texts)

Figure 2. Examples of Research Questions Student Teachers May Choose From

CONCLUSIONS

We set out with three questions that we would need to find answers to if we wanted to prepare student teachers appropriately for the technology-supported English language classroom. Our formats seem to offer a viable way in that they connect the concerns of school-based English language learning, of university-based initial teacher education, and of in-service teacher education in collaborative projects. If we wish to develop an appropriate knowledge base and also to bring about change at all three domains, the multiple and often differing perspectives from teachers, student teachers, learners, and teacher educators must be coordinated. This is why the socially mediated aspects of learning are of paramount importance in the process. As one of our student teachers put it:

> It took all of our creativity and social skills to come to terms with the complexity of factors involved in ICT-supported classrooms *and* our seminar. But now that it is done my sense of achievement is awesome and I am very proud when I look at our project on the website. An inspiring experience to get an idea of the potential technology offers for language learning and a feeling that it actually can be done. (Anja, Portfolio, summer term 2001).

REFERENCES

Barnes, A., & Murray, L. (1999). Developing the pedagogical information and communications technology competence of modern foreign languages teacher trainees. Situation: all change and plus ca change [Electronic version]. *Journal of Technology for Teacher Education, 8*(2), 165–180. Retrieved Nov. 8, 2004, from http://www.triangle.co.uk/jit/.

Belz, J. (2002). Social dimensions of telecollaborative foreign language study [Electronic version]. *Language Learning and Technology, 6*(1), 60–81. Retrieved Nov. 8, 2004, from www.llt.msu.edu.

Belz, J., & Müller-Hartmann, A. (2003). Teachers as intercultural learners: negotiating German-American telecollaboration along the institutional fault line. *Modern Language Journal, 87*(1), 71–89.

Berge, Z. (1995). Facilitating computer conferencing: Recommendations from the field. *Educational Technology, 36*(1), 22–29.

Breen, M., & Littlejohn, A. (2000). *Classroom decision-making. Negotiation and process syllabuses in practice.* Cambridge: Cambridge University Press.

Brush, T., Igoe, A., Brinkerhoff, J., Glazewski, K., Ku, H.-Y., & Smith, C. (2001). Lessons from the field. Integrating technology into preservice teacher education [Electronic version]. *Journal of Computing in Teacher Education 17*(4), 16–20 (Online). Retrieved Nov. 8, 2004, from http://www.iste.org/jcte/PDFs/te17416bru.pdf.

Cuckle, P., Clarke, S., & Jenkins, I. (2000). Students' information and communications technology skills and their use during teacher training [Electronic version]. *Journal of Information Technology for Teacher Education, 9*(1), 9–22. Retrieved Nov. 8, 2004, from http://www.triangle.co.uk/pdf/validate.asp?j=jit&vol=9&issue=1&year=2000&article=Cuckle_JITT_9_1.

Davis, N. (2000). Information technology for teacher education at its first zenith: The heat is on! [Electronic version]. *Journal of Information Technology for Teacher Education, 9*(3), 277–286. Retrieved Nov. 8, 2004 from http://www.triangle.co.uk/pdf/validate.asp?j=jit&vol=9&issue=3&year=2000&article=Editorial_JITT_9_3.

Dawson, K., & Norris, A. (2000). Preservice teachers' experiences in a K-12/University technology-based field initiative [Electronic version]. *Journal of Computing in Teacher Education, 17*(1), 4–12. Retrieved Nov. 8, 2004, from http://www.iste.org/jcte/PDFs/te17104daw.pdf.

Ellis, R. (2003). *Task-based Language Learning and Teaching.* Oxford: Oxford University Press.

Freeman, D., & Johnson, K. (1998). Reconceptualizing the knowledge-base of language teacher education. *TESOL Quarterly, 32,* 397–417.

Fullan, M. (1993). *Change forces. Probing the depths of educational reform.* London: The Falmer Press.

Gabel, P. (1997). *Lehren und Lernen im Fachpraktikum Englisch. Wunsch und Wirklichkeit.* Tübingen: Narr.

Jayroe, T., Ball, K., & Novinski, M. (2001). Professional development partnerships integrating educational technology. *Journal of Computing in Teacher Education, 18*(1), 12–18.

Johnson, K. (2002). Second Language Teacher Education. *TESOL Matters, 12*(2), 1 & 8.

Kohonen, V. (1992). Experiential language learning: Second language learning as cooperative learner education. In D. Nunan (Ed.), *Collaborative language learning and teaching* (pp. 14–39). Cambridge: Cambridge University Press.

Krainer, K., & Posch, P. (Eds.). (1996). *Lehrerfortbildung zwischen Prozessen und Produkten. Hochschullehrgänge „Pädagogik und Fachdidaktik für LehrerInnen" (PFL): Konzepte, Erfahrungen und Reflexionen.* Bad Heilbrunn: Klinkhardt.

Kramsch, C., & Thorne, S. (2002). Foreign language learning as global communicative practice. In D. Block & D. Cameron (Eds.), *Language learning and teaching in the age of globalization* (pp. 83–100). New York: Routledge.

Lantolf, J. (Ed.). (2000). *Sociocultural theory and second language learning.* Oxford: Oxford University Press.

Legutke, M. (2005). Redesigning the Foreign Language Classroom. A Critical Perspective on Information Technology and Educational Change." In C. Davison (ed.). *Information Technology and Innovation in Language Education.* Hong Kong: Hong Kong University Press, 127–148.

Legutke, M., Müller-Hartmann, A., & Schocker-v. Ditfurth, M. (2001). Mediale Lernumgebungen im Schnittfeld von Lehrerausbildung und Lehrerfortbildung. In H. Decke-Cornill (Ed.), *Fremdsprachenunterricht in medialen Lernumgebungen* (pp. 81–92). Frankfurt: Lang.

Legutke, M., & Thomas, H. (1991). *Process and experience in the language classroom.* Harlow: Longman.

Marcovitz, D. (1999). Support for information technology in schools: The roles of student teachers [Electronic version]. *Journal of Information Technology for Teacher Education 8*(3), 361–374. Retrieved Nov. 8, 2004, from http://www.triangle.co.uk/jit/.

Milken Exchange on Education Technology. (1999). *Will new teachers be prepared to teach in a digital age? A national survey on information technology in teacher education.* Retrieved Nov. 8, 2004, from http://www.mff.org/pubs/ME154.pdf.

Moving West: Life of Native Americans today. (2001). Retrieved Nov. 8, 2004 from http://www.vib-bw.de/tp7/wwwprojekte/pr_movw_fr.htm.

Müller-Hartmann, A. (2000). The role of tasks in promoting intercultural learning in electronic learning networks. *Language Learning & Technology* 4(2), 129–147.

Müller-Hartmann, A., & Schocker-v. Ditfurth, M. (2004). *Introduction to English Language Teaching.* Stuttgart: Klett.

Müller-Hartmann, A., & Schocker-v. Ditfurth, M. (in press). Technology-enhanced project work in pre-service language teacher education to support autonomous student teacher learning. In C. Wai Meng (Ed.), *Autonomous foreign language learning.* Singapore: Singapore University Press.

National Council for Accreditation of Teacher Education Task Force on Technology and Teacher Education. (1997). *Technology and the new professional teacher. Preparing for the 21st century classroom.* Washington, DC: NCATE. Retrieved Nov. 8, 2004, from www.ncate.org/accred/projects/tech/tech-21.htm.

Pope, C., & Golub, J. (2000). Preparing tomorrow's English language arts teachers today: Principles and practices for infusing technology [Electronic version]. *Contemporary Issues in Technology and Teacher Education* 1(1). Retrieved Nov. 8, 2004, from http://www.citejournal.org/vol1/iss1/currentissues/english/article1.htm.

Preparing Tomorrow's Teachers to Use Technology (PT3) program. (2002). Retrieved Nov. 8, 2004, from http://www.pt3.org/.

Rösler, D. (2000). Foreign language learning with the new media: Between the sanctuary of the classroom and the open terrain of natural language acquisition [Electronic version]. *German as a Foreign Language, 1,* 16–31. Retrieved Nov. 8, 2004, from http://www.gfl-journal.de/1-2000/roesler.html.

Schocker-v. Ditfurth, M. (2001). *Forschendes Lernen in der fremdsprachlichen Lehrerbildung. Grundlagen, Erfahrungen, Perspektiven.* Tübingen: Narr.

Schocker-v. Ditfurth, M., & Legutke, M. (2002). Visions of what is possible or lost in complexity? How student teachers experience collaborative, media-enhanced learning-to-teach environments. *English Language Teaching Journal,* 56(2), 162–171.

Sherwood, C. (1993). Australian experiences with the effective classroom integration of information technology: Implications for teacher education. *Journal of Information Technology for Teacher Education,* 2(2), 167–179.

Stenhouse, L. (1975). *An introduction to curriculum research and development.* London: Heinemann.

Tella, S. (1991). *Introducing international communications networks and electronic mail into foreign language classrooms.* Helsinki: University of Helsinki.

Thomas, J., & Cooper, S. (2000). Teaching technology: A new opportunity for pioneers in teacher education [Electronic version]. *Journal of Computing in Teacher Education, 17,* 1. Retrieved Nov. 8, 2004, from http://www.iste.org/jcte/PDFs/te17113tho.pdf.

Vygotsky, L. (1978). *Mind in society: The development of higher psychological processes.* Cambridge: Harvard University Press.

Warschauer, M. (Ed.). (1996). *Telecollaboration in foreign language learning.* Honolulu, HI: University of Hawai'i Second Language Teaching and Curriculum Center.

Warschauer, M. (1999). *Electronic literacies. Language, culture, and power in online education.* Mahwah: Lawrence Erlbaum.

Weilburger Erklärung. (2002). Retrieved Nov. 8, 2004, from http://lernen.bildung.hessen.de/interkulturell/euro-sprachen/material/.

Widdowson, H. (1990). *Aspects of language teaching.* Oxford: Oxford University Press.

Willis, J., & Mehlinger, H. (1996). Information technology and teacher education. In J. Sikula, T. Buttery, & E. Guyton (Eds.), *Handbook of research on teacher education* (pp. 978–1029). New York: Simon & Schuster Macmillan.

Willis, J. (1996). *A framework for task-based learning.* Harlow: Longman.

AUTHOR INDEX

A
Abbs, B. 299
Abdulaziz, M. 49
Abello, P. 363
Abeysekera, R. 825
Accardo, A. 1082
Achebe, C. 678
Adams, G. 649
Adams, J. 180
Adams, L. 287
Adamson, B. 104
Addis, C. 22
Adolphs, S. 839
Agarwal, J. 61
Agnello, M. 904
Ahlgren, I. 50
Ahmed, M. 839
Akamatsu, N. 1050, 1099
Alatis, J. 49, 285, 348, 1001, 1027
Alderson, J. 469, 481, 502, 957
Alexander, B. 1029, 1047
Alexander, N. 40, 49
Alexander, P. 49
Alexander, R. 134, 210
Alfred, G. 1047
Allan, K. 856
Allan, M. 389
Allan, Q. 957
Allen, P. 285, 286, 483
Allwright, D. 984, 999, 1082
Almon, C. 678
Almond, R. 519
Altman, H. 742
Alvarez, A.

Alvarez, H. 637
Alvermann, D. 1014
Amin, N. 84, 689, 1047
Ammar, A. 284
Ammon, U. 134, 149, 165
Anderson, A. 299
Anderson, B. 34, 197, 678, 887
Anderson, G. 1000, 1047
Anderson, J. 197, 330
Anderson, M. 758
Andrew, D. 930
Andrews, S. 957
Angelil-Carter, S. 665
Angelova, M. 887
Ansre, G. 49
Anzaldúa, G. 1012, 1014
Aoki, N. 742
Aphek, E. 839
Appadurai, A. 1047
Appel, G. 690
Applebaum, S. 679, 1015
Archibald, J. 824
Argyris, C. 411, 1000
Arkoudis, S. 376, 502, 517
Arnaud, J. 34
Arnberg, L. 165
Arndt, V. 957, 1066
Arnett, J. 649
Arredondo, J. 652
Arthur, B. 246
Artin, G. 638
Arva, V. 957
Asato, J. 637
Ashworth, M. 197, 266, 313

Askehave, I. 940
Aston, G. 299
Atkey, S. 824
Atkinson, D. 61, 887, 889, 984, 986, 1047
Atkinson, J. 1026
Atkinson, P. 985
Atkinson, T. 1082
Au, A. 469
Au, K. 689
Auer, P. 246
Auerbach, E. 34, 84, 284, 689, 1000, 1047
August, D. 689
Austin, J. 284, 1047
Ayers, W. 1016
Azurmendi, M. 266

B

Bachman, L. 285, 454, 469, 482, 517, 518
Bachoc, E. 266
Baddeley, A. 839
Badger, R. 940
Bahns, J. 839
Bailey, B. 678
Bailey, K. 482, 984, 999, 1000, 1082
Bailey, R. 22, 1051
Baker, C. 119, 165, 389, 547
Baker, K. 34, 180, 182, 715
Baker, R. 454
Baker, S. 72, 73
Bakhtin, M. 401, 636, 887, 1047
Balazs, G. 1082
Balester, V. 915
Baley, R. 678
Ball, K. 1137
Ball, S. 267
Ballard, B. 887
Bamgboṣe, A. 38, 49, 141, 149
Bamworth, R. 940
Bandura, A. 330
Banerjee, J. 481, 502, 518
Banks, C. 652, 689
Banks, J. 652, 689
Bankston, C. 645, 653
Bannan-Ritland, B. 758
Bannerji, H. 197
Baquedano-López, P. 637
Barahona, B. 34
Barfield, A. 742
Barker, T. 915
Barnes, A. 1137
Barnes, D. 715, 742, 889
Barnett, R. 1082
Baron, D. 180
Baron, N. 904

Barratt-Pugh, C. 454, 502, 518
Barritt, L. 502
Barro, A. 1051
Barron-Hauwaert, S. 165
Barrs, M. 454
Barry, H. 643, 652
Barson, J. 915
Barthes, R. 1047
Bartholomae, D. 401
Barton, D. 313, 401
Barton, L. 1083
Basena, D. 758
Bassano, S. 1000
Basturkmen, H. 518
Bates, E. 794
Bateson, M. 1014
Batson, T. 916
Baugh, J. 34, 180
Baumeister, R. 649
Bayley, R. 984
Baynham, M. 377
Baynham, N. 940
Bazerman, C. 401, 547, 887, 940, 1047
Beacco, J. 149
Beardsmore, H. 165, 267
Beasley, V. 887
Beaty, E. 744
Beauvillain, C. 246
Beck, I. 840
Beck, J. 761
Beck, U. 1082
Becker, W. 809
Beglar, D. 840
Behar, R. 1098
Bejar, I. 482
Belcher, D. 547, 887, 888
Bell, D. 285
Bell, J. 1014
Bellack, A. 715
Belmore, N. 915
Belsey, C. 1047
Belz, J. 1047, 1137
Beneke, J. 149
Benesch, S. 401, 482, 665, 666, 689, 887, 1047
Benner, P. 1065
Bennett, C. 1000
Benson, D. 1026
Benson, M. 666
Benson, P. 742
Bereiter, C. 285, 794, 1065
Berge, Z. 1123, 1137
Berkenkotter, C. 887, 940
Berliner, D. 1065

Berns, M. 149, 165, 482
Bernstein, B. 210, 547, 1082, 1111
Bernstein, R. 180
Berry, J. 649
Berry, R. 957
Berthoud, R. 210
Berwick, R. 484
Beveridge, M. 718
Bhabha, H. 649, 1047
Bhatia, V. 401, 411, 547, 666, 940
Bialystok, E. 246
Biava, T. 679
Biber, D. 482, 715, 856, 871
Bickel, B. 1123
Bickley, G. 469
Biesenbach-Lucas, S. 758
Bigelow, B. 715
Biott, C. 1000
Birdsong, D. 824
Birkales, G. 180
Bissoondath, N. 1047
Black, P. 502, 518
Blackledge, A. 680, 1047, 1051
Blair, M. 210
Blaise, C. 1014
Blaustein-Epstein, A. 180
Bley-Vroman, R. 300
Bloch, J. 758
Block, D. 134, 547, 1047
Blommaert, J. 34, 134, 180
Bloomfield, L. 246
Bloor, T. 957
Blue, G. 743
Blum-Kulka, S. 871
Blundell, L. 299
Bock, H. 887
Boden, D. 1026
Boersma, P. 794
Boggs, G. 689
Bohman, J. 638
Bokamba, E. 49
Boling, E. 810
Bolitho, R. 149, 957, 959
Bolter, J. 758
Bonanno, H. 888
Bond, T. 455
Bondebjerg, I. 134
Bongaerts, T. 246, 824
Booth, D. 482
Borg, S. 957, 1065, 1082
Borg, W. 985
Borko, H. 1065
Borman, K. 649, 652

Bosco, F. 285
Bostwick, R. 71
Boswood, T. 411
Bottery, M. 1082
Bottomly, Y. 437
Boud, D. 743
Bourdieu, P. 134, 180, 531, 679, 689, 887, 904, 1047, 1082, 1098
Bourne, J. 210, 267, 636, 1111
Boxer, D. 871
Boykin, A. 1098
Boyle, A. 482
Brabazon, T. 1123
Braine, G. 401, 679, 887, 957, 1047
Bramley, P. 407, 411
Brazil, D. 856
Breen, M. 285, 454, 502, 518, 715, 743, 1000, 1082, 1137
Bremer, K. 149
Brennan, M. 1083
Brenner, J. 930
Bridgeman, B. 482, 483
Brilliant-Mills, H. 984
Brindley, G. 411, 437, 454, 469, 482, 518, 1000
Brinkerhoff, J. 1137
Brinkerhoff, R. 404, 411
Brinton, S. 376
Britton, B. 794
Britton, J. 285, 715
Broadfoot, P. 454, 518, 520
Brock, M. 1083
Brock-Utne, B. 49
Broeder, P. 149, 165
Bronfenbrenner, U. 700
Brookes, A. 743
Brookfield, S. 743
Brookhart, S. 1065
Brooks, F. 715
Brophy, J. 731, 957
Broselow, E. 824
Brousseau, K. 1000
Brown, A. 469, 482, 502
Brown, C. 824
Brown, G. 299
Brown, H. 1047
Brown, J. 71, 518
Brown, K. 758, 809
Brown, S. 104
Brownell, J. 454
Brumfit, C. 149, 285, 957, 1000
Bruner, J. 689, 715, 718, 1014
Brush, T. 1137

Bruton, A. 285, 299
Brutt-Griffler, J. 22, 84, 134, 149, 531, 1047
Bryson, B. 22
Bryson, P. 1001
Bull, P. 1029
Bullough, R. 1065
Bunnell, T. 389
Bunting, E. 363
Burbules, N. 915
Burgess, S. 940
Burnaby, B. 197
Burns, A. 856, 1000, 1082
Burstein, J. 484
Burt, E. 197
Burt, H. 299
Burt, M. 636
Burton, D. 871
Butler, F. 454, 482
Butler, J. 1047, 1048
Butler, Y. 809
Buttjes, D. 149
Button, G. 1026
Byram, M. 149, 1047, 1048, 1051
Byrd, P. 482

C
Cadman, K. 887
Cadorath, J. 871
Cain, A. 1050
Cain, C. 637
Calderhead, J. 412, 1065, 1082, 1083
Calderón, M. 649
Calhoun, E. 1000
Cameron, D. 34, 134, 412, 904, 1048
Cameron, K. 758
Campbell, D. 331
Campbell, W. 267
Camps, D. 887, 889
Canagarajah, A. 34, 71, 227, 636, 666, 984, 1048
Canale, M. 285, 715
Candelier, M. 149, 957
Candlin, C. 285, 401, 412, 666, 887, 1000, 1048, 1082
Candy, P. 743
Cantoni, G. 34
Carder, M. 389
Carey, L. 437
Carey, P. 482, 484
Carger, C. 1014
Carlgren, I. 1082
Carlisle, R. 824
Carlson, R. 469

Carpenter, P. 794
Carr, D. 1026
Carr, J. 1048
Carr, W. 1000, 1083
Carranza, I. 180
Carrell, P. 285, 482
Carroll, J. 482
Carroll, S. 856
Carson, J. 483
Carter, K. 1014
Carter, R. 149, 839, 857, 871, 872, 957
Caruso-Shade, D. 1123
Carver, R. 794
Casale, J. 330
Casanave, C. 547, 666, 887, 888, 1048
Casey, K. 1014
Cash, D. 916
Casllister, T. 915
Castaños, F. 278, 287
Castells, M. 904
Cazden, C. 636, 715
Celce-Murcia, M. 285, 856, 871
Cenoz, J. 150, 165, 166
Centrie, C. 650
Chafe, W. 871
Chaika, E. 1048
Chaiklin, S. 637, 716
Chalhoub-Deville, M. 482
Chambers, J. 150
Chamoiseau, P. 1014
Chamot, A. 267, 330, 331, 389, 840
Chan, A. 1098
Chandler, P. 957
Chang, J. 363
Chang, P. 1014
Chang, Y. 888
Chang-Wells, G. 718
Chapelle, C. 482, 518, 519, 758, 984
Charge, N. 482
Charpentier, J. 34
Chascas, S. 809
Chase, G. 888
Chaudenson, R. 134
Chavez, L. 180
Cheah, Y. 497, 502
Chen, J. 503
Cheng, L. 518, 531
Cherry, R. 888
Cherryholmes, C. 1048
Chesla, C. 1065
Cheung, K. 1099
Chiseri-Strater, E. 888
Chisman, F. 181
Chiu, M. 637

Choi, C. 461, 469
Choi, I. 84, 482
Chomsky, N. 246, 285, 299, 794, 856
Christensen, C. 1123
Christensen, J. 1065
Christian, D. 180, 267
Christie, F. 547, 715, 716, 856, 940
Christison, M. 1000
Christopher, E. 872
Chu, W. 809
Chun, D. 758, 915
Churchill, S. 197, 267
Cicourel, A. 1026
Cisneros, S. 1014
Claiborne, R. 23
Clanchy, J. 887
Clandinin, D. 1014
Clapham, C. 469, 481, 482, 518, 957
Clark, C. 1083
Clark, E. 794
Clark, F. 502
Clark, H. 794
Clark, J. 454
Clark, R. 888, 957
Clarke, D. 1065
Clarke, S. 518, 547, 1137
Claxton, G. 518, 1082
Clayman, S. 1026
Clayton, J. 716
Cleland, B. 267, 268
Clifford, J. 650, 1099
Cline, F. 482, 483
Clive, J. 23
Cloud, N. 456
Cluver, A. 34
Clyne, M. 166, 904
Coady, J. 794, 839
Cobb, T. 957, 958
Cochran, C. 916
Cochran-Smith, M. 1000
Coe, R. 401
Coehlo, E. 1099
Coffin, C. 313, 858
Cohen, A. 503, 517, 743, 839
Cohen, E. 731
Cohen, J. 331
Cohen, L. 984
Cole, M. 637
Coleman, H. 85
Coleman, J. 237, 246
Coles, R. 1014
Colhoun, E. 1049
Collier, J. 1000

Collier, V. 50, 210, 228, 268, 331, 348, 363, 690, 715, 810
Collins, J. 180
Collins, K. 210
Collins, P. 689
Collot, M. 915
Combs, M. 180, 348
Commins, L. 469
Conchas, G. 650
Condon, W. 503, 519
Coniam, D. 4671, 810
Conle, C. 1014
Connelly, F. 1014
Connolly, J. 651
Connor, U. 401, 547, 666, 940, 1048
Connor-Linton, J. 482
Conrad, S. 482, 856
Constas, M. 1048
Cook, G. 150, 299, 871
Cook, T. 331
Cook, V. 84, 150, 166, 246, 285, 679, 856, 1048
Cooke, D. 1048
Cooper, A. 412
Cooper, R. 267
Cooper, S. 1138
Cope, B. 650, 774, 888, 904, 930, 940
Coppari, P. 455, 456
Coppetiers, R. 246
Corbel, C. 437, 758, 1123
Corbett, J. 1048
Corbin, J. 986
Corno, L. 731
Corsaro, W. 984
Corson, D. 197, 809, 1048, 1099
Cortazzi, M. 85
Costa, A. 313
Coté, J. 650
Cotterall, S. 743
Coughlan, P. 299
Coulmas, F. 150
Coulthard, R. 717, 873
Coupland, J. 871
Coupland, N. 150, 872
Courchêne, R. 186, 197, 1038, 1048
Covington, M. 731
Cowan, P. 1014
Crabbe, D. 743
Crabtree, B. 984
Craig, A. 888
Craig, C. 1014
Crandall, J. 267, 376, 389
Crawford, J. 85, 180, 181, 227, 267, 636

Creese, A. 210, 376, 1111
Creswell, J. 984
Criper, C. 49
Crites, S. 1014
Crocker, L. 502
Crookes, G. 85, 287, 299, 1001
Crow Dog, M. 1014
Crow, N. 1065
Crump, S. 1123
Crystal, D. 120, 134, 166, 181, 210, 531, 904, 915
Csizér, K. 150
Cuckle, P. 1137
Cuevas, G. 267
Culler, J. 1048
Cumming, A. 197, 455, 456, 482, 1001
Cummings, O. 412
Cummins, J. 34, 49, 166, 181, 197, 227, 267, 285, 286, 331, 348, 363, 389, 455, 483, 636, 650, 689, 715, 758, 769, 774, 809, 888, 904, 916, 1048, 1099, 1111
Cunningham, A. 809
Cunningham, D. 1123
Cunningham, S. 299
Curran, C. 247, 285
Currie, P. 888
Curry-Rodriguez, J. 268
Cutler, A. 794
Czarniawska, B. 1014

D
Dabbagh, N. 758
Dale, M. 330
Dale, T. 267
Dall'Alba, G. 740, 744
Dallas, D. 809
Dalton, J. 437
Dam, L. 743, 1000, 1082
Darder, A. 650, 715
Darling-Hammond, L. 958
Datta, M. 210
Davidson, A. 650
Davidson, F. 482, 483
Davidson, J. 1026
Davies, A. 518, 531, 716
Davies, B. 636
Davies, L. 760
Davis, B. 1123
Davis, J. 1015
Davis, K. 181, 984
Davis, N. 1137
Davison, C. 267, 268, 376, 377, 389, 455, 502, 518, 547, 986, 1100

Dawson, K. 1137
Day, C. 1083
Day, E. 636
de Bot, K. 149
de Jong, J. 483
de Kanter, A. 180
de Klerk, G. 34
de Silva Joyce, H. 856, 1000
de Smedt, K. 794
de Swaan, A. 135
Deakin-Crick, R. 518
Debski, R. 758, 915, 1123
DeCarrico, J. 857
Dehaene-Lambertz, G. 824
Dei, G. 1099
DeKeyser, R. 789, 794
Del Rio, P. 638
Deleuze, G. 1048
Delgado-Gaitan, C. 689
Delpit, L. 715, 1051, 1099, 1100
Demick, B. 85
Dendrinos, V. 135
Deneire, M. 150
Denicolo, P. 1083
Denzin, N. 984, 1014
dePyssler, B. 653
Derewianka, B. 454, 455, 502, 518, 715, 856, 940, 941
Derrida, J. 1048
Desai, R. 61
Deville, C. 482, 985
Devitt, S. 760
Devlin, B. 181, 716
Devy, G. 61
Dewey, J. 743, 1015
Dewey, M. 150
Di Cola, J. 331
Di Pietro, J. 285
Dias, P. 940
Diaz, R. 247
Diaz, S. 637
DiCerbo, K. 348
Dick, W. 437
Dicker, S. 1048
Dickinson, L. 743
Dijkstra, T. 794
Dillon, J. 715
DiMatteo, A. 916
Dirven, R. 49
Disick, R. 438
Dison, A. 888
Dison, L. 888
Dixon, C. 716, 717, 985

Doan, L. 905
Dodd, N. 49
Doiz, A. 167
Donahue, T. 34, 181
Donaldson, M. 715
Donato, R. 651, 690, 715
Donmall, G. 958
Donmall-Hicks, G. 958
Dorfman, A. 1015
Dörnyei, Z. 150, 285, 731, 743, 871
Doughty, C. 285, 299, 518, 758, 856, 1026, 1028, 1029
Doughty, P. 150
Douglas, D. 412, 482, 483
Draper, J. 181
Dresemann, B. 150
Drew, M. 930
Drew, P. 1026
Dreyfus, H. 758
Dreyfus, S. 758
Droeschel, Y. 150
Drucker, P. 1123
Drury, H. 889
Dryfoos, J. 650
du Gay, P. 637, 651
Du, P. 90, 105
Dudley-Evans, N. 412
Dudley-Evans, T. 401, 666, 940, 941
Duff, P. 120, 198, 299, 650, 984, 985, 1027, 1112
Dufficy, P. 941
Dugan, N. 794
Duke, N. 810
Dulay, H. 636
Dulay, M. 299
Dunkel, P. 482, 758
Dunn, W. 700
Dupoux, E. 824
Duran, R. 717
Duranti, A. 651, 1026
Durham, M. 150
Dutcher, N. 166
Dutertre, A. 1001
Dykman, E. 650
Dyson, A. 636

E

Earl, L. 34
Early, M. 198, 313, 985
Easterby-Smith, M. 412
Eckman, F. 824
Economou, D. 889
Edelenbos, P. 518
Edelsky, C. 689
Edge, J. 958, 985, 1001
Edmondson, W. 150
Edmonston, B. 182
Edwards, D. 715
Edwards, V. 531, 1112
Egan, K. 700
Eggington, W. 24, 691, 1047–1049, 1052
Eggins, S. 856, 872, 941
Ehrlich, S. 1048
Ehrman, M. 731
Eignor, D. 482, 484
Eimas, P. 794, 795
Eisner, E. 985
Elbaz, F. 1065, 1083
Elbaz-Luwisch, F. 1015
Eldaw, M. 839
Elder, C. 470, 483
Eliot, C. 761
Elley, W. B. 802, 809, 834, 839
Elley, W. G. 285
Elliott, J. 700, 1001
Ellis, A. 759, 809
Ellis, G. 1083
Ellis, M. 412
Ellis, N. 794
Ellis, R. 247, 2901, 348, 518, 840, 856, 958, 1027, 1137
Ellis, S. 454
Ellsworth, E. 1050
Elman, J. 794
Elson, N. 483
Ely, C. 759
Endres, S. 759
Engeström, Y. 637
English, L. 888
Enright, M. 483
Epp, L. 483
Epstein, A. 679
Eraut, M. 412
Erdoes, R. 1014
Erduran, S. 520
Erickson, M. 889
Ericsson, K. 1065
Erikson, E. 650
Erling, S. 150
Ernst, G. 872
Espinosa, P. 690
Esses, V. 197
Etxeberria, F. 166
Evans, L. 1123
Evans, R. 267, 268
Ewen, D. 181
Extra, G. 165

F
Faderman, L. 650
Fafunwa, A. 49
Faigley, L. 916
Fairclough, N. 34, 49, 650, 888, 930, 958, 985
Falodun, J. 300
Faltis, C. 689
Falvey, P. 469, 470
Fardon, R. 49
Feak, C. 942, 943
Featherstone, M. 85
Feez, S. 941
Feinberg, W. 650
Feldman, C. 247
Feldman, S. 652
Felix, U. 759
Ferguson, C. 181
Ferguson, P. 1001, 1082
Ferguson, R. 456
Fessler, R. 1065
Feuerverger, G. 1015
Fielding, L. 809
Fillmore, L. 331, 348, 638, 691, 810
Fine, G. 650
Fine, M. 652, 653
Finegan, E. 856
Finer, D. 824
Firmat, G. 1015
Firth, A. 150, 152, 299, 872, 1027
Firth, J. 285
Fishman, J. 34, 120, 181
Flavell, J. 743
Fleming, D. 197, 1048
Fleming, M. 149, 1047, 1048
Fletcher, J. 483
Flewelling, J. 470
Floriani, A. 715
Flower, L. 794
Flowerdew, J. 402, 872, 888, 1083
Flynn, L. 916
Fodor, J. 794
Fok, O. 809
Forester, J. 34
Forey, G. 412
Forman, E. 637, 638
Forsyth, D. 731
Foster, P. 299, 301
Fotus, S. 285
Foucault, M. 34, 531, 650, 1049, 1083
Fox, H. 666, 888
Fox, J. 1123
Fox, R. 1123
Fradd, S. 716

Francis, G. 872
Fránquiz, M. 635, 637
Franson, C. 1112
Fraser, B. 731
Freebairn, I. 299
Freebody, P. 547, 905
Freedman, A. 547, 548, 940, 941
Freeman, D. 72, 285, 286, 348, 363, 377, 958, 1001, 1015, 1065, 1083, 1137
Freeman, R. 985
Freeman, Y. 363
Freire, P. 85, 285, 502, 689, 743, 904, 1049
Fremer, J. 503
Fries, C. 285
Fröhlich, M. 285, 288
Frommer, J. 915
Fujishima, N. 666
Fulcher, G. 483
Fulford, R. 197
Fullan, M. 377, 455, 1137
Fuller, F. 412
Funabashi, Y. 71
Furlong, J. 1083
Furniss, G. 49

G
Gabel, P. 1137
Gabrielsen, G. 1000, 1082
Gagné, A. 470
Gairns, R. 839
Gall, J. 985
Gall, M. 985
Gallard, P. 331
Gallardo, F. 166
Gallas, K. 715
Gallego, M. 904
Gallegos, B. 1047
Gallimore, R. 638, 717
Gan, D. 1100
Gándara, P. 261, 266, 268
Ganderton, R. 759
García Lecumberri, M. 163, 165–167
García Mayo, M. 163, 165–167
García, A. 266, 268
García, E. 260, 268, 355, 363, 643, 650, 688, 690
García, O. 32, 35
Gardner, H. 363
Gardner, R. 197, 872
Gardner, S. 518, 519
Gardner-Chloros, P. 34
Garfinkel, H. 1027
Garrett, P. 151, 958
Gartner-Clough, P. 1124

Garton, J. 1123
Garvey, C. 314
Gaskill, W. 1027
Gass, S. 286, 287, 300, 794, 1027, 1030
Gates, P. 1082
Gawlitta, K. 135
Geddes, M. 300, 743
Gee, J. 314, 637, 650, 689, 888, 904, 1049, 1083, 1099, 1123
Gee, S. 941
Geertz, C. 888, 1015
Gegeo, D. 35, 36
Genesee, F. 120, 165, 166, 247, 268, 286, 518, 825
Geoghegan, W. 1123
George, J. 23
Gernsbacher, M. 794
Gersten, B. 1001
Gersten, R. 363
Geva, E. 809
Ghadirian, S. 759
Gibbons, P. 715, 856
Gibson, M. 650, 985, 1112
Giddens, A. 1082, 1083
Gilbert, G. 402
Giles, H. 150, 650
Gill, G. 840
Gillborn, D. 210, 455, 650, 1112
Gillespie, M. 35
Giltrow, J. 1049
Gimenez, T. 1083
Gingrich, N. 181
Ginther, A. 483
Ginther, L. 483
Gipps, C. 455, 518, 520
Giroux, H. 1049, 1083
Glas, C. 520
Glazewski, K. 1137
Glenwright, P. 470
Glesne, C. 985
Glynn, S. 794
Gnutzmann, C. 150, 166
Godwin-Jones, B. 754, 759
Goethals, M. 150
Goldstein, T. 652, 679, 985, 986, 1049, 1099
Golebiowski, Z. 759
Gollin, S. 402, 889
Golub, J. 1138
Gomes de Matos, F. 247
Gomez, E. 456
Gong, Y. 104
Gonzales, R. 34
González-Nueno, M. 239, 247

Good, T. 731
Goodfellow, R. 760
Goodman, K. 716
Goodman, S. 856
Goodman, Y. 716
Goodson, I. 1065
Goodwin, C. 1027
Goossens, L. 650
Gordon, C. 484
Gore, J. 690, 1001, 1066
Görlach, M. 150
Gorsuch, G. 71
Goswami, D. 1001
Gotanda, N. 637
Goto, S. 651
Gottlieb, M. 456
Gough, L. 331
Goulden, R. 839
Gout, A. 824
Grabe, W. 285, 314, 482, 794, 888, 941, 1049
Graddol, D. 135, 150, 181, 210, 904
Graham, J. 483
Grainger, J. 246, 794
Gramkow Andersen, K. 150
Granger, C. 905, 1049
Granger, S. 150
Grant, C. 1100
Grant, L. 470, 482, 483
Grant, R. 689, 691
Granville, S. 888
Graves, K. 455, 456, 1001
Gray, J. 85
Green, A. 518
Green, C. 868, 872
Green, J. 716, 717, 985
Greenbaum, S. 150, 857
Greenberg, K. 483
Greene, M. 689, 1015
Gregg, K. 1027
Gregory, E. 210
Gremmo, M. 743
Griffin, P. 455, 470
Grigorenko, E. 700
Grin, F. 135
Groom, N. 942
Grosjean, F. 166, 247, 679
Grossberg, L. 651
Grossman, P. 377, 1065
Grumet, M. 1015
Grundy, P. 149, 743
Grundy, S. 1001
Guattari, F. 1048
Guba, E. 518

Gudykunst, W. 651
Guest, E. 23
Gumperz, J. 150, 651, 1049
Gunn, M. 518
Guth, G. 36
Gutiérrez, K. 716, 985
Gutiérrez, R. 367, 368, 377

H
Haas, T. 402
Habermas, J. 35, 1083
Haegeman, P. 150
Hafner, K. 916
Haimd, N. 759
Hakuta, K. 247, 679, 689, 809
Halasek, K. 915
Hale, G. 483
Halio, M. 916
Hall, G. 651
Hall, J. 716, 985, 1049
Hall, K. 1049
Hall, S. 85, 197, 637, 651, 679, 1099
Halliday, M. 300, 314, 402, 547, 716, 856, 888, 930, 941
Halsey, A. 1001
Halter, R. 286
Hamblin, A. 412
Hamilton, J. 412
Hamilton, M. 401
Hammarberg, W. 167
Hammersley, M. 985
Hammond, J. 455, 716, 856, 941
Hamp-Lyons, L. 412, 481, 483, 502, 503, 519, 530, 531
Hanchanlash, C. 389
Hansen, J. 651, 666
Hao, Y. 104
Hardman, F. 959
Hardt, M. 135
Hargreaves, A. 1083
Harklau, L. 377, 651, 666, 985, 1049
Harlech-Jones, B. 49
Harlen, W. 519
Harley, B. 286, 300, 483, 824
Harré, R. 377, 636
Harrington, M. 794
Harris, D. 389
Harris, J. 402, 888, 1065
Harris, R. 35, 197, 268, 286, 547, 1049, 1112
Harris, S. 871
Harris, V. 691
Harris, Z. 1027
Harrold, D. 470

Hart, J. 227
Hartman, K. 916
Hartmann, R. 150
Hartup, W. 651
Harvey, P. 957
Hasan, R. 314, 774, 856, 872, 941
Hasebrink, U. 149
Hatch, E. 286, 872
Hatch, J.A. 1006, 1015
Hatcher, P. 809
Haugen, E. 247
Havranek, G. 286
Hawisher, G. 904, 916
Hawkins, E. 150, 958
Hawley, W. 1065
Hayakawa, S. 181
Haycraft, J. 958
Hayden, M. 389
Hayes, J. 794
Hazenberg, S. 839
He, A. 485, 1027
He, M. 1015, 1016
Healy, D. 743
Heath, C. 1027
Heath, S. 651, 904, 985
Hebdige, D. 651
Hegelheimer, V. 759
Heine, B. 49
Held, D. 85, 197, 679
Heller, M. 85, 651, 1049, 1099
Helt, M. 482
Hémard, D. 759
Henriques, J. 637
Henry, A. 941
Henry, F. 197
Henze, R. 651, 690
Herdina, P. 166
Heritage, J. 1026, 1027
Hermerschmidt, M. 888
Hernandez, J. 402
Hernández, R. 644, 651
Heron, J. 731
Herr, K. 1000
Herrimen, M. 377
Herrmann, A. 1123
Hester, H. 454
Heugh, K. 49
Hewlett, L. 888
Higa, M. 840
Higuchi, T. 71
Hiley, D. 638
Hill, K. 469, 484
Hinds, J. 547, 941
Hinett, K. 520

Hingley, W. 1050
Hinkel, E. 402, 1049
Hinton, L. 181
Hird, B. 1082
Hirsch, E. 181
Hirvela, A. 888
Hitchcock, G. 985, 1001
Hjarvad, S. 135
Hoddinott, D. 268
Hodge, R. 314, 930
Hoey, M. 872
Hoffman, E. 679, 1015
Hoffmann, C. 151, 166
Hogan, S. 438
Höglin, R. 135
Höjlund, G. 49
Holec, H. 743, 759
Holland, D. 227, 637
Hollander, E. 151
Holliday, A. 61, 227, 402, 985, 1049, 1083
Hollingsworth, H. 1065
Hollingsworth, S. 904, 1015
Hollqvist, H. 151
Hollway, W 637
Holmes, J. 888
Honey, J. 23, 181
Hong, T. 1100
Hood, S. 503, 1000
Hook, P. 731
Hooks, B. 1015
Hooper, H. 313, 314
Hooper, J. 957
Hope, M. 1083
Hopkins, D. 1001
Hopper, R. 1027
Horenczyk, G. 651
Hornberger, N. 120, 167, 1049
Horowitz, D. 402, 666
Horst, M. 286
Houghton, D. 666
House, H. 454, 502, 518
House, J. 135, 151
Hoven, D. 759
Howard, U. 1123
Howatt, A. 23, 286
Howie, D. 377
Hsia, S. 1083
Hsu, J. 759
Hu, H. 518
Huber, J. 1015
Huberman, A. 986
Huberman, M. 1065
Huckin, T. 547, 839, 887, 940, 941

Huddleston, R. 857
Hudelson, S. J. 685, 689
Hudson, C. 454, 456, 502, 518
Hudson, T. 455, 483, 518
Huebner, T. 181
Huerta-Macías, A. 506, 509, 519
Hufeisen, B. 165, 167
Hughes, A. 519
Hughes, D. 985, 1001
Hughes, J. 1026
Hughes, R. 149, 872
Huhta, A. 483, 503
Hull, D. 1123
Hull, G. 888
Hüllen, W. 135, 151
Hulme, C. 809
Hulstijn, J. 794, 795, 840
Humphrey, S. 857
Hunston, S. 872
Hunt, A. 840
Hunter, J. 637, 1099
Huot, B. 503
Hurd, S. 743
Hurst, D. 377, 389
Hurtado, A. 650
Hutchby, I. 872
Hutchinson, T. 104, 412
Hutchison, B. 1001
Huxur, G. 314
Hyerle, D. 314
Hyland, F. 503
Hyland, K. 402, 503, 887, 888, 941
Hyltenstam, K. 50, 300
Hyman, R. 715
Hymes, D. 286, 872
Hyon, S. 941

I
Ianco-Worrall, A. 247
Ibrahim, A. 637, 679, 1049, 1099
Iedema, R. 857
Igoa, C. 1015, 1099
Ihnatko, T. 888
Ilieva, R. 198, 1049
Illich, I. 743
Inbar, O. 810
Intemann, F. 150, 166
Ip, K. 809
Ito, K. 71
Ivanič, R. 875, 877, 881, 882, 884–889, 1046, 1049
Iverson, G. 824
Iwashita, N. 469, 470, 483

J

Jackson, A. 650
Jacobs, A. 794
Jacobs, U. 930
Jacobson, R. 247
Jacoby, S. 1018, 1029
Jadeja, R. 61
James, A. 151, 167, 651
James, C. 151, 742, 958
James, I. 1099
James, M. 519
James-Williams, S. 1099
Jamieson, J. 4884, 758
Janks, H. 1049
Jaramillo, A. 363
Jarvis, J. 872
Jarvis, S. 247, 1001
Javed, S. 759
Jayaram, N. 61
Jayroe, T. 1137
Jefferson, G. 872, 873, 1029
Jenkins, I. 1137
Jenkins, J. 135, 151, 152, 167, 247, 547
Jenkins, S. 23, 941
Jensen, L. 376
Jernudd, B. 181
Jessner, U. 150, 1667
Jewitt, C. 210, 930
Jiménez, R. 363
Jiminez, M. 181
Jin, L. 85
Johansson, S. 856
John, S. 890
Johns, A. 268, 401, 402, 666, 857, 889, 941
Johnson, C. 412
Johnson, J. 72
Johnson, K. 286, 377, 958, 1052, 1065, 1083, 1137
Johnson, M. 314, 794, 1123
Johnson, P. 650
Johnson, R. 120, 121, 268
Johnston, B. 1049, 1052
Johnston, M. 857
Johnstone, R. 286
Jonassen, D. 314, 759
Jonasses, D. 759
Jones, B. 1123
Jones, C. 889, 1123
Jones, F. 731
Jones, J. 888, 889
Jones, K. 905
Jones, L. 731
Jones, S. 119, 165, 389, 482, 483

Jones, V. 300
Jonietz, P. 389
Jordan, S. 1051
Jordan, R. 931, 941
Joshi, P. 61
Jung, S. 85
Jusczyk, P. 795
Just, M. 794

K

Kachru, B. 35, 61, 120, 151, 167, 181, 227, 679, 958
Kachru, Y. 679
Kagan, R. 181
Kalantzis, M. 650, 774, 888, 904, 930, 940
Kamana, K. 35
Kanagy, R. 300
Kanfer, R. 731
Kanno, Y. 72, 679, 1015
Kantor, R. 4884
Kapadia, S. 61
Kaplan, A. 1015
Kaplan, R. 23, 61, 794, 888, 889, 941
Kaplan, W. 198
Karavas-Doukas, K. 104, 519
Karl, J. 470
Karmiloff-Smith, A. 794
Karp, S. 715
Karumanchery, L. 1099
Kasermann, M. 716
Kashoki, M. 49
Kasper, G. 151, 247, 1027
Kato, S. 72
Katz, A. 456
Katz, M. 985
Kay, H. 941
Kay, S. 300
Kayman, M. 135
Keane, S. 363
Kecskes, I. 167, 247
Keep, C. 1123
Kellerman, E. 151, 247
Kellner, D. 904
Kelly, G. 743
Kelm, O. 759, 916
Kember, D. 1001
Kemmis, S. 1000, 1001, 1083
Kemp, F. 915
Kempf, S. 689
Kempler, D. 638
Kenning, M. 1123
Kenny, B. 743
Kenyon, D. 470, 484
Kere-Levy, M. 810

Kern, R. 759, 916, 1123
Kerr, P. 958
Khan, J. 61
Khan, R. 1050
Kheimetz, N. 679
Kiang, P. 651
Kiesler, S. 916
Kim, K. 85
Kim, R. 651
Kincheloe, J. 1049
Kinginger, C. 679
Kingston, M. 1015
Kirkpatrick, D. 412
Kirsch, I. 483, 484
Kirshner, D. 638, 1052
Kitamura, T. 72
Kleinsasser, R. 287
Klesmer, H. 809
Kliebard, H. 715
Kloss, H. 181
Knapp, K. 150, 151, 152, 1049
Knapp, M. 689
Knapp, P. 940
Knapp-Pothoff, A. 151
Knight, M. 363
Knijnik, G. 1001
Knobel, M. 904
Knowles, G. 181
Knowles, J. 1065
Knowles, M. 743
Knowles, V. 198
Kobayashi, M. 985
Kobayashi, S. 181
Kobayashi, Y. 679
Koda, K. 483
Koedinger, K. 759
Kohonen, V. 743, 1137
Kolb, D. 743
Kommers, P. 759
Komter, M. 872
Kontra, M. 135
Kordon, K. 151
Koshik, I. 1027, 1029
Kouritzin, S. 679
Kourtis-Kazoullis, V. 763, 770, 771, 772, 774
Kowal, M. 286
Kozol, J. 689
Kozulin, A. 716
Krainer, K. 1137
Kramer, M. 666
Kramsch, C. 85, 135, 247, 455, 679, 872, 985, 1049, 1083, 1137

Krashen, S. 35, 181, 268, 286, 300, 636, 651, 795, 809, 857, 958, 1027
Krauss, M. 181
Kress, G. 314, 759, 857, 889, 904, 930, 940, 941, 1049
Kreuter, B. 716
Kroll, B. 483
Kroskrity, P. 651
Ku, H. 1137
Kubanek-German, A. 518, 519
Kubota, R. 23, 85, 198, 689, 889, 941, 1050
Kuczaj, S. 700
Kuhl, J. 731
Kumaravadivelu, B. 286, 1050
Kunieda, M. 72
Kunnan, A. 484, 519
Küpper, L. 331
Kwan, A. 809
Kwon, O. 85
Kymlicka, W. 198

L
Labov, W. 247, 872
Lachat, M. 455
Lachicotte, W. 637
Lado, R. 286
Ladson-Billings, G. 1050
Lafond, L. 1050
Lakey, J. 210
Lakoff, G. 314
Lam, C. 809
Lam, E. 916
Lam, J. 872
Lam, W. 759
Lamb, C. 994, 1002
Lamb, M. 104
Lamb, T. 744, 745
Lambert, R. 181
Lambert, W. 247, 809
Lamy, M. 760
Landsman, L. 700
Langston, M. 916
Lanier, J. 1065
Lankshear, C. 904, 1123
Lantolf, J. 300, 690, 700, 717, 1050, 1137
Lapkin, S. 288, 301, 717
Larsen-Freeman, D. 72, 286, 348
Larson, R. 637, 716
Lasagabaster, D. 167
Lash, S. 1082
Lather, P. 1050
Latour, B. 402

Laurillard, D. 760
Laver, J. 872
Lawrence-Lightfoot, S. 1015
Lazaraton, A. 984, 985, 1027, 1028
Lazarus, R. 651
Le Page, R. 34
Lea, M. 889
Leather, J. 985
Lebauer, R. 872
Lebiere, C. 794
Lee, C. 716
Lee, D. 872
Lee, I. 810
Lee, J. 85
Lee, O. 716
Lee, S. 651
Lee, Y. 480, 481, 484
Leech, G. 840, 856, 857, 958
Legenhausen, L. 743, 744
Legutke, M. 744, 1137, 1138
Leibhammer, N. 930
Leibowitz, B. 889
Leith, D. 179, 181
Leki, I. 666, 986
Lemke, J. 716, 930
Lenneberg, E. 72
Leontiev, A. 700
Lerner, G. 1028
Lesaux, N. 809
Lesznyák, A. 144, 151
Leung, C. 197, 315
Leung, K. 809
Leung, S. 484
Leung, W. 810
Levelt, W. 795
Levin, J. 905
Levine, J. 210, 1112
Levine, T. 810
Levinson, B. 214, 227
Levy, M. 758, 760, 810
Lewin, K. 731, 1001
Lewin, L. 470
Lewis, M. 837, 840, 1123
Li, E. 744
Li, L. 104
Li, P. 198
Li, X. 1015
Liang, X. 314
Libben, G. 744
Lidz, C. 700
Lieberman, A. 1065
Lieberman, P. 377
Liebkind, K. 651
Lightbown, P. 2888, 300, 519, 760

Lillis, T. 889
Lin, A. 690, 1050, 1099
Lin, L. 716
Lincoln, Y. 518, 984, 1014
Lincoln-Porter, F. 717
Lindblad, S. 1082
Lindemann, B. 167
Lindholm, K. 180
Lindholm-Leary, K. 348
Lindsay, D. 166
Linell, J. 717
Lionnet, F. 247
Lippi-Green, R. 35, 679, 1099
Lippitt, R. 731
Litowitz, B. 637
Little, D. 744, 760, 857
Little, J. 377, 1065, 1083
Littlejohn, A. 743, 1137
Littlewood, W. 286, 744
Liu, D. 104
Liu, J. 651
Liu, L. 104
Llurda, E. 247
Lo Bianco, J. 181, 182, 268, 455
Lockhart, C. 1002, 1083
Lockwood, J. 412
Loewen, S. 518
Logan, G. 789, 795
Loh Fook Seng, P. 23
Long, M. 72, 247, 286, 287, 300, 348, 716, 760, 857, 958, 1001, 1028
Longacre, R. 314
Longhi-Chirlin, T. 810
Lopez, L. 167
Lopriore, L. 455, 456
Lor, W. 742
Lorsch, J. 377
Lortie, D. 377, 1066, 1083
Loschky, L. 300
Losey, K. 986
Lotherington, H. 904, 905
Louhiala-Salminen, L. 151
Low, M. 314
Lowenberg, P. 35
Lubelska, D. 36
Lucas, T. 651, 690
Lüdi, G. 151
Lugard, F. 23
Luk Hung-Kay, B. 23
Luk, J. 1050
Luke, A. 905, 941, 1099
Luke, C. 690
Lukes, M. 228, 638
Lukhele, R. 484

Lumley, T. 412, 454, 470, 502, 503, 518
Luoma, S. 518
Luria, A. 857
Lynch, B. 519, 531, 1050
Lynch, T. 872
Lyotard, J. 1071, 1083
Lyster, N. 986
Lyster, R. 287, 300
Lytle, S. 1000

M

Mabrito, M. 916
Macaire, D. 149
Macaulay, T. 23
MacDonald, J. 389
Macias, R. 182
MacIntosh, A. 402
Macken, M. 942
Macken-Horarik, M. 856
Mackenzie, P. 389
Mackey, A. 287, 300
Mackrell, G. 840
Maclear, K. 1099
Maclennan, C. 503
MacPherson, S. 1050
MacSwan, J. 348
MacWhinney, B. 795
Madood, T. 210
Mager, R. 437
Maggisano, C. 1015
Magnan, S. 1000
Magoto, J. 1123
Maharaj, S. 651
Maher, J. 72
Mahoney, K. 348
Maier, P. 942
Mair, C. 134, 1050
Makarec, K. 247
Malakoff, M. 167, 247
Malderez, A. 731
Malobonga, V. 484
Malone, M. 456
Man, E. 810
Manes, J. 50
Manion, L. 984
Mann, S. 743
Mansfield, S. 760
Mansour, G. 49
Manyak, P. 637
Marchart, O. 905
Marchenkova, L. 1049
Marcovitz, D. 1137
Marcus, G. 1099

Marinova-Todd, S. 72
Markee, N. 104, 412, 1001, 1028
Markus, H. 679
Marrow, A. 1001
Marshall, C. 986
Marshall, D. 72
Marshall, S. 649
Martin, J. 314, 547, 716, 850, 856, 857, 940, 942
Martin-Jones, M. 905
Marton, F. 744
Masats, D. 151
Masters, J. 993, 1001
Masuhara, H. 149
Mateene, K. 49
Mathew, R. 1001
Matsuda, P. 889
Matsuo, N. 301
Matthiessen, C. 314
Mattis, W. 197
Matute-Bianchi, M. 651
Maungedzo, R. 930
Mauranen, A. 151, 548, 942
May, L. 484
May, S. 268, 1050
Maybin, J. 716
Mayes, J. 759
Mazrui, A. 35
McCarthy, L. 889
McCarthy, M. 840, 857, 871, 872
McCarty, T. 35, 36, 135, 228
McCombs, B. 731
McConnell, D. 72
McCormick, M. 690
McCormick, W. 182
McDermott, R. 637, 716
McDonough, K. 287, 300
McGrath, I. 470, 744, 745
McGrew, T. 85, 197, 679
McGroarty, M. 690
McHoul, A. 1028
McKay, P. 268, 455, 456, 503, 519, 548, 716
McKay, S. 637, 651, 690, 986, 1050, 1099
McKeown, M. 840
McLaren, P. 198, 716
McLaughlan, T. 1123
McLaughlin, M. 651
McLean, M. 287
McLeod, P. 795
McLuhan, M. 905
McMahill, C. 679
McMeniman, M. 267

McMillan, J. 503
McNamara, T. 198, 456, 470, 4884, 519, 700, 1050
McNeill, A. 957, 958
McNess, E. 520
McNiff, J. 1001
McPake, J. 210, 1111
McPherson, P. 760, 1001
McQuillan, J. 35
McTaggart, R. 1001, 1083
Meacham, S. 690
Meara, P. 840
Measor, L. 1066
Mechling, J. 650
Meddleton, I. 840
Medgyes, P. 679, 957, 958
Medway, P. 940, 941
Meek, M. 268
Meeuwis, M. 152
Mehan, B. 716
Mehan, H. 690, 916, 1028
Mehler, J. 794
Mehlinger, H. 1138
Mehnert, U. 300
Meierkord, C. 151, 152, 1049
Melander, B. 135
Melanson, Y. 1015
Melis, I
Meloni, C. 761, 917
Mencken, H. 182
Mennen, S. 824
Mercer, N. 715, 716, 718
Mercuri, A. 248
Merriam, S. 986
Merten, M. 890
Messick, S. 456, 484, 519, 531
Met, M. 268
Meyer, L. 228, 331
Mhando, E. 49
Michaels, S. 716
Midy, J. 34
Mignolo, W. 23
Miklosy, K. 679
Miles, M. 986
Miles, S. 1083
Miller, C. 942
Miller, E. 548, 1030
Miller, J. 679, 795, 986, 1001
Miller, W. 975, 984
Mills, S. 637
Milroy, J. 35, 531
Milroy, L. 35, 531
Milton, J. 402, 840
Milton, M. 1082

Min, P. 651
Mincham, L. 503
Miner, S. 182
Minick, N. 637, 638
Mintzes, J. 314
Mirza, H. 210, 1112
Mishler, E. 1001
Mislevy, R. 519
Missler, B. 167
Mistry, J. 638
Mitchell, K. 198
Mitchell, R. 700, 857, 957, 1000
Miura, I. 71
Modiano, M. 151, 167
Moerman, M. 1028
Mohammed, S. 49
Mohan, A. 268
Mohan, B. 268, 314, 315, 377, 519, 717, 986, 1100
Moje, E. 652
Mok, J. 503
Moll, L. 363, 637, 690, 717
Mollaun, P. 482, 484
Mollin, S. 152
Monbiot, G. 135
Monoson, P. 470
Monroe, P. 23
Montero-Sieburth, M. 653
Montone, C. 180
Moon, R. 840
Moor, P. 299
Moore, H. 198, 456, 548
Moran, C. 363, 916
Moran, P. 1050
Morbey, M. 905
Morgan, B. 198, 1050, 1052
Morgan, C. 1050
Morgan, M. 182
Mori, J. 986, 1028
Morita, N. 986
Morris, L. 958
Morris, P. 104
Mosenthal, P. 483, 1014
Moses, D. 61
Mosier, C. 638
Moss, P. 484
Motteram, G. 760, 1123
Moya, P. 652
Mtana, N. 49
Mufwene, S. 135
Mukherjee, B. 198
Mulcahy-Ernt, P. 482, 483
Muldoon, M. 1001
Mulkay, M. 402

Müller-Hartmann, A. 1137, 1138
Mumby, J. 412
Muñez, V. 643, 645, 652
Mura, D. 679
Muraven, M. 649
Murphey, T. 731
Murphy, D. 1002
Murphy, E. 389
Murphy, R. 198
Murray, D. 690, 760
Murray, H. 152, 958
Murray, L. 1137
Mustafa, Z. 942
Muth, D. 794
Myers, G. 402, 942
Myles, F. 700, 857

N
Na, J. 85
Nagashima, Y. 72
Nagy, W. 840
Nakahama, Y. 300
Nakamura, K. 72
Nakaone, T. 1028
Nardi, B. 1124
Nathan, G. 247
Nation, I. 840
Nation, P. 744, 829, 830, 839, 840
Nattinger, J. 857
Nazroo, J. 210
Ndebele, N. 679
Negri, A. 135
Nel, K. 930
Nelson, C. 1050
Nettle, D. 905
Neumann, A. 1015
Neuwirth, C. 916
Newfield, D. 930
Newmark, L. 958
Newport, E. 72
Newton, I. 315
Newton, P. 503
Ng, R. 198
Ng, S. 810
Nguyen, A. 363
Nguyen, H. 1030
Nias, J. 1066
Nicholas, H. 287, 300, 519
Nichols, R. 1002
Nicholson, A. 758
Nickerson, C. 412
Niemann, Y. 652
Nieto, S. 690, 717, 1051, 1100
Nightingale, P. 887

Nihlen, A. 1000
Nissan, S. 482
Nityadandanam, I. 61
Nix, M. 742
Nix, P. 470
Noble, A. 503
Noble, G. 652, 940
Noddings, N. 1016
Noguchi, M. 73
Norris, A. 1137
Norris, C. 1051
Norris, D. 794
Norris, J. 287
North, B. 484
Norton, B. 35, 85, 198, 531, 637, 666, 679, 680, 690, 700, 986, 1051, 1100
Norton Peirce, B. 85, 680, 1051
Noullet, M. 36
Novak, J. 314
Novakovich, J. 680
Novinski, M. 1137
Nowakowski, J. 1123
Noyes, P. 957
Nunan, D. 287, 412, 437, 742, 744, 760, 872, 984, 1000, 1002
Nunberg, G. 182
Nurius, P. 679
Nuttall, J. 957

O
O' Donnell-Allen, C. 707, 717
O' Loughlin, K. 499, 500, 502, 503, 505, 508, 510, 514, 517, 519
O' Malley, J. 253, 267, 317, 318, 325, 328, 330, 331, 381, 389, 451, 452, 456, 837, 838, 840
O' Malley, M. 267
O' Sullivan, B. 505, 515, 519
Oakes, J. 717
Obler, L. 287
Obondo, M. 50
Ochs, E. 638, 1029
Odlin, T. 857
Ogborn, J. 930
Ogbu, J. 652, 1112
Ogulnick, K. 650
Ohta, A. 1028
Oja, S. 1002
Oliver, R. 716, 1082
Olneck, M. 652
Olsen, J. 1083
Olsen, L. 228, 363, 690
Olsen, M. 1015
Olsher, D. 1029

Olshtain, E. 856
Olson, D. 717
Olson, L. 652
Oltman, P. 484
Omaggio-Hadeley, A. 1000
Omanson, R. 840
Or, C. 810
Or, W. 744
Orellana, M. 680
Orlikowski, W. 943
Ortega, L. 287, 300
Osborn, T. 1051
Ota, H. 73
Othman-Yahya, S. 50
Otsu, Y. 73
Ovando, C. 348
Owston, R. 902, 904
Oxford, R. 760

P
Pahl, J. 411
Paiewonsky, E. 363
Pakir, A. 61, 1051
Palfreyman, D. 744, 958
Palloff, R. 760
Palmer, A. 285, 454
Palmquist, M. 916
Paltridge, B. 857, 889, 942
Palys, T. 986
Panova, I. 287
Papp, T. 167, 247
Paradis, J. 940
Paradis, M. 247, 795
Parakrama, A. 182
Pare, A. 940
Parisi, D. 794
Park, Y. 85, 760
Parks, S. 315
Parmar, R. 1123
Passel, J. 182
Pasta, D. 182
Patel, S. 61
Patel, Y. 61
Pattinois, D. 717
Pavlenko, A. 679, 680, 700, 1047, 1051
Pawley, A. 840
Pea, R. 760
Peal, E. 247
Pearce, J. 150
Pearson, P. 809
Pease-Alvarez, L. 638, 690, 759, 1016
Peck, A. 1002
Peck, J. 869, 872
Pegrum, M. 135

Peirce, B. 85, 484, 548, 680, 1051, 1100
Pelham, L. 809
Pemberton, R. 744
Pennycook, A. 23, 35, 61, 85, 152, 182, 287, 402, 531, 666, 690, 889, 905, 916, 1051
Penz, H. 152
Percy, A. 890
Perdue, C. 247
Perez, B. 690
Perkins, J. 182
Perrett, G. 856, 942
Perry, T. 1051, 1100
Persinger, M. 247
Peshkin, A. 228, 985
Peters, R. 247
Petersen, A. 652
Petersen, M. 135
Peterson, B. 715
Peterson, J. 35
Peterson, N. 915
Peterson, P. 1015, 1083
Peyton, J. 916
Phelps, R. 456, 759
Phillion, J. 1015, 1016
Phillips, D. 1016
Phillips, M. 1124
Phillips, T. 717
Phillipson, R. 23, 35, 50, 61, 73, 85, 134, 135, 152, 182, 402, 531, 905, 958
Phinney, J. 650, 652
Piatt, B. 182
Pica, T. 291, 297, 299, 300, 311, 315, 705, 717, 1023, 1026, 1028, 1029
Pick, S. 652
Pickering, L. 871
Pienemann, M. 857
Piepho, H. 152
Pierce, B. 198
Pierson, H. 744
Piller, I. 680, 1051
Pimsleur, P. 840
Pinar, W. 1016
Pinker, S. 300, 795
Pinney, T. 23
Pintrich, P. 731
Planken, B. 246, 824
Plass, J. 758
Plum, G. 401, 856, 887
Plunkett, K. 794, 795
Polacco, P. 363
Polanyi, L. 873
Polkinghorne, D. 1016
Pollard, J. 248

Pölzl, U. 152
Pomerantz, A. 1029
Pon, G. 652, 986
Poon, W. 412
Pope, C. 1138
Popham, D. 840
Popkewitz, T. 1083
Pople, M. 840
Porter, J. 402, 889
Porter, P. 287, 1028
Porter, R. 35, 182, 456
Portes, A. 652
Posch, P. 1137
Postlethwaite, T. 810
Powell, W. 484
Powers, D. 482
Poynting, S. 652
Poynton, C. 1051
Prabhu, N. 23, 247, 873, 958
Pratt, E. 916
Pratt, K. 760
Pratt, M. 889
Preisler, B. 135, 152
Pressley, M. 331, 810
Price, S. 1051
Pride, J. 35
Prior, P. 402, 548, 666, 889
Prodromou, L. 152
Pryor, J. 504, 520
Prys Jones, S. 119, 165, 389
Psathas, G. 1029
Puetter, S. 760
Pula, J. 503
Pullum, G. 857
Purani, T. 61
Purania, T. 61
Purpura, J. 519
Pusey, M. 456
Putnam, R. 1065
Putney, L. 691, 717
Pütz, M. 50

Q
Quay, S. 167
Quirk, R. 120, 151, 167, 845, 857, 958

R
Raimes, A. 484
Rajan, R. 23
Ramanathan, V. 61, 889, 984, 986, 1051
Ramey, D. 182
Ramirez, J. 182
Rampton, B. 35, 197, 268, 547, 652, 1049, 1051, 1112

Rannut, M. 182
Ranta, L. 287, 288, 300
Raphael, T. 689
Rasmussen, C. 1123
Raso, E. 503
Raymond, P. 656, 663, 664, 666
Rayson, P. 840
Raz, J. 744
Read, J. 519, 839
Rea-Dickins, P. 5120
Reagan, T. 85, 1051
Redfern, A. 1112
Redman, S. 839, 840
Reed, D. 503
Reed, M. 718
Rees, T. 197
Reich, R. 1124
Reid, W. 377
Reiman, A. 1066
Renandya, W. 24
Reppen, R. 482, 942
Resnick, L. 503
Resnick, M. 503
Reyes, A. 652
Reyes, M. 637
Reyhner, J. 35
Reynolds, M. 437
Riazantseva, A. 887
Riazi, A. 1050
Riazi, M. 1099
Ribé, R. 744
Rice, C. 135
Ricento, T. 35, 135, 182
Richards, J. 285, 287, 437, 873, 1002, 1083
Richards, K. 985, 986, 1001
Richterich, R. 412
Rickford, J. 760
Ridge, S. 50
Riley, P. 743, 744
Ringbom, H. 167
Risager, K. 1048
Rixon, S. 520
Rizzo, T. 984
Roberge, B. 1016
Roberts, B. 745
Roberts, C. 149, 150, 857, 1051
Roberts, D. 377
Roberts, M. 484
Roberts, S. 228
Robertson, R. 85
Robinson, J. 872, 1029, 1050
Robinson, M. 872
Robinson, P. 287, 300, 958
Robinson, W. 957

Robson, M. 1065
Roca, A. 182
Rochín, R. 644, 651
Rodriguez, R. 1016
Rodriguez, V. 652
Rodriguez-Brown, F. 637
Roelofs, A. 795
Roessel, R. 35
Roger, D. 1029
Rogers, C. 731, 744
Rogers, E. 760
Rogers, J. 1002
Rogers, P. 412
Rogers, T. 518
Rogoff, B. 638
Rohl, M. 454, 502, 518
Rohlen, T. 73
Rolls, E. 795
Romaine, S. 287, 905
Romero, A. 652
Ronowicz, E. 1051
Roschelle, J. 760
Rose, M. 888
Roseberry, R. 941
Rosenau, P. 1051
Rosenberger, L. 150
Rosenfeld, M. 484
Rosenthal, D. 652
Rosewell, L. 744
Rosiak, J. 1014
Rösler, D. 1138
Ross, G. 718
Ross, K. 810
Ross, S. 484
Rossell, C. 182
Rossiter, C. 182
Rossman, G. 986
Roth, A. 1027
Rotheram-Borus, M. 653
Rothery, J. 716, 942
Rothkopf, D. 135
Rouse, J. 1051
Routh, M. 840
Rowe, M. 717
Rowntree, D. 437
Rubagumya, C. 50, 167
Rubin, J. 182
Ruhlen, M. 50
Ruiz, R. 690
Rumbaut, R. 652
Russell, P. 840
Russo, R. 331
Rutherford, J. 637
Ryan, K. 482

Ryle, G. 958
Rymes, B. 716

S
Sacks, H. 873, 1029
Sadtono, E. 470
Sagasta, P. 167
Said, E. 85, 1051, 1100
Sainsbury, M. 456
Salaberry, R. 760
Salomon, G. 700
Salters, M. 437
Samarajiwa, C. 825
Samarin, W. 152
Samimy, K. 84
Samuda, V. 285, 287, 300
Sanaoui, R. 470, 840
Santiago, E. 1016
Santos, M. 637
Santos, T. 482, 889
Sapuppo, M. 456
Sarangi, S. 377
Sarap, M. 1051
Sato, K. 287
Sauvé, V. 1051
Savignon, S. 287
Saville, N. 484, 519
Saville-Troike, M. 700, 986
Say, A. 363
Sayers, D. 758, 774, 809, 916
Scardamalia, M. 285, 794, 1065
Scarino, A. 454, 456, 503
Schafer, R. 1016
Schecter, R. 1051
Schecter, S. 198, 652, 984, 986
Schedl, M. 483, 484
Scheerens, J. 520
Schegloff, E. 873, 1029
Schellekens, P. 744
Schieffelin, B. 183
Schiffrin, D. 873
Schifini, A. 363
Schils, E. 246, 824
Schlegel, A. 652
Schmid-Schoenbein, G. 1124
Schmidt, K. 651
Schmidt, R. 795
Schmitt, D. 840
Schmitt, N. 839, 840
Schmuck, P. 731
Schmuck, R. 731
Schneider, B. 649, 652
Schneider, M. 666
Schneider, S. 182

Schocker-v. Ditfurth, M. 970, 1125–1127, 1129, 1131, 1134, 1137, 1138
Schoepfle, G. 315
Scholes, R. 1051
Schön, D. 1000, 1083
Schonell, F. 840
Schultz, J. 916
Schunk, D. 331, 731
Schutz, A. 1029
Schutz, E. 1029
Schwab, J. 1002, 1016
Schwartz, J. 1029
Schwartz, M. 915
Schwarz, H. 1124
Schwienhorst, K. 760
Scollon, R. 690, 889, 942, 1051
Scollon, S. 690, 942, 1051
Scott, C. 520
Scott, K. 520
Scott, M. 411, 942
Scotton, C. 50
Scovel, T. 652, 825
Searle, J. 287
Seedhouse, P. 300, 301, 873, 1030
Segalowitz, N. 287, 795
Segul, J. 794
Seidlhofer, B. 136, 151, 152, 959
Selfe, C. 904
Seliger, H. 286
Selinker, L. 35, 794
Sengupta, S. 471
Senior, R. 731
Seo, J. 85
Shanahan, T. 637
Shannon, S. 182, 638, 1016
Shapard, R. 680
Shavelson, R. 437
Shaw, B. 840
Shaw, J. 36
Shaw, P. 135, 959
Shea, C. 1052
Sheeran, Y. 889
Shemesh, M. 810
Shen, B. 105
Shen, F. 890
Shen, M. 247
Shermis, M. 484
Sherwood, C. 1138
Shetzer, H. 761, 916, 917
Shield, L. 760
Shih, T. 652
Shilcock, R. 299
Shin, H. 85
Shirahata, T. 73

Shohamy, E. 503, 520, 531, 810
Shorrock, S. 1065
Short, D. 315, 455, 456, 690
Shrinivas, R. 61
Shubert, W. 1016
Shulman, L. 959, 1084
Shulz, R. 760
Shusterman, R. 638
Siegal, M. 666, 941
Siegel, J. 35
Siegel, L. 800, 809
Sikes, P. 1066
Silc, K. 758
Siles, M. 651
Silva, T. 889, 890, 942
Silverman, D. 986
Simich-Dudgeon, C. 267
Simmons, D. 744
Simon, P. 182
Simonot, M. 149
Simons, H. 1112
Simpson, J. 882, 884, 889
Sinclair, B. 745
Sinclair, J. 717, 857, 873
Singh, M. 1124
Singh, R. 825
Singleton, D. 167, 760
Siskin, L. 377
Sizmur, S. 456
Skehan, P. 248, 288, 2901, 484
Skillen, J. 890
Skinner, D. 637
Skourtou, E. 622, 763, 766, 774
Skutnabb-Kangas, T. 50, 136, 152, 182, 268, 363, 690, 905
Slade, D. 856, 872, 942
Slater, T. 315
Sleeter, C. 1016, 1100
Slimani, A. 873
Smagorinsky, P. 716, 717
Smith, C. 1137
Smith, D. 1016
Smith, F. 287, 715
Smith, J. 483, 503, 1065
Smith, L.E. 146, 152
Smith, L.M. 1016
Smith, M. 412, 492, 497, 503, 504, 1000, 1006
Smith, N. 857
Smith, P. 210
Smith, R. 744
Smith, W. 504
Smoke, T. 402, 666
Smulyan, L. 1002

Snow, C. 36, 72, 1100
Snow, M. 268, 376
Snyder, I. 760
Sökmen, A. 841
Soled, S. 470
Solomon, R. 652
Solsken, J. 638, 690, 986
Somekh, B. 1002
Soni, P. 61
Sonntag, S. 182
Soto, L. 1016
Sower, C. 1052
Spack, R. 666, 890
Spada, N. 2888, 300, 519, 760, 986
Spanos, G. 267, 330
Spence-Brown, R. 520
Spencer, J. 50
Spencer, M. 652
Spodark, E. 1124
Spolsky, B. 484, 504, 520, 531, 810
Spradley, J. 315
Sprinthall, L. 1066
Sprinthall, N. 1066
Sproull, L. 916
Sridhar, K. 152
Sridhar, S. 152, 680
Stanley, T. 198
Stansfield, C. 470
Starfield, S. 666, 890, 1052
Stawychny, M. 483
Steel, D. 469, 957
Stein, P. 930, 1052
Steinberg, L. 519
Steinberg, S. 1049
Steinkopf, M. 1124
Stenglin, M. 857
Stenhouse, L. 1002, 1138
Stephan, L. 36
Stephens, C. 840
Stephens, L. 690
Stern, H. 248, 288
Stern, M. 761
Stern, P. 437
Stern, R. 483
Sternberg, R. 700
Stevens, G. 182
Stevens, R. 454
Stevick, E. 228
Stewart, F. 23
Stewart, G. 198
Stewner-Manzanares, G. 331
Stierer, B. 716
Stiggins, R. 504
Stillman, J. 1001

Stivers, T. 1030
St. John, E. 910, 916
St. John, M. 392, 399, 401, 403, 412, 655, 666, 931, 940
Stobbe, J. 363
Stock, P. 502
Stodolsky, S. 377
Stokes, J. 299
Stoller, F. 1049
Stone, C. 700
Stone, L. 716
Strauss, A. 986
Street, B. 36, 889, 905, 1051, 1052
Strei, G. 36
Strevens, P. 402
Strickland, D. 1002
Strong, R. 438
Strong-Krause, D. 456
Stubbs, M. 402, 1030
Sturtridge, G. 300, 743
Suárez-Orozco, C. 640–645, 652
Suárez-Orozco, M. 637, 640–645, 652
Sugimoto, T. 905
Sullivan, B. 484, 519
Sullivan, N. 916
Sullivan, P. 1083
Sun, C. 105
Sung, K. 85
Sunga, N. 24
Suomi, B. 482
Sure, K. 50
Susser, B. 23
Sussex, R. 1124
Suzuki, Y. 73
Svartvik, J. 857
Swaffer, J. 1000
Swain, M. 73, 120, 121, 267, 268, 285, 286, 288, 2901, 483, 717, 856, 857
Swales, J. 402, 412, 548, 667, 888, 890, 940, 942, 943
Swanson, D. 652
Swartz, R. 315
Sweeting, A. 23
Syder, F. 829, 840
Sykes, G. 470, 958

T
Tabar, P. 652
Taborn, S. 873
Tabors, P. 1100
Tabouret-Keller, A. 34
Tadajeu, M. 50
Tajfel, H. 652, 1052
Tang, C. 86

Tang, G. 315
Tang, K. 484
Tang, R. 518, 890
Tanner, C. 1065
Tao, H. 872
Tao, P. 810
Tapia, J. 637
Tardy, C. 1049
Tarver, H. 183
Tator, C. 197
Taylor, C. 268, 4884, 638
Taylor, G. 887
Taylor, L. 482
Teasdale, A. 437, 504, 520
Teel, K. 731
Teeple, G. 198
Tejeda, C. 637
Tella, S. 916, 917, 1138
Tenorio-Coscarelli, J. 363
Terdiman, R. 1052
Teuben-Rowe, S. 691
Teutsch-Dwyer, M. 680
Thaler, M. 1002
Tharp, R. 638, 717
Tharu, S. 61
Thavenius, C. 745
Theodoridis, T. 774
Thesen, L. 667, 680, 890
Thew, C. 313
Thikoo, M. 24
Thomas, A. 454, 456
Thomas, C. 470
Thomas, D. 246
Thomas, H. 744, 1137
Thomas, J. 1138
Thomas, S. 520
Thomas, W. 50, 210, 228, 268, 331, 348, 690, 810
Thompson, G. 288, 864, 873
Thompson, J. 389
Thompson, M. 348
Thompson, P. 152, 942
Thornbury, S. 873, 959
Thorne, S. 700, 857, 1137
Thornton, G. 150
Thurrell, S. 871
Thwaite, A. 1082
Tickoo, M. 167
Tidmarsh, C. 520
Tigchelaar, A. 1050
Tinajero, J. 363
Tinker Sachs, G. 1002
Tinkham, T. 841
Tlusty, N. 1001

Tochon, F. 1016
Tollefson, J. 24, 36, 50, 135, 181, 531
Tomasello, M. 700
Tomkins, G. 198
Tomlin, R. 857
Tomlinson, B. 149, 957
Tonkyn, A. 856
Toogood, S. 734, 742, 744
Toohey, K. 531, 638, 700, 717, 986, 1002, 1016, 1051, 1052, 1100, 1112
Torigai, K. 73
Torr, J. 717
Torrance, H. 504, 520
Torres-Guzman, M. 690
Tosi, A. 389
Tough, A. 745
Tough, J. 717
Townsend, H. 269
Trahey, M. 301
Triggs, P. 520
Trimble, L. 402
Trivett, N. 890
Trudeau, P. 198
Truscello, D. 1123
Truscott, J. 288
Tsatsarelis, C. 930
Tse, L. 35
Tsuda, Y. 73, 136
Tsui, A. 135, 470, 471, 873, 959, 1066
Tu, W. 85
Tucker, G. 809
Tung, C. 471
Tunstall, P. 520
Turbee, L. 745
Turkle, S. 1124
Turnbull, M. 288
Turner, C. 483
Turner, D. 1050
Turner, J. 482
Turner, T. 760
Turner-Bisset, R. 959
Tyler, A. 300
Tyler, R. 438

U
Uchida, Y. 985
Umaña-Taylor, A. 640, 643, 652
Unsworth, L. 718
Unz, R. 269
Upshur, J. 518
Urwin, C. 637
Ushioda, E. 745
Usui, N. 73

V

Vaipae, S. 73
Valdés, G. 228, 653, 810, 1016
Valdes, J. 1052
Valdez, G. 1123
Valdez Pierce, L. 456
Valencia, J. 166
Valenzuela, A. 1100
Valette, R. 438, 520
Valli, L. 1065
Valsiner, J. 700
Vamdatta, D. 61
van Dam, J. 985
van der Silk, F. 824
van der Veer, R. 700
van Dijk, T. 315
van Ek, J. 438
van Els, T. 150
van Essen, A. 959
van Langenhove, L. 377
van Leeuwen, T. 314, 857, 930
van Lier, L. 151, 300, 301, 718, 873, 986, 1002, 1030
van Manen, M. 1016
van Nus, M. 412
van Patten, B. 301
Vandenberghe, R. 1065
Vandrick, S. 1052
Vang, T. 363
Vansia, K. 61
Vaquerano, F. 34
Varela, E. 285, 299, 331
Vargas, L. 653
Varghese, M. 1052
Varonis, E. 1030
Varro, G. 34
Vasquez, O. 638, 1016
Vass, A. 731
Vasseur, M. 149
Veel, R. 315, 377, 716, 858
Veltman, C. 183
Venezky, R. 905
Venn, C. 637
Ventola, E. 402, 548, 873
Verduin, J. 1002
Verhoeven, L. 810
Vidal, N. 744
Vieira, F. 745
Vigil, J. 653
Villarruel, F. 653
Villenas, S. 653
Vilmar, F. 135
Vincent, D. 905
Virdee, S. 210

Visser, J. 1124
Viswanathan, G. 24
Vitanova, G. 1049
Vocate, D. 700
Voller, P. 742, 745
Vollmer, G. 653
Vollmer, H. 152
Von Hoene, L. 679
Vukela, V. 45, 50
Vyas, H. 61
Vygotsky, L. 288, 331, 638, 690, 700, 718, 745, 774, 1138

W

Wadsworth, Y. 1002
Wagner, J. 150, 152, 299, 1027
Wagner, S. 484
Wagner, J. 139, 144, 150, 152, 296, 299, 1022, 1023, 1027
Wainer, H. 484
Wakefield, P. 313
Walberg, H. 731
Walkerdine, V. 637, 638, 1052
Wall, D. 469, 481, 504, 530
Wallace, C. 86, 484
Wallace, M. 1002, 1084
Walqui, A. 364
Walsh, C. 364, 718
Walsh, S. 873, 959
Walters, A. 412
Wandersee, J. 314
Wang, Q. 105
Wang, W. 1050, 1099
Wang, Y. 917
Ware, P. 917
Waring, R. 829, 840, 841
Warschauer, M. 745, 760, 761, 905, 916, 917, 1138
Watahomigie, L. 36
Watenburg, T. 61
Waters, A. 402, 485
Watson-Gegeo, K. 35, 36, 986
Watts, R. 135, 152, 873
Weasenforth, D. 758
Webb, C. 888
Webb, V. 49, 50
Weber, R. 810
Webster, A. 718
Wedell, M. 105
Weeden, P. 520
Weedon, C. 638, 653, 690, 1052
Wegerif, R. 718
Wei, L. 105
Weiner, M. 246

Author Index

Weininger, M. 760
Weinstein, G. 690
Weinstein, N. 1124
Weir, C. 484, 485, 519, 520
Weir, R. 700
Weis, L. 653
Wells, G. 718, 774, 986, 1052
Wendel, J. 301
Wenden, A. 743, 745
Wenger, E. 637, 638, 680, 700, 941, 1050, 1112
Wennerstrom, A. 943
Werner, O. 315
Werry, C. 1124
Wertsch, J. 638, 700
Wesche, M. 288, 376, 485
West, C. 690
West, M. 841
Wheeler, S. 744
Whelan, K. 1015
Whisler, J. 731
White, G. 940
White, J. 286
White, L. 288, 301, 825
White, M. 198
White, R. 301, 731, 1066
Whiteley, W. 49
Whiting, C. 1083
Whitmore, K. 637
Whittaker, S. 1124
Whitty, G. 1083, 1084
Widdicombe, S. 166
Widdowson, H. 86, 152, 153, 167, 269, 288, 301, 438, 873, 943, 1052, 1138
Wideman, H. 902, 904
Wigglesworth, J. 301
Wiley, T. 183, 228, 638
Wilgoren, J. 183
Wiliam, D. 502, 504, 518, 520
Wilkins, D. 248, 288, 412, 438
Wilkinson, A. 718
Wilkinson, R. 136
Willett, J. 638, 690, 986, 1112
Willetts, K. 267
Willey, B. 1030
Williams, A. 267, 269, 455, 518
Williams, C. 269, 1052
Williams, E. 856
Williams, G. 857, 858, 941
Williams, J. 288, 299, 518, 856
Williams, S. 167, 1099
Williamson, J. 959
Willig, A. 183
Willing, K. 412

Willis, A. 691
Willis, D. 301, 858
Willis, J. 301, 1138
Willows, D. 809
Wilmut, J. 520
Wilson, A. 840
Wilson, S. 470
Wilson, T. 1030
Wilson, W. 35, 36
Wilson-Keenan, J. 690, 986
Wink, J. 691
Winter, J. 520
Winter, R. 1002
Wisniewski, R. 1015
Witherell, C. 1016
Witt, D. 809
Wlodkowski, R. 731
Wolfson, W. 50
Woloshyn, V. 331
Wong, A. 810
Wong, C. 810
Wong, J. 1030
Wong, K. 809
Wong, P. 198
Wong, S. 637, 651, 689, 691, 986, 1052, 1099
Wong, S.C. 182, 1099
Wong Scollon, S. 1051
Wong, S.L. 651, 690
Wong-Fillmore, L. 348, 691
Wong-Scollon, S. 942
Woods, D. 1084
Woods, P. 1066
Woodward, T. 1084
Woodward-Kron, R. 890
Woolard, K. 36, 183
Woolf, B. 761
Woolgar, S. 402
Woolverton, S. 689
Worswick, C. 810
Wortham, S. 986
Wray, A. 841
Wray, D. 959
Wright, S. 36, 153
Wright, T. 959
Wrigley, H. 36, 181
Wu, K.Y. 471
Wulff, H. 653

X

Xiong, G. 650
Xu, J. 105
Xu, Y. 893, 896, 897, 904, 905

Y

Yager, T. 653
Yallop, C. 1051
Yamashita, S. 71
Yang, J. 1100
Yanow, D. 269
Yashiro, K. 72
Yates, J. 943
Yates, S. 917
Yeager, B. 717
Yee, P. 1100
Yelland, G. 248
Yngve, V. 873
Yon, D. 1100
Yoshida, K. 73
Young, J. 198
Young, L. 246
Young, R. 485, 745, 1029, 1030, 1052
Yow, V. 1016
Ytsma, J. 167
Yu, H. 1087, 1089, 1097, 1100
Yu, T. 105
Yuan, Y. 293, 297, 301
Yuen, S. 182
Yule, G. 299
Yung, H. 810

Z

Zabaleta, F. 266
Zambrano, A. 34
Zamel, V. 485, 890, 1052
Zammit, S. 716
Zeichner, K. 1001, 1066, 1084
Zelasko, N. 183
Zentella, A. 653
Zhang, R. 104
Zhang, S. 105
Zhang, Y. 105
Zhang, Z. 105
Zhao, J. 105
Zhenhua, H. 905
Zhou, L. 105
Zhou, M. 653
Zimmerman, B. 331
Zimmerman, C. 840
Zimmerman, D. 1026
Zine, J. 1099
Zinn, H. 183
Zoppis, C. 744
Zuber-Skerritt, O. 1002
Zubrow, D. 916
Zuengler, J. 548, 653, 986

SUBJECT INDEX

A
aboriginal students 448
academic 211, 212, 216–220, 222–228, 233, 234, 317–321, 329–331, 333–341, 343–355, 357–359, 391–396, 475–479, 655–660, 665–667, 681–689, 701–707, 709, 797–810, 875–891, 940–942, 1086–1090
  concepts 234, 319, 321, 325, 327, 349, 351, 352, 354, 355, 357, 359, 658, 702, 779, 797, 800, 801, 803, 806, 890, 917
  coursework 347
  development 161–163, 233, 234, 253, 317–321, 327, 328, 334–338, 340, 341, 343–345, 357–359, 365, 380, 381, 412, 616, 619, 681, 685–688, 701, 702, 797–802, 807, 808, 888–890
  disciplines 307, 368, 395, 400, 473, 709, 854, 877, 878, 883, 937, 973, 1034, 1070
  discourse 233, 309, 310, 312, 314, 315, 335, 368, 395, 396, 619, 620, 655, 662, 663, 665–667, 701–707, 709–715, 781, 873, 875–879, 884–886, 888–890, 916, 917, 976, 977
  discourse communities 368, 393, 869, 877–879, 886, 890
  discourse socialization 980, 986
  English 211–214, 216–220, 222–228, 233, 234, 264–267, 317–319, 333–355, 357–359, 380–382, 385–387, 401–403, 455–458, 483–485, 632–635, 665–667, 797–801, 803–810, 887–891, 940–943, 1086–1090
  genres (*see also* genre structure; genre-based approach) 377, 395, 396, 398, 400, 401, 536, 547, 620, 655, 659, 665, 666, 702, 716, 869, 876–879, 883, 884, 886, 887, 931, 932, 934, 937, 938, 942, 943
  language 222–226, 252–256, 317–321, 329–331, 333–341, 343–349, 351–355, 384–387, 475–479, 483–485, 632–636, 665, 666, 679–685, 700–705, 713–717, 797–810, 824, 876–880, 887–891, 937–942
  language development 50, 69, 166, 217, 223, 233, 310, 317–319, 325, 327, 335, 336, 340, 357, 363, 367, 412, 454, 619, 634, 701
  language learning 233, 234, 253, 254, 286, 287, 312, 317–319, 330, 331, 348, 384, 389, 483, 484, 616, 617, 632, 633, 666, 669, 679–681, 701–703, 707–709, 713–715, 763, 809
  learning 218, 224–226, 233, 234, 253–255, 267, 314, 315, 317–321, 327–331, 333, 334, 337, 338, 384–386, 615–617, 619, 620, 632–635, 679–681, 701–705, 707–709, 711–717, 802–805, 888–891
  literacies 399, 401, 402, 666, 781, 875–877, 883, 884, 886, 888–891, 900, 902, 905, 917, 941
  registers 352–354, 392, 635, 701, 702,

798, 800, 804, 808
researchers 195, 211, 395, 396, 398, 401, 477, 619, 645, 655, 656, 665, 706, 781, 886, 887, 968, 978, 995, 997, 998, 1034, 1070, 1078
writing 58, 61, 279, 350–353, 392–394, 401, 402, 477, 483, 484, 547, 548, 662, 663, 666, 781, 794, 797–801, 807, 808, 875–891, 912–914, 934, 940–943, 980
accent discrimination 9, 32, 35, 679, 825, 1094, 1099
accountability 10, 193, 211, 213, 220, 222, 223, 260, 406, 408, 415, 416, 440, 441, 444, 447, 450, 451, 453, 456, 457, 508, 967, 968, 998, 999, 1103
accountability-driven standards 447, 450
acculturation 335, 386, 545, 641, 643, 644, 646, 649, 651
acoustic
  information 787, 791
  input 791
acquired systems 949
acquisition (*see also* L1 acquisition; second language acquisition studies) 8, 155, 157, 158, 160–163, 165–167, 274–276, 284–292, 296–301, 333–335, 348–350, 516–518, 625, 626, 633–639, 716, 717, 783–795, 824, 825, 839–841, 848, 849, 856, 857, 1025–1028
  academic knowledge of English 335
  of ESL (*see* English as a second language) 350, 382, 383, 388, 416, 440, 490, 619, 625, 631, 633
  of language and literacy 633, 758
acquisition-rich 949
action research (*see also* ethnographic research; experimental research; qualitative research; quantitative research) 203, 759, 760, 911, 965, 977, 987–1002, 1067, 1074–1077, 1082, 1083
activity 133, 134, 290, 291, 295, 305–307, 361, 374, 375, 393, 394, 511, 512, 514, 515, 619, 629, 630, 635, 637, 638, 640, 641, 693–699, 705, 727–729, 947, 948, 976, 1046
adjacency pair 867
adolescence 616, 639–643, 649–652
adolescent
  identity 641–643, 645, 648, 649

immigrants 641, 646, 1049
adult
  education 34, 35, 235, 403, 404, 410, 411, 417, 421, 422, 431, 432, 436, 438, 657, 743
  literacy 27, 477, 689
Adult Migrant Education Services (AMES), Australia 411
Advisory Committee of Teacher Education and Qualifications (ACTEQ), Hong Kong 461–464, 466
affective filter 949
African-Caribbean 201
agent of change (*see* change agent) 688, 1059, 1131, 1133, 1059, 1064
alternative 4, 25, 26, 34, 37, 45, 85, 163, 215, 216, 222, 224, 306, 307, 419, 420, 493, 494, 501, 506, 507, 519–521, 537, 1042, 1043, 1073–1075, 1077, 1078
  assessment (*see* assessment) 419, 420, 493, 494, 501, 506, 507, 509, 519, 530
  pedagogies 1043, 1073, 1074
American Educational Research Association (AERA) 331, 469, 481, 1014, 1016
American War of Independence 187
Americanization 123, 129, 167, 215, 216, 220, 224, 1093
analytical thinking 1075
anecdotes 141, 869, 933, 975
applied
  linguistics (AL) 135, 136, 150–153, 284–288, 299–301, 331, 391, 392, 401, 402, 481–484, 517–520, 716, 717, 839, 840, 871, 872, 940–942, 957, 958, 966, 967, 984–987, 1000, 1001, 1027–1030, 1033–1035, 1047–1052
  research 337, 419, 963
apprenticeship 372, 377, 546, 547, 638, 686, 690, 704, 882, 887, 890, 1054, 1056
Argentina 5, 7, 107–121, 352
articulation 17, 250, 261, 330, 370, 381, 388, 422, 500, 790, 795, 813, 921, 986, 1074, 1075
Asian Americans 644, 645, 647, 648, 651, 652
Asian Canadian 647
assessment (*see also* benchmarks; testing) 94–96, 99, 101, 102, 206–209, 311–315, 415–422, 431–434, 436, 437,

Subject Index 1167

443–445, 447–471, 475–478, 480–485, 487–520, 529–531, 533, 534, 697–700, 928–930, 939, 1101–1104, 1106, 1107
  alternative 419, 420, 489, 493, 494, 501, 503, 506, 507, 509, 519, 520, 530
  dynamic assessment 419, 420, 494, 496, 512, 515, 619, 684, 699, 700, 898, 1110
  formative assessment (*see also* summative assessment) 94, 95, 99, 101, 419, 420, 447, 450, 489, 491, 492, 498, 499, 504–509, 511, 513–520, 1102
  frameworks 313, 314, 410, 418–421, 454, 455, 476, 490, 502, 505, 506, 509, 510, 512, 513, 517, 518, 520, 684
  functions 508, 509, 514
  innovations 488, 495, 502, 510
  instruction-embedded assessment 511
  instruments 327, 434, 449, 457, 462–464, 466, 487, 488, 656, 894, 1045
  paradigm 415, 418, 421, 422, 441, 460, 499, 504, 506, 508, 512, 513, 520, 684, 699
  performance 99, 298, 328, 329, 339, 417, 418, 421, 425, 432–434, 436, 437, 452, 456–459, 461, 477, 478, 482–485, 489–491, 497–500, 502, 503, 507, 508, 515, 698–700
  practices 49, 52, 198, 206, 313, 315, 366, 413, 419, 420, 449, 450, 452, 453, 487–489, 502, 503, 510, 513–515, 518, 530, 531, 534, 922, 928, 929
  procedures 193, 325, 418, 419, 432, 445, 448, 451, 459, 460, 507, 509, 510, 512, 518, 530, 1103, 1134
  summative assessment 94, 99, 419, 420, 450, 491, 498, 505, 508, 509, 513–515, 517, 519, 1102
Assessment Reform Group, UK 516, 517
assimilation 38, 174, 180, 189, 215, 218, 219, 221, 224, 258, 261, 335, 363, 448, 641, 650, 985
assimilationist 128, 224, 631, 645
assisted performance 619, 628, 703
asynchronous
  communication 762, 779
  environments 896, 900
attention 33, 63, 87, 107, 143, 164, 206, 208, 233, 254, 264, 265, 319, 320, 329, 330, 419, 487, 488, 792, 793, 931–933,

935, 945, 946, 1019, 1020
attentive silence 1093–1095
attitudinal roles 970, 1113, 1114, 1116
attraction 133, 720, 729
attribution 171, 306, 729
audience expectations 932, 937
auditory discrimination task 815, 817
Australia 156, 157, 196, 197, 249, 250, 259, 260, 266, 365, 366, 376, 377, 417, 418, 421, 443–445, 448, 449, 455, 456, 469, 470, 473–475, 495, 496, 502, 503, 517–520, 540, 541, 759, 760, 875, 876
Australian Council of TESOL Associations (ACTA) 268, 269, 1123
Austria 137, 155, 379, 380, 824
authentic
  communication 3, 754, 922
  language 621, 748, 752, 753, 873
  literacy tasks 979
  tasks 1114
authenticity 35, 80, 139, 399, 416, 477, 506, 511, 512, 520, 615, 718, 742, 752, 753, 824, 870, 1073, 1074, 1136
authorial
  meanings 1036
  self 881
authoring systems 1119, 1124
authoritarian leadership 724
autobiographical self 881
autocratic leadership 724
automatic word recognition 793
automatization 789, 795
autonomous
  classrooms 738
  learners 621, 744, 1129
  learning 621, 706, 739–741, 743–745, 915, 1071, 1128
  mode 620, 725, 726
  models of literacy 892, 900
autonomously-controlled tasks 738
autonomy 189, 277, 355, 435, 436, 620, 621, 623, 718, 725, 726, 728, 733–745, 750, 759, 760, 806, 946, 1002, 1036, 1046, 1051, 1069, 1079
  in English language teaching 733, 736, 741
  in language learning 733, 734, 738, 739, 742–745
autonomy-related practices 734, 735

B
back-channel utterances 866
backtracking 792
Bangalore Project 16
basic interpersonal communicative skills (BICS) 252, 353
behavioral objectives 423, 426, 437
behaviorism (*see also* cognitivism; constructivism) 422
behaviorist approaches 421
behaviorist-based teaching 1132
benchmark test (*see also* assessment) 458, 464, 467, 468
benchmarks 112, 195, 197, 260, 268, 416, 440, 444, 447, 448, 455, 456, 461–464, 466, 468–470, 483, 490, 502, 517, 518, 955, 1072
benchmark-setting 955
bilingual
 class 338, 343, 1088
 contexts 8, 1046
 education 8, 9, 33–36, 49, 50, 109–111, 119–121, 161, 162, 164, 165, 167, 172–175, 180–183, 219–221, 255, 256, 260–262, 264–269, 330, 331, 345, 346, 389, 459, 688–690, 809, 810
 principles 894
 programs 8, 64, 111, 112, 161, 174, 212, 221, 225, 263, 318, 330, 345, 346, 352, 448
 students 72, 162, 220, 311, 340, 364, 618, 634, 678, 679, 681–685, 687, 1107
 and trilingual programs xxiii
bilingualism 8, 16, 50, 71–73, 162–167, 174–176, 189–191, 241, 242, 246, 247, 255, 256, 267, 379, 385, 387–389, 676, 679, 680, 685, 794, 795, 894, 895, 901, 902
 additive bilingualism 44, 71, 111, 165, 166, 379, 387, 388, 895, 901, 902
biliteracy 635, 690, 1049
biographical methods 741
biolinguistic diversity 894
Black Stylized English (BSE) 675
branching onsets 820
British Council 16, 23, 49, 107, 110, 112–114, 119, 125, 132, 135, 150, 170, 181, 210, 241, 246, 502, 520, 742, 743, 1000
British National Corpus (BNC) 870

BSE (*see* Black Stylized English) 675

C
CA (*see* conversation analysis) 864, 865, 867–870, 1017–1026, 1031
CACD (*see* computer-assisted classroom discussion) 908–910, 914
CALL (*see* computer-assisted language learning) 3, 621, 622, 743, 747–749, 751, 752, 757–761, 915, 1113, 1117, 1118, 1120, 1122–1124
Cambodian 648
Canada 9, 10, 156, 157, 160, 182, 183, 185–198, 249, 250, 287, 288, 303, 304, 459, 470, 473, 474, 483, 674–677, 770, 771, 809–811, 1015, 1039–1042, 1047–1050, 1085, 1086, 1098, 1099
Canadian Constitution Act (CCA) 189
Canadian Language Benchmarks (CLB) 195, 197, 483, 490, 517, 518
Cantonese 352, 533, 534, 540–542, 631, 803, 968, 1011, 1012, 1057, 1065, 1086–1094, 1097
case studies 6, 70, 198, 314, 366, 377, 389, 400, 409, 412, 520, 615, 640, 658, 665, 666, 876, 877, 922, 923, 973, 979, 982, 983
casual conversation 143, 856, 860, 865, 866, 869, 872, 936, 966
Center for Applied Linguistics, USA 180, 310, 313, 364, 470, 689, 690
certification tests 459
change agent 1059
chat rooms 798
No Child Left Behind (NCLB) 10, 211, 215, 222, 228, 416, 491, 495, 497, 523, 525, 527, 529, 531
China (also PRC) 5, 6, 22, 64, 85, 87–93, 95, 100, 101, 103–105, 125, 156, 239, 289, 312, 403, 456, 457, 501, 502, 809, 810, 980, 1003, 1004, 1015
Chomsky 239, 241, 246, 273, 285, 289, 299, 694, 777, 779, 784, 785, 794, 846–849, 852–857, 1034
Chomsky's Universal Grammar 1034
chunking 880
class discussions 543, 658, 977, 979, 991, 1004
classificatory systems 535
classroom 280–288, 372–376, 417–420,

Subject Index 1169

487–520, 625–638, 700–709, 713–731, 907–910, 912–917, 968–971, 973–979, 981–986, 994–996, 999–1005, 1027, 1028, 1050–1058, 1075–1077, 1089–1094, 1104–1108, 1125–1138
approaches   6, 7, 27, 90, 287, 419, 420, 505, 506, 509, 510, 706, 757, 758, 843, 883, 937, 939–941, 949, 950, 964, 973–975, 985, 986, 1069, 1075, 1076, 1127
assessment   193, 206–208, 267, 268, 314, 315, 329, 417–420, 433, 434, 443, 457–459, 463–465, 468–470, 487–520, 530, 619, 700, 929, 930, 939, 1101, 1102, 1104, 1107
communication   239, 258, 399, 401, 402, 700, 715, 717, 748, 759, 760, 779, 888, 907, 908, 910, 913–917, 920, 942, 943, 969, 970, 976, 977, 984–986, 1125
context   206, 231, 232, 314, 402, 419, 420, 442, 499, 500, 506, 514, 515, 622, 634, 700–702, 706, 714–717, 719, 720, 941, 969, 970, 987, 1001–1003, 1005
discourse   90, 299, 300, 311, 312, 315, 402, 463, 514, 515, 519, 520, 547, 619, 620, 634–637, 701–715, 717, 718, 862–864, 871–873, 888, 889, 909, 910, 916, 917, 976, 977, 982–986
discourse processes   866
environment   48, 253, 255, 265, 286, 335, 367, 411, 620, 622, 716, 717, 719–721, 723, 725–727, 729–731, 760, 761, 763, 799, 1085, 1128, 1129
ethos   713, 888
interaction   275, 286, 287, 464, 465, 633, 634, 700, 701, 707–709, 714, 715, 717, 721, 741, 754, 863, 864, 872, 873, 908, 909, 915, 916, 963, 964, 966, 975–977, 985, 986, 1027, 1028
learning   252–255, 280–287, 299–301, 433–435, 487–497, 499–504, 510–520, 619, 620, 625–638, 700–709, 711–720, 733–735, 741–744, 757–761, 968–971, 984–987, 999–1005, 1050–1052, 1125–1128, 1131–1138
management   81, 222, 509, 720, 731, 735, 739, 943, 988, 1002, 1056, 1060, 1085, 1105
management strategies   1082
observations   61, 80, 206, 219, 255, 323, 358, 398, 661, 664, 963, 976, 977, 979, 981, 983, 990, 1010, 1092
pedagogy   6, 34, 48, 85, 89, 112, 232, 254, 255, 264, 267, 285, 635, 636, 715, 716, 763, 767, 926, 941, 942, 1050, 1081, 1082, 1104–1107
practices   13, 25, 47, 48, 355, 372, 373, 375, 392, 398, 399, 401, 419, 420, 487–489, 502, 503, 513–515, 518, 625–637, 706, 707, 922, 963–965, 982–986, 1075, 1076
research (see classroom-based research) 276, 283, 284, 629, 747, 757, 914, 964, 973, 974, 975, 977, 978, 982, 983, 985, 994, 995, 1000–1082
teaching   90, 150, 151, 254, 255, 281–289, 372–376, 462, 463, 491–497, 502–504, 715, 856, 857, 915–917, 939–941, 957, 958, 968–971, 999–1003, 1050–1058, 1064, 1065, 1075–1077, 1104–1108, 1129–1132
Classroom Action Research Network (CARN)   992
classroom-based
  courses   735
  research   922
  studies   420, 978, 983
clinical psychology   617, 639–641
CLT (see communicative language teaching) 78, 79, 232, 271–284, 287, 1071, 1127
clusters   443, 618, 669, 671, 748, 821–824, 964, 974, 988
CMC environments   752
coaches   1115
codas   820
code choices   647
coded data   983
code-switching   170, 242–244, 246, 635, 778, 1097
coercive relations of power   33, 706, 972, 1037
cognitive
  activity   619, 705, 855
  development   163, 247, 318, 336, 338, 340, 343–345, 629, 630, 638, 690, 788, 791
  learning models   318
  processes of language acquisition   631
  psychology   72, 273, 279, 283, 330
  science   779, 783, 786, 792, 793

cognitive academic language proficiency
    (CALP) 163, 353
cognitively complex questions 712
cognitively-challenging tasks 704, 969,
    1105
cognitive-social model 319
cohesive
    devises 694
    linguistic references 909
collaboration (*see also* interaction) 227,
    234, 320, 357–359, 363, 365–367, 369,
    373–377, 389, 399, 417, 443, 515, 621,
    629, 637, 752, 753, 967, 968, 1046,
    1047, 1076, 1077
collaborative
    activity 515, 629, 630, 635
    basis 999
    critical inquiry 753, 765, 911
    dialogue 301, 513, 705, 717, 857
    learning 387, 517, 717, 739, 744, 753,
        754, 760, 765, 802, 902, 903, 909,
        1061, 1123
    pedagogies 235, 391, 398, 399
    relations of power 903, 972
    roles 235, 368, 374, 635, 969, 1105,
        1115
    support 1068
    teaching 234, 365, 366, 368, 373, 374,
        376, 915, 1104, 1105
    work 365–369, 374–376, 516
collegial development 1078, 1080, 1082
collegiality 997, 1061, 1080
collocation 830, 833, 857, 953
colonial
    language policy 13, 15, 38, 40
    privilege 1044
colonialism 4, 13, 15, 17–19, 21–23, 35, 50,
    61, 75, 76, 83, 85, 531, 672, 1051,
    1088, 1097, 1098
colonialist discourses 23, 35, 61, 79, 85,
    531, 1051
colonization 65, 77, 107, 124, 156
command of English 78, 110, 111, 113, 118,
    674
commitment control strategies 728
common literacy standards 444, 447
communication 66–68, 91–94, 127–134,
    136–138, 144–147, 149–152, 155–158,
    170, 239, 240, 398–402, 408–412, 694,
    748, 749, 777–779, 887–899, 907–917,
    920–922, 1048–1052, 1111–1113,
    1125–1128
communicative
    abilities 67, 79, 115, 147, 271, 276, 279,
        400, 928
    action 1076
    activity 694, 705, 845
    approach 91, 271, 298, 753, 760, 804,
        1083
    behavior (*see also* behaviorism) 26, 393,
        936
    competence 66, 67, 77, 78, 93, 115, 162,
        254, 255, 273, 285–287, 312, 429, 475,
        476, 483, 622, 672, 715, 717, 758, 779,
        868, 893
    competencies 898, 903
    flexibility 659
    functions 274, 861, 862, 872
    language learning 742
    language pedagogy 285, 868
    language teaching (CLT) 64, 78, 232,
        239, 271–273, 275, 277, 279, 281, 283,
        285–290, 392, 751, 760, 804, 857, 869,
        871, 872, 922, 967
    methodology 274, 285, 1126
    needs 234, 253, 391, 398, 526, 780, 855,
        898, 932
    options 647
    practices 278, 283, 392, 398–400, 647,
        779, 920, 928
    problems 694
    strategies 1030
    styles 647
community
    literacies 400, 892
    of practice (COP) 231, 633, 638, 670,
        1046
comparative education 23, 104, 658, 689
competencies 114, 195, 227, 278, 279, 395,
    405, 408, 412, 416, 417, 421, 424–426,
    428, 431, 433, 437, 438, 452, 459, 736,
    898, 1132, 1133
    in education 1071
competency-based programs 424
comprehensible input 274–276, 279, 281,
    300, 717, 752, 769, 848, 949, 1023,
    1028
comprehension-based activities 295
compulsory education 97, 99, 100, 104,
    105, 114, 115

Subject Index

computer 242, 313, 476, 479, 480, 482–484, 621, 622, 747–760, 762, 767, 768, 781, 863, 864, 899, 904, 905, 907–910, 912–917, 953, 954, 1114, 1115, 1117, 1118, 1123–1125, 1130–1134
  adaptive testing 480, 482
  corpora 397, 480, 953, 954, 1070
  labs 749
  literacy 233, 303, 313, 622, 747, 749, 756, 758–760, 781, 904, 905, 907, 914–916, 1123
  support teacher 1117
  technology 3, 100, 484, 621, 622, 747–751, 753, 755–760, 904, 907, 915–917, 954, 1071, 1114, 1121, 1123–1125, 1127, 1130, 1131, 1133, 1137
computer-assisted
  classroom discussion (CACD) 781, 907, 908, 910
  instruction 622, 747, 749–751, 753, 756–758
  language learning (CALL) 621, 742, 747, 752, 758–760, 1117
computer-based
  activities 1127
  approaches 748, 755
  instruction (CBI) 748, 753, 755
  technologies 313, 747, 750, 751, 755, 756, 758
  training 748
computerized spellchecking 899
computer-mediated
  communication (CMC) 471, 748, 757, 762, 767, 781, 905, 907, 912–917
  communication literacy 914
  language learning 1132
  messages 909
  writing 781, 907
computer-supported
  learning environments 1125
  project seminars 1131
  projects 1133
concordancing tools 954, 956
connectionism 785, 793, 794
connectionist
  approach to learning 785
  architecture 785, 786
conscious knowledge 787, 813
consciousness 48, 80, 169, 198, 250, 285, 295, 300, 306, 399, 669, 689, 693, 695, 992
consciousness-raising tasks 285, 300
consonant 787, 789, 813, 821–823
  clusters 821–823
constructivism (see also behaviorism; cognitivism) 235, 395, 539
constructivist
  approaches 622, 737, 758, 1114
  view of learning 499, 750
  views of teaching 1126
consultants 213, 399, 462, 463, 466–468, 1115
content 58, 59, 114–116, 118–121, 231–234, 251–254, 266–268, 281–284, 303, 309–315, 317–321, 323–325, 345, 346, 357–359, 366–369, 373–377, 428, 429, 431–437, 803–808, 1119–1122, 1126–1129
  analysis (see also discourse analysis) 29, 253, 262, 281, 284, 310–313, 325, 381, 400, 478, 868, 869, 931, 942
  and assessment standards 417, 421
content-based
  instruction 119, 268, 284, 290, 366, 376
  language teaching 119, 167, 1085
content-language integration approach 252
context 6–11, 157–160, 199–201, 231–234, 252–256, 402, 403, 446, 447, 506, 537–540, 621, 622, 714–717, 734–740, 777–781, 797–800, 849–852, 856, 857, 937–942, 1005, 1021–1023, 1069–1073
  of culture 303, 649, 933, 935, 1037
context-dependent 419
context-free 498
context-sensitive 1039
contextual features 494, 538, 861, 975
contingency 710, 853, 915, 1119
contingent responses 712
contrastive rhetoric 235, 391, 392, 394, 395, 401, 547, 938, 940, 1039, 1047, 1048
control 219, 220, 240, 241, 292, 293, 296, 297, 318, 319, 329, 330, 522, 523, 529, 530, 615, 695, 708, 713, 724–726, 728, 729, 737, 738, 743, 744, 750, 851, 990, 1056
conversation 63, 64, 70, 71, 245, 246, 369, 371, 372, 715, 716, 752–754, 798, 799, 801, 802, 804–806, 859, 860, 863–866,

868, 869, 872, 873, 900, 966, 1017–1019, 1021–1023, 1025, 1027–1032
analysis (CA) 143, 150, 246, 647, 781, 859, 864, 865, 868, 869, 872, 873, 966, 975, 978, 983, 1017–1019, 1021–1023, 1025, 1027–1031
analysts 865, 869, 1018, 1019, 1021, 1022
conversational
 competence 868
 exposure 111
 fluency 351, 352, 701, 779, 797, 799–801, 805
 style 860
conversation-analysis-for-second-language-acquisition (CA-for-SLA) 1022
cooperative
 action research 992
 learning 99, 310, 314, 970, 1085, 1128, 1134
 learning activities 1085
core identities 65
coronal node 816, 817
corpora of language data 954
corporate
 position 1116
 universities 1119, 1124
corpus
 linguistics 146, 954
 of spoken language 870
 studies 853
corpus-based 151, 777, 840, 870, 871, 917
corrective feedback 275, 277, 278, 286, 287, 300, 760, 845, 948
Council of Europe 134, 146, 147, 149, 150, 152, 421, 425–427, 437, 442, 454, 734, 743, 759
covert error correction 790
Creole 28, 107, 115, 126, 143, 321, 644, 646, 1013
critic 1115
critical 25–29, 31, 32, 34–36, 47–49, 61, 83–85, 312–315, 391–395, 615–619, 650–653, 655, 656, 660–662, 665, 666, 685, 686, 689–691, 713–716, 763–766, 769–773, 1036–1052, 1097–1100
 applied linguistics 61, 85, 313, 315, 392, 402, 517, 519, 530, 531, 615, 650, 652, 689, 690, 824, 941, 967, 986, 992, 1048, 1050–1052

approaches 4, 6, 27, 36, 85, 169, 233, 235, 303, 391, 392, 531, 615–617, 690, 691, 706, 855, 883, 971, 1034, 1041, 1045
contrastive rhetoric 235, 391, 392, 394, 938, 1048
curriculum 36, 40, 69, 83, 250, 267, 313, 314, 392, 408, 444, 455, 493, 619, 665, 686, 714, 764, 765, 971, 972, 1000, 1015, 1016
discourse analysis 132, 235, 391, 392, 615, 650, 748, 976, 977, 1049–1051
discourse studies 645
EAP (*see* English for academic purposes) 402, 656, 665, 883, 1044
engagement 400, 512, 650, 911, 1046, 1116
ethnography 61, 235, 391–393, 617, 636, 651, 655, 656, 658, 660, 666, 905, 977, 978, 984, 986, 1045, 1098, 1099, 1112
language awareness 49, 854, 888, 947, 957, 958, 1094
language studies 26, 85, 531, 666, 1051
language testing 455, 474, 493, 517, 519, 520, 530, 531, 616, 1050
linguistics 49, 61, 85, 233, 303, 313–315, 392, 488, 517, 519, 531, 615, 650, 652, 689, 690, 824, 856, 938, 1048, 1050–1052
literacy 27, 28, 34–36, 178, 400, 401, 444, 445, 455, 689, 691, 749, 763–766, 769, 856, 876, 887, 888, 891–893, 901, 902, 905, 971, 972, 1012, 1014, 1015
multiculturalists 1042
pedagogy 6, 23, 34, 48, 75, 83–85, 250, 401, 616, 618, 636, 666, 686, 689–691, 715, 716, 753, 763–766, 971, 972, 1041–1044, 1050, 1051
period 40, 68, 69, 72, 178, 652, 747, 814, 824, 825, 832
period hypothesis 68, 69, 814, 824
reflexive practices 1043, 1044
reflexivity 966, 1041, 1043–1045, 1078
stance 395, 660, 707, 1074, 1076
theory 4, 26, 27, 31, 34, 35, 85, 197, 228, 313, 392, 401, 415, 639, 689, 742, 743, 824, 825, 855, 905, 1034, 1046–1048, 1050, 1051
thinking skills 233, 303, 312, 313, 452, 706, 713, 807

cross disciplinary conversation 376
cross-cultural
 communication 350, 1085
 comparison 306
cross-generational 642
crossings 650, 1035, 1079
cross-institutional communication 1128
cross-national 128, 439, 475, 642
cultural
 capital 77, 132, 133, 176, 397, 688, 875, 1088, 1093
 competence 444, 851, 1022
 congruence 709
 determinism 21
 difference 489, 650, 765, 919, 921, 922, 928, 941
 formations 15
 hybridity 1035
 identities 85, 133, 170, 197, 198, 202, 216, 227, 637, 645–647, 651, 679, 706, 893, 895, 898
 inequality 661
 instrumentalism 169
 meanings 233, 303
 ownership 870
 practices 205, 393, 397, 515, 534, 537, 539, 540, 698, 1039, 1042, 1051
 resources 629, 637
 specificity 18
 studies 152, 186, 197, 218, 538, 639, 645–647, 651, 679, 778, 1049, 1050, 1099, 1133, 1134, 1136
culturally
 appropriate curricula 1079
 specific context 706
culture 49, 50, 78, 79, 112, 113, 175–177, 196–198, 356–359, 394, 395, 419, 487–503, 637–641, 648–653, 921–924, 933, 984, 985, 1009, 1011–1016, 1021, 1022, 1033–1035, 1037–1052, 1098–1100
curriculum 87–89, 95–105, 107–114, 199–204, 206–210, 246–269, 355, 356, 365–369, 372–377, 406–412, 437–445, 454–456, 493, 494, 517–520, 684–687, 757–760, 807–809, 999–1002, 1014–1016, 1101–1112
 approaches 6, 7, 36, 87, 103, 162, 219, 232, 254, 256, 260, 368, 420, 421, 424, 425, 432, 433, 622, 706, 757, 758, 939, 940, 971, 992, 993
 change 7, 10, 82, 90, 96, 100–104, 118, 120, 165, 203, 259, 262, 284, 440, 441, 987, 999, 1001, 1069, 1110, 1111, 1126
 de facto curriculum 524, 529
 dynamic curriculum 10, 231, 254, 496, 979, 1080, 1110
 evaluation 93, 100, 104, 118, 253, 265, 268, 313, 320, 325, 327, 407, 408, 412, 413, 415, 420, 421, 424, 425, 431–433, 435, 517, 518, 992
 inquiry-based curriculum 619
 materials 87, 88, 103, 105, 164, 191, 195, 206, 208, 232, 251, 252, 318, 320, 327, 355, 386, 409, 410, 432, 433, 441–443, 484, 493
 planning 35, 105, 146, 253, 254, 301, 319, 366, 369, 372, 403, 407, 408, 423, 424, 431, 441, 497, 509, 1080, 1085, 1109
 practices 16, 77, 89, 93, 204, 206, 232, 250, 262, 355, 365–369, 372, 373, 510, 513, 534, 618, 622, 684, 685, 928, 1063
 theory 105, 118, 120, 235, 287, 313, 349, 355, 377, 392, 403, 410, 412, 454, 456, 503, 504, 511, 939, 940, 992, 1002
customization 1122

D

data-based language analysis 953
declarative knowledge 955
decolonization 13, 35
decolonized 1040
deconstructionism 1044
deep structure 341, 450, 1034
 of mind 1034
 of standards 450
default practices 1017
deficit model 497, 676
delayed communication 907
democratic
 approaches to assessment 530
 leadership 725
demographic
 changes 188, 191, 192
 research 617, 655–657
denominator 1024, 1025
descriptive ethnography 660

developmental
  path 540, 799, 1054, 1058, 1062, 1064
  stage 639, 1115
dialects 28, 126, 129, 158, 176, 179, 190, 243, 368, 444, 627, 647, 845, 870
diasporic identities 1035
digital
  divide 622, 755, 761, 917
  interfaces 891
  literacies 893, 897, 902
  text 899
disciplinary
  microworlds 884
  problems 1057, 1058
discoursal
  self 881
  strategies 884
discourse 303–305, 309–315, 391–400, 536–539, 545–547, 619, 620, 662, 663, 701–715, 777–781, 859–873, 875–880, 884–886, 888–891, 908–910, 930–932, 934–940, 975–977, 982–986, 1026–1030, 1049–1052
  analysis 33, 34, 235, 310–314, 391–393, 396, 397, 402, 484, 662, 663, 717, 861, 864, 868, 869, 872, 873, 888, 931, 975–977, 982, 983, 986, 1027–1031, 1049–1051
  classroom discourse 252, 287, 299, 300, 373, 401, 402, 419, 463, 511, 514, 515, 519, 520, 619, 620, 634–637, 701–709, 713–718, 862–864, 871–873, 909, 910, 976, 977, 982–986, 1027, 1028
  community 34, 112, 141, 178, 367, 396, 399, 402, 539, 545, 546, 635–637, 666, 764, 778, 781, 873, 875–878, 885, 886, 889, 890, 1068
  context 9, 81, 150, 210, 253, 284, 303, 305, 314, 514, 515, 701, 702, 706, 714, 715, 777, 778, 850, 851, 856, 857, 872, 873, 879, 880, 935, 937–940
  in English 9, 34, 75, 79, 111, 124, 125, 130, 131, 146, 149, 151, 214, 300, 314, 315, 400, 401, 418, 419, 473, 477, 478, 828, 894, 896
  of globalization 75, 81, 115, 893, 1070
  markers 545, 861, 862, 872, 873, 983
  of meetings 738
  norms 126, 130, 131, 146, 179, 395, 709, 713, 781, 869, 877, 878, 885, 891, 897, 898, 900, 1041, 1046, 1076
  practices 75, 84, 303–305, 313–315, 373, 375, 391–394, 396, 397, 400, 487, 514, 515, 634, 635, 637, 707, 876–879, 975–977, 982–986, 1043, 1058, 1080, 1081
  structure 251, 279, 307, 311, 314, 538, 539, 546, 708, 717, 778, 780, 806, 853, 859, 861, 864, 872, 873, 876, 878, 1030
  systems 284, 303, 314, 335, 394, 396, 419, 487, 488, 659, 861, 868, 878, 930, 938, 947, 966
discourse-based contexts 935
discursive
  construction 198, 373, 376, 377, 1047, 1050
  perspectives 1046
disengagement 1054
disintermediation 1121
display-based teaching 863
disruptive technology 1121
distance learning 735, 743, 749, 750, 758
domain 7, 37, 46, 126, 131, 146, 212, 434, 456, 476, 522, 699, 814, 857, 894, 909, 922, 929, 983, 1023–1025
dominance of tests 524
dominant variety of English 1042
dual language instruction 255
dynamic qualifications 1133

E
EAL (*see* English as an additional language) xxi, 10, 200, 202, 206–209, 265, 921, 928, 968, 969, 1101–1111
EAP (*see* English for academic purposes) 393–395, 415, 431, 617, 655, 656, 658–660, 663–665, 735, 751, 876, 883–887, 1044
  curricula 658, 659
early
  adopter group 1119
  majority 1116
ecological validity 974
economic globalization 76
education 20–23, 31–52, 103–105, 107–121, 164–167, 195–203, 255–269, 386–389, 421–425, 452–456, 469–471, 685–690, 715–719, 963–976, 1047–1055, 1082–1089, 1097–1107, 1110–

1120, 1123–1127, 1136–1138
educational
  anthropology 639
  attainment 10, 199–201, 203, 205, 207, 209, 656
  computing 1114, 1119
  disadvantage 663
  discourse 704, 742, 872
  integration 249, 257
  linguists 948
  opportunities 202, 366
  psychology 693, 698, 699, 720, 725, 729, 740, 759, 794, 1007
  reform 10, 11, 107, 108, 114, 115, 121, 162, 163, 436, 503, 618, 631, 637, 656, 681, 734, 735, 764, 999, 1083, 1137
  sectors 1119
  studies 73, 620, 719, 1003, 1013
EFL (*see* English as a foreign language) xxi, xxii, xxv, 21, 76, 78–80, 82, 108, 112–116, 118, 119, 121, 138, 139, 158, 167, 239, 380, 415, 417, 439, 442, 443, 448, 450, 452, 453, 462, 511, 661, 763, 834, 845, 895, 951, 952, 954, 956, 970, 971, 983–985, 1035, 1072, 1126, 1127, 1130–1134, 1136
  learners 439
  standards 417, 439, 442, 443, 453
electronic 120, 121, 129, 165, 247, 348, 412, 748, 749, 755, 758–761, 767, 773, 781, 808, 896, 904, 905, 907–910, 912–917, 939, 1123, 1124, 1137, 1138
  discourses 412, 908
  feedback 755, 909, 910, 917
  literacy 749, 758–760, 781, 808, 904, 905, 907, 914–916, 1123
  text types 1120
electrophysiological data 822
elementary schools 38, 63, 64, 68–73, 78, 222, 234, 312, 323, 328, 344, 349, 363, 527, 905
ELF (*see* English as lingua franca) xxi, xxii, 8, 132, 137–142, 144, 145, 147–149
ELLs (*see* English language learners) 211, 212, 215, 218, 223, 226, 227, 639, 640, 642–649, 655–657, 660, 661, 663–665, 806, 973, 974–976, 978, 979, 982, 983
ELT (*see* English language teaching) xxi, xxv, xxviii, 3–7, 9, 10, 13, 15–17, 19, 22, 25–33, 63, 67, 69, 70, 75–79, 83,

84, 87, 88, 90–92, 96, 102, 103, 107, 108, 118, 119, 130, 132, 155, 199, 209, 210, 231–235, 238, 403, 404, 406–410, 414–417, 419, 420, 439, 449, 441–445, 448–454, 498, 521, 534, 655, 656, 658, 733, 734, 735, 736, 741, 749, 777–782, 843–845, 849, 891, 893, 894, 896–898, 901–903, 919, 928, 929, 931, 946, 951, 954, 955, 963–968, 970–972, 987, 992, 994, 996, 999, 1003, 1033, 1037, 1038, 1040–1047, 1067, 1068, 1070, 1072–1074, 1114, 1118–1120, 1125
  classroom 29, 897, 928, 929
  curriculum design 235, 403, 408
  professional discourse community 951
  standards 417, 439–443, 445, 448–454
  workplace design and evaluation 409
e-mail 754, 755, 758, 760, 772, 860, 907, 908, 910–917, 1127, 1134, 1135
  communication 760, 907, 910–913, 915–917
  exchanges 908, 910–912, 916
emancipatory models 992
emerging demographics 196
EMI (*see* English medium instruction) 803, 804, 805, 807, 808
emic perspectives 973, 974, 977
emoticons 896, 899, 913
emotion control strategies 729
empirical research 143, 145, 289, 376, 439, 441, 448, 454, 474, 497, 625, 636, 737, 977, 987, 1000
empirical-analytical techniques 1043
empirically grounded understanding 1023
employment standards 421, 422
enculturation 393, 666, 902
England 13, 16, 72, 73, 110, 181, 199–203, 209, 210, 249, 250, 257, 259, 262–269, 348, 364–367, 373, 444, 445, 531, 647, 1049, 1100–1104, 1109–1111
English
  for Academic Purposes (EAP) 314, 376, 380, 393, 401, 402, 483, 485, 617, 655, 666, 689, 735, 798, 876, 887, 888, 890, 917, 941, 942, 1044, 1047
  as an additional language (EAL) 10, 163, 164, 199, 200, 202, 204, 207, 208, 210, 265, 268, 380, 455, 456, 510, 517, 520, 618, 735, 921, 968, 1101, 1111, 1112
  as an official language 65, 71–73, 78, 84

deficiency 657
education 14, 63, 64, 66–69, 71, 72, 75, 78, 82, 83, 85, 96, 105, 669, 929
　as a European lingua franca 141, 149, 151, 167
　as a foreign language (EFL) 76, 113, 146, 157, 158, 165–167, 250, 285, 417, 418, 439, 473, 474, 482, 484, 774, 825, 895, 945, 983, 1004
　for general purposes 661
　as a global language 48, 75, 76, 85, 107, 115, 120, 126, 134, 135, 150, 151, 166, 181, 671, 672, 893, 895, 900, 904, 967, 1049
　grammar 89, 201, 954
　imperialism 63, 65, 1048
　language education 32, 87, 419, 458, 490, 505, 748, 940, 973, 974, 1080
　language immersion 71, 112, 657
　language learners (ELLs) 30, 209, 211, 214, 226, 231, 233, 234, 310, 336–339, 341, 345, 346, 349, 350, 416, 417, 456, 630–634, 655, 663, 665, 666, 675, 676, 973, 974
　language teaching (ELT) 15, 83–85, 92–94, 103–105, 213–215, 223–227, 231, 232, 299–301, 416, 417, 518, 521, 747, 855–857, 931, 1000, 1003–1007, 1009, 1013, 1014, 1047–1050, 1123, 1124
　as a lingua franca (ELF) 7, 8, 128, 130, 132, 135–141, 143, 145–149, 151–153, 156, 415, 870
　medium instruction (EMI) 5, 1055
　medium school 201, 351, 352
　monolingual ideologies 644
　proficiency 17, 25, 27, 65, 66, 81, 92, 111, 113, 174, 193–195, 212, 216, 217, 219, 223, 351, 354, 357, 359, 360, 473–475, 798
　as a second language (ESL) 13, 48, 72, 127, 146, 155, 200–202, 267, 268, 313–315, 318, 331, 376, 377, 443, 444, 456, 517, 518, 533, 809, 895, 1100, 1111, 1112
　sociolects 870
　for Specific Purposes (ESP) 151, 234, 245, 265, 268, 391, 393, 395, 397, 399, 401, 402, 404, 411, 412, 547, 665, 782, 887, 888, 890, 931, 940–942
Englishization 123, 129, 132, 134, 135, 137
English-only 6, 9, 25, 27, 28, 33, 34, 43, 75, 76, 78–83, 85, 135, 152, 177, 180, 182, 219, 225, 227, 228, 337, 338, 343, 1089, 1090
　environment 336, 338, 1089
　instruction 6, 9, 25, 27, 28, 33, 34, 43, 75, 76, 79, 83, 225, 226, 338, 682
　policy 6, 33, 34, 43, 73, 75, 76, 78–83, 135, 152, 177, 182, 219, 227, 337, 531, 684, 1089
English-speaking 10, 11, 108, 109, 111, 112, 124, 125, 129, 174, 187, 189, 213, 216, 219–221, 249, 333, 334, 337, 338, 343, 349–354, 379, 382, 674–677, 799, 800
　ability 453, 799, 1093
　contexts 123, 211, 221, 318, 330, 333, 334, 417, 418, 453, 674, 799, 968, 1003, 1005
　environment 200, 334, 338, 345, 379, 417, 439, 701, 799, 834, 1013, 1102
environment control strategies 729
epistemological
　assumptions 234, 368, 376
　foundations of applied linguistics 1034
　framework 1024
　grounds 891, 893
　practices 883
　shift 891
epistemology (*see also* naturalistic enquiry) 262, 374, 844
error correction 30, 790, 791
ESL
　bandscales 440, 442–445, 450, 453, 455, 456, 490, 498, 510
　classroom 84, 198, 287, 321, 402, 666, 678, 689, 758, 760, 872, 926, 979, 1001, 1050
　educators 196, 262, 321, 444
　learners 204, 232, 249–251, 253, 255, 257, 259–261, 263, 265, 267, 269, 314, 365, 366, 376, 439, 443–445, 447, 448, 453, 631, 704
　learning 443, 446, 625, 631, 633, 636, 637, 679, 903, 1049, 1099
　pedagogy 250–254, 366
　programs 185–187, 189–191, 193, 195–197, 217, 219, 226, 288, 352, 380, 382, 388, 389, 424, 448, 1040, 1050

Subject Index

teachers 10, 86, 203, 207, 227, 234, 257, 266, 320, 321, 323, 344, 345, 365–370, 373–376, 383, 384, 386, 388, 433, 443, 688, 1055
ESP (*see* English for Specific Purposes) 234, 235, 245, 265, 391–401, 403, 404, 408–411, 431, 751, 782, 828, 931–933
  genre analysis 931
  language training curriculum 404
essayist-text literacy 876
ethical review boards 977
ethics 15, 34, 420, 483, 484, 518, 531, 1045, 1049, 1065
ethnic
  affiliations 617, 641, 664
  identity formation 641
ethnography 61, 235, 391–393, 411, 514, 617, 636, 647, 649–651, 655, 656, 658, 660, 665, 666, 975, 977, 978, 984–986, 1005–1007, 1023, 1027–1029, 1098, 1099
  case studies 658, 666
  data 660, 968, 977, 978, 986, 1019, 1098
  descriptions 656, 658, 1097
  findings 657, 1098
  methods 975, 984–986, 1097
  monitoring 204, 992
  research 234, 235, 391, 393, 411, 617, 649, 655–658, 968, 975, 977, 978, 984–986, 1005–1007, 1014, 1015, 1019, 1023, 1027–1029, 1099
  study 61, 393, 650, 660, 666, 872, 977, 978, 985, 986, 1029, 1045, 1047
  techniques 393, 514, 660, 986, 1019, 1023
ethnolinguistic
  identity 640, 649, 650
  minority groups 31, 642
ethnomethodological approach 1018
etic perspectives 977, 1018
EU (*see* European Union) 7, 123, 126–129, 131, 133, 134, 138
European immigration 108
European Union (EU) 7, 123, 127, 134, 135, 137, 142, 143, 150, 156, 165, 256, 421, 673
Europeanization 123, 134
evaluation strategies 740, 1085
evaluative 307, 377, 385, 670, 720, 748, 988, 1027

evidence-based practices 1071
exchange structure
  analysis 861, 868
  models 864
exchanges 66, 88, 222, 278, 314, 423, 425, 542, 543, 546, 622, 708, 710, 712–714, 725, 781, 862–865, 867, 907, 908, 910–912, 1132
ex-colonial languages 37, 39–41, 43
exemplary practices 994
expectancy of success 727
experience-based
  decision-making 1078
  skill 499
experiential
  function 849
  learning 706, 739, 743, 1132
  metafunctions 706, 846
expert teacher 1055
explicit 205, 206, 233, 234, 274, 275, 277, 290, 291, 319, 320, 329, 425, 535, 537, 539, 540, 778, 779, 783, 787, 788, 791–795, 831–833, 853, 854, 878, 879, 938, 939, 950, 951
  grammar instruction 779, 783, 793, 800
  knowledge 205, 252, 320, 397, 425, 537, 619, 714, 779, 783, 787, 788, 791–793, 795, 823, 833, 836, 938, 946, 950, 951, 957
  language instruction 290, 291, 794, 795, 979
  learning 205, 206, 276, 277, 319, 320, 328, 329, 516, 539, 619, 620, 698, 723, 753, 754, 768, 779, 783, 784, 788, 792–795, 831–833, 836, 837, 854, 938, 939, 1004, 1005
  pedagogy 205, 208, 766, 783, 809, 833, 885, 1106, 1111
  roles 1113, 1114
exploratory 151, 464, 520, 651, 690, 713, 810, 872, 902, 903, 967, 968, 976, 995, 1007, 1076–1078, 1082, 1083, 1114
  media 1114
  practice 713, 967, 968, 1076–1078, 1082, 1083
  talk 713, 872
  work 872, 967, 1076–1078, 1082, 1083
Exploratory Practice Centre 1077, 1082
expositions 536, 933
expression plane 850

external examiners 54
extracurricular activities 721
extralinguistic
  differences 1039
  factors 1036
extrinsic conditions 1036

F
face-to-face discussion 908–910, 970
facilitator 205, 514, 620, 725, 726, 731, 750, 998, 1108, 1114, 1115, 1117, 1122, 1123, 1129
faculty resistance 1116
familial conflict 641
Federal Law of Education (FLE) 107, 108, 111, 114, 116, 118
feedback 275, 277, 278, 286, 287, 291, 292, 296, 300, 419, 420, 425, 463, 491, 492, 498–500, 503, 508–511, 516, 517, 519, 520, 712, 729, 730, 845, 846, 862, 909, 910
female linguistic rights 140
feminism (also feminist) 198, 677, 1047, 1048
field 158, 159, 231, 305–309, 311, 391, 392, 394, 395, 397–401, 415–420, 477, 478, 534, 535, 739–743, 747–749, 843–846, 851, 852, 964–966, 980–983, 994–997, 999, 1007, 1008, 1010–1012
filter 673, 722, 949, 950
first
  class 912, 1116, 1134, 1135
  language (L1) 27, 44, 68, 69, 144, 173, 238–241, 243–246, 258, 259, 289, 290, 344, 345, 351–355, 359, 360, 394, 780, 813, 823, 936, 1070, 1072, 1090, 1091
FLE (*see* Federal Law of Education)
fluency 55, 77, 137, 162, 175, 195, 260, 272, 276, 285, 292–294, 297, 298, 301, 351, 352, 427, 478, 494, 783, 792–795, 799–801
  and accuracy 272, 276, 285, 293, 297, 301, 478
  promoting activities 792, 793
focus on form (FonF) 233, 281, 285–288, 299–301, 312, 518, 845, 856, 857, 932, 948, 956, 958, 1071
follow-up 164, 206, 462, 862, 864, 865, 909, 950, 1018, 1022, 1080, 1127
Ford Teaching Project 992

foreign language 66, 71–73, 87–89, 104, 105, 110, 113–116, 123–125, 133–135, 137, 138, 155–158, 162, 163, 165–167, 175, 283–289, 383–385, 673, 742–744, 915–917, 1124–1127, 1137, 1138
  classroom 3, 5, 68, 116, 165, 166, 283, 284, 286–288, 300, 513, 731, 735, 744, 763, 915–917, 985, 1000, 1004, 1005, 1050, 1125–1127, 1137, 1138
  education 41, 66–69, 71–73, 87–89, 104, 105, 107, 110, 113–116, 124, 125, 164–167, 181, 182, 283–285, 314, 315, 417, 915–917, 984, 985, 1049–1051, 1083, 1084, 1124–1127, 1137, 1138
  teacher 78, 103, 104, 284, 285, 287, 288, 417, 436–438, 511, 742, 744, 840, 916, 917, 945, 952, 984, 985, 1000, 1049, 1050, 1057, 1083, 1084, 1124–1127, 1137, 1138
  teacher education 284, 285, 389, 417, 471, 744, 916, 917, 952, 984, 1015, 1083–1085, 1125–1127, 1137, 1138
foreign-born students 657
formal register 876, 881
form-focused instruction 276, 283, 287
frequency 113, 155, 253, 292, 397, 778, 785, 790, 794, 798, 799, 801, 805, 806, 828, 830, 833, 836, 839, 840, 867, 1025
fricative 821
full
  access 813, 820, 822, 823, 848
  transfer 813, 820, 823
function 8, 26, 124–126, 130, 131, 138, 146, 148, 180, 221, 232, 237, 239, 240, 296, 297, 695–698, 722, 723, 726, 727, 828, 844, 849, 850, 1131, 1132
functional
  linguistic analyses 983
  roles 970, 1113, 1114, 1116, 1117, 1119
  roles for teachers 1116
  variation 140, 853
functional/notional model of English proficiency 474

G
gang affiliations 645
gendered identities 618, 641, 669, 671, 677
generalist teachers 1120
generalizability theory 480

generative
  grammar 786
  linguistics 784, 785
  theory 846, 848
generic
  approach 660
  structures 702
genre 58, 305, 308, 309, 311, 313–315, 392, 396, 397, 401, 402, 533–541, 544, 545, 547, 548, 716, 778, 781, 782, 851, 852, 856, 857, 869, 870, 887–890, 931–943, 1061
  structures 1061
genre-based approach 935–938, 941, 942
genres 305, 306, 308, 313–315, 394–402, 428, 429, 480, 481, 535–539, 545, 547, 716, 778, 781, 782, 856, 857, 869, 870, 876–879, 883, 884, 886, 887, 913, 926, 927, 931–943
gestures 170, 209, 425, 451, 538, 838, 920–922, 1019, 1020, 1028, 1036
global
  communications 1040, 1118
  community 672, 676, 870, 1068
  English 75, 83, 84, 123, 126–128, 132, 134, 135, 143, 152, 169, 895
  hypermedia 1113, 1115, 1117, 1119, 1121, 1123
  imperialism of English 22
  inequality 17, 18
  language 48, 75, 76, 85, 107, 115, 120, 126, 134, 135, 150, 151, 166, 171, 181, 671, 672, 871, 891, 893, 895, 900, 904, 967
  networks 75, 781, 891
  spread of English 18, 19, 76
globalization 32, 75–77, 79, 81, 84–86, 96, 115, 123, 124, 127–129, 134, 135, 137, 150, 153, 170, 178, 197, 200, 415, 416, 904, 905, 1047–1049
goals 33, 45, 65–67, 83, 211, 212, 221, 222, 224–227, 231–233, 237–241, 243–247, 280, 281, 320–323, 428–432, 434, 440, 443, 444, 493–496, 513, 721, 722, 726–729
government-initiated
  policy 440
  standards 440, 442
grades 53, 54, 56–60, 68–71, 75, 76, 79, 95, 99, 100, 163, 212, 310, 311, 321, 323, 324, 352, 383–385, 429, 729, 730, 768, 799–801, 923, 924, 1092–1094
grammar 6, 67, 68, 77, 89–92, 140, 141, 273–276, 285–288, 300, 301, 308–310, 314, 777–780, 783–786, 793–795, 813, 814, 843–858, 869–871, 932, 933, 939–941, 950–958, 1070, 1071
  checkers 1115
  instruction 6, 67, 68, 77, 92, 254, 273–275, 279, 280, 285, 287, 288, 295, 300, 301, 314, 622, 744, 753, 779, 783, 793, 800, 848, 849
grammar-translation method 67, 68, 89, 92
grammatical
  information 793, 847
  metaphor 307–309, 1035
  patterns 702
  terminology 951, 957
graphic
  literacy across languages 310, 315
  representation 309, 311
gratifying function 730
grounded
  accounts 983
  analysis 975, 1021
  theory (see also empirical research) 197, 986, 1074
  understanding 1023
group 201–208, 275, 276, 324, 325, 327–329, 351, 352, 361, 370–372, 467, 620, 640–648, 656, 657, 719–727, 731, 919, 920, 927, 1001, 1002, 1028, 1092–1097, 1104–1108, 1134, 1135
  cohesiveness 620, 719–723, 726, 1129
  dynamics 4, 238, 620, 642, 719, 720, 726, 731, 991, 1001, 1093, 1095
  norms 144, 324, 395, 500, 620, 645, 647, 719, 722, 723, 726, 1046
  roles 144, 257, 285, 371, 405, 498, 617, 620, 647, 712, 717, 719, 722–724, 969, 1096, 1114, 1119
  work 144, 145, 203, 206–208, 351, 352, 495, 496, 498, 640, 642, 645, 647, 712, 720–724, 772, 1028, 1057, 1058, 1091, 1092, 1094–1097, 1102, 1105–1108, 1134, 1135
group-orientedness 724
group-sensitive teaching practice 726
guided participation 628, 638
guides 29, 30, 215, 247, 1115

H

Hallidayan linguistics 1034
hedging 402, 868, 888
heritage language 224, 225
hierarchical mode 620, 725
higher education 52, 61, 76, 85, 89, 124, 125, 130, 131, 136, 182, 344, 376, 470, 474, 482, 485, 493, 503, 526–528, 547, 887–890
high-proficiency 791
high-stakes 213, 223, 417, 457–461, 463–465, 467, 469, 471, 491, 504, 528, 618, 684, 900, 972, 1096
  assessment 417, 457–471, 504, 505
  tests 223, 417, 457, 458, 460, 462, 463, 467, 528, 900, 972
high-track classes 979
Hong Kong 14, 15, 23, 351, 403–405, 407–412, 454–458, 461–465, 467–471, 491–494, 496, 502–504, 533, 534, 540–542, 742–745, 797, 798, 802, 803, 806–810, 1086–1089, 1091, 1092, 1098, 1099
Hong Kong Examination and Assessment Authority (HKEAA) 496
hybrid
  learning context 634
  register 709, 710
hypermedia 759, 907, 908, 959, 1113, 1115, 1117, 1119, 1121, 1123
  text types 1113
hypertext 756

I

ICT (*see* Information and Communication Technologies) 748, 749, 778, 891, 898, 899, 902, 969, 970 1113, 1114, 1116–1120, 1122, 1125–1136
  environment 1113, 1118
ICT-supported
  classrooms 1128, 1136
  context 1128
  EFL classroom 1127, 1131, 1132
  environments 1128, 1129
  learning environments 1127, 1131
  school-based projects 1135
ideational meanings 305, 307, 312, 868, 869
identity 185, 186, 195–198, 616–620, 625–633, 635–653, 655, 656, 660–666, 669–671, 673–675, 677–685, 705, 706, 887–890, 925–928, 985, 986, 1011–1016, 1041–1044, 1046–1052, 1071–1073, 1099, 1100, 1108–1112
  functions 133, 135, 152, 178, 231, 778, 923, 925
  negotiation 72, 170, 616, 625, 627, 670, 678–680, 706, 876, 965, 1046, 1047
  positioning 539, 616, 618, 627, 628, 632, 636, 646, 648, 661, 778, 1046
  processes 170, 195, 198, 435, 625, 626, 636, 640–643, 646, 648, 649, 705, 763, 887, 888, 1043, 1068, 1072, 1073, 1081
ideological models of literacy 892
IELTS (*see* International English Language Testing System) 474–480, 524
imagined communities 32, 34, 72, 197, 617, 618, 669–673, 675, 677–680, 887
imitation 245, 693, 696, 697, 880, 885, 1132
immersion education 110, 120, 121, 180, 181, 266, 268, 290
immigration 9, 80, 108, 109, 160, 172, 176, 182, 185–188, 190–195, 197, 198, 215, 220, 224, 259, 261, 502, 631, 641–643, 651, 652, 656, 657
  policy 9, 188
imperial
  language 13
  power 13, 18
imperialism 17, 18, 22, 23, 34, 35, 46, 50, 61, 63, 65, 71, 73, 84, 85, 128, 130, 135, 149, 152, 182, 213, 893, 894, 1097, 1098
implicit 4, 26–28, 31, 32, 214, 239, 244, 277, 287, 300, 353, 366, 376, 427, 512, 698, 699, 779, 783, 788, 789, 791–795, 1117, 1118
  knowledge 239, 244, 353, 354, 366, 376, 529, 764, 779, 783, 786, 788, 789, 791–793, 795, 936
  learning 27, 31, 32, 277, 287, 300, 354, 376, 533, 698, 757, 764, 779, 783, 784, 788, 792–795, 856, 1104
  roles 722, 1113, 1114
independent 8, 37, 39, 40, 113, 126, 137, 193, 195, 329, 352, 388, 394, 426, 427, 443, 444, 621, 721, 735, 736, 744, 788, 903

Subject Index

construction 195, 788, 790, 851
learning 37, 194, 329, 388, 426, 427, 620, 621, 735, 736, 744, 745, 788, 800, 837, 903, 1037, 1059
India 5, 16, 23, 24, 51–53, 55, 57, 59, 61, 124, 156, 188, 201, 241, 672, 1044
indigenous
languages 5, 34, 35, 37–47, 49, 157, 171, 179, 672, 755, 972
populations 453
individual
cognitive phenomenon 1024
plurilingualism 137, 147, 148
individualism 21, 27, 61, 180, 194, 441, 739, 889, 976, 1040
individualization 438, 739, 742, 743, 1114
individualized voice 881
individualizing discourse 1037
inductive analysis 980, 983
information 291–294, 312, 318–320, 405–407, 425–427, 429, 430, 434–436, 451–454, 477–480, 490–492, 507, 508, 688, 689, 766, 767, 771, 772, 784–793, 801, 897–904, 1113, 1114, 1118, 1137, 1138
Information and Communication Technologies (ICT) 622, 781, 891, 898, 907, 969, 1113
information
economy 4, 9, 621, 735, 893, 1113, 1114, 1118, 1121, 1122
literacy 319, 634, 704, 749, 756, 760, 764, 772, 791, 891, 895, 898–904, 914, 915, 972, 1015, 1052, 1122
revolution 492, 891, 897, 899
superhighway 895, 899
inhibitive silence 1093–1095
initial survival and exploration phase 1053
initiating 712, 850, 862, 865, 886, 890, 909, 1107
initiation-response-evaluation (IRE) 975
initiation-response-feedback (IRF) 708, 864
inner circle of countries 51
insider-outsider dichotomy 663
inquiry-based teaching 754
in-service 96, 284, 380, 466, 492, 687, 745, 953, 956, 959, 1058, 1067, 1072–1074, 1079, 1083, 1097, 1131, 1136
professional qualification program 1058

provision 96, 1072, 1073, 1079
trainees 953, 956, 1131
training 96, 380, 466, 745, 1073, 1074, 1131
institutional
discourses 648, 1043
talk 966, 1017, 1018
varieties of talk 966, 1017, 1025
instruction 3–11, 24–38, 40–46, 50–55, 66–72, 111, 112, 160–164, 212–215, 271–276, 278–291, 299–301, 319–321, 323, 324, 345–347, 380–383, 431–439, 696–699, 747–760, 797–800, 807–810
instructional
conversations 357, 358, 709
designers 1115, 1120
materials 195, 213, 330, 433, 738
methods 109, 162, 214, 222, 225, 915
technologies 756
instrumental value 727
integrated digitalization 902
integration 7, 50, 66, 90, 119, 123, 127, 128, 132, 139, 151, 185, 186, 232, 249–253, 256–258, 268, 271, 310, 311, 313–315, 1125, 1126, 1130
integrative 311, 314, 727, 751
evaluation 311, 314
value 727
integrator 1122
intelligence quotient (IQ) 244, 698, 699, 783, 794
intentions of introducing tests 522
interaction 275, 276, 278, 283, 284, 286, 287, 289–291, 293–296, 299–301, 627–629, 633, 634, 700–703, 707–710, 714–718, 751–755, 872, 873, 908, 909, 966, 975–977, 985, 986, 1017–1020, 1023–1030
interactional
behaviors 1017
hypothesis 275, 284
options 708
patterns 709, 716
scaffolding 705
interactionist sociolinguistics 1097
interactive 214, 255, 279, 285, 290, 291, 293, 294, 319, 346, 357, 420, 515, 529, 530, 658, 702, 707, 758–760, 765–767, 854, 855, 1026, 1027, 1128
approaches 214, 279, 285, 291, 357, 420,

421, 854, 855
process   214, 255, 515, 529, 658, 851, 855, 937, 952
teaching   215, 255, 279, 285, 357, 515, 529, 658, 702, 759, 766, 855, 937, 952, 1106
intercultural communication   128, 130, 142, 147, 150–152, 170, 639, 640, 646, 685, 690, 942, 1051, 1052, 1079, 1126
interculturality   1035, 1042
interdisciplinary   391, 400, 401, 403–405, 407, 409, 411, 719, 886, 1034
approach   403, 405, 407, 409, 411, 719
research   391, 400–404, 719, 886
interethnic communication   1079, 1081
intergenerational conflict   641
intergroup competition   722
interlanguage (IL)   30, 35, 47, 151, 240, 241, 274, 277, 286, 287, 292, 294, 296, 299, 300, 676, 785, 813, 824, 947–949, 1023, 1025, 1028
knowledge   241, 947, 948, 1023
speakers   240, 241, 277, 676, 824
internalization   437, 619, 631, 693, 695–698, 700
international   6–8, 19, 20, 34–36, 49, 50, 64, 65, 67–73, 77, 78, 110–116, 120, 121, 128–130, 132–135, 138, 140–152, 165–167, 169, 170, 181–183, 234, 379–389, 648–653, 1203, 1204
communication   17, 19, 32, 64, 66, 67, 115, 116, 129, 130, 132, 133, 138, 142, 146, 147, 149–152, 170, 247, 387, 525, 527, 685, 690, 911, 912
language   6–8, 19, 23, 32, 34–37, 49, 50, 64–66, 68–73, 110–113, 115, 116, 132–135, 140–152, 165–167, 181–183, 379–389, 455, 456, 520, 521, 525–527, 895, 896, 958
students   70, 71, 90, 96, 101, 112–115, 234, 314, 351, 352, 362, 379–389, 448, 474, 475, 651, 652, 658, 659, 664, 665, 690, 799, 804, 911, 912, 980
International English Language Testing System (IELTS)   474
internationalization   84, 125
Internet   4, 6, 64, 75, 84, 85, 100, 111, 169, 749, 755, 759–763, 765–774, 894–897, 901, 904, 905, 907, 913–917, 1114, 1117–1123, 1133–1135

communication   129, 673, 748, 749, 759, 762, 767, 861, 894, 896–898, 901, 904, 905, 907, 913, 915–917, 1127
interpersonal   239, 252, 305, 307, 353, 398, 430, 442, 616, 619, 620, 622, 706, 713, 714, 719, 720, 724, 731, 849, 850, 866, 869, 876
function   239, 619, 849, 850, 876
language   239, 252, 305, 353, 398, 442, 619, 620, 622, 623, 706, 713, 714, 719, 731, 849, 868, 869, 871, 876, 878, 879, 996, 1072, 1079
meanings   252, 868, 869
metafunctions   706, 849, 850
interpretative activity   1126
intertextual   539, 778, 876, 879, 880, 888, 1036
intertextuality   131, 397, 539, 756, 778, 781, 875, 879, 881, 883, 887–889, 930, 1047
intrinsic value   52, 727
intuitive practice   1075
investment   381, 408, 529, 625, 627, 628, 637, 651, 662, 669, 671, 678, 690, 986, 1041, 1051, 1054, 1089, 1099, 1100
involuntary minority groups   644
IQ (*see* intelligence quotient)   244, 698, 699, 783, 784
IRE (*see* Individual-Response-Evaluation)   915, 975, 979
IRF (*see* Individual-Response-Feedback)   708, 709, 711–713, 716, 909
sequence   712, 909, 986
IT industry professional   1115
iterative
analysis   983
process   995
IT-supported English language teaching   1127

J

Japan   5, 6, 21, 23, 63–67, 69–73, 78, 85, 156, 157, 170, 181, 301, 380, 412, 677–679, 742, 1028
Japanese identity   65, 73
joint construction   205, 851

K

K-12 school years   52
kindergartens (also pre-schools)   78

knowledge 303–309, 311–315, 317–320, 349–357, 365–369, 374–377, 397–404, 493–498, 522–524, 701–705, 739–741, 782–789, 791–795, 828–831, 938–942, 945–959, 965–969, 1068–1075, 1107–1112, 1125–1132
  about language (KAL) 101, 112, 282, 714, 740, 938, 946, 950, 953–959, 1005, 1006, 1108
  in action 469, 965, 995, 1070, 1075
  construction 130, 205, 303, 307, 309, 377, 396, 398, 402, 469, 537, 616, 650, 689, 697, 701, 705, 764, 765, 985, 1048, 1049
  economies 203
  framework 97, 190, 233, 301, 303, 306, 313, 315, 319, 320, 366, 369, 426, 495, 725, 766, 779, 792, 798, 883, 1105
  providers 1115
  structures (KSs) 92, 190, 233, 252, 268, 303–307, 309, 311, 313–315, 388, 395, 412, 425, 513, 621, 702, 707, 744, 766, 813, 814

L

L1 (*see* first language) 8, 9, 27–29, 33, 69, 71, 75, 76, 111, 112, 130, 132, 139, 143, 144, 152, 155, 156, 158, 159, 165, 218, 232, 238, 241–244, 246, 247, 255–257, 263, 264, 271, 274, 275, 280, 281, 311, 334–338, 340, 341, 343, 345, 346, 382, 402, 447, 542, 696, 697, 783, 785, 790, 791, 793, 794, 799, 802, 813–816, 818, 820, 821–824, 838, 846, 848, 885–887, 915, 950, 984
  acquisition 274, 790, 791
L2 (*see* second language) x, 8, 61, 68, 69, 72, 80, 111, 112, 132, 138, 143, 144, 155, 158, 159, 164, 231–233, 237–246, 253–256, 260, 263, 271–284, 303, 311, 333–339, 341–343, 345–347, 353, 393, 539, 615, 619, 639, 674, 676, 677, 693, 699, 701, 703–705, 708, 710, 712–714, 719–721, 727, 728, 753, 757, 763, 779, 780, 782–785, 788, 790–794, 800, 802, 811, 813–815, 817, 820, 821–824, 834, 838, 843, 845, 848, 854, 855, 885–887, 915, 945–947, 949–952, 954–956, 977, 980, 984, 1037, 1039, 1046, 1087
la langue 1034

la parole 1034
LA (*see* Language Awareness) 945–947, 950–954, 956
labial 813, 818
laggards 1116
laissez-faire leadership 724
language 3–11, 22–56, 63–73, 75–97, 107–116, 123–153, 155–167, 169–183, 188–228, 237–269, 271–293, 295–301, 333–341, 343–361, 379–389, 391–412, 415–440, 442–471, 473–485, 498–519
  acquisition 8, 155, 157, 158, 160–163, 165–167, 274–276, 284–290, 296–301, 333–335, 348–350, 516–518, 625, 626, 633–639, 783–787, 791–795, 824, 825, 839–841, 848, 849, 856, 857, 1025–1028
  acquisition process 8, 947
  analysis 31–36, 104, 286, 287, 310–314, 391, 392, 396, 449, 508–510, 517–519, 547, 548, 670–672, 868–870, 872, 873, 931–934, 952, 953, 966, 981–983, 1017, 1022–1025, 1027–1030
  analyst 132, 947, 1032
  assessment processes 419, 498, 505, 512, 514, 515
  awareness (LA) 49, 116, 147, 149, 151, 153, 159, 165, 167, 232, 237, 244, 286, 387, 433, 513, 945–949, 951–953, 955, 957–959
  benchmarking 404, 455, 457, 464, 469, 470
  choice 39, 44, 52, 88, 116, 128, 180, 203, 245, 260, 305–307, 310, 410, 445, 446, 460, 646, 647, 677, 847, 920, 921, 1127
  competence 66, 67, 115, 131, 133, 202, 239–241, 243, 244, 254, 255, 273, 274, 285–287, 317, 404, 410, 429, 436, 437, 475, 476, 672, 673, 717, 921, 922, 947
  context 6–9, 157–160, 199–201, 231–234, 252–256, 402, 403, 447, 454–457, 506, 621, 622, 637–639, 714–717, 737, 738, 777–781, 797–800, 849–851, 856, 857, 933, 937–942, 1005
  curriculum 6, 7, 87–89, 95–105, 110–114, 247–269, 365–369, 375–377, 403, 404, 406–408, 410–412, 437–440, 442–444, 454–456, 503, 504, 517–520, 757–760, 807–809, 1000–1002, 1015,

1016, 1101–1107
development   15, 16, 45–50, 87–91, 252–259, 286–292, 317–321, 334–338, 343–345, 372–377, 454–456, 481–484, 514–519, 697–702, 739–745, 797–802, 807–811, 967–972, 1067–1072, 1074–1083, 1101–1107
diversity   32, 127, 128, 132–134, 181, 182, 199–201, 208, 213–215, 261, 527, 666, 685, 690, 717, 767, 809, 810, 894, 921, 968, 969, 1000, 1001, 1099, 1100
ecology   7, 8, 11, 123, 127, 128, 134, 135, 182, 514, 632, 700, 893, 895, 985
education   31–52, 71–73, 103–105, 109–121, 164–167, 179–183, 255–258, 265–269, 453–456, 469–471, 688–690, 715–719, 957–959, 965–976, 984–986, 1047–1052, 1082–1085, 1097–1107, 1123–1127, 1136–1138
of empowerment   281, 666, 677, 689, 912, 996
features   111, 112, 141–146, 148, 232, 233, 253, 273, 274, 311, 320–322, 329, 330, 396–398, 410, 535, 538–540, 778, 789, 790, 812, 813, 851, 859–861, 933–938, 1078
function   8, 26, 124, 125, 131, 138, 146, 221, 232, 237, 239, 240, 292, 296, 297, 385, 419, 435, 508, 512, 619, 844, 849, 850
ideology   4, 6, 23–27, 29–36, 65, 82, 83, 103, 128, 130, 133, 170, 172, 174, 177, 180, 182, 183, 225, 261, 854, 856
of instruction   4–7, 11, 14, 25–34, 37, 38, 40–46, 48, 50–52, 55, 71, 75, 76, 111, 160, 161, 163, 164, 380, 439, 763, 798, 799, 808–810, 1085–1087
instructor   70, 194, 909, 1129
knowledge   93, 94, 243–246, 303–305, 311–315, 317–320, 352–355, 401–404, 522–524, 701–703, 739–741, 764–766, 782–789, 791–795, 811–814, 828–830, 945–951, 953–959, 965–969, 1068–1072, 1125–1127
learning   246–261, 283–288, 317–321, 327–331, 432–439, 510–520, 619–623, 625–640, 693–720, 733–745, 747–755, 757–761, 763–769, 934–943, 999–1007, 1009–1016, 1047–1052, 1099–1107, 1123–1128, 1131–1138

learning tasks   719, 738, 744
minority status   220, 642, 651
norms   35, 111, 123, 126–128, 130, 131, 140, 143, 146, 147, 149, 151, 165, 179, 232, 241, 330, 620, 722, 723, 781, 895, 897, 898
output   30, 118, 301, 319, 516, 615, 705, 708, 711, 717, 753, 757, 789, 848, 851, 857, 950
points   4–7, 9, 22, 26, 27, 32, 55, 65, 66, 92, 356–358, 537, 538, 626, 627, 632, 660, 661, 702, 705, 706, 708, 802, 803, 806, 807, 948, 949, 964, 965
policy   3–11, 33–40, 42–50, 71–73, 75, 76, 78, 79, 81–83, 127–129, 133–135, 146–149, 174, 175, 177, 178, 180–183, 199–201, 249, 250, 257–259, 262–265, 267–269, 467–471, 527–529
practices   5, 25–27, 38, 47–52, 232–234, 303, 313–315, 365–368, 391–394, 396–403, 487–489, 513–515, 616, 617, 625–637, 645–648, 887–889, 928, 929, 982–986, 1042–1044, 1049–1051
proficiency   65, 66, 101, 102, 110, 111, 155, 156, 158–166, 193–195, 223–226, 278–281, 349–354, 435–437, 458, 459, 469, 470, 473–479, 481–485, 487–489, 505–507, 528–530, 797–804, 806–809, 947, 948
proficiency testing   221, 470, 515
as a resource for meaning   305, 312, 315
socialization   83, 144, 231, 233, 303, 305, 633, 638, 641, 651, 652, 666, 670, 674, 759, 781, 854, 891, 892, 968, 978, 981–986
as system   950
systems   101, 102, 133, 158–160, 204, 256, 309, 416, 418–420, 444, 522, 523, 525, 527, 528, 688, 689, 753, 754, 786, 827, 847, 848, 895–897, 947, 1123, 1124
teacher   365–370, 415–423, 457–459, 461–471, 507–512, 514–520, 630–635, 707–713, 741–745, 861–864, 898–901, 945–959, 966–972, 994–996, 999–1002, 1066–1072, 1074–1085, 1102–1108, 1123–1129, 1136–1138
teacher development programs   83, 1074, 1079
teacher education   49, 50, 257, 284, 285,

Subject Index 1185

376, 377, 417, 421–423, 433, 461, 462, 469–471, 916, 917, 957–959, 963–972, 1002, 1015, 1016, 1082–1085, 1097–1099, 1125–1127, 1129, 1131–1133, 1136–1138
  teaching 37–52, 77–97, 99–105, 111–116, 146–153, 223–227, 231–234, 271–291, 297–301, 365–369, 517–525, 930–942, 945–959, 967–972, 999–1007, 1009–1016, 1047–1052, 1075–1085, 1099–1112, 1123–1129
  user 39, 84, 128, 132, 152, 214, 240–247, 426, 443, 748, 754, 762, 871, 896, 913, 947, 953, 966, 1051
  varieties 3, 25–33, 35, 51, 78, 107, 115, 133, 141, 142, 147, 149, 150, 152, 156, 157, 250, 526–528, 767, 859, 863, 895, 896, 966
large scale testing (*see also* assessment) 487
large-scale corpora 854
late majority 1116
leadership styles 719, 724, 726
learner 274, 275, 277, 278, 291, 292, 422–425, 431–434, 488–491, 498–501, 506–511, 514–519, 615–617, 619–623, 724–728, 736–745, 750, 752–754, 833–835, 845, 846, 902, 903, 948–953, 1127–1129
  achievement 212, 225, 321, 337, 339, 348, 350, 434, 489, 494, 506, 508, 509, 515, 518, 616, 626, 650, 719, 730, 731, 1101
  autonomy 277, 620, 621, 728, 734, 736–745, 750, 759, 760
  beliefs 725, 727, 739, 740, 743, 745, 950, 952
  development 159, 238, 255, 274, 277, 292, 296, 320, 336, 424, 425, 431, 432, 444, 500, 515–519, 546, 616, 618, 619, 717, 739–743, 745
  identities 196, 616, 617, 620, 629, 632, 636, 639, 642, 644–646, 648, 649, 670, 671, 676, 898, 900, 1111
  learnability 784
  training 196, 432, 437, 517, 518, 621, 734, 739, 742, 743, 745, 951–953, 955, 1120
  learner-centered 28, 92, 162, 272, 275, 277, 278, 281, 320, 493, 731, 742, 902, 910,

1042, 1127, 1129
  activities 278, 493, 902
  approaches 28, 162, 1127
  teaching 128, 275, 277
learner-centeredness 750
learner-computer interaction 754
learner-learner interaction 754
learner-text interaction 754
learning 246–255, 299–301, 317–321, 327–331, 432–439, 487–503, 510–520, 619–623, 625–637, 699–720, 733–745, 747–755, 757–761, 763–769, 836–841, 999–1006, 1009–1013, 1099–1111, 1120–1129, 1131–1138
  activity 115, 134, 231, 259, 511, 512, 515, 619, 629, 630, 635, 637, 638, 693–695, 697–699, 705, 727, 728, 765, 766, 845, 855, 947, 948, 953, 976
  contexts 10, 11, 32, 33, 90, 203, 204, 207–209, 215, 317, 318, 367, 377, 393, 506, 507, 519, 520, 616, 617, 633–635, 672, 714–716, 891, 892, 934, 935, 1005–1007, 1126–1128
  management systems 1117
  strategies 94, 97, 101, 203, 204, 208–210, 233, 246, 247, 252–254, 317–321, 328–331, 429, 511, 728, 729, 739, 740, 759, 760, 802, 803, 833, 834, 837–840, 1107, 1108, 1110, 1111
  style coordinators 1115
  styles 207, 374, 387, 412, 490, 500, 627, 716, 719, 735, 750, 759, 861, 937, 950, 1123
  teaching 90, 91, 93–97, 99–101, 231–234, 280–288, 299–301, 491–496, 747–754, 831–837, 855–858, 934–942, 967–972, 999–1007, 1009–1016, 1047–1052, 1055–1057, 1061–1065, 1075–1081, 1099–1108, 1123–1128
learning-to-teach studies 1126, 1131
legibility conditions 847, 848
legitimate peripheral participation 628, 637, 700, 941, 1050
LEP (*see* limited English proficiency) xxi, xxii, 217, 222, 266, 683, 971, 1037
level of development 725, 849
lexemes 789, 790, 829
lexical
  entry 789
  feedback signals 866

items 91, 131, 697, 790, 847, 853
knowledge 793, 830, 831, 839
lexico-grammar 850
lexicon 4, 20, 165, 635, 789, 790, 795, 841, 847, 866, 867, 898
lexis 205, 273, 306, 310, 513, 536, 540, 710, 777, 853, 869, 876
lifelong learning 515, 517, 518, 743, 1203
Likert-scale 640
limited English proficiency (LEP) 266, 351, 676, 1037, 1093
linear
  order 790
  reading 792
lingua franca 7, 8, 76, 107, 108, 110, 111, 123, 124, 128, 130, 132, 133, 135–141, 143, 145–153, 156, 158, 167, 240, 415, 526, 527, 777, 870, 895
linguistic 6–8, 32–35, 113–115, 125–142, 158–161, 199–202, 273–276, 279–281, 334–339, 399–403, 533–540, 681, 682, 688–691, 843–846, 851–854, 893, 894, 907–911, 1085, 1086, 1088–1091, 1096–1099
  anthropology 646, 1034
  awareness 47, 108, 131, 133, 140, 147, 151, 159, 160, 167, 232, 234, 237, 242, 303, 388, 782, 945, 948, 949, 957–959, 1094
  capital 132, 133, 176, 380, 397, 688, 893, 1036, 1088, 1089, 1093
  colonialism 17–19, 23, 35, 50, 61, 85, 531, 1088, 1097, 1098
  competence 7, 67, 77, 115, 126, 128, 131, 133, 240, 244, 273, 274, 285, 392, 410, 509, 544, 545, 632, 676, 779, 823, 824
  corpora 397, 777, 779
  and cultural backgrounds 356
  description 137, 139, 141, 305, 309, 514, 840, 844, 861, 936, 1039
  discrimination 29, 32, 50, 182, 257, 335, 815, 825, 968, 1085, 1098, 1099
  diversity 7, 10, 35, 63, 69, 123, 127, 128, 132–134, 136, 149, 182, 199, 200, 207, 208, 213, 223, 684, 685, 690, 767, 893, 894, 968, 969
  factors 129, 201, 223, 334, 335, 400, 534, 755, 948, 1036
  features 108, 141, 146, 158, 273, 279, 309, 320, 392, 395, 397, 410, 534, 535,
538–540, 778, 845, 846, 851, 852, 861, 933, 935, 936
  identities 30, 198, 200, 216, 227, 387, 539, 616, 618, 625, 626, 646, 648, 671, 675, 682, 689, 690, 706, 778, 1098, 1099, 1111
  imperialism 17, 18, 22, 23, 34, 35, 46, 50, 61, 63, 65, 71, 73, 84, 85, 128, 130, 135, 149, 152, 182, 227, 893, 894, 1097, 1098
  input 163, 274, 275, 279, 539, 630, 754, 757, 778, 802, 848, 851, 949, 1028
  models 34, 45, 73, 135, 147, 161, 167, 255, 273, 410, 512, 533, 534, 539, 786, 958, 1046, 1099, 1115
  pluralism 175, 1040
  practices 41, 47, 48, 50, 61, 77, 84, 305, 392, 400–403, 513, 514, 533, 534, 625, 626, 630, 632, 634, 635, 646, 647, 684, 893, 894, 1088, 1098, 1099
  profile 41, 199
  repertoires 147, 630
  resources 6, 7, 79, 147, 209, 241, 305, 309, 387, 397, 512, 514, 618, 625, 626, 630, 634, 635, 684, 685, 704, 851, 852, 920, 1088
  socialization 305, 534, 641, 651, 854, 968
  tensions 7, 47, 1085, 1086, 1088, 1089, 1091, 1093, 1096, 1097
  units 115, 392, 694, 812, 844, 935
  variation 29, 30, 140, 141, 399, 400, 940, 941
linguistically deficient 673
linguistically-mixed groups 1092, 1095, 1096
linguists 3, 4, 31, 34, 69, 126, 139, 239, 271–276, 278, 282, 545, 699, 702, 783, 784, 787, 844, 856, 859, 1025, 1026, 1033
listening
  comprehension 77, 318, 331, 476, 480, 658, 759
  skills pedagogy 866
literacies (also multiple literacies) 36, 83, 86, 180, 312–314, 394, 399–402, 650, 666, 690, 749, 758, 761, 781, 875–877, 883, 884, 888–895, 897, 898, 900–905, 1122, 1123
literacy 27–29, 33–36, 199–210, 260–262,

Subject Index 1187

350–358, 387, 388, 399–402, 443–445, 455, 456, 517–519, 632–638, 681–686, 689–691, 716–718, 763–767, 875–878, 883–905, 914–916, 940–942, 1011–1015
  acquisition 27, 29, 210, 284, 285, 388, 518, 547, 626, 633, 634, 636, 637, 666, 716, 717, 758, 800, 839, 857, 878, 886, 890, 984
    to adults 9, 1122
  education 34–37, 42, 44, 196, 197, 209, 210, 227, 259, 260, 267, 268, 313, 444, 455, 456, 689, 690, 716–718, 809, 887–891, 898, 902–905, 930, 1014, 1015, 1110–1112
  learning 204–210, 260–262, 284, 285, 303, 447, 517–519, 615, 616, 626, 629, 632–638, 690, 691, 716–718, 749, 757–760, 763, 764, 773, 774, 856–858, 890–892, 900–905, 1011–1014
  pedagogy 34, 85, 205, 208, 225, 285, 547, 616, 618, 635, 637, 650, 666, 686, 689–691, 763–767, 774, 887, 888, 903–905, 971, 972
  practices 27, 55, 58, 61, 391, 392, 400, 401, 518, 534, 618, 629, 633–637, 646, 647, 684, 685, 876, 877, 883–886, 891–893, 903–905, 922, 928, 982–984
local articulations 1035, 1037
localization 76
localized pedagogical expertise 81
logocentric context 922
longitudinal study 182, 369, 510, 840
low-proficiency 791
low-track mainstream classes 979

M

mainstream 10, 203–205, 207–212, 216–221, 223–225, 234, 249–255, 257–269, 313–315, 343–346, 365–369, 373, 375–377, 381, 383, 384, 674–677, 978, 979, 985, 986, 1104–1109, 1111, 1112
  approach 209, 251–253, 257, 265, 267, 314, 331, 389, 1026, 1104
  curriculum 10, 146, 199, 200, 204, 207, 209, 210, 212, 232, 234, 248–253, 255–269, 313, 314, 343, 365–369, 375–377, 701, 979, 980, 1101, 1104, 1111, 1112

mainstreaming 207, 217, 257–259, 314, 369, 377, 969, 979, 1101, 1104, 1108, 1109, 1112
managerial role 1129
mandated assessment policies 510
marginalization 131, 179, 525–527, 617, 641, 642, 644, 810, 965, 981, 983, 1037, 1068, 1074, 1079
meaning-based instruction 275, 276
meaning-focused activity 948
measure of language proficiency 505
mediated
  action 628–630
  classroom practices 625
medium
  of communication 138, 170, 200
  of education 44, 701
  of instruction 4–6, 14, 25–29, 31–34, 38, 41–45, 48, 50–52, 71, 92, 111, 135, 164, 256, 351, 352, 417, 439, 462, 803, 809, 810
mentor teacher 321, 754, 1064, 1118
mentoring 321, 754, 1061
message redundancy 710
metacognitive 118, 158, 254, 328, 728, 738, 740, 745, 839, 884, 886, 948
  awareness 738, 884, 948
  control strategies 728, 729
  knowledge 158, 740, 745, 947, 948
metadiscourse 394, 538, 547, 778, 864
metalanguage 397, 547, 766, 938, 951
metalinguistic
  awareness 162, 163, 167, 247, 705, 948, 951, 957
  knowledge 469, 705, 791, 957, 958
metaphoric roles 969, 1113–1115
methodology 27, 29, 30, 61, 84, 100, 105, 116, 191, 192, 194, 220, 246, 247, 274, 285–287, 300, 759, 760, 973, 974, 1002, 1017, 1018, 1082, 1083, 1120
microcontexts 875
micro-ethnographic approach 1022
micro-level
  acts 864
  analyses 973, 974, 976, 977, 983
middle ground 1038
migration (*see also* immigration) 32, 57, 181, 186, 198, 400, 653, 656, 657, 666, 1079
minimalist program 846–848

minimum language standards 464
minority stereotype 648
mixed
  methods 983
  mode 1121
mode 242, 292, 305, 311, 500, 534–536, 538, 540, 545, 546, 620, 704, 710, 725, 726, 737, 741, 778, 779, 849, 850, 920–922, 924, 925, 929
  continuum 704, 710, 778
model
  minority 644, 648, 651, 1099
  texts 937
modeling 205, 206, 246, 320, 323, 329, 535, 704, 722, 723, 759, 794, 795, 851, 914, 942, 1034
modernism 189, 891
modes of facilitation 725
modifier 1122
modularity issue 784
monitoring
  acquisition 621, 736
  work 1096
monocultural instruction 707
monoculturalism 130, 131, 618, 678
monolingual 5, 8, 10, 18, 37, 110, 127, 128, 138, 158–160, 162, 201, 211, 224, 231, 237, 240–243, 280, 634, 635, 675, 676, 683, 684
monologic instruction 707
morphology 335, 697, 705, 753, 780, 814, 823, 844, 846
mother tongue (*see* language) xxii, 4, 5, 15, 22, 31, 34, 35, 37, 41–43, 46, 47, 49, 52, 107, 115, 131, 138, 164, 167, 173, 188, 215, 216, 232, 234, 238, 247, 257, 260, 333, 338, 339, 340, 341, 343, 345–347, 350, 351, 379, 380, 381–385, 387, 388, 534, 787, 790, 861
motivating classroom
  environment 719–721, 723, 725, 727, 729, 731
motivation 93, 94, 138, 142, 150, 162, 201, 216, 255, 256, 283, 522, 620, 621, 652, 669, 670, 707, 726–729, 731, 742, 743, 752, 911, 912, 1063, 1064
motivational
  dimensions 728
  psychology 620, 719, 726, 729
  teaching practice 719, 726, 729

motivators 1115
moves 4, 65, 96, 123, 171, 173, 175, 177, 180, 206, 291, 308, 410, 490, 616, 712, 716, 855, 862–864, 883
multicultural
  contexts 348
  education 652, 689, 690, 706, 713, 717, 1100, 1102
  language 690, 986
  urban classrooms 632
multiculturalism 176, 180, 186, 189, 190, 197, 198, 265, 268, 893, 895, 901, 976, 1006, 1015, 1016, 1039, 1040, 1044, 1047, 1049, 1050, 1102
multiethnic schools 203, 1093
multilingual
  approach 46, 47
  authors 677
  classrooms 210, 268, 678, 941, 1093, 1094, 1111
  communities 160, 689, 1088
  contexts 201, 203, 204, 208, 209, 258, 386, 894, 1047, 1051, 1086
  education 165–167, 1097
  literacies 892, 905
  and multicultural 5, 37, 40, 45, 47, 63, 64, 66, 72, 166, 167, 210, 303, 524, 618, 679, 688
  policy 48, 49
  schools 160, 208, 968, 1049, 1085–1088, 1091, 1093, 1094, 1097–1099
  speaker 158, 159, 676
multilingualism 7, 45–47, 49, 50, 64, 114, 123, 127, 135, 137, 147, 148, 150, 151, 159, 165–167, 169, 170, 201, 263, 264, 679, 680, 892–894, 901, 902, 1051
multiliteracies 650, 683, 684, 690, 764, 766, 767, 774, 778, 781, 808, 891–893, 895, 897–901, 903–905, 919, 920, 927–930, 939, 940
Multiliteracies Project 808, 920, 928, 929
multimedia 6, 100, 309, 735, 748, 751, 758, 760, 767, 781, 901, 905, 907, 912–914, 929, 939, 984, 1117, 1118, 1128
  center teacher 1117
  literacies 914
multimodal
  assessment 929
  classrooms 921, 930
  contexts 891

discourse 781, 919, 930
pedagogies 779, 782, 919–923, 925–929, 1052
work 928
multimodalism 893, 896, 902
multimodality 312, 415, 778, 781, 854, 897, 904, 919, 922, 926–929
multiple 8, 9, 158, 170, 256, 257, 395, 396, 418, 449, 460, 530, 544, 545, 632, 636, 637, 645–647, 656, 657, 892, 893, 904, 905, 919–922, 975, 976, 984–986, 1098, 1099
choice questions 474, 656
cultural identities 170, 645, 646
identities 9, 170, 387, 616, 618, 625, 626, 632, 636, 637, 645–647, 649, 651, 657, 669, 671, 677, 885, 985, 986, 1033, 1098, 1099, 1111
language 8, 9, 158, 170, 256, 257, 303, 317, 423, 460, 469, 525, 529, 530, 627, 628, 632, 669, 767, 779, 857, 919–922, 941, 1098, 1099
linguistic codes 625, 634
literacies 400, 877, 892, 904, 905, 941, 1099, 1122
semiotic modes 779, 919, 920
sources of authority 1068
worlds 626, 637, 893, 904, 921, 968, 1087, 1089, 1098
multiskilled individuals 1120
mundane conversation 1017

N

narratives 23, 69, 252, 523, 627, 630, 635, 648, 650, 651, 653, 869, 879, 895, 933, 980, 1003, 1005, 1009, 1012–1015, 1043
nasal 813, 821
national assessment 193, 512
National Council for Accreditation of Teacher Education (NCATE) 1125, 1138
for Language in Education (NCLE) 946
national identities 671, 672
National Literacy Strategy (NLS) 204, 207, 210, 1111
native speaker competence 241
native-like pronunciation 68, 353, 815
native-speaker (NS) (*see also* near-native speakers) 8, 127, 139, 140, 143, 148, 231, 385, 756, 782, 801, 945, 954, 957, 1037, 1072
fallacy 954
nativism 784, 793
naturalistic 510, 824, 863, 864, 870, 964, 974, 994, 1034, 1121
enquiry 994
patterns 864, 964
spoken materials 870
nature of test performance 505
NCATE (*see* National Council for Accreditation of Teacher Education) 1125, 1138
NCLB (*see* No Child Left Behind) 10, 11, 211, 212–215, 222–226, 416, 491, 497
NCLE (*see* National Council for Language in Education) 946, 958
near-native speakers (*see also* native-speakers) 240, 246, 815
needs analysis 235, 391, 392, 406, 411, 478, 617, 658, 665, 883
research 658
negotiation of meaning 143, 146, 170, 281, 291, 292, 296, 297, 299, 300, 634, 705, 708, 711, 754, 851, 1030, 1060, 1127
neo-behaviorist discipline 694
neo-colonialism 17, 22
neologisms 898, 1035
Netherlands 73, 124, 127, 157, 389, 483, 758–760, 783, 824, 959, 984, 986
neurobiological function 786
neurocognitive
mechanics 793
studies 788
new literacies 891, 892, 900, 904, 905, 1099
New London Group 684, 690, 766, 767, 774, 892, 903, 905, 920
new rhetoric 401, 539, 547, 778, 782, 931–934, 936, 941, 942
New Zealand 156, 157, 186, 379, 418, 424, 473, 474, 525, 1050
nihilism 1044
NNS (*see* non-native speaker) 78, 79, 80, 945, 947, 949, 950, 952, 954, 955, 956, 1037, 1042
nomadology 1035, 1048
non-accent 1094
non-native 84, 85, 134, 135, 139–143, 146–148, 150–152, 156, 157, 166, 167,

242, 243, 291, 384, 458, 676, 814–817, 870, 871, 876, 877, 880, 881, 885, 942, 957, 958, 1027, 1028
dialects 870
speaker (NNS) 78, 151, 242, 278, 291, 300, 676, 820, 885, 1027, 1028
speaker (NNS) teachers 78, 886
users 140, 146, 867, 871
norm 10, 30, 78, 128, 149, 158, 159, 199, 200, 241, 245, 324, 328, 330, 339, 416, 424, 489, 494, 495, 617, 722, 723, 968, 969
norm-building procedure 723
norm-referenced testing 495
North American functionalists 849
noun phrase (NP) 784, 847
NP (*see* noun phrase) 784, 847
NS (*see* native-speakers) 75–82, 945, 949, 954, 955, 956, 1027
nuclear exchange 712
numerator 1024, 1025

O

objectives-driven curricula 423
observation 16, 43, 104, 139, 142, 147, 174, 252, 272, 274, 288, 315, 356, 452, 642, 643, 659, 988, 1013, 1044, 1045, 1061
Office for Standards in Education (OFSTED), England 268, 455, 1103, 1112
official
 curricula (*see* curriculum) 109
 language of instruction 1087
 language (*see* language) xxiii, 6, 9, 33, 37, 39, 40, 42, 43, 44, 46, 51, 65, 66, 71–73, 78, 84, 108, 110, 148, 155, 157, 161, 162, 172, 175, 176, 180, 182, 185, 186, 188, 189, 190, 524, 525, 527, 921, 1087
 participatory rights 707
online 246, 481, 748–750, 753–755, 758–761, 777, 784, 786, 787, 829, 833, 840, 860, 896, 897, 899, 900, 905, 907–909, 913–917, 951, 1114–1123, 1137, 1138
 communications 896, 913, 916, 1118, 1137
 contact 1119
 degree programs 1115
 discussion 749, 755, 908, 909, 914, 915, 1114, 1115, 1117
 education 759–761, 899, 905, 915, 917, 1114–1116, 1118, 1119, 1137, 1138
 learning environments 1117, 1120
 tutorial 1115
online-forum 900, 1135
open-ended questions 979
opposition 22, 33, 61, 174, 395, 463, 636, 661, 664, 666, 672, 937, 984, 1039, 1098
oppositional stance 1116
optimal
 language learning 701
 leadership style 620, 724
oral
 academic presentations 977
 assessment 463
 proficiency 79, 80, 278, 279, 312, 314, 324, 483–485, 502, 519, 868, 873
 proficiency interview 312, 868
ordinary conversation 966, 1017–1019, 1025
orientalism 13, 18, 21, 79, 85, 1051, 1098, 1100
orthographic input 791
outcomes-based
 approach 442
 assessment 445, 454, 461, 469, 513, 518, 999
 curriculum 440, 445
outer circle 51, 61, 120, 141, 151, 156, 167, 958
overt correction 790

P

packages 386, 702, 1118, 1119
palatal 811, 818, 819, 824
 fricatives 819
 stops 818, 819, 824
panel chair 1058–1061, 1064
paper-and-pencil tests 418, 460, 465, 467
paradigmatic assumptions 1034
paralinguistic 425, 1039
parallel distributed processing (PDP) 786
parameters theory 846
participatory
 action research 992, 995, 999, 1000, 1002
 model 500
patterns 3, 17, 21, 89, 243, 290, 294, 303,

308, 312, 335, 361, 394, 453, 454, 616, 709, 716, 785, 786, 853, 854, 975, 976
pedagogic 55, 130, 146, 153, 204–206, 210, 250, 251, 254, 256, 261–265, 294, 297–301, 368, 391, 445–447, 533, 534, 543, 948, 949, 1070, 1071, 1073–1075
  appropriacy 393
  content knowledge (PCK) 366, 368, 374, 948
  freedom 265
  grammars 787, 844, 845
  imperialism 1070, 1073
  knowledge 205, 256, 261, 265, 303, 366, 368, 374, 376, 447, 513, 787, 948, 949, 951, 967, 1069–1071, 1073–1075
  potential 146, 294, 951, 1075
  relations 366, 376
  structure 205, 299, 301, 844
pedagogies of transformation 1037, 1043
pedagogy 48, 49, 83–85, 249–255, 285–287, 618, 619, 684–687, 689–691, 715, 716, 763–768, 774, 840, 841, 866–871, 903–905, 919–921, 926–929, 970–972, 1041–1044, 1046–1051, 1081–1083, 1104–1107
peer 202, 216, 217, 233, 311, 329, 340, 347, 353, 418, 516, 517, 628–630, 642, 645, 647, 651, 909–911, 981, 983–985, 1087–1089, 1104, 1105
  groups 329, 347, 628, 642, 645
  social capital 1087–1089
  teaching 202, 418, 494, 517, 661, 726, 801, 916, 969, 1085, 1104, 1105
peer-feedback 909, 910
perception 40, 66, 133, 185, 186, 201, 247, 307, 350, 352, 392, 489, 501, 541, 542, 621, 660, 694, 695, 780, 794, 795, 817–819, 822–824
performance 99, 292–294, 296–301, 327–329, 339, 340, 407–410, 416–418, 421–426, 428, 431–434, 436–438, 440–444, 452, 456–461, 473–480, 482–485, 488–491, 497–500, 505–508, 698–700
  criteria 425, 431, 461, 479, 498, 500, 507, 513, 1096
  standards 97, 98, 120, 223, 339, 416, 417, 421–424, 428, 431, 433, 434, 436–444, 447, 449, 452, 458, 461, 479, 497, 498, 507, 510, 513

performance-based curriculum 428, 437
performative utterances 1037
performativity 984, 1035–1037, 1051, 1071, 1074, 1077, 1082
permanent residents 63, 657
personal
  autonomy 733, 745
  literacies 892
phatic exchanges 864
phenomenological approach 1018
phonemes 786, 787, 790, 815–817, 821
  coronal phonemes 817
phonetic information 791
phonetics 89, 94, 97, 247, 791, 824, 1059
  epenthetic vowel 822, 823
phonological
  structure 811, 812
  theory 811, 821, 825
phonology 131, 135, 143–145, 151, 167, 219, 247, 273, 335, 616, 777, 779, 780, 799, 800, 811, 813, 815, 817, 819, 821, 823–825
  allophones 815
  alveolar distinction 818, 819
  alveolar ridge 818
pivot move 712
place of articulation 813
placement 193, 209, 354, 358, 478, 504, 506, 523, 655, 664, 665, 683, 1104
plagiarism 781, 875, 876, 879, 880, 883, 885, 887–889, 907, 909, 913, 914, 916
plan 6, 78, 95, 128, 133, 134, 185, 192, 197, 203, 242, 293, 319, 343, 357, 365, 366, 404, 423, 789, 790, 1075, 1135, 1136
policy directions 63, 65, 67, 69, 71, 73
political 4, 5, 17–19, 31–36, 39–41, 76–78, 87, 88, 123, 126, 127, 161, 171–178, 185, 186, 257, 393–395, 521–523, 630, 631, 662, 663, 893–897, 996, 1040, 1044, 1045
population mobility 199, 200
portfolio assessment (*see* assessment) 420, 490, 493, 494, 498, 509
positivism (*see also* empirical research) 395, 1035, 1071
positivist research 1039
positivistic
  assumptions 966, 1034
  inquiry 1034

postcolonial
  contexts 141, 661, 671, 672
postcolonialism (*see also*
  colonialism) 1044
Postgraduate Certificate in Education
  (PCED) 1058
post-alveolar segments 817
post-method pedagogy 272, 282, 286
postmodern
  literacies 898, 902
  perspectives 645, 1040, 1083
postmodernism 645, 646, 652, 669, 891,
  1035, 1044, 1046, 1048, 1051, 1052
postsecondary
  contexts 655
  institutions 617, 655–657, 660, 665
  settings 655–657, 659–661, 663, 665,
    667
poststructural
  ideas 1037, 1041, 1046
  researchers 1042
  teachers 1043, 1045
poststructuralism 639, 669, 976,
  1033–1035, 1037–1039, 1041,
  1043–1047, 1049, 1051
poststructuralist theory 632, 638, 653, 690,
  1052
practical classroom teaching 1054
practice 199, 200, 204–208, 262–265, 271–
  273, 275–279, 303–308, 502–505,
  516–519, 625–630, 635–638, 716–719,
  741–744, 758–760, 892–895, 953–959,
  963–965, 997–999, 1044–1052, 1073–
  1084, 1108–1112
practitioner research 28, 987, 1000
pragmatic
  competence 151, 239, 273, 717
  functionalism 849
PRC (*see* China) 89
prefix 813, 836
preschools (*see* kindergarten) 85, 220, 352,
  675, 982, 1100
prescriptive 376, 394, 416, 423, 448, 812,
  937, 967, 1064, 1110
preservice 356, 376, 517, 687, 777,
  951–953, 956, 1001, 1016, 1097, 1125,
  1131, 1137
  courses 777, 952, 953, 956, 1125, 1131
  teachers 356, 376, 517, 951, 953, 1001,
    1097, 1125, 1131, 1137

TEFL training (*see* teaching English as a
  foreign language) 951
  trainees 951, 953, 956, 1131
  training 356, 376, 517, 777, 951–953,
    1131, 1137
primary
  language 166, 218, 349, 354, 363, 454,
    513, 880, 1085, 1086, 1095, 1096
  schools (*see* elementary schools) 6, 41,
    42, 87, 88, 93, 95, 96, 99, 104, 133,
    159, 162–164, 166, 204, 288, 442, 463,
    464, 468, 510, 519, 547, 798, 803–805,
    807, 869, 923, 946, 957, 1055, 1062,
    1066, 1111, 1112
Prism Model 333–335, 337, 338, 341–347
private speech 693, 696, 697, 700
problem-based learning 903
problem-posing 618, 686, 902, 1043
procedural
  dimensions 953, 955, 956
  TLA (*see* teacher language awareness)
    955
procedures 118, 147, 187, 193, 202, 205,
  272, 274, 282, 289, 298, 418, 419, 451,
  459, 460, 507, 509, 510, 530, 1076–
  1078, 1103, 1104, 1126–1128
process of self-regulation 146
process-oriented 713, 719, 1077, 1104
professional
  autonomy 946, 1079
  development 112, 113, 209, 210, 356,
    358, 372–376, 381, 386, 418–420,
    431–433, 435, 436, 443, 491, 492, 494,
    495, 497–500, 967, 968, 1052–1057,
    1059–1068, 1070, 1076–1078, 1083
  evaluation 458
  identity 368, 967, 969, 1067, 1071, 1073,
    1078–1081, 1111
  knowledge 404, 410, 412, 449, 512, 846,
    957, 968, 969, 1015, 1082, 1101, 1105,
    1108–1111
  participation 1043
  relationships 203
  standards 207, 210, 315, 416, 433, 443,
    470, 474, 476, 946, 953–955, 969,
    1107
professionalism 130, 131, 404, 433, 435,
  437, 441, 946, 968, 1067, 1069, 1072,
  1074, 1076, 1079, 1080, 1082, 1083
proficiency 65, 66, 79–81, 110, 111, 155,

Subject Index 1193

156, 158–166, 193–195, 216–219, 221–226, 278–281, 349–354, 435–437, 452–455, 458, 459, 469, 470, 473–479, 481–485, 487–489, 505–507, 797–804, 806–809
program standards 421, 431, 437, 438
project learning 739
pronunciation 29, 68, 78, 143, 151, 166, 246, 335, 353, 425, 465, 466, 541, 634, 780, 800, 812, 814, 815, 822–825, 829, 1057
proposition 33, 172, 175, 259, 261–263, 265, 266, 268, 341, 343–345, 348, 535, 695, 798, 843, 852
prosody 781, 859
prototypicality 932
psychoanalytic theories 632, 641
psycholinguistics 151, 152, 166, 247, 248, 280, 295, 694, 794, 795, 843, 855, 1034
 psycholinguistic approach, perspective 233, 289
psychometric 415, 419, 475, 482, 504, 507, 511–514, 520, 522, 640, 973
psychosocial
 processes 640
 theorists 641
public examinations 465, 467, 1088
pushed language 712

Q

qualitative research 298, 506, 518, 760, 886, 964, 965, 973–975, 978, 983–986, 994, 1014, 1016, 1027, 1097, 1126
quality assurance 945, 1060, 1061, 1086
quantitative research 964, 974–976, 1024
queer theory 1041, 1050

R

racial
 conflict 191
 minority groups 642
 tensions 1085, 1086, 1088, 1092–1095, 1097
racialized discourses 1093
racism 29, 31, 80, 85, 189, 197, 198, 201, 315, 644, 650, 926–928, 968, 976, 982, 1044, 1085, 1095, 1097, 1098, 1102
rational thinking 695
real-time communication 779, 907

recounts 305, 869, 933
reductionist curriculum (*see* curriculum) 703, 706
reference grammars (*see* grammar) 844, 845
reflection 118, 213, 215, 258, 303, 304, 320, 358, 373, 374, 386, 453, 494, 507, 523, 546, 621, 686, 698, 1035, 1074–1077, 1082, 1083
reflective
 conversation 754, 760, 1075
 methods 741
 practice 873, 959, 1067, 1074–1078, 1084
 practitioner 741, 1066, 1083
 thinking 1075
reflexivity 966, 978, 1041, 1043–1045, 1069, 1078, 1080
regional variation 950
register 158, 169, 243, 246, 307, 353, 359, 400, 425, 429, 465, 704, 705, 709, 710, 715, 716, 830, 833, 845, 857, 871, 941, 942
 of science 705
register-meshing 709
re-imagining 689
re-intermediation 1121, 1122
relational imitation 1132
remedial 206, 219, 345, 347, 381, 644, 682, 883
 students 345, 883
repair practices 966, 1017, 1018
representation 171, 309, 311, 644, 645, 647, 648, 651, 663, 664, 759, 781–785, 787, 788, 792, 793, 817, 823, 847, 881, 919–922, 924, 925, 928, 929, 984, 1033
representational resources 684, 779, 919, 920, 922, 924, 928, 929
research 25–29, 104, 105, 286–291, 297–301, 393–406, 410–412, 481–484, 517–520, 633–637, 655–658, 715–720, 757–760, 963–968, 972–979, 981–1003, 1005–1011, 1013–1016, 1023–1029, 1074–1077, 1130–1136
resistance 4, 22, 42, 64, 80, 83–85, 128, 374, 449, 637, 648, 651, 652, 661, 664, 669, 671, 678, 679, 689, 980–982, 1043–1045
response 80, 81, 178, 254–256, 287, 288,

475, 543, 544, 666, 708, 807, 862, 864, 872, 889, 897, 898, 915, 916, 920, 921, 932–934, 987, 1027–1029, 1074, 1075
responsibility   10, 34, 48, 52, 96, 112, 191, 192, 194, 207, 216, 355, 363, 366, 481, 742, 743, 1069, 1070, 1079, 1103, 1107, 1128, 1129
retrospective self-evaluation   620, 727, 729
rewards   26, 212, 222, 223, 226, 491, 721, 728–730, 833, 878, 998
rhetoric   14, 15, 17, 19, 58, 76, 79, 80, 127, 264, 391, 392, 394, 395, 401, 402, 538, 539, 547, 844, 931–934, 936, 938, 940–942, 1047, 1048, 1119, 1120
rhetorical
  analyses   392, 395
  purpose   852, 932
  structure   933
role identity   1097
roleplay   749
rules of pronunciation   812

S

scaffolding   280, 310, 311, 319, 355, 357, 451, 511, 512, 540, 619, 623, 686, 703, 705, 711, 715, 716, 726, 754, 807, 851, 856
schema   201, 252, 1054
schematic structure   933
school   6–11, 41–45, 66–72, 87–102, 104, 105, 109–114, 159–166, 199–212, 215–228, 265–269, 317–321, 333–369, 372–377, 379–389, 439–443, 797–801, 1054–1065, 1085–1092, 1096–1104, 1108–1112
  curriculum   6, 7, 87–89, 93, 97–105, 109–111, 202–204, 248–253, 255–259, 263–269, 318–320, 355, 356, 358, 359, 365–368, 403, 404, 439–442, 686, 687, 701, 702, 803–805, 807, 808, 1101–1106
  literacies   314, 650, 892, 900, 902, 904, 905, 914, 1049
school-aged learners   439–441, 443, 445, 447, 449, 451, 453, 455, 710
school-based
  assessment   496, 502, 509, 518
  curriculum development   999
  materials development   1059

school-wide pedagogical interventions   1096
science discourse   702
scientific
  concepts   702
  method   283, 975
Scotland   160, 1082, 1102
SCT (*see* socio-cultural theory)   693–695, 697, 699
second language (L2)   155–159, 237–241, 265–268, 284–288, 298–301, 347–351, 516–520, 700, 701, 715–719, 758–760, 794, 795, 809–811, 822–825, 887–890, 914–917, 939–942, 957–959, 1000–1004, 1026–1029, 1047–1051
  education programs   185, 186, 189
  acquisition (SLA)   8, 157, 158, 165, 166, 247, 274, 284–291, 298–301, 348–350, 482, 516–518, 625, 626, 638, 639, 716, 717, 783, 792–795, 824, 825, 839–841, 856, 857, 966, 1026–1028
  classrooms   198, 201, 213, 285, 287, 300, 318, 347–349, 446, 461, 616, 625, 632, 633, 856, 857, 916, 917, 936, 937, 939, 941, 984, 985, 1049, 1050
  competence   16, 115, 166, 202, 207, 231, 237, 239, 241, 244, 246, 274, 285–287, 317, 437, 444, 483, 717, 823, 824, 984, 985
  curriculum   110, 247–249, 253, 257, 267, 268, 366, 367, 376, 377, 439, 440, 443, 444, 454–456, 484, 485, 517–519, 687, 701, 758–760, 809, 915–917, 939, 940, 1000–1002, 1111, 1112
  grammar   241, 267, 274, 276, 285–288, 300, 301, 310, 314, 402, 705, 783, 794, 795, 813, 822, 823, 843, 856, 857, 939, 940, 957, 958, 1048, 1050, 1051
  learning   267, 268, 284–288, 299–301, 317–319, 331, 515–520, 631–633, 669–671, 679, 680, 700, 701, 715–719, 743, 758–761, 792–795, 839–841, 856–858, 915–917, 939–942, 1010–1013, 1048–1051
  literacy   199–201, 207, 210, 267, 268, 313–315, 387, 388, 443, 444, 447, 455, 456, 517–519, 626, 632, 633, 689, 690, 716–718, 758–760, 856, 857, 887, 888, 914–916, 940–942, 1011, 1012

phonology 616, 779, 780, 799, 811, 815, 823–825
syllabus 16, 120, 247, 274, 286, 287, 300, 402, 437, 743, 809, 941, 959
user 240, 241, 243–247, 871, 966, 1051
writing 61, 394, 401, 402, 454, 455, 482–484, 491, 547, 548, 666, 760, 783, 794, 875, 876, 880, 881, 887–890, 907–910, 912, 914–917, 940–942, 984, 985, 1047, 1048
secondary schools 7, 67, 68, 77, 81, 87–90, 92, 93, 99, 100, 103, 104, 189, 194, 200, 204, 206, 222, 266, 312, 364, 366, 367, 376, 377, 807–810
segmental 812, 823
segments 9, 449, 460, 812, 813, 815–818, 868, 870, 1022
segregation 174, 178, 215, 224, 641, 647, 969, 1107
self-access 734, 735, 738, 739, 743–745, 954, 956, 969, 1118
  centre 734, 744
  learning 735, 738, 739, 743–745, 969, 1118
  multimedia resource centers 735
self-assessment 329, 420, 432, 434, 436, 511
self-correction 711, 873, 1029
self-directed speaking 694
self-evaluation of teacher talk (SETT) 952
self-management of learning 736, 738, 739
self-motivating strategies 728
semantic
  activity 860
  plane 850
semiotic 300, 309, 398, 617, 638, 646–648, 774, 779, 782, 851, 854, 872, 897, 919–921, 925, 928, 930, 941, 966, 1014
  activity 309, 398, 779, 920, 928, 966, 1036
  practices 398, 617, 646–648, 779, 782, 920, 928, 1036
  production 928, 1036
separation 28, 35, 311, 641, 1095, 1132
sibilant 813
signalling 152
signifier 1035
silent period 451, 700, 1091
simplification 708, 806, 1039

simplified tasks 703
site 16, 84, 169, 218, 388, 656, 682, 687, 701, 750, 760, 808, 921, 922, 966, 970, 999, 1033, 1041, 1042, 1046, 1052
situated learning theory 670
skilled work force 238
skills-based instruction 634
SLA (*see* second language acquisition) 26–28, 139, 150, 158, 164, 237, 241, 247, 265, 274–276, 278, 284, 287, 290, 296, 299, 300, 333, 335, 345, 506, 516, 533, 626–628, 630, 633, 636, 639, 649, 670, 676, 701, 705, 748, 753, 757, 789, 811, 848, 851, 855, 1017, 1019, 1022–1026, 1034, 1037
social 30, 31, 261–267, 303–311, 391–398, 615–620, 625–643, 645–653, 681–691, 694–701, 715–720, 763–766, 853–857, 891–898, 919–925, 930–942, 970–976, 1026–1030, 1033–1037, 1048–1053, 1087–1089
  awareness 47, 48, 233, 242, 373, 386, 393, 396, 452, 537, 641, 708, 713, 718, 808, 912, 942, 959, 973, 974, 996, 1094
  construction 130, 139, 185, 198, 227, 309, 319, 396, 398, 402, 519, 536, 538, 546, 616, 627, 641, 764, 765, 1018, 1019, 1027
  context 9, 92, 231, 305, 314, 318, 319, 402, 447, 538, 539, 638, 639, 642, 643, 649, 650, 715, 716, 856, 857, 891, 892, 920–922, 933, 935, 937–942, 987, 988
  differences 139, 158, 173, 178, 185, 200, 224, 257, 305, 319, 395, 615, 616, 639, 643, 647, 673, 963, 964, 990, 1033, 1036
  integration 66, 139, 232, 249, 250, 257, 258, 262, 304, 313, 315, 641, 673, 679, 905, 978, 1126
  practices 5, 25–27, 47, 48, 170, 249, 250, 303–309, 313–315, 391, 392, 400, 401, 514, 515, 616–618, 625–630, 632–636, 646–648, 684, 685, 876, 883, 891–895, 1018, 1042
  processes 9, 116, 123, 170, 257, 258, 307, 308, 318, 319, 335, 397, 398, 514, 625, 626, 642, 643, 646, 648, 649, 705, 892, 987, 988, 1023, 1068, 1072, 1073
  psychology 395, 617, 620, 637, 639–641,

646, 649, 651, 690, 695, 698, 699, 716, 718–720, 731, 857, 1007, 1034
relationships 13, 47, 48, 144, 145, 254, 305, 386, 395, 397, 430, 515, 516, 615, 617, 619, 626, 636, 661, 682, 695, 707, 764, 765
roles 26, 144, 242, 307, 617, 618, 627, 629, 632, 633, 678, 707, 715, 741, 964, 971, 1030, 1052, 1096, 1113, 1114, 1117, 1122, 1123
semiotics 781, 873, 919, 930, 1051
theory of language 396, 699, 854, 919, 933
variation 30, 31, 235, 391, 398, 853, 940, 941, 950
social-contextual 975
socially
constructed 626, 628, 636, 655, 656, 665, 693, 877, 934
distributed cognition 1024
oriented research 644
socially-mediated cognitive development 630
social-semiotic systems 851
societal multilingualism 137, 147, 148
society for information technology and teacher education (SITE) 1130
sociocognitive
psychological 703
traditions 701
sociocultural 24, 27, 214, 218, 231–233, 294–296, 334–336, 343–346, 452, 615, 619, 625–632, 637, 638, 693, 699–701, 705, 715–718, 766, 857, 1046
approach 232, 233, 289, 294, 296, 305, 693, 695, 697, 699, 700, 716, 854, 1022
identity 231, 434, 619, 625–628, 631, 632, 635, 637, 638, 640, 643, 705, 1041, 1046
perspectives 233, 289, 415, 625, 626, 628, 631, 691, 700, 716, 718, 742, 857, 941, 985, 1046
processes 232, 334–336, 338, 341, 346, 348, 625, 626, 640, 700, 705, 774, 855, 941, 952
theoretical framework 640, 952
theory (SCT) (*see also* Vygostkian theory) 26, 27, 227, 233, 280, 284, 295, 300, 415, 615, 619, 628, 629, 640,

693, 699, 700, 717, 718, 766, 855, 857, 1046, 1050
socio-educational 5, 52, 60
contexts 976
practices 5, 51, 52, 60
problems 973
sociohistorical theories 626
sociolinguistics 30, 134, 135, 151, 152, 156, 166, 273, 335, 429, 647, 672, 674, 860, 872, 976, 983, 1034, 1039, 1041, 1048, 1049, 1097
norms 1039
perspectives 976, 1048
practices 976, 983
sociology 23, 34, 35, 49, 50, 85, 151, 152, 181, 267, 392, 395, 531, 547, 639, 643, 650, 651, 666, 723, 860, 878, 889, 890, 1018, 1019
sociopolitical 3, 4, 11, 17, 33, 36, 79, 181–183, 434, 495, 631, 661, 690, 706, 707, 717, 964, 976, 985, 1100
conflict 17, 33
context 4, 11, 36, 660, 690, 717, 985, 1100
elites 394
statement 707
sociopsychological frames 1041
socio-rhetorical communities 875
South Africa 4, 31, 34, 44–47, 83, 85, 444, 455, 525, 661, 672, 676, 680, 781, 782, 875, 876, 919, 921, 922, 926, 927, 929, 930, 984
South Korea 77, 78
Southampton KAL project 950
Spanish-speaking ethnic groups 643
speaking rights 713, 862
specialist 10, 203, 204, 207–209, 219, 251, 257, 260, 286, 363, 366–369, 374, 376, 386, 387, 399, 400, 410, 704, 1101, 1105, 1107, 1108, 1119, 1120
discourse 399, 704
language teachers 10, 285, 1085, 1119
teaching software 1120
speech 30, 144, 145, 149, 150, 176–179, 278, 477, 478, 480, 481, 634, 635, 693–697, 700, 786, 787, 789–795, 844, 860, 861, 869–872, 894–896, 979, 980, 1017, 1018, 1025, 1091–1093
behavior 180, 242, 627, 696, 1025
communities 48, 126, 140, 149, 170, 635,

Subject Index 1197

  869, 887, 895, 896, 921, 1081, 1093
 exchange systems 1017, 1025
 segmentation 791, 793
spiraling curriculum 979
spoken 25, 26, 37, 126, 143, 144, 146, 156, 157, 223, 237, 425–429, 443, 535–537, 702–704, 714, 715, 780–782, 804, 805, 854–857, 859–861, 865–873, 923–925, 936
 corpora 781, 845, 854, 859, 870, 953
 discourse 146, 149, 171, 251, 463, 478, 536, 539, 619, 620, 702–704, 714, 715, 780, 781, 828, 829, 839, 854, 856, 857, 859, 861–863, 865, 869–873
 interaction 143, 144, 146, 426, 427, 429, 443, 519, 778, 855, 859, 864, 868, 870, 872, 1017
 language 25, 26, 126–128, 143–146, 156, 157, 237, 251, 426–429, 463, 483, 525, 535–537, 619, 620, 714, 715, 778–782, 795, 799, 800, 854–861, 868–873, 921–925, 979, 980
 language use 146, 426, 427, 697, 828, 859, 860, 938, 979
spread of English 4, 7, 13, 17–19, 24, 32, 63, 69, 76, 127, 129, 135, 149, 151, 156, 170, 474, 526, 967, 972
stabilization phase 1053
stakeholder involvement 407, 457, 458, 464
standard 19, 20, 25–34, 61, 78, 79, 126, 128, 145, 146, 178, 179, 181–183, 203, 214, 224, 225, 307, 324, 327–329, 423, 427–430, 450–452, 462, 463, 647
 deviations 324, 328, 329
 English 8, 19, 20, 23, 25–34, 61, 78–80, 126, 128, 145–147, 152, 178, 179, 181, 182, 214, 218–220, 224, 225, 462, 527, 672, 673, 677, 870, 871
 language 19, 20, 25–34, 51, 61, 78–80, 126–128, 178, 179, 181–183, 214, 224, 225, 247, 385, 427–430, 462, 463, 527, 531, 672, 673, 763, 764, 1091, 1099–1101
 language ideology 26, 27, 29–34, 183, 1094
 written English 214, 312, 429, 921
standardized 10, 25, 29, 35, 87, 211, 212, 223, 226, 264, 324, 327, 329, 330, 339, 344, 350–352, 416, 453, 498, 499, 506, 524
 assessment 327, 339, 358, 416, 432, 453, 456, 489, 497–499, 506, 507, 512, 514, 898, 915
 measures of achievement 506
 multiple-choice tests 498
 test scores 358, 501
standards 97, 98, 222, 223, 310, 311, 313–315, 416, 417, 420–425, 427–431, 433–464, 469, 470, 495–498, 507, 509, 510, 512, 513, 517, 519, 520, 895, 946, 953–955, 998, 999, 1103, 1104
 approach 267, 310, 376, 422–424, 428, 430, 433, 435–437, 441–445, 448, 451, 495, 497, 507, 513, 953, 969, 999, 1002
 for literacy 260
 for teacher certification 457, 458
 for workplace 421, 422
standards-based 213, 315, 417, 421, 423, 425, 427, 429, 431, 433, 435–437, 440, 442, 445, 455, 497
 approaches 420, 421, 423, 425, 427, 429, 431, 433, 435, 437
 movement 417, 421, 428, 431, 435–437, 440
 reform 417, 436, 440, 442, 455
state-wide exams 54
statistical processes 195
stereotype 5, 63, 644, 648, 651
stigmatization 632, 647, 648
stigmatized varieties 28, 29, 31, 32
strategies 22, 23, 94, 151, 152, 203–210, 213, 214, 223, 224, 233, 252–255, 317–321, 328–331, 728, 729, 739, 740, 759, 760, 833, 834, 836–840, 884, 885, 980–983, 1078–1080, 1095, 1107–1111
strategy training 742, 838
stretched language 712
structural accuracy 846
structure 5, 93, 94, 192–194, 205, 251, 290, 295, 296, 306, 307, 311, 371, 410, 534, 535, 537–539, 806, 807, 811, 812, 820–823, 843–847, 859–861, 931–933, 971, 972
structure-based
 production tasks 295
 teaching 251, 276
student 257–260, 310, 311, 333–336, 355–

360, 502–504, 540, 616–618, 626–628, 662–664, 697, 698, 703, 705–712, 725–731, 764, 765, 799, 800, 875–890, 907–911, 968–972, 979–981, 1129–1138
  agency 207, 323, 660, 663, 927
  interaction 82, 278, 420, 423, 465, 510, 516, 627, 658, 703, 705, 707, 709, 710, 712, 714, 716, 721, 752, 908, 909, 1028
student-centered
  educational thought 733
  learning 753, 1114, 1115
student-student interaction 703
subject 16, 110–112, 163, 164, 208–210, 251–255, 365–369, 372–377, 384–387, 399, 463, 464, 533–538, 540–547, 701, 702, 803–808, 813, 945–948, 950, 951, 953–956, 1070, 1104–1107
  content 10, 164, 234, 251–253, 281, 284, 310, 319, 321, 366–369, 373–376, 381, 385, 428, 429, 459, 463, 702, 803, 804, 806–808, 948
  disciplines 367–369, 372–374, 709, 878, 1070
  positions 372, 375, 1037
  specialists 210, 321, 365–369, 373–376, 386, 399, 409, 436, 478, 483, 1072
subjectivity 133, 135, 180, 645, 682, 850, 854, 978, 998, 1014, 1036, 1037, 1042, 1047, 1049
subject-matter knowledge 945–947, 950, 953–956
subject-related
  discourse 704, 714
  registers 704
subject-specific approach 950
subjugated knowledges 1037
summative feedback 419, 509
Sweden 37, 131, 135, 138, 352
syllabic segmentation 791
syllabification 820
syllable 789, 791, 812, 820–822, 844
  boundaries 791, 822
  structure 789, 812, 820–822
symbolic
  architectures 784
  capital 669, 1036
symbolism 784, 793, 923
symmetrical interaction patterns 294

synchronous communication 762, 909
syntax 20, 68, 219, 242, 243, 294, 299, 335, 353, 705, 753, 769, 777, 780, 801, 812, 814, 823, 824, 846, 853, 1028, 1029
systematic 26, 29, 32, 92, 107, 112, 115, 130, 131, 191, 243, 263, 264, 304, 315, 392, 404, 416, 418, 539, 540, 844, 845, 1059
  analysis 29, 131, 392, 540, 975, 983
  descriptions 975
systemic functional linguistics (SFL) 233, 252, 303, 305, 306, 309, 313, 373, 396, 535, 538, 619, 701, 702, 851, 887, 933, 941, 983, 1051

T
talk-in-interaction 966, 1017–1019, 1023–1025, 1028, 1029
target language 3, 25, 27, 29, 31, 32, 78, 79, 178, 276, 277, 279–281, 283, 284, 461, 462, 627, 628, 639, 640, 752, 753, 807, 808, 848, 949, 950, 955, 956, 970, 1127, 1128
task 233, 280, 281, 283, 284, 287–301, 318–320, 423–425, 452, 462, 463, 476–478, 483, 519, 520, 619, 666, 703, 704, 721–725, 729, 730, 738, 752–754, 815–817, 1136–1138
task-based
  assessment (TBA) 320, 460, 519
  learning (TBL) 16, 239, 299, 301, 1138
  research 298
teachability hypothesis 849
teacher 75–84, 203–210, 365–377, 415–424, 457–459, 461–471, 507–512, 707–717, 739–745, 861–864, 898–903, 945–959, 963–972, 994–1002, 1052–1057, 1061–1089, 1093–1099, 1102–1108, 1117–1134, 1136–1138
  assessment 311, 404–406, 412, 413, 415–422, 436, 437, 449–453, 457–459, 463, 464, 466, 467, 469–471, 487–492, 495, 496, 498–500, 502, 504, 505, 507–520, 533, 534, 929, 1103, 1104, 1106, 1107
  autonomy 436, 620, 621, 725, 733, 739–745, 750, 946, 1002, 1069, 1079
  cognition 300, 636, 782, 952, 956, 957, 1052, 1082, 1084
  courses 209, 266, 399, 415, 433, 437,

Subject Index 1199

489, 496, 659, 777, 952–954, 956, 958, 970, 979, 1012, 1054, 1055, 1085, 1125, 1126, 1130, 1131
curriculum 6, 7, 95, 96, 103, 104, 206, 257, 266, 355, 356, 365–368, 372–377, 437, 438, 440, 503, 504, 509–511, 709, 710, 958, 959, 970–972, 992, 999–1002, 1014–1016, 1103–1108
development 49, 50, 82, 83, 318, 319, 323, 344, 345, 356, 357, 374–377, 418–422, 433, 516–519, 533, 534, 543, 544, 739–743, 952–954, 956, 967, 968, 999–1001, 1052–1057, 1059, 1061–1083
education 49, 50, 81–83, 375–377, 389, 421–424, 436–438, 458–462, 469–471, 741–745, 957–959, 963–972, 1001, 1002, 1014–1016, 1052–1055, 1064–1066, 1082–1089, 1097–1100, 1125–1127, 1129–1133, 1136–1138
as entrepreneur 1115
feedback 277, 278, 296, 374, 419, 420, 457, 463, 465, 489, 491, 492, 503, 508–511, 516, 520, 542, 708, 712, 729, 730, 845, 846, 862, 917
interaction 82, 205, 217, 231, 254, 278, 296, 301, 305, 420, 464, 465, 510, 707, 709, 710, 714, 741, 872, 873, 908, 909, 1026–1028, 1127
intervention 204, 209, 255, 620, 719, 965, 1095
language awareness (TLA) 782, 945, 947, 949, 951, 953, 955, 957, 959
metalinguistic awareness 163, 948, 951, 957
professionalism 433, 437, 946, 968, 1067, 1069, 1072, 1074, 1076, 1079, 1080, 1082, 1083
programs 6, 83, 103, 284, 285, 406, 416, 417, 421–423, 431, 436, 437, 459, 491, 492, 749, 750, 952, 954, 955, 968, 1043, 1077–1079, 1097, 1098, 1125, 1126, 1129–1131
reflection 213, 373, 374, 453, 708, 965, 968, 972, 1001, 1074–1076, 1082, 1085
research 418–420, 453, 454, 510–512, 515–517, 741, 742, 757, 919, 950–952, 956–958, 963–965, 967–973, 991–1002, 1014–1016, 1065–1067, 1069–

1071, 1074–1077, 1082–1087, 1097–1099, 1124–1127, 1130–1136
as researcher 398, 916, 996, 1002
roles 259, 285, 1114, 1127, 1129
standards 207, 208, 222, 223, 416, 417, 420–424, 431, 433, 434, 436–438, 440, 441, 443, 449–454, 457–463, 469, 470, 509, 510, 512, 519, 520, 946, 954, 955, 958, 959, 969, 1103, 1104
thinking 207, 314, 509, 713, 945, 994, 1004, 1008, 1045, 1065, 1067, 1069, 1074–1076, 1082–1084, 1092
training providers 207, 208
teacher-based assessment 416, 418, 419, 453, 489, 499, 510, 518
teacher-centered methods 1128
teacher-student interactions 616, 627, 703, 709, 851
teaching
English as a foreign language (TEFL) 146, 945
English as a second language (TESL) 155, 267, 376, 958, 1111
literature 271, 385, 926
methodology (*see also* teaching methods) 27, 29, 84, 105, 220, 239, 246, 286, 287, 300, 315, 415, 719, 857, 994, 1002
style 1063
technical
economy 178
language 702
technologies 233, 303, 313, 474, 480, 502, 621–623, 629, 630, 747, 748, 750, 751, 755–758, 781, 891, 898, 907, 915, 916, 937, 969, 970, 1113, 1114, 1120–1123
technology
enhanced language learning 748
integration 1130
resource people 1115
TEFL (see teaching English as a foreign language) 945, 947, 951, 952, 954, 955, 1060
metalanguage 951
tenor 305, 311, 535, 545, 849, 852
tertiary settings 511, 876, 1116, 1119
TESL (*see* teaching English as a foreign language) 197, 288, 470, 483, 679, 905, 951, 986, 1015, 1048
TESOL Quarterly 34, 35, 84–86, 198,

285–287, 299, 300, 331, 376, 377, 481–484, 636–638, 665–667, 679, 680, 856, 857, 871–873, 889, 890, 941, 983–986, 998–1002, 1026–1028, 1049–1052, 1098–1100

TESOL (*see* teaching English to speakers of other languages) xxi, 23, 34, 60, 84, 150, 166, 182, 198, 266, 278, 299, 310, 311, 415, 417, 418, 421, 422, 428, 431–434, 436, 441, 443, 453, 510, 512, 513, 678, 801, 978, 983, 994, 995, 998, 1038, 1041, 1085,

Test of English as Foreign Language (TOEFL)   64, 113, 418, 473–483, 524, 528

tests   10, 92–95, 99–101, 104, 222–226, 323–325, 327, 339–341, 350–352, 417, 418, 457–460, 462–470, 473–484, 487–490, 492–494, 496–498, 501–506, 519–525, 527–531, 951

text   205, 206, 305–309, 311, 312, 314, 397, 398, 536–540, 545–547, 752–757, 777–781, 797, 798, 801, 802, 804–808, 828, 829, 849–855, 879–881, 913–916, 932–936, 940–942, 1010, 1011, 1120–1122

  analysis   309, 311, 397, 400, 402, 538, 540, 548, 748, 853, 872, 888, 910, 916, 932–934, 940, 1007, 1022, 1023, 1058, 1136

  coherence   305, 538, 778, 792

  types   206, 305, 306, 308, 477, 478, 481, 547, 755, 756, 778, 807, 850, 860, 861, 914, 933, 936, 984, 1113, 1120–1122

textbooks   5, 6, 13, 18, 25, 29, 30, 40, 51, 52, 55, 57–59, 61, 84, 89–92, 95, 100–103, 308–310, 661, 766–768, 770, 771, 804, 805, 974, 975

textual   61, 135, 181, 305, 400, 534, 538, 539, 545, 622, 715, 759, 764, 778, 849, 850, 869, 879, 880, 883–887, 928, 929, 934–937, 1046, 1047

  function   849, 850

  information   764, 849, 850, 937

  meanings   622, 764, 850, 868, 869

theory   26, 27, 271–275, 299, 300, 309, 310, 391, 392, 538–540, 619, 636–640, 650–653, 689–691, 693–695, 697–700, 715–718, 741–743, 794, 795, 845–848, 851–857, 939–941, 963, 964, 1050–1052

thinking   21–23, 61, 160, 172, 179, 233, 261, 303, 310, 312–315, 452, 493, 503, 509, 546, 765, 807, 940, 1075, 1083, 1084

third

  ground   919, 921, 922, 928

  party   1122

TLA (*see* teacher language awareness)   782, 945–956

traditional   6, 7, 77, 221, 379, 380, 415, 416, 418, 419, 522, 622, 623, 698, 699, 763, 764, 766, 768–770, 774, 777, 779–782, 843–846, 863, 864, 910, 923–925, 1127–1130

  grammar   77, 92, 251, 402, 622, 661, 738, 744, 764, 768, 769, 777, 779, 780, 843–847, 853, 855, 924, 939

  grammar teaching   661, 768

  testing   221, 415, 416, 419, 497, 501, 512, 522, 619, 698, 699

transactions   51, 182, 410, 426, 429, 430, 862, 863, 869

transcript   924, 1019–1021, 1026, 1031, 1032

transcription   410, 781, 859, 865, 1020, 1022, 1031, 1032

transcultural identities   645

transculturation   1035, 1042, 1052

transformational grammar   273, 538, 778

transformative   5, 48, 622, 669, 684, 689, 696, 707, 753, 763, 765–768, 774, 903, 924, 928, 971, 972, 997, 1043, 1044, 1052, 1079–1081

  language pedagogy   669, 766

  pedagogy   5, 48, 669, 707, 753, 763–768, 774, 903, 928, 971, 972, 1043, 1044

transitional bilingual education   345, 346

transitions   663, 889, 979, 982, 1068, 1073

transmission   7, 11, 113, 210, 368, 481, 637, 751, 767, 768, 878, 902, 903, 953, 971, 972, 1114, 1126

  approaches   7, 368, 971, 1114

  education   7, 210, 637, 768, 902, 903, 1126

  knowledge transmitter   6, 101, 861, 971, 1132

transnational   125, 380, 646, 648, 1035, 1040

  identities   256

triangulation 507, 973–976
t-tests 325
turn-taking 709, 865–867, 873, 966, 979, 1017, 1018, 1029
two-way bilingual education 255, 256, 264

U

UK (also United Kingdom) 9, 10, 49, 50, 124–126, 199–201, 227, 237, 249, 250, 300, 314, 315, 389, 407, 520, 679, 735, 794, 795, 858, 859, 945, 946, 1047–1049, 1051, 1052, 1101, 1102
unilinear stage model 641
United Kingdom (UK) 7, 9, 130, 160, 187, 246, 379, 418, 422, 424, 444, 453, 473, 505, 534, 650, 781, 875, 876, 903, 1101, 1102
United States of America (USA) 781, 875, 876, 895
universal grammar (UG) 784, 785, 813, 822, 844, 848, 856, 1034, 1048
universities 49, 52, 54, 67, 76, 89, 125, 129, 400–403, 454, 455, 473–477, 479, 481, 482, 656–659, 662–664, 878, 879, 887–889, 1057, 1058, 1130–1132, 1134, 1135
University of Cambridge Local Examinations Syndicate (UCLES) 112, 113, 433, 438, 457, 460, 475, 482, 959
university entrance 6, 63, 67, 194, 417, 473, 534

V

validity 325, 347, 348, 416–420, 440, 444, 445, 448–453, 456–458, 460, 461, 476–478, 482–484, 494, 495, 501, 502, 505–508, 510, 512, 517–519, 521, 522, 531, 974, 975, 998
variation 26, 29–32, 93, 111, 140, 141, 144, 158, 170, 193, 218, 232, 235, 398–400, 416, 417, 439, 642, 871, 937, 940, 941, 950
velum 818
verb phrase (VP) 843, 847
verbal
  description 1021, 1031
  narratives 925
  participation 1093

vernacular
  education 14, 51
  medium 52, 54, 55
Vietnam 32, 36, 1003
Vietnamese 30, 35, 249, 650, 653, 674, 1003
virtual
  information exchange 901
  space 894, 895, 899
visible pedagogy 205
visual literacy 622, 756, 854, 930
vocabulary 20, 67, 90, 92–94, 97, 99, 145, 171, 201, 251–253, 335, 742–744, 758, 759, 779, 780, 793–795, 797–808, 827–841, 910, 911, 935, 951
  profiles 318, 951, 958
  teaching and learning 97, 232, 764, 780, 827, 829, 831, 833, 835, 837, 839–841, 898, 935, 1000
voice 8, 55, 57, 58, 60, 135, 144, 145, 149, 181, 225, 243, 492, 686, 806, 881, 883–885, 887–889, 896, 897, 1031, 1043, 1111
voluntary immigrants 644
VP (*see* verb phrase) 847
Vygotskian theory (*see also* sociocultural theory) 716, 851

W

wash out effect 1054
web
  designer 1115
  pages 749, 773, 907, 912, 922, 1119–1121
  traffic 891
Web-based bulletin 907
web-based cultural studies 1134
web-conferencing 1127
well-formed sentences 784
Wits Multiliteracies Reasearch Group 919, 930
word retrieval skills 783
working conditions 967, 1053, 1069
workplace English 403, 404
World Englishes 51, 61, 123, 126–129, 135, 140, 149, 150, 152, 153, 167, 415, 672, 954, 958, 959, 1039, 1050
world language 19, 20, 110, 134, 152, 525, 526, 531, 672, 678, 1050

World Wide Web 749, 759, 762, 767, 856, 907, 912, 916
writing 57, 58, 60, 61, 278, 279, 392–395, 401, 402, 409, 474–477, 480–484, 545–548, 662, 663, 666, 781, 788–794, 797–801, 875–891, 907–917, 929–935, 940–943, 979–982, 1061, 1062
  assignments 659, 662, 878, 914, 980, 981, 1096
written language 26, 35, 116, 146, 203, 205, 251, 353, 355, 403, 536, 619, 714, 777, 856, 859–861, 871, 872, 896, 897, 923, 924, 979

X

xenophobic 646

Z

zero proficiency 68
zone of proximal development (ZDP) (*see also* Vygotsky) 619, 623, 628, 629, 634, 636, 686, 693, 697, 700, 703, 717, 764, 766, 857, 1132
ZPD (*see* zone of proximal development) 619, 620, 629, 630, 693, 697–699, 703, 710, 764, 766

Springer International Handbooks of Education

Volume 1

International Handbook of Educational Leadership and Administration
Edited by Kenneth Leithwood, Judith Chapman, David Corson,
Philip Hallinger, and Ann Hart
ISBN 0-7923-3530-9

Volume 2

International Handbook of Science Education
Edited by Barry J. Fraser and Kenneth O. Tobin
ISBN 0-7923-3531-7

Volume 3

International Handbook of Teachers and Teaching
Edited by Bruce J. Biddle, Thomas L. Good, and Ivor L. Goodson
ISBN 0-7923-3532-5

Volume 4

International Handbook of Mathematics Education
Edited by Alan J. Bishop, Ken Clements, Christine Keitel, Jeremy Kilpatrick,
and Collette Laborde
ISBN 0-7923-3533-3

Volume 5

International Handbook of Educational Change
Edited by Andy Hargreaves, Ann Leiberman, Micheal Fullan,
and David Hopkins
ISBN 0-7923-3534-1

Volume 6

International Handbook of Lifelong Learning
Edited by David Aspin, Judith Chapman, Micheal Hatton,
and Yukiko Sawano
ISBN 0-7923-6815-0

Volume 7

International Handbook of Research in Medical Education
Edited by Geoff R. Norman, Cees P.M. van der Vleuten, and David I. Newble
ISBN 1-4020-0466-4

Volume 8

Second International Handbook of Educational Leadership and Administration
Edited by Kenneth Leithwood and Philip Hallinger
ISBN 1-4020-0690-X

Volume 9

International Handbook of Educational Evaluation
Edited by Thomas Kellaghan and Daniel L. Stufflebeam
ISBN 1-4020-0849-X

Volume 10

Second International Handbook of Mathematics Education
Edited by Alan J. Bishop, M.A., (Ken) Clements, Christine Keitel,
Jeremy Kilpatrick, and Frederick K.S. Leung
ISBN 1-4020-1008-7

Volume 11

The International Handbook of Educational Research in the Asia-Pacific Region
Edited by J.P. Keeves and R. Watanabe
ISBN 978-1-4020-1007-1

Volume 12

International Handbook of Self-Study of Teaching and Teacher Education Practices
Edited by J. John Loughran, Mary Lynn Hamilton, Vicki Kubler LaBoskey,
and Tom L. Russell
ISBN 978-1-4020-1812-1

Volume 13

International Handbook of Educational Policy
Edited by Nina Bascia, Alister Cumming, Amanda Datnow, Kenneth Leithwood,
and David Livingstone
ISBN 978-1-4020-3189-2

Volume 14

International Handbook of Virtual Learning Environments
Edited by Joel Weiss, Jason Nolan, Jeremy Hunsinger, and Peter Trifonas
ISBN 978-1-4020-3082-0

Volume 15

International Handbook of English Language Teaching
Edited by Jim Cummins and Chris Davison
ISBN 0-387-46300-3

Printed in the United States of America